SUMMARY

ITALIAN WINES 2011
GAMBERO ROSSO®

Gambero Rosso Holding S.p.A.
via Enrico Fermi, 161 - 00146 ROMA
tel. 06/551121 - fax 06/55112260
www.gamberorosso.it - email: gambero@gamberorosso.it

Senior Editors
Gianni Fabrizio
Eleonora Guerini
Marco Sabellico

SPECIAL Contributors
Antonio Boco
Dario Cappelloni
Giuseppe Carrus
Paolo De Cristofaro
Paolo Zaccaria

Regional Coordinators
Nino Ajello
Alessandro Bocchetti
Goffredo D'Andrea
Nicola Frasson
Massimo Lanza
Giorgio Melandri
Gianni Ottogalli
Nereo Pederzolli
Pierpaolo Rastelli
Carlo Ravanello
Leonardo Romanelli
Riccardo Viscardi

Main Contributors
Francesco Beghi
Sergio Bonanno
Michele Bressan
Pasquale Buffa
Dioniso Castello
Giacomo Mojoli
Franco Pallini
Marco Tonelli

Other Contributors
Filippo Apollinari
Rudina Arapi
Gilberto Arru
Enrico Battistella
Maura Bertorello
Andrea Bezzecchi
Teodosio Buongiorno
Sergio Ceccarelli
Valentina Congiu
Mario Demattè
Giovanni De Vecchis
Antonello Edonista
Gianfranco Fassina
Maurizio Fava
Loredana Greco
Giovanna La Molinara
Cristiana Lauro
Marco Manzoli
Maurizio Manzoni
Leonardo Marco
Nicola Massa
Enrico Melis
Enzo Merz
Daniele Montano
Vanni Muraro
William Nesto
Renato Orlando
Michelangelo Palermo
Luca Panunzio
Cinzia Pesci
Alessio Pietrobattista
Augusto Piras
Silvano Prompicai
Helmut Riebschlaeger
Francesca Rossi
Maurizio Rossi
Lorenzo Ruggeri
Herbert Taschler
Cinzia Tosetti
Paolo Trimani
Vincenzo Vernocchi
Stefano Zaghini

Editorial Coordinator
Giuseppe Carrus

Editorial Secretary
Giulia Sciortino

Layout
Gianna Petrucci

Translations Coordinated and Edited by
Giles Watson

Translators
Angela Arnone
Helen Donald
Rachel Fell
Juliet Hammond-Smith
Dave Henderson
Stephen Jackson
Allyson McKay
Sarah Ponting
Simon Tanner
Giles Watson
Ailsa Wood

Editor-in-Chief
Daniele Cernilli

Publisher
Gambero Rosso Inc.
President Sergio Cellini
636 Broadway – Suite 111 – New York, NY 10012
tel.- +1-212-253-5853 fax +1-212-253-8349
email: gamberousa@aol.com

Distribution
USA and Canada
by Antique Collectors' Club, Eastworks, 116
Pleasant St #18, Easthampton, MA 010207, USA;
UK and Australia by Antique Collectors' Club Ltd
Sandy Lane, Old Martlesham, Woodbridge,
Suffolk IP12 4SD - United Kingdom

The final edit of Italian Wines
was completed on 14 September 2010

ISBN 978-88-8971-182-8

printed in Italy for Gambero Rosso Holding S.p.A.
in January 2010 by
Puntoweb s.r.l., Ariccia, Rome

THE GUIDE

If anyone had told us in 1987 that 24 years later we would still be writing Italian Wines, we wouldn't have believed them. Yet here we are. Back then, we profiled 500 wineries and just 1,500 wines. Today, there are five times as many cellars and almost 13 times as many wines. In 1987, there were 32 Three Glass awards; this time there are about 400 while the ratio of prize-winners to wines tasted has remained almost the same. If we consider the enormous improvements in winemaking, this means we are much stricter now than we were in 1987. In fact, everything has changed. The pioneering spirit, the desire to rebuild the image of Italian wine, which the previous year has been shattered by the methanol scandal, the individual passion and a certain guilelessness provided the impulse that drove the first Guide's designers and compilers. All that is in the past. We have emerged from a period of construction that has seen new producers, new wine styles and new growing areas assert themselves and another of destruction that sometimes hastily shelved local techniques, vines and traditions. We saw a war machine sweep everything in its path to one side in the name of an often misconstrued modernism. The crises of 2001 and 2008 brought us all back down to earth. In recent times, over-ambitious wine styles and price tags have been scaling back. Over the years, the Guide has been following all this, seeking as far as possible not to take sides but to note what is going on and assess it using parameters that have had to adjust to the reality they were evaluating. The return to a more authentic, less glamorous, way of making wine, if only in the manner in which it is proposed to wine lovers, is a sign of the times that we salute with pleasure. It marks the recovery of a material culture and genuine added value that sets this world apart from all other sectors of food and agriculture. The award for Winery of the Year to Francesco Valentini and his absolutely stunning, "farmer's" wines underlines precisely this, and how it is possible to combine sensory values with respect for the territory and its heritage in viticulture and vinification. Also inspired by tradition was the award of the Red of the year to the Brunello di Montalcino Riserva '04 from Franco Biondi Santi. The award for the best sparkling wine returns to Franciacorta and goes for the first time to Le Marchesine for the Franciacorta Brut Secolo Novo '05. Other awards went to Günther Kerschbaumer for the Valle Isarco Sylvaner R '09 and to the Albana di Romagna Passito A R Riserva '06 from Cristina Geminiani's Zerbina for their sense of belonging to their territory. They received White of the Year and Sweet of the Year. Behind the awards lie exceptional performances but not just that. And at a time when there are calls from all sides to go beyond mere sensory characteristics and reward emblematic, territorial or natural wines, allow us to point out that we have been doing just that for 24 years. But with one small difference: for us, wines must above all be good in the hedonistic sense. The rest is secondary. We were before we had to be, in a sense. We should also point out very strongly that almost all the wineries reviewed and evaluated were visited in all of these years by a team of contributors of whom we are deeply proud. The were selected for their competence and honesty. They know that tasting and evaluating wines is an arduous task that entails a duty to respect the work of other people, conscious that the job will not solve the problems of humanity. All they are doing is putting their skills at the service of our readers. One final sign of the times. This year, more than 50 award-winning wines cost less than €15 in wine shops. We feel we should stress this point. It is not true that you need to spend a fortune in order to enjoy wines of exceptional quality. At least, not in Italy. Once again, we would like to

THE GUIDE

describe how we went about this vast sensory exploration of Italian wine. We had to bring forward the starting date again but the sheer number of wines tasted – almost 25,000 – made this inevitable. Our panels were already at work in the regions in early May. In each region, sometimes in individual provinces, and almost always at official institutions, we began to taste the wines collected by the consortiums, chambers of commerce and regional wine cellars that collaborated with us and monitored our operations. All the bottles were masked and inspected at comparative tastings with others of the same type and vintage. The venues where we worked and which we thank most sincerely, we hope without omission, are the following: the consortiums of Chianti Classico, Brunello and Rosso di Montalcino, Vino Nobile di Montepulciano, Vernaccia di San Gimignano, Chianti Rufina, Colli Fiorentini, Cortona, Morellino di Scansano, Montecucco, Monteregio di Massa Marittima, Gavi, Asti, Nebbioli dell'Alto Piemonte, Franciacorta, Oltrepò Pavese, Lugana, Valtellina, Soave, Valpolicella, the Enoteca Regionale del Roero, the Enoteca Regionale del Monferrato, the Enoteca Regionale di Nizza Monferrato, the Enoteca Regionale La Serenissima di Gradisca d'Isonzo, the Enoteca Regionale dell'Emilia Romagna, the Enoteca Regionale del Lazio, the Ente Vini Bresciani, the Istituto Agronomico Mediterraneo di Valenzano, the Istituto Marchigiano di Tutela Vini di Majolati Spontini, the Italian Sensory Analysis Centre at Matelica, Bolzano chamber of Commerce, Avellino Chamber of Commerce, the Genova Chamber of Commerce, the Trento Chamber of Commerce, the Cagliari Chamber of Commerce, the Perugia Chamber of Commerce the Umbria Regional Coordination of Wine and Oil Trails, Vinea at Offida and the Anteprima group at Lucca. Then there are the Wine Trails of Carmignano, the Wine Trails of Arezzo, the Union of Basilicata Chambers of Commerce at Matera and various privately owned facilities, the Réserve at Caramanico in Abruzzo, the Le Due Sorelle restaurant at Messina and the La Canonica restaurant at Casteldimezzo near Pesaro, the Cala de' Medici marina at Rosignano, the Hotel Carpe Diem at Montaione, Faenza Fiere and the Millésimes company. In the first stage of tasting, we used marks out of 100 and selected about 1,500 wines which went through to the Three Glass finals. These wines obtained a score of at least Two Red Glasses. It was a massive effort, followed by meetings of the Three Glass panel made up of leading regional panellists, which evaluated the wines in the final. Again, tasting was blind. In all, this involved two weeks of tastings, all carried out at Gambero Rosso's Città del Gusto headquarters in Rome. Taking part in the tastings were the three senior editors, Marco Sabellico, Eleonora Guerini and Gianni Fabrizio, editor-in-chief Daniele Cernilli, with, according to their assigned areas, Nino Aiello, Alessandro Bocchetti, Antonio Boco, Dario Cappelloni, Paolo De Cristofaro, Giuseppe Carrus, Goffredo D'Andrea, Nicola Frasson, Massimo Lanza, Giorgio Melandri, Gianni Ottogalli, Nereo Pederzolli, Pierpaolo Rastelli, Carlo Ravanello, Leonardo Romanelli, Riccardo Viscardi and Paolo Zaccaria.

Daniele Cernilli, Gianni Fabrizio, Eleonora Guerini and Marco Sabellico.

THREE GLASSES 2011

VALLE D'AOSTA		
Valle d'Aosta Chambave Moscato Passito Prieuré '08	La Crotta di Vegneron	37
Valle d'Aosta Chardonnay Cuvée Bois '08	Les Crêtes	40
Valle d'Aosta Chardonnay Élevé en Fût de Chêne '09	Anselmet	36
Valle d'Aosta Petite Arvine V. Rovettaz '09	F.lli Grosjean	39
Valle d'Aosta Pinot Gris '09	Lo Triolet	40
Valle d'Aosta Torrette Sup. V. de Torrette '06	Di Barrò	38
PIEDMONT		
Alta Langa Zero Cantina Maestra Ris. '04	Enrico Serafino	174
Barbaresco Camp Gros '06	Tenute Cisa Asinari dei Marchesi di Grésy	94
Barbaresco Ovello V. Loreto '07	Albino Rocca	161
Barbaresco Pora '06	Ca' del Baio	75
Barbaresco Ris. '05	Sottimano	175
Barbaresco S. Stefanetto '07	Piero Busso	73
Barbaresco Sorì Paitin '07	Paitin	147
Barbaresco V. Manzola '06	Fiorenzo Nada	143
Barbaresco Vanotu '07	Pelissero	149
Barbaresco Vign. in Montestefano Ris. '05	Produttori del Barbaresco	55
Barbaresco Vign. Starderi '07	La Spinetta	176
Barbera d'Asti Pomorosso '07	Coppo	101
Barbera d'Asti Sup. Alfiera '07	Marchesi Alfieri	48
Barbera d'Asti Sup. Nizza '07	Tenuta Olim Bauda	146
Barbera d'Asti Sup. Nizza Acsé '07	Scrimaglio	172
Barbera d'Asti Sup. Nizza Sotto la Muda '07	Paolo Avezza	54
Barbera d'Asti Sup. Nizza V. dell'Angelo '07	Cascina La Barbatella	56
Barbera del M.to Sup. Bricco Battista '07	Giulio Accornero e Figli	46
Barbera del M.to Sup. Pico Gonzaga '07	Castello di Uviglie	89
Barolo '06	Bartolo Mascarello	136
Barolo Arione '06	Enzo Boglietti	63
Barolo Bric del Fiasc '06	Paolo Scavino	171
Barolo Bricco Cogni '04	Michele Reverdito	159
Barolo Bricco Pernice '05	Elvio Cogno	95
Barolo Broglio Ris. '04	Schiavenza	171
Barolo Brunate '06	Mario Marengo	134
Barolo Brunate-Le Coste '06	Giuseppe Rinaldi	160
Barolo Bussia Ris. '01	Pianpolvere Soprano	151
Barolo Cannubi '06	Michele Chiarlo	92
Barolo Cannubi Boschis '06	Luciano Sandrone	167
Barolo Casa E. di Mirafiore Ris. '04	Fontanafredda	112
Barolo Cascina Francia '06	Giacomo Conterno	98
Barolo Cerretta '06	Giovanni Rosso	164
Barolo Gavarini V. Chiniera '06	Elio Grasso	122
Barolo Ginestra '06	Paolo Conterno	99
Barolo Le Rocche del Falletto '04	Bruno Giacosa	117
Barolo Liste '05	Giacomo Borgogno & Figli	64
Barolo Margheria '06	Azelia	54
Barolo Monfortino Ris. '02	Giacomo Conterno	98
Barolo Monvigliero '06	F.lli Alessandria	47
Barolo Monvigliero Ris. '04	Castello di Verduno	90
Barolo Ornato '06	Pio Cesare	152
Barolo Prapò '06	Bricco Rocche - Bricco Asili	70
Barolo Rocche '06	Renato Ratti	157
Barolo Rocche '06	Vietti	184
Barolo Rocche dei Brovia '06	Brovia	72
Barolo Rocchettevino '06	Gianfranco Bovio	66
Barolo Sarmassa '06	Marchesi di Barolo	133
Barolo Sorano Coste & Bricco '06	Ascheri	53
Barolo Terlo Ravera '06	Abbona	44
Barolo V. Rionda '06	Luigi Pira	153
Barolo V. Rionda Ris. '04	Vigna Rionda - Massolino	184
Barolo Vign. Rocche '06	Renato Corino	102
Barolo Vignolo Ris. '04	F.lli Cavallotto – Tenuta Bricco Boschis	91
Boca '06	Le Piane	151
Carema Et. Nera '05	Ferrando	110
Colli Tortonesi Timorasso Filari di Timorasso '07	Luigi Boveri	66
Colli Tortonesi Timorasso Pitasso '08	Claudio Mariotto	135
Colli Tortonesi Timorasso Sterpi '08	Vigneti Massa	186
Dogliani Bricco Botti '07	Pecchenino	149
Dogliani Vecchie V. Pirochetta '08	Cascina Corte	82
Erbaluce di Caluso La Rustìa '09	Orsolani	146
Gattinara '06	Torraccia del Piantavigna	180
Gattinara Vign. Osso S. Grato '06	Antoniolo	51
Gattinara Vign. S. Francesco '06	Antoniolo	51
Gavi del Comune di Gavi Minaia '09	Nicola Bergaglio	60
Gavi del Comune di Gavi Monterotondo '08	Villa Sparina	187

THREE GLASSES 2011

Langhe Arborina '08	Elio Altare - Cascina Nuova	49
Langhe Bianco Hérzu '08	Ettore Germano	116
Langhe Nebbiolo '08	Ca' Viola	76
Langhe Nebbiolo Costa Russi '07	Gaja	114
Langhe Nebbiolo Sorì Tildìn '07	Gaja	114
Lessona Omaggio a Quintino Sella '05	Sella	173
M.to Rosso La Mandorla '07	Luigi Spertino	176
Moscato d'Asti Tenuta del Fant '09	Tenuta Il Falchetto	108
Nebbiolo d'Alba V. Colla '07	Fabrizio Battaglino	57
Piemonte Moscato d'Autunno '09	Paolo Saracco	168
Roero Braja Ris. '07	Deltetto	106
Roero Mompissano Ris. '07	Cascina Ca' Rossa	76
Roero Printi Ris. '07	Monchiero Carbone	139
Roero Ròche d'Ampsèj Ris. '06	Matteo Correggia	103
LIGURIA		
Colli di Luni Vermentino Costa Marina '09	Ottaviano Lambruschi	211
Colli di Luni Vermentino Lunae Et. Nera '09	Cantine Lunae Bosoni	209
Riviera Ligure di Ponente Pigato Cycnus '09	Poggio dei Gorleri	214
Riviera Ligure di Ponente Vermentino '09	Maria Donata Bianchi	205
Riviera Ligure di Ponente Vermentino Le Serre '08	Tommaso Lupi & C.	211
Rossese di Dolceacqua Bricco Arcagna '08	Terre Bianche	216
Rossese di Dolceacqua Sup. Vign. Posau '08	Maccario Dringenberg	212
LOMBARDY		
Franciacorta Brut '05	Enrico Gatti	242
Franciacorta Brut Cabochon '05	Monte Rossa	248
Franciacorta Brut Extrême Palazzo Lana '05	Guido Berlucchi & C.	227
Franciacorta Brut Secolo Novo '05	Le Marchesine	246
Franciacorta Collezione Brut '05	Cavalleri	236
Franciacorta Cuvée Annamaria Clementi '03	Ca' del Bosco	231
Franciacorta Extra Brut '04	Ferghettina	240
Franciacorta Extra Brut Ris. Vintage '04	La Montina	249
Franciacorta Gran Cuvée Pas Operé '04	Bellavista	226
Franciacorta Pas Dosé QdE Ris. '04	Il Mosnel	250
Franciacorta Satèn Magnificentia	Uberti	259
Lugana Sup. Sel. Fabio Contato '06	Provenza	255
OP Barbera Castello di Cigognola '07	Castello di Cigognola	236
OP Pinot Nero Brut Cl. 1870 '06	F.lli Giorgi	243
OP Pinot Nero Cl. Nature	Monsupello	247
OP Pinot Nero Giorgio Odero '07	Frecciarossa	241
OP Pinot Nero Noir '07	Tenuta Mazzolino	246
TdF Chardonnay '07	Ca' del Bosco	231
Valtellina Sforzato Albareda '08	Mamete Prevostini	254
Valtellina Sfursat 5 Stelle '07	Nino Negri	251
Valtellina Sup. Sassella Ris. '06	Aldo Rainoldi	256
TRENTINO		
Granato '07	Foradori	285
Teroldego Rotaliano Maso Cervara '07	Cavit	282
Trento Altemasi Graal Brut Ris. '03	Cavit	282
Trento Balter Ris. '04	Nicola Balter	280
Trento Brut Domini '05	Abate Nero	280
Trento Brut Letrari Ris. '05	Letrari	287
Trento Extra Brut Perlé Nero '04	Ferrari	285
Trento Giulio Ferrari Riserva del Fondatore Brut '01	Ferrari	285
Trento Methius Brut Ris. '04	F.lli Dorigati	283
ALTO ADIGE		
A. A. Gewürztraminer Movado '09	Cantina Produttori Andriano	300
A. A. Gewürztraminer Kastelaz '09	Elena Walch	305
A. A. Gewürztraminer Nussbaumer '09	Cantina Tramin	328
A. A. Lagrein Abtei Ris. '07	Cantina Convento Muri-Gries	318
A. A. Lagrein Linticlarus Ris. '07	Tiefenbrunner	327
A. A. Lagrein Scuro Mirell '08	Tenuta Waldgries - Christian Plattner	330
A. A. Moscato Giallo Passito Serenade '07	Cantina di Caldaro	302
A. A. Moscato Giallo Passito Sissi Graf von Meran '08	Cantina Vini Merano	317
A. A. Pinot Bianco Dellago '09	Cantina Produttori Santa Maddalena/ Cantina Produttori Bolzano	324
A. A. Pinot Bianco Sirmian '09	Cantina Nals Margreid	318
A. A. Pinot Bianco Strahler '09	Stroblhof	325
A. A. Santa Maddalena Cl. '09	Pfannenstielhof - Johannes Pfeifer	320
A. A. Sauvignon Praesulis '09	Gumphof - Markus Prackwieser	309
A. A. Sauvignon Sel. Flora '09	Cantina Girlan	307
A. A. Sauvignon St. Valentin '09	Cantina Produttori San Michele Appiano	323
A. A. Terlano Pinot Bianco DeSilva '09	Peter Sölva & Söhne	324
A. A. Terlano Pinot Bianco Eichhorn '09	Manincor	316
A. A. Terlano Pinot Bianco Vorberg Ris. '07	Cantina Terlano	326
A. A. Valle Isarco Pinot Grigio '09	Köfererhof - Günther Kershbaumer	312
A. A. Valle Isarco Riesling Praepositus '08	Abbazia di Novacella	300

THREE GLASSES 2011

A. A. Valle Isarco Sylvaner '09	Garlider - Christian Kerchbaumer	307
A. A. Valle Isarco Sylvaner R '09	Köfererhof - Günther Kershbaumer	312
A. A. Valle Isarco Veltliner '09	Hoandlhof - Manfred Nössing	311
A. A. Valle Isarco Veltliner '09	Kuenhof - Peter Pliger	314
A. A. Valle Isarco Veltliner '09	Hannes Baumgartner Strasserhof	325
A. A. Valle Venosta Riesling '09	Falkenstein - Franz Pratzner	306
A. A. Valle Venosta Riesling '09	Tenuta Unterortl - Castel Juval	329
VENETO		
Amarone della Valpolicella Cl. Calcarole '06	Guerrieri Rizzardi	370
Amarone della Valpolicella '06	Corte Sant'Alda	362
Amarone della Valpolicella '06	Fattoria Garbole	368
Amarone della Valpolicella Campo dei Gigli '06	Tenuta Sant'Antonio	392
Amarone della Valpolicella Cl. '06	Allegrini	339
Amarone della Valpolicella Cl. '03	Cav. G. B. Bertani	344
Amarone della Valpolicella Cl. '06	Brigaldara	348
Amarone della Valpolicella Cl. Campomasua '05	Massimino Venturini	401
Amarone della Valpolicella Cl. Casa dei Bepi '05	Viviani	407
Amarone della Valpolicella Cl. Sergio Zenato '05	Zenato	408
Amarone della Valpolicella Cl. Vaio Armaron Serègo Alighieri '05	Masi	375
Amarone della Valpolicella Cl. Vign. Monte Ca' Bianca '05	Lorenzo Begali	343
Amarone della Valpolicella Cl. Vign. Monte Sant'Urbano '06	F.lli Speri	395
Bianco di Custoza Mael '09	Corte Gardoni	361
Breganze Cabernet Vign. Due Santi '08	Vigneto Due Santi	404
Cartizze Brut V. La Rivetta '09	Villa Sandi	406
Colli Berici Cabernet Vign. Pozzare '07	Piovene Porto Godi	387
Colli Euganei Cabernet Borgo delle Casette Ris. '06	Il Filò delle Vigne	365
Colli Euganei Cabernet Sauvignon Ireneo Capodilista '07	La Montecchia - Emo Capodilista	379
Custoza Sup. Amedeo '08	Cavalchina	357
Custoza Sup. Ca' del Magro '08	Monte del Frà	378
Lugana Sup. Molceo '08	Ottella	386
Montello e Colli Asolani Il Rosso dell'Abazia '07	Serafini & Vidotto	395
P. di Valdobbiadene Extra Dry Giustino B. '09	Ruggeri & C.	391
P. di Valdobbiadene Grave di Stecca Brut '09	Nino Franco	385
Recioto di Gambellara '07	La Biancara	344
Soave Cl. Calvarino '08	Leonildo Pieropan	386
Soave Cl. Campo Vulcano '09	I Campi	353
Soave Cl. Contrada Salvarenza Vecchie Vigne '08	Gini	368
Soave Cl. Monte Fiorentine '09	Ca' Rugate	352
Soave Cl. Staforte '08	Prà	388
Soave Cl. Vign. di Foscarino '08	Inama	370
Soave Sup. Il Casale '09	Agostino Vicentini	402
Valpolicella Sup. '06	Marion	374
Valpolicella Sup. Roccolo Grassi '07	Roccolo Grassi	390
FRIULI VENEZIA GIULIA		
Carso Malvasia '07	Kante	448
Carso Malvasia Non Filtrato '08	Skerk	473
COF Friulano '09	Ronchi di Manzano	466
COF Friulano V. Cinquant'Anni '08	Le Vigne di Zamò	483
COF Il Friulano '08	Ronc di Vico	464
COF Merlot Filip '06	Miani	455
COF Rosazzo Bianco Terre Alte '08	Livio Felluga	442
COF Rosso Sacrisassi '08	Le Due Terre	441
COF Sauvignon Zuc di Volpe '09	Volpe Pasini	485
COF Verduzzo Friulano '08	Davino Meroi	454
Collio Bianco '09	Edi Keber	448
Collio Bianco Broy '09	Eugenio Collavini	434
Collio Bianco Fosarin '09	Ronco dei Tassi	467
Collio Braide Alte '08	Livon	451
Collio Friulano '09	Colle Duga	435
Collio Friulano '09	Thomas Kitzmüller	449
Collio Friulano '09	Marega	453
Collio Friulano '09	Franco Toros	477
Collio Friulano '09	Villa Russiz	484
Collio Friulano Vigna del Rolat '09	Dario Raccaro	462
Collio Malvasia '09	Doro Princic	461
Collio Sauvignon Ronco delle Mele '09	Venica & Venica	480
Friuli Aquileia Pinot Bianco '09	Ca' Bolani	429
Friuli Isonzo Friulano '08	Borgo San Daniele	424
Friuli Isonzo Pinot Bianco '09	Mauro Drius	440
Friuli Isonzo Sauvignon Piere '08	Vie di Romans	481
Mario Schiopetto Bianco '07	Schiopetto	471
Pinot Grigio Gris '08	Lis Neris	451
Prulke '08	Zidarich	486
Rosso Gravner '04	Gravner	446
Vintage Tunina '08	Jermann	447

THREE GLASSES 2011

EMILIA ROMAGNA		
Albana di Romagna Passito AR Ris. '06	Fattoria Zerbina	529
Albana di Romagna Secco Codronchio '08	Fattoria Monticino Rosso	516
C. P. Vin Santo Albarola Val di Nure '00	Conte Otto Barattieri di San Pietro	500
Colli di Faenza Sangiovese Mantignano Vecchie Vigne Ris. '04	Il Pratello	520
Lambrusco di Sorbara del Fondatore '09	Chiarli 1860	506
Macchiona '06	La Stoppa	523
Reggiano Lambrusco Secco Concerto '09	Ermete Medici & Figli	515
Sangiovese di Romagna Sup. Avi Ris. '07	San Patrignano	521
Sangiovese di Romagna Sup. Il Nespoli Ris. '07	Poderi dal Nespoli	519
Sangiovese di Romagna Sup. Michelangiolo Ris. '07	Calonga	503
Sangiovese di Romagna Sup. Petrignone Ris. '07	Tre Monti	524
Sangiovese di Romagna Sup. Primo Segno '08	Villa Venti	529
Sangiovese di Romagna Sup. Pruno Ris. '07	Drei Donà Tenuta La Palazza	510
TUSCANY		
Ansonaco dell'Isola del Giglio '09	Altura	535
Bolgheri Camarcanda '07	Ca' Marcanda	549
Bolgheri Rosso Sup. Grattamacco '07	Podere Grattamacco	592
Bolgheri Sapaio Sup. '07	Podere Sapaio	641
Bolgheri Sassicaia '07	Tenuta San Guido	638
Bolgheri Sup. Castello di Bolgheri '07	Castello di Bolgheri	564
Bolgheri Sup. Ornellaia '07	Tenuta dell'Ornellaia	612
Brunello di Montalcino '05	Castello Romitorio	571
Brunello di Montalcino '05	Poggio Antico	622
Brunello di Montalcino Greppone Mazzi '05	Tenimenti Ruffino	634
Brunello di Montalcino Le Lucere Ris. '04	San Filippo	637
Brunello di Montalcino Madonna del Piano Ris. '04	Tenuta Val di Cava	657
Brunello di Montalcino Poggio all'Oro Ris. '04	Castello Banfi	561
Brunello di Montalcino Ris. '04	Biondi Santi - Tenuta Il Greppo	544
Brunello di Montalcino Ris. '04	Canalicchio di Sopra	552
Brunello di Montalcino Ris. '04	Capanna	553
Brunello di Montalcino Ris. '04	Caprili	555
Brunello di Montalcino Ris. '04	Sesti - Castello di Argiano	645
Brunello di Montalcino Tenuta Nuova '05	Casanova di Neri	560
Brunello di Montalcino Tradizione '04	Tenuta Vitanza	662
Brunello di Montalcino Ugolaia '04	Lisini	597
Camartina '07	Querciabella	629
Carmignano Ris. '07	Piaggia	617
Carmignano Villa di Capezzana '07	Tenuta di Capezzana	554
Cepparello '07	Isole e Olena	594
Chianti Cl. '08	Poggio al Sole	621
Chianti Cl. '08	Spadaio e Piecorto	647
Chianti Cl. Capraia Ris. '07	Rocca di Castagnoli	632
Chianti Cl. Castello di Brolio '07	Barone Ricasoli	541
Chianti Cl. Castello di Fonterutoli '07	Castello di Fonterutoli	566
Chianti Cl. Il Poggio Ris. '06	Castello di Monsanto	567
Chianti Cl. Montegiachi Ris. '07	Agricoltori del Chianti Geografico	534
Chianti Cl. Rancia Ris. '07	Fattoria di Felsina	586
Chianti Cl. Ris. '06	Castello di Cacchiano	565
Chianti Cl. Ris. '07	Castello di Radda	568
Chianti Cl. Ris. '07	Castello di Volpaia	570
Chianti Cl. Riserva di Famiglia '07	Famiglia Cecchi	572
Chianti Cl. Vign. S. Marcellino '07	Rocca di Montegrossi	633
Chianti I Tre Borri Ris. '07	Fattoria Corzano e Paterno	582
Colline Lucchesi Tenuta di Valgiano '07	Tenuta di Valgiano	658
Commendator Enrico '07	Fattoria Lornano	598
Cortona Syrah Migliara '07	Tenimenti Luigi D'Alessandro	649
Dofana '07	Fattoria Carpineta Fontalpino	556
Flaccianello della Pieve '07	Tenuta Fontodi	588
Fontalloro '07	Fattoria di Felsina	586
Fontissimo '06	Fattoria Le Fonti	588
Galatrona '08	Fattoria Petrolo	616
Guidalberto '08	Tenuta San Guido	638
I Sodi di San Niccolò '06	Castellare di Castellina	561
Il Pareto '07	Tenute Ambrogio e Giovanni Folonari	587
Le Pergole Torte '07	Montevertine	609
Lupicaia '07	Castello del Terriccio	563
Messorio '07	Le Macchiole	600
Montecucco Grotte Rosse '07	Salustri	635
Montecucco Sangiovese Lombrone Ris. '06	Colle Massari	578
Nobile di Montepulciano Asinone '07	Poliziano	627
Nobile di Montepulciano Ris. '06	Poderi Boscarelli	545
Nobile di Montepulciano Ris. '06	Fattoria del Cerro	574

THREE GLASSES 2011

THREE GLASSES 2011

CAMPANIA		
Centomoggia '08	Terre del Principe	814
Cupo '08	Pietracupa	810
Falerno del Massico Bianco V. Caracci '08	Villa Matilde	818
Fiano di Avellino '09	Colli di Lapio	800
Fiano di Avellino '08	Ciro Picariello	810
Fiano di Avellino Pietracalda '09	Feudi di San Gregorio	804
Fiano di Avellino Vigna della Congregazione '08	Villa Diamante	817
Greco di Tufo '09	Cantine dell'Angelo	799
Greco di Tufo '09	Pietracupa	810
Greco di Tufo Tornante '09	Vadiaperti	816
Greco di Tufo V. Cicogna '09	Benito Ferrara	804
Montevetrano '08	Montevetrano	808
Taurasi '06	Di Prisco	802
Taurasi '05	Perillo	809
Taurasi '06	Urciuolo	816
Taurasi Radici '06	Mastroberardino	807
Taurasi Radici Ris. '04	Mastroberardino	807
Taurasi Vigna Cinque Querce Ris. '05	Salvatore Molettieri	808
Terra di Lavoro '08	Galardi	805
PUGLIA		
Castel del Monte Rosso V. Pedale Ris. '07	Torrevento	856
Gioia del Colle Muro Sant'Angelo Contrada Barbatto '07	Chiaromonte	845
Gioia del Colle Primitivo 16 '07	Polvanera	852
Masseria Maime '08	Tormaresca	855
Nero '07	Conti Zecca	857
Primitivo di Manduria Es '08	Gianfranco Fino	848
Primitivo La Signora '07	Morella	850
Rasciatano Nero di Troia '08	Rasciatano	853
Salice Salentino Rosso Donna Lisa Ris. '06	Leone de Castris	848
Salice Salentino Rosso Selvarossa Ris. '07	Cantine Due Palme	846
BASILICATA		
Aglianico del Vulture Basilisco '07	Basilisco	830
Aglianico del Vulture Macarico '07	Macarico	835
Aglianico del Vulture Titolo '08	Elena Fucci	834
CALABRIA		
Cirò Rosso Duca Sanfelice Ris. '08	Librandi	867
Moscato Passito '09	Luigi Viola	870
SICILY		
Cabernet Sauvignon '08	Tasca d'Almerita	895
Cartagho Mandrarossa '08	Settesoli	894
Cometa '09	Planeta	892
Etna Rosso '07	Cottanera	882
Etna Rosso Archineri '08	Pietradolce	891
Etna Rosso Santo Spirito '08	Tenuta delle Terre Nere	895
Etna Rosso Sciarakè '08	Destro	883
Faro Palari '08	Palari	890
Harmonium '08	Firriato	887
Marsala Vergine Ris. '81	Carlo Pellegrino	891
Nero d'Avola Versace '08	Feudi del Pisciotto	886
Neromàccarj '07	Gulfi	888
Sàgana '08	Cusumano	883
Saia '08	Feudo Maccari	886
Tancredi '07	Donnafugata	884
SARDINIA		
Alghero Marchese di Villamarina '05	Tenute Sella & Mosca	920
Barrua '07	Agricola Punica	908
Cannonau di Sardegna Dule Ris. '07	Giuseppe Gabbas	914
Cannonau di Sardegna Mamuthone '08	Giuseppe Sedilesu	920
Cannonau di Sardegna Vinìola Ris. '07	Cantina Sociale Dorgali	913
Carignano del Sulcis Is Arenas Ris. '07	Sardus Pater	919
Gerione '07	Feudi della Medusa	913
Turriga '06	Argiolas	909
Vermentino di Gallura Sup. Thilibas '09	Pedres	918
Vermentino di Gallura Vigna'ngena '09	Capichera	909
Vernaccia di Oristano Ris. '99	F.lli Serra	921

THE BEST

RED OF THE YEAR
BRUNELLO DI MONTALCINO RISERVA '04 - BIONDI SANTI

WHITE OF THE YEAR
A.A. SYLVANER R '09 - KÖFERERHOF

SPARKLER OF THE YEAR
FRANCIACORTA BRUT SECOLO NOVO '05 - LE MARCHESINE

SWEET OF THE YEAR
ALBANA DI ROMAGNA PASSITO AR RIS. '06 - FATTORIA ZERBINA

WINERY OF THE YEAR

VALENTINI

BEST VALUE FOR MONEY

VERDICCHIO DEI CASTELLI DI JESI CL. SUP. '09 - PIEVALTA

OENOLOGIST OF THE YEAR

RUBEN LARENTIS

GROWER OF THE YEAR

WALTER MASSA

UP-AND-COMING WINERY

POLVANERA

AWARD FOR SUSTAINABLE VITICULTURE

SANDI SKERK

XII

THREE GLASSES 2011

UNDER €15

When we had concluded tastings this year, even we were surprised to see how many of the prize-winning wines were on sale at affordable prices. These last few economically difficult years have been an excellent deterrent for the over-ambitious price hikes we had previously witnessed. Nevertheless, 52 affordables out of 402 great wines is impressive. After consulting our calculators, we were worked it out to be 13 per cent of the total. This could well be the way to beat the crisis. Great wines that everyone can afford. Next to each wine you will find an average retail price expressed in euros, which will of course vary slightly from wine shop to wine shop. But finding 20 great wines in the €10 band was a pleasant surprise. For us as well as you.

A. A. Pinot Bianco Sirmian '09	Cantina Nals Margreid	**Alto Adige**
A. A. Pinot Bianco Strahler '09	Stroblhof	**Alto Adige**
A. A. Santa Maddalena Cl. '09	Pfannenstielhof - Johannes Pfeifer	**Alto Adige**
A. A. Valle Isarco Sylvaner '09	Garlider - Christian Kerchbaumer	**Alto Adige**
A. A. Valle Isarco Veltliner '09	Kuenhof - Peter Pliger	**Alto Adige**
A. A. Valle Isarco Veltliner '09	Hannes Baumgartner Strasserhof	**Alto Adige**
Albana di Romagna Secco Codronchio '08	Fattoria Monticino Rosso	**Emilia Romagna**
Bianco di Custoza Mael '09	Corte Gardoni	**Veneto**
Cannonau di Sardegna Dule Ris. '07	Giuseppe Gabbas	**Sardinia**
Cannonau di Sardegna Mamuthone '08	Giuseppe Sedilesu	**Sardinia**
Cartagho Mandrarossa '08	Settesoli	**Sicily**
Castel del Monte Rosso V. Pedale Ris. '07	Torrevento	**Puglia**
Chianti Cl. '08	Spadaio e Piecorto	**Tuscany**
Cirò Rosso Duca Sanfelice Ris. '08	Librandi	**Calabria**
COF Friulano '09	Ronchi di Manzano	**Friuli Venezia Giulia**
Colli di Faenza Sangiovese Mantignano Vecchie Vigne Ris. '04	Il Pratello	**Emilia Romagna**
Collio Bianco Fosarin '09	Ronco dei Tassi	**Friuli Venezia Giulia**
Collio Friulano '09	Colle Duga	**Friuli Venezia Giulia**
Collio Friulano '09	Thomas Kitzmüller	**Friuli Venezia Giulia**
Collio Friulano '09	Marega	**Friuli Venezia Giulia**
Custoza Sup. Amedeo '08	Cavalchina	**Veneto**
Custoza Sup. Ca' del Magro '08	Monte del Frà	**Veneto**
Dogliani Vecchie V. Pirochetta '08	Cascina Corte	**Piedmont**
Erbaluce di Caluso La Rustia '09	Orsolani	**Piedmont**
Fiano di Avellino '08	Ciro Picariello	**Campania**
Frascati Sup. Epos '09	Poggio Le Volpi	**Lazio**
Friuli Aquileia Pinot Bianco '09	Ca' Bolani	**Friuli Venezia Giulia**
Friuli Isonzo Pinot Bianco '09	Mauro Drius	**Friuli Venezia Giulia**
Gioia del Colle Primitivo 16 '07	Polvanera	**Puglia**
Grechetto Poggio della Costa '09	Sergio Mottura	**Lazio**
Greco di Tufo '09	Cantine dell'Angelo	**Campania**
Greco di Tufo '09	Pietracupa	**Campania**
Greco di Tufo Tornante '09	Vadiaperti	**Campania**
Lambrusco di Sorbara del Fondatore '09	Chiarli 1860	**Emilia Romagna**
Montepulciano d'Abruzzo '08	Villa Medoro	**Abruzzo**
Montepulciano d'Abruzzo Vignafranca '07	F.lli Barba	**Abruzzo**
Moscato d'Asti Tenuta del Fant '09	Tenuta Il Falchetto	**Piedmont**
Nebbiolo d'Alba V. Colla '07	Fabrizio Battaglino	**Piedmont**
Offida Pecorino Ciprea '09	San Savino - Poderi Capecci	**Marche**
Piemonte Moscato d'Autunno '09	Paolo Saracco	**Piedmont**
Reggiano Lambrusco Secco Concerto '09	Ermete Medici & Figli	**Emilia Romagna**
Riviera Ligure di Ponente Pigato Cycnus '09	Poggio dei Gorleri	**Liguria**
Sangiovese di Romagna Sup. Primo Segno '08	Villa Venti	**Emilia Romagna**
Soave Cl. Campo Vulcano '09	I Campi	**Veneto**
Soave Cl. Monte Fiorentine '09	Ca' Rugate	**Veneto**
Soave Sup. Il Casale '09	Agostino Vicentini	**Veneto**
Torgiano Bianco Torre di Giano V. il Pino Ris. '08	Lungarotti	**Umbria**
Verdicchio dei Castelli di Jesi Cl. Salmariano Ris. '07	Marotti Campi	**Marche**
Verdicchio dei Castelli di Jesi Cl. Sup. Pallio di S. Floriano '09	Monte Schiavo	**Marche**
Verdicchio dei Castelli di Jesi Cl. Sup. Pievalta '09	Pievalta	**Marche**
Verdicchio di Matelica Meridia '07	Belisario	**Marche**
Vermentino di Gallura Sup. Thilibas '09	Pedres	**Sardinia**

XIII

THE EDITOR'S "PLUS" WINES

This year, as I did last time, I want to point out to readers a number of wines – just 32 of them – that particularly impressed me. All of them were awarded Three Glasses by the entire tasting panel but these were wines that appealed to me for reasons of my own. Some are major classics. Four were Wine of the Year award-winners in various categories. Some are very traditional in style. Others are modern. But all are representative of their territories and, crucially, impeccably made, at least in my opinion. There are some seriously expensive bottles and others that are very affordable. One, the Montepulciano d'Abruzzo from Villa Medoro, costs just over six euros in the stores. It all goes to show that you don't need to spend a fortune to drink superb wine. Very much a sign of the times.

Daniele Cernilli

Albana di Romagna Passito AR Ris. '06	Zerbina	**Emilia Romagna**
A. A. Gewürztraminer Kastelaz '09	Elena Walch	**Alto Adige**
A. A. Valle Isarco Sylvaner R '09	Köfererhof - Günther Kershbaumer	**Alto Adige**
Amarone della Valpolicella Vajo Armaron '05	Serego Alighieri - Masi	**Veneto**
Barolo La Rocche del Falletto Ris. '04	B. Giacosa	**Piedmont**
Barolo Monfortino Ris. '02	G. Conterno	**Piedmont**
Barolo '06	B. Mascarello	**Piedmont**
Bolgheri Sassicaia '07	San Guido	**Tuscany**
Brunello di Montalcino Ris. '04	Biondi Santi	**Tuscany**
Camartina '07	Querciabella	**Tuscany**
Cervaro della Sala '08	Castello della Sala	**Umbria**
Chianti Classico Rancia Ris. '07	Felsina	**Tuscany**
COF Sauvignon Zuc di Volpe '09	Volpe Pasini	**Friuli Venezia Giulia**
Cupo '08	Pietracupa	**Campania**
Franciacorta Brut Secolo Novo '05	Le Marchesine	**Lombardy**
Gattinara Osso San Grato '06	Antoniolo	**Piedmont**
I Sodi di San Nicolò '06	Castellare	**Tuscany**
Le Pergole Torte '07	Montevertine	**Tuscany**
Langhe Costa Russi '07	Gaja	**Piedmont**
Marsala Vergine Ris. '81	Pellegrino	**Sicily**
Montepulciano d'Abruzzo '08	Villa Medoro	**Abruzzo**
Montepulciano d'Abruzzo '06	Valentini	**Abruzzo**
Montepulciano d'Abruzzo San Calisto '07	Valle Reale	**Abruzzo**
Montiano '08	Falesco	**Lazio**
Primitivo di Manduria Es '08	Fino	**Puglia**
Rosso Gravner '04	Gravner	**Friuli Venezia Giulia**
Rosso Piceno Sup. Roggio del Filare '07	Velenosi	**Marche**
Sangiovese di Romagna Sup. Avi '06	San Patrignano	**Emilia Romagna**
Taurasi Radici Ris. '04	Mastroberardino	**Campania**
Trebbiano d'Abruzzo Castello di Semivicoli '08	Masciarelli	**Abruzzo**
Trento Giulio Ferrari Riserva del Fondatore Brut '01	Ferrari	**Trentino**
Veneroso '07	Tenuta di Ghizzano	**Tuscany**

THREE GREEN GLASSES

Our special mentions for Three Glass wines from wineries that show particular attention for the environment has been a great success. There has been much interest in our Three Green Glasses and we see them as a litmus test indicating a shift in the attitude of many producers and consumers to the relationship of agriculture and the environment. This year, the survey we sent to wineries contained an extra page with questions formulated after talks with growers from the Italian Federation of Independent Viticulturists who apply sustainable viticulture methods in order to throw light on these issues. When we totted up, an impressive 83 of our 2011 Three Glass winners, eight more than last time and more than 20 per cent of the total, were green. This classification includes certified organic and biodynamic growers as well as those who comply with the following criteria:

1. Avoidance of systemic and high chemical-impact products in the vineyard.
2. Processing only of grapes sourced from estate-owned, or leased, or directly controlled, vineyards.
3. Guaranteed control by winery of all stages of production.
4. Rejection of winemaking practices that alter the characteristics of the vintage or variety.
5. Respect for the environment through elimination of most invasive practices such as the use of difficult-to-biodegrade materials, irrigation or the construction of territory-inappropriate cellars.
6. The use of traditional training systems and prevalently local varieties, vinified in full respect of their most typical characteristics.
7. Rejection of mechanized pruning and harvesting systems.
8. Rejection of stabilizing substances apart from sulphur dioxide.
9. Utilization of renewable energy sources.
10. Application of organic control of vine parasites.

A. A. Lagrein Scuro Mirell '08	Tenuta Waldgries - Christian Plattner	**Alto Adige**
A. A. Terlano Pinot Bianco Eichhorn '09	Manincor	**Alto Adige**
A. A. Valle Isarco Sylvaner '09	Garlider - Christian Kerchbaumer	**Alto Adige**
A. A. Valle Isarco Veltliner '09	Kuenhof - Peter Pliger	**Alto Adige**
A. A. Valle Venosta Riesling '09	Falkenstein - Franz Pratzner	**Alto Adige**
Aglianico del Vulture Macarico '07	Macarico	**Basilicata**
Aglianico del Vulture Titolo '08	Elena Fucci	**Basilicata**
Amarone della Valpolicella '06	Corte Sant'Alda	**Veneto**
Ansonaco dell'Isola del Giglio '09	Altura	**Tuscany**
Barbaresco Sorì Paitin '07	Paitin	**Piedmont**
Barbera d'Asti Sup. Nizza Acsé '07	Scrimaglio	**Piedmont**
Barbera del M.to Sup. Bricco Battista '07	Giulio Accornero e Figli	**Piedmont**
Barbera del M.to Sup. Pico Gonzaga '07	Castello di Uviglie	**Piedmont**
Barolo Brunate-Le Coste '06	Giuseppe Rinaldi	**Piedmont**
Barolo Bussia Ris. '01	Pianpolvere Soprano	**Piedmont**
Barolo Cerretta '06	Giovanni Rosso	**Piedmont**
Barolo Vignolo Ris. '04	F.lli Cavallotto – Tenuta Bricco Boschis	**Piedmont**
Bolgheri Rosso Sup. Grattamacco '07	Podere Grattamacco	**Tuscany**
Brunello di Montalcino '05	Poggio Antico	**Tuscany**
Brunello di Montalcino Ris. '04	Biondi Santi - Tenuta Il Greppo	**Tuscany**

THREE GREEN GLASSES

Camartina '07	Querciabella	**Tuscany**
Cannonau di Sardegna Mamuthone '08	Giuseppe Sedilesu	**Sardinia**
Carso Malvasia '07	Kante	**Friuli Venezia Giulia**
Carso Malvasia Non Filtrato '08	Skerk	**Friuli Venezia Giulia**
Castel del Monte Rosso V. Pedale Ris. '07	Torrevento	**Puglia**
Chianti Cl. Ris. '07	Castello di Volpaia	**Tuscany**
COF Friulano V. Cinquant'Anni '08	Le Vigne di Zamò	**Friuli Venezia Giulia**
COF Merlot Filip '06	Miani	**Friuli Venezia Giulia**
COF Rosso Sacrisassi '08	Le Due Terre	**Friuli Venezia Giulia**
COF Sauvignon Zuc di Volpe '09	Volpe Pasini	**Friuli Venezia Giulia**
Colli di Faenza Sangiovese Mantignano Vecchie Vigne Ris. '04	Il Pratello	**Emilia Romagna**
Colli Tortonesi Timorasso Sterpi '08	Vigneti Massa	**Piedmont**
Colline Lucchesi Tenuta di Valgiano '07	Tenuta di Valgiano	**Tuscany**
Collio Bianco '09	Edi Keber	**Friuli Venezia Giulia**
Collio Bianco Broy '09	Eugenio Collavini	**Friuli Venezia Giulia**
Collio Friulano '09	Thomas Kitzmüller	**Friuli Venezia Giulia**
Collio Friulano '09	Franco Toros	**Friuli Venezia Giulia**
Dogliani Vecchie V. Pirochetta '08	Cascina Corte	**Piedmont**
Etna Rosso Santo Spirito '08	Tenuta delle Terre Nere	**Sicily**
Fiano di Avellino Pietracalda '09	Feudi di San Gregorio	**Campania**
Fiano di Avellino Vigna della Congregazione '08	Villa Diamante	**Campania**
Flaccianello della Pieve '07	Tenuta Fontodi	**Tuscany**
Gioia del Colle Muro Sant'Angelo Contrada Barbatto '07	Chiaromonte	**Puglia**
Gioia del Colle Primitivo 16 '07	Polvanera	**Puglia**
Granato '07	Foradori	**Trentino**
Grechetto Poggio della Costa '09	Sergio Mottura	**Lazio**
Harmonium '08	Firriato	**Sicily**
Kurni '08	Oasi degli Angeli	**Marche**
Langhe Arborina '08	Elio Altare - Cascina Nuova	**Piedmont**
M.to Rosso La Mandorla '07	Luigi Spertino	**Piedmont**
Macchiona '06	La Stoppa	**Emilia Romagna**
Masseria Maime '08	Tormaresca	**Puglia**
Molise Don Luigi Ris. '08	Di Majo Norante	**Molise**
Montecucco Grotte Rosse '07	Salustri	**Tuscany**
Montecucco Sangiovese Lombrone Ris. '06	Colle Massari	**Tuscany**
Montello e Colli Asolani Il Rosso dell'Abazia '07	Serafini & Vidotto	**Veneto**
Montepulciano d'Abruzzo '06	Valentini	**Abruzzo**
Montepulciano d'Abruzzo Cerasuolo '09	Valentini	**Abruzzo**
Montepulciano d'Abruzzo Cocciapazza '07	Torre dei Beati	**Abruzzo**
Moscato Passito '09	Luigi Viola	**Calabria**
Nero d'Avola Versace '08	Feudi del Pisciotto	**Sicily**
Neromàccarj '07	Gulfi	**Sicily**
Offida Pecorino Ciprea '09	San Savino - Poderi Capecci	**Marche**
Prulke '08	Zidarich	**Friuli Venezia Giulia**
Rasciatano Nero di Troia '08	Rasciatano	**Puglia**
Recioto di Gambellara '07	La Biancara	**Veneto**
Riviera Ligure di Ponente Vermentino '09	Maria Donata Bianchi	**Liguria**
Roero Mompissano Ris. '07	Cascina Ca' Rossa	**Piedmont**
Roero Printi Ris. '07	Monchiero Carbone	**Piedmont**
Roero Ròche d'Ampsèj Ris. '06	Matteo Correggia	**Piedmont**
Rosso di Montalcino '07	Poggio di Sotto	**Tuscany**
Rosso Gravner '04	Gravner	**Friuli Venezia Giulia**
Saia '08	Feudo Maccari	**Sicily**
Sangiovese di Romagna Sup. Avi Ris. '07	San Patrignano	**Emilia Romagna**
Sangiovese di Romagna Sup. Primo Segno '08	Villa Venti	**Emilia Romagna**
Soave Cl. Vign. di Foscarino '08	Inama	**Veneto**
Terra di Lavoro '08	Galardi	**Campania**
Trebbiano d'Abruzzo '08	Valentini	**Abruzzo**
Valle d'Aosta Torrette Sup. V. de Torrette '06	Di Barrò	**Valle d'Aosta**
Valturio '08	Valturio	**Marche**
Veneroso '07	Tenuta di Ghizzano	**Tuscany**
Verdicchio dei Castelli di Jesi Cl. Sup. Pievalta '09	Pievalta	**Marche**
Verdicchio dei Castelli di Jesi Cl. Vigna Novali Ris. '07	Terre Cortesi Moncaro	**Marche**

STARS

A total of 137 wineries have won at least ten Three Glass awards in the 24 editions of Italian Wines. They are the elite, the aristocracy, in short the very top flight of Italian wine. In first place, it's that man again, Angelo Gaja, with 47 awards and a stuning four Stars. Ca' del Bosco and La Spinetta are in second place with 35 prizes and Three Stars each, followed by the rest. This year, there are 17 new entries: Cataldi Madonna in Abruzzo, Antoniolo and Cisa Asinari dei Marchesi di Gresy in Piedmont, Monsupello and Monte Rossa in Lombardy, Ca' Rugate, Gini, Masi and Viviani in Veneto, Kuenhof in Alto Adige, Livon, Raccaro and Ronco dei Tassi in Friuli, Fattoria di Petrolo in Tuscany, Umani Ronchi in Marche, Villa Matilde in Campania and Firriato in Sicily.

★★★★

47

Gaja (Piedmont)

★★★

35

Ca' del Bosco (Lombardy)
La Spinetta (Piedmont)

★★

29

Elio Altare - Cascina Nuova (Piedmont)

26

Allegrini (Veneto)
Castello di Fonterutoli (Tuscany)
Fattoria di Felsina (Tuscany)
Valentini (Abruzzo)

23

Castello di Ama (Tuscany)

22

Marchesi Antinori (Tuscany)
Giacomo Conterno (Piedmont)
Masciarelli (Abruzzo)
Poliziano (Tuscany)
Tenuta San Guido (Tuscany)
Cantina Produttori San Michele Appiano (Trentino Alto Adige)
Villa Russiz (Friuli Venezia Giulia)

21

Bellavista (Lombardy)
Castello della Sala (Umbria)
Domenico Clerico (Piedmont)
Ferrari (Trentino Alto Adige)
Feudi di San Gregorio (Campania)
Gravner (Friuli Venezia Giulia)
Jermann (Friuli Venezia Giulia)
Planeta (Sicily)

20

Girolamo Dorigo (Friuli Venezia Giulia)
Tasca d'Almerita (Sicily)
Cantina Tramin (Trentino Alto Adige)
Vie di Romans (Friuli Venezia Giulia)

★

19

Livio Felluga (Friuli Venezia Giulia)
Tenuta dell'Ornellaia (Tuscany)

18

Cascina La Barbatella (Piedmont)
Castello Banfi (Tuscany)
Tenuta Fontodi (Tuscany)
Bruno Giacosa (Piedmont)
Isole e Olena (Tuscany)
Leonildo Pieropan (Veneto)
Tenimenti Ruffino (Tuscany)
Schiopetto (Friuli Venezia Giulia)

17

Argiolas (Sardinia)
Querciabella (Tuscany)
Paolo Scavino (Piedmont)

16

Barone Ricasoli (Tuscany)
Arnaldo Caprai (Umbria)
Castello del Terriccio (Tuscany)
Matteo Correggia (Piedmont)
Romano Dal Forno (Veneto)
Elio Grasso (Piedmont)
Miani (Friuli Venezia Giulia)
Nino Negri (Lombardy)
Cantina Produttori Santa Maddalena/
Cantina Produttori Bolzano (Trentino Alto Adige)

15

Michele Chiarlo (Piedmont)
Cantina Produttori Colterenzio (Trentino Alto Adige)
Elena Walch (Trentino Alto Adige)
Mastroberardino (Campania)
Montevetrano (Campania)
Venica & Venica (Friuli Venezia Giulia)
Le Vigne di Zamò (Friuli Venezia Giulia)

STARS

★

14

Roberto Anselmi (Veneto)
Bricco Rocche - Bricco Asili (Piedmont)
Ca' Viola (Piedmont)
Cantina di Caldaro (Trentino Alto Adige)
Aldo Conterno (Piedmont)
Conterno Fantino (Piedmont)
Falesco (Umbria)
Les Crêtes (Valle d'Aosta)
Giuseppe Quintarelli (Veneto)
Tenuta San Leonardo (Trentino Alto Adige)
Luciano Sandrone (Piedmont)
Tenute Sella & Mosca (Sardinia)
Serafini & Vidotto (Veneto)
Uberti (Lombardy)
Roberto Voerzio (Piedmont)
Fattoria Zerbina (Emilia Romagna)

13

Avignonesi (Tuscany)
Casanova di Neri (Tuscany)
Gioacchino Garofoli (Marche)
Maculan (Veneto)
Montevertine (Tuscany)
Ronco del Gelso (Friuli Venezia Giulia)
Cantina Terlano (Trentino Alto Adige)
Franco Toros (Friuli Venezia Giulia)
Tua Rita (Tuscany)
Vietti (Piedmont)

12

Abbazia di Novacella (Trentino Alto Adige)
Castellare di Castellina (Tuscany)
Castello dei Rampolla (Tuscany)
Cusumano (Sicily)
Foradori (Trentino Alto Adige)
Edi Keber (Friuli Venezia Giulia)
Lis Neris (Friuli Venezia Giulia)
Le Macchiole (Tuscany)
Cantina Convento Muri-Gries (Trentino Alto Adige)
Palari (Sicily)
Vigna Rionda - Massolino (Piedmont)

★

11

Produttori del Barbaresco (Piedmont)
Brancaia (Tuscany)
Luigi Cataldi Madonna (Abruzzo)
Còlpetrone (Umbria)
Donnafugata (Sicily)
Tenute Ambrogio e Giovanni Folonari (Tuscany)
La Massa (Tuscany)
Fiorenzo Nada (Piedmont)
Pecchenino (Piedmont)
Prunotto (Piedmont)
Fattoria Le Pupille (Tuscany)
Albino Rocca (Piedmont)
Bruno Rocca (Piedmont)
Podere Rocche dei Manzoni (Piedmont)
San Patrignano (Emilia Romagna)
Cantina di Santadi (Sardinia)
Sottimano (Piedmont)
Volpe Pasini (Friuli Venezia Giulia)

10

Gianfranco Alessandria (Piedmont)
Antoniolo (Piedmont)
Benanti (Sicily)
Bucci (Marche)
Ca' Rugate (Veneto)
Tenute Cisa Asinari dei Marchesi di Grésy (Piedmont)
Tenuta Col d'Orcia (Tuscany)
Poderi Luigi Einaudi (Piedmont)
Firriato (Sicily)
Marchesi de' Frescobaldi (Tuscany)
Gini (Veneto)
Tenuta J. Hofstätter (Trentino Alto Adige)
Kuenhof - Peter Pliger (Trentino Alto Adige)
Livon (Friuli Venezia Giulia)
Malvirà (Piedmont)
Franco M. Martinetti (Piedmont)
Masi (Veneto)
Monsupello (Lombardy)
Monte Rossa (Lombardy)
Fattoria Petrolo (Tuscany)
Dario Raccaro (Friuli Venezia Giulia)
Ronco dei Tassi (Friuli Venezia Giulia)
Umani Ronchi (Marche)
Villa Matilde (Campania)
Viviani (Veneto)

HOW TO USE THE GUIDE

WINERY INFORMATION

ANNUAL PRODUCTION
HECTARES UNDER VINE
VITICULTURE METHOD
METHODS INDICATED: CONVENTIONAL, CERTIFIED ORGANIC, CERTIFIED BIODYNAMIC OR ORGANIC (IF NOT CERTIFIED)

SYMBOLS

○ WHITE WINE
⊙ ROSÉ
● RED WINE

RATINGS

🍷 MODERATELY GOOD TO GOOD WINES IN THEIR RESPECTIVE CATEGORIES
🍷🍷 VERY GOOD TO EXCELLENT WINES IN THEIR RESPECTIVE CATEGORIES
🍷🍷 VERY GOOD TO EXCELLENT WINES THAT WENT FORWARD TO THE FINAL TASTINGS
🍷🍷🍷 EXCELLENT WINES IN THEIR RESPECTIVE CATEGORIES
🍷🍷🍷+ AWARD-WINNING WINES SELECTED BY THE EDITOR

WINES RATED IN PREVIOUS EDITIONS OF THE GUIDE ARE INDICATED BY WHITE GLASSES (🍸, 🍸🍸, 🍸🍸🍸), PROVIDED THEY ARE STILL DRINKING AT THE LEVEL FOR WHICH THE ORIGINAL AWARD WAS MADE.

STAR ★

INDICATES WINERIES THAT HAVE WON TEN THREE GLASS AWARDS FOR EACH STAR

PRICE RANGES

1 up to €3.50
2 from €3.51 to €5.00
3 from €5.01 to €7.50
4 from €7.51 to €13.00
5 from €13.01 to €20.00
6 from €20.01 to €30.00
7 from €30.01 to €40.00
8 more than €40.00

ASTERISK *

INDICATES ESPECIALLY GOOD VALUE

NOTE

PRICES INDICATED REFER TO AVERAGE PRICES IN WINE STORES.
PRICE RANGES INDICATED FOR WINES WITH WHITE GLASSES (RATED IN PREVIOUS EDITIONS OF THE GUIDE) TAKE INTO ACCOUNT APPRECIATION OVER TIME WHERE APPROPRIATE.

ABBREVIATIONS

A. A.	Alto Adige
C.	Colli
Cl.	Classic
C.S.	Cantina Sociale (co-operative winery)
Cant.	Cellar
CEV	Colli Etruschi Viterbesi
Cast.	Castello (castle)
COF	Colli Orientali del Friuli
Cons.	Consorzio (consortium)
Coop.Agr.	Cooperativa Agricola (farming co-operative)
C. B.	Colli Bolognesi
C. P.	Colli Piacentini
Et.	Etichetta (label)
M.	Metodo
M.to	Monferrato
OP	Oltrepò Pavese
P.R.	Peduncolo Rosso (red bunchstem)
P.	Prosecco
Rif. Agr.	Riforma Agraria (agrarian reform)
Ris.	Riserva
Sel.	Selezione
Sup.	Superiore
TdF	Terre di Franciacorta
V.	Vigna (vineyard)
Vign.	Vigneto (vineyard)
V. T.	Vendemmia Tardiva (late harvest)

35

VALLE D'AOSTA

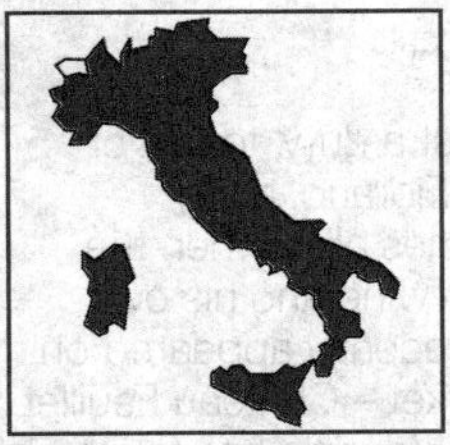

Geography and a significant tourism sector combine in Valle d'Aosta to put agriculture in the back seat. Wine, however, has considerable prestige, particularly when it comes together with tourism in local restaurants. That is why, every year, attention swings onto this region and its remarkable talent for winemaking. Valle d'Aosta wine producers have been reminding us of their existence for the last ten years or so now and how generations before them clawed back from the mountains a few square yards of land to cultivate, and to maintain, at enormous sacrifice, the dry stone walls that support these meagre, high-altitude vine-clad terraces. They remind us how difficult the daily life of a grower is in such a hostile environment, and how having the courage to set up your own winery is no small thing. The properties themselves are mostly small, some with tiny cellars under the stairs, risking money that forces the family into finding other, more substantial sources of income. Despite all this, regional wine is here on form again this year. Last year's success looked like a one-off yet here we are again praising the magnificent six of the Valle d'Aosta. The region's innate ability to make quality white wines has outshone itself. Chardonnay and Pinot Gris have already shown how well they do in Valle d'Aosta. Charrère of Les Crêtes, Martin of Lo Triolet and Anselmet wines seem unstoppable. Now for the first time Three Glasses have gone to the region's emblematic indigenous white grape, petite arvine. The Grosjean family have achieved this with their Valle d'Aosta Petite Arvine Vigne Rovettaz '09. Three Glasses also went to Crotta di Vegneron, a co-operative that has been a driving force for viticulture in Chambave and Nus. This year, the prize went to its most representative wine: Valle d'Aosta Chambave Moscato Passito Prieuré '08. Among so many prize-winning whites, the best surprise in the absence of the Fumin, which suffered from the difficult 2008 vintage, was that the highest award went to the region's most popular red grapes, petit rouge and vien de Nus. Above all, the award goes to the historic Torrette vineyard and the family that has kept it alive, in Di Barrò's Valle d'Aosta Torrette Supérieur Vigne de Torrette '06. Broadening this discussion to non-Three Glass winners, we report new producers already taking up the baton – the Vallets from Feudo di San Maurizio, the Fioranos from Château Feuillet, the Ottins, the Quinsons and many others – and the return of co-operative wineries, which have helped shape the history of wine in this region. Caves Coopératives de Donnas at Donnas and, particularly, the Cave Coopérative de l'Enfer and the legendary Enfer d'Arvier.

Anselmet

FRAZ. LA CRÊTE, 194
11018 VILLENEUVE [AO]
TEL. 3484127121
www.maisonanselmet.vievini.it

CELLAR SALES
PRE-BOOKED VISITS

ANNUAL PRODUCTION 35,000 bottles
HECTARES UNDER VINE 5
VITICULTURE METHOD Conventional

The Anselmet winery can be found in the historic area of Torrette, between Saint Pierre and Villeneuve. Giorgio is at the helm, ably supported by dad, the legendary Renato. Now firmly established as a leading Valle d'Aosta estate, Anselmet markets a wide range of wines that embody their territory of origin and Valle d'Aosta tradition. The opening of the new cellar has enabled their potential to be expressed to the full.

No one actually doubted it, but Anselmet did not disappoint expectations. Chardonnay Elevé en Fût de Chêne '09 can flaunt Three Glasses again this year. It is a refined, elegant wine, astonishing in its aromas which show flowery and fruity notes balanced by scents of sweet spices to make it one of the best Chardonnays in the country. We would need much more space to describe all Anselmet's top-quality wines so we will just mention the most interesting: the Pinot Gris '09, which has great structure and personality, the intense, meaty Merlot Le Pèllerin '08, the complex Le Prisonnier, from petit rouge, cornalin and fumin grapes, and the Syrah Henri '08.

○ Valle d'Aosta Chardonnay Élevé en Fût de Chêne '09	▼▼▼	6
● Valle d'Aosta Merlot Le Pèllerin '08	▼▼	5
○ Valle d'Aosta Pinot Gris '09	▼▼	5
● Valle d'Aosta Syrah Henri '08	▼▼	6
● Le Prisonnier	▼▼	6
○ Stéphanie	▼▼	4
○ Valle d'Aosta Petite Arvine '09	▼▼	5
● Valle d'Aosta Torrette Sup.	▼▼	6
○ Valle d'Aosta Chambave Muscat '09	▼	5
● Valle d'Aosta Cornalin Boblan '09	▼	6
○ Valle d'Aosta Müller Thurgau '09	▼	4
● Valle d'Aosta Torrette '09	▼	5
○ Valle d'Aosta Chardonnay Élevé en Fût de Chêne '08	▽▽▽	6
○ Valle d'Aosta Chardonnay Élevé en Fût de Chêne '07	▽▽▽	6
○ Valle d'Aosta Chardonnay Élevé en Fût de Chêne '06	▽▽▽	6

Le Château Feuillet

LOC. CHÂTEAU FEUILLET
11010 SAINT-PIERRE [AO]
TEL. 0165903905
www.chateaufeuillet.vievini.it

ROOMS AND FOOD

ANNUAL PRODUCTION 25,000 bottles
HECTARES UNDER VINE 5
VITICULTURE METHOD Organic

It's a pleasure, not just a duty, to talk or write about Maurizio Fiorano, a shy professional who comes alive when the conversation shifts to wine and his own bottles. Having only recently appeared on the Valle d'Aosta market – Château Feuillet was set up in 1997 – Maurizio has taken his wines up to a standard of excellence. Château Feuillet now turns out wines of impeccable quality, gracing the region's wine scene with impressive consistency.

The Petite Arvine '09 is again splendid this year. Its bright straw yellow heralds intense, refined fragrances of apricots followed by citrus, a rich, powerful palate braced by supporting acidity and a salty note which enriches the subtly long finish. Fumin '08 is an intense, brilliant ruby red with a good nose of red fruits and light vegetality, full tannins, good length and caressing fullness. The Torrette '09 is interesting. Bright ruby red with youthful purple highlights introduce intense aromas with a lovely earthy, smoky note on a background of fruit. Supple, not too heavy structure makes the wine very drinkable. The Syrah and the Moscato, both from '09, are agreeable.

● Valle d'Aosta Fumin '08	▼▼	5
○ Valle d'Aosta Petite Arvine '09	▼▼	4
● Valle d'Aosta Torrette '09	▼▼	4
● Valle d'Aosta Torrette Sup. '08	▼▼	4
○ Valle d'Aosta Chardonnay '09	▼	4
○ Valle d'Aosta Jaline	▼	6
○ Valle d'Aosta Moscato Bianco '09	▼	4
● Valle d'Aosta Syrah '09	▼	4
○ Valle d'Aosta Chardonnay '08	▽▽	4*
○ Valle d'Aosta Chardonnay '07	▽▽	4
● Valle d'Aosta Fumin '06	▽▽	4
● Valle d'Aosta Fumin '05	▽▽	4*
○ Valle d'Aosta Petite Arvine '08	▽▽	4*
● Valle d'Aosta Torrette '06	▽▽	4*
● Valle d'Aosta Torrette Sup. '06	▽▽	4

Coopérative de l'Enfer

VIA CORRADO GEX, 65
11011 ARVIER [AO]
TEL. 016599238
www.coenfer.it

CELLAR SALES
PRE-BOOKED VISITS

ANNUAL PRODUCTION 50,000 bottles
HECTARES UNDER VINE N.A.
VITICULTURE METHOD Conventional

Enfer d'Arvier was one of the first wines to be awarded Valle d'Aosta DOC status, in 1972. The vineyards from which it comes lie in the municipality of Arvier, where the valley forms a natural amphitheatre allowing the vines to grow in the best conditions. The aspect, permanently facing the sun, has earned the site the name "inferno". In 1978, the Coopérative de l'Enfer, or Co-Enfer, was set up to manage all winemaking activities, including bottling and marketing.

The Enfer d'Arvier Bio '08 Etichetta Verde is excellent, stylish and complex, with delicious vegetal and spicy fragrances. Pinot Grigio Soleil Couchant '09 is equally good, with delicate fruity hints reminiscent of pears. Co-Enfer takes part in the spumante marketing programme with the Caves Cooperatives of Morgex and Crotta di Vegneron: the range presented was good, with the fruity, well-balanced Brut Caronte, from petit rouge grapes, outstanding, presenting an interesting shade of pink and remarkably fresh-tasting. The 4478, which is the height in metres of Monte Cervino, aka the Matterhorn, is worth tasting, with nice berry aromas suggesting forest floor.

● Valle d'Aosta Enfer d'Arvier Bio Et. Verde '08	▼▼	4
⊙ Caronte Brut M. Cl.	▼▼	5
○ Valle d'Aosta Pinot Gris Soleil Couchant '09	▼▼	3
⊙ 4478	▼	5
⊙ Ancestrale Sec.	▼	4
● Valle d'Aosta Enfer d'Arvier '09	▼	4
● Valle d'Aosta Enfer d'Arvier Sup. Clos de L'Enfer '08	▼	5
● Valle d'Aosta Mayolet Vins de Seigneurs '09	▼	4
● Valle d'Aosta Enfer d'Arvier '06	▽▽	4
● Valle d'Aosta Enfer d'Arvier '05	▽▽	4*
● Valle d'Aosta Enfer d'Arvier '04	▽▽	4*
● Valle d'Aosta Enfer d'Arvier '03	▽▽	5
● Valle d'Aosta Enfer d'Arvier Clos de Enfer '05	▽▽	5
● Valle d'Aosta Mayolet Vins de Seigneurs '07	▽▽	4
● Valle d'Aosta Mayolet Vins de Seigneurs '06	▽▽	4*

La Crotta di Vegneron

P.ZZA RONCAS, 2
11023 CHAMBAVE [AO]
TEL. 016646670
www.lacrotta.it

CELLAR SALES
PRE-BOOKED VISITS
FOOD

ANNUAL PRODUCTION 300,000 bottles
HECTARES UNDER VINE 39
VITICULTURE METHOD Conventional

One of the first villages in Valle d'Aosta recognized by the dukes of Savoy was Chambave, which can take credit for one of the most fascinating wines of the entire Valle d'Aosta, the Moscato subsequently known as Chambave. Everyone has vines in this area, and when the co-operative was started in 1980, many contributed to the oenological fortunes of the area straight away. If moscato bianco is the overall driving force behind production, the selection of wines on the market is broad and varied, thanks to the work of the dynamic oenologist Andrea Costa and chairman Elio Comaz.

Andrea Costa impressed us last year with the ever-typical Fumin Esprit Follet, intense in colour and aroma. This year, he charmed us with Moscato Passito Prieuré '08, which easily won our coveted Three Glasses for its rare elegance and wonderful nut aromas followed by a perfectly balanced palate. Some years ago, the cellar put its money on the red Chambave. This year's results with Quatre Vignobles '08 have amply repaid anyone who put their faith in it. The Cuvée Particulière del Nus Malvoisie '08 and the ever-impressive Muscat Secco '09 did well. Don't miss Nus Supérieur Crème '08.

○ Valle d'Aosta Chambave Moscato Passito Prieuré '08	▼▼▼	6
● Valle d'Aosta Chambave Sup. Quatre Vignobles '08	▼▼	4*
● Valle d'Aosta Fumin Esprit Follet '08	▼▼	5
○ Valle d'Aosta Chambave Muscat '09	▼▼	4*
○ Valle d'Aosta Nus Malvoisie Cuvée Particulière '08	▼▼	5
● Valle d'Aosta Nus Sup. Crème '08	▼▼	4
○ Valle d'Aosta Chambave Muscat Attente '06	▼	6
● Valle d'Aosta Nus '09	▼	4
○ Valle d'Aosta Nus Malvoisie '09	▼	4
● Valle d'Aosta Pinot Noir '09	▼	4
● Valle d'Aosta Fumin Esprit Follet '07	▽▽▽	5*
○ Valle d'Aosta Chambave Moscato Passito Prieuré '07	▽▽	6
● Valle d'Aosta Chambave Sup. Quatre Vignobles '07	▽▽	4*

Di Barrò

LOC. CHÂTEAU FEUILLET, 8
11010 SAINT-PIERRE [AO]
TEL. 0165903671
www.vievini.it

CELLAR SALES
PRE-BOOKED VISITS

ANNUAL PRODUCTION 17,000 bottles
HECTARES UNDER VINE 2
VITICULTURE METHOD Organic

Ever since they began growing grapes, winery owner Elvira Rini and her husband Andrea Barmaz chose to pursue quality. Visitors are fascinated by the way they work even more than by the great wines. Elvira and Andrea are charming and always willing to help. Each wine is discussed and explained, with insight and respect. The winery lies in the heart of the Torrette area and Di Barrò was one of the first to carry this denomination. Elvira and Andrea's wines are always full of character and personality, and reflect careful farming that respects the environment.

Di Barrò has gone overboard with reds this year. Torrette Supérieur Vigne de Torrette '06, with balsamic and fruity aromas, shows powerful and complex with velvety tannins, which is how it won Three Glasses. This is the first award for the normally unpretentious Torrette. The Torrette Supérieur Clos de Château Feuillet '07 is also good, with even more exquisite aromas, evoking violets and fruit, with unusual peppery overtones. The Syrah Vigne de Conze '08 is also interesting, with characteristic scents of white pepper followed by ripe red fruit jam and elegantly posed tannins. The dried-grape Lo Flapì and the Pinot Gris '09 are both good.

● Valle d'Aosta Torrette Sup. V. de Torrette '06	▼▼▼	7
● Valle d'Aosta Torrette Sup. Clos de Château Feuillet '07	▼▼	5
● Valle d'Aosta Syrah V. de Conze '08	▼▼	5
○ Lo Flapì	▼	6
○ Valle d'Aosta Pinot Gris '09	▼	4
○ Lo Bien Flapì '06	▽▽	7
○ Valle d'Aosta Chardonnay '08	▽▽	4*
● Valle d'Aosta Fumin '07	▽▽	5
● Valle d'Aosta Fumin '06	▽▽	5
● Valle d'Aosta Mayolet V. de Toule '07	▽▽	4*
● Valle d'Aosta Syrah V. de Conze '07	▽▽	5
● Valle d'Aosta Torrette '07	▽▽	4

Caves Cooperatives de Donnas

VIA ROMA, 97
11020 DONNAS [AO]
TEL. 0125807096
www.donnasvini.it

CELLAR SALES
PRE-BOOKED VISITS

ANNUAL PRODUCTION 150,000 bottles
HECTARES UNDER VINE 26
VITICULTURE METHOD Conventional

The Romans left a road at Donnas, where the mild Alpine climate enables cultivation of plants such as olives, lemons, palms and mimosa, as well as grapevines. Napoleon himself sampled the wine of Donnas. And it is to preserve these noble viticultural traditions that in 1971 a group of wine growers, having obtained DOC recognition for Donnas (the first in Valle d'Aosta), set up a co-operative to protect and guarantee the wine's quality and authenticity. The co-operative works mainly with the local biotype of nebbiolo, called picotendro.

It is always a pleasure to taste the Donnas Nebbiolo. The Napoléon '06 is bright ruby, tending to garnet red and the nose is intense and complex, its nice fruit balanced by dried fruit, forest floor and tobacco. The full palate unveils dense, enfolding tannins that extend the finish. Donnas Supérieur Vieilles Vignes Cavour '06 is a bright, fresh garnet ruby with an intense nose of tobacco, dried flowers and liquorice on a background of oak. Dense on the palate, its powerful, juicy tannins are only slightly dried by the oak but the long finish augurs well. The simpler basic Donnas, also '06, is good.

● Valle d'Aosta Donnas Napoléon '06	▼▼	5
● Valle d'Aosta Donnas Sup. Vielles Vignes Cavour '06	▼▼	5
● Valle d'Aosta Donnas '06	▼	4
● Valle d'Aosta Donnas '04	▽▽	4*
● Valle d'Aosta Donnas Napoléon '04	▽▽	5
● Valle d'Aosta Donnas Napoléon '02	▽▽	4
● Valle d'Aosta Donnas Napoleone '03	▽▽	4*
● Valle d'Aosta Donnas Sup. Napoleone '03	▽▽	5
● Valle d'Aosta Donnas Sup. Vieilles Vignes '05	▽▽	5
● Valle d'Aosta Donnas Sup. Vieilles Vignes '03	▽▽	5
● Valle d'Aosta Donnas Sup. Vielles Vignes Cavour '04	▽▽	5
● Valle d'Aosta Donnas Sup. Vielles Vignes Cavour '02	▽▽	5

Feudo di San Maurizio

FRAZ. MAILLOD, 44
11010 SARRE [AO]
TEL. 3383186831
www.feudo.vievini.it

CELLAR SALES
PRE-BOOKED VISITS

ANNUAL PRODUCTION 40,000 bottles
HECTARES UNDER VINE 6
VITICULTURE METHOD Conventional

We still think of this as a young winery but more than 20 years have passed since Michel Vallet was able to put his passion for wine into practice by starting up the Feudo di San Maurizio in 1989. The winery is constantly growing but all this activity does not distract Michel from his land and his tradition. As you often read in literature about Valle d'Aosta wine, interest in indigenous vines is high, although they are often difficult to grow for obvious reasons of climate and the vineyards which can only be tended by hand.

Among the wines Michel presented, the local petit rouge-based Torrette '08 is particularly agreeable, presenting an intense, bright ruby red, its nose is intense and down to earth, with nice dark berries, damp earth and faint green notes, a satisfying, succulent palate with a mildly acidulous finish, good length and excellent character. The Gewürztraminer Grapillon '09 is nice. Brilliant in colour with intense roses and grapefruit, it has poise on the palate. The Chardonnay '08 is beautifully drinkable.

● Valle d'Aosta Torrette '08	▼▼	4
○ Valle d'Aosta Chardonnay '08	▼▼	4
○ Valle d'Aosta Gewurtraminer Grapillon '09	▼▼	5
● Valle d'Aosta Cornalin '09	▼	5
● Valle d'Aosta Fumin '07	▼	6
● Pierrots '07	▽▽	6
○ Valle d'Aosta Chardonnay '06	▽▽	4*
● Valle d'Aosta Fumin '06	▽▽	5
● Valle d'Aosta Mayolet '07	▽▽	5
○ Valle d'Aosta Müller Thurgau '08	▽▽	4*
● Valle d'Aosta Torrette '07	▽▽	4
● Valle d'Aosta Torrette Sup. '07	▽▽	5

F.lli Grosjean

VILLAGGIO OLLIGNAN, 1
11020 QUART [AO]
TEL. 0165775791
www.grosjean.vievini.it

CELLAR SALES
PRE-BOOKED VISITS

ANNUAL PRODUCTION 90,000 bottles
HECTARES UNDER VINE 10
VITICULTURE METHOD Conventional

One of the favourite destinations on the hill of Quart, close to Aosta, is the winery of the Grosjean family. The brothers' handwriting is on the bottle labels but the success of the wines here can be attributed to the whole family, an extended but cohesive unit that has made consistency and reliability the hallmarks of their work.

The wines reflect Valle d'Aosta. The Grosjeans live up to expectations created by prizes won in recent years with their traditional, native Fumin. Three Glasses again for an indigenous white which reflects its provenance, the Petite Arvine Vigne Rovettaz '09, a bright, intense, fruity wine which proffers apricots and tangerines then a fresh-tasting, well-balanced palate. Fumin Vigne Rovettaz '08 is great, if not as exciting as last year. It's a stunning purple with an intense nose of dark berry fruit and bark on a vegetal background. The palate is powerful and layered, with still youthful extract but also very lingering and full of character.

○ Valle d'Aosta Petite Arvine V. Rovettaz '09	▼▼▼	5
● Valle d'Aosta Cornalin V. Rovettaz '09	▼▼	4
● Valle d'Aosta Fumin V. Rovettaz '08	▼▼	6
● Valle d'Aosta Pinot Noir '09	▼▼	4
● Valle d'Aosta Mayolet '09	▼	4
○ Valle d'Aosta Muscat Petit Grain '09	▼	5
● Valle d'Aosta Fumin '06	▽▽▽	5
● Valle d'Aosta Fumin V. Rovettaz '07	▽▽▽	6
● Valle d'Aosta Cornalin V. Rovettaz '06	▽▽	4
○ Valle d'Aosta Pinot Gris V. Creton '08	▽▽	5
○ Valle d'Aosta Pinot Gris V. Creton '07	▽▽	5
○ Valle d'Aosta Pinot Gris V. Creton '06	▽▽	4*
● Valle d'Aosta Pinot Noir V. Tzeriat '07	▽▽	5
● Valle d'Aosta Torrette Sup. V. Rovetta '06	▽▽	4*
● Valle d'Aosta Torrette Sup. V. Rovettaz '07	▽▽	4*

★ Les Crêtes

LOC. VILLETOS, 50
11010 AYMAVILLES [AO]
TEL. 0165902274
www.lescretes.it

CELLAR SALES
PRE-BOOKED VISITS

ANNUAL PRODUCTION **230,000 bottles**
HECTARES UNDER VINE **25**
VITICULTURE METHOD **Conventional**

It's never easy to meet expectations,. not even for this winery. Les Crêtes has crowned the '08 Cuvée Bois a Three Glass accolade again this year, which brings the haul to 12 now. Every year, there is something new and interesting. Last year, it was the official induction into the winery management of the daughters Eleonora and Elena, who so have so staunchly supported the legendary, indefatigable Constantino. This year, the Grosjeans have started the winery extension, which includes expanding the existing building to meet domestic demand.

As ever, the Chardonnay Cuvée Bois '08 is wonderfully harmonious and well balanced, with intense, refined fragrances of acacia blossom, followed by nice spicy toastiness then hazelnuts. The satisfyingly rich, enfolding palate is still slightly marked by the oak. Fumin '08 is utterly thrilling, with intense, refined aromas that evoke fresh dark fruit veined with delicate black olives. Outstanding length is backed up by rich structure and cushiony tannins.

○ Valle d'Aosta Chardonnay Cuvée Bois '08	3 black	7
● Valle d'Aosta Fumin '08	2 black	6
● Valle d'Aosta Syrah Coteau La Tour '08	2 black	5
○ Valle d'Aosta Chardonnay '09	2 black	4
○ Valle d'Aosta Petite Arvine '09	2 black	4*
○ Neblù	1 black	6
● Valle d'Aosta Pinot Noir '09	1 black	4
● Valle d'Aosta Torrette '09	1 black	4
○ Valle d'Aosta Chardonnay Cuvée Bois '07	3 white	7
○ Valle d'Aosta Chardonnay Cuvée Bois '06	3 white	7
○ Valle d'Aosta Chardonnay Cuvée Frissonnière Les Crêtes Cuvée Bois '05	3 white	7
○ Valle d'Aosta Chardonnay Cuvée Frissonnière Les Crêtes Cuvée Bois '04	3 white	6
○ Valle d'Aosta Chardonnay Cuvée Frissonnière Les Crêtes Cuvée Bois '03	3 white	6
● Valle d'Aosta Fumin Vigne La Tour '02	3 white	6

Lo Triolet

LOC. JUNOD, 7
11010 INTROD [AO]
TEL. 016595437
www.lotriolet.vievini.it

CELLAR SALES
PRE-BOOKED VISITS

ANNUAL PRODUCTION **30,000 bottles**
HECTARES UNDER VINE **3**
VITICULTURE METHOD **Conventional**

Marco Martin's Lo Triolet estate is in the delightful village of Introd. This is where he revived the forgotten and often underrated vine, pinot grigio. In the 1990s, much laborious work was done on the expansion and renewal of the vineyards but the steady, competent way in which it was done has been rewarded by results at both national and international level. A few years ago, Lo Triolet acquired some vineyards in Nus, a village at the mouth of the Aosta valley, to focus on the typical local red grapes, with excellent results of course.

The steel-aged Valle d'Aosta Pinot Gris '09 that Marco presented this year is a wonderfully complex wine. Brilliant in the glass, it proffers intense aromas of lovely pear-like fruit offset by sweetish notes. The barrique-aged Pinot Gris is equally fine but needs a little time to achieve perfect balance. The Coteau Barrage '08 has gorgeous wafts of dark fruit with nice spice and fabulous character. Don't miss the Fumin '08.

○ Valle d'Aosta Pinot Gris '09	3 black	5
○ Valle d'Aosta Pinot Gris Élevé en Barriques '09	2 black	5
● Valle d'Aosta Rouge Coteau Barrage '08	2 black	5
● Valle d'Aosta Fumin '08	2 black	4
○ Mistigri '09	1 black	6
○ Vallèe d'Aoste Gewurztraminer '09	1 black	4
○ Valle d'Aosta Pinot Gris '08	3 white	4*
○ Valle d'Aosta Pinot Gris '05	3 white	4*
○ Mistigri '06	2 white	6
○ MonAtout '07	2 white	4
● Valle d'Aosta Coteau Barrage '06	2 white	5
○ Valle d'Aosta Pinot Gris '07	2 white	4
○ Valle d'Aosta Pinot Gris Élevé en Barriques '08	2 white	5
○ Valle d'Aosta Pinot Gris Élevé en Barriques '07	2 white	5
● Valle d'Aosta Rouge Coteau Barrage '07	2 white	5

Cave du Vin Blanc de Morgex et de La Salle

FRAZ. LA RUINE
CHEMIN DES ÎLES, 19
11017 MORGEX [AO]
TEL. 0165800331
www.caveduvinblanc.com

CELLAR SALES
PRE-BOOKED VISITS

ANNUAL PRODUCTION 170,000 bottles
HECTARES UNDER VINE 20
VITICULTURE METHOD Conventional

Wine is the last thing you expect find at the foot of Mont Blanc. This charming area, however, is where Gianluca Telloli skilfully interprets what the highest vineyards in Europe have to offer. The ideal base for spumante, which is now this winery's forte, is the prié blanc grape which, still on ungrafted vines, even manages to produce what is one of the most typical still wines of Valle d'Aosta, Blanc de Morgex et de La Salle. The co-operative, set up in 1989 and backed strongly by Fr Bougeat, continues to be the engine for the designation's production.

Although the cellar has focused particularly on spumante, some marketed under the Quatremillemetres label and mentioned in the Co-Enfer profile, still wines are not ignored. This year, we especially liked the Blanc de Morgex Vini Estremi '09, with its intense aromatics evoking aniseed and Alpine flowers. The fresh-tasting, flavoursome Piagne '09 is another Morgex with refined scents of apple and a caressing finish. The Rayon '09, which shows fresh, delicate, beautifully flowery and minerally, is now an established wine. Among the sparkling versions, the Brut '07 is simple and pleasing, with marked aromas, and the Extra Brut '07 is thinner and more acid.

○ Valle d'Aosta Blanc de Morgex et de La Salle La Piagne '09	▼▼	4
○ Valle d'Aosta Blanc de Morgex et de La Salle Rayon '09	▼▼	4
○ Valle d'Aosta Blanc de Morgex et de La Salle Vini Estremi '09	▼▼	4
○ Valle d'Aosta Blanc de Morgex et de La Salle '09	▼	3
○ Valle d'Aosta Blanc de Morgex et de La Salle M. Cl. Brut '07	▼	5
○ Valle d'Aosta Blanc de Morgex et de La Salle M. Cl. Extra Brut '07	▼	5
○ Valle d'Aosta Blanc de Morgex et de La Salle Brut Millesimé '07	▽▽	5
○ Valle d'Aosta Blanc de Morgex et de La Salle Rayon '08	▽▽	4*
○ Valle d'Aosta Blanc de Morgex et de La Salle Rayon '07	▽▽	4

La Vrille

LOC. GRANGEON, 1
11020 VERRAYES [AO]
TEL. 0166543018
www.lavrille-agritourisme.com

CELLAR SALES
PRE-BOOKED VISITS
ROOMS AND FOOD

ANNUAL PRODUCTION 10,000 bottles
HECTARES UNDER VINE 2
VITICULTURE METHOD Organic

Hervé Deguillame settled in Valle d'Aosta in 1990 after eight years at sea. With great-grandparents from Valle d'Aosta, he found his vocation while retracing his origins by working with vines and the land. Hervé planted his first vineyard in 1991, with moscato bianco, and managed to purchase the abandoned vineyard that four generations before had belonged to his family. He was later able to acquire, with 50 separate purchases, the former vineyards that stand in an eye-catching amphitheatre around the accommodation facilities that Hervé runs with his wife Luciana.

Muscat Flétri is lovely, though not as wonderful as last year. Its elegant nose and good structure accompany sweetness offset by sharp acidity. While La Vrille is known for great dried-grape wines, this year it has had great success with its Fumin '07, from the local grape of the same name. The brilliant, very varietal colour is a prelude to fantastic varietal aromas, made more complex by scents of balsam wood set against good fruit, and the elegant palate has heft. The Cornalin '08 and traditional dry Muscat di Chambave, with typical flower and fruit notes leading to a poised palate, are both good.

○ Valle d'Aosta Chambave Muscat Flétri Passito '08	▼▼	6
● Valle d'Aosta Fumin '07	▼▼	5
● Valle d'Aosta Cornalin '08	▼▼	4
○ Valle d'Aosta Chambave Muscat '08	▼	5
○ Valle d'Aosta Chambave Muscat Flétri Passito '07	▽▽▽	5*
○ Valle d'Aosta Chambave Muscat '07	▽▽	4
○ Valle d'Aosta Chambave Muscat '06	▽▽	4*
○ Valle d'Aosta Chambave Muscat Flétri Passito '06	▽▽	5
● Valle d'Aosta Fumin '06	▽▽	5

Brégy & Gillioz

VIA VERGNOD, 7
11010 SAINT-PIERRE [AO]
TEL. 0041763786668
www.grain-noble.ch

In the village of Saint Pierre, north of Aosta, André Brégy and Pierre André Gillioz work a three-hectare vineyard with just one variety, petite arvine. From this beautifully situated vineyard with a drip irrigation system comes Référence, a terrific wine with scents of dried apricots and honey.

○ Référence	🍷🍷	6

Diego Curtaz

FRAZ. VISERAN, 61
11020 GRESSAN [AO]
TEL. 0165251079
www.diegocurtazvini.it

Quality wines are expected from Diego Curtaz nowadays. Once again, his Torrette '09 hit the mark with its distinct, typical fruity aromas. Equally varietal is the Petit Rouge '09, a subtly elegant, fresh-tasting and easy to drink wine. The Dï Noutro is a little under par and not as interesting as last year.

● Valle d'Aosta Torrette '09	🍷🍷	4*
○ Dï Noutro	🍷	4
● Valle d'Aosta Petit Rouge '09	🍷	4

Les Granges

FRAZ. LES GRANGES, 8
11020 NUS [AO]
TEL. 0165767229
www.lesgrangesvini.it

The wines from this dynamic cellar are always good. The Fumin '08 is tremendous, with lovely overtones of berry fruit sweetened by notes of tobacco and harmony on the palate. The dried-grape version of Nus Malvoisie Flétri '08 has pleasing hints of honey and robust alcohol.

● Valle d'Aosta Fumin '08	🍷🍷	6
○ Valle d'Aosta Nus Malvoisie Flétri '08	🍷🍷	6
○ Valle d'Aosta Nus Malvoisie '09	🍷	4

Institut Agricole Régional

RÉGION LA ROCHÈRE, 1A
11100 AOSTA
TEL. 0165215811
www.iaraosta.it

Andrea Barmaz's arrival was long awaited and results are exciting. The winery's star is shining brightly again. We thought the Petite Arvine '09 was the most successful wine with its elegant hints of citrus and apricot-like fruit and well-balanced finish. The other wines are all well made.

○ Valle d'Aosta Petite Arvine '09	🍷🍷	4
○ Perce-Neige	🍷	4
○ Valle d'Aosta Pinot Gris '09	🍷	4

Elio Ottin

LOC. TORRENT DE MAILLOD, 4
11020 QUART [AO]
TEL. 0165774111
elio.ottin@gmail.com

Elio Ottin will tell you how he plants varieties to suite soil types and site climates. Indigenous grapes – petite arvine, petit rouge and fumin – are preferred. We loved the Petite Arvine '09's citrussy, flowery aromas and powerful, complex palate backed up by vibrant acidity to balance out the alcohol.

○ Valle d'Aosta Petite Arvine '09	🍷🍷	4
● Valle d'Aosta Torrette Sup. '08	🍷🍷	4
● Valle d'Aosta Pinot Noir '09	🍷	4

Pierre Philippe Quinson

LOC. TORRENT DE MAILLOD, 4
11020 QUART [AO]
TEL. 3485501979
pierreq@libero.it

Pierre Philippe Quinson left Valle d'Aosta to train as a vet and returned as an oenologist. In 2005, he planted his first vines on leased land at Quart, produced the Beato Emerico, and then at the Masarèn vineyard in Sarre, from very old native vines alongside barbera and dolcetto.

● Masarèn '09	🍷🍷	4*
● Valle d'Aosta Beato Emerico '09	🍷	3*

43

PIEDMONT

Piedmont wine is bowed but not broken. Inevitably, the region was caught up in the latest crisis, which has left it ravaged by the economic equivalent of a hurricane. Moscato seems to be holding up but Barbera, which accounts for 35 per cent of the region's area under vine, is struggling and nebbiolo, including Piedmont's aristocrats, Barolo and Barbaresco, is little better off. Over the past year, grape prices have plummeted and producers, desperate to clear their cellars for the new vintage, have been forced to slash prices. This is neither the place nor the time to discuss the mistakes that have led to this parlous situation, which has exacerbated the effects of the economic crisis. Yet as so often is the case, extreme challenges have produced astonishing individuals. Last year's tour de force with 84 Three Glass prizes may not have been matched but nonetheless there are 81 wines and 78 wineries on our podium. It shows that Piedmontese producers refuse to be disheartened and continue to release magnificent wines, as the many other wineries that came close to a third Glass also testify. Unsurprisingly, nebbiolo-based wines account for the lion's share with some 60 awards across the various designations – 35 Barolos, ten Barbarescos, six Nebbiolo dell'Alto Piemontes, five Roeros and similar, and four Langhe wines – but we note that Barbera makes steady progress every year. This time, there were eight awards: six Barbera d'Astis and two Barbera del Monferratos. However, Piedmont also confirmed it is a region that can bring out the best in less obvious varieties, both native and international. We would point out some interesting new developments. At last, we have a top award for an Alta Langa wine – the Riserva Zéro '04 from Enrico Serafino – the designation it is hoped will be the locomotive for Piedmont's sparkling wines. For the first time, the prize-winners include a dry Erbaluce di Caluso – Rustìa '09 from Orsolani – and a Pinot Nero fermented on the skins, the Monferrato Rosso La Mandorla '08 by Spertino. The peaks reached by dolcetto and cortese indicate that these varieties have their respective heartlands in Dogliani and Gavi. But the most heart-warming news is the return to Three Glasses of Moscato d'Asti with the following labels: Piemonte Moscato d'Autunno '09 from Paolo Saracco and Moscato d'Asti Tenuta del Fant '09 della Tenuta Il Falchetto from the Forno family. All in all, our review shows that the Piedmont of wine may be down but it is not out, with 13 wineries winning Three Glasses for the first time. In conclusion, we want to applaud the naturally farmed estates that won top honours.

Abbona

B.TA SAN LUIGI, 40
12063 DOGLIANI [CN]
TEL. 0173721317
www.abbona.com

CELLAR SALES
PRE-BOOKED VISITS

ANNUAL PRODUCTION 250,000 bottles
HECTARES UNDER VINE 45
VITICULTURE METHOD Conventional

The Abbona winery is a charming, original piece of architecture; an excellent example of elegant modernity well integrated with its surroundings. The large cellar, with a wide variety of different sized barrels, is worth a visit. This year, the wide range of wines presented by Marziano Abbona is joined by a vintage Metodo Classico Rosé that will delight even the most demanding lovers of fizz. The rest of the wines maintain excellent quality across the board.

The Barolo Terlo Ravera '06, a sound Novello vineyard selection, romps off with Three Glasses thanks to an elegant aromatic profile ranging from incense and sweet spice to red berry fruit. The well-rounded palate shows firm, progressive tannins, ushering in a youthful, fruit-driven finish. The Barolo Pressenda '06 opens on fresh notes of cinchona and liquorice with aniseed hints, leading into a deep, complex palate that gives well-behaved tannins and great class on the finish. The Dogliani Papà Celso '08, in line with the recent DOCG regulations requiring the exclusive use of dolcetto and at least one year's ageing before release, is as marvellous as ever.

● Barolo Terlo Ravera '06	▼▼▼	7
● Barolo Pressenda '06	▼▼	7
● Dogliani Papà Celso '08	▼▼	5
● Barbera d'Alba Rinaldi '08	▼▼	5
● Dolcetto di Dogliani San Luigi '09	▼▼	4*
○ Langhe Bianche Cinerino '09	▼▼	5
● Nebbiolo d'Alba Bricco Barone '08	▼▼	4
⊙ Spumante M. Cl. Extra Brut Duemilasei '06	▼▼	6
● Barolo Pressenda '00	▽▽▽	7
● Dogliani Papà Celso '07	▽▽▽	5
● Dogliani Papà Celso '06	▽▽▽	5
● Dogliani Papà Celso '05	▽▽▽	4*
● Dolcetto di Dogliani Papà Celso '04	▽▽▽	4*
● Dolcetto di Dogliani Papà Celso '00	▽▽▽	4
● Barbera d'Alba Rinaldi '07	▽▽	4

Anna Maria Abbona

FRAZ. MONCUCCO, 21
12060 FARIGLIANO [CN]
TEL. 0173797228
www.annamariabbona.it

CELLAR SALES
PRE-BOOKED VISITS

ANNUAL PRODUCTION 58,000 bottles
HECTARES UNDER VINE 10
VITICULTURE METHOD Conventional

Anna Maria Abbona and Franco Schellino's winery is an interesting landmark in Dogliani wine country. Their vineyards, situated at considerable altitudes, confer unique character. The wines may seem somewhat austere and closed when young, but careful ageing can coax out surprising depth and complexity. Dolcetto is the cornerstone of their competitively priced range of wines.

Awaiting the Langhe Rosso Cadò '07, to be released next year, we tried a range of dolcetto-based wines. The Dogliani Maioli '08 combines lashings of fruit with good strength and nice tannins, and we liked the drinkable, acidity-edged Langhe Dolcetto '09. The Dolcetto di Dogliani Sorì dij But '09 has great personality and length, made more interesting by its dry finish. This intermediate version is not loved by the guides but it is the biggest seller. San Bernardo has overpowering oak to the detriment of varietal fruit. This edition sees the official baptism of the appealing, incisively acidic Langhe L'Alman '09, from a vineyard of three-year-old riesling.

● Dogliani Maioli '08	▼▼	4
● Dolcetto di Dogliani Sorì dij But '09	▼▼	4*
● Dogliani San Bernardo '07	▼	5
○ Langhe Bianco L'Alman '09	▼	5
● Langhe Dolcetto '09	▼	3
● Dogliani Maioli '07	▽▽	4*
● Dogliani Maioli '06	▽▽	4*
● Dogliani San Bernardo '06	▽▽	5
● Dolcetto di Dogliani Sorì dij But '08	▽▽	4
● Dolcetto di Dogliani Sorì dij But '07	▽▽	4
● Langhe Nebbiolo '07	▽▽	4*
● Langhe Rosso Cadò '07	▽▽	5
● Langhe Rosso Cadò '06	▽▽	5

F.lli Abrigo

LOC. BERFI
VIA MOGLIA GERLOTTO, 2
12055 DIANO D'ALBA [CN]
TEL. 017369104
www.abrigofratelli.com

CELLAR SALES
PRE-BOOKED VISITS

ANNUAL PRODUCTION 60,000 bottles
HECTARES UNDER VINE 20
VITICULTURE METHOD Conventional

Fratelli Abrigo is run by Ernesto, his sister Mariarita, Ernesto's children, Silvia and Walter, and the oenologist Emanuele Antona. The family arrived in Diano d'Alba in 1935 from Barbaresco. Fathers used to buy good vineyards to leave to their children as a guarantee for a brighter future and the Berfi holding was purchased by the current owner's grandfather for this very reason. Their heritage is dolcetto, and the main Abrigo labels comprise various incarnations of the variety. Also noteworthy are the extremely attractive prices.

While awaiting the Diano d'Alba Superiore Vigna Pietrin '09 selection, scheduled for release next year, the best label presented was the Diano d'Alba Rocche dei Berfi '09. This concentrated wine with marked notes of red berry fruit on the nose shows good body and harmony. A pleasant drinker, it is distinguished by a fine almondy finish over a fruit and alcohol base. We also liked the quaffable Nebbiolo d'Alba Tardiss '08. The Barbera d'Alba '09 is in the same style, focusing on freshness and immediate appeal, although somewhat to the detriment of complexity.

● Diano d'Alba Rocche dei Berfi '09	🍷🍷	3*
● Nebbiolo d'Alba Tardiss '08	🍷🍷	5
● Barbera d'Alba '09	🍷	3
● Barbera d'Alba La Galùpa '08	🍷	4
● Diano d'Alba '09	🍷	3
○ Langhe Chardonnay Temp dër Fiù '09	🍷	3
● Barbera d'Alba La Galùpa '07	🍸🍸	4*
● Barbera d'Alba La Galùpa '06	🍸🍸	4
● Barbera d'Alba Piasusa '07	🍸🍸	3*
● Diano d'Alba Bric Tumlin '07	🍸🍸	3*
● Diano d'Alba Intreccio '07	🍸🍸	3*
● Diano d'Alba Sup. V. Pietrìn '08	🍸🍸	4
● Langhe Rosso Tambuss '05	🍸🍸	5

Orlando Abrigo

VIA CAPPELLETTO, 5
12050 TREISO [CN]
TEL. 0173630232
www.orlandoabrigo.it

CELLAR SALES
PRE-BOOKED VISITS
ROOMS AND FOOD

ANNUAL PRODUCTION 80,000 bottles
HECTARES UNDER VINE 18
VITICULTURE METHOD Conventional

Giovanni Abrigo carries on the work of his father Orlando with dedication and passion, as we see in the wines, which confirm their high standards. The range is fairly modern, with extract-rich Barbarescos aged in small wood. The Abrigo vineyards are situated at significant altitudes, close to nebbiolo's limit, and the winery also provides on-site holiday accommodation. Lovers of the Langhe will find five elegantly furnished double rooms and a pool with a view.

Even if it failed to pick up any top awards, this was the estate's best performance ever, with a wide range of consistently good products. The ruby red Barbaresco Vigna Rongalio Rocche Meruzzano '07 proffers raspberry, spice and tobacco over a tar backdrop. On the palate, this fine interpretation shows elegance, length and nice alcoholic warmth. The '07 Montersino has delicious fruit, with meek, close-woven tannins and a full, fleshy finish. The '07 Barbera Mervisano also made our finals with its lovely concentration and finesse. The Barbaresco Rocche Meruzzano '07 boasts ripe fruit, attractive spice and a mouthfilling, powerful palate, with slightly grainy tannins.

● Barbaresco Montersino '07	🍷🍷	7
● Barbaresco Rocche Meruzzano V. Rongallo '07	🍷🍷	7
● Barbera d'Alba Mervisano '07	🍷🍷	5
● Barbaresco Rocche Meruzzano '07	🍷🍷	6
○ Langhe Bianco D'Amblè '09	🍷🍷	4
● Langhe Nebbiolo Settevie '08	🍷🍷	4
● Langhe Rosso Livraie '06	🍷🍷	5
● Nebbiolo d'Alba Valmaggiore '08	🍷🍷	6
○ Langhe Chardonnay Très '09	🍷	4
● Barbaresco '02	🍸🍸	6*
● Barbaresco Montersino '05	🍸🍸	6
● Barbaresco Rocche Meruzzano V. Rongallo '06	🍸🍸	7
● Barbaresco V. Rongallo '04	🍸🍸	6
● Barbaresco V. Rongallo '03	🍸🍸	6

Giulio Accornero e Figli

Ca' Cima, 1
15049 Vignale Monferrato [AL]
tel. 0142933317
www.accornerovini.it

CELLAR SALES
PRE-BOOKED VISITS
ROOMS

ANNUAL PRODUCTION 100,000 bottles
HECTARES UNDER VINE 22
VITICULTURE METHOD Organic

Much has been said about the history and characteristics of this winery but we should stress that in the Monferrato Casalese area, families like the Accorneros are synonymous with terroir. This often misused term makes sense among these hills, with their mix of territory, site climates and human values, and the resulting wines embody a whole system. All this translates into Three Glasses for the Bricco Battista, with two other wines making it through to the finals and an excellent Barbera Giulin hard on their heels.

The dense ruby Bricco Battista '07 is masterly, giving cherry jam and notes of plain chocolate, a powerful, alcoholic palate and a reprise of fruit on the finish. Barbera Cima '04 shows a dense, youthful ruby hue, with spice and notes of plum paving the way for a powerful, concentrated palate. We were impressed with the Grignolino '09, whose varietal traits were enhanced by a good growing year. Giulin is superbly harmonious, with an evolved, fruity nose leading to an intense, lingering palate. Casorzo Brigantino has intense wild berries and florality while the palate's residual sugar and acidity are nicely balanced. The Freisa La Bernardina provides pleasant drinking.

● Barbera del M.to Sup. Bricco Battista '07	▼▼▼	6
● Barbera del M.to Sup. Cima '04	▼▼	7
● Grignolino del M.to Casalese Bricco del Bosco '09	▼▼	4*
● Barbera del M.to Giulin '08	▼▼	4
● Casorzo Brigantino '09	▼▼	4
● M.to Freisa La Bernardina '09	▼▼	4
● Casorzo Passito Pico '06	▼	4
○ M.to Bianco Fonsina '09	▼	4
● M.to Girotondo '08	▼	6
● Barbera d'Asti Bricco Battista '97	▽▽▽	5
● Barbera del M.to Sup. Bricco Battista '04	▽▽▽	6
● Barbera del M.to Sup. Bricco Battista '99	▽▽▽	6
● Barbera del M.to Sup. Bricco Battista '98	▽▽▽	6
● M.to Rosso Centenario '06	▽▽▽	6

Marco e Vittorio Adriano

fraz. San Rocco Seno d'Elvio, 13a
12051 Alba [CN]
tel. 0173362294
www.adrianovini.it

CELLAR SALES
PRE-BOOKED VISITS

ANNUAL PRODUCTION 90,000 bottles
HECTARES UNDER VINE 20
VITICULTURE METHOD Conventional

The fine winery of the brothers Marco and Vittorio Adriano is proving to be one of the best Langhe for quality and peaks of excellence. The merit goes to its Barbarescos, from the Bricco and Frati vineyards, for the Sanadaive, and Basarin at Neive, which since 2004 has also been used for the Riserva. They are all aged in 35-40 hectolitre Slavonian oak barrels. The range is completed by a series of affordable wines based on moscato, sauvignon, dolcetto, barbera and freisa.

Once again, the Adriano brothers came within a whisker of top honours with their Barbaresco Basarin Riserva '05, whose crisp, focused fruit is further lifted by elegant green notes and florality. In the mouth it is equally fresh and immediate, and just a touch more mid-palate flesh would make it really outstanding. Only slightly less impressive are the '07 Barbaresco Sanadaive and Basarin. The former is a tad closed and shows slightly dusty tannins while the latter has impetus and breadth but could do with a touch more complexity.

● Barbaresco Basarin Ris. '05	▼▼	6
● Barbaresco Basarin '07	▼▼	5
● Barbaresco Sanadaive '07	▼▼	5
● Langhe Freisa '09	▼▼	4
● Langhe Nebbiolo '08	▼▼	4
● Barbera d'Alba Sup. '08	▼	4
● Dolcetto d'Alba '09	▼	4
○ Langhe Bianco Basaricò '09	▼	4
● Barbaresco Basarin '06	▽▽	5*
● Barbaresco Basarin Ris. '04	▽▽	6
● Barbaresco Sanadaive '06	▽▽	5*
● Barbaresco Sanadaive '05	▽▽	6
● Barbera d'Alba Sup. '07	▽▽	4*
● Barbera d'Alba Superiore '06	▽▽	4
● Langhe Nebbiolo '07	▽▽	4*

Claudio Alario

VIA SANTA CROCE, 23
12055 DIANO D'ALBA [CN]
TEL. 0173231808
aziendaalario@tiscali.it

CELLAR SALES
PRE-BOOKED VISITS

ANNUAL PRODUCTION 40,000 bottles
HECTARES UNDER VINE 10
VITICULTURE METHOD Conventional

Claudio Alario's winery is something of a benchmark around Diano. His plots, some of which are at Serralunga and Verduno, allow him to present an impressive range that mirrors the best of Langhe's stylistic traits. Balance, harmony and great drinkability distinguish all the wines produced by this interesting winery. As a rule, the Dolcettos provide more traditional easy drinking, while the Barolos tend to be released while their oak is still evident.

Claudio Alario took home Three Glasses last year with his Barolo but this Diano producer never neglects his first love, Dolcetto. This year, we were particularly taken with the Costa Fiore '09 and the '09 Montagrillo. The former brims with fruit on the nose, giving ripe red berries and a beefily structured palate with no rough edges. The Montagrillo gives headier, more approachable fruit over a well-rounded palate and a delicious, nicely balanced finish. The Barolo Sorano opens with intense, elegant aromas ranging from sweet spice to raspberry, and shows dense, powerful progression in the mouth, despite the assertive tannins.

● Barolo Sorano '06	▼▼	8
● Diano d'Alba Costa Fiore '09	▼▼	4*
● Barbera d'Alba Valletta '08	▼▼	5
● Barolo Riva '06	▼▼	7
● Diano d'Alba Montagrillo '09	▼▼	4*
● Nebbiolo d'Alba Cascinotto '08	▼▼	5
● Diano d'Alba Pradurent Sup. '08	▼	4
● Barolo Sorano '05	▽▽▽	8
● Barbera d'Alba Valletta '07	▽▽	5
● Barolo Riva '05	▽▽	7
● Barolo Sorano '04	▽▽	8
● Diano d'Alba Costa Fiore '08	▽▽	4*
● Diano d'Alba Costa Fiore '06	▽▽	4
● Diano d'Alba Montagrillo '06	▽▽	4
● Diano d'Alba Pradurent Sup. '07	▽▽	4

F.lli Alessandria

VIA B. VALFRÉ, 59
12060 VERDUNO [CN]
TEL. 0172470113
www.fratellialessandria.it

CELLAR SALES
PRE-BOOKED VISITS

ANNUAL PRODUCTION 60,000 bottles
HECTARES UNDER VINE 12
VITICULTURE METHOD Conventional

Brothers Gian Battista and Alessandro are united by much more than work; for them, Barolo is nothing short of a calling. Their various vineyard selections share common traits, also due to the exclusive use of large wood. The Monforte and Verduno vineyards produce traditional, rounded wines. Their pride is the winery, already praised 150 years ago by Camillo Benso, Conte di Cavour, who awarded it a gold medal for its modern production methods. This remains a family business, with wives and children helping out in the 18th-century mansion that serves as a base.

The Barolo Monvigliero '06 has particularly elegant aromas of tobacco and rose petals, leading into an outstanding, meaty palate, with soft if still slightly green tannins. This is a Three Glass wine of length and clarity. The Gramolere '06, from the vineyard of the same name in Monforte, has more incisive tannins and solid, impressive structure. The delightful San Lorenzo '06 also offers refined notes of incense and already mellow tannins in a mid-weight body. There was a fine performance from the complex, perfectly balanced Barbera d'Alba Superiore Priòra '07.

● Barolo Monvigliero '06	▼▼▼+	7
● Barbera d'Alba Sup. La Priora '07	▼▼	5
● Barolo Gramolere '06	▼▼	7
● Barolo S. Lorenzo '06	▼▼	7
● Barolo '06	▼▼	6
● Langhe Nebbiolo Prinsiot '08	▼▼	4
● Langhe Rosso Luna '07	▼▼	5
● Verduno Pelaverga '09	▼▼	4
● Barolo Gramolere '05	▽▽▽	7
● Barolo Monvigliero '00	▽▽▽	7
● Barolo Monvigliero '95	▽▽▽	7
● Barolo S. Lorenzo '04	▽▽▽	7
● Barolo S. Lorenzo '01	▽▽▽	7
● Barolo S. Lorenzo '97	▽▽▽	7
● Barolo Monvigliero '05	▽▽	7

★ Gianfranco Alessandria

LOC. MANZONI, 13
12065 MONFORTE D'ALBA [CN]
TEL. 017378576
www.gianfrancoalessandria.com

CELLAR SALES
PRE-BOOKED VISITS

ANNUAL PRODUCTION 35,000 bottles
HECTARES UNDER VINE 7
VITICULTURE METHOD Conventional

A quarter century has passed since Gianfranco Alessandria decided to follow his father Giuseppe's advice and open his own winery in Monforte. The risk paid off, thanks above all to his well-received Barberas and Barolos. Consistency and style have grown with each vintage. The style is modern and drinkable, with lots of fruit and the use of new oak. Gianfranco started out with five hectares, and now has two more. This means he can personally tend the rows and the winery, with the help of his wife Bruna and daughter Vittoria.

We mentioned the Barbera Vittoria '07 in last year's edition, but didn't actually taste it until this year. It was well worth the wait. Great finesse and an impenetrable hue frame rich plum and dark berry fruit on the nose, followed by a marvellously full-bodied palate with just a hint of oak. The rough, grainy tannins of the Barolo San Giovanni '06, together with its clean aromas and luscious fruit, mark it out for ageing. The attractive Barolo '06 displays a meaty palate with less evident tannins. L'Insieme '07 comes from a blend of the classic Langhe varieties: nebbiolo, barbera and dolcetto.

● Barbera d'Alba Vittoria '07	🍷🍷	6
● Barolo S. Giovanni '06	🍷🍷	8
● Barbera d'Alba '09	🍷🍷	4*
● Barolo '06	🍷🍷	7
● Dolcetto d'Alba '09	🍷🍷	4*
● Langhe Nebbiolo '08	🍷🍷	5
● Langhe Rosso L'Insieme '07	🍷🍷	6
● Barbera d'Alba Vittoria '98	🍸🍸🍸	6
● Barolo '93	🍸🍸🍸	8
● Barolo S. Giovanni '04	🍸🍸🍸	8
● Barolo S. Giovanni '01	🍸🍸🍸	8
● Barolo S. Giovanni '00	🍸🍸🍸	8
● Barolo S. Giovanni '99	🍸🍸🍸	8
● Barolo S. Giovanni '98	🍸🍸🍸	8
● Barolo S. Giovanni '97	🍸🍸🍸	8
● Barolo S. Giovanni '05	🍸🍸	8

Marchesi Alfieri

P.ZZA ALFIERI, 28
14010 SAN MARTINO ALFIERI [AT]
TEL. 0141976015
www.marchesialfieri.it

CELLAR SALES
PRE-BOOKED VISITS
ROOMS

ANNUAL PRODUCTION 100,000 bottles
HECTARES UNDER VINE 25
VITICULTURE METHOD Conventional

The winery of the San Martino sisters at San Germano is situated in the municipal district of San Martino Alfieri, in the baroque Castello Alfieri. The first document that speaks of vineyards on the family lands, on the hills rolling down towards the Tanaro plain, dates back to 1377. The most important variety here is barbera, both in terms of quantity, seeing that it accounts for 15 of the 25 hectares under vine, and quality, as it is the base for the estate's leading wines.

Take a great Barbera vintage like '07, add a winery with great traditions and perfect soil, and you get Three Glasses for the Barbera d'Asti Superiore Alfiera '07. Opening on rich dark berry fruit, tobacco, cocoa and spice, it continues elegant and layered on the palate, showing fresh and full-bodied. The long finish is underpinned by nice acidity. As usual, the other wines are well made, particularly the Barbera d'Asti La Tota '08, boasting fruit and spice despite the difficult growing year, followed by a fleshy, mouthfilling palate and a long, savoury finish. The Monferrato Rosso Sostegno '08, from 70 per cent barbera topped up with pinot nero, offers crisp wild berry fruit.

● Barbera d'Asti Sup. Alfiera '07	🍷🍷🍷	6
● Barbera d'Asti La Tota '08	🍷🍷	4
● M.to Rosso Sostegno '08	🍷🍷	4*
● M.to Rosso Costa Quaglia '07	🍷	5
● Piemonte Grignolino Sansoero '09	🍷	4
● Barbera d'Asti Sup. Alfiera '05	🍸🍸🍸	6
● Barbera d'Asti Sup. Alfiera '01	🍸🍸🍸	6
● Barbera d'Asti Sup. Alfiera '00	🍸🍸🍸	6
● Barbera d'Asti Sup. Alfiera '99	🍸🍸🍸	6

Giovanni Almondo

VIA SAN ROCCO, 26
12046 MONTÀ [CN]
TEL. 0173975256
www.giovannialmondo.com

CELLAR SALES
PRE-BOOKED VISITS

ANNUAL PRODUCTION 80,000 bottles
HECTARES UNDER VINE 15
VITICULTURE METHOD Conventional

Domenico Almondo is one of the growers who has contributed most to developing the potential of this area. The composition of Domenico's vineyards, around half planted to arneis, shows that he considers himself above all a white wine maker but his range includes all the traditional Roero wines. The well-aspected vineyards are situated at altitudes of between 250 and 380 metres, on sandy or limestone soils.

As usual, the range presented this year is extremely good, starting with the intensely fruity Roero Bric Valdiana '08, which does however lacks a little aromatic complexity. The generous palate reveals initially juicy tannins, which become slightly grainier on the long finish. The delightful Barbera d'Alba Valbianchera '08 shows fresh and elegant, with fine mineral and cinchona notes. The two '09 Arneises, Vigne Sparse and Bricco delle Ciliegie, were below par, presenting pleasant but a touch too simple.

● Barbera d'Alba Valbianchera '08	🍷🍷	5
● Roero Bric Valdiana '08	🍷🍷	6
○ Roero Arneis Bricco delle Ciliegie '09	🍷	4
○ Roero Arneis V. Sparse '09	🍷	4
● Roero Bric Valdiana '07	YYY	6
● Roero Bric Valdiana '03	YYY	6
● Roero Bric Valdiana '01	YYY	6
● Roero Bric Valdiana '00	YYY	6

★★★ Elio Altare
Cascina Nuova

FRAZ. ANNUNZIATA, 51
12064 LA MORRA [CN]
TEL. 017350835
www.elioaltare.com

PRE-BOOKED VISITS

ANNUAL PRODUCTION 55,000 bottles
HECTARES UNDER VINE 10
VITICULTURE METHOD Organic

Elio Altare's love for Langhe goes hand-in-hand with his interest in Burgundy and pinot nero, explaining why he adopted methods unknown in Piedmont 30 years ago, such as barrique ageing and short maceration times. Without realizing it, Altare has become the leader of a new way of making Barolo in a modern style, with wines that are enjoyable only a few years after harvest. Today, this revolutionary prefers to spend his time in the vineyard, taking care of ten hectares in Langhe or his rows on the cliffs at Riomaggiore.

As a result of the vineyard being battered by hail, the Barolo Arborina is absent this year. Fortunately, the elegant Langhe Arborina '08 is a marvellous expression of nebbiolo, offering finely spiced, pervasive aromas and blackberry fruit with a hint of balsam, sustained by great harmony on the palate, which has evident but not green tannins. This extremely enjoyable Three Glass stunner has fine ageing potential. We also loved the '06 Barolo, which is a touch more austere on the palate and requires ageing. Another high in this excellent range is the barbera-cased Langhe Larigi '08, a particularly rich wine despite what was generally a disappointing year for the variety.

● Langhe Arborina '08	🍷🍷🍷	8
● Barolo '06	🍷🍷	7
● Langhe Larigi '08	🍷🍷	8
● Barbera d'Alba '09	🍷🍷	5
● L'Insieme '08	🍷🍷	7
● Langhe La Villa '08	🍷🍷	8
● Dolcetto d'Alba '09	🍷	4
● Barolo Vign. Arborina '01	YYY	8
● Barolo Vign. Arborina '00	YYY	8
● Barolo Vign. Arborina '99	YYY	8
● Barolo Vign. Arborina '98	YYY	8
● Langhe La Villa '06	YYY	8
● Langhe La Villa '99	YYY	8
● Langhe Larigi '07	YYY	8
● Langhe Larigi '04	YYY	8

Antichi Vigneti di Cantalupo

VIA MICHELANGELO BUONARROTI, 5
28074 GHEMME [NO]
TEL. 0163840041
www.cantalupo.net

CELLAR SALES
PRE-BOOKED VISITS

ANNUAL PRODUCTION 200,000 bottles
HECTARES UNDER VINE 35
VITICULTURE METHOD Conventional

Alberto Arlunno and his family have always managed to get the best out of the local morainic hills, thanks to their extensive knowledge of the Novara area. Breclema, Carella, Livelli and Baraggiola are just some of the vineyards which contribute to the wines of Antichi Vigneti di Cantalupo. Most of the winery's 34 hectares are planted to nebbiolo spanna and the rest have small quantities of vespolina, uva rara, greco, arneis and chardonnay.

The range of wines from Ghemme just lacked that little extra something but were nevertheless impressive, displaying great variety in style and territorial character. Once again, we thought the Ghemme '06 was the most expansive and approachable, with rusty notes of roots and dried flowers over well-integrated tannins, fading slightly on the finish. The two '04 selections show more marked tertiary aromas. Ghemme Signore di Bayard has a fantastic nose of oriental spices and herbs, with notes of blood-rich meat, while the Ghemme Collis Breclemae is more brooding, with disclosing infused flowers and dried fruits. Both are in the grip of austere tannins that time should soften.

● Ghemme '06	▼▼	5
● Ghemme Collis Breclemae '04	▼▼	7
● Ghemme Signore di Bayard '04	▼▼	6
○ Carolus '09	▼▼	4*
⊙ Colline Novaresi Nebbiolo Il Mimo '09	▼	4
● Colline Novaresi Vespolina Villa Horta '08	▼	3
● Ghemme '05	▽▽▽	5
● Ghemme Collis Breclemae '00	▽▽▽	7
○ Carolus '08	▽▽	4
● Colline Novaresi Primigenia '06	▽▽	3*
● Ghemme Collis Carellae '04	▽▽	6
● Ghemme Signore di Bayard '03	▽▽	6
● Ghemme Signore di Bayard '01	▽▽	6
● Ghemme Signore di Bayard '01	▽▽	6

Antico Borgo dei Cavalli

VIA DANTE, 54
28010 CAVALLIRIO [NO]
TEL. 016380115
www.vinibarbaglia.it

CELLAR SALES
PRE-BOOKED VISITS

ANNUAL PRODUCTION 20,000 bottles
HECTARES UNDER VINE 3
VITICULTURE METHOD Conventional

The extraordinary renaissance of wines from northern Piedmont is due above all to a constant generational turnover, with the wisdom of experienced growers meeting the enthusiasm of youth. We find a perfect example in the history of Antico Borgo dei Cavalli, a small winery established in 1946 by Mario Barbaglia and today run by his son Sergio and granddaughter Silvia. In addition to the classic range of wines based on nebbiolo, uva rara, croatina, vespolina and erbaluce, they have new ideas, especially for spumantes.

Once again, we saw a solid overall performance from Antico Borgo dei Cavalli, with no fewer than four wines of real class, starting with the two classic-method sparklers, the Curticella Caballi Regis Brut from erbaluce, and from uva rara, the Curticella Rosé Brut. The Colline Novaresi Uva Rara Lea '09 is vigorous and earthy while the erbaluce-only Colline Novaresi Bianco Lucino '09 is fresh and juicy. We have to admit that we were a touch disappointed with the Boca '06. Although it is well typed and austere, we know that Sergio and Silvia can do a great deal more in terms of depth and density.

● Boca '06	▼▼	6
○ Colline Novaresi Bianco Lucino '09	▼▼	4
○ Curticella Caballi Regis Brut	▼▼	5
⊙ Curticella Rosé Brut Uva Rara	▼▼	6
● Colline Novaresi Uva Rara Lea '09	▼	3
● Boca '04	▽▽	6
○ Colline Novaresi Bianco Lucino '07	▽▽	4
○ Colline Novaresi Bianco Lucino '06	▽▽	4
● Colline Novaresi Nebbiolo Il Silente '06	▽▽	5
● Colline Novaresi Uva Rara Lea '07	▽▽	3*
● Colline Novaresi Vespolina Ledi '07	▽▽	4
● Colline Novaresi Vespolina Ledi '06	▽▽	4
● Colline Novaresi Vespolina Ledi '04	▽▽	4*
○ Curticella Caballi Regis Brut M. Cl. '05	▽▽	5

★ Antoniolo

c.so Valsesia, 277
13045 Gattinara [VC]
tel. 0163833612
antoniolovini@bmm.it

CELLAR SALES
PRE-BOOKED VISITS

ANNUAL PRODUCTION 60,000 bottles
HECTARES UNDER VINE 12
VITICULTURE METHOD Conventional

The Nebbiolos of Rosanna, Alberto and Lorella Antoniolo are quite simply national treasures. Their incredible longevity is no bar to uncorking them immediately in all their uncontainable energy. They perfectly evoke the atmosphere of legendary vineyards such as San Francesco, Osso San Grato, Castelle, and Borelle. These Gattinaras redefine the concepts of purity and flavour, and render discussions about vinification, ageing, tradition and modernity superfluous.

The wines presented every year by the Antoniolos are simply out of this world. The '06 Gattinaras, San Francesco and Osso San Grato, as in previous years, are up there with the world's best wines. The former is earthy, balsamic and apparently more subtle while the latter, although more closed on the nose, with juniper and faint suggestions of white-fleshed fruits, is utterly mouthfilling even in small sips, thanks to almost overpowering acidity and incredibly vibrant, yet perfectly extracted, tannins. The icing on the cake is that the Gattinara '06 and the Gattinara Castelle '06 are very much like them in constitution and sense of place. A brilliant all-round performance.

● Gattinara Vign. Osso S. Grato '06	▼▼▼+	7
● Gattinara Vign. S. Francesco '06	▼▼▼	6
● Gattinara '06	▼▼	6
● Gattinara Vigneto Castelle '06	▼▼	6
⊙ Coste della Sesia Rosato Bricco Lorella '09	▼	4
○ Erbaluce di Caluso '09	▼	4
● Gattinara Vign. Castelle '00	ΥΥΥ	7
● Gattinara Vign. Castelle '99	ΥΥΥ	7
● Gattinara Vign. Osso S. Grato '05	ΥΥΥ+	7
● Gattinara Vign. Osso S. Grato '04	ΥΥΥ	7
● Gattinara Vign. Osso S. Grato '01	ΥΥΥ	7
● Gattinara Vign. S. Francesco '05	ΥΥΥ	7
● Gattinara Vign. S. Francesco '03	ΥΥΥ	7
● Gattinara Vign. S. Francesco '01	ΥΥΥ	6

Anzivino

c.so Valsesia, 162
13045 Gattinara [VC]
tel. 0163827172
www.anzivino.it

CELLAR SALES
PRE-BOOKED VISITS
ROOMS AND FOOD

ANNUAL PRODUCTION 60,000 bottles
HECTARES UNDER VINE 11
VITICULTURE METHOD Conventional

The union of tradition and modernity has projected the winery of Emanuele and Alessandro Anzivino into the elite of the north Piedmont wine scene. In the late 1990s, they decided to move from Milan to Gattinara and renovate an old distillery. Thus began an adventure in which innovative wines such as Nemesi, a blend of nebbiolo, merlot and syrah, or Caplenga, from nebbiolo, croatina and bonarda, rub shoulders with more traditional products from nebbiolo, blended with croatina, vespolina or bonarda.

Two wines in the final and various others hard on their heels are the mark of a winery in fine fettle. The first high point is Bramaterra Riserva '04, with intense, elegant aromas of sweet tobacco, liquorice and rust swathing a close-woven, meaty palate, just a touch closed on the finish. The other ace up the Anzivino sleeve is Coste della Sesia Faticato '06, an original dried-grape Nebbiolo – think Sfursat – that mingles jammy fruit with bay-led medicinal herbs, concealing slightly harsh tannins on the generous, glycerine-rich palate.

● Bramaterra Ris. '04	▼▼	5
● Coste della Sesia Nebbiolo Faticato '06	▼▼	6
● Bramaterra '06	▼▼	4
● Coste della Sesia Nebbiolo '05	▼▼	4*
● Gattinara '06	▼▼	5
● Caplenga	▼	3
● Nemesi	▼	3
● Bramaterra '05	ΥΥ	4
● Bramaterra '03	ΥΥ	5*
● Bramaterra '02	ΥΥ	5*
● Bramaterra '01	ΥΥ	5*
● Coste della Sesia Faticato '03	ΥΥ	7
● Gattinara '04	ΥΥ	5
● Gattinara Ris. '03	ΥΥ	6

Araldica Vini Piemontesi

V.LE LAUDANO, 2
14040 CASTEL BOGLIONE [AT]
TEL. 014176311
www.araldicavini.com

CELLAR SALES
PRE-BOOKED VISITS

ANNUAL PRODUCTION 6,000,000 bottles
HECTARES UNDER VINE 900
VITICULTURE METHOD Conventional

Araldica is a large co-operative bringing together 300 growers for a total of 900 hectares under vine. Situated on the borders of the provinces of Asti and Alessandria, its main varieties are barbera and cortese, even if it vinifies practically all the typical grapes of this part of Piedmont. Over the years, commitment to quality has been evident above all in the production of solid Gavis.

Araldica performed well overall, particularly with those Gavis. The subtle, elegant Gavi La Lancellotta '09 hinges on floral aromas and white-fleshed fruits, while the Gavi del Comune di Gavi Nuovo Quadro '09 shows vibrant almond veined with minerally gunflint over a palate of great pulp and backbone. There is perhaps a tad too much residual sweetness but it is well balanced and flaunts fine acidity. The Gavi '09 has body and acid thrust to underpin a long, zesty finish with an almond twist. Equally good is the exuberantly fruity, tannic Langhe Nebbiolo Castellero '06, which gives intense blackberries and cinchona.

○ Gavi '09	🍷🍷	3*
○ Gavi del Comune di Gavi Nuovo Quadro '09	🍷🍷	4
○ Gavi La Lancellotta '09	🍷🍷	4
● Langhe Nebbiolo Castellero '06	🍷🍷	4
○ Monferrato Bianco Camillona '09	🍷	4
○ Moscato d'Asti '09	🍷	3
○ Roero Arneis Sorilaria '09	🍷	4
● Barbera d'Asti Sup. D'Annona '07	🍷🍷 (white)	4*
● Barbera d'Asti Sup. Rive '04	🍷🍷 (white)	4*
● Langhe Nebbiolo Castellero '05	🍷🍷 (white)	4*

Tenuta dell'Arbiola

LOC. ARBIOLA
REG. SALINE, 67
14050 SAN MARZANO OLIVETO [AT]
TEL. 0141856194
www.arbiola.it

CELLAR SALES
PRE-BOOKED VISITS
FOOD

ANNUAL PRODUCTION 100,000 bottles
HECTARES UNDER VINE 20
VITICULTURE METHOD Conventional

Last year Tenuta dell'Arbiola was acquired by Saiagricola and after changing hands it is back in the main section of the Guide. Barbera is the most widely planted variety in the chalky-sandy soils of the hillside vineyards overlooking the Nizza valley, with small plots of moscato, cabernet sauvignon, merlot, pinot nero, chardonnay and sauvignon.

The change in management has had no effect on the hierarchy of the winery's products. Barbera d'Asti Superiore Nizza Romilda XII '07 is still the cellar's most interesting label and went through to the finals thanks to its deeply concentrated aromatics of fruit followed by rhubarb and printer's ink, then a rounded palate of structure and impressive acidity. Although still oaky, it vaunts a dynamic finish in which wild red berry fruit returns to the fore. Moscato d'Asti Ferlingot '09 has great character, combining lovely lime, white-fleshed fruit and rosemary on the nose with a fragrant, long, well-balanced palate.

● Barbera d'Asti Sup. Nizza Romilda XII '07	🍷🍷	6
○ Moscato d'Asti Ferlingot '09	🍷🍷	4
● Barbera d'Asti Sup. Nizza Romilda IX '04	🍷🍷 (white)	5
● Barbera d'Asti Sup. Nizza Romilda VII '01	🍷🍷 (white)	6
● Barbera d'Asti Sup. Nizza Romilda VIII '03	🍷🍷 (white)	6
● Barbera d'Asti Sup. Nizza Romilda X '05	🍷🍷 (white)	6

L'Armangia

FRAZ. SAN GIOVANNI, 122
14053 CANELLI [AT]
TEL. 0141824947
www.armangia.it

CELLAR SALES
PRE-BOOKED VISITS

ANNUAL PRODUCTION 85,000 bottles
HECTARES UNDER VINE 10
VITICULTURE METHOD Conventional

Armangia started operations in 1988, when Ignazio Giovine took over and extended the family vineyards. Ignazio's production philosophy pays particular attention to tending the rows. The environmental compatibility criteria adopted in the vineyards are in fact much stricter than those prescribed under European law. The soil is totally grassed and defence against parasites involves limited intervention using only copper and quarried sulphur-based products.

The return of the Barbera d'Asti Superiore Nizza Titon '07 coincides with Ignazio Giovine's return to the top flight of the DOCG. Titon reveals crisp, elegant fruit on the nose, with cherry and pepper notes leading the way, followed by a touch of earthiness. On the palate, good harmony and freshness make up for its lack of power and it ends long and focused. We also liked the Monferrato Rosso Pacifico '06, a blend of 45 per cent nebbiolo and practically all the black grapes grown on the estate, with a smoky nose and austere yet bright, juicy palate showing good length and nice, close-knit tannins, and the drinkably fresh, citrussy Moscato d'Asti Il Giai '09.

● Barbera d'Asti Sup. Nizza Titon '07	2 black glasses	4*
● M.to Rosso Pacifico '06	2 black glasses	4
○ Moscato d'Asti Il Giai '09	2 black glasses	3*
● Barbera d'Asti Sopra Berruti '08	2 white glasses	3*

Ascheri

VIA PIUMATI, 23
12042 BRA [CN]
TEL. 0172412394
www.ascherivini.it

CELLAR SALES
PRE-BOOKED VISITS
ROOMS AND FOOD

ANNUAL PRODUCTION 240,000 bottles
HECTARES UNDER VINE 40
VITICULTURE METHOD Conventional

Not many wineries in Langhe can combine quality and quantity. One that has managed to do so is the Ascheri family operation in Bra, which also houses the Muri Vecchi restaurant and a delightful hotel. The 40 hectares under vine are spread over three districts: Sorano at Serralunga; Rivalta, on the border of La Morra and Verduno; and Montelupa, the hillside vineyard that gives its name to the wines obtained from the syrah and viognier grown there. The products are modern in form but show highly traditional substance.

A magnificent version of the Barolo Sorano Coste e Bricco deservedly brought Three Glasses back to the Ascheris. The perfectly focused fruit and balsam accompany a palate of great vitality, underpinned by luxuriant, precise tannins. This spectacular bottle is joined in an impressive range by a more territorial than varietal Langhe Rosso Montalupa Syrah '06. We also liked the big, crunchy Langhe Arneis Cristina Ascheri '09 while the Nebbiolo d'Alba Fontanelle '08 still needs time but shows promise.

● Barolo Sorano Coste & Bricco '06	3 black glasses	7
○ Langhe Arneis Cristina Ascheri '09	2 black glasses	4*
● Langhe Rosso Montalupa '06	2 black glasses	6
● Nebbiolo d'Alba Fontanelle '08	2 black glasses	4
● Barolo Pisapola '06	1 black glass	6
● Dolcetto d'Alba Nirane '09	1 black glass	4
● Dolcetto d'Alba S. Rocco '09	1 black glass	4
○ Gavi del Comune di Gavi '09	1 black glass	4
○ Langhe Montalupa Bianco Viognier '06	1 black glass	5
○ Moscato d'Asti '09	1 black glass	4
● Nebbiolo d'Alba Bricco S. Giacomo '08	1 black glass	4
● Verduno Pelaverga '09	1 black glass	4
● Barolo Sorano '00	3 white glasses	6*
● Barolo Sorano '03	2 white glasses	6*
● Barolo Sorano Coste & Bricco '04	2 white glasses	7

Paolo Avezza

REGIONE MONFORTE, 62
14053 CANELLI [AT]
TEL. 0141822296
www.paoloavezza.com

CELLAR SALES
PRE-BOOKED VISITS

ANNUAL PRODUCTION 20,000 bottles
HECTARES UNDER VINE 7
VITICULTURE METHOD Conventional

Established in 1956, this winery was redesigned in 2001 to produce quality wines by Paolo Avezza, the third generation of the family to run it. It's a small-scale operation with only seven hectares under vine on chalky soil with a fair amount of sand and silt. As tradition demands, the main variety here is barbera but international varieties such as pinot nero and chardonnay also get a look-in. Results in the last couple of years prove that the Avezza family have made the right decisions.

The Avezza family can feel rightly satisfied with a highly deserved Three Glass prize in only their second year in the Guide. The Barbera d'Asti Superiore Nizza Sotto La Muda '07 shows intense aromas of rain-soaked earth, liquorice, abundant berry fruit and spice, accompanying a somewhat stiff, but fleshy palate with elegant tannins. The lingering finish is dominated by notes of autumn leaves and aromatic herbs. The attractive Barbera d'Asti '09 displays ripe plum on the nose, followed by a fresh, well-balanced palate, in which acidity nicely underpins good body. The other wines are well managed, and particular attention is devoted to developing Paolo's beloved spumantes.

● Barbera d'Asti Sup. Nizza Sotto la Muda '07	🍷🍷🍷	5*
● Barbera d'Asti '09	🍷🍷	3*
○ Alta Langa Brut '06	🍷	5
● Dolcetto d'Asti Sup. '09	🍷	3
○ Moscato d'Asti La Commenda '09	🍷	3
○ Piemonte Chardonnay Bricco della Croce '09	🍷	4
● Barbera d'Asti '07	YY	3*
● Barbera d'Asti Nizza Sotto la Muda '06	YY	5*

Azelia

FRAZ. GARBELLETTO
VIA ALBA-BAROLO, 53
12060 CASTIGLIONE FALLETTO [CN]
TEL. 017362859
l.scavino@azelia.it

CELLAR SALES
PRE-BOOKED VISITS

ANNUAL PRODUCTION 52,000 bottles
HECTARES UNDER VINE 12
VITICULTURE METHOD Conventional

Luigi Scavino's every move is observed by his 21-year-old son Lorenzo, who seems set on following in his footsteps. This will be no mean feat since the Barolos are all outstanding, with well-gauged oak and lovely fruit across the range. Nor should we forget the history of this winery, which was established in 1920 in Castiglione Falletto. The focus of the vineyard holding is shifting towards Serralunga d'Alba, as Luigi has always loved the soil and climate of the area, home to the Margheria, San Rocco and Voghera Brea crus.

Recent vintages have been more fruit-driven, showing less oak than in the past. The well-rounded, deep Barolo Margheria '06 has hints of tobacco and dried herbs on the nose. True to the best tradition of Serralunga in its sumptuous palate, it has lashings of character and thoroughly deserves Three Glasses. The '06 San Rocco, also from Serralunga, is warmer and more alcoholic while the traditional Bricco Fiasco '06 from Castiglione Falletto is soft and velvety. The potent Barolo Voghera Brea Riserva '04 still seems somewhat closed and its oak is a bit too evident.

● Barolo Margheria '06	🍷🍷🍷	8
● Barolo Bricco Fiasco '06	🍷🍷	8
● Barolo S. Rocco '06	🍷🍷	7
● Barbera d'Alba Vign. Punta '08	🍷🍷	5
● Barolo '06	🍷🍷	7
● Barolo Voghera Brea Ris. '04	🍷🍷	8
● Dolcetto d'Alba Bricco dell'Oriolo '09	🍷🍷	4
● Barolo '91	YYY	8
● Barolo Bricco Fiasco '01	YYY	8
● Barolo Bricco Fiasco '95	YYY	8
● Barolo Bricco Fiasco '93	YYY	8
● Barolo S. Rocco '99	YYY	8
● Barolo Voghera Brea Ris. '01	YYY	8
● Barbera d'Alba Vign. Punta '07	YY	5
● Barolo Bricco Fiasco '05	YY	8

Antonio Baldizzone Cascina Lana

c.so Acqui, 187
14049 Nizza Monferrato [AT]
tel. 0141726734
www.cascinalanavini.it

CELLAR SALES

ANNUAL PRODUCTION 60,000 bottles
HECTARES UNDER VINE 18
VITICULTURE METHOD Conventional

Cascina Lana, the lovely winery of Antonio Baldizzone and his wife Graziana Rizzoli, boasts some of the best vineyards in the area, all grouped together on the hills lying on the border of the municipalities of Nizza Monferrato and Acqui Terme, where they enjoy an ideal south-east aspect. The wines are extremely well typed, and fully live up to our quality expectations for this area, especially the Barberas, and in particular the Barbera from the Nizza subzone.

We loved the concentrated Barbera d'Asti Superiore Nizza '07, offering plums, coffee beans and spice on the nose with nicely balanced fruit and spice, over a potent, rich palate. This extremely well-rounded, long wine is still young but promises well. Almost as good is the Monferrato Rosso Vën ëd Michen '08, a broodingly dark 60-40 blend of barbera and cabernet sauvignon with tobacco, cinchona, black berry fruit and garden vegetables on a nose that leads into a rounded, juicy palate with slightly over-evident alcohol and a long finish. Both the citrussy Moscato d'Asti '09 and the uncomplicated, fruity Barbera d'Asti La Cirimela '09 are clean and attractive.

● Barbera d'Asti Sup. Nizza '07	🍷🍷	5
● M.to Rosso Vën ëd Michen '08	🍷🍷	5
● Barbera d'Asti La Cirimela '09	🍷	3
○ Moscato d'Asti '09	🍷	3
● Barbera d'Asti l'Anniversario '07	ŸŸ	5
● Barbera d'Asti Sup. Nizza '06	ŸŸ	5
● Barbera d'Asti Sup. Nizza '05	ŸŸ	5
● Barbera d'Asti Sup. Nizza '01	ŸŸ	5

★ Produttori del Barbaresco

via Torino, 54
12050 Barbaresco [CN]
tel. 0173635139
www.produttoridelbarbaresco.com

CELLAR SALES
PRE-BOOKED VISITS
ROOMS

ANNUAL PRODUCTION 500,000 bottles
HECTARES UNDER VINE 100
VITICULTURE METHOD Conventional

This is not only one of Italy's best co-operative wineries, it is one of the most enlightened in terms of pricing. Consistency throughout the range and peaks of excellence prompt us to rank Produttori del Barbaresco as one of the top operations in Langhe, or elsewhere for that matter. It brings out the best of over 100 hectares of vineyards farmed by 53 members, all planted to nebbiolo. The style is classic and traditional in the best sense of the word, thanks to long macerations and extended ageing in large wood.

Tasting together the nine Barbaresco Riservas, produced by the winery only in favourable years, is a perfect way to acquaint yourself with how the characters of the most famous DOCG vineyards change over the various vintages. A cool growing year like '05, for example, translates into an airier, franker Rabajà than usual, into medicinal herbs and austere tannins in the Pora, and into the sharp thrust of the Asili. As is often the case, at the top of the ladder is the multi-faceted Montestefano, whose spices and smoke are followed by a potent, meaty palate with unfaltering control and harmony. The Langhe Nebbiolo '08 is superb.

● Barbaresco Vign. in Montestefano Ris. '05	🍷🍷🍷	6
● Barbaresco Vigneti in Asili Ris. '05	🍷🍷	7
● Barbaresco Vigneti in Pora Ris. '05	🍷🍷	7
● Barbaresco Vigneti in Rabajà Ris. '05	🍷🍷	7
● Langhe Nebbiolo '08	🍷🍷	4*
● Barbaresco '06	🍷🍷	6
● Barbaresco Vigneti in Moccagatta Ris. '05	🍷🍷	7
● Barbaresco Vigneti in Montefico Ris. '05	🍷🍷	7
● Barbaresco Vigneti in Ovello Ris. '05	🍷🍷	7
● Barbaresco Vigneti in Pajé Ris. '05	🍷🍷	7
● Barbaresco Vigneti in Rio Sordo Ris. '05	🍷	7
● Barbaresco Vign. in Montefico Ris. '00	ŸŸŸ	6*
● Barbaresco Vign. in Montestefano Ris. '04	ŸŸŸ	6*
● Barbaresco Vign. in Montestefano Ris. '01	ŸŸŸ	6
● Barbaresco Vign. in Pajé Ris. '01	ŸŸŸ	6*
● Barbaresco Vign. in Rio Sordo Ris. '01	ŸŸŸ	6*

★ Cascina La Barbatella

S.DA ANNUNZIATA, 55
14049 NIZZA MONFERRATO [AT]
TEL. 0141701434
sonvico.barbatella@libero.it

CELLAR SALES
PRE-BOOKED VISITS

ANNUAL PRODUCTION 22,000 bottles
HECTARES UNDER VINE 4
VITICULTURE METHOD Conventional

Established in 1982 by Angelo Sonvico and recently acquired by the Perego family, Cascina La Barbatella has for many years been a leading light among quality Asti growers thanks to an approach based on elegance and well-focused aromas. Situated in one of the most beautiful areas with excellent growing conditions on the hills of Nizza Monferrato, its vineyards face south and south-east in three plots, with vines aged between 25 and 50 years old. Nizza is produced using only the oldest vines.

Angelo Sonvico's leaving gift was the '07 Barbera d'Asti Superiore Nizza La Vigna dell'Angelo, which earned the winery its 18th Three Glass award. This intense, characterful Nizza shows a plum and cherry nose over a classic, well-orchestrated palate, with finesse and aristocratic character, great length and complexity. Almost as good is the Monferrato Rosso Sonvico '07, a 50-50 blend of barbera and cabernet sauvignon, giving blackcurrant, tobacco and spices on the nose, preceding a powerful, juicy palate and a lingering, tangy finish. The rest of the wines are good.

● Barbera d'Asti Sup. Nizza V. dell'Angelo '07	▼▼▼	6
● M.to Rosso Sonvico '07	▼▼	6
● Barbera d'Asti La Barbatella '09	▼▼	4
○ M.to Bianco Noè '09	▼	4
● Barbera d'Asti Sup. Nizza V. dell'Angelo '01	▽▽▽	7
● M.to Rosso Mystère '01	▽▽▽	7
● M.to Rosso Sonvico '06	▽▽▽	6
● M.to Rosso Sonvico '04	▽▽▽	6
● M.to Rosso Sonvico '03	▽▽▽	7
● M.to Rosso Sonvico '00	▽▽▽	7
● M.to Rosso Sonvico '98	▽▽▽	7

Barni

VIA FORTE, 63
13862 BRUSNENGO [BI]
TEL. 015985977
filippo.barni@alice.it

CELLAR SALES
PRE-BOOKED VISITS

ANNUAL PRODUCTION 20,000 bottles
HECTARES UNDER VINE 5
VITICULTURE METHOD Conventional

Filippo Barni is one of the most original growers in the Biella area, where he started out as a grower and artist in the mid-1990s. The six hectares of the splendid Mesola amphitheatre are planted with century-old vines of croatina, nebbiolo, uva rara and erbaluce using the traditional maggiorina training system. The small plot in Brusnengo is planted to erbaluce and chardonnay. The wines in this compact range share a unique, lively and eclectic style in a natural idiom.

This is a comeback for Barni's wines to a full profile, with two real gems that impressed at our finals. The intense bright gold Cantagal '07, from erbaluce grapes part-dried for five months, offers candied peel, crème caramel, saffron and peaches in syrup. In the mouth it is sweet and viscous but loses nothing in freshness and character. The Bramaterra Vigna Doss Pilun '05 also did well. The notes of medicinal herbs, liquorice and rust are utterly varietal and the palate is lively and racy, although perhaps somewhat predictable.

● Bramaterra V. Doss Pilun '05	▼▼	5
○ Cantagal '07	▼▼	7
○ Albaciara Bianco '09	▼▼	4
● Bramaterra '05	▼▼	5
● Coste della Sesia Rosso Torrearsa '05	▼▼	5
● Bramaterra V. Doss Pilun '04	▽▽	5
● Bramaterra V. Doss Pilun '03	▽▽	5
● Bramaterra V. Doss Pilun '02	▽▽	5
○ Cantagal '06	▽▽	7
○ Cantagal '04	▽▽	7
○ Cantagal '03	▽▽	7
● Coste della Sesia Rosso Mesolone '02	▽▽	5
● Coste della Sesia Rosso Torrearsa '02	▽▽	5

Batasiolo

FRAZ. ANNUNZIATA, 87
12064 LA MORRA [CN]
TEL. 017350130
www.batasiolo.com

PRE-BOOKED VISITS

ANNUAL PRODUCTION 2,500,000 bottles
HECTARES UNDER VINE 107
VITICULTURE METHOD Conventional

There has been much talk over the last year of the new Boscareto Resort, built amidst the Serralunga vineyards by Batasiolo to attract wine tourists and gourmets. The Dogliani family hope this ambitious project will give a further boost to the Langhe, and complement one of the area's largest operations in terms of the range and quantity of wines produced. There are only Nebbiolos from some of the best vineyards but also whites, spumantes, Moscatos and a whole series of labels with an accomplished, assertive style.

Batasiolo fail to repeat last year's top accolade but the overall performance was extremely sound. The best performers were the Barolo Corda della Briccolina and the Barolo Vigneto Bofani '06, both of which made the finals and were appreciated for their authentic sense of terroir. The former displays dried flowers and raspberry on the nose; the latter medicinal herbs and tobacco. Both, however, reveal austere tannins, fine-grained but lacking support from the pulp. Also pleasing are the Gavi del Comune di Gavi Granée '09 and the Langhe Rosso '08, from dolcetto, barbera and nebbiolo.

● Barolo Bofani '06	▼▼	8
● Barolo Corda della Briccolina '06	▼▼	8
● Barolo '06	▼▼	7
● Barolo Boscareto '06	▼▼	8
● Barolo Cerequio '06	▼▼	8
● Barolo Ris. '04	▼▼	7
○ Gavi di Gavi Granée '09	▼▼	4
● Langhe Rosso '08	▼▼	4
● Barbaresco '07	▼	6
● Barbera d'Alba Sovrana '08	▼	5
● Dolcetto d'Alba Bricco di Vergne '09	▼	4
○ Gavi '09	▼	4
○ Langhe Bianco Sunsì '09	▼	5
○ Langhe Chardonnay Morino '08	▼	6
○ Langhe Chardonnay Serbato '09	▼	4
○ Moscato d'Asti Bosc dla Rei '09	▼	4
● Barolo Boscareto '05	▽▽▽	8
● Barolo Corda della Briccolina '88	▽▽▽	8

Fabrizio Battaglino

LOC. BORGONUOVO
VIA MONTALDO ROERO, 44
12040 VEZZA D'ALBA [CN]
TEL. 0173658156
www.battaglino.com

CELLAR SALES
PRE-BOOKED VISITS

ANNUAL PRODUCTION 17,000 bottles
HECTARES UNDER VINE 4
VITICULTURE METHOD Conventional

Fabrizio Battaglino's small winery, in its second year in the Guide, proved its worth and enjoyed further success. His vineyards of arneis, barbera and nebbiolo are planted on sandy soil at an altitude of 350 metres in the Colla and Munbèl hills, in the municipality of Vezza d'Alba. The wines produced are typical of the territory: Roero Arneis, Roero, Nebbiolo d'Alba, Barbera d'Alba and Langhe Rosso.

We saw a quantum leap forward by Fabrizio Battaglino, who walked off with Three Glasses for his Nebbiolo d'Alba Colla '07, a stylish, complex wine offering tobacco, spice, raspberry and dried flowers over a refreshing, elegant palate with well-integrated, close-woven tannins and a long finish. But that's not all, seeing that another two wines made our finals. The velvet-smooth Roero Sergentin '07 boasts rich red fruits on the nose, although it still has a touch too much oak, while the Roero Arneis '09 combines mineral notes and white-fleshed fruits on the nose with great grip and thrust on the palate. The remaining wines are pleasant.

● Nebbiolo d'Alba V. Colla '07	▼▼▼	4*
○ Roero Arneis '09	▼▼	4*
● Roero Sergentin '07	▼▼	4*
● Nebbiolo d'Alba '07	▼▼	4*
● Barbera d'Alba V. Munbèl '07	▼	4
● Langhe Rosso Ancreus '07	▼	4
● Barbera d'Alba V. Munbèl '06	▽▽	4*
● Nebbiolo d'Alba V. Colla '06	▽▽	4*
● Roero '06	▽▽	4*
○ Roero Arneis '08	▽▽	3*

Luigi Baudana

FRAZ. BAUDANA, 43
12050 SERRALUNGA D'ALBA [CN]
TEL. 0173613354
www.baudanaluigi.com

CELLAR SALES
PRE-BOOKED VISITS

ANNUAL PRODUCTION 25,000 bottles
HECTARES UNDER VINE 4
VITICULTURE METHOD Conventional

For this year, we felt Luigi Baudana's wines still deserved a place in the main section. As we mentioned last year, he has decided to hand over the running of the winery to G.D.Vajra from Barolo. We are well aware of Aldo Vajra's professionalism and experience and are sure that this small estate at Serralunga will continue to thrive, building on the solid foundations laid by Luigi and Fiorina Baudana.

This year, the two Barolo '06s complement each other with their distinct interpretations of the wine. The deep garnet Barolo Cerretta unfolds on the palate with sweet spice and red berry fruit, offset by appealingly supple tannins, to finish powerful and very long. The deep-hued, bright Barolo Baudana offers aromas of tobacco and raspberry, followed by a rich, juicy attack on the palate. It is just slightly mouth-drying on the finish and lacks the roundness of its stablemate. We also liked the fresh, well-balanced Langhe Chardonnay '09.

●	Barolo Cerretta '06	[2 black glasses]	7
●	Barolo Baudana '06	[2 black glasses]	7
○	Langhe Chardonnay '09	[2 black glasses]	4*
●	Barbera d'Alba Donatella '05	[2 white glasses]	5
●	Barolo '05	[2 white glasses]	6
●	Barolo Baudana '05	[2 white glasses]	7
●	Barolo Baudana '04	[2 white glasses]	7
●	Barolo Cerretta Piani '05	[2 white glasses]	7
●	Barolo Cerretta Piani '04	[2 white glasses]	7
●	Dolcetto d'Alba Baudana '06	[2 white glasses]	4

Bava

S.DA MONFERRATO, 2
14023 COCCONATO [AT]
TEL. 0141907083
www.bava.com

CELLAR SALES
PRE-BOOKED VISITS
ROOMS

ANNUAL PRODUCTION 500,000 bottles
HECTARES UNDER VINE 50
VITICULTURE METHOD Conventional

The winery, at Cocconato d'Asti, has several plots in Monferrato and Langhe. It dates back to 1911, and is now run by Roberto, Giulio and Paolo Bava. They produce various lines of still wines, in particular from barbera and malvasia, plus Alta Langa metodo classico spumantes from the Giulio Cocchi vineyard, owned by the Bava family.

We loved the Barbera d'Asti Superiore Nizza Piano Alto '07, whose pervasive bouquet is dominated by red stone fruits and spice. A long, taut, austere palate shows good pulp. Although not typical, it is hard not to like. We enjoyed the Barolo Scarrone '05, with raspberry and cinchona on the nose followed by mature notes on the tight-knit, balanced palate. The Alta Langa Brut Bianc d'Bianc '05 has sumptuous butter and white-fleshed fruit on the powerful, creamy nose but a touch too much sweetness in the mouth. Lastly, the Alta Langa Brut Toto Corde '06 shows rounded, complex notes of damson, honey, hazelnut and crusty bread leading into a poised palate.

●	Barbera d'Asti Sup. Nizza Piano Alto '07	[2 black glasses]	5
○	Alta Langa Brut Bianc 'd Bianc Giulio Cocchi '05	[2 black glasses]	6
○	Alta Langa Toto Corde Giulio Cocchi '06	[2 black glasses]	5
●	Barolo Scarrone '05	[2 black glasses]	7
⊙	Alta Langa Brut Rösa Giulio Cocchi '06	[1 black glass]	6
○	Moscato d'Asti Bass Tuba '09	[1 black glass]	4
○	Piemonte Chardonnay Thou Bianc '09	[1 black glass]	4
⊙	Alta Langa Brut Rösa Giulio Cocchi '04	[2 white glasses]	6
●	Barbera d'Asti Libera '07	[2 white glasses]	4*
●	Barbera d'Asti Sup. Stradivario '01	[2 white glasses]	7
●	Barolo Scarrone '04	[2 white glasses]	7

Bel Colle

FRAZ. CASTAGNI, 56
12060 VERDUNO [CN]
TEL. 0172470196
www.belcolle.it

CELLAR SALES
PRE-BOOKED VISITS

ANNUAL PRODUCTION 180,000 bottles
HECTARES UNDER VINE 10
VITICULTURE METHOD Conventional

The Barolo Monvigliero and the Monvigliero Riserva from the Bel Colle winery are produced at Verduno, a district better known for Pelaverga than nebbiolo-based wines. Actually, Bel Colle's Verduno Pelaverga is always one of the best but the winery has also been producing sound Barolos, Barbarescos, Barberas and Dolcettos for a good 34 years, led by its owners, Franco Pontiglione and Giuseppe Priola. The oenologist Paolo Torchio is a versatile wine technician and an essential part of the Bel Colle set-up.

The focused Barbera Le Masche from the splendid '07 vintage brims with fruit and acidity. An appealing Roero Monvijè '07 shows elegant, composed power while well-integrated tannins make the Nebbiolo d'Alba Bricco Reala '07 even more interesting. The '06 Barolo Monvigliero's turn comes next year but the Riserva Monvigliero '04 lived up to its reputation. Its tertiary aromas are already developed, with liquorice and tar combining in a classic profile while on the palate, balance, length and tannins come to the fore. The Barolo '06, a blend from two Verduno vineyards, Boscato and Neirane, is a lightweight version of the previous wine, laden with raspberry fruit.

● Barolo '06	▼▼	6
● Barolo Monvigliero Ris. '04	▼▼	7
● Barbaresco Roncaglie '07	▼▼	6
● Barbera d'Alba Sup. Le Masche '07	▼▼	5
● Dolcetto d'Alba '09	▼▼	4*
○ Langhe Chardonnay Le Masche '09	▼▼	4*
● Nebbiolo d'Alba Bricco Reala '07	▼▼	4*
● Roero Monvijé '07	▼▼	5
● Verduno Pelaverga '09	▼▼	4*
○ Roero Arneis '09	▼	4
● Barbaresco Roncaglie '06	▽▽	6
● Barbera d'Alba Le Masche '06	▽▽	4*
● Barolo Boscato '04	▽▽	6
● Barolo Boscato '03	▽▽	6
● Barolo Monvigliero '05	▽▽	6
● Barolo Monvigliero '01	▽▽	6*

Bera

VIA CASTELLERO, 12
12050 NEVIGLIE [CN]
TEL. 0173630194
www.bera.it

CELLAR SALES
PRE-BOOKED VISITS

ANNUAL PRODUCTION 130,000 bottles
HECTARES UNDER VINE 22
VITICULTURE METHOD Conventional

Walter Bera, who has been running the centuries-old family winery since the 1980s, is one of the most interesting big names in Moscato d'Asti. Thanks to his deep love of the territory, he has briskly managed to create a solid operation producing not only great sweet wines but also a large range of traditional reds, as well as dry whites and sparklers, all at competitive prices.

The exquisite Moscato Su Reimond, from an old vineyard, has concentration and creamy softness with ripe peach, citrus fruit and honey. The basic version is fresher and simpler, with apples, lime and florality. The Asti '09 has breadth on the nose and a fresh palate. The barbera-heavy Sassisto '07 is as good as ever, with hints of coffee, glossy tannins and fine balance. The plush, flavoursome Barbera La Lena '07 is very juicy. The earthy, fruit-driven Barbera d'Asti '08 and youthful Nebbiolo Alladio '06 with its freshly milled black pepper are well made. Last up are the solid Barbaresco '06, which still needs to smooth out, and the well-typed Dolcetto and Barbera d'Alba '09.

○ Moscato d'Asti Su Reimond '09	▼▼	4*
○ Alta Langa Bera Brut '04	▼▼	5
○ Asti '09	▼▼	4*
● Barbaresco '06	▼▼	6
● Barbera d'Alba Sup. La Lena '07	▼▼	4*
● Barbera d'Asti '08	▼▼	4*
● Langhe Sassisto '07	▼▼	5
○ Moscato d'Asti '09	▼▼	4*
● Barbera d'Alba '09	▼	4
● Dolcetto d'Alba '09	▼	4
● Langhe Nebbiolo Alladio '06	▼	5
● Barbera d'Alba Sup. La Lena '04	▽▽	4*
○ Moscato d'Asti '08	▽▽	4
○ Moscato d'Asti Su Reimond '08	▽▽	4
○ Moscato d'Asti Su Reimond '06	▽▽	4*

Cinzia Bergaglio

via Gavi, 29
15060 Tassarolo [AL]
tel. 0143342203
la.fornace@virgilio.it

CELLAR SALES
PRE-BOOKED VISITS

ANNUAL PRODUCTION 25,000 bottles
HECTARES UNDER VINE 5
VITICULTURE METHOD Conventional

Italy is often criticized for its plethora of labels, with even small wineries offering a disproportionate number of products. This premise serves to introduce the only two wines presented by this virtuous producer from Gavi. Both are full of character, taut and deep in the mouth with no excess or superfluity, and seamless progression. The tempting prices also deserve a mention.

The intense, subtle Gavi del Comune di Gavi Grifone delle Roveri '09 offers floral notes over a mineral backdrop which is beginning to come through. It is just a touch youthful, with some notes of fermentation still present, and shows medium weight in the mouth, where it is harmonious, fresh but not acidic, soft and long. The Gavi La Fornace '09, a classic of the designation, opens to fruit and spring flowers, paving the way for a clean-tasting, pleasantly fresh but not overpowering palate, characterized by a lovely sweet almond finish.

○ Gavi del Comune di Gavi Grifone delle Roveri '09	▼▼	3*
○ Gavi La Fornace '09	▼▼	3*
○ Gavi del Comune di Gavi Grifone delle Roveri '08	▽▽	3*
○ Gavi del Comune di Tassarolo La Fornace '08	▽▽	3*

Nicola Bergaglio

fraz. Rovereto
loc. Pedaggeri, 59
15066 Gavi [AL]
tel. 0143682195
nicolabergaglio@alice.it

CELLAR SALES
PRE-BOOKED VISITS

ANNUAL PRODUCTION 120,000 bottles
HECTARES UNDER VINE 15
VITICULTURE METHOD Conventional

This historic winery is located at Rovereto, one of the best growing areas in the whole of Gavi. The range hinges around a few wines, all based on cortese, a variety whose qualities this winery expresses to the full year in, year out. When young, the wines can at times be somewhat unapproachable, but with correct ageing achieve wonderful complexity.

Historic Bergaglio finally earns Three Glasses, thanks to the wine from its equally historic vineyard, Minaia. The superb Gavi del Comune di Gavi Minaia '09 plays on dominant notes of white-fleshed fruit, flowers and country herbs. Its characteristic, albeit subdued, mineral tones are just beginning to develop and will continue to improve for many years. On the palate, it is juicy, long, vibrant, and fresh but not acidic. A delight right through to the finish, where its notes of flint are accompanied by rich, sweet almond. Slightly simpler but not without character and drinkability is the Gavi del Comune di Gavi '09, a classic example of its type.

○ Gavi del Comune di Gavi Minaia '09	▼▼▼	5
○ Gavi del Comune di Gavi '09	▼▼	4
○ Gavi del Comune di Gavi '08	▽▽	4*
○ Gavi del Comune di Gavi '07	▽▽	3*
○ Gavi del Comune di Gavi Minaia '08	▽▽	4*
○ Gavi del Comune di Gavi Minaia '07	▽▽	4*

Bersano

P.zza Dante, 21
14049 Nizza Monferrato [AT]
tel. 0141720211
www.bersano.it

CELLAR SALES
PRE-BOOKED VISITS

ANNUAL PRODUCTION 2,600,000 bottles
HECTARES UNDER VINE 240
VITICULTURE METHOD Conventional

Bersano is a long-established winery with no fewer than 11 holdings scattered around Langhe, Monferrato and the Alessandria area. These comprising an impressive series of vineyards, including some of the finest in Piedmont. Despite substantial production figures, the cellar manages to offer high-quality wines with a real sense of place, in particular in the Conti della Cremosina line.

We applauded a fine encore from this great winery, which owns some of the finest barbera vineyards in the whole of the Asti area. Whilst awaiting the Barbera Generala '08, we tried the well-managed Arturo Bersano Brut Riserva '07 with its floral notes and yeastiness and fine length, and the lingering, intensely vibrant Barbera d'Asti Cremosina '08, which finds a nice balance of oak and ripe fruit. We also liked the Moscato d'Asti San Michele '09 with loads of lime and sage, and the uncomplicated, drinkable Arturosé Brut '07.

○ Arturo Bersano Brut Ris. '07	5
● Barbera d'Asti Cremosina '08	4
⊙ Arturosé Brut '07	5
○ Moscato d'Asti San Michele '09	4
● Barbaresco Mantico '03	6
● Barbera d'Asti Sup. Generala '07	6
● Barbera d'Asti Sup. Generala '03	6
● Barbera d'Asti Sup. Generala '01	7
● Monferrato Rosso Pomona '04	6

Guido Berta

loc. Saline, 53
14050 San Marzano Oliveto [AT]
tel. 0141856193
www.guidoberta.com

CELLAR SALES
PRE-BOOKED VISITS

ANNUAL PRODUCTION 30,000 bottles
HECTARES UNDER VINE 11
VITICULTURE METHOD Organic

Guido Berta continues to produce quality wines. His winery, based at San Marzano Oliveto, has 12 hectares under vine, all situated in the same municipality, with some vines as old as 50 years, planted on limestone and clay soils with aspects ranging from south-east to south-west. Barbera is Guido Berta's star, with moscato and chardonnay in supporting roles.

Guido Berta again made our finals with his top wine, Barbera d'Asti Superiore Nizza Canto di Luna '07. Opening with sweet wood, black berry fruit, tobacco and rain-soaked earth, it leads into a lingering, fruity palate with bags of character and tannins well tucked in. A wine of great class. The basic Barbera d'Asti Superiore '07 is also extremely well executed, with typical ripe, yet fresh fruit and a supple palate braced by good acidity but free of astringency or harshness. Lastly, we should mention the excellent Moscato d'Asti '09, where moss, peach and sage are backed up by a finely balanced, fresh palate.

● Barbera d'Asti Sup. Nizza Canto di Luna '07	5
● Barbera d'Asti Sup. '07	4
○ Moscato d'Asti '09	4
● Barbera d'Asti Sup. Canto di Luna '05	4
● Barbera d'Asti Sup. Canto di Luna '04	4

Eugenio Bocchino

FRAZ. SANTA MARIA
LOC. SERRA, 96A
12064 LA MORRA [CN]
TEL. 0173500358
www.eugeniobocchino.it

CELLAR SALES
PRE-BOOKED VISITS

ANNUAL PRODUCTION 30,000 bottles
HECTARES UNDER VINE 6
VITICULTURE METHOD Conventional

Eugenio and his wife Cinzia are Barolo outsiders. Their winery is a fairly new operation but with plenty of potential. A decade in La Morra has seen them adopt a traditional style, although they do use new technologies and French oak. They are not afraid to use barriques, and have learned to exploit them to advantage, as the Nebbiolo d'Alba La Perucca clearly shows. The couple promise that their operation will stay family run and compact, with just over five hectares at La Morra, Verduno, Roddi and Alba.

The fine La Morra vineyard brings us the Barolo La Serra '06, which is already fairly open on the nose, proffering somewhat one-dimensional red berry fruit, dried flowers and sweet tobacco, followed by powerful alcohol on the palate and rough, grainy tannins. This is clearly one to lay down. The complex Nebbiolo d'Alba La Perucca '06 opens with liquorice and leather on the nose, followed by lots of pulp and flesh in the mouth. The Langhe Nebbiolo Roccabella shows clearer signs of oak ageing, with spices to the fore. The sound Langhe Suo di Giacomo '06, based on barbera, nebbiolo and cabernet sauvignon, boasts intense vegetal and fruit aromas over a hefty, well-structured palate.

● Barolo La Serra '06	2 black glasses	7
● Langhe Nebbiolo Roccabella '06	2 black glasses	6
● Langhe Rosso Suo di Giacomo '06	2 black glasses	6
● Nebbiolo d'Alba La Perucca '06	2 black glasses	6
● Barbera d'Alba '07	2 white glasses	4*
● Barbera d'Alba '05	2 white glasses	4*
● Barolo La Serra '05	2 white glasses	8
● Barolo La Serra '04	2 white glasses	7
● Barolo La Serra '03	2 white glasses	7
● Barolo Lu '05	2 white glasses	7
● Barolo Lu '04	2 white glasses	7
○ Langhe Sas '06	2 white glasses	4
● Nebbiolo d'Alba La Perucca '05	2 white glasses	6
● Nebbiolo d'Alba La Perucca '04	2 white glasses	6

Alfiero Boffa

VIA LEISO, 50
14050 SAN MARZANO OLIVETO [AT]
TEL. 0141856115
www.alfieroboffa.com

CELLAR SALES
PRE-BOOKED VISITS
ROOMS

ANNUAL PRODUCTION 100,000 bottles
HECTARES UNDER VINE 25
VITICULTURE METHOD Certified organic

In this San Marzano Oliveto operation, the search for quality has always involved vinifying grapes from the individual vineyards separately. This focus on crus continues to give excellent results. Alfiero Boffa grows mainly barbera, and to a much lesser extent moscato and pinot nero, in vineyards situated at San Marzano Oliveto, Moasca and Nizza Monferrato.

The Barbera d'Asti Superiore Nizza La Riva '07 is the best in a splendid range from Alfiero Boffa. Initially limited to oak and tobacco, it then unfolds, showing sour cherry and ginger over a long, consistent palate. Boffa's other vineyard selections are also interesting. Barbera d'Asti Superiore Collina della Vedova '07 has intense notes of dark berry fruit and cocoa powder over a well-structured, powerful palate, offset by fresh acidity. The Barbera d'Asti Superiore Muntrivé '08 has tones of cinchona and a nicely fleshy, if somewhat immature palate, a common trait of '08 Barberas. Lastly, the fresh, supple Barbera d'Asti Superiore Cua Longa '08 proffers blackberries on the nose.

● Barbera d'Asti Sup. Nizza V. La Riva '07	2 black glasses	5
● Barbera d'Asti Sup. Collina della Vedova '07	2 black glasses	5
● Barbera d'Asti Sup. V. Cua Longa '08	2 black glasses	5
● Barbera d'Asti Sup. V. Muntrivé '08	2 black glasses	5
● Barbera d'Asti Sup. V. More '08	1 black glass	5
● Barbera d'Asti Sup. Nizza V. La Riva '01	2 white glasses	5
● Barbera d'Asti Sup. V. More '07	2 white glasses	5*
● Barbera d'Asti Sup. V. Muntrivé '05	2 white glasses	5

Enzo Boglietti

VIA FONTANE, 18A
12064 LA MORRA [CN]
TEL. 017350330
www.enzoboglietti.com

CELLAR SALES
PRE-BOOKED VISITS
ROOMS

ANNUAL PRODUCTION 90,000 bottles
HECTARES UNDER VINE 23
VITICULTURE METHOD Conventional

Boglietti's Barolos are a conscious attempt to make, using small wood, modern, concentrated wines that don't need long ageing. The brothers have vineyards in the southernmost strip of the Barolo production zone. The big news is the production of around 43 hectolitres of Barolo Riserva from the finest plots. The '04 Riserva is produced almost exclusively from the Fossati vineyard. Enzo and Gianni, who still rely on their indefatigable father Renato, share the work in the rows, winery and office. They dedicate their free time to the fine agriturismo they have opened in Sinio.

The superb Barolo Arione '06 fully deserved its Three Glasses. Red fruit and spice hold sway over elegant toastiness on the nose, and despite some harshness on the palate, there is enough pulp to ensure magnificent development. All the Barolos are aged for around two and a half years in a variety of barrels. The Riserva gets four years: 18 months in small wood, one year in 15-hectolitre barrels and a few months' final assemblage in 43-litre barrels. The result is classy, full of character and already drinking nicely. The Barolo Case Nere and Fossati '06 are sound, if still a touch oaky. The Barbera selections and the Langhe Buio will be released in 2011.

● Barolo Arione '06	3 black glasses	8
● Barolo Ris. '04	2 black glasses	8
● Barolo Case Nere '06	2 black glasses	8
● Barolo Fossati '06	2 black glasses	8
● Dolcetto d'Alba Tigli Neri '09	2 black glasses	4
● Langhe Cabernet V. Talpone '07	2 black glasses	7
● Langhe Merlot V. Talpone '07	2 black glasses	7
● Langhe Nebbiolo '09	2 black glasses	5
● Dolcetto d'Alba '09	1 black glass	4
● Barolo Arione '05	3 white glasses	8
● Barolo Brunate '01	3 white glasses	8
● Barolo Brunate '97	3 white glasses	8
● Barolo Case Nere '04	3 white glasses	8
● Barolo Case Nere '99	3 white glasses	8
● Barolo Fossati '96	3 white glasses	7

Bondi

S.DA CAPPELLETTE, 73
15076 OVADA [AL]
TEL. 0143821369
www.bondivini.it

CELLAR SALES
PRE-BOOKED VISITS

ANNUAL PRODUCTION 20,000 bottles
HECTARES UNDER VINE 7
VITICULTURE METHOD Conventional

Domenico Bondi and his children make reliable wines. We were getting used to seeing their wines in the final tastings and noted their absence this time. Sadly, '08 was not a great vintage for Dolcetto di Ovada, and so the results, although good, are not up to the usual high standards. We still hope to see an Ovada winery bring home top honours in the future with dolcetto, a variety that still has much potential to express in this area.

Ruvrin '07, a Barbera del Monferrato Superiore, combines an impenetrable hue with intense cocoa powder and cinchona, followed by a concentrated, fleshy palate with a beautifully lingering finish. D'Uien, a Dolcetto di Ovada Superiore '08, reveals its youth in its hue and fruity aromas. The palate has good structure, with slightly husky tannins emerging on the finish. The Dolcetto Nani '08 offers jammy aromas and alcohol on the nose, echoed on the lengthy palate. Le Guie '08, a Monferrato Rosso from barbera and dolcetto, has a powerful nose, matched by the palate. The obtrusive tannins still need some time to integrate on the finish.

● Dolcetto di Ovada Nani '08	2 black glasses	3
● Dolcetto di Ovada Sup. D'Uien '08	2 black glasses	4
● M.to Barbera Ruvrin Sup. '07	2 black glasses	4
● Monferrato Rosso Le Guie '08	1 black glass	4
● Dolcetto di Ovada Nani '07	2 white glasses	3*
● Dolcetto di Ovada Sup. d'Uien '07	2 white glasses	4
● M.to Barbera Ruvrin Sup. '06	2 white glasses	4
● M.to Rosso Le Guie '07	2 white glasses	4

Borgo Maragliano

REG. SAN SEBASTIANO, 2
14051 LOAZZOLO [AT]
TEL. 014487132
www.borgomaragliano.com

CELLAR SALES
PRE-BOOKED VISITS

ANNUAL PRODUCTION **220,000 bottles**
HECTARES UNDER VINE **21**
VITICULTURE METHOD **Conventional**

This estate in Loazzolo, with 21 hectares under vine in the Asti part of Langhe, is situated at an altitude of between 350 and 450 metres on a natural terrace that enjoys an outstanding site climate. The sandy, tufa and limestone soils are free of clay, and this, together with the good aspect, give Carlo Galliano's wines real finesse. The main varieties grown are moscato, chardonnay and pinot nero.

Three Glasses eluded Carlo Galliano this year but he confirmed his rank as one of Italy's leading producers of fizz. The Giuseppe Galliano Brut '06, from 80 per cent pinot nero topped up with chardonnay, has complex, well-orchestrated aromas, from crusty bread to damson and dried fruits. The lingering palate reveals power, balance and depth. The Francesco Galliano Blanc de Blancs '07 has layered balsam, floral and cake, complemented by a rich creamy palate that signs off with acid thrust and a bitterish finish. The Moscato d'Asti La Caliera '09 is also splendid, offering lively citrus and sage over a fresh, poised palate, with good acidity underpinning the luscious fruit.

○ Francesco Galliano Blanc de Blancs '07	5*
○ Giuseppe Galliano Brut '06	5*
○ Moscato d'Asti La Caliera '09	4*
○ El Calié '09	3*
○ Moscato Borgo Maragliano '09	4
○ Giuseppe Galliano Brut Ris. '01	5*
○ Francesco Galliano Blanc de Blancs '06	5*
○ Giuseppe Galliano Brut M. Cl. '04	5
○ Loazzolo Borgo Maragliano V. T. '04	6
○ Loazzolo Borgo Maragliano V. T. '01	6
○ Moscato d'Asti La Caliera '08	4*

Giacomo Borgogno & Figli

VIA GIOBERTI, 1
12060 BAROLO [CN]
TEL. 017356108
www.borgogno.com

CELLAR SALES
PRE-BOOKED VISITS

ANNUAL PRODUCTION **110,000 bottles**
HECTARES UNDER VINE **15**
VITICULTURE METHOD **Conventional**

Barolo and Borgogno are practically synonymous in Langhe. The foundation stone bears the date 1761 and Italian unity was toasted with a Borgogno Barolo in 1861. Today, in the original winery, renovated by the new owners, Eataly, visitors can buy bottles from 1961 onwards. Long ageing is in fact one of this winery's most laudable habits, as is the stiff, austere demeanour of their wines, which make no concessions to those looking for soft early drinkers.

Vigna Liste '05 perfectly embodies the classic traits of Barolo from Barolo and of the historic Borgogno winery, taking home Three Glasses by virtue of its dried flowers on the nose and the noble austerity of a powerful, delightfully tannic palate. The fine Riserva '04 is just a touch less lively, showing a leaner style based more on tannins than fruit pulp. The basic Barolo '05 is concentrated and strong in alcohol while the Barbera d'Alba Superiore '08, with cherry and rain-soaked earth on the nose, is pure pleasure. The Dolcetto '09 and Barbera d'Alba '08 are well made.

● Barolo Liste '05	8
● Barolo Ris. '04	8
● Barbera d'Alba Sup. '08	5
● Barolo '05	7
● Barbera d'Alba '08	4
● Dolcetto d'Alba '09	4
● Barolo Cl. '98	8
● Barbera d'Alba Sup. '07	5
● Barolo '04	8
● Barolo '03	8
● Barolo Cl. '03	8
● Barolo Cl. '01	8
● Barolo Liste '04	8
● Barolo Liste '03	8

Boroli

LOC. MADONNA DI COMO, 34
12051 ALBA [CN]
TEL. 0173365477
www.boroli.it

CELLAR SALES
PRE-BOOKED VISITS

ANNUAL PRODUCTION **200,000 bottles**
HECTARES UNDER VINE **32**
VITICULTURE METHOD **Conventional**

Silvano and Elena Boroli have really pulled the stops out, managing to turn Cascina Bompè in Madonna di Como into a solid operation in less than 20 years. They have a second facility, La Brunella, in Castiglione Falletto, where they produce Barolo, for a total of 32 hectares under vine. Most of the production is now dealt with by their son Achille, helped by oenologist Enzo Alluvione. Those who want the full experience can stop at the Locanda del Pilone, their fine renovated farmhouse with rooms and a restaurant.

Although they turned out a fine range this year, the Boroli family didn't quite achieve their usual heights of excellence. The two selections of '06 Barolo we tasted are still very young, and the polyphenols are not yet perfectly integrated. Better of the two is the Cerequio, thanks to its delicious fruit pulp, which does much to counter the harsh tannins. The Villero meanwhile offers purists the aromatic complexity and solidity of old-style Barolos and the less complex standard '06 has the merit of achieving good overall harmony. Among the other wines, a rich Barbera Fagiani '07 stands out for its warmth and well-rounded palate.

● Barbera d'Alba Sup. Fagiani '07	TT	6
● Barolo '06	TT	7
● Barolo Cerequio '06	TT	8
● Barolo Villero '06	TT	8
○ Moscato d'Asti Aureum '09	T	4
● Barolo Villero '01	YYY	8
● Barolo Villero '00	YYY	8
● Barbera d'Alba Sup. Fagiani '06	YY	6
● Barolo '05	YY	7
● Barolo Cerequio '04	YY	8
● Barolo Cerequio '04	YY	8
● Barolo Cerequio '03	YY	8
● Barolo Villero '05	YY	8
● Barolo Villero '03	YY	8
● Barolo Villero Ris. '00	YY	8

Francesco Boschis

FRAZ. SAN MARTINO DI PIANEZZO, 57
12063 DOGLIANI [CN]
TEL. 017370574
www.marcdegrazia.com

CELLAR SALES
PRE-BOOKED VISITS

ANNUAL PRODUCTION **40,000 bottles**
HECTARES UNDER VINE **11**
VITICULTURE METHOD **Conventional**

The Boschis family manages this interesting ten-hectare operation in the Dogliani area with a sure hand. Dolcetto is at the heart of the range presented, although the winery is no slouch with the other local varieties. The various interpretations of Dolcetto all show distinctive character, the result of combining tradition with no-nonsense modernity. The variety is too often underrated and its great potential snubbed. Prices at Boschis are very competitive.

Dogliani Vigna dei Prey '08 is on a par with the Dogliani Sorì San Martino '08, both just missing top honours. Complex and aristocratic, with an almost impenetrable purple-tinged ruby hue, Vigna dei Prey is dominated by spicy notes but the tucked-in tannins are fresh. The finer Sorì San Martino gives black berry fruit with tobacco and spice on the finish. The sauvignon-only Langhe Bianco Vigna del Garisin '09 flaunts a brilliant greenish straw before wafts of cinnamon and coffee beans mingle with elegant peaches and white-fleshed fruits. The well-managed Barbera d'Alba Le Masserie '07 presents a bright purple ruby and opens with vibrant, ripe fruit but shows a touch too much oak.

● Dogliani Sorì S. Martino '08	TT	4*
● Dogliani V. dei Prey '08	TT	4*
● Barbera d'Alba Sup. Le Masserie '07	TT	5
● Dolcetto di Dogliani Pianezzo '09	TT	4*
○ Langhe Bianco V. dei Garisin '09	TT	4
● Piemonte Grignolino '09	T	4
● Barbera d'Alba Le Masserie '06	YY	5
● Dogliani Sorì S. Martino '06	YY	4
● Dogliani V. dei Prey '07	YY	4*
● Dogliani V. dei Prey '06	YY	4
● Dogliani V. del Ciliegio '05	YY	4
● Dolcetto di Dogliani Pianezzo '08	YY	4*
● Dolcetto di Dogliani Pianezzo '07	YY	4
● Dolcetto di Dogliani Sup. V. del Ciliegio '06	YY	4
● Dolcetto di Dogliani V. Sorì San Martino '07	YY	4

Luigi Boveri

LOC. MONTALE CELLI
VIA XX SETTEMBRE, 6
15050 COSTA VESCOVATO [AL]
TEL. 0131838165
www.boveriluigi.com

CELLAR SALES
PRE-BOOKED VISITS

ANNUAL PRODUCTION 60,000 bottles
HECTARES UNDER VINE 15
VITICULTURE METHOD Conventional

Luigi Boveri runs this large winery in the Tortona area with determination. The new cellar lets him work more efficiently, since he follows the entire production process himself, from tending the rows to the promotion of the wines. His 15 hectares, with some plots around 70 years old, yield a sound range of well-priced wines with a real sense of terroir.

The beautifully hued greenish straw Filari di Timorasso '07 has a delightful nose of hydrocarbons against a mineral backdrop and citrus fruit, leading to a palate of spectacular power and balance. Poggio delle Amarene '07, an intense Barbera, reveals complexity at each stage of tasting. The Barbera Vignalunga '07 has character and complexity but fairly grainy tannins on the finish. We enjoyed the Boccanera '09, a Barbera that wants to finish top of the class. The range is completed by the Timorasso Derthona '08 and a pleasant Cortese Vigna del Prete '09.

○ Colli Tortonesi Timorasso Filari di Timorasso '07	3 (black)	5
● Colli Tortonesi Barbera Poggio delle Amarene '07	2 (black)	4*
● Colli Tortonesi Barbera Boccanera '09	2 (black)	3*
● Colli Tortonesi Barbera Vignalunga '07	2 (black)	6
○ Colli Tortonesi Cortese Vigna del Prete '09	1 (black)	3
○ Colli Tortonesi Timorasso Derthona '08	1 (black)	4
● Colli Tortonesi Barbera Boccanera '08	2 (white)	3*
● Colli Tortonesi Barbera Poggio delle Amarene '06	2 (white)	4
● Colli Tortonesi Barbera Poggio delle Amarene '06	2 (white)	4*
● Colli Tortonesi Barbera Vignalunga '06	2 (white)	6
● Colli Tortonesi Barbera Vignalunga '05	2 (white)	6
● Colli Tortonesi Barbera Vignalunga '04	2 (white)	6
○ Colli Tortonesi Bianco Filari di Timorasso '05	2 (white)	5
○ Colli Tortonesi Timorasso Derthona '07	2 (white)	4
○ Colli Tortonesi Timorasso Filari di Timorasso '06	2 (white)	5

Gianfranco Bovio

FRAZ. ANNUNZIATA
B.TA CIOTTO, 63
12064 LA MORRA [CN]
TEL. 017350667
www.boviogianfranco.com

CELLAR SALES
PRE-BOOKED VISITS

ANNUAL PRODUCTION 60,000 bottles
HECTARES UNDER VINE 10
VITICULTURE METHOD Conventional

Gianfranco Bovio started out with three hectares in 1976 and now has 20 but he has also grown in quality. Famous as a Langhe restaurant owner, with the Belvedere in La Morra, a beacon for gourmets the world over, Gianfranco has shared his commitment to winemaking with Walter Porasso since the early 1980s. After the '08 harvest, most of the dolcetto was pulled out to make room for nebbiolo.

Although viewed as the winery's basic Barolo, the outstanding Rocchettevino '06 took Three Glasses. Its elegant nose of medicinal herbs, tobacco and red fruit leads to a rich, dense, yet unassertive palate with balanced softness and tannins. The forward Barolo Parussi Riserva '03 gives dried flowers but is fading slightly as a result of the hot growing year. Also good are the Barolo '06 Gattera and Arborina, still a tad rough on the palate but already giving lashings of fruit and spice. The range also includes a complex, mature Barbera Regiaveja '05 and an aromatic Langhe Bianco '09, from chardonnay and sauvignon. Last up are a Nebbiolo and a Barbera, both fresh and varietal.

● Barolo Rocchettevino '06	3 (black)	6*
● Barolo Bricco Parussi Ris. '03	2 (black)	8
● Barolo Gattera '06	2 (black)	7
● Barbera d'Alba Il Ciotto '09	2 (black)	4*
● Barbera d'Alba Regiaveja '05	2 (black)	5
● Barolo Arborina '06	2 (black)	7
○ Langhe Bianco '09	2 (black)	4*
● Langhe Nebbiolo '09	1 (black)	5
● Barolo Bricco Parussi Ris. '01	3 (white)	7
● Barolo V. Arborina '90	3 (white)	8
● Barolo V. Arborina '05	2 (white)	7
● Barolo V. Arborina '04	2 (white)	7
● Barolo V. Arborina '03	2 (white)	7
● Barolo V. Gattera '05	2 (white)	7
● Barolo V. Gattera '04	2 (white)	7
● Barolo V. Gattera '03	2 (white)	7

Braida

S.DA PROVINCIALE, 9
14030 ROCCHETTA TANARO [AT]
TEL. 0141644113
www.braida.it

CELLAR SALES
PRE-BOOKED VISITS

ANNUAL PRODUCTION 600,000 bottles
HECTARES UNDER VINE 53
VITICULTURE METHOD Organic

Today, the oenologists Beppe and Raffaella Bologna continue in their quest for quality and innovation, fuelled by a tireless passion for this area and for barbera, inherited from their parents, Giacomo and Anna. The vineyards are spread over five municipalities: Rocchetta Tanaro, Costigliole d'Asti, Castelnuovo Calcea, Mango and Trezzo Tinella, with clay, limestone and sandy hillside soils ranging from medium to loose-textured.

Perhaps only the Bologna family could achieve results like these in a difficult growing year such as '08. The Barbera d'Asti Bricco della Bigotta shows complex aromatics of tobacco, rain-soaked earth and ripe black berry fruit. On the palate, power and length are accompanied by freshness and character. The Barbera d'Asti Bricco dell'Uccellone is still a touch youthful, offering notes of oak, tobacco and plum, although the fruit-laden palate shows well-gauged tannins and a tasty, fresh finish. Lastly, the Barbera d'Asti Ai Suma is still closed and difficult to read, but has black berry fruit with good acidity and flavour. The rest of the wines are well made and reliable.

● Barbera d'Asti Ai Suma '08	**YY**	8
● Barbera d'Asti Bricco dell'Uccellone '08	**YY**	7
● Barbera d'Asti Bricco della Bigotta '08	**YY**	7
● Barbera d'Asti Montebruna '08	**YY**	4
● Grignolino d'Asti '09	**YY**	4
○ Langhe Bianco Il Fiore '09	**Y**	4
○ Langhe Chardonnay Asso di Fiori '08	**Y**	5
● M.to Rosso Il Bacialé '08	**Y**	4
○ Moscato d'Asti V. Senza Nome '09	**Y**	4
● Barbera d'Asti Ai Suma '04	YYY	7
● Barbera d'Asti Bricco dell'Uccellone '05	YYY	7
● Barbera d'Asti Bricco della Bigotta '07	YYY	7
● Barbera d'Asti Bricco della Bigotta '06	YYY	7

Brema

VIA POZZOMAGNA, 9
14045 INCISA SCAPACCINO [AT]
TEL. 014174019
vinibrema@inwind.it

CELLAR SALES
PRE-BOOKED VISITS

ANNUAL PRODUCTION 140,000 bottles
HECTARES UNDER VINE 20
VITICULTURE METHOD Conventional

Brema is a family business that has been operating in the area since the 19th century and is now run by Ermanno and Alessandra Brema. This fine winery has always been committed to quality, and produces wines in the traditional mould. Native varieties, particularly barbera but also dolcetto and moscato, take pride of place and the vineyards are in various municipalities: Incisa Scarpaccino, Nizza Monferrato, Mombaruzzo and Fontanile d'Asti.

The quality of the wines is matched by the cellar's ability to maintain high standards. The Barbera d'Asti Superiore Nizza A Luigi Veronelli '07 shows hints of smoke, incense, dark berry fruit and sweet spice, ushering in a full-bodied, yet fresh palate which closes long with all the good acidity of a true Barbera. The two Dolcetto d'Astis are also superb: Montera '09 has blackberry and blueberry over a well-stuffed palate, and the generous Vigna Impagnato '08 offers with lovely fruit, although with a touch too much oak. The vibrant Moscato d'Asti Mariasole '09 opens with fresh herbs and peppermint over chlorophyll, to continue harmonious and long in the mouth.

● Barbera d'Asti Sup. Nizza A Luigi Veronelli '07	**YY**	7
● Dolcetto d'Asti Montera '09	**YY**	4*
● Dolcetto d'Asti V. Impagnato '08	**YY**	4
○ Moscato d'Asti Mariasole '08	**YY**	4
● Barbera d'Asti Sup. Nizza A Luigi Veronelli '06	YYY	7
● Barbera d'Asti Sup. Bricco della Volpettona '03	YY	6
● Barbera d'Asti Sup. Bricco della Volpettona '01	YY	6

Giacomo Brezza & Figli

VIA LOMONDO, 4
12060 BAROLO [CN]
TEL. 0173560921
www.brezza.it

CELLAR SALES
PRE-BOOKED VISITS
ROOMS AND FOOD

ANNUAL PRODUCTION 80,000 bottles
HECTARES UNDER VINE 16
VITICULTURE METHOD Conventional

Enzo Brezza may be young, but his winery has been operating in Barolo for over 130 years. There's also a family restaurant and hotel, a Mecca for Nebbiolo pilgrims. The style is traditional, with long macerations and medium-large wood. Enzo also chairs the Albeisa association, which is using the characteristic Langhe bottle to promote the area's best products. Champions of tradition maybe, but the fourth generation of the Brezza family is also interested in the new, as is evident from their trips to Australia, contacts with local winemakers, and the glass stoppers for Nebbiolo, Dolcetto and Barbera.

The most famous vineyard in Barolo gives us a delightfully classic Cannubi '06 with close-knit, faintly assertive tannins and a complex nose led by balsamic notes and raspberries. The Barolo Bricco Sarmassa '06 has even more pervasive, evolved aromatics, with dried flowers and sweet tobacco, while the extract is slightly more intrusive. Although sound, the Barolo Sarmassa '06 is still rather too austere and needs a few years' ageing. Despite the disappointing vintage for this variety, the Barbera Cannubi Muscatel '08 is one of the year's best.

● Barolo Bricco Sarmassa '06	▼▼	8
● Barolo Cannubi '06	▼▼	7
● Barbera d'Alba Cannubi Muscatel '08	▼▼	5
● Barolo Sarmassa '06	▼▼	7
● Dolcetto d'Alba S. Lorenzo '09	▼▼	4
● Langhe Nebbiolo '09	▼▼	4
● Barbera d'Alba Santa Rosalia '09	▼	4
● Langhe Freisa Santa Rosalia '09	▼	4
● Langhe Rosso '07	▼	5
● Barolo Cannubi '01	▽▽▽	7
● Barolo Sarmassa '05	▽▽▽	7
● Barolo Sarmassa '04	▽▽▽	7
● Barolo Sarmassa '03	▽▽▽	7
● Barolo Bricco Sarmassa '04	▽▽	8
● Barolo Bricco Sarmassa '01	▽▽	8
● Barolo Cannubi '05	▽▽	7

Bric Cenciurio

VIA ROMA, 24
12060 BAROLO [CN]
TEL. 017356317
www.bricenciurio.com

CELLAR SALES
PRE-BOOKED VISITS

ANNUAL PRODUCTION 45,000 bottles
HECTARES UNDER VINE 13
VITICULTURE METHOD Conventional

The Pittatore and Sacchetto families love both banks of the Tanaro. In fact, one part of the estate is in Barolo, the other in Roero at Castellinaldo, and the wines reflect these two souls. White grapes give their best in Roero Arneis while black grapes thrive in Barolo. The wines are technically perfect, and have real character too, thanks to the dedication of the family that has run the winery since 1994. In some cases, such as the Langhe Nebbiolo, the cellarman has been a little heavy-handed with the oak.

The fruity, mid-structured Barolo '06 lacks development on the palate while the more complex, characterful Coste di Rose '06 is slightly penalized by rustic notes and grainy tannins. Tropical fruit and citrus fruit characterize the splendidly soft, long Roero Arneis Sito dei Fossili '08. The current version of Roero Arneis also passed muster. The excellent Barbera Naunda '07 has swapped the oak that dominated previous vintages for plum, black berry fruit and sweet spice leading into a potent, long, refreshing palate.

● Barbera d'Alba Naunda '07	▼▼	5
○ Roero Arneis Sito dei Fossili '08	▼▼	4*
● Barbera d'Alba '08	▼▼	4*
● Barolo '06	▼▼	6
● Barolo Coste di Rose '06	▼▼	7
○ Roero Arneis '09	▼▼	4*
○ Sito dei Fossili V.T. '07	▼▼	6
● Langhe Nebbiolo '06	▼	5
● Barbera d'Alba '07	▽▽	4*
● Barolo '05	▽▽	6
● Barolo Costa di Rose '05	▽▽	7
● Barolo Costa di Rose '04	▽▽	7
● Langhe Rosso Rosso di Caialupo '06	▽▽	5
● Langhe Rosso Rosso di Caialupo '05	▽▽	5
○ Roero Arneis Sito dei Fossili '07	▽▽	4*

Bricco del Cucù

Loc. Bricco, 10
12060 Bastia Mondovì [CN]
tel. 017460153
www.briccocucu.com

CELLAR SALES
PRE-BOOKED VISITS

ANNUAL PRODUCTION 50,000 bottles
HECTARES UNDER VINE 10
VITICULTURE METHOD Conventional

The attractive name of this small family-owned estate immediately recalls the picturesque and relatively unknown farming environment of the Mondovì Langhe. Dario Sciolla manages his approximately 10 hectares with a firm, rigorous hand. His deeply territorial wines can be a bit rugged and introverted in their youth, but maturing brings out their true character. They are honestly and competitively priced.

Consistency – a sense of place – pervades the list. Prestigious, yes. A real winner, no. Perhaps because we tasted the wines very young, often just after bottling. The Dogliani Bricco San Bernardo '08 and Langhe Rosso Superboum '07 jostle for supremacy. The first shows the typical tannic structure and power of Dogliani's best dolcetto grapes enhanced by the elegance and freshness of those from the Bastìa Mondovì zone. The second is notable for its complex aromas – refreshing, vegetal sensations of forest floor – and succulent palate. The Livor '09 from arneis and sauvignon also shows well with unusual nettle and fresh herb notes and harmonious palate.

● Dogliani Bricco S. Bernardo '08	▼▼	4*
● Dolcetto di Dogliani '09	▼▼	4*
○ Langhe Bianco Livor '09	▼▼	3*
● Langhe Dolcetto '09	▼▼	3*
● Langhe Rosso Diavolisanti '08	▼▼	4*
● Langhe Rosso Superboum '07	▼▼	5
● Dogliani Bricco S. Bernardo '07	▽▽	4
● Dolcetto di Dogliani '08	▽▽	4*
● Dolcetto di Dogliani '07	▽▽	4*
● Dolcetto di Dogliani '05	▽▽	3*
● Dolcetto di Dogliani Sup. Bricco S. Bernardo '06	▽▽	4*
● Langhe Rosso Diavolisanti '07	▽▽	4*
● Langhe Rosso Diavolisanti '05	▽▽	4*

Bricco Maiolica

fraz. Ricca
via Bolangino, 7
12055 Diano d'Alba [CN]
tel. 0173612049
www.briccomaiolica.it

CELLAR SALES
PRE-BOOKED VISITS

ANNUAL PRODUCTION 90,000 bottles
HECTARES UNDER VINE 20
VITICULTURE METHOD Conventional

Beppe Accomo's estate stands out for its coherence and professional reliability. This grower takes Langhe's best varieties and turns them into major wines, paying particular attention to varietal cleanliness. Accomo eschews any strained interpretations or intervention that might hide the distinctive characteristics of the territory.

If the Diano d'Alba Superiore Sorì Bricco Maiolica is not as good as last year, blame the vintage. Less fleshy, the '08 is still great, complex with tobacco, red berry fruit, cinchona and liquorice notes. The superb pure merlot Langhe Filius '06 has currants and truffle, power, fullness and liveliness. The classic Nebbiolo d'Alba Cumot '07 is very territorial with a long, harmonious finish. The young powerful Barbera Vigna Vigia '07 shows all the richness of its generous year. The two whites did well: the more approachable chardonnay/sauvignon Rolando '09 has a rich, beeswax and honey personality while the Pensiero Infinito '06 is deeper, more reticent, almost complete.

● Barbera d'Alba Sup. V. Vigia '07	▼▼	5
● Diano d'Alba Sup. Sörì Bricco Maiolica '08	▼▼	4*
● Nebbiolo d'Alba Cumot '07	▼▼	5
● Dolcetto di Diano d'Alba '09	▼▼	4*
○ Langhe Bianco Pensiero Infinito '06	▼▼	6
○ Langhe Bianco Rolando '09	▼▼	4
● Langhe Rosso Filius '06	▼▼	6
● Langhe Rosso Tris '08	▼▼	4*
● Barbera d'Alba '08	▼	4
● Langhe Nebbiolo '08	▼	4
● Langhe Rosso Lorié '06	▼	6
● Barbera d'Alba V. Vigia '98	▽▽▽	5
● Diano d'Alba Sup. Sörì Bricco Maiolica '07	▽▽▽	4*
● Barbera d'Alba Sup. V. Vigia '06	▽▽	5
● Diano d'Alba Sup. Sörì Bricco Maiolica '06	▽▽	4
○ Langhe Bianco Pensiero Infinito '05	▽▽	6

Bricco Mondalino

REG. MONDALINO, 5
15049 VIGNALE MONFERRATO [AL]
TEL. 0142933204
www.briccomondalino.it

CELLAR SALES
PRE-BOOKED VISITS

ANNUAL PRODUCTION **80,000 bottles**
HECTARES UNDER VINE **13**
VITICULTURE METHOD **Conventional**

Bricco Mondalino lies in Vignale in Mondalino on a steep slope with a magnificent view of the surrounding hills as far as the Alps. The cellar started operating in 1973, when the Gaudio family began to bottle. Prior to this, they had sold it in bulk to wholesalers or to private customers. The estate offers a broad range of products, all rigorously based on indigenous grape types.

Barbera d'Asti Il Bergantino '07 shows a very intense ruby colour, aromas of blackberry and plum, and a rich, enfolding palate with a lingering finish. The Barbera Zerolegno '08 has an intense nose and a soft, weighty palate. The pale ruby Grignolino Bricco Mondalino offers pepper and vegetal notes, a full-bodied palate with good tannins and a longish finale. Molignano, a Malvasia di Casorzo, bubbles into the glass with a rich bouquet of flowery and forest fruit aromas and a consistent, balanced palate. The Cortese is a simple wine that reflects its variety and the basic Grignolino '09 is fairly balanced but falls prey to rather rugged tannins at the back.

● Barbera d'Asti Il Bergantino '07	▼▼	4
● Barbera del M.to Zerolegno '08	▼▼	4
● Grignolino del M.to Casalese Bricco Mondalino '09	▼▼	4
● Malvasia di Casorzo Molignano '09	▼▼	4
● Grignolino del M.to Casales '09	▼	4
○ M.to Casalese Cortese '09	▼	3
● Barbera d'Asti Il Bergantino '06	▽▽	4
● Barbera del M.to Zerolegno '07	▽▽	4*
● Barbera del M.to Zerolegno '06	▽▽	4*
● Grignolino del M.to Casalese Bricco Mondalino '08	▽▽	4
● Grignolino del M.to Casalese Bricco Mondalino '07	▽▽	4*
● Malvasia di Casorzo d'Asti Molignano '07	▽▽	4*

★ Bricco Rocche - Bricco Asili

VIA MONFORTE, 63
12060 CASTIGLIONE FALLETTO [CN]
TEL. 0173282582
www.ceretto.com

CELLAR SALES
PRE-BOOKED VISITS

ANNUAL PRODUCTION **45,000 bottles**
HECTARES UNDER VINE **18**
VITICULTURE METHOD **Conventional**

As usual, we list the Ceretto family labels together. Both of their estates founded in 1978 at Castiglione Falletto and Barbaresco are dedicated exclusively to the queens of Langhe DOCGs. The Barolos bear the prestigious names of Bricco Rocche, Brunate, Prapò and, soon, Cannubi; the Barbarescos come from Bricco Asili and Bernardot. Short macerations and barrique-ageing produce modern wines that, especially in recent years, are anything but predictable in the glass.

It wasn't so much the Barolo Prapò's Three Glasses that impressed us as the way in which it developed. Week after week, the '06 gradually shed its more oaky tones to reveal greater depth and authority. This is evident in its clear, refreshing fruit with undertones of citrus fruit and spices, and above all in its wide-reaching but full-flavoured, dry but authentic palate. A absolute triumph. The juicy, crisp Barbaresco Bricco Asili '07 with elegant, graceful tannins is in a similar vein. The Barbaresco Bernardot '07 is slightly more evolved.

● Barolo Prapò '06	▼▼▼	8
● Barbaresco Bernardot '07	▼▼	8
● Barbaresco Bricco Asili '07	▼▼	8
● Barolo Bricco Rocche '06	▼▼	8
● Barolo Brunate '06	▼▼	8
● Barbaresco Bricco Asili '99	▽▽▽	8
● Barbaresco Bricco Asili '89	▽▽▽	8
● Barbaresco Bricco Asili '86	▽▽▽	8
● Barbaresco Bricco Asili '85	▽▽▽	8
● Barolo Bricco Rocche '00	▽▽▽	8
● Barolo Bricco Rocche '89	▽▽▽	8
● Barolo Brunate '90	▽▽▽	8
● Barolo Prapò '05	▽▽▽	8
● Barolo Prapò '83	▽▽▽	8

Francesco Brigatti

VIA OLMI, 31
28019 SUNO [NO]
TEL. 032285037
www.vinibrigatti.it

CELLAR SALES
PRE-BOOKED VISITS

ANNUAL PRODUCTION 20,000 bottles
HECTARES UNDER VINE 6
VITICULTURE METHOD Conventional

Francesco Brigatti is a one-man band. Owner, oenologist and fruitmaker of the estate that bears his name, he astounds every year for the solid, distinctive range he produces from his five-hectare (plus one he rents) estate in the zone of Suno in the Colline Novaresi. He grows nebbiolo, uva rara, vespolina, bonarda, barbera and erbaluce and matures his wines in casks of varying sizes. The wines are unfussy and approachable.

Brigatti earns a full profile thanks to another range of high-quality wines led by his most famous labels, both of which featured largely in our final tastings. The Colline Novaresi Nebbiolo MötZiflon '07 aged for 20 months in large barrels and stands out for the delicacy of its flowery, slightly grassy nose. These aromas are echoed on the sharpish palate that only lacks that final push. Every bit as elegant is the Colline Novaresi Nebbiolo Motfrei '07, whose barrique ageing gives it a spicy note, but the tobacco, liquorice and violet framework is classic. Richness of flavour and tannic strength are the hallmarks of the sleek, balanced palate.

● Colline Novaresi Nebbiolo Mötfrei '07	▼▼	4*
● Colline Novaresi Nebbiolo MötZiflon '07	▼▼	4*
● Colline Novaresi Uva Rara '09	▼▼	4*
○ Costabella '07	▼▼	6
● Colline Novaresi Barbera Campazzi '08	▼	4
○ Colline Novaresi Bianco Mottobello '09	▼	4
● Colline Novaresi Vespolina '09	▼	4
● Colline Novaresi Barbera '06	YY	4
● Colline Novaresi Barbera V. Campazzi '07	YY	4
● Colline Novaresi Nebbiolo V. Mötfrei '06	YY	4
● Colline Novaresi Nebbiolo V. Mötfrei '04	YY	4*
● Colline Novaresi Rosso MötZiflon '06	YY	4*
● Colline Novaresi Rosso MötZiflon '04	YY	4
● Colline Novaresi V. MötZiflon '05	YY	4*

Vitivinicola Broglia

LOC. LOMELLINA, 22
15066 GAVI [AL]
TEL. 0143642998
www.broglia.eu

CELLAR SALES
PRE-BOOKED VISITS

ANNUAL PRODUCTION N.A.
HECTARES UNDER VINE 57
VITICULTURE METHOD Conventional

The Broglia family estate has both beauty and quality, a happy coupling evident in its stunning natural setting and the quality of the winemaking in all its labels. Cortese, a variety that is too often underrated, comes into its own here. The Bruno Broglia selection is obtained from very prestigious old vines and is regularly cited as a point of reference for its territory of origin.

The Gavi del Comune di Gavi Bruno Broglia '09 has yet to develop fully, and its early release does not leave room for full expression of its aromas. However, when left to breathe it reveals a nose led by spring flower aromas and a palate that has yet to find balance, showing soft and acid at the same time. A few months in the bottle will produce a very gratifying wine. The Meirana '09 is youthful and fermentative, its refreshing palate a foil to the overall sensation of sweet fruitiness. The rest of the wines on offer are well-styled, starting with the easy-drinking Roverello Rosé.

○ Gavi del Comune di Gavi Bruno Broglia '09	▼▼	6
○ Gavi del Comune di Gavi La Meirana '09	▼▼	4
⊙ Gavi Brut Rosé Roverello	▼	5
○ Gavi del Comune di Gavi Roverello '09	▼	4
● M.to Rosso Le Pernici '09	▼	4
○ Gavi del Comune di Gavi Bruno Broglia '08	YYY	6
○ Gavi del Comune di Gavi Bruno Broglia '07	YYY	6
○ Gavi del Comune di Gavi Bruno Broglia '06	YY	5
○ Gavi del Comune di Gavi Bruno Broglia '05	YY	5
○ Gavi del Comune di Gavi Bruno Broglia '04	YY	5
○ Gavi del Comune di Gavi Bruno Broglia '03	YY	5
○ Gavi del Comune di Gavi La Meirana '08	YY	4
○ Gavi del Comune di Gavi La Meirana '07	YY	4

Brovia

via Alba-Barolo, 54
12060 Castiglione Falletto [CN]
tel. 017362852
www.brovia.net

CELLAR SALES
PRE-BOOKED VISITS

ANNUAL PRODUCTION 60,000 bottles
HECTARES UNDER VINE 18
VITICULTURE METHOD Conventional

Brovia is a style. What else would you expect from a family that has made wine in Langhe since 1863? If Barolo is the heart of their production, evolving as they acquired plots in the best zones, the Castiglione Falletto cru is its life blood and embodies a philosophy: big personality, identical vinification, but each bottle distinctive. These are austere wines, hard to appreciate in their youth.

This year's range is top-class. The Rocche '06 is true to its vineyard and earns Three Glasses for its spicy nose and elegant, full-flavoured palate with marked but not overwhelming tannins and enormously enjoyable drinkability. The Villero '05 is more intense and a bit more evolved in its dried flower aromas. The palate is moderately powerful but grainy tannins make it rather hard. The Garblét Sué '06's red berry aromas give way to tobacco and tar, a very elegant palate and a dryish finish. The Ca' Mia '06 from Serralunga grapes is also good, if dominated by tannins that will mellow with time. The Dolcetto and the Barbera d'Alba, both '08, are textbook stuff.

● Barolo Rocche dei Brovia '06	3 (black)	8
● Barolo Garblèt Sué '06	2 (black)	8
● Barolo Villero '05	2 (black)	8
● Barbera d'Alba Sorì del Drago '08	2 (black)	4
● Barolo Ca' Mia '06	2 (black)	8
● Dolcetto d'Alba Vignavillej '08	2 (black)	4
● Barolo Ca' Mia '00	3 (white)	8
● Barolo Ca' Mia '96	3 (white)	8
● Barolo Monprivato '90	3 (white)	8
● Barbera d'Alba Sorì del Drago '04	2 (white)	4*
● Barolo Ca' Mia '05	2 (white)	8
● Barolo Ca' Mia '04	2 (white)	8
● Barolo Garblèt Sué '04	2 (white)	7
● Barolo Rocche dei Brovia '04	2 (white)	8
● Barolo Villero '04	2 (white)	8

Renato Buganza

loc. Cascina Garbinotto, 4
12040 Piobesi d'Alba [CN]
tel. 0173619370
www.renatobuganza.it

CELLAR SALES
PRE-BOOKED VISITS

ANNUAL PRODUCTION N.A.
HECTARES UNDER VINE 10
VITICULTURE METHOD Conventional

The Buganza family practises a viticulture that respects nature, dedicated exclusively to the cultivation of Piedmont's typical varieties: arneis, barbera, dolcetto, nebbiolo, the only exception being chardonnay. The estate consists of two farms, Garbianotto and Gerbore. This year this small operation makes its debut in the main section of the Guide.

Overall, the Buganzas' wines gave a fine performance. The tour de force is the Roero Gerbole '07, which offers complex notes of cinnamon, pencil lead and raspberry. It's a tad rustic, but shows lots of flesh and nice supporting acidity. The rest of the range shows well. The Barbera d'Alba Gerbole '07 has aromas of cinchona and tobacco and a fluent, fruity palate. Roero Bric Paradis '07 offers fruity notes with hints of balsam and wood resin and a complex palate still in thrall to the oak. Barbera d'Alba Vigna Veja '07 hints at tobacco, cherry and spice and has a long, dynamic palate. Last but not least, the elegant, balanced Roero Arneis dla Trifula '09 gives fruit and flower aromas.

● Roero Gerbole '07	2 (black)	5
● Barbera d'Alba Gerbole '07	2 (black)	4
● Barbera d'Alba V. Veja '07	2 (black)	4
● Langhe Rosso '07	2 (black)	4
○ Roero Arneis dla Trifula '09	2 (black)	4
● Roero Bric Paradis '07	2 (black)	5
○ Claudette Brut	1 (black)	5
● Barbera d'Alba V. Veja '06	2 (white)	4*
● Langhe Rosso '04	2 (white)	4*
● Roero Bric Paradis '05	2 (white)	5
● Roero Bric Paradis '04	2 (white)	5

G. B. Burlotto

via Vittorio Emanuele, 28
12060 Verduno [CN]
tel. 0172470122
www.burlotto.com

CELLAR SALES
PRE-BOOKED VISITS

ANNUAL PRODUCTION 60,000 bottles
HECTARES UNDER VINE 12
VITICULTURE METHOD Conventional

Marina Burlotto, Giuseppe Alessandria and their oenologist son Fabio are heirs to the legacy of Commander Giovanni Battista, who founded one of the most beautiful estates in Verduno in the late 1800s. Half of its 12 hectares are dedicated to nebbiolo (Monvigliero, Neirane, Breri, Rocche dell'Olmo in Verduno, Cannubi in Barolo), while the rest are divided between barbera, dolcetto, pelaverga, sauvignon and freisa. The wines are traditional in style and the Barolos age in 35 and 50-hectolitre barrels.

As always, the wines on offer are solid and complex. From the Barolos, we were very impressed yet again by the fundamentally tonic nature of Acclivi '06, a selection obtained from Verduno's best vineyards. Its nobly grassy elements are unmistakeable but it loses out to rather sandy tannins. The Barolo '06 is much more than a simple basic wine while the Vigneto Cannubi '06 has a taut, subtle profile but flags a bit in the follow-through. Among the other labels we have a spectacular Barbera d'Alba Aves '08, and a model Langhe Rosso Mores '07, from equal parts of nebbiolo and barbera.

● Barbera d'Alba Aves '08	▼▼	5*
● Barolo Acclivi '06	▼▼	7
● Barolo '06	▼▼	7
● Barolo Vign. Cannubi '06	▼▼	7
● Langhe Freisa '08	▼▼	4
● Langhe Mores '07	▼▼	5
● Langhe Nebbiolo '08	▼▼	4
⊙ Elatis Rosato	▼	5
○ Langhe Bianco Viridis '09	▼	4
● Barolo Acclivi '05	▽▽	7
● Barolo Acclivi '04	▽▽	7
● Barolo Vign. Monvigliero '04	▽▽	7
○ Langhe Bianco Dives '07	▽▽	4*
● Verduno Pelaverga '08	▽▽	4*

Piero Busso

via Albesani, 8
12052 Neive [CN]
tel. 017367156
www.bussopiero.com

CELLAR SALES
PRE-BOOKED VISITS

ANNUAL PRODUCTION 30,000 bottles
HECTARES UNDER VINE 8
VITICULTURE METHOD Conventional

This fine family estate is run by Piero, Lucia and their children Pierguido and Emanuela. Here we have Barbaresco in all its versions united by a complexity that requires time to show its full character. The vineyards have very low yields and follow a supervised control management system that allows nature to more or less run its course. This philosophy extends to the cellar, where Piero uses a light hand in the vinification and maturation processes. The result is a line-up of very powerful, complex wines.

The superb Barbaresco Santo Stefanetto '07 won Three Glasses for its balsamic nose with lovely liquorice undertones, rich palate with solid, smooth tannins and a characterful finish. The sound Barbaresco Gallina '06 throws an intense, gamey nose, big personality on the palate and youthful boisterousness. The enjoyable Barbaresco Borgese '07 has a dried flower and tobacco nose with hints of tar, and a powerful palate with dense tannic texture. The Barbaresco Mondino '07 is pleasant, more open but less dynamic. Barbera d'Alba Santo Stefanetto '07 comes from a magnificent harvest. It has spice and plum aromas with notes of rain-soaked earth and a big, juicy, very drinkable palate.

● Barbaresco S. Stefanetto '07	▼▼▼	8
● Barbaresco Borgese '07	▼▼	7
● Barbaresco Gallina '06	▼▼	8
● Barbera d'Alba S. Stefanetto '07	▼▼	6
● Barbaresco Mondino '07	▼▼	6
● Barbera d'Alba V. Majano '08	▼▼	4
○ Langhe Bianco '09	▼▼	4
● Langhe Nebbiolo '08	▼▼	5
● Barbaresco Gallina '05	▽▽▽	8
● Barbaresco S. Stefanetto '04	▽▽▽	8
● Barbaresco S. Stefanetto '03	▽▽▽	8
● Barbaresco S. Stefanetto '01	▽▽▽	8
● Barbaresco S. Stefanetto '00	▽▽▽	8
● Barbaresco Borgese '06	▽▽	7
● Barbaresco S. Stefanetto '06	▽▽	8

Ca' Bianca

REG. SPAGNA, 58
15010 ALICE BEL COLLE [AL]
TEL. 0144745420
www.cantinacabianca.it

CELLAR SALES
PRE-BOOKED VISITS

ANNUAL PRODUCTION 650,000 bottles
HECTARES UNDER VINE 39
VITICULTURE METHOD Conventional

This estate belonging to the Gruppo Italiano Vini (GIV) lies in Monferrato in Alessandria, a little-known corner of the country. It follows GIV's philosophy to the letter: to produce quality wines that reflect the characteristics of the territory and offer them at competitive prices. Easier said than done, but Ca' Bianca has proved highly adept at meeting expectations.

Despite the challenging '08 growing year, the estate has produced some very fine Barberas. The Barbera d'Asti Superiore Antè Linea Tenimenti shows intense sensations of coffee and tobacco with lovely fruity nuances. Barbera d'Asti Superiore Chersì Linea Tenimenti offers concentrated aromas of tobacco and black berry fruit with confident notes of cocoa powder and spice. The other Linea Tenimenti labels are also well-typed: the fresh-tasting, supple Barbera d'Asti Teis '09 revels in cherry aromas, the Roero Arneis '09 is firmly structured and refreshing with intense pears and dried flowers and the Gavi '09 offers pleasing hints of ripe apple fruit.

● Barbera d'Asti Sup. Antè Linea Tenimenti '08	▼▼	4
● Barbera d'Asti Sup. Chersì Linea Tenimenti '08	▼▼	6
● Barbera d'Asti Teis Linea Tenimenti '09	▼	4
○ Gavi Linea Tenimenti '09	▼	4
○ Roero Arneis Linea Tenimenti '09	▼	4
● Barbera d'Asti Sup. Chersì '07	▽▽	5
● Barbera d'Asti Sup. Chersì '06	▽▽	5
● Barbera d'Asti Sup. Chersì '05	▽▽	5
● Barbera d'Asti Sup. Chersì '04	▽▽	5
● Barbera d'Asti Sup. Chersì '03	▽▽	5

Ca' d' Gal

FRAZ. VALDIVILLA
S.DA VECCHIA DI VALDIVILLA, 1
12058 SANTO STEFANO BELBO [CN]
TEL. 0141847103
www.cadgal.it

CELLAR SALES
PRE-BOOKED VISITS
ROOMS AND FOOD

ANNUAL PRODUCTION 60,000 bottles
HECTARES UNDER VINE 8
VITICULTURE METHOD Conventional

Dynamic, passionate Alessandro Boido belongs to a group of producers bent on relaunching Moscato, a wine that has never quite received its just desserts. His vines, some of them 50 years old, grow on the sandy slopes of Santo Stefano Belbo and produce an ageable Moscato. Sceptical? Go to one of his Vigna Vecchia tastings; the beautiful agriturismo at Valdivilla next to the cellar is an added bonus. The rainbow Alessandro has chosen for his web site reflects his colourful, sparkling world.

We were very impressed by the three labels we tasted. Our pick is the very sound Moscato Vigna Vecchia '09, bright, seductive straw yellow with a nose redolent of flowery, citrussy nuances and a fresh palate showing balanced sweetness. The Asti is a fine example of how to make a wine of a widely enjoyed yet often underrated DOCG. Very quaffable, it offers refreshing tones with fragrant notes of shortcrust pastry and wonderful lingering length on the palate. As ever, the very elegant Moscato Lumine '09 shows the lovely varietal notes of its grape.

○ Moscato d'Asti V. Vecchia '09	▼▼	5
○ Asti '09	▼▼	4*
○ Moscato d'Asti Lumine '09	▼▼	4*
○ Asti '07	▽▽	4
○ Asti	▽▽	4
● Langhe Rosso Pian del Gaje '03	▽▽	4
○ Moscato d'Asti Lumine '08	▽▽	4
○ Moscato d'Asti Lumine '07	▽▽	4
○ Moscato d'Asti Lumine '06	▽▽	4
○ Moscato d'Asti V. Vecchia '07	▽▽	5
○ Moscato d'Asti V. Vecchia '06	▽▽	5
○ Moscato d'Asti V. Vecchia '05	▽▽	5

Ca' del Baio

VIA FERRERE, 33
12050 TREISO [CN]
TEL. 0173638219
www.cadelbaio.com

CELLAR SALES
PRE-BOOKED VISITS

ANNUAL PRODUCTION **100,000 bottles**
HECTARES UNDER VINE **25**
VITICULTURE METHOD **Conventional**

Paola, Valentina and Federica are the fourth generation of Grassos at Ca' del Baio, a lovely Treiso estate founded by great-grandfather, Luigi. Today, they and their parents Giulio and Luciana give a modern slant to a great tradition. They regularly update their range, creating Barbarescos of rare precision, splendour and territorial character. The Marcarini, Valgrande, Asili and Pora crus are household names. The wines mature in barriques, some new, 900-litre casks and medium barrels.

Giulio Grasso's cellar forges ahead full steam. We have some real gems nestling among the less luminous offerings, from the Moscato D'Asti 101 '09 to the Langhe Nebbiolo Bric del Baio '09 and the Barbera d'Alba Giardin '08. Then there is the usual prestigious list of Barbarescos dominated by a Pora '06 of exceptional integrity and breadth, showing aromas of citrus fruit, liquorice and fruit so crisp you could almost crunch it. The Asili '07 is a tad atypical in its notes of plum and Mediterranean style. Together with the close-knot, tangy Valgrande '07, it romped into our final tastings.

● Barbaresco Pora '06	TTT	7
● Barbaresco Asili '07	TT	6
● Barbaresco Valgrande '07	TT	6
● Barbaresco Marcarini '07	TT	6
● Barbera d'Alba Giardin '08	TT	4
● Langhe Nebbiolo Bric del Baio '08	TT	4
○ Moscato d'Asti 101 '09	TT	4
● Barbera d'Alba Paolina '08	T	4
● Dolcetto d'Alba Lodoli '09	T	4
● Barbaresco Asili '06	YYY	6
● Barbaresco Pora '04	YYY	7
● Barbaresco Valgrande '04	YYY	6
● Barbaresco Valgrande '99	YYY	6
● Barbera d'Alba Paolina '07	YY	4*

Ca' Rome' - Romano Marengo

S.DA RABAJÀ, 86/88
12050 BARBARESCO [CN]
TEL. 0173635126
www.carome.com

CELLAR SALES
PRE-BOOKED VISITS

ANNUAL PRODUCTION **30,000 bottles**
HECTARES UNDER VINE **5**
VITICULTURE METHOD **Conventional**

In 1980, wine merchant Romano Marengo began to make Langhe wines in a small cellar. The results were so good that he bought some Barolo and Barbaresco plots and brought in his children, Giuseppe and Paola. Their flagship, Maria di Brun after Romano's mother, is a traditional Barbaresco aged in big barrels and bottled only in the best years. The wines are austere: rigorous in their youth but very ageworthy.

Stamped by their terroir, the wines have developed a very interesting varietal definition over the years. Treat yourself to a bottle of Barbaresco Maria di Brun and see for yourself. The intense, lively Barolo Cerretta '06 has red berry fruit and spicy aromas with faint hints of tar followed by a surprisingly soft palate for a Serralunga cru but eminently drinkable and impressively long. The slightly simpler Barolo Rapet '06 gives cocoa powder and a less assertive but impeccable, substantial palate. The superb Barbaresco Chiaramanti '07 is quite open, displaying lovely raspberry sensations mid nose. The palate is juicy and fruity, showing powerful yet already very enjoyable.

● Barbaresco Chiaramanti '07	TT	7
● Barolo V. Cerretta '06	TT	8
● Barbaresco Maria di Brun '07	TT	8
● Barbaresco Sorì Rio Sordo '07	TT	7
● Barbera d'Alba La Gamberaja '08	TT	5
● Barolo Rapet '06	TT	8
● Langhe Nebbiolo Calimpia '07	TT	6
● Barbaresco Chiaramanti '06	YY	7
● Barbaresco Maria di Brun '06	YY	8
● Barbaresco Sorì Rio Sordo '06	YY	7
● Barbera d'Alba La Gamberaja '07	YY	5
● Barolo Rapet '05	YY	8
● Barolo Rapet '03	YY	7
● Barolo V. Cerretta '05	YY	8
● Barolo V. Cerretta '04	YY	7

Cascina Ca' Rossa

LOC. CASCINA CA' ROSSA, 56
12043 CANALE [CN]
TEL. 017398348
www.cascinacarossa.com

CELLAR SALES
PRE-BOOKED VISITS

ANNUAL PRODUCTION 60,000 bottles
HECTARES UNDER VINE 15
VITICULTURE METHOD Organic

The enthusiasm, passion and sheer dedication of Angelo Ferrio have brought this estate a series of successes. Meticulous work in vineyards on the steep, sandy terrain so typical of Roero, has enabled him to create wines with big personalities and a fine sense of place. Angelo has two crus among his various plots, Audinaggio and Mompissano, from which he obtains the jewels in his crown, his Roeros.

This year, it is the Roero Riserva Mompissano '07 that takes home Three Glasses for its aromas of dried flowers, tobacco and spice, and its complex, very deep palate with bags of fruit, lovely balance, acid grip and length. Roero Audinaggio '08 came very close, showing its customary elegance, clear notes of flowers and red berry fruit, and stylish, taut palate full of crunchy fruit. The well-made Roero Arneis Merica '09 offers notes of wisteria and apple-like fruit, a rather rustic but gutsy palate with backbone, and an almondy finish. The Langhe Nebbiolo '08 is harmonious, fresh and richly fruity.

● Roero Mompissano Ris. '07	3 black glasses	6
● Roero Audinaggio '08	2 black glasses	6
● Langhe Nebbiolo '08	1 black glass	4
○ Roero Arneis Merica '09	1 black glass	4
● Barbera d'Alba Mulassa '04	3 glasses	6
● Barbera d'Alba Mulassa '99	3 glasses	6
● Roero Audinaggio '07	3 glasses	6
● Roero Audinaggio '06	3 glasses	6
● Roero Audinaggio '01	3 glasses	6

★ Ca' Viola

B.TA SAN LUIGI, 11
12063 DOGLIANI [CN]
TEL. 017370547
www.caviola.com

CELLAR SALES
PRE-BOOKED VISITS
ROOMS AND FOOD

ANNUAL PRODUCTION 50,000 bottles
HECTARES UNDER VINE 10
VITICULTURE METHOD Conventional

Beppe Caviola looks after an awful lot of bottles. As an oenologist, he tours Italy advising prestigious cellars on their many wines. Langhe and Dogliani are home to his own 50,000 bottles and Ca' Viola is his world: cellar, laboratory and a small but perfectly appointed hotel for visitors. Wine is Beppe's life and his own are a tribute to his technical precision and viticulturist's heart. An innovator, he is experimenting with big barrels and spontaneous fermentations.

Three Glasses go to a magnificent Langhe Nebbiolo '08, a project to revamp a low-key DOCG. Very elegant aromas led by black berry fruit announce an enveloping, harmonious, well-structured palate, and a long, crisp finish. The Dolcetto d'Alba Barturot '09 is from Montelupo and defies anyone who thinks Dolcetto is a simple wine dominated by a fruity nose and a tannic palate. Barbera d'Alba Bric du Luv '08 is top of its vintage, an enchanting wine notable for its almost perfect balance on the palate and acidity kept nicely in check by sound structure.

● Langhe Nebbiolo '08	3 black glasses	6
● Barbera d'Alba Bric du Luv '08	2 black glasses	6
● Dolcetto d'Alba Barturot '09	2 black glasses	5
● Barbera d'Alba Brichet '09	2 black glasses	5
● Dolcetto d'Alba Vilot '09	2 black glasses	4*
● Barbera d'Alba Bric du Luv '07	3 glasses	6
● Dolcetto d'Alba Barturot '07	3 glasses	5
● Dolcetto d'Alba Barturot '05	3 glasses	5
● Dolcetto d'Alba Barturot '01	3 glasses	5
● Dolcetto d'Alba Barturot '98	3 glasses	5
● Langhe Rosso Bric du Luv '05	3 glasses	6
● Langhe Rosso Bric du Luv '03	3 glasses	6
● Langhe Rosso Bric du Luv '01	3 glasses	6
● Langhe Rosso Bric du Luv '99	3 glasses	6

Marco Canato

FRAZ. FONS SALERA
LOC. CA' BALDEA, 18/2
15049 VIGNALE MONFERRATO [AL]
TEL. 0142933653
www.canatovini.it

CELLAR SALES
PRE-BOOKED VISITS

ANNUAL PRODUCTION 30,000 bottles
HECTARES UNDER VINE 11
VITICULTURE METHOD Conventional

Marco and Roberto Canato maintain consistent quality across their range and regularly rise to greatness with their Rapet or Baldea. This Guide sees the Rapet return to our finals, while the '08 Baldea came close. Proof positive that the brothers are on the right track. Despite the enormous chore of replacing the vines ravaged by flavescence dorée, they forge ahead.

Rapet has a deep ruby colour, complex red berry fruit, cocoa powder and spice aromas, and lovely balance on the palate with fabulous progression and lots of pulp. Baldea shows complexity, character and concentration throughout. The 50 Anni '07 from 70 per cent barbera with freisa and grignolino was launched in magnums for the estate's 50th anniversary. It offers notes of spice, red berry fruit and tobacco, a firm entry on the palate and quite an intense finish. The Grignolino '09 has a flowery nose with vegetal, spicy nuances while the well-made palate is balanced with solid tannins. The simple Gambaloita '09 is a harmonious, balanced Barbera ideal for daily drinking.

● Barbera del M.to Sup. Rapet '07	▼▼	4*
● 50 Anni '07	▼▼	4
● Barbera del M.to Sup. La Baldea '08	▼▼	4
● Grignolino del M.to Casalese Celio '09	▼▼	4*
● Barbera del M.to Gambaloita '09	▼	3
● 50 Anni '06	▽▽	4
● Barbera del M.to La Birbona '08	▽▽	3*
● Barbera del M.to Sup. La Baldea '06	▽▽	4*
● Barbera del M.to Sup. La Baldea '03	▽▽	3*
● Barbera del M.to Sup. Rapet '06	▽▽	4
● Barbera del M.to Sup. Rapet '05	▽▽	4*
● Grignolino del M.to Casalese Celio '08	▽▽	4*
● Grignolino del M.to Casalese Celio '07	▽▽	4*
● Barbera del M.to Gambaloita '08	▽	3

Cantina del Pino

S.DA OVELLO, 31
12050 BARBARESCO [CN]
TEL. 0173635147
www.cantinadelpino.com

ANNUAL PRODUCTION 35,000 bottles
HECTARES UNDER VINE 7
VITICULTURE METHOD Conventional

Renato Vacca's is a beautiful, functional estate. With his father, he used to be a member of the Produttori del Barbaresco but struck out on his own in 1997. He devotes much of his energy to Barbaresco and the consistency of style of his labels have become a point of reference of the territory. His Ovello comes from up to 70-year-old vines. The wines tend to the classic in their tannic structure but show rather a modern bent in their aromatics.

The three labels on offer this year confirm Renato Vacca as a master of Barbaresco. Ovello '06 is young as yet, and gives little away, but displays alcohol on both nose and palate despite a caressing, velvety fruit element. The superb and powerful Albesani '06 shows still rather rugged tannins. The elegant, fruity Barbaresco '07 is a model of the type and is much readier and more satisfying than its very sound elder siblings. The Langhe Nebbiolo '08 is a mid-structured, extremely elegant wine. The Dolcetto is well-made with clear, candid fruitiness. We also liked the still rather closed Barbera d'Alba '08.

● Barbaresco '07	▼▼	6
● Barbaresco Albesani '06	▼▼	7
● Barbaresco Ovello '06	▼▼	7
● Barbera d'Alba '08	▼▼	5
● Dolcetto d'Alba '09	▼▼	4
● Langhe Nebbiolo '08	▼▼	4
● Barbaresco '04	▽▽▽	6*
● Barbaresco '03	▽▽▽	5*
● Barbaresco Albesani '05	▽▽▽	7
● Barbaresco Ovello '99	▽▽▽	6
● Barbaresco '05	▽▽	6*
● Barbaresco Ovello '05	▽▽	7
● Barbaresco Ovello '04	▽▽	7

La Caplana

VIA CIRCONVALLAZIONE, 4
15060 BOSIO [AL]
TEL. 0143684182
lacaplana@email.it

CELLAR SALES
PRE-BOOKED VISITS

ANNUAL PRODUCTION **100,000 bottles**
HECTARES UNDER VINE **2**
VITICULTURE METHOD **Conventional**

No surprises here. With yet another fine performance, Caplana offers further proof of a will to produce high-quality cortese, barbera and dolcetto-based wines that represent the territory. The Guido family who own this estate, and include various agronomists and oenologists among their members, supervise every process themselves.

As it did last year, the Dolcetto di Ovada Narciso dominates the range. The '08 is intense and generous on the nose, elegant on the palate. The basic Dolcetto also shows well, bright purple in colour with cassis sensations introducing a palate with rather rustic tannins but great structure. The Gavi del Comune di Gavi is harmonious throughout, ditto the basic Gavi, which has a fruity nose and a long, fresh palate. The Gavi Vignavecchia offers notes of citrus and apple fruit, firm structure and a lengthy finish. The Barbera d'Asti '08 is an approachable wine with alcohol-rich aromas that give way to fruit and lovely acidity on the palate.

● Dolcetto di Ovada Narciso '08	TT	3*
● Dolcetto di Ovada '09	TT	3*
○ Gavi del Comune di Gavi '09	TT	4
○ Gavi Vigna Vecchia '09	TT	3
● Barbera d'Asti '08	T	3
○ Gavi '09	T	3
● Barbera d'Asti Rubis '06	YY	3*
● Barbera d'Asti Rubis '05	YY	3*
● Dolcetto di Ovada Narciso '07	YY	3*
● Dolcetto di Ovada Narciso '06	YY	3*
○ Gavi del Comune di Gavi '08	YY	4
○ Gavi del Comune di Gavi '07	YY	4*
○ Gavi del Comune di Gavi V. Vecchia '07	YY	3*
○ Gavi V. Vecchia '08	YY	3*

Tenuta Carretta

LOC. CARRETTA, 2
12040 PIOBESI D'ALBA [CN]
TEL. 0173619119
www.tenutacarretta.it

CELLAR SALES
PRE-BOOKED VISITS
ROOMS AND FOOD

ANNUAL PRODUCTION **400,000 bottles**
HECTARES UNDER VINE **70**
VITICULTURE METHOD **Conventional**

The Miroglio family bought this large estate in 1985. Forty of its 100 hectares are planted to vine and records date it back to the 12th century. Based in Roero, it also has plots in Langhe, next to Piobesi d'Alba, including 2.5 hectares in Cannubi in Barolo, Poderi Tavoleto in San Rosso Seno d'Elvio and Cascina Bordino at Treiso. The wines range from classic Roero bottles to Barbaresco and Barolo.

In the face of so many prestigious Langhe wines, it was the homelier Roero Bric Paradiso '08 that graced our finals thanks to a very refined raspberry, tobacco and flowery bouquet and a powerful, full palate showing lovely balance and seamless tannic texture. The two Barbaresco '07s also cut quite a swath. Garassino has dense, well-integrated tannins and a long, velvety finish stuffed with fruit. The fresh, pleasant Cascina Bordino hints at tobacco and red berry fruit. We also tried two '06 Barolos: Vigneti In Cannubi recalls tar and cinchona and has a thick, velvety palate, rather dark and austere. The more flowery Cascina Ferrero has good body but is not terribly exciting.

● Roero Bric Paradiso '08	TT	5
● Barbaresco Cascina Bordino '07	TT	7
● Barbaresco Garassino '07	TT	6
● Barolo Cascina Ferrero '06	TT	6
● Barolo Vign. in Cannubi '06	TT	8
○ Roero Arneis V. Canorei '09	T	5
● Barolo Vign. in Cannubi '00	YYY	8
● Barbaresco Cascina Bordino '03	YY	7
● Barbaresco Cascina Bordino '01	YY	7
● Barolo Vign. in Cannubi '01	YY	8
● Roero Sup. Bric Paradiso '03	YY	5

La Casaccia

VIA D. BARBANO, 10
15034 CELLA MONTE [AL]
TEL. 0142489986
www.lacasaccia.biz

CELLAR SALES
PRE-BOOKED VISITS

ANNUAL PRODUCTION 25,000 bottles
HECTARES UNDER VINE 7
VITICULTURE METHOD Certified organic

The Rava husband and wife team put their agricultural knowledge to good use and continue to improve the quality of their wines. Their flagships, Barbera del Monferrato Bricco del Bosco and Barbera d'Asti Calichè, appear in turn at our finals and Il Poggeto, a Grignolino, is also one of the best of its type. The range focuses on the classic, local Monferrato varieties and does much to promote this territory.

The very pleasant Bricco del Bosco '07 is a deep ruby Barbera Superiore presenting aromas of cherry and plum shot through with intense spice. The palate caresses, showing very harmonious. Opaque ruby in colour, the Calichè '07 offers vegetal, spicy sensations and a fairly concentrated, rich palate. Poggeto '09 has a bright, pale ruby appearance and a true-to-type nose that unveils aromas spice with flowery, fruity nuances. The intense palate has marked tannins. Vigna Monfiorenza is a lively Freisa revealing flowery notes with traces of pepper and quite a balanced palate with a bit of a rustic finish.

● Barbera del M.to Sup. Bricco del Bosco '07	▼▼	4*
● Barbera d'Asti Sup. Calichè '07	▼▼	4
● Grignolino del M.to Casalese Poggeto '09	▼▼	3*
● M.to Freisa Monfiorenza '09	▼	3
● Barbera d'Asti Sup. Calichè '06	▽▽	5
● Barbera d'Asti V. Sant'Anna '07	▽▽	4*
● Barbera del M.to Sup. Bricco del Bosco '06	▽▽	5
● Grignolino del M.to Casalese Poggeto '08	▽▽	3*
● Grignolino del M.to Casalese Poggeto '07	▽▽	4*
● Grignolino del M.to Casalese Poggeto '06	▽▽	4*

Casalone

VIA MARCONI, 100
15040 LU [AL]
TEL. 0131741280
www.casalone.it

CELLAR SALES
PRE-BOOKED VISITS

ANNUAL PRODUCTION 50,000 bottles
HECTARES UNDER VINE 10
VITICULTURE METHOD Conventional

This estate sits on Bricco Santa Maria in Lu Monferrato and the Casalone family has been here since the 18th century. Several big labels are missing from this year's line-up, including the Monferrato Rosso Rus and the Barbera d'Asti Rubermillo but this did not detract from the overall performance. The Bricco Morlantino '07 more than made up for their absence and marched straight into our final tastings.

Bricco Morlantino '07 presents an almost opaque ruby appearance and a layered nose of plum, pepper and tobacco with mineral nuances. The palate is powerful and concentrated. The Malvasia Greca Monemvasia '09 reveals elegant, complex aromas and a palate of character and personality, finishing intense. Vendemmia Tardiva '07 from the same variety has a youthful character, a deep straw yellow hue tending to gold and concentrated notes of citrus peel that give way to wood resin. The palate is powerful, full and well balanced. Up last we have the La Caplëtta '09, a pale ruby Grignolino with fruity, spicy nuances, a harmonious palate and almost too-soft tannins.

● Barbera del M.to Bricco Morlantino Sup. '07	▼▼	4*
○ Monemvasia '09	▼▼	4
○ Monemvasia V. T. '07	▼▼	4
● Piemonte Grignolino La Capletta '09	▼	3
● Barbera d'Asti Rubermillo '07	▽▽	4
● Barbera d'Asti Rubermillo '05	▽▽	4*
● Barbera del M.to Bricco Morlantino Sup. '06	▽▽	4*
● M.to Rosso Rus '07	▽▽	4*
● M.to Rosso Rus '06	▽▽	4
● M.to Rosso Rus '05	▽▽	4*
○ Monemvasia '08	▽▽	4
○ Monemvasia V. T. '06	▽▽	5
● Monferrato Rosso Fandamat '07	▽▽	4

Cascina Adelaide

via Aie Sottane, 14
12060 Barolo [CN]
tel. 0173560503
www.cascinaadelaide.com

CELLAR SALES
PRE-BOOKED VISITS

ANNUAL PRODUCTION 50,000 bottles
HECTARES UNDER VINE 9
VITICULTURE METHOD Conventional

Its charming style and organic lines make this one of Langhe's most modern estates. Entrepreneur Amabile Drocco has turned the talents that have served him so well in other sectors to Barolo and the plots of his farmer father. His wines, Barolos and the simpler offerings, are all good. His vineyard and cellar staff work to create an elegant, balanced range and have turned the spotlight on a little-known cru, Preda, whose tufaceous and grey calcareous marl soils produce delicious wines.

The Barolo Cannubi '06 shows an intense, mature nose and a palate that starts out soft and easy to become harder in the finish. The Barolo Preda '06 is similar in style to the previous edition but drier in its tannins. The very modern Barolo Fossati '05 has strong oaky aromas on both nose and palate with nice spicy nuances. The simple Barolo 4 Vigne '06 is enjoyable and well made, with no peaks on nose or palate. Fresh on the palate and plummy in its aromas, the Barbera d'Alba Amabilin is a pleasant, easy-going wine that belies the impetuous nature of the wonderful '07 growing year.

● Barolo Cannubi '06	2 black glasses	8
● Barbera d'Alba Sup. Amabilin '07	2 black glasses	6
● Barolo Fossati '05	2 black glasses	8
● Barolo Preda '06	2 black glasses	8
● Barolo 4 Vigne '06	1 black glass	7
● Barbera d'Alba Sup. Amabilin '06	2 white glasses	6
● Barbera d'Alba Sup. V. Preda '07	2 white glasses	5
● Barbera d'Alba Sup. V. Preda '04	2 white glasses	5
● Barolo 4 Vigne '05	2 white glasses	7
● Barolo Cannubi '05	2 white glasses	8
● Barolo Fossati '04	2 white glasses	8
● Barolo Per Elen Ris. '01	2 white glasses	8
● Barolo Preda '05	2 white glasses	8
● Barolo Preda '04	2 white glasses	8

Cascina Bongiovanni

fraz. Uccellaccio
via Alba Barolo, 4
12060 Castiglione Falletto [CN]
tel. 0173262184
www.cascinabongiovanni.it

CELLAR SALES
PRE-BOOKED VISITS

ANNUAL PRODUCTION 35,000 bottles
HECTARES UNDER VINE 6
VITICULTURE METHOD Conventional

The indefatigable Davide Mozzone carries on the work started by his grand-father Giovanni and mother Olga. He produces 30,000 bottles from little more than six hectares and personally oversees vineyard and cellar. Barolo Pernanno is missing from the roll-call this year but we advise you to taste it anyway. It comes from a plot that is around 50 years old and ages in small barrels.

The 2006 growing year was so good that Davide decided to focus on just one Barolo label, opting not to produce his prestigious Pernanno selection. The well-made Barolo '06 runs the gamut from fruit to cinchona, tobacco to dried roses and a very firmly structured palate with close-knit tannic texture leading into a refreshing finish. The Langhe Faletto '08 is a balanced blend of barbera, nebbiolo and cabernet that harmoniously weds the cabernet's vegetal notes with barbera's fruity flesh, while the nebbiolo adds elegant tannic structure. The two '09 Dolcettos, Alba and Diano d'Alba, are up to their usual standards.

● Barolo '06	2 black glasses	6*
● Barbera d'Alba '08	2 black glasses	5
● Dolcetto d'Alba '09	2 black glasses	4*
● Dolcetto di Diano d'Alba '09	2 black glasses	4*
● Langhe Rosso Faletto '08	2 black glasses	5
○ Langhe Arneis '09	1 black glass	4
● Barolo Pernanno '01	3 white glasses	7
● Barbera d'Alba '07	2 white glasses	5
● Barolo '03	2 white glasses	6
● Barolo Pernanno '05	2 white glasses	7
● Barolo Pernanno '04	2 white glasses	7
● Dolcetto di Diano d'Alba '08	2 white glasses	4
● Langhe Rosso Faletto '07	2 white glasses	6
● Langhe Rosso Faletto '05	2 white glasses	5

Cascina Bruciata

s.da Rio Sordo, 46
12050 Barbaresco [CN]
tel. 0173638826
www.cascinabruciata.it

CELLAR SALES
PRE-BOOKED VISITS

ANNUAL PRODUCTION 30,000 bottles
HECTARES UNDER VINE 7
VITICULTURE METHOD Conventional

Cascina Bruciata's top selection is Rio Sordo, in the heart of Barbaresco. The vineyard's wines have great personality and are much sought-after by the dealers for the major bottling houses. Carlo Balbo's family took over in 1880 and his passion for the territory runs deep. Guido Martinetti is the oenologist. The estate (literally "burnt farm") is named for an arson incident in the late 1800s that forced the incumbent owner to sell up.

The Balbos are blessed with first-class vineyards and we never expect anything less than brilliance from them. The range is unrivalled and offers a fine, typical overview of Langhe wines and varieties. Barbaresco Rio Sordo '07 is the product of an early-ripening harvest and expresses all the elements of very ripe grapes. Aromas of forest fruit and dried flowers dominate, while the soft tannins are flanked by the alcohol's reassuring sweetness. Unusually, the Cannubi Muscatel '06 also presents soft and pliable, with no hint of excess hardness. From the two '09 Dolcettos, we preferred Rian's approachability to the rather undisciplined power of Rio Sordo.

● Barbaresco Rio Sordo '07	2 black glasses	6
● Barolo Cannubi Muscatel '06	2 black glasses	7
● Dolcetto d'Alba Rian '09	2 black glasses	4*
● Barbaresco '06	1 black glass	6
● Dolcetto d'Alba Vign. Rio Sordo '09	1 black glass	4
● Barbaresco '05	2 white glasses	6
● Barbaresco '04	2 white glasses	6
● Barbaresco Rio Sordo '06	2 white glasses	6
● Barbaresco Rio Sordo '05	2 white glasses	6
● Barbaresco Rio Sordo '03	2 white glasses	6
● Barbaresco Rio Sordo Ris. '04	2 white glasses	7
● Dolcetto d'Alba Vign. Rio Sordo '08	2 white glasses	4*
● Dolcetto d'Alba Vign. Rio Sordo '07	2 white glasses	4
● Langhe Nebbiolo Vign. dell'Usignolo '07	2 white glasses	4

Cascina Castlet

s.da Castelletto, 6
14055 Costigliole d'Asti [AT]
tel. 0141966651
www.cascinacastlet.com

CELLAR SALES
PRE-BOOKED VISITS

ANNUAL PRODUCTION 240,000 bottles
HECTARES UNDER VINE 22
VITICULTURE METHOD Organic

Mariuccia Borio is the driving force behind Cascina Castlet in Costigliole d'Asti. She has grassed the vineyards, joined a project to re-introduce birds to the territory as a natural insect deterrent and set about salvaging traditional varieties on the verge of extinction, such as uvalino. Respect for the environment and quality are her watchwords. Her seven vineyards stand on clay and limestone.

This year, the Barbera d'Asti Superiore Passum '07 is very fine. Taking advantage of what was a superb year for Barberas, it shows great character from its intense aromas of red fruit, tobacco and rain-soaked earth through to the very rich, vigorous palate whose alcohol is well buttressed by tannins and acidity. The Monferrato Rosso Policalpo '06, a blend of 60 per cent barbera and cabernet sauvignon, is also well made, long and harmonious in its aromas of pencil lead and tobacco. The basic Barbera d'Asti '09 is fresh, acidulous and easy-drinking but nicely fleshy. The Barbera d'Asti Superiore Litina '07 from an old vineyard is classic with notes of earth and black berry fruit.

● Barbera d'Asti Sup. Passum '07	2 black glasses	6
● Barbera d'Asti '09	2 black glasses	4*
● Barbera d'Asti Sup. Litina '07	2 black glasses	4
● M.to Rosso Policalpo '06	2 black glasses	5
○ Moscato d'Asti '09	1 black glass	4
○ Piemonte Chardonnay A Taj '09	1 black glass	4
● Barbera d'Asti Sup. Passum '05	2 white glasses	5
● Barbera d'Asti Sup. Passum '05	2 white glasses	5
● Barbera d'Asti Sup. Passum '04	2 white glasses	5
● Barbera d'Asti Sup. Passum '03	2 white glasses	5
● M.to Rosso Policalpo '03	2 white glasses	5
○ Piemonte Moscato Passito Avié '07	2 white glasses	5

Cascina Chicco

VIA VALENTINO, 144
12043 CANALE [CN]
TEL. 0173979411
www.cascinachicco.com

CELLAR SALES
PRE-BOOKED VISITS

ANNUAL PRODUCTION 270,000 bottles
HECTARES UNDER VINE 28
VITICULTURE METHOD Conventional

This solid Roero estate belonging to Enrico and Marco Faccenda is 60 years old. It makes the traditional wines of the zone but with a modern slant. Recent years have seen major investments in the vineyards and a new cellar. Today, Cascina Chicco owns plots in Canale, Vezza d'Alba, Castellinaldo, Castagnito and Monforte d'Alba, where it cultivates arneis, nebbiolo, barbera, favorita and brachetto.

This year's performance was rather low-key for the Faccenda family but they still placed one wine on our final tasting table. Roero Montespinato '08 displays aromas of ripe red berry fruit followed by nuances of tobacco and sweet spice. The palate is powerful with rich fruity flesh and a long finish that is ever so slightly overripe. The always well-made Arcass '08 is obtained from late-harvested arneis. It offers notes of raisin and botrytis, plus a full, chewy palate sustained by good acidity that refreshes the long finish. The rest of the production is well-managed, lacking just that extra something that we have come to expect from this estate.

● Roero Montespinato '08	▼▼	4*
○ Arcass V. T. '08	▼▼	5
● Roero Valmaggiore Ris. '07	▼▼	5
○ Langhe Favorita '09	▼	4
● Nebbiolo d'Alba Mompissano '08	▼	5
○ Roero Arneis Anterisio '09	▼	4
○ Arcàss Passito '04	▽▽▽	5
● Nebbiolo d'Alba Mompissano '99	▽▽▽	5
○ Arcàss Passito '06	▽▽	5
○ Arcàss Passito '05	▽▽	5
● Roero Valmaggiore '05	▽▽	5
● Roero Valmaggiore '04	▽▽	5
● Roero Valmaggiore Ris. '06	▽▽	5

Cascina Corte

FRAZ. SAN LUIGI
B.TA VALDIBERTI, 33
12063 DOGLIANI [CN]
TEL. 0173743539
www.cascinacorte.it

CELLAR SALES
PRE-BOOKED VISITS
ROOMS

ANNUAL PRODUCTION 30,000 bottles
HECTARES UNDER VINE 5
VITICULTURE METHOD Certified organic

The legendary Sandro Barosi is right at home in the vineyard. All the years he spent with Slow Food found practical application in 2001 and after a lifetime spent flying round the world he now has his feet firmly on the ground. He adheres to organic methods, territoriality and quality. Dolcetto is king in Dogliani and Sandro releases it in various guises. The cellar is still under construction but Sandro's great adventure continues.

Dogliani Pirocchetta Vecchie Vigne '08 won Cascina Corte its first Three Glasses. Young but already highly enjoyable, it will age splendidly. This label is living proof that Dolcetto is not a simple wine, giving black berry fruit and cocoa powder aromas, a potent, full palate finishing long, with freshness and almondy notes. The lovely Dolcetto di Dogliani '09 is a perfect exemplar of its DOCG. An exquisite nose led by blackberry and cocoa powder is the prelude to tight-woven but not invasive tannic texture and a pleasantly fresh, juicy finish. Of the '08s, we preferred the Langhe Nebbiolo to the Barbera, which is still a bit hard and acidulous.

● Dogliani Vecchie V. Pirochetta '08	▼▼▼	4*
● Dolcetto di Dogliani '09	▼▼	3*
● Langhe Nebbiolo '08	▼▼	5
● Piemonte Barbera '08	▼	4
● Dogliani V. Pirochetta '07	▽▽	4*
● Dogliani V. Pirochetta '06	▽▽	4
● Dolcetto di Dogliani '08	▽▽	3*
● Dolcetto di Dogliani '07	▽▽	3*
● Dolcetto di Dogliani '06	▽▽	4*
● Langhe Nebbiolo '07	▽▽	5
● Langhe Nebbiolo '06	▽▽	5
● Piemonte Barbera '06	▽▽	4*

Cascina Cucco

LOC. CUCCO
VIA MAZZINI, 10
12050 SERRALUNGA D'ALBA [CN]
TEL. 0173613003
www.cascinacucco.com

CELLAR SALES
PRE-BOOKED VISITS

ANNUAL PRODUCTION 60,000 bottles
HECTARES UNDER VINE 12
VITICULTURE METHOD Conventional

The headquarters of the Stroppiana family, entrepreneurs from Piedmont of worldwide fame, is worth a visit in a beautifully maintained, charming building just outside the municipality of Serralunga. This estate is fairly new, but with each passing year it achieves more impressive results. The style of the wines is a fine balance between classicism and modernity.

The Stroppianas did not disappoint us in this edition of the Guide, presenting a harmonious range of wines designed to satisfy a broad drinking public. The Barolo Cerrati Vigna Cucco '06 still has a very young nose that slowly opens out to reveal notes of tobacco and pencil lead enhanced by a well-orchestrated hint of oak. The palate is notable for its firm but balanced structure and velvety tannins. Similar in vein, the Cerrati '06 is slightly drier in its tannins. The Barolo di Serralunga '06 is readier for the corkscrew and less dynamic. From the rest of the range, we liked the Barbera Superiore '08.

	Glasses	
● Barbera d'Alba Sup. '08	2 black	5
● Barolo Cerrati '06	2 black	6
● Barolo Cerrati V. Cucco '06	2 black	7
● Barolo di Serralunga '06	2 black	6
○ Langhe Chardonnay '09	2 black	4*
● Langhe Rosso Mondo '08	2 black	5
● Barbera d'Alba '09	1 black	4
● Dolcetto d'Alba Vughera '09	1 black	4
● Barbera d'Alba Sup. '07	2 white	5
● Barbera d'Alba Sup. '05	2 white	5
● Barolo Cerrati '05	2 white	6
● Barolo V. Cucco '04	2 white	7
● Barolo V. Cucco '03	2 white	7
● Langhe Rosso Mondo '07	2 white	5

Cascina Fonda

LOC. CASCINA FONDA, 45
12056 MANGO [CN]
TEL. 017377156
www.cascinafonda.com

CELLAR SALES
PRE-BOOKED VISITS
ROOMS

ANNUAL PRODUCTION 120,000 bottles
HECTARES UNDER VINE 12
VITICULTURE METHOD Conventional

Secondino Barbero was an unassuming moscato grower who sold his fruit to the great Asti houses between 1963 and 1988. His sons Marco and Massimo set about bottling the fruit of their vineyards and soon began to attract the attention of the market with their high-quality range of wines. Their Moscato d'Asti and Asti Spumante are unfailingly clean, never over-elaborate and never too rich. In short, they are a delight to drink.

This year's notes are rather brief. In addition to the Asti Metodo Classico Driveri, the Passito and house reds (a Piemonte Brachetto, a Dolcetto d'Alba and a few bottles of Barbaresco) are all missing in action. Luckily for us, the three wines we sampled are fine examples of the quality and quantity that Cascina Fonda's production has achieved. The Moscato d'Asti Bel Piano '09 has intense, vivid notes of sage and a balanced palate that clearly favours the freshness of the acid sensations over enveloping sugar elements. The cuve close Asti Bel Piasì '09 offers faint, elegant notes of chlorophyll as the prelude to a sleek palate.

	Glasses	
○ Asti Bel Piasì '09	2 black	4*
○ Moscato d'Asti Bel Piano '09	2 black	4*
○ Langhe Arneis '09	1 black	4
○ Asti '07	2 white	4*
○ Asti Bel Piasì '08	2 white	4*
○ Asti Driveri M. Cl. '05	2 white	6
● Barbaresco Bertola '04	2 white	6
○ Moscato d'Asti Bel Piano '08	2 white	4*
○ Moscato d'Asti Bel Piano '07	2 white	4*
○ Moscato d'Asti V. Il Piano '06	2 white	4
● Piemonte Brachetto '06	2 white	4
○ Piemonte Moscato Passito '04	2 white	5

Cascina Garitina

via Gianola, 20
14040 Castel Boglione [AT]
tel. 0141762162
www.cascinagaritina.it

CELLAR SALES
PRE-BOOKED VISITS

ANNUAL PRODUCTION 180,000 bottles
HECTARES UNDER VINE 26
VITICULTURE METHOD Conventional

Gianluca Morino runs his old family estate with care and passion. He owns 13 hectares in Castel Boglione and directly manages another ten in the municipalities of Castelnuovo Calcea, San Marzano Oliveto and Calamandrana. The deep, medium-textured soil tends to clay and is rich in organic matter. Needless to say, Barbera is the chief variety grown, with 70 per cent of the vineyards dedicated to its cultivation. The rest contain dolcetto, pinot nero, cabernet sauvignon, merlot and brachetto.

Rather a disappointing performance this year from Gianluca's estate: our hero has accustomed us to better. However, he did offer us some sound, well-made wines to taste. The Barbera d'Asti Superiore Nizza Neuvsent '07 presents dark notes of black olives, tobacco, brandied cherries and plums while the palate is austere yet full of character with tight-woven tannins and a long finish showing bags of personality. The rest of the range is well typed but lacks its usual verve.

● Barbera d'Asti Sup. Nizza Neuvsent '07	▼▼	5
● Barbera d'Asti Bricco Garitta '09	▼	4
● Barbera d'Asti Sup. Vign. in Caranti '07	▼	4
● Barbera d'Asti Sup. Neuvsent '02	▽▽	5
● Barbera d'Asti Sup. Nizza Neuvsent '05	▽▽	5
● Barbera d'Asti Sup. Nizza Neuvsent '04	▽▽	5
● Barbera d'Asti Sup. Nizza Neuvsent '01	▽▽	5

Cascina Gilli

via Nevissano, 36
14022 Castelnuovo Don Bosco [AT]
tel. 0119876984
www.cascinagilli.it

CELLAR SALES
PRE-BOOKED VISITS

ANNUAL PRODUCTION 140,000 bottles
HECTARES UNDER VINE 23
VITICULTURE METHOD Conventional

Mention freisa within the context of contemporary Piedmont winemaking and someone will say Cascina Gilli. Gianni Vergnano, owner of this estate in lower Monferrato, and his staff were the first to dedicate themselves to the renaissance of a grape type that many consider to be a minor variety. The vineyards lie in the municipalities of Castelnuovo Don Bosco and Passerano Marmorito, and their base of marly clay also supports barbera, bonarda and malvasia.

The Freisas are traditionally the estate's most interesting bottles. This year, we also have a Barbera. Freisa d'Asti Vivace Luna di Maggio '09 shows intense fruity aromas with hints of black pepper-led spice. The palate has varietal bitterish notes and lots of fruit in the long finish. The Freisa d'Asti Vigna del Forno '08 rather falls prey to its difficult growing year and tends more towards red berry fruit and tobacco on the nose. The palate is light and pleasant. Barbera d'Asti Vigna delle More '08 offers gamey notes with red berry fruit sensations and a full, flavoursome palate. The finish is a tad over-alcoholic.

● Barbera d'Asti V. delle More '08	▼▼	4*
● Freisa d'Asti V. del Forno '08	▼▼	4*
● Freisa d'Asti Vivace Luna di Maggio '09	▼▼	3*
● Barbera d'Asti Sebrì '08	▼	5
○ Piemonte Chardonnay Rafé '09	▼	3
● Barbera d'Asti V. delle More '06	▽▽	4*
● Barbera d'Asti V. delle More '04	▽▽	4*
● Freisa d'Asti Arvelé '03	▽▽	4*
● Freisa d'Asti V. del Forno '07	▽▽	4*

Cascina La Maddalena

FRAZ. SAN GIACOMO
LOC. PIANI DEL PADRONE, 257
15078 ROCCA GRIMALDA [AL]
TEL. 0143876074
www.cascina-maddalena.com

CELLAR SALES
PRE-BOOKED VISITS
ROOMS

ANNUAL PRODUCTION 30,000 bottles
HECTARES UNDER VINE 4
VITICULTURE METHOD Conventional

Cascina La Maddalena's five hectares of vineyards are home to dolcetto, barbera and merlot. Production focuses on dolcetto and barbera, indigenous varieties that reveal some very interesting characteristics on these slopes. Wine tourists will be interested to know that the estate also features a bed & breakfast with three bedrooms and a large apartment.

As for many Ovada estates, the Dolcetto '09 is very successful: the year clearly favoured the variety. Bright purple, it has elegant blackberry and cocoa powder, and a soft palate with a very long finish. The Barbera '08 also shows well, its cherry and tobacco notes turning soft and fleshy on the palate. The Dolcetto Superiore Migulle '08 has a mature colour and nose while the palate offers smooth tannins and a fairly lengthy finish. The Dolcetto Bricco del Bagatto '07 has a very youthful hue, an estery nose and alcoholic warmth on the palate. The Barbera Rossa d'Ocra '07 exhibits evolved aromas at every stage of tasting, as does the Monferrato Rosso Bricco del Padrone '08.

● Barbera del M.to '08	🍷🍷	3*
● Dolcetto di Ovada '09	🍷🍷	3*
● Barbera del M.to Rossa d'Ocra '07	🍷	4
● Dolcetto di Ovada Bricco del Bagatto '07	🍷	4
● Dolcetto di Ovada Migulle Sup. '08	🍷	5
● M.to Rosso Bricco del Padrone '08	🍷	4
● Dolcetto di Ovada '08	YY	3*
● Dolcetto di Ovada '07	YY	3
● Dolcetto di Ovada Bricco del Bagatto '06	YY	4
● Dolcetto di Ovada Bricco del Bagatto '05	YY	4*
● M.to Rosso Bricco della Maddalena '04	YY	5
● M.to Rosso La Decima Vendemmia '06	YY	6
● M.to Rosso Pian del Merlo '07	YY	4
● Barbera del M.to '06	Y	3

Cascina Roera

FRAZ. BIONZO
VIA BIONZO, 32
14055 COSTIGLIOLE D'ASTI [AT]
TEL. 0141968437
www.cascinaroera.com

CELLAR SALES
PRE-BOOKED VISITS

ANNUAL PRODUCTION 20,000 bottles
HECTARES UNDER VINE 7
VITICULTURE METHOD Organic

Claudio Rosso and Piero Nebiolo continue the adventure they embarked upon in 2002. In their plots fanning out around the cellar at Bionzo near the castle of Costigliole, they grow the typical varieties of the zone, mainly barbera but also freisa, nebbiolo, arneis, cortese and chardonnay. Vineyard management is organic so there is cover cropping but no insecticides, just copper and sulphur.

Claudio and Piero aspire to produce natural wines with a very distinctive character. The Barbera d'Asti '08 presents notes of brandied cherries and tobacco followed by an austere but rich palate showing the warmth of the alcohol. The finish is long but somewhat dried by tannins. Cardin, a table wine obtained from a pleasant barbera and nebbiolo blend, made an interesting debut. Red berry fruit and ginger grace the nose, while the palate exhibits notes of pencil lead and cinchona. The Piemonte Chardonnay Le Aie '09 is clean with apple-like sensations.

● Barbera d'Asti '08	🍷🍷	3*
● Cardin	🍷🍷	5
○ Piemonte Chardonnay Le Aie '09	🍷	4
● Barbera d'Asti Sup. Cardin '05	YY	4
● Barbera d'Asti Sup. Cardin '04	YY	4*
● Barbera d'Asti Sup. Cardin Sel. '04	YY	5
● Barbera d'Asti Sup. S. Martino '05	YY	4
● M.to Rosso V. Piva '05	YY	4

Francesca Castaldi

via Novembre, 6
Briona [NO]
tel. 0321826520
francesca_castaldi@libero.it

CELLAR SALES
PRE-BOOKED VISITS

ANNUAL PRODUCTION **10,000 bottles**
HECTARES UNDER VINE **6**
VITICULTURE METHOD **Conventional**

The Castaldis' deep bond with the territory goes back 200 years. In the mid 1990s, Francesca's passion for the land and vine led her back to join her brother Giuseppe on their 6.5 hectares. The plots lie on the southernmost edge of a morainic hill, where the plateau widens and slopes gently down to the rice fields. The estate is not certified but does not use pesticides or herbicides. Next year will see completion of the new cellar in the centre of Briona at the historic family home below the Sforza castle.

Currently, the Castaldis vinify only part of their crop so production stands at around 10,000 bottles a year. The range comprises several labels of the classic local monovarietals but for their first appearance in the Guide they offered us just two to taste: the Fara '06 and the Colline Novaresi Bianco '09. The first matures for 26 months in 900-litre casks and arrived like a bolt from the blue to sweep up a resounding Three Glasses. Its winning attributes are character, a complex nose and elegant tannic texture. The erbaluce-based white is uncomplicated and harmonious.

● Fara '06	🍷🍷	5
○ Colline Novaresi Bianco '09	🍷🍷	3*

Renzo Castella

via Alba, 15
12055 Diano d'Alba [CN]
tel. 017369203
renzocastella@virgilio.it

CELLAR SALES
PRE-BOOKED VISITS

ANNUAL PRODUCTION **25,000 bottles**
HECTARES UNDER VINE **10**
VITICULTURE METHOD **Conventional**

This interesting estate in Diano d'Alba shows its colours exclusively in shades of dolcetto for this edition of the Guide. We admire the quality and rigour displayed by the young, enthusiastic owner and loudly applaud his decision to release only the very best wines onto the market in this time of crisis. Castella products are confidently dynamic, occasionally tart, and have a character that distinguishes them in a world of labels that often tend to be over-standardized and difficult to differentiate.

In the absence of an '08 version of the Nebbiolo and Barbera d'Alba – Renzo did not consider the growing year up to par – we only tasted the two versions of Dolcetto di Diano '09 for this edition of the Guide. We recommend both. The forthright Rivolia displays intense fruit and youthful alcohol on the nose. The palate has great structure and length but moderate concentration. The basic Diano d'Alba '09 is simpler and clean, the lighter flesh making the tannins slightly more marked and rugged.

● Dolcetto di Diano d'Alba '09	🍷🍷	3*
● Dolcetto di Diano d'Alba Rivolia '09	🍷🍷	3*
● Dolcetto di Diano d'Alba '08	🍷🍷 (white)	3*
● Dolcetto di Diano d'Alba Rivolia '07	🍷🍷 (white)	3*
● Dolcetto di Diano d'Alba V. della Piadvenza '07	🍷🍷 (white)	3*
● Dolcetto di Diano d'Alba V. della Piadvenza '06	🍷🍷 (white)	3*
● Dolcetto di Diano d'Alba V. della Rivolia '08	🍷🍷 (white)	3
● Dolcetto di Diano d'Alba V. della Rivolia '06	🍷🍷 (white)	3*
● Dolcetto di Diano d'Alba V. della Rivolia '05	🍷🍷 (white)	3*
● Dolcetto di Diano d'Alba V. La Sorda '05	🍷🍷 (white)	3*
● Nebbiolo d'Alba V. Madonnina '06	🍷🍷 (white)	4
● Nebbiolo d'Alba V. Madonnina '05	🍷🍷 (white)	4

Castellari Bergaglio

FRAZ. ROVERETO, 136
15066 GAVI [AL]
TEL. 0143644000
www.castellaribergaglio.it

CELLAR SALES
PRE-BOOKED VISITS

ANNUAL PRODUCTION 70,000 bottles
HECTARES UNDER VINE 12
VITICULTURE METHOD Conventional

Whatever Gavi's ups and downs, it owes a great deal to this important, long-established estate run by Marco Bergaglio. A desire to relaunch the territory and the selection of various plots that he interprets according to their individual characteristics are the driving force behind his interesting range of wines. Here, cortese comes to the fore in all its manifestations. Unlike those who opt for easy, acid freshness, the estate style is rooted in power, sweetness and structure.

The Gavi del Comune di Gavi Rolona is a highly distinctive, concentrated wine with delightful aromas of camomile and honey. The potent palate shows lots of flesh with no concessions to sweetness. Matured at length in barrel and bottle, Pilin '06 shows all of its customary opulence and fullness. The aromas of butter and spice on the nose are mirrored on a palate that is rather rich but very well made and designed to please those for whom freshness and acidity are not the be all and end all.

○ Gavi del Comune di Gavi Rolona '09	▼▼	4
○ Gavi Pilìn '06	▼▼	5
○ Gavi del Comune di Tassarolo Fornaci '09	▼	4
○ Gavi del Comune di Gavi Rolona '07	▽▽	4
○ Gavi del Comune di Gavi Rolona '04	▽▽	4
○ Gavi del Comune di Gavi Rovereto '04	▽▽	4
○ Gavi del Comune di Gavi Rovereto Vignavecchia '08	▽▽	4
○ Gavi del Comune di Gavi Rovereto Vignavecchia '07	▽▽	4
○ Gavi del Comune di Tassarolo Fornaci '08	▽▽	4
○ Gavi del Comune di Tassarolo Fornaci '07	▽▽	4
○ Gavi del Comune di Tassarolo Fornaci '06	▽▽	4*
○ Gavi del Comune di Tassarolo Fornaci '05	▽▽	4*

Castello del Poggio

LOC. POGGIO, 9
14100 PORTACOMARO [AT]
TEL. 0141202543
www.poggio.it

CELLAR SALES
PRE-BOOKED VISITS

ANNUAL PRODUCTION 800,000 bottles
HECTARES UNDER VINE 158
VITICULTURE METHOD Conventional

What a good year for this big estate, owned by the Zonin family! Over the years, the property has expanded through the acquisition of the Rocca Cerrina, Cascinot, Poggio and Orto farmsteads to build up a significant vineyard holding. The rows are mainly at Portacomaro with a few plots in Santa Margherita near Costigliole d'Asti. Moscato is the dominant variety here, followed by brachetto, grignolino, barbera, dolcetto, chardonnay, freisa and merlot. The terrain is silt and sand.

The Piedmont estate put on a fine performance. The Barbera d'Asti '07 exhibits classic notes of tobacco, sweet spice, earth and black berry fruit followed by a palate that may not be huge but is very balanced, fresh, long and pleasantly drinkable. We were most impressed by the Moscato d'Asti Vigneti Castello del Poggio '09 and Grignolino d'Asti '09. The former displays elegant aromas of peach, sage, lime and apple fruit, and a harmonious palate with a long, delicate finish that nicely offsets sweetness with acidity. The second has notes of currant and rain-soaked earth and a fresh, consistent palate with nice flesh.

● Barbera d'Asti '07	▼▼	4
● Grignolino d'Asti '09	▼▼	4*
○ Asti	▼	4
● M.to Dolcetto '08	▼	4
● Barbera d'Asti '05	▽▽	4*

Castello di Neive

VIA CASTELBORGO, 1
12052 NEIVE [CN]
TEL. 017367171
www.castellodineive.it

PRE-BOOKED VISITS

ANNUAL PRODUCTION 150,000 bottles
HECTARES UNDER VINE 28
VITICULTURE METHOD Conventional

With the lion's share of the Santo Stefano di Neive cru, this estate could almost be termed a monopoly. Owner Italo Stupino knows it and aims to make this a selling point for the entire Barbaresco territory, and of course his wines. Aged long and requiring time, they are not modern or easy-drinking but true to themselves. Those who know how to appreciate them also know they are worth waiting for. The estate is worth a visit just for the castle and the cellar full of large casks.

The Barbaresco Santo Stefano '07 has bags of character on the nose of spice, dried flowers and strawberry, and palate, where strong alcohol fails to dent its succulence and acid base. The Barbaresco '07 gives medicinal herbs and liquorice leading to a well-structured palate whose tannins are also softened by alcohol. The Mattarello enjoys an elegant, harmonious swansong. After the '09 edition, it will drop the variety from the label to become a simple Superiore. The sound Dolcetto d'Alba Basarin '09 needs a bit longer in bottle to mellow those tannic edges and is much more powerful than the Messoirano '09.

● Barbaresco S. Stefano '07	▼▼	7
● Barbaresco '07	▼▼	6
● Barbera d'Alba Sup. Mattarello '08	▼▼	5
● Dolcetto d'Alba Basarin '09	▼▼	4
● Dolcetto d'Alba Messoirano '09	▼▼	4
○ Piemonte Pinot Nero Brut '06	▼▼	6
○ Castello di Neive Passito '08	▼	6
○ Langhe Arneis Montebertotto '09	▼	4
● Barbaresco S. Stefano Ris. '01	▽▽▽	8
● Barbaresco S. Stefano Ris. '99	▽▽▽	8
● Barbaresco S. Stefano '06	▽▽	7
● Barbaresco S. Stefano '05	▽▽	6
● Barbaresco S. Stefano '04	▽▽	6
● Barbaresco S. Stefano Ris. '04	▽▽	8
● Barbera d'Alba Mattarello '07	▽▽	5

Tenuta Castello di Razzano

FRAZ. CASARELLO
LOC. RAZZANO, 2
15021 ALFIANO NATTA [AL]
TEL. 0141922124
www.castellodirazzano.it

CELLAR SALES
PRE-BOOKED VISITS

ANNUAL PRODUCTION 200,000 bottles
HECTARES UNDER VINE 38
VITICULTURE METHOD Conventional

This estate has its nerve centre in a noble residence dating back to the end of the 17th century, which houses the ageing cellars and a series of rooms and reception halls to entertain visitors. The entire structure underwent major renovation, completed in 2005. This estate has long been a point of reference for Monferrato winemaking thanks to its superb range of magnificent Barberas.

Quality is good across the board. The splendid Barbera Campasso '07 presents a dense, opaque ruby and oaky notes with lots of room for the fruit. The palate is firmly structured and balanced. Barbera Valentino Caligaris '07's slightly toastier aromas echo on the very concentrated, no-nonsense palate. In the complex, layered Barbera Eugenea '07 notes of plum and cocoa powder meld into pleasant coffee nuances and the powerful, alcoholic palate finishes very long. Del Beneficio '08 has a very youthful appearance and spicy aromas from its sojourn in oak. The potent palate shows lots of flesh and mirrors the oak-derived aromas at the back.

● Barbera d'Asti Sup. Campasso '07	▼▼	4
● Barbera d'Asti Sup. Beneficio '08	▼▼	5
● Barbera d'Asti Sup. Eugenea '07	▼▼	5
● Barbera d'Asti Sup. V. Valentino Caligaris '07	▼▼	5
○ Piemonte Chardonnay Costa al Sole '09	▼▼	3*
● Grignolino del M.to Casalese Pianaccio '09	▼	3
● Barbera d'Asti Sup. Beneficio '06	▽▽	5
● Barbera d'Asti Sup. Campasso '06	▽▽	4*
● Barbera d'Asti Sup. Eugenea '06	▽▽	5
● Barbera d'Asti Sup. Eugenea '05	▽▽	4*
● Barbera d'Asti Sup. V. del Beneficio '07	▽▽	5
● Barbera d'Asti Sup. V. Valentino Caligaris '06	▽▽	5
● Barbera d'Asti Sup. V. Valentino Caligaris '05	▽▽	5

Castello di Tassarolo

CASCINA ALBORINA, 1
15060 TASSAROLO [AL]
TEL. 0143342248
www.castelloditassarolo.it

CELLAR SALES
PRE-BOOKED VISITS

ANNUAL PRODUCTION 130,000 bottles
HECTARES UNDER VINE 20
VITICULTURE METHOD Certified organic

History and tradition are the hallmarks of this important Gavi estate. With the technical support of the very able Vincenzo Munì, Massimiliana Spinola walks a biodynamic path. The wines require a little extra effort to be fully understood, but they're worth it. Cortese, a multi-faceted variety, shows personality and complexity in all the versions on offer.

In addition to classic spring flower aromas, the Gavi del Comune di Tassarolo Spinola '09 also offers hints of almond on the nose. The typical palate errs more on the side of power than elegance and has a long, slightly bitterish finish that recalls the almond nuances. The Gavi del Comune di Tassarolo Il Castello '09 exhibits flowery notes with undertones of dried fruit and a fresh touch of aniseed. The well-structured palate displays good length and an even tangier finish than the Spinola.

○ Gavi del Comune di Tassarolo Il Castello '09	2 black glasses	4
○ Gavi del Comune di Tassarolo Spinola '09	2 black glasses	3*
○ Gavi Castello di Tassarolo '08	2 glasses	4*
○ Gavi Castello di Tassarolo '07	2 glasses	4
○ Gavi Tassarolo S '08	2 glasses	3*
○ Gavi Tassarolo S '07	2 glasses	3
○ Gavi Vign. Alborina '07	2 glasses	5*
○ Gavi Vign. Alborina '06	2 glasses	5
● M.to Rosso Cuvée dei Marchesi Spinola '06	2 glasses	4
● M.to Rosso No Sulphites '08	2 glasses	4*

Castello di Uviglie

VIA CASTELLO DI UVIGLIE, 73
15030 ROSIGNANO MONFERRATO [AL]
TEL. 0142488132
www.castellodiuviglie.com

CELLAR SALES
PRE-BOOKED VISITS

ANNUAL PRODUCTION 80,000 bottles
HECTARES UNDER VINE 25
VITICULTURE METHOD Organic

Castello di Uviglie's vineyards face south or south-west and have a mainly limestone and clay base, with two exceptions: Bricco, home of the grapes for the Pico Gonzaga, faces south and has marly clay soil; and Bricco del Conte, from which the wine of the same name is obtained, faces south-west with medium-textured, alkaline soil. We applaud Simone Lupano for his fine work in cellar and vineyard and the impressive results he has achieved.

The dense, opaque ruby Pico Gonzaga '07 presents oaky, intensely fruity aromas, a powerful, concentrated palate with lots of pulp and a never-ending finish. A mouthfilling, satisfying, fruit-brimming Three Glass champ. For the second year, Le Cave reached our finals. This elegant Barbera '08 has a plum and cocoa powder nose and an intense, enveloping palate. Grignolino San Bastiano is bright, pale ruby with a rich, concentrated nose, a palate of characterful tannins and a very long finish. The Bricco del Conte shows fabulous nose-palate balance while the estery, alcoholic Monferrato 1491 from albarossa still needs to smooth out its oaky edges.

● Barbera del M.to Sup. Pico Gonzaga '07	3 black glasses	5*
● Barbera del M.to Sup. Le Cave '08	2 black glasses	4*
● Grignolino del M.to Casalese San Bastiano '09	2 black glasses	4*
● Barbera del M.to Bricco del Conte '09	2 black glasses	4*
● M.to Rosso 1491 '07	2 black glasses	5
○ M.to Bianco San Martino '09	1 black glass	4
● M.to Freisa La Costa '09	1 black glass	4
○ Piemonte Chardonnay Ninfea '09	1 black glass	4
● Barbera del M.to Sup. Le Cave '07	3 glasses	5
● Barbera del M.to Sup. Le Cave '05	2 glasses	4*
● Barbera del M.to Sup. Pico Gonzaga '06	2 glasses	5
● Barbera del M.to Sup. Pico Gonzaga '04	2 glasses	5
● Grignolino del M.to Casalese San Bastiano '06	2 glasses	3*
● M.to Rosso 1491 '06	2 glasses	5

Castello di Verduno

VIA UMBERTO I, 9
12060 VERDUNO [CN]
TEL. 0172470284
www.castellodiverduno.com

CELLAR SALES
PRE-BOOKED VISITS
ROOMS AND FOOD

ANNUAL PRODUCTION 50,000 bottles
HECTARES UNDER VINE 7
VITICULTURE METHOD Conventional

The history of this cellar is the history of Barolo. In 1838, Carlo Alberto of Savoy commissioned a great nebbiolo wine and the Burlottos have maintained the tradition since the early 1900s, when the marriage of Gabriella to fourth-generation Barbaresco producer Franco Bianco expanded the range. The vineyards are legendary – Massara and Monvigliero for Barolo; Faset and Rabajà for Barbaresco – and the wines are released after regulations dictate. The pelaverga, dolcetto and barbera-based offerings also impress.

Barolo Monvigliero Riserva '04 is a triumph, winning a very sophisticated Three Glasses for the delicate, spicy aromas typical of the prestigious Verduno cru's best years, full flavour and long aromatic length. The Barolo Massara '05 is a dense, slightly evolved garnet with lovely liquorice notes and quite austere, rugged tannins that make it less elegant than the Monvigliero or Rabajà. The confident Barbaresco '07 reflects its rich, gutsy vintage and the fragrant Barbaresco Rabajà '05 recalls tobacco and cinchona, its full palate owing its elegance and length to impressive extract and acidity.

● Barolo Monvigliero Ris. '04	▼▼▼	8
● Barbaresco Rabajà '05	▼▼	7
● Barbaresco '06	▼▼	6
● Barbera d'Alba Bricco del Cuculo '08	▼▼	7
● Barolo Massara '05	▼▼	7
● Verduno Basadone '09	▼▼	4
● Barbaresco Rabajà '04	▽▽▽	7
● Barolo Massara '01	▽▽▽	7
● Barbaresco '05	▽▽	6
● Barbera d'Alba Bricco del Cuculo '07	▽▽	7
● Barolo Massara '04	▽▽	7
● Barolo Massara Ris. '99	▽▽	7
● Barolo Monvigliero '02	▽▽	7
● Barolo Monvigliero Ris. '03	▽▽	8
● Langhe Nebbiolo '07	▽▽	4

La Caudrina

S.DA BROSIA, 21
12053 CASTIGLIONE TINELLA [CN]
TEL. 0141855126
www.caudrina.it

CELLAR SALES
PRE-BOOKED VISITS

ANNUAL PRODUCTION 200,000 bottles
HECTARES UNDER VINE 30
VITICULTURE METHOD Conventional

The Dogliottis run this major estate in Castiglione Tinella with energy and high professional standards. Year after year, their consistent range of high-quality labels has earned them a reputation with those who appreciate this wine type. The various interpretations of Moscato are diverse and complementary, showcasing the true potential of this captivating, unique variety.

This year, the Moscato d'Asti La Caudrina '09 – a historic point of reference for the type – dominated our tastings with a top performance. Its straw-yellow colour and dense mousse are the prelude to a citrus fruit and apple nose, a palate with well-gauged sugar and a long, gratifying finish. Galeisa '09 offers clearly defined aromas and a refreshing, weighty palate. Asti la Selvatica '09, an archetype of its category, is one of the best versions we have seen in recent years, displaying compact perlage and impressive length.

○ Moscato d'Asti La Caudrina '09	▼▼	4*
○ Asti La Selvatica '09	▼▼	4
○ Moscato d'Asti La Galeisa '09	▼▼	4
○ Asti La Selvatica '07	▽▽	4*
● Barbera d'Asti La Solista '07	▽▽	4
● Barbera d'Asti La Solista '06	▽▽	4*
● Barbera d'Asti Sup. Montevenere '05	▽▽	5
○ Moscato d'Asti La Caudrina '08	▽▽	4
○ Moscato d'Asti La Caudrina '07	▽▽	4*
○ Moscato d'Asti La Galeisa '08	▽▽	4
○ Moscato d'Asti La Galeisa '06	▽▽	3*
○ Piemonte Moscato Passito Redento '04	▽▽	5

F.lli Cavallotto Tenuta Bricco Boschis

loc. Bricco Boschis
s.da Alba-Monforte
12060 Castiglione Falletto [CN]
tel. 017362814
www.cavallotto.com

CELLAR SALES
PRE-BOOKED VISITS

ANNUAL PRODUCTION 100,000 bottles
HECTARES UNDER VINE 26
VITICULTURE METHOD Organic

Young Alfio, Giuseppe and Laura are the fifth generation to produce quality wines on this estate. They are proud of their large, spacious cellar on the Bricco Boschis slopes, which has room for many more than the 100,000 bottles it houses. The Cavallottos prefer to fill it with big barrels for lengthy ageing. Long macerations, old vines and natural vineyard techniques also add to the classic nature of the range. What this estate lacks in pedigree it makes up for in consistency and style.

The magnificent Vignolo Riserva '04 has notes of red berry fruit shading gently into sweet tobacco. The tannins on the exhilarating, mouthfilling palate lend structure without descending into astringency. We gave it a brimming Three Glasses. Bricco Boschis Vigna San Giuseppe Riserva '04 has similar characteristics but is slightly softer and already very enjoyable on the palate. The quite different Barolo Bricco Boschis '06 offers elegance and superb complexity but at this time tends largely towards fruit and extract. Barbera d'Alba Vigna del Cuculo '06 is even better than usual.

● Barolo Vignolo Ris. '04	🍷🍷🍷	8
● Barbera d'Alba Bricco Boschis V. del Cuculo '06	🍷🍷	5
● Barolo Bricco Boschis '06	🍷🍷	8
● Barolo Bricco Boschis V. S. Giuseppe Ris. '04	🍷🍷	8
● Dolcetto d'Alba V. Scot '09	🍷🍷	4
● Langhe Freisa Bricco Boschis '08	🍷🍷	4
● Dolcetto d'Alba V. Melera '08	🍷	4
● Barolo Bricco Boschis '05	YYY+	7
● Barolo Bricco Boschis '04	YYY	8
● Barolo Bricco Boschis V. S. Giuseppe Ris. '01	YYY	8
● Barolo Bricco Boschis V. S. Giuseppe Ris. '00	YYY	8
● Barolo Bricco Boschis V. S. Giuseppe Ris. '99	YYY	8
● Barolo V. S. Giuseppe Ris. '89	YYY	8
● Barbera d'Alba V. del Cuculo '05	YY	5
● Barolo Vignolo Ris. '01	YY	8

Ceretto

loc. San Cassiano, 34
12051 Alba [CN]
tel. 0173282582
www.ceretto.com

CELLAR SALES
PRE-BOOKED VISITS

ANNUAL PRODUCTION 900,000 bottles
HECTARES UNDER VINE 87
VITICULTURE METHOD Conventional

This year, we profile the flagship wines of this historic brand established in 1937 by the Ceretto family. It now also embraces Bricco Rocche Bricco Asili and Vignaioli di Santo Stefano but these have their own Guide profiles. The San Cassiano ad Alba estate produces almost a million bottles from just over 80 hectares. The rich, varied range includes wines obtained from traditional varieties such as arneis, nebbiolo, dolcetto and barbera and less conventional grape types like riesling, merlot and syrah.

We note another fine performance from Ceretto's wines. The Barbaresco Asji '07 missed the final by a whisker. Its exuberant impact is enhanced by sweet and ripe yet refreshing fruitiness and an enfolding palate with soft tannins but the finish is not overly long. The Langhe Bianco Arbarei '08, a pure Riesling vinified in stainless steel, showed well again. It weds body with eloquence and closes elegantly. Barolo Zonchera '06 shows more muscle than complexity. One step below we have the Nebbiolo d'Alba Bernardina '08 and the Barbera d'Alba Piana '09.

● Barbaresco Asij '07	🍷🍷	8
● Barolo Zonchera '06	🍷🍷	8
○ Langhe Bianco Arbarei '08	🍷🍷	5
● Barbera d'Alba Piana '09	🍷	6
● Dolcetto d'Alba Rossana '09	🍷	5
● Langhe Rosso Monsordo '08	🍷	6
● Nebbiolo d'Alba Bernardina '08	🍷	6
● Barolo Zonchera '05	YY	8
● Barolo Zonchera '04	YY	6
○ Langhe Arbarei '07	YY	5
○ Langhe Bianco Arbarei '06	YY	5
○ Langhe Bianco Arbarei '05	YY	5
● Langhe Rosso Monsordo '06	YY	6
● Langhe Rosso Monsordo '05	YY	5
● Langhe Rosso Monsordo '04	YY	5

Erede di Armando Chiappone

S.DA SAN MICHELE, 51
14049 NIZZA MONFERRATO [AT]
TEL. 0141721424
www.eredechiappone.com

CELLAR SALES
PRE-BOOKED VISITS
FOOD

ANNUAL PRODUCTION 35,000 bottles
HECTARES UNDER VINE 10
VITICULTURE METHOD Conventional

The Chiappone family has worked its plots on the San Michele slopes just above Nizza Monferrato for three generations. Today, with Daniele at the helm, its limited production is all about quality. The vineyards lie at an altitude of 250-300 metres on a base of clay, marl and limestone and are largely given over to barbera with some freisa, dolcetto, cortese and favorita.

Barbera d'Asti Superiore Nizza Ru '06 comes out a year later than most others in Nizza. Aromas of black berry fruit, spice and tobacco announce a full, weighty palate that is very, very long and well sustained by acidity, even if the alcohol is a tad exuberant. The Barbera d'Asti Brentura '08 is also very well made. Young as yet, it exhibits fruity notes of plum and cherry with undertones of cinchona on the nose, and a varietal if rather rustic palate full of flesh and good acidity to give it a dash of energy. We also liked the Freisa d'Asti Sanpedra '06 for its tobacco, flowers and dried fruit sensations and powerful tannins that tend to leave the finish rather dry.

● Barbera d'Asti Sup. Nizza Ru '06	2 glasses (black)	5
● Barbera d'Asti Brentura '08	2 glasses (black)	4*
● Freisa d'Asti Sanpedra '06	1 glass (black)	3
● Barbera d'Asti Sup. Nizza Ru '04	2 glasses (white)	5
● Barbera d'Asti Sup. Nizza Ru '03	2 glasses (white)	5

★ Michele Chiarlo

S.DA NIZZA-CANELLI, 99
14042 CALAMANDRANA [AT]
TEL. 0141769030
www.chiarlo.it

CELLAR SALES
PRE-BOOKED VISITS

ANNUAL PRODUCTION 950,000 bottles
HECTARES UNDER VINE 100
VITICULTURE METHOD Conventional

Known across the world, the Chiarlo family's dynamic estate is on a continuing quest for the highest possible quality. Their range of wines is extensive and covers almost all the main types and DOCGs of southern Piedmont. Over the years, we have watched their steady march, the results of which are clear to see from their basic offerings to their most prestigious Barolo selections.

The very refined, elegant Barolo Cannubi '06 shows clear notes of spice and sweet tobacco with red berry fruit nuances. The palate is full but not over the top and the structure does not rely on extraction, muscle power or mouth-drying tannins. This classic, textbook interpretation of a historic cru earned the Chiarlos another Three Glass trophy. The Cerequio '06 is harder and more assertive but hints at excellent development potential. The Barbera d'Asti Superiore Nizza La Court '07 stopped just shy of top marks. Combined with that varietal fruit, its earthiness and minerality lend prestigious and complexity. The palate is not too long but shows elegance and balance.

● Barolo Cannubi '06	3 glasses (black)	8
● Barbera d'Asti Sup. Nizza La Court '07	2 glasses (black)	6
● Barolo Cerequio '06	2 glasses (black)	8
● Barbaresco Asili '07	2 glasses (black)	7
● Barolo Tortoniano '06	2 glasses (black)	6
○ Gavi del Comune di Gavi Rovereto '09	2 glasses (black)	4
● Barbera d'Asti Sup. Cipressi della Court '08	1 glass (black)	4
● M.to Rosso Montald '08	1 glass (black)	5
○ Moscato d'Asti Nivole '09	1 glass (black)	3
● Barbera d'Asti Sup. Nizza La Court '06	3 glasses (white)	6
● Barbera d'Asti Sup. Nizza La Court '03	3 glasses (white)	6
● Barbera d'Asti Sup. Nizza La Court '01	3 glasses (white)	6
● Barbera d'Asti Sup. Nizza La Court '00	3 glasses (white)	6
● Barolo Cannubi '04	3 glasses (white)	8
○ Gavi Fornaci di Tassarolo '90	3 glasses (white)	5

Quinto Chionetti & Figlio

B.TA VALDIBERTI, 44
12063 DOGLIANI [CN]
TEL. 017371179
www.chionettiquinto.com

CELLAR SALES
PRE-BOOKED VISITS

ANNUAL PRODUCTION 84,000 bottles
HECTARES UNDER VINE 15
VITICULTURE METHOD Conventional

One of Langhe's last, great gurus, Quinto shuns modern fads for practical methods that produce natural, upfront wines that bow only to the weather. Witness his results over the years: the Briccolero and San Luigi vie for supremacy, both vinified in steel and kept outside the recent Dogliani DOCG. Wines for immediate drinking in the Piedmont tradition, they also age well. Chionetti believes in long-lived Dolcettos and we agree: they are best drunk three to five years after harvest.

Once again, the Dolcetto di Dogliani Briccolero '09 proved more complex than the San Luigi. It presents an attractive, bright purplish colour, a potent nose rich in dark, ripe fruit aromas and led by notes of cocoa powder. The classic palate has an almondy finish. With its close-knit, tempting tannic texture, this is without doubt one of the great Dogliani Dolcettos. The '09 San Luigi shows robust alcohol with clear fruity sensations and unexpected hints of tobacco.

● Dolcetto di Dogliani Briccolero '09	🍷🍷	4*
● Dolcetto di Dogliani S. Luigi '09	🍷🍷	4*
● Dolcetto di Dogliani Briccolero '07	YYY	4*
● Dolcetto di Dogliani Briccolero '04	YYY	4*
● Dolcetto di Dogliani Briccolero '08	YY	4*
● Dolcetto di Dogliani Briccolero '06	YY	4*
● Dolcetto di Dogliani Briccolero '05	YY	4*
● Dolcetto di Dogliani S. Luigi '08	YY	4
● Dolcetto di Dogliani S. Luigi '07	YY	4*
● Dolcetto di Dogliani S. Luigi '06	YY	4*

Cieck

FRAZ. SAN GRATO
VIA BARDESONO
10011 AGLIÈ [TO]
TEL. 0124330522
www.cieck.it

CELLAR SALES
PRE-BOOKED VISITS

ANNUAL PRODUCTION 100,000 bottles
HECTARES UNDER VINE 20
VITICULTURE METHOD Conventional

Versatility and Caluso erbaluce go hand in hand in Cieck wines. The variety is presented in all versions: still, sparkling and dried-grape. The basic and Misobolo mature in stainless steel; the T selection in big barrels. Calliope and San Giorgio sojourn on the yeasts for 36 months and have been recently joined by a Brut Rosé obtained from neretto di San Giorgio. Nebbiolo, freisa and barbera complete the ampelographic picture of an estate that has always been on the cutting edge, not least with its pricing.

All nine labels presented are seriously good and testify louder than words to the achievements of this lovely estate belonging to Domenico Caretto and Lia Falconieri. The Rosé Brut '06 and the Erbaluce di Caluso Misobolo '09 both missed our highest accolade by a mere whisker. The first displays red berry fruit elegance with faint yeasty, smoky sensations to develop full and well-paced on the palate while the latter defies a challenging growing year to offer a profile of captivating freshness and linearity, falling off slightly only in the finish.

○ Erbaluce di Caluso Misobolo '09	🍷🍷	4*
⊙ Rosé Brut	🍷🍷	4
● Canavese Nebbiolo '07	🍷🍷	4
● Canavese Rosso Cieck '07	🍷🍷	3*
● Canavese Rosso Cieck Neretto '07	🍷🍷	4*
○ Erbaluce di Caluso '09	🍷🍷	3*
○ Erbaluce di Caluso Calliope Brut '06	🍷🍷	5
○ Erbaluce di Caluso Passito Alladium '04	🍷🍷	5
○ Erbaluce di Caluso S. Giorgio Brut '06	🍷🍷	5
○ Caluso Brut Calliope '01	YY	5*
○ Caluso Brut Calliope '00	YY	5*
○ Caluso Brut S. Giorgio '00	YY	4*
○ Erbaluce di Caluso Misobolo '08	YY	4*
○ Erbaluce di Caluso Passito Alladium Ris. '01	YY	6
○ Erbaluce di Caluso T '07	YY	4
○ Erbaluce di Caluso V. Misobolo '01	YY	3*

★ Tenute Cisa Asinari dei Marchesi di Grésy

S.DA DELLA STAZIONE, 21
12050 BARBARESCO [CN]
TEL. 0173635222
www.marchesidigresy.com

CELLAR SALES
PRE-BOOKED VISITS

ANNUAL PRODUCTION 200,000 bottles
HECTARES UNDER VINE 35
VITICULTURE METHOD Conventional

To illustrate the quality of the work carried out by this winery, we'd like to describe a large blind tasting of the 1999 vintage, held in January 2010. The Barbarescos presented by Alberto de Grésy astounded everyone, demonstrating the extraordinary, noble character of nebbiolo, combined with a rare potential for development, capable of offering complexity and unique sensations.

Barbaresco Camp Gros '06 is superb, with a stylish, concentrated, complex nose of herbs in the sun and fresh raspberries and a firmly structured palate with an incredibly elegant tannic weave. We awarded it Three Glasses. The magnificent Barbaresco Gaiun '06 displays notes of incense against a spicy background laced with hints of wood. On the palate, the nicely continuous, assertive tannins are not yet absolutely balanced. Langhe Sauvignon '09, long one of the area's best whites, deserves a special mention. It has a complex nose of peaches and sage, and a remarkably balanced buttery palate with good acidity. The release of several important reds has wisely been postponed.

● Barbaresco Camp Gros '06	▼▼▼	8
● Barbaresco Gaiun '06	▼▼	8
● Barbaresco Martinenga '07	▼▼	8
○ Langhe Sauvignon '09	▼▼	4*
● Dolcetto d'Alba Monte Aribaldo '09	▼▼	4
○ Langhe Bianco Villa Giulia '09	▼▼	4
● Langhe Rosso Villa Martis '07	▼▼	5
○ Moscato d'Asti La Serra '09	▼▼	4
○ Langhe Chardonnay '09	▼	4
● Langhe Nebbiolo Martinenga '09	▼	5
● Barbaresco Camp Gros '05	▽▽▽	8
● Barbaresco Camp Gros '01	▽▽▽	8
● Barbaresco Camp Gros '00	▽▽▽	8
● Barbaresco Camp Gros '99	▽▽▽	8
● Barbaresco Gaiun '04	▽▽▽	8

★★ Domenico Clerico

LOC. MANZONI, 67
12065 MONFORTE D'ALBA [CN]
TEL. 017378171
domenicoclerico@libero.it

PRE-BOOKED VISITS

ANNUAL PRODUCTION 30,000 bottles
HECTARES UNDER VINE 21
VITICULTURE METHOD Conventional

Domenico Clerico has been a great innovator of the Barolo style, with his ability to transform high-quality grapes into generous, exuberant wines that require carefully calibrated ageing to reveal their full complexity. In addition to the various Barolo vineyard selections, the rest of the list is consistently good.

The release of the promising '04 vintage of the famous Barolo Percristina has been delayed until next year and it will not be labelled Riserva. Barolo Ciabot Mentin Ginestra '06 is modern, with well-integrated oak that imparts hints of sweet spices. The stylish, elegant palate is already enjoyable, showing soft, close-knit tannins and good length. Barolo Pajana '06 has nice structure but is still a little immature and requires further bottle ageing to assimilate the sweet, toasty notes of the barrique. Langhe Arte '08, from nebbiolo with a dash of barbera, which in many vintages has been among the area's best blends, is sound but not stunning.

● Barolo Ciabot Mentin Ginestra '06	▼▼	8
● Barolo Pajana '06	▼▼	8
● Barbera d'Alba Trevigne '08	▼▼	4
● Langhe Dolcetto Visadì '09	▼▼	4*
● Langhe Nebbiolo Capismee '09	▼▼	5
● Langhe Rosso Arte '08	▼▼	6
● Barolo Ciabot Mentin Ginestra '05	▽▽▽	8
● Barolo Ciabot Mentin Ginestra '04	▽▽▽	8
● Barolo Ciabot Mentin Ginestra '99	▽▽▽	8
● Barolo Percristina '01	▽▽▽	8
● Barolo Percristina '99	▽▽▽	8
● Barolo Percristina '98	▽▽▽	8
● Barolo Percristina '97	▽▽▽	8
● Barolo Percristina '96	▽▽▽	8
Langhe Arte '96	▽▽▽	6

Elvio Cogno

via Ravera, 2
12060 Novello [CN]
tel. 0173744006
www.elviocogno.com

CELLAR SALES
PRE-BOOKED VISITS

ANNUAL PRODUCTION 70,000 bottles
HECTARES UNDER VINE 13
VITICULTURE METHOD Conventional

The extraordinary premises alone deserve a visit for the winery's dominant position, original architecture, warm, evocative atmosphere and welcoming spirit. It is managed by the dynamic couple of Nadia Cogno and Walter Fissore. Vineyards are managed to strict standards and the cellar is suitably equipped for the production of a range of wines whose stylistic definition and local character becomes more convincing every year.

Barolo Bricco Pernice '05, from the Ravera cru, won Three Glasses at its first release for its complex nose of spices, tar and white truffle, and a rich, not excessively powerful palate that unveils great class and length. The elegant, confident Barolo Ravera '06 is more open on the nose of dried herbs and sweet tobacco than on the dynamic, medium-long palate. Langhe Bianco Anas-cëtta '09, recently included in the Langhe DOC thanks to the efforts of the Cogno family, is aged in steel and has a fresh citrus nose with hints of pennyroyal, and a slightly salty, long, vibrant palate.

● Barolo Bricco Pernice '05	🍷🍷🍷	8
● Barolo Ravera '06	🍷🍷	8
○ Langhe Bianco Anas-cëtta '09	🍷🍷	4*
● Barbera d'Alba Bricco dei Merli '08	🍷🍷	5
● Barolo Cascina Nuova '06	🍷🍷	6
● Dolcetto d'Alba V. del Mandorlo '09	🍷🍷	4*
● Langhe Rosso Montegrilli '08	🍷🍷	5
● Barolo Ravera '04	YYY	7
● Barolo Ravera '01	YYY	7
● Barolo V. Elena '04	YYY	8
● Barolo V. Elena '01	YYY	8
● Barolo V. Elena '99	YYY	8
● Barbera d'Alba Bricco dei Merli '07	YY	5
● Barolo Ravera '05	YY	8
● Barolo V. Elena '03	YY	8

Colle Manora

s.da Bozzole, 5
15044 Quargnento [AL]
tel. 0131219252
www.collemanora.it

CELLAR SALES
PRE-BOOKED VISITS

ANNUAL PRODUCTION 70,000 bottles
HECTARES UNDER VINE 20
VITICULTURE METHOD Conventional

Giorgio Schön's estate has long been a good performer at our tastings, with a steadily increasing number of wines reaching our finals, demonstrating its steady improvement. This year's list did not include Albarossa Ray, which was a finalist last time. However, we were assured that it will make a comeback in grand style next year.

Barbera Manora '07 has a deep ruby hue and an elegant nose of fruit and spice, followed by a firmly structured palate with plenty of flesh. Palo Alto '06, from pinot nero, cabernet sauvignon and merlot, has a stylish, pervasive nose, accompanied by a long palate with an alluring tannic weave. Monferrato Rosso Barchetta '07, from cabernet sauvignon, merlot and barbera, is balanced and nicely harmonious. Bianco Mimosa '09, a monovarietal Sauvignon Bianco, has clear varietal notes perceptible in all stages of tasting.

● Barbera d'Asti Sup. Manora '07	🍷🍷	5
○ M.to Bianco Mimosa '09	🍷🍷	4
● M.to Rosso Barchetta '07	🍷🍷	6
● M.to Rosso Palo Alto '06	🍷🍷	6
● Barbera del M.to Pais '08	🍷	4
○ M.to Bianco Mila '08	🍷	6
● Barbera d'Asti Sup. Manora '06	YY	5
● Barbera del M.to Manora '05	YY	5
● Barbera del M.to Manora '04	YY	5
● Barbera del M.to Pais '06	YY	4*
○ M.to Bianco Mimosa '06	YY	4*
● M.to Rosso Palo Alto '05	YY	6
● M.to Rosso Ray '07	YY	5

Collina Serragrilli

LOC. SERRAGRILLI
VIA SERRAGRILLI, 30
12057 NEIVE [CN]
TEL. 0173677010
www.serragrilli.it

CELLAR SALES
PRE-BOOKED VISITS

ANNUAL PRODUCTION **100,000 bottles**
HECTARES UNDER VINE **15**
VITICULTURE METHOD **Conventional**

The three Lequio sisters are a good example of an all-female winery and are continuing the philosophy of high quality that has allowed them to make a name for themselves on the crowded Langhe wine scene. All the wines share a style that is a good blend of classic and modern, which becomes more and more distinctive each year. All are extremely drinkable and faithfully reflect the terroir.

Barbaresco Serragrilli '07 is fresh, fruity and spicy; the palate is fairly dry, but complex and balanced, with a long finish still displaying a little oak, making it a very enjoyable modern interpretation of the DOCG. Basarin '07 does not reveal the youthfulness of the vines too much, with an open, tar and fruit nose and a supple palate that is somewhat simple but well balanced. The highly drinkable Barbera d'Alba '07 is characterized by cherries and alcohol, with a very supple, fresh palate. Barbera Grillaia '08, however, is still a little heavily oaked and requires a few more months before it reaches its full potential.

● Barbaresco Serragrilli '07	▼▼	6
● Barbaresco Basarin '07	▼▼	6
● Barbera d'Alba '07	▼▼	4
● Barbera d'Alba Grillaia '08	▼	4
● Dolcetto d'Alba '09	▼	4
● Barbaresco Basarin '06	▽▽	6
● Barbaresco Basarin '04	▽▽	6
● Barbaresco Serragrilli '06	▽▽	6
● Barbaresco Serragrilli '05	▽▽	6
● Barbera d'Alba '06	▽▽	4
● Barbera d'Alba Grillaia '07	▽▽	4
● Langhe Grillorosso '06	▽▽	4
● Langhe Grillorosso '05	▽▽	4*

La Colombera

S.C. VHO, 7
15057 TORTONA [AL]
TEL. 0131867795
www.lacolomberavini.it

CELLAR SALES
PRE-BOOKED VISITS

ANNUAL PRODUCTION **50,000 bottles**
HECTARES UNDER VINE **20**
VITICULTURE METHOD **Conventional**

This interesting winery in the Tortona area is competently run by the Semino family, whose new generation, represented by daughter Elisa, promotes the products with great enthusiasm and dynamism. The style of the wines closely echoes the characteristics of the terroir, particularly in the various interpretations of Timorasso. These are never overly rich or excessive, displaying admirable drinkability and fresh flavour.

The magnificent list commences with Montino '08, a bright straw Timorasso boasting a stylish nose of petrol, citrus fruit and resin, and a potent, fleshy palate with good attack. Timorasso Derthona '08 is equally delicious, its nose alternating citrus, vegetal and mineral notes, and an exceptionally balanced palate with a very intense finish. Vegia Rampana is a splendid Barbera '08, which has a complex, well-orchestrated nose, accompanied by an elegant, powerful palate with a fruity finish. Stylish to a fault, the mouthwatering Barbera Elisa '08 offers finesse on nose and palate. The range is completed by the good Croatina Archè '08 and Cortese Bricco Bartolomeo '09.

○ Colli Tortonesi Timorasso Derthona '08	▼▼	5
● Colli Tortonesi Rosso Vegia Rampana '08	▼▼	4*
○ Colli Tortonesi Timorasso Il Montino '08	▼▼	6
● Colli Tortonesi Croatina Arché '08	▼▼	4*
● Colli Tortonesi Rosso Elisa '08	▼▼	5
○ Colli Tortonesi Bricco Bartolomeo '09	▼	3
○ Colli Tortonesi Timorasso Il Montino '06	▽▽▽	5
○ Colli Tortonesi Bricco Bartolomeo '08	▽▽	3*
○ Colli Tortonesi Timorasso Derthona '07	▽▽	5
○ Colli Tortonesi Timorasso Derthona '06	▽▽	5
● Colli Tortonesi Rosso Elisa '07	▽▽	5
● Colli Tortonesi Rosso Vegia Rampana '07	▽▽	4
○ Colli Tortonesi Timorasso Il Montino '07	▽▽	6
● Piemonte Barbera Elisa '05	▽▽	4

Il Colombo - Barone Riccati

VIA DEI SENT, 2
12084 MONDOVÌ [CN]
TEL. 017441607
www.ilcolombo.com

CELLAR SALES
PRE-BOOKED VISITS

ANNUAL PRODUCTION 14,000 bottles
HECTARES UNDER VINE 3
VITICULTURE METHOD Certified organic

Those unaware of the Langhe Monregalesi area are missing out on an extraordinary, unspoiled corner of Piedmont, with vineyards, meadows and woods. This delightful landscape is the setting for Il Colombo, its vineyard of the same name overlooked by a handsome 18th-century building. The Riccati family started making wine here in 1991 and in 2006 the estate was bought by the Norwegian couple Britt and Theo Holm, who entrusted the winery to Sabina Bosio and her husband Bruno Chionetti. They are flanked by consultant oenologist Beppe Caviola.

The chief variety is dolcetto, which the winery interprets very well, as testified by La Chiesetta '09, which is a bright, deep ruby with a complex nose of violets, tobacco and juicy fruit. The palate is equally full, with a weighty mouthfeel and a very long finish. Dolcetto Langhe Monregalesi Superiore Il Colombo '08, from a slightly less generous vintage, is nearly as good. It's dominated by more austere notes, initially cinchona, then flowers and red berry fruit. The close-woven tannins are smooth and well tucked in, giving the long finish class and complexity. Langhe Rosso Monteregale '07 is lean and austere, lacking a little balance because of still-prominent oak.

● Dolcetto delle Langhe Monregalesi La Chiesetta '09	TT	3*
● Dolcetto delle Langhe Monregalesi Sup. Il Colombo '08	TT	4*
● Langhe Rosso Monteregale '07	T	4
● Dolcetto delle Langhe Monregalesi Il Colombo '98	YYY	4
● Dolcetto delle Langhe Monregalesi Il Colombo '97	YYY	4
● Dolcetto delle Langhe Monregalesi La Chiesetta '08	YY	3*
● Dolcetto delle Langhe Monregalesi La Chiesetta '07	YY	3*
● Dolcetto delle Langhe Monregalesi La Chiesetta '06	YY	3*
● Langhe Rosso Monteregale '06	YY	4

★ Aldo Conterno

LOC. BUSSIA, 48
12065 MONFORTE D'ALBA [CN]
TEL. 017378150
www.poderialdoconterno.com

ANNUAL PRODUCTION 120,000 bottles
HECTARES UNDER VINE 25
VITICULTURE METHOD Conventional

There is no need to remind our readers what the estate founded in 1969 by Aldo Conterno, and now headed by his sons Franco and Stefano, represents for Italian wine. The family vineyards in Bussia's Romirasco, Cicala and Colonello vineyards have given rise to some of the most classic and ageworthy Nebbiolos in history, commencing with the unrivalled Granbussia Riserva. Today, the flagship wines have a more complex, modern character.

Once again we had to postpone our eagerly awaited tasting of Barolo Granbussia Riserva '04 but we consoled ourselves with a fine trio of Barolo '06 wines. The group is headed by Bussia Cicala, from the Monforte grand cru, which is virile with plenty of stuffing. It displays nice verve, releasing fresher hints of orange and bay leaf as it opens up, following brooding notes of coffee and incense. Bussia Colonello is similarly generous and cosseting but with a finish slightly dried by alcohol and prominent tannins. Bussia Romirasco '06 is a little static but promises very well.

● Barolo Cicala '06	TT	8
● Barolo Colonnello '06	TT	8
● Barbera d'Alba Conca Tre Pile '07	TT	6
● Barolo Romirasco '06	TT	8
● Langhe Nebbiolo Il Favot '06	TT	7
○ Langhe Chardonnay Bussiador '07	T	6
● Barolo Bussia Soprana '86	YYY	5
● Barolo Bussia Soprana '85	YYY	5
● Barolo Gran Bussia Ris. '01	YYY	8
● Barolo Gran Bussia Ris. '95	YYY	8
● Barolo Gran Bussia Ris. '90	YYY	8
● Barolo Romirasco '04	YYY	8
● Barolo Vigna del Colonnello '88	YYY	6
● Barolo Vigna del Colonnello '82	YYY	6

Diego Conterno

Montà, 27
12065 Monforte d'Alba [CN]
tel. 0173789265
www.diegoconterno.it

CELLAR SALES
PRE-BOOKED VISITS

ANNUAL PRODUCTION 40,000 bottles
HECTARES UNDER VINE 6
VITICULTURE METHOD Conventional

This small, recently founded estate is a good example of how, even at the leisurely pace of viticulture, it is possible to achieve high-quality results in a fairly short span of time. The fruits of the precious experience accumulated by Diego Conterno have allowed him to create a small but highly convincing range. We were impressed by the stylistic definition of the wines presented, which focus on terroir.

The estate's debut speaks for itself, with two wines reaching our finals and another two just missing out. Nebbiolo Baluma '08 is particularly well made, concentrated and stylish, with an elegant nose of raspberries, dried flowers and liquorice. The potent, mouthfilling palate shows good attack and impressive balance. Barbera Ferrione '07 is an almost inky dark ruby, with nice varietal stamping and a rich, chewy palate. All in all, it's a fine example from a good vintage. Barolo le Coste '06 has an attractive nose of fruit and oak, and a silky, close-knit tannic weave, accompanied by a very long palate, while the Barolo '06 is a shade less complex and still seems youngish.

● Barolo Le Coste '06	2 black glasses	7
● Nebbiolo d'Alba Baluma '08	2 black glasses	4*
● Barbera d'Alba Ferrione '07	2 black glasses	4
● Barolo '06	2 black glasses	7

★★ Giacomo Conterno

loc. Ornati, 2
12065 Monforte d'Alba [CN]
tel. 017378221

PRE-BOOKED VISITS

ANNUAL PRODUCTION 60,000 bottles
HECTARES UNDER VINE 17
VITICULTURE METHOD Conventional

Although not the oldest Barolo winery, the family have been making and selling wine here since the 1700s, with the first sales of bottled wines around 1920 when Monfortino was released. Since then, it has never faltered. Following his grandfather Giacomo and his father Giovanni, it is now Roberto's turn to perpetuate work in the vineyard and the art of the cellar. In these temples of wine, change happens very slowly, but this year we had a surprise: three additional hectares under vine at Serralunga d'Alba expanded the estate with the 2008 harvest.

This year we started with a very big Monfortino '02. Bear in mind that the 2002 vintage was considered one of the most difficult of the last 20 years. Nevertheless, going against all the rules of common sense and at the risk of damaging his credibility, Roberto stuck his neck out and declared that it would become a legendary vintage. An extra year in wood has resulted in the greatest Monfortino that we can remember. Barolo Cascina Francia, with its granitic tannic structure but velvety texture, and its complex aromas of mint, tobacco and liquorice, is in turn one of the great Barolos from the '06 vintage.

● Barolo Cascina Francia '06	3 black glasses	8
● Barolo Monfortino Ris. '02	3 black glasses +	8
● Barbera d'Alba Cascina Francia '08	2 black glasses	6
● Barbera d'Alba Cerretta '08	2 black glasses	6
● Langhe Nebbiolo Cerretta '08	2 black glasses	8
● Barolo Cascina Francia '05	3 white glasses +	8
● Barolo Cascina Francia '04	3 white glasses	8
● Barolo Cascina Francia '01	3 white glasses	8
● Barolo Cascina Francia '00	3 white glasses	8
● Barolo Monfortino Ris. '01	3 white glasses	8
● Barolo Monfortino Ris. '00	3 white glasses	8
● Barolo Monfortino Ris. '99	3 white glasses	8
● Barolo Monfortino Ris. '97	3 white glasses	8
● Barolo Monfortino Ris. '96	3 white glasses	8

Paolo Conterno

VIA GINESTRA, 34
12065 MONFORTE D'ALBA [CN]
TEL. 017378415
www.paoloconterno.com

PRE-BOOKED VISITS

ANNUAL PRODUCTION 55,000 bottles
HECTARES UNDER VINE 11
VITICULTURE METHOD Conventional

This small estate confidently continues its quest for excellence. The Ginestra di Monforte cru is a top-quality terroir, as many have rightly claimed. Its wines have distinctive depth and sensory complexity worthy of the finest in the world. The style of the various bottles uncorked for our tastings was again balanced and well calibrated.

Barolo Ginestra '06 earned Conterno its third Three Glass award, with a generous, pervasive nose of dried roses and cinchona against a delicate background of oak, and a potent, balanced palate with still-prominent tannins and an austere finish. Barolo Ginestra Riserva '04 is highly convincing, although the nose is still rather closed, displaying timid notes of tobacco, spices and a slightly oaky background, while the powerful palate is characterized by attractive tannins that are slightly dusty and drying.

● Barolo Ginestra '06	TTT	8
● Barolo Ginestra Ris. '04	TT	8
● Barbera d'Alba Ginestra '08	TT	5
● Barolo Riva del Bric '06	TT	7
● Langhe Nebbiolo '08	TT	5
● Langhe Nebbiolo Bric Ginestra '07	TT	6
● Barbera d'Alba Bricco Sant'Ambrogio '09	T	4
● Barolo Ginestra '05	YYY	8
● Barolo Ginestra Ris. '01	YYY	8
● Barbera d'Alba Ginestra '07	YY	5
● Barbera d'Alba Ginestra '06	YY	5
● Barolo '05	YY	7
● Barolo Ginestra '04	YY	8
● Barolo Ginestra Ris. '03	YY	8
● Langhe Nebbiolo '07	YY	5

★ Conterno Fantino

VIA GINESTRA, 1
12065 MONFORTE D'ALBA [CN]
TEL. 017378204
www.conternofantino.it

PRE-BOOKED VISITS

ANNUAL PRODUCTION 140,000 bottles
HECTARES UNDER VINE 25
VITICULTURE METHOD Organic

This renowned estate is one of the best-known producers of quality wines in Italy and indeed anywhere. It has achieved fame through many years of unflagging work that has been distinguished by stylistic consistency since the 1980s, testifying to a far-sightedness that has been richly rewarded by the world's consumers. Although none of the wines presented this year won our top accolade, average quality is excellent.

Barolo Sorì Ginestra '06 is concentrated, with hints of raspberries, sweet tobacco and liquorice, accompanying a modern, full-bodied palate with fruity pulp, smooth, velvety tannins and a focused finish. Barolo Vigna del Gris '06 has a nose of dark berry fruit, like blackberries, and faint citrus notes, against a delightful background of tobacco. The palate is already well balanced, thanks to a close-knit but not vegetal tannic weave. Barolo Mosconi '06 is characterized by prominent oak and rather rough, invasive tannins. It needs further bottle ageing. Langhe Rosso Monprà '07, from mainly nebbiolo and barbera, is a great version of this classic Langhe wine.

● Barolo Sorì Ginestra '06	TT	8
● Barolo V. del Gris '06	TT	8
● Langhe Rosso Monprà '07	TT	6
● Barolo Mosconi '06	TT	8
● Dolcetto d'Alba Bricco Bastia '09	TT	4*
○ Langhe Chardonnay Bastia '08	TT	6
○ Langhe Chardonnay Prinsipi '09	T	4
● Barolo Sorì Ginestra '00	YYY	8
● Barolo Sorì Ginestra '99	YYY	8
● Barolo Sorì Ginestra '98	YYY	8
● Barolo V. del Gris '04	YYY	8
● Barolo V. del Gris '01	YYY	8
● Barolo V. del Gris '97	YYY	8
● Barolo Sorì Ginestra '05	YY	8
● Barolo V. del Gris '05	YY	8

Contratto

via G. B. Giuliani, 56
14053 Canelli [AT]
tel. 0141823349
www.contratto.it

CELLAR SALES
PRE-BOOKED VISITS

ANNUAL PRODUCTION 300,000 bottles
HECTARES UNDER VINE 55
VITICULTURE METHOD Conventional

The distinguishing characteristics of this legendary Piedmont winery can be fully understood by visiting its charming headquarters in the centre of Canelli. Some of the wines, like For England, are part of Italian sparkling winemaking history and continue to offer a reliable, original taste experience.

Contratto has returned to making top-rate sparklers, of a quality that had long been absent. Proof is in the Giuseppe Contratto Brut Riserva '02, disgorged in 2010 after almost eight years on the lees. It is complex and full, with a pervasive nose of wholemeal, honey and ripe white-fleshed fruit, and a dry, no-nonsense palate with remarkable structure and good, fresh acidity. Asti De Miranda Metodo Classico '07 is also very good and has gained finesse and elegance year after year, although slightly at the expense of the mouthfilling richness of the first vintages. For England Pas Dosé '07 is very well made while Barolo Cerequio '06 is sound, but still marked by oak.

○ Asti De Miranda M. Cl. '07	▼▼	7
○ Giuseppe Contratto Brut Ris. '02	▼▼	6
● Barolo Cerequio '06	▼▼	8
○ For England Pas Dosé '07	▼▼	6
⊙ For England Rosé '07	▼	6
○ Asti De Miranda M. Cl. '00	YYY	6
○ Asti De Miranda M. Cl. '97	YYY	6
○ Asti De Miranda M. Cl. '96	YYY	6
● Barolo Cerequio '99	YYY	8
● Barolo Cerequio Tenuta Secolo '97	YYY	8
○ Spumante M. Cl. Brut Ris. Giuseppe Contratto '96	YYY	6
○ Asti De Miranda M. Cl. '06	YY	6
● Barolo Cerequio '05	YY	8

Vigne Marina Coppi

via Sant'Andrea, 5
15051 Castellania [AL]
tel. 3385360111
www.vignemarinacoppi.com

CELLAR SALES
PRE-BOOKED VISITS

ANNUAL PRODUCTION 20,000 bottles
HECTARES UNDER VINE 4
VITICULTURE METHOD Conventional

This estate's wines are especially delicate and aromatic thanks to the sandy soils of marine origin, in which you can still find fossil shells. The Guyot-trained vines are planted at 5,000 per hectare in a well-aspected position on the hilltop. Here Francesco Bellocchio, the grandson of the best-loved champion cyclist of all times, makes high-quality red and white wines with the aid of consultant oenologist Franco Cordero. Francesco initially had high hopes for the Favorita but it is actually the Timorasso and Barbera that are giving the most interesting results.

Timorasso Fausto '08 made it into our finals with its good varietal stamping and a full, very balanced palate. The pleasant, mature Barbera I Grop '07 is a bright, deep ruby, with a nose of fruit, tobacco and coffee, and a nicely acidic, full-bodied palate ending in a very vibrant finish. Castellania '08 is an enjoyable Barbera with reasonable balance and nice concentration, while Sant'Andrea '09 is a sound, uncomplicated Barbera. The delightful Favorita Marine '09 is also worth uncorking.

○ Colli Tortonesi Timorasso Fausto '08	▼▼	7
● Colli Tortonesi Barbera Castellania '08	▼▼	5
● Colli Tortonesi Barbera I Grop '07	▼▼	6
● Colli Tortonesi Barbera Sant'Andrea '09	▼▼	4
○ Colli Tortonesi Favorita Marine '09	▼	6
● Colli Tortonesi Barbera Castellania '07	YY	5
● Colli Tortonesi Barbera I Grop '06	YY	5
● Colli Tortonesi Barbera Sant'Andrea '08	YY	4
● Colli Tortonesi Barbera Sant'Andrea '07	YY	4*
○ Colli Tortonesi Favorita Marine '07	YY	5
● Colli Tortonesi Favorita Marine '06	YY	5
○ Colli Tortonesi Favorita Marine '06	YY	5

Coppo

via Alba, 68
14053 Canelli [AT]
tel. 0141823146
www.coppo.it

CELLAR SALES
PRE-BOOKED VISITS

ANNUAL PRODUCTION 420,000 bottles
HECTARES UNDER VINE 56
VITICULTURE METHOD Conventional

Founded in 1892, the estate owned by the Coppo family is a benchmark for Monferrato winemaking and the only cellar, here in Moscato country, to focus on dry wines and Metodo Classico sparklers. The wines are made from traditional Piedmontese grape varieties, with the important exception of chardonnay and pinot nero, largely from the vineyards that the Coppos own or manage on the hillsides around Canelli.

Monteriolo was missing this year but Coppo presented a first-rate series of Barberas. Barbera d'Asti Pomorosso '07 has great character with slightly sweet oak-derived notes of vanilla and cinnamon and overtones of dark berry fruit. Structure on the palate is firm, with good flesh and acidity, and a truly endless finish. Barbera d'Asti Superiore Nizza Riserva di Famiglia '04 is also very good, giving roasted coffee beans, cherries and plums against a background of incense, as is Barbera d'Asti Camp du Rouss '08, which displays attractive fruity freshness and an austere, tannic finish. The sparklers are excellent, as usual, while the rest of the list is well made.

● Barbera d'Asti Pomorosso '07	▼▼▼	7
● Barbera d'Asti Camp du Rouss '08	▼▼	4*
● Barbera d'Asti Sup. Nizza Riserva della Famiglia '04	▼▼	8
● Barbera d'Asti L'Avvocata '09	▼▼	4*
○ Coppo Brut Ris. '05	▼▼	6
● Langhe Rosso Mondaccione V.V. '06	▼▼	7
○ Luigi Coppo Brut	▼▼	5
● M.to Alterego '07	▼▼	6
○ Gavi La Rocca '09	▼	4
○ Moscato d'Asti Moncalvina '09	▼	4
● Barbera d'Asti Pomorosso '05	▽▽▽	7
● Barbera d'Asti Pomorosso '04	▽▽▽	7
● Barbera d'Asti Pomorosso '03	▽▽▽	7
● Barbera d'Asti Pomorosso '01	▽▽▽	7
○ Piemonte Chardonnay Monteriolo '06	▽▽▽	6
○ Piemonte Chardonnay Monteriolo '05	▽▽▽	6

Giovanni Corino

fraz. Annunziata, 24b
12064 La Morra [CN]
tel. 0173509452

CELLAR SALES
PRE-BOOKED VISITS

ANNUAL PRODUCTION 40,000 bottles
HECTARES UNDER VINE 8
VITICULTURE METHOD Conventional

Giuliano Corino knows the Langhe area like the back of his hand and his name is a guarantee for all lovers of great, noble Piedmontese wines. Corino's wines have excellent ageing prospects but also reveal great drinkability while young. Clarity and cleanliness are their stylistic hallmarks but without masking the characteristics of the grapes.

Barolo Vecchie Vigne '05 is again a first-rate wine, with a nicely open nose of spices and red berries, and a very alluring, not particularly potent, palate that presents velvety with medium length. Only a small number of bottles of Barolo Arborina '06 were produced after a severe hailstorm but the wine has a sweet nose of dried flowers and tobacco, accompanied by close-woven, slightly grainy tannins and a finish with only slightly less personality than the Vecchie Vigne. The evergreen Barolo Vigna Giachini '06 has always been the estate's signature wine and vaunts a similar style, with slightly more structure and pervasiveness on the palate.

● Barolo V. Giachini '06	▼▼	8
● Barolo Vecchie Vigne '05	▼▼	8
● Barolo Vign. Arborina '06	▼▼	8
● Barbera d'Alba '09	▼▼	4
● Barolo '06	▼▼	7
● Langhe Nebbiolo '09	▼▼	4
● Dolcetto d'Alba '09	▼	4
● Barbera d'Alba V. Pozzo '96	▽▽▽	8
● Barolo Rocche '01	▽▽▽	8
● Barolo Rocche '90	▽▽▽	8
● Barolo V. Giachini '89	▽▽▽	8
● Barolo Vecchie Vigne '99	▽▽▽	8
● Barolo Vecchie Vigne '98	▽▽▽	8
● Barolo V. Arborina '05	▽▽	8
● Barolo V. Giachini '05	▽▽	8
● Barolo Vecchie Vigne '04	▽▽	8

Renato Corino

FRAZ. ANNUNZIATA - B.TA POZZO, 49A
12064 LA MORRA [CN]
TEL. 0173500349
renatocorino@alice.it

CELLAR SALES
PRE-BOOKED VISITS

ANNUAL PRODUCTION 35,000 bottles
HECTARES UNDER VINE 7
VITICULTURE METHOD Conventional

The bond between man and the land is frequently cited as the finest expression of an estate's agricultural vocation. You only need to meet Renato Corino and shake his powerful hand to comprehend the vigour and power of labour contained in his wines. The estate's small production is characterized by consistently high quality, power, elegance and, above all, the great care lavished on the raw materials.

This year, Corino announced that, as from the '05 vintage, the magnificent Barolo Vecchie Vigne will become a Riserva, with five years of ageing. Consequently we will report on it next year. The other sad piece of news is that Barolo Arborina '06 will never be released, following a violent hailstorm. Barolo Vigneto Rocche '06 is astounding and took Three Glasses for its sweet spices, red berries and liquorice, combined with an austere, powerful palate with slightly drying, but not rough, tannins. Barolo '06 boasts great finesse and delicate tannins, in the classic La Morra style, while Barbera d'Alba Vigna Pozzo '07 is weighty and extracted, but has character and balance.

● Barolo Vign. Rocche '06	3 black glasses	8
● Barbera d'Alba V. Pozzo '07	2 black glasses	6
● Barolo '06	2 black glasses	6
● Nebbiolo d'Alba '08	2 black glasses	4*
● Barbera d'Alba '09	1 black glass	4
● Dolcetto d'Alba '09	1 black glass	4
● Barolo Vign. Rocche '04	3 white glasses	8
● Barolo Vign. Rocche '03	3 white glasses	8
● Barbera d'Alba V. Pozzo '06	2 white glasses	6
● Barbera d'Alba V. Pozzo '05	2 white glasses	6
● Barolo Vecchie Vigne '04	2 white glasses	8
● Barolo Vign. Arborina '05	2 white glasses	7
● Barolo Vign. Arborina '04	2 white glasses	8
● Barolo Vign. Rocche '05	2 white glasses	8

Cornarea

VIA VALENTINO, 150
12043 CANALE [CN]
TEL. 017365636
www.cornarea.com

CELLAR SALES
PRE-BOOKED VISITS
ROOMS

ANNUAL PRODUCTION 90,000 bottles
HECTARES UNDER VINE 15
VITICULTURE METHOD Certified organic

The Bovone family's estate is located in a scenic position on the Cornarea hill, crowned by a country house that is home to both the winery and handsome guest accommodation. Cornarea was the first winery in Roero to focus on arneis, a native grape variety that it vinifies in many different versions: dry, dried-grape, late-harvest and sparkling. The only other variety planted is nebbiolo, used to produce Roero and Nebbiolo d'Alba.

The Govone estate did this year, except for its best-known wine, Roero Arneis '09, which was not as good as usual. The nose is less well-defined and the palate is pleasant but short palate, lacking in depth. We liked Tarasco Passito '06, a monovarietal Arneis, with a concentrated, stylish nose offering classic beeswax, sultanas and elegant oxidized overtones, and a rich, long, charmingly fresh palate. Roero '07 is also good, with plenty of fruit, albeit still masked by oak on the nose, and a velvety, cosseting palate. Equally attractive is the Nebbiolo d'Alba '07, which is slightly huskier but with good texture and notes of tobacco and dark berry fruit.

● Nebbiolo d'Alba '07	2 black glasses	5
● Roero '07	2 black glasses	5
○ Tarasco Passito '06	2 black glasses	6
○ Andrè '07	1 black glass	6
○ Roero Arneis '09	1 black glass	5
● Nebbiolo d'Alba '06	2 white glasses	4*
● Nebbiolo d'Alba '05	2 white glasses	4
● Roero '06	2 white glasses	6
● Roero '05	2 white glasses	4
○ Roero Arneis '08	2 white glasses	4*
○ Tarasco Passito '05	2 white glasses	6

★ Matteo Correggia

LOC. GARBINETTO
VIA SANTO STEFANO ROERO, 124
12043 CANALE [CN]
TEL. 0173978009
www.matteocorreggia.com

CELLAR SALES
PRE-BOOKED VISITS

ANNUAL PRODUCTION 120,000 bottles
HECTARES UNDER VINE 20
VITICULTURE METHOD Organic

The estate founded by Matteo Correggia, who passed away in 2001, is located between Canale and Santo Stefano Roero and is now diligently run by his widow Ornella Costa. It is planted mainly to nebbiolo and barbera, but the sandy, very loose soils, poor in clay and silt and typical of Roero, are also home to arneis, sauvignon, cabernet, merlot and other native and international grape varieties. Over the past few years, Ornella has invested heavily in organic farming and the current results seem to confirm the wisdom of her choice.

We were very pleased to see Roero Riserva Roche d'Ampsej win Three Glasses again. The '06 vintage is both rich and austere, with tobacco, tar, dried flowers and dark berry fruit, echoed on a full, juicy, complex palate with good length. Nebbiolo d'Alba La Val dei Preti '08 is also very good, minerally and still a little oaky on the nose but with a complex, fresh, fragrant palate. Langhe Rosso Le Marne Grigie '06, from the estate's international red grape varieties – cabernet sauvignon and franc, merlot, syrah and petit verdot – is well made, potent and very concentrated while Barbera d'Alba Marun '08 is pleasant with good fruit, although the vintage has cramped its complexity.

● Roero Ròche d'Ampsèj Ris. '06	▼▼▼	7
● Nebbiolo d'Alba La Val dei Preti '08	▼▼	6
● Barbera d'Alba Marun '08	▼▼	6
● Langhe Rosso Le Marne Grigie '06	▼▼	7
● Anthos '09	▼	4
● Barbera d'Alba '08	▼	4
○ Roero Arneis '09	▼	4
● Barbera d'Alba Marun '04	▽▽▽	6
● Barbera d'Alba Marun '99	▽▽▽	6
● Roero Ròche d'Ampsèj '04	▽▽▽	7
● Roero Ròche d'Ampsèj '01	▽▽▽	8
● Roero Ròche d'Ampsèj '00	▽▽▽	8
● Roero Ròche d'Ampsèj '99	▽▽▽	8

Giuseppe Cortese

S.DA RABAJÀ, 80
12050 BARBARESCO [CN]
TEL. 0173635131
www.cortesegiuseppe.it

CELLAR SALES
PRE-BOOKED VISITS

ANNUAL PRODUCTION 50,000 bottles
HECTARES UNDER VINE 8
VITICULTURE METHOD Conventional

Giuseppe Cortese has built the success of his small estate on the dual foundations of terroir and stylistic consistency, making it a benchmark for the Barbaresco area. Eight hectares in the heart of the legendary Rabajà cru make a difference, especially if they become the inspiration for authentic, traditional wines aged in large and medium barrels. The rest of the range is classic in style, featuring Barbera, Dolcetto and two Chardonnays.

Giuseppe Cortese's flagship wine, Barbaresco Rabajà Riserva, has been missing from the past few editions of our Guide. Its younger sibling Rabajà '07, however, almost makes up for its absence, showing powerfully fruity and balsamic, although its development is rather too subtle. Further ageing could coax out more elegance. In contrast, Barbera d'Alba Morassina '07 displays very powerful development, with a long finish of incense and cocoa powder, while Barbera d'Alba '09 is suppler but equally concentrated, giving dark fruit but very pleasant.

● Barbaresco Rabajà '07	▼▼	6
● Barbera d'Alba '09	▼▼	4*
● Barbera d'Alba Morassina '07	▼▼	5
● Dolcetto d'Alba Trifolera '09	▼	4
○ Langhe Chardonnay '09	▼	4
● Langhe Nebbiolo '08	▼	5
● Barbaresco Rabajà Ris. '96	▽▽▽	8
● Barbaresco Rabajà '06	▽▽	6
● Barbera d'Alba '07	▽▽	4*
● Barbera d'Alba '06	▽▽	4
● Barbera d'Alba Morassina '06	▽▽	5
● Barbera d'Alba Morassina '05	▽▽	5
● Dolcetto d'Alba Trifolera '07	▽▽	4
● Langhe Nebbiolo '07	▽▽	5

Clemente Cossetti

VIA GUARDIE, 1
14043 CASTELNUOVO BELBO [AT]
TEL. 0141799803
www.cossetti.it

CELLAR SALES
PRE-BOOKED VISITS
ROOMS AND FOOD

ANNUAL PRODUCTION 600,000 bottles
HECTARES UNDER VINE 22
VITICULTURE METHOD Organic

This year we awarded the Cossetti family's estate our full profile for the first time. The winery is an example of how quantity can be successfully combined with quality. Its vineyards, on average over 30 years old, are located in Castelnuovo Belbo and face south and south-east. Barbera is the prevalent grape variety but chardonnay, cortese and dolcetto are also grown. The soil is clay based, with some iron and magnesium.

Barbera d'Asti Superiore Nizza '07 reached our finals. It focuses on elegance and freshness, with a well-defined nose of dark berry fruit and spices and a delicate, very harmonious palate with a long, balanced finish. Grignolino d'Asti '09 is also very well made, proffering red fruits and hazelnuts, which is echoed on the juicy palate with its balanced finish, despite slight residual sugar. The rest of the list is good, from the spicy Ruché di Castagnole Monferrato '08 to the fresh, fruity Barbera d'Asti Venti di Marzo '09 and the bottled cherry-themed Barbera d'Asti La Vigna Vecchia '08.

● Barbera d'Asti Sup. Nizza '07	🍷🍷	5
● Grignolino D'Asti '09	🍷🍷	3*
● Barbera d'Asti La Vigna Vecchia '08	🍷	3
● Barbera d'Asti Venti di Marzo '09	🍷	4
● Ruchè di Castagnole Monferrato '09	🍷	4
● Barbera d'Asti La Vigna Vecchia '07	ΥΥ	3*
● Barbera d'Asti Sup. Nizza '04	ΥΥ	5
● Barbera d'Asti Venti di Marzo '08	ΥΥ	3*

Stefanino Costa

B.TA BENNA, 5
12046 MONTÀ [CN]
TEL. 0173976336
www.ninocosta.eu

ANNUAL PRODUCTION N.A.
HECTARES UNDER VINE 7
VITICULTURE METHOD Conventional

Following its debut in the last edition of our Guide, this year we awarded Stefanino Costa's estate our full profile. The vineyards, some of which are 40 years old, are situated at Canale, Montà and Santo Stefano Roero, on mainly sandy soils at altitudes from 360 to 400 metres above sea level. The vine stock is exclusively native, particularly arneis, nebbiolo and barbera, which faithfully reflect the typical characteristics of the terroir thanks to attentive work in the vineyard and the cellar.

We very much liked Roero Bric del Medic '07, which reached our finals. It has a concentrated, lively nose, offering good fruity notes and balsamic hints, and a potent, complex, full palate with tannins that are still slightly rough and a long, fruit-laden finish. Barbera d'Alba Superiore Bric Cichin '07 is well made. It flaunts cocoa powder, red fruit and aromatic herbs, accompanied by a fresh, full, vibrant palate, which is not, however, perfectly balanced revealing slightly edgy tannins. Roero Arneis Bric Sarun '09 is sound, showing uncomplicated and pleasant, with notes of white-fleshed fruits.

● Roero Bric del Medic '07	🍷🍷	4
● Barbera d'Alba Sup. Bric Cichin '07	🍷🍷	4
○ Roero Arneis Bric Sarun '09	🍷	4
● Barbera d'Alba Sup. Bric Cichin '06	ΥΥ	4
● Roero Bric del Medic '06	ΥΥ	4

Daniele Coutandin

b.ta Ciabot, 12
10063 Perosa Argentina [TO]
tel. 0121803473
ramie.countadin@alpimedia.it

PRE-BOOKED VISITS

ANNUAL PRODUCTION 4,000 bottles
HECTARES UNDER VINE 1
VITICULTURE METHOD Conventional

In a wine world characterized by high-sounding proclamations and ready-made definitions, we often hear talk of mountain viticulture, heroically practised to grow vines in particularly difficult conditions. This small, family-run estate is an emblematic example, as its rigorous, demanding work manages to produce charming, original wines, first and foremost Ramìe, made from old local grape varieties.

The return of Ramìe, the estate's symbol, which was not released last year because of wine-related red tape, also marks the Coutandin family's return to our full profile. Vinified from old native varieties grown at altitudes between 650 and 800 metres above sea level, it was mistakenly considered an oenological relic, while it is actually one of the most original products of the entire Piedmont wine scene. The '07 vintage is small but extraordinarily good. Its aromas of bark and blueberries against a pleasantly vegetal backdrop and a full palate give it a wild, untamed personality that makes it absolutely unique.

● Pinerolese Ramìe '07	🍷🍷	5
● Barbichè '05	YY	4*
● Barbichè '04	YY	4*
● Barbichè '03	YY	4*
● Pinerolese Ramìe '06	YY	5
● Pinerolese Ramìe '05	YY	5
● Pinerolese Ramìe '04	YY	5
● Pinerolese Ramìe '03	YY	5

Dacapo

s.da Asti Mare, 4
14040 Agliano Terme [AT]
tel. 0141964921
www.dacapo.it

CELLAR SALES
PRE-BOOKED VISITS

ANNUAL PRODUCTION 43,000 bottles
HECTARES UNDER VINE 8
VITICULTURE METHOD Organic

Paolo Dania and Dino Riccomagno have been producing wines that faithfully reflect the terroir for 13 years. This is why they have chosen to concentrate on barbera, the area's principal grape variety, and cultivate it using organic methods, investing great effort in the vineyard. In addition to barbera, the estate also grows smaller percentages of nebbiolo, pinot nero, merlot and ruché.

Barbera d'Asti Superiore Vigna Dacapo '07 is very convincing, showing an inky, almost black, ruby with a sensational, concentrated nose that proffers notes of cinchona, rain-soaked earth and spices, against a background of plums and cocoa powder. The palate is firmly structured, with good acidity and length, although still young and closed, requiring further ageing. Monferrato Rosso Cantacucco '08, from 70 per cent pinot nero and 30 per cent nebbiolo, is well made, with a nose of violets, cloves and red berry fruit, echoed on the pleasantly fresh palate that has a long finish of blackberries and blueberries. Barbera d'Asti Sanbastian'08 is sound but reflects the poor vintage.

● Barbera d'Asti Sup. Nizza V. Dacapo '07	🍷🍷	5
● M.to Rosso Cantacucco '08	🍷🍷	6
● Barbera d'Asti Sanbastiàn '08	🍷	4
● Barbera d'Asti Sup. Nizza V. Dacapo '03	YY	5
● Barbera d'Asti Sup. Nizza V. Dacapo '01	YY	5
● M.to Rosso Tre '04	YY	6

Damilano

VIA ROMA, 31
12060 BAROLO [CN]
TEL. 017356105
www.cantinedamilano.it

CELLAR SALES
PRE-BOOKED VISITS

ANNUAL PRODUCTION **420,000 bottles**
HECTARES UNDER VINE **48**
VITICULTURE METHOD **Conventional**

This important, dynamic estate can currently count on some of the finest crus at Barolo: Cannubi, Brunate, Cerequio and Liste, making it a benchmark for aficionados in Italy and abroad. The renovation of the winery has contributed to a new sense of hospitality, combining impressive dimensions with a classically innovative style.

All the 2006 Barolos are characterized by their oak ageing, which lays spicy notes on the attractive fruity base. The very good Cannubi is already well balanced, velvety and extremely enjoyable, with a nose of red berry fruit and a mouthfilling palate without any sharp edges. Cerequio is a little more solidly built and assertive, the fruity flesh contrasting nicely with the tannins. Brunate is more complex with excellent balance and a distinctly long finish, while Liste is a little harder and edgier. Finally, Lecinquevigne successfully fulfils its appointed role as an earlier-drinking Barolo. The other wines on the list are all very sound and uncomplicated.

● Barolo Brunate '06	🍷🍷	8
● Barolo Cannubi '06	🍷🍷	8
● Barolo Cerequio '06	🍷🍷	8
● Barolo Lecinquevigne '06	🍷🍷	7
● Barolo Liste '06	🍷🍷	8
● Barbera d'Alba La Blu '08	🍷	5
● Barbera d'Asti '09	🍷	4
● Dolcetto d'Alba '09	🍷	4
○ Langhe Arneis '09	🍷	4
● Nebbiolo d'Alba '08	🍷	5
● Barolo Cannubi '04	YYY	8
● Barolo Cannubi '01	YYY	8
● Barolo Cannubi '00	YYY	8
● Barolo Brunate Cannubi '05	YY	8
● Barolo Cannubi '05	YY	8
● Barolo Liste '05	YY	8

Deltetto

C.SO ALBA, 43
12043 CANALE [CN]
TEL. 0173979383
www.deltetto.com

CELLAR SALES
PRE-BOOKED VISITS

ANNUAL PRODUCTION **170,000 bottles**
HECTARES UNDER VINE **21**
VITICULTURE METHOD **Conventional**

Founded in 1953, this family-run winery is now competently headed by Antonio Deltetto, a grower who loves to experiment. The extensive list includes Metodo Classico sparklers, which have occupied much of Antonio's time in recent years, as well as the typical local wines. In addition to the Roero wines from vineyards in the municipalities of Canale, Castellinaldo and Santo Stefano Roero, the estate also makes Barolo.

Deltetto won Three Glasses again this year with the splendid Roero Braja Riserva '07. It has a nose of tobacco, liquorice and rain-soaked earth, and an elegant, balanced palate with notes of red berries, velvety tannins and a long finish, supported by good acidity. Barbera d'Alba Superiore Bramé '08 is well made, offering concentrated cherry and blackberry fruit with spicy notes, and a full-flavoured, balanced palate with a good acidity. Deltetto Extra Brut Riserva '07, from 60 per cent pinot nero and 40 per cent chardonnay, is equally good, giving honey, wholemeal and crusty bread, and a fresh palate with a long, fruity finish. The rest of the list is well made.

● Roero Braja Ris. '07	🍷🍷🍷	5
● Barbera d'Alba Sup. Bramé '08	🍷🍷	4
○ Deltetto Extra Brut Ris. '07	🍷🍷	6
● Barolo Sistaglia '06	🍷	6
○ Deltetto Brut	🍷	5
⊙ Deltetto Extra Brut Rosé	🍷	6
○ Roero Arneis S. Michele '09	🍷	4
● Barbera d'Alba Sup. Rocca delle Marasche '04	YYY	6
● Barbera d'Alba Sup. Rocca delle Marasche '07	YY	6
● Barbera d'Alba Sup. Rocca delle Marasche '06	YY	6
● Barbera d'Alba Sup. Rocca delle Marasche '05	YY	6
○ Roero Arneis S. Michele '08	YY	4*

Destefanis

VIA MORTIZZO, 8
12050 MONTELUPO ALBESE [CN]
TEL. 0173617189
www.marcodestefanis.it

CELLAR SALES
PRE-BOOKED VISITS

ANNUAL PRODUCTION 60,000 bottles
HECTARES UNDER VINE 12
VITICULTURE METHOD Conventional

Montelupo Albese is a little village perched on the hilltops above Alba, offering a spectacular view of a lesser-known corner of Langhe. Marco Destefanis's estate of about 12 hectares yields excellent grapes that he uses to make characterful wines: Barbera, Nebbiolo, Chardonnay and, above all, Dolcetto, with the first-rate Vigna Monia Bassa sourced from old vineyards. The entire range is very attractively priced.

The wines that we tasted performed very well, showing good progress since last year. Following the unfortunate '08 vintage, Dolcetto Vigna Monia Bassa, made from the grapes of old vines, has returned with a dark, inky hue, a remarkably complex nose and a full palate with plenty of fruity pulp. Nebbiolo '07 is less convincing. It shows the typical varietal notes of the vintage, focusing on sweet tobacco and fresh balsamic overtones. Blackberries and plums are the distinguishing characteristics of the weighty, but balanced, Dolcetto Bricco Galluccio '09. The list is completed by the sound Langhe Rosso '08, from barbera, nebbiolo and cabernet, and two easy-drinking whites.

● Dolcetto d'Alba V. Monia Bassa '09	▼▼	4*
● Nebbiolo d'Alba '07	▼▼	4*
● Dolcetto d'Alba Bricco Galluccio '09	▼▼	3*
● Langhe Rosso '08	▼▼	4
○ Langhe Arneis '09	▼	2
○ Langhe Chardonnay '09	▼	2
● Barbera d'Alba Bricco Galluccio '06	∇∇	4*
● Dolcetto d'Alba Bricco Galluccio '08	∇∇	3*
● Dolcetto d'Alba Bricco Galluccio '07	∇∇	3*
● Dolcetto d'Alba Bricco Galluccio '06	∇∇	2
● Dolcetto d'Alba V. Monia Bassa '07	∇∇	4*
● Dolcetto d'Alba V. Monia Bassa '06	∇∇	3*
● Langhe Rosso '07	∇∇	4*
● Nebbiolo d'Alba '06	∇∇	4

Gianni Doglia

VIA ANNUNZIATA, 56
14054 CASTAGNOLE DELLE LANZE [AT]
TEL. 0141878359
www.giannidoglia.it

CELLAR SALES
PRE-BOOKED VISITS

ANNUAL PRODUCTION 60,000 bottles
HECTARES UNDER VINE 7
VITICULTURE METHOD Conventional

The capable, dynamic Gianni Doglia confidently runs a small estate that, year after year, becomes more convincing, thanks to the improving quality of the entire limited range of wines. Moscato d'Asti remains the estate's flagship but the greatest progress has been made by the red wines, which are now excellent. All the wines presented have a smooth, fresh palate without excessive concentration, oak or superfluous notes.

Meticulous, non-invasive work in the vineyard is translated into pure, forthright wines focusing on finesse. Barbera d'Asti Superiore has prominent fruit and sweet spices, and a nice, balanced palate with fair length, especially considering its vintage. Barbera d'Asti Boscodonne '09, which has always been the estate's flagship, along with Moscato, is very good, with a lively, focused nose of blackberries and a juicy, easy-drinking, but not simple, palate. Moscato d'Asti '09 has elegant, complex notes of peaches and sage, and a fairly solid palate lightened by good acidity. Elegance over richness. The release of the merlot-based Monferrato Rosso has been postponed.

● Barbera d'Asti Boscodonne '09	▼▼	4*
● Barbera d'Asti Sup. '08	▼▼	5
○ Moscato d'Asti '09	▼▼	4
● Barbera d'Asti Sup. '07	∇∇	5
● Barbera d'Asti Sup. '06	∇∇	5
● M.to Rosso "!" '06	∇∇	6
● M.to Rosso "!" '05	∇∇	5
● M.to Rosso "!" '04	∇∇	5
● M.to Rosso "!" '03	∇∇	5
○ Moscato d'Asti '08	∇∇	4*
○ Moscato d'Asti '07	∇∇	4*
○ Moscato d'Asti '06	∇∇	4*

★ Poderi Luigi Einaudi

B.TA GOMBE, 31/32
12063 DOGLIANI [CN]
TEL. 017370191
www.poderieinaudi.com

CELLAR SALES
PRE-BOOKED VISITS
ROOMS

ANNUAL PRODUCTION 250,000 bottles
HECTARES UNDER VINE 55
VITICULTURE METHOD Conventional

This old estate has successfully kept pace with the times by pursuing an intelligent balance of tradition and innovation. The stunning winery deserves a visit simply to enjoy the gorgeous scenery. However, the pleasure is intensified by tasting the wines that, year after year, have achieved enviable consistency. From Dolcetto to the Barolo crus, the estate expresses all the qualities of the Langhe.

Barolo Costa Grimaldi '06 is elegant, with fruity notes of strawberries and raspberries against a background of subtle, well-calibrated oak and a fresh, potent, alcoholic palate with attractive tannins already nicely balanced by firm structure. Barolo nei Cannubi '06 came very close to our top accolade by faithfully reflecting its terroir with a complex, forthright nose of red berries and sweet spices. Barolo Terlo '06 is currently the edgiest of the trio, with rather prominent oak and alcohol on the nose and a sound but not particularly elegant palate that lacks personality as the tannins are still harsh. Release of Langhe Luigi Einaudi '07 has been postponed until next year.

● Barolo Cannubi '06	2 black glasses	8
● Barolo Costa Grimaldi '06	2 black glasses	8
● Dogliani V. Tecc '08	2 black glasses	5
● Barolo Terlo '06	2 black glasses	7
● Dogliani I Filari '08	2 black glasses	5
● Dolcetto di Dogliani '09	2 black glasses	4*
● Langhe Nebbiolo '08	2 black glasses	4
● Piemonte Barbera '08	1 black glass	5
● Barolo Costa Grimaldi '05	3 white glasses	8
● Barolo Costa Grimaldi '01	3 white glasses	8
● Barolo nei Cannubi '00	3 white glasses	8
● Barolo nei Cannubi '99	3 white glasses	8
● Barolo nei Cannubi '98	3 white glasses	8
● Dogliani V. Tecc '06	3 white glasses	5
● Langhe Rosso Luigi Einaudi '04	3 white glasses	6
● Langhe Rosso Luigi Einaudi '99	3 white glasses	6

Tenuta Il Falchetto

FRAZ. CIOMBI
VIA VALLE TINELLA, 16
12058 SANTO STEFANO BELBO [CN]
TEL. 0141840344
www.ilfalchetto.com

CELLAR SALES
PRE-BOOKED VISITS

ANNUAL PRODUCTION 190,000 bottles
HECTARES UNDER VINE 34
VITICULTURE METHOD Conventional

This interesting estate owned by the Forno brothers, with an area of over 30 hectares, confidently pursues quality and consistency. The efforts lavished on bringing out the best of the moscato grape – a frequently underrated gem of Italy's ampelographic crown – translate into several versions, all of which are highly convincing. We have also noticed the consistent growth in quality of the reds, headed by Barbera, with well-balanced products offering great value for money.

Moscato Tenuta del Fant '09 performed exceptionally well, earning Three Glasses. It has an alluring, complex nose over a refreshing palate with nicely balanced sweetness and an incredibly long finish. Moscato Ciombi '09 is slightly less complex but still very convincing and appealing. From the reds, we liked the sound Barbera d'Asti Bricco Paradiso '07, which vaunts a well-calibrated nose of ripe red berries and a freshly acidic palate, while the refreshing, easy-drinking Barbera d'Asti Pian Scorrone '09 faithfully reflects its terroir.

○ Moscato d'Asti Tenuta del Fant '09	3 black glasses	4*
○ Moscato d'Asti Ciombi '09	2 black glasses	4*
● Barbera d'Asti Pian Scorrone '09	2 black glasses	3*
● Barbera d'Asti Sup. Bricco Paradiso '07	2 black glasses	6
● Barbera d'Asti Sup. Bricco Paradiso '06	2 white glasses	6
● Barbera d'Asti Sup. Bricco Paradiso '05	2 white glasses	6
● Barbera d'Asti Sup. Lurëi '07	2 white glasses	4*
● M.to Rosso La Mora '07	2 white glasses	4*
● M.to Rosso Solo '07	2 white glasses	5
○ Moscato d'Asti Ciombi '08	2 white glasses	4*
○ Moscato d'Asti Tenuta del Fant '08	2 white glasses	4*
○ Moscato d'Asti Tenuta del Fant '07	2 white glasses	4*
○ Moscato d'Asti Tenuta del Fant '06	2 white glasses	3*

Favaro

S.DA CHIUSURE, 1BIS
10010 PIVERONE [TO]
TEL. 012572606
www.cantinafavaro.it

CELLAR SALES
PRE-BOOKED VISITS

ANNUAL PRODUCTION 18,000 bottles
HECTARES UNDER VINE 3
VITICULTURE METHOD Conventional

The interest attracted by Camillo and Benito Favaro in recent years is generated by meticulous work in the vineyard and cellar but also by their passion for the world's great wines. Their three-hectare estate has an annual production of just 18,000 bottles, comprising traditional wines based on erbaluce – including Le Chiusure, aged exclusively in steel, and 13 Mesi, aged for a year in barriques – and several innovative ones, such as the Basy, F2 and Rossomeraviglia table wines made with the addition of unusual grape varieties for this area, such as freisa and syrah.

Once again it was Erbaluce di Caluso Le Chiusure that came close to our finals. The '09 version offers an usual combination of grip and saltiness, although it suffers from a nose dominated by primary notes and a slightly diluted finish after a difficult vintage. We were less enthusiastic about Erbaluce di Caluso 13 Mesi '08, which has fullness and freshness, but the oak currently gives it an excessively toasty character. Basy '08, a table wine from barbera and syrah, is just a little stiff, but spirited with nice flesh, as is F2, a monovarietal Freisa.

○ Erbaluce di Caluso Le Chiusure '09	▼▼	4*
● Basy '08	▼▼	4*
○ Caluso Passito Sole d'Inverno '05	▼▼	6
○ Erbaluce di Caluso 13 Mesi '08	▼▼	4*
● F2 '08	▼▼	4*
● Basy '03	▽▽	4
○ Caluso Passito Sole d'Inverno '00	▽▽	7
○ Erbaluce di Caluso '06	▽▽	4*
○ Erbaluce di Caluso 13 Mesi '07	▽▽	4
○ Erbaluce di Caluso Le Chiusure '08	▽▽	4*
○ Erbaluce di Caluso V. delle Chiusure '01	▽▽	4*
○ Erbaluce di Caluso V. delle Chiusure '00	▽▽	3*
● Rossomeraviglia '07	▽▽	6
○ Sole d'Inverno '00	▽▽	6

Giacomo Fenocchio

LOC. BUSSIA, 72
78675 MONFORTE D'ALBA [CN]
TEL. 017378675
www.giacomofenocchio.com

CELLAR SALES
PRE-BOOKED VISITS

ANNUAL PRODUCTION 80,000 bottles
HECTARES UNDER VINE 13
VITICULTURE METHOD Conventional

The Fenocchio brothers' estate is no newcomer to the production of well-typed, juicy wines. It offers Barbera, Dolcetto, Freisa and, above all, great Nebbiolos that elegantly reflect the characteristics of prestigious crus such as Cannubi in Barolo, Villero in Castiglione Falletto and Bussia in Monforte – also available in a Riserva version in great vintages – without pursuing excessive extraction. Long maceration and prolonged ageing in 350 to 500-litre Slavonian oak barrels are key to a style that is becoming increasingly popular among wine lovers and professionals.

This year the exemplary performance of the estate's wines earned it our full profile. The group of finalists commences with Barolo Bussia '06, whose slight initial uncertainty does not impair the development of berry fruit, liquorice and ginseng, which is made even more alluring by a saline note and complemented by a crisp, meaty palate with well-balanced acidity and tannins. Villero '06 is also very good, showing more powerful and clenched but equally elegant. The trio is completed by Cannubi '06, with great fruity character and a slightly warm finish.

● Barolo Bussia '06	▼▼	7
● Barolo Cannubi '06	▼▼	7
● Barolo Villero '06	▼▼	7
● Barbera d'Alba Sup. '08	▼▼	4*
● Barolo Bussia Ris. '04	▼▼	8
● Langhe Nebbiolo '08	▼▼	4
● Dolcetto d'Alba '09	▼	4
● Langhe Freisa '08	▼	4

Ferrando

VIA TORINO, 599
10015 IVREA [TO]
TEL. 0125633550
www.ferrandovini.it

CELLAR SALES
PRE-BOOKED VISITS

ANNUAL PRODUCTION 50,000 bottles
HECTARES UNDER VINE 7
VITICULTURE METHOD Conventional

The prestigious Piedmontese Carema zone is actually an enclave in Valle d'Aosta. Although it shares the climate and scenery of the small Alpine region, its ampelographic heritage is entirely Piedmontese. Indeed, Roberto Ferrando's legendary estate is the realm of mountain nebbiolo, of which it is the best-known and loved producer. The Ivrea-based winery makes a classic range from seven hectares of vineyards, comprising not only Nebbiolo but also Barbera and Erbaluce di Caluso, in all possible versions.

Carema wines constantly walk the very thin line that divides elegant interpretations from excessively lean and light-bodied ones unable to sustain the hefty tannins of high-altitude nebbiolo. However, when delicacy meets austerity, the result is very exciting, as illustrated by Ferrando's Carema Etichetta Nera '05. The nose offers an uninterrupted succession of dry flowers, medicinal herbs and antique wood while the palate is potent and movingly elegant, due to its velvety but incisive tannins. There are also two splendid versions of Carema Etichetta Bianca '06 and Erbaluce di Caluso Cariola '09.

● Carema Et. Nera '05	▼▼▼	7
● Carema Etichetta Bianca '06	▼▼	5
○ Erbaluce di Caluso Cariola '09	▼▼	4*
● Canavese Rosso La Torrazza '08	▼▼	4*
○ Erbaluce di Caluso Brut La Torrazza '06	▼▼	5
○ Erbaluce di Caluso La Torrazza '09	▼▼	4*
● Carema Et. Nera '01	▽▽▽	6
○ Caluso Passito Vign. Cariola '04	▽▽	6
○ Caluso Passito Vign. Cariola '03	▽▽	6
○ Caluso Passito Vign. Cariola '02	▽▽	6
● Carema Et. Nera '04	▽▽	7
● Carema Et. Nera '03	▽▽	7
● Carema Et. Nera '00	▽▽	6
○ Solativo V. T. '04	▽▽	5

Roberto Ferraris

FRAZ. DOGLIANO, 33
14041 AGLIANO TERME [AT]
TEL. 0141954234
www.robertoferraris.it

CELLAR SALES
PRE-BOOKED VISITS

ANNUAL PRODUCTION 45,000 bottles
HECTARES UNDER VINE 9
VITICULTURE METHOD Conventional

Barbera is the principal grape variety of Roberto Ferraris's small estate at Agliano Terme, an area particularly suited to the variety. The low yields, ideal site climates, age of the vines – some of which 70 years old – and white soils combine to yield very high-quality wines. However, smaller amounts of grignolino, freisa and dolcetto are also grown.

Barbera d'Asti Superiore Riserva del Bisavolo is one of the best '08 Barberas we tasted this year, with elegant tobacco, cherries, dried flowers and liquorice, and a not particularly rich but fresh, continuous palate with an aristocratic finish. The basic Barbera d'Asti '09 is also very good, giving plums, pencil lead and tobacco followed by an austere, full-bodied palate. Monferrato Rosso Grixa '08, a balanced Nebbiolo with a concentrated, reassuring nose of liquorice, raspberry jam and dried flowers, and sweet, close-knit tannins, is well made, like the other two Barbera d'Astis, the simpler, fruity Superiore La Cricca '08 and the tobacco and cherry-themed Nobbio '08.

● Barbera d'Asti '09	▼▼	3*
● Barbera d'Asti Sup. Riserva del Bisavolo '08	▼▼	4*
● Barbera d'Asti Nobbio '08	▼▼	4*
● Barbera d'Asti Sup. La Cricca '08	▼▼	5
● Monferrato Grixa '08	▼▼	5
● Barbera d'Asti Nobbio '06	▽▽	4*
● Barbera d'Asti Sup. La Cricca '07	▽▽	4*
● Barbera d'Asti Sup. La Cricca '05	▽▽	4
● Barbera d'Asti Sup. La Cricca '03	▽▽	5*
● Barbera d'Asti Sup. La Cricca '01	▽▽	5*
● Barbera d'Asti Sup. Riserva del Bisavolo '06	▽▽	5

Fabio Fidanza

via Rodotiglia, 55
14052 Calosso [AT]
tel. 0141826921
www.castellodicalosso.it

CELLAR SALES
PRE-BOOKED VISITS

ANNUAL PRODUCTION 21,000 bottles
HECTARES UNDER VINE 7
VITICULTURE METHOD Conventional

This year Fabio Fidanza's small estate earned a full profile. It has always produced good Barberas, for its vineyards are situated in Calosso, which is particularly well-suited for the cultivation of the variety. Fidanza's wines are modern and well made but with great personality, which nicely reflects the vintage.

The estate's production is increasingly convincing, particularly in the case of the '07 vintage. The Barbera d'Asti Superiore Sterlino '07 actually reached the finals, thanks to a highly complex nose of rain-soaked earth, cinchona and dark berry fruit, and potent, tannic fruit-rich palate with full flavour and a long, characterful finish. Barbera d'Asti '08 put up a less impressive performance, which is not surprising considering the difficult vintage. However, it is supple with good fruit.

● Barbera d'Asti Sup. Sterlino '07	TT	6
● Barbera d'Asti '08	T	3
● Barbera d'Asti '06	YY	3*
● Barbera d'Asti Sterlino Castello di Calosso '05	YY	5
● Barbera d'Asti Sup. Sterlino '06	YY	5
● M.to Rosso Que Duàn '07	YY	4*

Fontanabianca

via Bordini, 15
12057 Neive [CN]
tel. 017367195
www.fontanabianca.it

CELLAR SALES
PRE-BOOKED VISITS

ANNUAL PRODUCTION 50,000 bottles
HECTARES UNDER VINE 14
VITICULTURE METHOD Organic

This family-run estate covers approximately 15 hectares of vineyards, which yield wines with a well-defined character and consistently high quality, year after year, thanks to meticulous selection of the grapes. The mainstay of the list is Barbaresco, in various versions, and the modern style focuses on varietal trueness and elegance. All the wines have always offered particularly good value for money.

Barbaresco Bordini Sorì Burdin '07 does not have a particularly concentrated nose but it is already fairly complex and elegant, with notes ranging from dried flowers to wild berries. The palate is attractively full with surprisingly well-behaved tannins that develop into a slightly soft finish. Barbaresco Serraboella '07 reflects its warm vintage with a nose of herbs in the sun mingling with faint gamey notes. Warm and full on the palate, it has slightly drying tannins on the finish. The magnificent Barbera d'Alba Brunet '07 has an inky hue and a nose of cocoa powder, plums and cinchona, accompanied by a big, powerful, long palate that is still very youthful.

● Barbaresco Sorì Burdin '07	TT	7
● Barbera d'Alba Brunet '07	TT	5
● Barbaresco Serraboella '07	TT	6
○ Langhe Arneis '09	T	4
● Barbaresco Serraboella '06	YYY	7
● Barbaresco Sorì Burdin '05	YYY	7
● Barbaresco Sorì Burdin '04	YYY	7
● Barbaresco Sorì Burdin '01	YYY	7
● Barbaresco Sorì Burdin '98	YYY	7
● Barbaresco '05	YY	6
● Barbaresco Sorì Burdin '06	YY	7
● Barbera d'Alba Brunet '05	YY	5
● Barbera d'Alba Brunet '04	YY	4*

Fontanafredda

via Alba, 15
12050 Serralunga d'Alba [CN]
tel. 0173626111
www.fontanafredda.it

CELLAR SALES
PRE-BOOKED VISITS
ROOMS AND FOOD

ANNUAL PRODUCTION 6,500,000 bottles
HECTARES UNDER VINE 85
VITICULTURE METHOD Conventional

This historic Serralunga estate is run by Giovanni Minetti and owned by the Monte dei Paschi di Siena foundation, Oscar Farinetto and Luca Baffigo Filangieri. Since 2010 the winery has been called Casa E. di Mirafiore Fontanafredda, in tribute to its original name. This change has inspired a new project and a new product line developed according to natural protocols, including the Barolo Riserva and Barolo Lazzarito Vigna La Delizia. With an annual production of almost 7,000,000 bottles, the range has very few rivals in Italy.

Although Alta Langa Metodo Classico, Moscato d'Asti, Barbera and Dolcetto are all very good, once again this year Fontanafredda's top wines were Barolo and Barbaresco. Barolo Casa E. di Mirafiore Riserva '04 effortlessly took Three Glasses. It is a discerningly modern wine that drinks compact and well sustained, without ever faltering. Barbaresco Coste Rubin '07 also performed very well, presenting confident and chewy with plenty of freshness to enliven the palate. Barolo Serralunga '06 is equally good, with a less sensational nose but an impressively solid palate.

● Barolo Casa E. di Mirafiore Ris. '04	▼▼▼	8
● Barbaresco Coste Rubin '07	▼▼	6
● Nebbiolo d'Alba Marne Brune '08	▼▼	4*
○ Alta Langa V. Gatinera Brut '04	▼▼	6
○ Asti Galarej '09	▼▼	4*
● Barolo Paiagallo V. La Villa '06	▼▼	8
● Barolo Serralunga d'Alba '06	▼▼	6
● Barolo V. La Rosa '06	▼▼	8
● Diano d'Alba La Lepre '09	▼▼	4
○ Moscato d'Asti Moncucco '09	▼▼	4
○ Roero Arneis Pradalupo '09	▼	4
● Barolo Lazzarito V. La Delizia '04	▽▽▽	8
● Barolo Lazzarito V. La Delizia '01	▽▽▽	8
● Barolo Lazzarito V. La Delizia '99	▽▽▽	8
● Barolo V. La Rosa '04	▽▽▽	8
● Barolo V. La Rosa '00	▽▽▽	8

Forteto della Luja

reg. Candelette, 4
14051 Loazzolo [AT]
tel. 014487197
www.fortetodellaluja.it

CELLAR SALES
PRE-BOOKED VISITS

ANNUAL PRODUCTION 60,000 bottles
HECTARES UNDER VINE 9
VITICULTURE METHOD Certified organic

This small winery in the Asti part of Langhe has made respect for the environment its guiding principle. Indeed, Silvia and Gianni Scaglione have created a WWF nature reserve on their estate, where they produce organic wines, and have equipped it with a solar power plant. Their wines faithfully reflect the terroir through the use of mainly native grape varieties, grown chiefly on limestone and marl soils.

Although the estate didn't perform as well as last year, its wines are still good. Loazzolo Vendemmia Tardiva Piasa Rischei '07 focuses more on finesse than power, with pleasant notes of apple and pineapple and a long, balanced finish. Monferrato Rosso Le Grive '08, from nebbiolo and pinot nero, is also good, with a concentrated nose of cinchona-laced blackberries and plums and a palate that is potent, long and juicy, although perhaps a little lacking in personality. Moscato d'Asti Piasa San Maurizio '09 is well made, showing supple, simple and citrussy, as is the aromatic Piemonte Brachetto Pian dei Sogni '08, which gives morello cherries and wild strawberries.

○ Loazzolo Forteto della Luja Piasa Rischei '07	▼▼	7
● M.to Rosso Le Grive '08	▼▼	5
○ Moscato d'Asti Piasa San Maurizio '09	▼	4
⊙ Piemonte Brachetto Forteto Pian dei Sogni '08	▼	6
○ Loazzolo Piasa Rischei '97	▽▽▽	7
○ Loazzolo Piasa Rischei '00	▽▽	7
○ Loazzolo Piasa Rischei '99	▽▽	7
○ Loazzolo Piasa Rischei V.T. '06	▽▽	7

Gabutti - Franco Boasso

B.TA GABUTTI, 3A
12050 SERRALUNGA D'ALBA [CN]
TEL. 0173613165
www.gabuttiboasso.com

CELLAR SALES
PRE-BOOKED VISITS
ROOMS

ANNUAL PRODUCTION **30,000 bottles**
HECTARES UNDER VINE **6**
VITICULTURE METHOD **Conventional**

The heart of the winery founded in 1970 by the Boasso family is located in Serralunga, with just over four hectares under vine in the vineyards of Gabutti, Meriame and Margheria. These plots are used for the production of the Barolo crus of the same names, vinified in the traditional manner and aged in medium-sized barrels, recognizable by their winning combination of elegance and austerity. The range is completed by Barbera and Dolcetto, as well as the Moscato, Arneis and Langhe Rosso of the Grappoli line, which is also the name of the family's delightful farmstay accommodation.

Barolo Margheria '06 failed to repeat last year's success by a hair's breadth. It is nonetheless a very consistent, personal interpretation of one of Serralunga's finest vineyards, which is ideal for the production of nebbiolo with long development. This time, however, its proverbial austere tannins are possibly too severe and not adequately balanced by fruit. Nevertheless, it has an exceptionally alluring nose of medicinal herbs, cinchona and spices. Barolo Gabutti '06 is less mature and needs more time to develop its acid-tannic backbone, but it too displays admirable breadth and aromatic complexity. Barolo Serralunga '06 is full flavoured and earthy.

● Barolo Margheria '06	▼▼	6
● Barbera d'Alba '08	▼▼	4*
● Barolo Gabutti '06	▼▼	6
● Barolo Serralunga '06	▼▼	6
● Dolcetto d'Alba Meriame '09	▼▼	3*
● Langhe Rosso Grappoli '08	▼▼	4
○ Moscato d'Asti Grappoli '09	▼▼	4*
○ Roero Arneis Grappoli '09	▼	4
● Barolo Margheria '05	▽▽▽	6*
● Barbera d'Alba '07	▽▽	4*
● Barolo Gabutti '05	▽▽	6
● Barolo Serralunga '05	▽▽	6
● Barolo Serralunga '04	▽▽	6
● Dolcetto d'Alba Meriame '08	▽▽	4*

Gaggino

S.DA SANT'EVASIO, 29
15076 OVADA [AL]
TEL. 0143822345
www.gaggino.it

CELLAR SALES
PRE-BOOKED VISITS

ANNUAL PRODUCTION **150,000 bottles**
HECTARES UNDER VINE **20**
VITICULTURE METHOD **Conventional**

The quality of Gabriele Gaggino's wines has improved, earning the estate a full profile, which is essential to describe the work of this dynamic wine man. Last year Gabriele launched a new project, entrusting the commercial side of the business to two relatives who are experts in marketing, Franco Sorgato and Massimo Tresoldi, and continuing to manage vineyard and the cellar himself. He is aided in this task by Giovanni Bailo, the estate's consultant oenologist since 2000. The work of the close-knit team has made the winery a legend with lovers of rich, ageworthy Dolcettos.

This year the estate presented a magnificent list, with two wines reaching our finals and a series of other first-rate bottles. We started with Ticco '07, a Barbera with an inky ruby hue, a nose of fruit, spice and vegetal notes and a potent, juicy palate. Dolcetto Il Convivio '09 charmed us with a complex, pervasive nose that is a prelude to a splendidly balanced, elegant palate. The second Dolcetto, Sant'Evasio '08, closely resembles Convivio, but is slightly more evolved. Cortese Madonna della Villa '09 is pleasant and fragrant, while Cuimarö Bianc '09, a monovarietal Sauvignon Blanc, is very interesting.

● Dolcetto di Ovada Il Convivio '09	▼▼	4*
● M.to Rosso Il Ticco '07	▼▼	5
○ Cortese dell'Alto M.to Madonna della Villa '09	▼▼	5
● Dolcetto di Ovada Sup. Sant' Evasio '08	▼▼	4
○ Monferrato Bianco Cuimaro '09	▼▼	4
● Barbera del M.to La Zarina '06	▽▽	3*
● Dolcetto di Ovada Il Convivio '08	▽▽	3
● Dolcetto di Ovada Il Convivio '07	▽▽	3*
● Dolcetto di Ovada Il Convivio '06	▽▽	3*
● Dolcetto di Ovada Sup. S. Evasio '04	▽▽	4*
○ Piemonte Chardonnay La Pagliuzza '08	▽▽	3

★★★★ Gaja

via Torino, 18
12050 Barbaresco [CN]
tel. 0173635158
info@gajawines.com

ANNUAL PRODUCTION 300,000 bottles
HECTARES UNDER VINE 92
VITICULTURE METHOD Conventional

As Gaja is one of the most celebrated names in wine worldwide, it is particularly difficult to find adjectives and descriptions that have not already been used to describe it. Still, it is a fact that Gaja wines are always absolutely exemplary in style and seductiveness. Tasted young, they display an immediately recognizable exuberance and generosity but it is only after appropriate ageing that they develop their full potential in terms of depth and complexity.

Langhe Nebbiolo Costa Russi '07 performed brilliantly, with a flawlessly elegant, complex nose of red fruit, tobacco and smoke, and an outstanding palate with exceptionally full structure, stylish tannins, discreet, refreshing acidity and a remarkably long finish. The unforgettable Langhe Nebbiolo Sorì Tildin '07 is similar but spicier. San Lorenzo is another subtle, slightly more tannic, variation on the theme. Barbaresco '07 is exceptionally polished, with tobacco and berries, faint hints of oak and alluring tannins, which are big but not rough. Sperss '06, from Serralunga, is sound and very hefty. Although still a little edgy on the palate, it is destined for greatness.

● Langhe Nebbiolo Costa Russi '07	▼▼▼+	8
● Langhe Nebbiolo Sorì Tildin '07	▼▼▼	8
● Barbaresco '07	▼▼	8
● Langhe Nebbiolo Sorì S. Lorenzo '07	▼▼	8
● Langhe Nebbiolo Sperss '06	▼▼	8
● Langhe Nebbiolo Conteisa '06	▼▼	8
● Barbaresco '04	▽▽▽	8
● Langhe Nebbiolo Costa Russi '05	▽▽▽	8
● Langhe Nebbiolo Costa Russi '05	▽▽▽	8
● Langhe Nebbiolo Costa Russi '04	▽▽▽	8
● Langhe Nebbiolo Costa Russi '03	▽▽▽	8
● Langhe Nebbiolo Sorì S. Lorenzo '06	▽▽▽	8
● Langhe Nebbiolo Sorì S. Lorenzo '03	▽▽▽	8
● Langhe Nebbiolo Sorì S. Lorenzo '01	▽▽▽	8
● Langhe Nebbiolo Sorì Tildin '06	▽▽▽+	8
● Langhe Nebbiolo Sperss '04	▽▽▽	8

Filippo Gallino

fraz. Madonna Loreto
Valle del Pozzo, 63
12043 Canale [CN]
tel. 017398112
www.filippogallino.com

CELLAR SALES
PRE-BOOKED VISITS

ANNUAL PRODUCTION 82,000 bottles
HECTARES UNDER VINE 14
VITICULTURE METHOD Conventional

The Gallino family have long represented an authentic, rigorous style of viticulture, firmly tied to the terroir, with no bells or whistles. The approach is aimed at achieving quality while respecting tradition in the vineyard – where arneis, barbera and nebbiolo feature – and adopting a skilfully modern style in the cellar. The small wood used for ageing never detracts territorial expression. Filippo and Gianni Gallino's meticulous attention to detail makes us fret every year. They always bottle their wines at the last possible moment for our tastings – the phases of the moon can't be reset! – but we must say that the results more than justify the wait.

Roero '08 has a complex, delicate, balanced nose with great character, featuring notes of ink and pencil lead alongside the classic raspberry. The palate is powerful, although slightly over-extracted, and the tannins on the long finish are assertive. Langhe Nebbiolo Licin '08 is pleasant and elegant, despite being slightly weighed down by a faint vegetal note. All three Barbera d'Albas are very well made: the Superiore and the Eleine, both '08, and the basic vintage, which is very pleasant and well typed.

● Roero '08	▼▼	5
● Barbera d'Alba '09	▼▼	4
● Barbera d'Alba Sup. '08	▼▼	5
● Langhe Nebbiolo Licin '08	▼▼	5
● Barbera d'Alba Elaine '08	▼	5
○ Roero Arneis '09	▼	4
● Barbera d'Alba Sup. '05	▽▽▽	5
● Barbera d'Alba Sup. '04	▽▽▽	5
● Roero '06	▽▽▽	6
● Roero Sup. '03	▽▽▽	6
● Roero Sup. '01	▽▽▽	6

Gancia

c.so Libertà, 66
14053 Canelli [AT]
tel. 01418301
www.gancia.it

CELLAR SALES
PRE-BOOKED VISITS

ANNUAL PRODUCTION 30,000,000 bottles
HECTARES UNDER VINE N.A .
VITICULTURE METHOD Conventional

This legendary name in Italian winemaking, which became famous for its sparklers, remains the Gancia family's pride and joy, despite having embarked on the parallel production of still wines with Tenute dei Vallarino about ten years ago. The vineyards are located in the province of Asti and are planted with a wide array of varieties – moscato, chardonnay, sauvignon, barbera, nebbiolo, merlot, etc. – that are used to make an equally wide range of wines.

Gancia presented us with a list of first-rate wines, particularly the Metodo Classico sparklers. Cuvée 18 Brut is complex and balanced, with vibrant acidity. The following wines are also well made: Cuvée 18 Brut Rosé, with austere acidity but a delicate nose of strawberries and roses; Asti Cuvée 24 Metodo Classico '08, themed by custard and citrus fruit; and the two Barbera d'Astis, Superiore Nizza Bricco Asinari '07, which is very complex but has to absorb its oak, and the lively, pleasant Superiore La Ladra '07, which is perhaps a touch simple.

○ Cuvée 18 M. Cl. Brut	▼▼	5
○ Asti M. Cl. Cuvée 24 '08	▼▼	6
● Barbera d'Asti La Ladra '07	▼▼	4
● Barbera d'Asti Sup. Bricco Asinari '07	▼▼	6
⊙ Cuvée 18 M. Cl. Brut Rosé	▼▼	5
○ Asti Cuvée Platinum '09	▼	4
○ Asti Modonovo '09	▼	4
● Barbera d'Asti Filovia '09	▼	4
○ Asti Camillo Gancia M. Cl. '06	▽▽	6
○ Asti Camillo Gancia M. Cl. '05	▽▽	6

Tenuta Garetto

s.da Asti Mare, 30
14041 Agliano Terme [AT]
tel. 0141954068
www.garetto.it

CELLAR SALES
PRE-BOOKED VISITS

ANNUAL PRODUCTION 100,000 bottles
HECTARES UNDER VINE 20
VITICULTURE METHOD Conventional

Alessandro Garetto's estate is a solid one that skilfully interprets its terroir. There are approximately 18 hectares under vine, almost all of which are situated on the hill behind the winery. This well-aspected location faces south and south-west, and its limestone and marl soil is home to vineyards between 60 and 70 years old, as well as two more recent ones. Most of the estate is given over to barbera – 80 per cent of the area under vine – while the remaining 20 per cent is split between chardonnay, dolcetto and grignolino.

The winery continues to be one of the most consistent and reliable in the entire Asti area. Barbera d'Asti Superiore Nizza Favà is by now a regular in our finals. Its '07 vintage has coffee, mulberries, cinchona and plum jam, and a deep, highly concentrated palate with dense fruit, supported by good acidity. Barbera d'Asti Superiore In Pectore '08 is also very well made, showing blackberry jam and wild berries, as is the complex Barbera d'Asti Tra Neuit e Dì '09, with its pervasive nose of fresh dark berry fruit and long finish. Grignolino d'Asti 'L Giget '09 is as pleasant and supple as ever.

● Barbera d'Asti Sup. Nizza Favà '07	▼▼	5
● Barbera d'Asti Sup. In Pectore '08	▼▼	4
● Barbera d'Asti Tra Neuit e Dì '09	▼▼	3*
● Grignolino d'Asti 'L Giget '09	▼	3
● Barbera d'Asti Sup. Nizza Favà '04	▽▽▽	5
● Barbera d'Asti Sup. Favà '03	▽▽	5
● Barbera d'Asti Sup. Favà '02	▽▽	5
● Barbera d'Asti Sup. In Pectore '07	▽▽	4*
● Barbera d'Asti Sup. In Pectore '06	▽▽	4*
● Barbera d'Asti Sup. Nizza Favà '06	▽▽	5
● Barbera d'Asti Sup. Nizza Favà '05	▽▽	5

Antonia Gazzi

STRADA DA GAVARRA, 12
14049 NIZZA MONFERRATO [AT]
TEL. 0141793512
azienda.gazzi@virgilio.it

CELLAR SALES
PRE-BOOKED VISITS

ANNUAL PRODUCTION 10,000 bottles
HECTARES UNDER VINE 2
VITICULTURE METHOD Conventional

Antonia Gazzi and Sergio Mariani moved to Nizza Monferrato from Milan in 1993, with the specific intention of producing high-quality wine. Armed with the necessary enthusiasm and tenacity, they first opted not to uproot the old vineyards, which date from 1937 and 1947. They are excellently aspected and tended by hand on mixed tufa and sandy soil with cover cropping. The winery was one of the first, back in 2000, to use the name Nizza on its flagship wine.

This year Antonia presented us with two vintages of Barbera d'Asti Superiore Nizza Praiot. The '07 is one of the best Barberas we tasted, with great personality, a rich nose of fruit and spices and a firmly structured palate that is still slightly austere but very full flavoured and long. We were also enchanted by the '06 vintage, which has a nose of tobacco, cinchona, rain-soaked earth and bottled cherries, accompanied by a fresh, relaxed finish with prominent notes of cherries, and Barbera d'Asti Praiot '07, sourced from the lower part of the vineyard and displaying exuberant sensations of morello cherries leading to a powerful, balanced palate.

● Barbera d'Asti Sup. Nizza Praiot '07	🍷🍷	6
● Barbera d'Asti Praiot '07	🍷🍷	4*
● Barbera d'Asti Sup. Nizza Praiot '06	🍷🍷	6
● Barbera d'Asti Praiot '98	🍸🍸	4

Ettore Germano

LOC. CERRETTA, 1
12050 SERRALUNGA D'ALBA [CN]
TEL. 0173613528
www.germanoettore.com

CELLAR SALES
PRE-BOOKED VISITS
ROOMS

ANNUAL PRODUCTION 70,000 bottles
HECTARES UNDER VINE 14
VITICULTURE METHOD Conventional

Sergio Germano is a dynamic, friendly Langhe wine man who confidently runs this important estate which, year after year, scales new peaks of quality and reliability. The product range includes the main local DOC and DOCG wines, several illustrious crus and is rounded off – unusually – by some first-rate whites from choice growing country in upper Langhe.

This year the estate's wines were exceptional. Langhe Bianco Hérzu '08, an elegant monovarietal Riesling, won our top accolade, showing delicate, terse, mineral, long and very fresh. The majestic Barolo Lazzarito '04, in its first great vintage, is practically on a par, with a deep, focused nose of cinnamon, liquorice and sweet tobacco, and a characterful palate that ends on assertive but not invasive tannins. Barolo Cerretta '06 is rich and very fruity, with a meaty background note adding complexity. Finally, there is the austere, masculine Barolo Prapò '06 and a magnificent version of Langhe Rosso Balàu '07, a blend of mainly Dolcetto with barbera and merlot.

○ Langhe Bianco Hérzu '08	🍷🍷🍷	6
● Barolo Cerretta '06	🍷🍷	8
● Barolo Lazzarito Ris. '04	🍷🍷	8
● Barolo Prapò '06	🍷🍷	8
● Langhe Rosso Balàu '07	🍷🍷	5
● Barbera d'Alba V. della Madre '07	🍷🍷	6
● Barolo Serralunga '06	🍷🍷	7
● Dolcetto d'Alba Pradone '09	🍷🍷	4
○ Langhe Bianco Binel '08	🍷🍷	5
○ Langhe Chardonnay '09	🍷🍷	4*
● Langhe Nebbiolo '08	🍷🍷	5
● Barolo Cerretta '05	🍸🍸🍸	8
● Barolo Cerretta '01	🍸🍸🍸	7
● Barolo Prapò '04	🍸🍸🍸	7
○ Langhe Chardonnay '08	🍸🍸	4

Attilio Ghisolfi

LOC. BUSSIA, 27
12065 MONFORTE D'ALBA [CN]
TEL. 017378345
www.ghisolfi.com

CELLAR SALES
PRE-BOOKED VISITS

ANNUAL PRODUCTION 45,000 bottles
HECTARES UNDER VINE 6
VITICULTURE METHOD Conventional

This small family-run estate in the municipality of Monforte d'Alba offers a limited but very high-quality range of wines. Over the years, Gianmarco Ghisolfi has become impressively consistent. The style of his wines is not conducive to approachability but instead expresses a complexity and depth that emerge with careful sensory analysis.

The alluring Visette '06 – which added the name Bussia after the official institution of the Barolo subzones – is fairly mature and open, with slightly jammy raspberry notes and a particularly full, continuous palate. The very long finish features a modern-style hint of oak. Barolo Bussia '06, which is aged traditionally in large barrels, is sound but slightly harder and closed, with prominent tannins. Langhe Nebbiolo '07 is a truly pleasant surprise. While neither simple nor approachable, as so many wines of its kind are, it is not a Barolo clone either. Instead, it is more drinkable with very pleasant, layered fruit. The other wines had not been bottled when we tasted.

● Barolo Bussia Bricco Visette '06	TT	7
● Barbera d'Alba Maggiora '07	TT	4
● Barolo Bussia '06	TT	6
● Barolo Bricco Visette '05	YYY	7
● Barolo Bricco Visette '01	YYY	7
● Barolo Fantini Ris. '01	YYY	8
● Langhe Rosso Alta Bussia '01	YYY	6
● Langhe Rosso Alta Bussia '00	YYY	6
● Langhe Rosso Alta Bussia '99	YYY	6
● Barbera d'Alba V. Lisi '06	YY	5
● Barolo '05	YY	6
● Langhe Rosso Alta Bussia '06	YY	6

★ Bruno Giacosa

VIA XX SETTEMBRE, 52
12057 NEIVE [CN]
TEL. 017367027
www.brunogiacosa.it

ANNUAL PRODUCTION 500,000 bottles
HECTARES UNDER VINE 22
VITICULTURE METHOD Conventional

Bruno Giacosa is one of the greatest legends of quality Italian wines. The estate's superb Barbarescos and Barolos are highly sought after by every connoisseur, lover and collector of world-class fine wines. It is hard to find the right words to describe their style, for it is the terroir that does the talking, offering different but always absolutely fascinating emotions every time. Bruno himself is a living monument who, now in his 80s, continues to produce magnificent wines.

Le Rocche del Falletto di Serralunga '04 is probably the finest Barolo of recent years, on a par with Barbaresco Asili '96 and Barolo Collina Rionda '89. It won Three Glasses for its complex, stylish tobacco, dried flowers and raspberries, and a lengthy palate with good development and close-knit tannins. The excellent Asili '07, from one of the greatest Barbaresco crus, is already fairly open, fruity and enjoyable but its firm palate will allow long ageing. Barbaresco Santo Stefano, from Bruno's other renowned cru, is slightly more closed and austere. Rosé Extra Brut '07, from pinot nero, made its debut this year, showing the cellar can turn out Metodo Classico sparklers, too.

● Barolo Le Rocche del Falletto '04	TTT+	8
● Barbaresco Asili '07	TT	8
● Barbaresco Santo Stefano '07	TT	8
● Nebbiolo d'Alba Valmaggiore '08	TT	6
○ Roero Arneis '09	TT	5
⊙ Spumante Extra Brut Rosé Bruno Giacosa '07	TT	6
● Barbaresco Asili '05	YYY+	8
● Barbaresco Asili Ris. '04	YYY	8
● Barbaresco Rabajà Ris. '01	YYY	8
● Barbaresco Santo Stefano '01	YYY	8
● Barolo Falletto '04	YYY	8
● Barolo Falletto '01	YYY	8
● Barolo Falletto '00	YYY	8
● Barolo Le Rocche del Falletto '05	YYY	8
● Barolo Le Rocche del Falletto Ris. '01	YYY	8

Carlo Giacosa

s.da Ovello, 9
12050 Barbaresco [CN]
tel. 0173635116
www.carlogiacosa.it

CELLAR SALES
PRE-BOOKED VISITS

ANNUAL PRODUCTION 40,000 bottles
HECTARES UNDER VINE 5
VITICULTURE METHOD Conventional

This small winery run by Maria Grazia Giacosa and her family, continues to make rapid progress with its good-value quality wines, which are improving year after year. The whole range is highly recommended, particularly the Barbarescos, which display excellent character and are destined to be among of the best of their kind in a few years' time.

Allowing Barbaresco Montefico to age for an extra year looks like a wise decision. The '06 vintage emerged in all its splendour this year and its innate delicacy makes it easy to forget the power and extract of Langhe Nebbiolos. Its elegant tannins support a complex nose of raspberries and tobacco, accompanied by salty hints. Narin '07 is more approachable, while maintaining a generous, mouthfilling character. The rest of the range offers wines that are excellent value for money, particularly Barbera Mucin '09.

●	Barbaresco Montefico '06	2 black	6
●	Barbaresco Narin '07	2 black	5
●	Barbera d'Alba Lina '08	2 black	4*
●	Barbera d'Alba Mucin '09	2 black	4*
●	Dolcetto d'Alba Cuchet '09	2 black	3*
●	Langhe Nebbiolo Maria Grazia '08	2 black	4*
●	Barbaresco Montefico '05	2 white	6
●	Barbaresco Narin '06	2 white	6*
●	Barbaresco Narin '05	2 white	6*
●	Barbaresco Narin '04	2 white	6
●	Barbera d'Alba Lina '07	2 white	4*
●	Barbera d'Alba Lina '06	2 white	4
●	Barbera d'Alba Mucin '07	2 white	4*
●	Dolcetto d'Alba Cuchet '08	2 white	4
●	Dolcetto d'Alba Cuchet '07	2 white	4*

F.lli Giacosa

via XX Settembre, 64
12057 Neive [CN]
tel. 017367013
www.giacosa.it

CELLAR SALES
PRE-BOOKED VISITS

ANNUAL PRODUCTION 500,000 bottles
HECTARES UNDER VINE 50
VITICULTURE METHOD Conventional

This winery is much larger than many other local producers. Winemaking methods range from small wood to concrete vats, allowing it to craft products in a style that blends modernity and tradition. The extensive range is includes the main local DOC and DOCG wines at particularly competitive prices.

Barbaresco Basarin Vigna Gian Matè '07 has a balsamic nose with dried flowers and firm, slightly rough tannins. Basarin '07 is less hefty but almost as balanced, with a similar nose. Barolo Bussia '06 has classic liquorice and raspberries, austere tannins and good flesh. Aged for an extra year, Barolo Vigna del Mandorlo '05 gives charming wafts of tobacco, red fruit and cinchona, and a long, warm alcoholic palate. Barbera d'Alba Maria Gioana '07 has oak and bottled cherries, and good acidity that lends the full-bodied palate subtlety. Langhe Chardonnay Ca' Lunga '08 has classic oak from barrel ageing, and a pleasant, well-made, medium-length palate with good complexity.

●	Barbaresco Basarin V. Gian Matè '07	2 black	6
●	Barolo Bussia '06	2 black	6
●	Barbaresco Basarin '07	2 black	6
●	Barbera d'Alba Maria Gioana '07	2 black	5
●	Barolo V. Mandorlo '05	2 black	7
○	Langhe Chardonnay Ca' Lunga '08	2 black	5
○	Langhe Chardonnay Rorea '09	1 black	4
○	Roero Arneis '09	1 black	4
●	Barbaresco Basarin '06	2 white	6
●	Barbaresco Basarin V. Gian Matè '05	2 white	6
●	Barbaresco Gian Matè '04	2 white	6
●	Barbera d'Alba Madonna di Como '06	2 white	4*
●	Barbera d'Alba Maria Gioana '06	2 white	5
●	Barolo V. Mandorlo '04	2 white	7

Raffaele Gili

LOC. PAUTASSO, 7
12050 CASTELLINALDO [CN]
TEL. 0173639011

CELLAR SALES
PRE-BOOKED VISITS

ANNUAL PRODUCTION 52,000 bottles
HECTARES UNDER VINE N.A .
VITICULTURE METHOD Conventional

Raffaele Gili's winemaking estate was founded in 1993 at Castellinaldo. Most of these vineyards are in Bric Angelino and Bric Poiero, and planted mainly to traditional varieties – arneis, favorita, barbera, bonarda and nebbiolo – with cabernet sauvignon recently added. The small range of wines released aims at faithfully interpreting the terroir.

Among Raffaele Gili's wines, the best performance came from Nebbiolo d'Alba Sansivé '07, which went into our finals. Stylish with lovely spice and tobacco notes, this wine has a rich, well-structured palate with tannins well tucked in and a long, fruity finish. Another good wine is the Roero Bric Angelino '07 which shows a bouquet of dried flowers, tar and spice followed by a consistent, nicely textured palate, slightly marked by oak and lacking necessary acidity to give proper length and depth. The other labels submitted are all well crafted.

● Nebbiolo d'Alba Sansivé '07	▼▼	4*
● Roero Bric Angelino '07	▼▼	5
● Barbera d'Alba Castellinaldo '07	▼	5
● Barbera d'Alba Pautasso '08	▼	4
● Langhe Nebbiolo '09	▼	4
● Langhe Rosso L'Assemblato '07	▼	5
○ Roero Arneis '09	▼	4
● Barbera d'Alba Pautasso '07	▽▽	4*
● Nebbiolo d'Alba Sansivé '06	▽▽	4*
● Roero Bric Angelino '03	▽▽	5

Giovanni Battista Gillardi

CASCINA CORSALETTO, 69
12060 FARIGLIANO [CN]
TEL. 017376306
www.gillardi.it

CELLAR SALES
PRE-BOOKED VISITS

ANNUAL PRODUCTION 35,000 bottles
HECTARES UNDER VINE 7
VITICULTURE METHOD Conventional

Though not as famous as Barolo or Barbaresco, the Dogliani zone has some great operations, estates capable of exploiting the potential of their terroir through native or, in some cases, less traditional varieties. Among these, the Gillardi family faithfully interprets Dolcetto, a wine that ages in the new, efficient cellar. Alongside this, the Gillardis make a fairly large array of frequently excellent wines with less intimate ties to the territory.

Giacolino Gillardi again shows his dolcetto-making prowess. Cursalet '09 is one of the best in the past few years. Captivating right from the bright purple colour, this wine caresses the nose with refined black berry fruit lifted by tobacco and cocoa powder. The palate is a minor masterpiece of balance, giving savouriness and agility to a wine of considerable heft. Sourced from the youngest vineyards with not quite as good exposure, the less full-bodied Vigna Maestra '09 is fresher, edgier and marked by fruit that is less rich and juicy. From the new generation, this year we tasted the best Merlot ever here, for the first time labelled as Langhe, Il Merlò '07.

● Dolcetto di Dogliani Cursalet '09	▼▼	4*
● Langhe Rosso Merlò '07	▼▼	7
● Dolcetto di Dogliani Vign. Maestra '09	▼▼	4*
● Langhe Rosso Harys '08	▼▼	7
● Harys '00	▽▽▽	7
● Harys '99	▽▽▽	7
● Harys '98	▽▽▽	7
● Dolcetto di Dogliani Cursalet '08	▽▽	4
● Dolcetto di Dogliani Cursalet '07	▽▽	4*
● Dolcetto di Dogliani Vign. Maestra '08	▽▽	4*
● Langhe Rosso Harys '07	▽▽	7
● Langhe Rosso Harys '06	▽▽	7
● Langhe Rosso Yeta '07	▽▽	5

Cascina Giovinale

S.DA SAN NICOLAO, 102
14049 NIZZA MONFERRATO [AT]
TEL. 0141793005
www.cascinagiovinale.com

CELLAR SALES
PRE-BOOKED VISITS

ANNUAL PRODUCTION **25,000 bottles**
HECTARES UNDER VINE **7**
VITICULTURE METHOD **Conventional**

For around 30 years, Anna and Bruno Ciocca have managed this venerable estate. Their seven hectares of vineyards spread across the hill of San Nicolao, 260 metres above sea level, facing south and south-west. The main variety is Barbera, along with smaller amounts of cabernet sauvignon, dolcetto and moscato. All Cascina Giovinale vineyards fall inside the Nizza Monferrato subzone.

The Barbera d'Asti Superiore Nizza Anssèma '07 wins a place in our finals again this year. The intense, complex nose presents refined aromas of spice, tobacco, cherry and black berry fruit, while the palate, though not very rich, shows harmony, finesse and a long, succulent, full-flavoured finish. But the growing season shows on the Barbera d'Asti Superiore '08, which is less brilliant than usual, with cinchona, rain-soaked earth and shades of plum, mid body and slightly blurred in the finish. Finally, the Piemonte Cortese Naiss '09 is simple and pleasant.

● Barbera d'Asti Sup. Nizza Anssèma '07	2 black glasses	5
● Barbera d'Asti Sup. '08	1 black glass	4
○ Piemonte Cortese Naiss '09	1 black glass	4
● Barbera d'Asti Sup. Nizza Anssèma '06	2 white glasses	5*
● Barbera d'Asti Sup. Nizza Anssèma '05	2 white glasses	5
● Barbera d'Asti Sup. Nizza Anssèma '04	2 white glasses	5

La Gironda

S.DA BRICCO, 12
14049 NIZZA MONFERRATO [AT]
TEL. 0141701013
www.lagironda.com

CELLAR SALES
PRE-BOOKED VISITS

ANNUAL PRODUCTION **40,000 bottles**
HECTARES UNDER VINE **8**
VITICULTURE METHOD **Conventional**

Dedicatedly managed by Agostino Galandrino and his family, this small estate in Nizza Monferrato has for years continued to reward their efforts at producing top quality wines. The vineyards are in an area especially well suited to producing barbera, the variety that goes into the estate's showcase wine. Other native varieties include dolcetto, moscato and cortese.

We liked the Barbera d'Asti Superiore Nizza Le Nicchie '07. It's still a bit masked by oak but shows floral, balsamic aromas with good grip and acidity on a dynamic palate with notes of cherry and cinchona. The well-crafted Monferrato Chiesavecchia '07 is an unusual blend of 40 per cent cabernet franc with 20 per cent each of merlot, nebbiolo and barbera that throws with a still oaky cinchona-themed nose and a palate with great pulp, richness, dense tannins and a dynamic finish. The Barbera d'Asti La Gena '08 has tobacco and printer's ink, alcohol and a long, expansive palate. The Moscato d'Asti '09 is subtle and flowing.

● Barbera d'Asti Sup. Nizza Le Nicchie '07	2 black glasses	5
● M.to Rosso Chiesavecchia '07	2 black glasses	4*
● Barbera d'Asti La Gena '08	1 black glass	4
○ Moscato d'Asti '09	1 black glass	4
● Barbera d'Asti La Gena '06	2 white glasses	4*
● Barbera d'Asti Sup. Nizza Le Nicchie '06	2 white glasses	5
● Barbera d'Asti Sup. Nizza Le Nicchie '05	2 white glasses	5
● Barbera d'Asti Sup. Nizza Le Nicchie '04	2 white glasses	5
● Barbera d'Asti Sup. Nizza Le Nicchie '03	2 white glasses	5

La Giustiniana

FRAZ. ROVERETO, 5
15066 GAVI [AL]
TEL. 0143682132
www.lagiustiniana.it

CELLAR SALES
PRE-BOOKED VISITS

ANNUAL PRODUCTION 200,000 bottles
HECTARES UNDER VINE 39
VITICULTURE METHOD Conventional

A historic label in Gavi, Giustiniana has the size and character to excel both locally and nationally. With valuable assistance from Enrico Tomalino, the Lombardini family estate has shown increasing continuity, something seen again this year in the whole array submitted, Il Nostro Gavi '08 in particular. The general stylistic profile, modelled on the local terroir, combines with overall harmony and great drinkability, the real added value of great white wines.

The Gavi del Comune di Gavi Il Nostro Gavi '08 does justice to the underrated cortese variety. The fresh, youthful nose has echoes of almonds and minerality while the palate shows the extra year's ageing, producing a white wine that is complex, clean, elegant and concentrated with minerals returning in the harmonic finish. The Gavi del Comune di Gavi Montessora '09 is also a winner. The elegant nose features white-fleshed fruit, aniseed and pennyroyal. The structured, caressing palate is even richer and fuller than the Nostro Gavi, with good length but fruit a tad less pure. For lovers of slightly sparkling wines, the well-made cortese-based Roverì is enjoyable.

○ Gavi del Comune di Gavi Il Nostro Gavi '08	2 black glasses	5
○ Gavi del Comune di Gavi Montessora '09	2 black glasses	5
○ Gavi del Comune di Gavi Lugarara '09	1 black glass	4
○ Roverì Bianco	1 black glass	3
○ Gavi del Comune di Gavi Il Nostro Gavi '07	3 white glasses	5
○ Gavi del Comune di Gavi Il Nostro Gavi '06	2 white glasses	5
○ Gavi del Comune di Gavi Il Nostro Gavi '04	2 white glasses	5
○ Gavi del Comune di Gavi Lugarara '08	2 white glasses	4
○ Gavi del Comune di Gavi Lugarara '07	2 white glasses	4
○ Gavi del Comune di Gavi Montessora '08	2 white glasses	5
○ Gavi del Comune di Gavi Montessora '07	2 white glasses	5
● M.to Rosso Just '05	2 white glasses	6
● Piemonte Barbera Grangiarossa '07	2 white glasses	4*
● Piemonte Barbera Grangiarossa '05	2 white glasses	3

Cantina del Glicine

VIA GIULIO CESARE, 1
12052 NEIVE [CN]
TEL. 017367215
www.cantinadelglicine.it

CELLAR SALES
PRE-BOOKED VISITS

ANNUAL PRODUCTION 45,000 bottles
HECTARES UNDER VINE 4
VITICULTURE METHOD Organic

A visit to Adriana Mazzi and Roberto Bruno's estate is worth the trip to Neive for the lovely, brick and stone, underground 17th-century winery, as well as the warm welcome. Above all, you can taste an array of traditional Langhe wines that stay absolutely true to their territory, especially the Barbarescos, sourced from the Currà and Marcorino vineyards. Vignesparse is a blend from various sites.

Cantina del Glicine once again postpones the appointment with our top prize but this year's tasting shows this goal is not far off. The best wine, the Barbaresco Currà '07, opens on clear fruit and spice with a distinct touch of rosemary. The palate is more contradictory because vigorous acidity tends to reinforce the slightly sandy tannins. Once again the major theme of the Marcorino '07 is freshness of fruit. Nuances of strawberry and pennyroyal return on the palate, but without triggering that change of pace we were looking for.

● Barbaresco Currà '07	2 black glasses	6
● Barbaresco Marcorino '07	2 black glasses	6
● Barbera d'Alba Sup. La Dormiosa '07	2 black glasses	5
● Barbera d'Alba La Sconsolata '08	1 black glass	4
● Dolcetto d'Alba Olmiolo	1 black glass	4
● Nebbiolo d'Alba Calcabrume '08	1 black glass	4
○ Roero Arneis Il Mandolo	1 black glass	4
● Barbaresco Curà '05	2 white glasses	6
● Barbaresco Currà '06	2 white glasses	6
● Barbaresco Marcorino '06	2 white glasses	6
● Barbaresco Marcorino '05	2 white glasses	6*
● Barbera d'Alba La Sconsolata '07	2 white glasses	4
● Barbera d'Alba La Sconsolata '06	2 white glasses	4*
● Barbera d'Alba Sup. La Dormiosa '06	2 white glasses	5
● Barbera d'Alba Sup. La Dormiosa '05	2 white glasses	5

★ Elio Grasso

LOC. GINESTRA, 40
12065 MONFORTE D'ALBA [CN]
TEL. 017378491
www.eliograsso.it

CELLAR SALES
PRE-BOOKED VISITS

ANNUAL PRODUCTION 75,000 bottles
HECTARES UNDER VINE 14
VITICULTURE METHOD Conventional

Elio Grasso deserves his place in the hall of Langhe greats. Flanked by his wife Marina and recently their son Gianluca, he is one of the few winemakers capable of bringing traditionalists and modernists together with his powerful, multi-faceted Barolos. The Ginestra Vigna Casa Matè and Gavarini Vigna Chiniera age in 25-hectolitre Slavonia oak, and Runcot Riserva ages in barrique, but the stylistic thread goes far beyond technique, beautifully embodying three splendid vineyards at Monforte.

It was precisely this transverse quality, brought to its highest level, that shines through in the Barolo Gavarini Vigna Chiniera '06, one more Three Glass winner for Elio Grasso's estate. You have to rummage around smoky, resinous impressions before you discover a fruit with rare texture and integrity, then fully savour it in a palate that is young yet highly accessible. Only the details place the other Barolos a step below this. The Ginestra Vigna Casa Matè '06 has a rugged but carefree style while Runcot Riserva '04 shows perfectly digested oak and flows with finesse and seamlessly integrated tannins.

● Barolo Gavarini V. Chiniera '06	**YYY**	8
● Barbera d'Alba V. Martina '07	**YY**	5
● Barolo Ginestra V. Casa Maté '06	**YY**	8
● Barolo Rüncot Ris. '04	**YY**	8
● Dolcetto d'Alba dei Grassi '09	**YY**	4*
● Barolo Gavarini V. Chiniera '01	YYY	8
● Barolo Gavarini V. Chiniera '00	YYY	8
● Barolo Gavarini V. Chiniera '99	YYY	8
● Barolo Ginestra V. Casa Maté '05	YYY	8
● Barolo Ginestra V. Casa Maté '04	YYY	8
● Barolo Ginestra V. Casa Maté '03	YYY	8
● Barolo Rüncot '01	YYY	8
● Barolo Rüncot '00	YYY	8
● Barolo Rüncot '99	YYY	8

Silvio Grasso

FRAZ. ANNUNZIATA
CASCINA LUCIANI, 112
12064 LA MORRA [CN]
TEL. 017350322

CELLAR SALES

ANNUAL PRODUCTION 70,000 bottles
HECTARES UNDER VINE 11
VITICULTURE METHOD Conventional

The Grasso family works little more than ten hectares and turns excellent raw material into a range of high-quality wines. With a broad choice of Barolo crus available, Federico may give slightly different interpretations and turn to various uses. The Bricco Luciani represents the top label, guaranteeing rather interesting longevity. Excellent results also frequently come from other labels sourced from different vineyards, as well as the Barbera d'Alba Fontanile, aged long before release to market.

The Barolo Bricco Luciani '06, aged in new barriques, is built around brooding notes of cinchona and dark berries and drinks tannic and powerful, with a long finish. The powerful Giachini '06, like the Pì Vigne aged for two years in pre-used barriques, shows a pinch more acidity, held in place by rich pulp. The celebrated Ciabot Manzoni '06, aged in new barriques, shows spice and lots of rugged tannins that recover nicely in the harmonious finish thanks to good fruity pulp. The Barolo Turné '06 is the most traditional, aged only in large ovals after long maceration. The '06 version is especially tannic and robust.

● Barolo Bricco Luciani '06	**YY**	8
● Barolo Ciabot Manzoni '06	**YY**	8
● Barolo Giachini '06	**YY**	7
● Barbera d'Alba Fontanile '06	**YY**	5
● Barolo Pì Vigne '06	**YY**	6
● Barolo Turné '06	**YY**	7
● Dolcetto d'Alba '09	**YY**	4
● Barolo Bricco Luciani '01	YYY	8
● Barolo Bricco Luciani '96	YYY	8
● Barolo Bricco Luciani '95	YYY	8
● Barolo Bricco Luciani '90	YYY	8
● Barolo Bricco Luciani '05	YY	8
● Barolo Ciabot Manzoni '04	YY	8
● Barolo L'André '04	YY	7
● Barolo Turné '05	YY	7

Bruna Grimaldi

via Roddino
12050 Serralunga d'Alba [CN]
tel. 0173262094
www.grimaldibruna.it

CELLAR SALES

ANNUAL PRODUCTION 60,000 bottles
HECTARES UNDER VINE 10
VITICULTURE METHOD Conventional

Bruna Grimaldi and Franco Fiorino manage this interesting family-run operation in Serralunga and Grinzane Cavour. The stylistic profile of all the wines presented shows a sense of territory and respect for the variety with no excess or exaggeration. Among lesser-known labels, this is still one of the most interesting to discover and explore. We should also mention the wines are sold at sensible prices.

In this edition, Bruna Grimaldi presented us with a pleasing new item. After the power of Barolo from Serralunga – Badarina is one of the lesser known grand crus in the municipality – we can savour the delicacy of a wine from Grinzane Cavour. The '06 vintage was the first for Barolo Camilla. Sourced from vines around ten years old, it cannot compete with its big brother for depth or structure, but is still harmonious and pleasant. Top of the class is the '06 Badarina, a complex, camphor and liquorice red with a dense yet well-distributed tannic weave.

● Barolo Badarina '06	▼▼	7
● Barbera d'Alba Sup. Scassa '08	▼▼	4*
● Barolo Camilla '06	▼▼	6
○ Langhe Chardonnay Valscura '09	▼▼	4*
● Nebbiolo d'Alba Briccola '08	▼▼	4*
● Dolcetto d'Alba V. S. Martino '08	▼	4
● Barbera d'Alba Sup. Scassa '07	▽▽	4
● Barbera d'Alba Sup. Scassa '06	▽▽	4*
● Barbera d'Alba Sup. Scassa '05	▽▽	4*
● Barolo Badarina V. Regnola '05	▽▽	7
● Barolo Badarina V. Regnola '04	▽▽	7
● Barolo Badarina V. Regnola '03	▽▽	6*
● Nebbiolo d'Alba Briccola '07	▽▽	4
● Nebbiolo d'Alba Briccola '06	▽▽	4*

Giacomo Grimaldi

via Luigi Einaudi, 8
12060 Barolo [CN]
tel. 0173560536
ferruccio.grimaldi@libero.it

CELLAR SALES
PRE-BOOKED VISITS

ANNUAL PRODUCTION 50,000 bottles
HECTARES UNDER VINE 11
VITICULTURE METHOD Conventional

With around ten hectares in Barolo and Novello, this family estate is one of the most consistent and reliable operations in the zone. Year after year, the progress in quality and ever-greater varietal definition in the wines, along with their attractive prices, constitute corroboration of Ferruccio Grimaldi's estate's good health. If this is not enough, we could also add the fact he owns plots in some little known but first-rate vineyards and treats nebbiolo with a loving hand.

The Barolo Sotto Castello di Novello '06 failed by a whisker to repeat last year's success. The nose of liquorice, tobacco and medicinal herbs expresses all the complexity of nebbiolo with solid, austere beauty that reminds you of the essence of this great wine. Le Coste '05 seems more straightforward, with distinct aromas of raspberry upfront and less depth with a finish unable to offer length. Some of the basic wines were penalized by the '08 harvest. Sourced from a beautiful vineyard at Vezza d'Alba in Roero, the Nebbiolo d'Alba Valmaggiore this year surpasses, in density and body, the more famous Barbera Fornaci from the same vintage.

● Barolo Le Coste '05	▼▼	7
● Barolo Sotto Castello di Novello '06	▼▼	7
● Barbera d'Alba Fornaci '08	▼▼	5
● Barbera d'Alba Pistìn '09	▼▼	4*
● Barolo '06	▼▼	6
● Dolcetto d'Alba '09	▼▼	4*
● Nebbiolo d'Alba Valmaggiore '08	▼▼	5
● Barolo Sotto Castello di Novello '05	▽▽▽	7
● Barbera d'Alba Fornaci '07	▽▽	5
● Barbera d'Alba Fornaci '06	▽▽	5
● Barolo Le Coste '05	▽▽	7
● Barolo Le Coste '04	▽▽	7
● Barolo Le Coste '03	▽▽	7

Sergio Grimaldi - Ca' du Sindic

LOC. SAN GRATO, 15
12058 SANTO STEFANO BELBO [CN]
TEL. 0141840341
grimaldi.sergio@virgilio.it

CELLAR SALES
PRE-BOOKED VISITS

ANNUAL PRODUCTION 45,000 bottles
HECTARES UNDER VINE 10
VITICULTURE METHOD Conventional

Reliable quality at the top of its class and reasonable prices are the features that sum up this lovely operation managed by Sergio Grimaldi, with valuable collaboration from his wife Angela and son Paolo. This area is historically linked with moscato, which can be superb here. Efforts with barbera and brachetto, used in other wines in the range, also show reliability and well thought-out ideas about winemaking and territorial expression.

We begin our round-up with two excellent versions of Moscato d'Asti, both '09. The Capsula Oro and Capsula Argento are set apart by their bright, straw yellow colour, good definition on a nose brimming with flowers and lime aromas, and fresh, appealing drinkability. The Capsula Oro shows a bit more complex with greater length. The Brachetto '09 presents well-calibrated colour, outstanding rose sensations and a fresh, vibrant attack on the palate. The deep, juicy Barbera San Grato '07 gives earth and ripe plums, and the variety's signature balance of structure and acidity.

○ Moscato d'Asti Ca' du Sindic Capsula Oro '09	▼▼	4*
● Barbera d'Asti '07	▼▼	4*
● Barbera d'Asti San Grato '07	▼▼	4*
○ Moscato d'Asti Ca' du Sindic Capsula Argento '09	▼▼	3*
● Piemonte Brachetto '09	▼▼	3*
● Barbera d'Asti San Grato '06	▽▽	4*
● Barbera d'Asti San Grato '05	▽▽	4*
○ Moscato d'Asti Ca' du Sindic Capsula Argento '08	▽▽	3*
○ Moscato d'Asti Ca' du Sindic Capsula Argento '07	▽▽	3*
○ Moscato d'Asti Ca' du Sindic Capsula Argento '06	▽▽	3*
○ Moscato d'Asti Ca' du Sindic Capsula Oro '08	▽▽	4*
○ Moscato d'Asti Ca' du Sindic Capsula Oro '07	▽▽	4*
○ Moscato d'Asti Ca' du Sindic Capsula Oro '06	▽▽	4*
○ Piemonte Moscato Passito Montaldi '06	▽▽	6

La Guardia

POD. LA GUARDIA, 74
15010 MORSASCO [AL]
TEL. 014473076
www.laguardiavini.it

CELLAR SALES
PRE-BOOKED VISITS

ANNUAL PRODUCTION 150,000 bottles
HECTARES UNDER VINE 40
VITICULTURE METHOD Conventional

The Priarone family produces many wines. Every new Guide misses some that were not released to market that year but the labels produced are still numerous. The gamut of varieties runs from the native barbera, dolcetto, brachetto and moscato before continuing with the internationals cabernet sauvignon, pinot nero, merlot and chardonnay. This edition of the Guide features two Monferrato Rossos, the Sacro e Profano and Innominato, two products at the top of estate's list for many years.

Among the wines submitted, we appreciated the Doppio Rosso '07, from barbera and dolcetto, which is intense on the nose and powerful on the rich palate. The 805 '07 is a Monferrato Rosso from merlot and cabernet sauvignon. An impenetrable garnet frames aromas of cassis and sweet spice. The powerful palate is still fruity and long. Barbera Ornovo '07 sports a deep ruby red and an intense nose followed by a powerful, concentrated palate. The Dolcetto Villa Delfini '06 has structure and coherence but the oak is very present even on the palate. The Gamondino '07 has a nice young colour and intense fruity aromas, but reveals rather husky tannins on the palate.

● Barbera del M.to Ornovo '07	▼▼	4
● Doppio Rosso '07	▼▼	5
● M.to Rosso 805 '07	▼▼	5
● Dolcetto di Ovada Sup. Il Gamondino '07	▼	4
● Dolcetto di Ovada Sup. Villa Delfini '06	▼	4
● Figlio di un Bacco Minore	▼	4
○ Piemonte Chardonnay Villa Delfini '09	▼	4
● Barbera del M.to Ornovo '06	▽▽	4
● Barbera del M.to V. di Dante '05	▽▽	5
● Dolcetto di Ovada Sup. Bricco Riccardo '06	▽▽	4
● M.to Rosso Innominato '06	▽▽	5
● M.to Rosso Sacro e Profano '05	▽▽	5
○ Piemonte Chardonnay Villa Delfini '07	▽▽	4

Clemente Guasti

C.SO IV NOVEMBRE, 80
14049 NIZZA MONFERRATO [AT]
TEL. 0141721350
www.guasti.it

CELLAR SALES
PRE-BOOKED VISITS

ANNUAL PRODUCTION 120,000 bottles
HECTARES UNDER VINE 30
VITICULTURE METHOD Conventional

Founded in 1946 by Clemente Guasti, today the winery is passionately, skilfully run by his children, Alessandro and Andrea. The estate is divided into four holdings, three in the Nizza Monferrato area and one at Mombaruzzo. The fairly broad range of wines runs from sparklers to reds but special attention goes to barbera. The leading variety in this area is produced in many versions, from current-vintage Nizza wines to the "chinata" style, aromatized with cinchona bark.

This year, Guasti presented the '06 version of its top Barbera. Barbera d'Asti Superiore Nizza Barcarato proffers a nose with nice intensity and fruity notes of cherry with a thread of cinchona and tobacco. The palate is powerful, juicy, acidic and compact, marked by the austerity typical of the vintage. The Barbera d'Asti Superiore Fonda S. Nicolao shows a bit smaller and more mature in its sensations of tobacco, spice and dried herbs. The harmonious palate has a long, savoury finish. The supple Grignolino d'Asti '09 has notes of red berries, and Moscato d'Asti Santa Teresa '09 is subtle and floral. Both are well made.

● Barbera d'Asti Sup. Cascina Fonda San Nicolao '06	▼▼	5
● Barbera d'Asti Sup. Nizza Barcarato '06	▼▼	6
● Grignolino d'Asti '09	▼	4
○ Moscato d'Asti Santa Teresa '09	▼	4
● Barbera d'Asti Sup. Barcarato '04	▽▽	6
● Barbera d'Asti Sup. Nizza Barcarato '04	▽▽	6

Hilberg - Pasquero

VIA BRICCO GATTI, 16
12040 PRIOCCA [CN]
TEL. 0173616197
www.hilberg-pasquero.com

CELLAR SALES
PRE-BOOKED VISITS

ANNUAL PRODUCTION 23,000 bottles
HECTARES UNDER VINE 6
VITICULTURE METHOD Organic

A natural approach to agriculture, the decision to make only reds, although not yet Roero, and low-run selections mean, on the one hand, that each bottle gets maniacal care and on the other, makes this estate an anomaly in a wine world shifting to bigger numbers. Michelangelo "Miclo" Pasquero and Annette Hilberg have for years been committed to making their vineyards consistent with their biodynamic vision. And that vision is not a publicity stunt. It springs from daily observation among the rows and a visceral love of the land.

Despite a vintage year as unfavourable as 2008, the estate has released a series of interesting, convincing wines starting with the Nebbiolo d'Alba. The elegant aromas foreground raspberry with the help of delicate spicy notes leading into a taut, linear palate with no excess, well-orchestrated, long and refined. The nose of the Langhe Nebbiolo reveals a touch of raspberry jam and liquorice. The lively palate has a bright freshness with a mid-bodied base and long, pleasant finish. The two Barbera d'Albas, the Superiore '08 and slightly simpler '09, both have great character.

● Barbera d'Alba Sup. '08	▼▼	6
● Langhe Nebbiolo '08	▼▼	6
● Nebbiolo d'Alba '08	▼▼	6
● Barbera d'Alba '09	▼▼	4
● Vareij Rosso '09	▼	4
● Barbera d'Alba Sup. '98	▽▽▽	6
● Barbera d'Alba Sup. '97	▽▽▽	6
● Nebbiolo d'Alba '06	▽▽▽	6
● Nebbiolo d'Alba '05	▽▽▽	6
● Nebbiolo d'Alba '04	▽▽▽	6
● Nebbiolo d'Alba '03	▽▽▽	6
● Nebbiolo d'Alba '01	▽▽▽	6
● Nebbiolo d'Alba '00	▽▽▽	6
● Nebbiolo d'Alba '99	▽▽▽	6

Icardi

LOC. SAN LAZZARO
S.DA COMUNALE BALBI, 30
12053 CASTIGLIONE TINELLA [CN]
TEL. 0141855159
www.icardivini.it

CELLAR SALES
PRE-BOOKED VISITS

ANNUAL PRODUCTION 352,000 bottles
HECTARES UNDER VINE 75
VITICULTURE METHOD Certified biodynamic

Year after year, the great array of wines from this operation grows richer in character and originality. The battery ranges across many designations, representing a good part of Piedmont winemaking. The size of the vineyard holding is remarkable with plots scattered across Piedmont. The decision to use fully biodynamic growing methods with wines from Cascina San Lazzaro adds another positive note to the generous professional commitment of Claudio Icardi.

Still a bit shy on the nose but very promising, the barbera-based Langhe Rosso Dadelio '06 mingles cinchona and ripe plums before the full yet not excessive palate features surprising length. We were particularly struck by the nebbiolo-led Langhe Pafoj '07 featuring balsamic and tobacco notes, and a serious tannic weave that precedes the deep, intense closing. The Barolo '06 has the character of a great Barolo. The convincing, original Dadelio Bianco is rich and structured yet undemanding, with a nose defined by notes of melon and apricot. The Barbera Surì di Mù '08 adheres closely to the peculiarities of the variety, finding a nice balance of pulp and acidity.

● Barolo Parej '06	▼▼	7
● Langhe Rosso Dadelio Cascina San Lazzaro '06	▼▼	6
● Langhe Rosso Pafoj '07	▼▼	6
● Barbaresco Montubert '07	▼▼	8
● Barbera d'Alba Surì di Mù '08	▼▼	6
● Barbera d'Asti Nuj Suj '08	▼▼	6
○ Dadelio Bianco - Cascina San Lazzaro	▼▼	6
○ M.to Bianco Pafoj '09	▼▼	6
○ Moscato d'Asti La Rosa Selvatica '09	▼▼	4
● Dolcetto d'Alba Rousori '09	▼	4
● Barbera d'Asti Nuj Suj '07	▽▽	6
● Barolo Parej '05	▽▽	8
● Barolo Parej '04	▽▽	8
○ Moscato d'Asti La Rosa Selvatica '08	▽▽	5

Isabella

FRAZ. CORTERANZO
VIA GIANOLI, 64
15020 MURISENGO [AL]
TEL. 0141693000
info@isabellavini.com

CELLAR SALES
PRE-BOOKED VISITS
ROOMS AND FOOD

ANNUAL PRODUCTION 120,000 bottles
HECTARES UNDER VINE 26
VITICULTURE METHOD Conventional

Never a man to sit back, Gabriele Calvo continues to supervise the entire chain of wine production with good results. We did not taste the Bric Stupui this year since it wasn't produced in '06 but look forward to tasting this wine next year in the '07 version. The new item here is the Jagaem '02, a late-harvest Sauvignon that, after ageing for years, was at last considered ready for release to market. In search of a name for this wine, the Calvos opted to dedicate it to their children so Jagaem combines the initials of their names.

The Barbera Truccone '08 presents an intense ruby red. The nose has cherry and spice aromas on slightly vegetal notes, and the intense, caressing palate has a long finale. The Grignolino Monte Castello wears a pale ruby red and shows characteristic fruit over spiciness introducing a pulpy palate with concentration and elegant tannins. The Jagaem '02 is a deep gold running to amber. The nose is intense and layered thanks to aromas from the long oak ageing that leave room for apricot and honey. The powerful, alcoholic palate is balanced thanks to acidity that gives good support to the residual sugar.

● Barbera d'Asti Truccone '08	▼▼	4
● Grignolino del M.to Casalese Montecastello '09	▼▼	4*
○ M.to Bianco Jagaem V.T. '02	▼▼	5
● Barbera del M.to Vivace Bricco Montemà '09	▼	3
● M.to Freisa Vivace Sobric '09	▼	3
○ Piemonte Chardonnay Carpe Diem '08	▼	4
● Barbera d'Asti Bric Stupui '04	▽▽	5
● Barbera d'Asti Sup. Bric Stupui '05	▽▽	5
● Barbera d'Asti Truccone '06	▽▽	4*
● Barbera del M.to Bricco Montemà Tardivo '05	▽▽	4
● Grignolino del M.to Casalese Montecastello '06	▽▽	4*
● Monferrato Freisa Bioc '05	▽▽	4*

Isolabella della Croce

REG. CAFFI, 3
14051 LOAZZOLO [AT]
TEL. 014487166
www.isolabelladellacroce.it

CELLAR SALES
PRE-BOOKED VISITS

ANNUAL PRODUCTION 60,000 bottles
HECTARES UNDER VINE 15
VITICULTURE METHOD Organic

The Isolabella della Croce family's operation is in the main section of our Guide for 2011. Though founded only nine years ago, the estate boasts 50-year-old vineyards located up to 500 metres above sea level on very steep slopes. The winery deals mostly with moscato and barbera, grown alongside cabernet franc, merlot, pinot nero, cortese and chardonnay, and the wines are in a modern idiom.

Further confirmation that those who worked well in the Nizza Monferrato subzone in 2007 vintage found extraordinary opportunities to create great wines. This year, we enjoyed the Barbera d'Asti Superiore Nizza Augusta '07. Stylish fruit, with upfront raspberry aromas, leads into a palate that is full, rich, consistent, fresh and well orchestrated. The well-managed Moscato d'Asti Valdiserre '09 has tropical fruit tones, and great power and length on the palate. The well-typed Barbera d'Asti Maria Teresa '08 shows black berries and tobacco, the sauvignon-based Monferrato Bianco Solum '09 is simple and varietal, and the Piemonte Chardonnay '09 presents clean and supple.

● Barbera d'Asti Sup. Nizza Augusta '07	🍷🍷	5
○ Moscato d'Asti Valdiserre '09	🍷🍷	4
● Barbera d'Asti Maria Teresa '08	🍷	4
○ M.to Bianco Solum '09	🍷	4
○ Piemonte Chardonnay '09	🍷	4
● Barbera d'Asti Sup. Nizza Augusta '06	🥂🥂	5
○ Loazzolo Solio '05	🥂🥂	6
● M.to Rosso Superlodo '06	🥂🥂	6

Iuli

FRAZ. MONTALDO
VIA CENTRALE, 27
15020 CERRINA MONFERRATO [AL]
TEL. 0142946657
www.iuli.it

CELLAR SALES
PRE-BOOKED VISITS
ROOMS

ANNUAL PRODUCTION 35,000 bottles
HECTARES UNDER VINE 8
VITICULTURE METHOD Organic

For years this small co-operative, excellently managed by Fabrizio Iuli, has been a beacon in the hills of Val Cerrina. A steady crescendo now peaks in this exceptional line-up. We must acknowledge those who, with great self-sacrifice, are promoting a territory that has always been taken a back seat to neighbouring areas viewed as more prestigious.

From half and half nebbiolo and barbera, the Malidea '07 has a cinchona, spice and tobacco nose, a magnificent tannic weave and a long, velvety finish. Barabba '07 is grand at every stage. A near impenetrable purple-tinged ruby ushers in spice and leather against a fruity background, and a powerful palate supported by perfect acidity. The Rossore from the same year has striking finesse and aromatic progression on the nose and the palate unfolds harmoniously. A wine of personality. The Nino '08, a monovarietal Pinot Nero, shows clear varietal characteristics, just slightly over-developed. Finally, the pleasant Barbera Umberta '08 is well made all round.

● Barbera del M.to Sup. Barabba '07	🍷🍷	6
● Barbera del M.to Sup. Rossore '07	🍷🍷	4*
● M.to Rosso Malidea '07	🍷🍷	6
● Barbera del M.to Umberta '08	🍷🍷	4
● M.to Rosso Nino '08	🍷🍷	6
● Barbera del M.to Sup. Barabba '04	🥂🥂🥂	6
● Barbera del M.to Sup. Barabba '06	🥂🥂	6
● Barbera del M.to Sup. Barabba '03	🥂🥂	6
● Barbera del M.to Sup. Rossore '06	🥂🥂	4*
● Barbera del M.to Sup. Rossore '05	🥂🥂	5
● Barbera del M.to Umberta '07	🥂🥂	4*
● M.to Rosso Nino '07	🥂🥂	5

Tenuta Langasco

FRAZ. MADONNA DI COMO, 10
12051 ALBA [CN]
TEL. 0173286972
www.tenutalangasco.it

PRE-BOOKED VISITS

ANNUAL PRODUCTION 50,000 bottles
HECTARES UNDER VINE 22
VITICULTURE METHOD Conventional

This reliable estate is in the municipality of Alba, in the village of Madonna di Como, a splendid hilly area overlooking the capital of Langhe. Vineyard production concentrates on the characteristic varieties for this area: dolcetto, barbera, and nebbiolo. For years, Claudio Sacco and his family have achieved great results and now they have earned a full profile.

The best wine submitted was a seriously good Nebbiolo Sorì Coppa with a deep, vivid colour and fresh raspberry and liquorice aromas over aniseed. The enveloping attack on the palate is a nice balance of tannic weave and fruit. This simple Nebbiolo has nothing to envy ore important designations. Sourced from Madonna di Como, the Dolcetto Vigna Miclet '09 is sound and unveils a splendid, bright purple colour. The nose has clear black berries and a deep, alcohol-rich progression. The Barbera '08 shows a dark ruby red, good density on the palate and surprising structure, especially in view of the vintage.

● Nebbiolo d'Alba Sorì Coppa '08	🍷🍷	5
● Barbera d'Alba Madonna di Como '08	🍷🍷	4
● Dolcetto d'Alba Madonna di Como V. Miclet '09	🍷🍷	3*
● Barbera d'Alba Madonna di Como '07	🍷🍷 (white)	4
● Barbera d'Alba Madonna di Como '06	🍷🍷 (white)	4*
● Barbera d'Alba Madonna di Como '05	🍷🍷 (white)	4*
● Dolcetto d'Alba Madonna di Como '06	🍷🍷 (white)	3*
● Dolcetto d'Alba Madonna di Como V. Miclet '08	🍷🍷 (white)	3*
● Nebbiolo d'Alba Sorì Coppa '07	🍷🍷 (white)	5
● Nebbiolo d'Alba Sorì Coppa '06	🍷🍷 (white)	5
● Nebbiolo d'Alba Sorì Coppa '05	🍷🍷 (white)	5
● Nebbiolo d'Alba Sorì Coppa '04	🍷🍷 (white)	4

Gianluigi Lano

FRAZ. SAN ROCCO SENO D'ELVIO
S.DA BASSO, 38
12051 ALBA [CN]
TEL. 0173286958
lano.vini@tiscali.it

CELLAR SALES
PRE-BOOKED VISITS

ANNUAL PRODUCTION 40,000 bottles
HECTARES UNDER VINE 6
VITICULTURE METHOD Conventional

The family-run Lano estate continues to turn out reliability and excellent value for money in all their labels. Gianluigi Lano, with help from skilled oenologist Gianfranco Cordero, gives the best interpretation to fruit from an area on the edge of Barbaresco's most famous towns, but no less interesting and rich in potential for this. The style shows Gianfranco's ongoing search for varietal frankness and elegance.

Taking advantage of an extra year's ageing, the '06 Barbaresco shows nicely mature aromas, characterized by sun-dried grass and tobacco. The pleasant palate has fairly soft tannins but poorly defined character. The excellent quality Barbera d'Alba Fondo Prà '07 is classic, dark and rich in cherry and plum jam, and the powerful, harmoniously fresh palate shows good length. The exceptionally clean, fruity aromas of the Dolcetto d'Alba Ronchella '09 reveal blackberries and the pleasing palate closes on bitter almonds in a context of robust alcohol, power and outstanding personality.

● Barbera d'Alba Fondo Prà '07	🍷🍷	4*
● Barbaresco '06	🍷🍷	6
● Dolcetto d'Alba '09	🍷🍷	3*
● Dolcetto d'Alba Ronchella '09	🍷🍷	4*
● Barbera d'Alba '08	🍷	3
○ Langhe Favorita '09	🍷	3
● Langhe Freisa '09	🍷	3
● Barbaresco '05	🍷🍷 (white)	6
● Barbera d'Alba Altavilla '07	🍷🍷 (white)	4
● Barbera d'Alba Altavilla '06	🍷🍷 (white)	4*
● Barbera d'Alba Fondo Prà '06	🍷🍷 (white)	4
● Barbera d'Alba Fondo Prà '04	🍷🍷 (white)	4
● Dolcetto d'Alba Ronchella '07	🍷🍷 (white)	4*
● Langhe Rosso Samuele '06	🍷🍷 (white)	4

Ugo Lequio

VIA DEL MOLINO, 10
12057 NEIVE [CN]
TEL. 0173677224
www.ugolequio.it

CELLAR SALES
PRE-BOOKED VISITS

ANNUAL PRODUCTION 25,000 bottles
HECTARES UNDER VINE N.A .
VITICULTURE METHOD Conventional

Ugo Lequio is a great expert in Langhe terroirs. Long experience helps him select top-quality raw material. Though production in not huge, every label represents consistently solid value. The stylistic profile is well calibrated with no excesses or superfluous flourishes. You can taste the cellarability in an old bottle of Barbaresco Gallina: definitely an interesting, positive experience.

The Barbaresco Gallina '07 shows a classic approach. The nose is loaded with spice and tobacco, the broad structure on the palate is soft, thanks to good alcohol, and the finish is long and harmonious. A bit more acidity and extract would have racked up the wine's scores. The dark purple Barbera d'Alba Superiore Gallina '07 has a complex nose with appealing incense, plums and rain-soaked earth before the superb palate shows splendid freshness, softening what would have been opulence without this measured acidity. Sourced from the same vineyard, the extremely clear Barbera Gallina '08 is fresh and enjoyable, but the poor growing year has left cracks in the structure.

● Barbaresco Gallina '07	2 black glasses	6
● Barbera d'Alba Sup. Gallina '07	2 black glasses	5
● Barbera d'Alba Gallina '08	2 black glasses	4
● Dolcetto d'Alba '09	2 black glasses	4
○ Langhe Arneis '09	2 black glasses	4
● Barbaresco Gallina '06	2 white glasses	6
● Barbaresco Gallina '05	2 white glasses	6
● Barbaresco Gallina '04	2 white glasses	6
● Barbera d'Alba Sup. Gallina '06	2 white glasses	5
● Barbera d'Alba Sup. Gallina '05	2 white glasses	4*
● Dolcetto d'Alba '05	2 white glasses	4*
● Langhe Nebbiolo '08	2 white glasses	5
● Langhe Nebbiolo '06	2 white glasses	5*

Cascina Luisin

S.DA RABAJÀ, 34
12050 BARBARESCO [CN]
TEL. 0173635154
cascinaluisin@tiscali.it

PRE-BOOKED VISITS

ANNUAL PRODUCTION 30,000 bottles
HECTARES UNDER VINE 7
VITICULTURE METHOD Conventional

With their solid farming heritage, the Minuto family make wines that never stray from their original terroir. The deep character in these bottles frequently requires some patience but the propensity for ageing is an added value. The Barbaresco has excellent texture and the Barbera, sourced from old vines, is the star of the list. Unfortunately, we were unable to taste the Barbaresco '06 since it has practically sold out.

The successful Barbaresco Rabajà '07 is dark and already proffers smoke and tar on the nose. The traditional palate is austere and very classic. The intense Barbaresco Sorì Paolin '07 is a step behind with a bouquet of spice and red berries. The palate is juicy yet still a bit rigid because of the close-knit, austere tannins. The Barolo Leon '06 is very much already open, with nearly evolved notes on the nose that lead to cocoa powder and sun-dried herbs, but the palate is still trying to balance alcohol and tannins. The other wines are well made. The Barbera Asili is slightly penalized in this '08 version by an undistinguished vintage and overpowering oak.

● Barbaresco Rabajà '07	2 black glasses	7
● Barbaresco Sorì Paolin '07	2 black glasses	7
● Barbera d'Alba Asili '08	2 black glasses	5
● Barolo Leon '06	2 black glasses	7
● Dolcetto d'Alba Bric Trifüla '09	1 black glass	4
● Langhe Nebbiolo Maggiur '08	1 black glass	5
● Barbera d'Alba Asili '00	3 white glasses	6
● Barbera d'Alba Asili '99	3 white glasses	6
● Barbera d'Alba Asili Barrique '97	3 white glasses	6
● Barbaresco Rabajà '04	2 white glasses	7
● Barbaresco Sorì Paolin '05	2 white glasses	7
● Barbaresco Sorì Paolin '04	2 white glasses	7
● Barbera d'Alba Asili '06	2 white glasses	5
● Barbera d'Alba Asili '05	2 white glasses	6

La Luna del Rospo

FRAZ. SALERE, 38
14041 AGLIANO TERME [AT]
TEL. 0141954222
www.lalunadelrospo.it

ANNUAL PRODUCTION 45,000 bottles
HECTARES UNDER VINE 9
VITICULTURE METHOD Certified organic

In 1994, wine enthusiasts Michael Schaffer and Renate Schütz, originally from Bavaria, decided to become winemakers and purchased a lovely estate and house at Agliano Terme. Since then. they have focused their winery on native varieties and organic methods, targeted barbera, and grown from three hectares at the start to nearly ten today. Vines are on average over 40 years old and planted on limestone shale soils.

Michael and Renate decided to give another year in bottle to their showcase wine. So this year they return to the Guide with the Barbera '06. The Barbera d'Asti Bric Rocche has aromas of earth and pencil lead with shades of cinchona and printer's ink on the nose while the palate reflects the vintage and shows austere and rich in acidity with a long finish that is still compact but promising. The Barbera d'Asti Solo per Laura is instead marked by oak with notes of black berries and tobacco. On a par is the Barbera d'Asti Silente '08 has balsamic, fruity tones and a powerful, well-balanced palate with a long, characterful finish.

● Barbera d'Asti Bric Rocche '06	▼▼	4*
● Barbera d'Asti Silente '08	▼▼	4*
● Barbera d'Asti Solo per Laura '06	▼▼	5
● Grignolino d'Asti '08	▼	3
● Barbera d'Asti Bric Rocche '05	▽▽	4*
● Barbera d'Asti Bric Rocche '04	▽▽	4*
● Barbera d'Asti Solo per Laura '05	▽▽	5
● Barbera d'Asti Solo per Laura '04	▽▽	5
● Grignolino d'Asti '07	▽▽	3*
● M.to Rosso Gli Storni '04	▽▽	5

Malabaila di Canale

FRAZ. MADONNA DEI CAVALLI, 19
12043 CANALE [CN]
TEL. 017398381
www.malabaila.com

CELLAR SALES
PRE-BOOKED VISITS

ANNUAL PRODUCTION 80,000 bottles
HECTARES UNDER VINE 22
VITICULTURE METHOD Conventional

Founded 25-years ago, Malabaila is a great winemaking estate with 22 hectares planted to nebbiolo, barbera, brachetto, dolcetto, arneis, and favorita, in other words, all the typical Roero varieties. In the past few years, the estate has put in place vineyard management to avoid as far as possible the use of chemical products and herbicides.

The richer, more complex 2007 vintage was released this year and the simpler, ready to drink 2008 was postponed till next year. The Barbera d'Alba Mezzavilla '07 reached our finals thanks to a bouquet of remarkable finesse and intensity, with cherry, tobacco and spice, and a harmonic, pleasing palate, rich in fruit with a long finish. Two other good wines are the Nebbiolo d'Alba Bric Merli '07 has tobacco, liquorice and raspberry on the nose, and a long, powerful palate with tannins that are still harsh yet well supported by fruit. Roero Castelletto '07 has less than typical vegetal and coffee tones and a close-knit palate with excessively tough tannins.

● Barbera d'Alba Mezzavilla '07	▼▼	4
● Nebbiolo d'Alba Bric Merli '07	▼▼	4
● Roero Castelletto '07	▼▼	5
○ Langhe Favorita '09	▼	4
○ Roero Arneis '09	▼	4
○ Roero Arneis Pradvaj '09	▼	4
● Barbera d'Alba Mezzavilla '08	▽▽	4*
● Barbera d'Alba Mezzavilla '05	▽▽	4*
● Roero Castelletto Ris. '05	▽▽	5
● Roero Sup. Castelletto '04	▽▽	5

★ Malvirà

LOC. CANOVA
VIA CASE SPARSE, 144
12043 CANALE [CN]
TEL. 0173978145
www.malvira.com

CELLAR SALES
PRE-BOOKED VISITS
ROOMS AND FOOD

ANNUAL PRODUCTION 350,000 bottles
HECTARES UNDER VINE 40
VITICULTURE METHOD Organic

Massimo and Roberto Damonte, owners of this beautiful Roero estate, are committed to top quality on all fronts, from their wines to the hospitality at the splendid Villa Tiboldi. The several crus on this recently expanded estate – Trinità, Renesio, Saglietto and San Michele – are vinified separately to bring out their characteristic features. The result is a broad range of territory-focused wines.

The Damonte brothers were not able to submit some wines this year. A landslip caused problems with the new cellar and led to delays in bottling. Among the labels presented, those that reached our finals include: the Roero Renesio Riserva '07, with notes of tobacco, aromatic herbs and liquorice, and an elegant palate with juicy tannins and lovely acidity; and the Roero Arneis Trinità '09, with floral, citrus and spicy shades followed by a rich, taut palate with remarkable length and aromatic clarity. The other labels are well crafted, from the pleasant, fruity Roero Arneis '09 to the Barbera d'Alba Superiore San Michele '06, which has great structure and character.

○ Roero Arneis Trinità '09	TT	4
● Roero Renesio Ris. '07	TT	6
● Barbera d'Alba Sup. S. Michele '06	TT	5
○ Roero Arneis '09	TT	4
○ Langhe Sauvignon '09	T	4
○ Roero Arneis Saglietto '09	T	4
● Roero Mombeltramo Ris. '05	YYY	6
● Roero Renesio Ris. '05	YYY	6
● Roero Sup. Mombeltramo '04	YYY	6
● Roero Sup. Mombeltramo '00	YYY	6
● Roero Sup. Trinità '03	YYY	6
● Roero Sup. Trinità '01	YYY	6

Giovanni Manzone

VIA CASTELLETTO, 9
12065 MONFORTE D'ALBA [CN]
TEL. 017378114
www.manzonegiovanni.com

CELLAR SALES
PRE-BOOKED VISITS

ANNUAL PRODUCTION 40,000 bottles
HECTARES UNDER VINE 8
VITICULTURE METHOD Conventional

A real Langhe winemaker, Giovanni Manzone is passionate about his work. At his estate in Monforte d'Alba, he is responsible for rediscovering the fine Gramolere vineyard and the unfashionable Rossese Bianco. His wines reflect the most authentic country traditions and have great development potential. The new cellar is almost ready and during our visit, Giovanni showed us a nice discovery, a pure mountain spring a few metres from the bottle cellar.

The Manzone family makes three exceptional Barolos from the Gramolere vineyard at Monforte. The Gramolere '06 has broad, complex aromas – dried flowers and tobacco over white truffle – and the powerful, restless tannins of the Barolos of yesteryear. Less rich in pulp and even more austere, the Riserva '04 is less complex than its younger brother. Bricat '06, also from Gramolere but different soils, has enormous power. The dense, almost chewy style is nicely brought out by this estate's traditional vinification. A shade below this is the Barolo Castelletto '06, which has problems expressing the same powerful personality and depth.

● Barbera d'Alba Sup. La Serra '07	TT	5
● Barolo Bricat '06	TT	7
● Barolo Le Gramolere '06	TT	7
● Barolo Le Gramolere Ris. '04	TT	8
● Barolo Castelletto '06	TT	6
● Dolcetto d'Alba La Serra '08	TT	4*
○ Langhe Bianco Rosserto '08	TT	4
● Langhe Nebbiolo Il Crutin '08	TT	4
● Barbera d'Alba '08	T	4
● Dolcetto d'Alba Le Ciliegie '09	T	3
● Barolo Bricat '05	YYY	7
● Barolo Le Gramolere '04	YYY	7
● Barolo Le Gramolere Ris. '01	YYY	8
● Barolo Le Gramolere Ris. '00	YYY	8
● Barolo Le Gramolere Ris. '99	YYY	8

Paolo Manzone

LOC. MERIAME, 1
12050 SERRALUNGA D'ALBA [CN]
TEL. 0173613113
www.barolomeriame.com

CELLAR SALES
PRE-BOOKED VISITS
ROOMS

ANNUAL PRODUCTION 80,000 bottles
HECTARES UNDER VINE 10
VITICULTURE METHOD Conventional

This recently founded winery, managed by the skilled Paolo Manzone, combines great wines with a delightful agriturismo. This successful match, along with the scenic landscape, makes a visit worthwhile. The wines are concentrated into just a few labels, but the number is slowly increasing and value for money is a given.

That high note failed to come again this year. The two '06 Barolos are in the lead. Meriame, from a great vineyard at Serralunga, still seems austere, with rugged tannins and fairly complex tobacco and liquorice. The forest floor aromatics and sweet weight of alcohol make the '06 Barolo Serralunga already more accessible. The two new Langhe Rossos have opposing characters: Luvì '08, from 85-15 nebbiolo and dolcetto, is complex and austerely Nebbiolo-like. The more modern and international Ardì, a dolcetto and barbera blend, foregrounds rich pulp and sweet fruit. The classic Langa Nebbiolo, Barbera and Dolcetto are simpler.

● Barolo Meriame '06	**YY**	7
● Barolo Serralunga '06	**YY**	6
● Langhe Rosso Ardì '09	**YY**	4*
● Langhe Rosso Luvì '08	**YY**	4
● Nebbiolo d'Alba Mirinè '08	**YY**	4
● Barbera d'Alba Fiorenza '09	**Y**	4
● Dolcetto d'Alba Magna '09	**Y**	4
● Barbera d'Alba Fiorenza '08	YY	4*
● Barbera d'Alba Fiorenza '07	YY	4*
● Barolo Meriame '05	YY	7
● Barolo Meriame '04	YY	7
● Barolo Serralunga '05	YY	6
● Dolcetto d'Alba Magna '08	YY	4*
● Nebbiolo d'Alba Mirinè '07	YY	5
● Nebbiolo d'Alba Mirinè '06	YY	5

Poderi Marcarini

P.ZZA MARTIRI, 2
12064 LA MORRA [CN]
TEL. 017350222
www.marcarini.it

CELLAR SALES
PRE-BOOKED VISITS
ROOMS

ANNUAL PRODUCTION 108,000 bottles
HECTARES UNDER VINE 20
VITICULTURE METHOD Conventional

You do not become one of the standard bearers of Langhe tradition by accident. Luisa Marcarini and Manuel Marchetti know this well, heirs to a glorious history handed down through a series of extraordinary mainly nebbiolo-based wines. The Barolos bear the name of two magnificent La Morra vineyards, Brunate and La Serra, and show their origins from their star-bright hue. Long macerations and patient ageing in 20 to 40-hectolitre oak impart a sense of terroir to these phenomenally cellarable wines.

A bright, pale garnet-ruby, breezy whiffs of tobacco, liquorice and rose petals, and a palate that is sharp-edged yet velvety, earthy and aristocratic describe a great classic Nebbiolo. This successful Barolo Brunate '06 has everything except perhaps that extra structure and depth. The same vintage Barolo La Serra has a slightly more developed style, giving tobacco, spice, dried flowers and root vegetables on the textbook nose but the long finish turns a bit bitterish, in part because of slightly emphatic acidity.

● Barolo Brunate '06	**YY**	7
● Barolo La Serra '06	**YY**	7
● Barbera d'Alba Ciabot Camerano '08	**YY**	4*
● Dolcetto d'Alba Boschi di Berri '09	**YY**	4
● Langhe Nebbiolo Lasarin '09	**YY**	4*
● Dolcetto d'Alba Fontanazza '09	**Y**	4
○ Moscato d'Asti '09	**Y**	4
● Barolo Brunate '05	YYY	7
● Barolo Brunate '03	YYY	8
● Barolo Brunate '01	YYY	7
● Barolo Brunate '99	YYY	7
● Barolo Brunate '96	YYY	7
● Barolo Brunate Ris. '85	YYY	7
● Dolcetto d'Alba Boschi di Berri '96	YYY	5

Marchesi di Barolo

VIA ROMA, 1
12060 BAROLO [CN]
TEL. 0173564400
www.marchesibarolo.com

CELLAR SALES
PRE-BOOKED VISITS
FOOD

ANNUAL PRODUCTION 1,500,000 bottles
HECTARES UNDER VINE 156
VITICULTURE METHOD Conventional

This historic estate, successful in both Piedmont and across Italy, is one of the best-known labels of Italian wine worldwide. Production covers all the main Langhe designations and the most important product is Barolo, in different versions. The stylistic profile is a nice of balance of classic and modern. Special mention goes to the intelligent prices of all the wines submitted.

The Barolo Sarmassa '06 repeated last year's success and again won Three Glasses. This elegant wine has a lovely, shimmering ruby, juicy fruit up front with spice and sweet tobacco close behind, and a classic note of tar at the back. The attack and body are powerful despite the fact the tannins are still a tad grainy. Right behind this, the Cannubi '06 stands out for finesse, complexity and a long finish. Here again a bit of roughness emerges in the tannins. Never betraying its terroir, the Coste di Rose '06 is subtler and less fat yet shows clear elegance. This year, the always excellent but slightly muted Vigneti di Proprietà '06 is sold exclusively in magnums.

● Barolo Sarmassa '06	8
● Barolo Cannubi '08	8
● Barolo Coste di Rose '06	7
● Barolo Vign. di Proprietà in Barolo '06	8
● Barbaresco Serragrilli '07	6
● Barbera d'Alba Paiagal '08	5
● Barolo Ris. '04	8
● Dolcetto d'Alba Madonna di Como '09	4*
● Nebbiolo d'Alba Michet '08	5
● Dolcetto d'Alba Boschetti '08	5
● Barolo Estate Vineyard '97	8
● Barolo Estate Vineyard '90	8
● Barolo Ris. Grande Annata '99	7
● Barolo Sarmassa '05	8
● Barolo Vign. di Proprietà in Barolo '98	8

Marchesi Incisa della Rocchetta

VIA ROMA, 66
14030 ROCCHETTA TANARO [AT]
TEL. 0141644647
www.lacortechiusa.it

CELLAR SALES
PRE-BOOKED VISITS
ROOMS AND FOOD

ANNUAL PRODUCTION 40,000 bottles
HECTARES UNDER VINE 27
VITICULTURE METHOD Conventional

This family with a long winemaking tradition has vineyards in the hills of the Rocchetta Tanaro zone and the area around the national park of the same name. Barbara Incisa della Rocchetta and her son Filiberto Massone manage the estate with input from oenologist Donato Lanati. Wines and varieties have expanded over the years and today the stock includes find barbera, pinot nero, merlot, grignolino and arneis.

Overall production is convincing from Marchesi Incisa della Rocchetta, particularly the Barbera d'Asti Superiore Sant'Emiliano '07. The highly complex bouquet shows sensations of cherry, cinchona, tobacco and spice, and the austere, full palate has great character and length with no softness. The well-crafted Barbera d'Asti Valmorena '09 is stylish with notes of red berries and tobacco, great development and length. The Grignolino d'Asti '09 is spicy and a tad edgy but varietal and full-bodied. Monferrato Chiaretto Futurosa '09, a 65-35 blend of barbera and pinot nero is intense and fruity, but almost tannic, with no concessions to sweetness.

● Barbera d'Asti Sup. Sant'Emiliano '07	5
● Barbera d'Asti Valmorena '09	4
● Grignolino d'Asti '09	4
⊙ M.to Chiaretto Futurosa '09	3*
● Barbera d'Asti Sup. Sant'Emiliano '06	5
● Barbera d'Asti Sup. Sant'Emiliano '05	5
● Barbera d'Asti Sup. Sant'Emiliano '04	5
● Barbera d'Asti Sup. Sant'Emiliano '03	5

Marenco

P.ZZA VITTORIO EMANUELE, 10
15019 STREVI [AL]
TEL. 0144363133
www.marencovini.com

CELLAR SALES
PRE-BOOKED VISITS

ANNUAL PRODUCTION 300,000 bottles
HECTARES UNDER VINE 80
VITICULTURE METHOD Conventional

Strevi is located on the left bank of the River Bormida, around six kilometres from Acqui Terme. This terroir is especially suited for viticulture in the average altitude of the hills, the aspects and the centuries-old winemaking experience of families like the Marencos.

The new versions of Albarossa Red Sunrise and Barbera d'Asti Superiore Ciresa are missing this year but will be reviewed in future editions of the Guide. Outstanding wines include the aromatic Pineto '09, a standard-cork Brachetto with dried flower and rose petal aromas then nice balance of residual sugar and acidity. The dried-grape Passrì Pineto Brachetto Passito has a rich, intense nose and good length on the palate. The intense ruby red Marchesa Dolcetto d'Acqui '09 has jammy notes on the nose and tannins that are husky in the finish. The Carialoso is a harmonic, pleasant-drinking, white table wine. The Moscato d'Asti Strevi is aromatic and intense.

Wine	Glasses	Price
● Brachetto d'Acqui Pineto '09	2 (black)	5
○ Carialoso	1 (black)	4
● Dolcetto d'Acqui Marchesa '09	1 (black)	4
○ Moscato d'Asti Strevi '09	1 (black)	4
● Passrì Pineto	1 (black)	6
● Barbera d'Asti Sup. Ciresa '06	2 (white)	6
● Brachetto d'Acqui Pineto '07	2 (white)	4
● Dolcetto d'Acqui Marchesa '08	2 (white)	4*
● Dolcetto d'Acqui Marchesa '07	2 (white)	4
● M.to Albarossa Red Sunrise '07	2 (white)	5
○ Moscato d'Asti Scrapona '08	2 (white)	4
○ Moscato d'Asti Scrapona '07	2 (white)	4
○ Strevi Passrì di Scrapona '06	2 (white)	6

Mario Marengo

VIA XX SETTEMBRE, 34
12064 LA MORRA [CN]
TEL. 017350115
marengo1964@libero.it

CELLAR SALES
PRE-BOOKED VISITS

ANNUAL PRODUCTION 25,000 bottles
HECTARES UNDER VINE 4
VITICULTURE METHOD Conventional

The Marengo family has been making wine in La Morra for four generations since the estate was founded in 1899. Mario, father of the current owner Marco, was a small wine producer. The generational handover represented genuine change. What once could have been called a hobby has been transformed into a full-scale operation. Marco believes in his work and intervenes as little as possible in the cellar, never follows fashion and never uses clarification, filtration or cultured yeasts, even when the wine would permit them. He has also acquired rare skills with ageing barrels.

The Brunate selection gives us another splendid version. The '06 easily won Three Glasses. The nose and palate are exceptional in both complexity and elegance as tobacco, cinchona, liquorice and dried flowers unfurl their appeal. The Bricco Viole '06 is more close-knit and lacks the innate harmony of its big brother, but is still an utterly respectable Barolo, featuring austere tannins that tend to soften in the long finish. There was a nice showing from the Barbera d'Alba Pugnane '08. Its cherry, violet and incense tones are persuasive, the tannins vigorous and sweet tannins lend great drinkability.

Wine	Glasses	Price
● Barolo Brunate '06	3 (black)	7
● Barbera d'Alba Pugnane '08	2 (black)	4*
● Barolo Bricco Viole '06	2 (black)	7
● Dolcetto d'Alba '09	2 (black)	4*
● Nebbiolo d'Alba Valmaggiore '08	2 (black)	4
● Barolo Brunate '05	3 (white)	7
● Barolo Brunate '04	3 (white)	7
● Barbera d'Alba Pugnane '07	2 (white)	4*
● Barolo Bricco Viole '05	2 (white)	7
● Barolo Bricco Viole '04	2 (white)	7
● Dolcetto d'Alba '08	2 (white)	4
● Dolcetto d'Alba '07	2 (white)	4*
● Nebbiolo d'Alba Valmaggiore '07	2 (white)	4*
● Nebbiolo d'Alba Valmaggiore '06	2 (white)	4*

Claudio Mariotto

S.da per Sarezzano, 29
15057 Tortona [AL]
tel. 0131868500
www.claudiomariotto.it

CELLAR SALES
PRE-BOOKED VISITS

ANNUAL PRODUCTION 100,000 bottles
HECTARES UNDER VINE 32
VITICULTURE METHOD Conventional

This major operation has made significant contributions to the visibility of Tortona with a wealth of sound labels. Year after year, Claudio Mariotto convinces consumers thanks to the growing definition he gives even his simplest wines, not to mention the complexity and character of his top bottles, especially Timorasso and Barbera, the standard-bearers of this much-appreciated territory.

This magisterial version of Timorasso Pitasso '08 is an intense straw yellow. The nose offers white-fleshed fruits over minerals and the richness and depth on the palate highlight an aristocratic finish with rare length. Three deliciously drinkable Glasses. Introduced by a floral bouquet, showing citrus aromas and mineral notes, the '08 Derthona is a balanced, harmonious Timorasso with an intense finish. Vho is an intriguing Barbera '08 and an impeccable example of the wine type. The well-typed, intense Braghè '09, from freisa, is better than sound. We close this range with a serious Montemirano '08 from croatina.

○ Colli Tortonesi Timorasso Pitasso '08	▼▼▼	6
● Colli Tortonesi Rosso Vho '08	▼▼	5
○ Colli Tortonesi Timorasso Derthona '08	▼▼	5
● Colli Tortonesi Rosso Braghè '09	▼▼	4
● Colli Tortonesi Rosso Montemirano '08	▼▼	6
○ Colli Tortonesi Bianco Pitasso '06	▽▽▽	6
○ Colli Tortonesi Bianco Pitasso '05	▽▽▽	5
○ Colli Tortonesi Bianco Pitasso '04	▽▽▽	5
○ Colli Tortonesi Bianco Derthona '06	▽▽	5
○ Colli Tortonesi Bianco Derthona '05	▽▽	5
● Colli Tortonesi Rosso Poggio del Rosso '04	▽▽	6
● Colli Tortonesi Rosso Vho '06	▽▽	5
○ Colli Tortonesi Timorasso Derthona '07	▽▽	5
○ Colli Tortonesi Timorasso Pitasso '07	▽▽	6

★ Franco M. Martinetti

via San Francesco da Paola, 18
10123 Torino
tel. 0118395937
www.francomartinetti.it

PRE-BOOKED VISITS

ANNUAL PRODUCTION 150,000 bottles
HECTARES UNDER VINE 4
VITICULTURE METHOD Conventional

Franco Martinetti looks for elegance, balance and expression when he designs a new wine. The labels produced today represent a broad range of designations and all are impeccably crafted. A tireless ambassador for himself and his winemaking decisions, Franco surrounds himself with skilled producers who guarantee rigorous selection from all the contributing estates.

The top wines, Gavi Minaia '09, Barolo Marasco '06 and Barbera d'Asti Montruc '08, again just missed Three Glasses. The Gavi Minaia shows stylish, elegant aromas and a complete structure with a long finish but the oak is still there on nose and palate. We'll be back in a year. The Barolo is rather reticent on the nose, with still slightly simple fruit, and tight on the palate, though lovely structure shows through. The Barbera Montruc lacks the full-body of the best vintages but still satisfies with an approachably fresh nose and palate. The all-timorasso Martin and the chardonnay and pinot nero Metodo Classico Quarantatre have lost some richness, gaining finesse and drinkability.

● Barbera d'Asti Sup. Montruc '08	▼▼	6
● Barolo Marasco '06	▼▼	8
○ Gavi Minaia '09	▼▼	6
○ Colli Tortonesi Bianco Martin '08	▼▼	7
○ Colli Tortonesi Derthona Timorasso Biancofranco '09	▼▼	7
○ Gavi del Comune di Gavi '09	▼▼	5
● M.to Rosso Sul Bric '08	▼▼	7
○ Quarantatre Brut '05	▼▼	6
● Barbera d'Asti Bric dei Banditi '09	▼	4
● Colli Tortonesi Rosso Georgette '08	▼	6
● Colli Tortonesi Rosso Lauren '08	▼	6
● Barbera d'Asti Sup. Montruc '06	▽▽▽	6
● Barbera d'Asti Sup. Montruc '01	▽▽▽	6
● Barolo Marasco '01	▽▽▽	8
● Barolo Marasco '00	▽▽▽	8
● M.to Rosso Sul Bric '00	▽▽▽	6

Bartolo Mascarello

VIA ROMA, 15
12060 BAROLO [CN]
TEL. 017356125

CELLAR SALES
PRE-BOOKED VISITS

ANNUAL PRODUCTION 30,000 bottles
HECTARES UNDER VINE 5
VITICULTURE METHOD Conventional

It is difficult to find anything new to say about this historic winery in the town centre of Barolo. Descriptions tend to go along the lines of tradition and respect for the original terroir. After some hesitation, following the disappearance of the unforgettable Bartolo, wines from the latest vintage are highly convincing, adding a new verve to the great texture we have observed over the years.

The refined, complex Barolo '06 gives tobacco accompanying a light but clear touch of raspberry. The excellent palate is well structured yet not excessive, the tannins upfront but delicate. The finish is lingering, pure and wonderfully integrated. This great Barolo, already completely enjoyable now, shows more elegance compared to previous vintages, achieved mainly thanks to greater poise in the very ripe, balanced tannins. Production of other classic wines from this area is limited but those with the good luck to find them will taste some excellent examples of the classic Dolcetto, Barbera and Freisa.

● Barolo '06	▼▼▼+	8
● Barolo '05	▽▽▽	8
● Barolo '01	▽▽▽	8
● Barolo '99	▽▽▽	8
● Barolo '98	▽▽▽	8
● Barolo '89	▽▽▽	8
● Barolo '83	▽▽▽	8
● Barbera d'Alba '07	▽▽	5
● Barbera d'Alba Vign. S. Lorenzo '06	▽▽	5
● Barolo '04	▽▽	8
● Langhe Freisa '07	▽▽	5
● Langhe Freisa '06	▽▽	4

Giuseppe Mascarello e Figlio

VIA BORGONUOVO, 108
12060 MONCHIERO [CN]
TEL. 0173792126
www.mascarello1881.com

CELLAR SALES
PRE-BOOKED VISITS

ANNUAL PRODUCTION 50,000 bottles
HECTARES UNDER VINE 17
VITICULTURE METHOD Conventional

Fashions and trends never affect the style of wines from Mauro and Giuseppe Mascarello, the latest generations at an estate that has embodied Langhe tradition since the late 19th century, not just Barolo, but also Barbera, Dolcetto, and Freisa from long macerations and ageing in large barrels. Apparently subtle, rarefied right from the colour and at times surprising in their aromatics, they travel through time as few other wines, frequently offering unforgettable experiences to wine lovers with patient.

Once again, we must rely on the wine's ability to unfold completely over time because we found Mauro Mascarello's Barolo rather difficult to decode. Both the Monprivato and the Santo Stefano di Perno '05 have no trouble showing their usual firmness but some blurred elements on the nose and a tad too much tannic huskiness make them over-cautious for now. The same goes for the Ca' 'd Morissio Riserva '03, a selection from the michet clone in the Monprivato vineyard. Though a lovely interpretation of the vintage, the sweet attack contrasts with the edgy finish. The Barbera d'Alba Scudetto '05 is a big success.

● Barbera d'Alba Sup. Scudetto '05	▼▼	6
● Barolo Monprivato '05	▼▼	8
● Barolo Monprivato Cà d' Morissio Ris. '03	▼▼	8
● Barolo S. Stefano di Perno '05	▼▼	8
● Barbera d'Alba Sup. Codana '06	▼▼	7
● Barbera d'Alba Sup. S. Stefano di Perno '06	▼▼	6
● Dolcetto d'Alba Bricco '08	▼▼	4
● Dolcetto d'Alba S. Stefano di Perno '08	▼▼	4*
● Langhe Nebbiolo '07	▼▼	6
● Barolo Monprivato '01	▽▽▽	8
● Barolo Monprivato '85	▽▽▽	8
● Barolo S. Stefano di Perno '98	▽▽▽	8
● Barolo Villero '96	▽▽▽	8
● Barolo Monprivato Ca' d' Morissio '01	▽▽	6
● Barolo S. Stefano di Perno '04	▽▽	8

Tenuta La Meridiana

via Tana Bassa, 5
14048 Montegrosso d'Asti [AT]
tel. 0141956172
www.tenutalameridiana.com

CELLAR SALES
PRE-BOOKED VISITS

ANNUAL PRODUCTION **90,000 bottles**
HECTARES UNDER VINE **11**
VITICULTURE METHOD **Organic**

The Bianco family still manages this historic estate founded over a century ago. Vineyards enjoy good south-east to south-west exposure and stand in soils of marl with layers of tufa and clay. Tenuta La Meridiana grows several international varieties, including a small vineyard of malaga, but the strong point of production is barbera, aged traditionally in large ovals as well as in modern versions with time in barriques.

Good wines include the Barbera d'Asti Superiore Nizza Tra la Terra e il Cielo '07 with aromas running from black cherry to cloves and a palate that is powerful yet well supported by acidity, and the Barbera d'Asti Vitis '08 with cinchona, tobacco and rain-soaked earth, and a full, savoury palate with a long, cherry-like finish. Finally, a mention goes to La Malaga, a sweet wine from malaga only, with aromas of wild strawberries and flowers.

● Barbera d'Asti Sup. Nizza Tra La Terra e Il Cielo '07	▼▼	5
● Barbera d'Asti Vitis '08	▼▼	3*
● La Malaga '09	▼▼	4
● Barbera d'Asti Le Gagie '08	▼	4
● Barbera d'Asti Sup. Nizza Tra La Terra e Il Cielo '05	▽▽	5
● Barbera d'Asti Sup. Nizza Tra La Terra e Il Cielo '04	▽▽	5
● Barbera d'Asti Sup. Nizza Tra La Terra e Il Cielo '03	▽▽	5

Noceto Michelotti

s.da Bogliona, 15/17
14040 Castel Boglione [AT]
tel. 0141762170
www.nocetomichelotti.com

CELLAR SALES
PRE-BOOKED VISITS

ANNUAL PRODUCTION **120,000 bottles**
HECTARES UNDER VINE **32**
VITICULTURE METHOD **Conventional**

Estate owners Graham Kresfelder and Margret Schratt pay great attention to the vineyards as well as the cellar at their modern operation in upper Monferrato, a sort of natural amphitheatre of sand and limestone soils, with substantial lime and clay, where vines have a south and south-west exposure. The most important variety is naturally barbera, but many other vines are also grown here.

Nizza has now become the leading wine from Noceto Michelotti. The Barbera d'Asti Superiore Nizza Montecanta '07 wins a place in our finals for the second year running thanks to a rich bouquet with wafts of black cherry, cocoa powder and sweet spice, and a long, broad palate that is complex and caressing, yet still flaunts acidity and character. Also convincing is the Barbera d'Asti Superiore Montecanta '07, which shows fresh, pepper-led spice aromas and a varietal palate with vibrant acidity that supports the long, fruity finish. The rest of the range is well made.

● Barbera d'Asti Sup. Nizza Montecanta '07	▼▼	5
● Barbera d'Asti Sup. Montecanta '07	▼▼	5
● Barbera d'Asti Strada del Sole '07	▼	4
● M.to Rosso Montecanta '07	▼	4
● M.to Rosso Strada del Sole '08	▼	4
● Monferrato Rosso '07	▼	4
○ Piemonte Chardonnay Montecanta '08	▼	4
● Barbera d'Asti '05	▽▽	4*
● Barbera d'Asti Sup. Montecanta '05	▽▽	5
● Barbera d'Asti Sup. Nizza Montecanta '06	▽▽	5

Moccagatta

S.DA RABAJÀ, 46
12050 BARBARESCO [CN]
TEL. 0173635228

CELLAR SALES
PRE-BOOKED VISITS

ANNUAL PRODUCTION 60,000 bottles
HECTARES UNDER VINE 12
VITICULTURE METHOD Conventional

The winery of brothers Franco and Sergio Minuto is a beacon for Barbaresco aficionados. Care in the vineyards and meticulous use of oak for fermentation bring out all the potential from around 12 hectares on their property. The style of these wines sometimes can seem extreme but greater varietal definition comes with time in bottle.

Moccagatta Barbarescos have a modern style with rich personalities and oak-veined aromatics. The most successful is the '07 Barbaresco Bric Balin thanks to elegant aromatics and serious structure but the tannins are still slightly drying. The Barbaresco Basarin '07 lacks that power but is already more balanced, harmonic and easy drinking. Powerful brushes of oak on the nose of the Barbaresco Cole '07 accompany forward notes and aromatics veined with dried herbs while the tannins on the palate are not yet completely balanced. Of the two Chardonnays, at the moment we prefer the freshness of the '09 to the opulence of the Buschet '08.

● Barbaresco Bric Balin '07	ΨΨ (black)	7
● Barbaresco Basarin '07	ΨΨ (black)	7
● Barbaresco Cole '07	ΨΨ (black)	7
○ Langhe Chardonnay '09	ΨΨ (black)	4
○ Langhe Chardonnay Buschet '08	Ψ (black)	6
● Barbaresco Bric Balin '05	ΨΨΨ	7
● Barbaresco Bric Balin '04	ΨΨΨ	7
● Barbaresco Bric Balin '01	ΨΨΨ	8
● Barbaresco Cole '97	ΨΨΨ	8
● Barbaresco Basarin '06	ΨΨ	7
● Barbaresco Basarin '05	ΨΨ	7
● Barbaresco Bric Balin '06	ΨΨ	7
● Barbaresco Cole '06	ΨΨ	7
● Barbaresco Cole '05	ΨΨ	7
● Barbaresco Cole '04	ΨΨ	7

Mauro Molino

FRAZ. ANNUNZIATA
B.TA GANCIA, 111
12064 LA MORRA [CN]
TEL. 017350814
www.mauromolino.com

CELLAR SALES
PRE-BOOKED VISITS

ANNUAL PRODUCTION 50,000 bottles
HECTARES UNDER VINE 10
VITICULTURE METHOD Conventional

The new generation of Molinos continues the family dedication to quality and the local terroir. This estate has many plots of Barolo, small holdings in major vineyards with different features and nuances, producing a range of wines each with a precise personality in a modern stylistic idiom. In the cellar, barriques of various ages are used as well as less usual large French oak barrels.

This year the spotlight shines on the two Barolos, the Gallinotto and the Vigna Conca from the good '06 harvest. The first is very elegant, though marked by powerful toast and dried herbs on the nose, the caressing palate foregrounding alcohol and tannins. Vigna Conca is bigger with intense sweet sensations of oak and ripe red berries followed by a long finish that is not drying. The Barolo Gancia may not be that intense on pouring but it opens up with decent fruit. Nonetheless, the palate is drier and more clenched in the finish. The ever imposing Barbera d'Alba Vigna Gattera was not bottled because of the difficult '08 growing season.

● Barolo V. Conca '06	ΨΨ (black)	8
● Barolo V. Gallinotto '06	ΨΨ (black)	7
● Barbera d'Alba '09	ΨΨ (black)	4
● Barolo '06	ΨΨ (black)	6
● Barolo V. Gancia '06	ΨΨ (black)	8
● Langhe Nebbiolo '09	ΨΨ (black)	4
● Dolcetto d'Alba '09	Ψ (black)	4
● Barbera d'Alba V. Gattere '00	ΨΨΨ	6
● Barbera d'Alba V. Gattere '97	ΨΨΨ	6
● Barolo V. Conca '00	ΨΨΨ	8
● Barolo V. Conca '97	ΨΨΨ	8
● Barolo V. Conca '96	ΨΨΨ	8
● Barolo V. Gallinotto '01	ΨΨΨ	8
● Barbera d'Alba V. Gattere '07	ΨΨ	6
● Barolo Rocche dell'Annunziata '05	ΨΨ	8
● Barolo V. Gancia '05	ΨΨ	8

Monchiero Carbone

via Santo Stefano Roero, 2
12043 Canale [CN]
tel. 017395568
www.monchierocarbone.com

CELLAR SALES
PRE-BOOKED VISITS

ANNUAL PRODUCTION 150,000 bottles
HECTARES UNDER VINE 18
VITICULTURE METHOD Organic

Francesco Monchiero is the driving force behind this successful winery founded in the 1990s by his parents Marco Monchiero and Lucetta Carbone. Today the estate has holdings in the municipalities of Canale, Vezza d'Alba and Priocca, and in some of the best vineyards in the area. On the hill of Frailin, planted to nebbiolo, the cellar sources the estate showcase Roero Printi and Monbirone, where they plant barbera, and Renesio, where arneis fills the rows. Focus is almost exclusively on Roero varieties.

The Roero Printi Riserva won Three Glasses and proved one of the best wines in the designation, a benchmark of style for Roero. The '07 vintage show intense and complex with an elegant bouquet of raspberry, tobacco, spice and balsamic aromas before the fruit-forward, consistent palate has great tannic density and a long finish well supported by acidity. Also in the finals was the citrus and mineral Roero Arneis Cecu d'la Biunda '09 with notes of white-fleshed fruits and a rich, long palate. The Roero Srü '08 shows spice and black olive tapenade with a clean, fresh palate and good structure. The other labels are well made.

● Roero Printi Ris. '07	▼▼▼	6
○ Roero Arneis Cecu d'la Biunda '09	▼▼	4
● Roero Srü '08	▼▼	5
● Barbera d'Alba MonBirone '08	▼▼	5
○ Roero Arneis Re cit '09	▼▼	4
○ Langhe Bianco Tamardì '09	▼	4
○ Langhe Favorita '09	▼	4
● Langhe Nebbiolo Regret '08	▼	4
● Roero Printi '04	▽▽▽	6
● Roero Printi '00	▽▽▽	6
● Roero Printi '99	▽▽▽	7
● Roero Printi Ris. '06	▽▽▽	6
● Roero Srü '06	▽▽▽	5

Monfalletto Cordero di Montezemolo

fraz. Annunziata, 67
12064 La Morra [CN]
tel. 017350344
www.corderodimontezemolo.com

CELLAR SALES
PRE-BOOKED VISITS

ANNUAL PRODUCTION 220,000 bottles
HECTARES UNDER VINE 35
VITICULTURE METHOD Organic

This major Piedmont estate, perhaps even more famous abroad than in Italy, is part of the history of great Langhe wines. With around 35 hectares, it is among the largest, most complete operations in the area. Barolo is king. Several versions are proposed in a well-tried style that aims for an intelligent balance of tradition and modernity.

From the famous Villero vineyard at Castiglione Falletto, the layered Barolo Enrico VI '06 is still unforthcoming. The palate has powerful tannins, a long finale and good structure but not yet enough complexity. The austere Barolo Monfalletto '06 has assertive tannins and an alcoholic finish. Bricco Gattera '06 is already evolving. Nice liqueur fruits and light oak precede a less structured palate that is almost too soft for its age. Barbera Funtanì '07 has opulent fruit and good freshness while the '08 barrique-aged Chardonnay Elioro gives tropical fruit and a caressing palate. The other wines are sound but Barolo is the focus here.

● Barbera d'Alba Sup. Funtanì '07	▼▼	6
● Barolo Enrico VI '06	▼▼	8
● Barolo Monfalletto '06	▼▼	7
● Barolo V. Bricco Gattera '06	▼▼	8
○ Langhe Chardonnay Elioro '08	▼▼	5
○ Brut Montezemolo	▼	6
● Dolcetto d'Alba '09	▼	4
○ Langhe Arneis '09	▼	4
● Langhe Nebbiolo '09	▼	5
● Barolo Enrico VI '04	▽▽▽	8
● Barolo Enrico VI '03	▽▽▽	8
● Barolo V. Bricco Gattera '99	▽▽▽	8
● Barolo V. Enrico VI '00	▽▽▽	8
● Barolo V. Enrico VI '97	▽▽▽	8
● Barolo V. Bricco Gattera '05	▽▽	8

Montaribaldi

FRAZ. TRE STELLE
S.DA NICOLINI ALTO, 12
12050 BARBARESCO [CN]
TEL. 0173638220
www.montaribaldi.com

CELLAR SALES
PRE-BOOKED VISITS

ANNUAL PRODUCTION 70,000 bottles
HECTARES UNDER VINE 21
VITICULTURE METHOD Conventional

The Taliano family manages this large estate at Barbaresco. The broad range of wines includes all the main Langhe designations stops in Asti and Roero. The lion's share is Barbaresco but the other wines are also good. We also salute the reasonable prices.

Raspberry on the agreeable Barbaresco Palazzina '07 ushers in an austere, long palate. The Barbaresco Sörì Montaribaldi '07 gives stylish spice and tobacco upfront then a still aggressively tannic palate. The harmonic, fruity Barbera d'Alba Frere '09, the muscular Dolcetto Vagnona '09, the complex, fruity Langhe Nicolini '09 from equal parts of nebbiolo, barbera and dolcetto and the Langhe Nebbiolo Gambarin '08 are sound. Barbera Frere '09 is already balanced and drinkable. The unlucky vintage holds back the woody Barbera dü Gir '08 but the rich '09 harvest yielded a full, buttery Chardonnay Stissa d'le Favole '09.

●	Barbaresco Palazzina '07	ΨΨ (black)	5*
●	Barbaresco Ricü '05	ΨΨ (black)	7
●	Barbaresco Sörì Montaribaldi '07	ΨΨ (black)	6
●	Barbera d'Alba dü Gir '08	ΨΨ (black)	4
●	Barbera d'Alba Frere '09	ΨΨ (black)	3*
●	Dolcetto d'Alba Vagnona '09	ΨΨ (black)	3*
●	Langhe Nebbiolo Gambarin '08	ΨΨ (black)	4
●	Langhe Rosso Nicolini '09	ΨΨ (black)	4
●	Barbera d'Asti La Consolina '09	Ψ (black)	3
○	Langhe Chardonnay Stissa d'le Favole '09	Ψ (black)	3
○	Roero Arneis Capural '09	Ψ (black)	4
●	Barbaresco Ricü '04	ΨΨ (white)	7
●	Barbaresco Sörì Montaribaldi '04	ΨΨ (white)	6
●	Barbera d'Alba dü Gir '07	ΨΨ (white)	5
●	Barbera d'Alba dü Gir '06	ΨΨ (white)	5

Monti

LOC. SAN SEBASTIANO
FRAZ. CAMIE, 39
12065 MONFORTE D'ALBA [CN]
TEL. 017378391
www.paolomonti.com

CELLAR SALES
PRE-BOOKED VISITS

ANNUAL PRODUCTION 50,000 bottles
HECTARES UNDER VINE 11
VITICULTURE METHOD Organic

Pier Paolo Monti's estate started out in the late 1990s, riding the tide of interest in Langhe wines. But the value of the land and people also shone through and quality proved in easy reach. The finest of the estate's vineyards, Bussia Sottana, is hardly a discovery. Pier Paolo restricts himself to coaxing out the fruit with aromatic clarity and personality on the palate.

When we find a wine of absolute quality produced from native varieties, we are certainly not afraid to mention it. In this round of tastings, the most successful wine from Monti was the Langhe Dossi Rossi '07 from 40-40-20 cabernet, merlot and nebbiolo, all wrapped in a nice, bright ruby red. The nose gives intense, refined pipe tobacco and currants but the palate impressed even more, as happens frequently in these wines. The initial explosion is followed by a pause, then thrusting progression leads into a long, well-orchestrated finish.

●	Barbera d'Alba '07	ΨΨ (black)	6
●	Langhe Dossi Rossi '07	ΨΨ (black)	6
●	Barolo '06	ΨΨ (black)	8
●	Barolo Bussia '06	ΨΨ (black)	8
○	Langhe Bianco L'Aura '08	ΨΨ (black)	5
●	Nebbiolo d'Alba '07	ΨΨ (black)	5
●	Barbera d'Alba '06	ΨΨ (white)	6
●	Barolo '05	ΨΨ (white)	8
●	Barolo '04	ΨΨ (white)	7
●	Barolo Bussia '05	ΨΨ (white)	8
●	Barolo Bussia '04	ΨΨ (white)	8
○	Langhe Bianco L'Aura '07	ΨΨ (white)	5
●	Langhe Rosso Dossi Rossi '04	ΨΨ (white)	6
●	Nebbiolo d'Alba '06	ΨΨ (white)	5

Cascina Morassino

S.DA BERNINO, 10
12050 BARBARESCO [CN]
TEL. 0173635149

CELLAR SALES
PRE-BOOKED VISITS

ANNUAL PRODUCTION 20,000 bottles
HECTARES UNDER VINE 4
VITICULTURE METHOD Conventional

"A talent for longevity" might be the ideal motto for this family estate with great potential. The range reflects Langhe in the depth and rich expression of features shared by all the territory's wines. Ovello and Morassino are the two outstanding vineyard selections from the Bianco family estate, now firmly in the hands of the talented Roberto. Estate style aims for elegance, keeping oak from medium to large casks firmly under control.

That magnificent vineyard facing the hill of Albesani produces the Barbaresco Ovello '07 with a rich nose of spice and red fruit. The robust palate is almost massive and pleasantly tannic right up to the long finish in a version worthy of this famous vineyard. Morassino is a vineyard bordering Ovello and facing Neive and '07 Barbaresco shows traditional fruit, moderate structure and a tad more subtlety than its big brother. It has the advantage of being enjoyable now, though it lacks those evolved notes of a great Nebbiolo.

● Barbaresco Ovello '07	two black glasses	7
● Barbaresco Morassino '07	two black glasses	7
● Barbera d'Alba Vignot '08	two black glasses	5
● Dolcetto d'Alba '09	two black glasses	4
● Langhe Nebbiolo '08	two black glasses	5
● Langhe Rosso '08	two black glasses	5
● Barbaresco Morassino '06	two white glasses	7
● Barbaresco Morassino '05	two white glasses	7
● Barbaresco Ovello '06	two white glasses	7
● Barbaresco Ovello '05	two white glasses	7
● Barbaresco Ovello '04	two white glasses	7
● Barbaresco Ovello '03	two white glasses	7
● Barbera d'Alba Vignot '07	two white glasses	5*
● Dolcetto d'Alba '08	two white glasses	4

Stefanino Morra

VIA CASTAGNITO, 50
12050 CASTELLINALDO [CN]
TEL. 0173213489
www.morravini.it

CELLAR SALES
PRE-BOOKED VISITS

ANNUAL PRODUCTION 65,000 bottles
HECTARES UNDER VINE 10
VITICULTURE METHOD Conventional

Stefanino Morra's vineyards are in Vezza d'Alba, Castellinaldo and Canale. His wines are the result of scrupulous labour in the vineyards as well as the cellar, where his parents, his wife Edda and brother-in-law Gianni all help. The classic Roero arneis, barbera and nebbiolo dominate production and create a series of characterful wines with a personal style.

Morra confirms his wines' quality. In particular, his '07 Roero went into the finals. This deep, complex wine serves up tobacco, raspberry and dried flowers, a palate rich in fruit, well-knit if slightly tough tannins and a long, fresh, bright finish. The interesting Barbera d'Alba Castlè '07 gives cinchona, spice and black cherry followed by light, blood-rich hints and a fresher, juicier palate. The slightly husky Barbera d'Alba Castellinaldo '07 still has nice fruity pulp and rich acidity in support of the structure and the austere Roero Srai Riserva '06 is nicely paced with notes of dried figs, raspberry and incense.

● Roero '07	two black glasses	5
● Barbera d'Alba Castellinaldo '07	two black glasses	5
● Barbera d'Alba Castlè '07	two black glasses	6
● Roero Srai Ris. '06	two black glasses	6
○ Roero Arneis Vign. S. Pietro '08	one black glass	5
● Barbera d'Alba Castlè '06	two white glasses	5
● Castellinaldo Barbera d'Alba '03	two white glasses	5*
● Roero '06	two white glasses	5
● Roero Srai '04	two white glasses	6
● Roero Srai '03	two white glasses	6
● Roero Sup. '03	two white glasses	4*

F.lli Mossio

FRAZ. CASCINA CARAMELLI
VIA MONTÀ, 12
12050 RODELLO [CN]
TEL. 0173617149
www.mossio.com

CELLAR SALES
PRE-BOOKED VISITS

ANNUAL PRODUCTION 50,000 bottles
HECTARES UNDER VINE 10
VITICULTURE METHOD Conventional

This interesting, family-run estate in the scenic town of Rodello, just by Alba, makes straightforward, moreish wines that brim with rustic authenticity and reflect their local terroir. A major producer of quality Dolcetto, Mossio has managed to carve a niche for itself, showing reliability and consistency thanks to serious work in the vineyards and methodical care in the cellar.

Convincingly consistent quality was obvious in all the labels tasted. As on other occasions, the Dolcetto was outstandingly well made and achieved excellence in the dense, impenetrable Bricco Caramelli '09. The nose unveils deep vinous notes and ripe fruit then expands into a progression that is powerful yet not tiring. Only a bit less complex is the '09 Piano delli Perdoni with its blackberries, still slightly rough tannins and good length on the finish. Outstanding among the other wines was the robustly structured Barbera '07, nicely set off by its refreshing acidity.

● Dolcetto d'Alba Bricco Caramelli '09	2 glasses (black)	4*
● Barbera d'Alba '07	2 glasses (black)	5
● Dolcetto d'Alba Piano delli Perdoni '09	2 glasses (black)	4*
● Nebbiolo d'Alba '06	2 glasses (black)	5
● Langhe Rosso '07	1 glass (black)	5
● Dolcetto d'Alba Bricco Caramelli '00	3 glasses (white)	4
● Barbera d'Alba '06	2 glasses (white)	5
● Dolcetto d'Alba Bricco Caramelli '08	2 glasses (white)	4
● Dolcetto d'Alba Bricco Caramelli '07	2 glasses (white)	4
● Dolcetto d'Alba Bricco Caramelli '06	2 glasses (white)	4*
● Dolcetto d'Alba Piano delli Perdoni '08	2 glasses (white)	4*
● Dolcetto d'Alba Piano delli Perdoni '07	2 glasses (white)	4*
● Langhe Rosso '06	2 glasses (white)	5
● Langhe Rosso '05	2 glasses (white)	5

Mutti

LOC. SAN RUFFINO, 49
15050 SAREZZANO [AL]
TEL. 0131884119

ANNUAL PRODUCTION 55,000 bottles
HECTARES UNDER VINE 15
VITICULTURE METHOD Conventional

With degrees in agronomy and oenology, Andrea Mutti is a qualified estate manager. He was one of the pioneers in promoting this territory and its timorasso variety. Andrea strives for a personal style but with the greatest respect possible for the features of each specific terroir. During early phases, these wines may seem a bit introverted but with proper ageing, they reveal superb sensations when they are finally uncorked.

Deep straw yellow shading into gold heralds the fruit-led nose of the Timorasso Castagnoli '08, followed by a rich, long-lingering palate. The standard-label Barbera BoscoBarona has distinct varietal tones and a supple palate that toughens up a tad in the finish. From a sauvignon blanc base, the Colli Tortonesi Bianco Sull'Aia '09 is as distinctive in its aromatics as it is on the palate yet overall seem slightly weighed down by rather listless acidity.

● Colli Tortonesi Rosso Boscobarona '09	2 glasses (black)	3
○ Colli Tortonesi Timorasso Derthona Castagnoli '08	2 glasses (black)	5
○ Colli Tortonesi Bianco Sull'Aia '09	1 glass (black)	4
○ Colli Tortonesi Bianco Castagnoli '06	2 glasses (white)	5
○ Colli Tortonesi Bianco Castagnoli '05	2 glasses (white)	5
○ Colli Tortonesi Bianco Castagnoli '04	2 glasses (white)	5
○ Colli Tortonesi Bianco Castagnoli '03	2 glasses (white)	5
○ Colli Tortonesi Bianco Sull'Aia '08	2 glasses (white)	4
● Colli Tortonesi Rosso Rivadestra '05	2 glasses (white)	5
● Colli Tortonesi Rosso S. Ruffino '07	2 glasses (white)	5
● Colli Tortonesi Rosso S. Ruffino '04	2 glasses (white)	5
○ Colli Tortonesi Timorasso Derthona Castagnoli '07	2 glasses (white)	5

Ada Nada

LOC. ROMBONE
VIA AUSARIO, 12B
12050 TREISO [CN]
TEL. 0173638127
www.adanada.it

CELLAR SALES
PRE-BOOKED VISITS

ANNUAL PRODUCTION N.A.
HECTARES UNDER VINE N.A .
VITICULTURE METHOD Conventional

This interesting estate has around ten hectares under vine in the scenic town of Treiso and combines winemaking with a welcoming agriturismo. The various versions of Barbaresco reveal special attention to the sense of place of each wine and stylistic profiles show a desire to respect tradition. The price list offers good value for money.

With release of the Barbaresco postponed, we tasted a nice Valeirano '06 with fruit, leather and balsam. The caressing palate is warm yet fresh and has a frank, clean finish. Cichin '06 has the same complexity on the nose but favours classic liquorice and more austere tannins. A tad less elegant is the powerful Barbaresco Elisa '06 with aromas of dried herbs, rain-soaked earth and mushroom-like vegetality. The powerful, alcoholic palate has roughish tannins. A nice wine in spite of the difficult '08 harvest, the Barbera d'Alba Vigna'd Pierin gives fresh fruit and oak while the long, clean palate has none of excessive green notes the vintage has given other wines.

● Barbaresco Valeirano '06	▼▼	7
● Barbaresco Cichin '06	▼▼	7
● Barbaresco Elisa '06	▼▼	7
● Barbera d'Alba Vigna 'd Pierin '08	▼▼	4
● Langhe Nebbiolo Serena '09	▼▼	5
● Dolcetto d'Alba Autinot '09	▼	4
● Barbaresco Cichin '05	▽▽	7
● Barbaresco Elisa '04	▽▽	7
● Barbaresco Elisa '03	▽▽	7
● Barbaresco Valeirano '05	▽▽	7
● Barbera d'Alba V. 'd Pierin '06	▽▽	5
● Dolcetto d'Alba Autinot '07	▽▽	4
● Dolcetto d'Alba Autinot '06	▽▽	4

★ Fiorenzo Nada

LOC. ROMBONE
VIA AUSARIO, 12C
12050 TREISO [CN]
TEL. 0173638254
www.nada.it

CELLAR SALES
PRE-BOOKED VISITS

ANNUAL PRODUCTION 40,000 bottles
HECTARES UNDER VINE 7
VITICULTURE METHOD Conventional

Bruno Nada, with help from his son Danilo who has gradually settled into the operation, and vineyard supervision by his brilliant father Fiorenzo, manages this small but famous estate in the town of Treiso with energy and absolute precision. The stylistic profile of the wines shows recognizable character in the form of serious structure and elegance.

The stupendous Barbaresco Manzola '06 – the wine reviewed last year was actually from '05 – has a classic profile, in part from ageing in large barrels. Dried flowers, cinchona and red fruits usher in great structure and concentration in the mouth prevailing over temptations to finesse. We gave it Three elegant, refined Glasses. The Barbaresco Rombone '07 is taking a year off in barrel, along with the Seifile, so we'll be back next year. After this slow-down, Bruno will release his showcase selections with a year's more ageing from 2011. As ever, the other wines are pleasant and among the best in their respective categories.

● Barbaresco V. Manzola '06	▼▼▼	7
● Langhe Nebbiolo '08	▼▼	4*
● Barbera d'Alba '08	▼▼	5
● Dolcetto d'Alba '09	▼▼	4
● Barbaresco '01	▽▽▽	7
● Barbaresco Rombone '06	▽▽▽	8
● Barbaresco Rombone '05	▽▽▽	8
● Barbaresco Rombone '04	▽▽▽	8
● Barbaresco Rombone '99	▽▽▽	8
● Langhe Rosso Seifile '01	▽▽▽	8
● Seifile '93	▽▽▽	8
● Barbaresco V. Manzola '05	▽▽	7
● Langhe Rosso Seifile '06	▽▽	8

Cantina dei Produttori Nebbiolo di Carema

VIA NAZIONALE, 32
10010 CAREMA [TO]
TEL. 0125811160
www.saporipiemontesi.it

CELLAR SALES
PRE-BOOKED VISITS

ANNUAL PRODUCTION 65,000 bottles
HECTARES UNDER VINE 17
VITICULTURE METHOD Conventional

If Carema is a spiritual home for those searching out wines that shun the usual mellow, fruity style, it is thanks to operations such as Produttori Nebbiolo di Carema, which has kept alive a challenging, to put it mildly, tradition in less fortunate times. The co-operative has 79 members, who farm some 17 hectares of tiny pergola-trained plots carved out of the mountainsides. Label colours distinguish the wines: black for the standard Carema and white for the selection, both aged three years in large oak.

The Cantina will soon rise to the top step of the awards podium, since once again its Carema Etichetta Bianca misses by just a hair's breadth. The '06 momentarily perplexes with tertiary impressions of humus and roots but then beautiful fruit of rare purity and vibrancy makes its entrance. Utterly delicious in the mouth, it builds a fine progression of deceptive lightness and suppleness, while the alcohol pulls back a tad and slightly slows the finish. Carema Etichetta Nera '06 is fully its equal but nose and tannins are both closed for business at the moment, waiting for more relaxing times ahead.

● Carema Et. Bianca '06	2 black glasses	4*
● Carema Et. Nera '06	2 black glasses	4*
● Carema Et. Bianca '05	2 black glasses	4
● Carema '05	2 white glasses	4
● Carema '04	2 white glasses	4
● Carema Barricato '01	2 white glasses	5
● Carema Et. Bianca '98	2 white glasses	4*
● Carema Et. Bianca Barricato '97	2 white glasses	5
● Carema Et. Bianca Ris. '99	2 white glasses	4*
● Carema Et. Nera '01	2 white glasses	4*
● Carema Ris. '04	2 white glasses	4*
● Carema Ris. '02	2 white glasses	4
● Carema Ris. '01	2 white glasses	4

Angelo Negro & Figli

FRAZ. SANT'ANNA, 1
12040 MONTEU ROERO [CN]
TEL. 017390252
www.negroangelo.it

CELLAR SALES
PRE-BOOKED VISITS

ANNUAL PRODUCTION 250,000 bottles
HECTARES UNDER VINE 60
VITICULTURE METHOD Conventional

The Negro family runs one of Roero's leading estates. Dating back to the 17th century, Angelo Negro & Figli combines a varied line of wines with a remarkable level of quality. The entire family is involved in all phases of the operation, which grows only grapes traditional to the area. They focus on the classics of Roero but you can't ignore what they do with Barbaresco, sourced from vineyards in the commune of Neive.

Again this year, two wines reached our finals. Blossoms and plum introduce Roero Arneis Perdaudin '09, which progresses through a full body with nervy spine to a long, well-fruited conclusion. Tobacco leaf and black liquorice open Roero Sudisfà Riserva '07. Its notable length is marked by rich fruit and good body but the finish has slightly drying tannins. The remaining wines are all well crafted. Roero Arneis Serra Lupini '09 displays apricot and spring blossoms while Barbaresco Cascinotta '07 offers rich fruit and wild herbs and liquorice. The Arneis Giovanni Negro Extra Brut '06 is floral and tasty while Barbera d'Alba Superiore La Nanda '06 glories in cinchona and tobacco.

○ Roero Arneis Perdaudin '09	2 black glasses	4
● Roero Sudisfà Ris. '07	2 black glasses	6
● Barbaresco Cascinotta '07	2 black glasses	6
● Barbera d'Alba Sup. La Nanda '06	2 black glasses	4
○ Roero Arneis Giovanni Negro Extra Brut '06	2 black glasses	5
○ Roero Arneis Serra Lupini '09	2 black glasses	4
● Roero Prachiosso '07	1 black glass	5
● Roero Sudisfà '04	3 white glasses	6
● Roero Sudisfà '03	3 white glasses	6
● Barbaresco Basarin '06	2 white glasses	6
● Barbera d'Alba Bertu '06	2 white glasses	5
● Barbera d'Alba Bric Bertu '05	2 white glasses	5
● Barbera d'Alba Bric Bertu '04	2 white glasses	5
● Roero Sudisfà Ris. '06	2 white glasses	6
● Roero Sudisfà Ris. '05	2 white glasses	6

Andrea Oberto

B.TA SIMANE, 11
12064 LA MORRA [CN]
TEL. 017350104
obertoandrea@libero.it

CELLAR SALES
PRE-BOOKED VISITS

ANNUAL PRODUCTION 100,000 bottles
HECTARES UNDER VINE 16
VITICULTURE METHOD Conventional

The wines of Andrea and Fabio Oberto are always distinctive, particularly in their youth, for their sensory exuberance and extraordinary structure, along with their generous, clean-edged aromatics. This is all made possible by fruit that is treated with expertise and utter respect. The Barolo '06 selections are the winery's most sublime creations, deep, complex wines that reveal their full expressivity only after appropriate bottle ageing.

Barolo Vigneto Brunate '06 showcases the classic attributes of this cru with a few modern touches, such as generous fruit and notes of spice. In the mouth, it is seductive, smooth and refined. Barolo Vigneto Albarella '06 is just as tasty, but in a modern key, with smoky oak and a fairly accessible structure. Barolo Rocche '06 is pleasurable but still somewhat closed and hard-edged while the soundly made standard Barolo shows evolved and medium bodied. The quality of the 2007 vintage has delayed release of Barbera d'Alba Giada '07 and the other selections, too, are undergoing additional maturation. The Dolcetto and the standard Barbera are both fine and quaffable.

● Barolo Vign. Albarella '06	▼▼	8
● Barolo Vign. Brunate '06	▼▼	8
● Barolo '06	▼▼	7
● Barolo Vign. Rocche '06	▼▼	8
● Barbera d'Alba '09	▼	4
● Dolcetto d'Alba '09	▼	4
● Barbera d'Alba Giada '00	▽▽▽	6
● Barbera d'Alba Giada '97	▽▽▽	6
● Barbera d'Alba Giada '96	▽▽▽	6
● Barolo Vign. Albarella '01	▽▽▽	8
● Barolo Vign. Brunate '05	▽▽▽	8
● Barolo Vign. Rocche dell'Annunziata '96	▽▽▽	8
● Barolo '05	▽▽	7
● Barolo Vign. Albarella '05	▽▽	8
● Barolo Vign. Rocche dell'Annunziata '05	▽▽	8

Oddero Poderi e Cantine

FRAZ. SANTA MARIA
VIA TETTI, 28
12064 LA MORRA [CN]
TEL. 017350618
www.oddero.it

CELLAR SALES
PRE-BOOKED VISITS

ANNUAL PRODUCTION 110,000 bottles
HECTARES UNDER VINE 35
VITICULTURE METHOD Certified organic

With over 35 hectares of vineyards, just under half planted to nebbiolo for Barolo, Mariacristina and Mariavittoria Oddero's estate is one of the Langhe's most important, and not only for its numbers. Oddero's vineyard portfolio includes the likes of Villero and Rocche in Castiglione Falletto, Brunate in La Morra, Mondoca di Bussia Soprana in Monforte and Vigna Rionda in Serralunga, all world-class crus rendered in a dry, refined fashion, all well tempered in a sapient mix of small and large oak.

The diva did not reach the high note perhaps, but the chorus performed well. The '06 Barolos need a bit more time since, in contrast to their exuberant stuffing and promising veins of flavour and personality, the noses seemed to us somewhat compressed aromatically and the tannins muted. The most expressive is Barolo Rocche di Castiglione '06, but the standard Barolo is certainly no slouch either. Barolo Vigna Rionda Riserva '04 is up to snuff with its austerity and powerful tannicity but a combination of cinchona bark, brine and underbrush makes for a too-dark palette. The stylish, citrussy Moscato d'Asti Cascina Fiori '09 is one of the best of its kind.

● Barolo Rocche di Castiglione '06	▼▼	8
● Barolo V. Rionda Ris. '04	▼▼	8
○ Moscato d'Asti Cascina Fiori '09	▼▼	4*
● Barbaresco Gallina '07	▼▼	7
● Barolo '06	▼▼	6
● Barolo Villero '06	▼▼	7
● Dolcetto d'Alba '09	▼▼	4*
● Langhe Nebbiolo '08	▼▼	4
○ Langhe Chardonnay Collaretto '09	▼	4
● Barbaresco Gallina '04	▽▽▽	7
● Barolo Mondoca di Bussia Soprana '04	▽▽▽	8
● Barolo Mondoca di Bussia Soprana '97	▽▽▽	8
● Barolo V. Rionda '01	▽▽▽	8
● Barolo V. Rionda '00	▽▽▽	8
● Barolo V. Rionda '98	▽▽▽	8

Tenuta Olim Bauda

VIA PRATA, 50
14045 INCISA SCAPACCINO [AT]
TEL. 0141702171
www.tenutaolimbauda.it

CELLAR SALES
PRE-BOOKED VISITS

ANNUAL PRODUCTION 144,000 bottles
HECTARES UNDER VINE 30
VITICULTURE METHOD Conventional

Today, siblings Diana, Dino and Gianni Bertolino run the winery, which comprises various properties in different municipalities in the Asti area. The vineyards, on various soil types, are planted primarily to barbera and moscato but the internationals are present too, witness chardonnay. Most of the vineyards were planted between the 1950s and 1980s, and are farmed according to sustainable agriculture dictates, which limit use of chemicals and prohibit chemical weed killers.

Barbera d'Asti Superiore Nizza still shines, with the '07 again taking home the Three Glasses. Intense and complex, emanating fragrant cigar leaf, wild cherry, cinchona and pencil lead, it displays a dense fullness on the refined palate, balanced by electric acidity that supports the finish. Other wines are hardly less impressive. Barbera d'Asti Superiore Le Rocchette '08 starts with tobacco, red berry and pepper, then a lengthy progression features pulpy fruit and tannins a tad rough yet. Barbera d'Asti La Villa '09 shows uncomplicated, crisp and fruity, and Piemonte Chardonnay I Boschi '08 is dense and forceful, but refreshing and mineral-veined as well, and has fine potential.

● Barbera d'Asti Sup. Nizza '07	▼▼▼	6
● Barbera d'Asti La Villa '09	▼▼	4
● Barbera d'Asti Sup. Le Rocchette '08	▼▼	5
○ Piemonte Chardonnay I Boschi '08	▼▼	4
○ Gavi del Comune di Gavi '09	▼	4
○ Moscato d'Asti Centive '09	▼	4
● Barbera d'Asti Sup. Nizza '06	▽▽▽	6
● Barbera d'Asti Sup. Le Rocchette '07	▽▽	5
● Barbera d'Asti Sup. Le Rocchette '06	▽▽	5
● Barbera d'Asti Sup. Nizza '05	▽▽	5

Orsolani

VIA MICHELE CHIESA, 12
10090 SAN GIORGIO CANAVESE [TO]
TEL. 012432386
www.orsolani.it

CELLAR SALES
PRE-BOOKED VISITS

ANNUAL PRODUCTION 150,000 bottles
HECTARES UNDER VINE 20
VITICULTURE METHOD Conventional

These annual tastings are really an erbaluce festival for Orsolani. Gian Luigi and his family pour most of their research efforts into this main Canavese grape, including sparkling wine experimentation in the 1960s, the idea of a dry vineyard selection worthy of ageing, and limiting the oxidative tendency of the naturally dried passito version. Their 20 hectares of vineyards, planted to barbera, nebbiolo and neretto as well, are distributed over morainic hills with sandy, clayey and gravelly soils.

We tasted only a few Orsolani wines but they were delicious. La Rustìa '09 earned the distinction of winning Three Glasses for Erbaluce di Caluso, an often undervalued grape, and that in a far from easy growing year. The first sip showed us a wine that vaunts an impressive interleaving of dense fruit and genuine minerality. It may open in a minor key but then well-focused aromas of apple and pear, wild flowers and gunflint pour out, followed by a profound, aristocratic palate. Fine marks for Caluso Brut Cuvée Tradizione '05, made of erbaluce, a firmly structured classic-method sparkler that drives on clean and dry.

○ Erbaluce di Caluso La Rustìa '09	▼▼▼	4*
○ Caluso Passito Sulé '05	▼▼	6
○ Caluso Brut Cuvée Tradizione '05	▼▼	5
● Canavese Rosso Acini Sparsi '08	▼	4
○ Caluso Passito Sulé '04	▽▽▽	6
○ Caluso Passito Sulé '98	▽▽▽	6
○ Caluso Bianco Vignot S. Antonio '06	▽▽	5
○ Caluso Passito Sulé '02	▽▽	6
○ Caluso Passito Sulé '00	▽▽	6
○ Caluso Passito Sulé '99	▽▽	6
○ Caluso Spumante Brut Cuvée Tradizione Gran Ris. '03	▽▽	6
○ Caluso Spumante Brut Gran Ris. '99	▽▽	6
○ Erbaluce di Caluso Passito Sulé '01	▽▽	8
○ Erbaluce di Caluso Vignot S. Antonio '04	▽▽	5
○ Erbaluce di Caluso Vignot S. Antonio '03	▽▽	5

Paitin

LOC. BRICCO
VIA SERRA BOELLA, 20
12052 NEIVE [CN]
TEL. 017367343
www.paitin.it

CELLAR SALES
PRE-BOOKED VISITS
ROOMS

ANNUAL PRODUCTION 80,000 bottles
HECTARES UNDER VINE 17
VITICULTURE METHOD Organic

Although not well known in Italy, Pasquero Elia's family winery is one the best interpreters of Barbaresco, with almost 30 years experience now. Over recent years, the winery has undergone profound renewal, with a new cellar a few years ago and the vineyards too have been enlarged and updated. All of Giovanni and Silvano Elia's wines are sourced from the family's vineyards, which are mostly around their cellar at Bricco near Neive.

After a three-year hiatus, Barbaresco Sorì Paitin '07 wins Three Glasses again. What most impresses is its elegance and complexity, although it parades the richness and density that have always been the hallmark of both winery and terroir. A multi-faceted presentation of fruit and spice opens on subtle hints of iron rust, and concludes with a long-lingering, velvety sensation, the perfect foil to its dense-packed tannins. The '06 vintage of Sorì Paitin, from the oldest vineyards, falls short of the same mouthfeel, showing instead a certain tannic astringency purists will like. Barbaresco Serra '06 is by nature less refined and complex, and its tannins here are less delicate.

● Barbaresco Sorì Paitin '07	▼▼▼	6
● Barbaresco Sorì Paitin Vecchie Vigne '06	▼▼	8
● Barbaresco Serra '07	▼▼	6
● Barbera d'Alba Serra '09	▼▼	4
● Barbera d'Alba Sup. Campolive '08	▼▼	5
● Dolcetto d'Alba Sorì Paitin '09	▼▼	4
● Langhe Paitin '08	▼▼	4
○ Langhe Arneis Elisa '09	▼	4
● Nebbiolo d'Alba Ca Veja '08	▼	5
● Barbaresco Sorì Paitin '04	▽▽▽	6
● Barbaresco Sorì Paitin '97	▽▽▽	7
● Barbaresco Sorì Paitin Vecchie Vigne '04	▽▽▽	8
● Barbaresco Sorì Paitin Vecchie Vigne '01	▽▽▽	8
● Barbaresco Sorì Paitin Vecchie Vigne '99	▽▽▽	8
● Langhe Paitin '97	▽▽▽	6

Armando Parusso

LOC. BUSSIA, 55
12065 MONFORTE D'ALBA [CN]
TEL. 017378257
www.parusso.com

CELLAR SALES
PRE-BOOKED VISITS

ANNUAL PRODUCTION 120,000 bottles
HECTARES UNDER VINE 23
VITICULTURE METHOD Organic

Marco Parusso, whose placid exterior belies a volcanic, battle-ready spirit, runs this prestigious Langhe operation with his sister Tiziana. Their array of extraordinary terroirs, together with a particularly well-equipped cellar, allow Armando and Tiziana to transform the finest-quality fruit into a broad and complete portfolio of wines in a distinctive style, showing a judicious balance between classic and modern styles.

The compelling Barolo Mariondino '06 is intensely fruity, conveying impressions of peach pit and sweet tobacco. A very powerful palate offers dry tannins and a finish that is still somewhat austere. Spices and red berry fruit introduce the fine Bussia '06, with sweet oak wafting in the background. It enters to a smooth, but huge, energy-driven palate, and concludes with a lengthy tannin-edged finale. Oak marks Barolo Le Coste-Mosconi '06 on both nose and palate but its power and elegance presage improvement in the bottle. Barbera d'Alba Vecchie Vigne '07 intrigues with dried plum and chocolate on nose and palate, its dense fabric enlivened by a refreshing acidity.

● Barbera d'Alba Sup. Vecchie Vigne Ornati '07	▼▼	6
● Barolo Bussia '06	▼▼	8
● Barolo Mariondino '06	▼▼	8
● Barolo Le Coste Mosconi '06	▼▼	8
● Barolo Vign.Castiglione Falletto e Monforte D'Alba	▼▼	7
○ Langhe Bianco '09	▼▼	4
● Langhe Nebbiolo '08	▼▼	5
● Barbera d'Alba Ornati '09	▼	5
● Dolcetto d'Alba Piani Noci '09	▼	4
○ Langhe Bianco Bricco Rovella '08	▼	6
● Barbera d'Alba Sup. '00	▽▽▽	6
● Barolo Bussia V. Munie '99	▽▽▽	8
● Barolo Bussia V. Munie '97	▽▽▽	8
● Barolo Le Coste Mosconi '03	▽▽▽	8
● Barolo Vecchie Vigne in Mariondino Ris. '99	▽▽▽	8

Massimo Pastura Cascina La Ghersa

via San Giuseppe, 19
14050 Moasca [AT]
tel. 0141856012
www.laghersa.it

CELLAR SALES
PRE-BOOKED VISITS

ANNUAL PRODUCTION 185,000 bottles
HECTARES UNDER VINE 22
VITICULTURE METHOD Conventional

Over the past few years, this historic Asti-area operation, now directed by Massimo Pastura, has seen some deep changes, among them the steep increase in the number of wines produced. They now have three lines, Selezione Vigneti Unici di Massimo Pastura, the Classici di Cascina La Ghersa, and the Cascina La Ghersa – Linea Piagè. Their focus is on Piedmont's classic grapes, with barbera the favourite.

Massimo Pastura's passion and energy do not seem to have brought the desired results. We were not completely impressed with the wines of the Selezione Vigneti Unici. Barbera d'Asti Superiore Nizza Vignassa '07 is well balanced and convincing, fruity and tobacco-scented, with a structure still somewhat constricted, yet lengthy and impressive. Equally good is Barbera d'Asti Superiore Camparò '08, showing good varietal earthiness and dark berry fruit, with a supple, crisp and approachable mouth. Grignolino d'Asti Spineira '09 is sound, with red berry and tasty grip, as is Barbera d'Asti Superiore Muascae '07, with evolved notes of bottled cherries.

● Barbera d'Asti Sup. Camparò '08	🍷🍷	4
● Barbera d'Asti Sup. Nizza Vignassa '07	🍷🍷	5
● Barbera d'Asti Sup. Muascae '07	🍷	7
● Grignolino d'Asti Spineira '09	🍷	4
● Barbera d'Asti Sup. Nizza Vignassa '04	YY	6
● Barbera d'Asti Sup. Nizza Vignassa '03	YY	6

Agostino Pavia e Figli

fraz. Bologna, 33
14041 Agliano Terme [AT]
tel. 0141954125
www.agostinopavia.it

CELLAR SALES
PRE-BOOKED VISITS
ROOMS

ANNUAL PRODUCTION 75,000 bottles
HECTARES UNDER VINE 9
VITICULTURE METHOD Conventional

This historic family winery concentrates almost totally on the barbera variety. Their few hectares of well-aspected vineyard are planted in sandy-clay soils, with some in clay-marl. The Pavia family identified three cru vineyards, Bricco Blina, Moliss and Marescialla, which are vinified and matured with three different protocols, the first in steel, the second large oak, and the third in barriques

The winery produces a line-up of admirable solidity and consistent quality. The standard-bearer is again Barbera d'Asti Superiore La Marescialla '07, with intense notes of ripe plum, tobacco leaf, incense and spice, then a rich, succulent mouth and fine length on the finish. Barbera d'Asti Superiore Moliss '07 is very well crafted, releasing cigar tobacco and bottled cherries. Tasty, pulpy fruit stands out on the palate but the tannins are a tad severe. On the same quality rung is Grignolino d'Asti '09. It shines with an intense florality, along with hints of pepper and cinchona. The palate is notably varietal; the tannins dense and slightly obstreperous.

● Barbera d'Asti La Marescialla '07	🍷🍷	5
● Barbera d'Asti Sup. Moliss '07	🍷🍷	4
● Grignolino d'Asti '09	🍷🍷	3*
● Barbera d'Asti Bricco Blina '08	🍷	4
● Barbera d'Asti Casareggio '09	🍷	3
● Barbera d'Asti Bricco Blina '06	YY	4*
● Barbera d'Asti La Marescialla '04	YY	5
● Barbera d'Asti Sup. La Marescialla '06	YY	5
● Barbera d'Asti Sup. Moliss '06	YY	4
● Barbera d'Asti Sup. Moliss '05	YY	4

★ Pecchenino

B.TA VALDIBERTI, 59
12063 DOGLIANI [CN]
TEL. 017370686
www.pecchenino.com

CELLAR SALES
PRE-BOOKED VISITS
ROOMS

ANNUAL PRODUCTION 90,000 bottles
HECTARES UNDER VINE 25
VITICULTURE METHOD Conventional

Brothers Attilio and Orlando Pecchenino forge on with no false steps on their admirable professional journey. Both nationally and internationally, this wine family has achieved widespread respect that gives them one of the most recognizable names in the Langhe. The preferred vehicle for their operation is dolcetto but in recent years we have come to appreciate what they have achieved with the noble but difficult nebbiolo grape as well.

It might surprise that the Peccheninos have so soon succeeded with Barolo, too, but whoever is familiar with their history-making Dolcetto Sirì d'Jermu will understand the subtleties they exercise in creating the archetype of an elegant, smooth Dolcetto. It is the amazing Dogliani Bricco Botti '07, however, that won Three Glasses, a wine that seems to have squared the oenological circle. But the Peccheninos add to that by trotting out two of the finest '06 Barolos of the entire area, the complex Le Coste and the appealing, silk-smooth San Giuseppe. And for good measure, they have released one of the rare great Barberas of the barbera-challenging 2008 growing year.

● Dogliani Bricco Botti '07	▼▼▼	5
● Barbera d'Alba Quass '08	▼▼	5
● Barolo Le Coste '06	▼▼	7
● Barolo S. Giuseppe '06	▼▼	7
● Dogliani Sirì d'Jermu '08	▼▼	5*
● Dolcetto di Dogliani S. Luigi '09	▼▼	4
● Langhe Nebbiolo V. Botti '08	▼	5
● Barolo Le Coste '05	▽▽▽	7
● Dogliani Sirì d'Jermu '06	▽▽▽	5
● Dolcetto di Dogliani S. Luigi '00	▽▽▽	4
● Dolcetto di Dogliani Sirì d'Jermu '03	▽▽▽	5
● Dolcetto di Dogliani Sirì d'Jermu '01	▽▽▽	5
● Dolcetto di Dogliani Sirì d'Jermu '99	▽▽▽	5
● Dolcetto di Dogliani Sirì d'Jermu '96	▽▽▽	5
● Dolcetto di Dogliani Sup. Bricco Botti '04	▽▽▽	5

Pelissero

VIA FERRERE, 10
12050 TREISO [CN]
TEL. 0173638430
www.pelissero.com

CELLAR SALES
PRE-BOOKED VISITS

ANNUAL PRODUCTION 250,000 bottles
HECTARES UNDER VINE 35
VITICULTURE METHOD Conventional

Giorgio Pelissero heads this influential Langhe cellar, well known both in Italy and abroad. The dynamism that has marked his efforts here has gone to make Pelissero one of Barbaresco's most consistent and reliable names. The wine portfolio, which is quite broad, includes some of Piedmont's most important denominations. Compelling interpretations of Barbaresco are well complemented by the performances of other categories, Dolcetto in particular.

Barbaresco Vanotu '07 has character to spare, with aromas alternating between fruit and spice, backgrounded by sweet tobacco leaf. An ultra-rich palate is already plush, with poised tannins and pulpy fruit . This is a firmly structured, already enjoyable Three Glasses. Dolcetto d'Alba Augenta '09, always a stand-out in its class, has great structure. Dark berry and even cocoa powder emerge, segueing into dense concentration in the mouth, with abundant bright fruit, through to a finish edged in tasty tannins. Barbaresco Nubiola is just a bit more approachable and tasty than Tulin, both 2007s. Though sound, the latter seems a bit stiff without enough fruit to soften its lines.

● Barbaresco Vanotu '07	▼▼▼	8
● Dolcetto d'Alba Augenta '09	▼▼	4*
● Barbaresco Nubiola '07	▼▼	6
● Barbaresco Tulin '07	▼▼	7
● Barbera d'Alba Piani '09	▼▼	4
● Langhe Nebbiolo '09	▼▼	5
● Langhe Rosso Long Now '08	▼▼	6
● Dolcetto d'Alba Munfrina '09	▼	4
○ Langhe Favorita Le Nature '09	▼	3
● Barbaresco Vanotu '06	▽▽▽	8
● Barbaresco Vanotu '01	▽▽▽	8
● Barbaresco Vanotu '99	▽▽▽	8
● Barbaresco Vanotu '97	▽▽▽	8
● Barbaresco Vanotu '95	▽▽▽	8
● Barbaresco Nubiola '06	▽▽	6

Cascina Pellerino

LOC. SANT'ANNA, 93
12043 MONTEU ROERO [CN]
TEL. 0173978171
www.cascinapellerino.com

CELLAR SALES
PRE-BOOKED VISITS

ANNUAL PRODUCTION **50,000 bottles**
HECTARES UNDER VINE **8**
VITICULTURE METHOD **Conventional**

Cascina Pellerino, owned by Cristiano Bono and Roberto Ghione, has seen its line-up extended substantially over recent years in response to market demands for product diversity. Cheek by jowl with the expected area classics, nebbiolo, arneis, barbera and dolcetto, we find internationals such as chardonnay and cabernet. The vineyards are distributed across Canale, Santo Stefano Roero, Vezza d'Alba and Monteu Roero, where the cellar is located.

Cascina Pellerino turned in good performances, needing only a further small step up to be in the top ranks in the designation. Roero Vicot '07 is redolent of toasty oak, roast espresso bean and spices, which do tend to carpet the fruit a bit. The mouth has force, complexity and impressive length but oak seems to stick out everywhere. On the same quality rung is Roero Andrè '08, with agreeable pine resin, red berry and Mediterranean scrubland, showing clean and fruity overall. Its strong suit is not structure but it is pleasurable and easy drinking. Roero Arneis Boneur '09 offers varietal apple with hints of almond. There's a rich mouth and a long, lean finish.

● Roero André '08	🍷🍷	5
○ Roero Arneis Boneur '09	🍷🍷	4
● Roero Vicot '07	🍷🍷	6
● Barbera d'Alba Diletta '08	🍷	4
○ Felizia Brut	🍷	6
○ Langhe Favorita Lorena '09	🍷	4
● Barbera d'Alba Sup. Gran Madre '05	🍷🍷 (white)	5
● Roero Leoni '04	🍷🍷 (white)	6
● Roero Leoni '03	🍷🍷 (white)	6
● Roero Vicot '06	🍷🍷 (white)	6
● Roero Vicot '05	🍷🍷 (white)	5
● Roero Vicot '03	🍷🍷 (white)	5*

Elio Perrone

S.DA SAN MARTINO, 3BIS
12053 CASTIGLIONE TINELLA [CN]
TEL. 0141855803
www.elioperrone.it

PRE-BOOKED VISITS

ANNUAL PRODUCTION **150,000 bottles**
HECTARES UNDER VINE **13**
VITICULTURE METHOD **Conventional**

The Perrone family has long been interpreting the Asti area. This is the domain of moscato but barbera can turn in fine performances as well. Their estate vineyards now number a dozen, scattered about the hillsides in well-aspected positions that yield grapes of fine character. The fruit is vinified separately according to location but the wines are few, mostly dedicated to just these two varieties.

Among the wines we tasted, all finely crafted and with distinctive personalities, Clartè '09 stood out, a true Moscato d'Asti, except in the indication on the label. Apple, peach and musk crowd the nose, closely followed by a seductive palate and sweetness well held in check by zesty acidity. Moscato Sourgal '09 unleashes a creamy mousse and a truly refreshing palate with impressive staying power. Among the reds, Tasmorcan, the standard Barbera, is to be recommended, with complementary smoothness and acidity. Ripe, juicy fruit stands out in Barbera Mongovone '08, which offers fragrant red berry fruit and cocoa powder, and bright fruit that makes it such an enjoyable quaffer.

○ Clartè '09	🍷🍷	4*
● Barbera d'Asti Sup. Mongovone '08	🍷🍷	6
● Barbera d'Asti Tasmorcan '09	🍷🍷	4*
○ Moscato d'Asti Sourgal '09	🍷🍷	4*

Le Piane

LOC. LE PIANE
VIA CERRI, 10
28010 BOCA [NO]
TEL. 3483354185
www.bocapiane.com

CELLAR SALES
PRE-BOOKED VISITS

ANNUAL PRODUCTION 30,000 bottles
HECTARES UNDER VINE 7
VITICULTURE METHOD Conventional

The story here begins with Christoph Künzli, a Swiss importer bewitched by the beauty of the area, and with Antonio Cerri, the venerable grape-grower from whom he purchased the farm in 1998. Parcel after parcel, Künzli gathered together six and a half hectares, among them some old vineyards trained to the old local "maggiorina" pergola system and planted to nebbiolo, croatina, uva rara and vespolina. His best-known wine is Boca, aged three years in 25 to 28-hectolitre Slavonian oak casks.

Le Piane's stylistic journey seems to us to have now reached full maturity. Confirmation is an original yet consistent Boca. This '06 leads us down earthier, more austere paths than usual, our guide being a tannic suite of incredible density and fleshiness, and yet the nose brings us firmly back to the familiar high road of citrus, wild fennel and volcanic ash. An easy Three Glasses go to this effort. An absolutely worthy colleague is Colline Novaresi Piane '07, largely croatina with some nebbiolo, with its youthful succulent intensity, and Colline Novaresi La Maggiorina '09, with its seductive, compelling warmth.

● Boca '06	▼▼▼	7
● Colline Novaresi Le Piane '07	▼▼	6
● Colline Novaresi La Maggiorina '09	▼▼	4
● Boca '05	▽▽▽	7
● Boca '04	▽▽▽	7
● Boca '03	▽▽▽	7
● Boca '01	▽▽	7
● Boca '00	▽▽	5
● Colline Novaresi La Maggiorina '08	▽▽	4*
● Colline Novaresi La Maggiorina '06	▽▽	4*
● Colline Novaresi La Maggiorina '05	▽▽	3*
● Colline Novaresi Le Piane '06	▽▽	6
● Colline Novaresi Le Piane '05	▽▽	6
● Colline Novaresi Le Piane '04	▽▽	6

Pianpolvere Soprano

LOC. BUSSIA, 32
12065 MONFORTE D'ALBA [CN]
TEL. 017378421
www.pianpolveresoprano.it

ANNUAL PRODUCTION N.A.
HECTARES UNDER VINE 9
VITICULTURE METHOD Organic

Pianpolvere Soprano is a magnificent vineyard known for centuries for its production of great nebbiolo grapes – the name refers to a powder magazine dating back to the Napoleonic period. The Migliorini family, after purchasing the estate in 1998, have always kept its production separate from the celebrated grapes of Poderi Rocche dei Manzoni. Rodolfo Migliorini cut his professional teeth here, dedicating himself to organic and biodynamic viticulture, implemented manually.

Only a single wine, obviously a Barolo, is sourced from three hectares of old vines, and made only in the years considered better than simply good, so this profile will not appear every year in the Guide. To make the selection even more complex, Rodolfo decided to produce only a Riserva, a full seven years from the harvest. This Barolo Bussia '01 is richly perfumed, particularly with dark berry fruit and dried violets. The palate is monumental, but already rather supple and harmonious, full-volumed and compelling, a truly great Barolo. It is not easy to find, since it is exported pretty much across the globe, but it is worth seeking out.

● Barolo Bussia Ris. '01	▼▼▼	8

Pio Cesare

VIA CESARE BALBO, 6
12051 ALBA [CN]
TEL. 0173440386
www.piocesare.it

PRE-BOOKED VISITS

ANNUAL PRODUCTION **400,000 bottles**
HECTARES UNDER VINE **52**
VITICULTURE METHOD **Conventional**

Pio Cesare, the historic Alba-area cellar active since 1881, is one of Italy's most respected wine names globally. The complex in which it operates alone deserves a visit. Production philosophy leans heavily towards the classic, without running after quick-pleasing, obvious styles. Rather, Pio Cesare brings to its wines, particularly its Barolo and Barbaresco cru selections, a modernist stylistic imprint, made up of fairly intense tonalities and refined scents of oak in the wines' first years.

We want to note first off that this year we tasted a fabulous Chardonnay Piodilei '08. Barolo Ornato '06 deserves Three Glasses for the exuberant, cleanly delineated fruit that accompanies its classic notes of liquorice. Tannins on the palate are still fairy rough but they enjoy the covering support of a magnificent, juicy, pulp-rich structure. Overall, this is certainly the most classic edition that we have tasted in years. Barolo '06 is more austere, in a notably lean style, but very well put together and pleasurable. Among the many other very fine Pio Cesare offerings, we recommend the more than solid Barbera Fides '07, as well as, obviously, the two famous Barbarescos.

● Barolo Ornato '06	🍷🍷🍷	8
● Barolo '06	🍷🍷	8
○ Langhe Chardonnay PiodiLei '08	🍷🍷	6
● Barbaresco '06	🍷🍷	8
● Barbaresco Il Bricco '06	🍷🍷	8
● Barbera d'Alba Fides '07	🍷🍷	6
○ Langhe Nebbiolo '07	🍷🍷	4
● Barbera d'Alba '08	🍷	6
○ Gavi '09	🍷	4
○ Langhe Arneis '09	🍷	4
● Langhe Rosso Il Nebbio '09	🍷	5
○ Piemonte Chardonnay L'Altro '09	🍷	4
● Barbaresco Il Bricco '97	ϒϒϒ	8
● Barolo Ornato '05	ϒϒϒ	8
● Barolo Ornato '89	ϒϒϒ	8

Pioiero

CASCINA PIOIERO, 1
12040 VEZZA D'ALBA [CN]
TEL. 017365492
www.pioiero.com

CELLAR SALES
PRE-BOOKED VISITS

ANNUAL PRODUCTION **35,000 bottles**
HECTARES UNDER VINE **9**
VITICULTURE METHOD **Conventional**

The Rabino family cellar is located in the commune of Vezza d'Alba, near Castellinaldo and Castagnito. All of their wines are sourced from vineyards on the hill that gives its name to the property, planted in largely clay-limestone soils. Pioiero's wines, from varieties traditional to Roero, are markedly traditional in approach and directed to the strictest possible expression of their terroir of origin.

We very much liked Roero Arneis Cascina Pioiero '09, with its bright, emphatic apricot and citrus, nicely infused with delicate florality. The palate shows juicy succulence, with a well-calibrated, lengthy development and plenty of grip for good support. Roero '07 is well crafted, with enviable tobacco leaf and red berry fruit shot through with delicious spice. The body is rich but somewhat dried by a bit too much oak. The floral Langhe Favorita '09 is also well made, with complementary apple and peach, a reaching, harmonious finish, and a structure that is fairly impressive for the variety. Nebbiolo d'Alba '08 is right on the money, straightforward, fluid and nicely fruity.

○ Langhe Favorita '09	🍷🍷	3
● Nebbiolo d'Alba '08	🍷🍷	4
● Roero '07	🍷🍷	4
● Roero Sup. '04	ϒϒ	4*
● Roero Sup. '01	ϒϒ	4*

Luigi Pira

via XX Settembre, 9
12050 Serralunga d'Alba [CN]
tel. 0173613106
pira.luigi@alice.it

CELLAR SALES
PRE-BOOKED VISITS

ANNUAL PRODUCTION 50,000 bottles
HECTARES UNDER VINE 10
VITICULTURE METHOD Conventional

The ten hectares of vineyards cared for by the Pira family constitute a true collection of super-crus. All of Serralunga's proverbial power and depth, so unique, so unmatchable, are displayed in the stuffing and texture of the wines the Piras make. In the past, a tad too much oak did muffle some varietal notes but recent vintages have brought improved calibration and growing harmony among components. All of Pira's wines have astounding life-spans.

From one of the justly famous Langhe vineyards comes Barolo Vigna Rionda '06. Still fairly closed, it shows little action yet from its sweet tobacco and red berry but the body is fantastically vibrant, with emphatic tannins well inserted in fleshy fruit right through to the lengthy finish. It gets Three massive, classic Glasses. The more expressive Barolo Marenca '06 begins its release of liquorice within aromas of utter finesse. The tannins appear quickly, austere but not hard and the development is admirably compelling. Margheria '06 is more tannic, severe and closed but all signs are for a long, lovely life. Barbera and Nebbiolo '08 are superb base wines, rich and bright.

● Barolo V. Rionda '06	▼▼▼	8
● Barolo V. Marenca '06	▼▼	8
● Barolo V. Margheria '06	▼▼	7
● Barbera d'Alba '08	▼▼	5
● Barolo '06	▼▼	6
● Langhe Nebbiolo '08	▼▼	5
● Barolo V. Marenca '01	▽▽▽	8
● Barolo V. Marenca '97	▽▽▽	8
● Barolo V. Rionda '04	▽▽▽	8
● Barolo V. Rionda '00	▽▽▽	8
● Barbera d'Alba '07	▽▽	5
● Barolo V. Margheria '05	▽▽	7
● Barolo V. Rionda '05	▽▽	8
● Barolo Vign. Marenca '04	▽▽	8
● Barolo Vign. Margheria '04	▽▽	7

E. Pira & Figli

via Vittorio Veneto, 1
12060 Barolo [CN]
tel. 017356247
www.pira-chiaraboschis.com

CELLAR SALES
PRE-BOOKED VISITS

ANNUAL PRODUCTION 20,000 bottles
HECTARES UNDER VINE 4
VITICULTURE METHOD Certified organic

Among women in the wine world, Chiara Boschis is both an influence and a role model. You can run across her out in her magnificent vineyards, meet her in her "work outfit" doing jobs in the wine cellar and admire her elegant professionalism in presenting her wines. Recent tastings of older Barolo vintages have evidenced their propensity for adding uncommon complexity and depth. Among her winery's assets is the gorgeous parcel in Cannubi, which obviously yields the same-named Barolo.

Barolo Cannubi '06 is strikingly fruity and evolved on the nose over a full body and structure that is elegant, tannic and lengthy, though not particularly powerful. Barolo Via Nuova '06 first presents a tasty duet of sweet tobacco and fruit, then a near-endless, though not huge, development, even if less complex than Cannubi. Again, it is just a hair's breadth from the highest award but rest assured we have not heard the last from this 2006. The modern-styled Barbera d'Alba Superiore '08 is spicy and medium-bodied but somewhat oak-marked. The pulp-rich, succulent Dolcetto d'Alba '09 is delicious, uncomplex and eminently drinkable.

● Barolo Cannubi '06	▼▼	8
● Barolo Via Nuova '06	▼▼	8
● Barbera d'Alba Sup. '08	▼▼	5
● Dolcetto d'Alba '09	▼▼	4*
● Barolo '94	▽▽▽	8
● Barolo Cannubi '05	▽▽▽	8
● Barolo Cannubi '00	▽▽▽	8
● Barolo Cannubi '97	▽▽▽	8
● Barolo Cannubi '96	▽▽▽	8
● Barbera d'Alba '07	▽▽	6
● Barbera d'Alba '06	▽▽	6
● Barolo Cannubi '04	▽▽	8
● Barolo Via Nuova '05	▽▽	8
● Barolo Via Nuova '04	▽▽	8
● Dolcetto d'Alba '07	▽▽	5

Poderi Colla

loc. San Rocco Seno d'Elvio, 82
12051 Alba [CN]
tel. 0173290148
www.podericolla.it

PRE-BOOKED VISITS

ANNUAL PRODUCTION 150,000 bottles
HECTARES UNDER VINE 26
VITICULTURE METHOD Conventional

Poderi Colla's wines, which range from reds and whites to sparkling, clearly demonstrate both local traditions and expressive bonds with their terroirs. They turned in outstanding performances. The line-up of wines we tasted evidences impressive linearity and coherence with respect to the philosophy that Poderi Colla adheres to: nothing in excess, ageing in large oak, depth without excessive concentration and everything gauged to allow the fruit to convey into the wine its innermost essence.

Barolo Bussia Dardi Le Rose '06 hinges on red berry fruit and signature dried flowers while the palate puts elegance and harmony before naked power, to which its tannins make a valued contribution. Barbaresco Roncaglie '07 opens stylishly traditional and complex while the mouth is self-confident, sunny and delicious, thanks to its overall balance. An intensely rich Bricco del Drago '07 offers evolved spiciness, then pure succulence in the mouth, a tasty pairing of pulpy dolcetto and complex nebbiolo fruit. We very much liked the Riesling for its complex, minerally nose and rich palate, with its judicious acidity. All of these wines will benefit from more cellaring.

● Barbaresco Roncaglie '07	TT	7
● Barolo Bussia Dardi Le Rose '06	TT	7
● Langhe Bricco del Drago '07	TT	5
● Barbera d'Alba Costa Bruna '08	TT	4
○ Langhe Bianco Riesling '09	TT	4
● Nebbiolo d'Alba '08	TT	5
● Barolo Bussia Dardi Le Rose '99	YYY	7
● Barbaresco Roncaglie '06	YY	7
● Barolo Bussia Dardi Le Rose '05	YY	7
● Barolo Bussia Dardi Le Rose '04	YY	7
● Langhe Bricco del Drago '06	YY	5
● Langhe Bricco del Drago '04	YY	5
● Langhe Rosso Bricco del Drago '03	YY	5

Paolo Giuseppe Poggio

via Roma, 67
15050 Brignano Frascata [AL]
tel. 0131784929
cantinapoggio@tiscali.it

CELLAR SALES
PRE-BOOKED VISITS

ANNUAL PRODUCTION 18,000 bottles
HECTARES UNDER VINE 3
VITICULTURE METHOD Conventional

Paolo Poggio makes just a few wines but all are consistent and bear extremely competitive price tags. That makes it easy to recommend a visit to the cellar, a small operation in the Colli Tortonesi. Poggio's dedication has brought him impressive results, which simply seem to get better with every passing year. He focuses much of his attention on coaxing the best from the croatina grape, which along with timorasso, should command wider appreciation and development.

The team leader here is Campo La Bà '08, a sparkling ruby Barbera that lays out fruit and spice converging beautifully on a palate of admirable consistency and balance. A near-opaque ruby introduces Barbera Derio '07, whose aromatic spice and fruit precede power and intensity in the mouth. We liked Timorasso Ronchetto '08, with its evolved notes and good fruit, followed by appreciable harmony and full body. Campogallo '09 is a richly fragrant Cortese with relaxed, pleasurable approachability. Don't overlook the barbera-only Teo. After a difficult year, Prosone '08 from croatina didn't quite reach previous levels of performance.

● Colli Tortonesi Barbera Campo La Bà '08	TT	3*
● Colli Tortonesi Barbera Derio '07	TT	4
○ Colli Tortonesi Ronchetto '08	TT	4
○ Colli Tortonesi Cortese Campogallo '09	T	2
● Colli Tortonesi Rosso Prosone '08	T	3
● Teo	T	3
● Colli Tortonesi Barbera Campo La Bà '07	YY	2*
● Colli Tortonesi Barbera Derio '06	YY	4
● Colli Tortonesi Barbera Derio '04	YY	4*
○ Colli Tortonesi Ronchetto '06	YY	3
○ Colli Tortonesi Ronchetto '05	YY	3*
● Colli Tortonesi Rosso Prosone '07	YY	2*
● Colli Tortonesi Rosso Prosone '06	YY	2
● Colli Tortonesi Rosso Prosone '05	YY	2*

Pomodolce

via IV Novembre, 7
15050 Montemarzino [AL]
tel. 0131878135
www.pomodolce.it

CELLAR SALES
PRE-BOOKED VISITS

ANNUAL PRODUCTION 1,500 bottles
HECTARES UNDER VINE 4
VITICULTURE METHOD Certified organic

Pomodolce is a small, family operation in a beautiful setting in Val Curone. It not only produces terrific wines but hosts a highly respected family restaurant as well. The organically raised wines exhibit impressive body and personality, exuding a very marked impression of terroir. The whites evince an intense minerality and the reds fine spice-laden fruit. Kudos as well for the sober, original label style.

Grue '08 heads the team here, a refined Timorasso with mineral-edged citrus, apple and pear, followed by a rich, juicy mouth veined with a magisterial acidity. Timorasso Diletto '08 gets equally high marks for its intensity, power and volume at every step of its presentation. Fontanino '07 is a well-balanced but emphatic Croatina whose barrel-ageing still leaves a few too many signs. Barbera Marsèn '07 is stylishly redolent of cherry and tobacco while the nebbiolo Niali '06 is uncomplicated but well proportioned and delicious.

○ Colli Tortonesi Timorasso Derthona Diletto '08	▼▼	4
○ Colli Tortonesi Timorasso Grue '08	▼▼	6
● Colli Tortonesi Croatina Fontanino '07	▼▼	4
● Colli Tortonesi Barbera Marsén '07	▼	5
● Colli Tortonesi Rosso Niali '06	▼	5
○ Colli Tortonesi Timorasso Derthona Grue '07	▽▽▽	5
● Colli Tortonesi Barbera '05	▽▽	4*
○ Colli Tortonesi Bianco Diletto '06	▽▽	4
○ Colli Tortonesi Bianco Diletto '05	▽▽	5
● Colli Tortonesi Rosso '04	▽▽	5
○ Colli Tortonesi Timorasso Derthona Diletto '07	▽▽	5

Marco Porello

c.so Alba, 71
12043 Canale [CN]
tel. 0173979324
www.porellovini.it

CELLAR SALES
PRE-BOOKED VISITS

ANNUAL PRODUCTION 100,000 bottles
HECTARES UNDER VINE 15
VITICULTURE METHOD Conventional

The Porello family has been operating this cellar for three generations, constantly intent on meticulous vineyard management. That has yielded them wines with remarkable character, eloquently expressive of their terroir. All are made from local grapes: arneis, favorita, barbera, nebbiolo and brachetto. Vinification and bottling are done at Canale, where the main winery is, while the ageing is at the nearby cellar in Castello di Guarene.

Roero Torretta '07 continues to stand out as one of the finest products in the denomination. A spacious nose combines fragrant tobacco, liquorice and wild red berries, followed by juicy sapidity in a mouth noteworthy for its finesse, with dense tannins that build a lengthy finish. After earthy notes lift tasty cherry and redcurrant, Barbera d'Alba Mommiano '09 develops plenty of supple, crisp fruit. Nebbiolo d'Alba '08 is a subtle medley, intertwining tobacco, liquorice and rose petals but with tannins a bit out of kilter with respect to its structure. Langhe Favorita '09 is crisply aromatic, nicely proportioned and delicious right now.

● Roero Torretta '07	▼▼	5
● Barbera d'Alba Mommiano '09	▼▼	4*
○ Langhe Favorita '09	▼▼	3
● Nebbiolo d'Alba '08	▼▼	4
● Barbera d'Alba Filatura '08	▼	5
○ Roero Arneis Camestrì '09	▼	4
● Roero Torretta '06	▽▽▽	5*
● Roero Torretta '04	▽▽▽	5
● Barbera d'Alba Filatura '07	▽▽	5
● Barbera d'Alba Filatura '06	▽▽	5
○ Roero Arneis Camestrì '07	▽▽	4*
● Roero Torretta '05	▽▽	5

Ferdinando Principiano

VIA ALBA, 19
12065 MONFORTE D'ALBA [CN]
TEL. 0173787158
www.ferdinandoprincipiano.it

CELLAR SALES
PRE-BOOKED VISITS

ANNUAL PRODUCTION 50,000 bottles
HECTARES UNDER VINE 8
VITICULTURE METHOD Conventional

Ferdinando Principiano is one of the Langhe's nouvelle vague exponents. The family operation has been active since the early 1900s but Ferdinando has radically updated production during the last seasons, abandoning chemical fertilizers and weedkillers, and adopting natural wild yeasts. The wines of course reflect this natural, artisanal methodology, exhibiting at times unusual sensory profiles, further underscoring the edgy personalities of the Serralunga hills, where most of the nebbiolo is grown.

We did notice the absence of Barolo Boscaret, the Principiano wine that we felt has expressed itself most consistently over recent years. Barolo Ravera '06 is a more than worthy stand-in but perplexing in more than one way. An emphatically evolved nose, displaying fruit preserves and tea leaves, is paired with an impetuous palate with energy-charged tannins and acidity. Barolo Serralunga '06 travels along the same track: dried grass and moist earth are farther along the evolution curve than is suggested by a subtle but still unsoftened palate.

● Barolo Ravera '06	▼▼	7
● Barolo Serralunga '06	▼▼	6
● Dolcetto d'Alba S. Anna '09	▼▼	4*
● Barbera d'Alba Laura '09	▼	4
● Langhe Nebbiolo Coste '09	▼	4
● Barolo Boscareto '93	▽▽▽	8
● Barbera d'Alba La Romualda '07	▽▽	6
● Barbera d'Alba La Romualda '06	▽▽	6
● Barbera d'Alba La Romualda '05	▽▽	6
● Barolo Boscareto '05	▽▽	7
● Barolo Boscareto '04	▽▽	8
● Barolo Serralunga '05	▽▽	6
● Dolcetto d'Alba S. Anna '08	▽▽	4*
● Langhe Nebbiolo Coste '08	▽▽	4

★ Prunotto

REG. SAN CASSIANO, 4G
12051 ALBA [CN]
TEL. 0173280017
www.prunotto.it

PRE-BOOKED VISITS

ANNUAL PRODUCTION 600,000 bottles
HECTARES UNDER VINE 55
VITICULTURE METHOD Conventional

This glory of Alba winemaking has known increasing success since 1923. From 1963, one of its innovations was to put on the wine labels the name of the individual source crus, a move which contributed so much to the entire Langhe wine industry. The Florentine house of Marchesi Antinori has owned Prunotto for 20 years now and has constantly enlarged its roster of vineyards. The wine portfolio is extremely broad and notable for its fine quality-price ratio.

Barolo Bussia '06, from the celebrated Monforte cru, is for all its classic nebbiolo traits hard to simply label as a traditional Barolo, its fruit showing so generous and so immediately appealing. Barbera Nizza Costamiòle, from the rich '07 vintage, is massive but not heavy, crunchy yet refreshing and crisp, and a fine example of a modernist, concentrated Barbera crafted with a sapient hand. The nose on Barbaresco Bric Turot '06 was fortunate in its extra year's ageing, since the aromas are spacious and ripe, but alcohol marks a somewhat rough-edged mouth. The remaining wines are well made, particularly Nebbiolo '07, from the Occhetti cru in Roero.

● Barbera d'Asti Sup. Nizza Costamiòle '07	▼▼	6
● Barolo Bussia '06	▼▼	8
● Barbaresco Bric Turot '06	▼▼	7
● Barolo '06	▼▼	7
● Nebbiolo d'Alba Occhetti '07	▼▼	5
● Barbaresco '07	▼	6
● Barbera d'Asti Fiulòt '09	▼	4
● Dolcetto d'Alba '09	▼	4
● Dolcetto d'Alba Mosesco '08	▼	4
○ Moscato d'Asti '09	▼	4
● Barbera d'Asti Costamiòle '99	▽▽▽	6
● Barolo Bussia '01	▽▽▽	8
● Barolo Bussia '99	▽▽▽	8
● Barolo Bussia '98	▽▽▽	8
● Barolo Bussia '96	▽▽▽	8
● Barolo Cannubi '85	▽▽▽	6

La Querciola

LOC. PIANCERRETO, 85/TER
12060 FARIGLIANO [CN]
TEL. 0713737026
www.laquerciola.com

CELLAR SALES
PRE-BOOKED VISITS

ANNUAL PRODUCTION 80,000 bottles
HECTARES UNDER VINE 25
VITICULTURE METHOD Conventional

The name of La Querciola is inspired by a copse of oaks, now all too rare in the Langhe. The winery also has vineyards in the municipality of Barolo. Bruno Chionetti, who runs this operation, has always had a passion for Dolcetto but he extended his expertise to Barolo as well, without losing any of his magic touch. Next year will also see the release of Bruno's Langhe Bianco, which is all riesling renano, a grape that is yielding outstanding results in these hills. But dolcetto is still king.

The lovely Dogliani Cornole '08 initially delivers cinchona and cocoa powder, then insistent fragrant fruit. Powerful tannins make themselves felt in the mouth and a quite distinctive finish stretches out nicely. Dolcetto di Dogliani Carpeneta '09 is only a step behind, strutting sweet tobacco and refined red berry fruit. The mouth is full and satisfying but the conclusion still shows somewhat green. And now to the Barolos, Chionetti's latest conquest. The longish Donna Bianca '06, an assemblage of the Costa di Rose and Boschetti crus, privileges harmony over power, with sweet oak finessing tar and cinchona, while Costa di Rose '06, though not intense, is marked by vibrant energy.

● Barolo Donna Bianca '06	▼▼	6
● Dogliani Cornole '08	▼▼	4*
● Barolo Costa di Rose '06	▼▼	7
● Dolcetto di Dogliani Carpeneta '09	▼▼	4*
● Langhe Rosso Barilin '08	▼▼	4
● Langhe Rosso Chicchivello '09	▼	3*
● Barolo Donna Bianca '05	▽▽	6
● Barolo Donna Bianca '04	▽▽	6
● Dogliani Cornole '07	▽▽	4
● Dolcetto di Dogliani Carpeneta '08	▽▽	4

Renato Ratti

FRAZ. ANNUNZIATA, 7
12064 LA MORRA [CN]
TEL. 017350185
www.renatoratti.com

CELLAR SALES
PRE-BOOKED VISITS

ANNUAL PRODUCTION 300,000 bottles
HECTARES UNDER VINE 40
VITICULTURE METHOD Conventional

The complex that houses this historic Langhe producer's operations offers a telling example of how considerable size and modern stylistics can be integrated, architecturally speaking, into the surrounding landscape. Pietro Ratti, who has just assumed the chair of the Consorzio di Tutela del Barolo e del Barbaresco, continues his family's long traditions, all his efforts bring characterized by unrelenting dedication.

Barolo Rocche '06 flaunts toasty oak, tobacco and rose petals, complemented by dense, non-astringent tannins on its powerful palate. Three Glasses go to this classically austere, cellarable champion. Barolo Marcenasco '06, youthful, fruity and spicy, unfurls long, tannin-lined progression. Barolo Conca '06 combines Rocche's toastiness and Marcenasco's fruit. It has a touch too much oak and edginess to its tannins but the texture is spot on. Tannins and pulpy fruit combine for an exuberant Dolcetto d'Alba Colombè '09. The sauvignon I Cedri di Villa Pattono '08, suggesting sage and laurel, is alcoholically warm and less rich than the '07. Nebbiolo d'Alba Ochetti '08 is pleasurable.

● Barolo Rocche '06	▼▼▼	8
● Barolo Conca '06	▼▼	8
● Barolo Marcenasco '06	▼▼	7
● Dolcetto d'Alba Colombè '09	▼▼	4*
○ Monferrato Bianco I Cedri di Villa Pattono '08	▼▼	4*
● Nebbiolo d'Alba Ochetti '08	▼▼	5
● Barolo Rocche Marcenasco '84	▽▽▽	8
● Barolo Rocche Marcenasco '83	▽▽▽	8
● Barolo Conca '05	▽▽	8
● Barolo Conca Marcenasco '04	▽▽	8
● Barolo Marcenasco '05	▽▽	7
● Barolo Rocche '05	▽▽	8
● Barolo Rocche Marcenasco '04	▽▽	8
● Nebbiolo d'Alba Ochetti '07	▽▽	5

Ressia

via Canova, 28
12052 Neive [CN]
tel. 0173677305
www.ressia.com

CELLAR SALES
PRE-BOOKED VISITS

ANNUAL PRODUCTION 25,000 bottles
HECTARES UNDER VINE 6
VITICULTURE METHOD Conventional

Fabrizio Ressia directs this small operation in the Barbaresco area. Wine quality is consistent and high, the style a textbook reflection of local terroir and the price tags are reasonable and competitive, all excellent reasons for searching out Ressia's wines. The iconic bottle here is Barbaresco Canova, sourced from the easternmost cru vineyard in the Neive district.

Overall, we did not see a repetition of last year's exceptional results but it is well known that quite a few Barbarescos suffered the effects of the heat in the summer of 2007 and that the 2008 barbera harvest was marked by persistent rainfall. Barbaresco Canova '07 is sound and pleasurable, with dried flowers and marmalade already rather noticeable. The palate is fairly smooth but a tad alcoholic, despite decent acidity. Dark cherry backgrounds emphatic balsam in Barbera d'Alba Canova Superiore '08, followed by a rich palate that is somewhat unsettled by noticeable oak.

● Barbaresco Canova '07	TT	6
● Barbera d'Alba Sup. Canova '08	TT	4
○ Evien '09	TT	4
● Dolcetto d'Alba Canova '09	T	4
● Barbaresco Canova '06	YYY	6*
● Barbaresco Canova '05	YY	6
● Barbaresco Canova '04	YY	6
● Barbera d'Alba Canova '07	YY	4
● Barbera d'Alba Sup. Canova '07	YY	4*
● Dolcetto d'Alba Sup. Canova '06	YY	3
○ Evien '08	YY	4*
○ Evien Oro '07	YY	4
● Langhe Nebbiolo Gepù '06	YY	5

F.lli Revello

fraz. Annunziata, 103
12064 La Morra [CN]
tel. 017350276
www.revellofratelli.it

CELLAR SALES
PRE-BOOKED VISITS

ANNUAL PRODUCTION 65,000 bottles
HECTARES UNDER VINE 12
VITICULTURE METHOD Organic

Revello represents a happy combination of high-quality wine production and agriturismo activities. Their painstaking attention to detail is obvious in the hospitality and tasting areas, as well as in their modern, rational wine cellar. Carlo and Enzo Revello are utterly committed to their craft, producing a line of bright, appealing and firmly structured wines. The use of oak is improving the proportions of all of the wines we tasted.

Barolo Rocche dell'Annunziata '06 almost took home the top award. Its spacious, modernist nose showcases harmonious spice and red berries, and poise also marks the palate. Not particularly muscular, it is savoury and elegant, with a steady tannin-edged development. Finesse characterizes Barolo Vigna Gattera '06. It opens to smooth spice and raspberry, and then rugged but not aggressive tannins, finishing long. Barolo Vigna Giachini '06 exudes refined evolved impressions. The tannins are still somewhat rough and dusty but its succulence and length augur for good ageing. Both Vigna Conca and the standard '06, though less complex, are well crafted, the first offering rich spice.

● Barolo Rocche dell'Annunziata '06	TT	8
● Barolo V. Gattera '06	TT	7
● Barolo V. Giachini '06	TT	8
● Barbera d'Alba '09	TT	4*
● Barbera d'Alba Ciabot du Re '08	TT	6
● Barolo '06	TT	6
● Barolo V. Conca '06	TT	8
● Dolcetto d'Alba '09	TT	4*
● Langhe Nebbiolo '09	TT	5
● Barbera d'Alba Ciabot du Re '05	YYY	6
● Barbera d'Alba Ciabot du Re '00	YYY	7
● Barolo '93	YYY	8
● Barolo Rocche dell'Annunziata '01	YYY	8
● Barolo Rocche dell'Annunziata '00	YYY	8
● Barolo Rocche dell'Annunziata '97	YYY	8
● Barolo V. Conca '99	YYY	8

Michele Reverdito

FRAZ. RIVALTA
B.TA GARASSINI, 74B
12064 LA MORRA [CN]
TEL. 017350336
www.reverdito.it

CELLAR SALES
PRE-BOOKED VISITS

ANNUAL PRODUCTION 70,000 bottles
HECTARES UNDER VINE 18
VITICULTURE METHOD Conventional

This young operation, with superb vineyard resources ranging from nebbiolo through pelaverga, is determinedly stalking the highest quality possible at an impressive pace. All of the wines we tasted demonstrated an expressive vigour and varietal clarity truly among the best in the area. Last but certainly not least, accolades for very judicious price tags. Winemaking protocols differ widely, and depend on Reverdito's judgement, while cask conditioning varies significantly both in time and in type of barrel.

Three Glasses go for the first time to young Michele Reverdito. He has fine nebbiolo vineyards at La Morra and in Serralunga, with some vines in Verduno as well. The beribboned wine, Barolo Bricco Cogni '04, hails from a 40-year-old La Morra vineyard. It matured two years in barriques, another year in large wood, then considerable time in the bottle. It is as complex as one could want, with rich chocolate on the nose, a firm-structured yet smooth palate, showing dense and long-lingering. The other Barolos are very good indeed. Barbera Butti '07 is terrific. It still bears the signs of its two years in barriques but is already elegant.

● Barolo Bricco Cogni '04	▼▼▼	7
● Barbera d'Alba Butti '07	▼▼	4*
● Barbera d'Alba Delia '06	▼▼	5
● Barolo '06	▼▼	6
● Barolo Codane '06	▼▼	6
● Barolo Moncucco '05	▼▼	6
● Langhe Nebbiolo Simane '08	▼	4
● Verduno Pelaverga '09	▼	4
● Barbera d'Alba '07	▽▽	4
● Barolo Badarina '05	▽▽	6
● Barolo Codane '05	▽▽	6
● Barolo Moncucco '04	▽▽	6
● Barolo Serralunga '04	▽▽	6
● Dolcetto d'Alba Sup. Formica '07	▽▽	4
● Langhe Nebbiolo Simane '07	▽▽	4

Carlo Daniele Ricci

VIA MONTALE CELLI, 9
15050 COSTA VESCOVATO [AL]
TEL. 0131838115
www.aziendaagricolaricci.com

CELLAR SALES
PRE-BOOKED VISITS
ROOMS AND FOOD

ANNUAL PRODUCTION 30,000 bottles
HECTARES UNDER VINE 8
VITICULTURE METHOD Conventional

This dynamic operation in the Tortona area happily combines fine winemaking with equally fine agriturismo activities. Year after year, Carlo Daniele Ricci produces an array of wines that display rich personalities, often quite original, and admirably reflect their terroirs. At times, they are somewhat mute in the first months after bottling but their depth and intense flavours eventually shine.

A lively straw yellow introduces Terre del Timorasso '08, followed by an aromatic duet of fruit and toasty oak; the mouth already exhibits fine balance and length. Bonarda El Matt '08 is appealing, with pungent impressions of fresh greens veining its fruit. There is fine weight and pulp in the mouth while intense flavours compensate for a rough patch or two on the finish. The deep ruby Elso '07 is a Croatina with a broad nose and well-proportioned palate. Completing the team is the nebbiolo and barbera San Martino '07, which nods more to power than finesse.

○ Colli Tortonesi Terre del Timorasso '08	▼▼	4
● Colli Tortonesi Rosso Elso '07	▼	4
● Colli Tortonesi Rosso S. Martino '07	▼	4
● Piemonte Bonarda El Matt '08	▼	3
● Colli Tortonesi Barbera Castellania '06	▽▽	5
○ Colli Tortonesi Bianco S. Leto '03	▽▽	5
● Colli Tortonesi Rosso Elso '05	▽▽	4
● Colli Tortonesi Rosso S. Martino '06	▽▽	5
○ Colli Tortonesi Terre del Timorasso '07	▽▽	4
○ Colli Tortonesi Terre del Timorasso '05	▽▽	4
○ Colli Tortonesi Terre del Timorasso '04	▽▽	4
● Piemonte Bonarda El Matt '07	▽▽	4*

Giuseppe Rinaldi

via Monforte, 3
12060 Barolo [CN]
tel. 017356156
rinaldimarta@libero.it

CELLAR SALES
PRE-BOOKED VISITS

ANNUAL PRODUCTION **35,000 bottles**
HECTARES UNDER VINE **6**
VITICULTURE METHOD **Organic**

A historic cellar and a original wine man are the two faces of this operation, located inside a striking early-1900s building in the Barolo hills. Every bottle crafted by Beppe Rinaldi is imbued with a classic spirit and bespeaks his deep reverence for the local land. These days, when so much discussion now centres around the rediscovery and further development of traditional winemaking, the labours of "Citrico" are finally finding general appreciation and recognition.

Barolo Brunate-Le Coste '06 is a marvel. An intense wine, it parades refined raspberry and tobacco leaf alongside the classic spiciness of the nebbiolo grape. Though not huge, the palate has juicy tannins and a harmonious, lingering finish. Yes, there are some tartrates in suspension but wines here are not filtered nor do they receive much clarification. Three Glasses to the classic school of Barolo. Cannubi San Lorenzo-Ravera '06 is only slightly less complex. Its tannins show some bite but the palate makes a strong statement overall. For the lovers of real Freisa, without fizzy frippery, here is an extraordinary example, proffering rich raspberry, pepper and perfect tannins.

● Barolo Brunate-Le Coste '06	▼▼▼	8
● Barolo Cannubi S. Lorenzo-Ravera '06	▼▼	8
● Langhe Freisa '08	▼▼	5
● Langhe Nebbiolo '08	▼▼	5
● Barolo Brunate-Le Coste '01	▽▽▽	7
● Barolo Brunate-Le Coste '00	▽▽▽	7
● Barolo Brunate-Le Coste '97	▽▽▽	7
● Barolo Cannubi S. Lorenzo-Ravera '04	▽▽▽	7
● Barbera d'Alba '07	▽▽	4
● Barbera d'Alba '06	▽▽	4*
● Barolo Brunate-Le Coste '05	▽▽	7
● Barolo Brunate-Le Coste '04	▽▽	7
● Barolo Cannubi S. Lorenzo-Ravera '05	▽▽	7
● Barolo Cannubi S. Lorenzo-Ravera '04	▽▽	7
● Langhe Nebbiolo '07	▽▽	5

Rizzi

via Rizzi, 15
12050 Treiso [CN]
tel. 0173638161
www.cantinarizzi.it

CELLAR SALES
PRE-BOOKED VISITS
ROOMS

ANNUAL PRODUCTION **50,000 bottles**
HECTARES UNDER VINE **35**
VITICULTURE METHOD **Conventional**

This large, family winery in the Barbaresco district is showing increasing consistency year after year. The carefully honed Dellapiana style displays a profound respect for local traditions and for the classic approach. They use large oak almost exclusively. In addition to their prestigious Barbaresco crus, the other wines are well made and show clean-edged definition.

Barbaresco Rizzi '06 is intense and multi-faceted, combining sweet tobacco and spices with crisp hints of star anise. Spacious and admirably structured, it has pulpy fruit that checks the austere tannins on the finish. Still youthful, it is already delicious. The nose on Barbaresco Nervo Fondetta '07 releases both ripe fruit and dried flowers but it is mostly the palate that conveys appreciable elegance, with measured tannins and a smooth, untroubled finish. Barbaresco Pajoré '07 is the opposite, the elegance of the nose contrasted by overall astringency in the mouth. Chardonnay '09 impresses with its rich tropical fruit and citrus on the nose.

● Barbaresco Rizzi '06	▼▼	6
● Barbaresco Nervo Fondetta '07	▼▼	6
● Barbaresco Pajorè '07	▼▼	6
● Barbera d'Alba '08	▼▼	4
● Dolcetto d'Alba '09	▼▼	4
○ Langhe Chardonnay '09	▼▼	4
○ Moscato d'Asti '09	▼	4
● Barbaresco '05	▽▽	6
● Barbaresco Nervo Fondetta '06	▽▽	6
● Barbaresco Nervo Fondetta '05	▽▽	6
● Barbaresco Pajorè '06	▽▽	6
● Barbaresco Pajorè '05	▽▽	6
● Barbaresco Rizzi Boito '06	▽▽	6
● Barbaresco Rizzi Boito '05	▽▽	6

★ Albino Rocca

s.da Ronchi, 18
12050 Barbaresco [CN]
tel. 0173635145
www.roccaalbino.com

CELLAR SALES
PRE-BOOKED VISITS

ANNUAL PRODUCTION 130,000 bottles
HECTARES UNDER VINE 23
VITICULTURE METHOD Conventional

The Barbarescos of Angelo and Paola Rocca are tangible proof of the anachronistic silliness of reducing everything to an artificial traditonalist-modernist dichotomy. The Roccas perform brief macerations, and use barriques, only some new, as well as Austrian 20-hectolitre casks. Their wines are consistent winners, displaying the character of crus such as Ovello and Ronchi without neglecting the other members of their growing team, including Dolcetto, Cortese, Barbera, Chardonnay and Moscato.

Ovello Vigna Loreto '07 seems to be one of those Barbarescos that finds all heads nodding. Earthy, balsamic impressions offers glimpses of yellow-fleshed fruit, with generosity and tautness in fine tension on the palate, which shows both upfront tannins and rich appeal. It received an uncontested Three Glasses. The Rocca's fine hand with the '07 vintage continues apace with a dense, approachable Barbaresco '07, and with Vigneto Brich Ronchi, deliciously crunchy, with spice and dried rose petals preceding a caressing palate that is also self-confident and cleanly tannic.

● Barbaresco Ovello V. Loreto '07	🍷🍷🍷	7
● Barbaresco Duemilasette '07	🍷🍷	6
● Barbaresco Vign. Brich Ronchi '07	🍷🍷	7
● Barbera d'Alba Gepin '08	🍷🍷	5
● Dolcetto d'Alba Vignalunga '09	🍷🍷	4*
○ Piemonte Cortese La Rocca '09	🍷🍷	5
● Barbera d'Alba '09	🍷	4
○ Langhe Chardonnay da Bertü '09	🍷	4
○ Moscato d'Asti '09	🍷	4
● Nebbiolo d'Alba Duemilaotto '08	🍷	4
● Barbaresco Vign. Brich Ronchi '05	🍸🍸🍸	7
● Barbaresco Vign. Brich Ronchi '03	🍸🍸🍸	7
● Barbaresco Vign. Brich Ronchi '00	🍸🍸🍸	7
● Barbaresco Vign. Brich Ronchi Ris. '04	🍸🍸🍸	8
● Barbaresco Vign. Loreto '04	🍸🍸🍸	7

★ Bruno Rocca

via Rabajà, 60
12050 Barbaresco [CN]
tel. 0173635112
www.brunorocca.it

CELLAR SALES
PRE-BOOKED VISITS

ANNUAL PRODUCTION 60,000 bottles
HECTARES UNDER VINE 15
VITICULTURE METHOD Conventional

Bruno Rocca is one of the great names in the wines of Piedmont and indeed of Italy. His restructured cellar is set in a fascinating landscape of unequalled beauty. His wines are hailed throughout the world, recognizable for their very personal style, made up of modernity, exuberance and impeccable structure. Though seductive in their youth, they harbour proven potential for longevity and stunning maturity.

An intense Barbaresco Rabajà '07 displays spicy oak but in an overall context that is crisp and clean, accompanied by alluring impressions of cocoa and liquorice. The palate is notable for its power and lushness, which dense tannins render just a tad austere. The nose on Barbaresco Maria Adelaide '06 still preserves some severity, backgrounded by dried herbs, cinchona, roast espresso and roots while the mouth is still overtly astringent and tannic but its length and build presage rewards for patience. Barbaresco Coparossa '07 shows much the same while Barbaresco '07 is more approachable, its structure fairly balanced and tannins in check.

● Barbaresco Coparossa '07	🍷🍷	8
● Barbaresco Maria Adelaide '06	🍷🍷	8
● Barbaresco Rabajà '07	🍷🍷	8
● Barbaresco '07	🍷🍷	7
● Barbera d'Alba '08	🍷🍷	6
● Barbera d'Asti '08	🍷🍷	5
○ Langhe Chardonnay Cadet '09	🍷🍷	5
● Langhe Rosso Rabajolo '08	🍷🍷	6
● Dolcetto d'Alba Vigna Trifolè '09	🍷	4
● Langhe Nebbiolo Fralù '08	🍷	5
● Barbaresco Coparossa '04	🍸🍸🍸	8
● Barbaresco Maria Adelaide '04	🍸🍸🍸	8
● Barbaresco Maria Adelaide '01	🍸🍸🍸	8
● Barbaresco Rabajà '01	🍸🍸🍸	8

Rocche Costamagna

VIA VITTORIO EMANUELE, 8
12064 LA MORRA [CN]
TEL. 0173509225
www.rocchecostamagna.it

CELLAR SALES
PRE-BOOKED VISITS
ROOMS

ANNUAL PRODUCTION 85,000 bottles
HECTARES UNDER VINE 14
VITICULTURE METHOD Conventional

The Locatelli family winery, with an absolutely gorgeous home cellar complex including charming guest rooms, is one of the Langhe's top producers for quality and reliability. Their interpretation of Barolo is in admirable tension between tradition and modernity, with deep, cleanly delineated wines of distinction. The rest of the considerable line of wines is just as impressive and all turned in good performances this year.

Barolo Rocche dell'Annunziata Bricco Francesco '06 stood out at our tastings, thanks to its refined nose of crisp red berries and some first hints of tobacco leaf. The proportions are admirable right through a finish that is just a tad drying. We mistakenly mentioned Barbera d'Alba Superiore Rocche delle Rocche '07 last year. This splendid vintage is markedly savoury, juicy and lengthy with juniper and smoky impressions enriching clean-edged, emphatic notes of fruit. Standing out among the other offerings are an elegant Barolo Rocche dell'Annunziata '06, the nicely varietal Langhe Nebbiolo Roccardo '09, a powerful Dolcetto Rùbis '09 and a well-fruited Dolcetto Murrae '09.

● Barbera d'Alba Sup. Rocche delle Rocche '07	5
● Barolo Bricco Francesco Rocche dell'Annunziata '06	7
● Barolo Rocche dell'Annunziata '06	6
● Dolcetto d'Alba Murrae '09	4*
● Dolcetto d'Alba Rùbis '09	4*
● Langhe Nebbiolo Roccardo '09	4
● Barbera d'Alba Annunziata '08	4
○ Langhe Arneis '09	4
⊙ Osé '09	4
● Barolo Rocche dell'Annunziata '04	6
● Barbera d'Alba Annunziata '07	4
● Barolo Bricco Francesco Rocche dell'Annunziata '05	7
● Barolo Bricco Francesco Rocche dell'Annunziata '04	7
● Barolo Rocche dell'Annunziata '05	6
● Dolcetto d'Alba Rùbis '08	4

★ Podere Rocche dei Manzoni

LOC. MANZONI SOPRANI, 3
12065 MONFORTE D'ALBA [CN]
TEL. 017378421
www.rocchedeimanzoni.it

CELLAR SALES
PRE-BOOKED VISITS

ANNUAL PRODUCTION 250,000 bottles
HECTARES UNDER VINE 40
VITICULTURE METHOD Conventional

Rodolfo Migliorini continues directing with a sure hand this large and prestigious operation, fortunate to have such a well-equipped and attractive headquarters. The extensive line of Roche dei Manzoni wines demands careful attention along the many steps of wine production. The style here is open, warm and exuberant. The bottles are seductive in their youth but capable of yielding great emotions after appropriate cellaring.

The most complex among the Barolos is Barolo Vigna Cappella di Santo Stefano, spicy and balsamic but well fruited as well. A rich, firmly structured palate offers tannins already well tucked in, followed by a lengthy finale. Barolo Big 'd Big shows a bit more fruity and appealing, smooth and easily approachable. Aromatic spice marks Barolo Vigna d'la Roul but it is a bit edgier than the previous two. A fine line of sparkling wines includes the excellent Valentino Brut Zero Riserva '02, which shows sensory complexity and a creamy mousse. The latest arrival is Valentino Brut Zero Rosé, mostly pinot nero with a little chardonnay. This '05 delivers rich red berry fruit.

● Barolo V. Big 'd Big '06	8
● Barolo V. Cappella di S. Stefano '06	8
● Barolo V. d'la Roul '06	8
○ Valentino Brut Zero Ris. '02	6
● Barbera d'Alba Sorito Mosconi '06	6
○ Langhe Chardonnay L'Angelica '06	8
○ Valentino Brut Ris. Elena '05	6
⊙ Valentino Brut Zero Rosé Ris. '05	8
● Barolo V. Big 'd Big '99	8
● Barolo V. Cappella di S. Stefano '01	8
● Barolo V. Cappella di S. Stefano '96	8
● Langhe Rosso Quatr Nas '99	7
● Langhe Rosso Quatr Nas '96	8
○ Valentino Brut Zero Ris. '98	6

Flavio Roddolo

FRAZ. BRICCO APPIANI
LOC. SANT'ANNA, 5
12065 MONFORTE D'ALBA [CN]
TEL. 017378535

ANNUAL PRODUCTION 22,500 bottles
HECTARES UNDER VINE 6
VITICULTURE METHOD Conventional

Flavio Roddolo is a fine example of a laconic grower who shuns the limelight, loving his life as he personally tends his vines as though they were his garden. His estate is in Bricco Appiani, geographically outside the DOCG, the first outpost of Alta Langa. Flavio makes deep-souled wines that can seem closed in their youth but with time reveal real emotional treasures. Responding to consumers, Roddolo is delaying release dates, giving the wine more months, at times a year.

Barolo Ravera '05 is complex, intense yet refined, proffering classic impressions such as tar and liquorice over a base of red berry fruit. The tannins appear a tad rough but not at all harsh and they indicate a rich, long life ahead. The cabernet Langhe Bricco Appiani '05 hasn't been this intriguing in years. It shows enormous character, sober and austere, with spice and tar grounding dark berry fruit. The mouth, too, almost shuns smoothness, gaining in uncompromising genuineness. Sourced from the first hill outside the Barolo zone, Nebbiolo '06 is magnificent, with a multi-layered bouquet and a complex, tannin-rich palate.

● Barolo Ravera '05	▼▼	6
● Langhe Rosso Bricco Appiani '05	▼▼	6
● Nebbiolo d'Alba '06	▼▼	5
● Barbera d'Alba Sup. Bricco Appiani '05	▼▼	5
● Dolcetto d'Alba '08	▼▼	3*
● Dolcetto d'Alba Sup. '07	▼▼	4*
● Barolo Ravera '04	▽▽▽	6
● Barolo Ravera '01	▽▽▽	6
● Barolo Ravera '97	▽▽▽	6
● Bricco Appiani '99	▽▽▽	6
● Barbera d'Alba '05	▽▽	4*
● Dolcetto d'Alba '07	▽▽	3*
● Dolcetto d'Alba Sup. '04	▽▽	4*
● Langhe Rosso Bricco Appiani '04	▽▽	6

Ronchi

S.DA RONCHI, 23
12050 BARBARESCO [CN]
TEL. 0173635156
info@aziendaagricolaronchi.it

CELLAR SALES
PRE-BOOKED VISITS

ANNUAL PRODUCTION 25,000 bottles
HECTARES UNDER VINE N.A .
VITICULTURE METHOD Conventional

The '07 Barbaresco Ronchi, sourced from the east and south east-facing nebbiolo vineyard of the same name, will be another year coming onto the market. Giancarlo Rocca, who directs this small family winery, believes that this can only improve the sensory expressivity of this invaluable wine. The line-up we tasted this year testified, as it always has, to the consistently high quality that makes Ronchi one of the most reliable producers in the area.

In the temporary absence of Ronchi, we tasted the very impressive Barbaresco '07. After a youthful garnet, the nose shines with ripe red berry fruit along with the first hint of already refined and complex evolved impressions of tar and tobacco leaf. The mouthfeel is soft, particularly considering its age, thanks to a suite of glossy, caressing tannins, free of any roughness or bitterness, and the finish shows tremendous class. Barbera d'Alba Terlé '08 is a well-behaved offspring of what has been correctly referred to as a difficult year for barbera. Fruity and supple, with crisp, pulpy fruit, it is an utterly delicious quaffer. Don't miss the elegant Dolcetto '09.

● Barbaresco '07	▼▼	6
● Barbera d'Alba Terlé '08	▼▼	4
● Dolcetto d'Alba '09	▼▼	4
○ Langhe Chardonnay '08	▼	4
● Barbaresco '05	▽▽	6
● Barbaresco '04	▽▽	6
● Barbaresco Ronchi '06	▽▽	6*
● Barbaresco Ronchi '05	▽▽	6
● Barbera d'Alba Terlé '07	▽▽	4
● Barbera d'Alba Terlé '06	▽▽	4
● Dolcetto d'Alba '07	▽▽	5
○ Langhe Chardonnay '05	▽▽	4

Giovanni Rosso

Loc. Baudana, 6
12050 Serralunga d'Alba [CN]
Tel. 0173613340
www.giovannirosso.com

CELLAR SALES
PRE-BOOKED VISITS

ANNUAL PRODUCTION 55,000 bottles
HECTARES UNDER VINE 10
VITICULTURE METHOD Organic

This winery at famous Serralunga has gone in a few years from being a new emerging cellar to being one of the most impressive producers in Langhe. Davide Rosso directs all activities, after the death last year of his talented father, Giovanni. Davide's philosophy mirrors a respect for local tradition as he strives to coax out every bit of character from the local terroir. In their youth, the wines show a bit introverted and rough but with cellaring they unveil surprising complexity.

We were able to taste only a very few wines this year but it is a pleasure to see this winery receive its first Three Glasses for an absolutely ringing Barolo Cerretta '06. It parades spacious scents of medicinal herbs, spices, dried blossoms and red berry fruit, then exhibits on the palate the qualities that make Serralunga crus famous: superb structure and firm tannins well supported by dense stuffing. This is a wine that will improve over many, many years. Barolo La Serra is always a prestigious wine, it too guaranteeing years of evolution, but at the moment it is in the grip of clenched tannins that will need some in the bottle to relax.

●	Barolo Cerretta '06	▼▼▼	8
●	Barolo La Serra '06	▼▼	8
●	Barbera d'Alba Donna Margherita '08	▼▼	4
●	Barolo Serralunga '06	▼▼	6
●	Barbera d'Alba Donna Margherita '07	▽▽	4
●	Barbera d'Alba Donna Margherita '06	▽▽	4
●	Barolo Cerretta '05	▽▽	8
●	Barolo Cerretta '04	▽▽	8
●	Barolo Cerretta '03	▽▽	8
●	Barolo La Serra '05	▽▽	8
●	Barolo La Serra '04	▽▽	8
●	Barolo Serralunga '05	▽▽	6
●	Barolo Serralunga '04	▽▽	6
●	Dolcetto d'Alba Le Quattro Vigne '08	▽▽	4*

Rovellotti

Interno Castello, 22
28074 Ghemme [NO]
Tel. 0163841781
www.rovellotti.it

CELLAR SALES
FOOD

ANNUAL PRODUCTION 70,000 bottles
HECTARES UNDER VINE 16
VITICULTURE METHOD Organic

There can be no more coherent relationship than that between Antonello Rovellotti and his line of wines. This celebrated Ghemme producer is as tempestuous and brilliant as his wines are unpredictable. Traditionals such as nebbiolo and vespolina grow cheek by jowl with foreigners such as cabernet, merlot and pinot nero, displaying classic interpretations alongside notions of more recent inspiration. It is always an enriching experience to meet him in his fabulous cellar in ancient Ricetto.

That genius-like, idiosyncratic stamp seems particularly evident is this year's line-up of wines. Ghemme Chioso dei Pomi '05 sets the paradigm, putting a massive, concentrated body against evolved aromatics and overly harsh tannins. Colline Novaresi Vespolina Ronco al Maso '09 is in many ways far more polished. It still has to digest some oak but its floral and balsamic finish gives more than a ray of hope. Colline Novaresi Bianco Il Criccone '09 also turned in a good performance, establishing an intriguing dialogue between evolved notes of dried fruit and nuts on the one hand and almost piercing acidity on the other.

○	Colline Novaresi Bianco Il Criccone '09	▼▼	4*
●	Colline Novaresi Vespolina Ronco al Maso '09	▼▼	3*
●	Ghemme Chioso dei Pomi '05	▼▼	6
⊙	Colline Novaresi Nebbiolo Valplazza '09	▼	4
●	Colline Novaresi Nebbiolo Valplazza '07	▽▽	4
●	Colline Novaresi Vespolina '05	▽▽	3*
●	Colline Novaresi Vespolina Ronco al Maso '07	▽▽	3*
●	Ghemme Chioso dei Pomi '04	▽▽	6
●	Ghemme Chioso dei Pomi '03	▽▽	6
●	Ghemme Chioso dei Pomi '01	▽▽	6
●	Ghemme Costa del Salmino Ris. '04	▽▽	6
●	Ghemme Ris. '98	▽▽	6
●	Sciatò Muloeta '05	▽▽	5
●	Sciatò Muloeta '04	▽▽	5

Podere Ruggeri Corsini

LOC. BUSSIA CORSINI, 106
12065 MONFORTE D'ALBA [CN]
TEL. 017378625
www.ruggericorsini.com

CELLAR SALES
PRE-BOOKED VISITS

ANNUAL PRODUCTION 60,000 bottles
HECTARES UNDER VINE 10
VITICULTURE METHOD Conventional

Loredana Addari and Nicola Argamante are totally dedicated to this small cellar in Monforte d'Alba, a terroir that often infuses into its Barolos intense aromas, considerable weight, and a potential for fine evolution in the bottle. The Podere Ruggeri Corsini house style has grown in quality and reliability over the years. But with so many well-known producers here in the neighbourhood, this cellar is better recognized abroad than in Italy, where it seems known only to a passionate and lucky few.

Of the two 2006 Barolos, we preferred Corsini. Sourced from 25 to 45-year-old vineyards, it currently displays a fairly austere character, manifesting itself in some tannic rigidity, but this is simply the stuff of youth. Its pulpy richness and long, savoury finale augur a long and happy future. San Pietro, too, suffers a tad from its youth but it lacks the stuffing of its elder brother and is thus caught in a tighter tannic grip. The powerful, rich Langhe Rosso Autenzio is all albarossa. Finally come the three local classics: the tannic but pleasureable Langhe Nebbiolo '08; Barbera d'Alba '09, fruit-filled and delicious; and the down-to-earth, approachable Dolcetto d'Alba '09.

● Barolo Corsini '06	2 black glasses	6
● Barbera d'Alba '09	2 black glasses	4*
● Barolo S. Pietro '06	2 black glasses	6
● Langhe Rosso Autenzio '07	2 black glasses	5
● Dolcetto d'Alba '09	1 black glass	4
○ Langhe Bianco '09	1 black glass	4
● Langhe Nebbiolo '08	1 black glass	4
● Barbera d'Alba Armujan '07	2 white glasses	4
● Barolo Corsini '05	2 white glasses	6
● Barolo S. Pietro '05	2 white glasses	6
● Dolcetto d'Alba '08	2 white glasses	4
● Langhe Nebbiolo '07	2 white glasses	4
● Langhe Nebbiolo '06	2 white glasses	4

Josetta Saffirio

LOC. CASTELLETTO, 39
12065 MONFORTE D'ALBA [CN]
TEL. 0173787278
www.josettasaffirio.com

CELLAR SALES
PRE-BOOKED VISITS

ANNUAL PRODUCTION 25,000 bottles
HECTARES UNDER VINE 6
VITICULTURE METHOD Conventional

The Josetta Saffirio cellar has an interesting history. It put out a couple of memorable vintages of Barolo in the late1980s, then closed up after a year or two. Almost 20 years later, Sara Vezza, Saffirio's daughter, opened up again and, with the assistance of her father, took up where things had left off. They have a scant five hectares of vineyard which, with a new, rational cellar, allow a modest production and a good quality level.

Our plaudits go to Langhe Bianco '08, first of all because we're speaking here of rossese bianco, which has suffered almost total abandonment. Appearing a luminous straw yellow, it boasts intense smoke, pine resin and honey plus a finish that is sharp-edged and lengthy. Langhe Alna Rosso '08 is nearly as impressive, showing rich and delicious on the nose but austere and lean in the mouth. The Saffirio stars, though, are still its Barolos. Persiera '06 flaunts complex aromatics of tobacco, raspberry and dried blossoms, followed by nobly tannic development. Riserva '04 is a step behind, even though its firm tannins promise a fine future.

● Barolo Persiera '06	2 black glasses	8
● Barolo Persiera Ris. '04	2 black glasses	8
○ Langhe Bianco '08	2 black glasses	4*
● Barolo '06	2 black glasses	7
● Langhe Rosso Alna Rosso '08	2 black glasses	5
● Barbera d'Alba '08	1 black glass	4
● Barolo '89	3 white glasses	8
● Barolo '88	3 white glasses	8
● Barbera d'Alba '07	2 white glasses	4
● Barolo '05	2 white glasses	6
● Barolo '04	2 white glasses	6
● Barolo Persiera '05	2 white glasses	8
● Barolo Persiera '04	2 white glasses	8
● Langhe Nebbiolo '07	2 white glasses	5

Cascina Salicetti

VIA CASCINA SALICETTI, 2
15050 MONTEGIOCO [AL]
TEL. 0131875192
www.cascinasalicetti.it

CELLAR SALES
PRE-BOOKED VISITS

ANNUAL PRODUCTION 25,000 bottles
HECTARES UNDER VINE 16
VITICULTURE METHOD Conventional

Salicetti enjoys a memorable setting since this family wine estate lies all in one beautiful spot, with 15 hectares of fine vineyards surrounding the cellar. Oenologist Anselmo, who also runs the operation, puts out a portfolio of very impressive wines that are fairly approachable, with a well-calibrated balance between varietal aromatics and fresh, flavourful palates. Price tags, too, are pegged nicely to wine quality.

A pale, luminous straw yellow with tinges of green announces Timorasso Ombra di Luna '08, then aromatic mineral and spice lead to a palate that is imposing but well proportioned and a lengthy finish. Barbera Punta del Sole '07 is another team star, its purple-rimmed, intense ruby complemented by pungent black pepper, spice and sweet tobacco. The mouth impresses with its balance and succulently rich pulp. Timorasso Derthona '08 is straightforward and nicely balanced while Rugras '07, an evolved Dolcetto, shows emphatic and complex. The final team members are Dolcetto Di Marzi '08 and Cortese Montarlino '09.

● Colli Tortonesi Barbera Punta del Sole '07	▼▼	5
○ Colli Tortonesi Timorasso Ombra di Luna '08	▼▼	5
● Colli Tortonesi Dolcetto Rugras '07	▼▼	3
○ Colli Tortonesi Timorasso Derthona '08	▼▼	4
● Colli Tortonesi Dolcetto Di Marzi '08	▼	3
● Colli Tortonesi Barbera Morganti '07	▽▽	4
● Colli Tortonesi Barbera Morganti '06	▽▽	4
○ Colli Tortonesi Cortese Montarlino '07	▽▽	4
● Colli Tortonesi Rosso Il Seguito '07	▽▽	4
○ Colli Tortonesi Timorasso Derthona '07	▽▽	4*
○ Colli Tortonesi Timorasso Ombra di Luna '07	▽▽	5
○ Colli Tortonesi Timorasso Ombra di Luna '06	▽▽	5
○ Colli Tortonesi Timorasso Ombra di Luna '05	▽▽	3

San Fereolo

LOC. SAN FEREOLO
B.TA VALDIBÀ, 59
12063 DOGLIANI [CN]
TEL. 0173742075
www.sanfereolo.com

PRE-BOOKED VISITS

ANNUAL PRODUCTION 46,000 bottles
HECTARES UNDER VINE 12
VITICULTURE METHOD Organic

Near Dogliani, the gateway to the Langhe, there is the tiny, octagonal church of San Fereolo, and right next to it Nicoletta Bocca built her cellar in 1992. A wine lover, she arrived from Milan knowing little of this world but she thirsted for knowledge. After a few years of an organic approach to grape-growing, she shifted to biodynamics, all with the goal of minimizing intrusions in the vineyard and cellar and of producing terroir-driven wines.

Dolcetto di Dogliani Valdibà '09 is the star but unfortunately it was the only Dolcetto ready to be tasted for this edition. Deep and vibrant, it parades gorgeous classic notes of blackberry and almond, then enters somewhat dry, since the tannins, though measured, are a bit stiff. In sum, a wine to return to. The only other wine we tasted was Langhe Austri '07, a barbera with a little nebbiolo. Here again we see some imbalance, with exuberant aromas of black berry fruit and forceful alcohol on the palate. It needs some further months to tamp down its tannins and gain equilibrium but rich stuffing and fruit are already road signs for a promising path to future excellence.

● Dolcetto di Dogliani Valdibà '09	▼▼	4*
● Langhe Rosso Austri '07	▼▼	5
● Dolcetto di Dogliani S. Fereolo '99	▽▽▽	4
● Dolcetto di Dogliani S. Fereolo '97	▽▽▽	4
● Langhe Rosso Austri '03	▽▽▽	5
● Langhe Rosso Brumaio '97	▽▽▽	5
○ Coste di Riavolo '07	▽▽	4
● Dogliani '07	▽▽	4*
● Dogliani '06	▽▽	4*
● Dolcetto di Dogliani Sup. 1593 '03	▽▽	5
● Dolcetto di Dogliani Valdibà '08	▽▽	4*
● Langhe Rosso Austri '06	▽▽	5
● Langhe Rosso Il Provinciale '07	▽▽	5

Tenuta San Sebastiano

CASCINA SAN SEBASTIANO, 41
15040 LU [AL]
TEL. 0131741353
www.dealessi.it

CELLAR SALES
PRE-BOOKED VISITS

ANNUAL PRODUCTION 70,000 bottles
HECTARES UNDER VINE 10
VITICULTURE METHOD Conventional

San Sebastiano is located along the road leading from Lu Monferrato towards Mirabello. From the winery, there is an enchanting view over the estate vineyards, which are almost all around the cellar. Here Roberto De Alessi jealously watches over his offspring, from the vineyards into the cellar, and the results he achieves are impressive. The line-up we tasted was outstanding, with Barbera Mepari on the top rung.

Here is an exceptional version of Barbera Mepari '07, showing a luminous but almost opaque ruby and with richly fragrant tanned leather and other evolved impressions. The palate fairly explodes with intense tactile sensations that go on forever. Sol-Do '07 is a garnet-tending ruby with initial cinchona soon shading to an evolved headiness. Its tannins are noticeable and the conclusion quite rich. Passito LV '08, from part-dried moscato grapes, parades apricot and honey then fashions a wondrous balance between crisp acidity and smooth sweetness. In the more simple cabernet and merlot Dalera '06, berries and spice are followed in the mouth by fine proportion and length.

● Barbera del M.to Sup. Mepari '07	▼▼	5
○ M.to Bianco LV Passito '08	▼▼	4
● M.to Rosso Sol-Do '07	▼▼	4
● M.to Rosso Dalera '06	▼	4
● Piemonte Grignolino '08	▼	3
● Barbera del M.to '08	▽▽	3*
● Barbera del M.to Sup. Mepari '06	▽▽	5
● Barbera del M.to Sup. Mepari '05	▽▽	4*
● Grignolino del M.to Casalese '07	▽▽	3*
○ LV Passito '07	▽▽	4
● M.to Rosso Dalera '05	▽▽	6
● M.to Rosso Dalera '04	▽▽	4
● M.to Rosso Sol-Do '06	▽▽	4*
● M.to Rosso Sol-Do '05	▽▽	4*

★ Luciano Sandrone

VIA PUGNANE, 4
12060 BAROLO [CN]
TEL. 0173560023
www.sandroneluciano.com

CELLAR SALES
PRE-BOOKED VISITS

ANNUAL PRODUCTION 95,000 bottles
HECTARES UNDER VINE 25
VITICULTURE METHOD Conventional

Luca Sandrone could be said to be the modernist most loved by traditionalists, were we to adopt the current Langhe clichés. The reason is that Sandrone, here assisted by daughter Barbara and brother Luca, is able to fashion his expressive Barolo crus with powers that go far beyond mere winemaking techniques. In any case, both his Cannubi Boschis and Le Vigne macerate some ten days, then mature 24 months in 500-litre tonneaux. And much the same is true of his Barbera and Dolcetto.

Barolo Cannubi Boschis conquers its umpteenth laurel crown, in one of the best interpretations of the generous but by no means uniform 2006 vintage. Noble hints of oak join citron and red pepper, enriching still further beguiling notes of bouquet garni and wild red berry. But it is the mouth that makes the difference, exhibiting textbook extraction and leaving a precious memory of perfect roundness. Barolo Le Vigne '06 is a near-twin, which shows just a shade darker in its blackberry, cocoa and incense. It is full and powerful, with an unyielding but pleasurable tautness. We tasted Barbera d'Alba '08 as well.

● Barolo Cannubi Boschis '06	▼▼▼	8
● Barbera d'Alba '08	▼▼	6
● Barolo Le Vigne '06	▼▼	8
● Barolo Cannubi Boschis '05	▽▽▽	8
● Barolo Cannubi Boschis '04	▽▽▽	8
● Barolo Cannubi Boschis '03	▽▽▽	8
● Barolo Cannubi Boschis '01	▽▽▽	8
● Barolo Cannubi Boschis '00	▽▽▽	8
● Barolo Le Vigne '99	▽▽▽	8
● Barbera d'Alba '07	▽▽	6
● Barolo Le Vigne '05	▽▽	8
● Barolo Le Vigne '04	▽▽	8
● Nebbiolo d'Alba Valmaggiore '07	▽▽	6

Cantine Sant'Agata

REG. MEZZENA, 19
14030 SCURZOLENGO [AT]
TEL. 0141203186
www.santagata.com

CELLAR SALES
PRE-BOOKED VISITS

ANNUAL PRODUCTION 150,000 bottles
HECTARES UNDER VINE 11
VITICULTURE METHOD Conventional

Brothers Claudio and Franco Cavallero direct this reputable cellar, owned by the same family for a century now, focusing on the natives: barbera, cortese, grignolino, nebbiolo and ruché. The Cavalleros have devoted much research to this last grape, an aromatic variety that shows quite distinctive characteristics in this area, and over the past few years they have utilized it in a number of their wines.

Monferrato Genesi '07 unites two varieties, barbera and ruché in a 60-40 blend. The nose is stylish, redolent of tobacco, black pepper and raspberry, while the palate is mid-bodied with a fabulous tannin-laced development and a lengthy finish that is austere, but judiciously so. Barbera d'Asti Superiore Altea '07 turns to cinchona and cocoa powder over a foundation of dried plum and blackberry, then builds a palate of significant power and character, but with tannins that seem a tad grainy. Ruché di Castagnole Monferrato Il Cavaliere '09 releases classy wild roses and black liquorice. The tannins are well integrated on a full, spacious palate and the finish gleams with character.

● Barbera d'Asti Sup. Altea '07	▼▼	4
● M.to Rosso Genesi '07	▼▼	6
● Ruché di Castagnole M.to Il Cavaliere '09	▼▼	4*
● Grignolino d'Asti Miravalle '09	▼	4
● Ruché di Castagnole M.to Pro Nobis '09	▼	5
● Barbera d'Asti Sup. Altea '06	▽▽	4*
● Barbera d'Asti Sup. Cavalé '07	▽▽	5
● Ruché di Castagnole M.to 'Na Vota '08	▽▽	4
● Ruché di Castagnole M.to 'Na Vota '07	▽▽	4*
● Ruché di Castagnole M.to Pro Nobis '06	▽▽	5
● Ruché di Castagnole M.to Pro Nobis '05	▽▽	5

Paolo Saracco

VIA CIRCONVALLAZIONE, 6
12053 CASTIGLIONE TINELLA [CN]
TEL. 0141855113
info@paolosaracco.it

CELLAR SALES
PRE-BOOKED VISITS

ANNUAL PRODUCTION 400,000 bottles
HECTARES UNDER VINE 40
VITICULTURE METHOD Conventional

This historic operation at Castiglione Tinella reaches its third generation in the person of Paolo Saracco. Since 1986, he has infused it with energy, building the vineyards to their current 14 separate parcels, each with different exposures, elevations and soils, and enlarging the cellar to handle the increased production. There are some still wines, two whites and a fascinating Pinot Nero, but they put out 500,000 bottles yearly of Moscato d'Asti and the outstanding Moscato d'Autunno selection.

We always expect that Moscato d'Autunno will be good. But the '09 goes far beyond that, routing its competitors, thanks to harmonious proportions, magnificent, non-cloying aromatics and, finally, to its outstanding structure, all auguring it a bright future. A smooth, seductive Three Glasses. The lovely Moscato d'Asti '09 is creamy, fresh and irresistibly delicious. So is the promising, notably varietal Pinot Nero '08, impressing with velvety spice and gracious body. The ripe fruit and deliciously bitterish finish on Chardonnay Prasué '09 brings to mind a delicately complex, French-like minerality. The very young Riesling '09 pleases for its crisp, fresh mouth and fine structure.

○ Piemonte Moscato d'Autunno '09	▼▼▼	4*
○ Moscato d'Asti '09	▼▼	4
○ Langhe Chardonnay Prasuè '09	▼▼	4
● M.to Rosso Pinot Nero '08	▼▼	5
○ M.to Bianco Riesling '09	▼	4
○ Langhe Chardonnay Prasuè '07	▽▽	4
○ Langhe Chardonnay Prasuè '06	▽▽	4
● M.to Rosso Pinot Nero '06	▽▽	5
● M.to Rosso Pinot Nero '05	▽▽	5
○ Moscato d'Asti '08	▽▽	4
○ Moscato d'Asti '07	▽▽	4
○ Moscato d'Asti '06	▽▽	4
○ Piemonte Moscato d'Autunno '08	▽▽	4*
○ Piemonte Moscato d'Autunno '07	▽▽	4*

Roberto Sarotto

via Ronconuovo, 13
12050 Neviglie [CN]
tel. 0173630228
www.robertosarotto.com

CELLAR SALES
PRE-BOOKED VISITS

ANNUAL PRODUCTION 150,000 bottles
HECTARES UNDER VINE 50
VITICULTURE METHOD Conventional

The dynamic Roberto Sarotto runs a large operation, producing almost all the main Piedmont designations. That means lots of labels offering sound, reliable quality across the board. The winery's success rests on its vineyards, some owned, others leased, in fine wine country in each of the designations. The wines' style revolves around straightforward, well-managed, easy drinking. They are also invitingly priced.

Roberto Sarotto's list is long and the wines vary widely in type and price. He started with moscato at the historic winery at Neviglie, and now has three separate production facilities: Tenuta Manenti at Gavi for Cortese; Neive for Barbaresco; and Novello for Barolo. The '06 vintage was a good one for Roberto's Barolo. Audace is intense, complex, tannin-rich and full of character while Briccobergera '05 shows over-evolved on the nose and young on the palate. The '06 Barbarescos also turned out better than the '05s. Gaia Principe '06 is plush and firm while the Riserva '05 from the same vineyard is more evolved, although the tannins have yet to unbend.

● Barolo Audace '06	2 black glasses	6
● Barbaresco Gaia Principe '06	2 black glasses	6
● Barbaresco Gaia Principe Ris. '05	2 black glasses	7
● Barbera d'Alba Elena '08	2 black glasses	4*
● Barolo Bricco Bergera '05	2 black glasses	6
○ Gavi del Comune di Gavi Aurora '09	2 black glasses	4*
○ Gavi del Comune di Gavi Bric Sassi '09	2 black glasses	4*
○ Gavi del Comune di Gavi Campo dell'Olio '09	2 black glasses	5
● Langhe Rosso Enrico I '06	2 black glasses	6
● Barbera d'Alba Briccomacchia '08	1 black glass	4
● Dolcetto d'Alba San Ponzio '09	1 black glass	4
○ Moscato d'Asti Solatìo '09	1 black glass	4
● Barbaresco Gaia Principe Ris. '04	2 white glasses	7
● Barolo Audace Ris. '00	2 white glasses	7
● Langhe Rosso Enrico I '03	2 white glasses	5

Scagliola

via San Siro, 42
14052 Calosso [AT]
tel. 0141853183
www.scagliola-sansi.com

CELLAR SALES
PRE-BOOKED VISITS

ANNUAL PRODUCTION 140,000 bottles
HECTARES UNDER VINE 23
VITICULTURE METHOD Conventional

This historic, family-run winery, located in the Calosso hills, offers a range of consistently excellent wines. Barbera and moscato take pride of place, but plantings also include dolcetto, nebbiolo, brachetto, grignolino, cortese, cabernet and chardonnay. The vineyards are situated 300-400 metres above sea level, on medium-textured limestone and clay soils or sandy marl.

Barbera d'Asti Superiore Sansì Selezione '07 made our finals. Concentrated yet fresh, it boasts coffee, cocoa, bramble jelly and black cherries. We liked Moscato d'Asti Volo di Farfalle '09 for its classic citrus, peach and sage over an intense, rich palate, although the finish is slightly too sweet. Barbera d'Asti Frem '09 gives quinine and blackberry over an attractively full-bodied, refreshing palate. Also good are the Barbera d'Asti Superiore Sansì '08, with evolved aromas of cinnamon and red fruit, and the rich, juicy Monferrato Rosso Azörd '07, an equal-parts blend of barbera, cabernet sauvignon and nebbiolo, which lacks a little character.

● Barbera d'Asti Sup. SanSì Sel. '07	2 black glasses	8
○ Asti Moscato Volo di Farfalle '09	2 black glasses	5
● Barbera d'Asti Frem '09	2 black glasses	5
● Barbera d'Asti Sup. SanSì '08	2 black glasses	7
● M.to Rosso Azörd '07	2 black glasses	6
○ Asti Moscato Primo Bacio '09	1 black glass	4
● Barbera d'Asti Sup. SanSì Sel. '01	3 white glasses	7
● Barbera d'Asti Sup. SanSì Sel. '00	3 white glasses	7
● Barbera d'Asti Sup. SanSì Sel. '99	3 white glasses	7

La Scamuzza

CASCINA POMINA, 17
15049 VIGNALE MONFERRATO [AL]
TEL. 0142926214
www.lascamuzza.it

CELLAR SALES
PRE-BOOKED VISITS

ANNUAL PRODUCTION 15,000 bottles
HECTARES UNDER VINE 6
VITICULTURE METHOD Conventional

Thanks to the excellent results achieved with the latest wines from the '07 and '08 vintages, Laura Zavattaro has regained a position in the Guide more in line with the quality of her products. This estate in Vignale Monferrato has been operating since 1971, but has only been producing wine since 1973. It owns 40 hectares, of which around six are under Guyot-trained vines. The varieties planted are barbera, grignolino and cabernet sauvignon.

The fantastic, impenetrable ruby Barbera Vigneto della Amorosa '07 proffers black berry fruit, spice and tobacco on the nose, ushering in a muscular, heavy palate with a lingering finish. The charming Bricco San Tomaso '08 is a blend of barbera and cabernet sauvignon with an extremely complex nose that unfurls mature notes of plum and blackberry over pencil lead and cocoa powder. On the powerful, sumptuous palate, there is a nice vegetal finish, nicely counterpointed by the acidity. Last up is the attractive, well-balanced Grignolino Tumas '08, which shows evolved, tertiary aromas over a fairly uncomplicated, tidy palate.

● Barbera del M.to Sup. Vign. della Amorosa '07	▼▼	5
● M.to Rosso Bricco S. Tomaso '08	▼▼	5
● Grignolino del M.to Casalese Tumas '08	▼	4
● Barbera del M.to Baciamisubito '03	▽▽	4*
● Barbera del M.to Sup. Vign. della Amorosa '06	▽▽	5
● Barbera del M.to Sup. Vign. della Amorosa '05	▽▽	6
● Barbera del M.to Sup. Vign. della Amorosa '03	▽▽	6
● Grignolino del M.to Casalese Tumas '07	▽▽	4*
● M.to Rosso Bricco S. Tomaso '07	▽▽	5
● M.to Rosso Bricco San Tomaso '04	▽▽	5
● Monferrato Rosso Bricco San Tomaso '05	▽▽	5

Giorgio Scarzello e Figli

VIA ALBA, 29
12060 BAROLO [CN]
TEL. 017356170
www.barolodibarolo.com

CELLAR SALES
PRE-BOOKED VISITS

ANNUAL PRODUCTION 25,000 bottles
HECTARES UNDER VINE 6
VITICULTURE METHOD Conventional

This family-run winery, situated just outside the centre of Barolo, concentrates its efforts on just a few serious labels. A perfect example is the Barolo Vigna Merenda, from grapes grown in a plot in the prestigious Sarmassa vineyard. The other soils are also in extremely good wine country and produce wines with a markedly traditional style, at their best after appropriate ageing. Prices are extremely reasonable.

The Barolo Merenda '06's best feature is its penetrating nose of incense and quinine combined with vegetal aromas and faint hints of truffle. On the palate, it shows austere, with severe tannins and outstanding length. Those prepared to wait will reap rewards. The '06 Barolo can be considered the younger brother of the more famous Vigna Merenda. It shows impressive structure and rough tannins on the palate but lacks similar depth of extract. The '07 Barbera d'Alba has tar on the nose against a backdrop of ripe black berry fruit, preceding a chewy palate with somewhat sweet fruit but austere overall. The range is completed by a tannin-rich, fruity Dolcetto '08.

● Barolo V. Merenda '06	▼▼	7
● Barbera d'Alba Sup. '07	▼▼	5
● Barolo '06	▼▼	6
● Dolcetto d'Alba '08	▼	4
● Barolo V. Merenda '99	▽▽▽	6
● Barbera d'Alba Sup. '06	▽▽	5
● Barbera d'Alba Sup. '05	▽▽	5
● Barolo '05	▽▽	6
● Barolo '04	▽▽	6
● Barolo V. Merenda '05	▽▽	7
● Barolo V. Merenda '04	▽▽	7
● Dolcetto d'Alba '06	▽▽	4
● Langhe Nebbiolo '07	▽▽	4*

★ Paolo Scavino

FRAZ. GARBELLETTO
VIA ALBA-BAROLO, 59
12060 CASTIGLIONE FALLETTO [CN]
TEL. 017362850
e.scavino@libero.it

CELLAR SALES
PRE-BOOKED VISITS

ANNUAL PRODUCTION 100,000 bottles
HECTARES UNDER VINE 20
VITICULTURE METHOD Conventional

Enrico Scavino is a scrupulous producer and a great experimenter. Controversially, he introduced rotofermenters into Langhe and used small wood. Enrico's latest passion is his custom-made steel vats for submerged-cap fermentation. Enrico is now looking for more personality in his Barolo, and is returning to medium-large barrels and prolonged maceration. The winery is a stunning Langhe château, with an elegant barrique cellar and maturation area. Barolo Bricco Ambrogio, sourced from Roddi d'Alba, will soon be joined by a Barolo di Verduno and a Barolo di Serralunga.

The superb series of Barolos is led by the exceptional Bric del Fiasco '06, vaunting focused raspberry and blackcurrant fruit. On the dense, velvety palate we find good length and a rare, elegant personality. This is quite simply a masterpiece. Three other Barolos stand out in this magnificent range: the Riserva Rocche dell'Annunziata '04, the Carobric and the Cannubi, and a superb Barbera d'Alba '07.

● Barolo Bric del Fiasc '06	▼▼▼	8
● Barolo Cannubi '06	▼▼	8
● Barolo Carobric '06	▼▼	8
● Barolo Rocche dell'Annunziata Ris. '04	▼▼	8
● Barbera d'Alba Affinato in Carati '07	▼▼	6
● Barolo '06	▼▼	8
● Barolo Bricco Ambrogio '06	▼▼	8
○ Langhe Bianco '09	▼▼	4
● Langhe Nebbiolo '07	▼▼	6
○ Langhe Sorriso '08	▼▼	6
● Dolcetto d'Alba '09	▼	4
Barolo '84	▽▽▽	6
● Barolo Cannubi '92	▽▽▽	6
● Barolo Rocche dell'Annunziata Ris. '01	▽▽▽	8
● Barolo Rocche dell'Annunziata Ris. '97	▽▽▽	8
● Barolo Rocche dell'Annunziata Ris. '96	▽▽▽	8

Schiavenza

VIA MAZZINI, 4
12050 SERRALUNGA D'ALBA [CN]
TEL. 0173613115
www.schiavenza.com

CELLAR SALES
PRE-BOOKED VISITS
FOOD

ANNUAL PRODUCTION 35,000 bottles
HECTARES UNDER VINE 8
VITICULTURE METHOD Conventional

We would like to express our heartfelt sympathy to Luciano Pira and Maura Alessandria for the loss of their son Umberto. It's a thought we are sure we share with all the wine lovers who over the years have had the chance to visit Schiavenza, maybe stopping at the family restaurant and finding in the wines the indomitable character of Serralunga's uncompromising Nebbiolo. Prapò, Bricco Cerretta, Broglio and Perno di Monforte are four great vineyard selections, given serious ageing in medium-sized barrels.

We never cease to be amazed at how Schiavenza's Barolos manage to hint at their immense stature despite being some of slowest to open up and unbend. A case in point is the Barolo Prapò '06, is earthy and compact but also promises fantastic development, or the Bricco Cerretta '06, with hard, uncompromising tannins, lifted by rich stuffing. The most approachable seems to be the Broglio Riserva '04, aided by longer ageing. There are no flabby tannins to be expected here but reassuring wafts of citrus and cocoa powder soften the texture.

● Barolo Broglio Ris. '04	▼▼▼	6
● Barolo Bricco Cerretta '06	▼▼	6
● Barolo Prapò '06	▼▼	6
● Barolo Perno '06	▼▼	6
● Barolo Prapò Ris. '04	▼▼	6
● Barolo Broglio '05	▽▽▽	6
● Barolo Broglio '04	▽▽▽	6
● Barbera d'Alba Perno '06	▽▽	4
● Barbera d'Alba Perno '05	▽▽	4
● Barolo '04	▽▽	6
● Barolo Bricco Cerretta '04	▽▽	6
● Barolo Prapò '05	▽▽	6
● Dolcetto d'Alba Sorì '08	▽▽	4*
● Dolcetto d'Alba Vughera '08	▽▽	4*

Scrimaglio

Alessandria, 67
14049 Nizza Monferrato [AT]
tel. 0141721385
www.scrimaglio.it

CELLAR SALES
PRE-BOOKED VISITS

ANNUAL PRODUCTION **700,000 bottles**
HECTARES UNDER VINE **20**
VITICULTURE METHOD **Certified organic**

This Nizza Monferrato winery, established in the 1920s, continues to produce quality wines. The Barbera is the flagship of in a wide range of products, divided into a classic line and fashion wines, made using mostly, but not exclusively, native varieties. Organic methods accompany experiments in biodynamic farming and ISO 14001 environmental certification, in compliance with an eco-friendly philosophy.

The Scrimaglio family wins its first Three Glasses thanks to the Barbera d'Asti Superiore Nizza Acsé '07. Intense black berry fruit aromas, smoke, spice and balsamic minty notes are followed by a well-balanced, rich palate. Tight-knit and fresh-tasting, it offers Barbera's trademark acidity, ending on a long crunchy red fruit finish. The other Barberas are all well made, from the fruity, well-balanced Barbera d'Asti Superiore RoccaNivo '08 with hints of autumn leaves, showing great length and character, and the attractively drinkable Barbera d'Asti Superiore Fiat '07, with earth, tobacco and cherry, to the focused, fresh-tasting Barbera d'Asti Nowood '09.

● Barbera d'Asti Sup. Nizza Acsé '07	▼▼▼	6
● Barbera d'Asti NoWood '09	▼▼	4*
● Barbera d'Asti Sup. Fiat '07	▼▼	5
● Barbera d'Asti Sup. RoccaNivo '08	▼▼	4*
● Barbera d'Asti NoCork '09	▼	4
● Barbera d'Asti Sup. Acsé '04	▽▽	6
● Barbera d'Asti Sup. Acsé '03	▽▽	6
● Barbera d'Asti Sup. Crôutin '06	▽▽	6
● Barbera d'Asti Sup. Nizza Acsé '05	▽▽	6
● Barbera d'Asti Sup. Nizza Acsé '01	▽▽	6

Mauro Sebaste

fraz. Gallo
via Garibaldi, 222bis
12051 Alba [CN]
tel. 0173262148
www.maurosebaste.it

CELLAR SALES
PRE-BOOKED VISITS

ANNUAL PRODUCTION **150,000 bottles**
HECTARES UNDER VINE **25**
VITICULTURE METHOD **Conventional**

With around 25 well-tended hectares, this winery produces a selection of extremely reliable Piedmont wines. The range goes from whites to the area's classic reds: Dolcetto, Freisa, Nebbiolo and Barolo. Prestigious vineyard selections complete an excellent assortment worthy of the best estates, and clearly reflect the professionalism and passion of the owners.

Barolo Brunate has Riserva status from '06 so we'll have to wait two more years. Serralunga gives us a solidly built, sound Barolo Prapò '06, whose intense, earthy notes, liquorice and dried flowers usher in a surefooted palate with firm extract. Barolo Monvigliero from Verduno, also '06, is more approachable, thanks to a softer palate. From the hills overlooking Alba to the south comes a fruity, warm Dolcetto, the '09 Santa Rosalia. Barbera Centobricchi is not prize-winning material but has a classy palate. The Nebbiolo '08 Paris still shows evident oak while the well-styled Arneis '09 is an easy drinker. The well-rounded Barbera '07 has good body.

● Barbera d'Alba Sup. Centobricchi '08	▼▼	5
● Barolo Monvigliero '06	▼▼	7
● Barolo Prapò '06	▼▼	8
● Dolcetto d'Alba S. Rosalia '09	▼▼	4
○ Gavi '09	▼	4
● Nebbiolo d'Alba Parigi '08	▼	5
○ Roero Arneis '09	▼	4
● Barolo Brunate '05	▽▽	8
● Barolo Brunate '03	▽▽	7
● Barolo Monvigliero '05	▽▽	7
● Barolo Monvigliero '04	▽▽	7
● Barolo Prapò '05	▽▽	8
● Barolo Prapò '04	▽▽	8
● Langhe Freisa Sylla '08	▽▽	4

F.lli Seghesio

loc. Castelletto, 19
12065 Monforte d'Alba [CN]
tel. 017378108
az.agricolaseghesio@libero.it

CELLAR SALES
PRE-BOOKED VISITS

ANNUAL PRODUCTION 60,000 bottles
HECTARES UNDER VINE 10
VITICULTURE METHOD Conventional

Unfortunately, we open with the sad news of the death of Aldo, who with his brother Richard took the winery into Langhe's top flight. The out of the way Seghesio winery, surrounded by its own vineyards but also by plots owned by various prestigious Barolo producers, commands a wonderful view over some of the best wine country in Serralunga. Those who have never tried the fine wines offered by this winery may be attracted by its consistent quality and low prices. Apart from Barolo, Seghesio has a serious Barbera d'Alba, often one of the best of its kind.

In this round of tasting, we only had the chance to taste the thoroughly sound, deep-hued Barolo La Villa '06. The nose proffers raspberries and tobacco with light, elegant spice, over powerful tannins held in by good overall structure and a very long, perhaps over-assertive, finish. This will become a great Barolo. We are awaiting the Barbera d'Alba Vigneto della Chiesa '07, which promises real fireworks from a magnificent vintage.

● Barolo Vign. La Villa '06	🍷🍷	7
● Barbera d'Alba Vign. della Chiesa '00	YYY	6
● Barbera d'Alba Vign. della Chiesa '97	YYY	6
● Barolo Vign. La Villa '04	YYY	7
● Barolo Vign. La Villa '99	YYY	7
● Barolo Vign. La Villa '91	YYY	7
● Barbera d'Alba Vign. della Chiesa '06	YY	5
● Barolo Vign. La Villa '05	YY	7

Sella

via IV Novembre, 130
13060 Lessona [BI]
tel. 01599455
www.tenutesella.it

CELLAR SALES
PRE-BOOKED VISITS

ANNUAL PRODUCTION 80,000 bottles
HECTARES UNDER VINE 20
VITICULTURE METHOD Conventional

You can't say you know northern Piedmont until you have tried wines from Sella, the historic estate dating back to the 17th century. Bright and sophisticated, these are wines with a pure, deep style that perfectly reflects the diversity of the various zones. The sandy soil of Lessona is interpreted in one basic wine and two selections, while I Porfidi from Bramaterra pays tribute to its very different, porphyry soil. Vespolina, croatina and uva rara flank nebbiolo in the vineyards, and in the cellar large barrels rub shoulders with barriques of various ages.

Our finals saw Lessona triumph, starting with the '07, whose balance and complexity make it far more than a basic wine. With San Sebastian Zoppo '06, we move into crisper, spicier country, with red fruit and white pepper highlighting its territorial origins. L'Omaggio a Quintino Sella '05 is right up there with Italy's best wines this year. Rose petals and medicinal herbs give even further depth to a nose of rare beauty, perfectly echoed on a palate of superlative finesse.

● Lessona Omaggio a Quintino Sella '05	🍷🍷🍷	7
● Lessona '07	🍷🍷	6
● Lessona S. Sebastiano allo Zoppo '06	🍷🍷	7
● Bramaterra '07	🍷🍷	6
● Coste della Sesia Rosso Orbello '09	🍷🍷	4*
○ Coste della Sesia Bianco Doranda '09	🍷	4
⊙ Coste della Sesia Rosato Majoli '09	🍷	4
● Bramaterra I Porfidi '05	YYY	6
● Bramaterra I Porfidi '03	YYY	6
● Lessona S. Sebastiano allo Zoppo '04	YYY	6
● Lessona S. Sebastiano allo Zoppo '01	YYY	6
● Bramaterra I Porfidi '04	YY	6
● Coste della Sesia Rosso Casteltorto '06	YY	5
● Lessona '06	YY	5
● Lessona Omaggio a Quintino Sella '04	YY	7
● Lessona S. Sebastiano allo Zoppo '05	YY	6

Enrico Serafino

C.SO ASTI, 5
12043 CANALE [CN]
TEL. 0173979485
www.enricoserafino.it

CELLAR SALES
PRE-BOOKED VISITS

ANNUAL PRODUCTION 450,000 bottles
HECTARES UNDER VINE 13
VITICULTURE METHOD Conventional

The new start for Enrico Serafino's winery under the wing of Campari is most evident in the Cantina Maestra line of wines, which include the best selections of Roero wines and classic-method wines from Alta Langa. All the wines presented are extremely drinkable and show a fine sense of place. Special praise goes to the team managing the production chain, demonstrating that the quality and professionalism of a company's staff is fundamental to its success.

Lorenzo Barbero and Paolo Giacosa's hard work, with the unconditional support of Campari, has finally been rewarded with their first, well-deserved Three Glasses, assigned to the Zero '04. The award is for one of the winery's main products, classic-method sparkling wine from the Alta Langa DOC. This classy sparkler is the result of a strict selection of grapes, mostly pinot nero with small amounts of chardonnay, and combines beautifully taut acidity with a sharply-focused, complex nose. The vibrant, compelling Alta Langa Brut '05, wrongly listed in the last edition of the Guide, is just a touch simpler.

Wine	Glasses	
○ Alta Langa Zero Cantina Maestra Ris. '04	3 black glasses	5
○ Alta Langa Brut Cantina Maestra '05	2 black glasses	5
● Nebbiolo d'Alba Diauleri Cantina Maestra '08	2 black glasses	4*
● Barbera d'Alba Bacajé Cantina Maestra '09	2 black glasses	4*
● Barbera d'Alba Parduné Cantina Maestra '07	2 black glasses	5
● Roero '07	2 black glasses	4*
○ Roero Arneis Canteiò Cantina Maestra '09	2 black glasses	4
● Roero Pasiunà Cantina Maestra '07	2 black glasses	5
○ Roero Arneis '09	1 black glass	4
● Barbera d'Alba Sup. Parduné Cantina Maestra '05	2 white glasses	5
● Roero Pasiunà Cantina Maestra '06	2 white glasses	5
● Roero Pasiunà Cantina Maestra '05	2 white glasses	5
● Roero Sup. Pasiunà '04	2 white glasses	4*

Poderi Sinaglio

FRAZ. RICCA
VIA SINAGLIO, 5
12055 DIANO D'ALBA [CN]
TEL. 0173612209
www.poderisinaglio.it

CELLAR SALES
PRE-BOOKED VISITS
ROOMS AND FOOD

ANNUAL PRODUCTION 44,000 bottles
HECTARES UNDER VINE 13
VITICULTURE METHOD Conventional

The dynamic brothers, Bruno and Silvano Accomo run this interesting, yet little-known winery in the Diano area, which combines a farm holiday centre with the production of quality wine. The traditional wines of the Langhe – Nebbiolo, Dolcetto and Barbera – are worthily represented, and offer reliable quality at extremely reasonable prices.

The intense Dolcetto di Diano d'Alba '09 gave a fine performance, flaunting a great classic style with lashings of succulent fruit in the mouth, for a mouthfilling, satisfying drink. Refreshing and vinous, it shows excellent tannins and a lingering, appealing finish. We will have to wait another year for the Sorì Bric Maiolica '09 selection. The '08 Barbera d'Alba Vigna Erta also behaved well, with cherry to the fore supported by complex spice and tending towards sweetness on the finish. The Langhe Rosso Sinaij '07, from barbera, freisa and nebbiolo, aged in barrique for a year. Territorial and down-to-earth but original on the palate, it has incisive tannins and a long, spicy finish. The white version, made from chardonnay and sauvignon, has body, but is still oak-heavy.

Wine	Glasses	
● Barbera d'Alba V. Erta '08	2 black glasses	4
● Dolcetto di Diano d'Alba '09	2 black glasses	3*
● Langhe Nebbiolo '09	2 black glasses	4*
● Langhe Rosso Sinaij '07	2 black glasses	5
○ Langhe Bianco Boccabarile '08	1 black glass	4
○ Langhe Chardonnay '09	1 black glass	4
● Barbera d'Alba V. Erta '07	2 white glasses	4*
● Barbera d'Alba V. Erta '06	2 white glasses	4
● Diano d'Alba Sörì Bric Maiolica '07	2 white glasses	4
● Dolcetto di Diano d'Alba '07	2 white glasses	3
● Dolcetto di Diano d'Alba Sorì Bricco Maiolica '08	2 white glasses	4*
● Langhe Nebbiolo '08	2 white glasses	4
● Langhe Rosso Sinaij '06	2 white glasses	5

La Smilla

VIA GARIBALDI, 7
15060 BOSIO [AL]
TEL. 0143684245
www.lasmilla.it

CELLAR SALES

ANNUAL PRODUCTION 100,000 bottles
HECTARES UNDER VINE 6
VITICULTURE METHOD Conventional

The overall quality of La Smilla products is ever more convincing. After years of performing well, the Bosio winery has earned a reputation as one of the most reliable in Gavi. The grapes used for the wines are exclusively native: barbera, dolcetto and cortese.

Barbera Calicanto opens the range with an intriguing '07. Its vivid garnet hue anticipates aromas of red fruit and floral notes, echoed in the pulp-rich mouth. The fruity Dolcetto Ovada '08 shows lovely nose-palate harmony and the Barbera del Monferrato '08 combines intense fruit aromas with up-front acidity on the palate. The Gavi '09 has varietal cortese aromas and good balance on the palate. The Gavi del Comune di Gavi '09 highlights an evolved nose and velvety entry on the palate with a long finish. The bright Bergi '08 proffers intense blossom and aromatic herbs that usher in good concentration and flavour in the mouth, although the oak too assertive.

● Barbera del M.to Calicanto '07	🍷🍷	4
● Dolcetto di Ovada '08	🍷🍷	3*
○ Gavi '09	🍷🍷	3*
● Barbera del M.to '08	🍷	3
○ Gavi del Comune di Gavi '09	🍷	3
○ Gavi I Bergi '08	🍷	4
● Dolcetto di Ovada '07	🍸🍸	3*
● Dolcetto di Ovada Nsè Pesa '07	🍸🍸	4*
● Dolcetto di Ovada Nsè Pesa '06	🍸🍸	4*
○ Gavi '08	🍸🍸	3*
○ Gavi del Comune di Gavi '08	🍸🍸	3*
○ Gavi del Comune di Gavi '07	🍸🍸	3*
○ Gavi I Bergi '07	🍸🍸	4
○ Gavi I Bergi '06	🍸🍸	4

★ Sottimano

LOC. COTTÀ, 21
12052 NEIVE [CN]
TEL. 0173635186
www.sottimano.it

CELLAR SALES
PRE-BOOKED VISITS

ANNUAL PRODUCTION 65,000 bottles
HECTARES UNDER VINE 14
VITICULTURE METHOD Conventional

Don't judge by appearances. Barriques don't necessarily mean modernist wines. The Barbarescos produced by Rino Sottimano and his son Andrea need to be tasted to be believed. They have been some of the best in the DOCG for years. When young, they show marked extract and compact tannins but ageing reveals a bright style, reflecting the distinctive traits of vineyard selections such as Currà, Cottà, Fausoni and Pajorè. In the best vintages, the Sottimanos produce a Barbaresco Riserva, flanked by Dolcettos, Barberas and Brachettos.

After last year's fantastic debut, it is once again the Barbaresco Riserva that emerges from a consistently high-quality range. The cool growing year is reflected in the light fruit, corroborated by elegant vegetal and floral notes. Youth is even more evident on the palate, where the tannins bite without compromising lively drinkability. From the '07s we prefer, as often happens, the great finesse of Pajorè and the remarkable thrust of Cottà to the timid Fausoni and long, austere Currà. We were also impressed by the Langhe Nebbiolo '08 and the Barbera d'Alba Pairolero '08.

● Barbaresco Ris. '05	🍷🍷🍷	8
● Barbaresco Cottà '07	🍷🍷	8
● Barbaresco Pajoré '07	🍷🍷	8
● Barbaresco Currà '07	🍷🍷	8
● Barbaresco Fausoni '07	🍷🍷	8
● Barbera d'Alba Pairolero '08	🍷🍷	5
● Langhe Nebbiolo '08	🍷🍷	5
● Dolcetto d'Alba Bric del Salto '09	🍷	4
● Maté '09	🍷	4
● Barbaresco Cottà '05	🍸🍸🍸	8
● Barbaresco Cottà '99	🍸🍸🍸	7
● Barbaresco Currà '04	🍸🍸🍸	7
● Barbaresco Pajoré '01	🍸🍸🍸	7
● Barbaresco Pajoré '00	🍸🍸🍸	7
● Barbaresco Ris. '04	🍸🍸🍸	8

Luigi Spertino

via Lea, 505
14047 Mombercelli [AT]
tel. 0141959098
www.luigispertino.it

CELLAR SALES
PRE-BOOKED VISITS

ANNUAL PRODUCTION 40,000 bottles
HECTARES UNDER VINE 9
VITICULTURE METHOD Organic

The organic winery run by the Spertino family produces a range of quality wines from both native and international grape varieties, grown in small plots scattered around the towns of Mombercelli – home to the estate and the La Mandorla hill, from which the eponymous line of products originates – Vinchio, Nizza Monferrato, Moncalvo, Castagnole Monferrato, Portacomaro, Penango and Canelli. Aspects are generally favourable, ranging from south-east to south-west, and the vines are up to 50 years old.

Luigi and Mauro Spertino seem to like winning awards, and in the absence of the Barbera La Mandorla, Three Glasses went to their least conventional wine, the Pinot Nero Monferrato Rosso La Mandorla '07. It shows intense on the nose, with characteristic notes of wet dog and berries, while the fruit-rich palate is fresh, powerful and mouthfilling, with silky tannins and length nicely underpinned by acid thrust. We liked the classic, red fruits-themed Grignolino d'Asti '09, which shows fresh, pulpy and acidic, and the Barbera d'Asti '08, still closed on the nose, with hints of black fruit and spices finding it hard to emerge, over a juicy, full palate.

● M.to Rosso La Mandorla '07	▼▼▼	6
● Barbera d'Asti '08	▼▼	5
● Grignolino d'Asti '09	▼▼	4
● Barbera d'Asti Sup. La Mandorla '07	▽▽▽	8
● Barbera d'Asti '06	▽▽	4*
● Barbera d'Asti '05	▽▽	4*
● Barbera d'Asti '04	▽▽	4*
● Barbera d'Asti '03	▽▽	4*
● Barbera d'Asti Sup. La Mandorla '06	▽▽	6

★★★ La Spinetta

via Annunziata, 17
14054 Castagnole delle Lanze [AT]
tel. 0141877396
www.la-spinetta.com

PRE-BOOKED VISITS

ANNUAL PRODUCTION 550,000 bottles
HECTARES UNDER VINE 100
VITICULTURE METHOD Conventional

The instantly recognizable style of this consolidated winery has played a decisive role in the affirmation of Spinetta in markets around the world. The wines produced range from Moscato and the various Asti designations to vineyard selections of Barbaresco and Barolo. Giorgio Rivetti, the operation's heart and soul, continues to be an important professional benchmark for the growth of quality in Italian wine.

The 2007 growing year was excellent for Barbaresco. The superb Starderi has raspberry, liqueur cherries and oak spice, followed by a delicious, concentrated palate of caressing fruit. Impressive ripe fruit and spices on the Barolo Campè '06 precede a full, weighty palate of assertive tannins and upfront alcohol. As it breathes, lovely tobacco and dried flowers emerge, boding well for the future. Pin '08, from 65 per cent nebbiolo and 35 per cent barbera is top level. Oak provides faintly sweet, spicy aromas on the nose while on the thrusting, dense palate, nebbiolo tannins give magnificent structure. The superlative Barbera d'Asti Superiore Bionzo is a classic.

● Barbaresco Vign. Starderi '07	▼▼▼	8
● Barbaresco Vign. Valeirano '07	▼▼	8
● Barbera d'Asti Sup. Bionzo '08	▼▼	7
● Barolo Campè '06	▼▼	8
● M.to Rosso Pin '08	▼▼	7
● Barbaresco Vign. Bordini '07	▼▼	8
● Barbaresco Vign. Gallina '07	▼▼	8
● Barbera d'Alba Gallina '08	▼▼	7
● Langhe Nebbiolo '08	▼▼	6
○ Moscato d'Asti Bricco Quaglia '09	▼▼	4
○ Piemonte Chardonnay Lidia '08	▼▼	7
● Barbera d'Asti Ca' di Pian '08	▼	5
○ Langhe Bianco Sauvignon '07	▼	7
○ Piemonte Moscato Passito Oro '05	▼	7
● Barbaresco Vign. Starderi '05	▽▽▽	8
● Barbera d'Asti Sup. Bionzo '07	▽▽▽	7
● M.to Rosso Pin '06	▽▽▽	7

Luigi Tacchino

VIA MARTIRI DELLA BENEDICTA, 26
15060 CASTELLETTO D'ORBA [AL]
TEL. 0143830115
www.luigitacchino.it

CELLAR SALES
PRE-BOOKED VISITS

ANNUAL PRODUCTION 120,000 bottles
HECTARES UNDER VINE 10
VITICULTURE METHOD Conventional

Romina and Alessio skilfully manage the heritage left to them by their father and grandfather. Theirs is an inheritance of experience, passion and sacrifice. Much has been done in the Ovada area in recent years but it is young people like the Tacchinos who can give these hills the boost they still need to achieve the status they deserve. The Dolcetto di Ovada makes our finals with increasing frequency. Sooner or later, quality is bound to reap rewards.

Du Riva '07 vaunts an intense hue and blackberry aromas followed cocoa powder over a stylish palate with good structure and a velvety finish. The impenetrably hued Monferrato Di Fatto '07 opens on tobacco and blackcurrant, echoed on the palate, and supported by good tannins. The '09 Barbera boasts a purple hue with bright tints, accompanying focused fruit and ripe cherry on the nose, and beautiful balance in the mouth. The Barbera '08 Albarola is compromised by the growing year. Although pleasant, it is tannic and shows evident signs of barrel maturation. The drinkable Gavi di Gavi '09 is well-balanced. Marsenca '09 is a very drinkable Cortese.

● Dolcetto di Ovada Sup. Du Riva '07	▼▼	4*
● Barbera del M.to '09	▼▼	4
● M.to Rosso Di Fatto '07	▼▼	5
● Barbera del M.to Albarola '08	▼	4
○ Cortese dell'Alto M.to Marsenca '09	▼	3
○ Gavi del Comune di Gavi '09	▼	4
● Barbera del M.to '08	▽▽	4
● Barbera del M.to '07	▽▽	4
● Barbera del M.to Albarola '07	▽▽	4*
● Dolcetto di Ovada '07	▽▽	4
● Dolcetto di Ovada Du Riva '06	▽▽	4*
○ Gavi del Comune di Gavi '08	▽▽	4
● M.to Rosso Di Fatto '06	▽▽	5

Michele Taliano

C.SO A. MANZONI, 24
12046 MONTÀ [CN]
TEL. 0173976512
www.talianomichele.com

CELLAR SALES
PRE-BOOKED VISITS

ANNUAL PRODUCTION 60,000 bottles
HECTARES UNDER VINE 12
VITICULTURE METHOD Conventional

Divided between Langhe and Roero, the Taliano family's winery offers a wide range of labels. Roero production is concentrated in the vineyards of the central-northern side of Monti, an area that yields wines of great freshness and minerality. In the Langhe, the Taliano family owns Cascina Moreno, a farm situated between Barbaresco and Treiso, where they grow barbera, nebbiolo, dolcetto and moscato.

The Roero Ròche dra Bòssora Riserva '07 repeats the excellent showings of past years, hinting at red fruit and spices and with a lovely fruit-rich palate, its close-knit tannins and long juicy finish sustained by good acidity. We also enjoyed Nebbiolo d'Alba Blagheur '08, whose fine scents of raspberry, tobacco and sweet spices lead into a palate that still needs to unfold but is well balanced and fruity. The multi-faceted Barbaresco Ad Altiora '07 impressed with its rich tobacco and raspberry and good body, although the tannins are still a touch grainy. Overall, the other labels are well made.

● Roero Ròche dra Bòssora Ris. '07	▼▼	5
● Barbaresco Ad Altiora '07	▼▼	6
● Nebbiolo d'Alba Blagheur '08	▼▼	4
● Barbaresco Teramia Ris. '04	▼	6
● Barbera d'Alba A Bon Rendre '09	▼	4
● Barbera d'Alba Laboriosa '07	▼	4
● Langhe Rosso Tam Nan '07	▼	4
○ Roero Arneis Sernì '09	▼	4
● Barbaresco Ad Altiora '03	▽▽	6
● Roero Ròche dra Bòssora '05	▽▽	5
● Roero Ròche dra Bòssora '04	▽▽	5
● Roero Ròche dra Bòssora Ris. '06	▽▽	5

Tenuta La Tenaglia

S.DA SANTUARIO DI CREA, 5C
15020 SERRALUNGA DI CREA [AL]
TEL. 0142940252
www.latenaglia.com

CELLAR SALES
PRE-BOOKED VISITS

ANNUAL PRODUCTION 100,000 bottles
HECTARES UNDER VINE 30
VITICULTURE METHOD Conventional

The historic estate of Monferrato Tenaglia has been involved in the production of wine since the 17th century. Even then, this area was considered excellent for viticulture and was the source of high-quality wines. Now the company produces a range mainly from native varieties, and the quality of the final product is reflected in the range tasted for this edition of the Guide.

The excellent '09 Grignolino, through to the finals thanks to elegant aromas of pepper-lace flowers and fruits and a vibrant palate, shows assertive pulp and tannins. The superb, bright ruby Barbera 1930 '07 reveals elegant cherry and tobacco aromas with hints of spice over a well-orchestrated, intense palate. The Bricco Crea shows bright ruby with youthful tones while cherry and tobacco on the nose precede a firm, lingering palate. The exquisite Chardonnay '09 shows its youth, starting with its green-tinged straw and aromas of white-fleshed fruits leading to personality and presence in the mouth. We should also mention the Barbera del Monferrato '09.

● Barbera del M.to Sup. 1930 - Una Buona Annata '07	▼▼	6
● Grignolino del M.to Casalese '09	▼▼	4*
● Barbera d'Asti Bricco Crea '09	▼▼	4
○ Piemonte Chardonnay '09	▼▼	4
● Barbera del M.to '09	▼	4
● Barbera d'Asti Emozioni '99	YYY	7
● Barbera d'Asti Emozioni '07	YY	6
● Barbera d'Asti Giorgio Tenaglia '07	YY	5
● Barbera d'Asti Giorgio Tenaglia '06	YY	5
● Barbera del M.to Sup. Tenaglia è... '06	YY	4
● Grignolino del M.to Casalese '08	YY	4*
● Grignolino del M.to Casalese '07	YY	4
● M.to Rosso Olivieri '07	YY	6

Terralba

FRAZ. INSELMINA
15050 BERZANO DI TORTONA [AL]
TEL. 013180403
www.terralbavini.com

CELLAR SALES
PRE-BOOKED VISITS

ANNUAL PRODUCTION 45,000 bottles
HECTARES UNDER VINE 15
VITICULTURE METHOD Conventional

The winery headquarters, located in a picturesque landscape, is the centrepiece of a fine farming and winemaking operation which, year after year, gains a growing number of admirers. Stefano Daffonchio produces a set of interesting wines, whose strong personality can make them difficult to read but which can, after appropriate ageing, display notable qualities of depth and complexity, worthy of the best terroirs.

The range is led by Timorasso Stato '08, a well co-ordinated wine with concentrated aromas, where minerality accompanies wood resin and white-fleshed fruits. The palate is powerful, alcoholic and lingering. Derthona '08 shows amazing finesse on the nose and superb overall nose-palate harmony. Both the Barberas display interesting traits but Identità '08 goes one better than Terralba '07 with its greater freshness and balance. We also liked Vigna di Mezzo '07, from croatina and moradella, and La Vetta '07, a moradella monovarietal.

○ Colli Tortonesi Timorasso Derthona '08	▼▼	5
○ Colli Tortonesi Timorasso Stato '08	▼▼	6
● Piemonte Barbera Identità '08	▼▼	4
● Colli Tortonesi Barbera Terralba '07	▼	6
● Colli Tortonesi Rosso V. di Mezzo '07	▼	8
● La Vetta '07	▼	4
○ Colli Tortonesi Bianco Stato '05	YY	6
○ Colli Tortonesi Bianco Stato '04	YY	6
○ Colli Tortonesi Bianco Stato '03	YY	5
● Colli Tortonesi Rosso Montegrande '06	YY	5
● Colli Tortonesi Rosso Terralba '06	YY	6
● Colli Tortonesi Rosso V. di Mezzo '06	YY	5
○ Colli Tortonesi Timorasso Derthona '07	YY	5
○ Colli Tortonesi Timorasso Derthona '06	YY	5
● Piemonte Barbera Identità '07	YY	5

Terre da Vino

VIA BERGESIA, 6
12060 BAROLO [CN]
TEL. 0173564611
www.terredavino.it

CELLAR SALES
PRE-BOOKED VISITS

ANNUAL PRODUCTION 5,500,000 bottles
HECTARES UNDER VINE 4,500
VITICULTURE METHOD Conventional

The architectural design of the winery by Gianni Arnaudo from Cuneo has been the source of heated debate because of its size and impact on the landscape. What is certain is that it shows just what a modern wine headquarters can be, offering visitors an all-encompassing experience covering all the phases of growing, winemaking and direct sales. The range of wines offered, including the Barolo Essenze and the justly famous Barbera La Luna e i Falò, is reliable and reasonably priced.

The intense, estery Barolo Essenze '06 offers big, powerful tannins, dense, subtle fruit and excellent ageing potential. The traditional Barolo Paesi Tuoi '06 is very similar, with clean, layered liquorice and dried herbs. It shows austere on the palate but presents upfront fruit that provides balance. Both the captivating Barberas come from the difficult '08 vintage, with the Croere convincing on the nose thanks to cherries, spice and pencil lead, while La Luna e i Falò is just a tad simpler, with toasty notes accompanying fruit and rain-soaked earth. The classic Barbaresco La Casa in Collina '07 is already elegant, giving dried rose petals echoed on the finish.

● Barolo Essenze '06	▼▼	7
● Barolo Paesi Tuoi '06	▼▼	6
● Barbaresco La Casa in Collina '07	▼▼	6
● Barbera d'Alba Sup. Croere '08	▼▼	5
● Barbera d'Asti Sup. La Luna e i Falò '08	▼▼	4
○ Gavi del Comune di Gavi Masseria dei Carmelitani '09	▼▼	4
● Langhe Nebbiolo La Malora '08	▼▼	5
○ M.to Bianco Tra Donne Sole '09	▼▼	4*
○ Piemonte Moscato Passito La Bella Estate Oro '07	▼▼	5
○ Roero Arneis La Villa '09	▼	4
● Barbera d'Alba Sup. Croere '07	▽▽	5
● Barbera d'Alba Sup. Croere '06	▽▽	5
● Barbera d'Asti Sup. La Luna e i Falò '07	▽▽	4
● Barbera d'Asti Sup. Nizza Martlet '06	▽▽	5
● Barolo Essenze '04	▽▽	7

Terre del Barolo

VIA ALBA-BAROLO, 5
12060 CASTIGLIONE FALLETTO [CN]
TEL. 0173262053
www.terredelbarolo.com

CELLAR SALES
PRE-BOOKED VISITS

ANNUAL PRODUCTION 2,500,000 bottles
HECTARES UNDER VINE 610
VITICULTURE METHOD Conventional

This important Langhe winemaking project dates back to 1959. Over the years the winery, now run by Matteo Bosco, has become a large co-operative, especially considering the local production context, composed mainly of small family estates. The types offered cover all the major designations of the area and prices are competitive.

This year's result was outstanding, despite the absence of the Barolo vineyard selections, with an '06 vintage to remember: intense traditional, focused and already complex on the nose, followed by a moderately powerful, well-balance palate with graceful tannins and a satisfying finish. The difficult '08 vintage did no favours for the year's wines, which are normally excellent. Nevertheless, the agronomists and oenologists managed to produce admirable versions of Nebbiolo, Barbera and Dogliani. The Dogliani was particularly impressive. The basic '09s are great for everyday drinking and can also be purchased, like all the others, in the well-organized winery shop.

● Barolo '06	▼▼	6
● Barbera d'Alba Valdisera '08	▼▼	3*
● Dogliani '08	▼▼	4*
● Nebbiolo d'Alba '08	▼▼	4*
● Barbera d'Alba '09	▼	3
● Dolcetto d'Alba '09	▼	3
● Dolcetto d'Alba Castello '08	▼	4
● Dolcetto di Diano d'Alba '09	▼	4
● Dolcetto di Diano d'Alba Cascinotto '08	▼	4
● Barbera d'Alba Valdisera '07	▽▽	3*
● Barolo Cannubi '04	▽▽	7
● Barolo Monvigliero '04	▽▽	6
● Barolo Rocche Ris. '01	▽▽	6
● Barolo Rocche Ris. '99	▽▽	6
● Dogliani '07	▽▽	4

La Toledana

LOC. SERMOIRA,5
15066 GAVI [AL]
TEL. 014188551
www.latoledana.it

PRE-BOOKED VISITS

ANNUAL PRODUCTION N.A.
HECTARES UNDER VINE 28
VITICULTURE METHOD Conventional

This is the brightest star in the constellation of companies owned by Gianni Martini, a dynamic entrepreneur whose career started out in Gavi, no less, and has seen him become one of Italy's largest producers. La Toledana is a beautiful estate, featuring a villa with two towers, known locally as "tuledon", hence the winery's name. All the vineyards are planted to cortese, and all the wines produced are Gavi DOCGs.

The best of the bunch in our opinion is the Gavi del Comune di Gavi La Toledana '09, a white that although young, offers aromas ranging from chlorophyll to yellow damsons, and achieves a mineral complexity that will develop over time. The palate offers pervasive, pleasantly salty acidity. More evolved and austere, but also interesting, is the full-bodied Gavi del Comune di Gavi Raccolto Tardivo '09, which is slightly masked by oak, although not overpoweringly so. The Gavi La Doria '09 is well-managed while the Gavi del Comune di Gavi Castello La Toledana '06 is complex but a tad over-evolved and bitterish.

○ Gavi del Comune di Gavi La Toledana '09	🍷🍷	5
○ Gavi del Comune di Gavi La Toledana V.T. '09	🍷🍷	6
○ Gavi del Comune di Gavi Castello Toledana '06	🍷	6
○ Gavi La Doria '09	🍷	4

Torraccia del Piantavigna

VIA ROMAGNANO, 69A
28074 GHEMME [NO]
TEL. 0163840040
www.torracciadelpiantavigna.it

CELLAR SALES
PRE-BOOKED VISITS

ANNUAL PRODUCTION 90,000 bottles
HECTARES UNDER VINE 40
VITICULTURE METHOD Conventional

When your name means "vineyard planter", your destiny is clear. Piantavigna was the surname of the Francoli brothers' maternal grandfather. In 1990, they opened this operation with over 40 hectares spread over six zones in the provinces of Novara and Vercelli, entirely planted to nebbiolo, vespolina and erbaluce. In the cellar, collaboration with Giuseppe Caviola has led to the creation of a wide, varied range of wines, the most serious of which often reveal inimitable focus and sense of place to those prepared to be patient.

This fine winery in Ghemme has takes home its third Three Glasses, the second in a row for the Gattinara. The '06 version bewitched us with its profile, which manages to be youthful and tertiary at the same time. Walnuts, candied fruit, cocoa powder and white peach combine in a cascade of sensations held together by notes of iron filings, encored on the satisfying, austere palate, where sweet fruit and tightly woven tannins lead into a long, slightly salty finish. A touch more development, together with more persistently austere tannic, places the Ghemme from the same vintage just a step lower, but the whole range is outstanding.

● Gattinara '06	🍷🍷🍷	6
● Ghemme '06	🍷🍷	6
○ Colline Novaresi Bianco Erbavoglio '09	🍷🍷	4
● Colline Novaresi Nebbiolo Ramale '07	🍷🍷	5
● Colline Novaresi Nebbiolo Tre Confini '08	🍷🍷	4
● Colline Novaresi Vespolina La Mostella '08	🍷🍷	4*
⊙ Colline Novaresi Nebbiolo Rosato Barlan '09	🍷	5
● Gattinara '05	YYY	6
● Ghemme '04	YYY	6
● Gattinara '04	YY	6
● Gattinara '03	YY	6
● Gattinara '01	YY	6
● Ghemme '05	YY	6

Giancarlo Travaglini

VIA DELLE VIGNE, 36
13045 GATTINARA [VC]
TEL. 0163833588
www.travaglinigattinara.it

CELLAR SALES
PRE-BOOKED VISITS

ANNUAL PRODUCTION 250,000 bottles
HECTARES UNDER VINE 42
VITICULTURE METHOD Conventional

With nearly 60 hectares out of a designation total of about 110 under vine, the Travaglini family is the majority stakeholder in the Gattinara DOCG. This extraordinary heritage is reflected in wines with distinctive lightness and depth, and great ageing potential. The three Gattinaras, from different vineyards, type and duration of barrel maturation, are joined by a Nebbiolo from overripe grapes, Il Sogno, and a Coste della Sesia Nebbiolo.

In the '06, Travaglini gives us one of the best Gattinara vintages ever: pure joy on the nose, with its pot pourri of strawberries and incense, autumn leaves and ginseng. On the palate is tangible proof that great wines can be dense, youthful and austere yet at the same time approachable and seductively drinkable. This splendid performance is matched by an equally versatile Gattinara Riserva '05 of great breadth, with hints of cherry and black pepper encored on an exceptionally intense palate. Sogno, a Nebbiolo from overripe grapes with vigorous tannins, unleashes an attack that is nothing short of spectacular.

● Gattinara '06	▼▼	5
● Gattinara Ris. '05	▼▼	6
● Coste della Sesia Nebbiolo '08	▼▼	4*
● Il Sogno '06	▼▼	8
● Gattinara Ris. '04	▽▽▽	6
● Gattinara Ris. '01	▽▽▽	6
● Gattinara Tre Vigne '04	▽▽▽	6
● Gattinara '04	▽▽	5*
● Gattinara '03	▽▽	5
● Gattinara '01	▽▽	5*
● Gattinara Ris. '00	▽▽	6
● Gattinara Ris. '99	▽▽	6
● Gattinara Ris. '97	▽▽	6
● Gattinara Tre Vigne '01	▽▽	6

G. D. Vajra

LOC. VERGNE
VIA DELLE VIOLE, 25
12060 BAROLO [CN]
TEL. 017356257
www.gdvajra.it

CELLAR SALES
PRE-BOOKED VISITS

ANNUAL PRODUCTION 220,000 bottles
HECTARES UNDER VINE 50
VITICULTURE METHOD Organic

The extended Vajra family is a fine example of sticking to tradition and connection to the land. The winery is worth visiting both for its interesting architecture and for the warm welcome you will receive. Wines share a common style, based on poise, authenticity and elegance, which can satisfy even the most demanding wine lovers. The operation has recently grown in size, having taken over the Luigi Baudana winery in Serralunga d'Alba, a move that will bear fruit in coming years.

Although not present at our finals, the whole Vajra range is captivating, with now familiar points of excellence in Barolo Bricco delle Viole, the Barbera Superiore and Langhe Bianco. The fourth champion, Dolcetto d'Alba Coste & Fossati, had not yet been released at the time of tasting. The Barolo Bricco delle Viole '06 shows vibrant on the nose, with classic fruit notes, paving the way for a firmly structured, still slightly tannic palate and a long, focused, stylish finish. The complex Barbera d'Alba Superiore '07 displays great complexity on the nose, with plum accompanying spices and earthy notes to introduce a beautifully rich but not too soft palate.

● Barbera d'Alba Sup. '07	▼▼	6
● Barolo Bricco delle Viole '06	▼▼	8
○ Langhe Bianco Pétracine '09	▼▼	6
● Barolo Albe '06	▼▼	7
● Dolcetto d'Alba '09	▼▼	4*
● Langhe Freisa Kyè	▼▼	6
● Langhe Nebbiolo '08	▼▼	5
○ Moscato d'Asti '09	▼▼	5
● Barbera d'Alba '08	▼	5
● Barbera d'Alba Sup. '01	▽▽▽	5
● Barolo Bricco delle Viole '05	▽▽▽	8
● Barolo Bricco delle Viole '01	▽▽▽	8
● Barolo Bricco delle Viole '00	▽▽▽	8
● Barolo Bricco delle Viole '99	▽▽▽	8
○ Langhe Bianco '02	▽▽▽	5

Cascina Val del Prete

S.da Santuario, 2
12040 Priocca [CN]
tel. 0173616534
www.valdelprete.com

CELLAR SALES
PRE-BOOKED VISITS

ANNUAL PRODUCTION 50,000 bottles
HECTARES UNDER VINE 13
VITICULTURE METHOD Organic

The characteristic varieties of Roero are the protagonists in this historic Priocca winery run by Mario Roagna, who has taken over the operation begun by his parents in the 1970s. Arneis, nebbiolo and barbera are grown naturally in the vineyards surrounding the winery: Mario went biodynamic some years ago. The result is a range of excellently typed wines whose aim is to express their terroir to the full.

This was a decidedly off-form year for Mario Roagna's winery, compared to the standards he had accustomed us to. We liked the Roero Bricco Medica '07, with its aromas of ripe black berry fruit, spices, tobacco, a tannic palate and good length but lacking the balance and aromatic freshness it needed to be fully convincing. Also good is the Nebbiolo d'Alba Vigna di Lino '08, whose nose still shows a tad too much oak, but good fruit and attractive hints of cocoa powder. The palate echoes the nose but suffers from somewhat mouth-drying tannins. The two Barberas presented are well executed.

Wine	Glasses	Score
● Nebbiolo d'Alba V. di Lino '08	2 black glasses	5
● Roero Bricco Medica '07	2 black glasses	6
● Barbera d'Alba '08	1 black glass	4
● Barbera d'Alba Serra de' Gatti '09	1 black glass	4
● Nebbiolo d'Alba V. di Lino '00	3 white glasses	5
● Roero '04	3 white glasses	7
● Roero '03	3 white glasses	7
● Roero '01	3 white glasses	7
● Roero '00	3 white glasses	6

Mauro Veglio

fraz. Annunziata
cascina Nuova, 50
12064 La Morra [CN]
tel. 0173509212
www.mauroveglio.com

CELLAR SALES
PRE-BOOKED VISITS

ANNUAL PRODUCTION 60,000 bottles
HECTARES UNDER VINE 13
VITICULTURE METHOD Organic

The delightful landscape of Annunziata at La Morra is home to this fine winery, well managed by Mauro Veglio and his wife Daniela. Over the years, their project, which unites personal and professional aspirations, has brought excellent results. Modern stylistic consistency, achieved through a rigorous selection of raw materials and the confident use of oak, is evident in all the wines presented.

The excellent Barolo Rocche dell'Annunziata '06 opens with tobacco, raspberry and cinchona, leading to good thrust, close-knit tannins and superb length. The Barolo Castelletto '06 is woodier but also more potent, with assertive, spiky tannins. This needs a few more years. The more approachable Barolo Gattera '06 offers dried herbs and tobacco over well-behaved tannins and a roundish finish. The uncomplicated Barolo '06 shows well-typed aromatics and structure. Barolo Vigneto Arborina '06 and Barbera d'Alba Cascina Nuova '08 were not produced because of bad weather. The inviting Langhe Rosso L'Insieme '07 is a 40-30-30 blend of nebbiolo, cabernet sauvignon and barbera.

Wine	Glasses	Score
● Barolo Castelletto '06	2 black glasses	7
● Barolo Vign. Rocche dell'Annunziata '06	2 black glasses	8
● Barbera d'Alba '09	2 black glasses	4*
● Barolo '06	2 black glasses	6
● Barolo V. Gattera '06	2 black glasses	7
● Langhe Nebbiolo Angelo '08	2 black glasses	5
● Langhe Rosso L'Insieme '07	2 black glasses	7
● Dolcetto d'Alba '09	1 black glass	4
● Barbera d'Alba Cascina Nuova '99	3 white glasses	5
● Barbera d'Alba Cascina Nuova '96	3 white glasses	5
● Barolo V. Rocche '96	3 white glasses	7
● Barolo Vign. Arborina '01	3 white glasses	7
● Barolo Vign. Arborina '00	3 white glasses	7
● Barolo Vign. Gattera '05	3 white glasses	7
● Barbera d'Alba Cascina Nuova '07	2 white glasses	6

Eraldo Viberti

FRAZ. SANTA MARIA
B.TA TETTI, 53
12064 LA MORRA [CN]
TEL. 017350308
www.eraldoviberti.com

CELLAR SALES
PRE-BOOKED VISITS

ANNUAL PRODUCTION 27,000 bottles
HECTARES UNDER VINE 5
VITICULTURE METHOD Conventional

This small winery concentrates on a limited range of wines, selecting its grapes with great care and striving get the most out of the terroir. Its versions of Barolo, Barbera and Dolcetto, the three classic wines of the area, are a perfect balance of classic style, varietal identity, sense of place and a modern use of barriques. The wines may be over-assertive in youth, particularly the well-known Barbera Vigna Clara, but they always reflect Eraldo Viberti's commitment.

The sound Barolo Rocchettevino '06 is classic, clean and extremely true to type, playing more on its stylish aromatics, also deriving from barrel maturation, than on potency in the mouth. The tannins, already fairly mellow and rounded, give a velvety sensation to the lingering finish. It is worth noting that for the first time the winery specifies the vineyard of origin on the label. The Barbera d'Alba Vigna Clara '07 has loads of fruit and oak, with rich, concentration on the palate, just slightly to the detriment of balance, nicely reflecting the characteristics of what was an abundant harvest for barbera.

● Barbera d'Alba V. Clara '07	▼▼	5
● Barolo Rocchettevino '06	▼▼	7
● Barolo '93	YYY	8
● Barbera d'Alba V. Clara '06	YY	5
● Barbera d'Alba V. Clara '05	YY	6
● Barbera d'Alba V. Clara '04	YY	6
● Barolo '05	YY	7
● Barolo '04	YY	7
● Barolo '03	YY	7
● Dolcetto d'Alba '06	YY	3*

Vicara

CASCINA MADONNA DELLE GRAZIE, 5
15030 ROSIGNANO MONFERRATO [AL]
TEL. 0142488054
www.vicara.it

CELLAR SALES
PRE-BOOKED VISITS

ANNUAL PRODUCTION 180,000 bottles
HECTARES UNDER VINE 53
VITICULTURE METHOD Certified biodynamic

This is one of the leading wineries in the Monferrato Casalese Vicara area and never fails to provide us with excellent products. In this edition of the Guide, there were no fewer than three wines in the final tastings chasing the top award, led by a splendid Grignolino, a type that has never won Three Glasses. The outstanding overall quality achieved by Vicara was evident not only in the Barberas but also in the Freisa, often considered a lesser variety, which in versions such as this '09 reveals its true potential.

We applauded the masterful Grignolino, which combines a pale ruby hue with garnet hints and fruit aromas moving into pepper and roses. This is followed by harmony on the palate, with fine-grained tannins and a lingering finish. The impenetrable ruby Barbera Cantico della Crosia '07 unveils attractive oak quickly followed by plum and spice, while big pulp and attractive acidity come together in a beautifully lingering finish. The admirable deep ruby Vadmò '06 proffers light toast in prelude to wonderfully intense fruit and the poised, velvety palate finishes long. The balanced Freisa '09's complex, intense nose is complemented by faint prickle on the palate.

● Barbera del M.to Sup. Cantico della Crosia '07	▼▼	5
● Barbera del M.to Sup. Vadmò '06	▼▼	4*
● Grignolino del M.to Casalese '09	▼▼	4*
● M.to Freisa '09	▼▼	4
● Barbera del M.to Vivace '09	▼	4
● Barbera del M.to Volpuva '09	▼	4
○ M.to Bianco Airales '09	▼	4
⊙ M.to Rosato Chiaretto '09	▼	3
● Barbera del M.to Sup. Cantico della Crosia '06	YY	5
● Barbera del M.to Sup. Vadmò '05	YY	4*
● Barbera del M.to Vivace '08	YY	4
● Barbera del M.to Volpuva '08	YY	4
● Grignolino del M.to Casalese '08	YY	4
● Grignolino del M.to Casalese '07	YY	4

★ Vietti

P.ZZA VITTORIO VENETO, 8
12060 CASTIGLIONE FALLETTO [CN]
TEL. 017362825
www.vietti.com

CELLAR SALES
PRE-BOOKED VISITS

ANNUAL PRODUCTION 250,000 bottles
HECTARES UNDER VINE 35
VITICULTURE METHOD Conventional

The death of Alfredo Currado is a blow to all wine lovers. He was one of the first oenologists in Piedmont to vinify grapes from individual vineyards separately while traditionally in the Langhe, Barolo and Barbaresco were almost always blended. This was in the early 1960s and Vietti's vineyards were Rocche and Masseria, before the acquisitions in Brunate, Lazzarito, Villero. They make a formidable range, flanked by some of the best examples of Barbera d'Alba and Barbera d'Asti, not to mention Moscato, Arneis and Dolcetto.

A few years ago, Luca Currado took over the running of the winery from his father Alfredo and he has given us impressively consistent with peaks of excellence. This round of tastings was no exception, with a hat-trick of spectacular '06 Barolos. The Brunate is having difficulty digesting its oak but it has the confidence and earthiness of the best vintages. The same holds true for the Lazzarito, which still needs to metabolize its exuberant alcohol and cutting acidity. The Rocche, however, is already Three Glass material, thanks to its roots and balsam aromas leading to concentrated, sweet fruit, and a lingering, almost piquant finish.

● Barolo Rocche '06	TTT	8
● Barolo Brunate '06	TT	8
● Barolo Lazzarito '06	TT	8
● Barbaresco Masseria '07	TT	8
● Barbera d'Alba Scarrone '08	TT	6
● Barbera d'Alba Tre Vigne '08	TT	5
● Barbera d'Asti Tre Vigne '08	TT	5
● Langhe Nebbiolo Perbacco '07	TT	4
● Barolo Castiglione '06	T	7
● Dolcetto d'Alba Tre Vigne '09	T	4
○ Roero Arneis '09	T	4
● Barbera d'Asti Sup. Nizza La Crena '03	YYY	6
● Barolo Lazzarito '05	YYY+	8
● Barolo Lazzarito '04	YYY	8
● Barolo Rocche '01	YYY	8
● Barolo Villero Ris. '01	YYY	8

★ Vigna Rionda - Massolino

P.ZZA CAPPELLANO, 8
12050 SERRALUNGA D'ALBA [CN]
TEL. 0173613138
www.massolino.it

CELLAR SALES
PRE-BOOKED VISITS

ANNUAL PRODUCTION 100,000 bottles
HECTARES UNDER VINE 19
VITICULTURE METHOD Conventional

Brothers Franco and Roberto Massolino produce around 100,000 bottles from just over 20 hectares of the traditional Langhe varieties: dolcetto, chardonnay, moscato, barbera and of course nebbiolo. And this is not just any old nebbiolo, but the nebbiolo that on the slopes of Serralunga becomes the ingredient for Barolos of proverbial intensity and tannic power, with long ageing in mind. The current version is joined by the vineyard selections Parafada, the only one with some barrique ageing, Margheria and naturally Vigna Rionda.

The fantastic '04 Vigna Rionda Riserva from Franco and Roberto Massolino already deserves a place among the Barolo greats. Still young and restless, it already unveils a nose already has almost medicinal aromas of roots, herbs, bath salts and cinnamon, preparing the palate for a satisfying, massive yet silky impact, full of thrust and reluctant to fade. Faced with such brilliance, it's easy to forget the austere, yet finely structured Parafada '06, or the Margheria '06, with a solid, compact profile that lacks a little assertiveness in its tannins. We also liked the very good Barolo '06.

● Barolo V. Rionda Ris. '04	TTT	8
● Barolo Margheria '06	TT	8
● Barolo Parafada '06	TT	8
● Barbera d'Alba '09	TT	4
● Barbera d'Alba Gisep '08	TT	6
● Barolo '06	TT	6
● Dolcetto d'Alba '09	TT	4*
● Langhe Nebbiolo '07	TT	5
○ Moscato d'Asti di Serralunga '09	TT	4*
○ Langhe Chardonnay '09	T	4
● Barolo Margheria '05	YYY	8
● Barolo Parafada '04	YYY	8
● Barolo V. Rionda Ris. '01	YYY	8
● Barolo V. Rionda Ris. '99	YYY	8
● Barolo V. Rionda Ris. '98	YYY	8
● Barolo V. Rionda Ris. '97	YYY	8

I Vignaioli di Santo Stefano

LOC. MARINI, 26
12058 SANTO STEFANO BELBO [CN]
TEL. 0141840419
www.ceretto.com

CELLAR SALES
PRE-BOOKED VISITS

ANNUAL PRODUCTION 335,000 bottles
HECTARES UNDER VINE 40
VITICULTURE METHOD Conventional

Moscato, in its various forms, is the cornerstone of this important winery, set up in 1976. The cellar continues to bring out the best in the variety and the area, and remains a reliable benchmark of quality and style. The number of bottles produced is remarkable, helping to ensure national and international visibility for these first-rate labels.

Of the two wines tasted this year, the Moscato d'Asti stands out for its character and varietal definition. The '09 has a creamy, persistent mousse, and displays fresh citrus with hints of peach and sage on the nose. The palate is not too sweet and subtle elegance paves the way for a long, inviting finish. The drinkable Asti '09 unveils a delicate yellow colour shading into pale green. It's perhaps a touch lightweight but sustained by well-dosed acidity.

O Moscato d'Asti '09	TT	5
O Asti '09	T	6
O Asti '07	YY	4
O Asti '06	YY	4*
O Asti '05	YY	4*
O Moscato d'Asti '08	YY	5
O Moscato d'Asti '07	YY	4
O Moscato d'Asti '06	YY	4
O Moscato d'Asti '05	YY	4
O Piemonte Moscato Passito IL '04	YY	5
O Piemonte Moscato Passito IL '03	YY	5
O Piemonte Moscato Passito IL '02	YY	5

Vignaioli Elvio Pertinace

LOC. PERTINACE, 2
12050 TREISO [CN]
TEL. 0173442238
www.pertinace.it

CELLAR SALES
PRE-BOOKED VISITS

ANNUAL PRODUCTION 200,000 bottles
HECTARES UNDER VINE 60
VITICULTURE METHOD Conventional

Compared to other Italian co-operatives, often criticized for their size and lack of quality, Vignaioli Elvio Pertinace is a small operation, with around 70 professionally managed hectares under vine. Barbaresco, in a number of versions, rules the roost, and is also competitively priced. The range also includes other traditional Langhe wines, all well executed.

The youthfully hued '07 Barbaresco Marcarini gives lashings of fruit and medicinal herbs, with faint hints of liquorice in the background. On the palate, it shows nicely soft and mouthfilling, although not very rich. The '07 Barbaresco Nervo is even more generous on the nose, with cinchona and tobacco over a base of red berry fruit, followed by a potent palate that presents more serious and austere than the Marcarini. The Castellizzano '07 is a touch over-evolved, with obtrusive alcohol and excessive softness. The sound Dolcetto Vigneto Nervo '09 offers focused blackberry fruit with hints of cocoa powder, leading to great power and rich fruit on the palate.

● Barbaresco Castellizzano '07	TT	6
● Barbaresco Marcarini '07	TT	6
● Barbaresco Nervo '07	TT	6
● Dolcetto d'Alba Vigneto Nervo '09	TT	4
● Barbaresco '07	T	6
● Barbera d'Alba '08	T	4
● Dolcetto d'Alba '09	T	4
● Dolcetto d'Alba Castellizzano '09	T	4
● Langhe Nebbiolo '08	T	4
● Barbaresco Marcarini '05	YY	6
● Barbaresco Nervo '05	YY	6
● Barbaresco Vign. Marcarini '06	YY	6
● Barbaresco Vign. Nervo '06	YY	6
● Barbera d'Asti Gratia Plena '06	YY	4*
● Dolcetto d'Alba Castellizzano '07	YY	4

Vigne Regali

VIA VITTORIO VENETO, 76
15019 STREVI [AL]
TEL. 0144362600
www.castellobanfi.it

PRE-BOOKED VISITS

ANNUAL PRODUCTION 2,000,000 bottles
HECTARES UNDER VINE 76
VITICULTURE METHOD Conventional

The Banfi winery is located at Strevi Banfi, a town some 30 kilometres from the provincial capital of Alessandria, and about six kilometres from Acqui Terme, in a hilly area between 160 and 250 metres above sea level. This is home to moscato and brachetto grapes, which are processed directly on site, where the cellars and sparkling wine production facilities are situated. This practice, as in Canelli, dates back to the mid 19th century.

Vigne Regali has extensive experience with sparkling wines but also in the management of typical Piedmont red grape varieties. The Barbera Banin '07, for example, shows character, boasting fruit aromas over good acidity on the palate. The harmonious, well-balanced Dolcetto L'Ardi '09 opens with heady alcohol and blackberry, continuing on the attractive palate with velvety tannins. We saw a fine performance from the Gavi Principessa Gavia '09, which alternates flowers and fruit with fine mineral notes. A series of well-made sparklers starts with the Banfi Brut, followed by the '04 Cuvée Aurora and the Tener, finishing with the fragrant Brachetto.

○ Alta Langa Cuvée Aurora '04	▼▼	6
○ Banfi Brut Talento	▼▼	4
● Barbera d'Asti Sup. Vign. Banin '07	▼▼	6
● Dolcetto d'Acqui L'Ardì '09	▼▼	4
○ Gavi Principessa Gavia '09	▼▼	4
○ Moscato d'Asti Strevi '09	▼▼	4
○ Tener Brut	▼▼	4
⊙ Alta Langa Cuvée Aurora Rosé '07	▼	6
● Brachetto d'Acqui Rosa Regale '09	▼	5
● Barbera d'Asti Sup. Vign. Banin '06	▽▽	6
● Barbera d'Asti Vign. Banin '05	▽▽	6
● Brachetto d'Acqui Vign. La Rosa '08	▽▽	5
● Dolcetto d'Acqui L'Ardì '08	▽▽	4
○ Moscato d'Asti Strevi '08	▽▽	4

Vigneti Massa

P.ZZA G. CAPSONI, 10
15059 MONLEALE [AL]
TEL. 013180302
vignetimassa@libero.it

CELLAR SALES
PRE-BOOKED VISITS

ANNUAL PRODUCTION 80,000 bottles
HECTARES UNDER VINE 20
VITICULTURE METHOD Organic

The terms "grower" and "terroir" are often misused. They are however entirely appropriate when you are talking about Walter Massa, a creative, rebellious figure with few peers in Italian wine. This passionate promoter of his native Tortona has managed to attract attention to an area that until a few years ago was almost entirely neglected. Walter's wines reflect his uncompromising character. Deep and complex, they are not always approachable in youth, but with time can give marvellous, original sensations.

The magnificent '08 version of Timorasso Sterpi offers a complex bouquet of grapefruit and white-fleshed fruit preceding a powerfully generous, long, harmonious palate. Next on our list was Timorasso Derthona '08, which has a serious nose and a caressing palate but fails to scale the heights of Sterpi. The thoroughly enjoyable Monleale '07 is a splendid Barbera, and without doubt one of the most representative of the Tortona area. We were surprised by the Cerreta '03, a barbera-heavy blend we hadn't tasted for years that shows tertiary, evolved aromas and excellent length.

○ Colli Tortonesi Timorasso Sterpi '08	▼▼▼	7
● Colli Tortonesi Barbera Monleale '07	▼▼	6
○ Colli Tortonesi Timorasso Derthona '08	▼▼	6
● Colli Tortonesi Cerreta '03	▼▼	6
○ Colli Tortonesi Timorasso Costa del Vento '08	▼▼	7
● Colli Tortonesi Freisa Pietra del Gallo '09	▼	4
○ Colli Tortonesi Moscato Muscatè '09	▼	3
○ Colli Tortonesi Bianco Costa del Vento '05	▽▽▽	8
○ Colli Tortonesi Bianco Sterpi '04	▽▽▽	7
● Colli Tortonesi Rosso Bigolla '98	▽▽▽	7
○ Colli Tortonesi Timorasso Derthona '06	▽▽▽	6
○ Colli Tortonesi Timorasso Sterpi '07	▽▽▽	7
● Colli Tortonesi Monleale '06	▽▽	6
● Colli Tortonesi Monleale Bigolla '05	▽▽	7
○ Colli Tortonesi Timorasso Derthona '07	▽▽	6

Villa Giada

Reg. Ceirole, 10
14053 Canelli [AT]
tel. 0141831100
www.andreafaccio.it

CELLAR SALES
PRE-BOOKED VISITS
ROOMS

ANNUAL PRODUCTION 190,000 bottles
HECTARES UNDER VINE 25
VITICULTURE METHOD Conventional

Andrea Faccio's vineyards comprise three estates grouped together around farmhouses: Cascina Ceirole, the original winery headquarters, at Canelli; Cascina del Parroco at Calosso; and Cascina Dani at Agliano Terme. The extensive range of wines is divided into two lines: those from individual vineyards and the Surì ed Ajan. Barbera is flanked by other typical varieties, some native such as moscato, dolcetto and nebbiolo, others international.

The Barbera d'Asti Superiore La Quercia is one of the best '08 Barberas presented this year. After the varietal aromas of rain-soaked earth, with hints of tar and black berry fruit, there follows a zesty, rounded palate, nicely underpinned by acidity and a lingering, harmonious finish. We also liked the well-executed Barbera d'Asti Superiore Nizza Bricco Dani '07, with its deep bouquet, showing lovely plum, sweet oak spiciness and tobacco over a dense, chewy palate, held in balance by spirited acidity. Equally good is the modern-styled Barbera d'Asti Ajan '08, with toast, tobacco and spice on the nose, over a tight-knit, dense palate brimming with fruit.

● Barbera d'Asti Sup. La Quercia '08	▼▼	4*
● Barbera d'Asti Ajan '08	▼▼	4*
● Barbera d'Asti Sup. Nizza Bricco Dani '07	▼▼	5
● Barbera d'Asti Ajan '09	▼	4
● Barbera d'Asti Sup. Nizza Dedicato a '06	▼	6
● Gamba di Pernice '07	▼	4
○ Mo.to Bianco I Surì '09	▼	3
● Monferrato Rosso Treponti '07	▼	4
○ Moscato d'Asti Ceirole '09	▼	4
● Barbera d'Asti Sup. Bricco Dani '05	▽▽	5
● Barbera d'Asti Sup. Nizza Bricco Dani '05	▽▽	5
● Barbera d'Asti Sup. Nizza Bricco Dani '04	▽▽	5

Villa Sparina

fraz. Monterotondo, 56
15066 Gavi [AL]
tel. 0143633835
www.villasparina.it

PRE-BOOKED VISITS
ROOMS AND FOOD

ANNUAL PRODUCTION 450,000 bottles
HECTARES UNDER VINE 56
VITICULTURE METHOD Conventional

The estate combines a site of exceptional beauty and charm with excellent wines across the board. This picture perfectly portrays the work of the Moccagattas, who over the years has managed to make an important name for itself in Piedmont and beyond. Stylistically, the wines express a real sense of place, achieving complexity and drinkability at the same time.

The Gavi del Comune di Gavi Monterotondo '08 earned Three Glasses, with a particularly elegant entry on the nose that proffers minerality over spring flowers. The decidedly rich, almost fat, palate is perfectly offset by acidity and displays much more impressive structure than is usually found in this designation. From next year, the lively, vibrant, taut Monferrato Rosso Rivalta, from barbera, will take advantage of the new DOCG appellation, Barbera del Monferrato Superiore. The '07 gives ripe red berries, sweet tobacco and plum, leading to a powerful palate with confident but unobtrusive acidity and great overall character.

○ Gavi del Comune di Gavi Monterotondo '08	▼▼▼	7
● M.to Rosso Rivalta '07	▼▼	7
● Barbera del M.to Sup. '08	▼▼	4
○ Gavi del Comune di Gavi '09	▼▼	4
○ M.to Bianco Montej '09	▼▼	3
● Barbera del M.to Montej '09	▼	3
⊙ M.to Chiaretto Montej Rosé '09	▼	3
○ Villa Sparina Brut M. Cl.	▼	5
○ Gavi del Comune di Gavi Monterotondo '07	▽▽▽	6
● M.to Rosso Rivalta '04	▽▽▽	6
● M.to Rosso Rivalta '00	▽▽▽	6
● M.to Rosso Rivalta '99	▽▽▽	6
○ Gavi del Comune di Gavi Monterotondo '06	▽▽	6
● M.to Rosso Rivalta '06	▽▽	6

Cantina Sociale di Vinchio Vaglio Serra

REG. SAN PANCRAZIO, 1
14040 VINCHIO [AT]
TEL. 0141950903
www.vinchio.com

CELLAR SALES
PRE-BOOKED VISITS

ANNUAL PRODUCTION 1,000,000 bottles
HECTARES UNDER VINE 320
VITICULTURE METHOD Conventional

This great co-operative winery brings together about 220 members and makes an extremely wide range of products – over 30 – from quality wines to simpler labels for everyday drinking. The vineyards are concentrated in Vinchio, Vaglio Serra, Incisa Scapaccino, Cortiglione and Nizza Monferrato. Barbera is the main variety and the one with which this winery has achieved its greatest successes.

The Nizza from this important co-operative winery is released to market a year after most others. We loved the Barbera d'Asti Superiore Nizza Laudana '06, with its intense, complex aromas of tobacco, cherries in alcohol and liquorice preceding a well-orchestrated palate and a long finish buttressed by good acidity. The Barbera d'Asti Superiore Vigne Vecchie '07 has plum and earth tones but is still dominated by oak. The mid-bodied palate has somewhat aggressive tannins. Barbera d'Asti Vigne Vecchie 50 '08 shows pervasive notes of sweet spices and liqueur fruit on the nose, followed by a full-bodied and long, if slightly rustic, palate.

● Barbera d'Asti Sup. Nizza Bricco Laudana '06	TT	5
● Barbera d'Asti Sup. Vigne Vecchie '07	TT	5
● Barbera d'Asti Vigne Vecchie 50 '08	TT	4
● Barbera d'Asti Sorì dei Mori '09	T	3
● Monferrato Dolcetto Colle Sangiorgio '09	T	3
● Monferrato Rosso Tutti per Uno '06	T	5
○ Moscato d'Asti Valamasca '09	T	3
● Barbera d'Asti Sup. Sei Vigne Insynthesis '01	YYY	7
● Barbera d'Asti Sup. Sei Vigne Insynthesis '04	YY	7
● Barbera d'Asti Sup. Sei Vigne Insynthesis '03	YY	7
● Barbera d'Asti Sup. Vigne Vecchie '03	YY	5
● Barbera d'Asti Sup. Vigne Vecchie '01	YY	5

Virna

VIA ALBA, 73/24
12060 BAROLO [CN]
TEL. 017356120
www.virnabarolo.it

CELLAR SALES
PRE-BOOKED VISITS

ANNUAL PRODUCTION 60,000 bottles
HECTARES UNDER VINE 12
VITICULTURE METHOD Conventional

Despite their surname, the Borgognos of the Virna winery are not as well-known as the other members of this historic Barolo family, but sisters Virna and Ivana, aided by their father Ludovico, are the third generation to bottle the wine. With Virna's arrival on the scene, the operation has changed direction. There's a new winery and a traditional style but none of the past lack of aromatic focus. Yields are also limited, with the 12 hectares under vine at Barolo, Monforte d'Alba and Novello producing around 70,000 bottles a year. Virna is now aided by her husband and colleague Gianni Abrigo from Treiso but is determined to maintain her own distinctive style.

Consistency and a series of outstanding Barolos have finally earned Virna a full profile. We especially liked the '06 Preda Sarmassa, a well-judged blend of grapes from various soils. On the nose, complex red fruit, tobacco and rhubarb precede caressing tannins on a well-rounded, already velvety palate. The Cannubi Boschis '06, with sweet spice, aniseed and liquorice wrapped up in silky tannins, confirms the innate finesse of this vineyard selection. The austere Riserva Preda Sarmassa '04 seems to be in a phase of transition. A fine range is completed by a full-flavoured, powerful Barbera San Giovanni '07. The fresh-tasting Barbera '08 is also well executed.

● Barolo Preda Sarmassa '06	TT	6
● Barbera d'Alba '08	TT	4
● Barbera d'Alba Sup. San Giovanni '07	TT	5
● Barolo Cannubi Boschis '06	TT	6
● Barolo Preda Sarmassa Ris. '04	TT	7
● Nebbiolo d'Alba '08	T	4
● Barolo '04	YY	6
● Barolo '03	YY	6
● Barolo Cannubi Boschi '04	YY	6
● Barolo Cannubi Boschis '05	YY	6
● Barolo Cannubi Boschis '04	YY	6
● Barolo Cannubi Boschis '03	YY	6
● Barolo Preda Sarmassa '05	YY	6
● Barolo Preda Sarmassa '04	YY	6

Gianni Voerzio

s.da Loreto, 1
12064 La Morra [CN]
tel. 0173509194
voerzio.gianni@tiscali.it

VENDITA DIRETTA
VISITA SU PRENOTAZIONE

PRODUZIONE ANNUA 60.400 bottiglie
ETTARI VITATI 12.00
VITICOLTURA Organic

The range of wines offered by this established Langhe winery extends from Barolo to Moscato, and caters for just about all tastes. The style is instantly recognizable, consistent over time and gives guaranteed longevity. The grower's hand is evident in all of the labels and the cellar has long been a benchmark.

The youthfully ruby Barolo La Serra '06 offers vegetal aromas and ripe black berry fruit, accompanied by soft, fleshy, jammy notes on the potent palate. This is a very personal wine. Intense, brooding, spicy and fairly full-bodied, the Barbera d'Alba della Luna '08 Ciabot is particularly well executed, especially considering the difficult vintage. The Langhe Nebbiolo Ciabot della Luna '08 has character but lacks particular finesse. Ripe fruit and spring flowers distinguish the Langhe Arneis Bricco Cappellina '09, which unveils a balanced palate and an attractive fresh vein with goodish body, leading to a pleasantly bitterish finish. The simpler wines in the range are well managed.

● Barolo La Serra '06	🍷🍷	8
● Barbera d'Alba Ciabot della Luna '08	🍷🍷	5
○ Langhe Arneis Bricco Cappellina '09	🍷🍷	5
● Langhe Nebbiolo Ciabot della Luna '08	🍷🍷	6
● Dolcetto d'Alba Rocchettevino '09	🍷	4
● Langhe Freisa Sotto I Bastioni '09	🍷	4
○ Moscato d'Asti Vignasergente '09	🍷	5
● Barolo La Serra '98	YYY	8
● Barolo La Serra '97	YYY	8
● Barolo La Serra '96	YYY	8
● Barbera d'Alba Ciabot della Luna '07	YY	5
● Barbera d'Alba Ciabot della Luna '06	YY	5
● Barolo La Serra '05	YY	8
● Barolo La Serra '04	YY	8

★ Roberto Voerzio

loc. Cerreto, 1
12064 La Morra [CN]
tel. 0173509196

ANNUAL PRODUCTION 35,000 bottles
HECTARES UNDER VINE 17
VITICULTURE METHOD Conventional

Roberto Voerzio is one of the most famous producers in Langhe. His approach results in wines of remarkable character and personality, distinguished by great concentration and fruit sweetness, not to mention a sometimes cavalier use of oak. His vineyards include major crus at La Morra and Barolo, such as Brunate, Rocche, Torriglione, Capalot, Cerequio, La Serra, and Sarmassa. The vines are managed to obtain extremely low yields of around 2,000-2,500 bottles per hectare, using natural methods with no chemicals. Only native yeasts are used in the winery.

For several years, Roberto has not sent us samples for tasting. This year, we have been unable to find and taste the wines, since they are not yet on sale.

● Barbera d'Alba Vign. Pozzo dell'Annunziata Ris. '99	YYY	8
● Barbera d'Alba Vign. Pozzo dell'Annunziata Ris. '96	YYY	8
● Barolo Brunate '99	YYY	8
● Barolo Brunate '98	YYY	8
● Barolo Brunate '96	YYY	8
● Barolo Cerequio '96	YYY	8
● Barolo Rocche dell'Annunziata Torriglione '00	YYY	8
● Vignaserra '96	YYY	6

La Ballerina

FRAZ. TANA, 8
14048 MONTEGROSSO D'ASTI [AT]
TEL. 0141 956118
www.laballerina.it

This small family estate mainly grows native varieties. We very much liked the '09 Barbera del Monferrato L'Inquieto, which has an intense fruity nose, good structure and nice acidity. We also enjoyed the '05 Barbera d'Asti La Notte, with its earthy, cinchona notes and austere, relatively long palate.

● Barbera d'Asti La Notte '05	🍷🍷	4
● Barbera del Monferrato L'Inquieto '09	🍷🍷	4
● Barbera d'Asti GB '07	🍷	4

Osvaldo Barberis

B.TA VALDIBÀ, 42
12063 DOGLIANI [CN]
TEL. 017370054
www.osvaldobarberis.com

This interesting family estate has seven hectares at Dogliani and a second plot in Monforte. The range covers the main Langhe designations and two wines stand out. The '08 Dogliani Puncin is a masterfully interpreted Dolcetto and the '08 Nebbiolo Muntajà has impressive character, depth and style.

● Dogliani Puncin '08	🍷🍷	4*
● Barbera d'Alba Castella '08	🍷🍷	5
● Dolcetto di Dogliani Valdibà '09	🍷🍷	4*
● Nebbiolo d'Alba Muntajà '08	🍷🍷	5

Cascina Barisél

REG. SAN GIOVANNI, 30
14053 CANELLI [AT]
TEL. 0141824848
www.barisel.it

It wasn't a great vintage for Cascina Barisél. The '08 Barbera d'Asti is good, with spicy, cherry and tobacco aromas and a mid-bodied, well-balanced palate with good fruit and acidity. The fragrant, fruity '09 Moscato d'Asti is enjoyable, the '09 Monferrato Biano Foravía respectable and the Favorita fruity.

● Barbera d'Asti '08	🍷🍷	4*
○ M.to Bianco Foravìa '09	🍷	3
○ Moscato d'Asti '09	🍷	4

Davide Beccaria

VIA GIOVANNI BIANCO, 3
15039 OZZANO MONFERRATO [AL]
TEL. 0142487321
www.beccaria-vini.it

Three wines stood out at Beccaria. The '09 Frisa Lilàn has a fruity nose, elegant tannins, well-typed palate and pleasantly bitter finish. Young varietal characteristics dominate in the easy-drinking '09 Barbera Evoè. Last up is the '09 Grignò, from grignolino, with a fairly simple nose and soft palate.

● M.to Freisa Lilàn '09	🍷🍷	3*
● Barbera del M.to Evoè '09	🍷	3
● Grignolino del M.to Casalese Grignò '09	🍷	3

Bianchi

VIA ROMA, 37
28070 SIZZANO [NO]
TEL. 0321810004
www.bianchibiowine.it

This Sizzano estate makes high-quality wines organically. The entire range is exceptional but several wines outshine the rest. The balanced '06 Gattinara Vigneto Valferana is meaty and the '07 Ghemme flaunts iron-like minerality. The '05 Sizzano is spicy and slightly astringent.

● Gattinara Vign. Valferana '06	🍷🍷	5
● Ghemme '07	🍷🍷	5
● Sizzano '05	🍷🍷	4*

Massimo Bo

FRAZ. SANT'ANNA
VIA SANT'ANNA, 19
14055 COSTIGLIOLE D'ASTI [AT]
TEL. 0141961891
bo.massimo@hotmail.com

The '08 Barbera d'Asti Superiore Costiliolae is beautiful. It has intense cherry, tobacco, cocoa and spice, a complex palate and good acidity supporting a long, savoury finish. The '09 Barbera d'Asti Arbuc is well made and varietal while the rich '09 Moscato d'Asti is traditional, with candied peel aromas.

● Barbera d'Asti Sup. Costiliolae '08	🍷🍷	4
● Barbera d'Asti Arbuc '09	🍷	3
○ Moscato d'Asti '09	🍷	4

Bussia Soprana

LOC. BUSSIA, 81
12065 MONFORTE D'ALBA [CN]
TEL. 039305182
www.bussiasoprana.it

Bussia Soprana did well. The '07 Pinot Nero Rile Nero almost made it into the finals for its long, well-defined finish. The '07 Barbera Vigna del Re is equally good, offering cherries and sour cherries, meaty fruit, nice acidity and a good finish. The '08 Pinot Nero and '09 Pinot Grigio Dama d'Oro are varietal.

- ● Barolo Vigna Colonnello '06 🍷🍷 8
- ● Barbera d'Alba Mosconi '07 🍷🍷 5
- ● Barolo Gabutti della Bussia '06 🍷🍷 8
- ● Barolo Mosconi '06 🍷🍷 8

Ca' Nova

VIA SAN ISIDORO, 1
28010 BOGOGNO [NO]
TEL. 0322863406
www.cascinacanova.it

In 1996, Giada Codecasa decided to leave Milan and a career in law for a life in the hills above Novara. The family now manages a magnificent country hotel and around nine hectares of vines. They grow the classic varieties to make modern wines. Top of the line-up is a wonderfully persistent Ghemme '05.

- ● Ghemme '05 🍷🍷 5
- ○ Colline Novaresi Bianco Rugiada '09 🍷 4
- ⊙ Colline Novaresi Nebbiolo Aurora '09 🍷 4

La Ca' Növa

S.DA OVELLO, 4
12050 BARBARESCO [CN]
TEL. 0173635123
lacanova@libero.it

Ca' Nova, owned by the Rocca brothers, has 14 hectares of vines in Bric Mentina at Montefico and Montestefano di Barbaresco, all dedicated to the classic Langhe varieties. The Montestefano comes across as well-orchestrated but already evolved while the still-young Bric Mentina needs more time.

- ● Barbaresco Montestefano '07 🍷🍷 6
- ● Barbaresco Bric Mentina '07 🍷 6
- ● Dolcetto d'Alba '09 🍷 4

Carussin

REG. MARIANO, 27
14050 SAN MARZANO OLIVETO [AT]
TEL. 0141831358
www.carussin.it

The Ferro family has run this biodynamic estate specializing in indigenous varieties since 1927. The '08 Barbera d'Asti La Tranquilla tops the list. It's complex and elegant, with tobacco, tar and fruit notes, and a rich, tannic palate. The rest of the range is very decent.

- ● Barbera d'Asti La Tranquilla '08 🍷🍷 5
- ● Barbera d'Asti Lia Vì '08 🍷 4
- ○ Moscato d'Asti Filari Corti '09 🍷 4

Cascina Ballarin

FRAZ. ANNUNZIATA, 115
12064 LA MORRA [CN]
TEL. 017350365
www.cascinaballarin.it

The Viberti family's list is a good bet for lovers of Langhe wines. The range is headed by two Barolos, which we found slightly less elegant than usual. The '06 Bussia is quite powerful and has adequate structure but we found the alcohol in the '06 Bricco Rocca's lingering finish to be slightly drying.

- ● Barolo Bussia '06 🍷🍷 8
- ● Langhe Rosso Ballarin '07 🍷🍷 5
- ● Barolo Bricco Rocca '06 🍷 8

Cascina Christiana

S.DA SAN MICHELE, 24
14049 NIZZA MONFERRATO [AT]
TEL. 0141725100
www.cascinachristiana.com

Barbera is the mainstay of this tiny Monferrato estate. The easy-drinking '08 Barbera d'Asti La Mòta is good with red berries, tobacco and spices on the nose and a well-orchestrated, crisp, leisurely palate. The other wines are also well made.

- ● Barbera d'Asti Sup. La Mòta '08 🍷🍷 5
- ● Barbera d'Asti Reiss '09 🍷 3
- ● M.to Rosso Balôss '08 🍷 5

Cascina Flino

via Abelloni, 7
12055 Diano d'Alba [CN]
tel. 017369231
silvana.bona@uvetitn.it

Cascina Flino near Diano is sometimes unjustly underrated but it offers consistently reliable quality. The entire range was very convincing but the vibrant, harmonious '08 Nebbiolo, the '06 Barolo San Lorenzo, which is bursting with character, and the well-structured, acidity-braced '08 Barbera, took the lead.

● Barbera d'Alba Flin '08	🍷🍷	4*
● Barolo San Lorenzo '06	🍷🍷	5
● Diano d'Alba V. Vecchia '09	🍷🍷	4*
● Nebbiolo d'Alba '08	🍷🍷	4*

Cascina lo Zoccolaio

loc. Boschetti, 4
12060 Barolo [CN]
tel. 014188551
www.cascinalozoccolaio.it

Cascina Lo Zoccolaio, on the road from Barolo to Monforte, is the jewel in the Martini brothers' crown. The well-made '06 Barolo Riserva is powerful, rich in fruit and beautifully crisp while the '07 Barbera d'Alba Suculé is well typed, earthy and impressively supported by acidity.

● Barbera d'Alba Suculé '07	🍷🍷	5
● Barolo Ravera '06	🍷🍷	7

Cascina Montagnola

s.da Montagnola, 1
15058 Viguzzolo [AL]
tel. 0131898558
www.cascinamontagnola.com

Timorasso was the highlight of Cascina Montagnola's range. The '08 Morasso opens with intense wood resins and flint. The mouth is rich and its complexity enhanced by the wine's sheer harmony. The '07 Rodeo is inky black with strong oak aromas and a concentrated palate. The '09 Dunin is a very pleasant Cortese.

○ Colli Tortonesi Timorasso Morasso '08	🍷🍷	5
● Colli Tortonesi Barbera Rodeo '07	🍷🍷	6
○ Colli Tortonesi Cortese Dunin '09	🍷	4

Castello di Gabiano

via Defendente, 2
15020 Gabiano [AL]
tel. 0142945004
www.castellodigabiano.com

Castello di Gabiano has produced another range of high-quality wines. Adornes reached the final for its harmonious nose and palate. The 85-15 barbera and pinot nero Gavius has a complex nose and juicy palate. The '07 Rubino di Cantavenna has cinchona and tobacco then a full palate.

● Barbera d'Asti Sup. Adornes '07	🍷🍷	6*
● M.to Rosso Gavius '07	🍷🍷	4
● Rubino di Cantavenna '07	🍷🍷	4
● Grignolino del M.to Casalese Il Ruvo '09	🍷	4

Castello di Tagliolo

via Castello, 1
15070 Tagliolo Monferrato [AL]
tel. 014389195
www.castelloditagliolo.com

The castle's ancient makes a range of still whites and reds and three sparklers, one a cuve close wine. One of the two Metodo Classicos is a rosé. The Rosso Nobile barbera and cabernet sauvignon blend and the Metodo Classico Rosé stood out. The Brut Riserva del Marchese and '08 Dolcetto d'Ovada were less incisive.

● M.to Rosso Nobile '05	🍷🍷	4
⊙ Rosé Brut	🍷🍷	5
● Dolcetto di Ovada '08	🍷	3
○ Riserva del Marchese Brut	🍷	5

Cave di Moleto

reg. Moleto, 4
15038 Ottiglio [AL]
tel. 0142921468
www.moleto.it

The Cave di Moleto estate did really well with the 2008 vintage. Their '08 Mulej cabernet and merlot blend is deep in colour, with youthful highlights and a spicy, fruity nose that opens onto a powerful, austere palate. The '08 Bricco Prera is very concentrated, with a fruity nose and caressing, fleshy palate.

● Barbera del M.to Bricco della Prera '08	🍷🍷	4
● M.to Rosso Mulej '08	🍷🍷	5
● Barbera del M.to Procchio '08	🍷	4
● Monferrato Rosso Pieve di San Michele '08	🍷	3

OTHER WINERIES

Le Cecche

via Moglia Gerlotto, 10
12055 Diano d'Alba [CN]
tel. 017369323
www.lececche.com

Belgian doctor Jan De Bruyne pursues his winemaking dream with confidence. The range spans several designations, all of which have personality and finesse, from the '06 Serralunga Barolo to the mainly dolcetto Langhe Rosso, which is deep ruby red and balanced. The '08 Barbera and '09 Diano are both nice.

● Barbera d'Alba '08	🍷🍷	4*
● Barolo '06	🍷🍷	7
● Diano d'Alba '09	🍷🍷	3*
● Langhe Rosso '08	🍷🍷	4*

La Chiara

loc. Vallegge, 24
15066 Gavi [AL]
tel. 0143642293
www.lachiara.it

Family-run La Chiara was established in 1975. The property spans 39 hectares, of which ten are vineyards, with couple leased. Reds dominated with the '09 Barbera Bricco Bicocco surprising for its harmonious nose and palate. The enjoyable cabernet sauvignon, barbera and dolcetto Monferrato Nabarì is complex.

● Barbera del M.to Bricco Bicocco '09	🍷🍷	2*
● M.to Rosso Nabarì '08	🍷🍷	4
○ Gavi del Comune di Gavi La Chiara '09	🍷	3
○ Gavi del Comune di Gavi Vign. Groppella '08	🍷	4

Colombo

Reg. Cafra, 172
14051 Bubbio [AT]
tel. 0144852807
www.colombovino.it

Antonio Colombo acquired the 12-hectare estate on the stunning slopes of Valle Bormida at Bubbio in 2003. Today, his son Andrea is in charge with help from winemaker Giandomenico Negro and has made on of the best Pinot Neros in Italy. We tasted the first two vintages, opting for the elegant 2006 over the rich 2007.

● M.to Rosso Apertura '06	🍷🍷	6
● M.to Rosso Apertura '07	🍷🍷	6

Antica Cascina Conti di Roero

Val Rubiagno, 2
12040 Vezza d'Alba [CN]
tel. 017365459
www.oliveropietro.it

This historic estate is making its Guide debut with some fine wines. The '06 Barbera d'Alba Superiore Cascina Valmenera is intense, with beautiful fruit and spice. The '06 Roero is packed with energy and finesse giving red fruits aromas and a lengthy finish. The '09 Roero Arneis is crisp and floral.

● Barbera d'Alba Sup. Cascina Valmenera '06	🍷🍷	5
● Roero '06	🍷🍷	5
○ Roero Arneis '09	🍷🍷	4
○ Langhe Favorita '09	🍷	4

La Corte - Cusmano

regione Quartino, 7
Calamandrana [AT]
tel. 014176910
www.cusmano.it

This estate is based in Calamandrana but has vineyards in other villages. This is its first time in the Guide. We especially liked the '06 Barbera d'Asti Superiore Nizza Archincà, which was intense, with oaky, cocoa powder, chestnut and prunes. The palate is structured with balanced acidity supporting the fruit.

● Barbera d'Asti Sup. Nizza Archincà '06	🍷🍷	4
● Barbera d'Asti La Grissa '08	🍷	4

Costa dei Platani

s.da Maggiora, 89
15011 Acqui Terme [AL]
tel. 014456253
www.costadeiplatani.it

The new owner of Costa dei Platani, Marco Vicentini, is very enthusiastic about his outdoor lifestyle choice. He has numerous projects, most aimed at developing the business, but the cellar is to continue along its established path.

● Barbera del M.to Sup. Maggiora '06	🍷🍷	5
● M.to Rosso Madrigale '06	🍷🍷	6

Crealto

via Marconi, 3
14020 Cossombrato [AT]
tel. 0141905204
valerio.quarello@libero.it

La Querello has had a change of name and owners. Two wine enthusiasts from Genoa, Luigi and Eleonora Armanino, are now beavering away passionately. We have little to say until we see how the estate develops. This year's wines were excellent, as usual, but they are still the work of Carlo Quarello at this stage.

- ● Barbera d'Asti V. Cré '09 — 🍷🍷 4
- ● Grignolino del M.to Casalese Cré Marcaleone '09 — 🍷🍷 4

Giovanni Daglio

via Montale Celli, 10
15050 Costa Vescovato [AL]
tel. 0131838262
giovanni.daglio@tiscali.it

Giovanni Daglio did well this year with one wine making it into the finals. The '08 Timorasso Cantico opens with an intense nose onto a dense, character-laden palate. The compact ruby red '08 Barbera Basinas has spice, fruit and oak that converge in a potent, harmonious palate with a very intense finish.

- ○ Colli Tortonesi Timorasso Cantico '08 — 🍷🍷 5
- ● Colli Tortonesi Barbera Basinas '08 — 🍷🍷 4*
- ○ Colli Tortonesi Cortese Vigna del Re '09 — 🍷 3
- ● Colli Tortonesi Dolcetto Nibiò '08 — 🍷 4

Sergio Degiorgis

via Circonvallazione, 3
12056 Mango [CN]
tel. 014189107
www.degiorgis-sergio.com

Patrizia and Sergio Degiorgis cultivate around 11 hectares of vines on hillslopes in the Alba Langhe bordering on Asti. Once again, the '09 Moscato d'Asti Sorì del Re was the most interesting, giving balanced sweetness and acidity. The '08 Barbera d'Alba has middling body but shows crisp and easy to drink.

- ● Barbera d'Alba '08 — 🍷🍷 5
- ○ Moscato d'Asti Sorì del Re '09 — 🍷🍷 4
- ● Dolcetto d'Alba Bricco Peso '09 — 🍷 4
- ○ Moscato d'Asti '09 — 🍷 4

Tenuta dei Fiori

fraz. Rodotiglia
via Valcalosso, 3
14052 Calosso [AT]
tel. 0141853819
www.tenutadeifiori.com

Valter Bosticardo only presented one wine this year. The '07 Barbera d'Asti Superiore Rusticard 1933 features black fruit, cinchona, tobacco and oak. The palate is impressively structured, with a long finish and sombre overtones of tanned hides and alcohol.

- ● Barbera d'Asti Sup. Rusticardi 1933 '07 — 🍷🍷 6

Giovanni e Lorenzo Frea

fraz. San Rocco
12040 Montaldo Roero [CN]
tel. 017240254

We liked the wines presented by this Montaldo estate. The '09 Langhe Nebbiolo is harmonious, with nice red berry notes, a fruity palate and character-laden finish. The pleasant '08 Roero Muschiavin givees tobacco, raspberry, spices and velvety tannins.

- ● Langhe Nebbiolo '09 — 🍷🍷 4
- ● Roero Muschiavin '08 — 🍷🍷 5
- ○ Roero Arneis '09 — 🍷 4

Funtanin

via Torino, 191
12043 Canale [CN]
tel. 0173979488
www.funtanin.com

This estate has played an important role in Roero wine. Managed by the Sperone brothers, Funtanin makes authentically interpreted wines. The two Barberas are very convincing, with the '09 being generous and a little husky. The '07 Ciabot Pierin is slightly more complex. The '09 Arneis Vigna Pierin di Soc is varietal.

- ● Barbera d'Alba '09 — 🍷🍷 4
- ● Barbera d'Alba Ciabot Pierin '07 — 🍷🍷 5
- ○ Roero Arneis Pierin di Soc '09 — 🍷🍷 4
- ● Roero Bricco Barbisa '07 — 🍷 5

Pierfrancesco Gatto

VIA VITTORIO EMANUELE II, 13
14030 CASTAGNOLE MONFERRATO [AT]
TEL. 0141292149
vinigatto@libero.it

In the Guide for the second time, Gatto has eight hectares of vines in Castagnole Monferrato, Montemagno and Refrancore. The '07 Barbera d'Asti Superiore Iolanda is good, featuring cocoa, sweet spices, plums, cinchona and a powerful, austere palate backed by crisp acidity. The '08 Barbera d'Asti Serra is nice.

- ● Barbera d'Asti Sup. Iolanda '07 — 🍷🍷 4
- ● Barbera d'Asti Vigna Serra '08 — 🍷 4

La Ghibellina

FRAZ. MONTEROTONDO, 61
15066 GAVI [AL]
TEL. 0143686257
www.laghibellina.it

La Ghibellina's wines were good again this year. The '07 Nero del Montone barbera, merlot blend has concentrated colour, an exuberant nose and a caressing, fleshy palate. The '07 Gavi Brut Metodo Classico has a complex nose and an intense palate. The line-up closes with the Gavi del Comune di Gavis.

- ● M.to Rosso Nero del Montone '07 — 🍷🍷 5
- ○ Gavi del Comune di Gavi Altius '08 — 🍷🍷 5
- ○ Gavi del Comune di Gavi Brut '07 — 🍷🍷 5
- ○ Gavi del Comune di Gavi Mainìn '09 — 🍷 4

La Giribaldina

REG. SAN VITO, 39
14042 CALAMANDRANA [AT]
TEL. 0141718043
www.giribaldina.com

It was not a great year for the Colombo estate, which mainly produces barbera blends. We particularly liked the '07 Barbera d'Asti Superiore Nizza Cala delle Mandrie, which is dominated by jam aromas and a very rich palate. The other wines are all respectable.

- ● Barbera d'Asti Sup. Nizza Cala delle Mandrie '07 — 🍷🍷 5
- ○ M.to Bianco Ferro di Cavallo '09 — 🍷 4
- ● Piemonte Barbera Fruizzante Pavonessa '09 — 🍷 3

Incisiana

VIA SANT'AGATA, 10/12
14045 INCISA SCAPACCINO [AT]
TEL. 0141747113
www.incisiana.com

Florian Oelssner and Eckhard Fischer produce 18,000 bottles from their organic five-hectare vineyard. We would like to highlight the '08 Barbera d'Asti with tobacco and cherry jam, and a supple, fresh palate. The other wines are all well made.

- ● Barbera d'Asti '08 — 🍷🍷 4
- ● Barbera d'Asti Sup. Zerosso '05 — 🍷 6
- ● M.to Rosso Merlotone '06 — 🍷 6

Ioppa

VIA DELLE PALLOTTE 10
28078 ROMAGNANO SESIA [NO]
TEL. 0163833079
www.viniioppa.it

Giampiero and Giorgio Ioppa's small operation has a long tradition with the main Novara wine types, to which they give a modern touch. The '04 Ghemme Santa Fé is concentrated but somewhat one-dimensional. The '07 Colline Novaresi Nebbiolo is juicier and more relaxed, with a leisurely tobacco-veined finish.

- ● Colline Novaresi Nebbiolo '07 — 🍷🍷 5
- ● Ghemme Bricco Balsina '05 — 🍷🍷 6
- ● Ghemme Santa Fè '04 — 🍷🍷 5
- ○ San Grato Bianco '09 — 🍷 3

Lodali

VIA RIMEMBRANZA, 5
12050 TREISO [CN]
TEL. 0173638109
www.lodali.it

This interesting Treiso family estate has a long history of producing territorial wines of integrity. The '07 Barbaresco Lorens unveils nice, very slightly forward varietal notes. The '06 Barolo Lorens is nice and complex with plenty of length and an extended finish.

- ● Barbaresco Lorens '07 — 🍷🍷 6
- ● Barolo Lorens '06 — 🍷🍷 6

Malgrà
LOC. BAZZANA
VIA NIZZA, 8
14046 MOMBARUZZO [AT]
TEL. 0141725055
www.malgra.it

The '07 vintage was not the Malgrà estate's best. The Barbera d'Asti Superiore Nizza Mora di Sassi features incense, plum and tobacco, then a rich palate with good length that is unfortunately completely masked by the wood. The '07 Barbera d'Asti Superiore Gaiana is simple and supple but finishes slightly bitter.

● Barbera d'Asti Sup. Nizza Mora di Sassi '07 ŸŸ 6
● Barbera d'Asti Sup. Gaiana '07 Ÿ 4

Marcalberto
VIA PORTA SOTTANA, 9
12058 SANTO STEFANO BELBO [CN]
TEL. 0141844022
marcalbertopc@libero.it

This small estate is to all intents a craft winery and produces exclusively classic-method sparkling wines. Experience and passion are key to the wines, each of which has a its own personality. The '05 Brut is profound and complex, the rosé tempting and vinous, and the prices all very. very good.

○ Marcalberto Brut '05 ŸŸ 6
○ Marcalberto Brut ŸŸ 5
⊙ Marcalberto Brut Rosé ŸŸ 5

Marchese Luca Spinola
LOC. CASCINA MASSIMILIANA
15066 GAVI [AL]
TEL. 0143682514
www.marcheselucaspinola.it

Andrea Spinola's estate confirmed it can produce high-quality wines with this brilliant '09 Gavi Tassarolo, a wine that offers great value for money. The bouquet is amazingly complex and the mouth well balanced, elegantly savoury and exceptionally persistent. The '09 Gavi di Gavi has an elegant nose and good body.

○ Gavi del comune di Tassarolo '09 ŸŸ 3*
○ Gavi del Comune di Gavi '09 ŸŸ 4
○ Gavi di Gavi Tenuta Massimiliana '09 Ÿ 4

Le Marie
VIA SANDEFENDENTE, 6
12032 BARGE [CN]
TEL. 0175345159
info@lemarievini.eu

Valerio Raviolo produces some impressive wines from nebbiolo, barbera, dolcetto, bonarda and freisa, and has replanted several old local clones. The barbera and nebbiolo '07 Debarges gives aristocratic tobacco over minerality and then elegant tannins. The '07 Barbera Colombé is denser and caressing, if less elegant.

● Pinerolese Barbera Colombè '07 ŸŸ 4*
● Pinerolese Debàrges '07 ŸŸ 3*
○ Blanc de Lissart Ÿ 4

Mazzoni
VIA ROMA, 73
28010 CAVAGLIO D'AGOGNA [NO]
TEL. 0322806612
www.vinimazzoni.it

The Mazzoni family has a long history in wine but it was Tiziano who relaunched the estate just over ten years ago. Today, the top wine is Ghemme and the '06 shows complex and structured, with a long aromatic finish. Mazzoni's elegant Passito Le Masche is one of the best dried-grape wines in the zone.

● Ghemme dei Mazzoni '06 ŸŸ 5
○ Passito Le Masche ŸŸ 5

F.lli Molino
LOC. AUSARIO
VIA AUSARIO, 5
12050 TREISO [CN]
TEL. 0173638384
www.molinovini.com

This family estate is set in the picturesque hills of Treiso. The wines are good and the prices civilized. We most liked the elegant '07 Barbaresco Teorema and the '09 Barbera d'Asti Loreto, which is a wonderfully well-balanced combination of flesh and acidity.

● Barbaresco Teorema '07 ŸŸ 6
● Barbera d'Asti Loreto '09 ŸŸ 4*
● Barbaresco Ausario '07 Ÿ 6
● Dolcetto d'Alba Le Querce '09 Ÿ 3

Franco Mondo

REG. MARIANO, 33
14050 SAN MARZANO OLIVETO [AT]
TEL. 0141834096
www.francomondo.net

Franco Mondo grows mostly barbera on his 13-hectare estate, with some moscato, dolcetto and cortese. This year, the '06 Barbera d'Asti Superiore Nizza Vigna delle Rose and the '09 Barbera d'Asti are worthy of mention. The former is floral, with nice oak and a long, powerful palate; the latter gives ripe fruit.

● Barbera d'Asti Sup. Nizza V. delle Rose '06	🍷🍷	5
● Barbera d'Asti '09	🍷	3

Montalbera

MONTALBERA, 1
14030 CASTAGNOLE MONFERRATO [AT]
TEL. 0119433311
www.montalbera.it

Montalbera puts effort into Ruché so it is no surprise that the '09 Ruché di Castagnole Monferrato La Tradizione is very good, unfurling wild roses and liquorice aromatics and a powerful palate with a long finish. The well-balanced, fruity '08 Barbera d'Asti Lequilibrio is also excellent.

● Barbera d'Asti L'Equilibrio '08	🍷🍷	4
● Ruchè di Castagnole M.to La Tradizione '09	🍷🍷	4
● Barbera d'Asti La Ribelle '09	🍷	4

Tenuta Montemagno

VIA CASCINA VALFOSSATO, 9
14030 MONTEMAGNO [AT]
TEL. 014163624
www.tenutamontemagno.it

This 70-hectare estate near Asti has ten under vines. There's a broad range of wines, most of which are made from indigenous varieties. The two Barberas are harmonious, concentrated and fleshy. The '08 Violae is a barbera, syrah and ruché blend with an intense, expansive nose, powerful palate and long finish.

● Barbera D'Asti Austerum '08	🍷🍷	5
● Barbera d'Asti Mysterium '07	🍷🍷	5
O M.to Bianco Musae '09	🍷🍷	4
● M.to Rosso Violae '08	🍷🍷	5

La Morandina

LOC. MORANDINI, 11
12053 CASTIGLIONE TINELLA [CN]
TEL. 0141855261
www.lamorandina.com

This interesting estate produces everything from Moscato, its flagship wine, to Barbaresco. The range is very reliable and good throughout. Although slightly less successful than in the past, the '09 Moscato has a satisfying, vibrant palate despite being slightly too lean.

O Moscato d'Asti '09	🍷🍷	4
● Barbera d'Asti Cinque Vigne '08	🍷	4
O Langhe Chardonnay '09	🍷	5

Giuseppe Negro

VIA GALLINA, 22
12052 NEIVE [CN]
TEL. 0173677468
www.negrogiuseppe.com

Once again this small winery in Neive did well. The wines are stylistically convincing and well defined with a strong sense of place. The Barbera has well-balanced fruit and pulp while the two '07 Barbarescos are moderately modern. Gallina is fuller and softer; Pian Cavallo is stiffer and more cellarable.

● Barbaresco Gallina '07	🍷🍷	6
● Barbaresco Pian Cavallo '07	🍷🍷	6
● Barbera d'Alba Pulin '08	🍷🍷	4*

Lorenzo Negro

FRAZ. S. ANNA
FRAZ. SAN ANNA, 55
12040 MONTEU ROERO [CN]
TEL. 017390645
www.negrolorenzo.com

This small estate produces only local wines. The '06 Roero Riserva San Francesco has a beautifully elegant nose led by spices and raspberries. The not particularly full palate is fresh and consistent. The '07 Barbera d'Alba is pleasant and harmonious, with a long finish.

● Barbera d'Alba '07	🍷🍷	4*
● Roero San Francesco Ris. '06	🍷🍷	5
● Langhe Nebbiolo '08	🍷	4
● Langhe Rosso Arbesca '07	🍷	4

Nervi

c.so Vercelli, 117
13045 Gattinara [VC]
tel. 0163833228
www.gattinara-nervi.it

This historic winery near Vercelli, now owned by the Gruppo Sitindustrie and Malgrà, only presented one wine. The '04 Gattinara Podere dei Ginepri presents a fresh, rust-edged bouquet. The palate is rich and powerful, despite a slightly closed, bitter finish.

- ● Gattinara Podere dei Ginepri '04 — 🍷🍷 6

Cantina Sociale di Nizza

via Alessandria, 57
14049 Nizza Monferrato [AT]
tel. 0141721348
www.nizza.it

This co-operative winery presented several good wines. We particularly liked the '07 Barbera d'Asti Superiore 50 Vendemmie with its ripe berry fruit aromas and potent palate, and the '07 Barbera d'Asti Superiore Nizza Ceppi Vecchi, which offers tobacco and jam then remarkable structure.

- ● Barbera d'Asti Sup. 50 Vendemmie '07 — 🍷🍷 4*
- ● Barbera d'Asti Sup. Nizza Ceppi Vecchi '07 — 🍷🍷 4
- ● Barbera d'Asti Sup. Magister '08 — 🍷 4

Pace

fraz. Madonna di Loreto
Cascina Pace, 52
12043 Canale [CN]
tel. 0173979544
aziendapace@infinito.it

This was not a great year for the Negro brothers' estate. We liked the '07 Roero Riserva, which is deep and generous, with raspberry, tobacco and dried flowers. The slightly too alcoholic palate is enormously well structured with nice fruit, although the tannins are still a little grainy.

- ● Roero Ris. '07 — 🍷🍷 5
- ● Barbera d'Alba '08 — 🍷 4
- ○ Roero Arneis '09 — 🍷 4

Fabrizio Pinsoglio

fraz. Madonna dei Cavalli, 31bis
12050 Canale [CN]
tel. 0173968401
fabriziopinsoglio@libero.it

Pinsoglio's wines always have strong territorial traits. Take the '07 Roero Riserva, which is nice and savoury, with good structure and supporting acidity. The '09 Roero Arneis Vigna Malinat is well made, with floral notes, white-fleshed fruits aromas and a soft, clean finish.

- ● Roero Ris. '07 — 🍷🍷 5
- ○ Roero Arneis Vign. Malinat '09 — 🍷 3

Podere Macellio

via Roma, 18
10014 Caluso [TO]
tel. 0119833511
www.erbaluce-bianco.it

In recent years, Renato and Daniele Bianco have focused their efforts on erbaluce in the hope of relaunching this indigenous variety. We especially enjoyed the '02 Caluso Passito, which is youthful and bright although the finish is slightly short. The Erbaluce di Caluso Pas Dosé is beautifully dynamic.

- ○ Caluso Passito '02 — 🍷🍷 5
- ○ Erbaluce di Caluso Spumante M. Cl. Pas Dosé — 🍷🍷 5*
- ○ Erbaluce di Caluso '09 — 🍷 3

Post dal Vin - Terre del Barbera

fraz. Possavina
via Salie, 19
14030 Rocchetta Tanaro [AT]
tel. 0141644143
www.postdalvin.com

No need to guess which variety this estate focuses on. We very much liked the '08 Barbera d'Asti Superiore BriccoFiore, which offers intense cinchona, plum and cocoa aromas, a powerful palate and leisurely finish. The '09 Barbera d'Asti Maricca and the '08 Barbera d'Asti Superiore Castagnassa are also very pleasant.

- ● Barbera d'Asti Sup. BriccoFiore '08 — 🍷🍷 3*
- ● Barbera d'Asti Maricca '09 — 🍷 3
- ● Barbera d'Asti Sup. Castagnassa '08 — 🍷 4

OTHER WINERIES

Giovanni Prandi

FRAZ. CASCINA COLOMBÈ
VIA FARINETTI, 5
12055 DIANO D'ALBA [CN]
TEL. 017369248
www.prandigiovanni.it

This estate is best known for offering good value for money. This year, we especially liked the Dolcettos. The '09 is outstandingly juicy and deep, with a confident, but not overbearing, structure. The '09 Sorì Cristina is more austere.

● Dolcetto di Diano Sorì Colombè '09	🍷🍷	3*
● Dolcetto di Diano Sorì Cristina '09	🍷🍷	4*
● Barbera d'Alba '08	🍷	4
● Nebbiolo d'Alba Colombè '08	🍷	4

Produttori del Gavi

VIA CAVALIERI DI VITTORIO VENETO, 45
15066 GAVI [AL]
TEL. 0143642786
cantina.prodgavi@libero.it

The Cantina Produttori del Gavi's '09 range of cortese-based whites is again excellent. The Gavi G is a fine example of the type, offering an elegant nose and full-bodied, intense palate. The GG has a fruity nose, with flinty notes, and a lovely long, savoury palate.

○ Gavi del Comune di Gavi GG '09	🍷🍷	4
○ Gavi G '09	🍷🍷	4*
○ Gavi Il Forte '09	🍷	4
○ Gavi Primi Grappoli '09	🍷	4

La Raia

S.DA MONTEROTONDO, 79
15067 NOVI LIGURE [AL]
TEL. 0143743685
www.la-raia.it

Raia boasts 110 hectares and is one of the largest estates in the Gavi zone. There are 32 hectares of vineyards and annual production is around 80,000 bottles of Gavi and Barbera. We were impressed by the '09 Gavi, which has a fruity, mineral nose and a powerful, crisp palate.

○ Gavi '09	🍷🍷	4
○ Gavi Pisè '08	🍷	4
● Piemonte Barbera '09	🍷	4

Rattalino

S.DA GIRO DEL MONDO, 4
12050 BARBARESCO [CN]
TEL. 3492155012
www.massimorattalino.it

Massimo Rattalino acquired his five hectares at Barbaresco and Novello piece by piece. His oak-aged Barolo Trentacinque and Barbaresco Quarantatre are modern in style, with broad fruit and spice aromas, while his Barolo Trentaquattro and Barbaresco Quarantadue are more traditional, with livelier tannins.

● Barolo Trentacinque '05	🍷🍷	7
● Barbaresco Quarantadue '06	🍷🍷	6
● Barolo Trentaquattro '05	🍷🍷	7
● Barbaresco Quarantatre '06	🍷	6

Eraldo Revelli

LOC. PIANBOSCO, 29
12060 FARIGLIANO [CN]
TEL. 0173797154
www.eraldorevelli.com

This historic Dogliani estate produces various Dolcettos but we were most convinced by the '08 Dogliani San Matteo, which is generous, very succulent and astoundingly long. The pleasant '08 Langhe Rosso La Basarisca is mostly barbera with some dolcetto. The '09 Dolcetto Autin Lungh is huskier, savoury and intense.

● Dogliani S. Matteo '08	🍷🍷	5
● Langhe Rosso La Basarisca '08	🍷🍷	5
● Dolcetto di Dogliani Autin Lungh '09	🍷	5
● Dolcetto di Dogliani Otto Filari '09	🍷	4

Cascina Salerio

S.DA SALERIO, 16
14055 COSTIGLIOLE D'ASTI [AT]
TEL. 0141966294
casalerio@alice.it

Cascina Salerio did very well again this year. The '09 Monferrato Rosso Aqua, from 70 per cent cabernet sauvignon and 30 per cent barbera, offers rich fruit and an uncomplicated soft, fleshy palate with acidity and length. The plum and cocoa '08 Monferrato Rosso Fuoco is from 70-30 barbera and cabernet sauvignon.

● M.to Rosso Aqua '09	🍷🍷	3*
● M.to Rosso Fuoco '08	🍷🍷	4*

San Bartolomeo

LOC. VALLEGGE
CASCINA SAN BARTOLOMEO, 26
15066 GAVI [AL]
TEL. 01436431280
fulviobergaglio@alice.it

This historic Gavi estate is back in the Guide after several years. We are pleased to welcome Fulvio Bergaglio back with his '09 Pelöia, which almost made the finals. It gives chlorophyll and white fruits with mineral undertones and a potent, very harmonious palate. The '09 Gavi is also very decent.

○ Gavi '09	TT	3*
○ Gavi del Comune di Gavi Pelöia '09	TT	4*

Tenuta San Pietro

LOC. SAN PIETRO, 2
15067 TASSAROLO [AL]
TEL. 0143342422
www.tenutasanpietro.it

Best of the vast San Pietro range is the excellent '09 Gavi Il Mandorlo with its almonds and minerality, elegant structure and fleshy palate. The San Pietro Gavi is complex. The '08 Nero San Pietro has the same mix of albarossa, barbera and cabernet sauvignon. The sound '08 Orma Romea is from nibiô, a dolcetto clone.

○ Gavi del Comune di Tassarolo Il Mandorlo '09	TT	5
○ Gavi di Tassarolo San Pietro '09	TT	4
● M.to Nero San Pietro '08	TT	4
● M.to Orma Romea '08	TT	7

Giacomo Scagliola

REG. SANTA LIBERA, 20
14053 CANELLI [AT]
TEL. 0141831146
www.scagliolagiacomo.it

Giacomo Scagliolo again presented an excellent Moscato d'Asti. The '09 Santa Libera has intense citrus and lime, a rich, elegant palate and the right acidity to balance the fat, leisurely finish. The rest of the range is also well made.

○ Moscato d'Asti Santa Libera '09	TT	4*
● Barbera d'Asti Vigna dei Mandorli '08	T	4
○ Cortese Alto Monferrato '09	T	3

Simone Scaletta

LOC. MANZONI, 61
12065 MONFORTE D'ALBA [CN]
TEL. 3484912733
www.viniscaletta.com

This promising little family estate produces the main Langhe designations. The labels include an '06 Barolo Chirlet, which offers a complex nose and full-bodied, characterful palate. The nose and savoury, fruit-filled palate are in nice balance on the '08 Barbera Sarsera. The '08 Nebbiolo is nicely varietal.

● Barbera d'Alba Sarsera '08	TT	5
● Barolo Chirlet '06	TT	7
● Langhe Nebbiolo Autin 'd Madama '08	TT	5

Antica Casa Vinicola Scarpa

VIA MONTEGRAPPA, 6
14049 NIZZA MONFERRATO [AT]
TEL. 0141721331
www.scarpavini.it

This historic estate has a varied range. The '07 Barberesco Tettineive, with its raspberry, tobacco, and liquorice, and complex, finely structured, lingering palate is convincing. We also like the '07 Barbera d'Asti, which offers plum and cocoa powder, vibrant acidity and a full, lingering finish.

● Barbaresco Tettineive '07	TT	8
● Barbera d'Asti CasaScarpa '07	TT	4*
● M.to Rosso RossoScarpa '07	T	4
● Nebbiolo d'Alba Bric du Nota '07	T	5

La Spinosa Alta

C.NE SPINOSA ALTA 6
15038 OTTIGLIO [AL]
TEL. 0142921372
lanzani.vini@tin.it

This is La Spinosa Alta's second Guide profile. Barbera d'Asti Superiore '07 has a good nose and great follow-through. The '07 La Punta is interesting, offering intense fruit, faint oak and a fleshy, alcoholic finish. Tenebroso, from 90-10 nebbiolo and barbera, and Monferrato Rosso Les Celliers du Roi are well made.

● Barbera D'Asti Sup. '07	TT	4*
● Barbera del M.to Sup. La Punta '07	TT	4
● M.to Rosso Les Celliers du Roi Ris. '07	TT	4
● M.to Rosso Tenebroso '07	TT	4

OTHER WINERIES

Giuseppe Stella
S.DA BOSSOLA, 8
14055 COSTIGLIOLE D'ASTI [AT]
TEL. 0141966142
stellavini@libero.it

Beppe Stella's estate built on its previous performance. The '08 Barbera d'Asti Superiore Bricco Fubine - Il Vino del Maestro is rich, fruity, generous and boasts a harmonious finish while the '09 Freisa d'Asti Convento is intense, with pepper, tobacco, raspberries, fresh acidity, a leisurely palate and tannic finish.

● Barbera d'Asti Sup. Bricco Fubine Il Vino del Maestro '08	🍷🍷	5
● Freisa d'Asti Convento '09	🍷🍷	4*
● Grignolino d'Asti Sufragio '09	🍷	4

Traversa - Cascina Bertolotto
REG. ROCCHETTA 1
15018 SPIGNO MONFERRATO [AL]
TEL. 014491551
www.cascinabertolotto.it

The Traversa family did well with their Dolcetto d'Acqui, despite the failings of the 2008 vintage. La Muiètte has a complex nose and fleshy palate. La Cresta is pretty rugged but this makes it no less enjoyable. The dried moscato Surì di Bertolotto is slightly less incisive, as is Il Barigi, from cortese grapes.

● Dolcetto d'Acqui La Cresta '08	🍷🍷	4
● Dolcetto d'Acqui La Muiètte '08	🍷🍷	4
○ M.to Bianco Il Barigi '09	🍷	4
○ Surì di Bertolotto	🍷	6

F.lli Trinchero
VIA GORRA, 49
14048 MONTEGROSSO D'ASTI [AT]
TEL. 0141956167
www.fllitrincherovino.com

Fratelli Trinchero makes its Guide debut. The '07 Barbera d'Asti Superiore Rico made the finals with its intense cherries and plums, rich palate supported by good acidity, healthy minerality and long, fruity finish. The '09 Barbera d'Asti La Trincherina is uncomplicated and very likeable.

● Barbera d'Asti Sup. Rico '07	🍷🍷	4*
● Barbera d'Asti La Trincherina '09	🍷	3

Laura Valditerra
S.DA MONTEROTONDO, 75
15067 NOVI LIGURE [AL]
TEL. 0143321451
laura@valditerra.it

Laura Valditerra's glorious wines are enviably reliable. The brilliant '09 Vigna del Lago made the finals with its imposing structure and very complex, mineral nose reminiscent of wild flowers, followed by a harmonious, intense palate and leisurely finish. The '09 Tenuta Merlassino is less complex.

○ Gavi V. del Lago '09	🍷🍷	4*
○ Gavi Tenuta Merlassino '09	🍷🍷	4

La Vecchia Posta
VIA MONTEBELLO, 2
15050 AVOLASCA [AL]
TEL. 0131876254
lavecchiaposta@virgilio.it

La Vecchia Posta presented a slightly inferior selection this year, with a disappointing Rebelot merlot, pinot nero and dolcetto blend and '08 Timorasso Il Selvaggio, less successful than in past years. The '09 Dolcetto Teraforta did very well. It has intense fruit, decent balance and a tannic finish.

● Colli Tortonesi Dolcetto Teraforta '09	🍷🍷	3*
● Colli Tortonesi Rosso Rebelot '08	🍷	4
○ Colli Tortonesi Timorasso Il Selvaggio '08	🍷	4

Giacomo Vico
VIA TORINO, 80
12043 CANALE [CN]
TEL. 0173979126
www.giacomovico.it

The Vico family did superbly this time. The '08 Langhe Nebbliolo unveils tobacco and dried flowers, with supple, close-knit tannins. The '07 Roero is mature and well structured, with tobacco and raspberry jam aromas. The fruity '08 Barbera d'Alba is well made and the easy-drinking '09 Roero Arneis is enjoyable.

● Barbera D'Alba '08	🍷🍷	4
● Langhe Nebbiolo '08	🍷🍷	4
● Roero '07	🍷🍷	5
○ Roero Arneis '09	🍷	4

Il Vignale

LOC. LOMELLINA
VIA GAVI, 130
15067 NOVI LIGURE [AL]
TEL. 014372715
www.ilvignale.it

The Cappelletti husband and wife team gave us their '09 Gavi Vigne Alte this year. The deep straw yellow Vigne Alte tempts with flowers and white peaches backed by intense minerals, a fleshy, caressing palate and lovely leisurely finish. A Gavi for the cellar.

O Gavi Vigne Alte '09	🍷🍷	4

Villa Fiorita

VIA CASE SPARSE, 2
14034 CASTELLO DI ANNONE [AT]
TEL. 0141401231
www.villafiorita-wines.com

The Rondolino family recently celebrated 25 years at the Villa Fiorita estate. In the absence of any '08 Barberas, we liked the '09 Grignolino d'Asti delle Querce with its black pepper spice and fresh, leisurely palate. The pinot nero-only '07 Monferrato Rosso Abaco is uncomplicated but well made.

● Grignolino d'Asti Pian delle Querce '09	🍷🍷	3*
● Monferrato Rosso Abaco '07	🍷	3

La Zerba

S.DA PER FRANCAVILLA, 1
15060 TASSAROLO [AL]
TEL. 0143342259
www.la-zerba.it

The Lorenzi family gave us a treat. The splendid '09 Gavi Terraross is intense throughout, with a complex nose and savoury, generous body in the mouth. The '09 Gavi La Zerba is no lightweight, showing white-fleshed fruits and mineral notes leading into a rich, powerful palate that complements the nose exquisitely.

O Gavi Terrarossa '09	🍷🍷	3*
O Gavi La Zerba '09	🍷🍷	3*

LIGURIA

After the great results achieved by Liguria in the 2010 edition of the Guide – going from two Three Glass awards in 2009 to six – you might think this success was tied to a coincidence or, at best, a particularly favourable growing season. We do not want to stir up controversy so we will restrict ourselves to merely stating the numbers, which more than anything else do justice to this region's winemaking. Last year 50 estates submitted 259 wines. This time there were more than 358, sent in by 69 estates, nearly a 40 per cent increase. This is quite comforting because it means that in Liguria, where small and very small estates have always been around and producers in general have an unassuming, reserved character, an epochal change is under way, bringing attention to these extraordinary artisans. Those concerned are aware of this and refuse to remain passive spectators. Producers in Liguria clearly have no problems selling their products. They could easily remain here in their region where the population triples for several months of the year thanks to tourism. Tourists rarely leave without tasting a nice glass of Pigato, Vermentino, Dolceacqua, Cinque Terre or other wines. The number of Three Glass awards has increased to seven this year, and the number landing in our finals has grown to 21, underlining that currently Ligurian wine is on a roll. The numbers may seem small when compared to great wine regions like Tuscany or Piedmont but it is large when you consider Liguria's small population of just under 1,650,000, its land area of 70 per cent forest, and production of around 200,000 hectolitres of wine in a good year. To put it another way, barely 0.4 per cent of Italy's total. Top award winners include: from the Colli di Luni Lambruschi, a delicious Vermentino Costa Marina '09 and Lunae Bosoni with the Vermentino Lunae Etichetta Nera '09. Along the Riviera di Ponente come another two Vermentinos, the '09 by Maria Donata Bianchi and Le Serre '09 by Lupi. Poggio dei Gorleri defends the honour of Pigato with an excellent Cycnus '09. In closing, there are two extraordinary Rossese di Dolceacquas, Bricco Arcagna '08 from Terre Bianche and Superiore Vigneto Posau di Maccario Dringenberg. Several estates unfortunately remain out of the Guide, some although they have produced quality wines in the past. Either they are still at the beginning of their adventures or so small as to never go beyond the limited local area. We refer here to G.B. Parma, the only distiller in Liguria, Francesca Mozer's Lunisiana Soul, Cantina di Nonno Pescetto, Terra di Bargon with an excellent Sciacchetrà and the two historic micro-estates in the Ventimiglio area, Perrino and Terra dei Doria.

Massimo Alessandri

via Costa Parrocchia
18028 Ranzo [IM]
tel. 018253458
www.massimoalessandri.it

CELLAR SALES
PRE-BOOKED VISITS
FOOD

ANNUAL PRODUCTION 30,000 bottles
HECTARES UNDER VINE 6
VITICULTURE METHOD Conventional

We found further proof that Massimo's decision to plant and grow the non-native viognier and roussanne alongside traditional varieties on his six hectares under vine at altitudes of between 280 and 400 metres was a winning one. Meticulously tended and personally supervised by Massimo himself, the plots under vine produce wonderful fruit.

With the return of the Viorus '08, from roussanne and viognier, we can again savour the complex aroma of a product fermented in tonneaux with leisurely lees stirring. The caressing nose has citrus and summer flowers and the palate has a marked, full-flavoured length. Other than this, Massimo made a good showing with the Pigato Vigne Vegie '08, with almondy tones accompanying the usual rosemary and sage aromas. In the absence of the red Ligustico, Massimo submitted a red A' Seiana '08 with close-knit fullness on the nose and a complex Bordeaux structure. The Pigato '09 and Vermentino '09 Costa de Vigne are also well made.

○ Viorus Costa de Vigne '08	▼▼	6
● A' Seiana '08	▼▼	6
○ Riviera Ligure di Ponente Pigato Vigne Vegie '08	▼▼	5
○ Riviera Ligure di Ponente Pigato Costa de Vigne '09	▼	4
○ Riviera Ligure di Ponente Vermentino Costa de Vigne '09	▼	4
● A' Seiana '07	▽▽	6
● A' Seiana '06	▽▽	6
● Ligustico '07	▽▽	6
● Ligustico '05	▽▽	6
○ Riviera Ligure di Ponente Pigato Vigne Vegie '07	▽▽	5
○ Riviera Ligure di Ponente Pigato Vigne Vegie '06	▽▽	5
○ Viorus '07	▽▽	6

Laura Aschero

p.zza Vittorio Emanuele, 7
18027 Pontedassio [IM]
tel. 0183710307
lauraaschero@uno.it

CELLAR SALES
PRE-BOOKED VISITS

ANNUAL PRODUCTION 60,000 bottles
HECTARES UNDER VINE 3
VITICULTURE METHOD Conventional

Near Pontedassio, on the first hills that protect the Imperia hinterland from the northern winds, Marco Rizzo continues the work of his mother, Laura Aschero, founder of an estate that now produces over 60,000 bottles. Marco has carried on his mother's philosophy, maintaining a healthy balance between tradition and modernity. He makes the typical wines from this territory, Vermentino, Pigato and Rossese, and intends to work on the range, further refining its quality.

The '09 vintage again proved Marco's showcase product is still Vermentino, thanks to the intensity on the refined, elegant nose that hinges on citrus and apricot. This refreshing, lively wine shows great length on the palate. More complex on the nose, with a bouquet of ripe peaches and yellow-fleshed fruits, the Pigato '09 may be a bit forward on the palate. The '09 Rossese continues to show a grassy note we tasted in the past. It's not unpleasant but it does block development on the palate.

○ Riviera Ligure di Ponente Vermentino '09	▼▼	4
○ Riviera Ligure di Ponente Pigato '09	▼	4
● Riviera Ligure di Ponente Rossese '09	▼	4
○ Riviera Ligure di Ponente Pigato '08	▽▽	4*
○ Riviera Ligure di Ponente Pigato '06	▽▽	4
● Riviera Ligure di Ponente Rossese '07	▽▽	4
○ Riviera Ligure di Ponente Vermentino '08	▽▽	4*
○ Riviera Ligure di Ponente Vermentino '07	▽▽	4
○ Riviera Ligure di Ponente Vermentino '06	▽▽	4

La Baia del Sole

FRAZ. LUNI ANTICA
VIA FORLINO, 3
19034 ORTONOVO [SP]
TEL. 0187661821
www.cantinefederici.com

CELLAR SALES
PRE-BOOKED VISITS

ANNUAL PRODUCTION 140,000 bottles
HECTARES UNDER VINE 22
VITICULTURE METHOD Conventional

Isa and Giulio Federici's vineyards spread across the hillsides in the municipalities of Ortonovo and Castelnuovo Magra, overlooking the ruins of the ancient city of Luni a few steps from the Roman amphitheatre, with sunny exposure, cooled year round by breezes from the north. In around a quarter of a century, results have been stupendous thanks to the Federici family's scrupulous care in both the vineyards and cellar.

All the labels submitted were good, although the Vermentino '09 from the Sarticola vineyard stands out. Its iodine aroma, combined with wafts of citrus and spring flowers, leads into a pleasant vortex of long-lingering sensations that fuse with an extended fragrant finish. The Vermentino Solaris '09 may be better executed than the last wine but without the inspiration. Oro d'Isée '09 is an elegant wine with structured quality. The Rosso Forlino '09 is also good with well-supported body, elegant structure and soft tannins.

○ Colli di Luni Vermentino Sarticola '09	▼▼	5
○ Colli di Luni Gladius '09	▼	3
○ Colli di Luni Vermentino Oro d'Isée '09	▼	4
○ Colli di Luni Vermentino Solaris '09	▼	4
● Rosso Forlino '09	▼	4
● Colli di Luni Terre D'Oriente '06	▽▽	5
○ Colli di Luni Vermentino Sarticola '08	▽▽	5
○ Muri Grandi Golfo dei Poeti '08	▽▽	3*

Maria Donata Bianchi

LOC. VALCROSA
VIA MEREA
18013 DIANO ARENTINO [IM]
TEL. 0183498233
www.aziendagricolabianchi.com

CELLAR SALES
PRE-BOOKED VISITS
ROOMS

ANNUAL PRODUCTION 25,000 bottles
HECTARES UNDER VINE 4
VITICULTURE METHOD Organic

After their long ago experience with the small winery in the centre of Diano Castello, where Emanuele's father, Pietro, carried out his first tests with varieties from the Rhône valley, Maria Donata and Emanuele Trevia purchased a ten-hectare plot in the municipality of Diano Arentino, planted new vineyards and established their own winery. Syrah and grenache have been added to the traditional vermentino and pigato whites.

As it did two years ago, the Vermentino in the '09 edition hit the spot and won a well-deserved Three Glasses. Richly fruity and featuring an intense vein of acidity, it shows all the characteristics of the terroir, in particular medicinal and aromatic herb aromas and those savoury mouthfilling minerals that make this a real one-of-a-kind. In contrast, the '09 Pigato struggles a bit to find as clearly characteristic and convincing a path as its high-scoring cousin. Emanuele has put a lot into the '08 Mattana from syrah and grenache but although it has elegance and good structure, the wine fell short of expectations this year.

○ Riviera Ligure di Ponente Vermentino '09	▼▼▼	5
○ Riviera Ligure di Ponente Pigato '09	▼▼	5
● La Mattana '08	▼	6
○ Riviera Ligure di Ponente Vermentino '07	▽▽▽	4*
● Bormano '07	▽▽	5
● La Mattana '06	▽▽	6
○ Riviera Ligure di Ponente Pigato '07	▽▽	5*
○ Riviera Ligure di Ponente Pigato '06	▽▽	5
○ Riviera Ligure di Ponente Vermentino '08	▽▽	5
○ Riviera Ligure di Ponente Vermentino '06	▽▽	4*

Luigi Bianchi Carenzo

Via I. Lantero, 19
18013 Diano San Pietro [IM]
tel. 0183429072

CELLAR SALES
PRE-BOOKED VISITS

ANNUAL PRODUCTION **10,000 bottles**
HECTARES UNDER VINE **1**
VITICULTURE METHOD **Conventional**

We got to know Luigi Bianchi Carenzo as the owner of popular bar in the centre of Diano Marina. He candidly confessed to us that, by leaving his children to run the business during the day, he could dedicate himself to his passion for vineyards, and then take back the reins of his bar in the afternoon. A man of great passion, he has installed a lot of new technology at his estate, in the field as well as the cellar, leaving nothing to chance. The results are there in the glass.

His wines deserve much more than a simple mention – though we felt the '09 vintage was not one of the best – for the sensible cleanliness of the range and the attentive management of the terroir's characteristics. We rediscovered the fragrant freshness of aromas in the Vermentino '09 and the golden warmth, accompanied by tangy fragrance and velvety body, in the Pigato '09. Nicely structured, yet slightly below par compared to earlier versions, the Rossese '09 has delicate aromas but is unable to compensate for structure that is a tad too lightweight.

○ Riviera Ligure di Ponente Vermentino '09	▼▼	4*
○ Riviera Ligure di Ponente Pigato '09	▼	4
● Riviera Ligure di Ponente Rossese '09	▼	4
○ Riviera Ligure di Ponente Pigato '08	▽▽	4*
○ Riviera Ligure di Ponente Pigato '07	▽▽	4
○ Riviera Ligure di Ponente Pigato '06	▽▽	4
○ Riviera Ligure di Ponente Vermentino '08	▽▽	4*
● Riviera Ligure di Ponente Vermentino '07	▽▽	4*
○ Riviera Ligure di Ponente Vermentino '06	▽▽	4

BioVio

fraz. Bastia
via Crociata, 24
17031 Albenga [SV]
tel. 018220776
www.biovio.it

CELLAR SALES
PRE-BOOKED VISITS

ANNUAL PRODUCTION **40,000 bottles**
HECTARES UNDER VINE **4**
VITICULTURE METHOD **Certified organic**

The saga of the family of Gio Batta Vio, nicknamed Aimone, is all in his determined wife Chiara and their three wonderful daughters: Caterina, Camilla and Carolina. This close-knit, harmonious quintet grows aromatic herbs, well-suited to the Albenga plain, and also conscientiously produces excellent local grapes that are skilfully processed at the small winery. They are now at the top of local wine production. The first harvest was in 2000 and since then their wines have slowly acquired surprising personality while still respecting the traditions of Liguria.

From the wines we tasted, the '09 Vermentino Aimone is so characteristic that it is now instantly recognizable, thanks to rich, very personal aromas of medicinal and aromatic herbs, brought out by splendid acidity and clean minerality. The Pigato Bon in da Bon '09 rewards us with all the sunny opulence of its variety, and is organized here around first-rate nose-palate structure, revealing touches of ripe yellow-fleshed peach, damson and subtle apricot fruit. Though well crafted, the Granaccia Gigò fruit: 09 still needs a bit more work.

○ Riviera Ligure di Ponente Pigato Bon in da Bon '09	▼▼	4*
○ Riviera Ligure di Ponente Vermentino Aimone '09	▼▼	4*
● Bacilò '09	▼	4
● Granaccia Gigò '09	▼	4
○ Riviera Ligure di Ponente Pigato Marixe '09	▼	4
○ Riviera Ligure di Ponente Pigato Bon in da Bon '08	▽▽	4
○ Riviera Ligure di Ponente Pigato Bon in da Bon '06	▽▽	4*
○ Riviera Ligure di Ponente Pigato Marixe '08	▽▽	4*
● Riviera Ligure di Ponente Rossese Bastiò '07	▽▽	4
○ Riviera Ligure di Ponente Vermentino '07	▽▽	4
○ Riviera Ligure di Ponente Vermentino Aimone '08	▽▽	4*
○ Riviera Ligure di Ponente Vermentino Aimone '06	▽▽	4*

Enoteca Bisson

c.so Gianelli, 28
16043 Chiavari [GE]
tel. 0185314462
www.bissonvini.it

CELLAR SALES
PRE-BOOKED VISITS

ANNUAL PRODUCTION 80,000 bottles
HECTARES UNDER VINE 10
VITICULTURE METHOD Organic

We have already mentioned how Piero Lugano transferred his valuable personal experience to growing and winemaking, moving in little more than 30 years from an initial commercial phase to his own well-defined production, after having struggled to acquire the marvellous vineyards overlooking the Gulf of Paradiso and the cliffs of Cinque Terre. Piero is responsible for replanting many native varieties, in particular bianchetta genovese and ciliegiolo, revitalizing their cultivation with low environmental impact systems. His skills at the winery have done, and continue to do, the rest.

The Vermentino Vigna Intrigoso and Bianchetta Ü Pastine '09 showed something extra compared to the other wines. The first is a singular interpretation of the variety that favours the palate over the nose and produces a wine rich in texture and warm with complex structure while the latter recovers the best in the olfactory profile of bianchetta, a variety that, if well produced as in this case, can offer great minerality and a first rate flower and fruit bouquet. Though well made, the Granaccio and Ciliegiolo didn't impress particularly7.

○ Golfo del Tigullio Bianchetta Genovese Ü Pastine '09	🍷🍷	4
○ Golfo del Tigullio Vermentino V. Intrigoso '09	🍷🍷	4
⊙ Golfo del Tigullio Ciliegiolo '09	🍷	3
○ Golfo del Tigullio Vermentino Vigna Erta '09	🍷	4
● Il Granaccio '08	🍷	6
● Tre Vigne '09	🍷	4
● Braccorosso Granaccia Barrique '07	YY	5
○ Cinque Terre Marea Costa du Campu '07	YY	5
○ Cinque Terre Sciacchetrà '04	YY	6
○ Golfo del Tigullio Vermentino V. Erta '08	YY	4
○ Golfo del Tigullio Vermentino V. Intrigoso '07	YY	4
● Il Granaccio '06	YY	5
○ Marea Tardiva '06	YY	5

Bruna

fraz. Borgo
via Umberto I, 81
18020 Ranzo [IM]
tel. 0183318082
www.brunapigato.it

CELLAR SALES
PRE-BOOKED VISITS

ANNUAL PRODUCTION 46,000 bottles
HECTARES UNDER VINE 7
VITICULTURE METHOD Conventional

To reach the Bruna estate, you have to leave the main road that runs along Arroscia, linking the provinces of Savona and Imperia, and takes you to Borgo di Ranzo. Here over the past few years Francesca and her husband Roberto have chosen to continue the work begun by her father Riccardo, affectionately called "u Baccan" ("boss" in the local dialect). They have chosen to continue working these beautiful vineyards, which are not on the valley floor but higher up in the sun-drenched south-facing hills. The pair's courageous life choice came straight from the heart.

Proving its consistent high quality, U Baccan has won the Three Glass award in five editions of the Guide but the '08 only came close. The classic bouquet of citrus and aromatic herbs is not accompanied by the usual density, although this wine still shows great character. We also expected something more from the Rosso Pulin '08, a well-crafted blend of grenache, syrah, cinsault and barbera that lacks a little bite on this occasion. The two standard-label Pigatos, Russeghine and Maje, are well up to snuff and offer clean, fresh interpretations of typical local products.

○ Riviera Ligure di Ponente Pigato U Baccan '08	🍷🍷	6
● Rosso Pulin '08	🍷🍷	5
○ Riviera Ligure di Ponente Pigato Le Russeghine '09	🍷	4
○ Riviera Ligure di Ponente Pigato Maje '09	🍷	4
● Riviera Ligure di Ponente Rossese '09	🍷	4
● Rosso Bansigu '09	🍷	4
○ Riviera Ligure di Ponente Pigato U Baccan '07	YYY	6
○ Riviera Ligure di Ponente Pigato U Baccan '06	YYY	5
○ Riviera Ligure di Ponente Pigato U Baccan '05	YYY	5
○ Riviera Ligure di Ponente Pigato U Baccan '04	YYY	5
○ Riviera Ligure di Ponente Pigato U Baccan '03	YYY	5
● Rosso Pulin '06	YY	5

Buranco

VIA BURANCO, 72
19016 MONTEROSSO AL MARE [SP]
TEL. 0187817677
www.burancocinqueterre.it

CELLAR SALES
PRE-BOOKED VISITS
ROOMS

ANNUAL PRODUCTION 18,000 bottles
HECTARES UNDER VINE 2
VITICULTURE METHOD Conventional

Two hectares in Cinque Terre can seem enormous when you are used to measuring property in square metres. The Grillo family has dealt with this situation for three years in their vineyard with unstable, dry stone walls, breath-taking slopes and terraces ripped from the mountains overlooking the sea. These hectares produce traditional white grape varieties, bosco, vermentino and albarola, which mature aromatic notes of Mediterranean herbs and citrus, and the less traditional varieties syrah and cabernet sauvignon, which have adapted perfectly to the marine environment.

The Grillos proposed a respectable range of wines again this year. Mojou '08 surprised us with its extraordinary richness of Mediterranean aromas and fresh acidity. This tangy, clean wine is deep and uncompromising. The even fresher Cinque Terre Bianco '09 has long progression with fragrances of rock herbs, solid structure with nice length and a pleasantly bitterish finish.

○ Cinque Terre Bianco '09	▼▼	5
○ Mojou '08	▼▼	5
○ Cinque Terre '07	YY	5
○ Cinque Terre Mangioa '07	YY	6
● Cinque Terre Rosso '08	YY	5
○ Cinque Terre Sciacchetrà '07	YY	8
○ Cinque Terre Sciacchetrà '06	YY	8
○ Cinque Terre Sciacchetrà '04	YY	8

Cantine Calleri

LOC. SALEA
REG. FRATTI, 2
17031 ALBENGA [SV]
TEL. 018220085
postmaster@cantinecalleri.com

ANNUAL PRODUCTION 90,000 bottles
HECTARES UNDER VINE N.A.
VITICULTURE METHOD Conventional

Cavalier Aldo Calleri's winery now has over 40 years' experience here on the first range of foothills bordering the great Albenga plain to the north. To the three native varieties of pigato, vermentino and rossese, which have always taken root here virtually spontaneously, Marcello Calleri, who personally tends the vineyards and cellar, has added ormeasco from the nearby valley of Arroscia.

While the Vermentino '09 has maintained its pre-eminent position thanks to fragrant aromas and a pleasant salty vein, the Ormeasco di Pornassio '08 has earned a place of honour for its good structure, dense body and distinct aromas of mountain berries. The Saleasco '09 was less intriguing than the previous vintage but we liked the somewhat subdued Vermentino I Murazzi '09 because of the usual fresh mouthfeel and great length on the nose and palate.

● Ormeasco di Pornassio '08	▼▼	4
○ Riviera Ligure di Ponente Vermentino '09	▼▼	4
○ Riviera Ligure di Ponente Vermentino I Murazzi '09	▼▼	4
○ Riviera Ligure di Ponente Pigato '09	▼	4
○ Riviera Ligure di Ponente Pigato Saleasco '09	▼	4
○ Riviera Ligure di Ponente Pigato '07	YY	4*
○ Riviera Ligure di Ponente Pigato '06	YY	4*
○ Riviera Ligure di Ponente Pigato Saleasco '08	YY	4*
○ Riviera Ligure di Ponente Pigato Saleasco '06	YY	4*
○ Riviera Ligure di Ponente Vermentino '08	YY	4*
○ Riviera Ligure di Ponente Vermentino I Muzazzi '08	YY	4
○ Riviera Ligure di Ponente Vermentino I Muzazzi '07	YY	4

Cantine Lunae Bosoni

FRAZ. ISOLA DI ORTONOVO
VIA BOZZI, 63
19034 ORTONOVO [SP]
TEL. 0187669222
www.cantinelunae.com

CELLAR SALES
PRE-BOOKED VISITS

ANNUAL PRODUCTION **450,000 bottles**
HECTARES UNDER VINE **55**
VITICULTURE METHOD **Conventional**

Across many centuries, Paolo Bosoni has inherited the know-how and skill brought to Luni by Roman legionnaires, veterans of bloody battles with the Apuan Ligurians and Carthaginians. They were the ones who centuriated the land and planted vines where none had existed, and where today Paolo tends around 55 hectares with his large family.

All the wines submitted earned good scores but, naturally, the leader was the Vermentino Lunae Etichetta Nera '09. Its aromas range seamlessly from spring flowers to aromatic herbs, shifting through ripe fruit and expanding with resounding richness to prepare the palate for tasting. The lovely mouthfeel is rich in citrussy minerality. More oaky, and perhaps slightly more suited for meditative sipping, the Cavagino '09 unveils soft vanilla tones from its oak ageing. Uncomplicated immediacy is the strong suit of the Onda di Luna '09 and Nicolò V '06 won us over with intense ripe red berry notes.

- ○ Colli di Luni Vermentino Lunae Et. Nera '09 — 5
- ○ Colli di Luni Vermentino Cavagino '09 — 6
- ● Colli di Luni Niccolò V '06 — 5
- ○ Colli di Luni Onda di Luna '09 — 5
- ● Horae '08 — 6
- ○ Colli di Luni Vermentino Lunae Et. Nera '08 — 4
- ● Colli di Luni Niccolò V '05 — 5
- ○ Colli di Luni Onda di Luna '08 — 5
- ○ Colli di Luni Vermentino Cavagino '08 — 6*
- ○ Colli di Luni Vermentino Lunae Et. Grigia '08 — 4

Cascina Nirasca

FRAZ. NIRASCA
VIA ALPI, 3
18026 PIEVE DI TECO [IM]
TEL. 0183368067
www.cascinanirasca.com

CELLAR SALES
PRE-BOOKED VISITS

ANNUAL PRODUCTION **22,000 bottles**
HECTARES UNDER VINE **3**
VITICULTURE METHOD **Conventional**

Along the road that climbs toward Col di Nava and the first ridges of the Ligurian Alps, you pass through Pieve di Teco, one of the historic villages founded along a trading route that still connects Piedmont with the sea. Here, Marco Temesio and Gabriele Maglio have established a lovely operation comprising three hectares of vineyards, some owned and some leased, in the hills between 400 and 500 metres above sea level, and a cellar with modern equipment.

In contrast with last year, the Vermentino has stepped to the fore with the '09 vintage, confirming a mountain trend that has made the variety more interesting generally than the Pigato. We could say that its varietal aromas, all with a vein of florality, prevails over the structural fullness, giving us a fresh, seductive wine. In the Pigato, we note the lovely, zesty Mediterranean feel on both the nose and palate, and a delicately bitterish, salty close. The still young but really promising Pornassio '09 is also remarkable.

- ○ Riviera Ligure di Ponente Vermentino '09 — 4
- ○ Riviera Ligure di Ponente Pigato '09 — 4
- ● Ormeasco di Pornassio '09 — 4
- ⊙ Ormeasco di Pornassio Sciac-Trà '09 — 4
- ● Ormeasco di Pornassio '05 — 4*
- ● Ormeasco di Pornassio Sup. '07 — 4*
- ● Ormeasco di Pornassio Sup. '06 — 4
- ● Ormeasco di Pornassio Sup. '05 — 4*
- ○ Riviera Ligure di Ponente Pigato '08 — 4*
- ○ Riviera Ligure di Ponente Vermentino '07 — 4
- ● Senso '05 — 5
- ● Senso '04 — 5

Walter De Batté

VIA TRARCANTU, 25
19017 RIOMAGGIORE [SP]
TEL. 0187920127

CELLAR SALES

ANNUAL PRODUCTION 15,000 bottles
HECTARES UNDER VINE 5
VITICULTURE METHOD Organic

One of the most combative Ligurian winemakers, Walter De Battè has fought his toughest battles on the impossible cliffs of Cinque Terre, where in five years he has reclaimed around two hectares of vineyard for his estate, ripped piece by piece from the steep slopes, creating terraces held back by those famous dry stone walls. Walter is one of the partners in the Prima Terra project, begun with Riccardo Canesi and Pierfrancesco Donati, producing red and white wines partly sourced from estate vineyards in Val di Vara and Val di Magra.

The Cinque Terre '08 is rich in tones of ripe fruit and spice but there is no lack of mineral and pencil lead. The sumptuous Sciacchetrà shows pleasant oaky notes, rich extract, lively fresh acidity and complex aromas of dried figs and bitter almond. The whites from Val Magra, Harmoge '08 and Carlaz '08, have acquired lightness and, thanks to a more skilled use of oak, an easier, more approachable drinkability. The '08 Rossi Tonos from sangiovese, canaiolo and ciliegiolo and '07 Cerico from grenache and syrah are always elegant, forthright and clean.

○ Cinque Terre '08	5
○ Carlaz '08	5
○ Cinque Terre Sciacchetrà '06	8
● Tonos '08	5
● Çerico '07	5
○ Harmoge '08	5
● Bozòlo '07	5
○ Carlaz '07	5
● Çerico '05	5
○ Cinque Terre '07	5
○ Cinque Terre Sciacchetrà '03	8
○ Harmoge '06	5

Durin

VIA ROMA, 202
17037 ORTOVERO [SV]
TEL. 0182547007
www.durin.it

CELLAR SALES
PRE-BOOKED VISITS

ANNUAL PRODUCTION 140,000 bottles
HECTARES UNDER VINE 15
VITICULTURE METHOD Conventional

The great battle for Antonio Basso, grandson of estate founder Isidoro, nicknamed "Durin", was to definitively eliminate the indiscriminate cultivation characteristic of Valle Arroscia and obtain his current area under vine by acquiring new vineyards. Today, the estate produces a broad line of wines, all very respectable, with a total output of nearly 150,000 bottles.

Pigato, that most typical of local wines, can clearly reach peaks of excellence. The S-cianchi '09 made far and away the best showing with its caressing golden colour, citrussy fragrances led by grapefruit and bergamot with hints of sage, and an almost pebbly minerality that recalls spring water. The Pigato, Vigna Braie and A' Matetta, from vermentino and pigato, all from '09, are not far behind. Further down the list, the '09 Vermentinos lack those great aromas we loved in the last vintage. The red Matti '08, dolcetto, grenache and barbera, and Rossese Sempre are always good quality but a bit less assertive.

○ Riviera Ligure di Ponente Pigato I S-cianchi '09	4*
○ A' Matetta '09	5
○ Riviera Ligure di Ponente Pigato '09	4
○ Riviera Ligure di Ponente Pigato V. Braie '09	4
● Riviera Ligure di Ponente Rossese '09	4
● I Matti '08	5
○ Riviera Ligure di Ponente Vermentino '09	4
○ Riviera Ligure di Ponente Vermentino Lunghèra '09	4
○ A' Matetta '08	5
● I Matti '07	5
○ Riviera Ligure di Ponente Pigato I S-cianchi '08	4*
○ Riviera Ligure di Ponente Vermentino '08	4*
○ Riviera Ligure di Ponente Vermentino '07	4
○ Riviera Ligure di Ponente Vermentino Lunghèra '08	4*

Ottaviano Lambruschi

via Olmarello, 28
19030 Castelnuovo Magra [SP]
tel. 0187674261
ottavianolambruschi@libero.it

ANNUAL PRODUCTION 30,000 bottles
HECTARES UNDER VINE 5
VITICULTURE METHOD Conventional

Ottaviano Lambruschi could be called, with good reason, a maestro of Vermentino in Lunigiana. He's a maestro who, having believed in this variety to the point of desperation, acquired the Sarticola vineyard and later two wooded hectares near Costa Marina, all in the name of this his first love. In his five hectares of excellent vineyards torn from a hostile land, this determined man from Lunigiana who today, with help from his son Fabio, has achieved goals unthinkable only three decades ago at the time of his earliest releases.

This year, the Vermentino Costa Marina '09 has taken the place of its cousin Sarticola '09 in the race for Three Glasses. The difference in quality was actually not that great but the joyous pulp in the former fails to appear in the latter and, although both are supported by a persistent acid vein, the Costa Marina revels in a broad, multi-faceted bouquet of hedgerow and yellow-fleshed fruit and quite different, well-rounded minerality. Unfortunately, Ottaviano's class is not so obvious in the red wines and his Maniero '08, although nicely made, failed to convince entirely.

○ Colli di Luni Vermentino Costa Marina '09	▼▼▼	5
○ Colli di Luni Vermentino Sarticola '09	▼▼	4
● Colli di Luni Rosso Maniero '08	▼	4
○ Colli di Luni Vermentino Sarticola '08	▽▽▽	4*
○ Colli di Luni Vermentino Alessandro '05	▽▽	4*
○ Colli di Luni Vermentino Costa Marina '08	▽▽	4*
○ Colli di Luni Vermentino Costa Marina '07	▽▽	4*
○ Colli di Luni Vermentino Costa Marina '06	▽▽	4*
○ Colli di Luni Vermentino Costa Marina '05	▽▽	4*

Tommaso Lupi & C.

via Mazzini, 9
18026 Pieve di Teco [IM]
tel. 018336162
www.vinilupi.it

CELLAR SALES
PRE-BOOKED VISITS

ANNUAL PRODUCTION 140,000 bottles
HECTARES UNDER VINE N.A.
VITICULTURE METHOD Conventional

Tommaso Lupi founded his estate in Pieve di Teco around 50 years ago to supply wine to customers at his Osteria di Oneglia, now the Enoteca. The arrival of his children at the winery has allowed him to grow and make the leap in quality that has led him to become a major figure. Clearly Tommaso was far-sighted in recognizing a perfect territory for wine production in this corner of Liguria, squeezed tight between the sea and the first ridges of the Ligurian Alps.

Le Serre, the mouthfilling Vermentino submitted again this year in the '08 version, showed as impressively as its already very sound predecessor. The tangy, warm progression won us over right from the first sip and the palate flaunts freshness, minerality and delicately fragrant tones with touches of apple, pear and a light waft of citron. The Vermentino '09 and Pigato '09 are excellently crafted, in line with the strictest local winemaking standards. Vignamare '06, from vermentino and pigato, is a bit less serious, although soundly made.

○ Riviera Ligure di Ponente Vermentino Le Serre '08	▼▼▼	5
○ Riviera Ligure di Ponente Pigato '09	▼▼	4
○ Riviera Ligure di Ponente Vermentino '09	▼▼	4
○ Vignamare '06	▼▼	5
● Ormeasco di Pornassio Sup. Le Braje '06	▼	5
○ Riviera Ligure di Ponente Vermentino Le Serre '07	▽▽▽	5
○ Colli di Luni Pigato '08	▽▽	4*
○ Colli di Luni Vermentino '08	▽▽	4*
○ Riviera Ligure di Ponente Pigato '04	▽▽	4*
○ Riviera Ligure di Ponente Pigato Le Petraie '05	▽▽	5
○ Riviera Ligure di Ponente Vermentino '05	▽▽	4*
○ Vignamare '05	▽▽	5

Maccario Dringenberg

via Torre, 3
18036 San Biagio della Cima [IM]
tel. 0184289947
maccariodringenberg@yahoo.it

CELLAR SALES
PRE-BOOKED VISITS

ANNUAL PRODUCTION 20,000 bottles
HECTARES UNDER VINE N.A.
VITICULTURE METHOD Conventional

They say that since Goetz Dringenberg came to Vallecrosia – the "closed valley" in the local dialect – he has not been able to leave. We do not know if he couldn't find the way back to his native Germany or if he was smitten by the graces of a local architect, and grower in her free time, named Giovanna Maccario. It is clear that the graft of his Teutonic pragmatism onto the valley has been an excellent fillip and has contributed to the distinct improvement in the Rossese di Dolceacqua made here, its historic homeland.

Though the Dolceacqua Vigneto Luvaira Superiore '08 had to pull up at Two Glasses, the Dolceacqua Vigneto Posau Superiore from the same vintage easily sailed on and reached Three Glasses. Appealing right from its ruby red colour, it develops a rich bouquet that runs from blueberry, blackberry and blackcurrant wild berries to more pungent spicy and aromatic notes. Having shed last season's huskiness, this wine shows a complex, almost aristocratic, structure where the counterpoint of richness and length interweave to create an impressive tapestry.

● Rossese di Dolceacqua Sup. Vign. Posau '08	▼▼▼	5
● Rossese di Dolceacqua Sup. Vign. Luvaira '08	▼▼	5
● Rossese di Dolceacqua '09	▼	4
● Rossese di Dolceacqua Sup. Vign. Luvaira '07	▽▽▽	5
● Rossese di Dolceacqua Sup. Vign. Posau '07	▽▽	3

Il Monticello

via Groppolo, 7
19038 Sarzana [SP]
tel. 0187621432
www.ilmonticello.vai.li

CELLAR SALES
PRE-BOOKED VISITS
ROOMS

ANNUAL PRODUCTION 55,000 bottles
HECTARES UNDER VINE 10
VITICULTURE METHOD Organic

In the early 1980s, when electronic engineer Pierluigi Neri inherited land in the hilly area north of Sarzana, and returned to his old passion of making wine, he could never have imagined that this would become his sons' main activity. With help from their mother Maria Antonietta, Davide and Alessandro have led this estate winery to the top of the winemaking tree in the Luni area.

Poggio Paterno '08, an already recognized Vermentino, proves a great wine and showed well in our finals. The distinct, elegant nose reveals skilful use of oak that elegantly combines with fruit and fresh, citrussy notes. The excellent progression is fresh and lively. Rupestro Rosso '09 remains one of the most pleasant local reds, despite a slightly rigid tannic weave but only because of its recent release.

○ Colli di Luni Vermentino Poggio Paterno '08	▼▼	4
● Colli di Luni Rosso Rupestro '09	▼	4
○ Colli di Luni Vermentino '09	▼	4
● Colli di Luni Rosso Poggio dei Magni '05	▽▽	4
● Colli di Luni Rosso Poggio dei Magni '01	▽▽	4
○ Colli di Luni Vermentino '08	▽▽	4*
○ Colli di Luni Vermentino Poggio Paterno '07	▽▽	4*
○ Colli di Luni Vermentino Poggio Paterno '06	▽▽	4

Conte Picedi Benettini

VIA MAZZINI, 57
19038 SARZANA [SP]
TEL. 0187625147
www.picedibenettini.it

CELLAR SALES
PRE-BOOKED VISITS
ROOMS

ANNUAL PRODUCTION 30,000 bottles
HECTARES UNDER VINE N.A.
VITICULTURE METHOD Conventional

In Sarzana, when they say "Conte" they can only mean Conte Papirio Picedi Benettini, or "Nino" for short. A noble family going back to 1056, the Picedis lived at their ancestral residence, "il Palà", in Arcola from the early 16th century. Subsequently, the family moved to Baccano where they built Villa Chioso, a typical post-Renaissance construction surrounded by a vast, hilly estate of about 150 hectares. About three hectares were set aside for special crops and enclosed by a high wall to make a "chioso" (cf "clos" in French).

Vermentino Stemma '09 has finally exploded in all its potential and did well at our finals. Aside from the customary citrussy aromas of citron and lemon, this selection from the best estate grapes also displays elegant tones of white peach and green apple, presenting zesty, appealing and minerally in the mouth on closing. Unfortunately, we could not taste the Rosso Gran Baccano from the new vintage but Bianco Villa Il Chioso '09 and, even more so, Vermentino Il Chioso '09 complete an interesting array. The easy-drinking Ciliegiolo '09 hews to a local tradition.

○ Colli di Luni Vermentino Stemma '09	TT	4*
○ Colli di Luni Bianco Villa Il Chioso '09	TT	4*
○ Colli di Luni Vermentino Il Chioso '09	TT	3*
⊙ Ciliegiolo '09	T	4
○ Colli di Luni Vermentino '09	T	4
○ Ruzzese '09	T	4
● Colli di Luni Rosso Gran Baccano '08	YY	4*
● Colli di Luni Rosso Gran Baccano '07	YY	4
○ Colli di Luni Vermentino Stemma '08	YY	4*
○ Colli di Luni Vermentino Stemma '07	YY	4
○ Passito del Chioso '08	YY	5

La Pietra del Focolare

FRAZ. ISOLA
VIA DOGANA, 209
19034 ORTONOVO [SP]
TEL. 0187662129
www.lapietradelfocolare.it

CELLAR SALES
PRE-BOOKED VISITS

ANNUAL PRODUCTION 30,000 bottles
HECTARES UNDER VINE 7
VITICULTURE METHOD Organic

Stefano Salvetti and Laura Angelini recall their first plot of land in 1997 came from the "lovely Signora Francesca", owner of an old country house and the Bacchiano farm, a hectare of land planted to vines and olives. Our heroes leased this corner of paradise. Today, the Salvettis directly manage seven hectares under vine, six of these planted only to vermentino – located around Sarzana, Ortonovo and Castelnuovo Magra – and the rest to sangiovese, canaiolo and, more recently, merlot.

Competition between the Augusto, Villa Linda and Solarancio '09 Vermentinos, sourced from three different vineyards, ended in favour of the Solarancio for various reasons. The accentuated minerality is fully expressed thanks to the acid vein that irresistibly, insistently, shows off the variety's trademark flowers and fruit, structure and fullness, unveiling a charming bitter note in the closing. Both the Linda and the Augusto are good, as well as, the Rosso Saltamasso, released by Salvetti to complete the range.

○ Colli di Luni Vermentino Solarancio '09	TT	6
● Colli di Luni Rosso Saltamasso '08	T	5
○ Colli di Luni Vermentino Augusto '09	T	4
○ Colli di Luni Vermentino Villa Linda '09	T	5
○ Colli di Luni Vermentino Augusto '08	YY	4*
○ Colli di Luni Vermentino Augusto '06	YY	4
○ Colli di Luni Vermentino Solarancio '08	YY	5
○ Colli di Luni Vermentino Solarancio '07	YY	5
○ Colli di Luni Vermentino Solarancio '06	YY	5
○ Colli di Luni Vermentino Solarancio '04	YY	4*
○ Colli di Luni Vermentino Villa Linda '05	YY	4*
○ Colli di Luni Vermentino Viva Luce '05	YY	4*

Poggio dei Gorleri

FRAZ. GORLERI
VIA SAN LEONARDO
18013 DIANO MARINA [IM]
TEL. 0183495207
www.poggiodeigorleri.com

CELLAR SALES
PRE-BOOKED VISITS
ROOMS

ANNUAL PRODUCTION **60,000 bottles**
HECTARES UNDER VINE **9**
VITICULTURE METHOD **Conventional**

Gorleri is one of the most scenic of the small villages around Diano – "Communitas Diani" during the Middle Ages – and offers a stunning view of the Gulf and the Ligurian Alps. The owners of the estate, the Merano family, knew how to profit from this and built a lovely agriturismo for holiday stays, as well as investing in wine production. Their cellar is one of the most interesting in the region and boasts state-of-the-art equipment.

The Meranos never venture into international wines and remain thoroughly focused on native varieties. As always, Pigato tells its own story. The Cycnus '09 and Albium '09 clearly show how much pigato can give but the sunny, clear, golden spectrum of hues in the former already distances it from the second even before you raise the wine to the nose. A dazzling explosion of citrus and fines herbs fragrances introduces a palate that impresses on entry with extraordinary freshness and a barely hinted-at vein of ash and salt that lend the fruit complexity. Three Glasses. The Vermentino Vigna Sorì '09 is more than sound.

○ Riviera Ligure di Ponente Pigato Cycnus '09	▼▼▼	4*
○ Riviera Ligure di Ponente Pigato Albium '09	▼▼	5
○ Riviera Ligure di Ponente Vermentino V. Sorì '09	▼▼	4
● Ormeasco di Pornassio Peinetti '09	▼	4
○ Riviera Ligure di Ponente Vermentino '09	▼	4
○ Riviera Ligure di Ponente Pigato Cycnus '08	▽▽▽	4*
○ Riviera Ligure di Ponente Pigato Albium '08	▽▽	5
○ Riviera Ligure di Ponente Pigato Albium '07	▽▽	5
○ Riviera Ligure di Ponente Pigato Albium '06	▽▽	5
○ Riviera Ligure di Ponente Vermentino '08	▽▽	4*
○ Riviera Ligure di Ponente Vermentino Apricus '08	▽▽	5
○ Riviera Ligure di Ponente Vermentino Apricus '07	▽▽	5
○ Riviera Ligure di Ponente Vermentino V. Sorì '08	▽▽	4*

Cascina Praié

S.DA CASTELLO, 20
17051 ANDORA [SV]
TEL. 019602377
www.cascinapraievino.it

CELLAR SALES
PRE-BOOKED VISITS

ANNUAL PRODUCTION **40,000 bottles**
HECTARES UNDER VINE **8**
VITICULTURE METHOD **Conventional**

The nautical skills of Thor Heyerdhal, the great Norwegian anthropologist who lived for many years in Colla Micheri a few steps from Cascina Praiè, was clearly an education for Massimo Viglietti and Anna Maria Corrent, helping to guide them safely through the hazardous seas of Ligurian wine production. Tending eight hectares of "fasce" or terraces on the hills overlooking Andora and Laigueglia is anything but easy. Always keen to experiment, Massimo and Anna create their labels here, some from traditional grapes and others from imported varieties.

We felt the Ros'è '09 was very sound this year. From barbarossa, grenache and mourvèdre, it presents a delightfully intense rosé with an excellent floral bouquet and fresh, long progression. While waiting for the new vintage of Ardesia, from rossese and cabernet, we enjoyed the pleasant fruit and nice Mediterranean character of the Vermentino Colla Micheri '09. We expected something more from the Pigato Il Canneto '09 and Cervo Rosso '08.

○ Riviera Ligure di Ponente Vermentino Colla Micheri '09	▼▼	4
⊙ Ros'è '09	▼▼	4
● Cervo Rosso '08	▼	4
○ Riviera Ligure di Ponente Pigato Il Canneto '09	▼	4
● Ardesia '06	▽▽	4
● Ardesia '05	▽▽	5
○ Riviera Ligure di Ponente Pigato Il Canneto '05	▽▽	4*
○ Riviera Ligure di Ponente Vermentino Colla Micheri '07	▽▽	5
○ Riviera Ligure di Ponente Vermentino Le Cicale '07	▽▽	4*
○ Riviera Ligure di Ponente Vermentino Le Cicale '05	▽▽	4*
● Sciurbì '05	▽▽	4*
● Sciurbì '04	▽▽	4*

Sancio

via Laiolo, 73
17028 Spotorno [SV]
tel. 019743255
cantinasancio@libero.it

CELLAR SALES
PRE-BOOKED VISITS
ROOMS AND FOOD

ANNUAL PRODUCTION 37,000 bottles
HECTARES UNDER VINE 4
VITICULTURE METHOD Conventional

Climbing up to the Sancio estate, located in a panoramic spot on the heights overlooking Spotorno, can be a breathtaking experience. Over the years, the structure has been expanded and a larger cellar dug into the rock, alongside a small restaurant featuring specialties from the Ligurian hills. You will always find Riccardo Sancio busy somewhere in the vineyard or cellar. His never-failing attention gives the wines a very personal stamp.

This year, we thought the Pigato '09 was very good, even more so considering the fact that '09 was anything but an ideal growing year for the variety. Riccardo's version puts its best foot forward with rich aromas of ripe fruit and medicinal herbs before the palate shows softly full, elegantly dry and rich in pleasing sensations in the finish. The Pigato Cappellania '09 is along the same lines, drinking tangy and compelling, while the Vermentino '09 and Mataosso '09 – the latter an unusual wine obtained from the lumassina variety – are enjoyably drinkable but not excessively complex.

○ Riviera Ligure di Ponente Pigato '09	▼▼	4*
○ Riviera Ligure di Ponente Pigato Cappellania '09	▼▼	4
○ Lumassina Mataosso '09	▼	3
○ Riviera Ligure di Ponente Vermentino '09	▼	4
○ Il Bacioccio Passito	▽▽	6
○ Riviera Ligure di Ponente Pigato '07	▽▽	4
○ Riviera Ligure di Ponente Pigato '06	▽▽	4*
○ Riviera Ligure di Ponente Pigato Cappellania '07	▽▽	4
○ Riviera Ligure di Ponente Pigato Cappellania '06	▽▽	5
○ Riviera Ligure di Ponente Pigato Cappellania '05	▽▽	5
● Riviera Ligure di Ponente Rossese '06	▽▽	4

Luigi Sartori

fraz. Leca
reg. Torre Pernice, 3
17031 Albenga [SV]
tel. 018220042
sartoripigato@libero.it

CELLAR SALES

ANNUAL PRODUCTION 75,000 bottles
HECTARES UNDER VINE 10
VITICULTURE METHOD Conventional

Torre Pernice still stands today near Albenga. An iron structure built during the Middle Ages to counter the Saracen invasions that brought destruction to the city at the end of the first millennium. Rows of vines extend around this tower in the largest plain in Liguria, the Piana di Albenga, formed by the confluence of the rivers Arroscia and Neva. Some say long-established, ungrafted vines of pigato still exist in this loose, sedimentary earth, since phylloxera never affected its coarse, pebbly soils.

Yet again, Luigi Sartori and his wife Bianca Dulbecco did better with their dried-grape "passito" wines than the classics from the Riviera di Ponente. We refer here to the rossese-based Rosato Passito Rosa di Aleramo '09, which impressed with fresh, balanced notes of wild roses and, even more so, generous wafts of ripe blackberry, raspberry and cassis forest fruits. The Oro di Aleramo '09 is proof, if there is still any need, of the pigato variety's versatility, in this case giving salty, aromatic support to the wine, cosseting the elegant, softly layered structure. The Rossese, Pigato and Vermentino '09 are all good.

○ Oro di Aleramo '09	▼▼	7
⊙ Passito Rosa di Aleramo '09	▼▼	5
○ Riviera Ligure di Ponente Pigato Torre Pernice '09	▼	5
● Riviera Ligure di Ponente Rossese Torre Pernice '09	▼	4
○ Riviera Ligure di Ponente Vermentino Torre Pernice '09	▼	4
● Antico Rubino di Aleramo	▽▽	5
○ Oro di Aleramo	▽▽	7
⊙ Passito Rosa di Aleramo	▽▽	5

Terre Bianche

LOC. ARCAGNA
18035 DOLCEACQUA [IM]
TEL. 018431426
www.terrebianche.com

CELLAR SALES
PRE-BOOKED VISITS
ROOMS

ANNUAL PRODUCTION **61,000 bottles**
HECTARES UNDER VINE **8**
VITICULTURE METHOD **Conventional**

Many years ago, when the Rondelli brothers took their courage in both hands and founded the Terre Bianche estate, many thought they would never succeed. One reason for this is that their plots of vines and olive trees are spread across a ridge so high you might think life there was impossible, not only for plants but humans as well. Another factor was the innovative approach the two brothers took to growing and processing, which were regarded as unthinkable at the time. But the Rondellis were an outstanding success and today Filippo carries on the business begun by his father Claudio and uncle Paolo.

After years of production and constant improvement, the historic Bricco Arcagna Dolceacqua '08 deservedly won Three Glasses. A charming bright ruby colour, with caressing tones of coastal medicinal herbs and soft aromas of berries from the Alpine foothills, this champion gives a full-textured mouthfeel and elegant tannins, well tucked into the broad structure and nicely supported by alcohol, and close-knit, fresh minerality. The Pigato '09 is a worthy partner, very representative of the vintage, opulent in its bouquet and full-flavoured in the mouth. Bianco Arcana '08 from pigato and vermentino is good, as are the other labels.

● Rossese di Dolceacqua Bricco Arcagna '08	▼▼▼	6
○ Riviera Ligure di Ponente Pigato '09	▼▼	4
○ Arcana Bianco '08	▼	5
○ Riviera Ligure di Ponente Vermentino '09	▼	4
● Rossese di Dolceacqua '09	▼	4
○ Arcana Bianco '07	▽▽	5
● Arcana Rosso '06	▽▽	6
● Arcana Rosso '03	▽▽	5
○ Riviera Ligure di Ponente Vermentino '07	▽▽	4*
● Rossese di Dolceacqua '08	▽▽	4*
● Rossese di Dolceacqua '07	▽▽	4*
● Rossese di Dolceacqua Bricco Arcagna '07	▽▽	5
● Rossese di Dolceacqua Bricco Arcagna '06	▽▽	5

Cascina delle Terre Rosse

VIA MANIE, 3
17024 FINALE LIGURE [SV]
TEL. 019698782

CELLAR SALES
PRE-BOOKED VISITS

ANNUAL PRODUCTION **30,000 bottles**
HECTARES UNDER VINE **4**
VITICULTURE METHOD **Organic**

Arriving at the plateau of Le Manie, behind Finale Ligure, is an unforgettable experience, whether you climb up from the town on the coast or leave the Autostrada dei Fiori motorway at Spotorno. Here in 1985, Vladimiro Galluzzo decided to relaunch the family estate by investing in new structures and above all quality. Over the years, he has achieved major results and made a clear contribution to the growth of the entire area.

Here again at Terre Rosse, the '09 growing season seems to have been favourable to Pigato only in certain sites. The Apogeo clearly shows complex construction, rich in all sorts of ripe, apricot and damson-led, yellow-fleshed fruit, its great tanginess contained in a soft, satisfying mouthfeel and well supported by a subtle acid vein. The nicely crafted Vermentino '09 has rich, interesting aromas but has a less substantial structure than before. We expected more from the lumassina-only Acerbina '09 and the grenache, rossese and barbera-based Solitario '08 but we can wait.

○ Apogeo '09	▼▼	5
○ Riviera Ligure di Ponente Vermentino '09	▼▼	5
○ L'Acerbina '09	▼	5
○ Per Paola '09	▼	8
○ Riviera Ligure di Ponente Pigato '09	▼	5
● Solitario '08	▼	8
○ Riviera Ligure di Ponente Pigato '99	▽▽▽	5
○ L'Acerbina '08	▽▽	4*
○ Le Banche '08	▽▽	8
○ Riviera Ligure di Ponente Pigato '08	▽▽	5
○ Riviera Ligure di Ponente Pigato '07	▽▽	5
○ Riviera Ligure di Ponente Pigato '06	▽▽	5
● Solitario '07	▽▽	8
● Solitario '05	▽▽	6

Alta Via
LOC. ARCAGNA
18035 DOLCEACQUA [IM]
TEL. 0184488230

From five hectares near the Ligurian Alps comes Dapprimo '08, a blend of rossese, carignano and syrah with expansive progression, lively spice and clear notes of overripe berries. Close behind, the red Grai '06 is a monovarietal Carignano, intense on nose and mouth. The Rosarosae '09 is sound.

● Dapprimo '08	🍷🍷	4
● Grai '06	🍷🍷	5
⊙ Rosarosae '09	🍷	4

Anfossi
FRAZ. BASTIA
VIA PACCINI, 39
17031 ALBENGA [SV]
TEL. 018220024
www.aziendaagrariaanfossi.it

In addition to excellent DOP Ligurian basil, Mario Anfossi produces wines with a family tradition. The Vermentino '09 and Rossese '09 are pleasant but the Pigato '09 with its broad medicinal bouquet of camomile, mint and sage surprised us so much we gave it a very respectable mark.

○ Riviera Ligure di Ponente Pigato '09	🍷🍷	4
● Riviera Ligure di Ponente Rossese '09	🍷	4
○ Riviera Ligure di Ponente Vermentino '09	🍷	4

Tenuta Anfosso
C.SO VERBONE, 175
18036 SOLDANO [IM]
TEL. 0184289906
www.tenutaanfosso.it

High up between San Biagio and Soldano, you can see the vineyards of Alessandro and Marisa Anfosso. We were impressed by the Rossese Superiore '08 which, despite some roughness, has softened with broad berry aromas. Rossese Vigneto Luvaira is enjoyable for its expansive aromatics and pleasant body.

● Rossese di Dolceacqua Sup. '08	🍷🍷	4*
● Rossese di Dolceacqua Luvaira Sup. '08	🍷🍷	5

Riccardo Arrigoni
LOC. MIGLIARINI
VIA SARZANA, 224
19126 LA SPEZIA
TEL. 0187504060
www.awf2000.com

Pagni Vini boasts four generations of production with properties scattered across Liguria and San Gimignano in Tuscany. The Vermentino Vigna del Prefetto '09 is quite sound but our tasters preferred the traditional Sciacchetrà '00 with its elegant notes of dried figs, caramel and almond.

○ Cinque Terre Sciacchetrà '00	🍷🍷	8
○ Colli di Luni Vermentino V. del Prefetto '09	🍷	4

Samuele Heydi Bonanini
VIA SAN ANTONIO, 72
19017 RIOMAGGIORE [SP]
TEL. 0187920959
www.possa.it

We continue to admire Samuele Heydi Bonanini for his daily labours in the difficult Cinque Terre environment. We liked his Sciacchetrà '08, now firing on all cylinders again, and the Cinque Terre '09 shows floral finesse and intense minerality. The Passito La Rinascita '08 is still a tad fragile.

○ Cinque Terre '09	🍷🍷	7
○ Cinque Terre Sciacchetrà '08	🍷🍷	8
● Passito La Rinascita '08	🍷	8

Cantina Bregante
VIA UNITÀ D'ITALIA, 47
16039 SESTRI LEVANTE [GE]
TEL. 018541388
www.cantinebregante.it

We were exhilarated by the rich aromatics and lingering hints of Bulgarian rose in the reliable Moscato '09 and the equally good Ciliegiolo '09, which unfurls a swath of lovely aromas and fresh, harmonious flavours.

○ Golfo del Tigullio Moscato '09	🍷🍷	4
● Golfo del Tigullio Ciliegiolo '09	🍷	4

Enoteca Andrea Bruzzone

VIA BOLZANETO, 94/96/98
16162 GENOVA
TEL. 0107455157
www.andreabruzzonevini.it

Thanks to Andrea Bruzzone, the small Val Polcèvera DOC has survived. Treipaexi '09 is rich and full, and the '09 Coronata is a sound wine, with delicate aromas and good body. We also enjoyed the traditional Bianchetta Genovese '09 for its lingering notes of flowers and aromatic herbs.

● Val Polcèvera Rosso Treipaexi '09	🍷🍷	3
○ Val Polcèvera Bianchetta Genovese '09	🍷	3
○ Val Polcèvera Coronata '09	🍷	4

Altare Bonanni De Grazia Campogrande

VIA DI LOCA, 189
19017 RIOMAGGIORE [SP]
TEL. 3384063383
info@5terre-marmar.com

Antonio Bonanni has chosen to give a new stamp to his wines, avoiding the use of systemic and chemical products, restricting himself to sulphur, copper and the invaluable advice of the great Elio Altare. On tasting, his Cinqueterre shows very nice tanginess and remarkable length.

○ Cinque Terre '09	🍷🍷	8

Cascina Feipu dei Massaretti

FRAZ. BASTIA
REG. MASSARETTI, 7
17031 ALBENGA [SV]
TEL. 018220131
www.paginegialle.it/massaretti

Founded by Pippo and Iole Parodi, this estate is now managed by their son-in-law Mirko. We liked the impressive Pigato La Palmetta '09, with its marked minerality and delicate aromas of medicinal herbs. The genuinely fresh Rossese '09 also earned unanimous approval.

○ Riviera Ligure di Ponente Pigato La Palmetta '09	🍷🍷	4
● Riviera Ligure di Ponente Rossese d'Albenga '09	🍷	4

Cheo

VIA A. DEL SANTO, 48
19018 VERNAZZA [SP]
TEL. 0187821189
cheochea@hotmail.com

Those near inaccessible vineyards clinging to the slopes of Vernazza produce wines with great character and are, in fact, among the finest products of viticulture in Cinque Terre. Cheo '09 flaunts typical iodine notes and powerful tanginess. The '07 Sciacchetrà has great dried apricot and candied citrus.

○ Cinque Terre Cheo '09	🍷🍷	4
○ Cinque Terre Sciacchetrà '07	🍷🍷	8
○ Cinque Terre Perciò '09	🍷	4

Cantina Cinqueterre

FRAZ. MANAROLA
LOC. GROPPO
19010 RIOMAGGIORE [SP]
TEL. 0187920435
www.cantinacinqueterre.com

All the wines from this co-operative are good but the Sciacchetrà '07 is a real thoroughbred, with candied apricot and a pleasant acidity that softens the sweet fruity notes. The '09 Costa de Sèra vineyard selection is also sound, with clear spring flowers and intense balsamic notes.

○ Cinque Terre Sciacchetrà '07	🍷🍷	7
○ Cinque Terre Costa de Sèra di Riomaggiore '09	🍷🍷	4
○ Cinque Terre '09	🍷	4
○ Cinque Terre Costa da Posa di Volastra '09	🍷	4

La Colombiera

LOC. MONTECCHIO, 92
19030 CASTELNUOVO MAGRA [SP]
TEL. 0187674265

The Vermentino from Colombiera is always good quality and we love the fresh citrussy notes and convincing structure. Rosso Terrizzo '07 from sangiovese, ciliegiolo, canaiolo and other varieties confirms the quality of the '06, with good body and full aromas.

● Colli di Luni Rosso Terrizzo '07	🍷	4
○ Colli di Luni Vermentino '09	🍷	4

Fontanacota

via Dolcedo,121
18100 Imperia
tel. 0183293456
www.fontanacota.it

Wines from Maria Antonietta Berta are all good quality. The '09 Pigato shows the usual great aromatic profile, supported by nice acidity and accompanied by pleasant fruity notes. The Vermentino '09 is knowingly elegant but the Pornassio '09 never quite reaches the quality of the past.

○ Riviera Ligure di Ponente Pigato '09	🍷🍷	4*
● Ormeasco di Pornassio '09	🍷	4
○ Riviera Ligure di Ponente Vermentino '09	🍷	4

Foresti

via Braie, 223
18033 Camporosso [IM]
tel. 0184292377
www.forestiwine.it

Only one or two hesitations on the nose slow down Marco Foresti's wines, from 20 hectares of vineyards on the western riviera. The Vermentino I Soli '09 convinced us with interesting mineral notes and a hedgerow bouquet, on a par with the nicely structured Pigato '09. The Dolceacqua Superiore '08 must improve more.

○ Riviera Ligure di Ponente Pigato I Soli '09	🍷	4
○ Riviera Ligure di Ponente Vermentino I Soli '09	🍷	4
● Rossese di Dolceacqua Sup. '08	🍷	4

Forlini Cappellini

loc. Manarola
via Riccobaldi, 45
19010 Riomaggiore [SP]
tel. 0187920496
forlinicappellini@libero.it

This estate is long established at Manarola. We liked the Sciacchetrà '05 for its elegant length, almondy tones and characteristic myrtle, strawberry tree and bay leaf aromas of Mediterranean herbs. The Cinque Terre '09 also shows remarkable tanginess, no hesitation and good mineral density.

○ Cinque Terre '09	🍷🍷	5
○ Cinque Terre Sciacchetrà Ris. '05	🍷🍷	8

Gajaudo

loc. Bunda
s.da Provinciale, 7
18030 Imperia
tel. 0184208095
www.cantinagajaudo.com

The Gajaudos operate not far from Dolceacqua. Giulio Gajaudo has increased his efforts with rossese and the results have been swift in coming. The Rossese di Dolceacqua '09 has become more elegant, both on the nose and palate, but manages to maintain a structure that is all softness and balance.

● Dolceacqua Rossese '09	🍷🍷	4
○ Riviera Ligure di Ponente Vermentino '09	🍷	5

Giacomelli

via Palvotrisia, 134
19030 Castelnuovo Magra [SP]
tel. 0187674155

The Vermentino Boboli '08 from Roberto Petacchi shows it has plenty of attitude. This wine's zesty minerality is accompanied by great intensity on the nose of pleasant citrussy notes. Behind this, the newly introduced Vermentino Pianacce '08 is persuasive, proffering broad aromas and delicate body.

○ Colli di Luni Vermentino Boboli '08	🍷🍷	5
○ Colli di Luni Vermentino Pianacce '08	🍷	5

Tenuta Giuncheo

loc. Giuncheo
18033 Camporosso [IM]
tel. 0184288639
www.tenutagiuncheo.it

Arnold Schweizer built his cellar inside a bunker above Camporosso where we tasted the excellent Selezione '07, a dry, lively blend of Syrah and Bordeaux. The Rossese '08 is also pleasant, with broad aromas and rich varietal touches, and the Vermentino '09 appeals with its fruity notes.

● Rossese di Dolceacqua '08	🍷🍷	4
● Selezione '07	🍷🍷	4
● Lunico '07	🍷	5
○ Riviera Ligure di Ponente Vermentino '09	🍷	4

Ka Manciné

FRAZ. SAN MARTINO
P.ZZA OTTO LUOGHI, 36
18036 SOLDANO [IM]
TEL. 0184289089
www.kamancine.it

Maurizio Anfosso has only been selling his wines for a few years, but already shows good quality. The Beragna '09, with its bouquet of berries, drinks beautifully involving nose and palate in a vortex of fresh aromatic herbs, as does the Dolceacqua Galeae '09, which seems a bit less intense.

- ● Rossese di Dolceacqua Beragna '09 🍷🍷 4
- ● Rossese di Dolceacqua Galeae '09 🍷 5

Maixei

LOC. REGIONE PORTO
18035 DOLCEACQUA [IM]
TEL. 0184205015
www.maixei.it

"Maixei" are those dry stone walls holding up the terraces where rossese grapes are grown. From the range released by this co-operative, we point out the personality of the Vermentino '09 with its supple citrus notes, and the Rossese Superiore '08, which has a more reflective, ripe red berry-soaked timbre.

- O Dolceacqua Rossese Sup. '08 🍷🍷 5
- ● Riviera Ligure di Ponente Vermentino '09 🍷 4

Paganini

LOC. CHIAZZARI, 15
17024 FINALE LIGURE [SV]
TEL. 335211931
www.cantinapaganini.it

Gian Riccardo Paganini continues his personal campaign on behalf of the dry stone walls and vineyards that cling to the rocks overlooking Finale Ligure. The wines he makes repay his efforts. His Pigato '09 pairs pleasant citrussy hints with compelling iodine and salty notes from the nearby sea.

- O Riviera Ligure di Ponente Pigato '09 🍷 4

Gino Pino

FRAZ. MISSANO
VIA PODESTÀ, 31
16030 CASTIGLIONE CHIAVARESE [GE]
TEL. 0185408036
pinogino.az.agricola@tin.it

With the '09 harvest, Antonella Pino has managed to create an excellent Bianchetta Genovese '09, coaxing lovely citrussy aromas and zesty mineral density from this traditional variety. The sensual nose-palate harmony of his Moscato is by now a well-established item.

- O Golfo del Tigullio Bianchetta Genovese '09 🍷🍷 4
- O Golfo del Tigullio Moscato '09 🍷🍷 5

Danila Pisano

VIA SAN MARTINO, 20
18036 SOLDANO [IM]
TEL. 0184208551
danila.pisano@alice.it

With the '08 vintage, the Pisano estate shows its strength lies not only in the long-established Savoia vineyard but also the other plots on their property. A bit less rough than the previous vintage, the '08 Dolceacqua Superiore offers notes of red berries with pleasant spice and remarkable length.

- ● Rossese di Dolceacqua Sup. '08 🍷🍷 4
- ● Rossese di Dolceacqua V. Savoia '08 🍷 5

Poggi dell'Elmo

C.SO VERBONE, 135
18036 SOLDANO [IM]
TEL. 0184289148
guglielmi.g@libero.it

On retasting wines from Giovanni Guglielmi, we rediscover a constant quality underlining his commitment and skill. The aromas and restrained texture give the Dolceacqua '09 an even more approachable drinkability. The aroma-rich Dolceacqua Elmo '08 offers pleasing tannins and velvety structure.

- ● Rossese di Dolceacqua '09 🍷🍷 4
- ● Rossese di Dolceacqua Elmo '08 🍷 4

La Ricolla

via Garibaldi, 12/2
16040 Ne [GE]
tel. 0185337087
laricolla@alice.it

This year, the Vermentino Filiscano from Daniele Parma has less grip but we enjoyed the '09 Tolceto, a blood-red wine from sangiovese and ciliegiolo that regales the nose with deliciously distinct aromas, offering one or two surprising fragrances, and drinks wonderfully well.

○ Golfo Del Tigullio Vermentino Fliscano '09 — 🍷 4
● Tolceto Rosso '09 — 🍷 4

Le Rocche del Gatto

fraz. Salea
reg. Ruato, 4
17031 Albenga [SV]
tel. 3355223547
www.lerocchedelgatto.it

Luigi Crosa di Vergagni and his wife Chiara impressed us this year with an excellent Vermentino '09 that gives swaths of pleasant salty notes preceding fruity, floral nuances. The warm, balanced palate has good acidity and takes its leave with admirable reluctance.

○ Riviera Ligure di Ponente Vermentino '09 — 🍷🍷 4*

Santa Caterina

via Santa Caterina, 6
19038 Sarzana [SP]
tel. 0187629429
andrea.kihlgren@alice.it

Andrea Kihlgren owns eight hectares of vineyards distributed across various holdings. His Giuncaro '09, from a mix of tocai, sauvignon and vermentino, stands out for its rich aromas and fresh progression. The Santa Caterina '07 from sangiovese and merla is also sound.

○ Giuncaro '09 — 🍷🍷 4
● Santa Caterina '07 — 🍷 4

Tenuta Selvadolce

Selva Dolce, 14
18012 Bordighera [IM]
tel. 3492225844
www.selvadolce.it

Facing the sea a few kilometres from the French border, Selvadolce covers seven hectares, of which one and a half are planted to vines farmed biodynamically by Leonello Anello. The excellent Selvadolce Rosso '08 sparked interest thanks to its generosity and cleanliness.

● Selvadolce Rosso '08 — 🍷🍷 5
○ Riviera Ligure di Ponente Rucantù '08 — 🍷🍷 6

Agostino Sommariva

via Mameli, 1
17031 Albenga [SV]
tel. 0182559222
www.oliosommariva.it

Sommariva deserves a visit for the beautiful shop inside the medieval walls of Albenga, along with the old olive press and cellar. One of the wines worth buying is the tangy, mineral Pigato '09 with intense aromas of aromatic herbs and broom.

○ Riviera Ligure di Ponente Pigato '09 — 🍷 4

Podere Terenzuola

via Vercalda, 14
54035 Fosdinovo [MS]
tel. 0187680030
www.terenzuola.com

Terenzuola was founded at Fosdinovo by Luigi Giuliani. In 1906, his far-sighted grandson Ivan conceived a project spanning several regions as a producer in Luni, Candia and Cinque Terre. This year we very much liked the firmly structured Sciacchetrà '07, which unveils warm, soft aromas.

○ Cinqueterre Sciacchetrà '07 — 🍷🍷 8

Innocenzo Turco

VIA BERTONE, 7A
17040 QUILIANO [SV]
TEL. 0192000026
www.innocenzoturco.it

A specialist in Granaccia di Quiliano, Turco this year excited us with a truly remarkable Pigato. The '09 vintage yielded a leisurely, elegant wine. Its complex nose has fruity, floral tones and the round, harmonic palate reveals great depth.

○ Riviera Ligure di Ponente Pigato '09 ꝟꝟ 4

Valdiscalve

LOC. REGGIMONTI
SP 42
19011 BONASSOLA [SP]
TEL. 0187818178
www.vermenting.com

The vermentino, albarola and bosco grown at Reggimonti near Bonassola join forces to create the Vigna Reggimonti. This tangy, fresh wine has a palette of Mediterranean aromas, as does the slightly broader Vigna del Salice, whose more intense aromatics open broader horizons on the palate.

○ Colline di Levanto Bianco Verment Ing V. Salice '09 ꝟꝟ 4
○ Colline di Levanto Bianco Verment Ing V. Reggimonti '09 ꝟ 4

La Vecchia Cantina

FRAZ. SALEA
VIA CORTA, 3
17031 ALBENGA [SV]
TEL. 0182559881

Umberto Calleri is an older gentleman whose passion for wine has never faded. His Vermentino '09 gives balsam and an incomparable richness of spring flowers and ripe fruit. We loved the faithful interpretation of the terroir offered by the '09 Pigato.

○ Riviera Ligure di Ponente Pigato '09 ꝟ 4
○ Riviera Ligure di Ponente Vermentino '09 ꝟ 4

Claudio Vio

FRAZ. CROSA, 16
17032 VENDONE [SV]
TEL. 018276338
claudio.vio@libero.it

With the '08 Grottu, Claudio Vio has reproduced the great quality of the '06 and '07 vintages. Evident overripeness and time on the skins have given this white structure and character without upsetting the varietal fruit and flower profile of Pigato.

○ U Grottu '08 ꝟꝟ 5
○ Riviera Ligure di Ponente Vermentino '09 ꝟ 4

Vis Amoris

LOC. CARAMAGNA
S.DA MOLINO JAVÈ, 23
18100 IMPERIA
TEL. 3483959569
visamoris@libero.it

Roberto and Rossana Zappa surprised us with their Pigato Sogno. The '09 shows great depth on the nose, good salinity and a pleasing peach and apricot finish, outclassing the renowned Vigna Domè '09, which failed to deliver the character and full body to which we had grown accustomed.

○ Riviera Ligure di Ponente Pigato Sogno '09 ꝟꝟ 6
○ Riviera Ligure di Ponente Pigato V. Domè '09 ꝟ 5

Cooperativa Viticoltori Ingauni

VIA ROMA, 1
17037 ORTOVERO [SV]
TEL. 0182547127

This is one of the few co-operatives in Liguria. Under the guiding hand of president Enrico Massimo, the cellar is producing encouraging results. We spotlight the velvety, well-structured '09 Pornassio and particularly the classic, rich-textured Pigato, a tangy wine that does brilliantly here.

● Riviera Ligure di Ponente Ormeasco di Pornassio '09 ꝟ 4
○ Riviera Ligure di Ponente Pigato '09 ꝟ 4

LOMBARDY

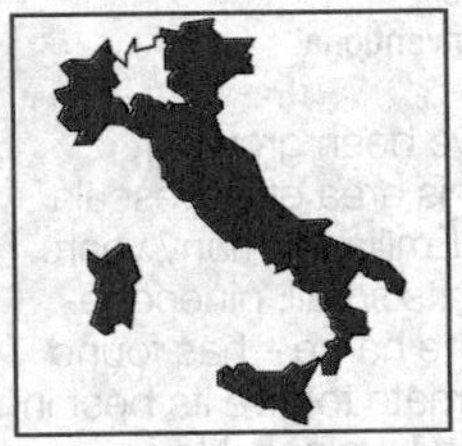

This was an exceptional year, not least for the excellent wines submitted to our tastings. It was Lombardy's best-ever performance, with an impressive 21 Three Glasses. This calls for celebration and there are plenty of sparkling wines to choose from. If we had to pick just one area, it would probably be Franciacorta, which marked its 50th anniversary with 12 Three Glasses. It was in 1961 that Franco Ziliani, Guido Berlucchi and Giorgio Lanciani refermented the first 1,000 bottles of Pinot di Franciacorta, the forerunner of today's Franciacorta DOCG. We could toast in Berlucchi's Franciacorta Palazzo Lana Brut Extrême '05, which won our top accolade again. Franciacorta has plenty of winners: Ca' del Bosco's Franciacorta Cuvée Annamaria Clementi '03 and Terre di Franciacorta Chardonnay '07; Bellavista's Franciacorta Gran Cuvée Pas Operé '04; Il Mosnel's Franciacorta Pas Dosé QdE Ris. '04; Gatti's Franciacorta Brut '05; Monte Rossa's Franciacorta Brut Cabochon '05; Cavalleri's Franciacorta Brut Collezione '05, and Ferghettina and La Montina's Franciacorta Extra Bruts '04. Sparkler of the Year went to Le Marchesine's extraordinarily elegant Franciacorta Brut Secolo Novo '05. However, Lombardy is not just Franciacorta. Oltrepò also took Three Glass awards for OP Pinot Nero Brut Nature by Monsupello, whose founder Carlo Boatti sadly died this year; Fratelli Giorgi's '06 Pinot Nero Brut 1870; Frecciarossa's OP Pinot Nero Giorgio Odero '07; Mazzolino's OP Pinot Nero Noir; and Castello di Cignola's OP Barbera Castello di Cigognola '07. This performance, unthinkable just a few years ago, is founded on extensive research. The Centro Vitivinicolo di Ricerca e Sperimentazione at Riccagioia will soon be inaugurated, offering top-level European training oenology and sparkling winemaking in particular. Across the region, Provenza's Lugana Superiore Selezione Fabio Contato '06 represents an area coming on fast in quality and where red wines from native varieties are set to emerge over the coming years. Finally, there's Valtellina, the land of heroic viticulture. This year it vaunts three great wines: two Valtellina Sforzatos – Nino Negri's classic 5 Stelle '07 and Mamete Prevostini's Albareda '08 – and, for the first time, a Valtellina Superiore, Rainoldi's splendid Sassella Riserva '06, underscoring the efforts of an area that does not believe in resting on its laurels. This spirit is characteristic of Lombardy in general. Without it, Guido Berlucchi and Franco Ziliani's 1,000 bottles would never have become a serious proposition. Today Franciacorta has an annual production of approximately ten million bottles and Lombardy is one of Italy's key wine regions. And all in the space of just 50 years.

Marchese Adorno

VIA CORIASSA, 4
27050 RETORBIDO [PV]
TEL. 0383374404
www.marcheseadorno-wines.it

CELLAR SALES
PRE-BOOKED VISITS

ANNUAL PRODUCTION **200,000 bottles**
HECTARES UNDER VINE **85**
VITICULTURE METHOD **Conventional**

This winery in western Oltrepò is destined to become one of the benchmarks for the entire area in the next few years. Owned by the Adorno family since 1834, the turning point came in 1997 with the last descendent of the line, Marchese Marcello, who decided to invest an impressive sum for the complete restoration of the beautiful winery and the entire business. All that was missing was the helmsman, and this gap was filled several months ago by the experienced Francesco Cervetti.

This year's list is thoroughly decent. Pinot Nero Rile Nero '07 almost made it to our finals. Aromas of dark berry fruit mingle with attractive notes of liquorice, spice and almond. The palate is satisfying, with a very long, well-defined finish. Barbera Vigna del Re '07 is equally good, with fragrant notes of black cherry and a fruity, chewy palate with perfect acidity and, once again, a nice finish. The basic Pinot Nero '08 and Pinot Grigio Dama d'Oro '09 are very pleasant and varietal. Bonarda '09 is a good, sound wine while Merlot Cliviano '08 is well made with typical peppery notes.

● OP Barbera V. del Re '07	2 black	6
● OP Bonarda Vivace Costa del Sole '09	2 black	4
○ OP Pinot Grigio Dama D'Oro '09	2 black	4
● OP Pinot Nero '08	2 black	5
● OP Pinot Nero Rile Nero '07	2 black	6
● Cliviano '08	1 black	4
● Cliviano '06	2 white	4
● OP Barbera V. del Re '05	2 white	6
● OP Barbera V. del Re '04	2 white	6
● OP Bonarda Frizzante '07	2 white	4*
○ OP Pinot Grigio Dama D'Oro '08	2 white	4*

Agnes

VIA CAMPO DEL MONTE, 1
27040 ROVESCALA [PV]
TEL. 038575206
www.fratelliagnes.it

CELLAR SALES
PRE-BOOKED VISITS

ANNUAL PRODUCTION **70,000 bottles**
HECTARES UNDER VINE **16**
VITICULTURE METHOD **Conventional**

The Agnes family have been growing Pignola Bonarda in this area of Rovescala near the border with Emilia for many years. Here the variety, with its small, pinecone-like berries – hence the name – has found the ideal soils and climate to give its best in both still and sparkling versions. Now Sergio and Cristiano continue the family tradition with great passion, accompanied by commendable consistency of quality and style consistency.

As in almost all our tastings, the top performer was the pure pignola Poculum '08 with an almost impenetrable ruby hue and a full, varied balsamic nose of almonds and vanilla, and a rounded, firm palate with smooth tannins. Millennium '07 is more traditional, having had an extra year in wood. The nose offers intriguing chocolate and mint, which accompany the attractive, full-flavoured, sound fruit. The two 2009 sparkling Bonardas are equally good, with Cresta del Ghiffi showing smoother. Both are clean with ripe tannins. The other wines are good, including the new Metodo Martinotti Pindesa fermented with brief skin contact.

● Poculum '08	2 black	5
● OP Bonarda Frizzante Campo del Monte '09	2 black	3*
● OP Bonarda Frizzante Cresta del Ghiffi '09	2 black	3*
● OP Bonarda Millenium '07	2 black	5
● OP Bonarda Possessione del Console '09	1 black	3
⊙ Pinot Nero Brut Martinotti Pindesa Rosé	1 black	4
● Vignazzo '06	1 black	3
● OP Bonarda Campo del Monte '06	2 white	3*
● OP Bonarda Campo del Monte '05	2 white	3*
● OP Bonarda Cresta del Ghiffi '06	2 white	3*
● OP Bonarda Cresta del Ghiffi '05	2 white	3*
● OP Bonarda Frizzante Cresta del Ghiffi '08	2 white	3*
● OP Bonarda Millenium '05	2 white	5
● Rosso Poculum '01	2 white	5

Anteo

LOC. CHIESA
27040 ROCCA DE' GIORGI [PV]
TEL. 038599073
www.anteovini.it

CELLAR SALES
PRE-BOOKED VISITS

ANNUAL PRODUCTION 240,000 bottles
HECTARES UNDER VINE 26
VITICULTURE METHOD Conventional

Trento Cribellati founded the winery in 1981 in a beautiful area between the upper Valle Scuropasso and the upper Valle Versa, about 380 metres above sea level, and named it after the mythological giant Antaeus, son of the earth goddess Gaea. Almost all its vineyards are planted to pinot nero for Metodo Classico sparklers, which are now made by Trento's children Piero and Antonella.

The elegant, complex Riserva del Poeta '03, dedicated to the memory of Trento Cribellati, nearly took Three Glasses for its aromatic herbs, good body and a long finish. Nature '05, whose '03 vintage won Three Glasses, is excellent again, showing taut with impressive backbone, as a good undosed monovarietal Pinot Nero should, and enhanced by tantalising balsam. The intense, mineral Rosé '05 is equally breathtaking. From this year, it is vintage-dated, although it cannot yet carry the Cruasé designation, applicable from the '07 harvest. The basic Brut is more straightforward but still appealing. The rest of the list is good, with an interesting red Pinot Nero Ca' dell'Oca '05.

○ OP Pinot Nero Brut Cl. Nature Écru '05	▼▼	5
○ OP Pinot Nero Brut Cl. Riserva del Poeta '03	▼▼	6
⊙ OP Pinot Nero Brut Cl. Rosé '05	▼▼	5
● OP Bonarda Frizzante Staffolo '09	▼▼	4*
○ OP Pinot Nero Brut Cl.	▼▼	5
⊙ OP Pinot Nero Brut Martinotti Rosé	▼▼	4*
● OP Pinot Nero Ca' dell'Oca '05	▼▼	4
○ OP Pinot Nero Brut Martinotti	▼	4
○ OP Pinot Nero Brut Cl. Nature Écru '03	▽▽▽	5
○ OP Pinot Nero Brut Cl. Nature Écru '02	▽▽	5
○ OP Pinot Nero Brut Cl. Nature Ecru '00	▽▽	5
○ OP Pinot Nero Brut Cl. Riserva del Poeta '99	▽▽	6
○ OP Pinot Nero Brut Nature Écru '04	▽▽	5*
○ OP Pinot Nero Brut Riserva del Poeta '02	▽▽	6

Antica Fratta

VIA FONTANA, 11
25040 MONTICELLI BRUSATI [BS]
TEL. 030652068
www.anticafratta.it

CELLAR SALES
PRE-BOOKED VISITS

ANNUAL PRODUCTION 360,000 bottles
HECTARES UNDER VINE N.A.
VITICULTURE METHOD Conventional

Antica Fratta at Monticelli Brusati has belonged to Berlucchi since 1979 and, unlike its parent company, has always been engaged in the production of Franciacorta. Housed in a handsome 19th-century building featuring a huge underground cellar with four tunnels arranged in a cross, the winery has earned the nickname "el cantinù", meaning the big cellar. Run by Cristina Ziliani for several years now, with a separate staff and vineyards from the parent company, Antica Fratta produces around 350,000 bottles of Franciacorta and Curtefranca a year.

The most interesting wine this year is the non-vintage Franciacorta Brut, which displays a very clean style. It shows a bright straw yellow, with a creamy mousse and fine bead. The nose opens on delicate notes of apples and pears, developing hints of cakes, vanilla and yeast. On the palate it is dry, zesty and full, with a long fruit and mineral finish. It is one of the finest of its kind. The Satèn is naturally softer, but equally well defined, with hints of apricot. Brut Essence '05 is rich and interesting, the Rosé '06 version less so.

○ Franciacorta Brut	▼▼	5
○ Franciacorta Essence Brut '05	▼▼	6
○ Franciacorta Satèn	▼▼	6
● Curtefranca Rosso Ragnoli '07	▼	4
⊙ Franciacorta Essence Rosé '06	▼	6
⊙ Franciacorta Rosé	▼	6
○ Franciacorta Antica Fratta Brut	▽▽	5
○ Franciacorta Brut '04	▽▽	6
○ Franciacorta Brut '03	▽▽	5
⊙ Franciacorta Essence Rosé '05	▽▽	6
● TdF Rosso Ragnoli '06	▽▽	4*
● TdF Rosso Ragnoli '05	▽▽	5

Barone Pizzini

LOC. TIMOLINE
VIA BRESCIA, 3A
25050 CORTE FRANCA [BS]
TEL. 0309848311
www.baronepizzini.it

CELLAR SALES
PRE-BOOKED VISITS
ROOMS

ANNUAL PRODUCTION 340,000 bottles
HECTARES UNDER VINE 47
VITICULTURE METHOD Certified organic

Barone Pizzini, founded in 1870, is owned by a group of Brescia businessmen and managed by the talented Silvano Brescianini. His hard work and determination have turned it into a model winery and an example of eco-compatible architecture. It was the first in Franciacorta to convert to organic farming, generating its own energy, purifying its water and recycling its waste. It has spawned to several other operations: Tenuta del Barco in Puglia, Podere Ghiaccioforte in Tuscany, and Pievalta in Marche, all of which are managed using natural methods to make the most of the local varieties.

The flagship wine, Franciacorta Bagnadore, hadn't been disgorged when we were tasting. However, we enjoyed the excellent Franciacorta Brut, which is bright straw yellow with an elegant mousse, a complex mineral nose and a sharp tangy palate, and the very good Extra Dry brimming with juicy fruit and just the right amount of sweetness on the fresh, nutty palate. We also liked Chardonnay Polzina '09, with notes of vanilla and white peach and good structure, and the rich, balanced Curtefranca Rosso '08, with pleasant aromas of autumn leaves. The Rosé, Satèn and Dosage Zero are less alluring than usual but well made.

● Curtefranca Rosso '08	▼▼	4
○ Franciacorta Brut	▼▼	5
○ Franciacorta Extra Dry	▼▼	6
○ Polzina Bianco '09	▼▼	4
○ Franciacorta Dosage Zero	▼	5
⊙ Franciacorta Rosé	▼	6
○ Franciacorta Satèn	▼	6
○ Franciacorta Brut Nature Bagnadore '04	▽▽	6
○ Franciacorta Extra Brut Bagnadore '03	▽▽	6
○ Franciacorta Extra Brut Bagnadore '02	▽▽	6
○ Franciacorta Satèn '01	▽▽	6
● San Carlo '07	▽▽	6

★★ Bellavista

VIA BELLAVISTA, 5
25030 ERBUSCO [BS]
TEL. 0307762000
www.bellavistawine.it

PRE-BOOKED VISITS

ANNUAL PRODUCTION 1,300,000 bottles
HECTARES UNDER VINE 184
VITICULTURE METHOD Conventional

Bellavista was founded during the 1970s by successful businessman Vittorio Moretti and today it heads the Terra Moretti Holding group, with estates in Lombardy and Tuscany. Now, with over 180 hectares of splendid vineyards, it is the jewel in the group's crown and one of the most respected names in Italian wine worldwide. Oenologist and general manager Mattia Vezzola has skilfully interpreted the terroir, creating a unique style with Moretti which focuses on finesse and elegance. It is a benchmark for the designation and an inspiration to subsequent wineries.

Although we may have tasted slightly fewer wines than usual this year, Moretti's cuvées gave us the same deep satisfaction. Three well-deserved Glasses went to Gran Cuvée Pas Operé '04, elegant and floral on the nose, juicy, fresh and close-woven in the mouth with good progression and a full flavour accompanied by a long apricot-themed finish. Gran Cuvée Satèn's soft, estery floral elegance almost earned it our highest accolade. The juicy, fresh Curtefranca Uccellanda '07 reached the finals for the first time, with perfectly integrated oak. Curtefranca del Convento dell'Annunciata '07 and all the other wines were very good, as usual.

○ Franciacorta Gran Cuvée Pas Operé '04	▼▼▼	8
○ Franciacorta Gran Cuvée Satèn	▼▼	7
○ TdF Bianco Uccellanda '07	▼▼	6
○ Curtefranca Bianco '09	▼▼	4
○ Franciacorta Brut	▼▼	6
○ TdF Bianco Convento dell'Annunciata '07	▼▼	6
○ Champenois Pas Operé '85	▽▽▽	5
○ Cremant '88	▽▽▽	5
○ Franciacorta Champenois Grand Cuvée Brut '88	▽▽▽	5
○ Franciacorta Extra Brut Vittorio Moretti '02	▽▽▽+	8
○ Franciacorta Gran Cuvée Brut '04	▽▽▽	7
○ Franciacorta Gran Cuvée Brut '02	▽▽▽	7
○ Franciacorta Gran Cuvée Brut '99	▽▽▽	6
○ Franciacorta Gran Cuvée Pas Operé '00	▽▽▽	7
○ Franciacorta Gran Cuvée Pas Operé '99	▽▽▽	7

F.lli Berlucchi

LOC. BORGONATO
VIA BROLETTO, 2
25040 CORTE FRANCA [BS]
TEL. 030984451
www.berlucchifranciacorta.it

CELLAR SALES
PRE-BOOKED VISITS

ANNUAL PRODUCTION 400,000 bottles
HECTARES UNDER VINE 70
VITICULTURE METHOD Conventional

Berlucchi is part of the local heritage. It is one of the legendary names of Franciacorta, where the noble family has always owned farmland and vineyards. Pia Donata Berlucchi, with the aid of her daughter Tilli Rizzo and oenologist Cesare Ferrari, enthusiastically runs the winery for her four siblings. The winery boasts 70 hectares of vineyards in the best wine areas of the designation, such as Torbiato di Adro and Borgonato di Corte Franca. The cellar is situated next to the handsome family home, a beautiful 16th-century-style building.

The firm, full-bodied Franciacorta Brut '06 went straight through to our finals for its elegance, smoothness and balance, and intriguing, deep, mineral sensations. The Rosé from the same vintage confirms that it is one of the best in the designation, showing creamy, flavoursome and satisfying. The Brut 25 is a rung above last year's version, with good backbone, depth and balance. Satèn '06 is a good example of its kind: creamy, smooth and fruity, with delicate hints of medicinal herbs. Pas Dosé '06 is elegant and taut while Brut Casa delle Colonne '05 is complex and rich. The rest of the list is very good.

○ Franciacorta Brut '06	▼▼	5*
○ Franciacorta Brut 25	▼▼	4*
○ Franciacorta Casa delle Colonne Brut '05	▼▼	6
○ Franciacorta Pas Dosé '06	▼▼	6
⊙ Franciacorta Rosé '06	▼▼	5
○ Franciacorta Satèn '06	▼▼	6
○ TdF Bianco Dossi delle Querce '07	▼▼	4
○ TdF Bianco '09	▼	3
● TdF Rosso '08	▼	3
○ Franciacorta Brut '05	▽▽	5
○ Franciacorta Brut '04	▽▽	5
○ Franciacorta Pas Dosé '05	▽▽	6
○ Franciacorta Satèn '05	▽▽	6
○ Franciacorta Satèn '03	▽▽	6
● TdF Rosso Dossi delle Querce '05	▽▽	4*

Guido Berlucchi & C.

LOC. BORGONATO
P.ZZA DURANTI, 4
25040 CORTE FRANCA [BS]
TEL. 030984381
www.berlucchi.it

CELLAR SALES
PRE-BOOKED VISITS
ROOMS AND FOOD

ANNUAL PRODUCTION 5,000,000 bottles
HECTARES UNDER VINE 600
VITICULTURE METHOD Conventional

In 1961, oenologist Franco Ziliani, just back from a trip to France, convinced his friends Guido Berlucchi and Giorgio Lanciani to referment 1,000 bottles by the classic method. At the time, the trio did not foresee the full implications of the experiment. They called the wine Pinot di Franciacorta and set in motion a process that, in 50 years, has brought international renown to the area and the wineries subsequently founded in what is now one of the zones of excellence of Italian winemaking. Berlucchi & Co. has become one of Italy's leading wineries so "Happy Anniversary"!

Following a period of purchasing grapes from other sparkling wine designations, such as Trentino and Oltrepò, Berlucchi is now synonymous with Franciacorta. This is confirmed by Brut Extrême Palazzo Lana '05, from 100 per cent pinot nero, which again won Three Glasses. It's a very deep wine, with plenty of backbone and minerality. The extraordinary Satèn Cuvée 61 is almost as good and went to our finals. The Rosé and Brut from the same range are also nice. The 2007 vintage of Cellarius Brut and Rosé is excellent, as is Cuvée Imperiale Vintage '03, but Cuvée Imperiale Brut, the winery's workhorse, with an annual production that runs to millions of bottles, delicious, too.

○ Franciacorta Brut Extrême Palazzo Lana '05	▼▼▼	7
○ Franciacorta Satèn Cuvée 61	▼▼	5
○ Cellarius Brut '07	▼▼	6
⊙ Cellarius Brut Rosé '07	▼▼	6
○ Cuvée Imperiale Brut	▼▼	5
○ Cuvée Imperiale Brut Vintage '03	▼▼	7
○ Franciacorta Brut Cuvée 61	▼▼	5
⊙ Franciacorta Brut Rosé Cuvée 61	▼▼	6
⊙ Cuvée Imperiale Max Rosé	▼	5
○ Franciacorta Brut Extrême Palazzo Lana '04	▽▽▽	7
○ Cellarius Brut '06	▽▽	6
⊙ Cellarius Rosé '06	▽▽	6
○ Franciacorta Cuvée Storica 61	▽▽	5
○ Franciacorta Satèn Brut '04	▽▽	6
○ Franciacorta Satèn Palazzo Lana '04	▽▽	7

Bersi Serlini

Loc. Cereto
via Cereto, 7
25050 Provaglio d'Iseo [BS]
tel. 0309823338
www.bersiserlini.it

CELLAR SALES
PRE-BOOKED VISITS

ANNUAL PRODUCTION 220,000 bottles
HECTARES UNDER VINE 32
VITICULTURE METHOD Conventional

The winery was founded in 1886, when the Bersi Serlini family purchased this old ecclesiastical property, which was a grange of the nearby monastery of San Pietro in Lamosa. Today the winery is one of the most handsome in the area, and it is situated next to the medieval building, reminding us of the estate's ancient wine tradition. The family business is run by Maddalena, a keen wine enthusiast, with the help of her sister Chiara.

This year, the estate's wines again stand out for their high average quality. We are convinced that Maddalena and her staff are very close to scaling the heights. Extra Brut Riserva '03 has great personality, a bright straw-yellow hue, a very fine bead and a nose that unfurls with soft fruity notes before developing more mineral, complex sensations. Its elegant palate echoes the nose, opening elegantly and continuing spirited and lingering. The Satèn is also alluring, with notes of tropical and kiwi fruit, and Cuvée n.4 '05 is as good as ever. Don't miss Demi Sec Nuvola, with nice notes of tarte tatin, and the tangy Rosa Rosae. The basic Brut is good..

○ Franciacorta Brut Cuvée n. 4 '05	2 black glasses	5
⊙ Franciacorta Brut Rosa Rosae	2 black glasses	6
○ Franciacorta Demi Sec Nuvola	2 black glasses	5
○ Franciacorta Extra Brut Ris. '03	2 black glasses	6
○ Franciacorta Satèn	2 black glasses	6
○ Franciacorta Brut	1 black glass	6
○ Franciacorta Brut Cuvée n. 4	2 white glasses	6
○ Franciacorta Brut Cuvée n. 4	2 white glasses	6
○ Franciacorta Brut Vintage '02	2 white glasses	8
○ Franciacorta Brut Vintage '01	2 white glasses	6
○ Franciacorta Brut Vintage Ris. '02	2 white glasses	7
○ Franciacorta Extra Brut '02	2 white glasses	6
○ Franciacorta Extra Brut Ris. '02	2 white glasses	6
○ Demi Sec Nuvola	1 white glass	6

F.lli Bettini

Loc. San Giacomo
via Nazionale, 4a
23036 Teglio [SO]
tel. 0342786068
bettvini@tin.it

CELLAR SALES
PRE-BOOKED VISITS

ANNUAL PRODUCTION 200,000 bottles
HECTARES UNDER VINE 15
VITICULTURE METHOD Conventional

This year's tasting offers confirmation of Pietro Bettini's commitment to quality. Part of the credit for this is due to the area in which his vineyards are situated, Valgella, which is increasingly emerging as a terroir with unique characteristics.

Sforzato '07 has a complex nose with notes of aromatic herbs and stewed berry fruit, good structure and a smooth, warm palate with a long finish. Made from late-harvest nebbiolo grapes, with the canes cut in mid October, Vigna La Cornella '06 has a sound nose, dominated by fruit, and good overall balance. The palate is full and juicy with an elegant finish. The easy-drinking Sassella Reale '06 is fresh with a nose of flowers and red berry fruits, accompanied by a racy, full-flavoured palate. Prodigio '06 is good, offering a nose of spring flowers and ripe plum and a balanced palate with smooth tannins and a lingering finish.

● Valtellina Sfursat '07	2 black glasses	7
● Valtellina Sup. Inferno Prodigio '06	2 black glasses	5
● Valtellina Sup. Sassella Reale '06	2 black glasses	5
● Valtellina Sup. Valgella V. La Cornella '06	2 black glasses	5
● Valtellina Sfursat '06	2 white glasses	7
● Valtellina Sfursat '05	2 white glasses	7
● Valtellina Sfursat '04	2 white glasses	7
● Valtellina Sup. Inferno Prodigio '05	2 white glasses	5
● Valtellina Sup. Inferno Prodigio '04	2 white glasses	5
● Valtellina Sup. Sant'Andrea '06	2 white glasses	5
● Valtellina Sup. Sassella Reale '04	2 white glasses	5
● Valtellina Sup. Valgella V. La Cornella '05	2 white glasses	5

Bisi

LOC. CASCINA SAN MICHELE
FRAZ. VILLA MARONE, 70
27040 SAN DAMIANO AL COLLE [PV]
TEL. 038575037
www.aziendagricolabisi.it

CELLAR SALES
PRE-BOOKED VISITS

ANNUAL PRODUCTION 100,000 bottles
HECTARES UNDER VINE 30
VITICULTURE METHOD Conventional

It's a shame that there aren't more men like Claudio Bisi in the wine world! He is enthusiastic, dependable, determined, modest and quality-focused. Founded by Claudio in 1926, with the aid of Leonardo Valenti this winery has taken great steps forward and now offers a convincing range, which is missing perhaps only a Metodo Classico in the uncompromising Bisi style.

Barbera Roncolongo is a regular feature in our finals. The '07 version shows deep ruby with exceptionally pleasant notes of wild berries and cherries accompanied by an array of spices and cocoa powder, good acidity and great depth. Cabernet Sauvignon Primm '07 is similar in style, with subtle vegetal notes. The bottle-fermented Ultrapadum, an equal blend of barbera and croatina, is as good as ever while Malvasia Passita Villa Marone '06, the area's finest dessert wine, is simply spectacular. Pinot Nero Calonga '07 is well typed, with an increasingly elegant nose and nicely calibrated oak. Riesling and Bonarda '09 are impeccable.

○ Bianco Passito Villa Marone '06	▼▼	5
● OP Barbera Roncolongo '07	▼▼	5
● OP Bonarda Frizzante '09	▼▼	3*
● OP Cabernet Sauvignon Primm '07	▼▼	5
● OP Pinot Nero Calonga '07	▼▼	5
○ OP Riesling '09	▼▼	3*
● Ultrapadum '08	▼▼	4
● OP Barbera Roncolongo '06	▽▽	5
● OP Barbera Roncolongo '05	▽▽	5
● OP Barbera Roncolongo '04	▽▽	5
● OP Barbera Roncolongo '03	▽▽	5
● OP Barbera Roncolongo '01	▽▽	5
● OP Cabernet Sauvignon Primm '01	▽▽	5
● OP Cabernet Sauvignon Primm '00	▽▽	5

Tenuta Il Bosco

LOC. IL BOSCO
27049 ZENEVREDO [PV]
TEL. 0385245326
www.ilbosco.com

CELLAR SALES
PRE-BOOKED VISITS

ANNUAL PRODUCTION 1,000,000 bottles
HECTARES UNDER VINE 150
VITICULTURE METHOD Conventional

This winery is the Zonin family's Oltrepò estate, founded over 20 years ago in Zenevredo on land that once belonged to the convent of Santa Maria Teodote, after which its Bonarda is now named. Piedmontese oenologist Piernicola Olmo has devised a more modern style for Bonarda, smoother and fruitier, as well as convincing the Zonins to focus on pinot nero and sparkling wines with the 152 hectares of vines. Soon several old vintages of Metodo Classico will be released following patient ageing on the lees.

While awaiting these old vintages, which are very promising based on our advance tastings, the new wines this year are two younger Metodo Classicos, both '07, in white and Cruasé versions. They are called Oltrenero and are both fresh, fairly uncomplicated and very enjoyable, particularly as an aperitif or to accompany light dishes. Bonarda Teodote '09 is always among the most fragrant and fruity in Oltrepò. The sparklers also include several Charmat-method wines: the two fresh, fragrant Phileos and the new Vyper, which is more straightforward. Pinot Nero Pelato '07 needs bottle ageing to find the right balance.

● OP Bonarda Vivace Teodote '09	▼▼	3*
⊙ OP Pinot Nero Brut Cruasè Oltrenero '07	▼▼	5
○ OP Pinot Nero Brut M. Cl. Oltrenero '07	▼▼	6
○ OP Pinot Nero Brut Martinotti Philèo	▼▼	4
⊙ Phileo Rosè Brut Martinotti	▼▼	3*
○ OP Pinot Nero Brut Vyper	▼	5
● OP Pinot Nero Poggio Pelato '07	▼	5
● OP Barbera Vivace '07	▽▽	3*
● OP Bonarda Vivace '08	▽▽	4*
● OP Bonarda Vivace '06	▽▽	3*
● OP Bonarda Vivace '03	▽▽	4
○ OP Brut Cl. Il Bosco '98	▽▽	5
○ OP Malvasia Frizzante '01	▽▽	3

Bosio

LOC. TIMOLINE
VIA MARIO GATTI
25040 CORTE FRANCA [BS]
TEL. 030984398
www.bosiofranciacorta.it

CELLAR SALES
PRE-BOOKED VISITS

ANNUAL PRODUCTION 100,000 bottles
HECTARES UNDER VINE 23
VITICULTURE METHOD Conventional

Cesare Bosio is an agronomist with perfect knowledge of the terroir while his sister Laura, an economics graduate, is responsible for sales and marketing. Despite their youth, the brother-and-sister team have achieved superior quality in the space of a few years and their success continues to grow. Cesare and Laura commenced their adventure only a decade ago, when they started to purchase vineyards for their small family estate, and now have over 20 hectares. The Bosios then built a handsome cellar with the very latest equipment.

Franciacorta Extra Brut Boschedòr made it into our finals, where it scored well for its impeccable mousse, complex nose of fruit, vanillaed oak and medicinal herbs, and a firm, full palate with good development and a lingering finish. The Bosios' commitment is confirmed by an excellent Franciacorta Brut, which shows savoury, compact and balanced; the elegant Rosé, giving by red berry fruit and vanilla; and a Satèn with soft notes of vanilla and butter but also nice freshness. The still wines include the smooth Curtefranca Rosso Zenighe '06, which has attractive extract.

	Glasses	
○ Franciacorta Extra Brut Boschedòr '05	2 (black)	5
○ Franciacorta Brut	2 (black)	5
⊙ Franciacorta Rosé	2 (black)	5
○ Franciacorta Satèn	2 (black)	5
● TdF Rosso Zenighe '06	2 (black)	4
○ Franciacorta Extra Brut Boschedòr '04	2 (white)	5
○ Franciacorta Extra Brut Boschedòr '03	2 (white)	5
○ Franciacorta Satèn	2 (white)	6
● TdF Rosso Zenighe '05	2 (white)	4*

Ca' dei Frati

FRAZ. LUGANA
VIA FRATI, 22
25019 SIRMIONE [BS]
TEL. 030919468
www.cadeifrati.it

CELLAR SALES
PRE-BOOKED VISITS
ROOMS AND FOOD

ANNUAL PRODUCTION 1,400,000 bottles
HECTARES UNDER VINE 120
VITICULTURE METHOD Conventional

The Dal Cero family have always been grape growers and have concentrated their efforts on promoting Lugana, which owes much of its recent fame to their work. Ca' dei Frati has 110 hectares of vineyards in finest parts of the DOC zone, for which it is a benchmark, and its wines are successfully exported all over the world. Igino Dal Cero is a keen oenologist always seeking new potential in his wines, which are a model of cellarability and elegance.

Lugana Brolettino almost repeated the success of the last vintage. An attractive bright yellowish green, with a clear, concentrated nose of apricot and damson and well-integrated new oak and vanilla, it unfurls a complex, juicy palate supported by a fresh swath of acidity and an elegant finish of aromatic herbs and balsam. Lugana I Frati '09 has a complex, vibrant nose with crisp florality and fruit echoed on a palate with good backbone, smoothness and minerality. We are sure that it will improve over the next few years in the Selezione Vecchie Annate range. The red Ronchedone '07, from sangiovese, marzemino and cabernet, is excellent, as is the rest of the list.

	Glasses	
○ Lugana Brolettino '08	2 (black)	4*
○ Lugana I Frati '09	2 (black)	4*
○ Cuvée dei Frati Brut '07	2 (black)	5
○ Pratto '08	2 (black)	5
● Ronchedone '07	2 (black)	5
○ Tre Filer '07	2 (black)	4
⊙ Riviera del Garda Bresciano I Frati Chiaretto '09	1 (black)	4
○ Lugana Brolettino '07	3 (white)	4*
○ Lugana I Frati '08	2 (white)	4*
○ Lugana I Frati Sel. Vecchie Annate '04	2 (white)	5
○ Pratto '07	2 (white)	5
● Ronchedone Grande Annata '04	2 (white)	6
○ Tre Filer '06	2 (white)	5

★★★ Ca' del Bosco

VIA ALBANO ZANELLA, 13
25030 ERBUSCO [BS]
TEL. 0307766111
www.cadelbosco.it

CELLAR SALES
PRE-BOOKED VISITS

ANNUAL PRODUCTION 1,350,000 bottles
HECTARES UNDER VINE 149
VITICULTURE METHOD Conventional

Ca' del Bosco is one of the top estates in Italian winemaking. Founded in the early 1970s, it now boasts 150 hectares of vineyards and produces just under a million excellent bottles of Franciacortas and still wines. The winery has a cutting-edge cellar that increasingly resembles an art gallery, as its talented president Maurizio Zanella intends. Maurizio, who has created a personal style with his wines, is one of the pioneers of modern Franciacorta and is now also president of the Franciacorta protection consortium.

The perfect, tried-and-tested mechanism behind the winery headed by oenologist Stefano Capelli has once again worked its magic. Two wines took our top accolade, confirming Ca' del Bosco's leadership role. They were the exceptionally good Annamaria Clementi '03, which is invigorating with alluring freshness and backbone, and the truly full-bodied, balanced Chardonnay '07, every bit as good as the whites of Burgundy. While the 2006 vintages are still resting in stacks, we enjoyed an excellent, palate-cossetting Cuvée Prestige and a very good Curtefranca Bianco '09.

○ Franciacorta Cuvée Annamaria Clementi '03	▼▼▼	8
○ TdF Chardonnay '07	▼▼▼	8
○ Curtefranca Bianco '09	▼▼	5
○ Franciacorta Brut Cuvée Prestige	▼▼	6
⊙ Franciacorta Cuvée Prestige Rosé	▼	7
○ Franciacorta Cuvée Annamaria Clementi '02	▽▽▽	8
○ Franciacorta Cuvée Annamaria Clementi '01	▽▽▽	8
○ Franciacorta Cuvée Annamaria Clementi '99	▽▽▽	8
○ Franciacorta Cuvée Annamaria Clementi '98	▽▽▽	8
○ Franciacorta Cuvée Annamaria Clementi '97	▽▽▽	8
○ Franciacorta Dosage Zéro '05	▽▽▽	7
○ Franciacorta Dosage Zéro '03	▽▽▽	7
○ Franciacorta Dosage Zéro '00	▽▽▽	8
○ Franciacorta Satèn '02	▽▽▽	7
○ TdF Chardonnay '02	▽▽▽	8

Ca' del Gè

FRAZ. CA' DEL GÈ, 3
27040 MONTALTO PAVESE [PV]
TEL. 0383870179
www.cadelge.it

CELLAR SALES
PRE-BOOKED VISITS

ANNUAL PRODUCTION 180,000 bottles
HECTARES UNDER VINE 45
VITICULTURE METHOD Conventional

Enzo Padroggi's death has left a void in Oltrepò and in all those who knew this man. Enzo was always ready to banter and debate, naturally in front of a glass of good wine, perhaps in his tasting room built on to a corner of his house, from which he occasionally took "special" bottles: oddities, experiments or old vintages. He was a man with a great love and enthusiasm for wine, which he conveyed to his daughters Sara and Stefania, who have now taken his place.

This year the Metodo Classico reached our finals for the second time running. It shows golden with a nose of cakes and citrus fruit, and a concentrated palate with an intriguing mineral vein and an impressively full finish. The two 2009 Rieslings are both good, giving peaches, flowers and tropical fruits, although we slightly preferred the more lingering Filagn Long. While not particularly complex or long, Pinot Nero '09 is nicely varietal and fragrant. Bonarda Vivace '09 and Chardonnay '09 are forthright and well typed.

○ OP Pinot Nero Brut Cl. '06	▼▼	5
● OP Bonarda La Fidela '04	▼▼	4
○ OP Riesling '09	▼▼	2*
○ OP Riesling Italico Filagn Long '09	▼▼	3*
○ Chardonnay '09	▼	3
● OP Bonarda Vivace '09	▼	3
● OP Pinot Nero '09	▼	4
● Dolcetto Tormento '97	▽▽	4
● OP Barbera '06	▽▽	2*
○ OP Pinot Nero Brut Cl. '05	▽▽	4
○ OP Riesling '08	▽▽	2*
○ OP Riesling '06	▽▽	2*
○ OP Riesling Italico Filagn Long '08	▽▽	3*
○ OP Riesling Renano V. Marinoni '04	▽▽	5

Ca' di Frara

VIA CASA FERRARI, 1
27040 MORNICO LOSANA [PV]
TEL. 0383892299
www.cadifrara.it

CELLAR SALES
PRE-BOOKED VISITS

ANNUAL PRODUCTION 400,000 bottles
HECTARES UNDER VINE 46
VITICULTURE METHOD Conventional

For many years Ca' di Frara has been a guarantee for those seeking quality wines in Oltrepò. Following the work commenced by his father Tullio, with the aid of his mother Daniela and brother Matteo, Luca Bellani has given the family winery a highly distinctive character. He has achieved this with a new cellar and vine stock combined with meticulous study of the vineyards, clones and woods. Luca imbues the natural weight of Oltrepò wines with the elegance and finesse that do not always emerge from a terroir whose maximum potential has yet to be fully expressed.

The Oltre il Classico project is the great adventure upon which the Bellanis have embarked in recent years. The fragrant, elegant Rosé Riserva '04 has a deep onionskin hue, nice complexity and impressive grip and backbone, making it a Pinot Nero Rosé in a class of its own. The other rosé, which now vaunts the Cruasé DOCG, is also very pleasant, showing fresh and fruity, as is the Blanc de Blancs with its notes of tropical fruits. The winery's classic Frater '07 is splendidly concentrated, balanced and fragrant while Riesling Apogeo '09 is floral, well defined and elegant. However, the entire range impresses.

⊙ OP Pinot Nero Brut Oltre il Classico Rosé Ris. '04	TT	6
● OP Rosso Il Frater Ris. '07	TT	6
○ Oltre il Classico Blanc de Blancs	TT	5
⊙ OP Pinot Nero Brut Oltre il Classico Cruasè	TT	5
● OP Pinot Nero Il Raro Nero '07	TT	5
○ OP Riesling Renano Apogeo Raccolta Tardiva '09	TT	4*
● OP Pinot Nero Pinot '09	T	5
● Io Rosso '03	YY	5
○ OP Pinot Grigio Raccolta Tardiva '04	YY	4
⊙ OP Pinot Nero Brut Oltre il Classico Rosé	YY	5
● OP Pinot Nero Il Raro '01	YY	5
○ OP Riesling Renano Apogeo Raccolta Tardiva '07	YY	4*
○ OP Riesling Renano Apogeo Raccolta Tardiva '06	YY	4*

Ca' Lojera

LOC. ROVIZZA
VIA 1886, 19
25019 SIRMIONE [BS]
TEL. 0457551901
www.calojera.com

CELLAR SALES
PRE-BOOKED VISITS

ANNUAL PRODUCTION 160,000 bottles
HECTARES UNDER VINE 18
VITICULTURE METHOD Conventional

Husband-and-wife team Ambra and Franco Tiraboschi are keen enthusiasts of country living and Lugana wine, to which they dedicate all their energy. Several years ago they purchased a handsome farmstead in Sirmione, where they built a state-of-the-art cellar and gradually added 18 hectares of vineyards. Their mission is to bring out the best in the wine and its terroir and their attentive, unhurriedly released selections once again reveal the potential for ageing of this excellent white.

Lugana del Lupo '08 is a good example of the winery's philosophy. It is a very generous, firmly structured white, released a year after harvest, which vaunts impressive fruit, but above all is starting to display the complex minerality and richness of flavour typical of the wine and the terroir. On the nose it offers fruit, flowers and fresh citrus, while the palate is well defined, balanced and taut, with great potential for ageing. Lugana Superiore '08 is elegantly evolved and attractively concentrated, while Lugana '09 is brimming with fruity freshness. Monte della Guardia Rosato '09 is fruity and easy drinking.

○ Lugana del Lupo '08	TT	5
○ Lugana '09	TT	4*
○ Lugana Sup. '08	TT	5
⊙ Monte della Guardia Rosato '09	T	3
○ Lugana '08	YY	4*
○ Lugana Riserva del Lupo '07	YY	5
○ Lugana Riserva del Lupo '06	YY	5
○ Lugana Sup. '06	YY	5
○ Lugana Sup. '05	YY	5
○ Ravel '05	YY	5

Il Calepino

via Surripe, 1
24060 Castelli Calepio [BG]
tel. 035847178
www.ilcalepino.it

CELLAR SALES
PRE-BOOKED VISITS

ANNUAL PRODUCTION 200,000 bottles
HECTARES UNDER VINE 15
VITICULTURE METHOD Conventional

Calepino is unquestionably the most interesting and varied estate in the province of Bergamo for quality and range. Although Metodo Classico sparklers are the leading wines on the list in an area in which this wine type is little esteemed, still wines made from the area's more established varieties, cabernet sauvignon, merlot and chardonnay, nonetheless always achieve high scores.

Riserva Fra' Ambrogio is still the best sparkler and immediately recognizable with its champagne-style development, notes of cakes and candied fruit, full palate and clean, well-defined finish. The Non Dosato is equally good, giving medicinal herbs, sage and basil, accompanied by impressive backbone and cleanliness. Clarity and intensity also characterize the Rosé, although it has a different aromatic profile, built around wild berries. Valcalepio Bianco Surie '08 is minerally, with attractive development, and Valcalepio Rosso '08 is also good, with nice structure and a nose of blueberries. Epias, a dried-grape wine from chardonnay, is as intriguing as ever.

⊙ Brut Cl. Non Dosato '05	▼▼	5
○ Brut Cl. Ris. Fra' Ambrogio '04	▼▼	5
⊙ Brut Cl. Rosé '04	▼▼	5
○ Chardonnay Epias	▼▼	6
○ Valcalepio Bianco Surie '08	▼▼	4
● Valcalepio Rosso '08	▼▼	4
○ Brut Cl. Il Calepino	▼	5
○ Brut Cl. Fra' Ambrogio Ris. '02	▽▽	5
○ Brut Cl. Il Calepino '05	▽▽	5
○ Brut Cl. Il Calepino '02	▽▽	4
⊙ Brut Cl. Rosé Il Calepino '05	▽▽	5
● Kalòs '04	▽▽	7
● Kalòs '00	▽▽	6
○ Valcalepio Bianco '08	▽▽	3*

Camossi

via Metelli, 5
25030 Erbusco [BS]
tel. 0307268022
www.camossi.it

CELLAR SALES

ANNUAL PRODUCTION 60,000 bottles
HECTARES UNDER VINE 24
VITICULTURE METHOD Conventional

During the early 1990s, the Camossi family converted their farm into a winery and produced their first bottles of Franciacorta in 1996. Today the cellar is manned by brothers Claudio and Dario, with the assistance of their parents and 85-year-old grandfather. The estate now has 24 hectares of vineyards, located in Erbusco, where the winery is based, Paratico and Provaglio, and a thoroughly decent production in terms of both quality and quantity.

Claudio and Dario's Franciacorta Extra Brut '06 made it through to our finals, where it performed well flaunting an elegant nose of aromatic herbs, with well-defined hints of apples and pears, and a tangy, smooth palate supported by fine acidity and a gentle sparkle. The smooth, supple Satèn offers a stylish nose of citrus fruit and vanilla, good body and firm structure, while the non-vintage Brut is fruity with attractive minerality. Franciacorta Rosé is goodish.

○ Franciacorta Extra Brut '06	▼▼	5
○ Franciacorta Brut	▼▼	5
○ Franciacorta Satèn	▼▼	4
⊙ Franciacorta Rosé	▼	5

Cantrina

FRAZ. CANTRINA
VIA COLOMBERA, 7
25081 BEDIZZOLE [BS]
TEL. 0306871052
www.cantrina.it

CELLAR SALES
PRE-BOOKED VISITS

ANNUAL PRODUCTION **25,000 bottles**
HECTARES UNDER VINE **6**
VITICULTURE METHOD **Conventional**

Cantrina is a small estate of just under six hectares in Bedizzole in Valtènensi, in the Lombard hinterland of Lake Garda. It is enthusiastically and creatively managed by Cristina Inganni, who is also vice-president of the Consorzio della Valtènensi, and Diego Lavo, with the aid of consultant oenologist Celestino Gaspari. Named after the hamlet in which it is located, the winery started off with vineyards planted mainly to international varieties but over the years local varieties have gradually been added.

Cantrina's wines are interesting. Nepomuceno '06 is a nice deep ruby with concentrated overripe red and black berries, freshly mown hay and a hint of capsicum. The smooth, full palate has plenty of fruit and evolving tannins. Groppello '09 is very elegant, well typed and supple, and the white Rinè '08, from chardonnay, incrocio Manzoni and riesling, is as interesting as ever, presenting firm and fresh, with well-integrated new oak. Il Sole di Dario, a sweet dried-grape wine from sauvignon, sémillon and riesling, is excellent, giving tropical fruit. Libero Esercizio di Stile Rosato '09 and Eretico '07, a red dried-grape wine from pinot nero, are both interesting.

● Garda Cl. Groppello '09	TT	4*
● Nepomuceno '06	TT	6
○ Rinè '08	TT	4*
○ Sole di Dario '06	TT	6
● Eretico '07	T	6
⊙ Libero Esercizio di Stile Rosato '09	T	4
● Garda Cl. Groppello '08	YY	4
● Nepomuceno Esercizio 5 '05	YY	6
○ Rinè '07	YY	4
○ Sole di Dario	YY	6

Cascina la Pertica

LOC. PICEDO
VIA ROSARIO, 44
25080 POLPENAZZE DEL GARDA [BS]
TEL. 0365651471
www.cascinalapertica.it

CELLAR SALES
PRE-BOOKED VISITS

ANNUAL PRODUCTION **40,000 bottles**
HECTARES UNDER VINE **11**
VITICULTURE METHOD **Certified biodynamic**

Several years ago, successful businessman Ruggero Brunori decided to found an estate to produce wine his way, using natural systems with a low environmental impact. Over the years, the input of winery manager Andrea Salvetti has helped this take hold and today the estate's 14 hectares in the morainic hills overlooking Lake Garda are farmed biodynamically. The mainly clay soils give the wines structure and freshness.

While awaiting the new Cabernet Le Zalte, still ageing in the cellar, we tasted Papuc '09, an intriguing deep ruby Marzemino with an elegant nose of black and red berry fruit and hints of dried roses, spice and chocolate. On the palate it's firm and highly drinkable. The delicately tannic Groppello Il Colombaio '09 is equally sound and focuses on elegance and balance. Ronco del Garda '09 is a pleasant red with a fruity nose of citrus and cocoa powder, and a fresh, supple palate. We liked Garda Chardonnay Le Sincette '09, which presents straw yellow with coppery highlights and a full-flavoured almondy palate. Chiaretto '09 and Garda Rosso '07 are both good.

○ Garda Chardonnay Le Sincette '09	TT	4*
● Garda Cl. Groppello Il Colombaio '09	TT	4*
● Il Marzemino Papüc '09	TT	4*
⊙ Garda Cl. Chiaretto Le Sincette '09	T	4
● Garda Cl. Rosso Le Sincette '07	T	5
● Ronco del Garda '09	T	3
● Garda Cabernet Le Zalte '07	YYY	7
● Garda Cabernet Le Zalte '06	YY	7
● Garda Cl. Groppello Il Colombaio '08	YY	4
● Garda Cl. Groppello Il Colombaio '07	YY	4*
● Garda Cl. Rosso Le Sincette '05	YY	5
○ Le Sincette Bianco '08	YY	4

CastelFaglia

FRAZ. CALINO
LOC. BOSCHI, 3
25046 CAZZAGO SAN MARTINO [BS]
TEL. 059812411
www.cavicchioli.it

CELLAR SALES
PRE-BOOKED VISITS

ANNUAL PRODUCTION 250,000 bottles
HECTARES UNDER VINE 20
VITICULTURE METHOD Conventional

The Cavicchiolis are a famous Modena wine family with a passion for sparklers – they also own Bellei Spumanti – and are renowned for their Lambruscos. A few years ago they set up this winery in Franciacorta, purchasing the historic property at the foot of the Faglia castle in Calino with around 20 hectares of vineyards in a well-aspected position on the hillside, approximately 300 metres above sea level. Output is high, in quantity and quality, and the wine is made entirely from estate-grown grapes.

The winery's oenologist Sandro Cavicchioli offers a wide range divided into several different lines. We especially liked the Blanc de Blancs of the Monogram range with its well-defined fruity notes, creamy effervescence and lingering aromas. Brut Monogram Magnum stands out for its attractive notes of toast and hazelnuts, fresh palate and overall balance. The well-made, varietal Rosé and Satèn of the same range are a rung below. The same two products are better in the Castelfaglia range and the other wines are well made.

○ Franciacorta Blanc de Blancs Monogram	▼▼	5
○ Franciacorta Brut Monogram Magnum	▼▼	6
⊙ Franciacorta Rosé Brut	▼▼	6
○ Franciacorta Satèn	▼▼	6
○ Curtefranca Bianco Prestigio '09	▼	4
● Curtefranca Rosso Prestigio '08	▼	4
○ Franciacorta Brut	▼	5
○ Franciacorta Extra Brut	▼	5
⊙ Franciacorta Rosé Monogram	▼	6
○ Franciacorta Satèn Monogram	▼	6
○ Franciacorta Monogram Brut Cuvée Giunone	▽▽	6
○ Franciacorta Satèn	▽▽	6
○ Franciacorta Satèn Blanc de Blancs	▽▽	6
○ Franciacorta Satèn Monogram	▽▽	6

Castello Bonomi

VIA SAN PIETRO, 46
25030 COCCAGLIO [BS]
TEL. 0307721015
www.tenutabonomi.it

CELLAR SALES
PRE-BOOKED VISITS

ANNUAL PRODUCTION 148,000 bottles
HECTARES UNDER VINE 17
VITICULTURE METHOD Conventional

The handsome Art Nouveau villa at the centre of the estate, on the slopes of the natural circus of Monte Orfano in the southern reaches of Franciacorta, gives this winery a château-like air. The surrounding vineyards are high-density, low-yield plantings, mostly on terraces that rise to almost 300 metres above sea level and are surrounded by woodland. This is ideal territory for vines, which yield excellent base wines for Franciacortas. Recently purchased by the Paladin family, a famous name in the Veneto wine world, the estate is currently having a makeover.

The feather in the winery's cap is Brut Cru Perdu, a 70-30 blend of chardonnay and pinot nero from a recently revived old vineyard. It ages on the lees for over two and a half years, followed by six months in bottle, and shows a handsome bright greenish-yellow with a fresh nose of aromatic herbs and red berry fruit and a vibrant, invigorating, zesty, full palate. Franciacorta Rosé is excellent, with attractive notes of raspberries and wild strawberries, while the smooth, creamy Satèn is perhaps a little overwhelmed by new oak. Curtefranca Rosso Cordelio '07 is firm with good structure.

○ Franciacorta Brut Cru Perdu	▼▼	8
● Curtefranca Rosso Cordelio '07	▼▼	5
⊙ Franciacorta Rosé	▼▼	6
○ Franciacorta Satèn	▼▼	6
○ Franciacorta Brut	▼	6
○ Franciacorta Brut Cru Perdu '05	▽▽	6
○ Franciacorta Extra Brut Lucrezia '01	▽▽	8
○ TdF Bianco Curtefranca Solicano '07	▽▽	4*
○ TdF Bianco Curtefranca Solicano '06	▽▽	4
○ TdF Bianco Curtefranca Solicano '04	▽▽	4
● TdF Rosso Curtefranca Cordelio '06	▽▽	5
● TdF Rosso Curtefranca Cordelio '05	▽▽	5
● TdF Rosso Curtefranca Cordelio '04	▽▽	5

Castello di Cigognola

P.ZZA CASTELLO, 1
27040 CIGOGNOLA [PV]
TEL. 0385284828
www.castellodicigognola

CELLAR SALES
PRE-BOOKED VISITS

ANNUAL PRODUCTION 40,000 bottles
HECTARES UNDER VINE 17
VITICULTURE METHOD Conventional

Castello di Cignola, owned by the Moratti family, is a historic property in the foothills overlooking the Po valley. The estate currently grows only barbera grapes, used to make two different wines: one aged with more oak and a younger wine. However, its manager Emilio De Filippi and Gianmarco Moratti, under the supervision of Riccardo Cotarella, are planning to expand the range gradually, adding Pinot Nero and Metodo Classico wines.

For the third year running, the flagship Barbera – simply called Castello di Cignola, although the 2005 vintage of the same wine went by the name of Poggio della Maga – easily earned Three Glasses. The stylistic features of the '07 match those of its predecessors: top-quality oak, very pleasant vanilla and spice that do not mask the fruity notes of slightly overripe cherries, and a very long finish with hints of cinchona and liquorice. Barbera Dodicidodici '08 has very ripe fruit and is simpler and highly drinkable.

● OP Barbera Castello di Cigognola '07	TTT	7
● OP Barbera Dodicidodici '08	TT	5
● OP Barbera Castello di Cigognola '06	YYY	7
● OP Barbera Poggio Della Maga '05	YYY	8
● OP Barbera '04	YY	6
● OP Barbera '03	YY	6
● OP Barbera Dodicidodici '07	YY	5
● OP Barbera Dodicidodici '06	YY	5

Cavalleri

VIA PROVINCIALE, 96
25030 ERBUSCO [BS]
TEL. 0307760217
www.cavalleri.it

CELLAR SALES
PRE-BOOKED VISITS

ANNUAL PRODUCTION 250,000 bottles
HECTARES UNDER VINE 43
VITICULTURE METHOD Conventional

Cavalleri was already an important name in Franciacorta in the mid 15th century. The family have always been landowners and growers, although the winery wasn't founded until the late 1960s with the establishment of the designation. Giovanni Cavalleri was the driving force and one of the most representative figures of the zone from its foundation until recently. This family-run estate's flagship wine is named after him. Today the winery is headed by his daughter Giulia, aided by a skilled team that works in a handsome state-of-the-art cellar.

While awaiting the new Collezione Esclusiva, we recommend the Three-Glass-winning Brut Collezione '05, an extraordinarily well-defined, balanced Franciacorta that is impressively dense and long, one of the finest examples of its type. Pas Dosé '06 is almost as good, with attractive floral hints on the nose and a savoury, edgy palate with a long finish. The Satèn is again among the best of its kind, with delicate, velvety notes of white-fleshed fruits, which are even more prominent in the Blanc de Blancs, where they meld with good acidity. The other wines are well made.

○ Franciacorta Collezione Brut '05	TTT	7
○ Franciacorta Pas Dosé '06	TT	6
○ Curtefranca Bianco '09	TT	4
○ Curtefranca Bianco Rampaneto '08	TT	5
● Curtefranca Rosso Tajardino '07	TT	6
○ Franciacorta Brut Blanc de Blancs	TT	6
⊙ Franciacorta Collezione Rosé '05	TT	7
○ Franciacorta Satèn	TT	6
● Curtefranca Rosso '08	T	4
○ Franciacorta Au Contraire Pas Dosé '01	YYY	8
○ Franciacorta Brut Collezione Esclusiva Giovanni Cavalleri '01	YYY	8
○ Franciacorta Collezione Brut '99	YYY	6
○ Franciacorta Collezione Brut '94	YYY	6
○ Franciacorta Collezione Esclusiva Brut '99	YYY	8

Clastidio Ballabio

via San Biagio, 32
27045 Casteggio [PV]
tel. 0383805728
www.ballabio.net

CELLAR SALES
PRE-BOOKED VISITS

ANNUAL PRODUCTION 26,000 bottles
HECTARES UNDER VINE 27
VITICULTURE METHOD Conventional

In 1905, Brianza-born Angelo Ballabio discovered this splendid corner of Oltrepò, fell in love with it and founded the winery that still bears his name. Laden with history and international awards, Ballabio was a benchmark for quality wines throughout the 20th century. Now the glorious estate is owned by businessman Filippo Nevelli, who has very clear ideas about its comeback in grand style, including the production of high-quality olive oil.

The winery has embraced the collective name Cruasé that identifies rosé Metodo Classico from 100 per cent pinot nero. Its Cruasé '07 has an attractive pale onionskin and an elegant nose of wild berries with aromatic herbs and gentian faithfully reflected on the impressively balanced palate with nice fruity body. Bonarda Vivace Vigna delle Cento Pertiche is very good with earthy local flavour. It boasts a medium ruby hue and a nose of plums and wild berries. Pinot Nero Clastidium '08 is interesting and very true to type, while Narbusto, a monovarietal Merlot, is pleasant.

● Clastidium di Pinot Nero '08	▼▼	4
● Narbusto '09	▼▼	4
● OP Bonarda Vivace Vigna Delle Cento Pertiche '09	▼▼	4
⊙ OP Pinot Nero Brut Cl. Cruasé '07	▼▼	5
⊙ Pinot Nero Rosé Clastidium '09	▼	4
● Clastidium di Pinot Nero '07	▽▽	4*
● OP Bonarda Vivace Delle Cento Pertiche '08	▽▽	4*
● OP Bonarda Vivace Le Cento Pertiche '02	▽▽	3
● OP Bonarda Vivace Le Cento Pertiche '01	▽▽	3*
● OP Bonarda Vivace Le Cento Pertiche '00	▽▽	3*

Battista Cola

via Indipendenza, 3
25030 Adro [BS]
tel. 0307356195
www.colabattista.it

CELLAR SALES
PRE-BOOKED VISITS

ANNUAL PRODUCTION 60,000 bottles
HECTARES UNDER VINE 10
VITICULTURE METHOD Conventional

The Colas' strength lies in their ten hectares of beautifully aspected vineyards on the slopes of Monte Alto, between Adro and Cortefranca. With the aid of consultant oenologist Alberto Musatti, each year Stefano Cola presents an array of first-rate cuvées and excellent red and white Curtefrancas. The winery was founded by his father Battista and during the mid 1980s acquired modern equipment and started to purchase new vineyards for the production of Franciacorta.

Stefano's range of Franciacortas is always good. The winery's pride and joy is its Dosage Zéro Etichette Storica, in this case the '06 vintage. An exemplary Franciacorta, it shows elegant and well-profiled, zesty and refreshing, with a nose bursting with white-fleshed fruit and aromatic herbs preceding a cosseting palate with good development and a long mineral finish. It is flanked by the Brut '06, with a fruity nose with hints of balsam and an attractive evolved style. The trio is completed by a very pleasant Satèn that, while not particularly clean on the nose, offers an exceptionally expressive palate. The basic Brut is very decent.

○ Franciacorta Dosage Zéro Etichetta Storica '06	▼▼	6
○ Franciacorta Brut '06	▼▼	5
○ Franciacorta Brut	▼▼	5
○ Franciacorta Satèn '06	▼▼	6
● Curtefranca Rosso '07	▼	3
○ Franciacorta Extra Brut	▼	5
○ Chardonnay '08	▽▽	4*
○ Franciacorta Brut '02	▽▽	6
○ Franciacorta Dosage Zéro Etichetta Storica '05	▽▽	5
○ TdF Bianco Sel. '94	▽▽	3
○ TdF Bianco V. Tinazza '01	▽▽	4*
● TdF Rosso Tamino '03	▽▽	4*

Contadi Castaldi

LOC. FORNACE BIASCA
VIA COLZANO, 32
25030 ADRO [BS]
TEL. 0307450126
www.contadicastaldi.it

CELLAR SALES
PRE-BOOKED VISITS

ANNUAL PRODUCTION 900,000 bottles
HECTARES UNDER VINE 130
VITICULTURE METHOD Conventional

Contadi Castaldi is the second estate founded by the Moretti family in Franciacorta. Based on the merchant-producer model, it was established to extend the group's range of Franciacortas without involving Bellavista. Over the years, it has developed a formula whereby the Contadi Castaldi team oversees the vineyards of its suppliers, in this sense operating like a large agricultural company. Today, the 120 contracted hectares yield an impressive 750,000 top-quality bottles. Production has recently been entrusted to oenologist Gian Luca Uccelli.

The wine that most impressed us during this year's tastings was Dosaggio Zero '06, which performed well in our finals with its perfectly integrated effervescence, rich fruit, good backbone and impressive overall balance. The range also flaunts a trio of stylistically exemplary wines, comprising a full Brut with good minerality, a smooth, juicy Satèn that is dynamic and refreshing, and a Rosé '06 with delightful wild strawberries and raspberries. Curtefranca Bianco '09 is as well made as ever, although Satèn Soul '03 is slightly over-evolved and less alluring than usual.

○ Franciacorta Dosage Zéro '06	▼▼	6
○ Curtefranca Bianco '09	▼▼	4*
○ Franciacorta Brut	▼▼	5
⊙ Franciacorta Rosé '06	▼▼	6
○ Franciacorta Satèn '06	▼▼	6
● Curtefranca Rosso '07	▼	4
⊙ Franciacorta Rosé	▼	5
○ Franciacorta Soul Satèn '03	▼	7
○ Pinodisé	▼	6
⊙ Franciacorta Brut Rosé '05	▽▽	6
⊙ Franciacorta Brut Rosé	▽▽	5
○ Franciacorta Satèn	▽▽	6
○ Franciacorta Soul Satèn '01	▽▽	7
○ Franciacorta Zéro '05	▽▽	6

Costaripa

VIA COSTA, 1A
25080 MONIGA DEL GARDA [BS]
TEL. 0365502010
www.costaripa.it

CELLAR SALES
PRE-BOOKED VISITS

ANNUAL PRODUCTION 300,000 bottles
HECTARES UNDER VINE 36
VITICULTURE METHOD Conventional

Renowned as one of the most talented Italian oenologists – and sparkling winemakers – Mattia Vezzola also finds time for the estate set up by his grandfather and after whom he is named. It is located in Moniga, on Lake Garda, where the soil and site climates are ideal for viticulture, a far northern strip of Mediterranean vegetation, where vineyards alternate with citrus trees and olive groves. Over the years, Costaripa has expanded to its impressive 36 hectares under vine, from which Mattia makes a wide range of local wines.

Groppello Maim is the estate's most interesting wine. It is also one of the best attempts to make a native red that emphasizes finesse and suppleness, a sort of little Burgundy. Judging by its well-defined aromas of red and black berry fruits, it's not far off. However, sparklers are in Mattia's blood and our favourite this year was the Brut Riserva '04 with its elegant floral nose and zesty, creamy palate. Chiaretto Molmenti '09 is an atypical rosé, which focuses not only on youthful fruitiness but aspires to more complex, mineral aromas with age. All the other wines are well made.

○ Costaripa Brut Ris. '04	▼▼	5
● Garda Cl. Groppello Maim '08	▼▼	5
⊙ Costaripa Brut Rosé	▼▼	5
⊙ Garda Cl. Chiaretto Molmenti '09	▼▼	5
⊙ Garda Cl. Chiaretto Molmenti '09	▼▼	5
● Garda Cl. Groppello Castelline '09	▼▼	4*
○ Costaripa Brut	▼	5
⊙ Garda Cl. Chiaretto Rosamara '09	▼	4
● Garda Cl. Rosso Campostarne '08	▼	4
● Garda Marzemino Mazane '09	▼	4
○ Lugana Pievecroce '09	▼	4
● Garda Cabernet Sauvignon Pradamonte '07	▽▽	5
⊙ Garda Cl. Chiaretto Molmenti '08	▽▽	5
● Garda Cl. Groppello Vign. Le Castelline '08	▽▽	4*
● Garda Marzemino Mazane '08	▽▽	4*
● Marzemino Le Mazane '08	▽▽	4

Dirupi

loc. Madonna di Campagna
via Grumello, 1
23020 Montagna in Valtellina [SO]
tel. 3472909779
www.dirupi.com

ANNUAL PRODUCTION N.A.
HECTARES UNDER VINE 4
VITICULTURE METHOD Conventional

All the ingredients were there: enthusiasm, expertise, a pinch of madness, willingness and great love for the land and for growing. Good wines were the natural consequence. This is how the story of Davide Fasolini and Pierpaolo Di Franco, young oenologists and Dirupi's founders, commenced. The estate has almost four hectares of vineyards divided into 18 lots, situated between 400 and 650 metres above sea level, all with Guyot-trained vines, part of which are currently being converted to organic farming methods.

This is estate is likely to represent the dynamic young face of Valtellina winemaking in the near future, as demonstrated by a great Nebbiolo that reached our finals: Dirupi Riserva '07 is a brilliant prototype of what this terroir can produce. With a production run of around 3,000 bottles, it aged in large barrels for two years and a further year in bottle. The concentrated nose offers notes of Alpine flowers and the complex, velvety palate has unusual grip and richness of flavour. Dirupi '08 is very good, with a concentrated floral nose and a rounded, liquorice-veined palate. Olé! is fresh, fruity and alluring while Nebbiolo '09 has a well-made, flavoursome palate.

● Valtellina Sup. '08	▼▼	5
● Valtellina Sup. Ris. '07	▼▼	7
● Nebbiolo Olè '09	▼▼	5
● Nebbiolo Olè '07	▽▽	5

Doria

loc. Casa Tacconi, 3
27040 Montalto Pavese [PV]
tel. 0383870143
www.vinidoria.com

CELLAR SALES
PRE-BOOKED VISITS
ROOMS AND FOOD

ANNUAL PRODUCTION 120,000 bottles
HECTARES UNDER VINE 28
VITICULTURE METHOD Certified organic

The Doria family, represented by Giuseppina with the support of her children and Viterbo oenologist-cum-cellar master Daniele Manini, run this gem of an estate in the western part of Montalto Pavese, on the road that leads down to Calvignano. The prevalently white soil is suited to the cultivation of white grape varieties, particularly riesling renano, which is the winery's pride and joy. Meticulous care in vineyards and cellar, plus the rediscovery of old traditions, are the cornerstones of production.

And speaking of old traditions, the winery uses only chestnut barrels from central Italy for its Barbera AD. The result is unique, with aromas reminiscent of chestnut flour, along with spice and liquorice, which enhance a wine with firm acid backbone and a strong personality. It is a bottle that you either love or hate. We love it, year after year. Riesling Roncobianco '07 has reached the stage where the last primary notes are fading, replaced by clear mineral and petrol ones. Bonarda Vivace '09 and the Contessa riesling-based sparkler are good. Brut Martinotti, from pinot nero, and Rosso Riserva Roncorosso '07 are a rung below.

○ Contessa Brut Martinotti	▼▼	6
● OP Barbera A.D. '07	▼▼	5
● OP Bonarda Frizzante '09	▼▼	4*
○ OP Riesling Renano Roncobianco '07	▼▼	5
○ OP Pinot Nero Brut Martinotti Querciolo	▼	5
● OP Rosso Roncorosso Ris. '07	▼	4
● OP Barbera A.D. '06	▽▽	5
● OP Barbera A.D. '05	▽▽	5
● OP Bonarda Vivace '06	▽▽	4*
○ OP Pinot Nero in bianco Querciolo '03	▽▽	4
○ OP Riesling Renano Roncobianco '03	▽▽	4
● OP Rosso Roncorosso '03	▽▽	4
● Rosso A.D. Memorial '04	▽▽	6

Sandro Fay

LOC. SAN GIACOMO DI TEGLIO
VIA PILA CASELLI, 1
23030 TEGLIO [SO]
TEL. 0342786071
elefay@tin.it

CELLAR SALES
PRE-BOOKED VISITS

ANNUAL PRODUCTION 38,000 bottles
HECTARES UNDER VINE 13
VITICULTURE METHOD Conventional

Although it's generally not a great idea to change a winning team, the roles have changed at Fay and, with Sandro's approval, his son Marco is playing an increasingly important role in the rapid progress of this farsighted winery. That's not all, because a new generation of producers is emerging in Valtellina. Marco Fay is one of them and indeed a benchmark, particularly in terms of viticultural research. In short, he is mapping out Valtellina's future.

Carteria '07 came within a hair's breadth of Three Glasses. This monovarietal Nebbiolo, made from grapes grown 450 metres above sea level in the heart of the Valgella zone on Guyot-trained vines harvested in mid September, has a balsamic nose with notes of dried flowers and a concentrated, fresh, balanced palate that finishes long. Cà Morei '07 has warm, complex aromas and full-bodied texture, supported by excellent acidity and balance. The elegantly austere Nebbiolo '07 was a pleasant surprise, displaying a fruity nose with aromatic herbs and a complex palate with lingering liquorice. Glicene '07 has a fragrant, complex nose and a characterful palate with good acidity.

● Nebbiolo '07	▼▼	4
● Valtellina Sup. Valgella Carterìa '07	▼▼	5
● Valtellina Sup. Sassella Il Glicine '07	▼▼	5
● Valtellina Sup. Valgella Ca' Morèi '07	▼▼	5
● Valtellina Sforzato Ronco del Picchio '02	▽▽▽	7
● La Faya '06	▽▽	5
● La Faya '05	▽▽	5
● Valtellina Sforzato Ronco del Picchio '06	▽▽	7
● Valtellina Sforzato Ronco del Picchio '05	▽▽	7
● Valtellina Sup. Sassella Il Glicine '06	▽▽	5
● Valtellina Sup. Sassella Il Glicine '05	▽▽	5
● Valtellina Sup. Valgella Ca' Morèi '06	▽▽	5
● Valtellina Sup. Valgella Carterìa '06	▽▽	5
● Valtellina Sup. Valgella Carterìa '05	▽▽	5

Ferghettina

VIA SALINE, 11
25030 ADRO [BS]
TEL. 0307451212
www.ferghettina.it

CELLAR SALES
PRE-BOOKED VISITS

ANNUAL PRODUCTION 350,000 bottles
HECTARES UNDER VINE 120
VITICULTURE METHOD Conventional

The Gatti family's adventure commenced in 1990, when Roberto, who had previously worked as cellarmaster in other Franciacorta wineries, decided to purchase the first four hectares in Erbusco. Today, Roberto and his wife Andreina, together with their children, oenologist Laura and student oenologist Matteo, manage 120 hectares of vineyards in six different municipalities of the designation and produce their wines in their well-equipped new cellar in Adro. Ferghettina has made excellent wines for many years and is one of the benchmarks for the designation.

This year, the inevitable Three Glasses rewarded the excellent Extra Brut '04, with its very fine bead, a captivatingly complex nose of ripe fruit, honey and vanilla, and an alluringly elegant, balanced, juicy palate The Satèn '06 is one of the best of its kind and manages to be smooth and cosseting without losing anything in freshness or drinkability thanks to the crisp, well-defined fruit that accompanies a long citrus finish. The Brut '06 is complex and layered while Franciacorta Brut and Curtefranca Bianco are very well made.

○ Franciacorta Extra Brut '04	▼▼▼	6
○ Franciacorta Satèn '06	▼▼	6
○ Curtefranca Bianco '09	▼▼	4
○ Franciacorta Brut '06	▼▼	6
○ Franciacorta Brut	▼▼	6
● Curtefranca Rosso '07	▼	4
⊙ Franciacorta Rosé '06	▼	6
○ Franciacorta Extra Brut '02	▽▽▽	6
○ Franciacorta Extra Brut '98	▽▽▽	6
○ Franciacorta Satèn '04	▽▽▽	6
○ Franciacorta Satèn '99	▽▽▽	6
○ Franciacorta Satèn '97	▽▽▽	5*
○ Franciacorta Satèn '05	▽▽	6

Le Fracce

FRAZ. MAIRANO
VIA CASTEL DEL LUPO, 5
27045 CASTEGGIO [PV]
TEL. 038382526
www.lefracce.com

CELLAR SALES
PRE-BOOKED VISITS

ANNUAL PRODUCTION 180,000 bottles
HECTARES UNDER VINE 40
VITICULTURE METHOD Conventional

This handsome estate is set in splendid grounds, with a building housing old carriages, vintage cars and more. The average level of the wines is always very good, although they tend to lack the extra something that would allow them access to our finals. The estate's longstanding wines have been joined by white and rosé Metodo Classico sparklers, which are now stacked in the dark, patiently awaiting the right moment for release. The tastings with disgorgement "à la volée" were promising.

Riesling Landò has returned to the high level of several years ago. The '09 vintage is floral and zesty with a faint mineral note destined to become more prominent over the years. Rosso Cirgà '05 is as good as ever, with attractive red berry fruit accompanied by an array of spices, roasted coffee beans, tobacco and liquorice, and a very long finish. Bonarda Vivace Rubiosa '09 is among the best from Oltrepò, showing a bright ruby with notes of blueberry. Bohemi '04, the estate's flagship wine, requires further bottle ageing for the oak to settle but prospects are good. Barbera Garboso '08, in contrast, is already excellent, showing well defined, fragrant and very pleasant.

● Garboso '08	2 black glasses	4*
● OP Bonarda Frizzante La Rubiosa '09	2 black glasses	4*
○ OP Riesling Landò '09	2 black glasses	4*
● OP Rosso Bohemi '04	2 black glasses	6
● OP Rosso Cirgà '05	2 black glasses	5
○ OP Pinot Grigio Levriere '09	1 black glass	4
● OP Pinot Nero '06	1 black glass	5
● Barbera Garboso '06	2 white glasses	4*
● OP Bonarda La Rubiosa '06	2 white glasses	4*
● OP Bonarda La Rubiosa '05	2 white glasses	4
● OP Pinot Nero '03	2 white glasses	6
● OP Rosso Bohemi '03	2 white glasses	6
● OP Rosso Bohemi '01	2 white glasses	6
● OP Rosso Cirgà '04	2 white glasses	5

Frecciarossa

VIA VIGORELLI, 141
27045 CASTEGGIO [PV]
TEL. 0383804465
www.frecciarossa.com

CELLAR SALES
PRE-BOOKED VISITS

ANNUAL PRODUCTION 150,000 bottles
HECTARES UNDER VINE 20
VITICULTURE METHOD Conventional

The Odero family's estate is one of Oltrepò's oldest and most illustrious, with a villa dominating the valley and a cellar. There's an old part and a newer one, situated exactly on the 45th parallel, considered the ideal latitude for viticulture around the world. The villa also has a large, welcoming new tasting room on the top floor. The winery has always stood out chiefly for its high-quality reds.

Indeed, this year Giorgio Odero '07, a red Pinot Nero, took our top accolade, a feat it had already achieved in 2005. It's a classy wine that shows terroir-true with handsome balsamic notes, deep and well typed. Le Praielle '07, a Barbera DOC, is very good and exceptional value for money. Fragrant, fruity and exuberant, it will not disappoint fans of this oft-underrated grape. The current Riesling Gli Orti and Bonarda Vivace Dardo are both very well typed. Uva Rara – one of the few instances of separate fermentation of this native variety – and the sparkling white Nai are pleasant.

● OP Pinot Nero Giorgio Odero '07	3 black glasses	6
● OP Barbera Le Praielle '07	2 black glasses	3*
● OP Bonarda Vivace Dardo '09	2 black glasses	3*
○ OP Riesling Renano Gli Orti '09	2 black glasses	4*
○ Nai '09	1 black glass	4
● Uva Rara '09	1 black glass	4
● OP Pinot Nero Giorgio Odero '05	3 white glasses	6
● OP Bonarda Vivace Dardo '06	2 white glasses	4*
● OP Pinot Nero Giorgio Odero '06	2 white glasses	6
● OP Pinot Nero Giorgio Odero '03	2 white glasses	5
● OP Pinot Nero Giorgio Odero '00	2 white glasses	5
○ OP Riesling Renano Gli Orti '08	2 white glasses	4*

Gatta

via San Rocco, 33/37
25064 Gussago [BS]
tel. 0302772950
www.agricolagatta.com

CELLAR SALES
PRE-BOOKED VISITS

ANNUAL PRODUCTION 100,000 bottles
HECTARES UNDER VINE 25
VITICULTURE METHOD Conventional

Mario Gatta continues the tradition commenced in the 1970s by his father Angelo, who planted the first vines. The vineyard still yields today a wine that has been given Angelo's nickname, "Negus". Mario is flanked by his brother Sergio, his wife Donatella and their sons Nicola and Giuseppe, who form a close-knit team that deals with everything, from tending the 25 hectares of vines at Cellatica and Gussago, on the westernmost slopes of Franciacorta, to marketing the wines.

From time to time, the Gattas offer freshly disgorged old vintages, which are generally very interesting cuvées. This is true of Brut Riserva Arcano '97, a deep, complex, minerally wine. The "recent" wines include an excellent Rosé Extra Brut, with an enchanting nose of wild strawberries and a lean but not stringy palate, which is invigorating and supple. Franciacorta Brut is full flavoured, smooth and rounded, with a slightly evolved finish, but we were less keen on the Extra Brut, which we found a little edgy. Cellatica Negus '03, which we had already tasted last year, is sound and Terre Bianco Febo '05 is good.

○ Franciacorta Brut	▼▼	4
○ Franciacorta Brut Arcano Ris. '97	▼▼	7
⊙ Franciacorta Extra Brut Rosé	▼▼	5
○ Franciacorta Dosage Zéro	▼	5
○ TdF Curtefranca Febo '05	▼	3
● Balench '00	▽▽	5*
● Cellatica Sup. Negus '03	▽▽	4
○ Febo '98	▽▽	4
○ Franciacorta Brut Arcano '94	▽▽	7
○ Franciacorta Brut Satèn '99	▽▽	5
○ Franciacorta Satèn '97	▽▽	5
● TdF Rosso Curtefranca '01	▽▽	4*

Enrico Gatti

via Metelli, 9
25030 Erbusco [BS]
tel. 0307267999
www.enricogatti.it

CELLAR SALES
PRE-BOOKED VISITS

ANNUAL PRODUCTION 120,000 bottles
HECTARES UNDER VINE 17
VITICULTURE METHOD Conventional

Lorenzo Gatti and his sister Paola, with her husband Enzo Balzarini, have taken over from their father Enrico, who founded this estate in 1975. They have made it into a genuine boutique winery, with an exceptionally well-equipped cellar, whose wines are produced exclusively from their 17 hectares of vineyards. The Franciacortas have made firm structure and elegant minerality the estate's hallmarks. In spite of the relatively low annual production of just over 120,000 bottles, this Erbusco winery has become one of the top names in Franciacorta.

Once again, the Gattis have won our top accolade, this time with an excellent Franciacorta Brut '05, a monovarietal Chardonnay aged on the lees for five years. It is a deep, enthralling, multifaceted wine with exceptional balance that shows refreshing and elegant with a lingering finish. Nature is almost as good, to the extent of "risking" another Three Glass award. Another Blanc de Blancs, it is incredibly fresh with a balanced, fruity finale. Satèn '06 is complex, dense and smooth in classic Gatti style. The Brut is very decent and the Rosé well made.

○ Franciacorta Brut '05	▼▼▼	5
○ Franciacorta Nature	▼▼	6
○ Franciacorta Brut	▼▼	5
○ Franciacorta Satèn '06	▼▼	6
⊙ Franciacorta Rosè	▼	6
○ Franciacorta Satèn '05	▽▽▽	6
○ Franciacorta Satèn '03	▽▽▽	6
○ Franciacorta Satèn '02	▽▽▽	6
○ Franciacorta Satèn '01	▽▽▽	5
○ Franciacorta Satèn '00	▽▽▽	6
○ Franciacorta Brut	▽▽	5*
○ Franciacorta Satèn '98	▽▽	5

F.lli Giorgi

FRAZ. CAMPONOCE, 39A
27044 CANNETO PAVESE [PV]
TEL. 0385262151
www.giorgi-wines.it

CELLAR SALES
PRE-BOOKED VISITS

ANNUAL PRODUCTION 1,600,000 bottles
HECTARES UNDER VINE 30
VITICULTURE METHOD Conventional

It has been very interesting to watch this winery develop over the past few years. Antonio Giorgi and his oenologist brother, the late Gianfranco, laid the groundwork for high-quality production despite the large numbers involved. You'll never come across a flawed wine by Fratelli Giorgi, even in their most economical labels, and the enthusiasm of Fabiano, Antonio's son, has allowed the winery to achieve ever-higher standards of quality.

Metodo Classico has always been the family's passion. The complex 1870 '06 has repeated the Three Glasses won last year by the '05 with its remarkable backbone and fullness. It's an ideal wine to drink through the meal. The other Metodo Classicos are also better this year – the Gianfranco Giorgi white and the Cruasé, both '07 – showing more complex and vibrant. Buttafuoco Storico Vigna Casa del Corno '06 is the very first of its kind to reach our finals. It has aromas of mint and chocolate, with charming overripe notes. There's not enough room to describe the other wines but the scores do the talking.

○ OP Pinot Nero Brut Cl. 1870 '06	▼▼▼	6
● OP Buttafuoco Storico Casa del Corno '06	▼▼	4
● OP Bonarda Frizzante La Brughera '09	▼▼	4*
⊙ OP Pinot Nero Brut Cl. Cruasé Gianfranco Giorgi '07	▼▼	5
○ OP Pinot Nero Brut Cl. Gianfranco Giorgi '07	▼▼	6
○ OP Riesling Il Bandito '09	▼▼	5
● OP Sangue di Giuda '09	▼▼	4
● Vigalòn '09	▼▼	3*
○ Fusion	▼	4
○ OP Malvasia Frizzante	▼	3
○ OP Pinot Nero Extra Dry Cuvée Eleonor Martinotti	▼	4
⊙ OP Pinot Nero Extra Dry Cuvée Eleonor Rosé Martinotti	▼	4
● OP Pinot Nero Giorginero '09	▼	4
● OP Pinot Nero Monteroso '07	▼	5
○ OP Pinot Nero Brut Cl. 1870 '05	▽▽▽	6

Conte Carlo Giorgi di Vistarino

FRAZ. SCORZOLETTA, 82/84
27040 PIETRA DE' GIORGI [PV]
TEL. 038585117
www.contevistarino.it

CELLAR SALES
PRE-BOOKED VISITS

ANNUAL PRODUCTION 550,000 bottles
HECTARES UNDER VINE 180
VITICULTURE METHOD Conventional

Conte Vistarino means Valle Scuropasso, which in turn means the home of Italian Pinot Nero. Indeed, it was the Conti Vistarino and the Gancias who first planted French clones for white-wine fermentation in this area of Oltrepò. This zone is the source of the grapes that for decades maintained the high international reputation of Italian sparklers, long before the rise of Franciacorta. With dozens of farms and a 200-hectare estate, approximately half of which is under vine, there is no lack of raw material for high-quality products.

Pernice '07, a red Pinot Nero, reached our finals and only just missed out on a repeat of last year's Three Glasses. It is a very well typed, highly characteristic wine with earthy, almost dark notes of fine wild berry fruit and tannins that require further bottle ageing to achieve perfect balance. All the sparklers are made from 100 per cent pinot nero. The 1865 '05 stands out for its development, complexity and elegance, with an intriguing sage note, while the Cruasé '07 is distinctly more spirited, with prominent citrus. The other wines are impeccable, particularly the Sangue di Giuda.

● OP Pinot Nero Pernice '07	▼▼	4
○ OP Pinot Nero Brut Cl. 1865 '05	▼▼	5
⊙ OP Pinot Nero Brut Cl. Cruasué Saignée della Rocca '07	▼▼	4
● OP Bonarda L'Alcova '09	▼	3
● OP Buttafuoco Monte Selva '08	▼	3
● OP Pinot Nero Costa del Nero '08	▼	3
● OP Sangue di Giuda Costiolo '08	▼	3
● OP Pinot Nero Pernice '06	▽▽▽	4*
⊙ OP Pinot Nero Brut Cl. Cruasué Saignée della Rocca '07	▽▽	4
● OP Pinot Nero Costa del Nero '07	▽▽	3*
● OP Pinot Nero Costa del Nero '04	▽▽	3*
● OP Pinot Nero Pernice '05	▽▽	5
● OP Pinot Nero Pernice '04	▽▽	5
○ OP Riesling 7 Giugno '07	▽▽	4

Isimbarda

LOC. CASTELLO
CASCINA ISIMBARDA
27046 SANTA GIULETTA [PV]
TEL. 0383899256
www.tenutaisimbarda.it

CELLAR SALES
PRE-BOOKED VISITS

ANNUAL PRODUCTION 110,000 bottles
HECTARES UNDER VINE 40
VITICULTURE METHOD Conventional

The estate's name is derived from the Marchesi Isimbardi, landowners and grape farmers who settled here in the middle of the Oltrepò winemaking area at the end of the 17th century. The estate managed by Daniele Zangelmi, in the foothills of the zone, boasts 36 hectares under vine with different soils, ranging from limestone marl, ideal for white grapes, to more clay-rich soils in sunnier positions, suitable for croatina and barbera, while pinot nero is grown on the higher land.

Riesling Vigna Martina has been Isimbarda's flagship wine for years. Vertical tastings show that it is at its best four or five years from harvest. When young, like this '09 vintage, it has citrus and rosemary-led aromatic herbs while the minerality that emerges later is still barely perceptible. Varmei, from 80 per cent incrocio Manzoni plus chardonnay and pinot grigio fermented in small casks, is also very good, balanced and fragrant. The interesting Pinot Nero Vigna del Cardinale '07 is invigorating and varietal. The Bonarda is as good as ever and from the other reds we preferred the approachable Monplò to the Montezavo, which is still too young.

● OP Bonarda Vivace V. delle More '09	▼▼	4*
● OP Pinot Nero V. del Cardinale '07	▼▼	5
○ OP Riesling Renano Vigna Martina '09	▼▼	4*
● OP Rosso Monplò '07	▼▼	4*
○ Varméi '09	▼▼	4*
○ OP Pinot Nero Brut Martinotti	▼	4
● OP Rosso Montezavo Ris. '07	▼	5
● OP Bonarda Vivace '00	▽▽	3*
○ OP Riesling Renano Vigna Martina '08	▽▽	4*
○ OP Riesling Renano Vigna Martina '06	▽▽	4
○ OP Riesling Renano Vigna Martina '02	▽▽	4
● OP Rosso Monplò '05	▽▽	4*
● OP Rosso Monplò '03	▽▽	4
● OP Rosso Monplò '01	▽▽	4*

Cantina Sociale La Versa

VIA F. CRISPI, 15
27047 SANTA MARIA DELLA VERSA [PV]
TEL. 0385798411
www.laversa.it

CELLAR SALES
PRE-BOOKED VISITS

ANNUAL PRODUCTION 5,000,000 bottles
HECTARES UNDER VINE 1,300
VITICULTURE METHOD Conventional

Much has changed this year at the historic co-operative winery in Santa Maria della Versa, starting with its manager. Francesco Cervetti, the man who restored La Versa's wines, and particularly its sparklers, to the splendour of the days in which they were served on transatlantic liners, has been replaced by the Piedmontese Corrado Cavallo, who had already spent a couple of years at the winery at the end of the 1990s. He has clear ideas and ambitions to raise quality yet further.

Testarossa Principio was absent this year – it will be released in 2011 as Principio – and Testarossa Rosé wasn't ready either. La Versa's reputation for sparklers is maintained chiefly by the classic Testarossa '05, a handsome, firm Pinot Nero with a nose of cakes and aromatic herbs and a full, lengthy palate. We just preferred the white Cuvée Storica, with notes of hazelnut, to the simpler, less distinctive rosé version. The average standard of several traditional '09 Oltrepò wines is also excellent: Bonarda, Sangue di Giuda and the exemplary Moscato di Volpara. Pinot Nero Liutajo del Re '07 still has very assertive tannins.

○ Brut Cl. Cuvée Storica	▼▼	5
● OP Bonarda Frizzante Ca' Bella '09	▼▼	4*
○ OP Moscato di Volpara Frizzante I Roccoli '09	▼▼	3*
○ OP Pinot Nero Cuvée Testarossa Brut '05	▼▼	5
● OP Sangue di Giuda I Roccoli '09	▼▼	4*
● OP Barbera Le Piane '08	▼	4
⊙ OP Pinot Nero Brut Cuvée Storica Rosé	▼	4
● OP Pinot Nero Liutajo Del Re '07	▼	5
○ Cuvée Testarossa Brut Principio '03	▽▽	8
○ Cuvée Testarossa Principio '01	▽▽	8
⊙ OP Pinot Nero Rosé Cuvée Testarossa Brut '05	▽▽	6
○ OP Pinot Nero Testarossa Principio '00	▽▽	8

Lantieri de Paratico

LOC. COLZANO
VIA SIMEONE PARATICO, 50
25031 CAPRIOLO [BS]
TEL. 030736151
www.lantierideparatico.it

CELLAR SALES
PRE-BOOKED VISITS

ANNUAL PRODUCTION 150,000 bottles
HECTARES UNDER VINE 17
VITICULTURE METHOD Conventional

The Lantieri de Paratico are an old Franciacorta family. Fabio Lantieri lives in the historic home at Capriolo. Fabio continues an old tradition, producing an attentively crafted range of Franciacortas and local wines from the grapes of his 17 hectares of vineyards, most of which are located next to the modern cellar.

The '06 vintage of Brut Arcadia is once again the estate's top sparkler. Made from a cuvée of Chardonnay with 30 per cent Pinot Nero, it ages for several months in small casks before refermentation and lees ageing, which generally lasts four years. It is an elegant, balanced wine with a firmly structured palate and a concentrated nose of vanilla, fruit, attractive oak and aromatic herbs. Lantieri also makes a very good creamy Satèn, alluringly smooth with hints of vanilla, lemon verbena and hazelnut. The round, juicy, fruit-packed Arcadia Rosé is very decent while the Brut and Extra Brut are good.

⊙ Franciacorta Arcadia Rosé	▼▼	6
○ Franciacorta Brut Arcadia '06	▼▼	6
○ Franciacorta Satèn	▼▼	5
● Curtefranca Rosso Colzano '07	▼	5
○ Franciacorta Brut	▼	5
○ Franciacorta Extra Brut	▼	5
○ Franciacorta Brut Arcadia '05	▽▽	6
○ Franciacorta Brut Arcadia '04	▽▽	6
○ Franciacorta Brut Arcadia '02	▽▽	6
○ Franciacorta Brut Arcadia '01	▽▽	6
● TdF Rosso Colzano '04	▽▽	5
● TdF Rosso Colzano '03	▽▽	5

Majolini

LOC. VALLE
VIA MANZONI, 3
25050 OME [BS]
TEL. 0306527378
www.majolini.it

CELLAR SALES
PRE-BOOKED VISITS

ANNUAL PRODUCTION 160,000 bottles
HECTARES UNDER VINE 20
VITICULTURE METHOD Conventional

The Majolini family own an industrial group of international stature but in the mid 1980s they felt the need to return to their farming roots. They renovated the beautiful farmstead in Ome and its holdings, marking the beginning of the Majolini adventure and, headed by Ezio – now flanked by his grandson Simone – the winery soon became one of the most important of the designation, with 20 hectares of wonderful vineyards, mainly around Ome, and a large, handsome, state-of-the art winery adorned with the last sculpture by Aligi Sassu, who was a family friend.

Brut Electo '05 performed well in our finals, displaying a very fine bead and a creamy mousse, accompanied by a nose that opens with complex, evolved notes of honey and spring flowers, subsequently disclosing white-fleshed fruits and vanilla. The palate offers soft fruity notes, creamy effervescence and attractive complexity. Franciacorta Brut has personality and a fresh attack followed by characteristic deeper, almost tertiary, notes of antique wood, wax and vanilla. We thought the Satèn and the Rosé Altera were a little less spectacular, with attractive fullness and good backbone, but slightly over-evolved.

○ Franciacorta Brut Electo '05	▼▼	8
○ Franciacorta Brut	▼▼	7
⊙ Franciacorta Rosé Altera	▼	6
○ Franciacorta Satèn	▼	6
○ Franciacorta Brut Electo '00	▽▽▽	7
○ Franciacorta Brut Electo '99	▽▽▽	6
○ Franciacorta Brut Electo '97	▽▽▽	6
○ Franciacorta Aligi Sassu Pas Dosé '03	▽▽	8
○ Franciacorta Electo Brut '01	▽▽	7
○ Franciacorta Pas Dosé Aligi Sassu '05	▽▽	8
○ Franciacorta Pas Dosé Aligi Sassu '99	▽▽	6
○ Franciacorta Satèn Ante Omnia '03	▽▽	8

Le Marchesine

VIA VALLOSA, 31
25050 PASSIRANO [BS]
TEL. 030657005
www.lemarchesine.it

CELLAR SALES
PRE-BOOKED VISITS

ANNUAL PRODUCTION 400,000 bottles
HECTARES UNDER VINE 40
VITICULTURE METHOD Conventional

The Biattas are an old family documented in the Brescia area since the 12th century. Loris skilfully runs the winery founded in the mid 1980s by his father Giovanni, and has enlarged and replanted the family vineyards. The cellar in Passirano produces wine exclusively from the grapes of the estate's 40 hectares under vine, with the aid of French consultant oenologist Jean-Pierre Valade.

The Biattas presented another winning wine this year, Brut Secolo Novo '05, which took our Sparkler of the Year award. Made from chardonnay grown on the Santissima hill in Gussago, it offers complex tertiary notes and attractive oak, with intriguing layers of hazelnut, white-fleshed fruit, peanut butter and aromatic herbs. The palate is creamy, continuous and elegant. Brut '05, from a vineyard at the foot of Monte Orfano, is also very good, with rich tropical fruit and fresh balance. The non-vintage Brut shows exemplary cleanliness and varietal stamping, and a long, balanced finish of ripe fruit, while the Extra Brut has fine concentrated citrus notes and a soft finale.

○ Franciacorta Brut Secolo Novo '05	TTT+	8
○ Franciacorta Brut '05	TT	6
○ Franciacorta Brut	TT	5
○ Franciacorta Extra Brut	TT	6
○ Curtefranca Bianco '09	T	4
● Curtefranca Rosso '08	T	4
⊙ Franciacorta Brut Rosé '06	T	6
○ Franciacorta Satèn	T	6
○ Franciacorta Brut '04	YYY	6
○ Franciacorta Brut '01	YY	6
○ Franciacorta Brut Secolo Novo '00	YY	7
○ Franciacorta Satèn '02	YY	6

Tenuta Mazzolino

VIA MAZZOLINO, 26
27050 CORVINO SAN QUIRICO [PV]
TEL. 0383876122
www.tenuta-mazzolino.com

CELLAR SALES
PRE-BOOKED VISITS

ANNUAL PRODUCTION 100,000 bottles
HECTARES UNDER VINE 25
VITICULTURE METHOD Conventional

There is an air of Burgundy at the splendid Mazzolino estate, run by Sandra Bragiotti with Burgundian oenologist Jean-François Coquard and Greek-born French consultant Kyriakos Kynigopoulos. France is present in the limited number of grape varieties and wines, clear ideas and, following the local trend, now also sparkling wine production. The winery will increasingly concentrate on pinot nero in all its forms, and several vineyards will probably be replanted in the near future.

Noir remains the flagship wine and the '07 vintage won our Three Glasses for the second year running. Showing a deep ruby tending to garnet, it has the usual notes of coffee and chocolate that enhance, rather than mask, the definition of the fruit. The long finish also features notes of violets and liquorice. Cabernet Corvino is as good as ever: fragrant and spicy without excessive grassiness but with very well-defined fruit. Chardonnay Blanc '08 is also very good and while not a local variety, this vintage has finally found the right balance between tropical fruit and oak. This year saw the debut of the Cruasé, a coppery Metodo Classico with attractive top notes of wild berries.

● OP Pinot Nero Noir '07	TTT	6
● OP Cabernet Sauvignon Corvino '07	TT	5
○ OP Chardonnay Blanc '08	TT	4
⊙ OP Pinot Nero Brut Cruasé Mazzolino	TT	4
○ Brut Cl. Mazzolino Blanc de Blancs	T	4
○ Camarà '09	T	3
● OP Bonarda Mazzolino '09	T	4
● OP Pinot Nero Noir '06	YYY	6
● OP Bonarda Mazzolino '07	YY	4*
● OP Cabernet Sauvignon Corvino '05	YY	4
○ OP Chardonnay Blanc '03	YY	4
● OP Pinot Nero Noir '05	YY	6
● OP Pinot Nero Noir '02	YY	6
● Terrazze '05	YY	3*

★ Monsupello

VIA SAN LAZZARO, 5
27050 TORRICELLA VERZATE [PV]
TEL. 0383896043
www.monsupello.it

CELLAR SALES
PRE-BOOKED VISITS

ANNUAL PRODUCTION 280,000 bottles
HECTARES UNDER VINE 48
VITICULTURE METHOD Conventional

We are saddened by the death of Carlo Boatti, one of the first men to believe in Oltrepò's potential and a contributor to the foundation of the consortium. Carlo also made Monsupello a benchmark for the designation's winemakers. We sincerely hope that his wife Carla and his children Laura and Pierangelo are able to continue his invaluable work.

The list of sparklers is extensive and excellent as usual, although the rest of the production is also noteworthy. This year we awarded Three Glasses to Nature, a great Pinot Nero Metodo Classico with exemplary balance and focus. The more complex champagne-style Ca' del Tava and the floral, mineral Rosé are no less impressive, while the elegant, full Classese '03, the only vintage sparkler, is also very good. Even the basic Brut earned an excellent score for its appealing zestiness. Finally, we were enchanted by the unique, crisp Bonarda Vaiolet '09.

○ OP Pinot Nero Cl. Nature	TTT	5
⊙ Brut Rosé	TT	5
○ OP Brut Cl. Cuvée Ca' del Tava	TT	7
○ Chardonnay '09	TT	4*
● OP Bonarda Vivace Vaiolet '09	TT	4*
○ OP Brut Cl. Classese '03	TT	6
○ OP Pinot Nero Brut Cl.	TT	5
○ Pinot Grigio '09	TT	4*
○ Riesling Renano '09	TT	4*
● OP Barbera I Gelsi '07	T	4
● Pinot Nero Junior '09	T	4
⊙ Brut Rosé	YYY	5*
○ OP Brut Cl. Cuvée Ca' del Tava	YYY	7
○ OP Pinot Nero Cl. Nature	YYY	5

Marchesi di Montalto

LOC. COSTA GALLOTTI, 5
27040 MONTALTO PAVESE [PV]
TEL. 0383870358
www.marchesidimontalto.it

CELLAR SALES
PRE-BOOKED VISITS

ANNUAL PRODUCTION 50,000 bottles
HECTARES UNDER VINE 100
VITICULTURE METHOD Conventional

When we received the samples from this hitherto unfamiliar winery for the first time several years ago, we were so struck by the average quality of its products that we immediately decided to assign it a full profile, with an array of Two Glass wines. We subsequently got to know the owner, Gabriele Marchesi, and learnt about the ups and downs that led to several mistakes and the difficulties arising from the many farms scattered over a 100-hectare estate. However, the winery now seems to be on the right path.

Monsaltus '07, from botrytized riesling italico grapes, is a wine with few equals in Italy. Its intense nose ranges from saffron to aromatic herbs over an equally rich palate. There is a noticeable change in the Metodo Classico sparklers: Cuvée 100 '07 is balsamic, smooth and alluring; Cruasé Costadelvento '07 is a concentrated rosé with notes of wild berries and citrus and good grip; and Tersilio Marchesi Fondatore '04 has more complex notes of cake and a firm finish. The excellent Riesling Passiré '08 from part-dried grapes is concentrated and fragrant. The rest of the list is good.

○ OP Riesling Italico Monsaltus '07	TTT	4
● OP Pinot Nero Brut Cruasè Costadelvento '07	TT	5
○ OP Pinot Nero Brut Tersilio Marchesi Ris. '04	TT	6
○ OP Pinot Nero Cuveè 100 Brut '07	TT	5
○ OP Riesling Passirè '08	TT	7
● OP Barbera Bandera '07	T	4
● OP Pinot Nero Ca' Nuè '09	T	3
● OP Rosso Re Nero Ris. '03	T	5
○ OP Riesling Brut Martinotti	YY	4*
○ OP Riesling Italico Monsaltus '04	YY	4
○ OP Riesling Italico Monsaltus '03	YY	4
○ OP Riesling Italico Monsaltus V. T. '06	YY	5

★ Monte Rossa

FRAZ. BORNATO
VIA MONTE ROSSA, 1
25040 CAZZAGO SAN MARTINO [BS]
TEL. 030725066
www.monterossa.com

CELLAR SALES
PRE-BOOKED VISITS

ANNUAL PRODUCTION 500,000 bottles
HECTARES UNDER VINE 70
VITICULTURE METHOD Conventional

Monte Rossa is located on the Bornato hill and its modern cellars stand alongside the handsome 17th-century home of the Rabotti family. The estate, founded by Paolo Rabotti and Paola Rovetta in the 1970s and now competently run by their son Emanuele, is one of the leading names in the history of this prestigious young DOCG. The Rabottis manage approximately 70 hectares of vineyards, both estate-owned and leased, and have concentrated their production exclusively on Franciacortas for several years now. Their cuvées are among the best around.

After five years of bottle ageing, Cabochon. '05 earned Three vibrant Glasses. A distinctive wine with a distinctive personality, it presents compact, powerful and stylish, with a nose of honey, vanilla and marmalade and a firm, full-bodied palate that is perfectly, elegantly balanced, deep and cosseting. This year saw the debut of the new Extra Brut Salvadek '06, with a striking designer label. It is another very good Franciacorta, made exclusively from chardonnay grapes from the winery's oldest vineyard, and shows full, balanced and long. However, the entire list of wines is very rewarding, from the Brut PR, with smoky notes, to the savoury Satèn Sansevé and the Prima Cuvée.

○ Franciacorta Brut Cabochon '05	▼▼▼	7
○ Franciacorta Extra Brut Salvadek '06	▼▼	6
○ Franciacorta Brut P. R.	▼▼	6
○ Franciacorta Prima Cuvée	▼▼	5
⊙ Franciacorta Rosé P. R.	▼▼	6
○ Franciacorta Satèn Sansevé	▼▼	6
○ Franciacorta Prima Cuvée Brut	▼	5
○ Franciacorta Brut Cabochon '04	▽▽▽	7
○ Franciacorta Brut Cabochon '01	▽▽▽	7
○ Franciacorta Brut Cabochon '99	▽▽▽	8
○ Franciacorta Brut Cabochon '98	▽▽▽	6
○ Franciacorta Extra Brut Cabochon '93	▽▽▽	6
○ Franciacorta Satèn	▽▽▽	6
○ Franciacorta Satèn	▽▽▽	6

Montelio

VIA D. MAZZA, 1
27050 CODEVILLA [PV]
TEL. 0383373090
montelio.gio@alice.it

CELLAR SALES
PRE-BOOKED VISITS
ROOMS AND FOOD

ANNUAL PRODUCTION 130,000 bottles
HECTARES UNDER VINE 27
VITICULTURE METHOD Conventional

Montelio means Sun Mountain, which reveals a lot about the vineyards of this historic estate owned by sisters Giovanna and Caterina Brazzola and long overseen by the great Mario Maffi, a talented oenologist and Oltrepò wine historian. We highly recommend a tour of the winery, which also offers accommodation. Maffi will explain everything that has happened here, and not only in relation to winemaking. A visit to the cellar, which houses a spectacular collection of old wines, is also a must.

The wines presented this year include the still Barbera '08 and the semi-sparkling Bonarda Vivace '09. Both are very varietal, the former with well-controlled acidity and the latter with fine-grained tannins and both are accompanied by clean-tasting notes of wild berries. La Stroppa, a pleasant Charmat-method sparkler, is fragrant. Two of the winery's classics, Müller Thurgau La Giostra '07 and Pinot Nero Costarsa '05, are a rung below, with rather evolved notes.

○ Brut Martinotti La Stroppa	▼▼	4
● OP Bonarda Frizzante '09	▼▼	3*
○ OP Riesling Italico '09	▼▼	3*
○ Müller Thurgau La Giostra '07	▼	3
○ Noblerot '07	▼	5
● OP Pinot Nero Costarsa '05	▼	5
● Comprino Rosso '06	▽▽	3*
○ Müller Thurgau La Giostra '06	▽▽	3*
● OP Barbera '08	▽▽	3*
● OP Barbera '07	▽▽	3*
● OP Bonarda Frizzante '08	▽▽	3*
● OP Bonarda Frizzante '06	▽▽	3*
● OP Bonarda Frizzante '05	▽	3*

Montenisa

FRAZ. CALINO
VIA PAOLO VI, 62
25046 CAZZAGO SAN MARTINO [BS]
TEL. 0307750838
www.antinori.it

PRE-BOOKED VISITS

ANNUAL PRODUCTION 220,000 bottles
HECTARES UNDER VINE 60
VITICULTURE METHOD Conventional

In 1999, Marchesi Antinori decided to start producing Franciacortas and bought this fine estate from the Conti Maggi. It now boasts 60 hectares of completely replanted vineyards overlooking Lake Iseo from the hamlet of Calino, where the house and cellar stand. The winery is run by Allegra, Alessia and Albiera Antinori and is named after Mount Nysa, which Greek mythology identifies as the birthplace of the god Bacchus.

Antinori's apprenticeship in Franciacorta is clearly over. The release of the Contessa Maggi '02 cuvée sanctions Montenisa's entry into the select group of the zone's best wineries. This wine only just missed our top accolade, with deep, well-defined fruit, complex mineral notes of antique wood and raisins, and true character. The Satèn '04 again showed itself to be a savoury, top-quality cuvée, compact and creamy, while the balanced, complex, close-focused Brut is also excellent.

○ Franciacorta Brut Contessa Camilla Maggi '02	▼▼	7
○ Franciacorta Brut	▼▼	6
○ Franciacorta Satèn '04	▼▼	7
○ Franciacorta Brut	▽▽	6
○ Franciacorta Brut	▽▽	5
○ Franciacorta Brut Contessa Camilla Maggi '01	▽▽	7
○ Franciacorta Brut Contessa Camilla Maggi '00	▽▽	7
○ Franciacorta Satèn '03	▽▽	7
○ Franciacorta Satèn '02	▽▽	7
○ Franciacorta Satèn	▽▽	7

La Montina

VIA BAIANA, 17
25040 MONTICELLI BRUSATI [BS]
TEL. 030653278
www.lamontina.it

CELLAR SALES
PRE-BOOKED VISITS

ANNUAL PRODUCTION 450,000 bottles
HECTARES UNDER VINE 72
VITICULTURE METHOD Conventional

The Bozza brothers' winery, purchased in the early 1980s, is a historic estate named after the Montini family, from which Pope Paul VI hailed. Oenologist Cesare Ferrari, agronomists Alceo Totò and Rocco Marino, and Michele Bozza, who co-ordinates sales, form a close-knit management team that has boosted both the quantity and quality of production in recent years. Over 60 hectares of vineyards in prime wine country and a constantly expanding state-of-the-art cellar have allowed La Montina to achieve excellent results.

While achieving important goals is rewarding, the Bozzas and their team are showing that they are now ready to establish themselves permanently at the top of the designation. Confirmation of this comes from the sumptuous Extra Brut Riserva '04, which is assertive, full, savoury and almost salty, but possesses extraordinary vitality. Creamy effervescence and sound fruit helped it to earn Three Glasses. The rest of the list is also impressive, with quality ranging from good to excellent, from the Brut '06 with attractive notes of tropical fruits, to the edgy, mineral Extra Brut, the entry-level Brut and the still wines.

○ Franciacorta Extra Brut Ris. Vintage '04	▼▼▼	7
● Curtefranca Rosso dei Dossi '07	▼▼	4
○ Franciacorta Brut '06	▼▼	6
○ Franciacorta Brut	▼▼	5
○ Franciacorta Extra Brut	▼▼	5
⊙ Franciacorta Rosé Demi Sec	▼▼	5
○ Curtefranca Palanca '09	▼	4
○ Franciacorta Satèn	▼	6
○ Franciacorta Brut '05	▽▽▽	6
○ Franciacorta Brut '04	▽▽	5
○ Franciacorta Brut '99	▽▽	6
○ Franciacorta Brut '98	▽▽	6
○ Franciacorta Extra Brut '02	▽▽	5
○ Franciacorta Extra Brut '01	▽▽	5

Monzio Compagnoni

VIA NIGOLINE, 18
25030 ADRO [BS]
TEL. 0307457803
www.monziocompagnoni.com

CELLAR SALES
PRE-BOOKED VISITS

ANNUAL PRODUCTION 250,000 bottles
HECTARES UNDER VINE 30
VITICULTURE METHOD Conventional

Marcello Monzio Compagnoni arrived in Franciacorta a few years ago following his wine experience in Valcalepio, where his original operation continues. In the space of a few years, he has purchased 30 hectares of fine vineyards, which he tends personally, and a sophisticated cellar at Adro. Painstaking selection of the grapes and extraordinary care lavished on every stage of fermentation and refermentation have enabled him to create extremely cuvées, which confidently occupy the upper echelons of the DOCG.

With wineries in two different zones, Monzio Compagnoni offers an extensive range. The savoury Extra Brut '06 performed very well in our finals, showing smooth and elegant, with attractive balsamic notes and a long finish. Notes of vanilla, butter and cakes distinguish the Satèn '06, which is one of the best of its kind, while the Brut from the same vintage has fine stylistic cleanliness and minerality. The Rosé '06 is less convincing, but we liked the Moscato di Scanzo Don Quijote and the Valcalepio Rosso Colle della Luna.

○ Franciacorta Extra Brut '06	🍷🍷	6
○ Franciacorta Brut '06	🍷🍷	5
○ Franciacorta Satèn '06	🍷🍷	6
● Moscato di Scanzo Don Quijote	🍷🍷	6
● Valcalepio Rosso Colle della Luna '06	🍷🍷	4
○ Curtefranca Bianco Ronco della Seta '09	🍷	4
⊙ Franciacorta Rosé '06	🍷	6
○ TdF Curtefranca Bianco della Seta '08	🍷	5
○ Valcalepio Bianco Colle della Luna '09	🍷	3
● Valcalepio Rosso di Luna '07	🍷	5
● Valcalepio Rosso Rosso Luna '07	🍷	5
○ Franciacorta Extra Brut '04	🍸🍸🍸	6
○ Franciacorta Extra Brut '03	🍸🍸🍸	6

Il Mosnel

LOC. CAMIGNONE
VIA BARBOGLIO, 14
25040 PASSIRANO [BS]
TEL. 030653117
www.ilmosnel.com

CELLAR SALES
PRE-BOOKED VISITS
FOOD

ANNUAL PRODUCTION 250,000 bottles
HECTARES UNDER VINE 40
VITICULTURE METHOD Conventional

Il Mosnel is one of Franciacorta's most handsome wineries. It is housed in a perfectly restored 17th-century building with the very latest cellar equipment at Passirano di Camignone, surrounded by vineyards on a single 40-hectare plot, which is unusual in this area. Giulio and Lucia Barzanò have taken over from their mother Emanuela Barboglio the reins of the estate, which has been in the family since 1836 but has focused exclusively on wine since the late 1960s.

QdE stands for "questione di etichetta" and refers to a label graphics award organized by Il Mosnel. It's also the name of an excellent Riserva '04 Dosage Zero, which shone at our finals. It flaunts personality and freshness, extraordinary stylistic cleanliness, a complex floral nose with lavender notes and a very deep, well-orchestrated palate. We gave it Three Glasses. Satèn '06 nearly did the same, showing soft and creamy with refreshing tropical notes. The excellent list also includes a superb Extra Brut Emanuela Barboglio '06, which is balanced and floral, and Pas Dosé Parosé, an elegant rosé from 70 per cent pinot nero and chardonnay with impressive acid backbone.

○ Franciacorta Pas Dosé QdE Ris. '04	🍷🍷🍷	7
○ Franciacorta Satèn '06	🍷🍷	6
○ Curtefranca Bianca Campolarga '09	🍷🍷	4
● Curtefranca Fontecolo Rosso '07	🍷🍷	4
○ Franciacorta Brut	🍷🍷	5
○ Franciacorta Extra Brut Emanuela Barboglio '06	🍷🍷	6
⊙ Franciacorta Pas Dosé Parosé '06	🍷🍷	6
○ Sebino Passito Sulif '08	🍷🍷	6
○ Franciacorta Pas Dosé	🍷	5
○ Franciacorta Satèn '05	🍸🍸🍸	6
○ Franciacorta Satèn '00	🍸🍸	6
○ Franciacorta Satèn '98	🍸🍸	6

Muratori - Villa Crespia

VIA VALLI, 11
25030 ADRO [BS]
TEL. 0307451051
www.fratellimuratori.com

CELLAR SALES
PRE-BOOKED VISITS

ANNUAL PRODUCTION 350,000 bottles
HECTARES UNDER VINE 60
VITICULTURE METHOD Conventional

The Muratori brothers are entrepreneurs from Brescia with a great passion for wine. They have turned this passion into a business by entrusting Professor Francesco Iacono with an ambitious project to create a chain of top-quality estates in Lombardy, Tuscany and Campania. Faithful to the principle of "one terroir, one wine", Iacono focuses exclusively on sparklers at Villa Crespia in Franciacorta, with its 60 hectares of vineyards and state-of-the-art winery. There are numerous versions from various vineyards planted according to in-depth zoning studies of the area.

This year it was a new cuvée that upheld the winery's honour at our finals. We refer to Franciacorta Dosaggio Zero Riserva Francesco Iacono '02, a highly complex, deep wine that is very fresh and mineral, made from a cuvée of Chardonnay from a vineyard in Erbusco, given brief skin contact and then aged on the lees for over seven years. The rest of the range is first-rate, as usual, from the fruity, close-focused Satèn Cesonato to the dense, biscuity Brut Novalia, the floral Brut Miolo, with notes of lavender and aromatic herbs, and the Rosé Brolese Extra Brut, which displays good backbone and firm structure.

○ Franciacorta Extra Brut Francesco Iacono Ris. '02	▼▼	8
○ Franciacorta Brut Miolo	▼▼	5
○ Franciacorta Brut Novalia	▼▼	5
⊙ Franciacorta Rosé Extra Brut Brolese	▼▼	6
○ Franciacorta Satèn Brut Cesonato	▼▼	6
○ Franciacorta Dosaggio Zero Numerozero	▼	6
○ Franciacorta Brut Miolo	▽▽	5
○ Franciacorta Brut Novalia	▽▽	6
○ Franciacorta Dosaggio Zero Cisiolo '04	▽▽	6
○ Franciacorta Dosaggio Zero Cisiolo '03	▽▽	6
○ Franciacorta Miolo	▽▽	6

★ Nino Negri

VIA GHIBELLINI
23030 CHIURO [SO]
TEL. 0342485211
www.ninonegri.it

CELLAR SALES
PRE-BOOKED VISITS
FOOD

ANNUAL PRODUCTION 800,000 bottles
HECTARES UNDER VINE 36
VITICULTURE METHOD Conventional

This winery is over 110 years old. Founded by Nino Negri in 1897, it has shaped the history of viticulture and winemaking in Valtellina. Negri has always been far-sighted in respect to its viticultural assets and during the 1980s it became part of the Gruppo Italiano Vini, soon emerging as the group's most prestigious estate. Credit for this goes to its accomplished staff and manager-oenologist Casimiro Maule, who was the first to bring out the extraordinary potential of the area's Nebbiolo to the full.

Sfursat 5 Stelle '07 once again took Three Glasses for its proverbial elegance, complex nose of bottled cherries and red-fruits jam and austere, full, perfectly balanced palate. The traditional Sfursat '07 has a nose of fresh flowers and ripe plums, a concentrated palate with fresh acidity, and a deep finish. Fracia '07 is excellent, with a spicy nose and a warm, close-knit palate, and Quadrio '07 is fruity with an almondy palate. Sasso Rosso '07 is distinctive and well made and Mazer '07 is good, giving spring flowers and a firm palate. Le Tense '07 has a complex nose and a balanced palate but we felt that the supple white Ca' Brione '09 was perhaps a little tired.

● Valtellina Sfursat 5 Stelle '07	▼▼▼	8
● Valtellina Sfursat '07	▼▼	7
● Valtellina Sup. Fracia '07	▼▼	8
● Valtellina Sup. Grumello Vigna Sassorosso '07	▼▼	5
● Valtellina Sup. Inferno '06	▼▼	5
● Valtellina Sup. Mazer '07	▼▼	5
● Valtellina Sup. Quadrio '07	▼▼	4
● Valtellina Sup. Sassella Le Tense '07	▼▼	5
○ Ca' Brione '09	▼	6
● Valtellina Sfursat '05	▽▽▽	8
● Valtellina Sfursat '04	▽▽▽	7
● Valtellina Sfursat '03	▽▽▽	7
● Valtellina Sfursat 5 Stelle '06	▽▽▽	8
● Valtellina Sfursat 5 Stelle '03	▽▽▽	8

Pietro Nera

via IV Novembre, 43
23030 Chiuro [SO]
tel. 0342482631
www.neravini.com

CELLAR SALES
PRE-BOOKED VISITS

ANNUAL PRODUCTION 700,000 bottles
HECTARES UNDER VINE 40
VITICULTURE METHOD Conventional

This winery has acquired experience over many years. It was founded in the 1940s and today, after patiently uniting the vineyards, the Nera estate covers an area of approximately 40 hectares. Family run, under the skilled leadership of Pietro Nera with the aid of sons Stefano and Simone, it continues to represent an important page in Valtellina's winemaking history.

Nera's debut in the Guide this year is spectacular with a highly interesting list of wines. It includes an exemplary Sforzato '05 with a complex, close-focused nose, tight-knit tannins and a long, elegant finish. Inferno Riserva '05 is very good, with mineral and tobacco notes on the nose and an austere, pleasingly acid-veined palate. Signorie '05 offers notes of pencil lead and peat, accompanied by a dry, linear palate with a long finish, while the classic Grumello Riserva '04 has a fruity nose and is highly drinkable. Inferno Efesto '07 and Sassella Alisio '06 are both well made with pleasantly refreshing acidity.

● Valtellina Sforzato '05	TT	6
● Valtellina Sup. Grumello Ris. '04	TT	5
● Valtellina Sup. Inferno Ris. '05	TT	5
● Valtellina Sup. Signorie '05	TT	5
● Valtellina Sup. Inferno Efesto '07	T	4
● Valtellina Sup. Sassella Alisio '06	T	4
● Valtellina Sforzato '01	YY	6
● Valtellina Sforzato '00	YY	6
● Valtellina Sforzato '99	YY	6
● Valtellina Sup. Inferno E'festo '02	YY	4*
● Valtellina Sup. Inferno Efesto '00	YY	4
● Valtellina Sup. Inferno Ris. '02	YY	5
● Valtellina Sup. Sassella Alisio '00	YY	4
● Valtellina Sup. Sassella Ris. '00	YY	5

Olivini

loc. Demesse Vecchie, 2
25015 Desenzano del Garda [BS]
tel. 0309910268
www.olivini.net

CELLAR SALES
PRE-BOOKED VISITS

ANNUAL PRODUCTION 130,000 bottles
HECTARES UNDER VINE 26
VITICULTURE METHOD Conventional

Giovanni, Giorgio and Giordana Olivini are three young siblings from a dynasty with other business interests, who decided to convert the family land into a modern winery. In the space of a few years, the operation made the transition from hobby to quality production, with the help of oenologist Antonio Crescini. Today Olivini boasts 26 hectares of fine vineyards and a thoroughly decent list, topped by the Lugana Brut.

Again this year, we were impressed by the Merlot Notte a San Martino '06, a full-bodied red made from overripe grapes that lays out a lush nose of chocolate and dark berries and a rounded, balanced palate. However, the Olivinis, who specialize in sparkling Lugana, also propose an elegant '06 version that is exceptionally refreshing and minerally. The same qualities can be found in the Lugana '09, although it is somewhat lacking in weight. Garda Rosé Brut Metodo Classico is a very good bright rosé with an attractive nose of wild strawberries and currants followed by a fresh, savoury palate.

⊙ Garda Brut Rosé M. Cl.	TT	5
○ Lugana Brut M. Cl. '06	TT	5
● Notte a San Martino '06	TT	5
○ Condolcezza	T	5
⊙ Garda Chiaretto Cl. '09	T	4
○ Lugana '09	T	3
● Garda Rosso Cl. '05	YY	3*
○ Lugana Brut M. Cl. '06	YY	5
● Notte a San Martino '05	YY	5

Pasini - San Giovanni

FRAZ. RAFFA
VIA VIDELLE, 2
25080 PUEGNAGO SUL GARDA [BS]
TEL. 0365651419
www.pasiniproduttori.it

CELLAR SALES
PRE-BOOKED VISITS

ANNUAL PRODUCTION 300,000 bottles
HECTARES UNDER VINE 36
VITICULTURE METHOD Conventional

Founded 50 years ago, this lovely family estate is now run by the third generation, Luca and Paolo. Today it is a leading winery with land from Lugana to Valtenesi and offers the typical wines of the Garda area, made from the grapes of its 36 hectares in various zones. Groppello is the star of this area, and Pasini pays tribute to the variety with an excellent interpretations. However, the estate also offers new wines aimed at exploring the potential of all the territory's signature grapes.

This year our favourite was the classic Groppello Riserva del Vigneto Arzane '07, one of the finest expressions of the variety. It has an alluring, fresh nose of berries, with top notes of cherries and blackberries, and a balanced palate with sound fruit and smooth tannins. A retasting of San Gioan I Carati '00, from cabernet and groppello, revealed complex tertiary aromas, proof of ageing potential. We were enchanted by two elegant, juicy, mineral Metodo Classico cuvées: Ceppo 326 Brut '06 and Ceppo 326 Rosé '06, both from chardonnay and groppello. Brut Lugana Metodo Classico and Centopercento Brut, from groppello, are good. The rest of the long list is interesting.

● Garda Cl. Groppello Vign. Arzane Ris. '07	▼▼	4*
⊙ Ceppo 326 Rosé M. Cl.	▼▼	5
○ Ceppo Brut 326 M. Cl.	▼▼	5
⊙ Garda Cl. Chiaretto Il Chiaretto '09	▼▼	4*
○ 100% Brut M. Cl.	▼	5
● Garda Cl. Groppello Il Groppello '09	▼	4
○ Lugana Brut	▼	4
○ Lugana Il Lugana '09	▼	4
● Garda Cl. Groppello Il Groppello '08	▽▽	4*
● Garda Cl. Groppello Vign. Arzane Ris. '06	▽▽	4*
● Garda Cl. Groppello Vign. Arzane Ris. '04	▽▽	4*
● Garda Cl. Rosso Sup. Cap del Priù '05	▽▽	4*
○ Lugana Il Lugana '08	▽▽	4*
○ Lugana Il Lugana '07	▽▽	4*
● San Gioan Rosso I Carati '05	▽▽	4*
● San Gioan Rosso I Carati '00	▽▽	4

Andrea Picchioni

FRAZ. CAMPONOCE, 8
27044 CANNETO PAVESE [PV]
TEL. 0385262139
www.picchioniandrea.it

CELLAR SALES
PRE-BOOKED VISITS

ANNUAL PRODUCTION 60,000 bottles
HECTARES UNDER VINE 10
VITICULTURE METHOD Organic

Under the guidance of Andrea Picchioni, the entire family contributes to the dedication that has allowed this little winery in Canneto Pavese to make a name for itself, year after year, as one of the most interesting in the entire Oltrepò. Its austere reds, destined for long ageing and based mainly on croatina, have recently been joined by exciting sparklers, with a new surprise each year.

Speaking of surprises, the most interesting this year is Profilo, a sparkler from pinot nero with approximately 20 per cent chardonnay. Following the presentation of the '97 and '98 vintages, it would have been logical to expect the '99. Instead, Picchioni has released a '94, whose 15 years on the lees have given it a delightfully complex nose and good length without detracting from its freshness. Rosso d'Asia, from 90 per cent croatina, is fruity with characteristic balsamic notes. Buttafuoco Riva Bianca '06 is more closed but promises well for the future. The other wines are less memorable, including Pinot Nero Arfena '08, which is somewhat lacking in backbone.

○ OP Profilo Brut Nature M. Cl. '94	▼▼	7
● Monnalisa '06	▼▼	5
● OP Buttafuoco Bricco Riva Bianca '06	▼▼	5
● Rosso d'Asia '06	▼▼	5
● OP Bonarda Vivace '09	▼	4
● OP Buttafuoco Luogo della Cerasa '08	▼	4
● OP Pinot Nero Arfena '08	▼	5
● OP Sangue di Giuda '09	▼	3
● OP Bonarda '07	▽▽	3*
● OP Bonarda Vivace '06	▽▽	3*
○ OP Profilo Brut Nature M. Cl. '98	▽▽	6
○ OP Profilo Brut Nature M. Cl. '97	▽▽	6
● OP Sangue di Giuda '06	▽▽	3*
● Rosso d'Asia '05	▽▽	5

Plozza

VIA SAN GIACOMO, 22
23037 TIRANO [SO]
TEL. 0342701297
www.plozza.com

CELLAR SALES
PRE-BOOKED VISITS

ANNUAL PRODUCTION 450,000 bottles
HECTARES UNDER VINE 28
VITICULTURE METHOD Conventional

Andrea Zanolari is increasingly present alongside his father Mario in running and overseeing Plozza. That might be one reason why the production philosophy is increasingly austere, capable of offering an elegant and faithful interpretation of local traditions and the terroir. Evidence of this comes from the various Riservas and, in particular, Sforzato Vin da Ca'.

Vin da Cà '06 almost took Three Glasses. Three months of thorough drying of the grapes and 30 months in large barrels and casks have conferred notes of tobacco and candied fruit. The palate is elegant and structured, with intriguingly full flavour. Numero Uno '06 has a concentrated, spicy nose of ripe plums and cloves and a close-knit, almondy palate with a lingering finish. The alluringly plush Passione Barrique '05 has a seductive nose and a powerful, full-bodied palate with smooth tannins. Sassella La Scala '06 offers a nose of berry fruit and a full palate with elegant tannins. Inferno Riserva '06 has toast and coffee, and a dry, full-flavoured palate with a long finish.

● Valtellina Numero Uno '06	2 black glasses	8
● Valtellina Sforzato Vin da Cà '06	2 black glasses	6
● Passione Barrique '05	2 black glasses	7
● Valtellina Sup. Inferno Ris. '06	2 black glasses	5
● Valtellina Sup. Sassella La Scala Ris. '06	2 black glasses	4
● Valtellina Numero Uno '01	3 white glasses	8
● Passione Barrique '04	2 white glasses	7
● Valtellina Numero Uno '05	2 white glasses	8
● Valtellina Sforzato Vin da Cà '05	2 white glasses	6
● Valtellina Sforzato Vin da Cà '04	2 white glasses	6
● Valtellina Sup. Grumello Ris. '05	2 white glasses	4
● Valtellina Sup. Grumello Ris. '04	2 white glasses	4*
● Valtellina Sup. Inferno Ris. '05	2 white glasses	5
● Valtellina Sup. Inferno Ris. '04	2 white glasses	5
● Valtellina Sup. Sassella La Scala Ris. '05	2 white glasses	4
● Valtellina Sup. Sassella La Scala Ris. '04	2 white glasses	4*

Mamete Prevostini

VIA LUCCHINETTI, 63
23020 MESE [SO]
TEL. 034341522
www.mameteprevostini.com

CELLAR SALES
PRE-BOOKED VISITS

ANNUAL PRODUCTION 160,000 bottles
HECTARES UNDER VINE 18
VITICULTURE METHOD Conventional

This winery's history is closely tied up with the personal story of Mamete Prevostini, and the professional success he has achieved in recent years. He has been president of the Consorzio Vini Valtellina for the past two years, which have been marked by focus on the strategic value of the land, as well as agronomic research and experimentation. Confirmation of this is offered by the slogan chosen by the consortium to describe the process, "from the glass to the vineyard", stressing the added value of Valtellina's soil and terroir.

The full-bodied Albareda '08 no longer merely flexes its muscles. This time, it took our top accolade for its unique nose of dates and dried figs and perfectly gauged acidity. Corte di Cama '08 is plush and cosseting, with a delicate nose. Riserva '06 is a quintessential Nebbiolo, Sommarovina '08 has a fragrant nose and a long finish, Sassella '08 is good, with a delicate nose and a balanced palate, and Grumello '08 is full, fresh and fruity. Nebbiolo Botonero '09 and Nebbiolo Santarita '09 are forthright, easy-drinking wines. The intriguing Rosato '09, from nebbiolo, is savoury, suggesting wild roses, while Opera '10, from chardonnay and sauvignon, is supple and fragrant.

● Valtellina Sforzato Albareda '08	3 black glasses	7
● Nebbiolo Ris. '06	2 black glasses	5
● Valtellina Sforzato Corte di Cama '08	2 black glasses	6
● Valtellina Sup. Grumello '08	2 black glasses	4
● Valtellina Sup. Sassella '08	2 black glasses	4
● Valtellina Sup. Sassella Sommarovina '08	2 black glasses	5
● Botonero '09	1 black glass	3
○ Opera Bianco '09	1 black glass	5
⊙ Rosato '09	1 black glass	4
● Valtellina Santarita '09	1 black glass	4
● Valtellina Sforzato Albareda '06	3 white glasses	7
● Valtellina Sforzato Albareda '05	3 white glasses	7
● Valtellina Sforzato Albareda '04	3 white glasses	7
● Valtellina Sforzato Albareda '03	3 white glasses	7
● Valtellina Sforzato Albareda '00	3 white glasses	7

Provenza

VIA DEI COLLI STORICI
25015 DESENZANO DEL GARDA [BS]
TEL. 0309910006
www.provenzacantine.it

CELLAR SALES
PRE-BOOKED VISITS

ANNUAL PRODUCTION 1,500,000 bottles
HECTARES UNDER VINE 120
VITICULTURE METHOD Conventional

Fabio and Patrizia Contato are taking management of the family winery founded by their father Walter in the 1960s very seriously. Today Provenza boasts over 100 hectares of manicured vineyards in Valtenesi and Lugana. The top-quality grapes, vinified vineyard by vineyard, drive a prestigious range of wines that have carved out an important place for themselves among the finest producers in Lombardy and beyond. Over the past few vintages, Provenza wines have achieved greater definition and intensity, as attested by many awards.

Three well-deserved Glasses went to Lugana Superiore Fabio Contato '06, which stands out for its soft, rich, sweet floral nose, with ripe apple-like notes and hints of vanilla. On the palate it is concentrated, rich and smooth, but supported by a bright vein of acidity that makes it exceptionally drinkable. The long finish is reminiscent of apples and pears. Lugana Molin '09 also went through to our finals. It is slightly simpler, but equally enjoyable, with lively notes of sage and tropical fruit. The trio of Luganas is completed by the excellent Tenuta Maiolo '09, which offers sound fruit and attractive tanginess. The quality of the rest of the range is good.

○ Lugana Sup. Sel. Fabio Contato '06	▼▼▼	6
○ Lugana Molin '09	▼▼	5
● Garda Cl. Rosso Negresco '08	▼▼	5
● Garda Cl. Rosso Sel. Fabio Contato '07	▼▼	6
● Garda Rosso Tenuta Maiolo '09	▼▼	4*
○ Lugana Brut Ca' Maiol '07	▼▼	5
○ Lugana Tenuta Maiolo '09	▼▼	4
● Garda Cl. Groppello Tenuta Maiolo '09	▼	4
○ Lugana Prestige '09	▼	3
○ Sebastian Brut	▼	4
⊙ Sebastian Rosè	▼	4
○ Lugana Sel. Fabio Contato '07	▽▽▽	6
○ Lugana Sel. Fabio Contato '08	▽▽	6
○ Lugana Sup. Sel. Fabio Contato '05	▽▽	5
⊙ Sebastian Rosè '07	▽	4

Francesco Quaquarini

LOC. MONTEVENEROSO
VIA CASA ZAMBIANCHI, 26
27044 CANNETO PAVESE [PV]
TEL. 038560152
www.quaquarinifrancesco.it

CELLAR SALES
PRE-BOOKED VISITS

ANNUAL PRODUCTION 650,000 bottles
HECTARES UNDER VINE 60
VITICULTURE METHOD Certified organic

The Quaquarini family have chosen to make organic wines, without taking things to extremes. They have a strong bond with their land at Monteveneroso, a beautiful secluded hamlet in the municipality of Canneto Pavese. The head of the family, Francesco, is leaving more and more space to his children. Umberto, an oenologist, and Maria Teresa have repaid his trust by carrying on his work. This explains why a fairly large estate, at least for the fragmented Oltrepò area, is able to produce wines that continue to improve year after year.

One of the winery's greatest strengths is again its Classese, which is close-focused and well defined. It's a sound, reliable sparkling Pinot Nero with no pretensions to extreme sophistication. The estate's Sangue di Giudas have always been a guarantee. Both the Vigna Acqua Calda and the basic '09 are concentrated, fragrant and alluring, with the former displaying slightly better length and aromatic variation. Pinot Nero Blau '07 is well made and very varietal. While hardly explosive, it boasts very good balance. Bonarda Vivace '09 and Barbera Poggio Anna '08 are both nicely made, fragrant and varietal.

● OP Barbera Poggio Anna '08	▼▼	4*
● OP Bonarda Frizzante '09	▼▼	3*
● OP Pinot Nero Blau '07	▼▼	4
○ OP Pinot Nero Brut Classese	▼▼	4*
● OP Sangue di Giuda '09	▼▼	4*
● OP Sangue di Giuda Acqua Calda '09	▼▼	4*
● OP Bonarda Frizzante '03	▽▽	3
● OP Buttafuoco '00	▽▽	2*
● OP Pinot Nero Blau '05	▽▽	4*
● OP Sangue di Giuda '08	▽▽	3*
● OP Sangue di Giuda '07	▽▽	3*
● OP Sangue di Giuda '06	▽▽	3*
● OP Sangue di Giuda Acqua Calda '04	▽▽	4

Aldo Rainoldi

via Stelvio, 128
23030 Chiuro [SO]
tel. 0342482225
www.rainoldi.com

CELLAR SALES
PRE-BOOKED VISITS

ANNUAL PRODUCTION 220,000 bottles
HECTARES UNDER VINE 10
VITICULTURE METHOD Conventional

In contrast to what is happening in many other winemaking areas, a generational change seems to be under way in Valtellina as talented youngsters take over. Everything remains in the family and under close control, but Peppino Rainoldi, the winery's owner, has invested heavily in his nephew. Aldo maintains relations with foreign markets, but first and foremost deals with the estate's longstanding growers.

It is the year of the Riservas at Rainoldi. Sassella '06 won Three Glasses for its rare finesse and austere, complex, close-focused nose. The palate is elegant, firm and full of character. Inferno '06 is very good, with intense aromas of plum and a dry, continuous, acidity-lengthened palate. Crespino '06 has a deep nose of iodine and a dynamic palate, with hints of gentian, fresh acidity and nice length. The Sforzato '07 is good, with a complex, close-focused nose and an elegant, continuous palate. Grumello '06 is gutsy and a tad gamey, with genuine structure and length while Ghibellino '09 has a complex nose and a full-flavoured, pleasantly fresh palate.

●	Valtellina Sup. Sassella Ris. '06	▼▼▼	6
●	Valtellina Sfursat '07	▼▼	6
●	Valtellina Sup. Crespino '06	▼▼	6
●	Valtellina Sup. Inferno Ris. '06	▼▼	6
●	Valtellina Sup. Grumello '06	▼▼	4
○	Ghibellino '09	▼	5
●	Valtellina Sfursat Fruttaio Ca' Rizzieri '06	▽▽▽	7
●	Valtellina Sfursat Fruttaio Ca' Rizzieri '02	▽▽▽	7
●	Valtellina Sfursat Fruttaio Ca' Rizzieri '00	▽▽▽	7
●	Valtellina Sfursat Fruttaio Ca' Rizzieri '98	▽▽▽	6
●	Valtellina Sfursat Fruttaio Ca' Rizzieri '97	▽▽▽	6
●	Valtellina Sfursat Fruttaio Ca' Rizzieri '95	▽▽▽	5
●	Valtellina Sfursat Fruttaio Ca' Rizzieri '04	▽▽	7
●	Valtellina Sup. Crespino '05	▽▽	6
●	Valtellina Sup. Inferno Ris. '05	▽▽	6

Ricci Curbastro

via Adro, 37
25031 Capriolo [BS]
tel. 030736094
www.riccicurbastro.it

CELLAR SALES
PRE-BOOKED VISITS
ROOMS

ANNUAL PRODUCTION 240,000 bottles
HECTARES UNDER VINE 26
VITICULTURE METHOD Conventional

Agronomist and oenologist Riccardo Ricci Curbastro has skilfully managed the family estate since the 1980s. Today it boasts almost 30 hectares of vineyards and a handsome cellar in the historic villa at Capriolo. His commitment has earned the winery a place among the very best of the zone. Riccardo also plays an important role in the wine world. He has been president of the Consorzio del Franciacorta and is currently president of FederDoc and the European Federation of Origin Wines, the umbrella organization for European wine consortia.

The estate's extensive list occasionally features the release of recently disgorged older vintages labelled MR, Museum Release. One of these, Satèn '04, distinguished itself in our finals with alluring hawthorn and gooseberry and velvety tones of vanilla, medicinal herbs and elderflower. Dosaggio Zero Gualberto '04 also reached the finals with attractive evolved minerality and plenty of backbone. We loved the healthy fruit of the supple, balanced, invigorating Extra Brut '06. The excellent non-vintage Brut is rounded, fresh and long while the juicy, mineral Extra Brut MR '03 is very sound. Curtefranca Santella del Grom '06 was the best of the still wines this year.

○	Franciacorta Dosaggio Zero Gualberto '04	▼▼	6
○	Franciacorta Satèn Brut M.R. '04	▼▼	6
●	Curtefranca Rosso Santella del Gröm '06	▼▼	4
○	Franciacorta Brut	▼▼	5
○	Franciacorta Extra Brut '06	▼▼	5
○	Franciacorta Extra Brut M.R. '03	▼▼	6
○	Franciacorta Satèn	▼▼	5
○	Curtefranca Bianco '09	▼	3
●	Curtefranca Rosso '07	▼	3
⊙	Franciacorta Brut Rosé	▼	6
○	Franciacorta Demi Sec	▼	5
○	Pinot Bianco Sebino '09	▼	5
○	TdF Curtefranca V. Bosco Alto '07	▼	4
○	Franciacorta Brut	▽▽	5
○	Franciacorta Extra Brut '05	▽▽	5
○	Franciacorta Extra Brut '03	▽▽	5*
○	Franciacorta Extra Brut '05	▽	5

Ronco Calino

FRAZ. TORBIATO
LOC. QUATTRO CAMINI
VIA FENICE, 45
25030 ADRO [BS]
TEL. 0307451073
www.roncocalino.it

PRE-BOOKED VISITS

ANNUAL PRODUCTION 60,000 bottles
HECTARES UNDER VINE 10
VITICULTURE METHOD Conventional

In 1996, Paolo Radici decided to purchase the handsome villa at Torbiato di Adro that had belonged to pianist Arturo Benedetti Michelangeli. It is surrounded by about ten hectares of vines, which provide the raw material for the small, meticulously crafted production of the new, very modern cellar. Ronco Calino offers a complete range crafted with the advice from Professor Leonardo Valenti of the University of Milan.

Our favourite was the Brut '06, a remarkably elegant, balanced cuvée with a fine bead and a complex nose of ripe fruit and camomile-led medicinal herbs. On the palate, it shows plush and full flavoured. Brut 120 '99 has aged for ten years on the lees and is complex and mineral, with plenty of backbone. The refreshing Brut offers notes of hawthorn blossom and citrus fruit while the soft, full Curtefranca Rosso '06 has good structure. Pinot Nero l'Arturo '07 and Rosé Radijan are both a little under par this year.

● Curtefranca Rosso '06	▼▼	5
○ Franciacorta Brut '06	▼▼	6
○ Franciacorta Brut	▼▼	5
○ Franciacorta Brut Centoventi '99	▼▼	8
○ Curtefranca Bianco '08	▼	4
⊙ Franciacorta Brut Rosé Radijan	▼	6
○ Franciacorta Satèn	▼	5
○ Passito Solmé	▼	6
● Pinot Nero L'Arturo '07	▼	6
○ Franciacorta Brut '05	▽▽	6
○ Franciacorta Brut '01	▽▽	6
○ TdF Bianco '03	▽▽	4*
● TdF Rosso '04	▽▽	5
● TdF Rosso '03	▽▽	5

Tenuta Roveglia

LOC. ROVEGLIA, 1
25010 POZZOLENGO [BS]
TEL. 030918663
www.tenutaroveglia.it

CELLAR SALES
PRE-BOOKED VISITS

ANNUAL PRODUCTION 250,000 bottles
HECTARES UNDER VINE 61
VITICULTURE METHOD Conventional

Roveglia is a handsome estate owned by the Swiss Zweifel Azzoni family. There are about 60 hectares of vineyards in the Lugana district, almost all planted to turbiana. In these clayey soils, the variety yields elegant, deep wines, spurring on the efforts of winery manager Paolo Fabiani and oenologist Flavio Prà. In recent years, the estate's wines, particularly the Luganas, have found their place among the best in the DOC, thanks to scrupulous field selection and sophisticated cellar techniques.

Lugana Filo di Arianna '08 deservedly featured in our finals. It is an opulent white, made with late-harvest grapes from the estate's oldest vineyards, and flaunts a nose of ripe fruit and flowers, with refreshing green notes, and a smooth, firmly structured palate showcasing sound fruit and ending in a long mineral, citrussy finish. Vigne di Catullo '08 is also first rate, appearing more spirited and supple, but still offering complex depth, while Lugana Limne '09 has crisp notes of fresh fruit and a close-focused, full, fruity palate. Garda Classico Rosato Miti '09, the white Ocros '08 and particularly the Lugana Brut, with charming floral and fruity notes, are all sound.

○ Lugana Sup. Filo di Arianna '08	▼▼	5
○ Lugana Brut	▼▼	4
○ Lugana Limne '09	▼▼	4*
○ Lugana Sup. Vigne di Catullo '08	▼▼	4
⊙ Garda Cl. Rosato Miti '09	▼	4
○ Ocros Bianco '08	▼	4
○ Lugana '08	▽▽	4*
○ Lugana '07	▽▽	4*
○ Lugana Sup. Filo di Arianna '06	▽▽	5
○ Lugana Sup. Filo di Arianna '05	▽▽	5
○ Lugana Sup. Vigne di Catullo '07	▽▽	4*
○ Lugana Sup. Vigne di Catullo '06	▽▽	4*
○ Lugana Sup. Vigne di Catullo '05	▽▽	4

San Cristoforo

VIA VILLANUOVA, 2
25030 ERBUSCO [BS]
TEL. 0307760482
www.sancristoforo.eu

CELLAR SALES
PRE-BOOKED VISITS

ANNUAL PRODUCTION 80,000 bottles
HECTARES UNDER VINE 12
VITICULTURE METHOD Conventional

Bruno Dotti and his wife Claudia Cavalleri run this Erbusco winery, which they purchased in 1992, with great dedication. Over the years, the estate has slowly expanded the area under vine to 12 hectares while the cellar has been modernized and rebuilt below ground. Today, annual production is around 80,000 bottles, which is expected to rise to 100,000 once the new vineyards start producing fruit.

Brut '06 is a deep, dense Franciacorta with an attractively delicate nose of hazelnut and honey, accompanied by an elegant, balanced, fresh palate. The Pas Dosé from the same vintage is more elegant and delicate but shows finesse, close-focused fruit and an attractive mineral finish. San Cristoforo Uno '06 is a full-bodied Merlot with hints of grass and spice on the nose and a juicy, close-knit palate. The Franciacorta Brut and the Rosé are both good.

○ Franciacorta Brut '06	▼▼	5
○ Franciacorta Pas Dosé '06	▼▼	6
● San Cristoforo Uno '06	▼▼	5
○ Franciacorta Brut	▼	5
⊙ Franciacorta Rosé	▼	5
● TdF Curtefranca Rosso '08	▼	4
○ Franciacorta Brut '03	▽▽	6
○ Franciacorta Pas Dosé '05	▽▽	6
○ Franciacorta Pas Dosé '04	▽▽	6
○ TdF Bianco '05	▽▽	3*
○ TdF Bianco '03	▽▽	4*
○ TdF Bianco '01	▽▽	3*
● TdF Curtefranca Rosso '03	▽▽	4*

Podere San Giorgio

LOC. CASTELLO, 1
27046 SANTA GIULETTA [PV]
TEL. 0383899168
www.poderesangiorgio.it

CELLAR SALES
PRE-BOOKED VISITS
FOOD

ANNUAL PRODUCTION 250,000 bottles
HECTARES UNDER VINE 24
VITICULTURE METHOD Conventional

This handsome estate with a 16th-century tower and a cellar dating from approximately the same period has belonged to the Perdomini family from Milan for the past 32 years, during which they have completely renovated it. Responsibility for production has been entrusted to various people, with mixed fortunes, but now, with the new generation represented by Elena Perdomini, the winery seems on right track. Actually, San Giorgio had put its money on a classic-method rosé well before the consortium launched the idea of Cruasé.

We'll commence with the Metodo Classico rosé, a Cruasé that lives up to those from the good old days. It has a coppery hue, with a concentrated nose of fruit and aromatic herbs followed by a palate with good backbone and a close-focused, fragrant finish. Bonarda Vivace Rebecca '09 has the distinctive vibrant medium-ruby hue of central Oltrepò wines and clean-tasting aromas of blueberries, then by very well-calibrated tannins. Titanium '07 is based on cabernet sauvignon and offers its typical grassy notes, along with spice, liquorice and wild berries. The Pinot Grigio '09 and Pinot Nero '07 are pleasant but not quite as good as past vintages.

● OP Bonarda Vivace Rebecca '09	▼▼	4*
⊙ OP Pinot Nero Brut Cl. Cruasé Castel San Giorgio	▼▼	5
● Titanium '07	▼▼	5
○ OP Pinot Grigio Argento Vivo '09	▼	4
● OP Pinot Nero Re Nero '07	▼	5
○ OP Pinot Grigio Argento Vivo '08	▽▽	4*
● OP Pinot Nero Re Nero '06	▽▽	4*

Travaglino

LOC. TRAVAGLINO, 6A
27040 CALVIGNANO [PV]
TEL. 0383872222
www.travaglino.it

CELLAR SALES
PRE-BOOKED VISITS

ANNUAL PRODUCTION 220,000 bottles
HECTARES UNDER VINE 80
VITICULTURE METHOD Conventional

This is one of Oltrepò's historic quality-oriented wineries. It was also one of the first to focus on improving the estate's vineyard selections. Vineyard management has undergone several changes but the concept is still the same: planting the right grapes in the right soils. This may seem a basic concept but quite often it has been neglected in Oltrepò. Here the soil is largely chalk and limestone, ideal for white grapes and varieties used for the production of sparklers.

One of those sparkling wines, the Classese '05, reached our finals, thanks to its concentrated, varied nose with notes of cakes and its full palate with impressive backbone and a very long finish. Once again Riesling Campo della Fojada '09 took Two Glasses, with its trademark notes of aromatic herbs – particularly sage and mint – and its commendably clean, slightly mineral palate. The Monteceresino, now Cruasé DOCG, is also good, with a charming nose of red berry fruit and attractively mineral palate. The rest of the list is good, with the Cuvée 59 worthy of special mention.

○ OP Pinot Nero Brut Classese '05	▼▼	5
⊙ OP Pinot Nero Brut Cl. Cruasè Monteceresimo '07	▼▼	4
○ OP Riesling Campo della Fojada '09	▼▼	4*
○ OP Gran Cuvée Brut	▼	5
○ OP Pinot Nero Brut Cl. Cuvée 59 '05	▼	5
● OP Pinot Nero Pernero '09	▼	4
● OP Pinot Nero Poggio della Buttinera '06	▼	5
○ OP Pinot Nero Brut Classese '04	▽▽	5
○ OP Pinot Nero Brut Cl. Cuvée 59 '06	▽▽	5
⊙ OP Pinot Nero Brut Rosé Monteceresino	▽▽	5
○ OP Riesling Campo della Fojada '08	▽▽	4
○ OP Riesling Campo della Fojada '05	▽▽	4
○ OP Riesling Campo della Fojada '04	▽▽	4
○ OP Riesling Campo della Fojada '00	▽▽	3*

★ Uberti

LOC. SALEM
VIA E. FERMI, 2
25030 ERBUSCO [BS]
TEL. 0307267476
www.ubertivini.it

PRE-BOOKED VISITS

ANNUAL PRODUCTION 180,000 bottles
HECTARES UNDER VINE 24
VITICULTURE METHOD Conventional

The Ubertis settled in Franciacorta in the late 18th century. Over the years, Agostino and his wife Eleonora have created one of the most esteemed wineries in the zone and beyond. The vineyards, their pride and joy, are mostly in Erbusco, like the famous, meticulously tended Comarì del Salem, a sort of Lombard grand cru. Agostino and Eleonora are flanked by their daughter Silvia, a graduate in oenology with experience abroad. The trio's expertise is accompanied by an authentic passion for wine, and Franciacorta in particular. Silvia's sister Francesca runs the hospitality side of the business.

The Three Glass award for Satèn Magnificentia this year is the Ubertis' 14th. It is fully deserved, for this historic cuvée is exceptionally complex, offering a nose of ripe plums and apricots, cakes and vanilla, with delicate citrus and herbal notes. On the palate it is the very epitome of Satèn: creamy, fruity, soft and perfectly balanced. Non Dosato Sublimis '04 vaunts impressive complexity, with hazelnut and biscuits on the nose and a solid, ripe, full-flavoured palate. Comarì del Salem Extra Brut is as charming as ever, with multi-layered structure and stylistic cleanliness. Quality throughout the list is also good.

○ Franciacorta Satèn Magnificentia	▼▼▼	6
○ Franciacorta Extra Brut Comarì del Salem '05	▼▼	7
○ Franciacorta Non Dosato Sublimis '04	▼▼	7
○ Curtefranca Bianco Maria Medici '06	▼▼	5
○ Franciacorta Brut Francesco I	▼▼	6
○ Franciacorta Extra Brut Francesco I	▼▼	6
○ Curtefranca Bianco '09	▼	4
● Curtefranca Rosso '08	▼	4
⊙ Franciacorta Brut Rosé Francesco I	▼	6
● Rosso dei Frati Priori	▼	5
○ Franciacorta Brut Comarì del Salem '00	▽▽▽	7
○ Franciacorta Extra Brut Comarì del Salem '03	▽▽▽	7
○ Franciacorta Extra Brut Comarì del Salem '02	▽▽▽	7
○ Franciacorta Extra Brut Comarì del Salem '01	▽▽▽	7
○ Franciacorta Extra Brut Comarì del Salem '98	▽▽▽	7

Vanzini

FRAZ. BARBALEONE, 7
27040 SAN DAMIANO AL COLLE [PV]
TEL. 038575019
www.vanzini-wine.com

CELLAR SALES
PRE-BOOKED VISITS

ANNUAL PRODUCTION 600,000 bottles
HECTARES UNDER VINE 22
VITICULTURE METHOD Conventional

When it comes to making the most typical wines of the region, the Vanzini brothers have few rivals in Oltrepò. In particular, pressure tanks for refermentation hold no secrets for them and, year after year, their Bonardas, Sangue di Giudas and Charmat-method sparklers are among the best of the zone. The quality of the pinot nero grapes from this area of San Damiano al Colle is so high that a return to the production of classic-method wines is planned for the near future.

The Vanzinis are the holders of a record. Their semi-sparkling Bonarda is the first ever to reach our finals. Actually, it would have been impossible not to select such a fragrant wine, with aromas of raspberry-led forest fruits and violets, soft, alluring tannins, good balance and perfect concentration. It also offers the same excellent value for money as the rest of the range. Sangue di Giuda '09 is equally good and again one of the best of the zone, with crisp fruit that comprises an unusual banana note. The two Charmat-method Extra Dry sparklers are impeccable, and the rest of the list is very good.

● OP Bonarda Frizzante '09	▼▼	3*
● OP Barbaleone '05	▼▼	6
● OP Sangue di Giuda '09	▼▼	4*
○ Pinot Nero Spumante Extra Dry Martinotti	▼▼	4*
⊙ Pinot Nero Spumante Extra Dry Martinotti Rosé	▼▼	4*
● OP Barbera '09	▼	4
○ OP Moscato Spumante	▼	3
○ OP Pinot Grigio '09	▼	4
● OP Barbera '08	▽▽	4*
● OP Barbera '06	▽▽	3*
● OP Barbera Vigna Preda '00	▽▽	5
● OP Sangue di Giuda '08	▽▽	4*
● OP Sangue di Giuda '07	▽▽	4*
● OP Sangue di Giuda '05	▽▽	4*

Vercesi del Castellazzo

VIA AURELIANO, 36
27040 MONTÙ BECCARIA [PV]
TEL. 038560067
vercesidelcastellazzo@libero.it

CELLAR SALES
PRE-BOOKED VISITS

ANNUAL PRODUCTION 80,000 bottles
HECTARES UNDER VINE 15
VITICULTURE METHOD Conventional

Montù Beccaria is quintessential terroir for the cultivation of black grapes. Here the Vercesi family, whose surname is very common in the area, have scrupulously been producing their various vineyard selections for many years, first in beautiful Castellazzo, which offers stunning views over the Versa and Po valleys, and now in the more modern cellar built a few years ago at the bottom of the valley. Obviously, they have not abandoned the family home. The wines are austere and tannic, requiring several years to emerge.

While Fatila '03 has achieved perfect balance between body and tannins, the '04 – albeit already very good with almondy notes and prominent tannins – requires further bottle ageing to reach its best. However, the Clà that we tasted this year is the best ever. Indeed, the '08 vintage has yielded an exceptionally tasty Barbera with sound, crisp fruit, attractive balsamic notes and a long, supple finish, which fully deserved Two Glasses. Pinot Nero Luogo dei Monti '07, which is sublimely well typed in the best vintages, seems to struggle a little, but earned Two Glasses for its promise. All the other wines are good, including Pezzalunga '09, which offers outstanding value.

● OP Barbera Clà '08	▼▼	4*
● OP Bonarda Fatila '03	▼▼	5
● OP Bonarda Vivace Luogo della Milla '09	▼▼	3*
● OP Pinot Nero Luogo dei Monti '07	▼▼	4*
● OP Rosso Pezzalunga '09	▼▼	3*
● Bacca Rossa '09	▼	2
○ OP Pinot Nero in Bianco Gugiarolo '09	▼	3
● OP Barbera Clà '07	▽▽	4
● OP Barbera Clà '06	▽▽	4*
● OP Barbera Clà '05	▽▽	4
● OP Bonarda Fatila '03	▽▽	5
● OP Rosso Pezzalunga '06	▽▽	3*
● Rosso del Castellazzo '04	▽▽	5
● Rosso del Castellazzo '03	▽▽	5

Bruno Verdi

VIA VERGOMBERRA, 5
27044 CANNETO PAVESE [PV]
TEL. 038588023
www.verdibruno.it

CELLAR SALES
PRE-BOOKED VISITS

ANNUAL PRODUCTION 100,000 bottles
HECTARES UNDER VINE 9
VITICULTURE METHOD Conventional

This is one of Oltrepò's most reliable wineries. Paolo Verdi started working alongside his father, after whom the estate is still named, as a child and following Bruno's untimely death, he took over responsibility for the cellar, encouraged by his prodigious mother Carla. Step by step, Paolo has built up a complete range of wines that has continued to improve over the years to its current level.

The most notable new features this year are the absences, for Paolo Verdi has decided to age both Rosso Riserva Cavariola, which regularly makes it through to our finals, and Riesling Vigna Costa, for an extra year. However, the estate still won Two Glasses with Bonarda Vivace '09, which has excellent fragrance, sound fruit, balance and drinkability. Vergomberra Brut '06 is one of the best ever, showing full flavoured, balsamic, edgy and concentrated. It's an excellent through-the-meal Metodo Classico. It's difficult to find fault with the rest of the list, which ranges from the very fragrant Sangue di Giuda Paradiso '09 to the Barbera del Marrone '07 with attractive balsam.

● OP Bonarda Vivace Possessione di Vergombera '09	🍷🍷	4*
● OP Barbera Campo del Marrone '07	🍷🍷	4
○ OP Brut Cl. Vergomberra '06	🍷🍷	5
● OP Buttafuoco '09	🍷🍷	4*
○ OP Moscato Volpara '09	🍷🍷	3*
● OP Sangue di Giuda Dolce Paradiso '09	🍷🍷	3*
○ OP Pinot Grigio '09	🍷	4
● OP Pinot Nero '08	🍷	4
● OP Rosso Cavariola Ris. '06	🍸🍸	5
● OP Rosso Cavariola Ris. '05	🍸🍸	5
● OP Rosso Cavariola Ris. '04	🍸🍸	5
● OP Rosso Cavariola Ris. '03	🍸🍸	5
● OP Rosso Cavariola Ris. '02	🍸🍸	5
● OP Rosso Cavariola Ris. '99	🍸🍸	5

Giuseppe Vezzoli

VIA COSTA SOPRA, 22
25030 ERBUSCO [BS]
TEL. 0307267579
eveniogv@libero.it

CELLAR SALES
PRE-BOOKED VISITS

ANNUAL PRODUCTION 130,000 bottles
HECTARES UNDER VINE 40
VITICULTURE METHOD Conventional

Several years ago, Giuseppe Vezzoli made a major life choice and closed his business to run his father Attilio's five-hectare vineyard. Subsequently, the property grew into an operation with 40 hectares under vine, estate-owned and leased, and an annual production of over 130,000 bottles. Giuseppe's wines are made with the aid of longstanding Franciacorta consultant oenologist Cesare Ferrari and are renowned for their consistent high quality.

Although Vezzoli's cuvées may not have reached their absolute peak this year, we were impressed by Franciacorta Brut Nefertiti '04, whose greatest charms are its fullness and structure, and we liked its complex nose, with hints of honey and vanilla, and its balanced palate. Nefertiti Extra Brut '04 has an attractively complex nose with smoky notes over hints of tropical fruit and an alluring fresh, fruity finish. The Brut '06 is rich and velvety, with green notes and hints of camomile, and a balanced, harmonious palate, while the basic Brut is good.

○ Franciacorta Brut '06	🍷🍷	6
○ Franciacorta Brut Nefertiti '04	🍷🍷	7
○ Franciacorta Extra Brut Nefertiti Dizeta '04	🍷🍷	7
○ Franciacorta Brut	🍷	6
○ Franciacorta Satèn	🍷	6
○ Franciacorta Brut '03	🍸🍸	6
○ Franciacorta Brut '01	🍸🍸	6
○ Franciacorta Brut '99	🍸🍸	6
○ Franciacorta Brut '98	🍸🍸	6
○ Franciacorta Brut Nefertiti '00	🍸🍸	7
○ Franciacorta Extra Brut Nefertiti Dizeta '03	🍸🍸	7
⊙ Franciacorta Rosé Brut	🍸🍸	6
○ Franciacorta Satèn '04	🍸🍸	6

Villa

via Villa, 12
25040 Monticelli Brusati [BS]
tel. 030652329
www.villafranciacorta.it

ROOMS AND FOOD

ANNUAL PRODUCTION 310,000 bottles
HECTARES UNDER VINE 37
VITICULTURE METHOD Conventional

Villa is a beautiful little hamlet in the municipality of Monticelli Brusati that Alessandro Bianchi purchased in the 1960s, together with approximately 100 hectares of surrounding countryside, and subsequently renovated. Today, the estate boasts almost 40 hectares under vine, including the Gradoni vineyard planted on the dry-stone terraces of the Madonna della Rosa hill. Management is in the capable hands of Paolo Pizziol and the complex also offers country accommodation.

This year we liked the good Brut '06, with its nose of tropical fruits, fine bead and creamy mousse, which offers plenty of fruity pulp and a delicate citrussy finish. Satèn '06 is plush and creamy, brimming with notes of vanilla and cake, followed by a full-flavoured, continuous palate and a long finish. Brut Cuvette '05 closely resembles a Satèn, with its notes of tropical fruit and vanilla. Both the slightly over-evolved Rosé '06 and the Demi Sec are good while Rosso Gradoni '06 was our favourite from the still wines.

● Curtefranca Rosso Gradoni '06	🍷🍷	5
○ Franciacorta Brut '06	🍷🍷	5
○ Franciacorta Brut Cuvette '05	🍷🍷	6
○ Franciacorta Satèn '06	🍷🍷	6
● Curtefranca Rosso '07	🍷	4
⊙ Franciacorta Rosé Brut '06	🍷	6
⊙ Franciacorta Rosé Demi Sec	🍷	5
○ Franciacorta Brut '05	ΥΥ	5
○ Franciacorta Brut '02	ΥΥ	5*
⊙ Franciacorta Rosé '05	ΥΥ	6
⊙ Franciacorta Rosé Demi Sec '03	ΥΥ	6
○ Franciacorta Satèn '04	ΥΥ	6

Chiara Ziliani

via Franciacorta, 7
25050 Provaglio d'Iseo [BS]
tel. 030981661
www.cantinazilianichiara.it

PRE-BOOKED VISITS

ANNUAL PRODUCTION 210,000 bottles
HECTARES UNDER VINE 17
VITICULTURE METHOD Conventional

Chiara Ziliani is a motivated young businesswoman who owns a handsome modern winery on a morainic hill about 250 metres above sea level, surrounded by 15 hectares of vineyards in Provaglio d'Iseo. In addition to the beautiful landscape, the high-density, low-yield vineyards managed to ensure low environmental impact are well worth a visit. Chiara produces a wide range of wines in three product lines. However, the one closest to her heart is undoubtedly the Satèn, of which she offers several versions.

This year we particularly liked the Brut Ziliani C '06, which proffers attractive notes of acacia honey, vanilla and apple jelly on the nose and is satisfyingly continuous, fresh and full on the palate. Satèn Ziliani C has a smoky nose but the palate is creamy, fresh and invigorating, like Rosé Conte di Provaglio, which is attractively full, with classic notes of wild berries and vanilla, and a savoury, assertive finish with fresh fruit. Brut Duca d'Iseo has citrussy tones and attractive minerality while the distinguishing characteristic of the Satèn in the same range is florality. Brut Conte di Provaglio is impressively continuous on the palate, and the other wines are all good.

○ Franciacorta Brut Conte di Provaglio	🍷🍷	4
○ Franciacorta Brut Duca d'Iseo	🍷🍷	4
⊙ Franciacorta Brut Rosé Conte di Provaglio	🍷🍷	5
○ Franciacorta Brut Ziliani C '06	🍷🍷	5
○ Franciacorta Satèn Duca d'Iseo	🍷🍷	5
○ Franciacorta Satèn Ziliani C	🍷🍷	5
⊙ Franciacorta Brut Rosé Ziliani C	🍷	5
○ Franciacorta Brut Ziliani C	🍷	5
○ Franciacorta Satèn Conte di Provaglio	🍷	4
⊙ Franciacorta Brut Rosé Ziliani C	ΥΥ	5
○ Franciacorta Satèn	ΥΥ	5
○ Franciacorta Satèn Conte di Provaglio	ΥΥ	5

OTHER WINERIES

Al Rocol

VIA PROVINCIALE, 79
25050 OME [BS]
TEL. 0306852542
www.alrocol.com

Gianluigi Vimercati lovingly tends his 9 hectares of vineyards in Ome, which yield a well-crafted range of Franciacortas and still wines. We picked out the excellent Extra Brut Castellini '06, with fresh balsamic, fruity notes, and Brut Ca' del Luf '06, which we liked for its solid structure and nice oak.

○ Franciacorta Extra Brut Castellini '06	🍷🍷	6
○ Franciacorta Brut Ca' del Luf '06	🍷🍷	5
○ Franciacorta Satèn Martignac	🍷	5
● TdF Rosso Roncat '06	🍷	5

Riccardo Albani

LOC. CASONA
S.DA SAN BIAGIO, 46
27045 CASTEGGIO [PV]
TEL. 038383622
www.vinialbani.it

Riccardo Albani's philosophy is strict organic farming and his wines must thus be judged in this light. This year he did not present the Riesling, one of his winery's top bottles, but Rosso Riserva Vigne della Casona '04 has plenty of fruit and very evolved notes.

● OP Rosso Vigne della Casona Ris. '04	🍷	5

Tenuta degli Angeli

FRAZ. SANTO STEFANO
VIA FARA, 2
24060 CAROBBIO DEGLI ANGELI [BG]
TEL. 035687130
www.tenutadegliangeli.it

Oro degli Angeli is a table wine made from dried moscato giallo. Once again, it is very pleasant, with notes of candied citron and mandarin and good backbone. Barbariccia '06 has well-calibrated oak, while the Metodo Classico is well made, with notes of aromatic herbs. Valcalepio Bianco Triplok '09 is nice.

○ Oro degli Angeli Passito '06	🍷🍷	5
● Valcalepio Rosso Barbariccia '06	🍷🍷	4
○ Spumante Brut Cl. degli Angeli	🍷	5
○ Valcalepio Bianco Triplok '09	🍷	4

Antica Tesa

LOC. MATTINA
VIA MERANO, 28
25080 BOTTICINO [BS]
TEL. 0302691500

The Noventa family keeps the honour of this small designation high with Botticino Vigna del Gobbio '06, from old vines, which gives pervasive blackberries and dark berry fruit with pleasant hints of attractive oak accompanied by a complex, elegant, full-bodied palate. One of the province's finest reds.

● Botticino Vigna del Gobbio '06	🍷🍷	6

AR.PE.PE.

VIA DEL BUON CONSIGLIO, 4
23100 SONDRIO
TEL. 0342214120
www.arpepe.com

Rocce Rosse '99 is complex with minerality, a taut, full-flavoured palate and a very long finish. Ultimi Raggi '04 has a pervasive nose of cherries and a warm, cossetting palate. The richly extracted Rosso di Valtellina '07 has a nose of tobacco and prunes, and a lingering finish.

● Rosso di Valtellina '07	🍷🍷	4
● Valtellina Sup. Sassella Rocce Rosse Ris. '99	🍷🍷	6
● Valtellina Sup. Sassella Ultimi Raggi '04	🍷🍷	7

Avanzi

VIA TREVISAGO, 19
25080 MANERBA DEL GARDA [BS]
TEL. 0365551013
www.avanzi.net

Avanzi is a legendary name in Garda winemaking and its fine estate in Sirmione produces numerous wines. We singled out an excellent Groppello '09, which is soft, fresh and elegantly tannic, and a decent, beefy Garda Rosso '08. The other wines are well made.

● Garda Cl. Groppello Giovanni Avanzi '09	🍷🍷	4*
⊙ Garda Brut Rosé '09	🍷	3
● Garda Cl. Sup. Rosso '08	🍷	4
○ Lugana Sirmione '09	🍷	4

Barbacarlo - Lino Maga

s.da Bronese, 3
27043 Broni [PV]
tel. 038551212
barbacarlodimaga@libero.it

Take it or leave it: Barbacarlo is an unconventional wine. Each taste of Lino Maga's creation is a surprise, varying from bottle to bottle, and from year to year. In our glass this year we enjoyed a wine with close-focused notes of dark berry fruit and an almondy finish.

● Barbacarlo '08	🍷🍷	6

Luciano Barberini

Via Emilia, 93
27050 Redavalle [PV]
tel. 038574164
www.barberinilucianovini.it

Castlà '08, from croatina and pinot nero, has a nose of red berries and an alluring palate. Montecastello '08, from barbera and cabernet sauvignon, is attractive with perceptible residual sugar, and the chewy Bonarda Vivace Poggio della Monsella '09 has blueberries. Pinot Grigio Costa dei Figli '09 is well made.

● Castlà '08	🍷🍷	3*
● Montecastello '08	🍷	4
● OP Bonarda Vivace Poggio della Monsella '09	🍷	3
○ Pinot Grigio Costa dei Figli '09	🍷	2

Barboglio De Gaioncelli

fraz. Colombaro
via Nazario Sauro
25040 Corte Franca [BS]
tel. 0309826831
www.barbogliodegaioncelli.it

The Costa family own 15 hectares of fine vineyards in Corte Franca that produce excellent grapes for their cuvées. This year we liked the Satèn, with complex minerality, the plush Brut and the charming Franciacorta Extra Dry with its subtle sweetness.

○ Franciacorta Brut	🍷	5
○ Franciacorta Extra Dry	🍷	4
○ Franciacorta Saten	🍷	5

La Basia

loc. La Basia
via Predefitte, 31
25080 Puegnago sul Garda [BS]
tel. 0365555958
www.labasia.it

Elena Parona's estate was founded in the hills of Valtènesi in 1975. It now has 20 hectares of vineyards and a consistently high-quality range. Both the solidly built Gropello '08 and the Chiaretto '09, with fresh vegetal and fruity notes, are sound, while the balanced Martì '06 is decent, with fine tannins.

● Garda Cl. Sup. Martì '06	🍷🍷	4
● Garda Groppello La Botte Piena '08	🍷🍷	3
⊙ Garda Cl. Chiaretto La Moglie Ubriaca '09	🍷	4

Cantina Sociale Bergamasca

via Bergamo, 10
24060 San Paolo d'Argon [BG]
tel. 035951098
www.cantinabergamasca.it

Valcalepio Rosso Orologio '08, is a wine that offers outstanding value, along with spicy notes and good fruit. Moscato Giallo Suite '09 is fresh and citrussy. This year Riserva Akros '06 was slightly below par, showing balance but less weight than usual. Schiava '09 is a pleasant, easy-drinking rosé.

● Valcalepio Rosso Orologio '08	🍷🍷	3*
○ Moscato Giallo Suite '09	🍷	3
⊙ Schiava '09	🍷	3
● Valcalepio Rosso Akros Ris. '06	🍷	4

Conti Bettoni Cazzago

via Marconi, 6
25046 Cazzago San Martino [BS]
tel. 0307750875
www.contibettonicazzago.it

Again this year, Vincenzo Bettoni Cazzago's Satèn is very good, with a close-focused nose of fruit and vanilla, a carefully calibrated palate and a finish with well-defined notes of fruit and toast. The non-vintage Brut displays pleasant savouriness and nice overall balance.

○ Franciacorta Satèn	🍷🍷	6
○ Franciacorta Brut	🍷	6

OTHER WINERIES

Bonaldi - Cascina del Bosco

LOC. PETOSINO
VIA GASPAROTTO, 96
24010 SORISOLE [BG]
TEL. 035571701
www.cascinadelbosco.it

Riserva Cantoalto '06 was the estate's best wines again this year, with attractive aromas of wild berries, spice and good depth. The Brut Metodo Classico has nice backbone and aromas of tropical fruit while Valcalepio Rosso '07 lays out fruit and a charming nose of hay and aromatic herbs.

- ● Valcalepio Rosso Cantoalto Ris. '06 — TT 5
- O Bonaldi Brut M. Cl. — T 5
- ● Valcalepio Rosso '07 — T 3

Borgo La Gallinaccia

VIA IV NOVEMBRE, 15
25050 RODENGO SAIANO [BS]
TEL. 030611314
www.borgolagallinaccia.it

This small estate in Rodengo Saiano has distinguished itself with the quality of its wines. We very much liked Colmo dei Colmi '07, a balanced, firmly structured, compact Bordeaux blend, and the Franciacorta Brut is also excellent. Both the Pas Dosé and the Satèn are sound.

- ● Colmo dei Colmi '07 — TT 5
- O Franciacorta Brut — TT 5
- O Franciacorta Pas Dosè — T 5
- O Franciacorta Satèn — T 5

La Boscaiola

VIA RICCAFANA, 19
25033 COLOGNE [BS]
TEL. 0307156386
www.laboscaiola.com

Giuliana Cenci crafts fine still wines and Franciacortas on the lovely family estate in Cologne. We singled out a juicy, vanillaed Satèn with close-focused aromas of white-fleshed fruits and aromatic herbs, a comfortingly balanced Brut and the pleasant Terre di Franciacorta Bianco Giuliana C. '08.

- O Franciacorta Satén — TT 6
- O TdF Bianco Giuliana C. '08 — TT 4
- O Franciacorta Brut — T 5

Alessio Brandolini

FRAZ. BOFFALORA, 68
27040 SAN DAMIANO AL COLLE [PV]
TEL. 038575232
www@alessiobrandolini.com

This very young estate presented several interesting wines for its Guide debut. The fragrant Bonarda Vivace '09 offers outstanding value for money, Soffio '08 is a juicy still Bonarda with lively tannins, while the red Beneficio '07, from barbera and croatina briefly aged in oak, has notes of plums.

- ● OP Bonarda Il Soffio '08 — TT 3*
- ● OP Bonarda Vivace '09 — TT 3*
- ● Beneficio '07 — T 2

Bredasole

LOC. BREDASOLE
VIA SAN PIETRO, 44
25030 PARATICO [BS]
TEL. 035910407
www.bredasole.it

The Ferrari brothers and consultant oenologist Corrado Cugnasco produce still wines and Franciacortas. Franciacorta Brut is very good, showing fresh, balsamic and mineral, as is the Nature, all invigorating savouriness and good pressure. Curtefranca Spigolato '07 is nice and the soft Demi Sec Demì is good.

- O Franciacorta Brut — TT 4
- O Franciacorta Nature — TT 5
- ● Curtefranca Rosso Spigolato '07 — T 5
- O Franciacorta Demi Sec Demi — T 6

Luciano Brega

FRAZ. BERGAMASCO, 7
27040 MONTÙ BECCARIA [PV]
TEL. 038560237
www.lucianobrega.it

Gran Montù, a legendary classic-method rosé, scored well for its convincing nose and full, balanced palate. Bonarda Casapaia – vintage not declared but it's an '08 – has very intense tertiary notes, while Bonarda Vivace '09 offers pleasant wild berries.

- ⊙ Gran Montù Brut Rosé — TT 4*
- ● OP Bonarda Vivace '09 — TT 3*
- ● OP Bonarda Casapaia '08 — T 4

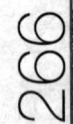

Cantina Sociale di Broni
via Sansaluto, 81
27043 Broni [PV]
tel. 038551505
www.bronis.it

Quality at Cantina di Broni has risen. This year, our favourites were Bonarda Vivace '09, with well-defined fruit, and the varietal Pinot Nero '07, both from the Bronis Selezione range. The Metodo Classicos are good. We just preferred the Cruasé, with attractive red fruit. The estate produces other fine wines.

● OP Bonarda Frizzante Bronis Sel. '09	🍷🍷	3*
● OP Pinot Nero Bronis Sel. '07	🍷🍷	3*
⊙ OP Pinot Nero Brut Cl. Cruasé	🍷🍷	4
○ OP Pinot Nero Classese Bronis	🍷	4

La Brugherata
fraz. Rosciate
via G. Medolago, 47
24020 Scanzorosciate [BG]
tel. 035655202
www.labrugherata.it

Doglio Riserva '06 is very sound, showing full, balanced and moderately grassy, with good tannins. Moscato di Scanzo Doge '07 is very good, its pervasive nose ushering in nice equilibrium. Valcalepio Bianco '09 and Valcalepio Rosso '08 are both well typed although we slightly preferred the Bianco's nose.

● Moscato di Scanzo Passito Doge '07	🍷🍷	8
○ Valcalepio Bianco Vescovado del Feudo '09	🍷🍷	4*
● Valcalepio Rosso Doglio Ris. '06	🍷🍷	5
● Valcalepio Rosso Vescovado '08	🍷	4

Bulgarini
loc. Vaibò, 1
25010 Pozzolengo [BS]
tel. 030918224
www.vini-bulgarini.com

The Bulgarini family lovingly tend 20 hectares of vineyards at Pozzolengo and make a carefully crafted range of local wines. This year, we thought the Lugana Superiore Ca' Vaibò '08 was excellent, with floral aromas and fresh, firm structure. Rosso Gerumi '06, from cabernet, merlot and marzemino is very sound.

● Guerumì '06	🍷🍷	5
○ Lugana Sup. Cà Vaibò '08	🍷🍷	4*

Ca' del Santo
loc. Campolungo, 4
27040 Montalto Pavese [PV]
tel. 0383870545
www.cadelsanto.it

Laura Bozzi's Bonarda Vivace Grand Cuvée '09 is very varietal, with remarkably fragrant sound fruit. 50+50 is a very balanced IGT red wine from equal parts of pinot nero and cabernet sauvignon, with notes of black pepper spice. OP Rosso Riserva Carolo '06 is well made, with a forthright nose.

● 50 + 50 '08	🍷🍷	4*
● OP Bonarda Vivace Grand Cuvée '09	🍷🍷	4*
● OP Rosso Carolo Ris. '06	🍷	4

Ca' Tessitori
via Matteotti, 15
27043 Broni [PV]
tel. 038551495
www.catessitori.it

Released for the first time this year, Sauvignon Agolo '09 has a convincing nose, balance and acidity, making it aromatic but not cloying. The uncomplicated, easy-drinking OP Rosso Borghesa '09 is good, with delicate floral notes, Bonarda Vivace '00 has good texture and OP Pinot Nero Brut Cl is very fresh.

○ Agolo '09	🍷🍷	3*
● OP Rosso Borghesa '09	🍷🍷	4*
● OP Bonarda Frizzante '09	🍷	3
○ OP Pinot Nero Cl. Brut	🍷	5

Calvi
fraz. Vigalone, 13
27044 Canneto Pavese [PV]
tel. 038560034
www.andreacalvi.it

Andrea Calvi's Bonarda Vivace '09 is refreshing and well made, with generous residual sugar, while we were pleasantly surprised by the aromatic complexity, attack and personality of the undosed Pinot Nero Metodo Classico. Barbera Tre '06 is very evolved, with a typical nose.

● OP Bonarda Vivace '09	🍷🍷	3*
○ OP Pinot Nero Brut	🍷🍷	5
● OP Barbera Tre '06	🍷	4

OTHER WINERIES

Caminella
via Dante Alighieri, 13
24069 Cenate Sotto [BG]
tel. 035941828
www.caminella.it

Valcalepio Rosso Ripa di Luna '07 shows an attractive deep ruby, then a balsamic nose and a nicely textured palate with fine-grained tannins. The white Verde Luna, from chardonnay, sauvignon blanc and pinot bianco, has a florality-led nose while the goodish Metodo Classico offers tropical notes.

○ Brut Cl. Ripa di Luna '07	🍷	5
● Valcalepio Rosso Ripa di Luna '07	🍷	4
○ Verde Luna Bianco '08	🍷	4

Le Cantorìe
fraz. Casaglio
via Castello di Casaglio, 24/25
25064 Gussago [BS]
tel. 0302523723
www.lecantorie.it

The Bontempi family own attractive hillside vineyards in Gussago, where they produce excellent Franciacortas and still wines in their modern cellar. This year our favourites were Balenc '06, a Bordeaux blend with berries and firm structure, the soft, full Cellatica Giulia '07, and the good Satèn Armonia.

○ Franciacorta Satèn Armonia	🍷🍷	6
● Rosso Balenc '06	🍷🍷	4
● Cellatica Rosso Sup. Giulia '07	🍷	4

Cascina San Pietro
fraz. Calino di Cazzago San Martino
via San Pietro, 30
25040 Cazzago San Martino [BS]
tel. 035912448
www.cascinaspietro.it

Giuseppe Pecis offers an extensive range of good Franciacortas and territory-dedicated wines. This year we particularly liked Franciacorta Extra Brut Terè dei Trici '06, with its complex nose of fruit and spices, and its savoury, juicy palate. The Franciacorta Brut is sound.

○ Franciacorta Extra Brut Terè dei Trici '06	🍷🍷	6
○ Franciacorta Brut	🍷	5

Cantina di Casteggio
via Torino, 96
27045 Casteggio [PV]
tel. 0383806311
www.cantinacasteggio.it

Following its merger with Cantina di Broni, we have provisionally assigned this estate a short profile. However, the wines that we tasted reveal an intention to maintain high quality. The concentrated, balsamic Cruasé Postumio is excellent, Pinot Grigio '09 is varietal, and Malvasia Secca '09 is fragrant.

○ OP Pinot Grigio '09	🍷🍷	4
⊙ OP Pinot Nero Brut Cl. Cruasé Postumio	🍷🍷	4*
○ OP Malvasia '09	🍷	3*

Castello di Grumello
via Fosse, 11
24064 Grumello del Monte [BG]
tel. 0354420817
www.castellodigrumello.it

The well-made Valcalepio Moscato Passito '03 is decidedly better than the 2002 vintage in aromatics and length, giving cinnamon and spices. Valcalepio Rosso Colle Calvario Riserva '05 has an attractive nose, good body, firm structure and nice smooth tannins while Valcalepio Bianco '09 is a fresh easy drinker.

● Valcalepio Moscato Nero Passito '03	🍷🍷	6
● Valcalepio Rosso Colle del Calvario Ris. '05	🍷🍷	6
○ Valcalepio Bianco '09	🍷	3

Castello di Gussago
via Manica, 24
25064 Gussago [BS]
tel. 0302525267
www.castellodigussago.it

The Gozio family have a long history of winemaking and produce a carefully crafted range from their 14 hectares on the Santissima hill at Gussago. Both the zesty Brut and the rounded, firmly structured Curtefranca Rosso Pomaro '05 are very good.

○ Curtefranca Bianco Malandrino '08	🍷🍷	5
● Curtefranca Rosso Pomaro '05	🍷🍷	5
○ Franciacorta Brut	🍷🍷	5

Castello di Luzzano

LOC. LUZZANO, 5
27040 ROVESCALA [PV]
TEL. 0523863277
www.castelloluzzano.it

We liked the balanced, easy-drinking Carlino '09, a fragrant still Bonarda with raspberries and cherries. Although still young, Rosso Riserva 270 '07 is potentially interesting, offering cherries and plums, then smooth tannins, while the Bonarda '09 and Pinot Nero Umore Nero '09 are fragrant and varietal.

● OP Bonarda Carlino '09	🍷🍷	4*
● OP Rosso Luzzano 270 Ris. '07	🍷🍷	6
● OP Bonarda Frizzante '09	🍷	3
● OP Pinot Nero Umore Nero '09	🍷	4

Il Cipresso

VIA CERRI, 2
24020 SCANZOROSCIATE [BG]
TEL. 0354597005
www.ilcipresso.info

Scanzo Serafino's Moscato is always one of the finest and the '07 vintage is no exception, with a charming nose of blueberry jam and good acid backbone. Riserva Bartolomeo '06 is very grassy and evolved while the easy-drinking Valcalepio Rosso Dionisio '08 has a fragrant nose of wild berries.

● Moscato di Scanzo Serafino '07	🍷🍷	7
● Valcalepio Rosso Bartolomeo Ris. '06	🍷	5
● Valcalepio Rosso Dionisio '08	🍷	4

Citari

FRAZ. SAN MARTINO DELLA BATTAGLIA
LOC. LOC. CITARI, 2
DESENZANO DEL GARDA [BS]
TEL. 3457137064
citari.artemisinformatica.com

This winery's Garda Rosso '08 is compact and full. There are also two carefully crafted Luganas from two different vineyards, La Conchiglia and La Sorgente, both '09. We prefer the former, which is a little richer and softer.

● Garda Cl. Rosso '08 '08	🍷🍷	4
○ Lugana Vign. La Conchiglia '09	🍷	4
○ Lugana Vign. La Sorgente '09	🍷	4

Civielle

VIA PERGOLA, 21
25080 MONIGA DEL GARDA [BS]
TEL. 0365502002
www.civielle.com

Founded in 1979, this co-operative winery receives the grapes of 45 small growers. Its comprehensive range includes the fragrant, zesty Lugana Biocòra '09, which shows edgy and mineral. The supple Groppello Pergola '09 has rich fruit, full flavour and silky-smooth tannins. Chiaretto '09 is a pleaser.

○ Lugana Biocòra '08	🍷🍷	4
⊙ Garda Cl. Chiaretto Selene '09	🍷	3
● Garda Cl. Groppello Pergola '08	🍷	4

Comincioli

LOC. CASTELLO
VIA ROMA, 10
25080 PUEGNAGO SUL GARDA [BS]
TEL. 0365651141
www.comincioli.it

Gianfranco Comincioli's estate specializes in Groppello and farms nine hectares of vines. Zephir '08 is deep and intriguing while Gropel Mì '05 is complex and firm. Try the white Perlì '09, from rare local varieties erbamat and trebbiano della Valtènesi, which delivers rich fruit and citrus.

● Riviera del Garda Bresciano Gropèl Mì '05	🍷🍷	5
● Riviera del Garda Bresciano Groppello Zephir '08	🍷🍷	5
○ Perlì '09	🍷	4

Cornaleto

VIA CORNALETTO, 2
25030 ADRO [BS]
TEL. 0307450507
www.cornaleto.it

Luigi Lancini has become Franciacorta's antiquarian, never tiring of presenting recent disgorgements of old vintages. This year, while awaiting an old vintage, we picked out an exceptionally well-made Satèn, which showed soft, deep and veined with balsamic notes. The non-vintage Brut is sound.

○ Franciacorta Satèn '04	🍷🍷	6
○ Franciacorta Brut	🍷	4

OTHER WINERIES

La Costa
FRAZ. COSTA
VIA CURONE, 15
23888 PEREGO [LC]
TEL. 0395312218
www.la-costa.it

La Costa is synonymous with research and experimentation in the field of natural agriculture. Solesta '08, a riesling renano and chardonnay blend, has a delicate nose and a savoury palate with good progression. Serìz '07, from merlot, cabernet and syrah, is firm, with sound fruit and well-calibrated oak.

- ● Serìz '07 — 2 glasses, 5
- ○ Solesta '08 — 2 glasses, 4

Delai
VIA MORO, 1
25080 PUEGNAGO SUL GARDA [BS]
TEL. 0365555527

This year, Sergio Delai offered us a very pleasant, fruity, sparkling Rosé, the appealing, slightly sparkling Chiaretto '09, with raspberry aromas, and the goodish Gropello Mogrì '08, which has sound fruit and delicate tannins.

- ⊙ Delai Rosé '09 — 2 glasses, 4
- ⊙ Garda Bresciano Chiaretto '09 — 1 glass, 4
- ● Garda Bresciano Groppello Mogrì '08 — 1 glass, 4

Le Due Querce
VIA SAN LORENZO, 24
25050 OME [BS]
TEL. 0354829930
www.duequerce.net

Gian Paolo Mensi has revived a family tradition in Ome, and makes a nicely crafted range of Franciacortas and still wines from his estate vineyards. They are high-quality products, as demonstrated by the firm, complex Brut Luis with aromas of toast and biscuits, and the good Terre di Franciacorta Rosso '08.

- ○ Franciacorta Brut 'Luis '06 — 2 glasses, 5
- ● TdF Rosso '08 — 1 glass, 3

Luca Faccinelli
CHIURO [SO]
TEL. 3470807011
www.lucafaccinelli.it

Valtellina Superiore '07 is the result of a good idea, teamwork and a well-assorted array of skills. The wine is close-focused, fruity and pervasive on the nose, then well-balanced and full in the mouth, with a seamless finish.

- ● Valtellina Sup. Ortensio Lando '07 — 2 glasses, 5

Lorenzo Faccoli & Figli
VIA CAVA, 7
25030 COCCAGLIO [BS]
TEL. 0307722761
az.faccoli@libero.it

The Faccoli brothers lovingly tend their vineyards at Coccaglio, which yield well-crafted Franciacortas. This year we liked the Brut, with complex yeastiness and minerality, and Dosage Zero '05, which proffers a wonderful layered palate supported by good acid backbone.

- ○ Franciacorta Brut — 2 glasses, 5
- ○ Franciacorta Dosage Zero '05 — 2 glasses, 6
- ○ Franciacorta Extra Brut — 1 glass, 5

Feliciana
LOC. FELICIANA
25010 POZZOLENGO [BS]
TEL. 030918228
www.feliciana.it

Massimo Sbruzzi runs an attractive farm holiday centre and makes a very good range of wines. His Lugana Sercè '08 is delicious, showing concentration and bursting with floral and vanilla notes, then a full, deep, lingering palate. The Chiaretto '09 is fresh, lean and supple.

- ○ Lugana Sercè '08 — 2 glasses, 4
- ⊙ Garda Classico Chiaretto '09 — 1 glass, 3

Fiamberti

VIA CHIESA, 17
27044 CANNETO PAVESE [PV]
TEL. 038588019
www.fiambertivini.it

Although both Metodo Classicos are well made, we preferred the deep-hued Cruasé, with its fresh, fragrant palate. Bonarda Frizzante Vigna Bricco della Sacca '09 recovers very well from a faltering start. Pinot Nero Nero '08 is varietal, pleasant and uncomplicated.

- ● OP Bonarda Frizzante Bricco della Sacca '09 — 🍷🍷 4
- ⊙ OP Pinot Nero Brut Cl. Cruasé — 🍷🍷 5
- ○ OP Pinot Nero Brut Cl. Fiamberti — 🍷 5
- ● OP Pinot Nero Nero '08 — 🍷 4

La Fiòca

FRAZ. NIGOLINE
VIA VILLA, 13B
25040 CORTE FRANCA [BS]
TEL. 0309826313
www.lafioca.com

La Fiòca is owned by the Gatti family and offers a range of interesting wines from the estate's vineyards. We selected a compact, close-focused, non-vintage Brut, which shows creamy and lingering with balsamic hints and supporting acidity, and a well-defined Rosé, which is a little short on structure.

- ○ Franciacorta Brut — 🍷🍷 5
- ⊙ Franciacorta Rosé — 🍷 5

Franca Contea

VIA VALLI, 130
25030 ADRO [BS]
TEL. 0307451217
www.francacontea.it

Luigi, Michele and Andrea Cavalleri use natural farming methods for their vineyards at Adro, Corte Franca and Provaglio. The winery is young, but very promising. Proof of this came at our tastings in the excellent Satèn '06, which has a complex, spicy nose and a long, juicy palate. The '06 Brut is also good.

- ○ Franciacorta Satèn '06 — 🍷🍷 5
- ○ Franciacorta Brut '06 — 🍷 5

Emilio Franzoni

FRAZ. SERA
VIA CAVOUR, 10
25082 BOTTICINO [BS]
TEL. 0302691071
www.franzonivini.it

The Franzonis specialize in the production of Botticino, of which they offer two versions, from the grapes of their estate's vineyards. La Foja d'Or '03 is an invigorating red that is not too evolved but boasts good, firm structure. La Foja '04 is suppler, fresher and easier drinking, although still sturdy.

- ● Botticino Foja d'Or Ris. '03 — 🍷 5
- ● Botticino La Foja '04 — 🍷 4

Fattoria il Gambero

FRAZ. CASE NUOVE
27045 SANTA MARIA DELLA VERSA [PV]
TEL. 038579268
www.fattoriailgambero.it

This year Vittorio Ferrario's estate presented just two wines. Alborada '09 is as always one of Oltrepò's best semi-sparkling Bonardas, fragrant and fruity, with good weight and balance. Riesling Kafir '07, which spends its last year of ageing partially in acacia barrels, has less prominent evolved notes.

- ● OP Bonarda Frizzante Alborada '09 — 🍷🍷 4*
- ○ OP Riesling Italico Kafir '07 — 🍷 4

I Gessi - Fabbio De Filippi

FRAZ. FOSSA, 8
27050 OLIVA GESSI [PV]
TEL. 0383896606
igessifabbio@libero.it

This is Defilippi Fabbio's debut in our Guide. Oliva Gessi, as its name suggests, is an area with chalky soils ideal for riesling, and Riesling I Gessi '09 is convincingly racy, giving sage and citrus fruit. Bonarda Vivace '09 is good and fragrant, while Cruasé Maria Cristina '07 is uncomplicated and fruity.

- ● OP Bonarda Vivace '09 — 🍷🍷 3*
- ○ OP Riesling Italico '09 — 🍷🍷 3*
- ⊙ OP Pinot Nero Brut Cl. Cruasé Maria Cristina '07 — 🍷 4

OTHER WINERIES

Nunzio Ghiraldi

FRAZ. LUGANA DI SIRMIONE
VIA CHIODI, 34
25019 SIRMIONE [BS]
TEL. 0309906612
www.nunzioghiraldi.it

Nunzio Ghiraldi specializes in Luganas, of which he offers two versions. The Superiore '09 is excellent, showing very intense, fresh and juicy, with full flavour and a long finish of more complex toast and mineral notes. Lugana '08 is just as good, although it focuses more on fruit and fresh citrus.

○ Lugana Il Gruccione '08	🍷🍷	4*
○ Lugana Sup. Il Gruccione '09	🍷🍷	4*

La Costa di Ome

VIA PIANELLO, 16
25050 OME [BS]
TEL. 030652271
info@lacostadiome.it

Giampaolo Papì and Giovanna Vezzoli have salvaged the family's vines and are now managing them organically. They have also carved a cellar out of the rock. Their Satèn is soft and elegant, with attractive vanilla and citrus, while the sturdy Terre di Franciacorta Rosso '07 has a nose of blackberries.

○ Franciacorta Satèn	🍷	4
● TdF Rosso '07	🍷	3

La Fiorita

VIA MAGLIO, 14
25020 OME [BS]
TEL. 030652279
www.lafiorita.bs.it

The Bono family are farmers and livestock breeders who lovingly tend five hectares under vine that yield a well-made range of wines. We enjoyed four Franciacortas: the mature, complex Paolo Bono Brut '04 and the simpler, but nonetheless pleasant, well-made Brut, Extra Brut and Satèn.

○ Franciacorta Brut '04	🍷🍷	5
○ Franciacorta Brut	🍷	4
○ Franciacorta Dosaggio Zero	🍷	5
○ Franciacorta Satèn	🍷	5

La Valle

VIA SANT'ANTONIO, 4
25050 RODENGO SAIANO [BS]
TEL. 0307722045
www.vinilavalle.it

Based in a fine 19th-century farmstead at Rodengo Saiano, La Valle proves its worth year after year. Regium '04 is elegant, firm and complex, with a long, chamois-soft finish. The Rosé is full, fragrant and one of the best that we tasted this year while the Satèn is velvety and well typed.

○ Franciacorta Brut Regium '04	🍷🍷	6
⊙ Franciacorta Rosé	🍷🍷	5
○ Franciacorta Satèn	🍷🍷	6
○ Franciacorta Brut Primum	🍷	5

Lazzari

VIA MELLA, 49
25020 CAPRIANO DEL COLLE [BS]
TEL. 0309747387
www.lazzarivini.it

Giovanni Lazzari and his family are devoted to this small Brescian DOC, of which they produce around 40,000 bottles a year. This year we singled out a good, juicy Marzemino, which showed fruity, soft and succulent, and a very elegant Capriano del Colle '07 that is soft, full and fresh, with smooth tannins.

● Capriano del Colle Rosso '07	🍷🍷	3*
● Marzemino '09	🍷🍷	3

Leali di Monteacuto

FRAZ. MONTEACUTO
VIA DOSSO, 5
25080 PUEGNAGO SUL GARDA [BS]
TEL. 0365651291
antonio.leali@genie.it

The Leali family produce classic Garda wines on their estate. This year the Rebo Montagü '08 is excellent, with notes of red and dark berries, chocolate and spices. The Riesling '09 is fresh and close-focused while the Groppello '08 is stylish, full-flavoured and elegantly tannic.

○ Garda Riesling '09	🍷🍷	4
● Rebo Montagü '08	🍷🍷	4
● Garda Bresciano Groppello '08	🍷	4

Locatelli Caffi
via A. Moro, 6
24060 Chiuduno [BG]
tel. 035838308
www.locatellicaffi.it

Valcalepio Bianco '09 is very fresh and enjoyable, with notes of peaches, apricots and bananas, good structure and a nice finish. Valcalepio Rosso Riserva '06 is not particularly complex, but very pleasant, with compact, sound fruit. Valcalepio Rosso '08 is fragrant and easy drinking.

O Valcalepio Bianco '09	YY	3*
● Valcalepio Rosso Ris. '06	YY	4*
● Valcalepio Rosso '08	Y	3

Longhi de Carli
via Verdi, 6
25030 Erbusco [BS]
tel. 0307760280
www.longhi-decarli.com

Alessandro Longhi's estate boasts 13 hectares of vineyards in Erbusco, in the heart of the designation. His wines include a very soft, fruity Franciacorta Satèn, with intense vanilla notes, and the interesting Brut Cuvée Giacomo '05, which has decent complexity and a slightly bitterish finish.

O Franciacorta Brut Cuvee Giacomo '05	Y	6
O Franciacorta Satèn	Y	6

Cantina Lovera
via Lovera, 14a
25030 Erbusco [BS]
tel. 0307760491
www.cantinalovera.it

The Betella family produce well-honed Franciacortas in Lovera, a district of the municipality of Erbusco. Don't miss their Satèn Adamantis, which is complex and velvety, with attractive notes of croissant and vanilla followed by a savoury finish. The creamy, supple Brut Merum is also good.

O Franciacorta Satèn Adamantis	YY	5
O Franciacorta Brut Merum	Y	5

Lurani Cernuschi
via Convento, 3
24031 Almenno San Salvatore [BG]
tel. 035642576
www.luranicernuschi.it

Opis is an interesting white, from the much underrated incrocio Manzoni grape. It has fragrant tropical notes with mineral hints, good development and a long finish. Valcalepio Rosso Tornago '07 is pleasant, with typical grassy notes. Valcalepio Bianco Amisa '09 is distinguished by a very attractive nose.

O Opis '09	YY	4*
O Valcalepio Bianco Amisa '09	Y	3
● Valcalepio Rosso Tornago '07	Y	4

Eligio Magri
via Colle dei Pasta, 8a
24060 Torre de' Roveri [BG]
tel. 0354528868
www.eligiomagri.it

Patrizio is as good as ever, with the '07 vintage showing intense with hints of vanilla, spices, hay and pepper, good attack and a nicely lingering finish. Lucelio '07, a Moscato Giallo with citrus fruit and white peaches, is interesting, while Valcalepio Rosso Lyr '07 is well made and fairly uncomplicated.

O Moscato Giallo Lucelio '07	YY	3*
● Patrizio '07	YY	4
● Valcalepio Rosso Lyr '07	Y	4

Marangona
loc. Antica Corte Ialidy
25010 Pozzolengo [BS]
tel. 030919379
www.marangona.com

The Marangona estate in Pozzolengo has 25 hectares of fine vineyards in the Lugana DOC zone farmed for low environmental impact. This year, the Rosso table wine is very good, with rich fruit, full flavour and elegant tannins. The Rosato '09 is fresh and savoury and the Lugana '09 is well made.

● Rosso Marangona	YY	4
O Lugana '09	Y	4
⊙ Rosato Marangona '09	Y	4

Martilde

FRAZ. CROCE, 4A/1
27040 ROVESCALA [PV]
TEL. 0385756280
www.martilde.it

Bonarda Zaffo '06 has the typical profile of an aged Bonarda, with prominent but elegant tannins and notes of jam and wild berries. Of the two '09 wines we tasted, we slightly preferred the Bonarda, with its violets and blackberries, although the Barbera was also pleasant, offering clear cherry notes.

● OP Bonarda '09	🍷🍷	4*
● OP Bonarda Zaffo '06	🍷🍷	5
● OP Barbera '09	🍷	4

Mirabella

VIA CANTARANE, 2
25050 RODENGO SAIANO [BS]
TEL. 030611197
www.mirabellavini.it

Mirabella was founded in 1979 by a group of Brescia businessmen led by Teresio Schiavi. It is now a solid estate with 50 hectares of vineyards managed by Francesco Bracchi. This year, we enjoyed the new Cuvée Dom, the excellent Dosaggio Zero, and the first-rate Rosé. The Satèn and the Brut are both sound.

○ Franciacorta Dosaggio Zero Dom	🍷🍷	6
⊙ Franciacorta Rosé Brut	🍷🍷	5
○ Franciacorta Brut	🍷	5
○ Franciacorta Satèn	🍷	5*

Cantine Francesco Montagna

VIA CAIROLI, 67
27043 BRONI [PV]
TEL. 038551028
www.cantinemontagna.it

Bonarda Vivace Viti di Luna '09 is fragrant and Moscato Frizzante Viti di Luna '09 is clean, fresh and exceptionally pleasant. The Metodo Classicos are interesting and we particularly liked Pinot Nero Brut Cuvée Tradizione, which shows golden with a fairly complex nose.

● OP Bonarda Frizzante Viti di Luna '09	🍷🍷	3*
○ OP Moscato Frizzante Viti di Luna '09	🍷🍷	3*
○ OP Pinot Nero Brut Cl. Cuvée Tradizione	🍷🍷	4
⊙ OP Pinot Nero Rosé Brut Cl.	🍷	4

Monte Cicogna

VIA DELLE VIGNE, 6
25080 MONIGA DEL GARDA [BS]
TEL. 0365503200
www.montecicogna.it

The Materossi family's winery is housed in an old farmstead on a hilltop overlooking Lake Garda. Agronomist Alessandro and his brother Cesare presented a sound Lugana '09, which is fresh and juicy, Chiaretto Siclì '09 with alluring raspberry notes, and above all the wonderfully deep Garda Rubiniere '07.

● Garda Cl. Rosso Sup. Rubinere '07	🍷🍷	4
⊙ Garda Cl. Chiaretto Siclì '09	🍷	4
● Garda Cl. Rosso Groppello Beana '08	🍷	4
○ Lugana S. Caterina '09	🍷	4

Tenuta Montedelma

VIA VALENZANO, 23
25050 PASSIRANO [BS]
TEL. 0306546161
www.montedelma.it

Pietro Berardi invests great passion in the family estate and offers an array of interesting wines. This year we singled out the very good, plush Pas Dosé '06, with plenty of fruit, a rounded Satèn with a fresh citrussy nose, and a pale but very pleasant Rosé.

○ Franciacorta Pas Dosé '06	🍷🍷	6
⊙ Franciacorta Rosé	🍷	5
○ Franciacorta Satèn	🍷	6

Montenato Griffini

VIA SPARANO, 13/14
27040 BOSNASCO [PV]
TEL. 0385272904
www.montenatogriffini.it

Barbara Faravelli Santambrogio's estate makes few wines and not every year, so it is not always in the Guide, although the average quality, particularly of croatina-based products, is always high. We could not overlook the excellent Pinot Nero '08, which is deep and fragrant with a well-typed nose.

● OP Pinot Nero '08	🍷🍷	4*

Monterucco

VALLE CIMA, 38
27040 CIGOGNOLA [PV]
TEL. 038585151
www.monterucco.it

The dry Malvasia Valentina '09 stands out for its citrus fruit and mint, and its deep nose and palate, while the Classese is always good and flavoursome, and would have repeated last year's Two-Glass feat had it shown a little more drive on the palate. Bonarda Vivace Vigna Il Modello '09 has assertive extract.

○ Malvasia Valentina '09	🍷🍷	4*
● OP Bonarda Vivace V. Il Modello '09	🍷	3
○ OP Pinot Nero Brut Classese	🍷	4

Il Montù

VIA MARCONI, 10
27040 MONTÙ BECCARIA [PV]
TEL. 0385262252
www.ilmontu.com

This year, the historic Montù Beccaria winery presented another good list of sparklers. Blanc da Noir is balanced and rounded, with nice backbone and a good finish. Rosé da Noir has notes of wild berries and citrus fruit with a concentrated nose. Extra Dry '06 is well calibrated, with intriguing red apples.

○ OP Pinot Nero Extra Dry '06	🍷🍷	5
○ Pinot Blanc da Noir	🍷🍷	5
⊙ Pinot Rosé da Noir	🍷🍷	5

Nettare dei Santi

VIA CAPRA, 17
20078 SAN COLOMBANO AL LAMBRO [MI]
TEL. 0371200523
www.nettaredeisanti.it

Franco Riccardi '07 is an IGT Bordeaux blend with a bright ruby hue, clear bell peppers, sun-dried hay and black pepper, and a full, meaty palate with fruity pulp and a long finish. The drinkable San Colombano '08 is well balanced and the fragrant Chardonnay Mombrione lacks only a touch of acidity.

● Franco Riccardi Sel. Mombrione '07	🍷🍷	5
○ Chardonnay Sel. Mombrione '09	🍷	3
● San Colombano '08	🍷	4

Olmo Antico

VIA MARCONI, 8
27040 BORGO PRIOLO [PV]
TEL. 0383872672
www.olmoantico.it

Organic farming and extreme wines are Paolo Baggini's trademarks. 14 Ottobre is a sparkling Croatina with a concentrated nose, Olmo Bianco '09 is a very evolved Riesling with notes of aromatic herbs, Merlot Giorgio Quinto '07 is good and forthright, and P. Nera '07 is a bright Pinot Nero with hints of jam.

● Croatina 14 Ottobre '09	🍷🍷	4*
● Giorgio Quinto '07	🍷	6
● La P. Nera '07	🍷	5
○ Olmo Bianco '09	🍷	4

Pedrinis

LOC. SANTO STEFANO
VIA SGARUGA, 19
24060 CAROBBIO DEGLI ANGELI [BG]
TEL. 0354259111
www.pedrinis.it

This is a Guide newcomer with several good wines. Felix '06 is a Valcalepio Rosso with distinct overripe notes, a nose of chocolate and spices, and a nice fruity palate. Moscato Giallo Thomas '07 is good, with typical citrus notes. Moscato Passito Betinus '06 is very typical, although short on acidity.

○ Thomas '07	🍷🍷	6
● Valcalepio Rosso Felix '06	🍷🍷	4
● Valcalepio Passito Betinus '06	🍷	6

Perla del Garda

FRAZ. ESENTA
LOC. BELLINO
25017 LONATO [BS]
TEL. 0309102021
ettore.prandini@libero.it

This young winery has 25 hectares of fine vineyards on the hillsides at Lonato, a modern cellar and plenty of enthusiasm. Lugana Madreperla is always good and this year the '08 vintage showed piquant, fruity and mineral. The complex Madonna della Scoperta '07 is decent while Garda Chardonnay Brut is good.

○ Garda Chardonnay Brut	🍷🍷	4
○ Lugana Madreperla '08	🍷🍷	4
○ Lugana Sup. Madonna della Scoperta '07	🍷	4

OTHER WINERIES

Piccolo Bacco dei Quaroni

FRAZ. COSTAMONTEFEDELE
27040 MONTÙ BECCARIA [PV]
TEL. 038560521
www.piccolobaccodeiquaroni.it

Laura Brazzoli and Mario Cavalli's Barbera Gustavo '07 is very fragrant and enjoyable. We were also impressed by Elos '08, a Malvasia Passita whose citrus notes are accompanied by intriguing wafts of petrol. The Buttafuoco '06, is very evolved, while the coppery Cruasé has a highly distinctive style.

○ Malvasia Passita Elos '08	🍷🍷	5
● OP Barbera Gustavo '07	🍷🍷	4
● OP Buttafuoco Vign. Ca' Padroni '06	🍷	3
⊙ OP Pinot Nero Brut Cl. Cruasé	🍷	4

Pietrasanta

VIA SFORZA, 55/57
20078 SAN COLOMBANO AL LAMBRO [MI]
TEL. 0371897540
carlopietrasanta@mivlombardia.com

Although Pietrasanta's San Colombano Riserva '04 is fairly rustic, reflecting the terroir, it is an interesting wine, with fruity pulp accompanied by unusual liquorice, rhubarb and medicinal herbs. The San Colombano '08 is simpler, characterized by notes of pepper and good length.

● San Colombano Ris. '04	🍷🍷	5
● San Colombano '08	🍷	4

Pilandro

FRAZ. SAN MARTINO DELLA BATTAGLIA
LOC. PILANDRO, 1
25010 DESENZANO DEL GARDA [BS]
TEL. 0309910363
www.pilandro.it

The Lavelli family tend 16 hectares of vineyards in San Martino, following an age-old tradition. They specialize in Luganas, of which they offer many versions. Arilica '08 is noteworthy, with elegant overtones of quince, while the excellent Terecrea '09 is fresher and crisper. The sparkling version is elegant.

○ Lugana Arilica '08	🍷🍷	4
○ Lugana Brut	🍷🍷	4
○ Lugana Trecrea '09	🍷🍷	4*

Pratello

VIA PRATELLO, 26
25080 PADENGHE SUL GARDA [BS]
TEL. 0309907005
www.pratello.com

This old winery at Padenghe produces a wide range of Garda wines. We very much liked the concentrated, full-bodied Nero per Sempre '09, from rebo and carmenère, and the elegant Discobolo '09. Lugana Catulliano '09 and the Brut Rosé are also very good.

● Garda Cl. Groppello Discobolo '09	🍷🍷	4
○ Lugana Catulliano '09	🍷🍷	4
● Nero per Sempre '09	🍷🍷	5
⊙ Pratello Brut Rosé '09	🍷🍷	4*

Quadra

VIA SANT'EUSEBIO, 1
25033 COLOGNE [BS]
TEL. 0307157314
www.quadrafranciacorta.it

The Ghezzi family have many business interests in Italy and Argentina. Founded in 2003, this estate presented an excellent Franciacorta Brut with savoury, mineral notes and an interesting Satèn, which showed fresh, fruity and plush. Dosso Oriane '05 is again good.

○ Franciacorta Brut '06	🍷🍷	5
○ Franciacorta Satèn	🍷🍷	6
● TdF Curtefranca Rosso Dosso Oriane '05	🍷🍷	5

Redaelli de Zinis

VIA N.H. UGO DE ZINIS, 10 (VIA BASSE SOTTO)
25080 CALVAGESE DELLA RIVIERA [BS]
TEL. 030601001
www.dezinis.it

This old estate's meticulously tended vineyards extend around the 18th-century house. Groppello '06 is interesting and pleasantly complex while the Groppello Cru '09 is fresher and more approachable. The Chiaretto '09 is as sound as ever and the white from the same vintage is also good.

● Garda Cl. Groppello Poggio dei Sassi Ris. '06	🍷🍷	4
○ Garda Cl. Bianco '09	🍷	4
⊙ Garda Cl. Chiaretto '09	🍷	4
● Garda Cl. Groppello Cru di Moniga '09	🍷	4

Riccafana

via Facchetti, 91
25033 Cologne [BS]
tel. 0307156797
www.riccafana.com

The Fratus family's estate offers a range of Franciacortas and clean, well-made local wines. This year we singled out an excellent, zesty, juicy Satèn and a Brut with impressive intensity, pulp and freshness. The Rosé, with notes of wild strawberries, was below par, showing somewhat over-evolved.

○ Franciacorta Brut	🍷🍷 5
○ Franciacorta Satèn	🍷🍷 4
⊙ Franciacorta Rosé	🍷 5

Ricchi

fraz. Ricchi
via Festoni, 13d
46040 Monzambano [MN]
tel. 0376800238
www.cantinaricchi.it

Chardonnay Meridiano '09, aged in large wooden barrels for 6 months, has very plush notes of tropical fruit. Le Cime, from partially dried garganega and moscato giallo grapes, is highly concentrated, with an alluring nose, while Merlot Carpino '06 is very well typed with hints of pepper and dark berry fruit.

○ Garda Chardonnay Meridiano '09	🍷🍷 4*
○ Le Cime Passito '08	🍷🍷 5
● Garda Merlot Carpino '06	🍷 5

Riva di Franciacorta

loc. Fantecolo
via Carlo Alberto, 19
25050 Provaglio d'Iseo [BS]
tel. 0309823701
www.rivadifranciacorta.it

The Riva family have bought over 30 hectares of fine vineyards and renovated an old house, fitting it out with modern winemaking kit. We liked the long, close-focused Franciacorta Satèn, with fresh citron, a Rosé with tempting overtones of blackberries and cherries, and the well-made Longobardo '07.

○ Franciacorta Satèn	🍷🍷 6
○ Franciacorta Rosé	🍷 5
● Terre di Franciacorta Longobardo '07	🍷 3

Tenuta San Francesco

via Scazzolino, 55
27040 Rovescala [PV]
tel. 029085141
www.alziati.it

Annibale Alzati's estate is characterized by traditionally made wines with highly original names. The results are often excellent, as shown by the aromatic complexity of Gaggiarone '04, the fragrance of Bonarda Vivace '09 and the forthright tannins of Dispensator de' Triboli '07, all from bonarda di Rovescala.

● Gaggiarone '04	🍷🍷 6
● OP Bonarda Vivace Garzoncello Scherzoso '09	🍷🍷 3*
● Dispensator de' Tripoli '07	🍷 4

Poderi di San Pietro

via Monti, 35
20078 San Colombano al Lambro [MI]
tel. 0371208050
www.poderidisanpietro.it

We liked the concentrated San Colombano Rosso di Valbissera '06, which has ripe fruit and good length. The spicy Belvedere '07 is a monovarietal Merlot with firm structure and notes of hay and coffee. Coffee also features in the simpler bouquet of the heady, easy-drinking Collada '08.

● Belvedere '07	🍷🍷 5
● San Colombano Rosso di Valbissera '06	🍷🍷 5
● San Colombano Collada '08	🍷 4

Tenuta Scarpa Colombi

via Groppallo, 26
27049 Bosnasco [PV]
tel. 0385272081
www.colombiwines.com

The pleasant, fragrant Bonarda Vivace Morgana '09 has a nose of blueberries while the VSQ Blanc de Blancs gives citrus and very ripe tropical fruit. Brut Martinotti Cuvée has peach notes and plenty of backbone and Pinot Grigio Rivaclara '08 is varietal with delicate mineral overtones.

● OP Bonarda Frizzante Morgana '09	🍷🍷 3*
○ Brut Cl. Blanc de Blancs	🍷 5
○ OP Pinot Grigio Rivaclara '08	🍷 3
○ OP Pinot Nero Brut Martinotti Cuvée di Famiglia	🍷 3

Cantine Selva Capuzza

FRAZ. SAN MARTINO DELLA BATTAGLIA
LOC. SELVA CAPUZZA
25010 DESENZANO DEL GARDA [BS]
TEL. 0309910381
www.selvacapuzza.it

The Formentini family's estate offers sound Garda DOC wines. This year, we picked out the excellent, long, full-flavoured Lugana Superiore Menasasso '09, the first-rate Garda Rosso '08, and the vibrant, fruity San Martino della Battaglia Campo del Solio '08.

● Garda Cl. Rosso '08	🍷🍷	4
○ Lugana Sup. Menasasso '09	🍷🍷	5
○ San Martino della Battaglia Campo del Soglio '08	🍷🍷	4

Lo Sparviere

VIA COSTA, 2
25040 MONTICELLI BRUSATI [BS]
TEL. 030652382
www.losparviere.com

This fine estate at Monticelli Brusati, with 30 hectares under vine, belongs to the Gussalli Berettas, an old family of Italian entrepreneurs. The elegant, invigorating Brut '06 has floral notes and plenty of pulp while the Extra Brut has creamy effervescence and fruit, which fades into a long mineral finish.

○ Franciacorta Brut '06	🍷🍷	5
○ Franciacorta Extra Brut	🍷🍷	5
○ Franciacorta Satèn	🍷	5

Vincenzo Tallarini

VIA FONTANILE, 7/9
24060 GANDOSSO [BG]
TEL. 035834003
www.tallarini.com

Tallarini offered two interesting Moscato Passitos. The Valcalepio '04, released in a decanter-style bottle, is very good, with evolved notes of spice, cinchona and rhubarb while the Moscato di Scanzo '06 has more conventional fruit preserves. Riserva San Giovannino '05 is pleasant and fairly concentrated.

● Moscato di Scanzo Passito '06	🍷🍷	7
● Valcalepio Moscato Passito '04	🍷🍷	6
● Valcalepio Rosso San Giovannino Ris. '05	🍷	5

Benedetto Tognazzi

FRAZ. CAIONVICO
VIA SANT' ORSOLA, 161
25135 BRESCIA
TEL. 0302692695
www.tognazzivini.it

Growers for three generations, the Tognazzis about ten years ago bought new vineyards in Lugana and built a new cellar. This year we particularly liked the sound Vigne di Mattina '07, which is balanced and velvety with delicate tannins. Cobio '07 is more approachable and vibrant while the Lugana '09 is decent.

● Botticino Vigne di Mattina '07	🍷🍷	3*
● Botticino Cobio '07	🍷	4
○ Lugana Cascina Ardea '09	🍷	4

La Tordela

VIA TORRICELLA, 1
24060 TORRE DE' ROVERI [BG]
TEL. 035580172
www.latordela.it

Valcalepio Rosso Campo Roccoli Vecchi Riserva '05 is a great red and the best of its kind, showing warm, cosseting and well balanced. Both the 2008 Bergamasca IGT wines are pleasant, with good structure, although we slightly preferred the Cabernet, which has a closer-focused nose.

● Valcalepio Rosso Campo Roccoli Vecchi Ris. '05	🍷🍷	5
● Cabernet Sauvignon Bergamasca '08	🍷🍷	3*
● Merlot '08	🍷	3

Torrevilla

VIA EMILIA, 4
27050 TORRAZZA COSTE [PV]
TEL. 038377003
www.torrevilla.it

The Cruasé is appealingly uncomplicated, Pinot Nero Fraseggio di Cadé '05 has rather prominent tannins, and Martinotti Novemesi is always very fragrant.

⊙ OP Pinot Nero Brut Cruasé	🍷	4
○ OP Pinot Nero Brut Martinotti Novemesi La Genisia	🍷	3
● OP Pinot Nero Fraseggio di Cadè '05	🍷	4

OTHER WINERIES

Pietro Torti

FRAZ. CASTELROTTO, 9
27047 MONTECALVO VERSIGGIA [PV]
TEL. 038599763
www.pietrotorti.it

Sandro Torti's Bonarda Vivace '09 is again one of the best for fragrant, sound fruit. Fagù '09 is an interesting Chardonnay that is very aromatic, Barbera Campo Rivera '06 requires further bottle ageing to acquire balance while Riesling Italico Moglialunga '09 is pleasant and floral.

○ Fagù '09	🍷🍷 3*
● OP Bonarda Vivace '09	🍷🍷 3*
● OP Barbera Campo Rivera '06	🍷 4
○ OP Riesling Italico Moglialunga '09	🍷 3

Cantina Sociale Val San Martino

VIA BERGAMO, 1195
24030 PONTIDA [BG]
TEL. 035795035
www.cantinavalsanmartino.com

This co-operative winery's Valcalepio Rosso Riserva '06 is overripe with a nose of coffee and chocolate laced with grassy notes, firm structure and a good finish. Bianco della Bergamasca has overtones of banana, while Rosso della Bergamasca hinges on plums. Both are uncomplicated, easy-drinking wines.

● Valcalepio Rosso Ris. '06	🍷🍷 5
○ Val San Martino Bianco '09	🍷 3
● Val San Martino Rosso '08	🍷 3

Vigna Dorata

FRAZ. CALINO
VIA SALA, 80
25046 CAZZAGO SAN MARTINO [BS]
TEL. 0307254275
www.vignadorata.it

Luciana Mingotti's cellar at Calino makes fine still wines and Franciacortas which performed well again this year. We recommend the charming, chamois-soft Satèn's attractive apricot notes, or the Franciacorta Brut, which is soft, close woven and well dosed, with an elegant aftertaste of marrons glacés.

○ Franciacorta Brut	🍷🍷 5
○ Franciacorta Satèn	🍷🍷 5
○ Franciacorta Extra Brut	🍷 5

Visconti

VIA C. BATTISTI, 139
25015 DESENZANO DEL GARDA [BS]
TEL. 0309120681
www.luganavisconti.it

Franco Visconti continues the family tradition with a legendary name that has celebrated its centenary. The crisp, fruity, full-flavoured Lugana Visconti '09 is excellent, the classic Etichetta Nera '09 is extremely drinkable and the other wines are decent.

⊙ Garda Cl. Chiaretto '09	🍷 4
○ Lugana Brut M. Cl.	🍷 5
○ Lugana Collo Lungo Et. Nera '09	🍷 4
○ Lugana Visconti '09	🍷 5

Zamichele

VIA ROVEGLIA PALAZZINA, 2
25010 POZZOLENGO [BS]
TEL. 030918631
cantinazamichele@libero.it

This small winery at Pozzolengo may not produce many wines but its Luganas are first rate. Once again Gardè '08, aged in oak, was excellent, with attractive density, sound fruit and good balance.

○ Lugana Gardè '08	🍷🍷 4*

Emilio Zuliani

VIA TITO SPERI, 28
25080 PADENGHE SUL GARDA [BS]
TEL. 0309907026
www.vinizuliani.it

Zuliani is a legendary name in Garda winemaking and production is meticulously vinified from estate-grown grapes. Chiaretto Pink Dream '09 is excellent, with notes of blueberry and raspberry and a full-flavoured, satisfying palate. The sparkling Garda Rosé, which is also called Pink Dream now, is well made.

⊙ Garda Cl. Chiaretto Pink Dream '09	🍷🍷 4*
⊙ Garda Cl. Rosé Pink Dream	🍷 3

TRENTINO

This is not a favourable moment for Trentino winemaking. Some accidents along the way have struck several large co-operative wineries and upset, to say the least, the region's system of winemaking co-operatives that has always been the backbone of the sector. Certainly other operations, such as Cavit for example, continue to reap successes in the market, but lately some problems have undoubtedly emerged among Trentino's splendid vineyards. Some of the handful of small producers are still fascinated by viticulture's new frontiers of biodynamics and natural winemaking while the rest hew to a precise grammar of winemaking based on whistle-clean musts, varietal aromas and crisply defined, if not particularly complex, aromatics. In the end, sparkling wines remain the great specialty of Trentino winemaking. We have no quibbles at all with the spumante sector, where the region's estates have for years been right at the top of the national tree. The prize for Sparkler of the Year goes to the '01 Giulio Ferrari and Oenologist of the Year is Ruben Larentis, the craftsman in the Giulio Ferrari cellar, which says it all about the excellence of regional sparkling wines, now all tucked safely under the great umbrella of the Trento DOC designation. But Ferrari is not the only one calling the shots. Once again, Cavit won Three Glasses, along with Abate Nero, Methius and Balter. One particular winemaker who has shown all his mastery is Nello Letrari. With more than 60 harvests behind him, this historic Italian sparkling winemaker took Three Glasses with a Trento DOC that is emblematic of the designation and truly inspirational for ambitious young producers. Trentino wine has all it takes to keep making better and better still and, especially, sparkling wines. On the still wine front, there was no San Leonardo, which will be released in the new vintage only at the end of 2011, but we did enjoy a splendid '07 version of Granato '07 Elisabetta Foradori, the first-ever edition after the total conversion of production to biodynamics, and the Teroldego Maso Cervara, again from '07 and again from Cavit. Only nine wines won prizes in the end, two fewer than last year, underlining that there were some less-than-memorable vintages of white wines on show this time.

Abate Nero

FRAZ. GARDOLO
SPONDA TRENTINA, 45
38014 TRENTO
TEL. 0461246566
www.abatenero.it

CELLAR SALES
PRE-BOOKED VISITS

ANNUAL PRODUCTION **70,000 bottles**
HECTARES UNDER VINE **65**
VITICULTURE METHOD **Conventional**

This vintage has been especially fortunate for Abate Nero. This small yet influential Trentino sparkling wine house has operated for more than 30 years on the left bank of the river Avisio, not far from Lavis. Luciano Lunelli and his staff have turned out a series of high-quality cuvées. Credit goes to the staff's constant dedication in the cellar and time-tested experience in selecting grapes from vineyards in the high hills to make only the best.

All the Trentos from this estate have distinct personality and finesse as their connecting thread. It is difficult to rank these by appeal, considering three made it into our finals. The big, complex Cuvée dell'Abate Riserva '05 is great but Three Glasses this year went to the invigorating, dynamic Domini '05, a monovarietal Chardonnay with lovely savouriness, subtle texture and great length. We also liked the captivating, easy-drinking Extra Brut '07. The Brut '07 and Extra Dry '07 are both enjoyable and well crafted.

○ Trento Brut Domini '05	🍷🍷🍷	6
○ Trento Abate Nero Extra Brut '07	🍷🍷	5*
○ Trento Brut Cuvée dell'Abate Ris. '05	🍷🍷	7
○ Trento Abate Nero Brut '07	🍷🍷	5
○ Trento Abate Nero Extra Dry '07	🍷🍷	5
○ Trento Brut Cuvée dell'Abate Ris. '04	YYY	7
○ Trento Brut Cuvée dell'Abate Ris. '03	YYY	6
○ Trento Brut Cuvée dell'Abate Ris. '02	YYY	6
○ Trento Brut Cuvée dell'Abate Ris. '01	YYY	6

Nicola Balter

VIA VALLUNGA II, 24
38068 ROVERETO [TN]
TEL. 0464430101
www.balter.it

CELLAR SALES
PRE-BOOKED VISITS

ANNUAL PRODUCTION **80,000 bottles**
HECTARES UNDER VINE **10**
VITICULTURE METHOD **Conventional**

Apparently this estate is a country retreat in the pine forests overlooking the city of Rovereto. The vineyards are tended like gardens, suspended between the green of the conifers and blue of the sky. Nicola Balter is a wine man to his boots and knows how perfect this place is for viticulture for he has worked here his for many years. Initially specializing in red wines, Nicola has always had an immense passion for sparkling wines and yet again his bottles did not disappoint.

The Riserva '04 is back in the limelight, winning Three Glasses and proving to be one of the most uncompromising, truly convincing sparklers submitted this year. This classic 80-20 blend of chardonnay and pinot nero is irresistible on both nose and the full, velvety palate. Enjoyable but much simpler than other editions, the Trento Brut is traditional, slightly tart and easy drinking. The 2008 growing year was no better for red wines at Balter than it was anywhere else, as shown by the Barbanico, which is still closed, tannic, and slightly astringent. The Lagrein-Merlot '09 is well made.

○ Trento Balter Ris. '04	🍷🍷🍷	6
○ Balter Brut	🍷	4
● Barbanico '08	🍷	5
● Lagrein-Merlot '09	🍷	4
○ Trento Balter Ris. '01	YYY	6
○ Trento Balter Ris. '03	YY	6
○ Trento Balter Ris. '02	YY	6

Bellaveder

LOC. MASO BELVEDERE
38010 FAEDO [TN]
TEL. 0461650171
www.bellaveder.it

CELLAR SALES
PRE-BOOKED VISITS

ANNUAL PRODUCTION 37,000 bottles
HECTARES UNDER VINE 8
VITICULTURE METHOD Conventional

The Bellaveder estate has only had a few harvests on the sunny, lower slopes of Faedo, not far from the university structure of the recently established oenology department at the San Michele all'Adige wine school. Owner Tranquillo Lucchetta is constantly busy on the estate, along with a young technical staff. A number of varieties are planted here, though chardonnay and teroldego are the darlings of the production.

This small yet promising estate makes a good– completely new – Trento and the Teroldego shows enviable character and backbone. The Trento '06 is young, actually still very young, but shows the freshness and complexity of a future champion. The Teroldego Mas Picol '09, a Teroldego from outside the DOC zone, won us over right away for the finesse of its bouquet. A long, savoury palate shows nice tannins and an easy-drinking appeal. This wine should not be underestimated: it's pleasant now but destined to improve. Though correct, the other wines show the cracks left by the age of the vine stock and some inexperience. But Lucchetta is aiming for higher things in the future.

● Teroldego Mas Picol '09	**YY**	4
○ Trento Brut '06	**YY**	5
● Trentino Lagrein Nansum '07	**Y**	5
○ Trentino Pinot Bianco '09	**Y**	4
● Rosso Bellaveder '05	YY	4*
● Teroldego Mas Picol '07	YY	4*
○ Trentino Chardonnay '07	YY	4*
○ Trentino Chardonnay '06	YY	4*

Conti Bossi Fedrigotti

VIA UNIONE, 43
38068 ROVERETO [TN]
TEL. 0464439250
www.bossifedrigotti.com

CELLAR SALES
PRE-BOOKED VISITS

ANNUAL PRODUCTION 180,000 bottles
HECTARES UNDER VINE 40
VITICULTURE METHOD Conventional

This is one of the Trentino operations that have written the history of wines from the Dolomites. Bossi Fedrigotti has harvested its grapes since 1697, always in the area around Rovereto, in hillside plots or along the river Adige. For some time now, the estate has been under the management of Gruppo Masi, well-known producers from Valpolicella. A convergence of view involving the three Bossi Fedrigotti siblings and the Verona winery led to this decision, which has yielded excellent results.

The Fojaneghe Rosso '07 shows great quality. The wine, a beacon for winemaking even outside Trentino, is a Bordeaux-style blend, from 45 per cent merlot, 40 per cent cabernet sauvignon and a small proportion of teroldego with a broad bouquet and an intense, juicy palate veined with minerality and braced by remarkable freshness and energy. The other 2009s submitted were fair, from the Trentino Marzemino to the Trentino Gewürztraminer and Valdadige Pinot Grigio.

● Fojaneghe Rosso '07	**YY**	6
○ Trentino Gewürztraminer '09	**Y**	4
● Trentino Marzemino '09	**Y**	4
○ Valdadige Pinot Grigio '09	**Y**	4
● Fojaneghe Rosso '06	YY	6
● Teroldego '06	YY	5*
● Trecento '04	YY	4
● Trentino Marzemino '04	YY	4*
● Trentino Sup. Marzemino Sel. Campobove '04	YY	4

Cavit

VIA DEL PONTE DI RAVINA, 31
38040 TRENTO
TEL. 0461381711
www.cavit.it

CELLAR SALES
PRE-BOOKED VISITS

ANNUAL PRODUCTION 65,000,000 bottles
HECTARES UNDER VINE 5,700
VITICULTURE METHOD Conventional

The Cavit consortium is a winemaking landmark in Trentino. Innovation and the defence of local typicality have developed within a commercial dynamic that has taken the operation right to the top of the Italian market in sheer business numbers, yet Cavit has always been careful to safeguard the interests of its more than 6,000 member growers and manage its widespread holdings. No other co-operative this big manages to accomplish as much.

Cavit submitted two absolutely top wines this year to win a brace of Three Glass awards. The first is another endorsement for Trento Altemasi Graal Brut Riserva, the '05, a sparkling wine with alluring vigour, tamed by impeccable vinification, great suppleness and the unmistakeable imprint of ripe apples with an acidulous note of mountain fruit. The second, an amazing Teroldego Rotaliano Maso Cervara '07, is austere, succulent, and seamless in its progression, its close-knit texture rich in aromatic shades. From the rest of the range, special mentions goes to the Nosiola '09 and Müller Thurgau '09 from the Bottega Vinai line, as well as the charming Vino Santo Arèle '99.

● Teroldego Rotaliano Maso Cervara '07	🍷🍷🍷	5
○ Trento Altemasi Graal Brut Ris. '03	🍷🍷🍷	7
○ Trentino Vino Santo Arèle '99	🍷🍷	8
○ Trentino Müller Thurgau Bottega Vinai '09	🍷🍷	4*
○ Trentino Nosiola Bottega Vinai '09	🍷🍷	3*
○ Trentino Pinot Grigio Bottega Vinai '09	🍷	4
● Trentino Rosso Quattro Vicariati '06	🍷	5
○ Trento Altemasi Graal Brut '01	(🍷🍷🍷)	7
○ Trento Altemasi Graal Brut Ris. '02	(🍷🍷🍷)+	7
○ Trento Altemasi Graal Brut Ris. '00	(🍷🍷🍷)	6
○ Trento Altemasi Graal Brut Ris. '97	(🍷🍷🍷)	6
○ Trento Altemasi Graal Brut Ris. '96	(🍷🍷🍷)	7
○ Trento Altemasi Graal Brut Ris. '95	(🍷🍷🍷)	6

Cesconi

FRAZ. PRESSANO
VIA MARCONI, 39
38015 LAVIS [TN]
TEL. 0461240355
www.cesconi.it

CELLAR SALES
PRE-BOOKED VISITS

ANNUAL PRODUCTION 130,000 bottles
HECTARES UNDER VINE 21
VITICULTURE METHOD Conventional

The Cesconis are a guarantee. Competent and highly professional, they are also always open to innovation or a return to farming methods that are more respectful of nature. The estate sprawls across two distinct zones: the hill of Lavis and the Arco hollow from Drò in the direction of Lake Garda. The vineyards are managed without forcing and take full advantage of the characteristics of the soil. White varieties are planted above Lavis, near the winery, and reds toward Garda.

The Cesconis have always worked well but it can't do much about poor growing years. Recent harvests may not have favoured the flagship wines but they still impress with their outstanding personality. Olivar '08, a successful blend of pinot bianco, pinot grigio and chardonnay, pays the price of an indifferent vintage year and is less intriguing than usual. The same goes for the Rosso del Pivier '07; a merlot with ten per cent cabernet franc. It shows good texture but is still more closed and immobile than it has been for some time. The other wines are also experiencing a closed phase, from the Rosso Cesconi '07 to the Nosiola '08.

○ Olivar '08	🍷🍷	5
● Rosso del Pivier '07	🍷🍷	6
○ Prabi Bianco '08	🍷🍷	4*
● Moratèl '07	🍷	4
○ Nosiola '08	🍷	4
● Rosso Cesconi '07	🍷	5
○ Olivar '07	(🍷🍷🍷)	5
○ Olivar '05	(🍷🍷🍷)	5
○ Olivar '01	(🍷🍷🍷)	5

Marco Donati

via Cesare Battisti, 41
38016 Mezzocorona [TN]
tel. 0461604141
donatimarcovini@libero.it

CELLAR SALES
PRE-BOOKED VISITS

ANNUAL PRODUCTION 90,000 bottles
HECTARES UNDER VINE 20
VITICULTURE METHOD Conventional

Marco Donati has the serious expression of a classic winemaker, a country gentleman constantly moving around his vineyards scattered across Trentino. His main focus is on Teroldego and vines of this variety stand around the cellar set up inside a 15th-century structure. The estate produces a broad range, though Teroldego is still the feather in their cap.

The dynamic Donati estate produced good results starting with the Vino del Maso '09 from 70-15-15 teroldego, lagrein and merlot. Broodingly dark aromatics of forest floor and spice introduce a meaty, austere wine with a supple, balanced palate. The main estate wine also showed good quality, despite the rather unfavourable growing season. Teroldego Rotaliano Sangue di Drago '08 has a character and drinkability that in any case mark it our as one of the best from the vintage. The rest of the production is good, as always.

● Teroldego Rotaliano Sangue del Drago '08	▼▼	6
● Vino del Maso Rosso '09	▼▼	4
● Teroldego Rotaliano Bagolari '09	▼	5
⊙ Trentino Lagrein Rosato Fratte Alte '09	▼	4
○ Trentino Müller Thurgau Albeggio '09	▼	4
○ Trentino Nosiola Sole Alto '08	▼	4
● Teroldego Rotaliano Sangue del Drago '98	▽▽▽	4
● Teroldego Rotaliano Sangue del Drago '04	▽▽	6
● Teroldego Rotaliano Sangue del Drago '03	▽▽	6
● Teroldego Rotaliano Sangue del Drago '02	▽▽	6
● Teroldego Rotaliano Sangue del Drago '01	▽▽	6

F.lli Dorigati

via Dante, 5
38016 Mezzocorona [TN]
tel. 0461605313
www.dorigati.it

CELLAR SALES
PRE-BOOKED VISITS

ANNUAL PRODUCTION 100,000 bottles
HECTARES UNDER VINE 13
VITICULTURE METHOD Conventional

At their winery in the heart of Mezzocorona, the Dorigatis continue the work begun by their forebears a century and a half ago. Cellarmen even before they were growers, the Dorigatis brought out the best in Teroldego, recovered Rebo and blazed the trail for the planting of white grape varieties. They make good wines and sell them at honest prices but for some years now the greatest satisfaction has come from their sparkling wine production. Now, they are aiming for even higher goals.

The Trento Methius has nothing to fear from the competition in terms of style or reliable quality and the 2004 version smoothly picked up Three Glasses. Methius introduces notes of wood resin on a background of crusty bread that lend elegance despite rich structure on the palate that will enable the wine to withstand further time in bottle. Teroldego Rotaliano Diedri '07 is massive on entry, with an explosive bouquet and solid, dry palate that unfolds more powerful than succulent. The easy-drinking Trentino Rebo '07 has savoury tones and the rest of production showcases the uncomplicated appeal of simple wines.

○ Trento Methius Brut Ris. '04	▼▼▼	7
● Teroldego Rotaliano Diedri Ris. '07	▼▼	6
● Teroldego Rotaliano '08	▼	4
● Trentino Rebo '07	▼	4
○ Trento Methius Brut Ris. '03	▽▽▽	7
○ Trento Methius Brut Ris. '02	▽▽▽	7
○ Trento Methius Brut Ris. '00	▽▽▽	7
○ Trento Methius Brut. Ris. '98	▽▽▽	7

Endrizzi

LOC. MASETTO, 2
38010 SAN MICHELE ALL'ADIGE [TN]
TEL. 0461650129
www.endrizzi.it

CELLAR SALES
PRE-BOOKED VISITS

ANNUAL PRODUCTION 500,000 bottles
HECTARES UNDER VINE 40
VITICULTURE METHOD Conventional

Care for these vineyards can be measured by counting the bird nests. There are 30 or so per hectare, built among the rows and small beds of medicinal herbs. This is the most eye-catching sign of the Endrici family's production philosophy, for 125 years committed to tending their vineyards in the hills of San Michele all'Adige, Faedo and Castel Monreale. Today, the Endricis aim to produce quality wines with low-impact farming techniques, maintaining eco-sustainability in the vineyards.

While waiting for the new version of the Gran Masetto, a Teroldego from grapes dried on rush mats, the top wines from the estate include the stylish yet approachable Trento Endrizzi Brut Riserva '05, an unhurriedly dynamic 60-40 blend of chardonnay and pinot nero, and the soft, savoury Trentino Pinot Nero Pian di Castello '08 with its rich fruit. The other wines submitted are well made and getting better, from the Masetto Bianco '08 to the Trentino Nosiola Tradizione '08.

● Trentino Pinot Nero Pian di Castello '08	TT	5
○ Trento Endrizzi Brut Ris. '05	TT	5
○ Masetto Bianco '08	T	4
○ Trentino Chardonnay Tradizione '09	T	3
○ Trentino Nosiola Tradizione '09	T	4
● Gran Masetto '06	YY	7
● Gran Masetto '05	YY	7
● Teroldego Rotaliano Maso Camorz Ris. '04	YY	4

Giuseppe Fanti

FRAZ. PRESSANO
P.ZZA DELLA CROCE, 3
38015 LAVIS [TN]
TEL. 0461240809
vignaiolo@virglilio.it

PRE-BOOKED VISITS

ANNUAL PRODUCTION 20,000 bottles
HECTARES UNDER VINE 4
VITICULTURE METHOD Organic

Alessandro Fanti is an authentic winemaker. He works his small family estate in the hills above Lavis, attending to every detail from vineyard to cellar with simplicity, honesty and courtesy. He is also among the promoters of I Dolomitici, a new association of a dozen producers who have committed to extending use of organic and biodynamic growing methods.

All four wines submitted are distinct. First up is the Portico '07, a Bordeaux-style wine with added teroldego, shows as refined as it is full-bodied with soft tannins and a caressing finish. Another good drinking wine is the minerally, savoury Chardonnay '08. With its good structure, it is one of the best Chardonnays we tasted from Trentino. The Incrocio Manzoni '08 is good – we mistakenly reviewed it in the previous edition of the Guide. In closing, the chardonnay, riesling, nosiola and incrocio Manzoni Pritianum '08 is complex and well orchestrated but should be left to age for another year or two.

○ Chardonnay '08	TT	4
● Portico Rosso '07	TT	4
○ Incrocio Manzoni '08	TT	4
○ Pritianum '08	T	5
○ Incrocio Manzoni '05	YY	4
○ Incrocio Manzoni '05	YY	4
● Portico Rosso '06	YY	4*
○ Pritianum '07	YY	5
○ Pritianum '05	YY	5

★★ Ferrari

VIA PONTE DI RAVINA, 15
38100 TRENTO
TEL. 0461972311
www.cantineferrari.it

CELLAR SALES
PRE-BOOKED VISITS
FOOD

ANNUAL PRODUCTION 4,600,000 bottles
HECTARES UNDER VINE 120
VITICULTURE METHOD Conventional

Trento, Ferrari and Lunelli are a winning trio for anyone who loves good drinking, especially classic-method sparklers. The vineyards are located in the hills near Trento, where chemicals are practically banished, the balance of the vines is respected and yields per hectare reduced. The vines are tended by a close-knit, energetic team and the young oenologist Ruben Larentis – co-director alongside Mauro Lunelli – crafts the profiles of all the wines.

This time Ferrari doubled its Three Glasses. The Riserva del Fondatore '01, the spumante dedicated to Giulio Ferrari, had no problems with the high notes and won yet another prize thanks to the breadth of its aromatics, acid grip and depth that are practically unique on the Italian landscape. The big news here is that even the Perlé Nero '04, a long-lingering, complex, monovarietal Pinot Nero with citron notes, won rave reviews and another Three Glasses. But that's not all. The chardonnay-only Riserva Lunelli '03 played well right to the end. As usual, all the other Trentos are better than just sound, with a lovely performance from the Perlé Rosé '06.

○ Trento Extra Brut Perlé Nero '04	▼▼▼	8
○ Trento Giulio Ferrari Riserva del Fondatore Brut '01	▼▼▼+	8
○ Trento Brut Lunelli Ris. '03	▼▼	8
⊙ Trento Brut Perlé Rosé '06	▼▼	8
○ Trento Brut	▼▼	6
○ Trento Brut Maximum	▼▼	6
○ Trento Brut Perlé '05	▼▼	7
○ Giulio Ferrari '94	▽▽▽	8
○ Trento Brut Perlé '02	▽▽▽	6
○ Trento Giulio Ferrari '97	▽▽▽	8
○ Trento Giulio Ferrari '96	▽▽▽	8
○ Trento Giulio Ferrari '95	▽▽▽	8
○ Trento Giulio Ferrari Riserva del Fondatore Brut '00	▽▽▽	8
○ Trento Giulio Ferrari Riserva del Fondatore Brut '99	▽▽▽	8

★ Foradori

VIA DAMIANO CHIESA, 1
38017 MEZZOLOMBARDO [TN]
TEL. 0461601046
www.elisabettaforadori.com

CELLAR SALES
PRE-BOOKED VISITS

ANNUAL PRODUCTION 160,000 bottles
HECTARES UNDER VINE 23
VITICULTURE METHOD Certified biodynamic

Elisabetta Foradori is considered the first lady of Teroldego and the woman who revived the fortunes of this wine. Not content with this, she took on another challenge and combined this rigorously interpreted biodynamic farming. She radically changed the stylistic imprint of all her wines, equipping her cellar with small clay amphorae from Georgia for experiments with nosiola and teroldego. Finally, she is also the founder of I Dolomitici, a group of Trentino winemakers who use natural growing methods.

None of Elisabetta's wines are listed in the 2010 edition of the Guide. She skipped the vintage so she could present wines created with her new vinification methods. The technique has clearly changed but the Foradori style, her stamp, is still noticeable and how. The marvellous Granato '07 may have an unusual range of balsamic, subtly pepper-led aromatics but the structure is perfectly in line with previous "traditional" versions. The basic Teroldego Rotaliano '07 is more immediate and easily approachable and the Myrto '09, now a monovarietal Incrocio Manzoni 6.0.13, was designed to be released in a few years' time.

● Granato '07	▼▼▼	8
● Teroldego Rotaliano Foradori '07	▼▼	5
○ Myrto '09	▼	5
● Granato '04	▽▽▽	7
● Granato '03	▽▽▽	7
● Granato '02	▽▽▽	7
● Granato '01	▽▽▽	7
● Granato '00	▽▽▽	7
● Granato '99	▽▽▽	5

Grigoletti

VIA GARIBALDI, 12
38060 NOMI [TN]
TEL. 0464834215
www.grigoletti.com

CELLAR SALES
PRE-BOOKED VISITS

ANNUAL PRODUCTION **60,000 bottles**
HECTARES UNDER VINE **7**
VITICULTURE METHOD **Conventional**

The Grigolettis have been making wine for generations in Vallagarina from only grapes grown around Nomi in vineyards wrested from the river Adige on ancient floodland. Everything is done as a family, from the fields to sales, with times and methods in the best country tradition. We should add that the Grigolettis focus not just on the vineyards. Recently, they renovated the cellar as well.

This year, the most convincing wine was the Retiko '08, a blend of chardonnay, sauvignon and incrocio Manzoni. With its well-gauged blend and broad aromas of citron and citrus, supported by a serious structure, this wine will be best in a few years. The Grigolettis' flagship wine is the Trentino Merlot Antica Vigna, but the 2008 growing season hurt many winemakers and results of the quirky vintage are evident in the glass. The Antica Vigna does its best, but nothing can change the quality of the growing season. The other wines are simple and country-style with always-honest pricing and a genuinely drinkable appeal.

○	Retiko '08	▼▼	5
●	Trentino Merlot Antica Vigna di Nomi '08	▼▼	5
●	Gonzalier '07	▼	5
○	San Martim V.T. '08	▼	5
○	Retiko '06	▽▽	5
●	Trentino Merlot Antica Vigna di Nomi '07	▽▽	5
●	Trentino Merlot Antica Vigna di Nomi '05	▽▽	5
●	Trentino Merlot Antica Vigna di Nomi '04	▽▽	5

La Vis/Valle di Cembra

VIA CARMINE, 7
38034 LAVIS [TN]
TEL. 0461440111
www.la-vis.com

CELLAR SALES
PRE-BOOKED VISITS
ROOMS AND FOOD

ANNUAL PRODUCTION **6,500,000 bottles**
HECTARES UNDER VINE **1,500**
VITICULTURE METHOD **Conventional**

At a difficult point in its history, Gruppo La Vis is still the leading co-operative winemaking enterprise with more than a thousand member growers. Among the top ten Italian winemaking groups in terms of turnover, La Vis has maintained its ability to provide great support to its members, their land and their wines.

Because of the difficult growing season, the Ritratto Bianco '08 is perhaps less appealing than other editions but it is still in the front rank of white wines from Trentino. The interesting Trentino Superiore Pinot Nero Vigna di Saosent '08 shows how well the variety does in Valle di Cembra. The savoury, mineral Müller Thurgau Ritratti '09 has aromas of new-mown hay-led, fresh, graceful aromatics. Kudos goes to the Trentino Nosiola Maso Rosabel '09 and Trentino Traminer Maso Clinga '09 but the Ritratto Rosso, from teroldego and lagrein, was penalized by the 2008 vintage year.

○	Ritratto Bianco '08	▼▼	5
○	Trentino Müller Thurgau Ritratti '09	▼▼	4
●	Trentino Pinot Nero V. di Saosent '08	▼▼	5
●	Ritratto Rosso '08	▼	5
○	Trentino Nosiola Maso Rosabel '09	▼	4
○	Trentino Pinot Grigio Ritratti '09	▼	5
○	Trentino Sauvignon Maso Tratta '09	▼	4
○	Trentino Traminer Aromatico Maso Clinga '09	▼	5
○	Ritratto Bianco '07	▽▽▽	5
●	Ritratto Rosso '03	▽▽▽	5
●	Ritratto Rosso '91	▽▽▽	4
○	Trentino Pinot Grigio Ritratti '95	▽▽▽	4

Letrari

VIA MONTE BALDO, 13/15
38068 ROVERETO [TN]
TEL. 0464480200
www.letrari.it

CELLAR SALES
PRE-BOOKED VISITS

ANNUAL PRODUCTION 150,000 bottles
HECTARES UNDER VINE 23
VITICULTURE METHOD Conventional

Nello Letrari has more than 60 harvests behind him and is rightfully considered the grand old man of Trentino wine. Enthusiastic about his work, Nello has a passion for sparklers that has spurred him on to tackle new challenges. While the estate is now practically in the hands of his children, Lucia and Paolo Emilio, Nello saves himself for his spumante and the Letraris are experiencing something of a surge with precisely this type of wine. In fact, they are considering converting most of their production to Trento DOC.

The Letraris' choice to devote themselves to the world of sparklers seems to have been a winner. Two Trentos from this lovely winery in Rovereto reached our finals and one, the Riserva '05, won Three Glasses. This wine is perfectly in line with the Trentino spumante profile but shows genuinely exclusive, exciting verve and sensory perceptions. Just as good is the Pas Dosé, the latest creation and already an outstanding bottle. But the still wines are another matter. Nello's children should perhaps pay more attention to his suggestions, above all by cutting the range and concentrating just a couple of reds, like the Marzemino and Moscato Rosa, and one or two whites.

○ Trento Brut Letrari Ris. '05	▼▼▼	6
○ Trento Dosaggio Zero '07	▼▼	5
● Trentino Moscato Rosa '07	▼▼	7
○ Trento Brut Letrari '07	▼▼	5
● Ballistarius '05	▼	6
● Trentino Rosso Maso Lodron '06	▼	4
● Ballistarius '01	▽▽	6
● Trentino Moscato Rosa '03	▽▽	7
○ Trento Brut Ris. '99	▽▽	6
○ Trento Riserva del Fondatore '98	▽▽	6
○ Trento Riserva del Fondatore 976 '00	▽▽	8
○ Trento Riserva del Fondatore 976 '99	▽▽	8

Maso Furli

LOC. FURLI, 32
38015 LAVIS [TN]
TEL. 0461240667
masofurli@alice.it

CELLAR SALES
PRE-BOOKED VISITS

ANNUAL PRODUCTION 18,000 bottles
HECTARES UNDER VINE 4
VITICULTURE METHOD Organic

Marco Zanoni is on the threshold of radical change in the vineyard. One of the promoters of I Dolomitici, the group of Trentino growers that tend their vineyards according to biodynamic and natural criteria, Marco tries never to force the progress of the season and cycles of the vines. Alongside this, he applies ultra-modern vinification techniques, like crushing in nitrogen-saturated bell jars, and uses equipment of his own invention.

Though he started out making white wines, Marco again sent a Bordeaux-style red to the finals. The '07 Rosso Furli is concentrated, rich and tannic but should be left to age in bottle for a few years. Among the whites, the intriguing Chardonnay '08 shows remarkable complexity on the nose, then savoury and refined in the mouth with a pleasant, velvety finish. It is no accident that for years this Chardonnay has been one of the most imitated in the Dolomites. Less on target are the Traminer and Sauvignon, which though usually outstanding remain a bit muted. More evidence that the 2008 vintage was forgettable around here.

● Maso Furli Rosso '07	▼▼	5
○ Incrocio Manzoni '08	▼	5
○ Trentino Chardonnay '08	▼	5
○ Trentino Sauvignon '08	▼	5
○ Trentino Traminer Aromatico '08	▼	5
● Maso Furli Rosso '05	▽▽	5
● Maso Furli Rosso '04	▽▽	5
● Maso Furli Rosso '03	▽▽	5
○ Trentino Sauvignon '04	▽▽	5
○ Trentino Sauvignon '03	▽▽	5
○ Trentino Traminer Aromatico '05	▽▽	5

MezzaCorona

VIA DEL TEROLDEGO, 1
38016 MEZZOCORONA [TN]
TEL. 0461616399
www.mezzacorona.it

CELLAR SALES
PRE-BOOKED VISITS

ANNUAL PRODUCTION **30,000,000 bottles**
HECTARES UNDER VINE **3,500**
VITICULTURE METHOD **Conventional**

Results from MezzaCorona are surprising. With profits growing despite the crisis in the wine sector, this winery invests over €20 million a year in innovations in the vineyards as well as renewable energy sources, with solar panels that power winemaking equipment. At the same time, the operation has inaugurated a bottling plant with a potential of 50 million units a year, all this without forgetting its inseparable ties as a co-operative winery and attention to safeguarding local production.

The Teroldego Rotaliano Nos '05 reached our finals. This "Superteroldego" shows remarkable structure and fruity richness but the traditional Riserva is also always great, though it may need a bit more time in bottle to knit together. The most successful wine from the Castel Firmian line is the particularly fragrant Trentino Müller Thurgau '09. Best of the sparklers was the fresh, fragrant Flavio. The other wines are well crafted, from the Trento Talento Cuvée 28 to the Rosé and many other still wines, including the Pinot Grigio produced by MezzaCorona in enormous quantities, enough to make it the world leader in this type.

● Teroldego Rotaliano Nos Ris. '05	6
○ Trento Rotari Flavio Ris. '04	7
● Teroldego Rotaliano Ris. '07	5
○ Trentino Müller Thurgau Castel Firmian '09	4
○ Trentino Pinot Grigio '09	3
○ Trento Rotari Cuvée 28	5
⊙ Trento Rotari Rosé	5
● Teroldego Rotaliano Nos Ris. '04	6
● Teroldego Rotaliano Ris. '05	5
○ Trento Rotari Flavio Ris. '03	7
○ Trento Rotari Flavio Ris. '02	7

Casata Monfort

VIA CARLO SETTE, 21
38015 LAVIS [TN]
TEL. 0461246353
www.cantinemonfort.it

CELLAR SALES
PRE-BOOKED VISITS

ANNUAL PRODUCTION **140,000 bottles**
HECTARES UNDER VINE **40**
VITICULTURE METHOD **Conventional**

Monfort's base of operations is the historic winery in the heart of Lavis, though the welcome centre is at Maso Cantanghel, a charming structure within the walls of a First World War fortress in the hills of Trento at the entrance to Valsugana. The Simonis manage these two structures with the same professionalism they show in the vineyards, where they are bringing back old grape varieties, as well as in their ventures with classic-method sparkling wines and challenging varieties like pinot nero.

The Simonis divide their products into two lines, in keeping with the two estate sites. We liked the Pinot Nero Casata Monfort '07 with its rich bouquet and a palate that is succulent, concentrated and austere, perhaps slightly closed but still promising, and the savoury, minerally Sauvignon Vigna Piccola Maso Cantanghel '09, which is very varietal. The always outstanding Trento DOC is long on the palate, and has fresh, floral aromas on the nose, then turns creamy in the mouth. The Teroldego and onionskin Pinot Grigio from the Casata Monfort line, and the Traminer Aromatico Vigna Caselle from the Maso Cantanghel line, are some of the other well-made wines submitted.

○ Sauvignon V. Piccola Maso Cantanghel '09	4
● Trentino Pinot Nero Casata Monfort '07	5
○ Trento Brut '06	5
● Teroldego Rotaliano Casata Monfort '09	4
○ Trentino Pinot Grigio Casata Monfort '09	4
○ Trentino Traminer Aromatico V. Caselle Maso Cantanghel '09	5
○ Blanc de Sers '06	4
○ Trentino Chardonnay '08	4
● Trentino Pinot Nero Maso Cantanghel '06	5
○ Trento Brut '05	5

Pisoni

FRAZ. PERGOLESE DI LASINO
LOC. SARCHE
VIA SAN SIRO, 7A
38070 LASINO [TN]
TEL. 0461564106
www.pisoni.net

CELLAR SALES
PRE-BOOKED VISITS

ANNUAL PRODUCTION **40,000 bottles**
HECTARES UNDER VINE **16**
VITICULTURE METHOD **Organic**

Inspired by Stefano and encouraged by his father Arrigo, the Pisoni estate has decided to slowly convert to biodynamic agriculture. The Pisonis have been making wine for nearly two centuries, tending their plots at various altitudes around the winery. Since the still wines are under experimentation, they decided to submit only the Trentos, two spumantes produced with passion and experience acquired since the 1960s.

From a chardonnay base with small amounts of pinot nero, the two Pisoni family sparkling wines were convincing, both showing fragrant, graceful, fluent and fresh-tasting. In particular we liked the nicely dry Extra Brut Riserva '04 with nice acid backbone and a long, bell-clear finish. The curious, inviting Rosé offers lovely notes of red fruit on the nose that shade slowly into a soft, oaky finish.

○ Trento Extra Brut Ris. '04	🍷🍷	5*
⊙ Trento Rosé Brut '07	🍷🍷	6
○ Trentino Vino Santo '98	YY	7
○ Trentino Vino Santo '97	YY	7
○ Trentino Vino Santo '83	YY	6
○ Trento Extra Brut Ris. '03	YY	5
○ Trento Extra Brut Ris. '01	YY	5

Pojer & Sandri

LOC. MOLINI, 4
38010 FAEDO [TN]
TEL. 0461650342
www.pojeresandri.it

CELLAR SALES
PRE-BOOKED VISITS

ANNUAL PRODUCTION **250,000 bottles**
HECTARES UNDER VINE **25**
VITICULTURE METHOD **Conventional**

Mario Pojer and Fiorentino Sandri never cease to amaze us. Not just because of the continuous evolution of their work as growers and winemakers – from the new equipment in the cellar to the hybrid vines growing in upper Valle di Cembra, near Grumes – but also for the courageous positions they have taken on Trentino wines and the role of winemakers and co-operatives. They believe in the sort of Trentino winemaking that defends itself not with big numbers but with how much care is lavished on the vineyards so as to obtain wines with a clear identity.

Wines from Mario Pojer and Fiorentino Sandri give a good overall performance, in particular the Rosso Faye '07 from cabernet sauvignon and franc, merlot and lagrein, and the Besler Biank '05, from sauvignon, pinot bianco, incrocio Manzoni and kerner. Both these wines are characterful and extremely pleasant, though unusual in style and produced with cutting-edge winemaking technology that involves washing bunches before crushing in a nitrogen-saturated environment. The Bianco Faye, Pinot Nero, Sauvignon and two sparklers are always convincing. The curious, yet cleverly made, Filii is a blend of riesling, müller thurgau, kerner and incrocio Manzoni with around nine per cent alcohol.

○ Besler Biank '05	🍷🍷	5
● Rosso Faye '07	🍷🍷	6
○ Bianco Faye '07	🍷🍷	6
○ Cuvée Extra Brut	🍷🍷	5
○ Essenzia Vendemmia Tardiva '07	🍷🍷	5
● Pinot Nero Rodel Pianezzi Ris. '06	🍷🍷	5
○ Sauvignon '09	🍷🍷	5
○ Filii '09	🍷	4
○ Nosiola '09	🍷	4
○ Bianco Faye '01	YYY	5
● Rosso Faye '05	YYY	6
● Rosso Faye '00	YYY	6

Pravis

LOC. LE BIOLCHE, 1
38076 LASINO [TN]
TEL. 0461564305
www.pravis.it

CELLAR SALES
PRE-BOOKED VISITS

ANNUAL PRODUCTION 200,000 bottles
HECTARES UNDER VINE 32
VITICULTURE METHOD Conventional

Make way for the new generation in the cellar and vineyard is the watchword at Pravis. Fresh from her oenology degree, Erika Pedrini has officially taken the place of her father Domenico, and Alessio Chistè, a recent graduate of San Michele all'Adige, is involved mostly in the vineyard. The estate has small vineyards scattered across Valle dei Laghi in the Brenta and Garda Dolomites. They were among the first to revive old native varieties, such as groppello di Revò, negrara, goldtraminer and cavallotta, and to use overripe white varieties to create personal, characterful wines.

Stravino di Stravino '07 from various overripe white varieties put on a convincing performance. After emerging from acacia barrels and stainless steel, this minerally wine has notes of jasmine and dates and a soft close lifted by rich alcohol. The Sauvignon Teramara and classic Nosiola Le Frate, both '09s, are two other representative products this year. The '08 Destrani from Franconia shows rustic and acidulous for an old-style country wine. The first harvest of Traminer Cros del Mont still shows the young age of the vines. The shiraz-based Syrae is well crafted but pays the price of a difficult '06 growing season.

○ Stravino di Stravino '07	5
○ Nosiola Le Frate '09	5
○ Sauvignon Atesino Teramara '09	5
● Destrani '08	4
● Syrae '06	5
○ Trentino Traminer Aromatico Cros del Mont '09	5
○ Stravino di Stravino '99	6
● Fratagranda '02	5
○ Stravino di Stravino '04	5
○ Trentino Vino Santo Arèle '97	7

Eugenio Rosi

VIA TAVERNELLE, 3B
38060 VOLANO [TN]
TEL. 0464461375
www.vignaioli.trentino.it

CELLAR SALES
PRE-BOOKED VISITS

ANNUAL PRODUCTION 18,000 bottles
HECTARES UNDER VINE 6
VITICULTURE METHOD Certified organic

Eugenio Rosi defines himself as a flamboyant artisan. With a group of friends, he started I Dolomitici, a new biodynamic group that uses his very personal winemaking techniques to create assertive wines by vinifying various white varieties in the red wine style to creating a dry Marzemino by harvesting overripe grapes or even a sweet version, of the kind that was fashionable back when Venice was an independent republic.

This time, the Cabernet Franc '08 is the best from Eugenio Rosi's philosophical production concepts. This dark, full, complex red opens up little by little, winning you over with power as well as elegance. Esegesi, his Bordeaux-blend red, reveals the shortcomings of the vintage. The '06 growing season in Vallagarina was not exactly memorable. Now we come to the Marzemino. Rosi uses this common local variety to make the Poiema '07 and Dòron '06, the former, from overripe grapes, is tannic and spicy while the second, from part- dried grapes, is more for meditative sipping.

● Cabernet Franc '08	6
● Esegesi '06	5
● Dòron '06	6
● Poiema '07	5
● Dòron '00	6
● Esegesi '05	5
● Esegesi '04	5

Cantina Rotaliana

VIA TRENTO, 65B
38017 MEZZOLOMBARDO [TN]
TEL. 0461601010
www.cantinarotaliana.it

CELLAR SALES
PRE-BOOKED VISITS

ANNUAL PRODUCTION 1,000,000 bottles
HECTARES UNDER VINE 330
VITICULTURE METHOD Conventional

Cantina Rotaliana has for some time been an example of highly professional production with an increasing sense of place, in which quantity and quality co-exist without friction. Grapes are contributed by an array of member growers proud of being the stewards of Campo Rotaliano, vineyards that were renowned even during the Middle Ages. The positive market response is forcing the winery to expand while fully respecting the special qualities of the fruit processed.

Since the missing Clesurae is still ageing, we most enjoyed the traditional Teroldego Rotaliano Riserva '07, as stylish in the attack on the palate as it is confident and caressing, and splendid value for money. Not bad either are the tangy, rounded Trentino Chardonnay '09 and Trentino Moscato Giallo '09. This latter wine type may occasionally be neglected but this version is bracing, sincere and ready to drink. The other wines are invariably good quality, particularly the whites. Everyone is waiting for that small parcel of wines "left on the lees" to be transformed into a Trento DOC sparkler by the director and oenologist, Leonardo Pilati.

● Teroldego Rotaliano Ris. '07	▼▼	5
○ Trentino Chardonnay '09	▼▼	4*
○ Trentino Moscato Giallo '09	▼▼	4*
○ Thamè Bianco '09	▼	5
○ Trentino Pinot Bianco '09	▼	4
○ Trentino Pinot Grigio '09	▼	4
● Teroldego Rotaliano Clesurae '06	▽▽▽	6
● Teroldego Rotaliano Clesurae '02	▽▽▽	6
● Teroldego Rotaliano Clesurae '99	▽▽▽	6
● Teroldego Rotaliano Ris. '04	▽▽▽	4
● Teroldego Rotaliano Clesurae '05	▽▽	6
● Teroldego Rotaliano Clesurae '04	▽▽	6
● Teroldego Rotaliano Clesurae '03	▽▽	6
● Teroldego Rotaliano Ris. '05	▽▽	5

★ Tenuta San Leonardo

FRAZ. BORGHETTO ALL'ADIGE
LOC. SAN LEONARDO
38060 AVIO [TN]
TEL. 0464689004
www.sanleonardo.it

CELLAR SALES
PRE-BOOKED VISITS

ANNUAL PRODUCTION 145,000 bottles
HECTARES UNDER VINE 21
VITICULTURE METHOD Conventional

Tenuta San Leonardo proves that climate, terrain and humans can interact. Located in the heart of Campi Sarni, where vines have been grown since before the year 1000, the residence of the Marchesi Guerrieri Gonzaga is a major bulwark of wine culture. Carlo Guerrieri Gonzaga and his son Anselmo respect the balance of nature and continue their experiments without forcing, always and only starting from red grape varieties: cabernet sauvignon and franc, merlot and a historic carmenère.

Courage, astuteness and new market sectors. The growing season failed to convince the Marchesi Guerrieri Gonzaga, who decided not to produce either the San Leonardo or Villa Gresti and instead went for a less challenging wine, albeit one still underwritten by the estate trademark. So we tasted the Terre di San Leonardo, from an equal blend of cabernet and merlot, which is in fact an absolutely enthralling wine that also offers good value. It was a masterstroke. Terre di San Leonardo '06 has a lovely ruby red colour, fruity, balsamic notes and a structure that is supple yet at the same time gutsy. It will improve in bottle for a few years yet.

● Terre di San Leonardo '06	▼▼	4
● San Leonardo '05	▽▽▽	8
● San Leonardo '04	▽▽▽	8
● San Leonardo '03	▽▽▽	8
● San Leonardo '01	▽▽▽	8
● San Leonardo '00	▽▽▽	8
● San Leonardo '99	▽▽▽	8
● San Leonardo '97	▽▽▽	5
● San Leonardo '96	▽▽▽	5
● Villa Gresti '03	▽▽▽	7

Istituto Agrario Provinciale San Michele all'Adige

via Edmondo Mach, 1
38010 San Michele all'Adige [TN]
tel. 0461615252
www.ismaa.it

CELLAR SALES
PRE-BOOKED VISITS

ANNUAL PRODUCTION 250,000 bottles
HECTARES UNDER VINE 60
VITICULTURE METHOD Conventional

The "Istituto" – as oenologists call it – has written the recent history of wines in the Dolomites. The foundation now looks to the future, acquiring university status and orchestrating the reorganization plans for the wine sector of the Trento provincial authority. At San Michele all'Adige, they are accustomed to tackling crises, aiming for innovation and educating students to make by wine by focusing on the land and not the market. The winery makes various lines of wines, all as interesting as the research carried out there.

The '06 version of the Trento spumante dedicated to the school's founder has not repeated last year's success but still remains one of the best in the category with an enviable versatility. Two whites from the Monastero line are also good quality: the Trentino Chardonnay '09 and Trentino Riesling '09. The latter is distinctly mineral and should be drunk in all its commanding complexity in a few years' time. One of the best of the Trentino Pinot Biancos tasted this year is the Istituto's '09, with notes of white-fleshed fruits and near perfect technique. The other wines from the range are well typed.

○ Trentino Pinot Bianco '09	2 black glasses	4*
○ Trento Mach Riserva del Fondatore '06	2 black glasses	6
○ Trentino Riesling Monastero '09	2 black glasses	4
○ Trentino Chardonnay Monastero '09	1 black glass	4
○ Trentino Pinot Grigio '09	1 black glass	4
● Trentino Pinot Nero '08	1 black glass	5
○ Trento Mach Riserva del Fondatore '04	3 white glasses	6
○ Trentino Bianco Monastero '05	2 white glasses	5
● Trentino Rosso Monastero '04	2 white glasses	6
○ Trento Mach Riserva del Fondatore '02	2 white glasses	5
○ Trento Mach Riserva del Fondatore '01	2 white glasses	5

Vallarom

fraz. Masi, 21
38063 Avio [TN]
tel. 0464684297
www.vallarom.it

CELLAR SALES
PRE-BOOKED VISITS

ANNUAL PRODUCTION 40,000 bottles
HECTARES UNDER VINE 7
VITICULTURE METHOD Organic

Changing in order to continue winemaking as their life's choice, Barbara and Filippo Scienza are modifying the entire agricultural set up on their scenic estate located in the so-called "Little Dolomites" facing Castel Avio. Changing means forgetting traditional growing systems to apply organic and biodynamic methods. The Scienzas took this decision with courage and determination, combining it with an estate makeover to create space for the cellar and an agriturismo soon to be in operation.

In order to change, something must be sacrificed. So the wines are in a transitional phase, different from some of the styles we have become accustomed to. We were most convinced by the Campi Sarni '07, a Bordeaux blend with damp earth tones and a textured palate, supported by well-integrated tannins, with a balsamic finish. The classic Marzemino is pleasant, softer than other versions, and should be drunk while young. The pinot bianco, chardonnay, sauvignon and riesling Vadum Caesaris '09 lacks a little vitality. We are waiting for the new classic spumantes that are still in the cellar and hope in the next few years to find the Pinot Nero and Enantio more convincing.

● Campi Sarni Rosso '07	2 black glasses	5
○ Enantio '08	1 black glass	4
● Pinot Nero '07	1 black glass	5
● Trentino Marzemino '09	1 black glass	4
○ Vadum Caesaris '09	1 black glass	4
● Campi Sarni Rosso '05	2 white glasses	5
○ Chardonnay Vigneto Casetta '06	2 white glasses	5
● Syrah '04	2 white glasses	6

Villa Corniole

FRAZ. VERLA
VIA AL GREC', 23
38030 GIOVO [TN]
TEL. 0461695067
www.villacorniole.com

CELLAR SALES
PRE-BOOKED VISITS

ANNUAL PRODUCTION 70,000 bottles
HECTARES UNDER VINE 14
VITICULTURE METHOD Conventional

Villa Corniole is one of the few Trentino estates to have won us over with the improved quality and the personality of the wines submitted. The cellar is practically carved out of the porphyry, the signature red rock of Valle di Cembra. Vineyards are organized into various sectors: white grape varieties are grown at high altitudes on terraces supported by dry stone walls and the red grapes are to be found in plots on the valley floor, in the heart of the Campo Rotaliano.

One of our finalists comes from high-altitude vineyards that are perfect for white grape varieties. This enjoyable Trentino Chardonnay Lukin '06 is sourced from the hills of Avisio, near the estate of the same name. Fermented part in oak and part in stainless steel, it proffers a nose of great intensity with ripe fruit sensations, and palate is fresh and lively. Also convincing is the Teroldego Rotaliano 7 Pergole '06, sourced from Guyot-trained vineyards with half the yields per hectare called for by regulations. This appealing, spicy wine will age well. The standard-label Teroldego is pleasant, fresh and ready to drink. The other wines are all well crafted, above all the Müller Thurgau '09 and Lagrein '08.

○ Trentino Chardonnay Lukin '06	▼▼	5
● Teroldego Rotaliano 7 Pergole '06	▼▼	6
● Teroldego Rotaliano '08	▼	4
● Trentino Lagrein '08	▼	4
○ Trentino Müller Thurgau '09	▼	4
● Cimbro '06	▽▽	4
● Teroldego Rotaliano '07	▽▽	4
● Teroldego Rotaliano 7 Pergole '03	▽▽	6
○ Trentino Chardonnay Lukin '04	▽▽	5

Roberto Zeni

FRAZ. GRUMO
VIA STRETTA, 2
38010 SAN MICHELE ALL'ADIGE [TN]
TEL. 0461650456
www.zeni.tn.it

CELLAR SALES
PRE-BOOKED VISITS

ANNUAL PRODUCTION 190,000 bottles
HECTARES UNDER VINE 20
VITICULTURE METHOD Conventional

For nearly 40 years, brothers Andrea and Roberto Zeni have been a benchmark for Trentino winemaking. They have expanded their estate by purchasing plots in the hills of Lavis, keeping the cellar at the original headquarters on the right bank of the river Adige. Though in the beginning, they dealt almost exclusively with still white wines, for a few years now they have worked with red grapes, from moscato rosa to old varieties like rossara and all the way through to pinot nero and teroldego, focusing at the same time on sparkling winemaking.

The '05 Teroldego Pini vineyard selection, always the estate standard-bearer, once again went into the finals thanks to its outstanding personality and a dynamic, long-finishing palate as juicy as it is minerally. The curious Rossara '09 is unusual in both its mouthfeel and richness of flavour. The Moscato Rosa '08 is more captivating, with floral aromas and spicy flavours. The Trento Maso Nero Rosé '05 is good yet again, taking its name from a plot in the high hills above Lavis where the Zenis' famous vineyard is found. The other products are all sound.

● Teroldego Rotaliano Pini '05	▼▼	7
⊙ Rossara '09	▼▼	4*
⊙ Trentino Moscato Rosa '08	▼▼	5
⊙ Trento Maso Nero Rosé '05	▼▼	6
○ Trentino Nosiola Maso Nero '09	▼	4
● Trentino Pinot Nero Spiazol '07	▼	5
● Teroldego Rotaliano Pini '01	▽▽	7
● Teroldego Rotaliano Vign. Le Albere '07	▽▽	4
● Trentino Moscato Rosa '04	▽▽	7
○ Trento Brut '03	▽▽	6
○ Trento Zeni Brut Ris. '95	▽▽	6

Acino d'Oro

FRAZ. BORGHETTO ALL'ADIGE
LOC. SAN LEONARDO, 3
38060 AVIO [TN]
TEL. 0464689004

Villa Imperiale is a joint project between Marchese Carlo Guerrieri Gonzaga and Cavit. This blend of local varieties – teroldego and lagrein – with the more international cabernet and merlot creates an outstandingly Trentino-style wine of which nearly a half million bottles are released at tempting prices.

● Villa Imperiale '07 🍷🍷 3*

Bolognani

VIA STAZIONE, 19
38015 LAVIS [TN]
TEL. 0461246354
www.bolognani.com

Cellarmen with a passion for vines, the Bolognani brothers are planning new winemaking projects and redesigning their wines in both style and substance, selecting grapes from contributing growers and their own vineyards. The outstanding Dolomite-style Teroldego Armilo '08 is fragrant and nicely made.

● Teroldego Armilo '08 🍷🍷 4
○ Müller Thurgau '09 🍷 4
○ Nosiola '09 🍷 4

Borgo dei Posseri

LOC. POZZO BASSO, 1
38061 ALA [TN]
TEL. 0464671899
www.borgodeiposseri.com

For some years now, viticulture has been back on the mountain of Ala, where Margherita de Pilati and Martin Mainenti have built their winemaking estate. The minerally Sauvignon Furiel '09 shows bright aromatic tones on nose and palate. The Gewürztraminer Arliz '09 is well made and uncompromising.

○ Sauvignon Furiel '09 🍷🍷 5
○ Gewürztraminer Arliz '09 🍷 5
● Merlot Rocol '07 🍷 4

Cesarini Sforza

FRAZ. RAVINA
VIA STELLA, 9
38123 TRENTO
TEL. 0461382200
www.cesarinisforza.com

Apart from the organizational restructuring, the future of this major winemaker lies in the high-quality range of spumantes it turns out every year. We loved the Trento Aquila Reale Riserva '03, a fresh, complex chardonnay-based Blanc des Blancs. The other wines are all good.

○ Trento Aquila Reale Ris. '03 🍷🍷 8
⊙ Trento Tridentum Rosé 🍷🍷 5
○ Trento Tridentum '06 🍷 5

Cobelli

LOC. MASI DI SORNI, 22
38015 LAVIS [TN]
TEL. 3495259503

Brothers Devis and Tiziano Corbelli run this tiny estate. Although they have made wines for a few years, only now have they decided to bottle them. Their Teroldego Grill '08 is non-DOC but shows amazing character and power. The traditional Traminer Gèss '08 is full and broad. We await new surprises.

● Teroldego Grill '08 🍷🍷 6
○ Trentino Traminer Gèss '08 🍷🍷 5

Concilio

Z.I., 2
38060 VOLANO [TN]
TEL. 0464411000
www.concilio.it

Connected with the Cantina Sociale di Trento, this historic wine estate presents an interesting range of wines designed mainly for foreign sales. One of the first Trentino-made Bordeaux blends, Mori Vecio Riserva '06 shows rich and fruity on the nose, then good structure and softness on the palate.

● Trentino Mori Vecio Ris. '06 🍷🍷 4
● Teroldego Rotaliano Braide '08 🍷 4

Cantina d'Isera
via al Ponte, 1
38060 Isera [TN]
tel. 0464433795
www.cantinaisera.it

Cantina d'Isera is known as a Marzemino producer but this co-operative winery also vinifies other varieties to make approachable, value-for-money wines. For some years, they have also made a couple of excellent Trento spumantes that are now the top of the cellar's range.

○ Trento Brut '06	5
○ Trento Brut Ris. '05	6
● Trentino Marzemino '09	4
○ Trentino Pinot Grigio '09	4

De Vescovi Ulzbach
p.zza Garibaldi, 12
38016 Mezzocorona [TN]
tel. 0461605648
www.devescoviulzbach.it

Take your time and wines from this long-established winery, which only started bottling again a few harvests ago, are sure to win you over. The estate focuses everything on Teroldego, made with grapes that ripen right outside their door. This year, only the basic '08 version was submitted.

● Teroldego Rotaliano '08	4

Cipriano Fedrizzi
via 4 Novembre, 1
38017 Mezzolombardo [TN]
tel. 0461602328
fedrizzicipriano@alice.it

The Fedrizzis grow practically only teroldego in vineyards near the river Noce in the heart of the Campo Rotaliano. They have revived a historic label of Teroldego, the Tiroldigo, and produce a new version with this name. The Teroldego Due Vigneti '08 is always sound.

● Teroldego Rotaliano Due Vigneti '08	6
● Teroldego Rotaliano Tiroldigo '09	4

Francesco Moser
fraz. Meano
via Castel di Gardolo, 5
38040 Trento
tel. 0461990786
www.cantinemoser.com

For fans of cycling, he is the world champion in time trials and the Giro d'Italia but for a few seasons now Francesco Moser has given more and more attention to the vineyards around the country house where his estate is headquartered in his native Valle di Cembra, just above Gardolo.

○ Passito del Maso '08	5
○ Traminer '09	4

Furlani
loc. Povo
via Gabbiolo, 2
38100 Trento
tel. 3471474234
www.cantinafurlani.it

Last year was the debut and this year sees confirmation with two wines from Matteo Furlani, both of them blends. Alteo '09 is made from cabernet and merlot and Joe '09 is from traminer, chardonnay and müller thurgau. The still-developing Furlani Brut is closed and in search of an identity.

● Alteo '09	4
○ Furlani Brut	5
○ Joe '09	4

Gaierhof
via IV Novembre, 51
38030 Roverè della Luna [TN]
tel. 0461658514
www.gaierhof.com

The Gaierhof wine estate flanks the working family farm, Maso Poli above Lavis, for some time property of the Togn family. The Moscato Rosa '09 and two Müller Thurgaus are among their most interesting wines.

● Trentino Moscato Rosa '09	6
○ Trentino Müller Thurgau '09	3
○ Trentino Müller Thurgau dei Settecento '09	4

OTHER WINERIES

Longariva
FRAZ. BORGO SACCO
VIA R. ZANDONAI, 6
38068 ROVERETO [TN]
TEL. 0464437200
www.longariva.it

Up and down tastings relegated this lovely estate to a small profile. Winemaking couple Rosanna and Marco Manica have for years been top producers of good Trentino wines. Among the various wines tasted, we liked the Trentino Chardonnay Praistel '07. The rest of the range is well crafted.

- ○ Trentino Chardonnay Praistel '07 — 🍷🍷 5
- ● Trentino Lagrein '06 — 🍷 4

Mas dela Fam
LOC. RAVINA
VIA STELLA, 18
38122 TRENTO
TEL. 0461349114
www.masdelafam.it

Luca Boscheri has experience in the recording industry and an passion for growing vines. Vines planted at his estate on dizzying slopes at the southern edge of the city have given encouraging results, especially the Bordeaux-blend Rubio Rosso '07, which is succulent, full and fascinating.

- ● Rubio Rosso '07 — 🍷🍷 4*

Maso Bastie
LOC. BASTIE, 1
38060 VOLANO [TN]
TEL. 0464412747
www.masobastie.it

At this old estate located between Rovereto, Volano and Vallagarina, Giuseppe and Patrizia Torelli tend a single plot of 14 hectares under vine. The range includes a robust Bordeaux blend Bastie Alte '06 and several delicious sweet wines, above all the Trentino Moscato Rosa '09.

- ● Bastie Alte '06 — 🍷🍷 6
- ● Moscato Rosa '09 — 🍷🍷 6
- ● Pra' dei Fanti '09 — 🍷 5

Maso Bergamini
FRAZ. COGNOLA
LOC. BERGAMINI, 3
38050 TRENTO
TEL. 0461983079
www.masobergamini.com

Maso Bergamini is one of the most beautiful estates in the hills on the Calisio side of Trento. For years, it has been managed by Remo Tomasi, a winemaker and enthusiastic experimenter who farms organically and carefully makes wines with small parcels of grapes from his splendid, scenic vineyards.

- ⊙ Trentino Moscato Rosa '09 — 🍷 5

Maso Martis
LOC. MARTIGNANO
VIA DELL'ALBERA, 52
38121 TRENTO
TEL. 0461821057
www.masomartis.it

Maso Martis is a reliable wine estate and competent crafter of sparkling wines. Managed by the Stelzer family, its vineyards are located in one of the most beautiful spots in Trento. In fact, the Trentos are the most convincing products. Special mention goes to the rich, complex Trento Brut Riserva '04.

- ○ Trento Brut Ris. '04 — 🍷🍷 6
- ● Moscato Rosa '09 — 🍷 6
- ○ Trento Brut '07 — 🍷 6
- ⊙ Trento Brut Rosé '07 — 🍷 6

Mori - Colli Zugna
VIA DEL GARDA, 35
38065 MORI [TN]
TEL. 0464918154
www.cantinamoricollizugna.it

Strange but true, an exquisite Teroldego comes from the homeland of Marzemino. It has nothing to envy its more celebrated cousins and is sold at an amazingly good price. This Cavit group winery uses grapes from vineyards in Vallagarina and Garda, releasing a range that includes Trento spumantes.

- ● Terodelgo V. del Gelso '09 — 🍷🍷 3*
- ○ Trentino Chardonnay V. del Gelso '09 — 🍷 3

Pedrotti Spumanti

VIA ROMA, 2A
38060 NOMI [TN]
TEL. 0464835111
www.spumanti.it

The Pedrottis have been involved in wine since the early 20th century. For some years now, they have been producing classic sparklers and have had success with their honest, convincing Trento Rosé '06, further demonstration of the oenological, as well as business, skills of this small Vallagarina estate.

- ⊙ Trento Brut Pedrotti Rosé '06 — 🍷🍷 5

Redondèl

VIA ROMA, 28
38017 MEZZOLOMBARDO [TN]
TEL. 0461605861
www.redondel.it

Paolo Zanini has settled on cultivating and vinifying only teroldego from his vineyards in the heart of the Rotaliana plain. Painstaking selection makes his wines unique but don't worry about the unusual names. These are well-made wines that are constantly improving and promise much.

- ● Beatome '06 — 🍷🍷 7
- ⊙ Teroldego Rotaliano Assolto '09 — 🍷 4

Revì

VIA FLORIDA, 10
38060 ALDENO [TN]
TEL. 0461842557
www.revispumanti.com

The name comes from a good wine location in the area, hence Re Vin (wine king). The estate produces only a couple of versions of Trento spumante from selected local grapes, mainly chardonnay and pinot nero. There are fewer than 20,000 bottles, all in the finest Trentino sparkling winemaking tradition.

- ○ Trento Revì Brut '06 — 🍷🍷 5

Arcangelo Sandri

VIA VANEGGE, 4
38010 FAEDO [TN]
TEL. 0461650935
www.arcangelosandri.it

Arcangelo's young daughters, Nadia and Sonia, lack only experience. In the meantime, they have planted vineyards in the Faedo hills and paid even more attention to vinification. Tastings were encouraging yet uneven. The Chardonnay Canopi '09 was stood out.

- ○ Trentino Chardonnay I Canopi '09 — 🍷 4
- ○ Trentino Müller Thurgau Cosler '09 — 🍷 4
- ○ Trentino Traminer Razer '09 — 🍷 4

Armando Simoncelli

VIA NAVICELLO, 7
38068 ROVERETO [TN]
TEL. 0464432373
www.simoncelli.it

In the '07 edition, Navesèl is again the standard-bearer for the wines from this unfussy, competent winemaker, committed with his family to promoting Marzemino as well as crafting a creamy, fragrant classic-method sparkling wine. The other wines are all succulent yet simple.

- ● Trentino Rosso Navesèl '07 — 🍷🍷 4
- ○ Trentino Chardonnay '09 — 🍷 3
- ● Trentino Marzemino '09 — 🍷 4
- ○ Trento Brut — 🍷 5

Spagnolli

VIA G. B. ROSINA, 4A
38060 ISERA [TN]
TEL. 0464409054
www.vinispagnolli.it

Spagnolli submitted a Nosiola, Chardonnay and a couple of versions of Marzemino, the house wine at Isera, where generations of the family have worked. Hereabouts, they know how to grow native varieties with utterly reliable results. Always attentive to value for money, the Spagnollis produce well-made wines.

- ● Trentino Marzemino Don Giovanni '08 — 🍷 5
- ○ Trentino Nosiola '09 — 🍷 4

Toblino

FRAZ. SARCHE
VIA LONGA, 1
38070 CALAVINO [TN]
TEL. 0461564168
www.toblino.it

This reliable, well-managed co-operative winery focuses mostly on the local market and tourists at Lake Garda. Toblino a leader in production of a good-value Vino Santo but also produces some late-harvest wines from unusual varieties such as goldtraminer and kerner.

○ Trentino Vino Santo Puro '99	🍷🍷 7
○ Goldtraminer '09	🍷 4
○ Kerner '09	🍷 4
○ Trentino Traminer Aromatico '09	🍷 4

Villa Piccola

LOC. VILLA PICCOLA, 4
38010 FAEDO [TN]
TEL. 0461650420

Though small, you can safely list this estate among those that have brought fame to Faedo, the village above San Michele all'Adige. From around five hectares, Villa Piccola creates wines that have been improving for some time. This year, the spotlight fell on the fresh, fruity Chardonnay Argentarie '09.

○ Chardonnay Argentarie '09	🍷🍷 4
● Pinot Nero Silbrarii '08	🍷 5

Vivallis

VIA PER BRANCOLINO, 4
38068 NOGAREDO [TN]
TEL. 0464834113
www.vivallis.it

Co-operative winemaking in Trentino is in turmoil. Mergers are in the pipeline to overcome this crisis and reconnect wines to their original terroirs. This year, wines from Vivallis may have felt some stress but they still confirm their well-designed profiles and are still great value for money.

● Suseya Rosso '07	🍷 5
○ Trentino Bianco Ultreya '09	🍷 4
○ Trentino Nosiola V. Vallunga '09	🍷 4

Conti Wallenburg

LOC. MARTIGNANO
VIA BASSANO, 3
38040 TRENTO
TEL. 045913399
www.masowallenburg.it

In Martignano, above Trento, the Montresor family of wine entrepreneurs from Verona has rebuilt an old farmhouse, where the cellar is located, and planted vines on nearby terraces. Initial harvests have produced excellent results with the Trento DOC sparkler giving the most convincing performance.

○ Trento Corte Imperiale Brut	🍷🍷 5
○ Trentino Traminer Maria Adelaide '09	🍷 6

ALTO ADIGE

A quick snapshot of the region shows 26 Three Glasses and White of the Year for the '09 Sylvaner R from Günther Kershbaumer's Köfererhof estate. Alto Adige produced around 327,000 hectolitres in 2009 and the vintage was excellent for both whites and reds. Although this certainly contributed to the excellent performance, merit also goes to the producers for interpreting the vintage so well. The wines are distinctly richer and fuller than in 2008, but they are also lovely and fresh, despite respectable alcohol content from the hot weather. Overall, the region appears to be focusing increasingly on whites, with around 50 per cent of Alto Adige's vineyards now planted to white varieties. That said, there are also some good traditional reds such as Lagrein and Schiava, which happens to have won its first Three Glasses with the '09 Santa Maddalena from Johannes Pfeifer's Pfannenstielhof estate. Pinot Bianco is clearly the region's top wine, providing a total of six Three Glasses but several other types also offered pleasant surprises, such as Veltliner produced in Valle Isarco, which won three awards with wines that have finally reached the peak of their expression, We were also delighted to be able to award a Pinot Grigio Three Glasses again, which is no surprise, given what good a year it was for the type. Valle Venosta and Valle Isarco also confirmed their position as outstanding white-producing zones, in particular with new entry Strasserhof, but Oltradige also did very well with the Peter Sölva & Söhne estate, which won its first Three Glasses. The lower Adige valley also took advantage of the vintage. Lagreins have achieved outstanding stylistic maturity and complexity, some great sweet wines are being produced and there are also increasing numbers of organic and biodynamic producers so it would seem that all is well with the region. However, the situation is not quite that simple because although Alto Adige appears to have been less affected by economic crisis than other regions, some larger producers, and those with less well-structured sales networks, are feeling the pinch. Cellar door sales are helping to keep the more forward-thinking estates afloat. Yet in spite of this, the region is doing relatively well, mainly thanks to the many producers, big and small, who constantly seek to better themselves. The new Consorzio Vini Alto Adige, which encompasses almost all the region's producers, should give them helping hand.

★ Abbazia di Novacella

Fraz. Novacella
via dell'Abbazia, 1
39040 Varna/Vahrn [BZ]
tel. 0472836189
www.abbazianovacella.it

CELLAR SALES
PRE-BOOKED VISITS
FOOD

ANNUAL PRODUCTION 650,000 bottles
HECTARES UNDER VINE 20
VITICULTURE METHOD Conventional

Built in 1142, Abbazia di Novacella has become somewhat of a legend, renowned for its architecture and history. This lovely wine estate has used a biomass power plant for years. The estate still belongs to the Augustinians, but Urban von Kleblesberg, the director, and winemaker Celestino Lucin are the driving force behind its roaring success. Their Sylvaner, Veltliner and Kerner lead the line-up, but they also have a Riesling, Pinot Grigio and Sauvignon Blanc, with Lagrein and Pinot Nero in the reds.

As usual, it was very hard deciding which of the five finalists would be awarded Three Glasses. Which is more worthy: the mineral, salty, austere, richly profound '09 Sylvaner Praepositus or the '09 Veltliner Praepositus with its complex iodine notes and bold yet very well-balanced structure? In the end, we chose the '08 Riesling Praepositus, which is very dry, powerful, vibrant, and incredibly complex despite its youth. It also has excellent cellar potential. That said, the entire range, including the classic line, is full of personality and, above all, has a clearly defined, easily recognizable style.

○ A. A. Valle Isarco Riesling Praepositus '08	▼▼▼	6
○ A. A. Valle Isarco Kerner Praepositus '09	▼▼	5
○ A. A. Valle Isarco Müller Thurgau '09	▼▼	4*
○ A. A. Valle Isarco Pinot Grigio '09	▼▼	4*
○ A. A. Valle Isarco Sylvaner Praepositus '09	▼▼	5*
○ A. A. Valle Isarco Veltliner Praepositus '09	▼▼	5
● A. A. Lagrein Praepositus Ris. '07	▼▼	6
● A. A. Moscato Rosa Praepositus '09	▼▼	6
● A. A. Pinot Nero Praepositus Ris. '07	▼▼	6
○ A. A. Sauvignon Praepositus '09	▼▼	5
○ A. A. Valle Isarco Kerner '09	▼▼	4
○ A. A. Valle Isarco Sylvaner '09	▼▼	4
○ A. A. Valle Isarco Kerner Praepositus '05	▽▽▽	5*
○ A. A. Valle Isarco Riesling Praepositus '06	▽▽▽	5
○ A. A. Valle Isarco Sylvaner Praepositus '08	▽▽▽	5
○ A. A. Valle Isarco Sylvaner Praepositus '07	▽▽▽	5

Cantina Produttori Andriano

via Silberleiten, 7
39018 Terlano/Terlan [BZ]
tel. 0471257156
www.cantina-andriano.com

CELLAR SALES
PRE-BOOKED VISITS

ANNUAL PRODUCTION 300,000 bottles
HECTARES UNDER VINE 105
VITICULTURE METHOD Conventional

Everything has changed here at Andriano, from the labels, to the vineyard, production philosophy and wine style. Forty per cent of the vines, especially the cabernet and merlot, have been ripped out in favour of white varieties, although a single particularly good plot of merlot has been kept. From vineyard to bunch, the various product lines are rigorously selected and there is an almost obsessive devotion to preserving the characteristics of traditional varieties. In short, there is no mistaking the new Terlano style.

There has been quite a revolution at Andriano. Not only have the labels had a facelift but the wines themselves have also had a change for the better. The '09 Gewürztraminer Movado took Three Glasses, thanks to big structure partnered with a lovely crisp, relaxed palate, and there is more. From the powerful yet refreshing '08 Gewürztraminer Passito Juvelo to the full, juicy '07 Lagrein Tor di Lupo Riserva, all the wines are decent to excellent. Achieving such good results in just two years, Andriano is sure to play a leading role in the future.

○ A. A. Gewürztraminer Movado '09	▼▼▼	6
○ A. A. Gewurztraminer Passito Juvelo '08	▼▼	6
● A. A. Lagrein Tor di Lupo Ris. '07	▼▼	6
○ A. A. Gewürztraminer '09	▼▼	4*
● A. A. Lagrein Rubeno '09	▼▼	4*
● A. A. Merlot Gant Ris. '07	▼▼	6
○ A. A. Pinot Bianco '09	▼▼	4*
○ A. A. Pinot Grigio '09	▼▼	4
● A. A. Santa Maddalena '09	▼▼	4
○ A. A. Sauvignon Blanc Andrius '09	▼▼	6
○ A. A. Sauvignon Blanc Floreado '09	▼▼	4

Baron Widmann

ENDERGASSE, 3
39040 CORTACCIA/KURTATSCH [BZ]
TEL. 0471880092
www.baron-widmann.it

CELLAR SALES
PRE-BOOKED VISITS

ANNUAL PRODUCTION 35,000 bottles
HECTARES UNDER VINE 15
VITICULTURE METHOD Conventional

Andreas Widmann owns one of the leading estates in Oltradige. His quiet cordiality and courtesy are paired with absolute conviction in his wine-growing and winemaking methods. Andreas's wines whole-heartedly reflect his personal style. They are ripe with understated elegance and so subtle that they risk passing unobserved in a world where excess and flamboyance often dominate. But that is what makes Baron Widmann wines so likeable.

These wines are subtle masterpieces. They whisper rather than shout, which tends to go against current fashions. Their style is reserved yet convincing because it gives voice to both the varietal characteristics and the terroir. The Auhof vineyard '08 Rot cabernet sauvignon, franc and merlot blend reflects this philosophy exquisitely. This elegant red is distinguished by juicy, soft, sweet tannins, fresh yet delicate acidity and a seamless palate. The same goes for the '09 Gewürztraminer and the ever-delicious '09 Schiava, which has an alcohol content of just 12.5 per cent.

● Rot '08	2 black glasses	5
○ A. A. Gewürztraminer '09	2 black glasses	5
○ A. A. Pinot Bianco '09	2 black glasses	4
○ A. A. Sauvignon '09	2 black glasses	4
● A. A. Schiava '09	2 black glasses	4*
○ A. A. Weiss '09	2 black glasses	4
○ A. A. Gewürztraminer '08	2 white glasses	5*
○ A. A. Sauvignon '08	2 white glasses	4
○ A. A. Weiss '08	2 white glasses	4*

Josef Brigl

LOC. SAN MICHELE
VIA MADONNA DEL RIPOSO, 3
39057 APPIANO/EPPAN [BZ]
TEL. 0471662419
www.brigl.com

CELLAR SALES
PRE-BOOKED VISITS

ANNUAL PRODUCTION 2,000,000 bottles
HECTARES UNDER VINE 50
VITICULTURE METHOD Conventional

Ignaz and Josef Brigl own one of the oldest estates in Alto Adige and some of the finest vineyards in the entire province. The estate is oozing with tradition, dating from at least the early 14th century. However, the winery also deftly adapts to the demands of an increasingly difficult market. Brigl is bursting with potential, as yet not fully expressed.

These assured wines are well constructed, well typed and pretty well defined. However, this big estate seems to be missing that special something needed to make their good wines great. The '09 Lago di Caldaro Windegg is delicious, making the most of a good vintage with its fresh, delicately floral palate. The '07 Lagrein Briglhof is very pleasant but seems a little tired and lacking in the kind of energy you would expect for a great Lagrein. The '07 Pinot Nero Briglhof is more convincing with its fresh nose and slim-bodied, supple palate. The rest of the range is of a good level but there is definitely room for improvement.

● A. A. Lago di Caldaro Scelto Windegg Cl. Sup. '09	2 black glasses	4*
● A. A. Lagrein Briglhof Ris. '07	2 black glasses	5
● A. A. Pinot Nero Briglhof '07	2 black glasses	6
● A. A. Santa Maddalena Rielerhof '09	2 black glasses	4
● A. A. Pinot Nero Kreuzbichler '07	1 black glass	5
○ A. A. Sauvignon '09	1 black glass	4
○ A. A. Terlano Drei König Hof '09	1 black glass	4
● A. A. Lagrein Briglhof Ris. '06	2 white glasses	5
○ A. A. Sauvignon '08	2 white glasses	4

Cantina Produttori Burggräfler

via Palade, 64
39020 Marlengo/Marling [BZ]
tel. 0473447137
www.burggraefler.it

CELLAR SALES
PRE-BOOKED VISITS
ROOMS AND FOOD

ANNUAL PRODUCTION 1,220,000 bottles
HECTARES UNDER VINE 140
VITICULTURE METHOD Conventional

This historic winery has at long last merged with the nearby Cantina Vini Merano. The cellar master, Hansjörg Donà, who has been running the cellar since 1980, inherited 208 member growers. The two brands will remain distinct and the Burggräfler brand will continue to ensure the availability of wines that have recently acquired their own style, making the winery one of the best in Alto Adige.

An outstanding performance by the Burggräfler winery in Marlengo this year. The 1990 Pinot Bianco Privat, Sauvignon MerVin and Chardonnay Privat are the obvious stars in a range of whites that totally won us over, although we did have a few doubts about the reds. The Pinot Bianco is concentrated, almost sea-salt savoury, complex, and smoky with a lovely long finish. The Sauvignon is somewhat more austere but also very elegant, and the Chardonnay is one of the best of the vintage.

○ A. A. Chardonnay Privat '09	2 black glasses	4
○ A. A. Pinot Bianco Privat '09	2 black glasses	4*
○ A. A. Sauvignon MerVin '09	2 black glasses	5
○ A. A. Gewürztraminer Mern '08	2 black glasses	5
● A. A. Meranese Schickenburg '09	2 black glasses	4
● A. A. Pinot Nero Privat '08	1 black glass	4
○ Cuvée Wais '09	1 black glass	4
○ A. A. Pinot Bianco Privat '07	2 white glasses	4*
● A. A. Pinot Nero Privat '07	2 white glasses	4
○ A. A. Sauvignon MerVin '08	2 white glasses	5
○ Cuvée Wais '08	2 white glasses	4*

★ Cantina di Caldaro

via Cantine, 12
39052 Caldaro/Kaltern
tel. 0471963149
www.kellereikaltern.com

CELLAR SALES
PRE-BOOKED VISITS

ANNUAL PRODUCTION 1,900,000 bottles
HECTARES UNDER VINE 300
VITICULTURE METHOD Conventional

Cantina di Caldaro is one of the biggest wine operations in Alto Adige. This colossus is skilfully run by chair Armin Dissertori and cellarmaster Andreas Praest. The range embraces the most common types for the zone, including Lago di Caldaro, Cabernet Sauvignon, Pinto Bianco and Gewürztraminer, and also features a line of certified biodynamic wines called Solos. The unforgettable Moscato Giallo Passito Serenade is regularly one of the best sweet wines in Italy.

The apparent ease with which the Moscato Giallo Passito Serenade picks up Three Glasses, and the fact that it is regularly one of the top sweet wines in the country, are sure signs of the reliability of the cellar. This is undoubtedly due to winemaker Andrea Praest and chair Armin Dissertori, who now also heads the Consorzio Vini Alto Adige which encompasses almost all of the region's producers. In addition to their extraordinary dessert wine, the '09 Pinot Bianco Vial, '09 Lago di Caldaro Pfarrhof, '07 Cabernet Sauvignon Pfarrhof Riserva and '08 Sauvignon Castel Giovanelli are also excellent.

○ A. A. Moscato Giallo Passito Serenade '07	3 black glasses	7
● A. A. Cabernet Sauvignon Pfarrhof Ris. '07	2 black glasses	6
● A. A. Lago di Caldaro Scelto Pfarrhof '09	2 black glasses	4*
○ A. A. Pinot Bianco Vial '09	2 black glasses	4
○ A. A. Sauvignon Castel Giovanelli '08	2 black glasses	6
○ A. A. Chardonnay Castel Giovanelli '08	2 black glasses	6
○ A. A. Gewürztraminer Campaner '09	2 black glasses	5
○ A. A. Gewürztraminer Solos '09	2 black glasses	5
○ A. A. Kerner Carned '09	2 black glasses	4
● A. A. Schiava Solos '09	2 black glasses	4
○ A. A. Moscato Giallo Passito Serenade '06	3 white glasses	6
○ A. A. Moscato Giallo Passito Serenade '05	3 white glasses	6
○ A. A. Moscato Giallo Passito Serenade '04	3 white glasses	6

Castelfeder

VIA FRANZ HARPF, 15
39040 CORTINA/KURTINIG [BZ]
TEL. 0471820420
www.castelfeder.it

CELLAR SALES
PRE-BOOKED VISITS

ANNUAL PRODUCTION 400,000 bottles
HECTARES UNDER VINE 20
VITICULTURE METHOD Conventional

This large family estate has been managed since 1989 by Günther Giovanett, who moved the cellar to Cortina Sulla Strada del Vino, a small village with a long history of viticulture, growing mostly white varieties such as chardonnay, pinot grigio, sauvignon and gewürztraminer. In recent years, Günther has been joined by his son, Ivan, a talented 27-year-old with a passion for Pinot Nero and daughter, Ines, also a winemaker. All bodes well for Catstelfeder.

The Giovanett family's estate is one of the more interesting concerns to have emerged in recent years. The wines are well made, elegant and attractive, although they possibly lack that final touch of excellence. Two bottles made it to the finals, the '09 Pinot Grigio 15er and the Gewürztraminer Vom Lehm, which are both juicy, very crisp and vibrant. The range presented this year is generally very good, especially the Pinot Nero, although we just prefer the '08 Glener over the '07 Riserva Burgum Novum.

○ A. A. Gewürztraminer Vom Lehm '09	▼▼	4*
○ A. A. Pinot Grigio 15er '09	▼▼	4*
● A. A. Lagrein Burgum Novum Ris. '07	▼▼	5
⊙ A. A. Lagrein Rosato '09	▼▼	4
○ A. A. Pinot Bianco Vom Stein '09	▼▼	4*
● A. A. Pinot Nero Burgum Novum Ris. '07	▼▼	6
● A. A. Pinot Nero Glener '08	▼▼	4*
○ Kerner Lahn '09	▼▼	4
○ Sauvignon Raif '09	▼▼	4*
○ A. A. Gewürztraminer Endidae Passito '07	▽▽	6
○ A. A. Gewürztraminer Endidae Passito '05	▽▽	6
○ A. A. Gewürztraminer Vom Lehm '08	▽▽	4*

★ Cantina Produttori Colterenzio

LOC. CORNAIANO/GIRLAN
S.DA DEL VINO, 8
39057 APPIANO/EPPAN [BZ]
TEL. 0471664246
www.colterenzio.it

CELLAR SALES
PRE-BOOKED VISITS

ANNUAL PRODUCTION 1,600,000 bottles
HECTARES UNDER VINE 315
VITICULTURE METHOD Conventional

Schreckbichl or Colterenzio has strongly contributed to the history and success of Alto Adige wine. Luis and Wolfgang Reifer made, and still make, the fortunes of this reliable estate at Cornaiano, internationally renowned for great wines such as Cabernet Sauvignon Lafòa and a consistently realistic pricing policy.

This vintage is a mixed bag. Alongside well-structured, technically convincing wines with plenty of style, we found a couple of overly soft products that lacked grit. The '07 Lagrein Mantsch Praedium Riserva is very good, being incredibly austere yet complex and dynamic with masterful tannins. The same goes for an estate classic that is dividing critics and enthusiasts, the '09 Sauvignon Lafòa, which is already wonderfully complex despite its youth.

● A. A. Lagrein Mantsch Praedium Ris. '07	▼▼	5
○ A. A. Sauvignon Lafòa '09	▼▼	6
○ A. A. Chardonnay Altkirch '09	▼▼	4
● A. A. Merlot Siebeneich Praedium Ris. '07	▼▼	5
○ A. A. Pinot Bianco Weisshaus Praedium '09	▼▼	4
○ A. A. Riesling Harrer Praedium '09	▼▼	4
● A. A. Schiava Mentzenhof '09	▼▼	4*
○ A. A. Gewürztraminer '09	▼	4
○ A. A. Moscato Giallo Sand Praedium '09	▼	4
● A. A. Cabernet Sauvignon Lafòa '04	▽▽▽	7
● A. A. Cabernet Sauvignon Lafòa '03	▽▽▽	8
● A. A. Cabernet Sauvignon Lafòa '01	▽▽▽	8
● A. A. Cabernet Sauvignon Lafoa '00	▽▽▽	8
○ A. A. Chardonnay Cornell '00	▽▽▽	6
○ A. A. Gewürztraminer Cornell '05	▽▽▽	5

Cantina Produttori Cortaccia

S.DA DEL VINO, 23
39040 CORTACCIA/KURTATSCH [BZ]
TEL. 0471880115
www.cantina-cortaccia.it

CELLAR SALES
PRE-BOOKED VISITS

ANNUAL PRODUCTION **110,000 bottles**
HECTARES UNDER VINE **180**
VITICULTURE METHOD **Conventional**

Cantina Produttori di Cortaccia has one of the most solid co-operative winemaking traditions in Alto Adige. The company boasts a holding of some 180 hectares, including several plots in grand cru zones. One such is Freienfeld, near Cortaccia, which provides the cabernet sauvignon and cabernet franc grapes for one of the region's top reds, the excellent Cabernet. The co-operative's range includes a series of wines from the best vineyards and a good-quality basic line.

Unexciting results for this historic co-operative and, since a winery of this calibre could be expected to do better, we can only assume that things are not going quite as they should. Too many highs and lows, even from very famous wines, and a certain lack of personality, are their weak points this year. The excellent '08 version of Gewürztraminer Brenntal, which is crisp and elegant with a long, floral finish, contrasts strongly with a less convincing '07 Cabernet Freienfeld.

○ A. A. Gewürztraminer Brenntal '08	🍷🍷	6
● A. A. Cabernet Kirchhügel Ris. '08	🍷🍷	5
○ A. A. Sauvignon Kofl '09	🍷🍷	5
● A. A. Schiava Grigia Sonntaler '09	🍷🍷	4
○ Bianco Amrita V.T. '08	🍷🍷	7
● A. A. Cabernet Freienfeld '07	🍷	6
○ A. A. Chardonnay Pichl '09	🍷	4
● A. A. Lagrein Frauriegl '07	🍷	6
● A. A. Merlot Brenntal '07	🍷	6
● A. A. Moscato Rosa Rayas '08	🍷	6
○ A. A. Müller Thurgau Graun '09	🍷	4
○ A. A. Pinot Bianco Hofstatt '09	🍷	4
○ A. A. Gewürztraminer Brenntal '02	🍸🍸🍸	6
○ A. A. Gewürztraminer Brenntal '00	🍸🍸🍸	5
● A. A. Lagrein Scuro Fohrhof '00	🍸🍸🍸	5

Egger-Ramer

VIA GUNCINA, 5
39100 BOLZANO/BOZEN
TEL. 0471280541
www.egger-ramer.com

CELLAR SALES
PRE-BOOKED VISITS

ANNUAL PRODUCTION **100,000 bottles**
HECTARES UNDER VINE **14**
VITICULTURE METHOD **Conventional**

Skilled winegrowers Toni and Peter Egger manage this long-established estate in the Bolzano area with a sure hand. In recent years, their wines have steadily improved and prices thankfully have remained extremely accessible. The estate produces around 100,000 bottles covering all the local classics, headed by Lagrein and Santa Maddalena, which are consistently elegant and full of character.

The Egger Ramer range has seen a return to excellence. With all the traditional types for the Bolzano area present, Lagrein and Santa Maddelena head the selection, followed by a few decent whites. The wines are all well made, highly fragrant, characteristic and very reasonably priced. The '09 Santa Maddalena Reisegger is wonderfully succulent and the '08 Lagrein Tenuta Kristan elegant and crisp. The '07 and '06 Riserva Kristan were presented together and, despite their youth, both have character, although the '07 seems fuller and more concentrated. The surprising '09 Valle Isarco Müller Thurgau Sabbiolino is mineral, salty and linear.

● A. A. Lagrein Gries Tenuta Kristan '08	🍷🍷	5
● A. A. Lagrein Gries Tenuta Kristan Ris. '07	🍷🍷	5
● A. A. Lagrein Gries Tenuta Kristan Ris. '06	🍷🍷	5
⊙ A. A. Lagrein Rosato '09	🍷🍷	4*
● A. A. Santa Maddalena Cl. Reisegger '09	🍷🍷	4*
○ A. A. Valle Isarco Müller Thurgau Sabbiolino '09	🍷🍷	4
○ Nugget	🍷🍷	5
○ A. A. Gewürztraminer '09	🍷	4
● A. A. Lagrein Gries Tenuta Kristan Ris. '05	🍸🍸	5
● A. A. Lagrein Gries Tenuta Kristan Ris. '04	🍸🍸	5

★ Elena Walch

via A. Hofer, 1
39040 Termeno/Tramin
tel. 0471860172
www.elenawalch.com

CELLAR SALES
PRE-BOOKED VISITS

ANNUAL PRODUCTION 350,000 bottles
HECTARES UNDER VINE 30
VITICULTURE METHOD Conventional

For years at the absolute pinnacle of Alto Adige wine, this estate is managed by the assured Elena Walch. Overlooking Lake Caldaro and Kastelaz, Castel Ringberg is the ideal site for producing great wines, of which the Gewürztraminer Kastelaz and Lagrein Castel Ringberg Riserva are perfect examples. They are followed by a series of skilfully crafted whites such as Beyond the Clouds, Pinot Bianco Kastelaz and Bianco Passito Chashmere, which is a gewürztraminer and sauvignon blend.

The '09 Gewürztraminer Kastelaz once again took Three Glasses, which comes as no surprise given that it is a veritable classic for its type that takes full advantage of the good vintage and promises exceptionally long cellaring. This champion is supported by other impressive wines such as the '08 Beyond the Clouds, predominantly chardonnay with a small percentage of aromatic grapes, which has never been crisper. The increasingly focused '09 Pinot Bianco Kastelaz is also extremely worthwhile, as is the '09 Sauvignon Castel Ringberg.

○ A. A. Gewürztraminer Kastelaz '09	YYY+	6
○ A. A. Bianco Beyond the Clouds '08	TT	7
○ A. A. Pinot Bianco Kastelaz '09	TT	5
○ A. A. Sauvignon Castel Ringberg '09	TT	5
● A. A. Lago di Caldaro Castel Ringberg '09	TT	4
● A. A. Lagrein Castel Ringberg Ris. '06	TT	6
○ A. A. Chardonnay Cardellino '09	T	5
○ A. A. Resling Castel Ringberg '09	T	5
● Kermesse '06	T	7
○ A. A. Gewürztraminer Kastelaz '08	YYY+	6
○ A. A. Gewürztraminer Kastelaz '07	YYY	6
○ A. A. Gewürztraminer Kastelaz '06	YYY	6
○ A. A. Gewürztraminer Kastelaz '05	YYY	6
○ A. A. Gewürztraminer Kastelaz '04	YYY	6
● A. A. Lagrein Castel Ringberg Ris. '04	YYY	6

Erbhof Unterganzner Josephus Mayr

fraz. Cardano
via Campiglio, 15
39053 Bolzano/Bozen
tel. 0471365582
mayr.unterganzner@dnet.it

CELLAR SALES
PRE-BOOKED VISITS

ANNUAL PRODUCTION 65,000 bottles
HECTARES UNDER VINE 8
VITICULTURE METHOD Conventional

Situated at the eastern edge of the broad Bolzano basin, the Mayr-Unterganzner farm has a long history. It continues to release wonderful wines, especially reds, that are full of character, dense, concentrated, and even austere at times. Josephus Mayr puts his unique passion and skill to good use to make great wines, including his stunning Lagrein, Santa Maddalena and Cabernet. The Lamarein from part-dried lagrein grapes deserves a special mention as it is the only wine of its type in Alto Adige.

This vineyard is an example, and not just to Alto Adige. Josephus Mayr is professional with a sincere interest in anything to do with nature. Denying him Three Glasses is more likely to upset us than him, convinced as he is of his choices, and quite rightly. His wines are concentrated and the blends decidedly modern. However, his use of oak can upset the balance a little in poor years like 2008. The '08 Cabernet Riserva Kampill is austere, rather elegant and expansive, with aromatic fruit and good tannins. The '07 Lagrein Riserva is dense and concentrated but has a hard time unbending.

● A. A. Cabernet Kampill Ris. '08	TT	6
● A. A. Lagrein Scuro Ris. '07	TT	5
⊙ A. A. Lagrein Rosato Spät Gelesen '09	TT	4
● A. A. Santa Maddalena Cl. '08	TT	4
○ A. A. Sauvignon Platt & Pignat '09	TT	4
● Composition Reif '07	TT	7
● Lamarein '08	TT	7
● A. A. Lagrein Scuro Ris. '05	YYY	5
● A. A. Lagrein Scuro Ris. '01	YYY	5
● A. A. Lagrein Scuro Ris. '00	YYY	5
● A. A. Lagrein Scuro Ris. '99	YYY	5
● Lamarein '05	YYY	7

Erste+Neue

via delle Cantine, 5/10
39052 Caldaro/Kaltern
tel. 0471963122
www.erste-neue.it

CELLAR SALES
PRE-BOOKED VISITS

ANNUAL PRODUCTION 1,000,000 bottles
HECTARES UNDER VINE 320
VITICULTURE METHOD Conventional

Erste & Neue, one of the region's top co-operatives, is now Prima & Nuova, with new labels and graphics. They release over one million bottles in three lines, of which Puntay is the biggest. They produce almost all the traditional Alto Adige varieties and Lago di Caldaro has imposed itself as the estate's trademark wine. In recent years, they have also produced a first-class Pinot Bianco, Prunar, which is cellarmaster Gerhard Sanin's baby.

Schiava is the most important variety produced by the estate managed by Manfred Schullian. It is therefore no surprise that in a particularly good year like 2009 the various versions of Alto Adige's most widely grown variety attain rare heights. The Lago di Caldaro Puntay, Lago di Caldaro Leuchtenburg and Santa Maddalena Gröbnerhof are simply exquisite, showing very different personalities. As usual, the excellent '09 Pinot Bianco Prunar is one of the wines Gherard Sanin has most groomed. Although still very young, it has plenty of spirit.

	Glasses	
○ A. A. Gewürztraminer Puntay '09	2 (black)	6
● A. A. Lago di Caldaro Scelto Puntay '09	2 (black)	4*
○ A. A. Pinot Bianco Prunar '09	2 (black)	4*
○ A. A. Sauvignon Puntay '09	2 (black)	6
○ A. A. Anthos Bianco Passito '07	2 (black)	6
● A. A. Cabernet Puntay '07	2 (black)	6
○ A. A. Chardonnay Salt '09	2 (black)	4
● A. A. Lago di Caldaro Scelto Leuchtenburg '09	2 (black)	4*
● A. A. Merlot Puntay '07	2 (black)	6
○ A. A. Pinot Grigio Grauer '09	2 (black)	4
○ A. A. Riesling Rifall '09	2 (black)	5
● A. A. Santa Maddalena Gröbnerhof '09	2 (black)	4*
○ A. A. Sauvignon Stern '09	2 (black)	5
○ A. A. Sauvignon Puntay '06	3 (white)	5
○ A. A. Anthos Bianco Passito '05	2 (white)	6
○ A. A. Pinot Bianco Prunar '08	2 (white)	4*

Falkenstein - Franz Pratzner

via Castello, 15
39025 Naturno/Naturns [BZ]
tel. 0473666054
www.falkenstein.bz

CELLAR SALES
PRE-BOOKED VISITS

ANNUAL PRODUCTION 45,000 bottles
HECTARES UNDER VINE 7
VITICULTURE METHOD Organic

Falkenstein, at Naturno, Val Venosta, is worth visiting for a number of reasons. Firstly, for the stunning view over the valley; secondly, for some of the steepest and densest vineyards in Alto Adige; thirdly, for its winemaker, Franz Pratzner, who is a man of few words but much action. His German-style Riesling and Pinot Bianco are must-tastes but the Pinot Nero and Sauvignon are also very interesting.

We like Franz Pratzner. His wines can present a few slight defects but they have such great personality that it is easy to gloss over the occasional imperfection. His '09 Riesling won Three Glasses. The attack is still austere and the palate opens with stony, iodine and sea-salt aromas backed by powerful yet light structure. The Pinot Bianco is lean, but well-built and sharpish, distinctly mineral, with noticeable acidity. The '09 Sauvignon is simpler but still has enormous grip and crispness. We rather like the '07 Pinot Nero, which presents typical Valle Venosta smokiness with close-focused fruit that follows through into a consistently fine, minerality and flowers palate.

	Glasses	
○ A. A. Valle Venosta Riesling '09	3 (black)	6
○ A. A. Valle Venosta Pinot Bianco '09	2 (black)	5
● A. A. Valle Venosta Pinot Nero '07	2 (black)	6
○ A. A. Valle Venosta Gewürztraminer '09	2 (black)	5
○ A. A. Valle Venosta Sauvignon '09	2 (black)	5
○ A. A. Valle Venosta Pinot Bianco '07	3 (white)	5
○ A. A. Valle Venosta Riesling '08	3 (white)	6
○ A. A. Valle Venosta Riesling '07	3 (white)	6
○ A. A. Valle Venosta Riesling '06	3 (white)	6
○ A. A. Valle Venosta Riesling '05	3 (white)	6

Garlider Christian Kerchbaumer

via Untrum, 20
39040 Velturno/Feldthurns [BZ]
tel. 0472847296
www.garlider.it

CELLAR SALES
PRE-BOOKED VISITS

ANNUAL PRODUCTION 16,000 bottles
HECTARES UNDER VINE 4
VITICULTURE METHOD Organic

Christian Kerchbaumer is a competent young producer with a true passion for wine. He has set up new vineyards, projects and experiments in the cellar and uses of carefully dosed native yeasts. At the Garlider estate, whites dominate with a focus on the classic Valle Isarco types but there are also a few hundred bottles of the only Pinot Nero in the area. The wines are bursting with personality. They are natural, expressive and show notes usually associated with wines produced further south than Valle Isarco. That said, we are in the south of the valley at Veltruno.

This year there is no Veltliner as Christian Kerchbaumer decided to bottle it at the end of August, missing our deadline. Rest assured, we will review it next year. In the meantime, we will make do with a masterful Sylvaner, the '09 version of which has achieved a new stylistic maturity, making it as rich and powerful as usual but with balanced acidity and a very strong natural character. The other wines all follow in this vein and the elegant, savoury, complex '09 Müller Thurgau has just one defect: its varietal name.

○ A. A. Valle Isarco Sylvaner '09	TTT	4*
○ A. A. Valle Isarco Müller Thurgau '09	TT	4*
● A. A. Pinot Nero '08	TT	5
○ A. A. Valle Isarco Pinot Grigio '09	TT	5
○ A. A. Valle Isarco Veltliner '08	YYY	5*
○ A. A. Valle Isarco Veltliner '07	YYY	5
○ A. A. Valle Isarco Veltliner '05	YYY	4*

Cantina Girlan

loc. Cornaiano/Girlan
via San Martino, 24
39050 Appiano/Eppan [BZ]
tel. 0471662403
www.girlan.it

CELLAR SALES
PRE-BOOKED VISITS

ANNUAL PRODUCTION 1,200,000 bottles
HECTARES UNDER VINE 230
VITICULTURE METHOD Conventional

New cellar, new bottles, new labels and new managing director but the same reliable quality for this co-operative winery, whose style is more clearly defined than ever. That said, you know you're in good hands with Gherard Kofler and Oscar Lorandi in that respect. The wines are all extremely dense and technically confident, with increasing personality. And the prices? As reasonable as ever, which is no bad thing in these straitened times.

Although the cellar is still incomplete, and labels and bottles have been changed, this co-operative winery seems to be making a strong play for quality. This year's range is even stronger and more convincing, in part thanks to the good '09 harvest. The whites are austere, salty and linear, like the Sauvignon Flora, which comfortably lifted Three Glasses. It's wonderfully dynamic, with a fragrant palate with iodine notes that soften its lively varietal character. The same energy is there in the Plattenriegl Pinot Bianco and Pinot Grigio. The Gschleier and Faß Nr° 9 Schiavas are both magnificent, with the first being remarkable for its austerity and the second for its sheer quaffability.

○ A. A. Sauvignon Sel. Flora '09	TTT	5
○ A. A. Gewürztraminer Sel. Flora '09	TT	5
○ A. A. Pinot Bianco Plattenriegl '09	TT	4*
● A. A. Schiava Gschleier '09	TT	5*
○ 448 slm '09	TT	3*
○ A. A. Bianco Riserva '08	TT	5
○ A. A. Gewürztraminer '09	TT	4
○ A. A. Gewürztraminer Aimè '09	TT	4
● A. A. Lagrein Merlot Laurin '07	TT	4
● A. A. Lagrein Ris. '07	TT	6
○ A. A. Pinot Bianco '09	TT	4*
○ A. A. Pinot Grigio '09	TT	4*
● A. A. Pinot Nero Patricia '08	TT	4*
○ A. A. Sauvignon Indra '09	TT	4
● A. A. Schiava Faß N° 9 '09	TT	4*
○ A. A. Sauvignon Indra '08	YYY	4*
● A. A. Schiava Gschleier '90	YYY	4

Glögglhof - Franz Gojer

FRAZ. SANTA MADDALENA
VIA RIVELLONE, 1
39100 BOLZANO/BOZEN
TEL. 0471978775
www.gojer.it

CELLAR SALES
PRE-BOOKED VISITS

ANNUAL PRODUCTION 40,000 bottles
HECTARES UNDER VINE 6
VITICULTURE METHOD Conventional

Franz Gojer is knowledgeable, competent, likeable and very well-known. He started up in 1982, when he inherited the farm, along with some of the best, most classic wines in the Bolzano area. Glögglhof is situated on the slopes of striking Santa Maddalena, north of Bolzano, and produces very typical wines, headed by the wine named for the Santa Maddalena hill. Franz is a master at producing Santa Maddalena and his base version and Rondell selection are consistently among the best.

It is hard to find tastier Santa Maddalena wines than those of Glögglhof, especially with a vintage like the '09, which was ideal for schiava. The Santa Maddalena Rondell opens with berry fruits and spicy notes, then follows through into a perfectly balanced palate with simply exquisite progression. The basic Santa Maddalena is only marginally less good but the real surprise is the '09 Lagrein, which is austere and mineral but also elegantly fruity and distinctly spicy.

● A. A. Lagrein '09	🍷🍷	4*
● A. A. Santa Maddalena Rondell '09	🍷🍷	4*
● A. A. Lagrein Scuro Ris. '07	🍷🍷	5
● A. A. Santa Maddalena Cl. '09	🍷🍷	4*
● A.. A. Vernatsch Karneid '09	🍷🍷	3*
● A. A. Lagrein '08	🍷🍷 (white)	4*

Cantina Gries/Cantina Produttori Bolzano

FRAZ. GRIES
P.ZZA GRIES, 2
39100 BOLZANO/BOZEN
TEL. 0471270909
www.cantinabolzano.com

CELLAR SALES
PRE-BOOKED VISITS

ANNUAL PRODUCTION 1,500,000 bottles
HECTARES UNDER VINE 170
VITICULTURE METHOD Conventional

Gries, just south of Bolzano is the heart of production for this ancient, traditional Alto Adige red wine and the winery is one of the top producers of Lagrein Scuro. Riserva Prestige Line, the Collection Baron Carl Eyrl and the current-vintage Lagrein Griser do the type proud. The winery also produces other big wines such as the Moscato Rosa Rosis and the Merlot Otto Graf Huyn Riserva.

The winery is located in the heart of Gries, the biggest Lagrein area and, naturally, most attention is focused on this variety. The '08 vintage was devastated by a hailstorm that centred on Gries but although the structures of the Collection Baron Carl Eyrl and the Prestige Line Riserva were slightly slimmer, they nevertheless manage a solid profile with stylish tannins and unusual crispness, making for particularly pleasant drinking. A year later, the '09 Lagrein Grieser is quite simply delicious, a crisp, spicy and fleshy monument to its type.

● A. A. Lagrein Collection Baron Eyrl '08	🍷🍷	4*
● A. A. Lagrein Grieser Prestige Line Ris. '08	🍷🍷	6
● A. A. Lagrein Grieser '09	🍷🍷	4*
● A. A. Lagrein Merlot Mauritius '08	🍷🍷	7
⊙ A. A. Lagrein Rosato '09	🍷🍷	4*
● A. A. Merlot Collection Conte Huyn '08	🍷🍷	5
○ A. A. Moscato Giallo Vinalia '08	🍷🍷	8
● A. A. Pinot Nero '09	🍷🍷	4*
● A. A. Lagrein Scuro Prestige Line Ris. '06	🍷🍷🍷 (white)	6
● A. A. Lagrein Scuro Prestige Line Ris. '00	🍷🍷🍷 (white)	6
○ A. A. Moscato Giallo Vinalia '03	🍷🍷🍷 (white)	6
○ A. A. Pinot Bianco Collection Dellago '06	🍷🍷🍷 (white)	4*

Gummerhof - Malojer

VIA WEGGESTEIN, 36
39100 BOLZANO/BOZEN
TEL. 0471972885
www.malojer.it

CELLAR SALES
PRE-BOOKED VISITS

ANNUAL PRODUCTION 100,000 bottles
HECTARES UNDER VINE 6
VITICULTURE METHOD Conventional

Gummerhof was first documented as early as 1480. Once marooned in a sea of vineyards north of Bolzano, today the winery run by Elisabeth, Urban and Alfred Malojer largely concentrates on the area's typical reds, although there are also a couple of good whites. The wines are true to type but also remarkably elegant, thanks to hard work in the vineyard and solid winemaking techniques. The prices are, as always, very reasonable.

It was an up and down year for this historic estate. The '09 Santa Maddalena was excellent, with red berry fruit, violets and green almonds preceding a full, beefy palate. The other reds are all well made and very varietal but possibly a tad simple and marginally too husky. A special mention goes to the successful '09 Pinot Grigio Gur zu Sand, which is austere but also has wonderful mineral notes and impressive extension.

● A. A. Cabernet Ris. '07	TT	5
O A. A. Pinot Grigio Gur zu Sand '08	TT	4*
● A. A. Santa Maddalena Cl. '09	TT	4*
● A. A. Cabernet-Lagrein Bautzanum Cuvée Ris. '07	T	5
O A. A. Gewürztraminer Kui '09	T	4
● A. A. Lagrein Scuro Gummerhof zu Gries '08	T	4
● A. A. Lagrein Scuro Ris. '07	T	5
O A. A. Müller Thurgau '09	T	4
O A. A. Pinot Bianco '09	T	4
● A. A. Pinot Nero Gstrein '08	T	4
O A. A. Sauvignon Gur zu Sand '09	T	4
● A. A. Lagrein Scuro Ris. '05	YY	5
● A. A. Lagrein Scuro Ris. '04	YY	5

Gumphof - Markus Prackwieser

LOC. NOVALE DI PRESULE, 8
39050 FIÈ ALLO SCILIAR/
VÖLS AM SCHLERN [BZ]
TEL. 0471601190
www.gumphof.it

CELLAR SALES
PRE-BOOKED VISITS

ANNUAL PRODUCTION 4,000 bottles
HECTARES UNDER VINE 5
VITICULTURE METHOD Conventional

Markus Prackwieser is a passionate young winegrower with a small estate perched on a steep crag on the slopes of the Sciliar mountain. It's a few hundred metres from Valle Isarco, which nevertheless seems to have a strong influence on the wines. Whites are crisp and mineral, with rare personality and complexity, which Markus achieved through painstaking work in the vineyard. Gumphof produces Pinot Bianco, Sauvignon, Pinot Nero, Gewürztraminer and Schiava, which is still one of the best.

Talented Markus has won back Three Glasses for his particularly convincing Sauvignon Praesulis, which despite its youth is very powerful and mature, with a mixed vegetal mouth and acidity that nicely backs the solidly constructed, dynamic palate. This wine will age well. The taut, racy '09 Pinot Bianco Praesulis, which we have only found at Gumphof in the better years, is equally good. All the other wines are fine, especially the '09 Schiava, which is delightfully drinkable and an intriguing expression of the type.

O A. A. Sauvignon Praesulis '09	TTT	5
O A. A. Pinot Bianco Praesulis '09	TT	4*
O A. A. Gewürztraminer Praesulis '09	TT	5
O A. A. Pinot Bianco '09	TT	4*
● A. A. Pinot Nero '08	TT	5
● A. A. Schiava '09	TT	4*
O A. A. Pinot Bianco Praesulis '06	YYY	4*
O A. A. Sauvignon Praesulis '07	YYY	5*
O A. A. Sauvignon Praesulis '04	YYY	5*

Franz Haas

VIA VILLA, 6
39040 MONTAGNA/MONTAN [BZ]
TEL. 0471812280
www.franz-haas.it

CELLAR SALES
PRE-BOOKED VISITS

ANNUAL PRODUCTION 290,000 bottles
HECTARES UNDER VINE 50
VITICULTURE METHOD Conventional

The Haas estate at Montan is one of Alto Adige's most prestigious, internationally renowned wineries. Its fame is entirely due to Franz Haas and Luisa Manna, who year after year have built up a range of wines led by a superb Pinot Nero, Sauvignon and Moscato Rosa whose distinctive style, elegance, character and reliability are defining traits.

No less than four wines got through to the finals, all representatives of the main Alto Adige types, and the entire range is of rare technical quality and expression. Although it lacked a high note, probably because it was bottled late, the '09 Sauvignon is one of the best of the vintage. It is elegant, linear and dynamic. The '08 Manna, a 50 per cent riesling, 20 per cent gewürztraminer and chardonnay and 30 per cent sauvignon blend is still too young to express its complexity fully. The exquisite '08 Moscato Rosa is technically perfect, albeit possibly a little unambitious. The estate's flagship wine, the '08 Pinot Nero Schweizer, will come out next year.

● A. A. Moscato Rosa '08	TT	6
○ A. A. Pinot Bianco '09	TT	5
○ A. A. Sauvignon '09	TT	6
○ Manna '08	TT	5
○ A. A. Gewürztraminer '09	TT	5
○ A. A. Pinot Grigio '09	TT	4
● A. A. Pinot Nero '08	TT	5
● A. A. Schiava Gentile '09	TT	4
● A. A. Lagrein '08	T	5
● A. A. Pinot Nero Schweizer '02	YYY	6
● A. A. Pinot Nero Schweizer '01	YYY	6
○ Manna '07	YYY	5
○ Manna '05	YYY	5
○ Manna '04	YYY	5

Haderburg

FRAZ. BUCHOLZ
LOC. POCHI, 30
39040 SALORNO/SALURN [BZ]
TEL. 0471889097
www.haderburg.it

CELLAR SALES
PRE-BOOKED VISITS

ANNUAL PRODUCTION 80,000 bottles
HECTARES UNDER VINE 12
VITICULTURE METHOD Certified biodynamic

In 1977, Alois Ochsenreiter and his wife Christine were the first Alto Adige farmers to convert their grape and apple orchards into a sparkling wine estate. Their operation has always put the accent on quality and respecting both the vine's and the wine's natural rhythms. Alois manages the vineyard and the cellar, part of which sits under the family farmhouse. The property also includes the biodynamic Obermairlhof vineyard in Valle Isarco.

The sparkling '00 Hasmannhof Riserva is magnificent. Savoury, with the expected mature notes, it seems almost faded but the palate develops with impressive energy and expansion. The pear, brioche and herb-dominated nose precedes a leisurely, deep palate with good structure and appeal. The '09 Sylvaner Obermairl is perfectly executed, being concentrated, vibrant and with an impressive, gutsy palate. The rest of the range is consistently reliable.

○ A. A. Spumante Hausmannhof Ris. '00	TT	7
○ A. A. Valle Isarco Sylvaner Obermairl '09	TT	4
● A. A. Pinot Nero Hausmannhof '08	TT	5
○ A. A. Spumante Brut	TT	5
○ A. A. Spumante Pas Dosé '06	TT	6
○ A. A. Spumante Hausmannhof Ris. '97	YYY	7
○ A. A. Valle Isarco Sylvaner Obermairlhof '05	YYY	4*

Hoandlhof - Manfred Nössing

FRAZ. KRANEBIH
VIA DEI VIGNETI, 66
39042 BRESSANONE/BRIXEN [BZ]
TEL. 0472832672
www.manni-noessing.com

PRE-BOOKED VISITS

ANNUAL PRODUCTION 17,000 bottles
HECTARES UNDER VINE 4
VITICULTURE METHOD Conventional

Manni Nössing's has such a strong personality that his directness can make him seem a bit arrogant and unfriendly but one thing is for certain: his wines have unique character, grip and finesse. Manni's versions of typical Valle Isarco types, such as Veltliner, Sylvaner, Kerner and Müller Thurgau, are always distinctive and in many cases of very high quality. The news this year is that Manni has started working on Riesling and if effort equals results, we are in luck.

Manni Nössing's collaboration with Vincenzo Bambina has spurred him to continue his small but significant revolution. The wines are increasingly stylish, sharp, and linear but have also gained in character and complexity. Furthermore, the alcohol content has dropped considerably, making the wines, of which the '09 Kerner is a prime example with just 13.8 per cent alcohol, even more refreshing. We gave Three Glasses to an '09 Veltliner that is nothing less than sensational with its smoky nose and bright, deep palate, which is sharp as a razor. How far can it grow? For grow it surely will. The Sylvaner, Kerner and Müller Thurgau Sass Rigais are all exceptional.

○ A. A. Valle Isarco Veltliner '09	▼▼▼	5*
○ A. A. Valle Isarco Kerner '09	▼▼	5
○ A. A. Valle Isarco Müller Thurgau Sass Rigais '09	▼▼	5
○ A. A. Valle Isarco Sylvaner '09	▼▼	5*
○ A. A. Valle Isarco Kerner '06	▽▽▽	4*
○ A. A. Valle Isarco Kerner '05	▽▽▽	4*
○ A. A. Valle Isarco Kerner '03	▽▽▽	4*
○ A. A. Valle Isarco Kerner '02	▽▽▽	4
○ A. A. Valle Isarco Sylvaner '08	▽▽▽	5*
○ A. A. Valle Isarco Sylvaner '04	▽▽▽	4*
○ A. A. Valle Isarco Veltliner '07	▽▽▽	5

★ Tenuta J. Hofstätter

P.ZZA MUNICIPIO, 7
39040 TERMENO/TRAMIN
TEL. 0471860161
www.hofstatter.com

CELLAR SALES
PRE-BOOKED VISITS

ANNUAL PRODUCTION 720,000 bottles
HECTARES UNDER VINE 54
VITICULTURE METHOD Conventional

Martin Foradori runs one of the most modern, dynamic estates in the province, doing great work in vineyard and cellar. He has an eye for new market trends, and applies aggressive, wide-ranging marketing strategies, but still places a special focus on traditional varieties. Hofstätter produces some of the most famous wines in Alto Adige, starting with the Gewürztraminer Kolbenhof, one of the best of its type. The Pinot Nero Barthenau Vigna Sant'Urbano is excellent and the rest of the range excels.

Two wines made the finals this year. The first, the Gewürztraminer Kolbenhof, features curious saffron notes and a compact, salty, dynamic palate, despite being impressively powerful. The second, the '07 Pinot Nero Barthenau Vigna Sant'Urban, is a great Alto Adige classic, showing dynamic, elegant and pleasantly mineral with good acidity and fine-grained tannins. Not far behind is the '07 Pinot Nero Mazzon Riserva, which is very well made, although slightly less complex than its big brother.

○ A. A. Gewürztraminer Kolbenhof '09	▼▼	6
● A. A. Pinot Nero Barthenau V. S. Urbano '07	▼▼	8
● A. A. Pinot Nero Mazzon Ris. '07	▼	6
○ A. A. Gewürztraminer Kolbenhof '04	▽▽▽	5
○ A. A. Gewürztraminer Kolbenhof '03	▽▽▽	5
○ A. A. Gewürztraminer Kolbenhof '01	▽▽▽	6
○ A. A. Gewürztraminer Kolbenhof '99	▽▽▽	4
○ A. A. Gewürztraminer Kolbenhof '98	▽▽▽	4
● Yngram '00	▽▽▽	7

Tenuta Klosterhof Oskar Andergassen

LOC. CLAVENZ, 40
39052 CALDARO/KALTERN
TEL. 0471961046
www.garni-klosterhof.com

CELLAR SALES
PRE-BOOKED VISITS
ROOMS AND FOOD

ANNUAL PRODUCTION 20,000 bottles
HECTARES UNDER VINE 2
VITICULTURE METHOD Conventional

This small family winery managed by Oskar Andergassen is situated in a sunny spot surrounded by vineyards, just five minutes from the centre of Caldaro. The wines have a lean style that aims for elegance with balanced extract to create appropriately typed products. The estate's flagship Pinot Nero, the Pinot Bianco and Lago di Caldaro are all impeccably reliable.

Klosterhof has an extremely reliable, if limited, range. Once again, we were most convinced by the '07 Pinot Nero Panigl, from the vineyard of the same name at 450 metres above sea level in Caldaro. The wine is extremely clean, elegant, and mineral with fine-grained tannins and nice acidity. The '09 Pinot Bianco Trifall is very well made. It is succulent, full, and brightly mineral, which creates a very expansive palate. The '09 Rosato Summer from pinot nero is interesting and shows rare character for its type.

● A. A. Lago di Caldaro Plantaditsch '09	TT	4
○ A. A. Moscato Giallo '09	TT	4
○ A. A. Pinot Bianco Trifall '09	TT	4
● A. A. Pinot Nero Panigl '07	TT	6
⊙ Rosé Summer '09	TT	4
○ A. A. Gewürztraminer '09	T	4
○ A. A. Pinot Bianco Trifall '08	YY	4*
● A. A. Pinot Nero Panigl '04	YY	6

Köfererhof Günther Kershbaumer

FRAZ. NOVACELLA
VIA PUSTERIA, 3
39040 VARNA/VAHRN [BZ]
TEL. 0472836649
www.koefererhof.it

CELLAR SALES
PRE-BOOKED VISITS
FOOD

ANNUAL PRODUCTION 48,000 bottles
HECTARES UNDER VINE 6
VITICULTURE METHOD Conventional

The cellar has been extended and restructured under the old family farmhouse a few kilometres north of Bressanone and Günther Kershbaumer finally seems able to express its full potential, which is considerable. Powerful, yet elegant, well-balanced whites are the estate's mainstay, placing Köfererhof firmly at the top of Italian production. There is no end of choice, with Sylvaner, Kerner, Riesling, Pinot Grigio and Müller Thurgau.

We know Günther Kershbaumer, the Köfererhof and its wines but we were flabbergasted by the series this year. They were all exceptionally good. If you consider that even the '09 Müller Thurgau had an outstanding score, you can imagine the rest. The estate earned two Three Glasses for the '09 Pinot Grigio and the '09 Sylvaner R, which was also the Guide's White of the Year. The Sylvaner is bound to cause a buzz for years to come. It is potent but stylish, vibrant and caressing, showing smoky, stony and near-faultless poise. The Pinot Grigio is simply one of the best Italian wines tasted in recent years and it promises a very Alsatian future.

○ A. A. Valle Isarco Pinot Grigio '09	TTT	4*
○ A. A. Valle Isarco Sylvaner R '09	TTT+	5
○ A. A. Valle Isarco Kerner '09	TT	5
○ A. A. Valle Isarco Müller Thurgau '09	TT	4*
○ A. A. Valle Isarco Riesling '09	TT	5
○ A. A. Valle Isarco Sylvaner '09	TT	4*
○ A. A. Valle Isarco Veltliner '09	TT	4*
○ A. A. Valle Isarco Gewürztraminer '09	TT	5
○ A. A. Valle Isarco Sylvaner R '08	YYY+	5
○ A. A. Valle Isarco Sylvaner R '07	YYY	5
○ A. A. Valle Isarco Sylvaner R '06	YYY	5

Tenuta Kornell

FRAZ. SETTEQUERCE
VIA BOLZANO, 23
39018 TERLANO/TERLAN [BZ]
TEL. 0471917507
www.kornell.it

CELLAR SALES
PRE-BOOKED VISITS

ANNUAL PRODUCTION 60,000 bottles
HECTARES UNDER VINE 14
VITICULTURE METHOD Conventional

Twelve hectares of broken, clayey, sandy porphyry-rich soil huddled around the splendid estate buildings, a Mediterranean climate, vines planted between 1985 and 2005, owner Florian Brigl's passion and an intense relationship with nature. These are all elements that can be found in Kornell wines, which are loaded with character, not least because theirs is one of the region's best terroirs. And the cellar also offers great value for money.

The wines are very well made, expressive and full of character, for starters. Modern in style, they also reflect their variety and territory to the full. The '07 Lagrein Staves Riserva convinced us most this year. This exceptional wine is elegant, mineral and peppery in the nose before unfolding leisurely on the palate. The '09 Sauvignon Cosmas is also very expressive. The rest of the range, starting with the '09 Pinot Bianco Pinus, is more than decent.

● A. A. Lagrein Staves Ris. '07	▼▼	4*
○ A. A. Sauvignon Cosmas '09	▼▼	4
● A. A. Cabernet Sauvignon Staves '07	▼▼	6
● A. A. Merlot Staves Ris. '07	▼▼	6
○ A. A. Pinot Bianco Pinus '09	▼▼	4
● A. A. Lagrein Greif '08	▼	4
○ A. A. Sauvignon Cosmas '08	▽▽	4
○ A. A. Sauvignon Cosmas '07	▽▽	4*

Tenuta Kränzl - Graf Franz Pfeil

VIA PALADE, 1
39010 CERMES/TSCHERMS [BZ]
TEL. 0473564549
www.labyrinth.bz

CELLAR SALES
PRE-BOOKED VISITS

ANNUAL PRODUCTION 35,000 bottles
HECTARES UNDER VINE 6
VITICULTURE METHOD Certified organic

There has been a lot of hype about the globalization of the market, standardized tastes and the like. Well, anyone who is not comfortable with all that take refuge in Conte Franz Pfeil's Weingut Kränzl estate. This singular winemaker and grower has created a kind of environmental oasis at Tscherms, the valley that links Bolzano with Merano. The vineyards went organic from as early as 1985 and there is an extraordinary labyrinth of a garden that testifies to Franz's commitment to nature. The wines hew brilliantly to this philosophy. They are not technological, and can be disconcerting at times, but they are never boring.

Fun is the keynote here. Every year, there is a new surprise and this time it is the '00 Farnatzer. Who would have dreamed Franz would produce an aged dried-grape Schiava? After lengthy fermentation and maturation in wood for almost nine years, the wine is complex, with smoky notes, a touch of broom, candied orange peel and herbs. The palate is gutsy, with racy acidity and the finish is literally spiky. The '09 Schiava Baslan is smoky and floral, with a delicate, caressing palate, while the '09 Meranese Hügel is a touch thinner but deliciously drinkable.

○ Farnatzer '00	▼▼	8
● Schiava Baslan '09	▼▼	4*
● A. A. Meranese Hügel '09	▼▼	4*
○ A. A. Passito Dorado '08	▼▼	6
○ A. A. Pinot Bianco Helios '08	▽▽	5
● Schiava Baslan '07	▽▽	4*

★ Kuenhof - Peter Pliger

LOC. MARA, 110
39042 BRESSANONE/BRIXEN [BZ]
TEL. 0472850546
pliger.kuenhof@rolmail.net

CELLAR SALES
PRE-BOOKED VISITS

ANNUAL PRODUCTION 33,000 bottles
HECTARES UNDER VINE 6
VITICULTURE METHOD Organic

The new vineyards at Kuenhof are starting to bear fruit. Production is gradually increasing and the warehouse has been expanded. In this idyllic corner, the word crisis is unheard-of and Peter and Brigitte Pliger seem oblivious to many of the problems affecting other producers. Their wines are increasingly linear, pure and disarmingly natural but they have an iron character. The Riesling Kaiton is their flagship and their Sylvaner and Veltliner are no less interesting.

The Veltliner has possibly grown the most in recent years. "It's because the vines are older", explains Peter Pliger modestly. Whatever the reason, his '09 Veltliner easily deserves Three Glasses. This wine is stylish from the outset and has an elegant, floral and herb palate with an almost self-effacing but very lengthy finish. In a similar vein, the '09 Sylvaner is at once potent and supple, qualities it manages to combine in perfect proportions. The '09 Riesling Kaiton has achieved an almost zen-like minimalism. These wines may not be to everyone's taste but we like them, A lot.

○ A. A. Valle Isarco Veltliner '09	▼▼▼	5*
○ A. A. Valle Isarco Riesling Kaiton '09	▼▼	5
○ A. A. Valle Isarco Sylvaner '09	▼▼	5*
○ A. A. Valle Isarco Gewürztraminer '09	▼▼	5
○ A. A. Valle Isarco Riesling Kaiton '07	▽▽▽	5*
○ A. A. Valle Isarco Riesling Kaiton '05	▽▽▽	4*
○ A. A. Valle Isarco Sylvaner '08	▽▽▽	5
○ A. A. Valle Isarco Sylvaner '06	▽▽▽	4*
○ A. A. Valle Isarco Sylvaner '03	▽▽▽	4*
○ A. A. Valle Isarco Sylvaner '02	▽▽▽	4*
○ A. A. Valle Isarco Sylvaner V.T. '04	▽▽▽	4*
○ Kaiton '01	▽▽▽	4
○ Kaiton '99	▽▽▽	4

Cantina Laimburg

LOC. LAIMBURG, 6
39040 VADENA/PFATTEN [BZ]
TEL. 0471969700
www.laimburg.bz.it

PRE-BOOKED VISITS

ANNUAL PRODUCTION 160,000 bottles
HECTARES UNDER VINE 45
VITICULTURE METHOD Certified organic

This winery in Vadena is part of Bolzano's centre for agricultural testing, which is mainly involved in viticultural and wine-related research. The 45 hectares of vines are distributed throughout some of the best winemaking areas in Alto Adige, with different terrains and at differing altitudes. Laimburg presented two lines both good. The Vini del Podere line features traditional vintage wines but the Selezione Maniero wines are more unusual. The products are mostly oak aged and their names refer to the Ladine legends of the Dolomites.

Laimburg's reds are very interesting but we were less convinced by the whites. The '07 Pinot Nero Riserva Selyet opens with good fruit and a mineral palate with soft, fine-grained tannins then lovely thrust in the finish. The crisply mineral, elegant yet relaxed '06 Cabernet Sauvignon Sass Roà Riserva is also very good. On the other hand, the whites were a little heavy and alcoholic for our liking, possibly because they had been bottled very recently.

● A. A. Pinot Nero Selyèt Ris. '07	▼▼	5
● A. A. Cabernet Sauvignon Sass Roà Ris. '06	▼▼	6
○ A. A. Sauvignon Passito Saphir '07	▼▼	8
● Col de Réy '06	▼▼	7
○ A. A. Sauvignon Oyèll '08	▼	5
● A. A. Lagrein Scuro Barbagòl Ris. '00	▽▽▽	6
● A. A. Cabernet Sauvignon Sass Roà Ris. '04	▽▽	6
○ A. A. Gewürztraminer Elyònd '07	▽▽	5
● A. A. Pinot Nero Selyèt Ris. '06	▽▽	5
● A. A. Pinot Nero Selyèt Ris. '04	▽▽	5

Larcherhof - Fam. Spögler

via Rencio, 82
39100 Bolzano/Bozen
tel. 0471365034
larcherhof@yahoo.de

CELLAR SALES
FOOD

ANNUAL PRODUCTION 20,000 bottles
HECTARES UNDER VINE 5
VITICULTURE METHOD Conventional

The Spögler family only started bottling the wines of the small Larcherhof estate on the outskirts of Bolzano in 2008. We're happy to hear this as the wines, which include classic local types such as Lagrein, Merlot and Santa Maddalena, are fresh-tasting, elegant and full of personality. The whole range also happens to be very good value for money.

The wines of Larcherhof are one of this year's finds. All are very expressive and sincere, with a few true high points, such as one of the most interesting Pinot Grigios of the year, which has an elegant nose and succulent, mineral, and relaxed, yet well-balanced palate. The classic types for the Bolzano area account for most of the production. There's a spicy, fleshy, delightfully drinkable '09 Lagrein and a Schiava Grigia and Santa Maddalena that are fragrant, very fresh and full of character. The '07 Lagrein Riserva Rivelaun is interesting, if a tad husky.

● A.A. Lagrein '09	🍷🍷	4*
○ A.A. Pinot Grigio '09	🍷🍷	4*
● A.A. Santa Maddalena '09	🍷🍷	4*
● A.A. Schiava Grigia '09	🍷🍷	3*
● A.A. Lagrein Rivelaun Ris. '08	🍷	5

Loacker Schwarhof

loc. Santa Giustina, 3
39100 Bolzano/Bozen
tel. 0471365125
www.loacker.net

CELLAR SALES
PRE-BOOKED VISITS

ANNUAL PRODUCTION 60,000 bottles
HECTARES UNDER VINE 7
VITICULTURE METHOD Certified biodynamic

The Loackers are artists, philosophers of the vine and pioneering winemakers. For decades now, they have been producing biodynamic bottles and using homeopathy both in the vineyard and cellar. Their wines personify their approach. The Merlot Ywain, Lagrein Gran Lareyn, Pinot Nero Norital and Santa Maddalena Morit are some of the most interesting and most representative.

Biodynamic viticulture can be risky and it is therefore no surprise that again this year we saw some good to very good wines and others that are less convincing. The '07 Lagrein Gran Lareyn Riserva is highly unusual with an almost Bordeaux-like nose and a varietal, almost pushy, spiciness on the palate, combined with very stylish tannins and an aristocratic finish. It is very, very good. The '09 Santa Maddalena Morit makes the most of a good year, showing fragrant, succulent, and velvety.

● A. A. Lagrein Gran Lareyn Ris. '07	🍷🍷	5
● A. A. Merlot Ywain '08	🍷🍷	5
● A. A. Pinot Nero Norital '08	🍷🍷	5
● A. A. Santa Maddalena Cl. Morit '09	🍷🍷	4
● A. A. Lagrein Gran Lareyn '08	🍷	5
○ A. A. Sauvignon Blanc Tasnim '09	🍷	5
● A. A. Merlot Ywain '04	🥂🥂🥂	5*
● A. A. Lagrein Gran Lareyn '07	🥂🥂	5
● A. A. Pinot Nero Norital '07	🥂🥂	5*
● A. A. Pinot Nero Norital '06	🥂🥂	5
● A. A. Santa Maddalena Cl. Morit '07	🥂🥂	4*

H. Lun

VIA VILLA, 22/24
39044 EGNA/NEUMARKT [BZ]
TEL. 0471813256
www.lun.it

CELLAR SALES
PRE-BOOKED VISITS

ANNUAL PRODUCTION 300,000 bottles
HECTARES UNDER VINE 30
VITICULTURE METHOD Conventional

Founded in 1840, Lun is the oldest private winery in Alto Adige. Today, its headquarters are at Plattenhof in Egna and for several years it has been part of the Cantina Girlan, with technical guidance from cellarmaster Gherard Kofler. For years now, the wines, especially the famous Sandbichler range, which is only produced in the best vintages, have been of an extremely high standard and equally well priced.

The Lagrein Sandbichler Riserva put this estate on the map and helped make a name for Alto Adige wine. We were therefore very happy to see it in such fine form. There's a minerally, stylish nose and salty, peppery palate that is taut and very dynamic. Although still very young, this red promises to become very interesting with age. Their other red, the '07 Cabernet Sauvignon Riserva, is also very convincing. Fresh, fleshy, beautifully relaxed and very drinkable, it could do with a touch more complexity. The '09 Gewürztraminer Sandbichler and the '09 Pinot Grigio were the two best whites.

● A. A. Lagrein Sandbichler Ris. '07	TT	6
○ A. A. Bianco Sandbichler '09	TT	4
● A. A. Cabernet Sauvignon Ris. '07	TT	4
○ A. A. Gewürztraminer Sandbichler '09	TT	5
○ A. A. Pinot Grigio '09	TT	4*
● A. A. Santa Maddalena '09	TT	4
○ A. A. Chardonnay '09	T	4
○ A. A. Pinot Bianco '09	T	4
● A. A. Pinot Nero Sandbichler Ris. '07	T	4
○ A. A. Gewürztraminer Sandbichler '07	YY	5
● A. A. Lagrein Scuro Albertus Ris. '04	YY	5
○ A. A. Moscato Giallo Sandbichler Passito '06	YY	6

Manincor

SAN GIUSEPPE AL LAGO, 4
39052 CALDARO/KALTERN [BZ]
TEL. 0471960230
www.manincor.com

CELLAR SALES
PRE-BOOKED VISITS

ANNUAL PRODUCTION 220,000 bottles
HECTARES UNDER VINE 50
VITICULTURE METHOD Certified biodynamic

Count Michael Goëss-Enzenberg , the owner of this young estate set up in 1996 but built in the early 17th century, embraced biodynamic principles when he began making wine. The subsequent arrival of Helmuth Zozin, one of biodynamic viticulture's major supporters, constituted a turning point in the vineyard and cellar. The whites, represented by Pinot Bianco and Sauvignon, are elegant, stylish and apparently fragile, but with great personality. Their red counterparts, a Pinot Nero and a Merlot, have unmistakeable character.

Helmuth Zozin's trademark is everywhere. Manincor's wines have impressive definition and stylistic purity. For the moment this is most noticeable with the whites, which are all exquisitely elegant and natural. They are also technically impeccable. The '09 Terlano Pinot Bianco Eichhorn won Three Glasses. It is fruity, with delicate smoky aromas and a full, complex palate veined with salty, iodine notes. What most impresses is the length and depth of the finish. The '09 Terlano Sauvignon is incredibly stylish and the '09 Terlano Chardonnay Sophie boasts few rivals in Italy.

○ A. A. Terlano Pinot Bianco Eichhorn '09	TTT	5
○ A. A. Terlano Chardonnay Sophie '09	TT	5
○ A. A. Terlano Sauvignon '09	TT	5
○ Le Petit de Manincor '08	TT	6
● A. A. Lago di Caldaro Cl. Sup. Keil '09	TT	4
● A. A. Lagrein Rubatsch '08	TT	5
○ A. A. Moscato Giallo '09	TT	4
● A. A. Pinot Nero Mason '08	TT	6
● A. A. Pinot Nero Mason di Mason '08	TT	8
○ A. A. Terlano Réserve della Contessa '09	TT	4
● Castel Campan '07	TT	8
● Reserve del Conte '08	TT	4
● Cassiano '05	YY	6
● Castel Campan '05	YY	8

K. Martini & Sohn

loc. Cornaiano/Girlan
via Lamm, 28
39057 Appiano/Eppan [BZ]
tel. 0471663156
www.martini-sohn.it

CELLAR SALES
PRE-BOOKED VISITS

ANNUAL PRODUCTION 250,000 bottles
HECTARES UNDER VINE 30
VITICULTURE METHOD Conventional

K. Martini & Sohn in Cornaiano is one of the region's most consistent, solid estates. This mid-sized operation was established in 1976 by Karl Martini and his son Gabriel, and is now also run by the younger Lukas. Martini & Sohn have successfully combined technology and tradition to create an above-average range of wines. The Maturum and Palladium lines are Gabriel Martini's pride and joy but the whole list is very good and prices are reasonable.

It was a good year for this estate, which really does not surprise us, given its history. The wines are well-made and fairly expressive, with several interesting highlights. This year, we particularly liked the '09 Schiava Palladium, which opens on cinchona and cherry aromas to usher in a fresh, vibrant palate that expands unhurriedly into a refreshing finish. The '08 Pinot Nero Palladium is elegant and very well balanced throughout. The '09 Pinot Bianco Palladium shows good structure and a lively mineral component that makes for a particularly pleasing mouthfeel.

⊙ A. A. Lagrein Rosé Gries '09	🍷🍷	4*
● A. A. Lagrein Scuro Maturum '08	🍷🍷	6
● A. A. Lagrein-Cabernet Coldirus Palladium '08	🍷🍷	4
○ A. A. Pinot Bianco Palladium '09	🍷🍷	4
○ A. A. Pinot Grigio '09	🍷🍷	4
● A. A. Pinot Nero Palladium '08	🍷🍷	4
● A. A. Schiava Palladium '09	🍷🍷	4*
○ A. A. Chardonnay Maturum '09	🍷	6
○ A. A. Chardonnay Palladium '09	🍷	4
● A. A. Lagrein Scuro Rueslhof Gurnzan '09	🍷	4
● A. A. Lagrein Scuro Maturum '07	🥂🥂	6

Cantina Vini Merano

loc. Maia Bassa
via San Marco, 11
39012 Merano/Meran [BZ]
tel. 0473235544
www.meranerkellerei.com

CELLAR SALES
PRE-BOOKED VISITS

ANNUAL PRODUCTION 450,000 bottles
HECTARES UNDER VINE 140
VITICULTURE METHOD Conventional

Cantina Produttori di Merano is a small co-operative by Alto Adige standards, producing around 450,000 bottles from several vineyards in stunning locations. Under the guidance of cellarmaster Stefan Kapfinger, quality is improving at an exponential rate. The wines have an increasingly well-defined style, bold personality and, in some cases, they are also classic expressions of their terroir. To top this off, the range is all very favourably priced, from the super Graf Von Meran line to the fantastic Schiavas.

Stefan Kapfinger presented an outstanding range of wines this year, starting with the '08 Moscato Giallo Passito Sissi, which opens with complex aniseed and orange peel aromas, backed by a concentrated, sweet palate with vibrant, refreshing acidity and impressive length. The '09 Pinot Bianco Sonnenberg is smoky, crisp and elegant and this year is matched by a quirky '09 Kerner, which is clearly influenced by the unique Valle Venosta terroir that is starting to make a name for itself. The rest of the long list of products, starting with the magnificent '09 Schiava, is of a quality rarely equalled in Alto Adige.

○ A. A. Moscato Giallo Passito Sissi Graf von Meran '08	🍷🍷🍷	6
● A. A. Meraner St. Valentin '09	🍷🍷	3*
○ A. A. Sauvignon Graf Von Meran '09	🍷🍷	5*
○ A. A. Val Venosta Pinot Bianco Sonnenberg '09	🍷🍷	4*
○ A. A. Amadeus V. T. '08	🍷🍷	7
○ A. A. Gewürztraminer Graf Von Meran '09	🍷🍷	5
● A. A. Lagrein Segen Ris. '07	🍷🍷	5
○ A. A. Pinot Bianco '08	🍷🍷	4*
● A. A. Pinot Nero Zeno Ris. '07	🍷🍷	5
○ A. A. Riesling Graf von Meran '09	🍷🍷	5
○ A. A. Val Venosta Kerner '09	🍷🍷	4*
● A. A. Val Venosta Schiava Sonnenberg '09	🍷🍷	3
○ A. A. Val Venosta Pinot Bianco Sonnenberg '08	🥂🥂🥂	4*
○ A. A. Moscato Giallo Passito Sissi Graf von Meran '07	🥂🥂	7

★ Cantina Convento Muri-Gries

FRAZ. GRIES
P.ZZA GRIES, 21
39100 BOLZANO/BOZEN
TEL. 0471282287
www.muri-gries.com

CELLAR SALES
PRE-BOOKED VISITS

ANNUAL PRODUCTION 500,000 bottles
HECTARES UNDER VINE 30
VITICULTURE METHOD Conventional

The Muri Gries monastery has been producing wine since the early 15th century, making it one of the oldest wineries in the country. Cellarman Christian Werth took charge in 1988 and is still passionate about his job after more than two decades. The fruit of all his hard work is wines that are increasingly well defined with the Lagrein Abtei Riserva becoming a classic of its type, and a truly impeccable range of wines, from the Pinot Nero to the Pinot Bianco, Santa Maddalena and splendid Moscato Rosa.

"Best-ever" is a well-worn description but in the case of the '07 Lagrein Abtei Riserva there is no other way of describing the purity of this Lagrein, which seems to have risen well above the variety's natural limits. It is austere, elegant and mineral, with silky tannins and a lingering finish. And that is just for starters. The '08 Bianco Abtei is also exceptional. This 70 per cent pinot bianco and 30 percent pinot grigio blend is delicate but unfolds delightfully on the palate. For those not familiar with Christian Werth's skills, the '09 Telano Pinot Bianco will come as a surprise. It is linear, sharp and very well constructed.

● A. A. Lagrein Abtei Ris. '07	▼▼▼	6
○ A. A. Bianco Abtei Muri '08	▼▼	5
○ A. A. Terlano Pinot Bianco '09	▼▼	4*
● A. A. Lagrein '09	▼▼	4*
⊙ A. A. Lagrein Rosato '09	▼▼	4
● A. A. Moscato Rosa Abtei '08	▼▼	6
○ A. A. Pinot Grigio '09	▼▼	4
● A. A. Pinot Nero '09	▼▼	4
● A. A. Pinot Nero Abtei Muri Ris. '07	▼▼	6
● A. A. Santa Maddalena '09	▼▼	3*
● A. A. Schiava Grigia '09	▼▼	3*
● A. A. Lagrein Abtei Ris. '06	▽▽▽	5
● A. A. Lagrein Abtei Ris. '05	▽▽▽	5
● A. A. Lagrein Abtei Ris. '04	▽▽▽	5
● A. A. Lagrein Abtei Ris. '03	▽▽▽	5
● A. A. Lagrein Abtei Ris. '02	▽▽▽	5
● A. A. Lagrein Abtei Ris. '01	▽▽▽	5

Cantina Nals Margreid

VIA HEILIGENBERG, 2
39010 NALLES/NALS [BZ]
TEL. 0471678626
www.kellerei.it

CELLAR SALES
PRE-BOOKED VISITS

ANNUAL PRODUCTION 900,000 bottles
HECTARES UNDER VINE 150
VITICULTURE METHOD Conventional

The imminent opening of the new cellar does not seem to have distracted Harald Schraffl, the very young cellarmaster. The Cantina Nals Margreid is a star on Alto Adige's wine scene. Territory is increasingly noticeable in their wines, especially the whites. Their style is increasingly well defined and they are technically flawless thanks to rigorous grape selection. Three whites stand out – the Pinot Bianco Sirmian, the Sauvignon Mantele and the Pinot Grigio Punggl– equalled by the reds of the Baron Salvadori line and the unmissable Schiava Galea.

Harald Schraffl has put the fantastic '09 harvest to good use. His whites are mature, concentrated, powerful with almost salt-like minerality and acidity to match the big structure. In this sense, the Pinot Bianco Sirmian is exemplary. As elegant as expected, it also boasts impressive structure and stylistic maturity, making it one of the best whites tasted this year. We were surprised, if only up to a point, by the elegance and poise of the Pinot Grigio Punggl. The Sauvignon Mantele is made on the same lines although its vegetal notes need to soften a little to make it truly exceptional. The rest of the range, starting with the fantastic '09 Schiava Galea, is stellar.

○ A. A. Pinot Bianco Sirmian '09	▼▼▼	4*
○ A. A. Gewürztraminer Baron Salvadori '09	▼▼	6
● A. A. Lagrein Baron Salvadori Ris. '07	▼▼	6
○ A. A. Pinot Grigio Punggl '09	▼▼	4*
○ A. A. Sauvignon Mantele '09	▼▼	5
● A. A. Schiava Galea '09	▼▼	4*
● A. A. Cabernet Sauvignon Baron Salvadori Ris. '07	▼▼	6
● A. A. Cabernet Sauvignon Lafot '07	▼▼	5
○ A. A. Chardonnay Baron Salvadori '08	▼▼	6
○ A. A. Moscato Giallo Passito Baronesse '07	▼▼	7
○ A. A. Pinot Bianco Penon '09	▼▼	4*
○ A. A. Pinot Grigio '09	▼▼	4*
● A. A. Pinot Nero '08	▼▼	4
○ A. A. Sauvignon '09	▼▼	4*
● A. A. Schiava Gentile Pfeffersburger '09	▼▼	3*
○ A. A. Pinot Bianco Sirmian '08	▽▽▽	4*
○ A. A. Pinot Bianco Sirmian '07	▽▽▽	4*

Josef Niedermayr

LOC. CORNAIANO/GIRLAN
VIA CASA DI GESÙ, 15/23
39057 APPIANO/EPPAN [BZ]
TEL. 0471662451
www.niedermayr.it

CELLAR SALES
PRE-BOOKED VISITS

ANNUAL PRODUCTION 220,000 bottles
HECTARES UNDER VINE 35
VITICULTURE METHOD Conventional

Josef Niedermayr has done much to help the Alto Adige wine industry get back on its feet. His estate is reliable and very professionally run in consultation with Lorenz Martini. The Aureus, a part-dried white made from mainly chardonnay with a good percentage of sauvignon and a small amount of gewürztraminer, is one of the best sweet wines in Italy. Their classic Alto Adige wines are technically good and wonderfully true to type.

This estate has played an important role in Alto Adige wine so it is only natural that the classic types should be at their best. Let us start with the '08 Lagrein Gries, which despite a disappointing harvest, is austere and mineral, with fine tannins and a relaxed finish marked by lovely crunchy fruit. The delicious '09 Lagrein Gries Blacedelle is succulent, with exuberant spice and fruit. The '08 Aureus part-dried white, one of the region's most famous sweet wines, suffered slightly from a bad year. Its nose features lychees and citrus that introduce a concentrated, if one-dimensional palate, with citron peel and orange. The rest of the range is as good as ever.

● A. A. Lagrein Gries Ris. '08	▼▼	6
O A. A. Aureus '08	▼▼	7
● A. A. Lagrein Gries Blacedelle '09	▼▼	5
● A. A. Schiava Ascherhof '09	▼▼	4
O A. A. Sauvignon Lage Naun '09	▼	5
O A. A. Aureus '99	▽▽▽	6
O A. A. Aureus '98	▽▽▽	6

Niklaserhof - Josef Sölva

LOC. SAN NICOLÒ
VIA DELLE FONTANE, 31A
39052 CALDARO/KALTERN
TEL. 0471963432
www.niklaserhof.it

CELLAR SALES
PRE-BOOKED VISITS

ANNUAL PRODUCTION 45,000 bottles
HECTARES UNDER VINE 6
VITICULTURE METHOD Conventional

Niklaserhof is a reliable bet if you are looking for original, high-quality wines with character. Surrounded by vineyards in the small hamlet of San Nicolò above Caldaro, the estate features a stone cellar filled with wooden barrels, as if to demonstrate that tradition can successfully fuse with new technology and innovation. In recent years Niklaserhof has produced some excellent whites from vineyards located on high plots. The cellar has particularly groomed the Pinot Bianco, a type that is making a strong comeback in the region.

This year's selection was slightly uneven. We especially enjoyed the '08 Lagrein, which was strongly influenced by the vintage, making it lean and elegant, with good tannins and a fresh, dynamic mouth. The '09 Pinot Bianco is also well made, with good structure, linear impetus and a fresh, mineral finish. The rest of the range is definitely well made, although it does not attain the excellence we were used to with the Sölva line.

O A. A. Bianco Mondevinum Ris. '07	▼▼	5
● A. A. Lago di Caldaro Scelto Cl. '09	▼▼	3
● A. A. Lagrein '08	▼▼	4
O A. A. Pinot Bianco '09	▼▼	4*
O A. A. Bianco Mondevinum '05	▽▽	5
O A. A. Pinot Bianco Klaser '07	▽▽	4

Pacherhof - Andreas Huber

FRAZ. NOVACELLA
V.LO PACHER, 1
39040 VARNA/VAHRN [BZ]
TEL. 0472835717
www.pacherhof.com

CELLAR SALES
PRE-BOOKED VISITS
ROOMS AND FOOD

ANNUAL PRODUCTION **90,000 bottles**
HECTARES UNDER VINE **11**
VITICULTURE METHOD **Organic**

The Pacher farm, which dates from the 11th century, sits above the abbey at Novacella. The Hubers took over in 1849 and it was Joseph Huber who, with another farmer, first started growing grapes in Valle Isarco. In 1880, they brought several sylvaner and müller thurgau vines, the first whites to be planted in Bressanone, back from their travels around Europe. Today, another Josef and his son Andreas look after the seven hectares of estate-owned and four hectares of leased vineyards, producing lively, aromatic, elegant, sinewy wines, which they vinify in steel vats and big barrels. Their Riesling, Kerner, Sylvaner, Pinot Grigio and Müller Thurgau are all fabulous.

The '09 Alte Reben produced by Andreas Huber from the oldest sylvaner vineyard in Valle Isarco is delicious. The wine has an almost an almost tangy mineral nose and a full yet racy, sea-salty palate that is at once dynamic and deep. It must be said that all the Pacherhof whites have a very fresh, precise style with easy-drinker appeal. The '09 Pinot Grigio is a perfect example. This wine combines very varietal aromas with solid, full yet supple structure and plenty of energy. The Veltliner, Riesling and Kerner are all made in the same, very successful, vein.

O A. A. Valle Isarco Sylvaner Alte Reben '09	▼▼	6
O A. A. Valle Isarco Pinot Grigio '09	▼▼	5
O A. A. Valle Isarco Riesling '09	▼▼	5
O A. A. Valle Isarco Veltliner '09	▼▼	5
O A. A. Valle Isarco Kerner '09	▼	5
O A. A. Valle Isarco Sylvaner Ris. '08	▼	6
O A. A. Valle Isarco Riesling '04	▽▽▽	5
O A. A. Valle Isarco Sylvaner Alte Reben '05	▽▽▽	5
O A. A. Valle Isarco Riesling '08	▽▽	5
O A. A. Valle Isarco Riesling '07	▽▽	5
O A. A. Valle Isarco Sylvaner Alte Reben '08	▽▽	6

Pfannenstielhof Johannes Pfeifer

VIA PFANNESTIEL, 9
39100 BOLZANO/BOZEN
TEL. 0471970884
www.pfannenstielhof.it

CELLAR SALES
PRE-BOOKED VISITS

ANNUAL PRODUCTION **38,000 bottles**
HECTARES UNDER VINE **4**
VITICULTURE METHOD **Conventional**

Johannes Pfeifer is a grower through and through. The wines he produces from his four hectares of vines situated in the heart of the Lagrein production area are very big, with an extremely well-defined style. He produces around 40,000 bottles per year, all of which are very well-made reds, starting with Santa Maddalena, which here at Pfannenstielhof is uniquely successful. That said, the Lagrein Riserva and the newest addition, the Pinot Nero, are also anything but ordinary and beautifully typed.

Pfannenstielhof's '09 Santa Maddalena is the first Schiava to receive Three Glasses, excluding the '90 Gschleier from Girlan, which received them on retasting. For years, Johannes Pfeifer's wine has regularly placed amongst the best and '09 was an excellent vintage. Distinguished by its intense spicy fruit bouquet, it unfurls fresh, minerality and a varietal, almond-edged finish. The star is flanked by a series of other great wines such as the '07 Lagrein Riserva, which shows juicy and full fleshed, with elegant tannins and dynamic, spicy palate. The '07 Pinot Nero from grapes grown at 500 metres in Pianizza di Sotto, near Caldaro, is astonishingly elegant and precise.

● A. A. Santa Maddalena Cl. '09	▼▼▼	4*
● A. A. Lagrein Ris. '07	▼▼	5
● A. A. Pinot Nero '07	▼▼	5*
● A. A. Lagrein '09	▼▼	4
● A. A. Lagrein Scuro '08	▽▽	4*
● A. A. Lagrein Scuro Ris. '05	▽▽	5
● A. A. Pinot Nero '05	▽▽	5
● A. A. Santa Maddalena Cl. '08	▽▽	3*

Tenuta Ritterhof

s.da del Vino, 1
39052 Caldaro/Kaltern [BZ]
tel. 0471963298
www.ritterhof.it

CELLAR SALES
PRE-BOOKED VISITS

ANNUAL PRODUCTION 290,000 bottles
HECTARES UNDER VINE 8
VITICULTURE METHOD Conventional

This historic estate owned by the Roner family, which also owns the famous distillery, produces enjoyable, well-made wines at reasonable prices. The vineyards are scattered across some of the best wine zones around Caldaro and Termeno. In addition to seven hectares of estate-owned vineyards, Ritterhof also vinifies the grapes of around 40 regular growers. Star wines include the Gewürztraminer Crescendo, Lagrein Manus Riserva and Pinot Grigio.

Again this year, skilled winemaker Bernard Hannes presented a series of very good wines showing a return to reliability. We'll start with the estate's classic, the '09 Gewürztraminer Crescendo, which is regularly among the best. This year, it impressed with its elegance and poise, offering a fresher palate than is usual for the type. The '09 Pinot Grigio is fresh and perky while the best red was, to our minds, the austerely mineral '07 Pinot Nero Crescendo, which finishes nice and long. The '09 Lago di Caldaro and Santa Maddalena Schiavas were positively delicious.

O A. A. Gewürztraminer Crescendo '09	🍷🍷	5
O A. A. Pinot Grigio '09	🍷🍷	4
● A. A. Lago di Caldaro Scelto '09	🍷🍷	3*
● A. A. Lagrein Crescendo Ris. '06	🍷🍷	5
O A. A. Pinot Nero Crescendo '07	🍷🍷	6
● A. A. Santa Maddalena Perlhof '09	🍷🍷	4
O A. A. Sauvignon '09	🍷🍷	4
● Perlhof Crescendo '08	🍷🍷	5
O A. A. Gewürztraminer '09	🍷	4
● A. A. Cabernet Merlot Crescendo Ris. '06	YY	5
O A. A. Gewürztraminer Crescendo '07	YY	5
O A. A. Gewürztraminer Crescendo '05	YY	5

Röckhof - Konrad Augschöll

via San Valentino, 9
39040 Villandro/Villanders [BZ]
tel. 0472847130
roeck@rolmail.net

CELLAR SALES
PRE-BOOKED VISITS
FOOD

ANNUAL PRODUCTION 10,000 bottles
HECTARES UNDER VINE 4
VITICULTURE METHOD Conventional

Konrad Augschöll was one of the first growers around Chiusa to bottle his own wine. He cultivates around three hectares of steep vineyards at 600 to 700 metres at the 15th-century Röckhof farm on the road from Chiusa to Villandro. White grapes, mainly riesling and müller thurgau, account for half the stock while the other half are pinot nero and zweigelt, an old Austrian variety that is particularly cold-resistant and well suited to high-altitude vineyards. The reds are served at the family's delightful farm holiday centre.

We loved Röckhof's Riesling Viel Anders again this year. It is succulent, expressive, mineral and maybe ever so slightly husky but also dynamic and nice and long. This white is very natural and lively, although possibly still a bit young to be appreciated fully. As usual, the '09 Müller Thurgau is very good, this year presenting beautifully concentrated, which is not all that common in the estate's emblematic wine.

O A. A. Valle Isarco Riesling Viel Anders '09	🍷🍷	4*
O A. A. Valle Isarco Müller Thurgau '09	🍷🍷	4*
O Caruess '09	🍷🍷	4*
O A. A. Valle Isarco Riesling Viel Anders '08	YYY	4*
O A. A. Valle Isarco Müller Thurgau '08	YY	4*
O A. A. Valle Isarco Riesling '07	YY	4*

Hans Rottensteiner

FRAZ. GRIES
VIA SARENTINO, 1A
39100 BOLZANO/BOZEN
TEL. 0471282015
www.rottensteiner-weine.com

CELLAR SALES
PRE-BOOKED VISITS

ANNUAL PRODUCTION 450,000 bottles
HECTARES UNDER VINE 10
VITICULTURE METHOD Conventional

North-west of Bolzano, at the entrance to Val Sarentino, the historic estate of Toni and Hannes Rottensteiner is one of the most reliable wineries in the province. Their bottles are always technically excellent and full of personality. The list is naturally headed by local classics such as Lagrein and the always-excellent Santa Maddalena Premstallerhof, which has become a benchmark. The rest of the range is headed by the Gewürztraminer Passito Cresta.

Overall, this year was probably one of the best for this important estate. Although there wasn't a true high note, the range is very good, topped by the '07 Lagrein Grieser Select Riserva, which is succulent, elegant and minerally, with silky tannins. It progresses well and the fruity, spicy fruit combines with just the right acidity. Equally good is the '08 Gewürztraminer Passito Cresta is complex and very concentrated with good acidity to support the solid profile. Santa Maddalena Premstallerhof was delicious, as usual, and the '09 vintage outshone itself. The '09 Pinot Bianco Carnol is spot on, possessing great finesse and lovely minerals.

○ A. A. Gewürztraminer Passito Cresta '08	🍷🍷	6
● A. A. Lagrein Grieser Select Ris. '07	🍷🍷	5
● A. A. Santa Maddalena Cl. Premstallerhof '09	🍷🍷	4*
○ A. A. Gewürztraminer Cancenai '09	🍷🍷	5
○ A. A. Pinot Bianco Carnol '09	🍷🍷	4*
● A. A. Schiava Nobile Kristplonerhof '09	🍷🍷	3*
○ A. A. Chardonnay '09	🍷	4
⊙ A. A. Lagrein Rosato '09	🍷	4
● A. A. Lagrein Ris. '02	YYY	4*
○ A. A. Gewürztraminer Passito Cresta '06	YY	6
○ A. A. Gewürztraminer Passito Cresta '04	YY	6
● A. A. Lagrein Grieser Select Ris. '05	YY	5
● A. A. Lagrein Grieser Select Ris. '04	YY	5

Castel Sallegg

V.LO DI SOTTO, 15
39052 CALDARO/KALTERN [BZ]
TEL. 0471963132
www.castelsallegg.it

CELLAR SALES
PRE-BOOKED VISITS

ANNUAL PRODUCTION 120,000 bottles
HECTARES UNDER VINE 31
VITICULTURE METHOD Conventional

Georg von Kuenburg owns one of the most traditional historic estates in the province of Bolzano. For years, the name Sallegg was remembered almost exclusively for its famous Moscato Rosa. However, things are changing and the estate now offers a range of products, such as Lago di Caldaro, Lagrein and Pinot Grigio, that offer excellent quality with a very strong personality. Being passionate about wine, the Georg has found the ideal partner in the person of Matthias Hauser, which promises a bright future for the estate.

This estate in Caldaro is back on the right path after a few years in the wilderness. It is apparent that the extensive range now has a clear strategy and ideology. The Lago di Caldaro Bischofsleiten is one of the estate's flagships and one of Georg's passions. The '09 version opens with raspberry and spices while the palate is almost austere and very mineral, with a dynamic, fruity thrust. The excellent '09 Pinot Bianco and Pinot Grigio are both eloquently varietal.

● A. A. Lago di Caldaro Scelto Bischofsleiten '09	🍷🍷	4*
○ A. A. Pinot Grigio '09	🍷🍷	4*
○ A. A. Gewürztraminer '09	🍷🍷	4
● A. A. Lagrein Ris. '07	🍷🍷	5
○ A. A. Moscato Giallo Secco '09	🍷🍷	4
○ A. A. Pinot Bianco '09	🍷🍷	4*
● A. A. Lagrein Ris. '06	YY	5*
● A. A. Moscato Rosa '03	YY	7
○ A. A. Pinot Bianco '08	YY	4*

★★ Cantina Produttori San Michele Appiano

via Circonvallazione, 17/19
39057 Appiano/Eppan [BZ]
tel. 0471664466
www.stmichael.it

CELLAR SALES
PRE-BOOKED VISITS

ANNUAL PRODUCTION 2,200,000 bottles
HECTARES UNDER VINE 370
VITICULTURE METHOD Conventional

Much has been said about Cantina Produttori San Michele Appiano and their long-serving winemaker, Hans Terzer, who is a veritable pioneer in Alto Adige. The fact is that the wines have few rivals and there are several quite exquisite gems. The Sanct Valentin line, starting with the legendary Sauvignon, is one of Italy's oenological gems.

This co-operative winery is a battleship that navigates surely on troubled waters. However, we continue to be amazed at the apparent ease with which they manage to produce exceptionally fine wines. The Sauvignon Sanct Valentin is a portrait of the vintage. Last year, it was agile and fresh while this year it has an impressive sensory profile and a great future ahead. Hans quite dazzled us with the '09 Riesling Montiggl, which has never been better, and a compact, well-orchestrated '07 Pinot Nero Sanct Valentin.

○ A. A. Sauvignon St. Valentin '09	▼▼▼	6
○ A. A. Pinot Bianco Schulthauser '09	▼▼	4*
● A. A. Pinot Nero St. Valentin '07	▼▼	6
○ A. A. Riesling Montiggl '09	▼▼	4*
○ A. A. Sauvignon Lahn '09	▼▼	4*
● A. A. Cabernet Ris. '07	▼▼	5
○ A. A. Gewürztraminer St. Valentin '09	▼▼	6
○ A. A. Pinot Grigio Anger '09	▼▼	4
● A. A. Schiava Pagis '09	▼▼	4
○ A. A. Bianco Passito Comtess '05	▽▽▽	6
○ A. A. Sauvignon St. Valentin '08	▽▽▽	6
○ A. A. Sauvignon St. Valentin '07	▽▽▽	6
○ A. A. Sauvignon St. Valentin '06	▽▽▽	5
○ A. A. Sauvignon St. Valentin '05	▽▽▽	5
○ A. A. Sauvignon St. Valentin '04	▽▽▽	5
○ A. A. Sauvignon St. Valentin '02	▽▽▽	5

Cantina Produttori San Paolo

loc. San Paolo
via Castel Guardia, 21
39050 Appiano/Eppan [BZ]
tel. 0471662183
www.kellereistpauls.com

CELLAR SALES
PRE-BOOKED VISITS

ANNUAL PRODUCTION 1,000,000 bottles
HECTARES UNDER VINE 170
VITICULTURE METHOD Conventional

The Cantina Sociale di San Paolo is a lovely medium-sized operations in the delightful village of San Paolo near Appiano. All around is a stunning vine-clad landscape, in the heart of Oltradige. The wines are very solidly made presenting well-defined, technically flawless, very good quality and constantly improving, largely due to the efforts of winemaker Wolfgang Tratter. The Exclusiv and fledgling Passion lines are the jewels in the estate's mostly white crown.

The 2008 vintage will not stand out as one of the best in Alto Adige. Here at San Paolo they took the bold decision to release the white '08 Passion a year later. And they were right, because the wines are full of personality and technically outstanding. This is especially true of the Pinot Bianco and the Sauvignon, which are both very convincing, well balanced and consistent, if a little lean. From the reds, the '07 Pinot Nero Passion Riserve stands out. Its beautiful nose precedes an austere, mineral palate with resolved tannins and a deep, assertive finish. We love the Schiava Sarnerhof, particularly '09.

○ A. A. Pinot Bianco Passion '08	▼▼	5
○ A. A. Sauvignon Passion '08	▼▼	5
● A. A. Schiava Sarnerhof Exclusiv '09	▼▼	4*
○ A. A. Pinot Bianco Exclusiv Plötzner '09	▼▼	4
○ A. A. Pinot Grigio Exclusiv Egg Leiten '09	▼▼	4
● A. A. Pinot Nero Luziafeld Exclusiv '08	▼▼	5
● A. A. Pinot Nero Passion Ris. '07	▼▼	6
● A. A. Schiava Passion '08	▼▼	4
○ A. A. Gewürztraminer St. Justina Exclusiv '08	▽▽	5*
● A. A. Lagrein Scuro DiVinus Ris. '04	▽▽	6
○ A. A. Pinot Bianco Passion '07	▽▽	5

★ Cantina Produttori Santa Maddalena/ Cantina Produttori Bolzano

VIA BRENNERO, 15
39100 BOLZANO/BOZEN
TEL. 0471270909
www.cantinabolzano.com

CELLAR SALES
PRE-BOOKED VISITS

ANNUAL PRODUCTION 1,000,000 bottles
HECTARES UNDER VINE 130
VITICULTURE METHOD Conventional

This winery and its cellarmaster, Stefan Filippi, have been at the pinnacle of Italian wine for years. The flagship wine, Lagrein Riserva Taber, is consistently one of the nation's top reds. However, man cannot live by Lagrein alone so the winery also produces an excellent Chardonnay Kleinstein, a classic Sauvignon Mock, two Gewürztraminers – the basic and the Kleinstein – a must-taste Santa Maddalena Huck am Bach and an extraordinary Pinot Bianco Dellago, which have all been outstanding for years now. What is more, the entire range shows strong varietal stamping and character.

There was no '08 Taber after a terrible hailstorm devastated the vines in Gries. Stefan Filippi will have to content himself with just one Three Glass award for the '09 Pinot Bianco Dellago, which has risen to become a model for its fellows. This white is both powerful and complex, even though it was only bottled only a few months ago, and features white peach e citrus notes to support its compact structure, which also features fresh mineral notes. The '08 Cabernet Mumelter is elegance personified and seems to be returning to its former glory. The '09 Santa Maddalena Huck am Bach is deliciously fragrant. The rest of the range is also well above average.

○ A. A. Pinot Bianco Dellago '09	🍷🍷🍷	5
● A. A. Cabernet Mumelter Ris. '08	🍷🍷	7
○ A. A. Gewürztraminer Kleinstein '09	🍷🍷	6
○ A. A. Santa Maddalena Cl. Huck am Bach '09	🍷🍷	4*
○ A. A. Chardonnay Kleinstein '09	🍷🍷	5
● A. A. Lagrein Scuro Perl '08	🍷🍷	5
● A. A. Merlot Siebeneich Ris. '08	🍷🍷	6
● A. A. Pinot Nero Ris. '08	🍷🍷	6
● A. A. Santa Maddalena Cl. '09	🍷🍷	4*
○ A. A. Sauvignon Mock '09	🍷🍷	5
○ A. A. Valle Isarco Müller Thurgau '09	🍷🍷	4
○ A. A. Valle Isarco Silvaner '09	🍷🍷	4
● A. A. Lagrein Scuro Taber Ris. '07	YYY	7
● A. A. Lagrein Scuro Taber Ris. '05	YYY	6
● A. A. Lagrein Scuro Taber Ris. '04	YYY	6
● A. A. Lagrein Scuro Taber Ris. '02	YYY	7
● A. A. Lagrein Scuro Taber Ris. '01	YYY	6
○ A. A. Pinot Bianco Dellago '08	YYY	5
○ A. A. Pinot Bianco Dellago '07	YYY	5

Peter Sölva & Söhne

VIA DELL'ORO, 33
39052 CALDARO/KALTERN [BZ]
TEL. 0471964650
www.soelva.com

CELLAR SALES
PRE-BOOKED VISITS

ANNUAL PRODUCTION 75,000 bottles
HECTARES UNDER VINE 11
VITICULTURE METHOD Conventional

The Peter Sölva & Söhne estate in Caldaro was first documented in 1731. The Sölva family produces around 75,000 bottles per year, divided between the DeSilva and Amistar lines. Young Stephan Sölva, who works with winemaker Christian Belutti, seems to have very clear ideas about the style of wines he wants to produce, that is, fresh, elegantly varietal whites and ambitiously powerful reds. His wines are all bursting with character, beautifully made and altogether enchanting.

Stephan Sölva is not exactly what you would call shy. He has unshakeable faith in his work and his idea of wine. This year we liked the whites, especially the '09 Terlano Pinot Bianco DeSilva, sourced from the 50-year-old Kühebene vineyard on tableland near Caldaro at 500 metres. This wine has very good structure and is already complex, with white peach and sage aromas, a racy palate and unhurried progression for the estate's first Three Glasses. From the rest, in the DeSilva line the '09 Lago di Caldaro appeals and the '09 Sauvignon intrigues. We remain perplexed about the Amistar reds, which are a little too heavily oaked for our liking.

○ A. A. Terlano Pinot Bianco DeSilva '09	🍷🍷🍷	5
● A. A. Lago di Caldaro Cl. Sup. DeSilva Peterleiten '09	🍷🍷	4*
○ A. A. Sauvignon DeSilva '09	🍷🍷	5
● A.A. A. A. Schiava BellDèS '09	🍷🍷	3*
● A. A. Cabernet Franc Amistar '07	🍷	6
● Amistar Rosso '07	🍷	6
○ A. A. Sauvignon DeSilva '08	YY	5
○ A. A. Terlano Pinot Bianco DeSilva '07	YY	5
● Amistar Rosso '04	YY	6

Hannes Baumgartner Strasserhof

FRAZ. NOVACELLA
LOC. UNTERRAIN, 8
39040 VARNA/VAHRN [BZ]
TEL. 0472830804
www.strasserhof.info

CELLAR SALES
PRE-BOOKED VISITS
ROOMS AND FOOD

ANNUAL PRODUCTION 35,000 bottles
HECTARES UNDER VINE 4
VITICULTURE METHOD Conventional

Strasserhof, one of the oldest farms in Valle Isarco, has some of the northernmost vineyards in the province of Bolzano. Hannes Baumgartner's vineyard is in a breathtakingly beautiful location. In recent years, the Strasserhof wines have had a dramatic change in style, becoming fresher, more minerally and acquiring bite. The Veltliner, Riesling, Sylvaner, Kerner and Müller Thurgau are very tasty and available at reasonable prices.

Over the past two years, Hannes seems to have found the right track. His wines are increasingly centred, distinctive and marked by the terroir. The result of this journey is explosive, with six exceptionally good '09 wines, starting with the sumptuous Veltliner, which won Three Glasses for its elegant, almost rarefied structure, with smoky, mineral notes and a breathtaking palate, astonishing given how recently it was bottled. The '09 Riesling is equally good and wine will reveal its full potential over time. A star is born.

O A. A. Valle Isarco Veltliner '09	▼▼▼	4*
O A. A. Valle Isarco Riesling '09	▼▼	5*
O A. A. Valle Isarco Gewürztraminer '09	▼▼	5
O A. A. Valle Isarco Kerner '09	▼▼	5
O A. A. Valle Isarco Müller Thurgau '09	▼▼	4*
O A. A. Valle Isarco Sylvaner '09	▼▼	4*
O A. A. Valle Isarco Kerner '08	▽▽	4*
O A. A. Valle Isarco Kerner '06	▽▽	4*
O A. A. Valle Isarco Sylvaner '06	▽▽	4*

Stroblhof

LOC. SAN MICHELE
VIA PIGANÒ, 25
39057 APPIANO/EPPAN [BZ]
TEL. 0471662250
www.stroblhof.it

CELLAR SALES
PRE-BOOKED VISITS

ANNUAL PRODUCTION 30,000 bottles
HECTARES UNDER VINE 4
VITICULTURE METHOD Conventional

Stroblhof is located in the heart of the classic white wine zone of Appiano and boasts a very long viticultural tradition. Andreas Nicolussi-Leck has run the estate and the cellar since 1995 and in recent years has shown a maturity of style. His whites are full of character, if a little edgy when young. They tend to be austere but fresh, with energy h and enormous cellaring potential. Stroblhof produces some of the best Italian Pinot Neros and Pinot Biancos around, which is no surprise since Hans Terzer consults.

Andreas Nicolussi-Leck is a skilled producer who makes unique, never ordinary, wines. The only problem that they always need many months before they express their potential to the full. As usual, we liked the '09 Pinot Bianco Strahler, which is vibrant, with incisive acidity, a slim body and very solid structure. It will reveal a few pleasant surprises in the future but for now it will have to be content with Three Glasses. The Pinot Neros are always at the top, starting with the '07 Riserva, which is still very young, but fine, elegant and intriguingly austere while the '08 Pigeno reflects the cooler vintage.

O A. A. Pinot Bianco Strahler '09	▼▼▼	4*
● A. A. Pinot Nero Ris. '07	▼▼	6
O A. A. Chardonnay Schwarzhaus '09	▼▼	4
● A. A. Pinot Nero Pigeno '08	▼▼	5
O A. A. Sauvignon Nico '09	▼▼	5
● A. A. Pinot Nero Ris. '05	▽▽▽	6
O A. A. Gewürztraminer Pigeno '07	▽▽	5
O A. A. Pinot Bianco Strahler '08	▽▽	4*
O A. A. Pinot Bianco Strahler '07	▽▽	4*
O A. A. Pinot Bianco Strahler '06	▽▽	4*
● A. A. Pinot Nero Pigeno '04	▽▽	5
● A. A. Pinot Nero Ris. '06	▽▽	6

Taschlerhof - Peter Wachtler

LOC. MARA, 107
39042 BRESSANONE/BRIXEN [BZ]
TEL. 0472851091
www.taschlerhof.com

CELLAR SALES
PRE-BOOKED VISITS

ANNUAL PRODUCTION **26,500 bottles**
HECTARES UNDER VINE **4**
VITICULTURE METHOD **Conventional**

This small estate in Mara, a small hamlet south of Bressanone, is owned by Peter Wachtler, a driving force behind the success of Valle Isarco wines. The south-east-facing vineyards are surrounded by woodlands at around 550 metres. The wines are strongly typed, with excellent character and slightly less acidity than many other local bottles but with the bold mineral quality typical of Valle Isarco whites. For years, Sylvaner Lahner has been the estate's flagship wine.

Again with the '09 vintage, Sylvaner Lahner is Taschlerhof's top wine. The nose is dominated by thyme and Mediterranean herbs, which lead into an elegantly succulent, dynamic palate with good thrust. The '09 Riesling is also very well made and despite its tender age shows style. While it does not have great structure, it is nevertheless firm and fresh. The other whites need a touch more personality to sit up there with the two leading lights.

○ A. A. Valle Isarco Sylvaner Lahner '09	▼▼	5
○ A. A. Valle Isarco Riesling '09	▼▼	5
○ A. A. Valle Isarco Sylvaner '09	▼	4
○ A. A. Valle Isarco Kerner '07	▽▽	5
○ A. A. Valle Isarco Riesling '08	▽▽	6
○ A. A. Valle Isarco Sylvaner Lahner '08	▽▽	6
○ A. A. Valle Isarco Sylvaner Lahner '05	▽▽	5*

★ Cantina Terlano

VIA SILBERLEITEN, 7
39018 TERLANO/TERLAN [BZ]
TEL. 0471257135
www.cantina-terlano.com

CELLAR SALES
PRE-BOOKED VISITS

ANNUAL PRODUCTION **1,000,000 bottles**
HECTARES UNDER VINE **140**
VITICULTURE METHOD **Conventional**

Terlano's local and international success is no fluke and it's not just a question of territory. The wines come from a combination of hard work and passion, which runs to keeping detailed records of the grape production of each individual vine. The result is a range of wines, especially whites, that are appreciated around the world, not least because of their legendary cellaring potential. The Pinot Bianco and Sauvignon in the whites and the Lagrein and Schiava in the reds are all characterful, with a distinctive saline quality and depth.

Terlano produces some of the greatest white wines in the world in terms of complexity and that crucially important factor, cellaring potential. As usual, a raft of bottles went to the finals and awarding Three Glasses was even more difficult – and delicate – than usual. Not for the first time, we chose the Pinot Bianco Riserva Vorberg, but it was close. The '07 vintage is astoundingly enjoyable, with distinct white fruits aromas and delicate smoky notes, while the mouth is gutsy, salty, succulent and very deep. We would also like to mention that the '07 Lagrein Porphyr Riserva is one of the nicest we've tasted.

○ A. A. Terlano Pinot Bianco Vorberg Ris. '07	▼▼▼	5
● A. A. Lagrein Gries Ris. '07	▼▼	5*
● A. A. Lagrein Porphyr Ris. '07	▼▼	6
○ A. A. Terlano Chardonnay '96	▼▼	8
○ A. A. Terlano Chardonnay Kreuth '08	▼▼	4*
○ A. A. Terlano Nova Domus Ris. '07	▼▼	6
○ A. A. Terlano Sauvignon Quarz '08	▼▼	6
○ A. A. Terlano Sauvignon Winkl '09	▼▼	4*
○ A. A. Chardonnay Cl. '09	▼▼	4
○ A. A. Gewürztraminer Cl. '09	▼▼	4
○ A. A. Gewürztraminer Lunare '08	▼▼	6
○ A. A. Pinot Grigio '09	▼▼	4
● A. A. Santa Maddalena Haüsler '09	▼▼	4*
○ A. A. Terlano Cl. '09	▼▼	4*
○ A. A. Terlano Pinot Bianco Cl. '09	▼▼	4*
○ A. A. Terlano Pinot Bianco Vorberg Ris. '06	▽▽▽	5*
○ A. A. Terlano Pinot Bianco Vorberg Ris. '02	▽▽▽	4*
○ A. A. Terlano Sauvignon Quarz '05	▽▽▽	6

Thurnhof - Andreas Berger

LOC. ASLAGO
VIA CASTEL FLAVON, 7
39100 BOLZANO/BOZEN
TEL. 0471288460
www.thurnhof.com

CELLAR SALES
PRE-BOOKED VISITS

ANNUAL PRODUCTION 25,000 bottles
HECTARES UNDER VINE 4
VITICULTURE METHOD Organic

Andreas Berger is a careful, very reserved wine producer. His small estate on the outskirts of Bolzano makes mostly red wines but also produces one of the best Moscato Giallos in Alto Adige. Andreas's modern wines tend to be a little stiff in their youth, and need a couple of years in the bottle to shine, but they never lack personality. All the Bolzano area's wine types are shown here at their best.

This year, Andreas surprised us with a particularly good version of the Sauvignon 800, the 800 referring to the vineyard's elevation. The nose opens with clear elderberry aromas that lead into a fresh, vibrant, slightly vegetal palate with very leisurely progression. This a white of finesse rather than muscle. As usual the Lagrein Riserva is stiff to the point of austerity but the '07 vintage is fantastically poised and harmony. A deliciously perky '09 Moscato Giallo underlines the quality of the work done at Thurnhof.

○ A. A. Sauvignon 800 '09	▼▼	4*
● A. A. Cabernet Merlot Wienegg '06	▼▼	6
● A. A. Lagrein Ris. '07	▼▼	5
○ A. A. Moscato Giallo '09	▼▼	4*
● A. A. Santa Maddalena '09	▼▼	4
● A. A. Lagrein Ris. '04	▽▽	5
● A. A. Lagrein Scuro Ris. '02	▽▽	5
○ A. A. Sauvignon '08	▽▽	4

Tiefenbrunner

FRAZ. NICLARA
VIA CASTELLO, 4
39040 CORTACCIA/KURTATSCH [BZ]
TEL. 0471880122
www.tiefenbrunner.com

CELLAR SALES
PRE-BOOKED VISITS
FOOD

ANNUAL PRODUCTION 800,000 bottles
HECTARES UNDER VINE 23
VITICULTURE METHOD Conventional

The Tiefenbrunner winery is famous for being one of the first estates to sell Alto Adige wines outside the province of Bolzano. Credit goes to Herbert Tiefenbrunner, a charismatic wine man, and his most famous label, Feldmarschall von Fenner, a Müller Thurgau obtained from grapes grown at over 1,000 metres. Herbert's shrewd son Christof is now making elegant, subtle wines of sound construction that are anything but predictable.

Again this year a slew of wines made it through to the finals, with the key Alto Adige types all being represented, which testifies to the care and quality of work carried out on this leading estate. This year, the '07 Lagrein Linticlarus Riserva took Three Glasses. A supremely elegant wine, it flaunts a composure that seems to be a hallmark of just about all Tiefenbrunner's wines. The estate's '09 Müller Thurgau Feldmarschall von Fenner is a bit of a fetish of ours and is already very interesting, although possibly a little hard to pin down, with spicy saffron and structure not yet in place. A wine that will benefit from another few months in the cellar.

● A. A. Lagrein Linticlarus Ris. '07	▼▼▼	6
○ A. A. Chardonnay Linticlarus '08	▼▼	6
○ A. A. Gewürztraminer Castel Turmhof '09	▼▼	6
● A. A. Lagrein Castel Turmhof '08	▼▼	4*
● A. A. Pinot Nero Linticlarus Ris. '07	▼▼	6
○ Feldmarschall von Fenner zu Fennberg '09	▼▼	6
○ A. A. Chardonnay Castel Turmhof '09	▼▼	4
○ A. A. Cuvée Anna Castel Turmhof '09	▼▼	4
○ A. A. Gewürztraminer Linticlarus V.T. '08	▼▼	7
○ A. A. Sauvignon Kirchleiten '09	▼▼	5
● A. A. Schiava Grigia Castel Turmhof '09	▼▼	4*
○ A. A. Gewürztraminer Castel Turmhof '02	▽▽▽	5
○ Feldmarschall von Fenner zu Fennberg '08	▽▽▽	6
○ Feldmarschall von Fenner zu Fennberg '05	▽▽▽	5
○ Feldmarschall von Fenner zu Fennberg '06	▽▽	5
○ Feldmarschall von Fenner zu Fennberg '04	▽▽	5

★★ Cantina Tramin

S.da del Vino, 144
39040 Termeno/Tramin [BZ]
tel. 0471096633
www.cantinatramin.it

CELLAR SALES
PRE-BOOKED VISITS

ANNUAL PRODUCTION 1,500,000 bottles
HECTARES UNDER VINE 235
VITICULTURE METHOD Conventional

The Cantina Tramin at Termeno, run by one of Italy's greatest winemakers, William Stürz, boasts a spectacular new cellar and new labels but it still remains a benchmark for the province of Bolzano. The estate's reputation was secured by its most famous wine, Gewürztraminer Nussbaumer and the dried-grape version, Terminum, but there is a whole list of strongly typed, stylistically rigorous wines to back it up. From Pinot Bianco to Pinot Grigio, Lagrein and Schiava, there is not a single local type in which the winery does not excel.

Let us cut to the chase. The '09 Gewürztraminer Nussbaumer took Three Glasses for the 11th consecutive year. With great structure, complexity and balance, it presents all the elements of a memorable vintage. Pinot Grigio Unterebner highlights a memorable year for the type and the '08 Gewürztraminer Passito Terminum is pretty good in spite of an awful growing season. The so-called classic line is exceptionally expressive and the prices also happen to be exceptional. That's what sets Tramin apart from ordinary wineries.

○ A. A. Gewürztraminer Nussbaumer '09	🍷🍷🍷	6
○ A. A. Gewürztraminer Terminum V. T. '08	🍷🍷	6
● A. A. Lagrein '09	🍷🍷	4*
○ A. A. Pinot Grigio Unterebner '09	🍷🍷	5
○ A. A. Sauvignon '09	🍷🍷	4*
● A. A. Schiava Freisinger '09	🍷🍷	4*
○ A. A. Stoan '09	🍷🍷	5
○ A. A. Chardonnay '09	🍷🍷	4*
○ A. A. Gewürztraminer '09	🍷🍷	4*
○ A. A. Pinot Bianco '09	🍷🍷	4*
○ A. A. Pinot Grigio '09	🍷🍷	4*
● A. A. Schiava Hexenbichler '09	🍷🍷	4*
○ T Bianco '09	🍷	3*
○ A. A. Gewürztraminer Nussbaumer '08	YYY	6
○ A. A. Gewürztraminer Nussbaumer '07	YYY	5
○ A. A. Gewürztraminer Terminum V. T. '07	YYY	6
○ A. A. Gewürztraminer Terminum V. T. '06	YYY	8

Untermoserhof
Georg Ramoser

via Santa Maddalena, 36
39100 Bolzano/Bozen
tel. 0471975481
untermoserhof@rolmail.net

CELLAR SALES
PRE-BOOKED VISITS
ROOMS

ANNUAL PRODUCTION 35,000 bottles
HECTARES UNDER VINE 4
VITICULTURE METHOD Conventional

The hill of Santa Maddalena is a magical place and the home of a very skilled and passionate winemaker, Georg Ramoser, who is also a great guy. Untermoserhof, which was built in the 17th century, has been run by the Ramosers for the past three generations. The estate produces around 35,000 bottles of the local classics every year. The style is fairly modern but the wines are beautifully typed and territorial.

Georg Ramoser produces a limited number of wines, all classics for the Santa Maddalena zone and all good. We'll start with a champion in its category, the '09 Santa Maddalena, which has surprisingly complex structure, a fresh, fruity nose and a gutsy, full, mineral palate. The '07 Lagrein Riserva is very young but already enjoyable. Savoury, very peppery, long and deep, it unveils smooth tannins and perfectly balanced acidity. The current Lagrein is exceptionally pleasant and indicates that 2009 will be a great year for the variety.

● A. A. Santa Maddalena Cl. '09	🍷🍷	4*
● A. A. Lagrein Scuro '09	🍷🍷	4*
● A. A. Lagrein Scuro Ris. '07	🍷🍷	5
● A. A. Lagrein Scuro Ris. '03	YYY	5*
● A. A. Lagrein Scuro Ris. '06	YY	5
● A. A. Lagrein Scuro Ris. '01	YY	5

Tenuta Unterortl - Castel Juval

FRAZ. JUVAL, 1B
39020 CASTELBELLO CIARDES/
KASTELBELL TSCHARS [BZ]
TEL. 0473667580
www.unterortl.it

CELLAR SALES
PRE-BOOKED VISITS

ANNUAL PRODUCTION 30,000 bottles
HECTARES UNDER VINE 4
VITICULTURE METHOD Conventional

The estate is located in a spectacularly wild setting, perched on a precipice above Castelbello in Valle Venosta. The vineyards cling to several sheer ridges between 600 and 800 metres above sea level. And this is home to husband and wife team Martin and Ghisela Aurich. Their Riesling, Pinot Bianco and Pinot Nero are famous and whites in general are lean, incisive, solidly structured and remarkably pure and linear. Also worth trying are the delicious fruit brandies produced by energetic Martin and sold at the estate's small cellar-door shop.

As the years go by, Martin Aurich's wines seem to become increasingly pure and stylized, regardless of the vintage. The '09 Riesling, from a fine vintage, seems rather lean and the first impression is quite hard to define. Little by little, though, the wine's racy vigour peeks through in whistle-clean varietal flavours and marathon length. The '09 Pinot Bianco follows in the same vein, interleaving light and shade initially, then blossoming into a burst of fruit and iodine sensations. The surprise of the year is the '09 Müller Thurgau, which is a typical Valle Venosta wine and, more importantly, bears Martin Aurich's mark.

Wine	Glasses	Score
○ A. A. Valle Venosta Riesling '09	3 black	5
○ A. A. Valle Venosta Pinot Bianco '09	2 black	4*
○ A. A. Valle Venosta Riesling Windbichel V.T. '09	2 black	6
○ A. A. Valle Venosta Müller Thurgau '09	2 black	4*
● A. A. Valle Venosta Pinot Nero '08	2 black	5
○ Juval Glimmet '09	2 black	4
● Juval Gneis '09	2 black	4
○ A. A. Valle Venosta Pinot Bianco '07	3 white	4*
○ A. A. Valle Venosta Riesling '08	3 white	5
○ A. A. Valle Venosta Riesling '07	3 white	5*
○ A. A. Valle Venosta Riesling '04	3 white	5*
○ A. A. Valle Venosta Riesling '03	3 white	5*
○ A. A. Valle Venosta Riesling '00	3 white	4
○ A. A. Valle Venosta Riesling Windbichel '05	3 white	5
● A. A. Valle Venosta Pinot Nero '07	2 white	5

Cantina Produttori Valle Isarco

VIA COSTE, 50
39043 CHIUSA/KLAUSEN [BZ]
TEL. 0472847553
www.cantinavalleisarco.it

CELLAR SALES
PRE-BOOKED VISITS

ANNUAL PRODUCTION 650,000 bottles
HECTARES UNDER VINE 130
VITICULTURE METHOD Conventional

Founded in 1961, Cantina Produttori Valle Isarco is the youngest co-operative winery in Alto Adige. It brings together 130 member growers and a modern cellar at Chiusa. This is as far north as grapes will grow and the climate is not exactly clement. The harvest starts a lot later than in Oltradige so even the white grapes have to wait until at least the end of September. Thomas Dorfmann, the dynamic cellarmaster, maintains quality in a range of basic wines that are honest, fresh and value for money. The showcase Aristos wines have character, structure and longevity.

You can't go wrong buying Cantina Produttori Valle Isarco wine from the standard Classica or top Aristos lines. All wines are flawlessly made, with strong local characteristics and crisis-beating prices, so it comes as no surprise that the winery is riding high commercially. The only thing that stops the wines from moving on is their personality, which could possibly be a touch stronger. The '09 Gewürztraminer Aristos appeals with its elegant rather than powerful structure. The '09 Riesling and Kerner in the Aristos line are equally good.

Wine	Glasses	Score
○ A. A. Valle Isarco Gewürztraminer Aristos '09	2 black	5
○ A. A. Valle Isarco Kerner Aristos '09	2 black	4
○ A. A. Valle Isarco Riesling Aristos '09	2 black	5
○ A. A. Valle Isarco Kerner '09	2 black	4*
● A. A. Valle Isarco Klausener Laitacher '09	2 black	4*
○ A. A. Valle Isarco Pinot Grigio Aristos '09	2 black	5
○ A. A. Valle Isarco Sylvaner '09	2 black	4*
○ A. A. Valle Isarco Sylvaner Aristos '09	2 black	5
○ A. A. Valle Isarco Veltliner '09	2 black	4*
○ A. A. Valle Isarco Veltliner Aristos '09	2 black	5
○ A. A. Sauvignon Aristos '09	1 black	4
○ A. A. Valle Isarco Kerner Aristos '05	3 white	4*
○ A. A. Valle Isarco Veltliner Aristos '03	3 white	4*

Vivaldi - Arunda

via Paese, 53
39010 Meltina/Mölten [BZ]
tel. 0471668033
www.arundavivaldi.it

CELLAR SALES
PRE-BOOKED VISITS

ANNUAL PRODUCTION 90,000 bottles
HECTARES UNDER VINE N.A.
VITICULTURE METHOD Conventional

Joseph Reiterer is the doyen of sparkling wine in Alto Adige. He's also the chairman and a founding member of the Alto Adige Metodo Classico association. The winery is located in Meltina at 1,200 metres and is the highest sparkling wine cellar in Europe, if not the world. The cuvées are available as Arunda, or Vivaldi, depending on whether they are destined for the German-speaking or Italian-speaking market. All feature a high percentage of chardonnay when they are not pure Blanc de Blancs. Lengthy maturation on the lees makes these sparkling wines exceptionally elegant.

Joseph Reiterer's sparkling wines are always flawless. This year we tasted, or rather, relished, a 50-50 pinot nero, chardonnay Spumante Rosé blend with a very floral nose and pleasant, relaxed mouthfeel. The '05 Extra Brut Riserva is an elegant 60-40 blend chardonnay and pinot nero that presents fresh, with an intense mineral quality. Its only defect seems to be a slight lack in structure. The rest of the range is a lot better than average.

⊙ A. A. Spumante Rosé Brut	6
○ A. A. Spumante Extra Brut Arunda Ris. '05	6
⊙ Arunda Reiterer & Reiterer	6
○ A. A. Spumante Brut	5
○ A. A. Spumante Extra Brut Cuvée Marianna	6
○ A. A. Spumante Blanc de Blancs	6
○ A. A. Spumante Extra Brut Arunda Ris. '04	6

Tenuta Waldgries Christian Plattner

loc. Santa Giustina, 2
39100 Bolzano/Bozen
tel. 0471323603
www.waldgries.it

CELLAR SALES
PRE-BOOKED VISITS

ANNUAL PRODUCTION 50,000 bottles
HECTARES UNDER VINE 5
VITICULTURE METHOD Organic

In a few short years, young Christian Plattner has become one of the great names for Lagrein, Alto Adige's best-known red. His exceptionally well-structured Lagreins are modern in style but are also very well typed and harmonious. Christian's Santa Maddalena is one of the region's best and he is in the process of planting a vineyard with the original clones. The beautiful old farmhouse, which is also home to an interesting wine museum, sits squarely on the Santa Maddalena hill.

Despite the difficult 2008 vintage, Waldgries managed to produce an impressive Lagrein Mirell, which was so well made it just had to have Three Glasses. Succulent, minerally and austere, it unveils graphite and damp earth, good acidity and assertive progression. It is still very young but has plenty of wiggle room for improvement. The Santa Maddalena is delicious, as always. The 2009 vintage is particularly complex, which is quite unusual for the type, but not for Christian Plattner. The '09 Sauvignon is astonishing. Christian has dedicated a lot of effort to the wine type, and it shows. Fresh and juicy with nicely understated green notes, it has a unique elegance.

● A. A. Lagrein Scuro Mirell '08	7
● A. A. Lagrein Scuro Ris. '08	6
● A. A. Santa Maddalena Cl. '09	4*
○ A. A. Sauvignon '09	5
● A. A. Lagrein '09	4
● A. A. Moscato Rosa Passito '08	6
● A. A. Lagrein Scuro Mirell '07	7
● A. A. Lagrein Scuro Mirell '01	7
● A. A. Lagrein Scuro Mirell '06	7
● A. A. Moscato Rosa '05	6
● A. A. Moscato Rosa Passito '07	6
● A. A. Santa Maddalena Cl. '08	4*

OTHER WINERIES

Tenuta Baron Di Pauli
VIA CANTINE, 12
39052 CALDARO/KALTERN
TEL. 0471963696
www.barondipauli.com

This is one of the oldest, most beautiful estates around Caldaro. Its wines are modern, yes, but they are also elegant, well typed and aristocratic. The '08 Gewürztraminer Exilissi is powerful and the '09 Lago di Caldaro Kalkofen tasty. The '08 Lagrein Carano is fresh, meaty, minerally and long.

○ A. A. Gewürztraminer Exilissi '08	🍷🍷	7
● A. A. Carano Lagrein '08	🍷🍷	6
● A. A. Lago di Caldaro Cl. Sup. Kalkofen '09	🍷🍷	4

Bessererhof - Otmar Mair
NOVALE DI PRESULE, 10
39050 FIÈ ALLO SCILIAR/
VÖLS AM SCHLERN [BZ]
TEL. 0471601011
www.bessererhof.it

Otmar Mair's estate in Novale di Presule did well again. Bessererhof produces around 30,000 bottles from approximately ten hectares and this year they treated us to possibly the best Alto Adige Chardonnay we tasted. It's juicy, minerally, with well-managed wood and a relaxed, expressive palate.

○ A. A. Chardonnay Ris. '07	🍷🍷	4
○ A. A. Moscato Giallo '09	🍷🍷	4
○ A. A. Pinot Bianco '09	🍷	4

Braunbach
LOC. SETTEQUERCE
VIA PADRE ROMEDIUS, 5
39018 TERLANO/TERLAN [BZ]
TEL. 0471910184
www.braunbach.it

The Braunback farm produces 70,000 bottles from its well-groomed vineyards on the San Genesio hillside in the heart of the Santa Maddalena Classico zone. The '09 Sauvignon Calldiv is austere but savoury and full. The '07 Merlot Calldiv is full and juicy and the '06 Brut spumante is very well made.

● A. A. Merlot Calldiv Siebeneich '07	🍷🍷	5
○ A. A. Sauvignon Calldiv '09	🍷🍷	4
○ A. A. Spumante Von Braunbach Brut Ris. '06	🍷🍷	5

Brunnenhof - Kurt Rottensteiner
LOC. MAZZON
VIA DEGLI ALPINI, 5
39044 EGNA/NEUMARKT [BZ]
TEL. 0471820687
www.brunnenhof-mazzon.it

Kurt Rottensteiner is scrupulous, producing 20,000 bottles from his five-hectare vineyard in Mazzon. He has a veritable passion for Pinot Nero and his '07 Riserva, which is austere to the extreme, promises much. The excellent '09 Gewürztraminer is bursting with style and power.

○ A. A. Gewürztraminer '09	🍷🍷	5
● A. A. Pinot Nero Ris. '07	🍷🍷	6

Ferruccio Carlotto
VIA CLAUSER, 19
39040 ORA/AUER [BZ]
TEL. 0471810407
michelacarlotto@virgilio.it

Michela Carlotto manages her tiny estate with skill, producing just over 10,000 bottles from two hectares of vines. This year we only tried the '07 Pinot Nero Filari di Mazzon. As expected, it is elegant, with fine-grained tannins and an expansive palate.

● A. A. Pinot Nero Filari di Mazzon '07	🍷🍷	5

Castello Rametz
LOC. MAIA ALTA
VIA LABERS, 4
39012 MERANO/MERAN [BZ]
TEL. 0473211011
www.rametz.com

Again this year, the Schmid family's historic estate, which produces around 400,000 bottles per year, proved extremely reliable. The star was a very well-constructed '06 Cabernet Sauvignon, followed by a very convincing '09 Riesling and '07 Chardonnay Cesuret.

● A. A. Cabernet '06	🍷🍷	6
○ A. A. Riesling '09	🍷🍷	4
○ Chardonnay Cesuret '07	🍷🍷	5
○ A. A. Sauvignon '09	🍷	4

Peter Dipoli

LOC. EGNA/NEUMARKT
VIA VILLA, 5
39055 EGNA/NEUMARKT [BZ]
TEL. 0471813400
www.peterdipoli.com

Peter Dipoli is very well-known in the Alto Adige wine world. He is competent, passionate and delightfully argumentative. His '08 Sauvignon Voglar, which was wrongly mentioned in last year's Guide, is wonderfully linear and full of character, which bodes well for cellaring.

- ○ A. A. Sauvignon Voglar '08 ᵧᵧ 5
- ● A. A. Merlot-Cabernet Sauvignon Yugum '05 ᵧᵧ 5

Ebnerhof - Johannes Plattner

FRAZ. CARDANO
LOC. RENON
LASTE BASSE, 21
39053 BOLZANO/BOZEN
TEL. 0471365120
www.ebnerhof.it

The wines of this small organic winery, whose grapes are grown on 2.5 hectares belonging to the Plattner family, are strongly typed, forthright and technically very well made. At last we got to try the '09 Malvasia, which is savoury and very natural. The '09 Santa Maddalena and Sauvignon are as good as ever.

- ○ A. A. Sauvignon '09 ᵧᵧ 4
- ● A. A. Malvasia '09 ᵧᵧ 4
- ● A. A. Santa Maddalena '09 ᵧᵧ 4*

Glassierhof - Stefan Vaja

VIA VILLA, 13
39044 EGNA/NEUMARKT [BZ]
TEL. 3351031673
glassierhof@tin.it

Stefan Vaja's small organic winery in the lower Adige valley, which produces 15,000 bottles annually from 3.2 hectares of vineyards, is making its debut in the Guide. The two '08 reds presented, a Lagrein and a Cabernet Merlot Learn, are not bad, although they still need a bit more bottle time.

- ● A. A. Lagrein '08 ᵧᵧ 5
- ● A. A. Learn '08 ᵧ 5

Gottardi

LOC. MAZZON
VIA DEGLI ALPINI, 17
39044 EGNA/NEUMARKT [BZ]
TEL. 0471812773
www.gottardi-mazzon.com

This estate, which is adored by Alto Adige Pinot Nero aficionados, produces 50,000 bottles annually from nine hectares of vines. The '07 Pinot Nero Mazzon is bright, with silky tannins and unfolds purposefully to a soft finish with its customary elegance.

- ● A. A. Pinot Nero Mazzon '07 ᵧᵧ 6

Griesbauerhof
Georg Mumelter

VIA RENCIO, 66
39100 BOLZANO/BOZEN
TEL. 0471973090
www.tirolensisarsvini.it

It was an erratic year for this famed estate in Bolzano, which produces 35,000 bottles annually from just over three hectares of vines. The '09 Santa Maddalena and Lagrein are well typed and very tasty but the rest of the range is just average, which is rather disappointing for an estate with this kind of history.

- ● A. A. Lagrein '09 ᵧᵧ 4
- ● A. A. Santa Maddalena Cl. '09 ᵧᵧ 3*
- ● Isarcus '08 ᵧ 4

Happacherhof
Istituto Tecnico Agrario Ora

VIA DEL CASTELLO, 10
39040 ORA/AUER [BZ]
TEL. 0471810538
www.ofl-auer.it

This small organic estate, which is tied to the agricultural college at Ora, produces around 20,000 bottles annually. The range is well managed and the wines are very well typed. The '08 Lagrein Riserva and Merlot are both well made and worthy of mention.

- ● A. A. Lagrein Bioland Ris. '08 ᵧᵧ 5
- ● A. A. Merlot '08 ᵧᵧ 4

OTHER WINERIES

Kettmeir

via delle Cantine, 4
39052 Caldaro/Kaltern [BZ]
tel. 0471963135
www.kettmeir.com

The Kettmeir estate was founded in 1919 by Giuseppe Kettmeir. It is situated on the vine-clad hills above Caldaro and was incorporated into the Santa Margherita group several years ago. The '08 Chardonnay Reinerhof and '09 Pinot Bianco are very convincing, as is the sparkling Brut Athesis.

O A. A. Pinot Bianco '09	🍷🍷	4*
O A. A. Chardonnay Reinerhof '08	🍷🍷	5
O A. A. Müller Thurgau Athesis '09	🍷	5
O A. A. Spumante Brut Athesis	🍷	5

Kössler

via Castel Guardia, 21
39050 Appiano/Eppan [BZ]
tel. 0471662183
www.koessler.it

Kössler is owned by the Cantina Sociale di San Paolo and produces around 200,000 bottles a year, all of which are of medium to high quality, starting with the '09 Lagrein and Pinot Nero, which are particularly fresh and juicy. Among the whites, we liked the '09 Pinot Bianco and Pinot Grigio.

● A. A. Lagrein '09	🍷🍷	4
● A. A. Pinot Nero '09	🍷🍷	4
O A. A. Pinot Bianco '09	🍷	4
O A. A. Pinot Grigio '09	🍷	4

Kupelwieser

s.da del Vino, 24
39040 Cortina/Kurtinig [BZ]
tel. 0471809240
www.kupelwieser.it

This estate in Cortina produces approximately 80,000 bottles annually from ten hectares and has a strong reputation for quality. The honours lists is headed by a wonderfully fresh, elegant and leisurely '09 Sauvignon. The fresh-tasting, crisp floral '09 Müller Thurgau is particularly successful.

O A. A. Müller Thurgau Intenditore '09	🍷🍷	5
O A. A. Sauvignon Intenditore '09	🍷🍷	5
● A. A. Lagrein Intenditore '08	🍷	5

Alois Lageder

v.lo dei Conti, 9
39040 Magrè/Margreid [BZ]
tel. 0471809500
www.aloislageder.eu

Alois Lageder took Alto Adige wines to the world and this year has made a return to the Guide. His near-legendary Chardonnay Löwengang and Cabernet Sauvignon Cor Römigberg are once again gracing our pages. Other than these two, the Pinot Bianco Haberle also shone.

O A. A. Chardonnay Löwengang '07	🍷🍷	7
O A. A. Pinot Bianco Haberle '09	🍷🍷	5
● A. A. Cabernet Sauvignon Cor Römigberg '05	🍷🍷	8

Lieselehof - Werner Morandell

via Kardatsch, 6
39052 Caldaro/Kaltern [BZ]
tel. 0471965060
www.lieselehof.com

The two-hectare Liesele farm is one of the most interesting in the area. Werner Morandell farms organically and keeps experimental high-altitude plots planted with rare varieties. From the 10,000-odd bottles released, Sweet Claire from bronner, the '09 Gewürztraminer and Pinot Bianco are interesting.

O Julian '09	🍷🍷	4
O Sweet Claire '08	🍷🍷	7
O Gewürztraminer '09	🍷	5
O Pinot Bianco '09	🍷	4

Marinushof - Heinrich Pohl

s.da Vecchia, 9b
39020 Castelbello Ciardes/
Kastelbell Tschars [BZ]
tel. 0473624717
www.marinushof.it

The tiny Marinus farmstead is owned by Sabrina and Heiner Pohl. They cultivate less than a hectare of vines and produce just 5,000 bottles annually, all in the Valle Venosta style. The highlights this year are the exceptional '09 Pinot Bianco, Pinot Grigio, and Pinot Nero Rosé, and '09 Pinot Nero.

O A.A. Valle Venosta Pinot Bianco '09	🍷🍷	4
O A.A. Valle Venosta Pinot Grigio '09	🍷🍷	4*
● A.A. Valle Venosta Pinot Nero '08	🍷🍷	5
⊙ A.A. Valle Venosta Pinot Nero Rosé '09	🍷🍷	4

OTHER WINERIES

Lorenz Martini
LOC. CORNAIANO/GIRLAN
VIA PRANZOL, 2D
39057 APPIANO/EPPAN [BZ]
TEL. 0471664136
www.lorenz-martini.it

Lorenz Martini loves the classic method and since 1985 has allocated some of each harvest to sparkling wines. His Comitissa is a 50-50 pinot bianco and chardonnay blend. Around 15,000 bottles of the excellent Brut Riserva, aged for 40 months on the lees, are made each year. We tasted the '06.

○ A. A. Spumante Comitissa Brut Ris. '06	🍷🍷 6

Maso Thaler
VIA GLENO, 59
39040 MONTAGNA/MONTAN [BZ]
TEL. 0471819928
www.masothaler.it

Maso Thaler is a small estate in the lower Adige valley that produces 12,000 bottles a year from 3.5 hectares at between 630 and 720 metres above sea level. This year, we enjoyed the delicious '08 Pinot Nero, which is clean, elegant and very drinkable.

● A. A. Pinot Nero '08	🍷🍷 5

Messnerhof - Bernhard Pichler
LOC. SAN PIETRO, 7
39100 BOLZANO/BOZEN
TEL. 0471977162
www.messnerhof.net

Skilled winemaker Bernhard Pichler has been running his three-hectare estate since 1993 and produces around 15,000 bottles a year. His '09 Terlano Sauvignon is elegant and minerally while the Santa Maddalena of the same year is floral, beguiling and very drinkable.

● A. A. Santa Maddalena Cl. '09	🍷🍷 4
○ A. A. Terlano Sauvignon '09	🍷🍷 4

Ignaz Niedrist
LOC. CORNAIANO/GIRLAN
VIA RONCO, 5
39050 APPIANO/EPPAN [BZ]
TEL. 0471664494
ignazniedrist@rdmail.net

This year sees the return of a major figure in Alto Adige wine. Ignaz Niedrist was one of the first to go seriously for quality. His range is quite excellent, headed by the '07 Lagrein Berger Gei, which is close-knit and exceptionally stylish. The '09 Riesling and Pinot Bianco are also good, as is the '08 Pinot Nero.

● A. A. Lagrein Berger Gei '07	🍷🍷 5
● A. A. Pinot Nero '08	🍷🍷 5
○ A. A. Riesling Renano '09	🍷🍷 4*
○ A. A. Terlano Pinot Bianco '09	🍷🍷 4*

Nusserhof - Heinrich Mayr
VIA MAYR NUSSER, 72
39100 BOLZANO/BOZEN
TEL. 0471978388

Nusserhof, which means "hazelnut farm" is a small walled vineyard. The farm is entirely enclosed within stone walls and produces wines with a lot of character using traditional methods and a uniquely personal style. The '06 Lagrein Riserva and hard to find white '09 Blaterle are both characterful.

○ A. A. Blaterle '09	🍷🍷 4
● A. A. Lagrein Scuro Ris. '06	🍷🍷 5
● Elda	🍷 5

Obermoser H. & T. Rottensteiner
FRAZ. RENCIO
VIA SANTA MADDALENA, 35
39100 BOLZANO/BOZEN
TEL. 0471973549
www.obermoser.it

This small estate at Rencio near Bolzano produces consistently good wines. Heinrich Rottensteiner and his son Thomas obtain just 30,000 bottles from little over three hectares of vineyards. Their '07 Lagrein Grafenleiten Riserva is fabulous and one of the best of its vintage.

● A. A. Lagrein Scuro Grafenleiten Ris. '07	🍷🍷 5
● A. A. Lagrein '09	🍷🍷 4*
● A. A. Santa Maddalena Cl. '09	🍷🍷 4

Oberrautner - Anton Schmid

FRAZ. GRIES
VIA M. PACHER, 3
39100 BOLZANO/BOZEN
TEL. 0471281440
www.schmid.bz

Schmid Oberrautner is a typical family-run Alto Adige wine estate and is headed by Andreas Schmid and his son Florian. The location is Gries, in the heart of the Lagrein production zone, and Florian set his heart on making typical local wines that are both drinkable and reasonably priced.

● A. A. Lagrein Scuro Grieser '09	🍷🍷	4*
● A. A. Lagrein Scuro Villa Schmid '08	🍷🍷	4
● A. A. Santa Maddalena Steinbauer '09	🍷🍷	4*
● A. A. Merlot Tulledro '09	🍷	4

Tenuta Pfitscherhof Klaus Pfitscher

VIA GLENO, 9
39040 MONTAGNA/MONTAN [BZ]
TEL. 0471819773
www.pfitscher.it

The small Ansiz Pfitscher family estate in Montagna is skilfully managed by Klaus Pfitscher and obtains 50,000 bottles from five and a half hectares. This year, we point out the great '07 vintage of Pinot Nero Matan and a very good '09 Schiava Grigia Alter Stoass.

● A. A. Pinot Nero Matan '07	🍷🍷	6
● Cortazo '07	🍷🍷	6
● A. A. Schiava Grigia Alter Stoass '09	🍷	4

Thomas Pichler

VIA DELLE VIGNE, 4
39052 CALDARO/KALTERN [BZ]
TEL. 0471963094
www.thomas-pichler.it

This tiny estate in the Caldaro area has less than one hectare under vine and produces approximately 7,000 bottles a year. The uniquely savoury, elegant '09 Lago di Caldaro Olte Rebe is from grapes harvested in a vineyard over 70 years old and the '08 Lagrein Riserva Sond is fresh, with a pleasant huskiness.

● A. A. Lago di Caldaro Olte Reben '09	🍷🍷	4*
● A. A. Lagrein Sond Ris. '08	🍷🍷	5

Prälatenhof - Roland Rohregger

PIANIZZA DI SOTTO, 15A
39052 CALDARO/KALTERN
TEL. 0471962541
www.paelatenhof.it

Prälatenhof's Lago di Caldaro is simply one of the best we have ever tried. The estate makes a total of 15,000 bottles from two and a half hectares, which sadly included a mere 2,500 bottles of the splendid '09 Lago di Caldaro. A lucky few will be able to savour it. The '09 Sauvignon is also good.

● A. A. Lago Di Caldaro Cl. Sup. '09	🍷🍷	4*
○ A. A. Sauvignon Blanc '09	🍷	5

Walter Schullian

LOC. KALTERER HOEHE, 4
39052 CALDARO/KALTERN
TEL. 0471964858
www.lacus-wein.com

Walter Schullian, the legendary cellarmaster of Prima & Nuova, has set up his own small estate at Caldaro and is currently producing two reds. Lacus and Lacus Selection are Bordeaux blends whose first '08 vintage impressed us immensely.

● Lacus '08	🍷🍷	7
● Lacus Sel. '08	🍷🍷	8

Steinhauserhof Oxenreiter

LOC. POCHI, 37
39040 SALORNO/SALURN [BZ]
TEL. 0471889031
www.oxenreiter.net

This estate in the lower Adige valley is run by Anton Ochsenreiter and releases around 45,000 bottles from seven hectares of vines. In a bold comeback this year, it blew us away with the '09 Gewürztraminer and the Sauvignon Selection, both of which are incredibly well made.

○ A. A. Gewürztraminer Sel. '09	🍷🍷	6
○ A. A. Sauvignon Sel. '09	🍷🍷	5

OTHER WINERIES

Villscheiderhof - Florian Hilpold

PIAN DI SOTTO, 13
39042 BRESSANONE/BRIXEN [BZ]
TEL. 0472832037
villscheider@akfree.it

The Hilpold family manages this small farmstead in Valle Isarco with passion, producing under 5,000 bottles from one and a half hectares. The wines are powerful and rich but well balanced. The two Gewürztraminers – the '09 and the late-harvest '08 – are very interesting. The Sylvaner and Kerner are also nice.

○ A. A. Valle Isarco Gewürztraminer '09	🍷🍷	5
○ A. A. Valle Isarco Gewürztraminer VT '08	🍷🍷	5
○ A. A. Valle Isarco Kerner '09	🍷🍷	5
○ A. A. Valle Isarco Sylvaner '09	🍷🍷	4

Karl Vonklausner

VIA CASTELLANO, 30A
39042 BRESSANONE/BRIXEN [BZ]
TEL. 0472833700
www.vonklausner.it

This small estate in Valle Isarco farms two hectares of vineyards on the northern outskirts of Bressanone. Christian Vonklausner produced two particularly interesting wines this year, the '09 Sylvaner and Gewürztraminer. Both have exceptional elegance and are very well typed.

○ A.A. Sylvaner '09	🍷🍷	4*
○ A.A. Valle Isarco Gewürztraminer '09	🍷	4

Wilhelm Walch

VIA A. HOFER, 1
39040 TERMENO/TRAMIN [BZ]
TEL. 0471860103
www.walch.it

Wilhelm Walch's wines are a sure bet. The 600,000 bottles produced from 75 hectares of estate-owned and leased vines are sold at very good prices. We picked out a deliciously juicy, savoury '09 Lagrein and the very successful '09 Müller Thurgau and Schiava Grigia Plattensteig.

● A. A. Lagrein '09	🍷🍷	4*
○ A. A. Müller Thurgau '09	🍷🍷	3*
● A. A. Schiava Grigia Plattensteig '09	🍷🍷	4*
○ A. A. Pinot Bianco '09	🍷	4

Alois Warasin

LOC. CORNAIANO/GIRLAN
VIA COLTERENZIO, 1
39047 APPIANO/EPPAN [BZ]
TEL. 0471662462
weine.a.warasin@rolmail.net

This four-hectare estate at Cornaiano turns out 10,000 bottles a year. This time, the wines positively shone. The splendid '09 Sauvignon is stylish and vibrant, as usual. The '08 Pinot Nero Riserva is elegant and very pleasant and the '09 Schiav Schreckbichler and Pinot Bianco are very well made.

● A.A. Pinot Nero Ris. '08	🍷🍷	5
○ A.A. Sauvignon '09	🍷🍷	5
● A.A. Schiava Schreckbichler '09	🍷🍷	4
○ A.A. Pinot Bianco '09	🍷	5

Josef Weger

LOC. CORNAIANO
VIA CASA DEL GESÙ, 17
39050 APPIANO/EPPAN [BZ]
TEL. 0471662416
www.wegerhof.it

This Cornaiano winery produces 80,000 bottles a year. The series of great wines starts with the magnificent '09 Gewürztraminer Maso delle Rose and a vibrant, stylish '09 Pinot Bianco. The '05 Passito Rodon from part-dried gewürztraminer, pinot bianco, pinot grigio and sauvignon grapes is also terrific.

○ A. A. Gewürztraminer Maso delle Rose '09	🍷🍷	5
○ A. A. Pinot Bianco '09	🍷🍷	4*
○ Rodon Maso delle Rose '05	🍷🍷	6
● A. A. Lagrein '08	🍷	4

Peter Zemmer

S.DA DEL VINO, 24
39040 CORTINA/KURTINIG [BZ]
TEL. 0471817143
www.peterzemmer.com

The estate run by Helmuth Zemmer has maintained a high standard of quality for many years. This time, we want to highlight the stylishly savoury '07 Lagrein Reserve, which is excellent. The '09 Gewürztraminer Reserve is very well constructed, as is the '09 Pinot Bianco La Lot.

● A. A. Lagrein Reserve '07	🍷🍷	5
○ A. A. Gewürztraminer Reserve '09	🍷🍷	5
○ A. A. Pinot Bianco La Lot '09	🍷🍷	4
○ A. A. Chardonnay Reserve '08	🍷	5

VENETO

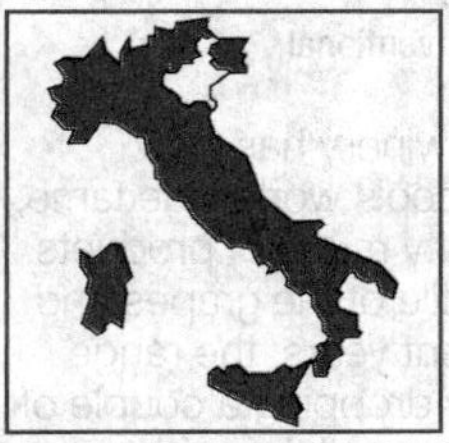

There's plenty of news from Veneto this year, and not just about prize-winning wineries and production areas. The headline grabber comes from the zones of Valpolicella, Asolo and Conegliano-Valdobbiadene, which have achieved the coveted DOCG status. Their stories are very different. In the first case two wines, Amarone and Recioto, have completed the journey they began many years ago and now take up their rightful positions at the very peak of Italian wine production. In the second instance, a wine – or more specifically an area – has achieved a result. The prosecco grape is no more and we can now only refer to it as glera, leaving room for a four-level designation. Prosecco and Prosecco di Treviso remain as DOC areas, leaving the "G" to Asolo – the former Prosecco del Montello and Colli Asolani DOCs – and Conegliano-Valdobbiadene, within which area the labels will also indicate leading subzones, such as the famous Cartizze or the lesser known but potential-rich Rive. These successful DOC zones also met with the approval of our tasting panels, reaping a plentiful crop of Three Glasses. In Valdobbiadene Nino Franco repeated his success, Villa Sandi's Cartizze Brut asserted its quality and Ruggeri made a comeback while Amarone is the region's locomotive. This style's driving power, based on the solid foundations of wineries that have been at the top for years, such as Allegrini, Speri or Tenuta Sant'Antonio, was enhanced this year by the new entry of Fattoria Garbole. The Valpolicellas were also on excellent form, and Marion is fast becoming this wine's most representative producer. Turning to white wines, we report an outstanding triple success for Custoza as Monte del Frà enters the region's elite. However Verona is not the only province with great quality. Colli Berici has taken off at last with a gorgeous Cabernet from Tommaso Piovene's winery while the Colli Euganei designation made its presence felt with an impressive, increasingly broad range. La Montecchia's Ireneo lined up alongside Filò delle Vigne, entering the Veneto Three Glass club with an extraordinary Cabernet. The now-classic zones like Soave, which retains its position as leading white production zone, include peaks of excellence such as Montello, with Serafini & Vidotto, and Breganze where the cousins Zonta seem unable to put a foot wrong. Lastly, Angiolino Maule, one of the greatest exponents of sustainable viticulture, thrashed the competition with a memorable Recioto di Gambellara.

Stefano Accordini

LOC. PEDEMONTE
VIA ALBERTO BOLLA, 9
37020 SAN PIETRO IN CARIANO [VR]
TEL. 0457701733
www.accordinistefano.it

CELLAR SALES
PRE-BOOKED VISITS

ANNUAL PRODUCTION 40,000 bottles
HECTARES UNDER VINE 11
VITICULTURE METHOD Conventional

At last the Accordinis' new winery sees the light in Mazzurega, with its first harvest this year. The building blends nicely into the surrounding hillside and environmental impact was an important factor in its design, from energy consumption to water recycling. These concerns begin in the vineyards: over the years long-abandoned "marogne", or dry-stone walls, and slopes have been recovered, providing this enchanting area with a more vibrant image and grapes of unquestionable high quality.

These grapes are transformed into an absolutely sound range of wines, in which the Amarone Acinatico '06 and its twin Recioto '07 stand out for their sensory expression. The former shows appreciable crisp, substantial fruit, its firm structure offset by mouthwatering acidity. The latter is more approachable and exuberant, and again the acidity of the traditional grapes adds lightness. The Valpolicella Ripasso '08 stands out for its harmony, while the Passo Rosso '08, a corvina-based blend with a touch of rondinella and Bordeaux varieties, shows firm, gutsy structure.

● Amarone della Valpolicella Cl. Acinatico '06	2 black glasses	8
● Recioto della Valpolicella Cl. Acinatico '07	2 black glasses	7
● Passo Rosso '08	2 black glasses	5
● Valpolicella Cl. Sup. Ripasso Acinatico '08	2 black glasses	6
● Valpolicella Cl. '09	1 black glass	4
● Amarone della Valpolicella Cl. Vign. Il Fornetto '95	3 white glasses	8
● Recioto della Valpolicella Cl. Acinatico '04	3 white glasses	7
● Recioto della Valpolicella Cl. Acinatico '00	3 white glasses	7
● Amarone della Valpolicella Cl. Acinatico '05	2 white glasses	8
● Amarone della Valpolicella Cl. Acinatico '04	2 white glasses	8
● Amarone della Valpolicella Cl. Acinatico '03	2 white glasses	8
● Passo Rosso '07	2 white glasses	6
● Recioto della Valpolicella Cl. Acinatico '06	2 white glasses	7
● Valpolicella Cl. Sup. Ripasso Acinatico '06	2 white glasses	5

Adami

FRAZ. COLBERTALDO
VIA ROVEDE, 27
31020 VIDOR [TV]
TEL. 0423982110
www.adamispumanti.it

CELLAR SALES
PRE-BOOKED VISITS

ANNUAL PRODUCTION 550,000 bottles
HECTARES UNDER VINE 11
VITICULTURE METHOD Conventional

The Adami brothers' winery has contributed to Prosecco's worldwide fame, thanks to a high-quality range of products that respects the profile of the grapes and the local area. In recent years, the range has been reduced by dropping a couple of labels, the Brut Waldaz and the Incrocio Manzoni, which somehow distracted attention from the more important Prosecco. Today, the product list focuses exclusively on the traditional local grape variety in all its variations interpretations.

On top form, naturally, are the wines from Valdobbiadene, in the new DOCG zone, in particular the Vigneto Giardino, the traditional family cru which never fails to express its class. The 2009 harvest has imbued the wine with a subtly floral hint, dotted with wisteria and lime, followed by a mouthwatering sensation of white-fleshed fruits. On the palate, there is a perfect blend of fizz, sugar and acidity. The Cartizze is very good, with its tropical, aromatic note, while the Bosco di Gica and Extra Dry Dei Casel, all '09, as ever are some of the most dependably fine wines of the whole designation.

○ Valdobbiadene Rive di Colbertaldo Vign. Giardino Dry '09	2 black glasses	4*
○ Cartizze '09	2 black glasses	5
○ Valdobbiadene Bosco di Gica Brut '09	2 black glasses	4*
○ Valdobbiadene Extra Dry Dei Casel '09	2 black glasses	4*
○ Treviso Garbèl Brut	1 black glass	4
○ Valdobbiadene Tranquillo Giardino '09	1 black glass	4
○ P. Frizzante di Treviso	1 black glass	4
○ Valdobbiadene Dry Vign. Giardino '08	2 white glasses	4*

Ida Agnoletti

LOC. SELVA DEL MONTELLO
VIA SACCARDO, 55
31040 VOLPAGO DEL MONTELLO [TV]
TEL. 0423620947
ettore.agnoletti@virgilio.it

CELLAR SALES
PRE-BOOKED VISITS

ANNUAL PRODUCTION 50,000 bottles
HECTARES UNDER VINE 6
VITICULTURE METHOD Conventional

Montello is a special place: a long, narrow, east-west strip of hillside enjoying the benefits of both sea and Alps, which provide a varied climate and endow its wines with a strong identity. The wines produced by Ida Agnoletti, who has run this little Selva del Montello winery for years with passion and perseverance, are no exception. The vineyards are situated on the southern foothills in an ideal location for the cultivation of the Bordeaux varieties which are her specialty.

The leading wine, Seneca '07, sourced from an old vineyard, impresses as usual with its subtle, never overstated range of aromas themed around a weave of fruit and aromatic herbs. The palate is light and taut. The more international and exuberant Ludwy '07 shows excellent texture. The two Merlots, '08 and La Ida '08, are also good. The former is more classic in style with strong hints of fines herbes and a firm, very straightforward palate. The other is warmer, more mature, and balanced, with a rich tangy flavour.

● Ludwy '07	▼▼	4*
● Montello e Colli Asolani Merlot '08	▼▼	3*
● Montello e Colli Asolani Merlot La Ida '08	▼▼	3*
● Seneca '07	▼▼	4*
○ Manzoni Bianco '08	▼	3
● Montello e Colli Asolani Cabernet Sauvignon '08	▼	3
○ Prosecco Frizzante P.S.L.	▼	3
● Ludwy '06	▽▽	4*
● Ludwy '05	▽▽	4
● Montello e Colli Asolani Merlot '07	▽▽	3*
● Seneca '06	▽▽	4*
● Seneca '05	▽▽	4

★★ Allegrini

VIA GIARE, 5
37022 FUMANE [VR]
TEL. 0456832011
www.allegrini.it

CELLAR SALES
PRE-BOOKED VISITS

ANNUAL PRODUCTION 900,000 bottles
HECTARES UNDER VINE 120
VITICULTURE METHOD Conventional

Although the Allegrini brothers' estate has always consisted of prestigious vineyards, they continue to invest in land, recovering high hillsides abandoned in the post-war period. The estate can thus guarantee stylishly fragrant, very high-quality grapes while safeguarding these forgotten hills by restoring the "marogne" dry-stone walls, as they have recently in the Mazzurega area, where the new ten-hectare vineyard continues a project begun at La Grola.

The wines give their usual classy performance with faultless interpretations of a still-strong tradition. Three pedigree champs lead the field, with a uniquely sound Amarone '06, firmly structured and sustained by masses of savouriness. Three Glasses. The '06 La Poja is a perfect blend of corvina fruit and solid Valpolicella structure with acidity and soft, smooth tannins. The Recioto '07 is an exuberant, fruity explosion with evident but nicely integrated sweetness. Alongside the traditional range we also recommend the interesting Bardolino '09.

● Amarone della Valpolicella Cl. '06	▼▼▼	8
● La Poja '06	▼▼	8
● Recioto della Valpolicella Cl. '07	▼▼	7
● Bardolino Cl. Le Barbere Naiano '09	▼▼	4*
● La Grola '07	▼▼	5
● Palazzo della Torre '07	▼▼	5
○ Soave '09	▼▼	4
● Valpolicella Cl. '09	▼▼	4*
● Amarone della Valpolicella Cl. '05	▽▽▽	8
● Amarone della Valpolicella Cl. '04	▽▽▽	8
● Amarone della Valpolicella Cl. '03	▽▽▽	8
● Amarone della Valpolicella Cl. '01	▽▽▽	8
● Amarone della Valpolicella Cl. '00	▽▽▽	8
● Amarone della Valpolicella Cl. '98	▽▽▽	8
● Amarone della Valpolicella Cl. '97	▽▽▽	8
● Amarone della Valpolicella Cl. '96	▽▽▽	8

Andreola Orsola

LOC. COL SAN MARTINO
VIA CAL LONGA, 52
31010 FARRA DI SOLIGO [TV]
TEL. 0438989379
www.andreolaorsola.it

CELLAR SALES
PRE-BOOKED VISITS

ANNUAL PRODUCTION 400,000 bottles
HECTARES UNDER VINE 20
VITICULTURE METHOD Conventional

The Andreola Orsola estate covers about 20 hillside hectares between Valdobbiadene and Conegliano, an area which has always produced mainly Prosecco as well as still. Naturally glera is Andreola's most widely vinified variety, interpreted in all the possible ways allowed by the production protocols for both the DOC and the new DOCG. As well as glera, the cellar is recovering the almost entirely abandoned native verdiso variety, which is also carving itself a significant niche.

The range is extensive although it has been rationalized with the advent of the new DOCG. Leading the field are four DOCG wines, including the fragrant, pear and wisteria-themed Cartizze, which we consider the best. Hot on its heels are the Brut and Extra Dry Dirupo. The former has more punch, thanks to lower sugar content, while the other is more stylish with a subtler flavour. The new Verv products, from vineyards in the province of Treviso, are simpler and more approachable. The list also includes some IGT wines.

O Cartizze	ΨΨ	6
O Valdobbiadene Brut Vign. Dirupo	ΨΨ	4
O Valdobbiadene Extra Dry Vign. Dirupo	ΨΨ	4
O Bollè Extra Dry	Ψ	4
O Treviso Verv Brut	Ψ	4
O Treviso Verv Extra Dry	Ψ	4
O Valdobbiadene Dry Mill. '09	Ψ	4
O Valdobbiadene Tranquillo Romit '09	Ψ	4
O Verdiso '09	Ψ	3

★ Roberto Anselmi

VIA SAN CARLO, 46
37032 MONTEFORTE D'ALPONE [VR]
TEL. 0457611488
www.anselmi.eu

CELLAR SALES
PRE-BOOKED VISITS

ANNUAL PRODUCTION 700,000 bottles
HECTARES UNDER VINE 70
VITICULTURE METHOD Conventional

Few producers have succeeded in representing an area the way Roberto Anselmi has since he took over the family estate. Today, over a decade since he emerged from the Soave DOC, his wines are still synonymous with fine quality and a benchmark for the whole zone. Anselmi's profound knowledge of everything to do with the winemaking sector, not only in production terms, enables him to make shrewd and often far-sighted decisions.

The well-established range is led by an excellent '08 version of Capitel Croce, a stylish white with a racy palate. The Capitel Foscarino '09, aged entirely in stainless steel, gives not just the usual broad range of sophisticated aromas but also an assertively gutsy, tangy flavour. The '09 San Vincenzo is a highly versatile white which tempts occasional drinkers and experienced tasters alike with its simplicity, flaunting a sophisticated fruity nose and a juicy, engaging palate.

O Capitel Croce '08	ΨΨ	5
O Capitel Foscarino '09	ΨΨ	4
O San Vincenzo '09	ΨΨ	4*
O Capitel Croce '06	ΨΨΨ	5
O Capitel Croce '05	ΨΨΨ	5
O Capitel Croce '04	ΨΨΨ	5
O Capitel Croce '03	ΨΨΨ	5
O Capitel Croce '02	ΨΨΨ	5
O Capitel Croce '01	ΨΨΨ	5
O Capitel Croce '00	ΨΨΨ	5
O Capitel Croce '99	ΨΨΨ	5
O Capitel Croce '07	ΨΨ	5
O Capitel Foscarino '07	ΨΨ	4*

Antolini

via Prognol, 22
37020 Marano di Valpolicella [VR]
tel. 0457755351
www.antolinivini.it

CELLAR SALES
PRE-BOOKED VISITS

ANNUAL PRODUCTION 40,000 bottles
HECTARES UNDER VINE 9
VITICULTURE METHOD Conventional

We are glad to welcome this estate's impressive entry to the Guide, demonstrating that the vitality of the Valpolicella zone can always produce interesting new wineries. We have tasted Antolini wines for years and believe they have finally achieved excellence. Since the early 1990s, brothers Pier Paolo and Stefano have scrupulously farmed nine hectares of hillside vineyards in the municipal areas of Marano, San Pietro in Cariano and Negrar, inspired by tradition and seeking to promote the local identity.

The Amarone '06, made from grapes grown in the Moròpio vineyard at an altitude of 350 metres on clayey land with no irrigation, impressed us with excellent tannins which enhance the wine's harmony and balance. The Amarone '06 from Ca' Coato, a Guyot-trained vineyard, unlike the rest which use the double pergola system, still lacks harmony on the nose but the palate is impressive both for its considerable texture and the balance. The rest of the range is characterized by a certain husky quality on the nose followed by vibrant progression on the palate.

● Amarone della Valpolicella Cl. Moròpio '06	TT	6
● Amarone della Valpolicella Cl. Ca' Coato '06	TT	7
● Recioto della Valpolicella Cl. '07	TT	5
● Valpolicella Cl. Sup. Ripasso '08	TT	4
● Theobroma '07	T	4
● Valpolicella Cl. '08	T	4
● Amarone della Valpolicella Cl. '04	YY	7
● Amarone della Valpolicella Cl. '03	YY	7
● Recioto della Valpolicella Cl. '06	YY	5

Balestri Valda

via Monti, 44
37038 Soave [VR]
tel. 0457675393
www.vinibalestrivalda.com

CELLAR SALES
PRE-BOOKED VISITS

ANNUAL PRODUCTION 50,000 bottles
HECTARES UNDER VINE 13
VITICULTURE METHOD Conventional

By now one of the leading names in the Soave zone, the Rizzotto family estate exports the whole world with increasing assurance and rock-solid quality. The strength of this range, which naturally focuses on Soave, is rooted in a moderately sized estate with vineyards situated in some of the designation's most interesting zones below Castelcerino, where Guido and his daughter Laura grow the grapes for the three whites, all characteristically subtle rather than strongly flavoured.

The Soave Classico '09 is a good white which combines fresh aromas with a dry, nicely structured palate. The Sengialta '09 and Lunalonga '08 are even more impressive. The former, barrel-aged, has fresh, floral and white-fleshed fruit aromas with a supple, nicely lingering palate. The other is barrique aged and on top form thanks to considerable breadth on the nose and a dry, sophisticated flavour. Turning to the sweet wines, we note a good performance from the Recioto di Soave Classico '07.

○ Soave Cl. Lunalonga '08	TT	4*
○ Soave Cl. Sengialta '09	TT	4*
○ Soave Cl. '09	TT	4
○ Recioto di Soave Cl. '07	T	6
○ Recioto di Soave Spumante '06	T	4
○ Soave Cl. '08	YY	4*
○ Soave Cl. '07	YY	4
○ Soave Cl. '06	YY	4
○ Soave Cl. '05	YY	3*
○ Soave Cl. Lunalonga '06	YY	4
○ Soave Cl. Lunalonga '05	YY	4
○ Soave Cl. Sengialta '08	YY	4*
○ Soave Cl. Sengialta '07	YY	4
○ Soave Cl. Sengialta '04	YY	4

Barollo

VIA RIO SERVA, 4B
35123 PREGANZIOL [TV]
TEL. 0422633014
www.barollo.com

PRE-BOOKED VISITS

ANNUAL PRODUCTION 50,000 bottles
HECTARES UNDER VINE 28
VITICULTURE METHOD Conventional

This young estate, founded about ten years ago, is passionately and capably managed by Nicola and Marco Barollo in Preganziol, in the Piave DOC zone, where they have carried forward a significant challenge. Their decision to work with leading agronomists and oenologists from the very first year of business has enabled them to make swift progress in the quality stakes, which was very clear from our tastings of their range.

Although quantities are still limited, the wines are split across a fairly wide range, with current vintage wines prominent, whites in particular. The most impressive wine, though, is Frank '08, a red based, predictably enough, on cabernet franc with fresh red berry aromas and a nice spicy character. The beautifully harmonious, balanced palate is juicy with smooth tannins. From the whites, we recommend the interesting '09 Pinot Grigio, which has a pleasantly approachable and performs best on the palate, which has good grip and a mouthwatering flavour.

● Frank '08	▼▼	5
○ Pinot Bianco '09	▼▼	5
○ Pinot Grigio '09	▼▼	5
○ Frater Bianco '09	▼	4
● Frater Rosso '09	▼	4
○ Manzoni Bianco '09	▼	5
○ Vintage Zero '08	▼	5
● Piave Merlot '04	▽▽	5
● Piave Merlot '03	▽▽	5
○ Pinot Bianco '08	▽▽	4
○ Pinot Grigio '08	▽▽	4
○ Pinot Grigio '05	▽▽	4

Cantina Beato Bartolomeo da Breganze

VIA ROMA, 100
36042 BREGANZE [VI]
TEL. 0445873112
www.cantinabreganze.it

CELLAR SALES
PRE-BOOKED VISITS

ANNUAL PRODUCTION 3,500,000 bottles
HECTARES UNDER VINE 8
VITICULTURE METHOD Conventional

Within a smallish DOC zone like Breganze, it was to be expected that a co-operative winery would play an even more important role than elsewhere. Over the last few years, the co-operative cellar in Via Roma has secured such a role in both quantity and quality terms. The journey has not been easy but today the winery offers products of absolute value with deep local roots. Credit is shared by executives and members who have joined forces in steering the winery towards top-quality products.

A very impressive performance from the '07 Kilò Riserva, a Cabernet with red berries and aromatic herbs on the nose, beautifully reflected on the palate with its long, mouthwatering flavour. The winery's strong point consists of two '07 Torcolatos: Bosco Grande is a very elegant interpretation with perfectly balanced sweetness; and a more engaging classic version with pleasingly husky progression. The Cabernet Bosco Grande '07 is coming on. It's from a franc clone that gives red berries and spice on the nose and a rounded, nicely supple palate.

● Breganze Cabernet Kilò Ris. '07	▼▼	5
● Breganze Cabernet Sup. Bosco Grande '07	▼▼	4
○ Breganze Torcolato '07	▼▼	6
○ Breganze Torcolato Bosco Grande Ris. '07	▼▼	5
○ Breganze Bianco Savardo '09	▼	4
● Breganze Cabernet Sup. Savardo '08	▼	4
○ Breganze Chardonnay Sup. Bosco Grande '08	▼	4
○ Breganze Vespaiolo Sup. Savardo '09	▼	4
○ Dolce San Giorgio	▼	4
● Ezzelino Rosso Passito '08	▼	5
● Breganze Cabernet Kilò Ris. '06	▽▽	5
● Breganze Cabernet Sup. Bosco Grande '06	▽▽	5
○ Breganze Torcolato '06	▽▽	6
○ Breganze Torcolato Bosco Grande Ris. '06	▽▽	5

Lorenzo Begali

VIA CENGIA, 10
37020 SAN PIETRO IN CARIANO [VR]
TEL. 0457725148
www.begaliwine.it

CELLAR SALES
PRE-BOOKED VISITS

ANNUAL PRODUCTION **60,000 bottles**
HECTARES UNDER VINE **8**
VITICULTURE METHOD **Conventional**

In ten years, Begali has become a truly iconic winery for its DOC – although it has retained its no-nonsense country soul. Just under ten hectares of vineyards surround the winery, partly on the plain and the rest on the east-facing hillside of Castelrotto, Ca' Bianca. Despite its small size, the winery has space for all production activities, with drying on the first floor, fermentation on the ground floor and ageing in small and medium-sized wood in the cellar below.

The wonderful Amarone Vigneto Monte Ca' Bianca '05 benefits from the cool vintage year to present a broad, sophisticated range of aromas. The palate is even more impressive and shows rare class, with cushiony tannins, unexpected length and nice suppleness for such a richly textured wine. A more mouthwatering and approachable style for the Amarone Classico '06 while the Recioto '07 is explosive as usual, with forward fruit and a racy, gutsy progression on the palate. We preferred the nicely full-bodied La Cengia '08 from the two Valpolicellas.

● Amarone della Valpolicella Cl. Vign. Monte Ca' Bianca '05	▼▼▼	8
● Amarone della Valpolicella Cl. '06	▼▼	7
● Recioto della Valpolicella Cl. '07	▼▼	7
● Valpolicella Cl. Sup. Ripasso Vign. La Cengia '08	▼▼	4*
● Valpolicella Cl. '09	▼	3
● Amarone della Valpolicella Cl. '03	▽▽▽	7
● Amarone della Valpolicella Cl. Vign. Monte Ca' Bianca '04	▽▽▽	8
● Amarone della Valpolicella Cl. Vign. Monte Ca' Bianca '03	▽▽▽	8
● Amarone della Valpolicella Cl. Vign. Monte Ca' Bianca '01	▽▽▽	7
● Amarone della Valpolicella Cl. Vign. Monte Ca' Bianca '00	▽▽▽	8
● Amarone della Valpolicella Cl. Vign. Monte Ca' Bianca '99	▽▽▽	8

Cecilia Beretta - Pasqua

LOC. SAN FELICE EXTRA
S.DA DELLA GIARA, 10
37131 VERONA
TEL. 0458432111
www.ceciliaberetta.it

CELLAR SALES
PRE-BOOKED VISITS

ANNUAL PRODUCTION **200,000 bottles**
HECTARES UNDER VINE **89**
VITICULTURE METHOD **Conventional**

This large Veronese winery offers impressive average quality despite its substantial production. The wines are not only excellent but also conform perfectly to the characteristics of this part of Veneto. Credit goes to the Pasqua brothers and all their technical staff. The brothers have consistently believed and invested in this area, while the winemaking staff have never been swayed by market trends, maintaining a precise, rigorous style, as the wines tasted this year demonstrate.

It was a remarkable overall performance from this winery, as one might guess from the list at the bottom of the page. While we are used to the richly fruity texture and smooth tannins of the Amarone Terre di Cariano '06, the Amarone Famiglia Pasqua put on a surprising performance in its debut '03 edition. The generous, predominantly red berry aromas are reflected on a firmly structured, powerful palate that moves nimbly to within a hair's breadth of our final tastings. There's a wide selection of Valpolicellas, all impressive, and all absolutely true to type.

● Amarone della Valpolicella Cl. Terre di Cariano '06	▼▼	8
● Amarone della Valpolicella Famiglia Pasqua '03	▼▼	7
● Morago Cabernet Sauvignon Pasqua '08	▼▼	4
● Picàie '07	▼▼	6
● Valpolicella Cl. Sup. Terre di Cariano '07	▼▼	4
● Valpolicella Cl. Villa Borghetti Pasqua '08	▼▼	5
● Valpolicella Sup. Ripasso '08	▼▼	5
● Valpolicella Sup. Ripasso Villa Borghetti Pasqua '08	▼▼	5
● Valpolicella Sup. Mizzole '07	▼▼	4
● Le Soraie Pasqua '07	▼	4
○ Soave Cl. Brognoligo '09	▼	3
● Amarone della Valpolicella Cl. Terre di Cariano '04	▽▽▽	8
● Amarone della Valpolicella Cl. Terre di Cariano '99	▽▽▽	7

Cav. G. B. Bertani

VIA ASIAGO,1
37023 GREZZANA [VR]
TEL. 0458658444
www.bertani.net

CELLAR SALES
PRE-BOOKED VISITS

ANNUAL PRODUCTION **2,000,000 bottles**
HECTARES UNDER VINE **200**
VITICULTURE METHOD **Conventional**

This estate, active for over 150 years, represents one of the long-established benchmarks of Valpolicella. Most astonishing of all is its inexhaustible vitality, demonstrated by the quality of the wines which is maintained and even improved on year after year. Bertani's production style focuses on elegance, inspired by experience of French winemaking acquired by the founders in the mid 19th century and transferred to Valpolicella on their return.

This year, Bertani presented its Amarone Classico '03. The 2002 was not produced because of unfavourable weather. In the '03, we encountered the usual, austere and characterful elegance, well worth Three Glasses, as the generous, subtle nose gradually released a swath of sensations ranging from ripe fruit to perceptions of balsam before the palate flaunted its customary taut, vibrant lightness. We were also impressed by the Soave Sereole '09 and Valpolicella Vigneto Ognisanti '07, both in line with the poised expression typical of the winery. The Secco Bertani '07 is firm, reliable and, like the rest of the range, flawless.

● Amarone della Valpolicella Cl. '03	▼▼▼	8
○ Soave Sereole '09	▼▼	4*
● Valpolicella Cl. Sup. Vign. Ognisanti '07	▼▼	4*
● Albion Cabernet Sauvignon Villa Novare '07	▼▼	6
○ Le Lave '08	▼▼	4
○ Lugana Le Quaiare '09	▼▼	4
● Recioto della Valpolicella Valpantena '07	▼▼	5
● Valpolicella Cl. Sup. Ripasso Villa Novare '07	▼▼	4
● Valpolicella Valpantena Secco Bertani '07	▼▼	5*
● Amarone della Valpolicella Cl. '01	▽▽▽	8
● Amarone della Valpolicella Cl. '00	▽▽▽	8
● Amarone della Valpolicella Cl. '99	▽▽▽	8
● Amarone della Valpolicella Cl. '98	▽▽▽	8
● Valpolicella Cl. Sup. Vign. Ognisanti '06	▽▽▽	4*

La Biancara

FRAZ. SORIO
C.DA BIANCARA, 14
36053 GAMBELLARA [VI]
TEL. 0444444244
www.biancaravini.it

CELLAR SALES
PRE-BOOKED VISITS

ANNUAL PRODUCTION **50,000 bottles**
HECTARES UNDER VINE **12**
VITICULTURE METHOD **Organic**

The estate is better known by the name of its owner, Angiolino Maule, than as La Biancara, further proof of Angelino's central role in the winery with his ideas and instincts. As a farmer first and wine producer second, he is always ready to challenge himself, while keeping the main focus on the vineyard, made of soil, grapes and hard human toil. The cellar takes second place but here, too, efforts aim to obtain sound wines that are as faithful to the terroir as possible.

This year's products are very impressive, starting with a gorgeous version of the Recioto di Gambellara from '07. This enchanting, generous wine is confidently complex on the nose and seems to have shed some of its past restlessness, expressing warm, mouthfilling sensations with exuberant sweetness and a long-lingering palate. The '08 Pico is almost like a Rhône wine with dried flowers and Mediterranean scrubland on the nose and a generous, mature palate. The Sassaia '09 is racier and the Masieri Bianco '09 is uncomplicated yet very characterful.

○ Recioto di Gambellara '07	▼▼▼	7
○ Pico '08	▼▼	5
○ Sassaia '09	▼▼	4*
● Canà Rosso '08	▼▼	4
○ Masieri Bianco '09	▼▼	3*
○ Pico '02	▽▽▽	4
○ Pico '07	▽▽	5
○ Pico '06	▽▽	5
○ Pico '04	▽▽	5
○ Recioto di Gambellara '02	▽▽	7
○ Sassaia '08	▽▽	4*
○ Sassaia '07	▽▽	4*
○ Sassaia '06	▽▽	4*

Desiderio Bisol & Figli

FRAZ. SANTO STEFANO
VIA FOLLO, 33
31049 VALDOBBIADENE [TV]
TEL. 0423900138
www.bisol.it

CELLAR SALES
PRE-BOOKED VISITS

ANNUAL PRODUCTION **1,300,000 bottles**
HECTARES UNDER VINE **100**
VITICULTURE METHOD **Conventional**

The longstanding Bisol family winery represents the evolution of this designation over the last 30 years, since after many years of business the activity has only really taken off in recent decades with an increase in vineyard surface area, bottle quantities and market share. Prices, however, have remained constant, neither taking advantage of times of plenty nor suffering excessively from the recent recession, which goes to show the wisdom of respecting human input and the value of the products.

As usual, the very well-stocked range is split into two lines, the cru and the Jeio, with less complex products made from grapes grown in various parts of the designation. The excellent Cartizze '09 is fragrant with white-fleshed fruit and flowers, showing both sweetness and a dry, classy finish on the palate. The Brut Crede and Dry Salis, both '09, are their usual elegant sparkling selves while the Vigneti del Fol '09 nearly went to our final tastings and is, as always, one of the most impressive Extra Dry sparklers in the area with sophisticated aromas and a dry, silky palate.

○ Cartizze '09	two black glasses	6
○ Valdobbiadene Brut Crede '09	two black glasses	5
○ Valdobbiadene Brut Jeio	two black glasses	4
○ Valdobbiadene Colmei Jeio Extra Dry	two black glasses	4
○ Valdobbiadene Dry Salis '09	two black glasses	5
○ Valdobbiadene Extra Dry Vigneti del Fol '09	two black glasses	5
○ Cartizze Jeio	one black glass	5
⊙ Jeio Cuvée Brut Rosé	one black glass	4
○ Jeio Cuvée Brut	one black glass	4
○ Prosecco Belstar Brut	one black glass	4
⊙ Talento Rosé Brut '05	one black glass	6
○ Cartizze '08	two white glasses	6
○ Valdobbiadene Brut Crede '08	two white glasses	5
○ Valdobbiadene Extra Dry Vigneti del Fol '08	two white glasses	5

F.lli Bolla

FRAZ. PEDEMONTE
VIA ALBERTO BOLLA, 3
37029 SAN PIETRO IN CARIANO [VR]
TEL. 0456836555
www.bolla.it

CELLAR SALES
PRE-BOOKED VISITS

ANNUAL PRODUCTION **15,000,000 bottles**
HECTARES UNDER VINE **350**
VITICULTURE METHOD **Conventional**

The history of winemaking in Verona is inseparable from that of this Pedemonte winery, which has for decades been synonymous with Veneto wine. Bolla has changed owners and fortunes, leading finally to its joining GIV last year. In recent times, quality has increased considerably and this trend was furthered when Cristian Scrinzi arrived to take the helm. This year's tasting confirms the way things are going and some wines came very close to our final tastings.

Heading our list of favourites are the Amarone Le Origini '07 and Valpolicella Le Pojane '08. The former has enjoyably ripe fruit, sweet cocoa powder on the nose and a firmly structured, dry palate with a good long finish. Le Pojane is a Valpolicella with generous sweet fruit aromas while the palate is well-sustained with taut, gutsy progression. The Soave Classico Tufaie '09 revives a glorious past of several years back when Bolla quite simply was white Veronese wine. The white-fleshed fruit and floral aromas are reflected on the slender, stylish palate.

● Valpolicella Cl. Sup. Le Pojane Ripasso '08	two black glasses	4
● Amarone della Valpolicella Cl. Le Origini '07	two black glasses	8
○ Soave Cl. Tufaie '09	two black glasses	4
● Bardolino Cl. '09	one black glass	4
○ Soave Cl. '09	one black glass	4
● Valpolicella Cl. '09	one black glass	4
● Amarone della Valpolicella Cl. '05	two white glasses	7
● Amarone della Valpolicella Cl. Capo di Torbe '05	two white glasses	8
● Amarone della Valpolicella Cl. Capo di Torbe '03	two white glasses	8
● Amarone della Valpolicella Cl. Le Origini '06	two white glasses	8
● Amarone della Valpolicella Cl. Le Origini '03	two white glasses	7
● Valpolicella Cl. Sup. Capo di Torbe '05	two white glasses	5
● Valpolicella Cl. Sup. Capo di Torbe '03	two white glasses	5
● Valpolicella Cl. Sup. Le Pojane Ripasso '06	two white glasses	4

Bonotto delle Tezze

FRAZ. TEZZE DI PIAVE
VIA DUCA D'AOSTA, 16
31020 VAZZOLA [TV]
TEL. 0438488323
www.bonottodelletezze.it

CELLAR SALES
PRE-BOOKED VISITS

ANNUAL PRODUCTION **40,000 bottles**
HECTARES UNDER VINE **50**
VITICULTURE METHOD **Conventional**

The Bonotto family estate has helped write the history of the Piave area since the time when wine production was often destined for little more than private consumption. Under the guidance of Antonio, Bonotto wine production has been rebuilt and this is now one of the most interesting local wineries, particularly in terms of quality. The grapes grown in the estate's own vineyards are still only partly used for bottled wines, which enables the winery to make extremely rigorous selections.

The range of wines presented has increased with the addition of a Prosecco and a Pinot Grigio, varieties which were not bottled until a couple of years ago. However the most significant wines are the reds, especially the Raboso Potestà '06 and Carmenere Barabane '08. The former gives red berries and spices on the nose, nicely reflected on the palate with assertive acidity and good length. The Camenere has milder aromas with distinct pepper and florality alongside the fruit. The medium-bodied palate opens out elegantly.

● Piave Carmenere Barabane '08	▼▼	4
● Piave Merlot Spezza '08	▼▼	4
● Piave Raboso Potestà '06	▼▼	5
○ Manzoni Bianco Novalis '09	▼	4
○ Treviso Brut	▼	4
○ Piave Chardonnay Oseada '09	▼	4
○ Piave Pinot Grigio Montesanto '09	▼	4
○ Manzoni Bianco Novalis '02	▽▽	4*
● Piave Merlot Spezza '07	▽▽	4*
● Piave Merlot Spezza '06	▽▽	4*
● Piave Merlot Spezza '03	▽▽	4
● Piave Raboso Potestà '05	▽▽	4
● Raboso Passito '07	▽▽	6

Borin Vini & Vigne

FRAZ. MONTICELLI
VIA DEI COLLI, 5
35043 MONSELICE [PD]
TEL. 042974384
www.viniborin.it

CELLAR SALES
PRE-BOOKED VISITS

ANNUAL PRODUCTION **140,000 bottles**
HECTARES UNDER VINE **28**
VITICULTURE METHOD **Conventional**

In recent years, this Monticelli estate has grown considerably in quality and today it is one of the most interesting in this lovely designation. The full-time involvement of their sons Francesco and Giampaolo has enabled Gianni and Teresa to extend the vineyards and purchase prestigious hillside locations in Arquà. Production focuses on the classic grapes of the designation, especially black varieties, creating a broad, well-balanced range of both simpler and more ambitious wines.

Zuan '08 is the most impressive wine, and how could it be otherwise? This is a Bordeaux blend in which cabernet sauvignon takes the lion's share and franc undertakes the task of embellishing the aromas with spicy sensations. The warm, mouthfilling palate is perfectly sustained by the acidity and dense tannic texture. The sunny Merlot Rocca Chiara Riserva '08 has sweet, approachable red fruit and a delicately caressing mouthfeel. While the Vigna Costa '08 reveals its usual grip, the Chardonnay Vigna Bianca '08 unfolds an astonishing medley of fruit and oak on a racy palate.

● Zuan '08	▼▼	6
● Colli Euganei Cabernet Sauvignon V. Costa '08	▼▼	4*
○ Colli Euganei Chardonnay V. Bianca '08	▼▼	4
● Colli Euganei Merlot Rocca Chiara Ris. '08	▼▼	4
○ Corte Borin '08	▼▼	4
○ Fiore di Gaia '09	▼▼	4*
○ Colli Euganei Fior d'Arancio '09	▼	4
○ Colli Euganei Pinot Bianco Monte Archino '09	▼	4
○ Colli Euganei Serprino '09	▼	3
● Colli Euganei Cabernet Sauvignon V. Costa '07	▽▽	4*
○ Fiore di Gaia '08	▽▽	4*
● Zuan '07	▽▽	6
● Zuan '06	▽▽	6
● Zuan '04	▽▽	6

F.lli Bortolin Spumanti

FRAZ. SANTO STEFANO
VIA MENEGAZZI, 5
31049 VALDOBBIADENE [TV]
TEL. 0423900135
www.bortolin.com

CELLAR SALES
PRE-BOOKED VISITS

ANNUAL PRODUCTION 300,000 bottles
HECTARES UNDER VINE 20
VITICULTURE METHOD Conventional

The Bortolin family has produced sparkling wines since the 1950s from the estate's own and bought-in grapes. Little has changed over the years. Generations succeed one another, the cellar is improved and new technology adopted but business continues as usual to focus on Charmat-method sparkling wines from prosecco (now glera) grapes. This Santo Stefano di Valdobbiadene winery aims to produce expressive wines in the different degrees of sweetness identified by the production protocol.

The Cartizze is a very good sparkling wine with magnificent aromas of lime blossom and white-fleshed fruits. The sweetness is perceptible on the supple, racy palate, which has good supporting acidity. The tropical, lively Rù is an approachable and very enjoyable Extra Dry and the interesting Colli di Conegliano Bianco '09 is subtly aromatic with good texture on the palate. The rest of the sparkling products are uncomplicated, light, fresh and drinkable.

○ Cartizze	▼▼	5
○ Valdobbiadene Extra Dry Rù	▼▼	4
○ Colli di Conegliano Bianco '09	▼	4
○ Valdobbiadene Brut	▼	4
○ Valdobbiadene Dry	▼	4
○ Valdobbiadene Extra Dry	▼	4
○ Vigneto del Convento Extra Brut	▼	4
○ Cartizze '07	▽▽	5
○ Cartizze Dry	▽▽	5
○ Valdobbiadene Brut '06	▽▽	4
○ Valdobbiadene Extra Dry '06	▽▽	4
○ Valdobbiadene Extra Dry Rù '06	▽▽	4

Bortolomiol

VIA GARIBALDI, 142
31049 VALDOBBIADENE [TV]
TEL. 0423974911
www.bortolomiol.com

CELLAR SALES
PRE-BOOKED VISITS

ANNUAL PRODUCTION 2,000,000 bottles
HECTARES UNDER VINE 5
VITICULTURE METHOD Conventional

A glance at the information at the top of the profile will explain the organization of this traditional Valdobbiadene winery and the whole designated zone, based on a large number of growers and fewer bottlers. A winery's quality is thus judged according to its technical skills but a good deal depends on the quality of the relationship with the grower. The Bortolomiol family has created an excellent network to produce a wide, totally sound range every year.

Many of the wines impressed us, in particular the Banda Rossa Extra Dry '09 for its generous aromas, mainly of spring flowers and apples. The beautifully harmonious palate is lifted by creamy effervescence. Lastly, we liked the Motus Vitae '08, dedicated to the winery founder and released after a year's delay. The aromas are obviously more mature and especially fruity while the palate is complex and remarkably tangy. Among the other wines, we recommend the excellent Cartizze.

○ Cartizze	▼▼	6
○ Valdobbiadene Brut Motus Vitae '08	▼▼	5
○ Valdobbiadene Dry Maior	▼▼	4
○ Valdobbiadene Extra Dry Banda Rossa '09	▼▼	4*
⊙ Filanda Rosé Brut	▼	4
○ Valdobbiadene Brut Prior	▼	4
○ Valdobbiadene Extra Dry Senior	▼	4
○ Valdobbiadene Frizzante Il Ponteggio	▼	4
○ Valdobbiadene Tranquillo Canto Fermo '09	▼	4
● Piave Cabernet Sauvignon Mormorò '07	▼	4
○ Ris. del Governatore Extra Brut '08	▼	4
○ Valdobbiadene Extra Dry Sel. Banda Rossa '06	▽▽	4
○ Ris. del Governatore Extra Brut '07	▽▽	4

Bosco del Merlo

VIA POSTUMIA, 14
30020 ANNONE VENETO [VE]
TEL. 0422768167
www.boscodelmerlo.it

CELLAR SALES
PRE-BOOKED VISITS

ANNUAL PRODUCTION 240,000 bottles
HECTARES UNDER VINE 96
VITICULTURE METHOD Organic

Owners Lucia, Carlo and Roberto Paladin are committed to developing their Venice estate but also to promoting the whole designation, which has too long relied on simple, moreish wines. Terms like rich texture, complexity and bottle ageing are rarely used in connection with Lison Pramaggiore: not so chez Paladin, where such considerations form the basis of all decisions. With about 100 hectares of vineyards, production focuses on the classics of the DOC, with some prestigious products alongside the simpler wines.

Among these finer products, we recommend three profoundly different but very impressive wines. The Turranio '09 has intense tropical, vegetal aromas and a tangy, supple, mouthwatering palate. The Roggio dei Roveri '07 has very nice floral and spicy aromas and stylish, slender structure in the mouth. Lastly, the 360 '07 is still very youthful, giving secondary aromas, while the palate reveals rich texture and ageing potential. There's been a style makeover for the fresher, fruitier Campo Camino '08 while the firm Vineargenti Riserva '05 returns to the DOC this year.

● 360 Ruber Capitae '07	▼▼	5
● Lison-Pramaggiore Refosco P. R. Roggio dei Roveri '07	▼▼	6
○ Lison-Pramaggiore Sauvignon Turranio '09	▼▼	4*
○ Lison-Pramaggiore Lison Cl. Juti '09	▼▼	4
● Lison-Pramaggiore Merlot Campo Camino '08	▼▼	4
● Lison-Pramaggiore Rosso Vineargenti Ris. '05	▼▼	6
○ Lison-Pramaggiore Pinot Grigio '09	▼	4
● 360 Ruber Capitae Rosso '04	▽▽	5
● Lison-Pramaggiore Refosco P. R. Roggio dei Roveri '05	▽▽	6
● Lison-Pramaggiore Refosco P. R. Roggio dei Roveri '04	▽▽	6
○ Lison-Pramaggiore Sauvignon Turranio '08	▽▽	4*
● Vineargenti Rosso '05	▽▽	6

Brigaldara

FRAZ. SAN FLORIANO
VIA BRIGALDARA, 20
37020 SAN PIETRO IN CARIANO [VR]
TEL. 0457701055
www.valpolicella.it/brigaldara

CELLAR SALES
PRE-BOOKED VISITS

ANNUAL PRODUCTION 200,000 bottles
HECTARES UNDER VINE 45
VITICULTURE METHOD Conventional

With over 40 hectares and 200,000 bottles released, Brigaldara is a significant winery for Valpolicella. But more important than statistics is the constant high level of quality shown by the wines. This standard is all the more appreciable given the consumer-friendly pricing policy. The style of the wines favours moderation and elegance over powerful structure while the winery's choices are inspired by territorial identity, as demonstrated by the two Amarones from different areas of origin.

Those two remarkable versions of Amarone are the Classico '06 and the Case Vecie '06. The latter is more concentrated with greater use of oak and a profound nose of good wild berry aromas and enthralling minerally hints. The plate is mouthwatering and moreish. Overripe fruit sensations of the Classico hint more clearly at the drying process but dried flowers and medicinal herbs refresh the aromas. The strikingly light palate consolidates a profile based on the subtlety of the fruit rather than its consistency, and the wine walked away with Three Glasses.

● Amarone della Valpolicella Cl. '06	▼▼▼	7
● Amarone della Valpolicella Case Vecie '06	▼▼	8
● Valpolicella Cl. Sup. Ripasso Il Vegro '07	▼▼	5
⊙ Dindarella '09	▼	4
○ Soave '09	▼	4
● Amarone della Valpolicella Case Vecie '03	▽▽▽	8
● Amarone della Valpolicella Case Vecie '00	▽▽▽	7
● Amarone della Valpolicella Cl. '05	▽▽▽	7
● Amarone della Valpolicella Cl. '99	▽▽▽	7
● Amarone della Valpolicella Cl. '98	▽▽▽	7
● Amarone della Valpolicella Cl. '97	▽▽▽	7
● Amarone della Valpolicella Case Vecie '05	▽▽	8
● Amarone della Valpolicella Case Vecie '04	▽▽	8
○ Passito Bianco '06	▽▽	5
● Recioto della Valpolicella Cl. '07	▽▽	7
● Valpolicella Cl. Sup. Ripasso Il Vegro '06	▽▽	5

Sorelle Bronca

FRAZ. COLBERTALDO
VIA MARTIRI, 20
31020 VIDOR [TV]
TEL. 0423987201
www.sorellebronca.com

CELLAR SALES
PRE-BOOKED VISITS

ANNUAL PRODUCTION 250,000 bottles
HECTARES UNDER VINE 20
VITICULTURE METHOD Certified organic

Ersiliana and Antonella Bronca's estate doesn't fit the classic profile for local properties, based on a dense network of growers and few or no estate-owned plots. But thanks in part to the tireless Piero Balcon, Antonella's husband, Bronca owns many hectares of vineyards and attention is slightly distracted from fizz in order to accommodate two still wines from the Conegliano DOC. The almost maniacal care in the vineyards is continued in the cellar, albeit with very limited interference.

The philosophy of maximum respect for the fruit applies to the production techniques used in the Particella 68, a spumante made from a single vineyard, identified in the land register as parcel 68, which is fermented directly from the must, thus restricting the use of sulphur and preserving the rounded, extraordinarily tangy flavour of the fruit. The excellent red Ser Bele '07 is fragrant with red berries and pencil lead, revealing rich texture supported by very sweet tannic structure. The other sparkling wines give their usual classy performance, especially the Brut.

● Colli di Conegliano Rosso Ser Bele '07	2 black glasses	6
○ Valdobbiadene Extra Dry Particella 68 '09	2 black glasses	5
○ Valdobbiadene Brut	2 black glasses	4*
○ Valdobbiadene Extra Dry	2 black glasses	4*
○ Colli di Conegliano Bianco Delico '07	2 white glasses	5
● Colli di Conegliano Rosso Ser Bele '06	2 white glasses	6
○ Valdobbiadene Brut '08	2 white glasses	4*
○ Valdobbiadene Extra Dry '08	2 white glasses	4*
○ Valdobbiadene Extra Dry Particella 68 '08	2 white glasses	5
● Colli di Conegliano Rosso Ser Bele '05	3 white glasses	6

Luigi Brunelli

VIA CARIANO, 10
37029 SAN PIETRO IN CARIANO [VR]
TEL. 0457701118
www.brunelliwine.com

CELLAR SALES
PRE-BOOKED VISITS
ROOMS

ANNUAL PRODUCTION 100,000 bottles
HECTARES UNDER VINE 12
VITICULTURE METHOD Conventional

Over 20 years ago, the Brunelli family's estate was one of the first in this area to shed its simple country image and leap into the spotlight thanks to the quality of its wines. All these years later, Luigi Brunelli's passion for his work has never wavered and this San Pietro winery is still one of the most respected hereabouts. Production focuses on the designation's reds, favouring a richly structured style but without losing sight of the supple profile typical of these traditional wines.

The Riserva Campo Inferi '05 is an Amarone that gives wild berries and aromatic herbs. The texture is firm and gutsy yet racily supple, leading to a long, mouthwatering finish. The two Valpolicellas are very good: the fruitier, fresher Praesel '08 and the more complex, edgy Pa' Riondo '08 both unveil the classic acidity typical of these traditional grapes. The Amarone '06 seeks to be approachable and uncomplicated with its fresh fruity sensations and well-controlled palate.

● Amarone della Valpolicella Cl. Campo Inferi Ris. '05	2 black glasses	8
● Amarone della Valpolicella Cl. '06	2 black glasses	8
● Valpolicella Cl. Sup. Campo Praesel '08	2 black glasses	4*
● Valpolicella Cl. Sup. Ripasso Pa' Riondo '08	2 black glasses	4*
● Corte Cariano Rosso '08	1 black glass	4
● Recioto della Valpolicella Cl. '08	1 black glass	6
● Amarone della Valpolicella Cl. Campo del Titari '97	3 white glasses	8
● Amarone della Valpolicella Cl. Campo del Titari '96	3 white glasses	8
● Amarone della Valpolicella Cl. Campo del Titari Ris. '04	2 white glasses	8
● Amarone della Valpolicella Cl. Campo del Titari Ris. '03	2 white glasses	8
● Amarone della Valpolicella Cl. Campo Inferi Ris. '04	2 white glasses	8

Tommaso Bussola

LOC. SAN PERETTO
VIA MOLINO TURRI, 30
37024 NEGRAR [VR]
TEL. 0457501740
www.bussolavini.com

CELLAR SALES
PRE-BOOKED VISITS

ANNUAL PRODUCTION 70,000 bottles
HECTARES UNDER VINE 19
VITICULTURE METHOD Conventional

Tommaso Bussola enjoys a well-founded reputation as one of the greatest exponents of Valpolicella's classic Recioto. But he is primarily a great producer with an original take on tradition, interpreted with personal sensitivity. Over time, the vine stock has been supplemented with the Montecchio property and the cellar space enlarged for maturing barrels and bottles. The winery style favours richly textured wines with more than a mere show of strength, as is clear from the slow cellar ageing process.

It would be hard not to begin with the flagship Recioto, which is always one of the most interesting wines from the designation. The '08 vintage of this wine is dark in colour, clearly indicating drying of the grapes, with stewed fruit aromas shot through with vibrant hints of cocoa powder and spices. The explosive sweetness on the palate is nicely supported by acidity and tannins through to a long finish. The Amarone '05 is also very good, warm and mouthfilling as ever, a style even more clearly reflected in the Valpolicella Ca' del Laito '05, sourced from the new Montecchio vineyards.

● Amarone della Valpolicella Cl. '05	2 black glasses	8
● Recioto della Valpolicella Cl. '08	2 black glasses	8
● Valpolicella Sup.Ripasso Ca' del Laito '05	2 black glasses	5
● Valpolicella Cl. '08	1 black glass	4
● Recioto della Valpolicella Cl. '04	3 glasses	7
● Recioto della Valpolicella Cl. BG '03	3 glasses	7
● Recioto della Valpolicella Cl. TB '04	3 glasses	8
● Recioto della Valpolicella Cl. TB '99	3 glasses	8
● Recioto della Valpolicella Cl. TB '95	3 glasses	8
● Amarone della Valpolicella Cl. '04	2 glasses	8
● Amarone della Valpolicella Cl. '03	2 glasses	8
● Recioto della Valpolicella Cl. '06	2 glasses	7

Ca' La Bionda

FRAZ. VALGATARA
LOC. BIONDA, 4
37020 MARANO DI VALPOLICELLA [VR]
TEL. 0456801198
www.calabionda.it

CELLAR SALES
PRE-BOOKED VISITS

ANNUAL PRODUCTION 110,000 bottles
HECTARES UNDER VINE 29
VITICULTURE METHOD Organic

Alessandro and Nicola Castellani, helped by their father Pietro, are among the most interesting winemakers in the designation. The production process is based on scrupulous management of vineyards, where invasive techniques have gradually been eliminated, while the cellar work ignores fashion to coax the highest possible expression from the wines. This latter decision may seem unimportant but at times it will move wine profiles away from the zone's norms while achieving great personality and excellent cellarability.

The excellent Amarone Ravazzol '06 is produced from grapes grown in a single, east-facing vineyard. Very ripe, sometimes stewed, fruit aromas give way to fresher hints of aromatic herbs and spices nicely reflected on the lean palate, supported by mouthwatering acidity. In the same style, the Amarone Classico '06 shows slightly less complex aromatics while the Valpolicella Casal Vegri '08 is still a little ruffled, as if in need of further bottle age to bring out the best.

● Amarone della Valpolicella Cl. Vign. di Ravazzol '06	2 black glasses	7
● Amarone della Valpolicella Cl. '06	2 black glasses	6
● Recioto della Valpolicella Cl. Vign. Le Tordare '07	2 black glasses	7
● Valpolicella Cl. Sup. Campo Casal Vegri '08	2 black glasses	5
● Amarone Cl. Vign. di Ravazzol Ris. Pietro Castellani '01	2 glasses	8
● Amarone della Valpolicella Cl. '04	2 glasses	6
● Amarone della Valpolicella Cl. Vign. di Ravazzol '05	2 glasses	7
● Amarone della Valpolicella Cl. Vign. di Ravazzol '03	2 glasses	7
● Recioto della Valpolicella Cl. Vign. Le Tordare '06	2 glasses	6
● Valpolicella Cl. Sup. Campo Casal Vegri '07	2 glasses	5

Ca' Lustra

LOC. FAEDO
VIA SAN PIETRO, 50
35030 CINTO EUGANEO [PD]
TEL. 042994128
www.calustra.it

CELLAR SALES
PRE-BOOKED VISITS

ANNUAL PRODUCTION 180,000 bottles
HECTARES UNDER VINE 25
VITICULTURE METHOD Certified organic

Franco Zanovello is a benchmark for the Colli Euganei, thanks to over 20 years' accumulated experience in the zone. With Ca' Lustra, he began producing simpler wines and built up year after year to a substantial range in which traditional bottles stand alongside more ambitious products, often among the most interesting in the area. The winery style for both reds and whites offers firmly structured palates, the logical expression of the warm, sunny Padua area.

The well-stocked range presented includes both simpler and more complex wines. Among the former, we recommend the rounded, mouthwatering, easy-drinking Merlot '08 while in the latter category, we note an excellent performance from the Merlot Sassonero '08 – fruitier, supported by nice acidity – and the more challenging Cabernet Girapoggio '07 with its tangy, harmonious palate. The sunny, mouthfilling Fior d'Arancio Passito '08 is impressive as ever while the newcomer Moscato di Retia '08 combines explosive sweetness with fresh acidity.

● Colli Euganei Cabernet Girapoggio '07	▼▼	5
○ Colli Euganei Fior d'Arancio Passito '08	▼▼	5
● Colli Euganei Merlot Sassonero '08	▼▼	5
● Colli Euganei Cabernet '08	▼▼	3*
● Colli Euganei Merlot '08	▼▼	3*
● Colli Euganei Rosso Natio '07	▼▼	5
○ Manzoni Bianco Pedevenda '09	▼▼	4*
● Marzemino Belvedere '09	▼▼	4
○ Moscato di Retia '08	▼▼	5
○ Moscato Secco 'A Cengia '09	▼▼	4
○ Colli Euganei Chardonnay Roverello '08	▼	3
○ Colli Euganei Pinot Bianco '09	▼	3
● Colli Euganei Cabernet Girapoggio '05	▽▽▽	5
○ Colli Euganei Fior d'Arancio Passito '07	▽▽▽	5
● Colli Euganei Merlot Sassonero Villa Alessi '05	▽▽▽	5
● Colli Euganei Cabernet Girapoggio '06	▽▽	5

Ca' Orologio

VIA CA' OROLOGIO, 7A
35030 BAONE [PD]
TEL. 042950099
www.caorologio.com

CELLAR SALES
PRE-BOOKED VISITS
ROOMS

ANNUAL PRODUCTION 27,000 bottles
HECTARES UNDER VINE 12
VITICULTURE METHOD Certified organic

On the slopes of Monte Cecilia, one of Veneto's southermost mountains, Ca' Orologio is part of the magnificent Villa Dondi dell'Orologio estate. In this charming setting, it is a treat to stroll with Maria Gioia Rosellini through organically farmed vineyards in the fertile Colli Euganei amongst the Mediterranean scrubland, broom and acacia. The products are based on the traditional local varieties, merlot and cabernet, which spread throughout the Colli area from the mid 19th century on.

The two reds, Relogio and Calaone, both '08, are now a guarantee of quality as outstanding exponents of the Euganei area. The former is a carmenère with a dash of cabernet sauvignon that gives remarkably generous fruit supported on the palate by sweet tannins and fresh acidity to extend and mellow the flavour. The acidity is even more forward in Calaòne, a traditional Bordeaux blend based mainly on merlot, which opens with an array of fresh berry aromas followed by a classy, light, elegant palate. The curious, racy raboso-based sparkler also deserves a mention.

● Colli Euganei Rosso Calaóne '08	▼▼	5*
● Relógio '08	▼▼	5
● Lunisóle '08	▼▼	5
⊙ Mezzo Rosato Brut M. Cl. '07	▼▼	5
○ Salaróla '09	▼▼	4
● Relógio '07	▽▽▽	5
● Relógio '06	▽▽▽	5
● Relógio '04	▽▽▽	5*
● Colli Euganei Rosso Calaóne '07	▽▽	5
● Colli Euganei Rosso Calaóne '06	▽▽	5
● Colli Euganei Rosso Calaóne '04	▽▽	4*
○ Salaróla '08	▽▽	4*

★ Ca' Rugate

via Pergola, 36
37030 Montecchia di Crosara [VR]
tel. 0456176328
www.carugate.it

CELLAR SALES
PRE-BOOKED VISITS

ANNUAL PRODUCTION **500,000 bottles**
HECTARES UNDER VINE **50**
VITICULTURE METHOD **Conventional**

When an estate achieves a generally very high standard of quality two things immediately come to mind: the quality of the territory and the lucidity with which the producer tackles everyday challenges. With wines from two areas as profoundly different as Soave and Valpolicella, covering both dry and sweet types, the character of Michele Tessari, the driving force of the family winery, is clearly reflected, providing an idea of his skill in interpreting wines and the local area.

A magnificent performance from the two Soave crus: the dynamic Monte Fiorentine '09 – with its usual Three Glasses – and the stylish Monte Alto '08. Hot on their heels is the San Michele. Turning to the Valpolicellas, it's hard to choose between the Amarone '06 and the '08 Campo Lavei. The former maintains a light, stylish profile despite its powerful structure, while the latter looks increasingly like a Valpolicella which has finally freed itself from Amarone. Lastly, the sweet wines, hovering between the enchanting sweetness of the La Perlara '08 and the spicy, gutsy L'Eremita '08. For the lucky few, there is a wonderful Corte Durlo, which we cannot review because so little is produces.

○ Soave Cl. Monte Fiorentine '09	▼▼▼	4*
● Amarone della Valpolicella '06	▼▼	8
● Recioto della Valpolicella L'Eremita '08	▼▼	6
○ Recioto di Soave La Perlara '08	▼▼	6
○ Soave Cl. Monte Alto '08	▼▼	4*
● Valpolicella Sup. Campo Lavei '08	▼▼	5
○ Soave Cl. San Michele '09	▼▼	3*
● Valpolicella Rio Albo '09	▼▼	3
● Valpolicella Sup. Ripasso '08	▼▼	5
○ Recioto di Soave La Perlara '07	▽▽▽	6
○ Soave Cl. Monte Fiorentine '08	▽▽▽	4*
○ Soave Cl. Monte Fiorentine '07	▽▽▽	4*
○ Soave Cl. Monte Fiorentine '06	▽▽▽	4*
○ Soave Cl. Monte Fiorentine '05	▽▽▽	4*
○ Soave Cl. Monte Fiorentine '04	▽▽▽	4*

Cambrago

fraz. San Zeno
via Cambrago, 7
37030 Colognola ai Colli [VR]
tel. 0457650745
www.cambrago.it

CELLAR SALES
PRE-BOOKED VISITS

ANNUAL PRODUCTION **120,000 bottles**
HECTARES UNDER VINE **14**
VITICULTURE METHOD **Conventional**

The vitality of a designation like Soave comes out in its top products, of course, but also in the growth of wineries emerging in the last ten years. The may be less well-known but offer a very high standard of quality, often at very interesting prices. We applaud an exemplary performance by Cambrago, owned by Bruno Fasoli and Cesare Sambugaro, with vineyards in both the Classico and DOC zones. Production is limited to two Soaves of reliable quality plus modest quantities of Recioto and Spumante.

The ever more impressive Soave Classico I Cerceni '09 made it through to our final tastings with fresh aromas of flowers and white-fleshed fruit, echoed with finesse on a palate with subtle, mouthwatering acidity. The simpler, more approachable Vigne Maiores '09 takes advantage of the versatility of the garganega grape, highlighting its fruitier, more delicate side. The Recioto '06 proffers a simpler, raisined aroma but gives its best performance on the palate, with marked but beautifully balanced sweetness.

○ Soave Cl. I Cerceni '09	▼▼	4*
○ Recioto di Soave I Cerceni '06	▼▼	6
○ Soave Vigne Maiores '09	▼▼	3*
○ Soave Brut I Cerceni	▼	4
● I Cerceni '05	▽▽	5
○ Recioto di Soave I Cerceni '05	▽▽	6
○ Recioto di Soave I Cerceni '04	▽▽	6
○ Soave Cl. I Cerceni '08	▽▽	4*
○ Soave Cl. I Cerceni '07	▽▽	4*
○ Soave Cl. I Cerceni '06	▽▽	3*
○ Soave Vigne Maiores '07	▽▽	3*

Giuseppe Campagnola

FRAZ. VALGATARA
VIA AGNELLA, 9
37020 MARANO DI VALPOLICELLA [VR]
TEL. 0457703900
www.campagnola.com

CELLAR SALES
PRE-BOOKED VISITS

ANNUAL PRODUCTION **4,800,000 bottles**
HECTARES UNDER VINE **110**
VITICULTURE METHOD **Conventional**

It is said that quality never goes hand-in-hand with large quantities, but luckily the reverse is sometimes true, and our tasting of Giuseppe Campagnola's wines was one of those occasions. The substantial production volume is divided into three lines with the Veronese wines at the top. In this case, few of the grapes are grown on the estate. Most are bought in from a network of growers, especially in the Marano valley, who are closely supervised throughout the season by the winery's team.

Our preference goes to the two Caterina Zardini wines, Amarone '06 and Valpolicella Superiore '08. The former perfectly reflects the features of the Marano valley, with subtle, piquant aromas nicely echoed on the palate, which opens out with supple lightness. In recent years, the Valpolicella has embraced a more generous, full-bodied style with a very well-rounded palate, although it has consequently lost much of the suppleness that characterized this wine until a few vintages ago. There were excellent performances from the other wines, especially the Recioto and the Ripasso, both '08.

● Amarone della Valpolicella Cl. Caterina Zardini '06	TT	7
● Valpolicella Cl. Sup. Caterina Zardini '08	TT	5
● Amarone della Valpolicella Cl. '07	TT	6
● Bardolino Cl. Roccolo del Lago '09	TT	4
● Recioto della Valpolicella Cl. Casotto del Merlo '08	TT	6
● Valpolicella Cl. Sup. Ripasso Le Bine '08	TT	4*
⊙ Bardolino Cl. Chiaretto Roccolo del Lago '09	T	4
○ Soave Cl. Vign. Monte Foscarino Le Bine '09	T	4
● Amarone della Valpolicella Cl. Caterina Zardini '04	YYY	7
● Amarone della Valpolicella Cl. Caterina Zardini '01	YYY	7
● Amarone della Valpolicella Cl. Caterina Zardini '99	YYY	7
● Valpolicella Cl. Sup. Caterina Zardini '05	YYY	4*
● Amarone della Valpolicella Cl. Caterina Zardini '05	YY	7
● Amarone della Valpolicella Cl. Caterina Zardini '03	YY	7

I Campi

VIA, SARMAZZA, 29A
37032 MONTEFORTE D'ALPONE [VR]
TEL. 0456175915
www.icampi.it

PRE-BOOKED VISITS

ANNUAL PRODUCTION **20,000 bottles**
HECTARES UNDER VINE **12**
VITICULTURE METHOD **Conventional**

Flavio Prà's commitment was clear from the first release of his wines, which immediately scaled the heights of quality for both designations embraced by the estate. Just three years later, the lovely new cellar is finished, blending perfectly with the farmlands of the Illasi valley renowned for its plentiful Valpolicella and Amarone wines. The red vineyards are located in the extended Valpolicella area while the only white produced comes from the western slope of the Soave Classico zone.

This year again, the most impressive wine was the very classy Soave Campo Vulcano '09, which secured Three Glasses for its generous range of aromas in which flowers and white-fleshed fruits presage the minerally features that will develop from the hints perceptible today. Its dry, vigorous palate is supported by fresh, vibrant acidity. The two Valpolicellas are different: the Campo Prognare '06, although generous and juicy, remains quite supple on the palate, while the Campo Ciotoli '08 offers a fresher, more vibrant profile in an excellent interpretation of a simple yet characterful wine.

○ Soave Cl. Campo Vulcano '09	TTT	4*
● Valpolicella Sup. Campo Prognare '06	TT	8
● Valpolicella Campo Ciotoli '08	TT	5
○ Soave Cl. Campo Vulcano '08	YYY	5
● Amarone della Valpolicella Campo Marna '04	YY	8
○ Soave Cl. Campo Vulcano '07	YY	5
● Valpolicella Cl. Campo Prognare '05	YY	8

Canevel Spumanti

LOC. SACCOL
VIA ROCCAT E FERRARI, 17
31049 VALDOBBIADENE [TV]
TEL. 0423975940
www.canevel.it

CELLAR SALES
PRE-BOOKED VISITS

ANNUAL PRODUCTION 600,000 bottles
HECTARES UNDER VINE 12
VITICULTURE METHOD Conventional

Over the years, this Saccol estate has kept up to date clear-headedly, spurning unsustainably rapid expansion even when the market seemed to be soaking up any kind of wine, and today it is on the frontline as the new DOCG is launched. With a larger vineyard area than most of its better-known colleagues, the estate produces a very sound range of exclusively sparkling wines in the Valdobbiadene designation. For consumers' benefit the labels show both the vintage year and annual production.

We note fine performances from all the products in '09, a more impressive year than we've seen in a while. The most widely stocked type is Extra Dry, with three different labels. Vigneto del Faè has white peaches and wisteria on the nose with a dry and outstandingly subtle palate while Il Millesimato combines very full fruity sensations and a firmer gutsy structure. The Extra Dry is simple and approachable. The Cartizze expresses mature aromas and a creamy palate while the Brut shows remarkable grip.

○ Cartizze '09	2 black glasses	6
○ Conegliano Valdobbiadene Brut '09	2 black glasses	4
○ Conegliano Valdobbiadene Il Millesimato '09	2 black glasses	4
○ Valdobbiadene Extra Dry '09	2 black glasses	4
○ Valdobbiadene Extra Dry Vign. del Faè '09	2 black glasses	4
○ Valdobbiadene Frizzante Vign. S. Biagio '09	1 black glass	4
○ Cartizze	2 white glasses	6
○ Cartizze	2 white glasses	6
○ Valdobbiadene Extra Dry Il Millesimato '08	2 white glasses	5
○ Valdobbiadene Extra Dry Il Millesimato '07	2 white glasses	5
○ Valdobbiadene Extra Dry Vign. del Faè	2 white glasses	4*

La Cappuccina

FRAZ. COSTALUNGA
VIA SAN BRIZIO, 125
37032 MONTEFORTE D'ALPONE [VR]
TEL. 0456175036
www.lacappuccina.it

CELLAR SALES
PRE-BOOKED VISITS
FOOD

ANNUAL PRODUCTION 300,000 bottles
HECTARES UNDER VINE 37
VITICULTURE METHOD Certified organic

Some choices are made with conviction, others out of expediency. The Tessari family's moves to embrace organic farming long before it was popular, and abandon the traditional pergola system in favour of vertical training throughout the vineyards, belong to the first category: far-sighted choices based on the awareness that only improvements in vineyard management can lead to higher quality, which we have witnessed regularly when tasting their wines or strolling through their land.

The extensive area under vine yields a range of excellent products: alongside Soaves are red wines like Campo Buri, a blend of oseleta and part-dried cabernet franc giving vibrant aromas and a remarkably rounded flavour. The San Brizio '08 is a generous Soave with complex aromas while Fontégo '09 displays the simpler, more fragrant features of the garganega grape. Most striking of all is the Arzìmo '08, for its subtle dried fruit aromas and beautifully balanced flavour that beautifully combines acidity and sweetness.

○ Recioto di Soave Arzìmo '08	2 black glasses	5
● Campo Buri '07	2 black glasses	5
● Carmenos Passito '08	2 black glasses	5
○ Soave Fontégo '09	2 black glasses	4*
○ Soave San Brizio '08	2 black glasses	4
● Madégo '09	1 black glass	4
○ Sauvignon '09	1 black glass	4
○ Soave '09	1 black glass	3
○ Arzìmo Passito '02	2 white glasses	5
● Campo Buri '02	2 white glasses	5
○ Soave Fontégo '04	2 white glasses	4
○ Soave San Brizio '03	2 white glasses	4

Casa Cecchin

via Agugliana, 11
36054 Montebello Vicentino [VI]
tel. 0444649610
www.casacecchin.it

CELLAR SALES
PRE-BOOKED VISITS

ANNUAL PRODUCTION 25,000 bottles
HECTARES UNDER VINE 6
VITICULTURE METHOD Conventional

After years of producing reliable, uncomplicated wines, the winery owned by Renato and his daughter Roberta is moving into a new area, striking out beyond the local markets and products towards a larger stage, where simplicity and authenticity are indispensable but no longer sufficient unto themselves. Hence the experimentation, agricultural rather than technological, with extended harvest times and part-drying of white grapes even for dry wines.

The most impressive wine is also a classic, the Durello Superiore '09, a wine which turns the features wrongly considered as the limitations of the durello grape – biting acidity and faint, simple aromas – into pluses. The wine displays subtle sensations of white-fleshed fruit and flowers on the nose with a vegetal hint emphasizing the rustic nature of the grape. The palate is energetic and dry with plenty of grip and a long, mouthwatering finish. In the same style, the Brut has considerable personality while from the Gambellara wines we especially liked the La Guarda '08.

○ Lessini Durello Sup. '09	2 Glasses (black)	3*
○ Lessini Durello Brut M. Cl. '05	2 Glasses (black)	4
○ Lessini Durello Passito Il Montebello '06	2 Glasses (black)	5
○ Lessini Durello Sup. Pietralava '08	2 Glasses (black)	4
○ Gambellara Cl. '09	1 Glass (black)	3
○ Gambellara Cl. La Guarda '08	1 Glass (black)	4
○ Recioto Cl. Gambellara Le Ginestre '06	1 Glass (black)	5
○ Gambellara Cl. La Guarda '07	2 Glasses (white)	3*
○ Lessini Durello Brut M. Cl. '04	2 Glasses (white)	4*
○ Lessini Durello Brut M. Cl. '03	2 Glasses (white)	4*
○ Lessini Durello Sup. '08	2 Glasses (white)	3*

Casa Roma

via Ormelle, 19
31020 San Polo di Piave [TV]
tel. 0422855339
www.casaroma.com

CELLAR SALES
PRE-BOOKED VISITS

ANNUAL PRODUCTION 200,000 bottles
HECTARES UNDER VINE 28
VITICULTURE METHOD Conventional

Gigi Peruzzetto runs the family estate near San Polo di Piave with his cousin Adriano. This occasionally over-generous area is known mainly for fresh-tasting, drinkable wines. Casa Roma differentiates its range, based on simple current vintage wines and a limited selection of more ambitious products. Although the area concentrates on merlot and cabernet, the most interesting wines are made from the traditional raboso and marzemina bianca grapes, to which a little Manzoni bianco is added.

At last a great version of Raboso – the '06 – reached our final tastings. Flowers and aromatic herbs on the nose, with lovely fruit in the background, give way to a stimulating rather than harsh varietal acidic vein on the palate, buoyed by well-honed tannins through to a long finish. The very good San Dordi '09 is a buttery but agile Manzoni Bianco. Finally, there was a good performance from the intensely spicy Carmenere '09 and the original Pro Fondo Rosso, a husky sparkling Raboso.

● Piave Raboso '06	2 Glasses (black)	5
○ Marzemina Bianca '09	2 Glasses (black)	3*
● Raboso Passito Callarghe '05	2 Glasses (black)	6
○ San Dordi '09	2 Glasses (black)	4
○ Manzoni Bianco '09	1 Glass (black)	3
● Piave Cabernet Sauvignon '09	1 Glass (black)	3
● Piave Carmenère '09	1 Glass (black)	3
○ Piave Pinot Grigio '09	1 Glass (black)	3
● Pro Fondo Rosso	1 Glass (black)	3
○ Verduzzo Passito '06	1 Glass (black)	3
○ Marzemina Bianca '08	2 Glasses (white)	3*
● Piave Raboso '05	2 Glasses (white)	5
○ San Dordi '08	2 Glasses (white)	4*

Michele Castellani

FRAZ. VALGATARA
VIA GRANDA, 1
37020 MARANO DI VALPOLICELLA [VR]
TEL. 0457701253
www.castellanimichele.it

CELLAR SALES
PRE-BOOKED VISITS

ANNUAL PRODUCTION 300,000 bottles
HECTARES UNDER VINE 40
VITICULTURE METHOD Conventional

The Castellani family winery in Valgatara has been extended and rendered more functional over the years by Michele, still firmly at the helm of the estate although his children have worked alongside him for some years. The products are divided into two lines, Ca' del Pipa and I Castei, both making the traditional wines of the Valpolicella area. The winery owns some of the extensive vineyards and manages others, growing the grapes used for a reliably good range of stylish products.

Particularly skilful workmanship went into the Recioto, again one of the best in the designation in the '08 vintage. Juicy fruit explodes on the nose and pronounced sweetness contrasts beautifully with the acidity and tannins. Of the two '06 Amarones, we preferred the Cinquestelle, with its compact appearance and aromas dominated by ripe red berries and spices, although the oak is still rather forward. The palate confirms expectations of firm structure and still ruffled power.

● Recioto della Valpolicella Cl. Monte Fasenara I Castei '08	TT	7
● Amarone della Valpolicella Cl. Campo Casalin I Castei '06	TT	8
● Amarone della Valpolicella Cl. Cinquestelle Collezione Ca' del Pipa '06	TT	8
● Valpolicella Cl. Sup. Ripasso Costamaran I Castei '08	T	5
● Valpolicella Cl. Sup. Ripasso San Michele Ca' del Pipa '08	T	5
● Recioto della Valpolicella Cl. Le Vigne Ca' del Pipa '99	YYY	7
● Amarone della Valpolicella Cl. Campo Casalin I Castei '05	YY	7
● Amarone della Valpolicella Cl. Le Vigne Ca' del Pipa '05	YY	8
● Recioto della Valpolicella Cl. Monte Fasenara I Castei '07	YY	7

Cantina del Castello

CORTE PITTORA, 5
37038 SOAVE [VR]
TEL. 0457680093
www.cantinacastello.it

CELLAR SALES
PRE-BOOKED VISITS

ANNUAL PRODUCTION 130,000 bottles
HECTARES UNDER VINE 12
VITICULTURE METHOD Conventional

For some years, Arturo Stocchetti has divided his time between running the estate and his role as chairman of the Consorzio del Soave. But the mandate does not distract him from winery business, indeed his broader vision of the Soave universe permits Arturo to focus more clearly on domestic matters. His choices are thus pondered ones and the winery style hews to the furrow of tradition, as we can see from the imperceptible prickle of the Ardens and even more in the lightness of the Soave.

We only tasted a few of the Cantina del Castello wines this year because Arturo felt that the two leading Soaves needed more ageing time. In the meantime, we enjoyed the Soave Classico Castello '09, displaying all the fragrant lightness this designation can offer in a mouthwateringly drinkable wine. The Ardens '08 is the last remaining example of what Recioto used to be decades ago: a sweet wine that undergoes a delicate second fermentation in the bottle, its softness refreshed by the light fizz.

○ Recioto di Soave Cl. Ardens '08	TT	5
○ Soave Cl. Castello '09	TT	4
○ Soave Cl. Sup. Monte Pressoni '01	YYY	4
○ Soave Cl. Acini Soavi '05	YY	5
○ Soave Cl. Carniga '07	YY	5
○ Soave Cl. Carniga '04	YY	4*
○ Soave Cl. Castello '08	YY	4
○ Soave Cl. Castello '07	YY	4*
○ Soave Cl. Pressoni '08	YY	4*
○ Soave Cl. Pressoni '07	YY	4
○ Soave Cl. Pressoni '06	YY	4*
○ Soave Cl. Pressoni '05	YY	4*

Cavalchina

FRAZ. CUSTOZA
LOC. CAVALCHINA
VIA SOMMACAMPAGNA, 7
37066 SOMMACAMPAGNA [VR]
TEL. 045516002
www.cavalchina.com

CELLAR SALES
PRE-BOOKED VISITS

ANNUAL PRODUCTION 450,000 bottles
HECTARES UNDER VINE 60
VITICULTURE METHOD Conventional

It all began in Custoza but today Franco and Luciano Piona manage three estates with skill and precision. The original winery focuses on fresh Garda wines while the Mantua estate at Monzambano grows international grapes alongside corvina and garganega, underlining a historic link with local winegrowing. The newest property, in Valpolicella, is cutting its teeth on wines that best represent the success and fame of the province of Verona: until now Valpolicellas; and Amarones from next year.

Amedeo is now a classic among great Italian white wines, an always impressive Custoza with very generous aromas and an elegant palate showing an impeccable blend of acidity, softness and oak. Three Glasses. The Garda Garganega Paroni '08 is brighter and more exuberant while among the Riviera wines we note the excellent performance of the Bardolino Santa Lucia '09 with its impressively rounded, light palate. The Corvina '08, Valpolicella Superiore Morari '08 and Garda Cabernet Sauvignon Il Falcone '07 never fail to make their presence felt. Last up is the '09 La Rosa, is a delightful, intensely fragrant sweet wine.

○ Custoza Sup. Amedeo '08	▼▼▼	4*
○ Garda Garganega Paroni La Prendina '08	▼▼	4
● Bardolino Sup. S. Lucia '09	▼▼	4
● Garda Cabernet Sauvignon Vign. Il Falcone La Prendina '07	▼▼	5
● Garda Corvina La Prendina '08	▼▼	4
○ Garda Sauvignon Valbruna La Prendina '08	▼▼	4
⊙ La Rosa Passito '09	▼▼	4
● Valpolicella Sup. Morari Terre d'Orti '08	▼▼	5
● Bardolino '09	▼	4
○ Custoza '09	▼	4
⊙ Feniletto La Prendina '08	▼	4
● Garda Merlot Faial La Prendina '07	▼	6
● Garda Merlot La Prendina '09	▼	3
○ Bianco di Custoza Sup. Amedeo '05	▽▽▽	4*
○ Bianco di Custoza Sup. Amedeo '04	▽▽▽	4*
○ Custoza Sup. Amedeo '07	▽▽▽	4*
○ Custoza Sup. Amedeo '06	▽▽▽	4*

Domenico Cavazza & F.lli

C.DA SELVA, 22
36054 MONTEBELLO VICENTINO [VI]
TEL. 0444649166
www.cavazzawine.com

CELLAR SALES
PRE-BOOKED VISITS

ANNUAL PRODUCTION 1,000,000 bottles
HECTARES UNDER VINE 150
VITICULTURE METHOD Conventional

Veneto's farming panorama is packed with a variety of wineries: some are large-scale, some have excellent quality, others offer encouraging prices. Obviously, perhaps, it is rare to find all three in one winery but the Cavazza brothers' estate does succeed in combining all three factors, thanks to two fine wine areas, Colli Berici and Gambellara, extensive, personally supervised vineyards and a pricing policy that never loses its bearings.

On its debut there is plenty to say about the Vin Santo di Gambellara Classico Capitel Santa Libera '03, an oxidized dried-grape wine based on garganega with sultanas and hazelnuts aromatics and perceptible but not excessive sweetness. The usual characterful performance from Colli Berici with the '08 Merlot, Cabernet and Syrah all on top form. Of the three we preferred the Cabernet for its generous aromas and fresh, compact flavour. Now two wines from Gambellara: the Creari '08 and La Bocara '09. The former displays very mature aromas and a rounded, powerful palate while the other is lighter and fresh-tasting.

● Colli Berici Cabernet Cicogna '08	▼▼	5
● Colli Berici Merlot Cicogna '08	▼▼	5
○ Gambellara Cl. Creari '08	▼▼	4
○ Gambellara Vin Santo Cl. Capitel S. Libera '03	▼▼	7
● Syrhae Cicogna '08	▼▼	5
○ Gambellara Cl. La Bocara '09	▼	4
● Colli Berici Cabernet Cicogna '07	▽▽	5
● Colli Berici Merlot Cicogna '07	▽▽	5
○ Gambellara Cl. Creari '07	▽▽	4
○ Gambellara Cl. La Bocara '08	▽▽	4*
○ Recioto di Gambellara Cl. Capitel S. Libera '07	▽▽	6
● Syrhae Cicogna '07	▽▽	5

Giorgio Cecchetto

FRAZ. TEZZE DI PIAVE
VIA PIAVE, 67
31028 VAZZOLA [TV]
TEL. 043828598
www.rabosopiave.com

CELLAR SALES
PRE-BOOKED VISITS

ANNUAL PRODUCTION **200,000 bottles**
HECTARES UNDER VINE **60**
VITICULTURE METHOD **Conventional**

The Piave DOC zone, between the foothills and the Adriatic, struggles to find its true vocation, cramped by very aggressive pricing policies and an awkwardly substantial presence of international varieties. But Giorgio and Cristina Cecchetto have a very clear vision and today their products are neatly divided into two ranges: the first offers simple, enjoyable current vintage wines; the second is based on the traditional local Raboso grape, together with a couple of vintages of an impressive Merlot.

The most interesting wines are those from raboso grapes: the powerful, mature Gelsaia '07, with its rich, soft profile enhanced by dried grapes aromas; and the Piave Raboso '06, which follows the more usual route of strong acidity and a more rigid profile. In the interesting Passito, powerful acidity plays a fundamental role in balancing the sweetness. Turning to the fresher wines, there was an excellent performance from the '09 Pinot Grigio, which chez Cecchetto, rises from obscurity on fragrant pear fruit and a harmonious palate.

● Gelsaia '07	▼▼	6
● Piave Raboso '06	▼▼	5
● Piave Raboso Passito	▼▼	5
○ Manzoni Bianco '09	▼	3
● Piave Cabernet Sauvignon '09	▼	3
● Piave Carmenère '09	▼	3
○ Piave Pinot Grigio '09	▼	3
● Piave Merlot Sante '07	▽▽	4
● Piave Merlot Sante '05	▽▽	4
● Piave Raboso '05	▽▽	5
● Piave Raboso '04	▽▽	5
● Piave Raboso Gelsaia '05	▽▽	6

Italo Cescon

FRAZ. RONCADELLE
P.ZZA DEI CADUTI, 3
31024 ORMELLE [TV]
TEL. 0422851033
www.cesconitalo.it

CELLAR SALES
PRE-BOOKED VISITS

ANNUAL PRODUCTION **800,000 bottles**
HECTARES UNDER VINE **115**
VITICULTURE METHOD **Conventional**

This traditional Ormelle estate regains a long profile, interpreting the Piave DOC with two lines: the well-known basic Tralcetto and a more ambitious line gradually winning shelf space and admirers. Domenico and sisters Gloria and Graziella have reduced the quantities of purchased grapes and converted to organic farming in the new plots, a far-sighted choice in an area whose strongpoint has always been large production quantities. The winery style aims for personality alongside drinkability.

The most impressive wine is an unfiltered Manzoni Bianco which is consequently slightly hazy and displays subtle aromas of flowers and white-fleshed fruit with a lovely hint of Mediterranean scrubland. The palate is even more impressive: generous and buttery yet slim-bodied and agile. The '08 Chieto is a very good blend of merlot and cabernet sauvignon with a fruity nose still marked by oak, offsetting a taut, nicely tangy palate. The Sauvignon '09 is mouthwatering.

● Chieto '08	▼▼	4
○ Manzoni Bianco '09	▼▼	6
○ Manzoni Bianco Svejo '09	▼	4
● Piave Raboso Rabià Ris. '06	▼	4
○ Piave Tai '09	▼	4
○ Sauvignon Mejo '09	▼	4
● Chieto '07	▽▽	4
○ Manzoni Bianco '08	▽▽	6
● Piave Cabernet La Cesura Ris. '05	▽▽	5
● Piave Merlot La Cesura Ris. '05	▽▽	5
● Piave Raboso Rabià Ris. '03	▽▽	6

Coffele

via Roma, 5
37038 Soave [VR]
tel. 0457680007
www.coffele.it

CELLAR SALES
PRE-BOOKED VISITS

ANNUAL PRODUCTION 110,000 bottles
HECTARES UNDER VINE 25
VITICULTURE METHOD Conventional

Although Alberto and Chiara Coffele's winery is still located in the centre of Soave, the old family property at Castelcerino has been renovated in recent years, overlooking most of the Classico growing zone and the Soave plain. Opposite the property's oldest vineyards, the house has been tastefully restored. It now includes a small lodge and a large grape-drying room, since this activity requires a large, clean space to keep fruit perfectly healthy even four months after the harvest.

The grapes dried at Castelcerino are used in the Recioto Le Sponde '08, a dried-grape wine of considerable stature with intense candied citrus peel and apricot aromas and a rounded, heady palate whose acidity perfectly contrasts the explosive sweetness. Soave Ca' Visco '09 is all about finesse. It's a subtle wine with restrained aromas ranging from flowers to white-fleshed fruit. The Alzari '08 displays a more mature, complex nose but still puts elegance before strength, like the simple, fragrant Classico '09.

○ Recioto di Soave Cl. Le Sponde '08	▼▼	6
○ Soave Cl. Ca' Visco '09	▼▼	4*
○ Soave Cl. '09	▼▼	4
○ Soave Cl. Alzari '08	▼▼	5
○ Chardonnay Castrum Icerini '07	▼	4
○ Soave Cl. Ca' Visco '05	▽▽▽	4*
○ Soave Cl. Ca' Visco '04	▽▽▽	4
○ Soave Cl. Ca' Visco '03	▽▽▽	4
○ Recioto di Soave Cl. Le Sponde '07	▽▽	6
○ Recioto di Soave Cl. Le Sponde '06	▽▽	6
○ Soave Cl. Alzari '07	▽▽	5
○ Soave Cl. Ca' Visco '08	▽▽	4*

Col Vetoraz

fraz. Santo Stefano
s.da delle Tresiese, 1
31040 Valdobbiadene [TV]
tel. 0423975291
www.colvetoraz.it

CELLAR SALES
PRE-BOOKED VISITS

ANNUAL PRODUCTION 800,000 bottles
HECTARES UNDER VINE 12
VITICULTURE METHOD Conventional

Over the last 30 years, the Prosecco universe has undergone many transformations, especially in technology terms but also in management of the market and image, as shown by the recent achievement of DOCG status. But a sound zone must be based on sound producers who know how to handle change. Vetoraz, which has long been one of the area's most important wineries, has focused entirely on producing high-quality wines through a dense network of growers and excellent cellar skills.

Again this year, the range presented by this Santo Stefano winery impressed the whole tasting panel. Our favourite was the Brut '09, a fresh, vibrant sparkling wine with aromas of white-fleshed fruit and lime flowers and a dry, nicely tangy palate. The '09 Cartizze, in contrast, opens out delicately with lovely tropical fruits and peaches while the mellow sweetness on the palate is met with good supporting acidity. We also liked the Extra Dry '09, which has less complexity, and the Millesimato Dry '09.

○ Cartizze '09	▼▼	6
○ Valdobbiadene Brut '09	▼▼	4*
○ Valdobbiadene Dry Millesimato '09	▼▼	4
○ Valdobbiadene Extra Dry '09	▼▼	4
○ Cartizze	▽▽	6
● Moraio Rosso '02	▽▽	5
○ Valdobbiadene Brut	▽▽	4*
○ Valdobbiadene Dry Millesimato '08	▽▽	4

Conte Collalto

via 24 Maggio, 1
31058 Susegana [TV]
tel. 0438738241
www.cantine-collalto.it

CELLAR SALES
PRE-BOOKED VISITS

ANNUAL PRODUCTION **800,000 bottles**
HECTARES UNDER VINE **141**
VITICULTURE METHOD **Conventional**

This traditional Susegana winery has always expressed the twin souls of its terroir, between the Piave river and the hills of the upper Treviso Marches. On one side is the breezy effervescence of Prosecco; on the other two firmly structured still reds based on merlot and cabernet, grown here for well over a century. The extensive vineyards are part of an even larger property which includes a splendid castle, a cattle farm and woodland, all in an enchanting, unspoilt setting.

Outstanding in the very broad range of wines, thanks to its originality and a bright, mouthwatering profile, is the '07 Wildbacher from a black grape of Austrian origin which has perfectly adapted to the Susegana area. The Rambaldo VIII '05 is a mature, mouthfilling Bordeaux blend while the Vinciguerra '05 favours a more traditional style, with its taut flavour and light palate. Turning to sparkling wines, we preferred the dry, punchy Brut and also recommend the original, mouthwateringly tropical Rosabianco, one of Professor Manzoni's many crossings, obtained from trebbiano and traminer.

● Colli di Conegliano Rosso Vinciguerra I '05	🍷🍷	4
● Incrocio Manzoni 2.15 '07	🍷🍷	3
○ Conegliano Valdobbiadene Brut	🍷🍷	4
● Rambaldo VIII '05	🍷🍷	6
● Wildbacher '07	🍷🍷	4
○ Chardonnay '09	🍷	3
○ Colli di Conegliano Bianco Schenella I '09	🍷	4
○ Manzoni Bianco '09	🍷	3
○ Conegliano Valdobbiadene Dry '09	🍷	4
○ Conegliano Valdobbiadene Extra Dry	🍷	4
● Piave Cabernet '07	🍷	3
● Piave Merlot '07	🍷	3
○ Pinot Grigio '09	🍷	3
○ Rosabianco '09	🍷	4
⊙ Rosé Extra Dry	🍷	4

Le Colture

fraz. Santo Stefano
via Follo, 5
31049 Valdobbiadene [TV]
tel. 0423900192
www.lecolture.it

CELLAR SALES
PRE-BOOKED VISITS
ROOMS

ANNUAL PRODUCTION **600,000 bottles**
HECTARES UNDER VINE **45**
VITICULTURE METHOD **Conventional**

Ruggeri is a common surname in Valdobbiadene, emphasizing the long-standing family connection with this area's sparkling wines. Having obtained the DOCG last year, the producers have had to show further development in quality, quite a challenge for a wine like Prosecco, which is renowned for being light and drinkable. If, as at Le Colture, there is practically complete control over all production phases, the task becomes easier and the results are there for all to see.

The range consists of four glera-based sparkling wines, all DOCG, and outstanding among these is the Cruner, a Dry whose generous, tropical aromas are refreshed by a subtle hint of citrus, nicely reflected on the beautifully creamy palate with its mellow sweetness. The enjoyably mouthwatering Pianer is less sweet and opens out more confidently while the Cartizze is soft and silky. The Faghèr is a gutsier Brut while the lovely Rosé is fresh and approachable.

○ Cartizze	🍷🍷	5
○ Valdobbiadene Dry Cruner	🍷🍷	4
○ Valdobbiadene Extra Dry Pianer	🍷🍷	4
○ Valdobbiadene Brut Faghèr	🍷	4
⊙ Rosé Dry	🍷	4

Corte Gardoni

Loc. Gardoni, 5
37067 Valeggio sul Mincio [VR]
tel. 0457950382
www.cortegardoni.it

CELLAR SALES
PRE-BOOKED VISITS

ANNUAL PRODUCTION **200,000 bottles**
HECTARES UNDER VINE **25**
VITICULTURE METHOD **Conventional**

Corte Gardoni is an original estate on the local winemaking scene. It began as a fruit farm but over the past decade, grapes have almost entirely replaced other crops and it is now a local benchmark. This background has created some real synergies. After harvesting, the grapes are left for a few days in huge cold stores once used for storing fruit. The grapes are cooled and then undergo cold maceration in order to enhance their rich array of aromas.

The Piccoli family scrupulously respect the vocation of the terroir for light, drinkable wines with a great personality. This objective is achieved in the Custoza Mael '09 and Bardolino Pradicà '08, both showing healthy fruit and finesse. The former is wonderfully approachable with white-fleshed fruits and floral aromas, unveiling a blend of grip and finesse on the palate that earned it Three Glasses. The Bardolino gives more complex mineral and black pepper sensations with an edgy, almost austere palate.

○ Bianco di Custoza Mael '09	▼▼▼	4*
● Bardolino Cl. Sup. Pradicà '08	▼▼	5*
● Becco Rosso '08	▼▼	4*
○ Custoza '09	▼▼	3*
○ Nichesole Vallidium '09	▼▼	4
⊙ Bardolino Chiaretto '09	▼	3*
● Bardolino Le Fontane '09	▼	3*
○ Bianco di Custoza Mael '08	▽▽▽	4*
⊙ Bardolino Chiaretto '08	▽▽	3*
● Bardolino Le Fontane '08	▽▽	3*
● Bardolino Sup. '06	▽▽	4
● Bardolino Sup. Pradicà '07	▽▽	5*
● Becco Rosso '07	▽▽	4*
○ Bianco di Custoza Passito Fenili '07	▽▽	6
○ Custoza '09	▽▽	3*
● Rosso di Corte '05	▽▽	5

Corte Rugolin

fraz. Valgatara
loc. Rugolin, 1
37020 Marano di Valpolicella [VR]
tel. 0457702153
www.corterugolin.it

CELLAR SALES
PRE-BOOKED VISITS

ANNUAL PRODUCTION **75,000 bottles**
HECTARES UNDER VINE **11**
VITICULTURE METHOD **Conventional**

Don't be fooled by Elena and Federico Coati's youth. Thanks to their experience, accumulated over the years at their father's side, Corte Rugolin has carved itself a very respectable niche in Valpolicella. The small estate owns about ten hectares of vineyards in fine locations, especially on Monte Danieli where the grapes are grown for the leading wine, an Amarone of the same name. Work in the cellar aims for a style that combines tradition with a sound, harmonious product.

The Amarone Monte Danieli '04 gave an outstanding performance with complex aromas of ripe, almost stewed fruit echoed by medicinal herbs. The beautifully handled texture is braced by a bright palate, which is never too massive despite its power. The Amarone Crosara delle Strie '06 is a touch lighter, deliberately made simpler and more approachable, while the rich, mouthfilling Ripasso '07 seems excessively influenced by the Amarone. The interesting Valpolicella '09 is refreshing and delightfully peppery.

● Amarone della Valpolicella Cl. Monte Danieli '04	▼▼	8
● Amarone della Valpolicella Cl. Crosara de le Strie '06	▼▼	7
● Valpolicella Cl. '09	▼▼	3*
● Valpolicella Cl. Sup. Ripasso '07	▼▼	5
● Amarone della Valpolicella Cl. Crosara de le Strie '05	▽▽	7
● Amarone della Valpolicella Cl. Crosara de le Strie '04	▽▽	6
● Amarone della Valpolicella Cl. Monte Danieli '03	▽▽	7
● Recioto della Valpolicella Cl. '03	▽▽	6
● Valpolicella Cl. Sup. Ripasso '06	▽▽	5
● Valpolicella Cl. Sup. Ripasso '05	▽▽	5
● Valpolicella Cl. Sup. Ripasso '04	▽▽	5

Corte Sant'Alda

LOC. FIOI
VIA CAPOVILLA, 28
37030 MEZZANE DI SOTTO [VR]
TEL. 0458880006
www.cortesantalda.it

CELLAR SALES
PRE-BOOKED VISITS

ANNUAL PRODUCTION 82,000 bottles
HECTARES UNDER VINE 17
VITICULTURE METHOD Certified organic

Marinella Camerani's winery is one of those that earned recognition for the extended Valpolicella area, east of Verona and brushing Soave. This area has always produced grapes, rather than wine, but it is rich in potential as demonstrated by Corte Sant'Alda, where zoning work and increasing respect for the environment have enabled Marinella to reach a high standard of quality and release expressive wines that reflect the features of the grapes and the hillslopes where they are grown.

The Amarone '06 and Campi Magri '07, both very good indeed, are on top form, showing distinct personality, which is never a given in Valpolicella. The Amarone picked up Three Glasses for its wild berry and aromatic herbs on the nose, ushering in a supple, taut palate flaunting remarkable structure and a long, unstoppable finish. The Campi Magri is more closed and almost shy but then opens out into spice and mineral hints reminiscent of corvina, and a taut, dry palate. The '09 Ca' Fiui '09 from grapes grown in the younger vineyards is as good as ever.

● Amarone della Valpolicella '06	▼▼▼	8
● Valpolicella Sup. Ripasso Campi Magri '07	▼▼	5
● Valpolicella Ca' Fiui '09	▼▼	4
○ Soave V. di Mezzane '09	▼	4
● Amarone della Valpolicella '00	▽▽▽	8
● Amarone della Valpolicella '98	▽▽▽	8
● Amarone della Valpolicella '95	▽▽▽	8
● Amarone della Valpolicella '90	▽▽▽	8
● Amarone della Valpolicella Mithas '95	▽▽▽	8
● Valpolicella Sup. '03	▽▽▽	6
● Valpolicella Sup. Mithas '04	▽▽▽	7
● Amarone della Valpolicella '04	▽▽	8
● Amarone della Valpolicella '03	▽▽	8
● Amarone della Valpolicella Mithas '04	▽▽	8
● Valpolicella Sup. Mithas '06	▽▽	7
● Valpolicella Sup. Ripasso Campi Magri '05	▽▽	5

Casa Coste Piane

FRAZ. SANTO STEFANO
VIA COSTE PIANE, 2
31040 VALDOBBIADENE [TV]
TEL. 0423900219
casacostepiane@libero.it

ANNUAL PRODUCTION 50,000 bottles
HECTARES UNDER VINE 6
VITICULTURE METHOD Conventional

Despite worldwide fame, Valdobbiadene remains a country area rooted in values as solid and hard to penetrate as the soil itself. So a character like Loris Follador is emblematic of this dual aspect: open to the world outside the wine sector, with artists often visiting the winery; but also close to tradition, to the extent that he is the last great exponent of the traditional "sur lie" Prosecco which undergoes second fermentation on the lees in the bottle.

The term "sur lie", however, can no longer be used under the new regulations so it has been renamed Naturalmente, a commercial term to indicate refermentation in bottle. Fresh, fruity aromas are picked up on the palate, where the wine displays its usual extraordinary grip and tangy flavour. One parcel of wine bottled with a crown cap has been downgraded to Glera and called Brichet but there is no substantial difference and it is practically impossible to tell two wines apart. The Extra Dry San Venanzio is particularly well-made.

○ Glera Frizzante Naturalmente Brichet	▼▼	4*
○ Valdobbiadene Extra Dry San Venanzio	▼▼	4
○ Valdobbiadene Frizzante Naturalmente	▼▼	4*
○ Valdobbiadene Frizzante Sur Lie	▽▽	4*
○ Valdobbiadene Frizzante Sur Lie	▽▽	3*
○ Valdobbiadene Frizzante Sur Lie	▽▽	3*

★ Romano Dal Forno

FRAZ. CELLORE
LOC. LODOLETTA, 1
37030 ILLASI [VR]
TEL. 0457834923
www.dalforno.net

CELLAR SALES
PRE-BOOKED VISITS

ANNUAL PRODUCTION 50,000 bottles
HECTARES UNDER VINE 25
VITICULTURE METHOD Conventional

Despite his success achieved over 30 years, Romano Dal Forno has always remained a countryman. Don't be intimidated by the imposing appearance of the cellar: it is simply a tool for transforming the grapes. In good weather, Romano will be out in the countryside, not in the winery waiting for visitors. His children are involved full-time in running the estate but Romano is still the guiding light, the first to get to work and the last to go home. A restless spirit in search of perfection.

The Valpolicella Superiore del Vigneto Monte Lodoletta '05 is the usual great Dal Forno red: inky dark with very vibrant aromas of red and black berry jam laced with spice and oak, tobacco and chocolate then a confidently muscular palate, flawed only by youth and rawness. After several years in the bottle, we expected to see some hint of ageing which, however, is only just beginning to emerge. Much the same applies to the Amarone Monte Lodoletta '04. It's a great wine in the making so we award no score this year. What is needed now is patience.

● Valpolicella Sup. Vign. di Monte Lodoletta '05	▼▼	8
● Amarone della Valpolicella Vign. di Monte Lodoletta '01	▽▽▽	8
● Amarone della Valpolicella Vign. di Monte Lodoletta '00	▽▽▽	8
● Amarone della Valpolicella Vign. di Monte Lodoletta '99	▽▽▽	8
● Amarone della Valpolicella Vign. di Monte Lodoletta '98	▽▽▽	8
● Amarone della Valpolicella Vign. di Monte Lodoletta '97	▽▽▽	8
● Amarone della Valpolicella Vign. di Monte Lodoletta '96	▽▽▽	8
● Amarone della Valpolicella Vign. di Monte Lodoletta '91	▽▽▽	8
● Valpolicella Sup. Vign. di Monte Lodoletta '04	▽▽▽	8

Luigino Dal Maso

C.DA SELVA, 62
36054 MONTEBELLO VICENTINO [VI]
TEL. 0444649104
www.dalmasovini.com

CELLAR SALES
PRE-BOOKED VISITS

ANNUAL PRODUCTION 500,000 bottles
HECTARES UNDER VINE 30
VITICULTURE METHOD Conventional

This Selva estate applies a shrewd policy of small steps, leading the Gambellara and Colli Berici areas inexorably towards winemaking fame. These small steps are, however, often supported by large investments in areas where focus on quality has not always paid off and niches can be hard to carve. Nicola, Anna and Silvia Dal Maso have refused to abandon the terroirs, and the grapes that have always identified them, but now interpret their terroir in a modern key, coaxing out the most exciting aspects.

Three wines made it to our final tasting, starting with a great version of the Riva del Molino '09, a Gambellara partly aged in large oak barrels which displays generous, still youthful aromas. The palate opens out classily ending in a long mouthwatering finish. The Ca' Fischele '09 is taut and edgy while the Colli Berici zone brings us a spicy, stylish Colpizzarda '08. From the same area come another three reds, all remarkably rounded and powerful: Terra dei Rovi '08 and Casara Roveri Merlot and Cabernet, both '07. But the biggest surprise was the '08 Montebelvedere for its fragrance and grip.

● Colli Berici Tocai Rosso Colpizzarda '08	▼▼	5
○ Gambellara Cl. Ca' Fischele '09	▼▼	3*
○ Gambellara Cl. Riva del Molino '09	▼▼	4*
● Colli Berici Cabernet Casara Roveri '07	▼▼	5
● Colli Berici Cabernet Montebelvedere '08	▼▼	4*
● Colli Berici Merlot Casara Roveri '07	▼▼	5
● Terra dei Rovi Rosso '08	▼▼	5
○ Gambellara Cl. '09	▼	2*
● Montemitorio '08	▼	3
○ Gambellara Cl. Riva del Molino '07	▽▽▽	4*
● Colli Berici Tocai Rosso Colpizzarda '07	▽▽	5
○ Gambellara Cl. Ca' Fischele '08	▽▽	3*
○ Gambellara Cl. Riva del Molino '08	▽▽	4*

De Stefani

VIA CADORNA, 92
30020 FOSSALTA DI PIAVE [VE]
TEL. 042167502
www.de-stefani.it

CELLAR SALES
PRE-BOOKED VISITS

ANNUAL PRODUCTION 250,000 bottles
HECTARES UNDER VINE 30
VITICULTURE METHOD Organic

The Piave designation includes many wineries producing simple, moreish reds and whites. But Alessandro De Stefani operates in different way. Although he works with a very wide range of labels, he has never sought lightness at all costs, preferring instead to ensure his wines have stature and depth. The grapes are grown on three estates: two on the plains along the Piave river; and the other on the hills at Refrontolo, which yields the marzemino grapes and those used in the sparkling wines.

De Stefani offers a very broad range of well-made wines, among which we preferred the Tai '09, a Tocai with aromas of yellow-fleshed fruit and lovely vegetal hints, then a buttery, pleasantly husky palate. The Soler '08 is a good if curious blend of part-dried marzemino with refosco, merlot and cabernet sauvignon that presents fruit-forward with a weighty palate while the Vitalys '09 is a medium-bodied, nicely supple Chardonnay. Kreda '08 is a Refosco with floral, peppery aromas and a refreshing flavour.

●	Soler '08	2 black glasses	5
○	Tai '09	2 black glasses	5
○	Vitalys '09	2 black glasses	4*
●	Cabernet Sauvignon '08	1 black glass	4
●	Carmerosso '08	1 black glass	5
●	Merlot Plavis '08	1 black glass	4
⊙	Metodo Zero Rosè Extra Dry	1 black glass	4
○	P. Extra Dry Metodo Zero	1 black glass	5
○	Pinot Grigio '09	1 black glass	4
●	Refosco P. R. Kreda '08	1 black glass	6
○	Venis '09	1 black glass	4
○	Olmera '08	2 white glasses	5
○	Passito Passut '06	2 white glasses	7
●	Soler '07	2 white glasses	5

F.lli Degani

FRAZ. VALGATARA
VIA TOBELE, 3A
37020 MARANO DI VALPOLICELLA [VR]
TEL. 0457701850
info@deganivini.it

CELLAR SALES
PRE-BOOKED VISITS

ANNUAL PRODUCTION 40,000 bottles
HECTARES UNDER VINE 6
VITICULTURE METHOD Conventional

Just a few hectares of vineyards producing limited quantities of evenly distributed wines sums up this Valgatara estate. Production focuses on designation wines with one fairly traditional line and the more ambitious La Rosta label. In recent years, the former has been revised and acquired more clearly defined aromas and fresher flavours, so the difference between the two lines has narrowed. Degani wines are never particularly or well extracted, tending to a more vigorous, dry style.

A good performance from the '08 Ripasso Cicilio, which slowly yields up its overripe red berry aromas streaked with vegetal hints. The palate expands into a husky finish as sugar takes a back seat. The Amarone La Rosta '07 pays the penalty for premature presentation but the range of aromas, now fairly uncomplicated with sweet, approachable fruit, promises to develop well. The palate is nicely tangy although the tannins are still a little assertive. We also liked the Valpolicella Superiore '08 with its simpler, softer style.

●	Amarone della Valpolicella Cl. La Rosta '07	2 black glasses	6
●	Valpolicella Cl. Sup. '08	2 black glasses	4
●	Valpolicella Cl. Sup. Cicilio Ripasso '08	2 black glasses	4*
●	Amarone della Valpolicella Cl. '07	1 black glass	7
●	Recioto della Valpolicella Cl. '08	1 black glass	5
●	Recioto della Valpolicella Cl. La Rosta '08	1 black glass	6
●	Valpolicella Cl. '09	1 black glass	3
●	Amarone della Valpolicella Cl. '06	2 white glasses	6
●	Amarone della Valpolicella Cl. '05	2 white glasses	6
●	Amarone della Valpolicella Cl. La Rosta '05	2 white glasses	6
●	Recioto della Valpolicella Cl. '06	2 white glasses	5
●	Recioto della Valpolicella Cl. La Rosta '06	2 white glasses	5
●	Valpolicella Cl. Sup. Cicilio Ripasso '06	2 white glasses	4*

Fasoli

FRAZ. SAN ZENO
VIA C. BATTISTI, 47
37030 COLOGNOLA AI COLLI [VR]
TEL. 0457650741
www.fasoligino.com

CELLAR SALES
PRE-BOOKED VISITS

ANNUAL PRODUCTION 300,000 bottles
HECTARES UNDER VINE 40
VITICULTURE METHOD Certified organic

Forty hectares producing only 300,000 bottles give a good idea of the meticulous work carried out by the Fasoli brothers in vineyards and cellar. Add to this organic farming certification and the die is cast. This estate pays great attention to the quality of the grapes and cellar work focuses on wines from the Soave and Valpolicella designations, along with some experimental labels, especially from international grapes, where part-drying is often involved.

The Pieve Vecchia '08 is a very impressive Soave in which oak and very ripe grapes are key. Rather than being heavy the palate, it drinks supple and winningly tangy. The interesting Amarone La Corte del Pozzo '04 gives textbook nose of nuts and spices while the palate reveals good body and well-gauged balance. As its name suggests, the garganega-only white Liber '08 is given freedom in the cellar to follow its natural course, which leads to complex aromas and a delicious flavour.

● Amarone della Valpolicella La Corte del Pozzo '04	▼▼	8
○ Liber Bianco '08	▼▼	4
○ Soave Pieve Vecchia '08	▼▼	5
● Pinot Nero Sande '05	▼	7
○ Soave Borgoletto '09	▼	4
● Valpolicella Cl. Ripasso La Corte del Pozzo '06	▼	5
○ Liber Bianco '07	▽▽	4
● Merlot Calle '07	▽▽	7
● Merlot Calle '06	▽▽	6
● Merlot Orgno '05	▽▽	7
○ Recioto di Soave S. Zeno '06	▽▽	6
○ Recioto di Soave S. Zeno '05	▽▽	6
○ Soave Borgoletto '08	▽▽	4*
○ Soave Borgoletto '06	▽▽	4*

Il Filò delle Vigne

VIA TERRALBA, 14
35030 BAONE [PD]
TEL. 042956243
www.ilfilodellevigne.it

CELLAR SALES
PRE-BOOKED VISITS

ANNUAL PRODUCTION 40,000 bottles
HECTARES UNDER VINE 18
VITICULTURE METHOD Conventional

Filò delle Vigne's 20-odd hectares of vineyards are situated along the southernmost slopes of the Colli Euganei, planted – according to aspect – with cabernet, merlot and some white grape varieties. Production is fairly limited in both labels and quantities, which bespeaks scrupulous care in vineyard and the cellar. Matteo Zanaica strives to use every corner of the small cellar in via Terralba to make sure each batch of wine matures in the best possible conditions.

The Three Glass-winning Borgo delle Casette Riserva '06 is a Cabernet Sauvignon with some Franc and Carmenère, all sourced from old vineyards, that supremely embodies the Mediterranean nature of the Colli Euganei. Rich red berry fruit with hints of scrubland and pencil lead stand out before the palate unveils nice concentration and a firm underpinning of acidity and tannin as it lingers harmoniously. The Cecilia di Baone Riserva '06, aged entirely in cement, is more approachable while the chardonnay-heavy blend Calto delle Fate '08 is rounded and stylish.

● Colli Euganei Cabernet Borgo delle Casette Ris. '06	▼▼▼	6
● Colli Euganei Cabernet Vigna Cecilia di Baone Ris. '06	▼▼	5
○ Il Calto delle Fate '08	▼▼	4
○ Colli Euganei Fior d'Arancio Spumante '09	▼	4
● Colli Euganei Cabernet Borgo delle Casette Ris. '05	▽▽	6
● Colli Euganei Cabernet Borgo delle Casette Ris. '04	▽▽	6
● Colli Euganei Cabernet Vigna Cecilia di Baone Ris. '04	▽▽	5
○ Colli Euganei Fior d'Arancio Luna del Parco '04	▽▽	6
○ Il Calto delle Fate '07	▽▽	6

Silvano Follador

FRAZ. SANTO STEFANO
LOC. FOLLO
VIA CALLONGA, 11
31040 VALDOBBIADENE [TV]
TEL. 0423900295
www.silvanofollador.it

CELLAR SALES
PRE-BOOKED VISITS

ANNUAL PRODUCTION 30,000 bottles
HECTARES UNDER VINE 4
VITICULTURE METHOD Organic

Last year's Three Glasses were the last steps on a journey that started ten years ago when the estate was still called Il Cardo but Alberta and Silvano already had their ideas straight. Maximum respect for the environment and the vines is their farming philosophy while cellar work aims to make the best of the grapes. The two wines produced not only differ in residual sugar content but also bring out the spirit of their terroir.

This year, the designation's "grand cru", Cartizze, has again made its mark with another admirable interpretation from the Follador winery. The family's refusal to add any sugar enables the wine to reveal the features of the terroir, with aromas of gooseberries and kiwi fruits, supported by remarkable tangy flavour and vibrant acidity as effervescence accentuates the palate's lightness. Only a short step behind is the Brut '09, a sparkling wine that follows the same route and emphasizes the simpler, more accessible features of the wine type without descending into banal softness.

○ Cartizze Brut '09	**YY**	5
○ Valdobbiadene Brut '09	**YY**	4*
○ Cartizze Brut '08	YYY	5

Le Fraghe

LOC. COLOMBARA, 3
37010 CAVAION VERONESE [VR]
TEL. 0457236832
www.fraghe.it

CELLAR SALES
PRE-BOOKED VISITS

ANNUAL PRODUCTION 90,000 bottles
HECTARES UNDER VINE 28
VITICULTURE METHOD Conventional

The estate's 28 hectares of vineyards enjoy a very favourable location in the north of the Bardolino designation beneath Mount Baldo, between the glacial Adige and Lake Garda hills. A dry climate with significant temperature variations and a variety of soils offers excellent winegrowing conditions. Well aware of the opportunities afforded by her land, Matilde Poggi works with the greatest sensitivity in both vineyards and cellar. The finesse and sober elegance of her wines are proof of this approach.

The Bardolino delle Fraghe gives an ample demonstration of Matilde's concept of wine. Approachable and food-friendly yet never commonplace, these wines also show an austere, elegant, complexity and minerality side. The '09 Garganega Camporengo's triumphantly firm flavour makes a lovely pair with the Bardolino, demonstrating the winery's steady growth in quality. We also liked the Chiaretto '09.

● Bardolino '09	**YY**	3*
○ Garganega Camporengo '09	**YY**	4*
⊙ Bardolino Chiaretto Ròdon '09	**YY**	3*
● Bardolino '08	YY	3*
● Bardolino '07	YY	3*
● Bardolino '06	YY	3*
⊙ Bardolino Chiaretto Ròdon '08	YY	3*
○ Camporengo Garganega Vendemmia a San Goffredo '04	YY	4
○ Garganega Camporengo '08	YY	4*
○ Garganega Camporengo '07	YY	4*
● Quaiare Cabernet '06	YY	5
● Quaiare Cabernet '03	YY	4

Marchesi Fumanelli

FRAZ. SAN FLORIANO
VIA SQUARANO, 1
37029 SAN PIETRO IN CARIANO [VR]
TEL. 0457704875
www.squarano.com

CELLAR SALES
PRE-BOOKED VISITS
FOOD

ANNUAL PRODUCTION 87,000 bottles
HECTARES UNDER VINE 45
VITICULTURE METHOD Conventional

Marchesi Fumanelli wines are released after ageing for an appropriate period to make them fully expressive and free of youthful exuberance. Lengthy maturation in glass is the finishing touch of a winemaking project that begins with scrupulous management of the vineyards, most located around the villa on the hillslopes between San Pietro and San Floriano. Work in the cellar is coordinated by Flavio Peroni, who aims to cosset the fruit and bring out its character to the greatest possible extent.

The decision to release the Amarone before the Valpolicella Superiore emphasizes the fact that this San Floriano winery follows different criteria to most others in the area. In this case, the results prove it was right. The Valpolicella Superiore '04 displays perfect maturity in broad, complex aromas of fruit intertwined with herbs, and a dry, harmonious finish. The Amarone '05 shows generously ripe aromas and bright acidity that lifts and lengthens the palate.

● Amarone della Valpolicella Cl. '05	▼▼	6
● Valpolicella Cl. Sup. '04	▼▼	4
● Valpolicella Cl. '09	▼	3
● Amarone della Valpolicella Cl. '04	▽▽	6
● Amarone della Valpolicella Cl. Octavius Ris. '03	▽▽	8
● Amarone della Valpolicella Ris. '03	▽▽	8
● Valpolicella Cl. '08	▽▽	3*
● Valpolicella Cl. Sup. Squarano '03	▽▽	6

Tenute Galtarossa

VIA ANDREA MONGA, 9
37029 SAN PIETRO IN CARIANO [VR]
TEL. 0456269600
www.tenutegaltarossa.com

PRE-BOOKED VISITS
ROOMS AND FOOD

ANNUAL PRODUCTION 20,000 bottles
HECTARES UNDER VINE 80
VITICULTURE METHOD Conventional

Between the hills of the town centre of San Pietro in Cariano and the village of Castelrotto is a small vineyard-clad plateau that slopes down towards the Adige river. Most of these vineyards – 80 hectares, in fact – belong to the Galtarossas, who work with the Gruppo Italiano Vini. Only the best grapes are destined for their two wines, an Amarone and a Valpolicella Superiore, while the rest of the fruit finds a different route to market.

Although slightly penalized by the early release, the wines still prove their worth. The fruit displayed in the Amarone '07 has a distinctly raisined, almost jammy tone but stays fresh thanks to subtle hints of aromatic herbs that are reflected on the firmly structured, fruity palate. In recent years, the Valpolicella Superiore Corte Colombara has lost a little of its lightness as it has veered towards the model of the Amarone, and the '08 has sweet, intensely fruity aromas and a dry, still cropped palate.

● Amarone della Valpolicella '07	▼▼	8
● Valpolicella Cl. Sup. Corte Colombara '08	▼▼	5
● Amarone della Valpolicella '06	▽▽	8
● Amarone della Valpolicella '05	▽▽	8
● Amarone della Valpolicella '04	▽▽	7
● Amarone della Valpolicella '03	▽▽	7
● Amarone della Valpolicella '01	▽▽	7
● Amarone della Valpolicella '00	▽▽	7
● Valpolicella Cl. Sup. Corte Colombara '07	▽▽	5
● Valpolicella Cl. Sup. Corte Colombara '06	▽▽	6
● Valpolicella Cl. Sup. Corte Colombara '04	▽▽	5
● Valpolicella Cl. Sup. Corte Colombara '03	▽▽	5
● Valpolicella Cl. Sup. Corte Colombara '02	▽▽	5
● Valpolicella Cl. Sup. Corte Colombara '01	▽▽	5

Fattoria Garbole

LOC. GARBOLE
VIA FRACANZANA, 6
37039 TREGNAGO [VR]
TEL. 0457809020
www.fattoriagarbole.it

CELLAR SALES
PRE-BOOKED VISITS

ANNUAL PRODUCTION 15,000 bottles
HECTARES UNDER VINE 6
VITICULTURE METHOD Conventional

Ettore and Filippo Finetto's estate is probably one of the furthest north in the designation, along the Illasi valley. The valley floor here consists of a thick layer of gravel tens of metres deep. The climate is cool and always breezy and as a result the grapes ripen over a week later than the norm for this area. Corvina, corvinone and rondinella take up most of the six hectares but a small corner is used to grow old local varieties for the blend of the three wines produced.

All the products share a distinguishing feature which can be summed up as a rich fruitiness, which imbues the powerful palate with vibrant, juicy vein of acidity. The exemplary Amarone '06 walked away with Three Glasses. Its considerable body is supported by the acidity, which endows it with lightness and grip. The Valpolicella Superiore '07, made with briefly dried grapes, shows a firmly structured yet supple body, while the Recioto '06 has a wide range of aromas with nuts following on from aromatic herbs and spices. This is a sweet, mouthfilling wine with bags of finesse.

Wine	Glasses	
● Amarone della Valpolicella '06	3 (black)	8
● Recioto della Valpolicella '06	2 (black)	6
● Valpolicella Sup. '07	2 (black)	6
● Amarone della Valpolicella '05	2 (white)	8
● Amarone della Valpolicella '04	2 (white)	8
● Amarone della Valpolicella '03	2 (white)	7
● Valpolicella Sup. '05	2 (white)	6

★ Gini

VIA MATTEOTTI, 42
37032 MONTEFORTE D'ALPONE [VR]
TEL. 0457611908
www.ginivini.com

CELLAR SALES
PRE-BOOKED VISITS

ANNUAL PRODUCTION 200,000 bottles
HECTARES UNDER VINE 30
VITICULTURE METHOD Conventional

It's hard to find anything new to say about Claudio and Sandro Gini's estate, which has been riding the crest of the wave for over 20 years. In fact, it was one of the first wineries to believe in this area's potential and see its efforts rewarded in our Guide. Today, their story starts a new chapter dedicated to red wines, officially still under wraps but to be announced imminently. For the Soave white wines, we note the usual meticulous work in the often very old vineyards, where some of the vines are up to 100 years old.

All the wines presented this year, focusing on the Soave designation, are very impressive. As usual, there are two house champs, Salvarenza and La Froscà. The former earned Three Glasses for a generous nose, showing enticing complexity with a harmonious blend of fruit, minerality and spiciness. A firmly structured palate, gutsier than past versions, takes you into a top class finish. The delicate, stylish La Froscà '09 shows aromas of flowers and white-fleshed fruits while the Recioto Col Foscarin '07 has citrus fruit and candied apricots on the nose and enough acidity to keep its explosive sweetness in check.

Wine	Glasses	
○ Soave Cl. Contrada Salvarenza Vecchie Vigne '08	3 (black)	5
○ Soave Cl. La Froscà '09	2 (black)	5
○ Recioto di Soave Col Foscarin '07	2 (black)	5
○ Soave Cl. '09	2 (black)	4
○ Soave Cl. Contrada Salvarenza Vecchie Vigne '07	3 (white)	5
○ Soave Cl. La Froscà '06	3 (white)	5
○ Soave Cl. La Froscà '05	3 (white)	5
○ Soave Cl. Sup. Contrada Salvarenza Vecchie Vigne '00	3 (white)	6
○ Soave Cl. Sup. Contrada Salvarenza Vecchie Vigne '95	3 (white)	5
○ Soave Cl. Sup. La Froscà '99	3 (white)	5
○ Soave Cl. Contrada Salvarenza Vecchie Vigne '06	2 (white)	5
○ Soave Cl. La Froscà '08	2 (white)	5

Gregoletto

FRAZ. PREMAOR
VIA SAN MARTINO, 83
31050 MIANE [TV]
TEL. 0438970463
www.gregoletto.com

CELLAR SALES
PRE-BOOKED VISITS

ANNUAL PRODUCTION 200,000 bottles
HECTARES UNDER VINE 15
VITICULTURE METHOD Conventional

The Gregoletto estate aims for a simplicity that only someone profound bonded to their land and winemaking can convincingly pull off. Small, apparently insignificant, daily decisions add up to determine the quality of wines whose greatness is based on everyday details. Gregoletto is here to show us this day-by-day quality, with no detail overlooked, guided by an instinct honed over years of hard toil.

This year, again, the most impressive product is the Prosecco Tranquillo '09, the epitome of an uncomplicated wine that nonetheless has the rare capacity to combine accessibility with unexpectedly generous aromas and flavour. The Manzoni Bianco '09 is as good as ever, with minerally aromas and juicy fruit. The Cabernet '08 is fruity, spicy and vibrant. Another paragon of rare approachability is the Prosecco Frizzante. A husky wine with a dry, tangy palate, it undergoes refermentation in bottle. The Extra Dry is vibrant while the rest of the extensive range is well up to snuff and adheres to the winery philosophy.

● Cabernet '08	2 black	4
○ Manzoni Bianco '09	2 black	4*
○ Conegliano Valdobbiadene Extra Dry	2 black	4
○ Conegliano Valdobbiadene Tranquillo '09	2 black	4*
○ Prosecco di Treviso Frizzante '09	2 black	4
● Merlot '08	1 black	4
○ Conegliano Valdobbiadene Extra Dry Monte Corbino	1 black	4
○ Pinot Bianco '09	1 black	4
○ Verdiso '09	1 black	4
● Cabernet '07	2 white	4
● Cabernet '06	2 white	4
○ Chardonnay '08	2 white	4
○ Chardonnay '07	2 white	4
○ Manzoni Bianco '08	2 white	4
○ Conegliano Valdobbiadene Tranquillo '08	2 white	4
○ Pinot Bianco '07	2 white	4

Grotta del Ninfeo

VIA BOSCHETTO, 6
37030 LAVAGNO [VR]
TEL. 0458980154
www.grottadelninfeo.it

CELLAR SALES
PRE-BOOKED VISITS

ANNUAL PRODUCTION 30,000 bottles
HECTARES UNDER VINE 27
VITICULTURE METHOD Conventional

The Fraccaroli family winery is in San Pietro di Lavagno, where Valpolicella Classica gives way to the broader Valpolicella designation, a less well-known zone with excellent potential. The extensive vineyards yield a limited but high-quality range based on Veronese tradition while the grapes from the six hectares in Soave are sold in bulk. Winery duties are shared out among all the siblings: sales and marketing for Luca, admin for Maria and vineyard management for Domenico, helped by their father Tiziano.

With input from consultant Giuseppe Carcereri, the winery has reached an admirable standard of quality in just a few years. The Amarone '05 stands out for its personality and generosity. It's closed on the nose, slow to yield its aromas, and rounded on the mouthfilling palate. The Ripasso '06 is similar, although it is less concentrated, while the Superiore '08 ha a very wide range of aromas, including fresher notes, and a supple, very stylish palate. The enjoyable Valpolicella '09 has a generally fresher profile with a sleek palate supported by acidity.

● Amarone della Valpolicella '05	2 black	7
● Valpolicella Sup. '08	2 black	4*
● Valpolicella Sup. Ripasso '06	2 black	5
● Valpolicella '09	1 black	3*
● Amarone della Valpolicella '03	2 white	6
● Valpolicella Sup. '03	2 white	5
● Valpolicella Sup. Ripasso '03	2 white	5

Guerrieri Rizzardi

VIA VERDI, 4
37011 BARDOLINO [VR]
TEL. 0457210028
www.guerrieri-rizzardi.it

CELLAR SALES
PRE-BOOKED VISITS

ANNUAL PRODUCTION 600,000 bottles
HECTARES UNDER VINE 100
VITICULTURE METHOD Conventional

When an estate possesses 100 hectares in the leading Veronese designations, technical skills and a very ambitious idea of what wine should be, the results are bound to come every year. At Guerrieri Rizzardi, it has been this way for a while, first in the Valpolicella estate and today at Bardolino, where the range is proving to be one of the most interesting in the area. All the wines across the board strive for elegance and adherence to the varietal typicality.

The Amarone Calcarole and Villa Rizzardi, both '06, have found their style: generosity and finesse on nose and palate for the more complex Amarone, which earned Three Glasses, while the Villa Rizzardi is fresher and crisper. A very interesting '08 version of Bardolino Munus follows the Pinot Nero path: generous, sophisticated aromas nicely reflected on the palate, which has more support from acidity than from tannin, and a very stylish overall result. All the products are impressive, particularly the juicy Ripasso Pojega '08 and the subtle Soave Costeggiola '09.

● Amarone della Valpolicella Cl. Calcarole '06	TTT	8
● Amarone della Valpolicella Cl. Villa Rizzardi '06	TT	7
● Bardolino Cl. Sup. Munus '08	TT	5
● Castello Guerrieri Rosso '07	TT	5
● Clos Roareti '08	TT	5
○ Soave Cl. Costeggiola '09	TT	4
● Valpolicella Cl. Sup. Ripasso Poiega '08	TT	4
● Bardolino Cl. Tacchetto '09	T	4
⊙ Rosa Rosae '09	T	4
● Amarone della Valpolicella Cl. Calcarole '03	YYY	8
● Amarone della Valpolicella Cl. Villa Rizzardi '04	YYY	7
● Valpolicella Cl. Sup. Ripasso Poiega '07	YYY	4*

Inama

LOC. BIACCHE, 50
37047 SAN BONIFACIO [VR]
TEL. 0456104343
www.inamaaziendaagricola.it

CELLAR SALES
PRE-BOOKED VISITS

ANNUAL PRODUCTION 420,000 bottles
HECTARES UNDER VINE 52
VITICULTURE METHOD Organic

Stefano Inama's wines have often been described as based on superlative cellar technique which enhances the sensory features of the grapes and brings them out to perfection. This is true, but there is more to it. Only rarely do we hear about Inama's vineyard management, involving 50 hectares in Soave and Colli Berici handled with respect for the environment and the vines themselves. The estate near Vicenza is organically farmed and things are progressing in the same direction at Soave.

Stefano presented a range that impressed for its quality and continuity this year. The Soave Du Lot '08 opens rich and fruity on the nose with a perfect fusion of yellow-fleshed fruit and oak, while the Foscarino '08, the Three Glass winner, is closed and slower to yield its aromas, but then lays out complexity and an unusually stylish palate. From the reds, we liked the Bradisismo '06, which expresses the sunny nature of the Colli Berici yet still has finesse and a supple, mouthwatering flavour. The very good Carmenere Più '07 expresses the explosive spiciness typical of locally grown carmenère grapes.

○ Soave Cl. Vign. di Foscarino '08	TTT	5
● Bradisismo '06	TT	6
○ Soave Cl. Vign. Du Lot '08	TT	5
● Carmenere Più '07	TT	4
○ Soave Cl. Vin Soave '09	TT	4*
○ Vulcaia Fumé '08	TT	6
○ Chardonnay '09	T	4
○ Vulcaia '09	T	4
○ Vulcaia Après '08	T	6
○ Sauvignon Vulcaia Fumé '96	YYY	6
○ Soave Cl. Vign. Du Lot '05	YYY	5
○ Soave Cl. Vign. Du Lot '01	YYY	5
○ Soave Cl. Vign. Du Lot '00	YYY	5
○ Soave Cl. Vign. Du Lot '99	YYY	5
○ Soave Cl. Vign. Du Lot '96	YYY	5

Lenotti

VIA SANTA CRISTINA, 1
37011 BARDOLINO [VR]
TEL. 0457210484
www.lenotti.com

CELLAR SALES
PRE-BOOKED VISITS

ANNUAL PRODUCTION 1,000,000 bottles
HECTARES UNDER VINE 55
VITICULTURE METHOD Conventional

Lenotti is one of the big estates typical of Lake Garda: over 50 hectares almost entirely dedicated to Bardolino producing around a million bottles a year. In the functional Via Santa Cristina winery, Giancarlo is in charge of production while his son Claudio runs the logistics and commercial side of the business, which is mainly focused on exports to overseas markets. A limited network of growers, supervised throughout the year, contribute the grapes for wines from other Veronese designations.

At 50,000 bottles, Le Olle is the Bardolino Superiore produced in greatest quantities in a style that aims to stay faithful to the profile of the type while offering a generous, nicely concentrated flavour. Mission accomplished, thanks to vibrant red berry and spice aromas and a rounded, agile palate. The Amarone '05 is closed and slow to yield up its aromas while the mid-bodied palate has a dry, mouthwatering flavour. The more approachable Ripasso '07 is nicely rounded and mouthfilling.

● Amarone della Valpolicella Cl. Di Carlo '05	▼▼	8
● Bardolino Cl. Sup. Le Olle '08	▼▼	4*
● Valpolicella Cl. Sup. Le Crosare Ripasso '07	▼▼	4
⊙ Bardolino Chiaretto Cl. '09	▼	4
● Bardolino Cl. '09	▼	4
○ Bianco di Custoza '09	▼	3
● Capomastro '08	▼	4
● Garda Cabernet Sauvignon Pramonte '07	▼	4
● Massimo '07	▼	4
● Valpolicella Cl. '09	▼	4
● Amarone della Valpolicella Cl. Di Carlo '03	▽▽	8
● Amarone della Valpolicella Cl. Di Carlo '01	▽▽	8
● Bardolino Cl. Sup. Le Olle '07	▽▽	4*
● Capo Mastro '05	▽▽	3
● Capomastro '07	▽▽	4*
○ Soave Cl. Capocolle '06	▽▽	4

Conte Loredan Gasparini

FRAZ. VENEGAZZÙ
VIA MARTIGNAGO ALTO, 23
31040 VOLPAGO DEL MONTELLO [TV]
TEL. 0438870024
www.venegazzu.com

CELLAR SALES
PRE-BOOKED VISITS
ROOMS

ANNUAL PRODUCTION 320,000 bottles
HECTARES UNDER VINE 80
VITICULTURE METHOD Organic

Montello is an isolated, soft-contoured hill between the Treviso pre-Alps and the plain, an area where wine has always been part of the local scene, albeit to a lesser extent than in other neighbouring areas. The first of very few estates to recognise the local potential was the Conte Loredan Gasparini winery, owned today by the Palla family. Their Capo di Stato has long been one of the best wines in Italy and Lorenzo Palla works with skill and passion to place this wonderful area in the spotlight.

Capo di Stato was again the most impressive wine this year thanks to vibrant aromatics of wild berries and mint, nicely reflected on the firmly structured, taut palate, which is supported by close-knit tannin. Slightly more approachable and simple is the Venegazzù della Casa '07, with red berry aromas and fresh vegetal hints that open out nicely on the palate. Without the simpler reds, a lovely version of the Manzoni Bianco '09 attracted our attention with its strikingly gutsy huskiness.

● Capo di Stato '07	▼▼	7
○ Manzoni Bianco '09	▼▼	4
● Venegazzù della Casa '07	▼▼	5
○ Asolo Brut	▼	4
● Capo di Stato '06	▽▽	7
● Capo di Stato '05	▽▽	6
● Capo di Stato '04	▽▽	6
● Capo di Stato '02	▽▽	6
● Falconera Rosso '06	▽▽	4
● Falconera Rosso '05	▽▽	4
○ Manzoni Bianco '08	▽▽	4*
● Venegazzù della Casa '06	▽▽	5
● Venegazzù della Casa '05	▽▽	5
● Venegazzù della Casa '04	▽▽	5

★ Maculan

via Castelletto, 3
36042 Breganze [VI]
tel. 0445873733
www.maculan.net

CELLAR SALES
PRE-BOOKED VISITS

ANNUAL PRODUCTION 900,000 bottles
HECTARES UNDER VINE 55
VITICULTURE METHOD Conventional

Maculan is worldwide representative of Italian winemaking thanks to the ever-impeccable standard of the products and the promotional work carried out by untiring communicator Fausto. He has created a mini Bordeaux here in the Breganze area, with merlot and cabernet representing its solid character and sweet wines – botrytized in favourable years – showing a suppler nature. Over the years, production has grown but the spirit remains the same, constantly pursuing the best possible quality.

This is a wide, well-established range although chez Maculan there are always surprises around the next corner. Without the sweet wines, we focused our attention on an excellent '08 version of Fratta, a Bordeaux blend which has become an Italian classic with its very ripe fruit and cocoa powder on the nose and weighty palate. The '08 Crosara, a monovarietal Merlot, follows the same style, although in this case the flavour is refreshed by acidity. The Brentino '08, excellent as ever, is again from Bordeaux varieties while the fragrant, well-typed Pinot Nero '08 is a very interesting wine.

● Breganze Rosso Crosara '08	**TT**	8
● Fratta '08	**TT**	8
● Breganze Pinot Nero '08	**TT**	4
● Brentino '08	**TT**	4*
● Madoro Passito '08	**TT**	6
○ Bidibi '09	**T**	4
○ Breganze Vespaiolo '09	**T**	4
● Cabernet '08	**T**	4
⊙ Costadolio '09	**T**	4
○ Dindarello '09	**T**	5
○ Ferrata Chardonnay '08	**T**	5
○ Ferrata Sauvignon '09	**T**	5
● Breganze Cabernet Sauvignon Palazzotto '05	YYY	5
● Breganze Cabernet Sauvignon Palazzotto '04	YYY	5*
● Fratta '01	YYY	8

Manara

fraz. San Floriano
via Don Cesare Biasi, 53
37029 San Pietro in Cariano [VR]
tel. 0457701086
www.manaravini.it

CELLAR SALES
PRE-BOOKED VISITS

ANNUAL PRODUCTION 75,000 bottles
HECTARES UNDER VINE 11
VITICULTURE METHOD Conventional

The Manaras, authentic exponents of Valpolicella tradition, own about ten hectares around San Floriano. At the Via Biasi cellar, which has been renovated and extended in recent years, their efforts are directed at reinterpreting the Valpolicella tradition, eliminating the decadent aspects and emphasizing a subtler profile with the hints of spice and racy acidity typical of the traditional grape varieties. Alongside Amarone, Valpolicella and Recioto are a couple of the cellar's own labels.

Although they did not reach our final tastings, Manara wines were very impressive, starting with the Amarone '06, a fine example of how a highly concentrated wine can also be light and drinkable. We note progress in the '07 Le Morete '07, a Valpolicella made using the ripasso technique to provide greater complexity on the nose and a mouthwatering, well-rounded palate. The Guido Manara '06, named for the father of the house, is a cabernet sauvignon-based blend using partly raisined grapes to achieve rich, ripe fruit without weighing down the palate.

● Amarone della Valpolicella Cl. '06	**TT**	6*
● Guido Manara '06	**TT**	6
● Valpolicella Cl. Sup. '07	**TT**	3
● Valpolicella Cl. Sup. Le Morete Ripasso '07	**TT**	4*
● Recioto della Valpolicella Cl. Moronalto '07	**T**	5
○ Strinà Passito '07	**T**	5
● Amarone della Valpolicella Cl. '00	YYY	6
● Amarone della Valpolicella Cl. '05	YY	6*
● Amarone della Valpolicella Cl. '04	YY	6
● Amarone della Valpolicella Cl. Postera '05	YY	6
● Guido Manara '05	YY	6
● Recioto della Valpolicella Cl. El Rocolo '06	YY	5
● Valpolicella Cl. Sup. '06	YY	3*
● Valpolicella Cl. Sup. Le Morete Ripasso '06	YY	4

Le Mandolare

LOC. BROGNOLIGO
VIA SAMBUCO, 180
37032 MONTEFORTE D'ALPONE [VR]
TEL. 0456175083
www.cantinalemandolare.com

CELLAR SALES
PRE-BOOKED VISITS

ANNUAL PRODUCTION 65,000 bottles
HECTARES UNDER VINE 20
VITICULTURE METHOD Conventional

The Soave area covers over 6,000 hectares in a highly varied network of estates in which grape-growers, bottlers and co-operative wineries interact as they compete for the vineyards. Many of the smaller farms are not yet able to bottle all their wine for commercial purposes so some of it is sold to external bottlers. It is natural that such estates, Le Mandolare among them, should then reserve their best grapes for their own wines, which are often of a high standard.

Despite the absence of Monte Sella, the winery's most representative product, our tastings at the Rodighiero winery went very well. This is also thanks to an excellent version of the Recioto Le Schiavette. The '07 is almost amber-toned with profound aromas of citrus and candied fruit laced with a minerally hint reminiscent of garganega grapes and followed by remarkable but not excessive sweetness on a palate with a warm Mediterranean profile. Of the two '09 Soaves, we preferred the Corte Menini, as we usually do, for its more generous aromas and firm, mouthwatering palate. The interesting Il Vignale '07 is a dry, gutsy dried-grape wine.

○ Il Vignale Passito '07	▼▼	5
○ Recioto di Soave Le Schiavette '07	▼▼	5
○ Soave Cl. Corte Menini '09	▼▼	3*
○ Brut Le Perle	▼	4
○ Soave Cl. Il Roccolo '09	▼	3
○ Recioto di Soave Cl. Le Schiavette '05	▽▽	5
○ Recioto di Soave Cl. Le Schiavette '04	▽▽	5
○ Recioto di Soave Le Schiavette '06	▽▽	5
○ Soave Cl. Corte Menini '08	▽▽	3*
○ Soave Cl. Il Roccolo '07	▽▽	3*
○ Soave Cl. Il Roccolo '06	▽▽	3*
○ Soave Cl. Il Roccolo '05	▽▽	3*
○ Soave Cl. Sup. Monte Sella '07	▽▽	4*
○ Soave Cl. Sup. Monte Sella '06	▽▽	4
○ Soave Cl. Sup. Monte Sella '02	▽▽	4

Marcato

VIA PRANDI, 10
37030 RONCÀ [VR]
TEL. 0457460070
www.marcatovini.it

CELLAR SALES
PRE-BOOKED VISITS

ANNUAL PRODUCTION 400,000 bottles
HECTARES UNDER VINE 50
VITICULTURE METHOD Conventional

In recent years, the quality of this Roncà winery's products has improved considerably. The new generation, now working full-time, has brought a wave of enthusiasm which manifests itself in a desire to experiment. Drying grapes for use in dry wines, or very long periods on the yeasts for sparkling wines, are just two of the techniques they are exploring. The opportunity of working in three different designations – Soave, Colli Berici and Lessini – enables the winery to present a broad, well-balanced range.

From Lessini comes a high calibre Brut hinting at significant developments for this area. The A.R. spends ten years on the yeasts and has emerged with a very complex nose and a firm-structured, harmonious palate. The two Soaves differ but are equally good: the Monte Tenda '09 is uncomplicated and mouthwatering while the '08 Il Tirso is more rounded and fruity, with good supporting oak. A well-stocked range from Colli Berici, headed by the very weighty Pianalto Riserva '06 while the Merlot Asinara La Giareta '07 and Tai Rosso Palladiano '08 reveal a more fragrant nature.

● Colli Berici Cabernet Pianalto Ris. '06	▼▼	7
● Colli Berici Merlot Vign. Asinara La Giareta '07	▼▼	4
○ Lessini Durello Brut M. Cl. A.R. '00	▼▼	6
● Palladiano La Giareta '08	▼▼	4
○ Soave Cl. Monte Tenda Le Barche '09	▼▼	4*
○ Soave Cl. Sup. Il Tirso '08	▼▼	4
○ Col Creo '08	▼	4
● Colli Berici Cabernet La Giareta '08	▼	4
○ Lessini Durello Brut I Prandi	▼	4
○ Soave Colli Scaligeri I Prandi '09	▼	4
○ Col Creo '07	▽▽	4*
● Colli Berici Cabernet Pianalto Ris. '02	▽▽	7
○ Lessini Durello Brut M. Cl. '02	▽▽	4
○ Lessini Durello Brut M. Cl. 36	▽▽	5
○ Lessini Durello Passito '04	▽▽	5
○ Soave Cl. Sup. Il Tirso '06	▽▽	4

Marion

FRAZ. MARCELLISE
VIA BORGO MARCELLISE, 2
37036 SAN MARTINO BUON ALBERGO [VR]
TEL. 0458740021
www.marionvini.it

PRE-BOOKED VISITS

ANNUAL PRODUCTION 40,000 bottles
HECTARES UNDER VINE 14
VITICULTURE METHOD Conventional

Nicoletta and Stefano Campedelli's winery began as a challenge less than 20 years ago but has rapidly established itself as one of the most interesting in the whole designation. Rigorous vineyard management and strict cellar selection set the standard very high early on, avoiding more commercial products to focus on high-profile wines. The delayed release of the first Amarone also demonstrates an intention to allow vineyards and experience to mature before tackling the most important wine.

This is a remarkable range of products with no weak links. Valpolicella Superiore is the type with the lowest commercial profile because of pressure from Amarone and Ripasso but at Marion, it plays a leading role. Generous aromas of red berries and aromatic herbs herald a beautifully taut, lingering palate which is clearly distinct from the Amarone profile. We gave it Three enthusiastic Glasses. As ever, the '06 Teroldego and Cabernet Sauvignon '05 are memorable, sophisticated interpretations of Veronese tradition using non-traditional grapes.

● Valpolicella Sup. '06	▼▼▼	5
● Cabernet Sauvignon '05	▼▼	5
● Calto '04	▼▼	5
○ Passito Bianco '02	▼▼	6
● Teroldego '06	▼▼	6
● Amarone della Valpolicella '03	▽▽▽	8
● Amarone della Valpolicella '01	▽▽▽	8
● Valpolicella Sup. '05	▽▽▽	5
● Amarone della Valpolicella '04	▽▽	8
● Cabernet Sauvignon '04	▽▽	5
● Cabernet Sauvignon '03	▽▽	5
● Teroldego '05	▽▽	6
● Teroldego '03	▽▽	6
● Valpolicella Sup. '04	▽▽	5
● Valpolicella Sup. '03	▽▽	6

Masari

LOC. MAGLIO DI SOPRA
VIA BEVILACQUA, 2A
36078 VALDAGNO [VI]
TEL. 0445410780
www.masari.it

CELLAR SALES
PRE-BOOKED VISITS

ANNUAL PRODUCTION 25,000 bottles
HECTARES UNDER VINE 4
VITICULTURE METHOD Organic

In the last century, the Agno valley underwent industrialization which reduced farming to a part-time activity where it did not disappear completely. Massimo Dal Lago and his wife Arianna have worked determinedly towards their objective of rediscovering this valley's country soul, devoting their time and passion to wine and drawing on their considerable professional and family experience. They only have a few hectares today but these yield some of the region's most interesting products.

Only three wines were presented this year, all beautifully made. Our favourite was the Doro '07, an original dried-grape wine which blends the fragrance of the garganega grape with the powerful acidity of durella to create a balance in which the sweetness and acidity enhance one another. The low alcohol content is an added bonus. The same blend in the '09 AgnoBianco produces fresh floral and white-fleshed fruits aromas and a dry, dynamic palate. The very good Masari '07, the winery's leading product, is a sound, crisp Bordeaux blend with a lingering finish.

○ Doro Passito Bianco '07	▼▼	6
○ AgnoBianco '09	▼▼	4
● Masari '07	▼▼	5
○ AgnoBianco '07	▽▽	4*
○ Doro Passito Bianco '06	▽▽	6
○ Doro Passito Bianco '05	▽▽	5
○ Doro Passito Bianco '04	▽▽	5
○ Doro Passito Bianco '03	▽▽	5
● Masari '06	▽▽	6
● Masari '05	▽▽	6
● San Martino '06	▽▽	4
● Vicenza Rosso San Martino '07	▽▽	4

★ Masi

FRAZ. GARGAGNAGO
VIA MONTELEONE, 26
37015 SANT'AMBROGIO DI VALPOLICELLA [VR]
TEL. 0456832511
www.masi.it

CELLAR SALES
PRE-BOOKED VISITS

ANNUAL PRODUCTION 6,800,000 bottles
HECTARES UNDER VINE 520
VITICULTURE METHOD Conventional

Credit for Valpolicella's worldwide fame is at least partly due to Sandro Boscaini who, in recent decades, has not only created products of excellent quality but has also been an effective communicator for the local area and its traditions wherever he travels. Almost seven million bottles per year released to market proudly display their roots in the traditions of this area north of Verona, expressing spicy aromas and bright, racy palates, indeed becoming benchmark wines for the whole zone.

An excellent range of products this year from the Gargagnago winery, headed up by a beautiful version of the Amarone Costasera Riserva '05, a focused red with firm structure. Even more impressive is the nicely textured, complex Vaio Armaron '05, which we wrongly reviewed last year and awarded Three Glasses to this time. The Valpolicella Anniversario 650 Anni '07 is very good, with overripe fruit and aromatic herbs on the nose and a full-bodied, nicely supple palate. Also outstanding are the Osar '05, a monovarietal Oseleta, and the Campofiorin '07. Both are characterful reds.

● Amarone della Valpolicella Cl. Vaio Armaron Serègo Alighieri '05	▼▼▼+	8
● Amarone della Valpolicella Cl. Costasera Ris. '05	▼▼	8
● Valpolicella Cl. Sup. Anniversario 650 Anni Serego Alighieri '07	▼▼	6
● Brolo di Campofiorin '07	▼▼	5
● Campofiorin '07	▼▼	5
● Osar '05	▼▼	5
○ Masianco '09	▼	4
○ Possessioni Bianco Serègo Alighieri '09	▼	4
● Amarone della Valpolicella Cl. Campolongo di Torbe '04	▽▽▽	8
● Amarone della Valpolicella Cl. Campolongo di Torbe '93	▽▽▽	6
● Amarone della Valpolicella Cl. Mazzano '01	▽▽▽	8
● Amarone della Valpolicella Cl. Mazzano '85	▽▽▽	8
● Amarone della Valpolicella Cl. Mazzano '83	▽▽▽	8
● Amarone della Valpolicella Cl. Costasera Ris. '04	▽▽	8
● Campofiorin '06	▽▽	5

Masottina

LOC. CASTELLO ROGANZUOLO
VIA BRADOLINI, 54
31020 SAN FIOR [TV]
TEL. 0438400775
www.masottina.it

CELLAR SALES
PRE-BOOKED VISITS

ANNUAL PRODUCTION 1,000,000 bottles
HECTARES UNDER VINE 44
VITICULTURE METHOD Conventional

The Dal Bianco family's estate deviates from the standard profile for this area dominated by wineries focusing on Treviso-style sparkling wines. At Masottina, the classic Prosecco products are joined by a broad, well-stocked range of white and red still wines to emphasize the area's twofold vocation. Over 40 hectares of vineyards provide the grapes for the more ambitions selections while the simpler wines are made using grapes bought in from growers whom the cellar monitors throughout the year.

The range of wines presented is broad and the outstanding bottles the Montesco and the Merlot Vigneto ai Palazzi Riserva, both '07. The former is a Bordeaux blend with generous aromas of fruit entwined with faint vegetal sensations and a medium-bodied, beautifully harmonious palate. The Merlot displays strikingly elegant aromas with a subtle palate and a lingering, succulent flavour. Just a step behind is its partner Cabernet Sauvignon '07, which has more distant aromas, slightly affected by the oak. Of the three glera-based sparkling wines, all from the new DOCG, we preferred the Extra Dry with its sophisticated citrussy hints.

● Colli di Conegliano Rosso Montesco '07	▼▼	6
○ Conegliano Valdobbiadene Extra Dry	▼▼	4
● Piave Cabernet Sauvignon Vign. ai Palazzi Ris. '07	▼▼	5
● Piave Merlot Vign. ai Palazzi Ris. '07	▼▼	5
○ Colli di Conegliano Bianco Rizzardo '08	▼	5
○ Manzoni Bianco '09	▼	4
○ Conegliano Valdobbiadene Extra Dry Rive di Ogliano '09	▼	4
○ Conegliano Valdobbiadene Brut	▼	4
● Piave Cabernet Sauvignon '09	▼	4
○ Piave Chardonnay Vign. ai Palazzi '09	▼	4
● Piave Merlot '09	▼	4
○ Piave Pinot Grigio '09	▼	4
● Colli di Conegliano Rosso Montesco '06	▽▽	6
● Piave Cabernet Sauvignon Vign. ai Palazzi Ris. '06	▽▽	5
● Piave Merlot Vign. ai Palazzi Ris. '06	▽▽	5

Roberto Mazzi

LOC. SAN PERETTO
VIA CROSETTA, 8
37024 NEGRAR [VR]
TEL. 0457502072
www.robertomazzi.it

CELLAR SALES
PRE-BOOKED VISITS

ANNUAL PRODUCTION 50,000 bottles
HECTARES UNDER VINE 8
VITICULTURE METHOD Conventional

Antonio and Stefano Mazzi's estate has been profoundly overhauled in the last 20 years. First the vineyards were replanted to new, more functional, patterns and some excellent plots abandoned after the Second World War were recovered. Then it was the cellar's turn; now it is more capacious to accommodate the casks needed to age all the wines. The Mazzis' decision to avoid flights of fancy demonstrates a commitment to tradition, which they interpret in a precise, clearly defined style.

Thanks to the Mazzi brothers' decision to age it for longer, the Amarone Punta di Villa '05 appeared more complex than in the past with layered aromas of tight-knit fruit and spice. The palate has settled down and drinks expansive, broad and silky. Both Valpolicellas are very good, although we just preferred the '07 Poiega, made using briefly dried grapes, which gives generous fruity aromas and succulent flavour. The entry-level Sanperetto '08 is perky and tangibly fresher.

● Amarone della Valpolicella Cl. Punta di Villa '05	8
● Valpolicella Cl. Sup. Vign. Poiega '07	5
● Valpolicella Cl. Sup. Sanperetto '08	4*
● Amarone della Valpolicella Cl. Castel '05	8
● Amarone della Valpolicella Cl. Punta di Villa '04	8
● Recioto della Valpolicella Cl. Le Calcarole '05	6
● Valpolicella Cl. Sup. '06	4*
● Valpolicella Cl. Sup. Sanperetto '07	4
● Valpolicella Cl. Sup. Vign. Poiega '06	5
● Valpolicella Cl. Sup. Vign. Poiega '05	5

Merotto

LOC. COL SAN MARTINO
VIA SCANDOLERA, 21
31010 FARRA DI SOLIGO [TV]
TEL. 0438989000
www.merotto.it

CELLAR SALES
PRE-BOOKED VISITS

ANNUAL PRODUCTION 450,000 bottles
HECTARES UNDER VINE 25
VITICULTURE METHOD Conventional

The advent of the new maxi-DOC, with DOCG recognition for the classic Valdobbiadene vineyards, has not caught Graziano Merotto unawares after decades of commitment to promoting the magnificent local hill country. The estate's extensive vineyard holding, plus the skill of an outstanding team, have enabled Graziano to turn out increasingly impressive wines, the result of a clear vision of how to achieve quality. Vineyard, cellar, distribution: nothing is left to chance.

With the new DOCG comes a new wine, a Brut from a single vineyard which is refermented directly from the must: the Cuvée del Fondatore Graziano Merotto '09. Very fine mousse and aromas of lime blossom and white peaches are, beautifully reflected on the gutsy and extremely lingering palate. Just a step behind it is the Bareta, emphasizing the light, upfront qualities of the type with equal finesse. The softer wines are very good, especially the Millesimato with its dry finish following the softness.

○ Valdobbiadene Brut Rive di Col San Martino Graziano Merotto '09	5
○ Cartizze Dry	6
○ Valdobbiadene Brut Bareta	4*
○ Valdobbiadene Dry Rive di Col San Martino Colmolina '09	4
○ Valdobbiadene Dry Rive di Col San Martino La Primavera di Barbara	4*
⊙ Grani Rosa di Nero Brut	4
○ Valdobbiadene Extra Dry Colbelo	4
○ Prosecco Passito Royam '09	6
○ Cartizze Dry	6
○ Valdobbiadene Dry Colmolina '08	4
○ Valdobbiadene Dry La Primavera di Barbara	4

Ornella Molon Traverso

FRAZ. CAMPO DI PIETRA
VIA RISORGIMENTO, 40
31040 SALGAREDA [TV]
TEL. 0422804807
www.ornellamolon.it

CELLAR SALES
PRE-BOOKED VISITS

ANNUAL PRODUCTION 350,000 bottles
HECTARES UNDER VINE 42
VITICULTURE METHOD Conventional

At a time when winemaking along the river Piave was an exclusively agricultural practice, for the farmers' own consumption or at most for limited sales to local customers, Ornella Molon invested in a project to turn her land into a prime wine zone. Over the decades, the estate has grown in all senses, and today it is one of the most exciting in eastern Veneto. From her more than 40 hectares, Ornella produces two lines, the more ambitious of which is named Ornella.

This line consists of a large number of wines, almost all monovarietal. The rich clayey soil yields great results from merlot, as the two house wines confirm every year. The '07 Merlot Ornella displays vibrant aromas of red berries and fines herbes, while the palate is full and harmonious. The Rosso di Villa '07 is spicier, marked by oak and still somewhat clenched. The Cabernet '07 is very good, particularly sound and succulent, as is the '09 Sauvignon '09, in one of its best versions, with intense vegetal hints and tropical fruit on the nose.

● Piave Cabernet Ornella '07	TT	5
● Piave Merlot Ornella '07	TT	5
● Piave Merlot Rosso di Villa '07	TT	6
○ Sauvignon Ornella '09	TT	4
○ Traminer Ornella '09	TT	4
● Vite Rossa Ornella '06	TT	5
○ Bianco di Ornella '07	T	5
○ Piave Chardonnay Ornella '09	T	4
● Piave Raboso Ornella '06	T	5
○ Vite Bianca Ornella '08	T	4
● Piave Cabernet Ornella '06	YY	5
○ Piave Chardonnay Ornella '08	YY	4*
● Piave Merlot Rosso di Villa '06	YY	6
● Piave Merlot Rosso di Villa '05	YY	6
● Piave Merlot Rosso di Villa '02	YY	6
● Vite Rossa Ornella '05	YY	5

Monte dall'Ora

LOC. CASTELROTTO
VIA MONTE DALL'ORA, 5
37029 SAN PIETRO IN CARIANO [VR]
TEL. 0457704462
www.montedallora.com

CELLAR SALES
PRE-BOOKED VISITS

ANNUAL PRODUCTION 35,000 bottles
HECTARES UNDER VINE 5
VITICULTURE METHOD Organic

This winery, lovingly managed by the Venturinis, was the most welcome surprise from Veneto in last year's edition. Happily, the wines have equalled, and indeed improved on, their performances this year, which suggests that yesterday's surprise will be a banker in the future. Valpolicella needs wineries like Monte dall'Ora, who respect and safeguard their land, with roots in tradition as well as an eye to the future. The decision to farm organically is gradually shifting to biodynamic farming.

We were very impressed with all the wines and two in particular: the Recioto Sant'Ulderico and the Amarone, both '06, supported by excellent texture and lovely fruit, with forward tannins. The greatest common feature of the wines is their harmonious character, which makes them eminently drinkable despite their strength, and definitely candidates for the cellar. Not to be overlooked are the Amarone Stropa '04, still a little closed on the nose but with a mouthfilling, densely woven palate, and the youthful Valpolicella Saseti '09, a winner in its category.

● Amarone della Valpolicella Cl. '06	TT	7
● Recioto della Valpolicella Cl. Sant' Ulderico '06	TT	6
● Amarone della Valpolicella Cl. Stropa '04	TT	8
● Valpolicella Cl. Saseti '09	TT	3*
● Amarone della Valpolicella Cl. '05	YY	7
● Amarone della Valpolicella Cl. Stropa '03	YY	8
● Recioto della Valpolicella Cl. Sant' Ulderico '04	YY	7
● Valpolicella Cl. Sup. '06	YY	5*
● Valpolicella Cl. Sup. Ripasso Saustò '06	YY	5

Monte del Frà

s.da per Custoza, 35
37066 Sommacampagna [VR]
tel. 045510490
www.montedelfra.it

CELLAR SALES
PRE-BOOKED VISITS

ANNUAL PRODUCTION 1,000,000 bottles
HECTARES UNDER VINE 178
VITICULTURE METHOD Conventional

Few people would have predicted such a swift transformation when, just a few years ago, Marica Bonomo joined this winery in Custoza, an area which traditionally produces very drinkable wines in large quantities. Marica persuaded the family to invest in a quality project, with input from Claudio Introini, a highly experienced winemaker from Valtellina. The improvements throughout the Garda-based range were echoed on the new Fumane estate, which now presents its new, enticing wines.

It was an impressive performance from this estate, led by a great Three Glass '08 version of Ca' del Magro, a Custoza with generous aromas of flowers and white-fleshed fruits, fresh acidity and a lovely tangy hint on the palate leading to a lingering finish. One step away from our final tastings was the Amarone '06, crafted in a style that goes more for finesse than strength, as is the case with the two '08 Valpolicella Superiores. The Ripasso is bright and spicy while its partner is fresher. Also coming along nicely are the Bardolino '09 and the Custoza '09, both simple but very enjoyable.

○ Custoza Sup. Ca' del Magro '08	🍷🍷🍷	4*
● Amarone della Valpolicella Cl. Tenuta Lena di Mezzo '06	🍷🍷	7
● Bardolino Cl. '09	🍷🍷	3*
○ Custoza '09	🍷🍷	4*
● Valpolicella Cl. Sup. Ripasso Tenuta Lena di Mezzo '08	🍷🍷	6
● Valpolicella Cl. Sup. Tenuta Lena di Mezzo '08	🍷🍷	5
● Valpolicella Cl. Tenuta Lena di Mezzo '09	🍷	4
● Amarone della Valpolicella Cl. Tenuta Lena di Mezzo '05	YY	7
● Amarone della Valpolicella Cl. Tenuta Lena di Mezzo '04	YY	7
○ Bianco di Custoza '07	YY	3*
○ Bianco di Custoza Sup. Ca' del Magro '06	YY	3*
○ Custoza Sup. Ca' del Magro '07	YY	4*
● Valpolicella Cl. Sup. Ripasso Tenuta Lena di Mezzo '07	YY	6
● Valpolicella Cl. Sup. Tenuta Lena di Mezzo '07	YY	5

Monte Fasolo

loc. Faedo
via Monte Fasolo, 2
35030 Cinto Euganeo [PD]
tel. 0429634030
www.montefasolo.com

CELLAR SALES
PRE-BOOKED VISITS

ANNUAL PRODUCTION 200,000 bottles
HECTARES UNDER VINE 72
VITICULTURE METHOD Conventional

Colli Euganei is one of Veneto's most interesting areas: warm and sunny with excellent temperature swings enabling Bordeaux varieties to ripen to a T. Each vine enjoys the best possible growing conditions on Monte Fasolo's 70-odd hectares of sunny, breezed-caressed hillsides. The large quantity of wine produced is only partly bottled, making it possible to carry out scrupulous selection starting in the vineyards, where only the best-suited slopes are used for the estate's wines.

The house champ is the Cabernet '07 grown at Podere Le Tavole, a red which expresses the fruity warm character of Colli Euganei but, thanks to the altitude, integrates fresh hints of aromatic herbs and mouthwatering acidity to streamline and lengthen the flavour. The sunny nature of the Colli Euganei explodes in the aromas of the Solone '06, with candied citrus peel and marzipan, mouthfilling sweetness and lovely acidity. The interesting Rusta '08 is an approachable red which reflects the nature of its terroir.

● Colli Euganei Cabernet Podere Le Tavole '07	🍷🍷	4*
○ Colli Euganei Fior d'Arancio Passito Solone '06	🍷🍷	6
● Colli Euganei Rosso Rusta '08	🍷🍷	4*
○ Colli Euganei Bianco Milante '07	🍷	4
⊙ Rosato '09	🍷	3
● Colli Euganei Cabernet Podere Le Tavole '06	YY	4*
● Colli Euganei Cabernet Podere Le Tavole '05	YY	4*
● Colli Euganei Cabernet Podere Le Tavole '04	YY	4*
○ Colli Euganei Dosaggio Zero M. Cl. '05	YY	6
○ Colli Euganei Fior d'Arancio Passito Solone '05	YY	5
○ Colli Euganei Fior d'Arancio Spumante '08	YY	4
● Colli Euganei Rosso Rusta '07	YY	4*
● Colli Euganei Rosso Rusta '05	YY	3*
○ Milante '07	YY	4
○ Milante '05	YY	4*
○ Milante Serie Oro '04	YY	4*

Monte Tondo

loc. Monte Tondo
via San Lorenzo, 89
37038 Soave [VR]
tel. 0457680347
www.montetondo.it

CELLAR SALES
PRE-BOOKED VISITS

ANNUAL PRODUCTION 160,000 bottles
HECTARES UNDER VINE 28
VITICULTURE METHOD Conventional

Gino Magnabosco's estate owns vineyards on the best hillsides of this large Veronese designation, like Monte Foscarino and Monte Tondo. The viticultural techniques used here have revised the traditional Veronese pergola training in a more restricted version that seeks to improve quality and provide grapes for better-quality wines. More recently, reds from neighbouring Valpolicella have joined the range, interpreted with the frankness typical of all Monte Tondo products.

From the Soaves, we preferred the two versions aged in oak, the Foscarin Slavinus and Casette Foscarin, both '08s. The former has generously sound aromas of flowers and white-fleshed fruits preceding a dry, firmly structured palate with good grip. Casette Foscarin displays riper notes on the nose and a more mature palate. The Monte Tondo '09 shows exemplary freshness. Valpolicella wines from the Campiano vineyards are increasingly impressive, especially the Amarone and Ripasso, both '06 and both crispy defined if a little husky.

○ Soave Cl. Casette Foscarin '08	2 black glasses	4*
○ Soave Cl. Sup. Foscarin Slavinus '08	2 black glasses	5
● Amarone della Valpolicella '06	2 black glasses	6
○ Soave Cl. Monte Tondo '09	2 black glasses	4
● Valpolicella Ripasso Campo Grande '06	2 black glasses	5
● Valpolicella San Pietro '08	1 black glass	4
○ Soave Cl. Monte Tondo '06	3 white glasses	4*
○ Soave Cl. Casette Foscarin '05	2 white glasses	4*
○ Soave Cl. Casette Foscarin '05	2 white glasses	4
○ Soave Cl. Casette Foscarin '04	2 white glasses	4*
○ Soave Cl. Monte Tondo '08	2 white glasses	4*
○ Soave Cl. Monte Tondo '07	2 white glasses	4*
○ Soave Cl. Sup. Foscarin Slavinus '07	2 white glasses	5
○ Soave Cl. Sup. Foscarin Slavinus '04	2 white glasses	5
○ Soave Cl. Sup. Foscarin Slavinus '03	2 white glasses	5

La Montecchia Emo Capodilista

via Montecchia, 16
35030 Selvazzano Dentro [PD]
tel. 049637294
www.lamontecchia.it

CELLAR SALES
PRE-BOOKED VISITS

ANNUAL PRODUCTION 110,000 bottles
HECTARES UNDER VINE 23
VITICULTURE METHOD Conventional

Giordano Emo Capodilista has brought together in a single structure two distinct Colli Euganei wineries: La Montecchia to the north and Conte Emo Capodilista with vineyards further south at Baone. He personally runs both of these estates with a single cellar at Selvazzano, on the old family holding. Thanks to their locations, the vineyards grow very different grapes – fragrant and edgy at Selvazzano, and sunnier, with firmer structure in Baone – providing a varied, very reliable range of products.

The wines tasted this year were excellent and four made it to the final tastings, one of which, Ireneo '07, won Three Glasses for its complex aromas of fruits and flowers, followed by a vibrant, nicely textured palate. Baon and Villa Capodilista, both '07, are two Bordeaux blends, the former mainly cabernet and the other merlot-based, emphasizing two different terroirs. Baon is sunny and crisp while the Villa Capodilista is more subtle and sophisticated. There's the usual explosion of candied citrus and dried flowers from the '08 Donna Daria, veined with impetuous sweetness and finishing long and dry.

● Colli Euganei Cabernet Sauvignon Ireneo Capodilista '07	3 black glasses	6
● Baon Capodilista '07	2 black glasses	6
○ Colli Euganei Moscato Fior d'Arancio Passito Donna Daria Capodilista '08	2 black glasses	6
● Colli Euganei Rosso Villa Capodilista '07	2 black glasses	6
● Colli Euganei Merlot '06	2 black glasses	5
○ Colli Euganei Moscato Fior d'Arancio Spumante '09	2 black glasses	4
● Colli Euganei Rosso Ca' Emo '08	2 black glasses	3*
● Godimondo Cabernet Franc '09	2 black glasses	4*
○ Colli Euganei Pinot Bianco '09	1 black glass	3
● Godimondo Carmenère '09	1 black glass	4
○ Piùchebello '09	1 black glass	4
● Turca	1 black glass	4
● Colli Euganei Rosso Ca' Emo '07	2 white glasses	3*
● Colli Euganei Rosso Villa Capodilista '06	2 white glasses	6

Monteforche

LOC. ZOVON
VIA ROVAROLLA, 2005
35030 VÒ [PD]
TEL. 3332376035

CELLAR SALES
PRE-BOOKED VISITS

ANNUAL PRODUCTION **19,000 bottles**
HECTARES UNDER VINE **4**
VITICULTURE METHOD **Organic**

Alfonso Soranzo owns this small Colli Euganei estate with five hectares of vineyards, mainly planted by his grandfather less than 40 years ago. At the turn of the century, Alfonso took over the winery, which had sold unbottled wine until then, moving in a new direction with great respect for the environment and viticulture to produce his first wines. A cellar little bigger than a cubbyhole and vineyards tended like a kitchen garden yield satisfactory results, as this year's tasting shows.

The excellent Vigna del Vento '07 is the only wine aged in oak, obtained from cabernet franc and merlot and very closed on the nose, where it is almost reluctant to express its aromas. After sufficient aeration, red berries and spices appear on the nose, to be nicely reflected on the firm-structured, compact palate. The Cabernet Franc '08 gives intense aromas of pepper and wild berries with a succulent, perky palate. The Vigneto Carantina '09 is a very interesting, gutsy and generous Garganega while the Cassiara '09 is a more fragrant, leaner blend of garganega and malvasia.

● Cabernet Franc '08	🍷🍷	5
○ Cassiara '09	🍷🍷	4*
● Vigna del Vento '07	🍷🍷	6
○ Vigneto Carantina '09	🍷🍷	5
○ Pinot Grigio '09	🍷	4
● Cabernet Franc '07	YY	4
○ Cassiara '08	YY	4
○ Vigneto Carantina '08	YY	4

Cantina Sociale di Monteforte d'Alpone

VIA XX SETTEMBRE, 24
37032 MONTEFORTE D'ALPONE [VR]
TEL. 0457610110
www.cantinadimonteforte.it

CELLAR SALES
PRE-BOOKED VISITS

ANNUAL PRODUCTION **2,000,000 bottles**
HECTARES UNDER VINE **1,300**
VITICULTURE METHOD **Conventional**

The Monteforte co-operative winery runs a very large vineyard holdings – over 1,000 hectares – but only bottles a very small part of the wine produced, enabling Gaetano Tobin to make impeccable selections of the best grapes to produce a range of fine wines beautifully representative of the Soave types. Over the last ten years, the winery's products have improved considerably, moving into the nearby areas of Lessinia, with the Durello, and Valpolicella, where the reds originate.

Outstanding among the many beautifully made Soaves presented was the Vigneto di Castellaro '08, the most ambitious wine, which was only a step away from our final tastings. Made entirely from grapes grown on Monte Castellaro, this wine is aged in wood and after two years it reveals intense aromas of yellow-fleshed fruit and flowers with seamlessly integrated oaky hints. The palate is firmly structured yet maintains the trademark supple qualities of this type. Hot on its heels are Clivus and Il Vicario, both '09, whose distinctive features are fresh aromas and a bright flavour.

○ Soave Cl. Clivus '09	🍷🍷	3*
○ Soave Cl. Il Vicario '09	🍷🍷	3*
○ Soave Cl. Sup. Vign. di Castellaro '08	🍷🍷	4*
● Amarone della Valpolicella Re Teodorico '06	🍷	6
○ Soave Cl. Terre di Monteforte '09	🍷	4
○ Soave Passo Avanti '08	🍷	4
● Amarone della Valpolicella Re Teodorico '04	YY	6
○ Recioto di Soave Cl. Il Sigillo I Vini del Chiostro '04	YY	5
○ Soave Cl. Clivus '08	YY	3*
○ Soave Cl. Clivus '07	YY	3*
○ Soave Cl. Clivus '06	YY	3*
○ Soave Cl. Il Vicario '08	YY	3*
○ Soave Cl. Il Vicario '07	YY	3*
○ Soave Cl. Sup. Vign. di Castellaro '05	YY	4*

Montegrande

via Torre, 2
35030 Rovolon [PD]
tel. 0495226276
www.vinimontegrande.it

CELLAR SALES
PRE-BOOKED VISITS

ANNUAL PRODUCTION 250,000 bottles
HECTARES UNDER VINE 23
VITICULTURE METHOD Conventional

Over just a few vintages, Raffaele Cristofanon has developed quality, rather than quantity, in the family estate. For years, consumers in Padua and its spa towns have been submerged in well-typed, unpretentious Colli Euganei crowd-pleasers so it took no small effort to polish up the image of one of the most active designations in Veneto. The first step was to overhaul vineyard management and today the grapes are tip-top. The quality of the leading wines has been racked up and there are definite improvements in the basic wines, too.

The Merlot '09 is emblematic of the improvement in the basic wines. The grape variety has been grown in the Colli Euganei for over 150 years and Cristofanon has been vinifying it for years as an easy-drinking red with ripe red berries on the nose and a firm, succulent palate. Even more impressive are the Sereo '07 and Vigna delle Roche '07. The former is a blend of the two cabernets, combining fruity hints with fresh aromatic herbs, while Roche is a merlot-heavy Bordeaux blend which uses a substantial dollop of franc to unfurl a lovely spicy aroma.

● Colli Euganei Cabernet Sereo '07	🍷🍷	4*
○ Colli Euganei Fior d'Arancio Passito '07	🍷🍷	6
● Colli Euganei Merlot '09	🍷🍷	3*
● Colli Euganei Rosso V. delle Roche '07	🍷🍷	4*
○ Castearo '09	🍷	3
○ Colli Euganei Bianco '09	🍷	3
● Colli Euganei Cabernet '09	🍷	3
○ Colli Euganei Chardonnay S. Giorgio '08	🍷	4
○ Colli Euganei Fior d'Arancio Spumante '09	🍷	3
○ Colli Euganei Pinot Bianco '09	🍷	3
● Colli Euganei Rosso '09	🍷	3
○ Castearo '08	YY	2*
● Colli Euganei Cabernet Sereo '06	YY	4*
● Colli Euganei Cabernet Sereo '05	YY	4*
○ Colli Euganei Fior d'Arancio Passito '06	YY	5
● Colli Euganei Merlot '07	YY	3*

Giacomo Montresor

via Ca' di Cozzi, 16
37124 Verona
tel. 045913399
www.vinimontresor.it

PRE-BOOKED VISITS

ANNUAL PRODUCTION 2,000,000 bottles
HECTARES UNDER VINE 150
VITICULTURE METHOD Conventional

A process of renewal is underway in this classic Verona winery, as we can clearly see from the new label design and even more from the wines, which are all fresher yet richer in texture. The very large estate grows the grape varieties used for the classic Veronese wines, primarily those from the Garda area, followed by products from nearby Valpolicella. Alongside this traditional range is another for wines made from international grape varieties.

Our tasting focused on the Veronese wines, starting with an excellent version of the Amarone Capitel della Crosara '06 with a fresh peppery nose reminiscent of corvinone grapes. The generous, succulent palate shows better integrated extract. The '06 Giacomo Montresor is fuller and more concentrated, as is the Valpolicella Castelliere delle Guaite '07, both of which display still -forward oaky hints. Turning to the whites, we enjoyed the tangy Custoza Monte Fiera '09 and the fresh-tasting, racy palate of the Lugana Gran Guardia '09.

● Amarone della Valpolicella Cl. Capitel della Crosara '06	🍷🍷	8
● Amarone della Valpolicella Giacomo Montresor '06	🍷🍷	8
○ Bianco di Custoza Vign. Monte Fiera '09	🍷🍷	5
○ Lugana Gran Guardia '09	🍷🍷	5
● Valpolicella Sup. Primo Ripasso Castelliere delle Guaite '07	🍷🍷	6
○ Lugana Campovalentino '09	🍷	4
○ Riesling n. 3 '09	🍷	5
○ Soave Cl. Capitel Alto '09	🍷	5
● Amarone della Valpolicella Cl. Capitel della Crosara '05	YY	8
● Amarone della Valpolicella Cl. Capitel della Crosara '04	YY	8
● Amarone della Valpolicella Cl. Castelliere delle Guaite '05	YY	8
● Amarone della Valpolicella Cl. Castelliere delle Guaite '04	YY	8

Marco Mosconi

via Paradiso, 5
37031 Illasi [VR]
tel. 0457834080
www.marcomosconi.it

CELLAR SALES
PRE-BOOKED VISITS

ANNUAL PRODUCTION 20,000 bottles
HECTARES UNDER VINE 6
VITICULTURE METHOD Conventional

The Illasi valley is famous for its generous Valpolicella and Amarone wines, but part of this area also falls within the Soave designation. Marco Mosconi's fairly young winery is located here, having carved itself a respectable niche in just a few years. The six hectares under vine consist of beautifully aspected old vines, particularly those used for Soave wines. The grapes are all processed here at the winery but only some of these are used for the estate's own wines, while the rest are sold wholesale.

The Soaves are the most impressive wines in Marco Mosconi's range although the Valpolicella is improving and the first Amarone will soon be bottled in the cellar. The Soave Rosetta '08 sourced from a single, 50-year-old vineyard releases stone fruits aromas with a nicely textured, lingering palate. The Corte Paradiso '09, fresher in style and produced in larger quantities, has an impressively taut palate. Also very good is the Valpolicella Superiore '07, giving beautifully concentrated fruit and mid body. The Recioto di Soave '07 is more succulent and alluring.

○ Recioto di Soave '07	▼▼	6
○ Soave Corte Paradiso '09	▼▼	4*
○ Soave Rosetta '08	▼▼	5
● Valpolicella Sup. '07	▼▼	5
● Recioto della Valpolicella '08	▼	6
○ Recioto di Soave '06	▽▽	6
○ Recioto di Soave '04	▽▽	6
○ Soave Corte Paradiso '08	▽▽	4
○ Soave Corte Paradiso '07	▽▽	4*
○ Soave Località Paradiso '06	▽▽	4

Mosole

loc. Corbolone
via Annone Veneto, 60
30029 Santo Stino di Livenza [VE]
tel. 0421310404
www.mosole.com

CELLAR SALES
PRE-BOOKED VISITS

ANNUAL PRODUCTION 220,000 bottles
HECTARES UNDER VINE 30
VITICULTURE METHOD Conventional

The winery is now halfway through a makeover begun by Lucio Mosole when Gianni Menotti took over the cellar. The basic wines have been improved, with fruitier generous texture and structure, while only some of the more ambitious wines have been fine-tuned so some classic riserva wines are still in the cellar. The typically clayey local soil is wonderful for growing tocai and merlot grapes and it is no coincidence that these are the leading varieties grown here at Mosole.

Again this year, tocai and merlot gave the Mosole range its sheen, especially the Ad Nonam '08 and Eleo '09. The red displays a range of aromas with generous fruity hints and fines herbes, and a slim-bodied, enjoyably expansive palate, whereas the white combines the typical buttery quality of tocai with sensations of sea breezes and scrubland, creating an extremely tangy flavour. The Hora Sexta '08 has found its style, all freshness and barely perceptible hints of oak, while the succulent Merlot '09 gives an excellent performance among the basic wines.

○ Lison-Pramaggiore Chardonnay Hora Sexta '08	▼▼	4
○ Lison-Pramaggiore Lison Eleo '09	▼▼	4*
● Lison-Pramaggiore Merlot '09	▼▼	4*
● Lison-Pramaggiore Merlot Ad Nonam '08	▼▼	5*
● Lison-Pramaggiore Cabernet Franc '09	▼	4
○ Lison-Pramaggiore Chardonnay '09	▼	4
○ Lison-Pramaggiore Pinot Grigio '09	▼	4
● Lison-Pramaggiore Refosco P. R. '09	▼	4
○ Lison-Pramaggiore Sauvignon '09	▼	4
○ Hora Sexta '07	▽▽	4*
○ Lison-Pramaggiore Eleo Bianco '08	▽▽	4*
● Lison-Pramaggiore Rosso Eleo '08	▽▽	4

Il Mottolo

LOC. LE CONTARINE
VIA COMEZZARE
35030 BAONE [PD]
TEL. 3479456155
www.ilmottolo.it

CELLAR SALES
PRE-BOOKED VISITS

ANNUAL PRODUCTION 15,000 bottles
HECTARES UNDER VINE 6
VITICULTURE METHOD Conventional

Sergio Fortin and Roberto Dalla Libera's winery, which began almost as a joke, is now among the leading estates in Colli Euganei, an area affected by the general renewal process sweeping the wine sector in recent years. The estate's six hectares are situated in a nicely aspected, breezy position in the southern Colli Euganei, between Baone and Arquà Petrarca. Like most other wineries in this area, production focuses on merlot and cabernet, grown here since the mid 19th century.

The best results come indeed from the merlot and cabernet and this is clearly shown by the Serro '07. A blend of these two grapes, it presents the rich fruitiness with which this zone endows its wines, without compromising on suppleness, grip or excellent texture. The simpler but equally well-typed Comezzara and Vigna Marè, both '08, are firm and mouthwatering. The richness of their texture is there as a component in the overall harmony rather than for its own sake. A very good Passito Vigna del Pozzo '08 has candied citrus aromas and explosive sweetness.

● Colli Euganei Rosso Serro '07	▼▼	4*
● Colli Euganei Cabernet V. Marè '08	▼▼	3*
○ Colli Euganei Fior d'Arancio Passito V. del Pozzo '08	▼▼	4
● Colli Euganei Merlot Comezzara '08	▼▼	3*
○ Le Contarine '09	▼	4
● Colli Euganei Cabernet V. Marè '07	▽▽	3*
● Colli Euganei Cabernet V. Marè '06	▽▽	3*
○ Colli Euganei Fior d'Arancio Passito V. del Pozzo '06	▽▽	5
● Colli Euganei Merlot Comezzara '07	▽▽	3*
● Colli Euganei Merlot Comezzara '06	▽▽	3*
● Colli Euganei Rosso Serro '06	▽▽	4*
○ Le Contarine '08	▽▽	3*

Musella

LOC. FERRAZZE
VIA FERRAZZETTE, 2
37036 SAN MARTINO BUON ALBERGO [VR]
TEL. 045973385
www.musella.it

CELLAR SALES
PRE-BOOKED VISITS
ROOMS

ANNUAL PRODUCTION 200,000 bottles
HECTARES UNDER VINE 43
VITICULTURE METHOD Organic

In a landscape overrun with building developments in the 1980s and 1990s, it is a pleasure to discover an unspoilt natural oasis like the Musella estate, a few kilometres from Verona. Maddalena Pasqua's vineyards seem to remind us that man can co-exist with nature and beauty without necessarily tipping the balance. Just over 40 hectares provide the grapes for the estate's whole range, hinging on Valpolicella reds plus an estate red and a white.

Two Amarones were presented this year. The extraordinary Riserva '06 has overripe fruit alongside the medicinal herbs on the nose with tobacco and lovely minerally sensations beautifully reflected on the firmly structured, acid-braced palate. The Senza Titolo '03, on the other hand, is a more extreme wine: presented after a long ageing, it presents generous and fruity with bags of structure. The equally good Ripasso '07 shows complex aromas of dried flowers and spice wrapped in fruit while the Vigne Nuove di Musella '08 is lighter and more agile.

● Amarone della Valpolicella Ris. '06	▼▼	7
● Valpolicella Sup. Ripasso '07	▼▼	4
● Amarone della Valpolicella Senza Titolo '03	▼▼	8
● Monte del Drago Rosso '06	▼▼	6
○ Bianco del Drago '09	▼	3
● Valpolicella Sup. Vigne Nuove di Musella '08	▼	4
● Amarone della Valpolicella '03	▽▽	6
● Amarone della Valpolicella Ris. '05	▽▽	7
● Amarone della Valpolicella Ris. '04	▽▽	7
● Monte del Drago Rosso '05	▽▽	6
● Monte del Drago Rosso '04	▽▽	6
● Recioto della Valpolicella '06	▽▽	6
● Valpolicella Sup. Ripasso '06	▽▽	4
● Valpolicella Sup. Vigne Nuove di Musella '07	▽▽	4
● Valpolicella Sup. Vigne Nuove di Musella '06	▽▽	4

Daniele Nardello

via IV novembre, 56
37032 Monteforte d'Alpone [VR]
tel. 0457612116
www.nardellovini.it

CELLAR SALES
PRE-BOOKED VISITS

ANNUAL PRODUCTION 30,000 bottles
HECTARES UNDER VINE 17
VITICULTURE METHOD Conventional

A glance at the details heading the profile will confirm that Daniele and Federica Nardello only bottle a small quantity of their wine. The winery is still very young and has not yet conquered sufficient market space to absorb all the wine they produce, so part is sold wholesale. The better aspected and older vineyards provide the grapes for the estate's own wines, all adhering closely to the designation in interpretations that allow for full expression of the grapes' characteristics.

Three Soaves, a Recioto and a new garganega and trebbiano-based white are the Nardello estate's wines. An excellent performance from the Vigna Turbian '09, a Soave with plenty of trebbiano that offers strikingly fresh, floral aromas and edgy, rangy palate. The Monte Zoppega '08 reveals softer notes, partly owing to barrel maturation and partly to the vineyard aspect, which makes the grapes richer and pares back their acidity. The soft, mouthfilling palate is highly personal. There was a good performance from the '09 Meridies, a simple, nicely drinkable Soave.

O Recioto di Soave Suavissimus '07	5
O Soave Cl. Meridies '09	3*
O Soave Cl. Monte Zoppega '08	4
O Soave Cl. V. Turbian '09	4*
O Blanc De Fe '09	4
O Recioto di Soave Suavissimus '06	6
O Recioto di Soave Suavissimus '05	7
O Soave Cl. Monte Zoppega '07	4*
O Soave Cl. V. Turbian '08	4*
O Soave Cl. V. Turbian '07	4*

Angelo e Figli Nicolis

via Villa Girardi, 29
37029 San Pietro in Cariano [VR]
tel. 0457701261
www.vininicolis.com

CELLAR SALES
PRE-BOOKED VISITS

ANNUAL PRODUCTION 200,000 bottles
HECTARES UNDER VINE 42
VITICULTURE METHOD Conventional

In recent decades, the Nicolis brothers' winery has grown noticeably, first with the purchase of new vineyards and then with the extension of the cellar, albeit at different times, as the spaces gradually became too small. The remarkable grape production makes scrupulous selection possible but despite the growing numbers, Beppe and Giancarlo Nicolis are in no hurry to put the new vintages on the market, and only release the wines they feel are ready.

This year, in fact, only two wines were presented, the Valpolicella '09 and a Superiore Ripasso, the Seccal '07. The winery style aims to give even current wines decent structure, and the Valpolicella is nicely fruity and mouthwatering. The Seccal, on the other hand, gives one of its most impressive performances with complex aromas ranging from ripe fruit to fines herbes, pepper and minerally hints, in a constantly changing cycle. The palate shows firm body without unduly aping the Amarone, and drinks dry and gutsy.

● Valpolicella Cl. Sup. Rip. Seccal '07	5
● Valpolicella Cl. '09	4
● Amarone della Valpolicella Cl. Ambrosan '98	8
● Amarone della Valpolicella Cl. Ambrosan '93	8
● Amarone della Valpolicella Cl. '05	7
● Amarone della Valpolicella Cl. '01	7
● Amarone della Valpolicella Cl. '00	7
● Amarone della Valpolicella Cl. Ambrosan '03	8
● Amarone della Valpolicella Cl. Ambrosan '01	8
● Amarone della Valpolicella Cl. Ambrosan '00	8
● Valpolicella Cl. Sup. Seccal '06	5
● Valpolicella Cl. Sup. Seccal '05	5

Nino Franco

via Garibaldi, 147
31049 Valdobbiadene [TV]
tel. 0423972051
www.ninofranco.it

CELLAR SALES
PRE-BOOKED VISITS
ROOMS

ANNUAL PRODUCTION 1,200,000 bottles
HECTARES UNDER VINE 2
VITICULTURE METHOD Conventional

Despite being arguably the world's best known and most important ambassador for Treviso sparkling wines, Primo Franco has never yielded to the influence of market trends and has always stuck to his own style. Not one bottle of Extra Dry, the most widely produced type in this area, is produced here because in Primo's opinion Prosecco can only be dry or soft. The winery's style aims for vibrant, sumptuous fruit which will stand up perfectly to a few years' ageing in the cellar.

Once again a memorable performance, crowned with Three Glasses, from the Grave di Stecca '09, a Brut made from a single, walled, clos-like vineyard, just above Valdobbiadene. The aromas emerge slowly, burgeoning into generous, sophisticated florality that initially dominates fruit that then gradually claims some space. The palate shows above average structure although the acidity and fizz lend considerable harmony. All the products are good, and we particularly liked the San Floriano and Primo Franco Dry, a tropical, mouthwatering spumante.

○ Valdobbiadene Grave di Stecca Brut '09	▼▼▼	6
⊙ Brut Rosé Faìve	▼▼	4
○ Cartizze	▼▼	5
○ Treviso Rustico Brut	▼▼	4
○ Valdobbiadene Brut	▼▼	4*
○ Valdobbiadene Dry Primo Franco '09	▼▼	4
○ Valdobbiadene V. della Riva di S. Floriano Brut	▼▼	4*
○ Valdobbiadene Grave di Stecca Brut '08	▽▽▽	6
○ Cartizze '07	▽▽	5
○ Valdobbiadene Brut Rive di S. Floriano '08	▽▽	4*
○ Valdobbiadene Dry Primo Franco '08	▽▽	4

Novaia

via Novaia, 1
37020 Marano di Valpolicella [VR]
tel. 0457755129
www.novaia.it

CELLAR SALES
PRE-BOOKED VISITS

ANNUAL PRODUCTION 32,000 bottles
HECTARES UNDER VINE 7
VITICULTURE METHOD Conventional

Now that he has concluded his long adventure with the Bolla winery, Giampaolo Vaona can devote all his time to his own estate, putting his experience alongside the exuberant enthusiasm of his son Marcello. Here at Vaona they know that the enchanting, undeveloped landscapes of the Marano valley produce sophisticated wines with moderate concentration compensated by intense aromas and vibrant palates. The products are organized into a basic line and a selection from the best vineyards.

The second, more ambitious, line includes the Valpolicella I Cantoni '07, which immediately foregrounds the varietal, intensely peppery aromas of corvinone with ripe, juicy red berries. The palate is nicely concentrated with a tangy, quite lingering flavour. Only just behind it is the Amarone Le Balze Riserva '05, confidently fruity and firmly structured, while the Corte Vaona '06 follows a more traditional style, with fruit and crushed herbs on the nose and a dry palate. Similar but obviously in a lighter key is the Ripasso '07.

● Valpolicella Cl. Sup. I Cantoni '07	▼▼	5
● Amarone della Valpolicella Cl. Corte Vaona '06	▼▼	6
● Amarone della Valpolicella Cl. Le Balze Ris. '05	▼▼	8
● Valpolicella Cl. Sup. Ripasso '07	▼▼	4*
● Recioto della Valpolicella Cl. Le Novaje '07	▼	5
● Amarone della Valpolicella Cl. Corte Vaona '05	▽▽	6
● Amarone della Valpolicella Cl. Le Balze '01	▽▽	8
● Amarone della Valpolicella Cl. Le Balze Ris. '03	▽▽	8
● Valpolicella Cl. '06	▽▽	3
● Valpolicella Cl. Sup. I Cantoni '06	▽▽	5
● Valpolicella Cl. Sup. I Cantoni '05	▽▽	5
● Valpolicella Cl. Sup. Ripasso '06	▽▽	4

Ottella

FRAZ. SAN BENEDETTO DI LUGANA
LOC. OTTELLA
37019 PESCHIERA DEL GARDA [VR]
TEL. 0457551950
www.ottella.it

CELLAR SALES
PRE-BOOKED VISITS

ANNUAL PRODUCTION 300,000 bottles
HECTARES UNDER VINE 30
VITICULTURE METHOD Conventional

In recent years, Francesco and Michele Montresor have rationalized their estate to create two distinct properties. Merlot, cabernet and corvina are now grown exclusively on the ten hectares at Ponti sul Mincio, while the grubbing up of these varieties at Lugana has made room in the vineyards for mass selection of old trebbiano clones. Production is now over 300,000 bottles per year and the winery style favours taut, edgy wines supported by acidity and with good ageing potential.

The increasingly impressive range is led by the Lugana Superiore Molceo '08, an effortless Three Glass winner, and the Prima Luce '07. The Lugana lays out fresh aromatics with white-fleshed fruit beautifully supported by flowers and tropical sensations, and a tangy, lingering and harmonious palate. The Prima Luce, a trebbiano-based dried grape wine, has very complex aromas of candied peel, dried flowers and minerally hints, while mature sensations play hide-and-seek on the buttery, characterful palate. There are two interesting reds: the fragrant, gutsy Campo Sireso '08 and the simpler but extremely enjoyable Gemei '09.

○ Lugana Sup. Molceo '08	▼▼▼	5
○ Prima Luce Passito '07	▼▼	6
● Campo Sireso '08	▼▼	5
● Gemei Rosso '09	▼▼	4
○ Lugana '09	▼▼	4*
○ Lugana Brut	▼	4
⊙ Roses Roses '09	▼	4
○ Vignenuove '09	▼	4
○ Lugana Sup. Molceo '07	▽▽▽	5
● Campo Sireso '05	▽▽	5
● Campo Sireso '04	▽▽	5
○ Lugana '08	▽▽	4*
○ Lugana Le Creete '08	▽▽	4*
○ Lugana Le Creete '07	▽▽	4*
○ Prima Luce Passito '02	▽▽	6

★ Leonildo Pieropan

VIA CAMUZZONI, 3
37038 SOAVE [VR]
TEL. 0456190171
www.pieropan.it

CELLAR SALES
PRE-BOOKED VISITS

ANNUAL PRODUCTION 400,000 bottles
HECTARES UNDER VINE 45
VITICULTURE METHOD Conventional

With 50-odd hectares of vineyards, the Pieropan family is able to manage the best batches of grapes while progressing slowly with a replanting programme to improve the extensive vineyards on the estate. The black grapes for the Ruberpan and the future Amarone are vinified in the cellar of the Villa Cipolla estate at Tregnago but the old restored building is no longer in use. Instead, the cellar now extends underground leaving the beautiful landscape in front of the villa unspoilt.

The Soaves still lead the field as ideal representatives of this large terroir. The Calvarino '08 is a pedigree wine as usual, proffering a fresh yet complex nose and a firmly structured palate with a long, gutsy flavour. The '08 La Rocca, now in its 30th vintage, reveals the more generous, mouthfilling side of this wine type, with ripe fruit and spices and impressively handled oak. The Soave Classico '09 is excellent every year, presenting simple and drinkable yet never run-of-the-mill. Lastly, there was a good performance from the sophisticated Ruberpan '06.

○ Soave Cl. Calvarino '08	▼▼▼	5
○ Soave Cl. La Rocca '08	▼▼	6
● Ruberpan '06	▼▼	5
○ Soave Cl. '09	▼▼	4*
○ Soave Cl. Calvarino '07	▽▽▽	5
○ Soave Cl. Calvarino '06	▽▽▽	5
○ Soave Cl. Calvarino '05	▽▽▽	5
○ Soave Cl. Calvarino '04	▽▽▽	5
○ Soave Cl. Calvarino '03	▽▽▽	5
○ Soave Cl. Calvarino '02	▽▽▽	5
○ Soave Cl. La Rocca '02	▽▽▽	6
○ Soave Cl. Sup. La Rocca '00	▽▽▽	6
○ Soave Cl. Sup. La Rocca '99	▽▽▽	6
○ Soave Cl. Sup. La Rocca '96	▽▽▽	6

Albino Piona

FRAZ. CUSTOZA
VIA BELLAVISTA, 48
37060 SOMMACAMPAGNA [VR]
TEL. 045516055
www.albinopiona.it

CELLAR SALES
PRE-BOOKED VISITS

ANNUAL PRODUCTION 500,000 bottles
HECTARES UNDER VINE 70
VITICULTURE METHOD Conventional

Production is gradually growing at Piona, in quality rather than in quantity, which is well-established. Having transferred all the activities to the new, functional cellar in Via Bellavista, Silvio, Monica, Alessandro and Massimo can now dedicate more attention to the leading wines, while continuing to produce the classic products which made the winery's fortune decades ago. The vineyards are mainly planted to grapes for the two lakeside designations, Bardolino and Custoza, with some digressions.

This year, the most impressive wine is a Custoza, although it could hardly be otherwise given the family tradition. It has earned Piona more visibility not only in the market but also in our Guide. The Custoza SP '09 is firmly based on the tradition of a few decades ago: uncompromising, made using the most natural methods as well as today's knowledge and technology. Intense aromas of flowers and white-fleshed fruit open the way for a wine with modest alcohol but bags of personality and a lingering flavour. The spicy Corvina '08 is very good.

○ Bianco di Custoza Passito La Rabitta '07	▼▼	6
○ Bianco di Custoza SP '09	▼▼	4*
● Campo Massimo Corvina Veronese '08	▼▼	4*
● Bardolino '09	▼	3
⊙ Bardolino Chiaretto '09	▼	3
○ Bianco di Custoza '09	▼	3*
● Campo Massimo Merlot '08	▼	4
● Bardolino '06	▽▽	3
⊙ Bardolino Chiaretto '04	▽▽	3*
○ Bianco di Custoza '07	▽▽	3*
○ Bianco di Custoza Sup. Campo del Selese '06	▽▽	3*
○ Bianco di Custoza Sup. Campo del Sèlese '01	▽▽	4
● Campo Massimo Corvina Veronese '07	▽▽	4*
● Campo Massimo Corvina Veronese '04	▽▽	3*

Piovene Porto Godi

FRAZ. TOARA
VIA VILLA, 14
36020 VILLAGA [VI]
TEL. 0444885142
www.piovene.com

CELLAR SALES
PRE-BOOKED VISITS

ANNUAL PRODUCTION 80,000 bottles
HECTARES UNDER VINE 32
VITICULTURE METHOD Conventional

Tommaso Piovene's winery is representative of the Colli Berici, isolated hill country south of Vicenza looking towards the nearby Colli Euganei. Since the mid 18th century, merlot and cabernet have been grown here alongside tocai rosso, the territory's unique signature variety. The cellar at Villaga develops through existing buildings in an enchanting labyrinth while the vineyards are part of the foothill area leading up to the summit of the hill overlooking the property.

Over the years, the vines have been planted in the most suitable locations and almost all the labels show the vineyard of origin today. The exception is the Polveriera '09, a Bordeaux blend made with estate-grown grapes that shows fresh, mouthwatering and very enjoyable. Richer in texture and complexity are the Merlot Fra i Broli '08, with a weighty palate supported by lively acidity, and the Cabernet Pozzare '07, to which we awarded Three Glasses. Glimpses of its rich extract are evident even on the nose and reveals a firm structure with bags of personality. Among the whites we recommend the good Garganega '09.

● Colli Berici Cabernet Vign. Pozzare '07	▼▼▼	5
● Colli Berici Merlot Fra i Broli '08	▼▼	5
○ Colli Berici Garganega Vign. Riveselle '09	▼▼	4
● Colli Berici Tai Rosso Vign. Riveselle '09	▼▼	4*
● Polveriera Rosso '09	▼▼	4*
○ Thovara Passito Bianco '08	▼▼	5
○ Colli Berici Pinot Bianco Polveriera '09	▼	4
○ Colli Berici Sauvignon Vigneto Fostine '09	▼	4
● Colli Berici Cabernet Vign. Pozzare '06	▽▽	5
● Colli Berici Merlot Fra i Broli '07	▽▽	5
● Colli Berici Merlot Fra i Broli '06	▽▽	5
● Colli Berici Tai Rosso Thovara '07	▽▽	6
● Colli Berici Tai Rosso Vign. Riveselle '08	▽▽	3
○ Thovara Passito Bianco '07	▽▽	5

Umberto Portinari

LOC. BROGNOLIGO
VIA SANTO STEFANO, 2
37032 MONTEFORTE D'ALPONE [VR]
TEL. 0456175087
portinarivini@libero.it

CELLAR SALES
PRE-BOOKED VISITS

ANNUAL PRODUCTION 30,000 bottles
HECTARES UNDER VINE 4
VITICULTURE METHOD Conventional

Umberto Portinari's small winery is in the village of Brognoligo, behind Monteforte d'Alpone, nestling in the Soave Classico hills. The family manages a handful of hectares with great passion, transforming the grapes into products with a distinctive yet simple country style, in which the unpredictability and pleasantly rustic nature of the garganega grape finds plenty of space. Naturally, the quality of the wines is not consistently high but their personality always makes an impression.

Only two Soaves were presented this year, both from '08. The Albare, for which the fruit-bearing cane is cut to increase concentration of the grapes, gives mature aromas mainly of yellow-fleshed fruit, with lovely vegetal hints that follow through on the firmly structured palate. The subtler Ronchetto shows fruity aromas with lovely floral and citrus sensations and a dry, satisfying palate. Perle d'Oro Brut is a simple Charmat-method sparkling wine with a fragrant, moreish flavour.

Wine	Glasses	Rating
O Soave Albare Doppia Maturazione Ragionata '08	2 (filled)	4
O Soave Cl. Ronchetto '08	2 (filled)	4
O Perle d'Oro Brut	1 (filled)	4
O Soave Albare Doppia Maturazione Ragionata '07	2 (outline)	4
O Soave Albare Doppia Maturazione Ragionata '06	2 (outline)	4
O Soave Albare Doppia Maturazione Ragionata '05	2 (outline)	4*
O Soave Albare Doppia Maturazione Ragionata '04	2 (outline)	4*
O Soave Cl. Ronchetto '07	2 (outline)	4*
O Soave Cl. Ronchetto '06	2 (outline)	4*
O Soave Cl. Ronchetto '05	2 (outline)	4*

Prà

VIA DELLA FONTANA, 31
37032 MONTEFORTE D'ALPONE [VR]
TEL. 0457612125
grazianopra@libero.it

CELLAR SALES
PRE-BOOKED VISITS

ANNUAL PRODUCTION 220,000 bottles
HECTARES UNDER VINE 20
VITICULTURE METHOD Conventional

Graziano Prà's beautiful estate covers much of the Soave Classico zone, where it has been a local benchmark for many years, and to a lesser extent the nearby Valpolicella designation where traditional Veronese wines are produced in full respect for the environment. While the whites show a mouthwateringly rich texture, the more sophisticated reds foreground natural aromatics with the gutsy tautness characteristic of corvina and corvinone.

Exemplary in this sense is the Valpolicella Morandina '07, which bucks the local trend with a colour that is not excessively intense and extremely fragrant spicy, undergrowth aromas followed by a dry, moderately weighty palate. The Monte Grande '09 and Staforte '08 are two very good Soaves which express their qualities in very different profiles. Monte Grande, aged in large casks, has a very nice fresh nose and the usual beautifully elegant palate while Staforte, a Three Glass star, aged unhurriedly in stainless steel and has acquired intriguingly complex aromatics with a ravishing note of savouriness on the palate.

Wine	Glasses	Rating
O Soave Cl. Staforte '08	3 (filled)	5
O Soave Cl. Monte Grande '09	2 (filled)	5
● Valpolicella Sup. Morandina '07	2 (filled)	6
O Soave Cl. '09	2 (filled)	4*
O Soave Cl. Colle S. Antonio '08	2 (filled)	5
● Valpolicella Sup. Ca' Morandina '08	1 (filled)	4
O Soave Cl. Monte Grande '08	3 (outline)	5
O Soave Cl. Monte Grande '06	3 (outline)	5
O Soave Cl. Monte Grande '05	3 (outline)	5
O Soave Cl. Monte Grande '04	3 (outline)	5
O Soave Cl. Monte Grande '03	3 (outline)	5
O Soave Cl. Monte Grande '02	3 (outline)	5
O Soave Cl. Staforte '06	3 (outline)	5*

★ Giuseppe Quintarelli

VIA CERÈ, 1
37024 NEGRAR [VR]
TEL. 0457500016
giuseppe.quintarelli@tin.it

CELLAR SALES
PRE-BOOKED VISITS

ANNUAL PRODUCTION 60,000 bottles
HECTARES UNDER VINE 12
VITICULTURE METHOD Conventional

This winery, probably more than any other in Veneto, represents the dream: a strongly defended sense of tradition and enormous patience while waiting for just the right moment to release the new wines. The wines are not produced every year, unless all the conditions are satisfactory and only in these circumstances can we taste the few bottles of Amarone or Recioto. Just over ten hectares yield minimal quantities: these eloquent statistics inadequately express the intimate, almost religious, relationship established with the wine in its long sojourn in the cellar as it waits for Giuseppe's OK.

The great qualities of the 2000 vintage, already clearly demonstrated by the Amarone last year, are replicated in the Amarone Selezione Giuseppe Quintarelli, which is further matured in the cellar before release ten years after the harvest. Profound, layered aromas, with hints of tobacco and spice following the fruit on the nose usher in a silky, long-lingering palate. The inimitable Alzero '00, from dried cabernet franc grapes, has an intensely spicy nose rich in stewed fruit, and a very personal harmonious palate veined with the subtle presence of softer sensations.

● Amarone della Valpolicella Cl. Sel. Giuseppe Quintarelli '00	🍷🍷	8
● Alzero '00	🍷🍷	8
● Primo Fiore '06	🍷🍷	5
● Amarone della Valpolicella Cl. '00	YYY	8
● Amarone della Valpolicella Cl. '98	YYY	8
● Amarone della Valpolicella Cl. '97	YYY	8
● Amarone della Valpolicella Cl. Ris. '83	YYY	8
● Amarone della Valpolicella Cl. Sup. Monte Cà Paletta '00	YYY	8
● Amarone della Valpolicella Cl. Sup. Monte Cà Paletta '93	YYY	8
● Amarone della Valpolicella Cl. Sup. Ris. '85	YYY	6
● Recioto della Valpolicella Cl. '95	YYY	8
● Recioto della Valpolicella Cl. Monte Ca' Paletta '97	YYY+	8
● Rosso del Bepi '96	YYY	8
● Valpolicella Cl. Sup. '99	YYY	8

Le Ragose

FRAZ. ARBIZZANO
VIA LE RAGOSE, 1
37020 NEGRAR [VR]
TEL. 0457513241
www.leragose.com

CELLAR SALES
PRE-BOOKED VISITS

ANNUAL PRODUCTION 150,000 bottles
HECTARES UNDER VINE 19
VITICULTURE METHOD Conventional

The Galli brothers' estate extends along the eastern ridge of the Negrar valley, at Arbizzano, above the winter fog line. Here, 20-odd hectares of vineyards produce a range consisting almost entirely of traditional wines that are accurately interpreted with no concessions to market trends. Marco's passion for this area and his grapes is clear as he describes them knowledgeably, offering his insightful take on what goes on in this, the most important designation in the province of Verona.

In the absence of both Amarones, we focused our attention on the Valpolicella Ripasso '07, which shows good concentration, dominated by red berries and spicy peppery hints, and then a dry, nicely taut profile on the palate. The Recioto '07 is even spicier and moderately sweet while the Galli brothers' version of Cabernet Sauvignon is highly original. There are generous, predominantly fruity aromas in the '05 and a surprisingly broad, harmonious palate with subtle sensations.

● Garda Cabernet Sauvignon '05	🍷🍷	5
● Recioto della Valpolicella Cl. '07	🍷🍷	6
● Valpolicella Cl. Sup. Ripasso '07	🍷🍷	4*
● Valpolicella Cl. '09	🍷	4
● Amarone della Valpolicella Cl. '88	YYY	8
● Amarone della Valpolicella Cl. '86	YYY	8
● Amarone della Valpolicella Cl. '04	YY	8*
● Amarone della Valpolicella Cl. '03	YY	7
● Amarone della Valpolicella Cl. Marta Galli '03	YY	8
● Recioto della Valpolicella Cl. '06	YY	6
● Valpolicella Cl. '08	YY	4*
● Valpolicella Cl. Sup. Le Sassine '05	YY	4
● Valpolicella Cl. Sup. Le Sassine Ripasso '04	YY	4*

Roccolo Grassi

VIA SAN GIOVANNI DI DIO, 19
37030 MEZZANE DI SOTTO [VR]
TEL. 0458880089
roccolograssi@libero.it

PRE-BOOKED VISITS

ANNUAL PRODUCTION 42,000 bottles
HECTARES UNDER VINE 14
VITICULTURE METHOD Conventional

Francesca and Marco Sartori have been among the most highly esteemed producers in Valpolicella since their first wines were released just over ten years ago. The strength of this young estate lies in its vineyards but the Sartoris are continually subjecting their approach to questions that arise from constant contact with the wine sector, talking with colleagues and tasting wines from many other places. Bottle ageing times are gradually becoming longer to let the wines mature adequately.

We tasted a full line-up this year with four wines, each better than the last. We'll start with the Amarone '06. Closed on the nose, it opens out slowly on the palate to show perfect handling of the substantial texture, actually growing in the glass. The Valpolicella Superiore '07 walked away with Three Glasses, opening out in an equally leisurely fashion into fresher aromas focusing, predictably enough, on red berry fruit. The palate is dry and firmly structured. Recioto '06 shows its usual concentrated sweetness and grip while the Soave Vigneto La Broia '08 has completely absorbed the oak and reveals a taut, lingering flavour.

● Valpolicella Sup. Roccolo Grassi '07	6
● Amarone della Valpolicella Roccolo Grassi '06	8
● Recioto della Valpolicella Roccolo Grassi '06	6
○ Soave Vign. La Broia '08	4*
● Amarone della Valpolicella Roccolo Grassi '00	8
● Amarone della Valpolicella Roccolo Grassi '99	8
● Valpolicella Sup. Roccolo Grassi '04	6
● Recioto della Valpolicella Roccolo Grassi '05	6
○ Soave Sup. La Broia '07	4*
● Valpolicella Sup. Roccolo Grassi '06	6

Roeno

VIA MAMA, 5
37020 BRENTINO BELLUNO [VR]
TEL. 0457230110
www.cantinaroeno.com

CELLAR SALES
PRE-BOOKED VISITS
ROOMS AND FOOD

ANNUAL PRODUCTION 80,000 bottles
HECTARES UNDER VINE 35
VITICULTURE METHOD Conventional

The narrow Valdadige winds from the province of Verona through the mountains towards Trento. There is little room for grapes to squeeze into what space is left here by the building developments, river and railway. On the other hand, the grapes grown hereabouts are extraordinary, thanks to the altitude, temperature variation and constant breezes. In just a few years, the Fugatti brothers' winery has earned itself a leading role in the designation with fresh-tasting, delicious wines of an excellent standard.

The Cristina late harvest is, as ever, the most impressive wine produced by the Fugatti brothers. The '07 version is citrussy with generous minerally sensations and an explosively sweet palate nicely controlled by acidity. Making its extraordinary debut is the Praecipuus '09, a Riesling grown at a high altitude that gives strikingly intense aromas of tropical fruit and benzene, with a lean, racy palate. There was a good performance from the Bordeaux blend Roeno '06, erroneously reviewed last year. Lastly, the whole range of simpler wines is showing progress.

○ Cristina V. T. '07	6
○ Praecipuus '09	5
● Rosso Roeno '06	5
● Valdadige Terra dei Forti Enantio '07	5
● La Rua Marzemino '09	4
○ Müller Thurgau Le Giarre '09	4*
● Teroldego I Dossi '09	4
○ Valdadige Chardonnay Le Fratte '09	4
○ Valdadige Pinot Grigio Tera Alta '09	4
○ Cristina V. T. '06	6
○ Cristina V. T. '05	6
● Valdadige Terra dei Forti Enantio '06	5
● Valdadige Terra dei Forti Enantio '05	5
○ Valdadige Terra dei Forti Pinot Grigio '08	4*

Ruggeri & C.

via Prà Fontana
31049 Valdobbiadene [TV]
tel. 04239092
www.ruggeri.it

PRE-BOOKED VISITS

ANNUAL PRODUCTION 1,000,000 bottles
HECTARES UNDER VINE 14
VITICULTURE METHOD Conventional

At this difficult time, with a market recession and new, huge designation to contend with, Paolo Bisol has chosen not to compromise or get involved in a price war. Instead, he has raised his game with an impressive range of products throughout. A strong, extensive network of growers, profound knowledge of the area and decades of experience have allowed him to take a leading role in launching the new DOCG. Tiptoeing into the business are his children Giustino and Isabella.

Vecchie Viti and Giustino B. are benchmark wines for the whole designation every year. The sparkling Giustino B. '09 won Three Glasses with its generous floral aromas and uncommonly stylish effervescence on the palate. Vecchie Viti '09 is a much firmer, tauter Brut made exclusively from vines over 80 years old that were discovered in supplier-growers' plots. It offers fresh aromas of apples and pears on the nose. The Extra Brut and Sessantanni, both '09, are excellent sparkling wines made from grapes grown in the heart of Valdobbiadene. The former is very dry while the Sessantanni is a celebration of the winery's 60 years of activity.

○ Valdobbiadene Extra Dry Giustino B. '09	3 (black)	5
○ Valdobbiadene Brut Vecchie Viti '09	2 (black)	5
○ Cartizze	2 (black)	5
○ L'Extra Brut '09	2 (black)	4
○ Valdobbiadene Brut Quartese	2 (black)	4*
○ Valdobbiadene Dry S. Stefano	2 (black)	4
○ Valdobbiadene Extra Dry Giall'Oro	2 (black)	4*
○ Sessantanni Exta Dry '09	2 (black)	4
○ Pinot Grigio Vign. Cornuda '09	1 (black)	4
○ Valdobbiadene Dry S. Stefano	3 (white)	4
○ L'Extra Brut '08	2 (white)	4
○ Valdobbiadene Brut Vecchie Viti '08	2 (white)	5
○ Valdobbiadene Extra Dry Giustino B. '08	2 (white)	5

Le Salette

via Pio Brugnoli, 11c
37022 Fumane [VR]
tel. 0457701027
www.lesalette.it

CELLAR SALES
PRE-BOOKED VISITS
ROOMS

ANNUAL PRODUCTION 130,000 bottles
HECTARES UNDER VINE 20
VITICULTURE METHOD Conventional

After years spent expanding his vine stock, Franco Scamperle is aiming for grand objectives no longer and has changed the winery's style, focusing on products of a high standard without, necessarily, making them in large quantities. Hence the decision to give up a small part of the vineyard in the extended designation, which helped keep the quantities high but also made it necessary to cross half the zone every day. Over the years, the cellar has been enlarged and become more functional, using the space available below the existing buildings.

The range has been well-established for years, and is closely bound up with traditional local wines, with outstanding quality from the Amarone Pergole Vece '06 and Ripasso I Progni. The former shows aromas of overripe fruit, fines herbes and spices while the palate is perfectly harmonious with a tangy, succulent flavour. The Ripasso '07 has a leaner profile traced with clear, fresh fruit aromas followed by a firmly structured palate and vigorous flavour. The Amarone La Marega '06 and Recioto Pergole Vece '07 display good texture but need further maturation.

● Amarone della Valpolicella Cl. Pergole Vece '06	2 (black)	8
● Valpolicella Cl. Sup. Ripasso I Progni '07	2 (black)	5
● Amarone della Valpolicella Cl. La Marega '06	2 (black)	6
● Ca' Carnocchio '07	2 (black)	5
● Recioto della Valpolicella Cl. Pergole Vece '07	2 (black)	6
● Recioto della Valpolicella Cl. Le Traversagne '07	1 (black)	6
● Valpolicella Cl. '09	1 (black)	4
● Amarone della Valpolicella Cl. Pergole Vece '05	3 (white)	8
● Amarone della Valpolicella Cl. Pergole Vece '95	3 (white)	8
● Amarone della Valpolicella Cl. La Marega '05	2 (white)	6
● Recioto della Valpolicella Cl. Pergole Vece '06	2 (white)	6
● Valpolicella Cl. Sup. Ripasso I Progni '06	2 (white)	5

La Sansonina

LOC. SANSONINA
37019 PESCHIERA DEL GARDA [VR]
TEL. 0457551905
www.sansonina.it

CELLAR SALES
PRE-BOOKED VISITS

ANNUAL PRODUCTION 21,000 bottles
HECTARES UNDER VINE 12
VITICULTURE METHOD Conventional

The Lugana area skims the southern banks of Lake Garda where the glacial hills give way to the extensive clay deposits that nurture the local turbiana grape. This is not the only variety to adapt beautifully to clayey land, as local country workers well know. Merlot, too, never fails to make a valuable contribution in this narrow strip of land between Veneto and Lombardy. At Sansonina, Carla Prospero proves a faithful exponent of both merlot and the traditional white Garda grape.

The Lugana '09, in only its second vintage, gives a clear indication of the qualities in the terroir. Predominant white-fleshed fruit on the nose is followed by herbaceousness reflected on a palate that opens out over a varietal vein of acidity into a lingering finish. The Merlot Sansonina '07 shows its Veronese side, its sweet, overripe fruit streaked with subtle hints of cocoa powder and spices. The palate is firm-bodied and juicy, again supported by taut acidity.

○ Lugana Sansonina '09	2 (black)	4*
● Sansonina '07	2 (black)	7
○ Lugana Sansonina '08	2 (outline)	4*
● Sansonina '06	2 (outline)	7
● Sansonina '05	2 (outline)	7
● Sansonina '04	2 (outline)	7
● Sansonina '03	2 (outline)	7
● Sansonina '01	2 (outline)	7

Tenuta Sant'Antonio

LOC. SAN ZENO
VIA CERIANI, 23
37030 COLOGNOLA AI COLLI [VR]
TEL. 0457650383
www.tenutasantantonio.it

CELLAR SALES
PRE-BOOKED VISITS

ANNUAL PRODUCTION 600,000 bottles
HECTARES UNDER VINE 95
VITICULTURE METHOD Conventional

Very few wineries have succeeded in accelerating the development of a territory but the Tenuta Sant'Antonio estate, owned by the Castagnedi family, is one of them. In a decade or so, they have managed to craft a precise interpretation of the extended Valpolicella zone, in a style typified by rich extract and sound aromas, and take viticulture into hitherto neglected areas. Today, the vine stock has grown to almost 100 hectares and the wines don't seem to have any chinks in their armour.

The Amarone Campo dei Gigli is now a classic in the designation. The '06, which won Three unequivocal Glasses, flaunts a range of aromas pivoting around healthy fruit while hints of spice and aromatic herbs accompany the palate through to a long, lingering finish. Although the Valpolicella Superiore La Bandina '07 is made using dried grapes and follows the same route as the Amarone, it emerges each year with an increasingly distinct image. Lastly, the Soave Monte Ceriani '08, aged in oak this year unlike previous editions, shows generous, quite stylish aromas and a vibrantly savoury palate.

● Amarone della Valpolicella Campo dei Gigli '06	3 (black)	8
○ Soave Monte Ceriani '08	2 (black)	4*
● Valpolicella Sup. La Bandina '07	2 (black)	5
● Valpolicella Sup. Ripasso Monti Garbi '08	2 (black)	4*
● Amarone della Valpolicella Campo dei Gigli '05	3 (outline)	8
● Amarone della Valpolicella Campo dei Gigli '04	3 (outline)	8
● Amarone della Valpolicella Campo dei Gigli '99	3 (outline)	8
● Amarone della Valpolicella Campo dei Gigli '98	3 (outline)	8
● Amarone della Valpolicella Campo dei Gigli '97	3 (outline)	8
○ Soave Monte Ceriani '05	3 (outline)	4*
● Valpolicella Sup. La Bandina '01	3 (outline)	6

Santa Margherita

VIA ITA MARZOTTO, 8
30025 FOSSALTA DI PORTOGRUARO [VE]
TEL. 0421246111
www.santamargherita.com

CELLAR SALES
PRE-BOOKED VISITS

ANNUAL PRODUCTION **12,500,000 bottles**
HECTARES UNDER VINE **N.D.**
VITICULTURE METHOD **Conventional**

Last year's positive impressions have been amply echoed this year. Santa Margherita seems to be rapidly claiming a more influential role on the Veneto wine scene. An increase in the estate's own vineyards makes it possible for the Fossalta-based winery to release leading wines obtained without purchased grapes, which however remain of fundamental importance for the less ambitious wines. The wines from both Valdadige and Alto Adige show significant improvement in quality.

Two of the most interesting wines, both white, come from Alto Adige. The Luna dei Feldi '09 is an original blend of chardonnay, müller thurgau and gewürztraminer which combines the structure, acidity and aromas of the three varieties with balanced, very enjoyable results. The Pinot Grigio Impronta del Fondatore '09 shows a more subdued profile as the vegetal, smoky sensations typical of the variety slowly emerge, to be followed by a savoury, satisfyingly long palate. From the Venetian flatlands comes a good '08 version of the distinctively and decidedly moreish Malbech.

○ A. A. Pinot Grigio Impronta del Fondatore '09	▼▼	4
○ Luna dei Feldi '09	▼▼	4*
● Malbech Impronta del Fondatore '08	▼▼	4*
○ Cartizze	▼	5
○ Valdobbiadene 52 Extra Dry	▼	4
○ Valdobbiadene Brut	▼	4
○ Valdobbiadene Extra Dry	▼	4
● Refosco P.R. Impronta del Fondatore '08	▼	4
○ Valdadige Pinot Grigio '09	▼	4
○ A. A. Pinot Grigio Impronta del Fondatore '08	▽▽	4*
○ Luna dei Feldi '07	▽▽	4
● Malbech '06	▽▽	4
● Malbech '05	▽▽	4*
● Merlot '07	▽▽	4*
● Refosco P.R. '07	▽▽	4

Santa Sofia

FRAZ. PEDEMONTE
VIA CA' DEDÉ, 61
37020 SAN PIETRO IN CARIANO [VR]
TEL. 0457701074
www.santasofia.com

PRE-BOOKED VISITS

ANNUAL PRODUCTION **550,000 bottles**
HECTARES UNDER VINE **N.D.**
VITICULTURE METHOD **Conventional**

Although during the history of the Guide we have witnessed the birth of many small wineries in the Verona area, and in Valpolicella in particular, we mustn't forget that larger estates present here for decades if not centuries have represented Verona worldwide. One of these is Santa Sofia, which has for many years been committed to all the designations in this province, thanks to the many estates scattered across the area which provide the grapes to be processed in the traditional Pedemonte winery.

The wines are presented quite slowly, so we are unlikely to see all the new vintages together. This year, we are missing the Amarone although the Montegradella '06 goes a long way towards making up for its absence. A generous nose with red berries and hints of medicinal herbs and spices introduces a lean palate with a succulent flavour. Also interesting is the '07 Ripasso, showing more complex, mature aromas and a softer palate. The rest of the range is always dependably good, both the traditional wines like the Custoza '09 and the more imaginative products.

● Valpolicella Cl. Sup. Montegradella '06	▼▼	5
● Valpolicella Sup. Ripasso '07	▼▼	4
○ Custoza Montemagrin '09	▼	3
○ Garda Pinot Grigio Le Calderare '09	▼	3
○ Lugana '09	▼	3
● Merlot Corvina '08	▼	3
● Predaia '03	▼	5
○ Recioto di Soave Cl. '07	▼	6
○ Soave Cl. Montefoscarino '09	▼	3
● Amarone della Valpolicella Cl. '05	▽▽	7
● Amarone della Valpolicella Cl. '04	▽▽	7
● Amarone della Valpolicella Cl. '01	▽▽	7
● Amarone della Valpolicella Cl. Gioé '03	▽▽	8
● Merlot Corvina '06	▽▽	3*
● Recioto della Valpolicella Cl. '06	▽▽	6
● Valpolicella Sup. Ripasso '06	▽▽	4

Santi

VIA UNGHERIA, 33
37031 ILLASI [VR]
TEL. 0456269600
www.carlosanti.it

CELLAR SALES
PRE-BOOKED VISITS

ANNUAL PRODUCTION 2,000,000 bottles
HECTARES UNDER VINE 70
VITICULTURE METHOD Conventional

When Amarone was relaunched on the lists of leading wineries, Santi stood out for its efforts to improve the quality of both this leading wine and the Valpolicella Superiore, which more than any other has been overshadowed by the Amarone phenomenon. Today, under the admirable guidance of the Gruppo Italiano Vini, Santi is among the best wineries in the area, with a critical production mass of around two million bottles, split across the various Veronese designations.

The Solane '08 is a splendid Valpolicella Ripasso which has always tried to present an image that is distinct from Amarone, highlighting the features of the traditional grape varieties. Its limpid ruby red heralds generous swath of wild berries and pepper, preceding a lean-bodied palate supported more by acidity than extract. The Amarone Proemio '07 is held back slightly by its premature release but has what it takes for a radiant future. Perfect fruit, tannin and acidity will achieve greater harmony from bottle ageing.

● Amarone della Valpolicella Proemio '07	▼▼	7
● Valpolicella Cl. Sup. Solane Ripasso '08	▼▼	4*
● Amarone della Valpolicella '07	▼▼	6
○ Soave Cl. Vign. di Monteforte '09	▼▼	4
⊙ Bardolino Chiaretto L'Infinito '09	▼	3
● Bardolino Cl. Vign. Ca' Bordenis '09	▼	4
● Valpolicella Cl. Le Caleselle '09	▼	4
● Amarone della Valpolicella Proemio '05	▽▽▽	7
● Amarone della Valpolicella Proemio '03	▽▽▽	7*
● Amarone della Valpolicella Proemio '00	▽▽▽	7
● Amarone della Valpolicella Proemio '06	▽▽	7
● Amarone della Valpolicella Proemio '04	▽▽	7
● Valpolicella Cl. Sup. Solane Ripasso '07	▽▽	4*
● Valpolicella Cl. Sup. Solane Ripasso '06	▽▽	4*
● Valpolicella Cl. Sup. Solane Ripasso '05	▽▽	4
● Valpolicella Cl. Sup. Solane Ripasso '04	▽▽	4*

Casa Vinicola Sartori

FRAZ. SANTA MARIA
VIA CASETTE, 2
37024 NEGRAR [VR]
TEL. 0456028011
www.sartorinet.com

PRE-BOOKED VISITS

ANNUAL PRODUCTION 15,000,000 bottles
HECTARES UNDER VINE 40
VITICULTURE METHOD Conventional

This classic Santa Maria di Negrar winery is now in its fourth generation. Andrea, Luca and Paolo have led the estate not only to remarkably good production standards but have also extended the vineyard holding. However, the big production numbers are founded on grapes purchased from local growers, as well as the partnership with Cantina di Colognola, which has worked very smoothly for several years now. The leading line is based on the classic Valpolicella wines, with one or two forays into neighbouring designations.

The top Sartori wines are missing as they are still maturing in the cellar but the Valpolicella Superiore Vigneti di Montegradella '07 steps in to fly the flag with wild berries and spices on the nose and a dry, taut flavour on a very pleasing palate. There's also a good performance from the Valpolicella Regolo '07, a Ripasso that gives more approachable ripe fruit and a generous but not overly voluminous palate. The Amarone Reius '06 is richer, still but nicely fresh, while the lighter wines from the Verona designations are dependably good.

● Amarone della Valpolicella Cl. Reius '06	▼▼	7
● Bardolino Cl. Ca' Nova '09	▼▼	4
● Valpolicella Cl. Sup. Vign. di Montegradella '07	▼▼	4*
● Valpolicella Sup. Ripasso Regolo '07	▼▼	4*
● Bardolino Cl. '09	▼	3*
○ Lugana '09	▼	3
○ Lugana La Musina '09	▼	4
○ Marani '08	▼	4
● Recioto della Valpolicella Cl. Rerum '08	▼	7
○ Soave Cl. '09	▼	3
○ Soave Cl. Sella '09	▼	4
● Valpolicella Cl. '08	▼	4
● Amarone della Valpolicella Cl. Corte Brà '04	▽▽	8
● Amarone della Valpolicella Le Vigne di Turano I Saltari '04	▽▽	8
● Valpolicella Sup. Ripasso Regolo '05	▽▽	4

★ Serafini & Vidotto

via Carrer, 8/12
31040 Nervesa della Battaglia [TV]
tel. 0422773281
serafinievidotto@serafinievidotto.com

CELLAR SALES
PRE-BOOKED VISITS

ANNUAL PRODUCTION 100,000 bottles
HECTARES UNDER VINE 21
VITICULTURE METHOD Organic

Activity never stops at Francesco Serafini and Antonello Vidotto's winery, which has promoted the image of Treviso and Veneto worldwide since the early 1990s, and today heads research into vineyard management that will reduce environmental impact without having to trust simply to luck. The range presented in recent years has been revised with the classic labels now flanked by simpler, lighter wines, often in the new half-litre format, which aims to promote awareness of wine consumption.

The top house wine and recipient of Three Glasses is again Rosso dell'Abazia, a cabernet sauvignon-heavy Bordeaux blend which has lost some of its distinctively exuberant aromatic quality over the years, acquiring instead greater depth and a firmer, more compact palate. The interesting Oltre il Rosso '07, another Bordeaux blend, is a great second wine, available in one-litre or half-litre formats. It's a ripe, fruity wine that caters for a taste for softness. The Pinot Nero '07 has a satisfying pale hue and subtle aromas followed by a firmer, more vibrant palate.

● Montello e Colli Asolani Il Rosso dell'Abazia '07	▼▼▼	6
● Montello e Colli Asolani Rosso Oltre il Rosso '07	▼▼	5
○ Oltre Il Bianco '09	▼▼	4
○ Treviso Bollicine di Prosecco	▼▼	4
● Pinot Nero '07	▼▼	6
⊙ Bollicine Rosé	▼	4
● Il Rosso dell'Abazia '02	▽▽▽	7
● Montello e Colli Asolani Il Rosso dell'Abazia '06	▽▽▽	6
● Montello e Colli Asolani Il Rosso dell'Abazia '05	▽▽▽	6
● Montello e Colli Asolani Il Rosso dell'Abazia '04	▽▽▽	6
○ Montello e Colli Asolani Extra Dry Bollicine di Prosecco	▽▽	4
● Montello e Colli Asolani Phigaia '06	▽▽	5*

F.lli Speri

loc. Pedemonte
via Fontana, 14
37020 San Pietro in Cariano [VR]
tel. 0457701154
www.speri.com

CELLAR SALES
PRE-BOOKED VISITS

ANNUAL PRODUCTION 350,000 bottles
HECTARES UNDER VINE 50
VITICULTURE METHOD Conventional

The Speri family winery perfectly mirrors the history of this magnificent Valpolicella area. With its extensive vineyards stretching into several municipal areas, experience Speri's its greatest strength. Through awareness of its roots and clear-focused objectives, the Via Fontana winery has been able to face the greatest challenges, coping with the evolution of taste in wine without repudiating tradition.

In recent years, Speri's flagship wine, Amarone Monte Sant'Urbano, has enhanced the strength and clarity of its aromas without losing any personality or grip. Three Glasses went to the '06 edition. The Valpolicella of the same name is also good, aiming as ever to maintain a distinct character from the Amarone, as is demonstrated by the light, bright '07 version. The '08 Ripasso is softer and more mouthwatering while the Recioto La Roggia '07 is all stylish wild berries and mint with acidity to offset the sweetness very nicely.

● Amarone della Valpolicella Cl. Vign. Monte Sant'Urbano '06	▼▼▼	8
● Recioto della Valpolicella Cl. La Roggia '07	▼▼	7
● Valpolicella Cl. Sup. Sant'Urbano '07	▼▼	5*
● Valpolicella Cl. Sup. Ripasso '08	▼▼	5
● Valpolicella Cl. '09	▼	4
● Amarone della Valpolicella Cl. Vign. Monte Sant'Urbano '04	▽▽▽	8
● Amarone della Valpolicella Cl. Vign. Monte Sant'Urbano '01	▽▽▽	8
● Amarone della Valpolicella Cl. Vign. Monte Sant'Urbano '00	▽▽▽	8
● Amarone della Valpolicella Cl. Vign. Monte Sant'Urbano '97	▽▽▽	8
● Amarone della Valpolicella Cl. Vign. Monte Sant'Urbano '95	▽▽▽	8
● Amarone della Valpolicella Cl. Vign. Monte Sant'Urbano '93	▽▽▽	8

I Stefanini

VIA CROSARA, 21
37032 MONTEFORTE D'ALPONE [VR]
TEL. 0456175249
www.istefanini.it

CELLAR SALES
PRE-BOOKED VISITS

ANNUAL PRODUCTION 80,000 bottles
HECTARES UNDER VINE 16
VITICULTURE METHOD Conventional

With only a few harvests under his belt, Francesco Tessari has a very clear vision of Soave and how this area should be interpreted. The wines are made exclusively from the estate's own vineyards, some on the hills of the classic zone and some on the plain. The latter yield grapes used exclusively for the basic Soave while the grapes grown on the hillslopes provide the winery's two vineyard selections, both sourced from Monte Tenda and both produced only in favourable years, to be released after lengthy bottle maturation.

At Tessari, the Soaves are not aged in oak. Long maturation on the lees in stainless steel enables the wines to acquire complex aromas and great expression in the mouth. The Monte de Toni '08, from the lowest vineyard with red, iron-rich soil, displays smoky aromas of ripe yellow-fleshed fruit, with a firm, vibrant, savoury palate. The Monte di Fice '08 hails from strongly basaltic soil and shows more tropical, exuberant aromas in which fruit takes the leading role. The palate is full-bodied and voluptuous.

O Soave Cl. Monte de Toni '08	▼▼	3*
O Soave Cl. Monte di Fice '08	▼▼	4*
O Soave Il Selese '09	▼	2*
O Soave Cl. Sup. Monte di Fice '07	YYY	3*
O Soave Cl. Monte de Toni '07	YY	3*
O Soave Cl. Sup. Monte di Fice '06	YY	3*
O Soave Il Selese '07	YY	2*
O Soave Il Selese '05	YY	3

David Sterza

LOC. CASTERNA
VIA CASTERNA, 37
37022 FUMANE [VR]
TEL. 0457704201
www.davidsterza.it

CELLAR SALES
PRE-BOOKED VISITS

ANNUAL PRODUCTION 20,000 bottles
HECTARES UNDER VINE 4
VITICULTURE METHOD Conventional

The journey of this Casterna winery, active for about a dozen years, towards improved quality has been very satisfying for David Sterza, who devotes his energy to the classic Valpolicella wines, with a little help from his cousin Paolo Mascanzoni. With only a few hectares in excellent prestigious locations, production is limited in quantity but has no weak points. The small, functional cellar blends into the village and consists of an invaluable first-floor grape-drying room, an underground vinification and ageing area and a shop on the ground floor.

In relatively few years of activity, the winery has abandoned the somewhat rustic style of the early years, acquiring integrity and definition while maintaining close contact with tradition. The very good Amarone '06, with its clear aromas of dried red berry fruits and spices, is a little gem of perfection on the palate, which is firm and sound, finishing dry. The Corvina '08, in which the grapes are briefly part-dried, is crisp and succulent while the '08 Ripasso shows approachable aromas of fruit and cocoa powder on the nose and nice supple movement over the palate.

● Amarone della Valpolicella Cl. '06	▼▼	6
● Corvina Veronese '08	▼▼	5
● Valpolicella Cl. Sup. Ripasso '08	▼▼	4
● Valpolicella Cl. '09	▼	3*
● Amarone della Valpolicella Cl. '05	YY	6*
● Amarone della Valpolicella Cl. '04	YY	6*
● Amarone della Valpolicella Cl. '03	YY	7
● Corvina Veronese '07	YY	5
● Recioto della Valpolicella Cl. '03	YY	6
● Valpolicella Cl. Sup. Ripasso '06	YY	4*
● Valpolicella Cl. Sup. Ripasso '05	YY	5
● Valpolicella Cl. Sup. Ripasso '03	YY	5

Suavia

FRAZ. FITTÀ DI SOAVE
VIA CENTRO, 14
37038 SOAVE [VR]
TEL. 0457675089
www.suavia.it

CELLAR SALES
PRE-BOOKED VISITS

ANNUAL PRODUCTION 100,000 bottles
HECTARES UNDER VINE 12
VITICULTURE METHOD Conventional

Few wineries can claims the charms of Suavia. This small estate has opted not to crank up quantities, despite its great success. With an exclusively female management team, led by sisters Arianna and Meri, Suavia allows its wines the appropriate time to mature in bottle before release, flying in the face of an impatient market that would rather see things speeded up. The style of the wines is evident from the basic version up. All convey a strong sense of place.

While Le Rive, a Soave aged in oak, was missing last year, this year it is the turn of the Monte Carbonare, which will be spending another year in the cellar. Thanks to longer ageing, the '07 Le Rive shows mature, very stylish aromas with yellow-fleshed fruit embracing faint hints of oak and more prominent minerally sensations. The palate is richly extracted and mouthfilling, with a soft, succulent flavour. The Soave Classico '09 displays its usual vibrant savouriness and edgy acidity. Complex aromas and perfectly integrated sweetness mark out the Recioto Acinatium '06.

O Recioto di Soave Acinatium '06	TT	6
O Soave Cl. '09	TT	4*
O Soave Cl. Le Rive '07	TT	5
O Soave Cl. Le Rive '02	YYY	5
O Soave Cl. Monte Carbonare '08	YYY	4*
O Soave Cl. Monte Carbonare '07	YYY	4*
O Soave Cl. Monte Carbonare '06	YYY	4*
O Soave Cl. Monte Carbonare '05	YYY	4*
O Soave Cl. Monte Carbonare '04	YYY	4
O Soave Cl. Monte Carbonare '02	YYY	4
O Soave Cl. Sup. Le Rive '00	YYY	5
O Soave Cl. Sup. Le Rive '98	YYY	5
O Recioto di Soave Acinatium '05	YY	6
O Soave Cl. '08	YY	4*

Tamellini

VIA TAMELLINI, 4
37038 SOAVE [VR]
TEL. 0457675328
piofrancesco.tamellini@tin.it

CELLAR SALES
PRE-BOOKED VISITS

ANNUAL PRODUCTION 160,000 bottles
HECTARES UNDER VINE 17
VITICULTURE METHOD Conventional

Estates like the one owned by brothers Gaetano and Piofrancesco Tamellini have made a significant contribution to kick-starting Soave, a designation as well-known as it is sluggish. These attentive exponents of the garganega grape and the variable nature of the Soave area managed to turn out a characterful, dependable range of products from the beginning. Their unmistakeable style, with rich extract and supple flavours, has developed from the old vines and unpredictable soil typical of the western slopes of the classic zone, where basalt soil gives way increasingly to limestone.

The '08 Le Bine de Costjola is a Soave showing mature aromas from the vineyard on, where the yields are distinctly low and the ripeness of the fruit is scrupulously nurtured. A long period in the cellar can only increase this wine's sunny, complex expressivity and the peachy fruit is joined in the '08 version by more complex hints of Mediterranean scrubland and dried flowers. Good grip on the soft, mouthfilling palate thanks to the acidity. Even more generous and succulent, the Recioto '07 counters sweetness with almost electric acidity. The Soave '09 is very good.

O Soave Cl. Le Bine de Costjola '08	TT	4*
O Recioto di Soave V. Marogne de Costjola '07	TT	6
O Soave '09	TT	4*
O Soave Cl. Le Bine '04	YYY	4*
O Soave Cl. Le Bine de Costjola '06	YYY	4*
O Soave Cl. Le Bine de Costjola '05	YYY	4*
O Recioto di Soave V. Marogne '04	YY	6
O Recioto di Soave V. Marogne '03	YY	6
O Soave '07	YY	4
O Soave '06	YY	4*
O Soave Cl. '08	YY	4*
O Soave Cl. Le Bine de Costjola '07	YY	4*

Tanorè

FRAZ. SAN PIETRO DI BARBOZZA
VIA MONT DI CARTIZZE, 3
31040 VALDOBBIADENE [TV]
TEL. 0423975770
www.tanore.it

CELLAR SALES
PRE-BOOKED VISITS

ANNUAL PRODUCTION 80,000 bottles
HECTARES UNDER VINE 8
VITICULTURE METHOD Conventional

Valdobbiadene is among the most enchanting areas of Italy. Its slopes are completely covered with vines, even where the slopes fall steeply down to the valley floor, and the hills are endlessly interspersed with sheer drops. The Follador siblings' winery clings to a hillside, overlooking the Cartizze area. The Folladors have always been careful interpreters of Prosecco and its hilly terrain. The range focuses on the traditional local variety, now called glera, and is organized according to the wines' sugar level in a fresh, approachable style.

Four labels were presented, in a fairly common line-up: a Brut, an Extra Dry, a Dry and a Cartizze. The first is a sparkling wine with a fresh, floral nose and a lean, citrussy, rather straightforward palate, while the Extra Dry displays forward apple and pear fruit with a pleasing, approachable flavour. As residual sugar increases, the wines become more impressive. For proof, taste the tropical fruits, mouthfilling Cartizze and to an even greater extent the Millesimato, with aromas of flowers and white-fleshed fruits, a stylish palate and dry finish.

○ Cartizze	🍷🍷	6
○ Valdobbiadene Extra Dry	🍷🍷	4
○ Valdobbiadene Il Tanorè Mill. Dry	🍷🍷	4
○ Valdobbiadene Brut	🍷	4

Giovanna Tantini

LOC. OLIOSI
VIA GOITO, 10
37014 CASTELNUOVO DEL GARDA [VR]
TEL. 0457575070
www.giovannatantini.it

CELLAR SALES
PRE-BOOKED VISITS

ANNUAL PRODUCTION 25,000 bottles
HECTARES UNDER VINE 12
VITICULTURE METHOD Conventional

Bardolino has for years been tagged as a DOC zone in recession. Today it is experiencing a great revival, owing to two closely connected factors. The first of these is the renewed market appeal of fresh, quaffable wines while the second and even more important reason is the growth in quality imposed by local estates. These are often new wineries, like this one managed with great passion by Giovanna Tantini, who has rapidly made it a benchmark for the whole DOC.

The excellent performance from the '09 Bardolino nearly took it to our finals. Nicely pale and brilliant, but still clear, in hue, it gives varietal wild berries and pepper-led spices on the nose, which are beautifully reflected on the savoury palate. Ettore is a Bordeaux blend. The '07 offers firm structure and rich extract not found in the Bardolino, emphasizing lovely fresh aromas and a compact palate, as well as good acidic grip. The Bardolino Chiaretto '09 is fragrant, succulent and very pleasing indeed.

● Bardolino '09	🍷🍷	4*
● Ettore '07	🍷🍷	5
⊙ Bardolino Chiaretto '09	🍷	4
● Bardolino '08	ΥΥ	4*
● Bardolino '07	ΥΥ	4*
● Bardolino '06	ΥΥ	4
● Ettore '06	ΥΥ	5
● Ettore '05	ΥΥ	7

F.lli Tedeschi

LOC. PEDEMONTE
VIA G. VERDI, 4
37029 SAN PIETRO IN CARIANO [VR]
TEL. 0457701487
www.tedeschiwines.com

CELLAR SALES
PRE-BOOKED VISITS

ANNUAL PRODUCTION 500,000 bottles
HECTARES UNDER VINE 38
VITICULTURE METHOD Conventional

The estate owned by Antonietta, Sabrina and Riccardo Tedeschi, still helped out by their father Lorenzo, is among the leading and best-known wineries in Valpolicella. The Tedeschis have made important purchases in recent years in the eastern area of the designation with the Maternigo estate, where part of the extensive acreage has been planted to vine. We'll see the fruits of this new venture next year but meanwhile we note the delayed release of the Amarone Monte Olmi. This difficult decision will allow the wine to mature properly before release.

Three very weighty Valpolicellas helped make up for the Amarone's absence, highlighting the area's typical gutsiness and grip, rather than opulence of texture. There were excellent performances from the Capitel San Rocco '08 and Capitel dei Nicalò '08, though we preferred the former, its red berries and vegetal aromas contrasting on the palate with very firm structure and a dry flavour with a lingering finish. The Nicalò is sounder and more approachable with a mouthwatering palate. Fabriseria '07 is more complex but will also become harmonious after further bottle ageing.

● Valpolicella Cl. Sup. Capitel dei Nicalò '08	TT	4*
● Valpolicella Sup. Capitel San Rocco Ripasso '08	TT	5*
● Amarone della Valpolicella Cl. '06	TT	6
● Recioto della Valpolicella Capitel Monte Fontana '05	TT	6
● Valpolicella Cl. Lucchine '09	TT	3
● Valpolicella Cl. Sup. La Fabriseria '07	TT	6
● Amarone della Valpolicella Cl. Capitel Monte Olmi '01	YYY	8
● Amarone della Valpolicella Cl. Capitel Monte Olmi '99	YYY	8
● Amarone della Valpolicella Cl. Capitel Monte Olmi '97	YYY	8
● Amarone della Valpolicella Cl. Capitel Monte Olmi '95	YYY	8
● Rosso della Fabriseria '97	YYY	6
● Amarone della Valpolicella Cl. Capitel Monte Olmi '05	YY	8

Viticoltori Tommasi

LOC. PEDEMONTE
VIA RONCHETTO, 2
37020 SAN PIETRO IN CARIANO [VR]
TEL. 0457701266
www.tommasiwine.it

CELLAR SALES
PRE-BOOKED VISITS

ANNUAL PRODUCTION 900,000 bottles
HECTARES UNDER VINE 165
VITICULTURE METHOD Conventional

After the recent increase in vineyards, the Tommasi family has developed a large, new cellar alongside the traditional base in Via Ronchetto. Spacious areas designed to improve handling of grapes and wines are very important for a winery producing almost a million bottles a year. Giancarlo Tommasi, who is gradually taking charge of the cellar, has effected a considerable leap in quality with the Valpolicella wines, in pursuit of a clearer, more fragrant style that still hews to tradition.

This improvement is particularly evident in the Amarone Classico '06 and Valpolicella Superiore Vigneto Rafael '08, showing much better defined aroma profiles in which clear, juicy fruit is complemented by satisfying by hints of spice. On the palate, the Amarone is richly but not excessively textured, with a light, succulent flavour, while the Rafael is firmly structured and bright. As usual, the Crearo della Conca d'Oro '08, a blend of cabernet franc, corvina and lightly dried oseleta, impressed us with rich extract and integrity. The Recioto '07 is mouthwatering and very long-lingering.

● Amarone della Valpolicella Cl. '06	TT	7
● Valpolicella Cl. Sup. Vign. Rafael '08	TT	5
● Amarone della Valpolicella Cl. Ca' Florian '06	TT	7
● Arele Rosso '08	TT	5
● Crearo della Conca d'Oro '08	TT	5
● Recioto della Valpolicella Cl. Fiorato '07	TT	6
○ Lugana Vign. San Martino Il Sestante '09	T	4
● Valpolicella Cl. Sup. Ripasso '08	T	5
● Amarone della Valpolicella Cl. '05	YY	7
● Amarone della Valpolicella Cl. '04	YY	7
● Amarone della Valpolicella Cl. Ca' Florian '05	YY	7
● Crearo della Conca d'Oro '07	YY	5*
● Crearo della Conca d'Oro '06	YY	5
● Valpolicella Cl. Sup. Ripasso '07	YY	5
● Valpolicella Cl. Sup. Vign. Rafael '07	YY	5

Trabucchi d'Illasi

LOC. MONTE TENDA
37031 ILLASI [VR]
TEL. 0457833233
www.trabucchidillasi.it

CELLAR SALES
PRE-BOOKED VISITS

ANNUAL PRODUCTION **70,000 bottles**
HECTARES UNDER VINE **15**
VITICULTURE METHOD **Certified organic**

Giuseppe and Raffaella Trabucchi's estate is situated along the ridge separating the areas of Soave and Valpolicella. This is not, strictly speaking, a borderline since the two designations often overlap hereabouts, allowing producers to work with both types. This is the case at Trabucchi, where the red Valpolicellas are joined by a mouthwatering Recioto di Soave when the growing year permits. The vineyards have been organically farmed for almost two decades out of respect for the grapes and surrounding land.

Only two wines were presented this year, both of a remarkably high standard. Recioto Terre del Cereolo is only produced in favourable years and the '06 displays intense aromas of red berries and spices, followed by an explosively sweet palate held in check through to the lingering finish by acidity and, above all, extract. The Valpolicella Terre di San Colombano '06 is more austere and profound with a lovely hint of fines herbes and pepper alongside the fruit, introducing a firm-bodied palate with a taut, dry flavour. The other wines are still maturing in the cellar, in pursuit of perfect harmony.

- ● Recioto della Valpolicella Terre del Cereolo '06 — TT 8
- ● Valpolicella Sup. Terre di S. Colombano '06 — TT 6
- ● Amarone della Valpolicella '04 — YYY 8
- ● Recioto della Valpolicella Cereolo '05 — YYY 8
- ● Valpolicella Sup. Terre di S. Colombano '03 — YYY 5*
- ● Amarone della Valpolicella Alberto Trabucchi '03 — YY 8
- ● Dandarin '05 — YY 6
- ● Recioto della Valpolicella '05 — YY 8
- ● Valpolicella Sup. Dandarin '04 — YY 5
- ● Valpolicella Sup. Terre del Cereolo '05 — YY 6
- ● Valpolicella Sup. Terre di S. Colombano '05 — YY 7

Cantina Sociale della Valpantena

FRAZ. QUINTO
VIA COLONIA ORFANI DI GUERRA, 5B
37034 VERONA
TEL. 045550032
www.cantinavalpantena.it

CELLAR SALES
PRE-BOOKED VISITS

ANNUAL PRODUCTION **7,500,000 bottles**
HECTARES UNDER VINE **600**
VITICULTURE METHOD **Conventional**

The development of a wine area always involves co-operative structures to some extent. Under the umbrella of such organizations, hundreds of different families and wine mentalities continually interact with each other. This Quinto operation has swiftly trained the efforts of its members in the direction of grape quality above all while in the cellar the technical team led by Luca Degani looks after winemaking. Over the years, the winery's style has increasingly focused on approachable, very drinkable and enjoyable wines.

The very wide range of products is almost entirely dedicated to Veronese tradition with DOC and IGT wines obtained from classic varieties. The two '08 Valpolicellas are the most impressive, both from the Torre del Falasco line. The Superiore has red berries and medicinal herbs on the nose and a medium-bodied, beautifully harmonious palate. The Ripasso is more pliant, dominated by red berries and hints of cocoa powder on the nose with a lovely soft palate with succulent flavour. The Recioto Tesauro '07 reveals nice sweetness and acidity.

- ● Valpolicella Sup. Ripasso Torre del Falasco '08 — TT 4
- ● Valpolicella Valpatena Sup. Torre del Falasco '08 — TT 4
- ● Amarone della Valpolicella '07 — T 6
- ● Amarone della Valpolicella Torre del Falasco '06 — T 7
- ○ Chardonnay Baroncino '09 — T 3
- ● Corvina Torre del Falasco '09 — T 2
- ○ Garganega Torre del Falasco '09 — T 2
- ○ Lugana Torre del Falasco '09 — T 3
- ● Recioto della Valpolicella Tesauro '07 — T 6
- ● Valpolicella Valpantena Ritocco '08 — T 4
- ● Amarone della Valpolicella Torre del Falasco '05 — YY 7
- ● Recioto della Valpolicella Tesauro '06 — YY 6
- ● Valpolicella Sup. Ripasso Torre del Falasco '07 — YY 4*

Cantina Sociale Valpolicella

via Ca' Salgari, 2
37024 Negrar [VR]
tel. 0456014300
www.cantinanegrar.it

CELLAR SALES
PRE-BOOKED VISITS

ANNUAL PRODUCTION 7,500,000 bottles
HECTARES UNDER VINE 500
VITICULTURE METHOD Conventional

Cantina Sociale della Valpolicella is the designation's leading co-operative winery, especially in terms of quality. This is not achieved exclusively in the cellar, as is demonstrated by ambitious growing projects aiming to improve production and achieve a more rational blend of grapes, based on their specific features. The guiding hand on the helm belongs to Daniele Accordini who, along with his staff, explores abandoned grape varieties and high hillside vineyards in the hope of endowing the wines with greater identity.

The range of wines presented this year was really impressive, starting with the quintessentially traditional Recioto. The '07 Vigneti di Moron, sourced from vineyards right behind the town of Negrar, unveils heady aromas of cherries, pepper and fines herbes. Exuberant sweetness on the palate has a lovely vein of acidity to streamline the flavour. Of the many Valpolicellas presented, we especially enjoyed the Verjago '06, a wine with a strong identity, spicy aromas and a vibrant, racy palate. There was a good performance from the Amarone '05, made from organically grown grapes.

● Recioto della Valpolicella Cl. Vign. di Moron Domini Veneti '07	TT	6
● Amarone della Valpolicella Cl. Biologico '05	TT	8
● Amarone della Valpolicella Cl. Domini Veneti '07	TT	6
● Amarone della Valpolicella Cl. Vign. di Jago Domini Veneti '04	TT	8
● Recioto della Valpolicella Cl. Domini Veneti '08	TT	6
● Valpolicella Cl. Sup. La Casetta di Ettore Righetti Domini Veneti '06	TT	5
● Valpolicella Cl. Sup. Verjago Domini Veneti '06	TT	6
● Valpolicella Cl. Sup. Ripasso Vign. di Torbe Domini Veneti '08	T	4
● Recioto della Valpolicella Cl. Vigneti di Moron Domini Veneti '01	YYY	6
● Recioto della Valpolicella Cl. Vign. di Moron Domini Veneti '06	YY	6

Massimino Venturini

fraz. San Floriano
via Semonte, 20
37020 San Pietro in Cariano [VR]
tel. 0457701331
www.viniventurini.com

CELLAR SALES
PRE-BOOKED VISITS
FOOD

ANNUAL PRODUCTION 90,000 bottles
HECTARES UNDER VINE 12
VITICULTURE METHOD Conventional

The Venturini brothers' winery came to the fore in the early 1990s when all of Valpolicella was experiencing a revival. Since then much has changed at the cellar and throughout the designation, but Mirco and Daniele have unwaveringly followed the path of a tradition that has never let them down, never yielding to a market that demands something new every year. The range exclusively focuses on traditional wines with a pleasantly husky character.

It's hard to choose between the two Amarones. Campomasua is the child of a single vineyard while the Classico reflects rigorous selection carried out in the other vineyards. The former wins Three Glasses in its '05 incarnation. Longer ageing in the cellar has imparted complex aromas in which overripe fruit embraces hints of crushed flowers and undergrowth. The palate shows considerable texture with smooth tannins and satisfying harmony. The '06 Classico is more youthful on the nose, with a taut, edgier palate. Back on excellent form, the Semonte Alto '06 gives complex aromas and a stylish flavour.

● Amarone della Valpolicella Cl. Campomasua '05	TTT	7
● Amarone della Valpolicella Cl. '06	TT	6
● Recioto della Valpolicella Cl. Le Brugnine '06	TT	6
● Valpolicella Cl. Sup. '07	TT	4
● Valpolicella Cl. Sup. Ripasso Semonte Alto '06	TT	4*
● Recioto della Valpolicella Cl. '07	T	6
● Valpolicella Cl. '09	T	3
● Amarone della Valpolicella Cl. '05	YY	6*
● Amarone della Valpolicella Cl. '04	YY	6
● Amarone della Valpolicella Cl. '03	YY	6*
● Amarone della Valpolicella Cl. Campomasua '03	YY	7
● Amarone della Valpolicella Cl. Campomasua '01	YY	7
● Recioto della Valpolicella Cl. Le Brugnine '04	YY	6
● Recioto della Valpolicella Cl. Le Brugnine '03	YY	6

Agostino Vicentini

FRAZ. SAN ZENO
VIA C. BATTISTI, 62C
37030 COLOGNOLA AI COLLI [VR]
TEL. 0457650539
vicentini@vinivicentini.com

CELLAR SALES
PRE-BOOKED VISITS

ANNUAL PRODUCTION 60,000 bottles
HECTARES UNDER VINE 14
VITICULTURE METHOD Conventional

The Vicentini family estate began as a fruit farm, as is often the case in this area. Grapes slowly took over from other crops although there is still a small but excellent production of cherries. In recent years, improvement in the quality of the grapes has been matched by work in the cellar and today Vicentini is one of the best producers in the whole designation. The Colognola ai Colli area lies in both the Valpolicella and Soave designations but the best results come from the latter.

Although we have become used to seeing excellent performances from Il Casale, which once again won Three Glasses, more recently Terre Lunghe has been receiving greater appreciation for its subtle aromas of white-fleshed fruit and flowers and even more so for its palate. The '09 is light, savoury, lingering and anything but commonplace. The '09 Il Casale makes the most of lower yields, showing a firmer, juicier profile that stays lean and taut. There's good news from Valpolicella with a characterful performance from the '06 Idea Bacco, a juicy, nicely balanced Superiore.

Wine	Glasses	Price
○ Soave Sup. Il Casale '09	3 (black)	5*
○ Soave Vign. Terre Lunghe '09	2 (black)	3*
○ Recioto di Soave '08	2 (black)	6
● Valpolicella Sup. Idea Bacco '06	2 (black)	6
● Valpolicella Sup. '07	1 (black)	4
○ Soave Sup. Il Casale '08	3 (white)	5
○ Soave Sup. Il Casale '07	3 (white)	5
○ Recioto di Soave '07	2 (white)	6
○ Soave Vign. Terre Lunghe '08	2 (white)	3*
○ Soave Vign. Terre Lunghe '07	2 (white)	3*

Vigna Ròda

VIA MONTE VERSA, 1569
35030 VÒ [PD]
TEL. 0499940228
www.vignaroda.com

CELLAR SALES
PRE-BOOKED VISITS

ANNUAL PRODUCTION 50,000 bottles
HECTARES UNDER VINE 17
VITICULTURE METHOD Conventional

Gianni Strazzacappa's estate stretches along the western ridge of the Colli Euganei around Vò, where the volcanic rocks are interspersed with alluvial deposits. This is red wine country, as is clear from the winery's distinctive, richly textured style. Production from the almost 20 hectares is gradually rising, in step with the growing fame of a winery establishing itself as one of the most interesting new operations in the Colli Euganei regional park.

The leading wine is Scarlatto, a merlot-heavy Bordeaux blend which gets more impressive every year, and the '07 came within a hair's breadth of our final tastings. Intense aromas of red berries and medicinal herbs and beautiful concentration on the palate with nicely integrated tannins. The Merlot and Cabernet, both '09, are more approachable, rich-textured wines. The Fior d'Arancio Passito Petali d'Ambra '07 gives aromas of candied citrus peel and spices which are nicely reflected on the palate with well-measured sweetness.

Wine	Glasses	Price
● Colli Euganei Cabernet Espero '09	2 (black)	4*
● Colli Euganei Merlot Il Damerino '09	2 (black)	3*
○ Colli Euganei Passito Fior d'Arancio Petali D'Ambra '07	2 (black)	5
● Colli Euganei Rosso Scarlatto '07	2 (black)	4*
○ Colli Euganei Bianco '09	1 (black)	4
○ Colli Euganei Chardonnay Cà Zamira '09	1 (black)	4
○ Colli Euganei Passito Fior d'Arancio Spumante '09	1 (black)	4
● Colli Euganei Rosso '09	1 (black)	4
● Colli Euganei Serprino '09	1 (black)	4
● Colli Euganei Merlot '08	2 (white)	3*
○ Colli Euganei Passito Fior d'Arancio '06	2 (white)	5
● Colli Euganei Rosso Scarlatto '06	2 (white)	4*

Vignale di Cecilia

LOC. FORNACI
VIA CROCI, 14
35030 BAONE [PD]
TEL. 042951420
www.vignaledicecilia.it

CELLAR SALES
PRE-BOOKED VISITS

ANNUAL PRODUCTION 20,000 bottles
HECTARES UNDER VINE 8
VITICULTURE METHOD Certified organic

Increasingly impressive wines are produced by Paolo Brunello at Vignale di Cecilia, located in the southern part of the Colli Euganei, in a small, west-facing amphitheatre. The local climate enables Bordeaux varieties to ripen perfectly while the white grapes are grown exclusively on the rented estate, which turns out a traditional combination of white wines including Moscato and an excellent if unexpected monovarietal Tocai. The quality of the wines is increasingly reliable thanks to the input of Andrea Boaretti.

Let's begin with the new wine, a monovarietal Tocai called Cocài. The '08 gives almondy aromas with minerally hints and yellow-fleshed fruit. The medium-bodied palate has a dynamic flavour. Benavides '09 is more closed and opens out only slowly into aromas of white-fleshed fruit with vibrant hints of sulphur, deriving from the volcanic nature of the local area. We admired the excellent performance from the '07 Passacaglia, a merlot-heavy Bordeaux blend that shows rich and fruity, with fines herbes and pencil lead on the nose and a sophisticated, nicely structured, long-lingering palate.

● Colli Euganei Rosso Passacaglia '07	TT	5
○ Benavides '09	TT	4
○ Cocài '08	TT	4
● Colli Euganei Rosso Covolo '08	TT	4
○ Benavides '08	YY	4*
○ Benavides '07	YY	4*
○ Folia '06	YY	5
● Colli Euganei Rosso Covolo '07	YY	4*
● Colli Euganei Rosso Covolo '06	YY	4*
● Colli Euganei Rosso Covolo '05	YY	4
● Colli Euganei Rosso Passacaglia '06	YY	5
● Colli Euganei Rosso Passacaglia '04	YY	5

Vignalta

VIA SCALETTE, 23
35032 ARQUÀ PETRARCA [PD]
TEL. 0429777305
www.vignalta.it

CELLAR SALES
PRE-BOOKED VISITS

ANNUAL PRODUCTION 280,000 bottles
HECTARES UNDER VINE 55
VITICULTURE METHOD Conventional

Vignalta was the first estate to promote the Colli Euganei around the world and is still the leading winery for the designation today. Vignalta's strength lies primarily in its extensive vineyards: over 50 hectares on the best slopes of the Colli Euganei regional park, where all varieties are suitably situated and the most favourably aspected areas have their own labels. The winery style is a delicate compromise of the rich features offered by the volcanic hill terrain and the elegance typical of great wines.

A slight delay in the presentation of the wines, to allow the leading products a little more maturation time, has left a few spaces in the list below but not in our overall evaluation of the range, in which all the wines are impressive. We applauded an excellent performance from the Arquà '06, from merlot grown on flaky red soil that endows it with very fruity character and extremely rich texture, as well as mouthwatering acidity, in a very weighty overall result. The new '06 Marrano from cabernet and merlot in equal parts showed well, with approachable fruit and a succulent, nicely textured palate.

● Colli Euganei Rosso Arquà '06	TT	6
○ Colli Euganei Chardonnay '08	TT	5
○ Colli Euganei Pinot Bianco '09	TT	4*
● Colli Euganei Rosso Venda '07	TT	4*
● Marrano '06	TT	5
○ Sirio '09	TT	4
● Colli Euganei Cabernet Ris. '90	YYY	6
● Colli Euganei Rosso Arquà '04	YYY	6
● Colli Euganei Rosso Gemola '01	YYY	6
● Colli Euganei Rosso Gemola '00	YYY	6
● Colli Euganei Rosso Gemola '99	YYY	6
● Colli Euganei Rosso Gemola '98	YYY	6

Le Vigne di San Pietro

via San Pietro, 23
37066 Sommacampagna [VR]
tel. 045510016
www.levignedisanpietro.it

CELLAR SALES
PRE-BOOKED VISITS

ANNUAL PRODUCTION 80,000 bottles
HECTARES UNDER VINE 20
VITICULTURE METHOD Conventional

Carlo Nerozzi's estate extends into the Bardolino and Custoza DOC zones, and more recently into Valpolicella at Valgatara and Moron, thanks to the ten or so hectares brought by new associate Giovanni Boscaini. The partners, assisted along the way by their friend and consultant Federico Giotto, demonstrate great unity of purpose. Whatever their origin, the wines produced share features, from the approachable Bardolino to the more ambitious Amarone. All are very enjoyable and show a strong link to the terroir and its traditions.

The range we tasted showed no weak spots. To the contrary, there are a few peaks of excellence. Our favourites were a fresh-tasting Bardolino '09 on one hand and on the other a more ambitious Bordeaux blend Refolà '05, which demonstrates the winery's flexibility. Clearly defined fruit in the Bardolino joins with a succulent, drinkable palate that picks up the spicy hints of black pepper to enhance complexity. The Refolà has a broad, clear nose on which red berries alternate with dried flowers, and a taut, savoury flavour. The Amarone '06, new this year, promises well with its harmonious flavour.

● Bardolino '09	▼▼	4*
● Refolà Cabernet Sauvignon '05	▼▼	7
● Amarone della Valpolicella '06	▼▼	7
⊙ CorDeRosa '09	▼▼	4*
○ Custoza '09	▼▼	4*
● Valpolicella Cl. Sup. '08	▼▼	5
● Valpolicella Cl. Sup. Rip. '08	▼▼	5
● Valpolicella '09	▼	4
● Refolà Cabernet Sauvignon '04	▽▽▽	7
○ Sud '95	▽▽▽	7
● Bardolino '08	▽▽	4*
⊙ CorDeRosa '08	▽▽	4*
○ Custoza '08	▽▽	4*
○ Due Cuori Passito '07	▽▽	6

Vigneto Due Santi

v.le Asiago, 174
36061 Bassano del Grappa [VI]
tel. 0424502074
vignetoduesanti@virgilio.it

CELLAR SALES
PRE-BOOKED VISITS

ANNUAL PRODUCTION 100,000 bottles
HECTARES UNDER VINE 18
VITICULTURE METHOD Conventional

For over 20 years now, cousins Adriano and Stefano Zonta have run the family estate just outside Bassano below the Valsugana. The quantities of grapes produced in the vineyards exceed the winery's requirements so they are able to replant when necessary and can face unpredictable weather conditions without much anxiety. The south-facing foothills with cool breezes from Valsugana enable the grapes to ripen perfectly, which is reflected in the fruity rich texture of the whole range.

Our favourite was the house flagship Cabernet Vigneto Due Santi '08, although the Rosso and Cabernet are catching it up in quality every year. Alongside red berries, the aromas hint at aromatic herbs and undergrowth, nicely reflected in the rich texture of the supple, very lingering and beautifully handled palate. Rosso and Cabernet, both '08, are only a tad more approachable, and very drinkable. The whites did well, especially the seductive Torcolato '07 and the dry Rivana '09, which offers good grip on the palate.

● Breganze Cabernet Vign. Due Santi '08	▼▼▼	5*
○ Breganze Bianco Rivana '09	▼▼	4
● Breganze Cabernet '08	▼▼	4*
● Breganze Rosso '08	▼▼	4*
○ Breganze Sauvignon '09	▼▼	4
○ Breganze Torcolato '07	▼▼	6
○ Malvasia Campo di Fiori '09	▼▼	4
○ Prosecco Extra Dry	▼	4
● Breganze Cabernet Vign. Due Santi '07	▽▽▽	5
● Breganze Cabernet Vign. Due Santi '05	▽▽▽	5
● Breganze Cabernet Vign. Due Santi '04	▽▽▽	5
○ Breganze Bianco Rivana '08	▽▽	4*
● Breganze Rosso '07	▽▽	4*
○ Breganze Sauvignon '08	▽▽	4*
○ Breganze Torcolato '06	▽▽	6
○ Malvasia Campo di Fiori '08	▽▽	4*

Villa Bellini

loc. Castelrotto di Negarine
via dei Fraccaroli, 6
37020 San Pietro in Cariano [VR]
tel. 0457725630
www.villabellini.com

CELLAR SALES
PRE-BOOKED VISITS

ANNUAL PRODUCTION 10,000 bottles
HECTARES UNDER VINE 3
VITICULTURE METHOD Certified organic

This small winery farms just three hectares in the Villa Bellini estate, on the Castelrotto hillside. Although limited in quantity, the products show strength that goes beyond commercial value. A profound quest for the characteristic features of local identity has always been the watchword and continued even when many other wineries adopted a more international style to pander to market tastes. Today, Cecilia Trucchi no longer walks this path alone, a path that is clearly marked out in her decision not to produce an Amarone.

After the grapes were lightly dried, the '07 Il Taso fermented in stainless steel with ambient yeasts and aged in tonneaux, some new and once-used. The traditional grape varieties are used, including some ancient varieties found among the older pergolas on the estate, and international varieties are banned. Cecilia's aim was to produce a wine that expressed the territorial features of Castelrotto as a possible Valpolicella territories. The aromas of fruit and spices are beautifully framed by a dry, almost austere palate.

● Valpolicella Cl. Sup. Il Taso '07	2 black glasses	6
● Amarone della Valpolicella Cl. '01	2 glasses	7
● Amarone della Valpolicella Cl. '00	2 glasses	7
● Amarone della Valpolicella Cl. '99	2 glasses	7
● Recioto della Valpolicella Cl. Uva Passa '06	2 glasses	7
● Recioto della Valpolicella Cl. Uva Passa '04	2 glasses	7
● Valpolicella Cl. Sup. Il Taso '06	2 glasses	6
● Valpolicella Cl. Sup. Il Taso '05	2 glasses	6
● Valpolicella Cl. Sup. Il Taso '04	2 glasses	6
● Valpolicella Cl. Sup. Il Taso '03	2 glasses	5
● Valpolicella Cl. Sup. Il Taso '02	2 glasses	4
● Valpolicella Cl. Sup. Il Taso '01	2 glasses	4

Villa Monteleone

fraz. Gargagnago
via Monteleone, 12
37020 Sant'Ambrogio di Valpolicella [VR]
tel. 0457704974
www.villamonteleone.com

CELLAR SALES
PRE-BOOKED VISITS
ROOMS

ANNUAL PRODUCTION 40,000 bottles
HECTARES UNDER VINE 7
VITICULTURE METHOD Conventional

In an area like Valpolicella, steamrollered by the success of Amarone, there are still estates like Villa Monteleone that have chosen not to expand but remain loyal to the path they mapped out years ago. Lucia Duran has never wavered from the project begun by her partner Antony Raimondi, known as the Prof, who was enamoured of this area and its wines. The winery's deep respect for Valpolicella is clear from the cellar itself, which blends into the hamlet of Gargnago, and the wines themselves which are as ripe and seductive as tradition demands.

This description fits the '06 Amarone, which displays aromas of cherries and cocoa powder on the nose and a palate that has yet to achieve perfect harmony, although all the conditions are in place. It is firm-bodied and still a little ruffled in sweetness, acidity and tannin but this will calm down after bottle ageing. The Valpolicella Ripasso Campo San Vito '08 is more balanced with generous fruit and fines herbes aromas and a dry, medium-bodied palate with a nicely moreish flavour. The simpler, fragrant Campo Santa Lena '09 is a deliciously drinkable Valpolicella.

● Amarone della Valpolicella Cl. '06	2 black glasses	8
● Valpolicella Cl. Sup. Campo S. Vito Ripasso '08	2 black glasses	5
● Valpolicella Cl. Campo S. Lena '09	1 black glass	4
● Amarone della Valpolicella Cl. '05	3 glasses	8
● Amarone della Valpolicella Cl. '04	2 glasses	8
● Amarone della Valpolicella Cl. '03	2 glasses	8
● Amarone della Valpolicella Cl. Campo S. Paolo '01	2 glasses	8
● Recioto della Valpolicella Cl. Pal Sun '05	2 glasses	6
● Valpolicella Cl. Sup. Campo S. Vito '04	2 glasses	5
● Valpolicella Cl. Sup. Campo S. Vito '03	2 glasses	5
● Valpolicella Cl. Sup. Campo S. Vito '02	2 glasses	5
● Valpolicella Cl. Sup. Campo S. Vito Ripasso '07	2 glasses	5
● Valpolicella Cl. Sup. Campo S. Vito Ripasso '06	2 glasses	5
● Valpolicella Cl. Campo S. Lena '08	1 glass	4

Villa Sandi

via Erizzo, 112
31035 Crocetta del Montello [TV]
tel. 0423665033
www.villasandi.it

CELLAR SALES
PRE-BOOKED VISITS
ROOMS AND FOOD

ANNUAL PRODUCTION 2,800,000 bottles
HECTARES UNDER VINE 302
VITICULTURE METHOD Conventional

Treviso is famous worldwide for its most representative wine, the focus of the new DOCG, Prosecco, interpreted in a variety of styles but always sparkling. As well as Conegliano and Valdobbiadene, the less renowned but excellent Montello area is also ideal for merlot and cabernet-based red wines. This is where we find Villa Sandi owned by the Moretti Polegato family, who have for many years produced still wines, Conegliano Valdobbiadene, and the classic method wines of the Opere Trevigiane line made in the cellars beneath the family's 17th-century Palladian villa.

Outstanding in the extensive range are the red Corpore '07 and the Cartizze Vigna La Rivetta, sourced from the vineyard of the same name. The red is a Bordeaux blend with aromas of red fruit, cocoa powder and pencil lead and a firm, silky sweet palate with nice tannic structure. The Cartizze, an original Brut interpretation highlighting the quality of both the wine and the terroir, earned Three Glasses for its superb grip, minerality and finesse. The Marinali Rosso '08, simpler and more approachable than the Corpore, and the Riserva di Opere Trevigiane '05, a nicely balanced, pinot nero and chardonnay-based Brut, are both impressive.

○ Cartizze Brut V. La Rivetta '09	3 black glasses	5
● Corpore '07	2 black glasses	6
● Marinali Rosso '08	2 black glasses	5
○ Opere Trevigiane Brut Ris. '05	2 black glasses	5
○ Valdobbiadene Dry Cuvée Oris	2 black glasses	4
○ Cartizze	1 black glass	6
● Filio	1 black glass	4
○ Marinali Bianco '09	1 black glass	5
○ Opere Trevigiane Brut	1 black glass	5
○ Valdobbiadene Brut '09	1 black glass	4
○ Valdobbiadene Extra Dry	1 black glass	4
● Piave Raboso '06	1 black glass	4
○ Avitus '08	2 white glasses	5
○ Cartizze Brut V. La Rivetta '08	2 white glasses	5
● Corpore '06	2 white glasses	6
● Marinali Rosso '07	2 white glasses	5
○ Opere Trevigiane Brut Ris. '04	2 white glasses	5

Villa Spinosa

loc. Jago dall'Ora
37024 Negrar [VR]
tel. 0457500093
www.villaspinosa.it

CELLAR SALES
PRE-BOOKED VISITS
ROOMS

ANNUAL PRODUCTION 45,000 bottles
HECTARES UNDER VINE 20
VITICULTURE METHOD Conventional

We have always been fascinated by this winery's ability to produce subtle, stylish, almost Burgundian wines in an area like Valpolicella, where exuberance is the name of the game. Making wines with these features using dried grapes, as in the Amarone, is no easy task, nor is it possible in many other wine areas. The secret lies in an ability to keep sight of the area's wealth of typical grapes and traditions. Completing the picture are the beautiful vineyards in the wonderful hillside locations of Negrar and Marano.

Elegance is the name of the game with the Valpolicella Superiore Figari '07. It offers a lively, appetizing hue, captivatingly generous aromas of overripe fruit with hints of sweet spices, and a sophisticated palate that shows silky, relaxed and not at all tight. The Amarone Anteprima '06 has an evolved nose with forward hints of cocoa powder and a strikingly mature, impressively dynamic palate. Equally charming is the Ripasso Jago '06, with its decadent aromas of chocolate and stewed fruit. The Valpolicella '08 is robust and uncomplicated.

● Valpolicella Cl. Sup. Figari '07	2 black glasses	4*
● Amarone della Valpolicella Cl. Anteprima '06	2 black glasses	6
● Valpolicella Cl. Sup. Ripasso Jago '06	2 black glasses	4
● Valpolicella Cl. '08	1 black glass	3
● Amarone della Valpolicella Cl. '01	2 white glasses	7
● Amarone della Valpolicella Cl. Anteprima '04	2 white glasses	6
● Valpolicella Cl. '07	2 white glasses	3*
● Valpolicella Cl. Sup. Figari '06	2 white glasses	4*
● Valpolicella Cl. Sup. Ripasso Jago '05	2 white glasses	4

Vigneti Villabella

FRAZ. CALMASINO
LOC. CANOVA, 2
37011 BARDOLINO [VR]
TEL. 0457236448
www.vignetivillabella.com

CELLAR SALES
PRE-BOOKED VISITS
ROOMS

ANNUAL PRODUCTION 500,000 bottles
HECTARES UNDER VINE 220
VITICULTURE METHOD Certified organic

Back to a full profile for the large Calmasino winery, a joint venture of the Cristoforetti and Delibori families, thanks to dependable fine quality products in a drinkable, rather than highly concentrated, style. The wines are sourced from the estate's extensive vineyards and are presented in decently assorted range where the Lake Garda DOCs take a front seat. The Villa Cordevigo project continues and today this beautiful building has become a splendid hotel.

The Amarone '05 is on top form after a lengthy stay in the cellar, giving intense wild berry and dried flower aromas and a relaxed palate with nice taut flavour. The Fiordilej '07 is a dried grape wine with striking aromas of candied citrus peel and dried apricots. The palate is conspicuously savoury, its sweetness is held in check by fresh acidity. The strongpoint of the Ripasso '07 is expression on the nose with overripe fruit echoed by hints of medicinal herbs and spices, while the lean-bodied palate has a nice harmonious flavour.

● Amarone della Valpolicella Cl. '05	🍷🍷	6
○ Fiordilej Passito '07	🍷🍷	6
● Valpolicella Cl. Sup. Ripasso '07	🍷🍷	4
⊙ Bardolino Chiaretto Cl. Pozzo dell'Amore '09	🍷	4
● Bardolino Cl. Sup. Terre di Cavagion '08	🍷	4
● Bardolino Cl. V. Morlongo '09	🍷	4
○ Lugana Ca' del Lago '09	🍷	4
○ Pinot Grigio V. di Pesina '09	🍷	4
○ Villa Cordevigo Bianco '07	🍷	5
○ Fiordilej '05	YY	4*
○ Lugana Ca' del Lago '07	YY	4
○ Villa Cordevigo Bianco '06	YY	5
● Villa Cordevigo Rosso '05	YY	6
● Villa Cordevigo Rosso '04	YY	6

★ Viviani

LOC. MAZZANO
VIA MAZZANO, 8
37020 NEGRAR [VR]
TEL. 0457500286
www.cantinaviviani.com

CELLAR SALES
PRE-BOOKED VISITS

ANNUAL PRODUCTION 70,000 bottles
HECTARES UNDER VINE 10
VITICULTURE METHOD Conventional

The high hillside hamlet of Mazzano in the municipal area of Negrar is one of the best terroirs in Valpolicella. Somewhat overlooked in the past because it had to co-exist with high-yield local production, it found a new lease of life when quality became the objective. Greatly admired Mazzano growers Claudio and Cinzia Viviani remain loyal to tradition yet are still able to stage their own wine renaissance, as is immediately apparent when walking through the rows of their new vineyard in front of the buildings.

The range presented this year is mouthwateringly good with three wines giving classy, characterful interpretations of the principal DOC types. The Amarone Casa dei Bepi '05 won Three Glasses for its customary harmonious concentration of fruit while the Valpolicella Campo Morar '07 offers a generous profile with silky tannins while avoiding similarities with the Amarone. Lastly, the '07 Recioto more than any other wine represents this area's tradition, offering vibrant, clear-cut aromas of wild berries and pepper ushering in assertive but beautifully balanced sweetness.

● Amarone della Valpolicella Cl. Casa dei Bepi '05	🍷🍷🍷	8
● Recioto della Valpolicella Cl. '07	🍷🍷	7
● Valpolicella Cl. Sup. Campo Morar '07	🍷🍷	6
● Amarone della Valpolicella Cl. '06	🍷🍷	6
● Amarone della Valpolicella Cl. Casa dei Bepi '04	YYY	8
● Amarone della Valpolicella Cl. Casa dei Bepi '01	YYY	8
● Amarone della Valpolicella Cl. Casa dei Bepi '00	YYY	8
● Amarone della Valpolicella Cl. Casa dei Bepi '98	YYY	8
● Amarone della Valpolicella Cl. Casa dei Bepi '97	YYY	8
● Valpolicella Cl. Sup. Campo Morar '05	YYY	6
● Valpolicella Cl. Sup. Campo Morar '01	YYY	6

Zenato

FRAZ. SAN BENEDETTO DI LUGANA
VIA SAN BENEDETTO, 8
37019 PESCHIERA DEL GARDA [VR]
TEL. 0457550300
www.zenato.it

CELLAR SALES
PRE-BOOKED VISITS

ANNUAL PRODUCTION 1,500,000 bottles
HECTARES UNDER VINE 70
VITICULTURE METHOD Conventional

The Zenato family estate has always been acknowledged as one of the best examples of the négociant, or grape merchant, tradition, producers who know the area and buy up the best parcels of fruit to vinify skilfully in their own cellars. But every year, the Zenatos make changes, buying property in the family homeland of Lugana and in Valpolicella, so that today they owns about 70 hectares. The estate's vineyards provide the grapes for all the leading selections while those used in the basic wines are purchased from growers who are monitored all year round.

The wines presented by the Zenatos this year are of an impressively high calibre. The Amarones are in different styles: the '06 Classico is concentrated and rich in extract, focusing more on texture than complexity, proffering appeal and approachability; and the Sergio Zenato '05 is more subdued, with depth on the nose and a palate whose the texture serves to imbue class and elegance. Three Glasses. We like the debut of the '06 Recioto della Valpolicella while from the whites, the Lugana San Benedetto '09, produced in substantial quantities, is astonishing as ever, showing assertive and very enjoyable.

● Amarone della Valpolicella Cl. Sergio Zenato '05	▼▼▼	8
● Amarone della Valpolicella Cl. '06	▼▼	8
○ Lugana S. Benedetto '09	▼▼	4*
○ Lugana Vign. Massoni Santa Cristina '09	▼▼	4
● Recioto della Valpolicella Cl. '06	▼▼	6
● Valpolicella Cl. Sup. '07	▼▼	4*
● Valpolicella Sup. Rip. Ripassa '07	▼▼	5
● Cabernet Sauvignon Santa Cristina '06	▼	4
○ Lugana Brut M. Cl.	▼	4
● Amarone della Valpolicella Cl. '05	▽▽▽	7
● Amarone della Valpolicella Cl. Sergio Zenato '03	▽▽▽	8
● Amarone della Valpolicella Cl. Sergio Zenato '00	▽▽▽	8
● Amarone della Valpolicella Cl. Sergio Zenato Ris. '98	▽▽▽	8

F.lli Zeni

VIA COSTABELLA, 9
37011 BARDOLINO [VR]
TEL. 0457210022
www.zeni.it

CELLAR SALES
PRE-BOOKED VISITS

ANNUAL PRODUCTION 1,000,000 bottles
HECTARES UNDER VINE 25
VITICULTURE METHOD Conventional

Although the Zeni brothers' estate is located at Bardolino, production is not limited to lakeside reds but also explores the surrounding designations. Grapes are bought in from growers who are supervised throughout the year. Even in the more structured wines, like those from nearby Valpolicella, the winery's signature style is a light, elegant palate with good personality. Production quantities are large and divided over several lines, all of which can be purchased at the cellar door sales outlet.

The Amarone Vigne Alte '07 is an impressive red with vibrant aromas of stewed red fruits and hints of spice, with oak remaining in the background. The subtle, harmonious palate is soft without excessive sugariness. The punchier Ripasso Marogne '08 is an extremely supple Valpolicella on the palate, supported by acidity rather than tannin. We also liked the Lugana Marogne '09, which gives simple fruity aromas contrasting with the nicely lively palate, and the dry Amarone Classico '07.

● Amarone della Valpolicella Cl. Vigne Alte '07	▼▼	7
● Valpolicella Sup. Ripasso Marogne '08	▼▼	4*
● Amarone della Valpolicella Cl. '07	▼	7
● Corvar Rosso '08	▼	5
● Costalago Rosso '08	▼	4
● Cruino Rosso '08	▼	5
○ Garganega Vigne Alte '09	▼	4
○ Lugana Marogne '09	▼	4
○ Lugana Vigne Alte '09	▼	4
● Recioto della Valpolicella Cl. Vigne Alte '08	▼	6
● Amarone della Valpolicella Cl. '88	▽▽▽	6
● Amarone della Valpolicella Cl. '05	▽▽	6
● Amarone della Valpolicella Cl. Vigne Alte '06	▽▽	7
● Recioto della Valpolicella Cl. Vigne Alte '07	▽▽	6

Zonin

via Borgolecco, 9
36053 Gambellara [VI]
tel. 0444640111
www.zonin.it

CELLAR SALES
PRE-BOOKED VISITS

ANNUAL PRODUCTION 23,000,000 bottles
HECTARES UNDER VINE 1,800
VITICULTURE METHOD Conventional

The statistics at the top of this Gambellara estate's profile are a truly impressive, accurately reflecting the Zonin universe. On this page we will focus on their Veneto products, which are firmly secured by three linchpins. The first is, of course, garganega, the Gambellara grape variety which characterizes the history of the winery. The next is prosecco, aka glera, the Treviso variety synonymous worldwide with fizz, and lastly nearby Valpolicella, which provides the well-structured reds.

Indeed, Valpolicella is the source of grapes for the Ripasso in a generously fruity '08 version, streaked through with lovely vegetal hints, nicely defined and reasonably long on the finish. The oaky hints are still rather forward in the red Berengario '06 from cabernet sauvignon and merlot, while the full-bodied palate shows very subtle supporting acidity. Turning to Gambellara, there was a lovely show from the Recioto Il Giangio '04, released only after a very long period of maturation. It's complex with a balanced palate.

● Berengario '06	▼▼	5
○ Recioto di Gambellara Cl. Il Giangio '04	▼▼	4
● Valpolicella Sup. Ripasso '08	▼▼	4
○ Gambellara Cl. Podere Il Giangio '09	▼	4
○ Prosecco Brut	▼	4
○ Prosecco Brut Special Cuvée	▼	3
○ Recioto di Gambellara Demi Sec	▼	4
● Amarone della Valpolicella '06	YY	6
● Amarone della Valpolicella '05	YY	6
● Amarone della Valpolicella '04	YY	6
● Amarone della Valpolicella '03	YY	6
● Valpolicella Sup. Ripasso '07	YY	4
● Valpolicella Sup. Ripasso '04	YY	4*
● Valpolicella Sup. Ripasso '03	YY	4*

Zymè

via Ca' del Pipa, 1
37029 San Pietro in Cariano [VR]
tel. 0457701108
www.zyme.it

CELLAR SALES
PRE-BOOKED VISITS

ANNUAL PRODUCTION 30,000 bottles
HECTARES UNDER VINE 16
VITICULTURE METHOD Conventional

The estate owned by Celestino Gaspari and Francesco Parisi has been growing one step at a time. First the vineyards, then the cellar and today the wines have been made over to offer a wide range of products closely linked to tradition both in the grapes used and cellar techniques. Although they are best known for vinifying oseleta grapes and producing dried-grape wines, today the winery has a fresh-tasting Valpolicella with a personality of its own. This youthful red flaunts fresh aromas and a vibrantly drinkable palate.

Our favourite was the '04 Amarone, released after a leisurely maturation, for its subtle, youthful aromas in which wild berries entwine with medicinal herbs and spices. The palate is even more impressive thanks to beautifully handled texture and fresh acidity that lengthens and streamlines the flavour. We enjoyed the Kairos '06, a sort of mature, mouthfilling Amarone made from several grape varieties. The Vigneti '07, another blend of local grapes, is generously fruity with a crisp, mouth-watering palate.

● Amarone della Valpolicella Cl. '04	▼▼	8
● I Vigneti '07	▼▼	6
● Kairos '06	▼▼	8
● Valpolicella Revirie '09	▼▼	4
○ Il Bianco From Black to White '09	▼	4
● Amarone della Valpolicella Cl. '03	YY	8
● Amarone della Valpolicella Cl. '01	YY	8
● Harlequin '03	YY	8
○ Il Bianco From Black to White '07	YY	4
● Kairos '05	YY	8
● Oseleta Oz '06	YY	7
● Oseleta Oz '03	YY	6

Astoria Vini
VIA CREVADA, 44
31020 REFRONTOLO [TV]
TEL. 04236699
www.astoria.it

After years in the financial sector, Luisella Benedetti has decided to go back to the land at the La Ghidina di Sirmione estate created by her grandmother Ancilla. We note a rapid increase in quality in the two excellent Luganas tasted this year, especially the Ella '09.

O Cartizze	🍷🍷 4
O Valdobbiadene Extra Dry '09	🍷🍷 4
O Conegliano Valdobbiadene Rive di Refontolo Casa Vittorino Brut '09	🍷 4

Bellenda
FRAZ. CARPESICA
VIA GIARDINO, 90
31029 VITTORIO VENETO [TV]
TEL. 0438920025
www.bellenda.it

As part of the new Prosecco DOCG, Bellenda is one of the most interesting estates in Conegliano, with a full range of sparkling wines. Outstanding among the classic-method wines are Saiph and the Vintage '03, as is the original Prosecco. we enjoyed the Brut from the Charmat-method range.

O Blanc de Blanc Saiph Extra Brut	🍷🍷 5
O Conegliano Valdobbiadene S.C. 1931 '08	🍷🍷 5
O Vintage Brut '03	🍷🍷 6
O Conegliano Valdobbiadene Brut San Fermo	🍷 4

Le Bertole
VIA EUROPA, 20
31049 VALDOBBIADENE [TV]
TEL. 0423975332
www.lebertole.com

Le Bertole is one of many estates to have flourished at Valdobbiadene in the last 20 years but the Bortolins have a much longer wine history. The Dry Supreme is a strikingly elegant Prosecco, giving fresh aromas of apples and pears over a savoury, harmonious palate. The Cartizze is more generous and mouthfilling.

O Cartizze	🍷🍷 6
O Valdobbiadene Supreme Dry	🍷🍷 5
O Valdobbiadene Brut	🍷 4
O Valdobbiadene Extra Dry	🍷 4

BiancaVigna
LOC. SAN PIETRO DI FELETTO
VIA CREVADA, 9/1
31010 SOLIGO [TV]
TEL. 0438801098
www.biancavigna.it

The Biancavigna winery is less than ten years old with a dozen or so available hectares of vineyards, half of which the estate owns. Production focuses on Prosecco, made exclusively from estate-grown grapes. There was a good performance from the Brut, with sophisticated aromas and a nicely textured palate.

O Conegliano Valdobbiadene Brut '09	🍷🍷 4
O P. Colli Trevigiani Brut	🍷 4
O P. Colli Trevigiani Extra Dry	🍷 4
O Valdobbiadene Extra Dry	🍷 4

Antonio Bigai
FRAZ. LISON
VIA CADUTI PER LA PATRIA, 29
30026 PORTOGRUARO [VE]
TEL. 336592660
www.amimanera.com

Even simpler wines still need bottle-ageing time so Toni Bigai has delayed release of his reds, leaving us only the whites, which brim with personality as usual from this winery. A Mi Manera '09 is floral and very drinkable. The Lison '09 is bright and buttery while the Malvasia '09 is pleasantly husky.

O A Mi Manera Bianco '09	🍷🍷 4
O Lison-Pramaggiore Lison Cl. '09	🍷🍷 4*
O Malvasia d'Istria '09	🍷 4

Borgoluce
LOC. MUSILE, 2
31058 SUSEGANA [TV]
TEL. 0438435287
www.borgoluce.it

The young Borgoluce winery has quickly carved itself a significant niche in the designation and its wines are increasingly impressive. Only a few were presented but all were excellent, starting with the Millesimato Extra Dry '09's apple and pear aromas and sophisticated, succulent palate. The Brut is elegant.

O Prosecco di Valdobbiadene Brut	🍷🍷 4
O Prosecco di Valdobbiadene Extra Dry '09	🍷🍷 4
O Prosecco di Valdobbiadene Extra Dry	🍷 4

LE ALTRE CANTINE

Le Carline

via Carline, 24
30020 Pramaggiore [VE]
tel. 0421799741
www.lecarline.com

Daniele Piccinin's vineyards are organically farmed to safeguard the environment and produce healthy wines. The Lison '09, a vibrantly firm white, stands out in the wide range for its generous texture and character. The Pinot Grigio '09 is in the style while the Cabernet '09 is lighter and fragrant.

○ Lison-Pramaggiore Lison '09	🍷🍷	3*
○ Lison-Pramaggiore Pinot Grigio '09	🍷🍷	3*
● Lison-Pramaggiore Cabernet Franc '09	🍷	3

Carpenè Malvolti

via Antonio Carpenè, 1
31015 Conegliano [TV]
tel. 0438364611
www.carpene-malvolti.com

This large Conegliano winery has always been a byword for Prosecco with its balanced range of excellent products. Of the many wines presented, some from outside the designation, the Treviso sparkling wines lead the field. The Brut is elegant, taut and succulent while the Extra Dry is more relaxed and savoury.

○ Conegliano Cuvée Brut	🍷🍷	5
○ Conegliano Cuvée Storica Extra Dry	🍷🍷	4
○ Conegliano Valdobbiadene Cuvée Oro Dry	🍷	4

Casa Geretto

via Vanoni, 3
30029 Santo Stino di Livenza [VE]
tel. 0421460253
www.geretto.it

The Geretto family has worked for years in the Lison Pramaggiore and Friuli Aquileia DOCs. The latter vineyards yield more satisfying results, as shown by the Refosco Vigne Vecchie '08, a red with deep aromas, medium body and a supple palate. The '08 Treuve Rosso is generous and savoury.

● Friuli Aquileia Refosco P.R. V. Vecchie Merk '08	🍷🍷	5
● Friuli Aquileia Rosso Treuve Merk '08	🍷	5

Case Paolin

via Madonna Mercede, 53
31040 Volpago del Montello [TV]
tel. 0423871433
www.casepaolin.it

The Pozzobon brothers are developing the family estate on the plains at Montello where glera and red Bordeaux varieties compete for space in the vineyards. The Rosso del Milio '08 has generous fruit and a firm, gutsy palate while the Brut is naturally lighter and more sophisticated.

○ Asolo Brut '09	🍷🍷	4*
● Montello e Colli Asolani Rosso del Milio '08	🍷🍷	4*
○ Santi Angeli Manzoni Bianco '08	🍷	4
○ Soér Passito '07	🍷	5

Castello di Lispida

via IV Novembre, 4
35043 Monselice [PD]
tel. 0429780530
www.lispida.com

The Colli Euganei DOC overlaps with the area's regional park, inside which Alessandro Sgaravatti's winery operates with due respect for its surroundings. The white Terralba '06 impresses, giving aromas of iodine and Mediterranean scrubland and a lovely savoury palate. The Montelispida '04 has rich texture.

○ Terralba '06	🍷🍷	6
● Montelispida '04	🍷	6

Gerardo Cesari

loc. Sorsei, 3
37010 Cavaion Veronese [VR]
tel. 0456260928
www.cesariverona.it

The Cesari estate has focused for years on the classic Valpolicella wines in a style characterized by roundness on the palate and complex aromas. Amarone Bosan is the best on the list, released only after lengthy maturation in the cellar. The '03 gives generous aromas and a firm, succulent palate.

● Amarone della Valpolicella Bosan '03	🍷🍷	8
● Amarone della Valpolicella Cl. '07	🍷🍷	6
○ Lugana Cento Filari '09	🍷	4
● Recioto della Valpolicella Cl. '07	🍷	6

LE ALTRE CANTINE

Colvendrà

via Liberazione, 39
31020 Refrontolo [TV]
tel. 0438894265
www.colvendra.it

The Della Colletta family have made wine for decades in the small town of Refrontolo halfway between Conegliano and Valdobbiadene. We enjoyed the Brut, a Prosecco with good expressive aromas and a dry, taut palate. The Dry Bepi '09 is also good, with a creamier, more mouthfilling flavour.

- ○ Conegliano Valdobbiadene Brut — 🍷🍷 4
- ○ Conegliano Valdobbiadene Rive di Refontolo Bepi Dry '09 — 🍷🍷 4
- ○ Conegliano Valdobbiadene Extra Dry — 🍷 4

Contrà Soarda

loc. Contrà Soarda, 26
36061 Bassano del Grappa [VI]
tel. 0424566785
www.contrasoarda.it

Mirco Gottardi owns one of the most interesting emerging wineries in the Breganze DOC zone, on the hills behind Bassano del Grappa. The cool breezes from nearby Valsugana contribute to the fragrant Vigna Corejo '07, a strikingly weighty Pinot Nero.

- ○ Breganze Torcolato '07 — 🍷🍷 6
- ● Vigna Correjo '07 — 🍷🍷 8
- ○ Il Pendio '08 — 🍷 4

Costozza

fraz. Costozza
p.zza da Schio, 4
36023 Longare [VI]
tel. 0444555099
www.costozza-villadaschio.it

Veneto's Colli Berici is a warm area where Bordeaux varieties, grown here for over a century, always ripen well. The Cabernet Sauvignon '08 has aromas of red fruit and forest floor with a firm, crisp palate. The Cabernet Franc '08 is simpler with fresh aromas and a bright palate.

- ● Cabernet Franc '08 — 🍷🍷 4
- ● Cabernet Sauvignon '08 — 🍷🍷 5
- ● Pinot Nero '09 — 🍷 4

F.lli Fabiano

via Verona, 6
37060 Sona [VR]
tel. 0456081111
www.fabiano.it

In recent years, the Fabianos have embarked on a search for higher product quality. We note an excellent performance from the winery's thoroughbred white Lugana I Fondatori '08, a simple yet singularly mouthwatering wine. We also like the '07 Amarone, which just lacks a pinch of extract.

- ○ Lugana Argillaia I Fondatori '08 — 🍷🍷 4
- ● Amarone della Valpolicella Cl. '07 — 🍷 7
- ○ Lugana Argillaia '09 — 🍷 4
- ● Valpolicella Cl. Sup. Ripasso '08 — 🍷 4

F.lli Farina

loc. Pedemonte
via Bolla, 11
37029 San Pietro in Cariano [VR]
tel. 0457701349
www.farinawines.com

The Farina family has worked in the Valpolicella area for decades, and the quality of the wines has risen considerably in recent years. Of the two Amarones we preferred the '06 for its traditional aromas and supple palate. The Riserva '04 has richer texture but less definition.

- ● Amarone della Valpolicella Cl. '06 — 🍷🍷 6
- ● Valpolicella Cl. Sup. Ripasso V. Montecorna '07 — 🍷🍷 4
- ● Amarone della Valpolicella Cl. Montefante Ris. '04 — 🍷 8

Giovanni Fattori

fraz. Terrossa
via Olmo, 6
37030 Roncà [VR]
tel. 0457460041
www.fattorigiovanni.it

Antonio Fattori's wines are increasingly impressive interpretations of Soave, an area with great potential. Soave Motto Piane '09, aged in oak, has lovely fresh, generous aromas and a succulent, harmonious palate. Its stablemate Recioto '08 is also interesting and reveals well-judged sweetness.

- ○ Recioto di Soave Motto Piane '08 — 🍷🍷 5
- ○ Soave Motto Piane '09 — 🍷🍷 4
- ○ Soave Cl. Danieli '09 — 🍷 4
- ○ Soave Cl. Runcaris '09 — 🍷 3

La Ghidina

LOC. DOSSOBUONO
VIA CADELLORA, 10
37062 VILLAFRANCA DI VERONA [VR]
TEL. 0458008721
www.ancillalugana.it

La Ghidina, better known as Ancilla, works in the Lugana designation straddling the provinces of Brescia and Verona along the southern shore of Lake Garda. There are three wines. Lugana Ancilla '08 stands out as generous, harmonious, rounded and juicy. We also like the fresher, more approachable Ella '09.

○ Lugana Ancilla '08	🍷🍷	4
○ Lugana Ella '09	🍷🍷	4*
○ Lugana La Ghidina '08	🍷	4

La Giaretta

FRAZ. VALGATARA
VIA DEL PLATANO, 12
37020 MARANO DI VALPOLICELLA [VR]
TEL. 0457701791
www.cantinalagiaretta.com

Valpolicella wines lend themselves to a variety of different interpretations, using the fresh grapes for fresh aromas and acidity, or dried grapes for richer, softer texture. At his Giaretta winery, Francesco Vaona favours a style whose most distinctive feature is rich extract.

● Amarone della Valpolicella Cl. '06	🍷🍷	6
● Amarone della Valpolicella Cl. I Quadretti '04	🍷🍷	8
● Valpolicella Cl. Sup. Ripasso '07	🍷	4

Latium

LOC. LEON
37030 MEZZANE DI SOTTO [VR]
TEL. 0457834037
www.latiummoriniit.it

We liked the Morini family's wines from the Illasi valley, where they make the classic Valpolicella and Soave products. In the former, more impressive group, Valpolicella Campo Prognai '07 stands out for its fruity profile and grip while the Amarone Campo Leon '05 unfurls very profound aromas.

● Amarone della Valpolicella Campo Leon '05	🍷🍷	7
● Valpoolicella Sup. Campo Prognai '07	🍷🍷	5
○ Soave Campo Le Calle '09	🍷	4

Firmino Miotti

VIA BROGLIATI CONTRO, 53
36042 BREGANZE [VI]
TEL. 0445873006
www.firminomiotti.it

Breganze is one of the lesser known Veneto DOCs but some exciting wineries work here. One of these is Franca Miotti's estate, whose leading wine is Torcolato. The '06 is a complex dried-grape wine that gives fruit aromas lifted by balsam and truffles followed by alluring but well-balanced sweetness.

● Breganze Cabernet '07	🍷🍷	4
○ Breganze Torcolato '06	🍷🍷	7
○ Breganze Bianco Le Colombare '09	🍷	4
● Breganze Rosso '07	🍷	4

Monte Faustino

VIA BURE ALTO
37029 SAN PIETRO IN CARIANO [VR]
TEL. 0457701651
www.fornaser.com

The Fornaser family has produced Valpolicella wines for decades and results are coming on. The Amarone '05 has textbook aromas of nuts and crushed flowers while the palate is rounded and voluptuous. The Ripasso La Traversagna '05 lays out a huskier nose with a dry, vibrant palate.

● Amarone della Valpolicella Cl. '05	🍷🍷	7
● Valpolicella Cl. Sup. Ripasso La Traversagna '05	🍷🍷	5
● Recioto della Valpolicella Cl. '05	🍷	6

Monte Zovo

LOC. ZOVO, 23A
37013 CAPRINO VERONESE [VR]
TEL. 0457281301
www.montezovo.com

In just a few years, the Cottini family winery has boosted production with steady improvements in quality. The most impressive wine again is the Amarone '07, which tempts with expressive fruit aromatics and a subtle palate. The Valpolicella Ripasso '08 is vibrant and generous.

● Amarone della Valpolicella '07	🍷🍷	8
● Valpolicella Sup. Ripasso '08	🍷🍷	4
● Bardolino '09	🍷	3
● Valpolicella '09	🍷	4

Montecariano

VIA VALENA, 3
37029 SAN PIETRO IN CARIANO [VR]
TEL. 0456838335
www.montecariano.it

The Gini family estate extends over extensive tableland behind San Pietro in Cariano. Alongside the traditional grape varieties is a small quantity of cabernet and, after brief raisining, it is used to make a red with lovely generous aromas, a firm structure and satisfying flavour.

- ● Puntara Cabernet Sauvignon '05 — 6
- ● Valpolicella Cl. '08 — 4*
- ● Valpolicella Cl. Sup. Corte Monte '05 — 5

Walter Nardin

LOC. RONCADELLE
VIA FONTANE, 5
31024 ORMELLE [TV]
TEL. 0422851622
www.vinwalternardin.it

The Nardin family estate extends over the Piave and Lison Pramaggiore DOC zones. The range is extensive. The '06 Rosso della Ghiaia, a Bordeaux blend with a dash of raboso, performs best on the palate with medium structure and a dry flavour. The rest of the list is dependably good.

- ● Rosso della Ghiaia La Zerbaia '06 — 5
- ○ Lison-Pramaggiore Lison La Zerbaia '09 — 5
- ○ Lison-Pramaggiore Pinot Grigio '09 — 4
- ○ Manzoni Bianco '09 — 4

Paladin

VIA POSTUMIA, 12
30020 ANNONE VENETO [VE]
TEL. 0422768167
www.paladin.it

Paladin is probably the most representative winery in the Lison Pramaggiore DOC , with extensive vineyards and a very high standard of quality. Malbech Gli Aceri '07 is the most exciting wine, as usual, with red fruit aromas and vegetal hints preceding a firm, nicely stylish palate.

- ● Malbech Gli Aceri '07 — 6
- ● Wine & Art Celiberti '06 — 8
- ○ Lison-Pramaggiore Pinot Grigio '09 — 4
- ● Lison-Pramaggiore Refosco P.R. '09 — 6

Il Pianzio

VIA PIANZIO, 66
35030 GALZIGNANO TERME [PD]
TEL. 0499130422
www.ilpianzio.it

The Colli Euganei is great wine country with warm, dry summers that enable the Bordeaux varieties to ripen perfectly. We gave a good mark to the Rosso Eremo '07 for its fruit-led aromas and a dry, nicely uncomplicated flavour. Even more impressive is the rounded, juicy Cabernet Sauvignon Jenio '08.

- ● Colli Euganei Cabernet Sauvignon Jenio '08 — 4
- ● Colli Euganei Rosso Eremo '07 — 4
- ○ Pianzio Aromatico '09 — 3

Luca Ricci

LOC. COLLALTO
VIA CUCCO, 27
31058 SUSEGANA [TV]
TEL. 0438980130
www.lefade.com

Luca Ricci produces two excellent reds here at Collalto, a small village near Susegana, surrounded by woods and vineyards. Busk '05 is a Merlot with an expressive nose and savoury, nicely textured palate. The Salariato '06 is a merlot-heavy Bordeaux blend with fresher aromas and a succulent flavour.

- ● BusK '05 — 5
- ● Salariato '06 — 5
- ○ Conegliano Valdobbiadene Le Fade Extra Dry — 4

Urbano Salvan

LOC. PIGOZZO
VIA MINCANA, 143
35020 DUE CARRARE [PD]
TEL. 049525841
www.salvan.it

The location of Giorgio Salvan's estate in front of the Colli Euganei bestows character and depth on its red wines. The good Merlot Riserva '07 is profound and complex with a savoury, satisfying flavour. There's a fresher, more supple palate for the Merlot '09 while the Cabernet Franc '09 gives spicy aromas.

- ● Colli Euganei Merlot Ris. '07 — 4*
- ● Colli Euganei Cabernet Franc '09 — 3*
- ● Colli Euganei Merlot '09 — 3*

LE ALTRE CANTINE

Tenuta San Basilio
via Monte Versa, 1348
35030 Vò [PD]
tel. 049994140
www.tenutasanbasilio.it

Colli Euganei is excellent wine country in a delightful regional park setting. Tenuta San Basilio's products hinge on Bordeaux varieties. The top wine is the excellent Rosso Fenice '07 a silkily crafted merlot-heavy blend. The Terre del Mosca '07 is weightier.

- ● Colli Euganei Rosso Fenice '07 — 4
- ● Terre del Mosca '07 — 4
- ○ Colli Euganei Bianco Fenice '08 — 4
- ○ Colli Euganei Fior d'Arancio Passito Oro Fenice '08 — 6

San Cassiano
Via San Cassiano, 17
37030 Mezzane di Sotto [VR]
tel. 0458880665
www.cantinasancassiano.it

Mirko Sella divides his production time between a wonderful extra virgin olive oil and wine. He has long enjoyed success with the oil and the wine is coming on a treat. The limited but excellent range of Valpolicellas includes a fresh, racy '09, a Superiore '07 and a richly textured Amarone '06.

- ● Amarone della Valpolicella '06 — 6
- ● Valpolicella '09 — 3*
- ● Valpolicella Sup. '07 — 5

San Rustico
fraz. Valgatara di Valpolicella
via Pozzo, 2
37020 Marano di Valpolicella [VR]
tel. 0457703348
www.sanrustico.it

The Campagnola brothers' estate has been active in Valpolicella for many years producing forthright wines firmly rooted in tradition. The Amarone Classico '05 has overripe fruit aromas and a savoury, nicely husky palate. The '06 Ripasso is softer and more mouthfilling. The Amarone Gaso '04 is well typed.

- ● Amarone della Valpolicella Cl. '05 — 6
- ● Amarone della Valpolicella Cl. Gaso '04 — 7
- ● Valpolicella Cl. Sup. Ripasso Gaso '06 — 4*

Tenuta Sant'Anna
loc. Loncon
via Monsignor P. L. Zovatto, 71
30020 Annone Veneto [VE]
tel. 0422864511
www.tenutasantanna.it

This large Generali group winery did well, led by a very impressive red. The Refosco del Peduncolo Rosso displays wild berries and spices on the nose, medium structure and considerable elegance. The new V8+ line comprises an extensive range of nicely made, fragrant Charmat-method sparkling wines.

- ● Lison-Pramaggiore Refosco P. R. '08 — 4
- ○ Valdobbiadene Sior Gino Dry V8+ '09 — 4
- ○ Valdobbiadene Sior Piero Extra Dry V8+ — 4
- ⊙ Sior Lele Rosé Brut — 4

Sutto
via San Lorenzetto, 9
31040 Salgareda [TV]
tel. 0422744063
www.sutto.it

The Sutto brothers' winery has grown considerably in just a few years. Only some of the grapes are used for the estate's wines, which are mainly reds. The very good Dogma '08 is a Bordeaux blend with complex aromas and a relaxed, savoury palate. The Cabernet Riserva '08 is crisp and mouthwatering.

- ● Dogma Rosso '08 — 5
- ● Piave Cabernet Ris. '08 — 4
- ● Piave Merlot Ris. '08 — 4
- ○ Manzoni Bianco '09 — 4

Le Tende
fraz. Colà di Lazise
via Tende, 35
37017 Lazise [VR]
tel. 0457590748
www.letende.it

Le Tende represents both the leading Garda DOCs, Bardolino and Custoza, with impressive results. The very good Bardolino Superiore '08 shows aromas of forest floor and aromatic herbs, with a racy but richly textured palate. The fresher Bardolino '09 and '09 Custozas are well crafted.

- ● Bardolino Cl. Sup. '08 — 3
- ● Bardolino Cl. '09 — 3*
- ○ Bianco di Custoza '09 — 3*
- ○ Bianco di Custoza Lucillini '09 — 3

Terre di Leone

LOC. PORTA
37020 MARANO DI VALPOLICELLA [VR]
TEL. 0456895040
www.terredileone.it

Terre di Leone is increasingly important in the Marano valley, a relatively unknown area which endows its wines with great finesse. This year, again, the best-made wine is the Amarone, the '06, with generous aromas and a sleek, succulent palate. The Valpolicella Superiore '07 is more closed but harmonious.

● Amarone della Valpolicella Cl. '06	🍷🍷	8
● Valpolicella Cl. Sup. '07	🍷🍷	6
● Dedicatum '07	🍷	6
● Valpolicella Cl. Sup. Ripasso '07	🍷	7

Luigi Valetti

LOC. CALMASINO DI BARDOLINO
VIA PRAGRANDE, 8
37010 BARDOLINO [VR]
TEL. 0457235075
www.valetti.it

The greatest difficulty for Bardolino producers is giving the wines rich texture and concentration without sacrificing their typical light, fragrant qualities. Valetti succeeds in this, releasing one of the best '08 Bardolino Superiores with wild berries and pepper on the nose and a crisp, succulent palate.

● Bardolino Cl. Sup. '08	🍷🍷	4
⊙ Bardolino Chiaretto Cl. '09	🍷	3
● Bardolino Cl. '09	🍷	3*
○ Bianco di Custoza '09	🍷	3*

Vaona

LOC. VALGATARA
VIA PAVERNO, 41
37020 MARANO DI VALPOLICELLA [VR]
TEL. 0457703710
www.vaona.it

The Vaona family estate at Valgatara, at the mouth of the Marano valley, farms ten or so hectares almost entirely dedicated to classic local varieties. The very good Amarone Pegrandi '06 is one of the most impressive wines in Valpolicella with overripe aromas and a succulent, supple palate.

● Amarone della Valpolicella Cl. Paverno '06	🍷🍷	6
● Amarone della Valpolicella Cl. Pegrandi '06	🍷🍷	6
● Valpolicella Cl. Sup. Ripasso Pegrand '08	🍷	4

Villa Erbice

VIA VILLA, 22
37030 MEZZANE DI SOTTO [VR]
TEL. 0458880086
agricolavillaerbice@virgilio.it

The Erbice brothers' estate covers 13 hectares in the Mezzane valley, most of which is dedicated to Valpolicella grapes. Amarone Tremenel '05 aged in small oak barrels and displays distinctive, complex aromas followed by a well-textured palate. The Ripasso '07 shows fresher aromas and a supple palate.

● Amarone della Valpolicella Vign. Tremenel '05	🍷🍷	7
● Valpolicella Sup. Ripasso '07	🍷🍷	5
● Valpolicella Sup. Vign. Montetombole '07	🍷	4

Zardetto Spumanti

VIA MARTIRI DELLE FOIBE, 18
31015 CONEGLIANO [TV]
TEL. 0438394969
www.zardettoprosecco.com

Zardetto was key in developing Treviso's sparkling wines in the 1980s. Today, with Fabio at the helm, the estate is reclaiming its rightful place with a broad, balanced range. The Dry Z shows faint, stylish aromas of apple and pear fruit with a soft, lingering flavour. The Brut B '09 is also good.

○ Conegliano Brut B '09	🍷🍷	4
○ Conegliano Dry Z	🍷🍷	4
○ Cartizze C n°5 '09	🍷	6
○ Conegliano Extra Dry X '09	🍷	4

Pietro Zardini

VIA DON P. FANTONI, 3
37029 SAN PIETRO IN CARIANO [VR]
TEL. 0456800589
www.pietrozardini.it

Pietro Zardini divides his time between his winery and consulting for local colleagues. The Amarone '05 is very good with nut aromas mingling with spice and fresh greens, followed by a very complex, harmonious palate. The Valpolicella and Lugana wines are simpler but very drinkable.

● Amarone della Valpolicella '05	🍷🍷	7
○ Lugana '09	🍷	4
● Valpolicella '08	🍷	3
● Valpolicella Sup. Ripasso Austero '06	🍷	5

FRIULI VENEZIA GIULIA

Friuli Venezia Giulia is superb white wine territory. For at least three decades, in all eight designated wine zones into which the region is divided, and particularly in the two hill areas, Collio and Colli Orientali del Friuli, wineries have been turning out fantastic bottles. The varieties used are both traditional, such as friulano (the former tocai friulano), ribolla, malvasia istriana, and internationals long established in the region, including pinot bianco and sauvignon. Since 1987, the Guide has been tracking Friuli's wine output, taking over from Luigi Veronelli who in earlier years rightly called this region the great homeland of Italian whites. The current edition of Italian Wines is the third to award 31 Three Glass prizes to Friuli Venezia Giulia's wines. Most of the winners come from Collio, but there are also plenty from Colli Orientali, Isonzo and, for the first time, Aquileia. But the revelation was the tiny wine zone of Carso, which picked up three top prizes as well as our Sustainable Viticulture accolade, which went to Sandi Skerk, one of the younger members of the DOC's band of extreme winemakers. We might also point out that Friuli Venezia Giulia is dominated to an inordinate extent by small-scale growers who look after their vineyards themselves and vinify their grapes perhaps with the aid of a cellarman but do not use consultants. It is no coincidence that there are no very large cellars in the region but small and medium-sized outfits abound, rarely farming more than 30 hectares or releasing more than 200,000 bottles a year. These are numbers that would make growers in neighbouring Veneto or Trentino smile. For some time, producers specialising in red wines and grapes have also been emerging. Many are based on merlot, which has been grown in Friuli for a century and a half and is pronounced hereabouts with the final "t". Traditional red grapes are also used, such as refosco, pignolo, schioppettino and less frequently tazzelenghe. Nor should we forget cabernet franc or cabernet sauvignon, although these appear to be losing ground, as are chardonnay and traminer aromatico. That seems to be the trend all across the region: more heritage varieties and more craft wines. Leading the movement are some particularly driven small-scale producers like Josko Gravner, Enzo Pontoni, who owns the Miani winery, Edi Kante, Gianni Del Fabbro of Ronc di Vico, Dario Raccaro and Fabio Coser of Ronco dei Tassi. Needless to say, the great names of Friulian wine, Silvio Jermann above all, who have in the past brought fame to this small but awesome north-eastern region, continue to add lustre to winemaking in Friuli Venezia Giulia.

Tenuta di Angoris

LOC. ANGORIS, 7
34071 CORMÒNS [GO]
TEL. 048160923
www.angoris.com

CELLAR SALES
PRE-BOOKED VISITS

ANNUAL PRODUCTION 850,000 bottles
HECTARES UNDER VINE 130
VITICULTURE METHOD Conventional

Tenuta di Angoris has 630 hectares around Cormòns, some 130 of which are under vine. Claudia, Marta and Massimo Locatelli carry on the good work begun by Luciano in the late 1970s, tending the rows and vinifying the grapes in a modern, well-equipped cellar that is heir to a three century-long tradition. The vines stand around an aristocratic home in the Friuli Isonzo DOC, in the Ronco Antico estate in the Collio and Stabili della Rocca in Colli Orientali del Friuli.

The range is split into two lines: Villa Angoris for wines from the Friuli Isonzo DOC and Vôs da Vigne for bottles sourced from hillslope plots. Expert agronomist Marco Simonit is in charge of the vineyards and work in the cellar is the responsibility of the estate's competent oenologist, Alessandro Del Zovo. The wines are very good this year. Ribolla Gialla Vôs da Vigne '09 repeated last year's performance in a spring flowers and fruit bouquet followed by a temptingly fresh-tasting palate. Pinot Grigio Vôs da Vigne is redolent of summer flowers while the Friulano Villa Angoris Brut 16 48 spumante are both excellent.

○ 1648 Brut '06	🍷🍷	4*
○ COF Ribolla Gialla Vôs da Vigne '09	🍷🍷	4*
○ Collio Pinot Grigio Vôs da Vigne '09	🍷🍷	4
○ Friuli Isonzo Friulano Villa Angoris '09	🍷🍷	4*
⊙ 1648 Rosé '06	🍷	6
○ COF Friulano Vôs da Vigne Selezione '09	🍷	5
○ COF Sauvignon Vôs da Vigne '09	🍷	5
● Friuli Isonzo Cabernet Franc Villa Angoris '09	🍷	4
● Friuli Isonzo Cabernet Sauvignon Villa Angoris '09	🍷	4
● Friuli Isonzo Merlot Villa Angoris '09	🍷	4
○ Friuli Isonzo Pinot Grigio Villa Angoris '09	🍷	4
● Friuli Isonzo Refosco P. R. Villa Angoris '09	🍷	4
○ Friuli Isonzo Sauvignon Villa Angoris '09	🍷	4
○ COF Bianco Spìule '07	🍸🍸	5
○ Collio Chardonnay Vôs da Vigne '08	🍸🍸	5
○ Friuli Isonzo Pinot Bianco Villa Angoris '08	🍸🍸	4*

Antonutti

FRAZ. COLLOREDO DI PRATO
VIA D'ANTONI, 21
33037 PASIAN DI PRATO [UD]
TEL. 0432662001
www.antonuttivini.it

CELLAR SALES
PRE-BOOKED VISITS

ANNUAL PRODUCTION 600,000 bottles
HECTARES UNDER VINE 17
VITICULTURE METHOD Conventional

Adriana and Lino, partners in life, also share the wine estate at Colloredo di Prato near Udine and Barbeano in the municipality of Spilimbergo, both in the Grave del Friuli DOC zone. They and their children Caterina and Nicola make up a fine team that has coaxed the best from the soil. The Antonuttis turn out an increasingly convincing range, managing to combine innovation with more than a hundred years of tradition.

Again, Traminer Aromatico Vis Terrae was top of the list. The '08 gives penetrating tropical aromatics and a creamily soft mouthfeel. We were also impressed by the '04 Cabernet Sauvignon Vis Terrae, which presents a deep ruby red, with varietal fruit on the estery nose and a powerful, savoury palate that signs off with a nice twist of bitterness. Best of the base line are the Friulano and the Sauvignon, both '09. The easy-drinking Friulano is utterly varietal on the nose and the Sauvignon has typically fresh, assertive fragrances laced with apricot.

● Friuli Grave Cabernet Sauvignon Vis Terrae '04	🍷🍷	4
○ Friuli Grave Friulano '09	🍷🍷	4
○ Friuli Grave Sauvignon '09	🍷🍷	4
○ Friuli Grave Traminer Aromatico Vis Terrae '08	🍷🍷	4
○ Friuli Grave Chardonnay Vis Terrae '09	🍷	4
● Friuli Grave Merlot Vis Terrae '05	🍷	4
○ Friuli Grave Pinot Grigio Vis Terrae '09	🍷	4
● Friuli Grave Refosco P. R. '08	🍷	4
○ Friuli Grave Chardonnay Vis Terrae '06	🍸🍸	4
○ Friuli Grave Pinot Grigio '08	🍸🍸	4*
○ Friuli Grave Pinot Grigio Vis Terrae '07	🍸🍸	4*
○ Friuli Grave Pinot Grigio Vis Terrae '06	🍸🍸	4
○ Friuli Grave Sauvignon '08	🍸🍸	4*
○ Friuli Grave Traminer Aromatico Vis Terrae '07	🍸🍸	4*

Aquila del Torre

FRAZ. SAVORGNANO DEL TORRE
VIA ATTIMIS, 25
33040 POVOLETTO [UD]
TEL. 0432666428
www.aquiladeltorre.it

CELLAR SALES
PRE-BOOKED VISITS
ROOMS

ANNUAL PRODUCTION 50,000 bottles
HECTARES UNDER VINE 18
VITICULTURE METHOD Conventional

Aquila del Torre has been growing grapes since the early 20th century. It was purchased in 1996 by the Ciani family, who quickly put in place an ambitious programme of vineyard conversion to promote the excellent native varietal biotypes on the estate. This is the northernmost edge of the Colli Orientali del Friuli, on the south-east slopes of the Savorgnano del Torre zone, celebrated as the home of Friuli's prestigious picolit grape.

Claudio Ciani laid the foundations and now his son Michele, who has completed a degree in agriculture and an internship in Alsace, looks after winemaking, separately fermenting grapes from the 16 plots into which the vineyards have been divided on the basis of soil and climate conditions. The Sauvignon from Vît dai Maz (the "madmen's vineyard"), so called because of its sheer slope, gives very fresh, concentrated medlar fruit. The pear and almond-fragranced Friulano stands out for varietal typicality, showing supple on the palate. Candied peel and fruit in syrup characterize the Picolit, which leaves luscious tropical fruit flavours in the mouth.

○ COF Friulano '09	🍷🍷	4
○ COF Picolit '07	🍷🍷	8
● COF Refosco P. R. '08	🍷🍷	4
○ COF Sauvignon Vit dai Maz '08	🍷🍷	6
● COF Merlot '08	🍷	4
○ COF Sauvignon '09	🍷	5
○ COF Friulano '08	🍸🍸	5
○ COF Picolit '06	🍸🍸	8
○ COF Picolit '03	🍸🍸	8
○ COF Picolit Oasipicolit '02	🍸🍸	8
● COF Refosco P. R. '07	🍸🍸	5
● COF Refosco P. R. SolSiRe '07	🍸🍸	5
○ COF Sauvignon Vit dai Maz '07	🍸🍸	5

Attems

FRAZ. CAPRIVA D'ISONZO
VIA AQUILEIA, 30
34070 GORIZIA
TEL. 0481806098
www.attems.it

CELLAR SALES
PRE-BOOKED VISITS

ANNUAL PRODUCTION 365,000 bottles
HECTARES UNDER VINE 50
VITICULTURE METHOD Conventional

Conte Sigismondo Douglas Attems was the man who in 1964 founded the Consorzio Vini del Collio, chairing the consortium for the rest of his life. Even today, the strict production protocol he insisted on safeguards the very high quality standards of the Collio DOC. In 2000, the estate broadened its horizons, hitching up with one of Italy's great wine dynasties, the Marchesi di Frescobaldi, a Florentine family that has been producing premium-quality wines for 30 generations.

Attems has always been particularly noted for whites of the kind that scrupulously reflect their territory. This time, the best of the bunch was Collio Bianco Cicinis '08. The name comes from the hill where the sauvignon, pinot bianco and friulano grapes in the blend were nurtured. Its lovely golden yellow ushers in peaches in syrup and jasmine scents while the slightly rustic palate has power, savouriness and penetration. The other wines are good.

○ Collio Bianco Cicinis '08	🍷🍷	5
○ Chardonnay '09	🍷	4
○ Collio Friulano '09	🍷	4
○ Collio Sauvignon '09	🍷	4
○ Pinot Grigio '09	🍷	4
○ Pinot Grigio Cupra Ramato '09	🍷	4
○ Ribolla Gialla '09	🍷	4
○ Collio Bianco Cicinis '07	🍸🍸	5
○ Collio Bianco Cicinis '06	🍸🍸	5
○ Collio Bianco Cicinis '05	🍸🍸	5
○ Collio Friulano '08	🍸🍸	4*
● Collio Merlot '06	🍸🍸	4
○ Collio Sauvignon '07	🍸🍸	4

Bastianich

LOC. GAGLIANO
VIA DARNAZZACCO, 44/2
33043 CIVIDALE DEL FRIULI [UD]
TEL. 0432700943
www.bastianich.com

CELLAR SALES
PRE-BOOKED VISITS

ANNUAL PRODUCTION 180,000 bottles
HECTARES UNDER VINE 40
VITICULTURE METHOD Conventional

Lidia Bastianich is the undisputed queen of Italian cooking in the Unites States. Forced to abandon her native Istria with her family after the Second World War, she carved out a career for herself as a cook, businesswoman and celebrity. Today, she and her son Joseph run a chair of successful restaurants from Manhattan to Las Vegas. Joe is an enthusiastic champion of Italian wine and a few years ago, also turned his hand to making it.

In fact, he maintains that wine is the driving force of his life. Here in Friuli at the cellar in Gagliano, near Cividale, consultant Emilio Del Medico has helped Joe make his Friulian dream come true in a stunning white wine. Joe knows that he is chasing a chimera but his great passion is Vespa Bianco, a blend of chardonnay, sauvignon and picolit. His baby has won major awards all over the globe and is at its peak a few years after the harvest.

○ Vespa Bianco '08	▼▼	6
○ COF Friulano Vigne Orsone '09	▼▼	4
● Calabrone '06	▼	8
○ COF Tocai Friulano Plus '02	YYY	5
○ Vespa Bianco '03	YYY	5
○ Vespa Bianco '01	YYY	5
○ Vespa Bianco '00	YYY	5
○ Vespa Bianco '99	YYY	5
○ COF Tocai Plus '06	YY	4
○ Malvasia Istriana '07	YY	5
○ Sauvignon "B" '07	YY	4
○ Vespa Bianco '07	YY	6
○ Vespa Bianco '06	YY	6
○ Vespa Bianco '05	YY	5
● Vespa Rosso '04	YY	6

Anna Berra

VIA RAMANDOLO, 29
33045 NIMIS [UD]
TEL. 0432790296
www.annaberra.it

CELLAR SALES
PRE-BOOKED VISITS

ANNUAL PRODUCTION 25,000 bottles
HECTARES UNDER VINE 6
VITICULTURE METHOD Conventional

Ivan Monai, young in years but old in growing experience, has for the past few years been running the estate founded by his mother at Ramandolo, on the slopes of Mount Bernadia, in the cooler northern part of Colli Orientali del Friuli. It might be a bit of an exaggeration to say that viticulture in these parts is heroic but it's certainly not easy. The mountain slopes are steep and all the work has to be done by hand. On top of that, the geography of the area favours hail, which is a disaster for the vines.

Unsurprisingly, the most territorial of the wines is Ramandolo but this year it wasn't released, evidently being in need of more cellar time. We did, however, tasted the entire Bernadia line, which impressed on our last visit. The Sauvignon is delicious, well defined and varietal on the grapefruit-laced aniseed and white peaches nose then savoury and juicy on the long-lingering palate. The Friulano is equally attractive. Penetrating varietal aromas led by nectarines usher in a supple palate. We also like the fresh, fragrant Chardonnay.

○ COF Sauvignon La Bernadia '09	▼▼	4*
○ COF Friulano La Bernadia '09	▼▼	4*
○ COF Chardonnay La Bernadia '09	▼	4
○ COF Friulano La Bernadia '08	YY	4*
● COF Refosco P. R. Ris. '03	YY	5
○ COF Sauvignon La Bernadia '08	YY	4*
○ Ramandolo '05	YY	5
○ Ramandolo Anno Domini '04	YY	6
○ Ramandolo Anno Domini '03	YY	6
○ Ramandolo Anno Domini '02	YY	6

Tenuta di Blasig

VIA ROMA, 63
34077 RONCHI DEI LEGIONARI [GO]
TEL. 0481475480
www.tenutadiblasig.it

CELLAR SALES
PRE-BOOKED VISITS

ANNUAL PRODUCTION 70,000 bottles
HECTARES UNDER VINE 16
VITICULTURE METHOD Conventional

Founded in 1788 by Domenico Blasig, this is one of the longest-established cellars in Friuli Venezia Giulia. We are now into the seventh generation and since 1989, the estate has been run by Elisabetta Bortolotto Sarcinelli, who gained experience in Germany and the United States before heading up this all-women team. It's a winning – if not deliberate, according to Elisabetta – combination Her dedication, skill and enthusiasm are applied to supervising all stages of production, from vineyard to winemaking, marketing and distribution.

Elisabetta's lieutenant for sales and public relations is the able Valentina Casula. Erica Orlandino looks after vineyard and cellar management. Again, our marks for Blasig wines were better than good, the highest going to a stunningly varietal Friulano '09 with rose-led floral fragrances, a true-to-type palate and a soft finish. The Malvasia confirmed its excellence with penetrating aromatics and gutsy savouriness in the mouth.

○ Friuli Isonzo Friulano '09	▼▼	4*
○ Friuli Isonzo Malvasia '09	▼▼	4*
● Friuli Isonzo Merlot '07	▼	4
● Friuli Isonzo Refosco P. R. '07	▼	4
● Tenuta di Blasig Rosso '05	▼	5
● Friuli Isonzo Cabernet '06	YY	4*
○ Friuli Isonzo Malvasia '08	YY	4*
○ Friuli Isonzo Malvasia '05	YY	4*
● Friuli Isonzo Merlot '06	YY	4*
● Friuli Isonzo Rive di Giare Refosco P. R. '05	YY	4*
● Friuli Isonzo Rive di Giare Refosco P. R. '04	YY	4*
○ Friuli Isonzo Tocai Friulano '04	YY	4*
○ Le Lule '03	YY	5
● Rosso Gli Affreschi '03	YY	5

La Boatina

VIA CORONA, 62
34071 CORMÒNS [GO]
TEL. 048160445
www.paliwines.com

CELLAR SALES
PRE-BOOKED VISITS
ROOMS

ANNUAL PRODUCTION 120,000 bottles
HECTARES UNDER VINE 62
VITICULTURE METHOD Conventional

La Boatina is part of Lorenzo Pali's Pali Wines group, which also includes Castello di Spessa, I Roncati and Distillerie De Mezzo. The location is Corona, a few kilometres from Cormòns, and the estate covers 80 hectares. For the past few years, La Boatina has been Pali Wines' trademark for all the group's Friuli Isonzo DOC wines. Although known for some time as a wine producer, the estate has comfortable bed and breakfast farmstay accommodation. Set among the rows, it's the ideal spot to discover the area's natural beauties.

Oenologist Domenico Lovat monitors winemaking with input from consultant Gianni Menotti. For some time, high quality has been a given in these parts. This year, the table shows whites only and the best of these, we thought, was the very fruity '09 Pinot Grigio with elegant, well-defined aromatics and a soft, well-poised palate. The white peach and peppermint Friulano '09 is a delicious easy-drinker while the '09 Pinot Bianco is upfront on the nose, closing stylishly long.

○ Friuli Isonzo Friulano '09	▼▼	4*
○ Friuli Isonzo Pinot Bianco '09	▼▼	4*
○ Friuli Isonzo Pinot Grigio '09	▼▼	4*
○ Friuli Isonzo Chardonnay '09	▼	4
○ Ribolla Gialla '09	▼	4
● Collio Rosso Picol Maggiore Ris. '01	YY	5
○ Friuli Isonzo Chardonnay '08	YY	4*
○ Friuli Isonzo Chardonnay '07	YY	4
○ Friuli Isonzo Friulano '08	YY	4*
○ Friuli Isonzo Pinot Bianco '07	YY	4*
○ Friuli Isonzo Pinot Grigio '07	YY	4
○ Friuli Isonzo Sauvignon '08	YY	4*
○ Friuli Isonzo Sauvignon '07	YY	4
○ Ribolla Gialla '08	YY	4*

Borgo Conventi

S.DA DELLA COLOMBARA, 13
24070 FARRA D'ISONZO [GO]
TEL. 0481888004
www.ruffino.it

CELLAR SALES

ANNUAL PRODUCTION 350,000 bottles
HECTARES UNDER VINE 30
VITICULTURE METHOD Conventional

Borgo Conventi is in the easternmost part of Friuli, in the province of Gorizia on the road that takes you from Gradisca to Farra d'Isonzo. Set up in 1975, it quickly asserted itself as a leading producer but the step change came in 2001, when the Tuscany-based Ruffino group took over the estate. Ruffino's centuries-long winemaking experience and commitment to boosting quality have given further impetus to Borgo Conventi's production.

As is often the case in these parts, production is split across the Collio and Friuli Isonzo DOCs with some vineyards on the flatlands and others in the hills. Managing both vineyards and cellars is oenologist Paolo Corso, the estate's technical director. Overall quality is impressive and the wines won very similar scores but we just preferred the '09 Isonzo Merlot for its penetrating wafts of blackberries and savoury, juicy palate. The '07 Schioppettino gives varietal spice over balsam with lots of energy on the fresh-tasting palate and the very varietal '09 Sauvignon reveals a whiff of fresh greens followed by savouriness in the mouth.

○ Collio Sauvignon '09	▼▼	4*
● Friuli Isonzo Merlot '09	▼▼	4*
● Schioppettino '07	▼▼	5
○ Collio Ribolla Gialla '09	▼	4
○ Friuli Isonzo Friulano '09	▼	4
○ Friuli Isonzo Pinot Grigio '09	▼	4
● Friuli Isonzo Refosco P. R. '09	▼	4
● Braida Nuova '91	YYY	7
○ Collio Bianco Colle Russian '06	YY	5
○ Collio Sauvignon '08	YY	5
○ Collio Sauvignon Colle Blanchis '08	YY	5
○ Friuli Isonzo Chardonnay '07	YY	4
○ Friuli Isonzo Friulano '08	YY	4*
○ Friuli Isonzo Pinot Grigio '07	YY	4
● Friuli Isonzo Refosco P. R. '08	YY	4*

Borgo del Tiglio

FRAZ. BRAZZANO
VIA SAN GIORGIO, 71
34070 CORMÒNS [GO]
TEL. 048162166

CELLAR SALES
PRE-BOOKED VISITS

ANNUAL PRODUCTION 35,000 bottles
HECTARES UNDER VINE 8
VITICULTURE METHOD Conventional

Nicola Manferrari's estate has only nine hectares under vine and output is a bare 35,000 bottles, with very low yields per vine. Over the years, it has become a beacon for many aficionados of Friulian wine in Italy and abroad. There's a wide range of labels on offer, starting with Collio Bianco Ronco della Chiesa and Collio Studio di Bianco, both complex, if oak-dominated in their youth. The other whites are more approachable, and we liked them a little bit more.

Our vote this time went to Collio Sauvignon '08. A powerful, varietal white, it proffers well-defined white peaches and aniseed. The '08 Collio Friulano del '08 is a touch more buttery and masked by oak, making up for this on the supple, structured palate with its bracing acidity. The '09 Verduzzo Friulano, released after nine years in the cellar, is special showing pale amber with a complex nut-led nose and full, rich palate that has no trace of sweetness. For the time being, the '09 Collio Chardonnay is less exciting as oak prevails.

○ Collio Sauvignon '09	▼▼	7
○ Collio Friulano '08	▼▼	7
○ Verduzzo Friulano '99	▼▼	7
○ Collio Chardonnay '08	▼	7
○ Collio Bianco Ronco della Chiesa '06	YYY	7
○ Collio Bianco Ronco della Chiesa '02	YYY	7
○ Collio Bianco Ronco della Chiesa '01	YYY	7
○ Collio Chardonnay '00	YYY	5
○ Collio Bianco '07	YY	6
○ Collio Bianco Ronco della Chiesa '07	YY	7

Borgo delle Oche

VIA BORGO ALPI, 5
33098 VALVASONE [PN]
TEL. 0434840640
www.borgodelleoche.it

CELLAR SALES
PRE-BOOKED VISITS

ANNUAL PRODUCTION 25,000 bottles
HECTARES UNDER VINE 7
VITICULTURE METHOD Conventional

Borgo delle Oche, officially constituted as recently as 2004, owes its name to the district where it is sited in the stunning medieval centre of Valvasone, in the province of Pordenone. The owner, Luisa Menini, has a degree in food technology and a genuine obsession with the care of her vineyards. She also looks after the estate paperwork. Luisa's task is to deliver perfect fruit to the agronomist and oenologist, Nicola Pittini, her partner in life as well as at work.

We enjoyed this year's offerings and Bianco Alba's '09 edition went to the finals, like its two predecessors. The part-dried traminer-based wine is flecked with amber and reveals intense fragrances of candied peel, honey and caramel. On the palate it is sheer delight, showing sweet, fragrant and incredibly long. The dry Traminer Aromatico '09 is also impeccably varietal while the friulano and verduzzo Bianco Lupi Terrae '08 is well up to snuff.

○ Bianco Alba '09	TT	6
○ Bianco Lupi Terrae '08	TT	5
● Merlot '08	TT	5
○ Terra & Cielo Brut	TT	5
○ Traminer Aromatico '09	TT	5
○ Pinot Grigio '09	T	5
● Refosco P. R. '08	T	5
○ Bianco Alba '08	YY	6
○ Bianco Alba '07	YY	5
○ Bianco Alba '06	YY	5
○ Bianco Lupi Terrae '07	YY	5
○ Pinot Grigio '07	YY	4
○ Traminer Aromatico '06	YY	4*

Borgo Judrio

VIA AQUILEIA, 79
33040 CORNO DI ROSAZZO [UD]
TEL. 0432755896
borgojudrio@alice.it

PRE-BOOKED VISITS

ANNUAL PRODUCTION 20,000 bottles
HECTARES UNDER VINE N.A.
VITICULTURE METHOD Conventional

Borgo Judrio evokes the hills that the river it is named after runs through. For centuries, this has been superb wine country. It was in 2007 that here at Corno di Rosazzo, in the heart of the Colli Orientali del Friuli DOC, the two Gigante brothers started out on their own winemaking adventure, giving birth to Borgo Judrio. Alberto is the owner and Ariedo, an expert oenologist, provides input in the cellar.

Gigante is a winery to watch. Last year, we noted that this is no nine-day wonder and in fact this year, the Gigantes sent another wine to our finals. The bottle in question is the Friulano, the region's signature native variety. Since it can no longer be called Tocai, producers appear to be vying with each other to make ever more impressive versions. The Gigantes' Friulano has a subtle, well-defined, varietal nose of thyme, spring flowers, mountain-cut hay and acacia honey followed by an elegantly clean, savoury palate. Their Sauvignon unveils a smoke-tinged varietal nose backed up by plenty of warmth and power.

○ COF Friulano '09	TT	4*
○ COF Sauvignon '09	TT	4*
○ COF Merlot '08	T	4
● COF Refosco P. R. '08	T	4
○ COF Ribolla Gialla '09	T	4
○ COF Friulano '08	YY	4*
● COF Refosco P. R. '06	YY	4*
○ COF Sauvignon '08	YY	4*

★ Borgo San Daniele

VIA SAN DANIELE, 16
34071 CORMÒNS [GO]
TEL. 048160552
www.borgosandaniele.it

CELLAR SALES
PRE-BOOKED VISITS

ANNUAL PRODUCTION 60,000 bottles
HECTARES UNDER VINE 18
VITICULTURE METHOD Conventional

Borgo San Daniele is a recently set up operation run by a brother-and-sister team, Mauro and Alessandra, who boldly took the life-changing decision to look after the vineyards they inherited from their grandfather. The name is taken from the district of Cormòns where they live. It's also where their cosy, welcoming winery is based.

Mauro's approach to viticulture aims for greatness with high-density, low-yield planting patterns, cover cropping and bunch thinning, a late harvest, skin contact for whites as well as reds, malolactic fermentation, extended lees contact and bottling without filtration. He is able to do all this thanks to the limited range of wines and his reward is another Three Glasses for his Friulano. The varietal '08 has concentrated aromatics and moments of extraordinary intensity on the palate. Another good performer was the pale onionskin Pinot Grigio '08, a fragrant, full-fruited wine that finds perfect poise on its savoury palate.

○ Friuli Isonzo Friulano '08	▼▼▼	5*
○ Friuli Isonzo Pinot Grigio '08	▼▼	5*
○ Arbis Blanc '06	▽▽▽	5
○ Arbis Blanc '05	▽▽▽	5
○ Friuli Isonzo Arbis Blanc '02	▽▽▽	5
○ Friuli Isonzo Friulano '07	▽▽▽	5*
○ Friuli Isonzo Pinot Grigio '04	▽▽▽	5
○ Friuli Isonzo Pinot Grigio '99	▽▽▽	5
○ Friuli Isonzo Tocai Friulano '03	▽▽▽	5
○ Friuli Isonzo Tocai Friulano '97	▽▽▽	5
● Gortmarin '03	▽▽▽	5
○ Arbis Blanc '07	▽▽	5
● Arbis Ros '06	▽▽	6
● Arbis Ros '05	▽▽	6

Borgo Savaian

VIA SAVAIAN, 36
34071 CORMÒNS [GO]
TEL. 048160725
stefanobastiani@libero.it

CELLAR SALES
PRE-BOOKED VISITS

ANNUAL PRODUCTION 40,000 bottles
HECTARES UNDER VINE 12
VITICULTURE METHOD Conventional

The premature death of Mario Bastiani has left a void at this small winery nestling in the shadow of Mount Quarin. But Mauro's son Stefano is an able, determined wine man and we are sure he will maintain the high quality standards set by his father and grandfather, Bruno, before him. The 12 hectares under vine stand around the district of Savaian, in the heart of the Collio, and in the Isonzo zone.

For the second year running, one of Stefano's wines went through to the finals. This time, it was the '07 Cabernet Franc, from a grape that has found a home from home in the dry and infertile, yet mineral salt and nitrate-rich, soil of Isonzo. The impenetrably deep ruby red shades into garnet before the black berry fruits and gamy notes of the bouquet remind you that this variety comes from Bordeaux. The palate is stylish and varietal. Stefano's pale onionskin Pinot Grigio '09 stands out for its bouquet but also has plenty of structure on the mouthfilling palate. We also enjoyed the slim-bodied, juicy '09 Friulano and Sauvignon.

● Friuli Isonzo Cabernet Franc '07	▼▼	4*
○ Collio Friulano '09	▼▼	4*
○ Collio Pinot Grigio '09	▼▼	4*
○ Collio Sauvignon '09	▼▼	4*
○ Collio Pinot Bianco '09	▼	4
○ Friuli Isonzo Traminer Aromatico '09	▼	4
○ Collio Chardonnay '04	▽▽	4*
○ Collio Friulano '08	▽▽	4*
● Collio Merlot '07	▽▽	4*
○ Collio Pinot Bianco '05	▽▽	4*
○ Collio Pinot Bianco '04	▽▽	4*
○ Collio Pinot Grigio '05	▽▽	4
○ Collio Sauvignon '08	▽▽	4*
○ Friuli Isonzo Traminer Aromatico '08	▽▽	4*

Cav. Emiro Bortolusso

via Oltregorgo, 10
33050 Carlino [UD]
tel. 043167596
www.bortolusso.it

CELLAR SALES
PRE-BOOKED VISITS

ANNUAL PRODUCTION **120,000 bottles**
HECTARES UNDER VINE **35**
VITICULTURE METHOD **Conventional**

We have been saying for some years that Bortolusso is the benchmark winery for the Friuli Annia DOC zone. Meanwhile, brother and sister Sergio and Clara keep up the good work. Located near the nature park of the Marano lagoon, the Bortolusso winery is strikingly attractive. The range, entirely sourced from the estate's own 35 hectares, is impressively good and remarkably well priced.

Sergio looks after the cellar, with invaluable input from consultant Luigino De Giuseppe, and the results are seriously good. For the second year running, the Bortolusso Malvasia went through to the finals for its elegant aromatics, gutsy character, savouriness and fine acid grip. But all the wines are great, from the soft, flower-themed '09 Chardonnay and juicy '09 Friulano to the taut '09 Sauvignon with its fresh greens fragrances.

○ Friuli Annia Malvasia '09	▼▼	3*
○ Friuli Annia Chardonnay '09	▼▼	3*
○ Friuli Annia Friulano '09	▼▼	3*
○ Friuli Annia Pinot Grigio '09	▼▼	3*
○ Friuli Annia Sauvignon '09	▼▼	3*
○ Friuli Annia Traminer Aromatico '09	▼	3
○ Friuli Annia Malvasia '08	▽▽	3*
○ Friuli Annia Malvasia '07	▽▽	3*
○ Friuli Annia Pinot Bianco '08	▽▽	3*
○ Friuli Annia Pinot Bianco '07	▽▽	3*
○ Friuli Annia Pinot Grigio '08	▽▽	3*
○ Friuli Annia Sauvignon '08	▽▽	3*
○ Friuli Annia Sauvignon '07	▽▽	3*

Rosa Bosco

via Roma, 5
33040 Moimacco [UD]
tel. 0432722461
www.rosabosco.it

CELLAR SALES
PRE-BOOKED VISITS

ANNUAL PRODUCTION **14,000 bottles**
HECTARES UNDER VINE **N.A.**
VITICULTURE METHOD **Conventional**

Rosetta Bosco, Rosetta to her friends, is one of the great ladies of wine whom we have praised in previous Guides for the passion and tenacity embodied in the only two wines she released: Boscorosso and Sauvignon Blanc, from rigorously selected, oak-fermented fruit. Last year, two new wines came along, eliciting unanimous plaudits. With the help of her son, the accomplished oenologist Alessio Dorigo, Rosetta now has four outstanding wines.

This year, Rosetta left her Boscorosso and Sauvignon Blanc ageing in the cellar, so we will be assessing them next time. For this guide, our attention focused on the Blanc de Blancs Brut spumante from chardonnay grown on the sun-blessed slopes of Rosazzo. The creamy, lingering mousse crowns a splendid golden yellow hue that reveals the constant rising streams of tiny bubbles. An invitingly complex, assertive bouquet mingles bergamot, peaches, pine resin, hazelnut and grilled bread before the caressingly appealing mouthfeel unveils distinct acidity and minerality.

○ Blanc de Blancs Brut	▼▼	6
○ Ribolla Gialla '09	▼▼	5
○ COF Sauvignon Blanc '02	▽▽▽	6
● COF Rosso Il Boscorosso '04	▽▽	7
● COF Rosso Il Boscorosso '03	▽▽	7
● COF Rosso Il Boscorosso '02	▽▽	7
● COF Rosso Il Boscorosso '00	▽▽	7
○ COF Sauvignon Blanc '06	▽▽	6
○ COF Sauvignon Blanc '05	▽▽	6
● Il Boscorosso '05	▽▽	7
○ Sauvignon Blanc '08	▽▽	6
○ Sauvignon Blanc '07	▽▽	6

Conte Brandolini

VIA VISTORTA, 82
33077 SACILE [PN]
TEL. 0434782490
www.vistorta.it

CELLAR SALES
PRE-BOOKED VISITS

ANNUAL PRODUCTION 250,000 bottles
HECTARES UNDER VINE 36
VITICULTURE METHOD Certified organic

Vistorta is a small village in western Friuli where the Brandolini family has owned a farm since 1780. In the 19th century, Guido Brandolini's remarkable far-sightedness turned the estate into an efficient, modern-minded operation. Since 1980, Brandino Brandolini d'Adda has been in charge. Previously he acquired experience at the family's other estate, Château Greysac in Médoc and has converted Vistorta along French lines.

With help from Georges Pauli, the oenologist at Château Gruaud-Larose, new plantings were made in the late 1980s to supplement the existing varieties. It is no coincidence that the choice fell on merlot, a grape originally from Gironde. Vistorta's Merlot, which won Three Glasses for five years running, quickly became one of Friuli's wine classics. This year, however, Brandolino decided not to present it, instead leaving it in the cellar for another year to acquire further complexity. Brandolino's brave decision shifted focus to the whites, enabling us to draw attention to the medlar and peach fruit-fuelled '09 Chardonnay, a very sound, complex offering with lots of freshness.

○ Friuli Grave Chardonnay '09	▼▼	3*
○ Friuli Grave Friulano '09	▼	4
○ Friuli Grave Sauvignon '09	▼	4
● Friuli Grave Merlot Vistorta '07	YYY	5
● Friuli Grave Merlot Vistorta '06	YYY	5
● Friuli Grave Merlot Vistorta '05	YYY	5
○ Friuli Grave Chardonnay '07	YY	3*
○ Friuli Grave Friulano '08	YY	4*
○ Friuli Grave Friulano '07	YY	4
○ Friuli Grave Pinot Grigio '07	YY	4
○ Friuli Grave Sauvignon '08	YY	4*
○ Friuli Grave Sauvignon '07	YY	4*
○ Friuli Grave Traminer Aromatico '07	YY	4*
● Treanni Rosso	YY	4

Branko

LOC. ZEGLA, 20
34071 CORMÒNS [GO]
TEL. 0481639826

CELLAR SALES
PRE-BOOKED VISITS

ANNUAL PRODUCTION 45,000 bottles
HECTARES UNDER VINE 7
VITICULTURE METHOD Conventional

This small, family-run winery takes its name from Branko Erzetic, father of the current owner Igor. The winery was set up in 1950 but its roots go further back because the Erzetic family has been growing grapes for a very long time. The vine stock is partly at Zegla, near the winery, with the remaining plots at Plessiva and Novalis, which are also superbly aspected Collio sites.

The Pinot Grigio, with its rich aromatics and plenty of structure, has long been the cellar's flagship wine. It's always one of the best around and the '09 edition is again one of Friuli's finest. The straw yellow precedes a varietal nose of citrus peel-veined fruit and the intriguing, caressing palate is utterly delicious. The Friulano '09 is pale green, crisply defined and true to type, giving wafts of peach and then a soft, concentrated mouthfeel.

○ Collio Pinot Grigio '09	▼▼	5
○ Collio Friulano '09	▼▼	5
● Red '08	▼	5
○ Collio Pinot Grigio '08	YYY	5*
○ Collio Pinot Grigio '07	YYY	5
○ Collio Pinot Grigio '06	YYY	5
○ Collio Pinot Grigio '05	YYY	5
○ Collio Chardonnay '08	YY	5
○ Collio Friulano '08	YY	5
○ Collio Friulano '07	YY	5
○ Collio Sauvignon '08	YY	5
○ Collio Sauvignon '06	YY	5
○ Collio Tocai Friulano '06	YY	5
● Red '07	YY	5

Livio e Claudio Buiatti

VIA LIPPE, 25
33042 BUTTRIO [UD]
TEL. 0432674317
www.buiattivini.it

CELLAR SALES
PRE-BOOKED VISITS

ANNUAL PRODUCTION 35,000 bottles
HECTARES UNDER VINE 8
VITICULTURE METHOD Conventional

Claudio Buiatti runs a small family operation he inherited from his father Livio. The cellar is right next to the family home in the centre of Buttrio and the vineyards sprawl over the rolling hills that lie between Buttrio and Premariacco, at "in Mont e Poianis". Claudio is aided by his wife Viviana, who welcomes guests to the winery and deals with the paperwork with skill born of long practice.

We have already pointed out the attention to vineyard management that has enabled Buiatti wines to enhance quality while continuing to represent excellent value for money. Quality, in fact, is now a given and the results have been quick to come. This time, we very much liked the '09 Friulano, a model of typicality with its peach and almond aromatics and gutsily fresh, savoury palate. Equally good is the '08 Refosco with its brooding, vaguely smoky nuances on the nose and intense, rich yet easy-drinking palate. The other wines are all appealing.

○ COF Friulano '09	two black glasses	4
● COF Refosco P. R. '08	two black glasses	4
● COF Cabernet '08	one black glass	4
● COF Merlot '08	one black glass	4
○ COF Picolit '07	one black glass	6
○ COF Pinot Grigio '09	one black glass	4
○ COF Sauvignon '09	one black glass	4
○ COF Friulano '07	two white glasses	4
● COF Refosco P. R. '07	two white glasses	4*
● COF Rosso Momon Ros Ris. '05	two white glasses	5
○ COF Sauvignon '08	two white glasses	4*
○ COF Sauvignon '07	two white glasses	4*
○ COF Tocai Friulano '04	two white glasses	4*

La Buse dal Lof

VIA RONCHI, 90
33040 PREPOTTO [UD]
TEL. 0432701523
www.labusedallof.com

CELLAR SALES
PRE-BOOKED VISITS

ANNUAL PRODUCTION 100,000 bottles
HECTARES UNDER VINE 25
VITICULTURE METHOD Conventional

Giuseppe Pavan set up this cellar at Prepotto in 1972. The name La Buse dal Lôf is Friulian for wolf's lair, a local place name for this long-noted wine zone. Currently, Michele Pavan is in charge. He aims to respect Friuli's heritage in vineyards and cellar, although that doesn't stop him using modern technology.

Buse dal Lôf stormed into the Guide as the '07 Schioppettino went straight through to the finals. It's a genuinely classy wine whose deep, garnet-flecked ruby red heralds penetratingly complex wafts of black-skinned forest fruits that shade into cocoa powder, pipe tobacco and pleasing hints of spice. The full-bodied palate is savoury and uncompromising. We also liked the deep-hued '07 Cabernet Sauvignon, which fuses red fruits and spice ahead of a fresh, well-balanced and deliciously juicy palate. Finally, the '09 Friulano is a paragon of typicality, but then so are all the others in this well-crafted range.

● COF Schioppettino '07	two black glasses	5
● COF Cabernet Sauvignon '07	two black glasses	4*
○ COF Friulano '09	two black glasses	4
○ COF Pinot Bianco In Bocca al Lupo '09	one black glass	4
● COF Refosco P. R. '08	one black glass	4
○ COF Ribolla Gialla '09	one black glass	4

Valentino Butussi

via Prà di Corte, 1
33040 Corno di Rosazzo [UD]
tel. 0432759194
www.butussi.it

CELLAR SALES
PRE-BOOKED VISITS
ROOMS

ANNUAL PRODUCTION 95,000 bottles
HECTARES UNDER VINE 16
VITICULTURE METHOD Organic

The Butussi wine story is made up of passing on experience, knowledge, hints and wrinkles from one generation to the next. Its roots are in the marl and sandstone of Prà di Corte at Corno di Rosazzo in the Colli Orientali del Friuli. The cellar made its name thanks to Valentino's son, Angelo, with his wife Pierina, who have passed the baton on to their four children. Now Tobia, Filippo, Mattia and Erika share the work in vineyard, cellar and office.

Once again, the Butussis sent two wines to the finals, confirming that the younger generation is on the right path. The '09 Friulano is simply excellent. Its lovely hue introduces upfront varietal aromas and a powerfully concentrated, full-bodied palate that still manages to be perky. Equally good is the '09 Sauvignon with its nose of elderflower, nettles and gunflint backed up by a long, vibrant palate. The nice, balsam-fragranced Pignolo '06 is true to type in the mouth and the deliciously tasty Picolit '07 is all elegance.

○ COF Friulano '09	▼▼	4*
○ COF Sauvignon '09	▼▼	4*
○ COF Picolit '07	▼▼	7
● COF Pignolo '06	▼▼	6
● COF Cabernet Franc '08	▼	4
● COF Cabernet Sauvignon '08	▼	4
○ COF Pinot Grigio '09	▼	4
● COF Refosco P. R. '09	▼	4
○ COF Ribolla Gialla '09	▼	4
○ COF Verduzzo Friulano '08	▼	4
○ COF Friulano '08	▽▽	4*
○ COF Picolit '06	▽▽	7
○ COF Tocai Friulano '05	▽▽	4*

Maurizio Buzzinelli

loc. Pradis, 20
34071 Cormòns [GO]
tel. 048160902
www.buzzinelli.com

CELLAR SALES
PRE-BOOKED VISITS
ROOMS AND FOOD

ANNUAL PRODUCTION 100,000 bottles
HECTARES UNDER VINE 24
VITICULTURE METHOD Conventional

Maurizio Buzzinelli's cellar is based at Pradis, near Cormòns, and sprawls over sun-kissed slopes looking over the Friulian countryside and on to the Adriatic. Maurizio and his wife Marzia decided to continue along the path grandfather Luigi took in 1937, when he settled here in the heart of Collio.

Maurizio himself tends the vines, mainly in the Collio DOC hill country but also on the Isonzo flatlands, where he grows mostly red-skinned varieties. The '09 vintage was a great one for his Friulano, from its lustrous hue to very varietal fruit-forward aromatics tinged with smokiness, and a soft mouthfeel braced by salt-edged acidity. The very approachable '09 Ribolla Gialla is outstandingly fresh, unveiling grapefruit, currants and gooseberries followed by a whistle-clean palate. Maurizio's '09 Sauvignon is citrussy on the nose and holds together well in the mouth while his '08 Refosco is more forward, showing concentrated and over-ripe aromas and juicy, savoury perceptions in the glass.

○ Collio Friulano '09	▼▼	4*
○ Collio Ribolla Gialla '09	▼▼	4*
○ Collio Sauvignon '09	▼▼	4*
○ Collio Pinot Bianco '09	▼	4
○ Collio Pinot Grigio '09	▼	4
● Friuli Isonzo Refosco P.R. '08	▼	4
○ Collio Chardonnay '04	▽▽	4
○ Collio Friulano '07	▽▽	4
○ Collio Malvasia Ronc dal Luis '08	▽▽	4*
○ Collio Pinot Grigio '08	▽▽	4*
○ Collio Tocai Friulano '06	▽▽	4
○ Collio Tocai Friulano '05	▽▽	4
○ Collio Tocai Friulano '04	▽▽	4
○ Collio Tocai Friulano Ronc dal Luis '06	▽▽	4

Ca' Bolani

VIA CA' BOLANI, 2
33052 CERVIGNANO DEL FRIULI [UD]
TEL. 043132670
www.cabolani.it

CELLAR SALES
PRE-BOOKED VISITS

ANNUAL PRODUCTION 2,500,000 bottles
HECTARES UNDER VINE 550
VITICULTURE METHOD Conventional

Tenuta Ca' Bolani, located in the heart of the Friuli Aquileia DOC, was purchased in 1970 by the Zonin family. They restored it to its former glory, reorganizing the vineyards, restoring the estate headquarters and building a modern, technology-packed cellar. The vineyards of Ca' Vescovo and Molin di Ponte, acquired respectively in 1980 and 1998, are also part of the holding. Ca' Bolani's 550 hectares under vine make it the estate with the largest vineyard holding in the region.

Management is in the hands of a very competent team. Oenologist Marco Rabino is in charge, helped out in the cellar by Roberto Marcolini while vineyard management is the domain of Gabriele Carboni. And the team is reaping the just rewards for its hard work. Pinot Bianco '09 more than deserved its Three Glasses, winning plaudits from our panel for its complex, penetrating fragrances and especially for its concentrated aromatics and fullness on the palate. The Refosco dal Peduncolo Rosso '08 and Sauvignon Aquilis '09 are also excellent.

○ Friuli Aquileia Pinot Bianco '09	🍷🍷🍷	4*
● Friuli Aquileia Refosco P. R. '08	🍷🍷	4*
○ Friuli Aquileia Sauvignon Aquilis '09	🍷🍷	4*
○ Friuli Aquileia Pinot Grigio '09	🍷	4
○ Friuli Aquileia Traminer Aromatico '09	🍷	4
○ Prosecco Ca' Bolani	🍷	3
● Friuli Aquileia Conte Bolani Gianni Zonin Vineyards '00	🍸🍸	6
○ Friuli Aquileia Friulano '08	🍸🍸	4*
● Friuli Aquileia Refosco P. R. Alturio Gianni Zonin Vineyards '05	🍸🍸	4*
○ Friuli Aquileia Sauvignon '08	🍸🍸	4*
○ Friuli Aquileia Sauvignon Tamànis Gianni Zonin Vineyards '08	🍸🍸	5*
○ Opimio Gianni Zonin Vineyards '01	🍸🍸	4*

Ca' Tullio & Sdricca di Manzano

VIA BELIGNA, 41
33051 AQUILEIA [UD]
TEL. 0431919700
www.catullio.it

CELLAR SALES
PRE-BOOKED VISITS

ANNUAL PRODUCTION 450,000 bottles
HECTARES UNDER VINE 78
VITICULTURE METHOD Conventional

Genuineness, experience, passion and quality are the priorities Paolo Calligaris has set for this estate. Grapes are estate-grown, some at Sdricca near Manzano, and vinified in the superb cellar at Aquileia, which is actually a beautifully converted tobacco drying house. One wing of the building is now a Taberna Romana decorated with amphorae, jars and impressive drapes. Diners can savour the atmosphere of imperial Aquileia as they stretch out on Roman dining couches.

The sandy terrain at Viola near Aquileia itself has long been a site for the cultivation of ungrafted traminer vines. Thanks to the skills of oenologist Francesco Visintin, this signature variety of the Aquileia DOC zone has been given a new lease of life. The true-to-type '09 Friulano from the Sdricca line is a fine bottle that offers toast, breadth, depth and complexity on the nose with a long, vibrantly savoury palate. We also liked the Ribolla Gialla '09 for its tropical fruits aromas and full, pleasingly citrussy, palate. Finally, the '08 Pignolo and '09 Traminer Viola are well up to standard.

○ COF Friulano Sdricca '09	🍷🍷	4*
● COF Pignolo Sdricca '08	🍷🍷	6
○ COF Ribolla Gialla Sdricca '09	🍷🍷	4*
○ Friuli Aquileia Traminer Viola '09	🍷🍷	4
○ COF Pinot Grigio Sdricca '09	🍷	4
○ COF Sauvignon Sdricca '09	🍷	4
○ Friuli Aquileia Muller Thurgau '09	🍷	4
○ Friuli Aquileia Pinot Grigio '09	🍷	4
● Friuli Aquileia Refosco Patriarca '09	🍷	4
○ Belladonna Sdricca	🍸🍸	6
○ COF Friulano Sdricca '08	🍸🍸	4*
● COF Pignolo Sdricca '06	🍸🍸	5
○ COF Pinot Grigio Sdricca '08	🍸🍸	4*
○ COF Verduzzo Friulano Sdricca '07	🍸🍸	6
○ COF Verduzzo Friulano Sdricca '06	🍸🍸	6
○ Friuli Aquileia Traminer Viola '08	🍸🍸	4*

Canus

VIA GRAMOGLIANO, 21
33040 CORNO DI ROSAZZO [UD]
TEL. 0432759427
www.canus.it

CELLAR SALES

ANNUAL PRODUCTION 35,000 bottles
HECTARES UNDER VINE 12
VITICULTURE METHOD Conventional

Canus is skilfully managed by Dario Rossetto with help from his sister Lara, who looks after administration and public relations. They were given the job by their father Ugo, a well-known businessman from Pordenone, who purchased the operation and passed his passion for viticulture on to them. The winery's curious name derives from a Latin word for grey hair, a trait that runs in the Rossetto family.

Dario's enthusiasm has blossomed in a few short years. His Refosco dal Peduncolo Rosso '07 is every bit as impressively varietal and appealing as last year's edition. Its lovely garnet-flecked ruby proffers complex aromas of forest fruits and spices, then a full, savoury and supple palate. Flowers and citrus are the aromatic themes of the poised '09 Ribolla Gialla, which drinks deliciously. All the other wines are well typed and worth uncorking.

● COF Refosco P. R. '07	🍷🍷	5
○ COF Ribolla Gialla '09	🍷🍷	4
○ COF Friulano '09	🍷	4
○ COF Malvasia '09	🍷	4
● COF Pignolo '07	🍷	6
○ COF Pinot Grigio '09	🍷	4
○ COF Sauvignon '09	🍷	4
○ COF Bianco Jasmine '07	YY	5
○ COF Bianco Jasmine '06	YY	4
○ COF Chardonnay '08	YY	4*
○ COF Pinot Grigio '06	YY	4
● COF Refosco P. R. '06	YY	5
○ COF Ribolla Gialla '07	YY	4
○ COF Ribolla Gialla Ribuele Blancie '07	YY	5
○ COF Sauvignon '06	YY	4
○ COF Tocai Friulano '06	YY	4*

Il Carpino

LOC. SOVENZA, 14A
34070 SAN FLORIANO DEL COLLIO [GO]
TEL. 0481884097
www.ilcarpino.com

CELLAR SALES
PRE-BOOKED VISITS

ANNUAL PRODUCTION 60,000 bottles
HECTARES UNDER VINE 16
VITICULTURE METHOD Organic

Franco and Anna Sosol set up their winery in 1987, at Borgo del Carpino between Oslavia San Floriano del Collio, right on the border with Slovenia. Now, their children Naike and Manuel help to run the estate, which is increasingly oriented to environmentally friendly viticulture. No chemical fertilizers are used among the rows and other treatments with natural products are kept to the bare minimum.

It's well known that winemaking in these parts is going back to its roots. Recently, the use of large Slavonian oak casks has become more widespread. Musts stay in contact with the skins for several days to coax out the more complex fragrances and flavours. However, the technique is not employed with fruit from the younger vineyards, which is fermented in steel. One such bottle is the '09 Ribolla Gialla Vigna Runc, a fresh, elegant bottle with penetrating aromas and a supple palate. Wines given skin contact are rich in colour, complex and concentrated on the nose, and structured on the palate, like the savoury, minerally Ribolla Gialla '07 with its hint of balsam.

○ Collio Ribolla Gialla V. Runc '09	🍷🍷	4*
○ Chardonnay '07	🍷🍷	5
○ Malvasia '07	🍷🍷	6
○ Pinot Grigio Vis Uvae '07	🍷🍷	6
○ Ribolla Gialla '07	🍷🍷	5
○ Bianco Runc '09	🍷	4
● Rosso Carpino '07	🍷	7
● Rubrum '99	YYY	8
○ Bianco Carpino '06	YY	5
○ Bianco Carpino '04	YY	5
○ Bianco Carpino '03	YY	5
○ Chardonnay '06	YY	5
○ Collio Malvasia Carpino '04	YY	6
○ Exordium '06	YY	6
○ Pinot Grigio Vis Uvae '06	YY	6

Casa Zuliani

VIA GRADISCA, 23
34070 FARRA D'ISONZO [GO]
TEL. 0481888506
www.casazuliani.com

CELLAR SALES
PRE-BOOKED VISITS

ANNUAL PRODUCTION 120,000 bottles
HECTARES UNDER VINE 21
VITICULTURE METHOD Conventional

There's a new wind blowing at Zuliani. The generational hand-overs initiated when Zuliano Zuliani set up the business in 1923 have been broken off. His great-grandson Federico Frumento, having taken on important managerial responsibilities in Liguria, has passed the estate on to Riccardo Monfardino. A Sardinian by birth and Friulian by adoption, Riccardo joined the winery a couple of years ago to work on the commercial side.

Nonetheless, the change of management has not had a major impact on a well-oiled organisational machine that boasts first-class technical staff. Giovanni Bigot is still in charge of the vineyards while Omar Caffar does an excellent job in the cellar. The Friulano repeated last year's success, confirming its excellence with penetrating, varietal aromatics and a rich, savoury palate with loads of concentration. The '07 Winter Chardonnay puts the accent on fruit over peanut butter with a full-flavoured palate. Tropical fruits are the keynote of the deep, vibrant Sauvignon Blanc '09.

○ Collio Friulano '09	2 black glasses	4*
○ Collio Sauvignon Blanc '09	2 black glasses	4
○ Winter Chardonnay '07	2 black glasses	5
○ Collio Chardonnay '09	1 black glass	4
○ Collio Malvasia '09	1 black glass	4
● Collio Merlot '07	1 black glass	5
○ Collio Pinot Grigio '09	1 black glass	4
○ Winter Sauvignon '08	1 black glass	5
● Winter Rosso '04	3 glasses	6
○ Collio Friulano '08	2 glasses	4*
○ Collio Friulano '07	2 glasses	4*
○ Collio Malvasia '05	2 glasses	4*
● Winter Rosso '03	2 glasses	5
○ Winter Sauvignon '05	2 glasses	5

Lino Casella

VIA ALBANA, 55
33040 PREPOTTO [UD]
TEL. 0432713429
info.casella@libero.it

ANNUAL PRODUCTION 16,000 bottles
HECTARES UNDER VINE 4
VITICULTURE METHOD Conventional

The recently founded Casella winery at Albana near Prepotto in the Colli Orientali del Friuli has plenty of history. Lino Casella may only have been in charge since 2006 but the estate is respected as Albana's historic winemaking memory. For such a young man, Lino has wide-ranging wine experience to help him run a cellar with lovely facilities and vineyards over 40 years old.

He turned out a great line-up this time, sending two reds from 2007 to our finals. His single-variety Merlot showed just how well the variety grows in this area. Its subtle nose of wild cherries and tobacco precedes an elegantly well-defined palate with lots of juicy savouriness. The sensory profile is similar in the Rosso Selezione dei Roseti, another merlot-based wine but this time blended with native tazzelenghe and schioppettino fruit. It's every bit as complex on the nose and supple in the mouth. Ripe apple fruit is the calling card of the '09 Friulano, which gives penetrating greens on the nose and then a gutsy palate.

● COF Merlot '07	2 black glasses	4*
● COF Rosso Sel. dei Roseti '07	2 black glasses	4*
○ COF Friulano '09	2 black glasses	4*
○ COF Ribolla Gialla '09	1 black glass	4
● COF Schioppettino '08	1 black glass	5
● COF Tazzelenghe '08	1 black glass	5
○ COF Bianco Sel. dei Roseti '07	2 glasses	4*
○ COF Pinot Bianco '07	2 glasses	4*
● COF Schioppettino '07	2 glasses	5
○ COF Tocai Friulano '06	2 glasses	4*
● Franconia '07	2 glasses	4*
● Franconia '06	2 glasses	4*

La Castellada

FRAZ. OSLAVIA, 1
34170 GORIZIA
TEL. 048133670

CELLAR SALES
PRE-BOOKED VISITS

ANNUAL PRODUCTION 23,000 bottles
HECTARES UNDER VINE 9
VITICULTURE METHOD Organic

Oslavia-based La Castellada was set up in 1985 when brothers Giorgio and Nicolò Bensa decided to bottle the wine the family obtained from its five hectares, which until then had only been sold at their father Giuseppe's trattoria. Little by little, the estate grew, gradually finding its own style of vinification in increasingly structured, complex wines that are always also natural, because Bensa viticulture is respectful of the environment.

Grapes, whether red or white, are given long skin contact, which gives rise to spontaneous fermentation and the extraction of tannins, natural antioxidants that make it possible to restrict the use of sulphites to a minimum. The wines are original, muscular, richly hued and excitingly fragrant. They evolve slowly, staying in oak for many years, but they thrill. Rosso della Castellada '04, for instance, reveals incredible finesse on nose and a palate so soft it seems almost sweet. The whites stand out for their colour, opulent aromatics and power on the palate.

● Collio Rosso della Castellada '04	▼▼	8
○ Collio Bianco della Castellada '06	▼▼	6
○ Collio Pinot Grigio '06	▼▼	6
○ Collio Ribolla Gialla '06	▼	6
○ Collio Sauvignon '06	▼	6
○ Bianco della Castellada '95	▽▽▽	6
○ Collio Bianco della Castellada '99	▽▽▽	6
○ Collio Bianco della Castellada '98	▽▽▽	6
○ Collio Chardonnay '94	▽▽▽	6
● Collio Rosso della Castellada '99	▽▽▽	8
○ Collio Sauvignon '93	▽▽▽	6
○ Collio Tocai Friulano '03	▽▽▽	6
○ Collio Bianco della Castellada '05	▽▽	6
○ Collio Ribolla Gialla '05	▽▽	6

Castello di Spessa

VIA SPESSA, 1
34070 CAPRIVA DEL FRIULI [GO]
TEL. 0481639914
www.paliwines.com

CELLAR SALES
PRE-BOOKED VISITS
FOOD

ANNUAL PRODUCTION 80,000 bottles
HECTARES UNDER VINE 28
VITICULTURE METHOD Conventional

Like all old manor houses, Castello di Spessa casts its spell over even the most distracted visitor. It's not just the elegance of the architecture or the beauty of the long-established parkland. There's also hundreds of years of history, people and events. In 1990, the current owner Loretto Pali started farming and at the same time gave the castle itself a makeover to turn it into a holiday complex complete with golf course and restaurant.

Underground is a communication bunker linking the castle to the cellar. Dating from 1939, it was used by occupying troops during the Second World War but today it is an ideal environment for ageing wines at constant temperature and humidity. We tasted the whites from the latest vintage and again two went through to the finals. The '09 Friulano gives scents of citron and elegantly assertive sensations in the mouth while the '09 Pinot Bianco is upfront on the nose with a gutsily appealing palate. Our congratulations to oenologist Domenico Lovat and his staff.

○ Collio Friulano '09	▼▼	5
○ Collio Pinot Bianco '09	▼▼	5
○ Collio Pinot Grigio '09	▼▼	5
○ Collio Ribolla Gialla '09	▼▼	5
○ Collio Sauvignon '09	▼▼	5
○ Collio Sauvignon Segrè '09	▼▼	6
● Collio Cabernet Sauvignon Rassauer '06	▼	5
○ Collio Pinot Bianco '06	▽▽▽	5
○ Collio Pinot Bianco '01	▽▽▽	4
○ Collio Sauvignon Segrè '03	▽▽▽	6
○ Collio Sauvignon Segrè '02	▽▽▽	6
○ Collio Tocai Friulano '05	▽▽▽	5
○ Collio Friulano '07	▽▽	5
○ Collio Ribolla Gialla '08	▽▽	5
● Collio Rosso Conte di Spessa '03	▽▽	6
○ Collio Sauvignon '08	▽▽	5

Castello Sant'Anna

LOC. SPESSA
VIA SANT'ANNA, 9
33043 CIVIDALE DEL FRIULI [UD]
TEL. 0432716289
centasantanna@libero.it

CELLAR SALES
PRE-BOOKED VISITS

ANNUAL PRODUCTION 20,000 bottles
HECTARES UNDER VINE 7
VITICULTURE METHOD Conventional

Castello Sant'Anna was founded in 1966 at Spessa near Cividale in the heart of the Colli Orientali del Friuli by Giuseppe Giaiotti, who left the world of industry for the countryside that had always attracted him. Giuseppe purchased what was once a noble Cividale family's vineyard-girt summer residence and set about restoring it. Andrea is now in charge and he carries on in the footsteps of his predecessors.

In recent years, Andrea has been busy building a new underground cellar that will give him plenty of space to work in and a constant temperature. This new Guide profile is well deserved and one wine even went on to our finals. The star is Andrea's superbly interpreted Sauvignon '09, a husky but fantastically fruit-driven, minerally wine that is spellbindingly assertive, savoury and complex. The '09 Friulano also has loads of intensity, freshness and balance. Finally, the Ribolla Gialla '09 is a model of varietal typicality and freshness.

○ COF Sauvignon '09	🍷🍷	4*
○ COF Friulano '09	🍷🍷	4*
○ COF Ribolla Gialla '09	🍷🍷	4*
● COF Merlot '07	🍷	5
● COF Pignolo '06	🍷	5
○ COF Pinot Grigio '09	🍷	4

Castelvecchio

VIA CASTELNUOVO, 2
34078 SAGRADO [GO]
TEL. 048199742
www.castelvecchio.com

CELLAR SALES
PRE-BOOKED VISITS

ANNUAL PRODUCTION 250,000 bottles
HECTARES UNDER VINE 40
VITICULTURE METHOD Conventional

Just above Sagrado, where the Carso tableland in the province of Gorizia offers lovely unspoiled corners of nature, stands Castelvecchio. The estate is managed with passion and professionalism by the Terraneo family, who enjoy a superb view that on clear days embraces the entire region. In the past, the area has seen glories and disasters. Today, the arid, rocky soil continues to pose awesome challenges, and sometimes unexpected opportunities.

The rocky substrate under a shallow layer of iron and limestone-rich red earth with little organic matter, the wind-swept climate and a late harvest yield a limited crop of grapes with absolutely unique characteristics. Cabernet franc and cabernet sauvignon from the '05 growing year fermented in oak and then three years' maturation in small and medium-sized wood went into Sagrado Rosso, a wine whose '05 vintage impressed our tasters. It has stuffing, personality, elegance and complexity as well as rich, spice-veined aromas that seem to linger for ever. The typically salty, faintly smoky Malvasia Istriana '09 is butter-smooth and excellent.

● Sagrado Rosso '05	🍷🍷	6
○ Carso Malvasia Istriana '09	🍷🍷	4
● Carso Cabernet Franc '07	🍷	5
● Carso Cabernet Sauvignon '07	🍷	5
○ Carso Sauvignon '09	🍷	4
○ Sagrado Bianco '08	🍷	5
● Carso Cabernet Sauvignon '05	🍸🍸	5
● Carso Cabernet Sauvignon '03	🍸🍸	5
○ Carso Malvasia Istriana '08	🍸🍸	4*
○ Carso Malvasia Istriana '07	🍸🍸	4
○ Carso Malvasia Istriana '06	🍸🍸	4
● Carso Merlot '04	🍸🍸	6
● Carso Merlot '03	🍸🍸	6
● Carso Refosco P. R. '06	🍸🍸	5
● Sagrado Rosso '03	🍸🍸	6

Marco Cecchini

LOC. CASALI DE LUCA
VIA COLOMBANI
33040 FAEDIS [UD]
TEL. 0432720563
www.cecchinimarco.com

CELLAR SALES
PRE-BOOKED VISITS

ANNUAL PRODUCTION **40,000 bottles**
HECTARES UNDER VINE **10**
VITICULTURE METHOD **Conventional**

This operation was little more than a hobby when Marco started out in 1998 with a single hectare at Faedis, in the Colli Orientali del Friuli. But our hero, who has a degree in economics and a great love of the outdoor life, was actually taking the first steps that would mark out his future. Now he has about ten hectares, half of which are planted to vines more than 40 years old.

Marco is helped out in the cellar by consultant Sonia Dell'Oste, who orchestrates a very well-matched team, ensuring continuity of the quality levels achieved. The Refosco dal Peduncolo Rosso '08 is impenetrably deep in hue, very true to type and complex on both nose and the full, juicy palate, which has lashings of personality. We could say the same of Careme '06, an estery, mouthfilling Bordeaux-inspired blend with a touch of refosco. Tove '09, a friulano-based white with some verduzzo, gives a convincing, tropical fruits nose.

○ COF Bianco Tovè '09	▼▼	4*
● COF Refosco P. R. '08	▼▼	4*
● COF Rosso Careme '06	▼▼	5
○ Pinot Grigio Vigneto Bellagioia '09	▼	4
○ COF Bianco Tovè '08	YY	4*
○ COF Bianco Tovè '06	YY	4*
○ COF Bianco Tovè '05	YY	4
○ COF Picolit '03	YY	6
● COF Refosco P. R. '07	YY	4*
○ COF Verduzzo Friulano Verlit '07	YY	5
○ COF Verduzzo Friulano Verlit '06	YY	5
○ Pinot Grigio Vigneto Bellagioia '08	YY	4*
○ Pinot Grigio Vigneto Bellagioia '07	YY	4*
○ Riesling '07	YY	4*

Eugenio Collavini

LOC. GRAMOGLIANO
VIA DELLA RIBOLLA GIALLA, 2
33040 CORNO DI ROSAZZO [UD]
TEL. 0432753222
www.collavini.it

CELLAR SALES
PRE-BOOKED VISITS

ANNUAL PRODUCTION **1,500,000 bottles**
HECTARES UNDER VINE **173**
VITICULTURE METHOD **Organic**

The Collavini winery is still named after Eugenio, who founded it in 1896. During the 1970s, the estate's holdings were extended by Manlio Collavini, who purchased a 16th-century noble residence in the centre of Rosazzo, which became the family home and location of the cellars. The quality turn-around came in 1996, with a comprehensive programme to modernize winemaking facilities and ensure the loyalty of the winery's supplier growers, who are monitored by a Collavini agronomist.

Today, Manlio Collavini continues to run the estate with his trademark entrepreneurial skills and help from his sons Luigi and Giovanni, while the cellar is in the capable hands of Walter Bergnanch, the man who created the blend of Collio Goriziano-grown chardonnay, friulano and sauvignon that goes into one of the most successful Collavini wines, Broy. This year's Three Glass award is Broy's fifth. In the glass, Broy faithfully reflects of its territory. Penetrating yellow peach and pineapple fruit introduce magnificently powerful, harmonious sensations in the mouth, where a wealth of flavours carry through to the endlessly long, savoury finale.

○ Collio Bianco Broy '09	▼▼▼	5*
○ COF Ribolla Gialla Turian '09	▼▼	6
○ Collio Pinot Grigio Villa Canlungo '09	▼▼	4*
○ Collio Sauvignon Blanc Fumât '09	▼▼	4*
● COF Refosco P. R. Pucino '09	▼	4
○ Collio Bianco Broy '08	YYY	5*
○ Collio Bianco Broy '07	YYY	5
○ Collio Bianco Broy '06	YYY	5
○ Collio Bianco Broy '04	YYY	5
○ Collio Bianco Broy '03	YYY	5
● COF Rosso Forresco '05	YY	6
● Collio Merlot dal Pic '05	YY	6
● Collio Merlot dal Pic '04	YY	6
○ Collio Pinot Grigio Black Label '07	YY	4*
○ Collio Sauvignon Blanc Fumât '08	YY	4*
○ Ribolla Gialla Brut '05	YY	6

Colle Duga

LOC. ZEGLA, 10
34071 CORMÒNS [GO]
TEL. 048161177
www.colleduga.com

CELLAR SALES
PRE-BOOKED VISITS

ANNUAL PRODUCTION 52,000 bottles
HECTARES UNDER VINE 9
VITICULTURE METHOD Conventional

Damina Princic's winery takes its name from the Colle Duga vineyard at Zegla, near Cormòns, in the Collio where the vines rub shoulders with their Slovenian counterparts in the Goriska Brda. Everyone in the family lends a hand, from Damian's father Luciano in the vineyard to his wife Monica in the office and their children Karin and Patrik when things are busy. Now and again, Damian likes to get an opinion on winemaking procedures from consultant Giorgio Bertossi but the powerful, dynamically savoury style of Colle Duga wines, which faithfully reflect their provenance, is all Damian's work.

This tirelessly passionate winemaker picked up another Three Glass prize for a simply stunning Collio Friulano '09. Whistle-clean, close-focused, very varietal and rich on eye and palate, it is an authoritative, extraordinarily long wine. Equally impressive are the '09 Collio Bianco, from sauvignon, chardonnay, friulano and malvasia, redolent of peppermint, and the Pinot Grigio from the same year, which proffers pears and bananas.

○ Collio Friulano '09	▼▼▼	4*
○ Collio Bianco '09	▼▼	5*
○ Collio Pinot Grigio '09	▼▼	4*
○ Collio Chardonnay '09	▼▼	4
● Collio Merlot '08	▼▼	5
○ Collio Sauvignon '09	▼▼	4
○ Collio Bianco '08	▽▽▽	5*
○ Collio Bianco '07	▽▽▽	5
○ Collio Tocai Friulano '06	▽▽▽	4*
○ Collio Tocai Friulano '05	▽▽▽	4*
○ Collio Chardonnay '08	▽▽	5
○ Collio Friulano '08	▽▽	4*
○ Collio Friulano '07	▽▽	4
○ Collio Pinot Grigio '08	▽▽	5
○ Collio Pinot Grigio '07	▽▽	5
○ Collio Pinot Grigio '05	▽▽	4

Colmello di Grotta

LOC. VILLANOVA
VIA GORIZIA, 133
34072 FARRA D'ISONZO [GO]
TEL. 0481888445
www.colmello.it

CELLAR SALES
PRE-BOOKED VISITS

ANNUAL PRODUCTION 100,000 bottles
HECTARES UNDER VINE 15
VITICULTURE METHOD Conventional

When Luciana Benatti created Colmello di Grotta in 1965, she set about restoring an abandoned farm settlement to its former glory while respecting local tradition. The wine produced was barely sufficient for the requirements of the family table and one or two lucky friends. When Luciana passed away, her daughter Francesca Bortolotto Possati, who inherited her mother's passion for viticulture, began to climb the region's quality ladder.

Colmello di Grotta's vine stock lies half in the Collio Goriziano and half in the Friuli Isonzo DOC zone and even though the two areas are adjacent, their soil types, and the wines they produce, are totally different. Francesca called in the wine skills of Fabio Coser to coax the best out of the territory and Fabio has duly highlighted the special features of both zones: the Collio wines are more structured and complex while Isonzo products are more seductively soft. The '09 Collio Pinot Grigio's intense, penetrating nose heralds a mouthfilling, structured palate with lots of body. The Isonzo Cabernet Sauvignon '08 is more straightforward, presenting soft, savoury, fresh and appealing.

○ Collio Pinot Grigio '09	▼▼	4*
● Friuli Isonzo Cabernet Sauvignon '08	▼▼	4*
○ Collio Bianco Sanfilip '08	▼	5
○ Collio Friulano '09	▼	4
○ Collio Ribolla Gialla '09	▼	4
○ Collio Sauvignon '09	▼	4
○ Collio Bianco Sanfilip '07	▽▽	5
○ Collio Pinot Grigio '08	▽▽	4*
○ Collio Sauvignon '08	▽▽	4*
● Friuli Isonzo Merlot '04	▽▽	4

Giorgio Colutta

via Orsaria, 32
33044 Manzano [UD]
tel. 0432740315
www.colutta.it

CELLAR SALES
PRE-BOOKED VISITS
ROOMS AND FOOD

ANNUAL PRODUCTION 130,000 bottles
HECTARES UNDER VINE 21
VITICULTURE METHOD Conventional

Giorgio Colutta has a medical degree and a great love of the land. Currently, he owns this estate, also known as Bandut, from the ancient name of one of the plots. The vineyards are at Buttrio, Manzano and Rosazzo, all within the prestigious Colli Orientali del Friuli Vine and Wine Park, and they are managed by the magisterial Antonio Maggio. The recently restructured cellars now include accommodations for customers and wine tourists.

There is an important newcomer in the person of Alessandro Sandrin, an oenologist with substantial experience in other Friulian cellars, despite his years. Alessandro is having a major impact on the wine style. Early results are excellent and bode well for the future. The Pinot Grigio '09 is fruit-forward and complex, unveiling a soft texture, good structure and long-lingering length. The '09 Sauvignon is headily alcoholic with varietal aromas and a fresh, free-flowing palate while the rest of the range is well typed and tasty.

○ COF Pinot Grigio '09	▼▼	4*
○ COF Sauvignon '09	▼▼	4*
○ COF Chardonnay '09	▼	4
○ COF Friulano '09	▼	4
○ COF Ribolla Gialla '09	▼	4
● COF Schioppettino '08	▼	5
○ COF Picolit '06	▽▽	8
○ COF Pinot Grigio '07	▽▽	4
● COF Schioppettino '07	▽▽	5
● COF Schioppettino '06	▽▽	5

Paolino Comelli

case Colloredo,8
33040 Faedis [UD]
tel. 0432711226
www.comelli.it

CELLAR SALES
PRE-BOOKED VISITS
ROOMS AND FOOD

ANNUAL PRODUCTION 60,000 bottles
HECTARES UNDER VINE 12
VITICULTURE METHOD Conventional

In 1946, Paolino Comelli was far-sighted enough to purchase an ancient hamlet of crumbling cottages in the hills at Colloredo di Soffumbergo in the municipality of Faedis, in the Colli Orientali del Friuli. He decided to convert it into a working farm and set about restructuring. But it is thanks to Pierluigi Comelli – Pigi to his friends – and his wife Daniela that it is now a farmstay complex of ravishing charm, complete with all mod cons and furnished in traditional Friulian style.

Now their children Nicola and Filippo are also involved in the business but the Comellis' wine successes are largely down to the invaluable consultancy input of Emilio Del Medico. The range goes from strength to strength and two went forward to this year's finals, where they very nearly won top honours. Rosso Soffumbergo '07 was repeating last year's visit and again showed appeal, fruit and persistence on the nose and soft-textured coherence in the mouth. The '09 Sauvignon is very much like its cousins of the Loire, the fresh greens and tropical fruits heralding very convincing structure on the palate and the '09 Pinot Grigio Amplius is excellent.

○ COF Sauvignon '09	▼▼	4*
● Rosso Soffumbergo '07	▼▼	5
○ COF Pinot Grigio Amplius '09	▼▼	4*
○ COF Friulano '09	▼	4
● COF Cabernet Sauvignon '05	▽▽	5
○ COF Chardonnay '06	▽▽	4
○ COF Friulano '07	▽▽	4*
● COF Merlot Jacò '06	▽▽	5
● COF Pignolo '05	▽▽	5
○ COF Sauvignon '07	▽▽	4
○ COF Tocai Friulano '06	▽▽	4
● Rosso Soffumbergo '06	▽▽	5
○ Verduzzo Friulano Eoos '07	▽▽	5

Dario Coos

LOC. RAMANDOLO, 5
33045 NIMIS [UD]
TEL. 0432790320
www.dariocoos.it

CELLAR SALES
PRE-BOOKED VISITS

ANNUAL PRODUCTION 45,000 bottles
HECTARES UNDER VINE 7
VITICULTURE METHOD Conventional

The Coos family has been making wine on the steep slopes at Ramandolo since the early 19th century, Dario, who set up the cellar in 1986, is the fifth generation of expert growers. Here in the north of the Colli Orientali del Friuli, where the hills are more like young mountains, nights are cold, days are warm, rainfall is substantial and verduzzo giallo has always featured in the vineyards. It's a vine that produces small clusters of sturdy, thick-skinned berries, ideal for overripening.

Since Ramandolo, and more recently Picolit, acquired DOCG status, these wines have become more prominent in the Coos range, and their quality has grown. Dario releases several types of Ramandolo and this year, we liked the '06 Romandus best. Its shimmering golden yellow unveils pear juice, honey and caramel aromatics before the intense sweetness is tempered by bright freshness, enhancing the wine's drinkability. We also loved the slightly more amber '07 Picolit with its hints of apricot jam, candied peel and honey. Also impressive is the complex, multi-faceted '08 Vindos Bianco blend of friulano, ribolla gialla and sauvignon.

○ COF Picolit '07	▼▼	7
○ Ramandolo Romandus '06	▼▼	6
○ Vindos '08	▼▼	4
○ Malvasia '09	▼	4
● Pignolo '08	▼	5
○ Ramandolo Il Longhino '07	▼	5
● Schioppettino '08	▼	5
○ COF Picolit '06	▽▽	7
○ Ramandolo '00	▽▽	5
○ Ramandolo Romandus '04	▽▽	6
○ Ramandolo Romandus '02	▽▽	6
○ Ramandolo V. T. '04	▽▽	5

Cantina Produttori di Cormons

VIA VINO DELLA PACE, 31
34071 CORMÒNS [GO]
TEL. 048161798
www.cormons.com

CELLAR SALES
PRE-BOOKED VISITS
ROOMS AND FOOD

ANNUAL PRODUCTION 2,250,000 bottles
HECTARES UNDER VINE 464
VITICULTURE METHOD Conventional

Back in the late 1960s, a group of far-sighted growers in Cormòns who even then could see that the future of wine was not a matter of fashion but depended on unremitting promotion of the territory. Luigi Soini, a cellarmaster at the time and currently director of this flourishing concern, has more than 200 growers supplying grapes from the region's five best DOC zones: Collio, Colli Orientali del Friuli, Carso, Friuli Isonzo and Friuli Aquileia.

Understandably enough, the range is very extensive but a special mention must go to the Vino della Pace, an emblem of universal peace, obtained from more than 600 different varieties, representing all five continents, cultivated at this Cormòns winery. Rodolfo Rizzi is in charge of winemaking and the results are excellent. This year, we like the bottles from Friuli Isonzo, particularly the fragrant, sumptuous '09 Friulano with its ripe fruits over vanilla and trademark almondiness at the back. The Collio Friulano unveils banana-like tropical fruits and a savoury, but slightly too alcoholic, palate.

○ Friuli Isonzo Friulano '09	▼▼	3*
○ Collio Friuliano '09	▼	3
○ Friuli Isonzo Malvasia Istriana '09	▼	3
○ Pinot Grigio Brut Gran Cuvée	▼	4
○ COF Ribolla Gialla '06	▽▽	4
○ Collio Tocai Friulano Rinascimento '04	▽▽	4*
○ Collio Tocai Friulano Rinascimento '03	▽▽	4*
○ Vino della Pace '02	▽▽	6

Conte D'Attimis-Maniago

VIA SOTTOMONTE, 21
33042 BUTTRIO [UD]
TEL. 0432674027
www.contedattimismaniago.it

CELLAR SALES
PRE-BOOKED VISITS

ANNUAL PRODUCTION 400,000 bottles
HECTARES UNDER VINE 85
VITICULTURE METHOD Conventional

Conte Alberto d'Attimis-Maniago Marchiò runs Tenuta Sottomonte, whic sprawls over the Buttrio hills in the Colli Orientali del Friuli DOC zone. This is one of Friuli's most ancient cellars, dating from 1585. One significant detail about this estate is that it is almost entirely planted to local biotypes that have adapted perfectly to the soil after long, patient selection of the varieties, international and native.

The family's 17th-century home at Maniago has just been restructured along with its stables. Currently, it is a hotel and restaurant. The cellars are at Buttrio, where Francesco Spitaleri's expert eye watches over them. We mentioned the attention focused by the estate on native varieties yet this year, the wine that scored highest was the '09 Sauvignon. The supremely elegant varietal nose gives way to a delicious, subtly orchestrated palate. The fruit-forward, mouthfilling Friulano '09 is also outstanding, showing varietal on nose and palate. Masculine tannins are the trademark of the liquorice and coffee Pignlo '06 while the Picolit '08 tempts the taste buds with wafts of caramel and confectioner's cream.

○ COF Friulano '09	▼▼	4*
○ COF Picolit '08	▼▼	8
● COF Pignolo '06	▼▼	8
○ COF Sauvignon '09	▼▼	4*
○ COF Bianco Ronco Broilo '07	▼	5
● COF Tazzelenghe '06	▼	7
○ COF Verduzzo Friulano '08	▼	5
○ COF Bianco Ronco Broilo '05	▽▽	5
○ COF Chardonnay '07	▽▽	5
○ COF Malvasia '06	▽▽	4*
● COF Pignolo '05	▽▽	6
● COF Rosso Vignaricco '05	▽▽	6
● COF Tazzelenghe '04	▽▽	6
● COF Tazzelenghe '03	▽▽	6

di Lenardo

FRAZ. ONTAGNANO
P.ZZA BATTISTI, 1
33050 GONARS [UD]
TEL. 0432928633
www.dilenardo.it

CELLAR SALES
PRE-BOOKED VISITS

ANNUAL PRODUCTION 600,000 bottles
HECTARES UNDER VINE 45
VITICULTURE METHOD Conventional

The Di Lenardo Vineyards winery is in the centre of Ontagnano, a village not far from Palmanova on the extensive Friulian flatlands. Massimo Di Lenardo is the go-getting proprietor who was canny enough to concentrate on export markets, particularly in North America, from the start. Today, about 80 per cent of production leaves Italy. The wines themselves often have entertaining names that reflect the jovial personality of their maker.

Over recent years, standards have been steadily improving across the board. Credit goes to Massimo, of course, but also to Giuliano Cattinelli, the estate oenologist. This time, two bottles went into our finals. The '09 Chardonnay gives a penetrating fruit-led bouquet that shades into butter and vanilla tones while the deep, savoury palate has fantastic personality. Ronco Nolè is a table wine from merlot, refosco and cabernet. Blended in the Bordeaux style, it gives a complex, balsamic nose and a full yet extremely elegant palate. The name is interesting. Ronco in Friulian is a hill and Nolè ("there isn't one" in Friulian) refers to the elevation-bereft plains of Friuli.

○ Chardonnay '09	▼▼	4*
● Ronco Nolè Rosso '08	▼▼	4*
○ Friuli Grave Friulano Toh! '09	▼▼	3*
● Merlot Just Me '08	▼▼	5
○ Verduzzo Pass the Cookies '09	▼▼	4*
○ Father's Eyes '09	▼	4
● Friuli Grave Refosco P. R. '09	▼	4
○ Friuli Grave Sauvignon Blanc '09	▼	3
○ Pinot Grigio '09	▼	3
○ Sarà Brut	▼	5
○ Chardonnay '08	▽▽	4*
○ Father's Eyes '08	▽▽	4*
○ Pinot Bianco '08	▽▽	3*
○ Pinot Grigio '08	▽▽	3*
○ Verduzzo Pass the Cookies '08	▽▽	4*

Carlo Di Pradis

LOC. PRADIS, 22BIS
34071 CORMÒNS [GO]
TEL. 048162272
www.carlodipradis.it

CELLAR SALES
PRE-BOOKED VISITS

ANNUAL PRODUCTION 80,000 bottles
HECTARES UNDER VINE 14
VITICULTURE METHOD Conventional

The 14 hectares under vine tended by Boris and David Buzzinelli are split equally between Collio and Friuli Isonzo, which is pretty much the norm for estates in the Cormòns area. The winery name is emblematic of the brothers' gratitude to their father, Carlo, who left them these wonderful plots at Pradis, where the brothers have built their cellar.

New developments this year include the restyled labels and the first release of Collio, a white blended from friulano, pinot grigio and pinot bianco. But we thought the '08 Scusse (the Friulian for skin) was even better. Its intense, smoke and mineral-veined bouquet leads into a solid, well-poised palate with attractive minerality. The '09 wines from the Collio DOC are great, as is the well-priced Sauvignon Isonzo '09.

O Collio Friulano Scusse '08	TT	5
O Collio '09	TT	4*
O Collio Friulano '09	TT	4*
O Collio Pinot Grigio '09	TT	4*
O Friuli Isonzo Sauvignon '09	TT	4*
O Collio Sauvignon '09	T	4
O Friuli Isonzo Chardonnay '09	T	4
O Friuli Isonzo Pinot Grigio '09	T	4
O Collio Friulano '08	YY	4*
O Collio Friulano Scusse '08	YY	5
O Collio Friulano Scusse '07	YY	5
O Collio Pinot Grigio '09	YY	4*
O Collio Pinot Grigio '08	YY	4*
O Collio Sauvignon '05	YY	4
O Collio Tocai Friulano '06	YY	4
O Collio Tocai Friulano '05	YY	4
O Friuli Isonzo Friulano BorDavi '08	YY	4*
O Friuli Isonzo Friulano BorDavi '07	YY	4*

Giovanni Donda

VIA MANLIO ACIDINIO, 4
33051 AQUILEIA [UD]
TEL. 043191185
www.vinidonda.it

CELLAR SALES

ANNUAL PRODUCTION 30,000 bottles
HECTARES UNDER VINE 7
VITICULTURE METHOD Organic

In 1924, Giovanni Donda from Scodovacca near Cervignano settled at Aquileia and purchased 13 hectares of spontaneous woodlands in the surrounding countryside. His son Bruno could see the potential and began to turn the woods into vineyards. Now Giovanni Donda has the job of bringing it all to fruition, a task he is carrying out superbly, as befits a territory where history, culture and wine tradition have always been inseparable.

Giovanni has entrusted winemaking to Giorgio Bertossi, a very experienced oenologist. For the second year running, the Sauvignon, now an estate flagship, went through to the finals. Greenish tinges enliven the hue of the '09 as sage and tomato leaf tempt the nose but it is the palate that thrills with its fullness, depth and sheer power. The '09 Chardonnay is penetratingly aromatic, fresh-tasting and vibrant. We also like the fruity '07 Refosco, as upfront on the palate as it is on the nose.

O Friuli Aquileia Sauvignon '09	TT	4*
O Friuli Aquileia Chardonnay '09	TT	4*
● Friuli Aquileia Refosco P. R. '07	TT	4*
O Friuli Aquileia Pinot Bianco '09	T	4
O Friuli Aquileia Pinot Grigio '09	T	4
O Friuli Aquileia Chardonnay '04	YY	4*
O Friuli Aquileia Pinot Bianco '08	YY	3*
O Friuli Aquileia Pinot Grigio '08	YY	4*
● Friuli Aquileia Refosco P. R. '06	YY	4*
● Friuli Aquileia Refosco P. R. '05	YY	4
O Friuli Aquileia Sauvignon '08	YY	4*
O Friuli Aquileia Sauvignon '07	YY	4
O Friuli Aquileia Sauvignon '05	YY	4

★★ Girolamo Dorigo

LOC. VICINALE
VIA DEL POZZO, 5
33042 BUTTRIO [UD]
TEL. 0432674268
www.montsclapade.com

CELLAR SALES
PRE-BOOKED VISITS
ROOMS

ANNUAL PRODUCTION 180,000 bottles
HECTARES UNDER VINE 40
VITICULTURE METHOD Conventional

The winery set up by Girolamo Dorigo in 1966 is today one of the benchmark operations for Friulian winemaking, even though the early days were tough. Girolamo was well aware of the territory's potential but equally conscious of regional wine at the time and took his cue from France. He was one of the first to increase planting densities, drastically cut cropping levels, ferment vineyard selections and use new small wood for ageing.

Girolamo is still very active on the estate but day-to-day management was handed over some time ago to his children Alessandra, who runs the office, and Alessio in the recently modernized cellar. The wines here are always good although this year a true stand-out was missing. The '07 Rosso Montsclapade showed the customary matière and personality, giving coffee and redcurrants then a powerful palate whose tannins have yet to unbend. The '09 Traminer is an attractive newcomer with varietal aromatics and a soft mouthfeel. All the other wines are better than good.

○ COF Chardonnay '09	▼▼	4*
○ COF Picolit '07	▼▼	7
● COF Pignolo di Buttrio '07	▼▼	8
● COF Refosco P. R. '08	▼▼	6
○ COF Ribolla Gialla '09	▼▼	4*
● COF Rosso Montsclapade '07	▼▼	7
○ COF Traminer '09	▼▼	4*
○ Dorigo Brut Cuvée	▼▼	5
● COF Refosco P. R. '07	▼	6
○ COF Sauvignon '09	▼	4*
● COF Montsclapade '99	▽▽▽	7
● COF Pignolo di Buttrio '03	▽▽▽	8
● COF Pignolo di Buttrio '02	▽▽▽	8
● COF Pignolo di Buttrio '01	▽▽▽	8
● COF Refosco P. R. Vign. Montsclapade '00	▽▽▽	6
● COF Rosso Montsclapade '06	▽▽▽	7
● COF Rosso Montsclapade '01	▽▽▽	7

Mauro Drius

VIA FILANDA, 100
34071 CORMÒNS [GO]
TEL. 048160998
www.driusmauro.it

CELLAR SALES
PRE-BOOKED VISITS

ANNUAL PRODUCTION 60,000 bottles
HECTARES UNDER VINE 15
VITICULTURE METHOD Conventional

The Drius family has lived at Cormòns for a long, long time and has always tilled the soil. For the Driuses are farmers through and through, proud of their craft and in love with the land that has always yielded its fruits in good times and bad. When Mauro Drius finished studying agriculture, he was a keen cattle farmer but milk quotas and mad cows have transformed him into a full time wine man.

He is assisted among the rows by his father Sergio and by his son Denis, who takes time off from his own studies to lend a hand. In previous Guides, we have pointed out Mauro's skills as a winemaker. It is important to note that he has won Three Glasses for several different wine types, underlining the excellent quality level of the entire range. This year, the top Drius wine was the '09 Friuli Isonzo Pinot Bianco, an intense, varietal, crisply defined wine on nose and palate. The subtly fragrances '07 Merlot is also great, proffering faint cocoa powder and tobacco and a characterful palate with lots of freshness and resolved tannins.

○ Friuli Isonzo Pinot Bianco '09	▼▼▼	4*
● Friuli Isonzo Merlot '07	▼▼	4*
○ Collio Friulano '09	▼▼	4*
○ Collio Sauvignon '09	▼▼	4*
○ Friuli Isonzo Bianco Vignis di Siris '07	▼▼	5*
○ Friuli Isonzo Chardonnay '09	▼	4
○ Collio Tocai Friulano '05	▽▽▽	4*
○ Collio Tocai Friulano '02	▽▽▽	4*
○ Friuli Isonzo Bianco Vignis di Siris '02	▽▽▽	4*
○ Friuli Isonzo Friulano '07	▽▽▽	4
○ Friuli Isonzo Malvasia '08	▽▽▽	4*
○ Collio Friulano '08	▽▽	4*
○ Friuli Isonzo Chardonnay '08	▽▽	4*
○ Friuli Isonzo Pinot Grigio '06	▽▽	4*

Le Due Terre

via Roma, 68b
33040 Prepotto [UD]
tel. 0432713189

CELLAR SALES
PRE-BOOKED VISITS

ANNUAL PRODUCTION 20,000 bottles
HECTARES UNDER VINE 5
VITICULTURE METHOD Organic

Due Terre is a small operation but one of Friuli Venezia Giulia's finest. It was founded in 1984 by Flavio Basilicata who makes a formidable team with Silvana Forte, demonstrating that passion and conviction, perhaps with a touch of inspiration, can coax spectacular results from just a few hectares. You can find our heroes at Prepotto in the Colli Orientali del Friuli, the home of Schioppettino.

The estate name comes from the subsoil, which is part limestone and part clay despite its small extent, while the wine name Sacrisassi was suggested by the discovery, during building work on the cellar, of stones that appear to have belonged to an ancient church. And it was the '08 Sacrisassi Rosso that repeated last year's exploit and swept up Three Glasses. A territory wine from a 50-50 blend of refosco and schioppettino redolent of black berry fruits, cinchona, rhubarb, liquorice and coffee introducing a splendidly muscular palate with a hint of spice on the lingering finish. Friulano and ribolla gialla go into the '08 Sacrisassi Bianco, a fresh, complex white that fills the palate.

● COF Rosso Sacrisassi '08	▼▼▼	7
○ COF Bianco Sacrisassi '08	▼▼	5
● COF Merlot '08	▼▼	7
● COF Pinot Nero '08	▼▼	5
○ COF Bianco Sacrisassi '05	▽▽▽	6
● COF Merlot '03	▽▽▽	6
● COF Merlot '02	▽▽▽	7
● COF Merlot '00	▽▽▽	7
● COF Rosso Sacrisassi '07	▽▽▽	7
○ COF Bianco Sacrisassi '07	▽▽	5
○ COF Bianco Sacrisassi '06	▽▽	5
● COF Merlot '07	▽▽	7
● COF Merlot '06	▽▽	5
● COF Pinot Nero '07	▽▽	5
● COF Rosso Sacrisassi '04	▽▽	7

Ermacora

fraz. Ipplis
via Solzaredo, 9
33040 Premariacco [UD]
tel. 0432716250
www.ermacora.com

CELLAR SALES
PRE-BOOKED VISITS

ANNUAL PRODUCTION 165,000 bottles
HECTARES UNDER VINE 25
VITICULTURE METHOD Conventional

Ermacora is a name that dates back to the days of the ancient Romans. The first bishop of Aquileia, who lived in the third century AD, was called Hermagoras and the Romans erected the stone bridge over the Natisone river on the road to Ipplis. It is in this Lombard settlement that brothers Dario and Luciano Ermacora make their wine at a family-run cellar with a rich heritage that respects its territory.

We have always admired the genuineness of Ermacora wines and their absolute varietal typicality, characteristics that are evident in this year's range. The '08 Picolit '08 is again the cellar's standard-bearer for the appeal and elegance of aromatics that hint at fruit jam, crème caramel, honey and macaroons. Creamy on the palate, it is also sweetish and incredibly long. The '08 Refosco dal Peduncolo Rosso is as varietal as they come, showing soft, savoury and poised on the palate. The faintly copper-hued '09 Pinot Grigio fills nose and palate with delicious fruit. Finally, the '06 Pignolo is intriguingly complex, juicy and unfolds convincingly on the palate and '09 Friulano is an upfront ambassador for its territory and variety.

○ COF Friulano '09	▼▼	4*
○ COF Picolit '08	▼▼	7
● COF Pignolo '06	▼▼	6
○ COF Pinot Grigio '09	▼▼	4*
● COF Refosco P. R. '08	▼▼	4*
○ COF Pinot Bianco '09	▼	4
○ COF Ribolla Gialla '09	▼	4
○ COF Sauvignon '09	▼	4
● COF Pignolo '00	▽▽▽	5
○ COF Friulano '08	▽▽	4*
○ COF Picolit '07	▽▽	7
● COF Pignolo '05	▽▽	6
● COF Pignolo '04	▽▽	6
● COF Pignolo '03	▽▽	6
● COF Refosco P. R. '07	▽▽	4*
○ COF Ribolla Gialla '08	▽▽	4*

Fantinel

FRAZ. TAURIANO
VIA TESIS, 8
33097 SPILIMBERGO [PN]
TEL. 0427591511
www.fantinel.com

CELLAR SALES
PRE-BOOKED VISITS

ANNUAL PRODUCTION 4,000,000 bottles
HECTARES UNDER VINE 300
VITICULTURE METHOD Conventional

The Fantinel winery's facilities, nestling in the countryside at Tauriano near Spilimbergo, are paragons of winemaking and hospitality. It all started in 1969 when Mario Fantinel purchased some plots at Dolegna in the Collio. His children further expanded the business and now the Fantinels have 300 hectares under vine. Marco, Stefano and Mariaelena, the third generation, release a range that has made its presence felt on the world's markets.

The Fantinels have branched out in the region and now also run the Sant'Helena estate in the Collio DOC, Roncaia in Colli Orientali del Friuli and Borgo Tesis in Friuli Grave. All are fine, territory-centred operations that grow their grapes in site climates that are ideal for ripening the fruit. Winemaking is the domain of the group's oenologists, Gianni Campo Dall'Orto and Adriano Copetti. The wines we tasted were all very appealing, the stand-out being the '09 Sant'Helena, a blend of friulano, pinot bianco and sauvignon with stylishly coherent fragrances and a fresh, impressively savoury palate.

○ Collio Bianco Sant'Helena '09	**YY**	5
○ Collio Chardonnay Sant'Helena '09	**Y**	5
○ Collio Friulano Sant'Helena '09	**Y**	5
○ Collio Pinot Grigio Sant'Helena '09	**Y**	5
○ Collio Sauvignon Sant'Helena '09	**Y**	5
● Friuli Grave Cabernet Sauvignon Sant'Helena '07	**Y**	5
● Friuli Grave Refosco P. R. Sant'Helena '07	**Y**	5
○ Collio Bianco Sant'Helena '08	YY	5
○ Collio Pinot Grigio Sant'Helena '08	YY	5
● Collio Rosso Sant'Helena '05	YY	5
○ Collio Sauvignon Sant'Helena '06	YY	5
○ Collio Tocai Friulano Sant'Helena '06	YY	5
● Friuli Grave Refosco P. R. Sant'Helena '06	YY	5

★ Livio Felluga

FRAZ. BRAZZANO
VIA RISORGIMENTO, 1
34071 CORMÒNS [GO]
TEL. 048160203
www.liviofelluga.it

PRE-BOOKED VISITS

ANNUAL PRODUCTION 800,000 bottles
HECTARES UNDER VINE 155
VITICULTURE METHOD Conventional

More than 70 years ago, Livio Felluga, looked up to as the patriarch of Friulian wine, moved from his native Isola d'Istria to start growing grapes in Friuli. During the 1950s, he opened his cellar at Brazzano near Cormòns and very shrewdly bought his first plots at Rosazzo. Today the estate is run by his four children and has 160 hectares in the Collio and Colli Orientali del Friuli hill country, 155 planted to vine.

Livio Felluga wines are known everywhere as the bottles with the distinctive map label, which was conceived by Livio back in 1956. Like the wines, the label was born of a love of the land and it has brought good fortune to the range, particularly the Rosazzo Bianco Terre Alte, one of the very few Italian whites to have achieved worldwide success. That helps to explain why it won Three Glasses. An extremely complex, penetrating nose of almonds and damsons takes you into a refined, savoury palate. Just a step behind are the '09 Sauvignon and '07 Picolit, the former being very varietal and the later harmoniously intense.

○ COF Rosazzo Bianco Terre Alte '08	**YYY**	7
○ COF Picolit '07	**YY**	8
○ COF Sauvignon '09	**YY**	5
○ COF Bianco Illivio '08	**YY**	5
○ COF Friulano '09	**YY**	5
○ COF Pinot Grigio '09	**YY**	5
● COF Refosco P. R. '07	**YY**	6
● COF Refosco P. R. '99	YYY	7
○ COF Rosazzo Bianco Terre Alte '07	YYY	8
○ COF Rosazzo Bianco Terre Alte '06	YYY	7
○ COF Rosazzo Bianco Terre Alte '04	YYY	7
○ COF Rosazzo Bianco Terre Alte '02	YYY	6
○ COF Rosazzo Bianco Terre Alte '01	YYY	6
● COF Rosazzo Sossò Ris. '01	YYY	7
○ Terre Alte '87	YYY	5

Marco Felluga

VIA GORIZIA, 121
34070 GRADISCA D'ISONZO [GO]
TEL. 048199164
www.marcofelluga.it

CELLAR SALES
PRE-BOOKED VISITS

ANNUAL PRODUCTION 600,000 bottles
HECTARES UNDER VINE 100
VITICULTURE METHOD Conventional

More than a century has passed since the first Felluga became involved in wine at Isola d'Istria on the seaside, the home of Malvasia and Refosco. Just after the Great War, destiny brought the family across the water to Grado, and then to Friuli. They are only a few kilometres apart but the scenery changes radically and with it the story of the Fellugas. Marco fell in love with Collio's exceptional wine potential and settled permanently.

He trained at the wine school in Conegliano and it is to him that we owe the innovation, focus on quality and experimentation that today are dedicatedly continued by his son Roberto, the fifth generation of wine Fellugas. A few years ago, Roberto launched a project to promote the longevity of Collio wines, which he releases several years after the harvest when they have acquired a certain maturity. It was his '07 Pinot Grigio Mongris Riserva that impressed us. We sent it to the finals for its crisp, complex, fruit-filled fragrances and above all for its seamlessly poised, full-bodied palate. The other wines are all very good but that's nothing new.

○ Collio Pinot Grigio Mongris Ris. '07	🍷🍷	5
○ Collio Bianco Molamatta '09	🍷🍷	5
○ Collio Chardonnay '09	🍷🍷	4*
○ Collio Friulano '09	🍷🍷	5*
● Collio Merlot Varneri '07	🍷🍷	4
○ Collio Ribolla Gialla '09	🍷🍷	5*
○ Collio Sauvignon '09	🍷🍷	4*
● Refosco P.R. Ronco dei Moreri '08	🍷🍷	5
○ Collio Pinot Grigio Mongris '09	🍷	4
○ Collio Bianco Molamatta '08	🍸🍸	5
● Collio Cabernet Sauvignon '06	🍸🍸	4*
● Collio Carantan '05	🍸🍸	6
○ Collio Chardonnay '08	🍸🍸	4*
○ Collio Friulano '08	🍸🍸	4*
● Collio Merlot Varneri '06	🍸🍸	4*
○ Collio Pinot Grigio '03	🍸🍸	4

Fiegl

FRAZ. OSLAVIA
LOC. LENZUOLO BIANCO, 1
34070 GORIZIA
TEL. 0481547103
www.fieglvini.com

CELLAR SALES
PRE-BOOKED VISITS

ANNUAL PRODUCTION 140,000 bottles
HECTARES UNDER VINE 30
VITICULTURE METHOD Conventional

The Fiegls have been living at Oslavia since 1782 and making wine since Valentino Fiegl was head of the household. Today, the 30 hectares are tended by Rinaldo, Giuseppe and Alessio, who have managed to bring the very best out of their fantastic patch of Collio. But another generation of Fiegls is on the way. Martin, Robert and Matej have completed their oenological studies and have thrown themselves into work on the estate with a will.

Best of the wines on offer this year was the Cuvée Rouge Leopold '04, leading a long list of Glass winners. It's an 80-20 blend of merlot with cabernet sauvignon. Unhurried ageing has given it penetrating, astonishingly complex aromatics that fuse fruit and spiciness over a basso continuo of balsam. The palate is soft, full and delicious. The '09 Ribolla Gialla gives pineapple-like tropical fruits, plenty of structure in the mouth and good acid grip. Merlot Leopold '05 is juicy and varietal while the Pinot Bianco '09 is remarkably concentrated, gutsy and caressing.

● Collio Cuvée Rouge Leopold '04	🍷🍷	6
● Collio Merlot Leopold '05	🍷🍷	5
○ Collio Pinot Bianco '09	🍷🍷	4
○ Collio Ribolla Gialla '09	🍷🍷	4
○ Collio Friulano '09	🍷	4
○ Collio Malvasia '09	🍷	4
○ Collio Pinot Grigio '09	🍷	4
○ Collio Pinot Grigio '04	🍸🍸🍸	4*
○ Collio Chardonnay '08	🍸🍸	4*
○ Collio Friulano '08	🍸🍸	4*
○ Collio Malvasia '06	🍸🍸	4
● Collio Merlot Leopold '04	🍸🍸	5
○ Collio Pinot Grigio '05	🍸🍸	4*
○ Collio Sauvignon '07	🍸🍸	4

Flaibani

VIA CASALI COSTA, 7
33043 CIVIDALE DEL FRIULI [UD]
TEL. 0432730943
www.flaibani.it

PRE-BOOKED VISITS

ANNUAL PRODUCTION 18,000 bottles
HECTARES UNDER VINE 4
VITICULTURE METHOD Conventional

This small winery started life in 1976, the year of the earthquake, an event with which the cellar's history entwines. Like many other native Friulians in exile, Pino Flaibani returned to his devastated homeland and decided to settle there. His work in publishing kept him in Milan but no sooner had he retired than he moved to Cividale in the Colli Orientali del Friuli and set about growing grapes.

With the unceasing support of his wife Dorina, and occasional help from sons Maurizio and Michele, Pino releases six wines, two white and four reds, a proportion that bucks the usual trend in the region. One of Pino's anchors is his go-getting daughter-in-law Bruna, who skilfully looks after sales and marketing. In previous Guides, we have praised the Flaibano reds but this time the top scorer was the '09 Friulano Riviere, a model of typicality with smoke-veined fruit and vegetal aromatics and a powerful, classically savoury palate. The onionskin-hued Pinot Grigio '09 is wonderfully intense and appealing.

○ COF Friulano Riviere '09	🍷🍷	4
● COF Merlot Seduzione Ris. '07	🍷🍷	5
○ Pinot Grigio '09	🍷🍷	4
● COF Cabernet Franc '08	🍷	4
● COF Cabernet Sauvignon '06	YY	4
● COF Cabernet Sauvignon Ris. '05	YY	4
● COF Schioppettino '07	YY	5
● Merlot Seduzione Ris. '05	YY	5
○ Riviere Bianco '07	YY	4

Adriano Gigante

VIA ROCCA BERNARDA, 3
33040 CORNO DI ROSAZZO [UD]
TEL. 0432755835
www.adrianogigante.it

CELLAR SALES
PRE-BOOKED VISITS

ANNUAL PRODUCTION 60,000 bottles
HECTARES UNDER VINE N.A.
VITICULTURE METHOD Conventional

Adriano Gigante's winery on the slopes of Rocca Bernarda near Corno di Rosazzo is absolutely representative of the Colli Orientali del Friuli DOC. It is associated with a wine that made the cellar's name back in 1957 when Adriano's grandfather Ferruccio realized he had an amazing vineyard, now known as "Storico", gave up his job as a miller and started growing grapes. Adriano has nurtured the plot, which continues to yield extraordinary fruit.

Aided in the office by his wife Giuliana, and in vineyard and cellar by his cousin Ariedo, Adriano releases a range of very high-quality wines. Yet again, the '09 edition of his Friulano Vigneto Storico earned a place in the finals, just missing out on the third Glass it has so often secured. The rich hue and sumptuous fragrances frame superb structure and a full body that closes on a twist of bitterness. The '09 Chardonnay '09 stands out for typicality and fullness while the '06 Picolit is simply delicious and the '07 Schioppettino is coherent and appealing.

○ COF Friulano Vign. Storico '09	🍷🍷	5
○ COF Chardonnay '09	🍷🍷	4*
○ COF Picolit '06	🍷🍷	7
○ COF Ribolla Gialla '09	🍷🍷	4*
● COF Schioppettino '07	🍷🍷	5
○ COF Verduzzo Friulano '07	🍷🍷	4*
● COF Merlot Ris. '06	🍷	6
● COF Pignolo '05	🍷	6
○ COF Pinot Grigio '09	🍷	4
○ COF Sauvignon '09	🍷	4
○ COF Tocai Friulano Vign. Storico '06	YYY	5
○ COF Tocai Friulano Vign. Storico '05	YYY	5
○ COF Tocai Friulano Vign. Storico '03	YYY	5

Gradis'ciutta

loc. Giasbana, 10
34070 San Floriano del Collio [GO]
tel. 0481390237
robigradis@libero.it

CELLAR SALES
PRE-BOOKED VISITS

ANNUAL PRODUCTION 60,000 bottles
HECTARES UNDER VINE 17
VITICULTURE METHOD Conventional

The Princic family has been making wine at Kosana in neighbouring Slovenia since 1780. The decline of the Habsburgs, the Great War and tenant farming brought great-grandfather Filip to Giasbana near San Floriano, in the heart of the Collio. His descendant Robert Princic knows what he wants. He loves this land, which is poor but richly rewards those who are prepared to work it passionately. Robert graduated in oenology and then joined the estate. For the past ten years, he has been managing Gradis'ciutta with flair.

Princic has always had an elegant way with Collio's classic whites but this time we especially liked the '07 Merlot. Invitingly bright and dense in hue, it gives well-defined strawberries and cherries that shade into tobacco and cocoa powder while the palate stands out for its stylish tannins and balance. Bratinis '08 is a blend of chardonnay, sauvignon and ribolla gialla that mingles pineapple-led tropical fruits with subtle wafts of aniseed. All the other wines are concentrated and juicy.

● Collio Merlot '07	🍷🍷	4*
○ Collio Bianco Bratinis '08	🍷🍷	4*
○ Collio Chardonnay '09	🍷🍷	4*
○ Collio Ribolla Gialla '09	🍷🍷	4*
● Collio Rosso Ris. '06	🍷🍷	5
○ Collio Friulano '09	🍷	4
○ Collio Pinot Grigio '09	🍷	4
○ Collio Sauvignon '09	🍷	4
○ Collio Bianco Bratinis '07	(🍷🍷)	4*
○ Collio Bianco del Tùzz '05	(🍷🍷)	4*
○ Collio Pinot Grigio '08	(🍷🍷)	4*
○ Collio Ribolla Gialla '08	(🍷🍷)	4*
○ Collio Ribolla Gialla '07	(🍷🍷)	4*
○ Collio Ribolla Gialla '06	(🍷🍷)	4

Grandi & Gabana

via Crosaris, 14
33050 Pocenia [UD]
tel. 0432777448
www.grandiegabana.it

CELLAR SALES
PRE-BOOKED VISITS

ANNUAL PRODUCTION 300,000 bottles
HECTARES UNDER VINE 94
VITICULTURE METHOD Conventional

Grandi & Gabana wines are crafted in the magnificent natural setting of the Latisana DOC zone. On the vast flatlands of Friuli at Paradiso, near Pocenia, is one of Gabeca's production hubs. The group's diversification policy sets great store by agriculture and food, where protection of the environment and consumer are paramount. The operation is located in the Fonte Paradiso mineral spring water protection zone, an area where polluting processes are banned.

The vineyards are under the supervision of agronomist Francesco Crivellaro while winemaking is the domain of oenologist Alessio Rossetto, who has a brand-new, well-equipped cellar. There are three distinct lines: Gran Cru, Terre d'Argilla and Borgo Crosaris, the last of which will appeal to the price-conscious. The '08 Pinot Bianco is crisply defined and coherent on the nose but above all gutsily fresh-tasting in the mouth. The Borgo Crosaris-label '09 Pinot Grigio, Bianco dello Stella and Rosso Amaranto are impressively well typed and appealing.

○ Bianco della Stella Borgo Crosaris '09	🍷🍷	3*
○ Friuli Latisana Pinot Bianco '08	🍷🍷	4*
○ Friuli Latisana Pinot Grigio Borgo Crosaris '09	🍷🍷	3*
● Rosso Amaranto Borgo Crosaris '09	🍷🍷	3*
○ Bianco di Villa Rem '08	🍷	4
● Friuli Latisana Cabernet Borgo Crosaris '09	🍷	3
○ Friuli Latisana Friulano '08	🍷	4
● Friuli Latisana Merlot Borgo Crosaris '09	🍷	3
● Friuli Latisana Refosco P. R. Borgo Crosaris '09	🍷	3
○ Friuli Latisana Friulano Sel. Grandi & Gabana '07	(🍷🍷)	4*
● Friuli Latisana Merlot Borgo Crosaris '08	(🍷🍷)	2*
● Friuli Latisana Refosco P. R. '06	(🍷🍷)	4*
○ Villa Rem '07	(🍷🍷)	4*

★★ Gravner

FRAZ. OSLAVIA
LOC. LENZUOLO BIANCO, 9
34070 GORIZIA
TEL. 048130882
www.gravner.it

ANNUAL PRODUCTION 39,000 bottles
HECTARES UNDER VINE 18
VITICULTURE METHOD Organic

We've been tasting Josko Gravner's wines for a long time – some of us for more than 30 years – and whatever the winemaking technique employed, they have always been exciting, driven by a production philosophy that shuns all compromise. Josko is an outstanding grower first and foremost and that is the explanation for many of his whites, amphora-fermented for over six months and aged in large wood for up to seven years. These amber gold jewels are obtained from super-healthy fruit using ancient techniques.

Because he wants to release his '03 Ribolla when he thinks it is good and ready, Josko only gave us one wine this time, and it was a red. Rosso Gravner is a merlot-heavy blend from the harvest of '04. The garnet ruby ushers in subtle, complex aromas of forest fruits veined with lighter hints of tobacco. Savoury and elegant on the palate, it has body, vibrancy and endless length as well as a deliciously agile drinkability. In other words, a Gravner-style red.

● Rosso Gravner '04	▼▼▼+	8
○ Breg '00	YYY	8
○ Breg '99	YYY	8
○ Breg Anfora '03	YYY	8
○ Breg Anfora '02	YYY	8
○ Collio Chardonnay Ris. '91	YYY	8
○ Ribolla Anfora '05	YYY	8
○ Ribolla Anfora '04	YYY	8
○ Ribolla Anfora '02	YYY	8
○ Ribolla Anfora '01	YYY	8

Iole Grillo

VIA ALBANA, 60
33040 PREPOTTO [UD]
TEL. 0432713201
www.vinigrillo.it

CELLAR SALES
PRE-BOOKED VISITS
ROOMS

ANNUAL PRODUCTION 40,000 bottles
HECTARES UNDER VINE 9
VITICULTURE METHOD Conventional

Anna Muzzolini is a dynamic businesswoman who for more than a decade has been running the estate her father Sergio set up in the 1970s. The winery at Albana, near Prepotto, in the Colli Orientali del Friuli has been carefully restored, revealing its lovely stone walls and a 18th-century residence. In the underground ageing cellars, the wines rest in casks of various sizes while outside there is a pretty farmstay waiting to welcome visitors and wine tourists.

Anna makes the business decisions but in vineyard and cellar she always shares the responsibility with the "irreplaceable" – as she calls him – Giuseppe Tosoratti. She can also call on the wine experience of Ramon Persello. When the vineyards were replanted, some of the international varieties were abandoned in favour of native grapes so it was no surprise to see an attractively fruity strawberry-themed Schioppettino '08, a wine of character with a vein of balsam and spice. Sauvignon is the only survivor of the international brigade and the '09 has a grassy nose and depth on the palate, if a tad too much sweetness. The '08 Refosco is juicy and mouthfilling.

● COF Refosco P. R. '08	▼▼	4
○ COF Sauvignon '09	▼▼	4
● COF Schioppettino '08	▼▼	5
○ COF Friulano '09	▼	4
● COF Merlot Ris. '06	▼	5
○ COF Ribolla Gialla '08	▼	4
● COF Merlot '03	YY	5
● COF Merlot Ris. '05	YY	5
● COF Refosco P. R. '06	YY	4
● COF Refosco P. R. '05	YY	4
○ COF Ribolla Gialla '07	YY	4*
● COF Rosso Guardafuoco '04	YY	5
○ COF Sauvignon '07	YY	4*
○ COF Sauvignon '06	YY	4
○ COF Tocai Friulano '06	YY	4

Albano Guerra

LOC. MONTINA
V.LE KENNEDY, 39A
33040 TORREANO [UD]
TEL. 0432715077
www.guerraalbano.it

CELLAR SALES
PRE-BOOKED VISITS

ANNUAL PRODUCTION 50,000 bottles
HECTARES UNDER VINE 7
VITICULTURE METHOD Conventional

The Albano Guerra estate is in the Colli Orientali del Friuli at Montina, near Cividale. Historical evidence shows that the area was highly esteemed as grape-farming country in classical times and indeed the site climates are ideal for producing distinctly aromatic, fragrant wines. Since 1997, Albano's son Dario has been in charge, implementing a policy of progressively raising quality.

Dario and his family are hospitable to a fault, which is an excellent reason to visit and sample one or two wines in the tasting room. Average quality has leapt forward in comparison with earlier editions of the Guide. The '09 Friulano is a paragon of typicality and delightfully flower-led, showing full, coherent and elegant on the palate. The '04 Rosso Riserva Gritul from merlot, refosco and pignolo has an austere, brooding nose before revealing unexpected freshness and a satisfying juiciness. Another fruity wine is the '07 Refosco, which is redolent of plums and supple on the deep palate. The '09 Sauvignon gives aniseed and alcohol with a full-flavoured palate.

○ COF Friulano '09	▼▼	4*
● COF Refosco P. R. '07	▼▼	5
● COF Rosso Gritul Ris. '04	▼▼	5
○ COF Sauvignon '09	▼▼	4*
○ COF Bianco Passiòn '08	▼	5
○ COF Pinot Grigio '09	▼	4
○ COF Bianco Passiòn '07	▽▽	5
○ COF Bianco Passiòn '06	▽▽	4*
● COF Cabernet Franc '00	▽▽	3
○ COF Friulano '07	▽▽	4
● COF Merlot '06	▽▽	4
● COF Refosco P. R. '06	▽▽	5

★★ Jermann

FRAZ. RUTTARS
LOC. TRUSSIO, 11
34070 DOLEGNA DEL COLLIO [GO]
TEL. 0481888080
www.jermann.it

ANNUAL PRODUCTION 750,000 bottles
HECTARES UNDER VINE 110
VITICULTURE METHOD Conventional

In 1881, founder Anton Jermann left Austria's Burgenland wine country to settle in Friuli. The estate thus has more than a century of history behind it but it was during the 1970s that the far-sighted Silvio Jermann put it on a path that has taken the Jermann name into the front rank of world wine production. The superb new facilities at Ruttars skilfully mingle technology with the local architectural heritage in a magical setting.

The original base at Villanova di Farra still houses the offices and makes the basic line of wines while Ruttars is where Capo Martino, Vignatruss, Dreams and Vintage Tunina are made. And yet again, Vintage Tunina, which last time earned a Plus, swept aside the competition to pick up Three Glasses for the '08 edition. The blend of sauvignon and chardonnay, "Friulified" with ribolla gialla, malvasia istriana and picolit, has become a classic. A penetrating nose of peaches and apricots leads into creamily elegant, well-structured sensations in the mouth. The temptingly off-dry Traminer Aromatico '09 is a delight.

○ Vintage Tunina '08	▼▼▼	8
○ Traminer Aromatico '09	▼▼	5*
○ Chardonnay '09	▼▼	5
● Pignacolusse '06	▼▼	6
○ Sauvignon '09	▼▼	5
○ Vinnae '09	▼▼	5
○ Capo Martino '08	▼	7
○ Capo Martino '05	▽▽▽	7
● Pignacolusse '00	▽▽▽	6
○ Vintage Tunina '07	▽▽▽+	8
○ Vintage Tunina '01	▽▽▽	8
○ Vintage Tunina '88	▽▽▽	7
○ Vintage Tunina '87	▽▽▽	7
○ Vintage Tunina '86	▽▽▽	7
○ W.... Dreams... ...... '06	▽▽▽	7
○ Where the Dreams Have No End '95	▽▽▽	5

Kante

FRAZ. SAN PELAGIO
LOC. PREPOTTO, 1A
34011 DUINO AURISINA [TS]
TEL. 040200255
kante.edi@libero.it

ANNUAL PRODUCTION 40,000 bottles
HECTARES UNDER VINE 13
VITICULTURE METHOD Organic

Edi Kante is synonymous with the Trieste Carso. He was the first, the trail-blazer, the man who took a wine zone everyone thought was challenging if not impossible to the attention of wine enthusiasts, planting his vines and making fine wines. The rock is unforgiving here but there are also the "doline", sinkholes where fertile soil has built up over time. All it takes is drive, decision and occasionally a little dynamite to create sun-kissed vineyards caressed by sea breezes and ventilated by the bora mountain winds.

Edi is an artist, brimming with ideas, and the undisputed leader of a group of youngsters keen to follow in his footsteps. A generous man with a word of advice for everyone, he is proud to have such influence. He loves his land, its rocks and its native varieties, the Vitovska and Terrano that have always been on his table, and the Malvasia that originally came from nearby Istria. It was the '07 Malvasia that this year rewarded all Edi's hard work. Wisteria edged with aniseed introduces a solid, sea-salt savoury palate with lots of body. Edi's '07 Sauvignon is equally, full, juicy and characterful.

O Carso Malvasia '07	▼▼▼	6
O Carso Sauvignon '07	▼▼	6
O Carso Chardonnay '07	▼▼	6
O Carso Vitovska '07	▼▼	6
O Carso Malvasia '06	▽▽▽	6
O Carso Malvasia '05	▽▽▽	6
O Carso Malvasia '98	▽▽▽	6
O Carso Sauvignon '92	▽▽▽	6
O Carso Sauvignon '91	▽▽▽	6
O Chardonnay '94	▽▽▽	6
O Chardonnay '90	▽▽▽	6
O Carso Chardonnay '06	▽▽	6
O Carso Sauvignon '04	▽▽	6
O Carso Vitovska '06	▽▽	6

★ Edi Keber

LOC. ZEGLA, 17
34071 CORMÒNS [GO]
TEL. 048161184
edi.keber@virgilio.it

CELLAR SALES
PRE-BOOKED VISITS

ANNUAL PRODUCTION 70,000 bottles
HECTARES UNDER VINE 10
VITICULTURE METHOD Organic

The Kebers are part and parcel of Zegla and Medana. Over the centuries, these border villages have belonged to several different states for one reason or another. People here have found themselves in Austria, then Italy, then Slovenia, and then back in Italy without having moved at all. Zegla is near Cormòns in the heart of the Collio Goriziano, and it is here that Edi Keber settled with his family, tirelessly committed to promoting the territory and recovering its traditions.

Collio has always meant superb white wine, often from blends of several varieties and it is that project that Edi has pursued for almost two decades. He doesn't claim to have invented anything but he is proud of rediscovering the past. Many other growers have followed his example. It is well known that to achieve his goal, Edi stopped making the Tocai Friulano that won him so much praise. Now, the grapes are a crucial part of his Collio, and this year the '08 version won Three Glasses. Sun-bright and temptingly fragrant, it gives broom-like florality and white peach fruit. In the mouth, it is simply awesome, presenting firm, savoury, vibrant and fantastically long.

O Collio Bianco '09	▼▼▼	5
O Collio Bianco '08	▽▽▽	5*
O Collio Bianco '04	▽▽▽	5
O Collio Bianco '02	▽▽▽	4
O Collio Tocai Friulano '07	▽▽▽	5
O Collio Tocai Friulano '06	▽▽▽	5
O Collio Tocai Friulano '05	▽▽▽	5
O Collio Tocai Friulano '03	▽▽▽	4*
O Collio Tocai Friulano '01	▽▽▽	4
O Collio Tocai Friulano '99	▽▽▽	4
O Collio Tocai Friulano '97	▽▽▽	4
O Collio Tocai Friulano '95	▽▽▽	4

Renato Keber

LOC. ZEGLA, 15
34071 CORMÒNS [GO]
TEL. 0481639844
www.renatokeber.it

CELLAR SALES
PRE-BOOKED VISITS
ROOMS

ANNUAL PRODUCTION 70,000 bottles
HECTARES UNDER VINE 15
VITICULTURE METHOD Conventional

Kebers have been living at Zegla since the second half of the 19th century. Here in the borderlands, wars have taken their toll of territory and families but the Kebers have lived through it all. When Renato completed his oenology studies in the early 1980s, he took over the estate and immediately set about stamping the wines with his personality. For years, he conducted trials to find the right symbiosis with the territory. Thanks to the support of his wife Savina, he has followed his own star, refusing to compromise.

Today, Renato proudly releases wines of personality and intensity shaped by his scrupulous care during production, and especially by lengthy ageing in bottle. Again this year, Renato sent one of his wines to our finals, the '06 Chardonnay from the Grici line. The rich colour heralds complex, penetrating fruit fragrances led by yellow peaches. The palate is full, savoury and characterful. In the '08 edition, Renato's Friulano Riserva is impeccably well typed with an intriguing grace note of smokiness, although the finish is a tad husky. And its counterpart with the Zegla label is equally impressive, despite a hint of bitterness.

○ Collio Chardonnay Grici '06	🍷🍷	6
○ Collio Friulano Ris. '08	🍷🍷	5
○ Collio Friulano Zegla '06	🍷	5
○ Collio Pinot Grigio Ris. '08	🍷	5
○ Collio Sauvignon Grici '06	🍷	6
○ Collio Friulano Zegla '05	🍸🍸🍸	5*
○ Collio Bianco Beli Grici '05	🍸🍸	4
● Collio Merlot Grici Ris. '03	🍸🍸	6
○ Collio Pinot Grigio '06	🍸🍸	4*
○ Collio Ribolla Gialla Extreme '06	🍸🍸	5
○ Collio Ribolla Gialla Extreme '05	🍸🍸	5
○ Collio Sauvignon '06	🍸🍸	4
○ Collio Sauvignon Grici '05	🍸🍸	6
○ Collio Tocai Friulano '06	🍸🍸	4

Thomas Kitzmüller

FRAZ. BRAZZANO
VIA XXIV MAGGIO, 56
34070 CORMÒNS [GO]
TEL. 048160853
www.kitzmuller.it

CELLAR SALES
PRE-BOOKED VISITS
ROOMS AND FOOD

ANNUAL PRODUCTION 23,000 bottles
HECTARES UNDER VINE 4
VITICULTURE METHOD Organic

This winery at Brazzano near Cormòns bears the name of its founder, Thomas Kitzmüller, who in 1987 started to farm the four hectares he owns, half in Collio and half in Isonzo. Thomas is a firm believer in integrated pest management and environment-friendly biological methods of plant protection. His cellar is in an 18th-century farm building which also houses a delightful farmstay called Mummelhaus.

Last time, we praised the great leap forward in quality at the estate and sent two Kitzmüller wines to the finals. This time, however, Thomas went one better, securing Three Glasses for his Friulano '09. It's a stunningly emblematic wine, giving intense damson and yellow peach fruit in an extremely well-typed profile of sustained fullness, savouriness and length. The faintly vegetal Sauvignon '09 is varietal to a fault in its sage and peppermint aromatics, elegant fragrances and hefty palate. The very pale Ribolla Gialla '09 is redolent of unripe fruits but has good stuffing and a satisfying palate. Yellow roses and white peaches are the keynotes of the fragrant Traminer Aromatico '09.

○ Collio Friulano '09	🍷🍷🍷	4*
○ Collio Sauvignon '09	🍷🍷	4*
○ Collio Ribolla Gialla '09	🍷🍷	4*
○ Collio Traminer Aromatico '09	🍷🍷	4*
○ Friuli Isonzo Friulano Corte Marie '09	🍷	3
○ Collio Friulano '08	🍸🍸	4*
○ Collio Ribolla Gialla '08	🍸🍸	4*
○ Collio Sauvignon '08	🍸🍸	4*
○ Collio Sauvignon '07	🍸🍸	4
○ Collio Tocai Friulano '06	🍸🍸	4
○ Collio Traminer Aromatico '08	🍸🍸	4*
○ Collio Traminer Aromatico '07	🍸🍸	4
○ Friuli Isonzo Friulano Corte Marie '08	🍸🍸	3*
○ Friuli Isonzo Tocai Friulano Corte Marie '06	🍸🍸	3*

Albino Kurtin

LOC. NOVALI, 9
34071 CORMÒNS [GO]
TEL. 048160685

CELLAR SALES
PRE-BOOKED VISITS

ANNUAL PRODUCTION 70,000 bottles
HECTARES UNDER VINE 11
VITICULTURE METHOD Conventional

Albino Kurtin's winery is at Novalis near Cormòns, in the celebrated vine-clad Collio amphitheatre that looks onto Slovenia. Albino says he grew up among the vines and enjoys a symbiotic relationship with the land. A defender of tradition who is open to innovation, he has managed to adapt to changes in the way he approaches his vineyards and his wines speak a new language born of the marriage between territory traditions and international taste.

He is flanked in the cellar by his son Alessio, who has completed his oenology studies and internships at several Italian estates. This year, the pair gave us an excellent range of wines. The '09 Pinot Grigio has faint onionskin highlights and ripe fruit aromas, including tropical fruits, with structure, typicality and an easy-drinking style. The '09 Malvasia is also fruit-led and varietal, preceding the savoury, faintly bitterish palate with wafts of wisteria. We liked the palate of the Friulano while Opera Prima Bianco '09 is a successful blend of pinot bianco, ribolla gialla and chardonnnay.

○ Collio Friulano '09	2 black glasses	4*
○ Collio Malvasia '09	2 black glasses	4*
○ Collio Pinot Grigio '09	2 black glasses	4*
○ Opera Prima Bianco '09	2 black glasses	4*
○ Collio Pinot Bianco '09	1 black glass	4
○ Collio Ribolla Gialla '09	1 black glass	4
○ Collio Friulano '08	2 white glasses	4*
○ Collio Malvasia '08	2 white glasses	4*
○ Collio Pinot Grigio '08	2 white glasses	4*
○ Collio Pinot Grigio '06	2 white glasses	3
○ Collio Sauvignon '07	2 white glasses	4
○ Collio Sauvignon '06	2 white glasses	3
● Diamante Nero '07	2 white glasses	4*
○ Opera Prima Bianco '07	2 white glasses	4

Vigneti Le Monde

LOC. LE MONDE
VIA GARIBALDI, 2
33080 PRATA DI PORDENONE [PN]
TEL. 0434622087
www.vignetilemonde.com

CELLAR SALES
PRE-BOOKED VISITS

ANNUAL PRODUCTION 120,000 bottles
HECTARES UNDER VINE 20
VITICULTURE METHOD Conventional

Vigneti Le Monde was set up in 1970 at Villa Giustinian in Portobuffolè, an ancient village recorded as long ago as 997 as a castle and river port belonging to the Venetian Republic. The vines grow on clay and limestone that is very different from the soil types in the Grave del Friuli DOC, where the terrain is usually gravelly. This is why Le Monde is considered to be a cru, where yields are very low and the average age of the vines is comfortably above 30 years.

Alex Maccan is an owner who knows his stuff and he has taken on a dynamic, and equally youthful, winemaker: Matteo Bernabei, son of the great Franco, one of Italy's best-known oenologists. The Maccan-Bernabei team has achieved fantastic results in double-quick time. We hope this will continue. The Refosco dal Peduncolo Rosso '09, standard-bearer of Friuli's native red varieties, stands out for its crisp, penetrating aromas and especially for its delightfully full body while the '09 Pinot Bianco fuses almonds with citrussy fragrances, showing savoury, stylish and subtle in the mouth.

○ Friuli Grave Pinot Bianco '09	2 black glasses	4*
○ Friuli Grave Pinot Grigio '09	2 black glasses	4
● Friuli Grave Refosco P. R. '09	2 black glasses	4
○ Friuli Grave Sauvignon '09	2 black glasses	4
● Friuli Grave Cabernet Franc '09	1 black glass	4
● Friuli Grave Cabernet Sauvignon '09	1 black glass	4
○ Friuli Grave Friulano '09	1 black glass	4
○ Friuli Grave Pinot Bianco '01	3 white glasses	4
○ Friuli Grave Bianco I Vasi '03	2 white glasses	4*
○ Friuli Grave Bianco Pujà '02	2 white glasses	4*
● Friuli Grave Cabernet Franc '02	2 white glasses	3*
● Friuli Grave Rosso Ca' Salice '04	2 white glasses	4

★ Lis Neris

via Gavinana, 5
34070 San Lorenzo Isontino [GO]
tel. 048180105
www.lisneris.it

CELLAR SALES
PRE-BOOKED VISITS

ANNUAL PRODUCTION 350,000 bottles
HECTARES UNDER VINE 54
VITICULTURE METHOD Conventional

Lis Neris, run by Alvaro Pecorari, is located in the centre of San Lorenzo Isontino, a few hundred metres from the vineyards, which extend over the loveliest part of a small plateau of deep gravel carried down from the eastern Alps by melting glaciers. The nearby Adriatic creates a Mediterranean-type climate with wide temperature fluctuations that encourage the grapes to ripen slowly, concentrating their aroma compounds.

The estate's turn-around came in 1981 with a new approach to production that focuses on quality. Alvaro has created his own distinctive winemaking style, hinging on softness and complexity. Yet again, he picked up Three Glasses for one of his bottles. It's the '08 Pinot Grigio Gris, the only wine of its type from the region to earn top honours. You'll thrill to its varietal typicality, fresh minerality and deliciously satisfying upfront palate. Another high scorer is the verduzzo and riesling '07 Tal Lùc, a very stylish sweet wine.

○ Pinot Grigio Gris '08	▼▼▼	5*
○ Tal Lùc '07	▼▼	7
○ Chardonnay Jurosa '08	▼▼	5
○ Confini '08	▼▼	6
○ Fiore di Campo '09	▼▼	4*
○ Friuli Isonzo Pinot Grigio '09	▼▼	4*
○ Lis '07	▼▼	6
○ Sauvignon Picol '08	▼	4
○ Fiore di Campo '06	▽▽▽	4
○ Friuli Isonzo Chardonnay Jurosa '00	▽▽▽	5
○ Friuli Isonzo Pinot Grigio Gris '01	▽▽▽	6
○ Lis '03	▽▽▽	6
○ Lis '99	▽▽▽	6
○ Pinot Grigio Gris '04	▽▽▽	5
○ Sauvignon Picol '06	▽▽▽	4
○ Tal Lùc '02	▽▽▽	7

★ Livon

fraz. Dolegnano
via Montarezza, 33
33048 San Giovanni al Natisone [UD]
tel. 0432757173
www.livon.it

CELLAR SALES
PRE-BOOKED VISITS
ROOMS

ANNUAL PRODUCTION 900,000 bottles
HECTARES UNDER VINE 175
VITICULTURE METHOD Conventional

The winery Dorino Livon set up in 1964 is at Dolegnano, a district of San Giovanni al Natisone, but the Livon Poggi group has vineyards all over Friuli and in other leading Italian wine zones. The Livon winery's celebrated winged woman trademark has been joined by: RoncAlto in Collio Goriziano, Villa Chiopris on the flatlands of Friuli, Borgo Salcetino in Tuscany and Colsanto in Umbria. Valneo and Tonino Livon are the men who created and run this impressive enterprise.

They have put the right people in the right positions. Each winery in the group now runs under its own steam as Valneo and Tonino supervise. In Friuli, the Livons have always relied on winemaker Rinaldo Stocco, who this year gave us a superb '08 Braide Alte and for the seventh time we gave it our top award. Sourced from the Braide Alte vineyard in Collio, it is an intriguing blend of Chardonnay, Sauvignon, Picolit and Moscato Giallo which displays all the power and finesse of the great Friulian whites. In short, a classic.

○ Collio Braide Alte '08	▼▼▼	5
● COF Refosco P. R. Riul '07	▼▼	5
○ Collio Bianco Solarco '09	▼▼	5
○ Collio Friulano Ronc di Zorz '09	▼▼	5
○ Collio Ribolla Gialla RoncAlto '09	▼▼	5
● TiareBlù '07	▼	5
○ Braide Alte '07	▽▽▽	6
○ Braide Alte '00	▽▽▽	6
○ Braide Alte '98	▽▽▽	6
○ Braide Alte '97	▽▽▽	6
○ Braide Alte '96	▽▽▽	6
● COF Refosco P. R. Riul '02	▽▽▽	5
○ COF Verduzzo Friulano Casali Godia '94	▽▽▽	5
○ Collio Sauvignon Valbuins '96	▽▽▽	5
● TiareBlù '00	▽▽▽	6

Tenuta Luisa

FRAZ. CORONA
VIA CORMONS, 19
34070 MARIANO DEL FRIULI [GO]
TEL. 048169680
www.viniluisa.com

CELLAR SALES
PRE-BOOKED VISITS

ANNUAL PRODUCTION 300,000 bottles
HECTARES UNDER VINE 79
VITICULTURE METHOD Conventional

Eddi Luisa and his wife make their wine in a lovely cellar at Corona near Nariano del Friuli, in the Isonzo DOC. Helping them are their sons, oenologist Michele and David, a qualified agronomist. The two generations bring together tradition and an ongoing quest for innovation while respecting both fruit and territory. This close-knit family makes a cocktail of enthusiasm, courage and far-sightedness that has driven the constant growth of Tenuta Luisa over the years.

Each stage of winemaking is monitored with passionate, scrupulous care, as you can appreciate if you uncork one of the bottles. The beautifully typed '08 Refosco dal Peduncolo Rosso went through to the finals for its no-nonsense aromatics and especially for its supple yet powerful palate. The '09 Sauvignon has depth and power on both nose and palate. The '09 Friulano is a paragon of stylish elegance with appealing citrus sensations in the mouth. Pinot Bianco '09 is well typed and well defined, flowing across the palate, while the '09 Sauvignon is faithful to its variety.

● Friuli Isonzo Refosco P. R. '08	●●	4*
○ Friuli Isonzo Friulano '09	●●	4*
○ Friuli Isonzo Pinot Bianco '09	●●	4*
○ Friuli Isonzo Sauvignon '09	●●	4*
○ Friuli Isonzo Chardonnay '09	●	4
○ Friuli Isonzo Pinot Grigio '09	●	4
○ Ribolla Gialla '09	●	4
○ Friuli Isonzo Tocai Friulano '03	○○○	4*
○ Chardonnay I Ferretti '07	○○	5
○ Friuli Isonzo Chardonnay '08	○○	4*
○ Friuli Isonzo Friulano '08	○○	4*
○ Friuli Isonzo Pinot Bianco '06	○○	4*
○ Friuli Isonzo Pinot Grigio '08	○○	4*
○ Friuli Isonzo Sauvignon '06	○○	4*
○ Friuli Isonzo Tocai Friulano '06	○○	4*
○ Friuli Isonzo Tocai Friulano '05	○○	4*

Magnàs

LOC. BOATINA
VIA CORONA, 47
34071 CORMÒNS [GO]
TEL. 048160991
www.magnas.it

CELLAR SALES
PRE-BOOKED VISITS
ROOMS AND FOOD

ANNUAL PRODUCTION 25,000 bottles
HECTARES UNDER VINE 10
VITICULTURE METHOD Conventional

The Magnàs farm estate is at Boatina, near Cormòns. It took off in the early 1970s when Luciano Visintin set out to put his personal stamp on the operation, drawing on his family's century and more of agricultural experience. Magnàs is the surname that this branch of the Visintin family has been known by for generations.

The winery has found continuity in Luciano's son Andrea, who looks after the entire production process from berry to bottle. The results are impressive and this time the '09 Friulano impressed our judges at the finals. Eye-catching in the glass, it proffers superbly typed upfront aromas that take you by the hand through a swath of fresh greens and ripe pears. The full, savoury palate is balanced and equally varietal. We also liked the subtly fragrant '09 Malvasia with its rose-led scents and punchy palate. Medlars and damsons on the '09 Chardonnay's nose lead into an attractively soft palate.

○ Friuli Isonzo Friulano '09	●●	4*
○ Friuli Isonzo Chardonnay '09	●●	4*
○ Friuli Isonzo Malvasia '09	●●	4*
● Friuli Isonzo Merlot '08	●	5
○ Friuli Isonzo Pinot Grigio '09	●	4
○ Friuli Isonzo Sauvignon '09	●	4
○ Friuli Isonzo Chardonnay '07	○○	4
○ Friuli Isonzo Friulano '08	○○	4*
○ Friuli Isonzo Malvasia '08	○○	5*
○ Friuli Isonzo Pinot Grigio '07	○○	4
○ Friuli Isonzo Pinot Grigio '06	○○	5
○ Friuli Isonzo Sauvignon '08	○○	4*
○ Friuli Isonzo Sauvignon '07	○○	4
○ Friuli Isonzo Sauvignon '06	○○	5
○ Friuli Isonzo Sauvignon '04	○○	5

Marega

VIA VALERISCE, 4
34070 SAN FLORIANO DEL COLLIO [GO]
TEL. 0481 884058
www.maregacollio.com

CELLAR SALES
PRE-BOOKED VISITS

ANNUAL PRODUCTION 52,000 bottles
HECTARES UNDER VINE 10
VITICULTURE METHOD Conventional

The Marega family settled at Valerisce, near San Floriano del Collio, back in 1905. With more than a century of winemaking under its belt, the cellar today is run by Livio and Giorgio. Our heroes deserve credit for rediscovering the holbar, a traditional, two to five-hectolitre cask of robinia, or false acacia, wood for whites while the brothers preferred oak for their reds. That was in 1988, when the decision looked like a gauntlet thrown down to technology.

Giorgio tends the vines while Livio looks after production and public relations. Their wines spend years in the holbars, going to market only when they are good and ready, but this time we liked the wines of the most recent vintage. Three went to the finals and the Friulano returned with Three Glasses. A fresh, varietal butter-rich wine, its deep hue is shot through with lovely greenish highlights. The '09 Sauvignon is complex, powerful and true to type while the penetrating Pinot Grigio '09 is as crisp and taut as you could wish.

○ Collio Friulano '09	🍷🍷🍷	4*
○ Collio Pinot Grigio '09	🍷🍷	4*
○ Collio Sauvignon '09	🍷🍷	4*
○ Collio Malvasia Istriana '06	🍷🍷	5
○ Collio Merlot '08	🍷🍷	4
● Collio Holbar Rosso '03	🥂🥂	6
○ Collio Malvasia Istriana '05	🥂🥂	5
○ Collio Pinot Grigio '08	🥂🥂	4
○ Collio Sauvignon '08	🥂🥂	4

Valerio Marinig

VIA BROLO, 41
33040 PREPOTTO [UD]
TEL. 0432713012
www.marinig.it

CELLAR SALES
PRE-BOOKED VISITS

ANNUAL PRODUCTION 25,000 bottles
HECTARES UNDER VINE 8
VITICULTURE METHOD Conventional

Valerio Marinig runs the classic Friulian family cellar his great-grandfather Luigi founded in 1921. Valerio, the fourth generation of Marinigs, looks after vineyards and cellar but his father Sergio is still very active, particularly among the rows. Valerio's mother Marisa is an admirable host for visitors while wife Michela does the books.

This year's profile highlights the progress Valerio's commitment has brought in just a few years, as we predicted in earlier Guides. The superb Sauvignon '09 is a stunner. Intensely fruity, showing white peach and mango-like tropical notes, it combines acid backbone with juiciness in the mouth. The lively, long-lingering '09 Pinot Bianco gives a complex palate of well-defined fragrances. Typicality on nose and palate is the hallmark of the fresh-tasting, savoury Friulano '09 while the subtly spicy '08 Schioppettino is an appealing easy drinker. Finally, the '08 Refosco offers well-crafted fragrances and a nicely tannic palate.

○ COF Sauvignon '09	🍷🍷	4*
○ COF Friulano '09	🍷🍷	4*
○ COF Pinot Bianco '09	🍷🍷	4*
● COF Refosco P. R. '08	🍷🍷	4*
● COF Schioppettino '08	🍷🍷	4*
● COF Cabernet Franc '08	🍷	4
● COF Cabernet Franc '07	🥂🥂	4*
○ COF Friulano '08	🥂🥂	4*
● COF Merlot '07	🥂🥂	4*
● COF Merlot '03	🥂🥂	4*
○ COF Pinot Bianco '07	🥂🥂	4
○ COF Pinot Bianco '06	🥂🥂	4
○ COF Sauvignon '07	🥂🥂	4
○ COF Sauvignon '06	🥂🥂	4

Masut da Rive

via Manzoni, 82
34070 Mariano del Friuli [GO]
tel. 048169200
www.masutdarive.com

CELLAR SALES
PRE-BOOKED VISITS

ANNUAL PRODUCTION 100,000 bottles
HECTARES UNDER VINE 20
VITICULTURE METHOD Conventional

Masut da Rive was created by Antonio Gallo, who ran it until the late 1930s. The property passed from father to son and today is in the hands of Fabrizio and Marco, sons of the great Silvano. Masut da Rive is in fact the nickname of the Gallo family, long established at Mariano del Friuli, and became the estate's name, too, when it ventured into the international market, above all to avoid stepping on the toes of the giant Gallo winery based at Sonoma, California.

We thought the best wine this time was the penetratingly fragranced almond and broom-laced '09 Pinot Bianco with its fruit and flower aromatics, satisfying savouriness and varietal typicality. The aromatic '09 Pinot Grigio is an elegant easy drinker while the savoury, aniseed-veined Sauvignon '09 is a wine with attitude. Cabernet Sauvignon '08 enfolds with its aromas and impresses with its power. Finally, the '07 Rosso Semidis is a Marlot the Gallos release only in the best growing years. It's well worth uncorking.

○ Friuli Isonzo Pinot Bianco '09	▼▼	4*
● Friuli Isonzo Cabernet Sauvignon '08	▼▼	4*
○ Friuli Isonzo Pinot Grigio '09	▼▼	4*
● Friuli Isonzo Rosso Semidis '07	▼▼	6
○ Friuli Isonzo Sauvignon '09	▼▼	4*
○ Friuli Isonzo Chardonnay '09	▼	4
○ Friuli Isonzo Friulano '09	▼	4
● Friuli Isonzo Merlot '08	▼	4
● Friuli Isonzo Refosco P. R. '08	▼	4
○ Friuli Isonzo Tocai Friulano '04	▽▽▽	4*
● Friuli Isonzo Cabernet Sauvignon '05	▽▽	4*
○ Friuli Isonzo Pinot Bianco '07	▽▽	4
○ Friuli Isonzo Pinot Grigio '08	▽▽	4*
● Friuli Isonzo Refosco P. R. '06	▽▽	4
○ Friuli Isonzo Rive Alte Tocai Friulano '05	▽▽	4*
○ Friuli Isonzo Sauvignon '07	▽▽	4

Davino Meroi

via Stretta, 7b
33042 Buttrio [UD]
tel. 0432674025
parco.meroi@virgilio.it

CELLAR SALES
PRE-BOOKED VISITS

ANNUAL PRODUCTION 20,000 bottles
HECTARES UNDER VINE 12
VITICULTURE METHOD Conventional

It was Davino, Paolo's father, who passed on to him the wine lore accumulated by grandfather Domenico in the gentle hills of Buttrio, where the Colli Orientali del Friuli begin. Paolo's skills at the grill of the Al Parco trattoria, where he serves mouth-watering steaks with traditional Friulian fare, are legendary but he is also an expert winemaker, with a rare craftsman's eye for gauging the new wood his wines will need.

Paolo learned his winemaking with his friend Enzo Pontoni of the Miani winery, who passed on his insights. The path Paolo mapped out is now being followed by oenologist Mirko Degan, who is also in charge of the vine stock. Last time, results were satisfactory but this year they are fantastic, as the Three Glass award to the '08 Verduzzo Friulano shows. Old gold in hue, it unfolds crunchy almond aromas with apricot jam and caramel preceding a very sweet, sound palate offset by fresh acidity and finishing long. Equally superb are the fresh, complex '08 Friulano and the zabaglione and confectioner's cream.

○ COF Verduzzo Friulano '08	▼▼▼	6
○ COF Friulano '08	▼▼	6
○ COF Picolit '08	▼▼	7
○ COF Chardonnay '07	▼▼	6
● COF Merlot Ros di Buri '07	▼▼	6
● COF Rosso Dominin '07	▼▼	8
● COF Rosso Nestri '07	▼▼	4*
○ COF Sauvignon '08	▼▼	5
● COF Rosso Dominin '06	▽▽	8
● COF Rosso Dominin '03	▽▽	8
● COF Rosso Dominin '02	▽▽	8
○ COF Sauvignon '07	▽▽	5
○ COF Tocai Friulano '06	▽▽	6
○ COF Verduzzo Friulano '07	▽▽	6

★ Miani

VIA PERUZZI, 10
33042 BUTTRIO [UD]
TEL. 0432674327
aletulissi@libero.it

CELLAR SALES
PRE-BOOKED VISITS

ANNUAL PRODUCTION 8,000 bottles
HECTARES UNDER VINE 16
VITICULTURE METHOD Organic

Our love for Enzo Pontoni remains sadly unrequited. The legendary wine man and owner of a tiny property at Buttrio in the Colli Orientali del Friuli never sends us his wines and we have to hunt for them in the shops, which is not always easy. But we are happy to do so. Enzo's bottles are simply superb and we feel it is a duty, as well as a pleasure, to discuss them in the Guide.

And when the wines are as good as this '06 Merlot Filip, the thrill is even greater as the complex, varietal nose mingles raspberries and tobacco with roasted almonds. Friulano Buri '08 reveals only faint suggestions of oak, showing elegant and very long, while the '09 Bianco Miani '09 and '08 Sauvignon Banel still have a little way to go. We'll be coming back for the Merlot Buri '06 next year. It looks like a genuine star but it is still too young for us to make a full appreciation.

● COF Merlot Filip '06	▼▼▼	8
○ COF Friulano Buri '08	▼▼	6
○ COF Miani Bianco '08	▼▼	7
○ COF Sauvignon Banel '08	▼▼	7
● Calvari '02	▽▽▽	8
○ COF Bianco '97	▽▽▽	7
● COF Merlot '02	▽▽▽	8
● COF Merlot '99	▽▽▽	8
● COF Merlot '98	▽▽▽	8
● COF Merlot Filip '04	▽▽▽	8
● COF Rosso '97	▽▽▽	8
○ COF Tocai Friulano '00	▽▽▽	7
○ COF Tocai Friulano '99	▽▽▽	7
○ COF Tocai Friulano '98	▽▽▽	7

Moschioni

LOC. GAGLIANO
VIA DORIA, 30
33043 CIVIDALE DEL FRIULI [UD]
TEL. 0432730210
info@moschioni.eu

PRE-BOOKED VISITS

ANNUAL PRODUCTION 40,000 bottles
HECTARES UNDER VINE 14
VITICULTURE METHOD Conventional

Michele Moschioni makes wine at Gagliano, a tiny village near Cividale del Friuli. Notoriously, Colli Orientali del Friuli is white wine country but for some time Michele has been impressing us with his red-only range, obtained by drying the grapes briefly before the crush. The wines are concentrated and alcoholic but wonderfully balanced.

As he waits for his children Alessia and Valentino to finish their studies, Michele tends the vineyards and vinifies the grapes on his own. Deservedly, his '07 Pignolo went through to the finals. Majestically impenetrable in the glass, it rolls out a fragrant medley of cocoa powder and pipe tobacco that gives way to liquorice-veined ripe red and black fruits and a broad, powerful palate with marvellous depth. The varietal Refosco '07 unveils crisp blackberries and spice followed by a beefy, well-extracted palate. Rosso Celtico, an estery 50-50 blend of merlot and cabernet sauvignon, is full flavoured and savoury.

● COF Pignolo '07	▼▼	8
● COF Refosco P. R. '07	▼▼	5
● COF Rosso Celtico '07	▼▼	6
● COF Rosso Reâl '07	▼	6
● COF Schioppettino '07	▼	7
● COF Rosso Celtico '04	▽▽▽	6
● COF Schioppettino '06	▽▽▽	7
● COF Pignolo '04	▽▽	8
● COF Pignolo Non Filtrato '03	▽▽	8
● COF Refosco P. R. '06	▽▽	5
● COF Rosso Bisest '05	▽▽	6
● COF Rosso Celtico '06	▽▽	6
● COF Rosso Celtico Non Filtrato '03	▽▽	6
● COF Rosso Reâl '06	▽▽	6
● COF Rosso Reâl '05	▽▽	6
● COF Schioppettino Non Filtrato '03	▽▽	7

Mulino delle Tolle

FRAZ. SEVEGLIANO
VIA MULINO DELLE TOLLE, 15
33050 BAGNARIA ARSA [UD]
TEL. 0432928113
www.mulinodelletolle.it

CELLAR SALES
PRE-BOOKED VISITS
ROOMS AND FOOD

ANNUAL PRODUCTION 100,000 bottles
HECTARES UNDER VINE 22
VITICULTURE METHOD Conventional

Aquileia is built on history and often archaeological remains turn up in the area. At Sedegliano, where Mulino delle Tolle stands at the crossroads of the ancient Via Postumia and Via Julia Augusta, discoveries include industrial quantities of wine amphorae, showing that wine was made here 2,000 years ago. Mulino delle Tolle has been making wine itself for generations but only began to bottle in 1988, thanks to Giorgio Bertossi.

Giorgio, an influential oenologist, and his cousin Elisio painstakingly restored the Casa Bianca, a farm complex that served as a lazar house in the 17th century was a customs post under the Habsburgs. From the excellent range, we picked out the green-flecked Sauvignon '09 whose particularly stylish varietal aromas introduce an easy-drinking palate with good structure. The Friulano '09 gives distinct peach aromas and a tangy, juicy palate. Bianco Palmade '09, from sauvignon, chardonnay and malvasia, hints at tropical fruit while the Chardonnay Brut has a creamy mousse and fresh citron fragrances.

○ Friuli Aquileia Friulano '09	▼▼	4*
○ Friuli Aquileia Sauvignon '09	▼▼	4*
○ Chardonnay Brut	▼▼	4*
○ Friuli Aquileia Bianco Palmade '09	▼▼	4*
○ Friuli Aquileia Chardonnay '09	▼	3
● Friuli Aquileia Refosco P. R. '08	▼	4
○ Friuli Aquileia Traminer Aromatico '09	▼	4
○ Friuli Aquileia Bianco Palmade '08	▽▽	4*
○ Friuli Aquileia Bianco Palmade '06	▽▽	4
○ Friuli Aquileia Bianco Palmade '05	▽▽	3
○ Friuli Aquileia Friulano '08	▽▽	4*
○ Friuli Aquileia Malvasia '06	▽▽	3*
○ Friuli Aquileia Malvasia '05	▽▽	3*
○ Friuli Aquileia Tocai Friulano '06	▽▽	3*
● Pignolo '06	▽▽	6

Muzic

LOC. BIVIO, 4
34070 SAN FLORIANO DEL COLLIO [GO]
TEL. 0481884201
www.cantinamuzic.it

CELLAR SALES
PRE-BOOKED VISITS

ANNUAL PRODUCTION 90,000 bottles
HECTARES UNDER VINE 15
VITICULTURE METHOD Conventional

In 1963, Giovanni Muzic's parents purchased the first five hectares of vineyard on the slopes of San Floriano del Collio, which they had been cultivating as tenant farmers. Today, Giovanni – known as Ivan to his friends – has 15 hectares that he loves to tend while his wife, Orieta, the driving force behind the operation, takes care of visitors. Their children Elija and Fabijan are finishing their oenology studies but both are already active in the cellar and in public relations.

The grapes that went into the '09 Malvasia come from a vineyard more than 50 years old. This is the first time they have been fermented separately and the wine duly went through to the finals. The lovely straw shimmers with greenish highlights, framing wafts of wisteria florality and medlar-like fruit before the palate shows juicy, concentrated and very minerally. The '09 Pinot Grigio suggests pears, elderflower and pine resin leading into a deliciously soft mouthfeel. Bric '08 is an impeccably well-typed blend of native friulano, malvasia istriana and ribolla gialla and the '09 Friulano and Ribolla Gialla flow nicely across the palate.

○ Collio Malvasia '09	▼▼	4*
○ Collio Bianco Bric '09	▼▼	4*
○ Collio Friulano V. Valeris '09	▼▼	4*
○ Collio Pinot Grigio '09	▼▼	4*
○ Collio Ribolla Gialla '09	▼▼	4*
○ Collio Sauvignon V. Pàjze '09	▼	4
● Friuli Isonzo Merlot '08	▼	4
○ Collio Bianco Bric '08	▽▽	4*
○ Collio Friulano V. Valeris '08	▽▽	4*
○ Collio Pinot Grigio '08	▽▽	4*
○ Collio Pinot Grigio '07	▽▽	4
○ Collio Sauvignon V. Pàjze '08	▽▽	4*
● Friuli Isonzo Cabernet Franc '06	▽▽	4
● Friuli Isonzo Merlot '07	▽▽	4*

Alessandro Pascolo

LOC. RUTTARS, 1
34070 DOLEGNA DEL COLLIO [GO]
TEL. 048161144
www.vinipascolo.com

CELLAR SALES
PRE-BOOKED VISITS

ANNUAL PRODUCTION 25,000 bottles
HECTARES UNDER VINE 7
VITICULTURE METHOD Conventional

Alessandro Pascolo is an enterprising wine producer who manages seven hectares of estate-owned vines. He is lucky enough to have had a grandfather, Angelo, who in the 1970 was shrewdly invested in land here on the sunny slopes of Ruttàrs, near Dolegna del Collio. There could have been no finer heritage to hand down to Alessandro, a man who loves nature and the outdoor life.

In fact, Alessandro has dedicated a wine on which he lavishes very special care to his grandfather; it is the Collio Bianco Agnul, from pinot bianco, friulano, malvasia and sauvignon. It's very much a wine of the territory, since blends like this are traditional to Collio. However, the wine we liked best this time was the rich-hued, penetratingly fragrant '09 Malvasia with its subtle flower-led aromatics, full body and distinct minerality. The '07 Merlot Selezione confirmed that this is a great wine. Its forward, faintly smoky fragrances usher in an agile, juicy palate. To round off, the '09 Pinot Grigio gives ripe berry and tropical fruits that are reprised on the caressingly full-bodied palate.

○ Collio Malvasia '09	▼▼	4*
● Collio Merlot Sel. '07	▼▼	5
○ Collio Pinot Grigio '09	▼▼	4*
○ Collio Bianco Agnul '08	▼	5
○ Collio Friulano '09	▼	4
○ Collio Sauvignon '09	▼	4
○ Collio Bianco Agnul '07	▽▽	4*
● Collio Merlot Sel. '06	▽▽	5
○ Collio Pinot Grigio '08	▽▽	4*

Pierpaolo Pecorari

VIA TOMMASEO, 36C
34070 SAN LORENZO ISONTINO [GO]
TEL. 0481808775
www.pierpaolopecorari.it

CELLAR SALES
PRE-BOOKED VISITS

ANNUAL PRODUCTION 130,000 bottles
HECTARES UNDER VINE 30
VITICULTURE METHOD Certified organic

Pierpaolo Pecorari's vineyards all lie in the Isonzo DOC zone, the triangle formed by Cormòns, Gorizia and Gradisca, although the cellar shuns the designation, preferring to release all its wines as IGT Venezia Giulia. The Pecoraris have been farming and making wine since time immemorial but Pierpaolo was responsible for the quality turning point that arrived in the early 1970s.

Aided in vineyard and cellar by his son Alessandro, Pierpaolo releases three lines: cask-conditioned wines that take their name from the place names of their vineyards (Olivers, Kolaus and Soris); the Altis line of wines aged on the lees in steel; and third line for more approachable everyday wines. In fact, we liked the everyday wines best this time. The '09 Chardonnay is beautifully typed, minerally, full and powerful. The Pinot Grigio from the same year tempts with its fragrances, creaminess and poise on the palate while the Sauvignon '09 is consistent and caressing.

○ Chardonnay '09	▼▼	4*
○ Pinot Grigio '09	▼▼	4*
○ Sauvignon Blanc '09	▼▼	4*
● Refosco P. R. '09	▼	4
○ Sauvignon Kolaus '08	▼	6
○ Sauvignon Kolàus '96	▽▽▽	5
● Merlot Baolar '03	▽▽	7
○ Pinot Bianco Altis '06	▽▽	5
○ Pinot Bianco Altis '04	▽▽	5
○ Pinot Grigio '04	▽▽	4*
○ Pinot Grigio Olivers '07	▽▽	6
○ Sauvignon Altis '07	▽▽	5
○ Sauvignon Altis '06	▽▽	5
○ Sauvignon Kolaus '07	▽▽	6

Petrucco

VIA MORPURGO, 12
33042 BUTTRIO [UD]
TEL. 0432674387
www.vinipetrucco.it

CELLAR SALES
PRE-BOOKED VISITS

ANNUAL PRODUCTION 80,000 bottles
HECTARES UNDER VINE 25
VITICULTURE METHOD Conventional

Lina and Paolo Petrucco's winery was born of their love of the land. The estate is in Colli Orientali del Friuli, at Buttrio di Monte, where their vineyards are steeped in history, having been planted by the Fascist leader Italo Balbo, who was married to Contessa Florio of Buttrio. Balbo, however, was never able to enjoy the wine since he was shot down over Tobruk in Libya in 1940. The vineyards bear his name today, Ronco del Balbo, the pride and joy of the Petruccos.

Paolo Petrucco is reaping the fruits of the step change he imposed on the winery a few years ago when he put a first-class vineyard and cellar team in place. Many of the wines scored seriously high marks and the '09 Pinot Grigio went on to our finals. Faintly coppery in the glass, it unveils intense, fruit-led elegance on the nose while the soft, poised palate is all appeal. The '09 Friulano and Ribolla Gialla drink wonderfully well while the '06 Pignolo and '07 Refosco give richness and power.

○ COF Pinot Grigio '09	▼▼	4*
○ COF Friulano '09	▼▼	4*
● COF Pignolo Ronco del Balbo '06	▼▼	6
● COF Refosco P. R. Ronco del Belbo '07	▼▼	5
○ COF Ribolla Gialla '09	▼▼	4*
○ COF Chardonnay '09	▼	4
○ COF Sauvignon '09	▼	4
○ COF Chardonnay '08	▽▽	4*
○ COF Friulano '08	▽▽	4*
● COF Merlot '06	▽▽	4
● COF Merlot Ronco del Balbo '06	▽▽	5
○ COF Picolit '07	▽▽	7
○ COF Picolit '02	▽▽	7
● COF Pignolo Ronco del Balbo '05	▽▽	6
● COF Refosco P. R. '06	▽▽	4
● COF Refosco P. R. Ronco del Belbo '06	▽▽	5

Petrussa

VIA ALBANA, 49
33040 PREPOTTO [UD]
TEL. 0432713192
www.petrussa.it

CELLAR SALES
PRE-BOOKED VISITS

ANNUAL PRODUCTION 60,000 bottles
HECTARES UNDER VINE 10
VITICULTURE METHOD Conventional

In 1986, Gianni and Paolo Petrussa opted to devote their energies to the family winery. Their parents were more than a little worried. Why give up secure jobs and a guaranteed income for the economic insecurity and sheer hard work of the vineyard? But the pair, true to the country origins of their forebears, were determined to make the break. Now that the generation change is complete, Giustina and Celestino are justly proud of their boys.

When we tasted this year, many of the wines had yet to go into bottle but we were able to try enough of them to confirm that Gianni and Paolo have achieved and maintain a level of excellence. They must be very happy to know that their '07 Schioppettino did so very well. Schioppettino is native to Prepotto and recently earned its own subzone. People round here are deeply proud of it. The subtle varietal fragrances of spice-veined red berry fruits over balsam introduces a deliciously full-bodied palate with nice savouriness.

● COF Schioppettino '07	▼▼	6
○ COF Chardonnay '08	▼▼	5
○ COF Sauvignon S. Elena '08	▼	4
● COF Cabernet '06	▽▽	4*
○ COF Chardonnay '07	▽▽	5
○ COF Chardonnay '06	▽▽	5
○ COF Friulano '07	▽▽	4
○ COF Pinot Bianco '08	▽▽	4*
○ COF Pinot Bianco '07	▽▽	4
○ COF Sauvignon '06	▽▽	4*
● COF Schioppettino '06	▽▽	6
● COF Schioppettino '04	▽▽	6
○ COF Tocai Friulano '06	▽▽	4*
○ Pensiero '06	▽▽	6

Roberto Picéch

LOC. PRADIS, 11
34071 CORMÒNS [GO]
TEL. 048160347
www.picech.it

CELLAR SALES
PRE-BOOKED VISITS
ROOMS

ANNUAL PRODUCTION 30,000 bottles
HECTARES UNDER VINE 7
VITICULTURE METHOD Conventional

The Picéchs are proud to have been a grape-growing family on the slopes of Pradis, near Cormòns, since 1920 and in 1963, they managed to purchase the vineyards they were tending. In those days, Egidio Picéch, known as "il Ribel" (the rebel), and his wife Jelka built up the estate that since 1989 has been managed by their son Roberto. Now that the new cellar has been finished, he can at last work in spaces proportionate to today's requirements.

Robert has chosen a challenging winemaking style, with increasingly long maceration on the skins, so that the Picéch range is acquiring an ever more personal style. A fine example is the Collio Bianco '07 named for his daughter Athena, obtained from friulano grapes and released only in magnums. Rich in colour and fragrances, it leads off with hazelnuts, spring flowers and grapeskins before the very appealing palate presents so structured it verges on huskiness. We like the subtly aromatic, smoke-veined Malvasia for its depth of palate and juiciness while the Collio Rosso '08 and '08 Bianco Jelka are reliably excellent.

○ Collio Bianco Athena '07	TT	8
○ Collio Bianco Jelka '08	TT	5
○ Collio Malvasia '09	TT	5
● Collio Rosso '08	TT	5
○ Collio Friulano '09	T	5
○ Collio Pinot Bianco '09	T	5
○ Collio Bianco Athena '05	YYY	8
○ Collio Bianco Jelka '99	YYY	4
○ Collio Friulano '08	YY	5
○ Collio Malvasia '08	YY	5
○ Collio Pinot Bianco '08	YY	5
○ Collio Pinot Bianco '07	YY	5
● Collio Rosso '07	YY	5
● Collio Rosso '03	YY	4
● Collio Rosso Ris. '06	YY	6

Vigneti Pittaro

VIA UDINE, 67
33033 CODROIPO [UD]
TEL. 0432904726
www.vignetipittaro.com

CELLAR SALES
PRE-BOOKED VISITS

ANNUAL PRODUCTION 500,000 bottles
HECTARES UNDER VINE 90
VITICULTURE METHOD Conventional

Piero Pittaro comes from a wine family with over 450 years of history. The cellar, which blends perfectly with its surroundings and the beautifully looked-after vineyards, is satisfyingly designed and popular with visitors because of the intriguing museum of wine-related exhibits. In the course of his career, Piero has been chair of the world oenologists, a title he hold for life.

For many years, he has had the invaluable collaboration of cellar director Stefano Trinco, an expert technician who has fine-tuned production of still wines and classic method sparklers. Scores this year show the standards of quality here at Pittaro. For the second year running, Pittaro Brut Etichetta Oro was the cellar's top wine. The recently disgorged '02 is an aristocratic Brut with forward fragrances, sumptuous aromatics and a tangy palate. Less challenging but equally agreeable are the Etichetta Argento and the Rosé Pink. Both have a lively, sophisticated mousse and poise in the mouth.

○ Pittaro Brut Et. Oro '02	TT	7
○ Pittaro Brut Et. Argento	TT	5
⊙ Pittaro Brut Pink	TT	5
○ COF Picolit Ronco Vieri '07	T	7
○ Friuli Grave Chardonnay Mousqué '09	T	4
○ Manzoni Bianco '09	T	4
● Moscato Rosa Valzer in Rosa '09	T	4
○ Ramandolo Ronco Vieri '07	T	5
○ Apicio '06	YY	5
○ COF Picolit Ronco Vieri '05	YY	7
○ Manzoni '08	YY	4*
● Moscato Rosa Valzer in Rosa '07	YY	4
○ Pittaro Brut Et. Oro '01	YY	7
○ Ramandolo Ronco Vieri '06	YY	5

Damijan Podversic

VIA BRIGATA PAVIA, 61
34170 GORIZIA
TEL. 048178217
www.damijangodversic.com

CELLAR SALES
PRE-BOOKED VISITS

ANNUAL PRODUCTION 23,000 bottles
HECTARES UNDER VINE 10
VITICULTURE METHOD Certified organic

Damijan Podversic runs a compact estate in Collio. Working with nature means knowing how to wait. That's how Damijan sees the farmer's craft and he has turned it into a philosophy of life. Yields per plant and per hectare are ridiculously low and Damijan uses no chemicals or pesticides. Nothing. Fermentation is on the skins for 90 days and oak maturation is unhurried. These are natural wines that ferment on their own lees and are bottled without clarification and, we would add, without compromise of any description.

Some may find these wines hard to comprehend but not us. There is nothing to understand. These are wines to love unreservedly. They slowly win you over and never let you go. Trust them. Let yourself go. Think of them as a new dance and let their rhythm guide you. Like the Kaplia '07 from malvasia, friulano and chardonnay, a complex, minerally wine of character with apricot-themed aromatics. Or the '07 Ribolla Gialla with its medley of ripe grape, fruit in syrup, sultana, quince and vanilla. Another wine of superb stuffing and personality.

○ Kaplja '07	▼▼	7
○ Ribolla Gialla '07	▼▼	6
○ Kaplja '06	▽▽	6
○ Kaplja '05	▽▽	6
○ Kaplja '04	▽▽	6
○ Ribolla Gialla '06	▽▽	6
○ Ribolla Gialla '03	▽▽	6
● Rosso Prelit '06	▽▽	6
● Rosso Prelit '04	▽▽	6
● Rosso Prelit '03	▽▽	6

Isidoro Polencic

LOC. PLESSIVA, 12
34071 CORMÒNS [GO]
TEL. 048160655
www.polencic.com

CELLAR SALES
PRE-BOOKED VISITS

ANNUAL PRODUCTION 120,000 bottles
HECTARES UNDER VINE 25
VITICULTURE METHOD Conventional

Michele, Elisabetta and Alex honour the memory of their father Isidoro and continue along the path he mapped out, enhancing the family plots by vinifying their fruit separately. Some years ago, they replanted a plot on the southern slope of Mount Quarin using rooted cuttings from family vines more than a century old. That is story behind Friulano Fisc, a wine that has earned the Polencic cellar many plaudits.

This year, the family sent three wines to our finals. The '09 Pinot Grigio proffers ripe, pear-led, white-fleshed fruits and a balanced, varietal palate that shows soft and structured. Collio Bianco Oblin Blanc '08 from chardonnay, ribolla gialla and sauvignon tempts the nostrils with peaches and yellow damsons, unveiling a savour, aromatic palate that finish long yet taut. All the other wines are excellent, particularly the '08 Fisc, which was let down only by its less than exciting growing year.

○ Collio Bianco Oblin Blanc '08	▼▼	5
○ Collio Pinot Grigio '09	▼▼	5
○ Collio Chardonnay '09	▼▼	4
○ Collio Friulano '09	▼▼	4
○ Collio Friulano Fisc '08	▼▼	5
○ Collio Pinot Bianco '09	▼	5
○ Collio Friulano Fisc '07	▽▽▽	5
○ Collio Pinot Bianco '07	▽▽▽	5
○ Collio Pinot Grigio '98	▽▽▽	4
○ Collio Tocai Friulano '04	▽▽▽	4*
○ Collio Bianco Oblin Blanc '07	▽▽	4
○ Collio Friulano '08	▽▽	4*
○ Collio Pinot Grigio '08	▽▽	5
○ Collio Pinot Grigio '07	▽▽	5
○ Collio Ribolla Gialla '07	▽▽	4*
○ Collio Sauvignon '07	▽▽	4*

Primosic

FRAZ. OSLAVIA
LOC. MADONNINA DI OSLAVIA, 3
34070 GORIZIA
TEL. 0481535153
www.primosic.com

CELLAR SALES
PRE-BOOKED VISITS

ANNUAL PRODUCTION 200,000 bottles
HECTARES UNDER VINE 31
VITICULTURE METHOD Conventional

The hill of Oslavia lies in the heart of the Collio DOC, a short distance from the towering Julian Alps and from the shores of the Adriatic. This location gives vineyards in Oslavia uniquely well-ventilated site climates with excellent temperature ranges. The Primosic family has lived here since the 19th century, when they sold wine to merchants who took it to Vienna, the capital of the Austro-Hungarian empire. Today, the winery is run by Silvestro with his sons Marko and Boris.

Marko takes care of marketing and distribution while Boris works with his father in vineyards and cellar. Primosic wine names often include the name of the vineyard they were sourced from, thanks to a major zoning project aimed at focusing attention on the vineyards. The '07 Ribolla Gialla di Oslavia presents a lovely golden yellow, brimming with ripe pears, sultanas and hazelnuts before the solidly structured, savoury sensations in the mouth. The fragrant, faintly copper-hued '09 Pinot Grigio Murno has a warm, caressing palate. Sauvignon Gmajne '09 has plenty of fragrance and taut acidity in the mouth while Chardonnay Gmajne '08 is stylish, well defined, savoury and nicely poised.

O Collio Chardonnay Gmajne '08	▼▼	5
O Collio Pinot Grigio Murno '09	▼▼	4*
O Collio Ribolla Gialla di Oslavia Ris. '07	▼▼	5
O Collio Sauvignon Gmajne '09	▼▼	5
O Collio Friulano Belvedere '09	▼	4
O Collio Picolit Ris. '06	▼	6
O Ribolla Gialla Think Yellow! '09	▼	5
O Collio Bianco Klin '04	▽▽	6
O Collio Bianco Klin Ris. '06	▽▽	6
O Collio Chardonnay Gmajne '05	▽▽	5
O Collio Friulano Belvedere '08	▽▽	4*
O Collio Ribolla di Oslavia Ris. '05	▽▽	5
O Collio Ribolla Gialla di Oslavia Ris. '06	▽▽	5
O Collio Sauvignon Blanc Gmajne '07	▽▽	5
O Ribolla Gialla Think Yellow! '08	▽▽	5

Doro Princic

LOC. PRADIS, 5
34071 CORMÒNS [GO]
TEL. 048160723
doroprincic@virgilio.it

CELLAR SALES
PRE-BOOKED VISITS

ANNUAL PRODUCTION 60,000 bottles
HECTARES UNDER VINE 10
VITICULTURE METHOD Conventional

The winery founded by Doro Princic in 1950 is run today by his son Alessandro, a genuine dirt-under-the-nails grape farmer. Sandro, as he is known, is as impressive a man as he looks. With his shrewd smile under his Austro-Hungarian moustache, he makes a wonderful team with his contagiously hospitable wife, Grazia. They are a well matched couple and both are good listeners who determinedly carry forward the mission undertaken by Doro, one of the great names in Collio winemaking.

Sandro has the knack of giving his wines a territorial imprint while bringing out the varietal characteristics of each. These are wines that win your heart. Take the '09 Malvasia, a penetratingly varietal bottle with an aromatic vein. It immediately reminds you of last year's release, which also won Three Glasses. The award goes to a wine that embodies a territory, hinting at sea breezes and rolling out a heady concentration of aromas and flavours. The same thrills are there in the Friulano and Pinot Bianco, both '09 and both Princic masterpieces.

O Collio Malvasia '09	▼▼▼	5*
O Collio Friulano '09	▼▼	5*
O Collio Pinot Bianco '09	▼▼	5*
O Collio Sauvignon '09	▼▼	5
O Collio Pinot Grigio '08	▼	5
O Collio Malvasia '08	▽▽▽	5
O Collio Pinot Bianco '07	▽▽▽	5
O Collio Pinot Bianco '05	▽▽▽	5
O Collio Pinot Bianco '04	▽▽▽	5
O Collio Pinot Bianco '02	▽▽▽	5
O Collio Tocai Friulano '06	▽▽▽	5
O Collio Tocai Friulano '93	▽▽▽	5
O Collio Friulano '08	▽▽	5
O Collio Pinot Bianco '08	▽▽	5
O Collio Pinot Grigio '08	▽▽	5

★ Dario Raccaro

FRAZ. RÒLAT
VIA SAN GIOVANNI, 87
34071 CORMÒNS [GO]
TEL. 048161425
az.agr.raccaro@alice.it

CELLAR SALES
PRE-BOOKED VISITS

ANNUAL PRODUCTION 27,000 bottles
HECTARES UNDER VINE 4
VITICULTURE METHOD Conventional

Dario Raccaro has no need of introductions. His name and wines are on everyone's lips. The main reason for this is a long-established vineyard, Vigna del Rolat, which was planted to tocai friulano at the turn of the 20th century. Subsequent replantings used scions from the same vineyard, maintaining the profile of the wines over the years. Some years ago, Dario managed to lease the vineyard, which he continues to tend with superb results.

The '09 growing year was a fantastic one for Friulano with ten single-variety wines from various designated areas picking up Three Glasses. Naturally, one of them was Dario's legendary Vigna del Rolat, which stepped up for its eighth top prize. The '09 thrills from the outset with penetrating, fruit-led aromatics subtly interweaving with green notes before the powerful, fresh palate reveals itself to be incredibly long and complex. In short, a classic. But the '08 Merlot also impresses, showing style, elegance and concentration as well-honed tannins perk up a palate brimming with fruit and spice.

○ Collio Friulano Vigna del Rolat '09	**YYY**	5
● Collio Merlot '08	**YY**	6
○ Collio Malvasia '09	**YY**	5
○ Collio Bianco '09	**Y**	5
○ Collio Bianco '03	YYY	5
○ Collio Bianco '02	YYY	4
○ Collio Friulano Vigna del Rolat '08	YYY	5
○ Collio Friulano Vigna del Rolat '07	YYY	5
○ Collio Tocai Friulano '05	YYY	5
○ Collio Tocai Friulano '04	YYY	5
○ Collio Tocai Friulano '01	YYY	4*
○ Collio Tocai Friulano '00	YYY	4
○ Collio Tocai Friulano Vigna del Rolat '06	YYY	5

La Rajade

LOC. PETRUS, 2
34070 DOLEGNA DEL COLLIO [GO]
TEL. 0481639273
www.larajade.it

CELLAR SALES
PRE-BOOKED VISITS

ANNUAL PRODUCTION 25,000 bottles
HECTARES UNDER VINE 6
VITICULTURE METHOD Conventional

La Rajade was founded only recently but incorporates a well-established farm that has always grown grapes and made wine. New owners Giuseppe Faurlin and Sergio Campeotto have chosen a name for the estate that reflects their approach. Rajade is the Friulian for sunbeam, the source of life and for the vine and its environment, and the name bespeaks their commitment to the territory.

Managing the estate is Diego Zanin, who may be on the young side but has a lot of experience under his belt. Diego looks after the vineyards, deals with public relations and oversees hospitality. In the cellar, he shares responsibilities with Andrea Romano Rossi, a very reliable oenologist of proven ability. Early results have been encouraging and bode well for the future. La Rajade turns out a fine selection of territory wines, the most outstanding of which is the Sauvignon. Intense fruit mingles on the nose with varietal tropical fruits and caramel before full body braced by acid backbone emerges in the mouth.

○ Collio Sauvignon '09	**YY**	5*
○ Collio Bianco '09	**Y**	4
○ Collio Friulano '09	**Y**	5
○ Collio Ribolla Gialla '09	**Y**	4
○ Collio Bianco Caprizi di Marceline '01	YY	4*
● Collio Cabernet Sauvignon Stratin '01	YY	5
○ Collio Chardonnay '01	YY	4
○ Collio Malvasia '08	YY	5
● Collio Merlot Ris. '97	YY	5
○ Collio Sauvignon '08	YY	5*
○ Collio Sauvignon '01	YY	4

Rocca Bernarda

FRAZ. IPPLIS
VIA ROCCA BERNARDA, 27
33040 PREMARIACCO [UD]
TEL. 0432716914
www.roccabernarda.com

CELLAR SALES
PRE-BOOKED VISITS

ANNUAL PRODUCTION 200,000 bottles
HECTARES UNDER VINE 43
VITICULTURE METHOD Conventional

Rocca Bernarda, constructed in 1567, was the family home of the noble counts Valvason Maniago. In 1977, the estate was bequeathed to the current owners, the sovereign Military Order of Malta, by Conte Gaetano Perusini. The past 500 years have traced the history of Friulian wine in the Rocca's cellars but the most significant pages were written by the counts Perusini Antonini and Picolit, the property's signature wine.

The special attention focused on Picolit has prompted estate manager Paolo Dolce to extend its sojourn in bottle. As a result, we were unable to taste it for this Guide. Instead, we were fascinated by another native wine, the '06 Pignolo, which we sent through to the finals. Its bright, impenetrable hue ushers in an intense red and black fruits bouquet that weaves in hints of liquorice and tar. The full-bodied, caressing palate proffers ripe, cushiony tannins. We also enjoyed the subtly varietal '09 Ribolla Gialla with its crisp citron and supple palate.

● COF Pignolo '06	▼▼	6
○ COF Friulano '09	▼▼	5*
○ COF Ribolla Gialla '09	▼▼	5*
○ COF Sauvignon '09	▼▼	5*
○ COF Chardonnay '09	▼	5
○ COF Pinot Grigio Ramato della Rocca '09	▼	5
● COF Merlot Centis '99	▽▽▽	6
○ COF Picolit '03	▽▽▽	8
○ COF Picolit '97	▽▽▽	8
○ COF Bianco Vineis '08	▽▽	4*
○ COF Bianco Vineis '07	▽▽	4
○ COF Friulano '08	▽▽	4*
○ COF Friulano '07	▽▽	4
● COF Merlot Centis '04	▽▽	5
○ COF Picolit '06	▽▽	8
○ COF Picolit '06	▽▽	8
○ COF Pinot Grigio Ramato della Rocca '06	▽▽	4

Paolo Rodaro

LOC. SPESSA
VIA CORMONS, 60
33040 CIVIDALE DEL FRIULI [UD]
TEL. 0432716066
paolorodaro@yahoo.it

CELLAR SALES
PRE-BOOKED VISITS

ANNUAL PRODUCTION 250,000 bottles
HECTARES UNDER VINE 45
VITICULTURE METHOD Conventional

The Rodaros have always been farmers. They were making wine in 1846 but the step change came when in the late 1960s and early 1970s brothers Luigi and Edo turned their modest operation into one of the most admired wineries in Colli Orientali del Friuli. Paolo Rodaro, the present owner, likes to refer to himself as a farmer from Spessa because he reckons that in the third millennium, the title is an honourable one.

Some red-skinned grapes are left in small cases to overripen in ventilated rooms, concentrating the aromas and providing the raw material for the Romain line. The '06 Refosco that strolled into our finals is one example. Well-defined fruit aromatics mingle with darker notes of saddle leather and fur, taking you into a full, juicy palate with good concentration and extract. The '09 Sauvignon is varietal, elegant and uncomplicated with a fresh, gutsy palate. Citrus-veined florality on nose and palate is the calling card of the '09 Ribolla Gialla and the Friulano from the same harvest is alcohol rich and citrussy, with a husky palate.

● COF Refosco P. R. Romain '06	▼▼	6
○ COF Friulano '09	▼▼	4*
○ COF Ribolla Gialla '09	▼▼	4*
○ COF Sauvignon '09	▼▼	4*
○ COF Verduzzo Friulano '08	▼▼	5
○ COF Malvasia '09	▼	4
● COF Refosco P. R. Romain '03	▽▽▽	7
○ COF Sauvignon Bosc Romain '96	▽▽▽	5
○ Ronc '00	▽▽▽	4
● COF Merlot Romain '06	▽▽	6
● COF Merlot Romain '02	▽▽	7
○ COF Picolit '04	▽▽	7
○ COF Verduzzo Friulano Pra Zenâr '06	▽▽	6
○ Ronc '02	▽▽	4*

Ronc di Vico

FRAZ. BELLAZOIA
CENTRALE, 5
33040 POVOLETTO [UD]
TEL. 0432565012
romcdivicobellazoia@libero.it

CELLAR SALES
PRE-BOOKED VISITS

ANNUAL PRODUCTION 8,000 bottles
HECTARES UNDER VINE 7
VITICULTURE METHOD Conventional

Ronc di Vico is at Bellazoia, near Povoletto, not far from Udine. Running the estate is the enthusiastic Gianni Del Fabbro and his son Lodovico, who inherited his name from the grandfather who created the winery. The duo take scrupulous care of the seven hectares under vine, half estate-owned and half leased, that extend over the hills at Faedis. The old vine stock awaiting skilled hands to convert it was a dream come true for the Del Fabbros and the start of a marvellous adventure.

It's not often that you discover a winery that has shot to the top of the ladder in a very short time. In this case, the secrets are enthusiasm, an instinct for quality and good advice from a winemaker friend. The first wine went into bottle in 2003 and you only have to glance at the scores to realise that Gianni has made lightning progress. Three of the wines went into the finals and the '08 Friulano came back with Three Glasses. Intense citrus and broom tempt the nose as crisp, fragrant freshness unfolds satisfyingly in the mouth. Superb.

○ COF Il Friulano '08	5*
● COF Refosco P. R. '07	7
● COF Titut Ros '07	6
○ COF Matec '07	6
○ COF Sauvignon '08	5
● COF Vico rosso '07	5

La Roncaia

FRAZ. CERGNEU
VIA VERDI, 26
33045 NIMIS [UD]
TEL. 0432790280
www.fantinel.com

CELLAR SALES
PRE-BOOKED VISITS

ANNUAL PRODUCTION 44,000 bottles
HECTARES UNDER VINE N.A.
VITICULTURE METHOD Conventional

La Roncaia, acquired by the Fantinel family in 1998, is at Cergneu near Nimis, in the extreme north of the Colli Orientali del Friuli DOC. This is Ramandolo country. The Fantinels' purchase was carefully thought out as the property has been producing wine for more than three decades and the premium-quality wines from densely planted vineyards nicely complemented the family estates in Collio and Grave del Friuli.

Gianni Campo Dall'Orto and Adriano Copetti oversee the group properties with outside help, in the case of La Roncaia, from the Terra&Vino team. Results are exciting and two wines went to our finals. The '07 Merlot mirrors last year's release with intense, attractive tones of caressing overripeness, rich aromatics and complex flavours. Bianco Eclisse '09, an unusual blend of sauvignon blanc and picolit, is fragrant, buttery and intense, unfolding bright and fresh on the palate.

○ COF Bianco Eclisse '09	5
● COF Merlot '07	5
○ COF Friulano '09	5
○ COF Picolit '07	6
○ Ramandolo '07	6
○ COF Bianco Eclisse '08	5
○ COF Bianco Eclisse '06	5
○ COF Bianco Eclisse '05	5
○ COF Friulano '08	5
○ COF Picolit '06	6
○ COF Ramandolo '06	6
○ COF Ramandolo '02	6
● COF Refosco Gheppio '01	6

Il Roncat - Giovanni Dri

LOC. RAMANDOLO
VIA PESCIA, 7
33045 NIMIS [UD]
TEL. 0432790260
www.drironcat.com

CELLAR SALES
PRE-BOOKED VISITS

ANNUAL PRODUCTION 50,000 bottles
HECTARES UNDER VINE 10
VITICULTURE METHOD Conventional

Giovanni Dri's name has always been linked with Ramandolo. Giovanni has lavished much effort on this supremely elegant sweet white, contributing to its renown and visibility in Italy and abroad. In fact, he was one of the promoters of the wine's DOCG status. His lovely cellar in the shadow of Mount Bernadia is a fine example of low environmental impact, rationality and organization and in it Giovanni turns out an impeccable range of territory wines.

Support has always been provided by his wife, Renata, who has now been joined by their daughters in the office and welcoming visitors. Top of the range is always Ramandolo, which in the Uve Decembrine '06 edition is on mid-season form. Pale amber introduces dried figs, stewed pears, honey and caramel followed by an entrancingly creamy-textured palate braced by refreshing acidity, to close long and sweet. Giovanni's dry wines are equally well crafted, showing upfront varietal typicality and a sense of place.

○ Ramandolo Uve Decembrine '06	▼▼	6
● COF Cabernet Il Roncat '08	▼	5
● COF Merlot '08	▼	4
● COF Pignolo Monte dei Carpini '07	▼	6
● COF Refosco '07	▼	5
○ Ramandolo '08	▼	5
○ COF Picolit Il Roncat '07	▽▽	8
○ COF Picolit Il Roncat '06	▽▽	8
● COF Schioppettino Monte dei Carpini '06	▽▽	5
○ Ramandolo Il Roncat '07	▽▽	6
○ Ramandolo Il Roncat '06	▽▽	6
○ Ramandolo Il Roncat '05	▽▽	6
○ Ramandolo Uve Decembrine '05	▽▽	6

Ronchi di Cialla

FRAZ. CIALLA
VIA CIALLA, 47
33040 PREPOTTO [UD]
TEL. 0432731679
www.ronchidicialla.it

CELLAR SALES
PRE-BOOKED VISITS

ANNUAL PRODUCTION 100,000 bottles
HECTARES UNDER VINE 23
VITICULTURE METHOD Conventional

Paolo and Dina Rapuzzi settled at Cialla in 1970. Theirs was a lifestyle choice for they came from a totally different background but their sons Pierpaolo and Ivan like to say they were born among the vines. Both youngsters have degrees in food technology and work with a will to promote the Cialla subzone, long acknowledged as outstanding wine country and home of several signature Friulian varieties, schioppettino above all.

Rapuzzi wines are released several years after the harvest following long, carefully monitored maturation. Ronchi di Cialla is one for the few wineries in Friuli, if not the only one, to include on its list perfectly conserved old and very old vintages of its wines. This year, three of the five wines presented went into the finals, where they impressed the judges. The Schioppettino is marvellously coherent, giving cinchona and cherries over a stylishly rich palate. The Picolit is a refined medley of appealing fragrances ushering in well-gauged fruit, sweetness and length. We also loved the Refosco for its wealth of minerality and vigorous extract.

○ COF Picolit di Cialla '07	▼▼	8
● COF Refosco P.R. di Cialla '06	▼▼	7
● COF Schioppettino di Cialla '06	▼▼	7
○ COF Cialla Bianco '08	▼▼	5
○ COF Verduzzo di Cialla '07	▼▼	6
● COF Schioppettino di Cialla '05	▽▽▽	7
○ COF Cialla Bianco '07	▽▽	5
○ COF Picolit di Cialla '06	▽▽	8
● COF Refosco P.R. di Cialla '05	▽▽	7
○ COF Verduzzo di Cialla '06	▽▽	6

Ronchi di Manzano

via Orsaria, 42
33044 Manzano [UD]
tel. 0432740718
www.ronchidimanzano.com

CELLAR SALES
PRE-BOOKED VISITS

ANNUAL PRODUCTION 300,000 bottles
HECTARES UNDER VINE 55
VITICULTURE METHOD Conventional

Ronchi di Manzano sprawls over 55 hectares in Colli Orientali del Friuli and is divided into two distinct production areas. Ronc di Scossai and Ronc di Subule are part of the Ronchi di Manzano after which the property is named and which stand around the two-floor underground cellar carved from the rock. The second zone lies further east at Ronc di Rosazzo. In charge is Roberta Borghese, a very dynamic woman of wine.

Roberta long ago realized how valuable these "ronchi", or hillslope vineyards, were and duly fell in love with them. She manages the entire production process herself and has accumulated a raft of recommendations and awards, which now include our Three Glasses. The winner is the Friulano '09, Roberta's most territorial wine. Star-bright in the glass, it unfurls florality and yellow peach-led fruit but it is the palate that stuns with its coherent freshness, tanginess and sheer appeal. The '09 Pinot Grigio is also a delight on the nose and caressingly juicy in the mouth. We also picked out the '08 Refosco and the Traminer Aromatico Fatato '09.

○ COF Friulano '09	▼▼▼	4*
○ COF Pinot Grigio '09	▼▼	4*
● COF Refosco P. R. '08	▼▼	4
○ COF Traminer Aromatico Fatato '09	▼▼	5
○ COF Rosazzo Bianco Ellègri '09	▼	4
● COF Rosazzo Rosso Braûros '06	▼	5
○ COF Sauvignon '09	▼	4
● COF Merlot Ronc di Subule '99	▽▽▽	5
● COF Merlot Ronc di Subule '96	▽▽▽	5
● COF Cabernet Sauvignon '07	▽▽	4
○ COF Friulano '08	▽▽	4
● COF Merlot Ronc di Subule '06	▽▽	5
○ COF Sauvignon '08	▽▽	4
○ COF Sauvignon '07	▽▽	4

Ronco Blanchis

via Blanchis, 70
34070 Mossa [GO]
tel. 0438492250
www.venegazzu.com

ANNUAL PRODUCTION 31,000 bottles
HECTARES UNDER VINE 10
VITICULTURE METHOD Conventional

The current owner of Ronco Blanchis is Giancarlo Palla, who a few years back bought the estate on the Blanchis hill at Mossa, one of the highest points in the Collio Goriziano DOC. Its fantastic exposure to sunlight has given it a reputation for outstanding wine that goes back to the days of the Austrian empire. Documents from 200 years ago show that the vineyards were supplying the noble Catterini de Herzberg family with excellent grapes.

Giancarlo Palla and his son Lorenzo wanted to get off to a flying start and hired the best local wine technicians and consultants. Ronco Blanchis makes only whites and the best of all is a lovely Friulano '09 that put on a fine show at our finals. The generous aromas proffer peach fruit veined with aniseed before the rich, full-bodied palate reveals a savoury side and a twist of bitterness. The tangy, no-nonsense '09 Chardonnay teases with hints of smokiness while the '09 Pinot Grigio gives satisfying fruit and flowers on nose and palate.

○ Collio Friulano '09	▼▼	4
○ Collio Chardonnay '09	▼▼	4*
○ Collio Pinot Grigio '09	▼▼	4*
○ Collio Sauvignon '09	▼	4
○ Collio Chardonnay '06	▽▽	4*
○ Collio Friulano '07	▽▽	4
○ Collio Pinot Bianco '08	▽▽	3*
○ Collio Pinot Grigio '08	▽▽	4*
○ Collio Pinot Grigio '07	▽▽	4
○ Collio Pinot Grigio '06	▽▽	4*
○ Collio Sauvignon '06	▽▽	4*
○ Collio Tocai Friulano '06	▽▽	4

★ Ronco dei Tassi

LOC. MONTE, 38
34071 CORMÒNS [GO]
TEL. 048160155
www.roncodeitassi.it

CELLAR SALES
PRE-BOOKED VISITS

ANNUAL PRODUCTION **100,000 bottles**
HECTARES UNDER VINE **18**
VITICULTURE METHOD **Conventional**

Ronco dei Tassi is at Montona, Cormòns, up against the slope of Mount Quarin that looks onto Slovenia. The winery was founded in 1989 by Fabio Coser, who worked at several other wine estates before purchasing his own property on the edge of a nature reserve and settling there with his family. The farmhouse was restructured and then a new cellar was built, the final touch being a tunnel carved into the rock of the mountain itself.

The star before the estate's name means that Ronco dei Tassi has earned Three Glasses ten times, a major milestone for a close-knit family team, comprising Fabio, his wife Daniela and their children Mattero and Enrico. Collio Bianco Fosarin is the wine that has won most awards. The '09 edition of this lovely pinot bianco, friulano and malvasia blend tempts with a complex swath of delicate fragrances laced with medlars and a hint of almondiness. The savoury, poised palate is long and genuinely elegant. We also liked the elegant nose of the fresh, juicy-tasting Sauvignon '09.

○ Collio Bianco Fosarin '09	🍷🍷🍷	4*
○ Collio Sauvignon '09	🍷🍷	5*
○ Collio Malvasia '09	🍷🍷	5
○ Collio Ribolla Gialla '09	🍷🍷	5
● Collio Rosso Cjarandon '07	🍷🍷	5
○ Collio Friulano '09	🍷	5
○ Collio Pinot Grigio '09	🍷	5
○ Collio Bianco Fosarin '08	🍸🍸🍸	4*
○ Collio Bianco Fosarin '07	🍸🍸🍸	4
○ Collio Bianco Fosarin '06	🍸🍸🍸	4
○ Collio Bianco Fosarin '04	🍸🍸🍸	4*
● Collio Rosso Cjarandon '01	🍸🍸🍸	5
● Collio Rosso Cjarandon '00	🍸🍸🍸	5
○ Collio Sauvignon '05	🍸🍸🍸	4*
○ Collio Sauvignon '98	🍸🍸🍸	4

★ Ronco del Gelso

VIA ISONZO, 117
34071 CORMÒNS [GO]
TEL. 048161310
www.roncodelgelso.com

CELLAR SALES
PRE-BOOKED VISITS

ANNUAL PRODUCTION **150,000 bottles**
HECTARES UNDER VINE **25**
VITICULTURE METHOD **Conventional**

Ronco del Gelso was created by Giorgio Badin, who continues to run it. The property is at Cormòns, just below the Collio hills, so the vineyards are registered in the Isonzo DOC and the infertile, dry, stony soil is ideal for cultivating grapes. When Giorgio started out in 1987, he had just two hectares under vine but the business has grown steadily. Now, he has 25 hectares and a new cellar that gives him complete freedom of operation.

Giorgio's wines have always been impeccably typed and whistle-clean, making them a benchmark for the new generation of Isonzo producers. It's no secret that they are regularly selected for our finals and frequently come back with Three Glasses. This year, our highest praise went to the Pinot Grigio Sot lis Rivis '09, an elegantly fragrant paragon of typicality with loads of fruit and a balanced, well-defined palate that reflects the variety. The '09 Malvasia impressed for its smoke-veined complexity on the nose and gutsy, mouthfilling palate. Friulano Toc Bas '09 is powerful, tangy and very varietal while the Merlot Sintesi dei Capitoli, with its plush tannins and generous fruit, is every bit as good.

○ Friuli Isonzo Malvasia '09	🍷🍷	4*
○ Friuli Isonzo Pinot Grigio Sot lis Rivis '09	🍷🍷	4*
○ Friuli Isonzo Friulano Toc Bas '09	🍷🍷	4*
● Friuli Isonzo Sintesi dei Capitoli Merlot '07	🍷🍷	5
○ Friuli Isonzo Chardonnay '08	🍷	4
○ Friuli Isonzo Pinot Bianco '09	🍷	4
○ Friuli Isonzo Riesling '09	🍷	4
○ Friuli Isonzo Traminer '09	🍷	4
● Friuli Isonzo Merlot '01	🍸🍸🍸	5
○ Friuli Isonzo Sauvignon '00	🍸🍸🍸	4
○ Friuli Isonzo Tocai Friulano '06	🍸🍸🍸	4*
○ Friuli Isonzo Tocai Friulano '05	🍸🍸🍸	4
○ Friuli Isonzo Tocai Friulano '04	🍸🍸🍸	4*
○ Friuli Isonzo Tocai Friulano '03	🍸🍸🍸	4*
○ Friuli Isonzo Tocai Friulano '01	🍸🍸🍸	4

Ronco delle Betulle

LOC. ROSAZZO
VIA ABATE COLONNA, 24
33044 MANZANO [UD]
TEL. 0432740547
www.roncodellebetulle.it

CELLAR SALES
PRE-BOOKED VISITS

ANNUAL PRODUCTION 70,000 bottles
HECTARES UNDER VINE 14
VITICULTURE METHOD Conventional

Since 1990, Ronco delle Betulle has been managed by the tenacious, enterprising Ivana Adami, now assisted by her son Simone. Together, they strive to focus on typicality in each wine, coaxing out the personality of the variety and above all offering a reading of the territory. The estate lies in the superb subzone of Rosazzo in the Colli Orientali del Friuli, home of the abbey celebrated for its efforts to protect native Friulian varieties.

Ivana follows each stage of production with an expert's skill and a woman's sensitivity, well aware that a wine's character derives first from the terroir and then from the hand of the winemaker. And she produces some gems, like the pinot bianco, chardonnay, sauvignon and friulano Rosazzo Bianco Vanessa '08, a rich-hued, complexly fragrant wine with punchy concentration on the savoury palate. The '07 Picolit is a masterpiece of finesse and elegance with delicious aromatics and plenty of persistence. Also impressive is the '09 Pinot Grigio, a fruit-forward, well-balanced wine with a soft mouthfeel. High marks went to the '09 Sauvignon, the '06 Rosazzo Rosso Narciso and the '08 Franconia.

○ COF Picolit '07	▼▼	6
○ COF Rosazzo Bianco Vanessa '08	▼▼	5
○ COF Pinot Grigio '09	▼▼	4*
● COF Rosazzo Rosso Narciso '06	▼▼	6
○ COF Sauvignon '09	▼▼	4*
● Franconia '08	▼▼	5
● COF Cabernet Franc '08	▼	5
● COF Merlot '07	▼	5
● COF Refosco P. R. '08	▼	5
○ COF Ribolla Gialla '09	▼	4
○ COF Rosazzo Bianco Vanessa '07	▽▽	5
● COF Rosazzo Pignolo '05	▽▽	7
● COF Rosazzo Rosso Narciso '04	▽▽	6
● COF Rosazzo Rosso Narciso '03	▽▽	6
○ COF Tocai Friulano '06	▽▽	4

Ronco di Prepotto

VIA BROLO, 45
33040 PREPOTTO [UD]
TEL. 0432281118
www.roncodiprepotto.com

CELLAR SALES
PRE-BOOKED VISITS

ANNUAL PRODUCTION 30,000 bottles
HECTARES UNDER VINE 6
VITICULTURE METHOD Conventional

The Ronco di Prepotto estate has belonged to the Macorig family since 1901. There are six hectares under vine on the hills overlooking Prepotto, in the Colli Orientali del Friuli, a marvellous wine area. Annibale Macorig and his son Giampaolo are refocusing their entire production to higher quality by cutting the number of labels and concentrating their efforts –and fruit – on a limited range of wines.

But clear ideas are not always enough; you need skill, as well. So the Macorigs hired expert oenologist Emilio Del Medico, who has taken the cellar to the top in just a few years. No self-respecting Prepotto winery lacks a Schioppettino and the Macorig '08 is a paragon of typicality with black berry fruits, pepper and clove spice, good savouriness and balance on a palate that closes elegantly on roasted coffee beans. Bianco Anatema '07 from friulano, malvasia istriana and riesling renano is a mature, complex wine with evolved aromatics, warm alcohol and a mouthfilling texture.

○ COF Bianco Anatema '07	▼▼	5
● COF Schioppettino '08	▼▼	5
○ COF Bianco Lavinia '04	▽▽	6
○ COF Bianco Lavinia '03	▽▽	6
● COF Rosso Zeus '06	▽▽	6
● COF Rosso Zeus '04	▽▽	6
● COF Rosso Zeus '03	▽▽	6
● COF Schioppettino '07	▽▽	4

Ronco Severo

VIA RONCHI, 93
33040 PREPOTTO [UD]
TEL. 0432713144

CELLAR SALES
PRE-BOOKED VISITS

ANNUAL PRODUCTION 32,000 bottles
HECTARES UNDER VINE 6
VITICULTURE METHOD Organic

Stefano Novello runs the winery that his father Severo set up in 1968 when he had the opportunity to purchase a few hectares at Prepotto, in the Colli Orientali del Friuli. A convinced proponent of organic and biodynamic farming. In practical terms, this means managing the vineyards with no chemicals apart from sulphur and copper, and making wine the traditional way, using no chemicals, selected yeasts or enzymes, and very low levels of sulphites. The goal is to make genuine wines while safeguarding a territory that belongs to everyone.

Stefano is an oenologist who has worked in California and New Mexico. He knows all about modern winemaking but eschews its methods. To avoid the need for preserving agents, he leaves the must in contact with the skins for several weeks, and sometimes for months, allowing the wine to extract the compounds that encourage cellarability, enhance colour and lend opulence to their fragrances. Yet again, Severo Bianco went through to the finals. Gold in colour and slightly hazy because it is unfiltered, it follows up the aromatic, alcohol-rich nose with a powerful, tangy palate. The rest of the range hews to the estate's philosophy and the wines continue to garner admirers for the integrity of their fruit.

O COF Severo Bianco '07	TT	5
O COF Friulano '08	TT	5
● COF Merlot Artiûl '07	TT	6
O COF Pinot Grigio '09	TT	5
● COF Refosco P.R. '07	TT	6
O COF Chardonnay '07	YY	5
O COF Friulano '07	YY	5
O COF Pinot Grigio '08	YY	4*
O Severo Bianco '07	YY	6

Roncùs

VIA MAZZINI, 26
34076 CAPRIVA DEL FRIULI [GO]
TEL. 0481809349
www.roncus.it

CELLAR SALES
PRE-BOOKED VISITS
ROOMS

ANNUAL PRODUCTION 35,000 bottles
HECTARES UNDER VINE 12
VITICULTURE METHOD Conventional

Roncùs is at Capriva del Friuli, in the heart of the Collio. It was founded by Marco Perco in 1985 when he decided to transform the family farm, which had always been multi-crop, into an estate dedicate exclusively to wine. Marco's aim has always been to bring out the sensory profile of each variety, taking his cue from the great whites of Alsace as he is convinced his own territory is a match for it.

His wines invariably have a minerality and concentration that require time to express themselves. These are wines that need patience, understanding and not too cool a serving temperature. We will withhold judgement on the malvasia, friulano and ribolla gialla Bianco Vecchie Vigne '07 as it is too soon to draw any conclusions but we did like the richly coloured, citrus-themed '08 Friulano and its full, savoury palate. The latest vintage of the Collio Bianco brims with fruits and greens that usher in a refined, characterful palate. Finally, the Sauvignon and Pinot Bianco from '08 are concentrated and satisfying.

O Collio Bianco '09	TT	4
O Collio Friulano '08	TT	5
O Pinot Bianco '08	TT	5
O Sauvignon '08	TT	5
O Roncùs Bianco Vecchie Vigne '01	YYY	6
O Collio Bianco Vecchie Vigne '06	YY	6
O Collio Bianco Vecchie Vigne '05	YY	6
O Collio Bianco Vecchie Vigne '04	YY	6
O Collio Friulano '07	YY	5
O Sauvignon '07	YY	5
● Val di Miez '06	YY	6

Russiz Superiore

VIA RUSSIZ, 7
34070 CAPRIVA DEL FRIULI [GO]
TEL. 048199164
www.marcofelluga.it

CELLAR SALES
PRE-BOOKED VISITS
ROOMS

ANNUAL PRODUCTION 200,000 bottles
HECTARES UNDER VINE 50
VITICULTURE METHOD Conventional

Russiz Superiore sprawls over the Collio Goriziano at Capriva del Friuli. Its history can be traced right back to the late 13th century. The eagle in the coat of arms derives from an emblem that belonged to the princes Torre Tasso, one of the first noble families to rule this area, who arrived in Friuli in 1273. A succession of noble crests, noble wines and noble families preceded the present owner Marco Felluga. Today, his son Roberto runs the estate with the entrepreneurial enthusiasm that he inherited from his father.

With the assistance of Raffaela Bruno, a brilliant oenologist, Roberto has carried forward a project to make long-lived whites and for the past few years his Riservas have been attracting praise. This year, we were stunned by the Sauvignon. The '06 Riserva is lustrous in hue yet still shimmers with flecks of green. The fruit-led aromatics are varietal and the rich, mouthfilling palate lingers. The peach and almond-themed current release is refined, beautifully typed and tempts the palate with its indelible savouriness. The complexly fragranced '07 Merlot is also fantastic, giving smooth tannins, fruit and spiciness.

● Collio Merlot '07	TT	5
○ Collio Sauvignon '09	TT	5
○ Collio Sauvignon Ris. '06	TT	6
● Collio Cabernet Franc '07	TT	5
○ Collio Pinot Bianco '09	TT	5
○ Collio Pinot Bianco Ris. '06	TT	6
○ Collio Pinot Grigio '09	TT	5
○ Horus '05	TT	7
○ Collio Bianco Col Disôre '09	T	6
○ Collio Friulano '09	T	5
○ Collio Bianco Russiz Disôre '01	YYY	6
○ Collio Bianco Russiz Disôre '00	YYY	5
○ Collio Pinot Bianco '07	YYY	5
○ Collio Sauvignon '05	YYY	5
○ Collio Sauvignon '04	YYY	6

Sant'Elena

VIA GASPARINI, 1
34072 GRADISCA D'ISONZO [GO]
TEL. 048192388
www.sant-elena.com

CELLAR SALES
PRE-BOOKED VISITS

ANNUAL PRODUCTION 130,000 bottles
HECTARES UNDER VINE 30
VITICULTURE METHOD Conventional

Sant'Elena, near Gradisca d'Isonzo, was founded in 1893 by the Klodic family but it was only converted to grape farming in the mid 1960s. Dominic Nocerino, a prominent importer of Italian wines into the United States, is the far-sighted, ambitious entrepreneur who in 1997 acquired the property with the declared objective of producing top-notch territory wines. With the help of extremely competent professionals, he has done so in double-quick time.

The cellar has up-to-the-minute equipment and is supervised by expert wine man, Maurizio Drascek. Dominic's whole range is impressive but most plaudits went to the '07 Merlot Ròs di Rôl, a vineyard selection from a very special plot on the estate. The complex bouquet ranges from fruit to cocoa powder and tobacco that return in the mouth, which is full and juicy yet very agile. The '09 Sauvignon tempts with fresh-baked bread and peach-like fruit before the palate shows fresh and vibrant. Finally, Rosso Quantum '07 is a juicy, balsamic, single-variety Pignolo from slightly dried grapes.

● Merlot '07	TT	5
● Merlot Ròs di Rôl '07	TT	7
● Quantum Rosso '07	TT	6
○ Sauvignon '09	TT	5
○ Bianco Mil Rosis '08	T	6
○ Pinot Grigio '09	T	5
● Tato '07	T	6
○ Bianco Mil Rosis '07	YY	6
● Merlot '06	YY	5
● Merlot '03	YY	5
○ Pinot Grigio '07	YY	5
○ Sauvignon '08	YY	5

★ Schiopetto

VIA PALAZZO ARCIVESCOVILE, 1
34070 CAPRIVA DEL FRIULI [GO]
TEL. 048180332
www.schiopetto.it

CELLAR SALES
PRE-BOOKED VISITS

ANNUAL PRODUCTION 177,050 bottles
HECTARES UNDER VINE 30
VITICULTURE METHOD Conventional

This long-established Collio Goriziano operation is based at Capriva del Friuli in an old archbishop's palace set among the vines. It was set up in 1965 by the legendary Mario Schiopetto, who was making his Friulian dream come true with German equipment and French finesse, concepts and techniques with which he had acquired familiarity on his frequent trips abroad. Today, his children run the show. Maria Angela is in charge of sales, Carlo deals with public relations and Giorgio, who is an oenologist and agronomist, makes the wine.

Mario Schiopetto introduced the concept of the garden-vineyard into Friuli, surrounding himself with an outstanding team of agronomists. A happy marriage of Colli Orientali del Friuli chardonnay with Collio friulano, harvested in 2007, brings us Mario Schiopetto Bianco. It's a splendid wine and a fitting tribute to Mario in its superb expression of both territories. Erroneously included in the 2009 Guide, it more than deserved its Three Glasses this year for its delightful colour, intriguing smoke-veined aromatics and a gutsy, savoury palate of impeccable, delicious typicality that lingers forever.

○ Mario Schiopetto Bianco '07	▼▼▼	6
○ Blanc des Rosis '07	YYY	5
○ Blanc des Rosis '06	YYY	5
○ Collio Pinot Bianco '00	YYY	5
○ Collio Sauvignon '97	YYY	5
○ Collio Tocai Friulano '00	YYY	5
○ Collio Tocai Friulano '95	YYY	5
○ Collio Tocai Friulano '88	YYY	5
○ Collio Tocai Friulano '87	YYY	5
○ Mario Schiopetto Bianco '03	YYY	6
○ Mario Schiopetto Bianco '02	YYY	6

La Sclusa

LOC. SPESSA
VIA STRADA DI SANT'ANNA, 7/2
33043 CIVIDALE DEL FRIULI [UD]
TEL. 0432716259
www.lasclusa.it

PRE-BOOKED VISITS

ANNUAL PRODUCTION 160,000 bottles
HECTARES UNDER VINE 35
VITICULTURE METHOD Conventional

Tita Tramuntin was the nickname of Giobatta Zorzettig, the patriarch of a generation of growers that has been active at Spessa near Cividale, in the Colli Orientali del Friuli, since 1963. There are rather a lot of Zorzettigs in the area so the estate was renamed La Sclusa after a stretch of the river Corno that runs through the vineyards. The family-run operation respects tradition, combining accumulated experience with modern winemaking techniques to produce wines with distinctive personalities.

Giobatta's heir Gino still helps out but handed management over to his three sons some time ago. Winemaking and public relations are in Germano's hands, Maurizio looks after the vines and Luciano takes care of the cellar. The fourth generation is also active. Laura keeps things ticking over in the office while Daniele helps out by looking after customers and handling deliveries. The wines we tasted this year are all good but the stand-out is an '09 Friulano that we sent to the finals for its upfront coherence and varietal aromatics, but above all for its elegance, concentration and finesse in the mouth. The juicy, savoury '08 Refosco flaunts beautifully gauged wood and we enjoyed the '08 Picolit. The other wines are good.

○ COF Friulano '09	▼▼	4*
○ COF Picolit '08	▼▼	7
● COF Refosco P. R. '08	▼▼	4
● COF Cabernet Franc '09	▼	4
○ COF Pinot Grigio '09	▼	4
○ COF Ribolla Gialla '09	▼	4
○ COF Friulano '08	YY	4
○ COF Picolit '06	YY	7
○ COF Picolit V. del Torrione '05	YY	7
● COF Refosco P. R. '07	YY	4
○ COF Ribolla Gialla '07	YY	4

Roberto Scubla

FRAZ. IPPLIS
VIA ROCCA BERNARDA, 22
33040 PREMARIACCO [UD]
TEL. 0432716258
www.scubla.com

CELLAR SALES
PRE-BOOKED VISITS

ANNUAL PRODUCTION **60,000 bottles**
HECTARES UNDER VINE **12**
VITICULTURE METHOD **Conventional**

This small winery is one of Friuli's jewels. Set up by Roberto Scubla in 1991, when he purchased a tumbledown farmhouse on the road leading up to Rocca Bernarda which he quickly transformed into an attractive country residence with adjoining cellar.

Every year, Roberto's wines are excellent and this time four went on to the finals. Yet again, Verduzzo Friulano Cràtis – the '07 on this occasion – stood out, nearly winning top honours. Its shimmering old gold is shot through with amber, framing apple juice, ripe fruit, nougat and caramel aromas. Pomèdes '08 is a show-stopping blend that marries the elegance of pinot bianco with the structure of friulano and the aromatics of riesling renano. The ribolla gialla and malvasia Speziale '09 is fresher, caressing the palate with its juiciness and the Sauvignon from the same vintage is marvellous.

○ COF Bianco Pomèdes '08	2 black glasses	6
○ COF Bianco Speziale '09	2 black glasses	4
○ COF Sauvignon '09	2 black glasses	4*
○ COF Verduzzo Friulano Cràtis '07	2 black glasses	6
○ COF Friulano '09	2 black glasses	4
● COF Cabernet Sauvignon '08	1 black glass	5
○ COF Pinot Bianco '09	1 black glass	4
● COF Rosso Scuro '07	1 black glass	5
○ COF Bianco Pomèdes '04	3 white glasses	5
○ COF Bianco Pomèdes '99	3 white glasses	5
○ COF Verduzzo Friulano Cràtis '06	3 white glasses	6
○ COF Verduzzo Friulano Cràtis '04	3 white glasses	6
○ COF Verduzzo Friulano Graticcio '99	3 white glasses	6

Renzo Sgubin

VIA FAET, 15
34071 CORMÒNS [GO]
TEL. 0481630297
info@renzosgubin.com

CELLAR SALES
PRE-BOOKED VISITS

ANNUAL PRODUCTION **30,000 bottles**
HECTARES UNDER VINE **11**
VITICULTURE METHOD **Conventional**

Renzo Sgubin set up this small family-run winery in 1997 on the land his father used to farm as a tenant and then managed to buy in the 1970s. The heart of the operation is at Pradis near Cormòns and Mount Quarin, where the Collio DOC meets Friuli Isonzo. It's wonderful wine country and there's a story to tell in every bottle. Renzo started bottling in 2003 and since then he has been steadily improving quality.

His partner Michela deals with hospitality and in the cellar, Renzo can call on the expert advice of Luigino De Giuseppe, a highly competent wine technician with experience all over Friuli and beyond. Every wine is a winner and the range is a triumph of drinkability and appeal. The '09 Malvasia is varietal, powerful and very aromatic. The Pinot Grigio gives elderflowers and acacia honey in an elegant, well-structure profile. Friulano, Sauvignon and Chardonnay '09 are true to type and the white 3,4,3 '08 blend proffers warm tropical sensations.

○ 3, 4, 3 '08	2 black glasses	4*
○ Friuli Isonzo Friulano '09	2 black glasses	4*
○ Friuli Isonzo Chardonnay '09	2 black glasses	4*
○ Friuli Isonzo Malvasia '09	2 black glasses	4*
○ Friuli Isonzo Pinot Grigio '09	2 black glasses	4*
○ Friuli Isonzo Sauvignon '09	2 black glasses	4*
○ 3, 4, 3 '07	2 white glasses	4
○ Friuli Isonzo Chardonnay '08	2 white glasses	4*
○ Friuli Isonzo Pinot Grigio '08	2 white glasses	4*
○ Friuli Isonzo Sauvignon '08	2 white glasses	4*

Giordano Sirch

VIA FORNALIS, 277
33043 CIVIDALE DEL FRIULI [UD]
TEL. 0432709835
www.sirchwine.com

ANNUAL PRODUCTION 50,000 bottles
HECTARES UNDER VINE 11
VITICULTURE METHOD Conventional

Giordano Sirch has always made wine for the local market at Cividale del Friuli, in the Colli Orientali, but his winery officially came into being only in 2002 thanks to his son Luca, who wanted to show it was possible to make excellent wines and sell them at reasonable prices. A modest ambition, perhaps, but Luca was aiming for subtly complex products that would bear the imprint of their territory.

Luca had invaluable help from his brother Pierpaolo, who with Marco Simonit set up the Preparatori d'Uva group, and although Pierpaolo is busy consulting up and down Italy, he still finds time to lend a hand on the family estate. In the cellar, Luca has consultancy input from Alessio Dorigo and the results are impressive. The superb Malvasia '09 very nearly won a third Glass for its heady roses and citrus fragrances and sumptuously aromatic palate. Friulano Mis Mas '09 sis all finesse and upfront fragrances followed by a fresh, tangy palate.. All the other wines are excellent, too. This was quite a performance.

○ Malvasia '09	🍷🍷	4*
○ COF Friulano Mis Mas '09	🍷🍷	3*
○ COF Pinot Grigio '09	🍷🍷	4*
○ COF Ribolla Gialla '09	🍷🍷	4*
○ COF Sauvignon '09	🍷🍷	4*
○ COF Friulano '09	🍷	4
○ COF Friulano '07	☐☐☐	4*
○ COF Friulano Mis Mas '08	☐☐	3*
○ COF Friulano Mis Mas '07	☐☐	3*
○ COF Sauvignon '08	☐☐	4*
○ COF Sauvignon '06	☐☐	4*

Skerk

FRAZ. SAN PELAGIO
LOC. PREPOTTO, 20
34011 DUINO AURISINA [TS]
TEL. 040200156
www.skerk.com

CELLAR SALES
PRE-BOOKED VISITS
FOOD

ANNUAL PRODUCTION 20,000 bottles
HECTARES UNDER VINE 6
VITICULTURE METHOD Certified organic

Anyone who talks about heroic viticulture without visiting the Carso DOC hasn't really grasped the concept. One of the finest exponents of this style of viticulture is Sandi Skerk, the wine man to whom we have awarded this year's prize for Sustainable Viticulture. The vines are tended by hand, the cellar is quite literally dug out of the Carso limestone and the vineyards look like suburban gardens gazing over the northernmost reaches of the Adriatic, and indeed of the Mediterranean.

All the wines are obtained with skin contact, and there is no filtration, so they can be slightly hazy and opalescent. Don't worry about this, though. Try them and give your taste receptors a treat. Let's start with the '08 Malvasia, a minor miracle of aromatics and savouriness. The Ograde '08 from vitovska, malvasia, sauvignon and pinot grigio is a lovely onionskin hue. The '08 Vitovska and Sauvignon are good while the distinctively intractable '08 Terrano is the only red in the range.

○ Carso Malvasia Non Filtrato '08	🍷🍷🍷	5
○ Carso Vitovska Non Filtrato '08	🍷🍷	5
○ Ograde Non Filtrato '08	🍷🍷	5
○ Carso Sauvignon Non Filtrato '08	🍷🍷	5
● Carso Terrano Non Filtrato '08	🍷	5
○ Carso Malvasia Non Filtrato '07	☐☐	5
○ Carso Malvasia Non Filtrato '06	☐☐	5
○ Carso Sauvignon Non Filtrato '06	☐☐	5
○ Carso Vitovska Non Filtrato '07	☐☐	5
○ Carso Vitovska Non Filtrato '06	☐☐	5

Edi Skok

LOC. GIASBANA, 15
34070 SAN FLORIANO DEL COLLIO [GO]
TEL. 0481390280
www.skok.it

CELLAR SALES
PRE-BOOKED VISITS

ANNUAL PRODUCTION 35,000 bottles
HECTARES UNDER VINE 11
VITICULTURE METHOD Conventional

The Skok family has always farmed and is deeply attached to tradition while still remaining open to innovation. Evidence of this is the new photovoltaic installation that produces sufficient energy to process the grapes, keep the refrigeration plant running and maintain the cellar at just the right temperature. Currently, Edi Skok and his sister Orietta are in charge and they make an irresistibly likeable team.

Not for the first time, the Skoks sent a wine to the finals. It was their '09 Pinot Grigio, a faintly coppery wine with penetrating yet complex, well-defined fragrances. The palate has plenty of stuffing and good minerality in a well-poised whole. The '09 Friulano Zabura, named after its vineyard, stood out for varietal typicality, tempting the nose with wafts of aniseed and delighting the palate with its vigour, savouriness and length. The very fine '08 Merlot gives intense ripe black berry fruits over tobacco and fur while the palate is full and temptingly tannic. Collio Bianco Pe Ar '08 is very aromatic, giving wafts of wild roses before the warm, soft-textured palate reveals good acid backbone.

○ Collio Pinot Grigio '09	🍷🍷	4*
○ Collio Bianco Pe Ar '08	🍷🍷	4
○ Collio Friulano Zabura '09	🍷🍷	4*
● Collio Merlot '08	🍷🍷	4
○ Collio Chardonnay '09	🍷	4
○ Collio Bianco Pe Ar '07	ΫΫ	5
○ Collio Chardonnay '08	ΫΫ	4*
○ Collio Friulano Zabura '08	ΫΫ	4*
○ Collio Pinot Grigio '07	ΫΫ	4
○ Collio Sauvignon '08	ΫΫ	4*
○ Collio Tocai Friulano Zabura '06	ΫΫ	4

Leonardo Specogna

VIA ROCCA BERNARDA, 4
33040 CORNO DI ROSAZZO [UD]
TEL. 0432755840
www.specogna.it

CELLAR SALES
PRE-BOOKED VISITS

ANNUAL PRODUCTION 100,000 bottles
HECTARES UNDER VINE 19
VITICULTURE METHOD Conventional

Leonardo Specogna founded the winery and today his grandsons Michele and Cristian are in charge. Their father Graziano and uncle Gianni took it upon themselves to extend the vine stock and pass on this lovely property on the slopes of Rocca Bernarda, halfway between Rosazzo and Cividale del Friuli, where generations of growers have shapes the terraced slopes, with the Julian Alps on one side and the Adriatic on the other.

Both brothers are qualified wine technicians and divide the work between them. Cristian deals with distribution and public relations, helping out Michele in the vineyards or cellar as required. The Specognas again sent a wine to our finals, a splendid '09 Sauvignon with a nose of varietal fruit and greens lifted by aniseed, leading into a savoury, long-lingering palate. Equally attractive is the complex, smoke-veined '06 Merlot Oltre, a wine of depth and personality. The '08 Picolit is deliciously sweet and the rest of the range is up to snuff.

○ COF Sauvignon '09	🍷🍷	4
● COF Merlot Oltre '06	🍷🍷	6
○ COF Picolit '08	🍷🍷	7
○ COF Friulano '09	🍷	4
○ COF Chardonnay '08	🍷	4
○ Pinot Grigio '09	🍷	4
○ COF Friulano '08	ΫΫ	4*
○ COF Friulano '07	ΫΫ	4
○ COF Chardonnay '07	ΫΫ	4*
○ COF Chardonnay '06	ΫΫ	4
● COF Merlot Oltre '05	ΫΫ	6
● COF Merlot Oltre '04	ΫΫ	6
● COF Pignolo '05	ΫΫ	5
○ COF Sauvignon '08	ΫΫ	4*

Oscar Sturm

LOC. ZEGLA, 1
34071 CORMÒNS [GO]
TEL. 048160720
www.sturm.it

CELLAR SALES
PRE-BOOKED VISITS

ANNUAL PRODUCTION 70,000 bottles
HECTARES UNDER VINE 10
VITICULTURE METHOD Conventional

Zegla is a series of gentle hills rising from the Collio Friulano towards Slovenia. Its perfectly isolated position gives it an ideal climate for growing grapes. In 1850, the Sturm family from the village of Andritz in Austria settled here. More recently, Oscar Sturm realized this was superb wine country and set up the estate, which he now runs with his sons Denis and Patrick. They are the new blood whose energy and enthusiasm have taken the Sturm winery to the top and kept it there.

Patrick is the younger of the two but makes all the decisions in the cellar. He's a determined wine man who demands results. His brother Denis, who has a degree in economics from the Bocconi university, has the task of promoting the estate's commercial profile. And the wines are again impressive. The '09 Pinot Grigio is an elegant medley of penetrating tropical aromas backed up by a deliciously buttery, mouthfilling palate. We also like the crisp, no-nonsense Chardonnay Andritz '09, which is gutsy yet refined in the mouth. The fruit and greens '09 Friulano and concentrated '08 Collio Bianco Andritz are both excellent.

○ Collio Pinot Grigio '09	▼▼	4*
○ Collio Bianco Andritz '08	▼▼	5
○ Collio Chardonnay Andritz '09	▼▼	4*
○ Collio Friulano '09	▼▼	4*
○ Collio Ribolla Gialla '09	▼	4
○ Collio Sauvignon '09	▼	4
○ Collio Sauvignon '06	▽▽▽	4
○ Collio Tocai Friulano '05	▽▽▽	4*
○ Collio Bianco Andritz '07	▽▽	5*
● Collio Merlot '06	▽▽	5
○ Collio Pinot Grigio '08	▽▽	4*
○ Collio Pinot Grigio '07	▽▽	4*
○ Collio Sauvignon '08	▽▽	4

Subida di Monte

LOC. MONTE, 9
34071 CORMÒNS [GO]
TEL. 048161011
www.subidadimonte.it

CELLAR SALES
PRE-BOOKED VISITS

ANNUAL PRODUCTION 60,000 bottles
HECTARES UNDER VINE 10
VITICULTURE METHOD Organic

Subida di Monte's lovely cellar dominates the Collio Goriziano that stretches from the river Isonzo to the Judrio. The vines bask in sunlight, protected by the sheltering Julian Alps and caressed by sea breezes from the Adriatic. The working spaces are modern in design. There's plenty of room for winemaking and hospitality in the winery built by the far-sighted lover of beautiful things Luigi Antonutti for his sons Cristian and Andrea, to whom he handed over some time ago.

The younger Antonuttis make no secret about wanting to make nature and territory-friendly wines. Only low environmental impact fungicides like sulphur and copper are applied. Production is well established at impressive levels on both the red and the white fronts. This time, we enjoyed a very fruity, mouthfilling Merlot '08, concentrated on the nose and very long on a full-bodied plate with loads of savouriness and personality. The Friulano '09 is a great wine, showing true to type on nose and palate. Our tasters also liked the other wines, particularly the Rosso Poncaia '07, a Merlot with a splash of Cabernet Franc, which gives nice cocoa powder nuances.

○ Collio Friulano '09	▼▼	4*
● Collio Merlot '08	▼▼	4*
○ Collio Pinot Grigio '09	▼	4
● Collio Rosso Poncaia '07	▼	5
○ Collio Sauvignon '09	▼	4
○ Collio Friulano '08	▽▽	4*
○ Collio Malvasia '07	▽▽	4
● Collio Merlot '06	▽▽	4
○ Collio Pinot Grigio '08	▽▽	4*
○ Collio Pinot Grigio '07	▽▽	4
○ Collio Pinot Grigio '06	▽▽	4
○ Collio Sauvignon '08	▽▽	4*
○ Collio Sauvignon '06	▽▽	4

Matijaz Tercic

LOC. BUKUJE, 9
34070 SAN FLORIANO DEL COLLIO [GO]
TEL. 0481884193
tercic@tiscalinet.it

CELLAR SALES
PRE-BOOKED VISITS

ANNUAL PRODUCTION 30,000 bottles
HECTARES UNDER VINE 12
VITICULTURE METHOD Conventional

Matijaz Tercic's winery is at San Floriano del Collio, right next door to Slovenia in the top righthand corner of Italy. The area has some of the finest site climates in the Collio thanks to an elevation that encourages a wide range of temperatures and exposes the vines to the influence of sea breezes from the nearby Adriatic. Members of the Tercic family have been making wine here for centuries.

Last time, we were delighted to report the first Three Glass award for the Tercic cellar and this time Matijaz's '08 Pinot Grigio went to the finals, where it almost repeated the feat. Subtle wafts of fresh and candied tropical fruits make way for broad, juicy sensations on a caressing, exciting palate. Also nice is the '08 Ribolla Gialla, an elegant essay in ripe white-fleshed fruits with lovely progression on the attractive, satisfying palate. Damsons and fresh almonds theme the '08 Pinot Bianco, which opens sweetish and signs off with a hint of bitterness. The sound Merlot from the previous vintage is a delight, presenting well defined on the nose and savoury on the palate.

○ Collio Pinot Grigio '08	TT	4*
○ Collio Ribolla Gialla '08	TT	4*
● Collio Merlot '07	TT	5
○ Pinot Bianco '08	TT	4
○ Collio Chardonnay '08	T	4
○ Collio Sauvignon '08	T	4
○ Friuli Isonzo Friulano '08	T	4
○ Collio Pinot Grigio '07	YYY	4*
○ Collio Bianco Planta '05	YY	5
○ Collio Chardonnay '07	YY	4*
● Collio Merlot '06	YY	5
○ Collio Sauvignon '07	YY	4*
○ Pinot Bianco '07	YY	4*
○ Vino degli Orti '07	YY	5

Franco Terpin

LOC. VALERISCE, 6A
34070 SAN FLORIANO DEL COLLIO [GO]
TEL. 0481884215
francoterpin@virgilio.it

CELLAR SALES
PRE-BOOKED VISITS

ANNUAL PRODUCTION 15,000 bottles
HECTARES UNDER VINE 10
VITICULTURE METHOD Organic

Franco Terpin is one of the increasingly appreciated band of Collio producers who farm organically or biodynamically. Like all of them, Franco has a profound love of his land. The Terpin winery is at San Floriano, where most of its vineyards are also located. The twisting road that leads to Franco's lair climbs through vineyards, woodland, cherry trees, meadows and fields.

Under-vine mowing, desuckering, bunch thinning and picking are all done manually. The philosophy is uncomplicated but it demands many sacrifices. Obviously, cellar management is of a piece with this approach. Fermentation with spontaneous yeasts, lengthy skin contact, no clarification and no filtering. That sums up Terpin wines. The '06 Ribolla Gialla is a lovely amber yellow, proffering candied peel and resin over saffron leading to a full, savoury palate. The old gold '07 Sauvignon gives smokiness and all the character of a white obtained with skin contact while softness offsets the tannic sensation.

○ Ribolla Gialla '06	TT	5*
○ Sauvignon '07	TT	5
○ Chardonnay '07	T	5
○ Eianco Jakot '07	T	5
○ Collio Ribolla Gialla '05	YYY	5*
○ Collio Chardonnay '06	YY	5
○ Collio Ribolla Gialla '04	YY	5
● Collio Rosso Stamas '05	YY	5
○ Collio Sauvignon '06	YY	5
○ Jakot Bianco '06	YY	5
○ Pinot Grigio Sialis '05	YY	6

Tiare - Roberto Snidarcig

LOC. SANT'ELENA
VIA MONTE, 58A
34071 CORMÒNS [GO]
TEL. 048160064
www.tiaredoc.com

CELLAR SALES
PRE-BOOKED VISITS
ROOMS

ANNUAL PRODUCTION 80,000 bottles
HECTARES UNDER VINE 10
VITICULTURE METHOD Conventional

Tiare started up in 1985 with just over a hectare of vines on the slopes of Mount Quarin, near Cormòns. Robserto Snidarcig, a man who can justly claim to have done it all on his own, has gradually extended the vine stock, which now covers ten hectares, and has built a new cellar a few hundred metres from the former border crossing at Vencò, on one of the roads leading into Slovenia. With his ever-active wife Sandra, Roberto also runs a lovely farmstay but most of his energy goes into the vineyard and cellar.

After a low-key start, Roberto scored well this year and nearly took top honours with his genuine, varietal '09 Sauvignon with is vibrantly tangy flavours. The '09 Chardonnay is equally impressive, giving damson-like fruit and almonds on the nose with a juicy, perkily fresh palate. The Isonzo DOC brings us Roberto's '09 Malvasia with complex fragrances and a very nice palate that holds together well. Finally, the '09 Pinot Grigio and Ribolla Gialla '09 are deliciously drinkable.

○ Collio Sauvignon '09	5
○ Collio Chardonnay '09	4
○ Collio Pinot Grigio '09	4
○ Friuli Isonzo Malvasia '09	4
○ Ribolla Gialla '09	4
○ Collio Friulano '09	4
○ Collio Pinot Bianco '08	4
● Friuli Isonzo Cabernet Sauvignon '07	4

★ Franco Toros

LOC. NOVALI, 12
34071 CORMÒNS [GO]
TEL. 048161327
www.vinitoros.com

CELLAR SALES
PRE-BOOKED VISITS

ANNUAL PRODUCTION 70,000 bottles
HECTARES UNDER VINE 10
VITICULTURE METHOD Organic

They say that wines reflect the personalities of their makers. When you uncork a bottle from Franco Toros, you get the impression of a self-effacing grower who likes to spend as much time as possible among his rows. And Franco is just like that. He uses the tools offered by technology to craft his wines but above all, he calls on the ancient lore that his family, like so many others, has accumulated over the generations. It was his forebear Edoardo who settled here at Novali, near Cormòns, back in 1900.

Franco's wines are always models of cleanliness, forthrightness, respect for variety and sheer drinkability. At first glance, they may seem uncomplicated but they soon unfold an astonishingly rich complexity. Awards galore, not always for the flagship products, confirm that Franco's entire range is fantastic. This year, Three Glasses went again to one of Franco's Friulanos, the emblematic '09. Subtle and well defined, it regales nose and palate with intriguing aromatics and satisfying minerality. The '09 Pinot Grigio is superb, giving ripe pears and elderflower blossom in an elegantly concentrated, caressingly creamy swath of sensations. Finally, the crisp aromas and muscular palate of the '07 Merlot reward investigation.

○ Collio Friulano '09	5*
● Collio Merlot '07	5*
○ Collio Pinot Grigio '09	5*
○ Collio Pinot Bianco '09	5
○ Collio Sauvignon '09	5
○ Collio Chardonnay '09	5
○ Collio Friulano '08	5*
○ Collio Pinot Bianco '08	5*
○ Collio Pinot Bianco '07	5
○ Collio Pinot Bianco '05	5
○ Collio Tocai Friulano '06	5
○ Collio Tocai Friulano '04	5
○ Collio Tocai Friulano '03	5

Torre Rosazza

FRAZ. OLEIS
LOC. POGGIOBELLO, 12
33044 MANZANO [UD]
TEL. 0422864511
www.torrerosazza.com

CELLAR SALES
PRE-BOOKED VISITS

ANNUAL PRODUCTION 350,000 bottles
HECTARES UNDER VINE 95
VITICULTURE METHOD Conventional

Torre Rosazza's home is the 18th-century Palazzo De Marchi, which houses the offices and cellars atop a hill in the municipality of Manzano, in Colli Orientali del Friuli. Having acquired the estate in 1974, Genagricola set to work to terrace the slopes and renew the vine stock. Management is in the hands of administrative director Enrico Raddi while public relations and distribution are the domain of Marco Zuliani.

The two superb terraced natural amphitheatres around Palazzo De Marchi are suntraps where vineyard manager Ennio Venuto grows fruit for the group oenologist, Luca Zaccarello. Luca's winemaking is evidently very effective because yet again Torre Rosazza sent a wine to the national finals. The stunner is the '09 Bianco Ronco di Masiero, a great blend of Pinot Grigio and Chardonnay with a dash of Picolit. Rich, penetrating tropical fruits and aniseed-fragrances lead into fresh, tangy perceptions. It was a very good year for the Friulano and Chardonnay, too, both showing varietal and fruit-led. The '08 Picolit is delicious.

○ COF Bianco Ronco del Masiero '09	▼▼	5*
○ COF Chardonnay '09	▼▼	4
○ COF Friulano '09	▼▼	4
○ Picolit '08	▼▼	6
● COF Cabernet Sauvignon '08	▼	5
○ COF Pinot Grigio '09	▼	4
● COF Rosso Bandaròs '07	▼	5
○ COF Friulano '08	▽▽	4*
○ COF Pinot Grigio '08	▽▽	4*
○ COF Ribolla Gialla '08	▽▽	4*
○ COF Sauvignon '08	▽▽	4*
○ Picolit '06	▽▽	6

La Tunella

FRAZ. IPPLIS
VIA DEL COLLIO, 14
33040 PREMARIACCO [UD]
TEL. 0432716030
www.latunella.it

CELLAR SALES
PRE-BOOKED VISITS

ANNUAL PRODUCTION 450,000 bottles
HECTARES UNDER VINE 80
VITICULTURE METHOD Conventional

La Tunella is a family winery, and a close-knit family at that with mum Gabriella watching over her two sons Massimo and Marco, and their respective wives Romina and Barbara. The Zorzettig property marches on in harmony, having achieved levels of excellence in recent years thanks to a blend of youthful energy, teamwork and the heritage of three generations of C olli Orientali del Friuli growers.

Massimo and Marco dedicated a memorable party to their beloved grandmother Linda, naming one of their wines after her. Linda '09 is probably the first native Friulian blend of malvasia and ribolla gialla. Varietal aromatics from both grapes alternate on the nose before the vibrantly supple palate unveils softness and fresh-tasting savouriness. But the best of the range is the '09 Biancosesto, the friulano and ribolla gialla blend that is the cellar's calling card. Smoky perceptions and minerality take you into a juicy, tangy palate. Finally, welcome to Valmasia '09, a tribute to the valley that yields the cellar's malvasia.

○ COF BiancoSesto '09	▼▼	5
○ COF Friulano '09	▼▼	4
○ COF LaLinda '09	▼▼	6
○ COF Ribolla Gialla Rjgialla '09	▼▼	4
○ COF Sauvignon '09	▼▼	4
● COF Malvasia Valmasia '09	▼	4
○ COF BiancoSesto '07	▽▽▽	5
○ COF BiancoSesto '06	▽▽▽	4*
○ COF BiancoSesto '08	▽▽	5
○ COF BiancoSesto '05	▽▽	4*
○ COF Chardonnay '07	▽▽	4
○ COF Friulano Selènze '08	▽▽	4*
○ COF Friulano Selènze '07	▽▽	4
● COF Rosso L'Arcione '05	▽▽	6

Valchiarò

fraz. Togliano
via dei Laghi, 4c
33040 Torreano [UD]
tel. 0432715502
www.valchiaro.it

CELLAR SALES
PRE-BOOKED VISITS

ANNUAL PRODUCTION 40,000 bottles
HECTARES UNDER VINE 12
VITICULTURE METHOD Conventional

In 1991, six partners with very different, non-wine, backgrounds founded Valchiarò at Torreano, near Cividale. They were united by two factors: friendship and a love of wine. We would add a third: a touch of recklessness, a very necessary element in ventures of this kind. In 2006, the friends took another step forward when they inaugurated their new, state-of-the-art cellar in an enchanting natural setting.

A lot of wine has flowed into and out of the barrels since 1991. Now, Valchiarò deservedly occupies a place in the front rank of the prestigious Colli Orientali del Friuli wine scene, thanks in no small part to Gianni Menotti, the gifted winemaker who continues to consult. This year, we didn't taste the Verduzzo Friulano, the wine we most liked on previous occasions, but the rest of the range is impressive. The '09 Sauvignon is redolent of elderflower and shows juicy yet restrained on the palate. Friulano Nexus '09 brings to mind Alpine meadow flowers, golden delicious apples, pears and thyme, with soft sensations and balance in the mouth. The brooding '06 Merlot Riserva gives spice over black berry fruits with a full, tangy palate.

○ COF Friulano Nexus '09	4*
● COF Merlot Ris. '06	5
○ COF Sauvignon '09	4*
○ COF Friulano '09	4
○ COF Pinot Grigio '09	4
○ COF Ribolla Gialla '09	4
○ COF Friulano Nexus '08	4*
● COF Refosco P. R. '04	4
○ COF Sauvignon '08	4*
○ COF Tocai Friulano '07	4
○ COF Verduzzo Friulano '07	4*
○ COF Verduzzo Friulano '06	4*
○ COF Verduzzo Friulano '05	4*

Valpanera

via Trieste, 5a
33059 Villa Vicentina [UD]
tel. 0431970395
www.valpanera.it

PRE-BOOKED VISITS

ANNUAL PRODUCTION 450,000 bottles
HECTARES UNDER VINE 55
VITICULTURE METHOD Conventional

Since it was set up, Valpanera has focused on promoting Refosco dal Peduncolo Rosso. This ancient, native Friuli Venezia Giulia grape has found an ideal habitat on the clay and sand soils of the Aquileia DOC. Giampietro Dal Vecchio has staked a lot on the grape, to the point that the entry to the estate he runs with his son is surmounted by a sign that says "Casa del Refosco" (Home of Refosco).

Luca Marcolini, the enterprising oenologist, made the estate's philosophy his own and his efforts were rewarded at our tastings. Two versions of his Refosco went through to the finals. The '06 Riserva reveals perfect handling of the new oak used for ageing. Rich, mouthfilling, sound and still fruity on the nose, it has power and elegance in the mouth. But the Superiore is stunning, with crisp, varietal aromatics and superb tannins while even the base Refosco is a wine of appeal and agility. Well done!

● Friuli Aquileia Refosco P. R. Ris. '06	5
● Friuli Aquileia Refosco P. R. Sup. '07	4*
● Friuli Aquileia Refosco P. R. '08	4*
○ Friuli Aquileia Chardonnay '09	4
○ Friuli Aquileia Sauvignon '09	4
○ Friuli Aquileia Verduzzo Friulano '08	4
○ Friuli Aquileia Chardonnay Carato '06	5
● Friuli Aquileia Refosco P. R. Ris. '05	5
● Friuli Aquileia Refosco P. R. Sup. '06	4*
● Friuli Aquileia Refosco P. R. Sup. '05	4
● Friuli Aquileia Rosso Alma '05	5

★ Venica & Venica

LOC. CERÒ, 8
34070 DOLEGNA DEL COLLIO [GO]
TEL. 048161264
www.venica.it

CELLAR SALES
PRE-BOOKED VISITS
ROOMS

ANNUAL PRODUCTION **240,000 bottles**
HECTARES UNDER VINE **37**
VITICULTURE METHOD **Conventional**

This year, the Venicas are celebrating 80 years since the foundation of their winery. In commemoration, they have personalized some magnums of Ronco delle Mele in elegant wooden presentation boxes stamped with the contract of sale, dated 1930. Gianni and Giorgio have grandfather Daniele to thank if they are now the proud owners of one of the region's leading wine estates. But then Gianni and Giorgio have done their bit, too.

The Venicas' success is linked to the obsessive care they have always lavished on their rows. Friuli's finest agronomists have scrutinized the rows to identify the most appropriate pruning techniques for each variety and plot. Again this year, the range scored impressively overall and once again the top of the list is the legendary Ronco delle Mele, in this case the '09. It is increasingly enthralling with each passing vintage. Citrus and elderflower aromatics introduce a truly distinctive palate. But the '09 Malvasia is also a stand-out for its wisteria notes and fluent, tangy palate. Other stars are the Chardonnay Ronco Bernizza and Sauvignon Ronco del Cerò, both '09s.

○ Collio Sauvignon Ronco delle Mele '09	▼▼▼	6
○ Collio Chardonnay Ronco Bernizza '09	▼▼	6
○ Collio Malvasia '09	▼▼	5
○ Collio Sauvignon Ronco del Cerò '09	▼▼	6
○ Collio Friulano Ronco delle Cime '09	▼▼	5
○ Collio Pinot Bianco '09	▼▼	5
○ Collio Pinot Grigio Jesera '09	▼▼	5
○ Collio Ribolla Gialla '09	▼▼	5
○ Collio Traminer Aromatico '09	▼	5
○ Collio Sauvignon Ronco delle Mele '08	▽▽▽	6
○ Collio Sauvignon Ronco delle Mele '07	▽▽▽	6
○ Collio Sauvignon Ronco delle Mele '05	▽▽▽	6
○ Collio Sauvignon Ronco delle Mele '02	▽▽▽	6
○ Collio Tocai Friulano Ronco delle Cime '06	▽▽▽	5
○ Collio Tocai Friulano Ronco delle Cime '02	▽▽▽	6

Paolo Venturini

VIA ISONZO, 135
34071 CORMÒNS [GO]
TEL. 048160446
www.venturinivini.it

CELLAR SALES
PRE-BOOKED VISITS

ANNUAL PRODUCTION **50,000 bottles**
HECTARES UNDER VINE **14**
VITICULTURE METHOD **Conventional**

Since 1976, Paolo Venturini has been running the estate set up by his father in the 1960s. The winery is based at Cormòns, where the Collio DOC meets the Isonzo, a famous territory for high-quality wines. Paolo has 14 hectares, at Pradis in Collio and at Bosc di Sot, Medea, in the Isonzo DOC. Paolo's efforts to marry the family traditions with new technology have been rewarded by results.

We have already praised the entire range in the past but this time there was genuine progress. Venturini and his friend oenologist Gianni Menotti's commitment and the application of Diego Mauric in the cellar have taken the winery into the big time with two wines going forward to the finals. The '09 Pinot Bianco opens on balsam, presenting very varietal, elegant and clean-lined. The rich-hued Friulano '09 offers very distinct varietal aromatics lifted by wafts of aniseed, backed up by a full, juicy, easy-drinking palate. The other excellent '09s are the wisteria-themed Malvasia, the Pinot Grigio and the Ribolla Gialla, both outstandingly stylish.

○ Collio Friulano '09	▼▼	4*
○ Collio Pinot Bianco '09	▼▼	4*
○ Collio Malvasia '09	▼▼	4
○ Collio Pinot Grigio '09	▼▼	4
○ Collio Ribolla Gialla '09	▼▼	4
○ Collio Chardonnay '09	▼	4
○ Collio Sauvignon '09	▼	4
○ Collio Malvasia '08	▽▽	4*
○ Collio Pinot Bianco '07	▽▽	4
○ Collio Sauvignon '08	▽▽	4*

La Viarte

VIA NOVACUZZO, 51
33040 PREPOTTO [UD]
TEL. 0432759458
www.laviarte.it

CELLAR SALES
PRE-BOOKED VISITS

ANNUAL PRODUCTION 100,000 bottles
HECTARES UNDER VINE 26
VITICULTURE METHOD Conventional

In 1973, Giuseppe Ceschin purchased 35 hectares in the Colli Orientali del Friuli hill country between Corno di Rosazzo and Prepotto, crowning his long-cherished dream of making wine. It was the beginning of an adventure, which he called La Viarte, the Friulian for springtime. The first wines were released in 1983 since it took a long time to terrace the slopes, establish the vineyards and build the cellar.

For some years, Giulio Ceschin has been managing the estate his parents Giuseppe and Carla set up. Giulio also chairs a group of Prepotto producers which has obtained recognition for the local Schioppettino variety as a separate subzone, Prepotto, of the Colli Orientali DOC. The '07 growing year was a good one and the well-crafted wines are all pleasers. The '09 Ribolla Gialla is very varietal, as is the tannic '06 Tazzelenghe, while Liende (Legend) '07, a blend of friulano and pinot bianco with a dash of sauvignon, riesling and ribolla gialla, is tangy, vigorous, fresh and remarkably supple.

○ COF Bianco Liende '07	🍷🍷	5
○ COF Friulano '09	🍷🍷	4
○ COF Ribolla Gialla '09	🍷🍷	4
● COF Schioppettino '07	🍷🍷	5
● COF Tazzelenghe '06	🍷🍷	6
○ COF Pinot Grigio '09	🍷	5
○ COF Sauvignon '09	🍷	4
○ COF Friulano '08	YY	4*
○ COF Pinot Bianco '08	YY	4*
○ COF Sauvignon '08	YY	4*
● COF Schioppettino '06	YY	5
○ Siùm '06	YY	6
○ Siùm '05	YY	6

★★ Vie di Romans

LOC. VIE DI ROMANS, 1
34070 MARIANO DEL FRIULI [GO]
TEL. 048169600
www.viediromans.it

CELLAR SALES
PRE-BOOKED VISITS

ANNUAL PRODUCTION 230,000 bottles
HECTARES UNDER VINE 44
VITICULTURE METHOD Conventional

The Gallo family's entry into the world of grapes and wine took place more than a century ago as first Basilio and then Stelio plied their trade. Since 1978, the operation has been run by Gianfranco, whose rigorous and sometimes bold choices, together with meticulous winemaking skills, have forged a very personal style. The splendid three-level Vie di Romans cellar at Mariano del Friuli was built in 1989.

Year after year, Gianfranco's wines flaunt an enviably reliable standard of quality. Released two years after the harvest, they are very territorial. Massive structure lets Gianfranco show off his prowess with small wood, especially in his whites. However, this time it was the steel-fermented Sauvignon Piere '08 that repeated last year's triumph and swept up Three Glasses. Complex, delicately varietal aromatics tempt you into a thoroughly convincing palate. Monumental. Fantastic fragrances took the '08 Flors di Uis, from malvasia, riesling and friulano, to within an ace of top honours.

○ Friuli Isonzo Sauvignon Piere '08	🍷🍷🍷	5*
○ Friuli Isonzo Bianco Flors di Uis '08	🍷🍷	5
○ Friuli Isonzo Chardonnay Ciampagnis Vieris '08	🍷🍷	5
○ Friuli Isonzo Friulano Dolée '08	🍷🍷	6
○ Friuli Isonzo Sauvignon Vieris '08	🍷🍷	6
○ Friuli Isonzo Chardonnay Vie di Romans '08	🍷🍷	6
○ Friuli Isonzo Malvasia Istriana Dis Cumieris '08	🍷🍷	5
○ Friuli Isonzo Pinot Grigio Dessimis '08	🍷🍷	5
Chardonnay '86	YYY	5
○ Dut'Un '02	YYY	7
Friuli Isonzo Chardonnay Ciampagnis Vieris '94	YYY	5
○ Friuli Isonzo Malvasia Istriana Dis Cumieris '06	YYY	5
○ Friuli Isonzo Rive Alte Sauvignon Piere '07	YYY	5*
○ Friuli Isonzo Sauvignon Vieris '04	YYY	5

Vigna del Lauro

LOC. MONTE, 38
34071 CORMÒNS [GO]
TEL. 048160155
www.vignadellauro.it

CELLAR SALES
PRE-BOOKED VISITS

ANNUAL PRODUCTION 60,000 bottles
HECTARES UNDER VINE 8
VITICULTURE METHOD Conventional

Vigna del Lauro was founded in 1994 by Fabio Coser, owner of Ronco dei Tassi, because of the need to flank those wines with more approachable, fresh-tasting products that offer very keen value for money, a demand that came with increasing insistence from Germany. Fabio looked around and settled on this vineyard surrounded by laurel trees, hence the name of the winery.

Other plots, some purchased and others leased, were added to the original holding and now the vine stock extends over ten hectares in the municipality of Cormòns, some in the Collio DOC and some in Isonzo. Fabio's winemaking skills are well known so these are top-class products. The '07 Merlot is astonishingly varietal, giving delicious cocoa powder and a balsamic note in the mouth that complements an elegantly full style that still manages to remain agile. We also loved the Friulano '09 for its trademark peaches and almonds over a refreshingly tangy palate. Citrus notes and complexity mark out the '09 Chardonnay while the '09 Sauvignon and Ribolla Gialla are fruit-led, well typed and seamless.

● Friuli Isonzo Merlot '07	2 black glasses	4*
○ Collio Friulano '09	2 black glasses	4*
○ Collio Ribolla Gialla '09	2 black glasses	4*
○ Collio Sauvignon '09	2 black glasses	4*
○ Friuli Isonzo Chardonnay '09	2 black glasses	4*
○ Collio Pinot Grigio '09	1 black glass	4
○ Collio Sauvignon '99	3 glasses	4
○ Collio Friulano '08	2 glasses	4*
○ Collio Friulano '07	2 glasses	4
○ Collio Pinot Grigio '07	2 glasses	4
○ Collio Ribolla Gialla '06	2 glasses	4*
○ Collio Sauvignon '08	2 glasses	4*
○ Collio Sauvignon '07	2 glasses	4*
● Friuli Isonzo Merlot '06	2 glasses	4*

Vigna Petrussa

VIA ALBANA, 47
33040 PREPOTTO [UD]
TEL. 0432713021
www.vignapetrussa.it

CELLAR SALES
PRE-BOOKED VISITS

ANNUAL PRODUCTION 30,000 bottles
HECTARES UNDER VINE 6
VITICULTURE METHOD Conventional

Vigna Petrussa is at Albana, a district of Prepotto, in the Colli Orientali del Friuli. Albana is the home of ribolla nera, a grape that has apparently always grown here. This is the native variety that yields Schioppettino, which is why the wine is a point of pride with local producers. Hilde Petrussa, who owns and manages Vigna Petrussa, campaigned for years to get the subzone recognized.

She must have been very proud when her Schioppettino did so well at our finals. Hilde lavishes great care on bunch thinning in July and then cuts the tip when the grapes begin to colour on the vine. Hand-picking in wooden cases is followed by part-drying until late in autumn. After wood ageing and maturation in glass, her '07 is very varietal, giving restrained aromatics and subtle notes of spice before the delicious palate unfolds its body and savouriness. Equally good is the more evolved, complex Refosco '06, all elegance in the mouth. We also noted fine performances by the Friulano '09 and Cabernet Franc '07.

● COF Refosco P. R. '06	2 black glasses	5
● COF Schioppettino '07	2 black glasses	5
● COF Cabernet Franc '07	2 black glasses	5
○ COF Friulano '09	2 black glasses	4
○ Richenza '08	1 black glass	5
○ COF Picolit '06	2 glasses	6
○ COF Picolit '05	2 glasses	6
○ COF Picolit '04	2 glasses	6
● COF Schioppettino '06	2 glasses	5
● COF Schioppettino '05	2 glasses	5
● COF Schioppettino '05	2 glasses	5
● COF Schioppettino '04	2 glasses	5
○ Richenza '05	2 glasses	5

Vigna Traverso

via Ronchi, 73
33040 Prepotto [UD]
tel. 0422804807
www.vignatraverso.it

CELLAR SALES
PRE-BOOKED VISITS

ANNUAL PRODUCTION 70,000 bottles
HECTARES UNDER VINE 45
VITICULTURE METHOD Conventional

Vigna Traverso, at Prepotto in Colli Orientali del Friuli, became part of the Molon Traverso portfolio in 1998 when the family, which owns a prominent Veneto-based operation, purchased the already well-known Ronco di Castagneto winery. Stefano, son of Ornella Molon and Giancarlo Traverso, is in charge and already he has shown that he can run a cellar, taking it to success in a very short time.

The cellar now being built near the vineyards will enable him to work more comfortably and efficiently. Results are impressive. The '09 Sauvignon stands out for its pineapple and mango-like tropical fruits veined with a hint of butter. Full body, depth and savouriness sign off with a lingering finale. Another excellent wine is the '08 Sottocastello, a friulano-heavy blend with chardonnay with penetrating, forward aromas and plenty of concentration. The Refosco '08 is well typed and the merlot-only Rosso Sottocastello '07 is also spot on.

○ COF Sauvignon '09	▼▼	4*
○ COF Bianco Sottocastello '08	▼▼	5
○ COF Friulano '09	▼▼	4*
● COF Refosco P. R. '08	▼▼	4*
● COF Rosso Sottocastello '07	▼▼	6
○ COF Pinot Grigio '09	▼	4
○ COF Ribolla Gialla '09	▼	4
● COF Rosso Troj '08	▼	5
● COF Cabernet Franc '07	▽▽	4*
○ COF Friulano '08	▽▽	4*
● COF Refosco P. R. '07	▽▽	4*
○ COF Ribolla Gialla '08	▽▽	4*
● COF Rosso Sottocastello '04	▽▽	7
○ COF Sauvignon '08	▽▽	4*
● COF Schioppettino '07	▽▽	5

★ Le Vigne di Zamò

loc. Rosazzo
via Abate Corrado, 4
33044 Manzano [UD]
tel. 0432759693
www.levignedizamo.com

CELLAR SALES
PRE-BOOKED VISITS

ANNUAL PRODUCTION 250,000 bottles
HECTARES UNDER VINE 67
VITICULTURE METHOD Organic

In 1978, Tullio Zamò set up the Vigne dal Leon winery on the slopes of Rocca Bernarda and then Abbazia di Rosazzo a few years later. His sons Silvano and Pierluigi followed in his footsteps and it was they who created Le Vigne di Zamò at Rosazzo, where they set their offices and superb hospitality facilities in a carefully restored farmhouse.

Everyone knows that old vines produce few bunches with incredible concentrations of aroma compounds and minerals. Well, vines more than half a century old give the Zamòs their most outstanding success. Yet again, Friulano Vigne Cinquant'Anni '08 earned Three Glasses for its imposing complexity, bringing out the best in the territory's most representative variety. Ronco dei Roseti '04, a Bordeaux blend with a splash of the local pignolo, charms with balsam-veined aromatics and vibrant, but not over-assertive, extract. Malvasia '08 and the chardonnay, sauvignon and riesling Ronco di Corte '08 are excellent.

○ COF Friulano V. Cinquant'Anni '08	▼▼▼	6
○ COF Malvasia '08	▼▼	5
● COF Rosazzo Ronco dei Roseti '04	▼▼	6
○ Ronco di Corte '08	▼▼	5
● COF Refosco P. R. Re Fosco '07	▼▼	6
○ COF Sauvignon '09	▼▼	5
○ COF Malvasia '00	▽▽▽	4
● COF Merlot V. Cinquant'Anni '06	▽▽▽	6
● COF Merlot V. Cinquant'Anni '99	▽▽▽	6
○ COF Rosazzo Bianco Ronco delle Acacie '01	▽▽▽	5
● COF Rosazzo Pignolo '01	▽▽▽	8
○ COF Tocai Friulano V. Cinquant'Anni '06	▽▽▽	6
○ COF Tocai Friulano V. Cinquant'Anni '00	▽▽▽	5
○ Ronco delle Acacie '93	▽▽▽	5
○ Ronco di Corte '87	▽▽▽	5

★★ Villa Russiz

VIA RUSSIZ, 6
34070 CAPRIVA DEL FRIULI [GO]
TEL. 048180047
www.villarussiz.it

CELLAR SALES
PRE-BOOKED VISITS

ANNUAL PRODUCTION 240,000 bottles
HECTARES UNDER VINE 40
VITICULTURE METHOD Conventional

Villa Russiz owes its foundation in 1869 to the foresight of the French count, Théodore de La Tour, and his Austrian wife, Elvine Ritter. Théodore was the first to sense the potential that would make Collio wines world-beaters. The current estate manager, Gianni Menotti, is the man who perhaps best knows the secrets of this terroir and its grapes, which he vinifies supremely well. Since 1988, Gianni has been running the property with passion, thanks to the La Tours, who left their estate to a charity. Income from the cellar in fact funds the Adele Cerruti foundation for children in need.

Gianni, who continues the work his father Edino carried out for 35 years, has the great merit of showing that a publicly owned enterprise can support itself independently, without finance from elsewhere. Villa Russiz means great wines and Gianni has had to find space in the trophy cupboard for his '09 Friulano's Three Glass award. Our judges noted its varietal typing, the extraordinarily crisp intensity that emerges on the nose and the power, harmony and bell-like clarity of the palate. The '09 Sauvignon de La Tour reaffirmed its class, presenting as a model of varietal character, and we also liked the gracefully contoured nose and consistency in the mouth of the Pinot Grigio '09.

○ Collio Friulano '09	▼▼▼	5*
○ Collio Pinot Grigio '09	▼▼	5*
○ Collio Sauvignon de La Tour '09	▼▼	6
● Collio Cabernet Sauvignon '08	▼▼	5
● Collio Merlot Graf de La Tour '07	▼▼	7
○ Collio Pinot Bianco '09	▼▼	5
○ Collio Ribolla Gialla '09	▼▼	5
○ Collio Malvasia '09	▼	5
○ Collio Sauvignon '09	▼	5
○ Collio Chardonnay Gräfin de La Tour '02	▽▽▽	6
● Collio Merlot Graf de La Tour '02	▽▽▽	7
○ Collio Pinot Bianco '07	▽▽▽	5
○ Collio Sauvignon de La Tour '08	▽▽▽	6
○ Collio Sauvignon de La Tour '05	▽▽▽	6
○ Collio Tocai Friulano '04	▽▽▽	5

Tenuta Villanova

LOC. VILLANOVA
VIA CONTESSA BERETTA, 29
34072 FARRA D'ISONZO [GO]
TEL. 0481889311
www.tenutavillanova.com

CELLAR SALES
PRE-BOOKED VISITS

ANNUAL PRODUCTION 800,000 bottles
HECTARES UNDER VINE 130
VITICULTURE METHOD Conventional

The date of foundation –1499 – is prominently displayed on the estate's perimeter wall. With more than 500 years of history, Tenuta Villanova is one of the bastions of Friulian winemaking. Far-sighted businessman Arnaldo Bennati purchased the property in 1932 and it is to this day managed by his wife Giuseppina Grossi Bennati, assisted by her nephew Alberto Grossi, who acts as general manager and has a very competent team working with him.

This is the only winery in Friuli with its own on-site distillery, which produces excellent grappa from the grape pressings. The Tenuta has fully 130 hectares under vine in the Collio and Isonzo DOC zones, where agronomist Altieri Chiappo is in charge, while the young but very experience oenologist Massimiliano Cattarin looks after the cellar. This year's range is well up to previous high standards, although there were no real stand-outs. The delicious, slightly copper-hued Pinot Grigio '09 gives stewed pears and apricots framing a full, well-poised palate. Finally, we enjoyed the excellent Traminer Aromatico '09 and the fragrantly tangy Ribolla Gialla, also '09.

○ Collio Ribolla Gialla '09	▼▼	5
○ Friuli Isonzo Pinot Grigio '09	▼▼	4
○ Friuli Isonzo Traminer Aromatico '09	▼▼	4
○ Collio Picolit '07	▼	7
● Friuli Isonzo Cabernet Sauvignon '07	▼	4
● Friuli Isonzo Refosco P. R. Colombara '07	▼	4
○ Collio Chardonnay Monte Cucco '97	▽▽▽	4
○ Collio Chardonnay Ronco Cucco '07	▽▽	5
○ Collio Friulano '08	▽▽	4*
○ Collio Friulano Ronco Cucco '07	▽▽	5
○ Collio Sauvignon Ronco Cucco '07	▽▽	5
○ Friuli Isonzo Chardonnay '07	▽▽	4
○ Friuli Isonzo Malvasia Saccoline '08	▽▽	4*
○ Friuli Isonzo Malvasia Saccoline '07	▽▽	4

Andrea Visintini

via Gramogliano, 27
33040 Corno di Rosazzo [UD]
tel. 0432755813
www.vinivisintini.com

CELLAR SALES
PRE-BOOKED VISITS

ANNUAL PRODUCTION 140,000 bottles
HECTARES UNDER VINE 28
VITICULTURE METHOD Conventional

The Visintini winery rises on the ruins of the feudal castle at Gramogliano, which was destroyed and rebuilt several times. Today, all that survives is a splendid watchtower with adjoining farmhouse. The operation was set up in 1973 by Andrea but today his children Oliviero, Cinzia and Palmira run the show with renewed enthusiasm, now that they have adequate working space in the restructured cellars. Old vines and the energy of youth make a winning combination.

Oliviero has always practised environment-friendly viticulture, keeping chemical treatments to a minimum and cutting the amount of fertilizer used, and with it nitrates entering the soil. Again this year we appreciated the genuineness and freshness of a range whose stand-out is the superbly well-defined, stylish '09 Sauvignon, whose varietal elderflowers, savouriness, juicy flavour and progression took it into the finals. The peaches and summer flowers of the '09 Friulano and a stylishly sumptuous palate also impressed. Finally, the faintly aromatic, soft-textured and fresh-tasting COF Bianco '09 scored well.

○ COF Sauvignon '09	▼▼	3*
○ COF Bianco '09	▼▼	3
○ COF Friulano '09	▼▼	3
● COF Merlot '08	▼	3
○ COF Pinot Grigio '09	▼	3
● COF Refosco P. R. '08	▼	4
● COF Merlot '07	▽▽	3*
● COF Merlot Torion Ris. '06	▽▽	4
○ COF Pinot Bianco '07	▽▽	3
○ COF Pinot Grigio '08	▽▽	3*
○ COF Ribolla Gialla '08	▽▽	3*
○ COF Sauvignon '07	▽▽	4
○ COF Sauvignon '06	▽▽	4

★ Volpe Pasini

fraz. Togliano
via Cividale, 16
33040 Torreano [UD]
tel. 0432715151
www.volpepasini.net

CELLAR SALES
PRE-BOOKED VISITS
ROOMS

ANNUAL PRODUCTION 400,000 bottles
HECTARES UNDER VINE 52
VITICULTURE METHOD Organic

The unremitting efforts of Emilio Rotolo and his son Francesco are bringing additional lustre to the range of Volpe Pasini wines. Add to that a cellar kept tidier than many front rooms, and vineyards in marvellous locations in the north-central part of Colli Orientali del Friuli, and you begin to see why Volpe Pasini is going from strength to strength. The whites are elegant and moderately alcoholic, the reds well structure and clearly stamped with their territory.

Sauvignon Zuc di Volpe '09 is a minor masterpiece. The varietal aromatics are not excessively "sauvage", background acidity is just right and the easy-drinking palate satisfies, lingering subtly at the back. The '09 Pinot Bianco and Friulano, also from the Zuc di Volpe line, are very good. We thought the best of the reds were the '07 Merlot Focus and Refosco. From the other more than just good whites, we picked out the '09 COF Sauvignon Volpe Pasini, which is fantastic value for money.

○ COF Sauvignon Zuc di Volpe '09	▼▼▼+	5*
○ COF Friulano Zuc di Volpe '09	▼▼	5
● COF Merlot Focus Zuc di Volpe '07	▼▼	5
○ COF Pinot Bianco Zuc di Volpe '09	▼▼	5
● COF Refosco P. R. Zuc di Volpe '07	▼▼	5
○ COF Chardonnay Zuc di Volpe '08	▼▼	5
○ COF Pinot Grigio Zuc di Volpe '09	▼▼	5
○ COF Ribolla Gialla Zuc di Volpe '09	▼▼	5
○ COF Sauvignon Volpe Pasini '09	▼▼	4*
○ COF Pinot Bianco Zuc di Volpe '08	▽▽▽	5
○ COF Pinot Bianco Zuc di Volpe '07	▽▽▽	5
○ COF Sauvignon Zuc di Volpe '05	▽▽▽	5
○ COF Sauvignon Zuc di Volpe '04	▽▽▽	5
○ COF Tocai Friulano Zuc di Volpe '06	▽▽▽	5

Francesco Vosca

FRAZ. BRAZZANO
VIA SOTTOMONTE, 19
34070 CORMÒNS [GO]
TEL. 048162135
www.voscavini.it

CELLAR SALES
PRE-BOOKED VISITS

ANNUAL PRODUCTION 30,000 bottles
HECTARES UNDER VINE 8
VITICULTURE METHOD Organic

Francesco Vosca farms at Brazzano, a district of Cormòns and right in the heart of Collio, a word we associate today with great wines, luxuriant countryside and enviable living standards. But Francesco can remember the 1960s, when poverty was rife here, many were forced to emigrate and he in his childhood had to dig the soil. The farm was converted in the 1990s, the cows were sold off and focus shifted to the vineyards and wine.

Francesco is helped in the office by his wife Anna, who also lends a meticulous hand in the vineyard, while in the cellar their son Gabriele is finding his feet, now that he has almost completed his education. The family is completed by Elisabetta, who looks after the books and public relations. The Voscas' teamwork has obtained surprising results, particularly with a marvellous '09 Malvasia redolent of wisteria and citrus over plus bay leaf, with a full, tangy flavour of great finesse. The '09 Isonzo DOC Sauvignon gives intense peaches and tropical fruits ushering in a delectably taut, deep palate.

○ Collio Malvasia '09	▼▼	4*
○ Collio Friulano '09	▼▼	4*
○ Collio Pinot Grigio '09	▼▼	4*
○ Friuli Isonzo Sauvignon '09	▼▼	4*
○ Friuli Isonzo Chardonnay '09	▼	4
○ Collio Friulano '08	YY	4*
○ Collio Friulano '07	YY	4
○ Collio Malvasia '06	YY	4
○ Collio Pinot Grigio '08	YY	4*
○ Collio Pinot Grigio '07	YY	4
○ Friuli Isonzo Chardonnay '08	YY	4*
○ Friuli Isonzo Sauvignon '07	YY	4

Zidarich

LOC. PREPOTTO, 23
34011 DUINO AURISINA [TS]
TEL. 040201223
www.zidarich.it

CELLAR SALES
PRE-BOOKED VISITS

ANNUAL PRODUCTION 18,000 bottles
HECTARES UNDER VINE 6
VITICULTURE METHOD Organic

The Zidarich winery in the heart of the Carso DOC dates from 1988. From its vantage point among the vines and Carso vegetation, the winery enjoys a stunning view over the Gulf of Trieste. And on this terrain, which contains lots of limestone and very little red earth, the innovative, very determined Benjamin Zidarich has revolutionized his father's estate, expanding what was only half a hectare under vine and putting the accent on native varieties.

The moderately continental tableland climate is swept by breezes from the Adriatic on one side and the cold, often violent, Bora winds from the other. Conditions like these restrict the choice of varieties but the native vitovska and terrano vines are always present. Traditional winemaking imposes bold choices: skin contact, native yeasts only, no filtration, no stabilization and an extended timescale. But determination has its just reward and Benjamin's Prulke '08, from vitovska, malvasia and sauvignon, duly won Three Glasses. Aroma-rich and fruity on the nose, it reveals stunning depth and savouriness in the mouth. Equally attractive is the complex merlot and terrano Ruje '04.

○ Prulke '08	▼▼▼	6
● Ruje '04	▼▼	7
○ Carso Malvasia '08	▼▼	6
● Carso Terrano '07	▼▼	6
○ Carso Vitovska '08	▼▼	6
○ Carso Malvasia '06	YYY	6
○ Carso Malvasia '07	YY	6
○ Carso Vitovska '07	YY	6
○ Carso Vitovska '06	YY	6
○ Carso Vitovska '05	YY	6
○ Prulke '07	YY	6
○ Prulke '06	YY	6
● Ruje '03	YY	7

Zof

FRAZ. SANT'ANDRAT DEL JUDRIO
VIA GIOVANNI XXIII, 32A
33040 CORNO DI ROSAZZO [UD]
TEL. 0432759673
www.zof.it

CELLAR SALES
PRE-BOOKED VISITS
ROOMS

ANNUAL PRODUCTION 90,000 bottles
HECTARES UNDER VINE 15
VITICULTURE METHOD Conventional

The Zof family has Austrian and Prussian roots but settled at Corno di Rosazzo in the Colli Orientali del Friuli more than a century ago. In the mid 1980s, Alberto Zof from the third-generation set up a wine estate, which his son Daniele now looks after. Meanwhile Alberto and his wife Angela manage a farmstay in the converted guest accommodation of an 18th-century villa adjoining the estate at Casali Gallo.

Right from the start, Daniele has focused on native varieties, adapting the vine stock and cutting the number of labels released. Results have duly arrived and Daniele's hard work has attracted praise for his reds as well as his whites. The '08 Schioppettino, from ribolla nera, and the Refosco dal Peduncolo Rosso from the same vintage obtained seriously good scores. The Schioppettino gives ripe fruit and sweet spice over a pleasingly gutsy palate while its fellow has a varietal nose and depth in the mouth. The whites from the last vintage and the '05 Pignolo are all worth uncorking.

● COF Refosco P.R. '08	▼▼	5
● COF Schioppettino '08	▼▼	5
○ COF Friulano '09	▼	4
● COF Pignolo Và Pensiero '05	▼	5
○ COF Ribolla Gialla '09	▼	4
○ COF Sauvignon '09	▼	4
○ COF Bianco Sonata '05	YY	4
○ COF Picolit '06	YY	6
○ COF Pinot Grigio '08	YY	4*
○ COF Ribolla Gialla '06	YY	4*
○ COF Sauvignon '08	YY	4*
○ COF Sauvignon '07	YY	4

Zuani

LOC. GIASBANA, 12
34070 SAN FLORIANO DEL COLLIO [GO]
TEL. 0481391432
www.zuanivini.it

VENDITA DIRETTA
VISITA SU PRENOTAZIONE

PRODUZIONE ANNUA 65.000 bottiglie
ETTARI VITATI 12.00
VITICOLTURA Convenzionale

Zuani è di Patrizia Felluga, la figlia d'arte di Marco, ed è l'espressione compiuta della sua filosofia, accumulata attraverso anni di esperienza tra vigneti e cantina. È una sfida quella che si è posta assieme ai due figli Antonio e Caterina: dedicarsi alla produzione di un solo vino, il Collio, quale espressione autentica di un territorio. Tutto ruota attorno ad un cru di esposizione eccezionale sui pendii di Giasbana, a San Floriano del Collio.

Nella vigna-giardino che contorna la cantina vengono allevati in parti uguali friulano, chardonnay, pinot grigio e sauvignon. Questi vitigni compongono il vino che viene poi vinificato in due diverse versioni: il Zuani Vigne, fresco e fruttato, viene prodotto interamente in vasche di acciaio termocondizionate, mentre quello della versione Zuani proviene da uve selezionate da vendemmia tardiva e matura in barrique francesi e americane. Naturalmente i due prodotti sono molto diversi: il primo è più immediato, fresco e di beva, mentre il secondo è più complesso, profuma di pesca gialla e mandorla e al palato è succoso, complesso e tipico. A noi piacciono entrambi.

DA TRADURRE

○ Collio Bianco Zuani '08	▼▼	6
○ Collio Bianco Zuani Vigne '09	▼▼	5
○ Collio Bianco Zuani Vigne '07	YYY	5
○ Collio Bianco Zuani '07	YY	6
○ Collio Bianco Zuani '06	YY	6
○ Collio Bianco Zuani '05	YY	6
○ Collio Bianco Zuani Vigne '08	YY	4*
○ Collio Bianco Zuani Vigne '06	YY	5

Alberice

VIA BOSCO ROMAGNO, 4
33040 CORNO DI ROSAZZO [UD]
TEL. 0422765571
www.tenutealeandri.it

Alberice is at Corno di Rosazzo in Colli Orientali del Friuli but belongs to Veneto-based Tenute Aleandri. We liked the palate-caressing depth of the Cabernet Franc and Refosco dal Peduncolo Rosso '07.

● COF Cabernet Franc '07	🍷🍷	4
● COF Refosco P. R. '07	🍷🍷	4
○ COF Ribolla Gialla '09	🍷	4
○ COF Sauvignon '09	🍷	4

Antico Broilo

VIA BROILO, 42
33040 PREPOTTO [UD]
TEL. 0432713082
www.anticobroilo.com

Giovanni Durì, known as Vanni, and his son Massimo run this small Prepotto operation. They grow four red-skinned grapes and two whites to make their compact range. The '07 Refosco and Schioppettino are textbook stuff, presenting complex, spicy and flavoursome.

● COF Refosco P. R. '07	🍷🍷	4*
● COF Schioppettino '07	🍷🍷	4*
● COF Pinot Nero '07	🍷	5
○ COF Ribolla Gialla '09	🍷	5

Tenuta Beltrame

FRAZ. PRIVANO
LOC. ANTONINI, 4
33050 BAGNARIA ARSA [UD]
TEL. 0432923670
www.tenutabeltrame.it

The Beltrames bought this estate, dating from the 15th century and once owned by the noble Antoninis, in 1991. Cristian Beltrame has beautifully restored it to its former glory. The long-aged wines are always exciting and the '09 Friulano is fruit-forward and powerful.

○ Friuli Aquileia Friulano '09	🍷🍷	4*
○ Friuli Aquileia Chardonnay Pribus '07	🍷	4
● Friuli Aquileia Merlot Ris. '06	🍷	4
● Tazzelenghe '06	🍷	4

Bidoli

FRAZ. ARCANO SUPERIORE
VIA FORNACE, 19
33030 RIVE D'ARCANO [UD]
TEL. 0432810796
www.bidolivini.com

Set up in 1924 by Alessandro Bidoli and currently managed by his grandchildren Arrigo and Margherita, who in 2002 turned Fornas dai Fradis, one of the region's oldest brick furnaces, into a new cellar. Best of the range is the excellently typed, tangily fresh Sauvignon '09.

○ Friuli Grave Sauvignon '09	🍷🍷	4*
● Friuli Grave Merlot Briccolo '07	🍷	4
○ Friuli Grave Pinot Grigio '09	🍷	3
● Friuli Grave Refosco P. R. Fornâs '06	🍷	4

Blason

VIA ROMA, 32
34072 GRADISCA D'ISONZO [GO]
TEL. 048192414
www.blasonwines.com

In their 18th-century residence at Gradisca d'Isonzo, Giovanni Blason combines his youthful enthusiasm with his father Augusto's experience. Their range maintains a good standard of quality. Well defined, uncomplicated and whistle-clean, Blason wines taste deliciously authentic.

● Friuli Isonzo Merlot '09	🍷	4
○ Friuli Isonzo Pinot Grigio '09	🍷	4
○ Malvasia '09	🍷	4

Borgo Magredo

LOC. TAURIANO
VIA BASALDELLA, 5
33090 SPILIMBERGO [PN]
TEL. 0422864511
www.borgomagredo.it

Borgo Magredo, set up in 1973 at Tauriano near Spilimbergo, stays true to the heritage of Grave del Friuli. Part of the Le Tenute di Genagricola group, the cellar turns out about a million bottles a year of well-made, unpretentious wines with genuine varietal stamping. At affordable prices.

○ Friuli Grave Chardonnay '09	🍷🍷	3*
○ Friuli Grave Sauvignon '09	🍷🍷	3*
○ Friuli Grave Friulano '09	🍷	3
● Friuli Grave Refosco P. R. '09	🍷	3

OTHER WINERIES

Emilio Bulfon

FRAZ. VALERIANO
VIA ROMA, 4
33094 PINZANO AL TAGLIAMENTO [PN]
TEL. 0432950061
www.bulfon.it

The Bulfon estate covers nine hectares in the hill country of Pordenone, planted exclusively to native varieties saved from almost certain extinction. The wines are genuine, uncomplicated and absolutely intriguing as they tell the story of another Friuli.

● Forgiarin '09	🍷🍷	4*
● Cianorie '09	🍷	4
● Piculit Neri '09	🍷	5
○ Ucelùt '09	🍷	5

Ca' Ronesca

LOC. LONZANO
CASALI ZORUTTI, 2
34070 DOLEGNA DEL COLLIO [GO]
TEL. 048160034
www.caronesca.it

Ca' Ronesca, set up in 1972 by Alcide Setten, has had a shot in the arm recently with the arrival of manager Claudio Tomadin and Trento-born oenologist Clizia Zambiasi, both young but with serious wine experience. There's plenty of energy in the air.

○ Collio Bianco Marnà '06	🍷🍷	5
○ Collio Pinot Grigio '09	🍷	4
○ Collio Ribolla Gialla '09	🍷	4
○ Collio Sauvignon Blanc '09	🍷	5

Paolo Caccese

LOC. PRADIS, 6
34071 CORMÒNS [GO]
TEL. 048161062
www.paolocaccese.com

Paolo Caccese's winery was set up at Cormòns in the 1950s by his father, an engineer with a huge passion for winemaking. Paolo's wines, like the subtly floral '09 Pinot Bianco, are renowned for their coherence and typicality.

○ Collio Pinot Bianco '09	🍷🍷	5*
● Collio Merlot '08	🍷	4
○ Collio Müller Thurgau '09	🍷	5
○ Collio Pinot Grigio '09	🍷	5

Cadibon

VIA CASALI GALLO, 1
33040 CORNO DI ROSAZZO [UD]
TEL. 0432759316
www.cadibon.com

Gianni Bon's family winery at Corno di Rosazzo has ten hectares in three DOCs: Colli Orientali, Grave and Colli. The '08 Refosco P.R. is straightforward but nicely savoury. Gianni's '09 Sauvignon from Grave is assertive and very varietal.

● COF Refosco P. R. '08	🍷🍷	4*
○ Friuli Grave Sauvignon '09	🍷🍷	4*
○ COF Pinot Grigio '09	🍷	4
○ COF Ribolla Gialla '09	🍷	4

Castello di Buttrio

VIA MORPURGO, 9
33042 BUTTRIO [UD]
TEL. 0432673015
www.castellodibuttrio.it

Castello di Buttrio, managed in the Colli Orientali del Friuli by Alessandra Felluga, daughter of the great Marco, specializes in serious wines from native grapes. Mille e una Botte '08 is deliciously sweet and the '09 Sauvignon is hews very much to type, showing juicy and cohesive.

○ COF Dolce Mille e una Botte '08	🍷🍷	4
○ COF Sauvignon '09	🍷🍷	5
○ COF Bianco Mon Blanc '09	🍷	4
○ COF Friulano '09	🍷	5

Castello di Rubbia

FRAZ. SAN MICHELE DEL CARSO
GORNJI VRH, 40
34070 SAVOGNA D'ISONZO [GO]
TEL. 0481882681
www.castellodirubbia.it

Castello di Rubbia draws on a wine heritage that goes back to the 16th century and the noble Egg family. Today at San Michele del Carso, Nata?a ?ernic manages 13 hectares. The Malvasia Leonard '07 is stunning. Concentration and butter-like aromas precede almost salty depth.

○ Leonard Malvasia '07	🍷🍷	6
● Terrano '08	🍷🍷	5

OTHER WINERIES

Duca Catemario di Quadri
LOC. GRAMOGLIANO
VIA DEL BARBARESCO, 11
33040 CORNO DI ROSAZZO [UD]
TEL. 0432753222
catemario@catemariowines.it

We were tasting Duca Catemario di Quadri wines for the first time. The winery is at Corno di Rosazzo in Colli Orientali del Friuli but there are also vines in Collio Goriziano. The subtle Sauvignon '09 gives white peaches and Cuccanea '09 is from friulano, pinot bianco and sauvignon.

○ Collio Sauvignon '09	🍷🍷	4
● COF Refosco P. R. '09	🍷	4
○ Collio Bianco Cuccanea '09	🍷	4
○ Collio Pinot Grigio '09	🍷	4

Colli di Poianis
VIA POIANIS, 34A
33040 PREPOTTO [UD]
TEL. 0432713185
www.collidipoianis.com

In 1991, Danilo and Gabriele Marinig made their father Paolino's dream come true. Today, Colli di Poianis farms 11 superb hectares under vine at Prepotto. The slightly rustic '09 Friulano is a punchy yet soft expression of its territory.

○ COF Friulano '09	🍷🍷	4*
○ COF Pinot Grigio '09	🍷	4
● COF Rosso Ronco della Poiana '08	🍷	5
● COF Schioppettino '09	🍷	6

Gianpaolo Colutta
VIA ORSARIA, 32A
33044 MANZANO [UD]
TEL. 0432510654
www.coluttagianpaolo.com

Giampaolo Colutta's Colli Orientali del Friuli estate has vineyards at Buttrio, Manzano and Premariacco for a total of about 30 hectares. Helping Giampaolo is his daughter Elisabetta. Their pleasingly varietal '05 Pignolo and fragrantly drinkable '09 Ribolla Gialla are great.

● COF Pignolo '05	🍷🍷	8
○ COF Ribolla Gialla '09	🍷🍷	4*
○ COF Picolit '08	🍷	7
○ COF Riesling '09	🍷	4

I Comelli
L.GO A.DIAZ, 8
33045 NIMIS [UD]
TEL. 0432790685
www.icomelli.com

The Comellis – Alessandro, Livia and their three children – run an agriturismo as well as their cellar so you can taste the wines with Friulian food in two very comfortable dining rooms. Ramandolo Ronc de Madalene '06 is refined, mouthfilling and delicious.

○ Ramandolo Ronc de Madalene '06	🍷🍷
○ COF Friulano '09	🍷
○ COF Pinot Grigio '09	🍷
○ Ramandolo '09	🍷

Crastin
LOC. RUTTARS, 33
34070 DOLEGNA DEL COLLIO [GO]
TEL. 0481630310

Sergio Collarig grows his grapes on the hills at Ruttars, in the Collio Goriziano on the border with Slovenia. He also runs the lovely Crastin farmstay estate. Wine quality is rising steadily. Look out for the varietal, sea salt-veined Ribolla Gialla.

○ Collio Ribolla Gialla '09	🍷🍷	4*
○ Collio Friulano '09	🍷	4
● Collio Merlot '08	🍷	4
○ Collio Pinot Grigio '09	🍷	4

Le Due Torri
LOC. VICINALE DEL JUDRIO
VIA SAN MARTINO, 19
33040 CORNO DI ROSAZZO [UD]
TEL. 0432759150
www.le2torri.com

Antonino Volpe has eight hectares of high-density vines in a sunny, well-ventilated part of the Grave del Friuli DOC. This year's Friulano is a masterpiece of penetrating, aniseed-laced typicality with a sound, savoury palate and good length.

○ Friuli Grave Friulano '09	🍷🍷	3*
○ Friuli Grave Sauvignon '09	🍷🍷	3*
○ Friuli Grave Chardonnay '09	🍷	3
● Pinot Nero '08	🍷	4

OTHER WINERIES

I Feudi di Romans
LOC. PIERIS
VIA CÀ DEL BOSCO, 16
34075 SAN CANZIAN D'ISONZO [GO]
TEL. 048176445
www.ifeudi.it

The estate has 160 hectares under vine, which are scheduled to grow in future. Severino Lorenzon set up the operation in the 1950s, Enzo continued and today Davide and Nicola lend a hand. The whites are impeccably typed, especially the crisp, upfront '09 Friulano.

○ Friuli Isonzo Friulano '09	🍷🍷	4
○ Friuli Aquileia Traminer Aromatico '09	🍷	4
○ Friuli Isonzo Pinot Grigio '09	🍷	4
○ Ribolla Gialla '09	🍷	4

Foffani
FRAZ. CLAUIANO
P.ZZA GIULIA, 13
33050 TRIVIGNANO UDINESE [UD]
TEL. 0432999584
www.foffani.it

Foffani dates from the 16th century and looks onto the square of the medieval village of Clauiano, just north of Aquileia on the Friulian plains. Giovanni and Elisabetta are the current incumbents. The intrigue TerVinum '09 is from merlot fermented off the skins and is well worth uncorking.

○ Friuli Aquileia Friulano '09	🍷	4
● Friuli Aquileia Merlot Ris. '06	🍷	4
○ Friuli Aquileia Pinot Grigio '09	🍷	4
○ Tervinum Bianco '09	🍷	5*

Forchir
FRAZ. FELETTIS
VIA CODROIPO, 18
33050 BICINICCO [UD]
TEL. 042796037
www.forchir.it

The Forchir philosophy is all there in the winery logo: Viticoltori in Friuli. The "grape growers in Friuli" have 220 low environmental impact hectares in three parts of Grave. The whites, particularly Pinot Bianco Campo dei Gelsi '09, are excellent.

○ Friuli Grave Pinot Bianco Campo dei Gelsi '09	🍷🍷	4*
○ Friuli Grave Sauvignon L'Altro '09	🍷	4
○ Friuli Grave Traminer Aromatico Glere '09	🍷	4

Conti Formentini
VIA OSLAVIA, 5
34070 SAN FLORIANO DEL COLLIO [GO]
TEL. 0481884131
www.contiformentini.it

Founded in 1520 at San Floriano del Collio, Conti Formentini is now part of Gruppo Italiano Vini, which has entrusted winemaking to Marco Del Piccolo. Furlanà means "speaking Friulian(o)" and evokes the typicality of the grape, as does the name Raiade (sunbeam) for Ribolla Gialla.

○ Collio Friulano Furlana '09	🍷🍷	4*
○ Collio Ribolla Gialla Raiade '09	🍷🍷	4*
○ Collio Chardonnay '09	🍷	4
○ Collio Pinot Grigio '09	🍷	4

Fossa Mala
V. BASSI 81
33080 FIUME VENETO [PN]
TEL. 0434957997
www.fossamala.it

At their villa at Fossa Mala near Fiume Veneto, nestling among the Grave vineyards, the Roncadin family have taken their vine stock from the initial six hectares to today's 30. The reds in particular offer complex aromatics and well-crafted personalities.

● Friuli Grave Cabernet Sauvignon '08	🍷🍷	4
● Friuli Grave Merlot '08	🍷🍷	4
● Friuli Grave Refosco P.R. '08	🍷	4
○ Friuli Grave Sauvignon '09	🍷	3

Jacùss
FRAZ. MONTINA
V.LE KENNEDY, 35A
33040 TORREANO [UD]
TEL. 0432715147
www.jacuss.com

Brothers Sandro and Andrea Jacuzzi work in tandem at their small property in Montina, at Torreano di Cividale in the Colli Orientali del Friuli. For many years, they have turned out unpretentious, beautifully typed wines that are paragons of sincerity.

● COF Cabernet Sauvignon '06	🍷	4
○ COF Friulano '09	🍷	4
○ COF Picolit '06	🍷	7
○ COF Verduzzo Friulano '06	🍷	5

Lupinc

FRAZ. PREPOTTO, 11B
34011 DUINO AURISINA [TS]
TEL. 040200848

Prepotto near Duino Aurisina stands on the sunny, wind-swept stone and earth of the Carso tableland. Matej Lupinc could see that these were the ingredients needed to make great wine and in 1970, he was the first to bottle it. The wines are genuine, clean, refined, aroma-rich and edged with salt.

○ Carso Malvasia '08	🍷🍷	4*
○ Carso Vitovska '08	🍷🍷	4*
○ Stara Brajda '08	🍷🍷	4*

Piera Martellozzo

VIA PORDENONE, 33
33080 SAN QUIRINO [PN]
TEL. 0434963100
www.martellozzo.com

The art of selection is part of Piera Martellozzo's family heritage. In her ongoing search for authenticity, her bold choices have taken her into the world of serious winemaking. Originally from Veneto, she found a second home, and the farmers to tend her rows, in Friuli.

○ Friuli Grave Dolce Fiola '09	🍷	4
● Friuli Grave Refosco P.R. '09	🍷	3
○ Friuli Grave Sauvignon '09	🍷	3
● Friuli Grave Tabbor '08	🍷	5

Micossi

LOC. SEDILIS
VIA NIMIS, 20
33017 TARCENTO [UD]
TEL. 0432783276
www.vignetimicossi.it

The Micossi family has run the estate now managed by Walter Revelant for three generations. There are only two and half hectares in the hills at Tarcento and Nimis, where the grapes are part-dried, and in the case of Ramandolo Late Harvest picked late.

○ COF Picolit '08	🍷🍷	6
○ Ramandolo Late Harvest '08	🍷🍷	6
● Schioppettino '08	🍷	5

Obiz

B.GO GORTANI, 2
33052 CERVIGNANO DEL FRIULI [UD]
TEL. 043131900
www.obiz.it

In 1997, Yunmani Bergamasco took over the Obiz farm estate near Aquileia. The first move was to restructure to boost the quality of production and the wines are now more than decent, the easy-drinking '08 Refosco showing ripe, smoky and deep on the nose.

○ Friuli Aquileia Friulano Tampia '09	🍷	4
● Friuli Aquileia Merlot Popone '08	🍷	4
○ Friuli Aquileia Pinot Grigio Fulvia Crescentina '09	🍷	3
● Friuli Aquileia Refosco P.R. Teodoro '08	🍷	4

Perusini

LOC. GRAMOGLIANO
VIA TORRIONE, 13
33040 CORNO DI ROSAZZO [UD]
TEL. 0432675018
www.perusini.com

I vigneti dell'azienda Perusini si estendono sui vocatissimi colli di Gramogliano, Rosazzo e Rocca Bernarda. È un'azienda storica per i Colli Orientali del Friuli, ed ora è affidata alla gestione di Teresa Perusini. La Ribolla Gialla '09 è fresca e agrumata. Il Cabernet Sauvignon '08 è lineare, semplice ma estremamente piacevole.
NON C'È IN DB

● COF Cabernet Sauvignon '08	🍷🍷	5
○ COF Ribolla Gialla '09	🍷🍷	4*
● COF Cabernet Franc '08	🍷	5
○ COF Chardonnay '09	🍷	4

Piè di Mont

LOC. PIEDIMONTE
VIA MONTE CALVARIO, 30
34170 GORIZIA
TEL. 0481391338
www.piedimont.it

Last time, we praised the fine debut by Roman Rizzi when we gave his classic method spumante high marks. Well, he's done it again, and this time the marks are even higher.

○ Piè di Mont Brut '07	🍷🍷	7

OTHER WINERIES

Pighin
FRAZ. RISANO
V.LE GRADO, 1
33050 PAVIA DI UDINE [UD]
TEL. 0432675444
www.pighin.com

Azienda fondata nel 1963 a Risano, nelle Grave del Friuli, integrata poi con 30 ettari sul Collio Goriziano. Dal 2004 è gestita totalmente da Fernando Pighin con la moglie Danila ed i figli Roberto e Raffaela. Il Villa Agricola Riserva '04 è balsamico, articolato, ha gran carattere. Il Friulano '09 è fruttato, integro e salmastro.

NON C'È IN DB

○ Friuli Grave Friulano '09	🍷🍷	4
● Friuli Grave Refosco P. R. '07	🍷🍷	4
● Friuli Grave Rosso Villa Agricola Ris. '04	🍷🍷	5
○ Collio Ribolla Gialla '09	🍷	4

Tenuta Pinni
VIA SANT'OSVALDO, 3
33098 SAN MARTINO AL TAGLIAMENTO [PN]
TEL. 0434899464
www.tenutapinni.com

Tenuta Pinni has deep roots in western Friuli. Brothers Francesco and Roberto personally supervise the vines and vinification in the cellars, dating from 1687. The upfront, well-typed whites are great value for money.

○ Chardonnay '09	🍷🍷	4*
○ Friuli Grave Friulano '09	🍷🍷	4*
○ Sauvignon '09	🍷🍷	4*
○ Pinot Grigio '09	🍷	3

Denis Pizzulin
BROLO,43
33040 PREPOTTO [UD]
TEL. 0432713425
www.pizzulin.com

Denis Pizzulin looks after 11 hectares of vines on the hills at Prepotto. His Guide debut comes with an intriguing, mouthfilling '06 Schioppettino Riserva. Rarisolchi '09 from pinot bianco and sauvignon gives aniseed and gooseberries with a juicy palate and the evocative '09 Friulano is nicely typed.

○ COF Friulano '09	🍷🍷	4
○ COF Rarisolchi Bianco '09	🍷🍷	4
● COF Schioppettino Ris. '06	🍷🍷	4
● COF Merlot '09	🍷	4

Plozner
VIA DELLE PRESE, 19
33097 SPILIMBERGO [PN]
TEL. 04272902
www.plozner.it

The winery founded by Lisio Plozner on the plains at Spilimbergo is now run by his granddaughter, wine woman Sabina Maffei, who acknowledges the courage of her forebear in planting vines on this stony terrain. Now, she is grateful. Granddad was right.

○ Friuli Grave Friulano '09	🍷🍷	4*
○ Moscabianca '09	🍷🍷	4*
● Friuli Grave Refosco P. R. '07	🍷	4
○ Friuli Grave Sauvignon '09	🍷	4

Polje
LOC. NOVALI, 11
34071 CORMÒNS [GO]
TEL. 047160660
www.conubia.com

The Polje winery at Novali, near Cormòns, has 12 hectares on a slope facing south east. The name comes from "polje", the Slovene name for the "dolina" sinkholes of the Carso plateau and Collio Goriziano. The '09 Friulano is crisp, juicy and lemony while the '09 Ribolla is all freshness.

○ Collio Friulano '09	🍷🍷	4
○ Collio Ribolla Gialla '09	🍷🍷	4
○ Collio Sauvignon '09	🍷	4
● Refosco P.R. '08	🍷	4

Teresa Raiz
LOC. MARSURE DI SOTTO
VIA DELLA ROGGIA, 22
33040 POVOLETTO [UD]
TEL. 0432679556
www.teresaraiz.it

Teresa Raiz was the grandmother of Paolo Tosolini, who now manages 15 hectares under vine in an excellently aspected location on the border of the Grave and Colli Orientali DOCs. Sovrey '08, from chardonnay, sauvignon and picolit, is redolent of caramel and delicious in the mouth.

○ Chardonnay Le Marsure '09	🍷🍷	4*
○ Sovrej '08	🍷🍷	4*
○ COF Pinot Grigio '09	🍷	4
○ COF Ribolla Gialla '09	🍷	4

Roncada

loc. Roncada, 5
34071 Cormòns [GO]
tel. 048161394
www.roncada.34x.com

Documents mention Roncada in the Collio Goriziano in 1882, when the lovely residence was built. In 1956, it was purchased by the Mattioni family and today has 25 hectares under vine. The '09 Ribolla Gialla and Friulano, and the '07 Merlot, impressed us.

○ Collio Friulano '09	4*
● Collio Merlot '07	5
○ Collio Ribolla Gialla '09	4*

Ronchi Rò delle Fragole

loc. Cime di Dolegna, 12
34070 Dolegna del Collio [GO]
tel. 0481639897
ronchiro.vini@tiscali.it

Ronchi Rò delle Fragole is a tiny operation on the slopes of Dolegna, in Collio. Since 2005, Romeo Rossi has patiently recovered the vineyards of friulano and sauvignon planted more than 30 years ago. Both wines are terroir-driven and deliciously fresh.

○ Collio Friulano '09	5
○ Collio Sauvignon '09	5

Ronco dei Folo

33020 Prepotto [UD]
tel. 055859811
www.tenutefolonari.com

Ronco dei Folo is the Friulian outpost of Ambrogio and Giovanni Folonari Tenute, a family active in wine since the late 18th century. Carefully selected Collio fruit goes into wines that reflect their territory to perfection.

○ Collio Pinot Grigio '09	4
○ Collio Ribolla Gialla '09	4
○ Collio Sauvignon '09	4
○ Collio Friulano '09	4

Ronco dei Pini

via Ronchi, 93
33040 Prepotto [UD]
tel. 0432713239
www.roncodeipini.it

Set up in 1969 by Giuseppe and Claudio Novello, Ronco dei Pini is based at Prepotto in the Colli Orientali del Friuli DOC but also owns vineyards at Zegla, in Collio Goriziano. We particularly liked the '07 Schioppettino, a well-typed, balsamic wine with plenty of vigour on the savoury palate.

● COF Schioppettino '07	5
○ Collio Sauvignon '09	4
○ Verduzzo Friulano Riccovino '08	6
○ Collio Chardonnay '09	4

Rubini

loc. Spessa
via Case Rubini, 1
33043 Cividale del Friuli [UD]
tel. 0432716141
www.villarubini.it

Villa Rubini is several centuries old but "only" started making wine in 1814. Leone and Rosa Rubini now have a tight-knit family team backed by oenologist Dimitri Pintar. The '09 Friulano is marvellously typed while the '08 Refosco dal Peduncolo Rosso is poised and structured.

○ COF Friulano '09	4*
● COF Refosco P.R. '08	4*
○ COF Pinot Grigio '09	4
● COF Rosso Anno Domini 1814 '07	5

San Simone

loc. Rondover
via Prata, 30
33080 Porcia [PN]
tel. 0434578633
www.sansimone.it

San Simone's quality has been appreciated for many years. Experimentation and tradition have always been the two mainstays of the Brisotto family. Refosco Re Sugano '08 is complex, sustained and satisfyingly spicy.

● Friuli Grave Refosco Re Sugano '08	4
● Friuli Grave Cabernet Franc Sugano '08	4
○ Friuli Grave Pinot Grigio '09	3
○ Friuli Grave Sauvignon '09	3

OTHER WINERIES

Sara e Sara
LOC. SAVORGNANO DEL TORRE
DEI MONTI, 5
33040 POVOLETTO [UD]
TEL. 0432666365
www.saraesara.com

Alessandro Sara's small family winery uses traditional methods, such as rack drying for grapes and vinification without filtration to ensure the soundness of the wines. Crei '08 is from verduzzo with a dash of botrytized friulano and sauvignon. Sheer delight.

○ COF Verduzzo Friulano Crei '08	5
○ COF Picolit '06	6
○ COF Friulano '08	4
● COF Rosso Il Rio Falcone '06	5

Scarbolo
FRAZ. LAUZACCO
V.LE GRADO, 4
33050 PAVIA DI UDINE [UD]
TEL. 0432675612
www.scarbolo.com

Valter Scarbolo likes to think of himself as a Friulian grape grower. He tends 25 hectares on the right bank of the Torre river in the Friulian flatlands. We very much liked the Refosco '06 and the current release of Friulano, as well as Pinot Grigio Ramato XL and the My Time white blend.

○ Friuli Grave Friulano '09	4*
● Friuli Grave Refosco P. R. '06	4*
○ Bianco My Time '07	4
○ Friuli Grave Pinot Grigio Ramato XL '08	4

Ferruccio Sgubin
VIA MERNICO, 8
34070 DOLEGNA DEL COLLIO [GO]
TEL. 048160452
info@ferrucciosgubin.it

The small family winery set up in 1960 by Ferruccio Sgubin at Mernico, Dolegna, on the border with Slovenia, is a haven of wind-tousled peace. The wines are of a piece, showing fresh, fragrant, well typed and true to their terroir.

○ Collio Friulano '09	4
○ Collio Pinot Bianco '09	4
○ Collio Ribolla Gialla '09	4
● Schioppettino '07	5

Skerlj
VIA SALES, 44
34010 SGONICO [TS]
TEL. 040229253
www.agriturismoskerlj.com

The winery at Sales on the Carso is where in 1965 Matej and Kristina Skerlj opened an "osmizza", a farm shop that today is a comfortable agriturismo. They use long macerations to make their concentrated, juicy, tannin and aroma-rich wines.

○ Malvasia '07	5
● Terrano '07	5
○ Vitovska '07	5

F.lli Stanig
VIA ALBANA, 44
33040 PREPOTTO [UD]
TEL. 0432713234
www.stanig.it

We are at Albana, near Prepotto in the Colli Orientali, where the Stanig estate has nine hectares. Federico and Francesco follow the example of grandfather Giuseppe with youthful enthusiasm. The wines did well, confirming their quality.

○ COF Malvasia Istriana '09	4*
● COF Merlot '07	4*
● COF Schioppettino '08	5*
○ COF Friulano '09	4

Terre di Ger
FRAZ. FRATTINA
S.DA DELLA MEDUNA, 17
33076 PRAVISDOMINI [PN]
TEL. 0434644452
www.terrediger.it

The Spinazzè family's lovely estate is in western Friuli. The cellar is modern and the rows stand on moderately loose, calcium-rich limestone between the villages of Chions and Frattina. Fruit and estery fragrances introduce a savoury, well-sustained palate on the '08 Merlot.

● Friuli Grave Merlot '08	3*
● El Masut '07	5
● Friuli Grave Cabernet Franc '08	3
○ Limine '08	5

Vidussi

VIA SPESSA, 18
34071 CAPRIVA DEL FRIULI [GO]
TEL. 048180072
www.vinimontresor.it

Vidussi is owned by the Montresor family. Most of the vines are in the Collio Goriziano, on the slopes from Capriva to Cormòns, and on to Rocca Bernarda. The expert Luigino De Giuseppe is in charge of winemaking and the excellent range reflects the varieties it is obtained from.

○ Collio Traminer Aromatico '09	🍷🍷	4*
○ COF Picolit Nato in Vigna '09	🍷	4
○ Collio Sauvignon '09	🍷	4
● Ribolla Nera o Schioppettino '09	🍷	4

Vigne Fantin Noda'r

LOC. ORSARIA
VIA CASALI OTTELIO, 4
33040 PREMARIACCO [UD]
TEL. 043428735
www.fantinnodar.it

Attilio Pignat bought Le Vigne Fantin Noda'r in 1991. The vines extend from the slopes of Buttrio towards Manzano and Premariacco, in Colli Orientali del Friuli. Top of the very respectable range is a tangy, gutsy Chardonnay '09.

○ COF Chardonnay '09	🍷🍷	4*
● COF Cabernet Sauvignon '09	🍷	4
○ COF Friulano '09	🍷	4
○ COF Ribolla Gialla '09	🍷	4

Villa de Puppi

VIA ROMA, 5
33040 MOIMACCO [UD]
TEL. 0432722461
www.depuppi.it

Count Luigi De Puppi owns the estate run by his children, Caterina and Valfredo. Most of the vines are at the estate's country house at Moimacco, but the holding includes ten more hectares in the hills of Rosazzo in the Colli Orientali. Tai Blanc is a fresh, well-typed and beautifully poised '09 Friulano.

○ Taj Blanc '09	🍷🍷	4*
● Cabernet '08	🍷	4
○ Sauvignon '09	🍷	4

Franco Visintin

VIA ROMA, 37
34072 GRADISCA D'ISONZO [GO]
TEL. 048199974

The quality of Franco Visintin's wines, his likeability and hospitality to all visitors keeps customers flocking to the cellar door in Gradisca d'Isonzo. The '09 Sauvignon and Chardonnay are the top whites while Franco's best red is Stàngja '06.

○ Friuli Isonzo Chardonnay '09	🍷🍷	4*
○ Friuli Isonzo Sauvignon '09	🍷🍷	4*
● Stàngja Rosso '06	🍷🍷	4*
● Friuli Isonzo Merlot '07	🍷	4

Maurizio Zaccomer

VIA SEDILIS, 31
33045 NIMIS [UD]
TEL. 0432790234
www.vinizaccomer.com

In the 1960s, Valentino Zaccomer created the winery that his son Maurizio runs with a special passion for Ramandolo, constantly improving grape-drying techniques and the use of wood for ageing. The '07 Ramandolo Settimo Cielo (Seventh Heaven) lives up to it name.

○ Ramandolo Settimo Cielo '07	🍷🍷
○ COF Picolit '07	🍷🍷
● COF Pignolo '07	🍷
○ Ribolla Gialla Brut	🍷

Zaglia

LOC. FRASSINUTTI
VIA CRESCENZA, 10
33050 PRECENICCO [UD]
TEL. 0431510320
www.zaglia.com

Giorgio Zaglia farms about 30 hectares between the Stella and Tagliamento rivers at Precenicco, in the Latisana DOC. His '09 Friulano is a medley of fruit and flowers, drinking long and slightly salty. Balsam on the nose and a rich, slightly astringent palate sum up the '08 Refosco.

○ Friuli Latisana Friulano '09	🍷🍷	3
● Friuli Latisana Refosco P.R. '08	🍷🍷	3
● Friuli Latisana Cabernet Franc Ris. '04	🍷	4
● Friuli Latisana Merlot '09	🍷	3

EMILIA ROMAGNA

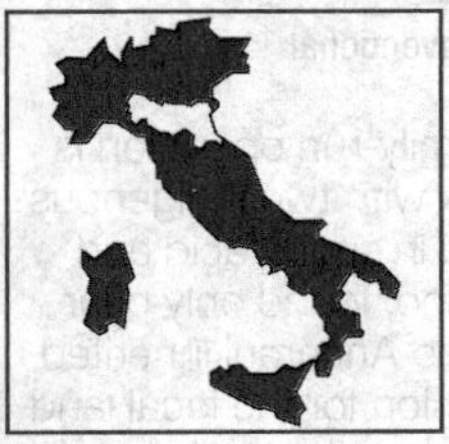

Emilia Romagna's Three Glasses awards failed to grow but the region is growing in the complexity of its wines, in interpreting its terroirs consistently and in establishing the language in which to express them. In the Colli Piacentini, La Stoppa strengthens its role as leader. It has never compromised the expressivity of its wines and has become the go-to operation for those searching for ways to express the character of these hills. Unfortunately, Piacenza still harbours too many wines that are overly technical or warped to fit presumed market imperatives, losing originality and gaining nothing in return. But producers here are slow to digest this lesson and the world of wine will be slow to turn its gaze here as long as the wines seem so stateless. Even the most traditional wines are often weak, one good example being a near-complete dearth of good Gutturnio Frizzantes. Barattieri's Vin Santo Albarola Val di Nure '00 signals that the Piacenza tradition of sweet wines is alive and well, here made with the oldest yeast mother in Italy, dating back to 1823. The Vin Santo of Vigoleno, in this edition for the first time, is also part of this tradition. The fine world of Emilia Lambrusco, though hit with a difficult vintage, merits its two Three Glasses and proves that serious commitment will bring excellent results. The producers who are taking their lead from their vineyards demonstrate that this is the key to high quality and an understanding of terroirs and of their diversity is fuelling a heartening local renewal. Colli Bolognesi producers are struggling to find the measure of their area, hampered by deteriorating results from the international grapes and by the growers' inability to study their wines for expressivity. Thus we see wines that are too formal, with little originality, dictated by formulas that ignore terroir. Romagna is in a growth phase, its wines showing more of a common character. Studies of soils and environments are revealing more every year. Results are not uniform but the general direction is clearly visible. The historic milestone is the award of Three Glasses to a Sangiovese Superiore, Villa Venti's Primo Segno '08, a first for a wine viewed as simple, a Sangiovese outside the Riserva category, and all that designation implies. Primo Segno comes from organic farming and winemaking tailored to the variety. Three Glasses go for the first time to an Albana Secco, too, Il Codronchio '08, re-opening the issue of this difficult but talented grape, with credible results until now only in sweet and passito versions. One of those sweet versions did in fact win the prestigious award of Sweet of the Year: Fattoria Zerbina's Albana di Romagna Passito Riserva AR '06. It's an extreme wine, born of years of hard work and quite extraordinary sensitivity.

Altavita - Fattoria dei Gessi

via Tranzano, 820
47023 Cesena [FC]
tel. 0547645996
www.altavita-wine.com

CELLAR SALES

ANNUAL PRODUCTION 20,000 bottles
HECTARES UNDER VINE 20
VITICULTURE METHOD Conventional

Altavita marries diverse careers and promotion of the local area, a shared passion of Cesena-based partners Enrico Giunchi, Maurizio Fuzzi and Stefania Migani. Agronomist Alessandro Giunchi, Enrico's brother, signed on as well. They produce two Sangioveses and a white, sourced from the partners' vineyards. The grapes are selected according to quality levels and terroir: some clayey soils, others looser and higher up, still others that show chalk, all located between Cesena and Saiano.

The project took off at a quick pace and we note a further step up in their overall quality. Tempora '07 competed in our finals. Glossy and elegant, with focused fruit and silky tannins, it would be smashing if shorn of some over-technical bits and had a tad more tautness. Evoca '08 displays enviable coherence and lean, ultra-elegant sinew. Sauvignon blanc, albana and trebbiano balance nicely in the citrussy, herbaceous Diapente '09, which fills but stays light on its feet. A lovely vein of acidity keeps the sweetness well in check in Solesia '08, pleasantly rustic and a classic of its kind.

● Sangiovese di Romagna Sup. Tempora Ris. '07	▼▼	5
○ Albana di Romagna Passito Solesia '08	▼▼	6
○ Diapente '09	▼▼	4
● Sangiovese di Romagna Sup. Evoca '08	▼▼	4
● Sangiovese di Romagna Sup. Evoca '07	▽▽	4*
● Sangiovese di Romagna Sup. Tempora Ris. '06	▽▽	5

Ancarani

via San Biagio Antico, 14
48018 Faenza [RA]
tel. 0546642162
www.viniancarani.it

CELLAR SALES
PRE-BOOKED VISITS
FOOD

ANNUAL PRODUCTION 30,000 bottles
HECTARES UNDER VINE 14
VITICULTURE METHOD Conventional

This modest-sized family-run operation is doing invaluable work with two indigenous varieties, albana, high in sugar, acid and tannin, and centesimino, found only near Faenza. Young Claudio Ancarani inherited his grandfather's passion for the local land and vineyards and he has thrown himself into a principled and committed promotion of his local area and its culture.

Uvappesa '08 is a red passito from centesimino. It shows classic aromas of rose petal and elderflower, with a dash of white pepper to give a pungent edge to tasty candied fruit. Equally fine is the dry version of the grape, Sâvignon Rosso '09, the local dialect name for centesimino. Its crisp-contoured nose hews to typicality, avoiding any flabby sweetness. Albana Santa Lusa '08 displays impressive thrust and self-confident tannins. Biagio Antico '09 is a fruity Sangiovese with a bright, supple mouth. Contrary perhaps to initial impressions, it makes a complex statement about the performance of sangiovese in the first line of hills.

○ Albana di Romagna Santa Lusa '08	▼▼	4
● Sangiovese di Romagna Biagio Antico Sup. '09	▼▼	4
● Sâvignon Rosso '09	▼▼	4
● Uvappesa '08	▼▼	4
○ Albana di Romagna Perlagioia '07	▽▽	4
○ Albana di Romagna Santa Lusa '07	▽▽	4
● Sangiovese di Romagna Biagio Antico Sup. '08	▽▽	4
● Sâvignon Rosso '08	▽▽	4
● Uvappesa '07	▽▽	4

Antica Corte Pallavicina

VIA SBRISI, 2
43010 POLESINE PARMENSE [PR]
TEL. 054296136
www.acpallavicina.com

CELLAR SALES
PRE-BOOKED VISITS
ROOMS AND FOOD

ANNUAL PRODUCTION 10,000 bottles
HECTARES UNDER VINE 4
VITICULTURE METHOD Conventional

A celebrated culatello sausage is but one part of the multi-faceted agricultural world of Antica Corte Pallavicina, which also includes a hotel and a restaurant. The four-hectare vineyard is dedicated to the revival of Fortana, the iconic wine of an area whose past production was either consumed locally or went to Cremona, through a port on the Po quite close to Corte itself. The wines of Massimo and Luciano Spigaroli cleave to tradition, straightforward, aromatic fellows with low alcohol and grippy acidity.

Fortana is best enjoyed in its first year, together with cold cuts, Parmesan cheese and the local wintertime dishes served in "scudlein", the still-ubiquitous local soup dishes. Metodo Classico Strologo '08 is a fine Fortana vinified off the skins and with 18 months sur lie; a bit countryish, it is nonetheless pleasingly distinctive. The ultra-aromatic Fortanella '09, made from the fortanella grape, is dry and straightforward, with good nerve and impressive drive on the palate. Fortana del Taro '09 is intriguing with a slightly sweet edge and generous dark cherry, raspberry and morello.

● Fortana del Taro '09	▼▼	3
● Fortanella '09	▼▼	3
○ Strologo Brut M. Cl. '08	▼▼	4

Ariola 1956

FRAZ. PILASTRO
LOC. CALICELLA DI PILASTRO
S.DA DELLA BUCA 5A
43010 LANGHIRANO [PR]
TEL. 0521637678
www.viniariola.it

CELLAR SALES
PRE-BOOKED VISITS
FOOD

ANNUAL PRODUCTION 600,000 bottles
HECTARES UNDER VINE 70
VITICULTURE METHOD Conventional

Marcello Ceci, after a career in wine retailing and working together with his brothers in the family's Ceci winery, finally pegged his future to wine production from his estate vineyards. In 2003, he purchased the historic Forte Rigoni Ariola, in the hills above Parma, pruned its name and launched winemaking and viticultural research. Ariola features sales of their wines along with their Casale del Groppone portfolio of agricultural products from local growers, particularly cheeses and cold cuts.

Overall, Ariola's wine line-up arouses less interest than usual. The best is the winery's classic Lambrusco, Marcello '09, one hundred per cent lambrusco maestri. It is an iconic, and appealing, representative of a specific style of Lambrusco, classic to the Parma area, and therefore full and fat, with a vein of sweetness and gobs of fruit. The all-maestri Angiol d'Or '09 is incredible value for the consumer, uncomplicated and straightforward, yet toothsome and worth more than a nod.

● Angiol d'Or Maestri in Purezza '09	▼▼	3
● Lambrusco Marcello '09	▼▼	4
● Lambrusco Gaspronero '09	▼	3
○ Forte Rigoni Malvasia Frizzante '08	▽▽	4
● Lambrusco Gaspronero '08	▽▽	3
● Lambrusco Marcello '08	▽▽	4*

Balìa di Zola

VIA CASALE, 11
47015 MODIGLIANA [FC]
TEL. 0546940577
bzolav@libero.it

CELLAR SALES
PRE-BOOKED VISITS

ANNUAL PRODUCTION 20,000 bottles
HECTARES UNDER VINE 6
VITICULTURE METHOD Conventional

Veruska Eluci purchased Balìa di Zola in 2003, then renovated the farm house, where her new winemaking cellar is now fully functioning. The largest estate vineyard, facing south to southwest, was partially replanted in 2004, with budwood from the old vines; the new vines are on their own roots, at 6,500 to the hectare. The winery still boasts some old vineyards, such as a one-hectare parcel beneath the Modigliana monastery. The soils are largely sandy marl, fairly loose-textured and rich in chalk.

The wine operation may be modest but the wines are impressively elegant, confirmed by our preview tasting of Riserva '08. Sangiovese di Romagna Balitore '09 is smashing, still youthful and spirited on the nose, then disciplined but supple in the mouth. The palate of sangiovese Redinoce '07 recovers nicely from too-heavy toast on the nose, achieving a crisp-edged elegance. Rosé Zolarosa '09, also sangiovese, offers a refreshing tang after a mineral-laced, fragrant bouquet.

● Redinoce '07	🍷🍷	5
● Sangiovese di Romagna Balitore '09	🍷🍷	4
⊙ Zolarosa Brut Rosé '09	🍷	4
● Redinoce '06	YY	5
● Redinoce '05	YY	5
● Redinoce '04	YY	5
● Sangiovese di Romagna Balitore '08	YY	4

Conte Otto Barattieri di San Pietro

VIA DEI TIGLI, 100
29020 VIGOLZONE [PC]
TEL. 0523875111
ottobarattieri@libero.it

CELLAR SALES
PRE-BOOKED VISITS

ANNUAL PRODUCTION 120,000 bottles
HECTARES UNDER VINE 34
VITICULTURE METHOD Conventional

The Barattieris were among the first to bring Piacenza's wines to the outside world in the days of the legendary semi-sparkling Sauvignon and long-serving cellarmaster Francesco Rossi. Unfortunately, the winery is currently in a slump, and Vin Santo is its only ace, sourced from the family's ancient and prestigious Mercati vineyard. But their close bond with the local terroir and that classically rustic winemaking touch could still be the cards to play for re-burnishing Piacenza's vinous heritage.

Albarola Val di Nure stands out among the rest of its teammates here, which are largely soulless. This wine was originally fermented, using traditional methods, from naturally dried malvasia di Candia aromatica grapes, and nothing has changed over nearly two centuries, including the yeast mother, which is from 1823. Albarola Val di Nure '00 lays out a cornucopia of zabaglione, cocoa powder, apricot, candied citrus, eucalyptus and tea, followed by a palate that is crisp-contoured and almost elegant when measured against the aromatic density that returns on the finish. A masterpiece, as always.

○ C. P. Vin Santo Albarola Val di Nure '00	🍷🍷🍷	8
○ C. P. Vin Santo Albarola Val di Nure '99	YYY+	8
○ C. P. Vin Santo Albarola Val di Nure '97	YYY	6
○ C. P. Vin Santo Albarola Val di Nure '96	YYY	6
○ C. P. Vin Santo Albarola Val di Nure '98	YY	8
● Il Faggio '05	YY	6

Le Barbaterre

LOC. BERGONZANO
VIA CAVOUR, 2A
42020 QUATTRO CASTELLA [RE]
TEL. 3358053454
www.barbaterre.com

CELLAR SALES

ANNUAL PRODUCTION 10,000 bottles
HECTARES UNDER VINE 9
VITICULTURE METHOD Certified organic

Barbaterre rises a stone's throw from Val d'Enza, in the first row of lovely hills that rise from Quattro Castella, right in the heart of the group of defensive fortresses erected by Matilde of Canossa. Massimo Bedogni and partner Erica have poured body and soul into the creation of this small but attractive winery. Their nine hectares of organically farmed vines, at an elevation of 350 metres, are planted in loose-textured soils rich in silt, marl and clay.

Not every wine hit the bull's-eye, but overall results are promising, displaying personality and originality. Take Sauvignon '07, an impressive non-disgorged sparkler. It shows a minerally nose, a tad sulphurous, then a dry, lean mouth that lengthens into a gorgeous, briny conclusion. The bottle-refermented Lambrusco dell'Emilia '09 shines too. Largely grasparossa with help from pinot nero, malbo gentile and salamino, it exhibits a wild, earthy edge that adds complexity to its taut brightness. Full marks to Orlando '06, a pinot nero blanc de noir whose four years sur lie yield a graceful reductive note and a rich, zippy palate.

○ Colli di Scandiano e Canossa Sauvignon '07	▼▼	3
● Lambrusco dell'Emilia '09	▼▼	3
○ Orlando '06	▼▼	3

Stefano Berti

LOC. RAVALDINO IN MONTE
VIA LA SCAGNA, 18
47100 FORLÌ
TEL. 0543488074
www.stefanoberti.com

CELLAR SALES
PRE-BOOKED VISITS

ANNUAL PRODUCTION 30,000 bottles
HECTARES UNDER VINE 8
VITICULTURE METHOD Conventional

Stefano Berti began making wine from his family's vineyards only after university but he is a grower in the strict sense, with his hands directly on the vines and winemaking. Of the winery's two terroirs, one, largely clay, faces south towards Bertinoro, and the other is a rocky, fluvial terrace above the Rabbi valley, whose exposure is not quite as favourable as its soils. Berti's two wines are both blends from various lots of fruit, selected according to the criterion of producing a top wine and a "second vin".

Calisto, sourced from an old two-hectare parcel of sangiovese, has changed course with the 2007. Once ripe, concentrated and oaky, it now shows more elegant and well defined. Although not exactly bright-edged yet, it does seem to indicate Stefano's passage from barriques to 400-litre tonneaux and the ever-decreasing role of other varieties in his Sangioveses. The mouth is ample, with admirable tannins, and the finish full-flavoured and vibrant. Ravaldo '09 is as reliable as ever.

● Sangiovese di Romagna Sup. Calisto Ris. '07	▼▼	5
● Sangiovese di Romagna Sup. Ravaldo '09	▼▼	4
● Sangiovese di Romagna Sup. Calisto '01	▽▽▽	5
● Sangiovese di Romagna Sup. Calisto '04	▽▽	5
● Sangiovese di Romagna Sup. Calisto '03	▽▽	5
● Sangiovese di Romagna Sup. Calisto Ris. '06	▽▽	5
● Sangiovese di Romagna Sup. Ravaldo '08	▽▽	4*
● Sangiovese di Romagna Sup. Ravaldo '07	▽▽	4*

Raffaella Alessandra Bissoni

loc. Casticciano
via Colecchio, 280
47032 Bertinoro [FC]
tel. 0543460382
www.vinibissoni.com

CELLAR SALES
PRE-BOOKED VISITS

ANNUAL PRODUCTION 25,000 bottles
HECTARES UNDER VINE 5
VITICULTURE METHOD Conventional

Raffaella Bissoni is determined and emotionally involved in her vineyards as only someone who spends her days working among the vine rows can be. The wines of her small operation are important ambassadors for Bertinoro and thus win recognition even beyond their inherent quality. For many years now, Raffaella has honed skills that turn out wines which are increasingly elegant and impressive, her slow, meditated progress ever more ready to capture subtleties and complexity.

The winery's five hectares are at 150 metres' elevation and the sangiovese is planted in the typical Bertinoro chalky soils. The older vineyards face north-east and north-west, the more recent plantings south. The wines demonstrate the quality of the vineyards but still lack energy in the mouth. More overall crispness, spontaneity and self-assurance would bump up the quality even higher. Vigna Collecchio '06 boasts an expressive nose and a full-flavoured, dry palate while Superiore '09 shows an impressive, taut typicality.

● Sangiovese di Romagna Sup. '09	🍷🍷	4
● Sangiovese di Romagna Sup. V. Collecchio Ris. '06	🍷🍷	5
○ Albana di Romagna Passito '06	🍷🍷	4*
○ Albana di Romagna Passito '04	🍷🍷	5
○ Albana di Romagna Passito '03	🍷🍷	4
● Sangiovese di Romagna Sup. '07	🍷🍷	4*
● Sangiovese di Romagna Sup. Ris. '06	🍷🍷	5
● Sangiovese di Romagna Sup. Ris. '05	🍷🍷	4
● Sangiovese di Romagna Sup. Ris. '04	🍷🍷	4*
● Sangiovese di Romagna Sup. Ris. '03	🍷🍷	4

Tenuta Bonzara

via San Chierlo, 37a
40050 Monte San Pietro [BO]
tel. 0516768324
www.bonzara.it

CELLAR SALES
PRE-BOOKED VISITS

ANNUAL PRODUCTION 70,000 bottles
HECTARES UNDER VINE 16
VITICULTURE METHOD Conventional

Back in 1963, Angelo Lambertini bought 100 hectares in the excellent San Chierlo di Monte San Pietro area with the goal of becoming one of the best producers in the area. He achieved that in 1975, when the legendary Luigi Veronelli recognized the superb characteristics in Bonzara's main wine, suggesting that it be called Bonzarone. Francesco Lambertini, a respected university lecturer, has directed the operation since 1986, assisted by oenologist Lorenzo Landi and by cellarmaster Mario Carboni.

Tenuta Bonzara wines, sourced from fairly high-elevation vineyards, have always stood out for their elegance. Pignoletto Vigna Antica '09 and Sauvignon Blanc Le Carrate '09 are the most impressive whites. Typicality and elegance duet nicely in the first, which leads with an unusual slaty mineral on the nose but then develops abundant fruit. Crisp, balsamic notes of tomato leaf introduce Le Carrate '09; a somewhat by-the-book palate nonetheless offers refreshing minerality. Rocca di Bonacciara '07's twelve months in barrique have left more than a trace of toasty oak but it still exudes a kind of refined charm.

○ C. B. Pignoletto Cl. V. Antica '09	🍷🍷	4
○ C. B. Sauvignon Sup. Le Carrate '09	🍷🍷	4
● C. B. Merlot Rocca di Bonacciara '07	🍷	5
● C. B. Cabernet Sauvignon Bonzarone '05	🍷🍷🍷	5
● C. B. Cabernet Sauvignon Bonzarone '97	🍷🍷🍷	5
● C. B. Cabernet Sauvignon Bonzarone '96	🍷🍷🍷	5
● C. B. Merlot Rocca di Bonacciara '95	🍷🍷🍷	5
● C. B. Cabernet Sauvignon Bonzarone '06	🍷🍷	5
○ C. B. Pignoletto Cl. V. Antica '07	🍷🍷	4*
○ C. B. Sauvignon Le Carrate '08	🍷🍷	3*
○ C. B. Sauvignon Sup. Le Carrate '07	🍷🍷	4*

Ca' Montanari

FRAZ. LEVIZZANO DI CASTELVETRO
VIA MEDUSIA, 32
41014 MODENA
TEL. 059741019
www.opera02.it

CELLAR SALES
ROOMS AND FOOD

ANNUAL PRODUCTION 70,000 bottles
HECTARES UNDER VINE 21
VITICULTURE METHOD Certified organic

Enrico Montanari and his son Mattia started this farming operation in Levizzano Rangone, close to Castelvetro. In addition to the 21 hectares of vineyard, their fantastic vinegar house produces DOP traditional Modena balsamic vinegar. They have eight rooms to let and a spacious hall where guests can dine on local fare: a variety of Parmesan cheeses, home-made pastas, air-cured Modena ham and cold cuts. It is a new development for the area, a winery that has become a multi-faceted visitor centre.

Ca' Montanari wines are sourced exclusively from the estate vineyards surrounding the winery, which are certified organic. They fuel Montanari's ambition to be an ambassador for the lambrusco grasparossa area. Opera 02 '09, grasparossa with 15 per cent salamino, is a Lambrusco in the most delicious sense of the term: straightforward, racy, taut, dry and clean-contoured, redolent of cherry but without vulgarity and rustic but in a countryish fashion. The all-grasparossa Opera Pura '09 exhibits a dry, vigorous mouth, with austere fruit and stylish aromas.

● Lambrusco Grasparossa di Castelvetro Opera Pura '09	🍷🍷	4
● Opera 02 Lambrusco di Modena '09	🍷🍷	4
● Opera 02 Lambrusco di Modena '08	YY	4*
● Opera Pura Lambrusco di Modena '08	YY	4*

Calonga

LOC. CASTIGLIONE
VIA CASTEL LEONE, 8
47100 FORLÌ
TEL. 0543753044
www.calonga.it

CELLAR SALES
PRE-BOOKED VISITS

ANNUAL PRODUCTION 30,000 bottles
HECTARES UNDER VINE 8
VITICULTURE METHOD Conventional

Maurizio Baravelli, his wife Monica and their three children, Lorenzo, Matteo and Francesco, direct this small operation with a sensitive hand as rare in Romagna as are his sandy soils. The eight hectares of vines lie in the foremost band of hills behind Forlì, planted at some 100 metres in sandy clay soils. The stratum is sandier in some areas, mixed with clay in others. Maurizio's leading wines are remarkable for their longevity.

Calonga's all-sangiovese star, Michelangiolo, sourced from the winery's oldest vineyard, is as impressive as ever and captures Three Glasses for the fifth year running. As usual it is a magical combination of full volume and supple energy. An almost earthy nose slowly reveals lean, finely focused fruit lifted by a subtle florality. Generous acidity and ultra-dense, expressive tannins maintain a vibrant tension, followed by a long and flavourful finish. An imposing body does nothing to detract from its essential elegance. Castellione '07, a spicy cabernet sauvignon, is massive but judiciously calibrated, with ripe, even tannins.

● Sangiovese di Romagna Sup. Michelangiolo Ris. '07	🍷🍷🍷	5
● Castellione Cabernet Sauvignon '07	🍷🍷	6
● Sangiovese di Romagna Sup. Michelangiolo Ris. '06	YYY	5
● Sangiovese di Romagna Sup. Michelangiolo Ris. '05	YYY	5
● Sangiovese di Romagna Sup. Michelangiolo Ris. '04	YYY	5
● Sangiovese di Romagna Sup. Michelangiolo Ris. '03	YYY	5
● Castellione Cabernet Sauvignon '06	YY	6
● Castellione Cabernet Sauvignon '03	YY	6

Casetto dei Mandorli

loc. Predappio Alta
via Umberto I, 21
47010 Predappio [FC]
tel. 0543922361
www.vini-nicolucci.it

CELLAR SALES
PRE-BOOKED VISITS

ANNUAL PRODUCTION **90,000 bottles**
HECTARES UNDER VINE **15**
VITICULTURE METHOD **Conventional**

Kudos to Alessandro Nicolucci for applying three generations of winemaking expertise to preserving a classic interpretation of sangiovese that succeeds in paring away hard edges and counterproductive excrescences. Of considerable help is Predappio Alta, a terroir long respected in Romagna and already famous in the 19th century for its dense-planted, bush-trained vines and for high wine quality. Casetto dei Mandorli serves as a benchmark throughout Romagna for Sangiovese matured in large casks.

Vigna del Generale '07 remains a classic for its austere, self-possessed style, a wine that can face the future unblinkingly. The nose displays a floral-edged minerality and the palate, supple but with a firm centre, shows fine depth. Tre Rocche '09, although down a rung from previous vintages and a tad less pure perhaps than we have come to expect, remains nonetheless impressive. Nero di Predappio '07 is a successful blend of sangiovese and refosco dal peduncolo rosso. Dry, tangy and crisp, it impresses more in the mouth than on the nose, and still more on the finish.

● Sangiovese di Romagna V. del Generale Ris. '07	🍷🍷	5
● Nero di Predappio '07	🍷🍷	5
● Sangiovese di Romagna Sup. Tre Rocche '09	🍷🍷	4
● Sangiovese di Romagna V. del Generale Ris. '05	YYY	5
● Nero di Predappio '06	YY	5
● Sangiovese di Romagna Sup. Tre Rocche '08	YY	4
● Sangiovese di Romagna V. del Generale Ris. '06	YY	5
● Sangiovese di Romagna V. del Generale Ris. '04	YY	5

Castelluccio

loc. Poggiolo di Sotto
via Tramonto, 15
47015 Modigliana [FC]
tel. 0546942486
www.ronchidicastelluccio.it

CELLAR SALES

ANNUAL PRODUCTION **90,000 bottles**
HECTARES UNDER VINE **14**
VITICULTURE METHOD **Conventional**

Castelluccio is one of Romagna's historic wineries. Claudio Fiore has directed it since 1999, continuing the work of his father Vittorio, who as a young man oversaw the winery's early extraordinary harvests. A restructuring of the vineyards, begun in 1999, has now started to yield good results. Fiore has reshaped the legendary lean, hard Ronchi wines into a style that is richer and more approachable, less austere and more expressive. The style is overtly international, spicy and full bodied.

Claudio Fiore decided not to present any wines this year, believing that he had not granted recent vintages the time they needed for appropriate maturation. So he has pushed back their release dates and the table below shows no new wines. Despite some criticism we have directed in recent years at Castelluccio for its excessively international style, this winery retains its importance in Romagna for its overall reliability and for its history.

○ Lunaria '08	YY	4
● Massicone '06	YY	5
● Massicone '04	YY	6
● Massicone '03	YY	6
● Ronco dei Ciliegi '04	YY	5
● Ronco dei Ciliegi '03	YY	6
○ Ronco del Re '06	YY	6
○ Ronco del Re '05	YY	6
● Ronco delle Ginestre '06	YY	6
● Ronco delle Ginestre '05	YY	6
● Ronco delle Ginestre '04	YY	6
● Sangiovese di Romagna Le More '07	YY	4*

Cavicchioli U. & Figli

via Canaletto, 52
41030 San Prospero [MO]
tel. 059812411
www.cavicchioli.it

CELLAR SALES
PRE-BOOKED VISITS

ANNUAL PRODUCTION 18,000,000 bottles
HECTARES UNDER VINE 150
VITICULTURE METHOD Conventional

Claudio, Federica and Sandro Cavicchioli direct this historic enterprise, which presents wines from another prominent winery as well, Francesco Bellei, the region's leading Metodo Classico producer. Cavicchioli's production has in recent years returned to fine quality, and some of its iconic wines, in particular the Sorbaras, compete regularly in our final tasting round. In fact, this San Prospero-based operation has historically enjoyed an intimate bond with the Sorbara growing area.

Ancestrale '09, a bottle-refermented Sorbara that is not disgorged, went to our final tasting. It is a multi-faceted, compelling wine that ranges from fragrant varietal fruit to the earthy, spice-edged notes typical of refermentation. With a palate that is spacious and sinewy, it projects an elegant, aromatic self-confidence. If Vigna del Cristo '09 opens with fruit that is a tad sweet and candyish. It is impressive in the mouth, its tension showcasing the qualities of a nervy acidity and well-calibrated tannins. The all-pignoletto Ancestrale Bianco '09 makes its debut, a very unusual and interesting wine with a bold vein of citrus from beginning to end.

● Lambrusco di Sorbara Rifermentazione Ancestrale Francesco Bellei '09	TT	5
● Lambrusco di Sorbara V. del Cristo '09	TT	4
○ Rifermentazione Ancestrale Bianco Francesco Bellei '09	TT	4
● Lambrusco di Sorbara Tre Medaglie '09	T	2
● Lambrusco Grasparossa di Castelvetro Amabile Tre Medaglie '09	T	2
● Lambrusco Salamino di Santa Croce Tre Medaglie '09	T	3
○ Brut Extra Cuvée Francesco Bellei	YY	5
● Lambrusco di Sorbara Contessa Matilde '07	YY	3
● Lambrusco di Sorbara Rifermentazione Ancestrale Francesco Bellei '08	YY	5
● Lambrusco di Sorbara V. del Cristo '08	YY	4*
● Lambrusco di Sorbara V. del Cristo '07	YY	4*
● Lambrusco Grasparossa di Castelvetro Amabile Tre Medaglie '08	YY	2
⊙ Rosé del Cristo Spumante '05	YY	6

Umberto Cesari

via Stanzano, 1120
40050 Castel San Pietro Terme [BO]
tel. 051941896
www.umbertocesari.it

CELLAR SALES
PRE-BOOKED VISITS

ANNUAL PRODUCTION 2,000,000 bottles
HECTARES UNDER VINE 128
VITICULTURE METHOD Conventional

In the early 1960s, it was difficult to buy into Umberto Cesari's dream of selling quality Romagna wines worldwide. But the dream came true in 1965 with his first releases and by the 1980s, the winery had grown to be one of Romagna's finest. Cesari began to travel the globe, creating international demand, a feat unique for the region. Today, he sells in 54 countries. Umberto is an unusual combination, a successful businessman who is also a fine winemaker.

The wines, rather than being terroir-driven, interpret Romagna in a way the international taste understands and can rely on. Laurento '07, after an initial hint of oak, builds an elegant palate with acceptable crispness. Liano '07 is a dense pairing of sangiovese and cabernet, on the whole fairly sweet with just a touch of dryness. Moma Rosso '08, from sangiovese, merlot and cabernet sauvignon, is as well-fashioned as ever, showing supple, fresh, fruity and with just the right level of spice. Following maturation in large wood, the Riserva di Sangiovese '06 lays out a splendidly smooth palate well complemented by elegance on the nose.

● Liano '07	TT	5
● Moma Rosso '08	TT	4
● Sangiovese di Romagna Laurento Ris. '07	TT	4
● Sangiovese di Romagna Ris. '07	TT	4
○ Moma Bianco '09	T	4
● Yemula '07	T	4
○ Albana di Romagna Passito Colle del Re '04	YY	5
● Liano '06	YY	5
● Liano '05	YY	5
● Moma Rosso '07	YY	4*
● Sangiovese di Romagna Laurento Ris. '06	YY	4
● Sangiovese di Romagna Ris. '06	YY	4*
● Tauleto Sangiovese '04	YY	6
● Yemula '06	YY	4

Chiarli 1860

via Daniele Manin, 15
41100 Modena
tel. 0593163311
www.chiarli.it

CELLAR SALES

ANNUAL PRODUCTION 600,000 bottles
HECTARES UNDER VINE 110
VITICULTURE METHOD Conventional

The Lambrusco world is largely inhabited by industrial-scale wines, using grapes and musts bought in from all over the area, but today it also vaunts ambitiously well-crafted wines, even in large, successful wineries such as Chiarli 1960. Anselmo and Mauro Chiarli invested in Villa Cialdini, which uses only estate fruit, sorbara at Sozzigalli and grasparossa at Castelvetro. The results have been excellent, with knock-on effect for the larger-scale producers as well.

Three Glasses go to Sorbara del Fondatore '09, a stunner partially bottle-fermented. Slightly hazy, since it isn't disgorged, and Janus-like in its complexity and austerity, it pours out floral and mineral impressions, while finely honed contours keep it driving forward. Equally thrusting is the impressive Vecchia Modena Premium '09, clean edged and aromatically refined. Vigneto Enrico Cialdini '09 boasts a distinctive nose of fruits and pungent earth before the creamy palate flows into a tightly-focused finale. Nivola '09, of salamino and grasparossa, is the modernist here, all emphatic fruit and soft contours.

● Lambrusco di Sorbara del Fondatore '09	▼▼▼	4*
● Lambrusco di Sorbara Vecchia Modena Premium MH '09	▼▼	4*
● Lambrusco Grasparossa di Castelvetro Vign. Enrico Cialdini '09	▼▼	4
● Nivola Lambrusco Scuro '09	▼▼	3
○ Moden Brut '09	▼	4
⊙ Rosè Brut '09	▼	4
● Lambrusco di Sorbara Vecchia Modena Premium '08	▽▽▽	3*
● Lambrusco di Sorbara del Fondatore '08	▽▽	4*
● Lambrusco di Sorbara Vecchia Modena Premium MH '07	▽▽	4*
● Lambrusco Grasparossa di Castelvetro Pruno Nero '08	▽▽	3*
● Lambrusco Grasparossa di Castelvetro Villa Cialdini '08	▽▽	4*
● Nivola Lambrusco Scuro '08	▽▽	3*
● Nivola Lambrusco Scuro	▽▽	3*
⊙ Rosé Brut	▽▽	4

Floriano Cinti

fraz. San Lorenzo
via Gamberi, 48
40037 Sasso Marconi [BO]
tel. 0516751646
www.collibolognesi.com

CELLAR SALES
PRE-BOOKED VISITS

ANNUAL PRODUCTION 95,000 bottles
HECTARES UNDER VINE 24
VITICULTURE METHOD Conventional

Floriano Cinti can be justly proud of his recently completed modern cellar, its temperatures geothermically-controlled, and of his 24 hectares of vineyards. Cinti has been growing grapes since 1992, and has long been a tireless and sensitive interpreter of the local terroir. He displays a rational, composed approach, two qualities in increasingly rare supply in the fast-paced world of wine.

If the straightforward style Cinti prefers works quite well with his native grapes, in particular his pignoletto, it falters somewhat with the internationals. The pignoletto gets no cold maceration, so no extracted bitterness. Two fine outcomes are worth mentioning, the pulpy verve both of Frizzante '09 and of the selection Sassobacco '09. In particular, the latter's lean, vibrant palate is a perfect foil to its rich, opulent nose. Barbera '08 shows clean, crisp flavours that are far more than merely simple.

○ C. B. Pignoletto Cl. Sassobacco '09	▼▼	4
○ C. B. Pignoletto Frizzante '09	▼▼	3
● C. B. Barbera '08	▼	4
● C. B. Barbera '07	▽▽	4*
● C. B. Barbera '06	▽▽	4
● C. B. Cabernet Sauvignon '06	▽▽	4
● C. B. Cabernet Sauvignon Sassobacco '05	▽▽	4
○ C. B. Chardonnay '08	▽▽	4*
○ C. B. Chardonnay '07	▽▽	3*
● C. B. Merlot Sassobacco '06	▽▽	4
○ C. B. Pignoletto Cl. Sassobacco '07	▽▽	4
○ C. B. Pinot Bianco '07	▽▽	3*

La Collina

VIA PAGLIA, 19
48013 BRISIGHELLA [RA]
TEL. 054683110
www.lacollina-vinicola.com

CELLAR SALES
PRE-BOOKED VISITS

ANNUAL PRODUCTION 10,000 bottles
HECTARES UNDER VINE 4
VITICULTURE METHOD Conventional

Located in one of the most beautiful hillside terroirs around Brisighella, La Collina has been run since 2002 by André Eggli, a German-speaking Swiss who travelled extensively in Italy and Spain in search of a place to set up his winemaking project. He produces but a single wine, Cupola, but his objective is to release a monovarietal Sangiovese that will express perfectly the hard but subtle character of this area and in a more international style. He also makes a superb extra virgin olive oil.

Cupola '07, half sangiovese and the remainder cabernet sauvignon and merlot, is a successful, dry, flavourful wine that flows uninterruptedly through to a nicely intriguing finish. Its one blemish is a bit of oak poking out. It is an impressive wine, no doubt about it, but everything here indicates that much more can be coaxed out of the potential of the sangiovese in order to compose a more original and expressive wine. We have full confidence that this will happen.

● Cupola '07	▼▼	6
● Colli di Faenza Sangiovese Cupola '06	▽▽	5
● Colli di Faenza Sangiovese Cupola '05	▽▽	5
● Colli di Faenza Sangiovese Cupola '04	▽▽	5

Leone Conti

LOC. SANTA LUCIA
VIA POZZO, 1
48018 FAENZA [RA]
TEL. 0546642149
www.leoneconti.it

CELLAR SALES
PRE-BOOKED VISITS

ANNUAL PRODUCTION 70,000 bottles
HECTARES UNDER VINE 17
VITICULTURE METHOD Conventional

Lying at the feet of the first band of hills behind Faenza, this historic operation was already putting out wines of considerable quality in the 1970s, benefitting from the lengthy history of viticulture in the area. Yes, Leone Conti interprets his profession as an opportunity to exercise his sensitivity rather than search for absolute quality but he gets outstanding performances every year from a number of his wines. The winery is also a benchmark for Albana, with its examples always superb.

Two wines stood out this year. Perhaps straightforward, they nonetheless competed in our final tasting round. Albana di Romagna Secco Progetto 1 '09 succeeds in expressing its varietal identity with a bright elegance. The tannins are a perfect foil to considerable depth and effectively complement a vein midway between citrus and honey coursing through the wine. Sangiovese '09 is a hurrah of typicality: on the nose, decent florality, then a thrusting palate, taut yet almost floating, from beginning to end. Chardonnay, sauvignon blanc, famoso and pinot bianco combine in Earth Hearth '09 to give a fine show, crisp and clean-edged. The all-centesimino Arcolaio '07 is fine, too.

○ Albana di Romagna Secco Progetto 1 '09	▼▼	4
● Sangiovese di Romagna '09	▼▼	3*
○ Earth Heart '09	▼▼	4
● Arcolaio '07	▼	5
○ Albana di Romagna Passito Nontiscordardime '06	▽▽	6
○ Albana di Romagna Progetto 1 '08	▽▽	4*
○ Albana di Romagna Secco Progetto 1 '07	▽▽	4*
○ An Ghin Gà '08	▽▽	4
○ Earth Heart '08	▽▽	4
○ LeOne '08	▽▽	4
○ Oro et Laboro	▽▽	5
● Sangiovese di Romagna Sup. Contiriserva Ris. '06	▽▽	5
● Sangiovese di Romagna Sup. Le Betulle '07	▽▽	4
○ Tu Chiamale se Vuoi Emozioni Lato B '07	▽▽	7

Corte Manzini

LOC. CÀ DI SOLA DI CASTELVETRO
VIA PER MODENA, 131/3
41014 CASTELVETRO DI MODENA [MO]
TEL. 059702658
www.cortemanzini.it

CELLAR SALES
PRE-BOOKED VISITS
ROOMS AND FOOD

ANNUAL PRODUCTION 80,000 bottles
HECTARES UNDER VINE 12
VITICULTURE METHOD Organic

This small family winery is in the lower Colli Modenesi hills, an area dedicated to lambrusco grasparossa. It prefers nutrient-poor hillslopes and has its own distinctive character, with well-structured tannins and an emphatic headiness. The Manzinis, totally committed growers, always bring in perfectly ripe fruit from their 12 estate hectares. They have honed their own personal style, with crisp-edged, fruity wines that need a full, rounded palate to be at their expressive best.

Corte Manzini's wines this year show less fruity and more austere. This is actually a positive change of style, signalling a welcome decrease in manipulation in the cellar. Two wines went to the final tasting round, L'Acino '09, showing crisp fruit joined to creamy suppleness in the mouth, and Lambrusco '09, countryish, but dynamic and elegant. Good marks too for Grasparossa Amabile '09 with clean, expressive dark cherry and everything in admirable balance right to the end. Bolla Rossa '09 was sound enough but seemed a touch tired in the fruit and stiff on the palate.

● Lambrusco Grasparossa di Castelvetro '09	4
● Lambrusco Grasparossa di Castelvetro L'Acino '09	4
● Lambrusco Grasparossa di Castelvetro Amabile '09	3
● Lambrusco Grasparossa di Castelvetro Bolla Rossa '09	3
● Lambrusco Grasparossa di Castelvetro '07	4*
● Lambrusco Grasparossa di Castelvetro Amabile '08	3*
● Lambrusco Grasparossa di Castelvetro L'Acino '08	4*
● Lambrusco Grasparossa di Castelvetro L'Acino '07	4*
● Lambrusco Grasparossa di Castelvetro Secco '06	4*
● Lambrusco Grasparossa di Castelvetro Secco L'Acino '06	4*

Crocizia

S.DA PER CROCIZIA, 7
43010 LANGHIRANO [PR]
TEL. 0521854450

CELLAR SALES

ANNUAL PRODUCTION 10,000 bottles
HECTARES UNDER VINE 5
VITICULTURE METHOD Certified organic

Fifteen years ago, the Rizzardi family decided to bring back to life an abandoned farm and Crocizia was the result. The five hectares of vines, farmed organically, lie on a natural terrace at 500 metres' elevation on the steep southern slope of the Parma watercourse, about a kilometre from the village of Pastorello. The earth has lain untouched for some 50 years so the soils have accumulated minerals and organic matter. Mostly chalk and marl, they impart a certain slatiness and marked acidity to the wines.

The Crocizia wines referment in the bottle, and the Rizzardi minimize cellar manipulations, avoiding, as they say on the label, additives, clarifying and stabilizing agents, cultured yeasts and enzymes. S'cètt '09, half lambrusco maestri and half barbera and croatina, is a dry, vibrant wine with an earthy edge and nervy acidity that drinks supple and very enjoyable. The dry Marc'Aurelio '09, all lambrusco maestri, is bursting with flavour and interest. Worth trying is Znèstra '09, mostly malvasia di Candia aromatica with a bit of moscato, with dried herbs and flowers infusing the bouquet.

● Marc'Aurelio '09	4
● S'cètt '09	4
○ Znèstra '09	3

Denavolo

FRAZ. DENAVOLO
LOC. GATTAVERA
29020 TRAVO [PC]
TEL. 3356480766
giulio.armani@gmail.it

CELLAR SALES

ANNUAL PRODUCTION 15,000 bottles
HECTARES UNDER VINE 3
VITICULTURE METHOD Organic

Giulio Armani has now focused his 30 years of experience on Val Trebbia, at the foot of Monte Denavolo, some 30 kilometres from Piacenza, in a very different terroir for him. High up at 500 metres, in marl-rich, rocky soils, he planted three hectares of white-wine varieties: ortrugo, malvasia di Candia aromatica, trebbiano romagnolo and marsanne, grapes with long histories of good results here. The difficult soils have yielded very interesting wines, helped by Armani's minimalist winemaking philosophy.

Denavolo produces two wines, each of which owes its distinctive character to a different vineyard. Dinavolo '07, which competed in our national final round, shows multi-faceted and complex, its hallmark a judicious, almost briny acidity. There are hints too of menthol, earth and citrus peel, plus an already well-integrated tannin. We liked energy-laden Dinavolino '09 as well, a crisp, slender charmer that slides into a surprisingly forceful finish.

O Dinavolo '07	🍷🍷 (black)	6
O Dinavolino '09	🍷🍷 (black)	4
O Dinavolo '05	🍷🍷 (white)	6
O Dinavolo '06	🍷🍷 (white)	6

Camillo Donati

LOC. AROLA, 32
43013 LANGHIRANO [PR]
TEL. 0521637204
camdona@tin.it

CELLAR SALES
PRE-BOOKED VISITS

ANNUAL PRODUCTION 70,000 bottles
HECTARES UNDER VINE 14
VITICULTURE METHOD Certified organic

In the early 1990s, Camillo Donati left a comfortable office job to take over his father's vineyards in Arola, 20 kilometres from Parma on the road to Langhirano, at an elevation of 250 metres. Helped by his niece Monia, he personally runs the 15-hectare estate vineyards, which yield very personal, exciting wines. He uses skin contact, natural fermentation temperatures and no chemicals, cultured yeasts or enzymes. Just great sensitivity.

The wines are all sparkling and bottle fermented. Its depth and elegance took La Mia Barbera '08 to our finals. Lean but stylish cherry animates the nose and tasty palate while a touch of headiness detracts nothing from its refinement. The dry, all-bonarda Ovidio '08 is distinctive and unexpected. An emphatic nose, vaunting blackberry and black pepper, leads to crunchy fruit on the palate and then to a hint of fresh vegetable in the finish. The golden-hued Mio Malvasia '08 allows the yeast to peek out, but the nose is delicate and floral. A pleasant bitterish note accompanies the dryness on the palate, while hints of citrus and candied fruit make for a tasty conclusion.

● La Mia Barbera '08	🍷🍷 (black)	3
● Il Mio Lambrusco '08	🍷🍷 (black)	4
O Il Mio Malvasia Dolce '08	🍷🍷 (black)	4
● Ovidio '08	🍷🍷 (black)	4
● Il Groppone d'Orlando '04	🍷🍷 (white)	4*
O Il Mio Malvasia Dolce '07	🍷🍷 (white)	4*
O Il Mio Sauvignon '07	🍷🍷 (white)	4*
● Lambrusco '06	🍷🍷 (white)	4*

Drei Donà Tenuta La Palazza

LOC. MASSA DI VECCHIAZZANO
VIA DEL TESORO, 23
47100 FORLÌ
TEL. 0543769371
www.dreidona.it

CELLAR SALES
PRE-BOOKED VISITS

ANNUAL PRODUCTION 130,000 bottles
HECTARES UNDER VINE 30
VITICULTURE METHOD Conventional

Claudio and Enrico Drei Donà figure among the longest-running operations in Romagna. Their vineyards are approaching maturity now and wine production is both reliable and impressive. The first modern vineyards date back to 1981, when Claudio Drei Donà decided to retire his lawyer's toga and dedicate himself to the family's farming properties, full of plans for a respected winery, along the lines of a small Bordeaux château.

Their Sangioveses serve as rare beacons in the region both for their unbroken consistency and for the respect that the Drei Donàs have always shown for Sangiovese's innate expressiveness. You can always rely on Pruno to reflect its terroir and represent one of the winery's best offerings, confirmed by the '07 winning Three Glasses. It boasts an utterly classic nose, a palate that thrusts forward, ripe tannins brimming with character, and an almost endless finale. The sangiovese Notturno '08, a chip off its elder brother, is styled for its refreshing crispness. Magnificat '07 is the winery's fine historic Cabernet Sauvignon and Tornese '08 is an excellent Chardonnay.

●	Sangiovese di Romagna Sup. Pruno Ris. '07	▼▼▼	6
○	Il Tornese Chardonnay '08	▼▼	4
●	Magnificat Cabernet Sauvignon '07	▼▼	6
●	Notturno Sangiovese '08	▼▼	4
○	Il Tornese Chardonnay '95	▽▽▽	6
●	Magnificat Cabernet Sauvignon '94	▽▽▽	6
●	Sangiovese di Romagna Sup. Pruno Ris. '06	▽▽▽	6
●	Sangiovese di Romagna Sup. Pruno Ris. '01	▽▽▽	5
●	Sangiovese di Romagna Sup. Pruno Ris. '00	▽▽▽	5
○	Il Tornese Chardonnay '07	▽▽	4*
○	Il Tornese Chardonnay '06	▽▽	5
●	Magnificat Cabernet Sauvignon '06	▽▽	6
●	Notturno Sangiovese '07	▽▽	4*
●	Sangiovese di Romagna Sup. Pruno Ris. '05	▽▽	6

Stefano Ferrucci

VIA CASOLANA, 3045/2
48014 CASTEL BOLOGNESE [RA]
TEL. 0546651068
www.stefanoferrucci.it

CELLAR SALES
PRE-BOOKED VISITS

ANNUAL PRODUCTION 95,000 bottles
HECTARES UNDER VINE 15
VITICULTURE METHOD Conventional

Ilaria Ferrucci took over the reins of the winery her father Stefano founded and in 2007 revolutionized its operation. The fruits are in fact slowly appearing but she is sticking to her plan, convinced of its long-term success. Change relies on renewal of the vineyards rather than on any short-cuts, and on the contributions of the talented winemaker, Federico Giotto, who focuses on research and consideration of all possibilities. The wines are showing the style Ferrucci is aiming at.

Stefano Ferrucci began the Domus Caia project some years ago when he was the first in Romagna to experiment with "appassimento", or natural drying of the grapes. Ilaria has kept faith with the original concept but has reduced the drying time, trying to respect as much as possible the delicacy of the sangiovese grape. The '07 is the most impressive of recent vintages, combining as it does Domus Caia's unique character with an overall elegance that glides through to a crisp, clean-edged conclusion. Centurione '09 gets high marks too. Dry and refreshing in the mouth, it's ready to enjoy, despite being a tad sweetish and oaky on the nose.

○	Albana di Romagna Passito Domus Aurea '08	▼▼	6
●	Sangiovese di Romagna Sup. Centurione '09	▼▼	4
●	Sangiovese di Romagna Sup. Domus Caia Ris. '07	▼▼	6
●	Sangiovese di Romagna Auriga '09	▼	3
○	Albana di Romagna Passito Domus Aurea '07	▽▽	6
○	Albana di Romagna Passito Domus Aurea '06	▽▽	6
●	Sangiovese di Romagna Sup. Domus Caia Ris. '04	▽▽	6
●	Sangiovese di Romagna Sup. Domus Caia Ris. '03	▽▽	6
●	Sangiovese di Romagna Sup. Domus Caia Ris. '06	▽▽	6
●	Sangiovese di Romagna Sup. Domus Caia Ris. '05	▽▽	6

Paolo Francesconi

LOC. SARNA
VIA TULIERO, 154
48018 FAENZA [RA]
TEL. 054643213
pfrancesconi@racine.ra.it

CELLAR SALES
PRE-BOOKED VISITS

ANNUAL PRODUCTION 15,000 bottles
HECTARES UNDER VINE 14
VITICULTURE METHOD Certified organic

Paolo Francesconi has been committed for some years now to a long-term programme of biodynamic production and naturally made wines. The red clay soils where his vineyards are planted are high quality but they don't yield fine results easily. After years of experience, though, Paolo's wines are generally consistent and are now beginning to exhibit the character that he has been striving for. The winery also produces an excellent extra virgin olive oil from the nostrana di Brisighella olive.

The '08 version of Limbecca, the winery's most straightforward Sangiovese, went to our finals last year but Francesconi is keeping back the '09 for additional bottle ageing. After a slightly blurred nose, the all-sangiovese Le Iadi '07 makes a terrific impression in the mouth, with clean lines and a taut progression. The tannins are nicely ripe and chewy, and the finish near endless. Idilio '08 is an Albana Passito with a multi-hued nose and a high dose of residual sugar that provides the perfect foil to its zingy acidity.

○ Albana di Romagna Passito Idillio '08	TT	5
● Sangiovese di Romagna Sup. Le Iadi Ris. '07	TT	5
● Symposium Merlot '08	T	4
● Colli di Faenza Rosso Miniato '07	YY	4
● D'Incanto	YY	5
● Impavido Merlot '06	YY	5
● Sangiovese di Romagna Sup. Le Iadi Ris. '06	YY	5
● Sangiovese di Romagna Sup. Limbecca '08	YY	4*
● Sangiovese di Romagna Sup. Limbecca '07	YY	4*
● Sangiovese di Romagna Sup. Limbecca '06	YY	4*

Maria Galassi

LOC. PADERNO DI CESENA
VIA CASETTE, 688
47023 CESENA [FC]
TEL. 054721177
www.galassimaria.it

CELLAR SALES
PRE-BOOKED VISITS

ANNUAL PRODUCTION 12,000 bottles
HECTARES UNDER VINE 18
VITICULTURE METHOD Certified organic

Galassi Maria is one of a new group of producers, often organic, who are shaking up Romagna with intriguing, stand-apart wines. The winery, located between San Vittore di Cesena and Bertinoro, has been in the Galassi family for 150 years. Its organically farmed vineyards stand on Bertinoro's hallmark soil, rich in chalk and seabed tufa, at an elevation of some 120 metres. The grapes go part to a local co-operative and part into the Galassi family's own production.

We were impressed by NatoRe Riserva '07, a wine with generous body, taut palate and dynamic progression. A touch of sweet oak on the nose doesn't compromise its rich but lean fruit. The mouth is all thrust and interest, with smooth, mellow tannins, and concludes with a flourish. NatoRe '08 is a tad vegetal on the nose but sound enough in the mouth. Beginning with the 2009 vintage, the wines will bear different names, NatoRe for the Reserve and Paternus for the Superiore. A Paternus '08 was released this year as well, of which we did not think too highly.

● Sangiovese di Romagna NatoRe Ris. '07	TT	6
● Sangiovese di Romagna NatoRe Sup. '08	T	4
● Sangiovese di Romagna Paternus '07	YY	4*
● Sangiovese di Romagna Sup. NatoRe '07	YY	4

Gallegati

VIA ISONZO, 4
48018 FAENZA [RA]
TEL. 0546621149
www.aziendaagricolagallegati.it

CELLAR SALES
PRE-BOOKED VISITS

ANNUAL PRODUCTION 15,000 bottles
HECTARES UNDER VINE 6
VITICULTURE METHOD Conventional

Cesare and Antonio Gallegati's small operation has become a point of reference in the Faenza area, thanks to their courageous decisions and impeccable vineyard management, reflecting both brothers' agricultural degrees. The estate lies in the first band of Faenza hills, a classic clay-soil area midway between the Senio and Lamone valleys. The wines, with their judicious balance of power and supple elegance, totally reflect this terroir and have become a benchmark for other local clay-grown Sangioveses.

The rich personality and classic style of Corallo Nero Riserva '07 propelled it into our finals. We appreciated its austerity and pure, dry sangiovese essence and its vibrancy in the mouth. Passito Albana Regina di Cuori Riserva '07 displays admirable typicality, with a nose marked by fig and apricot plus the classic lifting note that so animates the aromas. Corallo Blu Riserva '07, made of merlot and cabernet with a dollop of sangiovese, is succulent and dense, driven by a marked progression and good fruit, and always at its impressive best.

○ Albana di Romagna Passito Regina di Cuori Ris. '07	[2 black glasses]	6
● Sangiovese di Romagna Sup. Corallo Nero Ris. '07	[2 black glasses]	5
● Colli di Faenza Rosso Corallo Blu Ris. '07	[2 black glasses]	5
● Sangiovese di Romagna Sup. Corallo Nero Ris. '06	[3 glasses]	5
○ Albana di Romagna Passito Regina di Cuori '04	[2 glasses]	5
○ Albana di Romagna Passito Regina di Cuori Ris. '06	[2 glasses]	6
● Colli di Faenza Rosso Corallo Blu Ris. '06	[2 glasses]	5

Tenuta La Viola

VIA COLOMBARONE, 888
47032 BERTINORO [FC]
TEL. 0543445496
www.tenutalaviola.it

CELLAR SALES
PRE-BOOKED VISITS

ANNUAL PRODUCTION 35,000 bottles
HECTARES UNDER VINE 5
VITICULTURE METHOD Certified organic

Tenuta La Viola entered the modern era in 1998, when Stefano Gabellini took over the family winery on the death of his father. He was deeply aware of the significant potential represented by the Bertinoro area and enjoyed the advantage of his mother Lidia's dedicated and invaluable work in the vineyards, planted on the eastern slopes. In just a few years, Gabellini has turned the winery into one of the leading producers in the area.

Petra Honorii '07competed in the final tastings, thanks particularly to the thrusting energy that animates its cleanly defined mid palate, and to its full-bodied, crisp fruit. It still seems to be striving for something, however, perhaps a more ambitious reflection of terroir, and a nose free of all those sweet oak tones. Particella 25 '07, a blend of cabernet and merlot with ten per cent sangiovese, opens to a lean, herbaceous nose, yet shows elderflower and white peach, too. The mouth is bright, toothsome and dense, with already relaxed tannins, a bit overly seductive perhaps but refreshingly crisp.

● Sangiovese di Romagna Sup. Petra Honorii Ris. '07	[2 black glasses]	5
● Particella 25 '07	[2 black glasses]	6
● Sangiovese di Romagna Sup. Oddone '09	[1 black glass]	3
● Particella 25 '06	[2 glasses]	6
● Sangiovese di Romagna Sup. Il Colombarone '06	[2 glasses]	4*
● Sangiovese di Romagna Sup. Il Colombarone '05	[2 glasses]	4*
● Sangiovese di Romagna Sup. La Badia Ris. '03	[2 glasses]	5
● Sangiovese di Romagna Sup. Petra Honorii Ris. '06	[2 glasses]	5
● Sangiovese di Romagna Sup. Petra Honorii Ris. '05	[2 glasses]	5
● Sangiovese di Romagna Sup. Petra Honorii Ris. '04	[2 glasses]	5

Lini 910

LOC. CANOLO DI CORREGGIO
VIA VECCHIA CANOLO, 7
42015 CORREGGIO [RE]
TEL. 0522690162
www.lini910.it

CELLAR SALES
PRE-BOOKED VISITS

ANNUAL PRODUCTION 300,000 bottles
HECTARES UNDER VINE 25
VITICULTURE METHOD Conventional

Lini is a prestigious traditional Lambrusco label well known for its Metodo Classico, with which the Lini family began experimenting in the early 1960s. Now Alicia and Alberto, the new generation, have taken over with enthusiastic pride, continuing a business that is celebrating 100 years and so many stylistic periods. Their modest, high-quality operation produces traditional Reggio Emilia vinegar as well, made in 100 barrel-sets, now resting in a new vinegar house designed by Paolo Rizzato.

The Lini style, all about charm and finesse, can be seen at its best in the Metodo Classico but the family has held back its release this year. So we only have some of their Charmats to review. We liked the Lambrusco Rosé '09, from salamino and 20 per cent sorbara. It stages a fine duet between the earthy note of the first and the citrussy elegance of the second. The all-pinot nero Brut Pinot is equally refined, with stylish hazelnut wafting about and juicy sapidity in the mouth. Moscato Spumante '09 is classy and clean contoured, but Lambrusco Scuro '09, mostly salamino with some ancellotta and grasparossa, shows somewhat sweet and flattish.

○ In Correggio Brut Pinot '09	▼▼	4
⊙ In Correggio Lambrusco Rosato '09	▼▼	3
○ In Correggio Moscato Spumante '09	▼▼	4
● In Correggio Lambrusco Scuro '09	▼	4
○ In Correggio Brut M. Cl. '04	▽▽	5
○ In Correggio Brut M. Cl. '00	▽▽	5
⊙ In Correggio Brut Rosé M. Cl. '03	▽▽	5
● In Correggio Brut Rosso M. Cl. '05	▽▽	5
● In Correggio Brut Rosso M. Cl. '04	▽▽	5
● In Correggio Brut Rosso M. Cl. '03	▽▽	5

Luretta

LOC. CASTELLO DI MOMELIANO
29010 GAZZOLA [PC]
TEL. 0523971070
www.luretta.com

CELLAR SALES
PRE-BOOKED VISITS

ANNUAL PRODUCTION 250,000 bottles
HECTARES UNDER VINE 43
VITICULTURE METHOD Certified organic

Felice Salamini has the lively intelligence that at any moment can offer perspective-changing insights. His research is striking but Piacenza has only limited varieties and local wine traditions, so he blazes new trails and freely challenges established ways. What emerges is always reliable and intriguing. Salamini's adventure, beginning in 1992, is now shared by son Lucio, whose reserved character complements his father's exuberance. Their 43 hectares of vineyard are part in Val Luretta and part in Val Nure.

Luretta's white wines are generally reliable but the reds have shown uneven for a few years, with the latest vintages speaking a now-outdated stylistic language: overripe, over-done and over-oaked. On Attend les Invités Roncolino Riserva '07, only in magnum, is full-flavoured, nervy, elegant, with a stylish note of hazelnut lifting its complexity. Principessa '05, distinct from Principessa Brut, is a non-dosage Metodo Classico that is dry and fresh with an aromatic thread of chlorophyll. Malvasia Boccadirosa '09 shows an elegant, nicely contained typicality. Overall crispness animates Le Rane '06's refined sweetness and it boasts a rich tissue of mould from drying.

⊙ C. P. Brut Rosé On Attend les Invités Roncolino Ris. '07	▼▼	5
○ C. P. Malvasia Boccadirosa '09	▼▼	4
○ C. P. Malvasia Dolce Le Rane '06	▼▼	6
○ C. P. Pinot Nero M. Cl. Non Dosato Principessa '05	▼▼	4
⊙ C. P. Brut Rosé On Attend les Invités '07	▼	5
● C. P. Cabernet Sauvignon Corbeau '00	▽▽▽	6
⊙ C. P. Brut Rosé On Attend les Invités '04	▽▽	5
○ C. P. Chardonnay Selin Dl'Armari '07	▽▽	5
○ C. P. Chardonnay Selin dl'Armari '06	▽▽	5
○ C. P. Malvasia Boccadirosa '08	▽▽	4
○ C. P. Malvasia Boccadirosa '07	▽▽	4*
○ C. P. Sauvignon I Nani e Le Ballerine '08	▽▽	4

Gaetano Lusenti

LOC. CASE PICCIONI, 57
29010 ZIANO PIACENTINO [PC]
TEL. 0523868479
www.lusentivini.it

CELLAR SALES
PRE-BOOKED VISITS

ANNUAL PRODUCTION 120,000 bottles
HECTARES UNDER VINE 17
VITICULTURE METHOD Organic

Gaetano Lusenti lies in one of the Val Tidone's most spectacular spots, a short distance from Oltrepò Pavese, in a countryscape of gentle, vine-carpeted hills that march on forever. The Lusentis have a venerable bond with their land, and winemaking skills that few can equal in the area. Ludovica, herself from a farming family, represents the point of encounter between agricultural traditions and winemaking modernity, and thus was entrusted the task of safeguarding the character that incarnates those traditions.

The most interesting wine we tasted was Bianca Regina '08, from malvasia given a brief maceration on the skins. The aromatics typical of the variety are in display on the nose, including honey, tea leaves and eucalyptus, while the palate, crisply dry, exhibits impeccable balance. Il Piriolo '08 is stunningly rich, moderately tannic and even conjures up walnutskin and hazelnut. Although over-oaked at too many points, including the finish, Cresta al Sole '07 has its attractions, and Gutturnio Frizzante '09 is clean-edged and refreshing.

● C. P. Gutturnio Sup. Cresta al Sole '07	🍷🍷	4
○ C. P. Malvasia Bianca Regina '08	🍷🍷	4
○ C. P. Malvasia Passito Il Piriolo '08	🍷🍷	6
● C. P. Gutturnio Frizzante '09	🍷	3
● C. P. Gutturnio Frizzante '08	🍷🍷	3*
● C. P. Gutturnio Frizzante '07	🍷🍷	3*
○ C. P. Malvasia Bianca Regina '07	🍷🍷	4
○ C. P. Malvasia V. T. Bianca Regina '06	🍷🍷	4*
○ C. P. Malvasia V. T. Bianca Regina '05	🍷🍷	4*
⊙ C. P. Pinot Nero Spumante Rosé '00	🍷🍷	5
● Vigna Martin '07	🍷🍷	4*
● Vigna Martin IV '08	🍷🍷	4

Giovanna Madonia

LOC. VILLA MADONIA
VIA DE' CAPPUCCINI, 130
47032 BERTINORO [FC]
TEL. 0543444361
www.giovannamadonia.it

CELLAR SALES
PRE-BOOKED VISITS
FOOD

ANNUAL PRODUCTION 45,000 bottles
HECTARES UNDER VINE 12
VITICULTURE METHOD Conventional

Giovanna Madonia has her own style, which may seem confused but is actually remarkably coherent. She dislikes and avoids all set parameters and prefers to work unencumbered, without clichés. For example, when she grew tired of graphic artists' label proposals, she worked out her own in pencil and completed them with sketches by Altan. Her winery is one of the most solid in Romagna, and one of the most promising in the Bertinoro area. Soils in the area are rich in chalk and "spungone", or seabed tufa.

Giovanna Madonia's vineyards are planted in Monte Maggio, one of the most inland areas. In fact, ripening can occur as many as ten days later here than on slopes facing the sea. Sangiovese Ombroso Riserva '07, apart from a blurred point or two, displays an intriguing, multi-faceted character. An austere nose, replete with mineral and earthy impressions, is followed by rich, dense tannins and marked progression, all fuelled by vibrant acidity. The '08 is a good vintage for Fermavento, which takes its time in the glass, then opens out in all of its firm-structured authenticity.

● Sangiovese di Romagna Sup. Ombroso Ris. '07	🍷🍷	5
● Sangiovese di Romagna Sup. Fermavento '08	🍷🍷	4
● Sangiovese di Romagna Sup. Ombroso Ris. '06	🍷🍷🍷	5
● Sangiovese di Romagna Sup. Ombroso Ris. '01	🍷🍷🍷	5
○ Albana di Romagna Passito Chimera '03	🍷🍷	5
● Sangiovese di Romagna Sup. Fermavento '07	🍷🍷	4
● Sangiovese di Romagna Sup. Fermavento '05	🍷🍷	4*
● Sangiovese di Romagna Sup. Fermavento '04	🍷🍷	4*
● Sangiovese di Romagna Sup. Ombroso Ris. '05	🍷🍷	5
● Sangiovese di Romagna Sup. Ombroso Ris. '04	🍷🍷	5
● Sangiovese di Romagna Sup. Ombroso Ris. '03	🍷🍷	5
● Sterpigno Merlot '03	🍷🍷	6

Ermete Medici & Figli

LOC. GAIDA
VIA NEWTON, 13A
42040 REGGIO EMILIA
TEL. 0522942135
www.medici.it

CELLAR SALES
PRE-BOOKED VISITS

ANNUAL PRODUCTION 800,000 bottles
HECTARES UNDER VINE 60
VITICULTURE METHOD Conventional

The Medici family traditionally vinifies bought-in grapes but their high-quality wines are made from their own grapes as well, grown in skilfully managed estate vineyards. Giorgio Medici has carried out significant research into vinification and Medici wines today, which are increasingly impressive, represent the fruition of programmes conducted with commitment and professionalism. Their cru-based philosophy, an approach innovative and rare in the world of Lambrusco, is showing astonishing results.

Three Glasses once again go to Concerto, the winery's most iconic label. The '09, all salamino, vaunts a no-nonsense nose, here and there somewhat countryish but clean-contoured and fruit laden. The sapidity and rhythmic progression in the mouth are magisterial, right through to a dry, rich finish. Assolo '09 offers notes that are particularly husky and rustic this year with fruit that seems barely domesticated. The palate though, distinctive and expressive, is as complex as one could wish. The classic-method Granconcerto '08, all salamino and disgorged in 2010, is clean and creamy, with exquisite harmony on the palate.

● Reggiano Lambrusco Secco Concerto '09	▼▼▼	3*
● Reggiano Assolo '09	▼▼	3*
⊙ Granconcerto Brut M. Cl. '08	▼▼	4
● Reggiano Lambrusco Secco Libesco '09	▼▼	3
○ Colli di Scandiano e di Canossa Malvasia Daphne '09	▼	3
● Reggiano Lambrusco Secco I Quercioli '09	▼	2
● Reggiano Lambrusco Concerto '08	▽▽▽	3*

Monte delle Vigne

LOC. OZZANO TARO
VIA MONTICELLO, 13
43046 COLLECCHIO [PR]
TEL. 0521309704
www.montedellevigne.it

CELLAR SALES
PRE-BOOKED VISITS

ANNUAL PRODUCTION 250,000 bottles
HECTARES UNDER VINE 45
VITICULTURE METHOD Conventional

Andrea Ferrari and Paolo Pizzarotti's operation is one of the most interesting in the Parma hills. The partners have not spared resources on high-quality vineyards, now in full production, and on a modern, totally functional underground cellar. Their ambition is to produce quality still wines, thus divergent from the local traditions, but wines that nevertheless interpret traditional local varieties, such as barbera, bonarda and malvasia di Candia aromatica.

Monte delle Vigne wines are well made, even though they currently suffer from a lack of personality. Barbera '06 shows good stuffing but too much wood is sticking out, sweet at the outset and bitterish at the end, which chokes off any possible ambitions. We found the barbera and bonarda Monte delle Vigne Rosso '08 interesting. A touch evolved on the nose but with good depth and a nice earthy note, it releases plenty of appealing energy in the mouth, which is crisp and clean as well. Intrusive oak returns in Nabucco '08, made mostly from barbera helped by merlot, but the fruit in the mouth is tasty enough and the progression is taut.

● Barbera '06	▼▼	4
● Colli di Parma Rosso Monte delle Vigne '08	▼▼	4
● Nabucco '08	▼▼	5
○ Callas Malvasia '09	▼	5
● Colli di Parma Rosso Frizzante '09	▼	3
● Lambrusco '09	▼	3
○ Callas Malvasia '08	▽▽	5
○ Callas Malvasia '07	▽▽	5
● Colli di Parma Rosso '06	▽▽	4*
● Lambrusco '08	▽▽	3*
● Lambrusco '07	▽▽	3*
● Nabucco '06	▽▽	5

Roberto Monti

via Montecchio, 54
48013 Brisighella [RA]
tel. 054681701
robertomonti5@virgilio.it

ANNUAL PRODUCTION 4,000 bottles
HECTARES UNDER VINE 12
VITICULTURE METHOD Conventional

Young Paolo Monti, who works with his father in managing the winery's 12 hectares of vineyards, decided some years ago to vinify some of the grapes that were going to a local co-operative. His sensitivity and dedication are now yielding some very good wines, reflecting their local terroir quite well. This is even more to his credit when one notes the difficult terrain, between Faenza and the village of Brisighella: almost pure clay, giving rise to a striking, ravine-riven landscape.

The two Roberto Monti wines we tasted were both excellent, albeit less courageous than those from the '07 vintage, since we missed that extra bit of tension, of personality even. Still, they testify to extraordinary work in the vineyards, which expresses itself in the quality of the texture and tannins. Millo '08 surprises with an unexpected vegetal hint while the palate is impressive indeed, taut yet rich in mouthfeel and pulp, sliding into a finish on a minor key. Iaia Riserva '08 shows warmth on the nose, with cocoa powder and dried plum, and velvety mouthfeel, though the palate is just a shade drying.

● Colli di Faenza Rosso Iaia Ris. '08	🍷🍷	4
● Sangiovese di Romagna Sup. Millo '08	🍷🍷	4
● Colli di Faenza Rosso Iaia Ris. '07	YY	4*
● Sangiovese di Romagna Sup. Millo '07	YY	4*

Fattoria Monticino Rosso

via Montecatone, 7
40026 Imola [BO]
tel. 054240577
www.fattoriadelmonticinorosso.it

CELLAR SALES
PRE-BOOKED VISITS

ANNUAL PRODUCTION 70,000 bottles
HECTARES UNDER VINE 18
VITICULTURE METHOD Conventional

Monticino Rosso is one of the northernmost wineries in Romagna with a climate so special that Mussolini had a sanatorium built here in the1930s. The Zeoli brothers are scrupulous growers with a strong bond to their area, as testified by the huge number of loyal local customers of their unbottled wines. This trade is most advantageous, since it allows Monticino Rosso to bottle solely the wines they feel are their best.

The Zeolis are helped by Giancarlo Soverchia, who is working with them to improve their red wines. The goal is a complexity that so far we have not found very impressive, as stated in past Guides. But it's another world with the whites. There were Three Glasses for Albana di Romagna Codronchio '08, the first dry Albana to win a top prize. Late picking has given it a multi-layered nose of honey, passion fruit, spring blossoms and a thread of botrytis while the palate is crisp-edged and elegant, with ultra-generous acidity and an impression of bright cleanness. Albana Secco '09 is also lovely, spacious and clean, with fine depth and freshness at every moment.

○ Albana di Romagna Secco Codronchio '08	🍷🍷🍷	4*
○ Albana di Romagna Secco '09	🍷🍷	3
○ Albana di Romagna Secco '08	YY	3*
○ Albana di Romagna Secco '06	YY	3*
○ Albana di Romagna Passito '06	YY	5
○ Albana di Romagna Secco Codronchio '07	YY	4
○ Albana di Romagna Secco Codronchio '04	YY	4*
● Colli d'Imola Cabernet Sauvignon Pradello Ris. '04	YY	4
○ Colli d'Imola Pignoletto '08	YY	3*
● Sangiovese di Romagna Sup. '06	YY	3*

Fattoria Moretto

VIA TIBERIA, 13B
41014 CASTELVETRO DI MODENA [MO]
TEL. 059790183
www.fattoriamoretto.it

CELLAR SALES

ANNUAL PRODUCTION 12,000 bottles
HECTARES UNDER VINE 7
VITICULTURE METHOD Certified organic

Fausto Altariva directs this small operation founded in the early 1990s. It lies in the heart of the lambrusco grasparossa growing area, at an elevation of some 200 metres, and cultivates seven hectares of vines, all certified organic. No cultured yeasts or sulphur dioxide are used in production and fermentations take place in pressure autoclaves, followed by up to three months' maturation on the fine lees to encourage the development of complexity in the wine.

Moretto's philosophy requires the vinification of each vineyard separately, in order to coax out the characteristics of the various soils, which differ markedly from each other. The south-facing Vigna Canova is the winery's least clayey vineyard, and it yielded Vigna Canova '09. A clean, bright and austerely dry wine, it boasts a creamy mouthfeel well complemented by a vibrant acidity. Monovitigno '09 is sourced from a vineyard planted in 1968 to old clones of grasparossa. Its hallmarks are the smoothness of its tannins and its crisp freshness. The intriguing Grasparossa '09, dry and straightforward, is countryish and rustic in the most positive meaning for those terms.

- Lambrusco Grasparossa di Castelvetro V. Canova '09 — ΨΨ 4
- Lambrusco Grasparossa di Castelvetro '09 — ΨΨ 4
- Lambrusco Grasparossa di Castelvetro Monovitigno '09 — ΨΨ 4

Gianfranco Paltrinieri

FRAZ. SORBARA
VIA CRISTO, 49
41030 BOMPORTO [MO]
TEL. 059902047
www.cantinapaltrinieri.it

CELLAR SALES

ANNUAL PRODUCTION 60,000 bottles
HECTARES UNDER VINE 15
VITICULTURE METHOD Conventional

This small winery, founded in the1920s, is in Cristo, in the heart of the sorbara growing area. Alberto Paltrinieri and his wife Barbara Galassi, plus the rest of the family, personally manage the winemaking and 15 hectares of vineyards, vinifying only their own grapes. They belong to a small group of producers who determinedly preserve the subtly varietal, minerally style of Sorbara, an identity much appreciated today, and which represents one of the most intriguing styles in the varied Lambrusco panorama.

Leclisse '09, a selection of sorbara made at Cristo di Sorbara, shows those classic floral, minerally notes. It is crisp on the palate but lacks the depth of previous versions. We found Fermentazione in Bottiglia '09 interesting as well, displaying a multi-faceted, exotic bouquet that was quite complex, and spicy to boot. The palate is nicely balanced. Sant'Agata '09 and La Piria '09 were sound enough, but not much more than that, since both showed signs of overripeness, so we missed the balance and freshness in the mouth that we expected.

- Lambrusco di Sorbara Leclisse '09 — ΨΨ 4
- Lambrusco di Sorbara Fermentazione in Bottiglia '09 — ΨΨ 3
- Lambrusco di Sorbara La Piria '09 — Ψ 2
- Lambrusco di Sorbara Sant'Agata '09 — Ψ 3
- Lambrusco di Sorbara Leclisse '08 — ΥΥ 4*
- Lambrusco di Sorbara La Piria '08 — ΥΥ 2*
- Lambrusco di Sorbara Sant'Agata '08 — ΥΥ 3*

Tenuta Pennita

LOC. TERRA DEL SOLE
VIA PIANELLO, 34
47011 CASTROCARO TERME [FC]
TEL. 0543767451
www.lapennita.it

CELLAR SALES
PRE-BOOKED VISITS
ROOMS

ANNUAL PRODUCTION 50,000 bottles
HECTARES UNDER VINE 25
VITICULTURE METHOD Conventional

The Tumidei family has owned Tenuta Pennita since the 1970s. It lies just a couple of steps from Terra del Sole, the Renaissance ideal city which the Medicis constructed in 1564 and which served as the boundary between Tuscany and Romagna. Their main vineyards are in Monte Poggiolo, at about 170 metres' elevation, planted mostly in chalk-clay soils, with abundant transformed clays. In addition to its wines, La Pennita produces a widely admired estate-produced olive oil.

It is true that their olive oil is this modest operation's most important product but the 2008 grape harvest gave Gianluca Tumidei a good reason for a wine project that would show off to its best advantage a fine group of vineyards, with plenty there to make a fine selection. And thus La Pennita '08 went immediately to our final round, a pure, vibrant Sangiovese that exhibits a palate with enviable character and distinctiveness. The nose is lean and austere, almost rebarbative, but showing impressive depth. TerredelSol '07 is undeniably well made, rich and deep, but perhaps a tad too soft and evolved.

● Sangiovese di Romagna Sup. La Pennita '08	3
● Sangiovese di Romagna Sup. TerredelSol Ris. '07	4
○ Albana di Romagna Passito Nedda '03	5*
● Edmeo '04	5
● Edmeo '03	5
● Edmeo '02	5*
● Sangiovese di Romagna Ris. '05	4
● Sangiovese di Romagna Terredelsol '04	4
● Sangiovese di Romagna Terredelsol '03	4*

Tenuta Pertinello

S.DA ARPINETO PERTINELLO, 2
47010 GALEATA [FC]
TEL. 0543983156
www.tenutapertinello.altervista.org

CELLAR SALES

ANNUAL PRODUCTION 30,000 bottles
HECTARES UNDER VINE 9
VITICULTURE METHOD Conventional

Tenuta Pertinello lies high up in the Valle del Bidente, with its nine hectares of vines planted in sandy-marl soils at 350 to 430 metres. Moreno Mancini bought the operation in 2006, convinced of its potential for quality. Pertinello had always produced just one wine but since 2008, when Fabrizio Moltard joined the business, it has made three, the additions being Sasso and Il Bosco. The former is an all-sangiovese Riserva from the oldest vineyard while the latter is a simpler offering.

Luigi Martini, who tends the vineyards and cellar with passion and skill, personifies continuity here and every year brings in astonishingly healthy fruit to the cellar. Pertinello '07 leans to the sober and dry. We missed some of the vibrancy of previous editions but it is reliable and genuine. Il Bosco '09, the winery's most uncomplicated label, is a stainless steel sangiovese helped with a bit of merlot. It is very quaffable, clean and agile, nicely fragrant, and with appreciable energy.

● Colli della Romagna Centrale Sangiovese Pertinello '07	4
● Sangiovese di Romagna Il Bosco '09	4
● Colli della Romagna Centrale Sangiovese Pertinello '05	4
● Sangiovese di Romagna Il Bosco '08	4

Poderi dal Nespoli

LOC. NESPOLI
VILLA ROSSI, 50
47012 CIVITELLA DI ROMAGNA [FC]
TEL. 0543989637
www.poderidalnespoli.com

CELLAR SALES
PRE-BOOKED VISITS

ANNUAL PRODUCTION 300,000 bottles
HECTARES UNDER VINE 52
VITICULTURE METHOD Conventional

Poderi dal Nespoli is a well-established Romagna estate near the village of Cusercoli, high up the Valle del Bidente. It utilizes grapes from its more than 50 hectares of vineyards, planted part in clay, part in sandy marl soils. The house style has always privileged elegance over power. Fabio Ravaioli still holds the reins, even after the arrival of new partners and capital. Outgoing and clear-sighted, he has always ensured that the wines reflect their local terroir.

Il Nespoli '07 shrugged off a hot year to hew to its wonted elegance and subtlety, displaying a fine balance of acidity and tannins. High-elevation sangiovese flaunts both tasty fruit and flamboyance, but always within bounds. Overall, it is a sharply delineated, focused pleasure. Prugneto is all about fruit and this '09 vintage is particularly impressive, although this label is always a house classic and quite reliable. Full and lean in the mouth, it shows appreciable suppleness from first to last. Borgo dei Guidi '07, a blend of sangiovese, cabernet sauvignon and raboso del Piave, has a full, warm bouquet and a crisply complex palate.

● Sangiovese di Romagna Sup. Il Nespoli Ris. '07	▼▼▼	5
● Borgo dei Guidi '07	▼▼	6
● Sangiovese di Romagna Sup. Prugneto '09	▼▼	4
● Sangiovese di Romagna Sup. Il Nespoli Ris. '06	▽▽▽	5
● Borgo dei Guidi '06	▽▽	6
● Borgo dei Guidi '04	▽▽	6
○ Da Maggio Chardonnay '07	▽▽	3*
● Sangiovese di Romagna Prugneto '07	▽▽	4*
● Sangiovese di Romagna Prugneto '06	▽▽	4*
● Sangiovese di Romagna Sup. Il Nespoli Ris. '05	▽▽	5
● Sangiovese di Romagna Sup. Prugneto '08	▽▽	4*
● Sangiovese di Romagna Sup. Santodeno '08	▽▽	3

Il Poggiarello

LOC. SCRIVELLANO DI STATTO
29020 TRAVO [PC]
TEL. 0523957241
www.ilpoggiarellovini.it

CELLAR SALES
PRE-BOOKED VISITS

ANNUAL PRODUCTION 100,000 bottles
HECTARES UNDER VINE 18
VITICULTURE METHOD Conventional

Back in the1980s, Franco Illari of the Antica Osteria del Teatro awakened a passion for wine in then-young Stefano, Massimo and Paolo Perini. Today, Quattro Valli and Poggiarello comprise an initiative to add to the family's long-time winemaking activity a winery reflecting new ideas, with ambitious, challenging goals. The vineyards, initially laid out by Fregoni and Scienza, enjoy uniform, optimal exposures, and they are now at an age that shows terrific potential for high quality.

The wines we tasted this year evidence in general a heavy winemaking hand that blunts their expressiveness and reflection of terroir, with the first noticeable culprit being a too-heavy load of oak. Perticato Valandrea '09, 55 per cent barbera and 45 per cent bonarda, turned in the best performance. Still, 12 months in barriques have left their mark on the nose and toasty oak somewhat mutes its pulpy, fragrant fruit. On the white side, the clean and refreshing Perticato Il Quadri '09 acquits itself well.

● C. P. Gutturnio Perticato Valandrea '09	▼▼	4
○ C. P. Sauvignon Perticato Il Quadri '09	▼▼	5
○ C. P. Malvasia Perticato Beatrice Quadri '09	▼	5
● Colli Piacentini Gutturnio La Barbona Ris. '08	▼	5
● C. P. Barbera 'L Piston '08	▽▽	4
● C. P. Barbera 'L Piston '07	▽▽	4*
● C. P. Cabernet Sauvignon Perticato Il Novarei '06	▽▽	6
● C. P. Gutturnio La Barbona Ris. '07	▽▽	5
● C. P. Gutturnio La Barbona Ris. '06	▽▽	5
● C. P. Gutturnio Perticato Valandrea '08	▽▽	4
● C. P. Gutturnio Perticato Valandrea '07	▽▽	4*
○ C. P. Malvasia Perticato Beatrice Quadri '08	▽▽	5
● Colli Piacentini Cabernet Sauvignon Perticato del Novarei '07	▽▽	6
○ Colli Piacentini Chardonnay Perticato La Piana '07	▽▽	5

Il Pratello

via Morana, 14
47015 Modigliana [FC]
tel. 0546942038
www.ilpratello.net

CELLAR SALES
PRE-BOOKED VISITS

ANNUAL PRODUCTION 20,000 bottles
HECTARES UNDER VINE 6
VITICULTURE METHOD Certified organic

The road to Pratello climbs gradually and tortuously from Modigliana along the Ibola river to reach a wild area where bracken and chestnuts grow among the broom. This elevation of some 600 metres is at the limits of vine-growing with its harsh climate and often thin, sandy soils. Up here, Emilio Placci planted sangiovese back in 1991. A winegrower who grows and makes his wines with no consultants or chemical help, he clings to the idea that wine is also a style of life, one in harmony with nature.

Il Pratello keeps available several vintages of the same wine, since they boast a longevity that has few local peers. Three Glasses go to Mantignano Vecchie Vigne '04, lean but deep in the mouth, and with a nose offering generous minerality and earthiness. Both energy and elegance are in full evidence and still-fragrant fruit is wonderfully integrated, adding to the wine's complexity. Morana '08 is subtle and supple. After crisp, almost peppery fruit on the nose, the wine takes off in the mouth, propelled into a crisp finish. Le Campore '06 is a tad husky but its complexity merits full respect. All-merlot Calenzone '04 shows tarry and dark, then fresh and relaxed in the mouth.

● Colli di Faenza Sangiovese Mantignano Vecchie Vigne Ris. '04	▼▼▼	4*
● Colli di Faenza Rosso Calenzone '04	▼▼	6
○ Le Campore '06	▼▼	4
● Sangiovese di Romagna Morana '08	▼▼	3
● Colli di Faenza Sangiovese Badia Raustignolo Ris. '03	▽▽	6
● Colli di Faenza Sangiovese Mantignano Ris. '04	▽▽	4*
○ Le Campore '05	▽▽	4*
● Sangiovese di Romagna Morana '06	▽▽	3*

Vigne di San Lorenzo

via Campiume, 6
48013 Brisighella [RA]
tel. 3391137070
www.campiume.it

CELLAR SALES
PRE-BOOKED VISITS
ROOMS AND FOOD

ANNUAL PRODUCTION 10,000 bottles
HECTARES UNDER VINE 3
VITICULTURE METHOD Certified organic

Filippo Manetti turned the ancient village of Campiume, in a gorgeous location in Valle del Lamone, just north of Brisighella, into his residence, a winery, and five guest rooms. His philosophy aims at living in harmony with nature and his wines reflect that. The vineyards are farmed organically and the wines are made without chemical assistance and with natural, unforced timeframes. At times perhaps they stray from formal parameters, but they are filled with character and emotions.

Campiume Riserva '07 is a wine that requires time and patience. The 2007 season was hot and since Manetti makes his wines to reflect their vintage, his sangiovese came in big and sweet. So we have a different Campiume here, less minerally and more fruity. It is still taut and sharp-edged in the mouth but with a lot more body to slow down the progression. The more vibrant San Lorenzo '07 starts off tarry and austere on the nose but a bit of time coaxes out fruit that is refined and multi-faceted. Its elegance is appealing but the palate is notable above all for its breadth and uninterrupted, driving energy.

● San Lorenzo '07	▼▼	5
● Sangiovese di Romagna Sup. Campiume Ris. '07	▼▼	5
● Fieni '06	▽▽	6
● San Lorenzo '06	▽▽	5
● Sangiovese di Romagna Sup. Campiume Ris. '06	▽▽	5

Tenimenti San Martino in Monte

via San Martino in Monte
47015 Modigliana [FC]
tel. 3292984507
www.sanmartinoinmonte.com

ANNUAL PRODUCTION 4,000 bottles
HECTARES UNDER VINE 6
VITICULTURE METHOD Conventional

Romagnolo Maurizio Costa returned to his roots from his childhood Rome with a deeply felt, fascinating project that many friends are involved in as well. San Martino in Monte is high up above Modigliana but the wines are made at another winery. Francesco Bordini, who rightly suggested that Costa's funds should go rather into the vineyards, oversees every step of the winemaking process. The results are already quite good, and the new, totally underground cellar promises to make that leap permanent.

The winery may have Romagna's oldest vineyard, dated to 1922 from its grafting method and human memory. The vines have been restored and wine made since 2002. Final results lie in the future but quality seems impressive in cold seasons and more difficult in warmer ones. Vigna alle Querce '07 is a case in point. Made from sangiovese, merlot, syrah and cabernet franc, it seems just too sweet overall and its abundance of fruit a tad too far beyond ripe. Quite successful though is Vigna della Signora '08, from chardonnay musquet, sauvignon blanc and riesling. Fine as ever, this is a fresh, driving offering, yet broad and deep at the same time, with good proportion on all fronts.

● Sangiovese di Romagna Sup. V. 1922 Ris. '07	**TT**	7
● Vigna alle Querce '07	**TT**	5
○ Vigna della Signora '08	**TT**	6
● Sangiovese di Romagna Sup. V. 1922 Ris. '06	YY	7
● Sangiovese di Romagna V. 1922 '05	YY	7
● Sangiovese di Romagna V. 1922 '04	YY	7
● Vigna alle Querce '06	YY	5
● Vigna alle Querce '05	YY	5
● Vigna alle Querce '03	YY	6

★ San Patrignano

via San Patrignano, 53
47853 Coriano [RN]
tel. 0541362111
www.sanpatrignano.org

PRE-BOOKED VISITS

ANNUAL PRODUCTION 500,000 bottles
HECTARES UNDER VINE 110
VITICULTURE METHOD Organic

The community of San Patrignano, founded by Vincenzo Muccioli in 1978, is now Europe's leading community for recovering drug addicts. On Vincenzo's death, son Andrea took over direction of the community. His passion for wine has transformed one activity into a multi-faceted, ambitious initiative. The vineyards cover 110 hectares of limestone and clay soils on the Coriano hills overlooking the Rimini coast, where the airy slopes offer optimal conditions for both Sangiovese and Bordeaux varieties.

Stefano Longhi has recently converted the vineyards to organic farming, and some to biodynamic. Experiments continue, including vinifications without cultured yeasts or chemical additions, plus ageing in large oak. This is welcome news, since in the past oak has been too apparent. Avi Riserva '07, all sangiovese, is extremely impressive for the subtle elegance of its style and its stand-out character. A lean minerality makes for a fine nose and a well-proportioned palate drives long, impressively forceful without being hard-muscled. The nicely spicy Montepirolo '07, from cabernet sauvignon, merlot and cabernet franc, shows deep and rich, with all components well gauged.

● Sangiovese di Romagna Sup. Avi Ris. '07	**TTT**+	6
● Colli di Rimini Cabernet Montepirolo '07	**TT**	6
○ Aulente Bianco '09	**TT**	4
● Aulente Rosso '09	**TT**	4
○ Vie '09	**TT**	5
● Colli di Rimini Cabernet Montepirolo '06	YYY	6
● Colli di Rimini Cabernet Montepirolo '04	YYY	6
● Colli di Rimini Cabernet Montepirolo '01	YYY	6
● Colli di Rimini Rosso Noi '04	YYY	6
● Sangiovese di Romagna Sup. Avi Ris. '06	YYY	6
● Sangiovese di Romagna Sup. Avi Ris. '05	YYY	6
● Sangiovese di Romagna Sup. Avi Ris. '01	YYY	6
● Sangiovese di Romagna Sup. Avi Ris. '00	YYY	6

San Valentino

FRAZ. SAN MARTINO IN VENTI
VIA TOMASETTA, 13
47900 RIMINI
TEL. 0541752231
www.vinisanvalentino.com

CELLAR SALES
PRE-BOOKED VISITS
ROOMS

ANNUAL PRODUCTION 140,000 bottles
HECTARES UNDER VINE 28
VITICULTURE METHOD Conventional

San Valentino lies in the first rank of Rimini's hills, where the airy marine climate tames alike summer heat and winter cold. Giovanni Mascarin bought the property in 1990, but it was only in 1997 that he and his sister Valeria decided to make quality wine. Fabrizio Moltard took over winemaking and success followed quickly, with full-volumed, beguiling wines, perfect for the markets abroad. Roberto Mascarin runs the operation today, and Benoit De Coster the winemaking, but nothing has changed.

The objective of Mascarin and De Coster is international: clean, powerful pleasers. Their wines are interesting, even if they lack perhaps a reflection of their terroir. We thought Terra di Covignano Riserva '07 one of the best recent vintages, particularly for its lively acidity, which nicely structures the large body. The nose is less impressive, showing slight overripeness, with an impression somewhere between espresso bean and cocoa powder. Eclissi di Sole '08, a blend of sangiovese and syrah with a dash of montepulciano, evidences a sound winemaking hand, with dynamic progression in the mouth, but an obvious desire for sweet fruit on the nose does not make for sophistication.

● Eclissi di Sole '08	🍷🍷	5
● Sangiovese di Romagna Sup. Terra di Covignano Ris. '07	🍷🍷	6
● Sangiovese di Romagna Sup. Scabi '09	🍷	4
● Sangiovese di Romagna Sup. Terra di Covignano Ris. '05	YYY	6
● Sangiovese di Romagna Sup. Terra di Covignano Ris. '03	YYY	5
● Sangiovese di Romagna Sup. Terra di Covignano Ris. '02	YYY	5
● Sangiovese di Romagna Sup. Terra di Covignano Ris. '01	YYY	5
● Sangiovese di Romagna Sup. Terra di Covignano Ris. '04	YY	5

Tenuta Santini

FRAZ. PASSANO
VIA CAMPO, 33
47853 CORIANO [RN]
TEL. 0541656527
www.tenutasantini.com

CELLAR SALES
PRE-BOOKED VISITS

ANNUAL PRODUCTION 30,000 bottles
HECTARES UNDER VINE 22
VITICULTURE METHOD Conventional

Rimini's first hills, between the Valmarecchia and the Marche border, are warm and well ventilated, already influenced by the nearby Adriatic, and carpeted with vast wheat fields punctuated by olive groves and vineyards. Tenuta Santini, near the coast but removed from the swarming sea resorts, nestles in an area with still-pristine culture, dialect and customs. In 2001, the deeply committed Sandro Santini, together with his uncle, redirected the family winery towards a higher-quality future.

As we wrote previously, Tenuta Santini's wines did make an initial quality leap. They are still reliable and enjoyable but they are having difficulty finding the right language, and have yet to rise to the desired level of distinction. Two Glasses go to the least complicated wine, Beato Enrico '09, with clean lines, good fruit on the nose and grip in the mouth. Not extraordinary, certainly, but absolutely well crafted. Battarreo '08 too merits Two Glasses, a cabernet and merlot partnership with some sangiovese. It displays fruit, elegance and good interest in the mouth. We were less pleased with Cornelianum '07, with too much sweet fruit and oak, and just too manipulated.

● Battarreo '08	🍷🍷	4
● Sangiovese di Romagna Sup. Beato Enrico '09	🍷🍷	4
● Sangiovese di Romagna Sup. Cornelianum Ris. '07	🍷	5
● Battarreo '06	YY	4
● Battarreo '04	YY	4*
● Battarreo '03	YY	4*
● Sangiovese di Romagna Sup. Beato Enrico '08	YY	4*
● Sangiovese di Romagna Sup. Beato Enrico '07	YY	4*
● Sangiovese di Romagna Sup. Beato Enrico '06	YY	4*
● Sangiovese di Romagna Sup. Cornelianum Ris. '06	YY	5
● Sangiovese di Romagna Sup. C ornelianum Ris. '05	YY	5

La Stoppa

LOC. ANCARANO
29029 RIVERGARO [PC]
TEL. 0523958159
www.lastoppa.it

CELLAR SALES
PRE-BOOKED VISITS
FOOD

ANNUAL PRODUCTION 160,000 bottles
HECTARES UNDER VINE 32
VITICULTURE METHOD Certified organic

La Stoppa is a respected Colli Piacentini operation. Over a century ago, Gian Carlo Ageno intuited the potential of these nutrient-poor soils and experimented with high-quality viticulture, using French varieties. The Pantaleoni family bought the property in 1973. Today, Elena Pantaleoni is the soul of the operation and Giulio Armani oversees the vineyards and winemaking. The best results currently come from indigenous grapes, and the wines reflect the maturity of the vineyards planted by Elena.

Three Glasses go to Macchiona '06, a barbera and bonarda blend that vaunts a bright palate and a nose that gradually absorbs evolved impressions to reveal lean, intriguing minerality. Barbera '06 earned a place in our final tasting round. Tarry, deep and elegant, it drives bullet-like in the mouth, leaving a contrail of tasty mineral. Malvasia, trebbiano and ortrugo are given very lengthy macerations on the skins to produce Ageno '06, which offers tons of tannins and youthful verve. It also manages to avoid over-facile aromatics that so often slide into excessive sweetness. Cabernet Sauvignon Stoppa '02 opens to gunflint and tobacco leaf, then builds a long, supple progression.

● Macchiona '06	▼▼▼	5
○ Ageno '06	▼▼	5
● C. P. Barbera della Stoppa '06	▼▼	5
● C. P. Cabernet Sauvignon Stoppa '02	▼▼	5
● C. P. Cabernet Sauvignon Stoppa '96	▽▽▽	5
○ C. P. Malvasia Passito V. del Volta '06	▽▽▽	6
○ C. P. Malvasia Passito V. del Volta '04	▽▽▽	6
○ C. P. Malvasia Passito V. del Volta '03	▽▽▽	5
○ C. P. Malvasia Passito V. del Volta '97	▽▽▽	5
● Macchiona '05	▽▽▽	5
○ Buca delle Canne '06	▽▽	7
● C. P. Cabernet Sauvignon Stoppa '06	▽▽	5
● C. P. Gutturnio '07	▽▽	4*
○ C. P. Malvasia Passito V. del Volta '07	▽▽	6

La Tosa

LOC. LA TOSA
29020 VIGOLZONE [PC]
TEL. 0523870727
www.latosa.it

CELLAR SALES
PRE-BOOKED VISITS

ANNUAL PRODUCTION 120,000 bottles
HECTARES UNDER VINE 13
VITICULTURE METHOD Conventional

In 1984, the Pizzamiglio family, with roots in Milan, brought a small revolution to the Colli Piacentini when they produced non-sparkling wines and obsessed over high quality in their vineyards. La Tosa puts out well-crafted bottles because nothing is left to chance and every step receives almost maniacal attention. The result is a very recognizable style, even if the wines rarely reveal the qualities of their Val Nure terroir, which is overlain by a thoroughgoing, even heavy-handed, fruitiness.

Vignamorello '09, one of the most appealing editions ever, reached our finals, thanks to its crisp fruit, seductive mouthfeel, juicy pulp and emphatic flavours. Although the oak shows somewhat and the tone is a tad sweet, it's clean and sound, lacking only that snap of originality to push it to the top step. Gutturnio '09 performs well, with clean fruit, but is weighed down by too much sweetness. The '09 version of Malvasia Sorriso di Cielo is more refreshing than past editions. Its contours are clean and flavours rich, and it is delicious overall.

● C. P. Gutturnio Vignamorello '09	▼▼	5
● C. P. Gutturnio '09	▼▼	4
○ C. P. Malvasia Sorriso di Cielo '09	▼▼	4
● C. P. Cabernet Sauvignon Luna Selvatica '08	▼	6
○ C. P. Malvasia Passito L'Ora Felice '09	▼	5
○ C. P. Valnure Riodeltordo '09	▼	3
● C. P. Cabernet Sauvignon Luna Selvatica '06	▽▽▽	6
● C. P. Cabernet Sauvignon Luna Selvatica '04	▽▽▽	6
● C. P. Cabernet Sauvignon Luna Selvatica '97	▽▽▽	5
● C. P. Cabernet Sauvignon Luna Selvatica '07	▽▽	6
● C. P. Gutturnio '08	▽▽	4
● C. P. Gutturnio Vignamorello '08	▽▽	5
○ C. P. Malvasia Sorriso di Cielo '08	▽▽	4
○ C. P. Valnure Rio del Tordo '08	▽▽	3*

Tre Monti

loc. Bergullo
via Lola, 3
40026 Imola [BO]
tel. 0542657116
www.tremonti.it

CELLAR SALES
PRE-BOOKED VISITS

ANNUAL PRODUCTION 180,000 bottles
HECTARES UNDER VINE 50
VITICULTURE METHOD Conventional

Sergio Navacchia bought Tre Monti, where sons David and Vittorio have been fully involved since 1986. One holding, with the cellar, is at Serra, in the Imola hills, and the other, at Petrignone in the hills near Forlì, has the historic Thea vineyard. The Serra soils are largely clay, with some areas of silt and others rich in active lime, and the albana grape thrives here. Petrignone shows more transformed clays, with up to 20 per cent sand, and a stony fluvial bench emerges here and there in the sangiovese vineyards.

Petrignone Riserva '07, an almost electric sangiovese, brings home Three Glasses. Vivacious and stylish overall, the mouth shows nicely dry and the tannins are glossy and self-confident. Particularly impressive is Thea Riserva '08, supple and spacious, yet at the same time austere and quite complex. We thought the whites were down a note, showing a tad tired and somewhat burdened. The exception is Vigna della Rocca '09, which got good marks for its citrussy nose. The mouth is rich enough but needs a bit more acidic grip. Campo di Mezzo '09, straightforward and consistent, has an attractive peppery edge to the nose.

● Sangiovese di Romagna Sup. Petrignone Ris. '07	▼▼▼	4
○ Albana di Romagna Secco V. della Rocca '09	▼▼	4
● Sangiovese di Romagna Sup. Thea Ris. '08	▼▼	5
○ Colli d'Imola Chardonnay Ciardo '09	▼	4
● Sangiovese di Romagna Sup. Campo di Mezzo '09	▼	4
● Colli di Imola Boldo '97	▽▽▽	4
● Sangiovese di Romagna Sup. Petrignone Ris. '06	▽▽▽	4
○ Albana di Romagna Passito Casa Lola '07	▽▽	5
○ Albana di Romagna Secco V. della Rocca '08	▽▽	4
○ Colli d'Imola Bianco Thea Bianco '06	▽▽	5
● Colli d'Imola Boldo '07	▽▽	4
● Sangiovese di Romagna Sup. Campo di Mezzo '08	▽▽	4
● Sangiovese di Romagna Sup. Thea Ris. '07	▽▽	5

Vallona

fraz. Fagnano
via Sant'Andrea, 203
40050 Castello di Serravalle [BO]
tel. 0516703333
fattorie.vallona@serravallewifi.net

CELLAR SALES
PRE-BOOKED VISITS

ANNUAL PRODUCTION 90,000 bottles
HECTARES UNDER VINE 29
VITICULTURE METHOD Conventional

Maurizio Vallona is one of the pillars in the Colli Bolognesi and a grower in the strictest sense of the term, with a character to match. At home in vineyard and cellar, he shuns the limelight and says little in public. Vallona is one of the finest Colli Bolognesi white-wine producers, as you can see from his vineyards. In soils that are predominantly limestone and sand, a full 70 per cent of the vines are planted to white varieties.

Vallona's explore pignoletto, plus his mastery of winemaking, means that his most successful wines precisely reflect this new vinous frontier. The most impressive expression is Pignoletto Amestesso '06. With its vibrant nose and mineral-veined palate, it sets a new course for the area. Primedizione Cuvée '09, mostly pignoletto, is succulent and winds up to tension at the end, which makes for a dynamic wine. Among the international whites, Sauvignon Blanc '09 stands out, opening to tangy grapefruit and then developing a snappy, full-flavoured mid palate. From the reds, we liked Cabernet Sauvignon Diggioanni '07 overall but there is some lurking overripeness and alcoholic heat.

● C. B. Cabernet Sauvignon '09	▼▼	4
● C. B. Pignoletto Cl. Amestesso '06	▼▼	4
○ C. B. Sauvignon Blanc '09	▼▼	4*
○ Primedizione Cuvée 2009	▼▼	4
● Diggioanni Cabernet Sauvignon '07	▼	5
● C. B. Cabernet Sauvignon Sel. '99	▽▽▽	5
● C. B. Cabernet Sauvignon Sel. '97	▽▽▽	5
● C. B. Merlot Affederico '01	▽▽▽	5
● Diggioanni Cabernet Sauvignon '04	▽▽▽	5
● Diggioanni Cabernet Sauvignon '06	▽▽	5
○ Essè Brut Spumante	▽▽	4

Podere Vecciano

via Vecciano, 23
47852 Coriano [RN]
tel. 0541658388
www.poderevecciano.it

CELLAR SALES
PRE-BOOKED VISITS

ANNUAL PRODUCTION 70,000 bottles
HECTARES UNDER VINE 10
VITICULTURE METHOD Certified organic

Davide Bigucci's operation has grown continuously, and it now figures as one of the finest in the Colli Riminesi. This is a growing area with terrific potential but to break through it needs a group of talented and passionate producers. Bigucci's work in the vineyards is meticulous and he is smart not to be forcing results. Use of chemicals is kept at a minimum, his winemaking methods respect the qualities of the fruit and he tries as much as possible to let the natural process take its course.

D'Enio Riserva '07 competed in the final tastings, thanks to its supple, generous palate and appealingly dry crispness. A slightly dusty nose is the only cavil. With the '09, Montetauro continues to be enjoyable, even taking into account a slight lack of excitement in the mouth. It is Podere Vecciano's least complex offering but it acquits itself well up against VignaalMonte '07, which seems a touch warm in this edition.

● Sangiovese di Romagna Sup. D'Enio Ris. '07	▼▼	5
● Montetauro '09	▼▼	2*
● Sangiovese di Romagna Sup. VignalMonte '07	▼▼	4
○ Colli di Rimini Rebola VignalaGinestra '07	▽▽	4*
● Montetauro '08	▽▽	2*
● Sangiovese di Romagna Sup. D'Enio Ris. '06	▽▽	5
● Sangiovese di Romagna Sup. D'Enio Ris. '04	▽▽	5
● Sangiovese di Romagna Sup. D'Enio V.V. Ris. '06	▽▽	5
● Sangiovese di Romagna Sup. VignalMonte '06	▽▽	4*
● Vignalavolta '06	▽▽	4*

Francesco Vezzelli

fraz. San Matteo
via Canaletto Nord, 878a
41122 Modena
tel. 059318695
aavezzelli@gmail.com

CELLAR SALES

ANNUAL PRODUCTION 110,000 bottles
HECTARES UNDER VINE 15
VITICULTURE METHOD Conventional

This historic cellar is now run by Francesco Vezzelli, who looks after vines and winemaking, and by his son Roberto, who markets and sells it. The vineyards are in Sozzigalli, in the floodplains of the Secchia river. These loose, nutrient-poor soils are heaven for sorbara since they bring out its hallmark florality and minerality. The Vezzellis demonstrate a sure hand for this variety and they stuck to their subtler, elegant style even a few years back, when market voices demanded more powerful versions.

The Sorbara Enrico Vezzelli '09 selection is as fine as ever, redolent of slaty mineral and flowers, and with a stylish palate. Bricco di Checco, made of salamino and ancellotta, also repeats the pleasures of past vintages. The '09 nose leans to the floral, with violets and mulberry, plus wild blackberry. Although the acidity dips a bit, the mouth reflects a judicious balance between a firm structure and basic earthiness on the one hand and smoother, softer impressions on the other, characteristic of ancellotta. Equally sound is Rive dei Ciliegi '09, made with grasparossa bought in from two of Vezzelli's long-time growers. It is dry and crisply rustic, with loads of fruit.

● Lambrusco di Sorbara Enrico Vezzelli '09	▼▼	4
● Lambrusco Grasparossa di Castelvetro Rive dei Ciliegi '09	▼▼	4
● Lambrusco Il Bricco di Checco '09	▼▼	3
● Lambrusco di Sorbara Enrico Vezzelli '08	▽▽	4*
● Lambrusco Grasparossa di Castelvetro Rive dei Ciliegi '08	▽▽	4*
● Lambrusco Il Bricco di Checco '08	▽▽	2*

Vigne dei Boschi

VIA TURA, 7A
48013 BRISIGHELLA [RA]
TEL. 054651648
vignedeiboschi@alice.it

CELLAR SALES

ANNUAL PRODUCTION 19,000 bottles
HECTARES UNDER VINE 11
VITICULTURE METHOD Organic

Paolo Babini grows a few hectares biodynamically in the Valle del Lamone. The soils are marly sandstones, almost beyond the pale for viticulture, and in fact, Babini's vineyards are under siege by woods and naked river-devoured cliffs. His winery-laboratory has yielded good results for both sangiovese and understanding of the local terroir. Babini has energetically supported the valley zonation programme of the University of Milan and has become known locally as an expert on this area.

The wines are made in full respect for the growing year, with no help from technology or chemicals. We didn't taste the sangiovese Poggio Tura '06, which needs another year. Sedici Anime '08 is from riesling renano, vat-matured in cement. The nose is complex and mineral-edged, the palate spacious, and it cuts like a blade all the way through the mouth. The all-sauvignon blanc Borgo Casale '05 rested long in old oak and emerges in full expressive maturity. This ultra-refined wine almost hides behind a self-confident but subtle style, yet its engine is extraordinary acidity that is never green or vegetal. Nero Selva '06 is a floral pinot nero, dry in the mouth but full of interest.

○ Borgo Casale '05	2 black glasses	4
● Nero Selva '06	2 black glasses	5
○ Sedici Anime '08	2 black glasses	5
● Poggio Tura '05	3 white glasses	6
● Borgo Stignani '02	2 white glasses	4*
● Rosso per Te '06	2 white glasses	5
○ Sedici Anime '07	2 white glasses	5
● Sette Pievi '03	2 white glasses	5
● Sette Pievi '01	2 white glasses	5*

Produttori di Vigoleno

VIA LIBERTÀ, 1
29010 VERNASCA [PC]
TEL. 0523891225
www.vinsantodivigoleno.it

ANNUAL PRODUCTION N.A.
HECTARES UNDER VINE N.A .
VITICULTURE METHOD Conventional

Vigoleno is a gorgeous fortified hamlet, still perfectly intact within its walls. A small group of local producers proudly carries on the ancient tradition of Vin Santo. Vigoleno's version is made from indigenous grapes, mostly melara and santa maria, but with berverdino, trebbiano and marsanne as well, the latter called champagne locally. The grapes are harvested fairly early and naturally dried, then given extremely lengthy fermentations, and the wine aged, without any topping-up, for many years.

The Colli Piacentini DOC Vin Santo di Vigoleno is one of the smallest designations in Italy, and most of the production is family-sized, apart from Lusignani's almost 2,000 bottles. We included them all together in one profile under the municipality, since it would be difficult to give each wine a profile yet together they constitute an extraordinary corpus meriting attention. Lusignani's Vin Santo '00 went to our final round for its richness and aromatic breadth, offering dried fig and zabaglione, cheek by jowl with notes of espresso bean and candied citrus. Final round also for Enzo Perini's Vin Santo '02. It's fresh and deep, with zabaglione as well, and a quite classic character.

○ C.P. Vin Santo di Vigoleno Enzo Perini '02	2 black glasses	6
○ C.P. Vin Santo di Vigoleno Lusignani '00	2 black glasses	6
○ C.P. Vin Santo di Vigoleno Giuseppe Sesenna '03	2 black glasses	6
○ C.P. Vin Santo di Vigoleno Massimo Visconti '01	2 black glasses	6
○ C.P. Vin Santo di Vigoleno Paolo Loschi '03	2 black glasses	6
○ C.P. Vin Santo di Vigoleno Stefano Ballarini '02	2 black glasses	6

Villa Bagnolo

LOC. BAGNOLO
VIA BAGNOLO, 160
47011 CASTROCARO TERME [FC]
TEL. 0543769047
www.villabagnolo.it

CELLAR SALES

ANNUAL PRODUCTION 80,000 bottles
HECTARES UNDER VINE 15
VITICULTURE METHOD Conventional

Villa Bagnolo is located in the lower Colli Forlivesi, above Castrocaro Terme. Enjoying breezes from both plains and sea, it lies above an unusual salty clay that is used by a nearby thermal spa. Lombard businessman Vito Ballarati retired here with his family and poured into this project the considerable energy and creativity that had marked his professional life. Villa Bagnolo covers 54 hectares, 15 in vines, the majority sangiovese. The wines mature in large oak.

Riserva Bagnolo '07 turned in a terrific performance, with a taut but agile progression driving through its considerable volume. It does show a little sweet oak but that remains mostly below the radar. Sorgara '08 starts with a hardly varietal florality but the mouth, dry and fresh, finds just the right level of energy. Sassetto '09 is a fruity, fun quaffer with an intriguing peppery note. This simple, straightforward standard label is very well made. Alloro '08, from sangiovese, cabernet sauvignon and cabernet franc, evidences some tiredness in the fruit and too much softness but it does offer decided elegance of expression as well.

● Sangiovese di Romagna Sup. Bagnolo Ris. '07	▼▼	5
● Sangiovese di Romagna Sup. Sassetto '09	▼▼	4
● Sangiovese di Romagna Sup. Sorgara '08	▼▼	4
● Alloro '08	▼	5
● Alloro '07	▽▽	5
● Alloro '06	▽▽	5
● Sangiovese di Romagna Sup. Bagnolo Ris. '06	▽▽	5
● Sangiovese di Romagna Sup. Sassetto '06	▽▽	3*
● Sangiovese di Romagna Sup. Sorgara '07	▽▽	4

Villa Liverzano

FRAZ. RONTANA
VIA VALLONI, 47
48013 BRISIGHELLA [RA]
TEL. 054680461
www.liverzano.it

CELLAR SALES
PRE-BOOKED VISITS
ROOMS

ANNUAL PRODUCTION 10,000 bottles
HECTARES UNDER VINE 3
VITICULTURE METHOD Conventional

Following his success as a grower in Tuscany, Romagna-born Swiss citizen Marco Montanari came to Brisighella few years ago, intrigued with a region far removed from the wine-sector limelight. Rather than make wines that reflect their local terroir, Montanari pursues an elegant, original style, helped by sand-chalk soils that contribute stylishly unusual expressions even in sangiovese, as well as by his own immensely dedicated work in the vineyards. Villa Liverzano also has a striking country hotel.

Montanari did not present his Don '08 this year. It's getting another year in the bottle, in accord with his awareness over recent years of the very positive contribution of longer bottle ageing. We can only agree with him, since we retried Don '07 and found that it had improved tremendously compared to its showing shortly after bottling. We did very much like Rebello '08, a merlot and sangiovese partnering. A bit of reduction is soon gone and the wine opens up beautifully, with plenty of interest on all sides. The progression is marked by dynamic self-confidence and consistency, and it displays an abundance of zesty fruit from first to last.

● Rebello '08	▼▼	6
● Don '07	▽▽	6
● Don '06	▽▽	6
● Don '05	▽▽	6
● Don '04	▽▽	6
● Rebello '07	▽▽	6
● Rebello '06	▽▽	6
● Rebello '05	▽▽	6
● Rebello '04	▽▽	6
● Rebello '03	▽▽	5

Villa Papiano

via Ibola, 24
47015 Modigliana [FC]
tel. 0546941790
www.villapapiano.it

CELLAR SALES
PRE-BOOKED VISITS

ANNUAL PRODUCTION 25,000 bottles
HECTARES UNDER VINE 10
VITICULTURE METHOD Conventional

The ten-year-old Villa Papiano long ago won full respect and it is the now the flagship of a new phenomenon in Romagna, high-elevation estates that produce Sangioveses grown on marl-sandstone soils. The vineyards lie on the wooded southern slope of Monte Chioda, reaching as high as 500 metres. The wines here are elegant, becoming cleaner-edged and more linear every year, benefitting from the impressive distinctiveness gifted by these difficult soils when they are treated with due respect.

I Probi Riserva '07, austere on the nose, serious and straightforward, accurately mirrors its terroir. The progression is magisterial, as are its dry, lively flavours, the only small cloud being a clumsy sweetness on the nose and a mouth that is a shade too technical. Papiano di Papiano '07, mostly merlot with some sangiovese and other grapes, opens sweet and mature – think chocolate and spice – followed by appealing richness in the mouth. Le Tresche '09, made from all sauvignon blanc partly aged in oak, is juicy and complex, with lovely tropical notes and a zippy crispness in the mouth. Le Papesse '08, though a tad softish, is soundly made.

○ Le Tresche di Papiano '09	YY (black)	4
● Papiano di Papiano '07	YY (black)	5
● Sangiovese di Romagna I Probi di Papiano Ris. '07	YY (black)	4
● Sangiovese di Romagna Le Papesse di Papiano '08	Y (black)	4
● Papiano di Papiano '04	YYY	5
○ Le Tresche di Papiano '08	YY	4
● Papiano di Papiano '06	YY	5
● Papiano di Papiano '05	YY	5
● Sangiovese di Romagna I Probi di Papiano Ris. '06	YY	4*
● Sangiovese di Romagna I Probi di Papiano Ris. '05	YY	4
● Sangiovese di Romagna Le Papesse di Papiano '07	YY	4*
● Sangiovese di Romagna Le Papesse di Papiano '05	YY	4*

Villa Trentola

loc. Capocolle di Bertinoro
via Molino Bratti, 1305
47032 Bertinoro [FC]
tel. 0543741389
www.villatrentola.it

CELLAR SALES
PRE-BOOKED VISITS

ANNUAL PRODUCTION 45,000 bottles
HECTARES UNDER VINE 20
VITICULTURE METHOD Conventional

This estate, purchased in 1890 by Enrico Prugnoli, brought together three separate farms, Valle, Colombaia and Molino. The limestone clays and marine tufa, or "spungone", are classic to the Bertinoro area, and the Villa Trentola vineyards, trained to spurred cordon, are meticulously cared for. Owner Enrico Prugnoli is an agronomist and oversees the vines, while daughter Federica makes the wine, assisted by consultant Fabrizio Moltard.

We tasted only two wines this year. The missing team members are actually the simplest of the Villa Trentola's Sangioveses. Il Moro Riserva '07 is a fine Sangiovese di Romagna, its palate dry, clean-contoured and linear. Placidio '07, from 100 per cent merlot, is ultra-stylish. It takes off minerally and a bit reduced but then opens wide and lengthy in the mouth, displaying its charms in lovely subtle tones.

● Il Placidio '07	YY (black)	6
● Sangiovese di Romagna Sup. Il Moro di Villa Trentola Ris. '07	YY (black)	5
● Sangiovese di Romagna Sup. Il Moro di Villa Trentola '05	YY	5
● Sangiovese di Romagna Sup. Il Moro di Villa Trentola '03	YY	6
● Sangiovese di Romagna Sup. Il Moro di Villa Trentola '02	YY	5
● Sangiovese di Romagna Sup. Il Prugnolo di Villa Trentola '07	YY	4
● Sangiovese di Romagna Sup. Il Prugnolo di Villa Trentola '06	YY	4*
● Sangiovese di Romagna Sup. Placidio '04	YY	8
● Sangiovese di Romagna Ultimo Atto Sup. '08	YY	5

Villa Venti

LOC. VILLAVENTI DI RONCOFREDDO
VIA DOCCIA, 1442
47020 FORLÌ
TEL. 0541949532
www.villaventi.it

CELLAR SALES
PRE-BOOKED VISITS
ROOMS AND FOOD

ANNUAL PRODUCTION 18,000 bottles
HECTARES UNDER VINE 7
VITICULTURE METHOD Certified organic

Mauro Giardini and Davide Castellucci bought Villa Venti in 2002, and operate it along with their wives, sisters Manuela and Monica De Riva. The estate is at 160 metres' elevation, and the vineyards, organically farmed, are planted in transformed red and sandy yellow clays but the soils vary tremendously, even within individual vineyard blocks. The nearby sea tempers the climate of this inland hill area and increases the day-night temperature differences.

Villa Venti takes home Three Glasses for its Sangiovese di Romagna Superiore Primo Segno '08. Full-volumed in the mouth, it glories in vibrant, savoury fruit that contributes to a subtly constructed, super-stylish personality, a tribute to the potential of sangiovese. Felis Leo '07 is made of merlot, sangiovese and cabernet sauvignon. It opens immediately, delightfully protean in its energy and rhythmic progression, and exhibits a tasty mineral edge all the way through.

● Sangiovese di Romagna Sup. Primo Segno '08	▼▼▼	4
● Felis Leo '07	▼▼	4
● Sangiovese di Romagna Sup. Primo Segno '07	▽▽	4*

★ Fattoria Zerbina

FRAZ. MARZENO
VIA VICCHIO, 11
48018 FAENZA [RA]
TEL. 054640022
www.zerbina.com

CELLAR SALES
PRE-BOOKED VISITS

ANNUAL PRODUCTION 220,000 bottles
HECTARES UNDER VINE 33
VITICULTURE METHOD Conventional

Fattoria Zerbina has been one of Romagna's most dependable wineries for 20 years now, turning out quality in a linear, consistent style that well reflects the area, particularly for sangiovese. It has always demonstrated an obsessive dedication to the vineyards, treating the grapes with absolute respect, and now that the vines are fully mature, the wines express terrific quality and an immediately recognisable identity across the entire line, from the simplest wine to the most ambitious Riserva.

Three Glasses go to AR Riserva '06 and the Sweet of the Year. This is an extreme wine, with the grapes picked berry by berry, the culmination of years of efforts and of a sensibility rare indeed. Incredible density is accompanied by a crisp freshness that never loses its nerve, caressed by rich yet always stylish sensory impressions of saffron, apricot, spring flowers, figs. Scacco Matto '07 performs well, particularly refined and refreshing. Notes of botrytis emerge first, but a broad array of aromas gradually follows. Pietramora Riserva '07 is lean and austere, expressive of its terroir, and unleashes a near-endless finish. The fruit in Marzieno '06 shows somewhat impoverished.

○ Albana di Romagna Passito AR Ris. '06	▼▼▼+	8
○ Albana di Romagna Passito Scacco Matto '07	▼▼	7
● Marzieno '06	▼▼	6
● Sangiovese di Romagna Sup. Pietramora Ris. '07	▼▼	7
● Sangiovese di Romagna Il 500 '09	▼▼	3
● Sangiovese di Romagna Sup. Torre di Ceparano '07	▼	4
○ Albana di Romagna Passito Scacco Matto '01	▽▽▽	7
● Marzieno '04	▽▽▽	6
● Marzieno '03	▽▽▽	6
● Marzieno '01	▽▽▽	6
● Sangiovese di Romagna Sup. Pietramora Ris. '06	▽▽▽	7
● Sangiovese di Romagna Sup. Pietramora Ris. '04	▽▽▽	7
● Sangiovese di Romagna Sup. Pietramora Ris. '03	▽▽▽	7

Barbolini

LOC. CASINALBO
VIA FIORI, 40
41043 FORMIGINE [MO]
TEL. 059550154
www.barbolinicantina.it

Barbolini is a family operation in the foothills near Modena with 35 hectares of vineyard. Lancillotto '09, though showing a tad overripe, reveals an impressive mouth, spacious and crisp. Bellerofonte '09, with an earthy nose redolent of roots and moss, is simply delicious.

- ● Lambrusco di Sorbara Bellerofonte '09 — 🍷🍷 3*
- ● Lambrusco Grasparossa di Castelvetro Lancillotto '09 — 🍷🍷 3*

Casali Viticultori

FRAZ. PRATISSOLO
VIA DELLE SCUOLE, 7
42019 SCANDIANO [RE]
TEL. 0522855441
www.casalivini.it

Casale Viticoltori works 40 hectares of vineyard, four estate-owned and the rest leased, with varieties including spergola, marzemino and lambrusco. Pra di Bosso '09, from montericco, marani and salamino, is formidable, ambitious in its minerality, broad yet clean-edged and focused, and nicely dry.

- ● Reggiano Lambrusco Pra di Bosso '09 — 🍷🍷 3*

Cavim
Cantina Viticoltori Imolesi

FRAZ. SASSO MORELLI
VIA CORRECCHIO, 54
40026 IMOLA [BO]
TEL. 054255003
www.cavimimola.it

Cavim is a well-known co-operative whose wine has gone in bulk to local eateries but in recent years bottled products offer fine quality and popular price tags. Sangiovese di Romagna Superiore Moro di Serrafelina '09 is fragrant and generous while Chardonnay Blumanne '09 shows savoury and juicy.

- ○ Colli d'Imola Chardonnay Blumanne '09 — 🍷🍷 2*
- ● Sangiovese di Romagna Sup. Moro di Serrafelina '09 — 🍷🍷 3*
- ● Sangiovese di Romagna Sup. Moro di Serrafelina Ris. '07 — 🍷 3

Cantine Ceci

VIA PROVINCIALE, 99
43030 TORRILE [PR]
TEL. 0521810252
www.lambrusco.it

Ceci, near Parma, has purchased wine from the area and sold it under its own label since 1938. The wines are big and generous, consistently styled sweet and fruity, and quite appealing and expressive both on nose and palate.

- ● Otello Lambrusco Et. Nera '09 — 🍷🍷 3*
- ● Otello NerodiLambrusco '09 — 🍷🍷 4

Celli

VIA CARDUCCI, 5
47032 BERTINORO [FC]
TEL. 0543445183
www.celli-vini.com

Mauro Sirri directs Celli, near Bertinoro, and his simplest wines are the most impressive. I Croppi '09, Celli's iconic wine, appears amber with a rustic nose and cutting acidity. Le Grillaie '09 show less typicality than in the past, but it is soundly made, nicely dry and vivacious.

- ○ Albana di Romagna Secco I Croppi '09 — 🍷🍷 3*
- ● Sangiovese di Romagna Sup. Le Grillaie '09 — 🍷🍷 3*

Corte d'Aibo

VIA MARZATORE, 15
40050 MONTEVEGLIO [BO]
TEL. 051832583
www.cortedaibo.it

Corte d'Aibo vinifies only its own organically grown grapes. The reds show fine body but they evidence a touch of overripeness and too much oak. We liked the two Pignolettos. The '09 is marked by fresh vegetables on the nose and tasty fruit in the mouth. Montefreddo '09 is clean, complex and flavourful.

- ○ C. B. Pignoletto Cl. Montefreddo '09 — 🍷🍷 3*
- ○ Pignoletto '09 — 🍷🍷 2*

Il Cortile - Dall'Asta
LOC. CASATICO DI LANGHIRANO
S.DA DELLA NAVE, 14
43010 PARMA
TEL. 0521863576
info@cantinedallasta.com

Founded by Luigi Dall'Asta in 1910, Cortile-Dall'Asta is Parma's oldest winery. It originally made wines from its flat-land vineyards and bought-in fruit but now it sources from 15 hectares of estate hillside vineyards. Mefistofele '09, from maestri, is a fine offering, broad, fragrant and dry.

○ Colli di Parma Malvasia Dama Bianca M. Cl. '08 — 🍷🍷 4
● Lambrusco dell'Emilia Mefistofele '09 — 🍷🍷 2*

Fiorini
LOC. GANACETO
VIA NAZIONALE PER CARPI, 1534
41010 MODENA
TEL. 059386028
www.fiorini1919.com

Fiorini has nine hectares in the sorbara area, divided into three parcels, two with sorbara in fairly loose soils, the other with salamino in clay. In 1998, grasparossa was planted in the limestone hills of Maranello. Becco Rosso '09 is almost ancient in style: dry, earthy, minerally and nicely complex.

● Lambrusco di Sorbara Corte degli Attimi '09 — 🍷🍷 4*
● Lambrusco Grasparossa di Castelvetro Becco Rosso '09 — 🍷🍷 4*

Lusvardi
LOC. MOLINO DI GAZZATA
VIA CANALE PER REGGIO, 2
42018 SAN MARTINO IN RIO [RE]
TEL. 0522646516
www.lusvardi.it

Lusvardi is a small, innovative operation in San Martino in Rio, with vineyards at 40-50 metres in medium-textured, clayey soils. Their effervescent wines are made without adding sugar or must so they are clean and fruit-forward, on the light side, refreshing and flavourful in the mouth.

● Lusvardi Brut '09 — 🍷🍷 4*
⊙ Lusvardi Brut Rosé '09 — 🍷🍷 4*

Tenuta Masselina
LOC. SERRÀ
VIA POZZE, 1030
48014 CASTEL BOLOGNESE [RA]
TEL. 0545651004
www.masselina.it

The CEVICO co-operative established Masselina, with 12 hectares of vineyard in the hills between Faenza and Imola, as a kind of research laboratory. The sangiovese-cabernet 158 slm '09 boasts bright, expressive fruit and an elegant, flavour-rich palate while Chardonnay 147 slm '09 is fragrant and crisp.

○ 147 slm '09 — 🍷🍷 3*
● 158 slm '09 — 🍷🍷 3*

Orsi - San Vito
FRAZ. OLIVETO
VIA MONTE RODANO, 8
40050 MONTEVEGLIO [BO]
TEL. 051964521
www.vignetosanvito.it

Despite difficulties, Federico Orsi is committed to organic farming, and his first results are so good that his wines have been flying out the door. Vigna del Grotto '07is redolent of honey and blossoms, with a clean, briny edge to the mouth. Monte Rodano '08 is gamy and dry with thrusting energy.

● C. B. Cabernet Sauvignon Monte Rodano '08 — 🍷🍷 4*
○ C. B. Pignoletto Cl. V. del Grotto '07 — 🍷🍷 4*

Pezzuoli
VIA VIGNOLA, 136
41053 MARANELLO [MO]
TEL. 0536948800
www.pezzuoli.it

Pezzuoli makes wine solely from its 120 hectares of estate vineyards on its various properties in Modena's three separate lambrusco zones. Rosso Aurora '09 is fragrant, taut and lengthy. Tramonto Rosso '09 is broad and deep, sporting a gorgeous, clean-edged finish.

● Lambrusco di Sorbara Rosso Aurora '09 — 🍷🍷 4*
● Lambrusco Grasparossa di Castelvetro Tramonto Rosso '09 — 🍷🍷 4*

Fondo San Giuseppe

VIA TURA
48013 BRISIGHELLA [RA]
TEL. 3346018221
stefano.bariani@alice.it

Stefano Bariani farms five hectares organically, mostly white grapes. The vines are at 400 metres in loose, silty-marl soils, along with 11 hectares of woods. The trebbiano Tèra '09 builds an impressively taut, dry palate and Fiorile '08, an Albana, shows complexity on the nose and focus in the mouth.

○ Fiorile '08	🍷🍷	5
○ Tèra '09	🍷🍷	4*

Cantina Sociale Santa Croce

SS 468 DI CORREGGIO, 35
41012 CARPI [MO]
TEL. 059664007
www.cantinasantacroce.it

The Santa Croce co-operative boasts 100 years of history and puts out delicious monovarietal Salaminos every year from its grapes in the village of Santa Croce. The sober Tradizione '09 is the best of the line, with austere fruit, then a well-focused palate animated by a zippy acidity.

● Lambrusco Salamino di S. Croce Enoteca '09	🍷🍷	2*
● Lambrusco Salamino di S. Croce Tradizione '09	🍷🍷	2*

Cantina Sociale Settecani

VIA MODENA, 184
41014 CASTELVETRO DI MODENA [MO]
TEL. 059702505
www.cantinasettecani.it

Founded in 1923, the Settecani co-operative lies at the foot of the Modena Apennines and draws its grasparossa grapes from the hill areas. The fragrant, country-style Grasparossa '09 is lively and creamy, with well-focused fruit. Vigna del Re '09 is crisp and ultra-elegant.

● Lambrusco Grasparossa di Castelvetro Secco '09	🍷🍷	4*
● Lambrusco Grasparossa di Castelvetro Secco V. del Re '09	🍷🍷	4*

Alberto Tedeschi

VIA SAN MARTINO, 1
40011 ZOLA PREDOSA [BO]
TEL. 3465373919
www.albertotedeschi.it

Alberto Tedeschi is a grower who has original ideas about pignoletto. He makes just one wine, fermenting the grapes along with the stems in old wood vats and matures the wine 24 months on the lees. The '07 is a subtle, judiciously balanced proposition that shows minerally and elegant with cutting acidity.

○ Vigne Spungola Bellaria '07	🍷🍷	4

Cantina Valtidone

VIA MORETTA, 58
29011 BORGONOVO VAL TIDONE [PC]
TEL. 0523862168
www.cantinavaltidone.it

If Valtidone's red wines suffer in general from a lack of freshness and grip in the mouth, his whites are reliable. Armonia '09 is floral, fresh and well proportioned. Perlage shows fine depth and complexity, fragrant citrus and a touch of spice, then a long, rhythmic progression.

○ Brut Perlage	🍷🍷	5
○ C. P. Ortrugo Armonia Frizzante '09	🍷🍷	3*
○ C. P. Malvasia Frizzante Aurora '09	🍷	3

Villa di Corlo

LOC. BAGGIOVARA
S.DA CAVEZZO, 200
41100 MODENA
TEL. 059510736
www.villadicorlo.com

Maria Antonietta Munari's winery has two separate properties. The lambrusco is planted at Villa di Corlo, while Cà del Vento, high in the Reggio hills, grows the international varieties. Giaco '07, a Bordeaux blend, is impressive, as is Rosso Estella '09, made of grasparossa and salamino.

● Giaco a Cà del Vento '07	🍷🍷	4
● Rosso Estella Lambrusco '09	🍷🍷	3*
● Corleto Lambrusco '09	🍷	3

TUSCANY

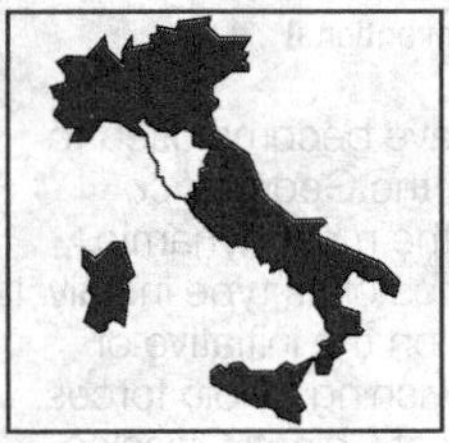

Even more Three Glasses went to Tuscany this year, taking the total to 67. This means second place again, behind Piedmont but the gap is closing. Improvement has come from better rounded vintages and enhanced definition that have enabled the various areas to express their individual characteristics to the full. This certainly applies to Chianti Classico, this year taking home the good result from designation and IGT wines – 12 apiece – that it deserves, given the huge potential of such a vast, complex area, whether the main grape is sangiovese or one of the non-native varieties. The fragrant simplicity of the 2008 vintage suggested that it would succeed in bringing out the lighter, more graceful aspects of the designation in wines that are naturally delicious, succulent, fresh-tasting wines, while 2007 had more of a proud look, all structure and austerity. But muscle power has left the spotlight so Bolgheri and Maremma no longer seem to be the models to follow wherever you may be making you wine. Speaking of the coast, here too the pursuit of elegance wins the day, even though the Mediterranean stamp and warm climate are an integral part, and indeed a strongpoint, of the intensifying search for differentiation. At Montalcino, the Brunello 2004 stands head and shoulders above the rest with Riserva and selections proving more impressive in the 2005 version, a lighter and therefore more challenging year for sangiovese, especially in some areas. Compensating for this lack of structure are two wonderful Rosso di Montalcino from one vintage, 2007, which are stylish and seductive, more in keeping with the grape variety. What we need to emphasize is a general trend towards enhanced precision, recognizability, territorial character and authenticity. Gradually and with difficulty, the message seems to be getting through that more original, authentic products bring success, especially on international markets. These small steps are evident, especially to those of us who taste all the region's wines every year. One obvious example of this, which can easily be noted while turning the pages of the Guide, is the necessary grouping together of several wineries owned by the same estate in one profile. While in the past we guaranteed separate profiles for the different production zones, serious space problems encountered this year have forced us to put them all together. This is a sign that new wineries with fine quality products are making progress. Good news, very good indeed.

Agricola Alberese

FRAZ. ALBERESE
LOC. SPERGOLAIA
58010 GROSSETO
TEL. 0564407180
www.alberese.com

CELLAR SALES
PRE-BOOKED VISITS
ROOMS

ANNUAL PRODUCTION **150,000 bottles**
HECTARES UNDER VINE **53**
VITICULTURE METHOD **Certified organic**

As well as enjoying a fantastic location in the Maremma nature park, the regional authority-owned winery appears to have set off on the road to fine quality. The range of wines has a clean style, not without typical features, and sells at affordable prices, which does no harm in times like these. Credit goes to the carefully considered decision to extensively upgrade cellar and vineyards, which led Agricola Alberese to release its first bottled products in 2003.

The Morellino di Scansano Barbicato '07, which made it through to the finals, is a sunny wine with rich, generous aromas and a warm, flavoursome palate. Also very good is the Morellino Pellegrone '08, which gives orange peel and spices leading into an enjoyable and nicely lively palate. The Morellino Serrata dei Cavalleggeri '09 is coherent and straightforward with a relaxed palate. The Castelmarino, a monovarietal Vermentino, is fragrant and uncomplicated, as is the rosé Scoglietto '09, made from sangiovese.

● Morellino di Scansano Barbicato '07	🍷🍷	6
● Morellino di Scansano Pellegrone '08	🍷🍷	4
● Morellino di Scansano Serrata dei Cavalleggeri '09	🍷	4
⊙ Scoglietto '09	🍷	4
○ Vermentino Castelmarino '09	🍷	4
● Morellino di Scansano '05	♡♡	4
● Morellino di Scansano Barbicato '04	♡♡	4
● Morellino di Scansano Pellegrone '06	♡♡	4*
● Morellino di Scansano Serrata dei Cavalleggeri '07	♡♡	4*

Agricoltori del Chianti Geografico

LOC. MULINACCIO, 10
53013 GAIOLE IN CHIANTI [SI]
TEL. 0577749489
www.chiantigeografico.it

CELLAR SALES
PRE-BOOKED VISITS
ROOMS

ANNUAL PRODUCTION **1,600,000 bottles**
HECTARES UNDER VINE **580**
VITICULTURE METHOD **Conventional**

In recent years, we have become used to excellent results from the Georgrafico co-operative, one of the most dynamic, best-organized wineries of its type in Italy. It was founded in 1961 on the initiative of Gaiole winegrowers wishing to join forces to protect the identity of Chianti Classico and reap the fruits of their labours. Today it numbers over 200 members, a top class expert oenological team and extensive vineyards across Chianti to Montalcino, Scansano and San Gimignano.

Another great version of the Chianti Classico Riserva Montegiachi, the '07, won Three Glasses. This wine is still maturing and needs time in bottle, of course, but the quality is already clear from the overall style: oaky hints on the nose blend perfectly with complex, profound floral and fruity aromas. The coherent flavour on the palate never cramps the original texture, which offers impressive territory-derived nuances. The Chianti Classico '08 is very enjoyable in its youthful freshness.

● Chianti Cl. Montegiachi Ris. '07	🍷🍷🍷	5
● Brunello di Montalcino Castello Tricerchi '05	🍷🍷	8
● Morellino di Scansano Le Preselle '09	🍷🍷	4*
● Chianti Cl. '08	🍷	4
● Chianti Cl. Contessa di Radda '08	🍷	5
● Chianti Colli Senesi '09	🍷	3
● Chianti Colli Senesi Torri Ris. '07	🍷	3
● Pulleraia '08	🍷	6
● Chianti Cl. Montegiachi Ris. '05	♡♡♡	5
● Chianti Cl. Contessa di Radda '04	♡♡	4
● Ferraiolo '04	♡♡	6
● Pulleraia '03	♡♡	5
● Pulleraia '01	♡♡	6
● Pulleraia '00	♡♡	4*
● Rosso di Montalcino Castello Tricerchi '07	♡	5

Podere l'Aione

LOC. AIONE, 12
56040 MONTECATINI VAL DI CECINA [PI]
TEL. 058830339
www.aione.ch

CELLAR SALES
PRE-BOOKED VISITS

ANNUAL PRODUCTION 18,000 bottles
HECTARES UNDER VINE 6
VITICULTURE METHOD Conventional

Owners Robert Walti and Doris Portner have set up a small winery capable of producing wines that develop confidently, in a precise, distinctive style. The winery, near the old village of Montecatini Val di Cecina, is situated in an enchanting natural setting. The vineyards include older vines, planted around 80 years ago, and more recent plantings at the considerable altitude of 500 metres above sea level.

The red Etico '07, from mainly merlot, is very well rounded, with aromas focusing on dark-coloured fruit and confident toasty hints. Despite a certain general maturity, the palate opens out and presses forward to show lively freshness in the finish. Also very good is the Salve Sangiovese '07 displays hints of spices and aromatic herbs such as lavender and curry leaves, with a silky body and nice progression. The Aione '07 shows red fruit and lavender while the palate finishes with slightly unripe, drying vegetal hints.

● Etico '07	▼▼	6
● Salve '07	▼▼	6
● Aione '07	▼	6
○ Montescudaio Vin Santo '03	▼	5
● Aione '03	▽▽	6
● Aione '01	▽▽	6
● Etico '06	▽▽	6
● Etico '05	▽▽	6
● Etico '04	▽▽	6
● Salve '05	▽▽	6

Altura

LOC. MOLINACCIO
58012 GIGLIO [GR]
TEL. 0564806041
www.arcobalena.net

CELLAR SALES
PRE-BOOKED VISITS
FOOD

ANNUAL PRODUCTION 6,000 bottles
HECTARES UNDER VINE 4
VITICULTURE METHOD Organic

Altura has a short history but ancient roots. It released its first wine ten years ago after a massive effort to recover an abandoned vineyard. Four hectares of terraces with huge rocks rising steeply above the sea, surrounded by aridity, wind, salt and blazing sunshine. With love and a little madness, Francesco Carfagna and his family saved this place from environmental and social decay and brought it back to life. A dozen-odd kilometres of rebuilt dry stone walls, grafting with native germ plasm, Guyot and bush-trained vines. All in full respect of the spirit of the place.

The first Three Glasses for Francesco Carfagna's Ansonaco in recognition of its personality and unique grape is also a tribute to the personal vision of a grower who practices biodynamic farming and protects biodiversity without propounding the theory. Almost 6,000 bottles per year produced without weedkiller, only hoes, manure and flowable sulphur. No clarification or filtration before bottling. This wine is the child of the wind and the salty air, flawed in some ways but versatile with a vibrant, profound, salty nose. The palate is powerful, generous, genuinely minerally, mouthfilling and very lingering.

○ Ansonaco dell'Isola del Giglio '09	▼▼▼	6
○ Ansonaco dell'Isola del Giglio '08	▽▽	6
○ Ansonaco dell'Isola del Giglio '07	▽▽	5
○ Ansonaco dell'Isola del Giglio '06	▽▽	5

Ampeleia

LOC. MELETA
58028 ROCCASTRADA [GR]
TEL. 0564567155
www.ampeleia.it

CELLAR SALES
PRE-BOOKED VISITS

ANNUAL PRODUCTION **120,000 bottles**
HECTARES UNDER VINE **40**
VITICULTURE METHOD **Conventional**

The Ampeleia project brings together three friends: Elisabetta Foradori, Thomas Widmann and Giovanni Podini, she a winegrower and the other two entrepreneurs, united by their deep passion for wine. The vineyards are at Fattoria di Meleta, a reference point in the 1980s for Maremma winemaking, which enjoyed less attention back then. Behind this project is uncompromising hard work, looking above all to the future and pursuing a personal, innovative style that reflects a whole terroir.

The Ampeleia '07, a blend of cabernet franc and sangiovese, shows sophisticated style with enthralling chocolate and cherry aromas heralding the firmly structured, sweet and succulent palate. Kepos '08 is a subtle, balanced, flavoursome and very supple blend of five Mediterranean varieties: grenache, mourvèdre, marselan, carignano and alicante, and proves perfectly able to deliver hints of terroir.

● Ampeleia '07	🍷🍷	6
● Kepos '08	🍷🍷	6
● Kepos '06	YYY	6
● Ampeleia '06	YY	6
● Ampeleia '05	YY	6
● Ampeleia '04	YY	6
● Kepos '07	YY	4

★★ Marchesi Antinori

P.ZZA DEGLI ANTINORI, 3
50123 FIRENZE
TEL. 05523595
www.antinori.it

PRE-BOOKED VISITS
ROOMS

ANNUAL PRODUCTION **20,000,000 bottles**
HECTARES UNDER VINE **2,200**
VITICULTURE METHOD **Conventional**

Antinori is one of the best-known names in Italian wine production, and how could it be otherwise when 26 generations have worked with wine over the last 600 years? Proving the point in terms of quality are an impressive number of vineyards producing wines in industrial quantities but which still show very strong links to the territory. A winery which cannot be overlooked, as capable today of setting the course as it was when it first produced the Tignanello, marking the beginning of a renaissance for this area.

Three Glasses again for the Solaia. This blend, based on cabernet sauvignon and sangiovese with a dash of cabernet franc, offers echoes of currants and strawberries on the nose with subtly fresh, clean vegetal hints. The dynamic palate and already relaxed tannins reflect a style that favours elegance and allure, leading to a long, dry finish. The '07 Tignanello, from a sangiovese-heavy blend, is also very good. Blackberry and raspberry mingles with hints of pipe tobacco and leather to introduce a very flavoursome palate, thanks to the balance of acidity and tannin, with a clean, rounded finish.

● Solaia '07	🍷🍷🍷	8
● Tignanello '07	🍷🍷	8
● Cortona Bramasole La Braccesca '07	🍷🍷	6
● Villa Antinori Rosso '07	🍷🍷	5
● Chianti Cl. Badia a Passignano Ris. '07	🍷	7
● Nobile di Montepulciano La Braccesca '07	🍷	5
● Santa Cristina '09	🍷	4
● Solaia '06	YYY	8
● Solaia '03	YYY	8
● Solaia '01	YYY	8
● Solaia '00	YYY	8
● Solaia '99	YYY	8
● Solaia '98	YYY	8
● Solaia '97	YYY	8
● Tignanello '05	YYY	8
● Tignanello '04	YYY	8

Argentiera

LOC. DONORATICO
VIA AURELIA, 410
57024 CASTAGNETO CARDUCCI [LI]
TEL. 0565773176
www.argentiera.eu

CELLAR SALES
PRE-BOOKED VISITS

ANNUAL PRODUCTION 400,000 bottles
HECTARES UNDER VINE 60
VITICULTURE METHOD Conventional

Argentiera, owned by the Fratini families, is now a benchmark winery in the Bolgheri area. The estate is situated in the southern part of the designation, with nicely aspected vineyards on varied terrain with good clay and stony soil. Meticulous cellar work does the rest and delivers flawlessly made wines for appreciative palates in a dynamic and very elegant style.

An impressive overall performance from the latest tasting, although a top note is missing. The Bolgheri Superiore '07, especially, fails to achieve the full complexity one would expect. It is nevertheless a very good wine, with curranty and floral aromas and a lingering, alluring palate. However, it is slightly marked by toasty sensations and assertive tannins which hold back progression a little. We liked the Bolgheri Villa Donoratico '07. It's earthy and fluent although here, too, the tannin is slightly intrusive.

● Bolgheri Sup. Argentiera '07	**YY**	8
● Bolgheri Villa Donoratico '07	**YY**	5
● Bolgheri Sup. Argentiera '06	YYY	8
● Bolgheri Sup. Argentiera '05	YYY	8
● Bolgheri Sup. Argentiera '04	YYY	8
● Bolgheri Poggio ai Ginepri '05	YY	4*
● Bolgheri Sup. Argentiera '03	YY	8
● Bolgheri Villa Donoratico '07	YY	5
● Bolgheri Villa Donoratico '05	YY	5
● Bolgheri Villa Donoratico '04	YY	5

Argiano

FRAZ. SANT'ANGELO IN COLLE
53024 MONTALCINO [SI]
TEL. 0577844037
www.argiano.net

PRE-BOOKED VISITS
ROOMS

ANNUAL PRODUCTION 350,000 bottles
HECTARES UNDER VINE 51
VITICULTURE METHOD Conventional

At last, signs of resurgence from this wonderful classic Montalcino estate. A magnificent location in the south-west part of the designation with over 50 hectares of beautifully sited vineyards, almost all south-facing with excellent ventilation. Density varies according to when the vineyards were planted, with the most recent close to 7,000 plants per hectare. The soil has plenty of stones on a clay base, typical for this area. The splendid historical winery buildings have been joined by a modern, efficient cellar.

We were most impressed by the Suolo '07, a monovarietal Sangiovese made from older vines. Nicely concentrated ruby red ushers in aromas ranging from fruity hints of morello cherries to medicinal herbs and sweet pipe tobacco. The close-woven texture offers compact tannins and lovely acidity for an excellent base worthy of a Brunello di Montalcino. We also liked the Solengo '07, a blend of syrah, merlot and cabernet sauvignon.

● Solengo '07	**YY**	8
● Suolo '07	**YY**	8
● Brunello di Montalcino '05	**Y**	7
⊙ L' O Rosato '09	**Y**	4
● Non Confunditur '08	**Y**	6
● Brunello di Montalcino Ris. '88	YYY	6
● Brunello di Montalcino Ris. '85	YYY	5
● Solengo '97	YYY	8
● Solengo '95	YYY	8
● Brunello di Montalcino '04	YY	7
● Brunello di Montalcino '02	YY	8
● Brunello di Montalcino '01	YY	7
● Rosso di Montalcino '07	YY	5
● Solengo '03	YY	8

★ Avignonesi

FRAZ. VALIANO DI MONTEPULCIANO
VIA COLONICA, 1
53040 MONTEPULCIANO [SI]
TEL. 0578724304
www.avignonesi.it

CELLAR SALES
PRE-BOOKED VISITS

ANNUAL PRODUCTION 700,000 bottles
HECTARES UNDER VINE 119
VITICULTURE METHOD Conventional

Avignonesi is a traditional name in the Nobile di Montepulciano area, with a history dating back to the 1970s when the first vineyards were planted in a dream of a location near the village of Valiano. The Vin Santos are perhaps the most intimately connected to Montepulciano, and the winery's strongpoint, but a very precise style has developed throughout the range in recent years, with the appearance of measured, well-balanced wines.

The Vin Santo and Vin Santo Occhio di Pernice, both '98, are outstanding. The former may well be the best Tuscan wine of its type while the latter reveals impressively weighty, concentrated texture. The Nobile '07 is well balanced with a very supple palate. The Cortona Desiderio '07, a monovarietal Merlot, lays out a well-stocked array of aromatics and firm structure while the Rosso di Montepulciano '09 is sweet and dependably good. The powerful '06 50 & 50, a blend of sangiovese and merlot made with the Chianti Capannelle winery, fails to relax.

○ Vin Santo '98	3 black glasses	8
● Vin Santo Occhio di Pernice '98	2 black glasses	8
● Cortona Desiderio '07	2 black glasses	7
● Nobile di Montepulciano '07	2 black glasses	5
● 50 & 50 Avignonesi e Capannelle '06	1 black glass	8
● Rosso di Montepulciano '09	1 black glass	4
● 50 & 50 Avignonesi e Capannelle '99	3 white glasses	8
○ Vin Santo '96	3 white glasses	8
○ Vin Santo '95	3 white glasses	8
○ Vin Santo '93	3 white glasses	8
● Vin Santo Occhio di Pernice '97	3 white glasses +	8
● Vin Santo Occhio di Pernice '93	3 white glasses	8
○ Vin Santo Occhio di Pernice '90	3 white glasses	8

Badia a Coltibuono

LOC. BADIA A COLTIBUONO
53013 GAIOLE IN CHIANTI [SI]
TEL. 0577746110
www.coltibuono.com

CELLAR SALES
PRE-BOOKED VISITS
ROOMS AND FOOD

ANNUAL PRODUCTION 950,000 bottles
HECTARES UNDER VINE 72
VITICULTURE METHOD Certified organic

An old abbey with a modern atmosphere, centuries of history behind up-to-date products, if you are looking for ever fresher, brighter and more natural wines. Emanuela Stucchi Prinetti, the astute manager of the family estate, has succeeded in converting the many hectares of vineyards to organic farming and has altered the feel of the wines, favouring a more drinkable style. Her new challenges include the Vin Santo Occhio di Pernice. The abbey is also a hospitality structure where cooking courses and jazz concerts are held in the summer.

Two of the many wines presented went through to the finals. The Chianti Classico RS '08 has cherry and strawberry fruit with minerally hints preceding a supple body, powerful acidity and an appetizing flavour with a lip-smacking finish. The nicely made Vin Santo Occhio di Pernice '03 shows vibrant aromas with hints of violets, blackberry and blackcurrant jam against light nuances of spice, and a full-bodied, softly generous palate with a long finish. The Trappoline '09, from chardonnay and sauvignon, is a nice surprise. Floral aromas with hints of banana and peach fruit introduce good structure, a flavoursome palate and a lingering finale.

● Chianti Cl. RS '08	2 black glasses	4*
○ Vin Santo del Chianti Cl. Occhio di Pernice '03	2 black glasses	6
● Chianti Cl. Ris. '07	2 black glasses	6
○ Trappoline '09	2 black glasses	4
○ Vin Santo del Chianti Cl. '04	2 black glasses	6
● Cancelli Sangiovese '09	1 black glass	3
● Chianti Cl. '08	1 black glass	5
● Chianti Cl. Cultus Boni '07	1 black glass	6
● Sangioveto '06	1 black glass	7
● Chianti Cl. '06	3 white glasses	5*
● Chianti Cl. Ris. '04	3 white glasses	6
● Sangioveto '95	3 white glasses	6
● Chianti Cl. Ris. '06	2 white glasses	6
● Chianti Cl. Ris. '05	2 white glasses	6

Fattoria di Bagnolo

LOC. BAGNOLO-CANTAGALLO
VIA IMPRUNETANA PER TAVARNUZZE, 48
50023 IMPRUNETA [FI]
TEL. 0552313403
www.bartolinibaldelli.it

CELLAR SALES
PRE-BOOKED VISITS

ANNUAL PRODUCTION 25,000 bottles
HECTARES UNDER VINE 10
VITICULTURE METHOD Conventional

Marco Bartolini Baldelli is to all intents and purposes a farming entrepreneur, with various interests throughout Tuscany although the main focus of his activities is Impruneta, an area well-known in the past for its extra virgin olive oil but which has gained an increasingly high reputation in the wine sector over the years. Credit also goes to the winery for the consistently high quality of the products, the result of painstaking manual work in cellar and vineyard.

The Chianti Colli Fiorentini '08 has a fresh, bright nose with hints of aromatic herbs then a warm, succulent, sweet palate with a lingering finish. The Capro Rosso '07, from sangiovese, colorino and cabernet sauvignon, has striking toastiness and spice on the nose. The palate is flavoursome, powerful and soft with a lovely dynamic finish. The Vin Santo Riserva '01 shows pale amber and aromas of hazelnuts, almonds and aromatic herbs, with a lovely, lingering sensation in the finish. The Chianti Colli Fiorentini Riserva '07 displays spices and wild berries while the mid-bodied palate is mouthwatering, not too powerful and a tad abrupt at the back.

● Capro Rosso '07	▼▼	5
● Chianti Colli Fiorentini '08	▼▼	4
○ Vin Santo del Chianti Ris. '01	▼▼	6
● Chianti Colli Fiorentini Ris. '07	▼	5
● Capro Rosso '06	▽▽	6
● Capro Rosso '05	▽▽	6
● Capro Rosso '04	▽▽	5
● Chianti Colli Fiorentini '07	▽▽	4*
● Chianti Colli Fiorentini '06	▽▽	4*
● Chianti Colli Fiorentini '05	▽▽	3*
● Chianti Colli Fiorentini Ris. '06	▽▽	5
● Chianti Colli Fiorentini Ris. '05	▽▽	5
● Chianti Colli Fiorentini Ris. '04	▽▽	5

I Balzini

LOC. PASTINE, 19
50021 BARBERINO VAL D'ELSA [FI]
TEL. 0558075503
www.ibalzini.it

PRE-BOOKED VISITS

ANNUAL PRODUCTION 50,000 bottles
HECTARES UNDER VINE 8
VITICULTURE METHOD Conventional

The estate owned by the D'Isantos has made important progress in safeguarding the environment: the newly built underground cellar has zero energy consumption for the basic lighting; the photovoltaic system covers 80 per cent of energy requirements; and the winery has chosen to reduce bottle weight by 200 grams and abandon polystyrene and plastic packaging. These factors demonstrate that it is possible to make wine while looking out for the local area. The winery's name derives from the little terraces, or "balzi", where the vineyards are planted.

The tastings show continuity in the quality of the wines. The very good Black Label '07, from cabernet sauvignon, sangiovese and merlot, has ripe aromas of blackberries, damson and cherries, livened up by spices, cinnamon and cloves. The succulent palate shows excellent weight, boisterous but not unruly tannins and a lovely dynamic finish. We also liked the White Label '07, from equal quantities of sangiovese and cabernet sauvignon, with a slew of wild berry aromas and hints of Mediterranean scrubland. The palate opens out nicely to reveal nice weighty texture and good length.

● I Balzini Black Label '07	▼▼	6
● I Balzini White Label '07	▼▼	5
● I Balzini Green Label '08	▼	4
● I Balzini Black Label '06	▽▽	6
● I Balzini Black Label '05	▽▽	6
● I Balzini Black Label '03	▽▽	6
● I Balzini Black Label '01	▽▽	6
● I Balzini Black Label '00	▽▽	7
● I Balzini White Label '06	▽▽	6
● I Balzini White Label '05	▽▽	6
● I Balzini White Label '04	▽▽	5
● I Balzini White Label '03	▽▽	5

Riccardo Baracchi

loc. San Martino
via Cegliolo, 21
52042 Cortona [AR]
tel. 0575612679
www.baracchiwinery.com

CELLAR SALES
PRE-BOOKED VISITS
ROOMS AND FOOD

ANNUAL PRODUCTION 75,000 bottles
HECTARES UNDER VINE 22
VITICULTURE METHOD Organic

It all began with the renovations to the villa that would become the Il Falconiere hotel. Following his wife Silvia's success in the fine food sector, it was almost a given that Riccardo Baracchi would go into winemaking, thanks to a healthy passion inculcated by a family wine tradition that involved his father and now his son Benedetto. Although only recently discovered, this area has a longstanding heritage so traditional varieties like trebbiano do well, along with the more innovative syrah.

Best this year is the syrah and cabernet sauvignon Ardito '07, with vibrant wafts of wild berries and spice followed by a weighty but not heavy structure, lovely tannic texture, a flavoursome back palate and reasonably good finish. Dominating the nose of the interesting Merlot Smeriglio '08 are red berries with hints of cinnamon while the soft, succulent palate has a relaxed finish. A nice '07 version of the Brut Rosé displays more clearly defined aromas and a generous, well-balanced body. The beautifully made Astore '09 is a monovarietal Trebbiano with flowers and fresh apple and peach fruit while the palate is impressively tasty and persistent.

● Ardito '07	▼▼	7
○ Astore '09	▼▼	4
● Cortona Smeriglio Merlot '08	▼▼	5
⊙ Spumante Brut Rosé '07	▼▼	8
● Cortona Smeriglio Sangiovese '08	▼	5
● Cortona Smeriglio Syrah '08	▼	5
● Ardito '05	▽▽	7
● Ardito '04	▽▽	6
● Cortona Smeriglio Merlot '07	▽▽	5
● Cortona Smeriglio Merlot '06	▽▽	5
● Cortona Smeriglio Merlot '05	▽▽	5
● Cortona Smeriglio Sangiovese '05	▽▽	5
● Cortona Smeriglio Sangiovese '04	▽▽	5
● Cortona Smeriglio Syrah '07	▽▽	5

Fattoria dei Barbi

loc. Podernovi, 170
53024 Montalcino [SI]
tel. 0577841111
www.fattoriadeibarbi.it

CELLAR SALES
PRE-BOOKED VISITS
FOOD

ANNUAL PRODUCTION 800,000 bottles
HECTARES UNDER VINE 90
VITICULTURE METHOD Conventional

Fattoria dei Barbi, owned by the Cinelli family since the 14th century, has produced Brunello di Montalcino wines since 1892. We recommend a visit to the buildings, highly evocative of a 20th century farm, also because current owner Stefano Cinelli has created a beautiful museum of rural civilization which takes a deeper look at Montalcino farming history. The farm is situated along the road to Castelnuovo dell'Abate with about 50 hectares of Brunello vineyards, in a rather cool and breezy area. The stony land, with a small clay and sand component, produces very stylish wines.

An excellent performance from the range tasted took two wines into the finals. The estate's cru, Brunello di Montalcino Vigna del Fiore '05, is nicely typed showing a floral, slightly fruity nose with quite vibrant, lingering hints of black cherries. Sculpted, mellow tannins, with acidity supporting the texture, lead to a generous finish. The Riserva '04 displays warmer aromas with hints of jam and pleasant tobacco. The vibrant palate is softened by lovely acidity.

● Brunello di Montalcino Ris. '04	▼▼	8
● Brunello di Montalcino V. del Fiore '05	▼▼	8
● Brunello di Montalcino '05	▼	6
● Brunello di Montalcino '04	▽▽	6
● Brunello di Montalcino '01	▽▽	6
● Brunello di Montalcino Ris. '01	▽▽	8
● Brunello di Montalcino Ris. '00	▽▽	8
● Brunello di Montalcino V. del Fiore '04	▽▽	8
● Brunello di Montalcino V. del Fiore '03	▽▽	8
● Brunello di Montalcino V. del Fiore '01	▽▽	7
● Brusco dei Barbi '08	▽▽	3*
● Morellino di Scansano Sole '07	▽▽	5

★ Barone Ricasoli

LOC. CASTELLO DI BROLIO
53013 GAIOLE IN CHIANTI [SI]
TEL. 05777301
www.ricasoli.it

CELLAR SALES
PRE-BOOKED VISITS
FOOD

ANNUAL PRODUCTION 2,000,000 bottles
HECTARES UNDER VINE 250
VITICULTURE METHOD Conventional

The Ricasoli family's history goes hand in glove with Chianti Classico, where it is still a benchmark winery. The extensive vineyards surround the splendid medieval castle of Brolio in the southern part of the designation, planted at altitudes between 200 and almost 500 metres, and have undergone extensive modernization. The wines have a modern style and very precise focus.

The Chianti Classico Castello di Brolio '07 is exemplary. The style hinges on sweet fruity and toasty components, which yield hints of morello cherries, vanilla and spice over a rather dark, close-woven basic texture. Three Glasses. The Chianti Classico Brolio '08 shows more or less similar features in a simpler context of fruit aromatics. The impressive Rocca Guicciarda Riserva '07 shows iron-like minerality and flavoursome tannins, not unlike the Colledilà '07, a textured monovarietal Sangiovese. The powerful Casalferro '07 gives new oak and alcohol in this single-variety Merlot version. The two whites from '09, Granello and Torricella, are both well focused.

● Chianti Cl. Castello di Brolio '07	▼▼▼	8
● Casalferro '07	▼▼	8
● Chianti Cl. Colledilà '07	▼▼	8
● Chianti Cl. Rocca Guicciarda Ris. '07	▼▼	6
● Chianti Cl. Brolio '08	▼	6
○ Granello '09	▼	6
○ Torricella '09	▼	6
● Casalferro '05	∇∇∇	8
● Casalferro '03	∇∇∇	6
● Casalferro '99	∇∇∇	6
● Chianti Cl. Castello di Brolio '06	∇∇∇	8
● Chianti Cl. Castello di Brolio '04	∇∇∇	8
● Chianti Cl. Castello di Brolio '03	∇∇∇	7
● Chianti Cl. Castello di Brolio '01	∇∇∇	7
● Chianti Cl. Castello di Brolio '00	∇∇∇	7
● Chianti Cl. Castello di Brolio '99	∇∇∇	7

Mattia Barzaghi

LOC. SAN DONATO, 13
53037 SAN GIMIGNANO [SI]
TEL. 0577941501
www.mattiabarzaghi.com

CELLAR SALES

ANNUAL PRODUCTION 45,000 bottles
HECTARES UNDER VINE 8
VITICULTURE METHOD Organic

Mattia Barzaghi is dynamic. He applies his ideas about vines and wine to the letter, his bottles have character and he uses modern techniques to communicate with the world about his winery. So when he arrived in the town of a hundred towers, a shake-up was in order. Mattia has been in this area since 2000 and worked for eight years in a local winery, learning about wine and laying the foundations for what he calls the "zeta project". He grows just two varieties, using organic methods: vernaccia for whites and sangiovese for the reds and rosés. Results are excellent.

The Riserva Cassandra '08 della Vernaccia makes it to our final tastings thanks to lovely complex aromas in which fresh, lively pear and peach-like fruit mingles with hints of nuts and forest floor. A firm, succulent, compelling palate shows clean and lingering. We liked the Zeta '09, initially reserved on the nose but more forthcoming on the palate, which unfolds savoury and weighty with a lingering flavour.

○ Vernaccia di S. Gimignano Cassandra Ris. '08	▼▼	5
○ Vernaccia di S. Gimignano Zeta '09	▼▼	4*
● Mezzanotte '09	▼	4
● Sorriso '09	▼	4
● Sciamano '07	∇∇	5
○ Vernaccia di S. Gimignano Cassandra Ris. '07	∇∇	5
○ Vernaccia di S. Gimignano Zeta '08	∇∇	4*
○ Vernaccia di S. Gimignano Zeta '07	∇∇	5

Fattoria di Basciano

V.LE DUCA DELLA VITTORIA, 159
50068 RUFINA [FI]
TEL. 0558397034
www.renzomasibasciano.it

CELLAR SALES
PRE-BOOKED VISITS

ANNUAL PRODUCTION **200,000 bottles**
HECTARES UNDER VINE **35**
VITICULTURE METHOD **Conventional**

Agronomist and winemaker Paolo Masi creates his wines in the Rufina area with commendably consistent quality, personally supervising the various stages of production and achieving excellent results thanks to his unflagging care and attention. He is also very skilled at selecting the grapes used to produce his two, always sound wines, Chianti Riserva and Erta e China, which also stands out as excellent value for money. The winery style is modern and not purely territory-bound.

Erta e China '08 is an equal blend of sangiovese and cabernet sauvignon with hints of blackberries and spice on the nose, a delicate, soft body with nicely integrated tannin and a pleasing, lingering finish. The '08 I Pini, from merlot, cabernet sauvignon and syrah, has distinctive aromas of pepper and animal skins, a weighty structure and spicy finish. The Vigna Il Corto '08, sangiovese with a splash of cabernet sauvignon, reveals pleasant vegetal hints on the nose and a hefty but slightly stiff body that relaxes into the finish. The two enjoyable Chianti Rufinas are richer in nicely handled tannins. The Vin Santo '04 will appeal to lovers of traditional style.

● Chianti Rufina '08	▼▼	3*
● Chianti Rufina Ris. '07	▼▼	5
● Erta e China '08	▼▼	3
● I Pini '08	▼▼	5
● Vigna Il Corto '08	▼▼	4
● Chianti Ris. '07	▼	3*
⊙ Rosato di Toscana '09	▼	2
○ Vin Santo del Chianti Rufina '04	▼	5
● Chianti Rufina '05	▽▽	3*
● Erta e China '07	▽▽	3*
● Erta e China '06	▽▽	3*
● I Pini '07	▽▽	5
● I Pini '06	▽▽	5
● Il Corto '06	▽▽	5
○ Vin Santo Rufina '03	▽▽	5
○ Vin Santo Rufina '02	▽▽	4

Belpoggio

FRAZ. CASTELNUOVO DELL'ABATE
LOC. BELLARIA
53024 MONTALCINO [SI]
TEL. 0423982147
www.belpoggio.it

ANNUAL PRODUCTION **30,000 bottles**
HECTARES UNDER VINE **5**
VITICULTURE METHOD **Conventional**

Belpoggio is in a sense a relaxation for the Martellozzo family, who have worked for a century in the Prosecco zone in Veneto. Five of the estate's ten hectares are planted with vineyards, a stone's throw from the enchanting abbey of Sant'Antimo. The soil is principally loose-packed with a very high proportion of marl to reduce the clay component. The small cellar uses advanced technology and medium-sized 30-hectolitre casks. Wines come from low-yield vineyards and careful bunch selection, and the aromas tend be fruity-led.

Both of the very impressive wines presented this year just fell short of our highest accolade. The Brunello '05 has a generous nose with balsamic hints enhancing the black cherries and yellow peaches and a nuance of tobacco to add an evolved sensation. The palate is close-knit and nicely dynamic with mellow extract and a lingering finish. The Rosso di Montalcino '08 is just as good with a vibrant, very fruity and lightly spiced nose. The palate is mouthwatering with sweet tannins and lovely acidity.

● Brunello di Montalcino '05	▼▼	7
● Rosso di Montalcino '08	▼▼	5
● Brunello di Montalcino '04	▽▽	7
● Brunello di Montalcino '03	▽▽	7

Podere Le Berne

loc. Cervognano
via Poggio Golo, 7
53040 Montepulciano [SI]
tel. 0578767328
www.leberne.it

CELLAR SALES

ANNUAL PRODUCTION 25,000 bottles
HECTARES UNDER VINE 6
VITICULTURE METHOD Conventional

Andrea Natalini is not about to be overawed by the flattering results obtained in the recent past and continues to work with the same level of commitment and passion in his vineyards at Cervognano, one of the leading crus in Montepulciano. His wines have achieved an extremely focused and well-defined style. They stand the test of time while remaining very drinkable with nicely typical features and bags of character.

The Nobile di Montepulciano '07 unveils faint but well-focused aromas and a succulent palate with lovely texture and nicely vigorous acidity. The very drinkable Rosso di Montepulciano '09 is a subtle, supple, flavoursome wine. The Nobile Riserva '06 is powerful and rich in texture but unable to relax on the palate, held back by the still-exuberant oak that also adds an excessively toasty aroma to the nose.

● Nobile di Montepulciano '07	▼▼	4
● Rosso di Montepulciano '09	▼▼	4
● Nobile di Montepulciano Ris. '06	▼	6
● Nobile di Montepulciano '06	▽▽▽	4
● Nobile di Montepulciano '05	▽▽	4*
● Nobile di Montepulciano '04	▽▽	4
● Nobile di Montepulciano Ris. '05	▽▽	6
● Nobile di Montepulciano Ris. '04	▽▽	6
● Nobile di Montepulciano Ris. '03	▽▽	6
● Rosso di Montepulciano '08	▽▽	4
● Rosso di Montepulciano '06	▽▽	4
● Rosso di Montepulciano '05	▽▽	4

Bindella

fraz. Acquaviva
via delle Tre Berte, 10a
53045 Montepulciano [SI]
tel. 0578767777
www.bindella.it

CELLAR SALES
PRE-BOOKED VISITS

ANNUAL PRODUCTION 120,000 bottles
HECTARES UNDER VINE 31
VITICULTURE METHOD Conventional

In recent years this estate, run by Rudolf Bindella at Acquaviva di Montepulciano, has often produced a range of wines with a dependable, well-established level of quality, achieving some peaks of absolute excellence. This is thanks to coherent decision-making strategies that have remained unaffected, on the whole, by the passing trends of almost 30 years. The cellar continues to release nicely varietal wines which stand the test of time.

The Nobile di Montepulciano I Quadri '07 is again well put-together, very characterful and unafraid of the passing of the years. The same applies to the Nobile Riserva '06, showing more austere stylistic features, especially in the earthy, dried flowers aromas and compact, flavoursome pace on the palate. The more approachable Nobile '07 probably needs time to settle down fully. The moreish white Gemella '09 is from sauvignon grapes while the very interesting Dolce Sinfonia is a creamy, dynamic Vin Santo Occhio di Pernice made from sangiovese and trebbiano.

● Nobile di Montepulciano I Quadri '07	▼▼	5
● Nobile di Montepulciano Ris. '06	▼▼	5
○ Vin Santo Dolce Sinfonia '06	▼▼	6
○ Gemella '09	▼	4
● Nobile di Montepulciano '07	▼	5
● Antenata '07	▽▽	6
● Nobile di Montepulciano '05	▽▽	6
● Nobile di Montepulciano I Quadri '06	▽▽	5
● Nobile di Montepulciano I Quadri '05	▽▽	5
● Nobile di Montepulciano I Quadri '04	▽▽	5
● Vallocaia '06	▽▽	6
● Vallocaia '04	▽▽	6

Biondi Santi - Tenuta Il Greppo

LOC. VILLA GREPPO, 183
53024 MONTALCINO [SI]
TEL. 0577848087
www.biondisanti.it

CELLAR SALES
PRE-BOOKED VISITS
ROOMS

ANNUAL PRODUCTION **80,000 bottles**
HECTARES UNDER VINE **25**
VITICULTURE METHOD **Organic**

The Tenuta del Greppo estate is, in some ways, a magical place. To drive down the cypress-lined avenue is to travel back through time into Montalcino's past. Franco Biondi Santi, a man of austere charm and old-fashioned class, is the operation's soul. The tour of the winery hews to a long-standing ritual, consisting of measured observations and memories of vintages and characters. Alongside the huge, old casks in the cellar are ten and 40-hectolitre casks, many of which are new.

All the wines presented were outstanding, and the Brunello Riserva '04 is a real show-stopper which will go down in history. A bright, moderately dense ruby red shimmers as it introduces classic aromas of ripe cherries with more mature sensations of tobacco and hints of leather and medicinal herbs. Plenty of acidity, supported by soft, mouthfilling tannin and a well-rounded, unforgettable finish in fact earned the wine our vote as Red of the Year. We also liked the very good Brunello di Montalcino '05 and Rosso di Montalcino '07.

● Brunello di Montalcino Ris. '04	TTT+	8
● Brunello di Montalcino '05	TT	8
● Rosso di Montalcino '07	TT	6
● Brunello di Montalcino '04	YYY	8
● Brunello di Montalcino '03	YYY	8
● Brunello di Montalcino '01	YYY	8
● Brunello di Montalcino '83	YYY	6
● Brunello di Montalcino Ris. '01	YYY	8
● Brunello di Montalcino Ris. '99	YYY	8
● Brunello di Montalcino Ris. '95	YYY	6

Borgo Salcetino

LOC. LUCARELLI
53017 RADDA IN CHIANTI [SI]
TEL. 0577733541
www.livon.it

CELLAR SALES
PRE-BOOKED VISITS

ANNUAL PRODUCTION **126,000 bottles**
HECTARES UNDER VINE **15**
VITICULTURE METHOD **Conventional**

The Livon family, well-known for its Friulian wines, has purchased several properties around Italy in recent years, setting up interesting estates in areas well-suited to red wine production. Borgo Salcetino, near Radda, is their Chianti holding. The beautiful slopes are planted to varieties both local, like sangiovese and canaiolo, and international, in the shape of merlot and cabernet sauvignon. You'll find only large casks in the cellar, as for reds at other Livon properties. The wines seem to be very good and distinctly personal, confirming substantial development.

The two Chianti Classicos are similar in style with unusual aromas: slightly gamy, reductive sensations with potential to develop over more stylish earthy aromas and still-perceptible hints of yeast. The Riserva Lucarello '07 is distinctly richer in texture with an impressively crisp, complex palate. The Chianti Classico '08 is less complex but quite delicious. Purists may turn up their noses but these are two profoundly gourmand reds. The sangiovese and merlot Rossole '08 is mellow and flavoursome.

● Chianti Cl. '08	TT	4
● Chianti Cl. Lucarello Ris. '07	TT	5
● Rossole '08	TT	4
● Chianti Cl. '03	YY	4
● Chianti Cl. '01	YY	4
● Chianti Cl. Lucarello Ris. '06	YY	5
● Chianti Cl. Lucarello Ris. '01	YY	5
● Chianti Cl. Lucarello Ris. '99	YY	5
● Rossole '06	YY	4
● Rossole '04	YY	5
● Rossole '00	YY	5
● Rossole '99	YY	5

Poderi Boscarelli

FRAZ. CERVOGNANO
VIA DI MONTENERO, 28
53045 MONTEPULCIANO [SI]
TEL. 0578767277
www.poderiboscarelli.com

CELLAR SALES
PRE-BOOKED VISITS

ANNUAL PRODUCTION **80,000 bottles**
HECTARES UNDER VINE **14**
VITICULTURE METHOD **Conventional**

Boscarelli may well represent the absolute benchmark for sangiovese production in the Montepulciano area. The estate, owned by the De Ferrari family since 1962, has never lost sight of the focus of this area where Vino Nobile production is fundamental, while endowing other wine types produced with character and personality. The wines show continuity of style and quality, the result of strict selections in the vineyard and cellar, and never bow to passing oenological trends.

While the IGTs from the Cervognano winery and the Nobile Nocio dei Boscarelli were absent from the roll-call, requiring another year's bottle ageing, the Nobile Riserva '06 gave a very good performance with well-defined aromas expressed in lush, sweetish fruit and a succulent palate, slightly held back by a hint of oak that has not yet been assimilated. The Nobile '07 is satisfying with just a few stiff corners to rub off. The Rosso di Montepulciano Prugnolo '08 is fragrant and nicely paced.

● Nobile di Montepulciano Ris. '06	▼▼▼	6
● Nobile di Montepulciano '07	▼▼	6
● Rosso di Montepulciano Prugnolo '08	▼	4
● Nobile di Montepulciano Nocio dei Boscarelli '04	▽▽▽	7
● Nobile di Montepulciano Nocio dei Boscarelli '03	▽▽▽	7
● Nobile di Montepulciano Nocio dei Boscarelli '01	▽▽▽	7
● Nobile di Montepulciano Ris. '88	▽▽▽	5
● Nobile di Montepulciano V. del Nocio Ris. '91	▽▽▽	7
● Boscarelli dei Boscarelli '06	▽▽	8
● Nobile di Montepulciano Nocio dei Boscarelli '06	▽▽	8
● Nobile di Montepulciano Nocio dei Boscarelli '05	▽▽	7
● Nobile di Montepulciano Ris. '03	▽▽	6

★ Brancaia

LOC. POPPI, 42
53017 RADDA IN CHIANTI [SI]
TEL. 0577742007
www.brancaia.com

CELLAR SALES
PRE-BOOKED VISITS
ROOMS

ANNUAL PRODUCTION **400,000 bottles**
HECTARES UNDER VINE **26**
VITICULTURE METHOD **Conventional**

The owners of the Brancaia estate, Swiss couple Brigitte and Bruno Widmer, are now celebrating 30 years of business in an area where they have played an important role since 1981. Barbara and Martin Kronenberg-Widmer manage the various business activities, including the Ilatraia estate in Maremma, purchased in 1998, a holiday centre as well as a farm. The wines always reveal a pursuit of softness and elegance, without neglecting the typical features of the terroir. a reduced selection was presented this year, but still very sound results.

The Tre '08, from sangiovese, merlot and cabernet sauvignon, uses grapes from both properties to proffer aromas of cinnamon and clove spice on a fruity base with toasted hints of oak, a soft, supple body and lingering, appetizing finish. The interesting new arrival, Bianco '09, a monovarietal Sauvignon, lays out aromas of honey, vanilla and white-fleshed fruit. The palate is warm, succulent, generous, nicely weighty and sweet, with further warmth in the finish. The Chianti Classico '08 is simpler and fairly good. Ilatraia gives intense, harmonious aromatics that usher in an outstanding palate whose solid, well-paced progression is bolstered by soft, flavoursome tannins.

● Ilatraia '08	▼▼	7
○ Bianco '09	▼▼	5
● Brancaia Tre '08	▼▼	5
● Chianti Cl. '08	▼	6
● Brancaia '99	▽▽▽	8
● Brancaia Il Blu '06	▽▽▽	7
● Brancaia Il Blu '05	▽▽▽	7
● Brancaia Il Blu '04	▽▽▽	7
● Brancaia Il Blu '03	▽▽▽	7
● Brancaia Il Blu '01	▽▽▽	7
● Brancaia Il Blu '00	▽▽▽	7
● Ilatraia '07	▽▽	7

Brunelli - Le Chiuse di Sotto

LOC. PODERNOVONE, 154
53024 MONTALCINO [SI]
TEL. 0577849337
www.giannibrunelli.it

CELLAR SALES
PRE-BOOKED VISITS
ROOMS AND FOOD

ANNUAL PRODUCTION 33,000 bottles
HECTARES UNDER VINE 6
VITICULTURE METHOD Conventional

Laura continues the work she shared with Gianni with great dedication. The vineyards are divided into two main blocks. one facing the winery, on the northern slope of Montalcino, well-known for subtle aromas and lovely acidity, and the other, Podernuovi, on the southern slope. The lands are similar, rich in stony material and with little clay, but the considerable difference in climate enables final blends with edgier, more complex profiles.

The Brunello di Montalcino Riserva '04 is excellent. The blend of grapes from two different locations brings us a captivating wine with alternating aromas of jammy fruit and a fresher, balsamic vein, as well as classic hints of tobacco and tar. The palate is sweet with mellow tannin and enlivened by a northern acidity. The stylish and very well-rounded finish beautifully reflects the aromas. The Brunello '05 is leaner and perfectly balanced with a refreshing palate and engaging aromas.

● Brunello di Montalcino Ris. '04	2 black	8
● Amor Costante '06	2 black	6
● Brunello di Montalcino '05	1 black	7
● Amor Costante '05	3 white	6
● Amor Costante '03	2 white	6
● Brunello di Montalcino '04	2 white	7
● Brunello di Montalcino '01	2 white	7
● Brunello di Montalcino '00	2 white	7
● Brunello di Montalcino Ris. '01	2 white	8

Bruni

FRAZ. FONTEBLANDA
LOC. LA MARTA, 6
58010 ORBETELLO [GR]
TEL. 0564885445
www.aziendabruni.it

CELLAR SALES
PRE-BOOKED VISITS

ANNUAL PRODUCTION 400,000 bottles
HECTARES UNDER VINE 36
VITICULTURE METHOD Conventional

The Bruni estate, founded in the early 1970s and managed today by brothers Marco and Moreno Bruni, produces generally well-made wines in a nicely drinkable, confident style which is occasionally overshadowed by excessive extract and use of oak. If this Fonteblanda winery manages to avoid these stylistic stumbles more systematically it will emerge on the Maremma winemaking scene with tangible margins of improvement.

The very good Morellino di Scansano Laire Riserva '08 shows nicely focused aromas with distinctive hints of spice fusing with peppery sensations. The powerful palate is supported by good acid backbone. Morellino Marteto '09 is rounded and flavoursome while the refreshing, racy Plinio '09, from vermentino and viognier, is fermented exclusively in stainless steel. The Perlaia '09, from vermentino and viognier slightly dried on the vine, is a little sedentary.

● Morellino di Scansano Laire Ris. '08	2 black	5
● Morellino di Scansano Marteto '09	2 black	4
○ Plinio '09	2 black	4
○ Vermentino Perlaia '09	1 black	4
○ Capalbio Bianco Vermentino Plinio '07	2 white	4*
● Morellino di Scansano Laire '04	2 white	5
● Morellino di Scansano Laire Ris. '07	2 white	5
● Morellino di Scansano Laire Ris. '05	2 white	5
● Morellino di Scansano Marteto '07	2 white	4*
● Morellino di Scansano Marteto '06	2 white	4
○ Vermentino Perlaia '08	2 white	4
○ Vermentino Perlaia '06	2 white	4

Le Buche - Cantine Olivi

LOC. LE BUCHE
VIA CASELFAVA, 25
53047 SARTEANO [SI]
TEL. 0578274066
www.lebuche.eu

CELLAR SALES
PRE-BOOKED VISITS
ROOMS AND FOOD

ANNUAL PRODUCTION 60,000 bottles
HECTARES UNDER VINE 30
VITICULTURE METHOD Conventional

By now there are very few remaining areas in Tuscany which are unsuited for wine, as demonstrated by Giuseppe Olivi's estate. In 1986, the first part of the project took off with the construction of a holiday centre before the winemaking adventure began in 1996, with the purchase of Podere Le Buche and involvement of Giuseppe's son Riccardo. The property had already been planted to vine but previously there had been no commitment to pursuing quality, which has now been remedied.

The best wine is Memento '07, a blend of syrah and sangiovese, with a fragrant, generous nose ranging from bay and sage-like aromatic herbs to blackberries, damson jam and spicy hints. The palate is firmly structured and mouthwatering, progressing nicely in step with the tannic weave to a crescendo finish. The newest arrival, Pugnitello '07, from the vineyard of the same name, also performed well with a succession of gamy animal skin aromas with tobacco and leather over a fruity base of wild berries. The stylish, coherent palate is lingering with good acidity.

● Memento '07	▼▼	7
● Pugnitello '07	▼▼	7
○ Coreno '09	▼	5
● Le Buche '07	▽▽	6
● Memento '06	▽▽	7

Tenuta del Buonamico

LOC. CERCATOIA
VIA PROVINCIALE DI MONTECARLO, 43
55015 MONTECARLO [LU]
TEL. 058322038
www.buonamico.it

CELLAR SALES
PRE-BOOKED VISITS
ROOMS

ANNUAL PRODUCTION 130,000 bottles
HECTARES UNDER VINE 29
VITICULTURE METHOD Conventional

The Tenuta del Buonamico estate changed hands a couple of years ago and is now owned by the Fontana family. Of course this new direction has been marked by changes and innovations, especially the renewal of some vineyards and the technical staff, and structural modernizations like the lovely new tasting room. The wines remain excellent and consequently the winery, too, remains one of the most prestigious in the area, now with new energy.

The Cercatoja Rosso '07, from a composite blend of sangiovese, syrah, cabernet and merlot, shows confidently grassy aromas with clear hints of bell peppers and a relaxed, tangy palate. Also impressive is the Il Fortino Syrah '07, which offers a mature, chewy style as well as considerable balance and the classic spicy aromas. The white wines are less successfully focused.

● Cercatoja Rosso '07	▼▼	6
● Il Fortino Syrah '07	▼▼	6
● Montecarlo Rosso '09	▼	3
● Cercatoja Rosso '06	▽▽	6
● Cercatoja Rosso '04	▽▽	5
● Cercatoja Rosso '99	▽▽	6
● Il Fortino Syrah '06	▽▽	6
● Il Fortino Syrah '00	▽▽	7
● Il Fortino Syrah '98	▽▽	7
● Montecarlo Rosso '08	▽▽	3
● Montecarlo Rosso '07	▽▽	3*
● Villa Lombardi '07	▽▽	4

Buondonno Casavecchia alla Piazza

Loc. La Piazza, 37
53011 Castellina in Chianti [SI]
tel. 0577749754
www.buondonno.com

CELLAR SALES
PRE-BOOKED VISITS
ROOMS

ANNUAL PRODUCTION 35,000 bottles
HECTARES UNDER VINE 8
VITICULTURE METHOD Certified organic

The estate owned by Gabriele Buondonno and Valeria Sodano, Neapolitan agronomists enamoured of Tuscany, has an illustrious history since it was once the property of Lionardo Buonarroti, Michelangelo's nephew. The current owners came here in 1988 and were among the first to convert their estate to organic farming, a philosophy they love to discuss with other Tuscan and Piedmontese colleagues with whom they organize new ways of working together. As well as producing wine, olive oil and grappa, the estate includes holiday accommodation.

The very good Chianti Classico Riserva '07 gives vanilla, raspberry and currant-led red berries, and assorted spices. The palate is flavoursome, weighty and succulent with nicely blended, mouthwatering tannins and a finish with good staying power. The Chianti Classico '08 is also good, giving mint-refreshed fruitiness, a supple structure with subtle tannins and a nicely flavoursome finish. The captivating Campo ai Ciliegi '07, from syrah with merlot and sangiovese, has a variety of aromas such as pepper, leather and tobacco, and a good, confident attack on the flavoursome, lingering palate with perceptible but nicely tucked in tannins.

● Chianti Cl. Ris. '07	🍷🍷 6
● Campo ai Ciliegi '07	🍷🍷 6
● Chianti Cl. '08	🍷🍷 4
● Campo ai Ciliegi '03	🍷🍷 5
● Campo ai Ciliegi '00	🍷🍷 5
● Chianti Cl. '01	🍷🍷 5

La Busattina

Fraz. San Martino sul Fiora
loc. Busattina
58050 Manciano [GR]
tel. 0564607840
busattina@libero.it

CELLAR SALES
PRE-BOOKED VISITS
ROOMS AND FOOD

ANNUAL PRODUCTION 10,000 bottles
HECTARES UNDER VINE 4
VITICULTURE METHOD Certified biodynamic

Emilio Falcione and his wife Elisabetta began their winemaking adventure in the early 1990s when they purchased La Busattina: 25 hectares at an altitude of 460 metres with four and a half hectares under vine, some planted in the 1970s and the rest in 2002. From organic the estate moved on to biodynamic farming in 1997, thanks to the boost given to this method by Australian agronomist Alex Podolinsky. In 2000, La Busattina began bottling and today is proud of its distinctive style and quality with well-balanced, generally elegant wines.

Once the slightly evolved sensation dissipates, Terre Eteree '06, a blend of sangiovese and ciliegiolo, displays rounded, luxuriant fruit aromas and a refreshing, edgy palate. The Ciliegiolo '07 has subtle aromas and pleasantly spiky tannins which enhance the very drinkable flavour. The San Martino 210 '08, a blend of trebbiano, malvasia and ansonica, is juicy and dynamic with good acidity and a lovely tangy sensation at the back.

● Sovana Rosso Terre Eteree '06	🍷🍷 4
● Ciliegiolo '07	🍷🍷 6
○ San Martino 210 '08	🍷🍷 4

Ca' del Vispo

LOC. LE VIGNE
VIA DI FUGNANO, 31
53037 SAN GIMIGNANO [SI]
TEL. 0577943053
www.cadelvispo.it

CELLAR SALES
PRE-BOOKED VISITS

ANNUAL PRODUCTION 150,000 bottles
HECTARES UNDER VINE 23
VITICULTURE METHOD Conventional

A return to the Guide a few years on for the estate owned by Massimo Daldin, originally from Trento. His parents fell in love with San Gimignano and moved to Tuscany, selling their wine estate back home and buying another in Vernaccia territory. Having taken over the running of the winery, Massimo reorganized and perfected the farming methods, thanks to experience gained while travelling and visiting other areas and producers. In 1997, he began selling his own wines.

The best wine this year was the Vernaccia Vigna in Fiore '09, a selection aged in oak with hints of peaches, honey and almonds on the nose and a fresh, lively, long-lingering palate with a mouthwatering finish. Of the many reds produced, first mention goes to the Rovai '07, an equal blend of sangiovese, cabernet sauvignon and merlot, with spicy aromas of vanilla and cloves over a fruity cherry base. The palate is well balanced with blended tannins and a lingering finish. The rest of the range is also worth uncorking.

● Rovai '07	2 black glasses	5
○ Vernaccia di S. Gimignano V. in Fiore '09	2 black glasses	4
● Chianti Colli Senesi '09	1 black glass	3
● Cruter '07	1 black glass	5
● Fondatore '07	1 black glass	5
● Basolo '02	2 white glasses	4
● Cruter '01	2 white glasses	4
● Cruter '00	2 white glasses	4*
● Fondatore '00	2 white glasses	4
● Rovai '01	2 white glasses	4

Ca' Marcanda

LOC. SANTA TERESA, 272
57022 CASTAGNETO CARDUCCI [LI]
TEL. 0173635158
info@gajawines.com

ANNUAL PRODUCTION 380,000 bottles
HECTARES UNDER VINE 100
VITICULTURE METHOD Conventional

Angelo Gaja's Bolgheri estate is more dynamic and on better form than ever, showing the utmost respect for the terroir and various high points. The estate is situated in Castagneto Carducci, with about 100 hectares of land and a futuristic cellar making a discreet and unobtrusive yet pleasing impression. Rather than a stopper to seal in the characteristics of the territory, the Gaja style is like a detonator that releases them to their best advantage.

The Bolgheri Superiore Camarcanda '07, a blend of merlot and cabernet sauvignon with a little franc, is a beautifully rounded red, perfectly focused on elegant aromas of red fruit and grassy hints, as well as sensations of spices and rose water. The same weave on the palate reflects sophisticated and skilful handling of the expressive strength and energy, leading up to a perfectly tannic finish with generous leathery hints and a touch of tobacco. Three Glasses. The Promis '08 from merlot, syrah and sangiovese is also very stylish with a fruity nose showing gamy hints and a fresh, succulent palate with a lingering finish.

● Bolgheri Camarcanda '07	3 black glasses	8
● Brunello di Montalcino Pieve di Santa Restituta '05	2 black glasses	8
● Promis '08	2 black glasses	6
● Bolgheri Camarcanda '01	3 white glasses	8
● Magari '03	3 white glasses	7
● Bolgheri Camarcanda '06	2 white glasses	8
● Bolgheri Camarcanda '05	2 white glasses	8
● Bolgheri Camarcanda '04	2 white glasses	8
● Magari '07	2 white glasses	7
● Magari '06	2 white glasses	8
● Magari '05	2 white glasses	8
● Magari '01	2 white glasses	8
● Promis '07	2 white glasses	6
● Promis '06	2 white glasses	8
● Promis '05	2 white glasses	8
● Promis '03	2 white glasses	6

Tenuta Le Calcinaie

LOC. SANTA LUCIA, 36
53037 SAN GIMIGNANO [SI]
TEL. 0577943007
www.tenutalecalcinaie.it

CELLAR SALES
PRE-BOOKED VISITS

ANNUAL PRODUCTION 60,000 bottles
HECTARES UNDER VINE 10
VITICULTURE METHOD Certified organic

A lovely performance from the winery owned by Simone Santini, passionate winegrower who graduated from Siena as a wine technician and decided to produce his own. In 1986, Simone planted his first vineyard and began to make wines regularly from 1993 onwards. He converted the vineyards to organic farming methods in 1995 and gained certification for organic vinification in 2001. Construction of the cellar enabled him to complete a high-quality production cycle.

The standard-label Vernaccia is right on the mark as aromas of fresh herbs alternate with citrus peel and hints of almonds and a lively, dynamic palate with a succulent finish. The Riserva Vigna ai Sassi '07, more relaxed and serene, has almost opulent aromas, a weighty, soft palate with generous flavour and a lingering salty sensation. Among the reds the Teodoro '07, an equal blend of sangiovese, merlot and cabernet sauvignon, stands out for its captivating aromatic bouquet of bay leaves, Mediterranean scrubland and wild berries, and firm, mouthwatering palate with decent length. The Chianti Colli Senesi is well typed if not especially thrilling.

● Teodoro '07	▼▼	5
○ Vernaccia di S. Gimignano '09	▼▼	4
○ Vernaccia di S. Gimignano V. ai Sassi '07	▼▼	4
● Chianti Colli Senesi '09	▼	4
● Teodoro '06	▽▽	5
○ Vernaccia di S. Gimignano V. ai Sassi '06	▽▽	4
○ Vernaccia di S. Gimignano V. ai Sassi '05	▽▽	4
○ Vernaccia di S. Gimignano V. ai Sassi '04	▽▽	4
○ Vernaccia di S. Gimignano V. ai Sassi '03	▽▽	4

Camigliano

LOC. CAMIGLIANO
VIA D'INGRESSO, 2
53024 MONTALCINO [SI]
TEL. 0577816061
www.camigliano.it

CELLAR SALES
PRE-BOOKED VISITS
ROOMS

ANNUAL PRODUCTION 300,000 bottles
HECTARES UNDER VINE 92
VITICULTURE METHOD Organic

The small village of Camigliano owes its survival to the Ghezzi family, Milanese entrepreneurs with their hearts firmly in Montalcino. Gualtiero and Laura live here and dedicate their time and passion to promoting this corner of paradise. The south-west of the designation, towards Maremma, is swept by warm breezes from Grosseto that threaten to cause overripeness. This agronomical challenge is being met by new and now productive vineyards.

The designation wines are very good, the most impressive being the Brunello Gualto '04. Concentrated in hue, it gives vibrant ripe blackberry, morello cherry and blueberry fruit, with jammy overtones. The lovely acidity is astonishing while the tannins are still rather chafing, making the finish a little laboured. Also very interesting is Cabernet Campo ai Mori '07, displaying damson fruit and pencil lead on the nose with hints of orange peel, and a complex, nicely dynamic palate with lovely tannins.

● Brunello di Montalcino '05	▼▼	6
● Brunello di Montalcino Gualto Ris. '04	▼▼	8
● Rosso di Montalcino '08	▼▼	4
● Sant'Antimo Cabernet Sauvignon Campo ai Mori '07	▼▼	5
○ Moscadello di Montalcino Laura '08	▼	6
● Brunello di Montalcino '04	▽▽	6
● Brunello di Montalcino '03	▽▽	6
● Brunello di Montalcino '02	▽▽	6
● Brunello di Montalcino Gualto Ris. '01	▽▽	8
● Poderuccio '07	▽▽	4*
● Sant'Antimo Cabernet Sauvignon Campo ai Mori '06	▽▽	5

Campo alla Sughera

LOC. CACCIA AL PIANO, 280
57020 BOLGHERI [LI]
TEL. 0565766936
www.campoallasughera.com

CELLAR SALES
PRE-BOOKED VISITS

ANNUAL PRODUCTION 90,000 bottles
HECTARES UNDER VINE 16
VITICULTURE METHOD Conventional

This winery, founded in the late 1990s by Knauf, might be counted among those with a certain historical significance, given the extremely young area, although to tell the truth the wines have only been released for sale since 2004. The Campo alla Sughera estate consists of just over 15 hectares of specialized vineyards, mainly planted to cabernet sauvignon and franc, merlot, petit verdot for the reds, and vermentino, sauvignon blanc and chardonnay for the whites. All the wines in the range show dependable quality.

The Bolgheri Superiore Arnione '07 fails to match the standard of the previous version because of glitches on the nose that infiltrate the usual aromas of lush, balsam-enhanced fruit and spice. The very impressive Campo alla Sughera '06 is luxuriant, generous and weighty with a perfect entry on the palate and lovely finish. The Adeo '08 is also remarkably well focused.

● Bolgheri Rosso Adeo '08	▼▼	5
● Bolgheri Superiore Arnione '07	▼▼	7
● Campo alla Sughera '06	▼▼	8
○ Bolgheri Bianco Achenio '09	▼	6
○ Bolgheri Bianco Arioso '09	▼	6
● Bolgheri Superiore Arnione '06	▽▽▽	7
○ Arioso '06	▽▽	4
● Bolgheri Rosso Adeo '07	▽▽	5
● Bolgheri Rosso Adeo '06	▽▽	5
● Bolgheri Superiore Arnione '05	▽▽	7
● Bolgheri Superiore Arnione '04	▽▽	7
● Bolgheri Superiore Arnione '03	▽▽	7

Canalicchio - Franco Pacenti

LOC. CANALICCHIO DI SOPRA, 6
53024 MONTALCINO [SI]
TEL. 0577849277
www.canalicchiofrancopacenti.it

CELLAR SALES
PRE-BOOKED VISITS

ANNUAL PRODUCTION 30,000 bottles
HECTARES UNDER VINE 10
VITICULTURE METHOD Conventional

Canalicchio is a small estate in the northern part of the designation, overlooking Buonconvento. The land is very well suited to wine with clay giving way to stones and shale lentils making the soil looser and less compressed. The winery follows a classic style, using medium-sized casks in Slavonian oak and lengthy maceration with frequent pumping over during fermentation.

We note a good performance from these wines with the Brunello di Montalcino Riserva '04 coming very close to our highest accolade. Medium-intense ruby red precedes classic aromas including mature hints of tobacco and leather that amplify the fruity sensations of sour cherries and blackberries. The palate is somewhat penalized by still rather aggressive tannins, which will probably favour its ageing prospects, while the lingering finish reflects the aromas nicely. The Brunello di Montalcino '05 is also well made.

● Brunello di Montalcino Ris. '04	▼▼	8
● Brunello di Montalcino '05	▼▼	6
● Rosso di Montalcino '08	▼	4
● Brunello di Montalcino '04	▽▽▽	6
● Brunello di Montalcino '01	▽▽	6
● Brunello di Montalcino '00	▽▽	6*

Canalicchio di Sopra

LOC. CASACCIA, 73
53024 MONTALCINO [SI]
TEL. 0577848316
www.canalicchiodisopra.com

CELLAR SALES
PRE-BOOKED VISITS
ROOMS

ANNUAL PRODUCTION 55,000 bottles
HECTARES UNDER VINE 15
VITICULTURE METHOD Conventional

Quite a youthful team runs this winery, situated on very well-suited land in the northern part of the Montalcino designation at Canalicchio, a place name which has always been part of the annals of Montalcino. The winery philosophy is a simple one: don't ruin the good material from the vineyards in the cellar. And it's a traditional cellar with 30 and 50-hectolitre Slavonian oak barrels and non-invasive fermentation methods, gently transforming the fruits of labour in 15 hectares of vineyards.

The extremely good Brunello Riserva '04 again received Three Glasses, like its brother last year. A classic nose gives spice and tobacco aromas enhancing the ripe cherries. A confident entry on the palate, soft and subtle, reveals wonderful balance of acidity and silky, mellow tannins and velvety, rounded development to a very lingering finish. Also excellent is the Brunello '05, and the Rosso di Montalcino '08 is delicious.

● Brunello di Montalcino Ris. '04	🍷🍷🍷	8
● Rosso di Montalcino '08	🍷🍷	4*
● Brunello di Montalcino '05	🍷🍷	7
● Brunello di Montalcino '04	ƳƳƳ	7
● Brunello di Montalcino Ris. '01	ƳƳƳ	8
● Brunello di Montalcino '01	ƳƳ	6
● Brunello di Montalcino '00	ƳƳ	6
● Rosso di Montalcino '06	ƳƳ	5

Candialle

FRAZ. GREVE IN CHIANTI
VIA SAN LEOLINO, 71
50020 PANZANO [FI]
TEL. 055852201
www.candialle.com

PRE-BOOKED VISITS

ANNUAL PRODUCTION 20,000 bottles
HECTARES UNDER VINE 6
VITICULTURE METHOD Organic

Candialle is about 20 kilometres from Florence, near the Via Chiantigiana leading to Siena, in the south of the famous Conca d'Oro close to Panzano. The vineyards sprawl across an area at altitudes between 300 and 350 metres on typical marly soil with some alberese clay and rock. Most of the plots on the estate are planted to sangiovese, as well as less traditional varieties like syrah, petit verdot, merlot and cabernet.

The very good Chianti Classico '08, a monovarietal Sangiovese aged in barriques, has an enthralling, pervasive nose which perfectly combines oaky sensations with dynamic, crisp fruit and floral hints of gladiolus, as well as complex flinty nuances. The palate is also delightful, with uncommon grip and flavour. The '07 Ciclope is not bad either. Sangiovese with some merlot and syrah displays a beautifully mature nose with perfectly judged sweetness from caramelly sensations. This is followed by bay leaves, which return on the succulent, taut and profoundly dynamic palate.

● Chianti Cl. '08	🍷🍷	5
● Ciclope '07	🍷🍷	5
● Pli '07	🍷	7
● Chianti Cl. '05	ƳƳ	4
● Ciclope '06	ƳƳ	5
● Ciclope '04	ƳƳ	5

Capanna

LOC. CAPANNA, 333
53024 MONTALCINO [SI]
TEL. 0577848298
www.capannamontalcino.com

CELLAR SALES
PRE-BOOKED VISITS

ANNUAL PRODUCTION 70,000 bottles
HECTARES UNDER VINE 20
VITICULTURE METHOD Conventional

Patrizio Cencioni is a man of few words and great courage, as he has demonstrated by accepting the post of chairman of the consortium at such a difficult time. Over the years, he has modernized his winery in the north of the designation at the foot of Montosoli while maintaining a traditional style. About 12 hectares of vineyards grow grapes for Brunello while the recently rebuilt cellar contains beautiful wooden casks for fermenting red wines, and casks of different sizes up to 30 hectolitres.

This year, our Three Glasses go to the Brunello Riserva '04, a successful combination of terroir and winery style. Intense ruby and balsamic, spicy, liquorice sensations on the nose alongside ripe morello cherries introduce excellent length and integrity. A powerful entry on the palate is reminiscent of warmer areas, with the acidity of the northern zone supporting the texture. The tannins make their presence felt as the thrilling progression powers through to the very long finish. The Brunello '05 is also well made and lingers nicely lingering.

● Brunello di Montalcino Ris. '04	▼▼▼	8
● Brunello di Montalcino '05	▼▼	6
● Rosso di Montalcino '08	▼▼	4
○ Moscadello di Montalcino '08	▼	4
● Brunello di Montalcino Ris. '90	▽▽▽	6
● Brunello di Montalcino '04	▽▽	6

Capannelle

VIA CAPANNELLE, 13
53013 GAIOLE IN CHIANTI [SI]
TEL. 057774511
www.capannelle.com

CELLAR SALES
PRE-BOOKED VISITS
ROOMS

ANNUAL PRODUCTION 70,000 bottles
HECTARES UNDER VINE 16
VITICULTURE METHOD Conventional

Capannelle, in Chianti Classico, exemplifies a winery that has made modern style and new technology its hallmarks. The estate owned by James B. Sherwood, founder and shareholder of the Orient Express group, opened for business 40 years ago managed by Raffaele Rossetti. The original 17th century house was completely renovated and today includes a kitchen, frequently graced by great chefs, innovative tasting rooms where conferences on wine have been held, and an original temperature and humidity-controlled cellar where old vintages are stored for clients.

We especially liked Solare '06, based on sangiovese and malvasia nera, with minerally, pencil lead sensations followed by hints of leather and blackberry jam. The succulent palate has energy and salty sensations, nicely amalgamated tannins and an enthralling, very flavoursome finish. The 50&50 made in collaboration with the Avignonesi winery of Montepulciano from sangiovese and merlot, proffers spiciness with a soft palate and extended finish. The unusual and appetizing Chardonnay '08 has aromas of nutmeg-like spice, aromatic herbs led by sage and mint, and citrus peel. The palate is richly structured and dynamic with a lovely fresh finish and lingering tangy sensation.

○ Chardonnay '08	▼▼	8
● Solare '06	▼▼	8
● 50 & 50 Avignonesi e Capannelle '06	▼	8
● Chianti Cl. Ris. '07	▼	7
● 50 & 50 Avignonesi e Capannelle '99	▽▽▽	8
● 50 & 50 Avignonesi e Capannelle '97	▽▽▽	8
● 50 & 50 Avignonesi e Capannelle '04	▽▽	8
● 50 & 50 Avignonesi e Capannelle '03	▽▽	8
● 50 & 50 Avignonesi e Capannelle '01	▽▽	8
○ Chardonnay '06	▽▽	7
● Chianti Cl. Capannelle '01	▽▽	6
● Solare '04	▽▽	8

Tenuta Caparzo

LOC. CAPARZO
SP DEL BRUNELLO
53024 MONTALCINO [SI]
TEL. 0577848390
www.caparzo.it

CELLAR SALES
PRE-BOOKED VISITS
ROOMS

ANNUAL PRODUCTION 455,000 bottles
HECTARES UNDER VINE 80
VITICULTURE METHOD Conventional

This winery is a jewel set in the northern quadrant of Montalcino, surrounded by a crown of cypress trees. The 80-plus hectares of vineyards are still increasing with new purchases in the southern sector. The cellar and fermentation structures have recently undergone a complete makeover thanks to substantial investment based on a strong belief in its potential. The vineyards are located in various Montalcino crus like Montosoli in the north and Castelgiocondo to the west.

The most impressive wine for us was the Rosso di Montalcino La Caduta '07, made from grapes grown on tufaceous land in the western part of the designation. A classic ruby with a rounded, vibrant nose of lingering yellow peaches, morello cherries and spice precedes a palate with plenty of grip supporting the soft, stylish extract. Of the Brunellos presented our favourite was the '05, with slightly vegetal aromas over a base of nicely expressed cherry fruit and a palate supported well by acidity into a long, elegant finish.

● Rosso di Montalcino La Caduta '07	▼▼	5
● Brunello di Montalcino '05	▼▼	6
● Brunello di Montalcino Ris. '04	▼▼	8
● Ca' del Pazzo '06	▼▼	6
● Borgonero Borgo Scopeto '05	▼	5
● Chianti Cl. Borgo Scopeto '08	▼	4
● Rosso di Montalcino '08	▼	5
● Brunello di Montalcino La Casa '93	▽▽▽	7
● Brunello di Montalcino La Casa '88	▽▽▽	7
● Brunello di Montalcino '03	▽▽	7
● Brunello di Montalcino La Casa '04	▽▽	8
● Rosso Caparzo '07	▽▽	4*
● Rosso di Montalcino La Caduta '06	▽▽	5

Tenuta di Capezzana

LOC. SEANO
VIA CAPEZZANA, 100
59015 CARMIGNANO [PO]
TEL. 0558706005
www.capezzana.it

CELLAR SALES
PRE-BOOKED VISITS

ANNUAL PRODUCTION 600,000 bottles
HECTARES UNDER VINE 106
VITICULTURE METHOD Conventional

Capezzana is a rare case of an estate over 1,200 years old. A ninth-century parchment records a contract for land planted with vineyards. The original houses were built here in the early Renaissance by Monna Nera Bonaccorsi. Current owners, the Contini Bonaccossi family, began their wine project in the early 20th century with Alessandro, while his son, Ugo, ran the estate with great skill and experience until a few years ago, when he handed over the task of continuing the business to his children.

Three Glasses for the Carmignano Villa di Capezzana '07. Nicely relaxed mature aromas of tobacco and leather give way to ripe fruit, with a well-balanced, approachable and succulent palate closing in a lovely, well-rounded finish. The excellent Ghiaie della Furba '06 has spicy aromas and vibrant hints of ripe fruit. Tannins blend with the alcohol on a dynamic palate that finishes long. The old-style Villa di Trefiano '06 shows a slightly rugged palate but clearly defined, almost minty, aromas with enthralling savoury flavour. The Trebbiano '07 is a lovely surprise with its array of aromatics and flavours while the '08 Barco Reale is pleasant and approachable.

● Carmignano Villa di Capezzana '07	▼▼▼	5
● Ghiaie della Furba '06	▼▼	6
● Carmignano Villa di Trefiano '06	▼▼	6
○ Trebbiano '07	▼▼	5
● Barco Reale '08	▼	4
● Carmignano Villa di Capezzana '05	▽▽▽	5
● Carmignano Villa di Capezzana '99	▽▽▽	6
● Ghiaie della Furba '01	▽▽▽	6
● Ghiaie della Furba '98	▽▽▽	5
● Carmignano Villa di Capezzana '06	▽▽	5
● Carmignano Villa di Capezzana '04	▽▽	5
● Carmignano Villa di Capezzana '01	▽▽	5
● Carmignano Villa di Capezzana '00	▽▽	5*
● Ghiaie della Furba '05	▽▽	6
● Ghiaie della Furba '04	▽▽	6
● Ghiaie della Furba '03	▽▽	6
● Ghiaie della Furba '00	▽▽	6
● Ghiaie della Furba '99	▽▽	6

Caprili

LOC. SANTA RESTITUTA
53024 MONTALCINO [SI]
TEL. 0577848566
info@caprili.it

CELLAR SALES
PRE-BOOKED VISITS

ANNUAL PRODUCTION 60,000 bottles
HECTARES UNDER VINE 15
VITICULTURE METHOD Conventional

In the family-run Bartolomei winery, the three brothers look after the vineyards, cellar and sales. Their far-sighted father Alfo bought the estate back in 1965 and the first Brunellos were bottled in the late 1970s. Situated in a particularly favourable position, the estate has 15 hectares of vineyards at an altitude of about 300 metres on particularly loose, very stony land with a substrate of limestone and silicates. Vinification methods follow the classic format of about 25 days' fermentation and ageing in Slavonian oak casks containing more than 30 hectolitres.

The wines are all very interesting and the truly outstanding Brunello Riserva over 30-hectolitre 04 was awarded Three Glasses. Dense ruby and a rounded, clean, vibrant nose with morello cherries and cherry jam aromas softened by fresh balsam usher in a powerful palate that opens confidently. Generous, vigorous development is nicely supported by acidity and close-knit, never harsh tannins. The rounded, finish beautifully reprises the aromatics. Also very impressive is the Brunello '05 with its classic, lingering hints of cherries and yellow peaches.

● Brunello di Montalcino Ris. '04	YYY	8
● Brunello di Montalcino '05	YY	6

Podere Il Carnasciale

LOC. PODERE IL CARNASCIALE
52020 MERCATALE VALDARNO [AR]
TEL. 0559911142

ANNUAL PRODUCTION 7,000 bottles
HECTARES UNDER VINE 2
VITICULTURE METHOD Conventional

The wine that came about by accident. Curious agronomist Remigio Bordini was unable to identify a plant he found on the Colli Euganei and named it caberlot for its resemblance to both cabernet franc and merlot; creative German, Wolf Rogosky, enamoured by the wines of Vittorio Fiore, wished to entrust him with wine production on his estate in Valdarno. The meeting between the two was crucial. A rooted cutting no one would risk buying was planted and virgin land was turned over to the production of great wines. Today the estate is managed by Wolf's wife, Bettina.

The '07 version of the Caberlot is again outstanding, releasing an incredible variety of aromas from balsam and mint to more complex hints of chocolate and spice and crystal-clear wild berries with a slight vegetal hint. The palate is focused, soft and succulent, with tannins nicely tucked in, good fruity acid backbone and a long-lingering finish.

● Caberlot '07	YY	8
● Caberlot '05	YYY	8
● Caberlot '04	YYY	8
● Caberlot '00	YYY	8
● Caberlot '06	YY	8
● Caberlot '03	YY	8

Fattoria Carpineta Fontalpino

FRAZ. MONTAPERTI
LOC. CARPINETA
53019 CASTELNUOVO BERARDENGA [SI]
TEL. 0577369219
www.carpinetafontalpino.it

CELLAR SALES
PRE-BOOKED VISITS
ROOMS

ANNUAL PRODUCTION 100,000 bottles
HECTARES UNDER VINE 19
VITICULTURE METHOD Conventional

Carpineta Fontalpino, owned by Filippo and established oenologist Gioia Cresti, is at Montaperti, on the edge of the southern part of Chianti Classico. Here the soil is a mixture of clay and sand with plenty of pebbles. The wines are modern in style and highlight the profile of this generous area, which favours full ripening and yields vibrant, fleshy fruit.

After the winery's first Three Glasses last year, for the Do Ut Des '07, Montaperti did it again with the Dofana '07, a blend of sangiovese and petit verdot. A concentrated, rounded nose gives red and black fruit aromas, hints of balsam and still-forward oaky sensations. The juicy, mouthfilling palate is well-structured. The '08 Do Ut Des is slightly affected by a leaner vintage year, lacking the structure to achieve greater results. The Chianti Classico Fontalpino '08 is succulent, fragrant and nicely drinkable.

● Dofana '07	▼▼▼	8
● Do Ut Des '08	▼▼	6
● Chianti Cl. Fontalpino '08	▼▼	4
● Do Ut Des '07	▽▽▽	6
● Do Ut Des '06	▽▽	6
● Do Ut Des '05	▽▽	6
● Do Ut Des '04	▽▽	6
● Dofana '06	▽▽	8
● Dofana '04	▽▽	8

Casa al Vento

LOC. CASA AL VENTO
53013 GAIOLE IN CHIANTI [SI]
TEL. 0577749485
www.borgocasaalvento.com

CELLAR SALES
PRE-BOOKED VISITS
FOOD

ANNUAL PRODUCTION 30,000 bottles
HECTARES UNDER VINE 4
VITICULTURE METHOD Certified organic

Casa al Vento takes its name from the village in which it is situated, in the Gaiole area, and is the brainchild of owner Pino Gioffreda, whose iron will has created a perfect system here based on organic farming and attention to personal care, as shown by cooking and wellbeing courses held in the holiday centre. The wines tend to be fresh and drinkable, expressing the most elegant side of the Chianti Classico nature.

The wines at Casa al Vento all show a clean, fragrant style. This year again, the Chianti Classico '08 is very good, fresh and subtle with aromas of berries and medicinal herbs, and a clean, crisp, very drinkable palate with a deep succulent finish. A lovely version of the Chianti Classico Foho Riserva '07 has a more open nose displaying ripe fruit, damp earth, blood-rich aromas and a rounded, well-structured palate with nicely extracted tannins. There's also a lovely '07 version of Gaiolè, from sangiovese and merlot, with a fruity vegetal nose and nicely relaxed palate.

● Chianti Cl. Foho Ris. '07	▼▼	5
● Chianti Cl. Aria '08	▼▼	4
● Gaiolè '07	▼▼	5
● Chianti Cl. Aria '07	▽▽	4*
● Chianti Cl. Foho Ris. '06	▽▽	5
● Gaiolè '06	▽▽	5

Casa alle Vacche

FRAZ. PANCOLE
LOC. LUCIGNANO, 73A
53037 SAN GIMIGNANO [SI]
TEL. 0577955103
www.casaallevacche.it

CELLAR SALES
PRE-BOOKED VISITS

ANNUAL PRODUCTION 120,000 bottles
HECTARES UNDER VINE 22
VITICULTURE METHOD Conventional

A lovely example of continuity over the years from the Ciappi family. The remarkable series of labels this year again achieved excellent results without losing sight of value for money. The name derives from the 19th century term for a place where animals – "vacche" means cows – would rest, reflecting the production philosophy of working unhurriedly. Production is split between Vernaccia and various reds, especially Chianti Colli Senesi.

The best result this year comes from the Vernaccia Crocus Riserva '08, with very subtle aromas of fresh aromatic herbs and delicate hints of pear fruit. The palate is vigorous and weighty with a savoury, flavoursome finish. We also liked the '09 I Macchioni selection with more dynamic, vibrant aromas and a light, subtle, lingering flavour. The most impressive red was the very fruity Aglieno '08, made from sangiovese and merlot. Also good is the '08 Acantho, a fresh, balsamic Cabernet Sauvignon. The two Chianti Colli Senesi wines presented are well typed and beautifully drinkable while the Vernaccia '09 is simple but delicious.

● Acantho '08	▼▼	4*
● Aglieno '08	▼▼	4*
○ Vernaccia di S. Gimignano Crocus Ris. '08	▼▼	4*
○ Vernaccia di S. Gimignano I Macchioni '09	▼▼	4*
● Chianti Colli Senesi '09	▼	2
● Chianti Colli Senesi Cinabro Ris. '07	▼	4
○ Vernaccia di S. Gimignano '09	▼	2
● Aglieno '01	▽▽	4*
● Chianti Colli Senesi Cinabro Ris. '02	▽▽	4
● Chianti Colli Senesi Cinabro Ris. '01	▽▽	5
● S. Gimignano Rosso Acantho '04	▽▽	4
● S. Gimignano Rosso Acantho '03	▽▽	4
○ Vernaccia di S. Gimignano '08	▽▽	2*
○ Vernaccia di S. Gimignano '07	▽▽	2*
○ Vernaccia di S. Gimignano I Macchioni '09	▽▽	4*

Casa Emma

LOC. CORTINE
SP DI CASTELLINA IN CHIANTI, 3
50021 BARBERINO VAL D'ELSA [FI]
TEL. 0558072239
www.casaemma.com

CELLAR SALES
PRE-BOOKED VISITS

ANNUAL PRODUCTION 85,000 bottles
HECTARES UNDER VINE 21
VITICULTURE METHOD Conventional

Situated at an altitude of over 400 metres in the lovely hills of San Donato in Poggio, Casa Emma has been owned by the Bucalossi family for many years. As well as the vineyards, the estate includes a botanical garden surrounding the farmhouse and a cellar where the wines are aged in barriques. Bottles are released for sale when they have acquired their distinctive modern style, which is still quite uncompromising and embodies a certain territorial charm.

The Chianti Classico Riserva '07 is a good example. It's a red that is able to deliver pleasing aromas of red fruits and subtle spices despite the still quite evident oak from ageing. The dynamic palate is bound to achieve greater balance over time. The Chianti Classico '08, with even darker fruit, displays a beautiful mid palate with poised flavour and acidity. The Merlot Soloìo '07 is a little unfocused on the nose.

● Chianti Cl. '08	▼▼	4
● Chianti Cl. Ris. '07	▼▼	6
● Soloìo '07	▼	7
● Chianti Cl. Ris. '95	▽▽▽	4
● Chianti Cl. Ris. '93	▽▽▽	4
● Soloìo '94	▽▽▽	5
● Chianti Cl. '07	▽▽	4
● Chianti Cl. '06	▽▽	4*
● Chianti Cl. Ris. '05	▽▽	6
● Chianti Cl. Ris. '04	▽▽	6
● Soloìo '06	▽▽	7

Casa Sola

s.da di Cortine, 5
50021 Barberino Val d'Elsa [FI]
tel. 0558075028
www.fattoriacasasola.it

CELLAR SALES
PRE-BOOKED VISITS
ROOMS

ANNUAL PRODUCTION 75,000 bottles
HECTARES UNDER VINE 26
VITICULTURE METHOD Conventional

The estate is owned by the noble Gambaro family, who purchased it in 1960. In 1985, Giuseppe Gambaro decided to work full-time in the business and along with his wife Claudia began to learn about fermentation techniques and great wines from around the world. The cellar was modernized with more advanced machinery after the vineyards had been replanted. Subsequently, the houses on the estate were renovated to create a holiday centre.

The very good Riserva di Chianti Classico '07 has ripe fruit aromas of damson jam and cherries, perked up by hints of spice. The entry is rounded and firm on the palate with nicely blended tannins and an extended finish. The appetizing, alluring Vin Santo del Chianti Classico '01 shows a classic bouquet of nutty aromas, breadth, a soft, creamy structure and a delicious finish. The old-style Chianti blend including white-skinned grapes creates a fresh, moreish Amici '08 while the '06 Montarsiccio, from cabernet sauvignon, merlot and sangiovese, is a tad rugged with unfocused aromas.

● Chianti Cl. Ris. '07	🍷🍷	5
○ Vin Santo del Chianti Cl. '01	🍷🍷	6
● Montarsiccio '06	🍷	6
● Per gli Amici '08	🍷	3
● Chianti Cl. '03	ΥΥ	4
● Chianti Cl. Ris. '04	ΥΥ	6
● Montarsiccio '01	ΥΥ	6
● Montarsiccio '99	ΥΥ	7

Fattoria Casalbosco

fraz. Santomato
via Montalese, 117
84020 Pistoia
tel. 0573479947
www.fattoriacasalbosco.com

CELLAR SALES
PRE-BOOKED VISITS
ROOMS

ANNUAL PRODUCTION 120,000 bottles
HECTARES UNDER VINE 45
VITICULTURE METHOD Conventional

This estate near the Pistoiese Appennines has been owned by the Becagli family since 1960. Originally used as a country residence, it has been extensively renovated in recent years and today it is run by Mario Becagli's sons Massimo and Tommaso, who have changed the image and winemaking style. Many vineyards have been replanted, especially with international varieties, and the cellar as been modernized. The 150-plus hectares also include a holiday complex and extensive olive groves.

We were impressed by the Opus Magnum '06, a monovarietal Cabernet with minty, balsamic sensations over blueberry fruit and hints of spice. The tannins blend well with the alcohol on the firmly structured, well-balanced palate, with a tangy, crescendo finish. We also liked the classic Vin Santo '06: aromas dominated by dried fruit like hazelnuts and dried figs, and a velvety broad palate with a lingering, enjoyable finish. The flawless, well-typed Orchidea '07, merlot and cabernet sauvignon, has cherries and raspberries on the nose and a structure more balanced than powerful with a fairly lingering finish. The two Chiantis are nicely made, stylish and refreshing.

● Opus Magnum '06	🍷🍷	6
○ Vin Santo del Chianti Casalbosco '06	🍷🍷	6
● Chianti '09	🍷	3
● Chianti Porpora Ris. '07	🍷	4
● Orchidea '07	🍷	6
● Orchidea '06	ΥΥ	6

Fattoria Casaloste

via Montagliari, 32
50020 Panzano [FI]
tel. 055852725
www.casaloste.com

CELLAR SALES
PRE-BOOKED VISITS
ROOMS

ANNUAL PRODUCTION 55,000 bottles
HECTARES UNDER VINE 10
VITICULTURE METHOD Certified organic

Giovanni Battista D'Orsi, one of a group of Campania producers enamoured of Chianti Classico, moved here after finishing his agronomy and oenology studies in Naples. It was not long before this sangiovese addict converted all his vineyards to organic management and became a local pioneer. Giovanni's more structured wines always need time to breathe if they are to be tasted at their best.

Two finalists, no less. The complex aromatic profile of the Riserva Don Vincenzo '07 combines notes of Mediterranean scrub, coffee, toastiness and bramble jelly. We liked the palate's broad, dense entry, good progression and delightful finale. The aromatic profile of the equal parts sangiovese and merlot Inversus '07 reveals ripe cherry and plum fruit with a firm, round body that shows flavoursome and enfolding. The Riserva '07 is stiffer, with a mineral hint on the nose and a streamlined body slowed down by the tannins in the finale. The Chianti Classico '08 is simple, subtle and slightly edgy.

● Chianti Cl. Don Vincenzo Ris. '07	▼▼	7
● Inversus '07	▼▼	7
● Chianti Cl. '08	▼	5
● Chianti Cl. Ris. '07	▼	6
● Chianti Cl. Don Vincenzo Ris. '01	YYY	7
● Chianti Cl. '06	YY	5
● Chianti Cl. '04	YY	5
● Chianti Cl. '03	YY	5
● Chianti Cl. Ris. '04	YY	6
● Inversus '03	YY	6

Fattoria Le Casalte

fraz. Sant'Albino
via del Termine, 2
53045 Montepulciano [SI]
tel. 0578798246
www.lecasalte.com

CELLAR SALES
PRE-BOOKED VISITS

ANNUAL PRODUCTION 50,000 bottles
HECTARES UNDER VINE 13
VITICULTURE METHOD Conventional

Chiara Barioffi is the go-getting owner of Fattoria Le Casalte, one of the Montepulciano wineries that recently elbowed its way to the front of the crowded, competitive Tuscan winemaking scenario, thanks to a determinedly unwavering production philosophy. The wines now have distinct style features offering robust structure and plenty of personality but, above all, they are distinctly true to type.

The well-layered flower and spice aromas of the Nobile Quercetonda '07 pave the way for a powerful, compact palate tending to the mighty and compact, still somewhat held back by a few too many toasty notes. The Rosso Toscano '08 sangiovese and canaiolo blend is ever so drinkable, surprising us not just with its fragrance but also the very competitive price. The '07 Nobile is delicious and well defined; the Rosso di Montepulciano '08 simple and approachable.

● Nobile di Montepulciano Quercetonda '07	▼▼	6
● Rosso Toscano '08	▼▼	3*
● Nobile di Montepulciano '07	▼	5
● Rosso di Montepulciano '08	▼	4
● Nobile di Montepulciano Quercetonda '06	YYY	6
● Nobile di Montepulciano '06	YY	5
● Nobile di Montepulciano '04	YY	5
● Nobile di Montepulciano Quercetonda '04	YY	6
● Nobile di Montepulciano Quercetonda '03	YY	5
● Nobile di Montepulciano Quercetonda '01	YY	6
● Rosso Toscano '06	YY	2*
○ Vin Santo '97	YY	5

Casanova della Spinetta

LOC. CASANOVA
56030 TERRICCIOLA [PI]
TEL. 0587690508
www.la-spinetta.com

PRE-BOOKED VISITS

ANNUAL PRODUCTION **150,000 bottles**
HECTARES UNDER VINE **65**
VITICULTURE METHOD **Conventional**

The wines made by the lively enterprising Rivetti family from Piedmont are now right on track, having found their stylistic comfort zone. The winery is located between Pisa and Volterra, with a good 65 hectares of sangiovese, colorino and vermentino. A number of labels are in the pipeline, with two Riservas out next year. This season's newcomer is called Vermentino.

The three wines tasted this year included newcomer Vermentino, a very drinkable '09 with typical floral and white-fleshed fruits on the nose, and a fresh, full-flavoured palate. The Gentile di Casanova '06, pure prugnolo gentile, as sangiovese is also called, presents a vibrant colour with an intense, pervasive nose of clean, ripe red berries and Mediterranean scrub. The palate is succulent and persuasive. The monovarietal Colorino di Casanova '06 is already fragrant on the nose, with attractive spice and black berry preserve notes although the palate lacks some expansion, probably because the oak is still a little too evident.

● Il Colorino di Casanova '06	2 glasses (black)	5
○ Il Gentile di Casanova '06	2 glasses (black)	6
○ Vermentino '09	1 glass (black)	5
● Il Colorino di Casanova '05	2 glasses (white)	5
● Il Gentile di Casanova '05	2 glasses (white)	6
● Il Nero di Casanova '07	2 glasses (white)	5
● Nero di Casanova '04	2 glasses (white)	4

★ Casanova di Neri

POD. FIESOLE
53024 MONTALCINO [SI]
TEL. 0577834455
www.casanovadineri.com

CELLAR SALES
PRE-BOOKED VISITS

ANNUAL PRODUCTION **225,000 bottles**
HECTARES UNDER VINE **55**
VITICULTURE METHOD **Conventional**

Giacomo Neri has grown his winery into one of Montalcino's most famous, known worldwide, and visitors flock like pilgrims. New premises are on road from Torrenieri up to Montalcino so on clear days the bell tower of Siena's Piazza del Campo can be seen from the grape reception terrace. Neri's vineyards are all over the area, some to the north but mostly near the old Castelnuovo dell'Abate onyx quarry and on the eastern slope of lower central Sesta.

The true dependability of this winery can be noted in the quality of the '05 Brunello di Montalcino wines, both in our finals. We gave Three Glasses to Tenuta Nuova for its repeat performance as a modern wine but with some downscaling of the forceful oak of the past. The nose presents ripe fruit, morello cherry, wild cherry and blackberry, with hints of spicy balsam and oak. Tannins on the round, intense palate are noticeable but not mouth-drying and the finale is intense. The Brunello di Montalcino '05, replacing the Cerretalto selection, not produced in 2005, has a mildly smoky, spicy nose that enfolds the ripe blackberry. Its understated palate is intense and stylish.

● Brunello di Montalcino Tenuta Nuova '05	3 glasses (black)	8
● Brunello di Montalcino '05	2 glasses (black)	6*
● Pietradonice '07	2 glasses (black)	8
● Rosso di Montalcino '08	2 glasses (black)	5
● Sant'Antimo Rosso di Casanova di Neri '08	2 glasses (black)	4
● Brunello di Montalcino '00	3 glasses (white)	6
● Brunello di Montalcino Cerretalto '04	3 glasses (white)+	8
● Brunello di Montalcino Cerretalto '01	3 glasses (white)	8
● Brunello di Montalcino Cerretalto '99	3 glasses (white)	8
● Brunello di Montalcino Cerretalto '95	3 glasses (white)	8
● Brunello di Montalcino Cerretalto Ris. '88	3 glasses (white)	8
● Brunello di Montalcino Tenuta Nuova '01	3 glasses (white)	7
● Brunello di Montalcino Tenuta Nuova '99	3 glasses (white)	7
● Brunello di Montalcino Tenuta Nuova '97	3 glasses (white)	7
● Pietradonice '05	3 glasses (white)	8
● Sant'Antimo Pietradonice '01	3 glasses (white)	8
● Sant'Antimo Pietradonice '00	3 glasses (white)	8

★ Castellare di Castellina

LOC. CASTELLARE
53011 CASTELLINA IN CHIANTI [SI]
TEL. 0577742903
www.castellare.it

CELLAR SALES
PRE-BOOKED VISITS

ANNUAL PRODUCTION 180,000 bottles
HECTARES UNDER VINE 24
VITICULTURE METHOD Conventional

This is the most prestigious of the estates owned by wine buff, successful journalist and publisher, Paolo Panerai. The 24 hectares are in the municipality of Castellina, the heart of historic Chianti territory, also the homeland of the district's classiest long-lived Sangioveses, which Panerai calls Sangiovetos. Here wines hold up even when harvest time is hot, as it was in 2006, and the rather alcoholic results are distinctly muscular.

The '06 I Sodi di San Niccolò is perhaps the most impressive version we have ever tasted of this famous red from sangiovese topped up with malvasia nera. The growing year has enhanced the body but without sacrificing elegance and we expect the wine to evolve positively with time. Another agile, stylish wine is the Chianti Classico Riserva '07, from a less extreme season and which we prefer to the more distant Vigna Il Poggiale, also '07. The cabernet sauvignon-only Coniale '06, a red with some international feel, is also very rich and very young. We found the merlot Poggio ai Merli '08 to be more on the ball and the pleasant Chianti Classico '08 is very drinkable.

● I Sodi di San Niccolò '06	▼▼▼+	8
● Chianti Cl. Ris. '07	▼▼	5
● Chianti Cl. V. il Poggiale Ris. '07	▼▼	6
● Coniale '06	▼▼	7
● Poggio ai Merli '08	▼▼	8
● Chianti Cl. '08	▼	4
● Chianti Cl. V. il Poggiale Ris. '01	▽▽▽	6
● Chianti Cl. V. il Poggiale Ris. '00	▽▽▽	6
● Chianti Cl. V. il Poggiale Ris. '97	▽▽▽	6
● I Sodi di San Niccolò '05	▽▽▽+	8
● I Sodi di San Niccolò '04	▽▽▽	8
● I Sodi di San Niccolò '03	▽▽▽	8
● I Sodi di San Niccolò '02	▽▽▽	8
● I Sodi di San Niccolò '01	▽▽▽	8
● I Sodi di San Niccolò '98	▽▽▽	8
● I Sodi di San Niccolò '97	▽▽▽	8
● I Sodi di San Niccolò '95	▽▽▽	8

★ Castello Banfi

LOC. SANT'ANGELO SCALO
CASTELLO DI POGGIO ALLE MURA
53024 MONTALCINO [SI]
TEL. 0577840111
www.castellobanfi.com

CELLAR SALES
PRE-BOOKED VISITS
ROOMS AND FOOD

ANNUAL PRODUCTION 9,000,000 bottles
HECTARES UNDER VINE 850
VITICULTURE METHOD Conventional

The winery, owned by the Italian-American Marianis, makes top-notch wines for all budgets. This is significant for an estate of over 800 hectares, all under vine in the municipality of Montalcino, with 150 designation-registered. A pat on the back for those working in the various sectors, like agronomist Marmugi or cellar manager Buratti. The winery is coordinated by Enrico Viglierchio, who sails the ship with panache even in stormy waters.

We are happy to award Three Glasses again to the '04 Brunello Poggio all'Oro Riserva, released for the first time since the '99 vintage. A wine with great style and an intense nose of balsam, bramble jelly and cherries, its lays out honed tannins in the persuasive progression into a long-lingering finale. The '05 Brunello Poggio alle Mura, one of the best ever, is scrumptious, while the Brunello di Montalcino '05 is very well made.

● Brunello di Montalcino Poggio all'Oro Ris. '04	▼▼▼	8
● Brunello di Montalcino Poggio alle Mura '05	▼▼	8
● Brunello di Montalcino '05	▼▼	8
● Centine '08	▼▼	4*
● Cum Laude '07	▼▼	6
● Excelsus '07	▼▼	8
○ Moscadello di Montalcino Florus '08	▼▼	6
● Rosso di Montalcino '08	▼	6
○ San Angelo '09	▼	5
● Brunello di Montalcino Poggio all'Oro Ris. '95	▽▽▽	8
● Brunello di Montalcino Poggio all'Oro Ris. '90	▽▽▽	6
● Brunello di Montalcino Poggio all'Oro Ris. '88	▽▽▽	6
● Excelsus '93	▽▽▽	6
● Summus '95	▽▽▽	6
● Cum Laude '06	▽▽	6
○ Moscadello di Montalcino Florus '07	▽▽	6
● Summus '06	▽▽	8

Castello d'Albola

Loc. Pian d'Albola, 31
53017 Radda in Chianti [SI]
tel. 0577738019
www.albola.it

CELLAR SALES
PRE-BOOKED VISITS

ANNUAL PRODUCTION 800,000 bottles
HECTARES UNDER VINE 157
VITICULTURE METHOD Conventional

The Zonin family are leading Italian wine entrepreneurs and this Chianti estate is one of the biggest in this area. Named after Pian d'Albola where it is located, it looks onto the lovely Radda hillsides. Here there are some of the most famous plots in the designation. Skilled technical and administrative staff do the rest, ensuring aficionados receive impeccable wines with plenty of personality.

The sangiovese and cabernet Acciaiolo '07 was less awe-inspiring than other versions. The ripe fruit nose, with spice notes and emphatic oak, comes with a structured palate hindered by clenched tannins that still need to unbend. The Chianti Classico Riserva '06 is also still cropped and impenetrable. The fascinating, truly expressive pale amber Vin Santo '01 has sweet, fruity and spice aromas, with a warm, distinctive palate that unfolds its flavour and embraces the acid in an endless finale. The '09 Chardonnay has yellow peaches, spices and aromatic herbs on the nose.

● Acciaiolo '07	ΨΨ	7
○ Vin Santo del Chianti Cl. '01	ΨΨ	7
○ Chardonnay '09	Ψ	4
● Chianti Cl. Ris. '06	Ψ	5
● Acciaiolo '06	ΨΨΨ	7
● Acciaiolo '04	ΨΨΨ	7
● Acciaiolo '01	ΨΨΨ	7
● Acciaiolo '95	ΨΨΨ	6
● Acciaiolo '03	ΨΨ	7
● Acciaiolo '00	ΨΨ	7
● Chianti Cl. Ris. '05	ΨΨ	5
● Chianti Cl. Ris. '04	ΨΨ	5

★ Castello dei Rampolla

via Case Sparse, 22
50020 Panzano [FI]
tel. 055852001
castellodeirampolla.cast@tin.it

CELLAR SALES
PRE-BOOKED VISITS

ANNUAL PRODUCTION 90,000 bottles
HECTARES UNDER VINE 42
VITICULTURE METHOD Organic

Castello dei Rampolla is a Chianti Classico star for wines that express the territory's true character. The 42 hectares are located in the Panzano Conca d'Oro and are managed with total integrity, proved by the committed investment in organic management that began way back. These noble wines are up-to-the-minute precisely because they are so genuine.

This year there is no d'Alceo, the winery's flagship cabernet sauvignon and petit verdot, but we hardly missed it thanks to an outstanding Sammarco '06. The ample, complex nose is characterized by ripe, intense fruit with hints of iron filings and topsoil. The palate is structured and compact, with tannins still short-tempered enough to outweigh the acid but just give them time to unbend. The fragrant, juicy Chianti Classico '07 is delicious, with red berry and medicinal herb notes accompanying an ample, relaxed palate with a deep finale that closes just slightly bitter.

● Sammarco '06	ΨΨ	8
● Chianti Cl. '07	ΨΨ	5
● d'Alceo '04	ΨΨΨ	8
● d'Alceo '03	ΨΨΨ	8
● d'Alceo '01	ΨΨΨ	8
● d'Alceo '00	ΨΨΨ	8
● La Vigna di Alceo '99	ΨΨΨ	8
● La Vigna di Alceo '98	ΨΨΨ	8
● La Vigna di Alceo '97	ΨΨΨ	8
● Sammarco '05	ΨΨΨ	8
● Sammarco '85	ΨΨΨ	8

★ Castello del Terriccio

LOC. TERRICCIO
VIA BAGNOLI, 16
56040 CASTELLINA MARITTIMA [PI]
TEL. 050699709
www.terriccio.it

CELLAR SALES
PRE-BOOKED VISITS

ANNUAL PRODUCTION 350,000 bottles
HECTARES UNDER VINE 62
VITICULTURE METHOD Conventional

Terriccio is in a sort of paradise, an immense estate at the northern edge of Maremma with woodlands in the higher part, crops rolling downhill and olive groves and vineyards, graced with the southern-style charm of eucalyptus. The Serafini Ferri family arrived here at the end of the war and the winery has gradually become one of the most charismatic in Italian winemaking, with outstanding bottles that inspire the entire area.

The '07 Lupicaia is yet another Three Glasses and what is more has an even greater capacity than its predecessors to convey the winery's traits when it is poured. The intensity of this cabernet sauvignon, merlot and petit verdot blend is outstanding, ranging from wild berry to toasty notes that are still a little evident, then spice and a classic hint of balsam that gives the game away. The palate is a monument to texture and utter complexity. Watch out, however, as the Tassinaia '07 is well up to the challenge, with even more mentholated, balsamic aromas, a supple weave laced with iron-like minerality and electrifying flavour.

● Lupicaia '07	▼▼▼	8
● Tassinaia '07	▼▼	7
● Castello del Terriccio '06	▼▼	8
● Castello del Terriccio '04	▽▽▽	8
● Castello del Terriccio '03	▽▽▽	8
● Castello del Terriccio '01	▽▽▽	8
● Castello del Terriccio '00	▽▽▽	8
● Lupicaia '06	▽▽▽	8
● Lupicaia '05	▽▽▽	8
● Lupicaia '04	▽▽▽	8
● Lupicaia '01	▽▽▽	8
● Lupicaia '00	▽▽▽	8
● Lupicaia '99	▽▽▽	8
● Lupicaia '98	▽▽▽	8
● Lupicaia '97	▽▽▽	8
● Lupicaia '96	▽▽▽	8
● Lupicaia '95	▽▽▽	8
● Lupicaia '93	▽▽▽	8

Castello del Trebbio

VIA SANTA BRIGIDA, 9
50060 PONTASSIEVE [FI]
TEL. 0558304900
www.vinoturismo.it

CELLAR SALES
PRE-BOOKED VISITS

ANNUAL PRODUCTION 340,000 bottles
HECTARES UNDER VINE 52
VITICULTURE METHOD Conventional

We like the winery that Anna Baj Macario took over in 1968. It is a place of history where the Pazzi family plotted against the Medici, now an estate of almost 400 hectares growing not just vines but also saffron and, above all, olives. Anna's husband Stefano Casadei, a professional agronomist, manages the vines and the cellar, and produces wines elsewhere, including in Val di Cornia and Sardinia.

The finalist '06 Pazzesco, from 50-50 merlot and syrah, has an intriguing undergrowth, aromatic herbs and mixed fruits nose, solid attack and tannins meshing in the alcohol, with a crescendo finish. A tasty Merlot '07 has cherry, strawberry, red berries, cinnamon and cloves, a silky, fluent palate and good progression. The enticing Lastricato '07 gives complex laurel, mint, myrtle and blackcurrant aromas, intense attack, mighty body and solid tannins in a tangy finale. The Bianco della Congiura '09, a rare riesling, pinot grigio, incrocio Manzoni and viognier blend, has pear and white peach notes, a smooth, supple body and inviting acid backbone. The '09 Chianti is tasty.

● Pazzesco '06	▼▼	6
● Chianti Rufina Lastricato Ris. '07	▼▼	5
● Merlot '07	▼▼	6
○ Bianco della Congiura '09	▼	5
● Chianti '09	▼	2
○ Bianco della Congiura '07	▽▽	5
● Chianti Rufina Lastricato Ris. '06	▽▽	5
● Chianti Rufina Lastricato Ris. '04	▽▽	5
● Chianti Rufina Lastricato Ris. '03	▽▽	5
● Merlot '06	▽▽	6
● Pazzesco '04	▽▽	6
● Pazzesco '03	▽▽	6
● Rosso della Congiura '04	▽▽	7
● Rosso della Congiura '03	▽▽	7

★★ Castello di Ama

LOC. AMA
53013 GAIOLE IN CHIANTI [SI]
TEL. 0577746031
www.castellodiama.com

PRE-BOOKED VISITS

ANNUAL PRODUCTION 350,000 bottles
HECTARES UNDER VINE 90
VITICULTURE METHOD Conventional

This name in Chianti Classico, with 90 hectares in the hills between Gaiole and Radda, has produced some of the area's most iconic wines, including Merlot L'Apparita and the Chianti Classico crus Bellavista and La Casuccia. Life and business partners Marco Pallanti and Lorenza Sebasti run the winery with passion and skill recognized across the Italian wine world. We tasted only two wines as the selections need another year.

New entry Il Chiuso '09 is a sangiovese and pinot nero, a tasty, dangerously drinkable red blend inheriting a label that in the past indicated a pure Pinot Nero and is presented as the winery's stylishly simple basic product. The other wine we tasted is Chianti Classico Castello di Ama '07, still somewhat closed on the nose, recouping on the palate what is not yet available on the nose. We know Ama takes its time but it might be an idea to seek some aromatic expression for the early years.

Wine	Glasses	Price
● Chianti Cl. Castello di Ama '07	2 (red)	7
● Il Chiuso '09	2 (red)	5
● Chianti Cl. Bellavista '01	3	8
● Chianti Cl. Bellavista '99	3	8
● Chianti Cl. Bellavista '95	3	6
● Chianti Cl. Bellavista '90	3	8
● Chianti Cl. Castello di Ama '05	3	6
● Chianti Cl. Castello di Ama '03	3	6
● Chianti Cl. Castello di Ama '01	3	6
● Chianti Cl. Castello di Ama '00	3	6
● Chianti Cl. Castello di Ama '99	3	5
● Chianti Cl. La Casuccia '04	3	8
● Chianti Cl. La Casuccia '01	3	8
● Chianti Cl. La Casuccia '97	3	8
● l'Apparita Merlot '01	3	8
● l'Apparita Merlot '00	3	8
● V. l'Apparita Merlot '92	3	8
● V. l'Apparita Merlot '90	3	8

Castello di Bolgheri

LOC. BOLGHERI
S.DA LAURETTA, 7
57020 CASTAGNETO CARDUCCI [LI]
TEL. 0565762110
www.castellodibolgheri.eu

CELLAR SALES
PRE-BOOKED VISITS
ROOMS

ANNUAL PRODUCTION 60,000 bottles
HECTARES UNDER VINE 50
VITICULTURE METHOD Conventional

Recently Castello di Bolgheri has shown extraordinarily consistent quality, threading together a very persuasive series of excellent wines. It has become a reference point for consumers seeking the best local wines. The vineyards are located at the far north of the designation, where the sand and clay soils have a high gravel content. The cellars are to be found in the superb medieval castle that dominates the village.

The Bolgheri Superiore '07 has phenomenal impact and lashings of character. It's a red that combines to perfection intensity, a spicy, fruit-rich weave, extractive weight, sprightly evolution and length. Nor does it lack some intriguing quirky traits. In a word, it's one of the year's best and more than worthy of the Three Glasses.

Wine	Glasses	Price
● Bolgheri Sup. Castello di Bolgheri '07	3 (red)	7
● Bolgheri Sup. '05	2	8
● Bolgheri Sup. Castello di Bolgheri '06	2	8
● Bolgheri Varvàra '07	2	5
● Bolgheri Varvàra '06	2	5

Castello di Bossi

LOC. BOSSI IN CHIANTI
53019 CASTELNUOVO BERARDENGA [SI]
TEL. 0577359330
www.castellodibossi.it

CELLAR SALES
PRE-BOOKED VISITS

ANNUAL PRODUCTION 600,000 bottles
HECTARES UNDER VINE 124
VITICULTURE METHOD Conventional

Castello di Bossi comprises several estates in a number of Tuscany's most renowned terroirs. The owners, Marco and Maurizio Bacci, have vineyards in Montalcino, Maremma and Chianti Classico. Castelnuovo Berardenga is the biggest estate and the headquarters. The Baccis grow mainly classic sangiovese, of course, although they did add some prized and less obvious varieties as long as four decades ago.

The staggering sweet Vin San Laurentino '01, with its intense amber colour, has overripe fruit aromas that verge on quinine before returning to distinct hints of preserves. The palate is dense, sweet, well developed and tasty, with huge fullness and a stunning finale. The seductive Chianti Classico Riserva Berardo '07 is very rich, complex and juicy, although it has to be said that on the flavour front the simple Chianti Classico '08 is its equal. The fresh, lively Merlot Girolamo '07 is another success and a good example of its type.

○ San Laurentino '01	TT	8
● Chianti Cl. '08	TT	5
● Chianti Cl. Berardo Ris. '07	TT	6
● Girolamo '07	TT	8
● Brunello di Montalcino Renieri '05	T	8
● Rosso di Montalcino Renieri '08	T	5
○ Vento Vermentino Terre di Talamo '09	T	4
● Corbaia '03	YYY	7
● Corbaia '99	YYY	8
● Chianti Cl. Berardo Ris. '04	YY	6
● Chianti Cl. Berardo Ris. '03	YY	6
● Corbaia '01	YY	7
● Girolamo '04	YY	7
● Girolamo '03	YY	7
● Girolamo '01	YY	7
● Morellino di Scansano Tempo Terra di Talamo '07	YY	4
○ Vin San Laurentino '99	YY	8

Castello di Cacchiano

FRAZ. MONTI IN CHIANTI
LOC. CACCHIANO
53010 GAIOLE IN CHIANTI [SI]
TEL. 0577747018
cacchiano@chianticlassico.com

CELLAR SALES
PRE-BOOKED VISITS
ROOMS

ANNUAL PRODUCTION 120,000 bottles
HECTARES UNDER VINE 31
VITICULTURE METHOD Conventional

The Giovanni Ricasoli Firidolfi family own Castello di Cacchiano, located on a spectacular promontory in Monti in Chianti, municipality of Gaiole. The vaulted cellars are also here, as are some of the most interesting in the area, with traditional large barrels and tonneaux, surrounded by vineyards. The wines are some of the designation's most archetypal, and the better bottles will evoke the matchless magic of the most delicate, elegant Sangioveses.

One of the best bottles of recent years is the Chianti Classico Riserva '06, a quintessentially territorial red and a perfect combination of tradition and contemporary precision. Each note whispers blossom, morello cherry, a nuance of spice and game. The deep, vibrant palate is a masterpiece with exciting progression. The winery's pride and joy is its excellent Vin Santo '02 and its Chianti Classico '08 is very enjoyable.

● Chianti Cl. Ris. '06	TTT	6
● Chianti Cl. '08	TT	5
○ Vin Santo del Chianti Cl. '02	TT	7
● Chianti Cl. Millennio Ris. '90	YYY	5
● Chianti Cl. '06	YY	5
● Chianti Cl. '05	YY	5
● Chianti Cl. '03	YY	5
● Chianti Cl. '02	YY	4
● Chianti Cl. Ris. '01	YY	5
○ Vin Santo '00	YY	6
○ Vin Santo '99	YY	6
○ Vin Santo '98	YY	6
○ Vin Santo del Chianti Cl. '01	YY	7

★★ Castello di Fonterutoli

LOC. FONTERUTOLI
VIA OTTONE III DI SASSONIA, 5
53011 CASTELLINA IN CHIANTI [SI]
TEL. 057773571
www.fonterutoli.it

CELLAR SALES
PRE-BOOKED VISITS
ROOMS AND FOOD

ANNUAL PRODUCTION 710,000 bottles
HECTARES UNDER VINE 117
VITICULTURE METHOD Conventional

Fonterutoli and Chianti share many pages of history so aficionados have to know the winery well to understand this fascinating designation's past dynamics and current developments. As the Mazzeis have owned the place since the mid 1400s, they are a point of reference for the district and its wines. Today's wines are the offspring of this vineyard territory and cutting-edge cellaring techniques, achieving top quality despite the sheer amounts produced.

In this respect the '07 Chianti Classico Castello di Fonterutoli is an exemplary red and, youth notwithstanding, blends spicy and toasty notes that range through vanilla to coffee beans, nuanced with intense, caressing fruit. There is no tension and the ensuing harmony creates excellent balance. The '07 Siepi is another champion, an iconic merlot and sangiovese Supertuscan with a brooding profile, deep texture and huge extract. The Badiola '08 is not bad at all and we also like the wines from the Tenuta di Belguardo vineyards in Maremma.

● Chianti Cl. Castello di Fonterutoli '07	TTT	7
● Siepi '07	TT	8
● Tenuta di Belguardo '07	TT	6
● Badiola '08	TT	4*
⊙ Belguardo Rosé '09	T	5
● Chianti Cl. '08	T	5
● Chianti Cl. Ser Lapo Ris. '06	T	5
● Serrata di Belguardo '08	T	5
● Chianti Cl. Castello di Fonterutoli '04	YYY	7
● Chianti Cl. Castello di Fonterutoli '03	YYY	7
● Chianti Cl. Castello di Fonterutoli '01	YYY	7
● Chianti Cl. Castello di Fonterutoli '00	YYY	8
● Chianti Cl. Castello di Fonterutoli '99	YYY	8
● Siepi '06	YYY	8
● Siepi '05	YYY	8
● Siepi '03	YYY	8
● Siepi '01	YYY	8

Castello di Meleto

LOC. MELETO
53013 GAIOLE IN CHIANTI [SI]
TEL. 0577749217
www.castellomeleto.it

CELLAR SALES
PRE-BOOKED VISITS
ROOMS AND FOOD

ANNUAL PRODUCTION 480,000 bottles
HECTARES UNDER VINE 120
VITICULTURE METHOD Conventional

Medieval Castello di Meleto once belonged to the Vallombroso monastic order, then more recently to the famous Ricasoli family, but is now part of Viticola Toscana, a company that also owns Pieve di Spaltenna. The castle has about 3,000 hectares of terrain around it, with the vines planted on marl, alberese clay-limestone and marly limestone soil. The Spaltenna winery can boast about 60 hectares under vine.

The Riserva '07 Vigna Casi is a delight, not only for the densely woven texture of mature fruit and vanilla notes but also a captivating land-rooted feel with excellent suggestions of pencil lead, citrus fruit, rain-washed pebbles and roses. The sangiovese and merlot Meletino '07 has refreshing aromas and a crispy palate; the other reds are less precise in their oak-fruit symmetry.

● Chianti Cl. V. Casi Ris. '07	TT	6
● Meletino '07	TT	3*
● Chianti Cl. '08	T	5
● Chianti Cl. V. Poggiarso Ris. '07	T	6
● Chianti Cl. Ris. '03	YYY	5
● Chianti Cl. Pieve di Spaltenna '07	YY	4*
● Chianti Cl. Pieve di Spaltenna '06	YY	4*
● Chianti Cl. Pieve di Spaltenna '04	YY	4
● Chianti Cl. Pieve di Spaltenna '02	YY	4
● Chianti Cl. Pieve di Spaltenna '01	YY	4
● Chianti Cl. Ris. '01	YY	5
● Chianti Cl. Ris. '99	YY	4
● Chianti Cl. V. Casi Ris. '04	YY	5
● Rainero '04	YY	7
● Rainero '03	YY	7
○ Vin Santo del Chianti Cl. '00	YY	6

Castello di Monsanto

FRAZ. MONSANTO
VIA MONSANTO, 8
50021 BARBERINO VAL D'ELSA [FI]
TEL. 0558059000
www.castellodimonsanto.it

CELLAR SALES
PRE-BOOKED VISITS
ROOMS

ANNUAL PRODUCTION **450,000 bottles**
HECTARES UNDER VINE **72**
VITICULTURE METHOD **Conventional**

Considered revolutionary until recently for introducing quality as a concept to a conflict-ridden Chianti, Castello di Monsanto is now seen as a paradigm in this lovely part of Tuscany. Many innovations were the pioneer work of Fabrizio Bianchi, a wine mastermind who developed the area's great potential. Barberino Val d'Elsa has mainly marl soils. The wines, as we said, are now classics but still have a style of their own.

In the house reds it is quite often the precise tannins that make the difference since local grapes store up lots of polyphenols. The '06 Chianti Classico Riserva Il Poggio shows faultless tannins, which helps to make the wine even more persuasive and on-target than usual, without hindrances to its progression. What a red. It glows, it commands, bursting with nuanced aromas and chiaroscuros on the nose with its superb wafts of Mediterranean scrub, and on a palate so tasty and refreshing that it is almost perilously moreish.

● Chianti Cl. Il Poggio Ris. '06	▼▼▼	7
● Chianti Cl. '08	▼▼	5
● Chianti Cl. Ris. '07	▼▼	5
○ Fabrizio Bianchi Chardonnay '09	▼▼	5
● Nemo '08	▼▼	7
⊙ Fabrizio Bianchi Rosato '09	▼	5
● Chianti Cl. Il Poggio Ris. '88	▽▽▽	7
● Nemo '01	▽▽▽	7
● Chianti Cl. Il Poggio Ris. '04	▽▽	7
● Chianti Cl. Ris. '06	▽▽	5
○ Fabrizio Bianchi Chardonnay '06	▽▽	5
● Fabrizio Bianchi Sangiovese '99	▽▽	7
● Nemo '04	▽▽	7
● Tinscvil '00	▽▽	6

Castello di Poppiano

FRAZ. POPPIANO
VIA DI FEZZANA, 45
50025 MONTESPERTOLI [FI]
TEL. 05582315
www.conteguicciardini.it

CELLAR SALES
PRE-BOOKED VISITS

ANNUAL PRODUCTION **250,000 bottles**
HECTARES UNDER VINE **130**
VITICULTURE METHOD **Conventional**

Ferdinando and Titti Guicciardini run their business with laudable enthusiasm in a winery steeped in history. They work to achieve excellent results not only with traditional varieties but also with other vines that adapt well to the terrain. After modernizing the main winery, Guicciardini invested in the Massi di Mandorla estate, believing in Maremma before many others and making good wines there, too.

The Chianti Colli Fiorentini Riserva '07 has tobacco and leather notes underpinned by fruit while the vegetal palate has refined tannins that are not too rich. The Toscoforte '08 sangiovese, merlot and cabernet sauvignon blend has a fresh, spicy, sweet nose, plenty of power and a final flourish. The inviting Syrah '08, topped up with sangiovese, is warm, muscular, and satisfyingly long. The enjoyable Tricorno '08, from sangiovese with a syrah top-up, has a delicate nose and intact structure, tucked-in tannins and a lengthy finale.

● Chianti Colli Fiorentini Ris. '07	▼▼	5
● Syrah '08	▼▼	5
● Toscoforte '08	▼▼	4
● Tricorno '08	▼▼	6
● Chianti Colli Fiorentini Il Cortile '08	▼	4
○ Vin Santo della Torre Grande del Chianti '03	▼	5
● Chianti Colli Fiorentini Ris. '06	▽▽	5
● Colpetroso Massi di Mandorlaia '05	▽▽	5
● Morellino di Scansano Massi di Mandorlaia '06	▽▽	4*
● Morellino di Scansano Massi di Mandorlaia Ris. '04	▽▽	5
● Syrah '07	▽▽	5
● Syrah '06	▽▽	5
● Toscoforte '06	▽▽	4*

Castello di Querceto

LOC. QUERCETO
VIA A. FRANÇOIS, 2
50020 GREVE IN CHIANTI [FI]
TEL. 05585921
www.castellodiquerceto.it

CELLAR SALES
PRE-BOOKED VISITS
ROOMS

ANNUAL PRODUCTION **600,000 bottles**
HECTARES UNDER VINE **60**
VITICULTURE METHOD **Conventional**

When we say a territory expresses its traits through its wine, we mean wineries like this one, found in unexpected places; wineries with strong personalities that make their mark. The location of the Fracois family's vineyards is actually unique, on soils rich in manganese and alkaline earth metals at altitudes up to 530m. The cellars are also very interesting as they involved conversion of several rooms under the castle.

The modern-style Chianti Classico Riserva Il Picchio '07 is delicious again this year, opening on black cherry, blackberry and pencil lead before the fairly pulpy palate shows appreciable roundness. It's a warm, succulent, well-extracted wine but all this prevents it from unfolding completely. We'll wait and see. The '07 Chianti Classico Riserva is open and mature but despite its eloquence is slightly hindered by its exuberant, extract-rich palate whose tannins have yet to mellow out. The Chianti Classico '08 also has black berries and toastiness.

● Chianti Cl. Il Picchio Ris. '07	▼▼	6
● Chianti Cl. Ris. '07	▼▼	5
● Il Sole di Alessandro '06	▼▼	8
○ Vin Santo del Chianti Cl. '06	▼▼	5
● Chianti Cl. '08	▼	4
● La Corte '06	▼	7
● Chianti Cl. Il Picchio Ris. '06	▽▽	6
● Chianti Cl. Il Picchio Ris. '03	▽▽	6
● Chianti Cl. Ris. '06	▽▽	5
● Chianti Cl. Ris. '05	▽▽	5
● Chianti Cl. Ris. '04	▽▽	5
● Chianti Cl. Ris. '03	▽▽	5
● Chianti Cl. Ris. '01	▽▽	5
● La Corte '98	▽▽	7

Castello di Radda

LOC. IL BECCO
53017 RADDA IN CHIANTI [SI]
TEL. 0577738992
www.castellodiradda.it

CELLAR SALES
PRE-BOOKED VISITS

ANNUAL PRODUCTION **50,000 bottles**
HECTARES UNDER VINE **N.A .**
VITICULTURE METHOD **Conventional**

This impressive Castello di Radda hilltop winery faces the Chianti village of Radda to the east, more or less under Volpaia, another point of reference for this area. The vineyards have south-east and south-west exposure, and medium-textured, calcareous-clay soil with plenty of gravel, which guarantees the grapes achieve perfect phenolic ripeness. The wines age in French oak barriques and recently we have noticed enhanced texture and finesse.

The bottom line is that the Chianti Classico Riserva '07 is a spectacular red with aromas of wild strawberries, fresh flowers and citrus sweets, all marked out by their sheer finesse and depth. The palate is equally convincing with unbeatable progression, savouriness and sense of place. Three Glasses with a pedigree.

● Chianti Cl. Ris. '07	▼▼▼	6
● Chianti Cl. Poggio Selvale '06	▽▽	4*
● Chianti Cl. Poggio Selvale '05	▽▽	4*
● Chianti Cl. Poggio Selvale Ris. '04	▽▽	5

Castello di San Sano

FRAZ. SAN SANO
LOC. PALAZZINO
53013 GAIOLE IN CHIANTI [SI]
TEL. 0577746056
www.castellosansano.com

CELLAR SALES
PRE-BOOKED VISITS

ANNUAL PRODUCTION 200,000 bottles
HECTARES UNDER VINE 87
VITICULTURE METHOD Conventional

The winery is named after the small Gaiole in Chianti village where it is located and is owned by Calogero Calì, already in the Guide with his Rocca di Castagnoli and Tenuta di Capraia estates. The vineyards are on tableland with excellent exposure and stony soils. This is a working farm that also produces extra virgin olive oil and breeds Cinta Senese pigs. Its wines are feisty and combine precise tone with a genuine territorial feel.

There's another great performance from the '07 Chianti Classico Riserva Guarnellotto. The nose is still a tad reticent but is evolving nicely, and we have no doubts about the gripping, racy palate with its awesome progression. The '08 house white was a pleasant surprise for its honey, yellow-fleshed fruit and vanilla aromas, and the taut, nicely dynamic palate with tasty finale. The Borro al Fumo '07 sangiovese and cabernet blend is again savoury and relaxed.

● Chianti Cl. Guarnellotto Ris. '07	▼▼	5
● Borro al Fumo '07	▼▼	6
○ Sanzano '08	▼▼	5
● Chianti Cl. '08	▼	4
● Chianti Vign. della Rana '08	▼	4
● Borro al Fumo '04	▽▽	6
● Chianti Cl. '07	▽▽	4*
● Chianti Cl. '06	▽▽	4*
● Chianti Cl. '04	▽▽	4
● Chianti Cl. Guarnellotto Ris. '06	▽▽	5
● Chianti Cl. Guarnellotto Ris. '05	▽▽	5
● Chianti Cl. Guarnellotto Ris. '04	▽▽	5

Castello di Sonnino

VIA VOLTERRANA NORD, 6A
50025 MONTESPERTOLI [FI]
TEL. 0571609198
www.castellosonnino.it

CELLAR SALES
PRE-BOOKED VISITS

ANNUAL PRODUCTION 200,000 bottles
HECTARES UNDER VINE 45
VITICULTURE METHOD Conventional

Castello di Sonnino, or Montespertoli like its village, has an original 13th-century tower and a fine 17th-century palazzo. It was purchased by the Sonninos in the 19th century and many great names stayed here, from its owner Sidney Sonnino to Umberto I, Gabriele D'Annunzio and Giovanni Giolitti, to mention just a few. Documents in the castle library describe early 20th-century agriculture and innovations in Tuscan winemaking and olive growing.

We found the overall quality to be outstanding. The pure sangiovese Cantinino '07 performed well, its complex aromatic profile nuanced with black berries melting into balsamic and liquorice notes before the solid, soft-textured palate powers through to a savoury, succulent finale. The tasty Lo Schiavone '06 is an unusual, almost equal parts sangiovese and malbec blend with an opulent nose of bramble jelly and intense clove-led spice, a round body and long persistence. The San Leone '07, from merlot topped up with sangiovese and petit verdot, has a fresh, grassy aromatic profile, silky structure and a seamless, savoury palate.

● Cantinino '07	▼▼	5
● Lo Schiavone '06	▼▼	6
● San Leone '07	▼▼	7
● Chianti Montespertoli Castello di Montespertoli '07	▼	3
● Cantinino '06	▽▽	5
● Cantinino '05	▽▽	5
● Cantinino '04	▽▽	5
● Leone Rosso '08	▽▽	3*
● Leone Rosso '07	▽▽	3*
● Lo Schiavone '05	▽▽	6
● San Leone '04	▽▽	7

Castello di Vicchiomaggio

loc. Le Bolle
via Vicchiomaggio, 4
50022 Greve in Chianti [FI]
tel. 055854079
www.vicchiomaggio.it

CELLAR SALES
PRE-BOOKED VISITS

ANNUAL PRODUCTION 300,000 bottles
HECTARES UNDER VINE 33
VITICULTURE METHOD Conventional

The vineyards and the castle that gives the winery its name are on the Greve valley hillside. The business opened in the early 1960s when the Matta family arrived and converted it into an elegant holiday farm, with wine production becoming gradually more significant. The cellars are home both to barriques and large traditional casks used for different wines in a distinctive house style.

The Chianti Classico Riserva Agostino Petri da Vicchiomaggio '07 is very good, giving minerality and undergrowth that veer increasingly to grassy, vegetal notes of moss, plumped up by hints of sweet ripe fruit. The deep, crispy Riserva La Prima '07 is also first-rate with a great future ahead, like the sangiovese, cabernet and merlot blend Ripa delle More, which intriguingly weaves red and black forest fruits with undertones of balsam. The Merlot FSM '06 is well rounded, with hints of sweet fruit and tannins.

Wine	Glasses	Score
● Chianti Cl. Agostino Petri da Vicchiomaggio Ris. '07	2 black	6
● Chianti Cl. La Prima Ris. '07	2 black	7
● Chianti Cl. Gustavo Petri Ris. '07	2 black	7
● Chianti Cl. San Jacopo '08	2 black	5
● FSM '06	2 black	8
● Ripa delle More '07	2 black	8
● Ripa delle Mandorle '09	1 black	5
● FSM '04	3 white	8
● Ripa delle More '97	3 white	6
● Ripa delle More '94	3 white	5
● Chianti Cl. Agostino Petri Ris. '04	2 white	6
● Chianti Cl. La Prima Ris. '06	2 white	7
● FSM '05	2 white	8
● Ripa delle More '06	2 white	8
● Ripa delle More '99	2 white	6

Castello di Volpaia

loc. Volpaia
p.zza della Cisterna, 1
53017 Radda in Chianti [SI]
tel. 0577738066
www.volpaia.com

CELLAR SALES
PRE-BOOKED VISITS
ROOMS AND FOOD

ANNUAL PRODUCTION 250,000 bottles
HECTARES UNDER VINE 46
VITICULTURE METHOD Certified organic

Castello di Volpaia belongs to the Mascheroni Stianti family, who have preserved and enhanced the features of a lovely site that conveys Chianti's history, people, architecture and countryside, just as it did in the 11th century when the village was founded between two small valleys on the Florence-Siena border. The vines stand at elevations of up to 500 metres while the flawless, modern-style wines embody all the typicality of their terroir.

The pure sangioveto Chianti Classico Riserva '07, aged for two years in large Slavonian oak and in barrique, is sensational. Each component plays a part to make a marvellous whole. There are no false steps as fruit that is ripe yet refreshing merges with the earthy minerality notes accompanying both the aromas and the broad, deep palate with its massive flavour and infinite length. The other wines are noteworthy, including the Morello di Prile '09 from Prelius in Maremma, all proof of a general level with few equals in Tuscany.

Wine	Glasses	Score
● Chianti Cl. Ris. '07	3 black	6
● Chianti Cl. Il Puro Vign. Casanova Ris. '07	2 black	8
● Balifico '07	2 black	7
● Chianti Cl. '08	2 black	5
● Morello di Prile Prelius '09	2 black	4
● Chianti Cl. Coltassala Ris. '07	1 black	7
● Balifico '00	3 white	7
● Chianti Cl. Coltassala Ris. '04	3 white	7
● Chianti Cl. Coltassala Ris. '01	3 white	7
● Chianti Cl. Il Puro Vign. Casanova Ris. '06	3 white	8
● Balifico '06	2 white	7
● Chianti Cl. '99	2 white	4*
● Chianti Cl. Coltassala Ris. '03	2 white	7
● Chianti Cl. Coltassala Ris. '00	2 white	7
● Chianti Cl. Coltassala Ris. '99	2 white	6
● Chianti Cl. Ris. '05	2 white	6

Castello Romitorio

LOC. ROMITORIO, 279
53024 MONTALCINO [SI]
TEL. 0577847212
www.castelloromitorio.com

CELLAR SALES
PRE-BOOKED VISITS

ANNUAL PRODUCTION 150,000 bottles
HECTARES UNDER VINE 25
VITICULTURE METHOD Conventional

The delightful Castello di Romitorio stands at the end of a dirt track. The austere 14th-century manor is home to the renowned artist Sandro Chia, creator of the winery's labels. A close bond connects the terroir, the wine and the owner, and after a few off years, probably because of cellar reorganization, the winery is now back on form. Its 25 hectares are split between the land near the castle and a Castelnuovo dell'Abate plot that adds power to the finesse of the upper western area.

The first-rate Brunello '05 that took the Three Glasses has an ample, complex, intense nose with classic morello cherry notes interweaving with blossom and hints of balsamic and tobacco. The palate is elegant and the secret of its success is deceptive subtlety. The tannins are fine and mellow, acidity sustains the wine without getting carried away and clean-cut progression leads to a full, lingering finale with awesome nose-palate harmony.

● Brunello di Montalcino '05	▼▼▼	8
● Brunello di Montalcino Ris. '04	▼▼	8
● Rosso di Montalcino '08	▼▼	6
● Brunello di Montalcino Ris. '97	YYY	8
● Brunello di Montalcino '03	YY	8
● Morellino di Scansano Ghiaccio Forte '07	YY	6

Castelvecchio

LOC. SAN PANCRAZIO
VIA CERTALDESE, 30
50026 SAN CASCIANO IN VAL DI PESA [FI]
TEL. 0558248032
www.castelvecchio.it

CELLAR SALES
PRE-BOOKED VISITS
ROOMS AND FOOD

ANNUAL PRODUCTION 100,000 bottles
HECTARES UNDER VINE 27
VITICULTURE METHOD Conventional

The Rocchi family are deeply involved in their winery and annexed holiday farm facilities. The business is now firmly in the hands of Stefania and Filippo, who inherited a vineyard estate they have completely renovated over the years. Filippo is also committed to the cellars, his approach changing as he gained experience. Now he makes wines with personality but distinguishes between those for everyday consumption and high-end bottles.

The finalist was Il Brecciolino '07, a sangiovese, merlot and petit verdot blend with a herby, minty nose profile, spirited, hefty structure and a savoury, lingering finale. We also like the '07 Vigna La Quercia selection for its traditional cherry and plum fruit notes, solid structure and pleasing flavour. The solidity of the Chianti Colli Fiorentini '08 is appealing, with its fragrant nose and good supporting acidity. We found both the Chianti Santa Caterina '08 and San Lorenzo '09 chardonnay and trebbiano to be simpler than usual. The Vin Santo '99 is old school.

● Il Brecciolino '07	▼▼	6
● Chianti Colli Fiorentini V. La Quercia '07	▼▼	5
● Chianti Colli Fiorentini '08	▼	4
● Chianti Santa Caterina '08	▼	3
○ Colli dell'Etruria Centrale Vin Santo '99	▼	6
○ San Lorenzo '09	▼	3
● Chianti Colli Fiorentini '07	YY	4*
● Chianti Colli Fiorentini Il Castelvecchio '06	YY	4*
● Chianti Colli Fiorentini V. La Quercia Ris. '05	YY	5
● Il Brecciolino '06	YY	6
● Il Brecciolino '05	YY	6
● Numero Otto '07	YY	5
● Numero Otto '06	YY	5
● Vin Santo del Chianti Chiacchierata Notturna '03	YY	7

Famiglia Cecchi

LOC. CASINA DEI PONTI, 56
53011 CASTELLINA IN CHIANTI [SI]
TEL. 057754311
www.cecchi.net

PRE-BOOKED VISITS

ANNUAL PRODUCTION 7,200,000 bottles
HECTARES UNDER VINE 292
VITICULTURE METHOD Conventional

The Cecchi family shows the enduring bond some Tuscan aristocrats have with their land, vineyards and wine production. Noblesse aside, this winery has shown it cares about the quality of its wines by initiating and pursuing an extensive improvement scheme. Of course, with such large quantities some provisos are in order but in the more rigorous selections the wines are not only impeccable but also increasingly characterful.

The '07 Chianti Classico Riserva di Famiglia, for instance, with its accomplished nice of aromas that proffer sensations of mature fruit, refined spice and just a hint of grass in the background. The nose is already open and readable while the palate serious, vibrant and in parts austere palate promises long, positive evolution. The Coevo '07 is another ace with a mature, spicy nose and warm, hefty palate. True to its profile, it reveals a fair degree of overall elegance. The Chianti Classico Villa Cerna Riserva '07 is good, too.

● Chianti Cl. Riserva di Famiglia '07	🍷🍷🍷	6
● Coevo '07	🍷🍷	6
● Chianti Cl. Villa Cerna Ris. '07	🍷🍷	5
● Morellino di Scansano Val delle Rose '09	🍷🍷	3*
● Morellino di Scansano Val delle Rose Ris. '07	🍷🍷	5
● Chianti Cl. Dentro '08	🍷	4
○ Litorale Vermentino Val delle Rose '09	🍷	4
● Coevo '06	ΥΥΥ	6
● Chianti Cl. Riserva di Famiglia '06	ΥΥ	6
● Chianti Cl. Villa Cerna '07	ΥΥ	5
● Chianti Cl. Villa Cerna Ris. '05	ΥΥ	5
● Morellino di Scansano Ris. '05	ΥΥ	5
● Morellino di Scansano Val delle Rose Ris. '06	ΥΥ	5

Centolani

LOC. FRIGGIALI
S.DA MAREMMANA
53024 MONTALCINO [SI]
TEL. 0577849454
www.tenutafriggialiepietranera.it

CELLAR SALES
PRE-BOOKED VISITS
ROOMS

ANNUAL PRODUCTION 260,000 bottles
HECTARES UNDER VINE 43
VITICULTURE METHOD Conventional

This top-notch operation has over 40 hectares under vine, split across two vineyards. One is Friggiali, in western Montalcino, and the other is Pietranera, in the south-east at Castelnuovo dell'Abate, where the terrain is a unique lava soil rich in iron and heavy metals. The newly restored cellars use various sizes and types of casks to ensure optimum handling for each vintage. The winery complex is also striking, with welcoming agriturismo facilities.

We were unable to spot a champion this year but the range is more than adequate, including a well-honed, juicily elegant Brunello di Montalcino Riserva '04 with an intense finale. The two complex, land-rooted '05 Brunellos are solid, although we preferred the Pietranera and its ripe fruit nose with morello cherry and notes of tobacco, as its dense tannins are already mellow and the progression smooth, with a tasty finale. The Brunello Friggiali is somewhat edgy, with a lively tannin-acid component and a leaner structure.

● Brunello di Montalcino Tenuta Friggiali Ris. '04	🍷🍷	7
● Brunello di Montalcino Pietranera '05	🍷🍷	7
● Brunello di Montalcino Tenuta Friggiali '05	🍷🍷	7
● Rosso di Montalcino Pietranera '08	🍷	5
● Rosso di Montalcino Tenuta Friggiali '08	🍷	4
● Brunello di Montalcino Tenuta Friggiali '04	ΥΥΥ	6
● Brunello di Montalcino Tenuta Friggiali Ris. '99	ΥΥΥ	8
● Brunello di Montalcino Donna Olga '04	ΥΥ	8
● Brunello di Montalcino Tenuta Friggiali '03	ΥΥ	6
● Rosso di Montalcino Pietranera '07	ΥΥ	4*

La Cerbaiola

P.zza Cavour, 19
53024 Montalcino [SI]
tel. 0577848499
www.aziendasalvioni.com

CELLAR SALES
PRE-BOOKED VISITS

ANNUAL PRODUCTION 16,000 bottles
HECTARES UNDER VINE 4
VITICULTURE METHOD Conventional

Giulio and Mirella Salvioni are key figures in Brunello di Montalcino history whose versions of late 1980s vintages brought a new perspective to local potential. The winery increased its holding to today's four hectares on a single estate near the winemaking cellars at Le Cerbaie, in east Montalcino. The vines are about 420 metres above sea level and densities depend on when they were planted, with the most recent at 5,000 vines per hectare.

The '05 Brunello has a broad nose with clean sensations of morello cherry lifted by hints of tobacco and a vein of spice. The tannic weave is compact and mellow while the well-sustained progression is elegant and lingering, expanding in the finish. The '08 Rosso di Montalcino came up trumps with lots of fruit, nice yellow peach to the fore, an tasty progression assisted by refreshing acidity through to a lingering finale.

● Brunello di Montalcino '05	**YY**	8
● Rosso di Montalcino '08	**YY**	6
● Brunello di Montalcino '04	YYY	8
● Brunello di Montalcino '00	YYY	8
● Brunello di Montalcino '99	YYY	8
● Brunello di Montalcino '97	YYY	8
● Brunello di Montalcino '90	YYY	8
● Brunello di Montalcino '89	YYY	8
● Brunello di Montalcino '88	YYY	8
● Brunello di Montalcino '87	YYY	8
● Brunello di Montalcino '85	YYY	8
● Brunello di Montalcino '03	YY	8
● Brunello di Montalcino '01	YY	8
● Brunello di Montalcino '98	YY	8
● Rosso di Montalcino '07	YY	6

Cerbaiona

loc. Cerbaiona
53024 Montalcino [SI]
tel. 0577848660

CELLAR SALES

ANNUAL PRODUCTION 15,000 bottles
HECTARES UNDER VINE 3
VITICULTURE METHOD Conventional

This winery, with just over three hectares under vine, is famous for its exquisite Brunellos. The vineyard was planted back in 1977, on soil rich in gravel but with little clay, which increases significantly lower down. This is Le Cerbaie, an area at about 350 metres on the eastern slope of Montalcino with excellent exposure. Wine is fermented in cement tanks and aged in 30-hectolitre Slavonian oak casks.

The house champion this year is the '07 Rosso di Montalcino, which earned Three Glasses for its elegance. The nose, with lovely notes of blackberry and morello cherry, as well as a hint of liquorice, is exceptionally intense and clean. The palate gives full rein to Cerbaiona's traditional power. Stylish acidity and tannins sustain the wine's drinkability and progression before the finale expands in a lingering crescendo. The tasty Brunello '05 is elegant on nose and palate but is a tad unambitious.

● Rosso di Montalcino '07	**YYY**	8
● Brunello di Montalcino '05	**YY**	8
● Brunello di Montalcino '04	YYY+	8
● Brunello di Montalcino '01	YYY	8
● Brunello di Montalcino '99	YYY	8
● Brunello di Montalcino '97	YYY	8
● Brunello di Montalcino '90	YYY	8
● Brunello di Montalcino '88	YYY	8
● Brunello di Montalcino '85	YYY	8
● Brunello di Montalcino '03	YY	8
● Brunello di Montalcino '02	YY	8
● Brunello di Montalcino '98	YY	8
● Diego Molinari '06	YY	5
● Rosso di Montalcino '05	YY	5

Fattoria del Cerro

FRAZ. ACQUAVIVA
VIA GRAZIANELLA, 5
53040 MONTEPULCIANO [SI]
TEL. 0578767722
www.saiagricola.it

CELLAR SALES
PRE-BOOKED VISITS
ROOMS AND FOOD

ANNUAL PRODUCTION **850,000 bottles**
HECTARES UNDER VINE **170**
VITICULTURE METHOD **Conventional**

The Fattoria del Cerro winery, owned by Gruppo Fondiaria-SAI, has more production potential than most in the Montepulciano area. The winemaking project started in 1978 and the last 30 years or so have seen the estate become a leader on the Italian wine scene. Both the sales and technical departments were recently restructured extensively, with the latter now in the hands of oenologist Riccardo Cotarella.

The Nobile Riserva '06 is a distinctly well-crafted wine from its crisp, lingering aromas to its well-paced, nicely complex palate. The original colorino-only Caggio al Vescovo '07 is convincing and the poised, fluent Nobile '07 is also up to scratch. Vin Santo Sangallo '04 keeps its sweetness in check but lacks a little body. The rest of the range holds its own. The house flagship, Nobile Antica Chiusina, is having another year in glass and so was not available for this Guide.

● Nobile di Montepulciano Ris. '06	▼▼▼	5
○ Moscadello di Montalcino La Poderina '08	▼▼	6
● Caggio al Vescovo '07	▼▼	5
● Rosso di Montalcino La Poderina '08	▼▼	5
○ Braviolo '09	▼	2
● Brunello di Montalcino La Poderina '05	▼	7
● Brunello di Montalcino Poggio Banale La Poderina '04	▼	7
● Nobile di Montepulciano '07	▼	5
● Rosso di Montepulciano '09	▼	4
○ Vin Santo di Montepulciano Sangallo '04	▼	6
● Nobile di Montepulciano '90	▽▽▽	4*
● Nobile di Montepulciano Vign. Antica Chiusina '00	▽▽▽	7
● Nobile di Montepulciano Vign. Antica Chiusina '99	▽▽▽	7
● Nobile di Montepulciano Vign. Antica Chiusina '98	▽▽▽	7
● Nobile di Montepulciano Vign. Antica Chiusina '05	▽▽	7
● Nobile di Montepulciano Vign. Antica Chiusina '04	▽▽	7

Vincenzo Cesani

FRAZ. PANCOLE
VIA PIAZZETTA, 82D
53037 SAN GIMIGNANO [SI]
TEL. 0577955084
www.agriturismo-cesani.com

CELLAR SALES
PRE-BOOKED VISITS

ANNUAL PRODUCTION **100,000 bottles**
HECTARES UNDER VINE **20**
VITICULTURE METHOD **Certified organic**

The family winery of Letizia Cesani, president of the Consorzio di San Gimignano, left its flagship Luenzo and the Vernaccia Sanice selection to age for another year in bottle. The operation is undergoing a transition but this hasn't meant that the daily quest for quality is any less intense. Apart from grapes, the estate produces olives and a new crop, saffron, famous here in ancient times and now a firm favourite with gourmets worldwide.

We were very taken with the full-bodied Vernaccia di San Gimignano '09, which has fresh notes of ripe peach and pineapple-led fruit, a velvety entry on the palate and a gratifyingly lengthy finale. The rosé Serarosa '09 has captivating aromatics, with strawberry and raspberry to the fore, a satisfyingly rich but not heavy body, and palpable, lively acid sinew. The San Gimignano Cellori '06 sangiovese and merlot blend was a bit of a let-down this year, with ripe jam aromas and a palate still in the grip of stiff tannins.

○ Vernaccia di S. Gimignano '09	▼▼	4*
● San Gimignano Rosso Cellori '06	▼	5
⊙ Serarosa '09	▼	3
● Luenzo '99	▽▽▽	5
● Luenzo '97	▽▽▽	5
● Luenzo '02	▽▽	6
● Luenzo '01	▽▽	6
● Luenzo '00	▽▽	6
● San Gimignano Rosso Cellori '05	▽▽	5
● San Gimignano Rosso Cellori '03	▽▽	6
○ Vernaccia di S. Gimignano '08	▽▽	3*
○ Vernaccia di S. Gimignano '07	▽▽	3*
○ Vernaccia di S. Gimignano Sanice '07	▽▽	4*
○ Vernaccia di S. Gimignano Sanice '04	▽▽	4

Giovanni Chiappini

loc. Le Preselle
pod. Felciaino, 189b
57020 Bolgheri [LI]
tel. 0565765201
www.giovannichiappini.it

CELLAR SALES
PRE-BOOKED VISITS

ANNUAL PRODUCTION 40,000 bottles
HECTARES UNDER VINE 7
VITICULTURE METHOD Conventional

The winery opened back in the 1970s, so it could be seen as a long-standing local operation, but the winemaking watershed did not arrive until 1995. Today, there are five hectares under vine and other parts of the estate are set aside for olives and arable crops. The house style tends towards power and agreeably concentrated wines with more than a little depth and elegance.

The Lienà Cabernet Sauvignon is tasty, with close-woven aromas and flavours tending to darker notes but it does seem somewhat young and needs to unfold. The Bolgheri Superiore Guado dei Gemoli '07 is also excellent, a bit too open on the nose but with a flavoursome, austere palate. All the other wines, from the Bolgheris to the IGTs are right on target.

● Lienà Cabernet Sauvignon '07	2 black glasses	8
● Bolgheri Rosso Felciaino '09	2 black glasses	4
● Bolgheri Sup. Guado de' Gemoli '07	2 black glasses	7
● Bolgheri Rosso Ferrugini '08	1 black glass	
● Bolgheri Sup. Guado de' Gemoli '06	2 glasses	7
● Lienà Cabernet Franc '06	2 glasses	8
● Lienà Cabernet Franc '05	2 glasses	8
● Lienà Cabernet Franc '04	2 glasses	8
● Lienà Cabernet Sauvignon '06	2 glasses	8
● Lienà Cabernet Sauvignon '05	2 glasses	8
● Lienà Cabernet Sauvignon '04	2 glasses	8

Ciacci Piccolomini D'Aragona

fraz. Castelnuovo dell'Abate
loc. Molinello
53024 Montalcino [SI]
tel. 0577835616
www.ciaccipiccolomini.com

CELLAR SALES
PRE-BOOKED VISITS
ROOMS

ANNUAL PRODUCTION 200,000 bottles
HECTARES UNDER VINE 40
VITICULTURE METHOD Conventional

This time-honoured winery, along the Castelnuovo dell'Abate to Sant'Angelo in Colle road, has wonderful vines with south-east exposure and marl-rich Eocene soil. The offices are in Palazzo Piccolomini, where the old cellars can still be visited. Paolo and Lucia Bianchini run the winery and the new Montecucco estate, a seamless continuation of Montalcino for soil and site climates. The wine style is traditional, especially for designation-label bottles.

The excellent Brunello di Montalcino Santa Caterina d'Oro Riserva '04 has a fruity nose with notes of wild cherry preserve, tobacco and medicinal herbs. The palate has seductive tannins and intense progression, underpinned by decent acidity and the clean, juicy finale is engaging. The Sant'Antimo Fabius '07, a fruit-led, spicy pure Syrah, is another good effort, with taut body, a well-defined tannic weave and just the right amount of oak to round things off.

● Brunello di Montalcino Santa Caterina d'Oro Ris. '04	2 black glasses	8
● Sant'Antimo Fabius '07	2 black glasses	5
● Brunello di Montalcino V. di Pianrosso '98	3 glasses	7
● Brunello di Montalcino V. di Pianrosso '90	3 glasses	8
● Brunello di Montalcino V. di Pianrosso '88	3 glasses	8
● Brunello di Montalcino V. di Pianrosso Ris. '01	3 glasses	8
● Brunello di Montalcino V. di Pianrosso Ris. '99	3 glasses	8
● Brunello di Montalcino V. di Pianrosso Ris. '95	3 glasses	6
● Brunello di Montalcino '04	2 glasses	6
● Brunello di Montalcino V. di Pianrosso '04	2 glasses	7
● Brunello di Montalcino V. di Pianrosso '03	2 glasses	7
● Brunello di Montalcino V. di Pianrosso '01	2 glasses	8
● Montecucco Sangiovese '07	2 glasses	5
● Montecucco Sangiovese '06	2 glasses	5
● Sant'Antimo Ateo '06	2 glasses	5
● Sant'Antimo Fabius '06	2 glasses	6

Donatella Cinelli Colombini

LOC. CASATO PRIME DONNE
53024 MONTALCINO [SI]
TEL. 0577662108
www.cinellicolombini.it

CELLAR SALES
PRE-BOOKED VISITS
ROOMS AND FOOD

ANNUAL PRODUCTION **180,000 bottles**
HECTARES UNDER VINE **34**
VITICULTURE METHOD **Conventional**

A woman's winery owned by vivacious Donatella Cinelli Colombini, a lady of many interests and a born multi-tasker. She has 34 hectares mainly in northern Montalcino, with vines aged 15 years on average. The cellars are well-equipped with temperature-controlled vats and a range of casks in various sizes.

The compelling Brunello di Montalcino '05 made the finals for its complex aromas hinting at leather and tobacco. We waited a few minutes for the wine to reveal its fruit, spices and medicinal herbs. Although the progression is slowed by clenched, youthful tannins, acidity bolsters the palate. The '04 Brunello Riserva is not really up to snuff, showing quite rustic on the nose and failing to deliver the density on the palate that impressed us last year. The Prime Donne '05 is a modern-style selection.

● Brunello di Montalcino '05	▼▼	6
● Brunello di Montalcino Prime Donne '05	▼▼	7
● Brunello di Montalcino Ris. '04	▼	8
● Rosso di Montalcino '08	▼	5
● Brunello di Montalcino Prime Donne '01	▽▽▽	7
● Brunello di Montalcino '04	▽▽	6
● Brunello di Montalcino '03	▽▽	6
● Brunello di Montalcino Prime Donne '03	▽▽	7
● Il Drago e le Sette Colombe '05	▽▽	5
● Orcia Cenerentola '05	▽▽	6
● Rosso di Montalcino '06	▽▽	5

La Cipriana

LOC. CAMPASTRELLO, 176B
57022 CASTAGNETO CARDUCCI [LI]
TEL. 0565775568
www.lacipriana.it

PRE-BOOKED VISITS
ROOMS

ANNUAL PRODUCTION **35,000 bottles**
HECTARES UNDER VINE **8**
VITICULTURE METHOD **Conventional**

The Fabiani family opened their winery near Castagneto Carducci in 1975, making it one of the oldest in Bolgheri. Part of the vines are close to the cellars, in the Campastrello district, and the rest are along the Bolgherese provincial highway towards Bolgheri itself. The beautifully looked-after vineyards are now of an age to offer excellent results and deliver their varietal characteristics to the glass.

The Bolgheri Rosso San Martino '07 has very ripe fruit notes as well as some decidedly grassy nuances, traits that are mirrored on the palate along with perceptible sweet notes. The straightforward, less openly engaging Bolgheri Rosso '08 has more balance with its fresh, inviting aromas of ripe morello cherry and black pepper leading to a crunchy, flavoursome palate. The Bolgheri Vermentino Paguro '09 is uncomplicated and well typed.

● Bolgheri Rosso '08	▼▼	4
● Bolgheri Rosso Sup. San Martino '07	▼▼	7
○ Bolgheri Vermentino Paguro '09	▼	4
● Bolgheri Rosso Scopaio '02	▽▽	5
● Bolgheri Rosso Sup. San Martino '06	▽▽	7
● Bolgheri Rosso Sup. San Martino '05	▽▽	6
● Bolgheri Rosso Sup. San Martino '04	▽▽	6
● Bolgheri Rosso Sup. San Martino '03	▽▽	6

★ Tenuta Col d'Orcia

LOC. SANT'ANGELO IN COLLE
53020 MONTALCINO [SI]
TEL. 057780891
www.coldorcia.it

CELLAR SALES
PRE-BOOKED VISITS

ANNUAL PRODUCTION **800,000 bottles**
HECTARES UNDER VINE **142**
VITICULTURE METHOD **Conventional**

This is an impeccable Montalcino estate of 500 hectares, with more than 140 under vine for various designation wines and smart, efficient offices in Sant'Angelo Scalo. The functional cellars are state of the art and the barrel cellar has a range of cask sizes and oaks. The winery has been run by capable, skilled Edoardo Virano for 30 years, always with the full backing of the owners, the Marone Cinzano family.

The winery's reliability is in no doubt: it produced three finalists this year. Two are wines of non-native grapes and the third is the Brunello di Montalcino '05 with a classic, intense nose of deep, pervasive morello cherry. We liked the palate for the finesse of the tannins, and the finale for its sheer length. The house classic, the '05 Olmaia, is a very good Cabernet with attractive bell pepper notes, pencil lead and ripe fruit, where zest of citron lifts the black berry fruit.

● Brunello di Montalcino '05	▼▼	8*
● Olmaia '05	▼▼	7
● Sant'Antimo Nearco '06	▼▼	6
● Spezieri '09	▼▼	3*
● Rosso di Montalcino '08	▼	5
● Brunello di Montalcino Poggio al Vento Ris. '99	▽▽▽	8
● Brunello di Montalcino Poggio al Vento Ris. '97	▽▽▽	8
● Brunello di Montalcino Poggio al Vento Ris. '95	▽▽▽	8
● Brunello di Montalcino Poggio al Vento Ris. '90	▽▽▽	8
● Brunello di Montalcino Poggio al Vento Ris. '88	▽▽▽	8
● Brunello di Montalcino Poggio al Vento Ris. '85	▽▽▽	8
● Olmaia '01	▽▽▽	7
● Olmaia '00	▽▽▽	7
● Olmaia '94	▽▽▽	7

Col di Bacche

S.DA DI CUPI
58010 MAGLIANO IN TOSCANA [GR]
TEL. 0577738526
www.coldibacche.com

PRE-BOOKED VISITS

ANNUAL PRODUCTION **75,000 bottles**
HECTARES UNDER VINE **11**
VITICULTURE METHOD **Conventional**

Alberto Carnasciali's model cellar has asserted itself in Maremma winemaking without too much hullabaloo. It's a relatively recent operation, with the first vines planted in 1998 and the wines making their debut in 2004. Now its position is consolidated, and it is developing into something of an authority. There are no shortcuts behind this success. It is all down to the unflagging commitment of a master winemaker.

The Morellino di Scansano Rovente '08 is confirmed as the flagship wine, revealing refined aromas echoed perfectly by the roundish yet vibrant progression. Another favourite is the Cupinero '08, from merlot topped up with cabernet sauvignon, which gives clean varietal aromas and a full, fragrant palate. The '09 Morelllino, as always, is one of the best of its type and the new Col di Bacche wine, an '09 Vermentino, was always destined for instant success.

● Cupinero '08	▼▼	6
● Morellino di Scansano Rovente '08	▼▼	6
● Morellino di Scansano '09	▼▼	4
○ Vermentino '09	▼▼	4
● Morellino di Scansano Rovente '05	▽▽▽	5
● Cupinero '07	▽▽	6
● Cupinero '06	▽▽	6
● Cupinero '05	▽▽	6
● Cupinero '04	▽▽	6
● Morellino di Scansano '08	▽▽	4
● Morellino di Scansano '07	▽▽	4*
● Morellino di Scansano '06	▽▽	4
● Morellino di Scansano Rovente '07	▽▽	6
● Morellino di Scansano Rovente '06	▽▽	5

Colle Bereto

LOC. COLLE BERETO
53017 RADDA IN CHIANTI [SI]
TEL. 0554299330
www.collebereto.it

CELLAR SALES
PRE-BOOKED VISITS

ANNUAL PRODUCTION 60,000 bottles
HECTARES UNDER VINE 15
VITICULTURE METHOD Conventional

The winery belongs to the Pinzautis, who work in the fashion sector and acquired it as a country home to relax in. Bitten by the viticulture bug, however, they are now dedicated winemakers. The ancient village is documented as early as the 11th century. As well as pinot nero, by no means typical of Chianti, the winery now produces a small amount of Spumante Brut from the same grapes, starting a new trend that is spreading fast around the territory.

This year's best was Il Tocco '08, from merlot with a dash of sangiovese. The aromatics hinge around forest berries and assorted spices like cinnamon and cloves. The tasty entry on the palate is layered, broad, juicy and inviting. We liked the '08 Il Cenno '08, from pure pinot nero, which throws a tempting nose of blackcurrants, blackberries and aromatic herbs. The velvety body is a tad too slight, with a sweet but short finale. Both versions of Chianti Classico are slightly stalky.

● Il Tocco '08	🍷🍷	6
● Chianti Cl. '08	🍷	4
● Chianti Cl. Ris. '07	🍷	5
● Il Cenno '08	🍷	6
● Chianti Cl. '07	YY	4*
● Chianti Cl. '06	YY	4*
● Chianti Cl. '04	YY	4
● Chianti Cl. Ris. '06	YY	5
● Chianti Cl. Ris. '04	YY	5
● Chianti Cl. Ris. '03	YY	5
● Il Cenno '06	YY	6
● Il Tocco '06	YY	6

Colle Massari

LOC. POGGI DEL SASSO
58044 CINIGIANO [GR]
TEL. 0564990496
www.collemassari.it

CELLAR SALES
PRE-BOOKED VISITS

ANNUAL PRODUCTION 250,000 bottles
HECTARES UNDER VINE 83
VITICULTURE METHOD Certified organic

Colle Massari embarked on its wine adventure in 1998 with a series of significant investments to promote this nook of Maremma. Today, the operation is considered a leader locally and further afield, its success due to the significant vineyard holding, as well as the solid, ongoing advance of the wines. At the helm of this massively ambitious project is the energetic Claudio Tipa, president of the Consorzio del Montecucco.

The Montecucco Sangiovese Lombrone Riserva '06 is on its way to becoming a Maremma winemaking classic, revealing an intense, clean aromatic profile, and a full-bodied, well-paced palate. Three Glasses. The Montecucco Rosso Colle Massari Riserva '07 is also very tasty, with good aromatics and a precise, juicy palate. The Montecucco Rosso Rigoleto '09 is fragrant and drinkable. The '09 Montecucco Vermentino Le Melacce and '08 Montecucco Vermentino Irisse are both well made, with a sound, savoury note at the back. We enjoyed the '09 Grottolo, a sangiovese, ciliegiolo and montepulciano-based rosé.

● Montecucco Sangiovese Lombrone Ris. '06	🍷🍷🍷	7
● Montecucco Rosso Colle Massari Ris. '07	🍷🍷	5
⊙ Grottolo '09	🍷	4
● Montecucco Rosso Rigoleto '08	🍷	4
○ Montecucco Vermentino Irisse '08	🍷	5
○ Montecucco Vermentino Le Melacce '09	🍷	4
● Montecucco Sangiovese Lombrone Ris. '05	YYY	7
● Montecucco Sangiovese Lombrone Ris. '04	YYY	7
● Montecucco Rosso Colle Massari Ris. '06	YY	5
● Montecucco Rosso Colle Massari Ris. '05	YY	5
● Montecucco Rosso Colle Massari Ris. '04	YY	6
● Montecucco Rosso Rigoleto '06	YY	4*
○ Montecucco Vermentino Le Melacce '07	YY	4*

Collelungo

loc. Collelungo
53011 Castellina in Chianti [SI]
tel. 0577740489
www.collelungo.com

CELLAR SALES
PRE-BOOKED VISITS
ROOMS AND FOOD

ANNUAL PRODUCTION **40,000 bottles**
HECTARES UNDER VINE **20**
VITICULTURE METHOD **Conventional**

Overall, the Cattelan family winery performed well and confirms the excellent results of the last few years. This is concrete proof of all the effort they have put in since buying the business. The wines have scaled back their obsessive pursuit of modernity and now focus on territorial traits. Meanwhile, the holiday farm has been completed and the accommodations are now ready to welcome guests.

The Campo Cerchi Riserva '07 impressed with refreshing, well-integrated mentholated and balsamic notes, hints of liquorice, and bramble jelly, unveiling a full, tasty palate and agreeable progression on the succulent, expansive palate. The Alidoro '08 is also appreciable for its spicier aromatic component of round, lively fruit, and a far from clichéd juicy, generous palate with a lingering finish. The elegant, lavender florality-led bouquet of the '07 Riserva introduces more prominent tannins and a tasty finish. The Chianti Classico '08 has three trump cards: appeal on the nose, subtle drinkability and an enjoyable, juicy finale.

- Alidoro di Collelungo '08 — 5
- Chianti Cl. '08 — 4
- Chianti Cl. Campo Cerchi Ris. '07 — 6
- Chianti Cl. Ris. '07 — 5
- Chianti Cl. '07 — 4*
- Chianti Cl. '05 — 4
- Chianti Cl. '04 — 4
- Chianti Cl. Campo Cerchi Ris. '00 — 8
- Chianti Cl. Ris. '04 — 5
- Chianti Cl. Ris. '03 — 5
- Merlot '06 — 5

Colline San Biagio

loc. Bacchereto
via San Biagio 6/8
59015 Carmignano [PO]
tel. 0558717143
www.collinesanbiagio.it

CELLAR SALES
PRE-BOOKED VISITS
ROOMS

ANNUAL PRODUCTION **N.A.**
HECTARES UNDER VINE **N.A .**
VITICULTURE METHOD **Conventional**

This Carmignano winery makes an excellent debut in the Guide. The business started life in the holiday farm sector, with two renovated farmhouses, a late 13th-century monastery and a 15th-century building. Agricultural activities revolve mostly around wine and oil but there is also a thriving production of fruit preserves made using traditional methods.

We gave all three wines tasted good scores. The Sancta Blasii '07 has complex aromas with fruity notes of blackcurrant and cherry melding into green peppers and mint as the generous, round, warm palate takes you through to a long-lingering finale. The Carmignano '06 is more direct and accessible, with its mature, tertiary aromas where animal skins and hide encounter spices and aromatic herbs. The solid, well-balanced body has lingering echoes of overripeness. What sets the Donna Mingarda '08 apart is its freshness with minty and forest berry aromas, and the acid vein on the palate that adds vibrancy to its agile self-assurance.

- Carmignano '06 — 5
- Carmignano Sancti Blasii '07 — 5
- Donna Mingarda '08 — 5

Tenuta di Collosorbo

FRAZ. CASTELNUOVO DELL'ABATE
LOC. VILLA A SESTA, 25
53024 MONTALCINO [SI]
TEL. 0577835534
www.collosorbo.com

CELLAR SALES
PRE-BOOKED VISITS

ANNUAL PRODUCTION 100,000 bottles
HECTARES UNDER VINE 27
VITICULTURE METHOD Organic

The winery is in Sesta, authentic Montepulciano cru country, and has recently upped gear. The cool gravel-rich limestone terrain lies on a deep clay layer that helps to release water slowly in hot, dry periods, so the grapes ripen evenly. The 27-hectare estate produces several designation wines, with a prevalence of Brunello di Montalcino. Fermentation is traditional while Slavonian casks of ten to 50 hectolitres are used for ageing.

Some very persuasive Brunellos were presented this year, with the '05 a whisper ahead of the others, despite the vintage looking weaker on paper. There are classic wafts of wild cherry and morello cherry on the nose while the palate stands out for its stylish tannins and surprisingly close-knit, generous finale. Left to breathe briefly, the Riserva '04 shows massive body but there are a few rough edges caused by still raw tannins.

● Brunello di Montalcino '05	**ΨΨ**	7
● Brunello di Montalcino Ris. '04	**ΨΨ**	8
● Rosso di Montalcino '08	**ΨΨ**	5
● Brunello di Montalcino '03	ΨΨ	7
● Brunello di Montalcino '01	ΨΨ	6
● Brunello di Montalcino '00	ΨΨ	6
● Brunello di Montalcino Ris. '01	ΨΨ	8
● Brunello di Montalcino Ris. '98	ΨΨ	8
● Brunello di Montalcino Ris. '97	ΨΨ	8
● Rosso di Montalcino '01	ΨΨ	5
● Rosso Sorbus '02	ΨΨ	5
● Rosso Sorbus '01	ΨΨ	6

Contucci

VIA DEL TEATRO, 1
53045 MONTEPULCIANO [SI]
TEL. 0578757006
www.contucci.it

CELLAR SALES
PRE-BOOKED VISITS

ANNUAL PRODUCTION 100,000 bottles
HECTARES UNDER VINE 21
VITICULTURE METHOD Conventional

Generations of Contuccis have been winemakers and the winery is now run by Alamanno, past president of the Consorzio del Nobile and winemaking legend, not just in Montepulciano. Adamo Pallecchi, Contucci's cellarman for 50 years and a Montepulciano wine institution, manages the ancient cellars in the old town centre. Of course this sort of winery makes traditional wines that have no truck with fashion, even at the risk of stylistic flaws, as has occurred recently.

The Nobile Riserva '06 reached the finals. Its austere aromas but convincing progression on the palate thanks to tasty tannins and energetic acid verve. The two '07 Nobiles are also good. The Mulinvecchio has a pleasant floral nose with a lively, nuanced palate while the Pietra Rossa, in contrast, is a more textured wine with concentrated aromas and a dense, multi-layered palate.

● Nobile di Montepulciano Ris. '06	**ΨΨ**	6
● Nobile di Montepulciano Mulinvecchio '07	**ΨΨ**	6
● Nobile di Montepulciano Pietra Rossa '07	**ΨΨ**	5
● Nobile di Montepulciano '99	ΨΨ	5
● Nobile di Montepulciano Pietra Rossa '03	ΨΨ	5
○ Vin Santo '90	ΨΨ	4

La Corsa

S.DA VICINALE DEL PRATACCIONE, 19
58015 ORBETELLO [GR]
TEL. 0564880007
www.lacorsawine.it

PRE-BOOKED VISITS

ANNUAL PRODUCTION 15,000 bottles
HECTARES UNDER VINE 13
VITICULTURE METHOD Conventional

Successful manager Marco Bassetti and his wife Stefania Craxi got their winery off to a roaring start. The winemaking plan kicked off back in 1990, when they bought land for a vineyard that now covers 13 hectares. La Corsa can be found in southern Maremma, not far from Capalbio, and has shunned the local trend for international varieties, preferring sangiovese vines for their top-of-the-range wines.

The pure sangiovese Mandrione '08 has intense aromatics that range from lush fruit to healthy balsamic notes. Oak on the palate is balanced and the wine is succulent and agreeably boisterous. Another pure sangiovese is the Mandrone '07, with lighter aromas and refreshing, moreish flavours. The delicious Aghiloro '09 blend of sangiovese and petit verdot targets immediate drinkability.

● Mandrione '08	🍷🍷	6
● Aghiloro '09	🍷🍷	5
● Mandrione '07	🍷🍷	6

Fattoria Le Corti

LOC. LE CORTI
VIA SAN PIERO DI SOTTO, 1
50026 SAN CASCIANO IN VAL DI PESA [FI]
TEL. 055829301
www.principecorsini.com

CELLAR SALES
PRE-BOOKED VISITS
ROOMS AND FOOD

ANNUAL PRODUCTION 150,000 bottles
HECTARES UNDER VINE 50
VITICULTURE METHOD Conventional

Fattoria Le Corti, in the north of Chianti Classico, includes a grand Tuscan Renaissance-style villa, proof of the owners' blue-blooded origins. For years the winery was almost at a standstill until Duccio Corsini restored its former glory, his dedication contributing to the identification of the territory's wine profile. The 50 hectares or so under vine are on the hills above the Terzona torrent, a tributary of the Pesa which gives the valley its name.

Again we found the best wine to be the Chianti Classico Riserva Cortevecchia '07. Deep and refined, it is a successful fusion of Chianti's most authentic characteristics, from flowers to red berries, hints of earth to Mediterranean scrubland, creating along the way a mouthfilling, crunchy palate with very sweet fruit. The Chianti Classico A 101 Riserva '06 is pervasive, with ripe fruit, tobacco notes and a slightly decadent palate. The splendid Vin Santo Sant'Andrea '99 has aromas that go on for ever.

● Chianti Cl. Cortevecchia Ris. '07	🍷🍷	5
● Chianti Cl. Ris. A - 101 '06	🍷🍷	4*
○ Vin Santo del Chianti Cl. Sant'Andrea '99	🍷🍷	7
○ Vermentino Reius '09	🍷🍷	4
● Chianti Cl. Don Tommaso '07	🍷	6
● Chianti Cl. Le Corti '08	🍷	4
● Chianti Cl. Cortevecchia Ris. '05	YYY	5
● Chianti Cl. Don Tommaso '99	YYY	5
● Chianti Cl. Cortevecchia Ris. '06	YY	5
● Chianti Cl. Don Tommaso '05	YY	6
● Chianti Cl. Don Tommaso '04	YY	6
● Chianti Cl. Don Tommaso '00	YY	5
● Marsiliana '04	YY	6
● Marsiliana '03	YY	6
● Marsiliana '02	YY	6
● Marsiliana '01	YY	6

Fattoria Corzano e Paterno

FRAZ. SAN PRANCAZIO
VIA PATERNO, 8
50020 SAN CASCIANO IN VAL DI PESA [FI]
TEL. 0558248179
www.corzanoepaterno.it

CELLAR SALES
PRE-BOOKED VISITS
ROOMS

ANNUAL PRODUCTION 85,000 bottles
HECTARES UNDER VINE 16
VITICULTURE METHOD Conventional

The Fattoria di Corzano e Paterno is owned and managed by the Gelpke and Goldschmidt families. The enterprise is the result of combining two separate farms back in 1976 to produce oil, cheese and, of course, wine. The winery is less than 20 kilometres south-west of Florence, on the Via Cassia in Valle della Pesa. The vineyards lie on pebbly slopes and the wines reflect the traits of the terroir.

The pure sangiovese Riserva di Chianti I Tre Borri '07 is phenomenal with inspired, all-embracing mineral and earth notes. The flavour is astonishing and the lingering charm of the finish is sustained by some intriguing touches of iron filings. Equally good is the sangiovese, cabernet sauvignon and merlot blend Il Corzano '07 with austere incense, aromatic herbs like laurel and mint, hints of spice, all woven into a solid, juicy body with a silky tannic weave and a tasty, extended rising finale. The Chianti Terre di Corzano has a fresh palate; the '09 Il Corzanello is a very drinkable white from trebbiano, chardonnay and sémillon.

● Chianti I Tre Borri Ris. '07	▼▼▼	6
● Il Corzano '07	▼▼	6
● Chianti Terre di Corzano '08	▼	4
○ Il Corzanello '09	▼	4
● Il Corzano '05	▽▽▽	6
● Chianti I Tre Borri '99	▽▽	6
● Il Corzano '06	▽▽	6
● Il Corzano '04	▽▽	6
● Il Corzano '99	▽▽	6
○ Passito di Corzano '99	▽▽	7
○ Passito di Corzano '97	▽▽	7
○ Passito di Corzano '96	▽▽	7
○ Vin Santo '94	▽▽	6

Cupano

LOC. CAMIGLIANO
POD. CENTINE, 31
53024 MONTALCINO [SI]
TEL. 0577816055
www.cupano.it

CELLAR SALES
PRE-BOOKED VISITS

ANNUAL PRODUCTION 14,000 bottles
HECTARES UNDER VINE 4
VITICULTURE METHOD Organic

This little winery, created by Ornella Tondini and Lionel Cousin on the hill opposite Camigliano, has four hectares of designation vines and many aficionados. The vineyard uses biodynamic methods and wines are aged only in barriques and tonneaux. The soils are mainly pebble-rich arenaceous sand. Over the years, the use of oak has gained focus and is now, we feel, less invasive, probably because there is more attention to picking dates.

The wines we tasted this year are significant in this respect. Not just the Brunello '05, from a cooler growing season, where we appreciated the oak's toasty, spicy notes integrated with the clean morello cherry, but also other wines, like the Rosso di Montalcino '07, with its persuasive, refreshing nose of wild cherry and ripe black cherry plus some good sweet spice. The palate belies its origins in a more southerly estate and reveals good acidity sustaining the wine in the broad, consistent finish.

● Brunello di Montalcino '05	▼▼	8
● Rosso di Montalcino '07	▼▼	6
● Sant'Antimo Ombrone '07	▼▼	7
● Brunello di Montalcino '02	▽▽	8
● Rosso di Montalcino '05	▽▽	6
● Rosso di Montalcino '04	▽▽	6

La Cura

loc. Cura Nuova, 12
58024 Massa Marittima [GR]
tel. 0566918094
www.cantinalacura.it

CELLAR SALES
PRE-BOOKED VISITS

ANNUAL PRODUCTION 30,000 bottles
HECTARES UNDER VINE 5
VITICULTURE METHOD Conventional

La Cura, a small winery deep in the Monteregio di Massa Marittima DOC zone, typifies the potential of Italy's quality winemaking profession. This typical family winery is run by Enrico Corsi, tends his vines and cellars with passion. The wines seem to have evolved precise style traits and quality is both solid and consistent, confirming with each passing year that this is one of winemaking Maremma's most interesting operations.

Again, Merlot La Cura has emerged in the '08 vintage thanks to its warm, balsamic aromas, a worthy prelude to a dense yet well-paced palate. The solid Monteregio Breccerosse '09, with a fine salty tang in the finale, is another winner. The Monteregio Colle Bruno '09 flows nicely while the chardonnay, trebbiano and malvasia Trinus, despite its simplicity, is consistent.

● La Cura Merlot '08	🍷🍷	5
● Monteregio di Massa Marittima Rosso Breccerosse '09	🍷🍷	4
● Monteregio di Massa Marittima Rosso Colle Bruno '09	🍷	4
○ Trinus '09	🍷	4
● La Cura Merlot '07	YY	5
● La Cura Merlot '06	YY	5
● La Cura Merlot '04	YY	5
● Monteregio di Massa Marittima Rosso Breccerosse '06	YY	4
○ Predicatore '06	YY	5
○ Trinus '06	YY	4

Maria Caterina Dei

via di Martiena, 35
53045 Montepulciano [SI]
tel. 0578716878
www.cantinedei.com

CELLAR SALES
PRE-BOOKED VISITS
ROOMS

ANNUAL PRODUCTION 200,000 bottles
HECTARES UNDER VINE 55
VITICULTURE METHOD Conventional

Maria Caterina Dei has run the family winery since 1991. The business evolved from the initial 1964 purchase of the Bossona vineyard and, in 1973, of the Martiena property, now also the head offices. The first bottle arrived in 1985 and subsequent Dei wines have developed a far from secondary role in the Nobile di Montepulciano designation, thanks to a range of very drinkable products with solid structure and harmonious development.

The Nobile Bossona Riserva '06 is comforting in both its quality and its continuity of style, with well-defined aromas and a round, balanced palate. The Nobile '07 is quite delicious, with spice aromas and a racy, compelling flavour, and savoury tannins that are kept absolutely under control. Likewise the Sancta Catharina '08, a sangiovese, cabernet sauvignon, syrah and petit verdot blend, is muscular but relaxed, with a refreshing, seductive, consistent nose.

● Nobile di Montepulciano Bossona Ris. '06	🍷🍷	6
● Nobile di Montepulciano '07	🍷🍷	5
● Sancta Catharina '08	🍷🍷	6
● Nobile di Montepulciano Bossona Ris. '04	YYY	6
● Nobile di Montepulciano '06	YY	5
● Nobile di Montepulciano '04	YY	5
● Nobile di Montepulciano '01	YY	5
● Nobile di Montepulciano Bossona Ris. '03	YY	6
● Rosso di Montepulciano '08	YY	4
● Rosso di Montepulciano '07	YY	4
● Sancta Catharina '07	YY	6
● Sancta Catharina '06	YY	6

Diadema

VIA IMPRUNETANA PER TAVERNUZZE, 21
50023 IMPRUNETA [FI]
TEL. 0552311330
www.diadema-wine.com

CELLAR SALES
PRE-BOOKED VISITS
ROOMS

ANNUAL PRODUCTION 55,000 bottles
HECTARES UNDER VINE 9
VITICULTURE METHOD Conventional

Diadema has made its way into the Guide's full profiles. The operation belongs to Alberto Giannotti, an enthusiastic producer now more committed to his winery than to his hotel business. The Villa l'Olmo estate covers about 30 hectares, of which nine are under vine and a good part are olive groves. The family has owned this estate since the latter half of the 18th century and started dedicated viticulture in 2000, initially as a well-planned marketing project. The bottles are even decorated with Swarosky crystals.

The best wine is the Diadema Rosso '08, a sangiovese-heavy mix with cabernet sauvignon, merlot and syrah. Its nose is complex, redcurrants and raspberries backed by notes of vanilla and cinnamon leading into a soft-textured palate and lingering, juicy finish. The newest wine, Diadema D'Amare '07, a similar blend minus the syrah, is also good. It has clean tones showing mineral notes and hints of tobacco overlaying cherry-like fruitiness, while the palate has a lovely, coherent continuity of taste. The Diadema Bianco '09, from chardonnay, viognier and sauvignon blanc, is very good.

○ Diadema Bianco '09	▼▼	8
● Diadema D'Amare '07	▼▼	8
● Diadema Rosso '08	▼▼	8
○ Diadema Bianco '07	▽▽	8
● Diadema Rosso '07	▽▽	8
● Diadema Rosso '06	▽▽	8

I Fabbri

LOC. LAMOLE
VIA CASOLE, 52
50022 GREVE IN CHIANTI [FI]
TEL. 339412622
www.agricolaifabbri.it

CELLAR SALES
PRE-BOOKED VISITS

ANNUAL PRODUCTION 25,000 bottles
HECTARES UNDER VINE 9
VITICULTURE METHOD Conventional

Historical documents prove that this property has been in the Grassi family since the 17th century, and they have always produced wine and olive oil. Their passion has followed them over the generations and today the estate is run by sisters Susanna and Maddalena. The two strive to highlight the characteristics of the district of Lamole and have implemented a type of integrated vineyard management, intending to adopt organic growing methods in the future.

This year, we tasted two new Chianti Classicos, Olinto and Lamole, both excellent. The best wine is Riserva '07 with well-defined fruity aromas of blackberry and cherry and hints of pencil lead. A sound, juicy body leads to an excellent long finish. The Olinto '08 is also good, with aromatics centring on plum, a taut, lively and vigorous structure and good progression to a long finish. The other wines are less structured but very drinkable. The '08 Chianti Classico has slightly edgy tannins but rich texture, the Terre di Lamole '08 is soft and caressing and the Lamole is very much florality-led, easy-drinking and enjoyable.

● Chianti Cl. Olinto '08	▼▼	4
● Chianti Cl. Ris. '07	▼▼	5
● Chianti Cl. '08	▼	4
● Chianti Cl. Lamole '08	▼	4
● Chianti Cl. Terra di Lamole '08	▼	4
● Chianti Cl. '06	▽▽	4*
● Chianti Cl. '04	▽▽	4
● Chianti Cl. '03	▽▽	4
● Chianti Cl. Ris. '03	▽▽	5
● Chianti Cl. Terra di Lamole '06	▽▽	4*
● Chianti Cl. Terra di Lamole '03	▽▽	4

Fanti

FRAZ. CASTELNUOVO DELL'ABATE
POD. PALAZZO
53020 MONTALCINO [SI]
TEL. 0577835795
balfanti@tin.it

CELLAR SALES
PRE-BOOKED VISITS

ANNUAL PRODUCTION 200,000 bottles
HECTARES UNDER VINE 50
VITICULTURE METHOD Conventional

Over the last ten years, the winery has been totally restructured. It has also been expanding progressively and now has 50 hectares under vine on soils that are basically galestro limestone marl, all in the district of Castelnuovo dell'Abate. With the increase in vine stock, it became necessary to build a new cellar, set underground in the hill facing the abbey of Sant'Antimo. It's a spacious facility and is equipped with the latest technology.

There are several important changes, especially in the style of the wines. The '05 Brunello, possibly helped by a good growing year, has a certain finesse and elegance, very different to the muscular, highly concentrated style that was typical of these wines in the late 1990s and early 2000s. The nose is stylish and offers fresh overtones of black cherry, medicinal herbs and tanned leather. Lively tannins and vivacious acidity fill the mouth as the glycerine sweetness struggles to offset them as they surge through to a broad, consistent finish.

● Brunello di Montalcino '05	▼▼	6
○ Vin Santo '05	▼▼	6
● Rosso di Montalcino '08	▼	4
● Sant'Antimo Rosso Sassomagno '08	▼	4
● Brunello di Montalcino '00	▽▽▽	7
● Brunello di Montalcino '97	▽▽▽	7
● Brunello di Montalcino Ris. '95	▽▽▽	7
● Brunello di Montalcino '04	▽▽	7
● Brunello di Montalcino '03	▽▽	7
● Rosso di Montalcino '07	▽▽	5
● Sant'Antimo Rosso '07	▽▽	4*
○ Vin Santo '04	▽▽	5

Tenuta Farnete

FRAZ. COMEANA
VIA MACIA
59100 CARMIGNANO [PO]
TEL. 0571910078
www.enricopierazzuoli.com

CELLAR SALES
PRE-BOOKED VISITS

ANNUAL PRODUCTION 31,500 bottles
HECTARES UNDER VINE 8
VITICULTURE METHOD Conventional

Enrico Pierazzuoli manages two estates not far from each other but in very different territories. Tenuta Cantagallo, in Chianti Montalbano, was purchased in the 1970s and Tenuta Le Farnete, in Carmignano, was acquired in the early 1990s. Tenuta Cantagallo has an agriturismo as well as producing wine and olive oil. The winery's philosophy is set out in their motto: "A bottle of wine for every vine".

The Carmignano wines are the best. From the others, we liked the '09 Aleatico with its intense aromas of vanilla and wild berries preceding a round, creamily soft body taking you into a tangy finish. The sweet Vin Santo Millarium '05 is very good, with dried figs, dates and hazelnuts and a rich, caressing palate leading to a velvety, lingering finish. The two Carmignanos are both excellent. The Riserva '07 has powerful tertiary aromas while the '07 Carmignano throws powerful aromas of spices and aromatic herbs. Both these wines are full-bodied and succulent but the tannins are more pronounced in the older wine. The fresh Chianto Montalbano '09 is deliciously drinkable.

● Aleatico '09	▼▼	5
● Carmignano '08	▼▼	4
● Carmignano Ris. '07	▼▼	5
● Chianti Montalbano Tenuta Cantagallo '09	▼▼	3
○ Vin Santo Chianti Montalbano Millarium Ris. '05	▼▼	6
● Barco Reale '09	▼	4
● Chianti Montalbano Tenuta Cantagallo Ris. '07	▼	4
● Gioveto '07	▼	5
● Carmignano '07	▽▽	4*
● Carmignano Ris. '06	▽▽	5

Fassati

FRAZ. GRACCIANO
VIA DI GRACCIANELLO, 3A
53040 MONTEPULCIANO [SI]
TEL. 0578708708
www.fazibattaglia.it

CELLAR SALES
PRE-BOOKED VISITS

ANNUAL PRODUCTION 800,000 bottles
HECTARES UNDER VINE 70
VITICULTURE METHOD Conventional

Spartaco Sparaco, the legendary owner of Fazi Battaglia, was the first to realize that this early 20th century Montepulciano winery had great possibilities. He bought it in 1969 and set in on its way to becoming one of the most important operations in the Nobile di Montepulciano DOCG. Luca, Barbara and Chiara Gianotti, the children of Spartaco's daughter Maria Luisa, have been running Fassati since 1990 and about ten years ago they took over another Tuscan property, Tenuta Greto delle Fate in Maremma.

The Nobile di Montepulciano Gersemi '07 has vigorous fruity sensations, showing pleasant sweet tones on the nose and a juicy palate free of any spikiness. The delicious Nobile Pasiteo '07 has aromas that hit the mark and is sheer pleasure to drink. The Morellino '09 could genuinely become one of the best wines in its class. Nobile Salarco Riserva '06 has mature aromas with flavours slightly held back by the oak. The Vermentino Greto delle Fate '09 is straightforward and fresh.

● Morellino di Scansano Greto delle Fate '09	▼▼	4
● Nobile di Montepulciano Gersemi '07	▼▼	6
● Nobile di Montepulciano Pasiteo '07	▼▼	6
● Nobile di Montepulciano Salarco Ris. '06	▼	7
● Rosso di Montepulciano Selciaia '09	▼	4
○ Vermentino Greto delle Fate '09	▼	4
● Morellino di Scansano Greto delle Fate '08	▽▽	4
● Morellino di Scansano Greto delle Fate '07	▽▽	4*
● Nobile di Montepulciano Gersemi '06	▽▽	6
● Nobile di Montepulciano Pasiteo '03	▽▽	5
● Nobile di Montepulciano Salarco Ris. '05	▽▽	7
● Nobile di Montepulciano Salarco Ris. '04	▽▽	6

★★ Fattoria di Felsina

VIA DEL CHIANTI, 101
53019 CASTELNUOVO BERARDENGA [SI]
TEL. 0577355117
www.felsina.it

CELLAR SALES
PRE-BOOKED VISITS

ANNUAL PRODUCTION 430,000 bottles
HECTARES UNDER VINE 76
VITICULTURE METHOD Conventional

Felsina is in the southern-most part of the Chianti Classico DOCG, with property extending even further south, and captures the voluptuousness of the greatest Tuscan Sangioveses. The wines, particularly those of Castelnuovo Berardenga, can be very similar to Brunellos. Here the rocks gradually give way to clay of the Crete Senesi, in a varied landscape of great charm, as is often the case with borderlands. Felsina wines reflect these territories well in a benchmark style that is a glowing example of purity and personality.

The Fontalloro shows how these two areas, Chianti Classico and Chianti Colli Senesi can blend into a totally unique wine. For years, this pure Sangiovese has been exceptional and we think that the '07 vintage is one of the very best, a rare example of how body, power and warmth can be matched step by step by elegance, complexity and minerality. The Chianti Classico Riserva Rancia '07 is great and as always has more depth and directness, with comforting tangy notes of mineral and citrus fruit.

● Chianti Cl. Rancia Ris. '07	▼▼▼+	7
● Fontalloro '07	▼▼▼	7
● Chianti Cl. '08	▼▼	5
● Chianti Cl. Ris. '07	▼▼	5
○ I Sistri '08	▼▼	5
● Nero di Nubi Castello della Farnetella '06	▼▼	6
● Poggio Granoni Castello della Farnetella '07	▼▼	6
○ Vin Santo del Chianti Cl. '01	▼▼	6
● Chianti Colli Senesi Castello della Farnetella '08	▼	4
● Chianti Cl. Rancia Ris. '05	▽▽▽	6
● Chianti Cl. Rancia Ris. '04	▽▽▽	6
● Chianti Cl. Rancia Ris. '03	▽▽▽	6
● Chianti Cl. Rancia Ris. '00	▽▽▽	6
● Fontalloro '06	▽▽▽	7
● Fontalloro '05	▽▽▽	7
● Fontalloro '01	▽▽▽	6
● Fontalloro '99	▽▽▽	6
● Fontalloro '98	▽▽▽	6
● Maestro Raro '01	▽▽▽	6

Ferrero

FRAZ. SANT' ANGELO IN COLLE
LOC. PASCENA
53024 MONTALCINO [SI]
TEL. 0577844170
claudia.ferrero@gmail.com

CELLAR SALES
PRE-BOOKED VISITS

ANNUAL PRODUCTION 20,000 bottles
HECTARES UNDER VINE 6
VITICULTURE METHOD Conventional

This small winery near Sant'Angelo in Colle has shown once again how good it is. The owner is an oenologist who attended the wine school in Alba, one of the foremost in Italy. The winery has three well-exposed hectares within the designation area on soils that are clay mixed with limestone at an altitude of about 250 metres. French oak is preferred in the cellar, as it is sweeter. The owner's daughters are actively in the winery and are very keen to follow in their mother's footsteps.

We found their Brunellos very interesting and the Riserva '04 was one of our finalists. It has a traditional nose, where slight aromas of reduction give way to cherry and blackberry, enriched by overtones of spices and tobacco. The sweet attack follows through to a well-structured palate with a delightful tannic weave and good acidity giving a well-balanced finish. The Brunello '05 is approachable and easy drinking but just as complex. The nose is close-focused, with prominent cherry and slightly toasty notes, while the palate is well-balanced with a good tannic extraction going through to an engaging finish.

● Brunello di Montalcino Ris. '04	▼▼	8
● Brunello di Montalcino '05	▼▼	7
● Alicante '07	▼	6
● Rosso di Montalcino '08	▼	5
● Alicante '06	▽▽	6
● Brunello di Montalcino '04	▽▽	7
● Cabernet '06	▽▽	6
● Mo '06	▽▽	6
● Rosso di Montalcino '07	▽▽	5

★ Tenute Ambrogio e Giovanni Folonari

LOC. PASSO DEI PECORAI
VIA DI NOZZOLE, 12
50022 GREVE IN CHIANTI [FI]
TEL. 055859811
www.tenutefolonari.com

CELLAR SALES
PRE-BOOKED VISITS

ANNUAL PRODUCTION 1,000,000 bottles
HECTARES UNDER VINE 300
VITICULTURE METHOD Conventional

Ten years ago, Ambrogio and Giovanni Folonari left Ruffino to start their own independent wine business, acquiring several working wineries, such as Tenuta di Nozzole, at Greve in Chianti, and setting up others from scratch. Most of them are in Tuscany, with one exception, Ronco di Folo, which is in Friuli. Interestingly, each wine convincingly reflects the characteristics of the territory, thereby underlining how carefully the owners safeguard their wines' typicality.

The '07 Il Pareto, one of the very first Supertuscans, deserves its Three Glasses. Sourced from a single vineyard planted to cabernet sauvignon, it gives a balsamic, minty bouquet with fresh overtones of blueberry and delicate hints of red pepper. Its meaty, rounded attack and tannic weave unfold effectively to finish delightfully long and full of flavour. The very sound Cabreo La Pietra '08 is made with chardonnay grapes from one of the Tenute Cabreo vineyards and shows full of captivating smoky, spicy notes. A dynamic wine, it brims with warm, sweet flavours and finishes decidedly long.

● Il Pareto '07	▼▼▼	8
● Bolgheri Sup. Baia al Vento Campo al Mare '07	▼▼	5
● Nobile di Montepulciano Ris. Torcalvano '06	▼▼	6
● Brunello di Montalcino La Due Sorelle Ris. Tenuta La Fuga '04	▼▼	8
● Brunello di Montalcino Tenuta La Fuga '05	▼▼	7
○ Cabreo La Pietra '08	▼▼	6
● Chianti Cl. La Forra Ris. '07	▼▼	5
● Nobile di Montepulciano Torcalvano '07	▼▼	4*
● Chianti Cl. Nozzole '07	▼	4
○ Le Bruniche '09	▼	4
● Rosso di Montalcino Tenuta La Fuga '08	▼	5
● Rosso di Montepulciano Torcalvano '08	▼	4
● Cabreo Il Borgo '06	▽▽▽	6
● Il Pareto '04	▽▽▽	8
● Il Pareto '01	▽▽▽	8
● Il Pareto '00	▽▽▽	8
● Il Pareto '98	▽▽▽	7
● Il Pareto '97	▽▽▽	7

Fattoria Le Fonti

LOC. LE FONTI
50020 PANZANO [FI]
TEL. 055852194
www.fattorialefonti.it

CELLAR SALES
PRE-BOOKED VISITS

ANNUAL PRODUCTION 40,000 bottles
HECTARES UNDER VINE 8
VITICULTURE METHOD Conventional

We awarded Three Glasses to Fontissimo '06, the signature wine of this small Panzano-based winery run by the Schmitt Vitali family with passion and love since 1994. They did not send any wines to be tasted last year, and had to be left out of the Guide, but this time they have made a resounding comeback. Care was applied right from the start as all the vineyards were replanted and the cellar renovated. Sustainable growing methods have been the order of the day here since the get-go.

The award-winning wine is made from sangiovese, merlot and cabernet sauvignon and has a very assertive bouquet of well-integrated raspberries and redcurrants laced with hints of cinnamon and nutmeg, all delicately shaded with mint. The supple, rich body is well-balanced and full of succulence, the tannins well tucked in and the finish juicy. The Vigna della Lepre '07, from sangiovese with variable amounts of merlot, is a lovely surprise. Its fresh fruitiness is enhanced by hints of cloves in a soft structure where the entry is velvety acquiring vigour as it unfolds, to sign off with a clean, satisfying after-aroma. The good '07 Riserva has tertiary aromas and a meaty taste.

● Fontissimo '06	▼▼▼	6
● Chianti Cl. '07	▼▼	4
● Chianti Cl. Ris. '07	▼▼	5
● V. della Lepre '07	▼▼	3
● Fontissimo '05	▼	6
● Chianti Cl. Ris. '04	ΨΨ	5
● Fontissimo '04	ΨΨ	6
● Fontissimo '01	ΨΨ	6
● Fontissimo '99	ΨΨ	6
● Fontissimo '98	ΨΨ	5

★ Tenuta Fontodi

FRAZ. GREVE IN CHIANTI
VIA SAN LEOLINO, 89
50020 PANZANO [FI]
TEL. 055852005
www.fontodi.com

CELLAR SALES
PRE-BOOKED VISITS

ANNUAL PRODUCTION 300,000 bottles
HECTARES UNDER VINE 70
VITICULTURE METHOD Organic

The Manetti family owns the long-established Fontodi winery in Chianti Classico. This is one of those operations that in the past was able to innovate the local wines, becoming one of the great beacons of the area. It is located at Panzano, in the so-called Conca d'Oro, a subzone that produces powerful, sun-drenched wines of great longevity. The nature of this special territory convinced the Manettis to go organic.

The house Supertuscan, Flaccianello della Pieve '07, from a selection of the estate's best sangiovese, is superlative, presenting warmly powerful and richly concentrated. The nose is a triumph of red and black berry fruit in a medley of Mediterranean scrub, coffee and chocolate while the palate has lots of body, although it will need time to expand and reach its peak. The Chianti Classico Vigna del Sorbo '07 is excellent. In fact, we think it's even better than the '06. This is a wine of great impact that reflects the winery style, mingling very subtle spicy notes with sumptuous, fresh-tasting fruitiness.

● Flaccianello della Pieve '07	▼▼▼	7
● Chianti Cl. V. del Sorbo Ris. '07	▼▼	7
● Chianti Cl. V. del Sorbo Ris. '06	▼▼	7
● Syrah Case Via '07	▼▼	7
● Chianti Cl. V. del Sorbo Ris. '01	ΨΨΨ	7
● Chianti Cl. V. del Sorbo Ris. '90	ΨΨΨ	7
● Chianti Cl. V. del Sorbo Ris. '86	ΨΨΨ	6
● Chianti Cl. V. del Sorbo Ris. '85	ΨΨΨ	5
● Flaccianello della Pieve '05	ΨΨΨ	7
● Flaccianello della Pieve '03	ΨΨΨ	7
● Flaccianello della Pieve '01	ΨΨΨ	7
● Flaccianello della Pieve '00	ΨΨΨ	7
● Flaccianello della Pieve '91	ΨΨΨ	7
● Flaccianello della Pieve '90	ΨΨΨ	7
● Flaccianello della Pieve '88	ΨΨΨ	6
● Syrah Case Via '98	ΨΨΨ	7
● Syrah Case Via '95	ΨΨΨ	7

Podere La Fortuna

LOC. LA FORTUNA, 83
53024 MONTALCINO [SI]
TEL. 0577848308
www.tenutalafortuna.it

CELLAR SALES
PRE-BOOKED VISITS

ANNUAL PRODUCTION 60,000 bottles
HECTARES UNDER VINE 13
VITICULTURE METHOD Conventional

Father and son Gioberto and Angelo Zannoni are the driving force behind this winery. They share the same enthusiasm for their 13 hectares under vine and take the same pride in farming this "lucky" land. The vineyards are split between the north-eastern and the southern slopes of the district, on similar gravelly soils of Eocene origin. The cellar contains 35-hectolitre barrels and a few barriques with increasing numbers of 900-litre casks and macerations tend to be long.

The winery is very consistent and this year presented two Brunellos, both of which reached our finals. Their styles, however, are very different. The '05 Brunello has intensely fruity aromas of cherry and yellow peach, tinged with tobacco and sweet leather. Although this was not a great vintage, the palate is rich with mellow tannins that give plenty of depth to the wine. Wood makes a heavy impact on the Riserva '04 and the notes of cherry are joined by delicate spicy balsamic notes. It's a wine of imposing structure, underpinned by lovely acidity and close-knit tannins, with a very long, dense finish.

● Brunello di Montalcino '05	▼▼	7
● Brunello di Montalcino Ris. '04	▼▼	8
● Fortunello '09	▼▼	3*
● Rosso di Montalcino '08	▼	5
● Sant'Antimo La Fortuna '08	▼	5
● Brunello di Montalcino '04	▽▽▽	7
● Brunello di Montalcino '01	▽▽▽	7
● Brunello di Montalcino '03	▽▽	7
● Rosso di Montalcino '06	▽▽	5

Frascole

LOC. FRASCOLE, 27A
50062 DICOMANO [FI]
TEL. 0558386340
www.frascole.it

CELLAR SALES
PRE-BOOKED VISITS

ANNUAL PRODUCTION 55,000 bottles
HECTARES UNDER VINE 15
VITICULTURE METHOD Certified organic

The Lippi family are enthusiastic producers in the Rufina area and deserve credit for bringing the town of Dicomano to the world's attention. The vineyards of the designation start here, at the head of the valley where the rivers Comano and Sieve merge. Wine and olive oil play an important role on this estate and its agriturismo facilities, as does the environment. It is no coincidence that they have been farming organically for ten years.

We waited an extra year before tasting the '01 Vin Santo, a deep amber-coloured nectar with a cornucopia of aromas where walnuts and almonds blend with citrus fruit, honey, dates and figs. The palate is dense and succulent, with great personality and vitality. The two Chianti Rufinas are excellent. The '08 has balsamic, fruity aromas and firmly structured body with hard yet well-integrated tannins and a sapid finish. The Riserva '07 has austere aromas that fuse soft tanned leather, tobacco and dried flowers over a base of jam. The body is full with slightly stiff tannins but finishes fresh and long. Vènia '07, from sangiovese and merlot, is uncomplicated.

○ Vin Santo del Chianti Rufina '01	▼▼	8
● Chianti Rufina '08	▼▼	4
● Chianti Rufina Ris. '07	▼▼	5
● Vènia '07	▼	5
● Chianti Rufina '06	▽▽	4*
● Vènia '06	▽▽	5
● Vènia '04	▽▽	5
○ Vin Santo del Chianti Rufina '97	▽▽	8
○ Vin Santo del Chianti Rufina '96	▽▽	8

★ Marchesi de' Frescobaldi

via Santo Spirito, 11
50125 Firenze
tel. 05527141
www.frescobaldi.it

CELLAR SALES
PRE-BOOKED VISITS

ANNUAL PRODUCTION 9,000,000 bottles
HECTARES UNDER VINE 1,200
VITICULTURE METHOD Conventional

The Frescobaldi universe expands. We tasted wines from Costa di Nugola, an estate on the coast near Livorno of 127 hectares, 92 under vine. The Frescobaldi group includes eight Tuscan properties: the main Nipozzano estate; Castello di Pomino, Remole and Castiglioni in the province of Florence; Santa Maria and Ammiraglia in the Morellino di Scansano and Monteregio designations of Maremma; and Castelgiocondo at Montalcino. Other estates are Luce della Vita at Montalcino and Attems in Friuli.

The best wine is Chianti Rufina Riserva Montesodi '07, which has a complex nose where wild berries enfold notes of cinnamon and liquorice. The soft, full entry has a good density, the tannins are not over-spiky, and there is a long, savoury finish. The good-value Chianti Rufina Nipozzano Riserva '07 is the biggest surprise. It has a fresh, lively nose and the vigorous body combines with excellent. The '07 Mormoreto, from a blend of cabernet sauvignon, merlot, cabernet franc and petit verdot, has fresh, balsamic aromas, nice structure and assertive tannins before relaxing on the finish. We also like the citrussy Pomino Benefizio Riserva '08 and the Giramonte '07.

● Chianti Rufina Montesodi Ris. '07	▼▼	7
● Brunello di Montalcino Ripe al Convento Ris. Castelgiocondo '04	▼▼	8
● Chianti Rufina Nipozzano Ris. '07	▼▼	5
● Giramonte Rosso '07	▼▼	8
● Morellino di Scansano Pietraregia dell'Ammiraglia Ris. '07	▼▼	4
● Mormoreto '07	▼▼	8
○ Pomino Il Benefizio Ris. '08	▼▼	6
● Brunello di Montalcino Castelgiocondo '05	▼	7
● Brunello di Montalcino Luce della Vite '05	▼	8
⊙ Costa di Nugola Rosato '09	▼	3
● Costa di Nugola Syrah '08	▼	3
○ Costa di Nugola Vermentino '09	▼	3
● Morellino di Scansano Santa Maria '08	▼	4
○ Pomino Bianco '09	▼	4
● Rèmole '08	▼	3
● Tenuta di Castiglioni '08	▼	5

Gattavecchi

loc. Santa Maria
via di Collazzi, 74
53045 Montepulciano [SI]
tel. 0578757110
www.gattavecchi.it

CELLAR SALES
PRE-BOOKED VISITS

ANNUAL PRODUCTION 280,000 bottles
HECTARES UNDER VINE 40
VITICULTURE METHOD Conventional

Luca Gattavecchi, his brother Gionata and sister Daniela run the winery founded by their father Valente after the Second World War. Winemaking is carried out in two distinct locations, the original Gattavecchi cellar in the centre of Montepulciano and the modern premises of the Poggio alla Sala estate, in the subzone of Argiano. The former's production is aimed almost exclusively at the local market whereas Poggio alla Sala makes the more interesting wines.

Both '07 Nobiles are well-made and very enjoyable. The Gattavecchi is more austere while the Poggio alla Sala has a more captivating theme. The two '06 Riservas are equally sound, the Gattavecchi showing full of flavour and the Poggio alla Sala well-balanced and very vigorous. The Nobile Parceto '07 is also made at Poggio alla Sala and while the oak from ageing is there, it is never unduly prominent.

● Nobile di Montepulciano '07	▼▼	5
● Nobile di Montepulciano Parceto Poggio alla Sala '07	▼▼	6
● Nobile di Montepulciano Poggio alla Sala '07	▼▼	5
● Nobile di Montepulciano Poggio alla Sala Ris. '06	▼▼	6
● Nobile di Montepulciano Ris. '06	▼▼	6
● Nobile di Montepulciano '05	▽▽	5
● Nobile di Montepulciano Poggio alla Sala '06	▽▽	5
● Nobile di Montepulciano Poggio alla Sala '04	▽▽	5
● Nobile di Montepulciano Poggio alla Sala Ris. '03	▽▽	5
● Nobile di Montepulciano Riserva dei Padri Serviti '04	▽▽	5
● Nobile di Montepulciano Riserva dei Padri Serviti '03	▽▽	5

★ Tenuta di Ghizzano

FRAZ. GHIZZANO
VIA DELLA CHIESA, 4
56037 PECCIOLI [PI]
TEL. 0587630096
www.tenutadighizzano.com

CELLAR SALES
PRE-BOOKED VISITS
ROOMS

ANNUAL PRODUCTION 70,000 bottles
HECTARES UNDER VINE 20
VITICULTURE METHOD Organic

Ginevra Venerosi Pesciolini is from a family with long traditions. It is said that they built the tower of Ghizzano in 1370. The family agricultural properties, cellar and olive oil mill are set in a wonderful spot on the hills of Pisa, to the south-east of the town and its leaning tower. The climate is mild and the soils are marine in origin, silty-sand with clay. The wines have a great personality, perfectly reflecting the character of these territories and the growing methods used, which are as natural as possible.

Nambrot '07, from merlot with some cabernet franc and petit verdot, is complex, deep and full-bodied. The aromatic weave reveals raw meat, black-fleshed fruit and liquorice while the complex palateis full-bodied and warm, bolstered by close-knit, lively tannins. The sumptuously full Veneroso '07, from sangiovese and cabernet, has now scaled the absolute heights of quality, with elegance and satisfying depth. A fascinating wine that thoroughly deserves Three Glasses.

● Veneroso '07	▼▼▼+	6
● Nambrot '07	▼▼	7
● il Ghizzano '09	▼▼	4*
● Nambrot '06	▽▽▽	7
● Nambrot '06	▽▽▽	7
● Nambrot '05	▽▽▽	7
● Nambrot '04	▽▽▽	7
● Nambrot '03	▽▽▽	7
● Nambrot '01	▽▽▽	8
● Nambrot '00	▽▽▽	8
● Veneroso '04	▽▽▽	6
● Veneroso '01	▽▽▽	6
● il Ghizzano '08	▽▽	4*
● Veneroso '06	▽▽	6

I Giusti e Zanza

VIA DEI PUNTONI, 9
56043 FAUGLIA [PI]
TEL. 058544354
www.igiustiezanza.it

CELLAR SALES
PRE-BOOKED VISITS

ANNUAL PRODUCTION 84,000 bottles
HECTARES UNDER VINE 17
VITICULTURE METHOD Organic

Paolo Giusti's winery is a benchmark point for wines of the Pisa hills. The operation is continuously evolving, starting with substantial changes to how they approach viticulture, and now they are turning to organic methods that are sure to bring the best out in the territory. The soils are alluvial gravel and support many varieties, from sangiovese and syrah to merlot and cabernet sauvignon.

The Dulcamara '07 is excellent. This Bordeaux blend has a fascinating medley of black and green notes, where blueberry and blackberry combine with vegetal and mint-like balsamic sensations in a meaty, complex and very convincing palate of graceful, intense depth. The Nemorino Bianco '09 is very good but we were a bit disappointed in the '08 Belcore as its aromas are still not clearly defined and it tends to dry the mouth.

● Dulcamara '07	▼▼	6
○ Nemorino Bianco '09	▼▼	4
● Belcore '08	▼	4
● Nemorino Rosso '08	▼	4
● Belcore '07	▽▽	4
● Belcore '06	▽▽	4
● Dulcamara '06	▽▽	6
● Dulcamara '05	▽▽	6
● Dulcamara '04	▽▽	6
● Dulcamara '01	▽▽	6
● Dulcamara '00	▽▽	6
● PerBruno '06	▽▽	5
● PerBruno '05	▽▽	5
● PerBruno '04	▽▽	5

Podere Grattamacco

LOC. LUNGAGNANO
57022 CASTAGNETO CARDUCCI [LI]
TEL. 0565765069
www.collemassari.it

CELLAR SALES
PRE-BOOKED VISITS

ANNUAL PRODUCTION 80,000 bottles
HECTARES UNDER VINE 13
VITICULTURE METHOD Certified organic

Grattamacco was established in the late 1970s and today is in hands of Claudio Tipa, one of the most thorough, methodical entrepreneurs in the Italian wine world. The property lies on the ridge of a hill between Castagneto Carducci and Bolgheri, in a beautiful natural setting, where the vines grow on various soils of sandstone, limestone, marl and clay. Work in the cellar is carried out meticulously, with great care taken over every detail. The wines are never less than good and sometimes are absolutely excellent.

The '07 Grattamacco is a masterpiece, its structure always in balance with its aromatic complexity and depth of flavour. This is a wine that flaunts bewitching aromas of raspberry in a setting of earthy, finely spiced notes, and a creamy, velvety palate of great energy. A magnificently drinkable wine. The Alberello '07 is themed around flowers, spiciness and aromatic herbs. A deliciously tempting red, it is very easy to drink but by no means dull. The finish may be just a bit too alcoholic. The Bolgheri Rosso '08 and Grattamacco Bianco '09 are both pleasant.

● Bolgheri Rosso Sup. Grattamacco '07	▼▼▼	8
● Bolgheri Sup. L'Alberello '07	▼▼	7
○ Grattamacco '09	▼▼	5
● Bolgheri Rosso '08	▼	5
● Bolgheri Rosso Sup. Grattamacco '06	▽▽▽	8
● Bolgheri Rosso Sup. Grattamacco '05	▽▽▽	8
● Bolgheri Rosso Sup. Grattamacco '04	▽▽▽	8
● Bolgheri Rosso Sup. Grattamacco '03	▽▽▽	8
● Bolgheri Rosso Sup. Grattamacco '01	▽▽▽	8
● Bolgheri Rosso Sup. Grattamacco '99	▽▽▽	8
● Grattamacco '85	▽▽▽	8
● Bolgheri Rosso '07	▽▽	5
● Bolgheri Rosso '06	▽▽	5
● Bolgheri Sup. L'Alberello '06	▽▽	7
● Bolgheri Sup. L'Alberello '04	▽▽	7

Castelli del Grevepesa

FRAZ. MERCATALE IN VAL DI PESA
VIA GREVIGIANA, 34
50024 SAN CASCIANO IN VAL DI PESA [FI]
TEL. 055821911
www.castellidelgrevepesa.it

CELLAR SALES
PRE-BOOKED VISITS

ANNUAL PRODUCTION 5,800,000 bottles
HECTARES UNDER VINE 1,000
VITICULTURE METHOD Conventional

This co-operative winery has over 1,000 hectares, most within the Chianti Classico designation, and nearly 200 direct growers, making it the largest in the area. It was set up in 1965, largely due to the resolve of Gualtiero Armando Nunzi, who convinced several producers to join together and make the most of their combined vineyards. They apply an interesting internal classification system for members' plots, resulting in a range of exceptionally exciting, rigorously selected top-quality wines.

The wines we like best are two '07 selections of Chianti Classico from vineyards at Panzano and Lamole. The first in particular has fine, deeply appealing sensations on the nose and palate where velvety tones follow through to a very relaxed long finish. The second has grassy-spicy aromatics, at least initially. It is clearly well made but not so traditional or distinctive. The two Clemente VII selections are very mature and open.

● Chianti Cl. Lamole '07	▼▼	4
● Chianti Cl. Panzano '07	▼▼	4
● Chianti Cl. Clemente VII '08	▼	4
● Chianti Cl. Clemente VII Ris. '07	▼	5
● Chianti Cl. Castelgreve Lessenziale '07	▽▽	4*
● Chianti Cl. Castelgreve Lessenziale Ris. '06	▽▽	5
● Chianti Cl. Clemente VII Ris. '00	▽▽	5
● Coltifredi '01	▽▽	6
● Coltifredi '97	▽▽	6
● Gualdo al Luco '01	▽▽	6
● Gualdo al Luco '98	▽▽	6

Fattoria di Grignano

FRAZ. GRIGNANO
VIA DI GRIGNANO, 22
50065 PONTASSIEVE [FI]
TEL. 0558398490
www.fattoriadigrignano.com

CELLAR SALES
PRE-BOOKED VISITS

ANNUAL PRODUCTION 150,000 bottles
HECTARES UNDER VINE 50
VITICULTURE METHOD Certified organic

The Grignano winery, owned by the Inghirami family, forges on. It was established in the 15th century by the Gondi family on the site of the Castello di Vico, and before that of a Roman fortification, taking on its present appearance in the 18th century. The current owners bought the estate in 1972. It extends to over 600 hectares and there are seed crops and orchards, as well as vineyards and olive groves. The property is divided into 47 plots, each with its own history and characteristics.

The '08 Chianti Rufina is good. Its fresh notes of blueberry and redcurrant blend with spicy, cinnamon tones in balanced, succulent body. The palate is elegant and not overly powerful with tucked-in tannins and a long finish. The pleasant Vin Santo del Chianti Rufina '94 has been ageing unhurriedly. It is amber-coloured and brims with butter and nuts aromas followed by a caressingly soft palate with a well-balanced finish. The sangiovese and merlot Supertuscan Salicaria '05 has a stylish bouquet of cherries and redcurrants with a grace note of cloves. A generous palate presents tannins nicely in step with the alcohol and is in no hurry to end.

● Chianti Rufina '08	▼▼	4*
● Salicaria '05	▼▼	5
○ Vin Santo del Chianti Rufina Grignano '94	▼▼	5
○ Chardonnay '09	▼	3
● Chianti Rufina Poggio Gualtieri Ris. '03	▼	6
● Chianti Rufina Ris. '07	▼	5
● Pietramaggio Rosso '09	▼	2
● Chianti Cl. Poggio Gualtieri Ris. '00	▽▽	5
● Chianti Rufina '06	▽▽	3*
● Chianti Rufina '03	▽▽	3
● Chianti Rufina Ris. '06	▽▽	4*
● Chianti Rufina Ris. '05	▽▽	4*
● Chianti Rufina Ris. '04	▽▽	4
● Salicaria '03	▽▽	6
○ Vin Santo del Chianti Capsula Oro '01	▽▽	5

Tenuta Guado al Tasso

LOC. BELVEDERE, 140
57020 BOLGHERI [LI]
TEL. 0565749735
www.antinori.it

PRE-BOOKED VISITS

ANNUAL PRODUCTION 880,000 bottles
HECTARES UNDER VINE 300
VITICULTURE METHOD Conventional

Owned by the Antinori family, one of the most famous, prestigious dynasties in Italian wine, Tenuta Guado al Tasso has a formidable vineyard holding totalling 300 hectares. The vines are in the so-called Bolgheri amphitheatre at less than 60 metres' elevation, with very small temperature differences tempered by the influence of the sea. These are ideal conditions for the grape varieties grown planted, which ripen early.

The wines are modern in style and excellent in quality, the product of perfectly ripened fruit and generous use of new wood. One is the '07 Bolgheri Superiore Guado al Tasso, made in a style that highlights its toasty, vanilla notes yet still full-bodied and gutsy. Time in the cellar is sure to bring balance. The Bolgheri Bruciato '08 is less successful and while it has a certain richness, it is also rather unforthcoming. The Vermentino '09 gives distinct tropical fruits.

● Bolgheri Rosso Sup. Guado al Tasso '07	▼▼	8
● Bolgheri Rosso Bruciato '08	▼	5
○ Bolgheri Vermentino '09	▼	5
● Bolgheri Rosso Sup. Guado al Tasso '01	▽▽▽	8
● Bolgheri Rosso Sup. Guado al Tasso '90	▽▽▽	8
● Bolgheri Rosso Bruciato '02	▽▽	5
● Bolgheri Rosso Sup. Guado al Tasso '06	▽▽	8
● Bolgheri Rosso Sup. Guado al Tasso '05	▽▽	8
● Bolgheri Rosso Sup. Guado al Tasso '04	▽▽	8
● Bolgheri Rosso Sup. Guado al Tasso '03	▽▽	8
● Bolgheri Rosso Sup. Guado al Tasso '00	▽▽	8
○ Bolgheri Vermentino '08	▽▽	5

Fattoria Il Lago

FRAZ. CAMPAGNA, 18
50062 DICOMANO [FI]
TEL. 055838047
www.fattoriaillago.com

CELLAR SALES
PRE-BOOKED VISITS
ROOMS AND FOOD

ANNUAL PRODUCTION 60,000 bottles
HECTARES UNDER VINE 22
VITICULTURE METHOD Conventional

The Salimbeni family's winery has earned a place among the full Guide profiles with a series of top notch results and this year there are lots of new wines. The present owners bought the property in 1962. The estate has over 400 hectares and includes three villages, evidence that many people once lived here. The settlements have now been converted into a farmstay and a winery. The vineyards have been completely renewed in line with the ownership's desire to respect traditions and experiment with different grapes.

The best wine is the '08 Syrah, which has a lovely aromatic spectrum of wild berries and pepper edged with hints of tanned leather. Full-bodied on the palate, with nicely tapered tannins, it is underpinned by delightful acidity leading to a compelling finish. The Chianti Rufina '08 is very good. It sets out crisp, forthright aromas and then balance, body and succulence in the mouth. The imposing Pian de' Guardi '06, a pure Sangiovese with ripe blackberry jam and aromatic herbs, reveals soft flavours that expand in a long finish. The Pinot Nero '08 is appealing while the Rosé '09 and the Malvasia '09, from malvasia bianca, are uncomplicated easy drinkers.

● Chianti Rufina '08	▼▼	4*
● Pian de' Guardi '06	▼▼	5
● Syrah '08	▼▼	5
○ Malvasia Bianca '09	▼	4
● Pinot Nero '08	▼	6
⊙ Rosé '09	▼	4
○ Vin Santo del Chianti Rufina '03	YY	5

★ Isole e Olena

LOC. ISOLE, 1
50021 BARBERINO VAL D'ELSA [FI]
TEL. 0558072763
www.isoleolena.it

CELLAR SALES
PRE-BOOKED VISITS

ANNUAL PRODUCTION 200,000 bottles
HECTARES UNDER VINE 50
VITICULTURE METHOD Conventional

In 1976, Paolo De Marchi started his Isole e Olena project, albeit in his own way, remodelling the winery his father had bought near Barberino Val d'Elsa. It was a turning point for the Chianti Classico territory, helping to redefine the quality of winemaking in the area and in the process creating one of the loveliest wineries in Italy. As well as using traditional grapes, the cellar also obtains great results from less conventional varieties.

Cepparello is one of the very best Sangioveses to be found and over the years has stayed a splendid wine in a class of its own. Unsurprisingly, the '07 version thrilled our tasters. In fact, a few bottles should be in the cellar of anyone who loves these wines. The nose is sensational with an exceptionally fine texture, where dried flowers, spices, tanned leather, pencil lead and ripe cherry all flow together, linked by mineral, earthy tones as gripping progression on the palate introduces a succession of sensations. Monumental.

● Cepparello '07	▼▼▼	8
● Cabernet Sauvignon Collezione De Marchi '04	▼▼	8
○ Chardonnay Collezione De Marchi '08	▼	7
● Syrah Collezione De Marchi '06	▼	8
● Cabernet Sauvignon '90	YYY	6
● Cabernet Sauvignon '88	YYY	6
● Cepparello '06	YYY	8
● Cepparello '05	YYY	8
● Cepparello '03	YYY	8
● Cepparello '01	YYY	7
● Cepparello '00	YYY	7
● Cepparello '99	YYY	6
● Cepparello '88	YYY	6
● Cepparello '86	YYY	6
● Chianti Cl. '88	YYY	3
● Syrah '99	YYY	7

Lanciola

LOC. POZZOLATICO
VIA IMPRUNETANA, 210
50023 IMPRUNETA [FI]
TEL. 055208324
www.lanciola.it

CELLAR SALES
PRE-BOOKED VISITS

ANNUAL PRODUCTION 250,000 bottles
HECTARES UNDER VINE 40
VITICULTURE METHOD Conventional

The Guarneri family winery is thriving. Father and son have the same passion for wine, one working in the vineyards, the other promoting the range. The estate goes back to days of the Medici when it was owned by the Ricci family, who set up its initial agricultural and winemaking structure. Today, there are about 40 hectares under vine, a further 14 in the Chianti Classico area and 35 of olive groves. The Guarneris use grapes that are not always traditional for the territory and experiment with varieties such as pinot nero and cabernet sauvignon.

This year, we were particularly impressed by an absolutely traditional '05 Vin Santo, with amber tones and a persuasive nose where hazelnut, butter and almond blend together wonderfully and the sweet, full-bodied palate enfolds the senses, although it finishes rather quickly. Ricciobianco '08, a monovarietal Chardonnay, impressed us with its marked mineral tones fusing with fresh grassiness and spring flowers. The palate has good texture, backed by an acid backbone and a lip-smacking finish.

○ Ricciobianco '08	🍷🍷	5
○ Vin Santo del Chianti Colli Fiorentini '05	🍷🍷	6
● Chianti Cl. Le Masse di Greve Ris. '07	🍷	5
● Chianti Colli Fiorentini '08	🍷	3
● Riccionero '07	🍷	6
● Chianti Cl. Le Masse di Greve Ris. '06	YY	5
● Chianti Cl. Le Masse di Greve Ris. '04	YY	5
● Chianti Cl. V. Nuova '07	YY	4*
● Chianti Colli Fiorentini '06	YY	3*
○ Vin Santo del Chianti '04	YY	6

Lavacchio

VIA DI MONTEFIESOLE, 55
50065 PONTASSIEVE [FI]
TEL. 0558317472
www.fattorialavacchio.com

CELLAR SALES
PRE-BOOKED VISITS
ROOMS AND FOOD

ANNUAL PRODUCTION 100,000 bottles
HECTARES UNDER VINE 21
VITICULTURE METHOD Certified organic

The Lottero family winery is back in the Guide's full profiles. Originally from Genoa, the Lotteros chose to make wine here over 30 years ago. The property was founded in the 18th century by the Florentine Peruzzi family and then owned by the Marchesi Strozzi Sacrati from Mantua. As well as producing wine and olive oil, the operation has a restaurant and an agriturismo, as well as growing wheat and vegetables organically. Faye Lottero runs the estate, enthusiastically showing off pieces of its past, like the oil press with millstones and a working windmill.

The Chianti Rufina Cedro Riserva '07 has lovely fruity aromas and a sound, juicy body of the right density. The Fontegalli '06 is also good. The mix of merlot, cabernet sauvignon and sangiovese grapes reveals aromatic tones of ripe fruit and mixed spices, a soft, silky body and a deliciously long farewell. Oro del Cedro '09 is a late-harvest wine from traminer aromatico revealing fascinating aromas of saffron, tea and roses with a sweet, velvety mouthfeel and a lingering finish. Pachar '09 from chardonnay, viognier and sauvignon has pleasant mineral and flowery tones and an assertive acid backbone. The traditional '04 Vin Santo is enjoyable.

● Chianti Rufina Cedro Ris. '07	🍷🍷	5
● Fontegalli '06	🍷🍷	6
○ Oro del Cedro '09	🍷🍷	5
○ Pachar '09	🍷	5
○ Vin Santo del Chianti Rufina '04	🍷	5
○ Oro del Cedro '06	YY	6
○ Pachar '07	YY	5
○ Pachar '06	YY	4*
○ Pachar '05	YY	4
○ Vin Santo del Chianti Rufina '01	YY	5

Il Lebbio

LOC. SAN BENEDETTO, 11C
53037 SAN GIMIGNANO [SI]
TEL. 0577944725
www.illebbio.it

CELLAR SALES
PRE-BOOKED VISITS

ANNUAL PRODUCTION 80,000 bottles
HECTARES UNDER VINE 21
VITICULTURE METHOD Conventional

This winery takes its name from the Italian for the dwarf elder, a common plant that grows wild around San Gimignano..The Niccolinis are enthusiastic wine producers and recently started a farm holiday centre near Gambassi Terme. In addition to producing wine and extra virgin olive oil, they cultivate the very challenging saffron to obtain a high-quality local product.

Despite the large number of red wines on offer, we were most impressed by two Vernaccias. The '09 vintage has fresh aromas of basil and mint laced with almond, followed by structure with good texture, sustained by a distinct vein of acidity. The '09 Tropìe has ripe aromas with apricot and peach tones, minerality and a supple, broad palate that holds together well into a tangy, lingering finish. The reds are less exciting. Polito '07, from sangiovese and colorino, has a red fruits-only nose and well-distributed tannins but the finish is clenched. The Lendo '07, from cabernet sauvignon, montepulciano and merlot, has a soft texture but not enough length.

○ Vernaccia di S. Gimignano '09	▼▼	4*
○ Vernaccia di S. Gimignano Tropìe '09	▼▼	4*
● Chianti '08	▼	4
● Cicogio '09	▼	4
● Lendo '07	▼	4
● San Gimignano Rosso Polito '07	▼	6
● I Grottoni '03	▽▽	4
● Lendo '06	▽▽	4
● San Gimignano Rosso Polito '06	▽▽	6
○ Vernaccia di S. Gimignano '08	▽▽	3*
○ Vernaccia di S. Gimignano Tropìe '08	▽▽	4*
○ Vernaccia di S. Gimignano Tropìe '07	▽▽	4*
○ Vernaccia di S. Gimignano Tropìe '06	▽▽	4*

Cantine Leonardo da Vinci

VIA PROVINCIALE MERCATALE, 291
50059 VINCI [FI]
TEL. 0571902444
www.cantineleonardo.it

CELLAR SALES
PRE-BOOKED VISITS
ROOMS AND FOOD

ANNUAL PRODUCTION 4,000,000 bottles
HECTARES UNDER VINE 660
VITICULTURE METHOD Conventional

Cantine Leonardo is one of the largest Tuscan co-operative wineries, if we include their Montalcino cellar. In recent years, they have been very active. They have created new brands to break into foreign markets, something that has gained impetus after they started collaborating with the giant Gallo enterprise. A distribution company was set up to market Italian and non-domestic wines, a modern wine bar was opened and also a restaurant.

The wines presented this year are generally well-styled, taking into account the limitations of a certain simplicity of structure, especially in some wine types. At Montalcino, however, the wines are held back by monumental tannins and unfocused aromas. From this range of different wines, we liked the Chianti Da Vinci '09 whose the intense fruity aromas are perked up by spice and hints of liquorice. The palate is soft and refreshed by acidity, leading into a lingering, flavoursome finish. The '05 Vin Santo Tegrino is also good, with traditional aromatics and a sweet, enjoyable palate.

● Chianti Da Vinci '09	▼▼	3*
● Brunello di Montalcino Da Vinci '05	▼	7
● Chianti Da Vinci Ris. '07	▼	4
● Leonardo Rosso '09	▼	3
● Morellino di Scansano '09	▼	4
● Rosso di Montalcino Leonardo '08	▼	4
○ Ser Piero '09	▼	3
○ Vin Santo Tegrino '05	▼	5
● Brunello di Montalcino Da Vinci '03	▽▽	7
● Chianti Da Vinci '07	▽▽	3
● Merlot degli Artisti '05	▽▽	6
● Sant'Ippolito '07	▽▽	5
○ Ser Piero '07	▽▽	3

Tenuta di Lilliano

LOC. LILLIANO, 8
53011 CASTELLINA IN CHIANTI [SI]
TEL. 0577743070
www.lilliano.com

CELLAR SALES
PRE-BOOKED VISITS

ANNUAL PRODUCTION 250,000 bottles
HECTARES UNDER VINE 50
VITICULTURE METHOD Conventional

Chianti Classico lovers will be entranced by the fascinating Lilliano winery. Some of the bottles in its cellar are unbeatable and lovers of the Sangiovese from this territory will be highly impressed by the house style. Owned for generations by the Ruspoli family, this stunning winery is surrounded by exceptionally beautiful vineyards planted on alberese soil. Vinification and maturation methods are essentially traditional but reinterpreted in a modern idiom.

The exceptionally complex Chianti Classico Riserva '07 is one of the best wines in the designation. Its aromas foreground wild berries and field gladioli while its the spicy, balsamic tones still have to integrate fully. The palate reveals similar complex, soft sensations wrapped in a warm, alcoholic embrace with assertive tannins. The nice savoury Chianti Classico '08 has an iron filings theme and the '07 Anagallis, from sangiovese, colorino and merlot, is equally attractive with sensations of blackcurrants and nettles.

● Chianti Cl. Ris. '07	2 black glasses	5
● Anagallis '07	2 black glasses	6
● Chianti Cl. '08	2 black glasses	4
● Anagallis '06	2 glasses	6
● Anagallis '90	2 glasses	5
● Chianti Cl. '07	2 glasses	4*
● Chianti Cl. '06	2 glasses	4*
● Chianti Cl. Ris. '06	2 glasses	5
● Chianti Cl. Ris. '04	2 glasses	5
● Chianti Cl. Ris. '03	2 glasses	5

Lisini

FRAZ. SANT'ANGELO IN COLLE
POD. CASANOVA
53020 MONTALCINO [SI]
TEL. 0577844040
www.lisini.com

CELLAR SALES
PRE-BOOKED VISITS

ANNUAL PRODUCTION 81,000 bottles
HECTARES UNDER VINE 18
VITICULTURE METHOD Conventional

This ancient estate has been around since the early 16th century and has been making wine since 1930, although it was only in the 1960s that wine production really took off. The vineyards are not extensive with only about 15 hectares dedicated to Brunello and even less for Rosso and Sant'Antimo, all in superb locations. The soils are Eocene in origin and very gravelly, seamed with deep-buried clay that regulates its humidity. Temperature-controlled vats are used and the oak barrels are now renewed more frequently than in the past.

This year, we tasted a truly outstanding wine, the '04 Brunello Ugolaia. It gives generous, traditional aromas where tobacco and a flowery vein of oleanders and violets back up the wild cherry. The palate displays a remarkably deep, coherent simplicity, its close-knit, mellow tannins balanced by a fresh acidity and depth in the finish. The '05 Brunello di Montalcino is well made and, in line with a cooler year, is light-bodied.

● Brunello di Montalcino Ugolaia '04	3 black glasses	8
● Brunello di Montalcino '05	2 black glasses	8
● Brunello di Montalcino '90	3 glasses	6
● Brunello di Montalcino '88	3 glasses	6
● Brunello di Montalcino Ugolaia '01	3 glasses	8
● Brunello di Montalcino Ugolaia '00	3 glasses	8
● Brunello di Montalcino Ugolaia '91	3 glasses	8
● Brunello di Montalcino '04	2 glasses	7
● Brunello di Montalcino '03	2 glasses	7
● Brunello di Montalcino '01	2 glasses	7
● Rosso di Montalcino '06	2 glasses	5

Livernano

LOC. LIVERNANO, 67A
53017 RADDA IN CHIANTI [SI]
TEL. 0577738353
www.livernano.it

CELLAR SALES
PRE-BOOKED VISITS
ROOMS AND FOOD

ANNUAL PRODUCTION 50,000 bottles
HECTARES UNDER VINE 12
VITICULTURE METHOD Organic

Livernano's path took a completely new direction in 1990, after it was bought by the current owner, Robert Cuillo. Changes brought clear improvements to vineyard and cellar and the village of Livernano was totally renovated. The estate's lands are farmed organically, respecting the territory and the local grapes, on soils that are mainly marl with some albarese and sandstone. The wines are rich and fleshy with strong overtones of oak from ageing in small casks.

The '07 Livernano is the direct result of a style that uses carefully selected cabernet sauvignon and merlot with a small amount of sangiovese. A wine of great impact, it is still getting to grips with excessive toasty notes but does flaunt delightful energy on the palate, which will make it very enjoyable in future years. The dark, tight-knit and distinctly spicy aromatics are reminiscent of the Rhône valley. The '07 Puro Sangue is another a top-quality wine, a pure Sangiovese with a vanillaed nose and incisive thrust on the palate. The Chianti Classico Riserva '07 is sweet with aromas of black cherry and blueberry.

● Livernano '07	▼▼	7
○ Anima '08	▼▼	4
● Chianti Cl. Ris. '07	▼▼	5
● Puro Sangue '07	▼▼	6
● Chianti Cl. '07	▼	4
● Chianti Cl. Ris. '04	▽▽▽	5
● Livernano '05	▽▽▽	7
● Livernano '03	▽▽▽	8
● Livernano '99	▽▽▽	8
● Livernano '98	▽▽▽	8
● Livernano '97	▽▽▽	8
● Chianti Cl. '06	▽▽	4*
● Livernano '00	▽▽	8
● Puro Sangue '00	▽▽	7

Fattoria Lornano

LOC. LORNANO, 11
53035 MONTERIGGIONI [SI]
TEL. 0577309059
www.fattorialornano.it

CELLAR SALES
PRE-BOOKED VISITS

ANNUAL PRODUCTION 100,000 bottles
HECTARES UNDER VINE 48
VITICULTURE METHOD Conventional

Fattoria di Lornano has earned its first Three Glasses with the '07 Commedator Enrico, from sangiovese and merlot. The Taddei family has owned this estate, where houses and main buildings cluster around an ancient ninth century church, for at least three generations. Pope Innocent III granted the church administrators the additional privilege of managing the surrounding parishes and their agricultural lands. The estate fell into private hands in the mid 1500s and the present-day structure goes back to the second half of the 18th century.

The Commendator Enrico has a complex suite of aromas where the toastiness of oak blends with coffee, chocolate and sensations of jam and blackberry. Entry is soft and almost creamily caressing, with tapered, close-knit tannins and a long, well-sustained finish. The other wines are less successful, particularly on the nose, where they lack cleanliness, yet they do reveal, by and large, captivating notes of minerals and aromatic herbs. The elegant, easy-drinking Le Bandite '08 is richer but edgy on the palate and the Riserva struggles to contain its tannins.

● Commendator Enrico '07	▼▼▼	5
● Chianti Cl. '08	▼	4
● Chianti Cl. Le Bandite '08	▼	4
● Chianti Cl. Ris. '07	▼	4
● Chianti Cl. '03	▽▽	4
● Chianti Cl. Ris. '06	▽▽	4
● Chianti Cl. Ris. '01	▽▽	5
● Commendator Enrico '05	▽▽	5
● Commendator Enrico '04	▽▽	5
● Commendator Enrico '01	▽▽	5
○ Vin Santo del Chianti Cl. '01	▽▽	6

Luiano

LOC. MERCATALE VAL DI PESA
VIA DI LUIANO, 32
50024 SAN CASCIANO IN VAL DI PESA [FI]
TEL. 055821039
www.luiano.it

CELLAR SALES
PRE-BOOKED VISITS
ROOMS

ANNUAL PRODUCTION 150,000 bottles
HECTARES UNDER VINE 25
VITICULTURE METHOD Conventional

The Luiano farm gets its name from a legend that Janus Bifrons lived in the forest where the winery now stands. This became know as the wood of Janus, in Latin "lucus Iani", and from there came its present-day name. The founder, Antonio Palombo, is from Naples and arrived with his wife Licia to put into practice his viticulture and oenology studies. Today, he is helped out by their children. Antonio bought and restructured a medieval hamlet and completely replanted the vineyards between 1996 and 2005.

We liked the Lui '07, a grape blend of cabernet sauvignon, merlot and colorino, which gives powerful aromas of ripe fruit where plum, redcurrant and cherry follow one another in quick succession. The entry is generously powerful and leads to a well-sustained, delicious finish. The Chianti Classico '08 is good. It is very fresh and lively on the nose with assertive flowery notes and delicate spicy notes before the taut, smooth, never smothering palate ends on a rising finish. The Riserva '07 is held back by extract and the RossoAssai '09, with intense, tempting aromas, is well styled and easy drinking.

● Lui '07	▼▼	5
● Chianti Cl. '08	▼▼	4
● Chianti Cl. Ris. '07	▼	4
● RossoAssai '09	▼	3
● Lui '04	▽▽	5
● Sangiò '06	▽▽	4

I Luoghi

LOC. CAMPO AL CAPRIOLO, 201
57022 CASTAGNETO CARDUCCI [LI]
TEL. 0565777379
www.iluoghi.it

PRE-BOOKED VISITS

ANNUAL PRODUCTION 15,000 bottles
HECTARES UNDER VINE 4
VITICULTURE METHOD Certified organic

Stefano Granata and Paola De Fusco own one of the most interesting young wineries in the Bolgheri area. It was established around the year 2000 and its style is very personal, a long way from the norm in this territory. The owners are actively involved in all the agricultural and winemaking procedures, tending the rows with obsessive care and using very natural cellar methods. There are only three and a half hectares under vine, in plots that are vinified separately to only make very few bottles. Look out for them.

Campo al Fico '07 is spectacular. It still has a touch of toastiness but underneath is a wine of enormous energy, with a taut, deep palate bursting with dynamic freshness. The '07 Podere Ritorti is not far behind, revealing itself to be a fascinating wine with delicious aromatic herbs and raspberries preceding a broad savoury palate.

● Bolgheri Sup. Campo al Fico '07	▼▼	8
● Bolgheri Sup. Podere Ritorti '07	▼▼	5
● Bolgheri Sup. Campo al Fico '06	▽▽	8

★ Le Macchiole

via Bolgherese, 189a
57020 Bolgheri [LI]
tel. 0565766092
www.lemacchiole.it

PRE-BOOKED VISITS
FOOD

ANNUAL PRODUCTION 100,000 bottles
HECTARES UNDER VINE 22
VITICULTURE METHOD Conventional

Eugenio Campolmi set up Le Macchiole in 1983 and after his premature death in 2002, his wife Cinzia Merli took over, successfully pressing ahead with his project. The watchword is the same: promote the winery's plots by producing great monovarietal wines. The wines define the wine history of Bolgheri as much today as they have in the past.

In our opinion, the top wine from the range is the '07 Messorio, a monovarietal Merlot whose a sensuous nose brims with chocolate and liqueur cherries, nicely integrated into the wood. The palate is magnificent, displaying perfectly executed texture with prominent but mellow tannins. The '07 Paleo is just a step below; it's an evidently well-made Cabernet Franc that has a tad too much alcohol in the finish. A whirlwind of black fruits, white pepper and lavender make up a great '07 Scrio, from syrah grapes, with complex, very long-lingering drinkability. The '08 Paleo Bianco is intense and delicately spicy.

● Messorio '07	▼▼▼	8
● Paleo Rosso '07	▼▼	8
● Scrio '07	▼▼	8
○ Paleo Bianco '08	▼▼	6
● Bolgheri Rosso Sup. Paleo '97	ΨΨΨ	8
● Bolgheri Rosso Sup. Paleo '96	ΨΨΨ	8
● Bolgheri Rosso Sup. Paleo '95	ΨΨΨ	8
● Messorio '06	ΨΨΨ	8
● Messorio '01	ΨΨΨ	8
● Messorio '99	ΨΨΨ	8
● Messorio '98	ΨΨΨ	8
● Messorio '97	ΨΨΨ	8
● Paleo Rosso '03	ΨΨΨ	8
● Paleo Rosso '01	ΨΨΨ	8
● Scrio '01	ΨΨΨ	8

La Madonnina - Triacca

loc. Strada in Chianti
via Palaia, 39
50027 Greve in Chianti [FI]
tel. 055858003
www.triacca.com

PRE-BOOKED VISITS

ANNUAL PRODUCTION 600,000 bottles
HECTARES UNDER VINE 100
VITICULTURE METHOD Conventional

La Madonnina is at Strada in Chianti, in the municipality of Greve, and belongs to the small Triacca group. This Swiss family owns other Tuscan estates and one in Valtellina. The cellars are in the outstanding Villa Franchi and the vineyards feature mainly with sangiovese, cabernet and merlot and were planted in the late 1970s and early 1980s. This Chianti winery seems to be the most successful in the group and overall offers good wines.

The '07 Felcinaia, from cabernet, merlot and sangiovese grapes, is good. The initially powdery nose becomes cleaner and shows a delightful palette of wild berry and mint aromatics before the well-made palate shows clean and soft but rather predictable. Il Mandorlo '07, from sangiovese and cabernet grapes, is excellent, unfolding with fascinating tertiary aromas. The Chianti Classico Riserva '07 is not bad at all, with spicy, medicinal, even slightly vegetal, overtones and the Bello Stento '08 is soft and mature. We really like the Nobile di Montepulciano '07.

● Chianti Cl. Bello Stento '08	▼▼	4
● Chianti Cl. Ris. '07	▼▼	4
● Falcinaia '07	▼▼	6
● Il Mandorlo '07	▼▼	4
● Nobile di Montepulciano '07	▼▼	4
● Nobile di Montepulciano Poderuccio '07	▼	5
● Chianti Cl. Ris. '04	ΨΨΨ	4
● Chianti Cl. Bello Stento '03	ΨΨ	4
● Chianti Cl. Ris. '06	ΨΨ	4*
● Chianti Cl. Ris. '05	ΨΨ	4*
● Chianti Cl. Ris. '03	ΨΨ	4
● Il Mandorlo '01	ΨΨ	5
● Nobile di Montepulciano Fattoria Santa Venere '06	ΨΨ	5

Malenchini

LOC. GRASSINA
VIA LILLIANO E MEOLI, 82
50015 BAGNO A RIPOLI [FI]
TEL. 055642602
www.malenchini.it

CELLAR SALES
PRE-BOOKED VISITS

ANNUAL PRODUCTION 90,000 bottles
HECTARES UNDER VINE 17
VITICULTURE METHOD Conventional

Our review for this winery owned by the Malenchini family is nearly identical to last year's. All the wines are good level and value for money is shrewdly gauged. The owner, Marina, is the president of the Consorzio del Chianti Colli Fiorentini, a young, dynamic operation emerging in Italy's extensive and varied wine panorama. The winery is based in the Medici villa of Lilliano, a building of great charm near Florence, in the family for over two centuries. The winery is run enthusiastically by Marina's daughter Diletta.

The best wine this year is Bruzzico '07, from cabernet sauvignon and sangiovese, with crisp, well-focused aromas of cherries and wild berries, rounded off by hints of spices. The palate has nice balance palate with succulent tannins and its rich flavour finishes long. The Chianti Colli Fiorentini '08 is good, with a simple nose and a supple, fresh structure. The wines in the Daily Quality line are well-made and focus on drinkability while the Vin Santo '04 is traditional in its aromas and soft-textured body.

● Bruzzico '07	**YY**	5
● Chianti Colli Fiorentini '08	**Y**	4
○ Daily Quality Bianco '09	**Y**	3
● Daily Quality Rosso '09	**Y**	3
○ Vin Santo Chianti Colli Fiorentini '04	**Y**	5
● Bruzzico '06	YY	5
● Bruzzico '05	YY	5
● Bruzzico '04	YY	5

Mannucci Droandi

FRAZ. MERCATALE VALDARNO
VIA ROSSINELLO E CAMPOLUCCI, 79
52020 MONTEVARCHI [AR]
TEL. 0559707276
www.mannuccidroandi.com

CELLAR SALES
PRE-BOOKED VISITS

ANNUAL PRODUCTION 70,000 bottles
HECTARES UNDER VINE 35
VITICULTURE METHOD Certified organic

In a kind of family saga, Roberto Mannucci Droandi follows in the footsteps of his forebears, who were growers in the Carmignano area and the Borro estate until the mid 1800s. When he took up winemaking, Roberto got his wife Maria Grazia and nephews Andrea and Matteo on board to help preserve the family's viticultural heritage. Initially, Roberto cultivated traditional grapes and then started experimenting with forgotten varieties. After many trials and selections, he started making wine.

Results vary year by year and one of the best things Roberto does is to let nature back in to play its part in viticulture. The best wines are the Barsaglina '08 and the Foglia Tonda, also '08. The former has clean, grassy tones, where hints of aromatic herbs and a faint spiciness mix as the supple, racy body rounds off with a long finish. The Foglia Tonda has surprising tones of green pepper and ripe fruitiness, the tannins nicely offset by the alcohol, and a long, succulent finish. The '05 Vin Santo is good. Its hazelnut and dates precede a soft, dense entry and a sweetly delicious finish. The two Chiantis have clean aromas and forthright palates. Both are good.

● Barsaglina '08	**YY**	5
● Foglia Tonda '08	**YY**	5
○ Vin Santo del Chianti Cl. Ceppeto '05	**YY**	6
● Chianti Cl. Ceppeto '07	**Y**	4
● Chianti Colli Aretini '08	**Y**	3
● Campolucci '06	YY	5
● Campolucci '03	YY	5
● Campolucci '01	YY	5
● Chianti Cl. Ceppeto '04	YY	4*
● Chianti Colli Aretini '05	YY	3*
● Chianti Colli Aretini '04	YY	3*
● Foglia Tonda '07	YY	5

Fattoria Mantellassi

LOC. BANDITACCIA, 26
58051 MAGLIANO IN TOSCANA [GR]
TEL. 0564592037
www.fatt-mantellassi.it

CELLAR SALES
PRE-BOOKED VISITS

ANNUAL PRODUCTION 550,000 bottles
HECTARES UNDER VINE 60
VITICULTURE METHOD Conventional

This Maremma cellar has a winemaking history spanning four decades and, through the pioneering dedication of Ezio Mantellassi, has greatly contributed to the success of Morellino in Italy and around the world. Today, the winery is run by his sons Aleardo and Giuseppe, who continue to produce wines in the distinctive Mantellassi style, which is a benchmark of typicality for sangiovese grown in southern Tuscany.

We tasted one of the best versions ever of Querciolaia '07, from alicante, which is called "uva spagna" here. The aromas are well-defined and have a certain sweetness that leads into a dense, juicy mouth. The very drinkable Morellino San Giuseppe '09 is similar in style to the '09 Morellino Mentore, although the latter is simpler and less focused. The Morellino Le Sentinelle Riserva '07 is austere and slightly too taut.

● Querciolaia '07	2 black glasses	5
● Morellino di Scansano San Giuseppe '09	2 black glasses	4
● Morellino di Scansano Le Sentinelle Ris. '07	1 black glass	5
● Morellino di Scansano Mentore '09	1 black glass	4
● Morellino di Scansano Le Sentinelle Ris. '06	2 glasses	5
● Morellino di Scansano Le Sentinelle Ris. '05	2 glasses	5
● Morellino di Scansano Le Sentinelle Ris. '04	2 glasses	5
● Morellino di Scansano Mentore '08	2 glasses	4
● Morellino di Scansano San Giuseppe '08	2 glasses	4
● Morellino di Scansano San Giuseppe '06	2 glasses	4
● Morellino di Scansano San Giuseppe '02	2 glasses	4
● Querciolaia '05	2 glasses	5
● Querciolaia '04	2 glasses	5
● Querciolaia '01	2 glasses	5

Il Marroneto

LOC. MADONNA DELLE GRAZIE, 307
53024 MONTALCINO [SI]
TEL. 0577849382
www.ilmarroneto.com

CELLAR SALES
PRE-BOOKED VISITS

ANNUAL PRODUCTION 20,000 bottles
HECTARES UNDER VINE 6
VITICULTURE METHOD Organic

The one-time lawyer Alessandro Mori has been running Il Marroneto for years with boundless enthusiasm. The winery is located to the north-west of Montalcino, at an altitude of about 350 metres, and the cellar is in the base of a beautiful 13th-century tower, once part of the auxiliary fortifications of Montalcino, surrounded by the vineyard. The wines are traditional, elegant and emblematic of this cooler area of Montalcino. The soils are principally sandstone and play their part in producing wines that are not too structured.

The excellent Brunello di Montalcino '05 comes from the winery's Madonna delle Grazie cru. It is pale ruby in colour and has a traditional nose with well-defined, intense aromas of tanned leather and tobacco mingling with light, fascinating notes of medicinal herbs. Entry on the palate is not over-powerful but is well sustained by good acidity and very relaxed tannins that have mellowed with long ageing, first in wood and then in bottle. This is a wine of rare finesse and elegance, finishing intense and very long-lasting, in keeping with a wine that is in a class of its own.

● Brunello di Montalcino Madonna delle Grazie '05	2 black glasses	8
● Brunello di Montalcino '05	2 black glasses	7
● Rosso di Montalcino Ignaccio '07	1 black glass	5
● Brunello di Montalcino '03	2 glasses	7
● Brunello di Montalcino '01	2 glasses	7
● Brunello di Montalcino Madonna delle Grazie '04	2 glasses	8
● Brunello di Montalcino Madonna delle Grazie '01	2 glasses	8
● Brunello di Montalcino Madonna delle Grazie '00	2 glasses	8

Cosimo Maria Masini

VIA POGGIO AL PINO, 16
56028 SAN MINIATO [PI]
TEL. 0571465032
www.cosimomariamasini.it

CELLAR SALES
PRE-BOOKED VISITS

ANNUAL PRODUCTION 35,000 bottles
HECTARES UNDER VINE 17
VITICULTURE METHOD Organic

Cosimo Maria Masini is a young producer whose delightful winery is set in the valley of the river Arno, facing the rolling hills of San Miniato. The estate practices organic agriculture, growing grapes on soils that are marine in origin and full of fossils. The climate here is ideal, moderated by sea breezes and the tramontana winds that help keep the grapes sound. The wines have character, which in some cases gets the better of the rather obsessive quest for the perfect style.

Talking of which, we found the red Nicolò '07, from cabernet sauvignon and franc grapes, absolutely delicious. It has typical aromas that are markedly grassy, shading into refreshing hints of camphor. The rich, caressing fruit has good flavour, texture and length. The Cosimo '07, predominantly from sangiovese, also reveals herbaceousness but its palate dull and rustic. From the whites, we like the tangy, peppery Daphnè '08 best.

● Nicolò '07	🍷🍷 (red)	5
● Cosimo '07	🍷 (red)	6
○ Daphnè '08	🍷 (red)	5
○ Annick '08	🍷🍷	4
○ Annick '07	🍷🍷	4*
○ Annick '06	🍷🍷	4
● Cosimo '06	🍷🍷	6
○ Daphnè '07	🍷🍷	5
● Nicole '06	🍷🍷	4*
● Nicolò '06	🍷🍷	5

★ La Massa

VIA CASE SPARSE, 9
50020 PANZANO [FI]
TEL. 055852722
info@fattorialamassa.com

PRE-BOOKED VISITS

ANNUAL PRODUCTION 110,000 bottles
HECTARES UNDER VINE 25
VITICULTURE METHOD Conventional

We really cannot keep the Panzano-based winery out of this year's Guide even though its owner, maybe wishing to make a point, refused to send us any wines to taste. We try and find the bottles for ourselves but sometimes cannot find both the wines produced in time for our tastings. This year, we were able to taste Giorgio Primo '07 during an event at Panzano and so can review it. However, we should say that we discovered La Massa years ago and have given the cellar many awards.

The Giorgio Primo '07 is a really good wine. It may not represent its territory, as it is now made from only 50 per cent sangiovese plus 40 per cent merlot and ten per cent cabernet sauvignon and petit verdot, but this is the most successful vintage of recent years. Its bright garnet red introduces complex aromas of fruit together with tobacco and sweet wood. We were particularly delighted by the dense, fine-grained tannins, which are very similar to those of a Bordeaux. It's a very well-made international-style red. With a touch more grip and sense of territory it may replicate past glories.

● Giorgio Primo '07	🍷🍷 (red)	8
● Chianti Cl. Giorgio Primo '01	🍷🍷🍷	8
● Chianti Cl. Giorgio Primo '00	🍷🍷🍷	7
● Chianti Cl. Giorgio Primo '99	🍷🍷🍷	7
● Chianti Cl. Giorgio Primo '98	🍷🍷🍷	7
● Chianti Cl. Giorgio Primo '97	🍷🍷🍷	7
● Chianti Cl. Giorgio Primo '96	🍷🍷🍷	7
● Chianti Cl. Giorgio Primo '95	🍷🍷🍷	7
● Chianti Cl. Giorgio Primo '94	🍷🍷🍷	7
● Chianti Cl. Giorgio Primo '93	🍷🍷🍷	7
● Giorgio Primo '03	🍷🍷🍷	8
● La Massa '01	🍷🍷🍷	5

Mastrojanni

FRAZ. CASTELNUOVO DELL'ABATE
POD. LORETO SAN PIO
53024 MONTALCINO [SI]
TEL. 0577835681
www.mastrojanni.com

CELLAR SALES
PRE-BOOKED VISITS

ANNUAL PRODUCTION 80,000 bottles
HECTARES UNDER VINE 24
VITICULTURE METHOD Conventional

Founded in 1975, Mastrojanni is one of the longest-established wineries in Montalcino. It is set in a beautiful position, at 400 metres above sea level in the south-west corner of the district, dominated by the massive form of Mount Amiata, a defence from bad weather coming from the west. The very loose silty, limestone soil helps produce long-living, tannic wines with fine aromas. The operation is owned by the Illy family who have recently carried out refurbishment of its cellar, buying new equipment for fermentation and barrels for ageing.

The wines presented are going through a transitional year following on from the previous management. The Brunello di Montalcino '05 is in the traditional house style and has a graceful nose with rather intense notes of flowers and white cherries. In the mouth, its delightful acidity underpins slim body with fine-grained tannins and the elegant progression moves to a clean finish. The intensely fruity Rosso di Montalcino '08 is well made with lively tannins.

● Brunello di Montalcino '05	▼▼	7
● Rosso di Montalcino '08	▼	5
● Brunello di Montalcino '97	▽▽▽	7
● Brunello di Montalcino '90	▽▽▽	7
● Brunello di Montalcino Ris. '88	▽▽▽	7
● Brunello di Montalcino Schiena d'Asino '93	▽▽▽	7
● Brunello di Montalcino Schiena d'Asino '90	▽▽▽	7
● Brunello di Montalcino '04	▽▽	7
● Brunello di Montalcino Schiena d'Asino '04	▽▽	8
● Brunello di Montalcino V. Schiena d'Asino '01	▽▽	8
● San Pio '05	▽▽	5

Melini

LOC. GAGGIANO
53036 POGGIBONSI [SI]
TEL. 0577998511
www.cantinemelini.it

CELLAR SALES
PRE-BOOKED VISITS

ANNUAL PRODUCTION 4,000,000 bottles
HECTARES UNDER VINE 145
VITICULTURE METHOD Conventional

The Melini winery goes back to 1705 when the wealthy Melini family from Val di Sieva founded their wine house at Pontassieve. The first wine was Vermiglio, a good red if consumed locally but it did not take to being transported. They initially experimented with pasteurization and then decided to use the flasks invented by Paolo Carrai. After changing hands several times, Melini now belongs to the Gruppo Italiano Vini, which also owns Machiavelli, a winery specializing in Chianti Classico also reviewed here this year.

The Chianti Classico Riserva La Selvanella '07 again went into the finals. Ruby red, it proffers a nose of tertiary tobacco and tanned leather, combined with a ripe fruitiness and cherry jam. The entry on the palate is substantial, with prominent tannins in a sound body underpinned by acidity. The finish is full of flavour and very long. The Chianti Classico Granaio is good, with a set of aromas that foreground ripe, plum-led fruit interweaving with fresh, flowery notes before the palate shows meaty and flavoursome with well-integrated acidity and a lingering finish. The '07 Vigna di Fontalle Riserva di Machiavelli is tantalizing.

● Chianti Cl. La Selvanella Ris. '07	▼▼	6
● Chianti Cl. Granaio '08	▼▼	4
● Chianti Cl. V. di Fontalle Ris. Machiavelli '07	▼▼	6
● Chianti Cl. Solatìo del Tani Machiavelli '08	▼	4
● Chianti San Lorenzo '09	▼	4
● I Coltri '09	▼	3
○ Vernaccia di S. Gimignano Le Grillaie '09	▼	4
● Chianti Cl. La Selvanella Ris. '06	▽▽▽	6
● Chianti Cl. La Selvanella Ris. '03	▽▽▽	5
● Chianti Cl. La Selvanella Ris. '01	▽▽▽	5
● Chianti Cl. La Selvanella Ris. '00	▽▽▽	5
● Chianti Cl. La Selvanella Ris. '99	▽▽▽	6
● Chianti Cl. La Selvanella Ris. '90	▽▽▽	5
● Chianti Cl. La Selvanella Ris. '05	▽▽	6
● Chianti Cl. La Selvanella Ris. '04	▽▽	7

Fattoria Michi

via San Martino, 34
55015 Montecarlo [LU]
tel. 058322011
www.fattoriamichi.it

PRE-BOOKED VISITS

ANNUAL PRODUCTION 130,000 bottles
HECTARES UNDER VINE 16
VITICULTURE METHOD Conventional

In the small area of Montecarlo, Fattoria Michi has always been important. The estate was owned by the Michi family until 2005 and is now run by a company that has decided to follow the same strategies and concentrate on the grapes that give the best results locally, focusing mainly on whites. Since buying the winery, the new owners have started upgrading it, in particular the cellar, and they have also started importing wines as well as producing them.

From the wines presented, the one that stood out was the only red, Montecarlo '09. It hinges mainly on aromatic freshness, with very strong sensations of well-defined fruit on the nose, while the not overly powerful palate is very enjoyable, ending on a lingering, juicy finish. The '09 Vermentino is also very good. Its ripe white-fleshed-fruit, minerals and florality combine deliciously in a well-layered, savoury structure. Vigna del Cavaliere '09, a blend of chardonnay, sauvignon and vermentino, is still young and fails to unbend completely in the mouth. The Montecarlo Bianco '09 is uncomplicated and enjoyable.

● Montecarlo Rosso '04	▼▼	4
○ Vermentino '09	▼▼	4
○ Dorato '07	▼	5
○ Montecarlo Bianco '09	▼	4
○ Vigna del Cavaliere '09	▼	5
○ Malie '05	▽▽	4
○ Montecarlo Bianco '05	▽▽	4
○ Vecchie Vigne '07	▽▽	4*
○ Vigna del Cavaliere '07	▽▽	5

Mocali

loc. Mocali
53024 Montalcino [SI]
tel. 0577849485
azmocali@tiscali.it

CELLAR SALES
PRE-BOOKED VISITS

ANNUAL PRODUCTION 120,000 bottles
HECTARES UNDER VINE 14
VITICULTURE METHOD Conventional

Tiziano Ciacci runs this lovely estate. Its position is excellent on a small terrace above the church of Santa Restituta in the western part of Montalcino at about 350 metres above sea level. The marly soil enjoys excellent ventilation so the rows only require minimal treatment. The wines have styles determined by the wood they age in, such as the 900-litre casks used for Vigna delle Raunate, and all the wines are vinified in wooden barrels with temperature-control systems and in stainless steel vats. The overall quality is rising.

Two of the wines reached our finals. The first was Brunello di Montalcino Vigna delle Raunate Riserva '04, which has a varietal nose. After breathing in the glass for a short period, it unveils tobacco, damp leather and notes of cherry jam. The palate is tantalizing with fresh acidity, underpinning massive extract. The tannins are mellow, the finish full and enfolding. This Brunello is not particularly elegant but it does have great personality. The '08 Rosso di Montalcino is very different, throwing a well-defined nose of fruity blackberries and somewhat jammy ripe cherries, followed by an intense, complex palate that finishes juicily.

● Brunello di Montalcino V. delle Raunate Ris. '04	▼▼	8
● Rosso di Montalcino '08	▼▼	4*
● Mirus '07	▼▼	6
● Brunello di Montalcino '05	▼	6
● Brunello di Montalcino Ris. '04	▼	8
● I Piaggioni '08	▼	4
● Brunello di Montalcino '04	▽▽	7
● Brunello di Montalcino '03	▽▽	7
● Brunello di Montalcino Ris. '01	▽▽	7
● Brunello di Montalcino V. delle Raunate '04	▽▽	8
● Brunello di Montalcino V. delle Raunate Ris. '01	▽▽	8
● I Piaggioni '05	▽▽	4*

Il Molino di Grace

LOC. IL VOLANO LUCARELLI
50022 PANZANO [FI]
TEL. 0558561010
www.ilmolinodigrace.com

CELLAR SALES
PRE-BOOKED VISITS

ANNUAL PRODUCTION 210,000 bottles
HECTARES UNDER VINE 44
VITICULTURE METHOD Organic

Molino di Grace started making good wines right from the start and now is a sound, well-run winery. In its ten years of activity, it has been able to carve an important space for itself in the crowded, complex world of Chianti. The winery is the work of Clifford and Donna Meneghetti Weaver and is located in the municipality of Gaiole. Here, they grow grapes and produce wines in a modern style, full of expression and generous, ripe fruit, and are careful in choosing when to use small, medium or large-sized wooden casks and barrels.

We liked the Chianti Classico '08 with its fascinating aromas that blend rocky, mineral notes with austere, dark-fleshed fruit and sensations of blood-rich meat and iron. The palate is nicely rounded with a solid backbone of flavour and freshness framed by delightful dark, yet lively, sensations. The very successful Chianti Classico Riserva '07 has lovely sandalwood spice, lavender and dark citrus fruit in a savoury, consistent palate. We were not convinced by the '07 Sangiovese Gratius.

● Chianti Cl. '08	▼▼	5
● Chianti Cl. Ris. '07	▼▼	5
● Gratius '07	▼	7
● Chianti Cl. Il Margone Ris. '05	▽▽▽	7
● Chianti Cl. Il Margone Ris. '04	▽▽▽	7
● Chianti Cl. Ris. '01	▽▽▽	5
● Gratius '04	▽▽▽	7
● Gratius '00	▽▽▽	7
● Chianti Cl. Il Margone Ris. '06	▽▽	7
● Chianti Cl. Il Margone Ris. '01	▽▽	6
● Chianti Cl. Il Margone Ris. '99	▽▽	5
● Chianti Cl. Ris. '04	▽▽	6
● Gratius '01	▽▽	7

Montauto

LOC. SANTA BARBARA DI MONTAUTO
58014 MANCIANO [GR]
TEL. 3383833928
www.montauto.org

CELLAR SALES
PRE-BOOKED VISITS

ANNUAL PRODUCTION N.A.
HECTARES UNDER VINE 11
VITICULTURE METHOD Conventional

Montauto extends across 200 hectares, 11 of which are under vine. The estate is managed by Riccardo Lepri and has a particular leaning towards whites. This is partly because many of the numerous wines produced are from white grapes and also because there is a considerable variation in temperature between day and night in this corner of Maremma. This is something that also significantly influences the character of reds produced by this Manciano-based winery.

Sovana Rosso '09 is all flowery aromas and lip-smacking palate, sensations also displayed by the pleasant, slightly more complex Tiburzio '07, from sangiovese and alicante. The Bianco di Pitigliano '09 is approachable and enjoyable, marked out by a lovely tanginess. The Enos I '09 has a very natural vein of acidity and is an elegant, lively wine from sauvignon only. The Gessaia '09, also from sauvignon, and the Maremma Bianco '09, from vermentino and malvasia, are both well made.

○ Bianco di Pitigliano '09	▼▼	3
○ Enos I '09	▼▼	5
● Sovana Rosso '09	▼▼	3
● Tiburzio '07	▼▼	5
○ Gessala '09	▼	4
○ Maremma Bianco '09	▼	4
○ Montauto Sauvignon '05	▽▽	4

Tenuta di Montecucco

LOC. MONTECUCCO
58044 CINIGIANO [GR]
TEL. 0564999029
www.tenutadimontecucco.it

CELLAR SALES
PRE-BOOKED VISITS
ROOMS

ANNUAL PRODUCTION **150,000 bottles**
HECTARES UNDER VINE **32**
VITICULTURE METHOD **Certified organic**

Collemassari SpA now owns the Tenuta di Montecucco, located in an old convent and extending across 700 hectares, of which 32 are under vine. The winery is in the heart of the Montecucco DOC, hence its name, and has been influential in the success of the designation since the DOC was created in 1998. Recently, the estate has been carefully renovated, including upgrading the cellar, parts of whose walls date back to the 12th century.

Montecucco Le Coste '07 is a very successfully made wine with finely spiced aromas and a subtle palate of great liveliness. The Montecucco Sangiovese Rigomoro Riserva '06 is more austere, with solid structure and aromas of dark berry fruit and chocolate. The '08 Montecucco Rosso Passonaia is delightful and utterly enjoyable.

● Montecucco Sangiovese Le Coste '07	▼▼	5
● Montecucco Rosso Passonaia '08	▼▼	4
● Montecucco Sangiovese Rigomoro Ris. '06	▼▼	4
● Montecucco Rosso Passonaia '03	▽▽	4
● Montecucco Sangiovese Le Coste '06	▽▽	5
● Montecucco Sangiovese Rigomoro Ris. '05	▽▽	6
● Montecucco Sangovese Le Coste '04	▽▽	5

Fattoria Montellori

VIA PISTOIESE, 1
50054 FUCECCHIO [FI]
TEL. 0571260641
www.fattoriamontellori.it

CELLAR SALES
PRE-BOOKED VISITS
FOOD

ANNUAL PRODUCTION **330,000 bottles**
HECTARES UNDER VINE **55**
VITICULTURE METHOD **Conventional**

Alessandro Nieri is a trail-blazer for many reasons. He believed in this territory before others, basing his views on the experience he acquired from his father and grandfather, who pioneered the winery. Alessandro has used international grapes carefully with good results and above all he started making classic-method sparkling wines when many thought this was sheer folly. In the light of what is going on today in Tuscan wine, where they even make sparkling wines from sangiovese, Alessandro was obviously just ahead of his time.

Salamartano '07, from cabernet sauvignon, cabernet franc and merlot, reached our finals. It has complex aromas where fruitiness combines with the clove and liquorice spice and delicious hints of cocoa. The full, attractively nuanced palate then expands into an extensive, succulent finish. The Dicatum '07, a pure Sangiovese, is very good and has a bouquet of cherry and plum over hints of aromatic herbs, while the succulent body is full but not tired, with well-integrated tannins and long length. The amber-flecked Vin Santo '03 offers subtle fragrances of hazelnut, honey and nuts become a delicious, velvety sweetness in the mouth.

● Salamartano '07	▼▼	6
○ Bianco dell'Empolese Vin Santo '03	▼▼	6
● Dicatum '07	▼▼	6
○ Mandorlo '09	▼	3
○ Montellori Pas Dosé '06	▼	5
○ Sant'Amato '09	▼	4
● Chianti Fattoria Le Caselle '06	▽▽	3*
● Dicatum '03	▽▽	5
● Salamartano '04	▽▽	6
● Salamartano '99	▽▽	6
○ Sant'Amato '02	▽▽	4*
○ Sant'Amato '00	▽▽	3*
● Tuttosole '06	▽▽	5
● Tuttosole '05	▽▽	6

Fattoria di Montemaggio

LOC. MONTEMAGGIO
53017 RADDA IN CHIANTI [SI]
TEL. 0577738820
www.montemaggio.com

CELLAR SALES
PRE-BOOKED VISITS

ANNUAL PRODUCTION 24,000 bottles
HECTARES UNDER VINE 8
VITICULTURE METHOD Organic

Montemaggio is a small winery that always releases satisfying wines. Currently, the estate is converting to organic methods after spending years weighing up how best to respect the territory and so improve the wines. The name comes from Monte Maggiore, the highest hill in the area, on which there was once very probably a guard tower to defend the road between Siena and Florence. As well as the vineyards, the estate also farms the olive groves planted on some of the land.

We were impressed by the '07 Torre di Montemaggio, a pure Merlot where mineral tones and pencil lead mingle with hints of wild berries and enjoyable spices. Sensations on the palate are pleasant and generous yet fresh and lively, while the finish is savoury and succulent. The '07 Riserva is good, the green notes aromas of forest floor being offset by hints of fruit preserve. The full, lively palate is assertive and juicy with delightful after-aromas of Mediterranean scrubland. The '08 Chianti Classico is an uncomplicated easy drinker, if something of a lightweight, while the Rosé '09 is fresh and perky.

● Chianti Cl. Ris. '07	▼▼	5
● Torre di Montemaggio '07	▼▼	6
● Chianti Cl. '08	▼	5
⊙ Rosé di Montemaggio '09	▼	4
● Chianti Cl. '06	▽▽	5*
● Chianti Cl. Ris. '01	▽▽	5
● Torre di Montemaggio '06	▽▽	6
● Torre di Montemaggio '04	▽▽	5
● Torre di Montemaggio '03	▽▽	5

Montenidoli

LOC. MONTENIDOLI
53037 SAN GIMIGNANO [SI]
TEL. 0577941565
www.montenidoli.com

ROOMS

ANNUAL PRODUCTION 120,000 bottles
HECTARES UNDER VINE 24
VITICULTURE METHOD Certified organic

Many years ago, Elisabetta Fagiuoli decided to settle in San Gimignano and one of her plans was to make wine from the grapes growing in the vineyard behind her house. Several harvests later, she became a full-time grower. Her closeness to the land and her vineyard has meant that Elisabetta now lives and works in tune with nature and its cycles. Her wines reflect this and today Montenidoli is one of the most important wineries in Tuscany.

Elisabetta interprets Vernaccia in her own way, making very personal wines. The Fiore '08 has fragrant, flowery aromas and a fresh savouriness while the opulent, gratifying Tradizionale '08 is golden in colour with tones of ripe fruit and grape skin. Finally, the '06 Carato, aged in new wood, is a unique, vigorous wine with tones of white chocolate, aniseed and vanilla. Templare '06 is an unusual but alluring blend of vernaccia, trebbiano, malvasia bianca, sémillon, verdicchio and grechetto from very old vines that have always grown here in San Gimignano, once the home of the Knights Templar.

○ Vernaccia di S. Gimignano Carato '06	▼▼	5
⊙ Canaiuolo '09	▼▼	4*
● Chianti Colli Senesi Il Garrulo '07	▼▼	4
○ Il Templare '06	▼▼	5
● Sono Montenidoli '04	▼▼	7
○ Vernaccia di S. Gimignano Fiore '08	▼▼	4*
○ Vernaccia di S. Gimignano Tradizionale '08	▼▼	4*
● Chianti Colli Senesi '07	▼	5
○ Vernaccia di S. Gimignano Carato '05	▽▽▽	6
○ Vernaccia di S. Gimignano Carato '02	▽▽▽	6
⊙ Canaiuolo '08	▽▽	4*
● Chianti Colli Senesi Il Garrulo '06	▽▽	4
○ Vernaccia di S. Gimignano Carato '04	▽▽	6
○ Vernaccia di S. Gimignano Fiore '07	▽▽	4*
○ Vernaccia di S. Gimignano Tradizionale '07	▽▽	4*
○ Vernaccia di S. Gimignano Tradizionale '06	▽▽	4*

★ Montevertine

LOC. MONTEVERTINE
53017 RADDA IN CHIANTI [SI]
TEL. 0577738009
www.montevertine.it

PRE-BOOKED VISITS

ANNUAL PRODUCTION 75,000 bottles
HECTARES UNDER VINE 15
VITICULTURE METHOD Conventional

Montevertine is a legend in its own time. It has enormous vision and is always one step ahead with a canny knack for predicting the all right moves. Le Pergole Torte is the emblematic wine both of this estate belonging to the Manetti family and of quality that speaks of the Chianti Classico territory, true to itself since its launch in 1971, ever modern and ever unique.

The '07 is another magnificent vintage for Le Pergole Torte. Graceful notes of dried flowers and fresh red strawberry and forest fruits red berries mingle with hints of iron filings and pencil lead on the nose. The palate is sharpish and appealing, showing soft yet taut, and the style is never forgotten once tasted. A very long, triumphant finish rounds off this stunning Three Glass winner. The '07 Montevertine is by design even more insubstantial, almost evasive, in style but its brightness and brilliance make it an absolute gem, its aromas recalling flowers, arbutus and mountain herbs. The Pian del Ciampolo '08 has a big palate, excellent progression and a delicate finish.

● Le Pergole Torte '07	TTT+	8
● Montevertine '07	TT	6
● Pian del Ciampolo '08	TT	4
● Le Pergole Torte '04	YYY	8
● Le Pergole Torte '03	YYY	8
● Le Pergole Torte '01	YYY	8
● Le Pergole Torte '99	YYY	8
● Le Pergole Torte '92	YYY	8
● Montevertine '04	YYY	6
● Montevertine '01	YYY	6

Moris Farms

LOC. CURA NUOVA
FATTORIA POGGETTI
58024 MASSA MARITTIMA [GR]
TEL. 0566918010
www.morisfarms.it

CELLAR SALES
PRE-BOOKED VISITS
ROOMS

ANNUAL PRODUCTION 400,000 bottles
HECTARES UNDER VINE 71
VITICULTURE METHOD Conventional

Adolfo Parentini, now flanked by his son Giulio, has steered Moris Farms firmly to the position it enjoys today. What with Fattoria Poggetti in the Monteregio di Massa Marittima DOC and Poggio la Mozza in the Morellino di Scansano DOCG, they farm quite a few hectares of vines. The Parentinis owe much of their success to the Avvoltore, which debuted with the 1988 version. Over the years, it has grown to develop a sound, confident style, keeping pace with the evolution of its vineyard of origin, Poggio all'Avvoltore.

The Avvoltore '07 comes from a blend of sangiovese, cabernet sauvignon and syrah, proffering aromas of ripe fruit and Mediterranean scrub. It has dense tannic texture and rather too many toasty sensations, but shows lovely acidity that lends it succulence and energy. We also liked the Morellino Riserva '07 with its warm aromas and lovely mouthfeel. The rest of the range is reliable.

● Avvoltore '07	TT	6
● Morellino di Scansano Ris. '07	TT	5
● Monteregio di Massa Marittima Rosso '07	T	4
● Morellino di Scansano '09	T	4
● Avvoltore '06	YYY	6
● Avvoltore '04	YYY	6
● Avvoltore '01	YYY	6
● Avvoltore '00	YYY	6
● Avvoltore '99	YYY	6
● Morellino di Scansano '08	YY	4
● Morellino di Scansano Ris. '06	YY	5
● Morellino di Scansano Ris. '05	YY	5

La Mormoraia

LOC. SANT'ANDREA, 15
53037 SAN GIMIGNANO [SI]
TEL. 0577940096
www.mormoraia.it

ELLAR SALES
PRE-BOOKED VISITS
ROOMS

ANNUAL PRODUCTION 170,000 bottles
HECTARES UNDER VINE 30
VITICULTURE METHOD Conventional

Over the years, the Passoni family from Milan has fashioned a small corner of paradise at La Mormoraia, taking the old farm buildings and transforming them into a state-of-the-art cellar. Here, they are realizing their dream of producing great wines from their 30 hectares of vineyards nestling in one of the most beautiful panoramas in the world. Indeed, their Vernaccia Riserva has long been a point of reference for the territory.

The magnificent Riserva '08 is no exception. It lays out all its fullness and complexity right from the start as hints of medicinal herbs and vanilla on the nose underscore the clean, clear fruity aromas that echo confidently and lingeringly across the palate. The Vernaccia '09 is savoury, fresh and juicy. The Ostrea Grigia '09, a vernaccia and sauvignon mix, is always interesting and shows lovely mineral richness. In anticipation of the reds that require a longer period of ageing, we tasted an excellent Syrah '08, fresh, full and spicy, and a pleasantly refreshing, fruity San Gimignano Sangiovese '07.

○ Vernaccia di S. Gimignano Ris. '08	▼▼	5
○ Ostrea Grigia '09	▼▼	4
● Syrah '08	▼▼	4*
○ Vernaccia di S. Gimignano '09	▼▼	4
● San Gimignano Sangiovese '07	▼	4
● Chianti Colli Senesi '08	▽▽	4*
● Chianti Colli Senesi '07	▽▽	4*
● Mitylus '06	▽▽	6
● Mitylus '05	▽▽	6
● Neitea '07	▽▽	5
● Neitea '06	▽▽	5
● San Gimignano Merlot '07	▽▽	5
● San Gimignano Merlot '06	▽▽	5
○ Vernaccia di S. Gimignano Ris. '07	▽▽	5
○ Vernaccia di S. Gimignano Ris. '06	▽▽	5

Tenute Niccolai - Palagetto

VIA MONTEOLIVETO, 46
53037 SAN GIMIGNANO [SI]
TEL. 0577943090
www.tenuteniccolai.it

CELLAR SALES
PRE-BOOKED VISITS
ROOMS

ANNUAL PRODUCTION 350,000 bottles
HECTARES UNDER VINE 100
VITICULTURE METHOD Conventional

Luano Niccolai, a successful entrepreneur who grew up in the country, is the driving force behind Tenute Niccolai. Feeling the urge to go back to these roots, he founded this, the first hub, in San Gimignano. Today, the estate also has properties in the zones of Montecucco and in Montalcino. Luano's daughter Sabrina and her husband Mario now run things on the agricultural side and also manage the agriturismo and the olive growing. The San Gimignano property has its own olive press.

The many labels presented show very well-styled palates with aromas that have yet to define themselves in terms of clarity and cleanliness. However, it is very clear that the quality of the fruit is very high and this promises excellent results. The cream of the crop this year is the Vernaccia Riserva '06. Its austere nose unfurls notes of honey, dried flowers and pineapple jam, and soft body showing lovely density, strong acid backbone and a mouthwatering finish. From the whites, we liked the I'Niccolò '09 from vermentino, chardonnay and sauvignon for its refreshing aromas of aromatic herbs and fresh, enjoyable palate.

○ Vernaccia di S. Gimignano Ris. '06	▼▼	5
○ I'Niccolò '09	▼	5
● Montecucco Rosso Solleone Pian de' Cerri '07	▼	4
● San Gimignano Sangiovese Uno di Quattro '07	▼	4
● San Gimignano Sottobosco '06	▼	5
● San Gimignano Syrah Uno di Quattro '06	▼	4
○ Vernaccia di S. Gimignano Il Palagetto '09	▼	3
○ Vernaccia di S. Gimignano V. Santa Chiara '09	▼	4
● Brunello di Montalcino La Bellarina '03	▽▽	7
● San Gimignano Sottobosco '05	▽▽	5
● San Gimignano Sottobosco '03	▽▽	5
● San Gimignano Syrah Uno di Quattro '05	▽▽	7
○ Vernaccia di S. Gimignano Ris. '02	▽▽	4
○ Vernaccia di S. Gimignano Ris. '01	▽▽	4

Fattoria Nittardi

LOC. NITTARDI
53011 CASTELLINA IN CHIANTI [SI]
TEL. 0577740269
www.nittardi.com

CELLAR SALES
PRE-BOOKED VISITS

ANNUAL PRODUCTION 90,000 bottles
HECTARES UNDER VINE 29
VITICULTURE METHOD Conventional

Fattoria di Nittardi numbers Michelangelo Buonarroti among its previous owners and is rightly considered part of the region's heritage. It now belongs to the Fermfert Canali family, who have given a real boost to the winemaking, cultural and artistic capacities of this stunning estate. The house, cellar and vineyards lie in a natural rift of rare, entrancing beauty. The modern, characterful wines adhere to a philosophy of fullness and stylistic precision combined with depth and personality.

This is a great year for the Chianti Classico Casanova di Nittardi '08, a deep, chewily delicious wine with sensations that move from classic red fruit aromas to greener notes that sometimes overstep the line into grassiness. The Riserva '07 is first-class. Nectar Dei '07 from cabernet, merlot and syrah is good but still needs to find balance as its oak tends to overwhelm it at the moment. Ad Astra '07 from the Maremma is better integrated from this point of view.

● Ad Astra '07	▼▼	5
● Chianti Cl. Casanuova di Nittardi '08	▼▼	5
● Chianti Cl. Ris. '07	▼▼	7
● Nectar Dei '07	▼▼	7
● Chianti Cl. Ris. '98	▽▽▽	7
● Chianti Cl. Casanuova di Nittardi '06	▽▽	5
● Chianti Cl. Ris. '05	▽▽	7
● Chianti Cl. Ris. '04	▽▽	7
● Chianti Cl. Ris. '00	▽▽	7
● Chianti Cl. Ris. '99	▽▽	7
● Nectar Dei '06	▽▽	7
● Nectar Dei '05	▽▽	7
● Nectar Dei '03	▽▽	6

Nottola

FRAZ. GRACCIANO
VIA BIVIO DI NOTTOLA, 9A
53040 MONTEPULCIANO [SI]
TEL. 0578707060
www.cantinanottola.it

CELLAR SALES
PRE-BOOKED VISITS
ROOMS AND FOOD

ANNUAL PRODUCTION 135,000 bottles
HECTARES UNDER VINE 23
VITICULTURE METHOD Conventional

Founded in 1992, Nottola is owned by Giuliano Giomarelli, who has just finished reorganizing the whole estate. This restructuring is already bearing fruit and has swept away any doubts that may have lingered in the past to place it squarely among the best artisan wine producers. The wines are well made and have an approach that favours balance and drinkability. The grapes are cultivated with care and there is no forcing or exaggeration in the cellar.

The Anterivo '07, a sangiovese and merlot blend, is a Supertuscan with concentrated but not too heavy aromas and a dynamic, poised palate showing good structure. The Nobile '07 has a generous, clean nose and a tasty, eminently drinkable palate. The Rosso di Montepulciano '08 is perhaps one of the best of its kind, a richly extracted wine with a bright, delicious flavour. PerGloria '09, a white obtained from a novel blend of vermentino and pinot bianco, is enjoyable. The '05 Vin Santo is austere and anything but cloying.

● Anterivo '07	▼▼	6
● Nobile di Montepulciano '07	▼▼	5
● Rosso di Montepulciano '08	▼▼	4
○ PerGloria '09	▼	3
○ Vinsanto di Montepulciano '05	▼	6
● Nobile di Montepulciano '03	▽▽	5
● Nobile di Montepulciano '02	▽▽	5
● Nobile di Montepulciano V. del Fattore '02	▽▽	5
● Rosso di Montepulciano '05	▽▽	4

Podere Orma

via Bolgherese
57022 Castagneto Carducci [LI]
tel. 0575477857
www.tenutasetteponti.it

ANNUAL PRODUCTION 26,000 bottles
HECTARES UNDER VINE 5
VITICULTURE METHOD Conventional

In just a few short years, the high-profile style of Antonio Moretti's Bolgheri estate has carved a prominent, well-respected niche for itself in this very prestigious wine area. Production is limited, the vineyards face south-west, and the deep earth is made up of pebbles and clay. His other estates – Tenuta Setteponti also in Tuscany and Feudo Maccari in Sicily – have their own profiles in this year's edition of the Guide.

The Orma '07, obtained from its usual blend of equal parts cabernet franc and merlot, is a magnificent benchmark red for the territory. Elegant and deep, it presents deliciously crunchy fruit and a graceful yet full-bodied palate of wondrous profundity and a wealth of light and dark tones. The Three Glass award was a formality.

● Orma '07	3 glasses (black)	7
● Orma '06	3 glasses (white)	7
● Orma '05	2 glasses (white)	7

★ Tenuta dell'Ornellaia

fraz. Bolgheri
via Bolgherese, 191
57022 Castagneto Carducci [LI]
tel. 056571811
www.ornellaia.it

PRE-BOOKED VISITS

ANNUAL PRODUCTION 730,000 bottles
HECTARES UNDER VINE 97
VITICULTURE METHOD Conventional

Tenuta dell'Ornellaia is the embodiment of an ideal, a tribute to Italian wine that stands with the very best players on the international stage. Founded in 1981, its vineyards and cellar are located on the properties of Ornellaia and Bellaria, north-west of Bolgheri. These terrains comprise alluvial, volcanic and marine soil and the varieties cultivated are the classic grape types of the zone. The wines are truly exceptional.

Our pick of this year's crop is the extraordinary '07 version of the Ornellaia. Three instant, outstanding Glasses. Very young as yet, it already fascinates with its delicious aromas of coffee beans and black cherries laced with subtle grassy, spicy nuances that frame a rich, creamy palate with incomparable texture and never-ending length. The Masseto '07 also gives a fine performance, even if it is a tad over-exuberant in its toastiness and a little unruly in its tannins. The excellent Bolgheri Rosso Serre Nuove '08 is warm and embracing, just a step behind the '08 Le Volte.

● Bolgheri Sup. Ornellaia '07	3 glasses (black)	8
● Masseto '07	2 glasses (black)	8
● Bolgheri Rosso Serre Nuove '08	2 glasses (black)	7
● Le Volte '08	1 glass (black)	4
● Bolgheri Sup. Ornellaia '02	3 glasses (white)	8
● Bolgheri Sup. Ornellaia '01	3 glasses (white)	8
● Bolgheri Sup. Ornellaia '99	3 glasses (white)	8
● Bolgheri Sup. Ornellaia '98	3 glasses (white)	8
● Bolgheri Sup. Ornellaia '97	3 glasses (white)	8
● Masseto '04	3 glasses (white)	8
● Masseto '01	3 glasses (white)	8
● Masseto '00	3 glasses (white)	8
● Masseto '99	3 glasses (white)	8
● Masseto '98	3 glasses (white)	8
● Masseto '97	3 glasses (white)	8
● Masseto '95	3 glasses (white)	8
● Masseto '94	3 glasses (white)	8

Siro Pacenti

LOC. PELAGRILLI, 1
53024 MONTALCINO [SI]
TEL. 0577848662
pacentisiro@libero.it

PRE-BOOKED VISITS

ANNUAL PRODUCTION 80,000 bottles
HECTARES UNDER VINE 20
VITICULTURE METHOD Conventional

Giancarlo Pacenti's avant-garde cellar has long been a point of reference for Brunello aficionados. His ongoing experiments with casks and vinification techniques provide a sounding board for the entire territory. One of the first champions of barrique-ageing, Giancarlo was also one of the first to appreciate the importance of diversifying his sources of grapes and to this end acquired several hectares on the south-east slopes. Even his fermenting vats are carefully researched and he developed them himself.

The big news this year from this estate is the presentation of a new wine, the Brunello PS '04. Ruby in appearance, it proffers very fresh cherry-led fruit aromas before the refined palate unfolds with sustained acidity that tends to tail off slightly in the finish. All in all, a classic example of a wine from these northern zones. Immensely elegant tannins and good length complete the picture. The first-class Rosso di Montalcino '08 shows intense fruity notes with faint spicy, balsamic hints. The palate is edgy but continuous, extremely close-knit and has a long, lingering finish.

● Brunello di Montalcino PS '04	2 black glasses	8
● Rosso di Montalcino '08	2 black glasses	6
● Brunello di Montalcino '05	2 black glasses	8
● Brunello di Montalcino Ris. '04	1 black glass	8
● Brunello di Montalcino '97	3 white glasses	8
● Brunello di Montalcino '96	3 white glasses	8
● Brunello di Montalcino '95	3 white glasses	8
● Brunello di Montalcino '88	3 white glasses	8
● Brunello di Montalcino '04	2 white glasses	8
● Brunello di Montalcino '03	2 white glasses	8
● Brunello di Montalcino '01	2 white glasses	8

Fattoria Il Palagio

FRAZ. CASTEL SAN GIMIGNANO
LOC. IL PALAGIO
53030 COLLE DI VAL D'ELSA [SI]
TEL. 0577953192
www.ilpalagio.com

CELLAR SALES
PRE-BOOKED VISITS

ANNUAL PRODUCTION 500,000 bottles
HECTARES UNDER VINE 90
VITICULTURE METHOD Conventional

This Tuscan estate was annexed to the Zonins' empire in 1979. Once the property of the Marchesi Tortoli Matteucci, it extends over approximately 350 hectares and includes 15 hectares of olive groves in addition to those planted to vine. Local varieties vernaccia and sangiovese account for the lion's share, but there are also international grape types, mainly destined for their whites. The wines from Maremma, such as the Morellino di Scansano, are sold under the same label.

This year, the all-sangiovese '07 Arnolfo di Cambio rules the roost. Austere and dark on the nose, it opens out to reveal gorgeous fruit notes. Entry on the palate is not huge but gradually develops into a lingering embrace, signing off with an appealingly long finish. The Vernaccia Le Ginestrelle '09 shows clean, offering subtle notes of white peach and pineapple perked up by lively refreshing acidity. The remaining two whites are a bit more predictable: Chioppaia '09, a Chardonnay, and the '09 Melaia, a Sauvignon that has more marked acidity.

● Arnolfo di Cambio '07	2 black glasses	5
○ Vernaccia di San Gimignano Le Ginestrelle '09	2 black glasses	4*
● Chianti Cellini '08	1 black glass	3
○ Chioppaia '09	1 black glass	4
○ Melaia '09	1 black glass	3
● Arnolfo di Cambio '03	2 white glasses	5
○ Il Palagio Sauvignon '06	2 white glasses	4
○ Il Palagio Sauvignon '05	2 white glasses	4
○ Il Palagio Sauvignon '03	2 white glasses	4
○ Il Palagio Sauvignon '02	2 white glasses	4*
○ Il Palagio Sauvignon '01	2 white glasses	3*
○ Il Palagio Sauvignon '00	2 white glasses	3*
○ Vernaccia di S. Gimignano La Gentilesca '01	2 white glasses	4

La Palazzetta

FRAZ. CASTELNUOVO DELL'ABATE
VIA BORGO DI SOTTO
53020 MONTALCINO [SI]
TEL. 0577835631
www.palazzettafanti.com

CELLAR SALES
PRE-BOOKED VISITS
ROOMS

ANNUAL PRODUCTION 50,000 bottles
HECTARES UNDER VINE 11
VITICULTURE METHOD Conventional

In the short time since he started bottling in 1988, Flavio Fanti has positioned his estate well. Shy and reserved, he produces wines much like himself that need time to open out and show their true personality. The vineyards stand in a single block around the cellar where they are easy to manage. The soil is pebbly and moderately loose-packed. Flavio's cellar is Spartan, containing the bare minimum, including ten and 25-hectolitre barrels for maturing the Brunello and 900-litre casks for the Rosso.

The wines put on a fine show with the Brunello Riserva '04 picking up Three Glasses. The fruity, classic nose offers notes of morello and wild cherry, ripe blackberry and a gorgeous balsamic vein laced with sweet tobacco. The entry is confident, leaving little room for sweetness, the tannins are elegant but discernible, well supported by the acidity as the palate powers into a very long finish. The Rosso di Montalcino '08 is also first-class, flaunting the sweet, spicy legacy of its cask-conditioning without detracting from the clear notes of red berry fruit.

● Brunello di Montalcino Ris. '04	🍷🍷	8
● Brunello di Montalcino '05	🍷🍷	6
● Rosso di Montalcino '08	🍷🍷	4
● Brunello di Montalcino Ris. '97	🍷🍷🍷	8
● Brunello di Montalcino '04	🍷🍷	6
● Brunello di Montalcino '03	🍷🍷	7
● Brunello di Montalcino Visconti '04	🍷🍷	7

Marchesi Pancrazi Tenuta di Bagnolo

FRAZ. BAGNOLO
VIA MONTALESE, 156
50045 MONTEMURLO [PO]
TEL. 0574652439
www.pancrazi.it

CELLAR SALES
PRE-BOOKED VISITS

ANNUAL PRODUCTION 12,000 bottles
HECTARES UNDER VINE 6
VITICULTURE METHOD Conventional

The Marchesi Pancrazi operation owns two estates in the Prato area, a villa in Bagnolo and a farm in San Donato. The first rather accidentally became home to pinot nero but it has revealed a potential hitherto unsuspected in this zone. At San Donato, the winery has relaunched colorino, an indigenous variety that had long been marginalized but has now come back into favour with a large number of producers.

Only one Pinot Nero, the '08, was offered for tasting. Its fascinating, complex nose melds blueberries and currants with very intense sensations of cinnamon and clove. Entry on the palate is expansive but not sensuous, full with no sign of tannic coarseness, and has a long, lip-smacking finish. The San Donato '08, also from pinot nero with gamay, is a pleasant, approachable wine with very assertive aromas of cherry and strawberry, the odd trace of aromatic herbs and a rich, tasty palate. Tuscany rarely provides us with a rosé like Villa di Bagnolo '09. It presents a lovely combination of flowery and forest fruit aromas and a generous, mouthwateringly savoury palate.

● Pinot Nero Villa di Bagnolo '08	🍷🍷	6
⊙ Pinot Nero Villa di Bagnolo Rosato '09	🍷🍷	4
● San Donato '08	🍷🍷	4
● Pinot Nero Villa di Bagnolo '07	🍷🍷	6
● Pinot Nero Villa di Bagnolo '04	🍷🍷	7
● Pinot Nero Villa di Bagnolo '01	🍷🍷	6

Giovanni Panizzi

FRAZ. SANTA MARGHERITA
LOC. RACCIANO, 34
53037 SAN GIMIGNANO [SI]
TEL. 0577941576
www.panizzi.it

CELLAR SALES
PRE-BOOKED VISITS
ROOMS

ANNUAL PRODUCTION 300,000 bottles
HECTARES UNDER VINE 67
VITICULTURE METHOD Conventional

Once again Panizzi swept the board, this time with the Vernaccia Riserva '07. Giovanni Panizzi stays on as director, although the ownership has changed hands. His decision pays tribute to the work he has done over the years, first as a grower and then as president of the consortium, to relaunch the image of a wine teetering on the brink of obscurity. He teased out unsuspected potential from this variety, including ageability. We have a new line of reasonably priced single-variety reds.

The '07 Riserva is notable for its broad-ranging, varied aromas that mingle fruit with flowery and spicy nuances. The body is elegant yet not evanescent, balanced, and impressively long. Matured in large wood, the Vernaccia Evoè '07 also shows well. It's a bit more mainstream in its aromas of almond and flowers, and exhibits powerful but not excessive structure on the long, tangy palate. The Vigna Santa Margherita '09 selection stands out for its elegance and poise, unfurling a range of aromas that is both refined yet assertive.

○ Vernaccia di S. Gimignano Ris. '07	▼▼▼	6
○ Vernaccia di S. Gimignano Evoè '07	▼▼	5
○ Vernaccia di San Gimignano V. Santa Margherita '09	▼▼	4
● Cabernet Sauvignon '09	▼	3
⊙ Ceraso Rosa '09	▼	3
● Chianti Colli Senesi Vertunno Ris. '07	▼	4
● Merlot '09	▼	3
⊙ Rosato '09	▼	3
● Rosso di Montalcino '08	▼	4
○ Vernaccia di S. Gimignano '09	▼	4
○ Vernaccia di S. Gimignano Ris. '05	▽▽▽	6
○ Vernaccia di S. Gimignano Ris. '98	▽▽▽	6
○ Vernaccia di S. Gimignano Ris. '06	▽▽	6
○ Vernaccia di San Gimignano V. Santa Margherita '07	▽▽	4*
○ Vernaccia di San Gimignano V. Santa Margherita '05	▽▽	4

Tenuta La Parrina

FRAZ. ALBINIA
S.DA VICINALE DELLA PARRINA
58010 ORBETELLO [GR]
TEL. 0564862636
www.parrina.it

PRE-BOOKED VISITS
ROOMS AND FOOD

ANNUAL PRODUCTION 200,000 bottles
HECTARES UNDER VINE 55
VITICULTURE METHOD Certified organic

La Parrina, owned by Franca Spinola, extends over an impressive 450 hectares along the Tyrrhenian coast in a glorious setting. Out of this total, 55 hectares are planted to sangiovese, cabernet sauvignon, merlot, trebbiano, vermentino, ansonica, chardonnay and sauvignon. In addition to ripening the grapes to perfection, the Mediterranean climate gives their wines a distinctive character.

La Parrina's wines are always well made. This year, we were particularly taken by the '08 Radaia, a pure Merlot and the estate's first vineyard selection. Fruity tones of very ripe blackberries and raspberries dominate the nose, where oaky notes are still in evidence. The palate is full and caressing, although the tannins have yet to smooth out completely. The Parrina Rosso Muraccio '09 from sangiovese also gives a good performance. Fresh aromas of red berry fruit and grass are the prelude to a juicy, very drinkable palate with a clean finish. The Ansonica '09 is a flower-themed easy drinker.

○ Ansonica Costa dell'Argentario '09	▼▼	4
● Parrina Rosso Muraccio '08	▼▼	4
● Radaia '08	▼▼	7
● Parrina Rosso '09	▼	4
○ Vermentino '09	▼	4
● Radaia '07	▽▽	7
● Radaia '06	▽▽	7
● Radaia '04	▽▽	7

Petra

LOC. SAN LORENZO ALTO, 131
57028 SUVERETO [LI]
TEL. 0565845308
www.petrawine.it

CELLAR SALES
PRE-BOOKED VISITS

ANNUAL PRODUCTION 310,000 bottles
HECTARES UNDER VINE 98
VITICULTURE METHOD Conventional

This beautiful Suvereto estate belongs to the Terra Moretti Group and is run by Francesca, Vittorio's daughter. The 100 hectares of vineyard are dedicated to producing wines of absolute quality. They enjoy Mediterranean site climates and are home to mainly sangiovese, cabernet sauvignon, merlot, a bit of syrah and alicante, and the white malvasia, trebbiano, clarette and vermentino for the sweet wine.

The range offered by Petra is good as ever and the flagship Petra '07 from cabernet sauvignon and merlot graced our finals. Its generous, embracing nose is led by ripe red and black berry fruit, jammy notes of the berries, hints of balsam and delicate traces of oak. The palate is similar in style: concentrated, succulent, soft and seductive. It could do with a touch more acid backbone, though. The Quercegobbe '07 from 100 per cent merlot has a spicy nose with mature notes and hints of grilled peppers before the palate shows still rather clenched tannins. Val di Cornia Ebo '07 from sangiovese, cabernet sauvignon and merlot is fragrant and fruity.

● Petra Rosso '07	▼▼	8
● Quercegobbe '07	▼▼	7
● Val di Cornia Ebo '07	▼▼	4
● Petra Rosso '04	▽▽▽	8
● Petra Rosso '06	▽▽	8
● Quercegobbe '06	▽▽	7
● Quercegobbe '05	▽▽	7

★ Fattoria Petrolo

FRAZ. MERCATALE VALDARNO
LOC. GALATRONA
VIA PETROLO, 30
52021 BUCINE [AR]
TEL. 0559911322
www.petrolo.it

ROOMS

ANNUAL PRODUCTION 60,000 bottles
HECTARES UNDER VINE 31
VITICULTURE METHOD Conventional

A star for Luca Saintjust's estate. For the tenth time, it scales the dizzying Three Glass heights with just one wine. Luca's adventure started with merlot, which is perfectly at home on the gentle slopes of Petrolo. The secret of his success lies in his quest for beauty, for sheer exquisiteness as a way of life. The Boggina is living proof of this, not that we need any. Named for its vineyard, this Sangiovese is produced in extremely limited quantities and is sadly difficult to get your hands on.

But the real revelation this year is the '01 San Petrolo, a sort of evolution of Vin Santo with lower alcohol and taut acidity. It's an absolute masterpiece. The Galatrona '08 is a thoroughbred. It presents a generous nose mingling forest fruit with chocolate and spice as well as some fresh notes to lend it elegance. Entry on the palate is velvety, full and weighty, with sharp acidity that ensures unexpected length. The Boggina '07 is still a bit rigid but shows indisputable character. Torrione '08, a pure Sangiovese, is always enjoyable.

● Galatrona '08	▼▼▼	8
○ San Petrolo '01	▼▼	8
● Boggina '07	▼▼	8
● Torrione '08	▼▼	6
● Galatrona '07	▽▽▽	8
● Galatrona '06	▽▽▽	8
● Galatrona '05	▽▽▽	8
● Galatrona '04	▽▽▽	7
● Galatrona '01	▽▽▽	8
● Galatrona '00	▽▽▽	8
● Galatrona '99	▽▽▽	7
● Galatrona '98	▽▽▽	7

Piaggia

LOC. POGGETTO
VIA CEGOLI, 47
59016 POGGIO A CAIANO [PO]
TEL. 0558705401
www.piaggia.com

ANNUAL PRODUCTION 75,000 bottles
HECTARES UNDER VINE 15
VITICULTURE METHOD Conventional

Mauro Vannucchi runs this estate together with his daughter Silvia. They picked up another Three Glasses this year, an exceptional result if you consider the small size of the property and the consistently high level of quality. The estate takes its name from the vineyard from which it was launched and the wines have undergone an interesting stylistic change from concentrated, mature, almost opulent products to territorial. The lovely richness on the palate has remained unchanged.

The laurel wreath goes to the Carmignano Riserva '07. Still intense ruby in colour, it has a complex cornucopia of aromas, starting with dried flowers and forest fruits to move on to nuances of pepper and juniper. Entry on the palate is warm and enveloping with plush tannins nicely distributed across the structure and a long, lingering, very alluring finish. The Carmignano Sasso '08 also shows very well. The nose hints at more balsamic, minty tones over a fruity base of cherry then the palate is full-bodied and well-balanced with a refreshing acid vein and a juicy finish.

● Carmignano Ris. '07	▼▼▼	6
● Carmignano Sasso '08	▼▼	5
● Carmignano Ris. '99	YYY	6
● Carmignano Ris. '98	YYY	6
● Carmignano Ris. '97	YYY	5
● Carmignano Sasso '07	YYY	5
● Il Sasso '01	YYY	5
● Carmignano Ris. '06	YY	6
● Carmignano Ris. '05	YY	6
● Carmignano Ris. '04	YY	6
● Carmignano Sasso '06	YY	5
● Carmignano Sasso '05	YY	5
● Carmignano Sasso '04	YY	5

Piancornello

LOC. PIANCORNELLO
53024 MONTALCINO [SI]
TEL. 0577844105
piancorello@libero.it

CELLAR SALES
PRE-BOOKED VISITS

ANNUAL PRODUCTION 50,000 bottles
HECTARES UNDER VINE 10
VITICULTURE METHOD Conventional

Claudio Monaci, a calm, sensitive man, runs the family estate with passion. His ten hectares of vines lie deep in south-west Montalcino, just above the plain leading to Orcia. The sedimentary soil is full of marine fossils and pebbles, giving it a loose texture and good drainage. Despite the small cellar, Claudio moves easily through the barriques stacked two or three high. Vinification is carried out in stainless steel and a small part in oak, and malolactic fermentation is directly in the barrique.

The Rosso di Montalcino '08 is great. The nose reveals strong fruity notes of wild and morello cherries and blackberries with faint balsamic undertones. The generous palate is perked up by acidity that lingers on through the long finish. The Brunello Riserva '04 is a complex wine. The impressively structured palate is nicely buttressed by abundant tannins and surprising acidity while the nose foregrounds curious evolved sensations. There is no Brunello '05: Claudio opted not to produce it as he didn't deem the growing year good enough.

● Rosso di Montalcino '08	▼▼	4*
● Brunello di Montalcino Ris. '04	▼▼	8
● Brunello di Montalcino '99	YYY	7
● Brunello di Montalcino '04	YY	7
● Brunello di Montalcino '03	YY	7
● Brunello di Montalcino '01	YY	7
● Brunello di Montalcino '00	YY	7
● Brunello di Montalcino '97	YY	7
● Brunello di Montalcino '96	YY	6
● Brunello di Montalcino Piancornello '03	YY	7
● Brunello di Montalcino Ris. '01	YY	7
● Rosso di Montalcino '05	YY	4
● Rosso di Montalcino '03	YY	5

Fattoria di Piazzano

VIA DI PIAZZANO, 5
50053 EMPOLI [FI]
TEL. 0571994032
www.fattoriadipiazzano.it

CELLAR SALES
PRE-BOOKED VISITS
ROOMS AND FOOD

ANNUAL PRODUCTION 75,000 bottles
HECTARES UNDER VINE 34
VITICULTURE METHOD Conventional

The Fattoria di Piazzano has been in the Becattini family since 1948. Its founder, Otello, was an industrialist from Prato. He retired here to become a farmer and indulge his passion for astronomy in the observatory he built on the estate. The origins of this place go back to the Palaeolithic era and the name Piazzano derives from the Roman occupation of the territory of Empoli. As well as vines, the estate grows various types of olives and produces honey.

We were offered a broad range of labels to taste this year. The single-variety Colorino '08 offers fresh, grassy aromas, notes of black berry fruit including plum and blackberry, solid body with vibrant tannins, a well-managed acid vein and a finish that builds. The Ventoso '09 from sangiovese with malvasia nera and canaiolo is an enjoyable wine notable for the clarity of its aromas and a pleasing mouthfeel thanks to its soft, tight body with well-integrated supporting acidity. The Chiantis are deliciously drinkable.

● Colorino '08	3*
● Ventoso '09	3*
● Chianti '09	3
● Chianti Rio Camerata Ris. '08	4
● Merlot '07	4
● Sangiovese '07	4
● Chianti '05	3*
● Chianti Ris. '98	4
● Piazzano Sangiovese '06	5
● Piazzano Syrah '06	5
● Piazzano Syrah '05	5

Tenute Piccini

LOC. PIAZZOLE, 25
53011 CASTELLINA IN CHIANTI [SI]
TEL. 057754011
www.tenutepiccini.it

PRE-BOOKED VISITS

ANNUAL PRODUCTION 10,000,000 bottles
HECTARES UNDER VINE 130
VITICULTURE METHOD Conventional

Tenute Piccini is one of Tuscany's largest estates. Founded by Angiolo in 1882 on seven hectares at Poggibonsi, it was his son Mario who launched it commercially when he took over in 1925 and started to export wine to France and Germany. In the 1960s, Pierangelo introduced new products. Today, Mario and Martina are at the helm and have consolidated the Piccini image, managing production on the properties of Villa al Cortile in Montalcino, Tenuta Moraia in Maremma and Valiano in Chianti Classico.

The Bolgheri '08 performs well, offering intense fruity aromas with hints of toastiness and mixed spice, a soft body with nice pressure and a warm, lip-smacking finish. We also liked Il Pacchia '09 produced in Maremma from sangiovese and merlot. It presents more mature but clean notes on the nose, a full, dense body with nice juicy progression and a rising finish. The Brunello di Montalcino '05 is austere and subtle, the Chianti Classico Riserva '06 is solid and the Saccente '07 from alicante with a little merlot is very enjoyable indeed.

● Bolgheri Rosso Pietracupa Tenuta Moraia '08	4*
● Il Pacchia Tenuta Moraia '09	3*
● Brunello di Montalcino Villa al Cortile '05	6
● Chianti Cl. Ris. Valiano '06	5
● Saccente Tenuta Moraia '07	3
● Brunello di Montalcino Villa al Cortile '03	6
● Chianti Cl. Ris. '05	4*

La Pieve

LOC. LA PIEVE
VIA SANTO STEFANO
50050 MONTAIONE [FI]
TEL. 0571697934
info@lapieve.net

CELLAR SALES
PRE-BOOKED VISITS
ROOMS

ANNUAL PRODUCTION 60,000 bottles
HECTARES UNDER VINE 18
VITICULTURE METHOD Certified organic

The Tognettis stride along, producing results that show they are going in the right direction. They consistently offer us a high-quality range from their 18 hectares of vineyards where they cultivate largely traditional grape types – sangiovese with some colorino, ciliegiolo and canaiolo – and also international varieties, which form the basis of their keynote wines. The estate features an agriturismo in the renovated old farm buildings.

Once again this year, the '08 Il Gobbo Nero from 100 per cent syrah is top dog. Its measured nose recalls pepper and mixed spice with very assertive cherry undertones. The palate shows well-rounded structure and develops steadily to reveal backbone and pleasant length. We also liked the Rosso del Pievano '07, this year based on a merlot-heavy blend with cabernet sauvignon and cabernet franc. It has fresh minty, balsamic aromas with notes of blueberry and currant. The palate displays soft, silky body with lovely tannic texture, a well-integrated acid vein and a juicy finish. Both Chiantis are agreeable, easy-drinking wines with subtle yet elegant aromas.

● Il Gobbo Nero '08	▼▼	4*
● Rosso del Pievano '07	▼▼	4*
● Chianti '09	▼	3
● Chianti Fortebraccio '08	▼	4
● Chianti '07	▽▽	3*
● Chianti '03	▽▽	3*
● Chianti '00	▽▽	2*
● Chianti Cl. La Pieve '06	▽▽	3*
● Chianti Cl. La Pieve '05	▽▽	3*
● Chianti Fortebraccio '01	▽▽	4*
● Il Gobbo Nero '07	▽▽	4*
● Rosso del Pievano '06	▽▽	4*
● Chianti Fortebraccio '06	▽	3*

Il Pinino

LOC. PODERE PININO, 327
53024 MONTALCINO [SI]
TEL. 0577849381
www.pinino.com

CELLAR SALES
PRE-BOOKED VISITS

ANNUAL PRODUCTION 85,000 bottles
HECTARES UNDER VINE 16
VITICULTURE METHOD Organic

Max Hernandez and Andrea Gamon, the two partners who own this estate, continue to work tirelessly. They have secured planning permission to build their new cellar and work is due to start in the new year. The 16 hectares have a fairly loose base of sandstone and clay. The only wines made are Montalcino designation products aged in medium-sized barrels of up to 30 hectolitres. The style is fairly traditional with fresh, fragrant fruit. This year sees a new recruit to the ranks, a brand new Brunello Riserva, Pinone.

The new boy debuted to a fanfare and earned a place on our final tasting table. Intense ruby in appearance, it offers a generous nose still somewhat in thrall to the oak but with gorgeous notes of sweet spice and faint balsamic tones. The fruity vein is very clear, however, and led by ripe notes of cherry, wild cherry and a touch of blackberry. The close-knit, smooth tannins render the palate succulent and good acidity supports development into a classy finish. Just one Rosso di Montalcino '08 was offered for tasting but it proved expansive with clear, fruity aromas.

● Brunello di Montalcino Pinone Ris. '04	▼▼	8
● Brunello di Montalcino '05	▼	7
● Rosso di Montalcino '08	▼	5
● Brunello di Montalcino '04	▽▽	7
● Brunello di Montalcino '02	▽▽	7
● Brunello di Montalcino Clandestino '04	▽▽	7
● Rosso di Montalcino '06	▽▽	4
● Rosso di Montalcino '05	▽▽	4
● Rosso di Montalcino '04	▽▽	4

Podere Fortuna

VIA SAN GIUSTO A FORTUNA, 7
50037 SAN PIERO A SIEVE [FI]
TEL. 0558487214
www.poderefortuna.com

CELLAR SALES
PRE-BOOKED VISITS

ANNUAL PRODUCTION 10,000 bottles
HECTARES UNDER VINE 6
VITICULTURE METHOD Organic

Alessandro Brogi placed no fewer than two wines in the finals this year. He has put his money on pinot nero, a variety favoured for growers who like risks, planting it in Tuscany's territory of Mugello before he really knew what it would do. In addition to the two Pinot Neros, we tasted a very unusual passito that bowled us over. Ten years after replanting his vineyards, Brogi can now make a careful selection, row by row in the Burgundy fashion. We expect to see more new labels in the future.

The Fortuni '07 has fresh fruity notes of currants and blueberries with hints of cherries and faint spicy nuances. Entry on the palate is broad, full and holds up well, with acid backbone lending lovely freshness into a clear, clean finish. Campo de' Tre Filari '07 is obtained from equal parts of petit manseng, sauvignon blanc, traminer aromatico and malvasia rosa. Intoxicating and seductive, its rich, flower and spice sensations accompany a smooth, full body, with good breadth and texture, and a long, satisfying finish.

○ Campo de' Tre Filari '07	2 (black)	7
● Fortuni '07	2 (black)	6
● Coldaia '07	2 (black)	6
● Pinot Nero Coldaia '06	2	6
● Pinot Nero Coldaia '05	2	6
● Pinot Nero Fortuni '06	2	6
● Pinot Nero Fortuni '05	2	6

Poggerino

LOC. POGGERINO
53017 RADDA IN CHIANTI [SI]
TEL. 0577738958
www.poggerino.com

CELLAR SALES
PRE-BOOKED VISITS
ROOMS

ANNUAL PRODUCTION 60,000 bottles
HECTARES UNDER VINE 10
VITICULTURE METHOD Organic

This estate, the property of the Lanza family since the 1940s, has undergone several transformations over the years in terms of land and vineyards. It is located in a very beautiful zone ideal for viticulture on the highest slopes of Radda, at an altitude of around 500 metres. The soil is a mix of clay and big chips of marl, the vines are farmed organically and the big, solid wines flaunt impressive extraction.

Elegant and close-woven on the nose with gorgeous black and red fruit sensations, the Chianti Classico '07 shows bags of personality and good nose-palate consistency, although it is a little disrupted by very close-knit, tight tannins that can be rather mouth-drying. The Riserva Bugialla '07 is obtained from old sangiovese vines and macerates for more than two months on the skins to acquire its fine character. The nose shows aromatic concentration and intensity, its wealth of fruity aromas enveloped in assertive toasty tones. The well-extracted palate is warm and full but with a vein of alcohol and copious tannins.

● Chianti Cl. '07	2 (black)	4
● Chianti Cl. Bugialla Ris. '07	2 (black)	6
● Primamateria '06	2 (black)	6
● Chianti Cl. Ris. '90	3	5
● Primamateria '01	3	6
● Chianti Cl. '06	2	4*
● Chianti Cl. '04	2	4
● Chianti Cl. '01	2	4
● Chianti Cl. Bugialla Ris. '04	2	6
● Chianti Cl. Bugialla Ris. '00	2	6
● Chianti Cl. Bugialla Ris. '99	2	6
● Primamateria '00	2	6
● Primamateria '99	2	5

Poggio al Sole

loc. Badia a Passignano
s.da Rignana, 2
50028 Tavarnelle Val di Pesa [FI]
tel. 0558071850
www.poggioalsole.com

CELLAR SALES
PRE-BOOKED VISITS
ROOMS

ANNUAL PRODUCTION 80,000 bottles
HECTARES UNDER VINE 16
VITICULTURE METHOD Conventional

A old Swiss winemaking family from the Bündner Herrschaft area, the Davaz have brought their decades of experience to bear in the Chianti Classico. The eldest son, Johannes, put in his time as a grower and cellarman before studying oenology and now runs the estate single-handed. The south-facing vineyards lie at altitudes of 320-480 metres and the cellar is highly efficient. The wines have a modern style that allows free reign to the characteristics of the territory and all have lovely, expressive appeal. Watch this space.

The Chianti Classico '08 gave a stellar performance. There's a trace of pear drops on the nose, with just a smidgeon too much sweetness, but after that it is an anthem to all the most wonderful elements of the DOCG. Notes of earth and rock, morello cherry and flowers; a deep palate, at times vertical and very sharp. Hats off to this Three Glass champ. The other wines also show well. Casasilia '07 is dynamic and delicious but still masked by toasty notes, the Syrah '08 is precise and coherent while the Cabernet '07 is lively with nicely integrated fruit.

● Chianti Cl. '08	🍷🍷🍷	5
● Cabernet Sauvignon '07	🍷🍷	7
● Chianti Cl. Casasilia '07	🍷🍷	7
● Syrah '08	🍷🍷	7
● Chianti Cl. Casasilia '99	🍸🍸🍸	7
● Chianti Cl. Casasilia '98	🍸🍸🍸	7
● Chianti Cl. Casasilia '97	🍸🍸🍸	7
● Syrah '99	🍸🍸🍸	7
● Chianti Cl. '07	🍸🍸	5
● Chianti Cl. '03	🍸🍸	5
● Chianti Cl. Casasilia '04	🍸🍸	7
● Syrah '05	🍸🍸	7
● Syrah '03	🍸🍸	7
● Syrah '01	🍸🍸	7

Poggio al Tesoro

loc. Felciaino
via Bolgherese, 189b
57022 Bolgheri [LI]
tel. 0565773051
www.poggioaltesoro.it

CELLAR SALES

ANNUAL PRODUCTION 192,000 bottles
HECTARES UNDER VINE 50
VITICULTURE METHOD Conventional

Poggio al Tesoro has many hectares under vine distributed across various plots and the soil is composed of red sand with plenty of pebbles. The Allegrini family, long-time producers of great Verona reds, own this estate in partnership with well-known importer, Leonardo Lo Cascio. If their wines are anything to go by, their Bolgheri joint venture has a bright future. In a few short years, their reds have already earned a reputation for quality.

This year, Cabernet Franc Dedicato a Walter '07 excelled itself. This highly distinctive red offers intense notes of balsam and eucalyptus that meld perfectly with a dense but varied base of black berry fruit veined with exquisite spicy nuances of sandalwood. The consistent palate shows magnificent fullness, perfect maturity and superb aromatic length. The rest of the range is good.

● Dedicato a Walter '07	🍷🍷	6
● Bolgheri Sondraia '07	🍷🍷	6
● Mediterra '08	🍷🍷	4
○ Bolgheri Bianco Solosole '09	🍷	4
⊙ Bolgheri Rosato Cassiopea '09	🍷	4
○ Bolgheri Bianco Solosole '08	🍸🍸	5
● Bolgheri Sondraia '06	🍸🍸	6
● Dedicato a Walter '06	🍸🍸	6
● Dedicato a Walter '05	🍸🍸	6
● Mediterra '07	🍸🍸	5

Poggio Antico

LOC. POGGIO ANTICO
53024 MONTALCINO [SI]
TEL. 0577848044
www.poggioantico.com

CELLAR SALES
PRE-BOOKED VISITS
FOOD

ANNUAL PRODUCTION 120,000 bottles
HECTARES UNDER VINE 32
VITICULTURE METHOD Organic

Paola Gloder and Poggio Antico are one and the same: the estate has grown with and thanks to her. Several years ago, the vineyards were completely replanted at high vine density, and the cellar was renovated to make room for temperature-controlled, truncated cone-shaped fermenting vats that are the perfect foil to the casks of varying sizes used to mature the Brunellos. The wines speak for themselves.

Paola saw no fewer than two of her wines on our final tasting table this year, both of them '05s. Of the two, we preferred the Brunello di Montalcino '05 and awarded it Three overflowing Glasses. Clean, clear, intense aromas of blackberry, cherry, tobacco and leather announce a traditional style. The palate is rich and harmonious with smooth tannins and lovely acidity, a legacy of its high-altitude plots of origin. The finish is very long and embracing. Brunello Altero '05 displays fresher notes of fruit and balsam, a sweet, juicy palate and an equally thrilling finish.

● Brunello di Montalcino '05	▼▼▼	7
● Brunello di Montalcino Altero '05	▼▼	7
● Brunello di Montalcino Ris. '04	▼	8
● Madre '07	▼	7
● Rosso di Montalcino '08	▼	5
● Brunello di Montalcino '88	YYY	7
● Brunello di Montalcino '85	YYY	7
● Brunello di Montalcino Altero '04	YYY	7
● Brunello di Montalcino Altero '99	YYY	7
● Brunello di Montalcino Ris. '01	YYY	8
● Brunello di Montalcino Ris. '85	YYY	8
● Brunello di Montalcino '04	YY	7
● Brunello di Montalcino Altero '03	YY	7
● Madre '06	YY	6
● Rosso di Montalcino '07	YY	5

Poggio Argentiera

LOC. ALBERESE
S.DA BANDITELLA, 2
58010 GROSSETO
TEL. 0564405099
www.poggioargentiera.com

CELLAR SALES
PRE-BOOKED VISITS

ANNUAL PRODUCTION 200,000 bottles
HECTARES UNDER VINE 42
VITICULTURE METHOD Conventional

Since its foundation in 1998, Gianpaolo Paglia's estate has managed its vineyards and cellar expertly to become one of the best producers in the Maremma. The wines have a clear-cut style that favours mature fruitiness, a good dose of oak and powerful structure, yet they are also nice and fresh. According to Paglia, however, this is all about to change, as he plans to replace almost all of his barriques with large ovals for the upcoming vintage.

The balanced, rich fruity notes of the Morellino di Scansano Capatosta '08 announce a full, juicy palate. Maremmante '09 from syrah and alicante is approachable and very agreeable with crisp aromas and measured, tasty progression. The '09 Morellino di Scansano Bellamarsilia presents delicate and at times muddled aromatics but it makes up for this on the fragrant, fruity palate. The '09 Guazza from ansonica and vermentino is simple and coherent.

● Maremmante '09	▼▼	4
● Morellino di Scansano Capatosta '08	▼▼	6
○ Guazza '09	▼	3
● Morellino di Scansano Bellamarsilia '09	▼	4
● Finisterre '07	YYY	7
● Morellino di Scansano Capatosta '00	YYY	6*
● Finisterre '06	YY	7
● Finisterre '05	YY	7
● Maremmante '07	YY	4*
● Morellino di Scansano Bellamarsilia '07	YY	4*
● Morellino di Scansano Bellamarsilia '06	YY	4
● Morellino di Scansano Capatosta '07	YY	6
● Morellino di Scansano Capatosta '06	YY	6
● Morellino di Scansano Capatosta '05	YY	6

Poggio Bonelli

VIA DELL'ARBIA, 2
53019 CASTELNUOVO BERARDENGA [SI]
TEL. 0577355382
www.poggiobonelli.it

CELLAR SALES
PRE-BOOKED VISITS
ROOMS AND FOOD

ANNUAL PRODUCTION 230,000 bottles
HECTARES UNDER VINE 85
VITICULTURE METHOD Conventional

This estate is now part of Monte Dei Paschi di Siena's agricultural portfolio but has had several owners down the years. In medieval times it belonged to the Spennali family, then the Piccolominis and Landuccis who ran it, first solo then with the Crocis, until the 20th century. Poggio Bonelli started making wine in the 16th century and has grown in importance over the years. Today, it also produces extra virgin olive oil and boasts agriturismo facilities. When the bank took it over, they replanted the vineyards and renovated part of the cellar and farm buildings.

The Poggiassai '07, a blend of sangiovese with a little cabernet sauvignon, earns itself a Three Glass crown for its refined, elegant nose offering fresh notes of forest fruit ennobled by hints of spice. The palate is pleasantly enveloping and full with tannins that show superb alcohol and measured depth of flavour. The finish is mouthwatering. The Riserva '07 is also very good, showing earthy, jammy aromas with undertones of aromatic herbs. Entry on the palate is good, the progression taut and supple with well-integrated acid backbone and lively length.

● Poggiassai '07	▼▼▼	6
● Chianti Cl. Ris. '07	▼▼	6
● Chianti Villa Chigi Saracini '09	▼	4
● Tramonto d'Oca '07	▼	6
○ Vin Santo del Chianti Cl. '01	▼	6
● Poggiassai '06	▽▽▽	6
● Chianti Cl. Ris. '06	▽▽	6
● Chianti Cl. Ris. '05	▽▽	6
● Chianti Cl. Ris. '03	▽▽	6
● Poggiassai '05	▽▽	6
● Tramonto d'Oca '04	▽▽	6
● Tramonto d'Oca '03	▽▽	6

Fattoria Poggio Capponi

LOC. SAN DONATO A LIVIZZANO
VIA MONTELUPO, 184
50025 MONTESPERTOLI [FI]
TEL. 0571671914
www.poggiocapponi.it

CELLAR SALES
PRE-BOOKED VISITS

ANNUAL PRODUCTION 200,000 bottles
HECTARES UNDER VINE 37
VITICULTURE METHOD Conventional

Fattoria Poggio Capponi was founded in the 1400s. The landscape has always been dominated by vines and olive trees, a truly stunning setting that also features cypresses and fields of wheat. It is so beautiful, in fact, that the Taviani brothers chose it for the setting of their film "La notte di San Lorenzo". The estate is happy to experiment, most recently with a new sparkling wine process that can be used for small batches and has been very successful with vermentino.

This year they offered a fine range of wines for us to taste. The Tinorso '08 from merlot and syrah has lovely fruity notes of cherry and forest fruit and a very dynamic body with smooth tannins. The Sovente '09, a barrique-matured Chardonnay, is good giving aromas of citrus and ripe fruit. The palate is enveloping but not overly so and the finish long and mouthwatering. The '09 Bianco di Binto from equal parts vermentino, trebbiano and chardonnay stands out for its elegant notes of aromatic herbs and spring flowers, fine but well-distributed palate and understated yet lingering finish.

○ Bianco di Binto '09	▼▼	3*
○ Sovente '09	▼▼	4*
● Tinorso '08	▼▼	5
● Chianti '09	▼	3
● Chianti Montespertoli Petriccio '08	▼	4
● Chianti Poggio Capponi '07	▽▽	3*
○ Sovente '06	▽▽	4
○ Sovente '04	▽▽	4
○ Sovente '03	▽▽	4
● Tinorso '06	▽▽	5
● Tinorso '05	▽▽	5
● Tinorso '04	▽▽	5
● Tinorso '02	▽▽	5

Poggio di Sotto

FRAZ. CASTELNUOVO DELL'ABATE
LOC. POGGIO DI SOTTO
53024 MONTALCINO [SI]
TEL. 0577835502
www.poggiodisotto.com

CELLAR SALES
PRE-BOOKED VISITS
ROOMS

ANNUAL PRODUCTION 45,000 bottles
HECTARES UNDER VINE 12
VITICULTURE METHOD Certified organic

Piero Palmucci is a brusque man little given to compromise and set firmly in his convictions. He continues to produce wines of enormous personality from his cellar, wines that embody the more traditional Brunello style. The vines in his well-tended vineyards have a very low yield and lie at varying altitudes in front of Mount Amiata, enabling optimal management of the growing years. All the wines are matured in large barrels of Slavonian oak.

The Rosso di Montalcino '07 thrilled us with its stylistic definition and personality, so much so that we awarded it Three Glasses. The nose is classic, revealing notes of ripe red berry fruit, leather, tobacco and medicinal herbs, while the already mature tannins are delicate and the acidity is dynamic, ensuring endless progression to an alluring, lingering finish. The '04 Brunello Riserva shows very well, if ever so slightly tired, presenting complex aromas of fruit jam, pipe tobacco and new-mown hay.

Wine	Glasses	
● Rosso di Montalcino '07	3 black	7
● Brunello di Montalcino Ris. '04	2 black	8
● Brunello di Montalcino '05	2 black	8
● Brunello di Montalcino '04	3 white +	8
● Brunello di Montalcino '99	3 white	8
● Brunello di Montalcino Ris. '99	3 white	8
● Brunello di Montalcino Ris. '95	3 white	8
● Brunello di Montalcino '03	2 white	8
● Brunello di Montalcino '01	2 white	8
● Rosso di Montalcino '06	2 white	7

Poggio Molina

LOC. POGGIO MOLINA
52021 BUCINE [AR]
TEL. 0559789402
www.poggiomolina.it

CELLAR SALES
PRE-BOOKED VISITS

ANNUAL PRODUCTION 60,000 bottles
HECTARES UNDER VINE 16
VITICULTURE METHOD Conventional

This zone has only recently been discovered in wine terms. This matters little to Claudio Bossini, whose modern estate in Val d'Ambra focuses on international varieties such as cabernet sauvignon, merlot and cabernet franc. Claudio produces pleasing wines that do not necessarily reflect the territory but are beautifully precise and carefully crafted. His 16 hectares of vines fan out around the main house that dates back to the early 1700s.

Once again, Le Caldie leads the pack, this time in the '07 edition. Obtained from almost pure merlot with a small amount of cabernet sauvignon and sangiovese, it exhibits very confident fruity notes of currants and blackberries enhanced by vanilla nuances. The soft body shows supporting acidity, delicate tannins and a mouthwatering finish. We liked the '07 Lo Scopaio from cabernet franc, merlot and sangiovese. The refreshing nose hints at cherry and mint while the edgy but balanced palate ends in a fresh, enjoyable finish. The Vinobono '08 from 100 per cent sangiovese is a good everyday wine and very pleasant indeed.

Wine	Glasses	
● Le Caldie '07	2 black	6
● Lo Scopaio '07	2 black	5
● Vinobono '08	1 black	4
● Le Caldie '06	2 white	6
● Le Caldie '04	2 white	6
● Lo Scopaio '06	2 white	5
● Lo Scopaio '05	2 white	5
● Vinobono '05	2 white	4*

Podere Poggio Scalette

LOC. RUFFOLI
VIA BARBIANO, 7
50022 GREVE IN CHIANTI [FI]
TEL. 0558546108
www.poggioscalette.it

PRE-BOOKED VISITS

ANNUAL PRODUCTION 45,000 bottles
HECTARES UNDER VINE 15
VITICULTURE METHOD Organic

The Fiore family embarked on its winemaking adventure in 1991. Prior to this paterfamilias Vittorio had been, and still is, oenologist to other estates. But desiring to set up on his own, he and his wife bought this near-derelict property, restored the buildings and expanded the area planted to vine. He works alongside his son, Jurj, another oenologist, who lavishes all his time and passion into the estate.

This year, the Fiores presented a new wine, the Capogatto '07, a blend of cabernet franc, sauvignon, merlot and petit verdot that departs from estate traditions. It mingles fresh herbaceousness with clear minerality over fruit. The body is delicate, balanced, long and pleasurable. The sangiovese Carbonaione '07 graced our finals with complex spicy aromas hinting at cinnamon and cloves. The ample body has good weight, precise, well-defined tannins and captivating length in the finish. The superb Piantonaia '07, a pure Merlot, also made the finals for its black berry fruit and aromatic herb, balsam-veined bouquet, smooth, firmly structured body and long, savoury palate.

● Il Carbonaione '07	▼▼	7
● Piantonaia '07	▼▼	8
● Capogatto '07	▼▼	7
● Il Carbonaione '05	▽▽▽	7
● Il Carbonaione '03	▽▽▽	8
● Il Carbonaione '00	▽▽▽	8
● Il Carbonaione '98	▽▽▽	8
● Il Carbonaione '96	▽▽▽	8
● Il Carbonaione '04	▽▽	7
● Il Carbonaione '99	▽▽	8
● Piantonaia '05	▽▽	8
● Piantonaia '04	▽▽	8
● Piantonaia '03	▽▽	8

Poggio Torselli

VIA SCOPETI, 10
50026 SAN CASCIANO IN VAL DI PESA [FI]
TEL. 0558290241
www.poggiotorselli.it

CELLAR SALES
PRE-BOOKED VISITS

ANNUAL PRODUCTION 40,000 bottles
HECTARES UNDER VINE 28
VITICULTURE METHOD Conventional

Poggio Torselli, named in 1427, has belonged to Florence's most prestigious families: the Antinoris; the Corsinis and the Strozzis. Construction started under Lorenzo Merlini in the late 1600s and was completed in the early 1700s with a lovely terraced garden boasting water features, flower beds and hedges. When it was restored, the original concept was maintained with seasonal rotation of the plants to include antique roses, aromatic plants and perennials. The villa features the furniture of the period.

Once again, it is the white Monna Aldola, a pure Chardonnay, that we liked best. The '09 gives camomile tea, flowers and assorted fruit before a soft, mouthwatering front palate then breadth and long, enjoyable length. We also liked the '06 Raniero from 100 per cent merlot. Its mineral tones and forest fruits aromas are the prelude to a plush body with tannins that meld with the alcohol, lovely acid backbone and a delicious finish. The '01 Vin Santo is delightful, offering butter-like sensations with the odd trace of bitter apricot. Entry on the palate is creamy, sweet and caressing.

○ Monna Aldola '09	▼▼	4
● Raniero '06	▼▼	4
○ Vin Santo del Chianti Cl. '01	▼▼	5
● Chianti Cl. Ris. '07	▼	5
● Chianti Cl. '04	▽▽	4
○ Monna Aldola '07	▽▽	4*
○ Monna Aldola '06	▽▽	4
● Tieri del Fula '06	▽▽	4*
● Tieri del Fula '05	▽▽	4
● Tieri del Fula '04	▽▽	5

Il Poggiolo

LOC. POGGIOLO, 259
53024 MONTALCINO [SI]
TEL. 0577848412
www.ilpoggiolomontalcino.com

CELLAR SALES
PRE-BOOKED VISITS

ANNUAL PRODUCTION 40,000 bottles
HECTARES UNDER VINE 7
VITICULTURE METHOD Conventional

Rudy Cosimi is a dynamo, a former motorcycle champ with several European trophies to his name who now races cars. He also runs his family's estate, now smaller after he and his brother inherited it and shared it out. We are pleased to see that he has also reduced the number of labels. Rudy's seven hectares of vines, split equally between Brunello and Rosso, in north-west Montalcino where the soil is fresh and marly. The wines mature in French oak casks of varying sizes: barriques, 900-litre casks and traditional.

Best of the wines Rudy offered us for tasting this year was the '07 Rosso di Montalcino Quello Buono. Rich ruby in appearance, it presents generous aromas of red berry fruit, currant, morello and very ripe cherry, enhanced by balsamic notes absorbed from its oak-ageing. Entry on the palate is confident, with well-balanced tannins and acidity that accompany the palate into a dense, lingering finish. The two Brunello di Montalcinos are well made. The '05 is fresher and more elegant; the Riserva '04 is fuller and more complex.

● Rosso di Montalcino Quello Buono '07	**YY**	6
● Brunello di Montalcino '05	**YY**	7
● Brunello di Montalcino Ris. '04	**YY**	8
● Rosso di Montalcino '07	**Y**	5
● Brunello di Montalcino Il mio Brunello '04	YYY	8
● Brunello di Montalcino Terra Rossa '01	YYY	7
● Brunello di Montalcino '04	YY	7
● Brunello di Montalcino Beato '04	YY	8
● Brunello di Montalcino Beato '03	YY	8
● Brunello di Montalcino Beato '01	YY	8
● Rosso di Montalcino Quello Buono '06	YY	4
● Rosso di Montalcino Quello Buono '05	YY	4

Tenuta Il Poggione

FRAZ. SANT'ANGELO IN COLLE
LOC. MONTEANO
53024 MONTALCINO [SI]
TEL. 0577844029
www.tenutailpoggione.it

CELLAR SALES
PRE-BOOKED VISITS
ROOMS

ANNUAL PRODUCTION 500,000 bottles
HECTARES UNDER VINE 123
VITICULTURE METHOD Conventional

Poggione is part of Sant'Angelo in Colle and the Franceschi family, who have owned this historic estate for five generations. There are over 100 hectares of vineyards scattered across the various Montalcino designations with varying aspects and elevations. The soil types are all high-quality, medium-textured and pebbly. The beautiful new centre outside the village also has a modern, efficient oil press, and the air-conditioned cellar is on the technological cutting-edge. Fabrizio Bindocci runs the show.

This has been a bit of a watershed year for Poggione's wines, which are well made but don't include an out-and-out winner. Of those on offer, we particularly liked the Brunello Riserva '04, a classic, austere wine that will cellar very well. The clear nose recalls cherry and tobacco. Entry on the palate is good but progression is curbed by rather wishy-washy tannins that shackle development despite the body. The Brunello di Montalcino '05 is sound.

● Brunello di Montalcino '05	**YY**	7
● Brunello di Montalcino Ris. '04	**YY**	7
● Rosso di Montalcino '08	**Y**	4
● Brunello di Montalcino Ris. '97	YYY	8
● Brunello di Montalcino '04	YY	7
● Brunello di Montalcino '03	YY	7
● Brunello di Montalcino Ris. '03	YY	7
● Il Poggione '06	YY	4*
● Rosso di Montalcino '07	YY	4*

★★ Poliziano

LOC. MONTEPULCIANO STAZIONE
VIA FONTAGO, 1
53045 MONTEPULCIANO [SI]
TEL. 0578738171
www.carlettipoliziano.com

CELLAR SALES
PRE-BOOKED VISITS
FOOD

ANNUAL PRODUCTION 600,000 bottles
HECTARES UNDER VINE 140
VITICULTURE METHOD Conventional

Federico Carletti has been reappointed president of the Consortium of Vino Nobile and this will be his primary concern, given that over the last 20 years his estate has become a fixed point of reference in Tuscan winemaking and beyond. As well as achieving astonishing levels of consistency, year after year the wines also demonstrate a first-class level of quality.

The Nobile di Montepulciano Asinone won its 22nd Three Glass trophy, leaving no doubt as to the significance of this extraordinary wine. The Vin Santo '99 reaffirms its place as one of the best in its class. The '07 Le Stanze, a blend of cabernet sauvignon and merlot, is a juicy wine with fabulous depth. The muscular Mandrone di Lhosa '07 is obtained from a mix of cabernet sauvignon, alicante, petit verdot and carignano produced at Magliano in Tuscany. The Nobile '07 is well-made. The Morellino di Scansano, Rosso di Montepulciano and Cortona Merlot In Violas were not ready when we were tasting.

● Nobile di Montepulciano Asinone '07	3 black glasses	7
● Le Stanze '07	2 black glasses	8
○ Vin Santo di Montepulciano '99	2 black glasses	7
● Mandrone di Lohsa '07	2 black glasses	6
● Nobile di Montepulciano '07	1 black glass	5
● Le Stanze '03	3 white glasses	7
● Nobile di Montepulciano Asinone '06	3 white glasses	7
● Nobile di Montepulciano Asinone '05	3 white glasses	7
● Nobile di Montepulciano Asinone '04	3 white glasses	7
● Nobile di Montepulciano Asinone '03	3 white glasses	7
● Nobile di Montepulciano Asinone '01	3 white glasses	7
● Nobile di Montepulciano Asinone '00	3 white glasses	7
● Nobile di Montepulciano Asinone '99	3 white glasses	6

Pratesi

LOC. SEANO
VIA RIZZELLI, 10
59011 CARMIGNANO [PO]
TEL. 0558704108
www.pratesivini.it

PRE-BOOKED VISITS

ANNUAL PRODUCTION 60,000 bottles
HECTARES UNDER VINE 7
VITICULTURE METHOD Conventional

This estate harvested its first vintage in 1983, making it an important shaker and mover in the recent history of Carmignano wines. Filippo Pratesi owns it with his father Giampiero and from the outset he adopted innovative production techniques, planting up to 10,000 vines per hectare in an effort to plumb the real potential of the territory. The result is a series of concentrated, complex wines with big personality that may not achieve the best results all the time but do perform very well in the right years.

A case in point is the '07 Carmione, a blend of cabernet sauvignon, cabernet franc and merlot offering rich, opulent aromas that wed forest fruit to vanilla and spice, hinting at fresh, extremely intense notes of green pepper. The broad, concentrated palate exhibits smooth tannins and a very long finish. The Vigna di Carmio Riserva '07 is also very pleasant, a Carmignano with very clean aromas of flowers and cherries in syrup and vital, refreshing body on a graceful, elegant palate. The Carmignano '08 is very well made, showing lighter with stylish, relaxed body.

● Carmignano '08	2 black glasses	5
● Carmignano V. di Carmio Ris. '07	2 black glasses	6
● Carmione '07	2 black glasses	6
● Carmignano '01	2 white glasses	6
● Carmignano '00	2 white glasses	6
● Carmignano '99	2 white glasses	5

★ Fattoria Le Pupille

s.da Piagge del Maiano
58100 Grosseto
tel. 0564409517
www.fattorialepupille.it

CELLAR SALES
PRE-BOOKED VISITS

ANNUAL PRODUCTION 450,000 bottles
HECTARES UNDER VINE 70
VITICULTURE METHOD Conventional

Elisabetta Geppetti fully deserves her reputation as a leading light in Maremma wine, especially in the territory of Morellino di Scansano. She picked her first harvests in the early 1980s but it was the release of Saffredi almost 30 years ago that really put Fattoria Le Pupille on the map. Today, the estate has consolidated its position as a leader and is one of the most important producers in Italian winemaking.

The estate's flagship, the Saffredi '07, is obtained from a blend of cabernet sauvignon, merlot and alicante. This is a deeply alluring wine of extraordinary elegance presenting a complex, clearly articulated palette of aromatics and elegant, succulent character in the mouth. The Morellino Poggio Valente Riserva '07 also shows very well, displaying assertive tannins and limpid aromas. The Morellino di Scansano '09 is eminently drinkable while the rest of the range is absolutely dependable.

● Morellino di Scansano Poggio Valente Ris. '07	TT	6
● Saffredi '07	TT	8
● Morellino di Scansano '09	T	4
● Pelofino '09	T	3
○ Poggio Argentato '09	T	4
⊙ Rosa Mati '09	T	4
● Morellino di Scansano Poggio Valente '04	YYY	6
● Morellino di Scansano Poggio Valente '99	YYY	6
● Saffredi '04	YYY	8
● Saffredi '03	YYY	8
● Saffredi '02	YYY	8
● Saffredi '01	YYY	8
● Saffredi '00	YYY	8

La Querce

via Imprunetana per Tavarnuzze, 41
50023 Impruneta [FI]
tel. 0552011380
www.laquerce.com

CELLAR SALES
PRE-BOOKED VISITS

ANNUAL PRODUCTION 25,000 bottles
HECTARES UNDER VINE 8
VITICULTURE METHOD Conventional

Around ten years ago, Massimo Marchi's estate received an injection of energy thanks to director Marco Ferretti, who dedicated himself to relaunching a winery that had showed it could produce quality wines in the past. The eight hectares under vine have recently been completely replanted largely to sangiovese with some international varieties.

The sangiovese and colorino La Querce '07 is excellent. The fresh, aromatic nose shows minty, balsamic tones and clear currant and blueberry fruit. The soft, silky palate is well gauged and presents a clear acid vein and long, agreeable finish. The '07 M, a pure Merlot, made a successful debut. The nose is dominated by notes of forest fruits with clear minerality and delicious hints of spice. The structure is nicely soft and the palate is crisp and clean. The fine Chianti Colli Fiorentini La Torretta '08 has notes of cherry and blackberry, weighty body, perceptible but pleasant tannins and a dry finish. The '09 Chianti Sorrettole is uncomplicated and drinkable.

● La Querce '07	TT	5
● Chianti Colli Fiorentini La Torretta '08	TT	4
● M '07	TT	5
● Chianti Sorrettole '09	T	3
● La Querce '06	YY	5
● La Querce '05	YY	5
● La Querce '04	YY	5
● La Querce '03	YY	5

★ Querciabella

VIA BARBIANO, 17
50022 GREVE IN CHIANTI [FI]
TEL. 05585927777
www.querciabella.com

CELLAR SALES
PRE-BOOKED VISITS

ANNUAL PRODUCTION 330,000 bottles
HECTARES UNDER VINE 82
VITICULTURE METHOD Certified biodynamic

Querciabella is rightly considered one of the most beautiful estates in Chianti Classico. Every year it presents excellent, highly innovative wines and shows no signs of flagging. We would even go so far as to say that this estate on the Ruffoli hill is undergoing a sort of renaissance, rethinking its wines, their style, the varieties and the territory. The estate is now biodynamic and processes respect the natural environment and, of course, enhance the wines' characteristics in the glass.

The '07 Camartina, a celebrated red obtained from sangiovese and cabernet sauvignon aged in largely new French barriques, has a divine profile that alternates dark sensations of blueberry, black cherry, toastiness and coffee with a mellower, aromatically green soul that is fresh and balsamic. What follows is a monumental palate, creamy and very, very long. The Merlot Palafreno '07 is good and rich, mingling red and black berry fruits aromas with the customary grassy notes. The Chianti Classico '08 is crunchy and floral while the '08 Batàr offers notes of aromatic herbs and wild flowers.

● Camartina '07	▼▼▼+	8
○ Batàr '08	▼▼	7
● Chianti Cl. '08	▼▼	6
● Palafreno '07	▼▼	8
● Mongrana '08	▼	4
● Camartina '06	▽▽▽	8
● Camartina '05	▽▽▽	8
● Camartina '04	▽▽▽	8
● Camartina '03	▽▽▽	8
● Camartina '01	▽▽▽	8
● Camartina '00	▽▽▽	8
● Camartina '99	▽▽▽	8
● Camartina '97	▽▽▽	8
● Camartina '94	▽▽▽	8
● Camartina '88	▽▽▽	8
● Chianti Cl. Ris. '95	▽▽▽	5

Rasa - La Serena

POD. RASA I, 133
53024 MONTALCINO [SI]
TEL. 0577848659
la_serena@virgilio.it

CELLAR SALES
PRE-BOOKED VISITS

ANNUAL PRODUCTION 23,500 bottles
HECTARES UNDER VINE 8
VITICULTURE METHOD Conventional

Brothers Andrea and Marcello Mantengoli are very different but form a winning team on the family estate. Pragmatic Andrea runs the vineyards and cellar while creative Marcello takes care of labels and sales. The property lies in eastern Montalcino at the foot of the Cerbaie hills. The terrain is not so loose here, a more compact mixture of sandstone and clay with some limestone. The functional, beautiful new cellar designed by Marcello houses 20-hectolitre barrels and barriques used to age part of the Brunello.

The Brunello Gemini '04 is first-class and earns a place in our final tastings. The classic, balsamic nose displays notes of tobacco and very clear sensations of yellow peaches as well as classic cherry-like aromas. The palate shows delicate, elegant continuity but is somewhat curbed by its still edgy tannins. The '05 Brunello also did well, its key characteristics being lovely acidity and perfectly smooth tannins. Relaxed progression enhances the elegant soul of this wine.

● Brunello di Montalcino Gemini '04	▼▼	8
● Brunello di Montalcino '05	▼▼	7
● Rosso di Montalcino '08	▼	4
● Brunello di Montalcino '03	▽▽	7
● Brunello di Montalcino Gemini '01	▽▽	8
● Rosso di Montalcino '06	▽▽	4

Riecine

LOC. RIECINE
53013 GAIOLE IN CHIANTI [SI]
TEL. 0577749098
www.riecine.com

CELLAR SALES
PRE-BOOKED VISITS

ANNUAL PRODUCTION 45,000 bottles
HECTARES UNDER VINE 11
VITICULTURE METHOD Organic

American Gary J. Baumann bought Riecine in 1996 from John Dunkley, its late founder. Visionary oenologist Sean O'Callaghan runs the vineyards and cellar, where he has created a personal style outside the box of Chianti tradition – but he remains faithful to sangiovese – while still managing to exalt its essence. Old concepts; different name. Some plots lie below the cellar; others among woods at an altitude of 500 metres in Vertine at La Casina; yet more in Montecucco. All are managed biodynamically.

The wines are all deliciously juicy and deep. If anything, we have noted that hot growing years tend to reveal the odd note of overripeness when we tasted the wines in the cellar directly from the barriques. The Chianti Classico Riserva '06 is a case in point for it displays very obvious alcohol. The same goes for La Gioia, also '06, with its complement of grapes from Maremma, a warm, mouthfilling texture and fabulous progression.

● Chianti Cl. '07	2 black glasses	5
● Chianti Cl. Ris. '06	2 black glasses	6
● La Gioia '06	2 black glasses	7
● Chianti Cl. Ris. '99	3 glasses	8
● Chianti Cl. Ris. '88	3 glasses	6
● Chianti Cl. Ris. '86	3 glasses	5
● La Gioia '04	3 glasses	7
● La Gioia '01	3 glasses	7
● La Gioia '98	3 glasses	8
● La Gioia '95	3 glasses	8
● Chianti Cl. Ris. '98	2 glasses	5
● La Gioia '05	2 glasses	7
● La Gioia '03	2 glasses	7
● La Gioia '00	2 glasses	8
● La Gioia '99	2 glasses	8

Rietine

LOC. RIETINE, 27
53013 GAIOLE IN CHIANTI [SI]
TEL. 0577731110
www.rietine.com

CELLAR SALES
PRE-BOOKED VISITS

ANNUAL PRODUCTION 60,000 bottles
HECTARES UNDER VINE 13
VITICULTURE METHOD Conventional

Rietine, situated in a small Chianti village, belongs to husband and wife team Galina Lazarides and Mario Gaffuri. Over the years, it has evolved into quite an enterprise. Although they sell much of their production to the overseas market, Galina and Mario's wines remain typical and true to the territory where they have chosen to make their home after many years of working abroad.

The Riserva '07 gave a fine performance, its wide range of varied aromas running the gamut from cinnamon and cloves to more mature notes of blackberry and blueberry jam. Entry on the palate is broad and well sustained with ever so slightly rough tannins. The merlot-only Tiziano '07 starts on minty tones but opens out to reveal traces of pencil lead, leather and cherry. The caressing palate shows delicate tannic texture and a refreshing acid vein that lingers on into a long-lingering finish. The lighter-weight Chianti Classico '08 can still point to a decent profile of aromatic herbs mingled with plum and cherry sensations.

● Chianti Cl. Ris. '07	2 black glasses	5
● Tiziano '07	2 black glasses	6
● Chianti Cl. '08	1 black glass	4
● Chianti Cl. Ris. '04	3 glasses	5
● Chianti Cl. '03	2 glasses	4
● Chianti Cl. Ris. '99	2 glasses	5
● Tiziano '99	2 glasses	6

Rigoloccio

loc. Rigoloccio
via Provinciale, 82
58023 Gavorrano [GR]
tel. 056645464
www.rigoloccio.it

CELLAR SALES
PRE-BOOKED VISITS

ANNUAL PRODUCTION 50,000 bottles
HECTARES UNDER VINE 10
VITICULTURE METHOD Conventional

Rigoloccio takes its name from the largest pyrite mine in the mineral complex located in the nearby metalliferous hills of Gavorrano. Alberto Abati and Ezio Puggelli started their foray into Maremma winemaking in 2002 with the objective of creating a range of wines that is not just very well made but also very reasonably priced, a rare combination in today's market.

Sorvegliante '07 is obtained from a blend of cabernet sauvignon, cabernet franc and alicante. It presents clean, refreshing aromas with grassy overtones that melt into hints of spice. The palate is mouthwatering and soft. The Cabernet e Alicante '08 is a fragrant, harmonious wine while the Chardonnay e Fiano '09 is approachable and uncomplicated, if rather tangy.

● Cabernet Alicante '08	▼▼	4
● Il Sorvegliante '07	▼▼	5
○ Chardonnay Fiano '09	▼	4
● Cabernet Alicante '06	▽▽	4*
○ Chardonnay Fiano '07	▽▽	4*
○ Chardonnay Fiano '06	▽▽	4
● Il Sorvegliante '06	▽▽	5
● Il Sorvegliante '05	▽▽	5
● Merlot '06	▽▽	4*

Rocca delle Macìe

loc. Le Macìe, 45
53011 Castellina in Chianti [SI]
tel. 05777321
www.roccadellemacie.com

CELLAR SALES
PRE-BOOKED VISITS
ROOMS AND FOOD

ANNUAL PRODUCTION 4,500,000 bottles
HECTARES UNDER VINE 200
VITICULTURE METHOD Conventional

Today's wine lovers are hell-bent on rooting out small, even tiny, estates that produce a handful of bottles. Fair enough, rarity is the golden rule of collecting, but we believe there is still merit in estates that offer quality, labels that reflect their territory of origin and a clear identity. It shouldn't matter if they churn out thousands of bottles that are easily obtained and don't coast a fortune. Rocca delle Macìe is one such, and to our mind its mastermind Sergio Zingarelli is on the right track.

The Chianti Classico Riserva di Fizzano '06 is an absolutely splendid wine, for example. The nose mingles notes of cocoa powder with gorgeous tertiary aromas of leather and tobacco. The palate is still in the first throes of youth but is vigorous, showing acid verve and austere depth. Of the whites we tasted we particularly liked the Vernaccia '09 for its light notes hinting at white peach and pear followed up by nice backbone on the palate.

● Chianti Cl. Fizzano Ris. '06	▼▼	6
○ Vernaccia di S. Gimignano '09	▼▼	3*
● Chianti Cl. Granchiaia '08	▼	5
● Chianti Colli Senesi Rubizzo '09	▼	4
● Chianti Vernaiolo '09	▼	3
● Morellino di Scansano Campomaccione '09	▼	4
● Sasyr '08	▼	4
● Roccato '00	▽▽▽	7
● Roccato '99	▽▽▽	7
● Chianti Cl. Tenuta S. Alfonso '07	▽▽	5
● Roccato '05	▽▽	7
● Roccato '98	▽▽	7
● Ser Gioveto '06	▽▽	7
● Ser Gioveto '01	▽▽	7
● Ser Gioveto '00	▽▽	7

Rocca di Castagnoli

Loc. Castagnoli
53013 Gaiole in Chianti [SI]
tel. 0577731004
www.roccadicastagnoli.com

CELLAR SALES
PRE-BOOKED VISITS
ROOMS AND FOOD

ANNUAL PRODUCTION 356,000 bottles
HECTARES UNDER VINE 117
VITICULTURE METHOD Conventional

Two estates, one property: same extraordinary quality of wines. Or almost. Rocca di Castagnoli and Tenuta di Capraia share a common elegance based on clarity and precision, yet in the glass they portray two quite different viticultures: the high altitudes of Gaiole; and the heart of Castellina in Chianti. The estate's style does the rest as each year they present us with gems to taste, bottles of clearly defined, precise wines that reflect their territories of origin.

Our vote this year goes to the Chianti Classico Riserva '07 from Tenuta di Capraia. This magnificent wine of immense energy and depth offers a cornucopia of violets, morello cherries and leather aromas, duly delivering that vertical, acid component that we expect to see in all the great wines of this DOCG. Just a half-step behind comes the Poggio ai Frati Riserva '07, which is well made but more predictable. The spectacular Chianti Classico Tenuta di Capraia '08 gets a note of merit.

● Chianti Cl. Capraia Ris. '07	TTT	5
● Chianti Cl. Poggio ai Frati Ris. '07	TT	5
● Chianti Cl. Tenuta di Capraia '08	TT	4
● Buriano '06	TT	7
● Chianti Cl. Poggio ai Frati '08	TT	4
○ Molino delle Balze '09	T	5
○ Vin Santo del Chianti Cl. '01	T	8
● Chianti Cl. Poggio ai Frati Ris. '06	YYY	5*
● Chianti Cl. Poggio ai Frati Ris. '04	YYY	5
● Chianti Cl. Tenuta di Capraia Ris. '06	YYY	5*
● Chianti Cl. Tenuta di Capraia Ris. '05	YYY	5
● Stielle '00	YYY	8

Rocca di Frassinello

Loc. Giuncarico
58040 Gavorrano [GR]
tel. 056688400
www.roccadifrassinello.it

CELLAR SALES
PRE-BOOKED VISITS

ANNUAL PRODUCTION 180,000 bottles
HECTARES UNDER VINE 70
VITICULTURE METHOD Conventional

Rocca di Frassinello's oenological mission has consolidated its position in the Maremma wine world. It was founded by Paolo Panerai, editor, financier and owner of Castellare di Castellina. The estate embraces a large number of vineyards on the slopes facing the small village of Giuncarico and a beautiful cellar designed by Renzo Piano. The wines already display their own distinctive style and belong to an exclusive group of high-class wines produced along the Tuscan coast.

The Baffo Nero continues its undaunted course to excellence. Obtained from pure merlot again in the '08 version, it presents rich, harmonious aromas and a warm, fruity, embracing palate. The '08 Rocca di Frassinello is again a very classy wine with balsam, balance and elegance. The robust, intense Le Sughere di Frassinello '08 has gorgeous notes of Mediterranean scrub. The '08 Poggio alla Guardia is simpler but very vigorous. All three are produced from a mix of sangiovese, cabernet sauvignon and merlot in varying proportions.

● Rocca di Frassinello '08	TTT	6
● Baffo Nero '08	TT	6
● Le Sughere di Frassinello '08	TT	5
● Poggio alla Guardia '08	T	4
● Baffo Nero '07	YYY	6
● Rocca di Frassinello '06	YYY	6
● Rocca di Frassinello '05	YYY	7
● Le Sughere di Frassinello '07	YY	5
● Le Sughere di Frassinello '06	YY	5
● Poggio alla Guardia '06	YY	4*
● Rocca di Frassinello '07	YY	6

Rocca di Montegrossi

FRAZ. MONTI IN CHIANTI
53010 GAIOLE IN CHIANTI [SI]
TEL. 0577747977
www.roccadimontegrossi.it

CELLAR SALES
PRE-BOOKED VISITS

ANNUAL PRODUCTION 80,000 bottles
HECTARES UNDER VINE 18
VITICULTURE METHOD Certified organic

Rocca di Montegrossi belongs to Marco Ricasoli Firidolfi, a descendant of the family that has written some of the most important pages in Chianti history. The estate lies near Monti, not far from Gaiole, and its beautiful vineyards are cultivated on limestone soil of medium texture at an altitude of between 300 and 450 metres. Marco obtains his classic DOCGs from indigenous varieties and his wines, at once rich and luxuriant, are balanced and elegant.

Once again, Marco presented us with a sumptuous version of the Chianti Classico Vigneto San Marcellino based exclusively on sangiovese grown in the vineyard of the same name. The '07 is an extremely dense wine, presenting warm and chewy with very alluring modern notes enhanced by oaky aromas that lend it complexity and fullness. It's a cut above the '06. The Bordeaux blend Geremia '07 is good. Up last, the Chianti Classico '08 is rather overwhelmed by the oak and has a slightly bitter finish.

● Chianti Cl. Vign. S. Marcellino '07	▼▼▼	7
● Chianti Cl. Vign. S. Marcellino '06	▼▼	4
● Geremia '07	▼▼	6
● Chianti Cl. '08	▼	4
● Chianti Cl. Vign. S. Marcellino Ris. '99	▽▽▽	5
● Chianti Cl. '00	▽▽	4
● Chianti Cl. Vign. S. Marcellino Ris. '04	▽▽	6
● Chianti Cl. Vign. S. Marcellino Ris. '01	▽▽	6
● Geremia '03	▽▽	6
● Geremia '99	▽▽	6
○ Vin Santo del Chianti Cl. '02	▽▽	8
○ Vin Santo del Chianti Cl. '01	▽▽	8
○ Vin Santo del Chianti Cl. '00	▽▽	8
○ Vin Santo del Chianti Cl. '98	▽▽	8
○ Vin Santo del Chianti Cl. '97	▽▽	8

Rocca di Montemassi

FRAZ. MONTEMASSI
VIA SANT'ANNA
58036 ROCCASTRADA [GR]
TEL. 0564579700
www.roccadimontemassi.it

CELLAR SALES
PRE-BOOKED VISITS

ANNUAL PRODUCTION 400,000 bottles
HECTARES UNDER VINE 160
VITICULTURE METHOD Conventional

This Maremma estate belonging to the Zonin Group, one of the largest in Italy, debuted well. The cellar and vineyards are the result of a project launched in 1999 and nurtured patiently and naturally since then. It lies in the foothills of Montemassi in the heart of the "bitter" Maremma described by Luciano Bianciardi as being made of sweat and toil whether you are above the earth or beneath it. Today, Maremma has a more generous aspect and has rediscovered its wine vocation.

The '08 Rocca di Montemassi is a blend of merlot, cabernet sauvignon, petit verdot and syrah, the result of a collaboration with famed French oenologist Denis Dubourdieu. It combines intense, captivating aromas and a juicy palate. The Monteregio Sassabruna '08 is spot on with its clean nose and contrasty palate. The '09 Le Focaie, a pure Sangiovese, is balanced and vigorous. Calasole '09 from vermentino is fresh and easy drinking.

● Rocca di Montemassi '08	▼▼	6
● Monteregio di Massa Marittima Sassabruna '08	▼▼	4
○ Calasole '09	▼	4
● Le Focaie '09	▼	4

★ Tenimenti Ruffino

P.LE RUFFINO, 1
50065 PONTASSIEVE [FI]
TEL. 0556499717
www.ruffino.it

CELLAR SALES
PRE-BOOKED VISITS

ANNUAL PRODUCTION 14,500,000 bottles
HECTARES UNDER VINE 600
VITICULTURE METHOD Conventional

This big name in winemaking exports to almost every country in the world and has become a symbol of Italian wine and viticulture. There are estates in all the main zones of Tuscany, some of which – like Greppone Mazzi in Montalcino – represent the best of their designations. The others are Lodola Nuova in Montepulciano; Santedame, Gretole, Montemasso and Poggio Casciano in Chianti Classico; La Solatia in Monteriggioni, near Siena; and Borgo Convent in Friuli, featured in a separate profile in the section of the Guide dedicated to that region.

Brunello di Montalcino Greppone Mazzi '05 is a magnificent wine from an ordinary vintage, which scored very highly. Traditional in style, it combines an elegant nose of subtle morello cherry and tobacco with and a full but supple palate. Riserva Ducale Oro '06 is woodier than usual with a slightly over-evolved nose and clenched tannins, like Modus '07, from sangiovese with small additions of cabernet sauvignon and merlot. Urlo '07, an exotic blend of cabernet sauvignon, merlot, petit verdot and alicante, is very good, Nobile Lodola Nuova Riserva '06is good and reliable and the other wines are decent.

● Brunello di Montalcino Greppone Mazzi '05	🍷🍷🍷	7
● L'Urlo '06	🍷🍷	6
● Chianti Cl. Ris. Ducale Oro '06	🍷🍷	6
● Modus '07	🍷🍷	6
● Nobile di Montepulciano Lodola Nuova Ris. '06	🍷🍷	7
○ La Solatia Pinot Grigio '09	🍷	3
○ Libaio '09	🍷	3
● Nobile di Montepulciano Lodola Nuova '08	🍷	5
● Rosso di Montepulciano Lodola Nuova '09	🍷	4
● Chianti Cl. Ris. Ducale Oro '04	YYY	6
● Chianti Cl. Ris. Ducale Oro '01	YYY	6
● Chianti Cl. Ris. Ducale Oro '00	YYY	6
● Modus '04	YYY	6
● Romitorio di Santedame '00	YYY	8
● Romitorio di Santedame '99	YYY	7
● Romitorio di Santedame '98	YYY	6
● Romitorio di Santedame '97	YYY	6

Salcheto

LOC. SANT'ALBINO
VIA DI VILLA BIANCA, 15
53045 MONTEPULCIANO [SI]
TEL. 0578799031
www.salcheto.it

CELLAR SALES
PRE-BOOKED VISITS

ANNUAL PRODUCTION 130,000 bottles
HECTARES UNDER VINE 33
VITICULTURE METHOD Conventional

Winemaking at Michele Manelli's Salcheto estate, near Sant'Albino, brooks no compromise. Despite the difficulties involved, it appears to have paid off. Year after year, the challenging Salco Evoluzione project has achieved excellent results, and much experimentation has been carried out on Nobile di Montepulciano, leading to the release six years after harvest of a wine that confirms its excellent potential for ageing and staying power.

Nobile Salco Evoluzione '05 once again demonstrates the wisdom of this singular, daring decision in a vintage that can by no means be described as excellent. Its full, sculpted nose is followed by an alluring, deep, juicy palate. Nobile '07 is enjoyable, with a close-focused nose and a weighty, well-paced palate, while Rosso di Montepulciano '09 is uncomplicated and approachable, focusing on drinkability and fragrance.

● Nobile di Montepulciano Salco Evoluzione '05	🍷🍷	7
● Nobile di Montepulciano '07	🍷🍷	5
● Rosso di Montepulciano '09	🍷	4
● Nobile di Montepulciano '97	YYY	5
● Nobile di Montepulciano Salco Evoluzione '01	YYY	7
● Nobile di Montepulciano '06	YY	5
● Nobile di Montepulciano '05	YY	5
● Nobile di Montepulciano Salco Evoluzione '04	YY	7
● Nobile di Montepulciano Salco Evoluzione '03	YY	7

Salustri

FRAZ. POGGI DEL SASSO
LOC. LA CAVA
58040 CINIGIANO [GR]
TEL. 0564990529
www.salustri.it

CELLAR SALES
PRE-BOOKED VISITS
ROOMS

ANNUAL PRODUCTION 80,000 bottles
HECTARES UNDER VINE 12
VITICULTURE METHOD Certified organic

Poggi del Sasso, where this pioneer estate of the Montecucco DOC zone started making wine at the end of the 1990s, is a little village that probably never envisaged becoming a famous name in the wine world, thanks to one of its residents, Leonardo Salustri. Today the quality of its wines is among the highest and most consistent in the whole Maremma area, offering one of the finest interpretations of sangiovese, the quintessential Tuscan grape.

Year after year, Salustri's two different Montecucco vineyard selections offer striking varietal definition. Three Glasses went to Grotte Rosse '07, which has slightly more powerful tannins than the leaner, laid-back Santa Maria '07. Both have a very concentrated nose and a full, flavoursome palate. Narà '09, a monovarietal Vermentino, is very simple, yet enjoyable.

● Montecucco Grotte Rosse '07	**YYY**	6
● Montecucco Santa Marta '07	**YY**	5
○ Narà '09	**Y**	4
● Montecucco Santa Marta '06	YYY	5
● Montecucco Grotte Rosse '06	YY	6
● Montecucco Grotte Rosse '05	YY	6
● Montecucco Grotte Rosse '04	YY	6
● Montecucco Grotte Rosse '02	YY	6
● Montecucco Marleo '04	YY	4
● Montecucco Santa Marta '05	YY	5

Fattoria San Donato

LOC. SAN DONATO, 6
53037 SAN GIMIGNANO [SI]
TEL. 0577941616
www.sandonato.it

CELLAR SALES
PRE-BOOKED VISITS
ROOMS AND FOOD

ANNUAL PRODUCTION N.A.
HECTARES UNDER VINE 12
VITICULTURE METHOD Conventional

Fattoria San Donato has belonged to the Fenzi family since 1932. The hamlet was built in the Middle Ages, on the old Via Francigena, around the Romanesque parish church. Today several of the buildings have been converted into guest facilities. The watchtower houses the inn and the farm workers' homes are now self-catering accommodation while the winery is located in the central complex. The estate also produces extra virgin olive oil and saffron. Visitors receive a warm welcome and can participate in tastings accompanied by local specialities.

Vernaccia Benedetta Riserva '07 excelled in our tastings this year, displaying a complex nose in which ripe fruity notes of bananas and peaches mingle with hints of aromatic herbs and autumn leaves. On the palate it is full and juicy, with impressive consistency. Vin Santo '04 is also decent, with an alluring nose of figs and dates fusing with hazelnuts, and a full, creamy, velvety palate that finishes long. Vernaccia '09 is uncomplicated but fresh and racy, with striking floral overtones, while Merlot Arrigo '07 is more complex, although its tannins are still a little stiff.

○ San Gimignano Vin Santo '04	**YY**	5
○ Vernaccia di S. Gimignano Benedetta Ris. '07	**YY**	5
● San Gimignano Arrigo Merlot '07	**Y**	4
○ Vernaccia di S. Gimignano '09	**Y**	3
● Chianti Colli Senesi Fede Ris. '05	YY	4*
● Chianti Colli Senesi Fede Ris. '04	YY	4*
● Chianti Colli Senesi Fiamma '06	YY	4*
● Chianti Colli Senesi Fiamma '05	YY	4*
○ Vernaccia di S. Gimignano Angelica '05	YY	4*
○ Vin Santo '03	YY	4*

Fattoria San Fabiano Borghini Baldovinetti

LOC. SAN FABIANO, 33
52100 AREZZO
TEL. 057524566
www.fattoriasanfabiano.it

CELLAR SALES
PRE-BOOKED VISITS

ANNUAL PRODUCTION 700,000 bottles
HECTARES UNDER VINE 120
VITICULTURE METHOD Organic

The estate owned by Conte Gianluigi Borghini Baldovinetti de Bacci Venuti, whose ancestors include the family that commissioned the "Legend of the True Cross" fresco cycle in the chapel of San Francesco in Arezzo from Piero della Francesca, is imbued with history. However history also pervades the viticultural tradition, which commenced after the Second World War, and was consolidated during the years of Italy's economic miracle. The estate strives to imbue a sense of place in wines that communicate their territory and the experience of their producer.

Once again the top performer was Armaiolo '07, from sangiovese and cabernet sauvignon, with well-defined grassy notes, ripe dark berry fruit and clove-led spice. The firm, juicy palate unveils prominent close-knit tannins and a slightly tired but flavoursome finish. Piocaia '07, from the same grapes with the addition of merlot, also scored well. Surprisingly fresh and fruity fragrances precede a soft, weighty palate. Nobile di Montepulciano '07 is pleasant and Chianti Putto '09 is decent.

● Armaiolo '07	TT	7
● Piocaia '07	TT	4
● Chianti Putto '09	T	4
● Nobile di Montepulciano Poggio Uliveto '07	T	5
● Armaiolo '05	YY	5
● Armaiolo '00	YY	6
● Armaiolo '99	YY	6
● Nobile di Montepulciano Poggio Uliveto '05	YY	5
● Nobile di Montepulciano Poggio Uliveto '04	YY	4*
● Nobile di Montepulciano Poggio Uliveto '03	YY	4
● Nobile di Montepulciano Poggio Uliveto '02	YY	4
● Piocaia '03	YY	4
● Piocaia '01	YY	4*

San Fabiano Calcinaia

LOC. CELLOLE
53011 CASTELLINA IN CHIANTI [SI]
TEL. 0577979232
www.sanfabianocalcinaia.com

CELLAR SALES
PRE-BOOKED VISITS
ROOMS AND FOOD

ANNUAL PRODUCTION 160,000 bottles
HECTARES UNDER VINE 42
VITICULTURE METHOD Certified organic

This estate is owned by Guido Serio and his wife Isa, who purchased it in 1983. The villa and the cellars date back to the 11th century and were part of a medieval village. Guido and Isa immediately set to work, enthusiastically planting new vineyards and replanting the existing ones. They subsequently restored the cottages, transforming them into guest accommodation, and opened the inn, which serves local specialities.

The flagship wine, Cerviolo '06, a blend of sangiovese, cabernet sauvignon and merlot, put up the best performance, with a pleasant, complex nose featuring spicy, earthy notes and concentrated, rich fruit. Full body and firm structure on the cosseting, intense palate take you through to a pleasantly long, relaxed finish. Cerviolo Bianco '08, from chardonnay and sauvignon, is also very pleasant, with accentuated minerals and aromatic herbs, which give way to white-fleshed fruit. The well-rounded palate is lush and juicy, with an alluring zesty finish.

○ Cerviolo Bianco '08	TT	5
● Cerviolo Rosso '06	TT	7
● Cabernet Sauvignon '08	T	5
● Casa Boschino '08	T	4
● Chianti Cl. Cellole Ris. '07	T	6
● Cerviolo Rosso '00	YYY	7
● Cerviolo Rosso '99	YYY	6
● Cerviolo Rosso '98	YYY	6
● Chianti Cl. Cellole Ris. '00	YYY	6
● Cerviolo Rosso '04	YY	7
● Cerviolo Rosso '03	YY	7
● Chianti Cl. Cellole Ris. '06	YY	6
● Chianti Cl. Cellole Ris. '04	YY	6

San Felice

LOC. SAN FELICE
53019 CASTELNUOVO BERARDENGA [SI]
TEL. 05773991
www.agricolasanfelice.it

CELLAR SALES
PRE-BOOKED VISITS
ROOMS AND FOOD

ANNUAL PRODUCTION 1,200,000 bottles
HECTARES UNDER VINE 210
VITICULTURE METHOD Conventional

San Felice is a splendid Chianti producer belonging to the Allianz group, with over 200 hectares of vineyards in San Gusmé in the north-eastern part of the municipality of Castelnuovo Berardenga, not far from the Montalcino hamlet of Sant'Angelo in Colle, where its owns Campogiovanni. Constant experimentation and meticulously tended vineyards are features of both prestigious estates, making San Felice one of the leading names in Tuscan winemaking. The wines have great personality and some, like Vigorello, have been in production since 1968.

While the top end of the range suffered from the absence of the new Pugnitello this year, the estate's wines nonetheless performed well. Our favourite was the youthful Chianti Classico Poggio Rosso Riserva '06, which has a concentrated, well-typed nose and a full, confident palate, still a little clenched from oak and with a slightly bitterish finish. The same is true of Vigorello '06, a blend of sangiovese and cabernet sauvignon with 20 per cent merlot, whose enfolding, balsamic nose is accompanied by rather prominent oak on the palate. Brunello Campogiovanni '05, from a lesser vintage, is good, and Chianti Classico '08 is pleasant but again rather wooded.

● Chianti Cl. Poggio Rosso Ris. '06	[2 black glasses]	7
● Brunello di Montalcino Campogiovanni '05	[2 black glasses]	7
● Vigorello '06	[2 black glasses]	7
● Chianti Cl. '08	[1 black glass]	4
● Chianti Cl. Poggio Rosso Ris. '03	[3 white glasses]	6
● Chianti Cl. Poggio Rosso Ris. '00	[3 white glasses]	6
● Chianti Cl. Poggio Rosso Ris. '95	[3 white glasses]	5
● Chianti Cl. Poggio Rosso Ris. '90	[3 white glasses]	6
● Pugnitello '07	[3 white glasses]	7
● Pugnitello '06	[3 white glasses]	7
● Vigorello '97	[3 white glasses]	5

San Filippo

LOC. SAN FILIPPO, 134
53024 MONTALCINO [SI]
TEL. 0577847176
www.sanfilippomontalcino.com

ANNUAL PRODUCTION 50,000 bottles
HECTARES UNDER VINE 10
VITICULTURE METHOD Conventional

In a few years, Roberto Giannelli has managed to restore the reputation that San Filippo enjoyed in the early 1980s. The vineyards, located in the eastern part of Montalcino in the Cerbaie hills, enjoy superb aspects. They are situated about 250 metres and planted at a density of roughly 5,000 vines per hectare, on marly soil with a little clay. The entire winery has been renovated and the barrel stock has been completely renewed, as has the fermentation cellar, now equipped with temperature-controlled vats.

The excellent Brunello di Montalcino Le Lucere '04 took Three Glasses. It is an extremely traditional wine, with an intense, complex nose of golden-leaf tobacco, balsamic notes, strawberries, herbs and leather. On the palate it offers mellow tannins, enhanced by fragrant acidity, and full, deep finish. The Brunello '05 is well made, if a little light bodied, reflecting the vintage.

● Brunello di Montalcino Le Lucere Ris. '04	[3 black glasses]	8
● Brunello di Montalcino '05	[2 black glasses]	8
● Rosso di Montalcino Lo Scorno '08	[1 black glass]	5
● Sant'Antimo Staffato '07	[1 black glass]	6
● Brunello di Montalcino '03	[2 white glasses]	7
● Brunello di Montalcino Le Coste Ris. '01	[2 white glasses]	7
● Brunello di Montalcino Le Lucere '04	[2 white glasses]	7

San Giusto a Rentennano

FRAZ. MONTI IN CHIANTI
LOC. SAN GIUSTO A RENTENNANO, 20
53013 GAIOLE IN CHIANTI [SI]
TEL. 0577747121
www.fattoriasangiusto.it

CELLAR SALES
PRE-BOOKED VISITS

ANNUAL PRODUCTION 85,000 bottles
HECTARES UNDER VINE 29
VITICULTURE METHOD Certified organic

San Giusto a Rentennano, owned by the Martini Gigala family since the late 1950s, is one of Chianti Classico's finest wineries and is situated in the southern part of the zone. The vineyards are farmed organically and have different soils, with tufa predominating. The climate is generally warm and the wines are aged in small oak casks. Their development is always very authentic, natural and relaxed, immediately conjuring up images of the terroir.

Chianti Classico Riserva Le Baroncole, from sangiovese with a small amount of canaiolo, is as charming as ever. The '07 vintage lays out an alluring mineral aromatic profile, with pervasive, chewy notes of red fruit and hints of oriental spices adding complexity. There is still slightly too much toast but it will fade with time. Percarlo '06 is good, despite its fairly lively alcohol and tannins. La Ricolma '07 is full and ripe.

● Chianti Cl. Le Baroncole Ris. '07	TT	6
● La Ricolma '07	TT	8
● Percarlo '06	TT	8
● Chianti Cl. '08	T	5
● Percarlo '99	YYY	8
● Percarlo '97	YYY	8
● Percarlo '95	YYY	8
● Percarlo '88	YYY	8
● Chianti Cl. Le Baroncole Ris. '06	YY	6
● Chianti Cl. Le Baroncole Ris. '05	YY	6
● La Ricolma '04	YY	7
● Percarlo '05	YY	8
● Percarlo '04	YY	8
● Percarlo '03	YY	8

★★ Tenuta San Guido

FRAZ. BOLGHERI
LOC. CAPANNE, 27
57022 CASTAGNETO CARDUCCI [LI]
TEL. 0565762003
www.sassicaia.com

PRE-BOOKED VISITS
FOOD

ANNUAL PRODUCTION 610,000 bottles
HECTARES UNDER VINE 90
VITICULTURE METHOD Conventional

Sassicaia and Tenuta San Guido are a concrete example of how tradition is a dynamic concept. In this gravelly, oenologically obscure part of Tuscany, which nonetheless closely resembled the Graves area of Bordeaux, the planting of cabernet vines was considered exotic, as was the use of new fermentation and ageing methods. It wasn't until years later, with the release of the first vintage, 1968, that the whole world realized that this apparent folly had resulted in one of Italian wine's greatest oenological accomplishments.

Sassicaia '07 is one of the best vintages ever. It is a sumptuous, graceful red that manages to enhances its own distinctive features. In short, it is a wine of unrivalled class, in which every detail is focused on overall perfection, characterized by body, grip and flavour. This stunner is flanked by the sublime Guidalberto '08 with a delicate nose and a relaxed, crisp palate.

● Bolgheri Sassicaia '07	TTT+	8
● Guidalberto '08	TTT	7
● Le Difese '08	TT	5
● Bolgheri Sassicaia '06	YYY+	8
● Bolgheri Sassicaia '05	YYY	8
● Bolgheri Sassicaia '04	YYY	8
● Bolgheri Sassicaia '03	YYY	8
● Bolgheri Sassicaia '02	YYY	8
● Bolgheri Sassicaia '01	YYY	8
● Bolgheri Sassicaia '00	YYY	8
● Guidalberto '04	YYY	7
● Sassicaia '92	YYY	8
● Sassicaia '90	YYY	8
● Sassicaia '88	YYY	8
● Sassicaia '85	YYY	8
● Sassicaia '84	YYY	8
● Sassicaia '83	YYY	8

San Michele a Torri

VIA SAN MICHELE, 36
50020 SCANDICCI [FI]
TEL. 055769111
www.fattoriasanmichele.it

CELLAR SALES
PRE-BOOKED VISITS

ANNUAL PRODUCTION 200,000 bottles
HECTARES UNDER VINE 55
VITICULTURE METHOD Certified organic

This year one of the Nocentini family's wines reached our finals: Chianti Classico Riserva Tenuta La Gabbiola '07, from the Chianti Classico holding. However, the wines made by the main estate also performed well. Although winemaking is documented here from the late 1700s, the business really got under way in the 19th century. Since Paolo, the current owner, took over, great progress has been made wine and olive oil making, firstly with the decision to put organic farming methods in place in the vineyards and subsequently with increasing attention to work in the cellar.

The finalist has an attractive ruby hue and a nose of tobacco, leather, jam and hints of spice. There's a nice entry on the flavoursome, lively palate and a sustained, pleasant finish. Murtas '07, from sangiovese, colorino and cabernet sauvignon, has an alluringly complex nose of cloves and cinnamon with fruity notes of mint-veined raspberries and currants. Entry on the juicy, dynamic palate is soft and generous while the finish is full and lingering.

Wine	Glasses	
● Chianti Cl. Tenuta La Gabbiola '07	2 (black)	5
● Murtas '07	2 (black)	5
● Chianti Colli Fiorentini '08	1 (black)	3
● Chianti Colli Fiorentini S. Giovanni Novantasette Ris. '07	1 (black)	5
○ Colli dell'Etruria Centrale Vin Santo '05	1 (black)	5
● Chianti Cl. Tenuta La Gabbiola Ris. '04	2 (white)	5
● Chianti Colli Fiorentini S. Giovanni Novantasette Ris. '05	2 (white)	5
● Murtas '05	2 (white)	6
● Murtas '03	2 (white)	6
● Murtas '02	2 (white)	6
● Murtas '01	2 (white)	6

Fattoria San Pancrazio

LOC. SAN PANCRAZIO
VIA CERTALDESE, 63/65
50026 SAN CASCIANO IN VAL DI PESA [FI]
TEL. 0558248046
www.fattoriasanpancrazio.com

CELLAR SALES
PRE-BOOKED VISITS

ANNUAL PRODUCTION 150,000 bottles
HECTARES UNDER VINE 28
VITICULTURE METHOD Conventional

This estate has a long history, for the farm was built in 1388. It belonged to the Gianfigliazzi family until they died out and the parents of the current owner, Valentina Masti, bought it in 1978. For many years, it was only a property investment and country home but since 2000, when Valentina and her husband Simone Priami went to live in it, they have developed the winemaking side, replanting the vineyards and renovating the villa and its cellar.

This year, San Pancrazio presented us with Chianti Classico Riserva '07 and Chianti Classico '08, both very well made. The Riserva has an intriguing nose in which herbal notes, such as bay, rosemary and mint, mingle with ripe fruit like cherries and plums. Entry on the palate is full, complex and cosseting, with subtle tannins and a nice swath of acidity that enhances the full flavour, culminating in a progressive, lingering finish. The '08 vintage has a fruity nose of currants and blueberries, with hints of spices and violets, and a balanced palate with perfect structure and well-calibrated freshness.

Wine	Glasses	
● Chianti Cl. Ris. '07	2 (black)	6
● Chianti Cl. '08	2 (black)	4
● Chianti Cl. Ris. '06	2 (white)	5
● Merlot '05	2 (white)	6

San Polino

LOC. CASTELNUOVO DELL'ABATE
POD. SAN POLINO, 163
53024 MONTALCINO [SI]
TEL. 0577835775
www.sanpolino.it

CELLAR SALES
PRE-BOOKED VISITS

ANNUAL PRODUCTION **10,000 bottles**
HECTARES UNDER VINE **4**
VITICULTURE METHOD **Certified biodynamic**

This small winery gives lustre to the San Polo area on the south-eastern slope of Montalcino. The land under vine is gravelly with mainly sandy clay soil, which makes the wines elegant rather than powerful. Medium-sized barrels, barriques and tonneaux are used for ageing in the cellar. The winery employs strictly organic methods and is AIAB certified. Its wines, from a small area under vine, are classic in style but have a distinctive personality.

All three wines presented reached our finals. Despite the difficult '05 vintage, the two Brunellos are excellent and different. Brunello '05 has incredible finesse, with notes of spice and fresher, more approachable nuances of red berry fruit. The palate echoes the nose and is supported by good acidity, with an elegant finish. Helichrysum has warmer, more Mediterranean notes of myrtle and medicinal herbs while the fruit tends towards wild cherry and jam. It is denser on the palate, with good development, and although the tannins are not as mellow, they do not cramp the finish.

● Brunello di Montalcino '05	TT	7
● Brunello di Montalcino Helichrysum '05	TT	8
● Rosso di Montalcino '08	TT	5
● Brunello di Montalcino '04	YY	8
● Brunello di Montalcino Helichrysum '04	YY	8

San Polo

POD. SAN POLO DI PODERNOVI, 161
53024 MONTALCINO [SI]
TEL. 0577835101
www.poggiosanpolo.com

CELLAR SALES
PRE-BOOKED VISITS

ANNUAL PRODUCTION **150,600 bottles**
HECTARES UNDER VINE **17**
VITICULTURE METHOD **Organic**

San Polo, on the eastern slope of Montalcino, has a charming location, at the end of a long dirt track. The production of the new estate, headed by well-known Veneto winemaker Marilisa Allegrini, is excellent. This solid winery vaunts handsome high-density vineyards that are the result of meticulous studies carried out on soil, clones and rootstock. The innovative cellar is inspired by the principles of bioarchitecture and houses barrels of various sizes for ageing Brunello.

The wines that we tasted performed very well, particularly the young ones. Rubino '08 is deliciously easy drinking while the excellent Rosso di Montalcino '07 has a concentrated nose of cherries and blackberries and attractive spicy oak, accompanied by a vibrant, close-knit palate. Brunello Riserva '04 is also good, characterized by an intense but rather simple nose and a balanced, harmonious palate.

● Brunello di Montalcino Ris. '04	TT	8
● Rosso di Montalcino '07	TT	5
● Rubio '08	TT	4
● Brunello di Montalcino '05	T	7
● Brunello di Montalcino '04	YY	7
● Brunello di Montalcino '03	YY	7
● Brunello di Montalcino '99	YY	7
● Mezzopane '05	YY	6

San Quirico

LOC. PANCOLE, 39
53037 SAN GIMIGNANO [SI]
TEL. 0577955007
az.agr.sanquirico@libero.it

CELLAR SALES
PRE-BOOKED VISITS

ANNUAL PRODUCTION 200,000 bottles
HECTARES UNDER VINE 26
VITICULTURE METHOD Certified organic

Vernaccia di San Gimignano Isabella Riserva reached our finals, after having won Three Glasses last year, again confirming the wine's excellent ageing prospects. The estate has belonged to the Vecchione family since the mid-1800s and viticulture, along with olive growing, has always been one of its main activities. It started selling bottled wine in 1974 and subsequently obtained organic certification. Today it is run by Andrea with the aid of his daughter Isabella.

Our finalist boasts a fragrant nose in which notes of almond mingle with autumn leaves. Entry on the palate is low key, gradually becoming broader and more dynamic through to the full-flavoured, long finish. The Vernaccia '09 is simpler and more approachable, characterized by fruity notes of apples and spring flowers, elegant structure and full, not particularly lingering, flavour. In our tastings of the two reds, we liked the drinkability of the Chianti '09 and the austerity of San Gimignano Cabernet '05, which is slightly held back by tannins.

○ Vernaccia di S. Gimignano Isabella Ris. '05	▼▼	4
● Chianti Colli Senesi '09	▼	3
● San Gimignano Cabernet '05	▼	5
○ Vernaccia di S. Gimignano '09	▼	4
○ Vernaccia di S. Gimignano Isabella Ris. '04	▽▽▽	5
○ Vernaccia di S. Gimignano Isabella Ris. '99	▽▽	4

Podere Sapaio

LOC. LO SCOPAIO, 212
57022 CASTAGNETO CARDUCCI [LI]
TEL. 0565765187
www.sapaio.com

PRE-BOOKED VISITS

ANNUAL PRODUCTION 75,000 bottles
HECTARES UNDER VINE 25
VITICULTURE METHOD Conventional

Podere Sapaio was founded in 1999 by Massimo Piccin. Today it has a decent area under vine in the municipalities of Castagneto Carducci and Bibbona, on land formed by sandy sediment and alluvial deposits with well-drained chalky soils. The vineyards are planted with the classic varieties of the Bolgheri zone and the style of the wines is modern, with good overall balance and expressive complexity.

Bolgheri Superiore Sapaio '07 is simply marvellous. Its exceptionally complex nose derived from the aromatic concentration of perfectly ripe fruit, well integrated with clear notes of toast and spice. On the palate it displays alluring smoky notes but it was its weave and depth that impressed us most, enhancing the wine's complexity. Bolgheri Volpolo '08 is simpler but nonetheless very good.

● Bolgheri Sapaio Sup. '07	▼▼▼	7
● Bolgheri Volpolo '08	▼▼	5
● Bolgheri Sapaio Sup. '06	▽▽▽	7
● Bolgheri Sapaio Sup. '05	▽▽	7
● Bolgheri Sapaio Sup. '04	▽▽	7
● Bolgheri Volpolo '07	▽▽	5
● Bolgheri Volpolo '06	▽▽	5

Sassotondo

PIAN DI CONATI, 52
58010 SOVANA [GR]
TEL. 0564614218
www.sassotondo.it

CELLAR SALES
PRE-BOOKED VISITS

ANNUAL PRODUCTION 50,000 bottles
HECTARES UNDER VINE 12
VITICULTURE METHOD Certified organic

Located in Sorano and Pitigliano, this estate covers an area of 72 hectares with mainly tufa soil, as the area belongs to the volcanic basin of Lake Bolsena. The area under vine is ten hectares, planted mainly to ciliegiolo, followed by sangiovese and merlot, while a couple of hectares are dedicated to trebbiano, greco and sauvignon. Organic farming methods have been used here for many years, bearing witness to the deep respect for nature that fires agronomist Carla Benini and Edoardo Ventimiglia.

Sassotondo presented four wines to our tastings this year. Our favourite was the flagship San Lorenzo '07, with a distinctive peppery nose and a generous, juicy palate that is slightly overwhelmed by tannic oak. Sovana Superiore Franze '07 is good, with clean aromas and good texture, the new Tufo Rosso '09, from ciliegiolo and sangiovese, is delicious and Ciliegiolo '09 is well paced.

● San Lorenzo '07	**YY**	7
● Ciliegiolo '09	**Y**	4
● Sovana Rosso Sup. Franze '07	**Y**	5
● Tufo Rosso '09	**Y**	3
● Ciliegiolo '08	YY	4
● Ciliegiolo '07	YY	3*
● San Lorenzo '06	YY	7
● San Lorenzo '05	YY	7
● San Lorenzo '04	YY	6

Michele Satta

LOC. CASONE UGOLINO, 23
57022 CASTAGNETO CARDUCCI [LI]
TEL. 0565773041
www.michelesatta.com

CELLAR SALES
PRE-BOOKED VISITS

ANNUAL PRODUCTION 180,000 bottles
HECTARES UNDER VINE 28
VITICULTURE METHOD Conventional

Michele Satta is one of Bolgheri's most authentic winemakers and a very determined man with clear ideas. It all started at the end of the 1980s, when the first plot was purchased and the new cellar built. Many years have passed and the estate has made several new acquisitions, such as the Castagni and Poderini vineyards, but Michele's enthusiasm has remained the same, along with his decisions that sometimes go against local trends, commencing with his true veneration of sangiovese.

Cavaliere '06 is a monovarietal Sangiovese, with a complex nose of fruit preserve, tobacco and freshly mown hay. The same sensations are echoed on the palate, which vaunts evolved notes and tannins that are still rather stiff. Bolgheri Rosso Piastraia '07 is good with a nose of black and red berry fruit, aromatic herbs and lavender. It is full flavoured and gutsy, although still fairly tannic. Bolgheri Superiore I Castagni '07 is very open and ripe, perhaps not as good as usual, while Costa di Giulia '09 is a nicely aromatic white.

● Bolgheri Rosso Piastraia '07	**YY**	6
● Cavaliere '06	**YY**	8
● Bolgheri Rosso Sup. I Castagni '07	**Y**	8
○ Costa di Giulia '09	**Y**	5
● Bolgheri Rosso Piastraia '02	YYY	7
● Bolgheri Rosso Piastraia '01	YYY	7
○ Bolgheri Bianco '07	YY	4
● Bolgheri Rosso '06	YY	6
● Bolgheri Rosso Sup. I Castagni '06	YY	8
● Bolgheri Rosso Sup. I Castagni '05	YY	8
● Cavaliere '05	YY	8
○ Costa di Giulia '08	YY	5
○ Costa di Giulia '07	YY	5
● Diambra Rosso '07	YY	4

Savignola Paolina

VIA PETRIOLO, 58
50022 GREVE IN CHIANTI [FI]
TEL. 0558546036
www.savignolapaolina.it

CELLAR SALES
PRE-BOOKED VISITS
ROOMS

ANNUAL PRODUCTION 35,000 bottles
HECTARES UNDER VINE 6
VITICULTURE METHOD Conventional

This delightful little winery has long been owned by the Fabbri family, of which Paolina, one of the legendary figures of Chianti Classico, was a prominent member. It has a cool climate and is situated on the Greve hills at an average altitude of 330 metres. The full-flavoured wines have good, relaxed progression totally in keeping with the characteristics of the area. The classic local wines are made exclusively from traditional grape varieties.

Chianti Classico Riserva '07 is a real charmer with an intensely floral, delicately spiced nose featuring notes of wild strawberries. It is also delicious on the palate, which focuses on flavour rather than body, and has great length. Granaio '08, from sangiovese and merlot, is also good, although the toast aromas of the wood were still a little invasive at the time of tasting. Chianti Classico '08 is well made but has a bitterish finish.

● Chianti Cl. Ris. '07	🍷🍷	5
● Granaio '08	🍷🍷	5
● Chianti Cl. '08	🍷	4
● Chianti Cl. '03	YY	4
● Chianti Cl. Ris. '06	YY	5
● Chianti Cl. Ris. '05	YY	5
● Chianti Cl. Ris. '04	YY	5
● Chianti Cl. Ris. '03	YY	5
● Granaio '07	YY	5
● Granaio '06	YY	5
● Granaio '03	YY	5
● Granaio '02	YY	6
● Granaio '01	YY	6

La Selva

FRAZ. SAN DONATO - ALBINIA
LOC. FONTE BLANDA
SP 81 OSA, 7
58010 ORBETELLO [GR]
TEL. 0564885799
www.laselva-bio.eu

CELLAR SALES
PRE-BOOKED VISITS
ROOMS

ANNUAL PRODUCTION 200,000 bottles
HECTARES UNDER VINE 26
VITICULTURE METHOD Certified organic

Organic viticulture, a state-of-the-art cellar and special attention to old local varieties are the cornerstones of Karl Egger's production. These factors are flanked by a particularly fair pricing policy, making the Orbetello estate one of the most interesting on the Maremma wine scene, with a consistent and possibly excessively wide, range of balanced, pleasant wines.

Prima Causa '08, from cabernet sauvignon and merlot, is very good with a penetrating nose and a juicy palate. The peppery, flavoursome Ciliegiolo '08 is again possibly the best of its kind. Morellino '09 has a truly satisfying, relaxed palate while Morellino Colli dell'Uccellina '08 is a little stiffer and the rest of the list is reliable.

● Prima Causa '08	🍷🍷	6
● Ciliegiolo '08	🍷🍷	5
● Morellino di Scansano '09	🍷🍷	4
● Maremma Rosso '09	🍷	3
● Morellino di Scansano Colli dell'Uccellina '08	🍷	5
○ Vermentino La Selva '09	🍷	4
● Ciliegiolo '07	YY	5
● Ciliegiolo '06	YY	5
● Morellino di Scansano '07	YY	4*
● Morellino di Scansano Colli dell'Uccellina '06	YY	4*
● Prima Causa '06	YY	6
○ Vermentino La Selva '08	YY	4
○ Vermentino La Selva '07	YY	4*

Fattoria Selvapiana

LOC. SELVAPIANA, 43
50068 RUFINA [FI]
TEL. 0558369848
www.selvapiana.it

CELLAR SALES
PRE-BOOKED VISITS

ANNUAL PRODUCTION 220,000 bottles
HECTARES UNDER VINE 60
VITICULTURE METHOD Conventional

Fattoria di Selvapiana is one of Rufina's historic estates, founded during the Middle Ages and long the summer residence of Florence's bishops. It was purchased by the Giuntini Antinori family in 1827 and the current owner, Francesco, is the fifth generation. He has helped restore the Rufina designation to its former splendour, distinguishing itself on the vast Chianti wine scene as it already had at the time of Cosimo III de' Medici. Today it is run by Silvia and Federico Giuntini Masseti, who also oversee production of the Fattoria di Petrognano estate in the nearby Pomino DOC.

This year saw the debut of the intriguing Syrah '07, with a complex spicy nose of pepper and juniper, which mingle with cherries and currants, and end notes of tobacco. Entry on the palate is solid and juicy, with good grip and close-knit, well-integrated tannins and the finish is very attractive. Fornace '07, from merlot and cabernet sauvignon with a dash of sangiovese, is also very nice, with an inviting nose of menthol-lifted strawberries and plums. The palate opens soft, broad and tannic, following through to a long, appetizing finish.

● Fornace '07	▼▼	6
● Syrah '07	▼▼	5
● Chianti Rufina '08	▼	4
● Chianti Rufina Bucerchiale Ris. '07	▼	6
● Chianti Rufina '03	▽▽	4
● Chianti Rufina Bucerchiale '04	▽▽	6
● Chianti Rufina Bucerchiale Ris. '06	▽▽	6
● Chianti Rufina Bucerchiale Ris. '03	▽▽	6
● La Fornace '04	▽▽	6
● Pomino Fattoria di Petrognano '06	▽▽	4*
● Pomino Fattoria di Petrognano '04	▽▽	4
○ Vin Santo della Rufina '99	▽▽	6

Sensi

FRAZ. CERBAIA
VIA CERBAIA, 107
51035 LAMPORECCHIO [PT]
TEL. 057382910
www.sensivini.com

CELLAR SALES
PRE-BOOKED VISITS

ANNUAL PRODUCTION 2,000,000 bottles
HECTARES UNDER VINE 50
VITICULTURE METHOD Conventional

Pietro Sensi was the first of the family to enter the wine business, in 1895, selling his products at the local markets. His sons, Vittorio and Armido, founded Fratelli Sensi in 1919 and Vittorio's sons gave the business a further boost, conquering new markets after the Second World War. Widespread national distribution commenced in the mid 1970s while exports got firmly under way with the arrival of the fourth generation at the end of the 1980s. The family also owns Fattoria Calappiano in the Vinci area.

The list is extensive, topped by the Calappiano wines, commencing with Chianti Riserva Vinciano '07, which has a nose of red berry fruit, good body, well-integrated tannins and an attractive finish. Lungarno '08, from sangiovese with a small amount of colorino, is also very good, giving Mediterranean scrubland and dark berry fruit, stylish structure, balance and a convincing rising finish. Chianti Riserva '07 is a tasty, easy-drinking wine that is pleasantly uncomplicated and very traditional in style.

● Chianti Sensi Ris. '07	▼▼	5
● Chianti Vinciano Fattoria Calappiano Ris. '07	▼▼	5
● Lungarno Fattoria Calappiano '08	▼▼	6
● Brunello di Montalcino Boscoselvo '05	▼	8
● Chianti Vinciano '09	▼	5
● Mantello '08	▼	5
● Morellino di Scansano Arcere '09	▼	4
● Rosso di Montalcino Boscoselvo '08	▼	5
● Testardo '08	▼	5

Tenuta di Sesta

FRAZ. CASTELNUOVO DELL'ABATE
LOC. SESTA
53020 MONTALCINO [SI]
TEL. 0577835612
www.tenutadisesta.it

CELLAR SALES
PRE-BOOKED VISITS

ANNUAL PRODUCTION 150,000 bottles
HECTARES UNDER VINE 30
VITICULTURE METHOD Conventional

Giovanni Ciacci heads a handsome estate in the heart of the legendary Sesta cru, after which it is named, in the southern part of the zone in Sant'Angelo in Colle and Castelnuovo dell'Abate. The well-drained soil of the vineyards, which cover an area of approximately 30 hectares, is a mixture of limestone and tufa, with very little clay, while natural air circulation ensures exceptionally healthy fruit. The house style is compromise between tradition and innovation, particularly in its use of oak, for which it adopts medium-sized barrels.

One of the estate's Brunellos reached our national finals for the umpteenth time this year. The '05 vintage is excellent and closely reflects the terroir. On the nose it is varietal, with cherry jam and sound notes of peaches and tobacco. It's a fantastic wine considering the vintage, testifying to the fact that the terroir makes the difference. The firmly structured palate is surefooted and tannic, nicely balanced by acidity. We also liked the Riserva '04, which has slightly evolved notes.

● Brunello di Montalcino '05	▼▼	6
● Brunello di Montalcino Ris '04	▼▼	8
● Poggio d'Arna '08	▼	4
● Rosso di Montalcino '08	▼	4
● Brunello di Montalcino '04	▽▽	6
● Brunello di Montalcino '02	▽▽	6
● Brunello di Montalcino Ris. '01	▽▽	8
● Poggio d'Arna '07	▽▽	4
● Rosso di Montalcino '07	▽▽	4
● Rosso di Montalcino '06	▽▽	4*

Sesti - Castello di Argiano

FRAZ. SANT'ANGELO IN COLLE
LOC. CASTELLO DI ARGIANO
53024 MONTALCINO [SI]
TEL. 0577843921
www.sestiwine.com

CELLAR SALES
PRE-BOOKED VISITS

ANNUAL PRODUCTION 61,000 bottles
HECTARES UNDER VINE 9
VITICULTURE METHOD Conventional

Giuseppe Sesti continues to produce first-rate wines, year after year. The estate covers an area of around 100 hectares, with nine under vine. It is housed in a delightful location, in the 13th-century tower of Argiano castle that defended Camigliano, a junction on the road to the Maremma region. Work in the vineyard and the cellar is carried out in accordance with the phases of the moon, revealing the owner's love of astronomy. The wines are aged in small barrels of 15 to 30 hectolitres.

This year the estate's best-known wine put up an excellent performance. The quality of the '04 vintage and Riserva Phenomena's reliability make it a benchmark in Montalcino. Its label changes every year, each commemorating a particularly important astronomical phenomenon. The classic nose is well defined and close focused, with warm, caressing wild and morello cherries and blackberries, which mingle with spicy overtones of medicinal herbs and tobacco. The palate is in a class of its own, with close-knit mellow tannins and the typically low acidity of the zone, displaying good, rich development and a broad, lingering finish. Brunello '05 is also very good.

● Brunello di Montalcino Ris. '04	▼▼▼	8
● Brunello di Montalcino '05	▼▼	8
● Rosso di Montalcino '08	▼	5
○ Sauvignon '09	▼	5
● Brunello di Montalcino Phenomena Ris. '01	▽▽▽	8
● Brunello di Montalcino '04	▽▽	7
● Brunello di Montalcino Phenomena Ris. '03	▽▽	8
● Castello Sesti '06	▽▽	7
● Grangiovese '06	▽▽	5
● Rosso di Montalcino '06	▽▽	6
○ Sauvignon '08	▽▽	4
○ Sauvignon '07	▽▽	4

Tenuta Sette Ponti

LOC. VIGNA DI PALLINO
52029 CASTIGLION FIBOCCHI [AR]
TEL. 0575477857
www.tenutasetteponti.it

CELLAR SALES
PRE-BOOKED VISITS

ANNUAL PRODUCTION 230,000 bottles
HECTARES UNDER VINE 50
VITICULTURE METHOD Conventional

Antonio Moretti continues to reap success all over Italy, without forgetting Sette Ponti, the first of his wineries. The Arezzo estate covers an area of 250 hectares, including 50 under vine. Here Antonio's father Alberto decided to establish his country retreat, where he could hunt in the reserve with his friends. The estate already had a vineyard, sporadically tended by the Savoia family, its previous owners. Regular wine production commenced at the end of the 1950s but it wasn't until the arrival of Antonio, in the mid 1990s, that the estate adopted a new approach, focusing on quality and an international style.

Oreno '07, from merlot, cabernet sauvignon and sangiovese, is exceptionally good. The complex nose of tobacco, wild berries and spice introduces a generous, rounded palate with mellow tannins and a refreshing swath of acidity, ending in a clean, long finish. Crognolo '08, from sangiovese with small amounts of merlot and cabernet, is fresh and approachable while Anni '09, from viognier and sauvignon, is well made but not particularly exciting.

● Oreno '07	2 black glasses	8
● Crognolo '08	2 black glasses	5
● Poggio al Lupo '08	2 black glasses	5
○ Anni '09	1 black glass	4
● Oreno '05	3 white glasses	8
● Oreno '00	3 white glasses	6
○ Anni '08	2 white glasses	4*
● Crognolo '07	2 white glasses	5
● Crognolo '06	2 white glasses	5
● Crognolo '05	2 white glasses	5
● Morellino di Scansano Poggio al Lupo '07	2 white glasses	4
● Morellino di Scansano Poggio al Lupo '06	2 white glasses	4*
● Oreno '06	2 white glasses	8
● Oreno '03	2 white glasses	7
● Poggio al Lupo '06	2 white glasses	6
● Poggio al Lupo '05	2 white glasses	6
● Poggio al Lupo '03	2 white glasses	6

Solatione

FRAZ. MERCATALE VAL DI PESA
VIA VALIGONDOLI, 53A
50024 SAN CASCIANO IN VAL DI PESA [FI]
TEL. 055821623
www.solatione.it

CELLAR SALES
PRE-BOOKED VISITS

ANNUAL PRODUCTION 12,000 bottles
HECTARES UNDER VINE 6
VITICULTURE METHOD Conventional

This estate has been owned by the Giachi family since 1972. Wine production began immediately from the excellent sangiovese already planted in the vineyards but it was another 20 years before the first bottled wine was marketed in 1992. In addition to wine, the estate also makes olive oil, which is one of the finest in Chianti. For many years, the winery concentrated on the production of typical local products, such as Chianti Classico and Vin Santo, which receives special attention here, but recently it has also started experimenting with international grape varieties.

Riserva '07 is excellent, with an opulent, complex nose ranging from wild berries to pencil lead, tobacco and aromatic herbs. The broad, cosseting palate displays powerful attack, open tannins and a flavoursome finish. Rosso Ombroso '07 is a Chianti-style single-variety Merlot. It has a nose of cherries and strawberries, with well integrated notes of pencil lead and balsamic hints, and a smooth, complex palate with firm body, attractive freshness and a long, focused finish.

● Chianti Cl. '08	2 black glasses	4
● Chianti Cl. Ris. '07	2 black glasses	5
● Rosso Ombroso '07	2 black glasses	6
● Chianti Cl. '04	2 white glasses	4
● Chianti Cl. '02	2 white glasses	4
● Chianti Cl. Ris. '04	2 white glasses	5
● Chianti Cl. Ris. '01	2 white glasses	5

Le Sorgenti

LOC. VALLINA
VIA DI DOCCIOLA, 8
50012 BAGNO A RIPOLI [FI]
TEL. 055696004
www.fattoria-lesorgenti.com

PRE-BOOKED VISITS
ROOMS

ANNUAL PRODUCTION 40,000 bottles
HECTARES UNDER VINE 13
VITICULTURE METHOD Organic

Dynamism can generates quality. Take the Ferraris, who get consistently excellent results. The estate dates from the Middle Ages, but in 1585 the old hunting lodge was converted into a villa. It was given its current name in the late 19th century by Gaetano Leopoldi, cousin of the poet Giacomo. The current owners came from Emilia to dedicate themselves heart and soul to their new business, Gabriele in the vineyard and cellar, and Elisabetta managing the commercial side. Their son Filippo is studying oenology, ready to put his knowledge at the service of the family business.

Scirus '07, from cabernet sauvignon, merlot, malbec and petit verdot, reached our finals. It has an alluring, fresh nose of currants and balsamic notes, broad, soft structure, mellow, balanced tannins and a lingering finish. Sghiras '07, a chardonnay and sauvignon blend, is surprisingly lively with fresh citrus notes, hints of basil and white peaches, lean, lively body, balanced acidity and a very satisfying long finish.

● Scirus '07	2 black glasses	6
○ Sghiras '07	2 black glasses	5
● Chianti Colli Fiorentini Respiro '08	1 black glass	4
● Gaiaccia '08	1 black glass	5
● Chianti Colli Fiorentini Respiro '07	2 white glasses	4
● Chianti Colli Fiorentini Respiro '06	2 white glasses	4*
● Gaiaccia '07	2 white glasses	5
● Gaiaccia '06	2 white glasses	5
● Gaiaccia '05	2 white glasses	4
● Gaiaccia '04	2 white glasses	4
● Scirus '06	2 white glasses	6
● Scirus '05	2 white glasses	6
● Scirus '04	2 white glasses	6
● Scirus '03	2 white glasses	6
○ Sghiras '06	2 white glasses	5

Spadaio e Piecorto

VIA SAN SILVESTRO, 1
50021 BARBERINO VAL D'ELSA [FI]
TEL. 0558072915
spadaiopiecorto@tiscali.it

CELLAR SALES
PRE-BOOKED VISITS

ANNUAL PRODUCTION 60,000 bottles
HECTARES UNDER VINE 14
VITICULTURE METHOD Conventional

The Stefanelli brothers' winery earned our highest accolade for the first time this year with Chianti Classico '08. This excellent performance crowns years of work focused on attaining quality with an eye to price. The winery is situated on the border between the provinces of Florence and Siena and is housed in a small hamlet that was built in the 12th century. Along with the core activities of wine and olive oil production, it also offers holiday apartments in the municipality of Poggibonsi.

The winner of our Three Glasses boasts an invitingly clean, focused nose of cherries and plums with accentuated mineral notes, smooth body, well-integrated mellow tannins and acid backbone that ensures vigour and a full-flavoured, lingering finish. We also liked Piecorto '08, a monovarietal Sangiovese with a pervasive nose of wild berries and spices, firm structure and well-integrated tannins.

● Chianti Cl. '08	3 black glasses	4*
● Chianti Cl. Piecorto '08	2 black glasses	4
● Chianti Cl. Ris. '07	1 black glass	5
● Chianti Cl. Piecorto '06	2 white glasses	4*
● Pietra Forte '01	2 white glasses	4
● Pietra Rossa '05	2 white glasses	4*
● Pietra Rossa '04	2 white glasses	4

Tenuta di Sticciano

VIA DI STICCIANO, 207
50052 CERTALDO [FI]
TEL. 0571669191
www.tenutadisticciano.it

CELLAR SALES
PRE-BOOKED VISITS
ROOMS

ANNUAL PRODUCTION 80,000 bottles
HECTARES UNDER VINE 25
VITICULTURE METHOD Organic

This year we have awarded a full profile to the estate owned by Alessio Milioti, who personally oversees work in the cellar. The farm dates from the 17th century and winemaking is documented from around 1815. In addition to wine, 40 hectares of olive groves allow the production of various types of oil and the estate also makes honey. Farm holidays are also offered, with cookery lessons and other activities that allow guests contact with nature.

A wide array of wines was presented for our tastings. Chianti Riserva della Villa '07 is very good, vaunting a fresh nose of cherries and light earthy notes, racy body, prominent acidity and a long finish. Attimo '06, a blend of equal parts of syrah and merlot, is peppery with distinct gamey notes and fruity overtones of currants. The juicy, mouthfilling palate shows soft structure and a long finish. Cantastorie '06, from 50 per cent cabernet sauvignon and 50 per cent sangiovese, is a powerful wine with a nose of vanilla and cloves over blackberry jam. Entry on the palate is creamy, following through full bodied and well sustained.

● Attimo '06	▼▼	4
● Cantastorie '06	▼▼	5
● Chianti della Villa Ris. '07	▼▼	4*
● Chianti Casa La Fornace '09	▼	2
● Cantastorie '05	▽▽	5
● Cantastorie '01	▽▽	4
● Chianti della Villa Ris. '06	▽▽	4*
● Sysame '05	▽▽	4*

Tenimenti Angelini

LOC. VAL DI CAVA
53024 MONTALCINO [SI]
TEL. 057780411
www.tenimentiangelini.it

CELLAR SALES
PRE-BOOKED VISITS

ANNUAL PRODUCTION 900,000 bottles
HECTARES UNDER VINE 55
VITICULTURE METHOD Conventional

Tenimenti Angelini, the farming division of the well-known pharmaceutical group, owns several estates,. including Val di Suga in Montalcino and Tre Rose in Montepulciano. The former has recently completed the replanting of its vineyards and renovation of its production facilities, and boasts one of the zone's legendary vineyards, Vigna Spuntali, which yielded a sumptuous '05 vintage. Although Tre Rose has little new to offer, it remains a very reliable winery.

Montepulciano won the contest between the two estates this year, with its Nobile di Montepulciano Simposio '07 reaching our finals. The nose melds blackberry jam with unusual floral notes of roses and violet. Although the tannins are still young and prominent they will mellow in time, and the full finish lingers. The Montalcino estate's Brunello '05 is very good. It has a traditional nose, with notes of hay, tobacco and medicinal herbs, accompanied by an elegant palate of medium intensity, which is balanced and fairly long.

● Nobile di Montepulciano Simposio '07	▼▼	6
○ Vin Santo di Montepulciano Tenuta Tre Rose '99	▼▼	6
● Brunello di Montalcino '05	▼▼	5
● Nobile di Montepulciano Simposio Tenuta Tre Rose '07	▼▼	6
● Brunello di Montalcino V. Spuntali '04	▼	8
● Nobile di Montepulciano '07	▼	4
● Nobile di Montepulciano La Villa Tenuta Tre Rose '07	▼	6
● Rosso di Montalcino '08	▼	4
● Brunello di Montalcino V. del Lago '95	▽▽▽	8
● Brunello di Montalcino V. del Lago '93	▽▽▽	8
● Brunello di Montalcino V. del Lago '90	▽▽▽	8
● Brunello di Montalcino V. Spuntali '95	▽▽▽	8
● Brunello di Montalcino V. Spuntali '93	▽▽▽	8
● Brunello di Montalcino '04	▽▽	7
● Brunello di Montalcino V. Spuntali '03	▽▽	8
● Nobile di Montepulciano La Villa Tenuta Tre Rose '06	▽▽	6
● Nobile di Montepulciano Tenuta Tre Rose '06	▽▽	4*

Tenimenti Luigi D'Alessandro

via Manzano, 15
52042 Cortona [AR]
tel. 0575618667
www.tenimentidalessandro.it

PRE-BOOKED VISITS

ANNUAL PRODUCTION 100,000 bottles
HECTARES UNDER VINE 37
VITICULTURE METHOD Conventional

An estate's greatness can be judged above all by the consistency of its products, which is a distinguishing feature of the winery founded by the D'Alessandro family. One of the reasons is their unwavering belief in a hitherto unknown but high-quality terroir, where syrah has found an ideal habitat, making it possible to establish a solid project in which to invest. It has served as an example for the numerous producers who have subsequently set up business here, laying the bases for the creation of an exceptionally dynamic, evolving designation.

Once again the estate's best wines were its two leading Syrahs: Bosco '07 and, in particular, Migliara '07, which deservedly took Three Glasses. The first has dynamic, firm body that gradually relaxes, combined with an aromatic profile that is not yet fully expressed, while Migliara has marvellous spicy sensations, jam and nicely integrated notes of leather. On the palate it is well orchestrated and complex but not heavy, with a nice finish. Syrah '08 is more approachable, with an intense, fresh nose of fruit and flowers, and a simpler, more supple palate. Fontarca Viognier '08, is fresh and easy drinking, and Vin Santo '01 has a complex nose but a slightly lightweight finish.

● Cortona Syrah Migliara '07	▼▼▼	7
● Cortona Il Bosco '07	▼▼	7
● Cortona Syrah '08	▼▼	4
○ Fontarca Viognier '08	▼▼	5
○ Cortona Vin Santo '01	▼	7
● Cortona Il Bosco '06	▽▽▽	7
● Cortona Il Bosco '04	▽▽▽	7
● Cortona Il Bosco '03	▽▽▽	7
● Cortona Il Bosco '01	▽▽▽	7
● Podere Il Bosco '97	▽▽▽	5
● Cortona Il Bosco '05	▽▽	7
● Cortona Syrah '07	▽▽	4*
● Cortona Syrah Migliara '06	▽▽	8

Terenzi

loc. Montedonico
58054 Scansano [GR]
tel. 0564599601
www.terenzi.eu

CELLAR SALES
ROOMS

ANNUAL PRODUCTION 180,000 bottles
HECTARES UNDER VINE 30
VITICULTURE METHOD Conventional

The Terenzi estate, run by Florio, his wife Giuseppina and their son Federico, continues to achieve excellent results. It is a fresh new entry on the Maremma wine scene, whose products were released for the first time in 2007, concentrating from the outset on quality. The style of the wines of the Scansano-based estate focuses strongly on balance and drinkability, without excessive oak or extraction.

Morellino di Scansano Riserva '07 is extremely convincing, with a well-defined nose and a fragrant, flavoursome palate. Bramaluce '08, from sangiovese, syrah and alicante, is firm and juicy, with attractive menthol on the nose. The well-made Morellino '09, is focused, deep and exceptionally supple while Balbino '09, a monovarietal Vermentino, is pleasant and tangy.

● Morellino di Scansano '09	▼▼	3*
● Morellino di Scansano Ris. '07	▼▼	4
○ Balbino '09	▼▼	4
● Bramaluce '08	▼▼	5
○ Balbino '08	▽▽	4
● Bramaluce '07	▽▽	5
● Francesca Romana '07	▽▽	5
● Morellino di Scansano '08	▽▽	3*
● Morellino di Scansano Ris. '06	▽▽	4

Terre del Marchesato

FRAZ. BOLGHERI
LOC. SANT'UBERTO, 164
57020 CASTAGNETO CARDUCCI [LI]
TEL. 0565749752
www.fattoriaterredelmarchesato.it

CELLAR SALES
PRE-BOOKED VISITS

ANNUAL PRODUCTION 50,000 bottles
HECTARES UNDER VINE 10
VITICULTURE METHOD Conventional

After having taken over the family estate, founded during the 1950s, Maurizio Fuselli has managed to transform it into a handsome, well-organized winery in the Bolgheri zone, whose first official year of production is labelled with the 2003 vintage. The operation is based in Sant'Uberto, in the Ferrugini area, where the sandy soils are darker due to the presence of ferrous minerals and clay. The estate again confirmed its reliability, capable not only of producing impeccable wines but also highly original ones.

Marchesale '07 is a single-variety Syrah with a very concentrated nose and palate. The former is warm and spicy, dominated by notes of wild berry jam and chocolate, while the latter is powerfully extracted, with very stiff young tannins. Emilio Primo '08, from cabernet, merlot and syrah, is more delicate, disclosing fruit jelly combined with a refined blend of oriental spices. Cabernet Tarabuso '07 is elegant, with exquisite herbaceous overtones, and the two whites are good, although very different in style.

● Marchesale '07	▼▼	8
● Emilio Primo '08	▼▼	5
○ Emilio Primo Bianco '09	▼▼	6
● Tarabuso '07	▼▼	7
○ Papeo '08	▼	6
● Marchesale '06	▽▽	8
● Syrah del Marchesato '05	▽▽	8
● Tarabuso '06	▽▽	7
● Tarabuso '05	▽▽	6

Teruzzi & Puthod

LOC. CASALE, 19
53037 SAN GIMIGNANO [SI]
TEL. 0577940143
www.teruzzieputhod.it

CELLAR SALES
PRE-BOOKED VISITS

ANNUAL PRODUCTION 1,200,000 bottles
HECTARES UNDER VINE 90
VITICULTURE METHOD Conventional

This estate belongs to the Campari Group, a multinational that also owns several famous Italian wineries in Piedmont and Sardinia. The winery was founded by Enrico Teruzzi and Carmen Puthod in 1974 and plays a leading role in the zone, for it was one of those responsible for the international success of Vernaccia di San Gimignano. Although the flagship is still missing, despite the impressive dimensions and extensive list of wines, the estate finally appears to have completed its running-in period.

This year we found the red wines the most convincing, such as Peperino '07, from sangiovese and merlot, with alluring fruity notes of blueberries and morello cherries, accompanied by spicy sensations of pepper, a lean, juicy body and fresh, dynamic progression with a flavoursome finish. The latest arrival, Arcidiavolo '07, from sangiovese, alicante, cabernet sauvignon and petit verdot has a nose ranging from vegetal moss and mint to more intense tobacco and leather, bound together by overtones of cherry jam. It is soft and hefty on the palate, with a nice swathe of acidity and vibrant tannins, displaying good continuity.

● Arcidiavolo '07	▼▼	6
● Peperino '07	▼▼	4*
○ Terre di Tufi '09	▼▼	5
○ Vernaccia di S. Gimignano '09	▼▼	4*
● Peperino '05	▽▽	4
○ Terre di Tufi '08	▽▽	5
○ Terre di Tufi '07	▽▽	5
○ Terre di Tufi '05	▽▽	5
○ Terre di Tufi '01	▽▽	5
○ Terre di Tufi '99	▽▽	5
○ Vernaccia di S. Gimignano '08	▽▽	4*
○ Vernaccia di S. Gimignano '07	▽▽	4

Testamatta

VIA DI VINCIGLIATA, 19
50014 FIESOLE [FI]
TEL. 055597289
www.bibigraetz.com

PRE-BOOKED VISITS

ANNUAL PRODUCTION 500,000 bottles
HECTARES UNDER VINE 55
VITICULTURE METHOD Conventional

This year was rather low key for the estate owned by Bibi Greatz, an eclectic Florentine producer with an Israeli father and Norwegian mother. The flagship wine Testamatta, a monovarietal Sangiovese that made the estate's name, was missing from our tastings as it was still ageing in the cellar. Bugia, the barrique-aged Ansonica from the island of Giglio, was also absent. We can call it a pause for reflection while awaiting further developments in production, which also features special wines such as Vin Santo, a few bottles of which are occasionally released.

Colore '06, from mainly colorino and canaiolo, has a vegetal nose of autumn leaves and aromatic herbs against a background of blueberries and blackcurrants. The broad palate has stiff tannins, medium development and a full-flavoured finish. Grilli del Testamatta '08 , from sangiovese, colorino and canaiolo, has a focused nose of cherries and blackberries softened by spicy notes of pepper and fresh hints of mint. Entry on the palate is tasty, with good weight and balanced acidity, cruising through to a well-calibrated finish. Cicala del Giglio '09, an Ansonica aged exclusively in steel, has a fresh, floral nose, lean body, and good zesty flavour.

●	Colore '06	▼▼	8
●	Grilli del Testamatta '08	▼▼	6
○	Casamatta Bianco '09	▼	3
●	Casamatta Rosso '08	▼	3
○	Cicala del Giglio '09	▼	4
●	Colore '05	▽▽	8
●	Colore '03	▽▽	8
●	Testamatta '07	▽▽	8
●	Testamatta '06	▽▽	8
●	Testamatta '05	▽▽	8
●	Testamatta '04	▽▽	8
●	Testamatta '02	▽▽	8

Giuliano Tiberi

FRAZ. CASALGUIDI
VIA CASTEL BIAGINI, 23
51034 SERRAVALLE PISTOIESE [PT]
TEL. 0573527589
www.giulianotiberi.it

CELLAR SALES
PRE-BOOKED VISITS
ROOMS

ANNUAL PRODUCTION 25,000 bottles
HECTARES UNDER VINE 5
VITICULTURE METHOD Conventional

Making wine in uncharted territory is always courageous. But that is what Giuliano Tiberi did after having left his job as a chemist to dedicate himself to farming, investing in an estate in Montalbano, an area that is now making a name for itself among wine lovers following a long period of obscurity. Mindful of his youth in the Marche region, where his family owned a farm, Giuliano built a winery and an oil press. He seeks to preserve the traditional grape varieties that yield good results, without disdaining new ones.

Chianti Montalbano Imbricci '09 performed very well, displaying a fresh, lively floral nose with slightly earthy notes, firm, juicy body, and intriguing drinkability. Merli '08, a distinctive monovarietal Merlot, is also good, with characteristic notes of wild berries accompanied by liquorice and menthol. On the palate it is firm, juicy and cosseting, with a long, enjoyable finish.

●	Chianti Montalbano Imbricci '09	▼▼	3*
●	I Merli '08	▼▼	5
●	Le Vespe '08	▼	4
●	I Merli '05	▽▽	5

Tolaini

LOC. VALLENUOVA
SP 9 DI PIEVASCIATA, 28
53019 CASTELNUOVO BERARDENGA [SI]
TEL. 0577356972
www.tolaini.it

CELLAR SALES
PRE-BOOKED VISITS

ANNUAL PRODUCTION 250,000 bottles
HECTARES UNDER VINE 50
VITICULTURE METHOD Conventional

Pierluigi Tolaini's estate performed very well this year, with its flagship wine Picconero, a blend of merlot and cabernet sauvignon with a small amount of petit verdot, reaching our finals. Pierluigi is a singular character who emigrated to Canada as a young man and, after having done a plethora of humble jobs, founded the country's largest private transport company. In 1998, his love for Italy prompted him home to purchase land in Castelnuovo Beradenga, where he established the estate that bears his name. Pierluigi's philosophy foregrounds local varieties, flanked by international grapes, which are well suited to the Chianti zone.

Picconero '07 has a complex nose, with toasty notes interweaving with coffee, liquorice and attractive crisp fruit. The broad palate has a smooth, velvety attack with subtle, well-balanced tannins accompanying a very long, relaxed finish. Al Passo '07, from mainly sangiovese, is also pleasant, with a close-focused nose of cherries, cinnamon and cloves. The plush palate has good attack, with prominent fresh acidity, ensuring a nicely lingering finish.

● Picconero '07	**YY**	8
● Al Passo '07	**YY**	5
● Valdisanti '07	**Y**	6
● Al Passo '06	YY	5
● Picconero '06	YY	8
● Picconero '05	YY	8
● Picconero '04	YY	8
● Valdisanti '06	YY	6
● Valdisanti '05	YY	6
● Valdisanti '04	YY	6

Torraccia di Presura

LOC. STRADA IN CHIANTI
VIA DELLA MONTAGNOLA, 130
50027 GREVE IN CHIANTI [FI]
TEL. 0558588656
www.torracciadipresura.it

CELLAR SALES
PRE-BOOKED VISITS

ANNUAL PRODUCTION 200,000 bottles
HECTARES UNDER VINE 35
VITICULTURE METHOD Conventional

This winery has been owned by the Osti family since 1986 and once belonged to the estate of the 19th-century villa of La Presura. It is the first winery in Chianti Classico on the Via Chiantigiana connecting Florence with Siena. The family started by replanting the vineyards and subsequently built a new cellar on the spot believed to have been the site of a watchtower, after which the estate is named. It is interesting to note that it also produces a small amount of sparkling wine from chardonnay, trebbiano and malvasia.

Chianti Classico '08 is very good and reached our finals on the strength of its complex nose of ripe cherry and strawberry fruit with delicate minerality. On the palate it is pleasant and fresh, with a nicely lingering, full-flavoured finish. The two versions of Tarroco are less interesting, both held back by an over-reticent nose, while the '08 vintage is more straightforward, with the Riserva showing plenty of body but a rather closed palate.

● Chianti Cl. '08	**YY**	5
● Chianti Cl. Il Tarocco '08	**Y**	5
● Chianti Cl. Il Tarocco Ris. '07	**Y**	5
● Lucciolaio '06	**Y**	6
● Arcante '04	YY	6
● Chianti Cl. '03	YY	4
● Chianti Cl. Il Tarocco '03	YY	4
● Chianti Cl. Il Tarocco Ris. '05	YY	5
● Chianti Cl. Il Tarocco Ris. '04	YY	5
● Chianti Cl. Il Tarocco Ris. '03	YY	5
● Chianti Cl. Il Tarocco Ris. '01	YY	5
● Lucciolaio '04	YY	6

Fattoria Torre a Cona

loc. San Donato in Collina
50010 Rignano sull'Arno [FI]
tel. 055699000
www.villatorreacona.com

CELLAR SALES
PRE-BOOKED VISITS
ROOMS

ANNUAL PRODUCTION 30,000 bottles
HECTARES UNDER VINE 14
VITICULTURE METHOD Conventional

The winery owned by the Rossi di Montelera family in the Colli Fiorentini area, reconfirmed its usual high quality again this year. Extensive renovation has involved not only the winemaking side of the business, with the construction of a new cellar and the replanting of the vineyards, but also the guest facilities, with first-rate accommodation and a splendid tasting room housed in an old granary. The wines are characterized by a traditional style.

Torre a Cona's wines are always very elegant, in perfect keeping with their terroir. Vin Santo del Chianti Merlaia is stunning, with a full, pervasive nose of dried figs, almonds, citrus peel and a juicy, yet taut palate thanks to good underlying acidity. Terre di Cino '07, a monovarietal Sangiovese, has a fruity nose, with top notes of strawberries, and a fresh, fragrant, juicy palate. Chianti dei Colli Fiorentini '08, is deliciously easy drinking.

● Chianti Colli Fiorentini '08	Two Black Glasses	2
● Terre di Cino '07	Two Black Glasses	4
○ Vin Santo del Chianti Merlaia '04	Two Black Glasses	5
● Chianti Colli Fiorentini '07	Two White Glasses	2
● Terre di Cino '06	Two White Glasses	4
● Terre di Cino '05	Two White Glasses	4
● Terre di Cino '04	Two White Glasses	4
○ Vin Santo del Chianti Merlaia '03	Two White Glasses	5
○ Vin Santo del Chianti Merlaia '01	Two White Glasses	5

Le Torri di Campiglioni

via San Lorenzo a Vigliano, 31
50021 Barberino Val d'Elsa [FI]
tel. 0558076161
www.letorri.net

CELLAR SALES
PRE-BOOKED VISITS
ROOMS

ANNUAL PRODUCTION 150,000 bottles
HECTARES UNDER VINE 28
VITICULTURE METHOD Conventional

This winery was founded 30 years ago by a group of friends who decided to team together to launch a farm while, initially, continuing in their existing professions. Wine and olive oil were their first love, and have now been joined by guest facilities following the renovation of local farmhouses that can accommodate up to 40 people. Great attention has always been paid to the environment and the recent construction of a solar power plant enables the estate to generate most of its own energy.

The wine that impressed us this year was Meridius '07, from sangiovese with a small amount of merlot, which has a complex nose of spice-laced raspberries and cherries, soft, silky body, well-integrated tannins and a succulent finish. Villa San Lorenzo '07, from sangiovese only, also scored well, displaying balanced notes of assorted fruit preserves with mineral and balsamic hints, dynamic, fresh body and a concentrated, long, full palate. Vigliano '07, a monovarietal Cabernet Sauvignon, has balsamic and vegetal notes, with cooked green peppers and red berry fruit. The soft palate shows good attack, prominent tannins and an alluring, lingering finish.

● Meridius '07	Two Black Glasses	5
● Villa San Lorenzo '07	Two Black Glasses	6
● Chianti Colli Fiorentini '08	One Glass	4
● Chianti Colli Fiorentini Ris. '07	One Glass	5
● Vigliano '07	One Glass	6
● Magliano '04	Two White Glasses	6
● Vigliano '04	Two White Glasses	6

Fattoria La Traiana

LOC. TRAIANA, 16
52028 TERRANUOVA BRACCIOLINI [AR]
TEL. 0559179004
fatt.latraiana@libero.it

ANNUAL PRODUCTION N.A.
HECTARES UNDER VINE 60
VITICULTURE METHOD Certified organic

This year seems like a period of transition for Giandomenico Gigante's winery. Production as a whole is still sound, without peaks of excellence, but with the wines of the Val Cornia estate in top form. Perhaps it is just a pause for reflection by a producer who sought out forgotten local varieties to give his wines greater character and personality, and adopted organic farming techniques in the vineyards.

Tenuta Sasso Orlando's Sauvignon Blanc '09 is good, with green notes, white peaches and assorted citrus fruit, and a lively, spirited palate that is full and juicy with a flavoursome finish. Terra di Sasso '07, a monovarietal Cabernet Sauvignon, is stylish, with attractive notes of bell pepper and wild berries, firm, balanced body and a long finish. From the Terranuova Bracciolini estate, we preferred the young wines, like Alò '08, from sangiovese with small amounts of merlot and cabernet sauvignon, which has fruity notes of cherries and a lean, full-flavoured palate, and Chianti Superiore '08, with a more traditional nose and an enjoyable, smooth palate.

○ Sauvignon Blanc Sasso Orlando '09	▼▼	5
● Terra di Sasso Sasso Orlando '07	▼▼	5
● Alò '08	▼	4
● Campo Arsiccio '06	▼	6
○ Campogialli '08	▼	5
● Chianti Sup. '08	▼	4
● Pian del Pazzo '06	▼	6
● Campo Arsiccio '05	▽▽	6
● Pian del Pazzo '04	▽▽	6
● Pian del Pazzo '03	▽▽	6
● Terra di Sasso Sasso Orlando '06	▽▽	5
● Terra di Sasso Sasso Orlando '05	▽▽	5

Travignoli

VIA TRAVIGNOLI, 78
50060 PELAGO [FI]
TEL. 0558361098
www.travignoli.com

CELLAR SALES
PRE-BOOKED VISITS

ANNUAL PRODUCTION 250,000 bottles
HECTARES UNDER VINE 70
VITICULTURE METHOD Conventional

After many years at the helm of the Consorzio Chianti Rufina, the estate's owner Giovanni Busi has left to become president of the Consorzio del Chianti, the complex body that oversees the diverse area of Italy's largest DOCG, embracing several zones with their own distinct features. On the basis of the work carried out so far, the future looks very promising. The estate has ancient origins and traces of Etruscan camps, and has been used for the systematic cultivation of vines since the 12th century. In the 18th century, it was bought by the Busi family, who have run it ever since. In addition to wine, it also produces extra virgin olive oil.

This year there is a change in labelling. From the '07 vintage onwards, the Riserva has become Tegolaia, a name formerly used for an IGT wine. Its debut was impressive, its alluring nose combining fruity notes of plums and cherries with more evolved ones of tobacco, then a balanced palate, with juicy tannins and good acid backbone, and a very satisfying finish. Chianti Rufina '08 is well made and highly drinkable. A fresh, floral nose leads into simple structure. Gavignano '09, from chardonnay, is sound and floral, with hints of white peaches and a rich palate.

● Chianti Rufina Tegolaia Ris. '07	▼▼	5
● Chianti Rufina '08	▼	3
○ Gavignano '09	▼	3
● Calice del Conte '04	▽▽	6
● Chianti Rufina Ris. '04	▽▽	5
● Tegolaia '06	▽▽	5
● Tegolaia '04	▽▽	5
○ Vin Santo Chianti Rufina '01	▽▽	5
○ Vin Santo Chianti Rufina '00	▽▽	5

Tenuta di Trinoro

VIA VAL D'ORCIA, 15
53047 SARTEANO [SI]
TEL. 0578267110
www.trinoro.it

CELLAR SALES

ANNUAL PRODUCTION 40,000 bottles
HECTARES UNDER VINE 22
VITICULTURE METHOD Conventional

Andrea Franchetti accepts no compromises in his quest for absolute quality. His vineyards are cultivated exclusively with non-invasive techniques and the grapes are harvested as late as possible. Technological tricks are banished from the cellar, where fermentation takes place in concrete vats with the use of native yeasts, and ageing is carried out in carefully selected barriques. This refusal to compromise has transformed a remote corner of the south-eastern province of Siena into a little Bordeaux.

Needless to say, the results of our tastings are consistent with this scrupulous attention to detail. Tenuta di Trinoro '08, a blend of merlot, cabernet franc, cabernet sauvignon and petit verdot, won Three Glasses for its impressive power and ripe fruit, combined with great complexity entirely derived from the terroir. Le Cupole '08, the estate's "second vin", is made from the same blend of grapes but from younger vineyards, and shows rounded, ripe and nicely supple.

● Tenuta di Trinoro '08	▼▼▼	8
● Le Cupole di Trinoro '08	▼	6
● Tenuta di Trinoro '04	YYY	8
● Tenuta di Trinoro '03	YYY	8
● Le Cupole di Trinoro '07	YY	6
● Le Cupole di Trinoro '06	YY	6
● Le Cupole di Trinoro '05	YY	6
● Tenuta di Trinoro '07	YY	8
● Tenuta di Trinoro '06	YY	8
● Tenuta di Trinoro '05	YY	8

★ Tua Rita

LOC. NOTRI, 81
57028 SUVERETO [LI]
TEL. 0565829237
www.tuarita.it

PRE-BOOKED VISITS

ANNUAL PRODUCTION 110,000 bottles
HECTARES UNDER VINE N.A.
VITICULTURE METHOD Conventional

Tua Rita's wines are highly renowned, both in Italy and abroad. This fame was initially largely attributable to Redigaffi, a monovarietal Merlot that was the estate's flagship, but now has valid rivals for the title. Tua Rita produces modern, firmly structured, Mediterranean-style wines that faithfully reflect the terroir. The vineyards are located on the hills behind the cellar, which has a small annual production of cult wines.

Once again this year Redigaffi is Redigaffi and, according to tradition, won its umpteenth Three Glass award. Despite the theoretically uninspiring growing season, the '08 vintage is its usual full, voluptuous self, with attractive notes of dark berry fruit and chocolate with balsamic hints. The big-hitting palate is vibrant and firmly structured, supported by impressive acidity. Syrah '08 shows plenty of spice on the nose and firm and caressing on the palate. Giusto di Notri '08, from cabernet sauvignon and merlot, is fragrant and supple.

● Redigaffi '08	▼▼▼	8
● Giusto di Notri '08	▼▼	8
● Syrah '08	▼▼	8
● Perlato del Bosco Rosso '08	▼▼	6
● Rosso dei Notri '09	▼▼	6
○ Perlato del Bosco Bianco '09	▼	4
● Redigaffi '07	YYY	8
● Redigaffi '06	YYY	8
● Redigaffi '04	YYY	8
● Redigaffi '03	YYY	8
● Redigaffi '02	YYY	8
● Redigaffi '01	YYY	8
● Redigaffi '00	YYY	8
● Redigaffi '99	YYY	8
● Redigaffi '98	YYY	8

Uccelliera

FRAZ. CASTELNUOVO DELL'ABATE
POD. UCCELLIERA, 45
53020 MONTALCINO [SI]
TEL. 0577835729
www.uccelliera-montalcino.it

CELLAR SALES
PRE-BOOKED VISITS

ANNUAL PRODUCTION 50,000 bottles
HECTARES UNDER VINE 6
VITICULTURE METHOD Conventional

Andrea Cortonesi has been bitten by the building bug and work on the cellar and the apartments adjoining the estate never seems to cease. He has also opened a restaurant in Siena, near Piazza del Campo. However, there is no need to worry. Tastings revealed that he hasn't been neglecting his wines. Andrea lavishes meticulous care on the vineyards, located near the abbey of Sant'Antimo, 250 metres above sea level. Purchased in 1986 and subsequently expanded and partially replanted, they now cover an area of six and a half hectares at a density of 5,000 vines per hectare.

Brunello Riserva '04 is very good, with a ripe nose of cherry jam, hints of spice and a distinctive liquorice note. The powerful palate has firm structure and good acidity, although the tannins are still a little rough. Its muscular development ends in a complex but not yet perfectly relaxed finish. Further bottle ageing will help it achieve balance. Lovers of fresh, elegant wines will appreciate the highly drinkable Brunello '05, which displays good balance and fine-grained tannins.

● Brunello di Montalcino Ris. '04	▼▼	8
● Brunello di Montalcino '05	▼▼	8
● Rosso di Montalcino '08	▼	6
● Brunello di Montalcino Ris. '97	▽▽▽	8
● Brunello di Montalcino '03	▽▽	7
● Brunello di Montalcino '02	▽▽	7
● Brunello di Montalcino Ris. '01	▽▽	8
● Rapace '05	▽▽	6
● Rosso di Montalcino '07	▽▽	5

F.lli Vagnoni

LOC. PANCOLE, 82
53037 SAN GIMIGNANO [SI]
TEL. 0577955077
www.fratellivagnoni.com

CELLAR SALES
PRE-BOOKED VISITS
ROOMS

ANNUAL PRODUCTION 120,000 bottles
HECTARES UNDER VINE 21
VITICULTURE METHOD Certified organic

The estate owned by the Vagnoni brothers has swiftly recovered from a year of transition, with its Vernaccia Riserva I Mocali '08 reaching our finals and the entire list performing well. Founded in 1955, the farm grows not only grapes and olives, but also fruit and cereals. There's also guest accommodation and in 2007, when the new cellar was built, a drying room was included for the grapes destined for Vin Santo.

Our finalist has a complex nose, with prominent minerality mingling with white peaches and exotic fruit. Entry on the palate is full and convincing, continuing broad, juicy and long length. Vernaccia '09 is also very good, with aromatic notes of hedgerow, nuts and ripe apples and a vibrant, racy palate with a pleasant full-flavoured finish. The amber-hued Vin Santo '06 is first rate, presenting a complex, leisurely nose with stylish notes of dried figs, hazelnuts and dates, and a sumptuous, exceptionally elegant palate that drinks dense and full, with a well-defined finish. Both the rosé Pancolino '09 and Chianti Colli Senesi '08 are pleasant early drinkers.

○ Vernaccia di S. Gimignano I Mocali Ris. '08	▼▼	5
○ San Gimignano Vin Santo '06	▼▼	7
○ Vernaccia di S. Gimignano '09	▼▼	2
● Chianti Colli Senesi '08	▼	2
⊙ Il Pancolino '09	▼	2
● I Sodi Lunghi '04	▽▽	4
○ Vernaccia di S. Gimignano Mocali Ris. '06	▽▽	5
○ Vernaccia di S. Gimignano Mocali Ris. '05	▽▽	5
○ Vernaccia di S. Gimignano Mocali Ris. '04	▽▽	4
○ Vernaccia di S. Gimignano Mocali Ris. '03	▽▽	4
○ Vernaccia di S. Gimignano V. Fontabuccio '06	▽▽	4*
○ Vernaccia di S. Gimignano V. Fontabuccio '04	▽▽	3

Tenuta Val di Cava

LOC. VAL DI CAVA
53024 MONTALCINO [SI]
TEL. 0577848261
www.valdicava.it

PRE-BOOKED VISITS

ANNUAL PRODUCTION 57,000 bottles
HECTARES UNDER VINE 19
VITICULTURE METHOD Conventional

Val di Cava is situated in the northern part of Montalcino, at the foot of the renowned Montosoli hill. The vineyards practically form a single plot, at an average altitude of 300 metres, and cover an area of approximately 20 hectares, planted almost exclusively to Brunello. Mass selection has resulted in classic, not particularly high density, plantings. The recently expanded cellar houses barrels of various sizes – larger for Brunello – while fermentation takes place partly in wooden vats.

Brunello Madonna del Piano '04, named after the votive chapel in the middle of the vineyard, is excellent and won our Three Glasses. Brief aeration brings out the best of the nose, with spicy, floral overtones and toastiness enriching classic notes of leather and ripe cherries. The attractive palate displays fine terroir-driven acidity, high quality, mellow tannins, good continuity and a very long, focused finish. Brunello '05 is also well made, with well-defined fruit on the nose and a full-bodied palate, especially considering its vintage.

● Brunello di Montalcino Madonna del Piano Ris. '04	TTT+	8
● Brunello di Montalcino '05	TT	8
● Rosso di Montalcino '08	TT	5
● Brunello di Montalcino '04	YY	7
● Brunello di Montalcino '99	YY	8
● Brunello di Montalcino Madonna del Piano Ris. '03	YY	8
● Brunello di Montalcino Madonna del Piano Ris. '01	YY	8
● Brunello di Montalcino Madonna del Piano Ris. '99	YY	3
● Rosso di Montalcino '05	YY	4

Tenuta Valdipiatta

VIA DELLA CIARLIANA, 25A
53040 MONTEPULCIANO [SI]
TEL. 0578757930
www.valdipiatta.it

CELLAR SALES
PRE-BOOKED VISITS
ROOMS

ANNUAL PRODUCTION 120,000 bottles
HECTARES UNDER VINE 32
VITICULTURE METHOD Conventional

Year after year, the products of Miriam Caporali's estate have acquired a distinctive style, characterized by balance and elegance. The result is a range of characterful, coherent wines of consistently high quality, offering one of the clearest examples of the potential of sangiovese in Montepulciano for over 20 years. Today the estate offers visitors mini tasting courses held by its staff.

Nobile Vigna d'Alfiero '07 again proved to be in a class of its own, with a concentrated nose, good stuffing and nice complexity, although it is held back a little by slightly excessive oak. Balance and drinkability are the distinguishing characteristics of the flavoursome, fragrant Nobile '07. The same style, albeit slightly lower key, can be found in Rosso Montepulciano '08, which is extremely easy drinking.

● Nobile di Montepulciano '07	TT	5
● Nobile di Montepulciano V. d'Alfiero '07	TT	7
● Rosso di Montepulciano '08	T	4
● Nobile di Montepulciano Ris. '90	YYY	5
● Nobile di Montepulciano V. d'Alfiero '99	YYY	6
● Nobile di Montepulciano '06	YY	5
● Nobile di Montepulciano '05	YY	5
● Nobile di Montepulciano V. d'Alfiero '06	YY	7
● Nobile di Montepulciano V. d'Alfiero '05	YY	7
● Nobile di Montepulciano V. d'Alfiero '04	YY	7
● Pinot Nero '06	YY	6
○ Vin Santo di Montepulciano '04	YY	7

Tenuta di Valgiano

FRAZ. VALGIANO
VIA DI VALGIANO, 7
55018 LUCCA
TEL. 0583402271
www.valgiano.it

CELLAR SALES

ANNUAL PRODUCTION 70,000 bottles
HECTARES UNDER VINE 25
VITICULTURE METHOD Certified biodynamic

Valgiano nestles among the Lucca hills, in a spectacular natural setting. It is a sunny area, with a typically Mediterranean climate, which provides the perfect backdrop for the meticulous, loving labours of Moreno Pietrini and Laura di Collobaino, along with Saverio Petrilli, a leading figure in the Italian biodynamic movement, and everyone else who lives and works here. It is this magical union of man and nature, rather than the grape varieties used, that is the key to understanding the essence of Valgiano's wines.

Tenuta di Valgiano '07 è is a red with a unique appeal. It can certainly be described as changeable, and sometimes even capricious, but at the right moment it rewards the drinker with simply breathtaking authenticity and natural, tumultuous development. It is so rhythmic and vibrant, with endless flavour, that it simply not possible to describe in mere tasting notes. We unhesitatingly awarded it Three Glasses. Palistorti '08, with notes of iodine and rich aromatic herbs is also good and very long-lingering while Palistorti Bianco '09 has intensely yellow aromas and a slightly alcoholic palate.

●	Colline Lucchesi Tenuta di Valgiano '07	3 glasses (black)	7
○	Colline Lucchesi Palistorti Bianco '09	2 glasses (black)	5
●	Colline Lucchesi Rosso dei Palistorti '08	2 glasses (black)	5
●	Colline Lucchesi Tenuta di Valgiano '06	3 glasses +	7
●	Colline Lucchesi Tenuta di Valgiano '05	3 glasses	7
●	Colline Lucchesi Tenuta di Valgiano '04	3 glasses	7
●	Colline Lucchesi Tenuta di Valgiano '03	3 glasses	7
●	Colline Lucchesi Tenuta di Valgiano '01	3 glasses	8
○	Colline Lucchesi Palistorti Bianco '08	2 glasses	5
○	Colline Lucchesi Palistorti Bianco '07	2 glasses	5
●	Colline Lucchesi Palistorti Rosso '07	2 glasses	5
●	Colline Lucchesi Palistorti Rosso '06	2 glasses	5
●	Colline Lucchesi Rosso dei Palistorti '04	2 glasses	5
●	Colline Lucchesi Rosso dei Palistorti '03	2 glasses	5

Vecchie Terre di Montefili

VIA SAN CRESCI, 45
50022 PANZANO [FI]
TEL. 055853739
www.vecchieterredimontefili.com

CELLAR SALES
PRE-BOOKED VISITS

ANNUAL PRODUCTION 40,000 bottles
HECTARES UNDER VINE 14
VITICULTURE METHOD Conventional

In the year 1200, this estate was donated to the monks of Passignano abbey by the owners of the castle of Montefili. The castle's crest depicted a vine with a bunch of grapes, which shows that viticulture and winemaking flourished in the area even in antiquity. In 1979, the Acuti family from Prato purchased the property. During this period, many areas of Chianti were completely neglected, and here too it was necessary to plant new vineyards and totally rebuild the winery. The estate initially focused on sangiovese, later adding cabernet sauvignon.

Bruno di Rocca '06, from cabernet sauvignon and sangiovese, has an intense nose with fresh, vegetal notes and pleasant balsamic hints, accompanied by dark blackberry-like berry fruit. On the palate, it is full and juicy, displaying good backbone and structure and a long, flavoursome finish. The Riserva '06 is also very good, with earthy aromas and notes of tobacco, followed by plum jam, and an elegant, restrained palate.

●	Bruno di Rocca '06	2 glasses (black)	7
●	Chianti Cl. Ris. '06	2 glasses (black)	6
●	Anfiteatro '06	1 glass (black)	8
●	Chianti Cl. '07	1 glass (black)	5
●	Anfiteatro '03	3 glasses	8
●	Anfiteatro '94	3 glasses	8
●	Anfiteatro '05	2 glasses	8
●	Bruno di Rocca '05	2 glasses	7
●	Bruno di Rocca '04	2 glasses	8
●	Chianti Cl. '06	2 glasses	5

Castello di Velona

Loc. Velona
53024 Montalcino (SI)
TEL. 0577800101
www.castellodivelona.it

CELLAR SALES
PRE-BOOKED VISITS
ROOMS AND FOOD

ANNUAL PRODUCTION **N.A.**
HECTARES UNDER VINE **5**
VITICULTURE METHOD **Conventional**

A new farm concept has been created at Velona castle. It takes the form of a hotel housed in an 11th-century castle, with a first-rate restaurant and soon also a wellness centre. The vineyards are beautifully situated, overlooking Monte Amiata, approximately 400 metres above sea level in the far south-west of Montalcino, beyond Castelnuovo, on loose clay-based soils with plenty of gravel. Modern, high-density plantings ensure low yields per vine while the state-of-the art cellar is equipped with temperature-controlled vats and medium-sized barrels.

Both the wines presented were very good, although we preferred Rosso di Montalcino '07. Its full, complex nose offers notes of oleander, peaches and morello cherries, with well-calibrated oak. The full, concentrated palate is well orchestrated, attractive tannins and good acidity ensuring great drinkability. Brunello '05 has hints of wild strawberries and subtle vegetal notes on the nose, accompanied by an elegant palate with fine, well-integrated tannins.

● Brunello di Montalcino '05	🍷🍷	7
● Rosso di Montalcino '07	🍷🍷	5

I Veroni

VIA TIFARITI, 5
50065 PONTASSIEVE [FI]
TEL. 0558368886
www.iveroni.it

CELLAR SALES
PRE-BOOKED VISITS
ROOMS AND FOOD

ANNUAL PRODUCTION **80,000 bottles**
HECTARES UNDER VINE **15**
VITICULTURE METHOD **Organic**

Although the estate has been owned by the Malesci family since the end of the 19th century, it has medieval origins and was once among the feudal possessions of the noble Guidi family. In 1978, Laura Malesci, the current owner, started to renovate the cellars and the other buildings while expanding and modernizing the vineyards. Today, her work is continued by her son Lorenzo Mariani, a lawyer and wine enthusiast, who with the aid of agronomist Andrea Paoletti has embarked on the conversion of the vineyards to organic farming methods.

The Riserva '07 is as good as ever, unfurling an attractive fruity nose of currants and blueberries that mingle with wafts of Mediterranean scrubland. The nice entry on the palate introduces firm, juicy tannins and a generous, powerful finish. Vin Santo '03 has a striking nose in which bitterish notes of cinchona jostle with fruit, then good progression on the palate and a lingering finish. Chianti Rufina '08 is very easy drinking, but rendered slightly edgy by prominent tannins, while the Rosé '09 is fresh and enjoyable.

● Chianti Rufina Ris. '07	🍷🍷	5
○ Vin Santo del Chianti Rufina '03	🍷🍷	6
● Chianti Rufina '08	🍷	4
⊙ Rosé '09	🍷	4
● Chianti Rufina '06	🍷🍷 (outline)	4*
● Chianti Rufina '05	🍷🍷 (outline)	3*
● Chianti Rufina Ris. '06	🍷🍷 (outline)	5
● Chianti Rufina Ris. '04	🍷🍷 (outline)	4
○ Vin Santo del Chianti Rufina '02	🍷🍷 (outline)	6
○ Vin Santo del Chianti Rufina '99	🍷🍷 (outline)	5

Villa Cafaggio

via San Martino a Cecione, 5
50020 Panzano [FI]
tel. 0558549094
www.villacafaggio.it

CELLAR SALES
PRE-BOOKED VISITS

ANNUAL PRODUCTION 400,000 bottles
HECTARES UNDER VINE 40
VITICULTURE METHOD Conventional

The name of the estate is derived from Cahago, which denotes a fenced cultivated field. During the 15th century, it belonged to the Benedictine monks of Siena and was subsequently sold to various families, such as the Florentine Nicolinis, and the hospital of Santa Maria Nuova. At the beginning of the 19th century, the property passed to the Farkas family, who started to restore the cellars and replant the vineyards and olive groves. Today the estate is owned by the Lavis group.

Cortaccio '06, from cabernet sauvignon, performed well, with a complex nose of menthol, vegetal notes and bell pepper weaving with wild berries. Entry on the palate is firm, full and very tasty, continuing with well-calibrated tannins and a long finish. San Martino '06, a monovarietal Sangiovese, is also good, with a fruity nose of cherries and plums, good structure with well-distributed, fine-grained tannins, and a full-flavoured finish. The Riserva '07 has an evolved nose of leathery, earthy notes, but its prominent tannins clip the finish.

● Cortaccio '06	**YY**	8
● San Martino '06	**YY**	8
● Chianti Cl. Ris. '07	**Y**	5
● Chianti Cl. Ris. '03	YYY	6
● Cortaccio '01	YYY	8
● Cortaccio '97	YYY	6
● San Martino '00	YYY	8
● San Martino '99	YYY	7
● Chianti Cl. Ris. '06	YY	6
● Cortaccio '05	YY	8
● Cortaccio '04	YY	8
● San Martino '05	YY	8

Villa di Geggiano

loc. Ponte a Bozzone
via di Geggiano, 1
53019 Castelnuovo Berardenga [SI]
tel. 0577356879
www.villadigeggiano.com

CELLAR SALES
PRE-BOOKED VISITS

ANNUAL PRODUCTION 35,000 bottles
HECTARES UNDER VINE 8
VITICULTURE METHOD Certified organic

Villa di Geggiano and its stunning garden, dating from at least the 14th century, are national monuments and offer the rare opportunity to take a step back in time. The estate is named after the splendid property that, like the building, belongs to the Bianchi Bandinellis. It is just a few kilometres from Siena, in the southern part of Chianti Classico, where the climate is warmer and the soils are rich in tufa and silt, as well as the usual marl, and studded with cobbles. Certified organic farming methods are used in the vineyards while the wines are aged chiefly in French wood.

We found the Chianti Classico Riserva less convincing than usual this year. Although the '07 vintage is sound and juicy, it did not seem as deep or complex as the previous edition. In fact, we preferred the basic Chianti Classico '08, in which we immediately recognized the estate's hallmarks: a soft, complex nose of blueberries and raspberries with hints of spice, and a taut, vibrant, sometimes austere palate, with firm but perfect tannins.

● Chianti Cl. '08	**YY**	4
● Chianti Cl. Ris. '07	**YY**	6
● Chianti Cl. '07	YY	4*
● Chianti Cl. Ris. '06	YY	6
● Chianti Cl. Ris. '04	YY	6
● Chianti Classico Ris. '04	YY	5
● Geggiaiolo '06	YY	7

Villa Petriolo

via di Petriolo, 7
50050 Cerreto Guidi [FI]
tel. 057155284
www.villapetriolo.com

PRE-BOOKED VISITS

ANNUAL PRODUCTION 55,500 bottles
HECTARES UNDER VINE 14
VITICULTURE METHOD Conventional

The estate run by the Maestrelli sisters long ago chose to focus on total quality and this has led them to take increasingly focused decisions, particularly regarding ageing. Indeed, Chianti Rosae Mnemonis and Chianti Villa Petriolo will be released later than usual to complete ageing in the cellar. This year we tasted a new wine: Ser Berto '08, a monovarietal Merlot. The estate has been in the family for 40 years and the sisters have given a great boost to viticultural development and communication, associating the estate with literature through a competition and art, with exhibitions of works by contemporary artists.

L'Imbrunire '09, a monovarietal Canaiolo, reached our finals with an elegant, fresh nose of cherries and currants lifted by mint, and an excellent lean, balanced palate with a soft attack and a long finish. The other new entry is a Merlot, Ser Berto '08, which also scored well, offering minerals and pencil lead combined with fruity plum notes, and a firm palate with well-calibrated tannins and a full-flavoured subtle weave. Vin Santo '04 has a charming nose with alluring notes of honey and peach jam, and a soft, creamy, full palate with a long finish.

● L'Imbrunire '09	▼▼	5
● Ser Berto '08	▼▼	5
● Golpaja '07	▼	5
○ Vin Santo del Chianti '04	▼	6
● Chianti Rosae Mnemosis '08	▽▽	5
● Chianti Rosae Mnemosis '07	▽▽	5
● Chianti Rosae Mnemosis '06	▽▽	5
● Golpaja '06	▽▽	5
● Golpaja '05	▽▽	5
● Golpaja '04	▽▽	5
● L'Imbrunire '08	▽▽	5

Villa Pillo

via Volterrana, 24
50050 Gambassi Terme [FI]
tel. 0571680212
www.villapillo.com

CELLAR SALES
PRE-BOOKED VISITS

ANNUAL PRODUCTION 300,000 bottles
HECTARES UNDER VINE 40
VITICULTURE METHOD Conventional

The farm, dating from the Middle Ages, covers an area of over 450 hectares. It was bought by the American Dyson family in 1989, who restored the dwellings to their original splendour before renovating the vineyards and cellar, introducing innovative elements drawn from their experience in California. Their decision to use mainly international grape varieties was made on the basis of the terroir's profile. In addition to wine, the estate also produces olive oil and cereals.

Borgoforte '08, a blend of cabernet sauvignon and sangiovese with a little merlot, reached our finals for its concentrated nose of dark berry fruit, with hints of spice and toast, and its full-bodied, rich palate of balanced acidity and a long, flavoursome finish. Cypresses '08, a monovarietal Sangiovese, is also very good, giving cherry fruit, a soft, alluring palate and perfect length. Merlot Sant'Adele is pleasant, with a nose of wild berries and spices and an excellent, full-flavoured, rounded palate. Cingalino '09, an equal blend of cabernet franc and merlot, came as a surprise, showing fresh, enjoyable and agile but lingering.

● Borgoforte '08	▼▼	4*
● Cingalino '09	▼▼	2
● Cypresses '08	▼▼	4*
● Merlot Sant'Adele '08	▼▼	6
● Syrah '08	▼	6
● Vivaldaia '08	▼	6
● Borgoforte '06	▽▽	4*
● Borgoforte '05	▽▽	4
● Cypresses '07	▽▽	4*
● Merlot Sant'Adele '06	▽▽	6
● Merlot Sant'Adele '05	▽▽	6
● Syrah '07	▽▽	6
● Syrah '06	▽▽	6
● Syrah '05	▽▽	6
● Vivaldaia '06	▽▽	6
● Vivaldaia '05	▽▽	6

Villa Vignamaggio

VIA DI PETRIOLO, 5
50022 GREVE IN CHIANTI [FI]
TEL. 055854661
www.vignamaggio.com

CELLAR SALES
PRE-BOOKED VISITS
ROOMS AND FOOD

ANNUAL PRODUCTION **250,000 bottles**
HECTARES UNDER VINE **42**
VITICULTURE METHOD **Conventional**

This handsome estate covers an area of 160 hectares in the municipality of Greve in Chianti, including 42 hectares of east and south-west-facing vineyards altitudes between 42 and 330 metres. Most of the rows are planted to sangiovese, although the estate also grows cabernet franc, with vines over 40 years old. The cellar has naturally controlled temperature and humidity and houses both small casks and larger barrels.

This year, Gianni Nunziante's estate failed to achieve our highest accolade, which it has become accustomed to winning year after year. We are sure that it is an isolated episode. This winery is run with great competence. Our favourite wine was Obsession '07, a blend of merlot, cabernet sauvignon and sangiovese whose fresh, pervasive nose melds attractive dark berry fruit with balsam while the fragrant palate lacks a little depth because the tannins are excessively drying. Vignamaggio '07, a monovarietal Cabernet Franc, has a slightly harsh nose with little complexity and a juicy, nicely taut palate, although we'd have liked a bit more depth.

● Obsession '07	7
● Vignamaggio '07	8
● Chianti Cl. '08	5
● Chianti Cl. Monna Lisa Ris. '07	6
● Il Morino '08	3
● Vignamaggio '06	8
● Vignamaggio '05	8
● Vignamaggio '04	7
● Vignamaggio '01	7
● Vignamaggio '00	7

Tenuta Vitanza

FRAZ. TORRENIERI
POD. BELVEDERE, 145
52024 MONTALCINO [SI]
TEL. 0577832882
www.tenutavitanza.it

CELLAR SALES
PRE-BOOKED VISITS

ANNUAL PRODUCTION **160,000 bottles**
HECTARES UNDER VINE **16**
VITICULTURE METHOD **Conventional**

A new, amazingly efficient cellar with stunning architecture has allowed the winery to solve a few problems that arose in the past. Its vineyards are situated on two opposite slopes of Montalcino, some in the wide area east of Torrenieri, with clay soils rich in tufa and fossil material that aid drainage and aeration, and others in the far south-east, at Castelnuovo dell'Abate, where the temperatures are higher and the soils looser with plenty of marl. The cellar is equipped with barrels of all sizes and employs cutting-edge fermentation techniques.

This year, the estate performed very well at our tastings, with two wines reaching the finals. The first is the new Brunello di Montalcino Tradizione '04, whose name is derived from the use of 30 and 40-hectolitre barrels. It is extremely elegant, with alluring notes of bramble and blackberries accompanying distinct white cherries. The palate has fine body, carried by good acidity, while the exceptionally fine-grained tannins are already mellow and do not hold back the finish, which is intense and lingers.

● Brunello di Montalcino Tradizione '04	6
● Brunello di Montalcino '05	7
● Rosso di Montalcino '08	4
● Brunello di Montalcino Ris. '04	8
● Volare '07	3
● Brunello di Montalcino '00	7
● Brunello di Montalcino '03	7
● Brunello di Montalcino '01	7
● Brunello di Montalcino '98	8
● Brunello di Montalcino Ris. '01	8

Tenuta Vitereta

via Casanuova, 108/1
52020 Laterina [AR]
tel. 057589058
www.tenutavitereta.com

CELLAR SALES
PRE-BOOKED VISITS
ROOMS AND FOOD

ANNUAL PRODUCTION 80,000 bottles
HECTARES UNDER VINE 50
VITICULTURE METHOD Certified organic

This estate is worth a visit, if only to try to understand the philosophy that drives it, which attributes value not only to agricultural production as a whole but also to the concept of a return to the past. This translates into painstaking attention to detail, aimed at achieving high quality in every single product. The 50 hectares of vineyards are flanked by another 50 given over to meadows and pastures, as well as cereal crops – from corn and durum wheat to maize – alfalfa and olives. However, wines are the estate's true passion, and are never banal, if not always perfect.

It was the whites that intrigued us this year. Supremo '04 is an original interpretation of Vin Santo from trebbiano. It has a sweet nose with buttery notes, elegant body, an enfolding palate and a long finish that makes it a true delight for aficionados. Trebbiano '08 is made from 50 per cent dried grapes, whose must is aged in separate barriques. Pale amber introduces a nose of evolved minerality and fruit, and a full, flavoursome palate. Donna Aurora '08 is a very easy-drinking Chardonnay fermented in barrique, which unfurls a complex nose and good, but not excessive, structure. The two versions of Chianti are pleasant but nothing special.

○ Supremo '04	▼▼	8
○ Trebbiano di Toscana '08	▼▼	5
● Chianti Casarossa Ris. '07	▼	5
● Chianti Lo Sterpo '08	▼	4
○ Donna Aurora '08	▼	5
● Capitoni '06	▽▽	4
● Capitoni '05	▽▽	4*
● Ripa della Mozza '03	▽▽	5
○ Trebbiano di Toscana '07	▽▽	5
● Villa Bernetti '05	▽▽	5
● Villa Bernetti '04	▽▽	5
● Villa Bernetti '03	▽▽	5
○ Vin Santo '03	▽▽	8
○ Vin Santo del Chianti '04	▽▽	8

Viticcio

via San Cresci, 12a
50022 Greve in Chianti [FI]
tel. 055854210
www.fattoriaviticcio.com

CELLAR SALES
PRE-BOOKED VISITS
ROOMS

ANNUAL PRODUCTION 200,000 bottles
HECTARES UNDER VINE 35
VITICULTURE METHOD Organic

This estate belongs to Alessandro Landini, who inherited it from his engineer father Lucio, a man with close ties to his native land. After purchasing the winery in the 1960s – a dark period for Chianti Classico – the challenge was to create a high-quality product capable of reviving the image of Chianti, which had fallen out of favour. The results convinced Alessandro to take over the family business after graduating in business studies, in order to develop production further, always with an eye to quality.

This year, the best wine was Chianti Classico Beatrice Riserva '07, with a complex nose whose fruity base of blackberries and cherries is enhanced by spices. Entry on the palate is complex, very full and mouthfilling while the tannins meld perfectly with the alcohol, creating a rising finish. Prunaio '07, a single-variety Sangiovese, has a charming nose of wild berries but the palate is somewhat clenched. Monile '07, from mainly cabernet sauvignon, is a little lacking in balance.

● Chianti Cl. Beatrice Ris. '07	▼▼	6
● Chianti Cl. '08	▼	4
● Monile '07	▼	7
● Prunaio '07	▼	7
● Prunaio '99	▽▽▽	7
● Chianti Cl. '07	▽▽	4*
● Chianti Cl. '06	▽▽	4*
● Chianti Cl. '05	▽▽	4
● Chianti Cl. Beatrice Ris. '06	▽▽	6
● Chianti Cl. Ris. '05	▽▽	5
● Chianti Cl. Ris. '04	▽▽	5
● Greppicaia I Greppi '05	▽▽	6
● Prunaio '05	▽▽	7
● Prunaio '04	▽▽	7

Abbadia Ardenga

FRAZ. TORRENIERI
VIA ROMANA, 139
53028 MONTALCINO [SI]
TEL. 0577834150
www.abbadiardengapoggio.it

This is a good example of a medium size, local state-run winery. The Brunello is always reliable. We preferred the '05 Brunello di Montalcino with its clean nose of morello cherry with tobacco and myrtle. On the palate, its lovely acidity is coupled with time-honed tannins for a wine of delicious length.

● Brunello di Montalcino '05	🍷🍷 6
● Rosso di Montalcino '08	🍷 4

Abbazia di Monte Oliveto

VIA MONTEOLIVETO, 15
53037 SAN GIMIGNANO [SI]
TEL. 0577907136
www.monteoliveto.it

The location is splendid, right next to the abbey built in 1340 by the Olivetan monks. The best wine is the Vernaccia La Gentilesca '08, complex on the nose, with good body, great definition and zesty flavour. The '09 Vernaccia is simpler, giving fruitiness and easy structure braced by good acidity.

○ Vernaccia din San Gimignano La Gentilesca '08	🍷🍷 4
○ Vernaccia di S. Gimignano '09	🍷 4

Acquabona

LOC. ACQUABONA
57037 PORTOFERRAIO [LI]
TEL. 0565933013
www.acquabonaelba.it

The wines presented by this historic 14-hectare Elban winery are always decent. The Elba Rosso Riserva '07 is very good, showing fragrant with red fruit and Mediterranean scrub over a juicy palate with a clean finish. The '09 Elba Bianco evokes flowers and sage, then a savoury, well-orchestrated palate.

○ Elba Bianco '09	🍷🍷 3
● Elba Rosso Ris. '07	🍷🍷 5
● Aleatico dell'Elba '07	🍷 6
● Voltraio '08	🍷 5

Cantine Acquaviva

LOC. ACQUAVIVA DI MONTEPULCIANO
VIA DEL SANTO, 8
53045 MONTEPULCIANO [SI]
TEL. 0578809009
www.cantineacquaviva.com

Massimiliano Neri's winery had a good Guide debut. Aside from the quirky name, Eau de Vin N°0 is very convincing. The '08, from a blend of sangiovese, syrah, cabernet sauvignon and merlot, has stylish, well-focused aromas and lively follow-through on the poised, stylish palate.

● Eau de Vin N° 0 '08	🍷🍷 8

Podere Allocco

LOC. SEANO
VIA CAPEZZANA, 19
59015 CARMIGNANO [PO]
TEL. 0558705259
podereallocco@texfee.it

Wool entrepreneur Emilio Mannelli's adventure continues. Carmignano '08 is great: fresh and pleasing on the nose, elegant and structured in the mouth. The whites also did well. Trebbiano '08 has more depth while Bacano '09, from chardonnay and sauvignon, is an easy drinker with complex fragrances.

● Carmignano '08	🍷🍷 5
○ Bacano '09	🍷 4
⊙ Carmignano Ris. '07	🍷 5
○ Trebbiano '08	🍷 4

Altiero

LOC. MONTEFIORALLE
VIA SAN CRESCI, 58
50022 GREVE IN CHIANTI [FI]
TEL. 055853728
www.altieroinchianti.it

Paolo Baldini's winery lies beside Montefioralle village, in Radda in Chianti. The sangiovese grapes are from Bovoli, 400 metres above sea level, and age in second-use barriques. The '07 Riserva is terrific: beautifully made, with luscious red fruits, minerality and summery hints of forest and earth.

● Chianti Cl. Ris. '07	🍷🍷 5
● Chianti Cl. '08	🍷 4

OTHER WINERIES

Amantis

loc. Colombaio Birbe - Poggio Rineschi
58033 Castel del Piano [GR]
tel. 0577223051
azienda@agricolaamantis.com

Oenologist Paolo Vagaggini's wines are generous. Montecucco Sangiovese Riserva '06 is powerful and succulent while the bright Montecucco Rosso Birbanera '08 is more approachable. Iperione '07, from cabernet franc and sangiovese, is intense, powerful, youthful and perhaps for this reason, a little rigid.

- ● Montecucco Sangiovese Ris. '06 — 🍷🍷 5
- ● Iperione '07 — 🍷 7
- ● Montecucco Rosso Birbanera '08 — 🍷 4

Fattoria Ambra

via Lombarda, 85
59015 Carmignano [PO]
tel. 3358282552
www.fattoriaambra.it

Ambra focuses on territory and its wines have personality. The Carmignanos are good. Le Vigne Alte Riserva '07 has powerful structure, with distinct tannins well integrated with the alcohol. Santa Cristina in Pilli '08 has drinkability as its forte. The rest of the range is sound.

- ● Carmignano Le Vigne Alte di Montalbiolo Ris. '07 — 🍷🍷 5
- ● Carmignano V. S. Cristina in Pilli '08 — 🍷🍷 4
- ● Barco Reale '09 — 🍷 3
- ● Carmignano Elzana Ris. '07 — 🍷 5

Stefano Amerighi

fraz. Farneta
via di Poggiobello
52044 Cortona [AR]
tel. 0575648340
www.stefanoamerighi.it

An excellent debut for Stefano Amerighi and his Cortona Syrah '07. Stefano continues his family's farming tradition, concentrating on viticulture and biodynamic principles. The wine has focused aromas of red fruits, pepper and leather, and a teasingly complex palate with a soft attack that then picks up.

- ● Cortona Syrah '07 — 🍷🍷 6

Artimino

fraz. Artimino
v.le Papa Giovanni XXIII, 1
59015 Carmignano [PO]
tel. 0558751423
www.artimino.com

Once again, Vin Santo dominates the range from the winery made famous by the Villa dei Cento Camini. Occhio di Pernice '04, based on red grapes, has a broad palette of intense aromatics introducing a firm flavoursome palate with good length. The other wines are agreeable.

- ● Carmignano Villa Medicea Ris. '07 — 🍷🍷 5
- ● Vin Santo di Carmignano Occhio di Pernice '04 — 🍷🍷 6
- ● Barco Reale '09 — 🍷 3
- ● Carmignano Villa Artimino '08 — 🍷 4

Baccinetti

pod. Pian di Maggio
53024 Montalcino [SI]
tel. 0577839025
giovanni.pennoni@virgilio.it

In Giovanni Pennoni's winery everything is well organized and clearly thought out. The '05 Brunello has a classic evolved nose of restrained plums, leather, tobacco leaf and cherries. The palate is tasty, tannic and dynamic, with a very intense, caressing finish.

- ● Brunello di Montalcino Soporaia '05 — 🍷🍷 7

Tenuta Bacco e Petroio

loc. Sovigliana
via Villa Alessandri, 18
50059 Vinci [FI]
tel. 0571509583
www.baccoapetroio.it

The Pratellis have been here since 1963. We selected the most successful of their many bottles, like the fruit-led Chianti Vigna al Bosco '08, with its fresh nose, solid body, well-measured tannins and juicy finish. The '08 Rosso di Tufo, from sangiovese, canaiolo and merlot, is bright and quaffable.

- ● Chianti V. al Bosco '08 — 🍷🍷 3*
- ● Chianti Sagace Ris. '06 — 🍷 4
- ● Rosso di Tufo '08 — 🍷 2
- ● Sangiovese '08 — 🍷 3

Badia di Morrona
via del Chianti, 6
56030 Terricciola [PI]
tel. 0587656013
www.badiadimorrona.it

Around 90 hectares of vines in the Pisan hills make Gaslini Alberti's estate one of the largest in the area. Bianco Pisano di San Tropè Vin Santo '05 is concentrated on the nose, where it shows notes of nuts, then coherent and well-balanced on the mushrooms and autumn leaves-veined palate.

- ○ Bianco Pisano di San Torpè Vin Santo '05 — 5
- ● Chianti I Sodi del Paretaio '09 — 3
- ○ Felciaio '09 — 3
- ● VignAalta '06 — 6

Pietro Beconcini
fraz. La Scala
via Montorzo, 13a
56020 San Miniato [PI]
tel. 0571464570
www.pietrobeconcini.com

Careful selection of local vines enabled Pietro Beconcini to isolate a clone of sangiovese and one of malvasia nera, as well as find tempranillo in the vineyards. The sangiovese-only barrique-aged Reciso '07 is very good, showing toasty with solid body, confident tannins and a powerful finish.

- ● Il Reciso '07 — 6
- ● Ixe '08 — 4
- ● Maurleo '08 — 4
- ● Vigna Le NIcchie '06 — 6

Begnardi Sapori di Monteantico
loc. Monteantico
pod. Camporosso, 34
58030 Civitella Paganico [GR]
tel. 0564991030
www.begnardi.com

A successful debut for this Montecucco DOC winery of five hectares managed by brothers Luca and Michele Begnardi. The Montecucco Sangiovese Pigna Rossa Riserva '07 is absolutely delicious, a stylish, well-balanced wine, with complex aromas and confident, sustained flavour. A great discovery.

- ● Montecucco Sangiovese Pigna Rossa Ris. '07 — 6

Tenuta di Bibbiano
via Bibbiano, 76
53011 Castellina in Chianti [SI]
tel. 0577743065
www.tenutadibibbiano.com

Montornello stands out amongst the wines offered by the Morrocchesi family winery. It has a nice, well-measured nose, notes of pencil lead and leather and a tantalizing, full body with tannins well integrated with the alcohol. The rising finish is highly aromatic. The rest of the range is decent.

- ● Chianti Cl. Montornello '08 — 5
- ● Chianti Cl. '08 — 4
- ● Chianti Cl. V. del Capannino Ris. '07 — 6
- ● Domino '08 — 8

Il Borghetto
loc. Montefiridolfi
via Collina Sant'Angelo, 21
50026 San Casciano in Val di Pesa [FI]
tel. 0558244442
www.borghetto.org

Borghetto is one of the most popular of the latest generation of Chianti wineries with wine lovers, and with knowledgeable insiders. Unfortunately, the wines we tasted were a bit of a mixed bag so we are reserving judgement.

- ● Chianti Cl. Bilaccio '06 — 4*
- ● Chianti Cl. Ris. '05 — 7
- ● Collina 21 '06 — 4*

La Casa di Bricciano
loc. La Casa di Bricciano, 43
53013 Gaiole in Chianti [SI]
tel. 0577 749297
www.lacasadibricciano.it

This winery already has many admirers. This time, the '07 Ritrovo is excellent. It's a Supertuscan based on cabernet sauvignon and merlot. Forest fruits combine with hints of pepper and cinnamon, the palate is soft and silky and the finish powers along nicely. The Sangiovese '07 drinks well.

- ● Il Ritrovo '07 — 8
- ● Sangiovese '07 — 7

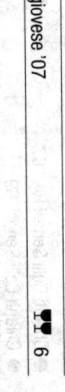

Caccia al Piano 1868

via Bolgherese, 279
57022 Castagneto Carducci [LI]
tel. 030984381
www.berlucchi.it

It was a good tasting for this Bolgheri winery, owned by the Guido Berlucchi group, with 20 hectares of vineyards in Castagneto Carducci. Overripe fruit for the Bolgheri Superiore San Biagio '07, with oak still evident. Balsam and a still-dry palate but great structure for Bolgheri Superiore Levia Gravia '06.

● Bolgheri Sup. Levia Gravia '06	🍷🍷	8
● Bolgheri Sup. San Biagio '07	🍷	8

Caiarossa

loc. Serra all'Olio, 59
56046 Riparbella [PI]
tel. 0586699016
www.caiarossa.com

Caiarossa forms part of the winery portfolio of Dutch entrepreneur Eric Albada Jelgersma. It is run on biodynamic lines. The wine we liked best bears the name of the cellar and is a complex blend. The '07 gives fresh herbs, eucalyptus and curry-like helichrysum and a dynamic palate.

● Caiarossa '07	🍷🍷	8

La Calonica

fraz. Valiano di Montepulciano
via della Stella, 27
53045 Montepulciano [SI]
tel. 0578724119
www.lacalonica.com

A short entry for La Calonica this year but then the Riserva wines were absent. The pleasant Nobile '07 is well orchestrated and full of flavour while the Rosso di Montepulciano '09 is very approachable. The fresh-tasting Cortona Sangiovese Calcinaio '09 is a fresh-tasting, soft-textured pleaser.

● Nobile di Montepulciano '07	🍷🍷	5
● Cortona Girifalco '07	🍷	6
● Cortona Sangiovese Calcinaio '09	🍷	4
● Rosso di Montepulciano '09	🍷	4

Camperchi

loc. La Cornia
via del Burrone, 38
52040 Civitella in Val di Chiana [AR]
tel. 0575440281
www.camperchi.com

The winery name refers to Hercules, once worshipped in these parts. The '07 Sangiovese is convincing, with firm, surefooted structure. On the nose, notes of wild strawberry stand out while the palate is well balanced by supporting acidity.

● Sangiovese '07	🍷🍷	6

Camporignano

fraz. Monteguidi
53031 Casole d'Elsa [SI]
tel. 0577963915
www.camporignano.it

The '07 Cerronero stands out. It's a blend of merlot and cabernet sauvignon with vibrant, well-defined aromas and a tasty, mouthfilling palate. The '08 Camporignano, from merlot and sangiovese, is easier drinking and the still stiffish sangiovese-only Mattaione '08 is austere.

● Camporignano '08	🍷🍷	3
● Cerronero '07	🍷🍷	6
● Mattaione '08	🍷	4

Canneto

via dei Canneti, 14
53045 Montepulciano [SI]
tel. 0578757737
www.canneto.com

The wines from Ottorino De Angelis's winery are impeccably made. The Nobile '07's nose is characterized by lovely earth-veined fruit leading on to a tasty, fresh palate. The Nobile Riserva '06 tastes a little tired from the oak. The '09 Rosso di Montepulciano is fluent and fresh-tasting.

● Nobile di Montepulciano '07	🍷🍷	5
● Nobile di Montepulciano Ris. '06	🍷	5
● Rosso di Montepulciano '09	🍷	4

Cappella Sant'Andrea

LOC. CASALE, 26
53037 SAN GIMIGNANO [SI]
TEL. 0577940456
www.cappellasantandrea.it

This small winery is carefully tended and managed by Antonella Leoncini, who has brought in her father and now her daughter Flavia to help run it. The Vernaccia Rialto '09 is the top wine, with tantalizing, layered aromatics and rounded, nicely satisfying body.

○ Vernaccia di S. Gimignano Rialto '09	🍷🍷	4
● Donna Flavia '09	🍷	4
● S. Gimignano Rosso Serreto '06	🍷	4
○ Vernaccia di S. Gimignano '09	🍷	3

Capua Winery

LOC. PIAN D'ARTINO 21
58014 MANCIANO [GR]
TEL. 0564601032
www.capuawinery.net

Some good wines here. Sangiovese Tutto Cuore '08 has stylish aromas and a relaxed, tasty palate. Well-focused aromas with green notes and a sleek palate characterize the cabernet franc Fiammante '08. The single-variety alicante Miosogno '08 has interesting aromas and good progression.

● Tutto Cuore '08	🍷🍷	5
● Fiammante '08	🍷	6
● Miosogno '08	🍷	6

Fattoria Casabianca

FRAZ. CASCIANO
LOC. MONTE PESCINI
53016 MURLO [SI]
TEL. 0577811026
www.fattoriacasabianca.it

Casabianca wines are very well made. The Chianti Colli Senesi Riserva '07 has taut progression way above average for its type. The Colli Senesi '09 is also enjoyable, showing more fluent and simpler. Sussingo '09, a blend of sangiovese and cabernet sauvignon, is approachable and tasty.

● Chianti Colli Senesi Ris. '07	🍷🍷	4*
● Chianti Colli Senesi '09	🍷	3
● Sussingo '09	🍷	3

Casale dello Sparviero Fattoria Campoperi

LOC. CASALE, 93
53011 CASTELLINA IN CHIANTI [SI]
TEL. 0577743228
www.casaledellosparviero.it

The winery takes its name from the 17th-century farmhouse around which it was built, where sparrowhawks (sparvieri) nested. Chianti Classico is the main wine, made in numerous versions. The best is the '07 Riserva with layered aromatics and a taut, savoury palate.

● Chianti Cl. Ris. '07	🍷🍷	5
● Chianti Cl. Ris. '06	🍷	5
● Chianti Cl. V. Paronza '08	🍷	5
● Rosso dello Sparviero '09	🍷	4

Casavyc

POD. CAMPOROMANO, 43
58054 SCANSANO [GR]
TEL. 3356880673
www.casavyc.it

Viviana Filocamo's wines are always interesting. Up and Down Duepertrenta '08, from syrah and grenache, offers lovely sensations with fresh, well-defined aromas and a fragrant, delicious palate. The '08 Morellino di Scansano 070707 is more solid but with rather too much toast.

● Up & Down Duepertrenta '08	🍷🍷	5
● Morellino di Scansano 070707 '08	🍷	7

Podere Casina

FRAZ. ISTIA D'OMBRONE
PIAGGE DEL MAIANO
58040 GROSSETO
TEL. 0564408210
www.poderecasina.com

A positive year for Rahel Kimmich and Marcello Pirisi. The Morellino '09 is agreeably fruity with dense aromas and fresh, relaxed progression while the sangiovese-based Aione '08 is earthy on the nose and well co-ordinated on the palate. The ..rah '08, from syrah grapes, is balsamic if a little rigid.

● Aione '08	🍷🍷	5
● Morellino di Scansano '09	🍷🍷	4
● ...rah '08	🍷	5

Tenuta Casteani

FRAZ. PODERE FABBRI
LOC. CASTEANI
58023 GAVORRANO [GR]
TEL. 056680060
www.casteani.it

A fine Guide debut for Marco Pelosi. Terra di Casteani '08 got our vote. It's a blend of sangiovese and merlot with intense fresh aromas and a soft, succulent palate. Sessanta '07, from sangiovese, merlot and alicante, is simpler but very drinkable. The '09 Rusada, a monovarietal sangiovese rosé, is fragrant.

● Terra di Casteani '08	🍷🍷 5
● 60 Sessanta '07	🍷 4
⊙ Rusada '09	🍷 3

Castel Pietraio

S.DA DI STROVE, 33
53035 MONTERIGGIONI [SI]
TEL. 057730020
www.castelpietraio.it

Baron Neri del Nero's winery joins the Guide. Adaileta '08 is a very fine barrique-aged Chardonnay with scents of ripe bananas and pineapple, lovely minerality, a full, enfolding body and a long finish. The Sindrada '09 is fresh, the Albertus '07 nice and the Chianti Colli Senesi '08 uncomplicated.

○ Adaileta '08	🍷🍷 4*
● Albertus '07	🍷 6
● Chianti Colli Senesi '08	🍷 3
○ Sindrada '09	🍷 3

La Castellaccia

VIA DI MONTAUTO, 18A
53037 SAN GIMIGNANO [SI]
TEL. 0577940426
www.lacastellaccia.it

It's the first time in the Guide for Alessandro Tofanari, a Florentine who decided to build in San Gimignano somewhere he could pursue his passions: horses and wine. The Vernaccia Murice '08 is very pleasing, with notes of citrus and ripe fruit, rich, tasty structure with nice vein of acidity.

○ Vernaccia di San Gimignano Murice '08	🍷🍷 4
● Chianti Colli Senesi '08	🍷 3
● I Giovenchi '08	🍷 4

Castellani

FRAZ. SANTA LUCIA
56025 PONTEDERA [PI]
TEL. 0587292900
www.castelwine.com

The Castellani family has four wineries in as many areas of Tuscany, starting with the Pisan hills, then Maremma and Chianti Classico. From the Campomaggio estate we have the '06 Rosso, based on sangiovese, cabernet and syrah, which cleanly made and delicious.

● Campomaggio Rosso '06	🍷🍷 5
● Chianti Sup. Poggio al Casone '07	🍷 3
● Genius Loci '07	🍷 4
○ Il Burchino '07	🍷 3

Fattoria Castellina

VIA PALANDRI, 27
50050 CAPRAIA E LIMITE [FI]
TEL. 057157631
www.fattoriacastellina.com

Fabio Montomoli owns the winery with his wife Elena, who looks after the farm holiday side. The move to biodynamics started in 2004 and is now complete. The wines are not always aromatically perfect but they do offer interesting sensations. The syrah-only Geos '07 is tannic, with a long, tasty finish.

○ Daino Bianco '07	🍷🍷 6
● Geos '07	🍷🍷 6
● Chianti Montalbano '07	🍷 4
○ Solare '09	🍷 4

Castello della Paneretta

LOC. MONSANTO
S.DA DELLA PANERETTA, 35
50021 BARBERINO VAL D'ELSA [FI]
TEL. 0558059003
www.paneretta.it

At Castello della Paneretta the passion for canaiolo has existed for a long time. The '07 monovarietal version convinced us with its fresh greens enhanced by hints of aromatic herbs, good concentration and smooth acid-veined palate dominated by a vein of acid and leading to a tasty, prolonged finish.

● Canaiolo '07	🍷🍷 6
● Solimpia '08	🍷 4
○ Vin Santo del Chianti Cl. '04	🍷 6

Castello delle Stinche

LOC. LAMOLE, 70
50022 GREVE IN CHIANTI [FI]
TEL. 0558547065
www.fattoriadilamole.it

This is a great little winery, with vines in the fascinating terroir of Lamole. We tried a very taut Chianti Classico Vigna Castello di Lamole Riserva '06 with a clean palate, good progression and very focused sense of place.

- Chianti Cl. V. Castello di Lamole Ris. '06 — ŸŸ 6

Castello di Gabbiano

FRAZ. MERCATALE VAL DI PESA
VIA GABBIANO, 22
50020 SAN CASCIANO IN VAL DI PESA [FI]
TEL. 055821053
www.castellogabbiano.it

This Mercatale Val di Pesa-based winery was not up to snuff this year. The '07 Chianti Classico Riserva is decent, with ripe fruit, bramble jelly and plum jam mingled with dried flowers and mixed herbs. There's power on the palate and a long, tasty finish. The sangiovese-only Bellezza '07 is a little rugged.

- Chianti Cl. Ris. '07 — ŸŸ 6
- Bellezza '07 — Ÿ 6

Castello di Selvole

FRAZ. VAGLIAGLI
LOC. SELVOLE, 1
53019 CASTELNUOVO BERARDENGA [SI]
TEL. 0577322662
www.selvole.com

There was a decent showing from Selvole wines but not that exciting. The Riserva is attractive, with ripe aromas plum jam laced with liquorice and coffee. Entry on the palate is broad and structured, with solid, powerful tannins while the finish is relaxed and nicely consistent.

- Chianti Cl. Ris. '07 — ŸŸ 4
- Chianti Cl. Ponte Rosso Ris. '07 — Ÿ 5
- Chianti Cl. San Martino a Selvoli '08 — Ÿ 4
- Sangiovese '08 — Ÿ 3

Castello Il Palagio

FRAZ. CAMPOLI
VIA CAMPOLI, 140
50024 SAN CASCIANO IN VAL DI PESA [FI]
TEL. 0558218157
www.palagio.net

IThe castle is used mainly for receptions. Overnight stays are also possible. The '08 Chianti Classico is good, with elegant fruit and green notes, a full, juicy body and a delicious finish. The rather rugged Riserva's sinew is held back by tannins in the finish. Torgentile '06 is rounded and ready to drink.

- Chianti Cl. '08 — ŸŸ 4
- Chianti Cl. Ris. '06 — Ÿ 5
- Torgentile '06 — Ÿ 6

Castello La Leccia

LOC. LA LECCIA
53011 CASTELLINA IN CHIANTI [SI]
TEL. 0577743148
www.castellolaleccia.com

Francesco Daddi runs this historic castle. The Chianti Classico Bruciagna '07 is great, very lively on the nose, with aromas of Mediterranean scrub, clean, clear fruit and minerality. It's juicy on the palate, showing vitality, well-embedded tannins and good length. The Chianti Classico '08 is stylish.

- Chianti Cl. Bruciagna '07 — ŸŸ 5
- Chianti Cl. '08 — Ÿ 4
- Vivaio del Cavaliere '09 — Ÿ 4

Castiglion del Bosco

LOC. CASTIGLION DEL BOSCO
53024 MONTALCINO [SI]
TEL. 0577807078
www.castigliondelbosco.it

The cleanness and complexity of the wines reflect the big investments made by the Ferragamo family. The modern winery is beautiful and blends into the landscape well. We liked the Brunello Campo del Drago '04 best for its vibrant nose of blackberry and cherry fruit, nice extract and good progression.

- Brunello di Montalcino Campo del Drago '04 — ŸŸ 8
- Brunello di Montalcino '05 — Ÿ 7
- Rosso di Montalcino '08 — Ÿ 5

Fattoria Cerbaia

S.DA DI CERBAIA, 16
50028 TAVARNELLE VAL DI PESA [FI]
TEL. 0558079148
www.aziendacerbaia.com

Newcomer Cerbaia also runs an agriturismo and makes olive oil. The Luigi Maria '08 is a lovely Bordeaux blend of merlot, cabernet sauvignon and petit verdot, with fresh mint and green capsicum, then dark berry fruit. The palate is warm and soft, with tannins tucked in and lingering length.

● Luigi Maria '08	♟♟	6
● Chianti Cl. '08	♟	4

Cima

FRAZ. ROMAGNANO
VIA DEL FAGIANO, 1
54100 MASSA
TEL. 0585831617
www.aziendagricolacima.it

The wines from the Cima estate are moulded by the 27 hectares or so of vineyards on the hills of Candia, between Massa and Carrara, on the lowest slopes that form the base of the Apuan Alps. Merlot Montervo '08 is subtly redolent of rose petals and wild cherries with a dynamic palate and good length.

● Montervo '08	♟♟	6
● Massaretta '08	♟	6
● Vermentino Nero '08	♟	6

Fattoria Colle Verde

FRAZ. MATRAIA
LOC. CASTELLO
55010 LUCCA
TEL. 0583402310
www.colleverde.it

This winery situated in the Matraia hills is generally reliable. Brania delle Ghiandaie '07 from sangiovese with a little syrah is decent with persuasive, albeit not yet fully defined, aromas and austere, linear palate but it is very satisfying drinking.

● Colline Lucchesi Rosso Brania delle Ghiandaie '07	♟♟	5

La Ciarliana

FRAZ. GRACCIANO
VIA CIARLIANA, 31
53040 MONTEPULCIANO [SI]
TEL. 0578758423
www.laciarliana.it

The wines from Luigi Frangiosa's winery maintain their good quality and stylistic definition but it is the basic Nobile that always stands out. The '07 version, too, is well balanced and delicious. The Nobile Vigna Scianello '06 is still held back by the oak.

● Nobile di Montepulciano '07	♟♟	5
● Nobile di Montepulciano V. Scianello '06	♟	6

Colle Santa Mustiola

VIA DELLE TORRI, 86A
53043 CHIUSI [SI]
TEL. 0578220525

Fabio Cenni looks after four hectares of sangiovese, with a little colorino here and there, used in small amounts for Poggio ai Chiari, the only wine the estate produces. It is a red with authentic character, a match for the great Sangioveses from classic areas, as the '05 shows, despite the middling vintage.

● Poggio ai Chiari '05	♟♟	7

Colognole

LOC. COLOGNOLE
VIA DEL PALAGIO, 15
50068 RUFINA [FI]
TEL. 0558319870
www.colognole.it

Brothers Cesare and Mario Coda Nunziante can rest assured. Their two characterful, territorial wines did well. The fresh-tasting '08 Chianti Rufina is better with Mediterranean scrub and dark berries, a firm but not heavy body and a nice, juicy finish. The Riserva del Don '07 is more rigid.

● Chianti Rufina '08	♟♟	4*
● Chianti Rufina Ris. del Don '07	♟	6

Il Colombaio di Santa Chiara

LOC. SAN DONATO, 1
53037 SAN GIMIGNANO [SI]
TEL. 0577942004
www.colombaiosantachiara.it

This year's offerings from the Logi brothers are not as stunning as last year's but still pass muster. Vernaccia is still their top wine, in this case the Riserva Albereta '08, with almondy nuances, white-fleshed fruits, a supple, taut body and nice zesty finish. The Vernaccia Selvabianca '09 is pleasing.

○ Vernaccia di S. Gimignano Albereta Ris. '08	🍷🍷	5
● Il Priore '08	🍷	4
● S. Gimignano Rosso Colombaio '07	🍷	5
○ Vernaccia di San Gimignano Selvabianca '09	🍷	4

La Colombina

VIA DEL LUOGO NUOVO, 1
53024 MONTALCINO [SI]
TEL. 0577849231
www.lacolombinavini.it

The vineyards are over ten years old and planted at 6,000 vines per hectare. The range is impressive with three wines outstanding. The '04 Brunello Riserva came top with clear peach, nice tobacco and leather. The palate is stylish, with good supporting acidity, resolved tannins and a long, elegant finish.

● Brunello di Montalcino '05	🍷🍷	7
● Brunello di Montalcino Ris. '04	🍷🍷	8
● San Martino '06	🍷🍷	6

Podere Concori

LOC. FIATTONE
VIA PROVINCIALE, 1
55027 GALLICANO [LU]
TEL. 0583766039
www.podereconcori.com

Melograno Rosso has come up trumps again, this time with the '08 vintage. A seductive wine with aromas of red fruits, medicinal herbs and green pepper, it has a lovely balsamic vein and the easy-drinking palate oozes finesse and flavour. Congratulations to Gabriele da Parato for his wonderful winemaking.

● Melograno Rosso '08	🍷🍷	5

Il Conventino

VIA DELLA CIARLIANA, 25B
53040 MONTEPULCIANO [SI]
TEL. 0578715371
www.ilconventino.it

The wines from Alberto Brini's organic winery are generally good and reflect their vintage. The Nobile Riserva '06 has strong fragrances of cherry and a confident, well co-ordinated palate. The Nobile '07 has good texture, although it is still a little clenched.

● Nobile di Montepulciano Ris. '06	🍷🍷	6
● Nobile di Montepulciano '07	🍷	5

Dalle Nostre Mani

VIA DEI CIPRESSI
50054 FUCECCHIO [FI]
TEL. 3395734846
www.dallenostremani.com

Winery owners Lapo Tardelli and Giulio Wilson Rosetti decided to make wines of provenance when they began converting the old vineyards to organic. The best is Toscoregio '08, from sangiovese and pugnitello, with fresh, earthy aromas, ripe fruit, solid body, good supporting acidity and clean, savoury finish.

● Toscoregio '08	🍷🍷	3*
● Arialdo '09	🍷	2
● Toscomagno '08	🍷	5

Tenuta degli Dei

VIA SAN LEOLINO, 56
50020 GREVE IN CHIANTI [FI]
TEL. 055852593
www.deglidei.it

Tommaso Cavalli's '07 is good. The blend varies each year but always includes merlot, cabernet franc and sauvignon, with petit verdot, alicante, and bouschet in varying amounts. The forceful aromas range from toast to coffee, with herbs and spices. Silky tannins take you into a rising finish.

● Cavalli Selection '07	🍷🍷	8

Fattoria Dianella Fucini

VIA DIANELLA, 48
50059 VINCI [FI]
TEL. 0571508166
www.fattoriadianella.it

The winery is named after poet and former owner Renato Fucini. This year, there's an excellent current Chianti, which has lovely fresh vibrant aromas and has a nice fruity after-aroma. Quite delicious drinking.

● Chianti '09	🍷🍷 3*
● Il Matto delle Giungaie '07	🍷 4
● Le Veglie di Neri '09	🍷 4

Fabrizio Dionisio

FRAZ. OSSAIA
LOC. IL CASTAGNO
52040 CORTONA [AR]
TEL. 063223541
www.fabriziodionisio.it

The Cuculaia Syrah '08 went straight to the finals. It's a wine that is only produced during great vintages, with lovely aromatics, hints of pepper and cinnamon which fuse seamlessly with the currants and cherry. The full palate is juicy and lively and the long rising finish has nice spiciness at the back.

● Cortona Syrah Cuculaia '08	🍷🍷 7
● Cortona Syrah Castagnino '08	🍷 4
⊙ Rosa del Castagno '09	🍷 4

Duemani

LOC. ORTACAVOLI
VIA COMUNALE DI VORNO, 9/4A
56046 RIPARBELLA [PI]
TEL. 0583975048
www.duemani.eu

The winery belonging to the famous oenologist Luca D'Attoma and Elena Celli is set in an amphitheatre of very clayey soil with plenty of stones. We were impressed by Duemani '07, from cabernet franc, which gives toast and ripeness veined with elegant herbaceousness and has lovely texture.

● Duemani '07	🍷🍷 8
● Altrovino '08	🍷 6
● Suisassi '07	🍷 8

Agricola Fabbriche

VIA FABBRICHE, 2-3A
52046 LUCIGNANO [AR]
TEL. 0575836152
www.agricolafabbriche.it

It was a good tasting overall for the Palma family wines. The sangiovese and merlot Camargi '08 is excellent this year, softer than last time, with aromatic herbs and black berry fruit, full, complex body and lovely finish. Vendemmia Tardiva Elis '09 enchants the nostrils and delights the palate.

● Camargi '08	🍷🍷 5
● Merlot '07	🍷 5
○ Vendemmia Tardiva Elis '09	🍷 5

Ficomontanino

LOC. FICOMONTANINO
53043 CHIUSI [SI]
TEL. 057821180
www.agricolaficomontanino.it

Lucumone is still the most interesting of the Giannelli family's wines. From cabernet sauvignon only, the '07 version is further confirmation of its elegance and balance. The Chianti Colli Senesi Tutulus '08 is well focused and delicious while the '08 Colli Senesi is fragrant and approachable.

● Lucumone '07	🍷🍷 5
● Chianti Colli Senesi '08	🍷 3
● Chianti Colli Senesi Tutulus '08	🍷 5

Fietri

LOC. FIETRI
53010 GAIOLE IN CHIANTI [SI]
TEL. 0577734048
www.fietri.com

This recently built winery is also an agriturismo. The Chianti Classico '08 did well, with pronounced fruit aromas that mingle currants and strawberries with spicy scents of pepper and juniper. Entry on the palate is bright with subtle tannins, well-integrated acidity and a juicy, generous finish.

● Chianti Cl. '08	🍷🍷 4
⊙ Rosato '09	🍷 4

Il Fitto

FRAZ. CIGNANO
LOC. IL FITTO, 126
52042 CORTONA [AR]
TEL. 0575648988
www.podereilfitto.com

Another Guide newcomer, Edda Billi and Franco Fierli's operation sent Cortona Syrah '08 to the finals. The concentrated nose melds spice with fruit and leather. The palate is solid but bright, its supporting acidity lending drinkability. The Rosso '08, from sangiovese with a little merlot, is enjoyably fresh.

- ● Cortona Syrah Il Fitto '08 4*
- ● Rosso di Toscana '08 3

Le Fonti

LOC. SAN GIORGIO
53036 POGGIBONSI [SI]
TEL. 0577935690
www.fattoria-lefonti.it

Vito Arturo '07 reached the finals. From sangiovese only, it unveils concentrated strawberry jam and fresh cherry, hints of mixed spice and some balsamic nuances. There's good weight on the generous palate, its acidity well integrated with the extract leading to a nice consistent finish.

- ● Vito Arturo '07 6
- ● Chianti Cl. '08 4
- ● Chianti Cl. Ris. '07 6
- ⊙ Rosato '09 3

Le Fonti a San Giorgio

VIA COLLE SAN LORENZO, 16
50025 MONTESPERTOLI [FI]
TEL. 0571609298
www.lefontiasangiorgio.it

The estate, which includes olive groves and visitor facilities, has belonged to the Giovannellis for three generations. The best of the wines is the Chianti Montespertoli Riserva I Fossili '07, with well-defined fruit and lively florality, sleek body, excellent progression, succulence and a long tasty finish.

- ● Chianti Montespertoli I Fossili Ris. '07 4*
- ● Chianti '09 3
- ● Chianti Montespertoli '07 3

Podere Forte

LOC. PETRUCCI, 13
53023 CASTIGLIONE D'ORCIA [SI]
TEL. 05778885100
www.podereforte.it

Guardiavigna remains the top wine of an estate now totally converted to organic farming. The '07, a blend of cabernet franc, merlot and petit verdot, is generous and vibrant. Both the Orcia Petruccino '08 and Orcia Petrucci '07 are stylish, though excessive toastiness in the latter upsets the overall balance.

- ● Guardiavigna '07 8
- ● Orcia Petrucci '07 8
- ● Orcia Petruccino '08 6

Fortediga

LOC. RIBOLLA
58036 ROCCASTRADA [GR]
TEL. 3393667707
www.fortediga.it

The Fortediga wines are powerful. The Cabernet Sauvignon – Syrah '08 is well made, fluent and balanced. The '07 Salebro, from cabernet sauvignon, is very concentrated on both nose and palate. The Vermentino '09 is full bodied, with good structure and a nice savoury touch in the finish.

- ● Cabernet Sauvignon - Syrah '08 5
- ● Salebro '07 5
- ○ Vermentino '09 4

Fattoria di Fugnano

VIA FUGNANO, 52
53037 SAN GIMIGNANO [SI]
TEL. 0577940012
www.fattoriadifugnano.com

The Fugnano estate dates back to the 13th century. Both winemaking and farmstay facilities are in operation here. The best wine is the '06 Donna Gina, a monovarietal Sangiovese with austere aromatics of bramble jelly and cinnamon and nutmeg spice followed by a broad, powerful body and a long finish.

- ● Donna Gina '06 4*
- ○ Vernaccia di San Gimignano '09 3

Eredi Fuligni

VIA SALONI, 33
53024 MONTALCINO [SI]
TEL. 0577848039
brunellofuligni@virgilio.it

The Brunello Riserva '04 is very well made with a classic nose of gently expressed cherry and tobacco. The palate has lovely structure, still a little stiff from clenched tannins, which hold back the development and blocks the finish. It will only improve with cellaring.

- ● Brunello di Montalcino Ris. '04 🍷🍷 8
- ● S. J. '08 🍷 5

Giannoni Fabbri

LOC. SAN MARCO IN VILLA, 2
52044 CORTONA [AR]
TEL. 3475883939
www.giannonifabbri.it

Marco Giannoni invests great energy in his 15-hectare estate, replanted over the years more densely and with new varieties. The results are not disappointing. The '03 Vin Santo is splendid, with amazing multi-faceted aromas, a big, caressing palate and a delicious lingering finish.

- ○ Cortona Vin Santo '03 🍷🍷 6
- ● Cortona Amato Syrah '08 🍷 4

Marchesi Ginori Lisci

FRAZ. PONTEGINORI
LOC. QUERCETO
56040 MONTECATINI VAL DI CECINA [PI]
TEL. 055210961
www.marchesiginorilisci.it

The Ginori winery lies on medium-textured soil, with plenty of clay and an underlying layer of gravel. Both the peppery, dynamic and very long Macchion del Lupo '07 and the velvet-soft Bordeaux blend Castello Ginori '06 are excellent.

- ● Castello Ginori '06 🍷🍷 5
- ● Montescudaio Macchion del Lupo '07 🍷🍷 4*

Podere Giocoli

VIA PENNA ALTA, 127C
52024 TERRANUOVA BRACCIOLINI [AR]
TEL. 3939850852
www.poderegiocoli.it

Fanciful names and labels there may be, but the varieties planted are soundly in line with tradition: albano, orpicchio or pugnitello. The best wine was the Ideoso '07, from sangiovese, pugnitello, pampadurrre and cabernet, tantalizes the nose and proffers solid flavour on the palate.

- ● Ideoso '07 🍷🍷 6
- ○ Baturlo '09 🍷 5
- ● Chianti Alione Ris. '08 🍷 5

Godiolo

VIA DELL'ACQUAPUZZOLA, 13
53045 MONTEPULCIANO [SI]
TEL. 0578757251
www.godiolo.it

Year after year, Franco Fiorini's winery shows that it has made the right decisions, releasing good wines that are so very drinkable. The Nobile '07 is delicious, if a tad thin, but very well balanced and tasty. The clean, well-typed Rosso di Montepulciano '08 is also good but perhaps just a little unexciting.

- ● Nobile di Montepulciano '07 🍷🍷 5
- ● Rosso di Montepulciano '08 🍷 4

Tenuta di Gracciano della Seta

FRAZ. GRACCIANO
VIA UMBRIA, 59
53045 MONTEPULCIANO [SI]
TEL. 0578708340
g.rigoli@agriconsulting.it

Piera Mazzucchelli's winery is one of the oldest around Montepulciano and the wines are rigorously austere. One such is the Nobile Riserva '06, with flowery aromas and subtle, savoury palate. The Nobile '07 is similar, with nice saltiness in the finish. The Rosso di Montepulciano '08 is uncomplicated.

- ● Nobile di Montepulciano Ris. '06 🍷🍷 5
- ● Nobile di Montepulciano '07 🍷 5
- ● Rosso di Montepulciano '08 🍷 4

Fattoria di Gratena

LOC. PIEVE A MAIANO
52100 AREZZO
TEL. 0575368664
www.gratena.it

Rosanna and Paolo Sieni's estate sails into the Guide thanks to the excellence of the Siro '07, from a variety that takes its name from the winery itself: gratena. The aromas on the nose are stunning and the palate shows excellent structure: a soft entry with bright tannins and a juicy rising finish.

● Siro '07	🍷🍷	6
● Chianti '07	🍷	4
● Chianti Rapozzo da Maiano '07	🍷	5
● Siro Passito '07	🍷	7

Podere Gualandi

LOC. POPPIANO
VIA RIPE, 19
50025 MONTESPERTOLI [FI]
TEL. 05582336
www.guidogualandi.com

Guido Gualandi, making his Guide debut, has always used natural methods. The Vinum '09 is successful. From malvasia lunga del Chianti and trebbiano coda di cavallo, it unfurls ripe, minerally, layered fruit and aromatic herbs, then solid body, savouriness, nicely gauged acidity and a lingering finish.

○ Vinum '09	🍷🍷	4*
● Chianti Colli Fiorentini Montebetti '07	🍷	4
● Gualandus '07	🍷	6
⊙ Rosato '09	🍷	3

Icario

VIA DELLE PIETROSE, 2
53045 MONTEPULCIANO [SI]
TEL. 0578758845
www.icario.it

The Cecchetti family makes good wines. The Rosso di Montepulciano '09, for example, has discreet, dense aromas with good progression. The Nobile '07 is good too, if a little marred by excess oak. The Nobile Vitaroccia '07 needs another year to mature.

● Rosso di Montepulciano '09	🍷🍷	4*
● Nobile di Montepulciano '07	🍷	5

Innocenti

FRAZ. TORRENIERI
LOC. CITILLE DI SOTTO, 45
53028 MONTALCINO [SI]
TEL. 0577834227
www.innocentivini.com

All the wines offered were very good, a sign of reliability and consistent quality. The Brunello Riserva '04 seemed the best for its nose of fruit and medicinal herbs, intense palate, good tannins and great development, with a finish to match. The Brunello '05 also passed muster.

● Brunello di Montalcino '05	🍷🍷	7
● Brunello di Montalcino Ris. '04	🍷🍷	8
● Vignalsole '06	🍷	5

Fattoria La Striscia

VIA DEI CAPPUCCINI, 3
52100 AREZZO
TEL. 057526740
www.lastriscia.com

This is a debut for the Occhini family winery near Arezzo in a 16th-century villa completed in the 18th century. Nowadays, it's an agriturismo and cookery school. The sangiovese, merlot and cabernet Occhini '07 is great, with complex forest fruits and spices, supple body and a rising finish.

● Occhini '07	🍷🍷	5
● Merlot '07	🍷	6

Maurizio Lambardi

POD. CANALICCHIO DI SOTTO, 8
53024 MONTALCINO [SI]
TEL. 0577848476
www.lambardimontalcino.it

These are great classic wines of northern Montalcino, perfectly reflecting their territory. Austere but uncomplicated, they have a few rough edges in youth. The '05 Brunello is well made, offering a layered nose of fruit, intriguing tobacco and herbs, good texture, tidy extract and a satisfying finish.

● Brunello di Montalcino '05	🍷🍷	6
● Rosso di Montalcino '08	🍷	4

Poderi Laura Berlucchi Fontemorsi

VIA DELLE COLLINE
50040 MONTESCUDAIO [PI]
TEL. 0583 349025
www.fontemorsi.it

The winery of Laura Berlucchi and partners Francesco Benasaglio, Roberto Ligasacchi and Carlo Sanvitale is at Montescudaio, on land that was once under the sea. The '07 Guadipiani from sangiovese and cabernet is excellent with plenty of extract and intensity.

- Guadipiani '07 — 🍷🍷 4
- Volterrano '07 — 🍷 4

Le Due Arbie

LOC. PIEVASCIATA
VIA COMUNELLA 2
53019 CASTELNUOVO BERARDENGA [SI]
TEL. 0577356982
agrisvi.siena@virgilio.it

This winery, which also has farmstay facilities, makes its Guide debut with a particularly interesting Riserva. The generous aromas are themed on earthiness and minerals, with after-aromas of tobacco, leather and bramble jelly. The attack on the palate is rounded and juicy, the tannins elegant.

- Chianti Cl. Parteno Ris. '06 — 🍷🍷 5

Villa Le Prata

LOC. LE PRATA, 261
53024 MONTALCINO [SI]
TEL. 0577848325
www.villaleprata.com

Benedetta Losappio runs this tiny estate in the north-east of Montalcino. The range shows well, with the Brunello '05 a model of sober modernity. The intense nose offers fruity notes of cherry and sour cherry with spice and cinnamon nuances. The structured palate ends in a generous finish.

- Brunello di Montalcino '05 — 🍷🍷 8
- Rosso di Montalcino Tirso '08 — 🍷🍷 5

La Lecciaia

LOC. VALLAFRICO
53024 MONTALCINO [SI]
TEL. 0583928366
www.lecciaia.it

Each year, this solid estate offers good quality. The Brunello Vigna Manapetra Riserva '04 is good, intense on the nose with clearly defined fruit. The layered palate has young but very compact tannins and a long, full finish. The other Riserva, the simple '04 and the Rosso '08 are all convincing.

- Brunello di Montalcino Ris. '04 — 🍷🍷 7
- Brunello di Montalcino V. Manapetra Ris. '04 — 🍷🍷 8
- Rosso di Montalcino '08 — 🍷🍷 4
- Brunello di Montalcino '05 — 🍷 6

Lunadoro

FRAZ. VALIANO DI MONTEPULCIANO
LOC. TERRAROSSA PAGLIERETO
53040 MONTEPULCIANO [SI]
TEL. 0578748154
www.lunadoro.com

Dario Cappelli's and Gigliola Cardinali's estate is known for well-made, very drinkable wines. The fragrant, lip-smacking Rosso di Montepulciano '08 is one of the best in its class. The Nobile '07 is good, especially on the palate. The sangiovese, trebbiano and malvasia Ricordo '08 is well made.

- Rosso di Montepulciano '08 — 🍷🍷 4*
- Nobile di Montepulciano '07 — 🍷 5
- Ricordo '08 — 🍷 4

Macchion dei Lupi

LOC. CAMPO AL DRAGO, 195
57028 SUVERETO [LI]
TEL. 0565845100
www.macchiondeilupi.it

Carlo Parenti's biodynamic estate debuted well. He presented two vintages of the same wine, Esperienze, obtained from a blend of sangiovese and cabernet sauvignon. The very interesting '06 has a full, intense nose and a nicely balanced palate. The '07 is a bit weaker and hints at overripeness.

- Esperienze '06 — 🍷🍷 5
- Esperienze '07 — 🍷 5

Podere Il Macchione

FRAZ. GRACCIANO
VIA PROVINCIALE, 18
53045 MONTEPULCIANO [SI]
TEL. 0578 758595
www.podereilmacchione.it

Nobile di Montepulciano's most faithful fans will know this name. Founded over 30 years ago, Podere Il Macchione disappeared from our tastings two decades ago but now makes an intriguing comeback in the Guide. The Nobile '07 is extremely full and rewarding; the Nobile '06 is also good, if a tad more rigid.

- Nobile di Montepulciano '07 — 🍷🍷 5
- Nobile di Montepulciano '06 — 🍷 5

Fattoria di Magliano

LOC. STERPETI, 10
58051 MAGLIANO IN TOSCANA [GR]
TEL. 0564593040
www.fattoriadimagliano.it

The cabernet sauvignon and merlot Poggio Bestiale '08 has generous aromas and a deep, juicy palate. The pure Syrah Perenzo '08 is full of balsamic notes but the palate is rather stiff. Morellino di Scansano Heba '09 is good and Sinarra '09 from sangiovese and petit verdot is very enjoyable.

- Poggio Bestiale '08 — 🍷🍷 6
- Morellino di Scansano Heba '09 — 🍷 4
- Perenzo '08 — 🍷 6
- Sinarra '09 — 🍷 5

La Mannella

LOC. LA MANNELLA, 322
53024 MONTALCINO [SI]
TEL. 0577848268
http://www.lamannella.it

Marco Cortonesi has a deep bond with his vineyards. He uses long macerations and matures his grapes fully. The well-made Brunello '05 has warm wild cherry notes and a continuous, layered palate. The Brunello di Montalcino Poggiarelli '05 is well-structured but still rather tight with clenched tannins.

- Brunello di Montalcino '05 — 🍷🍷 6
- Brunello di Montalcino I Poggiarelli '05 — 🍷🍷 8
- Rosso di Montalcino '08 — 🍷🍷 4

Stafania Mezzetti

LOC. TERONTOLA
VIA FOSSE ARDEATINE, 32 C
52044 CORTONA [AR]
TEL. 0575678528
www.vinimezzetti.it

Stefania Mezzetti's estate straddles two regions, Umbria and the zone of Cortona, from where she obtains her more prestigious bottles. Our pick this year is the Dardano Sangiovese '07, showing generous and focused in its clean, fruity aromas with a balanced, lively body.

- Cortona Dardano Sangiovese '07 — 🍷🍷 4
- Cortona Lucumone Cabernet Sauvignon '07 — 🍷 5
- Cortona Selvans Merlot '07 — 🍷 4

Le Miccine

LOC. LE MICCINE
SS TRAVERSA CHIANTIGIANA
53013 GAIOLE IN CHIANTI [SI]
TEL. 0577749526
www.lemiccine.com

The Meneghetti Weavers' estate offers a very well-made Riserva '07 with nice ripe fruity notes of blackberry and plum jam, soft spicy pepper, animal skins and leather. The soft, full body has light, delicate tannins, an acid vein nicely integrated with the alcohol and a long, lip-smacking finish.

- Chianti Cl. Don Alberto Ris. '07 — 🍷🍷 5

Poderi di Miscianello

LOC. PONTE A BOZZONE
SS CHIANTIGIANA, 408
53010 SIENA
TEL. 0577356840
www.miscianello.it

This estate comprises a small settlement, now an agriturismo. The one wine presented is superb. Chianti Classico '08 has rich, elegant, cherry-led fruit aromas with typical flowery nuances. The palate has good impact, light and soft, with smooth tannins, nice drinkability and a long, mouth-watering finish.

- Chianti Cl. '08 — 🍷🍷 4

Podere Monastero

LOC. MONASTERO
53011 CASTELLINA IN CHIANTI [SI]
TEL. 0577740273
www.poderemonastero.com

We can always count on Alessandro Cellai's wines. He offers just two labels this year: La Pineta from pinot nero and Campanaio from equal parts cabernet sauvignon and merlot. Both '08, they offer different interpretations of a small but elegant year with grip. The first is more refined; the second gutsier.

● Campanaio '08	🍷🍷	6
● La Pineta '08	🍷🍷	7

Azienda Agricola Montaioncino

VIA MONTAIONCINO, 1
50053 EMPOLI [FI]
TEL. 0571929334
www.montaioncino.it

Mauro Cartechini carries on the tradition started by his grandfather Duilio and his father. This year's pick of the crop is the Quinto '06, a pure barrique-aged Sangiovese, offering notes of ripe fruit, impressive body, tannins nicely fused with the alcohol and good length.

● Quinto '06	🍷🍷	4*
● Chianti '09	🍷	3
● Duilio '07	🍷	4
○ Vin Santo dell'Empolese '01	🍷	4

Montecalvi

VIA CITILLE, 85
50022 GREVE IN CHIANTI [FI]
TEL. 0558544665
www.montecalvi.com

The Bolli O'Byrnes' wines show well this year. Top dog is the Supertuscan Montecalvi Vielle Vigne '08 from sangiovese, cabernet sauvignon with other varieties depending on the year. It offers blackberry and blueberry jam, faint spicy nuances, and a lovely, elegant, measured palate of good length.

● Montecalvi V. V. '08	🍷🍷	7
● Chianti Cl. '08	🍷	5
● San Piero '08	🍷	8

Fattoria di Montecchio

FRAZ. SAN DONATO IN POGGIO
VIA MONTECCHIO, 4
50020 TAVARNELLE VAL DI PESA [FI]
TEL. 0558072907
www.fattoriamontecchio.it

Bit of a low-key performance from this Tavarnelle estate. We liked the pure Merlot La Papessa '07 for its pleasant notes of intense, ripe fruit, spicy nuances of cinnamon and clove, and full, smooth body with a long, lip-smacking finish. The two Chianti Classicos are well typed, if on the rugged side.

● La Papessa '07	🍷🍷	6
● Chianti Cl. '07	🍷	3
● Chianti Cl. Ris. '07	🍷	5

Monterotondo

LOC. MONTEROTONDO, 12
53013 GAIOLE IN CHIANTI [SI]
TEL. 0577 749089
www.agriturismomonterotondo.net

This small organic estate is in an old farmhouse restored in the 1990s. Its 3.5 hectares in Chianti Classico are almost all planted to sangiovese that ages in small and medium barrels. The splendid Chianti Classico Seretina Riserva '07 gives blackberries, blueberries and a deep, textured palate.

● Chianti Cl. Seretina Ris. '07	🍷🍷	5

Tenuta Monteti

VIA DELLA SGRILLA, 6
58011 CAPALBIO [GR]
TEL. 0564896160
www.tenutamonteti.it

Monteti '07, a cabernet sauvignon, petit verdot and cabernet franc blend with dash of alicante and merlot, is rich and complex. It offers focused aromas and a deep, juicy palate. The more approachable Caburnio '08 from cabernet sauvignon, alicante and merlot has a muzzy nose but a tasty palate.

● Monteti '07	🍷🍷	6
● Caburnio '08	🍷	4

Cantina Vignaioli del Morellino di Scansano

LOC. SARAGIOLO
58054 SCANSANO [GR]
TEL. 0564507288
www.cantinadelmorellino.it

Vin del Fattore '08 is a very typical Morellino with precise aromas of cherry and earth, and an elegant, well-paced palate. Morellino Roggiano '09 is good, showing more approachable and lip-smacking rather than scented. The more modern Morellino San Rabano '07 has ground coffee and a clean, fluent palate.

- ● Morellino di Scansano Vin del Fattore '08 — TT 4
- ● Morellino di Scansano Roggiano '09 — T 4
- ● Morellino di Scansano San Rabano '07 — T 5

Tenuta di Morzano

FRAZ. MORZANO
VIA DI MONTELUPO 69/71
50025 MONTESPERTOLI [FI]
TEL. 0571671021
www.vinnovo.it

Luciano and Francesca Mignolli's profile mirrors that of last year. Nicosole '08, a pure Syrah, convinces with its spicy aromas of pepper, cinnamon and clove laced with forest fruit. It shows racy body, vibrant tannins and a nice juicy finish. The two Chiantis are well-made and pleasing on the palate.

- ● Nicosole '08 — TT 5
- ● Chianti Montespertoli Emilio '08 — T 4
- ● Chianti Montespertoli Morzano Ris. '08 — T 4

La Mozza

LOC. MONTE CIVOLI
58051 MAGLIANO IN TOSCANA [GR]
TEL. 0432700943
www.bastianich.com

The Bastianich estate in Maremma did very well. The Aragone '07 is in fine fettle. Obtained from a blend of sangiovese, alicante, syrah and carignano, this fragrant wine has a very rewarding palate. The good Morellino I Perazzi '08 is precise in its aromas but perhaps lacking a bit in structure.

- ● Aragone '07 — TT 5
- ● Morellino di Scansano I Perazzi '08 — T 4

Tenute Silvio Nardi

LOC. CASALE DEL BOSCO
53024 MONTALCINO [SI]
TEL. 0577808269
www.tenutenardi.com

This historic estate lies in the north of the territory, a beautiful area with deer, boar and porcupine. This year sees a new Brunello, Poggio Doria '04, that needs time in bottle to achieve real balance and mellow its tannins. Good acidity makes for a layered palate. The '99 Vin Santo is first-class.

- ○ Vin Santo del Chianti '99 — TT 6
- ● Brunello di Montalcino '05 — T 6
- ● Brunello di Montalcino Poggio Doria '04 — T 7

No, vo' li'

VIA DI FONTECORNINO, 9
53045 MONTEPULCIANO [SI]
TEL. 0578799166
www.no-vo-li.it

Giuseppe Putzulu's estate makes its comeback to the Guide. La Scudiscia '06 from sangiovese, merlot and syrah presents truly captivating aromas and a mouth-watering, balanced palate. Cavernano '07 from sangiovese, cabernet sauvignon, merlot and syrah is simpler but good with a clean, fluent palate.

- ● La Scudiscia '06 — TT 6
- ● Cavernano '07 — T 5

O.T.

LOC. CAMPIGALLO
VIA PERETA
56040 CASALE MARITTIMO [PI]
TEL. 3483040076
www.otwine.com

The wine Oliviero Toscani produces on his family estate run by children Lola and Rocco is called OT. The '06, a blend of syrah, cabernet franc and petit verdot, shows an elegant nose with gorgeous notes of black pepper and a supple, harmonious palate that makes it extremely drinkable.

- ● OT Oliviero Toscani '06 — TT 7

Fattoria Ormanni

LOC. ORMANNI, 1
53036 POGGIBONSI [SI]
TEL. 0577937212
www.ormanni.it

Fattoria Ormanni lies between Poggibonsi and Castellina in Chianti and is considered traditional in Chianti Classico terms, partly because of its long association with Giulio Gambelli. Riserva Borro del Diavolo '06 is an absolute stunner of a wine: dark on the nose; sweet and chewy on the palate.

- ● Chianti Cl. Borro del Diavolo Ris. '06 🍷🍷 5
- ● Chianti Cl. '07 🍷 4

Padelletti

VIA PADELLETTI, 9
53024 MONTALCINO [SI]
TEL. 0577848314
www.padelletti.it

This historic estate with Claudia Padelletti in the cellar marches on. The very interesting Riserva '04 has a classic yellow peach, morello cherry and tobacco nose. The firm palate shows taut tannins and acidity, good length and fine extract at the back. The fine Brunello '05 is faintly vegetal on the nose.

- ● Brunello di Montalcino Ris. '04 🍷🍷 7
- ● Brunello di Montalcino '05 🍷 7

Il Palagione

VIA PER CASTEL SAN GIMIGNANO, 36
53037 SAN GIMIGNANO [SI]
TEL. 0577953134
www.ilpalagione.com

Despite the absence of some big hitters, Monica Rota and Giorgio Comotti always manage to put on a good show. Cream of this year's crop is Vernaccia Hydra '09 with a sage and almond nose, racy, dynamic, acidity-sustained body and a rising finish. Enif '09 from trebbiano and malvasia is simple and unusual.

- ○ Vernaccia di S. Gimignano Hydra '09 🍷🍷 4
- ● Chianti Colli Senesi Caelum '08 🍷 4
- ● Chianti Colli Senesi Draco Ris. '07 🍷 4
- ○ Enif '09 🍷 3

Panzanello

VIA CASE SPARSE, 86
50022 PANZANO [FI]
TEL. 055852470
www.panzanello.it

Panzanello dates back to the 1400s and produced wine and oil even then. Today it belongs to the Sommaruga family. The Chianti Classico '08 is a scented, fresh wine with a wonderful palate that embodies the aromas and pace of its territory. The Riserva '07 is oaky and tighter in its tannins.

- ● Chianti Cl. '08 🍷🍷 5
- ● Chianti Cl. Ris. '07 🍷 6

Poderi del Paradiso

LOC. STRADA, 21A
53037 SAN GIMIGNANO [SI]
TEL. 0577941500
www.poderidelparadiso.it

Graziella Cappelli's estate offers its usual array of labels topped by the Vernaccia '09. The charming aromatic bouquet displays notes of peach and almond enhanced by aromatic herbs. The body is lean and the palate vivid and full of flavour. The rest of the range is well managed.

- ○ Vernaccia di S. Gimignano '09 🍷🍷 3*
- ● Chianti Colli Senesi '08 🍷 3
- ● San Gimignano Bottaccio '07 🍷 5
- ○ Vernaccia di S. Gimignano Biscondola '09 🍷 4

Il Paratino

VIA DEI PARMIGIANI
57023 CECINA [LI]
TEL. 3388454571

Paratino di Cecina is run by youngsters from the local drug rehabilitation centre. The wine is genuinely excellent. Paratino '07 from cabernet franc has an intense ruby appearance, wide-ranging, complex, balsamic aromas and a silky, harmonious palate. This is a very serious bottle.

- ● Paratino '07 🍷🍷 5

Pasolini Dall'Onda

P.ZZA MAZZINI, 10
50021 BARBERINO VAL D'ELSA [FI]
TEL. 0558075019
www.pasolinidallonda.com

We have a fine performance from this estate which also has vineyards in Emilia Romagna and a first-rate production of extra-virgin olive oil. The Montepetri '09 is very good. It presents notes of camomile tea and spiciness, a weighty, succulent, supple palate that builds up into a delicious finish.

○ Montepetri '09	🍷🍷	4
● Chianti Cl. Sicelle '06	🍷	4
● Chianti Drove '08	🍷	3

Paterna - Cooperativa Agricola Valdarnese

LOC. PATERNA, 96
52028 TERRANUOVA BRACCIOLINI [AR]
TEL. 055977052
www.paterna.it

The co-operative estate headed by Marco Noferi proceeds apace. It is a farm and an agriturismo as well as a winery. The best bottle this year is the '03 Vin Santo, displaying intense hazelnut and almond aromas, hints of honey and dried fig and a caressing, sweet, velvety palate. The other wines are pleasant.

○ Vin Santo del Chianti '03	🍷🍷	5
● Chianti Colli Aretini '08	🍷	4
○ Il Terraio '09	🍷	4
● Vignanova '06	🍷	5

Petreto

VIA ROSANO, 196A
50012 BAGNO A RIPOLI [FI]
TEL. 0556519021

Alessandro Fonseca reaffirms the quality of his top wine, Pourriture Noble '06. Obtained from a blend of botrytized sémillon and sauvignon grapes, it presents a rich amber with generous aromas ranging from honey to orange peel and a long, sweet palate. The rest of the wines simple but well made.

○ Pourriture Noble '06	🍷🍷	6
● Bocciolè '07	🍷	5
● Chianti Colli Fiorentini '08	🍷	3
○ Podere Sassaie '09	🍷	4

Fattoria di Petroio

LOC. QUERCEGROSSA
VIA DI MOCENNI, 7
53019 CASTELNUOVO BERARDENGA [SI]
TEL. 0577328045
www.fattoriapetroio.it

The Lenzi family estate marches full-steam ahead, producing wines that faithfully reflect the characteristics of the territory. The Riserva '07 shows well, proffering lovely fruit ennobled by intense tobacco and leather. The sound body delivers well-defined tannins and an appetizing finish.

● Chianti Cl. Ris. '07	🍷🍷	5
● Chianti Cl. '07	🍷	4
● Poggio al Mandorlo '07	🍷	3

Pianirossi

LOC. PORRONA
POD. SANTA GENOVEFFA
58044 CINIGIANO [GR]
TEL. 0564990573
www.pianirossi.com

Once again it is the Pianirossi that impresses, this time in the '07 version. This blend of cabernet sauvignon, petit verdot and montepulciano has intense, delightful aromas and a deep, dense, fruity palate. The estate, also called Pianirossi, belongs to Stefano Sincini, CEO of Tod's.

● Pianirossi '07	🍷🍷	7

Agostina Pieri

FRAZ. SANT'ANGELO SCALO
LOC. PIANCORNELLO
53026 MONTALCINO [SI]
TEL. 0577844163
pieriagostina@libero.it

Success is a beautiful cellar in south-east Montalcino. The wines continue to show greater freshness on the nose. The Brunello '05 has intense, rich, clean aromas of morello cherry and cherry jam with classic hints of sweet tobacco. The palate is full, concentrated and enveloping with high-class tannins.

● Brunello di Montalcino '05	🍷🍷	8
● Sant'Antimo J & F '06	🍷🍷	5
● Rosso di Montalcino '08	🍷	5

OTHER WINERIES

Pietrafitta
LOC. CORTENNANO, 54
53037 SAN GIMIGNANO [SI]
TEL. 0577943200
www.pietrafitta.com

With origins in 961, this is one of the oldest estates in the territory of San Gimignano. Back then it was part of the Fosci fiefdom, property of Marchese Ugo Salico. Badge for best wine this year goes to Vernaccia La Costa Riserva '08 for its powerful, well-defined body and long, agreeable palate.

○ Vernaccia di S. Gimignano La Costa Ris. '08	🍷🍷	5
● Campidonne '08	🍷	4
○ Vernaccia di S. Gimignano '09	🍷	4
○ Vernaccia di S. Gimignano V. Borghetto '09	🍷	4

Pieve Santo Stefano
LOC. SARDINI
55100 LUCCA
TEL. 0585857996
www.pievedisantostefano.com

This year, we tasted the first wines from the Piccioli family, who have embarked on a massive reorganization of the vineyards, are building a new cellar and oil press, and are setting up a small local history museum. The '08 Lodovico is a full, complex wine with a spicy nose and a caressing palate.

● Colline Lucchesi Ludovico '08	🍷🍷	4
● Colline Lucchesi Villa Sardini '08	🍷	4

La Pievuccia
LOC. LA PIEVUCCIA
VIA SANTA LUCIA, 118
52043 CASTIGLION FIORENTINO [AR]
TEL. 0575651007
www.lapievuccia.it

This small estate comprises an agriturismo and an organic farm producing wine, oil and honey. This year's champ is the Vin Santo '05. Its cornucopia of aromas runs the gamut from dried fruit and nuts to notes of honey before presenting a seamless body and a lingering finish.

○ Vin Santo della Valdichiana '05	🍷🍷	6
● Balzanella Valdichiana '08	🍷	4
○ Chardonnay Valdichiana '09	🍷	3

Podere Ciona
LOC. MONTEGROSSI
53013 GAIOLE IN CHIANTI [SI]
TEL. 0577749127
www.podereciona.com

Le Diaccie is always the best of Franco Gatteschi's wines. The '07 version of this pure Merlot reveals a very elegant array of aromas in which minty, balsamic notes mingle with earthy, minerally tones over a fruity base. The weighty palate has delicate tannins, impressive acidity and good length.

● Le Diaccie '07	🍷🍷	6

Podere San Cristoforo
LOC. BAGNO
VIA DEL MULINO
58023 GAVORRANO [GR]
TEL. 3358212413
www.poderesancristoforo.it

This estate belonging to Lorenzo Zonin farms biodynamically. The pure petit verdot San Cristoforo '09 is lip-smacking and racy. Just as tasty, if a tad lightweight, are the Amaranto '09, a Sangiovese aged in oak for five months, and the Carandelle '09, also from sangiovese but oak-aged for 12 months.

● San Cristoforo '09	🍷🍷	5
● Amaranto '09	🍷	4
● Carandelle '09	🍷	4

Relais Poggio Borgoni
VIA CASSIA PER SIENA, 35
50026 SAN CASCIANO IN VAL DI PESA [FI]
TEL. 0558228119
www.relaispoggioborgoni.it

We see a promising debut in the Guide from this estate which also boasts a hotel and a restaurant. The three wines presented all did well. The Riserva Borromeo '07 has a rich nose of forest fruit, vanilla and toasty notes, and a long, full, velvety palate. We also liked the Chianti La Curva del Vescovo '07.

● Chianti Cl. Borromeo Ris. '07	🍷🍷	6
● Chianti Cl. La Curva del Vescovo '07	🍷🍷	5
● Poggio Borgoni '08	🍷	4

Tenuta Poggio Verrano

s.da Provinciale 9, km 4
58051 Magliano in Toscana [GR]
tel. 0564589943
www.poggioverrano.it

This year, Francesco Bolla proposed Dròmos '06, a sangiovese, cabernet sauvignon, cabernet franc and alicante blend that is juicy and expansive, if a bit alcoholic at the back. Dròmos L'Altro '07 from sangiovese has fresh red berry fruit and Mediterranean scrub but flags a bit because of drying tannins.

Wine	Glasses	Score
● Dròmos '06	2 glasses	7
● Dròmos L'Altro '07	2 glasses	8

Fattoria Poggiopiano

via di Pisignano, 28/30
50026 San Casciano in Val di Pesa [FI]
tel. 0558229629
www.fattoriapoggiopiano.it

The absence of their flagships Rosso di Sera and Chianti Classico La Tradizione meant the Bartolis stepped down to a short profile this year. Given their solidity and expertise, this will just be a temporary blip. The current Chianti Classico is fragrant and the new Taffetà '06 from all colorino is a bit tired.

Wine	Glasses	Score
● Chianti Cl. '08	2 glasses	4
● Taffetà '06	1 glass	8

La Porrona

loc. Montisi
53049 Torrita di Siena [SI]
tel. 0577845913
www.laporrona.it

Giuseppe Brusone's small estate in the province of Siena did well on its first appearance in the Guide. Brusone is also the name of its sole – at least for the moment – wine. The '06 from sangiovese with a little merlot has goodish, austere aromas and then reveals lovely energy and flavour as the palate unfolds.

Wine	Glasses	Score
● Brusone '06	2 glasses	5

La Porta di Vertine

loc. Casanuova di Paiolo
53013 Gaiole in Chianti [SI]
tel. 0577749577
www.laportadivertine.it

Porta di Vertine takes its name from its location in Gaiole with steep terrains with a very stony base. The varieties are traditional and age in large barrels. The bottles we tasted were variable and didn't convince us fully, but the good ones demonstrated all the allure and purity of the type.

Wine	Glasses	Score
● Chianti Cl. Ris. '07	2 glasses	6
⊙ Rosato '09	1 glass	4
● Sassi Chiusi '07	1 glass	6

Tenuta Le Potazzine

loc. Le Prata
53024 Montalcino [SI]
tel. 0577849406
www.lepotazzine.it

Giuseppe Gorelli's highly territorial wines come from meticulous vineyard selections, careful fermentation and shrewd ageing. His plots lie high up in western Montalcino. The Brunello '05 has fresh notes of white cherry with the growing year's vegetal and spicy hints, lovely acidity and compact tannins.

Wine	Glasses	Score
● Brunello di Montalcino Ris. '04	2 glasses	8
● Brunello di Montalcino '05	1 glass	8
● Rosso di Montalcino '08	1 glass	5

Provveditore

loc. Salaiolo
pod. Provveditore, 174
58054 Scansano [GR]
tel. 0564599237
www.provveditore.it

Provveditore, owned by Alessandro Bargagli, comprises 30 hectares of vines near Scansano at an altitude of 300 metres. The Morellino Primo Riserva '07's very fresh aromas range from ripe cherry to faint, rather vegetal nuances. The palate is lively, juicy and taut. Morellino '08 is delicious in its simplicity.

Wine	Glasses	Score
● Morellino di Scansano '08	2 glasses	4
● Morellino di Scansano Primo Ris. '07	2 glasses	5
● Morellino di Scansano Sassato '09	1 glass	3

Querce Bettina

LOC. LA CASINA DI MOCALI, 275
53024 MONTALCINO [SI]
TEL. 0577848588
www.quercebettina.it

This small western estate makes classic, complex wines. The Rosso di Montalcino '07 is a gem, showing compact, well-expressed aromas of spice and balsam with a consistent fruity vein of wild and morello cherry. The palate is intense and appealing with a long finish. The '05 Brunello is also lovely and fragrant.

● Rosso di Montalcino '07	4
● Brunello di Montalcino '05	7

Quercia al Poggio

FRAZ. MONSANTO
S.DA QUERCIA AL POGGIO, 4
50021 BARBERINO VAL D'ELSA [FI]
TEL. 0558075278
www.quercialpoggio.com

Quercia al Poggio stands in a lovely hamlet surrounded by woods in Barberino Val d'Elsa. The Chianti Classico Riserva '06 makes a huge impression. Warm and caressing, it offers gorgeous sensations of wild flowers. The Chianti Classico '08 is fresh, flowery and spicy.

● Chianti Cl. Ris. '06	5
● Chianti Cl. '08	5

La Rasina

LOC. RASINA, 132
53024 MONTALCINO [SI]
TEL. 0577848536
www.larasina.it

The wines of this small estate in eastern Montalcino are powerful with distinct oakiness in their early years. The late-released Brunello Divasco '04 has intense aromas of fruit and fruit jam, cherry, blackberry, cocoa powder and spice. The palate is full and still edgy with well made but youthful tannins.

● Brunello di Montalcino '05	7
● Brunello di Montalcino Il Divasco '04	8
● Rosso di Montalcino '08	5

La Regola

VIA A. GRAMSCI, 1
56046 RIPARBELLA [PI]
TEL. 0586698145
www.laregola.com

This year, the reds presented by the Nuti brothers seemed to be rather muddled. The best of the bunch is the Montescudaio Rosso Beloro '07, which shows ripe black berry fruit aromas on the nose and a well-paced, balsamic, enveloping palate with clear, confident tannins. The whites fare better.

○ Montescudaio Bianco Steccaia '09	4
● Montescudaio Rosso Beloro '07	7
○ Lauro Bianco '08	5

Il Rio

VIA DI PADULE, 131
50039 VICCHIO [FI]
TEL. 0558407904
ilriocerrini@libero.it

Paolo Cerrini's wines never disappoint. This goldsmith-turned-farmer in Mugello gave us two new wines, the pure Sauvignon Carabà '09 and the Terosé '09, a rosé from pinot nero. Ventisei '07, a very good Pinot Nero, has notes of currants and blueberries, delightful, fresh, enjoyable body and good length.

● Ventisei '07	5
○ Annita '09	5
○ Carabà '09	5
⊙ Terosé '09	4

Tenute delle Ripalte

LOC. RIPALTE
57031 CAPOLIVERI [LI]
TEL. 056594211
www.tenutadelleripalte.it

Piermario Meletti Cavallari has forsaken Bolgheri for the shores of Elba and 12 hectares planted to vermentino, grenache and aleatico on a huge estate of over 450. The impressive Alea Ludendo '05 is a distinctive Aleatico with lots of fruit jam and balsamic notes, and a palate at once dry and sweet.

● Elba Aleatico Alea Ludendo '05	7
○ Vermentino di Toscana '09	4

La Sala

LOC. PONTEROTTO
VIA SORRIPA, 34
50026 SAN CASCIANO IN VAL DI PESA [FI]
TEL. 055828111
www.lasala.it

Laura Baronti's lovely Vin Santo '03 has delightful notes of peachy dried fruit and nuts like hazelnut. Entry on the palate is broad, velvety and extremely satisfying. Campo all'Albero '07 from cabernet sauvignon and sangiovese also impresses with mint and alluring spice, a full, juicy body and nice vivacity.

● Campo all'Albero '07	6
○ Vin Santo del Chianti Cl. '03	6
● Chianti Cl. '08	4
● Chianti Cl. Ris. '07	6

Fattoria San Felo

LOC. PAGLIATELLI
58051 MAGLIANO IN TOSCANA [GR]
TEL. 056428481
www.fattoriasanfelo.it

Our pick of the wines Federico Vanni presented is the white Lux Lunae. Obtained from viognier, it offers complex notes of aromatic herbs and thyme and a deliciously tangy palate. We also liked the simpler but tasty Le Stoppaie '09 from vermentino. Morellino Lampo '09 and Riserva Dicioccatore '07 are well made.

○ Lux Lunae '09	4
○ Le Stoppaie '09	4
● Morellino di Scansano Dicioccatore Ris. '07	5
● Morellino di Scansano Lampo '09	4

San Giorgio

FRAZ. CASTELNUOVO DELL'ABATE
LOC. SAN GIORGIO
53020 MONTALCINO [SI]
TEL. 0272094585
www.tenutasangiorgio.it

We applauded the Brunello '05, a bottle from a challenging growing year. The nose is classic and slightly evolved, with notes of tobacco, leather and herbs. The elegant palate shows an integrated but rather too evident tannic-acid vein, while the finish has good length. Cacciacone '07 is fragrant.

● Brunello di Montalcino Ugolforte '05	7
● Cacciacone '07	6

San Giuseppe

LOC. CASTELNUOVO DELL'ABATE
POD. SAN GIUSEPPE, 35
53020 MONTALCINO [SI]
TEL. 0577835754
www.stelladicampalto.it

Stella di Campalto's biodynamic estate in Castelnuovo dell'Abate produces some very subtle wines. The well-made, elegant Brunello di Montalcino '05 displays sweet spicy notes that never mask the fruity nuances of white cherry and peach. The palate has acidity and well-behaved, tucked-in tannins.

● Brunello di Montalcino '05	8
● Rosso di Montalcino '07	6

Fattoria Santa Vittoria

LOC. POZZO
VIA PIANA, 43
52045 FOIANO DELLA CHIANA [AR]
TEL. 057566807
www.fattoriasantavittoria.com

Yet again it is the Vin Santo – this time the '04 – that thrilled us with its classic hints of dried figs, dates and hazelnut, big, enveloping body, silky texture and lingering length. The rest of the range is well made.

○ Valdichiana Vin Santo Ris. '04	6
● Leopoldo '07	5
● Poggio del Tempio '08	4
● Scannagallo '07	4

Vasco Sassetti

LOC. CASTELNUOVO ABATE
VIA BASSOMONDO, 7
53024 MONTALCINO [SI]
TEL. 0577835619
lanzini.massimo@tiscali.it

The late Vasco Sassetti was an institution at Castelnuovo dell'Abate in south-west Montalcino. The wines this year are excellent and the Brunello Riserva '04 is outstanding. Full and intense on the nose, it unveils a seamless palate with nice tannins and supporting acidity, and a full, vigorous finish.

● Brunello di Montalcino Ris. '04	8
● Brunelo di Montalcino '05	7

Scopetani

via Fiorentina, 33
50068 Rufina [FI]
tel. 0558397032
www.scopetani.it

The Chiantl Rufina Stellario Riserva '07 stands out among the wines offered by Gisella and Graziano Scopetani. Founded in 1930, this is one of the brightest estates in the territory. The star wine has alluring balsam over a fruity base, robust body with well-made tannins, strong acid backbone and a long finish.

● Chianti Rufina Stellario Ris. '07	🍷🍷	4*
● Chianti Rufina Risasso '08	🍷	2
● Chianti Rufina V. Macereto Ris. '07	🍷	4
● Chianti Scopetani '09	🍷	3

Sedime

pod. Sedime, 63
53026 Pienza [SI]
tel. 0578748436
capitoni.marco@libero.it

Marco Capitoni's Orcia Rosso Frasi is a very interesting wine. The '07 is obtained from sangiovese with small amounts of canaiolo and displays good mouthfeel and wonderful drinkability. Orcia Rosso Capitoni '08 from sangiovese and merlot is well made but its tannic weave is still rather rigid.

● Orcia Rosso Frasi '07	🍷🍷	5
● Orcia Rosso Capitoni '08	🍷	4

Serraiola

fraz. Frassine
loc. Serraiola
58025 Monterotondo Marittimo [GR]
tel. 0566910026
www.serraiola.it

The Lenzis' wines have character, notably the reds. The merlot, sangiovese and syrah Campo di Montecristo '08 is full and intense. Shiraz '08 also shows well with notes of scrub and a very – perhaps excessively – concentrated palate. Centrati il Monteregio Lentisco and Monteregio Cervone, both '09, are good.

● Campo Montecristo '08	🍷🍷	6
● Monteregio di Massa Marittima Cervone '09	🍷	4
● Monteregio di Massa Marittima Rosso Lentisco '09	🍷	4
● Shiraz '08	🍷	5

Signano

p.zza Sant'Agostino, 17
53037 San Gimignano [SI]
tel. 0577940164
signanno@casolaredibucciano.com

The Vernaccia Riserva '07 performs well. The complex, aromatic nose hints at spice, dried fruit and nuts while the sound, powerful body shows lovely length. The other two Vernaccias are simpler but have an appetising acid vein and a clean, crisp palate. The austere San Gimignano Rosso '05 is a bit mature.

○ Vernaccia di S. Gimignano Ris. '07	🍷🍷	5
● S. Gimignano Rosso '05	🍷	5
○ Vernaccia di S. Gimignano '09	🍷	4
○ Vernaccia di S. Gimignano Poggiarelli '09	🍷	4

I Sodi

fraz. Monti in Chianti
loc. I Sodi
53013 Gaiole in Chianti [SI]
tel. 0577747012
www.agrisodi.com

The Casinis' estate takes it name from its hard terrain. They offer a superb Vin Santo Riserva '04 with pleasant, bitter, vegetal aromas and evolved hints of dried fruit. Entry on the palate is big, dense and succulent, progressing very nicely into a positive finish. The two Chianti Classicos are well typed.

○ Vin Santo del Chianti Cl. Ris. '04	🍷🍷	6
● Chianti Cl. '08	🍷	4
● Chianti Cl. Ris. '07	🍷	5

Solaria - Cencioni

pod. Capanna, 102
53024 Montalcino [SI]
tel. 0577849426
www.solariacencioni.com

Patrizia Cencioni and her vineyards bring us two Brunellos this year. We preferred the Brunello 123 Riserva '04. The nose starts out closed but after a little aeration reveals notes of tobacco and leather. The palate is medium rich with a long, strong tannic-acid element. One for the cellar.

● Brunello di Montalcino 123 Ris. '04	🍷🍷	8
● Brunello di Montalcino '05	🍷	8

Fattoria Sorbaiano

LOC. SORBAIANO
56040 MONTECATINI VAL DI CECINA [PI]
TEL. 058830243
www.fattoriasorbaiano.it

Fattoria Sorbaiano lies a stone's throw from Montecatini Val di Cecina. This year's most convincing bottle is the Cabernet Franc '07. Initially veiled, the nose opens out to reveal attractive blueberry and spicy sensations. The pi?ce de résistance, however, is the palate: chewy and very deep.

- ● Cabernet Franc '07 — 🍷🍷 6

Casale dello Sparviero

LOC. CASALE, 93
53011 CASTELLINA IN CHIANTI [SI]
TEL. 0577743228
www.casaledellosparviero.it

This estate takes its name from its 17th-century hamlet where sparrow-hawks (sparvieri) used to nest. Production is rooted in the Chianti Classico and offers many versions of the wine. The best is the Riserva '07, which is complex in its aromas and full with nice pressure on the savoury palate.

- ● Chianti Cl. Ris. '07 — 🍷🍷 5
- ● Chianti Cl. V. Paronza '08 — 🍷 5
- ● Rosso dello Sparviero '09 — 🍷 4

Streda in Belvedere

VIA DI STREDA, 46
50059 VINCI [FI]
TEL. 0571729195
www.streda.it

The Lenzis' estate lies between Cerreto Guidi and Vinci, both zones long famous for their wines. Production is steady and we were very impressed by Duccio di Streda '07, a highly drinkable sangiovese-heavy wine with fresh, fruity impact. The intense, spicy Syrah '08 is a very rich, savoury and long.

- ● Duccio di Streda Rosso '07 — 🍷🍷 3*
- ● Casanova '09 — 🍷 4
- ● Chianti '09 — 🍷 3
- ● Syrah '08 — 🍷 6

Talenti

FRAZ. SANT'ANGELO IN COLLE
LOC. PIAN DI CONTE
53020 MONTALCINO [SI]
TEL. 0577844064
www.talentimontalcino.it

This stunning, picturesque estate opposite Sant'Angelo in Colle has been completely renovated. The vines fan out from the main building. Brunello Pian di Conte Riserva '04 lacks clarity on the nose, notably in its toasty tones, which also echo on a palate where dense tannins curb its development.

- ● Brunello di Montalcino Pian di Conte Ris. '04 — 🍷🍷 8
- ● Rispollo '08 — 🍷 3

Fattoria della Talosa

VIA PIETROSE, 15A
53045 MONTEPULCIANO [SI]
TEL. 0578758277
www.talosa.it

Thanks to serious work in cellar and vineyard, the Jacorossis' wines have been reliably sound for several years. The Nobile '07 is concentrated and robust but comes across very light on the palate. The very tasty Nobile Riserva '06 presents intense fruit enhanced by notes of ground coffee and tobacco.

- ● Nobile di Montepulciano '07 — 🍷🍷 5
- ● Nobile di Montepulciano Ris. '06 — 🍷🍷 6

Terre dei Fiori

LOC. MELOSELLA ZONA VII
S.DA GRILLESE, 1
58100 GROSSETO
TEL. 0564405457
www.tenutecosta.it

Terre dei Fiori is the Tuscan estate of Tenute Costa, which also has properties in Piedmont and Alto Adige. Morellino Ventaio '08 has an intense nose, firm structure and a good palate. The Morellino '08 is more predictable but drinks easily. The Vermentino '09 is tasty and coherent.

- ● Morellino di Scansano Ventaio '08 — 🍷🍷 5
- ● Morellino di Scansano '08 — 🍷 4
- ○ Vermentino '09 — 🍷 4

Tiberio

FRAZ. PENNA, 116A
52028 TERRANUOVA BRACCIOLINI (AR)
TEL. 0559172781
www.tiberiowine.com

Enzo Nocentini's estate debuts in the Guide. His family have been wine-makers since 1831 and production, based on native varieties, is firmly rooted in the territory. The results are good and we particularly liked the Canaiolo '07 with its fresh, vegetal nose laced with aromatic herbs and sound, supple body.

● Canaiolo '07	(2 glasses)	5
● Malvasia Nera '07	(1 glass)	5

La Togata

LOC. TAVERNELLE
S.DA DI ARGIANO - POD. PODERUCCIO
53024 MONTALCINO [SI]
TEL. 0668803000
www.brunellolatogata.com

Danilo Tonon's estate is back in the Guide with an excellent Brunello Riserva '04. The nose is rich, intense and clean with notes of ripe raspberry, morello cherry and faint balsam. The long palate shows lovely thick, smooth tannins. Progression is captivating; the long finish well-buttressed by acidity.

● Brunello di Montalcino La Togata Ris. '04	(2 glasses)	8
● Brunello di Montalcino La Togata '05	(2 glasses)	8
● Rosso di Montalcino '08	(1 glass)	5

Podere Torcilacqua

LOC. BADIA A PASSIGNANO
S.DA DI GREVE, 8
50028 TAVARNELLE VAL DI PESA [FI]
TEL. 0558071598
www.torcilacqua.it

Mauro Bianchi's estate in the famous Badia di Passignano also has olive groves and an agriturismo. Yet again, the cryptically named Merlot, Kai Zen, reigns supreme with fresh, fruity blueberry, vegetal hints of forest fruit and pencil lead. The palate is warm, balanced and not very big but deliciously long.

● Kai Zen '08	(2 glasses)	6
● Chianti Cl. '08	(1 glass)	4

Torre

LOC. VICO D'ELSA
P.ZZA TORRIGIANI, 15
50021 BARBERINO VAL D'ELSA [FI]
TEL. 0558073001
www.marchesitorrigiani.it

The wines produced by Marchesi Torrigiani, viticulturists since the 13th century, passed muster. Guidaccio '08 from sangiovese with some merlot and cabernet shows well. The austere nose combines notes of tobacco and blackberry jam with hints of spice. The body is firm, full and succulent.

● Guidaccio '08	(2 glasses)	6
● Chianti '08	(1 glass)	4
● Torre di Ciardo '08	(1 glass)	4

Valdarno Superiore

VIA PONTE ALLE FORCHE, 25A
52027 SAN GIOVANNI VALDARNO [AR]
TEL. 0559120413
www.valdarnosuperiore.it

the Guide in its 50th year. Principe della Treggiaia '07, an equal-parts blend of sangiovese, cabernet sauvignon and merlot, has nice fruity aromas of cherry and blackberry, juicy, harmonious body and excellent drinkability. The Chianti Superiore '07 is pleasant.

● Il Principe della Treggiaia '07	(2 glasses)	5
● Chianti Sup. '07	(1 glass)	4

Varramista

LOC. VARRAMISTA
VIA RICAVO
56020 MONTOPOLI IN VAL D'ARNO [PI]
TEL. 057144711
www.varramista.it

Despite its long history, it wasn't until the 1990s that this Pisa estate came into its own when Giovanni Alberto Agnelli inherited it from his grandfather Enrico Piaggio. Our pick is the Syrah Varramista '07: blackcurrant and pepper herald a complete, almost fumé palate with great body and lovely tannins.

● Varramista '07	(2 glasses)	7
● Frasca '07	(2 glasses)	5
● Chianti Monsonaccio '08	(1 glass)	4

Villa Corliano

LOC. BRUCIANESI
VIA DI CORLIANO, 4
50055 LASTRA A SIGNA [FI]
TEL. 0558734542
www.villacorliano.com

The Pancanis' Riserva Briccole '07 impressed us the most this year with its lovely complex bouquet. Its tertiary notes of tobacco and leather mingle with sensations of blackberry and plum jam. The solid palate shows sharp but well-integrated tannins and a nice fresh, juicy acid vein.

- Chianti Colli Fiorentini Briccole Ris. '07 🍷🍷 5
- Ghirigoro '08 🍷 5

Villa I Cipressi

LOC. VILLA I CIPRESSI
53024 MONTALCINO [SI]
TEL. 0577848640
www.villacipressi.it

Honey producer extraordinaire Huber Ciacci has turned his hand to winemaking and is doing very well. The Rosso di Montalcino '08 is delicious, in fact one of best of the year. Clear, fresh cherry and blackberry fruit introduces close-knit texture, elegant tannins, good continuity and an intense finish.

- Rosso di Montalcino '08 🍷🍷 4
- Brunello di Montalcino '05 🍷🍷 7

Villa Poggio Salvi

LOC. POGGIO SALVI
53024 MONTALCINO [SI]
TEL. 0577848486
www.biondisantispa.com

Engineer Tagliabue's estate proceeds slowly but surely. The two Brunellos are well made but we preferred the Brunello Riserva '04. The fruity nose presents close-focused notes of strawberry and yellow peach. The elegant palate is well supported by acidity and the extract is nicely gauged.

- Brunello di Montalcino '05 🍷🍷 7
- Brunello di Montalcino Ris. '04 🍷 7
- Il Tosco '07 🍷 4
- Rosso di Montalcino '08 🍷 4

Bandini Villa Pomona

LOC. POMONA
S.DA CHIANTIGIANA, 222
53011 CASTELLINA IN CHIANTI [SI]
TEL. 0577740930
www.fattoriapomona.it

The Raspi family owns this estate, carrying forward the legacy of Bandino Bandini, who in 1899 started a flourishing farm. The Riserva '07 is very good, giving fresh Mediterranean scrub and forest fruit, a vibrant, balanced body and a long, tangy finish. The Chianti Classico '08 is well styled and drinkable.

- Chianti Cl. Ris. '07 🍷🍷 5
- Chianti Cl. '08 🍷 4

Villa Sant'Andrea

LOC. MONTEFIRIDOLFI
VIA DI FABBRICA, 63
50020 SAN CASCIANO IN VAL DI PESA [FI]
TEL. 0558244254
www.villas-andrea.it

The Chianti Classico '08 did well with fresh, pleasingly intense fruit-like aromas. Entry on the palate is full and measured with well-distributed tannins, a strong acid vein and tangy finish. The Riserva '07 exhibits good structure, full body, assertive, roughish tannins and a slightly cropped finish.

- Chianti Cl. '08 🍷🍷 4
- Chianti Cl. Ris. '07 🍷 5

Villa Sant'Anna

LOC. ABBADIA
VIA DELLA RESISTENZA, 143
53045 MONTEPULCIANO [SI]
TEL. 0578708017
www.villasantanna.it

The Nobile '07 is as full and layered on the palate as it is fragrant on the nose. It is produced by the Fabroni family, a female dynasty led by Simona Ruggeri Fabroni with daughters Margherita and Anna. The Nobile Poldo '06 is still a bit rigid, and muddled on the nose and oak-dominated.

- Nobile di Montepulciano '07 🍷🍷 5
- Nobile di Montepulciano Poldo '06 🍷 6

MARCHE

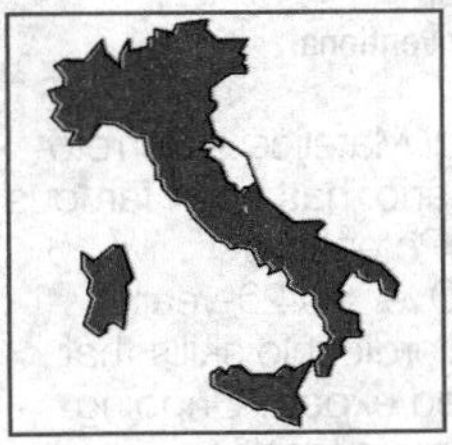

Results from Marche look to be extremely positive. The 17 Three Glass prizes overall constitute a number never achieved before and the prize for the Best Value for Money Wine goes to a Verdicchio, a wine type where good value is the rule rather than the exception. At the same time, we cannot play down the darker side of the picture, which is the shadow stretching threateningly over the Piceno area. Excluding the usual Kurni di Oasi degli Angeli and Roggio del Filare from the Velenosi estate, local reds remain prisoners of their own alcoholic and extractive generosity, sometimes associated with an aromatic phase that needs greater definition and finesse. Though the San Savino Ciprea continues to keep Offida Pecorino in the spotlight, the average quality of this DOC has taken a step back, blocked at wines that are less vibrant and harmonious compared to last season. One explanation could be difficulties associated with in the 2009 growing season. The Pesaro area seems to have shaken off the long torpor that has characterized it for too many years. Though lacking high points, the territory shows vitality and a few new names have appeared on the radar to complement Valturio, whose monovarietal Sangiovese of the same name is right on target. The province of Macerata has made progress. Aside from Matelica, which is always capable of producing Verdicchios with great style and an outstanding sense of terroir, we draw attention to an area that has been overshadowed by classic wine-producing parts of the region: Tolentino. With a great past, but little quality wine production, the town is home to the estate of Aldo Brachetti Peretti, an oil executive who, after various unsuccessful attempts, has finally managed to produce a wine as great as his ambitions. The '07 Pollenza shows austerity and a refined stylistic imprint. Ancona shines and proudly shows off its slew of awards for Jesi Verdicchios. Pievalta also wins plaudits as the wine that most delights both palate and purse, and furthermore it's from organically farmed grapes. Marotti Campi for the first time joins the club of prize-winning estates awarded at least one prize and many others show their sensitivity in interpreting the grape. Sensitivity is even more beautifully evident in two jewels from Conero: the resurgent '05 Dorico from Moroder and the Cumaro '08 from Umani Ronchi, winning their its Three Glass award after coming so close so many times. And the Lacrima is clearly coming on.

Aurora

loc. Santa Maria in Carro
c.da Ciafone, 98
63035 Offida [AP]
tel. 0736810007
www.viniaurora.it

CELLAR SALES
PRE-BOOKED VISITS
ROOMS

ANNUAL PRODUCTION 45,000 bottles
HECTARES UNDER VINE 8
VITICULTURE METHOD Certified organic

More than an estate or agriturismo, Aurora is a way of life. Being part of it means being immersed in a world of solidarity, sustenance and the joy of being together. All this inexhaustible energy comes from five partners who still share the same powerful motivation they had years ago when, in 1979, they joined together and set up a project with an almost utopian feel. A pioneer and promoter of organic methods, Aurora has its own sincere, humanistic vision of the land.

The Barricadiero '08 from montepulciano with a little cabernet and merlot is again the best wine. Austere and gutsy, the close-knit tannins lend character although the less incisive nose fails to hide a bit too much huskiness in a range of dark fruit and earthy tones. Close behind, the Rosso Piceno Superiore '08 offers temperamental generosity on the palate and better drinkability after the nose charms with echoes of burnt embers. From the whites, we liked the rustic sincerity of the Falerio '09 but were perplexed by the Fiobbo '08, a monovarietal Pecorino. Though powerful and long, is lacks momentum and the heavy nose is too muddled.

● Barricadiero '08	▼▼	5
● Rosso Piceno Sup. '08	▼▼	4*
● Rosso Piceno '09	▼▼	3*
○ Falerio dei Colli Ascolani '09	▼	2
○ Offida Pecorino Fiobbo '08	▼	4
● Barricadiero '06	▽▽▽	5
● Barricadiero '04	▽▽▽	5
● Barricadiero '03	▽▽▽	5*
● Barricadiero '01	▽▽▽	5
● Barricadiero '07	▽▽	5
● Barricadiero '05	▽▽	5
○ Offida Pecorino Fiobbo '07	▽▽	4*
○ Offida Pecorino Fiobbo '06	▽▽	4*
○ Offida Pecorino Fiobbo '04	▽▽	4*
● Rosso Piceno '08	▽▽	3*

Belisario

via Aristide Merloni, 12
62024 Matelica [MC]
tel. 0737787247
www.belisario.it

CELLAR SALES
PRE-BOOKED VISITS

ANNUAL PRODUCTION 820,000 bottles
HECTARES UNDER VINE 300
VITICULTURE METHOD Conventional

The Cantina Sociale di Matelica e Cerreto d'Esi, known as Belisario, has been famous for years for Roberto Potentini's winemaking talents. Over his 20-year career, Roberto has Verdicchio skills that make him a recognized expert. Ongoing experiments conducted in tandem with agronomist Mario Ghergo have been turned into successful wines: the cru concept for the Vigneti del Cerro vineyard, the use of barriques, now properly scaled back, for the Cambrugiano and organic management for Vigneti Belisario.

The '07 Meridia comes from ripe, acidity-rich verdicchio grapes fermented and aged in large cement vats, and left on the fine lees for more than a year. The resulting wine has a French air. Elegance and minerality mark every aspect, with charming dark and light effects and rare balance. In spite of the weak season, the convincing Cambrugiano Riserva '07 is still well gauged, long and precise. Always excellent, the Vigneti del Cerro '09 has a salty freshness and the Vigneti Belisario '09 is firm and complex. Outstanding among the reds is the San Leopardo '06, whose grassy, liquorice root notes return on a light, relaxed palate.

○ Verdicchio di Matelica Meridia '07	▼▼▼	4*
○ Verdicchio di Matelica Cambrugiano Ris. '07	▼▼	4*
● San Leopardo '06	▼▼	4*
○ Verdicchio di Matelica Terre di Valbona '09	▼▼	2*
○ Verdicchio di Matelica Vign. Belisario '09	▼▼	4*
○ Verdicchio di Matelica Vign. del Cerro '09	▼▼	3*
● Aeno '09	▼	4
○ Esino Bianco Ferrante '09	▼	2
○ Verdicchio di Matelica Cambrugiano Ris. '06	▽▽▽	4*
○ Verdicchio di Matelica Cambrugiano Ris. '02	▽▽▽	4*
○ Verdicchio di Matelica Vign. Belisario '05	▽▽	4*
○ Verdicchio di Matelica Vign. Belisario '04	▽▽	4*
○ Verdicchio di Matelica Vign. del Cerro '07	▽▽	3*
○ Verdicchio di Matelica Vign. del Cerro '06	▽▽	3*
○ Verdicchio di Matelica Vign. del Cerro '04	▽▽	3*

Bisci

via Fogliano, 120
62024 Matelica [MC]
tel. 0737787490
www.bisciwines.it

CELLAR SALES
PRE-BOOKED VISITS

ANNUAL PRODUCTION 100,000 bottles
HECTARES UNDER VINE 19
VITICULTURE METHOD Conventional

Pierino and Giuseppe Bisci began their activity in 1980. Since then they have lent their name to some of the most individual versions of Verdicchio di Matelica, distinguished by clear extractive richness and high alcohol. Time is an invaluable ally, softening their youthful exuberance. Recently, some indecision has translated into less defined wines with confused aromatic profiles. The arrival of oenologist Aroldo Bellelli seems to have helped overcome these problems. Let's hope the brothers can achieve more consistent quality.

Senex '03 proves time benefits whites from the Biscis. Surprisingly compact, considering it is from the hottest season in memory, the progression and complex features of this wine are sustained by aniseed and almonds. The full, caressing palate has an enduring, mellow finish. Vigneto Fogliano '07 is also rather good, though some incipient mature tones pull the nose toward echoes of dried fruit and liquorice. The interesting Verdicchio '09 shows its original terroir and has nice vitality on the palate. Some robust reds are also on the list. The most convincing is Piangifame '07, a monovarietal Sangiovese with ripe fruit on the nose and good development on the palate.

● Piangifame '07	▼▼	5
○ Verdicchio di Matelica '09	▼▼	4*
○ Verdicchio di Matelica Senex '03	▼▼	5
○ Verdicchio di Matelica Vign. Fogliano '07	▼▼	4*
● Rosso Fogliano '07	▼	4
○ Sauvignon '09	▼	5
● Villa Castiglioni '06	▼	5
● Rosso Fogliano '02	YY	3
○ Verdicchio di Matelica '04	YY	4*
○ Verdicchio di Matelica '03	YY	4*
○ Verdicchio di Matelica '02	YY	4*
○ Verdicchio di Matelica Senex '98	YY	5*
● Villa Castiglioni '03	YY	5
● Villa Castiglioni '01	YY	5

★ Bucci

fraz. Pongelli
via Cona, 30
60010 Ostra Vetere [AN]
tel. 071964179
www.villabucci.com

CELLAR SALES
PRE-BOOKED VISITS

ANNUAL PRODUCTION 120,000 bottles
HECTARES UNDER VINE 31
VITICULTURE METHOD Certified organic

Ampelio Bucci creates elegant, complex, long-lived Verdicchios. His Villa Bucci is a classic of the type, personal yet recognizable, and different from others. But the wine is not in our score sheet this year. In agreement with his famous consultant Giorgio Grai, Ampelio has postponed release so our date is moved to next year and the 2008 version. This loss is partially compensated by one of the rare appearances of its red namesake. Though lacking the same magnetism as the white, it has uncommon finesse and integrity.

The Villa Bucci '06 is made from 70 per cent montepulciano with sangiovese, sourced from the San Fortunato plot, a cru with vines over 40 years old. The delicate, mellow nose has crisp cherries and liquorice then the palate proffers measured tannins, breadth and lively energy, a perfect synthesis of complexity and drinkability. Only 5,000 units went into bottle. The 15,000 bottles of the more coherent Tenuta Pongelli are from equal amounts montepulciano and sangiovese, and boast the same easy drinking quality thanks to delicate tannins and full fruit. Finally, the Verdicchio '09 juggles flowers and fruit on the nose, and has a light, subtle, immediately enjoyable palate.

● Rosso Piceno Villa Bucci '06	▼▼	6
● Rosso Piceno Tenuta Pongelli '08	▼▼	4
○ Verdicchio dei Castelli di Jesi Cl. Sup. '09	▼▼	4
○ Verdicchio dei Castelli di Jesi Cl. Villa Bucci Ris. '07	YYY	7
○ Verdicchio dei Castelli di Jesi Cl. Villa Bucci Ris. '06	YYY	7
○ Verdicchio dei Castelli di Jesi Cl. Villa Bucci Ris. '05	YYY	6
○ Verdicchio dei Castelli di Jesi Cl. Villa Bucci Ris. '04	YYY	6
○ Verdicchio dei Castelli di Jesi Cl. Villa Bucci Ris. '03	YYY	6
○ Verdicchio dei Castelli di Jesi Cl. Villa Bucci Ris. '01	YYY	6
○ Verdicchio dei Castelli di Jesi Cl. Villa Bucci Ris. '00	YYY	6

Le Caniette

C.DA CANALI, 23
63038 RIPATRANSONE [AP]
TEL. 07359200
www.lecaniette.it

CELLAR SALES
PRE-BOOKED VISITS

ANNUAL PRODUCTION 60,000 bottles
HECTARES UNDER VINE 16
VITICULTURE METHOD Certified organic

Caniette has quite a long history of alternating generations. This is not unusual in Ripatransone, a vineyard-covered municipality where a good part of the economy is based on wine and agriculture. This estate's enviable stylistic consistency focuses on concentration, ripe fruit and powerful structure. The Vagnonis seem to be giving up the overripeness that gave the red wines monumental aromatics. Their bottles have always been distinctive, like the characterful of whites from native pecorino and passerina.

More specifically, we note the increasing originality of Iosonogaia. The latest version of this Pecorino is entirely fermented in barrique and has lost its invasive oak gaining savouriness, supported by a complex, multi-faceted nose. More normal, if we can say that, is the white Offida Passerina Lucrezia '09, which has subtle, floral aromas, yet shows backbone and refinement in the mouth. The just-released Nero di Vite '05 has intense liquorice, morello cherry and oaky spice while the palate is a concentrated mix ending on bitter chocolate. The elegant, fruity nose of the Rosso Bello '08 leads directly to a highly pleasing, succulent palate.

○ Offida Pecorino Iosonogaia non sono Lucrezia '08	[2 black glasses]	5
○ Offida Passerina Lucrezia '09	[2 black glasses]	4
● Rosso Piceno Nero di Vite '05	[2 black glasses]	7
● Rosso Piceno Rosso Bello '08	[2 black glasses]	4
○ Offida Passerina Vino Santo Sibilla Chimica '04	[2 white glasses]	6
○ Offida Passerina Vino Santo Sibilla Tiburtina '05	[2 white glasses]	6
○ Offida Pecorino Iosonogaia non sono Lucrezia '06	[2 white glasses]	5
○ Offida Pecorino Iosonogaia non sono Lucrezia '04	[2 white glasses]	5
● Rosso Piceno Morellone '03	[2 white glasses]	5
● Rosso Piceno Morellone '02	[2 white glasses]	5
● Rosso Piceno Nero di Vite '04	[2 white glasses]	7
● Rosso Piceno Nero di Vite '01	[2 white glasses]	7

La Canosa

C.DA SAN PIETRO, 6
63030 ROTELLA [AP]
TEL. 0736374556
www.lacanosaagricola.it

CELLAR SALES
PRE-BOOKED VISITS

ANNUAL PRODUCTION 120,000 bottles
HECTARES UNDER VINE 25
VITICULTURE METHOD Conventional

No matter how well planned, projects starting from scratch need time to fulfil their potential. Illva Saronno's Canosa has built a beautiful winery on the slopes of Mount Ascensione in a high, cool area with plenty of light. Vines are still generally young, and results are inconsistent, but a lot of effort goes into interpreting the terroir. The wines are good, and some reds are even excellent, but lack nuance and clear personality. Future efforts should be directed to remedying this.

Best on the list is Nullius '08, a flowers and fruit Sangiovese with an green notes and a measured, supple palate that avoids heaviness. The powerful, less supple Musè '08 is a meaty, alcoholic Montepulciano from ripe fruit. The nice Signator '08 has earthy aromas and is a bit husky but shows good progression. The usually outstanding Nummaria '08 was slightly blurred and seemed fatigued by an unrefined overripe tone on the nose that detracts from the palate. The same goes for Pekò '09, from an unlucky growing season, which is still full and fruity. The passerina Servator '09 gives flowers and acidity.

● Musè '08	[2 black glasses]	5
● Nullius '08	[2 black glasses]	5
● Rosso Piceno Signator '08	[2 black glasses]	4
○ Passerina Brut '09	[1 black glass]	4
○ Pekò '09	[1 black glass]	4
⊙ Rosé Brut '09	[1 black glass]	4
● Rosso Piceno Sup. Nummaria '08	[1 black glass]	4
○ Servator '09	[1 black glass]	4
● Musè '07	[2 white glasses]	5
● Nullius '07	[2 white glasses]	5
● Rosso Piceno Sup. Nummaria '07	[2 white glasses]	4*
● Rosso Piceno Sup. Nummaria '05	[2 white glasses]	4*
○ Servator '07	[2 white glasses]	4*

Casalfarneto

VIA FARNETO, 12
60030 SERRA DE' CONTI [AN]
TEL. 0731889001
www.casalfarneto.it

CELLAR SALES
PRE-BOOKED VISITS

ANNUAL PRODUCTION 500,000 bottles
HECTARES UNDER VINE 43
VITICULTURE METHOD Conventional

Acquired a few years ago by the Togni family, this estate is being reorganized after changing oenologists during the 2009 harvest. We have been following progress since Casalfarneto has a modern cellar and vineyards planted in one of the best growing areas on the left bank of the river Esino. Here the hills are rounder and the Verdicchio acquires a finesse and brilliance unmatched elsewhere in the designation. For now these features have not emerged completely but are well within reach.

As always, the whites are the most interesting. Fontevecchia '09 has sublime citrussy freshness on the nose and a clear, clean almond finish. It may lack some complexity but agility is guaranteed. The more modern Grancasale is more concentrated, also showing an excessively soft mid palate, because of residual sugars, that loses some verve and masks the varietal richness of flavour. But the succulence remains. A convincing red, the '09 Lacrima Rosae, shows sound and varietal on the nose and invigorating on the palate. The Tonos '07 is overripe on the nose, gives morello cherry on the alcoholic palate and finishes harsh.

● Lacrima di Morro d'Alba Rosae '09	▼▼	4*
○ Verdicchio dei Castelli di Jesi Cl. Sup. Fontevecchia '09	▼▼	4*
○ Verdicchio dei Castelli di Jesi Cl. Sup. Grancasale '09	▼▼	4
● Rosso Conero Tonos '07	▼	4
○ Verdicchio dei Castelli di Jesi Cl. Grancasale Ris. '06	▽▽	4
○ Verdicchio dei Castelli di Jesi Cl. Solustro '06	▽▽	3*
○ Verdicchio dei Castelli di Jesi Cl. Sup. Fontevecchia '08	▽▽	4*
○ Verdicchio dei Castelli di Jesi Cl. Sup. Fontevecchia '07	▽▽	4*
○ Verdicchio dei Castelli di Jesi Cl. Sup. Fontevecchia '06	▽▽	4*
○ Verdicchio dei Castelli di Jesi Cl. Sup. Grancasale '08	▽▽	4*

Casalis Douhet

LOC. PORTO POTENZA PICENA
VIA MONTECORIOLANO,11
62018 POTENZA PICENA [MC]
TEL. 0733688121
www.coriolano.com

CELLAR SALES
PRE-BOOKED VISITS

ANNUAL PRODUCTION 30,000 bottles
HECTARES UNDER VINE 40
VITICULTURE METHOD Conventional

The Casalis Douhet family, originally from Savoy, bequeathed this property to the Colosimo institute for the blind in Naples. The lovely estate on the Adriatic now belongs to the Campania regional authority. For some time, efforts to boost quality have shown good results, producing a clean, modern style with no excess or forcing. A little character is still lacking but this will come as more experience is gained by the young but capable Giuseppe Morelli, oenologist and technical director of the cellar.

Top wine is the '07 Coriolano from 45-40-15 cabernet sauvignon, montepulciano and merlot. Intense roses and spice precede an invigorating palate with good grip and flavourful tannins. Not far behind, the Giulio Douhet '08 shows ripe fruit sensations and a slightly overripe, soft, round palate. The fresh, enjoyable Colosimo '09, from half merlot with 40 per cent sangiovese and a bit of cabernet, is apparently simple but unveils captivating drinkability from a well-gauged structure and tidy floral hints. Less positive reviews go to the whites. The maceratino Brezzato '09 has backbone but slips away quickly and the chardonnay Oltremare '09 lacks thrust but is still big and fruity.

● Colli Maceratesi Rosso Colosimo '09	▼▼	3*
● Coriolano '07	▼▼	4*
● Rosso Piceno Giulio Douhet '08	▼▼	4*
○ Colli Maceratesi Bianco Brezzato '09	▼	3
○ Oltremare '09	▼	3
● Colli Maceratesi Rosso '03	▽▽	3*
● Coriolano '06	▽▽	4*
● Merlot '03	▽▽	3*
○ Oltremare Bianco '08	▽▽	3*
● Rosso '03	▽▽	4*
● Rosso Piceno Giulio Douhet '07	▽▽	4*

Maria Pia Castelli

C.DA SANT'ISIDORO, 22
63015 MONTE URANO [FM]
TEL. 0734841774
www.mariapiacastelli.it

CELLAR SALES
PRE-BOOKED VISITS

ANNUAL PRODUCTION **20,000 bottles**
HECTARES UNDER VINE **8**
VITICULTURE METHOD **Organic**

Enrico Bartoletti and Maria Pia Castelli planted their vineyards at good densities along the flatlands of the Tenna river valley, where they are tended like gardens and managed with biodynamically. The vines give low yields and reach sugar and phenolic ripeness earlier than elsewhere. In the cellar, Marco Casolanetti brings his own winemaking vision to production. These wines share a concentration that is not particularly showy but very characterful.

The Erasmo Castelli '08, from montepulciano only, was not ready for tasting so it will be reviewed next year. The sangiovese Orano '09 has good complexity on the nose and is ready right away instead of having to wait the usual three years after the harvest. Stella Flora is a macerated on the skins from pecorino, passerina, trebbiano and malvasia aromatica di Candia, fermented and aged in oak. With respect to the past, the '08 reveals some signs of incipient oxidation but with a flavourful, saline palate. A rosé from montepulciano and sangiovese, the Sant'Isidoro '09 is decent with an old-fashioned floral tone and soft, substantial palate.

● Orano '09	2 black glasses	4
○ Stella Flora '08	2 black glasses	6
⊙ Sant'Isidoro '09	1 black glass	3
● Erasmo Castelli '06	3 white glasses	6
● Erasmo Castelli '07	2 white glasses	6
● Erasmo Castelli '05	2 white glasses	6
● Erasmo Castelli '04	2 white glasses	6
● Erasmo Castelli '03	2 white glasses	6
● Erasmo Castelli '02	2 white glasses	6
● Orano '08	2 white glasses	4*
● Orano '06	2 white glasses	4*
○ Stella Flora '07	2 white glasses	6
○ Stella Flora '06	2 white glasses	6
○ Stella Flora '05	2 white glasses	6

Cantine di Castignano

C.DA SAN VENANZO, 31
63032 CASTIGNANO [AP]
TEL. 0736822216
www.cantinedicastignano.com

CELLAR SALES
PRE-BOOKED VISITS

ANNUAL PRODUCTION **350,000 bottles**
HECTARES UNDER VINE **520**
VITICULTURE METHOD **Conventional**

Castignano is a small inland town in Piceno where the hills begin to rise before becoming the Monti Sibillini. Ravines and woods criss-cross the pristine landscape. Vines have always been the keystone of the area's farming. The local co-operative winery, Cantine di Castignano, takes grapes from various producers and distributes well-made wines at favourable prices. Over the years, the customer base has been widened through a series of popular direct sales points in neighbouring provinces.

The abundance of pecorino, a variety that loves the foothill climate, means the cellar can produce some 80,000 well-priced units of Montemisio '09, an easy-drinker with pineapple and wild flowers. Never this good before, the well-focused Passerina '09 is gutsy and floral. The Rosso Picenos also prove their worth. Choose from the juicy, dynamic standard label or the denser, more mature Destriero '08. For those who love balanced, subtle flavours, the Templaria '08 from 70 per cent merlot with sangiovese is admirable, dynamic wine overlaid with fruit. The two young Falerios are simple, varietal and unambitious.

○ Offida Passerina '09	2 black glasses	2*
○ Offida Pecorino Montemisio '09	2 black glasses	2*
● Rosso Piceno '09	2 black glasses	1*
● Rosso Piceno Sup. Destriero '08	2 black glasses	2*
● Sangiovese '08	2 black glasses	2*
○ Falerio dei Colli Ascolani '09	1 black glass	1
○ Falerio dei Colli Ascolani Destriero '09	1 black glass	2
● Templaria '08	1 black glass	3
○ Falerio dei Colli Ascolani Destriero '08	2 white glasses	2*
○ Falerio dei Colli Ascolani Destriero '07	2 white glasses	2*
○ Gramelot '07	2 white glasses	3*
○ Offida Passerina '08	2 white glasses	2*
○ Offida Pecorino Montemisio '08	2 white glasses	2*
● Offida Rosso Gran Maestro '05	2 white glasses	4*
● Offida Rosso Gran Maestro '02	2 white glasses	4*
● Offida Rosso Gran Maestro '01	2 white glasses	4*
● Rosso Piceno '07	2 white glasses	1*

Ciù Ciù

LOC. SANTA MARIA IN CARRO
C.DA CIAFONE, 106
63035 OFFIDA [AP]
TEL. 0736810001
www.ciuciu.com

CELLAR SALES
PRE-BOOKED VISITS
ROOMS AND FOOD

ANNUAL PRODUCTION **445,000 bottles**
HECTARES UNDER VINE **98**
VITICULTURE METHOD **Certified organic**

The tireless Bartolomei brothers manage the largest areas under vine in Piceno. Their vast vineyard holdings are planted to local varieties, and wines have a style we could define as judiciously modern, careful to avoid the huskiness and heaviness that denote rough vinification. Over the past ten years, the range has always been highly reliable and shown a pleasantly fruity, soft style. It's still there this time but we noticed a less vibrant and personal character.

We tasted the '05 Oppidum, from slightly overripe montepulciano. Substantial and varietal, it gives tannins sheathed in a glycerine blanket that makes the palate rich, almost doughy, although this is a bit diluted by robust alcohol. Generally the most old-style in the group, the '08 Rosso Piceno Superiore Gotico shows modern sensations of black berry syrup with more freshness and intensity. From barbera, merlot and sangiovese, the San Carro '09 has bright, flamboyant fruit and is designed for immediate consumption. Among the whites, a soft weave emerges in the '09 Le Merlettaie, a Pecorino with yellow-fleshed fruit and meadow herbs. The Evoé '09 is subtle and balanced.

Wine	Glasses	
○ Evoé '09	2 black	3*
○ Offida Pecorino Le Merlettaie '09	2 black	4*
● Oppidum '05	2 black	5
● Rosso Piceno Sup. Gotico '08	2 black	4*
● Saggio '08	2 black	5
● San Carro '09	2 black	4*
○ Falerio dei Colli Ascolani Oris '09	1 black	3
● Rosso Piceno Bacchus '09	1 black	3
○ Offida Pecorino Le Merlettaie '07	2 white	4*
○ Offida Pecorino Le Merlettaie '06	2 white	4*
● Offida Rosso Esperanto '04	2 white	5
● Rosso Piceno Sup. Gotico '07	2 white	4*
● Rosso Piceno Sup. Gotico '06	2 white	4*
● Saggio Sangiovese '07	2 white	5
● Saggio Sangiovese '06	2 white	5

Tenuta Cocci Grifoni

LOC. SAN SAVINO
C.DA MESSIERI, 12
63038 RIPATRANSONE [AP]
TEL. 073590143
www.tenutaccoccigrifoni.it

CELLAR SALES
PRE-BOOKED VISITS

ANNUAL PRODUCTION **400,000 bottles**
HECTARES UNDER VINE **45**
VITICULTURE METHOD **Conventional**

Guido Cocci Grifoni passed away 11 July 2010. A symbol of viticulture in Piceno, for years Guido embodied the figure of an intransigent, terribly stubborn winemaker. These traits led him to be the first to bottle the Rosso Piceno Superiore and rediscover the robust pecorino variety, the latter found along cattle-droving trails. In Arquata del Tronto, he took the first cuttings to graft onto the newest vineyards in Ripatransone and began the spread of this native variety in Piceno.

A recent vertical tasting of the Offida Pecorino Podere Colle Vecchio, back to 1991, showed the longevity of this variety, which combines alcohol, extracts and high acidity. Marilena and Paola Cocci Grifoni decided to prolong ageing so we will review the '09 in the next Guide. We recommend the Vigna Messieri '06, a prototype of the traditional Rosso Piceno with an old-style profile on the nose – liquorice, morello cherry, earthy notes and spice – and a generous, well-developed palate. Rubinio '09 is enjoyable. The basic wines from passerina only scored well. The '09 Adamantea shows field herbs and a pleasantly bitter finish; Brut Gaudio Magno '09 is fragrant and coherent.

Wine	Glasses	
● Rosso Piceno Sup. V. Messieri '06	2 black	5
○ Offida Passerina Adamantea '09	2 black	4*
○ Falerio dei Colli Ascolani Le Torri '09	1 black	3
○ Falerio dei Colli Ascolani Vign. San Basso '09	1 black	3
○ Offida Passerina Gaudio Magno Brut '09	1 black	4
● Rosso Piceno Rubinio '09	1 black	3
○ Falerio dei Colli Ascolani Vign. San Basso '07	2 white	3
○ Offida Pecorino Podere Colle Vecchio '08	2 white	4*
○ Offida Pecorino Podere Colle Vecchio '07	2 white	4*
○ Offida Pecorino Podere Colle Vecchio '05	2 white	4*
○ Offida Pecorino Podere Colle Vecchio '04	2 white	4*
● Rosso Piceno Sup. Le Torri '06	2 white	3*
● Rosso Piceno Sup. V. Messieri '04	2 white	4*
● Rosso Piceno Sup. V. Messieri '02	2 white	4*

Collestefano

loc. Colle Stefano, 3
62022 Castelraimondo [MC]
tel. 0737640439
www.collestefano.com

CELLAR SALES
PRE-BOOKED VISITS

ANNUAL PRODUCTION 60,000 bottles
HECTARES UNDER VINE 10
VITICULTURE METHOD Certified organic

Fabio Marchionni created the Collestefano family estate and expanded it over the years but he has never lost his craftsmanship, which comes across in hands-on management, strictly organic methods and well-gauged production numbers. Over time, the Verdicchio has acquired a precise style of freshness, tanginess, aromatic clarity and a progressive ability to deliver unsuspected complexity with age. The prudent pricing policy has encouraged distribution and the wines regularly sell out.

The Collestefano perfectly reflects the progress of the season. The '09 is fresh on the nose whose varietal florality anticipates a linear palate, apparently lightweight yet capable of savoury length in the finish. A serious entry enhances drinking pleasure on a palate that should acquire great aromatic complexity in a few years' time. Fabio's experiments include small-batch vinifications. From a splendid lot of sauvignon grapes sourced on site, he has interpreted the French classic in a citrus theme with pleasant drinkability. For next year, Fabio has announced a Metodo Classico from verdicchio with a low production run.

○ Verdicchio di Matelica Collestefano '09	TT	4*
○ Sauvignon '09	TT	3*
⊙ Rosa di Elena '09	T	3
○ Verdicchio di Matelica Collestefano '07	YYY	4*
○ Verdicchio di Matelica Collestefano '06	YYY	4*
⊙ Rosa di Elena '08	YY	3*
○ Verdicchio di Matelica Collestefano '08	YY	4*
○ Verdicchio di Matelica Collestefano '05	YY	4*
○ Verdicchio di Matelica Collestefano '04	YY	4*
○ Verdicchio di Matelica Collestefano '03	YY	4*
○ Verdicchio di Matelica Collestefano '02	YY	4
○ Verdicchio di Matelica Collestefano '01	YY	4

La Cantina dei Colli Ripani

via Tosciano, 28
63038 Ripatransone [AP]
tel. 07359505
www.colliripani.it

CELLAR SALES
PRE-BOOKED VISITS

ANNUAL PRODUCTION 600,000 bottles
HECTARES UNDER VINE 900
VITICULTURE METHOD Certified organic

Active since 1977, Cantina dei Colli Ripani currently vinifies fruit from 450 partners throughout the countryside around Ripatransone. Production focuses on local designations where, in some cases, international varieties are grown alongside montepulciano, sangiovese and pecorino while the commercial line is divided between products labelled Colli Ripani, generally correct with modest price tags, and Pharus, aimed at greater satisfaction for real wine lovers and again good value for money.

After a few glitches, production has returned to commendably constant quality. Leading the pack is a splendid '07 version of Castellano, which has shed its old-fashioned style for a reserved modernity, exalting the pulpy fruit of the montepulciano while the 40 per cent sangiovese brings backbone and movement on the palate. High scores also go to the Leo Ripanus '06, from montepulciano and 40 per cent cabernet sauvignon, with a balsamic nose and intense, fruity flavour supported by perfectly extracted, sweet, dense tannins. The '09 Rugaro is the last of the winners, giving aromatic herbs on the nose then balanced alcoholic vigour well fused with the smooth, pleasant palate.

● Rosso Piceno Sup. Castellano '07	TT	3*
○ Offida Pecorino Rugaro '09	TT	3*
● Offida Rosso Leo Ripanus '06	TT	4*
○ Falerio dei Colli Ascolani Brezzolino '09	T	2
● Rosso Piceno Rupe Nero '09	T	1
○ Falerio dei Colli Ascolani Brezzolino '08	YY	2*
○ Falerio dei Colli Ascolani Brezzolino '07	YY	2*
○ Falerio dei Colli Ascolani Brezzolino '06	YY	2*
○ Offida Pecorino Rugaro '07	YY	3*
○ Offida Pecorino Rugaro '04	YY	3*
● Offida Rosso Leo Ripanus '03	YY	4*
● Offida Rosso Leo Ripanus '02	YY	4*
● Rosso Piceno Rupe Nero '07	YY	1*
● Rosso Piceno Sup. Castellano '06	YY	3*
● Rosso Piceno Sup. Castellano '01	YY	3*

Colonnara

via Mandriole, 6
60034 Cupramontana [AN]
tel. 0731780273
www.colonnara.it

CELLAR SALES
PRE-BOOKED VISITS

ANNUAL PRODUCTION **1,000,000 bottles**
HECTARES UNDER VINE **120**
VITICULTURE METHOD **Certified organic**

Colonnara has expanded its range, producing wines outside its 50-year tradition: Lacrima di Morro d'Alba, Offida Passerina and Pecorino, and Bianchello del Metauro. There is a clear desire for diversification and reflecting the region's winemaking heritage. Quality changes gear and register, getting higher when you move to the Verdicchio and sparklers, two recognized house specialities. But the real surprise is the return to quality of the Tornamagno, the historic label from this co-operative at Cupramontana.

The '04 Tornamagno from 60-40 montepulciano and sangiovese shows elegant balsam and spice then an austere, well-developed palate with a deep finish. From the sparklers, the Colonnara Metodo Classico '05 is more complex and intense than the cuve close wines. The fragrant, continuous Riserva Personalizzata is an extended Charmat wine released in fewer than 10,000 bottles. From the Verdicchios, soft, full Tùfico '07 is as good as ever but we'd like to see more dynamism. The Cuprese '09 is measured and well balanced but lacks some final staying power. Among wines from outside the zone, the supple, varietal Offida Pecorino '09 is well made.

○ Colonnara Brut M. Cl. '05	TT	5
○ Colonnara Brut Riserva Personalizzata '08	TT	4
○ Offida Pecorino '09	TT	4*
● Tornamagno '04	TT	4
○ Verdicchio dei Castelli di Jesi Cl. Sup. Cuprese '09	TT	4*
○ Verdicchio dei Castelli di Jesi Cl. Sup. Tùfico '07	TT	4
○ Bianchello del Metauro '09	T	3
○ Colonnara Brut Charmat	T	3
● Lacrima di Morro d'Alba '09	T	4
○ Offida Passerina '09	T	3
○ Verdicchio dei Castelli di Jesi Cl. Portonuovo '09	T	3
○ Verdicchio dei Castelli di Jesi Spumante Ubaldo Rosi Brut Ris. '04	YY	6

Il Conte Villa Prandone

c.da Colle Navicchio, 28
63033 Monteprandone [AP]
tel. 073562593
www.ilcontevini.it

CELLAR SALES
PRE-BOOKED VISITS

ANNUAL PRODUCTION **130,000 bottles**
HECTARES UNDER VINE **25**
VITICULTURE METHOD **Conventional**

Lu Kont (The Count) is the local nickname of the head of the Amilcare family, handed down to his sons. Despite the fact the De Angelis brothers' estate is in one of the areas historically best suited to montepulciano, it had never produced this as a monovarietal till now. The rest of the range is tied to the territory and the most typical varieties are produced in a soft, succulent, ripe fruit style encouraged by the hot climate in Monteprandone.

Lu Kont '07 comes from low-yield vines and ages almost two years in barrique and cement. This intense, juicy wine never disappoints and shows montepulciano's suitability for extractive wines with sweet, smooth tannic weight. The Zipolo '07 is still the benchmark red and has been for some years. Intensely fruity, this well-designed wine has robust, solid structure, though the tannins are still tight. Marinus '08, on the other hand, shows mature and expansive. Donello is an approachable, current-release Sangiovese, all fruit and flavour. Among the whites, the Navicchio '09 offers a fruity timbre on the nose and a soft, caressing flavour that is just a bit flat.

● Zipolo '07	TT	6
● Donello Sangiovese '09	TT	4
● Lu Kont '07	TT	6
● Rosso Piceno Sup. Marinus '08	TT	4
○ Cavaceppo Passerina '09	T	4
○ Falerio dei Colli Ascolani Aurato '09	T	2
○ Offida Passerina Passito L'Estro del Mastro '07	T	5
○ Offida Passerina Spumante Emmanuelmaria '09	T	4
○ Offida Pecorino Navicchio '09	T	4
● Rosso Piceno Conte Rosso '09	T	3
● Rosso Piceno Conte Rosso '08	YY	3*
● Rosso Piceno Conte Rosso '07	YY	3*
● Rosso Piceno Sup. Marinus '07	YY	4
● Zipolo '06	YY	6
● Zipolo '05	YY	6

Conti di Buscareto

FRAZ. PIANELLO
VIA SAN GREGORIO, 66
60010 OSTRA [AN]
TEL. 0717988020
www.contidibuscareto.com

CELLAR SALES
PRE-BOOKED VISITS

ANNUAL PRODUCTION 150,000 bottles
HECTARES UNDER VINE 70
VITICULTURE METHOD Conventional

There is no connection between Claudio Gabellini or Enrico Giacomelli and the Conti di Buscareto, an old local family whose history runs back to the mid 1400s. They may, however, share the desire to leave a mark on the various, scattered properties, each with its own characteristics. Verdicchio grows at Arcevia with pre-Apennine soil and climate. Lacrima nera comes from the best-suited zone of Morro d'Alba in the village of Sant'Amico. The other red varieties are at Camerata Picena, a warmer area near Conero and Mount San Vito.

The best wines are from Arcevia. The cool site climate gives the verdicchio elegance and poise, the two distinguishing features of Ammazzaconte '08. The bouquet is complex, floral and aniseed-laced before delicate smoky tones show framed in a deep, austere flavour. The current-vintage Verdicchio is less complex and aims for immediacy. Among the reds, the solid, nicely textured Bisaccione '07, from 70-30 montepulciano and cabernet sauvignon, is slightly held back by oak. As we wait for the selections, there were good showings from a well-typed Lacrima '09, the viscous Passito '08 and a flavourful, Charmat-method Brut Rosé, all from the fragrant native lacrima di Morro d'Alba.

○ Verdicchio dei Castelli di Jesi Ammazzaconte '08	▼▼	4*
● Bisaccione '07	▼▼	6
● Lacrima di Morro d'Alba '09	▼▼	4*
● Lacrima di Morro d'Alba Passito '08	▼▼	4
● Rosso Piceno '08	▼▼	3*
○ Verdicchio dei Castelli di Jesi '09	▼▼	3*
⊙ Rosa '09	▼	3
⊙ Rosé Brut '09	▼	4
● Lacrima di Morro d'Alba Compagnia della Rosa '04	▽▽	5
● Lacrima di Morro d'Alba Nicolò di Buscareto '04	▽▽	6
● Rosso Piceno '07	▽▽	3*
○ Verdicchio dei Castelli di Jesi '07	▽▽	3*
○ Verdicchio dei Castelli di Jesi '06	▽▽	3*
○ Verdicchio dei Castelli di Jesi '05	▽▽	3*
○ Verdicchio dei Castelli di Jesi Ammazzaconte '06	▽▽	4*

Tenuta De Angelis

VIA SAN FRANCESCO, 10
63030 CASTEL DI LAMA [AP]
TEL. 073687429
www.tenutadeangelis.it

CELLAR SALES

ANNUAL PRODUCTION 500,000 bottles
HECTARES UNDER VINE 50
VITICULTURE METHOD Conventional

De Angelis is a major Piceno grape producer that has historically made large quantities of wine sold in bulk. But in the 1990s, under the guidance of Quinto Fausti, the cellar began bottling local wines. In particular, the name has been linked with long-lived versions of Rosso Piceno Superiore and the polished structure of Anghelos, a sound Montepulciano softened with a pinch of Cabernet Sauvignon. This policy has not changed. To the contrary, it has been extended to designation white wines, which are selling well.

The showcase Anghelos '07 is faithful to its style. Deliberately majestic, full and pulpy yet not overripe, this wine has flavour and density melding with a finish of morello cherry and roast coffee beans. L'Oro '08 is just as sound. Though lacking the depth and tenacity of the Anghelos, it shares its density and volume. Simpler and more easily approachable, the Rosso Piceno Superiore '08 has a fruity, round palate. Among the whites, the Pecorino '09 repeats the good impression made by the '08 and, although from an unexciting vintage, is remarkably supple with lovely echoes of pineapple and almond. The subtle, acidulous Passerina '09 is a wine to open straight away.

● Anghelos '07	▼▼	5
○ Offida Pecorino '09	▼▼	3*
● Rosso Piceno Sup. '08	▼▼	3*
● Rosso Piceno Sup. Oro '08	▼▼	4
○ Falerio dei Colli Ascolani '09	▼	2
○ Offida Passerina '09	▼	3
○ Prato Grande '09	▼	2
● Rosso Piceno '09	▼	2
● Anghelos '01	▽▽▽	5
● Anghelos '99	▽▽▽	5
● Anghelos '05	▽▽	4
● Anghelos '04	▽▽	4
● Anghelos '03	▽▽	5
● Rosso Piceno Sup. Oro '04	▽▽	4

Degli Azzoni Avogadro Carradori

VIA DON MINZONI, 26
62010 MONTEFANO [MC]
TEL. 0733850219
www.degliazzoni.it

CELLAR SALES
PRE-BOOKED VISITS
ROOMS AND FOOD

ANNUAL PRODUCTION **100,000 bottles**
HECTARES UNDER VINE **130**
VITICULTURE METHOD **Conventional**

Degli Azzoni produces few bottles considering how hectares it has under vine. The explanation is in its long history of selling unbottled wine through busy sales points. Everyone in Macerata knows this winery, even those with no oenophile ambitions. For some time, under the direction of Filippo Degli Azzoni, the cellar has been shifting to high-quality bottled wines. The labels we tasted are good and sourced from the estate's vast vineyards.

Attention to native varieties is reflected in the table below. The two best wines come from only one variety each: montepulciano for the excellent Passatempo '08, with ripe fruit, a soft, relaxed flavour and still slightly oaky finish, and maceratino for the Colli Maceratesi Bianco '09, with a slightly aromatic nose in a vegetal setting, and a substantial, never boring palate. The blend of overripe grapes in Sultano '08 includes picolit and sauvignon with a preponderance of malvasia aromatica di Candia. Complex green sensations, candied tropical fruits and honey tones show on the nose and return on the changing, velvety palate.

● Cantalupo Rosso '08	▼▼	4*
○ Colli Maceratesi Bianco '09	▼▼	3*
● Passatempo '08	▼▼	6
○ Sultano '08	▼▼	4
○ Beldiletto Brut '08	▼	4
○ Cantalupo Bianco '09	▼	2
○ Bianco di Cantalupo '07	▽▽	3*
● Passatempo '07	▽▽	6
● Rosso Cantalupo '07	▽▽	4*
● Rosso Cantalupo '07	▽▽	4*
● Rosso Cantalupo '06	▽▽	3*
● Rosso Cantalupo '05	▽▽	4*
● Rosso Cantalupo '04	▽▽	4*
○ Sultano '07	▽▽	4*

Fattoria Dezi

C.DA FONTEMAGGIO, 14
63029 SERVIGLIANO [FM]
TEL. 0734710090
fattoriadezi@hotmail.com

CELLAR SALES
PRE-BOOKED VISITS
ROOMS

ANNUAL PRODUCTION **50,000 bottles**
HECTARES UNDER VINE **16**
VITICULTURE METHOD **Organic**

Dezi family holdings are at Servigliano and Santa Vittoria in Matenano, a rather different zone from classic areas in Piceno since it is more northern and closer to the Apennines than the Adriatic. Davide Dezi's skills with sangiovese and montepulciano ensure perfectly ripe grapes. His brother Stefano makes wines with definition and character that express their terroir and age magnificently, especially the Regina del Bosco, which lays out kaleidoscopic complexity as it matures.

From montepulciano only, Regina del Bosco '07 flaunts a beautiful nose of cocoa powder, spice and red fruit. The palate is meaty yet crisp, vital and even exuberant. We could mention the slight surplus of alcohol but time in glass will help relax the profile and give it harmony. Properly different, the Sangiovese Solo '08 has a smoky nose over ripe cherries and a penetrating palate with a warm tone, but slightly stiff closing. From montepulciano with small amounts of sangiovese, the Dezio '08 failed to open completely at our tastings, although it did show a succulent, taut, dark palate.

● Regina del Bosco '07	▼▼	7
● Solo Sangiovese '08	▼▼	7
● Dezio Vign. Beccaccia '08	▼▼	5
● Regina del Bosco '06	▽▽▽	7
● Regina del Bosco '05	▽▽▽	7
● Regina del Bosco '03	▽▽▽	6
● Solo Sangiovese '05	▽▽▽	7
● Solo Sangiovese '01	▽▽▽	6
● Solo Sangiovese '00	▽▽▽	6
● Dezio Vign. Beccaccia '06	▽▽	5
● Solo Sangiovese '07	▽▽	7
● Solo Sangiovese '06	▽▽	7

La Distesa

VIA ROMITA, 28
60034 CUPRAMONTANA [AN]
TEL. 0731781230
www.ladistesa.it

CELLAR SALES
PRE-BOOKED VISITS
ROOMS AND FOOD

ANNUAL PRODUCTION **10,000 bottles**
HECTARES UNDER VINE **3**
VITICULTURE METHOD **Organic**

Corrado Dottori is an unusual winemaker, cultured, passionate and stubborn. He is also a great writer. His works mix economy, sociology, holism, agronomy and rock music with a vision he applies to his own life. He lives with his wife and children in a corner of paradise, his agriturismo just below the hermitage of Romita di Cupramontana at the edge of the forest of Frati Bianchi. The vineyards and cellar are in the other direction, in the exceptional vineyard of San Michele. Corrado's wines are more spontaneous than anything else on the shelf today.

Using strictly organic methods, no yeasts, long fermentation and minimal technology, Corrado attempts to reproduce the aromas he remembers from his grandfather's vats. He seems happy with the Terre Silvate '09's mix of almonds, flowers and meadow herbs framed in a salt-veined palate. The Nur '08, from 40 per cent verdicchio with trebbiano and malvasia, aged on the skins, is a refined example of a natural wine. Intense notes of tea leaves and apricot accompany exuberantly vibrant pulp. More controversial is Gli Eremi Riserva '08 grips the palate and reveals a clear oxidative touch from the barriques. But this is a wine that ages magnificently.

- ○ Nur '08 — 4*
- ○ Verdicchio dei Castelli di Jesi Cl. Sup. Terre Silvate '09 — 3*
- ○ Verdicchio dei Castelli di Jesi Cl. Sup. Gli Eremi Ris. '08 — 4
- ○ Bianco 99 — 6
- ● Nocenzio '03 — 4*
- ● Nocenzio '02 — 4*
- ○ Nur '06 — 4
- ○ Verdicchio dei Castelli di Jesi Cl. Sup. Gli Eremi '03 — 4*
- ○ Verdicchio dei Castelli di Jesi Cl. Sup. Terre Silvate '07 — 3*
- ○ Verdicchio dei Castelli di Jesi Cl. Sup. Terre Silvate '06 — 3*
- ○ Verdicchio dei Castelli di Jesi Cl. Sup. Terre Silvate '05 — 3*

Fausti

C.DA CASTELLETTA, 15
63023 FERMO [FM]
TEL. 0734620492
faustivini@gmail.com

CELLAR SALES
PRE-BOOKED VISITS

ANNUAL PRODUCTION **65,000 bottles**
HECTARES UNDER VINE **11**
VITICULTURE METHOD **Organic**

Contrada Castelletta is a hill between the sea and Fermo that owes its name to a watchtower facing the Adriatic. Saracens are no longer a danger but the breezes that do cool down the Mediterranean temperatures even in the heat of the day. A great grower, Domenico D'Angelo protects his grapes and always makes well-crafted wines with a fruity intensity that never shades into overripeness or jammy notes. On the other hand, we should say this year the whites showed a slower pulse. We hope this is only temporary.

The Vespro shows high quality and is always competing for a third Glass. A blend of 70 per cent montepulciano, from a clone selected at Fermo, and the rest syrah, it shows elegant smoky, fruity notes. The stylish, well-knit tannic weave on the soft palate supports a long, consistent, decisive finish. Also sound is the monovarietal Syrah from a French clone, Perdomenico. The '08 lays out a convincing olfactory array of red fruit and pepper held together by the sweetness of the alcohol. The palate is vigorous, well defined and almost monumental but could perhaps have benefited from greater suppleness in the mouth. The '09 Fausto fails to shake off slightly too much roughness.

- ● Vespro '08 — 5
- ● Perdomenico Syrah '08 — 5
- ● Rosso Piceno Fausto '09 — 2
- ● Vespro '05 — 5
- ● Vespro '03 — 4*
- ○ Offida Pecorino Ale '08 — 3*
- ● Rosso Piceno Fausto '07 — 2*
- ● Rosso Piceno Fausto '06 — 3*
- ● Rosso Piceno Fausto '03 — 2*
- ● Vespro '07 — 5
- ● Vespro '06 — 5
- ● Vespro '04 — 5
- ● Vespro '02 — 4*
- ● Vespro '01 — 4

Fazi Battaglia

via Roma, 117
60031 Castelplanio [AN]
tel. 073181591
www.fazibattaglia.it

CELLAR SALES
PRE-BOOKED VISITS

ANNUAL PRODUCTION 3,000,000 bottles
HECTARES UNDER VINE 260
VITICULTURE METHOD Conventional

Titulus in the amphora bottle makes up 93 per cent of production. This historic label is bound up with the winery's identity. But this has not stopped trials of other techniques with Verdicchio, from overripening for the Massaccio to barriques for the San Sisto, yeasts for Le Moie and vineyard strategies for more consistent development of the Botrytis cinerea used in the Arkezia. This ongoing research has now produced results far beyond the formal typicality of the wine in the famous bottle.

Three Glasses go to the San Sisto '07, highly elegant on the nose, where nuts, minerality and hints of attractive oak tend to balsamic notes, and deep and tidy on the palate. The Massaccio '07 has a different impact, a tropical stamp in the fruit echoes and caressing glycerine that is never heavy and recovers savouriness at the back. Of the two current selections, we preferred the fruity, joyful Ekeos over the clearly varietal Le Moie, which has proper acid thrust. The Rie Verdi '09 is another experiment from adding 65 per cent riesling renano to verdicchio. Though citrussy and soft, it needs more grip. The dark, alcoholic Passo del Lupo '07 is not quite up to snuff.

○ Verdicchio dei Castelli di Jesi Cl. San Sisto Ris. '07	▼▼▼	5
○ Verdicchio dei Castelli di Jesi Cl. Sup. Massaccio '07	▼▼	5
○ Arkezia Muffo di S. Sisto '07	▼▼	7
○ Verdicchio dei Castelli di Jesi Cl. Sup. Ekeos '09	▼▼	5
○ Verdicchio dei Castelli di Jesi Cl. Sup. Le Moie '09	▼▼	4
● Conero Passo del Lupo Ris. '07	▼	5
○ Rie Verdi '09	▼	4
● Rosso Conero Ekeos '09	▼	5
○ Verdicchio dei Castelli di Jesi Cl. San Sisto Ris. '05	▽▽▽	5
○ Verdicchio dei Castelli di Jesi Cl. Sup. Massaccio '03	▽▽▽	4*
○ Verdicchio dei Castelli di Jesi Cl. Sup. Massaccio '01	▽▽▽	4
○ Verdicchio dei Castelli di Jesi Cl. Sup. Massaccio '00	▽▽▽	4

Fiorano

c.da Fiorano, 19
63030 Cossignano [AP]
tel. 073598446
www.agrifiorano.it

CELLAR SALES
PRE-BOOKED VISITS
ROOMS

ANNUAL PRODUCTION 30,000 bottles
HECTARES UNDER VINE 5
VITICULTURE METHOD Certified organic

The scenic view of the Fiorano winery, located below the agriturismo facility and residence of Paolo Beretta's family, opens onto a steep hilly amphitheatre where vines alternate with olive trees and farmed plots in a multi-coloured patchwork. Pecorino is planted in the coolest area; the sunnier slopes are reserved for sangiovese, montepulciano and some merlot. Organic growing methods create honest, well-defined wines that are sold at very fair prices.

The Pecorino Donna Orgilla '09 is becoming a benchmark for the type, thanks to a citrussy vitality that lends finesse to the flavour and savoury thrust to the back palate, all this accompanied by suppleness in the progression. The Terre di Giobbe '07 is as dark as ink and the light gamey whiffs on the nose quickly shift into morello cherry and damp earth. The palate shows the weight of the extracts and tannins are still slightly rough but adjusting. A perfect everyday wine is the sangiovese-based Fiorano '09 with floral aromas and a supple, delicate palate.

○ Offida Pecorino Donna Orgilla '09	▼▼	4*
● Rosso Piceno Sup. Terre di Giobbe '07	▼▼	4*
● Fiorano Sangiovese '09	▼	3
○ Donna Orgilla Pecorino '07	▽▽	4*
○ Offida Pecorino Donna Orgilla '08	▽▽	4*
● Rosso Piceno Sup. Terre di Giobbe '06	▽▽	4*
● Rosso Piceno Sup. Terre di Giobbe '05	▽▽	4*
● Ser Balduzio '04	▽▽	6

Cantine Fontezoppa

C.DA SAN DOMENICO, 24
62012 CIVITANOVA MARCHE [MC]
TEL. 0733790504
www.cantinefontezoppa.it

CELLAR SALES
PRE-BOOKED VISITS

ANNUAL PRODUCTION **150,000 bottles**
HECTARES UNDER VINE **35**
VITICULTURE METHOD **Conventional**

The three production sites produce a diversified range. Verdicchio comes from the Matelica vineyards, the only ones leased. Local lacrima, sangiovese, and maceratino along with internationals cabernet sauvignon, and merlot are grown in the hills overlooking the sea, behind Civitanova Marche. Inevitably, the terroir in the foothills of Serrapetrona also hosts the local vernaccia nera. Giovanni Basso has overseen vinification for a couple of years and respects the original territory with a successful modern style.

Vernaccia nera gives some surprising monovarietals. The ambitious Morò '06 may be a bit clenched but the '07 Falcotto has a clear, pleasant peppery nose that returns on the palate with power and finesse. Among the reds from the coast, the Carapetto '07 is a spicy, precise Cabernet Sauvignon, and the lacrima-based Dirosaediviola '07 has an intense floral bouquet and fresh, pleasantly tannic palate. The Annibal Caro '08, an equal blend of sangiovese and cabernet, has vegetal, blood-rich sensations on the nose and well-proportioned sweet fruit on the palate. The Ribona '09 is the best of its type and combines ripe fruit with an surprising pebbles, benzene and grapefruit aromatics.

● Annibal Caro '08	▼▼	5
● Carapetto '07	▼▼	5
○ Colli Maceratesi Ribona '09	▼▼	4*
● Dirosaediviola '07	▼▼	5
● Serrapetrona Falcotto '07	▼▼	5
○ Marche Bianco '09	▼	4
⊙ Piccinì '09	▼	4
● Serrapetrona Morò '06	▼	5
○ Verdicchio di Matelica '09	▼	4
● Carapetto '06	▽▽	5
○ Colli Maceratesi Ribona '08	▽▽	4*
● Marche Rosso '07	▽▽	2*
● Marche Rosso '06	▽▽	2*
● Mariné '07	▽▽	5
○ Verdicchio di Matelica '08	▽▽	4*

★ Gioacchino Garofoli

P.LE G. GAROFOLI, 1
60022 CASTELFIDARDO [AN]
TEL. 0717820162
www.garofolivini.it

CELLAR SALES
PRE-BOOKED VISITS

ANNUAL PRODUCTION **2,000,000 bottles**
HECTARES UNDER VINE **42**
VITICULTURE METHOD **Conventional**

The precision Carlo Garofoli uses to make his wines amazes us every time and not just for his magic with verdicchio. For years, we have celebrated his talents with the variety in labels like Podium and Serra Fiorese, absent this year for a greater period of ageing. We are equally surprised at his prowess when he ventures into new products. What is the latest? In its second release, a wonderful version of Brut Rosé Metodo Classico is Carlo's tribute to sparklers.

The montepulciano Brut Rosé Metodo Classico '07 has unexpected aromatic finesse reflected in the creamy effervescence. The verdicchio Riserva Metodo Classico '06 is also high quality. Among the still wines, Podium '08 breaks away and wins another Three Glasses for refined aromas and a marvellous mid palate. Macrina '09 gives penetrating smokiness in the most powerful version we can remember. From the reds, Agontano Riserva '07 lives up to its reputation as a thoroughbred Montepulciano, generous and impulsive now, but turning velvety over the next few years. Last comes Kòmaros '09, a top regional rosé with crisp fruit and irresistible drinkability.

○ Verdicchio dei Castelli di Jesi Cl. Sup. Podium '08	▼▼▼	5
● Conero Grosso Agontano Ris. '07	▼▼	5
⊙ Garofoli Brut Rosé '07	▼▼	5
○ Verdicchio dei Castelli di Jesi Cl. Sup. Macrina '09	▼▼	4*
○ Garofoli Brut Ris. '06	▼▼	5
⊙ Kòmaros '09	▼▼	3*
● Rosso Conero Piancarda '07	▼▼	4*
● Camerlano '06	▼	5
○ Dorato '08	▼	4
○ Garofoli Brut Charmat '09	▼	4
● Rosso Piceno Colle Ambro '07	▼	4
○ Verdicchio dei Castelli di Jesi Passito Brumato '06	▼	5
○ Verdicchio dei Castelli di Jesi Cl. Sup. Podium '07	▽▽▽	5*
○ Verdicchio dei Castelli di Jesi Cl. Sup. Podium '06	▽▽▽	5*
○ Verdicchio dei Castelli di Jesi Cl. Sup. Podium '04	▽▽▽	4*

Piergiovanni Giusti

loc. Montignano
via Castellaro, 97
60019 Senigallia [AN]
tel. 071918031
www.lacrimagiusti.it

CELLAR SALES
PRE-BOOKED VISITS

ANNUAL PRODUCTION **51,000 bottles**
HECTARES UNDER VINE **13**
VITICULTURE METHOD **Conventional**

Lacrima producers traditionally also plant a few rows of verdicchio. Jesi is not that far away and many areas lie in classic verdicchio territory. Growers also want to diversify. But the white wine spirit of the area has yet to convince Piergiovanni Giusti, whose exclusive dedication to Lacrima has made him an admired specialist. Production is low but much sought-after, in particular Luigino and Rubbjano. Shrewd ageing and a year in barrique never cramp the limpid aromatic profile.

The 4,500 bottles of Luigino '08 won the derby by a nose. From old vines, it has uncommon complexity for a Lacrima, giving black pepper, smokiness and black berry fruits over a concentrated palate founded on solid, slightly stiff, tannins with bright flavour. The Rubbjano '08, also 4,500 bottles, has more vivid, juicy fruit of peaches and morello cherries against light background touches of rose petals. The palate is invigorating, expansive, succulent and immediately pleasing. The Lacrima '09, aged six months in used barriques and large barrels, has energy and aromatic typicality without descending into caricature. Le Rose di Settembre '09 is also sound, with distinct florality.

● Lacrima di Morro d'Alba Sup. Luigino Vecchie Vigne '08	▼▼	5
● Lacrima di Morro d'Alba '09	▼▼	4*
● Lacrima di Morro d'Alba Rubbjano '08	▼▼	4
⊙ Le Rose di Settembre '09	▼	3
● Lacrima di Morro d'Alba '07	▽▽	3
● Lacrima di Morro d'Alba '06	▽▽	3*
● Lacrima di Morro d'Alba '05	▽▽	3*
● Lacrima di Morro d'Alba Luigino '06	▽▽	5
● Lacrima di Morro d'Alba Luigino '05	▽▽	5
● Lacrima di Morro d'Alba Luigino '04	▽▽	5
● Lacrima di Morro d'Alba Rubbjano '06	▽▽	4*
● Lacrima di Morro d'Alba Rubbjano '04	▽▽	4*
⊙ Le Rose di Settembre '06	▽▽	3*
⊙ Le Rose di Settembre '05	▽▽	3*

Luca Guerrieri

via San Filippo, 24
61030 Piagge [PU]
tel. 0721890152
www.aziendaguerrieri.it

CELLAR SALES
PRE-BOOKED VISITS
ROOMS AND FOOD

ANNUAL PRODUCTION **180,000 bottles**
HECTARES UNDER VINE **35**
VITICULTURE METHOD **Conventional**

Luca Guerrieri's wine estate is part of a broader agricultural group of vast holdings and lovely farms. Despite the potential of the recent past, these wines showed some indecision we could not ignore. With this year's tastings, the range finally shows a clearer overall vision, focusing on local designations and no-frills wines that present clean, essential and direct.

One of the best Bianchellos, the well-typed Celso '09, has flowers, meadow herbs and a fresh, balanced, palate. The surprisingly good Galileo '07 is a multi-faceted Sangiovese with a fruit, spice and flower bouquet, and a vibrant palate with gutsy tannins and nice movement. International tendencies show in the Guerriero Nero '08, an almost equal blend of sangiovese, merlot and cabernet. But this raw material has been skilfully managed. The flavourful palate has an appealing aromatic herb finish. Stepping down a level, we appreciated the immediacy of the Brut Rosé, a Charmat-method sangiovese, and the fruity Lisippo '09, an unusual blend of bianchello and verdicchio.

○ Bianchello del Metauro Celso '09	▼▼	3*
● Colli Pesaresi Sangiovese Galileo '07	▼▼	4
● Guerriero Nero '08	▼▼	4*
○ Bianchello del Metauro '09	▼	3
○ Colli Pesaresi Lisippo '09	▼	3
● Colli Pesaresi Sangiovese '09	▼	3
○ Guerrieri Brut '09	▼	4
⊙ Guerrieri Brut Rosé '09	▼	4
○ Bianchello del Metauro Celso '04	▽▽	4*
● Colli Pesaresi Sangiovese Galileo '00	▽▽	5
● Colli Pesaresi Sangiovese Galileo Ris. '00	▽▽	5
● Guerriero Nero '04	▽▽	4*

Fattoria Laila

via San Filippo sul Cesano, 27
61040 Mondavio [PU]
tel. 0721979353
www.fattorialaila.it

CELLAR SALES
PRE-BOOKED VISITS

ANNUAL PRODUCTION 130,000 bottles
HECTARES UNDER VINE 40
VITICULTURE METHOD Conventional

Andrea Crocenzi's winery straddles the provinces of Pesaro and Ancona but his vineyards are located in Corinaldo and the Moie district of Maiolati Spontini, planted mostly to verdicchio but also montepulciano and sangiovese, and the promontory of Conero, all montepulciano. This estate has always been attentive to ripening and its modern wines avoid the redundancy of overripeness in favour of clear aromas, supported by freshness and drive. Overall, the range is reliable although it lacks the high note that would crown years of hard work.

The Verdicchio Lailum Riserva is the best. The '08 shows crystalline aromas of citrus, spring flowers and green peaches, the palate is austere yet solid with a subtle yet persistent finale. Among the other good wines, Eklektikos '09 has a more varietal aniseed and almond flavour. The Classico Superiore '09 aims for persuasive fruit. Moving on to the reds, the Rosso Conero '09 shows fragrant morello cherry and a succulent palate. The same goes for the Rosso Piceno '09 with softer tannins and a rounder palate. Less open than last year, the concentrated Lailum Rosso '07 shows full fruit and balsamic echoes on the nose but is also rigid on the palate. Time will bring harmony.

○ Verdicchio dei Castelli di Jesi Cl. Lailum Ris. '08	▼▼	5
● Rosso Conero Fattoria Laila '09	▼▼	4*
● Rosso Piceno Fattoria Laila '09	▼▼	3*
● Rosso Piceno Lailum '07	▼▼	5
○ Verdicchio dei Castelli di Jesi Cl. Sup. '09	▼▼	3*
○ Verdicchio dei Castelli di Jesi Cl. Sup. Eklektikos '09	▼▼	4*
● Lailum '02	▽▽	5
● Lailum '01	▽▽	5
● Rosso Piceno Lailum '06	▽▽	5
● Rosso Piceno Lailum '05	▽▽	5
● Rosso Piceno Lailum '03	▽▽	5
○ Verdicchio dei Castelli di Jesi Cl. Lailum Ris. '07	▽▽	4*
○ Verdicchio dei Castelli di Jesi Cl. Lailum Ris. '04	▽▽	4

Luciano Landi

via Gavigliano, 16
60030 Belvedere Ostrense [AN]
tel. 073162353
www.aziendalandi.it

CELLAR SALES
PRE-BOOKED VISITS

ANNUAL PRODUCTION 100,000 bottles
HECTARES UNDER VINE 18
VITICULTURE METHOD Conventional

Belvedere Ostrense owes its name to the views over the nearby Adriatic and surrounding countryside, always well tended and lined with rows. These vineyards historically grow verdicchio and the red grape that "weeps" when ripe: lacrima. Luciano Landi's skill with the variety is not surprising, since he has always accentuated ripening to concentrate the structure, soften the impact of the tannins and support aromatic weight.

In Goliardo, Luciano strives to craft a red free of lacrima's sometimes excessive florality. He uses 80 per cent montepulciano with cabernet and merlot. This dark, concentrated wine offers ripe fruit and tight-knit tannins on a well-designed palate but lacking personality. The Gavigliano '08 Lacrima Superiore is better, condensing penetrating roses and cherries on a dense yet magically flavoursome palate. The basic Lacrima is fruity and robust with no aggressive astringency. The peppery Passito '08 shows cherry syrup and a clearly sweet finish with great staying power. The Verdicchio '09 is only fair, showing thirst quenching but quickly fading.

● Goliardo '08	▼▼	5
● Lacrima di Morro d'Alba '09	▼▼	3*
● Lacrima di Morro d'Alba Passito '08	▼▼	6
● Lacrima di Morro d'Alba Sup. Gavigliano '08	▼▼	4
● Ragosto '08	▼	4
○ Verdicchio dei Castelli di Jesi Cl. '09	▼	3
● Goliardo '07	▽▽	5
● Goliardo '03	▽▽	6
● Lacrima di Morro d'Alba '08	▽▽	3*
● Lacrima di Morro d'Alba Gavigliano '05	▽▽	4*
● Lacrima di Morro d'Alba Passito '06	▽▽	6
● Lacrima di Morro d'Alba Sup. Gavigliano '07	▽▽	4*
● Lacrima di Morro d'Alba Sup. Gavigliano '06	▽▽	4*
○ Verdicchio dei Castelli di Jesi Cl. '06	▽▽	3*

Leopardi Dittajuti

via Marina II, 24
60026 Numana [AN]
tel. 0717390116
www.conteleopardi.com

CELLAR SALES
PRE-BOOKED VISITS

ANNUAL PRODUCTION **250,000 bottles**
HECTARES UNDER VINE **44**
VITICULTURE METHOD **Conventional**

Vittorio Leopardi Dittajuti's vineyards breathe the salt spray from the Adriatic. Between Numana and Sirolo, they lend colour to a strip of Marche where white rock alternates with green nature and blue sea. The sauvignon grapes from this estate acquire a coastal personality. The whites were the most satisfying. Some montepulciano-based wines stammered a bit, showing excess oak and forced ripening of fruit, which darkens the aromatic profile and toughens the palate.

The Pigmento Riserva '07 shows cherries in alcohol and smoke on the nose while the round palate is refined and compact, slightly lacking in depth, but nicely reflecting the warmth of montepulciano. The Fructus '09 is consistent, enjoyable and easy going. The Casirano and Vigneti del Coppo, both '08s, are less focused. The Bianco del Coppo and Calcare, both '09s, are from all sauvignon. The former is vegetal and delicate with nice acidity; the Calcare has an intense nose of passion fruit, sage and citrus, then the palate is supple and salty with a reprise of the aromatics. The well-made Castelverde '09 is a country-style Verdicchio with good presence on the palate.

○ Bianco del Coppo Sauvignon '09	▼▼	4*
○ Calcare Sauvignon '09	▼▼	4*
● Conero Pigmento Ris. '07	▼▼	6
● Rosso Conero Fructus '09	▼▼	4*
○ Verdicchio dei Castelli di Jesi Cl. Castelverde '09	▼▼	4*
● Rosso Conero Casirano '08	▼	5
● Rosso Conero Vign. del Coppo '08	▼	4
○ Villamarina Brut	▼	4
○ Bianco del Coppo Sauvignon '08	▽▽	4*
○ Bianco del Coppo Sauvignon '07	▽▽	4*
● Conero Pigmento Ris. '06	▽▽	6
● Conero Pigmento Ris. '04	▽▽	6
● Rosso Conero Vign. del Coppo '02	▽▽	4*
○ Verdicchio dei Castelli di Jesi Cl. Castelverde '06	▽▽	4*

Roberto Lucarelli

loc. Ripalta
via Piana, 20
61030 Cartoceto [PU]
tel. 0721893019
www.laripe.com

CELLAR SALES
PRE-BOOKED VISITS

ANNUAL PRODUCTION **130,000 bottles**
HECTARES UNDER VINE **24**
VITICULTURE METHOD **Conventional**

Roberto Lucarelli has never surrendered to the idea of Bianchello del Metauro as a simple, docile, everyday wine to drink young. With his oenologist Aroldo Bellelli, he has persisted, paying attention to yields and the ripening curve of the grapes, and making prudent use of low temperatures in vinification. In the end, he has managed to impart a stature and personality we never thought possible. On the other hand, he still fails to convince us in his reds, often pointlessly over-extracted and marked by superfluous oak.

The Rocho '09 is a different Bianchello from the rest. The intense nose has appealing, well-integrated vegetal sensations as well as flowers and fresh fruit. The savoury, citrussy palate has good fluidity and staying power in the finish. Bianchello La Ripe '09 offers the same sensations but less intense and extremely pleasant drinkability. Fragrance and a slightly sweetish flavour mark out an easy-drinking Brut Extra Dry, the Esther. Soft but a bit predictable, the Chardonnay '09 made a decent debut.

○ Bianchello del Metauro La Ripe '09	▼▼	3*
○ Bianchello del Metauro Rocho '09	▼▼	4*
○ Chardonnay '09	▼	4
● Colli Pesaresi Sangiovese Insieme Ris. '07	▼	5
○ Esther Brut Extra Dry	▼	4
○ Bianchello del Metauro '01	▽▽	4*
○ Bianchello del Metauro La Ripe '08	▽▽	3*
○ Bianchello del Metauro La Ripe '07	▽▽	3*
○ Bianchello del Metauro La Ripe '06	▽▽	2*
○ Bianchello del Metauro Rocho '08	▽▽	4*
○ Bianchello del Metauro Rocho '07	▽▽	4
● Colli Pesaresi Sangiovese '01	▽▽	4
● Colli Pesaresi Sangiovese Goccione '06	▽▽	5
● Colli Pesaresi Sangiovese La Ripe '06	▽▽	3*

Stefano Mancinelli

VIA ROMA, 62
60030 MORRO D'ALBA [AN]
TEL. 073163021
www.mancinelli-wine.com

CELLAR SALES
PRE-BOOKED VISITS

ANNUAL PRODUCTION **150,000 bottles**
HECTARES UNDER VINE **25**
VITICULTURE METHOD **Conventional**

Stefano Mancinelli's sales outlet is popular and he admits to selling most of his production via local distribution. This reflects two aspects: the winery's central location, just outside the walls around the oldest part of Morro d'Alba, is fundamental. Second, and most important, Stefano Mancinelli holds a prestigious position in this DOC zone. He was the first to believe in Lacrima and his interpretations are still a benchmark for those looking to try their hand with the local variety.

Of the three versions submitted, the best is definitely the Lacrima Superiore '08, intensely floral with varietal roses upfront. The palate is soft and full, and the sandiness of the tannins comes out in the finish but is well controlled. The nicely made Lacrima '08 is a territorial wine with lots of energy and clear florality. Sensazioni di Frutto '09 is a Lacrima vinified by carbonic maceration. This special technique releases the full range of aromatics and the palate has good backbone and concentration. We close with the Verdicchio Classico Superiore '09, noteworthy for its curious coppery hue and nice flavour of fresh almonds.

● Lacrima di Morro d'Alba '08	▼▼	4
● Lacrima di Morro d'Alba Sensazioni di Frutto '09	▼▼	4
● Lacrima di Morro d'Alba Sup. '08	▼▼	4
○ Verdicchio dei Castelli di Jesi Cl. Sup. '09	▼▼	3
● Lacrima di Morro d'Alba Passito Re Sole '05	▽▽	5
● Lacrima di Morro d'Alba S. Maria del Fiore '06	▽▽	4*
● Lacrima di Morro d'Alba Sensazioni di Frutto '07	▽▽	4
● Lacrima di Morro d'Alba Sup. '06	▽▽	4*
● Lacrima di Morro d'Alba Sup. '05	▽▽	4*
● Terre dei Goti	▽▽	6
○ Verdicchio dei Castelli di Jesi Cl. S. Maria del Fiore '04	▽▽	3*
○ Verdicchio dei Castelli di Jesi Cl. Sup. S. Maria del Fiore '07	▽▽	3*
○ Verdicchio dei Castelli di Jesi Cl. Sup. S. Maria del Fiore '05	▽▽	3*
○ Verdicchio dei Castelli di Jesi Passito Stell '06	▽▽	5

Clara Marcelli

VIA FONTE VECCHIA, 8
63030 CASTORANO [AP]
TEL. 073687289
www.claramarcelli.it

ANNUAL PRODUCTION **N.A.**
HECTARES UNDER VINE **N.A .**
VITICULTURE METHOD **Certified organic**

Daniele and Emanuele Colletta are the soul of this winery, set up by their mother Clara Marcelli. Though not working in the cellar full time, both tend this long-established family property with 40-year-old vineyards. New plantings were added in 2002. Montepulciano dominates these rows of vines, though traditional pecorino, passerina and sangiovese also make an appearance. Since 1992, the operation has been managed organically. The wines already show great personality and have margins for further improvement.

The K'un '08 is a deep monovarietal Montepulciano with clear crunchy fruit. The mineral, lightly balsamic nose changes at every turn of the glass and the palate flows long and vibrant. The Rosso Piceno Superiore '08 lays out ripe fruit and spice, grafting the same aromas onto a meaty palate with sweet, solid tannins that mark the finish. The pecorino Irata '09 shows great shape by flaunting a complex nose of aniseed and an assertive, characterful, almost salty palate. This savouriness shows in another white, the Raffa '09, which hinges on varietal passerina florality shot through with pleasing citrus in a satisfyingly intense progression with great staying power.

● K'un '08	▼▼	4*
○ Offida Passerina Raffa '09	▼▼	4
○ Offida Pecorino Irata '09	▼▼	4
● Piceno Rosso Sup. '08	▼▼	4
● K'un '07	▽▽	4
● K'un '06	▽▽	4*
○ Offida Pecorino Irata '07	▽▽	4*
● Piceno Rosso Sup. '07	▽▽	4

Marotti Campi

VIA SANT'AMICO, 14
60030 MORRO D'ALBA [AN]
TEL. 0731618027
www.marotticampi.it

CELLAR SALES
PRE-BOOKED VISITS

ANNUAL PRODUCTION 170,000 bottles
HECTARES UNDER VINE 56
VITICULTURE METHOD Conventional

Lorenzo Marotti Campi has never betrayed verdicchio, the variety at home here in the hills of Morro d'Alba as well as Jesi, for the more widely planted lacrima. He reserves the same respect for both and has hired a recognized specialist in these varieties: Roberto Potentini. After long study, his top wines Salmariano and Orgiolo boast reliability, personality and charm, a sign that hard work, clear ideas and determination have finally paid off.

This superb all-verdicchio Salmariano Riserva '07, aged part in small oak, won Three Glasses for an imperious, untamed palate, full of flavour yet with a light, refined expression nose echoing smoke, citrus and aniseed. We should also mention the good Orgiolo '08, a peppery, aromatically intense Lacrima with succulent, polished tannins. The same skill was lavished on Rùbico. The basic version has a nose of violets and roses that return on the palate. Rùbico's white alter ego, the '09 Luzano, aims for the varietal typicality of almonds and a tangy finish. The Xyris '09 is a delicious, part-fermented Lacrima must with an irresistible floral fragrance.

○ Verdicchio dei Castelli di Jesi Cl. Salmariano Ris. '07	▼▼▼	4*
● Lacrima di Morro d'Alba Sup. Orgiolo '08	▼▼	4*
● Lacrima di Morro d'Alba Rùbico '09	▼▼	4
○ Verdicchio dei Castelli di Jesi Cl. Sup. Luzano '09	▼▼	3
● Xyris Mosto Parzialmente Fermentato '09	▼▼	4
○ Verdicchio dei Castelli di Jesi Cl. Albiano '09	▼	2
● Lacrima di Morro d'Alba Sup. Orgiolo '07	▽▽	4*
● Lacrima di Morro d'Alba Sup. Orgiolo '06	▽▽	4*
○ Verdicchio dei Castelli di Jesi Cl. Salmariano Ris. '06	▽▽	4*
○ Verdicchio dei Castelli di Jesi Cl. Sup. Luzano '08	▽▽	3*
○ Verdicchio dei Castelli di Jesi Cl. Sup. Luzano '07	▽▽	3*
○ Verdicchio dei Castelli di Jesi Cl. Sup. Luzano '06	▽▽	3*

La Monacesca

C.DA MONACESCA
62024 MATELICA [MC]
TEL. 0733672641
www.monacesca.it

CELLAR SALES
PRE-BOOKED VISITS

ANNUAL PRODUCTION 170,000 bottles
HECTARES UNDER VINE 27
VITICULTURE METHOD Conventional

In 1988, Mirum was released in a distinctive, long Rhine bottle that contained verdicchio, as well as small amounts of chardonnay and sauvignon. Actually, the wine was called Mirus. The root is from the name of the owner, Casimiro Cifola, aka Miro. To be honest, for many years this was not even a designation wine. Today, the wine has changed and is now a monovarietal Verdicchio in a Bordeaux bottle, proud of its type. But little has changed in its ability to promote the territory and its signature wine.

Aldo Cifola, Miro's son, makes a special edition of the emblematic wine: Mirum 20 Anni. In barely 6,600 bottles, 85 per cent '08 Mirum with older vintages. The nose is explosive and deep, and palate has a soft, broad entry, almost sweet in the presence of residual sugars fusing with the distinct alcoholic warmth that ushers in a long, layered finish. Three Glasses go to the standard version: the palate has unstoppable progression driven by the constant tension of acid backbone and softness. Just when the softness seems to prevail, a jolt from the salt and citrus closes the harmonious circle. The remarkable basic version has as much flavour and character as ever.

○ Verdicchio di Matelica Mirum Ris. '08	▼▼▼	5
○ Verdicchio di Matelica Mirum 20 Anni Ris. '08	▼▼	5
○ Verdicchio di Matelica '09	▼▼	4*
● Camerte '99	▽▽▽	5
○ Mirus '91	▽▽▽	5
○ Verdicchio di Matelica Mirum Ris. '07	▽▽▽	5*
○ Verdicchio di Matelica Mirum Ris. '06	▽▽▽	5
○ Verdicchio di Matelica Mirum Ris. '04	▽▽▽	5
○ Verdicchio di Matelica Mirum Ris. '02	▽▽▽	5
● Camerte '06	▽▽	5
○ Ecclesia Chardonnay '07	▽▽	4
○ Verdicchio di Matelica La Monacesca '08	▽▽	4*
○ Verdicchio di Matelica La Monacesca '07	▽▽	4*
○ Verdicchio di Matelica La Monacesca '06	▽▽	4*
○ Verdicchio di Matelica Mirum Ris. '03	▽▽	5

Monte Schiavo

FRAZ. MONTESCHIAVO
VIA VIVAIO
60030 MAIOLATI SPONTINI [AN]
TEL. 0731700385
www.monteschiavo.it

CELLAR SALES
PRE-BOOKED VISITS

ANNUAL PRODUCTION **1,800,000 bottles**
HECTARES UNDER VINE **115**
VITICULTURE METHOD **Conventional**

The Pieralisi family estate, Monte Schiavo, has beautiful vineyards in wonderful sites like Poggio San Marcello or Tassanare, in Rosora and Arcevia, in a high altitude, almost unpolluted zone. Over the years, it has always followed its own idea of quality, watching market trends, but never looking for quick profits. Research and innovation into Verdicchio have been constant. For the first time here, Three Glasses go to a white, the designation's emblematic wine. In the past only, the Rosso Conero Adeodato red has been honoured.

For 20 years, the Pallio di San Floriano has combined a sense of terroir with value for money. The splendid '09 vintage shows great energy and an electrifying backdrop of salt and almonds that recalls the variety. Coste del Molino '09 is a bit more dilute on the palate but presents savoury and austerely elegant. The ambitious Le Giuncare Riserva '08, 25 per cent barrique-aged, has tropical fruit, candied citrus and botrytis. The palate is a tad too soft but still full and flavourful. Nativo '07, an unfiltered Verdicchio aged long on the fine lees, has the same qualities with more backbone and harmony. From the reds, the fruity Conti Cortesi '08 has a precise, expansive palate.

○ Verdicchio dei Castelli di Jesi Cl. Sup. Pallio di S. Floriano '09	▼▼▼	4*
○ Verdicchio dei Castelli di Jesi Cl. Coste del Molino '09	▼▼	3*
● Rosso Conero Conti Cortesi '08	▼▼	4*
○ Verdicchio dei Castelli di Jesi Cl. Le Giuncare Ris. '08	▼▼	4*
○ Verdicchio dei Castelli di Jesi Cl. Sup. Nativo '07	▼▼	4*
● Esino Rosso Ruviano '08	▼	6
● Lacrima di Morro d'Alba Pansè '09	▼	4
● Rosso Piceno Sup. Sassaiolo '08	▼	3
○ Verdicchio dei Castelli di Jesi Cl. Ruviano '09	▼	3
○ Verdicchio dei Castelli di Jesi Cl. Le Giuncare Ris. '07	▽▽	4*
○ Verdicchio dei Castelli di Jesi Cl. Sup. Pallio di S. Floriano '08	▽▽	4*

Montecappone

VIA COLLE OLIVO, 2
60035 JESI [AN]
TEL. 0731205761
www.montecappone.com

CELLAR SALES
PRE-BOOKED VISITS

ANNUAL PRODUCTION **120,000 bottles**
HECTARES UNDER VINE **70**
VITICULTURE METHOD **Conventional**

Last year's well-deserved Three Glasses for the Utopia '07 represented proper recognition for the careful ongoing efforts of Gianluca and Alessandro Mirizzi. Gianluca has now decided to streamline his range of labels further. He could even trim away some more, but this is for him to decide. We limit ourselves to commenting on a solid range that always looks to the territory and gives a modern interpretation of the long winemaking tradition in Jesi.

Three Glasses again for the Utopia. The imposing '08 vintage has an intensely varietal nose and great integrity, also evident on a flavourful palate with attractive backbone, and a long salty finish with upfront bitter almonds, verdicchio's trademark. The Federico II '09 shows the same bearing as Utopia but with a less incisive step and a balanced palate showing savouriness and tidy aromas. The direct, essential Sauvignon Breccia '09 is citrussy and spirited, the complete opposite of the soft, fragrant, easy drinking Tabano Bianco '09, from half verdicchio with moscato and sauvignon. The juicy Tabano Rosso '08 and fragrant rosé Pergolesi 1710 '09 are two decent reds.

○ Verdicchio dei Castelli di Jesi Cl. Utopia Ris. '08	▼▼▼	5
○ La Breccia Sauvignon '09	▼▼	4*
⊙ Pergolesi 1710 '09	▼▼	4*
○ Tabano Bianco '09	▼▼	5
● Tabano Rosso '08	▼▼	5
○ Verdicchio dei Castelli di Jesi Cl. Sup. Federico II A.D. 1194 '09	▼▼	3
● Rosso Piceno '09	▼	4
○ Verdicchio dei Castelli di Jesi Cl. '09	▼	4
○ Verdicchio dei Castelli di Jesi Cl. Utopia Ris. '07	▽▽▽	5*
○ Esino Bianco Tabano '07	▽▽	5
○ La Breccia Sauvignon '08	▽▽	4*
○ La Breccia Sauvignon '06	▽▽	4*
○ Verdicchio dei Castelli di Jesi Cl. Sup. Montesecco '06	▽▽	4*
○ Verdicchio dei Castelli di Jesi Cl. Utopia Ris. '06	▽▽	5
○ Verdicchio dei Castelli di Jesi Cl. Utopia Ris. '04	▽▽	5

Alessandro Moroder

via Montacuto, 121
60029 Ancona
tel. 071898232
www.moroder-vini.it

PRE-BOOKED VISITS

ANNUAL PRODUCTION 140,000 bottles
HECTARES UNDER VINE 32
VITICULTURE METHOD Conventional

Maker of one of the most classic versions in the designation, Alessandro Moroder personifies the noblest vision of Montepulciano del Conero. He has never wavered from this in quality or because of market demands. Alessandro releases his wines when they are ready, in other words, after they have the chance to soften out their youthful exuberance and find their inner balance. Time particularly helps the Riserva Dorico, which only brings out its potential several years after the harvest, offering silky texture and complexity.

After 14 years, Dorico brings Three Glasses back to Moroder. The '05 vintage is still young but has elegant tannins that guarantee complexity for many years. Already perfect, the aromatic profile has upfront morello cherries shaded by aromatic herbs and oriental spice. The palate has personality and stylistic precision. The two Rosso Coneros come from two different yet complementary production philosophies. Aìon is easier, fruity and rounded but the Moroder is more along the lines of the Dorico. It doesn't have the same complexity but echoes the balanced concentration on the palate. BianConero '09 is a pleasant filtered sweet wine from moscato bianco and alicante nero.

● Conero Dorico Ris. '05	▼▼▼	6
● Rosso Conero Aiòn '08	▼▼	3*
● Rosso Conero Moroder '07	▼▼	4*
○ BianConero '09	▼	4
⊙ Rosa di Montacuto '09	▼	3
● Rosso Conero Dorico '93	▽▽▽	5
● Rosso Conero Dorico '90	▽▽▽	5
● Rosso Conero Dorico '88	▽▽▽	5
● Ankon '03	▽▽	6
● Conero Dorico Ris. '04	▽▽	6
● Rosso Conero Dorico Ris. '03	▽▽	6
● Rosso Conero Dorico Ris. '01	▽▽	6

Oasi degli Angeli

c.da Sant'Egidio, 50
63012 Cupra Marittima [AP]
tel. 0735778569
www.kurni.it

CELLAR SALES
PRE-BOOKED VISITS

ANNUAL PRODUCTION 5,000 bottles
HECTARES UNDER VINE 7
VITICULTURE METHOD Organic

Some believe that insanely concentrating yields and ripening of montepulciano, and ageing the wine twice in new oak, they can produce a Kurni. But even coming close to cloning Kurni is impossible. Kurni is the result of an ever-evolving vineyard project that exploits the finesse of the white limestone in the hills behind Cupramarittima and the latest biodynamic discoveries to create a terroir that cannot be reproduced. There is one, fundamental, variable: the winemaker with his interpretation of variety and territory.

A monovarietal montepulciano, the Kurni '08 has a beautiful nose, some might say lustrous, with black berry fruit, morello cherry, and touches of blood-rich meat and oriental spice. The power of the alcohol shows and is refreshed by spicy balsamic notes before a sumptuous palate shows concentrated but never fatiguing, with fruit that shifts from sweet and mouthfilling on entry to crunchy mid palate, then explodes when the sweet, sophisticated mass of extract takes control of the endless finish. Three Glasses.

● Kurni '08	▼▼▼	8
● Kurni '07	▽▽▽	8
● Kurni '04	▽▽▽	8
● Kurni '03	▽▽▽	8
● Kurni '02	▽▽▽	8
● Kurni '01	▽▽▽	8
● Kurni '00	▽▽▽	8
● Kurni '98	▽▽▽	8
● Kurni '97	▽▽▽	8
● Kupra '06	▽▽	8
● Kupra '05	▽▽	8
● Kurni '06	▽▽	8
● Kurni '05	▽▽	8

Borgo Paglianetto

LOC. PAGLIANO, 393
62024 MATELICA [MC]
TEL. 073785465
www.borgopaglianetto.it

VENDITA DIRETTA
VISITA SU PRENOTAZIONE

PRODUZIONE ANNUA **100.000 bottiglie**
ETTARI VITATI **18.00**
VITICOLTURA **Convenzionale**

Il progetto di Mario Bassilissi e della famiglia Roversi prende forma e sostanza. Titolari rispettivamente di Terra Vignata e Del Carmine, da tre anni hanno unito le forze sotto un'unica azienda, sita in contrada Pagliano, alle spalle di Matelica, in un'incantevole piccola valle. La cantina domina il più importante tra i vigneti, dove regna il verdicchio, ma trovano spazio anche montepulciano, sangiovese e altri vitigni a bacca rossa. Il rinnovato centro aziendale accoglie una funzionale sala degustazioni e vende, tra l'altro, una selezione di prodotti tipici.

Buonissimo il Vertis '08, etichetta di punta tra i bianchi: Verdicchio maturato in acciaio ha profumi eleganti, tra nuance di fiori e anice e una bocca che riesce a fondere succosità e potenza, tensione sapida e rigore aromatico. Tra i migliori Verdicchio di Matelica assaggiati quest'anno. A debita distanza si piazza il Petrara '08, elegante al naso ed equilibrato al palato pur senza l'argento vivo del precedente. Il Verdicchio Terra Vignata '09 è floreale, immediato, facile da bere, in virtù della sua allettante morbidezza. Con lo stesso nome c'è anche un rosso, sempre '09, ottenuto da un blend di sangiovese, lacrima e merlot, dal naso speziato e con un gusto agile, scorrevole, dalla piena corrispondenza tra naso e bocca, sfumante in un ricordo pepato.
TESTO NON IN DB

○ Verdicchio di Matelica Vertis '08	▼▼	4*
● Terravignata '08	▼▼	3
○ Verdicchio di Matelica Petrara '08	▼▼	3*
○ Verdicchio di Matelica Terra Vignata '09	▼▼	3*
● Colli Maceratesi Rosso Petrara '06	▽▽	3*
○ Verdicchio di Matelica Aja Lunga '05	▽▽	4*
○ Verdicchio di Matelica Aja Lunga '04	▽▽	4
○ Verdicchio di Matelica Aja Lunga '03	▽▽	3*
○ Verdicchio di Matelica Petrara '05	▽▽	3*
○ Verdicchio di Matelica Petrara '04	▽▽	3*
○ Verdicchio di Matelica Petrara '03	▽▽	2*
○ Verdicchio di Matelica Terra Vignata '08	▽▽	3*
○ Verdicchio di Matelica Vertis '07	▽▽	4*

Piantate Lunghe

FRAZ. CANDIA
VIA PIANTATE LUNGHE, 91
60131 ANCONA
TEL. 07136464
www.piantatelunghe.it

CELLAR SALES
PRE-BOOKED VISITS

ANNUAL PRODUCTION **30,000 bottles**
HECTARES UNDER VINE **12**
VITICULTURE METHOD **Conventional**

The Piantate Lunghe estate was the last to join the montepulciano club. Started in 2004 by the brothers Guido and Roberto Mazzoni, and Amedeo Giustini, the winery has always impressed with its modern, efficient style, transmitting all the variety's generosity without losing the finesse of the white limestone soils in Monte Conero. Located in a single plot at Angeli near Varano, a couple of kilometres from the Adriatic, the vineyards have excellent exposure and good breezes. These wines have style, precision and commendably constant quality.

The Rossini made another excellent showing and, though not receiving our highest award, the '07 version punches out its own special peach and ripe cherry fruit with extravagant confidence, softened by refined aromatic herbs. The palate maintains a ripeness of fruit and a compact tannic weave that lacks only a bit of expansion in the finish, which time in bottle will put right. The Rosso Conero '07 is simply the best in its category. The announces its juicy load of fruit run through with nuances of roasted coffee beans, later confirmed in a well-paced, dynamic palate that never disperses the energy of the tannins.

● Conero Rossini Ris. '07	▼▼	6
● Rosso Conero '07	▼▼	4
● Conero Rossini '06	▽▽▽	6
● Conero Rossini Ris. '05	▽▽▽	6
● Conero Ris. '04	▽▽	6
● Rosso Conero '06	▽▽	4*
● Rosso Conero '05	▽▽	4*

Pievalta

via Monteschiavo, 18
60030 Maiolati Spontini [AN]
tel. 0731705199
www.baronepizzini.it

CELLAR SALES
PRE-BOOKED VISITS

ANNUAL PRODUCTION **80,000 bottles**
HECTARES UNDER VINE **27**
VITICULTURE METHOD **Certified biodynamic**

When Barone Pizzini arrived in the hills of Verdicchio, there was no winery: only a run down farm and old, if enviably aspected, vineyards needing to be restored. Headquarters in Brescia called for a new philosophy of organic agriculture so a young oenologist, Alessandro Fenino, came in from Lombardy and joined this new operation. Today, after seven years of ever more convincing production, Pievalta wines proudly belong to their terroir, show personality and are almost shamelessly sincere, even more so since the shift to biodynamic viticulture.

Sourced from vineyards on the left bank at Moie near Maiolati Spontini, the surprising Pievalta '09 is great value for money. The spontaneous floral nose has yet to acquire finesse but is terribly sincere. The pervasive palate has fantastic vitality and a charming salty close. Slightly overripe grapes from San Paolo di Jesi, on the right bank of the Esino, create the monovarietal Verdicchio of the same name. Brushed by botrytis, this elegant wine has shifting hints of aromatic herbs and citrus peel. The Dominé '09 is a Verdicchio fermented without sulphites. Though it has good acid tangy grip, the wine raised questions about its aromatics and development.

Wine	Glasses	Score
○ Verdicchio dei Castelli di Jesi Cl. Sup. Pievalta '09	3 (black)	3*
○ San Paolo '06	2 (black)	4*
○ Perlugo Extra Brut	1 (black)	4
○ Verdicchio dei Castelli di Jesi Cl. San Paolo Ris. '05	2	5
○ Verdicchio dei Castelli di Jesi Cl. San Paolo Ris. '04	2	4*
○ Verdicchio dei Castelli di Jesi Cl. Sup. Dominè '08	2	4*
○ Verdicchio dei Castelli di Jesi Cl. Sup. Dominè '06	2	4
○ Verdicchio dei Castelli di Jesi Cl. Sup. Pievalta '06	2	3*
○ Verdicchio dei Castelli di Jesi Cl. Sup. Pievalta '05	2	3*

Il Pollenza

via Casone, 4
62029 Tolentino [MC]
tel. 0733961989
www.ilpollenza.it

CELLAR SALES

ANNUAL PRODUCTION **80,000 bottles**
HECTARES UNDER VINE **50**
VITICULTURE METHOD **Conventional**

Even the most ambitious projects, planned in every detail and executed without skimping, need time to produce significant results. Il Pollenza, born out of the desire of Aldo Brachetti Peretti to grow vines around his estate in Tolentino, today offers a high quality range of wines that are not territory-linked – no native varieties are planned – but do have an expressive style that shows off elegance, measured power and complexity. Bordeaux obviously inspires every aspect.

Three Glasses go to the '07 Il Pollenza from merlot and the two cabernets, which shows excellent complexity, finesse and depth. The fine weave of pencil lead, cedar wood, cassis and aromatic herbs leads to a precise, austere palate with great momentum and a radiant finish. The Cosmino '07 Cabernet Sauvignon mixes red fruit and green bell pepper notes with oriental spice as the dense tannic weave on the palate grafts onto alcohol-rich texture, delivering power and progression. Further down, the structure of the merlot Porpora '07 is a bit blocked by oak. A sweet Sauvignon, the refined Pius IX Mastai '08 offers hints of peaches in syrup.

Wine	Glasses	Score
● Il Pollenza '07	3 (black)	8
● Cosmino '07	2 (black)	5
○ Pius IX Mastai '08	2 (black)	6
● Porpora '07	2 (black)	4
○ Brianello '09	1 (black)	4
● Cosmino '03	2	5
● Il Pollenza '04	2	8
● Il Pollenza '03	2	8
● Il Pollenza '02	2	7
● Il Pollenza '01	2	7
○ Pius IX Mastai '06	2	6
○ Pius IX Mastai '03	2	6

Sabbionare

VIA SABBIONARE, 10
60036 MONTECAROTTO [AN]
TEL. 0731889004
sabbionare@libero.it

CELLAR SALES
PRE-BOOKED VISITS

ANNUAL PRODUCTION 30,000 bottles
HECTARES UNDER VINE 10
VITICULTURE METHOD Conventional

Sabbionare is one of the micro-estates in the area around Castelli di Jesi. The tiny size pays tribute to the spirit of this place and tradition, drawing strength from the craftsmanship of its operations. This world is made of word-of-mouth, trusted customers and friendly prices. This winery might escape some but an attentive eye never misses a great Verdicchio that defies the best in typicality, intensity and personality. We often take the long Rhine bottle of Sabbionare from the fridge with a subtle frisson of pleasure.

Here is more proof of the stature of the '09 Sabbionare, 10,000 bottles released. Despite the average growing year, the wine shows better than average quality distinguished by finesse on a nose of almonds, aniseed and flowers, along with the first hints of the minerality that comes with age. The taut, well-turned palate is long, almost tannic and salty. It's a wine that was released too quickly to market and will only show its full value over time. The Pratelli '09, 15,000 units bottled, is another wine that has you reaching for the bottle again because of its a refreshing interpretation of this classic type. But don't worry about that second bottle: the price tag is low.

○ Verdicchio dei Castelli di Jesi Cl. Sup. Sabbionare '09	▼▼	4*
○ Verdicchio dei Castelli di Jesi Cl. I Pratelli '09	▼▼	2*
○ Verdicchio dei Castelli di Jesi Cl. I Pratelli '07	▽▽	2*
○ Verdicchio dei Castelli di Jesi Cl. I Pratelli '06	▽▽	2*
○ Verdicchio dei Castelli di Jesi Cl. Sup. Sabbionare '08	▽▽	4*
○ Verdicchio dei Castelli di Jesi Cl. Sup. Sabbionare '07	▽▽	4*
○ Verdicchio dei Castelli di Jesi Cl. Sup. Sabbionare '06	▽▽	4*
○ Verdicchio dei Castelli di Jesi Passito '06	▽▽	4

Saladini Pilastri

VIA SALADINI, 5
63030 SPINETOLI [AP]
TEL. 0736899534
www.saladinipilastri.it

CELLAR SALES
PRE-BOOKED VISITS

ANNUAL PRODUCTION 800,000 bottles
HECTARES UNDER VINE 150
VITICULTURE METHOD Certified organic

The solid range this year from Saladini Pilastri is comforting. As well as a great Vigna Monteprandone '08, falling just short of perfection, the array of wines faithfully represents the territory. These coherent, sincere wines are come from many years of organic farming. Despite of long experience with montepulciano and sangiovese, there is also a nice line in local whites. We should also mention prices are right on target.

The elegant Vigna Monteprandone '08 shows good measure. The 30 per cent sangiovese gives an acid vein to the caressing, flavourful palate of the montepulciano for an international-style wine that is distinctly territorial. Pregio del Conte '08 is back on form. This unusual equal blend of aglianico and montepulciano gives chocolate, spice and red fruit over an invigorating palate with a long, complex finish. The Montetinello '08 has the usual generous palate and full fruit. Among the whites, the Pecorino '09 is succulent, and Passerina '09 has a spirited, sustained drinkability. The Falerio Vigna Palazzi '09, with meadow herbs and a harmonious palate, is one of the best of this type.

● Rosso Piceno Sup. V. Monteprandone '08	▼▼	5
○ Falerio dei Colli Ascolani V. Palazzi '09	▼▼	3*
○ Offida Passerina '09	▼▼	3*
○ Offida Pecorino '09	▼▼	3*
● Pregio del Conte '08	▼▼	5
● Rosso Piceno Sup. Montetinello '08	▼▼	4*
⊙ Consenso '09	▼	4
○ Falerio dei Colli Ascolani '09	▼	1*
● Rosso Piceno '09	▼	4
● Rosso Piceno Parnaso '08	▼	4
● Rosso Piceno V. Piediprato '08	▼	4
● Rosso Piceno Sup. V. Monteprandone '00	▽▽▽	4
○ Offida Pecorino '08	▽▽	3*
● Rosso Piceno Sup. V. Monteprandone '07	▽▽	5
● Rosso Piceno Sup. V. Monteprandone '04	▽▽	5

San Giovanni

C.DA CIAFONE, 41
63035 OFFIDA [AP]
TEL. 0736889032
www.vinisangiovanni.it

PRE-BOOKED VISITS

ANNUAL PRODUCTION **90,000 bottles**
HECTARES UNDER VINE **30**
VITICULTURE METHOD **Organic**

The San Giovanni estate constantly evolves with the ever-restless Gianni di Lorenzo. Labels come and go, as do early and late releases, new wines like the Marta Passerina Brut and passerina still wines. But we know these vineyards are well tended, vinifications precise and the various labels combine modern and tradition without forcing. The '07 Rosso Piceno Superiore Leo Guelfus was not present. We'll come back for it.

The lean vintage year has not bothered Pecorino Kiara '09. The customary intensity on the nose starts a sequence of meadow herbs, almond and delicate floral tones before the palate sketches a racy profile with fine progression. The fresh, simple Marta Brut flows nicely thanks to unassertive prickle. The Offida Passerina Marta '09 has chlorophyll and a palate designed for immediate enjoyability. There were more nuanced reviews for Zeii '05, whose liquorice sensations announce an accentuated arc of development, confirmed by an intense palate with unintegrated tannins and bitterness at the back. Proof that an honest wine rarely performs miracles when the season is unimpressive.

○ Offida Passerina Marta '09	▼▼	3*
○ Offida Pecorino Kiara '09	▼▼	4*
○ Falerio dei Colli Ascolani Leo Guelfus '09	▼	3
● Offida Rosso Zeii '05	▼	5
○ Passerina Brut Marta	▼	4
○ Falerio dei Colli Ascolani Marta '03	▽▽	4*
○ Offida Passerina Passito '04	▽▽	5
○ Offida Pecorino Kiara '08	▽▽	4*
○ Offida Pecorino Kiara '06	▽▽	4*
○ Offida Pecorino Kiara '04	▽▽	4*
● Offida Rosso Zeii '04	▽▽	5
● Offida Rosso Zeii '03	▽▽	5
● Rosso Piceno Sup. Leo Guelfus '06	▽▽	4*
● Rosso Piceno Sup. Leo Guelfus '04	▽▽	4*

Poderi San Lazzaro

C.DA SAN LAZZARO, 88
63035 OFFIDA [AP]
TEL. 0736889189
www.poderisanlazzaro.it

CELLAR SALES
PRE-BOOKED VISITS

ANNUAL PRODUCTION **45,000 bottles**
HECTARES UNDER VINE **8**
VITICULTURE METHOD **Certified organic**

Cellar space is limited and there are always too many vineyards when you have to do everything yourself. But Paolo Capriotti has the right stuff, real drive and clear ideas. Results are good even if sometimes, especially in the Grifola, the texture is over-generous. With more experience, we feel Paolo will succeed in taming montepulciano's generosity.

The naturally intense morello cherry and animal skins on the nose of the montepulciano-only Grifola '07 is underscored by a lift that is controlled yet present. The palate has all the force of powerful extracts and the alcohol is anything but restrained. A big wine that time will tame. The whiff of game on the nose of the more controlled Podere 72 '08 shifts into pulp and juice on the palate. We close the reds with the characterful, blood-rich Sangiovese Polesio '09. Finally, there's a successful Pecorino Pistillo '09, a small part fermented in 900-litre casks, which no longer briefly macerates on the skins. The nose has gained definition without losing salinity or backbone.

● Grifola '07	▼▼	5
○ Offida Pecorino Pistillo '09	▼▼	4*
● Rosso Piceno Sup. Podere 72 '08	▼▼	4*
● Polesio '09	▼▼	3
● Grifola '06	▽▽	5
● Grifola '05	▽▽	5
● Grifola '04	▽▽	5
○ Offida Pecorino Pistillo '08	▽▽	4*
○ Offida Pecorino Pistillo '07	▽▽	4*
○ Pistillo Pecorino '05	▽▽	4*
● Podere 72 '04	▽▽	4*
● Rosso Piceno Sup. Podere 72 '07	▽▽	4*
● Rosso Piceno Sup. Podere 72 '06	▽▽	4*
● Rosso Piceno Sup. Podere 72 '05	▽▽	4*

Fattoria San Lorenzo

via San Lorenzo, 6
60036 Montecarotto [AN]
tel. 073189656
az-crognaletti@libero.it

CELLAR SALES
PRE-BOOKED VISITS

ANNUAL PRODUCTION 100,000 bottles
HECTARES UNDER VINE 36
VITICULTURE METHOD Organic

Original comes to mind to describe wines from Fattoria San Lorenzo. Everything starts from Natalino Crognaletti's radical approach to winemaking: pampered vines, constant care in the cellar, (where Hartmann Donà also works, no chemicals and no shortcuts. The wines react accordingly, unveiling superb character. We should say they are not perfect. For example, Crognaletti's almost overripe concentration for his most important selections may raise eyebrows. But never forget that sincerity is the driving force behind the taste.

The San Lorenzo is a 1998. That's right. A 2,500-litre vat left for ten years on the fine lees, protected by the natural cold of the cellar. Only 3,000 bottles exist of this elegant, evolved wine, still full of nuances and salty tautness. The Vigna delle Oche Riserva '07 is penalized by too soft a structure but regains energy in the finish. A warm tone also shows in the Classico Superiore '08, which has more fluency on the palate. A sangiovese, montepulciano blend, the Vigneto Burello '07 is unexpectedly delicious, giving oregano on the nose and pervasive, sweet fruit mid palate. We like the frank, country-style Verdicchio Vigneto di Gino '09, which is rustic but vibrant.

○ Il San Lorenzo '98	🍷🍷	7
● Rosso Piceno Vigna Burello '07	🍷🍷	4*
○ Verdicchio dei Castelli di Jesi Cl. Sup. V. delle Oche '08	🍷🍷	4*
● Rosso Conero '07	🍷🍷	4
● Rosso Conero V. la Gattara '06	🍷🍷	4
○ Verdicchio dei Castelli di Jesi Cl. V. delle Oche Ris. '07	🍷🍷	5
○ Verdicchio dei Castelli di Jesi Cl. V. di Gino '09	🍷🍷	3*
○ Frigidus '03	🍷	5
● Vigneto del Solleone '05	🍷	6
○ Il San Lorenzo '97	YY	7
○ Verdicchio dei Castelli di Jesi Cl. Sup. V. delle Oche '07	YY	4*
○ Verdicchio dei Castelli di Jesi Cl. V. delle Oche Ris. '06	YY	5
○ Verdicchio dei Castelli di Jesi Cl. V. delle Oche Ris. '02	YY	5
● Vigneto del Solleone '02	YY	6
● Vigneto del Solleone '01	YY	6

San Savino - Poderi Capecci

loc. San Savino
via Santa Maria in Carro, 13
63038 Ripatransone [AP]
tel. 073590107
www.sansavino.com

CELLAR SALES
PRE-BOOKED VISITS

ANNUAL PRODUCTION 120,000 bottles
HECTARES UNDER VINE 32
VITICULTURE METHOD Organic

Simone Capecci's line-up has been broadly reworked. Practically no reds were submitted. We were expecting the prizewinning Sangiovese Fedus and sumptuous Montepulciano Quinta Regio, his two strikers. But this skilled winemaker from San Savino in Ripatransone won the match thanks to touches of class from the youngest wines: the talented Pecorino Ciprea and supple, racy Passerina Tufilla. It will be fun to watch the other wines hit the field next year and play on more difficult terrain.

The second Three Glass award in a row goes to Ciprea. The 2009 growing season was very different to the hot '08. Pecorino, a variety with a fairly unstable ripening curve, is sensitive to weather variations and reacts in kind. The cool 2009 season has produced a wine with a racy profile, sublime grip and linear development on the palate. The nose is resplendent in whistle-clean notes of citrus and white peaches, all swathed in a pervasive elegance that is never too obtrusive. Distinct acid backbone makes for a vibrant palate on the Tufilla '09, a monovarietal Passerina that may be aromatically less rich than the Ciprea but unfurls a dynamic through to savoury length on the finish.

○ Offida Pecorino Ciprea '09	🍷🍷🍷	4*
○ Offida Passerina Tufilla '09	🍷🍷	4*
● Fedus Sangiovese '06	YYY	5
● Moggio Sangiovese '98	YYY	6
○ Offida Pecorino Ciprea '08	YYY	4*
● Quinta Regio '01	YYY	6
● Quinta Regio '00	YYY	6
● Fedus Sangiovese '07	YY	5
● Fedus Sangiovese '05	YY	5
○ Offida Pecorino Ciprea '07	YY	4*
○ Offida Pecorino Ciprea '06	YY	4*
● Quinta Regio '03	YY	6
● Rosso Piceno Sup. Picus '06	YY	4*

Santa Barbara

B.GO MAZZINI, 35
60010 BARBARA [AN]
TEL. 0719674249
www.vinisantabarbara.it

CELLAR SALES
PRE-BOOKED VISITS

ANNUAL PRODUCTION 650,000 bottles
HECTARES UNDER VINE 40
VITICULTURE METHOD Conventional

Stefano Antonucci did not start out as a winemaker. He worked at a bank. Passion and his own touch of folly led him to run one of the most representative Marche estates. The wines aim for immediate communication through well-defined aromatics and supple drinkability for the whites, all from a verdicchio base. The reds, from blends of local and international varieties, show power, structure and aromatic intensity. The welcoming tasting hall at the winery in an old palazzo at Barbara is worth a visit.

The best-known wine, Vaglie '09, boasts enviable balance. The nose is deeply typical of Verdicchio with almond and lime blossom before the expansive, salty palate shows pure and supple with nicely gauged alcohol. With a pinch more complexity it would have been perfect. The Pathos '08, from equal parts of merlot, cabernet and syrah, has a soft palate and sweet, generous tannins but the vegetal, peppery nose is slightly puzzling. The better Maschio da Monte '08 is balsamic and slightly overripe on the nose but has a vibrant palate. We should mention the debut of a light-hearted, aromatic rosé, the Sensuade '09 from an blend of moscato rosso, vernaccia di Pergola and lacrima.

○ Verdicchio dei Castelli di Jesi Cl. Le Vaglie '09	▼▼	4*
● Pathos '08	▼▼	7
● Rosso Piceno Il Maschio da Monte '08	▼▼	6
⊙ Sensuade '09	▼▼	5
○ Verdicchio dei Castelli di Jesi Cl. Stefano Antonucci Ris. '08	▼▼	5
○ Passerina '09	▼	4
● Pignocco '09	▼	4
⊙ Stefano Antonucci M. Cl. Rosé	▼	5
● Stefano Antonucci Rosso '08	▼	5
○ Verdicchio dei Castelli di Jesi Cl. Tardivo Ma non Tardo '06	▼	6
● Vigna San Bartolo '08	▼	4
● Rosso Piceno Il Maschio da Monte '04	▽▽▽	5
○ Verdicchio dei Castelli di Jesi Cl. Le Vaglie '06	▽▽▽	4*
○ Verdicchio dei Castelli di Jesi Cl. Stefano Antonucci Ris. '06	▽▽▽	4*

Sartarelli

VIA COSTE DEL MOLINO, 24
60030 POGGIO SAN MARCELLO [AN]
TEL. 073189732
www.sartarelli.it

CELLAR SALES
PRE-BOOKED VISITS

ANNUAL PRODUCTION 290,000 bottles
HECTARES UNDER VINE 60
VITICULTURE METHOD Conventional

Verdicchio, and only verdicchio, enters Patrizio Chiacchierini and Donatella Sartarelli's winery. The choice is well considered. Montecarotto and Poggio San Marcello are the cradle of this Marche native and represent, along with Serra De' Conti, the best terroir on the left bank of the Esino. The magnificent vines at Coste del Molino and famous vineyard at Balciana, with a north-eastern aspect, produce fruit fermented only in stainless steel for distinctive wines with real character.

Grapes in the Balciana vineyard ripen on the vine until late November. The vineyard's autumn mist encourages botrytis, creating the unique qualities in the wine of the same name. The rich, opulent '08 is soft with residual sugar and a conspicuous helping of glycerine but still recovers savouriness and grip on the back palate. The nose regales candied citrus peel, thyme and toasted almond with imposing intensity. The Tralivio '08 is mature, tangy and juicy with power and alcoholic vigour that lend depth to the finish. The Classico '09 is true to its name, an example of almondy typicality and youthful, vibrant suppleness.

○ Verdicchio dei Castelli di Jesi Cl. Sup. Balciana '08	▼▼	6
○ Verdicchio dei Castelli di Jesi Cl. '09	▼▼	3*
○ Verdicchio dei Castelli di Jesi Cl. Sup. Tralivio '08	▼▼	4*
○ Verdicchio dei Castelli di Jesi Cl. Sup. Balciana '04	▽▽▽	6
○ Verdicchio dei Castelli di Jesi Cl. Sup. Contrada Balciana '98	▽▽▽	6
○ Verdicchio dei Castelli di Jesi Cl. Sup. Contrada Balciana '97	▽▽▽	6
○ Verdicchio dei Castelli di Jesi Cl. Sup. Contrada Balciana '95	▽▽▽	6
○ Verdicchio dei Castelli di Jesi Cl. Sup. Contrada Balciana '94	▽▽▽	6
○ Verdicchio dei Castelli di Jesi Cl. Sup. Balciana '07	▽▽	6

Selvagrossa

s.da Selvagrossa, 37
61020 Pesaro
tel. 0721202923
www.selvagrossa.it

CELLAR SALES
PRE-BOOKED VISITS

ANNUAL PRODUCTION **35,000 bottles**
HECTARES UNDER VINE **4**
VITICULTURE METHOD **Conventional**

Some surprising Marche wines come from Pesaro. We don't expect sensational news from this territory but this time, aside from good vibrations in the glass, we found an operation with passion and innovative ideas. Brothers Alessandro and Alberto Taddei are the prime movers. Alessandro manages the vineyards and cellar with advice from Vittorio and Jurij Fiore. An eminent sommelier, Alberto brings his professional experience to the assembly of the blends, as well as running foreign sales. Selvagrossa is a name to remember.

Great interest was sparked by the Poveriano '07, from only cabernet franc aged 16 months in barrique, with a dark liquorice and wet earth profile on the nose and a palate of character. It's austere almost to the point of stiffness but remarkably charming. Muschèn '08, from half sangiovese with 35 per cent merlot and cabernet franc, is more immediately enjoyable, thanks to stainless steel ageing that has brought out rich blueberry fruit, the juicy palate mirroring this well. A step below is Trimpilin '07, from sangiovese with ten per cent ciliegiolo, which has depth but is let down by overripe fruit and premature development.

● Muschèn '08	🍷🍷 (filled)	1*
● Poveriano '07	🍷🍷 (filled)	4
● Trimpilin '07	🍷 (filled)	4

Spinsanti

via Fonte Inferno, 11
60021 Camerano [AN]
tel. 071731797
catiaspinsanti@alice.it

CELLAR SALES
PRE-BOOKED VISITS
ROOMS AND FOOD

ANNUAL PRODUCTION **36,000 bottles**
HECTARES UNDER VINE **8**
VITICULTURE METHOD **Organic**

Catia Spinsanti's tiny estate is completely family run. She and her husband Andrea Gaggiotti tend their few hectares planted to montepulciano on the white limestone soils of Conero, with a few rows also reserved for sangiovese. This tradition is accepted both by the historic Rosso Conero DOC and by the recent Conero Riserva DOCG. Both allow up to 15 per cent of sangiovese. The small but well-organized cellar has vats of cement, stainless steel and various sizes of wood. Barriques are used for the showcase wine, Sassone.

The '07 Sassòne is a monovarietal Montepulciano from the oldest plot of vines and respects the pecking order that deems it superior to Camars. Fruity on the nose with ripe cherry and peach that return in the mouth, it progresses caressingly with no over-extraction or overripeness. Aged in large barrels, the Camars '08 has a more natural, direct expression. The few husky hints on the nose are pacified by a frank, old-fashioned character. It's a tad rough but it works.

● Rosso Conero Camars '08	🍷🍷 (filled)	4*
● Sassòne '07	🍷🍷 (filled)	5
● Rosso Conero Adino '08	🍷🍷	3*
● Rosso Conero Adino '07	🍷🍷	3*
● Rosso Conero Adino '06	🍷🍷	3
● Rosso Conero Adino '05	🍷🍷	3*
● Rosso Conero Camars '07	🍷🍷	4*
● Rosso Conero Camars '06	🍷🍷	4*
● Rosso Conero Camars '05	🍷🍷	4*
● Sassòne '06	🍷🍷	6
● Sassòne '05	🍷🍷	6
● Sassòne '04	🍷🍷	5
● Sassòne '03	🍷🍷	5
● Sassòne '01	🍷🍷	5

Silvano Strologo

VIA OSIMANA, 89
60021 CAMERANO [AN]
TEL. 071731104
www.vinorossoconero.com

CELLAR SALES
PRE-BOOKED VISITS

ANNUAL PRODUCTION **70,000 bottles**
HECTARES UNDER VINE **16**
VITICULTURE METHOD **Conventional**

Silvano Strologo's reds are immediately recognizable as the offspring of his beloved overripening. This unmistakeable style gives concentrated extract, clear alcohol and an enormously compact tannic weave. These upfront wines need years before they start to expand and reorganize their aromatics. When young they are dark, edgy and slow to emerge. We have said so many times, wishing for greater freshness in the standard-label Julius. But Silvano likes his wines like this and has every right to make them his way.

Two Glasses for the future go to the Decebalo Riserva '07, now closed behind sensations of cherries in alcohol and animal skins. Development will bring out the oregano and Mediterranean scrub already suggested and the dense palate has a warm, commanding timbre. We have less faith in the dry Traiano '06 with a nose marked by veiled, watery notes. Rosa Rosae '09 is a rosé from montepulciano, with a pinch of sangiovese, and gives great freshness in its hints of pomegranate and almond enhanced by a taut, savoury backbone. There is a debutant in Kalos '09, from 40-40-20 malvasia, trebbiano and moscato giallo, an aromatic white with a good nose and a clear, fruity mouthfeel.

● Conero Decebalo Ris. '07	🍷🍷	6
⊙ Rosa Rosae '09	🍷🍷	3*
○ Kalos '09	🍷	4
● Rosso Conero Traiano '06	🍷	5
● Rosso Conero Traiano '00	YYY	5
● Conero Decebalo Ris. '06	YY	6
● Conero Decebalo Ris. '05	YY	6
● Conero Decebalo Ris. '04	YY	6
○ Muscà	YY	5
● Rosso Conero Caesar '07	YY	4*
● Rosso Conero Julius '07	YY	4*
● Rosso Conero Julius '06	YY	4*
● Rosso Conero Traiano '05	YY	5
● Rosso Conero Traiano '02	YY	5

Tenuta di Tavignano

LOC. TAVIGNANO
62011 CINGOLI [MC]
TEL. 0733617303
www.tenutaditavignano.it

CELLAR SALES
PRE-BOOKED VISITS

ANNUAL PRODUCTION **100,000 bottles**
HECTARES UNDER VINE **30**
VITICULTURE METHOD **Conventional**

Any list of the best Verdicchios around today would have to include whites from Stefano Aymerich, sourced from a spectacular amphitheatre-shaped vineyard on a small piece of land governed by the province of Macerata but in character, proximity and history part of the terroir on the right bank of the river Esino. These powerful, savoury Verdicchios are designed by Pierluigi Lorenzetti. Montepulciano, sangiovese and a little cabernet are also among the vines grown.

It missed out on our highest prize but Misco Riserva '08 is still a top wine in the designation. The faintly vegetal nose has citrus and the palate has winning breadth but lacks complexity to match the superb '06 and '05 editions. A bit more bottle time would help. The other Misco, the Classico Superiore '09, is already open and well defined. Despite its youth, it impressed on nose and palate with close-knit texture and varietal aromatic complexity. The other two representatives are reliable and well priced. We prefer the penetrating Tavignano '09 over the green, extroverted Vigna Verde '09. We enjoyed the Rosso Picenos less. They're well made but lack elegance.

○ Verdicchio dei Castelli di Jesi Cl. Misco Ris. '08	🍷🍷	5
○ Verdicchio dei Castelli di Jesi Cl. Sup. Misco '09	🍷🍷	4*
○ Verdicchio dei Castelli di Jesi Cl. Sup. Tavignano '09	🍷🍷	3*
○ Verdicchio dei Castelli di Jesi Cl. Vigna Verde '09	🍷🍷	3*
● Rosso Piceno Castel Rosino '09	🍷	3
● Rosso Piceno Tavignano '08	🍷	4
○ Verdicchio dei Castelli di Jesi Cl. Misco Ris. '06	YYY	5*
○ Verdicchio dei Castelli di Jesi Cl. Misco Ris. '05	YYY	5
○ Verdicchio dei Castelli di Jesi Cl. Sup. Misco '06	YYY	4*
○ Verdicchio dei Castelli di Jesi Cl. Sup. Misco '08	YY	4
○ Verdicchio dei Castelli di Jesi Cl. Sup. Tavignano '08	YY	3*
○ Verdicchio dei Castelli di Jesi Cl. Vigna Verde '08	YY	3*

Fattoria Le Terrazze

via Musone, 4
60026 Numana [AN]
tel. 0717390352
www.fattorialeterrazze.it

CELLAR SALES
PRE-BOOKED VISITS

ANNUAL PRODUCTION **90,000 bottles**
HECTARES UNDER VINE **20**
VITICULTURE METHOD **Conventional**

Till a few years ago, Antonio Terni's wines had most modern style in the designation. Elegant definition, well-measured balance and international inspiration won two Three Glass awards at the same year, a first for Marche. But something has changed. Though still good, the wines seem in search of greater personality. The cracks are beginning to show. This is only be an interim period, we are sure, and hope the still-ageing Sassi Neri '07 marks a new start.

Vision of J is the cellar's best monovarietal Montepulciano selection, released only in major vintages. The latest is the '06. The nose has oregano and the concentrated palate, more full-bodied than elegant, shows overripe touches. Chaos '07, from 50-25-25 montepulciano, merlot and syrah, still has to absorb its oak. Dry tannins hold back the juicy, dynamic palate in the closing. Of the two Rosso Coneros, we preferred the Praeludium '09, with backbone, fruit and pervasive tannic sweetness. Always pleasant, the Donna Giulia Metodo Classico '07, from montepulciano and pinot nero fermented off the skins, shows wild strawberries and a palate of measured softness.

● Rosso Conero Visions of J '06	▼▼	7
● Chaos '07	▼▼	7
● Rosso Conero Praeludium '09	▼▼	3*
○ Donna Giulia Brut '07	▼	5
● Rosso Conero '08	▼	4
● Chaos '04	▽▽▽	6
● Chaos '01	▽▽▽	7
● Chaos '97	▽▽▽	7
● Conero Sassi Neri Ris. '04	▽▽▽	6
● Rosso Conero Sassi Neri '02	▽▽▽	6
● Rosso Conero Sassi Neri '99	▽▽▽	6
● Rosso Conero Sassi Neri '98	▽▽▽	6
● Rosso Conero Visions of J '01	▽▽▽	8
● Rosso Conero Visions of J '97	▽▽▽	8

Terre Cortesi Moncaro

via Boreale, 37
60036 Acquaviva Picena [AP]
tel. 073189245
www.moncaro.com

CELLAR SALES
PRE-BOOKED VISITS
FOOD

ANNUAL PRODUCTION **7,500,000 bottles**
HECTARES UNDER VINE **1,618**
VITICULTURE METHOD **Certified organic**

The well-organized Terre Cortesi began in 1964 but expanded enormously following the acquisition of co-operatives in Conero and Acquaviva Picena by the co-operative winery in Montecarotto. Thanks to this core of three wineries in the best growing areas, the range covers all the major regional designations. The wines have a unique fruity, intense style and polished palates with volume and flavour, but no rough edges. Often, they provide a revisitation of classic themes in a modern key.

Verdicchio Vigna Novali Riserva '07 is a superb expression of the rhythm, tangy depth and personality of grapes from Jesi and won Three Glasses. The characterful standard labels include a varietal, flavourful Fondiglie, the vegetal, appealing Verde Cà Ruptae, and the fresh, assertive drinkability of Le Vele. We liked Pecorino Ofithe '09, whose rosemary and almond echoes meld into fluent suppleness. The reds feature the juicy intensity of the Vigneti del Parco Riserva '07 and likeability of Monte Scuro Riserva '07 with finely woven tannins. From the Picenos, Terrazzano '08 put on a good debut. It's successful but a bit too formulaic with its vivid vanilla and morello cherry.

○ Verdicchio dei Castelli di Jesi Cl. Vigna Novali Ris. '07	▼▼▼	5
● Conero Vign. del Parco Ris. '07	▼▼	5
● Conero Cimerio Ris. '08	▼▼	4*
● Conero Monte Scuro Ris. '07	▼▼	4*
○ Offida Pecorino Ofithe '09	▼▼	4*
● Rosso Piceno Sup. Roccaviva '08	▼▼	4*
● Rosso Piceno Sup. Terrazzano '08	▼▼	4*
○ Verdicchio dei Castelli di Jesi Cl. Le Vele '09	▼▼	4*
○ Verdicchio dei Castelli di Jesi Cl. Sup. Fondiglie '09	▼▼	4*
○ Verdicchio dei Castelli di Jesi Cl. Sup. Verde Ca' Ruptae '09	▼▼	4*
○ Verdicchio dei Castelli di Jesi Passito Tordiruta '07	▼▼	7
○ Verdicchio dei Castelli di Jesi Cl. V. Novali Ris. '06	▽▽▽	5*
● Conero Vign. del Parco Ris. '06	▽▽	5

★ Umani Ronchi

via Adriatica, 12
60027 Osimo [AN]
tel. 0717108019
www.umanironchi.com

CELLAR SALES
PRE-BOOKED VISITS

ANNUAL PRODUCTION **3,300,000 bottles**
HECTARES UNDER VINE **230**
VITICULTURE METHOD **Conventional**

The Bernetti family estate has an international business. Present in most developed markets, its technically perfect wines have great personality and deep roots, driving trends but never following them. The vast vineyards are in various plots around Montecarotto, where the beautiful Le Busche vineyard is a grand cru, Cupramontana and Moie near Maiolati, specializing in verdicchio, and areas around Conero for red grapes. Extensive grape selection precedes production the substantial number of bottles.

Another double Three Glass award is close, given the integrity, consistency and power of the Plenio Riserva '07 and the elegant, supple measure of the '07 Pelago from equal parts montepulciano and cabernet sauvignon with ten per cent merlot. These two wines are multiple top award winners. Casal di Serra Vecchie Vigne '08 is sourced from a vineyard between 35 and 40-years old. Aniseed, citrussy freshness and minerality explode in elegant, overflowing savouriness. The Cùmaro Riserva '07 is a characterful, multi-layered Montepulciano with tannins that guarantee longevity. Maximo '07 from botrytized sauvignon shows tasty peaches in syrup.

● Conero Cùmaro Ris. '07	TTT	5
○ Verdicchio dei Castelli di Jesi Cl. Sup. Casal di Serra Vecchie Vigne '08	TTT	5
● Pelago '07	TTT	6
○ Verdicchio dei Castelli di Jesi Cl. Plenio Ris. '07	TT	5
○ Maximo '07	TT	5
● Rosso Conero Serrano '09	TT	4*
○ Verdicchio dei Castelli di Jesi Cl. Sup. Casal di Serra '09	TT	4
○ Verdicchio dei Castelli di Jesi Cl. Villa Bianchi '09	TT	4
● Pelago '06	YYY	6
○ Verdicchio dei Castelli di Jesi Cl. Plenio Ris. '06	YYY	5
○ Verdicchio dei Castelli di Jesi Cl. Plenio Ris. '05	YYY	5
○ Verdicchio dei Castelli di Jesi Cl. Plenio Ris. '04	YYY	5
○ Verdicchio dei Castelli di Jesi Cl. Plenio Ris. '03	YYY	5
○ Verdicchio dei Castelli di Jesi Cl. Plenio Ris. '02	YYY	4*
○ Verdicchio dei Castelli di Jesi Cl. Plenio Ris. '01	YYY	4*

Vallerosa Bonci

via Torre, 13
60034 Cupramontana [AN]
tel. 0731789129
www.vallerosa-bonci.com

CELLAR SALES
PRE-BOOKED VISITS

ANNUAL PRODUCTION **250,000 bottles**
HECTARES UNDER VINE **35**
VITICULTURE METHOD **Conventional**

Redistributing family shares of property has led to the creation of another estate, La Marca di San Michele, which is separate from Giuseppe Bonci's historic Vallerosa brand. But little has changed in the vineyard, although some parcels in the San Michele cru were lost, and nothing in the cellar. This year the wines again show the solid structure, elegance and alcoholic power that have characterized them for some time, making them icons of a classic, robust interpretation of the variety.

Pietrone Riserva '07 unfolds all its power and class on the nose with aniseed and nuts, and palate with a flavourful development slowed down by slightly dilute alcohol in the close. As personal and rhythmical as ever, the Le Case '07, part aged in oak, has soft, flavoursome progression. The San Michele '08 is less convincing than in other years. Alcoholic and slightly mature on the nose, the wine regains altitude on a finish that shows savoury length. Other worthwhile wines feature the fragrantly reliable Verdicchio Brut Charmat '08 and the fresh, sound Michelangiolo, an '07 Metodo Classico, which is a tad too simple.

○ Verdicchio dei Castelli di Jesi Cl. Pietrone Ris. '07	TT	5
○ Verdicchio dei Castelli di Jesi Cl. Sup. Le Case '07	TT	5*
○ Verdicchio dei Castelli di Jesi Cl. Sup. S. Michele '08	TT	5
● Casanostra '06	T	4
○ Verdicchio dei Castelli di Jesi Cl. Manciano '09	T	4
○ Verdicchio dei Castelli di Jesi Cl. Spumante Brut Charmat '08	T	4
○ Verdicchio dei Castelli di Jesi Passito Rojano '07	T	5
○ Verdicchio dei Castelli di Jesi Spumante Michelangiolo M. Cl. '07	T	4
○ Verdicchio dei Castelli di Jesi Cl. Pietrone Ris. '04	YYY	5
○ Verdicchio dei Castelli di Jesi Cl. Sup. Le Case '04	YYY	4*

Valturio

via dei Pelasgi, 10
61023 Macerata Feltria [PU]
tel. 0722728049
www.valturio.com

CELLAR SALES
PRE-BOOKED VISITS
ROOMS

ANNUAL PRODUCTION 40,000 bottles
HECTARES UNDER VINE 10
VITICULTURE METHOD Organic

Montefeltro is a lovely, unspoiled area, half in Marche and half in Romagna. Adriano Galli and his wife Isabella Santarelli have replanted vineyards here, following their instincts and trusting a centuries-old tradition. Their project to produce hillslope sangiovese, at between 400 and 500 metres, was implemented with intelligence and skill. The beautiful amphitheatre of perfectly managed, bush-trained vines, at 7,000 plants per hectare, is shaping an original, interesting identity.

The all-sangiovese Valturio '08 won Three Glasses for the second time in a row. The wine is incisive, full of energy, elegant, spirited and still a little vinous. The austere, spicy, fruit on the nose vibrates as if ready to take flight. The balanced palate is taut and long with intriguing acid strength. On the label of the Valturio is the famous image of a fantastic war machine in the shape of a dragon inserted into the military portrait painted by Roberto Valturio from Macerata Feltria for Sigismondo Malatesta in 1455. Another good wine, the Solco '08, from mostly rebo, is soft and more international.

● Valturio '08	▼▼▼	5
● Olmo '09	▼▼	4
● Solco '08	▼▼	5
● Valturio '07	▽▽▽	5
● Olmo '08	▽▽	4
● Valturio '06	▽▽	5

Velenosi

loc. Monticelli
via dei Biancospini, 11
63100 Ascoli Piceno
tel. 0736341218
www.velenosivini.com

CELLAR SALES

ANNUAL PRODUCTION 1,500,000 bottles
HECTARES UNDER VINE 135
VITICULTURE METHOD Conventional

Despite the crisis in consumption, every year we record a steady increase in production from Velenosi thanks to this estate's dynamic moves in the market. Successful penetration of a segment where competition is fierce requires a reliable range, fluent in a universal language. Angela Velenosi and her team succeed in reinventing modernity, giving the market what the market wants without selling the soul of the territory. To the contrary, the list features the region's main designations.

The excellent Roggio del Filare '07 won another Three Glasses, showing power, aromatic precision, a pervasive quality on the palate and impeccable design. This Rosso Piceno Superiore combines the pulp and tannic density from montepulciano with sangiovese's dynamism and elegance. Almost as good is the Ludi '07, a skilful blend of montepulciano, merlot and syrah with a Mediterranean nose and generous character. Brecciarolo Gold '07 cut the mustard with a close-knit weave, lightened by crunchy red fruit that lends irresistible drinkability. A tad sharper and simpler, the Brecciarolo '07 is a champion in value for money. The other wines are pleasant and intensely fragrant.

● Rosso Piceno Sup. Roggio del Filare '07	▼▼▼+	7
● Offida Rosso Ludi '07	▼▼	6
○ Falerio dei Colli Ascolani Vigna Solaria '09	▼▼	3*
○ Offida Pecorino '09	▼▼	4
● Querciantica Visciole	▼▼	4
● Rosso Piceno Sup. Brecciarolo '07	▼▼	3*
● Rosso Piceno Sup. Il Brecciarolo Gold '07	▼▼	5
○ Chardonnay Villa Angela '09	▼	4
● Lacrima di Morro d'Alba Querciantica '09	▼	4
○ Passerina Brut	▼	5
○ Passerina Villa Angela '09	▼	4
● Ludi '01	▽▽▽	6
● Ludi '00	▽▽▽	6
● Rosso Piceno Sup. Roggio del Filare '06	▽▽▽	7
● Rosso Piceno Sup. Roggio del Filare '05	▽▽▽	6
● Rosso Piceno Sup. Roggio del Filare '04	▽▽▽	6
● Rosso Piceno Sup. Roggio del Filare '03	▽▽▽	6
● Rosso Piceno Sup. Roggio del Filare '02	▽▽▽	5
● Rosso Piceno Sup. Roggio del Filare '01	▽▽▽	5

Vicari

VIA POZZO BUONO, 3
60030 MORRO D'ALBA [AN]
TEL. 073163164
www.vicarivini.it

CELLAR SALES
PRE-BOOKED VISITS

ANNUAL PRODUCTION 70,000 bottles
HECTARES UNDER VINE 12
VITICULTURE METHOD Conventional

Nazzareno Vicari has only been making wine since 1994 though his heritage is authentically country. He has passed these traditions on to his two children, Valentina and Vico. Valentina works with sales and publicity, and Vico is passionate about production. If he had his way, and we are not joking here, he would sleep in the cellar. Their arrival has brought new ideas, greater stylistic definition and reliability. Results prove they are right and there's scope for further improvement.

Vico has tried everything to fight the bitter, dry sensation of tannins in lacrima nera. In the Essenza '09, carbonic maceration gives spicy, floral intensity while in the Lacrima Superiore '08, slight overripening of the fruit translates into a juicy, vigorously alcoholic flavour with a long aromatic return on the finish. In Rustico '09, elimination of the grape seed during fermentation favours a fresh, substantial, drinkability with no bitterness. The good, dried-grape Passito Amaranto '08 shows pepper tones and the long, intense palate has calibrated sweetness. Verdicchio '09 is a bit too heavy. The Rosso Piceno '09 is better with a fruity, lively palate.

● Lacrima di Morro d'Alba Essenza del Pozzo Buono '09	▼▼	4*
● Lacrima di Morro d'Alba Passito Amaranto del Pozzo Buono '08	▼▼	4
● Lacrima di Morro d'Alba Rustico del Pozzo Buono '09	▼▼	4*
● Lacrima di Morro d'Alba Sup. del Pozzo Buono '08	▼▼	4
● Rosso Piceno del Pozzo Buono '09	▼▼	3*
○ Verdicchio dei Castelli di Jesi Cl. del Pozzo Buono '09	▼	3
● Lacrima di Morro d'Alba del Pozzo Buono '02	▽▽	4
● Lacrima di Morro d'Alba Essenza del Pozzo Buono '08	▽▽	4
● Lacrima di Morro d'Alba Sup. del Pozzo Buono '07	▽▽	4
● Rosso Piceno del Pozzo Buono '01	▽▽	4*

Vignamato

VIA BATTINEBBIA, 4
60038 SAN PAOLO DI JESI [AN]
TEL. 0731779197
www.vignamato.com

CELLAR SALES
PRE-BOOKED VISITS

ANNUAL PRODUCTION 55,000 bottles
HECTARES UNDER VINE 16
VITICULTURE METHOD Conventional

Vineyards surround the lovely Ceci family villa with cellar annexe and tasting hall. Home and business in the same building is common, especially when there's a family tradition and Maurizio's son Andrea continues the winemaker's art. The tidy cellar is all due to the feminine touch of Serenella, Maurizio's wife and factotum among the barrels and bottles. For many years, Giancarlo Soverchia has given technical guidance and creates powerful, enjoyable wines with a strong tie to this land between Staffolo and San Paolo di Jesi.

The Ambrosia Riserva '07 is a good example of the power of Verdicchio from this area. The palate shows alternating smoke and hazelnut and long dried fruit echoes in the close. Always sound, the steel-aged Versiano '09 is a classically intense Verdicchio with a delicious almondy flavour. Sourced from organic fruit, the Eos '09 has upfront acid backbone as well as a nice return of yellow-fleshed fruits. From the reds, the overripening in Campalliano '07 is still puzzling but we appreciate the tannic grip of the Rosolaccio '07. The lip-smacking RosAmato '09 rosé is redolent of flowers and white peaches.

○ Verdicchio dei Castelli di Jesi Cl. Ambrosia Ris. '07	▼▼	4*
● Esino Rosso Rosolaccio '07	▼▼	3*
⊙ RosAmato '09	▼▼	2*
○ Verdicchio dei Castelli di Jesi Cl. Eos '09	▼▼	2*
○ Verdicchio dei Castelli di Jesi Cl. Sup. Versiano '09	▼▼	4*
○ Verdicchio dei Castelli di Jesi Cl. Valle delle Lame '09	▼▼	3*
● Rosso Piceno Campalliano '07	▼	4
○ Verdicchio dei Castelli di Jesi Cl. Eos '08	▽▽	2*
○ Verdicchio dei Castelli di Jesi Cl. Sup. Versiano '08	▽▽	4*
○ Verdicchio dei Castelli di Jesi Cl. Valle delle Lame '08	▽▽	3*

Mario & Giorgio Brunori

v.le della Vittoria, 103
60035 Jesi [AN]
tel. 0731207213
www.brunori.it

The Brunoris are linked with San Nicolò, an exceptional vineyard in San Paolo di Jesi, and make elegant, long-lived Verdicchios. In the past few years, this wine has struggled to show it class but still has indisputable quality. Also convincing is the less brilliant Le Gemme '09, a well typed, coherent bottle.

○ Verdicchio dei Castelli di Jesi Cl. Sup. San Nicolò '09	🍷🍷	4*
● Lacrima di Morro d'Alba Alborada '09	🍷	3
○ Verdicchio dei Castelli di Jesi Cl. Le Gemme '09	🍷	3

Capinera

via Crocette, 12
62010 Morrovalle [MC]
tel. 0733222444
www.capinera.com

The Capinera brothers produce various labels at this lovely estate in Macerata and Civitanova Marche. The star is Cardinal Minio '07 from merlot, compact and fruity yet never cloying with polished tannins. Also decent is the soft, flavoursome chardonnay-based La Capinera '09.

● Cardinal Minio '07	🍷🍷	5
○ Chardonnay La Capinera '09	🍷	4

Carminucci

via San Leonardo, 39
63013 Grottammare [AP]
tel. 0735735869
www.carminucci.com

Carminucci is in an unusual position because some of the wines are not up to past standards, particularly Litora and Paccaosso. Among the best are the energy-filled Rosso Piceno Superiore Naumachos '08 and deliciously drinkable but simpler Grotte sul Mare '09. Falerio Naumachos '09 is subtle.

● Rosso Piceno Grotte sul Mare '09	🍷🍷	2*
● Rosso Piceno Sup. Naumachos '08	🍷🍷	4*
○ Falerio dei Colli Ascolani Naumachos '09	🍷	3

Castello Fageto

via Valdaso, 52
63016 Pedaso [FM]
tel. 0734931784
www.castellofageto.it

Claudio Di Ruscio's estate made a nice showing after changing oenologists. We note the usual skill with whites, in particular the tropical fruits Pecorino Fenèsia '09, and passerina Letizia '09 with its salty finish. The austere, intense Serrone '08 Bordeaux blend is the outstanding red.

○ Offida Pecorino Fenèsia '09	🍷🍷	4*
● Serrone '08	🍷🍷	5
○ Passerina Letizia '09	🍷	4
● Rosso Piceno Colle del Buffo '08	🍷	4

Enrico Ceci

via Santa Maria D'Arco, 7
60038 San Paolo di Jesi [AN]
tel. 0731779033
www.cecienrico.it

This small estate in San Paolo di Jesi makes one of the jewels of the designation, the Santa Maria d'Arco '09, with refined touches of aniseed, aromatic herbs and gunflint, and a crystalline palate with long aromatic staying power. The Rosso Piceno '08 of the same name is bit rough.

○ Verdicchio dei Castelli di Jesi Cl. Sup. Santa Maria d'Arco '09	🍷🍷	4*
● Rosso Piceno Santa Maria d'Arco '08	🍷	4

Giacomo Centanni

c.da Aso, 159
63010 Montefiore dell'Aso [AP]
tel. 0734938530
www.vinicentanni.it

From just north of Offida, Giacomo Centanni has submitted a couple of precise, sprightly interpretations. The expressive Offida Passerina has clear fruit and flower aromas and a monovarietal Montepulciano, the Montefloris '08, is smooth and balsamic. All are attractively priced.

● Montefloris '08	🍷🍷	4
○ Offida Passerina '09	🍷🍷	4
● Offida Pecorino '09	🍷	4
● Rosso Piceno Rosso di Forca '08	🍷	3

Colli di Serrapetrona
via Colli, 7/8
62020 Serrapetrona [MC]
tel. 0733908329
www.collidiserrapetrona.it

In the absence of their more important wines, Robbione and Sommo, Collequanto '08 had to hold the fort. There's pepper and a light touch of roses on the stylish, flavourful palate. The sparkling rosé Blink is light and carefree, again from vernaccia nera.

- ● Serrapetrona Collequanto '08 — 2 glasses 4*
- ⊙ Blink Brut '09 — 1 glass 4
- ⊙ Serrarosa '09 — 1 glass 3

Cantina Cològnola
loc. Cològnola
62011 Cingoli [MC]
tel. 0733616438
www.agrarialombardi.it

This estate did not submit the two major Ghiffa labels of Verdicchio that have made its name. The Labieno Riserva '07 flaunts a well-turned, solid, citrussy palate and Cingulum '08 is one of the best regional dried-grape wines, showing elegant and long with wafts of botrytis and liquorice.

- O Verdicchio dei Castelli di Jesi Cl. Labieno Ris. '07 — 2 glasses 5
- O Verdicchio dei Castelli di Jesi Passito Cingulum '08 — 2 glasses 6

Croce del Moro
via Tassanare, 4
60030 Rosora [AN]
tel. 0731814158
www.tassanare.it

The splendid Crocetta Riserva '05 from Bruno Cavallaro develops faultlessly with elegant minerality on the nose and liquorice on the palate. Pity only 1,000 bottles were produced. The '08 with the same name is well typed and expansive.

- O Verdicchio dei Castelli di Jesi Cl. Sup. Crocetta Ris. '05 — 2 glasses 5
- O Verdicchio dei Castelli di Jesi Cl. Sup. Crocetta '08 — 2 glasses 5

Andrea Felici
via Sant'Isidoro 28
62021 Apiro [MC]
tel. 0733611431
www.andreafelici.it

We have been watching Andrea and Leo Felici's powerful Verdicchios for some years now. This time they've got the right stuff. The great Cantico della Figura Riserva '07 is a full-flavoured selection that presents succulent yet fresh and minerally. The more immediate Andrea Felici is well typed and well paced.

- O Verdicchio dei Castelli di Jesi Cl. Il Cantico della Figura Ris. '07 — 2 glasses 5
- O Verdicchio dei Castelli di Jesi Cl. Sup. Andrea Felici '09 — 2 glasses 4

Fiorini
via Giardino Campioli, 5
61040 Barchi [PU]
tel. 072197151
www.fioriniwines.it

Fiorini is traditionally linked to Bianchello del Metauro. Tastings clearly show this is still the house speciality. Tenuta Campioli '09 displays flowers on a juicy palate and Sant'Ilario '09 is fragrant and racy. Among the reds, the Sirio, a standard label Sangiovese, flaunts flowers aplenty.

- O Bianchello del Metauro Tenuta Campioli '09 — 2 glasses 3*
- O Bianchello del Metauro V. Sant'Ilario '09 — 1 glass 2
- ● Colli Pesaresi Rosso Bartis '08 — 1 glass 4
- ● Colli Pesaresi Sangiovese Sirio '09 — 1 glass 3

Esther Hauser
c.da Coroncino, 1a
60039 Staffolo [AN]
tel. 0731770203
esther.hauser@piccoliproduttori.it

Though reviewed last year, Esther Hauser's reds have only recently been released to market. Retasting confirmed that, in this land of Verdicchios, the best red wines were the Ceppo and especially the Cupo. It presents steadfast and multi-faceted with refined tannins and rare craftsmanship.

- ● Il Ceppo '07 — 2 glasses (outline) 5
- ● Il Cupo '07 — 2 glasses (outline) 6

Ma.Ri.Ca.

via Acquasanta, 7
60030 Belvedere Ostrense [AN]
tel. 0731290091
www.cantinamarica.it

Over the past few years, this family run estate has sensitively interpreted lacrima and verdicchio. Tosius '09 contrasts meadow herbs and almond in a delicate yet at the same time tenacious palate. The aromas of the Ramosceto '09 are a summary of the variety's typicality.

- ● Lacrima di Morro d'Alba Ramosceto '09 🍷🍷 3*
- ○ Verdicchio dei Castelli di Jesi Cl. Sup. Tosius '09 🍷🍷 4*
- ○ Verdicchio dei Castelli di Jesi Cl. Tregaso '09 🍷 2

Malacari

via Enrico Malacari, 6
60020 Offagna [AN]
tel. 0717207606
www.malacari.it

Alessandro Starrabba's wines are identified by their meatiness, backbone and a note of iron on the nose. The Villa Malacari '08 has crisp fruit and still edgy tannins. The well-tempered Grigiano '07 has a stylish nose and great progression on a palate that reveals unexpected harmony.

- ● Conero Grigiano '07 🍷🍷 5
- ● Rosso Conero Villa Malacari '08 🍷 4

La Marca di San Michele

via Torre, 13
60034 Cupramontana [AN]
tel. 0731781183
www.lamarcadisanmichele.com

Alessandro and Beatrice Bonci manage six hectares of old verdicchio in the San Michele vineyard at Cupramontana. The elegant, minerally Capovolto '08 is an all-around Verdicchio. The developing Pigro Riserva '08 is slightly marked by ageing in ten-hectolitre oak casks but still shows savoury and expansive.

- ○ Verdicchio dei Castelli di Jesi Cl. Il Pigro Ris. '08 🍷🍷 6
- ○ Verdicchio dei Castelli di Jesi Cl. Sup. Capovolto '08 🍷🍷 4
- ○ Verdicchio dei Castelli di Jesi Cl. Sup. Capovolto '07 🍷🍷 4

Marchetti

fraz. Pinocchio
via di Pontelungo, 166
60131 Ancona
tel. 071897386
www.marchettiwines.it

Don't be fooled by the small profile for Maurizio Marchetti. This estate is one of the most precise in Conero though recent tastings have revealed a tad too much weight. The Verdicchios remain sound and the soft, full Tenuta del Cavaliere '09 is best for its great length on the palate.

- ○ Verdicchio dei Castelli di Jesi Cl. Sup. Tenuta del Cavaliere '09 🍷🍷 4
- ● Rosso Conero fresco '09 🍷 4
- ○ Verdicchio dei Castelli di Jesi Cl. '09 🍷 3

Valter Mattoni

c.da Pescolla
63030 Castorano [AP]
tel. 073687329

Valter La Roccia Mattoni makes a wine that resembles him: overwhelming. He produces 3,000 bottles of visceral, pulsating monovarietal Montepulciano that in some ways – alcohol, for example – goes over the top. It is a driven, direct reflection of a sun-blessed territory.

- ● Arshura '08 🍷🍷 5

Enzo Mecella

via Dante, 112
60044 Fabriano [AN]
tel. 073221680
www.enzomecella.com

Enzo Mecella is a historic winemaker who uses grapes from trusted growers. The wines can be inconsistent but in the right vintage year have class and longevity to spare. This is the case with the Verdicchio Casa Fosca Sotto le Querce '08, which personifies the subtle, progressive style of the best Matelicas.

- ○ Verdicchio di Matelica Casa Fosca Sotto le Querce '08 🍷🍷 5
- ○ Verdicchio di Matelica Pagliano '09 🍷🍷 5

Claudio Morelli

V.LE ROMAGNA, 47B
61032 FANO [PU]
TEL. 0721823352
www.claudiomorelli.it

Claudio Morelli's Bianchellos have always embodied the cru concept. If the Borgo Torre '09 – the best – is a product of the Fano hinterland, La Vigna delle Terrazze '09 comes from a fine vineyard on the Adriatic. All have savoury features, clean aromas and a distinct floral suppleness.

○ Bianchello del Metauro Borgo Torre '09	YY	4*
○ Bianchello del Metauro La Vigna delle Terrazze '09	Y	4
○ Bianchello del Metauro S. Cesareo '09	Y	3

La Muròla

C.DA VILLAMAGNA, 9
62010 URBISAGLIA [MC]
TEL. 0733506843
www.cantinalamurola.it

Located in one of the loveliest corners of Marche, the recently founded, high-quality La Murola estate has aroused great interest. The Vigna Monte '08 is an expansive, leisurely Montepulciano with vegetal shades marked by the youth of the vines. The Millerose '09 is a mouthwatering, great-drinking Sangiovese rosé.

○ Colli Maceratesi Ribona Andrea Baccius '09	YY	4*
⊙ Millerose '09	YY	3
● Vigna Monte '08	YY	4
○ Passerina '09	Y	3

Filippo Panichi

VIA SCIROLA, 37
63031 CASTEL DI LAMA [AP]
TEL. 0736815339
www.filippopanichi.it

Filippo Panichi shows commendable energy and dedication in both vineyards and the recently renovated cellar. There is still a lot of work to do, especially with the whites, but labels like the succulent, appetizing Polittico '08 show the way to quality.

● Rosso Piceno Sup. Polittico '08	YY	4*
● Rubens '07	Y	5

Alberto Quacquarini

VIA COLLI, 1
62020 SERRAPETRONA [MC]
TEL. 0733908180
www.quacquarini.it

Quacquarini is the Vernaccia. So deep are the ties and years spent producing this characteristic sparkler from Serrapetrona that the two terms are synonymous. Excellent quality has returned to the white wines, dominated by a peppery Colli della Serra '07. The fruity, flavourful Serrapetrona '08 is also good.

● Colli della Serra '07	YY	3
● Serrapetrona '08	YY	4
● Petronio '06	Y	5
● Vernaccia di Serrapetrona Dolce	Y	4

Rio Maggio

C.DA VALLONE, 41
63014 MONTEGRANARO [FM]
TEL. 0734889587
www.riomaggio.it

Simone Santucci is emerging from the uncertainty that dogged his reds and confused the aromas of the whites. While waiting for more improvement, we mention a Telusiano '09 with a rounded, elegant measure and a Rio '08 with a juicy weave. The nicely developed Pinot Nero '07 has cassis and aromatic herbs.

○ Falerio dei Colli Ascolani Telusiano '09	YY	4*
● Rosso Piceno Rio '08	YY	3
● Colle Monteverde Pinot Nero '07	Y	5

San Francesco

VIA SAN FRANCESCO, 4
63030 ACQUAVIVA PICENA [AP]
TEL. 0735764416
www.vinicherri.it

Though good in the recent past, the Cherri family estate hit a minor key this time. The few wines are correct but lack verve. The best, Pecorino Altissimo '09, has flavour, weight and pervasiveness. Oriente is a subtle, standard-label Falerio with elegant features but rushes too quickly over the palate.

○ Offida Pecorino Altissimo '09	YY	4
○ Falerio dei Colli Ascolani Oriente '09	Y	3
○ Offida Passerina Radiosa '09	Y	4

Santa Cassella

C.DA SANTA CASSELLA, 7
62018 POTENZA PICENA [MC]
TEL. 0733671507
www.santacassella.it

Whites from Santa Cassella have their own characteristic vegetal aromatic intensity, which lengthens the pleasure. Such is the balanced, enjoyable Colli Maceratesi Bianco '09 and the Donna Angela '09, markedly influenced by malvasia. The cabernet sauvignon Conte Leopoldo '08 is austere and compact.

○ Colli Maceratesi Bianco '09	(2 glasses) 3*
● Conte Leopoldo '08	(2 glasses) 4*
○ Donna Angela '09	(1 glass) 4

Fattoria Serra San Martino

VIA SAN MARTINO, 1
60030 SERRA DE' CONTI [AN]
TEL. 0731878025
www.serrasanmartino.com

Kirsten and Thomas Weydemann produce few bottles but all their wines show character with mature, multi-layered aromas and powerful structure. The best is the exuberant merlot-based Costa dei Zoppi '07, with slightly unbalanced tannins. Paonazzo '07, a spicy Syrah with a full-bodied palate, is also good.

● Costa dei Zoppi '07	(2 glasses) 5
● Il Paonazzo '07	(2 glasses) 6
● Lisippo '06	(1 glass) 8

Sparapani - Frati Bianchi

VIA BARCHIO, 12
60034 CUPRAMONTANA [AN]
TEL. 0731781216
www.fratibianchi.it

Despite the complicated growing year, Verdicchios from Pino Sparapani have not lost the artisan's touch that adds charm to the intrinsic power of the variety. Better of the two labels as always is the '09 Priore '09, with a lovely nose of aniseed and an elegant, measured palate that lacks a bit of depth.

○ Verdicchio dei Castelli di Jesi Cl. Salerna '09	(2 glasses) 4*
○ Verdicchio dei Castelli di Jesi Cl. Sup. Il Priore '09	(2 glasses) 4

La Staffa

VIA CASTELLARETA, 19
60039 STAFFOLO [AN]
TEL. 0731779810
www.vinilastaffa.it

Riccardo Baldi shows he can also make reds. Vivinaja '08, an 80-20 montepulciano and cabernet mix, has green streaks and a balsamic touch on spiky but flavoursome tannins. The '06 Rubinia is a mature, outgoing Montepulciano. The Rincrocca '08 is elegant and coherent, but a tad rigid at the back.

● Esino Rosso Vivinaja '08	(2 glasses) 2*
● Rubinia '06	(2 glasses) 5
○ Verdicchio dei Castelli di Jesi Cl. Sup. Rincrocca '08	(2 glasses) 3*
○ Verdicchio dei Castelli di Jesi Cl. '09	(1 glass) 2

Villa Grifoni

FRAZ. SAN SAVINO
C.DA MESSIERI,10
63038 RIPATRANSONE [AP]
TEL. 073590495
www.villa-grifoni.it

We were hoping for something more from Giuseppe Cocci Grifoni's estate, a rise in average quality across the range. Instead, we noted only an excellent Rosso Piceno Superiore '08 with a solid fruity vein and a decent Offida Passerina '09 that lays out citrus and more timid savouriness.

● Rosso Piceno Sup. '08	(2 glasses) 4*
○ Villa Grifoni Offida Passerina '09	(1 glass) 4

Villa Pigna

C.DA CIAFONE, 63
63035 OFFIDA [AP]
TEL. 073687525
www.villapigna.com

In the range from Villa Pigna, only Vellutato '09, a Montepulciano with fresh fruit and a highly pleasing palate, is in step with the best. We sensed difficulty in expression from the Rozzano '08 as well as the Cabernasco '07. Let's hope this is just a passing phase.

● Vellutato '09	(2 glasses) 3*
● Rosso Piceno Sup. Vergaio '08	(1 glass) 4

UMBRIA

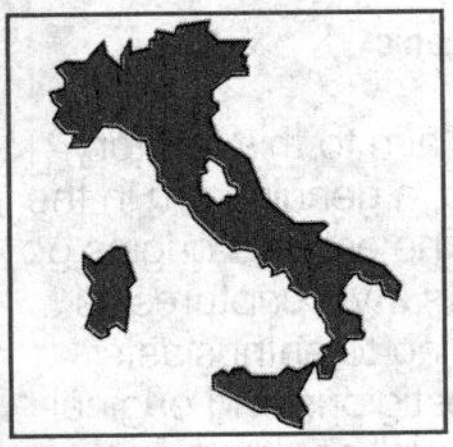

During Italy's oenological renaissance, Umbria could have been taken as a model of how the wine scene was evolving throughout the country. In a very short time, archaic production methods were replaced by exceptionally high quality, although there was at times a tendency to follow the latest fashions, surrendering a degree of territorial identity, losing some of the wines' individuality and loosening ties with winemaking traditions in the various areas. Many wineries and wines left the cellar under the banner of modernity, which certainly helped the sector to expand, although there was a move towards utilizing international grape varieties, outside their benchmark designations. It soon became necessary to face an ever-changing market, grappling with new terminology and tackle the looming threat of standardization. Things are changing slowly but surely. The traditional designations are creeping back into favour, as are several forgotten grape varieties, and alongside better winemaking practices there is greater care in the vineyard and a clear desire to produce wines with a precise sense of place. The obsession with red wines in a region historically known for its whites seems to have run its course. There has been a revival of white grape varieties and the recovery of large areas of vineyards. Grechetto is fashionable once again, as is trebbiano spoletino, one of the oldest native varieties with great potential, which produces minerally, long-lived wines. Several Orvieto producers have resumed their battle to revive a territory and a designation that are extraordinarily fascinating and have a rich winemaking history. This is why we have awarded four Three Glass prizes this year, which is unusual for the region. Next to a big-hitting Cervaro della Sala '08, undeniably great but with no surprises, other wines have achieved absolute excellence: the '08 Torgiano Bianco Vigna il Pino from Cantine Lungarotti, and two Orvieto Classico Superiore, "IL" '09 from Decugnano dei Barbi and the Campo del Guardiano '07, from Palazzone. The situation is less clear-cut in the red wine areas of Montefalco and Sagrantino, owing partly the rapid appearance of many new wineries. Here the wines have immense potential, especially if they are taken at face value as wines to lay down needing many years to reach their peak of maturation. The current market situation is complicated and will only improve if goals are identified and necessities turned into opportunities. Returning to the quality of the wines, we were unsurprised by the outstanding, reliable 25 Anni '07 Caprai, by the well-established Perticaia '07, by the return of the great Colle Grimaldesco '06 Tabarrini, by the first top award for Della Cima '06 Villa Mongalli and by the repeat performance of Adanti '06, one of the regions's most traditional wines.

Adanti

LOC. ARQUATA
06031 BEVAGNA [PG]
TEL. 0742360295
www.cantineadanti.com

CELLAR SALES
PRE-BOOKED VISITS

ANNUAL PRODUCTION 150,000 bottles
HECTARES UNDER VINE 30
VITICULTURE METHOD Conventional

Picture a manor house not far from the village of Bevagna, hosting the cellar, vineyards extending across the surrounding hills over some of the best wine-growing territories in the area, including the Colcimino vineyard, large barrels and casks where the wines are aged and a relaxed, deeply traditional style. This is Adanti, a traditional winery as brilliant today as in the past, through the work of the men and women who interpret its characteristics in a modern key.

The Montefalco Sagrantino '06 is exceptional, aged as always in 30-hectolitre barrels and 900-litre casks, its relaxed notes and exquisite aromatic spectrum making it truly unusual, a wine that whispers rather than one that shouts. It has a deep, genuine taste with earthy, natural overtones, and a flavoursome finish of fine-grained tannins. We found it even better than the cellar's new wine, Domenico '05, produced from the Colcimino grapes, whose profile is still somewhat undefined, with a slightly coarse tannic weave.

● Montefalco Sagrantino Arquata '06	▼▼▼	6
● Montefalco Sagrantino Il Domenico '05	▼▼	5
○ Colli Martani Grechetto '09	▼▼	3
○ Montefalco Bianco '09	▼	3
● Montefalco Sagrantino Arquata '05	▽▽▽	6
● Montefalco Sagrantino Arquata '01	▽▽	6
● Montefalco Sagrantino Passito Arquata '05	▽▽	7
● Montefalco Sagrantino Passito Arquata '04	▽▽	7

Antonelli - San Marco

LOC. SAN MARCO, 60
06036 MONTEFALCO [PG]
TEL. 0742379158
www.antonellisanmarco.it

CELLAR SALES
PRE-BOOKED VISITS
ROOMS

ANNUAL PRODUCTION 300,000 bottles
HECTARES UNDER VINE 45
VITICULTURE METHOD Organic

Antonelli asserts its claim to this territory, the hills of San Marco, a genuine cru in the zone of Montefalco. The estate's origins go far back in time and its style captures its distinctive traits, offering to enthusiasts some of the most prestigious and original Sagrantino wines, as well as other local reds, such as the Montefalco Riserva. Organic growing methods and maturation in cellar, often in large barrels, help these sumptuous wines develop naturally.

Montefalco Sagrantino Chiusa di Pannone, from a walled vineyard, is the leading label. The '05 wine is extraordinary, true to its own inherently elegant style, although when we carried out our tastings it failed to repeat the performance of the previous vintage because of little gaps in the palate and tannic weave. Montefalco Rosso Riserva '07 is very good, as we would expect, it has class and a rigid profile, revealing a delicious fruit alongside its elegant spiciness. The Rosso di Montefalco '08 and the Grechetto '09 are both excellent, while the Contrario '08, from sagrantino grapes, strikes a chord.

● Montefalco Rosso Ris. '07	▼▼	5
● Montefalco Sagrantino Chiusa di Pannone '05	▼▼	7
○ Colli Martani Grechetto '09	▼▼	3
● Montefalco Rosso '08	▼▼	4*
● Baiocco '08	▼	3
● Contrario '08	▼	4
● Montefalco Sagrantino Chiusa di Pannone '04	▽▽▽	7
● Montefalco Rosso Ris. '06	▽▽	5
● Montefalco Rosso Ris. '05	▽▽	5
● Montefalco Sagrantino '04	▽▽	6

Argillae

Loc. Pomarro, 45
05010 Allerona [TR]
tel. 0763624604
www.argillae.it

CELLAR SALES
PRE-BOOKED VISITS

ANNUAL PRODUCTION **50,000 bottles**
HECTARES UNDER VINE **70**
VITICULTURE METHOD **Conventional**

The winery owned by the Bonollo, Di Cosimo and Ascenzi families is based in the hills to the north-west of Orvieto, between the towns of Allerona and Ficulle, where the soil is clay mixed with sand and limestone, with the typical gullies found in this area. The vines grow at altitudes of 350 to 500 metres above sea level. As this area would indicate, the whites are the most convincing wines, although we would have expected a bit more personality.

We were again delighted with the Grechetto '09, a wine of a certain elegance made from the local grape. Delicate flowery perfumes are woven with tones of grapefruit and plum, while the palate has distinctive almond overtones and a certain depth of acidity and savouriness. The simple Orvieto '09 is not bad, hinging on exuberant youthful freshness, an easy-drinking wine with a great taste. The Panata '09 convinced us less than in other years. This Chardonnay aged in steel and barrique is a little forced, and the palate has too much alcohol. The Sinuoso '09, from merlot and cabernet, is only mediocre.

○ Grechetto '09	▼▼	4
○ Orvieto '09	▼▼	3
○ Panata '09	▼▼	4
● Sinuoso '09	▼	3
○ Grechetto '08	▽▽	4*
○ Panata '08	▽▽	4*

Barberani - Vallesanta

Loc. Cerreto
05023 Baschi [TR]
tel. 0763341820
www.barberani.it

CELLAR SALES
PRE-BOOKED VISITS

ANNUAL PRODUCTION **350,000 bottles**
HECTARES UNDER VINE **55**
VITICULTURE METHOD **Conventional**

The Barberani family owns a traditional Orvieto winery that has always shown a great dynamism. This is due to the crucial input of Bernardo and Niccolò, two energetic young brothers who are becoming more confident of their capabilities. The vineyards and cellar are on the hills around Lake Corbara, in prestigious sites with wonderful views. The wines reflect the estate's philosophy to enhance traditional designations while staying open to new ideas, especially for reds.

Once again the Calcaia '07 is very good, a Noble Rot classical blend of procanico, verdello, grechetto and sauvignon with typical aromas ranging from notes of tropical and dried fruit to sensations of soot and saffron. This is a sweet, sumptuous wine. The palate is slightly penalized by an acidity that, while good, does not contrast with the sugar sufficiently. Polvento '06 from sangiovese, merlot and cabernet grapes is superb, with a lovely aromatic impact that alternates fruity tones with and wild herbs. The Castagnolo '09 is great.

● Lago di Corbara Rosso Polvento '06	▼▼	4
○ Orvieto Cl. Sup. Calcaia '07	▼▼	6
○ Orvieto Cl. Sup. Castagnolo '09	▼▼	4*
● Lago di Corbara Rosso Villa Monticelli '04	▽▽▽	5
○ Grechetto '07	▽▽	4*
● Lago di Corbara Foresco '07	▽▽	4*
● Lago di Corbara Foresco '06	▽▽	4*
● Lago di Corbara Rosso Villa Monticelli '05	▽▽	5
○ Moscato Passito Villa Monticelli '06	▽▽	6
○ Orvieto Cl. Sup. Calcaia '06	▽▽	6
○ Orvieto Cl. Sup. Calcaia '05	▽▽	6
○ Orvieto Cl. Sup. Calcaia '04	▽▽	6
○ Orvieto Cl. Sup. Castagnolo '07	▽▽	4*
○ Orvieto Cl. Sup. Castagnolo '06	▽▽	4
○ Orvieto Cl. Sup. Pomaio Villa Monticelli '06	▽▽	5
○ Orvieto Cl. Sup. Pomaio Villa Monticelli '05	▽▽	5

Bigi

LOC. PONTE GIULIO
05018 ORVIETO [TR]
TEL. 0763315888
www.cantinebigi.it

PRE-BOOKED VISITS

ANNUAL PRODUCTION 4,100,000 bottles
HECTARES UNDER VINE 196
VITICULTURE METHOD Conventional

Established in 1880 by Luigi Bigi, this Orvieto winery has belonged for years to Gruppo Italiano Vini, which has helped it become one of the best organized operations in the area. Its whites are among the finest in the region with some interesting Orvietos and Grechettos, the main varieties of the designation. They have also introduced some good red wines.

The Grechetto Strozza Volpe never misses a beat. The '09 version is again a white full of light and dark tones, fine yet complex, with notes of ripe yellow apple, camomile and meadow flowers. It has a good flesh, with hints of honey, but stays delightfully refreshing. The Orvieto Classico '09 is delicious and we preferred it to the Torricella '09, a fuller wine but whose progression is less complex. From the reds, we preferred the Satriano '08 and the Vipra Rossa '09 is enjoyable and easy drinking.

○ Orvieto Cl. Secco '09	🍷🍷	3
● Sartiano '08	🍷🍷	4
○ Strozza Volpe Grechetto '09	🍷🍷	3
○ Orvieto Cl. Torricella '09	🍷	4
● Vipra Rossa '09	🍷	3
● Sartiano '07	ΥΥ	5
○ Strozza Volpe Grechetto '08	ΥΥ	3*

Blasi Bertanzi

LOC. SAN BENEDETTO
VIA CASE SPARSE, 64
06019 UMBERTIDE [PG]
TEL. 0758697891
www.cantineblasi.it

CELLAR SALES

ANNUAL PRODUCTION 35,000 bottles
HECTARES UNDER VINE 16
VITICULTURE METHOD Conventional

This is the biggest surprise of the year. Blasi Bertanzi has come from nowhere and parades a series of really good wines. Located in the mountainous Altotevere, near the town of Umbertide, where they grow typical regional grapes as well as other decidedly more exotic varieties. The wines are original, enjoyable and often unconventional.

The Regghia '08 is a convincing sangiovese, syrah and alicante mix aged in large wood, giving complex aromas of red and black berry fruit, chocolate, cep mushrooms, cedarwood and mustard. The palate holds together well, showing taut and balsamic with an austere finish. Rogaie '07 is an astonishing white that impressed with its chalky, intensely fruity aromas and also for its savoury palate, with delightful hints of medicinal herbs and aromatic traits. The Impronta '07 is also good.

● Impronta '07	🍷🍷	5
● Regghia '08	🍷🍷	5
○ Rogaie '07	🍷🍷	5

Bocale

loc. Madonna della Stella
via Fratta Alzatura
06036 Montefalco [PG]
tel. 0742399233
www.bocale.it

CELLAR SALES
PRE-BOOKED VISITS

ANNUAL PRODUCTION 15,000 bottles
HECTARES UNDER VINE 4
VITICULTURE METHOD Organic

Bocale is a small winery emerging on the Montefalco wine scene. Its name comes from the local pronunciation of the word "vocale", a two-litre jug used in the past both for wine and for oil. Bocale has also become the nickname of the Valentini family, who own the winery. After their forebears linked the name to the land, the younger generations are now reviving this bond with local viticulture.

The Montefalco Sagrantino '07, while still very young, seems to have found the right direction. Its nose brims with black berry fruits with prominent toasty notes, the palate showing warm and fleshy, with exuberant tannins still need to settle and a slight excess of alcohol. Without doubt, it will improve after ageing in bottle for a while. The Montefalco Rosso Antigniano 08 has a similar spectrum of aromatics: intensely fruity with toasty notes on the nose and still a little muzzy on the palate.

- ● Montefalco Rosso Bocale '08 🍷🍷
- ● Montefalco Sagrantino Bocale '07 🍷🍷
- ● Montefalco Sagrantino '06 🥂🥂 6

Brogal Vini

loc. Bastia Umbra
via degli Olmi, 9
06083 Perugia
tel. 0758001501
www.brogalvini.com

CELLAR SALES
PRE-BOOKED VISITS
ROOMS

ANNUAL PRODUCTION 3,000,000 bottles
HECTARES UNDER VINE 75
VITICULTURE METHOD Conventional

Antigniano Brogal Vini is a fairly ambitious project as it represents two of the most important areas in the region, and also two DOCGs, Torgiano and Montefalco. There is a total of 75 hectares under vine yielding three million bottles a year. Many wines achieve extremely satisfying results in a well-crafted, austere style and also offer great value for money.

Starting with the most important designations, two wines stand out: the Torgiano Rosso Riserva Santa Caterina '06 with its refreshing continuity and slight grassy notes, and the Montefalco Sagrantino Guado alle Chiavi '06, which shows full fruit on both nose and palate, with assertive toasty notes. The Torgiano Bianco Kirnao '09 is outstanding, a fragrant wine with an excellent mouthfeel and a good acid-sustained progression, while the Grechetto '09 has overtones of citrus fruits and flowers with delightful hints of wild thyme and an almond-washed finish.

- ○ Grechetto Antigniano '09 🍷🍷 4
- ● Montefalco Sagrantino Guado alle Chiavi Antigniano '06 🍷🍷 7
- ○ Torgiano Bianco Kirnao '09 🍷🍷 4
- ● Torgiano Rosso Santa Caterina Ris. '06 🍷🍷 6
- ○ Bizante Bianco '09 🍷 5
- ● Torgiano Rosso '07 🍷 4
- ● Torgiano Rosso Santa Caterina Ris. '04 🥂🥂 6

★ Arnaldo Caprai

LOC. TORRE
06036 MONTEFALCO [PG]
TEL. 0742378802
www.arnaldocaprai.it

CELLAR SALES
PRE-BOOKED VISITS

ANNUAL PRODUCTION **750,000 bottles**
HECTARES UNDER VINE **136**
VITICULTURE METHOD **Conventional**

Marco Caprai is the undisputed leader of the Montefalco wine scene. Through his experiments, passion and ability to interpret events, Sagrantino has emerged from the local consumption and has crossed regional and national boundaries, taking on its current role of a great wine to lay down. Marco has a clear mental image of what a wine should be, and what values should always be present, whether you like the wine or not.

The extremely warm harvest of '07 produced a very powerful, rich and caressing 25 Anni. This red should be left in the cellar as it is maintains its balance and strength without becoming pretentious or clumsy. The aromas evoke quinine, blackberry and blueberry and cocoa is clearly in evidence before the full palate unveils great tannic weight that will need further ageing to unbend. The second-tier wine, Collepiano '07, has spicy aromas and is excellent. The new Montefalco Rosso Vigna Flaminia Maremmana '07 is already one of the best in its category. The Anima Umbra Rosso '08, from sangiovese and canaiolo, is a splendid, great-value wine.

Montefalco Sagrantino 25 Anni '07	3 glasses	8
Montefalco Sagrantino Collepiano '07	2 glasses	7
Rosso Outsider '06	2 glasses	7
Anima Umbra Rosso '08	2 glasses	4
Colli Martani Grechetto Grecante '09	2 glasses	4
Montefalco Rosso '08	2 glasses	5
Montefalco Rosso Ris. '07	2 glasses	7
Montefalco Sagrantino Passito '07	2 glasses	8
Montefalco Vigna Flaminia Maremmana '07	2 glasses	
Anima Umbra Bianco '09	1 glass	4
Montefalco Sagrantino 25 Anni '06	3 white glasses	8
Montefalco Sagrantino 25 Anni '05	3 white glasses	8
Montefalco Sagrantino 25 Anni '04	3 white glasses	8
Montefalco Sagrantino 25 Anni '98	3 white glasses	8
Montefalco Sagrantino 25 Anni '97	3 white glasses	8
Montefalco Sagrantino 25 Anni '95	3 white glasses	8

Cardeto

FRAZ. SFERRACAVALLO
LOC. CARDETO
05018 ORVIETO [TR]
TEL. 0763340135
www.cardeto.com

CELLAR SALES
PRE-BOOKED VISITS

ANNUAL PRODUCTION **3,000,000 bottles**
HECTARES UNDER VINE **880**
VITICULTURE METHOD **Conventional**

Established in the late 1940s, Cardeto is one of the oldest co-operative wineries in the region and one of the most important for its production volumes. The vineyards cover nearly 900 hectares and are owned by over 350 member-growers from the main towns in the district: Orvieto, Porano, Baschi, Castiglione in Teverina, Civitella d'Agliano, Montecchio and Allerona. Cardeto also makes substantial quantities of Orvieto, one of Umbria's most important designations.

The Orvieto Classico Pierleone '09, from native grapes only, is splendid, combining the fine flowery aromas of mimosa and lime blossom with a masterly palate of great substance, freshness and depth. The Colbadia '09, from procanico grapes and a touch of sauvignon, is very interesting with its elegant aromas and fine almond-edged mouth, as are the simpler Orvieto Classico Superiore Febeo '09, the Chardonnay Soliano '09 and the Grechetto '09. All whites are good, eclipsing the reds: Nero della Greca '08, a monovarietal sangiovese but rather uncertain this year, Rupestro '09 and Alborato '09, to which we preferred the rosé version.

Colbadia '09	2 glasses	4
Grechetto '09	2 glasses	3
Orvieto Cl. Pierleone '09	2 glasses	3
Orvieto Cl. Sup. Febeo '09	2 glasses	4
Soliano '09	2 glasses	5
Alborato '09	1 glass	3
Alborato Rosato '09	1 glass	4
Nero della Greca '08	1 glass	5
Rupestro '09	1 glass	3
Arciato '06	2 white glasses	5
Arciato '05	2 white glasses	4
Nero della Greca '07	2 white glasses	5
Nero della Greca '07	2 white glasses	5
Nero della Greca '06	2 white glasses	5
Nero della Greca '05	2 white glasses	5
Rupestro '07	2 white glasses	3*

Carini

FRAZ. COLLE UMBERTO
S.DA DEL TEGOLARO
06133 PERUGIA
TEL. 0755829102
www.agrariacarini.it

CELLAR SALES
PRE-BOOKED VISITS

ANNUAL PRODUCTION 40,000 bottles
HECTARES UNDER VINE 10
VITICULTURE METHOD Conventional

The Carini winery is no longer a novelty. In double-quick time, it has carved out for itself a leading role on the Umbrian wine scene, with technically impeccable wines, modern in style and brimming with personality and elegance. The winery is on the slopes of Mount Terzio, between Perugia and Lake Trasimeno, in an enchanting setting filled by the Carini family with vines, olive groves, cinta senese pigs and more.

The Tegolare is again superlative. The '08 edition of the cellar's flagship, from merlot and cabernet sauvignon, has potential. The aromatics are quite dark, dominated by toasty notes, dark berries and pink pepper while the palate still lacks clarity but its fruity energy promises a shining future. Just look at how the '07 is today when initially it had seemed even more tousled. Poggio Canneto '09, from chardonnay and pinot bianco, has improved and after brief ageing in new oak for the first time. The Oscano '09, from sangiovese and gamay perugino, is splendid, intensely fruity, with a spice-rich nose and a warm, caressing palate.

● Tegolaro '08	▼▼	6
● Òscano '09	▼▼	4
○ Poggio Canneto '09	▼▼	4
● Tegolaro '07	▽▽	6
● Tegolaro '06	▽▽	6
● Tegolaro '05	▽▽	6
● Tegolaro '04	▽▽	6

La Carraia

LOC. TORDIMONTE, 56
05018 ORVIETO [TR]
TEL. 0763304013
www.lacarraia.it

CELLAR SALES
PRE-BOOKED VISITS

ANNUAL PRODUCTION 500,000 bottles
HECTARES UNDER VINE 119
VITICULTURE METHOD Conventional

The Carraia winery was founded in the late 1980s as a collaboration between grower Odoardo Gialletti and the oenologist Riccardo Cotarella. From the outset they set up a vast project to renew vineyard management and cellar techniques, using local varieties and international grapes, setting grechetto, sangiovese and montepulciano next to chardonnay, merlot and cabernet sauvignon.

We thought the best wine was Orvieto Classico Poggio Calvelli '09, for years a leading Orvieto and this year better than usual. Its flowery aromas lead to sensations of yellow and green apple; the palate attacks coherently and then is expansive, with a gutsy, grapefruity finish. The reds, Tizzonero '08, from sangiovese and montepulciano, where lovely gamey tones overlay dark, meaty fruit, and Giro di Vite '08, from montepulciano only, a delight of black berry fruit and shades of cocoa, are excellent. The Bordeaux blend Fobiano '08 is less convincing, while remaining typical. The Sangiovese '09, the Le Basque '09, from grechetto and viognier, and the Orvieto Classico '09 are decent.

○ Orvieto Cl. Poggio Calvelli '09	▼▼	3
● Fobiano '08	▼▼	5
● Giro di Vite '08	▼▼	5
● Tizzonero '08	▼▼	4
○ Le Basque '09	▼	4
○ Orvieto Cl. '09	▼	2
● Sangiovese '09	▼	3
● Fobiano '03	▽▽▽	5
● Fobiano '07	▽▽	5
● Fobiano '06	▽▽	5
● Fobiano '05	▽▽	5
● Fobiano '04	▽▽	5
● Giro di Vite '07	▽▽	5
● Giro di Vite '06	▽▽	5
● Giro di Vite '04	▽▽	5
○ Orvieto Cl. Poggio Calvelli '08	▽▽	3*
○ Orvieto Cl. Poggio Calvelli '07	▽▽	3*

Tenuta Castelbuono

LOC. BEVAGNA
VOC. FOSSATO, 20
06031 PERUGIA
TEL. 0742361670
www.cantineferrari.it

ANNUAL PRODUCTION 112,000 bottles
HECTARES UNDER VINE 32
VITICULTURE METHOD Conventional

Several wineries from outside the region have invested in the Sagrantino area. Among these, the Lunelli family from Trento, famous for bubbly, has linked its name to the most famous red wine area in Umbria. The vineyards are between the towns of Montefalco and Bevagna, which is also the home of the new cellar designed by the famous architect Arnaldo Pomodoro. The soil is silty clay and the wines age in 900-litre casks and large barrels.

Montefalco Sagrantino '06 is very interesting. The grapes are from vineyards in the municipality of Montefalco, selected in collaboration with the winemaking school at San Michele all'Adige and the wines are in the customary house style, where captivating aromas hint at red and black berry fruit with elegant spice, while the palate is austere. The wine still needs to unfold and the tannins, in particular, are still rather stiff, but the overall complexity bodes well for the future. We'll see when it's had some cellar time. However, we found the pale, mouth-drying Montefalco Rosso '08 less successful.

● Montefalco Sagrantino '06	🍷🍷	6
● Montefalco Rosso '08	🍷	4
● Montefalco Rosso '07	🍷🍷 (white)	4*
● Montefalco Rosso '06	🍷🍷 (white)	4*
● Montefalco Sagrantino '05	🍷🍷 (white)	6
● Montefalco Sagrantino '04	🍷🍷 (white)	6

★★ Castello della Sala

LOC. SALA
05016 FICULLE [TR]
TEL. 076386051
www.antinori.it

PRE-BOOKED VISITS

ANNUAL PRODUCTION 662,000 bottles
HECTARES UNDER VINE 160
VITICULTURE METHOD Conventional

When in the 1940s Marchesi Antinori decided to make a great white wine, their choice of where to buy land fell on Umbria. In the event, they chose an area historically renowned for its whites, the territory around Orvieto. The vineyards and cellar are on a tufaceous buff at over 500 metres above sea level, between the River Paglia and Mount Nibbio. This territory, together with the Antinoris' ideas and skills, produces one of Italy's most celebrated, long-living wines.

The '08 harvest produced another astounding Cervaro della Sala and this vintage may have a touch more dynamism. It is a wine of great impact, where the buttery, vanillaed notes from the oak are felt, especially when the wine is young, but cannot curb its magnificent, fine fruit, energy and minerality, while the powerful palate shows vibrant acidity and exceptionally long finish. The Chardonnay Bramito del Cervo '09, themed around green notes, is also extremely good. The Orvieto Classico Superiore San Giovanni della Sala '09, which has a lovely supple palate, is very good indeed.

○ Cervaro della Sala '08	🍷🍷🍷+	7
○ Bramito del Cervo '09	🍷🍷	4
○ Orvieto Cl. Sup. San Giovanni della Sala '09	🍷🍷	4
● Pinot Nero della Sala '07	🍷	6
○ Cervaro della Sala '07	🍷🍷🍷 (white)	7
○ Cervaro della Sala '06	🍷🍷🍷 (white)	7
○ Cervaro della Sala '05	🍷🍷🍷 (white)	7
○ Cervaro della Sala '04	🍷🍷🍷 (white)	7
○ Cervaro della Sala '01	🍷🍷🍷 (white)	6

Castello delle Regine

loc. Le Regine
via di Castelluccio
05022 Amelia [TR]
tel. 0744702005
www.castellodelleregine.com

CELLAR SALES
PRE-BOOKED VISITS
FOOD

ANNUAL PRODUCTION **350,000 bottles**
HECTARES UNDER VINE **87**
VITICULTURE METHOD **Conventional**

Castello delle Regine is one of the newest Umbrian wineries to have caught consumers' attention by offering high-quality wines in a precise style. The estate belongs to the Nodari family and boasts 400 hectares of land at the towns of Narni and Amelia, where international and traditional grapes of central Italy, such as sangiovese, are cultivated in the over 80 hectares under vine.

The Sangiovese Selezione del Fondatore '05 is one of the best wines of recent years. The nose shows refined tertiary hints of leather and spices with fresh red and black berry fruit and is a lip-smacking wine that follows through delightfully, only slightly held back by a tannic finish and a tad too much alcohol. The Merlot '07, one of the winery's thoroughbreds, is also very good, with tempting hints of chocolate and black berry fruit plus a large dose of toastiness. The Bianco delle Regine '09 is altogether lovely and the Rosso di Podernovo '07 is decent, while the Sangiovese Poggio delle Regine '08 and the Rosé delle Regine '09 are enjoyable but less exciting.

● Sangiovese Sel. del Fondatore '05	🍷🍷	6
○ Bianco delle Regine '09	🍷🍷	4
● Merlot '07	🍷🍷	7
● Rosso di Podernovo '07	🍷🍷	4
● Poggio delle Regine '08	🍷	5
⊙ Rosé delle Regine '09	🍷	4
● Merlot '05	ΥΥΥ	7
● Merlot '04	ΥΥΥ	7
● Merlot '03	ΥΥΥ	7
● Merlot '02	ΥΥΥ	6
● Merlot '01	ΥΥΥ	7
● Merlot '06	ΥΥ	7

Castello di Magione

via dei Cavalieri di Malta, 31
06063 Magione [PG]
tel. 075843542
www.castellodimagione.it

CELLAR SALES
PRE-BOOKED VISITS

ANNUAL PRODUCTION **120,000 bottles**
HECTARES UNDER VINE **44**
VITICULTURE METHOD **Conventional**

The Castello di Magione, clinging to a cliff over Lake Trasimeno, has a truly fascinating history. Owned by the Sovereign Military Order of Malta, the cellar has recently been relocated to the valley and is now housed in buildings that are less evocative but more suited to modern-day needs, while the wines remain decidedly interesting. The entire production, starting from Grechetto, seems to have found a perfect dimension. These wines have elegance and an identifiable house style.

We were impressed by the Carpaneto '08, which successfully combines the directness of sangiovese, the aromatic nuances of gamay perugino and the fruitiness of merlot. This is an evocative red, with notes of citrus fruit and earth, and charming grassy balsamic tones laced with benzene. The Nero dei Cavalieri '07 is also good, a crisp, flavoursome wine from pinot nero grapes. We liked the classy Grechetto Monterone, although this '09 edition is perhaps more substantial and mature than usual.

● Carpaneto '08	🍷🍷	4
○ C. del Trasimeno Grechetto Monterone '09	🍷🍷	4
● Nero dei Cavalieri '07	🍷🍷	5
○ Albaneta '09	🍷	4
○ C. del Trasimeno Grechetto Monterone '08	ΥΥ	4*
○ C. del Trasimeno Grechetto Monterone '07	ΥΥ	3*
○ C. del Trasimeno Grechetto Monterone '06	ΥΥ	3*
○ C. del Trasimeno Grechetto Monterone '05	ΥΥ	3*
○ C. del Trasimeno Grechetto Monterone '04	ΥΥ	3*

Fattoria Colle Allodole

LOC. COLLE ALLODOLE
06031 BEVAGNA [PG]
TEL. 0742361897
www.fattoriacolleallodole.it

CELLAR SALES

ANNUAL PRODUCTION 70,000 bottles
HECTARES UNDER VINE 12
VITICULTURE METHOD Conventional

Francesco Antano follows in the footsteps of his late father Milziade, a pioneer of Sagrantino, working with obstinacy and passion while putting his personal imprint on the estate with enthusiasm. This is, and remains, an artisan winery, with wonderful rare bottles that can kindle dreams in enthusiasts. At least, in those who pay attention to the wines and can wait long enough before opening the bottles laid down in their cellars.

Antano boasts many beautiful and well-located vineyards, starting from the Colleallodole cru, from which they obtain a limited production of the most enthralling Sagrantino. Unfortunately, the wines we were given to taste were still unintelligible, perhaps because not yet fully matured. We will therefore reserve judgement for future editions of the Guide. We will only review here the Montefalco Sagrantino Passito '07, as we consider it the best of this year. It has an intensely fruity nose where fine spices meet aromas of cigar and a powerful, compact mouth with depth, complexity and flawless tannins.

Wine	Glasses	Score
● Montefalco Sagrantino Passito '07	2 (black)	8
● Montefalco Sagrantino Colleallodole '06	3	7
● Montefalco Sagrantino Colleallodole '05	3	7
● Montefalco Rosso '07	2	5
● Montefalco Rosso '06	2	5
● Montefalco Rosso '05	2	5
● Montefalco Rosso Ris. '06	2	6
● Montefalco Rosso Ris. '05	2	6
● Montefalco Rosso Ris. '04	2	6
● Montefalco Sagrantino '06	2	6
● Montefalco Sagrantino '05	2	6
● Montefalco Sagrantino '04	2	6
● Montefalco Sagrantino Passito '06	2	5
● Montefalco Sagrantino Passito '05	2	5
● Montefalco Sagrantino Passito '04	2	5

★ Còlpetrone

LOC. MARCELLANO
VIA PONTE LA MANDRIA, 8/1
06035 GUALDO CATTANEO [PG]
TEL. 074299827
www.colpetrone.it

CELLAR SALES
PRE-BOOKED VISITS

ANNUAL PRODUCTION 250,000 bottles
HECTARES UNDER VINE 63
VITICULTURE METHOD Conventional

Còlpetrone, part of the Saiagricola group, has been for years a leading estate for wines of the area of Montefalco, starting with Sagrantino. Over the last year, changes within the company have resulted in the reorganization of many technical and managerial aspects and the winery has set out on a new path. It has well-established roots, consisting of a splendid cellar and southeast-facing vineyards in the district of Gualdo Cattaneo, where the soils are silty mixed with some clay.

The new technical staff has decided to delay presenting the most recent vintages of Sagrantino, in order to ensure that the wines can age further in the cellar. So, for now, no Sagrantino '07 and no Sagrantino Gold '06. We will see what happens next year. Meanwhile we can enjoy a lovely Montefalco Rosso '08, a wine that offers aromas of cocoa and small red berries, flowing to a supple, confident palate, and the always enticing Montefalco Sagrantino Passito. The '07 vintage has intense aromas of liquorice and blackberry and is quite tannic and sweet.

Wine	Glasses	Score
● Montefalco Rosso '08	2 (black)	4
● Montefalco Sagrantino Passito '07	2 (black)	6
● Montefalco Sagrantino '04	3	6
● Montefalco Sagrantino '03	3	6
● Montefalco Sagrantino '02	3	6
● Montefalco Sagrantino '01	3	6
● Montefalco Sagrantino '00	3	6
● Montefalco Sagrantino '99	3	6
● Montefalco Sagrantino '98	3	5
● Montefalco Sagrantino '97	3	5
● Montefalco Sagrantino '96	3	4
● Montefalco Sagrantino Gold '05	3	8
● Montefalco Sagrantino Gold '04	3	8

Custodi

LOC. CANALE
V.LE VENERE
05018 ORVIETO [TR]
TEL. 076329053
www.cantinacustodi.com

CELLAR SALES
PRE-BOOKED VISITS

ANNUAL PRODUCTION **50,000 bottles**
HECTARES UNDER VINE **37**
VITICULTURE METHOD **Conventional**

Gian Franco Custodi is one of the small host of the finest Umbrian winemakers, those who are devoted to their work rather than to random matters. Today he is helped by his daughters, undoubtedly easing his commitment towards the some 70 hectares owned by the family, 37 of which are under vine, to the cellar work and to the necessary commercial operations. The vineyards are located at Canale, and many fall under the Orvieto DOC.

The volcanic, tufaceous and clayey soil impart to these whites a distinctly fascinating character. By throwing a good growing year into the equation, the result is a really top notch Orvieto Classico Belloro '09. It gives minerally, nearly rocky aromas that combine with sensations of white tea, flowers and citrus fruit, while the gutsy palate is meaty and acid, followed by a bergamot-rinsed finish. The Piancoleto '09, from sangiovese and merlot grapes and aged only in stainless steel, is delicious in its simplicity. The Merlot Austero '08 is less successful.

Wine	Rating	Price
○ Orvieto Cl. Belloro '09	2 black glasses	2
● Piancoleto '09	2 black glasses	3
● Austero '08	1 black glass	4
● Austero '07	2 white glasses	4*
○ Orvieto Cl. Belloro '08	2 white glasses	2*
○ Orvieto Cl. Belloro '07	2 white glasses	2*
○ Orvieto Cl. Sup. Pertusa V. T. '07	2 white glasses	5

Decugnano dei Barbi

LOC. FOSSATELLO, 50
05019 ORVIETO [TR]
TEL. 0763308255
www.decugnano.it

CELLAR SALES
PRE-BOOKED VISITS

ANNUAL PRODUCTION **120,000 bottles**
HECTARES UNDER VINE **32**
VITICULTURE METHOD **Conventional**

Decugnano dei Barbi is one of the most beautiful wineries in Umbria. Its setting is paradisiacal, famous for wine production for over eight centuries, with marl and clay soils, marine in origin, full of oyster fossils and shells. The climate is ideal, well-ventilated and with big day-night temperature swings. The Barbi family has owned the estate since 1973. After several hesitant years, Decugnano may have regained its leading position on the regional wine scene.

The Orvieto Classico Superiore "IL" '09 is just simply delicious. It is still young, with enthralling primary aromas that express clear, vivid flowery and fruity sensations, giving way to more complex, mineral tones. The attack is solid and juicy, relaxed and lengthened by lovely acidity as the palate unfolds with almonds and aromatic herbs. The '08 "IL" from sangiovese, montepulciano and syrah is also very good, themed around dark fruit and chocolate, with still prominent toasty notes. The Maris '09, from chardonnay and grechetto and with aromas of mint and rosemary, is very enjoyable.

Wine	Rating	Price
○ Orvieto Cl. Sup. "IL" '09	3 black glasses	5
● "IL" Rosso '08	2 black glasses	5
○ Maris '09	2 black glasses	4
○ Decugnano Brut '04	1 black glass	5
● "IL" Rosso '06	2 white glasses	6
● Lago di Corbara "IL" '02	2 white glasses	6
● Lago di Corbara Decugnano Rosso '05	2 white glasses	4*
○ Orvieto Cl. Sup. "IL" '03	2 white glasses	5
○ Orvieto Cl. Sup. "IL" Sel. '04	2 white glasses	5

Italo Di Filippo

VOC. CONVERSINO, 153
06033 CANNARA [PG]
TEL. 0742731242
www.vinidifilippo.com

CELLAR SALES
PRE-BOOKED VISITS

ANNUAL PRODUCTION 200,000 bottles
HECTARES UNDER VINE 20
VITICULTURE METHOD Certified organic

The Di Filippo winery is in the municipality of Cannara, straddling two territories whose characteristics are reflected in the wines. The winery is committed to these lands and their approach is one of respect for traditions and the environment. For years, they have employed organic methods, making genuine wines with personality. Their range is vast, with several interesting bottles, while others are less convincing. There are some exciting, tasty reds and whites, starting with those from local grapes.

The Sagrantino '06 is very impressive, after sufficient airing to free it from feral reductive notes. Its development is earthy, full of flavour and dynamic in places, with fine-grained tannins. We also had some interesting tastings in the cellar of the Sagrantinos that will be released over the next few years. The minerally Grechetto Sassi d'Arenaria '09, with its yellow-fleshed fruit and wild flowers, is among the best whites, and the uncomplicated Colli Martani '09 is also pretty good.

○ Colli Martani Grechetto '09	▼▼	3
○ Colli Martani Grechetto Sassi d'Arenaria '09	▼▼	3
● Montefalco Rosso '07	▼▼	4
● Montefalco Rosso Sallustio '07	▼▼	4
● Montefalco Sagrantino '06	▼▼	6
● Villa Conversino Rosso '09	▼	3
○ Colli Martani Grechetto '08	▽▽	3*
● Montefalco Rosso Sallustio '06	▽▽	4*

Duca della Corgna

VIA ROMA, 236
06061 CASTIGLIONE DEL LAGO [PG]
TEL. 0759652493
www.ducadellacorgna.it

CELLAR SALES
PRE-BOOKED VISITS

ANNUAL PRODUCTION 280,000 bottles
HECTARES UNDER VINE 55
VITICULTURE METHOD Conventional

The renaissance Duca Ascanio della Corgna, a mercenary commander, architect and military engineer whose exploits made his land famous, is remembered in these wines from a project implemented to promote the winery's quality. The headlands of Castiglione del Lago with their limestone soil are the ideal base for this venture, covered by vines that over time have become one with the land, from grechetto to gamay del Trasimeno, a grape similar to grenache, and sangiovese.

It was a great year for the Colli del Trasimeno Rosso Riserva Corniolo '07, from mostly sangiovese, with a warm, intense heart evoking ripe plum, cocoa and leather and an accurate, expansive continuity in the mouth. The two Gamays are both splendid, the Etichetta Bianca '09 showing crisper and juicier and the Nera '07 is more intense, hinged on notes of oak and black pepper. The Grechetto Ascanio '09 is delicately flowery, with lovely ripe fruit, and the fleshy, energetic Colli del Trasimeno Grechetto Nuricante '09 is even better.

● C. del Trasimeno Rosso Corniolo Ris. '07	▼▼	5
○ Ascanio '09	▼▼	3
● C. del Trasimeno Gamay Divina Villa Et. Bianca '09	▼▼	4
● C. del Trasimeno Gamay Divina Villa Et. Nera '07	▼▼	4
○ C. del Trasimeno Grechetto Nuricante '09	▼▼	4
○ C. del Trasimeno Baccio del Bianco '09	▼	3
● C. del Trasimeno Baccio del Rosso '09	▼	3
○ Ascanio '08	▽▽	3*
● C. del Trasimeno Gamay Divina Villa Et. Bianca '08	▽▽	4*
● C. del Trasimeno Gamay Divina Villa Et. Nera '06	▽▽	4*
● C. del Trasimeno Rosso Corniolo Ris. '06	▽▽	5

Podere Fontesecca

VOC. FONTESECCA, 30
06062 CITTÀ DELLA PIEVE [PG]
TEL. 3496180516
www.fontesecca.it

CELLAR SALES
PRE-BOOKED VISITS
ROOMS

ANNUAL PRODUCTION 8,000 bottles
HECTARES UNDER VINE 3
VITICULTURE METHOD Certified organic

Fontesecca is Paolo Bolla's Umbrian winery, and is situated near the marvellous town of Città della Pieve, in an area bordering Tuscany. The pebbly, tufaceous clayey soils are marine in origin and full of shells. The estate is farmed organically and the vine stock comprises local varieties, which are clearly in symbiosis with the wonderful territory in which they grow.

These are still early days but this will not stop us celebrating one of the best '09 whites from Umbria. Made from the classical trio of trebbiano, grechetto and malvasia, this is an intense, fragrant wine, where notes of wild flowers interweave with hints of rock and minerals. It has a fleshy texture, with hints of yellow-fleshed fruit but above all, it is uplifted by a mouthwateringly delicate mineral vein. The PinoSangiovese '08 has a great personality.

○ Bianco Fontesecca '09	🍷🍷	4
● Pino Sangiovese '08	🍷🍷	5
● Ciliegiolo '09	🍷	5

Goretti

LOC. PILA
S.DA DEL PINO, 4
06132 PERUGIA
TEL. 075607316
www.vinigoretti.com

CELLAR SALES
PRE-BOOKED VISITS

ANNUAL PRODUCTION 400,000 bottles
HECTARES UNDER VINE 60
VITICULTURE METHOD Conventional

On the lovely hills of Pila, a few kilometres from Perugia, sits an ancient tower which wine tourists and regular clients identify with the Goretti winery. This estate has a long history and is known for admirably consistent quality both in its leading wines and in the value for money bottles. The style is precise and the tone modern. The family now also boasts a new property near Montefalco, Le Mura Saracene, at Pietrauta.

We could not taste the Perugia winery's signature wine, Arringatore, or those produced at Montefalco. They need a further year in the cellar. But the wines from the latest harvest were superlative, starting with the Grechetto Il Moggio '09, which was aged briefly in barrique. The aromatic fragrances are intense before the palate brilliantly hints at yellow-fleshed fruit and gunflint with a vivid, lip-smacking finish. The Fontanella Rosso '09 amazed us. It's one of the best from recent years, easy-drinking yet anything but dull, suffused with red fruits and paprika, and giving spice and pepper on the palate.

● Fontanella Rosso '09	🍷🍷	3
○ Il Moggio '09	🍷🍷	4
○ Chardonnay '09	🍷	3
○ Grechetto '09	🍷	2
○ Colli Perugini Chardonnay '08	🥂🥂	3*
● Colli Perugini Rosso L'Arringatore '06	🥂🥂	5
● Colli Perugini Rosso L'Arringatore '05	🥂🥂	5
● Colli Perugini Rosso L'Arringatore '04	🥂🥂	5
● Colli Perugini Rosso L'Arringatore '03	🥂🥂	5
● Colli Perugini Rosso L'Arringatore '01	🥂🥂	5
○ Il Moggio '08	🥂🥂	4*

Lamborghini

LOC. SODERI, 1
06064 PANICALE [PG]
TEL. 0758350029
www.lamborghinionline.it

CELLAR SALES
PRE-BOOKED VISITS
FOOD

ANNUAL PRODUCTION **132,000 bottles**
HECTARES UNDER VINE **32**
VITICULTURE METHOD **Conventional**

Purchased by Ferruccio Lamborghini in the 1970s, this delightful estate includes 100 hectares of land, a golf club, an agriturismo and, obviously, the vineyards and cellar. Since the 1990s, Patrizia Lamborghini, Ferruccio's daughter, has skilfully managed the estate, imparting a modern character to the often barrique-aged wines.

We could not taste the Campoleone '08, the winery's flagship red, as it will be presented next year. This means that the estate's marquee wine was missing. We were, however, able to taste both l'Era '08, a Sangiovese with toasty aromas, already rather mature and caressing, and the Trescone '08, from sangiovese, ciliegiolo and merlot, a more crisp, juicy and relaxed wine.

● Trescone '08	TT	4
● Era '08	T	4
● Campoleone '04	YYY	7
● Campoleone '01	YYY	6
● Campoleone '00	YYY	6
● Campoleone '99	YYY	6
● Campoleone '07	YY	6
● Campoleone '05	YY	6
● Campoleone '03	YY	6
● Campoleone '02	YY	6
● Campoleone '98	YY	5
● Campoleone '97	YY	5
● Era '07	YY	4*
● Torami '07	YY	5

Lungarotti

V.LE GIORGIO LUNGAROTTI. 2
06089 TORGIANO [PG]
TEL. 075988661
www.lungarotti.it

CELLAR SALES
PRE-BOOKED VISITS
ROOMS AND FOOD

ANNUAL PRODUCTION **2,900,000 bottles**
HECTARES UNDER VINE **310**
VITICULTURE METHOD **Conventional**

Giorgio Lungarotti conceived and established his winery in the 1960s and it still remains one of the most fascinating on the Italian wine scene. Uncompromisingly traditional, it combines impressive production volumes with high-quality wines, some of which are exceptional and often come from specific, separately vinified and bottled vineyards. The active family foundation is also responsible for setting up and managing the Museo del Vino at Torgiano.

Among the wines we tasted, we were especially impressed by the Torgiano Bianco Vigna il Pino Riserva '08, from trebbiano and grechetto grapes aged in barrique, partly because of some amazing repeat tastings of old vintages, which showed that this white has excellent development and ageing potential. Fine flowery and fruity aromas blend with lovely buttery notes, while the delicate palate has young, citrussy traits and over time will develop greater taste and complexity. Among the reds, the San Giorgio '05 and the incredible Rubesco '07 are both excellent.

○ Torgiano Bianco Torre di Giano V. il Pino Ris. '08	TTT	4*
● San Giorgio '05	TT	6
● Torgiano Rosso Rubesco '07	TT	4
○ Aurente '08	TT	5
● Montefalco Rosso '08	TT	4
● Montefalco Sagrantino '07	TT	6
○ Torgiano Bianco Torre di Giano '09	TT	3
○ Torveto '09	TT	4
● Toralco '08	T	5
● Torgiano Rosso Vigna Monticchio Ris. '05	YYY	6*
● Torgiano Rosso Vigna Monticchio Ris. '04	YYY	6
● Torgiano Rosso Vigna Monticchio Ris. '03	YYY	6
● Torgiano Rosso Vigna Monticchio Ris. '01	YYY	7
○ Torgiano Bianco Torre di Giano V. il Pino Ris. '07	YY	4*
○ Torgiano Bianco Torre di Giano V. il Pino Ris. '06	YY	4*
○ Torgiano Bianco Torre di Giano V. il Pino Ris. '04	YY	4*

Martinelli

voc. Sasso
via Madonna della Neve, 1
06031 Bevagna [PG]
tel. 0742362124
www.cantinemartinelli.com

CELLAR SALES
PRE-BOOKED VISITS

ANNUAL PRODUCTION 155,000 bottles
HECTARES UNDER VINE 20
VITICULTURE METHOD Conventional

The Martinelli winery is at Bevagna, one of the most symbolic towns for Sagrantino, and could nearly represent a new generation for the wines of the area. It is a young, modern operation, yet one that is able to produce wines that are well-made, gratifying and technically flawless, focused on a style that puts the accent on perfectly ripe fruit and ageing in barrique.

Because of the very warm '07 harvest, we tend to prefer the standard-label Sagrantino to the Saranna selection. The former has layered aromas centring on small wild berries and refreshing notes of bergamot, with a palate that is warm and soft, but not excessively so, and a coherent tannic weave, while the Saranna is less focused and has too much extract. The Gaite Rosso '09 is very convincing, from sangiovese, sagrantino and merlot grapes, enjoyable and full of flavour, while the Montefalco Rosso '08 is just a step below.

● Montefalco Sagrantino '07	🍷🍷	5
● Gaite Rosso '09	🍷🍷	4
● Montefalco Sagrantino Sel. Soranna '07	🍷🍷	7
● Montefalco Rosso '08	🍷	4
○ Gaite Bianco '08	ŸŸ	4*
● Gaite Rosso '08	ŸŸ	4*
● Montefalco Sagrantino '06	ŸŸ	5
● Montefalco Sagrantino '05	ŸŸ	5
● Montefalco Sagrantino '04	ŸŸ	5
● Montefalco Sagrantino '03	ŸŸ	6
● Montefalco Sagrantino '02	ŸŸ	6
● Montefalco Sagrantino Sel. Soranna '06	ŸŸ	7
● Montefalco Sagrantino Sel. Soranna '05	ŸŸ	7
● Montefalco Sagrantino Sel. Soranna '03	ŸŸ	7

Cantina Monrubio

fraz. Monterubiaglio
loc. Le Prese, 22
05014 Castel Viscardo [TR]
tel. 0763626064
www.monrubio.it

CELLAR SALES
PRE-BOOKED VISITS

ANNUAL PRODUCTION 900,000 bottles
HECTARES UNDER VINE 700
VITICULTURE METHOD Conventional

The Monrubio co-operative winery was established in the late 1950s at Castel Viscardo, near Orvieto. Here it remains, boasting a large number of member-growers who bring in an equally significant vineyard pool. Many of the grapes come from within the Orvieto and Orvieto Classico designations, but the cellar has shown that its skill with red-berried varieties, producing interesting reds from local and international grapes.

Palaia '08, a blend of cabernet, merlot and pinot nero, is again executed in a modern style, full of delicious fruity notes and an overall toastiness that was still to the fore when we tasted the wine, while the palate has a good taste and consistent tannins. From the whites, the Orvieto Classico Superiore Soana '09 is simply splendid. It has minerally, rocky aromas where yeasty notes are still in evidence and a complex palate, where sensations of mango flow into notes of mountain butter, drinking delicious, fresh and deep.

○ Orvieto Cl. Sup. Soana '09	🍷🍷	3*
● Palaia '08	🍷🍷	4
● Monrubio '07	ŸŸ	3*
● Monrubio '06	ŸŸ	3*
● Monrubio '05	ŸŸ	3*
● Monrubio '04	ŸŸ	3*
● Nociano '03	ŸŸ	4*
○ Orvieto Cl. Sup. Soana '08	ŸŸ	3*
○ Orvieto Cl. Sup. Soana '07	ŸŸ	3*
○ Orvieto Cl. Sup. Soana '06	ŸŸ	3
● Palaia '07	ŸŸ	4*
● Palaia '06	ŸŸ	4
● Palaia '05	ŸŸ	5
● Palaia '04	ŸŸ	5
● Palaia '03	ŸŸ	5

Moretti Omero

LOC. SAN SABINO, 19
06030 GIANO DELL'UMBRIA [PG]
TEL. 074290433
www.morettiomero.it

CELLAR SALES
PRE-BOOKED VISITS

ANNUAL PRODUCTION **30,000 bottles**
HECTARES UNDER VINE **8**
VITICULTURE METHOD **Certified organic**

Moretti Omero is a small, enthusiastic producer of extra virgin olive oil and wine. The estate's lands are at Giano dell'Umbria, near the Monti Martani, and they have been using organic growing methods since the early 1990s. The winery boasts certifications from ICEA (Institute for Ethical and Environmental Certification) and AIAB (Italian Association for Organic Agriculture). At their best, the wines show a distinct personality together with some very original touches.

We were overwhelmed by the white Nessuno '09, a blend of grechetto and malvasia aromatica, for its intense, lingering aromas that range from wild flowers to delicious yeasty notes. In the mouth, it is a marvel of taste, freshness and deep fleshiness. The Sagrantino '05 is also great, with a Bordeaux-type aromatic spectrum, and lovely taste and lip-smacking tannins. The Sagrantino '06 is good but a notch below the others. The rest of the range is interesting.

● Montefalco Sagrantino '05	**YY**	6
○ Nessuno '09	**YY**	4
● Montefalco Sagrantino '06	**YY**	6
○ Grechetto '09	**Y**	3
● Montefalco Rosso '07	**Y**	4
● Montefalco Sagrantino '02	YY	6
● Sagrantino di Montefalco '01	YY	6

La Palazzola

LOC. VASCIGLIANO
05039 STRONCONE [TR]
TEL. 0744609091
www.lapalazzola.it

ANNUAL PRODUCTION **150,000 bottles**
HECTARES UNDER VINE **36**
VITICULTURE METHOD **Conventional**

Stefano Grilli is a passionate, original and sometimes unpredictable producer. His talents have made La Palazzola what it is today: a place where anything can happen, in wine terms, and where they often conceive wines that are unusual in the regional context. And when La Palazzola shows the way, others then imitate. The estate in the Vascigliano countryside just outside Terni grows many grape varieties and makes many wines, ranging from reds to sparklers and even sweet wines.

Indeed, our favourite is a sweet wine, the Vin Santo '06. It has exceptionally complex aromas offering balsamic, wood resiny sensations with incense, integrating the profile of dried fruits, mainly figs, dates and apricots, while the taste is deep, but never over-sweet or sugary. The sparkling wines are, as usual, very good, and we liked the Riesling Brut '05, with its aromatic and creamy bubbles. The two reds are excellent, and we would like specifically to mention Rubino '07, which is sweetly spiced yet austere on the palate.

○ Vin Santo '06	**YY**	5
● Bacca Rossa Passito '07	**YY**	5
○ Gran Cuvée Brut '08	**YY**	5
○ Riesling Brut M. Cl. '05	**YY**	5
● Rubino '07	**YY**	5
● Syrah '08	**YY**	4
○ Gran Cuvée Brut '06	YY	5
○ Gran Cuvée Brut '05	YY	5
○ Gran Cuvée Brut '04	YY	5
● Le Petrare '06	YY	4*
● Merlot '05	YY	5
● Merlot '04	YY	5
● Merlot '99	YY	5
● Rubino '04	YY	5
○ Trebbiano Metodo Ancestrale '05	YY	5
○ V. T. da Uve Muffate '06	YY	4
● Vin Santo Bacca Rossa '05	YY	5

Palazzone

LOC. ROCCA RIPESENA, 68
05019 ORVIETO [TR]
TEL. 0763344921
www.palazzone.com

CELLAR SALES
PRE-BOOKED VISITS
ROOMS AND FOOD

ANNUAL PRODUCTION **120,000 bottles**
HECTARES UNDER VINE **25**
VITICULTURE METHOD **Conventional**

Giovanni Dubini is one of the most interesting, genuine Umbrian growers. He owns Palazzone, which takes its name from the splendid vine-girt, and vine-clad, building located at the centre of the estate. The winery is on the hilly slopes between Rocca Ripesena and Romitorio, only a few kilometres from Orvieto, at altitudes between 210 and 340 metres, aspected east and north-east. These plots are ideal for making great whites, provided the grower is as sensitive as Dubini.

Orvieto Classico Superiore Campo del Guardiano needs to age for several years after the harvest, distancing itself from the image of immediacy linked to the whites of the area. Indeed, the '90 is still exceptional and the '96 is a delight. The '07 edition is another top notch wine. This fantastic white evokes acacia honey, flowers, stone and chlorophyll, with a Mediterranean palate of ringingly flavoursome appeal. The Viognier L'Ultima Spiaggia '09 is also better than ever, with overtones of mineral, leather and white pepper. Terre Vineate '09, the Grechetto '09 and the red Armaleo '07 are all good.

○ Orvieto Cl. Sup. Campo del Guardiano '07	▼▼▼	5
○ L'Ultima Spiaggia '09	▼▼	4
● Armaleo '07	▼▼	8
○ Grechetto '09	▼▼	4
○ Orvieto Cl. Sup. Terre Vineate '09	▼▼	4
● Armaleo '06	▽▽	8
● Armaleo '05	▽▽	8
○ Grechetto '08	▽▽	4*
○ Grechetto '07	▽▽	4*
○ Muffa Nobilis '05	▽▽	6
○ Muffa Nobilis '03	▽▽	6
○ Orvieto Cl. Campo del Guardiano '05	▽▽	5
○ Orvieto Cl. Campo del Guardiano '04	▽▽	5
○ Orvieto Cl. Sup. Campo del Guardiano '06	▽▽	5
○ Orvieto Cl. Sup. Terre Vineate '08	▽▽	4*
○ Orvieto Cl. Sup. Terre Vineate '06	▽▽	4
○ Orvieto Cl. Sup. Terre Vineate '05	▽▽	4

F.lli Pardi

VIA GIOVANNI PASCOLI, 7/9
06036 MONTEFALCO [PG]
TEL. 0742379023
www.cantinapardi.it

CELLAR SALES
PRE-BOOKED VISITS

ANNUAL PRODUCTION **55,000 bottles**
HECTARES UNDER VINE **11**
VITICULTURE METHOD **Conventional**

The Pardi cellar is just below the walls encircling the town of Montefalco. The family has strong connections to the town and to its most valuable products: textiles and wine. For this reason the Pardi brothers decided some time ago to reconnect with the past, resuming the successful winemaking activities started in the early 20th century by their great grandparents, who even supplied wines to the Vatican. Today, the wines have a certain elegance and are more easy-drinking than id usual in this area.

The extreme warmth of the '07 vintage is strongly felt in the winery's reds, boosting the body, alcohol and aromatic characteristics of the wines. The Sagrantino has a vigorous fruity-floweriness, further enriched by the toasty notes given by the wood, and the Montefalco Rosso '08 has even more intense aromas, with overtones of dark fruit, pomegranate syrup and crushed flowers. The Montefalco Sagrantino Passito '07 is unsurprisingly splendid, with hints of chocolate and mint. The tangy Montefalco Bianco Colle di Giove '09, with notes of iodine, is excellent.

○ Montefalco Bianco Colle di Giove '09	▼▼	3
● Montefalco Sagrantino '07	▼▼	6
● Montefalco Sagrantino Passito '07	▼▼	6
● Montefalco Rosso '08	▼	4
● Montefalco Rosso '07	▽▽	4*
● Montefalco Rosso '06	▽▽	4*
● Montefalco Rosso '05	▽▽	4
● Montefalco Sagrantino '06	▽▽	6
● Montefalco Sagrantino '05	▽▽	6
● Montefalco Sagrantino '04	▽▽	6
● Montefalco Sagrantino '03	▽▽	6
● Montefalco Sagrantino Passito '03	▽▽	6
● Rosso di Montefalco '04	▽▽	4
● Rosso di Montefalco '03	▽▽	4*

Perticaia

via E. Cattaneo, 39
06035 Montefalco [PG]
tel. 0742379014
www.perticaia.it

CELLAR SALES
PRE-BOOKED VISITS

ANNUAL PRODUCTION 100,000 bottles
HECTARES UNDER VINE 15
VITICULTURE METHOD Conventional

Perticaia is an ancient word meaning "plough" and is linked to peasant culture. It is also the name of the winery near Montefalco owned by Guido Guardigli, a clear-headed and dedicated figure who supported the development in quality of Italian agriculture on many fronts. The cellar and vineyards are in the district of Casale, on soils containing medium-sized stones. The wines are flawless, and the Sagrantino is one of the finest in circulation.

The '07 harvest gifted this imposing red with a dash of extra body and power. Perticaia knows how to manage these qualities to perfection, producing a wine with elegant aromas of black berry fruit and spices, and a deep, supple palate. It may require slightly more time than usual before being opened. The new entry Montefalco Rosso Riserva '07 gave a great performance and, despite having aromas of reduction, it is spectacular on the palate. The Trebbiano Spoletino '09 is tempting and brilliant, and so is the Rosso '09, from sangiovese, colorino and merlot.

● Montefalco Sagrantino '07	▼▼▼	6
● Montefalco Rosso Ris. '07	▼▼	6
○ Trebbiano Spoletino '09	▼▼	4
● Umbria Rosso '09	▼	3
● Montefalco Sagrantino '06	▽▽▽	6
● Montefalco Sagrantino '05	▽▽▽	6
● Montefalco Sagrantino '04	▽▽▽	6
● Montefalco Rosso '07	▽▽	4*
● Montefalco Rosso '06	▽▽	4*
● Montefalco Rosso '05	▽▽	4
● Montefalco Rosso '04	▽▽	4
● Montefalco Sagrantino '03	▽▽	6
● Montefalco Sagrantino '01	▽▽	6
○ Trebbiano Spoletino '08	▽▽	4*
○ Trebbiano Spoletino '07	▽▽	4*

Pucciarella

loc. Villa di Magione
06063 Magione [PG]
tel. 0758409147
www.pucciarella.it

ANNUAL PRODUCTION 130,000 bottles
HECTARES UNDER VINE 50
VITICULTURE METHOD Conventional

Pucciarella is now one of the most interesting wineries in the Trasimeno zone. The cellar skilfully interprets both the wines of the area's traditional designations and others that are more modern and innovative. It starts in the vineyards, at Magione and Corciano, where the soils are full of stones and the average altitude is above 300 metres. Owned by the Cariplo Bank pension fund, it is one of the wineries of the area that has shown positive growth in recent years.

Best of the year goes to the fantastic Chardonnay Arsiccio '08, where yellow-fleshed fruit interacts with wood and the alluring palate is enriched by hints of stone but the finish is too alcoholic. The Agnolo '09 is very good, showing delicately aromatic with a fleshy palate and a sage-like finish. From the reds, the Bordeaux Empireo '08 has overtones of bitter chocolate, the mouth is dense but rather clenched, and the Berlingero '09 from sangiovese, merlot and gamay grapes, is uncomplicated and tasty. The classic-method Classico Ca' de Sass '07, from chardonnay grapes, is fragrant and the Vin Santo '06 is good.

○ Arsiccio '08	▼▼	4
○ C. del Trasimeno Bianco Agnolo '09	▼▼	4*
● C. del Trasimeno Rosso Berlingero '09	▼▼	4
○ C. del Trasimeno Vin Santo '06	▼▼	4
○ Ca' de Sass '07	▼▼	4
● Empireo '08	▼▼	4*
○ Arsiccio '07	▽▽	4*
○ C. del Trasimeno Bianco Agnolo '08	▽▽	4*
○ C. del Trasimeno Bianco Agnolo '07	▽▽	4*
● C. del Trasimeno Rosso Berlingero '05	▽▽	4
● C. del Trasimeno Rosso Sant'Anna Ris. '06	▽▽	5
○ C. del Trasimeno Vin Santo Eletto '04	▽▽	4*
○ Chardonnay Arsiccio '06	▽▽	4
● Empireo '07	▽▽	4*
● Empireo '06	▽▽	4*
● Empireo '05	▽▽	4*

Roccafiore

FRAZ. CHIOANO
LOC. COLLINA
06059 TODI [PG]
TEL. 0758942416
www.roccafiore.it

CELLAR SALES
PRE-BOOKED VISITS
ROOMS AND FOOD

ANNUAL PRODUCTION **80,000 bottles**
HECTARES UNDER VINE **13**
VITICULTURE METHOD **Organic**

The Baccarelli family owns Roccafiore, a young winery whose wines year by year acquire a stronger identity and personality. The vineyards are managed using organic growing methods and extend over the hills around Todi, on clay and sand soils. The virtually new cellar was designed constructed with skill and attention to every detail. At the moment, the whites are more successful while the reds still have to find a clearly defined style.

Fiordaliso '09, from grechetto and trebbiano spoletino, is a splendid wine with expressive appeal centred around its brilliant, fresh drinkability and a certain aromatic complexity. We loved the Fiorfiore '08, a delicate yet complex Grechetto di Todi with an enthralling weave, good flavour and personality that elegantly alternates aromas of soft toffee, nuances of honey and aromatic herbs. The Passito Collina d'Oro '07 is good.

○ Colli Martani Grechetto di Todi Fiorfiore '08	TT	4
○ Collina d'Oro Passito '07	TT	5
○ Fiordaliso '09	TT	3
● Roccafiore Rosso '08	T	4
○ Colli Martani Grechetto di Todi Fiorfiore '07	YY	4*
○ Fiordaliso '08	YY	3*

Scacciadiavoli

LOC. CANTINONE, 31
06036 MONTEFALCO [PG]
TEL. 0742371210
scacciadiavoli@tin.it

CELLAR SALES
PRE-BOOKED VISITS

ANNUAL PRODUCTION **200,000 bottles**
HECTARES UNDER VINE **32**
VITICULTURE METHOD **Conventional**

Scacciadiavoli, bought by the Panbuffetti family in the early 1950s, is one of the most beautiful estates in the region, with a marvellous cellar, a rare example of farm industry architecture built by Principe Ludovisi Boncompagni in the 19th century. The vineyards are on many hilly slopes around Montefalco, Gualdo Cattaneo and Giano at an altitude of about 400 metres on mainly clayey soils.

The Montefalco Sagrantino '07 needs to age in bottle a few more years so we didn't taste it. We did, however, taste the Montefalco '08 and found it largely positive. This red has a mature profile, showing intense, fruity aromas and flashes of slightly grassy tones. The palate gives similar sensations, showing full and sound, with a finish of lovely tannins and hints of crushed herbs. The Brut '07, from sagrantino and chardonnay, is very good, with fine citrussy aromas and hints of yeast and white peach followed by a harmonious, deep palate. The delicate, fresh Grechetto '09 is not bad, with nuances of yellow-fleshed fruit and mint, and a bittery finish.

○ Grechetto '09	TT	3
● Montefalco Rosso '08	TT	4
○ Spumante Brut '07	TT	4
● Montefalco Rosso '05	YY	4
● Montefalco Rosso '00	YY	4
● Montefalco Sagrantino '06	YY	6
● Montefalco Sagrantino '05	YY	6
● Montefalco Sagrantino '04	YY	6
● Montefalco Sagrantino '03	YY	6
● Montefalco Sagrantino '01	YY	6
● Montefalco Sagrantino Passito '06	YY	6
● Montefalco Sagrantino Passito '05	YY	6
● Montefalco Sagrantino Passito '03	YY	6
● Montefalco Sagrantino Passito '01	YY	6

Sportoletti

loc. Capitan Loreto
via Lombardia, 1
06038 Spello [PG]
tel. 0742651461
www.sportoletti.com

CELLAR SALES
PRE-BOOKED VISITS

ANNUAL PRODUCTION 233,000 bottles
HECTARES UNDER VINE 30
VITICULTURE METHOD Conventional

There can be little doubt that the winery owned by the Sportoletti brothers is the best place to taste Assisi DOC wines. The aim is for the world famous Assisi name to become known in the wine world, too. This cellar presses on with these and with other red and white IGT wines, renewing, and in some ways transforming, the concept of quality wine on the lovely Spello hills, introducing international varieties such as merlot, cabernet and chardonnay.

The Villa Fidelia Rosso '08, from merlot, cabernet sauvignon and franc aged for one year in barrique, is, as usual, the cellar's best red, although it is duller than other years. The aromas are mature and tertiary while the palate is less vibrant, albeit totally gratifying in its balance. Villa Fidelia Bianco '08 is more successful this time. Made from grechetto and chardonnay with the customary barrique ageing, it shows aromas of camomile and yellow flowers and has a relaxed, fluid, decidedly savoury palate. The intensely fruity Grechetto '09 and the Assisi Rosso '09, from sangiovese merlot and cabernet, are less reliable.

● Villa Fidelia Rosso '08	**YY**	6
○ Assisi Grechetto '09	**YY**	3
● Assisi Rosso '09	**YY**	4
○ Villa Fidelia Bianco '08	**YY**	4
○ Assisi Grechetto '07	YY	3*
○ Assisi Grechetto '04	YY	3*
● Assisi Rosso '08	YY	4*
○ Villa Fidelia Bianco '06	YY	4*
○ Villa Fidelia Bianco '05	YY	4
● Villa Fidelia Rosso '07	YY	6
● Villa Fidelia Rosso '06	YY	6
● Villa Fidelia Rosso '05	YY	6
● Villa Fidelia Rosso '04	YY	6
● Villa Fidelia Rosso '00	YY	7
● Villa Fidelia Rosso '99	YY	6

Giampaolo Tabarrini

fraz. Turrita
06036 Montefalco [PG]
tel. 0742379351
www.tabarrini.com

CELLAR SALES
PRE-BOOKED VISITS

ANNUAL PRODUCTION 70,000 bottles
HECTARES UNDER VINE 11
VITICULTURE METHOD Conventional

Giampaolo Tabarrini is one of the most original, brilliant winemakers in Umbria. He gets the best out of his grapes, thanks to his philosophy of clear, focused wines with no compromises. His vineyards are cultivated with obsessive care and the fruit is sometimes vinified and bottled separately, generating a large number of wines from the different crus. All are very different from each other, yet all have a certain richness and ripeness of fruit.

There may be small imbalances but there are also authentic masterpieces. One is the Sagrantino Colle Grimaldesco '06, which at last has achieved exceptional results. Amazingly complex aromas accompany good body and precisely extracted tannins. It is still very young and will excite at future tastings. Adarmando from trebbiano spoletino is just as good, unleashing a masterly set of aromas in this '08 edition where ripe tones of mango and tropical fruit mix with fresh notes of citron peel as lovely acidity melds with mineral sensations. The Montefalco Sagrantino Campo alla Cerqua '06, aged only in large barrels, is good, yet below expectations.

● Montefalco Sagrantino Colle Grimaldesco '06	**YYY**	6
○ Adarmando '08	**YY**	5
● Montefalco Sagrantino Campo alla Cerqua '06	**YY**	7
● Montefalco Rosso '08	**YY**	4
○ Adarmando '07	YYY	5*
● Montefalco Sagrantino Colle Grimaldesco '01	YYY	6
○ Adarmando '06	YY	4*
● Montefalco Sagrantino Colle alle Macchie '04	YY	8
● Montefalco Sagrantino Colle alle Macchie '03	YY	8
● Montefalco Sagrantino Colle Grimaldesco '05	YY	6
● Montefalco Sagrantino Colle Grimaldesco '04	YY	6
● Montefalco Sagrantino Colle Grimaldesco '03	YY	6
● Montefalco Sagrantino Colle Grimaldesco '02	YY	6

Terre de La Custodia

LOC. PALOMBARA
06035 GUALDO CATTANEO [PG]
TEL. 074292951
www.terredelacustodia.it

CELLAR SALES
PRE-BOOKED VISITS

ANNUAL PRODUCTION **1,000,000 bottles**
HECTARES UNDER VINE **118**
VITICULTURE METHOD **Conventional**

The Farchionis are thoroughbred entrepreneurs in food farming with a clear bent for olive oil production. In just in a short period, they have also created an interesting winemaking operation. Terre de La Custodia boasts a beautiful, brand new cellar in the town of Gualdo Cattaneo with vineyards located both here and at Montefalco and Todi, where most of the white grape varieties are grown. All the wines are coherent and technically flawless.

This year the novelty is the Brut Rosé '08. From sangiovese grapes, it has enthralling aromas of rose, medlar and light citrus notes, while in the mouth its fine, tasty sparkle follows through to a refreshing finish. The Montefalco Sagrantino '07 is excellent, showing intensely fruity with hints of tar and forest floor, and has a limpid palate and dense, focused tannins. Among the whites, we were impressed by the fine, deep Grechetto Plentis '08 and the Grechetto '09 with its full flavours. One notch below are the Montefalco Rosso '08 and the Collezione '09, from sangiovese, sagrantino and merlot.

⊙ Brut Rosé '08	🍷🍷	6
○ Colli Martani Grechetto '09	🍷🍷	4
○ Colli Martani Grechetto Plentis '08	🍷🍷	4
● Montefalco Sagrantino '07	🍷🍷	7
● Colli Martani Collezione '09	🍷	4
● Montefalco Rosso '08	🍷	5
● Collezione '05	YY	3*
○ Colli Martani Grechetto '07	YY	4*
○ Colli Martani Grechetto Plentis '05	YY	3*
● Montefalco Rosso '05	YY	4*
● Montefalco Sagrantino '06	YY	6
● Montefalco Sagrantino '05	YY	6
● Montefalco Sagrantino '04	YY	8
● Montefalco Sagrantino Exubera '05	YY	8
● Montefalco Sagrantino Exubera '04	YY	7
● Montefalco Sagrantino Exubera '03	YY	7
● Montefalco Sagrantino Passito Melanto '04	YY	7

Tiburzi

Z. A. PIETRAUTA
06036 MONTEFALCO [PG]
TEL. 0742379864
www.tiburzicantine.com

CELLAR SALES
PRE-BOOKED VISITS

ANNUAL PRODUCTION **70,000 bottles**
HECTARES UNDER VINE **8**
VITICULTURE METHOD **Conventional**

Tiburzi alternates convincing performances with other much less successful results, yet, when things work out, their wines are some of the best-made and most distinctive in the area. The cellar is very near to Montefalco while the vineyards cover an area of eight hectares, at the significant average altitude of about 450 metres above sea level. The house reds all have an assertive attack and they also have depth of taste and delightfully modulated aromatics.

The Montefalco Sagrantino Taccalite '06 is a jewel. Initially uncertain on the nose, it opens out confidently with overtones of coffee, veal liver, dark fruit and sensations of blood-rich meat. The palate is the best part, however. It attacks with fullness and then unbends with conviction, becoming light and graceful, following through to resolved, flavoursome tannins with delicious minerally glints and a clean freshness. The Maloperro '08, from sagrantino, tannat, merlot and sangiovese is amazing, with its unusual name and blend as well as solid progression focused on shades of mulberry and blueberry.

● Montefalco Sagrantino Taccalite '06	🍷🍷	6
● Maloperro '08	🍷🍷	5
○ Brigante '09	🍷	3
● Montefalco Sagrantino Taccalite '07	YY	6
● Montefalco Sagrantino Taccalite '04	YY	6
● Montefalco Sagrantino Taccalite '02	YY	6
● Montefalco Sagrantino Taccalite '01	YY	6
● Montefalco Santambrà '07	YY	4*
● Rosso Colle Scancellato '06	YY	3*

Todini

FRAZ. ROSCETO
VIA COLLINA, 29
06059 TODI [PG]
TEL. 075887122
www.cantinafrancotodini.com

CELLAR SALES
PRE-BOOKED VISITS
ROOMS AND FOOD

ANNUAL PRODUCTION **300,000 bottles**
HECTARES UNDER VINE **70**
VITICULTURE METHOD **Conventional**

The Todini family winery is a complex operation with many hectares of land. Most is planted to seed crops but a large part is under vine, there's a brand-new, functional cellar and an elegant hotel and restaurant. It is in the Collevalenza district, a stone's throw from Todi, in the centre of the Colli Martani DOC. Grechetto is grown here, together with many other varieties, reflecting the modern, dynamic nature of the estate.

Bianco del Cavaliere is a wine that extols the principle grape of the terroir. It is a monovarietal grechetto and the '09 is fascinating, full of complex, fruity sensations, bursting with yellow apple fragrances and lovely hints of sage-led aromatic herbs. The palate is fleshy, intense and full of vitality. Nero della Cervara '08 is just below expectations. A blend of cabernet franc, merlot and petit verdot, it gives muzzy aromas with invasive toasty notes and prominent tannins. These traits are repeated in the Rubro '08, a sangiovese that is still hard to read and masked by the wood it aged in.

○ Colli Martani Grechetto di Todi Bianco del Cavaliere '09	▼▼	4
● Nero della Cervara '08	▼▼	6
● Colli Martani Sangiovese Rubro '08	▼	5
○ Colli Martani Grechetto di Todi '05	▽▽	4*
○ Colli Martani Grechetto di Todi Bianco del Cavaliere '08	▽▽	4*
○ Colli Martani Grechetto di Todi Bianco del Cavaliere '07	▽▽	4*
○ Colli Martani Grechetto di Todi Bianco della Cervara '06	▽▽	4*
● Colli Martani Sangiovese Rubro '06	▽▽	5
● Colli Martani Sangiovese Rubro '04	▽▽	5
● Nero della Cervara '07	▽▽	6
● Nero della Cervara '05	▽▽	6
● Nero della Cervara '04	▽▽	6
● Nero della Cervara '03	▽▽	6

Tudernum

LOC. PIAN DI PORTO, 146
06059 TODI [PG]
TEL. 0758989403
www.tudernum.it

CELLAR SALES
PRE-BOOKED VISITS

ANNUAL PRODUCTION **1,600,000 bottles**
HECTARES UNDER VINE **7**
VITICULTURE METHOD **Conventional**

Tudernum is a leading Umbrian co-operative, ideal for those who are looking for well-made wines with personality and a good price-quality ratio. They can be found among the estate's traditional wines, including Grechetto di Todi and Montefalco Sagrantino, as many member-growers have good plots in the Montefalco area, and also among wines from international varieties, often vinified separately and with an impeccable clarity of style that unveils plenty of pleasant surprises.

Good news from the '07 vintage of Montefalco Sagrantino, one of the most convincing in its category, with a dark aromatic profile and clear hints of blackberry, pepper and salsify. The two '09 Grechettos are just as interesting, showing original and true to type. The basic version has great energy and skin tannins framed by intriguing rocky sensations and hints of aniseed. The Colle Nobile has character and a generous, ripe fruit, staying easy-drinking and fresh. The stiff, crunchy Rojano '07, from sangiovese, merlot and sagrantino is very good.

● Montefalco Sagrantino '07	▼▼	6
● Cabernet Sauvignon '09	▼▼	3
○ Colli Martani Grechetto di Todi '09	▼▼	3
○ Colli Martani Grechetto di Todi Colle Nobile '09	▼▼	4
● Rojano '07	▼▼	4
○ Colli Martani Bianco '09	▼	2
● Colli Martani Sangiovese '09	▼	3
● Merlot '09	▼	3
● Montefalco Rosso '08	▼	5
○ Colli Martani Grechetto di Todi Colle Nobile '08	▽▽	4*
● Merlot '08	▽▽	3*
● Merlot '07	▽▽	3*
● Montefalco Sagrantino Tudernum '06	▽▽	6
● Rojano '06	▽▽	4

Tenuta Le Velette

FRAZ. CANALE DI ORVIETO
LOC. LE VELETTE, 23
05019 ORVIETO [TR]
TEL. 076329090
www.levelette.it

CELLAR SALES
PRE-BOOKED VISITS

ANNUAL PRODUCTION 400,000 bottles
HECTARES UNDER VINE 109
VITICULTURE METHOD Conventional

Ensconced on the lovely plateau facing the rock of Orvieto, at the heart of the classic designations, Velette unites local tradition, the characteristics of the terroir and a dynamic approach. Work done by the Etruscans, the Romans and the Premonstratensian canons, who extended the cellars dug into the tufaceous rock, was continued by the noble Negronis and, from the mid 19th century, by the Felici family, ancestors of the current owners, Corrado and Cecilia Bottai.

The range includes the merlot-only Gaudio '07 with caressing aromas of black berry fruits, lavender, chocolate and toastiness. Its full, fleshy palate holds together well but it is slightly held back, the extract in particular, by still marked tones of wood and coffee. The Rosso di Spicca '09 is very good, foregrounding sensations of redcurrant, and the palate is crisp and tasty. Excellent among the '09 whites are the full-bodied, grapey Grechetto Sole Uve, the Lunato, with aromas of meadow grasses and flint, and the more aromatic, citrus-rich Berganorio.

● Gaudio '07	🍷🍷	5
○ Orvieto Cl. Sup. Lunato '09	🍷🍷	4
● Rosso Orvietano Rosso di Spicca '09	🍷🍷	3
○ Sole Uve '09	🍷🍷	4
○ Orvieto Cl. Berganorio '09	🍷	3
● Calanco '03	YYY	5
● Calanco '95	YYY	5
● Gaudio '03	YYY	5
● Accordo '06	YY	4*
● Accordo '05	YY	4*
● Calanco '05	YY	5*
● Calanco '01	YY	5
● Gaudio '05	YY	5
● Gaudio '04	YY	5
● Gaudio '01	YY	5
○ Orvieto Cl. Berganorio '08	YY	3*
○ Orvieto Cl. Sup. Lunato '08	YY	4*

Villa Mongalli

LOC. CAPPUCCINI
06031 BEVAGNA [PG]
TEL. 3485110506
www.villamongalli.com

ANNUAL PRODUCTION 70,000 bottles
HECTARES UNDER VINE 15
VITICULTURE METHOD Conventional

Villa Mongalli takes its name from a historic residence in the long-established park near the cellar which, although it is only a few years old, is a leading producer of Montefalco wines. It was founded by the Menghini family and boasts some of the best land in the district. There are 15 hectares under vine, at an average altitude of 370 metres, on light, warm, permeable, pebble and clay soils. Wines are aged in barrique and large barrels and all have a natural elegance.

The Montefalco Sagrantino Della Cima '06, which comes from the highest part of a vineyard near the winery, is an extraordinary red of complexity and finesse. Its aromas evoke black cherry, cedarwood and Mediterranean scrubland, leading to a flavoursome palate veined with Virginia tobacco while a hint of blood-red meat and delicious earthy tannins give it an extra touch of personality and weight. The Sagrantino Col Cimino '07 is wonderful, presenting more fluid and supple, yet still quite full bodied.

● Montefalco Sagrantino Della Cima '06	🍷🍷🍷	7
● Montefalco Sagrantino Col Cimino '07	🍷🍷	4
● Montefalco Rosso Le Grazie '08	🍷🍷	4
● Montefalco Sagrantino Pozzo del Curato '07	🍷🍷	5
● Col Cimino '06	YY	4*
● Col Cimino '05	YY	4*
● Montefalco Rosso Le Grazie '06	YY	4*
● Montefalco Rosso Le Grazie '04	YY	4*
● Montefalco Sagrantino Della Cima '05	YY	7
● Montefalco Sagrantino Della Cima '04	YY	7
● Montefalco Sagrantino Pozzo del Curato '07	YY	5
● Montefalco Sagrantino Pozzo del Curato '06	YY	5
● Montefalco Sagrantino Pozzo del Curato '05	YY	5
● Montefalco Sagrantino Pozzo del Curato '04	YY	5

Castello di Corbara

LOC. CORBARA, 7
05018 ORVIETO [TR]
TEL. 0763304035
www.castellodicorbara.it

The castle at Corbara gives its name to the winery. The property is impressive with 100 hectares under vine at altitudes between 100 and 350 metres in a splendid setting. The stand-out wine is Merlot De Coronis '07, an intense, crisp wine with a fruit-veined structure.

● Lago di Corbara Merlot De Coronis '07	🍷🍷	5
● Lago di Corbara Rosso '08	🍷🍷	5
○ Grechetto Podere Il Caio '09	🍷	3
○ Orzalume '08	🍷	4

Chiorri

LOC. SANT'ENEA
VIA TODI, 100
06132 PERUGIA
TEL. 075607141
www.chiorri.it

In the hills around Perugia, on a splendid terrace overlooking the valley, the Mariotti family lovingly runs the Chiorri winery. The wines are all good, well typed and have kept the traditional character that made them special for years. The Grechetto '09 is extremely well made.

○ Grechetto '09	🍷🍷	3*
● Vero Amore '08	🍷🍷	6
⊙ Colli Perugini Rosato '09	🍷	3
● Colli Perugini Rosso '08	🍷	4

Cirulli

SP DELLA SALA N. 6
05016 FICULLE [TR]
TEL. 0763324301
www.cirulliviticoltore.com

The Cirulli winery at Ficulle made a fine Guide debut. Its best wines are the 1861 San Valentino '08, a cabernet and merlot blend with enjoyably balsamic and ripe fruity overtones, and the Ritorto '09, from grechetto plus chardonnay, a lovely, deep wine, full of savouriness and freshness.

● 1861 San Valentino '08	🍷🍷	6
○ Ritorto '09	🍷🍷	6
○ Eliana '09	🍷	5
● Hedone Rosso '09	🍷	4

Collecapretta

LOC. TERZO LA PIEVE, 70
06049 SPOLETO [PG]
TEL. 0743268529
vittoriomattiolicollecapretta@yahoo.it

The Mattioli family's small cellar and vineyards stand in a unique setting on breathtakingly beautiful hills at altitudes from 400 to 550 metres. Their traditional approach has produced a stunning Trebbiano Spoletino Vigna Vecchia '08, with fascinating minerality, a savoury palate and deep acidity.

○ Vigna Vecchia '08	🍷🍷	4

Cantina Dionigi

VOC. MADONNA DELLA PIA, 92
06031 BEVAGNA [PG]
TEL. 0742360395
www.cantinadionigi.it

Roberto Dionigi owns one of the small traditional wineries in the area, making authentic, great-drinking wines, despite sometimes not being perfect. They are down-to-earth wines, some of them splendid like the fresh, crisp Grechetto '09 Vigna del Brillo and the vanillaed, tannin-rich Colle Sorragami '09.

○ Colli Martani Grechetto Colle Sorrogami '09	🍷🍷	5
○ Colli Martani Grechetto V. del Brillo '09	🍷🍷	4
● Merlot Passito Civico 92	🍷🍷	5
● Montefalco Rosso '08	🍷	4

Fanini

LOC. PETRIGNANO DEL LAGO
VOC. I CUCCHI
06070 CASTIGLIONE DEL LAGO [PG]
TEL. 0759528116
www.cantinafanini.it

Founded in 1972, the Fanini cellar is near Lake Trasimeno and the Tuscan borders. The whites are their best wines. The Chardonnay Robbiano '08, aged in barrique, is convincing, presenting intense, powerful and warm with fruity, toasty overtones. Equally pleasing is the Pinot Bianco Albello del Lago '09.

○ Chardonnay Robbiano '08	🍷🍷	4
○ C. del Trasimeno Bianco Albello del Lago '09	🍷	4

Cantina La Spina

FRAZ. SPINA
VIA EMILIO ALESSANDRINI, 1
06055 MARSCIANO [PG]
TEL. 0758738120
www.cantinalaspina.it

La Spina, near the village of the same name at Marsciano, is a small winery greatly esteemed in the region, and rightly so, as it releases genuine wines with distinctive flavour and style. The Rosso Spina '08, a fine, elegant Montepulciano, is again the best.

- ● Merlato '09 🍷🍷 3
- ● Rosso Spina '08 🍷🍷 5
- ● Cimaàlta '09 🍷 3
- ● Polimante '08 🍷 5

Madonna Alta

LOC. PIETRAUTA
VIA LUDOVICO ARIOSTO, 37
06036 MONTEFALCO [PG]
TEL. 0742356371
www.madonnalta.it

This winery near Montefalco belongs to the Ferraro family from Naples and often produces well-made wines, even though the style is currently changing towards generous, rounded fruit. The wines are always pleasant, beginning with the delightfully tasty Sagrantino '07.

- ● Montefalco Sagrantino '07 🍷🍷 6
- ○ Colli Martani Grechetto '09 🍷 4
- ● Falconero Rosso '09 🍷 4
- ● Montefalco Rosso '08 🍷 5

Madonna del Latte

LOC. SUGANO, 11
05018 ORVIETO [TR]
TEL. 0763217760
www.madonnadellatte.it

After travelling round Italy in search of the best wines and restaurants, Manuela Zardo and Hellmuth Zwecker set up their own wine project near Orvieto, on sand and limestone soil at over 400 metres above sea level. Wines come from non-native grapes such as viognier, cabernet sauvignon and franc.

- ● Sucano '08 🍷 6
- ○ Viognier '09 🍷 4

Monte Vibiano

LOC. MONTE VIBIANO VECCHIO DI MERCATELLO
VIA VITTORIO VENETO, 4
06072 MARSCIANO [PG]
TEL. 0758783386
www.montevibiano.it

The charming Monte Vibiano winery is putting in place a worthy project for zero carbon dioxide emissions, the outcome of a green revolution. Sadly, the wines are less original. Impeccably made and sometimes delicious they may be, but we expected more from this estate.

- ● Colli Perugini Rosso L'Andrea '06 🍷 6
- ● Colli Perugini Rosso Monvì '06 🍷 4
- ● Villa Monte Vibiano Rosso '08 🍷 2

Peppucci

LOC. SANT'ANTIMO
FRAZ. PETRORO, 4
06059 TODI [PG]
TEL. 0758947253
www.cantinapeppucci.com

The view of Todi is not the only reason why we like the Peppucci's new operation. The wines are flawless, despite being rather warm and mature. We like the relaxed Petroro 4 '09, from sangiovese, merlot and cabernet, and the new, finely textured Giovanni '08, a Merlot-heavy blend with Cabernet.

- ● Giovanni '08 🍷🍷 5
- ● Petroro 4 '09 🍷🍷 4*
- ● Alter Ego '07 🍷 6
- ○ Colli Martani Grechetto di Todi Montorsolo '08 🍷 4

Tenuta Poggio del Lupo

VOC. BUZZAGHETTO, 100
05011 ALLERONA [TR]
TEL. 0763628350
www.tenutapoggiodellupo.it

Every year Poggio del Lupo, owned by the Palato family, churns out successful, very well-made wines, with enviable consistency. The Silentis '07 is splendid. This monovarietal Montepulciano has a fascinating spicy progression and the meaty palate is controlled and deep, with no tannic burr.

- ○ Orvieto Novilunio '09 🍷🍷 3*
- ● Rosso Silentis '07 🍷🍷 5
- ○ Màrneo '09 🍷 4

Rocca di Fabbri

LOC. FABBRI
06036 MONTEFALCO [PG]
TEL. 0742399379
www.roccadifabbri.com

This was a below-par year for the wines from the well-established Rocca di Fabbri winery run by the Vitali sisters. The Sagrantino '07 has aromas of cherry and pepper and clove-led spice introducing a rather clenched palate. Rosso di Montefalco '08 lacks definition.

● Montefalco Rosso '08	🍷 5
● Montefalco Sagrantino '07	🍷 7

Romanelli

LOC. COLLE SAN CLEMENTE 129 A
06036 MONTEFALCO [PG]
TEL. 3479065613
www.romanelli.se

This new winery only has seven and a half hectares under vine but lays out its stall stressing care for the environment and natural wines. The robust, flavoursome Montefalco Rosso '07 is very good, as is the Jura-esque Grechetto '08. Sagrantino '07 is less convincing.

○ Colli Martani Grechetto '08	🍷🍷 4
● Montefalco Rosso '07	🍷🍷 4
● Montefalco Sagrantino '07	🍷 6
● Predara '08	🍷 4

Ruggeri

VIA MONTEPENNINO, 5
06036 MONTEFALCO [PG]
TEL. 0742379294

This year Ruggeri, a small, exciting winery in a particularly attractive hillslope site, did not present the Sagrantino '07. We had to console ourselves with a good Sagrantino Passito '07, bursting with ripe fruit leading to a warm palate, and the equally enjoyable Montefalco Rosso '08.

● Montefalco Rosso '08	🍷🍷 4
● Montefalco Sagrantino Passito '07	🍷🍷 6

Spoletoducale - Casale Triocco

LOC. PETROGNANO, 54
06049 SPOLETO [PG]
TEL. 074356224
www.spoletoducale.it

This well-established co-operative, midway between Montefalco and Spoleto, has a large number of member-growers and many hectares under vine, often planted to intriguing local varieties, from sagrantino to trebbiano spoletino.

○ Colli Martani Grechetto '09	🍷🍷 3*
● Montefalco Rosso Casale Triocco '08	🍷 4
○ Trebbiano Spoletino '09	🍷 3

Terre Margaritelli

FRAZ. CHIUSACCIA
LOC. MIRALDUOLO
06089 TORGIANO [PG]
TEL. 0757824668
www.terremargaritelli.com

The Margaritelli family own one of the few wineries where you can find good wines from Torciano. The estate covers more than 50 hectares on a hilly site in the district of Miralduolo. It's a young, dynamic operation and is growing steadily, as you can tell from the Torgiano Rosso Mirantico '08.

● Torgiano Mirantico '08	🍷🍷 4*
○ Greco di Renabianca '09	🍷 4
● Malot '08	🍷 4
● Roccascossa '08	🍷 3

Tenuta Vitalonga

LOC. MONTIANO
05016 FICULLE [TR]
TEL. 0763836722
www.vitalonga.it

The Maravalle family has built their wine business in the municipality of Ficulle on stunning hills. The wines are modern in style and use both local and international varieties. This year, they seemed a little tired, with evolved tones and still marked by toasty sensations.

● Elcione '08	🍷 4
● Terra di Confine '08	🍷 5

LAZIO

We start with some good news. A Frascati won Three Glasses for the first time this year. We chose the deserving Poggio Le Volpi's Frascati Superiore Epos '09 to break an inexplicable duck for the most famous district of a region where white wine accounts for about 70 per cent of total production. So for the second consecutive year after Antonello Coletti Conti's Cesanese del Piglio, a new wine and a new designation took home its first Three Glasses. Not that this result changes our opinion very much with regard to Lazio's overall winemaking culture. Last year we talked about cellars who focus "less on the quest for premier quality or territoriality than on producing clean, defect-free wines". The wines we tasted this year confirmed this impression to the point that we decided to cut the number of main profiles by two and add six short profiles. We thought this was more appropriate for the many wineries who make competent wines of very decent quality but in some cases are squeezed out by producers with bigger reputations whose products fail to match their fame. As far as the various production zones are concerned, Viterbo is evolving with a series of excellent wineries flanked by the recovery of truly territorial varieties like grechetto and aleatico. Frosinone is proudly enjoying the creation of its Cesanese del Piglio DOCG and has every intention of continuing along the path to improvement. We are confident that we will be seeing some results very soon. The province of Latina confirms its impressive solidity and quality. There may not have been the decisive leap ahead that we expected from several producers but there is certainly greater awareness of the potential of the vines, and the way to go to get the best from them. Moreover, if the only Rieti winery is obviously in good health, then the vineyard scenario in the province of Rome is also holding its own, as usual. An award for a Frascati is certainly a good sign, as is the actual Frascati consortium's work to encourage the various producers to seek quality, but it is still not enough for us to be persuaded that Castelli viticulture has shrugged off the economic and quality crisis that has been dragging it down for several years. For the other award-winning wines, it is total dejà vu with Sergio Mottura's Grechetto Poggio della Costa '09 and Falesco's Montiano '08. The former confirms just what extraordinary quality can be had from grechetto, in particular from Lazio's upper Tiber valley, and the latter shows how right the Cotarella family were to use merlot in the same area.

Marco Carpineti

LOC. CAPO LE MOLE
SP VELLETRI-ANZIO, KM 14,300
04010 CORI [LT]
TEL. 069679860
www.marcocarpineti.it

CELLAR SALES
PRE-BOOKED VISITS

ANNUAL PRODUCTION 100,000 bottles
HECTARES UNDER VINE 41
VITICULTURE METHOD Certified organic

That Marco Carpineti is a brave chap is proved by his decision to apply organic management using only native varieties and, recession notwithstanding, to create a new practical cellar that looks good and has the right technology. More recently, he embarked on the acquisition of new vineyards he tends personally and which will soon be ready to boost production and meet increased demand.

The two wines that made the finals are Marco's outstandingly opulent Moro '08, which is rich in tropical fruit, citron and sage, but some seemed a little tired so we will leave it to him to explain why. The other finalist is newcomer Marco Carpineti Brut '08, an all-bellone classic method wine opening new horizons for the variety with its perlage, crusty bread aromas and refined palate, everything a good sparkler should have. Three more well-made labels are the Cori Rosso Capolemole '08, with an almost explosive but not excessive palate, its fruit and spice promising to fuse in the future, the arciprete-only Collesanti '09 and Cori Bianco Capolemole '09, both fresh and tangy.

○ Marco Carpineti Brut '08	🍷🍷	4*
○ Moro '08	🍷🍷	4*
○ Collesanti '09	🍷🍷	3*
○ Cori Bianco Capolemole '09	🍷🍷	3*
● Cori Rosso Capolemole '08	🍷🍷	3*
⊙ Os Rosae '09	🍷	4
● Tufaliccio '09	🍷	3
○ Collesanti '07	🥂🥂	3*
○ Collesanti '06	🥂🥂	4
○ Cori Bianco Capolemole '06	🥂🥂	4*
○ Cori Bianco Capolemole '05	🥂🥂	4*
● Dithyrambus '03	🥂🥂	6
○ Moro '07	🥂🥂	4*
○ Moro '06	🥂🥂	4*
○ Moro '04	🥂🥂	3*

Casale del Giglio

LOC. LE FERRIERE
S.DA CISTERNA-NETTUNO KM 13
04100 LATINA
TEL. 0692902530
www.casaledelgiglio.it

CELLAR SALES
PRE-BOOKED VISITS

ANNUAL PRODUCTION 1,200,000 bottles
HECTARES UNDER VINE 125
VITICULTURE METHOD Conventional

Few in Lazio or elsewhere can compete with the Antonio Santarelli and Paolo Tiefentalher winery for large-scale production combined with sheer quality, both in flagship and routine wines. In an era of native grape revivals, they have kept faith for over 20 years with the international varieties chosen not to be trendy but after careful trialling to promote a then little-known area that now, uncoincidentally, teems with other wineries.

The rich, refined Mater Matuta is a regular at our finals but we are pleased to report that this year it is partnered by what is possibly the best ever Madreselva '07 Bordeaux blend, while the Cabernet Sauvignon '07 confirms leadership of the monovarietals. Overall, the standard is good. Nor can we ignore the success of the whites, with the floral Antinoo '08 right back where it should be, in perfect harmony with the oak. The Petit Manseng '09 surprised us with its hints of medlar and tropical fruits and the '09 Chardonnay is one of the best in the province.

● Madreselva '07	🍷🍷	5
● Mater Matuta '07	🍷🍷	7
○ Antinoo '08	🍷🍷	4
● Cabernet Sauvignon '07	🍷🍷	5
○ Chardonnay '09	🍷🍷	4*
○ Petit Manseng '09	🍷🍷	4*
⊙ Albiola '09	🍷	3
● Merlot '08	🍷	4
● Petit Verdot '08	🍷	4
○ Satrico '09	🍷	3
○ Sauvignon '09	🍷	4
● Shiraz '08	🍷	4
○ Antinoo '04	🥂🥂	4*
● Mater Matuta '00	🥂🥂	6
● Mater Matuta '98	🥂🥂	4

Casale della Ioria

P.ZZA REGINA MARGHERITA, 1
03010 ACUTO [FR]
TEL. 077556031
www.casaledellaioria.com

CELLAR SALES
PRE-BOOKED VISITS

ANNUAL PRODUCTION 70,000 bottles
HECTARES UNDER VINE N.A.
VITICULTURE METHOD Conventional

If the Cesanese del Piglio became the first Lazio DOCG, Paolo Perinelli played his part, not just for the quality of his wines but also with his skill at finding his way through the red tape. The rest comes from devoted care of his various vineyards, all on volcanic clay substrate hillsides with planting densities of about 5,000 vines per hectare. Oenologist Roberto Mazzer is a key figure in the cellar.

The winery regains its full profile thanks to a series of excellent wines, with the flagship Torre del Piano '08 rightly getting to the finals. Cesanese expresses its character fully, even in a rustic note that in no way mars the round, well-balanced palate. The same positive rustic note is there again in the basic Campo New '07, a significant newcomer with potential, which should be watched closely. The tasty, refreshing Passerina Colle Bianco '09 remains top of the whites while praise is due for the attempt to recover the rare native olivella di Esperia variety, with satisfactory results that can only improve.

● Cesanese del Piglio Torre del Piano '08	5
● Cesanese del Piglio Casale della Ioria '08	4*
● Cesanese del Piglio Campo Nuovo '07	5
○ Colle Bianco '09	3
● L'Olivella '08	4
● Cesanese del Piglio Casale della Ioria '05	4
● Cesanese del Piglio Casale della Ioria '01	4
● Cesanese del Piglio Torre del Piano '07	5
● Cesanese del Piglio Torre del Piano '05	5
● Cesanese del Piglio Torre del Piano '03	5
● Cesanese del Piglio Torre del Piano '01	5
● Cesanese del Piglio Torre del Piano '00	5
○ Colle Bianco '07	3*

Cincinnato

VIA CORI-CISTERNA KM 2
04010 CORI [LT]
TEL. 069679380
www.cantinacincinnato.it

CELLAR SALES
PRE-BOOKED VISITS

ANNUAL PRODUCTION 300,000 bottles
HECTARES UNDER VINE 400
VITICULTURE METHOD Certified organic

Twenty years ago, it was unthinkable that in Lazio, or in central-southern Italy overall, a co-operative winery could combine large-scale production and low prices with even just average quality. Cori managed this thanks to 250 members and growers, to president Nazareno Milita and oenologist Carlo Morettini, not to mention an admirable focus on native vines now repaid with some excellent results.

To get three different wines to three consecutive finals is a feat that shows how good the range now is. This year, we chose the full, flavoursome yet elegant Cori Rosso Raverosse '07, with fruit and spices already balanced. The previous finalists also performed well: Nero Buono '07, with blueberry, red berry and cinchona notes has a liveliness that will last, and the Bellone '08 is back with its refined nose profile and generous palate. Two more drinkable still wines, the Castore '09 and Cori Bianco Illirio '09, confirm bellone as the flagship grape here. The most convincing, however, is the Brut, a long, enjoyable yet unpretentious Charmat. The other two reds are not bad.

● Cori Rosso Raverosse '07	3*
○ Bellone '08	4*
● Nero Buono '07	4*
● Arcatura '08	4
○ Brut Cincinnato Spumante	2
○ Castore '09	2
○ Cori Bianco Illirio '09	3
● Pollùce '08	2
○ Bellone '06	4*
○ Cori Bianco Illirio '08	3*
● Cori Rosso Raverosse '02	3*
● Nero Buono '06	4*
● Rosso dei Dioscuri '05	2*

Colacicchi

VIA ROMAGNANO, 2
03012 ANAGNI [FR]
TEL. 064469661
info@trimani.com

ANNUAL PRODUCTION 27,000 bottles
HECTARES UNDER VINE 6
VITICULTURE METHOD Conventional

Two hesitant years relegated this proven winery to a short profile but this season the selection was superb, maybe the best ever. So past glory has now been recovered, proving the Trimani family should stick to its strategy and that 70 years ago Luigi Colacicchi was right to blend cesanese with Bordeaux varieties. It would be sad to lose wines that are part of Lazio's oenological history.

There is no doubt this year that Torre Ercolana '06 just missed top ranking. This full, elegant wine still has plenty of tannic sinew, perfect spice and lingers long. Little brother Schiaffo '08 also made the finals with the same cesanese, cabernet and merlot blend but without the oak, and perfect nose-palate symmetry in its cherry, wild berry and tobacco notes. The wine is designed to be consumed young but will age well. Two good Romagnanos include the cesanese and merlot Rosso '07 whose tertiary aromas are kicking off nicely, with tannins and oak blending well, and a very drinkable Bianco '09 blend of native grapes and chardonnay whose intense nose verges on aromatic.

● Schiaffo '08	▼▼	5
● Torre Ercolana '06	▼▼	7
○ Romagnano Bianco '09	▼▼	5
● Romagnano Rosso '07	▼▼	5
○ Romagnano Bianco '03	▽▽	4
● Romagnano Rosso '01	▽▽	5
● Schiaffo '02	▽▽	4
● Torre Ercolana '05	▽▽	7
● Torre Ercolana '04	▽▽	7
● Torre Ercolana '03	▽▽	7
● Torre Ercolana '01	▽▽	6

Antonello Coletti Conti

VIA VITTORIO EMANUELE, 116
03012 ANAGNI [FR]
TEL. 0775728610
www.coletticonti.it

CELLAR SALES
PRE-BOOKED VISITS

ANNUAL PRODUCTION 20,000 bottles
HECTARES UNDER VINE 20
VITICULTURE METHOD Conventional

In Anagni, the Coletti Conti family history is linked to the Church and nobility, above all the Caetanis, so it is no coincidence that the family estate is called La Caetanella. Antonello works enthusiastically on his wines, which he manages personally from berry to bottle. In the heart of DOCG country, the Cesaneses are obviously the prime focus, but there is interest in other, almost experimental, varieties.

The Romanico '08 was not as good as last year's but is still the area's best pure Cesanese. It's young but caressing and full, successfully bringing out red berries, spice and strong tannins, enhanced by balsamic oak. The way forward is confirmed by Hernicus '09, a basic Cesanese with hints of myrtle, red berries and evident but clean oak. There is also an excellent Cosmato '08, from cesanese and Bordeaux varieties, with great style and nose-palate symmetry. As always a subject of discussion, Arcadia '09, an unusual Incrocio Manzoni, is exuberant, over the top alcohol included. It lacks a little balance but intrigues in its own way. Another year in the bottle, perhaps?

● Cesanese del Piglio Romanico '08	▼▼	6
● Cesanese del Piglio Hernicus '09	▼▼	4
● Cosmato '08	▼▼	6
○ Arcadia '09	▼	4
● Cesanese del Piglio Romanico '07	▽▽▽	6
○ Arcadia '07	▽▽	4
● Cesanese del Piglio Hernicus '07	▽▽	4
● Cesanese del Piglio Hernicus '06	▽▽	4*
● Cesanese del Piglio Hernicus '05	▽▽	4
● Cesanese del Piglio Hernicus '04	▽▽	4
● Cesanese del Piglio Romanico '06	▽▽	6
● Cesanese del Piglio Romanico '05	▽▽	6
● Cosmato '03	▽▽	6

Colle Picchioni Paola Di Mauro

LOC. FRATTOCCHIE
VIA COLLE PICCHIONE, 46
00040 MARINO [RM]
TEL. 0693546329
www.collepicchioni.it

CELLAR SALES
PRE-BOOKED VISITS

ANNUAL PRODUCTION 100,000 bottles
HECTARES UNDER VINE 18
VITICULTURE METHOD Organic

The Di Mauro family winery is just outside Rome on the Via Appia to Marino, near Castel Gandolfo. It opened in 1976 and was run first by Paola and her son Armando, now joined by grandson Valerio. Despite producing small amounts, the winery is a quality icon in the Castelli Romani and the entire region, beginning with its various Marinos and its most famous product, the Vassallo Bordeaux blend.

Even in a tough year like 2008, Vassallo is again one of Lazio's best reds. It is a blend of 60 per cent merlot, 30 per cent cabernet sauvignon and cabernet franc, revealing aromas of red and black berries, nuanced with oriental spice, with a consistent, full, elegant palate and long finale. The well-made Marino Donna Paola '09 is full, with an aroma-led nose and good structure with pink grapefruit and almond on the palate. The rest are a little under par, with all wines well made but lacking the brilliance we are used to from this winery.

● Il Vassallo '08	▼▼	6
○ Marino Donna Paola '09	▼▼	4
● Collerosso '09	▼	3
○ Le Vignole '08	▼	5
○ Marino Coste Rotonde '09	▼	3
● Perlaia '09	▼	4
● Il Vassallo '05	▽▽▽	6
● Vigna del Vassallo '01	▽▽▽	6
● Vigna del Vassallo '00	▽▽▽	6
● Vigna del Vassallo '88	▽▽▽	5
● Vigna del Vassallo '85	▽▽▽	5
● Il Vassallo '07	▽▽	6
○ Le Vignole '07	▽▽	5
○ Le Vignole '06	▽▽	4*
○ Marino Coste Rotonde '08	▽▽	3*
○ Marino Donna Paola '08	▽▽	4
○ Marino Donna Paola '07	▽▽	4*
● Perlaia '08	▽▽	4

Paolo e Noemia D'Amico

FRAZ. VAIANO
LOC. PALOMBARO
01024 CASTIGLIONE IN TEVERINA [VT]
TEL. 0761948034
www.paoloenoemiadamico.it

CELLAR SALES
PRE-BOOKED VISITS

ANNUAL PRODUCTION 150,000 bottles
HECTARES UNDER VINE 26
VITICULTURE METHOD Conventional

Paolo and Noemia D'Amico's winery has been at the forefront of Lazio winemaking. In the heart of Tuscia, bordered by Lazio, Tuscany and Umbria, it stands over the gullies that are a main feature of this location. The enterprise is known for a series of international-style, mainly chardonnay-based, wines that have won many admirers. Most of the vineyards are on clay and limestone.

This is not the first year that we preferred the Chardonnay Calanchi di Vaiano '09, matured mainly in steel, to the barrique-conditioned Falesia '08. The former has a rich bouquet, ranging from saffron to Mediterranean scrub and citrus peel, with a rich palate of white-fleshed fruit notes but also significant acid grip. The Falesia, however, has milder tones both on the nose, with hints of butter and cinnamon, and on the consistent but not very gutsy palate. Pinot Nero Notturno dei Calanchi '08 is an interesting red whose balsamic, Peruvian bark, aromatic herb and black berry nose profile precedes a rich, full and very refreshing palate.

○ Calanchi di Vaiano '09	▼▼	4
○ Falesia '08	▼▼	5
● Notturno dei Calanchi '08	▼▼	6
● Villa Tirrena '07	▼▼	5
○ Orvieto Noe '09	▼	4
○ Seiano Bianco '09	▼	4
● Seiano Rosso '09	▼	4
○ Calanchi di Vaiano '08	▽▽	5
○ Calanchi di Vaiano '07	▽▽	5*
○ Calanchi di Vaiano '06	▽▽	4*
○ Falesia '07	▽▽	5
○ Falesia '06	▽▽	5
● Seiano Rosso '07	▽▽	4*

★ Falesco

LOC. SAN PIETRO
05020 MONTECCHIO [TR]
TEL. 07449556
www.falesco.it

CELLAR SALES
PRE-BOOKED VISITS
ROOMS

ANNUAL PRODUCTION **2,500,000 bottles**
HECTARES UNDER VINE **370**
VITICULTURE METHOD **Conventional**

This winery straddling Umbria and Lazio and owned by Renzo and Riccardo Cotarella, was founded at Montefiascone in 1979 and is renowned both in Italy and abroad. The estate's vineyards go from the hills near Lake Bolsena to those around Orvieto, on land with similar traits, the same geologic origins, in part volcanic and in part sedimentary, and similar climatic conditions. A further three hectares were bought at Gualdo Cattaneo specifically for Sagrantino di Montefalco.

This year the Montiano's '08 edition won Three Glasses for the 13th time. It's a monovarietal merlot with a full bouquet, where tones of tobacco and oriental spices combine with cherry and black berry fruit and the palate has great structure, presenting soft and fruity, with a long, complex finish. The ripe red fruity Montefalco Sagrantino 2R '07 is good, still tannic and impenetrable while Ferentano '08, a pure Roscetto, is aromatic and intense but, as always when released, still masked by oak. The standard of the wines and their excellent value for money makes Falesco one of Italy's most exciting wineries.

● Montiano '08	🍷🍷🍷+	6
○ Ferentano '08	🍷🍷	5
● Sagrantino di Montefalco 2R '07	🍷🍷	7
○ Est Est Est di Montefiascone Falesco '09	🍷🍷	2*
○ Est Est Est di Montefiascone Poggio dei Gelsi '09	🍷🍷	3*
● Pomele '09	🍷🍷	5
● Tellus '09	🍷🍷	4
● Vitiano Rosso '09	🍷🍷	4
● Marciliano '04	YYY	6
● Montiano '07	YYY	6
● Montiano '06	YYY	6
● Montiano '05	YYY	6
● Montiano '03	YYY	6
● Montiano '01	YYY	6
● Montiano '00	YYY	6
● Montiano '99	YYY	6
● Montiano '98	YYY	5
● Montiano '97	YYY	5

Fontana Candida

VIA FONTANA CANDIDA, 11
00040 MONTE PORZIO CATONE [RM]
TEL. 069401881
www.fontanacandida.it

CELLAR SALES
PRE-BOOKED VISITS
FOOD

ANNUAL PRODUCTION **5,000,000 bottles**
HECTARES UNDER VINE **97**
VITICULTURE METHOD **Conventional**

Fontana Candida, one of the most famous GIV-Gruppo Italiano Vini brands, is at Monteporzio in the heart of the Frascati designation. The vineyards are located at 200-400 metres above sea level, with typical pozzolana terrain, a volcanic ash that produces deep, mineral-rich, sandy soils. The winery processes estate-grown fruit and also works with 200 growers, supported all year round by in-house technical staff.

The Luna Mater project continues to be a success and produces one of the best Frascatis on the market. The '09 has spice and yellow-fleshed fruit aromas leading into a minerally, tangy palate, with good acid grip and a citrussy finale. The Frascati Superiore Santa Teresa '09 we tasted flaunts all the quality that has distinguished it for many years, with an aromatic, fruit-led nose, and a well-structured, refreshing and supple palate. There is a well-made Malvasia '09, with an enjoyably aromatic, varietal note. Back after a few years' absence is a tasty Kron '07 from merlot with 15 per cent sangiovese, giving crisp wild berry and tobacco notes.

○ Frascati Sup. Luna Mater '09	🍷🍷	5
○ Frascati Sup. Santa Teresa '09	🍷🍷	4*
● Kron '07	🍷🍷	5
○ Malvasia '09	🍷🍷	4*
○ Frascati Sup. Terre dei Grifi '09	🍷	3
○ Frascati Sup. Luna Mater '08	YY	5
○ Frascati Sup. Luna Mater '07	YY	6
○ Frascati Sup. Santa Teresa '07	YY	5
○ Malvasia '08	YY	4
○ Malvasia '07	YY	5

Marcella Giuliani

LOC. VICO MORICINO
VIA ANTICOLANA KM 5
03012 ANAGNI [FR]
TEL. 0644235908
www.aziendaagricolamarcellagiuliani.it

CELLAR SALES
PRE-BOOKED VISITS

ANNUAL PRODUCTION **31,000 bottles**
HECTARES UNDER VINE **10**
VITICULTURE METHOD **Certified organic**

If cesanese is now acknowledged as one of Italy's top native varieties, this is thanks to those who worked to bring it to the public eye, and have even been accused of internationalizing the grape. We feel these are merits that Marcella Giuliani and oenologist Riccardo Cotarella can be proud of. The winery continues with the project and has now converted to organic viticulture, having thoroughly modernized vineyards and cellars.

With all due respect to the flagship Dives, we would like to open with the other two reds, considered basic wines but whose quality is impressive. The drinkable, pleasing Graffio '09 from cabernet and petit verdot returns, still young but excellent, its tannins fully meshed with the oak. The Alagna '09 Cesanese also convinced us, not with might and muscle but with its crisp, lingering fruit. The Dives '08 is its usual full, intense self, the fruit still slightly veiled by the oak. Passerina Alagna Bianco '09 confirms its quality and the Rosato '09 is a real surprise. We rank it the best Lazio rosé for its freshness and strawberry and raspberry aromas.

● Cesanese del Piglio Alagna '09	TT	3*
● Cesanese del Piglio Dives '08	TT	5
● Il Graffio '09	TT	4*
⊙ Rosato Alagna '09	TT	3*
○ Alagna Bianco '09	T	3
○ Alagna Bianco '08	YY	3*
● Cesanese del Piglio Alagna '08	YY	3*
● Cesanese del Piglio Alagna '07	YY	3*
● Cesanese del Piglio Dives '07	YY	5
● Cesanese del Piglio Dives '06	YY	5
● Cesanese del Piglio Dives '05	YY	5
● Cesanese del Piglio Dives '04	YY	5
● Il Graffio '06	YY	4

Antica Cantina Leonardi

VIA DEL PINO, 12
01027 MONTEFIASCONE [VT]
TEL. 0761826028
www.cantinaleonardi.it

CELLAR SALES
PRE-BOOKED VISITS
ROOMS

ANNUAL PRODUCTION **100,000 bottles**
HECTARES UNDER VINE **37**
VITICULTURE METHOD **Certified organic**

The Leonardi family winery, founded in the early 1900s and now run by the third generation, Ugo and Maria Vittoria, confirms its recent progress. The wines are almost all from traditional vines on two estates, one 24 hectares at about 450 metres above sea level on the hills around volcanic Lake Bolsena, and the other 13 hectares in the municipality of Graffignano, on the Umbrian border.

It was one more step forward for the Leonardis, who went to the finals with an '09 Le Muffe. This singular 50-50 chardonnay and trebbiano blend gives nut and spice aromas, and a truly complex, lengthy palate with the candied apricot notes typical of noble rot. Grechetto Pensiero '09 is also delicious with white-fleshed fruit notes and good structure, as is the '09 Montefiascone Poggio del Cardinale Est Est Est with pervasive hints of aromatic herbs, tropical fruit and peach and a distinctly refreshing, enjoyable palate that shows simpler and tighter than expected. The other wines are well made.

○ Le Muffe '09	TT	5
○ Est Est Est di Montefiascone Poggio del Cardinale '09	TT	3*
○ Pensiero '09	TT	3*
● Don Carlo '07	T	4
○ Vivì '09	T	3
○ Est Est Est di Montefiascone Poggio del Cardinale '08	YY	3*
○ Le Muffe '08	YY	4
○ Pensiero '08	YY	3*
○ Pensiero '07	YY	3*

Sergio Mottura

LOC. POGGIO DELLA COSTA, 1
01020 CIVITELLA D'AGLIANO [VT]
TEL. 0761914533
www.motturasergio.it

CELLAR SALES
PRE-BOOKED VISITS
ROOMS AND FOOD

ANNUAL PRODUCTION **98,000 bottles**
HECTARES UNDER VINE **37**
VITICULTURE METHOD **Certified organic**

Sergio Mottura runs an organic winery up on the hills around Civitella d'Agliano, an area that was producing white grapes long before it was fashionable to do so. Add to this the low yield per vine, meticulous work in the cellar, respect for the typicality of grape and the territory, ongoing mass selection and the result is wines we consider to be some of the best in Italy.

Latour a Civitella was absent this year following the poor 2008 season so the Grechetto Poggio della Costa '09 stepped in to pick up Three Glasses for the second consecutive year. It has a delicate, floral nose with mineral and citrus peel nuances before the palate unfolds consistent, deep, crisp, very tangy and long. Great quality also from the Sergio Mottura Brut '05, the best version of recent years, and from a truly stylish classic-method Blanc des Blancs with aromas of crusty bread and biscuits leading into a rich, leisurely palate of flowers and white peaches. The rest of the range is tempting.

○ Grechetto Poggio della Costa '09	▼▼▼	4*
○ Sergio Mottura Brut '05	▼▼	6
○ Muffo '07	▼▼	6
● Nenfro '06	▼▼	5
○ Orvieto '09	▼▼	4
○ Orvieto V. Tragugnano '09	▼▼	4*
⊙ Civitella Rosato '09	▼	4
● Civitella Rosso '09	▼	4
○ Grechetto Latour a Civitella '06	▽▽▽	5*
○ Grechetto Latour a Civitella '05	▽▽▽	5*
○ Grechetto Latour a Civitella '04	▽▽▽	5*
○ Grechetto Latour a Civitella '01	▽▽▽	4
○ Grechetto Poggio della Costa '08	▽▽▽	4*
○ Grechetto Latour a Civitella '07	▽▽	5
○ Grechetto Poggio della Costa '07	▽▽	4*

Principe Pallavicini

VIA CASILINA KM 25,500
00030 COLONNA [RM]
TEL. 069438816
www.vinipallavicini.com

CELLAR SALES
PRE-BOOKED VISITS
FOOD

ANNUAL PRODUCTION **556,500 bottles**
HECTARES UNDER VINE **80**
VITICULTURE METHOD **Conventional**

Principe Pallavicini has been operating in Lazio since the 17th century with two estates, one in the Castelli Romani, the historic Tenuta Colonna with over 64 hectares under vine and the location of the winery's registered offices, cellars and ageing caves. The other is the Tenuta di Cerveteri in the lower Maremma, where the warm, dry site climates and very chalky, pebbly soil persuaded the winery to plant black-skinned grapes.

There is no doubt about the reliability of Principe Pallavicini wines, at least for the whites, but we admit that we were hoping for a quality leap that has not materialized. The Stillato '09, from a late harvest of malvasia puntinata is good, with acacia honey and candied apricot notes ushering in a rich, full palate with hints of fruit in syrup and marzipan. The 1670 '08 70-30 blend of malvasia puntinata and sémillon is enjoyable, with spice and floral notes, yellow-fleshed fruit and broom flowers. The same goes for the Frascati Superiore Poggio Verde '09, with jasmine on the nose and a substantial, refreshing palate. Despite various trials, the house reds have yet to shine.

○ 1670 '08	▼▼	5
○ Frascati Sup. Poggio Verde '09	▼▼	4*
○ Stillato '09	▼▼	5
● Casa Romana '07	▼	6
● Cesanese Amarasco '08	▼	5
● Moroello '07	▼	6
● Syrah '09	▼	4
○ 1670 '07	▽▽	5
○ 1670 '06	▽▽	5
● Moroello '05	▽▽	6
● Moroello '04	▽▽	6
○ Pagello '06	▽▽	4
● Soleggio '06	▽▽	4
○ Stillato '08	▽▽	5
○ Stillato '07	▽▽	5

Poggio Le Volpi

via Colle Pisano, 27
00040 Monte Porzio Catone [RM]
tel. 069426980
www.poggiolevolpi.it

CELLAR SALES
PRE-BOOKED VISITS

ANNUAL PRODUCTION **224,000 bottles**
HECTARES UNDER VINE **30**
VITICULTURE METHOD **Conventional**

Poggio Le Volpi was set up in 1996 by Felice Mergè. In under 15 years, it has established itself as one of the most interesting, dynamic Castelli Romani wineries. The desire to experiment and seek out new directions has enhanced the quality of the Monteporzio Catone vineyards, on volcanic soil at 400 metres, almost entirely planted to traditional varieties that yield wines with strong personalities.

For years, Felice Mergè's wines were a whisper away from the Three Glasses now awarded to his Superiore Epos '09, the first Frascati to gain this distinction. The full, layered bouquet has spice, oak, damson and citrus notes while the long, dynamic palate is consistent, tangy and with good acid grip. A surprising Frascati Cannellino has notes of candied apricot, saffron, nuts, and a long, refreshing palate. The well-made Baccarossa '08, from nero buono di Cori, has a very clean-cut aromatic profile; the full, quiet complex Donnaluce '09, a 60-30-10 blend of malvasia del Lazio, greco and chardonnay, has tropical fruits but not enough backbone and a sweetish finale.

○ Frascati Sup. Epos '09	▼▼▼	4*
○ Frascati Cannellino	▼▼	4*
● Baccarossa '08	▼▼	5
○ Donnaluce '09	▼▼	4
● Baccarossa '07	▽▽	5
● Baccarossa '06	▽▽	5
● Baccarossa '05	▽▽	6
○ Donnaluce '07	▽▽	4*
○ Donnaluce '06	▽▽	5
○ Frascati Sup. Epos '08	▽▽	4*
○ Frascati Sup. Epos '07	▽▽	4*
○ Frascati Sup. Epos '06	▽▽	5
○ Passito Odôs '06	▽▽	5
○ Passito Odôs '05	▽▽	4*

Sant'Andrea

loc. Borgo Vodice
via Renibbio, 1720
04010 Terracina [LT]
tel. 0773755028
www.cantinasantandrea.it

CELLAR SALES
PRE-BOOKED VISITS

ANNUAL PRODUCTION **200,000 bottles**
HECTARES UNDER VINE **70**
VITICULTURE METHOD **Conventional**

The Pandolfos can boast an adventurous past, having moved from Sicily to Tunisia, then settling in Terracina several decades ago. Here their presence is not only deep-rooted but also considered crucial for the promotion of the local moscato, first a table grape and now used for a prestigious DOC product. Sant'Andrea produces five types of Moscato di Terracina without compromising the other native vines.

Although there was no finalist to put the cherry on the cake, the winery's top bottles are excellent. Oppidum '09, an almost golden colour with precise varietal aromas is just a little heavy on the palate. Dune '08 successfully matches small wood with the aromatic malvasia grape. Finally, Il Sogno '07, a long, structured merlot and cesanese blend still has too much new oak at the moment. We were surprised, but not overly so, by the gutsy, balanced, enjoyable Templum '09 in one of its best versions ever. We also thought all three of the DOC Circeo Riflessi wines, particularly considering their price tag, while Oppidum Spumante '09 is well made, as usual.

○ Circeo Bianco Dune '08	▼▼	4*
● Circeo Rosso Il Sogno '07	▼▼	5
○ Moscato di Terracina Amabile Templum '09	▼▼	3*
○ Moscato di Terracina Secco Oppidum '09	▼▼	3*
○ Circeo Bianco Riflessi '09	▼	2
⊙ Circeo Rosato Riflessi '09	▼	2
● Circeo Rosso Riflessi '09	▼	2
○ Moscato di Terracina Secco Oppidum Spumante '09	▼	3
○ Circeo Bianco Dune '07	▽▽	4*
○ Circeo Bianco Dune '03	▽▽	4*
○ Moscato di Terracina Passito Capitolium '04	▽▽	3*
○ Moscato di Terracina Secco Oppidum '08	▽▽	3*
○ Moscato di Terracina Secco Oppidum '07	▽▽	3*

Sant'Isidoro

LOC. PORTACCIA
01016 TARQUINIA [VT]
TEL. 0766869716
www.santisidoro.net

CELLAR SALES
PRE-BOOKED VISITS

ANNUAL PRODUCTION 120,000 bottles
HECTARES UNDER VINE 57
VITICULTURE METHOD Conventional

The Palombi winery dates back to the late 1930s. Part of an 800-hectare estate on the Lazio stretch of the Maremma coast, it has 57 hectares of medium-textured clay soil mostly planted in the mid 1990s, all cordon trained and about ten kilometres from the sea between Tarquinia and Montalto di Castro. The main varieties are montepulciano, sangiovese, merlot and cabernet sauvignon for reds; trebbiano and chardonnay for whites.

With the Palombi flagship Soremidio absent, Forca di Palma '09 and Corithus '09 fly the colours in its place. The former is a 70-30 chardonnay and trebbiano toscano blend with a full bouquet of citrus, white blossom and white pepper notes, a consistent palate, good pressure and a finale of citron and tangerine peel. Corithus is half sangiovese with 30 per cent montepulciano and merlot, giving broodier notes of Peruvian bark, printer's ink and black berries followed by a palate with good texture but unexceptional dynamism. The simple, well-made Terzolo '09 is mainly cabernet sauvignon with ten per cent merlot.

● Corithus '09	TT	4*
○ Forca di Palma '09	TT	3*
● Terzolo '09	T	3
● Corithus '08	YY	4*
● Corithus '07	YY	4*
● Soremidio '07	YY	5
● Soremidio '06	YY	5
● Soremidio '05	YY	6

Trappolini

VIA DEL RIVELLINO, 65
01024 CASTIGLIONE IN TEVERINA [VT]
TEL. 0761948381
www.trappolini.com

CELLAR SALES
PRE-BOOKED VISITS

ANNUAL PRODUCTION 150,000 bottles
HECTARES UNDER VINE 25
VITICULTURE METHOD Conventional

The Trappolini family opened its winery in the early 1960s to sell unbottled wine but today has its own brand. It is now undoubtedly a key point of reference for the upper Tiber valley, offering an excellent range of wines that revolve around the area's most significant varieties, from sangiovese to grechetto and aleatico.

Trappolini wines offer very dependable quality and this year's results offer further proof. The finalist Paterno '08 is a stylish, balanced Sangiovese with cinchona and cherry notes, good fruit and nice structure. All the other wines are as reliable as ever, including Sartei '09, a tasty half-and-half blend of trebbiano and malvasia with pepper, rosemary and white peach on the nose, Cenereto '09, a montepulciano and sangiovese mix showing red berries and Mediterranean scrubland and a clean, somewhat simple but well-executed palate. Idea '09 is an Aleatico with notes of chocolate, black cherry and printer's ink followed by a full, rich palate whose sweetness is offset by acidity.

● Paterno '08	TT	4*
● Cenereto '09	TT	3*
● Idea '09	TT	4
○ Sartei '09	TT	2*
○ Brecceto '09	T	4
○ Est Est Est di Montefiascone '09	T	2
○ Orvieto '09	T	3
○ Brecceto '08	YY	4*
○ Brecceto '07	YY	4*
● Cenereto '08	YY	3*
● Cenereto '07	YY	3*
● Idea '08	YY	4
● Paterno '07	YY	4*
● Paterno '06	YY	4*
○ Sartei '08	YY	2*

Casale Cento Corvi

VIA AURELIA KM 45,500
00052 CERVETERI [RM]
TEL. 069903902
www.casalecentocorvi.com

No Giacchè as it was not yet bottled when we tasted but we liked Kantharos Bianco 09 from sauvignon with five per cent chardonnay, giving wood resin and jasmine, then a rich, iodine-veined palate with good acidity. The 60-40 merlot and syrah Kottabos Rosso '08 is well made, fruity and cinchona-edged.

○ Kantharos Bianco '09	🍷🍷	4*
● Kottabos Rosso '08	🍷	4
● Zilath Rosso '09	🍷	3

Casale Marchese

VIA DI VERMICINO, 68
00044 FRASCATI [RM]
TEL. 069408932
www.casalemarchese.it

The Frascati Superiore '09 has good floral and peach notes, and a well-structured, citrussy palate. The '08 Clemens is less complex this year but throws a lovely pineapple and stone fruit nose. Also good is the '09 Novum from merlot and cabernet sauvignon, with black cherries and cinnamon.

○ Frascati Sup. '09	🍷🍷	3
○ Clemens '08	🍷	4
● Novum '09	🍷	4

Castel de Paolis

VIA VAL DE PAOLIS
00046 GROTTAFERRATA [RM]
TEL. 069413648
www.casteldepaolis.it

This top Castelli Romani winery is under par this year. The aromatic, full-bodied Frascati Superiore '09 lacks definition while the Donna Adriana '09, a 50-40-10 blend of malvasia puntinata, viognier and sauvignon with citrus and white-fleshed fruit but lacks the expected complexity and depth.

○ Campo Vecchio Bianco '09	🍷	4
○ Donna Adriana '09	🍷	5
○ Frascati Cannellino '09	🍷	4
○ Frascati Sup. '09	🍷	4

Castello Torre in Pietra

VIA DI TORRIMPIETRA, 247
00050 FIUMICINO [RM]
TEL. 0661697070
www.castelloditorreinpietra.it

The wines from this large winery near Rome are well made and forthright. The '09 Chardonnay has generous peach notes but could be more feisty. Tarquinia Bianco '09 is floral and fluent, Syrah '08 has spice and wild berries while Tarquinia Rosato '09 is simple and appealing.

○ Chardonnay '09	🍷	3
● Syrah '08	🍷	4
○ Tarquinia Bianco '09	🍷	2
⊙ Tarquinia Rosato '09	🍷	2

Cavalieri

VIA MONTECAGNOLO, 16
00045 GENZANO DI ROMA [RM]
TEL. 069375807
www.cavalieri.it

Colli Lanuvini Superiore '09, with peach and melon notes, and a pleasing, simple citrussy palate, is the only wine from the designation in the Guide. The fruit-rich Rutilo '07, a 50-30-20 cesanese, montepulciano and cabernet sauvignon mix, has good texture. The Teresa '09 and Diomede '08 are well made.

○ Colli Lanuvini Sup. '09	🍷	2
○ Diomede '08	🍷	
● Rutilo '07	🍷	5
○ Teresa '09	🍷	3

Cantina Cerquetta

VIA DI FONTANA CANDIDA, 20
00040 MONTE PORZIO CATONE [RM]
TEL. 069424147
www.cantinacerquetta.it

The Ciuffas are back in with a good Frascati Superiore Antico Cenacolo '09, showing flowers and spice with a rich palate braced by acid backbone. Equally good is the '09 Frascati Superiore Ciuffa Style, with white-fleshed fruit, yellow blossom and saffron introducing a long, almondy finale.

○ Frascati Sup. Antico Cenacolo '09	🍷🍷	4
○ Frascati Sup. Ciuffa Style '09	🍷🍷	4

OTHER WINERIES

Damiano Ciolli
VIA DEL CORSO
00035 OLEVANO ROMANO [RM]
TEL. 069564547
www.damianociolli.it

Damiano Ciolli's wines are helping to redefine quality standards for the Cesanese di Olevano Romano designation. Cirsium '07 has toasty, tar and cherry aromas, and a mid-bodied palate with good black berry nuances and a sustained finale. The refreshing Silene '08 gives red berries.

● Cesanese di Olevano Cirsium '07	🍷🍷	5
● Cesanese di Olevano Silene '08	🍷	4

Colletonno
LOC. COLLETONNO
03012 ANAGNI [FR]
TEL. 0775769271
www.colletonno.it

This short profile is not a downgrade as standards are unchanged, with just the San Magno '08 less full and complex than usual. The youthful succulence of the Colle Ticchio '09 works well, however, as does the almond appeal of the malvasia, chardonnay and trebbiano Colle Sape '09.

● Cesanese del Piglio Colle Ticchio '09	🍷🍷	4*
● Cesanese del Piglio San Magno '08	🍷	4
○ Colle Sape '09	🍷	3

La Ferriera
LOC. ROSAMISCO
03042 ATINA [FR]
TEL. 0776610413
www.laferriera.it

Lucio Mancini's new winery now knows that a professional approach brings results. The two very different Forgiatos are equally good, with the '08 drinkable and fruity while the full Riserva '06 reveals mature spice and minerals. The Dorato '09, in contrast, has subtle, delicate floral notes.

● Atina Cabernet Forgiato '08	🍷🍷	5
● Atina Cabernet Forgiato Ris. '06	🍷🍷	5
○ Dorato '09	🍷	4

Donato Giangirolami
LOC. BORGO MONTELLO
VIA DEL CAVALIERE, 1414
04100 LATINA
TEL. 3358394890
www.donatogiangirolami.it

Donato Giangirolami has revamped his organic winery's range. We tasted a striking, well-co-ordinated Rezo '09 malvasia and grechetto blend, and a fruity Pancarpo '09 Syrah. The floral Grechetto has hints of spring, while the not too tannic, fruit-led Rubidio '09 is ready to drink.

● Pancarpo '09	🍷🍷	4
○ Rezo '09	🍷🍷	4*
○ Grechetto Bianco Propizio '09	🍷	4
● Rubidio '09	🍷	4

Gotto d'Oro
LOC. FRATTOCCHIE
VIA DEL DIVINO AMORE, 115
00040 MARINO [RM]
TEL. 0693022211
www.gottodoro.it

This large co-operative winery came up with the goods. The mid-bodied Malvasia del Lazio has a mint and aromatic herb nose, and a citron-veined, citrussy palate. The Marino Mitreo Taurus '08 is more complex, with flowers and stone fruits, but lacks crispness and has only average length.

● Castelli Romani Rosso '09	🍷	3
○ Malvasia del Lazio '09	🍷	3
○ Marino Mitreo Taurus '08	🍷	4
○ Marino Sup. '09	🍷	3

Podere Grecchi
S.DA SAMMARTINESE, 8
01100 VITERBO
TEL. 0761305671
www.poderegrecchi.com

Sergio Buzzi's recently founded cellar enters the Guide. Poggio Grecchi '09 from chardonnay and sauvignon is full and brimming with crisp citrus notes. Also good are the spring flowers '09 San Silvestro blend of grechetto and viognier and the '08 CEV Poggio Ferrone '08, with great fruit and stuffing.

○ Poggio Grecchi '09	🍷🍷	3
● CEV Poggio Ferrone '08	🍷	3
○ San Silvestro '09	🍷	2

OTHER WINERIES

Le Lase

LOC. RESANO
01028 ORTE [VT]
TEL. 0761281460
www.lelase.com

This young winery confirmed its success with a very complex incrocio Manzoni Zefiro '09 with yellow-fleshed fruits and aromatic herbs. The Goccia '09 Chardonnay with its attractive spice and the floral Semia '09 from pinot bianco, pinot grigio and chardonnay are both well made.

○ Zefiro '09	🍷🍷	4
○ Goccia '09	🍷	4
○ Semia '09	🍷	4

Isabella Mottura

LOC. RIO CHIARO, 1
01020 CIVITELLA D'AGLIANO [VT]
TEL. 3357077931
www.isabellamottura.com

Isabella Mottura's wines are noteworthy examples of the Colli Etruschi Viterbesi DOC. The delicious Violone Amadis '08 gives aromatic herbs, spices and rain-soaked earth, and a mid-bodied, fluent, fruit-led palate. The well-made Merlot Akemi '09 offers oriental spices and black berries.

● CEV Violone Amadis '08	🍷🍷	6
● CEV Merlot Akemi '09	🍷	4
● Siren '09	🍷	3
○ Tregoniano '09	🍷	4

I Pampini

LOC. ACCIARELLA
S.DA FOGLINO, 1126
04010 LATINA
TEL. 0773643144
www.ipampini.it

This young, organic, seaside winery impressed with a Cabernet Sauvignon Il Capitano '07 giving black berries, spices and coffee. All it needs is a dash more flesh and structure. Bellone Maroso '09 also appeals for its tropical fruits aromas and deep palate.

● Il Capitano '07	🍷🍷	4
○ Maroso '09	🍷🍷	4
○ Bellone '09	🍷	3
● Kubizzo '07	🍷	4

Monti Cecubi

C.DA PORCIGNANO, 3
04020 ITRI [LT]
TEL. 0771729177

Monte Cecubi is no newcomer and production is increasingly on song, using local grapes like abbuoto in a fruity Vinum Caecubum '08 and also varieties from nearby areas, like falanghina for a delicious Boccabianca '09, fiano for an equally tasty Cento Chiavi '09, and vermentino for the Amyclano '09.

○ Boccabianca '09	🍷🍷	4*
○ Cento Chiavi '09	🍷🍷	4*
○ Amyclano '09	🍷	4
● Vinum Caecubum '08	🍷	4

L'Olivella

VIA DI COLLE PISANO, 5
00044 FRASCATI [RM]
TEL. 069424527
www.racemo.it

The top Olivella wine this year is a Bombino '09, with hints of jasmine and stone fruits and a consistent palate with staying power. The nicely crafted Frascati Superiore Racemo '09 is pleasing, with notes of wisteria and citrus, as is the Tre Grome '08 for its lemon and white pepper aromas.

○ Bombino '09	🍷🍷	4*
○ Frascati Sup. Racemo '09	🍷	4
○ Tre Grome '08	🍷	5

La Pazzaglia

S.DA DI BAGNOREGIO, 4
01024 CASTIGLIONE IN TEVERINA [VT]
TEL. 0761947114
www.tenutalapazzaglia.it

The Verdecchia family did well. Corno '09 from grechetto topped up with pinot bianco and chardonnay is full, its stone fruits, saffron and white pepper nose preceding a simpler but appealing palate. Orvieto '09 has citrus and flower aromas with a fluent, fruity palate.

○ Il Corno '09	🍷🍷	4*
○ Orvieto '09	🍷	3
● Palagio '09	🍷	3

Pietra Pinta

S.P. PASTINE KM 20,200
04010 CORI [LT]
TEL. 069678001-9677151
www.pietrapinta.com

The Ferretti winery always shines and last year's Chardonnay '09 is back with weighty but stylish citron notes. There is also a varietal Malvasia Puntinata '09 and the interesting reds include an international Shiraz '08 as well as a native Nero Buono '08, both correct and drinkable.

○ Chardonnay '09	🍷🍷	4*
○ Malvasia Puntinata '09	🍷	4
● Nero Buono '08	🍷	4
● Shiraz '08	🍷	4

Tenuta di Pietra Porzia

VIA PIETRA PORZIA, 60
00044 FRASCATI [RM]
TEL. 069464392
www.tenutadipietraporzia.it

Tenuta di Pietra Porzia is back after a few years' absence thanks to some quality labels. The best are the varietal, aromatic Frascati Superiore Regillo Etichetta Bianca '09, with a long citrus finale, and the fresh, appealing, almondy Frascati Superiore '09 with its good fruit.

○ Frascati Sup. '09	🍷🍷	3
○ Frascati Sup. Regillo Et. Bianca '09	🍷🍷	4
○ Frascati Sup. Regillo Et. Nera '09	🍷	4
○ Malvasia del Lazio '09	🍷	4

Poggio alla Meta

VIA CHIARENZO - VILLA CIOFFI
03030 PESCOSOLIDO [FR]
TEL. 0776886135
www.poggioallameta.it

Another new entry from the Atina area with Professor Nicotina and Anselmo Cioffi working to promote local varieties. The interesting reds offer nice varietal versions of cabernet, ranging easily from younger, drinkable wines to the complex Vecchio '07. As usual, the Passerina is full and appealing.

● Atina Cabernet Il Giovane '09	🍷🍷	4*
● Atina Rosso alla Meta '08	🍷🍷	4*
● Atina Cabernet Il Vecchio Ris. '07	🍷	5
○ Piluc '09	🍷	3

Proietti

VIA MAREMMANA SUPERIORE, KM 2,800
00035 OLEVANO ROMANO [RM]
TEL. 069563376
agricolaproietti@yahoo.it

The Proietti winery enters the Guide, confirming the progress of Cesanese di Olevano Romano. The stylish Vignalibus '08 has a mineral, red berry and spice nose, and a long, taut finale. Passo di Brecciara '07 is more generous and structured, showing tannic with hints of blossom and ripe black berries.

● Cesanese di Olevano Romano Vignalibus '08	🍷🍷	*
● Cesanese di Olevano Romano Passo di Brecciara '07	🍷	5
● Passo di Brecciara '06	🍷	4
○ Villa Maina '09	🍷	3

Il Quadrifoglio

LOC. DOGANELLA DI NINFA
VIA ALESSANDRO III, 5
04012 CISTERNA DI LATINA [LT]
TEL. 069601530
ilquadrifoglio.ss@libero.it

Praise goes to the De Gregorios for their work. Reds based on montepulciano, blending superbly with cabernet in the nicely spiced Muro Pecoraro '08, and with petit verdot for the ambitious but off-centre Ottavione '06. Pezze di Ninfa '09, a floral Chardonnay with immediate impact, is nice.

● Muro Pecoraro '08	🍷🍷	4*
● Ottavione '06	🍷	5
○ Pezze di Ninfa '09	🍷	3

La Rasenna

VIA DELLA SCAGLIA
00059 SANTA SEVERA [RM]
TEL. 3924974478
www.larasenna.it

Francesco Gambini's new winery enters the Guide mainly for the fresh Moss '09, a rich, layered 70-30 moscato and sauvignon blend with acacia honey aromas and a long finale backed up by mineral notes. The Cabernet Franc '08 with hints of Mediterranean scrubland is good, as is the '08 Petit Verdot.

○ Moss '09	🍷🍷	3*
● Cabernet Franc '08	🍷	4
● Petit Verdot '08	🍷	4

Riserva della Cascina

LOC. FIORANO
VIA APPIA ANTICA, 560
00134 ROMA
TEL. 067917221
riservadellacascina@inwind.it

The Brannetti husband and wife team run an organic winery just outside Rome. This year, they sent some well-made, great value wines again. Castelli Romani Rosso '09 has blackberry and cherry aromas, with a pleasingly fluent, consistent palate. All the wines tasted were well made.

● Castelli Romani Rosso '09	🍷🍷	3*
○ Gallieno '08	🍷	4
○ Marino Sup. '09	🍷	3

Tenuta Ronci di Nepi

LOC. VALLE RONCI
01036 NEPI [VT]
TEL. 0761555125
www.roncidinepi.com

Ronci in Nepi produces good wines fairly steadily. The '07 Ronci, a spicy, fruit-led Cabernet Sauvignon with nice texture is good, as is the Oro di Nè '09 Chardonnay with mainly pineapple and grapefruit tropical fruits and a rich but vigorous palate with a fresh citrus finale.

○ Oro di Nè '09	🍷🍷	4*
● Ronci '07	🍷🍷	
○ Manti '08	🍷	4
● Veste Porpora '08	🍷	3

Cantine San Marco

LOC. VERMICINO
VIA DI MOLA CAVONA, 26/28
00044 FRASCATI [RM]
TEL. 069409403
www.sanmarcofrascati.it

San Marco presented seven different Frascatis. We liked the '09 Frascati Superiore Crio 10 whose name comes from the ten hours of pre-fermentation low-temperature skin contact. It gives tropical fruits, a refreshing, fruity palate and persistent finale. The other wines tasted were also well made.

○ Frascati Sup. Crio 10 '09	🍷🍷	4*
○ Frascati Sup. Crio 8 '09	🍷	3
○ Frascati Sup. De Notari Crio 12 '09	🍷	4
○ Frascati Sup. Solofrascati '09	🍷	4

Tenuta Santa Lucia

LOC. SANTA LUCIA
02047 POGGIO MIRTETO [RI]
TEL. 076524616
www.tenutasantalucia.com

Our favourite from the wines tasted at this Rieti cellar was Otio '08, a 40-30-30 montepulciano, cabernet sauvignon and merlot blend, with hints of black berries and mild spice, and a pleasing, medium-bodied, long palate. The well-made Colli della Sabina Collis Pollionis Rosso '09 has depth.

● Otio '08	🍷🍷	5
○ Colli della Sabina Collis Pollionis Bianco '09	🍷	4
● Colli della Sabina Collis Pollionis Rosso '09	🍷	4
○ Elodia '08	🍷	5

Stefanoni

LOC. ZEPPONAMI
VIA STEFANONI, 48
01027 MONTEFIASCONE [VT]
TEL. 0761827031
www.cantinastefanoni.it

It was a so-so year for Stefanoni but we still enjoyed the better than well-made wines, from the pleasant, peachy '09 Montefiascone Foltone Est Est Est to the textured '08 Rosso di Montanello sangiovese, montepulciano and ciliegiolo blend and the fruit-led Roscetto Colle de Poggeri '09.

○ Est Est Est Foltone '09	🍷	3
● L'Eatico '09	🍷	4
○ Roscetto Colle de Poggeri '09	🍷	3
● Rosso di Montanello '08	🍷	2

Giovanni Terenzi

LOC. LA FORMA
VIA FORESE, 13
03010 SERRONE [FR]
TEL. 0775594286
www.viniterenzi.com

Despite a short profile, the absence of Cesanese Vajoscuro and a disappointing Colle Forma '08, there was a reassuring Velobra '08 and an interesting new sangiovese grosso-based Quercia Rossa '08. As usual, Passerina Villa Santa '09 is nicely made, ready to uncork and with tautly acidic.

● Cesanese del Piglio Velobra '08	🍷🍷	4*
● Quercia Rossa '08	🍷🍷	6
● Cesanese del Piglio Colle Forma '08	🍷	5
○ Passerina Villa Santa '09	🍷	4

OTHER WINERIES

Terra delle Ginestre
SS 630 Ausonia, 59
04020 Spigno Saturnia [LT]
tel. 0771700297
www.terradelleginestre.it

Giulio Marrone's co-operative abandons its Stellaria to focus on a new bellone and moscato blend, a fresh, floral Letizia '09. Top wines are still the classic Il Generale '08, from rare native grapes, combining drinkability and impact, and the pleasing Invito '09 with its lingering aromas.

● Il Generale '08	🍷🍷 4
○ Moscato di Terracina Invito '09	🍷🍷 3*
○ Letizia '09	🍷 4

Tre Botti
s.da della Poggetta, 10
01024 Castiglione in Teverina [VT]
tel. 0761948930
www.trebotti.it

The Botti family can confirm things went the right way with a Bludom '09, an interesting Aleatico full of spice aromas, nutmeg and aniseed, a balanced, fruity palate, just the right sweetness and not too much extract. We also recommend the fresh, citrussy, Orvieto '09, which finishes long.

● Bludom '09	🍷🍷 5
○ Orvieto '09	🍷🍷 3*
● Castiglionero '08	🍷 4
● Tusco '08	🍷 3

Villa Gianna
b.go San Donato
s.da Maremmana
04010 Sabaudia [LT]
tel. 0773250034
www.villagianna.it

The Giannini winery had an off year although results are still convincing, especially the whites. We like the crisp, varietal Chardonnay '09 while the enjoyably uncomplicated Sauvignon '09 is offset by an intriguing but rather too muscular Innato '09. Rudèstro '08 is always well made.

○ Vigne del Borgo Chardonnay '09	🍷🍷 3*
○ Circeo Bianco Innato '09	🍷 4
● Rudèstro '08	🍷 3
○ Vigne del Borgo Sauvignon '09	🍷 3

Villa Simone
via Frascati Colonna, 29
00040 Monte Porzio Catone [RM]
tel. 069449717
www.pierocostantini.it

Our favourite this year is the uncomplicated, varietal Villa Simone Frascati Superiore '09 with almond notes, fullness, consistency and a long finish. The balsamic Syrah '08, rich, fruity Cesanese del Piglio '07 and a Frascati Superiore Villa dei Preti '09 with blossom and citrus are all well made.

○ Frascati Sup. '09	🍷🍷 3
● Cesanese del Piglio '07	🍷 3
○ Frascati Sup. Villa dei Preti '09	🍷 4
● Syrah '08	🍷 3

La Visciola
c.da Carcassano
03010 Piglio [FR]
tel. 0775501950
maccioccapiero@libero.it

Piero and Rosa Macciocca tread an arduous organic road. Results are still on their way but encouragement is in order. Ambient yeasts, maceration and no sulphites have created an extreme but interesting Passerina Donna Rosa, the '08 pipping the '09. The husky Cesanese is varietal.

○ Donna Rosa '08	🍷🍷 4
● Cesanese del Piglio Priore '08	🍷 5
○ Donna Rosa '09	🍷 4

Conte Zandotti
via Vigne Colle Mattia, 8
00132 Roma
tel. 0620609000
www.cantinecontezandotti.it

Conte Zandotti is back with a Frascati Superiore '09 that gives flowers, citrus and a complex, taut, minerally palate. We like the malvasia puntinata and trebbiano Aurora '09 blend, with its aromatic herbs, and the tannic, textured La Petrosa '08 from cabernet sauvignon and sangiovese.

○ Frascati Sup. '09	🍷🍷 4
○ Aurora '09	🍷 3
● La Petrosa '08	🍷
○ Malvasia del Lazio Rumon '09	🍷 4

ABRUZZO

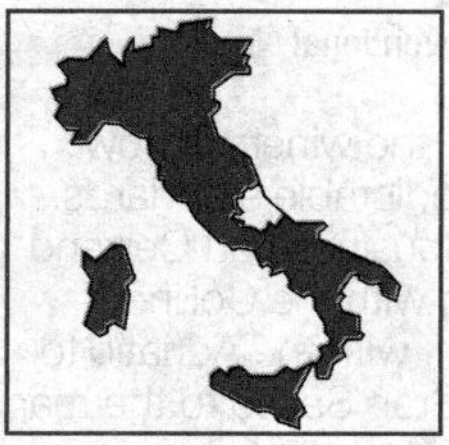

Abruzzo is one region where international varieties and globalization have not put down roots. We tasted several hundred wines and only about ten were made with grapes other than trebbiano, montepulciano, pecorino and one or two other minor varieties. At Controguerra, right in the north, there is a little cabernet but is used mainly for blending. On the other hand, territorial typing is taking place for Montepulciano and, to a lesser extent, of Trebbiano. Most of us now realize that the sturdiest reds with the most intense colour come from the Teramo hills. It is equally evident that more elegant Montepulcianos are produced inland, around Ofena, Capestrano and Popoli. Even more obviously, territory in many cases is helped along by talented regional winemakers. And to cap it all, we decided to give what is probably our most significant annual award, for Winery of the Year, to a legendary Abruzzo winemaker. Valentini, in Loreto Aprutino, is now in the capable hands of Francesco Paolo, who took over after the premature death of his father Edoardo. We received a trio of superb wines and had no choice but to give them all Three Glasses, which is unusual for this Guide. Alongside Valentini we have wines by Professor Luigi Cataldi Madonna from Ofena, Leonardo Pizzolo's Valle Reale in Popoli, and Marina Cvetic Masciarelli, another spiritual heir, in this case of her husband Gianni, who died two years ago tragically young. Then there are the Barbas, Federica Morricone, Adriana and Fausto's Torre dei Beati, also from Loreto Aprutino, and Cavalier Dino Illuminati, a line-up of enthusiastic, capable winemakers who pave the way for dozens of excellent wineries, some co-operatives, which make up the production backbone of one of Italy's most exciting wine regions. The vineyards are often stunning, with low pergolas, but increasingly we are seeing high training, too. Then there are two stars, two very interesting varieties, montepulciano and trebbiano, the latter expressing only in Abruzzo traits that are absolutely unknown elsewhere. Recently another unique variety has been added, pecorino, which in specific circumstances and when not over-exploited, endows wines with its own very special aromas of mango and passion fruit, reminiscent of certain exotic, untamed Sauvignons. Then there are minor native vines, especially passerina and cococciola. The last few vintages have seesawed, with 2006 and 2008 good on the whole; 2007 was hot; and 2009 was cool, but that was good for whites. It could have been worse, even if the climate is changing and average temperatures are rising. However this, sadly, is true everywhere.

Agriverde

LOC. CALDARI
VIA STORTINI, 32A
66020 ORTONA [CH]
TEL. 0859032101
www.agriverde.it

CELLAR SALES
PRE-BOOKED VISITS
ROOMS AND FOOD

ANNUAL PRODUCTION **700,000 bottles**
HECTARES UNDER VINE **65**
VITICULTURE METHOD **Certified organic**

Gutsy Giannicola Di Carlo has always targeted the leading edge for his winery. This year Ferrari elected it a top example of green agriculture in the presentation of a scheme the automotive producer is implementing at Maranello. The Agriverde project has 65 hectares under vine, managed totally by certified organic methods, a modern winery, a spa offering wine therapy, an elegant tourist farm with its own restaurant and, famously, attention to bio-architecture.

There were some very good labels this year, but they are not quite as exciting as usual. As expected, the Montepulciano Plateo is the most convincing, with its usual well-handled texture. This '05 vintage, however, is slightly dried by aggressive tannins. The aromas of the ambitious Solàrea '05, another Montepulciano, are quite masked by the oak and the remarkable structure dominated by tannins. The organic Natum range offers some good items like a rustic, gutsy, long Montepulciano d'Abruzzo '09, or the refreshing, well-typed Trebbiano '09. The Trebbiano Solarea '08 is a good effort with its exotic hints of vanilla and banana. Other wines are enjoyable and well made.

Wine	Glasses	
● Montepulciano d'Abruzzo Plateo '05	2 (black)	7
● Montepulciano d'Abruzzo Natum '09	2 (black)	4*
● Montepulciano d'Abruzzo Solàrea '05	2 (black)	5
○ Pecorino Riseis '09	2 (black)	4
○ Trebbiano d'Abruzzo Natum '09	2 (black)	4*
○ Trebbiano d'Abruzzo Riseis di Recastro '09	2 (black)	4
○ Trebbiano d'Abruzzo Solarea '08	2 (black)	5
○ Chardonnay Piane di Maggio '09	1 (black)	3
○ Trebbiano d'Abruzzo Piane di Maggio '09	1 (black)	3
● Montepulciano d'Abruzzo Plateo '04	3 (outline)	7
● Montepulciano d'Abruzzo Plateo '01	3 (outline)	7
● Montepulciano d'Abruzzo Plateo '00	3 (outline)	7
● Montepulciano d'Abruzzo Plateo '98	3 (outline)	6
● Montepulciano d'Abruzzo Solàrea '03	3 (outline)	5

Anfra

VIA COLLE MORINO, 8
64025 PINETO [TE]
TEL. 3471154504
www.anfra.it

CELLAR SALES
PRE-BOOKED VISITS
FOOD

ANNUAL PRODUCTION **30,000 bottles**
HECTARES UNDER VINE **10**
VITICULTURE METHOD **Conventional**

After last year's coup, the winery is now back at sound but predictable standards. Anfra is a very young business on Cerrano hill territory, bordering with the Colline Teramane. Its location, with the Adriatic to the front and Mount Gran Sasso to the rear, generates substantial day-night temperature differences, especially in summer and autumn, a good thing above all for white wines.

We sampled seven well-made, agreeable wines, with only a flagship missing as the Nero dei Due Mori '07 comes over as a little under par. This complex, mature Montepulciano has intense oak and dried tomato aromas, and a round, juicy palate but overdoes the tannins. The Borgo Santa Maria '09, the winery's back-up Montepulciano d'Abruzzo, has an evolved nose tinged with mild oak but a hearty, appealing palate. The Cerasuolo '09 is very good, intensely fruity and crisp, with definite strawberry aromas. Two of the most persuasive whites are Trebbiano d'Abruzzo '09. The Borgo Santa Maria has an evident toastiness and straightforward progression; the Trebbiano d'Abruzzo '09 is less complex.

Wine	Glasses	
⊙ Montepulciano d'Abruzzo Cerasuolo Borgo Santa Maria '09	2 (black)	4
● Montepulciano d'Abruzzo Nero dei due Mori '07	2 (black)	5
○ Trebbiano d'Abruzzo '09	2 (black)	4
○ Trebbiano d'Abruzzo Borgo Santa Maria '09	2 (black)	4*
● Montepulciano d'Abruzzo Borgo Santa Maria '09	1 (black)	4
○ Passerina '09	1 (black)	4
○ Pecorino '09	1 (black)	4
● Montepulciano d'Abruzzo Borgo Santa Maria '08	2 (outline)	4
● Montepulciano d'Abruzzo Nero dei due Mori '06	2 (outline)	5
○ Trebbiano d'Abruzzo '08	2 (outline)	4*

F.lli Barba

LOC. SCERNE DI PINETO
S.DA ROTABILE PER CASOLI
64020 PINETO [TE]
TEL. 0859461020
www.fratellibarba.it

CELLAR SALES
PRE-BOOKED VISITS
ROOMS

ANNUAL PRODUCTION 350,000 bottles
HECTARES UNDER VINE 68
VITICULTURE METHOD Conventional

This venerable Abruzzo agricultural enterprise confirms its stature as a regional leader. It can be found in Pineto, in the Colline Teramane, where it faces the sea with the Gran Sasso massif soaring in the background, the microclimate is perfect for general farming and for viticulture in particular. The large farm has about 70 hectares under vine, a sort of business in the business.

Barba's wines were a textbook tasting, with everyone agreeing on the caressing Vignafranca '07 and its well-defined, stylish notes. The full, commanding palate is also incredibly vibrant and balanced, with superbly woven tannins. The Trebbiano '07 is again traditional, with a subtle, varietal nose and a fruity, super-elegant palate. I Vasari is a Montepulciano is a vineyard selection with an old-fashioned flavour and this '07 version is amazingly complex. The delicate Bianco Vignafranca '08 is a pure Trebbiano, true to type and with great progression. An outstanding wine in the Colle Morino range is Etichetta Bianca '08, a Montepulciano with a very tempting price tag.

● Montepulciano d'Abruzzo Vignafranca '07	🍷🍷🍷	4*
● Montepulciano d'Abruzzo I Vasari '07	🍷🍷	6
○ Trebbiano d'Abruzzo '07	🍷🍷	5
○ Vignafranca Bianco '08	🍷🍷	4*
● Montepulciano d'Abruzzo Colle Morino '09	🍷🍷	3*
● Montepulciano d'Abruzzo Colle Morino Et. Bianca '08	🍷🍷	3*
○ Trebbiano d'Abruzzo Colle Morino '09	🍷🍷	2*
● Montepulciano d'Abruzzo Vignafranca '06	YYY	4*
○ Trebbiano d'Abruzzo '06	YYY	5*
● Montepulciano d'Abruzzo Vignafranca '05	YY	4*
● Montepulciano d'Abruzzo Vignafranca '04	YY	4
● Montepulciano d'Abruzzo Vignafranca '03	YY	4*
● Montepulciano d'Abruzzo Vignafranca '01	YY	4*

Tenute Barone di Valforte

C.DA PIOMBA, 11
64029 SILVI MARINA [TE]
TEL. 0859353432
www.baronedivalforte.it

CELLAR SALES
PRE-BOOKED VISITS

ANNUAL PRODUCTION 100,000 bottles
HECTARES UNDER VINE 42
VITICULTURE METHOD Conventional

Here on the Pescara hills looking out to sea on the border between the provinces of Pescara and Teramo, the Sorricchio family run a tight ship with lots of ambition. They have always cultivated vines but only recently got into marketing and bottling their own wines, in newly-built cellars. This year's wines are more persuasive than past efforts.

We tasted modern, approachable, well-made wines overall. The Montepulciano d'Abruzzo Riserva '07 is memorable for its complex, caressing aromas of red berries and a light, estery note; the palate has a rich, forceful texture and a close-knit tannic weave. The ambitious Colline Teramane Colle Sale '07, with evolved oaky and vanilla notes on the nose, is disappointing. The palate is concentrated and slightly sweet. We like the intense, enfolding Cerasuolo '09, with a classic note of bitter almond and a refreshing, fruity progression. The whites are less successful. The Passerina '09 is gently aromatic thanks to its attractive fragrances but has a Sauvignon feel.

● Montepulciano d'Abruzzo Ris. '07	🍷🍷	4*
⊙ Montepulciano d'Abruzzo Cerasuolo '09	🍷🍷	3*
● Montepulciano d'Abruzzo Colline Teramane Colle Sale '07	🍷	4
○ Passerina '09	🍷	4
○ Pecorino '09	🍷	4
● Montepulciano d'Abruzzo '08	YY	3*
○ Pecorino '08	YY	4*

Bove

via Roma, 216
67051 Avezzano [AQ]
tel. 086333133
bovevini@virgilio.it

CELLAR SALES
PRE-BOOKED VISITS

ANNUAL PRODUCTION **1,200,000 bottles**
HECTARES UNDER VINE **60**
VITICULTURE METHOD **Conventional**

This small Marsica winery has its premises in Avezzano, in an area not renowned for quality wines, but in the early 1900s was one of the region's chief wine reservoirs. Nonetheless, over the last few years we were surprised by some excellent wines at astonishing value for money. The range was limited, with just three wines tasted, but all scored very well.

The Indio '07 is a Montepulciano d'Abruzzo with an exotic name. It easily made our finals with its typical, concentrated wild cherry and cocoa powder aromas, and the right amount of oak incorporated in a full, exemplary palate profile in an attractively modern style. Poggio d'Albe '08 is less complex, a crisp, well-made Montepulciano characterized by intense red berries on the nose and a captivating, intense smoky note; the intense, layered mouthfeel is clean and subtle. Safari is a concentrated, up-to-the-minute Pecorino from the region's trendiest native variety, with cool citrus aromas and crisp acidity sustaining seamless progression.

● Montepulciano d'Abruzzo Indio '07	🍷🍷	4*
● Montepulciano d'Abruzzo Poggio d'Albe '08	🍷🍷	3*
○ Safari Pecorino '09	🍷🍷	3*
● Montepulciano d'Abruzzo Indio '04	ΥΥ	4*

Podere Castorani

c.da Oratorio
via Castorani, 5
65020 Alanno [PE]
tel. 0852012513
www.castorani.it

CELLAR SALES
PRE-BOOKED VISITS

ANNUAL PRODUCTION **1,000,000 bottles**
HECTARES UNDER VINE **100**
VITICULTURE METHOD **Certified organic**

The Trulli family's Alanno winery confirms its success with the ambitious Podere Castorani, inland of Pescara, bearing fruit, opting for organic viticulture, fermentation in cement vats and traditional winemaking methods that include using only a small manually operated grape press. Radical choices, but they got two wines a slot in the national finals.

Podere Castorani, a typical Montepulciano fermented in cement for some good old-fashioned nuances, has a varietal, intense nose and a full, feisty palate. The other Montepulciano, Coste delle Plaie '07, has outstanding texture and solidity; the tannic weave is complex but not too refined. The crisp, powerful Cerasuolo Cadetto '09 rosé lingers on the palate. Jarno is an ambitious, chancy interpretation of a Montepulciano from part-dried grapes, and this '06 is the best yet. The clean, well-typed Pecorino Amorino '09 stands out in the whites, as does Jarno Bianco, with the international appeal of tropical fruits and vanilla, with unusually lively progression for this genre.

● Montepulciano d'Abruzzo Costa delle Plaie '07	🍷🍷	4*
● Montepulciano d'Abruzzo Podere Castorani '06	🍷🍷	6
○ Jarno Bianco '08	🍷🍷	6
● Jarno Rosso '06	🍷🍷	7
⊙ Montepulciano d'Abruzzo Cerasuolo Cadetto '09	🍷🍷	3*
○ Pecorino Amorino '09	🍷🍷	4
○ Trebbiano d'Abruzzo Costa delle Plaie '09	🍷🍷	4
● Montepulciano d'Abruzzo Amorino '06	ΥΥ	4*
● Montepulciano d'Abruzzo Cadetto '08	ΥΥ	2*
○ Trebbiano d'Abruzzo Costa delle Plaie '08	ΥΥ	4*

★ Luigi Cataldi Madonna

Loc. Piano
67025 Ofena [AQ]
tel. 0862954252
cataldimadonna@virgilio.it

CELLAR SALES
PRE-BOOKED VISITS

ANNUAL PRODUCTION 260,000 bottles
HECTARES UNDER VINE 70
VITICULTURE METHOD Conventional

Gran Sasso's Corno Grande, the only Apennine glacier and backdrop to the Ofena plateau, brings the range of temperatures underpinning the fragrant wines from this 70-hectare estate. Luigi Cataldi Madonna, baron, philosopher and great winemaker, then works his own magic to preserve this oenological abundance in wines as traditional as they are contemporary.

The year's winning duo was almost a foregone conclusion. First the Pecorino that Cataldi Madonna began producing almost 20 years ago, even more intense in this '08, with deep bitter orange and passion fruit nuances. The palate has good structure with acidity through to the finish. Then the '07 Tonì, possibly the best yet, its typical, caressing aromas evoking quinine and liquorice, plus an elegant, complex palate. The inspired Piè delle Vigne Cerasuolo is its usual convincing self. The '08 Malandrino has set out to regain agility and lightness. And there's a special mention for this year's surprise, the three-litre bag-in-box, tempting wines at tempting prices.

● Montepulciano d'Abruzzo Tonì '07	▼▼▼	6
○ Pecorino '08	▼▼▼	6
● Montepulciano d'Abruzzo '08	▼▼	4*
⊙ Montepulciano d'Abruzzo Cerasuolo '09	▼▼	3*
⊙ Montepulciano d'Abruzzo Cerasuolo Piè delle Vigne '08	▼▼	5
● Montepulciano d'Abruzzo Malandrino '08	▼▼	5
○ Trebbiano d'Abruzzo '09	▼▼	3*
● Montepulciano d'Abruzzo Malandrino '06	▽▽▽	5
● Montepulciano d'Abruzzo Tonì '06	▽▽▽	6
● Montepulciano d'Abruzzo Tonì '04	▽▽▽	6
○ Pecorino '07	▽▽▽	6
○ Pecorino '06	▽▽▽	6
○ Pecorino '05	▽▽▽	6

Centorame

Loc. Casoli di Atri
via delle Fornaci, 15
64030 Atri [TE]
tel. 0858709115
www.centorame.it

CELLAR SALES
PRE-BOOKED VISITS

ANNUAL PRODUCTION 85,000 bottles
HECTARES UNDER VINE 8
VITICULTURE METHOD Conventional

Lamberto Centorame is the young manager of this tiny winery at Casoli d'Atri, located in the Teramo hill territory. The estate has a mere eight hectares of vines planted in clay soils overlooking the Adriatic where the sun is sometimes very hot indeed. The wines produced are very personal and focus on power. Not always refined in style, they are invariably intense.

Now David beats Goliath. The unfussy Trebbiano d'Abruzzo San Michele '09 made the finals for its varietal nose with smoky notes and secondary hints, and long, lingering, subtle palate. A great white. The flagship Castellum Vetus '07, an aspiring Colline Teramane, is less persuasive than usual. The sour cherry and cocoa powder on the nose are marred by alcohol; the full, concentrated flavour is let down by dry tannins and the tart, over-extracted finale. The Trebbiano Castellum Vetus is an oaky old-school white with a sweet, juicy palate sustained by a typically intact tangy note. The pecorino and sauvignon TuaPina is a modern white with nice, salt-veined progression.

○ Trebbiano d'Abruzzo San Michele '09	▼▼	3*
● Montepulciano d'Abruzzo Colline Teramane Castellum Vetus '07	▼▼	5
○ Trebbiano d'Abruzzo Castellum Vetus '08	▼▼	4
○ TuaPina '09	▼▼	4*
● Montepulciano d'Abruzzo San Michele '08	▼	4
● Montepulciano d'Abruzzo Colline Teramane Castellum Vetus '06	▽▽	5
● Montepulciano d'Abruzzo Colline Teramane Castellum Vetus '05	▽▽	5
● Montepulciano d'Abruzzo San Michele '07	▽▽	4*
● Montepulciano d'Abruzzo San Michele '06	▽▽	3*
● Montepulciano d'Abruzzo San Michele '05	▽▽	3*
○ Trebbiano d'Abruzzo Castellum Vetus '07	▽▽	4*
○ Trebbiano d'Abruzzo Castellum Vetus '06	▽▽	4*
○ Trebbiano d'Abruzzo San Michele '08	▽▽	3*

Col del Mondo

C.DA CAMPOTINO, 35C
65010 COLLECORVINO [PE]
TEL. 0858207831
www.coldelmondo.com

CELLAR SALES

ANNUAL PRODUCTION **45,000 bottles**
HECTARES UNDER VINE **12**
VITICULTURE METHOD **Conventional**

The Col del Mondo winery in Collecorvino gets a full profile this year for its interesting range of worthy wines. Some time ago, the estate, on the Pescara hills between the sea and the Apennines, began a policy of offering typical, balanced products at reasonable prices. In less than ten years, the business has carved a niche that is both modern and traditional in Abruzzo's competitive winemaking scenario.

The flagship is a Montepulciano d'Abruzzo '07, which went to the finals thanks to complex pencil lead notes alongside varietal cherry and cocoa powder. The full, subtle palate has first-rate texture, with crisp, well-balanced progression. Also worthy of note is an inspired Kerrias '06, a Montepulciano giving distinctive, refined red berry aromas and a classic feisty palate with tannins that are close-knit but not aggressive. From the whites, the Pecorino Kerrias '09 appeals with its lively pink grapefruit aromas that return nicely in the palate, flanked by delicious acidity. The Sunnae Trebbiano and Montepulciano, two good everyday wines, are less complex.

● Montepulciano d'Abruzzo '07	▼▼	4*
○ Kerrias Pecorino '09	▼▼	4*
● Montepulciano d'Abruzzo Kerrias '06	▼▼	5
● Montepulciano d'Abruzzo Sunnae '08	▼	3
○ Trebbiano d'Abruzzo Sunnae '09	▼	3
● Montepulciano d'Abruzzo '06	▽▽	4*
● Montepulciano d'Abruzzo '05	▽▽	4*
● Montepulciano d'Abruzzo Kerrias '04	▽▽	5
● Montepulciano d'Abruzzo Sunnae '06	▽▽	3*

Collebello - Cantine Marano

VIA DEL LAGO, 19
64081 TORTORETO [TE]
TEL. 0861501032
www.collebello.it

CELLAR SALES
PRE-BOOKED VISITS

ANNUAL PRODUCTION **30,000 bottles**
HECTARES UNDER VINE **17**
VITICULTURE METHOD **Certified organic**

We noted this impressive newcomer last year and were unable to include it in the Guide for lack of space. The wines we tasted this year were good enough to get Cantine Mara not just a place but a triumphant full profile. The vines are in the Colline Teramane and this young business concentrates on organic farming methods in the vineyard and vinification is as natural as possible.

The '07 Montepulciano d'Abruzzo Borgo Gaio reached our finals thanks to its varietal aromas. The intense hints of wild cherry and cocoa powder on the nose lead into a nicely sound, full and, dare we say feisty, texture, sustained by a seductive tannic weave. Polifemo '07 is the house Colline Teramane, an imposing Montepulciano with oak that is just a tad pushy but which slowly reveals a full, caressing structure. The Lui line, labelled as natural wine, includes a Montepulciano d'Abruzzo and a Trebbiano d'Abruzzo whose merit lies in rustic appeal. The '09 Pecorino Ginestra is rather more modern.

● Montepulciano d'Abruzzo Borgo Gaio '07	▼▼	3*
● Montepulciano d'Abruzzo Colline Teramane Polifemo '07	▼▼	5
● Montepulciano d'Abruzzo Lui '08	▼▼	4
○ Trebbiano d'Abruzzo Lui '09	▼▼	3*
○ Ginestra Pecorino '09	▼	4

Collefrisio

LOC. PIANE DI MAGGIO
66030 FRISA [CH]
TEL. 0859039074
www.collefrisio.it

PRE-BOOKED VISITS

ANNUAL PRODUCTION **200,000 bottles**
HECTARES UNDER VINE **36**
VITICULTURE METHOD **Certified organic**

This Ortona winery is no newcomer and sent a remarkable four wines to this year's finals. One of its estates is in the Ortona hills, looking out to sea, and the other is on the Chieti slopes, cooled by breezes off the Maiella massif. The territories are different and give Collefrisio distinctive, sound textures. We tasted wines created by this lushness and a modern style of viticulture that respects tradition.

The only basic thing about the Montepulciano d'Abruzzo Zero '08 is its price. Crisp aromas come with a juicy, full-flavoured palate, good length and a subtle weave. Montepulciano newcomer Morrecine '08 has traditional morello cherry and spice; the palate is still quite clenched but with a pleasing texture. An inspired '06 Montepulciano Collefrisio di Collefrisio has impressive, well-managed strength veiled by oak that will retreat with time. The Montepulciano Uno has well-typed, intense cocoa powder and wild cherries, and a full yet agile palate. Best whites are a subtle, terpenic Pecorino '09 and the varietal Trebbiano Zero. The Cerasuolo is as drinkable as ever.

● Montepulciano d'Abruzzo Collefrisio di Collefrisio '06	4*
● Montepulciano d'Abruzzo Morrecine '08	4*
● Montepulciano d'Abruzzo Uno '07	4*
● Montepulciano d'Abruzzo Zero '08	4*
⊙ Montepulciano d'Abruzzo Cerasuolo '09	4*
○ Pecorino '09	4
○ Trebbiano d'Abruzzo Zero '09	3*
● Montepulciano d'Abruzzo '05	4
● Montepulciano d'Abruzzo Uno '06	4
● Montepulciano d'Abruzzo Uno '05	4*
● Montepulciano d'Abruzzo Zero '07	4*
● Montepulciano d'Abruzzo Zero '06	4*
○ Pecorino '08	4
○ Trebbiano d'Abruzzo Uno '08	4
○ Trebbiano d'Abruzzo Uno '07	4*
○ Trebbiano d'Abruzzo Zero '08	3*

Colonnella

VIA VIBRATA, 72
64010 COLONNELLA [TE]
TEL. 0861714777
www.cantinacolonnella.it

CELLAR SALES
PRE-BOOKED VISITS

ANNUAL PRODUCTION **300,000 bottles**
HECTARES UNDER VINE **350**
VITICULTURE METHOD **Conventional**

Colonnella is a small Medieval village dominating the Tronto valley and marking where Abruzzo meets the Marche. Years back this co-operative winery began to pursue a quality policy, selecting grapes from the many Colline Teramane member growers. It is the only co-operative enterprise in this part of Abruzzo and we tasted excellent wines this year, offering great value for money.

The Cinque Colli '07 is a Controguerra Rosso montepulciano and cabernet blend with brisk, lively morello cherry notes that verge on complex and wild. The subtle, elegant flavour is sustained by fresh, spirited acidity and a tangy finale. The Barocco '05 Colline Teramane Montepulciano has overtones of ripe wild cherry and cocoa powder. The full-textured palate is managed with an agility that makes the wine pleasantly drinkable, despite the vintage. The commercial Clivis '09 is an approachable white from local passerina grapes. The simpler Le Rue passerina-based sparkler is more appealing with the bounteous mousse from refermentation. A very quaffable, affordable bubbly.

● Controguerra Rosso Ris. Cinque Colli '07	4*
● Montepulciano d'Abruzzo Colline Teramane Barocco '05	4
○ Clivis Passerina '09	3
○ Passerina Brut Le Rue	3

Contesa

c.da Caparrone, 4
65010 Collecorvino [PE]
tel. 0858205078
www.contesa.it

CELLAR SALES
PRE-BOOKED VISITS

ANNUAL PRODUCTION 200,000 bottles
HECTARES UNDER VINE 45
VITICULTURE METHOD Organic

Collecorvino's hills roll seamlessly from the Adriatic to Maiella in this interesting, ancient winemaking district. Contesa is a single 45-hectare estate with state-of-the-art cellars created by resolute Abruzzo oenologist Rocco Pasetti after he left his family's winery. Recently, the enterprise has grown in fame on the regional winemaking front for its reliable, quality range.

The Vigna Corvino '08 Montepulciano made our finals for its elegant wild cherry nose and full, clean palate, backed by poised acidity with good freshness. The Sorab '08 is a traditional Pecorino, tinged with oak but also with crisp grapefruit notes and rich, juicy flesh. We also like the Trebbiano d'Abruzzo '09, with its husky aromas and intense, drinkable flavour. The uncomplicated, amiable basic Pecorino was managed skilfully, as usual. The ambitious Montepulciano d'Abruzzo '06 was less persuasive, showing over-evolved with a tannin-heavy palate. Nerone '05, a big Montepulciano with big mouthfeel, is a bit of a mystery, showing stiff progression and still clenched.

● Montepulciano d'Abruzzo V. Corvino '08	▼▼	3*
○ Pecorino Sorab '08	▼▼	4
○ Trebbiano d'Abruzzo '09	▼▼	4*
● Montepulciano d'Abruzzo '06	▼	5
● Montepulciano d'Abruzzo Nerone '05	▼	5
○ Pecorino '09	▼	4
○ Trebbiano d'Abruzzo V. Corvino '09	▼	3
● Montepulciano d'Abruzzo '05	▽▽	5
● Montepulciano d'Abruzzo Amir '06	▽▽	5
⊙ Montepulciano d'Abruzzo Cerasuolo V. Corvino '08	▽▽	3*
● Montepulciano d'Abruzzo Nerone '04	▽▽	5
○ Pecorino '08	▽▽	4*
○ Pecorino Sorab '07	▽▽	5

Dino Illuminati

c.da San Biagio, 18
64010 Controguerra [TE]
tel. 0861808008
www.illuminativini.it

CELLAR SALES
PRE-BOOKED VISITS

ANNUAL PRODUCTION 1,200,000 bottles
HECTARES UNDER VINE 120
VITICULTURE METHOD Conventional

Controguerra is in the north of the Colline Teramane, almost on the Marche border. This is where the winery was founded and here Cavalier Dino Illuminati started his venture. Now 80, but with the stamina of a man half his age, Dino still runs his enterprise, ably assisted by his son Stefano. There are over 100 hectares under vine for a winery that has been producing unique, traditional wines since 1890.

The Zanna is a Three Glass habitué and may be the best Colline Teramane around. A classic Montepulciano from a lovely Abruzzo pergola planted over four decades ago. This '07 is even more layered, full and brimming with personality. The Lumen is a typical Controguerra Rosso cabernet and montepulciano blend. The nose is fresh and elegant, while the palate has excellent texture. Riparosso is a Montepulciano d'Abruzzo produced in impressive quantities with impeccable quality. The '09 is very varietal with crisp, pleasant wild cherry and cocoa powder notes. From the whites, we liked both the fresh, citrussy Costalupo '09, which is taut and drinkable, and the oak-aged Daniele.

● Montepulciano d'Abruzzo Colline Teramane Zanna Ris. '07	▼▼▼	6
● Controguerra Rosso Lumen Ris. '07	▼▼	6
○ Controguerra Bianco Costalupo '09	▼▼	3*
○ Controguerra Bianco Daniele '07	▼▼	5
● Montepulciano d'Abruzzo Ilico '08	▼▼	4
● Montepulciano d'Abruzzo Riparosso '09	▼▼	3*
○ Pecorino '09	▼▼	4*
⊙ Montepulciano d'Abruzzo Cerasuolo Campirosa '09	▼	3
● Montepulciano d'Abruzzo Colline Teramane Pieluni Ris. '01	▽▽▽	7
● Montepulciano d'Abruzzo Colline Teramane Zanna Ris. '06	▽▽▽	6
● Montepulciano d'Abruzzo Colline Teramane Zanna Ris. '05	▽▽▽	6
● Montepulciano d'Abruzzo Colline Teramane Zanna Ris. '01	▽▽▽	5

Lidia e Amato

c.da San Biagio, 2
64010 Controguerra [TE]
tel. 0861817041
www.lidiaeamatoviticoltori.com

CELLAR SALES
PRE-BOOKED VISITS

ANNUAL PRODUCTION **30,000 bottles**
HECTARES UNDER VINE **12**
VITICULTURE METHOD **Conventional**

This tiny but long-established Controguerra winery, opposite upper-crust Illuminati, has just a few hectares but is run with dedication by expert winemakers. Lidia Tavoletti and husband Amato name their wines after their grandchildren and look after both with care, lots of love and craftsmanship. This year they get a full profile for the overall quality of the wines tasted.

The mighty Controguerra Sebastian '07 montepulciano and cabernet blend is full and rich, with a striking, well-managed texture. It will evolve brilliantly. Colline Teramane Riccardo '07 is a mouthfilling, intense Montepulciano, with clean varietal wild cherry on the nose and slightly over-extracted tannins that clench the palate slightly. We also like the whites from native grapes. Elena is a single-variety Passerina, in the local tradition, and Greta is a classic Pecorino. Two whites that charm with their huskiness. Palù is an effective Trebbiano d'Abruzzo, underpinned by fresh notes and the well-managed Controguerra Bianco Lidia is quite good.

● Controguerra Sebastian '07	▼▼	4*
○ Controguerra Elena '09	▼▼	4*
○ Greta '09	▼▼	4
● Montepulciano d'Abruzzo Colline Teramane Riccardo '07	▼▼	5
○ Trebbiano d'Abruzzo Palù '09	▼▼	3*
○ Controguerra Lidia '09	▼	4
● Controguerra Sebastian '06	▽▽	4*
○ Greta '08	▽▽	4*
● Montepulciano d'Abruzzo Colline Teramane Riccardo '06	▽▽	4*
● Montepulciano d'Abruzzo Colline Teramane Riccardo '05	▽▽	4*
● Montepulciano d'Abruzzo Forty '07	▽▽	3*

Marina Cvetic

via San Silvestro, 10
66010 San Martino sulla Marrucina [CH]
tel. 087185241
www.masciarellidistribuzione.it

PRE-BOOKED VISITS

ANNUAL PRODUCTION **48,000 bottles**
HECTARES UNDER VINE **8**
VITICULTURE METHOD **Conventional**

Marina Cvetic Masciarelli's Teramo estate was her husband Gianni's pride and joy. There are eight hectares under vine and about 3,000 olive trees, in the municipalities of Corropoli and Controguerra, deep in the Colline Teramane. The project got under way with the 2003 harvest, starting with pure montepulciano. The winery, with its own cellars and management, is now independent of the parent company in San Martino sulla Marrucina.

Iskra is Russian for spark and a spark can start an idea, a business, even a revolution. Gianni Masciarelli may have had in mind a revolution of Teramo wines, making them even more soundly territorial. We feel the '05 vintage has completed the circle. It's a shame that Gianni did not live to taste this superb Montepulciano, which combines the power of local wines, from which it acquires a Bordeaux-like finesse, with close-knit but not aggressive tannins and a salty acidity that balances its impressive firmness. A small masterpiece that may not have a DOCG label but is still one of the best wines in this part of the region.

● Iskra '05	▼▼▼	5
● Iskra '04	▽▽	5
● Iskra '03	▽▽	5

★★ Masciarelli

via Gamberale, 1
66010 San Martino sulla Marrucina [CH]
tel. 087185241
www.masciarelli.it

CELLAR SALES
PRE-BOOKED VISITS

ANNUAL PRODUCTION 3,000,000 bottles
HECTARES UNDER VINE 420
VITICULTURE METHOD Conventional

Two years have passed since Gianni Masciarelli died and his splendid winery continues to produce top-quality wines. Much is due to the courage of his wife Marina Cvetic, whose hands-on dedication has guided a company making almost three million bottles, with over 400 hectares of vines scattered over much of Abruzzo and exporting halfway around the world. These are wines that can reach peaks of excellence but are always, whatever the case, reliable and good value for money.

No Villa Gemma '07 this year as it is maturing in oak and will not see the light until 2011. There is a sumptuous Castello di Semivicoli Trebbiano '08, however, which flaunts both power and agility. The reds include the Montepulciano d'Abruzzo and the new Marina Cvetic Merlot, both '07 and both intriguing. The Merlot comes from the Ofena vines and is a real surprise. Then there are two cask-aged whites, a Chardonnay and a Marina Cvetic Trebbiano, both '08, which are less oaky than in the past, but are still young. Lastly, there are the basic wines, well-crafted Montepulcianos and Trebbianos, and a successful white Villa Gemma '09, completing a varied and well-orchestrated range.

○ Trebbiano d'Abruzzo Castello di Semivicoli '08	▼▼▼+	6
○ Chardonnay Marina Cvetic '08	▼▼	6
● Merlot Marina Cvetic '07	▼▼	5
● Montepulciano d'Abruzzo Marina Cvetic '07	▼▼	5
○ Trebbiano d'Abruzzo Marina Cvetic '08	▼▼	6
● Montepulciano d'Abruzzo '09	▼▼	3*
○ Trebbiano d'Abruzzo '09	▼▼	3*
○ Villa Gemma Bianco '09	▼▼	4*
● Montepulciano d'Abruzzo Marina Cvetic '05	▽▽▽	5
● Montepulciano d'Abruzzo Villa Gemma '06	▽▽▽	8
● Montepulciano d'Abruzzo Villa Gemma '05	▽▽▽	8
● Montepulciano d'Abruzzo Villa Gemma '04	▽▽▽	8
○ Trebbiano d'Abruzzo Castello di Semivicoli '07	▽▽▽+	6
○ Trebbiano d'Abruzzo Castello di Semivicoli '05	▽▽▽	6

Mastrangelo

via Istonia, 81
66054 Vasto [CH]
tel. 3358390720
www.vinimastrangelo.com

CELLAR SALES
PRE-BOOKED VISITS

ANNUAL PRODUCTION 37,500 bottles
HECTARES UNDER VINE 6
VITICULTURE METHOD Conventional

The Mastrangelo winery in Vasto has carved itself a niche in the competitive Abruzzo winemaking scene in quite a short space of time. It has two estates: one on the Chieti hills looking out to sea, and the other in the classic Pescara territory of Loreto Aprutino. The traditional wines were more than usually enticing this year and their old-style rustic feel is the key to their charm.

The typical Tenimenti del Grifone '06 Montepulciano is nicely old fashioned, with a mature varietal nose and a tangy palate revealing a close-knit but not aggressive tannic weave. The vibrant Montepulciano d'Abruzzo Alma Dei '07 is lively, with clean hints of wild cherry and complex cocoa powder, but a surprisingly poised, full mouthfeel with long, concentrated structure. A worthy white is the Trebbiano d'Abruzzo L'Oro del Cardinale '07 for its well-meshed vanilla and oak notes, and elegant structure. The rustic aromas and a tart, over-evolved palate marked down the very old-school Pecorino Nuntius '09. Trebbiano '09 is fresh, agile and uncomplicated.

● Montepulciano d'Abruzzo Alma Dei '07	▼▼	4
● Montepulciano d'Abruzzo Tenimenti del Grifone '06	▼▼	5
○ Trebbiano d'Abruzzo L'Oro del Cardinale '06	▼▼	5
○ Nunthius '09	▼	4
○ Trebbiano d'Abruzzo '09	▼	4
● Montepulciano d'Abruzzo La Riserva del Vicario '04	▽▽	5
○ Trebbiano d'Abruzzo L'Oro del Cardinale '05	▽▽	5

Camillo Montori

LOC. PIANE TRONTO, 82
64010 CONTROGUERRA [TE]
TEL. 0861809900
www.montorivini.it

CELLAR SALES
PRE-BOOKED VISITS
ROOMS AND FOOD

ANNUAL PRODUCTION 600,000 bottles
HECTARES UNDER VINE 50
VITICULTURE METHOD Conventional

This winery, a byword for Colline Teramane and key in the creation of the DOCG, covers 50 hectares in northern Abruzzo, on the Tronto river border with the Marche. Run with sound country, it turns out traditional wines in the old Controguerra cellars so it is a surprise to see restyling of labels and names, perhaps in an attempt to find a slicker look for wines that appeal precisely for their classic style.

This year, there are five above-average labels. First up is an inspired Trend Riserva '06, a classic, solid Controguerra Rosso cabernet and montepulciano. Then there is a typical, pleasant Montepulciano Fonte Cupa '06, with caressing smoky notes while the oak where the wine matured has amalgamated with its full, juicy structure. Trend '09 is the new name for a Pecorino that was always one of the most minerally and interesting versions of this native grape. The Passerina is also as brisk and clear-cut as it should be. The traditional Trebbiano d'Abruzzo Fonte Cupa '09 is varietal and alcohol-led, standing out for its intense, nicely tangy progression.

○ Controguerra Passerina Trend '09	▼▼	4
● Controguerra Rosso Trend Ris. '06	▼▼	6
● Montepulciano d'Abruzzo Fonte Cupa '06	▼▼	5
○ Pecorino Trend '09	▼▼	4
○ Trebbiano d'Abruzzo Fonte Cupa '09	▼▼	4
○ Controguerra Passerina Trend '09	▽▽	4
⊙ Montepulciano d'Abruzzo Cerasuolo '08	▽▽	3*
● Montepulciano d'Abruzzo Colline Teramane Fonte Cupa '02	▽▽	5
○ Trebbiano d'Abruzzo Fonte Cupa '08	▽▽	4

Bruno Nicodemi

C.DA VENIGLIO
64024 NOTARESCO [TE]
TEL. 085895493
www.nicodemi.com

CELLAR SALES
PRE-BOOKED VISITS

ANNUAL PRODUCTION 200,000 bottles
HECTARES UNDER VINE 30
VITICULTURE METHOD Conventional

Nicodemi, on the Notaresco tableland in the Colline Teramane, has always been crucial to this district. It is a small winery confidently run in a traditional style by Elena and her brother Alessandro. The excellent estate vineyards are cared for with love and the wines are typified by their structure, fruit and weight, retaining a good balance despite being lavishly extracted.

The Notàri '07 Montepulciano Colline Teramane was our favourite, with complex, balsamic yet typical aromas. The tannins are close-knit and concentrated, with a cool acidity sustaining the structure. As always, the Neromoro is an extreme Montepulciano, the result of some heavy-duty extraction. The oak in this '06 vintage is noticeable but will tone down with time. The basic Montepulciano d'Abruzzo '08, with intense wild cherry on the nose, is a competent red, consistent but not overpowering, to knock back without a second thought. The varietal Notàri Bianco '09, an elegant Trebbiano d'Abruzzo, is good. The basic Trebbiano '09 this year is one of the soundest of its type.

● Montepulciano d'Abruzzo Colline Teramane Notàri '07	▼▼	5
● Montepulciano d'Abruzzo Colline Teramane Neromoro Ris. '06	▼▼	6
○ Trebbiano d'Abruzzo '09	▼▼	3*
○ Trebbiano d'Abruzzo Notàri '09	▼▼	4
● Montepulciano d'Abruzzo '08	▼	4
● Montepulciano d'Abruzzo Colline Teramane Neromoro Ris. '03	▽▽▽	6
● Montepulciano d'Abruzzo Colline Teramane Neromoro Ris. '04	▽▽	6
● Montepulciano d'Abruzzo Colline Teramane Notàri '06	▽▽	5
● Montepulciano d'Abruzzo Colline Teramane Ris. '00	▽▽	5

Pasetti

C.da Pretaro
via San Paolo, 21
66023 Francavilla al Mare [CH]
tel. 08561875
www.pasettivini.it

CELLAR SALES
PRE-BOOKED VISITS
ROOMS

ANNUAL PRODUCTION **500,000 bottles**
HECTARES UNDER VINE **40**
VITICULTURE METHOD **Conventional**

Mimmo and Franca Pasetti's thriving Francavilla al Mare winery does not seem to be suffering from the recession. The happy couple run a prospering business, reaping on-going success from the grapes grown at Pescosansonesco, at the foot of Gran Sasso, and at Capestrano, in Abruzzo's so-called oven. Wines from these estates are modern and popular with consumers, which is no bad thing.

The rich, powerful Montepulciano Hariman '05 has surprising symmetry. The nose has complex, stylish, smoky aromas; the palate is full and concentrated, sustained by a lovely tangy note. Pecorino Colle Civetta '09 is an excellent, stylish white, vinified completely in steel, and with fresh, terpenic, quite complex aromas. The Testarossa has always been one of the most reliable Montepulcianos around and the '06 has wild cherry on the nose, with a full, nicely husky palate. The pleasant, intense Cerasuolo '09 is one of the best in Abruzzo. Pecorino '09 is the winery's warhorse, its quality constant despite the thousands of bottles produced. The Trebbiano Zarachè '09 is well typed.

● Montepulciano d'Abruzzo Harimann '05	**YY**	7
○ Pecorino Pasetti Colle Civetta '09	**YY**	5
⊙ Montepulciano d'Abruzzo Cerasuolo Pasetti '09	**YY**	3*
● Montepulciano d'Abruzzo Tenuta di Testarossa '06	**YY**	5
○ Pecorino Pasetti '09	**Y**	4
○ Trebbiano d'Abruzzo Zarachè '09	**Y**	4
⊙ Montepulciano d'Abruzzo Cerasuolo Pasetti '08	YY	3*
● Montepulciano d'Abruzzo Harimann '04	YY	7
○ Trebbiano d'Abruzzo Zarachè '08	YY	4*

Emidio Pepe

via Chiesi, 10
64010 Torano Nuovo [TE]
tel. 0861856493
www.emidiopepe.com

CELLAR SALES
PRE-BOOKED VISITS
ROOMS

ANNUAL PRODUCTION **80,000 bottles**
HECTARES UNDER VINE **15**
VITICULTURE METHOD **Certified organic**

Emidio Pepe is one of the founding fathers of fine Abruzzo wine. In the 1970s, Mario Soldati held up Torano Nuova, in the Colline Teramane, as an example of modern wine production. Little has changed, with fermentation and maturation always in cement, followed by bottle ageing. Classic vineyard management is artfully unsophisticated and respects the quirks of each cru. Recently Sofia Pepe, who now runs the estate, has introduced biodynamics.

This year the pared-down list did well. The Trebbiano d'Abruzzo '08 is a delight, showing elegantly rustic with subtle floral notes on the nose, underpinned by varietal toastiness, and a refined, juicy palate already drinking well but promising even more. The '09 Cerasuolo is a classic Pepe rosé, with natural, evolved hints and a pleasant, refreshing palate. The Montepulciano d'Abruzzo '07 is enjoyable and very crisp for a Pepe. We left it to breathe and found hints of damp earth, then aromas of cherry and wild cherry. The cool, tangy progression aroused our curiosity, so we will see how it evolves.

● Montepulciano d'Abruzzo '07	**YY**	6
○ Trebbiano d'Abruzzo '08	**YY**	6
⊙ Montepulciano d'Abruzzo Cerasuolo '09	**YY**	6
● Montepulciano d'Abruzzo '98	YYY	8
● Montepulciano d'Abruzzo Bio '05	YY	8
● Montepulciano d'Abruzzo Colline Teramane '06	YY	8
○ Trebbiano d'Abruzzo '07	YY	6
○ Trebbiano d'Abruzzo '06	YY	6
○ Trebbiano d'Abruzzo '03	YY	6

Pietrantonj

via San Sebastiano, 38
67030 Vittorito [AQ]
tel. 0864727102
www.vinipietrantonj.it

CELLAR SALES
PRE-BOOKED VISITS

ANNUAL PRODUCTION **650,000 bottles**
HECTARES UNDER VINE **60**
VITICULTURE METHOD **Conventional**

The historic Vittorito winery is inland of Pescara, just under Maiella, and has been producing wine for about 200 years in this area. Pietrantonj's wines always make an impact, their mountain character coming through in a traditional feel and significant acidity. Backing this up is intact fruit and a typicality that can sometimes sacrifice elegance and approachability.

The Cerano '06 is a sound, full Montepulciano that shows robust and flavoursome but closes tart and clenched. Arboreo '07, the house's second Montepulciano, is clean, with red berries on the nose, but a tad overripe on the palate, which closes slightly tart. The rosé Cerasuolo Arboreo '09 is as good as ever, played out on vibrant strawberry hints and with gentle, persuasive continuity. From the whites, the Malvasia '09 is hardly a paragon of style but it is a pleasant, clean wine, even tautly elegant. The two Trebbiano d'Abruzzo house whites, Arboreo '09 and Cerano '09, are well made by no more, presenting rather unsophisticated.

○ Malvasia '09	🍷🍷	3*
● Montepulciano d'Abruzzo Arboreo '07	🍷🍷	5
● Montepulciano d'Abruzzo Cerano '06	🍷🍷	3*
⊙ Montepulciano d'Abruzzo Cerasuolo Arboreo '09	🍷🍷	2*
○ Trebbiano d'Abruzzo Arboreo '09	🍷	4
○ Trebbiano d'Abruzzo Cerano '09	🍷	4
● Montepulciano d'Abruzzo Arboreo '03	YY	2*
● Montepulciano d'Abruzzo Cerano '05	YY	3*
● Montepulciano d'Abruzzo Cerano '02	YY	4
○ Trebbiano d'Abruzzo Arboreo '08	YY	4

San Lorenzo

c.da Plavignano, 2
64035 Castilenti [TE]
tel. 0861999325
www.sanlorenzovini.com

CELLAR SALES
PRE-BOOKED VISITS

ANNUAL PRODUCTION **680,000 bottles**
HECTARES UNDER VINE **150**
VITICULTURE METHOD **Conventional**

This thriving border winery, astride the provinces of Teramo and Pescara, is managed with enthusiasm by the two young Galassos, descendants of a true Abruzzo wine dynasty. There are over 100 hectares under vine, ranging from classic native to international varieties. The wines are powerful and enterprising but sometimes chase market trends and thereby lose sight of the terroir's huge potential.

Again, this year's list was long, with 14 labels from a robust, mouthfilling Colline Teramane Riserva to more quaffable rosés, with every wine nuance in between. The Montepulciano Colline Teramane Riserva '06 Escol has grand texture but lacks finesse in the handling and the tannins are still clenched, with emerging new oak notes. The ambitious Oinos '07 is a full, rich, tasty Montepulciano Colline Teramane, with oak on the nose that may be difficult to absorb. The Antares '08 is a plush, fruity Montepulciano. We liked the white Pecorino '09, which is crisp, varietal and fresh, and the competent Trebbiano Sirio '09. A special mention for the fragrant, enjoyable Rosato '09.

● Montepulciano d'Abruzzo Colline Teramane Escol Ris. '06	🍷🍷	5
● Montepulciano d'Abruzzo Antares '08	🍷🍷	3*
● Montepulciano d'Abruzzo Colline Teramane Oinos '07	🍷🍷	5
○ Pecorino '09	🍷🍷	3*
⊙ Rosato '09	🍷🍷	2*
● Montepulciano d'Abruzzo Aldebaran '09	🍷	4
● Montepulciano d'Abruzzo Sirio '07	🍷	2*
○ Trebbiano d'Abruzzo Sirio '09	🍷	2*
○ Chardonnay Chioma di Berenice '07	YY	4*
● Montepulciano d'Abruzzo Antares '07	YY	3*
● Montepulciano d'Abruzzo Colline Teramane '03	YY	5
● Montepulciano d'Abruzzo Colline Teramane Oinos '06	YY	5
● Montepulciano d'Abruzzo Sirio '07	YY	2*

Nicola Santoleri

via dei Cavalieri, 20
66016 Guardiagrele [CH]
tel. 0871893301
www.nicolasantoleri.it

ANNUAL PRODUCTION **40,000 bottles**
HECTARES UNDER VINE **30**
VITICULTURE METHOD **Conventional**

The plucky offspring of that Abruzzo wine gentleman Nicola Santoleri have taken on a far from simple legacy, despite their youth. For many aficionados, Nicola's wines were an outright passion, embodying the noble integrity of a county heritage with many virtues and one or two imperfections. The great grapes from the historic Guardiagrele vines, on Maiella's Chieti foothills, are vinified traditionally, with few concessions to modernity.

The Crognaleto Riserva '98 is an old-school Montepulciano d'Abruzzo with layered cocoa powder and coffee notes, but also nice balsam. The palate is remarkable for its sound fruit, despite the vintage, and the mouthfilling progression typical of a great red, which reveals the wine is still very young. The Vigna Ladra is traditionally a more refreshing, open Montepulciano. The sweet, juicy texture has an appealing huskiness. This year, the Trebbiano Crognaleto '08 is especially appealing, with mineral aromas, and confirms it is one of the best of its sort.

● Montepulciano d'Abruzzo Crognaleto Ris. '98	🍷🍷	6
● Montepulciano d'Abruzzo V. Ladra '07	🍷🍷	5
○ Trebbiano d'Abruzzo Crognaleto '08	🍷🍷	5
● Montepulciano d'Abruzzo Crognaleto Ris. '00	🍷🍷	6
○ Trebbiano d'Abruzzo Crognaleto '07	🍷🍷	5

Strappelli

loc. Torri, 15
64010 Torano Nuovo [TE]
tel. 0861887402
www.cantinastrappelli.it

CELLAR SALES
PRE-BOOKED VISITS

ANNUAL PRODUCTION **60,000 bottles**
HECTARES UNDER VINE **10**
VITICULTURE METHOD **Certified organic**

The Strappelli family has been growing grapes for generations on a true terroir, the Villa Torri hillside at Torano Nuova, in the Colline Teramane. Gran Sasso lies to the east and the sea to the south of these ten hectares that have been totally converted to certified organic viticulture, with only traditional vines. The winemaking style refuses to be draw into modern excess and the wines are very well typed, with bags of character.

The Colle Trà '07, an inspired Colline Teramane Riserva, had no trouble getting into our finals thanks to its complex, crisp aromas, the result of long skin contact. There is quinine on the nose, but also traditional morello cherry, and the concentrated palate is full, with strikingly solid texture. The Montepulciano d'Abruzzo '07 has earth and ripe fruit aromas, while the palate reveals a full, spirited tannic weave. The whites include a Pecorino Soprano '09 with complex bitter orange and grapefruit. The crisp, clean Trebbiano d'Abruzzo '09 has easy, pleasant progression.

● Montepulciano d'Abruzzo Colline Teramane Colle Trà '07	🍷🍷	4*
● Montepulciano d'Abruzzo '07	🍷🍷	4*
○ Pecorino Soprano '09	🍷🍷	4*
○ Trebbiano d'Abruzzo '09	🍷	3
● Montepulciano d'Abruzzo '06	🍷🍷	4*
● Montepulciano d'Abruzzo '05	🍷🍷	4*
● Montepulciano d'Abruzzo Colline Teramane Celibe Ris. '03	🍷🍷	6
● Montepulciano d'Abruzzo Colline Teramane Celibe Ris. '04	🍷🍷	6

Terra d'Aligi

loc. Piazzano
via Piana La Fara, 90
66041 Atessa [CH]
tel. 0872897916
www.terradaligi.it

CELLAR SALES
PRE-BOOKED VISITS

ANNUAL PRODUCTION **550,000 bottles**
HECTARES UNDER VINE **50**
VITICULTURE METHOD **Conventional**

After last year's dubious efforts, the Spinelli family winery recovered its usual standard and earned a full Guide profile. The location is the Val di Sangro hill district in the province of Chieti at Atessa, where the wines are powerful, robust, perhaps lacking in finesse, but certainly well crafted and interesting. Terra d'Aligi almost always produces very successful wines in this style.

We tasted a most convincing Tatone '07 Montepulciano, presenting as solid and generous as usual. The varietal, balsamic aromas have a hint of oak woven into a muscular, refined texture. The second Montepulciano d'Abruzzo, Tolos '07, is also interesting with intense and quite unexpected bitter orange and Mediterranean herb notes on the nose. The palate has a complex yet agile structure. The Montepulciano d'Abruzzo '08 impressed with its power, drinking taut and full of character. The whites included an enjoyably refreshing, crisp Pecorino '09 and the Trebbiano d'Abruzzo '09 left us in no doubt with its lovely toasty, varietal nose and poised, juicy progression.

● Montepulciano d'Abruzzo Tatone '07	▼▼	4*
● Montepulciano d'Abruzzo '08	▼▼	3*
● Montepulciano d'Abruzzo Tolos '07	▼▼	6
○ Pecorino '09	▼▼	3*
○ Trebbiano d'Abruzzo '09	▼▼	3*
● Montepulciano d'Abruzzo Tolos '05	▽▽	6
● Montepulciano d'Abruzzo Tolos '03	▽▽	5
● Montepulciano d'Abruzzo Tolos '01	▽▽	5

Tiberio

c.da La Vota
65020 Cugnoli [PE]
tel. 0858576744
www.tiberio.it

CELLAR SALES
PRE-BOOKED VISITS

ANNUAL PRODUCTION **80,000 bottles**
HECTARES UNDER VINE **30**
VITICULTURE METHOD **Conventional**

The Tiberio family winery on Maiella's Pescara slopes is run mainly by Cristiana, despite her youth. She chose to produce unique, personal wines, forged by the temperatures that are a key factor here at harvest time. The wines come from the Cugnoli vineyards, between Maiella and Gran Sasso, and are vinified with modern methods that manage to preserve the traits imparted by the terroir's soil and weather conditions.

The Montepulciano '07 Althea reached the finals for its intense, caressing wild cherry and blueberry aromas. The palate is sweet, Mediterranean and very pleasing, sustained by good tannic weave and crisp acidity. The Montepulciano d'Abruzzo '08 is just a notch below, with clean, well-defined cherry notes and an intense, coherent palate. The whites include a striking Pecorino '09, already layered, subtle and with a good grapefruit note that suggests mineral development to come. The well crafted Trebbiano is more traditional, sustained by charred oak and hints of cultured yeasts. The Cerasuolo '09 is enjoyable.

● Montepulciano d'Abruzzo Althea '07	▼▼	5
● Montepulciano d'Abruzzo '08	▼▼	4*
○ Pecorino '09	▼▼	4
⊙ Montepulciano d'Abruzzo Cerasuolo '09	▼	4
○ Trebbiano d'Abruzzo '09	▼	4
● Montepulciano d'Abruzzo '07	▽▽	4*
● Montepulciano d'Abruzzo '06	▽▽	3*
● Montepulciano d'Abruzzo Althea '06	▽▽	5
● Montepulciano d'Abruzzo Althea '05	▽▽	5
○ Trebbiano d'Abruzzo '07	▽▽	4*

Cantina Tollo

VIA GARIBALDI, 68
66010 TOLLO [CH]
TEL. 087196251
www.cantinatollo.it

CELLAR SALES
PRE-BOOKED VISITS

ANNUAL PRODUCTION 12,500,000 bottles
HECTARES UNDER VINE 3,500
VITICULTURE METHOD Conventional

Cantina Tollo, simply the best of Abruzzo's many co-operative wineries and one of the region's top labels, has been producing quality for years, exploiting the significant potential of countless small contributors on the prosperous Chieti hills, from Mount Maiella down to the Adriatic. Year after year, this generous land gives impressively well-made wines that represent great value for money.

The simple Aldiano Riserva '07, a Montepulciano d'Abruzzo produced in large quantities, had no trouble reaching the finals with its elegant, caressing wild cherry and cocoa powder nose, and a full, subtle palate. There were also some surprises from the Hedòs, an inspired Cerasuolo '09 with an intense strawberry and almond nose, and a full, concentrated palate refreshed by a tangy finale. Colle Secco Rubino and Riserva are confirmed as two of the region's best Montepulcianos for their price bracket. The well-focused Pecorino '09 is nicely rustic and underpinned by an intense, enjoyable progression, with its usual tart finale. All the other wines on the very long list are well made.

● Montepulciano d'Abruzzo Aldiano Ris. '07	▼▼	4*
⊙ Montepulciano d'Abruzzo Cerasuolo Hedòs '09	▼▼	4*
● Montepulciano d'Abruzzo Colle Secco Ris. '07	▼▼	4*
● Montepulciano d'Abruzzo Colle Secco Rubino '07	▼▼	4*
○ Pecorino '09	▼▼	4*
○ Cretico Chardonnay '08	▼	5
● Montepulciano d'Abruzzo Valle d'Oro '08	▼	2*
○ Chardonnay Cretico '07	▽▽	5
● Montepulciano d'Abruzzo Aldiano '07	▽▽	4*
● Montepulciano d'Abruzzo Cagiòlo '06	▽▽	5
● Montepulciano d'Abruzzo Colle Secco Rubino '06	▽▽	4*
● Montepulciano d'Abruzzo Duecuori '07	▽▽	3*
○ Trebbiano d'Abruzzo Aldiano '08	▽▽	4*
○ Trebbiano d'Abruzzo Duecuori '08	▽▽	3*
○ Trebbiano d'Abruzzo Menir '07	▽▽	5

Torre dei Beati

C.DA POGGIORAGONE, 56
65014 LORETO APRUTINO [PE]
TEL. 3333832344
www.torredeibeati.it

CELLAR SALES
PRE-BOOKED VISITS

ANNUAL PRODUCTION 60,000 bottles
HECTARES UNDER VINE 17
VITICULTURE METHOD Certified organic

Torre dei Beati is a commendable winery, as modern as it is artisanal, in Loreto Aprutino with its landscape of vines and olive groves facing the Popoli gullies between Gran Sasso and Maiella. This is a splendid area with a long tradition of viticulture, where the few hectares are managed with a farmer's skill and traditional but never cautious cellaring technique. The passion of Fausto and Adriana Albanese produces interesting wines.

The Cocciapazza '07 won Three Glasses for its caressing, concentrated aromas and powerful, complex palate, with a slightly pinched texture that will relax with time, to reveal that it is a pedigree Montepulciano. Mazzamurello '07, the second Montepulciano selection, matures on fine lees is still unyielding but already suggests an elegant nose and imposing, vigorous structure. There is also the uncomplicated Montepulciano d'Abruzzo '08, with its refreshing wild cherry notes and a juicy, intrepid body. Rosa-ae '09 is one of the region's most individual Cerasuolos. The Pecorino '09 is the best ever thanks to varietal aromas and nice pulp refreshing the palate.

● Montepulciano d'Abruzzo Cocciapazza '07	▼▼▼	5
● Montepulciano d'Abruzzo '08	▼▼	4*
● Montepulciano d'Abruzzo Mazzamurello '07	▼▼	6
⊙ Montepulciano d'Abruzzo Cerasuolo Rosa-ae '09	▼▼	3*
○ Pecorino '09	▼▼	4
● Montepulciano d'Abruzzo '07	▽▽▽	4*
⊙ Montepulciano d'Abruzzo Cerasuolo Rosa-ae '08	▽▽	3*
● Montepulciano d'Abruzzo Cocciapazza '06	▽▽	5
● Montepulciano d'Abruzzo Mazzamurello '04	▽▽	5

La Valentina

VIA TORRETTA, 52
65010 SPOLTORE [PE]
TEL. 0854478158
www.fattorialavalentina.it

CELLAR SALES
PRE-BOOKED VISITS

ANNUAL PRODUCTION 350,000 bottles
HECTARES UNDER VINE 40
VITICULTURE METHOD Organic

One of the most established wineries on the Pescara hills once more showed its stuff although a top award eluded it. The two estates, the older on the hills behind the city of Pescara, and the more recent on the Maiella slopes at San Valentino in Abruzzo Citeriore, have very different soils that provide the Di Properzios with exceptional raw materials for original, idiosyncratic wines produced with organic methods and modern cellaring.

We have to acknowledge again this year that the most interesting wine tasted was the Spelt. The '06 Montepulciano d'Abruzzo is subtle, clean and layered, with balsamic and mineral notes barely veiled by oak that will presumably metabolize with time; the palate is round and enjoyably tangy. Bellovedere '07 was less convincing, with typical but more rustic notes, and a concentrated, tannic palate. The Montepulciano d'Abruzzo '08 is basic only in price, flaunting intense, caressing aromas and a succulent progression. The whites included a Pecorino '09 and a quaffable Trebbiano '09, an uncomplicated but very well made wine.

● Montepulciano d'Abruzzo Spelt '06	🍷🍷	5
● Montepulciano d'Abruzzo '08	🍷🍷	3*
● Montepulciano d'Abruzzo Bellovedere '07	🍷🍷	7
○ Pecorino '09	🍷	4
○ Trebbiano d'Abruzzo '09	🍷	3
● Montepulciano d'Abruzzo Bellovedere '05	YYY	7
● Montepulciano d'Abruzzo Spelt '05	YYY	5

★★ Valentini

VIA DEL BAIO, 2
65014 LORETO APRUTINO [PE]
TEL. 0858291138

ANNUAL PRODUCTION 40,000 bottles
HECTARES UNDER VINE 64
VITICULTURE METHOD Organic

Meet the Winery of the Year for Italian Wines 2011, which says a great deal about our opinion of Francesco Valentini and his magnificent wines. We also think his father Edoardo, a great grower and wine man, would have been proud of what his son has achieved. Vineyards at Loreto Aprutino, surrounded by Gran Sasso, Maiella and the Adriatic, and genuine wines made with time-honoured artisanal viticulture and simple methods from superb grapes.

A triple Three Glass winner. Not an easy feat in our Guide but we had no option, especially after Francesco decided to present all three house wines, which is quite rare these days. So we enjoyed a sumptuous Montepulciano d'Abruzzo '06. Powerful, agile, rustic yet elegant, complex but drinkable. A masterpiece that is ready to drink now but which will live for years. The splendidly complex Trebbiano d'Abruzzo '08 is one of Italy's great whites, with heady, charred oak notes, hints of wild flowers and a persuasively taut, zesty progression. The deliciously fragrant Cerasuolo '09 is young but long and savoury. Don't miss this rosé.

● Montepulciano d'Abruzzo '06	🍷🍷🍷+	8
⊙ Montepulciano d'Abruzzo Cerasuolo '09	🍷🍷🍷	7
○ Trebbiano d'Abruzzo '08	🍷🍷🍷	7
● Montepulciano d'Abruzzo '02	YYY	8
● Montepulciano d'Abruzzo '01	YYY	8
● Montepulciano d'Abruzzo '00	YYY	8
● Montepulciano d'Abruzzo '97	YYY	7
● Montepulciano d'Abruzzo '95	YYY	6
● Montepulciano d'Abruzzo '90	YYY	6
⊙ Montepulciano d'Abruzzo Cerasuolo '08	YYY	7
⊙ Montepulciano d'Abruzzo Cerasuolo '06	YYY	7
○ Trebbiano d'Abruzzo '05	YYY	7
○ Trebbiano d'Abruzzo '04	YYY	7
○ Trebbiano d'Abruzzo '02	YYY	7
○ Trebbiano d'Abruzzo '01	YYY	6
○ Trebbiano d'Abruzzo '00	YYY	6

Valle Reale

Loc. San Calisto
65026 Popoli [PE]
tel. 0859871039
www.vallereale.it

CELLAR SALES
PRE-BOOKED VISITS

ANNUAL PRODUCTION 522,800 bottles
HECTARES UNDER VINE 60
VITICULTURE METHOD Conventional

This developing inland Abruzzo winery has an estate in Popoli and one in Capestrano. Viticulture here is tough, in a mountain area no one thought could bring such results. The unique wines are distinctive and their fundamental hallmark is their elegance. It's all due to the tenacity of Leonardo Pizzolo, who loves this land and who, aided by oenologist Luciana Biondo, has taken courageous route of spontaneous fermentation without inoculated yeasts.

The Montepulciano San Calisto '07 is the best ever. On tasting, it reveals subtle, very clean aromas of wild strawberry and raspberry. The palate is not enormous but is refined, expansive, and even agile. The Trebbiano Vigneto di Capestrano '08 is a white that honours its native vine, a natural wine with a crisp, citrussy nose. The Valle Reale Montepulciano is modern, refreshing and in this '08 version hints at tomato and violet; the palate is clean and gutsy, with a nicely zesty finale. A new cru, the Sant'Eusanio '09, is a Montepulciano matured in steel, with an interestingly compact consistency. The simple, well-managed Vigne Nuove wines can be very good.

● Montepulciano d'Abruzzo San Calisto '07	TTT+	6
○ Trebbiano d'Abruzzo V. di Capestrano '08	TTT	5
● Montepulciano d'Abruzzo Valle Reale '08	TT	4*
● Montepulciano d'Abruzzo Vigne Nuove '09	TT	3*
● Montepulciano d'Abruzzo Sant'Eusanio '09	TT	4
⊙ Montepulciano d'Abruzzo Cerasuolo Vigne Nuove '09	T	3
● Montepulciano d'Abruzzo San Calisto '06	YYY+	6
● Montepulciano d'Abruzzo San Calisto '05	YYY	6
● Montepulciano d'Abruzzo San Calisto '04	YYY	6
● Montepulciano d'Abruzzo Valle Reale '06	YYY	4*
● Montepulciano d'Abruzzo San Calisto '03	YY	5
● Montepulciano d'Abruzzo Valle Reale '07	YY	4*
○ Trebbiano d'Abruzzo V. di Capestrano '07	YY	5

Valori

via Torquato al Salinello, 8
64027 Sant'Omero [TE]
tel. 086188461
vinivalori@tin.it

PRE-BOOKED VISITS

ANNUAL PRODUCTION 30,000 bottles
HECTARES UNDER VINE 16
VITICULTURE METHOD Conventional

To understand the Valori winery, you have to visit the Sant'Omero estate. The vineyard is tended as if it was a garden and in no way resembles the others round about. We are in the heart of the Colline Teramane, almost on the Marche border, and this territory produces complex, intense grapes that Luigi Valori processes with skill, assisted by partner Marina Cvetic Masciarelli's staff.

We received only three wines. The Montepulciano d'Abruzzo Vigna Sant'Angelo '07 is the flagship and a regular at our finals. It gives intense blueberry, wild cherry and cocoa powder on the nose, with a full, Mediterranean palate, sustained by a classic sea-salt acidity. The Inkiostro '07, from merlot only, is a classic southern Italian red, with bottled cherry on the nose and a round, tannic palate. The substantial texture has still to unfold but will evolve nicely with time. The alcoholic Trebbiano d'Abruzzo '09 is as varietal as it should be, with a crisp, consistent palate.

● Montepulciano d'Abruzzo V. Sant'Angelo '07	TT	5
● Inkiostro '07	TT	5
○ Trebbiano d'Abruzzo '09	TT	3*
● Montepulciano d'Abruzzo V. Sant' Angelo '03	YYY	5
● Inkiostro '05	YY	5
● Montepulciano d'Abruzzo V. Sant' Angelo '05	YY	5
● Montepulciano d'Abruzzo V. Sant' Angelo '04	YY	5
● Montepulciano d'Abruzzo V. Sant'Angelo '06	YY	5

Villa Medoro

FRAZ. FONTANELLE
64030 ATRI [TE]
TEL. 0858708142
www.villamedoro.it

CELLAR SALES
PRE-BOOKED VISITS

ANNUAL PRODUCTION 300,000 bottles
HECTARES UNDER VINE 100
VITICULTURE METHOD Conventional

The entrepreneurial verve and skills of a very young Federica Morricone are the reason for the international success this Atri winery reaped recently. The winery has state-of-the-art equipment, a good 92 hectares under vine on the southern slopes of the Colline Teramane, and a range of wines that astonishes, not least for their affordability, not to be sniffed at in these times of recession.

We were surprised to find that the best wine this year was the Montepulciano d'Abruzzo '08, a basic product at a truly honest price for a red of this calibre. It is masterfully made, powerful and agile, with good structure and drinkability. Also nice are the Adrano '07 Colline Teramane, unbelievably concentrated but with clean aromas, and a more rustic, traditional Rosso del Duca '08. The whites include a Chimera '09 trebbiano and falanghina blend and a Trebbiano d'Abruzzo '09, both delicious. The Cerasuolo '09 is fragrant and approachable. The debuting Pecorino '09 is interesting with varietal aromas and a gutsy palate.

● Montepulciano d'Abruzzo '08	▼▼▼+	3*
● Montepulciano d'Abruzzo Colline Teramane Adrano '07	▼▼	6
● Montepulciano d'Abruzzo Rosso del Duca '08	▼▼	4*
○ Chimera '09	▼▼	3*
⊙ Montepulciano d'Abruzzo Cerasuolo '09	▼▼	3*
○ Pecorino '09	▼▼	3*
○ Trebbiano d'Abruzzo '09	▼▼	3*
● Montepulciano d'Abruzzo '06	▽▽▽	3*
● Montepulciano d'Abruzzo Colline Teramane Adrano '06	▽▽▽	6
● Montepulciano d'Abruzzo Colline Teramane Adrano '05	▽▽▽	6
● Montepulciano d'Abruzzo Colline Teramane Adrano '04	▽▽▽	6
● Montepulciano d'Abruzzo Colline Teramane Adrano '03	▽▽▽	6

Ciccio Zaccagnini

C.DA POZZO
65020 BOLOGNANO [PE]
TEL. 0858880195
www.cantinazaccagnini.it

CELLAR SALES
PRE-BOOKED VISITS

ANNUAL PRODUCTION 1,200,000 bottles
HECTARES UNDER VINE 150
VITICULTURE METHOD Conventional

Years ago, Zaccagnini managed to square the quality versus quantity circle. This established winery has spoiled us with keynote wines that enjoy great commercial success. Here in Bolognano, on the Pescara hills, there are over 150 hectares of estate yielding native and international wines for every palate and preference, always combining a varietal stamp with appeal. We tasted a wide selection this year.

The Trebbiano San Clemente '08 impressed us with its intense, varietal aromas, the oak carefully gauged so the fruit is not masked. The Tralcetto is a lovely Montepulciano at a persuasive price, with hints of cherry and cocoa powder, and a pleasing, round flavour. Bianco di Ciccio is a persuasive, drinkable Trebbiano that shows clean and palatable. Yamada '09 is a full, dense Pecorino with typical almondy notes and generous, weighty palate. As usual, the Castello di Salle '07 is a sound, well-made Montepulciano. The other wines are well managed.

● Montepulciano d'Abruzzo Tralcetto '08	▼▼	3*
○ Trebbiano d'Abruzzo S. Clemente '08	▼▼	5
○ Bianco di Ciccio '09	▼▼	3*
● Montepulciano d'Abruzzo Castello di Salle '07	▼▼	4
⊙ Montepulciano d'Abruzzo Cerasuolo Myosotis '09	▼▼	4*
● Montepulciano d'Abruzzo Chronicon '07	▼▼	4*
● Montepulciano d'Abruzzo Cuvée dell'Abate '08	▼▼	3*
● Montepulciano d'Abruzzo S. Clemente Ris. '07	▼▼	6
○ Trebbiano d'Abruzzo Chronicon '09	▼▼	4*
○ Yamada '09	▼▼	4
● Montepulciano d'Abruzzo Castello di Salle '06	▽▽	4*
● Montepulciano d'Abruzzo S. Clemente '06	▽▽	6
● Montepulciano d'Abruzzo S. Clemente '05	▽▽	6

Barone Cornacchia
Villa Torri, 20
64010 Torano Nuovo [TE]
tel. 0861887412
www.baronecornacchia.it

Barone Cornacchia is a traditional Abruzzo winery that presented just a few wines. The taut, consistent Poggio Varano '07 Montepulciano d'Abruzzo has well-typed, fruit-forward notes. The Trebbiano d'Abruzzo '09 is uncomplicated, but fragrant and delicate.

● Montepulciano d'Abruzzo Poggio Varano '07	🍷🍷 4
○ Trebbiano d'Abruzzo '09	🍷 3

Nestore Bosco
c.da Casali, 147
65010 Nocciano [PE]
tel. 085847345
www.nestorebosco.com

The historic winery in the Pescara hills has been vinifying at Nocciano since 1897. We like the Pecorino '09, with varietal aromas and a lively, intense palate. The opulent reds are less successful. An ambitious Voluptuosus '06 Montepulciano has good texture but too much oak. Trebbiano '09 is well typed.

○ Pecorino '09	🍷🍷 4
● Montepulciano d'Abruzzo Voluptuosus '06	🍷 5
○ Trebbiano d'Abruzzo '09	🍷 4

Cerulli Irelli Spinozzi
loc. Casale 26
SS 150 del Vomano km 17,600
64020 Canzano [TE]
tel. 086157190
www.cerullispinozzi.it

This Canzano winery in the Colline Teramane disappointed, presenting few labels and with no top wines. Cortalto '09 is still one of the region's best Pecorinos, with a typical, intense nose and crisp citrus hints. The consistent, lively Montepulciano d'Abruzzo '09 is also good.

● Montepulciano d'Abruzzo '09	🍷🍷 3*
○ Pecorino Cortalto '09	🍷🍷 4

Chiarieri
c.da Granaro, 18
65019 Pianella [PE]
tel. 085973313
www.chiarieri.it

The performance of this traditional Pianella winery was up and down. Granaro '09 Montepulciano d'Abruzzo is convincing, with an intense fruit nose and poised progression. The well-made Cerasuolo Invidia '09 is pleasing and the fresh, varietal Trebbiano Granaro '09 interesting.

● Montepulciano d'Abruzzo Granaro '09	🍷🍷 3*
⊙ Montepulciano d'Abruzzo Cerasuolo Invidia '09	🍷 3
○ Trebbiano d'Abruzzo Granaro '09	🍷 3

Giuseppe Ciavolich
loc. Quattro Strade
c.da Cerreto, 37
66010 Miglianico [CH]
tel. 0871958797
www.ciavolich.com

A traditional Chieti hills winery whose Pecorino Aries '09 is the best on the list this year. Rustic, with fermentation aromas and fresh, juicy pulp in the mouth. We also like the upfront Trebbiano Ancilla '09. The intense, nicely crafted Ancilla '08 Cabernet Sauvignon is good.

○ Aries '09	🍷🍷 4
○ Ancilla '09	🍷 3
○ Trebbiano d'Abruzzo Ancilla '09	🍷 3

Citra
c.da Cucullo
66026 Ortona [CH]
tel. 0859031342
www.citra.it

There was the usual daunting line-up from Citra. The gutsy, full-flavoured Quis '08 Montepulciano has a sea-salt nose and lithely managed texture. Quid Trebbiano d'Abruzzo is good too, with smoky, varietal notes and refreshing length. The value-for-money Palio line is also striking.

● Montepulciano d'Abruzzo Quis '08	🍷🍷 4
○ Trebbiano d'Abruzzo Palio '09	🍷🍷 2*
○ Trebbiano d'Abruzzo Quid '09	🍷🍷 3*

Tenuta I Fauri

s.da Corta, 9
66100 Chieti
tel. 0871332627
www.tenutaifauri.it

I Fauri sent us a patchy selection that struggled to earn the marks it deserves. Trebbiano d'Abruzzo Santa Cecilia '09 has a tasty progression and shows energy despite oak veiling the nose. It may not be fashionable but it is well made. Pecorino dei Fauri '09 has a rustic nose and a relaxed, tangy palate.

- ○ Pecorino dei Fauri '09 4*
- ○ Trebbiano d'Abruzzo Santa Cecilia '09 4

Cantina Frentana

via Perazza, 32
66020 Rocca San Giovanni [CH]
tel. 087260152
www.cantinafrentana.it

Traditionally one of the better wineries on Abruzzo's complex co-operative scene, Frentana this year had an indifferent year. The '09 Panarda is a classy Montepulciano, showing fruity and balsamic with elegant juicy pulp, veiled by slightly dry tannins.

- ● Montepulciano d'Abruzzo Panarda '09 3*
- ○ Pecorino '09 3

Gentile

via del Giardino, 7
67025 Ofena [AQ]
tel. 0862956618
www.gentilevini.it

A transitional year for this Ofena winery. Orfeo is a Montepulciano d'Abruzzo with fruit-rich, well-typed notes that shows agile on the palate. Zeus '07, again Montepulciano d'Abruzzo, is muzzy and marred by a tart finale. The very rustic Trebbiano Ares has over-evolved aromas.

- ● Montepulciano d'Abruzzo Orfeo '08 4*
- ● Montepulciano d'Abruzzo Zeus '07 6
- ○ Trebbiano d'Abruzzo Ares '09 2

Lepore

c.da Civita, 29
64010 Colonnella [TE]
tel. 086170860
www.vinilepore.it

A poor turnout for this established Colline Teramane winery. Passera delle Vigne, from white passerina grapes, is rustic and slightly diluted by alcohol, but still fresh and drinkable. The Montepulciano d'Abruzzo is quite forward and perilously overripe. The Trebbiano '09 is decent.

- ○ Controguerra Passerina Passera delle Vigne '09 4*
- ● Montepulciano d'Abruzzo '08 4
- ○ Trebbiano d'Abruzzo '09 3

Antonio e Elio Monti

via Pignotto, 62
64010 Controguerra [TE]
tel. 086189042
www.vinimonti.it

Lack of space robbed this Controguerra winery of a full profile. Their Senior '05 is an inspired Colline Teramane, not too refined but mighty and tannic. The intense Rio Moro '07 Riserva is a Controguerra with tight-knit tannins. The well-typed Raggio di Luna '09 Chardonnay has a round, juicy palate.

- ○ Controguerra Bianco Raggio di Luna '09 3*
- ● Controguerra Rosso Rio Moro Ris. '07 5
- ● Montepulciano d'Abruzzo Senior '05 4

Peperoncino

loc. Piano
67025 Ofena [AQ]
tel. 0862761073
www.peperoncinovini.it

This supermarket brand, originally a Cataldi Madonna label, offers quality at a good price in sound wines with decent texture. The intense, refined Montepulciano Tritano '08 is superb, with a close-knit, relaxed tannic weave. The simpler Capestrano is a lean, drinkable Montepulciano.

- ● Montepulciano d'Abruzzo Tritano '08 3*
- ● Montepulciano d'Abruzzo Capestrano '08 2*
- ○ Trebbiano d'Abruzzo Capestrano '09 1*

La Quercia

C.DA COLLE CROCE
64020 MORRO D'ORO [TE]
TEL. 0858959110
www.vinilaquercia.it

A short profile this year for the successful Morro D'Oro winery. Sadly, the wines for this edition although sound were not up to past standards. The ambitious Colline Teramane '05 is the best, with typical cherry and quinine notes, and a juicy, zesty palate. The other wines are decent.

● Montepulciano d'Abruzzo Colline Teramane Mastrobono Ris. '05	🍷🍷	6
● Montepulciano d'Abruzzo '08	🍷	4
○ Trebbiano d'Abruzzo Prima Madre '09	🍷	4

Cantina Sangro

VIA PER SANTA MARIA IMBARO, 1
66022 FOSSACESIA [CH]
TEL. 087257412
www.cantinasangro.it

This co-operative winery in Fossacesia, located on the hills that slope down to the sea, is an old acquaintance of our Guide. Montepulciano Terra Regia is firing on all cylinders again this year. The Colle Cesi '08 Montepulciano is also good, as is the Kaleo '09, a sound, fresh Pecorino.

● Montepulciano d'Abruzzo Colle Cesi '08	🍷🍷	1*
○ Pecorino Kaleo '09	🍷🍷	2*
● Montepulciano d'Abruzzo Terra Regia '06	🍷	4

Santobono

P.ZZA DELLA VITTORIA, 16
66050 SAN BUONO [CH]
TEL. 3332887579

We noted this new Vasto winery's sound, traditional wines. The three labels we tasted are worthwhile and individual. The Lenzino Riserva is a Montepulciano with concentrated, caressing aromas, and a nice husky palate. The typical, juicy Trebbiano d'Abruzzo is deliciously enjoyable.

● Montepulciano d'Abruzzo Lenzino '08	🍷🍷	4*
● Montepulciano d'Abruzzo Lenzino Ris. '06	🍷🍷	5
○ Trebbiano d'Abruzzo '09	🍷🍷	3*

Cantine Talamonti

C.DA PALAZZO
65014 LORETO APRUTINO [PE]
TEL. 0858289039
www.cantinetalamonti.it

This modern winery releases interesting wines. Aternum is an old-school Trebbiano with oak and banana notes and the varietal palate is nicely dynamic, despite the substantial structure. Modà is a Montepulciano d'Abruzzo with clean, intense wild cherry notes and a palate with good tannic weave.

○ Trebbiano d'Abruzzo Aternum '08	🍷🍷	4
● Montepulciano d'Abruzzo Modà '09	🍷	3

Tenuta Ulisse

VIA SAN POLO, 40
66014 CRECCHIO [CH]
TEL. 0871306252
www.tenutaulisse.it

This Crecchio winery relies on proactive marketing to make its carefully made products popular. The wines are modern, inspired and sometimes slick but always engaging. The dynamic Montepulciano d'Abruzzo Unico '09 is true to type. The expansive, citrussy Pecorino '09 is also good and the rest well made.

● Montepulciano d'Abruzzo Unico '09	🍷🍷	3*
○ Pecorino Unico '09	🍷🍷	5
○ Cococciola Unico '09	🍷	5
○ Trebbiano d'Abruzzo Unico '09	🍷	5

Valle Martello

C.DA VALLE MARTELLO, 10
66010 VILLAMAGNA [CH]
TEL. 0871300330
www.vallemartello.net

A farm winery, managed with passion by the Mascis, Valle Martello struggles to make headway. The plain, well-typed wines are interesting but that is not enough. Brado is a consistent, heady Montepulciano. The Cococciola Brado '09, a white from a native grape, is appealing.

○ Brado Cococciola '09	🍷	3
● Brado Montepulciano '09	🍷	4

MOLISE

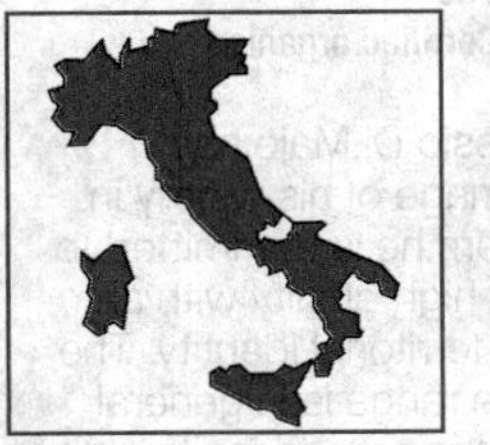

For several years, our introduction to this small region in the centre-south of Italy has been one of the most difficult to write. There are very few producers and only about 50 wines in the region. Crucially, there are very few wine areas of real interest. Molise is, after all, a mountainous area, and has always been defined by its forests and fields. Only the areas descending towards the Adriatic Sea in the north-east of the region are planted with vineyards and olive groves, which are often of a high quality. There is one outstanding figure in this small world: Alessio Di Majo, an exceptionally able wine producer who has been at the helm of his family's superb estate in Campomarino for over 20 years. Di Majo's specialities are Don Luigi, a Molise red from montepulciano and the native local grape tintilia, and Contado, a Molise Aglianico produced from vineyards situated as far north as these grapes can grow. Molise is therefore very much a borderland straddling the traditional wine areas of Irpinia and Lucania in Calabria and northern Puglia, the true domain of aglianico, and of Abruzzo and southern Marche, which are dominated by montepulciano. No good wine producing area in the world has only one producer and luckily there are other cellars, both old and new. These include Borgo di Colloredo, with its excellent Tintilia and Falanghina, followed closely by Cantine Salvatore, a cellar that specializes in Tintilia, and an absolute first, Antonio Valerio's San Nazzaro, a winery in the heart of Molise, at Monteroduni in the province of Isernia not far from the borders with Sannio, the ancient Samnium territory in the province of Benevento, and with Campania. This cellar produces Pentro d'Isernia, hitherto a virtually unheard of designation, with wines made from sangiovese and montepulciano. This is the first time that the number of Molise producers included in the Guide has reached double figures. There are now ten with other exciting prospects on the way, such as Cianfagna and its fantastic wine with a name redolent of alchemy, Tintilia Sator, as well as the well-established wineries that make up the backbone of Molise viticulture: Catabbo, Cipressi, Masseria Flocco, D'Uva and Terresacre at Montenero di Bisaccia, not far from the border with northern Puglia. They all play their part in defining this small world. Molise may not be all that significant in terms of its production but nonetheless it is an important region culturally, above all for its revival of tintilia, a local grape variety that promises to give wonderful results in the years ahead.

Borgo di Colloredo

LOC. NUOVA CLITERNIA
C.DA ZEZZA, 8
86042 CAMPOMARINO [CB]
TEL. 087557453
www.borgodicolloredo.com

CELLAR SALES
PRE-BOOKED VISITS
ROOMS AND FOOD

ANNUAL PRODUCTION 300,000 bottles
HECTARES UNDER VINE 60
VITICULTURE METHOD Conventional

The Di Giulio family continues its excellent work in the vineyards and cellar at Campomarino. Year after year, their unremitting hard work produces a range of well-made, high-quality wines. One of the most interesting things about the Di Giulios is their desire to establish a definite link between vineyard and individual wine, a fine example of estate strategy focused on coaxing the best out of the region's traditional grapes. This is something we wish to praise in this edition.

Whites take centre stage, as is often the case at Borgo di Colloredo. Molise Falanghina '09 has close-focused, caressing fruity overtones and lovely sapidity; Biferno Bianco Gironia '09, a blend of malvasia, trebbiano and bombino, reveals an elegant, consistent nose, followed by a rich, full palate that finishes on a pleasant aromatic note. Greco '09 is less fragrant and slightly more rustic than in previous years while Biferno Rosato Gironia '09 is straightforward but sound. The winery's new red, Molise Tintilia '08 is full-bodied with intense balsamic aromas but perhaps overdoes the oak.

○ Biferno Bianco Gironia '09	▼▼	4*
○ Molise Falanghina '09	▼▼	4*
● Molise Tintilia '08	▼▼	6
⊙ Biferno Rosato Gironia '09	▼	4
○ Greco '09	▼	3
○ Biferno Bianco Gironia '08	▽▽	4*
● Biferno Rosso Gironia '04	▽▽	4*
○ Greco '08	▽▽	3*
● Molise Montepulciano '06	▽▽	4*

Di Majo Norante

FRAZ. NUOVA CLITERNIA
C.DA RAMITELLI, 4
86042 CAMPOMARINO [CB]
TEL. 087557208
www.dimajonorante.com

CELLAR SALES
PRE-BOOKED VISITS

ANNUAL PRODUCTION 800,000 bottles
HECTARES UNDER VINE 85
VITICULTURE METHOD Certified organic

Year after year, Alessio Di Majo has strengthened the image of his winery in Campomarino, where he is committed to producing wines of high quality with an increasingly strong territorial identity. The standard across the range is in general high, especially for the reds, despite a poor year throughout the region.

The Molise Rosso Riserva Don Luigi '08 takes pride of place once again, with Three Glasses. This is a powerful, gutsy red with balsamic, smoky aromas, well-balanced and finishing with a clean, soft mouth. The Aglianico del Molise Riserva Contado '08 revealed a great structure, and its aromas of jam and wild cherry reflect its bond with the territory. The Molise Tintilia '07 is also good; it has a complex nose, with aromas of plum and toasted notes, finishing harmoniously in the mouth with well-dosed oak. The outstanding Molise Moscato Apianae '08 is a delightful, aromatic sweet wine, with aromas of bergamot and sweet saffron.

● Molise Don Luigi Ris. '08	▼▼▼	6
● Molise Aglianico Contado Ris. '08	▼▼	4*
○ Molise Apianae '08	▼▼	5
● Biferno Rosso Ramitello Ris. '08	▼▼	4
● Molise Tintilia '07	▼▼	5
○ Molì Bianco '09	▼	2
● Molì Rosso '09	▼	3
○ Molise Falanghina '09	▼	4
○ Molise Greco '09	▼	4
● Sangiovese '09	▼	3
● Molise Aglianico Contado '03	▽▽▽	4*
● Molise Aglianico Contado '99	▽▽▽	4*
● Molise Aglianico Contado Ris. '07	▽▽▽	4*
● Molise Don Luigi '05	▽▽▽	6
● Molise Don Luigi '99	▽▽▽	5
● Molise Don Luigi Ris. '06	▽▽▽	6

Cantine Salvatore

C.DA VIGNE
86049 URURI [CB]
TEL. 0874830656
www.cantinesalvatore.it

CELLAR SALES
PRE-BOOKED VISITS

ANNUAL PRODUCTION **60,000 bottles**
HECTARES UNDER VINE **15**
VITICULTURE METHOD **Conventional**

Cantine Salvatore keeps up its good work, expanding its range of wines whilst retaining the high levels achieved. The winery is based at Ururi, a hillside village surrounded by lovely vineyards and olive groves. Overall the wines are of a good, steady standard.

Molise Tintilia Rutilia '08 sends out all the right signals, an enjoyable, mouthfilling wine with an enfolding nose offering hints of violet and liquorice but the mouth is over-tannic. Molise Rosso Don Donà '07 is a new wine, mainly from montepulciano grapes, whose intense aromas are concentrated and evolved, indeed slightly overripe. In the mouth it is full-bodied and concentrated, with a lovely structure, giving way to a rather bitter finish. The white Molise Falanghina Nysias '09 is also good, with good backbone, intense aromas of ripe fruit and a full, concentrated, somewhat alcoholic palate. L'IndoVino '09 is a decent, uncomplicated, coherent red.

○ Molise Falanghina Nysias '09	▼▼	4*
● Molise Rosso Don Donà '07	▼▼	5
● Molise Tintilia Rutilia '08	▼▼	4
● L'IndoVINO '09	▼	3
○ Molise Falanghina Nysias '08	▽▽	4*
● Molise Tintilia Rutilia '07	▽▽	5

Valerio Vini - San Nazzaro

LOC. SELVOTTA
86075 MONTERODUNI [IS]
TEL. 0865493043
www.valeriovini.it

CELLAR SALES
PRE-BOOKED VISITS

ANNUAL PRODUCTION **30,000 bottles**
HECTARES UNDER VINE **1**
VITICULTURE METHOD **Conventional**

The only winery in the province of Isernia to be included makes a grand entrance in this year's Guide. Antonio Valerio is the face of the winery, a young entrepreneur who has taken over and blown life back into the neglected Cantina Sociale at Monteroduni. Antonio has also revived the practically extinct DOC Pentro.

In fact the winery's revelation this year is Pentro '08, a blend of montepulciano and sangiovese, and one of our finalists. This wine is a deep ruby red with intense aromas and a complex, enfolding nose, where hints of ripe fruit are followed by a tidy mouth, with a fleshy, rich structure. The range is completed with Molise Rosso Calidio '09, a basic, simple, easy-drinking wine, Molise Rosso Sannazzaro '08, a tangy, dense wine from montepulciano grapes and the white Fannia '09, a sharp, light Falanghina.

● Pentro di Isernia '08	▼▼	5
○ Fannia '09	▼	2
● Molise Rosso Calidio '09	▼	4
● Molise Rosso Sannazzaro '08	▼	4

Cantina Catabbo

C.DA PETRIERA
86046 SAN MARTINO IN PENSILIS [CB]
TEL. 0875604945
www.catabbo.it

The wines from Cantina Catabbo with splendid vineyards at San Martino in Pensilis are not up to previous standards. Molise Tintilia '08, the estate's signature wine, is worth mentioning: it has typical, spicy aromas but is somewhat dull and lacks concentration, despite last year's high quality.

- ● Molise Tintilia '08 — ŸŸ 5
- ○ Petriera Bianco '09 — Ÿ 3
- ● Petriera Rosso '09 — Ÿ 3

Cianfagna

C.DA BOSCO PAMPINI, 3
86030 ACQUAVIVA COLLECROCE [CB]
TEL. 0875970253
www.cianfagna.com

This year the best Tintilia was made by Vincenzo Cianfagna, a young producer truly enthusiastic about this native grape. His Molise Tintilia Sator '08 has aromas of plum and liquorice and a rich, full palate, where oak is not too prominent. An excellent result, rewarding great work in the vineyard.

- ● Molise Tintilia Sator '08 — ŸŸ 6

Cantine Cipressi

C.DA MONTAGNA
86030 SAN FELICE DEL MOLISE [CB]
TEL. 0874874535
www.cantinecipressi.it

The wines from San Felice-based Cantine Cipressi are decent but the Molise Tintilia Macchiarossa '08 wasn't firing on all cylinders, following up its varietal spiciness with a bitterish finish. The gutsy, full-bodied Aglianico Elkon '08 is very good, confirming aglianico can give great results here.

- ● Elkon Aglianico '08 — ŸŸ 4
- ● Molise Rosso Mekan '08 — Ÿ 4
- ● Molise Rosso Rumen '08 — Ÿ 3
- ● Molise Tintilia Macchiarossa '08 — Ÿ 5

D'Uva

C.DA RICUPO, 13
86035 LARINO [CB]
TEL. 0874822320
www.cantineduva.com

Angelo D'Uva's long-established winery is now back on form, following substantial renovation work on the cellar and superb adjoining agriturismo. The Molise Trebbiano Kantharos '09 is uncomplicated and coherent, and both the Molise Tintilia '08 and the Molise Rosso Ricupo '07 are well-made reds.

- ● Molise Rosso Ricupo '07 — Ÿ 4
- ● Molise Tintilia '08 — Ÿ 4
- ○ Molise Trebbiano Kantharos '09 — Ÿ 4

Masserie Flocco

C.DA DIFENSOLA
86045 PORTOCANNONE [CB]
TEL. 0875590032
www.masserieflocco.com

The Masserie Flocco winery at Portocannone still struggles to uphold its quality, despite an excellent Molise Rosso Podere di Sot '08. The best wine the cellar presented is an elegant, easy-drinking wine from montepulciano grapes. The Cabernet Sauvignon '09 is well-balanced, with typical varietal aromas.

- ● Cabernet Sauvignon '09 — ŸŸ 3
- ● Molise Rosso Podere di Sot '08 — ŸŸ 4*

Terresacre

C.DA MONTEBELLO
86036 MONTENERO DI BISACCIA [CB]
TEL. 0875960191
www.terresacre.net

The best wine from the up-and-coming Terresacre at Montenero near Bisaccia is Molise Rosso Rispetto '07, a minerally, balsamic wine of great structure and sapidity, it has excessive oak but finishes long and relaxed. Moravite Merlot '09 and Molise Rosso Neravite '08 are simple, easy-drinking wines.

- ● Molise Rosso Rispetto '07 — ŸŸ 5
- ● Molise Rosso Neravite '08 — Ÿ 3
- ● Moravite '09 — Ÿ 4

CAMPANIA

If you are one of those people who gets a thrill from statistical curiosities, then you'll find the next few pages very interesting reading. In a year when Campania beat its own record for Three Glasses – a very impressive 19 in this edition of the Guide – the scores overall are lower than in previous years and the number of winners fewer. But this is just one of the many contradictions we noted in an extremely dynamic, complex area that encompasses widely varying geography, site climates, styles and entrepreneurial activities. Never before have we encountered such a strong legacy after a challenging growing year as in this round of tastings; 2009 was a real test for most of the region's whites. But the difficulties of the vintage only go a short way towards explaining what we found: a growing gap not so much in quality but in the ambitions of top and less significant producers, and between well-established terroirs and those yet to forge an identity. On one hand, the average standard seems to be winding down; on the other, there are wines out there that not only get better every year but continue to develop character, in some cases highly distinctive personalities. The Greco di Tufos are a case in point and won a slew of prizes this time round. In contrast with other varieties, 2009 was a magnificent growing year for the reddest of the Irpinia's whites, which presents us with four splendid, unique interpretations. Gabriella Ferrara's Vigna Cicogna and Cantine dell'Angelo's di Tufo win their first much-deserved trophies while Vadiaperti's Tornante triumphs again and Pietracupa scores a double top with its Greco di Tufo and the '08 version of its Fiano Cupo selection. These are flanked by the Fiano di Avellino of the same vintage by Vigna della Congregazione and Ciro Picariello, the latter another fine first-time winner. The '09 Fiano di Avellinos did not fare so well, although Feudi di San Gregorio returns to top form with a surprising Pietracalda and the reliable Colli di Lapio. It was a mixed '06 in Taurasi territory but there was a fabulous hat-trick for Urciuolo, Di Prisco and Radici di Mastroberardino, whose classic Radici Riserva '04 earns it a double crown. The roll of honour concludes with two absolute gems from '05: Molettieri's Vigna Cinque Querce Riserva and Perillo's Taurasi, another sumptuous Three Glass debutante. After Irpinia, Caserta produced the best results, with the honours going again to the Terra di Lavoro in the '08 version, the same vintage as the Casavecchia Centomoggia from Terre del Principe and the Falerno Bianco Caracci from Villa Matilde. Salerno took home just one award for the eternally admirable Montevetrano, this one an '08.

Alois

LOC. AUDELINO
VIA RAGAZZANO
81040 PONTELATONE [CE]
TEL. 0823876710
www.vinialois.it

PRE-BOOKED VISITS

ANNUAL PRODUCTION **120,000 bottles**
HECTARES UNDER VINE **24**
VITICULTURE METHOD **Conventional**

We are very pleased to note the return to a full profile of the log-established Alois family of Caserta, well-known outside the winemaking world for their prestigious silk production. After a few tentative seasons, the Pontelatone winery returns on top form with a revised range and style. Carmine Valentino is now technical manager, while pallagrello, casavecchia and falanghina remain the principal varieties grown on the 14 estate-owned and ten leased hectares under vine.

The summary table only gives a partial idea of our reactions to Michele and Massimo Alois' wines this year. Looking past the scores, we were very encouraged by the progress made by the Pallagrello Nero Cunto '08 and Casavecchia Trebulanum '07. While both these wines show their own respective varietal features, they are also richly textured, opening out compact and dynamic over the initial framework established by the oak used for ageing, without forced interpretation or excessive extract. The Pallagrello Bianco Caiatì '09 shows a more mature profile and linear progression.

● Cunto '08	▼▼	5
● Trebulanum '07	▼▼	6
○ Pallagrello Bianco Caiatì '09	▼	4
● Campole '06	▽▽	4*
● Campole '05	▽▽	4
● Campole '04	▽▽	4
● Campole '03	▽▽	3*
○ Pallagrello Bianco Caiatì '07	▽▽	4*
● Pallagrello Nero '06	▽▽	4*
● Settimo '07	▽▽	4*
● Trebulanum '03	▽▽	5
● Trebulanum '02	▽▽	5

Antonio Caggiano

C.DA SALA
83030 TAURASI [AV]
TEL. 082774723
www.cantinecaggiano.it

CELLAR SALES
PRE-BOOKED VISITS
FOOD

ANNUAL PRODUCTION **150,000 bottles**
HECTARES UNDER VINE **23**
VITICULTURE METHOD **Conventional**

Antonio Caggiano has only just over 15 harvests under his belt but he is already considered a veteran of Irpinia winemaking. Back in 1994, he created one of the first Taurasi crus exclusively aged in barriques, Bordeaux style. Vigna Macchia dei Gotiis still the cutting edge of his solid, compact range. His son Pino and friend, Professor Luigi Moio, are always at his side. The estate's vineyards are all in the Taurasi designation in the Sala, Piano di Montevergine, Pezza dei Preti, San Pietro and Coste districts.

Once again, there was an impressive overall performance from Antonio Caggiano's wines. The whites stand out for their usual buttery, mouthfilling style with well-defined, well-absorbed oak. The Greco di Tufo Devon '09 displays a fruity, zesty sweetness as well as salty backbone. The Fiano di Avellino Béchar '09 is even better, contrasting its glycerine-themed entry with a subtle, flavoursome progression despite the slightly closed tannins. The Taurasi Vigna Macchia dei Goti '06 comes close to its best-ever version, showing extremely elegant with distinct smokiness.

○ Fiano di Avellino Béchar '09	▼▼	4
● Taurasi V. Macchia dei Goti '06	▼▼	6
○ Fiagre '09	▼▼	4
○ Greco di Tufo Devon '09	▼▼	4
● Taurasi V. Macchia dei Goti '04	▽▽▽	6
● Taurasi V. Macchia dei Goti '99	▽▽▽	7
○ Fiagre '07	▽▽	4*
○ Fiano di Avellino Béchar '08	▽▽	5
○ Greco di Tufo Devon '08	▽▽	5
○ Greco di Tufo Devon '06	▽▽	4*
● Irpinia Salae Domini '06	▽▽	6
● Irpinia Taurì '06	▽▽	4
● Taurasi V. Macchia dei Goti '05	▽▽	6

Cantine dell'Angelo

via Santa Lucia, 32
83010 Tufo [AV]
tel. 3384512965
www.cantinedellangelo.com

CELLAR SALES
PRE-BOOKED VISITS

ANNUAL PRODUCTION 18,000 bottles
HECTARES UNDER VINE 5
VITICULTURE METHOD Conventional

The umpteenth Irpinian fairytale ending, from the countryside of Tufo to Three well-deserved Glasses, as told by Maria Nuzzolo and Angelo Muto, the brains and hands behind the tiny, family-run Cantine dell'Angelo winery founded in 2006 after over 30 years' farming experience. The recipe seems as simple as it is successful: five hectares of vineyards in the village's most typical locations near the old sulphur mines; traditional fermentation in steel; and an essential style that enhances the salty, minerally components of the greco grape grown in these parts.

From the first winter tastings onwards, we had the impression that this would be one of the best Greco di Tufos of 2009. This glowing promise was not only fulfilled in subsequent months but was transformed into thrilling liquid emotion. Don't be put off by the initial depreciative impact – decanting might be a good idea – for the expressive key of this wine is a triumph of purity and energy. It displays unmistakeable hints of sulphur and white-fleshed fruits before the apparently slender palate with long-lingering salty sensations.

○ Greco di Tufo '09	🍷🍷🍷	4*

Viticoltori del Casavecchia

via Madonna delle Grazie, 28
81040 Pontelatone [CE]
tel. 0823659198
www.viticoltoridelcasavecchia.it

CELLAR SALES
PRE-BOOKED VISITS

ANNUAL PRODUCTION 35,000 bottles
HECTARES UNDER VINE 20
VITICULTURE METHOD Conventional

With 20 hectares of vineyards farmed by over 40 member growers, Viticoltori del Casavecchia is a very important winery in the Caserta and Campania production zones. Season after season, we find a wide range of wines with admirably coherent stylistic identity and pricing. This is all thanks to teamwork, orchestrated principally by Alfonso Cutillo, Battista Perrone and Maurizio Alongi. Casavecchia comes in three versions, one with beautifully gauged oak, one a rosé and the sweet Futo.

For once the most impressive wine was not Casavecchia Vigna Prea. The '07 is a lovely version, make no mistake, with hints of cigar smoke deepening the confident spice and flavoursome development, marked out with acidity rather than extract. But we preferred, by a whisker, the Casavecchia Corte Rosa '08, aged for 12 months in tonneaux, for its naturalness, strong tannins and oaky sensations nicely blended with the black fruit, streaked through with sulphur minerality. The Erta dei Ciliegi '09, made from casavecchia grapes with a little pallagrello nero and aged in stainless steel, is simpler, as expected, but equally coherent and full of pep.

● Corte Rosa '08	🍷🍷	4
● Erta dei Ciliegi '09	🍷🍷	3
● Futo '08	🍷🍷	5
● Vigna Prea '07	🍷🍷	5
○ Pallagrello Bianco '09	🍷	4
⊙ Sfizio Rosa '09	🍷	3
● Corte Rosa '06	🍷🍷	4*
● Erta dei Ciliegi '07	🍷🍷	3*
● Erta dei Ciliegi '06	🍷🍷	3*
● Futo '07	🍷🍷	5
○ Pallagrello Bianco '08	🍷🍷	4*
⊙ Sfizio Rosa '08	🍷🍷	3*
● Vigna Prea '06	🍷🍷	5
● Vigna Prea '05	🍷🍷	5

Colli di Lapio

VIA ARIANIELLO, 47
83030 LAPIO [AV]
TEL. 0825982184
www.collidilapio.it

CELLAR SALES
PRE-BOOKED VISITS

ANNUAL PRODUCTION **50,000 bottles**
HECTARES UNDER VINE **6**
VITICULTURE METHOD **Conventional**

Success and recognition haven't changed the spirit of the Romano family of Lapio one bit. No great speeches but plenty of teamwork: Clelia's strong-willed shyness, her husband Angelo's profound knowledge of the Irpinia area and the enthusiasm of their children Carmela and Federico; the grandchildren Chiara, Andrea and Alessandro will make do for now with the labels named after them. The Fiano di Avellino is aged in stainless steel while the Taurasi Vigna Andrea matures in mainly new barriques.

It would be challenging, to put it mildly, to top the exceptional performance of the Fiano di Avellino di Clelia in last year's Guide. But our predictions were belied by a '09 version which is even more astonishing, if that were possible, especially bearing in mind the troublesome growing year for this type. Compared to the best vintages, it lacks roundedness and depth in the mouth but makes up for it with impeccably coherent territoriality in layered hints of citrus fruit and aromatic herbs, and the marked iodine sensation mid palate. The Taurasi Vigna Andrea '06 is slightly overripe while the Irpinia Campi Taurasini Donna Chiara '08 is weighty.

○ Fiano di Avellino '09	▼▼▼	5
● Campi Taurasini Irpinia Donna Chiara '08	▼▼	5
● Taurasi V. Andrea '06	▼▼	6
○ Fiano di Avellino '08	▽▽▽+	5*
○ Fiano di Avellino '07	▽▽▽	5
○ Fiano di Avellino '05	▽▽▽	5
○ Fiano di Avellino '04	▽▽▽	5
● Campi Taurasini Irpinia Donna Chiara '07	▽▽	5
● Campi Taurasini Irpinia Donna Chiara '06	▽▽	5
● Campi Taurasini Irpinia Donna Chiara '06	▽▽	5
○ Fiano di Avellino '03	▽▽	5
● Taurasi V. Andrea '05	▽▽	6
● Taurasi V. Andrea '04	▽▽	6
● Taurasi V. Andrea '03	▽▽	6
● Taurasi V. Andrea '01	▽▽	6

Contrade di Taurasi

VIA MUNICIPIO, 39
83030 TAURASI [AV]
TEL. 0815442457
www.contradeditaurasi.it

CELLAR SALES
PRE-BOOKED VISITS

ANNUAL PRODUCTION **20,000 bottles**
HECTARES UNDER VINE **5**
VITICULTURE METHOD **Organic**

We highly recommend a visit to this winery to see for yourself the special features of the subzone east of this Irpinia town and in particular, to get to know everyone working at Contrade di Taurasi. This is a real dream team caring for the estate's five hectares using organic farming principles, with special attention paid to guided natural fermentation. The new crus will shortly be presented and the typical Taurasi style is succulent and relaxed. The wines are aged in five to 15-hectolitre casks.

Only Taurasi Riservas were presented for this edition. The '03 is charming and complex, only slightly penalized by slightly dry tannins. The '05 is just a step away from Three Glasses, probably held back only by its youthful aromatics and extract. However, the smoky, citrussy sensations enhanced by flavoursome, salty acidity suggest that this promises to become a characterful wine. We also liked the Greco Musc' '08 very much. This is the traditional name for rovello bianco grown on centuries-old starsete pergola-trained vines, and the wine shows aromas of wood resin, gunflint and musk with a piquant, flavoursome palate, very slightly pheolic in the finish.

● Taurasi Ris. '05	▼▼	7
○ Greco Musc' '08	▼▼	5
● Taurasi Ris. '03	▼▼	7
● Irpinia Aglianico '08	▼	4
● Taurasi '04	▽▽▽	7
● Aglianico '05	▽▽	4
● Irpinia Aglianico '07	▽▽	4*
● Taurasi '05	▽▽	7
● Taurasi '00	▽▽	6
● Taurasi '99	▽▽	7
● Taurasi Ris. '01	▽▽	7

Marisa Cuomo

via G. B. Lama, 16/18
84010 Furore [SA]
tel. 089830348
www.marisacuomo.it

CELLAR SALES
PRE-BOOKED VISITS
ROOMS AND FOOD

ANNUAL PRODUCTION **102,000 bottles**
HECTARES UNDER VINE **18**
VITICULTURE METHOD **Organic**

The estate owned by Marisa Cuomo and Andrea Ferraioli shows the characteristics of an artisanal winery. The estate's own three hectares are supplemented by another 14 farmed almost 40 growers in seven municipal areas over the Furore subzone. Dozens of grape varieties are used to produce white wines fermented in stainless steel, except for the Fiorduva, and reds aged in barriques, both the standard wines and the Riservas. These bottles are both characterful and ageable, an ideal combination of the earthy and maritime nature of these terraces wrested from the living rock.

The big news this year is that the Furore Bianco Fiorduva missed its sixth consecutive Three Glass award by a hair's breadth. The '09 is still a beautiful wine with the usual luxurious array of aromas, penalized only by a warmer, leaner finish than usual. The Ravello Bianco '09 also made the final tastings with magnificent savouriness supported by the falanghina and biancolella grapes. The whole range has achieved a very high standard, however, starting with the delightful Furore Rosso '09 and a dynamic, tannic Ravello Rosso Riserva '07 with its irresistibly iron-like minerality.

○ Costa d'Amalfi Bianco Ravello '09	▼▼	5
○ Costa d'Amalfi Fiorduva '09	▼▼	7
○ Costa d'Amalfi Bianco Furore '09	▼▼	5
● Costa d'Amalfi Rosso Furore '09	▼▼	5
● Costa d'Amalfi Rosso Furore Ris. '07	▼▼	7
● Costa d'Amalfi Rosso Ravello Ris. '07	▼▼	6
⊙ Costa d'Amalfi Rosato '09	▼	5
○ Costa d'Amalfi Fiorduva '08	▽▽▽	7
○ Costa d'Amalfi Fiorduva '07	▽▽▽	7
○ Costa d'Amalfi Fiorduva '06	▽▽▽	7
○ Costa d'Amalfi Fiorduva '05	▽▽▽	7
○ Costa d'Amalfi Fiorduva '04	▽▽▽	7
○ Costa d'Amalfi Bianco Furore '08	▽▽	5
● Costa d'Amalfi Rosso Furore Ris. '06	▽▽	7

D'Ambra Vini d'Ischia

fraz. Panza
via Mario D'Ambra, 16
80077 Forio [NA]
tel. 081907210
www.dambravini.com

CELLAR SALES
PRE-BOOKED VISITS

ANNUAL PRODUCTION **500,000 bottles**
HECTARES UNDER VINE **18**
VITICULTURE METHOD **Conventional**

Casa D'Ambra, founded in 1888, is one of the oldest estates in Campania and undoubtedly the most important in Ischia, the largest of the islands in the Gulf of Naples. At the helm, Andrea D'Ambra deserves credit for an image that harmoniously combines a winery symbolizing island tradition with a special vocation for innovation. On the one hand we have wines made from biancolella, forastera, piedirosso and guarnaccia and on the other, successful experimentation into the lesser-known Aegean varieties, and more recently other Campanian grapes like greco.

Few wines express the specific features, good and bad, of each vintage in Campania like those made at D'Ambra. The 2009 whites are impeccably measured and coherent, but too supple and essential in flavour. Best results come from the Ischia Forastera Euposia '09, rich in earthy and even black fruits aromas. The '09 Biancolellas have suffered more, both in the basic version and the Tenuta Frassitelli, though it is still a classy, original wine. The Ischia Rosso Dedicato a Mario D'Ambra '06 is very successfully typed, with tannic texture that is sound and compact if not overly sophisticated.

○ Ischia Biancolella Tenuta Frassitelli '09	▼▼	5
○ Ischia Forastera Euposia '09	▼▼	4
● Ischia Rosso Dedicato a Mario D'Ambra '06	▼▼	6
○ Ischia Biancolella '09	▼	4
○ Ischia Biancolella Calitto '09	▼	4
○ Ischia Biancolella Tenuta Frassitelli '90	▽▽▽	4
○ Ischia Bianco '08	▽▽	3*
○ Ischia Bianco Kyme '05	▽▽	5
○ Ischia Biancolella '08	▽▽	4
○ Ischia Biancolella '07	▽▽	4*
○ Ischia Biancolella Tenuta Frassitelli '08	▽▽	5
○ Ischia Biancolella Tenuta Frassitelli '07	▽▽	5
○ Ischia Biancolella Tenuta Frassitelli '06	▽▽	5
○ Ischia Forastera Euposia '07	▽▽	5

Viticoltori De Conciliis

LOC. QUERCE
84060 PRIGNANO CILENTO [SA]
TEL. 0974831090
www.viticoltorideconciliis.it

CELLAR SALES
PRE-BOOKED VISITS

ANNUAL PRODUCTION 150,000 bottles
HECTARES UNDER VINE 28
VITICULTURE METHOD Organic

Bruno De Conciliis shoulders a double burden of responsibility. On one hand, he wants to maintain the high-profile performances shown in recent years by the family winery while on the other being aware that for many years the cellar has been a benchmark for Cilento winemaking. Above all, it has inspired a varied group of small-scale producers and wine technicians who regard him as a motivational role model, starting with his natural farming principles. The principal varieties grown here are fiano and aglianico, which are released in various styles.

It isn't always easy to predict the immediate future development of the leading De Conciliis wines. They show unquestionably weighty extract but sometimes we are unable to perceive the pace and progression that would add excitement. This is basically our current reading of the Naima '06, which we probably tasted in a preliminary phase. Not far behind, the Cilento Aglianico Donnaluna '08 has a modern, Mediterranean feel supported and refreshed on the palate. Leading the field is the Ka!, which is quite simply the best special Campanian wine tasted this year.

○ Ka!	🍷🍷	6
● Donnaluna Aglianico '08	🍷🍷	4
● Naima '06	🍷🍷	7
● Bacioilcielo '09	🍷	4
○ Donnaluna Fiano '09	🍷	4
○ Perella Fiano '08	🍷	5
○ Selim Brut	🍷	4
● Naima '01	YYY	6
○ Ka! '06	YY	6
● Naima '05	YY	7
● Naima '04	YY	7
● Naima '03	YY	7
● Naima '02	YY	7
● Zero '05	YY	8

Di Prisco

C.DA ROTOLE, 27
83040 FONTANAROSA [AV]
TEL. 0825475738
www.cantinadiprisco.it

CELLAR SALES
PRE-BOOKED VISITS

ANNUAL PRODUCTION 100,000 bottles
HECTARES UNDER VINE 10
VITICULTURE METHOD Conventional

In many ways, Pasqualino Di Prisco is the emblematic Irpinian producer. A tireless grower, with deep ties to the land, less at ease among tasting tables and wine enthusiasts, and with the slightly pessimistic fatalism of true country folk. This sensitivity sometimes clashes with the awareness that he and his friend Carmine Valentino are caring for one of the best-performing wineries in the province, with peaks of excellence, and enjoy an ideal subzone for making supple, stylish wines.

Subtle vegetal and floral hints, spicy black pepper sensations and a fresh, fruity progression contrasting with succulent, crisp tannins. These are the features we have become used to in recent years with disarming regularity from the Di Prisco Taurasi. The generous but diverse '06 vintage year adds more austerity and perfectly extracted texture . Three Glasses, no discussions. The Greco di Tufo '09 came very close to this accolade with a simply complete profile that is reductive but interesting, with whiffs of sea breezes and mineral butteriness. The Fiano di Avellino '09 is subtle and flavoursome.

● Taurasi '06	🍷🍷🍷	6
○ Greco di Tufo '09	🍷🍷	4
○ Fiano di Avellino '09	🍷🍷	4
● Taurasi '05	YYY	6*
● Aglianico '03	YY	4
○ Fiano di Avellino '07	YY	4*
○ Fiano di Avellino '05	YY	4
○ Greco di Tufo '07	YY	4*
○ Greco di Tufo '06	YY	4*
○ Greco di Tufo '05	YY	4
○ Greco di Tufo Pietrarosa '07	YY	4
○ Greco di Tufo Pietrarosa '05	YY	4*
● Taurasi '04	YY	6
● Taurasi '03	YY	6
● Taurasi '02	YY	6

DonnaChiara

LOC. PIETRACUPA
VIA STAZIONE
83030 MONTEFALCIONE [AV]
TEL. 0825977135
www.donnachiara.it

CELLAR SALES
PRE-BOOKED VISITS
FOOD

ANNUAL PRODUCTION 100,000 bottles
HECTARES UNDER VINE 20
VITICULTURE METHOD Conventional

The project dreamt up by Irpinian entrepreneur Umberto Petitto to promote his family's winemaking heritage is certainly ambitious. On the frontline are his wife Chiara and daughter Ilaria, assisted by Angelo Valentino, and their task is to look after the complete range of Irpinian wines produced from the 20-hectare estate, with some additional purchases of selected grapes. The whites are aged in steel and typically fruity and buttery while the aglianico-based reds, from the Venticano and Torre Le Nocelle areas, show a definitely modern style.

We were looking forward with some curiosity to tasting Donnachiara's first Taurasi, from '06, and our impressions were somewhat contradictory. The fruity, pulpy texture is undoubtedly present but in this phase the wood used for ageing is still forward, creating an excessively severe, coffee sensation in the tannic texture. We had fewer doubts about the Fiano di Avellino '09, outgoing and multi-faceted with white-fleshed fruits and aromatic herbs, and a coherent palate despite a slightly sweetish sensation. Along the same lines, the Greco di Tufo '09, shows more tropical sensations with a slightly almondy finish.

○ Fiano di Avellino '09	TT	4
○ Greco di Tufo '09	TT	4
● Taurasi '06	TT	6
○ Falanghina del Beneventano '09	T	4
○ Fiano di Avellino '08	YY	4*
○ Fiano di Avellino '07	YY	4*
○ Greco di Tufo '08	YY	4*
● Irpinia Aglianico Preludio '07	YY	4
● Irpinia Aglianico Preludio '06	YY	4*

I Favati

P.ZZA DI DONATO
83020 CESINALI [AV]
TEL. 0825666898
www.cantineifavati.it

CELLAR SALES
PRE-BOOKED VISITS

ANNUAL PRODUCTION 60,000 bottles
HECTARES UNDER VINE 10
VITICULTURE METHOD Conventional

Piersabino and Giancarlo Favati, with wife Rosanna Petrozziello and technical assistance from Vincenzo Mercurio, form the solid team running this small estate of ten hectares under vine and about 60,000 bottles a year, released in a varied, coherent range of Irpinia wines. Alongside the classic wines are the Etichette Bianche labels, consisting of selections of greco and fiano harvested later and aged in stainless steel after cold maceration prior to fermenting. The aglianico-based reds show a dry, modern style.

After the successful experiments of '07, the Fiano di Avellino Pietramara Etichetta Bianca returns, a wine of unquestionable personality with astonishing hints of forest floor, herbs and incense, echoed on the palate with a sweet entry and bitterish finish. The Greco di Tufo Terrantica Etichetta Bianca '09 is even more surprising and closer to the mark. The nose opens with a beautiful blend of sulphur and tropical sensations with hints of cereals and spice, and a particularly buttery, piquant palate, just a little too phenolic in the finish. The Greco di Tufo Terrantica '09 is more relaxed and less complex. We recommend you try the fiano-based sparkling wines.

○ Greco di Tufo Terrantica Et. Bianca '09	TT	4
○ Fiano di Avellino Pietramara Et. Bianca '09	TT	4
○ Greco di Tufo Terrantica '09	TT	4
○ Cabrì Fiano Et. Bianca Extra Brut	T	
○ Cabrì Fiano Extra Dry	T	
○ Fiano di Avellino Pietramara '09	T	4
● Irpinia Campi Taurasini Cretarossa '08	T	4
○ Fiano di Avellino Pietramara '08	YY	4*
○ Fiano di Avellino Pietramara '06	YY	4
○ Fiano di Avellino Pietramara Et. Bianca '07	YY	4*
○ Greco di Tufo Terrantica '08	YY	4
● Irpinia Campi Taurasini Cretarossa '07	YY	4
● Taurasi Terzo Tratto '05	YY	5
● Taurasi Terzo Tratto '04	YY	5

Benito Ferrara

FRAZ. SAN PAOLO, 14A
83010 TUFO [AV]
TEL. 0825998194
www.benitoferrara.it

CELLAR SALES
PRE-BOOKED VISITS

ANNUAL PRODUCTION 45,000 bottles
HECTARES UNDER VINE 8
VITICULTURE METHOD Conventional

Few Greco di Tufo wines arouse contrasting opinions and impressions like the Vigna Cicogna made by Gabriella Ferrara and her husband Sergio, sentinels on their hilltop at San Paolo a Tufo. This magnificent location, with about two south-facing hectares on land rich in mineral salts and sulphur, is interpreted in a buttery, opulent style by the Ferraras, who sometimes resort to the Tufo tradition of late harvesting to balance out the high level of acidity in this Irpinian grape.

It is certainly no surprise that the Ferrara family have won their first Three Glasses. Weather conditions during the abbreviated '09 harvest already seemed ideal on paper for the Greco di Tufo Vigna Cicogna to achieve the squaring of the circle in a wine of this style. In a less generous year, the usual exuberant sugary component and extract are routed to a magnificent fusion of flavour and complexity with smoky aspects and an overall balance and structure which for once place the evolved aromas of honey and dried fruit in the background. Just a step behind, the basic Greco di Tufo '09 displays pounding acidity and assertive progression.

○ Greco di Tufo V. Cicogna '09	▼▼▼	5
○ Greco di Tufo '09	▼▼	4
○ Fiano di Avellino '09	▼	5
● Taurasi V. Quattro Confini '06	▼	6
○ Fiano di Avellino '08	▽▽	5
○ Greco di Tufo '08	▽▽	4
○ Greco di Tufo '06	▽▽	4*
○ Greco di Tufo V. Cicogna '08	▽▽	5
○ Greco di Tufo V. Cicogna '07	▽▽	5
○ Greco di Tufo V. Cicogna '06	▽▽	5
○ Greco di Tufo V. Cicogna '05	▽▽	5
○ Greco di Tufo V. Cicogna '04	▽▽	5

★★ Feudi di San Gregorio

LOC. CERZA GROSSA
83050 SORBO SERPICO [AV]
TEL. 0825986683
www.feudi.it

CELLAR SALES
PRE-BOOKED VISITS
FOOD

ANNUAL PRODUCTION 3,500,000 bottles
HECTARES UNDER VINE 216
VITICULTURE METHOD Certified organic

The winds of change are blowing at Sorbo Serpico, where 1986 saw the beginning of one of the most revolutionary adventures in the winemaking south of Italy. After a few seasons of transition, Feudi di San Gregorio seems to have regained its drive and vigour under the young and determined chairman Antonio Capaldo and vineyard manager Pierpaolo Sirch. The whites in particular, aged exclusively in stainless steel, now seem to present greater personality and coherence with the terroir in their freshness and harmony.

The range presented this year deserves to be tasted without preconceptions, starting with the vivid, juicy Fiano di Avellino '09, of which 500,000 bottles are produced. Only 30,000 were released of its elder brother, the Pietracalda '09, which won another Three Glasses for a very different interpretation to those we have been accustomed to. A yeasty sweetness is still present but integrated beautifully into a taut, coherent profile. The Greco di Tufo Cutizzi '09 has also changed its outlook. The best red tasted was the astonishing, spicy, earthy Aglianico del Vulture '07.

○ Fiano di Avellino Pietracalda '09	▼▼▼	5
● Aglianico del Vulture '07	▼▼	5
○ Greco di Tufo Cutizzi '09	▼▼	5
○ Dubl Greco Brut M.Cl. '06	▼▼	7
○ Fiano di Avellino '09	▼▼	4
⊙ Irpinia Ros'Aura '09	▼▼	4
● Pàtrimo '07	▼▼	8
● Taurasi '06	▼▼	6
○ Greco di Tufo '09	▼	4
● Irpinia Aglianico Rubrato '08	▼	4
○ Sannio Falanghina '09	▼	4
○ Sannio Falanghina Serrocielo '09	▼	4
○ Greco di Tufo Cutizzi '07	▽▽▽	4*
○ Greco di Tufo Cutizzi '06	▽▽▽	4*
● Irpinia Serpico '05	▽▽▽	8
● Serpico '04	▽▽▽	8

Galardi

FRAZ. SAN CARLO
SP SESSA-MIGNANO
81037 SESSA AURUNCA [CE]
TEL. 0823708900
www.terradilavoro.com

PRE-BOOKED VISITS

ANNUAL PRODUCTION 30,000 bottles
HECTARES UNDER VINE 10
VITICULTURE METHOD Certified organic

Fontana Galardi is a small estate at San Carlo near Sessa Aurunca, situated at about 400 metres on the summit of a cool hill surrounded by olive groves and woods of chestnut and oak. The volcanic and alluvial soil is very deep with a significant component of limestone and shale. These are the origins of the most famous blend of aglianico and piedirosso in Campanian winemaking, a legend thanks to the work of Luisa Murena, Arturo Celentano, Francesco and Dora Catello.

It is comes more naturally to compare a wine of such distinctive character with its own previous versions than with other Supercampanians. Over the years, the Terra di Lavoro '08 seems destined to embody the role of a successful wine that is in many ways atypical and difficult to place. For once the aromas catch you unawares with the undertow of black berry jam more than the distinctive volcanic smokiness, suggesting a transitory phase. This impression is confirmed on the palate which is currently suspended between ripe fruit and austere tannin, but shows unquestionably rich in texture.

● Terra di Lavoro '08	▼▼▼	8
● Terra di Lavoro '07	▽▽▽	8
● Terra di Lavoro '06	▽▽▽	8
● Terra di Lavoro '05	▽▽▽	8
● Terra di Lavoro '04	▽▽▽	8
● Terra di Lavoro '03	▽▽▽	7
● Terra di Lavoro '02	▽▽▽	7

Cantine Grotta del Sole

VIA SPINELLI, 2
80010 QUARTO [NA]
TEL. 0818762566
www.grottadelsole.it

CELLAR SALES
PRE-BOOKED VISITS

ANNUAL PRODUCTION 850,000 bottles
HECTARES UNDER VINE 42
VITICULTURE METHOD Conventional

Grotta del Sole is much more than a benchmark winery for the area south of Naples known as Campi Flegrei. In little more than 20 years, the Martusciello family has created a veritable war machine with an assortment ranging from the Sorrentina peninsula to Vesuvius, Beneventano and Irpinia, via Asprinio d'Aversa, which includes both sparkling and non-sparkling wines. Technical management is entrusted to Attilio Pagli and Francesco Martusciello Jr.

This year, as well as the usual performance from Grotta del Sole that put it at the peak of regional production, a red is also able to challenge the best in Campania and sailed through to the finals. The Piedirosso dei Campi Flegrei Montegauro Riserva '07 shows a weighty, mouthfilling palate and the extract you expect from a leading wine. The acidulous, fermentative aromas of the Falanghina dei Campi Flegrei '09 don't stop it being one of the best of the type and the Asprinio d'Aversa Brut is also back on form. One step behind are the Lettere della Penisola Sorrentina '09 and Falanghina dei Campi Flegrei Coste di Cuma '08.

● Campi Flegrei Piedirosso Montegauro Ris. '07	▼▼	4
○ Asprinio d'Aversa Brut	▼▼	4
○ Campi Flegrei Falanghina '09	▼▼	4
● Quarto di Sole '07	▼▼	5
● Aglianico '08	▼	4
○ Campi Flegrei Falanghina Coste di Cuma '08	▼	5
● Penisola Sorrentina Lettere '09	▼	4
○ Vesuvio Lacryma Christi Bianco '09	▼	4
○ Fiano di Avellino '07	▽▽	4*
○ Greco di Tufo Quarto di Luna '07	▽▽	5
● Quarto di Sole '05	▽▽	5
● Quarto di Sole '01	▽▽	5

La Guardiense

LOC. SANTA LUCIA, 104-105
82034 GUARDIA SANFRAMONDI [BN]
TEL. 0824864034
www.laguardiense.it

CELLAR SALES
PRE-BOOKED VISITS
FOOD

ANNUAL PRODUCTION **4,000,000 bottles**
HECTARES UNDER VINE **2,000**
VITICULTURE METHOD **Conventional**

Fifty years of history, about a thousand grower members, four million bottles a year and 2,000 hectares of vineyards. With these numbers to hand, it is easy to concede that La Guardiense is one of the leading co-operative wineries in southern Italy. Domizio Pigna at the helm and consultant winemaker Riccardo Cotarella have relaunched the winery into the Sannio elite with remarkable results in the basic wines, which sell at astonishingly affordable prices, as well as the Janare selections.

This year, there were no stand-outs to go forward to the finals but the whole range seems to be on top form, starting with the Sannio Piedirosso Cantone '08, which presents open and fleshy with wild berries and hints of balsam. The more complex, composed Guardiolo Aglianico Cantari Riserva '07 serves up toasty sensations which do not overpower the ripe, healthy fruit, developing into a mouthfilling, coherent palate. Guardiolo Rosso Riserva '07 is just as good, based on darker fruit but equally soft and persistent. The Sannio Greco Pietralata '09 from the Janare line stands out among the whites. It enters slightly yeasty but the blend of sweetness and zing is very successful.

● Guardiolo Aglianico Cantari Ris. '07	2 glasses (black)	5
● Guardiolo Rosso Ris. '07	2 glasses (black)	3
○ Sannio Greco Pietralata Janare '09	2 glasses (black)	4
● Sannio Piedirosso Cantone Janare '08	2 glasses (black)	5
● Guardiolo Aglianico Lucchero '08	1 glass (black)	4
○ Guardiolo Falanghina '09	1 glass (black)	3
○ Guardiolo Falanghina Senete Janare '09	1 glass (black)	4
○ Sannio Fiano '09	1 glass (black)	3
○ Sannio Fiano Colle di Tilio Janare '09	1 glass (black)	4
○ Sannio Greco '09	1 glass (black)	3
● Guardiolo Aglianico Cantari Ris. '06	2 glasses (white)	5
● Guardiolo Aglianico Sel. '08	2 glasses (white)	3*
● Guardiolo Aglianico Sel. '06	2 glasses (white)	3*
● Guardiolo Rosso Ris. '06	2 glasses (white)	3*
○ Sannio Fiano Colle di Tilio Janare '08	2 glasses (white)	4
○ Sannio Greco Pietralata Janare '08	2 glasses (white)	4*

Luigi Maffini

FRAZ. SAN MARCO
LOC. CENITO
84048 CASTELLABATE [SA]
TEL. 0974966345
www.maffini-vini.com

CELLAR SALES
PRE-BOOKED VISITS

ANNUAL PRODUCTION **95,000 bottles**
HECTARES UNDER VINE **15**
VITICULTURE METHOD **Conventional**

Luigi Maffini's wines are where the generous Cilento ambience meets the controlled rigour of the man who makes them. Aglianico and fiano are the varieties principally grown on the winery's 15 hectares for both the basic labels and modern-style selections with frequent initial oaky sensations which never penalize the palate overall. Perhaps they lack a touch of unpredictability at times but the range remains a solid point of reference for critics and enthusiasts alike.

In many ways, this was an unusual performance from the wines of Luigi Maffini. Probably a few bottles were tasted while in a less than ideal phase but both the leading wines fell a little short of our expectations. The Cenito '07 is affected by a slightly overripe, evolved nose and above all, by a rather severely astringent tannic finish. The Pietraincatenata '08 is still affected by the oak and shows somewhat unbalanced aromas of candied citrus peel and dried fruit with an almost buttery palate. The Kràtos '09, a Fiano aged in steel, is crisper and more dynamic.

● Cilento Aglianico Cenito '07	2 glasses (black)	6
○ Kràtos '09	2 glasses (black)	4
○ Pietraincatenata '08	2 glasses (black)	5
⊙ Denazzano Aglianico Rosato '09	1 glass (black)	4
● Klèos '08	1 glass (black)	4
● Cilento Aglianico Cenito '03	3 glasses (white)	6
○ Pietraincatenata '07	3 glasses (white)	5
○ Pietraincatenata '04	3 glasses (white)	5
● Cenito '01	2 glasses (white)	7
● Cilento Aglianico Cenito '06	2 glasses (white)	6
● Cilento Aglianico Cenito '05	2 glasses (white)	6
● Cilento Aglianico Cenito '04	2 glasses (white)	6
○ Pietraincatenata '06	2 glasses (white)	5
○ Pietraincatenata '05	2 glasses (white)	5

Masseria Felicia

FRAZ. CARANO
LOC. SAN TERENZANO
81030 SESSA AURUNCA [CE]
TEL. 0823935095
www.masseriafelicia.it

CELLAR SALES
PRE-BOOKED VISITS

ANNUAL PRODUCTION 25,000 bottles
HECTARES UNDER VINE 4
VITICULTURE METHOD Organic

Masseria Felicia makes a more than welcome return to the main section of our Guide with the same rigorous, artisanal style skilfully expressing the moods of aglianico-based Falerno in the San Terenzano area of Sessa Aurunca. Despite a change of hands in the technical department, now the responsibility of Vincenzo Mercurio, the red wines made by Maria Felicia Brini and her family are always distinctive for their remarkable weighty palates and insistent smoky sensations, partly from the territory and partly from the use of new oak casks.

Having reclaimed its rightful place in the long profiles Masseria Felicia also very nearly walked off with our highest accolade. This is thanks to the winery's most celebrated wine, the Falerno del Massico Rosso Etichetta Bronzo '07, which unleashes all its potential in aromas of blackberries, black pepper and cocoa powder followed by a seductive palate with a powerful but never rushed progression. We also enjoyed a substantial performance also from the Falerno del Massico Rosso Ariapetrina '07, with less sophisticated tannins but a generous, close-woven structure.

● Falerno del Massico Rosso Et. Bronzo '07	🍷🍷	6
● Falerno del Massico Rosso Ariapetrina '07	🍷🍷	4
○ Falerno del Massico Bianco Anthologia '09	🍷	4
● Falerno del Massico Rosso '08	🍷	4
● Piedirosso '09	🍷	
⊙ Rosalice '09	🍷	4
○ Sinopea '09	🍷	4
○ Falerno del Massico Bianco Anthologia '08	🍸🍸	4*
● Falerno del Massico Rosso '05	🍸🍸	4*
● Falerno del Massico Rosso Et. Bronzo '06	🍸🍸	6
● Falerno del Massico Rosso Et. Bronzo '05	🍸🍸	6
● Falerno del Massico Rosso Et. Bronzo '03	🍸🍸	6

★ Mastroberardino

VIA MANFREDI, 75/81
83042 ATRIPALDA [AV]
TEL. 0825614111
www.mastroberardino.com

CELLAR SALES
PRE-BOOKED VISITS
ROOMS AND FOOD

ANNUAL PRODUCTION 1,500,000 bottles
HECTARES UNDER VINE 340
VITICULTURE METHOD Conventional

A glorious, over 130 year-long, adventure in every bottle and a modern juggernaut launched at tomorrow's challenges. This special blending of past and future is part of the DNA of this most famous Irpinian winery, managed today by Piero Mastroberardino. Every year new wines show up, and the Mirabella estate looks increasingly like a research laboratory, as well as a venue for gourmet and sports event. This tireless energy is reflected in the style of the wines, with results that are not always easy to read.

As usual, the most striking aspect is the solid, reliable range of wines across all types, including the so-called basic lines. The reds are the most impressive, starting with a couple of Taurasis of a very high standard. Radici '06 has a modern feel with oak that is still blending in but the healthy fruit and coherent palate suggest positive ageing prospects. The Radici Riserva '04 leads us into completely different pastures, perceptibly evolved with tertiary aromas of wood resin, stewed fruit and forest floor, but is vibrant and austere on the palate with a still-clenched tannic structure.

● Taurasi Radici '06	🍷🍷🍷	6
● Taurasi Radici Ris. '04	🍷🍷🍷+	6
○ Fiano di Avellino Radici '09	🍷🍷	4
● Aglianico '08	🍷🍷	4*
○ Fiano di Avellino '09	🍷🍷	4
○ Greco di Tufo Novaserra '09	🍷🍷	4
● Irpinia Aglianico Redimore '08	🍷🍷	4
○ Greco di Tufo '09	🍷	4
○ Irpinia Falanghina Morabianca '09	🍷	4
⊙ Lacrimarosa '09	🍷	4
● Mastro d'Irpinia Rosso '09	🍷	3
○ Sannio Falanghina '09	🍷	4
○ Vesuvio Lacryma Christi Bianco '09	🍷	4
● Vesuvio Lacryma Christi Rosso '09	🍷	4
○ Greco di Tufo Novaserra '07	🍸🍸🍸	4*
○ Greco di Tufo Novaserra '06	🍸🍸🍸	4*
● Taurasi Naturalis Historia '04	🍸🍸🍸	7
● Taurasi Radici '05	🍸🍸🍸	6

Salvatore Molettieri

C.DA MUSANNI, 19B
83040 MONTEMARANO [AV]
TEL. 082763424
www.salvatoremolettieri.it

CELLAR SALES
PRE-BOOKED VISITS

ANNUAL PRODUCTION **66,000 bottles**
HECTARES UNDER VINE **13**
VITICULTURE METHOD **Conventional**

The Molettieri family and their Vigna Cinque Querce guard the secret of what are said to be the most extreme Taurasis in the designation. They are the result of rigorous work in the vineyard and the location in Montemarano, at an elevation of about 600 metres on a ridge facing north at many points where the harvest almost always takes place well into November. Structure and body off the charts, high alcohol content and untamed acidic and tannic energy: one of the most difficult balances to get right in winemaking.

We were as ever astonished by the firepower of the Molettieri family's Taurasis, which in their best versions combine flavour with, we dare say, drinkability. One such is the Cinque Querce Riserva '05, with its usual repertoire of opulent but never monolithic dark-skinned fruits streaked with earthy, balsamic, smoky and peppery aromas. These are echoed on the beautifully rounded, satisfying palate thanks to dense tannic texture that expands the flavour rather than holding it back, disguising the warm alcoholic embrace. For the time being, the Vigna Cinque Querce '06 is a more compressed and less blurry expression of a more generous vintage year.

● Taurasi Vigna Cinque Querce Ris. '05	🍷🍷🍷	8
● Taurasi Vigna Cinque Querce '06	🍷🍷	7
○ Fiano di Avellino Apianum '08	🍷	4
● Irpinia Aglianico Cinque Querce '08	🍷	5
● Taurasi Vigna Cinque Querce '05	YYY+	7
● Taurasi Vigna Cinque Querce '04	YYY	7
● Taurasi Vigna Cinque Querce '01	YYY	6
● Taurasi Vigna Cinque Querce Ris. '04	YYY	8
● Taurasi Vigna Cinque Querce Ris. '01	YYY	8
● Aglianico Cinque Querce '03	YY	5
● Aglianico Cinque Querce '02	YY	5
● Taurasi Vigna Cinque Querce '03	YY	8
● Taurasi Vigna Cinque Querce Ris. '03	YY	8
● Taurasi Vigna Cinque Querce Ris. '00	YY	7

★ Montevetrano

LOC. NIDO
VIA MONTEVETRANO, 3
84099 SAN CIPRIANO PICENTINO [SA]
TEL. 089882285
www.montevetrano.it

PRE-BOOKED VISITS

ANNUAL PRODUCTION **30,000 bottles**
HECTARES UNDER VINE **6**
VITICULTURE METHOD **Conventional**

This winery has obtained more Three Glass awards than any other in Campania, winning in every vintage year except in '94 and in the first two versions of'91 and '92, which were almost prototypes for the numbers bottled and type of vinification. This project has revolutionized the image of a whole region and stands today as a classic rather than an avant-garde operation. This was Silvia Imparato's dream and with the help of Riccardo Cotarella she has transformed an unusual Picentino-area blend of cabernet sauvignon, merlot and aglianico into a splendid land-rooted wine.

The umpteenth Three Glass prize for a Montevetrano, in the umpteenth version that offers a perfect snapshot of its vintage year. From a dry but variable pre-harvest summer, the '08 reaches the glass with ripe red fruit in the foreground and boisé sensations that slightly slow down the usual symphony of Mediterranean scrubland and volcanic ash. The palate hints at highly concentrated tannins which still need to mellow down fully but is immediately balanced by stylish, mouthfilling salty flavour sensations.

● Montevetrano '08	🍷🍷🍷	8
● Montevetrano '07	YYY+	8
● Montevetrano '06	YYY	8
● Montevetrano '05	YYY	8
● Montevetrano '04	YYY	8
● Montevetrano '03	YYY	8
● Montevetrano '02	YYY	8
● Montevetrano '01	YYY	8
● Montevetrano '00	YYY	8
● Montevetrano '99	YYY	8
● Montevetrano '98	YYY	8
● Montevetrano '97	YYY	8

Nanni Copè

VIA TUFO, 3
81041 VITULAZIO [CE]
TEL. 0823990529
www.nannicope.it

CELLAR SALES

ANNUAL PRODUCTION 7,500 bottles
HECTARES UNDER VINE 2
VITICULTURE METHOD Conventional

One life, many vines. This is the subtitle chosen by Giovanni Ascione to announce his new adventure as a wine producer at Castel Campagnano to colleagues and enthusiasts. This is a dream come true for one of wine and food journalism's brightest stars, a walking encyclopaedia of world wines. It all began with a two and a half hectare vineyard in Monticelli, with semi-pergola-trained vines growing mainly pallagrello nero with some aglianico and casavecchia. This is the blend used in the winery's only label, Sabbie di Sopra il Bosco.

Nanni Copè could not have made a more impressive debut. Not so much for sailing through to the final tastings as for his clear definition of the style and terroir he intends to explore. This is an elegant, minerally wine in the most authentic sense. Don't be deceived by the still in many ways youthful appearance of the fruit, or by the toasty sensation needing to blend in, because Sabbie di Sopra il Bosco '08 already lights up with dynamic, tangy features that open new horizons in expression for the typical grape varieties of the Colline Caiatine.

● Sabbie di Sopra il Bosco '08	🍷🍷	6

Perillo

C.DA VALLE, 19
83040 CASTELFRANCI [AV]
TEL. 082772252
cantinaperillo@libero.it

CELLAR SALES

ANNUAL PRODUCTION 20,000 bottles
HECTARES UNDER VINE 4
VITICULTURE METHOD Conventional

Don't be deceived by appearances. Michele Perillo's impassible mask hides the pride of a serious producer. Back in 1999, he decided to focus on the small family estate, helped by his friend Carmine Valentino, and immediately became a benchmark for the Castelfranci area. The light clay and limestone soil, centuries-old "raggiera" wheelspoke-trained vines and the aglianico clone known here as coda di cavallo are the ideal ingredients for austere, ageworthy Taurasis that require a great deal of patience.

Patience is the secret that has at last led Michele Perillo and Anna Maria Romano to their first well-deserved Three Glasses. Year by year, they took the measure of unpredictable material, honed the quality of the extract and gradually discovered the key to revealing an intriguing hardness which is not however an end in itself. We are thus able enjoy the Taurasi '05 in which a reductive style is not a problem. Instead, it seems to guarantee a radiant future thanks to unusually lively fruit and an astoundingly youthful progression that speaks straight to the heart.

● Taurasi '05	🍷🍷🍷	5
● Taurasi Ris. '04	🍷🍷	6
● Aglianico '04	🍷🍷 (white)	5
● Castelfranci '01	🍷🍷 (white)	5
○ Coda di Volpe '07	🍷🍷 (white)	5
● Taurasi '04	🍷🍷 (white)	5*
● Taurasi '03	🍷🍷 (white)	6

Ciro Picariello

VIA MARRONI
83010 SUMMONTE [AV]
TEL. 0825702516
www.ciropicariello.com

CELLAR SALES
PRE-BOOKED VISITS

ANNUAL PRODUCTION 50,000 bottles
HECTARES UNDER VINE 7
VITICULTURE METHOD Conventional

Ciro and Rita Picariello are among the few Irpinian producers to have succeeded in winning the approval of critics and enthusiasts alike since their first release of the Fiano di Avellino in 2004. This is a very special interpretation, a joint expression of the Summonte and Montefredane locations, aged in steel with minimal malolactic fermentation and released about one year after the harvest. Completing the range for now are smaller quantities of Greco di Tufo and Aglianico, as we await the monovarietal Summonte vineyard selection.

This Fiano di Avellino '08 is simply fantastic. From the very first tasting, it presented as the missing link between the no-frills linearity of the early releases and the subsequent pursuit of grace and focus shown in recent years. A slightly evolved initial sensation does not hold back the hints of peat, dried herbs, musk and even saffron and an almost botrytized note echoed on the palate with sweetness and flavour into a piquant, sharp, satisfying finish. It's irresistible now and further excitement is in store for those who wait.

○ Fiano di Avellino '08	**YYY**	4*
○ Fiano di Avellino '07	YY	4*
○ Fiano di Avellino '06	YY	4*
○ Fiano di Avellino '05	YY	4*

Pietracupa

C.DA VADIAPERTI, 17
83030 MONTEFREDANE [AV]
TEL. 0825607418
pietracupa@email.it

CELLAR SALES
PRE-BOOKED VISITS

ANNUAL PRODUCTION 35,000 bottles
HECTARES UNDER VINE 4
VITICULTURE METHOD Conventional

It was no unexpected feat that launched Pietracupa among the brightest stars in Italy's winemaking firmament. What Peppino Loffredo began in 1989 has been embellished by his son Sabino year after vintage year in a series of wines that show incredible coherence, character and faithful expression of the terroir. This has come about without any proclamations or posing, just day-by-day tasting and immense sensitivity. Fermentation was in steel only and the acidity carefully preserved for the Fiano and Greco, while the reds are not far behind.

The Greco di Tufo '09 earned its fourth Three Glasses in a row with almost disarming ease. A salty breeze peeps out from a prolonged, savoury palate with masterful definition. Keeping it company is a compelling version of Cupo, a monovarietal Fiano sourced from an old vineyard in Montefredane. The '08 renounces the opulence we were accustomed to in order to enhance the smoky minerality typical of the area, releasing a thirst-quenching, albeit very youthful, citrussy radiance. The Fiano di Avellino '09, which finishes a tad abruptly, also made the finals.

○ Cupo '08	**YYY**+	5
○ Greco di Tufo '09	**YYY**	4*
○ Fiano di Avellino '09	**YY**	4*
● Quirico '08	**YY**	5
● Taurasi '06	**YY**	6
○ Cupo '05	YYY	5
○ Cupo '03	YYY	4*
○ Greco di Tufo '08	YYY+	4*
○ Greco di Tufo '07	YYY	4*
○ Greco di Tufo '06	YYY	4*
○ Fiano di Avellino '08	YY	4*
○ Fiano di Avellino '07	YY	4*
○ Greco di Tufo "G" '03	YY	4
● Taurasi '05	YY	6
● Taurasi '04	YY	6

Tenuta Ponte

VIA CARAZITA, 1
83040 LUOGOSANO [AV]
TEL. 082773564
www.tenutaponte.it

CELLAR SALES
PRE-BOOKED VISITS

ANNUAL PRODUCTION **180,000 bottles**
HECTARES UNDER VINE **25**
VITICULTURE METHOD **Conventional**

Tenuta Ponte, founded in 1995, is a project involving five partners in Luogosano, supervised in the cellar by Carmine Valentino. The estate's 25 hectares are situated at Luogosano, Taurasi and Sant'Angelo all'Esca growing aglianico, coda di volpe, as well as a little merlot and sangiovese, while the fiano and greco grapes are bought in. The whites age in steel and the Taurasi for 12 months in barriques, some new, and another 12 in larger casks.

Precisely because we have grown used to a high standard from Tenuta Ponte in recent years, it seems natural to talk about a interlocutory performance here. The Taurasi '06 is the usual serious but relaxed interpretation with a smoky base nicely blending with hints of black cherries and eucalyptus. Although the palate displays significant tannic texture, it tends to lose momentum and the finish is bitterish. The Fiano di Avellino '09 is also juicy and dynamic but was still very compressed at the time of tasting. The Greco di Tufo '09 is more disappointing. An honourable mention for the Irpinia Campi Taurasini Carazita '07, one of the best-value reds from Irpinia.

○ Fiano di Avellino '09	TT	4*
● Taurasi '06	TT	4*
○ Greco di Tufo '09	T	4
● Irpinia Campi Taurasini Carazita '07	T	3
○ Coda di Volpe '06	YY	3
○ Fiano di Avellino '08	YY	4*
○ Fiano di Avellino '07	YY	4*
○ Fiano di Avellino '06	YY	4*
○ Fiano di Avellino '04	YY	4*
○ Greco di Tufo '08	YY	4*
○ Greco di Tufo '07	YY	4*
○ Greco di Tufo '06	YY	4*
○ Irpinia Coda di Volpe '07	YY	3*
● Taurasi '05	YY	4
● Taurasi '04	YY	4*
● Taurasi '03	YY	5

Quintodecimo

VIA SAN LEONARDO, 27
83036 MIRABELLA ECLANO [AV]
TEL. 0825449321
www.quintodecimo.it

CELLAR SALES
PRE-BOOKED VISITS
ROOMS

ANNUAL PRODUCTION **30,000 bottles**
HECTARES UNDER VINE **12**
VITICULTURE METHOD **Organic**

Experimentation continues at Quintodecimo, estate and vineyard at Mirabella chosen by Luigi Moio and his partner Laura Di Marzio for his adventure as a producer and academic. Aglianico, fiano, greco and falanghina, the principal varieties of the inland areas, are interpreted through work in the vineyards and cellar that aims to enhance the healthy fruit and ageing potential. These wines show a weighty contribution from the oak in the early phases and should improve with time.

The Falanghina Via del Campo continues to take our breath away. The'08 version came within a hair's breadth of the highest accolade thanks to very distinctive candied citrus peel, balsamic herbs and even saffron leading into a fully rounded palate with more successfully blended toasty sensations, we think, than the equally impressive Fiano di Avellino Exultet '08. Again, oakiness cools us a little towards the Taurasi Vigna Quintodecimo Riserva '05, which has beautiful texture but still lacks complexity because of liquorice and coffee in the long finish. The '07 Irpinia Aglianico Terra d'Eclano is again excellent.

○ Fiano di Avellino Exultet '08	TT	7
○ Via Del Campo Falanghina '08	TT	6
● Irpinia Aglianico Terra d'Eclano '07	TT	7
● Taurasi V. Quintodecimo Ris. '05	TT	8
○ Greco di Tufo Giallo D'Arles '08	T	7
○ Fiano di Avellino Exultet '07	YY	7
○ Fiano di Avellino Exultet '06	YY	7
○ Greco di Tufo Giallo D'Arles '07	YY	7
● Irpinia Aglianico Terra d'Eclano '06	YY	7
● Taurasi V. Quintodecimo Ris. '04	YY	8
○ Via Del Campo Falanghina '07	YY	6
○ Via Del Campo Falanghina '06	YY	6

Fattoria La Rivolta

C.DA RIVOLTA
82030 TORRECUSO [BN]
TEL. 0824872921
www.fattorialarivolta.com

CELLAR SALES
PRE-BOOKED VISITS
ROOMS

ANNUAL PRODUCTION 150,000 bottles
HECTARES UNDER VINE 29
VITICULTURE METHOD Certified organic

Knowing Paolo Cotroneo, we are convinced that he is certainly not content with leading what we have believed for the last few seasons to be the best winery in the Sannioarea, Fattoria La Rivolta. His greatest credit is having focused a formidable range of wines centred on the main Campania varieties, with the help of Vincenzo Mercurio. The whites always stand out for their coherent, clearly defined aromas while the leading reds are aged in small casks and show an austere, essential character.

Warmer years certainly benefit the Aglianico del Taburno Terra di Rivolta Riserva '07. It retraces the glories of '03 displaying memorable spicy, fleshy force enhanced by breezier floral hints. It just lacks a bit more depth and finesse in the extract to reach the highest step.
Distinctive as ever, Sogno di Rivolta '09 is a blend of falanghina, fiano and greco aged for four months in oak, perceptible in hints of aniseed and a rounded flavour but nicely blended with the fresher, saltier sensations. The Taburno Piedirosso '09 is enjoyably multi-faceted while the Taburno Falanghina '09 is serene and expressive.

● Aglianico del Taburno Terra di Rivolta Ris. '07	🍷🍷	6
○ Sogno di Rivolta '09	🍷🍷	4
○ Taburno Falanghina '09	🍷🍷	4
● Taburno Piedirosso '09	🍷🍷	4
● Aglianico del Taburno '07	🍷	4
○ Sannio Fiano '09	🍷	4
○ Taburno Greco '09	🍷	4
● Aglianico del Taburno Terra di Rivolta Ris. '06	🍸🍸	6
● Aglianico del Taburno Terra di Rivolta Ris. '04	🍸🍸	6
● Aglianico del Taburno Terra di Rivolta Ris. '03	🍸🍸	6
○ Sogno di Rivolta '08	🍸🍸	4
○ Sogno di Rivolta '07	🍸🍸	4*
○ Taburno Greco '08	🍸🍸	4*
● Taburno Piedirosso '08	🍸🍸	4*

Rocca del Principe

LOC. ARIANIELLO, 9
83030 LAPIO [AV]
TEL. 0825982435
roccadelprincipe@libero.it

CELLAR SALES
PRE-BOOKED VISITS

ANNUAL PRODUCTION 26,000 bottles
HECTARES UNDER VINE 4
VITICULTURE METHOD Conventional

Rocca del Principe's wonderful adventure is inextricably entwined with the characteristics of Fiano di Avellino grown on the slopes of Lapio, the small village which is uncoincidentally considered to be its spiritual home. Ercole Zarrella and his wife Aurelia Fabrizio, helped by Carmine Valentino, proudly enhance the subtle, typically tangy aromatics by taking special care over harvest times, preserving the backbone of acidity in their single wine, aged exclusively in stainless steel.

Every vintage year has its virtuous exceptions. While the average standard of '09 Fiano di Avellinos is not terribly exciting, Rocca del Principe's is about as good as they get. Once again, we see a profile almost like a mountain wine, with glimpses of citrussy hints behind the sensations of yeast, lemon verbena and sage. What's missing? Probably just a touch of depth because the slender, insistent palate emphasizes a breezy, salty energy right through to the well-typed, coherent finish.

○ Fiano di Avellino '09	🍷🍷	4*
○ Fiano di Avellino '08	🍸🍸🍸	4*
○ Fiano di Avellino '07	🍸🍸🍸	4*
○ Fiano di Avellino '06	🍸🍸	4*

Ettore Sammarco

via Civita, 9
84010 Ravello [SA]
tel. 089872774
www.ettoresammarco.it

CELLAR SALES
PRE-BOOKED VISITS

ANNUAL PRODUCTION 75,000 bottles
HECTARES UNDER VINE 10
VITICULTURE METHOD Conventional

The best-known estate in Ravello is named after its founder, Ettore Sammarco, who in 1962 decided to create his own brand to transform and sell the grapes from his one-hectare vineyard in Castiglione. Another ten hectares shared between 30 growers supply the grapes for a complete range of whites, reds and rosés from the Costa d'Amalfi. Although the list includes various varieties and types, the style is always dynamic and consistent with the features of the designation.

No wines went through to the finals this year but this gives us an opportunity to point out how enjoyable Ettore and Bartolo Sammarco's range of wines is. The Selva delle Monache and Vigna Grotta Piana are both a mirror-image of the Ravello Bianco '09. The former is sharper and more youthful while the other is more buttery and juicy, partly from ageing in barriques. In answer to this pair of whites are the two Ravello Selva delle Monache Rosso reds. The '08 just needs to lose some veiled aromas but the palate is rounded and powerful while the Riserva '06 has smoky, briary charm but falls away slightly in the closing stages.

○ Costa d'Amalfi Ravello Bianco Selva delle Monache '09	▼▼	4*
○ Costa d'Amalfi Ravello Bianco V. Grotta Piana '09	▼▼	5
● Costa d'Amalfi Ravello Rosso Selva delle Monache '08	▼▼	4
● Costa d'Amalfi Ravello Rosso Selva delle Monache Ris. '06	▼▼	5
⊙ Costa d'Amalfi Ravello Rosato Selva delle Monache '09	▼	4
○ Costa d'Amalfi Terre Sarecene Bianco '09	▼	4
○ Costa d'Amalfi Ravello Bianco Selva delle Monache '08	▽▽	4*
○ Costa d'Amalfi Ravello Bianco V. Grotta Piana '08	▽▽	5
● Costa d'Amalfi Ravello Rosso Selva delle Monache Ris. '05	▽▽	5
● Costa d'Amalfi Terre Sarecene Rosso '07	▽▽	4*

Sanpaolo - Magistra Vini

c.da San Paolo
83042 Atripalda [AV]
tel. 0825610307
www.cantinasanpaolo.i

CELLAR SALES
PRE-BOOKED VISITS

ANNUAL PRODUCTION 250,000 bottles
HECTARES UNDER VINE 15
VITICULTURE METHOD Conventional

The Irpinian winery owned by Magistravini, which takes its name from a district of Torreoni, is in many ways still be discovered. Under the management of Claudio Quarta, assisted by Vincenzo Mercurio, it has given impetus to new projects to emphasize the special features of a significant winemaking operation that combines big numbers and ambitions. After the four Falanghina selections, this year for the first time we are assessing two Fiano di Avellinos and a Greco di Tufo, also aged in steel.

The new selections bring the best results in this round of tastings, above all the Fiano di Avellino Montefredane '09, one of the best-typed leading wines of the vintage, with coherent emphasis of the typical smoky features of the hills and a taut, sharp palate. No less terroir-rooted, the Fiano di Avellino Lapio '09 has thyme, balsam and floral hints on the nose to lead us in the right direction. The Terra and Acqua '09 are our favourites of the four Falanghinas made from different soils: sandy (Acqua), limestone (Aria), volcanic (Fuoco) and clayey (Terra).

○ Fiano di Avellino Montefredane '09	▼▼	4*
○ Falanghina Acqua '09	▼▼	4
○ Falanghina Terra '09	▼▼	4
○ Fiano di Avellino Lapio '09	▼▼	4*
○ Falanghina Aria '09	▼	4
○ Falanghina del Beneventano '09	▼	3
○ Falanghina Fuoco '09	▼	4
○ Greco di Tufo Montefusco '09	▼	4
○ Irpinia Aglianico '08	▼	4
○ Suavemente Bianco '09	▼	4
● Taurasi '05	▼	6
○ Falanghina Aria '08	▽▽	4
○ Falanghina del Beneventano '08	▽▽	4
○ Falanghina Fuoco '08	▽▽	4
○ Fiano di Avellino '07	▽▽	4*
○ Greco di Tufo '07	▽▽	4*

Luigi Tecce

C.da Trinità
83052 Paternopoli [AV]
tel. 082771375
ltecce@libero.it

CELLAR SALES
PRE-BOOKED VISITS

ANNUAL PRODUCTION **5,000 bottles**
HECTARES UNDER VINE **4**
VITICULTURE METHOD **Conventional**

The term wine producer is not a good fit for Luigi Tecce, a young man whose charm and passion are contagious. In the late 1990s, he chose to literally live in symbiosis with his vines at Paternopoli. His Aglianico wines originate from vines dating back to the 1930s and trained in the classic Avellino wheelspoke pattern. Almost four hectares, distributed over the area bordering with Castelfranci, are interpreted by Luigi in a powerful, exuberant and highly recognizable style. The wines ferment in chestnut vats and aged for 12 months in 40 per cent new barrels.

The Taurasi Poliphemo '06 came very close to hitting the jackpot in its first finals. Despite the uncertain year, this is an opulent version which is enjoyable today and will be even more so in the future when it has had time to relax. For now, it is just held back by a slightly evolved acidulous sensation covering the nuanced aromas of dried herbs, incense and ripe red fruit. Magnificent pink pepper spice coats the palate, with biting, close-woven tannins that contrast slightly too much with the initial glycerine-sweet entry.

● Taurasi Poliphemo '06	2 black glasses	7
● Taurasi Poliphemo '05	2 white glasses	7

Terre del Principe

fraz. Squille
via SS. Giovanni e Paolo, 30
81010 Castel Campagnano [CE]
tel. 0823867126
www.terredelprincipe.com

CELLAR SALES
PRE-BOOKED VISITS

ANNUAL PRODUCTION **55,000 bottles**
HECTARES UNDER VINE **11**
VITICULTURE METHOD **Conventional**

Terre del Principe estate was founded by Manuele Piancastelli and Peppe Mancini in 2003 after the break-up with their former partners at Vestini Campagnano. With Luigi Moio still alongside them, they have never wavered in their desire to recover and promote practically extinct varieties like pallagrello and casavecchia, using them as a basis for modern, well-structured wines. The grapes are picked when at peak ripeness and the wines are aged in small oak barrels. There are two versions of Pallagrello Bianco: the Fontanavigna fermented in steel; and the barrique-aged Le Serole.

It was another good year for Terre del Principe, with Three Glasses going again to Casavecchia Centomoggia for an '08 that plays its classic, earthy, balsamic trump card again. It's hard to establish where the terroir features end and the influence of the oak begins. The palate broadens as it progresses, suggesting that the sharper corners emerging in the finish will eventually be rubbed off. The Pallagrello Nero Ambruco '08 displays a nose that is more layered but perhaps less sound, while the Vigna Piancastelli '07 is slightly too stiff.

● Centomoggia '08	3 black glasses	6
● Ambruco Pallagrello Nero '08	2 black glasses	6
○ Le Serole Pallagrello Bianco '09	2 black glasses	5
● V. Piancastelli '07	2 black glasses	7
● Castello delle Femmine '08	1 black glass	4
○ Fontanavigna Pallagrello Bianco '09	1 black glass	5
⊙ Roseto del Volturno '09	1 black glass	5
● Ambruco '06	3 white glasses	6
● Centomoggia '07	3 white glasses	6
● Ambruco Pallagrello Nero '08	2 white glasses	6
● Centomoggia '04	2 white glasses	6
○ Fontanavigna Pallagrello Bianco '07	2 white glasses	5
○ Le Serole Pallagrello Bianco '08	2 white glasses	5
○ Le Serole Pallagrello Bianco '03	2 white glasses	5
● V. Piancastelli '05	2 white glasses	7
● V. Piancastelli '04	2 white glasses	7

Terredora

VIA SERRA
83030 MONTEFUSCO [AV]
TEL. 0825968215
www.terredora.com

CELLAR SALES
PRE-BOOKED VISITS

ANNUAL PRODUCTION 1,200,000 bottles
HECTARES UNDER VINE 180
VITICULTURE METHOD Conventional

Few Irpinian wineries can count on a vine stock comparable to that of the large Terredora estate founded in 1993 by Walter Mastroberardino and co-run today with his children Paolo, Lucio and Daniela. From Montefusco to Lapio, Santa Paolina and Pietradefusi, some of the best locations in the province are the starting point for a well-stocked, reliable range that seems to favour a rounded, approachable style, especially in the white wines. The aglianico-based reds are more typified, especially after sufficient bottle-ageing.

Once again, it is the Greco di Tufo Loggia della Serra leading the vast range of Terredora wines. This is the label which seems most able to combine expression, contrast, softness and balance. The '09 presents foreground aromas of tropical fruit and almost toasted sensations while the palate does not disappoint, progressing with delicious savouriness. The tangy, austere Taurasi Fatica Contadina '05 is a little affected by the oak in this phase but already reveals definite personality. The Coda di Volpe '09 is very well made and the Irpinia Falanghina '09 is subtle and crisp.

○ Greco di Tufo Loggia della Serra '09	▼▼	4*
○ Coda di Volpe '09	▼▼	4*
● Taurasi Fatica Contadina '05	▼▼	6
● Aglianico '08	▼	4
○ Falanghina '09	▼	4
○ Fiano di Avellino Campo Re '08	▼	5
○ Fiano di Avellino Terre di Dora '09	▼	4
○ Greco di Tufo Terre degli Angeli '09	▼	4
○ Irpinia Falanghina '09	▼	4
● Taurasi Pago dei Fusi '05	▼	6
○ Fiano di Avellino Terre di Dora '06	YY	4*
○ Greco di Tufo Loggia della Serra '08	YY	4*
○ Greco di Tufo Terra degli Angeli '05	YY	4*
○ Greco di Tufo Terre degli Angeli '07	YY	4*

Torricino

LOC. TORRICINO
VIA NAZIONALE
83010 TUFO [AV]
TEL. 0825998119
www.torricino.com

CELLAR SALES
PRE-BOOKED VISITS

ANNUAL PRODUCTION 50,000 bottles
HECTARES UNDER VINE 10
VITICULTURE METHOD Certified organic

We have always had faith in the ideas of Stefano Di Marzo, owner of the Torricino estate in Tufo. His modern approach is inspired by the rural memories and traditions of his small village, where greco is much more than just a grape variety. The vineyards are located near the old sulphur mines and the buttery, richly extracted and sometimes a little evolved style of his first vintages seems to be undergoing a makeover. The whites are aged exclusively in steel while partly new barriques are used for the Aglianico and future Taurasi.

In the usual compact range, lacking the Raone this time, we were perhaps expecting more from the Greco di Tufo '09, particularly given the favourable growing year for the type. The freshness and juicy fruit are there, no doubt, but we are left with an impression of a version halfway between the subtle, taut 2008 and previous versions. In some ways, the Fiano di Avellino '09 is more impressive, showing generous, confident and balanced despite the long alcoholic finish. Irpinia Campi Taurasini '08 is nicely controlled and rigorous, just a little dusty in the tannic texture.

○ Fiano di Avellino '09	▼▼	4*
○ Greco di Tufo '09	▼▼	4*
● Irpinia Campi Taurasini Rosso '08	▼	4
● Aglianico '05	YY	4*
○ Fiano di Avellino '08	YY	4
○ Fiano di Avellino '07	YY	4*
○ Fiano di Avellino '06	YY	4*
○ Greco di Tufo '08	YY	4*
○ Greco di Tufo '07	YY	4*
○ Greco di Tufo '05	YY	4*
○ Greco di Tufo '04	YY	4*
○ Greco di Tufo Raone '07	YY	4*
○ Greco di Tufo Raone '05	YY	4*
○ Greco di Tufo Raone '04	YY	4

Urciuolo

FRAZ. CELZI
VIA DUE PRINCIPATI, 9
83020 FORINO [AV]
TEL. 0825761649
www.fratelliurciuolo.it

CELLAR SALES
PRE-BOOKED VISITS

ANNUAL PRODUCTION **100,000 bottles**
HECTARES UNDER VINE **25**
VITICULTURE METHOD **Conventional**

The estate managed by brothers Ciro and Antonello Urciuolo is one of the leading wineries in Campania and belongs to a select group that combines the pursuit of quality with availability and affordable prices. The whites, aged in steel with a long period on the fine lees, favour rich extract and generous texture. The reds, matured in casks of different sizes, are a hymn to the rigorous character of the aglianico grape, from Mirabella, Castelfranci and Montemarano.

The Taurasi '06 is more than a salute to the vintage. It is a minor, multi-dimensional masterpiece of power, perfectly accessible today but with potential for a journey decades long. The aromas develop in many directions, from hints of forest floor and roots to meaty and refined balsamic sensations with a tenacious hint of cocoa powder and black pepper. Fruity sweetness and weighty tannins move in unison towards an endless mouthfilling, velvet-soft finish. An excellent debut for the Greco di Tufo Faliesi '08, which has more breadth than linearity while the Fiano di Avellino '09 is still coming together.

● Taurasi '06	▼▼▼	6*
○ Fiano di Avellino '09	▼▼	4*
○ Greco di Tufo Faliesi '08	▼▼	4
● Aglianico '08	▼	3
○ Falanghina '09	▼	3
○ Greco di Tufo '09	▼	4
● Taurasi '05	▽▽▽	6
● Aglianico '07	▽▽	3*
● Aglianico '06	▽▽	3*
○ Fiano di Avellino '08	▽▽	4
○ Fiano di Avellino '07	▽▽	4*
○ Greco di Tufo '08	▽▽	4*
○ Greco di Tufo '07	▽▽	4*
● Taurasi '03	▽▽	6

Vadiaperti

C.DA VADIAPERTI
83030 MONTEFREDANE [AV]
TEL. 0825607270
www.vadiaperti.it

CELLAR SALES
PRE-BOOKED VISITS

ANNUAL PRODUCTION **50,000 bottles**
HECTARES UNDER VINE **8**
VITICULTURE METHOD **Conventional**

Aged only in steel with little racking, powerful reduction of aromas, generous sulphiting, malolactic fermentation reduced to a minimum, hard, linear, essential flavours without resort to softening with extract and glycerines. This is the Vadiaperti style, take it or leave it. Antonio and Raffaele Troisi's winery embodies the most extreme spirit of Irpinia in wines with sometimes frighteningly long embryonic phases, later bursting free like the true highlanders they are.

This information will be useful, we think, when faced with the vast range tested in this edition. At the time of tasting, the Fiano di Avellino and Greco di Tufo '09 were practically mute on the nose but showed fruity pulp and backbone. Much the same applies to the Greco di Tufo Tornante '09, a selection from Marotta di Montefusco. The change of pace on the palate, however, removes any remaining doubt that this is a great, authentic, craft-style Greco. Dry, tannic and sharp, the finish screams youth in every drop. From Montefredane comes the Fiano di Avellino Aipierti '08 selection, compressed on the nose once again but racy and stylish on the palate.

○ Greco di Tufo Tornante '09	▼▼▼	4*
○ Fiano di Avellino Aipierti '08	▼▼	4
○ Fiano di Avellino '09	▼▼	4
○ Greco di Tufo '09	▼▼	4
○ Irpinia Coda di Volpe '09	▼	4
○ Greco di Tufo Tornante '08	▽▽▽	4*
○ Falanghina '07	▽▽	4*
○ Fiano di Avellino '08	▽▽	4
○ Fiano di Avellino '07	▽▽	4*
○ Fiano di Avellino Aipierti '07	▽▽	4*
○ Greco di Tufo '08	▽▽	4
○ Greco di Tufo '05	▽▽	4*
○ Greco di Tufo Tornante '07	▽▽	4*
○ Irpinia Coda di Volpe '07	▽▽	4*
○ Irpinia Coda di Volpe '05	▽▽	2*

Vestini - Campagnano

FRAZ. SS. GIOVANNI E PAOLO
VIA BARRACCONE, 5
81013 CAIAZZO [CE]
TEL. 0823679087
www.vestinicampagnano.it

CELLAR SALES
PRE-BOOKED VISITS

ANNUAL PRODUCTION **38,000 bottles**
HECTARES UNDER VINE **6**
VITICULTURE METHOD **Certified organic**

In the grid below, you will find summaries of the wines from Vestini Campagnano and Poderi Foglia, the two estates owned by the Barletta and Quaranta families. The former, located at Caiazzo, is well-known to enthusiasts for the work begun in the 1990s to recover the pallagrello and casavecchia varieties under former partners Manuela Piancastelli and Peppe Mancini. Poderi Foglia, at Conca della Campania in the Galluccio area, presents a characteristic line of aglianico and falanghina-based wines which are excellent value for money.

The ranges presented by Vestini Campagnano and Poderi Foglia often result in contrasting results and comments. We know that the reds usually have an international feel, with emphatic use of oak and extract, yet some astonish us with their evolved sensations and tangy flavour, revealing unpredictable character. This is the case with Kajanero '08, a blend of pallagrello, casavecchia, aglianico and pizzutella. The Pallagrello Nero '07 is darker and more compressed while the best white is the Pallagrello Bianco '09 again, with supple aromas of apricots, aniseed and burnt wheat, and a buttery but refreshing palate.

● Kajanero '08	▼▼	3
○ Pallagrello Bianco '09	▼▼	5
● Pallagrello Nero '07	▼▼	6
● Connubio '06	▼	8
○ Galluccio Rosso Concarosso '08	▼	4
● Casa Vecchia '01	▽▽▽	5*
● Casa Vecchia '06	▽▽	6
● Casa Vecchia '05	▽▽	6
● Concarosso Poderi Foglia '06	▽▽	5
● Connubio '01	▽▽	7
○ Galluccio Falanghina Concabianco Poderi Foglia '08	▽▽	4
● Kajanero '06	▽▽	3*
○ Pallagrello Bianco '08	▽▽	5
● Pallagrello Nero '01	▽▽	5*

Villa Diamante

VIA TOPPOLE, 16
83030 MONTEFREDANE [AV]
TEL. 0825670014
www.villadiamante.eu

CELLAR SALES
PRE-BOOKED VISITS

ANNUAL PRODUCTION **15,000 bottles**
HECTARES UNDER VINE **3**
VITICULTURE METHOD **Certified organic**

For a few years now, Fiano di Avellino Vigna della Congregazione has no longer been the only wine produced here but it remains the standard-bearer for the Villa Diamante range. The wine originates from a vineyard of about four hectares on the Toppole hill at Montefredane, at just over 400 metres, on clay, shale and limestone soil. Antoine Gaita and Diamante Renna's interpretation employs a very much hands-off approach: no clarification or filtration, and a long ageing period in stainless steel.

There is something supernatural about the unpredictable performances of the leading Villa Diamante wines. This year brings us an astonishing '08. The initial impact is less typically Vigna della Congregazione than usual, referring to that special smoky, chestnut-like minerality which in this version hides among hints of Mediterranean scrubland, chlorophyll, and thistle honey. The palate is less sharp than usual but the salty sensation and substantial backbone of acidity give irresistible momentum. And the Three Glasses are back.

○ Fiano di Avellino Vigna della Congregazione '08	▼▼▼	5
○ Greco di Tufo V. dei Ciamillo '08	▼	4
● Irpinia Aglianico Rosso Pater Nobilis '06	▼	6
○ Fiano di Avellino Vigna della Congregazione '06	▽▽▽	5
○ Fiano di Avellino Vigna della Congregazione '04	▽▽▽	5
○ Fiano di Avellino Cuvée Enrico '00	▽▽	7
○ Fiano di Avellino Vigna della Congregazione '07	▽▽	5
○ Fiano di Avellino Vigna della Congregazione '05	▽▽	5
○ Fiano di Avellino Vigna della Congregazione '02	▽▽	5

★ Villa Matilde

SS Domitiana, 18
81030 Cellole [CE]
tel. 0823932088
www.villamatilde.it

CELLAR SALES
PRE-BOOKED VISITS
ROOMS AND FOOD

ANNUAL PRODUCTION 700,000 bottles
HECTARES UNDER VINE 120
VITICULTURE METHOD Conventional

Villa Matilde is a veteran of Caserta winemaking and driving force behind a renewal that has brought enthusiasts to the area where the legendary Falerno was produced in ancient times. At the helm are Salvatore and Maria Ida da Avallone, assisted by Riccardo Cotarella, and the wines based on falanghina, aglianico, piedirosso and primitivo are what we could call sensibly modern. With the purchase of the Tenuta di Altavilla estate in Irpinia, the range now includes Greco di Tufo, Fiano di Avellino and Taurasi.

It's impossible to comment on all the One-Glass-or-better wines presented for tasting this year by Villa Matilde. We note in particular the umpteenth impressive performance from the '09 Falanghina Tenuta Rocca dei Leoni, the region's best buy in the category, and a very well-typed Fiano di Avellino Tenute di Altavilla '09. Without the Camarato, the leading red is the Cecubo '08, made with primitivo and abbuoto, with slightly evolved but subtle aromas of briar and tobacco. A positive performance came from the Falerno del Massico Rosso '07 but towering above them all is the Falerno del Massico Bianco Caracci '08, which earned another Three Glasses.

○ Falerno del Massico Bianco V. Caracci '08	▼▼▼	5
● Cecubo '08	▼▼	5
○ Falanghina Tenuta Rocca dei Leoni '09	▼▼	4
● Falerno del Massico Rosso '07	▼▼	4
○ Fiano di Avellino Tenute di Altavilla '09	▼▼	4
● Aglianico Rocca dei Leoni '09	▼	3
○ Eleusi Falanghina Passito '08	▼	6
○ Falanghina di Roccamonfina '09	▼	4
○ Falerno del Massico Bianco '09	▼	4
● Taurasi Tenute di Altavilla '06	▼	6
⊙ Terre Cerase Tenuta Rocca dei Leoni '09	▼	3
○ Falerno del Massico Bianco V. Caracci '05	▽▽▽	5
○ Falerno del Massico Bianco V. Caracci '04	▽▽▽	4*
● Falerno del Massico Camarato '05	▽▽▽	7
● Falerno del Massico Camarato '04	▽▽▽	6
● Falerno del Massico Camarato '01	▽▽▽	6

Villa Raiano

loc. San Michele di Serino
Bosco Satrano, 1
83020 Serino [AV]
tel. 0825595663
www.villaraiano.it

CELLAR SALES

ANNUAL PRODUCTION 220,000 bottles
HECTARES UNDER VINE 20
VITICULTURE METHOD Conventional

Significantly, Villa Raiano regains its well-deserved ranking among the best producers in Campania. Now that work on the new cellar is complete and technical management is now in the hands of Fortunato Sebastiano, we see a winery on the move, greater land-rootedness in the wines and an evolving style. The bottles acquiring more grip and linearity and grip, as is already clear in the whites, all steel-aged.

The new labels are shaking up the reliable Villa Raiano range. Confidently through to the finals is the Fiano di Avellino Ventidue '09, named after the 22 kilometres separating the cellar from the Lapio vineyard where the fiano grows. Its distinctive features are aromatic herbs on the nose and a subtle but flavoursome palate. Very close behind is the Fiano di Avellino Alimata '09, emphasizing the Montefredane terroir and showing more closed on the nose with a sweeter palate, but perhaps just lacking a touch of depth. This same comment applies to Greco di Tufo Marotta '09, a selection from a Montefusco vineyard.

○ Fiano di Avellino Ventidue '09	▼▼	5
● Aglianico '08	▼▼	4
○ Fiano di Avellino Alimata '09	▼▼	5
○ Greco di Tufo Contrada Marotta '09	▼▼	5
○ Falanghina Beneventano '09	▼	4
○ Fiano di Avellino '09	▼	4
○ Greco di Tufo '09	▼	4
○ Fiano di Avellino '08	▽▽	4
○ Fiano di Avellino '05	▽▽	4*
○ Fiano di Avellino Ripa Alta '07	▽▽	5
○ Greco di Tufo '08	▽▽	4
○ Greco di Tufo '06	▽▽	4*
○ Greco di Tufo '05	▽▽	4
● Raiano '05	▽▽	5
● Taurasi Cretanera Ris. '03	▽▽	6

Agnanum

VIA VICINALE ABBANDONATA AGLI ASTRONI, 3
80125 NAPOLI
TEL. 3385315272
www.agnanum.it

Raffaele Moccia is one of the most authentic producers of Flegrei wines. From just over three hectares in the Astroni hills between Naples and Pozzuoli, he creates a series of wines designed to spend time in the cellar. The Falanghina dei Campi Flegrei Vigna del Pino '08 is a fine example.

○ Falanghina dei Campi Flegrei V. del Pino '08	🍷🍷	4
○ Falanghina dei Campi Flegrei '08	🍷	4
● Piedirosso dei Campi Flegrei V. delle Volpi '07	🍷	4

Aia dei Colombi

C.DA SAPENZE
82034 GUARDIA SANFRAMONDI [BN]
TEL. 0824817384
www.aiadeicolombi.it

We have often complimented the Pascale brothers on their deliciously fresh-tasting whites from falanghina and fiano. This year, we take our hats off to a very deep, classy Guardiolo Aglianico Colle dell'Aia Riserva '05, undoubtedly one of the best reds we tasted in the whole Sannio area.

● Guardiolo Aglianico Colle dell'Aia Ris. '05	🍷🍷	5
○ Guardiolo Falanghina '09	🍷	3
○ Guardiolo Falanghina Vignasuprema '08	🍷	4

Amarano

C.DA TORRE, 32
83040 MONTEMARANO [AV]
TEL. 082763351
www.amarano.it

First time in the Guide for a small estate that conveys the full power of the Montemarano terroir. Lucia Storti goes straight to the finals with her charming, sound Taurasi Principe Lagonessa '06 offering notes of cinchona, nutmeg, leather and a close-woven, creamy palate. One of the best of its year.

● Taurasi Principe Lagonessa '06	🍷🍷	5

Giuseppe Apicella

FRAZ. CAPITIGNANO
VIA CASTELLO SANTA MARIA, 1
84010 TRAMONTI [SA]
TEL. 089856209
www.giuseppeapicella.it

In 1977, Giuseppe Apicella opened the first cellar in town based on the largest area of vineyards on the Amalfi coast. Today, he is flanked by his children, Prisco and Fiorina, and their production veers more and more towards whites. Witness the splendid Tramonti Bianco Colle Santa Marina '09.

○ Costa d'Amalfi Tramonti Bianco '09	🍷🍷	4*
○ Costa d'Amalfi Tramonti Bianco Colle Santa Marina '09	🍷🍷	4*
● Piedirosso '09	🍷	4

Bambinuto

VIA CERRO
83030 SANTA PAOLINA [AV]
TEL. 0825964634
info@cantinabambinuto.com

Established in 2006 by Marilena Aufiero and her family, who had spent many years as growers, Bambinuto's limited production is mainly white. Once again it is the Greco di Tufo Picoli '09 that dominates, instantly recognisable if a tad overround and opulent.

○ Greco di Tufo Picoli '09	🍷🍷	5
○ Fiano di Avellino '09	🍷	4

Barone

VIA GIARDINO, 2
84070 RUTINO [SA]
TEL. 0974830463
www.cantinebarone.it

Giuseppe Di Fiore, Francesco Barone and Emanuele Perrella form the team at Barone, one of the most interesting estates in Cilento. This year's solid range is topped by the '09 Fiano Vestalis, a dense, complex wine fermented in 900-litre casks and matured in stainless steel for eight months.

○ Vestalis '09	🍷🍷	5
● Cilento Aglianico Pietralena '08	🍷	4
○ Cilento Fiano Vignolella '09	🍷	4
○ Marsia Bianco '09	🍷	2

OTHER WINERIES

Bianchini Rossetti
FRAZ. CASALE DI CARINOLA
VICO TENENTE TRABUCCO
81030 CARINOLA [CE]
TEL. 0823709187
www.bianchinirossetti.com

This small estate belonging to Tony Rossetti and Francesco Bianchini shows its potential with a classic blend of aglianico and piedirosso. Falerno del Massico Rosso Mille 880 '07 combines a full, modern impact and the progression of an austere, elegant wine with an irresistible salty vein.

● Falerno del Massico Rosso Mille 880 '07 ΥΥ 4

Boccella
VIA SANT'EUSTACHIO
83040 CASTELFRANCI [AV]
TEL. 082772574
giuseppebocella@hotmail.it

Founded as recently as 2005, the tiny estate of Raffaele Boccella and family is already a point of reference for those who love Taurasis with a strong artisan bent. Top of the list is the Sant'Eustachio '06, which once again won a place in our finals for its density and austerity, despite the odd unruly tannin.

● Taurasi Sant'Eustachio '06 ΥΥ 6

Brunigi Galco
LOC. CASCANO
NAZ. APPIA
81037 SESSA AURUNCA [CE]
TEL. 3270132435
www.brunigigalco.com

If the area of Falerno considers itself a leading light, then much of the credit goes to a group of small new estates which are determined to take the right direction. One such is Carmine Gatta's cellar, which has earned a Guide profile with an intense, territorial Falerno del Massico Rosso La Pera '07.

● Falerno del Massico La Pera '07 ΥΥ 5

Calafè
LOC. VIGNA
83030 PRATA DI PRINCIPATO ULTRA [AV]
TEL. 0825781010
www.calafe.it

A double round of applause for Benito Petrillo. Not only has he launched Calafè as one of the most interesting wines of the entire, crowded Irpinia wine scene, he is also helping to highlight the potential of Greco di Tufo as a cellarable wine. Witness the Ariavecchia '08 selection.

O Greco di Tufo Ariavecchia '08 ΥΥ 6
O Greco di Tufo '08 Υ 5

Il Cancelliere
C.DA IAMPENNE, 45
83040 MONTEMARANO [AV]
TEL. 082763557
www.ilcancelliere.it

The first Riserva produced by Cancelliere, a tiny artisan estate, comes in just over 500 bottles. Compared to the standard-label Nero Nè '05, the Riserva brings out Contrada Iampenne's earthy, smoky character. The acid and tannins have yet to find balance but this is an extremely alluring wine.

● Taurasi Nero Nè Ris. '05 ΥΥ 4
● Gioviano '07 Υ 4

Cantine del Mare
VIA CAPPELLA, IV TRAV. 6
80070 MONTE DI PROCIDA [NA]
TEL. 0815233040
www.cantinedelmare.it

This is one of the best surprises to come out of this year's tastings. The small estate rents about six hectares of vineyards around Monte di Procida, the highest point in Campi Flegrei. The Campi Flegrei Falanghina '09 and Piedirosso '08 show well, appetizing for their saltiness and aromatic poise.

O Campi Flegrei Falanghina '09 ΥΥ 4*
● Campi Flegrei Piedirosso '08 ΥΥ 4*
O Campi Flegrei Falanghina Sorbo Bianco '06 Υ 5
● Campi Flegrei Piedirosso Sorbo Rosso '06 Υ 5

I Capitani

via Bosco Faiano, 15
83030 Torre le Nocelle [AV]
tel. 0825969182
www.icapitani.com

We are pleased to see this lovely Irpinia estate belonging to Ciriaco Cefalo and his family back in the Guide. Surprisingly, this year's range is led by the label that is intended to be the estate's simplest, most approachable wine, the Irpinia Aglianico Guaglione '08, which combines softness with flesh.

- ● Irpinia Aglianico Guaglione '08 🍷🍷 4
- ● Irpinia Emè '07 🍷 5
- ● Taurasi Bosco Faiano '05 🍷 5

Cantina Capizzi

loc. Piedimonte di Sessa Aurunca
via Massicani, 18
81037 Sessa Aurunca [CE]
tel. 0823701186
info@cantinacapizzi.com

The group of estates that have set out to restore Falerno to its ancient splendour is growing fast. Gennaro and Silvio Capizzi's small cellar is one and brings us two Falerno Rosso '07s with body and structure. Pittacium has a slightly grassier finish while Don Gennaro shows more character and complexity.

- ● Falerno del Massico Don Gennaro '07 🍷🍷 5
- ● Falerno del Massico Pittacium '07 🍷 4

Alexia Capolino Perlingieri

via Marraioli, 58
82037 Castelvenere [BN]
tel. 0824971541
www.capolinoperlingieri.com

We have yet to see the full fruits of Alexia Capolino Perlingieri's labours to reclaim her family's wine heritage at Castelvenere. This year, Alexia offered us the first release of the Sannio Aglianico Talento, an '07 with good supporting acidity but a bit rough in its extract.

- ● Sannio Aglianico Talento '07 🍷🍷 4
- ● Sannio Rosso Sciascì '08 🍷 4
- ⊙ Sannio Vignarosa '09 🍷 4

La Casa dell'Orco

fraz. San Michele
via Limaturo, 52
83039 Pratola Serra [AV]
tel. 0825967038
www.lacasadellorco.it

The Musto family's estate offers a range of labels very distinctive for their soft, relaxed style. This is nowhere more obvious than in the smooth, succulent Fiano di Avellino '09 with its fragrant, tropical aromas. We also still like the dense, extract-rich Irpinia Coda di Volpe '09.

- ○ Fiano di Avellino '09 🍷🍷 4*
- ○ Greco di Tufo '09 🍷 4
- ● Irpinia Aglianico '09 🍷 4
- ○ Irpinia Coda di Volpe '09 🍷 3

Cautiero

c.da Arbusti
82030 Frasso Telesino [BN]
tel. 3387640641
www.cautiero.it

Four hectares and around 10,000 bottles a year are the credentials of this new entry, an organic estate at Frasso Telesino run by Fulvio Cautiero and Immacolata Cropano. Despite its rather muddled aromas and over-exuberant extract, we liked the forthright character of the '08 Sannio Aglianico Fois Rosso.

- ● Sannio Aglianico Fois Rosso '08 🍷🍷 3*
- ○ Sannio Falanghina Fois '09 🍷 3
- ○ Sannio Greco Trois '09 🍷 3

Tenuta del Cavalier Pepe

via Santa Vara
83040 Luogosano [AV]
tel. 082773766
www.tenutacavalierpepe.it

We believe that this ambitious project launched by the Milena Pepe has yet to show its true potential. Forty hectares produce around 250,000 bottles a year of the full range of Irpinia wines. The reds dominate at the moment and the Taurasi Opera Mia '06 shows very well on its debut performance.

- ● Taurasi Opera Mia '06 🍷🍷 6
- ● Irpinia Aglianico Terra del Varo '08 🍷 4
- ○ Irpinia Coda di Volpe Bianco di Bellona '09 🍷 4
- ● Irpinia Rosso Sanserino '08 🍷 4

Colle di San Domenico
SS Ofantina km 7,500
83040 Chiusano di San Domenico [AV]
tel. 0825985423
www.cantinecolledisandomenico.it

The range of wines produced by Colle San Domenico is solid as a rock. It may not have a single outstanding product but overall presents a united front, and the wines are released at great prices. The Greco di Tufo '09 is particularly good.

○ Greco di Tufo '09	🍷🍷	4
● Taurasi '05	🍷🍷	5
○ Fiano di Avellino '09	🍷	4
● Irpinia Aglianico '08	🍷	3

Colli di Castelfranci
c.da Braudiano
83040 Castelfranci [AV]
tel. 082772392
www.collidicastelfranci.com

The growing number of competitive Campania estates forces us to pick and choose and this year it is the turn of Colli di Castelfranci to sit on the short profile bench. If the wines are anything to go by, particularly the Greco di Tufo Grotte '09 and Taurasi Gagliardo '05. They'll be back in a full profile soon.

○ Greco di Tufo Grotte '09	🍷🍷	4
● Taurasi Gagliardo '05	🍷🍷	6
○ Fiano di Avellino Pendino '09	🍷	4
⊙ Irpinia Aglianico Rosato Crote '09	🍷	4

D'Antiche Terre - Vega
c.da Lo Piano - s.s. 7 bis
83030 Manocalzati [AV]
tel. 0825675358
www.danticheterre.it

Two very characterful editions of Taurasi '05 show just how important D'Antiche Terre is in the panorama of Irpinia winemaking. The standard label shows an almost primary fruitiness that the Il Vicario Riserva deepens with smoky, salty tones and a more austere palate.

● Taurasi '05	🍷🍷	6
● Taurasi Il Vicario Ris. '05	🍷🍷	5
● Irpinia Aglianico '08	🍷	
○ Irpinia Coda di Volpe '09	🍷	4

De Falco
via Figliola
80040 San Sebastiano al Vesuvio [NA]
tel. 0817713755
www.defalco.it

De Falco's wines gave their usual sound performance. The estate has yet to produce an out-and-out winner but the range shows no weak points whatsoever. The Falanghina del Beneventano '09 is sweet and lively while the Lacryma Christi Rosso'09 has supporting acidity and character.

● Aglianico del Beneventano '08	🍷	3
○ Falanghina del Beneventano '09	🍷	3
○ Vesuvio Lacryma Christi Bianco '09	🍷	4
● Vesuvio Lacryma Christi Rosso '09	🍷	4

Di Meo
c.da Coccovoni, 1
83050 Salza Irpina [AV]
tel. 0825981419
www.dimeo.it

We have come to expect high standards from the wines produced by the Di Meo brothers and would like to see a bit more intensity and character in the whites. The reds fare better, with a chewy, territorial Taurasi Riserva '04 and a modern Irpinia Rosso Don Generoso '06, which is slightly dusty on the finish.

● Taurasi Ris. '04	🍷🍷	6
○ Coda di Volpe '09	🍷	4
○ Fiano di Avellino '09	🍷	4
● Irpinia Rosso Don Generoso '06	🍷	8

La Dormiente
via Pezze, 2
82030 Torrecuso [BN]
tel. 0824872737
www.ladormiente.it

This lovely estate in Torrecuso is back after a year's sabbatical. It takes its name from the outline of the Taburno mountain, which in popular myth is likened to a sleeping (dormiente) woman. With Agnese Ariano and Lorenzo Nifo at the helm, the entire range has a relaxed expressivity that we love.

● Aglianico del Taburno '06	🍷🍷	4*
● Aglianico del Beneventano '09	🍷	4
○ Falanghina del Beneventano '09	🍷	3
○ Taburno Falanghina '09	🍷	4

Cantina Farro

FRAZ. BACOLI
LOC. FUSARO
VIA VIRGILIO, 16/24
80070 NAPOLI
TEL. 0818545555
www.cantinefarro.it

Michele Farro's estate gives its usual reliable performance. This year, we were particularly impressed by the whites. Campi Flegrei Falanghina '09 interprets its year with a subtle but well-sustained palate. The Campi Flegrei Falanghina Le Cigliate '08 selection is more intense with tertiary aromas.

○ Campi Flegrei Falanghina '09	🍷🍷	4*
○ Campi Flegrei Falanghina Le Cigliate '08	🍷🍷	5
● Campi Flegrei Piedirosso '09	🍷	4
⊙ Depié Rosé '09	🍷	4

Fontanavecchia

VIA FONTANAVECCHIA
82030 TORRECUSO [BN]
TEL. 0824876275
www.fontanavecchia.info

Libero Rillo, one of Sannio's best-known and loved estates, continues to stride ahead. The whites have a dry, fermentative style while the reds need time to smooth their oaky corners, although the Aglianico del Taburno Vigna Cataratte Riserva '06 is already interesting.

● Aglianico del Taburno V. Cataratte Ris. '06	🍷🍷	5
○ Sannio Fiano '09	🍷	3
○ Sannio Greco '09	🍷	4
○ Taburno Falanghina '09	🍷	3

Cantina Giardino

VIA PETRARA, 21B
83031 ARIANO IRPINO [AV]
TEL. 0825873084
www.cantinagiardino.com

Cantina Giardino presented us with just two labels to taste this year. The experiments of these brilliant interpreters of Irpinia wines include skin contact for whites, amphora-ageing, and sulphur-free vinification. Both the Aglianico Le Fole '08 and the Greco T'Ara Rà '08 show well.

● Le Fole '08	🍷🍷	4
○ T'Ara Rà '08	🍷🍷	6

Raffaele Guastaferro

VIA GRAMSCI
83030 TAURASI [AV]
TEL. 082539244
www.guastaferro.it

Raffaele Guastaferro's eyes mirror the determination of a man who knows he possesses a very special terroir that yields chewy, multi-faceted Taurasis. Witness the Primum '06 that offers one of the most stunning noses of its year, hinting at blackcurrant, olive, pepper and cinchona. The finish is ever-so-slightly dry.

● Taurasi Primum '06	🍷🍷	5

Iannella

VIA TORA
82030 TORRECUSO [BN]
TEL. 0824872392
www.cantineiannellainterfree.it

We like Iannella's wines because although they have rather international overtones, they are always juicy and constant across all types. This year our vote goes to the delicately vegetal, balsamic Sannio Piedirosso '08. The Taburno Falanghina '09 shows well, too.

● Sannio Piedirosso '08	🍷🍷	4*
○ Falanghina Spumante Extra Dry	🍷	4
○ Taburno Coda di Volpe '09	🍷	4
○ Taburno Falanghina '09	🍷	4

Marianna

VIA DEI VIGNETI, 5
83010 GROTTOLELLA [AV]
TEL. 0825671252
www.vinimarianna.it

The results garnered this year by this estate, founded by Ciriaco Coscia and run today by Luca Pierro and Raffaele Panarella, are no accident. The wines confirm our impression of overall quality with a Fiano di Avellino '09 that is one of the best options of its year and a typical Taurasi Riserva '05.

○ Fiano di Avellino '09	🍷🍷	4*
● Taurasi Ris. '05	🍷🍷	6
○ Irpinia Coda di Volpe '09	🍷	3
● Irpinia Piedirosso '08	🍷	3

Guido Marsella
VIA MARONE, 2
83010 SUMMONTE [AV]
TEL. 0825626555

It's been a few years since the able Guido Marsella sent us wines to taste but the year's panorama would not be complete without his Fiano di Avellino. Notably, the 2008 is a more direct, dynamic interpretation than usual with lovely citrussy aromas. Its only weakness is too much almondiness in the finish.

○ Fiano di Avellino '08 🍷🍷 4

Masseria Frattasi
VIA TORRE VARONI, 15
82016 MONTESARCHIO [BN]
TEL. 0823351740
www.masseriafrattasi.it

This estate owned by Pasquale Clemente and Caterina Cecere goes from strength to strength, and not just in the number of labels produced. The slope of Mount Taburno that faces Montesarchio offers whites with a strong salt and mineral slant. The Taburno Falanghina Donna Laura Riserva '08 is a perfect example.

○ Falanghina del Taburno Donna Laura Ris. '08 🍷🍷 5
● Taburno Aglianico Caudium '08 🍷🍷 4
● Orchis Purpurea '08 🍷 5
○ Taburno Falanghina Bonea '09 🍷 4

La Molara
C.DA PESCO
83040 LUOGOSANO [AV]
TEL. 082778017
www.lamolara.com

Taurasi de La Molara is one of the fruitiest, raciest interpretations of the DOCG thanks to the limestone terrain of Luogosano and, most of all, to the solid, balanced approach of this estate. Results are good, even with entry-level wines, the Naif Bianco '09 from falanghina and the Rosso '07 from aglianico.

● Taurasi Santa Vara '06 🍷🍷 6
● Irpinia Aglianico Campi Taurasini V. Claudia '07 🍷 4
○ Naif Bianco '09 🍷 4
● Naif Rosso '07 🍷 4

Cantina dei Monaci
FRAZ. SANTA LUCIA, 206
83030 SANTA PAOLINA [AV]
TEL. 0825964350
www.cantinadeimonaci.it

This small estate belonging to Angelo Carpenito and Maria Coppola has never come so close to winning its first trophy. The Greco di Tufo '09 has an irresistibly fresh, salty framework in perfect harmony with its smoky, nobly vegetal aromas. This almost muted style is also reflected in the Fiano di Avellino '09.

○ Greco di Tufo '09 🍷🍷 4*
○ Fiano di Avellino '09 🍷🍷 4

Monte di Grazia
VIA R. ORSINI, 36
84010 TRAMONTI [SA]
TEL. 089876906
www.montedigrazia.it

The young organic estate of Alfonso and Anna Arpino produces fewer than 10,000 bottles a year. Its two hectares are also home to a few plots of tintore, with vines over 100 years old. We particularly like the Monte di Grazia Rosso '07, which is sharpish for its year.

● Monte di Grazia Rosso '07 🍷🍷 5
● Monte di Grazia Rosso '05 🍷🍷 5
○ Bianco '09 🍷 4

Mustilli
VIA CAUDINA, 10
82019 SANT'AGATA DE' GOTI [BN]
TEL. 0823718142
www.mustilli.com

Leonardo and Paola Mustilli's historic estate continues its steady march to the peak of Sannio production. Take the Sant'Agata dei Goti Aglianico Cesco di Nece '07, an austere, varietal interpretation with notes of cinchona and tobacco. It is intense and caressing, despite its good bite of tannins.

● S. Agata dei Goti Aglianico Cesco di Nece '07 🍷🍷 5
○ S. Agata dei Goti Falanghina '09 🍷 4
● Sannio Aglianico Grifo di Rocca '08 🍷 4
○ Sannio Greco V. Fontanella '09 🍷 4

Lorenzo Nifo Sarrapochiello

VIA PIANA
82030 PONTE [BN]
TEL. 0824876450
www.nifo.eu

We admit to a weakness for the wines of Lorenzo Nifo Sarrapochiello, a young producer based at Ponte. Their natural expressiveness tends to compensate for the odd trace of aromatic rusticity, as demonstrated by the Aglianico del Taburno D'Erasmo Riserva '06. It is still developing but has excellent character.

- ● Aglianico del Taburno D'Erasmo Ris. '06 🍷🍷 5
- ⊙ Taburno Aglianico Rosato Màrosa '09 🍷 4
- ● Taburno Rosso Serrone '08 🍷 3

Nugnes

VIA VICINALE MASSERIA SS. APOSTOLI
81030 CARINOLA [CE]
TEL. 0815584386
www.aziendagricolanugnes.it

Flanked by children Gilemma and Orlando, Antonio Nugnes has set his sights high at his new estate. Our first tastings reveal an impressive range, particularly strong in terms of reds. We prefer the fluidity of the Falerno Rosso '08 to the toasty opulence of the Falerno del Massico Rosso Caleno Riserva '07.

- ● Falerno del Massico Calena Ris. '07 🍷🍷 5
- ● Falerno del Massico Rosso '08 🍷🍷 4
- ○ Falerno del Massico Bianco '09 🍷 4
- ○ Falerno del Massico Vite Aminea '09 🍷 4

Ocone

LOC. LA MADONNELLA
VIA DEL MONTE, 56
82030 PONTE [BN]
TEL. 0824874040
www.oconevini.it

Mimì Ocone is a living chapter of Sannio's wine history. His is also a leading light on today's scene. His modern estate is anchored in a solid range that appear deceptively simple, never extreme wines. A good example is the Taburno Falanghina Vigna del Monaco '09.

- ○ Taburno Falanghina V. del Monaco '09 🍷🍷 4
- ● Taburno Aglianico '06 🍷 4
- ● Taburno Aglianico Anastasi '06 🍷 5
- ○ Taburno Greco '09 🍷 4

Oppida Aminea - F.lli Muratori

LOC. EREMITA
82100 BENEVENTO
TEL. 0824334061
www.arcipelagomuratori.it

The Campania estate owned by the Franciacorta-based Muratori group continues to build on its quality. Oppida Aminea at Benevento is planted largely to falanghina, greco and fiano while Giardini Arimei at Forio d'Ischia is running new experiments with biancolella, forastera and other minor varieties.

- ○ Sannio Falanghina Caracena Tenuta Oppida Aminea '09 🍷🍷 4*
- ○ Giardini Arimei 🍷 6
- ○ Sannio Greco Caucino Tenuta Oppida Aminea '09 🍷 4

Fattoria Pagano

VIA DEI CILIEGI
81030 CARINOLA [CE]
TEL. 0823720550
www.fattoriapagano.com

Antonio Pagano's wines could not have made a more impressive debut. His Falerno Rossos flaunt a calm, virtuous character and shy away from display. A blood-rich meat note makes the Angelus '07 deeply alluring as it unfolds soft, caressing texture and a long balsamic finish.

- ● Falerno del Massico Angelus '07 🍷🍷 5
- ● Falerno del Massico Gaurasi '07 🍷🍷 4*

Palummo

LOC. LA STARZA
VIA DELLE CINQUE PIETRE
81045 GALLUCCIO [CE]
TEL. 3397461776
www.aziendapalummo.com

Flanked by Pasquale Telaro, Emanuela Palummo and Luciano Cinquanta run this three-hectare estate in Galluccio. The emphasis on fruitier, more vinous elements does not prevent their first reds from exhibiting sound, taut structure, most notably in the Galluccio Rosso Nesso '08.

- ● Galluccio Nesso '08 🍷🍷 3
- ● Petreo '08 🍷 3

Gennaro Papa

P.ZZA LIMATA, 2
81030 FALCIANO DEL MASSICO [CE]
TEL. 0823931267
www.gennaropapa.it

Gennaro and Antonio Papa are emerging ever more strongly as a point of reference for Falerno Primitivo. Credit goes to their rigorous selections and the Campantuono label that year after year shows consistently high quality. Despite the odd youthful indiscretion, the '08 already combines energy and weight.

● Falerno del Massico Primitivo Campantuono '08	6

La Pietra di Tommasone

VIA PROVINCIALE FANGO, 98
80076 LACCO AMENO [NA]
TEL. 0813330330
www.tommasonevini.it

Antonio Monti's beautiful estate deserves more space. It has been among the top Ischia cellars for several seasons now. Antonio experiments with blends in both his reds and whites but the results are typical and consistent. We recommend the Pignanera '07 from equal parts aglianico and montepulciano.

● Pignanera '07	7
● Pithecusa Rosso '08	5
○ Ischia Biancolella '09	4
○ Pithecusa Bianco '09	4

Andrea Reale

LOC. BORGO DI GETE
VIA CARDAMONE, 75
84010 TRAMONTI [SA]
TEL. 089856144
www.aziendaagricolareale.it

What a performance from the Reale family estate in Tramonti. Borgo di Gete '08 from pure tintore displays a customary fullness on the palate that needs time to integrate with the oaky notes. The Getis Rosato '09 is fabulous. Obtained from piedirosso with some tintore, it gets our vote as Campania's best rosé.

● Borgo di Gete '08	7
⊙ Getis Rosato '09	4
○ Aliseo '09	4
● Cardamone '09	5

Rocca dell'Angelo

LOC. SAN NICOLA
83030 VENTICANO [AV]
TEL. 0825965343
www.roccadellangelo.it

The province of Avellino is an endless source of surprise and innovation. Just look at Rocca dell'Angelo, a small estate that enters the Guide on its first try with a compact, spicy Taurasi '05. What it lacks in body it makes up for in aromatic complexity that ranges from incense to cocoa powder.

● Taurasi '05	5

Francesco Rotolo

VIA SAN CESARIO, 18
84070 RUTINO [SA]
TEL. 0974830050

With two of the most lustrous, raciest Fianos we tasted this year in the province of Salerno, Alfonso Rotolo makes a convincing return to the Guide. The Fiano '09 presents a crisp, harmonious profile and a finish of bitter herbs. The barrique-matured Valentina '09 selection is closer-knit and more caressing.

○ Fiano '09	4
○ Fiano Valentina '09	4
⊙ Rose d'Autunno '09	4

Russo

LOC. CARAZITA
VIA FONTANA DELLO SPALATRONE
83030 TAURASI [AV]
TEL. 069410405
www.cantinerussotaurasi.com

The premature demise of Ermanno Russo, founder of this lovely Taurasi estate, was a heavy blow for his family and wine lovers that knew this warm, passionate man. His daughter Marcella is more than capable of carrying on his excellent work, as this year's range of wines clearly shows.

● Taurasi Spalatrone '06	6
○ Falanghina Grandilla '09	4

OTHER WINERIES

San Francesco

FRAZ. CORSANO
VIA SOFILCIANO, 18
84010 TRAMONTI [SA]
TEL. 089876748
www.vinitenutasanfrancesco.it

Campania is a treasure trove that has yet to reveal all of its gems. Among these are the wines of San Francesco: austere, expansive reds and whites that embody the perfect fusion of earth and sea unique to this zone. A fine example is Tramonti Bianco Per Eva '09, which strolled into our finals.

○ Costa d'Amalfi Bianco Per Eva '09	🍷🍷	4
○ È Iss '07	🍷🍷	4
○ Costa d'Amalfi Tramonti Bianco '09	🍷	4
⊙ Costa d'Amalfi Tramonti Rosato '09	🍷	4

Fattoria Selvanova

LOC. SQUILLE
VIA SELVANOVA
81010 CASTEL CAMPAGNANO [CE]
TEL. 0823867261
www.selvanova.com

We have written for years about the rigorous efforts of Antonio Buono on his splendid estate in Castel Campagnano. He has yet to live up to his promise, however. Technically irreproachable, we would like to see a bit more character in his wines. The Aglianico Silicata '06 is excellent.

● Silicata '06	🍷🍷	6
● Aglianico Selvanova '06	🍷	7
● Sopralago '06	🍷	5
● Vignantica '08	🍷	4

Sorrentino

VIA CASCIELLO, 5
80042 BOSCOTRECASE [NA]
TEL. 0818584963
www.sorrentinovini.com

If we had to uncork a truly authentic Lacryma Christi, a bottle from this estate would probably come to mind. Focus, compactness and energy are the hallmark of Giuseppe Sorrentino's wines. With no recourse to pointless forcing of extract or aromas, they are eminently drinkable.

● Piedirosso Ver Sacrum '09	🍷🍷	3*
○ Falanghina Ver Sacrum '09	🍷	3
⊙ Vesuvio Lacryma Christi Rosato Ver Sacrum '09	🍷	3
● Vesuvio Lacryma Christi Rosso Ver Sacrum '09	🍷	3

Santiquaranta

C.DA TORREPALAZZO
82030 TORRECUSO [BN]
TEL. 0824876128
www.santiquaranta.it

The odd couple of cider producer Luca Baldino and Enrico De Lucia is behind this Santiquaranta estate. They are a disparate pair but form a close team that is building on quality year after year. Our pick of the wines on offer is the delicious Sannio Moscato '09.

○ Sannio Moscato '09	🍷🍷	4
● Aglianico Passito '08	🍷	6
○ Sannio Falanghina '09	🍷	4

La Sibilla

FRAZ. BAIA
VIA OTTAVIANO AUGUSTO, 19
80070 BACOLI [NA]
TEL. 0818688778
www.sibillavini.it

The fine estate belonging to the Di Meo family is one of the most impressive in the region. We like the relaxed, tempting style of the wines, especially the whites. The Campi Flegrei Falanghina '09 and the Cruna deLago '08 selection are undeniably minerally.

○ Campi Flegrei Falanghina '09	🍷🍷	4
○ Campi Flegrei Falanghina Cruna deLago '08	🍷🍷	5
● Campi Flegrei Piedirosso '01	🍷	4
○ Passito di Falanghina Passio '07	🍷	7

Tenuta Adolfo Spada

FRAZ. VAGLIE
SP 14 SESSA MIGNANO
81044 GALLUCCIO [CE]
TEL. 0823925709
www.tenutaspada.it

Brothers Ernesto and Vincenzo Spada see their lovely estate take an inevitable back seat this year. They are the creators of Gladius, one of the best reds to come out of Campania in recent years. It needs a bit more time in the cellar so we tasted a pleasant Fiorflòres '09, a pure Falanghina.

○ Fiorflòres '09	🍷🍷	4
○ Galluccio Gallicius Bianco '09	🍷	3
● Galluccio Gallicius Rosso '09	🍷	3

OTHER WINERIES

Cantina del Taburno
VIA SALA, 16
82030 FOGLIANISE [BN]
TEL. 0824871338
www.cantinadeltaburno.it

This is not what we have come to expect from the Cantina del Taburno. Fair enough, their two flagship reds, the Bue Apis and Delius, are absent yet again from the line-up but we still feel the range is a bit below par. The whites are balanced and drinkable but they are too one-dimensional and tend to lack bite.

- ○ Coda di Volpe Amineo '09 — 🍷 4
- ● Taburno Aglianico Fidelis '06 — 🍷 4
- ○ Taburno Falanghina '09 — 🍷 4
- ○ Taburno Falanghina Folius '07 — 🍷 5

Terre Irpine
C.DA PANTANELLE
P.ZZA MUNICIPIO, 6
83055 STURNO [AV]
TEL. 0825448774
www.terreirpine.it

Who said great wines only come from your own vines? Terre Irpine consistently features among our top Campania estates with a Taurasi produced from grapes it buys in from the Montemarano area. Compared to last year's magnificent version, the '06 is a little less expansive and complex.

- ● Taurasi '06 — 🍷🍷 5

Trabucco
VIA VITTORIO EMANUELE, 1
81030 CARINOLA [CE]
TEL. 0823737345
www.trabucconicola.it

Nicola Trabucco is a key player in the enthusiasm the area of Falerno has generated in recent years. His contribution is twofold: technical advice to many of the smaller estates; and the excellent wines he produces on his family's estate. The Falerno del Massico Rosso Erre '08 is a fine example.

- ● Falerno del Massico Rosso Erre '08 — 🍷🍷 4*
- ● Falerno del Massico Rosso Rapicano '08 — 🍷🍷 5

Antica Masseria Venditti
VIA SANNITICA, 120/122
82037 CASTELVENERE [BN]
TEL. 0824940306
www.venditti.it

Scoring systems and grids can't always do justice to everything we pick up during our tastings. A case in point is Nicola Venditti. Not only do his wines offer a very sound interpretation of the terroir of Castelvenere, they also display a sincere, authentic soul that never fails to thrill.

- ● Sannio Aglianico Marraioli '07 — 🍷🍷 4
- ● Sannio Rosso '08 — 🍷🍷 3*
- ● Sannio Barbera Barbetta '08 — 🍷 4
- ○ Sannio Falanghina Vàndari '09 — 🍷 4

Le Vigne di Raito
FRAZ. RAITO
SAN VITO, 9
84019 VIETRI SUL MARE [SA]
TEL. 089233428
www.levignediraito.com

Able and determined, Patrizia Malanga swells the ranks of that group of producers so expertly interpreting the wines of the Amalfi coast. As its name suggests, the cellar is at Raito. To date, it produces just one wine, the Ragis '07, whose strong Mediterranean character echoes across a measured, assertive palate.

- ● Ragis '07 — 🍷🍷 6

Volpara
FRAZ. TUORO
VIA PODESTI, 23
81037 SESSA AURUNCA [CE]
TEL. 0823938051
www.volparavini.it

Volpara follows last year's impressive performance with another triumphant showing, placing the Falerno del Massico Rosso Ri Sassi '07 in our finals. Fascinating topsoil and black olives announce a close-knit, austere palate that is full but not too heavy. We prefer it to Tuoro Riserva, also '07.

- ● Falerno del Massico Rosso Ri Sassi '07 — 🍷🍷 4
- ● Falerno del Massico Rosso Tuoro Ris. '07 — 🍷🍷 5

BASILICATA

The full extent of changes that have overtaken wine in Basilicata will soon become clear. Rankings and marks aside, there is at last a feeling of ferment and progress not just in average quality but more particularly in the style and expression of the wines. Progress may still be a little haphazard, and at times reluctant to use words such as diversity and difference in a positive sense, but it is essential to shake up an area that is too ready simply to rest on the laurels of occasional praise from critics or the market. The designation that is the focus of most activity is without doubt Aglianico del Vulture, with its solid, distinctive combination of terroir and grape, recently enhanced by the attribution of DOCG status. Around the ancient extinct Vulture volcano, there is a growing group of contenders old and new, families with a long viticultural tradition and new non-regional wine investors with deep pockets or enthusiasts embarking on a new life path. No definitive map of the area yet exists but there are more and more discussion groups on the qualities of aglianico grown on the various slopes of Mount Vulture, especially on what distinguishes classic areas from the sites that slope down towards Puglia. The number of growers adhering to the so-called natural trend is growing, as is the group of those who believe that the route to excellence does not necessarily entail savage thinning and concentrated, extract-stuffed wines, with or without a large dollop of oak. There's been a change, as can be seen from our tastings this year. Among the winners are again the Aglianico del Vulture Titolo '08 from Elena Fucci and the Aglianico del Vulture Basilisco '07 by Michele Cutolo while it is the first time for the Aglianico del Vulture Macarico '07 from Rino Botte, who has been a prime candidate for our highest award for several years. But many other wineries have taken a big step forward. Grifalco della Lucania and Michele Laluce make their first appearance among the winners and finalists: we thought their Aglianico del Vulture Damaschito '07 and Le Drude '06 were absolute stunners. The most opulent, oak-brushed Aglianicos are still to be found at Cantine del Notaio, Di Palma, Eubea and Vulcano & Vini, the group that took over Bisceglia; the most elegant wines are at Eleano and Paternoster, not forgetting Terre degli Svevi and Cantina di Venosa. Martino, Carbone and D'Angelo make up a really strong group of owners. The scene around Matera is more uncertain and has yet to find a proper identity in terms of varieties and production technique. Nonetheless, the potential already looks excellent from wineries such as Battifarano, Masseria Cardillo, Taverna and the new entry Tenuta Marino.

Basilisco

VIA PIAVE, 35
85022 BARILE [PZ]
TEL. 0972771033
basilisco@interfree.it

CELLAR SALES
PRE-BOOKED VISITS

ANNUAL PRODUCTION **45,000 bottles**
HECTARES UNDER VINE **10**
VITICULTURE METHOD **Conventional**

The wines of Basilisco are a tangible example of what aglianico can offer in terms of elegance, expansion and depth. The highly distinctive style is increasingly in evidence year after year, and celebrates the fruit obtained from the vines of the Contrada Macarico and Gelosia areas, in the countryside around Barile, and excellent use of oak. Above all they reflect the rigorous work of Michele Cutolo and Nunzia Calabrese, who have been assisting Lorenzo Landi since 2003.

From the rich, austere vintage of '07 comes an Aglianico del Vulture Basilisco that is in many ways both untypical and true to type. The inconsistencies are due to slower definition of aroma and a more vigorous tannic thrust than usual but we still found the familiar dynamic, tapered profile that again earns it Three Glasses. We are already anticipating great things for the '08, if it is anything like the Aglianico del Vulture Teodosio, a second-label wine according to the winery but not in its substance. There's more noticeable oak, but the hefty, characterful texture is excellent.

● Aglianico del Vulture Basilisco '07	TTT	6
● Aglianico del Vulture Teodosio '08	TT	4
● Aglianico del Vulture Basilisco '06	YYY	6
● Aglianico del Vulture Basilisco '04	YYY	6
● Aglianico del Vulture Basilisco '01	YYY	6
● Aglianico del Vulture Basilisco '05	YY	6
● Aglianico del Vulture Teodosio '07	YY	4

Bisceglia

C.DA FINOCCHIARO
85024 LAVELLO [PZ]
TEL. 097288409
www.agricolabisceglia.com

CELLAR SALES
PRE-BOOKED VISITS

ANNUAL PRODUCTION **400,000 bottles**
HECTARES UNDER VINE **55**
VITICULTURE METHOD **Certified organic**

The acquisition of the Bisceglia brand and winery by the Vulcano & Vini group is one of the biggest bits of news in the Vulture region in recent years. The new ownership has Paolo Zamparelli at the helm and five other members, with technical collaboration from Maurizio Angeletti and Giovanni Riviezzo. The range is unchanged for the moment, with a basic and premium Aglianico del Vulture, accompanied by a Syrah, a Chardonnay and a monovarietal Fiano, made in the usual succulent, well-orchestrated style.

New winery, same old Gudarrà, it should say, at least judging by the '07, sailed into the finals, missing top honours by a whisker. It is a very convincing version, exemplary in its definition of balsamic and tropical hints, backed up by healthy, well-ripened red fruit melded in a palate that lacks only a touch of drive. The Aglianico del Vulture Terra di Vulcano '08 is also looking good. It's an entry-level wine that does its duty more than adequately, displaying fine balance and power. The Armille Syrah '09 is well-managed and varietal while Bosco delle Rose Chardonnay '09 is soft and lively.

● Aglianico del Vulture Gudarrà '07	TT	5
● Aglianico del Vulture Terra di Vulcano '08	TT	3*
● Armille Syrah '09	T	4
○ Bosco delle Rose Chardonnay '09	T	4
○ Fiano Terre di Vulcano '09	T	4
● Aglianico del Vulture Gudarrà '05	YYY	5
● Aglianico del Vulture Gudarrà '04	YYY	5*

Cantine del Notaio
via Roma, 159
85028 Rionero in Vulture [PZ]
tel. 0972723689
www.cantinedelnotaio.com

CELLAR SALES
PRE-BOOKED VISITS

ANNUAL PRODUCTION 170,000 bottles
HECTARES UNDER VINE 27
VITICULTURE METHOD Certified biodynamic

The new vinification cellar has just been finished at Serra del Granato di Ripacandida but Gerardo Giuratrabocchetti's main operations centre is still at the marvellous maturing cellars carved out of the tufa at Rionero in Vulture. The range is constantly being expanded, with a series of aglianico-based wines at different stages of maturity, including some fermented without the skins and some spumante versions, produced from 27 biodynamically farmed hectares of the classic area. The reds are very distinctive with their depth and toasty opulence.

This year's tastings turned the wineries own rankings on their heads with one of the most successful versions of Aglianico del Vulture Il Repertorio to the fore. The '08 has a most intriguing spectrum of aromatics, from ripe dark berry fruit to dark spices and Mediterranean scrubland, but most of all, it unfolds balanced progression already quite well integrated with the oak, in spite of the clenched tannins. The oak is less attractive at this stage in the Aglianico del Vulture La Firma '07 and the Aglianico del Vulture Il Sigillo '06, which are rather too dry and monolithic despite their undoubted weight.

● Aglianico del Vulture Il Repertorio '08	2 black glasses	5
● Aglianico del Vulture Il Sigillo '06	2 black glasses	7
● Aglianico del Vulture La Firma '07	2 black glasses	7
○ Il Preliminare '09	2 black glasses	4
○ La Raccolta '09	2 black glasses	6
⊙ Il Rogito '08	1 black glass	5
● L'Atto '08	1 black glass	4
○ L'Autentica '08	1 black glass	6
○ La Stipula M. Cl. Brut '08	1 black glass	5
⊙ La Stipula Rosé M. Cl. '08	1 black glass	5
● Aglianico del Vulture La Firma '00	3 glasses	6
● Aglianico del Vulture La Firma '06	2 glasses	7
○ Il Preliminare '08	2 glasses	4
○ L'Autentica '06	2 glasses	6

Carbone
via Nitti, 48
85025 Melfi [PZ]
tel. 0972237866
www.carbonevini.it

CELLAR SALES
PRE-BOOKED VISITS

ANNUAL PRODUCTION 45,000 bottles
HECTARES UNDER VINE 18
VITICULTURE METHOD Conventional

This small Melfi winery is already a significant contender in the Vulture area, in spite of the youth of both estate and those running it. Luca and Sara Carbone are not content merely to build up their estate, starting with a plot of old vines in the upper part of Melfi; they are increasingly involved in a movement that aims to make this lovely area better known to wine professionals and enthusiasts. The new fermentation cellar is under construction but the splendid barrel cellar in the historic centre is the ideal setting for these information sessions.

This performance was hardly what we had been expecting, particularly from the Aglianico del Vulture Stupor Mundi '07, a Carbone standard-bearer. When we tasted it, the wine was probably still finding its feet with aromatics shifting towards a mature profile of bramble jelly, further enhanced by somewhat insistent hints of oak even on the palate, where the tannin seems slightly too big. We retasted an open bottle, which was more expansive, but for now we are cautiously sticking to Two Glasses.

● Aglianico del Vulture Stupor Mundi '07	2 black glasses	6
● Aglianico del Vulture Terra dei Fuochi '08	1 black glass	4
● Aglianico del Vulture 400 Some '07	2 glasses	5
● Aglianico del Vulture 400 Some '06	2 glasses	5
● Aglianico del Vulture Terra dei Fuochi '07	2 glasses	4*

D'Angelo

via Provinciale, 8
85028 Rionero in Vulture [PZ]
tel. 0972721517
www.dangelowine.com

CELLAR SALES
PRE-BOOKED VISITS

ANNUAL PRODUCTION **350,000 bottles**
HECTARES UNDER VINE **50**
VITICULTURE METHOD **Conventional**

It is certainly no accident that the winery run by Donato D'Angelo has become, for professionals and wine lovers, emblematic of the most genuine Aglianico del Vulture tradition. A long, glorious history that began in the post-war years plays a role in this but mostly it is the distinctiveness of a rigorous style that has hardly changed over the years, the result of long maceration and unhurried barrel ageing, for wines that demand care and patience. Some bottles are more modern in character but the spirit of the winery is decidedly classic.

It is a new line-up again for the D'Angelo family, with no Vigna Caselle or, sadly, Donato D'Angelo. These absences weigh heavily but only partially account for a rather disappointing performance. We recall much more convincing versions of Aglianico Canneto and Serra delle Querce, a blend of aglianico and merlot, than the'08s. More in line with the winery's usual style is the no-nonsense Aglianico del Vulture '08. Its nose is very much old style, with roots, earth and liquorice and the palate gushes with pressure and flavour, missing the final by a whisker.

● Aglianico del Vulture '08	▼▼	4
● Canneto '08	▼	5
● Serra delle Querce '08	▼	6
● Aglianico del Vulture V. Caselle Ris. '01	YYY	4*
● Aglianico del Vulture Donato D'Angelo '07	YY	5
● Aglianico del Vulture V. Caselle Ris. '04	YY	5
● Aglianico del Vulture Valle del Noce '07	YY	6
● Aglianico del Vulture Valle del Noce '05	YY	6
● Serra delle Querce '07	YY	6

Cantine Di Palma

c.da Scavoni
85028 Rionero in Vulture [PZ]
tel. 0972722891
www.cantinedipalma.com

CELLAR SALES
PRE-BOOKED VISITS

ANNUAL PRODUCTION **130,000 bottles**
HECTARES UNDER VINE **14**
VITICULTURE METHOD **Conventional**

Antonio Di Palma's winery is a solid, family-run affair, which has added on a further 13.5 hectares of vines in the Rionero and Barile area. Production concentrates entirely on Aglianico del Vulture, interpreted as a first and second-label wine. Il Nibbio Grigio aged almost exclusively in new barriques while second and third-use small barrels are used for Tenuta Piano Regio. In general, the wines are rich and concentrated, and will grow in complexity, opening out over time.

It is worth waiting a year to taste the Aglianico del Vulture Il Nibbio Grigio '07 again, the unique wine presented in this edition by Antonio Di Palma. It is still rather young and boisterous, especially in the oak department, but aeration reveals intact, close-knit fruit, enlivened by whiffs of balsam, which are nicely absorbed in the full-bodied, caressing palate. So, a very well-made modern Aglianico, which lacks just a hint of depth and, perhaps, unpredictability.

● Aglianico del Vulture Il Nibbio Grigio '07	▼▼	6
● Aglianico del Vulture Il Nibbio Grigio Et. Nera '03	YYY	6
● Aglianico del Vulture Il Nibbio Grigio Et. Nera '05	YY	6
● Aglianico del Vulture Tenuta Piano Regio '07	YY	4*
● Aglianico del Vulture Tenuta Piano Regio '05	YY	4*
● Aglianico del Vulture Tenuta San Savino '02	YY	5

Eleano

C.DA PIAZZOLLA, 10
85028 RIONERO IN VULTURE [PZ]
TEL. 0972722273
www.eleano.it

CELLAR SALES
PRE-BOOKED VISITS

ANNUAL PRODUCTION **26,000 bottles**
HECTARES UNDER VINE **5**
VITICULTURE METHOD **Conventional**

The little winery run by Alfredo Cordisco and Francesca Grieco is far more than a novelty for the Vulture area. Not only does the quality of its output put it in the front rank of Basilicata estates but the Aglianico's consistency of style, in a search for measured expansiveness rather than sheer muscle, is evident too, with a judicious contribution from the ageing casks of ten hectolitres or more. The five hectares of land from which Eleano produces around 30,000 bottles lie in Pian dell'Altare, in the Ripacandida area.

It will be even more difficult to call the Aglianico del Vulture Dioniso a second wine if it stays this good. The '07 version also gained a place in the finals for its juiciness and austerity, despite some lack of precision in aromas and its rigid closure. The Aglianico del Vulture Eleano '06 is more complete, splendid in its wealth of iron minerality and sea salt, showing taut and flavoursome. And as if that were not enough, here we have one of the best sweet wines of Basilicata, the dried-grape Moscato Bianco Ambra '08.

● Aglianico del Vulture Dioniso '07	TT	4
● Aglianico del Vulture Eleano '06	TT	6
○ Ambra '08	TT	5
● Aglianico del Vulture '05	YY	6
● Aglianico del Vulture Dioniso '06	YY	4*
○ Ambra Moscato '06	YY	4*

Eubea

S.DA PROVINCIALE, 8
85020 RIPACANDIDA [PZ]
TEL. 0972723574
www.agricolaeubea.com

CELLAR SALES
PRE-BOOKED VISITS

ANNUAL PRODUCTION **50,000 bottles**
HECTARES UNDER VINE **17**
VITICULTURE METHOD **Certified organic**

Eubea certainly didn't sneak back into the main section of our Guide. After being relegated to a small profile in last year's edition, when we'd managed to taste Eugenia Sasso's wines only as barrel samples, this year we found them in more dazzling form than ever. The three Aglianicos are interpreted in the usual powerful, full-flavoured style, sometimes with a degree of over-extraction, but very much in line with the selection work going on in the 17 hectares surrounding Ripacandida.

Eubea put on a great performance this year with two wines almost reaching maximum marks. While Aglianico del Vulture Ròinos is an old hand at our finals, the Aglianico del Vulture Riparossa is a surprise, especially considering the price. They are both from the '07 vintage and both are naturally characterized by the greater density and support of the Ròinos, which is offset in the Riparossa by a vibrant, delicious development of youthful, flowery and aromatic herbal tones. The Aglianico del Vulture Il Covo dei Briganti '07 is not far behind.

● Aglianico del Vulture Riparossa '07	TT	4*
● Aglianico del Vulture Ròinos '07	TT	6
● Aglianico del Vulture Il Covo dei Briganti '07	TT	5
● Aglianico del Vulture Ròinos '01	YYY	8
● Aglianico del Vulture Ròinos '06	YY	8

Elena Fucci

c.da Solagna del Titolo
85022 Barile [PZ]
tel. 0972770736
az.elenafucci@tiscali.it

CELLAR SALES
PRE-BOOKED VISITS

ANNUAL PRODUCTION **15,500 bottles**
HECTARES UNDER VINE **6**
VITICULTURE METHOD **Organic**

The first ten harvests are being celebrated at the Fucci estate, a landmark for a small property which has literally shot ahead in recent years, quickly becoming one of the undisputed beacons of wine in Basilicata. Thanks go to Salvatore and his daughter Elena, an oenologist, whose work goes into a single wine, Titolo, produced from an Aglianico vineyard covering six hectares located about 600 metres above sea level in Contrada Solagna del Titolo, harvested when fully ripe and aged in mostly new small wood.

Aglianico del Vulture Titolo assures us that it is truly in a class of its own through its sheer style. The '08 version shows us just why. Behind its material form, underlined by lush fruit and powerful, vigorous tannins, lies something quite different, which comes through on the nose in flashes of roots across balsam and iodine, confirmed in a creamy, rounded palate infused with fresh tastes. To sum up, it is a wine that only a cursory tasting could classify simply as modern. As the months pass, it even seems to lighten in pressure and length: Three emphatic Glasses.

● Aglianico del Vulture Titolo '08	YYY (red)	7
● Aglianico del Vulture Titolo '07	YYY+	7
● Aglianico del Vulture Titolo '06	YYY	6
● Aglianico del Vulture Titolo '05	YYY	6

Grifalco della Lucania

loc. Pian di Camera
85029 Venosa [PZ]
tel. 097231002
grifaicodellalucania@email.it

CELLAR SALES
PRE-BOOKED VISITS

ANNUAL PRODUCTION **60,000 bottles**
HECTARES UNDER VINE **18**
VITICULTURE METHOD **Certified organic**

The story of Fabrizio and Cecilia Piccin is unusual, to say the least. Now living in Basilicata after moving in 2003 to set up this new property from Tuscany, where they produced wine in the Chianti and Montepulciano area. They have 18 hectares in Ginestra, Maschito, Rapolla and Venosa, the vast majority given over to aglianico and under organic cultivation. The Grifalco reds are aged in large barrels and are notable for being extremely delicate and lustrous, without no concessions to flamboyance but favouring structure and flavour.

The reds presented this year by Grifalco are so much fun, starting with an Aglianico del Vulture Gricos '08 which only shares its price band with other basic wines. Aglianico del Vulture Grifalco '08 is even more invigorating and multi-faceted, with volcanic veins, good flavour and eclectic on the palate, with tannins managed for the long term. But it is the Aglianico del Vulture Damaschito '07 that was the real heart stopper at this tasting. It bowled us over with its iron minerality and flowery tone, adding in medicinal herbs with a backdrop of plenty of succulent, lively, crunchy red fruit slightly rawish at the back.

● Aglianico del Vulture Damaschito '07	YY (black)	5
● Aglianico del Vulture Gricos '08	YY (black)	3*
● Aglianico del Vulture Grifalco '08	YY (black)	4
● Aglianico del Vulture Gricos '07	YY	3*
● Aglianico del Vulture Grifalco '07	YY	4
● Aglianico del Vulture Grifalco '06	YY	4*

Michele Laluce

VIA ROMA, 21
85020 GINESTRA [PZ]
TEL. 0972646145
www.vinilaluce.it

CELLAR SALES
PRE-BOOKED VISITS

ANNUAL PRODUCTION **30,000 bottles**
HECTARES UNDER VINE **6**
VITICULTURE METHOD **Certified organic**

Michele Laluce's huge hands tell you more about this small craft-style winery a thousand words. It's a cellar that has grown in the shelter of the Laluce family's long winemaking tradition. The vines are in Ginestra, in the countryside of Serra del Tesoro at about 400 metres above sea level, and consist almost entirely of aglianico. Each wine has its own style, with a varied range of ageing curves, maceration times and maturations, which take place in stainless steel and oak casks of various sizes.

Once again, the wines presented by Michele Laluce are not for finicky noses or palates. Some lack of focus in the aromas and a certain degree of tannic rusticity are there in the mix but also incomparable character, pure and simple, whose strength lies in the naturalness of its expression and drinkability These are the finest qualities that we find in the Aglianico del Vulture Le Drude '06, an authoritative finalist with a generous nose ranging through plums, cocoa powder and hot spices. It could just do with a little more flesh to balance out the eager tannins but the citrus and salt tang gives momentum and length.

● Aglianico del Vulture Le Drude '06	🍷🍷	5
● Aglianico del Vulture Zimberno '06	🍷🍷	5
● S'Adatt '08	🍷	5
● Aglianico del Vulture Zimberno '02	YY	5
● S'Adatt '04	YY	4*

Macarico

P.ZZA CARACCIOLO, 7
85022 BARILE [PZ]
TEL. 0972771051
www.macaricovini.it

CELLAR SALES
PRE-BOOKED VISITS
ROOMS AND FOOD

ANNUAL PRODUCTION **22,000 bottles**
HECTARES UNDER VINE **5**
VITICULTURE METHOD **Certified organic**

The headquarters have changed but not the quality and style of the bijou winery of Rino Botte and Renato Abrami. The business still centres on splendid aglianico vineyards at Contrada Macarico, where the vines are planted almost 10,000 per hectare and rigorously pruned. The result can be seen in the estate's two wines. They are very concentrated and sometimes difficult to interpret in the first few months but over time seem to find new harmony and expansion, teasing out all their considerable potential.

We are pleased to have been supporters of the wines of Rino Botte and Renato Abrami. But we didn't need any great foresight to see that sooner or later Aglianico del Vulture Macarico would find the find the way to control its natural power and put it to good use in definition and depth. That is what we feel about the '07 version. This wonderfully smoky, sensuous but also gracefully extracted masterpiece deservedly won Three Glasses. The lovely Aglianico del Vulture Macarì '08, juicy and dynamic as usual, is a worthy runner-up.

● Aglianico del Vulture Macarico '07	🍷🍷🍷	6
● Aglianico del Vulture Macarì '08	🍷🍷	5
● Aglianico del Vulture '06	YY	6
● Aglianico del Vulture '05	YY	6
● Aglianico del Vulture Macarì '07	YY	5*
● Aglianico del Vulture Macarì '06	YY	5

Armando Martino

via Luigi Lavista, 2a
85028 Rionero in Vulture [PZ]
tel. 0972721422
www.martinovini.com

CELLAR SALES
PRE-BOOKED VISITS

ANNUAL PRODUCTION **300,000 bottles**
HECTARES UNDER VINE **15**
VITICULTURE METHOD **Conventional**

Martino returns to the main section of our Guide in top form and to the sound of clinking glasses. We have a good report from this historic estate of Rionero, but also, we believe, for the entire Vulture area. The whole range of aglianico-based wines has found new vigour and consistency, as testified by the fine balance between technical precision and a traditional feel we noted in the top wines. The grapes come from the estate's 15 hectares, plus targeted purchases from traditional suppliers.

From the broad range released by Armando and Carolin Martino, we are only considering the four wines they sent for tasting, all very persuasive. We were most impressed by the Aglianico del Vulture Oraziano '06, aged in stainless steel and barriques. It unveils classic forest fruits and spice mingling with citrus hints and hazelnuts, leading into a tangy, fresh-tasting palate with a close-knit, precise finish. The Donna Lidia Rosé '09, also aglianico, is excellent and is one of the region's best rosés for its sharpness and vibrancy.

● Aglianico del Vulture Oraziano '06	🍷🍷	6
⊙ Rosé Donna Lidia '09	🍷🍷	4
● Aglianico del Vulture Pretoriano '06	🍷	6
● Rosso Carolin '09	🍷	4
● Aglianico del Vulture Bel Poggio '05	YY	5
● Aglianico del Vulture Oraziano '05	YY	6
● Aglianico del Vulture Pretoriano '05	YY	6

Paternoster

c.da Valle del Titolo
85022 Barile [PZ]
tel. 0972770224
www.paternostervini.it

CELLAR SALES
PRE-BOOKED VISITS

ANNUAL PRODUCTION **150,000 bottles**
HECTARES UNDER VINE **20**
VITICULTURE METHOD **Certified organic**

For nearly 85 years, the name Paternoster has been a synonym for Basilicata excellence all over the world. From this glorious history we now see a winery that is totally forward-looking, having undertaken a painstaking assessment of all its facilities, old and new. This is a special moment, as can be sensed immediately in a wide, versatile range full of innovative stylistic interpretations alongside more classic expressions. Aglianico is the main variety, also available in the sparkling Barigliott version, and moscato, fiano and falanghina make up the rest.

There were no top prizes but it was a good round of tastings for Paternoster wines. With the Rotondo '07 only tasted from the barrel, all anticipation was concentrated on the Aglianico del Vulture Don Anselmo Riserva '06, which did not disappoint, hitting the mark for yet another place in the finals. It is probably in an in-between phase, which heightens the impression of plum and dried flowers evolution on the nose, and reveals extremely insistent tannin, later dried by alcohol in the finish. On the other hand, we would point out the terrifically good Aglianico del Vulture Synthesi '07.

● Aglianico del Vulture Don Anselmo Ris. '06	🍷🍷	7
● Aglianico del Vulture Synthesi '07	🍷🍷	4
● Barigliòtt '09	🍷	4
○ Biancorte '09	🍷	4
● Aglianico del Vulture Don Anselmo '94	YYY	5
● Aglianico del Vulture Don Anselmo Ris. '05	YYY+	7
● Aglianico del Vulture Rotondo '01	YYY	6
● Aglianico del Vulture Rotondo '00	YYY	6
● Aglianico del Vulture Rotondo '98	YYY	5*
● Aglianico del Vulture Rotondo '06	YY	6

Terre degli Svevi

LOC. PIAN DI CAMERA
85029 VENOSA [PZ]
TEL. 097231263
www.giv.it

CELLAR SALES
PRE-BOOKED VISITS
FOOD

ANNUAL PRODUCTION 240,000 bottles
HECTARES UNDER VINE 120
VITICULTURE METHOD Conventional

This is the Basilicata outpost of the Gruppo Italiano Vini group, one of the most important non-local investments made in Basilicata. Founded in 1998, Terre degli Svevi now has 120 hectares of vines on property in Venosa, Barile and Maschito, nearly all under aglianico, with a small amount of müller thurgau and traminer aromatico. Nunzio Capurso is in charge of production and his hand can be seen in wines that are solid and modern but never forced. The top reds are aged in barriques, only some of which are first use.

This year's tastings are pretty much in line with the results of last year. The most successful wine is again the Aglianico del Vulture Re Manfredi. The'07 version is decidedly tertiary on entry, midway between cherry jam and almonds, and proceeds deftly and drily over the palate with somewhat over-austere extract. In the same mould, but with more evolved, vegetal tones, the Aglianico del Vulture Serpara '06 is enlivened by resounding acidity. The Re Manfredi Bianco '09, from müller thurgau and traminer aromatico, is well made.

● Aglianico del Vulture Re Manfredi '07	▼▼	5
● Aglianico del Vulture Vign. Serpara '06	▼▼	6
○ Re Manfredi Bianco '09	▼	4
● Aglianico del Vulture Re Manfredi '05	▽▽▽	5
● Aglianico del Vulture Re Manfredi '99	▽▽▽	5*
● Aglianico del Vulture Vign. Serpara '03	▽▽▽	5*

Cantina di Venosa

LOC. VIGNALI
VIA APPIA
85029 VENOSA [PZ]
TEL. 097236702
www.cantinadivenosa.it

CELLAR SALES
PRE-BOOKED VISITS

ANNUAL PRODUCTION 800,000 bottles
HECTARES UNDER VINE 800
VITICULTURE METHOD Conventional

It always seems something of an understatement to refer to the Cantina di Venosa as one of the most important co-operative wineries in the south. Not that this diminishes its economic role in an area as difficult as Vulture or plays down the system that enables over 450 member growers to have their say on aglianico and the region. The fact is that the progress made in the last few years deserves attention, quite apart from any social factors, especially if we consider the winery's intelligent pricing policy.

This year's tastings perfectly reflected the hierarchy of Aglianico del Vulture in four versions made according to various ageing methods and use of oak. The most supple of these is the Vignali '08, together with the Bali'Aggio of the same vintage. Both are aged in barrels and stainless steel, showing a darker, more tertiary character than expected. Terre di Orazio '08, aged in large wood, is bursting with body and complexity and the barrique-aged Carato Venusio '07 even more so. It sailed easily into the finals with its flowery, spicy character, and slim-bodied richness of flavour.

● Aglianico del Vulture Carato Venusio '07	▼▼	5
● Aglianico del Vulture Terre di Orazio '08	▼▼	4
○ Dry Muscat Terre di Orazio '09	▼▼	3
● Aglianico del Vulture Bali'Aggio '08	▼	3
● Aglianico del Vulture Vignali '08	▼	3
○ D'Avalos Bianco '09	▼	4
● Aglianico del Vulture Carato Venusio '06	▽▽	6
● Aglianico del Vulture Terre di Orazio '07	▽▽	4*
● Aglianico del Vulture Vignali '07	▽▽	4*

Alovini

via Gramsci, 30
85013 Genzano di Lucania [PZ]
tel. 0971776372
www.alovini.it

Oronzo Alò, one of the proudest interpreters of Aglianico del Vulture, hails from Genzano di Lucania. Only two wines were presented this year. Aglianico del Vulture Le Ralle '08 has green notes but has a sweet, full palate and Le Ralle Rosato '09, from aglianico and montepulciano, is well-executed.

● Aglianico del Vulture Le Ralle '08	🍷🍷	3
⊙ Le Ralle Rosato '09	🍷	3

Francesco Bonifacio

c.da Piani di Camera
85029 Venosa [PZ]
tel. 097231436
www.cantinebonifacio.it

A single wine is enough to understand the importance of Francesco and Michele Bonifacio's production, from the 15-hectare winery they created in Venosa in 2003. The aglianico-only Sfida '09 is one of the region's best early-drinking reds. The fruit is close-focused and varied, the tannin stylish and pleasant.

● La Sfida '09	🍷🍷	2*

Masseria Cardillo

SS 407 Basentana km 97,5
75012 Bernalda [MT]
tel. 0835748992
www.masseriacardillo.it

Masseria Cardillo is the Matera winery that has probably been the most consistent at tastings over recent years. It's a good sign for a range that offers affordable wines, such as Vigna Giadì '08, a blend of sangiovese and primitivo that proffers a whiff of smoke and clear fruit that flows across the palate.

● Vigna Giadì '08	🍷🍷	3
● Aglianico del Vulture Rubra '03	🍷	5

Casa Maschito

via F. S. Nitti
85020 Maschito [PZ]
tel. 097233101
www.casamaschito.it

This is a happy Guide debut for Casa Maschito, a winery founded in 1999 by six young partners. Both wines offered have tertiary aromas but their character and measure override these. Aglianico del Vulture La Bottaia '05 is more subtle, Portale Adduca '05 more complex.

● Aglianico del Vulture Portale Adduca '05	🍷🍷	4
● Aglianico del Vulture La Bottaia '05	🍷	5

Cantine Cerrolongo

c.da Cerrolongo, 1
75020 Nova Siri [MT]
tel. 0835536174
www.cerrolongo.it

In Matera, an area still seeking to break through, the Battifarano family winery remains an undisputed point of reference. This is thanks to wines such as Matera Moro Torre Bollita, a blend of cabernet, primitivo and merlot. We preferred the '07 to the '08 for its greater complexity.

● Matera Moro Torre Bollita '07	🍷🍷	4
○ Chardonnay Toccacielo '09	🍷	4
● Matera Moro Torre Bollita '08	🍷	4
● Matera Primitivo Akratos '08	🍷	4

Ditaranto

via B. Spinoza, 44
75024 Montescaglioso [MT]
tel. 0835200993
www.ditarantovini.it

This winery of Angelo Mossuto and Antonio Ditaranto is still a novelty in the province of Matera. It has 22 hectares of land in Montescaglioso under the most common indigenous and international varieties. We particularly liked Matera Moro Il Cellerario '08 from a fairly solidly built range.

● Matera Moro Il Cellerario '08	🍷	4
● Portico '08	🍷	2

OTHER WINERIES

Iacovazzo
VIA SARAGAT, 42
75100 MATERA
TEL. 0835389054
www.tenute-iacovazzo.com

We will be following the progress over the next few years of this new winery, built by Giuseppe Iacovazzo on about 30 hectares of land in Matera. First tastings highlighted a more than agreeable Matera Greco Duetto '09, a varietal Sauvignon Bianco d'Autore '09 and a very sound Matera Moro Dionisio '09.

- ○ Bianco d'Autore '09 — 🍷 4
- ○ Matera Greco Duetto '09 — 🍷 4
- ● Matera Moro Dionisio '09 — 🍷 4

Lelusi
VIA CROCE, 3
85022 BARILE [PZ]
TEL. 024043805
www.lelusivini.com

Lelusi is a conflation of Letizia, Luca and Simona, the creative hands behind this young aglianico-only Barile winery. The best wine is Aglianico del Vulture Lelusi which in the '07 version flaunts great personality, with herbs, berries and hints of the sea creeping in, making for stylish, relaxed drinking.

- ● Aglianico del Vulture Lelusi '07 — 🍷🍷 6
- ● Aglianico del Vulture Shesh '08 — 🍷 4

Cantine Madonna delle Grazie
LOC. VIGNALI
VIA APPIA
85029 VENOSA [PZ]
TEL. 097235704
www.cantinemadonnadellegrazie.it

Giuseppe Latorraca's eight-hectare Venosa estate is no longer just a lovely surprise. Liscone and Messer Oto make an impressive pair of Aglianico del Vultures. The former, in the '07 version, is subtle and earthy, although seemingly simple while the second, the '08 vintage, is more modern.

- ● Aglianico del Vulture Liscone '07 — 🍷🍷 4
- ● Aglianico del Vulture Messer Oto '08 — 🍷🍷 4
- ⊙ Sagaris Rosato '09 — 🍷 4

Tenuta Marino
PIANO DELLE ROSE
85035 NOEPOLI [PZ]
TEL. 0835815978
www.tenutamarino.it

It did not take many tastings to get a feel for the potential of this umpteenth new winery in the province of Potenza, run by Francesco Marino with the help of Carmine Valentino. The monovarietal Syrah Terra Aspra Rossos stand out immediately. We found the '09 more complete than the '08.

- ● Terra Aspra Rosso '09 — 🍷🍷 4
- ● Matera Primitivo Terra Aspra '08 — 🍷 5
- ● Terra Aspra Rosso '08 — 🍷 4

Mastrodomenico
V.LE EUROPA, 5
85022 MATERA
TEL. 0972770108
www.vignemastrodomenico.com

The Barile area is one of the most prolific parts of Vulture for long-established and more recent estates. One of these is the small winery of the Mastrodomenico family, which releases Aglianico del Vulture Likos '07. It's a wine with a modern stamp, a its oaky exuberance offset by the structure.

- ● Aglianico del Vulture Likos '07 — 🍷 5

Musto Carmelitano
VIA PIETRO NENNI, 23
85020 MASCHITO [PZ]
TEL. 097233312
az.agricola@mustocarmelitano.it

We are willing to take a bet on this young, 15,000-bottle winery, guided by the firm hand of the wonderful Elisabetta Musto Carmelitano. For a start, Aglianico Pian del Moro and Serra del Prete '08 are outstanding for their compactness and verve.

- ● Pian del Moro '08 — 🍷🍷 4
- ● Serra del Prete '08 — 🍷🍷 4
- ● Maschitano Rosso '08 — 🍷 3

Ofanto

FRAZ. MONTICCHIO BAGNI
85020 RIONERO IN VULTURE [PZ]
TEL. 0972080289
www.ofantovini.it

There was another great performance by the winery of Ruggiero Potito, the only producer in the Monticchio Bagni area. From an original, varied range, we preferred the Tentazioni Moscato Dolce '09, for its penetrating suite of aromas leading on to a fresh palate.

○ Tentazioni Moscato Dolce '09	🍷🍷 4
● Aglianico del Vulture Emozioni '06	🍷 5

Tenuta del Portale

LOC. LE QUERCE
85022 BARILE [PZ]
TEL. 0972724691
tenutadelportale@tiscali.it

There was another well-chosen brace of wines this year from Tenuta del Portale. The Aglianico del Vulture '08 has a seemingly forward aromatic framework but flows over the palate well. Aglianico del Vulture Le Vigne a Capanno '08 is still very much an early drinker with more texture and energy.

● Aglianico del Vulture Le Vigne a Capanno '08	🍷🍷 5
● Aglianico del Vulture '08	🍷 4

Regio Cantina

LOC. PIANO REGIO
85029 VENOSA [PZ]
TEL. 3346966263
www.regiocantina.it

Year after year, Regio Cantina's Aglianico del Vulture Donpà confirms its status as one of the most typical and consistent reds of the region. The '07 version is wonderful for its Mediterranean traits of ripe cherry and spices, as well as its firm structure, soundly anchored by the usual close-knit tannins.

● Aglianico del Vulture Donpà '07	🍷🍷 5
● Aglianico del Vulture Genesi '07	🍷 4
● Aglianico del Vulture Solagna '08	🍷 3
○ Brinato '09	🍷 3

Vigneti del Vulture

C.DA PIPOLI
85011 ACERENZA [PZ]
TEL. 0971285061
www.vignetidelvulture.it

The Farnese group and Cantina Diomede took over the Consorzio Viticoltori Associati del Vulture buildings to establish a new winery that manages 56 hectares on lease near Acerenza in 2010. Judging by the Aglianico del Vulture Piano del Cerro Riserva '04, the future is assured.

● Aglianico del Vulture Piano del Cerro Ris. '04	🍷🍷 6
⊙ Pipoli Rosato Basilicata '09	🍷 4

PUGLIA

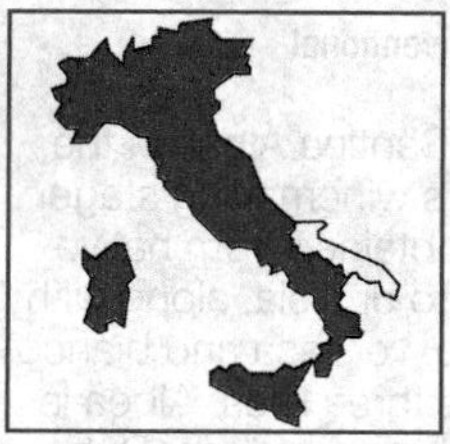

People often say it's harder to repeat a success than to achieve it in the first place but that's precisely what Puglia has done this year. Last time's overall progress has continued and we feel justified in calling this a consolidated trend. True, there aren't as many Three Glasses – only ten instead of 12 – but Puglia is still in double figures and, more important, there is a definite impression of continuity from the region's producers, in stark contrast to the situation not very long ago. In just a few years, native varieties have become the focus of Puglian winemaking and the high road to success and recognition outside the region. Major grapes are now being interpreted with greater precision of style. Primitivo, negroamaro and nero di Troia are presented in versions that make it easier to distinguish the sensory profile of the grape from territory-derived characteristics. The most exciting native is still primitivo, thanks in part to the step change in quality in the Gioia del Colle zone and in part to reinforced belief on the part of all the Manduria producers, aware now that their bottles have the potential to earn a place in the forefront of Italian winemaking. For nero di Troia, Castel del Monte remains key, even though true quality-oriented selection in terms of clones and sites is perhaps only now gaining momentum. Salento, as style parameters for negroamaro-based wines are being rethought, is still best represented by long-established names, at least as far as top-quality wines are concerned. Moving on to the award winners, we find a new winery, which unsurprisingly hails from the Gioia del Colle DOC. Polvanera, with its Gioia del Colle Primitivo 16 '07, joins two other new entries, the first release of Gioia del Colle Primitivo Muro Sant'Angelo Contrada Barbatto '07 from Chiaromonte and Primitivo La Signora '07 by Morella. All the other Three Glass winners are familiar names, starting with the fourth Primitivo, the '08 Primitivo di Manduria Es from Gianfranco Fino. There are two Nero di Troias, Castel del Monte Rosso Vigna Pedale Riserva '07 by Torrevento and Rasciatano Nero di Troia '08 from Rasciatano, and four mainly or only negroamaro-based wines: Salice Salentino Rosso Donna Lisa Riserva '06 by Leone de Castris; Salice Salentino Rosso Selvarossa Riserva '07 from Due Palme; Nero '07 by Conti Zecca and finally Masseria Maime '08 from Tormaresca. Crowning this excellent regional performance is the award for Up-and-Coming Winery, which went to Polvanera.

A Mano

5° TRAV. PROV. CASAMASSIMA, 8
70023 GIOIA DEL COLLE [BA]
TEL. 0803434872
www.amanowine.com

PRE-BOOKED VISITS

ANNUAL PRODUCTION 320,000 bottles
HECTARES UNDER VINE N.A.
VITICULTURE METHOD Certified organic

Elvira Sbalchiero from Friuli and Californian oenologist Mark Shannon run A Mano, one of the most exciting wineries in Gioia del Colle and, indeed, the whole of Puglia. Although they have no vines of their own, the couple keep a close eye on a series of plots, some with long-established bush-trained vines, and turn out a remarkably reliable range of premium wines.

Elvezia and Mark never miss a beat. The Primitivo A Mano '08 is fresh and taut, giving red stone fruits in a deliciously long, elegant, sensory experience that nearly earned a third Glass. Equally attractive is the Mediterranean scrubland-themed Negroamaro A Mano '08 with its hints of incense, echoed on a black fruits-led palate. The Fiano-Greco '09 is a 50-40-10 fiano minutolo, greco and fiano blend whose aromatic, jasmine-veined citrus aromatics make it one of Puglia's best whites. The negroamaro-based Rosato '09 proffers forest fruits and the easy-drinking Promessa Organic Syrah Merlot '09 is nicely crafted.

● Negroamaro A Mano '08	🍷🍷	3*
● Primitivo A Mano '08	🍷🍷	3*
○ Fiano - Greco '09	🍷🍷	3*
● Promessa Organic Syrah Merlot '09	🍷🍷	3*
⊙ Rosato A Mano '09	🍷🍷	3*
● Prima Mano '06	YY	5
● Primitivo '07	YY	3*

Cantina Albea

VIA DUE MACELLI, 8
70011 ALBEROBELLO [BA]
TEL. 0804323548
www.albeavini.com

CELLAR SALES
PRE-BOOKED VISITS

ANNUAL PRODUCTION 300,000 bottles
HECTARES UNDER VINE 40
VITICULTURE METHOD Conventional

Dante Renzini keeps Cantina Albea in the centre of the territory's winemaking stage. Most of the range is obtained from native grapes, especially nero di Troia, along with primitivo, negroamaro, verdeca and bianco d'Alessano. There are three lines. Albea is reserved for the flagship selections, Due Trulli and Terre del Sole.

Albea impresses with its solidity and reliable quality. The '08 is excellent in both the Raro blend of negroamaro and primitivo, which proffers morello cherries, red fruits and plum jam giving way to a long, full, palate with lashings of fruit, and Lui, a monovarietal Nero di Troia, which this year is a tad less fresh than in recent vintages but still has plenty of fruit and stuffing. The spice and red berry fruit Primitivo Petranera is very well made, if not particularly varietal, and the Petrarosa '09 rosé is soft with lush fruit. It's also from primitivo.

● Lui '08	🍷🍷	6
● Raro '08	🍷🍷	5
● Petranera '08	🍷🍷	4
⊙ Petrarosa '09	🍷🍷	4
● Lui '06	YYY	6
● Lui '05	YYY	6
● Lui '07	YY	6
● Lui '04	YY	6
● Petranera '07	YY	4

Apollonio

via San Pietro in Lama, 7
73047 Monteroni di Lecce [LE]
tel. 0832327182
www.apolloniovini.it

CELLAR SALES
PRE-BOOKED VISITS

ANNUAL PRODUCTION **1,200,000 bottles**
HECTARES UNDER VINE **50**
VITICULTURE METHOD **Conventional**

The Apollonio family winery dates from 1870 and for the past 15 years has been run by the fourth generation, brothers Marcello and Massimiliano. There are two lines, Apollonio and Rocca dei Mori, while most of the vineyards are bush-trained and stand on clay and limestone soil. The key theme of the range is the extended cask conditioning and very long maturation in bottle that the cellar lavishes on its top reds.

This traditional approach means that Apollonio wines go to market only when they are good and ready. It's no surprise, then, that the current release is the '04 vintage. Terragnolo Negroamaro is an intriguing medley of black fruits, spice and hazelnuts introducing a surprisingly fresh, stylish palate with great length. Good marks also went to the substantial, fruity Terragnolo Primitivo, which gives coffee and cherry aromatics and a slightly evanescent finish. Copertino's ripe black berry fruit fuses with a spicy palate and the relaxed Salice Salentino is forward but very good drinking.

● Terragnolo Negroamaro '04	▼▼	5
● Copertino '04	▼▼	4
● Salice Salentino '04	▼▼	4
● Terragnolo Primitivo '04	▼▼	5
○ Elfo Bianco '09	▼	3
● Elfo Negroamaro '09	▼	3
○ Laicale Chardonnay '08	▼	4
● Valle Cupa '04	▼	5

Cantele

sp Salice Salentino
San Donaci km 35,600
73010 Guagnano [LE]
tel. 0832705010
www.cantele.it

CELLAR SALES
PRE-BOOKED VISITS

ANNUAL PRODUCTION **1,800,000 bottles**
HECTARES UNDER VINE **150**
VITICULTURE METHOD **Conventional**

The Cantele family cellar has a broad range of wines from native and international grapes grown in various plots located mainly at Guagnano, Montemesola and San Pietro Vernotico. The feature that unites all the vineyards is their red soil. For several years, the Canteles have been combining quantity with quality, imbuing all their wines with appeal and easy-drinking character.

There were no top awards this year, although Cantele wines are still in the front rank of Puglian production. The '08 Amativo rolls out black fruits, cinchona and spice aromatics, followed by a juicy, effortlessly fruit-led palate. We also gave the thumbs-up to the '08 Manara Negroamaro, a full, substantial wine with lots of fruity freshness. Other well-made wines are the pleasing, balsam-veined '08 Varius and the easy-drinking '09 Negroamaro, subtly shaded with incense. Finally, the '09 Teresa Manara Chardonnay didn't quite live up to recent vintages, showing distinct oaky aromas and a slight lack of complexity in the mouth.

● Amativo '08	▼▼	5
● Teresa Manara Negroamaro '08	▼▼	4
◉ Negroamaro '09	▼▼	3*
● Varius '08	▼▼	4
● Alticelli Aglianico '08	▼	4
○ Chardonnay '09	▼	3
● Primitivo '08	▼	3
◉ Rosato Negroamaro '09	▼	3
● Salice Salentino Rosso Ris. '07	▼	3
○ Teresa Manara Chardonnay '09	▼	4
● Amativo '07	▽▽▽	5*
● Amativo '03	▽▽▽	5*
● Amativo '05	▽▽	5*
● Amativo '04	▽▽	5*

Carvinea

VIA PER SERRANOVA, 1
72012 CAROVIGNO [BR]
TEL. 0805862345
www.carvinea.com

ANNUAL PRODUCTION 35,000 bottles
HECTARES UNDER VINE 11
VITICULTURE METHOD Conventional

Carvinea is a new venture set up by Beppe De Maria to combine his passion for wine with his love of the uniquely fascinating territory of Salento. His spurred cordon-vines are young, only five years old, and grow on limestone and tufaceous soil while cropping levels for the montepulciano, petit verdot and aglianico vines, among others, are only about one kilogram per plant. In a nutshell, the estate's goal is uncompromising quality.

Carvinea got off to a good start and the '07 Sierma went through to our finals. This single-variety Aglianico flaunts great structure and a close-knit texture, proffering black-skinned stone fruits and spice, echoed on the fresh-tasting, well-made palate with its hefty extract. Sorma '07, an interesting, unusual blend of montepulciano and petit verdot, gives rich, ripe black fruits over fresh greens. The palate is a tad masked by the oak but reveals great body, nice fruit and attractive length. The aglianico and petit verdot Frauma '07 is well crafted, as is the montepulciano-only '07 Merula.

● Sierma '07	🍷🍷	4
● Sorma '07	🍷🍷	4
● Frauma '07	🍷	4
● Merula '07	🍷	4

Castello Monaci

C.DA MONACI
73015 SALICE SALENTINO [LE]
TEL. 0831665700
www.castellomonaci.it

CELLAR SALES
PRE-BOOKED VISITS
FOOD

ANNUAL PRODUCTION 2,200,000 bottles
HECTARES UNDER VINE 150
VITICULTURE METHOD Conventional

Just outside Salice Salentino is the evocative Norman-period Castello Monaci winery and the vine stock of this extensive Gruppo Italiano Vini-owned estate. The soil has two distinct layers, the upper level being more fertile and the deeper, rocky lower layer guaranteeing good drainage. Two lines, Castello Monaci and Feudo Monaci, make up the range. Both are obtained almost exclusively from native varieties to showcase the virtues of the territory.

The '08 Artas is less convincing than previous editions, confirming that the growing year was challenging, as we noticed last year in other '08s. Plums, red fruits and spices usher in a clean, free-flowing palate that is well made but could do with a little more of the grip and length that the wine usually delivers. But the various '09 monovarietals all performed well. Primitivo Pilùna mingles flowers and fresh red fruits, Negroamaro Maru's earthiness and wafts of juniper are veined with iodine while its nice balance is offset by decent acidity. Finally, the less complex Malvasia Nera Medos is a genuine delight with its hints of aromatic herbs.

● Artas '08	🍷🍷	6
● Maru '09	🍷🍷	4*
● Medos '09	🍷🍷	4
● Pilùna '09	🍷🍷	4*
● Salice Salentino Aiace Ris. '07	🍷	4
● Salice Salentino Liante '09	🍷	3
● Artas '07	🍷🍷🍷	6
● Artas '06	🍷🍷🍷	5
● Artas '05	🍷🍷🍷	5*
● Artas '04	🍷🍷🍷	5*

Giancarlo Ceci

C.DA SANT'AGOSTINO
70031 ANDRIA [BA]
TEL. 0883564938
www.agrinatura.net

ANNUAL PRODUCTION 500,000 bottles
HECTARES UNDER VINE 70
VITICULTURE METHOD Certified organic

Giancarlo Ceci's long-standing estate was one of the first organic operations in Puglia. Situated in the hinterland of Andria, it is turning out an exciting prospect among wine estates in the Castel del Monte area. A Mediterranean climate, oak woods and the commitment to nurturing the area's natural biodiversity contribute to wines that embody all that is good in the local territory.

In fact, Ceci's winery is a point of reference for the whole Castel del Monte district. The '08 Castel del Monte Rosso Parco Marano is remarkably precise and clean on the nose, where black berry fruit and incense herald a deliciously fresh palate brimming with stylishly elegant tannins, red berry fruits, Mediterranean scrubland and spiciness. Also well made is the earthy, currant-themed Castel del Monte Rosso Parco Grande '09, which is backed up by nice acid grip. However, the '07 Castel del Monte Rosso Felice Ceci is less successful. A muzzy nose precedes a palate that offers mainly ripe cherry fruit.

● Castel del Monte Rosso Parco Marano '08	¶¶	4
● Castel del Monte Rosso Parco Grande '09	¶¶	3*
● Castel del Monte Rosso Felice Ceci '07	¶	4
● Castel del Monte Rosso Parco Marano '06	♀♀	4
● Castel del Monte Rosso Parco Marano '05	♀♀	4
● Castel del Monte Rosso Parco Marano '04	♀♀	4

Chiaromonte

VIA PER SAMMICHELE Z.I.
70021 ACQUAVIVA DELLE FONTI [BA]
TEL. 080768575
www.vinichiaromonte.it

PRE-BOOKED VISITS

ANNUAL PRODUCTION 50,000 bottles
HECTARES UNDER VINE 27
VITICULTURE METHOD Certified organic

Nicola Chiaromonte is a firm believer in the quality of primitivo from Gioia del Colle. He is the latest generation of a winemaking family, the winery owner and house oenologist. In recent years, Nicola has released a string of excellent wines as he strives to promote the territory. That commitment is clear in his decision to vinify separately the fruit of his bush-trained vines from the best sites to create wines that are truly capable of communicating their provenance.

Currently, Nicola is exploring the potential of Gioia del Colle-grown primitivo and here is his first vineyard selection, Muro Sant'Angelo Contrada Barbatto '07, to confirm his skills and pick up a well-deserved Three Glasses. Steel fermentation and maturation have imbued it with power as well as savouriness, freshness and elegance. Black berry fruits and spices are bolstered by acidity that delivers truly outstanding length and persistence. A step behind are the other two Gioia del Colle Primitivos, the '07 Riserva, a red fruits and printer's ink fragranced wine with a very precise palate, and the Muro Sant'Angelo '06, which gives Mediterranean scrubland and a bright, crisp finish.

● Gioia del Colle Primitivo Muro Sant'Angelo Contrada Barbatto '07	¶¶¶	6
● Gioia del Colle Muro Sant'Angelo '06	¶¶	5
● Gioia del Colle Primitivo Ris. '07	¶¶	8
● Donna Carlotta '09	¶	5
● Elè '09	¶	5
● Gioia del Colle Primitivo Ris. '06	♀♀	8
● Gioia del Colle Primitivo Ris. '05	♀♀	7

Cantine Due Palme

VIA SAN MARCO, 130
72020 CELLINO SAN MARCO [BR]
TEL. 0831617909
www.cantineduepalme.it

CELLAR SALES
PRE-BOOKED VISITS

ANNUAL PRODUCTION **6,000,000 bottles**
HECTARES UNDER VINE **2,200**
VITICULTURE METHOD **Conventional**

Year after year, Cantine Due Palme confirms its status as one of the most influential co-operatives in the whole of Puglia. Founded in 1989, it stands out for its number of members, partly because it has recently incorporated two other co-operatives, and for the quality of its wines. This key player in Salento winemaking is very attentive to safeguarding the territory, Puglia's unique heritage, its native varieties and its bush-trained vineyards.

Currently led by Angelo Maci, Cantine Due Palme is one of Salento's leading wineries and garnered a fourth consecutive Three Glass prize for its Salentino Rosso Riserva '07, a wine of substance and structure, fragrant with Mediterranean scrubland and black olive tapenade. Brindisi Rosso '09 is another fine wine, following liquorice and morello cherry fragrances with a sumptuous palate of ripe red fruits. We liked the '09 Serre, a light, fresh, attractive all-sussumaniello wine that puts the accent on black-skinned stone fruits. Melarosa Extra Dry is a nicely made, well-poised Charmat-method sparkler from negroamaro that is perhaps a little too sweet.

● Salice Salentino Rosso Selvarossa Ris. '07	ΨΨΨ	5*
● Brindisi Rosso '09	ΨΨ	4
● Serre '09	ΨΨ	4
⊙ Melarosa Extra Dry '09	Ψ	4
● Salice Salentino Rosso Selvarossa Ris. '06	ΨΨΨ	5*
● Salice Salentino Rosso Selvarossa Ris. '05	ΨΨΨ	5*
● Salice Salentino Rosso Selvarossa Ris. '04	ΨΨΨ	4*
● Brindisi Rosso '07	ΨΨ	4
● Salice Salentino Rosso Selvarossa Ris. '03	ΨΨ	6
● Serre '08	ΨΨ	4

Eméra

VIA PROVINCIALE, 222
73010 GUAGNANO [LE]
TEL. 0832704398
www.cantineemera.it

PRE-BOOKED VISITS

ANNUAL PRODUCTION **200,000 bottles**
HECTARES UNDER VINE **40**
VITICULTURE METHOD **Conventional**

The Guagnano-based Eméra winery is part of the Magistravini project orchestrated by businessman Claudio Quarta. The vines stand on limestone and tufaceous soil in one of the finest growing areas for negroamaro and this year saw the new underground cellar come onstream. The top selections are released as the Anima line, comprising wines obtained from Salento's two main native grapes, negroamaro and primitivo.

And it is thanks primarily to the Anima wines that Paolo Quarta's estate earned its first full profile. Anima di Niuru Maru '08 unveils complex aromatics brimming with ripe black-skinned fruits and a substantial palate with tight-knit tannins well tucked in and a long finale that is just a hint too sweet. Anima di Primitivo '08 gives florality, coffee and rain-soaked earth that are reprised on the fresh, appealing palate. To round off, the richly fragranced Salice Salentino '08 is less complex on the palate and the '09 Amure, a chardonnay and malvasia bianca mix, serves up honey and jasmine.

● Anima di Niuru Maru '08	ΨΨ	3*
● Anima di Primitivo '08	ΨΨ	4
○ Amure '09	Ψ	3
● Salice Salentino '08	Ψ	4
● Anima di Niuru Maru '06	ΨΨ	4*
● Anima di Primitivo '07	ΨΨ	4*

Felline - Pervini

via Santo Stasi Primo - Z. I.
74024 Manduria [TA]
tel. 0999711660
www.racemi.it

CELLAR SALES
PRE-BOOKED VISITS

ANNUAL PRODUCTION 300,000 bottles
HECTARES UNDER VINE N.A.
VITICULTURE METHOD Certified organic

Gregory Perrucci's winery is still a bastion of Salentino winemaking tradition, recovering old vineyards of bush-trained vines planted on the area's characteristic red earth. There are two lines. Pervini is for everyday easy drinkers sold at affordable prices and Felline, sourced from the older vineyards, features territorial wines with a profound sense of place.

We were reassured by the usual rock-solid performances, starting with the '08 Vigna del Feudo with its cherry and briary fruit aromatics and a fresh, still youthful palate that will improve with cellaring. Primitivo di Manduria Segnavento '09 is attractive, well made and unveils nice acidity, lifted by distinct forest fruit aromas. Primitivo di Manduria Archidamo '08 is whistle-clean and full of crunchy fruit. We were particularly intrigued by the '07 Primitivo di Manduria Dolce Naturale Primo Amore's sound fruit and great balance of sweetness and acidity. As ever, the other labels on offer were more than just well made.

● Vigna del Feudo '08	5
● Primitivo di Manduria Archidamo '08	3*
● Primitivo di Manduria Dolce Naturale Primo Amore '07	4
● Primitivo di Manduria Segnavento '09	3*
● Alberello '09	3
● Primitivo di Manduria '08	4
○ Rufiano '09	4
⊙ Vigna Rosa '09	4
● Vigna del Feudo '06	5
● Vigna del Feudo '05	5

Feudi di San Marzano

via Regina Margherita, 149
74020 San Marzano di San Giuseppe [TA]
tel. 0999576100

CELLAR SALES
PRE-BOOKED VISITS

ANNUAL PRODUCTION 3,000,000 bottles
HECTARES UNDER VINE 500
VITICULTURE METHOD Conventional

Feudi di San Marzano was set up in 2003 and leases an impressive 500 hectares under vine, most on the red earth of the municipality of San Marzano. Native varieties account for almost the entire estate and several vineyards are still bush-trained. Estate staff look after them all year round.

The wines presented put the accent on appeal and luscious fruit. The '07 Primitivo di Manduria Sessantanni is redolent of wood, spice and black cherries that lead into a rich, intense palate with close-knit tannins and a hint too much sweetness. The Sud line bottles are good. Primitivo di Manduria '08 is clean-tasting and fruity while the '09 Primitivo Merlot '09 favours tobacco, coffee and black berry fruit. Negroamaro '09 has a dry spice and plum theme. Finally, Negroamaro F '08 stands out from the crowd for its fresh aromatic herbs nose and a taut, savoury palate with plenty of grip.

● Negroamaro F '08	6
● Negroamaro Sud '09	4*
● Primitivo di Manduria Sessantanni '07	6
● Primitivo di Manduria Sud '08	4*
● Primitivo Merlot Sud '09	4*
⊙ Negroamaro Rosato Sud '09	4

Gianfranco Fino

LOC. LAMA
VIA FIOR DI SALVIA, 8
74100 TARANTO
TEL. 0997773970
www.gianfrancofino.it

PRE-BOOKED VISITS

ANNUAL PRODUCTION **13,000 bottles**
HECTARES UNDER VINE **8**
VITICULTURE METHOD **Conventional**

Gianfranco Fino started out in 2004 when he purchased just over a hectare of bush-trained primitivo vines more than half a century old. Today, there are seven hectares under primitivo, all bush-trained and with the same average age as the original vineyard. There's also a hectare planted to negroamaro. The quality of the red soil, very low yields, scrupulous cellar work and a desire to make rich, structured wines have turned this recently established operation into an example for the region.

Gianfranco's style and approach to production are evident in his '08 range. Primitivo di Manduria Es again won Three Glasses this year for a sumptuously complex bouquet that hints at chocolate, Mediterranean scrubland and subtle sweet spice, following up with a juicy, full-bodied palate and a long, taut finish, brimming with crunchy fruit. The single-variety Negroamaro is another impeccably crafted high-flyer, showing elegantly complex with perceptions of plums, black damsons and briary fruit.

● Primitivo di Manduria Es '08	🍷🍷🍷+	7
● Jo '08	🍷🍷	7
● Primitivo di Manduria Es '07	🍸🍸🍸+	7
● Primitivo di Manduria Es '06	🍸🍸🍸	6
● Jo '07	🍸🍸	7
● Jo '06	🍸🍸	6
● Primitivo di Manduria Es '05	🍸🍸	6
● Primitivo di Manduria Es '04	🍸🍸	6

Leone de Castris

VIA SENATORE DE CASTRIS, 26
73015 SALICE SALENTINO [LE]
TEL. 0832731112
www.leonedecastris.com

CELLAR SALES
PRE-BOOKED VISITS
ROOMS AND FOOD

ANNUAL PRODUCTION **2,500,000 bottles**
HECTARES UNDER VINE **250**
VITICULTURE METHOD **Conventional**

Leone de Castris is one of the key estates in the history of Puglian wine. Founded in 1665, in 1925 it became the first cellar in the region to bottle its own wines. Production is wide-ranging with almost 30 labels, from classics to the various Salice Salentinos and the two versions of Five Roses, the first rosé bottled in Italy. The theme is tradition veined with modernity, aimed at the international market.

We loved the '06 Salice Salentino Rosso Donna Lisa Riserva, which won Three Glasses for its wafts of fresh red fruits, black olive tapenade and spices, complemented by an elegant, savoury palate that signs off long and fruity. Best of the rest, we thought, were the appealingly balsamic all-negroamaro '09 Elo Veni, the '09 Vigna Case Alte, a Sauvignon with a nose of fruit-tinged florality and a stylishly complex palate with good balance and varietal aromatics. Yet again, Five Roses 66° Anniversario '09, from negroamaro with a dash of malvasia nera, is one of Italy's finest rosés.

● Salice Salentino Rosso Donna Lisa Ris. '06	🍷🍷🍷	6
● Elo Veni '09	🍷🍷	4
⊙ Five Roses 66° Anniversario '09	🍷🍷	4
○ Vigna Case Alte '09	🍷🍷	4*
● Copertino '09	🍷	3
⊙ Five Roses '09	🍷	4
○ Messapia '09	🍷	3
⊙ Salice Salentino Brut Five Roses Metodo Cl. '08	🍷	5
● Salice Salentino Rosso Maiana '09	🍷	3
● Salice Salentino Rosso Donna Lisa Ris. '05	🍸🍸🍸	6
● Salice Salentino Rosso Donna Lisa Ris. '01	🍸🍸🍸	6
● Salice Salentino Rosso Donna Lisa Ris. '00	🍸🍸🍸	6
● Salice Salentino Rosso Donna Lisa Ris. '99	🍸🍸🍸	6

Lomazzi & Sarli

C.DA PARTEMIO, SS 7 BR-TA
72022 LATIANO [BR]
TEL. 0831725898
www.vinilomazzi.it

CELLAR SALES
PRE-BOOKED VISITS
ROOMS AND FOOD

ANNUAL PRODUCTION **1,000,000 bottles**
HECTARES UNDER VINE **150**
VITICULTURE METHOD **Conventional**

Lomazzi & Sarli belongs to the Dimastrodonato family. This year's production confirms its reputation for solidity and overall quality. The vineyards on the Brindisi plain are planted on alluvial soil at densities of 5-6,000 vines per hectare. One third are bush trained. Revamping the cellar is the next step and offers scope for further growth.

Although the Dimastrodonatos did not produce a real show-stopper, the range as a whole is very reliable. Nomas '07 is a very nice Sussumaniello with crisp, resin-veined aromatics lifted by spiciness and red berry fruits. In contrast, Brindisi Rosso Tenuta Partemio '08 is plum-themed and reveals great balance in the mouth. The citrussy '08 Primitivo Latias '08 is good, as is the Salice Salentino Tenuta Partemio '08, which is oakier but unfolds a long palate of crunchy fruit. Our round-up closes with the '07 Dimastrodonato, one of the finest Aleatico Dolce Naturale wines we tasted this year. Its dried roses and black berry fruits usher in a very appealing palate with just the right note of sweetness.

● Brindisi Rosso Tenuta Partemio '08	2 black glasses	3*
● Dimastrodonato '07	2 black glasses	5
● Latias '08	2 black glasses	4
● Nomas '07	2 black glasses	6
● Salice Salentino Tenuta Partemio '08	2 black glasses	3*
● Brindisi Rosso Solise '07	1 black glass	4
● Tenuta Partemio Negroamaro '08	1 black glass	3
● Tenuta Partemio Primitivo '08	1 black glass	3
● Latias '07	2 white glasses	4
● Nomas '05	2 white glasses	6
● Salice Salentino Tenuta Partemio '06	2 white glasses	3*

Masseria Li Veli

SP CELLINO-CAMPI, KM 1
72020 CELLINO SAN MARCO [BR]
TEL. 0831617906
www.liveli.it

CELLAR SALES
PRE-BOOKED VISITS
FOOD

ANNUAL PRODUCTION **350,000 bottles**
HECTARES UNDER VINE **33**
VITICULTURE METHOD **Certified organic**

The Falvo family acquired Masseria Li Veli near Cellino San Marco in 1999. Behind the move lay a desire to make native-grape wines using the traditional triangle-based "vigna latinae" planting pattern and low-pruned bush-trained vines, a system already put in place in the 19th century. After a few so-so years, results are now coming through.

The Falvos threw themselves into the new venture enthusiastically. Proof of success comes in the well-nuanced nose of the '08 Salice Salentino Pezzo Morgana Riserva '08, which gives scrubland, black berry fruits, cinchona and sweet spice and a still oak-veiled but very well made palate of crisp, crunchy fruit and savouriness. All it needs is time. Verdeca Askos '09 is intriguing with ripe tropical fruits and a dry, long palate that eschews sweetness while the '09 Passamante '09 is an attractively balsamic monovarietal Negroamaro with balance and a fresh, savoury finish.

● Salice Salentino Rosso Pezzo Morgana Ris. '08	2 black glasses	5
● Passamante '09	2 black glasses	3*
○ Verdeca Askos '09	2 black glasses	4
● Masseria Li Veli '07	1 black glass	6
● Orion '09	1 black glass	3
⊙ Rosato '09	1 black glass	3
● Passamante '07	2 white glasses	4*

Tenute Mater Domini

VIA DEI MARTIRI, 17/19
73012 CAMPI SALENTINA [LE]
TEL. 0832792442
www.tenutematerdomini.it

PRE-BOOKED VISITS

ANNUAL PRODUCTION 60,000 bottles
HECTARES UNDER VINE 40
VITICULTURE METHOD Conventional

The Semeraro family knows what it wants: to combine innovation in the vineyard with modern cellar technology and Salentino tradition to make a great wine. There are two estates, Masseria Casili and Masseria Fontanelle, and all the vines lie within the Salice Salentino designation so negroamaro is the principal variety. Although various planting patterns have been trialled, half of the vine stock is bush-trained in the traditional Puglian "alberello sciolto" style.

Salice Salentino Casili Riserva did well again and the '07 edition went through to the finals. A richly fragrant wine, it offers printer's ink, black berry fruits and fresh greens on the nose, followed by a toastier, spicier palate where liquorice, chocolate and coffee take you through to a long, fruit-led finale. Marangi Negroamaro '07 is less substantial but still vibrantly appealing with violet-led florality, nice poise and acidity in the mouth. Marangi Bianco '09 is a well-typed, uncomplicatedly citrus-themed Sauvignon.

● Salice Salentino Casili Ris. '07	YY	6
● Marangi Negroamaro '07	YY	4
○ Marangi Bianco '09	Y	4
● Marangi Negroamaro '06	YY	4
● Salice Salentino Casili Ris. '06	YY	6

Morella

VIA PER UGGIANO, 147
74024 MANDURIA [TA]
TEL. 0999791482
www.morellavini.com

CELLAR SALES
PRE-BOOKED VISITS

ANNUAL PRODUCTION 15,000 bottles
HECTARES UNDER VINE 13
VITICULTURE METHOD Conventional

Lisa Gilbee is an Australian oenologist whose main objective has always been to recover long-established bush-trained vineyards, especially of primitivo, in a red-earth zone that is one of the finest growing areas for the variety. Old vines, planted 50 to 80 years ago, are complemented by state-of-the-art cellar techniques that coax the best from the excellent grapes.

The Old Vines wine was not on parade this year so it was a great satisfaction for Lisa and her team to win Three Glasses for the other label obtained from long-established, bush-trained, red-earth vineyards. Primitivo La Signora '07 proffers black berry fruits, printer's ink, black olive tapenade and a hint of earthiness leading into a sumptuous, tight-knit palate with tautness, crunchy fruit and an iodine-themed finish. The wines from younger vineyards are equally good. Mezzanotte Rosso '09 is a blend of 70 per cent primitivo with petit verdot, cabernet sauvignon and negroamaro whose soft mouthfeel accompanies ripe fruit and scrubland aromatics. The '08 Primitivo Negroamaro Terre Rosse is a medley of spice and good fruit.

● Primitivo La Signora '07	YYY	6
● Mezzanotte Rosso '09	YY	4
● Primitivo Negroamaro Terre Rosse '08	YY	5
● Primitivo Malbek '08	Y	5
● Primitivo Old Vines '07	YYY	6
● Primitivo La Signora '05	YY	6
● Primitivo Old Vines '06	YY	6
● Primitivo Old Vines '05	YY	6
● Primitivo Old Vines '04	YY	6

Cosimo Palamà

VIA A. DIAZ, 6
73020 CUTROFIANO [LE]
TEL. 0836542865
www.vinicolapalama.com

CELLAR SALES
PRE-BOOKED VISITS

ANNUAL PRODUCTION **250,000 bottles**
HECTARES UNDER VINE **15**
VITICULTURE METHOD **Conventional**

The Palamà family winery was set up in 1936 and has bottled since 1990. The traditional bush-trained vines grow on medium-textured, limestone-based soil. Only native varieties are planted, such as malvasia bianca, malvasia nera, negroamaro, primitivo, montepulciano, verdeca and bianco d'Alessano. There are four lines and modernization of the cellar has given the wines better aromatic focus while maintaining a strong sense of place.

Which is comforting for a cellar that has firm links with its territory. Mavro '08, from 80 per cent negroamaro with malvasia nera di Lecce, may be less intriguing than last year's but is nonetheless solid, giving black fruits jam and spice fragrances and a soft, relaxed palate with good fruit and body, although the sweetish note at the back is excessive. The negoramaro-only '09 Metiusco Rosato is a delicious medley of flowers and red berry fruits. Vino D'Arcangelo '09, a deliberately rustic single-variety Malvasia Nera, deserves a special mention for its cherry jam and soft, mellow, sweet palate.

● Mavro '08	TT	4*
● Il Vino D'Arcangelo '09	TT	4
⊙ Metiusco Rosato '09	TT	3*
● Albarossa Primitivo '08	T	2*
● Metiusco Rosso '09	T	4
● Salice Salentino Rosso Albarossa '08	T	1*
● Mavro '07	YY	4*
● Mavro '06	YY	4
● Salice Salentino Rosso Albarossa '07	YY	1*

Pietraventosa

C.DA PARCO LARGO
70023 GIOIA DEL COLLE [BA]
TEL. 0805034436
www.pietraventosa.it

CELLAR SALES

ANNUAL PRODUCTION **10,000 bottles**
HECTARES UNDER VINE **5**
VITICULTURE METHOD **Certified organic**

Pietraventosa is a recently founded winery located west of Gioia del Colle and shares the passion for quality of the "new wave" of local cellars. For Marianna Annio, that means a small range of native-grape wines. Her organically farmed vines grow on about a metre of mineral-rich red soil resting on rock and yields are low. A new cellar completes the picture.

The wines presented confirm Marianna Annio and Raffaele Leo's commitment to quality. Gioia del Colle Riserva di Pietraventosa '07 is redolent of red berry fruits and scrubland. There's good structure and length on the palate, which is missing only a hint of pressure. The cellar's other two wines are well made. Ossimoro '07 from primitivo and aglianico is slightly muzzy on the nose but unveils a palate brimming with fruit and tucked-in tannins. Gioia del Colle Primitivo Allegoria '07 offers red berry fruits and aromatic herbs.

● Gioia del Colle Primitivo Riserva di Pietraventosa '07	TT	6
● Gioia del Colle Primitivo Allegoria '07	TT	4
● Ossimoro '07	TT	4
● Gioia del Colle Primitivo Ris. '06	YYY	5

Polvanera

s.da vicinale Lamie Marchesana, 601
70023 Gioia del Colle [BA]
tel. 080758900
www.cantinepolvanera.com

ANNUAL PRODUCTION 150,000 bottles
HECTARES UNDER VINE 30
VITICULTURE METHOD Certified organic

Filippo Cassano is one of the leading new wave producers of Gioia del Colle Primitivo. Polvanera is one of the largest estates in the designation, boasting five hectares of bush-trained vines about 60 years old. The whole range has a very precise style: the wines combine great power and structure with freshness and approachability, nicely embodying the Mediterranean spirit of the territory.

If anyone had any doubts about the quality of Filippo Cassano's wines, this year's offerings should dispel them. The two '07 Gioia del Colle Primitivos are among the most intriguing wines we tasted for this edition of the Guide. The 16 swept up Three Glasses for its fresh wafts of aromatic herbs, citrus and red fruits that introduce a fresh, savoury palate that fills the mouth, unfolding precisely with impressive length. A step behind was the full-bodied, complex 17, which gives rich spiciness and marked scrubland and plum aromas. Nor should we forget Auva '09, the best Fiano Minutolo we uncorked this year, or Syrma, an elegant sweet Moscato.

● Gioia del Colle Primitivo 16 '07	🍷🍷🍷	4*
● Gioia del Colle Primitivo 17 '07	🍷🍷	4*
○ Auva '09	🍷🍷	4
○ Syrma	🍷🍷	4
● Gioia del Colle Primitivo 16 '06	🍷🍷 (outline)	4
● Gioia del Colle Primitivo 17 '06	🍷🍷 (outline)	4*

Racemi

via Santo Stasi Primo - Z. I.
74024 Manduria [TA]
tel. 0999711660
www.racemi.it

CELLAR SALES
PRE-BOOKED VISITS

ANNUAL PRODUCTION 1,200,000 bottles
HECTARES UNDER VINE 150
VITICULTURE METHOD Certified organic

Gregory Perrucci's Racemi project aims to promote the native grapes, territories and grape-farming techniques of Salento, a goal he pursues by bringing together a group of small estates, all with vineyards that are still bush-trained. Masseria Pepe is near the coast, Sinfarosa stands on deep, black soil, Tenuta Pozzopalo has black and tufaceous soils, Torre Guaceto still grows varieties like ottavianello and sussumaniello, Torre Guaceto is in the nature reserve of the same name and Casale Bevagna is characterized by its red earth.

Gregory's group continues to be a point of reference for lovers of Salento's wines and long-established bush-trained vineyards. Primitivo di Manduria Giravolta Tenuta Pozzopalo '08 tempts the nose with fragrances of scrubland and lychee, showing fresh and flowing in the mouth. Torre Guaceto wines did well. Negroamaro Pietraluna '09 reveals flowers and black berry fruits that are echoed on the well-knit palate while Sussumaniello Sum '08 regales the senses with pepper spice, fruit and aromatic herbs. The attractively long, gutsy, malvasia nera-based Anarkos '09 from primitivo and negroamaro impressed with its sour cherries and minerality.

● Primitivo di Manduria Giravolta Tenuta Pozzopalo '08	🍷🍷	5
● Anarkos '09	🍷🍷	3*
● Pietraluna Torre Guaceto '09	🍷🍷	3*
● Susumaniello Sum Torre Guaceto '08	🍷🍷	5
⊙ Burlesque	🍷	4
● Zinfandel '08	🍷	4
● Anarkos '08	🍷🍷 (outline)	3*
● Ottavianello Dedalo Torre Guaceto '07	🍷🍷 (outline)	4
● Susumaniello Sum Torre Guaceto '07	🍷🍷 (outline)	5

Rasciatano

C.DA RASCIATANO
70051 BARLETTA [BA]
TEL. 0883510999
www.rasciatano.com

CELLAR SALES
PRE-BOOKED VISITS

ANNUAL PRODUCTION 30,000 bottles
HECTARES UNDER VINE 18
VITICULTURE METHOD Organic

Rasciatano, halfway between the coast and the hill country of Murgia, has been owned by the Porro family since the 17th century. Although until it was better known for the significant quantities of olive oil it produced, it has been winning friends in the world of Puglian wine, thanks to its very well-made Nero di Troia and Malvasia. The vineyards were planted between 1992 and 2002, and stand on sandy soil over strata of chalky stone.

Rasciatano Nero di Troia '08 regained Three Glass status with a brilliant performance. A red fruits, spice and liquorice nose ushers in a savoury, wonderfully fresh palate of sound fruit with enough pressure to take it through to the acidity-bolstered finish with a star anise and nutmeg theme. We were also impressed by the quality of the clean-tasting Rasciatano Malvasia Bianca '09 with its minerally complexity and notes of sage, lime blossom and citrus. Rasciatano Rosé '09, from montepulciano only, is well typed.

● Rasciatano Nero di Troia '08	🍷🍷🍷	7
○ Rasciatano Malvasia Bianca '09	🍷🍷	7
⊙ Rasciatano Rosé '09	🍷	5
● Rasciatano Nero di Troia '07	YYY	7
● Rasciatano Rosso '06	YY	7

Rivera

C.DA RIVERA, SP 231 KM 60,500
70031 ANDRIA [BA]
TEL. 0883560501
www.rivera.it

CELLAR SALES
PRE-BOOKED VISITS

ANNUAL PRODUCTION 1,400,000 bottles
HECTARES UNDER VINE 95
VITICULTURE METHOD Conventional

The estate set up in 1950 by Sebastiano De Corato and now run by his son Carlo continues to be a beacon for the Castel del Monte designation. Rivera's extensive range covers just about all the types permitted by the DOC regulations, whether reds, whites, rosés, blends or monovarietals. The spurred-cordon rows grow on limestone and tufaceous terrain on the Karst tableland of Murgia, a stone's throw from Frederick II's castle.

Castel del Monte Nero di Troia Puer Apuliae Riserva '07 unveils a rather complex nose whose distinct flowers and spice are laced with black berry fruits before the palate shows fairly coarse tannins and slightly over-assertive oak. We very much like the fresh, supple '08 Castel del Monte Nero di Troia Violante, with its sumptuous chocolate-laced fruit, and the all-bombino nero Castel del Monte Pungirosa '09 rosé, which gives varietal flowers and red berry fruits. As usual, the rest of the extensive range is well crafted.

● Castel del Monte Nero di Troia Puer Apuliae Ris. '07	🍷🍷	7
⊙ Castel del Monte Pungirosa '09	🍷🍷	3*
● Castel del Monte Rosso Violante '08	🍷🍷	4*
⊙ Castel del Monte Rosé '09	🍷	3
● Castel del Monte Rosso Rupicolo '08	🍷	3
○ Locorotondo '09	🍷	2
● Castel del Monte Nero di Troia Puer Apuliae '04	YYY	7
● Castel del Monte Nero di Troia Puer Apuliae '06	YY	7
● Castel del Monte Nero di Troia Puer Apuliae '05	YY	7

Tenute Rubino

VIA E. FERMI, 50
72100 BRINDISI
TEL. 0831571955
www.tenuterubino.com

CELLAR SALES
PRE-BOOKED VISITS

ANNUAL PRODUCTION **800,000 bottles**
HECTARES UNDER VINE **200**
VITICULTURE METHOD **Conventional**

The Rubino family has four separate estates, all located in the environs of Brindisi. Two, at Iaddico and Marmorelle, are only a few dozen metres from the sea while the Uggio and Punta Aquila holdings are on the tableland behind Brindisi. Most of the vineyards are spurred cordon-pruned and the rest are bush-trained. Planting densities range from 4,000 to 6,000 vines per hectare.

It wasn't the best of vintages for Tenute Rubino, considering the high standards achieved in recent years. Visellio '08 is a structure, juicy single-varietal Primitivo that hints at olives and currants but lacks the aromatic definition of previous editions. The cellar's workhorse '09 Marmorelle Rosso is well crafted. It's a flower and spice blend of negroamaro and malvasia nera while Saturnino '09 is a fresh, appealingly fruity rosé from negroamaro. But the sussamaniello-only '08 Torre Testa puzzled our tasters. It falls far short of the standard set by past editions.

● Marmorelle Rosso '09	▼▼	3*
⊙ Saturnino '09	▼▼	3*
● Visellio '08	▼▼	5
● Negroamaro '08	▼	4
● Torre Testa '08	▼	7
● Torre Testa '02	▽▽▽	6
● Torre Testa '01	▽▽▽	6
● Torre Testa '04	▽▽	6
● Torre Testa '03	▽▽	6
● Visellio '07	▽▽	5

Cosimo Taurino

SS 605
73010 GUAGNANO [LE]
TEL. 0832706490
www.taurinovini.it

CELLAR SALES
PRE-BOOKED VISITS

ANNUAL PRODUCTION **600,000 bottles**
HECTARES UNDER VINE **111**
VITICULTURE METHOD **Conventional**

Francesco and Rosanna Taurino's cellar hasn't quite found its feet again yet as its long spell in the shadows continues. Founded in 1970 by Cosimo Taurino, the estate was and is a point of reference for Puglian wine, especially with its legendary Patriglione. Production focuses on the traditional local varieties, starting with negroamaro, most of which comes from bush-trained vines.

The flagship wines, Patriglione, Notarpanaro and the more recent A Cosimo Taurino, were missing from the line-up but the bottles we uncorked were more than decent. The '08 7° Ceppo '08, sourced from the traditionally trained primitivo vines that are part of the Cosimo Taurino heritage, gives wafts of earthiness, incense and black berry fruits that are mirrored on the expansive ripe fruit palate. The stylistically similar '07 Salice Salentino Rosso Riserva '07 is on a par, flowing across the palate with cherry-like notes, and the nice negroamaro-only Scaloti '09 gives florality and good acid thrust.

● 7° Ceppo '08	▼▼	4
● Salice Salentino Rosso Ris. '07	▼▼	4
⊙ Scaloti '09	▼▼	3*
● Patriglione '94	▽▽▽	8
● Patriglione '88	▽▽▽	5
● Patriglione '85	▽▽▽	5
● A Cosimo Taurino '04	▽▽	5
● A Cosimo Taurino '03	▽▽	5
● A Cosimo Taurino '02	▽▽	5
● Notarpanaro '06	▽▽	4
● Patriglione '03	▽▽	7
● Patriglione '01	▽▽	7

Tormaresca

LOC. TOFANO
C.DA TORRE D'ISOLA
70055 BARI
TEL. 0883692631
www.tormaresca.it

PRE-BOOKED VISITS

ANNUAL PRODUCTION 2,000,000 bottles
HECTARES UNDER VINE 480
VITICULTURE METHOD Certified organic

Since the Antinoris set up Tormaresca in 1998, their Puglian stronghold has constantly grown and renewed itself in both the vineyards and in the cellar. There are two estates. Bocca di Lupo is located in Murgia within the Castel del Monte designation at about 250 metres above sea level, where the 130 hectares enjoy significant day-night temperature swings, and Masseria Maime in Salento extends over 350 hectares under vine along the Adriatic coast.

This time, the standard of quality from Tormaresca was truly impressive. Topping our score sheet was the '08 Negroamaro Masseria Maime, which picked up Three Glasses again. A sumptuously complex red, it proffers black-skinned stone fruits and printer's ink in a savoury, long-lingering sensory experience. Also excellent is Castel del Monte Aglianico Bocca di Lupo '07, an austere wine whose violets-led florality mingles with resin and cinchona, and the '08 Torcicoda, a gutsy, complex Primitivo with black-skinned forest fruits to the fore. Look out for the subtle, fruity '09 Castel del Monte Chardonnay Pietrabianca '09 and the attractively intense Calafuria '09 rosé.

● Masseria Maime '08	TTT	6
● Castel del Monte Aglianico Bocca di Lupo '07	TT	6
● Torcicoda '08	TT	5
⊙ Calafuria '09	TT	4
○ Castel del Monte Chardonnay Pietrabianca '09	TT	5
● Fichimori '09	T	4
○ Roycello '09	T	4
● Masseria Maime '07	YYY	5
● Masseria Maime '06	YYY	5
● Masseria Maime '05	YYY	5*
● Masseria Maime '04	YYY	5*
● Masseria Maime '02	YYY	5
● Masseria Maime '00	YYY	5*
● Torcicoda '01	YYY	5*

Torre Quarto

C.DA QUARTO, 5
71042 CERIGNOLA [FG]
TEL. 0885418453
www.torrequartocantine.it

CELLAR SALES
PRE-BOOKED VISITS
ROOMS AND FOOD

ANNUAL PRODUCTION 500,000 bottles
HECTARES UNDER VINE 45
VITICULTURE METHOD Conventional

Stefano Cirillo Farrusi's winery has a long, illustrious history stretching back to the 15th century and was already exporting its bottles in the 1930s. Recently, the focus on quality has led to a major effort to convert the vine stock and modernize the cellar. With the sole exception of chardonnay, all the varieties grown are native to Puglia.

It's certainly unusual that a Cerignola-based winery should have a Primitivo di Manduria as its flagship wine but for the past couple of years that has been the bottle from Torre Quarto that we have liked best. The '07 is a lovely product with a penetratingly deep bouquet led by black berry fruits and rain-soaked earth, which are reprised on the complex, spice and mineral palate with its cushiony tannins and long finish. We also liked the '09 Hirondelle, a fresh, full-bodied Greco that gives grapefruit, spices and spring flowers. The rest of the range is well made.

● Primitivo di Manduria Torre Quarto '07	TT	4*
○ Hirondelle '09	TT	3*
● Bottaccia '09	T	4
○ Claire '09	T	3
⊙ Guappo '09	T	3
○ Nina '09	T	3
● Rosso di Cerignola Quarto Ducale '07	T	4
● Sangue Blu '09	T	4
● Tarabuso '09	T	4
● Primitivo di Manduria Tarabuso '06	YY	4*
● Tarabuso '08	YY	4*

Torrevento

LOC. CASTEL DEL MONTE
SP 234 KM 10,600
70033 CORATO [BA]
TEL. 0808980923
www.torrevento.it

CELLAR SALES
PRE-BOOKED VISITS
ROOMS AND FOOD

ANNUAL PRODUCTION **2,500,000 bottles**
HECTARES UNDER VINE **400**
VITICULTURE METHOD **Certified organic**

Torrevento, in the northernmost part of Murgia, has belonged to the Liantonio family since 1948. The vineyards are planted at about 4,500 vines per hectare on the rocky limestone soil characteristic of Karst-type terrain. Despite its size and substantial production potential, the estate has for some time been certified organic, to which it adds ISO 14001 environmental quality certification.

The Liantonio brothers' operation continues to be one of the most exciting in the Castel del Monte designation. The nero di Troia-only '07 Castel del Monte Rosso Vigna Pedale Riserva again earned the Liantonios Three Glasses for its combination of elegance and attitude, showing well-honed tannins, a smooth palate and lots of fruit. Kebir '05, a 50-50 blend of nero di Troia and cabernet sauvignon, is a long, spicy and surprisingly fresh pleaser. Castel del Monte Rosato Primaronda '09 is impressively crafted and redolent of cherries, the hefty Nero di Troia Torre del Falco '08 holds together well and the Primitivo di Manduria Ghenos '08, grown outside its zone, is long and minerally.

● Castel del Monte Rosso V. Pedale Ris. '07	🍷🍷🍷	4*
● Kebir '05	🍷🍷	6
⊙ Castel del Monte Rosato Primaronda '09	🍷🍷	3*
● Primitivo di Manduria Ghenos '08	🍷🍷	4
● Torre del Falco '08	🍷🍷	4
○ Matervitae Fiano '09	🍷	4
○ Moscato di Trani Dulcis in Fundo '08	🍷	4
● Salice Salentino Rosso Faneros '08	🍷	4
● Castel del Monte Rosso V. Pedale Ris. '06	🍸🍸🍸	4*
● Castel del Monte Rosso V. Pedale Ris. '05	🍸🍸🍸	4*
● Castel del Monte Rosso V. Pedale Ris. '04	🍸🍸🍸	4*

Agricole Vallone

VIA XXV LUGLIO, 5
73100 LECCE
TEL. 0832308041
www.agricolevallone.it

PRE-BOOKED VISITS

ANNUAL PRODUCTION **516,000 bottles**
HECTARES UNDER VINE **170**
VITICULTURE METHOD **Certified organic**

The winery run by sisters Vittoria and Maria Teresa Vallone was created in 1934. There are three estates. Flaminio, outside Brindisi, lies entirely in the designated zone of the same name, Iore near San Pancrazio Salentino is registered as Salice Salentino DOC and Castelserranova at Carovigno, right on the Adriatic, is where the grapes are dried for Graticciaia and the dried-grape "passito" Passo de le Viscarde.

For the past couple of years, we have found the Graticciaia to be lacking some of its previous depth and complexity but that doesn't mean it's not an excellent wine with a distinctive style. As usual, the 2006 is a single-variety Negroamaro whose pale, garnet-flecked ruby heralds liquorice and plum jam aromatics and a traditionally expansive palate that signs off with a hint of liqueur cherries. Brindisi Rosso Vigna Flaminio Riserva '06 flows across the palate elegantly, serving up well-defined aromatics and the rest of the range is as reliable as ever.

● Brindisi Rosso V. Flaminio Ris. '06	🍷🍷	4
● Graticciaia '06	🍷🍷	7
⊙ Brindisi Rosato V. Flaminio '09	🍷	3
● Brindisi Rosso V. Flaminio '08	🍷	3
○ Corte Valesio '09	🍷	3
○ Passo de le Viscarde '06	🍷	5
● Salice Salentino Rosso Vereto Ris. '06	🍷	4
● Versante Negramaro '08	🍷	2*
● Graticciaia '03	🍸🍸🍸	7
● Graticciaia '01	🍸🍸🍸	7

Vetrere

FRAZ. VETRERE
SP MONTEIASI-MONTEMESOLA KM 16
74100 TARANTO
TEL. 0995661054
www.vetrere.it

CELLAR SALES
PRE-BOOKED VISITS

ANNUAL PRODUCTION **170,000 bottles**
HECTARES UNDER VINE **37**
VITICULTURE METHOD **Conventional**

The vineyards of sisters Annamaria and Francesca Bruni surround the estate villa, where the old cellar carved from the tufaceous rock has been converted into a modern winemaking facility. Renowned for its extra virgin olive oil, the estate has since 2002 also released an extensive range of top-quality wines from both native and international varieties. Recently, fiano minutolo has become increasingly important.

The sisters kept their ship of state on a steady course but there were no real highlights. Actually, we noted a new style in the wines, which tend to greater overall sweetness, something that raised one or two tasters' eyebrows. The quality is still there, of course, as is shown by the '09 Tempio di Giano. This pleasing Negroamaro gives flowers and balsam before signing off with red fruits. Cré '09 from fiano minutolo is also nice, opening on camomile and bitter honey and unfolding savoury and fresh, with plenty of acid backbone to bolster progression. Another wine to watch out for is Aureo Brut '08 from fiano minutolo, a dry, aroma-rich Italian-method sparkler with lots of appeal.

○ Cré '09	2 glasses	4
● Tempio di Giano '09	2 glasses	3*
○ Aureo Brut '08	1 glass	4
● Barone Pazzo '08	1 glass	4
○ Cré Vendemmia Tardiva '09	1 glass	5
● Livruni '09	1 glass	3
⊙ Taranta '09	1 glass	3

Conti Zecca

VIA CESAREA
73045 LEVERANO [LE]
TEL. 0832925613
www.contizecca.it

CELLAR SALES
PRE-BOOKED VISITS

ANNUAL PRODUCTION **2,000,000 bottles**
HECTARES UNDER VINE **320**
VITICULTURE METHOD **Conventional**

More than five centuries ago, the noble Zecca family from Naples moved onto these farmlands at Leverano in the heart of Salento. The operation embraces four estates, which produce four separate lines. Sarceno, Donna Marzia and Santo Stefano are at Leverano while Cantalupi lies in the Salice Salentino designation.

As ever, the range is impeccable, starting with the Nero '07, which again picked up Three Glasses. Red fruits and spices are the calling card of this 70-30 blend of negroamaro and cabernet sauvignon while the palate is still slightly masked by oak, although its pressure and sheer length are remarkable. Also excellent are the rich, fruit-forward Leverano Terra Riserva '06, the attractively spicy Cantalupi Negramaro '08, the supple, refreshing Primitivo '08 and the Malvasia Bianca '09, which finds just the right aromatic note. Finally, the Donna Marzia of everyday wines includes a well turned-out Rosso '08 and a fruitily aromatic Bianco '09.

● Nero '07	3 glasses	6
● Cantalupi Negramaro '08	2 glasses	3*
○ Donna Marzia Bianco '09	2 glasses	2*
● Donna Marzia Rosso '08	2 glasses	2*
● Leverano Rosso Terra Ris. '06	2 glasses	5
○ Malvasia Bianca '09	2 glasses	4*
● Primitivo '08	2 glasses	4*
⊙ Cantalupi Rosato '09	1 glass	3
● Salice Salentino Rosso Cantalupi '07	1 glass	4
● Nero '06	3 glasses (outlined)	6
● Nero '03	3 glasses (outlined)	6
● Nero '02	3 glasses (outlined)	6
● Nero '01	3 glasses (outlined)	6

Agrialp
SP Burgo Coccaro
72015 Fasano [BR]
tel. 0804827830
www.agrialp.it

Quality is the keynote again this year with a structured, cherry and printer's ink Sarzano '08 from primitivo and Locorotondo Monte Cannone '09, which presents appealingly savoury and fresh-tasting. Primitivo di Manduria Padula delle Monache '08 is fruity and whistle-clean.

○ Locorotondo Monte Cannone '09	🍷🍷	4*
● Sarzano '08	🍷🍷	4*
● Primitivo di Manduria Padula delle Monache '08	🍷	4

Masseria Altemura
c.da Palombara - SP 69
72028 Torre Santa Susanna [BR]
tel. 0831740485
www.masseriaaltemura.it

Masseria Altemura releases clean, well-crafted wines. We like the Negroamaro '08's violets, spice-laced red fruits and attractive, refreshing palate. The thinnish, flowery negroamaro Rosato '09 and easy-drinking primitivo-based Sasseo '08 are well typed.

● Negroamaro '08	🍷🍷	4
⊙ Rosato '09	🍷	4
● Sasseo '08	🍷	4

Antica Enotria
SP 65 c.da Risicata
71042 Cerignola [FG]
tel. 0885418462
www.anticaenotria.it

Antica Enotria is a certified organic estate whose best wine is the steel-aged Montepulciano Falù Rosso '08, a taut, savoury wine with intense sensations of red fruits and capers. Nero di Troia '07 is well-crafted and Puglia Rosso '08 is an easy drinker that slips down.

● Falù Rosso '08	🍷🍷	4*
● Nero di Troia '07	🍷	4
● Puglia Rosso '08	🍷	2

Antiche Terre del Salento
via Stefano Bizantino, 30
74024 Manduria [TA]
tel. 0999795879
www.anticheterredelsalento.it

Vincenza Dinoi has five hectares of bush-trained vines on Manduria's classic red earth, which give her just over 10,000 premium-quality bottles a year. Our favourite was the jasmine-fragranced Primitivo di Manduria Cerva Regia '07 with its wafts of black fruits and spices, good length and savouriness.

● Primitivo di Manduria Cerva Regia '07	🍷🍷	6
● Feudo del Conte '07	🍷	6

Cantine Botromagno
loc. Zona PIP
via Archimede, 22
70024 Gravina in Puglia [BA]
tel. 0803265865
www.botromagno.it

The whites were not presented but the cellar's reds impressed. The forest fruits and tar-themed Nero di Troia '07 is good, showing a precise palate, good fruit, staying power and freshness. Pier delle Vigne '06, the flagship 60-40 blend of aglianico and montepulciano, is full bodied and nuanced with leather and spices.

● Nero di Troia '07	🍷🍷	4
● Pier delle Vigne '06	🍷	5
⊙ Silvium '09	🍷	3
○ Verdeca di Gravina Spumante Brut	🍷	4

Sergio Botrugno
loc. Casale
via Arcione, 1
72100 Brindisi
tel. 0831555587
www.vinisalento.com

Sergio Botrugno's estate has about 30 hectares, three quarters planted with bush-trained vines. Negroamaro Patrunu Rò '09 is the stand-out for its fruit and Mediterranean scrubland introducing an attractively easy-drinking palate with good acidity. The other wines are well made.

● Patrunu Rò '09	🍷🍷	4*
● Brindisi Rosso Arcione '09	🍷	4
● Malvasia nera '09	🍷	3
● Seno di Ponente Rosso '09	🍷	3

C.a.l.o.s.m.

VIA PIETRO SICILIANI, 8
73058 TUGLIE [LE]
TEL. 0833598051
www.calosm.it

This year, rosés were in the spotlight at the Calò winery. Both are from negroamaro with 15 per cent malvasia nera. Villa Valentina Rosato '09 gives flower and wild strawberries with a nice sweetish palate while the dry, full Salmace '09 has lashings of red fruits.

⊙ Salmace '09	🍷🍷	3*
⊙ Villa Valentino Rosato '09	🍷🍷	2*
● Tisciano '08	🍷	3

Francesco Candido

VIA A. DIAZ, 46
72025 SAN DONACI [BR]
TEL. 0831635674
www.candidowines.it

Wines from Candido this year were well made, if less exciting than in the past. Immensum '08, a 70-30 blend of negroamaro and cabernet sauvignon, is nicely fruity, soft in the mouth and holds up well while the printer's ink and spice Duca d'Aragona '04 lacks a little depth and complexity.

● Duca d'Aragona '04	🍷🍷	5
● Immensum '08	🍷🍷	5
● Negroamaro De Vinis '07	🍷	3

Antiche Aziende Canosine

VIA SCONCORDIA
70053 CANOSA DI PUGLIA [BA]
TEL. 3289406102
www.anticheaziendecanosine.it

With the Tharen dried-grape wine missing, it was the Canosa Rossos that led the cellar back into the Guide. The spicy, cherry and blackberry Phatos Riserva '07 has good acid thrust and Aufidus '07 florality and black fruits lead into a fresh, vigorous palate of forest fruits aromatics.

● Canosa Rosso Aufidus '07	🍷🍷	4
● Canosa Rosso Pathos Ris. '07	🍷🍷	4
O Halbus '09	🍷	4
● Mherum '08	🍷	4

Cefalicchio

C.SO SAN SABINO, 6
70053 CANOSA DI PUGLIA [BA]
TEL. 0833617601
www.cefalicchio.it

Cefalicchio has been farmed biodynamically since 1992 and released beautifully made, characterful wines. We liked the clean, aromatic '09 Moscato Bianco Secco Jalal, an attractively fresh wine that holds together well. The fruit-led Montepulciano Vigne Alte '07 and the floral Ponte della Lama Rosato '09 are well typed.

O Jalal '09	🍷🍷	5
⊙ Ponte della Lama Rosato '09	🍷	4
● Vigne Alte '07	🍷	4

Coppi

CIR.NE SUD - II TRATTO
70010 TURI [BA]
TEL. 0808915049
www.vinicoppi.it

The long-established Coppi winery kept its short profile. We very much liked the morello cherry, black berry fruit and rain-soaked earth fragrances of the Primitivo '08, which has a clean, impressively persistent palate. The negroamaro-only Pellirosso '08 is uncomplicated but well made and Negroamaro '08 delivers wafts of Mediterranean scrubland.

● Primitivo '08	🍷🍷	2*
● Negroamaro '08	🍷	2*
● Pellirosso '08	🍷	2*

D'Alfonso del Sordo

C.DA SANT'ANTONINO
71016 SAN SEVERO [FG]
TEL. 0882221444
www.dalfonsodelsordo.it

It was a so-so year for D'Alfonso del Sordo. The wines are well executed but lack the brilliance of previous vintages. Merlot Doganera '07 is clean and appealingly fresh but a little too straightforward, the bombino-based Catapanus '09 is attractively aromatic while Nero di Troia Guado San Leo '08 has plenty to offer but lacks definition.

O Catapanus '09	🍷	3
● Doganera '07	🍷	6
● Guado San Leo '08	🍷	6
● San Severo Rosso Posta Arignano '09	🍷	3

d'Araprì

VIA ZANNOTTI, 30
71016 SAN SEVERO [FG]
TEL. 0882227643
www.darapri.it

D'Araprì is the only winery south of the river Po to specialize in classic method sparklers. The wine we liked this time was the Brut Rosé from 70 per cent montepulciano with pinot nero, a dry, savoury offering redolent of flowers and fresh-baked bread. The rest of the range is well made.

⊙ d'Araprì Brut Rosé	🍷🍷	6
○ d'Araprì Gran Cuvée XXI Secolo '04	🍷	6
○ d'Araprì Nobile Ris. '06	🍷	6
○ d'Araprì Pas Dosé	🍷	5

Erario

SS 7 PER MANDURIA - LECCE KM 1
74024 MANDURIA [TA]
TEL. 0999794407
info@agricolaerario.it

The small Erario co-operative – it has seven members farming 20 hectares – turned out a well-made range. We especially enjoyed the flowers and spice Primitivo di Manduria Chàrisma '08, although it is a tad sweet on the palate, and the malvasia and fiano Angelo Bianco 13 '09 for its tropical fruits, savouriness and nice fresh style.

○ Angelo Bianco 13 '09	🍷🍷	5
● Primitivo di Manduria Chàrismá '08	🍷🍷	5
● Brunera Negroamaro '09	🍷	3
● Primitivo di Manduria Diavolo Rosso '08	🍷	6

Ferri

VIA BARI, 347
70010 VALENZANO [BA]
TEL. 0804671753
www.cantineferri.it

The Ferri winery lies just outside the Gioia del Colle designated area. Wine to uncork are the Oblivio '08, a spice and orange peel Nero di Troia, and Aureus '08, an upfront citrus and flowers Chardonnay. The Primitivo Purpureus '07 is well made, as is the Duo Bianco '09, an unusual blend of garganega and chardonnay.

○ Aureus '08	🍷🍷	4
● Oblivio '08	🍷🍷	5
○ Duo Bianco '09	🍷	2*
● Purpureus '07	🍷	4

Tenuta Fujanera

C.DA QUADRONE DELLE VIGNE KM 2,500
VIA BARI
71100 FOGGIA
TEL. 0881630003
www.fujanera.it

Giusy Albano's winery did well again. Arrocco '09 is a fresh, savoury single-variety Nero di Troia with nice fruit, her rosé Re del Cuore '09 is a floral-themed blend of nero di Troia, sangiovese and montepulciano with appealing hints of green tea. Negroamaro Lamadàli '08 and Falanghina Bellalma '09 are well made.

● Arrocco '09	🍷🍷	4
⊙ Re del Cuore '09	🍷🍷	4
○ Bellalma '09	🍷	4
● Lamadàli '08	🍷	4

Duca Carlo Guarini

L.GO FRISARI, 1
73020 SCORRANO [LE]
TEL. 0836460288
www.ducacarloguarini.it

Duca Carlo Guarini is back in the Guide with Malìa '07, a lovely pepper-themed monovarietal Malvasia Nera with plenty of substance and a refreshing black fruits finish, and the negroamaro-only Nativo '08, with its cherry and spice nose introducing a long, fluent palate.

● Malìa '07	🍷🍷	4
● Nativo '08	🍷🍷	4
⊙ Campo di Mare '09	🍷	3
● Piutri '07	🍷	4

Masseria L'Astore

LOC. L'ASTORE
VIA G. DI VITTORIO, 1
73020 CUTROFIANO [LE]
TEL. 0836542020
www.lastoremasseria.it

Astore Masseria took a step back, presenting wines that are well made but less crisply defined than in recent vintages. Astore '07 is an aglianico and petit verdot mix with lots of fruit that lacks acid grip and comes across as over-extracted, while Jema '08 is a greens and wet earth-themed Primitivo.

● L'Astore '07	🍷🍷	5
⊙ Il Massaro Rosa '09	🍷	4
● Jema '08	🍷	4

Paolo Leo

VIA TUTURANO, 21
72025 SAN DONACI [BR]
TEL. 0831635073
www.paololeo.it

Paolo Leo is back in the Guide thanks mainly to his flagship '08 Orfeo, a rich, full-bodied Negroamaro with a clean palate and lots of fruit. Salice Salentino Rosso Limitone dei Greci '06 is also well crafted, giving evolved nutty aromatics on the nose but showing fresh and taut in the mouth, and the fragrant, upfront Fucsia '09 rosé is also nicely made.

● Orfeo '08	🍷🍷	5
⊙ Fucsia '09	🍷	4
● Salice Salentino Limitone dei Greci '06	🍷	4

Cantina Locorotondo

VIA MADONNA DELLA CATENA, 99
70010 LOCOROTONDO [BA]
TEL. 0804311644
www.locorotondodoc.com

Cantina del Locorotondo turns out several very decent wines, especially Cummerse Rosso '07, a well made plum and cherry blend of aglianico, nero di Troia and cabernet sauvignon with good length and fragrances. The other wines are well typed and appealing.

● Cummerse Rosso '07	🍷🍷	4
○ Locorotondo '09	🍷	4
● Primitivo di Manduria Terre di Don Peppe '08	🍷	6
○ Roccia Bianco '09	🍷	4

Alberto Longo

C.DA PADULECCHIA, SP 5
LUCERA-PIETRAMONTECORVINO KM 4
71036 LUCERA [FG]
TEL. 0881539057
www.albertolongo.it

Alberto Longo had an indifferent year. The wines on offer were well crafted but below the usual standard. Falanghina Le Fossette '09 proffers flowers and white-fleshed fruit, Cacc'e Mmitte di Lucera '09 is light and resiny while the '07 Syrah 04.07.07 has depth but lacks clarity. The falanghina-based Le Fossette Brut is nice.

○ Falanghina Le Fossette '09	🍷🍷	4
● Cacc'e Mmitte di Lucera '09	🍷	4
○ Le Fossette Brut	🍷	5
● Syrah 04.07.07. '07	🍷	4

Maria Marmo

C.DA COCEVOLA, SS 170
CASTEL DEL MONTE KM 9,900
70031 ANDRIA [BA]
TEL. 0883262489
www.tenutacocevola.com

This time, Castel del Monte Nero di Troia Vandalo '07 nearly made the final. It always impresses but its printer's ink, ripe black fruits, body and close-knit tannins lacked the taut acidity that usually accompanies them. The other wines are well typed.

● Castel del Monte Nero di Troia Vandalo '07	🍷🍷	7
● Castel del Monte Nero di Troia Rosso Cocevola '07	🍷	4
⊙ Castel del Monte Rosato '09	🍷	4

Menhir

VIA SCARCIGLIA, 18
73027 MINERVINO DI LECCE [LE]
TEL. 0836818191
www.cantinemenhir.com

Menhir showed again how reliable its quality is. We liked Numero Zero '08, a Negroamaro with fresh black fruits, earth and spice on the nose and plenty of fruit, body and volume in the mouth. Pass-0 '09 is also worth uncorking. It's a late harvest of fiano minutolo that unveils lavender and citrus.

● Numero Zero '08	🍷🍷	3*
○ Pass-0 '09	🍷🍷	3*
● Quota 29 '08	🍷	3
● Trelune '08	🍷	3

Mille Una

L.GO CHIESA, 11
74020 LIZZANO [TA]
TEL. 0999552638
www.milleuna.it

Mille Una had a less successful year. Primitivo Tretarante '07 gives evolved notes of red fruits and chocolate followed by a complex palate with over-assertive sweetness. Primitivo di Manduria Ori di Taranto '08 is uncomplicated and slips down easily while Maviglia '08 is a spicy, oxidative wine.

● Tretarante '07	🍷🍷	8
○ Maviglia '08	🍷	7
● Primitivo di Manduria Ori di Taranto '08	🍷	5

Azienda Monaci

LOC. TENUTA MONACI
73043 COPERTINO [LE]
TEL. 0832947512
www.aziendamonaci.com

Le Braci's absence affected Monaci's results but the wines we did taste were excellent. Girofle '09's palette of aromatics ranges from flowers to fresh fruit and the currants and raspberry-themed palate has plenty of oomph. I Censi '07 is clean-tasting, offering black fruits, capers and spice. Both are from negoramaro.

⊙ Girofle '09	🍷🍷	4
● I Censi '07	🍷🍷	5
● Copertino Rosso Eloquenzia '07	🍷	4

Casa Vinicola Nico

SPECCHIA
74011 CASTELLANETA [TA]
TEL. 0998491041
www.nicocasavinicola.it

The Nico family has been making wine at Castellaneta since 1935. The compact, crisply aromatic Aglianico '07 lays out coffee and spices while the Primitivo '08 gives red-skinned stone fruits and fresh green followed by a fruit-driven palate with a well-crafted but slightly mouth-drying finale.

● Aglianico '07	🍷🍷	4
● Primitivo '08	🍷🍷	4
○ Falanghina '09	🍷	3
● Vini Rudy - Primitivo - Sangue Arena '08	🍷	2*

Giovanni Petrelli

VIA VILLA CONVENTO, 33
73041 CARMIANO [LE]
TEL. 0832603051
www.cantinapetrelli.com

Giovanni Petrelli's cellar is back in the Guide. Salice Salentino Rosso Centopietre '08 proffers intriguing black fruits, spices and liquorice aromas but the appealingly fresh palate is less complex. Leucòs '09, a late harvest of moscato grapes, mingles roses with nut-like aromatics.

○ Leucòs '09	🍷🍷	4
● Salice Salentino Centopietre '08	🍷🍷	4
● Copertino Tre Archi '07	🍷	4
● Diecimila Tenuta Scozzi '07	🍷	4

Agricola Pliniana

C.DA BARCE
74024 MANDURIA [TA]
TEL. 0999794273
www.cantinepliniana.it

This influential co-operative winery has returned to these pages with a line-up of excellent Primitivo di Manduria bottles. Juvenis '07 is a deep, varietal wine with complex black fruits aromatics and Due Mari '06 is a delightful tipple with spice and figs echoed on the fresh, well-defined palate.

● Primitivo di Manduria Due Mari '06	🍷🍷	3*
● Primitivo di Manduria Juvenis '07	🍷🍷	4
● Primitivo di Manduria Priscus '07	🍷	4

Primis

VIA C. COLOMBO, 44
71048 STORNARELLA [FG]
TEL. 0885433333
www.primisvini.com

Crusta is back, having given its wines an extra year's maturation in bottle. The montepulciano-only '06 has a deep, richly extracted palate after unveiling sumptuous cherries, blackberries and eastern spices on the nose. The flowers and white-fleshed fruits Bombino Bianco '09 is another fine wine.

○ Bombino Bianco '09	🍷🍷	4
● Crusta '06	🍷🍷	5
● Nero di Troia '08	🍷	4
● Syrah '08	🍷	4

Rosa del Golfo

VIA GARIBALDI, 56
73011 ALEZIO [LE]
TEL. 0833281045
www.rosadelgolfo.com

Damiano Calò's long-established operation is one of the best-known in the region. This year, we liked the '09 Scaliere, a very well-typed Negroamaro redolent of cherry-led red fruits and spices that are picked up on the attractively fruit-forward palate. The nicely crafted, flower-themed Brut Rosé holds together well.

● Scaliere '09	🍷🍷	3*
○ Bolina '09	🍷	4
⊙ Brut Rosé	🍷	5
● Primitivo '08	🍷	4

OTHER WINERIES

L'Antica Cantina di San Severo

V.LE SAN BERNARDINO, 94
71016 SAN SEVERO [FG]
TEL. 0882221125
www.anticacantina.it

San Severo has 500 members who farm 1,000 hectares. We loved the '09 Nobiles Rosso, a plum jam, balsam-veined Nero di Troia with loads of fruit and mouthfilling appeal and the fresh, clean '09 San Severo Rosso Castrum '09, which offers spices and red berry fruits.

- ● Nobiles Rosso '09 🍷🍷 3*
- ● San Severo Castrum Rosso '09 🍷🍷 3*
- ○ San Severo Castrum Bianco '09 🍷 3

Santa Maria del Morige

FRAZ. CARPIGNANA
VIA DEL MARE, KM 2
73044 GALATONE [LE]
TEL. 3458592276
www.santamariadelmorige.com

The Conserva family winery interprets negroamaro in occasionally unusual ways. The classic, black cherry fruit-rich Cinabro '07 flows over the palate borne up by perky acidity whereas Murice Bianco '09, from negroamaro fermented off the skins, is attractively fresh but a little unchallenging.

- ● Cinabro '07 🍷🍷 4
- ○ Murice Bianco '09 🍷 4

Santi Dimitri

C.DA SANTI DIMITRI
VIA GUIDANO
73013 GALATINA [LE]
TEL. 0836565866
www.santidimitri.it

Vincenzo Vallone has bounced back into the Guide. Margìa '06 is a fragrant spice and red fruits blend of 60 per cent negroamaro with cabernet sauvignon and merlot. The fresh, supple Rosso '08 is a well-crafted Negroamaro and Cinciallegra Bianco '09, a 50-50 blend of chardonnay and sauvignon, is savoury and citrus-led.

- ● Margìa '06 🍷🍷 5
- ● Aruca Rosso '07 🍷 4
- ○ Cinciallegra Bianco '09 🍷 3
- ● Ruvezzo Rosso '08 🍷 3

Schola Sarmenti

VIA GENERALE CANTORE, 37
73048 NARDÒ [LE]
TEL. 0833567247
www.scholasarmenti.it

This year, we thought the best of Luigi Carlo Marra's wines was Artetica '06, a 70-30 blend of negroamaro and primitivo with cherry aromatics and a soft, fruit-rich mouthfeel that reveals a tad too much sweetness. Watch out for the Nardòs, too. Both the '07 Roccamora and the '05 Nerìo Riserva are spot on.

- ● Artetica '06 🍷🍷 6
- ● Critèra '07 🍷 4
- ● Nardò Nerìo Ris. '05 🍷 4
- ● Nardò Rosso Roccamora '07 🍷 3

Setteterre

VIA PER FAGGIANO, 228
74100 TARANTO
TEL. 0994527396
setteterre@hotmail.it

Setteterre's production is proving to be remarkably reliable. Primitivo di Manduria Vigna dell'Ora '08 is impressively concentrated and long, unveiling nice fresh black fruits and spices, whereas Uva Prigioniera '08 is an utterly traditional, expansive Negroamaro that flows effortlessly over the palate.

- ● Primitivo di Manduria V. dell'Ora '08 🍷🍷 6
- ● Uva Prigioniera '08 🍷🍷 5
- ● Primitivo di Manduria Diverso '08 🍷 6

Cantine Soloperto

SS 7 TER
74024 MANDURIA [TA]
TEL. 0999794286
www.soloperto.it

Soloperto is a benchmark for the Primitivo di Manduria designation. The wines we liked this year were the attractively savoury '08 Mono, which has excellent fruit, and the more traditional Patriarca '08. It's perhaps a whisker too sweet but its minerality and persistence are impressive.

- ● Primitivo di Manduria Mono '08 🍷🍷 5
- ● Primitivo di Manduria Patriarca '08 🍷🍷 5
- ● Primitivo di Manduria '08 🍷 3
- ● Primitivo di Manduria Rubinum 14° '08 🍷 4

Conte Spagnoletti Zeuli

FRAZ. MONTEGROSSO
C.DA SAN DOMENICO, SP 231 KM 60,000
70031 ANDRIA [BA]
TEL. 0883569511
www.contespagnolettizeuli.it

Conte Spagnoletti Zeuli is a long-standing Castel del Monte winery. Rosso Tenuta Zagaria Vignagrande '07 is a well-executed bottle from nero di Troia with floral aromas and cushiony tannins while Aglianico Ghiandara '06 shows more oak but flows through to a long finale underpinned by notes of cherry.

- ● Castel del Monte Aglianico Ghiandara '06 — 🍷🍷 4
- ● Castel del Monte Rosso Tenuta Zagaria Vignagrande '07 — 🍷🍷 4
- ○ Jody '09 — 🍷 4

Teanum

VIA SALVEMINI, 1
71010 SAN PAOLO DI CIVITATE [FG]
TEL. 0882551056
www.teanum.it

Teanum's Alta line again offers some very well-made wines like the attractively long currant jam and chocolate '08 Nero di Troia and the fresh-tasting, varietal '08 Cabernet Sauvignon '08 with its floral aromas and nice balance.

- ● Alta Cabernet Sauvignon '08 — 🍷🍷 4*
- ● Alta Nero di Troia '08 — 🍷🍷 4*
- ● Otre Primitivo '08 — 🍷 3
- ● San Severo Rosso Canticum '08 — 🍷 1*

Cantina Sociale Cooperativa Vecchia Torre

VIA MARCHE, 1
73045 LEVERANO [LE]
TEL. 0832925053
www.cantinavecchiatorre.it

Vecchia Torre is finding its way back to a fine level of quality. Our favourites this year were the two Salice Salentinos, the '06 Riserva, which proffers complex spice and incense aromatics before unveiling balance, length and fruitiness in the mouth, and the fresh, well-defined aromas of Vecchia Torre '08.

- ● Salice Salentino Rosso Ris. '06 — 🍷🍷 4
- ● Salice Salentino Vecchia Torre '08 — 🍷🍷 3*
- ● Leverano Rosso '08 — 🍷 3
- ● Primitivo Salento '08 — 🍷 3

Tenuta Viglione

VIA CARLO MARX, 44P
70029 SANTERAMO IN COLLE [BA]
TEL. 0803023927
www.tenutaviglione.it

Giovanni Zullo's cellar is one of the rising stars in Gioia del Colle. His '04 Primitivo Marpione Riserva follows florality with a fruity, close-woven palate of substance, ending long and taut. Rosso Rupestre '07 is a remarkably complex balsamic blend of 55 per cent primitivo with merlot.

- ● Gioia del Colle Rosso Marpione Ris. '04 — 🍷🍷 4
- ● Gioia del Colle Rosso Rupestre '07 — 🍷🍷 3*

Villa Mottura

P.ZZA MELICA, 4
73058 TUGLIE [LE]
TEL. 0833596601
www.motturavini.it

This time round, Villa Mottura's Moscato di Trani '07 is one of the best sweet wines in Puglia. Beautifully balanced, it serves up attractively well-defined quince and camomile flowers aromatics that are echoed on the palate. The Salice Salentino Rosso '07 is also very appealing, foregrounding a ripe plum and damson theme.

- ○ Moscato di Trani '07 — 🍷🍷 6
- ● Salice Salentino Rosso '07 — 🍷🍷 6
- ● Negroamaro Le Pitre '08 — 🍷 7
- ⊙ Rosé '09 — 🍷 5

Vinicola Mediterranea

VIA MATERNITÀ INFANZIA, 22
72027 SAN PIETRO VERNOTICO [BR]
TEL. 0831676323
www.vinicolamediterranea.it

Vincola Mediterranea is on form this year and we enjoyed the range of excellently made bottles. Particularly impressive are the Negroamaro Il Nobile '09, a poised, complex wine with just the right hint of bitterness in the long finish, and the likeable '09 Primitivo Febo, which foregrounds fruit.

- ● Negroamaro Il Nobile '09 — 🍷🍷 4
- ● Primitivo Febo '09 — 🍷🍷 3*
- ● Brindisi Rosso Il Visconte '08 — 🍷 4
- ● Primitivo di Manduria Primo Duca '07 — 🍷 4

CALABRIA

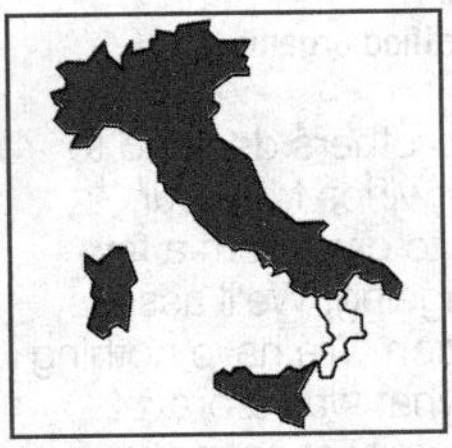

There have never been as many Calabrian wines in the final as this year, and we take it as a sign of the slow but constant improvement in the quality of wine production in the region. This impression is confirmed and backed up by the considerable number of wineries appearing in the Guide this year for the first time. Important news, obviously, but there is more. Our tastings confirmed the upwards trend in the province of Cosenza, which is competing with Cirò for regional leadership. And if the province of Cosenza has been making real progress in recent years, much of this is due to the work of the Vini della Calabria Citra consortium and its ever-dynamic founder and current chairman, Demetrio Stancati. It was he who managed to convince the Cosenza producers to form an association and above all to focus on producing quality wines. This farsighted, intelligent change of direction is beginning to bear fruit. Things are also happening in Cirò, where the average quality of the wines has improved. There have also been attempts by many wineries to modernize not just technically but also by adopting packaging more suited to the latest marketing trends. We are however less enthusiastic about the debate, at times extremely heated, regarding the adoption of new regulations for this historic DOC zone. The debate sees on one side the traditionalists, led by Nicodemo Librandi, who has invested so much energy, time and resources in bringing the best out of native varieties, and in particular gaglioppo. On the other side we have those who would like to extend the scope of the designation to include so-called international varieties. We feel it's a shame not to make the most of a varietal heritage such as Calabria's, whose range of native grape varieties is one of the largest in the entire Italian peninsula. There is little to report from the rest of the region and the situation in the Lamezia area appears to have become fossilized. Apart from the two historic brands Statti and Lento, which are doing well, there are no other figures on the horizon. In the province of Reggio Calabria, the little movement we saw in previous years seems to have died down. Production figures remain more or less the same as last year, in other words around 500,000 hectolitres, accounting for around one per cent of national production.

Roberto Ceraudo

LOC. MARINA DI STRONGOLI
C.DA DATTILO
88815 CROTONE
TEL. 0962865613
www.dattilo.it

CELLAR SALES
PRE-BOOKED VISITS
ROOMS AND FOOD

ANNUAL PRODUCTION 70,000 bottles
HECTARES UNDER VINE 20
VITICULTURE METHOD Certified organic

Roberto Ceraudo will soon be celebrating his 40th harvest but thanks to his unwavering passion for his land, he is as enthusiastic as ever. He has now been joined by his children: Giuseppe, who helps him in the rows and back at the winery; and Susy, who deals with the business side of things. The Dattilo estate covers 60 hectares in the countryside around Strongoli, in a well-aspected hillside area near the sea. Roberto Ceraudo was one of the first growers in Calabria to convert to organic farming.

On the whole, the wines presented this year performed well, starting with the Petraro '07, a blend of gaglioppo and cabernet sauvignon, which impressed us with its clean aromatic profile brimming with spices, aromatic herbs and an elegant note of bay leaves. We also found Doro Bè '06 interesting. This Magliocco from part-dried grapes offers refreshing acidity to support lovely honey and tobacco, balanced by impressive structure. The best white is Imyr '09, an elegant Chardonnay with attractive notes of tropical fruit perking up a long, leisurely finish.

● Doro Bè '06	▼▼	8
○ Imyr '09	▼▼	5
○ Petelia '09	▼▼	4
● Petraro '07	▼▼	6
● Dattilo '07	▼	4
⊙ Grayasusi Etichetta Argento '09	▼	5
⊙ Grayasusi Etichetta Rame '09	▼	4
○ Grisara '09	▼	5
○ Grisara '08	▽▽	5
○ Grisara '07	▽▽	5
○ Imyr '08	▽▽	5
● Petraro '06	▽▽	6

iGreco

C.DA GUARDAPIEDI
87062 CARIATI [CS]
TEL. 0983969441
www.igreco.it

CELLAR SALES
PRE-BOOKED VISITS
ROOMS AND FOOD

ANNUAL PRODUCTION 308,000 bottles
HECTARES UNDER VINE 80
VITICULTURE METHOD Certified organic

This year, the Greco brothers decided to exclude some of their wines from our selections, preferring to give them a few months' extra cellar ageing. We'll assess them for our next edition. We have nothing but appreciation for what was a brave move. This dynamic family of entrepreneurs started out in the olive oil business and their stated aim has always been to produce wines of matching quality, right from the first harvest, combining a modern style with a real sense of terroir.

Masino made it to the finals. This monovarietal Calabrese unveils sweet fruity notes on the nose and a savoury, well-behaved palate, where smooth tannins support ripe, succulent fruit. The delicious Catà '08 is a Gaglioppo with a tight-knit, intense aromatic profile, combining wild cherry with balsam and mineral notes. On the palate it shows plush and well-balanced. The refreshing, drinkable Savù '09, a rosé from Gaglioppo, shows aromas of red berry fruit over a fresh, lip-smacking palate. The fragrant Greco Filù '09 reveals fresh fruit on the nose and flows across the palate.

● Masino '09	▼▼	6
● Gaglioppo Catà '08	▼▼	4*
⊙ Gaglioppo Savù '09	▼	4
○ Greco Filù '09	▼	4
● Gaglioppo Catà '07	▽▽	3*
● Masino '08	▽▽	4
○ Riticella '08	▽▽	5

Cantine Lento

VIA DEL PROGRESSO, 1
88046 LAMEZIA TERME [CZ]
TEL. 096828028
www.cantinelento.it

CELLAR SALES
PRE-BOOKED VISITS

ANNUAL PRODUCTION **500,000 bottles**
HECTARES UNDER VINE **70**
VITICULTURE METHOD **Conventional**

Lento is a solid family business that in just over five years has managed to modernize without losing its character. This transformation has affected the size of the operation, which has grown considerably, and also the quality of the wines produced. Now the Lentos, with 70 hectares under vine on the Amato estate, are self-sufficient in production while their brand new, highly-equipped winery means they finally have the space and technology they need.

As always, the wines presented were excellent and the Lamezia Riserva '05 deservedly made the finals. Rounded and stylish, it shows a close-woven nose dominated by red fruit, with hints of balsam and printer's ink, followed by a long, appealing palate with bags of flavour and pulp. The Tisaloro '08, a mix of magliocco and merlot, shows a well-developed nose, with red fruit and hints of balsam leading to marvellous structure on the palate nicely counterpointed by acidity and tannins. The top white is the coherent, elegant Lamezia Greco '09, with a full-flavoured palate set off by refreshing acidity behind abundant floral aromas.

● Lamezia Ris. '05	2 black glasses	5
○ Lamezia Greco '09	2 black glasses	4
○ Passito '06	2 black glasses	5
● Tisaloro '08	2 black glasses	5
○ Contessa Emburga '09	1 black glass	4
○ Lamezia Bianco Dragone '09	1 black glass	4
⊙ Lamezia Rosato Dragone '09	1 black glass	4
● Lamezia Rosso Dragone '09	1 black glass	4
● Federico II '06	2 white glasses	5
● Federico II '05	2 white glasses	5
● Federico II '04	2 white glasses	5

Librandi

LOC. SAN GENNARO
JONICA 106
88811 CIRÒ MARINA [KR]
TEL. 096231518
www.librandi.it

CELLAR SALES
PRE-BOOKED VISITS

ANNUAL PRODUCTION **2,200,000 bottles**
HECTARES UNDER VINE **232**
VITICULTURE METHOD **Conventional**

When Nicodemo and Tonino Librandi decided to completely renovate their winery they made no concessions to fashion, nor were they tempted to cut corners to achieve quick results. Starting from their basic axiom, namely the link between native varieties and terroir, over the last decade they have gained immense experience in experimental vineyards, clonal selections and painstaking small-batch fermentations. Their goal is to select the best clones of Calabria's native varieties.

Judging by their Duca San Felice, which repeats last year's Three Glasses performance, the Librandis are clearly on the right track. The '08 vintage has given us a stylish wine, with graceful aromas, lashings of fruit and flowers notes on the nose and rare balance on the palate. The same holds true for the succulent, full Magliocco Magno Megonio '08, offering black berry fruit and spices on the nose. Gravello '08, a classic blend of gaglioppo and cabernet with Mediterranean aromas, is fresh, fruit-driven and leisurely on the palate. It also reached the finals. The Mantonico Efeso '09 was, as usual, great and the new gaglioppo sparkler, Almaneti '07 Rosé Brut, made a fine debut.

● Cirò Rosso Duca Sanfelice Ris. '08	3 black glasses	4*
● Gravello '08	2 black glasses	6
● Magno Megonio '08	2 black glasses	5
⊙ Almaneti Rosé Brut '07	2 black glasses	5
○ Critone '09	2 black glasses	4*
○ Efeso '09	2 black glasses	5
○ Le Passule '08	2 black glasses	6
⊙ Terre Lontane '09	2 black glasses	4*
○ Cirò Bianco '09	1 black glass	3
● Cirò Rosso Cl. '09	1 black glass	3
● Cirò Rosso Duca Sanfelice Ris. '07	3 white glasses	4*
● Cirò Rosso Duca Sanfelice Ris. '05	3 white glasses	4*
● Gravello '05	3 white glasses	5

Fattoria San Francesco

LOC. QUATTROMANI
88813 CIRÒ [KR]
TEL. 096232228
www.fattoriasanfrancesco.it

CELLAR SALES
PRE-BOOKED VISITS

ANNUAL PRODUCTION 300,000 bottles
HECTARES UNDER VINE 40
VITICULTURE METHOD Conventional

After a brief partnership with Montresor from Verona, Francesco Siciliani is back in the driving seat, having regained a controlling stake in his historic winery. We send him our best wishes, and are sure he will further develop a brand that has revolutionized modern winemaking in Cirò and Calabria. All the ingredients for growth are there: a united, well-integrated team of owners and staff, no fewer than 40 hectares under vine in the countryside around Cirò, and a recently renovated, modern, efficient winery.

The Cirò Rosso Classico Ronco dei Quattro Venti '08 shows great character, with jammy wild berries lifted by fine floral notes. On the palate it shows full-bodied and tight-knit, with glossy tannins and a goodish fruity finish. We also liked the Cirò Rosso Classico '09 with its fresh vegetal aromas and hints of spice and cinchona over a supple, refreshing palate of medium structure and good length. The clean, fresh, easy-drinking Pernicolò '09, from greco and chardonnay, offers floral notes on the nose and a refreshing, savoury palate.

⊙ Cirò Rosato Cl. Ronco dei Quattroventi '09	▼▼	5
● Cirò Rosso Cl. '09	▼▼	3*
● Cirò Rosso Cl. Ronco dei Quattroventi '08	▼▼	6
○ Brisi '07	▼	7
⊙ Cirò Rosato '09	▼	4
● Donna Madda '08	▼	5
○ Pernicolò '09	▼	4
● Cirò Rosso Cl. '08	▽▽	3*
● Cirò Rosso Cl. Donna Madda '05	▽▽	5
● Cirò Rosso Cl. Donna Madda '01	▽▽	5
○ Fata Morgana '07	▽▽	5

Senatore Vini

LOC. SAN LORENZO
88811 CIRÒ MARINA [KR]
TEL. 096232350
www.senatorevini.com

CELLAR SALES
PRE-BOOKED VISITS

ANNUAL PRODUCTION 250,000 bottles
HECTARES UNDER VINE 27
VITICULTURE METHOD Conventional

The Senatore brothers' Cirò winery has all it takes to move up to the next level and we are sure that even better results will soon be on their way. The Senatore family have been producing wine in Cirò for generations and in only a few years have completely modernized their operation. There have been changes both in the rows and the production facility. Much of the old vine stock has been replanted with spacing more suitable for modern viticultural methods, and a new winery has been built.

Arcano '07 is an austere, varietal, traditionally styled Cirò Rosso Classico Riserva offering jammy red berry fruit aromas echoed on the palate. We liked the lovely salmon pink Cirò Rosato Puntalice '09 with its distinct, fresh aromas of wild strawberries and white cherries interwoven with floral and mineral notes. This vibrant, savoury wine flows nicely across the palate. The attractive Alikia '09, an unusual blend of greco and gewürztraminer, displays the varietal aromas of the latter, while refreshing acidity on the palate balances its sweetness, and nicely counterpoints the rich, succulent fruit

○ Alikia '09	▼▼	4
⊙ Cirò Rosato Puntalice '09	▼▼	4*
● Cirò Rosso Cl. Arcano Ris. '07	▼▼	5
○ Cirò Bianco Alaei '09	▼	4
● Cirò Rosso Cl. Arcano '08	▼	4
● Gaglioppo Merlot '09	▼	4
● Nerello '08	▼	5
● Cirò Rosso Cl. Arcano '07	▽▽	4*
● Cirò Rosso Cl. Arcano '06	▽▽	4*
● Cirò Rosso Cl. Arcano Ris. '06	▽▽	5
● Ehos '06	▽▽	4*
● Gaglioppo Merlot '08	▽▽	4

Serracavallo

C.DA SERRACAVALLO
87043 BISIGNANO [CS]
TEL. 098421144
www.viniserracavallo.it

CELLAR SALES
PRE-BOOKED VISITS
FOOD

ANNUAL PRODUCTION 50,000 bottles
HECTARES UNDER VINE 30
VITICULTURE METHOD Conventional

Demetrio Stancati's love of wine is such that in the mid 1990s he gave up a brilliant career in medicine to dedicate his energies to the fine family winery. Not content, he rounded up local growers to set up the Consorzio dei Produttori della Calabria Citra, of which he is the chairman. He dedicates time and resources not only to the consortium, but also to developing native varieties, especially magliocco, with excellent results, as our tastings showed.

Two wines made the final this year. Vigna Savuco '06, a full-bodied but never overpowering monovarietal Magliocco, combines blackberry and currants on the nose, and compact, rounded fruit on the firmly-structured palate, without compromising drinkability. The other finalist was the elegant Terraccia '08, from magliocco and cabernet. Its intense, close-woven palate follows plum and wild cherry aromas, mingling with minerality and balsam. The lovely Zilì '09, a magliocco-sangiovese rosé, shows a fresh, savoury, supple palate behind abundant citrus fruit, Mediterranean herbs, raspberry and cherry.

● Terraccia '08	🍷🍷	5
● Vigna Savuco '06	🍷🍷	5
⊙ Zilì '09	🍷🍷	4
○ Besidiae '09	🍷	3
● Sette Chiese '09	🍷	4
● Terraccia '07	🥂	5
● Terraccia '06	🥂	5
● Terraccia '04	🥂	5
● Terraccia '03	🥂	5

Statti

C.DA LENTI
88046 LAMEZIA TERME [CZ]
TEL. 0968456138
www.statti.com

CELLAR SALES
PRE-BOOKED VISITS
FOOD

ANNUAL PRODUCTION 300,000 bottles
HECTARES UNDER VINE 55
VITICULTURE METHOD Conventional

The Statti brothers' winery is one of the operations that have made most progress over recent years, becoming a benchmark for the entire region. This has been made possible by significant investments, both in the vineyard and at the cellar. On their estate in Lamezia, the Stattis have managed to achieve extremely high, consistent quality. They missed out on Three Glasses this year by a whisker but hopefully will soon be taking home top honours.

Arvino '08, a blend of gaglioppo and cabernet sauvignon, reveals blackberries and mulberries on the nose, with beautifully integrated balsam and oak. The palate opens with fleshy, dark berry fruit, balanced by smooth tannins and lip-smacking acidity, leading to a long, leisurely finish. Black cherry and blackcurrant aromas distinguish Cauro '07, an elegant red from gaglioppo, magliocco and cabernet sauvignon with mellow tannins and juicy fruit on the palate. The zesty, drinkable Greco '09 shows supple structure and good grip, with nice fruit-flavour balance, and signs off with a long, mineral finish.

● Arvino '08	🍷🍷	4*
● Cauro '07	🍷🍷	5
○ Greco '09	🍷🍷	4*
● Gaglioppo Rosso '09	🍷	3
○ Lamezia Bianco '09	🍷	3
● Lamezia Rosso '09	🍷	3
● Arvino '07	🥂	4*
● Arvino '06	🥂	4*
● Arvino '05	🥂	4*
● Arvino '04	🥂	3*
● Cauro '06	🥂	5
● Cauro '05	🥂	5

Tenuta Terre Nobili

via Carigliato
87046 Montalto Uffugo [CS]
tel. 0984934005
www.tenutaterrenobili.it

CELLAR SALES
PRE-BOOKED VISITS
ROOMS

ANNUAL PRODUCTION **35,000 bottles**
HECTARES UNDER VINE **16**
VITICULTURE METHOD **Certified organic**

This winery was set up in the 1960s by Lidia Matera's father, Ennio. His passion for winemaking led him to give up his job as an engineer and become a full-time grower. At a tender age his daughter Lidia also caught the bug. Her mission is to get the best from the terroir and its varieties, producing fine wine while respecting the environment. It is no surprise, then, that Lidia was one of the first growers to go organic.

Alarico '09, a first-rate monovarietal Nerello, opens with seductive red berry fruit offset by beautifully aromatic oak and a fresh mineral vein. It shows good length and the sweetness is nicely underpinned by subtle tannins. Only slightly less complex is the elegant Magliocco Cariglio '09, with rich, juicy fruit. A full-flavoured, balsamic mouth follows attractive oak and fresh fruit on the nose. The Greco Santa Chiara '09 gives floral, mineral and plum notes on the nose, leading into a fresh palate with a pleasing citrus finish.

● Alarico '09	2 black glasses	5
● Cariglio '09	2 black glasses	4*
○ Santa Chiara '09	1 black glass	4
● Alarico '08	2 white glasses	4
● Alarico '07	2 white glasses	5
● Cariglio '07	2 white glasses	5
● Cariglio '01	2 white glasses	3*
○ Santa Chiara '08	2 white glasses	4

Luigi Viola

via Roma, 18
87010 Saracena [CS]
tel. 0981349099
www.cantineviola.it

CELLAR SALES
PRE-BOOKED VISITS

ANNUAL PRODUCTION **8,000 bottles**
HECTARES UNDER VINE **2**
VITICULTURE METHOD **Certified organic**

The Violas' estate comprises just a few hectares in the Parco del Pollino and a small, atmospheric winery housed in the town's old converted cinema. But there is also the undying passion and dedication of Luigi and his sons, Roberto, Alessandro and Claudio. We are particularly happy to see his well-deserved success, having followed his progress and encouraged him ever since he first told us, with his customary modesty, about his dream of reviving the forgotten traditional Moscato di Saracena.

With the superb '09 vintage of his Moscato, Luigi Viola took home Three Glasses for the third year running. This wine is nothing short of spectacular: a richly layered, extraordinary example of elegance, with intense, complex aromas of tropical fruit, dried figs, lavender, medicinal herbs and candied peel. Dense, fine-grained and deep, it shows exceptional length on the palate, where sharp acidity balances a sweetness that never cloys. This is quite simply poetry in a glass!

○ Moscato Passito '09	3 black glasses	7
○ Moscato Passito '08	3 white glasses	7
○ Moscato Passito '07	3 white glasses	7

Cantine Campoverde

LOC. CIPARSIA
87012 CASTROVILLARI [CS]
TEL. 0981415141
www.cantinecampoverde.it

Cosenza is clearly making headway, as confirmed by the second debut in this edition of a winery from the province. The interesting Magliocco '08 offers lots of fruit and flavour, as well as good length. Among the whites, we liked the Timpa del Principe '09, a fresh and highly drinkable blend of greco and mantonico.

○ Chardonnay '09	🍷 4
● Dolcedorme '09	🍷 4
● Magliocco '08	🍷 4
○ Timpa del Principe '09	🍷 4

Caparra & Siciliani

BIVIO SS JONICA 106
88811 CIRÒ MARINA [KR]
TEL. 0962371435
www.caparraesiciliani.it

Wines from this historic Cirò winery include a particularly impressive Volvito '07, a traditionally styled Cirò with varied aromas ranging from red berry fruit jam to leather and tobacco. The long, leisurely fruit-laden palate is underpinned by close-knit, lively tannins.

● Cirò Rosso Cl. Sup. Volvito '07	🍷🍷 4
○ Cirò Bianco Curiale '09	🍷 3
⊙ Cirò Rosato Le Formelle '09	🍷 3
● Cirò Solagi '08	🍷 3

Umberto Ceratti

VIA DEGLI UFFIZI, 5
89030 CARAFFA DEL BIANCO [RC]
TEL. 0964956008

The Cerattis are one of the few producers of Greco di Bianco left, and without doubt the best-known in the area. Their delightful Greco di Bianco '06 displays candied peel, camomile, dried figs and cakes on the nose, followed by a fresh-tasting, well-balanced, leisurely palate.

○ Greco di Bianco '06	🍷🍷 5

Colacino

VIA A. GUARASCI, 5
87054 ROGLIANO [CS]
TEL. 0984961034
www.colacino.it

Colacino, one of the very few wineries in the Savuto DOC zone, once more proved its worth. The Colle Barabba '08 convinced us with its spicy nose and succulent whole fruit in the mouth. The well-fruited Britto '07 shows green aromatic herbs and a chocolate-like nose.

● Savuto Sup. Britto '07	🍷🍷 5
● Savuto V. Colle Barabba '09	🍷🍷 4
● Amazio '09	🍷 4
○ Quarto '09	🍷 4

Donnici 99

C.DA VERZANO
87100 COSENZA
TEL. 0984781842
www.donnici99.com

From the wines presented by this interesting estate near Cozenza, the Audace Diverzano '08 is a cut above the rest. This blend of barbera and merlot boasts floral aromas of dried rose, geraniums and violets over well-structured, focused fruit on the palate, with a minty note on the long leisurely finish.

● Audace Diverzano '08	🍷🍷 3*
● Donnici Antico Diverzano '07	🍷🍷 4
● Ardente Diverzano '07	🍷 4
⊙ Fugace Diverzano '09	🍷 3

Cantina Enotria

LOC. SAN GENNARO
SS JONICA 106
88811 CIRÒ MARINA [KR]
TEL. 0962371181
www.cantinaenotria.com

The wines of this large co-operative are always reliable. The classy Riserva '07 Piana delle Fate marries red fruit with gardenia and eucalyptus, leading to sweetness on the dense palate and a satisfyingly fruit-rich finish. The easy-drinking Cirò Rosato '09 is fresh and fruity.

● Cirò Rosso Cl. Sup. Piana delle Fate Ris. '07	🍷🍷 4
○ Cirò Bianco '09	🍷 3
⊙ Cirò Rosato '09	🍷 3
● Cirò Rosso Cl. '08	🍷 4

Feudo dei Sanseverino

VIA VITTORIO EMANUELE, 108/110
87010 SARACENA [CS]
TEL. 098121461
www.feudodeisanseverino.it

The captivating Moscato Passito '05 lays out a complex aromatic profile, with fig jam, spicy panpepato, caramel and oriental spices. The sweet, lingering palate signs off with hints of toffee. The Moscato Passito '07 Mastro Terenzio proved to be slightly simpler and less fresh.

○ Mastro Terenzio '07	🍷🍷	6
○ Moscato Passito al Governo di Saracena '05	🍷🍷	5
● Lacrima Nera '07	🍷	4

Ippolito 1845

VIA TIRONE, 118
88811 CIRÒ MARINA [KR]
TEL. 096231106
www.ippolito1845.it

Our finals were graced by the Gaglioppo 160 Anni '07, produced to celebrate the 160th anniversary of this historic Cirò winery. Rich and strong, it proffers aromas of jammy cherry and plum, chocolate and tobacco. The dense, tannin-rich palate displays overripe sweetness, finishing long and spicy.

● 160 Anni '07	🍷🍷	6
● Cirò Rosso Cl. Ripe del Falco Ris. '98	🍷🍷	6
⊙ Cirò Rosato Mabilia '09	🍷	3
● Cirò Rosso Cl. Sup. Liber Pater '08	🍷	3

Tenuta Iuzzolini

LOC. FRASSÀ
88811 CIRÒ MARINA [KR]
TEL. 0962371326
www.tenutaiuzzolini.it

This estate produces well-executed wines, starting with the Cirò Rosso '08, whose fresh flowers and liquorice lead into a palate with good tannin-fruit balance. The interesting Madre Goccia '09, from greco and chardonnay, shows minerals and lashings of melon and peach fruit over a zesty, lingering palate.

○ Bristace '09	🍷🍷	7
● Cirò Rosso Cl. '08	🍷🍷	3*
● Artino '09	🍷	5
○ Madre Goccia '09	🍷	4

Malaspina

VIA PALLICA, 67
89063 MELITO DI PORTO SALVO [RC]
TEL. 0965781632
www.aziendavinicolamalaspina.com

This winery near Reggio Calabria is run by the Malaspina sisters. The interesting Rosato Rosaspina '09, a highly drinkable Gaglioppo, shows a fresh, tangy and approachable nose where red berry fruit accompanies an attractive hint of balsam. We also liked the complex, leisurely Passito Cannici '08.

○ Cannici Passito '08	🍷🍷	5
⊙ Rosaspina '09	🍷🍷	3
○ Micah '09	🍷	4
● Patros Pietro '07	🍷	5

Malena

LOC. PETRARO
SS JONICA 106
88811 CIRÒ MARINA [KR]
TEL. 096231758
www.malena.it

The best of a good range of wines from Malena was, as usual, the beautiful deep cerise Bacco Rosato '09, from gaglioppo. Red cherry, violet and fresh woodland aromas precede a well-managed palate with good structure and length, rounded off by a nicely refreshing, fruity finish.

⊙ Bacco Rosato '09	🍷🍷	4
⊙ Cirò Rosato '09	🍷	3
● Cirò Rosso Cl. '08	🍷	3
○ Similoro Bianco '09	🍷	4

Salvatore Marini

VIA TERMOPILI, 47
87069 SAN DEMETRIO CORONE [CS]
TEL. 0984947868
www.vinimarini.it

The Marini made a great start, with their Elaphe '08 making the finals straight away. This elegant, complex blend, based mainly on magliocco and aglianico, shows wild cherry, bitter orange, tamarind and chocolate on the nose. On the palate, elegant tannins offset impressive acidity.

● Elaphe '08	🍷🍷	5
● Korone '08	🍷🍷	4

Domenico Pandolfi

C.DA SODA, 30/32
87010 SARACENA [CS]
TEL. 0981349336
agripandolfi@live.it

This year's Guide sees the debut of Pandolfi, one of the promising new wineries in Saracena, home of Moscato Passito di Saracena. Quintessentially traditional, the Moscato '09, offers notes of quince, honey and medicinal herbs. While sweet and lingering, it shows refreshing acidity on the palate.

○ Moscato Passito di Saracena '09	🍷🍷 7

La Pizzuta del Principe

C.DA LA PIZZUTA, 1
88816 STRONGOLI [KR]
www.lapizzutadelprincipe.it

Welcome to the Guide to the Bianchi family, thanks to a fine performance from their Gaglioppo, Zingamaro '09. Fruit and Mediterranean herbs on the nose lead to a full, satisfying palate and attractive liquorice on the finish. The refreshing, drinkable Molarella '09 is a white with hints of blossom and sea air.

● Zingamaro '09	🍷🍷 4
⊙ Calastrazza '09	🍷 3
○ Molarella '09	🍷 3

Re Alarico

LOC. CONTRADA CANALE
87030 CAROLEI [CS]
TEL. 098436108
www.realarico.com

This Cosenza winery, only established five years ago, makes its debut in the Guide. The attractive Mentore '08, from magliocco canino, magliocco dolce and cabernet, is big on flavour and fruit, and shows goodish length. The herbaceous, floral Alisa '09, a white from montonico, has freshness on the palate.

○ Alisa '09	🍷 4
● Mentore '08	🍷 5
● Re Alarico '08	🍷 3
● Xenia '09	🍷 4

Santa Venere

LOC. TENUTA VOLTAGRANDE
SP 04 KM 10,00
88813 CIRÒ [KR]
TEL. 096238519
www.santavenere.com

The wines from this estate, which uses organic methods, are always spot on. The Riserva di Cirò Federico Scala '07 stood out, combining captivating floral notes and dark berry fruit with velvety elegance in the mouth. Speziale '09, an interesting red from marsigliana nera grapes, has a fresh, full-flavoured palate.

● Cirò Rosso Cl. Sup. Federico Scala Ris. '07	🍷🍷 5
● Speziale '09	🍷🍷 4
● Cirò Rosso Cl. '09	🍷 4
● Vurgadà '09	🍷 4

Domenico Spadafora

ZONA INDUSTRIALE, 18
87050 MANGONE [CS]
TEL. 0984969080
www.cantinespadafora.it

Spadafora is back in the Guide thanks to a fine performance from Solenero '08, a generous, fruit-fuelled magliocco-merlot blend, showing fine length and structure. The nose gives ripe wild berries and spices, swathed in refreshing balsam. The rest of the wines are well made.

● Solenero '08	🍷🍷 4*
● Donnici Ris. '05	🍷 4
⊙ Donnici Rosato V. Fiego '09	🍷 3
● Donnici Rosso V. Fiego '08	🍷 3

Stelitano

C.DA PALAZZI, 1
89030 CASIGNANA [RC]
TEL. 0964913023
stelitano@interfree.it

We loved Stelitano's Greco di Bianco '08, with its nose of tropical fruit, dates, topsoil and porcini mushrooms. In the mouth, fresh acidity balances the sweetness, and lovely liquorice notes emerge in the long, leisurely finish. The nice Mantonico '08 has intense nuts, citrus fruit, honey and figs.

○ Greco di Bianco '08	🍷🍷 7
○ Mantonico '08	🍷🍷 6

Terre del Gufo - Muzzillo

FRAZ. DONNICI INFERIORE
C.DA ALBO SAN MARTINO
87100 COSENZA
TEL. 3357725614
www.terredelgufo.com

The Magliocco Canino Timpamara '08 Selezione Sud Ovest made the finals thanks to a well-developed, complex nose, paving the way for focused, elegant fruit on the captivating palate. The youthful Donnici Portapiana '09 also has class, showing Mediterranean aromas over a refreshing, flavoursome palate.

- ● Timpamara Sel. Sud Ovest '08 — 🍷🍷 7
- ● Portapiana Donnici '09 — 🍷🍷 5

Terre di Balbia

C.DA MONTINO
87042 ALTOMONTE [CS]
TEL. 048161264
www.terredibalbia.it

The Venica-Caputo duo produce fine wines, especially Serramonte '07, an elegant blend of magliocco and sangiovese from 50-year-old vines. Dense and juicy in the mouth, but well balanced, it offers a close-focused nose bursting with cherry and blackberry fruit, followed by Mediterranean herbs and fresh-roasted coffee.

- ● SerraMonte '07 — 🍷🍷 7
- ● Balbium '08 — 🍷 4

Tramontana

LOC. GALLICO MARINA
VIA CASA SAVOIA, 156
89139 REGGIO CALABRIA
TEL. 0965370067
www.vinitramontana.it

The wines from this dynamic Reggio Calabria outfit are always reliable. The refreshing Pellaro '08 charms with its complex nose of red berry fruit, aromatic herbs and balsamic notes over a backdrop of liquorice, echoed on the finish. We liked the fresh, balsamic '07 Nerello 1890 with its fruit-infused finish.

- ● 1890 '07 — 🍷🍷 6
- ● Pellaro '08 — 🍷🍷 4*
- ● Costa Viola '08 — 🍷 4
- ● To Crasi '07 — 🍷 4

Val di Neto

C.DA MARGHERITA VIA DELLE MAGNOLIE
88900 SCANDALE [KR]
TEL. 096254079
www.cantinavaldineto.com

The technical staff at Val di Neto decided to leave the estate's top wines to age in the cellars. The best of those presented was Ferule '08, a blend of greco and chardonnay, whose attractive oak and tropical fruits encore in the mouth underpinned by refreshing acidity and a firm backbone.

- ○ Ferule '08 — 🍷🍷 4*
- ⊙ Amistà '09 — 🍷 4

Vigna de Franco

FRAZ. CIRÒ MARINA
SS 106 KM 279,800
88811 CROTONE
TEL. 3290732473
http://vignadefranco.blogspot.com/

We are pleased to mention this small Cirò winery, which produces a single wine from organically grown fruit. The Cirò 'A Vita '08 has a layered, elegant nose, offering rich, sun-drenched aromas. The lip-smacking palate shows real sinew and big, perfectly ripe fruit, supported by close-woven tannins.

- ● Cirò Rosso Cl. Sup. 'A Vita '08 — 🍷🍷 4*

Vinicola Zito

FRAZ. PUNTA ALICE
VIA SCALARETTO
88811 CIRÒ MARINA [KR]
TEL. 096231853
www.zito.it

The outstanding Cirò Rosso Classico '08 has a well-developed aromatic profile, brimming with red fruit, candied peel and Mediterranean herbs to counterpoint an austere, elegant palate. We also liked the well-crafted Cirò Riserva '07, with its balsamic, nicely balanced palate.

- ● Cirò Rosso Cl. Ris. '07 — 🍷🍷 4*
- ● Cirò Rosso Cl. Sup. '08 — 🍷🍷 4*
- ● Cirò Rosso Cl. Alceo '09 — 🍷 3
- ● Cirò Rosso Cl. Krimisa '08 — 🍷 4

SICILY

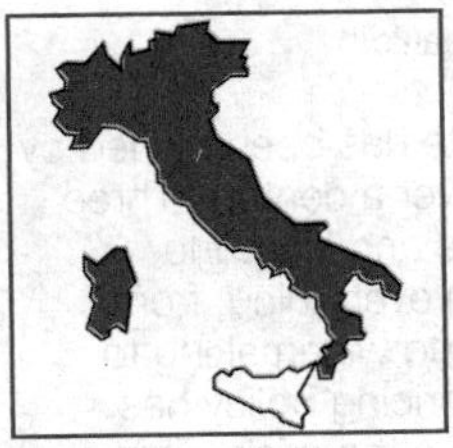

Sicily is the land of wine. This large, vine-clad island in the centre of the Mediterranean was perhaps home to the Oenotrians, who gave the Greek part of Italy its first name, Oenotria. The word's Greek root literally means "land of vines", which shows just how deep-rooted wine culture is here. This year's tastings saw a region strongly committed to quality making headway in international markets. Although turnover may have dropped, there have been gains in quantity. Sicily's once huge unbottled wine market has been hit by major losses, while bottled wine has recovered brilliantly from the 2008 crisis and in 2009 went over the €75,000,000 mark for the first time. Much of this wine is labelled IGT, a classification that has proved to be more versatile and practical than the DOC and DOCG designations. The latter two have lost five per cent per year over the last five years, compared to IGT wines, which have seen seven per cent growth. About 65 per cent of Sicily's production is accounted for by table wine and must, 30 per cent is IGT and less than five per cent DOC. If we also consider the number of vineyards pulled up over the last five years, it is clear that a move towards quality is the only option. In our 2011 edition, 15 wineries took Three Glasses. The biggest group was Etna Rosso, with Cottanera's '07, Pietradolce's Archineri '08, Terre Nere's Santo Spirito '08 and Destro's Sciarakè '08. These and Palari's classic Faro Palari '08 show a dynamic eastern Sicily and Etna, as has been evident for some years. The province of Trapani on the other side of the island, although accounting for 60 per cent of regional production, took just three top awards. Firstly, the extraordinary Marsala Vergine Riserva 1981 from Pellegrino, winning Three Glasses for the first time, and with a wine that is out of fashion and drunk much less than in the past, undeservedly, we feel. Since Italian unity began in Marsala, maybe this is the best wine to toast its 150th anniversary. It is joined by two great reds, Donnafugata's Tancredi '07 and Firriato's Harmonium '08. Palermo chimes in with Tasca d'Almerita and its classic Cabernet Sauvignon '08, while Cusumano offers Sàgana '08. From Agrigento, more specifically Menfi, we have Planeta's Cometa '09 and Settesoli's Cartagho Mandrarossa '08. To conclude, the province of Caltanissetta gives us Nero d'Avola Versace from Feudi del Pisciotto, Siracusa offers Saia '08 from Feudo Maccari and Ragusa has Gulfi's Neromàccarj '07. This first-rate series is a victory for technique, terroir and native varieties. Apart from the Tancredi, a blend of nero d'Avola with 30 per cent cabernet sauvignon, Regaleali's Cabernet Sauvignon and Planeta's not quite native Fiano, all the prize-winners are from traditional varieties, with nero d'Avola ruling the roost.

Abbazia Santa Anastasia

C.DA SANTA ANASTASIA
90013 CASTELBUONO [PA]
TEL. 091671959
www.abbaziasantanastasia.it

CELLAR SALES
PRE-BOOKED VISITS

ANNUAL PRODUCTION 650,000 bottles
HECTARES UNDER VINE 62
VITICULTURE METHOD Certified organic

This beautiful abbey was founded in the 12th century by Ruggero d'Altavilla, and flourished for centuries. The immense estate of over 300 hectares is spread over hillsides overlooking the sea and buffeted by its changing, tempestuous winds. We are in the magnificent Parco delle Madonie, near Castelbuono and its artistic treasures. Here, since 1980, the Lena family has moved from traditional to organic, and now biodynamic, farming.

The deep, mineral biodynamic Sens(i)nverso Nero d'Avola '08 confirms its character and reached our finals with its ripe, well-focused black cherry, liquorice and cocoa powder, backed up by silky, seductive tannins. We also loved Litra '07, from cabernet sauvignon, which gives delicious, intense balsam and blackcurrant, and the vibrant Montenero '08, from nero d'Avola, cabernet sauvignon and merlot, with good length and well-dosed oak. The biodynamic Sens(i)nverso Cabernet Sauvignon '08, with attractive fruit, is also admirable. The other wines pass muster.

● Sens(i)nverso Nero d'Avola '08	2 glasses (black)	6
○ Gemelli '09	2 glasses (black)	5
● Litra '07	2 glasses (black)	7
● Montenero '08	2 glasses (black)	5
● Passomaggio '08	2 glasses (black)	4
● Sens(i)nverso Cabernet Sauvignon '08	2 glasses (black)	6
○ Sinestesìa '09	2 glasses (black)	4*
● Syrah '09	2 glasses (black)	4*
○ Contempo Grillo '09	1 glass (black)	3
● Contempo Nero d'Avola '09	1 glass (black)	3
○ Zurrica '09	1 glass (black)	4
● Litra '04	3 glasses (white)	7
● Litra '01	3 glasses (white)	8
● Litra '00	3 glasses (white)	7
● Montenero '04	3 glasses (white)	5

Alessandro di Camporeale

C.DA MANDRANOVA
90043 CAMPOREALE [PA]
TEL. 092437038
www.alessandrodicamporeale.it

CELLAR SALES
PRE-BOOKED VISITS

ANNUAL PRODUCTION 150,000 bottles
HECTARES UNDER VINE 35
VITICULTURE METHOD Organic

This 35-hectare estate has been owned by the same family for over a century. Three brothers, Nino, Natale and Rosolino Alessandro, deal with everything, from growing, marketing and winemaking to sales. Their prudent pricing policy has enabled them to ignore the crisis. This small, reliable, family operation is loved by wine enthusiasts, and for some time has been using certified organic farming methods to produce natural wine.

The excellent, dark, lively ruby Kaid '08, from syrah, missed out on Three Glasses by a whisker. Layered and intense, it seduces with blackcurrant, ginger, liqueur cherries, cloves and mint. Potent, with lively, well-honed tannins, it unfolds in the mouth with balance and forthright character. The attractive, charming Kaid Vendemmia Tardiva '08, also from syrah, shows depth, offering sweet fruit and great length. The fleshy, fresh-tasting Catarratto Benedè, the sound, mature DonnaTà, from nero d'Avola, and the zesty, harmonious new arrival, the Kaid Sauvignon Blanc, are all impeccable fruits of the '09 harvest.

● Kaid '08	2 glasses (black)	5*
○ Benedè '09	2 glasses (black)	4*
● DonnaTà '09	2 glasses (black)	4
○ Kaid Sauvignon Blanc '09	2 glasses (black)	5*
● Kaid V. T. '08	2 glasses (black)	6
○ Benedè '08	2 glasses (white)	4*
● DonnaTà '07	2 glasses (white)	4*
● Kaid '07	2 glasses (white)	5
● Kaid '06	2 glasses (white)	5

Baglio del Cristo

C.DA FAVAROTTA
SS 123 KM 19,200
92023 CAMPOBELLO DI LICATA [AG]
TEL. 0922 877709
www.cristodicampobello.it

CELLAR SALES
PRE-BOOKED VISITS

ANNUAL PRODUCTION 300,000 bottles
HECTARES UNDER VINE 30
VITICULTURE METHOD Conventional

The estate has 30 hectares of vineyards on chalk and limestone soils in the breeze-cooled hills to the south of Campobello. The well-equipped winery is housed in the enclosed farmstead dedicated to an ancient crucifix, an icon of popular worship for centuries. The intention of Angelo Bonetta and his sons Carmelo and Riccardo is to emphasize the Sicilianness of their wines, regardless of whether native or international varieties are used.

For the second year running, Nero d'Avola Lu Patri '08 reached our finals with its abundant ripe fruit aromas, lifted by upfront balsam and sustained by a concentrated, well-rounded palate with vibrant, lingering fruit. The slightly overripe Syrah Lusirà '08 combines a nice spicy bouquet with solid structure, showing fresh on the palate with an attractive oak aftertaste. Judiciously dosed wood is also evident in the savoury, stylish elegance of Chardonnay Laudàri '09. We loved Adènzia '08, a blend of nero d'Avola, syrah and cabernet sauvignon, and the stylish, fresh C'D'C' Bianco Cristo di Campobello '09, from native varieties with a splash of chardonnay.

● Lu Patri '08	▼▼	6
● Adènzia Rosso '08	▼▼	4
○ Laudàri '09	▼▼	5
● Lusirà '08	▼▼	6
○ Adènzia Bianco '09	▼	4
○ C'D'C' Bianco Cristo di Campobello '09	▼	3
○ Lalùci '09	▼	4
○ Adènzia '08	▽▽	4*
○ Laudàri '07	▽▽	6
● Lu Patri '07	▽▽	6

Baglio di Pianetto

VIA FRANCIA
90030 SANTA CRISTINA GELA [PA]
TEL. 0918570002
www.bagliodipianetto.com

CELLAR SALES
PRE-BOOKED VISITS

ANNUAL PRODUCTION 400,000 bottles
HECTARES UNDER VINE 95
VITICULTURE METHOD Conventional

The Sicilian winery of Conte Paolo Marzotto can rely on two separate production facilities: the first at Pianetto, near Palermo, and the second at Contrada Baroni, near Noto. These two areas offer entirely different site climates but are both excellent wine country. The Noto terroir reflects the closeness of the sea and limestone soils with high levels of rock fragments. At Pianetto, meanwhile, the conditioning factor is the elevation of the vineyards, all about 600 metres above sea level, and the wide day-night temperature range.

As usual, the wines selected for our regional tastings were sound and well-managed. The Ramione '06, an elegant blend of Nero d'Avola and Merlot, nearly made the finals with its charming wild cherry, chocolate and fresh balsamic aromas. The plush, lingering Salici '05, a monovarietal Merlot, combines elegant medicinal herbs with fine cherry jam notes, returning on the palate to enliven the long finish. Shymer '08, a Shyraz-Merlot with glossy, smooth tannins, proffers red berry fruit on the nose. The fresh-tasting, elegantly crafted Viognier Ginolfo '09 has a lovely citrus finish.

○ Ginolfo '09	▼▼	5
● Ramione '06	▼▼	4*
● Salici '05	▼▼	4
● Shymer '08	▼▼	4*
● Chianu Carduni '06	▼	7
○ Ficiligno '09	▼	4
● Nero d'Avola '07	▼	4
● Ramione '04	▽▽▽	4*
● Chianu Carduni '05	▽▽	7
● Nero d'Avola '06	▽▽	4*
○ Piana del Ginolfo '08	▽▽	4*
● Ramione '05	▽▽	4*
● Shymer '07	▽▽	4*

Barbera

C.DA TORRENOVA, SP 79
92013 MENFI [AG]
TEL. 0925570442
www.cantinebarbera.it

CELLAR SALES
PRE-BOOKED VISITS
FOOD

ANNUAL PRODUCTION **100,000 bottles**
HECTARES UNDER VINE **15**
VITICULTURE METHOD **Conventional**

When her father set up the Barbera winery, Marilena was running her established accountancy firm at Menfi and when she went to the winery it was almost exclusively to deal with the accounts. Slowly, the winery began to take up more of her time and energy, and what started out as work became a passion. From that point on, there was no stopping her. First she closed her office, and then started to take an active role in running the operation. And it is thanks to this love affair that the Barbera winery, in her words "has become a real gem".

Once again, the wines from this, one of the most dynamic wineries in Sicily, are first rate. Merlot, petit verdot and nero d'Avola join forces for the Coda della Foce '08, proffering fruit aromas on the nose, which explode in the mouth, where they are nicely balanced by the silky, elegant tannins. The Merlot Azimut '08 has a generous, velvety nose of deep, ripe red berry fruit, encored on the lingering palate. We loved the intense, mineral Inzolia Dietro le Case '09, combining hints of aromatic herbs with a rich, refreshing, lingering palate.

● Coda della Foce '08	TT	6
○ Inzolia '09	TT	4*
⊙ La Bambina '09	TT	4*
● Menfi Cabernet Sauvignon La Vota '08	TT	5
○ Menfi Inzolia Dietro le Case '09	TT	4
● Menfi Merlot Azimut '08	TT	5
● Nero d'Avola '09	T	4
● Coda della Foce '05	YY	5
○ Inzolia '08	YY	4*
● Menfi Azimut '07	YY	4
● Menfi Coda della Foce '06	YY	5
○ Menfi Inzolia Dietro le Case '07	YY	4*

★ Benanti

VIA G. GARIBALDI, 475
95029 VIAGRANDE [CT]
TEL. 0957893438
www.vinicolabenanti.it

CELLAR SALES
PRE-BOOKED VISITS

ANNUAL PRODUCTION **180,000 bottles**
HECTARES UNDER VINE **50**
VITICULTURE METHOD **Conventional**

When everyone had lost faith in Etna's wines, once the pride of Sicily, Giuseppe Benanti, inspired by family memories, reclaimed abandoned terraces and started to experiment. If Etna is experiencing a new golden age, no one can deny that the brilliant Benanti was the first to believe in its potential and get the ball rolling again. The latest news from this famous winery, where his sons Antonino and Salvino now also work, is that they have acquired a further four hectares at Monte Serra. Their aim is to move forward, while respecting tradition.

The Etna Bianco Superiore Pietramarina '06, from carricante, missed out on Three Glasses by a whisker. This extraordinarily complex, charming wine shows minerality and honey, damsons, acacia blossom over fine acid structure, great character and personality. The Etna Rosso Serra della Contessa '08, from nerello mascalese and cappuccino, also made the finals. An elegant, austere wine characterized by hints of plum, pencil lead, sour cherry and spice, it shows rich, full, lively texture. The Etna Rosso Rovittello '07, from the same grapes as Serra, also impressed, as did Il Monovitigno Nerello Cappuccio '08. The rest of the wines are impeccable.

○ Etna Bianco Sup. Pietramarina '06	TT	7
● Etna Rosso Serra della Contessa '08	TT	8
○ Edelmio '08	TT	5
○ Etna Bianco di Caselle '09	TT	4*
● Etna Rosso di Verzella '07	TT	4
● Etna Rosso Rovittello '07	TT	6
● Il Drappo '08	TT	7
● Lamorèmio '06	TT	6
● Nerello Cappuccio Il Monovitigno '08	TT	6
● Nerello Mascalese Il Monovitigno '07	TT	6
○ Etna Bianco Sup. Pietramarina '04	YYY	7
● Etna Rosso Serra della Contessa '06	YYY	8
● Etna Rosso Serra della Contessa '04	YYY	8
● Etna Rosso Serra della Contessa '03	YYY	7
● Il Drappo '04	YYY	6

Vini Biondi

C.SO SICILIA, 20
95039 TRECASTAGNI [CT]
TEL. 0957633933
www.vinibiondi.it

CELLAR SALES
PRE-BOOKED VISITS

ANNUAL PRODUCTION 20,000 bottles
HECTARES UNDER VINE 14
VITICULTURE METHOD Organic

Ciro Biondi's passion for Etna is no coincidence: his family has produced wine here for over 100 years, exporting it successfully until the Second World War, which marked the beginning of a dark period for Etna winemaking. Rebirth began in 1999, starting with painstaking work in the rows, all at high elevation and bush-trained. The Monte Ilice vineyard, 900 metres above sea level with an incline of 50 per cent, is an excellent example of winegrowing in extreme conditions.

After the fantastic debut last year, the Etna Rosso M.I.'08 once more made our finals and just missed out on top honours. The expressive charm of the previous vintage makes way for extreme finesse on a nose of rarefied, complex spice and incense. Mineral notes encore on the palate, which shows noble structure, glossy tannins and a well-focused, leisurely finish. The Etna Rosso Outis '07 is extremely elegant on the nose, with almost austere ripe fruit that merges with an intriguing hint of iron filings. On the palate, it shows delicate, with fine-grained tannins and a pleasing finish.

● Etna Rosso M.I. '08	TT	6
● Etna Rosso Outis '07	TT	6
● Etna Rosso M.I. '07	YYY	6
● Etna Rosso Outis '05	YYY	6
○ Etna Bianco Outis '06	YY	5
● Etna Rosso Outis '06	YY	6
● Etna Rosso Outis '04	YY	6

Alice Bonaccorsi

LOC. PASSOPISCIARO
C.DA CROCE MONACI
95036 RANDAZZO [CT]
TEL. 095337134
www.valcerasa.com

PRE-BOOKED VISITS

ANNUAL PRODUCTION 35,000 bottles
HECTARES UNDER VINE 14
VITICULTURE METHOD Certified organic

We are in Contrada Crocemonaci near Randazzo, 800 metres above sea level, in a winery of 14 hectares, amidst lava stone terraces painstakingly cut from the hillside, offering splendid views of rumbling Etna and the enchanting Alcantara valley. A life decision brought Alice Bonaccorsi, agronomist and grower to live and work here, with her husband, Rosario Pappalardo. Their guiding principle is utmost respect for the land and its fruits, and organic certification is merely the starting point.

The superb Etna Bianco Noir '08 reached our finals. This blend of carricante with minnella, catarratto and insolia, comes from a vineyard with an average vine age of 50 years, with some over 100. A deep gold tinged with orange accompanies captivating dried wild flowers, beeswax, cedar, peach, apricot and pencil lead. This leads to a fleshy, fresh, summery palate with nice length. Also impressive is the Etna Rosso Crucimonaci '06, from nerello mascalese and cappuccio, showing intense, deep and fruity, with silky tannins. The citrussy carricante-based Etna Bianco Valcerasa '08, and the minerally Rocca delle Campane '07, from carricante and chardonnay, are also classy.

○ Etna Bianco Noir '08	TT	7
● Etna Rosso Crucimonaci '06	TT	7
○ Etna Bianco Valcerasa '08	TT	5
○ Rocca delle Campane '07	TT	4*
● Rossorelativo '08	TT	4*
○ Etna Bianco Valcerasa '05	YY	4*
● Etna Rosso Valcerasa '06	YY	5
● Etna Rosso Valcerasa '05	YY	4

Calatrasi

C.DA PIANO PIRAINO
90040 SAN CIPIRELLO [PA]
TEL. 0918576767
www.calatrasi.it

CELLAR SALES
PRE-BOOKED VISITS

ANNUAL PRODUCTION **2,000,000 bottles**
HECTARES UNDER VINE **890**
VITICULTURE METHOD **Certified organic**

Calatrasi has three production sites in Sicily, Puglia and Tunisia, for a total of 1,750 hectares. The modern wine concept tends to favour fresh, fragrant drinkable products with a sense of place that have sold in their millions all over the world. This impressive operation was established in 1980 by brothers Giuseppe and Maurizio Micciché, inspired by their father Vincenzo, who, like Maurizio, was a doctor with a passion for winemaking.

The complex, layered Terre di Ginestra 651 Nero d'Avola '08 easily made the finals with its lovely ripe plum and cherry aromas, alternating with black pepper, chocolate and wild rose. On the soft, lively palate it shows generous and leisurely, providing pleasurable drinking. The classy Terre di Ginestra Magnifico Syrah '08 is balsamic, spicy and juicy. The deep, brooding Terre di Ginestra Nero d'Avola '08 displays seductive hints of plum, morello cherry, cloves, iodine and porcini mushrooms. The other labels also performed well.

● Terre di Ginestra 651 Nero d'Avola '08	**ΨΨ**	5
○ Terre di Ginestra 651 Chardonnay '08	**ΨΨ**	5
● Terre di Ginestra Magnifico Syrah '08	**ΨΨ**	5
● Terre di Ginestra Nero d'Avola '08	**ΨΨ**	4*
○ Terre di Ginestra Catarratto '09	**Ψ**	4
○ Terre di Ginestra Magnifico Viognier '09	**Ψ**	4
● 'A Naca '06	ΨΨ	6
● Terre di Ginestra 651 '07	ΨΨ	5
● Terre di Ginestra 651 '06	ΨΨ	5
● Terre di Ginestra 651 Nero d'Avola '07	ΨΨ	5
● Terre di Ginestra FrancQ '08	ΨΨ	4
● Terre di Ginestra Magnifico '07	ΨΨ	5
● Terre di Ginestra Nero d'Avola '06	ΨΨ	4*

Cantina Viticoltori Associati Canicattì

C.DA AQUILATA
92024 CANICATTÌ [AG]
TEL. 0922829371
www.viticultoriassociati.it

CELLAR SALES
PRE-BOOKED VISITS

ANNUAL PRODUCTION **700,000 bottles**
HECTARES UNDER VINE **1,000**
VITICULTURE METHOD **Conventional**

This gem among Sicily's co-operative wineries was established over 40 years ago, and is managed with a firm hand by its astute chairman, Giovanni Greco. There are around 500 member growers, with 1,000 hectares of land in diverse wine areas, individually monitored by the technical staff. Over the years, they have invested significantly in technology, which has made it possible to successfully combine tradition with the latest vinification systems and respond to the challenges of the global market.

We saw another fine performance from the Aynat '07, a Nero d'Avola boasting elegant ripe plum and cherry fruit. On the palate it shows mouth filling, vigorous structure, sustained by vibrant tannins, reflecting excellent raw material and oak. Deep and compact, with well-defined nuances of plum and blueberry, the Aquilae Nero d'Avola '09 is intense and drinkable, as is the highly satisfying Aquilae Syrah '09, which proffers hints of pepper and ripe red berry fruit over a juicy, palate with well-honed tannins. Equally good are the fresh, tangy Aquilae Grillo and the soft, smooth Aquilae Merlot, both '09s.

○ Aquilae Catarrato '09	**ΨΨ**	3*
○ Aquilae Grillo '09	**ΨΨ**	3*
● Aquilae Merlot '09	**ΨΨ**	3*
● Aquilae Nero d'Avola '09	**ΨΨ**	3*
● Aquilae Syrah '09	**ΨΨ**	3*
● Aynat '07	**ΨΨ**	5
● Aquilae Cabernet Sauvignon '08	ΨΨ	3*
● Aquilae Merlot '08	ΨΨ	3*
● Aquilae Syrah '08	ΨΨ	3*
● Aynat '06	ΨΨ	5
● Scialo '07	ΨΨ	4*
● Scialo '06	ΨΨ	4*

Centopassi

VIA PORTA PALERMO, 132
90048 SAN GIUSEPPE JATO [PA]
TEL. 0918577655
www.cantinacentopassi.it

CELLAR SALES
PRE-BOOKED VISITS
ROOMS AND FOOD

ANNUAL PRODUCTION **300,000 bottles**
HECTARES UNDER VINE **60**
VITICULTURE METHOD **Certified organic**

Wine can be a means of redemption for a land exploited by the Mafia. In a project that deserves our admiration, two co-operative wineries, Placido Rizzotto – Libera Terra and La Pio La Torre, have joined forces in a consortium. They have been assigned over 400 hectares of land confiscated from Cosa Nostra in Alto Belice at Corleone, 60 of which are under vine. October 2009 saw the inauguration of the vinification plant at San Giuseppe Jato, also built on land seized from the Mafia.

The highly drinkable Centopassi Rosso '09, from nero d'Avola and perricone, opens on a flower and fruit nose, followed by attractive acidity in the mouth. The more complex, mature Nero d'Avola Argille di Tagghia Via '09 is dedicated to Peppino Impastato. After notes of pepper and red berry fruit, the Syrah Marne di Saladino '08, dedicated to Emanuele Basile, unveils a solid, consistent palate. Elegant hints of Mediterranean scrub, fresh almond and lovely, fragrant fruit distinguish the Catarratto Terre Rosse di Giabbascio '09, dedicated to Pio La Torre. The delicate, clean nose of the Centopassi Bianco '09, a blend of grillo and catarratto, leads to a fresh, zesty palate.

○ Catarratto Terre Rosse di Giabbascio '09	▼▼	4
● Centopassi Rosso '09	▼▼	4
● Nero d'Avola Argille di Tagghia Via '09	▼▼	4
● Syrah Marne di Saladino '08	▼▼	6
○ Centopassi Bianco '09	▼	4
○ Centopassi Placido Rizzotto Bianco '08	▽▽	3*
○ Centopassi Placido Rizzotto Catarratto '07	▽▽	3*
● Centopassi Placido Rizzotto Rosso '07	▽▽	3*
○ Rocce di Pietra Longa '08	▽▽	4*
○ Terre Rosse di Giabbascio '08	▽▽	4*

Tenuta Chiuse del Signore

C.DA CHIUSE DEL SIGNORE
SP LINGUAGLOSSA-ZAFFERANA KM 2
95015 LINGUAGLOSSA [CT]
TEL. 0942611340
www.gaishotels.com

CELLAR SALES
PRE-BOOKED VISITS

ANNUAL PRODUCTION **45,000 bottles**
HECTARES UNDER VINE **50**
VITICULTURE METHOD **Conventional**

About a decade ago, Sergio De Luca, a talented hotelier in Taormina, decided to renovate the winery he had inherited from his grandmother at Linguaglossa. This estate of around 60 hectares, now mostly under vine, is situated 600 metres above sea level, in some of the best wine country in the Etna foothills. He recovered all the bush-planted vines, some a century old, and the spectacular amphitheatre vineyard next to the historic winery with its old winepress.

The intensely deep, mouthfilling Serrantico '08 shows a nose of balsam, delicious blackberry and peppery potpourri. This velvety blend of merlot and syrah shows fine tannic texture on a long, clean palate. The NerEtna '08, from nerello mascalese and cappuccio, is a mineral-rich, fruit-laden nectar offering wonderful, satisfying drinkability. Nerello mascalese and a splash of merlot make up the Rasule Alte Rosso '09, which perfectly combines drinkability and complexity. On the attractive nose, fine hints of red berry fruit and aromatic herbs are to the fore.

● Serrantico '08	▼▼	6
● Etna Rosso NerEtna '08	▼▼	5
○ Rasule Alte Bianco '09	▼▼	4*
● Rasule Alte Rosso '09	▼▼	4*
● Pinot Nero '07	▼	7
● Pinot Nero '06	▽▽	7
● Rasule Alte Rosso '08	▽▽	4*
● Rasule Alte Rosso '07	▽▽	4*
● Rasule Alte Rosso '06	▽▽	4*
● Serrantico '07	▽▽	6
● Serrantico '06	▽▽	6
● Serrantico '05	▽▽	6

COS

SP 3 Agate-Chiaramonte km 14,300
97019 Vittoria [RG]
tel. 0932876145
www.cosvittoria.it

CELLAR SALES
PRE-BOOKED VISITS

ANNUAL PRODUCTION **160,000 bottles**
HECTARES UNDER VINE **25**
VITICULTURE METHOD **Organic**

"Titta" Cilia and Giusto Occhipinti, who have never lacked enthusiasm, dedication or a spirit of adventure, have now been producing fine wine for 30 years. Blessed with infinite curiosity and open minds, they have made their winery an experimental workshop, open to the new and never settling for second best. Today, the two friends, who have just inaugurated the new winery and an impressive amphora cellar, are two of the biggest names in natural wine production, based on respect for the land and its fruits.

Intense, with hints of sour cherry, Mediterranean herbs and iodine, the extremely drinkable Nero di Lupo '08, from nero d'Avola, is full-flavoured and supple. The excellent Cerasuolo di Vittoria Classico '08, from nero d'Avola and frappato, shows mineral and dynamic, with sweet notes of strawberry and redcurrants. The ruby Maldafrica '07, from cabernet sauvignon, nero d'Avola and merlot, has nice ripe fruit and impressive length. Equally attractive are the fresh, subtle Frappato '09 and the elegant, fleshy Ramì '09, from inzolia and grecanico.

● Cerasuolo di Vittoria Classico '08	▼▼	5
● Frappato '09	▼▼	4*
● Maldafrica '07	▼▼	5
● Nero di Lupo '08	▼▼	5
○ Ramì '09	▼▼	4*
● Pithos '08	▼	5
● Cerasuolo di Vittoria Classico '07	▽▽	5
● Cerasuolo di Vittoria Classico '06	▽▽	5
● Contrade Labirinto '04	▽▽	8
● Frappato '08	▽▽	4*
● Frappato '07	▽▽	4*
● Syre '05	▽▽	6

Cottanera

loc. Iannazzo
SP 89
95030 Castiglione di Sicilia [CT]
tel. 0942963601
www.cottanera.it

CELLAR SALES
PRE-BOOKED VISITS

ANNUAL PRODUCTION **300,000 bottles**
HECTARES UNDER VINE **55**
VITICULTURE METHOD **Conventional**

The Cambria family's fine estate has been producing wines on Etna for over 50 years. Around a decade ago, Gugliemo Cambria, who passed away recently, decided to completely restyle his products and focus on producing quality wines. Cottanera can now count not only on an extremely modern winery but also on 55 hectares of vineyards spread over a plateau 700 metres above sea level. This shift in policy has required time and energy but the flattering results show that it has paid off.

A great performance, and another Three Glasses, for the '07 Etna Rosso, from nerello mascalese and cappuccio. This wine shows a real sense of its volcanic terroir, integrating rich mineral, smoky notes with focused, elegant fruit. Full-flavoured and fresh, it has perfect nose-palate consistency, underpinned by silky tannins and a body of rare weight and length. The intense, deep, balsamic Mondeuse L'Ardenza '08, with close-woven, smooth tannins, missed top honours by a whisker. We also liked the mineral, dynamic Nerello Mascalese Fatagione '08, which is eminently quaffable.

● Etna Rosso '07	▼▼▼	6
● L'Ardenza '08	▼▼	5
● Fatagione '08	▼▼	5
● Grammonte '08	▼▼	5
○ Barbazzale Bianco '09	▼	3
● Barbazzale Rosso '09	▼	3
○ Etna Bianco '09	▼	4
● Nume '07	▼	5
● Sole di Sesta '07	▼	5
● Etna Rosso '06	▽▽▽	6
● Etna Rosso '05	▽▽▽	6
● Sole di Sesta '00	▽▽▽	7
● L'Ardenza '07	▽▽	5
● Nume '06	▽▽	5

★ Cusumano

C.DA SAN CARLO SS 113
90047 PARTINICO [PA]
TEL. 0918903456
www.cusumano.it

PRE-BOOKED VISITS

ANNUAL PRODUCTION **2,500,000 bottles**
HECTARES UNDER VINE **400**
VITICULTURE METHOD **Conventional**

In ten years, Alberto and Diego Cusumano's winery has gone from strength to strength, managing to make a name for itself on the difficult international markets. With estates in Salemi, Pachino, Butera and Piana degli Albanesi, they have managed to perfectly combine territoriality, impeccable product definition, modern marketing and well-judged, reasonable pricing. Their remarkable achievements, also in terms of image, have made this one of Sicily's leading wineries.

A monumental version of the Sàgana, from nero d'Avola, the '08, won Three Glasses with ease. Its impenetrable ruby hue immediately reveals its strong personality. The intense, beautiful notes of black mulberry, liquorice and topsoil, and the sumptuous, elegant tannins confirm its great class. Three other wines made the finals, proving the winery's good stylistic judgement: the charming, fruity Noà '08, from nero d'Avola, cabernet sauvignon and merlot; the sunny Mediterranean Cubia '09, from insolia; and the latest arrival, the silky, sweet Moscato dello Zucco '07, from moscato grapes, marking the return of a noble traditional Sicilian wine. The other labels are excellent.

● Sàgana '08	▼▼▼	5
○ Cubia '09	▼▼	4*
○ Moscato dello Zucco '07	▼▼	7
● Noà '08	▼▼	5
○ Angimbé '09	▼▼	4*
● Benuara '09	▼▼	4*
○ Jalé '09	▼▼	5
● Merlot '09	▼▼	4
● Nero d'Avola '09	▼▼	4*
● Pinot Nero '08	▼▼	5
⊙ Rosato '09	▼▼	3*
● Syrah '09	▼▼	4*
○ Alcamo Bianco '09	▼	3
○ Inzolia '09	▼	3
● Sàgana '07	▽▽▽	5
● Sàgana '06	▽▽▽	5

Destro

LOC. MONTELAGUARDIA
95036 RANDAZZO [CT]
TEL. 095937060
www.destrovini.com

ANNUAL PRODUCTION **N.A.**
HECTARES UNDER VINE **N.A.**
VITICULTURE METHOD **Conventional**

The Destro family winery, run by Antonino and his children Daniela and Giuseppe, covers 11 hectares and is situated 750 metres above sea level in Contrada Montelaguardia, near Randazzo. The vines are close to the ridges of the valley below Montenero, on the north-eastern slopes of Etna, and are buffeted by the changing winds throughout the day and night. Warehouses and renovated country villas house the vinification plants of this winery, which practices mainly natural farming methods.

The Etna Rosso Sciarakè '08, a monovarietal nerello mascalese, thoroughly deserved Three Glasses, captivating the panel with its splendid hints of violet, rose petals, black cherry and black pepper, against a backdrop of slate and clay. Juicy and perfectly balanced, it shows well-sculpted, lively tannins, and provides wonderfully enjoyable drinking. The Etna Bianco Isolanuda '09, a fine marriage of carricante and catarratto, also gave a fine performance. Zesty, with deliciously fresh notes of grass, acacia blossom and Mediterranean scrubland, its marked minerality makes it a satisfying, dynamic wine.

● Etna Rosso Sciarakè '08	▼▼▼	6*
○ Etna Bianco Isolanuda '09	▼▼	4*
● Etna Rosso Aspide '07	▼	4
● Etna Rosso Sciarakè '07	▽▽	5

★ Donnafugata

VIA SEBASTIANO LIPARI, 18
91025 MARSALA [TP]
TEL. 0923724200
www.donnafugata.it

CELLAR SALES
PRE-BOOKED VISITS

ANNUAL PRODUCTION 2,440,000 bottles
HECTARES UNDER VINE 328
VITICULTURE METHOD Conventional

The wines of Giacomo Rallo came as a shock to the then sleepy Sicilian wine industry when they made their debut back in 1983. Modern, well-made and drinkable, they eschewed the old Sicilian style of strong, structured wines. Almost 30 years after his arrival on the scene, which marked the beginning of the modern age in the region's winemaking, Donnafugata's wines continue to distinguish themselves for finesse and pleasureableness. Giacomo is now helped by his sons José and Antonio.

The winery champions, Mille e una Notte and Ben Ryé, are absent this year, left to age further in the cellars. The cadet of the dynasty, the Tancredi '07, stepped in to hold the fort, and performed so well it walked off with Three Glasses. This blend of nero d'Avola supported by cabernet sauvignon vaunts balsam, red berry fruit, tobacco and coffee aromas. On the soft, mouthfilling palate, it shows fine balance, thanks to the well-integrated, attractive oak. The whites also performed well. Ansonica Vigna di Gabri '09 is floral, refreshing and zesty, while the well-rounded, fruity Chardonnay La Fuga '09 reveals sea breeze and aromatic herbs.

Wine	Glasses	
● Tancredi '07	3 glasses	5
○ Contessa Entellina Chardonnay La Fuga '09	2 glasses	4
○ Contessa Entellina Chiarandà '08	2 glasses	6
○ Contessa Entellina V. di Gabri '09	2 glasses	4
○ Lighea '09	2 glasses	4
● Sedàra '09	2 glasses	4
● Contessa Entellina Milleunanotte '06	3 glasses (outline)	8
● Contessa Entellina Milleunanotte '05	3 glasses (outline)	8
● Contessa Entellina Milleunanotte '04	3 glasses (outline)	7
● Contessa Entellina Milleunanotte '03	3 glasses (outline)	7
● Contessa Entellina Milleunanotte '02	3 glasses (outline)	7
● Contessa Entellina Milleunanotte '01	3 glasses (outline)	7
● Contessa Entellina Milleunanotte '00	3 glasses (outline)	7
○ Passito di Pantelleria Ben Ryé '06	3 glasses (outline)	7

Duca di Salaparuta Vini Corvo

VIA NAZIONALE, SS 113
90014 CASTELDACCIA [PA]
TEL. 091945201
www.duca.it

CELLAR SALES
PRE-BOOKED VISITS

ANNUAL PRODUCTION 10,000,000 bottles
HECTARES UNDER VINE 155
VITICULTURE METHOD Conventional

The winemaking powerhouse created by the ILLVA group from Saronno brings together three iconic brands of Sicilian wine: Corvo, Duca di Salaparuta and Florio. Significant investments have built on the heritage of the two historic giants from Casteldaccia and Marsala, in particular the purchase of three estates in excellent wine country: Vajasindi, in Castiglione; Suor Marchesa, in Butera; and Risignolo at Salemi. They have an overall vision of Sicily's territory, whose fruits they purvey across the price range.

The premium line sees a fine performance on one hand from Duca Enrico, and the '06 vintage just missed the finals, with its fine, elegant aromatics around a mature, somewhat austere palate. On the other, the sumptuously sweet Malvasia delle Lipari Passito Florio '09 has nice hints of balsam. The well-crafted Grillo Kados Risignolo '09 shows focused notes of almond and hints of aniseed over weighty pulp and full flavour on the palate. The Nero d'Avola Passo delle Mule '08 shows consistent, intense varietal fruit while the Colomba Platino L '09 reveals lovely balance on the palate. We enjoyed the Zibibbo Liquoroso Morsi di Luce '07.

Wine	Glasses	
○ Colomba Platino L '09	2 glasses	4
● Duca Enrico '06	2 glasses	8
○ Florio Malvasia delle Lipari Passito '09	2 glasses	6
○ Florio Morsi di Luce '07	2 glasses	5
○ Kados Tenuta Risignolo '09	2 glasses	4
● Passo delle Mule Tenuta Suor Marchesa '08	2 glasses	4
⊙ Corvo Rosa '09	1 glass	4
● Corvo Rosso '08	1 glass	4
○ Florio Ambar Liquoroso Moscato	1 glass	4
○ Florio Passito di Pantelleria Liquoroso Zighidì	1 glass	4
○ Irmana Bianco '09	1 glass	4
● Irmana Rosso '09	1 glass	4
● Lavico Tenuta Vajasindi '07	1 glass	4
● Nawari Tenuta Vajasindi '07	1 glass	6
● Duca Enrico '03	3 glasses (outline)	7

Fatascià

VIA MAZZINI, 40
90139 PALERMO
TEL. 091332505
www.fatascia.com

PRE-BOOKED VISITS

ANNUAL PRODUCTION 390,000 bottles
HECTARES UNDER VINE 30
VITICULTURE METHOD Conventional

The winery started out in 2000 with a strip of the Abbazia Santa Anastasia estate, and soon became an independent operation run by Stefania Lena, who deals with production and technical decisions, and her husband Giuseppe Natoli, who looks after the commercial side of things. Fatascià is the name they give the blackcap on Pantelleria, and this symbol of dynamism and independence is perfectly suited to the couple's entrepreneurial spirit. They have been vinifying their grapes themselves for some years now, in Balestrate's historic Baglio Abate.

We saw another consistent performance from Stefania's wines: the nero d'Avola Almanera '08 shows great concentration, with an intense nose of red fruit and spice, over upfront tannins on the dense, muscular palate. Cherry jam and balsamic hints accompany a well-rounded, crisp palate on the Aliré '08, from nero d'Avola and syrah. The fine Syrah '09 vaunts floral scents and spice over a soft, vibrant palate. The Rosso del Presidente '08, from a 50-50 blend of cabernet franc and nero d'Avola, shows elegant toastiness on the nose. Its youth is still evident on the palate. The best of the whites is L'Enigma '09, a stylish, fresh-tasting blend of grillo, grecanico and inzolia.

● Aliré '08	**YY**	4
● Almanera '08	**YY**	4
○ L'Enigma '09	**YY**	4
● Rosso del Presidente '08	**YY**	5
● Syrah '09	**YY**	4
○ Inzolia & Grillo '09	**Y**	4
● L'Insolente Noir '08	**Y**	6
● Nero d'Avola '09	**Y**	3
● Almanera '01	YYY	3*
● Almanera '07	YY	4*
● Almanera '06	YY	4*
● L'Insolente '07	YY	7
● L'Insolente '06	YY	7
● Rosso del Presidente '07	YY	5

Tenuta di Fessina

LOC. CONTRADA ROVITTELLO
VIA NAZIONALE 120, 22
95012 CASTIGLIONE DI SICILIA [CT]
TEL. 057155284
www.cuntu.it

PRE-BOOKED VISITS

ANNUAL PRODUCTION 60,000 bottles
HECTARES UNDER VINE 15
VITICULTURE METHOD Organic

A further four hectares have recently been added to the estate in Castiglione di Sicilia owned by Silvia Maestrelli, a Tuscan winegrower, her husband Roberto Silva and the oenologist-agronomist Federico Curtaz. The vineyards are planted to nerello mascalese and are almost all over 60 years old. The new acquisition, which joins the land already managed at Segesta, in the province of Trapani, and at Noto, demonstrates how this good-natured, enthusiastic trio have fallen even deeper in love with Sicily, as they would be the first to admit.

The Etna Rosso Musmeci '08 almost took top honours. This successful marriage of nerello mascalese and cappuccio, from vines over a century old, fully confirms its class. On the nose, layered, focused notes of cherry, blackcurrant, sweet spices, dried roses and pencil lead pave the way for an exuberant palate, with lovely acidity supported by smooth, elegant tannins and great length. But our tastings showed that the whole of the winery's range is witnessing significant improvements in quality, as in the case of the fruit-heavy, pleasurable Etna Rosso Erse '09, the spicy Laeneo '09, from nerello cappuccio, and the vibrant Ero '09, from nero d'Avola.

● Etna Rosso Musmeci '08	**YY**	7
● Ero '09	**YY**	5*
● Etna Rosso Erse '09	**YY**	5*
● Laeneo '09	**YY**	5
○ Se '09	**Y**	4
● Etna Rosso Musmeci '07	YYY	7
● Etna Rosso Erse '08	YY	5

Feudi del Pisciotto

LOC. PISCIOTTO
93015 NISCEMI [CL]
TEL. 0577742903
www.castellare.it

PRE-BOOKED VISITS

ANNUAL PRODUCTION **220,000 bottles**
HECTARES UNDER VINE **50**
VITICULTURE METHOD **Organic**

Judging by the spectacular 18th-century winepress, which provides symbolic access to the modern winery, wine has always been made in Paolo Panerai's Sicilian estate. Its 50 or so hectares are situated in the countryside around Niscemi, and occupy a single hillside plot. Spectacular views can be had from the tower of the old farmstead. In agreement with the designers of the labels, a percentage of Feudi's profits has been earmarked to restore a Sicilian work of art, namely Eterno, Giacomo Serpotta's series of stucco sculptures in Palermo.

Repeating last year's excellent performance, the wines presented at our selections confirmed the great quality and extreme reliability of the whole range. Three Glasses went to the extraordinary Nero d'Avola Versace '08, an elegant wine with real character, which marries complex notes of blackcurrant and plum with hints of balsam, followed by tight-knit texture and admirable balance in the mouth. The delicious Frappato Carolina Marengo '08 made our finals, with its elegant blackberry and dark berry fruit over a fleshy, lively, well-balanced palate. The intense Grillo Carolina Marengo '08 is also impressive.

● Nero d'Avola Versace '08	YYY (black)	5
● Frappato Carolina Marengo '08	YY (black)	5
○ Baglio del Sole Inzolia Catarratto '09	YY (black)	3*
● Cabernet Sauvignon Missoni '08	YY (black)	5
○ Grillo Carolina Marengo '08	YY (black)	5
○ Baglio del Sole Inzolia '09	Y (black)	3
● Baglio del Sole Nero d'Avola '08	Y (black)	4
○ Chardonnay Alberta Ferretti '08	Y (black)	5
● Merlot Valentino '08	Y (black)	5
● Nero d'Avola Versace '07	YYY	5*
● Baglio del Sole Nero d'Avola '07	YY	4*
○ Chardonnay Alberta Ferretti '07	YY	5
● Frappato Carolina Marengo '07	YY	5
○ Grillo Carolina Marengo '07	YY	5

Feudo Maccari

C.DA MACCARI
SP PACHINO-NOTO, KM 13,500
96017 NOTO [SR]
TEL. 0931596894
www.feudomaccari.it

CELLAR SALES
PRE-BOOKED VISITS

ANNUAL PRODUCTION **166,000 bottles**
HECTARES UNDER VINE **50**
VITICULTURE METHOD **Organic**

We saw an excellent performance from the beautiful estate of Antonio Moretti, who ten years ago chose this location for a new adventure in the world of wine, after experience at the top in his native Tuscany. Feudo Maccari covers 160 hectares between Noto and Pachino, in one of the best wine areas in Sicily. Now that the modern winery is fully up and running, Antonio can better exploit the potential of 50 hectares of vineyards all planted with bush vines, according to traditional practice in this part of Sicily.

The simply amazing Saia '08 is the best vintage ever of this Nero d'Avola, offering attractive red fruit with charming, delicate swathes of balsam. On the palate, it shows austere, elegant and long, combining lovely freshness and majestic fruit in a close-knit structure with perfect maturity. Almost as good is the stylish Mahâris '08, from nero d'Avola, cabernet sauvignon and syrah, revealing a balsamic, mineral, spicy nose over a deep, lingering palate. We also liked their only white, the lively, drinkable Grillo '09, with its subtle tropical fruits and summer flowers.

● Saia '08	YYY (black)	5*
● Mahâris '08	YY (black)	7
○ Grillo '09	YY (black)	4*
● Nero D'Avola '09	YY (black)	4*
○ Sultana '09	YY (black)	6
⊙ Rosè di Nero D'Avola '09	Y (black)	4
● Saia '07	YYY	5*
● Saia '06	YYY	5
● Mahâris '07	YY	7
● Mahâris '06	YY	7
● Mahâris '05	YY	6
● ReNoto '07	YY	4*
● ReNoto Nero d'Avola '08	YY	4*
⊙ ReNoto Rosè '08	YY	3*

Feudo Principi di Butera

C.DA DELIELLA
93011 BUTERA [CL]
TEL. 0934347726
www.feudobutera.it

CELLAR SALES
PRE-BOOKED VISITS

ANNUAL PRODUCTION **800,000 bottles**
HECTARES UNDER VINE **180**
VITICULTURE METHOD **Conventional**

A painstakingly tended estate of 320 hectares, of which 180 are already under vine, is only a small portion of the vast tracts of land that belonged to the Principi di Deliella. This is the Zonin family's Sicilian adventure, and here, close to the sea, on the hillsides between Riesi and Butera, in 1997 they created a model farm, in keeping with the extraordinary beauty of the surrounding landscape. The admirably restored old enclosed farmstead, and the modern underground winery are full of atmosphere.

Since the Nero d'Avola Deliella was not ready for our tastings, this year's best wine was the debutante Symposio '07, a blend of cabernet sauvignon, merlot and petit verdot. Its intense garnet accompanies a well-rounded, complex nose, with blackberry and blueberry over balsam and cocoa powder. The leisurely, satisfying palate displays silky tannins. The elegant, Mediterranean Riesi '08, from nero d'Avola and syrah has impact, proffering ripe, juicy fruit. The Nero d'Avola '08 gave a first-rate performance, with delicious tones of cherry jam, as did the fresh, attractive Merlot '08. The rest of the wines are good.

● Merlot '08	TT	4
● Nero d'Avola '08	TT	4*
● Riesi '08	TT	4
● Symposio '07	TT	5
● Cabernet Sauvignon '08	T	4
○ Chardonnay '09	T	4
○ Insolia '09	T	4
● Syrah '08	T	4
● Cabernet Sauvignon '00	YYY	7
● Deliella '05	YYY	7
● Deliella '02	YYY	8
● Deliella '00	YYY	6
● Deliella '06	YY	7
● Nero d'Avola '07	YY	4*

★ Firriato

VIA TRAPANI, 4
91027 PACECO [TP]
TEL. 0923882755
www.firriato.it

CELLAR SALES
PRE-BOOKED VISITS

ANNUAL PRODUCTION **4,250,000 bottles**
HECTARES UNDER VINE **320**
VITICULTURE METHOD **Certified organic**

The countryside around Trapani, Etna, Castiglione di Sicilia, and the island of Favignana in the Egadi, are home to the three production centres of this important operation, run by Vinzia and Salvatore Di Gaetano. The couple are increasingly turning towards organic methods and the natural differentiation of individual wines from their various estates. The aim is to produce impeccable, well-made products that nicely express their terroir. All consumers and price ranges are catered for.

Yet another well-deserved Three Glasses for the Nero d'Avola Harmonium from Borgo Guarini. The '08 is a wine of incredible personality and character. Purplish and inky, with hints of blackberry, black plum, spice and autumn leaves, it combines power and vitality with wonderful drinkability. The extremely elegant Etna Rosso Cavanera Rovo delle Coturnie '08, from nerello mascalese and cappuccio, proffers delicate violets, black cherries and slate, and also came close to receiving top honours. The Camelot '08 from Baglio Sorìa, a blend of cabernet sauvignon and merlot, is on great form, and give balsam behind ripe currant and blackberry fruit. The other wines are all extremely good.

● Harmonium '08	TTT	6*
● Camelot '08	TT	6
● Etna Rosso Cavanera Rovo delle Coturnie '08	TT	6
○ Altavilla della Corte Grillo '09	TT	3*
● Altavilla della Corte Nero d'Avola Cabernet Sauvignon '08	TT	4
○ Chiaramonte Ansonica '09	TT	4*
● Chiaramonte Nero d'Avola '08	TT	4*
○ Etna Bianco Cavanera Ripa di Scorciavacca '09	TT	5
○ Passito L'Ecrù '08	TT	6
○ Quater Bianco '09	TT	5
● Quater Rosso '08	TT	5*
● Ribeca '08	TT	6
○ Santagostino Bianco Baglio Sorìa '09	TT	5
● Santagostino Rosso Baglio Sorìa '08	TT	5
● Harmonium '07	YYY	5*
● Harmonium '06	YYY	5*

Gulfi

C.DA PATRIA
97012 CHIARAMONTE GULFI [RG]
TEL. 0932921654
www.gulfi.it

PRE-BOOKED VISITS
ROOMS AND FOOD

ANNUAL PRODUCTION **180,000 bottles**
HECTARES UNDER VINE **75**
VITICULTURE METHOD **Certified organic**

The Gulfi winery developed around a fairly simple idea: rediscovering nero d'Avola in its native territory, to restore dignity and identity to both. Vito Catania, its driving force, recalls that when he was a boy, wine was never referred to in general terms, but identified by its district of origin. After a few years' "warming up", we now finally have the wines, no longer bearing generic names such as Nero d'Avola, but with the district of origin clearly specified on the label.

As usual, the quality of the products is extremely high, starting with the extraordinary Neromaccarj '07, that confidently takes home Three Glasses. Blackberry jam, forest floor and a nice iodine note come together in this soft, sensuous wine, made even more enjoyable by refreshing acidity. The other nero d'Avola vineyard selection, Nerobaronj '07, is satisfying and brimming with silky tannins. The winery's warhorse, the Rossojbleo '09, also from nero d'Avola, has a mineral nose with elegant hints of mulberry. This lively, fruit-infused wine is rendered even more drinkable by its close-woven, focused tannins.

● Neromàccarj '07	▼▼▼	6
● Nerobaronj '07	▼▼	6
● Rossojbleo '09	▼▼	4
○ Carjcanti '08	▼	5
● Cerasuolo di Vittoria '09	▼	4
● Reseca '06	▼	6
○ Valcanzjria '09	▼	4
● Neromàccarj '04	▽▽▽	6
● Nerosanlorè '05	▽▽▽	6
○ Carjcanti '07	▽▽	5
○ Carjcanti '06	▽▽	5
● Cerasuolo di Vittoria '08	▽▽	4*
● Nerobaronj '06	▽▽	6
● Neromàccarj '05	▽▽	6

Marabino

C.DA BUONIVINI
SP ROSOLINI - PACHINO KM 8,5
97017 NOTO [SR]
TEL. 3355284101
www.marabino.it

CELLAR SALES
PRE-BOOKED VISITS
ROOMS AND FOOD

ANNUAL PRODUCTION **130,000 bottles**
HECTARES UNDER VINE **27**
VITICULTURE METHOD **Certified organic**

The winery was established in 2002 by Nello Messina, who has now handed over its running to his son Pierpaolo. It operates alongside Natura Iblea, involved in organic farming for over 20 years, and the magnificent Relais Torre Marabino. The aim of the three complementary operations is to promote the territory through excellence. The vineyards, located in the Eloro and Noto DOC zones in the districts of Buonivini and Barone are being converted to biodynamic methods. The best is the nero d'Avola selection, Vigna di Archimede.

The Moscato della Torre '09 confirms last year's excellent results: intense, focused sage and rose interweave with mineral notes, conferring fine elegance on concentrated white peach fruit. Nose-palate consistency is perfect, with sweetness sustained by lively acidity. We loved the Eloro Nero d'Avola Archimede '08, showing concentrated ripe fruit and spice over a stylish, fleshy palate. The admirable Chardonnay Eureka '09 is overflowing with floral aromas, leading into fresh, generous fruit on the palate, rounded off by a lovely pineapple finish. The varietal character of the Noto Nero d'Avola '08 is commendable, while the Eloro Nero d'Avola Rosa Nera '09 is fresh and attractive.

● Eloro Archimede '08	▼▼	6
○ Moscato di Noto Moscato della Torre '09	▼▼	6
⊙ Eloro Rosa Nera '09	▼▼	4
○ Eureka '09	▼▼	4
● Noto Nero d'Avola '08	▼▼	4
● Don Paolo '06	▽▽	5
● Eloro Archimede '07	▽▽	5
● Eloro Archimede '06	▽▽	5
● Eloro Don Pasquale '07	▽▽	4*
○ Moscato di Noto Moscato della Torre '08	▽▽	6
○ Moscato di Noto Moscato della Torre '07	▽▽	6
○ Moscato di Noto Moscato della Torre '06	▽▽	6

Martinez

via Mazara, 29
91205 Marsala [TP]
tel. 0923981050
www.martinez.it

CELLAR SALES

ANNUAL PRODUCTION 400,000 bottles
HECTARES UNDER VINE 60
VITICULTURE METHOD Conventional

A story of 150 years spanning six generations indissolubly links the Martinez family to Marsala. In recent years, the wine has been trying to regain its centuries-old reputation and recover from its fall from favour, which has also affected those growers who strive for quality and to preserve the tradition of one of the best-known wines in the world. The case of this winery, currently run by the dynamic Carlo Martinez, is indicative, as it only releases ten per cent of its Riserva on the market.

The Vergine Riserva '95 made the finals thanks to a nose of superb complexity and finesse, with focused notes of carob, Virginia tobacco, medicinal herbs and hints of balsam. On the palate, it reveals excellent alcohol-acid balance with a long, clean finish. The Vergine Riserva Exito '82, whose name comes from the Spanish for "success", has a more essential, yet intense, elegant bouquet, followed by a pleasantly dry palate. The more classic Vergine '02 shows hazelnut, toastiness and orange marmalade. The Superiore Riserva Dolce has attractive hints of rhubarb and chocolate while the Superiore Riserva Secco shows gentian, green tea and bay leaves. Both are excellent.

O Marsala Vergine Ris. '95	▼▼	5
O Marsala Dolce Sup. Ris.	▼▼	3*
O Marsala Secco Sup. Ris.	▼▼	3*
O Marsala Vergine '02	▼▼	4*
O Marsala Vergine Exito Ris. '82	▼▼	6
O Laus Malvasia Liquoroso	▼	4
O Laus Zibibbo Liquoroso	▼	4
O Menhir Liquoroso	▼	3

Morgante

c.da Racalmare
92020 Grotte [AG]
tel. 0922945579
www.morgantevini.it

CELLAR SALES
PRE-BOOKED VISITS

ANNUAL PRODUCTION 335,000 bottles
HECTARES UNDER VINE 55
VITICULTURE METHOD Conventional

Grotte offers a landscape of rare charm, amidst abandoned sulphur mines, boundless fields of wheat, almond groves and vineyards. The Morgante family have been working here for generations and in 1994 started to produce their own wine. Nero d'Avola is their raw material and there is no temptation to introduce non-native varieties. Here, the variety expresses its character and generous intensity to the full. Antonio and his sons Carmelo and Giovanni have been supported in the rows since 1997 by the technical guidance of Riccardo Cottarella.

The Nero d'Avola Don Antonio '08's ninth appointment with Three Glasses is merely postponed. Although just missing the top award, it shows concentration, intensity and focused varietal notes of ripe fruit, nicely merging with mineral, balsamic tones of great finesse. The supple, elegant palate displays silky tannins and good finish. The Nero d'Avola '09 nearly made the finals and impressed us with its vitality and drinkability. The nicely fragrant "lightweight" Nero d'Avola, the Scinthilì '09, proffers a nose of cherries and capers with gorgeous fruit, and is best enjoyed chilled.

● Don Antonio '08	▼▼	5
● Nero d'Avola '09	▼▼	3*
● Schinthilì '09	▼▼	3*
● Don Antonio '07	▽▽▽	5
● Don Antonio '06	▽▽▽	5
● Don Antonio '03	▽▽▽	5
● Don Antonio '02	▽▽▽	5
● Don Antonio '01	▽▽▽	5
● Don Antonio '00	▽▽▽	6
● Don Antonio '05	▽▽	5
● Don Antonio '04	▽▽	5

★ Palari

LOC. SANTO STEFANO BRIGA
C.DA BARNA
98137 MESSINA
TEL. 090630194
www.palari.it

PRE-BOOKED VISITS

ANNUAL PRODUCTION **50,000 bottles**
HECTARES UNDER VINE **7**
VITICULTURE METHOD **Conventional**

The estate comprises seven hectares of steep land, with slopes often over 80 per cent, hemmed in by stone terracing. The vines, some very old, are bush-trained, and provide low yields of often unfamiliar varieties such as acitana and galatena. There is also the splendid 18th-century family villa, with views over the Strait of Messina, where an artisanal approach to vinification and maturation is adopted to produce the gems of architect, wine man and globetrotter Salvatore Geraci. Vital assistance is provided by his brother Giampiero and oenologist Donato Lanati.

The Faro Palari '08 wins the umpteenth Three Glasses of its stunning career. This blend is based on nerello mascalese, topped up with small amounts of acitana and galatena, as well as limited quantities of other local varieties. An intense garnet accompanies an extraordinary nose, with elegant notes of red and black berry fruit, mint and pencil lead. The palate is a velvety hymn to elegance, with great grip. It this profile that has made this a cult Italian wine. The superb Rosso del Soprano '08, from the same grapes as the Faro, also made the finals and shows seductive forest fruits, sorb apple and liquorice.

● Faro Palari '08	TTT	7
● Rosso del Soprano '08	TT	5*
● Faro Palari '07	YYY+	7
● Faro Palari '06	YYY	7
● Faro Palari '05	YYY	7*
● Faro Palari '04	YYY	8
● Faro Palari '03	YYY	7
● Faro Palari '02	YYY	7
● Faro Palari '01	YYY	7
● Faro Palari '00	YYY	7
● Rosso del Soprano '07	YYY	5

Passopisciaro

LOC. PASSOPISCIARO
VIA SANTO SPIRITO
95030 CASTIGLIONE DI SICILIA [CT]
TEL. 0578267110
www.passopisciaro.com

ANNUAL PRODUCTION **58,800 bottles**
HECTARES UNDER VINE **29**
VITICULTURE METHOD **Conventional**

Certain places and people seem destined to meet, and when they do, something unique is created. This is what happened with Etna and Andrea Franchetti of Tenuta di Trinoro. On the slopes of the volcano, between Randazzo and Castiglione, he found a new place to express his boundless passion for wine, and his utmost respect for local resources and traditions, which he contributed to promoting by organizing the Contrade event.

Passopisciaro '08, a blend of nerello mascalese from old vines on the northern slopes of Etna, is back in the finals with its complex bouquet of red berry fruit, iron filings and intriguing animal notes. On the palate, it is caressing, elegant and lingering. Contrada Porcaria '08, a vineyard selection from 80-year-old nerello mascalese planted on a plateau at 600-800 metres above sea level, is intense, sensual and meaty on the nose, unveiling great finesse and length on the finish. The elegant, nicely acidic Contrada Rampante '08 is from 100-year-old nerello mascalese vines. Equally charming are the other two nerello selections, Sciaranuova '08 and Chiappemacine '08.

● Contrada Porcaria '08	TT	8
● Passopisciaro '08	TT	6
● Contrada Chiappemacine '08	TT	7
● Contrada Rampante '08	TT	7
● Contrada Sciaranuova '08	TT	7
● Franchetti '08	TT	8
● Passopisciaro '04	YYY	6
● Franchetti '06	YY	8
○ Guardiola '07	YY	6
● Passopisciaro '07	YY	6
● Passopisciaro '06	YY	6
● Passopisciaro '05	YY	6
○ Passopisciaro Bianco '08	YY	6

Carlo Pellegrino

VIA DEL FANTE, 39
91025 MARSALA [TP]
TEL. 0923719911
www.carlopellegrino.it

CELLAR SALES
PRE-BOOKED VISITS

ANNUAL PRODUCTION **6,900,000 bottles**
HECTARES UNDER VINE **150**
VITICULTURE METHOD **Conventional**

With over 130 years of history behind it, Pellegrino forges ahead. The winery is run by descendants of the family, chairman Pietro Alagna, managing director Benedetto Renda and Massimo Bellina, Emilio Ridolfi, Paola Alagna and Caterina Tumbarello, who hold various other positions. There are two product lines, Carlo Pellegrino for the Marsalas and other fortified wines, and Duca di Castelmonte for the rest, coming from the three production facilities based in Marsala and Pantelleria.

Three Glasses go to the Riserva 1981, marking an important step in the rehabilitation of Marsala, which remained somewhat in the shade while other emerging names in Sicily hogged the limelight. It's impossible not to be impressed by the elegance and complexity of this Vergine, with tight-knit aromas of walnutskin, iodine and spice over dried fruits. On the palate, it shows authoritative and statuesque, with splendid acidity underpinning monumental structure. In the Duca di Castelmonte line, we liked the spicy, silky Tripudium '07, from nero d'Avola, syrah and cabernet sauvignon, and the Passito di Pantelleria Nes '08, from moscato, pleasantly piquant and well-focused on the palate.

○ Marsala Vergine Ris. '81	TTT+	8
● Dinari del Duca Syrah Duca di Castelmonte '07	TT	4
○ Passito di Pantelleria Nes Duca di Castelmonte '08	TT	6
○ Tripudium Bianco Duca di Castelmonte '09	TT	4
● Tripudium Rosso Duca di Castelmonte '07	TT	5
○ Dinari del Duca Grillo Duca di Castelmonte '09	T	4
● Dinari del Duca Nero d'Avola Duca di Castelmonte '07	T	4
○ Gibelè Duca di Castelmonte '09	T	4
○ Duca di Castelmonte Passito di Pantelleria Nes '06	YY	6
○ Passito di Pantelleria Nes '05	YY	6
● Tripudium Rosso Duca di Castelmonte '06	YY	5
● Tripudium Rosso Duca di Castelmonte '05	YY	5

Pietradolce

FRAZ. SOLICCHIATA
C.DA MONAGAZZI
95012 CASTIGLIONE DI SICILIA [CT]
TEL. 3484037792
www.pietradolce.it

CELLAR SALES
PRE-BOOKED VISITS
ROOMS AND FOOD

ANNUAL PRODUCTION **5,000 bottles**
HECTARES UNDER VINE **8**
VITICULTURE METHOD **Conventional**

Just over five years ago, the well-known nursery owners and wine collectors Michele and Mario Faro decided to change sides and start producing wine themselves, so they took in hand the family vineyards situated at Solicchiata and Passopisciaro, planted with 50-year-old bush vines in a plot 700 metres above sea level. The small, well-equipped winery is in Riposto, in one of their business premises. They will soon be taking the next step – building a new, larger winemaking facility next to a new vineyard.

Again this year there were Three authoritative Glasses for the extraordinarily elegant Etna Rosso Archineri '08, a monovarietal nerello mascalese. Intense, complex hints of wild berries, spice, charming florality and balsam develop over a backdrop of elegant mineral tones and well-integrated fine-grained oak. Follow-through on the palate is textbook stuff, with lashings of fruit backed up by tannins and acidity providing character, balance and great drinkability.

● Etna Rosso Archineri '08	TTT	5*
● Etna Rosso Archineri '07	YYY	5*

★★ Planeta

C.DA DISPENSA
92013 MENFI [AG]
TEL. 091327965
www.planeta.it

PRE-BOOKED VISITS

ANNUAL PRODUCTION 2,200,000 bottles
HECTARES UNDER VINE 390
VITICULTURE METHOD Conventional

Alessio, Francesca and Santi Planeta, who run the prestigious family brand that revolutionized winemaking in Sicily, have set themselves another challenge. After the estates at Menfi, Sambuca, Noto, Vittoria and, most recently Etna, at Castiglione di Sicilia, which produce wines with a real sense of place, the Planetas have acquired a plot at Capo Milazzo. Their aim is to produce Mamertino, a wine famous in Roman times. Considering their previous successes, wine lovers and critics have understandably high expectations.

Once again, the golden, light green-tinged Cometa '09, a monovarietal Fiano, walked away with Three Glasses. Stylish and layered, on the nose it proffers grapefruit, hazelnut, acacia blossom, honey and saffron. On the palate, this drinkable, seductive wine is assertive, surefooted, lively and creamy. A whole series of '08s also made the finals, from the plush, fleshy Chardonnay to the supple, balsamic Syrah and the intense, varietal Nero d'Avola Santa Cecilia. We were also impressed by the two latest arrivals: the fragrant Plumbago '08, from nero d'Avola, and the savoury, minerally Carricante '09. The other wines are excellent.

○ Cometa '09	🍷🍷🍷	6
○ Chardonnay '08	🍷🍷	6
● Santa Cecilia '08	🍷🍷	5
● Syrah '08	🍷🍷	5
○ Alastro '09	🍷🍷	4*
○ Carricante '09	🍷🍷	5
● Cerasuolo di Vittoria '09	🍷🍷	4*
● Merlot '08	🍷🍷	5
● Plumbago '08	🍷🍷	4
● Burdese '05	🍸🍸🍸	5*
● Burdese '03	🍸🍸🍸	5
○ Cometa '08	🍸🍸🍸	6
○ Cometa '05	🍸🍸🍸	5
● Merlot '04	🍸🍸🍸	5
● Santa Cecilia '06	🍸🍸🍸	5

Tenute Rapitalà

C.DA RAPITALÀ
90043 CAMPOREALE [PA]
TEL. 092437233
www.rapitala.it

CELLAR SALES
PRE-BOOKED VISITS

ANNUAL PRODUCTION 3,200,000 bottles
HECTARES UNDER VINE 175
VITICULTURE METHOD Conventional

A long love story unites Gigi Guarrasi and Hugues de la Gatinais as well as a great passion for Sicily and its wine. Their wonderful story continues with the new generation, represented by Laurent, who now runs the winery, which some years ago became part of Gruppo Italiano Vini. The estate has a selection of vineyards ideal for the production of quality wines on the hillsides rolling down from Camporeale towards Alcamo and the sea, with elevations of between 300 and 600 metres.

The '08 Solinero and Hugonis, respectively a Syrah and a blend of cabernet sauvignon and nero d'Avola, are still maturing so will have to wait until next year. The Chardonnay Conte Hugues '08 confirms its reliability, with a mature nose, tending towards austerity in its fine mineral hints integrated with unobtrusive oak. On the mouthfilling palate, it displays a Mediterranean warmth all its own. The extremely pleasing Catarratto-Chardonnay Casalj '09 proffers elegant floral notes over fresh, dense fruit. Intense ripe fruit and good balance on the palate distinguish the Nero d'Avola Campo Reale '09. The Bouquet '09, from grillo, sauvignon blanc and viognier, is very attractive.

○ Bouquet '09	🍷🍷	4
● Campo Reale Nero d'Avola '09	🍷🍷	4
○ Casalj '09	🍷🍷	4
○ Conte Hugues Bernard de la Gatinais '08	🍷🍷	5
○ Cielo d'Alcamo '08	🍷	6
● Nuhar '08	🍷	4
○ Piano Maltese Bianco '09	🍷	4
● Hugonis '01	🍸🍸🍸	7
● Solinero '03	🍸🍸🍸	6
● Solinero '00	🍸🍸🍸	6
● Hugonis '07	🍸🍸	6
● Hugonis '06	🍸🍸	6
● Solinero '06	🍸🍸	6

Riofavara

C.DA FAVARA
SP 49 ISPICA - PACHINO
97014 ISPICA [RG]
TEL. 0932705130
www.riofavara.it

CELLAR SALES
PRE-BOOKED VISITS

ANNUAL PRODUCTION 70,000 bottles
HECTARES UNDER VINE 16
VITICULTURE METHOD Certified organic

The turnaround for this winery came in 1994, when Massimo and Marianta Padova began to introduce strict quality criteria and to focus on the territory of Ispica and Val di Noto, with its deep-rooted traditional values. They started with nero d'Avola, which expresses its true character in these limestone soils. In addition to nero d'Avola, the 16 hectares under vine are planted to moscato bianco, the basic ingredient of Moscato di Noto, as well as inzolia, grecanico and chardonnay.

Eloro Sciavé '08, a selection from the winery's best plots of nero d'Avola, nearly made the finals for the second year running. Although less mature than the '07, it shows finesse and intensity, with ripe fruit swathed in balsam. On the solid, clean-tasting palate, good structure is underpinned by taut tannins. The Eloro '07 delights the nose with charming hints of sea breeze, leather and cherry jam, followed by a well-rounded palate. The Marzaiolo '09 is an impressive blend of inzolia, grecanico and chardonnay. Yellow-fleshed fruit, aniseed and elegant mineral notes encore on a lovely full-flavoured palate. The fruit-heavy Nero d'Avola San Basilio '08 provides pleasant drinking.

● Eloro '07	🍷🍷	4
● Eloro Nero d'Avola Sciavé '08	🍷🍷	5
○ Marzaiolo '09	🍷🍷	4
● San Basilio '08	🍷🍷	4
● Eloro Nero d'Avola Sciavé '07	YY	5
● Eloro Nero d'Avola Sciavé '06	YY	5
○ Marzaiolo '08	YY	4*
○ Marzaiolo '07	YY	4*
○ Moscato di Nota Notissimo '08	YY	4*
○ Moscato di Nota Notissimo '07	YY	4

Girolamo Russo

LOC. PASSOPISCIARO
VIA REGINA MARGHERITA, 78
95012 CASTIGLIONE DI SICILIA [CT]
TEL. 3283840247
www.girolamorusso.it

CELLAR SALES
PRE-BOOKED VISITS

ANNUAL PRODUCTION 12,500 bottles
HECTARES UNDER VINE 16
VITICULTURE METHOD Certified organic

A degree in literature and a piano diploma are unusual qualifications for a winemaker, yet the sensitivity and open-mindedness fostered by such an education are ideal for someone who wants to make great wines. Giuseppe Russo has succeeded brilliantly and his background clearly influenced his decision to focus on the strong territorial identity of Etna, embodied in his family's old vineyards at Castiglione di Sicilia and Randazzo.

The skill of a producer is measured in part in consistency of his results, and Giuseppe Russo has not disappointed. His Etna Rosso Feudo '08 reached the finals with a nose of great charm and complexity, showing clean red berry fruit and autumn leaves swathed in elegant balsam and spice. Mineral notes return on the authoritative palate to be exalted by plush, generous texture. The San Lorenzo '08 reveals admirable mineral finesse and generous fruit leading to a solid, aristocratic palate with a lingering finish. The trio rounds off with the Etna Rosso 'A Rina' '08, showing real maturity in an austere, well-crafted body. This is an impressive all-round performance.

● Etna Rosso Feudo '08	🍷🍷	6
● Etna Rosso 'A Rina' '08	🍷🍷	6
● Etna Rosso San Lorenzo '08	🍷🍷	6
● Etna Rosso Feudo '07	YYY	6
● Etna Feudo '06	YY	6
● Etna Rosso 'A Rina' '07	YY	5
● Etna Rosso 'A Rina' '06	YY	5
● Etna Rosso San Lorenzo '07	YY	6
● Etna Rosso San Lorenzo '06	YY	6

Settesoli

SS 115
92013 Menfi [AG]
tel. 092577111
www.mandrarossa.it

CELLAR SALES
PRE-BOOKED VISITS

ANNUAL PRODUCTION **20,000,000 bottles**
HECTARES UNDER VINE **6,500**
VITICULTURE METHOD **Conventional**

Settesoli is one of Europe's largest co-operative wineries. Established over 50 years ago, with time it has become one of the most dynamic and reliable producers in Sicily. It has been run since 1973 by Diego Planeta, who has skilfully managed its transformation – not an easy task for an operation that boasts no fewer than 6,500 hectares under vine, 2,300 member growers, and produces tens of millions of bottles.

Once again, the Mandrarossa wines are extremely convincing and the best of the range. Once again, Nero d'Avola Chartago, easily took top honours for an outstanding '08 vintage. This deep, weighty wine with a rich bouquet of extremely elegant incense, chocolate and attractive oak, shows lovely pulp, length and concentration in the mouth. The well-executed Bendicò '08, a blend of nero d'Avola, merlot and syrah, also flew into the finals. Austere, with stylish overtones of tobacco on the nose, it shows elegant, velvety and lingering on the palate. The rest of the range is excellent and available at extremely reasonable prices.

● Cartagho Mandrarossa '08	▼▼▼	4*
● Bendicò Mandrarossa '08	▼▼	4*
● Bonera Mandrarossa '08	▼▼	4*
○ Chardonnay Mandrarossa '09	▼▼	3*
○ Fiano Mandrarossa '09	▼▼	3*
○ Grecanico Mandrarossa '09	▼▼	3*
○ Seligo Bianco '09	▼▼	4*
● Seligo Rosso '08	▼▼	4*
● Cartagho Mandrarossa '06	▽▽▽	5
● Bendicò Mandrarossa '03	▽▽	4
● Bendicò Mandrarossa '01	▽▽	5
● Bonera Mandrarossa '04	▽▽	4*
● Cartagho Mandrarossa '07	▽▽	5
● Mandrarossa Cartagho '04	▽▽	5

Spadafora

via Ausonia, 90
90144 Palermo
tel. 091514952
www.spadafora.com

CELLAR SALES
PRE-BOOKED VISITS
ROOMS AND FOOD

ANNUAL PRODUCTION **260,000 bottles**
HECTARES UNDER VINE **95**
VITICULTURE METHOD **Conventional**

Founded by Don Pietro Spadafora, this historic Sicilian winery is now run by his son Francesco, for whom it has become a passion. He deals both with vineyard management and more strictly oenological matters. When he inherited it from his father, Virzì was a winery run the traditional way. But Francesco didn't lose heart and began to replant the old vineyards at densities more suitable for modern viticulture, modernized the winery and introduced temperature control and small wood for ageing.

As usual, Spadafora, with around 100 hectares under vine in the countryside around Monreale, gave a flattering performance. Syrah Sole dei Padri has evidently booked a permanent place in our finals, and the '07 Vintage shows great energy, with loads of balsam, spice and rich red berry fruit on the nose preceding a lively, lingering palate with a spectacular finish. The complex Schietto Syrah '06, with its nice Mediterranean notes and spice, shows dense and full-bodied on the palate, and also deservedly made it to the finals. The Syrah '08 is simpler than its big brothers but still extremely pleasurable.

● Schietto Syrah '06	▼▼	4*
● Sole dei Padri '07	▼▼	7
● Don Pietro Rosso '07	▼▼	4*
● Syrah '08	▼▼	5
○ Alhambra '09	▼	3
○ Don Pietro Bianco '09	▼	4
● Schietto Cabernet Sauvignon '06	▼	6
○ Schietto Chardonnay '09	▼	5
○ Schietto Grillo '09	▼	4
○ Schietto Chardonnay '05	▽▽	5
● Schietto Syrah '05	▽▽	5
● Sole dei Padri '06	▽▽	7
● Sole dei Padri '05	▽▽	7
● Sole dei Padri '04	▽▽	7

★★ Tasca d'Almerita

C.DA REGALEALI
90020 SCLAFANI BAGNI [PA]
TEL. 0916459711
www.tascadalmerita.it

CELLAR SALES
PRE-BOOKED VISITS
ROOMS AND FOOD

ANNUAL PRODUCTION 3,000,000 bottles
HECTARES UNDER VINE 500
VITICULTURE METHOD Conventional

It's always exciting to visit Regaleali, the Tascas' estate covering almost 500 hectares under vine in the countryside around Sclafani Bagni. Time seems to stand still here in this landscape of rare beauty, in softly rolling hills where vines alternate with olive trees. But it's only an impression, because Regaleali has always been a workshop, an exciting mine of ideas, where the family's vocation for viticulture has helped to write the history of wine in Sicily and further afield. Lucio is in fact the eighth generation of Tasca winemakers.

The quality of the range presented this year is superlative and starts off with the extraordinary '08 vintage of the Cabernet Sauvignon, one of the best ever. Blackberry, blackcurrant, wild cherry, iodine, pencil lead and balsamic notes weave together in a nose of rare complexity to return on the intense, incredibly long palate. The Tascante '08, a Nerello Mascalese from the new estate on Etna, made the finals on its debut for an elegant nose of peach and sour cherry. The other finalist, the Chardonnay '08, shows tropical fruit, medicinal herbs and a lovely savoury cleanness.

● Cabernet Sauvignon '08	▼▼▼	6
○ Chardonnay '08	▼▼	6
● Tascante '08	▼▼	6
● Camastra '08	▼▼	5
○ Contea di Sclafani Almerita Brut '07	▼▼	6
○ Contea di Sclafani Almerita Extra Brut '06	▼▼	6
● Cygnus '08	▼▼	5
○ Diamante d'Almerita '09	▼▼	6
○ Regaleali Bianco '09	▼▼	4*
● Regaleali Rosso '09	▼▼	4*
○ Tasca d'Almerita Whitaker Grillo '09	▼▼	4
● Cabernet Sauvignon '07	▽▽▽	6
○ Chardonnay '06	▽▽▽	6
● Contea di Sclafani Rosso del Conte '05	▽▽▽	7
● Contea di Sclafani Rosso del Conte '04	▽▽▽	7

Tenuta delle Terre Nere

C.DA CALDERARA
95036 RANDAZZO [CT]
TEL. 095924002
tenutaterrenere@tiscali.it

CELLAR SALES
PRE-BOOKED VISITS

ANNUAL PRODUCTION 120,000 bottles
HECTARES UNDER VINE 22
VITICULTURE METHOD Certified organic

Marc De Grazia's experience on Etna has been a series of incredible successes. His research on individual vineyards with old vine stock has led him to identify what can only be called crus, each offering enormous potential for expression. The Don Peppino vineyard, with ungrafted bush vines dating back to before 1870, is a real marvel but the other plots, at Guardiola, Calderara Sottana, Feudo di Mezzo and Santo Spirito have proved that they are equally able to deliver wines of exciting character.

The star of the '08 vintage is the Etna Rosso Santo Spirito, with its sublime, intense bouquet of stewed fruit, spice and beeswax, followed by extreme elegance and length in the mouth. The Vigna di Don Peppino shows slightly less depth but can point to a rounded, complex nose with nicely dosed oak over a velvety, warm palate. Our finals were also graced by Feudo di Mezzo, with its fine notes of geraniums and aromatic herbs, dense pulp and throbbing tannins. The Guardiola is floral, spicy and graceful while the Calderara Sottana is a touch huskier than usual. The Etna Rosso '09 was a lovely surprise. Stylish and complex, it shows weight, cleanliness and drinkability.

● Etna Rosso Santo Spirito '08	▼▼▼	7
● Etna Rosso Feudo di Mezzo Quadro delle Rose '08	▼▼	7
● Etna Rosso Prephilloxera La V. di Don Peppino '08	▼▼	8
○ Etna Bianco '09	▼▼	4
● Etna Rosso '09	▼▼	4
● Etna Rosso Calderara Sottana '08	▼▼	7
● Etna Rosso Guardiola '08	▼▼	7
○ Etna Bianco Le Vigne Niche '08	▼	7
⊙ Etna Rosato '09	▼	4
● Etna Rosso Feudo di Mezzo Quadro delle Rose '05	▽▽▽	7
● Etna Rosso Feudo di Mezzo Quadro delle Rose '04	▽▽▽	6
● Etna Rosso Prephilloxera La V. di Don Peppino '07	▽▽▽	8
● Etna Rosso Prephilloxera La V. di Don Peppino '06	▽▽▽	7

Valle dell'Acate

C.DA BIDINI
97011 ACATE [RG]
TEL. 0932874166
www.valledellacate.it

CELLAR SALES
PRE-BOOKED VISITS

ANNUAL PRODUCTION **450,000 bottles**
HECTARES UNDER VINE **100**
VITICULTURE METHOD **Organic**

The Jaconos are among the winemaking pioneers of Val di Noto and have been producing wine on their fine estate at Bidini, near the River Dirillo, for at least 200 years. For more than five years, the operation has been run by Gaetana, pharmacist by profession and wine woman by vocation, who chose the right moment to transform the historic winery into a business with a modern philosophy. This means focusing on native varieties, coaxing out their personalities to the full and keeping the market in mind.

The varietal, clean, highly drinkable Nero d'Avola Il Moro '08 made our finals for its rich whole fruit and glossy tannins. A champion in its category is the extremely pleasing Cerasuolo di Vittoria '08, from nero d'Avola and frappato, of which Gaetana is without doubt one of the best interpreters. The fragrant, captivating Il Frappato '09 offers wild strawberries and raspberries on the nose leading to a fresh, supple palate. The impeccable range, a source of great satisfaction to Valle dell'Acate, is completed by the fresh-tasting, zesty Insolia '09 and the '07, from insolia and chardonnay, with balsam and peaches that encore on the palate.

● Il Moro '08	ΨΨ (black)	4*
○ Bidis '07	ΨΨ (black)	5
● Cerasuolo di Vittoria '08	ΨΨ (black)	4*
● Vittoria Il Frappato '09	ΨΨ (black)	4*
○ Vittoria Insolia '09	ΨΨ (black)	3*
○ Zagra '09	ΨΨ (black)	4*
● Cerasuolo di Vittoria '07	ΨΨ	4
● Il Moro '07	ΨΨ	4
● Tanè '06	ΨΨ	6
● Tanè '05	ΨΨ	6
● Tanè '04	ΨΨ	6
● Tanè '03	ΨΨ	6
● Vittoria Il Frappato '08	ΨΨ	4*

Zisola

C.DA ZISOLA
96017 NOTO [SR]
TEL. 057773571
www.zisola.it

CELLAR SALES
PRE-BOOKED VISITS

ANNUAL PRODUCTION **120,000 bottles**
HECTARES UNDER VINE **21**
VITICULTURE METHOD **Conventional**

Filippo Mazzei, one of the best-known growers in Italy and whose family owns Castello di Fonterutoli, scoured Sicily for years, looking for a winery. But he didn't just want somewhere to make wine. He had always been in love with the island and above all sought a spiritual haven. In the end, he found it at Zisola, near Noto, a splendid estate with bush vines and a beautiful old farmstead with a citrus orchard.

Doppiozeta '07, an excellent blend of stringently selected nero d'Avola, syrah and cabernet franc, made our finals. An intense purplish hue ushers in an elegant, meaty but not overpowering nose, with complex aromatics led by mineral and balsamic notes. On the lively palate, it shows exemplary cleanness, with well-focused, rounded tannins. Simpler, but nevertheless extremely interesting, is the varietal, well-typed Nero d'Avola Zisola '08, offering distinct, elegant notes of ripe fruit, topsoil, spice and iodine that pave the way for a fresh, clean palate that delivers crisp, satisfying drinkability.

● Doppiozeta '07	ΨΨ (black)	7
● Zisola '08	ΨΨ (black)	5
● Doppiozeta '06	ΨΨ	8
● Nero d'Avola '06	ΨΨ	4*
● Nero d'Avola '05	ΨΨ	4
● Zisola '07	ΨΨ	6

OTHER WINERIES

Tenuta dell' Abate

via Kennedy, 46
93100 Caltanissetta
tel. 0934584188
tenutadellabate@hotmail.com

The Romano family winery has 60 hectares in the countryside around Caltanisetta. The best wine is the Terre del Palco Nero d'Avola '09. It has a fruity nose over a well co-ordinated palate, with glossy tannins and a consistent finish. The Insolia Lissandrello '09 has nice pulp behind floral and grassy notes.

● Terre del Palco Nero d'Avola '09	🍷🍷	4
○ Lissandrello '09	🍷	3
○ Terre del Palco Chardonnay '09	🍷	4
○ Terre del Palco Grillo Viognier '09	🍷	4

Abraxas

fraz. Bukkuram
via E. Albanese, 29
90139 Palermo
tel. 0916116832
www.abraxasvini.com

We were impressed by the performance of the winery owned by Calogero Mannino, a former minister of agriculture. The stylish, full-flavoured, vibrant Passito di Pantelleria Abraxas '07 has soft, sweet notes of dried apricots and candied orange peel. Just as good is the elegant Kuddia del Moro '07, from mondeuse.

● Kuddia del Moro '07	🍷🍷	6
○ Passito di Pantelleria Abraxas '07	🍷🍷	7
○ Kuddia del Gallo '09	🍷	4
○ Kuddia delle Ginestre '08	🍷	5

Goffredo Adragna

c.so Vittorio Emanuele, 71
91100 Trapani
tel. 092326401
www.tenuteadragna.it

Rocche Rosse '09, from cabernet sauvignon and syrah, boasts a beautifully intense, varietal nose, as cherry fruit nicely merges with vegetable notes of bell pepper and spice. On the palate, it shows fine texture and a velvety, lingering finish. The refreshing Chardonnay '09 gives spring flowers and aniseed.

○ Chardonnay '09	🍷🍷	4
● Rocche Rosse '09	🍷🍷	4
○ Inzolia '09	🍷	3
○ Marsala Ambra Semisecco Sup.	🍷	5

AgroGento

c.da Anguilla
92017 Sambuca di Sicilia [AG]
tel. 0423860930
www.agroargento.it

It was yet another good result for Timoleonte '07, the winery's top red, from nero d'Avola and other native varieties. The estery, nicely toasty nose precedes a crisp, structured palate with a lingering finish. The Grillo Calancùni '09 has delicate herbaceous and fruit aromas followed by a balanced palate.

● Timoleonte '07	🍷🍷	4
○ Calancùni '09	🍷	4
● Carrivàli '08	🍷	4

Ajello

c.da Giudeo
91025 Mazara del Vallo [TP]
tel. 091309107
www.ajello.info

We liked the Zibibbo '09, which gives intense, aromatics and a refreshing palate with a nice reprise of fruit, despite some wavering on the finish. The sweet Shams '09, from moscato, grillo, inzolia and catarratto, reveals lavender, citrus fruit and spring flowers on the nose, followed by excellent balance in the mouth.

○ Shams '09	🍷🍷	5
○ Zibibbo '09	🍷🍷	4
○ Bizir '09	🍷	4
⊙ Rosato '09	🍷	4

Al Cantàra

via Antonio Cecchi, 23
95100 Catania
tel. 095222644
www.al-cantara.it

'A Nutturna '08 is an unusual blend of grecanico and gewürztraminer grown at 1,000 metres. It shows intriguing minerally hydrocarbon notes and good acidity. We tried two vintages of Etna Rosso O'Scuru O'Scuru, the '07 and the '08. The latter is richer and overripe, the former a touch more austere and rustic.

○ 'A Notturna '08	🍷🍷	5
● Etna Rosso O' Scuru O' Scuru '08	🍷🍷	7
● Etna Rosso O' Scuru O' Scuru '07	🍷	7
● Muddichi di Suli '08	🍷	5

Avide

c.da Mastrella, 346
97013 Comiso [RG]
tel. 0932967456
www.avide.it

The '06 vintage of Nero d'Avola 3 Carati confirms its qualities with intense, layered fruit and balsam on the nose followed by weight and elegance in the mouth. We liked the fragrant simplicity of the Herea Frappato Rosé '09, fresher on the palate than the sumptuous, somewhat woody Riflessi di Sole '07.

● 3 Carati '06	🍷🍷	5
⊙ Herea Frappato Rosé '09	🍷🍷	3*
○ Herea Inzolia '09	🍷	3
○ Vittoria Riflessi di Sole '07	🍷	5

Biscaris

via Maresciallo Giudice, 52
97011 Acate [RG]
tel. 0932989206
www.biscaris.it

We saw a good debut for this small winery set in the heart of the Cerasuolo di Vittoria DOCG zone, which nicely reflects traditional styling. The Cerasuolo di Vittoria Principuzzu '07 has a complex bouquet with elegant spice over a harmonious palate. The Frappato Glorioso '08 is more immediate, fresh and fragrant.

● Cerasuolo di Vittoria Pricipuzzu '07	🍷🍷	4
● Glorioso Frappato '08	🍷🍷	4*
○ Achàtes Inzolia '09	🍷	4
● Hiscor '06	🍷	4

Bonavita

loc. Faro Superiore
c.da Corso
98158 Messina
tel. 0902932106
www.bonavitafaro.it

We liked the wines of the Scarfone family, whose small estate is situated at Faro Superiore and Curcuraci. The classy Faro '08, from nerello mascalese, cappuccio and nocera, has a seductive, intense garnet hue and pervasive aromas of blackberry, nutmeg and tobacco. This is a stylish, lively wine with silky tannins.

● Faro '08	🍷🍷	6
⊙ Rosato '09	🍷🍷	4*

Brugnano

c.da San Carlo, SS 113, km 307
90047 Partinico [PA]
tel. 0918783360
www.brugnano.it

Brugnano's wines are good. The well-executed blend of nero d'Avola and tannat, Naisi '08, showing intense, iron filings and raw meat on the nose over a velvety, hefty palate with prominent tannins. The grassy, drinkable Catarratto V90 '09 is well typed. Rosso V90 '08, from nero d'Avola and merlot, is more mature.

● Naisi '08	🍷🍷	4
○ Kue '09	🍷	4
○ V90 Bianco '09	🍷	3
● V90 Rosso '08	🍷	3

Buceci

via Unità d'Italia, 3
90035 Marineo [PA]
tel. 0918726367
www.bucecivini.it

We saw a good performance from Franco Calderone's winery, which has 50 hectares under vine farmed organically. The admirably intense Pinot Nero Millemetri '07 offers cosseting plums and cherries. The pleasing, well-balanced Merlot-Nero d'Avola '08 matches fruit on the nose with a juicy palate.

● Pinot Nero Millemetri '07	🍷🍷	6
● Liamà '06	🍷	6
● Merlot Nero d'Avola '08	🍷	4

Calabretta

via Bonaventura, 178a
95036 Randazzo [CT]
tel. 3284565050
www.calabretta.net

The Calabretta family grow grapes and make wine on Etna to natural farming and winemaking canons. This year, we appreciated the rustic elegance of the Nerello Mascalese Nonna Concetta '07, its complex bouquet brimming with tertiary aromas. The Carricante '07 displays fully ripe fruit and mineral notes.

○ Carricante '07	🍷🍷	4
● Nerello Mascalese Nonna Concetta '07	🍷🍷	5

Caruso & Minini

VIA SALEMI, 3
91025 MARSALA [TP]
TEL. 0923982356
www.carusoeminini.it

This winery from eastern Sicily has made real progress. The Cusora '09, a blend of chardonnay and viognier, shows clean peaches and appealing, fragrant fruit. The equally convincing Nero d'Avola Cutaja '08 offers intense, meaty aromas and balance in the mouth. The Cusora Rosso '08, from syrah and merlot, is good.

○ Cusora Bianco '09	🍷🍷	3
● Terre di Giumara Cutaja '08	🍷🍷	4
● Cusora Rosso '08	🍷	3
○ Terre di Giumara Isula '09	🍷	4

Casano

VIA A. CATALFO, 1
91025 MARSALA [TP]
TEL. 0923999314
www.casanovini.it

Francesco Intorcia runs his winery with passion. Established in 1940, it has always focused on Marsala and fortified wines. His intense, layered Vergine has an elegant, classic oxidized bouquet veined with iodine and walnutskin and a dry, lip-smacking, lingering palate. The Superiore Ambra Dolce is nice.

○ Marsala Ambra Dolce Sup.	🍷🍷	4
○ Marsala Vergine	🍷🍷	5
○ Grillo '09	🍷	3
○ Marsala Ambra Secco Sup.	🍷	4

Castellucci Miano

VIA SICILIA, 1
90029 VALLEDOLMO [PA]
TEL. 0921542385
www.castelluccimiano.it

The whites are on form: Shiarà '09, from high-altitude vineyards of bush-trained catarratto, shows an admirably complex nose, with fragrant, zesty focused fruit. Inzolia La Masa '08 proffers elegant notes of peach and weighty flesh. Appealing black cherry and great drinkability distinguish the PerricOne '07.

○ La Masa '08	🍷🍷	4
● PerricOne '07	🍷🍷	4
○ Shiarà '09	🍷🍷	5
● Maravita '07	🍷	6

Curto

SS 115 ISPICA - ROSOLINI KM 358
97014 ISPICA [RG]
TEL. 0932950161
www.curto.it

The Eloro Nero d'Avola Fontanelle '06 is one of the greatest examples of its type. Dense, full-bodied, austere and elegant, it shows juicy, pleasant fruit wrapped in silky, dynamic tannins. But Francesca Curto has other strings to her bow, such as the dry, well-typed, varietal Eloro Nero d'Avola '07.

● Eloro Fontanelle '06	🍷🍷	5*
● Eloro Nero d'Avola '07	🍷🍷	3*
⊙ Eloro Nero d'Avola Eos '09	🍷	3
○ Poiano '09	🍷	3

d'Alessandro

ZI AGRIGENTO CENTRO DIREZ. SAN BENEDETTO
92100 AGRIGENTO
TEL. 0642142640
www.dalmin.it

The Nero d'Avola Syrah '08 is the wine we most liked from the D'Alessandro family. It's deep and concentrated with sweet notes of spice and red berry fruit. All the other products presented are classy and well made, especially the varietal, fragrant Nero d'Avola and Grillo, both from '09.

● Nero d'Avola Syrah '08	🍷🍷	4*
○ Grillo '09	🍷	4
○ Inzolia '09	🍷	3
● Nero d'Avola '09	🍷	3

Di Giovanna

C.SO UMBERTO I, 137
92017 SAMBUCA DI SICILIA [AG]
TEL. 0925941086
www.digiovanna-vini.it

We liked the wines from Gunther and Klaus Di Giovanna. The Gerbino Rosso '08, from cabernet sauvignon, merlot, syrah and nero d'Avola, is graceful, fresh and intense with ripe fruit. Equally good are the racy Gerbino Chardonnay '09 and the captivating, cherry-infused Gerbino Rosato '09, from nero d'Avola.

○ Gerbino Chardonnay '09	🍷🍷	3
⊙ Gerbino Rosato '09	🍷🍷	3*
● Gerbino Rosso '08	🍷🍷	3*
○ Viognier '09	🍷	4

Gaspare Di Prima

via G. Guasto, 27
92017 Sambuca di Sicilia [AG]
tel. 0925941201
www.diprimavini.it

This year there was no Villamaura Syrah, the estate's top wine and often in our finals, but the Pepita Rosso '09, from nero d'Avola and syrah, cut a fine figure, showing hints of berries and aromatic herbs over a velvety, well-gauged palate. Gibilmoro Nero d'Avola '08 has lovely mulberry-led fruit and balsam.

● Pepita Rosso '09	🍷🍷	4*
○ Gibilmoro Chardonnay '09	🍷	4
● Gibilmoro Nero d'Avola '08	🍷	4
○ Pepita Bianco '09	🍷	4

Tenuta Enza La Fauci

c.da Mezzana-Spartà
98163 Messina
tel. 3476854318
www.tenutaenzalafauci.com

We saw a brilliant debut from the wines of Enza La Fauci, owner of a small naturally farmed estate. The excellent, minerally Faro Oblì '08, from nerello mascalese, cappuccio, nocera and nero d'Avola, offers captivating ripe fruit, and impressive balance of structure and fresh drinkability.

● Faro Oblì '08	🍷🍷	7
● Terre di Vento '08	🍷🍷	6

Feotto dello Jato

c.da Feotto
90048 San Giuseppe Jato [PA]
tel. 0918572650
www.feottodellojato.it

The best wine from this Monreale DOC estate is the Merlot Rosso di Turi '07. The rich, concentrated nose leads with oak and liqueur cherries, mirrored on the palate. The toasty oak tends to overwhelm the fruit both in the Syrah Sirae '07 and in the Nero d'Avola Fegotto '07.

● Monreale Rosso di Turi '07	🍷🍷	5
● Feotto Rosso '08	🍷	3
● Monreale Rosso Fegotto '07	🍷	4
● Monreale Sirae '07	🍷	5

Ferreri

c.da Salinella
91029 Santa Ninfa [TP]
tel. 092461871
www.ferrerivini.it

This year, the range is good. Best of the bunch is the Cabernet Sauvignon '08, with an austere, well-rounded palate and a concentrated nose. The Nero d'Avola '08 also shows class, its almost impenetrable dark ruby heralding an intense, minerally, elegant, fruit-heavy nose, encored on the palate.

● Cabernet Sauvignon '08	🍷🍷	5
● Nero d'Avola '08	🍷🍷	4*
○ Brasi Catarratto '08	🍷	5
○ Inzolia '09	🍷	4

Feudo Arancio

c.da Portella Misilbesi
92017 Sambuca di Sicilia [AG]
tel. 0925579000
www.feudoarancio.it

There are two new blends, Dalila '09 and Cantadoro '07, respectively a Grillo-Viognier and a Nero d'Avola-Cabernet Sauvignon. Passito Hekate '08 is a nice surprise, with intense, focused citrus and lavender aromas over a sweet, harmonious palate. We also liked the clean fruit and flowers of the Chardonnay '09.

○ Chardonnay '09	🍷🍷	4
○ Hekate Passito '08	🍷🍷	5
● Cantadoro '07	🍷	4
○ Dalila '09	🍷	4

Feudo Cavaliere

c.da Cavaliere Bosco
95126 Santa Maria di Licodia [CT]
tel. 3487348377
www.feudocavaliere.com

The Platania D'Antoni family have tended their vineyards on the southern slopes of Etna, situated 800 to 1,000 metres above sea level, since 1880. Nerello Mascalese Don Blasco '07 is stylish while the Etna Bianco Millemetri '09 shows aniseed and softness. The Etna Rosso Millemetri '08 is a tad over-evolved.

● Don Blasco '07	🍷🍷	5
○ Etna Bianco Millemetri '09	🍷🍷	4
⊙ Etna Rosato Millemetri '09	🍷	4
● Etna Rosso Millemetri '08	🍷	4

Feudo di Santa Tresa

S.DA COMUNALE MARANGIO, 35
97019 VITTORIA [RG]
TEL. 0932513126
www.santatresa.it

The wine our tasting panel most appreciated this year was the Rina Ianca '09, a well-balanced blend of grillo and viognier. Combining a brilliant gold with aromas of ripe pear, almond and oriental spices, it is lingering, fresh, dynamic and pleasurable. The other wines pass muster.

○ Rina Ianca '09	2 glasses	3*
● Cerasuolo di Vittoria '07	1 glass	4
● Frappato '09	1 glass	4

Feudo Montoni

C.DA MONTONI VECCHI
90144 CAMMARATA [AG]
TEL. 091513106
www.feudomontoni.it

The Vrucara '07 reached the finals with excellently co-ordinated complexity on the nose, offering plum, tar and elegant hints of balsam, and then a soft, ripe, lingering palate. The Nero d'Avola '08 is a simpler easy drinker, but remains true to the noble lineage of its raw material.

● Nero d'Avola Sel. Speciale Vrucara '07	2 glasses	6
● Nero d'Avola '08	2 glasses	4
○ Catarratto '09	1 glass	4

Fondo Antico

FRAZ. RILIEVO
VIA FIORAME, 54A
91100 TRAPANI
TEL. 0923864339
www.fondoantico.it

With its charming deep gold, accompanied by fresh, upfront yellow peaches, joined by sage and lavender, the late-harvest Baccadoro '08, from grillo and moscato, is the wine we most appreciated. The Grillo Parlante '09, from grillo, offers a savoury, fragrant palate with nice, lively acidity.

○ Baccadoro '08	2 glasses	4
○ Grillo Parlante '09	2 glasses	4*
● Il Canto di Fondo Antico '06	1 glass	5
● Nero d'Avola '09	1 glass	4

Cantine Foraci

C.DA SERRONI
91026 MAZARA DEL VALLO [TP]
TEL. 0923934286
www.foraci.it

The wines from this famous estate, which has long been using organic methods, are always good. The excellent Nero d'Avola Syrah '08 has ripe, concentrated fruit underpinned by driving, well-honed tannins. The lively, tangy O' Feo Inzolia '09, with fresh, sustained acidity, provides enjoyable drinking.

● Nero d'Avola Syrah '08	2 glasses	3*
○ Grillo '09	1 glass	3
○ O' Feo Inzolia '09	1 glass	3
● Satiro Danzante Nero d'Avola '08	1 glass	4

Tenuta Gorghi Tondi

C.DA SAN NICOLA
91026 MARSALA [TP]
TEL. 0923719741
www.gorghitondi.com

The wines from Annamaria and Clara Sala were very interesting, starting with the juicy Coste a Preola Rosso '08, from nero d'Avola and syrah, with surprising balance and structure. The '08 was a fine vintage for Riarso, a Passito di Pantelleria characterized by rich aromatics and taut acidity.

○ Chardonnay '09	2 glasses	4
● Coste a Preola Rosso '08	2 glasses	4*
○ Riarso '08	2 glasses	6
○ Kheirè '09	1 glass	4

Graci

LOC. PASSOPISCIARO
C.DA ARCURIA
95012 CASTIGLIONE DI SICILIA [CT]
TEL. 3487016773
www.graci.eu

Alberto Graci's Etna Rosso Quota 600 '08, from nerello mascalese, easily made our finals, thanks to supple, elegant structure nicely sustained by mineral notes and ripe peach. We liked the Etna Bianco Quota 600 '09, from carricante and catarratto, with its tropical fruit aromas.

● Etna Rosso Quota 600 '08	2 glasses	6
○ Etna Bianco Quota 600 '09	1 glass	5

Guccione
C.DA CERASA SP 102 BIS
90046 MONREALE [PA]
TEL. 0916116686
www.guccione.eu

Last year's success has not changed the strict methods adopted by this small biodynamic winery. Francesco and Manfredi Guccione maintained that their wines were not ready and needed a longer period of bottle ageing. Critics and aficionados will just have to do resign themselves and wait.

○ Lolik '07	🍸🍸🍸	4*
● Cerasa V.T. '08	🍸🍸	5
○ Girgis '07	🍸🍸	4*
○ Veruzza '07	🍸🍸	4*

Hauner
LOC. SANTA MARIA
VIA UMBERTO I
98050 LIPARI [ME]
TEL. 0909843141
www.hauner.it

We will always be grateful to Carlo Hauner for reproposing the greatness of Salina's wines. The Malvasia Passito '07 bearing his name is on fine form. A compact nose of medicinal herbs and tropical fruit leads to a firm, sweet but never cloying palate. Hierà '08, from alicante and calabrese, is fresh and mineral.

● Hierà '08	🍷🍷	4
○ Malvasia Passito Carlo Hauner '07	🍷🍷	7
● Rosso Antonello '06	🍷🍷	5
○ Salina Bianco '09	🍷🍷	4*

Intorcia
VIA MAZARA, 10
91025 MARSALA [TP]
TEL. 0923999133
www.intorcia.it

The Intorcia family have been producing Marsala for 80 years. We tried three, all well made, starting with the Vergine Soleras. Its elegant, complex aromas of sorb apple and cut hay return in a dry, full-flavoured palate. The Superiore G.D. "Garibaldi Dolce" is consistent and clean while the Superiore S.O.M. is well-typed.

○ Marsala Vergine Soleras	🍷🍷	5
○ Marsala G.D. Sup.	🍷	5
○ Marsala S.O.M. Sup.	🍷	4

Maggio
S.DA CENTRALE MARANGIO, 35
97019 VITTORIA [RG]
TEL. 0932984771
www.maggiovini.it

A fine performance from the Maggio family winery. Of the many wines presented this year, the complex Cerasuolo di Vittoria Vigna di Pettineo '07 stands out for its ripe fruit and silky soft palate. Amongae '07, an elegant, balsamic blend of Nero d'Avola and Cabernet Sauvignon is also first rate and structured.

● Amongae '07	🍷🍷	4
● Cerasuolo di Vittoria V. di Pettineo '07	🍷🍷	5
● Rasula Cabernet Sauvignon '07	🍷	4
● Rasula Nero d'Avola '08	🍷	4

Masseria del Feudo
C.DA GROTTAROSSA
93100 CALTANISSETTA
TEL. 0934856575
www.masseriadelfeudo.it

The Rosso delle Rose '07, a lovely blend of nero d'Avola and syrah, continues to give great satisfaction to Carolina and Francesco Cucurullo. With its intense, garnet-tinged ruby hue, it is a wine with fine character and freshness, perfectly mature and an extremely pleasurable drinker. The rest of the wines are good.

● Rosso delle Rose '07	🍷🍷	4*
○ Il Giglio Bianco '09	🍷	3
● Il Giglio Rosso '09	🍷	3

Miceli
C.DA PIANA SCUNCHIPANI, 190
92019 SCIACCA [AG]
TEL. 092580188
www.miceli.net

Passito di Pantelleria Nun '08 confirms its worth, offering lovely candied peel and an appealing whiff of smoke, followed by a well-developed, gentle palate. Another wine has been added to the winery's extensive range: Merlot Zirlio '08 is a easy-drinking red with pleasing fruit.

○ Moscato Passito di Pantelleria Nun '08	🍷🍷	6
○ Foravia '08	🍷	4
● Smodato '08	🍷	6
● Zirlio '08	🍷	4

Cantina Modica di San Giovanni

C.DA BUFALEFI
96017 NOTO [SR]
TEL. 0931573576
www.olioevinobufalefi.it

Once again, the labels of Alessandro Modica's winery are reliable and well managed. The well-typed, minerally Mamma Draja '09, from nero d'Avola, offers focused, refreshing fruit and appealing length. Equally good is the smooth Dolcenero '07, a dried-grape wine from nero d'Avola.

- ● Dolcenero '07 — 🍷🍷 6
- ⊙ Mamma Draja '09 — 🍷🍷 4*
- ○ Lupara '09 — 🍷 4

Cantine Mothia

VIA GIOVANNI FALCONE, 22
91025 MARSALA [TP]
TEL. 0923737295
www.cantine-mothia.com

The Bonomo winery is in an old building on the splendid Salt Road from Trapani to Marsala, where the grapes picked at the Stagnone nature park used to be collected. The most captivating wine is the sweet Grillo, Mulsum '08, giving intense sea breeze, quince and dried apricot aromas over a dense, rounded palate.

- ● Hammon '06 — 🍷🍷 4
- ○ Mulsum '08 — 🍷🍷 5
- ○ Saline '09 — 🍷 2
- ○ Vela Latina '09 — 🍷 4

Antica Tenuta del Nanfro

C.DA NANFRO SAN NICOLA LE CANNE
95041 CALTAGIRONE [CT]
TEL. 093360744
www.nanfro.com

Tenuta del Nanfro has around 50 hectares in the countryside around Caltagirone, farmed organically. The excellent Cerasuolo di Vittoria Sammauro '08 is fresh and fragrant, with lovely ripe fruit that unfolds beautifully in the mouth. The fine, easy-drinking Nero d'Avola Strade '08 is varietal and well balanced.

- ● Cerasuolo di Vittoria Sammauro '08 — 🍷🍷 4
- ● Strade Rosso '08 — 🍷🍷 4
- ● Frappato '09 — 🍷 4
- ○ Strade Bianco '09 — 🍷 4

Nicosia

VIA LUIGI CAPUANA
95039 TRECASTAGNI [CT]
TEL. 0957806767
www.cantinanicosia.it

This year Nicosia sent a good range of wines, starting with the Etna Rosso Fondo Filara '08, brimming with minerality on the nose and extract in the mouth. We also liked the Etna Bianco Fondo Filara '09 for its fresh, lively palate following blossom and white-fleshed fruits aromatics.

- ● Etna Rosso Fondo Filara '08 — 🍷🍷 4
- ○ Etna Bianco Fondo Filara '09 — 🍷 4
- ● Fondo Filara Nero d'Avola '08 — 🍷 4
- ● Sosta Tre Santi '07 — 🍷 6

Occhipinti

C.DA FOSSA DI LUPO
VIA DEI MILLE, 55
97019 VITTORIA [RG]
TEL. 0932868222
www.agricolaocchipinti.it

The dedicated Arianna Occhipinti farms her vines naturally and combines great technical expertise with genuine passion. The mineral SP 68 '09, from nero d'Avola and frappato, made the final with its mulberry and blackberry notes. The fresh-tasting, fragrant Il Frappato '08 is highly quaffable.

- ● SP 68 '09 — 🍷🍷 4*
- ● Il Frappato '08 — 🍷🍷 5
- ● Siccagno '07 — 🍷 6

Orestiadi

FRAZ. SANTA NINFA
LOC. C.DA SALINELLA
VIA A. GAGINI, 41
91029 GIBELLINA [TP]
TEL. 092469124
www.orestiadisrl.it

The name comes from a famous arts foundation and was chosen by the Ermes winery, which owns brands such as Marchese Montefusco and Barone Montalto. The Nero d'Avola Agamennone '08 impressed us with its cleanliness, complexity and concentration. The Grillo Egisto '09 is good, if rather Sauvignonesque.

- ● Agamennone '08 — 🍷🍷 4
- ○ Egisto Grillo '09 — 🍷🍷 4
- ● Marchese Montefusco Syrah '09 — 🍷🍷 4
- ● Merlot Rilento '09 — 🍷 3

Ottoventi

C.DA TORREBIANCA - FICO
91019 VALDERICE [TP]
TEL. 0923 1892880
www.cantinaottoventi.it

We saw a good debut from the Ottoventi winery, which earns a place in the Guide for its quality wines. Best of the whites is the '09 Grillo .8, flaunting aromatic herbs and summer flowers over a refreshing, lively palate. The dynamic, fruity Grillo '09 is equally captivating and offers a lovely almondy finish.

○ Grillo .8 '09	🍷🍷	4
○ Ottoventi Grillo '09	🍷🍷	5
● Nero d'Avola .20 '08	🍷	4
○ Ottoventi Bianco '09	🍷	4

Piana dei Cieli

C.DA BERTOLINO - SCIFITELLI
92013 MENFI [AG]
TEL. 092572060
www.pianadeicieli.com

Annalisa and Nino Giambalvo's Syrah '08 is back on track with delicious nutmeg, pepper and red berry fruit, leading to solid, fleshy elegance in the mouth. The mature, mineral Chardonnay Pizzo dei Corvi '09 has good texture on a fresh, elegant palate. The varietal Nero d'Avola '08 is young and uncomplicated.

○ Pizzo dei Corvi '09	🍷🍷	4
● Syrah '08	🍷🍷	4
● Nero d'Avola '08	🍷	4

Poggio di Bortolone

FRAZ. ROCCAZZO
VIA BORTOLONE, 19
97010 CHIARAMONTE GULFI [RG]
TEL. 0932921161
www.poggiodibortolone.it

We were disappointed to see no Cerasuolo Bortolone this year but Addamanera '06 was some consolation. This very Bortolone-style interpretation of Syrah shows marked tertiary aromas and seduces with notes of coffee, wax, moss and spice, paving the way for a warm, sunny palate just starting to decline.

● Addamanera '06	🍷🍷	4*

Porta del Vento

C.DA VALDIBELLA
90043 CAMPOREALE [PA]
TEL. 0916116531
www.portadelvento.it

Perricone is the leitmotiv of the new natural wines from Marco Sferlazzo. Splendid cherry, mineral elegance and length distinguish the MaQuè '09, a blend with 80 per cent nero d'Avola, which made the finals. MaQuè Perricone '09 lays out elegant swathes of fragrant fruit. The Rosé '09 offers quince and bright acidity.

● MaQuè '09	🍷🍷	4
● MaQuè Perricone '09	🍷🍷	5
⊙ MaQuè Rosé '09	🍷	4

Pupillo

C.DA LA TARGIA
96100 SIRACUSA
TEL. 0931494029
www.solacium.it

Pupillo deserves credit for relaunching Moscato di Siracusa, a wine that was dying out. Solacium '09 made the finals with its elegant orange blossom and honey leading to poised body and acidity in the mouth. We also liked the Pollio '09. It's less complex but has a fine nose.

○ Moscato di Siracusa Solacium '09	🍷🍷	6
○ Cyane '09	🍷🍷	4
○ Moscato di Siracusa Pollio '09	🍷🍷	6
● Re Federico '09	🍷	4

Cantine Rallo

VIA VINCENZO FLORIO, 2
91025 MARSALA [TP]
TEL. 0923721633
www.cantinerallo.it

Andrea Vesco's organic wines deliver consistent quality. The excellent, varietal Alcamo Nero d'Avola '09 is nicely drinkable, offering ripe, fragrant cherry and mulberry fruit. The captivating Marsala Soleras Riserva Venti Anni shows intense, elegant and soft. Equally good is the complex, lingering Chardonnay.

● Alcamo Nero d'Avola '09	🍷🍷	4*
○ Chardonnay '09	🍷🍷	4
○ Marsala Vergine Soleras Venti Anni Ris.	🍷🍷	6
○ Müller Thurgau '09	🍷	4

Rizzuto

c.da Piconello
92011 Cattolica Eraclea [AG]
tel. 091333081
www.rizzutoguccione.com

The bright ruby Piconello Cabernet Sauvignon Chiaro '07 is the thoroughbred of Ruggero Rizzuto's winery, with focused, rounded hints of wild berries, tobacco, myrtle and cloves. But we also appreciated the winery's two highly drinkable whites.

⊙ Piconello Cabernet Sauvignon Chiaro '07	🍷🍷	4*
○ Enzo '09	🍷	4
○ Piconello Grillo '09	🍷	4

Rocca d'Api

via Rocca d'Api, 72
95019 Zafferana Etnea [CT]
tel. 0957082594

Among the certified organic wines presented by the Castorina family, we particularly liked the elegant Etna Rosso Zero 1 '06, from nerello mascalese and cappuccio. Its minerality and ripe fruit reflect an extraordinary volcanic terroir. The other products are well managed.

● Etna Rosso Zero 1 '06	🍷🍷	5
○ Etna Bianco Le Moire '09	🍷	4
○ Etna Bianco Zero 1 '05	🍷	5
● Etna Rosso Le Moire '08	🍷	4

Sallier de la Tour

c.da Pernice
90144 Monreale [PA]
tel. 0916459711
www.tascadalmerita.it

The performance of Principe Filiberto's estate was excellent. Best of the range is the top-notch La Monaca '08, a monovarietal Syrah offering intense black pepper and cherry with compact, juicy fruit. We also liked the Le Bianche '09, from sémillon, viognier and sauvignon blanc.

● La Monaca '08	🍷🍷	5
○ Le Bianche '09	🍷🍷	5
● Cabernet '08	🍷	3
● Nero d'Avola '08	🍷	3

Emanuele Scammacca del Murgo

via Zafferana, 13
95010 Santa Venerina [CT]
tel. 095950520
www.murgo.it

The Scammacca family was the first to recommence sparkling wine production on Etna, building a modern winery and achieving excellent results. The Murgo Extra Brut '04, from selected nerello mascalese grapes, made the finals. Bottle refermentation imbues minerality and florality over a fresh, poised palate.

○ Murgo Extra Brut '04	🍷🍷	6
⊙ Etna Rosato '09	🍷🍷	4*
⊙ Murgo Brut Rosé '07	🍷🍷	4
● Tenuta Gelso Bianco '08	🍷🍷	3*

Scilio

c.da Arrigo
95015 Linguaglossa [CT]
tel. 095932822
www.scilio.com

Again this year the wines from this fine Etna winery are excellent. We liked the Etna Bianco '09, from carricante and catarratto, with its fresh, mineral palate and delicate fruit bouquet. The charming Sikélios '05, a red dried-grape wine from various native varieties, is velvety and lingering.

○ Etna Bianco '09	🍷🍷	4
● Sikélios Rosso '05	🍷🍷	5
⊙ Etna Rosato '09	🍷	4
● Etna Rosso '07	🍷	4

Solidea

c.da Kaddiuggia
91017 Pantelleria [TP]
tel. 0923913016
www.solideavini.it

The wines from this small Pantelleria winery are always great. The sweet, delightful Passito di Pantelleria '09 has citrus that encores elegantly on the palate. Sweet but not cloying, the Moscato di Pantelleria '09 is sustained by lovely, refreshing acidity. Like the others, the well-styled Ilios '09, is from moscato.

○ Moscato di Pantelleria '09	🍷🍷	5
○ Passito di Pantelleria '09	🍷🍷	6
○ Ilios '09	🍷	4

Tamburello

C.DA PIETRAGNELLA
90144 MONREALE [PA]
TEL. 0918465272
www.aziendetamburello.it

With its brooding garnet accompanying ripe, intense black cherry-led fruit, the '06 Monreale Pietragavina Perricone is the best wine produced by the winery run by Mirella Tamburello. The Monreale Nero d'Avola Pietragavina '06 is pleasing and well typed.

● Monreale Pietragavina Perricone '06	🍷🍷	4*
● Dagala Rosato '09	🍷	3
● Dagala Rosso '09	🍷	3
● Monreale Pietragavina Nero d'Avola '06	🍷	4

Terre di Giurfo

VIA PALESTRO, 536
97019 VITTORIA [RG]
TEL. 0957221551
www.terredigiurfo.it

It's nice to have the chance to try the same wine from the same vintage with and without cask conditioning, as we did with Terre di Giurfo's Cerasuolo di Vittoria Maskarìa '07. The unoaked version scored better, with its unblemished, attractively fragrant fruit. The Syrah Ronna '09 is also very good.

● Maskarìa '07	🍷🍷	4
● Ronna '09	🍷🍷	4
● Kuntari '07	🍷	4
● Maskaria Barricato '07	🍷	4

Terrelíade

LOC. SILENE
C.DA PORTELLA MISILBESI
92017 SAMBUCA DI SICILIA [AG]
TEL. 0421246281
www.terreliade.com

The wines from Gruppo Santa Margherita's Sambuca estate improve every year. The excellent Punenti '09, an elegant, well-typed, monovarietal Inzolia, shows fresh, tangy and fleshy on the palate. The mature, fruity, juicily supple Nirà '08, from Nero d'Avola, is equally good. The rest of the wines are more than decent.

● Nirà '08	🍷🍷	4*
○ Punenti '09	🍷🍷	4*
● Musia '08	🍷	4
○ Timpa Giadda '09	🍷	4

TerzaVia

VIA GIACINTO BRUZZESE, 28
91025 MARSALA [TP]
TEL. 3357725238
debartolirenato@gmail.com

Renato De Bartoli produces a small range of natural wines. We pick out Occidens '09, a characterful, minerally white from a complex blend of grecanico, catarratto, grillo and zibibbo, the flavoursome, succulent Amada '08, from tempranillo and nero d'Avola, and the fresh, tangy Lucido '09, from catarratto.

● Amada '08	🍷🍷	4*
○ Occidens '09	🍷🍷	4*
○ Lucido '09	🍷	4

Barone di Villagrande

VIA DEL BOSCO, 25
95025 MILO [CT]
TEL. 0957082175
www.villagrande.it

On its debut, the Etna Bianco Superiore Legno di Conzo '07 from carricante showed its class, personality and complexity. As usual, we were charmed by the minerally Etna Bianco Superiore '09, a monovarietal Carricante, offering subtle elegance with lively acidity and freshness.

○ Etna Bianco Legno di Conzo Sup. '07	🍷🍷	6
○ Etna Bianco Sup. '09	🍷🍷	4*
● Etna Rosso '08	🍷	4
○ Fiore di Villagrande '08	🍷	5

Vivera

C.DA MARTINELLA SP 59/IV
95015 LINGUAGLOSSA [CT]
TEL. 095643837
www.vivera.it

The Vivera winery has 45 organically farmed hectares under vine and three estates: on Etna, at Chiaromonte Gulfi and at Corleone. We liked the Etna Salisire '08, offering subtle flowers, aromatic herbs, citrus and pineapple. The other Etna white, A'mami '08, from carricante and chardonnay, is also good.

○ A'mami '08	🍷🍷	5
○ Etna Bianco Salisire '08	🍷🍷	5
○ Altrove '09	🍷	4
● Terra dei Sogni '08	🍷	4

SARDINIA

Average wine quality in Sardinia is up and there are plenty of high points. There are always at least eleven Three Glass awards and this year is no exception. Wines are good and prices very honest. In the north east, vermentino is at its best in Gallura, producing soft Mediterranean wines lifted by minerality, aromatic herbs and scrub while the hot '09 growing season seems not to have affected quality very much. Alongside vermentino, other traditional varieties might have disappeared, replaced by more fashionable internationals, had it not been for several brave winemakers. So we still have nuragus, nasco, malvasia or vernaccia to give us local labels and exciting flavours. Cannonau as always is the leading red and although it is catalogued as a single variety by the obsolete Sardegna DOC, actually varies different based from zone to zone and year to year. Mamoiada cannonau gives appealing, traditional wines while those from Ogliastra are fresh and lively. Steel-fermented Cannonaus from the '09 vintage are fragrant and vinous whereas riserva bottles from the excellent '07 harvest are mouthfilling, full-bodied and age-worthy. Carignano, a native of Sulcis sometimes on old, ungrafted vines, gives power and the '07 vintage brought us wines of stunning complexity. Still on the reds, it is nice to see the return of small-scale productions of grapes like cagnulari around Sassari, bovale inland and around Oristano, or monica in Campidano. These are only a few of the most famous actors on the Sardinian wine stage. We would also like to make a point to growers and winemakers on the island, merely an encouragement to do even better. There is no lack of tradition and more estates should leverage this to produce peaks of excellence, as well as good overall quality, so that they can compete head on equal terms with other Italian and even international wines. Competition is intensifying. Prize-winners this year include seven celebrated Sardinian wines: the Alghero Marchese di Villamarina '05 from Sella & Mosca, the '07 Cannonau di Sardegna Riservas Dule and Vinìola, respectively from Giuseppe Gabbas and Cantina di Dorgali, Carignano del Sulcis Is Arenas Riserva '07 from Sardus Pater, Barrua '07 from Agricola Punica, Gerione '07 from Feudi della Medusa, and Turriga '06 from Argiolas. To these we add four great newcomers: Cannonau di Sardegna Mamuthone '08 from Sedilesu, the '09 Vermentino di Gallura Superiores Thilibas and Vigna'ngena respectively from Pedres and Capichera and a fabulous Vernaccia di Oristano Riserva '99 from Fratelli Serra. This is a good start. Better things are sure to come.

6 Mura

VIA IS PASCAIS, 18
09010 GIBA [CI]
TEL. 0781964370
www.6mura.com

CELLAR SALES

ANNUAL PRODUCTION 150,000 bottles
HECTARES UNDER VINE 25
VITICULTURE METHOD Conventional

This young estate in Giba enters joins the front rank of major Sardinian wineries. Nor could it be otherwise considering the passion and commitment uniting the five friends who became partners in 6 Mura. You can taste this passion in their most important wine, named for the estate. The carignano is grown in vineyards with sandy plots and old, ungrafted, bush-trained vines. For now, we are dealing with a great wine that needs only a pinch more experience to become a regional point of excellence.

The 6 Mura Rosso IGT nearly took top honours. The nose already reveals its clearly Mediterranean imprint proffering aromas of spice, scrub, forest floor and red berries. The palate is soft and caressing, and the slightly excessive alcohol is immediately subdued by good acid backbone and savoury, flavourful finish. The rest of the wines are interesting and, though simpler, never boring, starting with a juicy, fragrant Carignano del Sulcis Giba '08 and ending with a fresh Vermentino di Sardegna Giba '09.

● 6 Mura Rosso '07	ΥΥ	5
● Carignano del Sulcis Giba '08	Υ	4
○ Vermentino di Sardegna Giba '09	Υ	4
● 6 Mura Rosso '06	ΥΥ	5
● 6 Mura Rosso '05	ΥΥ	5

Agricola Punica

LOC. BARRUA
09010 SANTADI [CI]
TEL. 0781941012
www.agripunica.it

PRE-BOOKED VISITS

ANNUAL PRODUCTION 130,000 bottles
HECTARES UNDER VINE 65
VITICULTURE METHOD Conventional

The Agricola Punica estate operates in Sulcis with around 65 hectares under vine. Carignano is the most-planted variety and main ingredient in blending the two wines produced. Low yields per hectare and careful grape selection characterize production headed up by Sebastiano Rosa, known mostly for managing Tenuta San Guido. Alongside carignano, also grown on several old, ungrafted vines, the estate's stock includes some international varieties, largely cabernet, as well as merlot and syrah.

The estate's showcase Barrua easily won Three Glasses, thanks to a good growing season, especially for carignano, and the estate's unswerving attention to this variety. The '07 shows off its Mediterranean character with notes of scrub, spice and red berries and a palate that combines nice softness with brilliant acidity, pushing through to a deep, extremely clean finish over a creamy, mouthfilling tannic weave. The Montessu '08 from 60% carignano with cabernet, syrah and merlot puts the accent more on ripe fruit with vegetal and balsamic shades and a juicy drinkability that is never overdone.

● Barrua '07	ΥΥΥ	7
● Montessu '08	ΥΥ	5
● Barrua '05	ΥΥΥ	6
● Barrua '06	ΥΥ	6

★ Argiolas

VIA ROMA, 28
09040 SERDIANA [CA]
TEL. 070740606
www.argiolas.it

CELLAR SALES
PRE-BOOKED VISITS
ROOMS

ANNUAL PRODUCTION 2,000,000 bottles
HECTARES UNDER VINE 230
VITICULTURE METHOD Conventional

A lot has been written about the Argiolas estate, perhaps because this is one of the island's most prestigious operations, or because prestige has comes year after year with investments, commitment and risks that set an example for other Sardinian wineries. But the real power behind this Serdiana-based winery is a great family that has made the most of the legacy left by the estate's founder, Antonio Argiolas. Everyone has their own job, from work in the vineyards to sales and marketing. The result is a successful, high-quality range of wines sold all over the world.

The estate's signature Turriga won Three Glasses once again. The '06 vintage, from 85 per cent cannonau with bovale, carignano and malvasia nera, is what you would expect from a great southern Italian wine. The complex impact on the nose layers notes of ripe red berries, cherry and plum over spicy nuances of sweet tobacco and cocoa powder. The sumptuous, caressing palate has tannins that assert their presence but are well integrated with serious body that draws the wine into a long finish. From the other wines, we mention two new arrivals, the Iselis Bianco '09 from nasco, and Iselis Rosso '08, a very convincing monica-based selection.

● Turriga '06	▼▼▼	7
○ Angialis '07	▼▼	6
● Antonio Argiolas 100 '08	▼▼	6
● Iselis Rosso '08	▼▼	4*
● Is Solinas '08	▼▼	4
○ Iselis Bianco '09	▼▼	4*
○ Vermentino di Sardegna Is Argiolas '09	▼▼	4*
● Cannonau di Sardegna Costera '09	▼	3
● Korem '08	▼	5
● Monica di Sardegna Perdera '09	▼	3
○ Nuragus di Cagliari S'Elegas '09	▼	2
⊙ Serralori Rosato '09	▼	2
○ Vermentino di Sardegna Costamolino '09	▼	3
○ Angialis '06	▽▽▽	5
● Turriga '05	▽▽▽	7
● Turriga '04	▽▽▽	8
● Turriga '02	▽▽▽	8
● Turriga '01	▽▽▽	8

Capichera

SS ARZACHENA-SANT'ANTONIO, KM 4
07021 ARZACHENA [OT]
TEL. 078980612
www.capichera.it

CELLAR SALES
PRE-BOOKED VISITS

ANNUAL PRODUCTION 250,000 bottles
HECTARES UNDER VINE 50
VITICULTURE METHOD Conventional

The Capichera estate knows how to bring out the best in Vermentino di Gallura. Founded in the early 1920s, the estate released its first bottles under the Capichera label in the 1980s and instantly changed perceptions of Vermentino. This rich wine had structure and cellarability that were difficult to find in the market at the time. Today the estate, managed by brothers Mario and Fabrizio Ragnedda, has 50 hectares under vermentino and carignano, grown in some vineyards in Sulcis. The whole line shows the same good quality. Paradoxically, we preferred some of the simpler wines.

Vermentino di Gallura Vigna'ngena '09 shows what we always like to find in a Vermentino from the north of the island. With complex impact on the nose in full Mediterranean style, it features notes of white-fleshed fruit, as well as nuances of mineral, citrus and aromatic herbs. Freshness frames the palate, making the wine elegant and stylish despite serious structure: Three Glasses. Another high scorer was the Mantenghja '06, a carignano-based red with charming notes of spice and wild berry fruit. The fresh, supple palate is good, only penalized for the time being by slight tannic astringency.

○ Vermentino di Gallura Vigna'ngena '09	▼▼▼	6
● Mantenghja '06	▼▼	8
● Assajè Rosso '07	▼▼	6
○ Capichera '08	▼▼	6
○ Capichera V.T. '08	▼	8
○ Santigaini '06	▼	8
○ Capichera '05	▽▽	8
○ Capichera V.T. '04	▽▽	8
● Mante'nghja '04	▽▽	8
○ Vermentino di Gallura Vigna 'Ngena '07	▽▽	7

Carpante

VIA GARIBALDI, 151
07049 USINI [SS]
TEL. 079380614
www.carpante.it

CELLAR SALES
PRE-BOOKED VISITS

ANNUAL PRODUCTION **30,000 bottles**
HECTARES UNDER VINE **8**
VITICULTURE METHOD **Conventional**

Carpante is a small estate founded in early 2003. Since then, it has found an important place on the Sardinian winemaking scene, thanks to a good range of native varieties and the fine wine country in which it operates. For this reason, we feel the time is right for this winery to make a leap in quality. Everything is in place to make wines that are not only well typed but also prestigious. It would be a pity not to make the most of the varieties, the exceptional terroir, with semi-limestone, clay soils and a breezy climate.

Cagnulari mixed with small amounts of bovale sardo and pascale give the '07 Carpante convincing fragrances of leather and tobacco, with echoes of currant and blueberry nuances. The supple, zesty palate is criss-crossed with acidity that refreshes the drinkability. Also very good is the Vermentino di Sardegna Longhera '09, showing fruity and citrussy with a slightly almond finish. Good though a bit under par, the Cagnulari '09 is warm with a slightly bitter taste, especially in the finish. The other wines are all well managed.

● Carpante '07	🍷🍷	5
○ Vermentino di Sardegna Longhera '09	🍷🍷	4*
● Cagnulari '09	🍷	4
● Lizzos '08	🍷	5
○ Vermentino di Sardegna Frinas '09	🍷	5
● Cagnulari '06	YY	4
● Cannonau di Sardegna '07	YY	4*
● Carpante '06	YY	5
○ Vermentino di Sardegna Frinas '08	YY	5

Giovanni Cherchi

LOC. SA PALA E SA CHESSA
07049 USINI [SS]
TEL. 079380273
www.vinicolacherchi.it

CELLAR SALES
PRE-BOOKED VISITS

ANNUAL PRODUCTION **170,000 bottles**
HECTARES UNDER VINE **30**
VITICULTURE METHOD **Conventional**

You can be confident when you buy wine from Giovanni Cherchi. The average quality produced at this winery in Usini has been great for years now, putting him into the front rank of island estates. This estate in the village of Logudoro, in the province of Sassari, was set up in the 1970s and includes 30 hectares under vine, most planted to vermentino and the rest to two reds, cannonau and cagnulari. Cherchi has clearly put his money on cagnulari, bringing new quality to a variety that might have disappeared without his perseverance.

We were most convinced this time by the Luzzana '08, an equal blend of cagnulari and cannonau, grown in hilly zones at around 200 metres above sea level. The complex nose gives roses and plums with plenty of green notes and balsam. The juicy, graceful palate shows nice freshness that satisfies without weighing down the wine. From the whites, we mention the two Vermentino di Sardegnas. Tuvaoes '09 is fresh, citrussy and floral while Pigalva '09 plays more off tones of white peach and wisteria. The other wines are all well made.

● Luzzana '08	🍷🍷	5
○ Vermentino di Sardegna Pigalva '09	🍷🍷	4*
○ Vermentino di Sardegna Tuvaoes '09	🍷🍷	4
○ Boghes '09	🍷	5
● Cagnulari '09	🍷	4
● Cannonau di Sardegna '08	🍷	4
○ Tokaterra	🍷	4
● Cagnulari '08	YY	4*
● Cagnulari '06	YY	5
● Cannonau di Sardegna '07	YY	4*
● Luzzana '06	YY	5
● Soberanu '06	YY	8
○ Vermentino di Sardegna Tuvaoes '08	YY	4*

Attilio Contini

VIA GENOVA, 48/50
09072 CABRAS [OR]
TEL. 0783290806
www.vinicontini.it

CELLAR SALES
PRE-BOOKED VISITS

ANNUAL PRODUCTION **700,000 bottles**
HECTARES UNDER VINE **70**
VITICULTURE METHOD **Conventional**

Founded in the late 1800s, the Contini estate is one of the most respected wineries on the island. It is located a few kilometres from Oristano so how could it not be good at making Vernaccia? Over a century after its foundation, fruit from the 70 hectares under vine produces over 700,000 bottles. Vineyards are scattered mostly around Oristano, with some in parts of Sardinia. This helps make a truly remarkable range of wines which includes old Riserva di Vernaccias as well as great reds and whites produced with the use of native varieties.

Vernaccia di Oristano Antico Gregori is as remarkable as ever, though not among the best. Made using the Solera method from a blend of old reserves of Vernaccia, it unveils outstanding intensity on a nose played off dried fruit, chestnut honey and medicinal herbs. The dry palate has good acidity and the finish offers the oxidized notes typical of this wine type. As for the rest, the reds are the most interesting: Nieddera '07, a vineyard selection, has charming earthy, ripe fruit notes; the Cannonau di Sardegna Sartiglia '08 is fresh with vegetal tones; and the Riserva '06 of Cannonau 'Inu is well typed and shows hints of violet, rose and ripe fruit.

○ Vernaccia di Oristano Antico Gregori	TT	7
● Cannonau di Sardegna 'Inu Ris. '06	TT	5
● Cannonau di Sardegna Sartiglia '08	TT	4*
● Nieddera Rosso '07	TT	4
○ Vermentino di Gallura Elibaria '09	TT	4*
● Cannonau di Sardegna Tonaghe '08	T	4
○ Karmis '09	T	4
⊙ Nieddera Rosato '09	T	3
● Rosso di Contini '09	T	4
○ Vermentino di Sardegna Pariglia '09	T	4
○ Vermentino di Sardegna Tyrsos '09	T	3
○ Vernaccia di Oristano Componidori '03	T	4
○ Pontis '00	YYY	5
○ Vernaccia di Oristano Ris. '71	YYY	5
○ Vermentino di Sardegna Salmastro Terre di Ossidiana '08	YY	4*
○ Vermentino di Sardegna Tyrsos '08	YY	3*

Ferruccio Deiana

LOC. SU LEUNAXI
VIA GIALETO, 7
09040 SETTIMO SAN PIETRO [CA]
TEL. 070749117
www.ferrucciodeiana.it

CELLAR SALES
PRE-BOOKED VISITS

ANNUAL PRODUCTION **458,000 bottles**
HECTARES UNDER VINE **74**
VITICULTURE METHOD **Certified organic**

Ferruccio Deiana would rather spend his time in the vineyard than the cellar. That cellar and most of the vineyards are located here in Settimo San Pietro, a few kilometres from the town and not far from Cagliari. There are further rows at Serdiana, part of estate expansion to the goal of 100 hectares. Traditional varieties from the south of the island are grown, planted in soils based strictly on the different varieties. This translates into a broad selection of top-quality wines.

The most convincing wine this year was Sileno '07. This Riserva di Cannonau di Sardegna offers all the most main characteristics of the variety. The nose proffers red berry fruit and currants, and the very soft palate also manages to be fresh, savoury and balsamic. This wine is simple yet never boring. The juicy, fragrant Monica di Sardegna Sanremy '09 has notes of currant and blueberry. Best of the whites is the Vermentino di Sardegna Donnikalia '09, with intense fruit on the nose followed by a lean palate and almond finish. We conclude with Oirad '09, a very aromatic sweet white from moscato, malvasia and nasco with hints of Mediterranean herbs.

● Cannonau di Sardegna Sileno Ris. '07	TT	5
● Monica di Sardegna Sanremy '09	TT	3*
○ Oirad '09	TT	6
○ Vermentino di Sardegna Donnikalia '09	TT	4*
● Cannonau di Sardegna Sanremy '09	T	4
○ Pluminus '09	T	7
○ Vermentino di Sardegna Arvali '09	T	4
● Ajana '02	YYY	7
● Ajana '05	YY	7
● Cannonau di Sardegna Sanremy '08	YY	4*
● Cannonau di Sardegna Sileno '08	YY	4*
● Cannonau di Sardegna Sileno Ris. '06	YY	5
○ Pluminus '08	YY	7
○ Pluminus '07	YY	7

Tenute Dettori

LOC. BADDE NIGOLOSU
07036 SENNORI [SS]
TEL. 079514711
www.tenutedettori.it

PRE-BOOKED VISITS
ROOMS AND FOOD

ANNUAL PRODUCTION **35,000 bottles**
HECTARES UNDER VINE **22**
VITICULTURE METHOD **Organic**

Alessandro Dettori has a simple production philosophy. Let nature runs its course in the vineyard. He preserves old, bush-trained vines, some ungrafted, and makes few changes in the cellar, using spontaneous fermentation, no selected yeasts and no sulphites. Alessandro takes pride in making wine outside the boxes of fashion and current winemaking dogma. Results can be hard to interpret. Sometimes we taste delightful products, wines you could write a poem to, but, as Dettori well knows, nature can play dirty tricks and defects show. But that's how Alessandro and his wines are made. Take them or leave them.

The Dettori Bianco '07 was the most convincing. A cloudy, amber yellow, it gives distinct notes of nuts, bitter honey and medicinal herbs. On the palate, savouriness nicely offsets the softness and the finish shows sensations weighed down a bit by oxidized tones. The most interesting red is Ottomarzo '07, a monovarietal Pascale that fermented in cement. The convincing nose has notes of ripe fruit, and palate is soft, caressing and warm. Special mention goes to Dettori's new creation, Chimbanta & Battoro '06, a sweet red from the monica variety harvested when overripe.

○ Dettori Bianco '07	**ΥΥ**	6
● Chimbanta & Battoro '06	**ΥΥ**	7
○ Moscadeddu '07	**ΥΥ**	7
● Ottomarzo '07	**ΥΥ**	6
● Chimbanta '07	**Υ**	6
○ Dettori Bianco Un anno dopo '06	ΥΥΥ	6
● Dettori Rosso '04	ΥΥΥ	8
● Tenores '03	ΥΥΥ	8
○ Dettori Bianco '06	ΥΥ	6
○ Moscadeddu '06	ΥΥ	6
○ Moscadeddu '05	ΥΥ	6
● Tenores '05	ΥΥ	8

Cantine Dolianova

LOC. SAN'ESU
SS 387 KM 17,150
09041 DOLIANOVA [CA]
TEL. 070744101
www.cantinedidolianova.it

CELLAR SALES
PRE-BOOKED VISITS

ANNUAL PRODUCTION **4,000,000 bottles**
HECTARES UNDER VINE **1,200**
VITICULTURE METHOD **Conventional**

Cantine di Dolianova boasts some serious numbers: 4,000,000 bottles produced from 1,200 hectares under vine, worked by 630 member growers who have for years made this co-operative winery in Campidano is one of the largest operations on the island. Having said that, it is nice to confirm that quantity corresponds to high quality in these well-priced wines. The wide range produced generally focuses on native varieties, though there is no lack of internationals, especially in the IGT labels.

The red wines were most convincing this year. The imposing structure of the Cannonau di Sardegna Blasio Riserva '06 emerges on the nose in sensations of chocolate, spice and vanilla, and the soft, caressing palate is tarnished only by a slight astringency in the finish. The other Cannonau di Sardegna '08, the Anzenas from the San Pantaleo line, is balanced and juicy on the palate and unveils a nose with precise notes of red berries and violets. Finally, the Terresicci '06 is interesting. This blend of barbera, syrah and montepulciano has a lingering, complex nose and the palate is structured, yet has good acidity.

● Cannonau di Sardegna Anzenas San Pantaleo '08	**ΥΥ**	3*
● Cannonau di Sardegna Blasio Ris. '06	**ΥΥ**	4*
● Terresicci '06	**ΥΥ**	6
● Falconaro '07	**Υ**	4
○ Karalis Brut	**Υ**	3
● Monica di Sardegna Arenada San Pantaleo '08	**Υ**	3
○ Montesicci '09	**Υ**	4
○ Moscato di Cagliari '08	**Υ**	4
○ Nuragus di Cagliari Perlas San Pantaleo '09	**Υ**	2
⊙ Sibiola Rosato '09	**Υ**	3
○ Vermentino di Sardegna Naeli '09	**Υ**	3
○ Vermentino di Sardegna Prendas San Pantaleo '09	**Υ**	3
● Cannonau di Sardegna Anzenas San Pantaleo '07	ΥΥ	3*
● Monica di Sardegna Arenada San Pantaleo '07	ΥΥ	3*

Cantina Sociale Dorgali

VIA PIEMONTE, 11
08022 DORGALI [NU]
TEL. 078496143
www.csdorgali.com

CELLAR SALES
PRE-BOOKED VISITS

ANNUAL PRODUCTION 1,600,000 bottles
HECTARES UNDER VINE 750
VITICULTURE METHOD Conventional

A lot of time has passed since 1953 when a group of growers in Dorgali founded Cantina di Dorgali. Today, this co-operative on the eastern coast of the island produces more than a million and a half bottles with an eye always focused on quality. The standard-bearer remains Cannonau, a wine that has always produced flattering results in this area. The arrival of internationally famous consultants has raised the quality bar as production matches native varieties to the profiles of the various terroirs.

For the second year running, the Cannonau di Sardegna Viniola Riserva '07 deservedly won Three Glasses. This is what you would expect from a Cannonau that flaunts elegance and touches of crisp, never too ripe, red berries over a soft, fresh, mineral palate that shows caressing, drinkable and never too heavy. Premio Hortos '07, the latest creation from Dorgali, is also worth uncorking. This cannonau and syrah blend offers a nose of fruit melding with spicy, balsamic notes that re-emerge on the fresh, savoury palate. The rest of the wines are well made.

● Cannonau di Sardegna Viniola Ris. '07	TTT	5*
● Premio Hortos '07	TT	6
● Cannonau di Sardegna V. di Isalle '09	TT	4*
● Cannonau di Sardegna Filieri '09	T	4
⊙ Cannonau di Sardegna Rosato Filieri '09	T	4
● Cannonau di Sardegna Tunila '09	T	3
● Noriolo '08	T	4
● Cannonau di Sardegna Viniola Ris. '06	YYY	5*
● Cannonau di Sardegna Filieri '08	YY	4*
● Cannonau di Sardegna V. di Isalle '08	YY	4*
● Cannonau di Sardegna V. di Isalle '07	YY	4*
● Filieri Rosso '07	YY	2*
● Fùili '07	YY	5
● Noriolo '07	YY	4*

Feudi della Medusa

LOC. SANTA MARGHERITA
POD. SAN LEONARDO, 15
09010 PULA [CA]
TEL. 0709259019
www.feudidellamedusa.it

CELLAR SALES
PRE-BOOKED VISITS
ROOMS AND FOOD

ANNUAL PRODUCTION 250,000 bottles
HECTARES UNDER VINE 75
VITICULTURE METHOD Conventional

The production philosophy at Feudi della Medusa is obvious. Go to the winery, see the structure and take a tour of the vineyards in the south of the island and around Sassari. Here everything is studied to create high quality wines. The vineyards have the best exposures and some host old, bush-trained vines. The state-of-the-art cellar and internationally famous consultants help produce excellent wines whose only defect is that they are sometime released too young. In other words, this way of making wine monitors what happens internationally while respecting traditional Sardinian varieties.

Gerione wins Three Glasses for the second year in a row. This could not have been otherwise considering it is one of the best versions ever. The'07, from cagnulari, cabernet franc and syrah, charmed us from the attack on the nose, with blueberry and myrtle peeking through Mediterranean scrubland aromas before the creamy palate serves up caressing extract and a deep, full-flavoured finish. The Cannonau di Sardegna '08 is also well typed with notes of rose and eucalyptus while the Crisaore '07, from cagnulari with a touch of bovale, gives sensations of leather and tobacco.

● Gerione '07	TTT	8
○ Aristeo '06	TT	6
● Cannonau di Sardegna '08	TT	5
● Crisaore '07	TT	6
○ Alba Nora '08	T	6
○ Vermentino di Sardegna Albithia '09	T	4
● Gerione '06	YYY	8
○ Alba Nora '07	YY	6
● Arrubias '06	YY	6
● Cannonau di Sardegna '07	YY	5
● Cannonau di Sardegna '06	YY	5
● Crisaore '06	YY	6
● Norace '06	YY	6

Giuseppe Gabbas

via Trieste, 65
08100 Nuoro
tel. 078433745
ggabbas@tiscali.it

PRE-BOOKED VISITS

ANNUAL PRODUCTION 70,000 bottles
HECTARES UNDER VINE 13
VITICULTURE METHOD Conventional

Giuseppe Gabbas is a genuine grape grower. Here in the heart of Barbagia, a few kilometres from Nuoro, an area particularly well suited to cannonau, Gabbas lovingly tends around 13 hectares of bush-trained vineyards, planted to the most important red variety on the island. Respect for this variety and appreciation of the terroir, two estate watchwords, are followed by careful vinification that produces wines with elegance and finesse difficult to find elsewhere.

By now, we are accustomed to superb quality from the Dule and so tasting the '07 vintage was merely pleasant confirmation. The Riserva di Cannonau Barbaricino proffers beautiful sensations on the clear, clean nose with a succession of juniper and red berries interleaved with hints of cherry and currant. Acidity dominates the palate with a nicely contrasting soft, caressing texture. Three Glasses. The Cannonau di Sardegna Lillové '09 is well made and authentic, just like the Avra '07, a sweet red from a base of overripe cannonau. The Arbeskia tasting is postponed till next year, when we expect a new monovarietal selection of Cannonau.

● Cannonau di Sardegna Dule Ris. '07	▼▼▼	5*
● Avra '07	▼▼	5
● Cannonau di Sardegna Lillové '09	▼	4
● Cannonau di Sardegna Dule Ris. '06	▽▽▽	5*
● Cannonau di Sardegna Dule Ris. '05	▽▽▽	4*
● Arbeskia '06	▽▽	5
● Cannonau di Sardegna Lillové '08	▽▽	4*
● Cannonau di Sardegna Lillové '07	▽▽	4*

Cantina Gallura

via Val di Cossu, 9
07029 Tempio Pausania
tel. 079631241
www.cantinagallura.com

CELLAR SALES
PRE-BOOKED VISITS

ANNUAL PRODUCTION 1,300,000 bottles
HECTARES UNDER VINE 350
VITICULTURE METHOD Conventional

When you hear talk of wine in Gallura, you think of Dino Addis, heart and soul of this nice co-operative at Tempio. Winemaker, agronomist and manager, Dino puts all his experience and passion into vinifying grapes delivered by the 135 partners of the winery. The result is output of over a million top-quality bottles at incredibly honest prices. Vermentino is the most grown variety and wines are obtained from careful vineyard selections. Other varieties are planted, including cannonau, nebbiolo and moscato di Tempio, this last producing an excellent sweet sparkling wine.

The most important wine in the range is Vermentino di Gallura Superiore Genesi '09. Citrus, floral and aromatic herb aromas convinced us on the nose, and the palate, despite the slightly sweet attack, shows good acid backbone that refreshes progression. Among the other Vermentino di Galluras, the Canayli '09 and Piras '09 are good, especially the latter. Despite the fact this may seem thinnish, it has pleasant minerality, lime and orange blossom. Final mention goes to the superb Moscato di Tempio Spumante, an estate classic and one of the best sweet sparklers on the island.

○ Vermentino di Gallura Sup. Genesi '09	▼▼	6
● Karana '09	▼▼	3*
○ Moscato di Tempio Pausania	▼▼	4*
○ Vermentino di Gallura Piras '09	▼▼	3*
○ Vermentino di Gallura Sup. Canayli '09	▼▼	4*
⊙ Campos '09	▼	3
● Cannonau di Sardegna Templum '08	▼	4
● Dolmen '07	▼	5
○ Ladas Brut	▼	3
○ Vermentino di Gallura Gemellae '09	▼	3
○ Zivula	▼	5
○ Vermentino di Gallura Sup. Genesi '08	▽▽▽	6
○ Vermentino di Gallura Gemellae '08	▽▽	3*
○ Vermentino di Gallura Piras '08	▽▽	3*
○ Vermentino di Gallura Sup. Canayli '08	▽▽	4*

Cantina del Giogantinu

VIA MILANO, 30
07022 BERCHIDDA [OT]
TEL. 079704163
www.giogantinu.it

CELLAR SALES
PRE-BOOKED VISITS

ANNUAL PRODUCTION 1,568,000 bottles
HECTARES UNDER VINE 320
VITICULTURE METHOD Conventional

Giogantinu is one of the many Sardinian co-operatives that confirm how well co-operative wineries perform on the island. It would be a pity not to properly exploit the special terroir In Gallura, especially with vermentino, so 350 member growers tend around 320 hectares of vineyards for a production of over a million and a half bottles. The broad range of wines gives priority to Vermentino, of course, but there is also room for excellent reds, mostly blends of international and native varieties.

The most convincing wines were the two Vermentino di Gallura Superiores. Aldia '09 offers aromas of cereals and white-fleshed fruits before the palate unveils a rich texture nicely balanced by freshness and tanginess. The Giogantinu '09, one of the list's great classics, foregrounds minerality with outstanding notes of wild flowers introducing a pleasant, vibrant palate. From the reds, we mention the succulence and heady aromas of the Cannonau di Sardegna Eja '08, and the merlot, carignano and muristellu Terra Saliosa '09, which boasts and excellent tannic weave and complex aromas.

● Cannonau di Sardegna Eja '08	▼▼	4
● Terra Saliosa '09	▼▼	4*
○ Vermentino di Gallura Sup. Aldia '09	▼▼	4*
○ Vermentino di Gallura Sup. Giogantinu '09	▼▼	3*
○ Giogantino Brut	▼	4
○ Lughente '05	▼	6
● Nastarrè '09	▼	3
○ Vermentino di Gallura '09	▼	3
○ Vermentino di Gallura Lunghente '09	▼	4
○ Vermentino di Gallura Sup. Aghiloia '09	▼	4
○ Vermentino di Gallura Tancaré '09	▼	3
● Terra Mala '05	▽▽	6
● Terra Saliosa '08	▽▽	4*
● Terra Saliosa '07	▽▽	4*
○ Vermentino di Gallura Sup. Aldia '08	▽▽	4*

Antichi Poderi Jerzu

VIA UMBERTO I, 1
08044 JERZU [OG]
TEL. 078270028
www.jerzuantichipoderi.it

CELLAR SALES
PRE-BOOKED VISITS

ANNUAL PRODUCTION 2,500,000 bottles
HECTARES UNDER VINE 750
VITICULTURE METHOD Conventional

Jerzu is a town in Ogliastra 500 metres above sea level on the eastern coast of Sardinia. Wine has always played a major role here, in particular Cannonau, which has its own subzone. The co-operative winery in Jerzu started during the 1950s and for some time has traded under the name Antichi Poderi. The new title coincides with a shift to quality-driven production from vineyard to fermentation. A million and a half bottles are sourced from 750 hectares under vine where vermentino, carignano and several international varieties are grown, as well as cannonau.

Again this year, the Cannonau di Sardegna Bantu '09 surprised us. This standard-label wine is fresh and juicy, which may be the reason for its success. The nose has upfront touches of wild strawberries, blueberries and currants before the pleasant palate shows refined tannins and a long, clean finish. It's a great wine for everyday drinking. Another red worth mentioning is Akratos '05, from a cannonau base, sourced from the oldest vineyard on the estate. The nose has outstanding aromas of scrubland, followed by a soft entry on the palate braced by an acid vein that makes for pleasant, elegant drinkability.

● Akratos '05	▼▼	6
● Cannonau di Sardegna Bantu '09	▼▼	3*
● Cannonau di Sardegna Josto Miglior Ris. '07	▼▼	5
○ Vermentino di Sardegna Telavè '09	▼▼	3*
● Cannonau di Sardegna Chuerra Ris. '07	▼	5
● Cannonau di Sardegna Marghìa '08	▼	4
● Monica di Sardegna Camalda '09	▼	4
○ Vermentino di Sardegna Lucean Le Stelle '09	▼	4
● Cannonau di Sardegna Josto Miglior Ris. '05	▽▽▽	5
● Cannonau di Sardegna Bantu '08	▽▽	3*
● Cannonau di Sardegna Chuerra Ris. '06	▽▽	5
● Cannonau di Sardegna Josto Miglior Ris. '06	▽▽	5
● Cannonau di Sardegna Marghìa '07	▽▽	4*
○ Vermentino di Sardegna Telavè '08	▽▽	3*

Masone Mannu

LOC. SU CANALE
SS 199 KM 48
07020 OLBIA
TEL. 078947140
www.masonemannu.com

CELLAR SALES
PRE-BOOKED VISITS

ANNUAL PRODUCTION 100,000 bottles
HECTARES UNDER VINE 18
VITICULTURE METHOD Conventional

In the seven years since this estate was founded, Masone Mannu has secured an important place on the island's winemaking scene. Overall quality is high and constantly increasing. At this point, we expect excellence from this Olbia winery and, considering the range of varieties and nature of the terroirs, we think this will not be long in coming. Most of the 18 hectares under vine are planted to vermentino with around four under cannonau, carignano, bovale sardo and malvasia. Carefully vinified, these whistle-clean wines reflect their original varieties and terroirs.

The most convincing white wine was the Vermentino di Gallura Costarenas Superiore '09. Despite the hot growing season, it shows beautiful mint and rosemary notes, followed by fruitiness and florality. The Gallura terroir emerges in grand style on the palate in savouriness, minerality and sea salt sensations. Reds include an excellent Cannonau di Sardegna '08, with heady alcohol, fruit and green notes on the nose before the fresh, juicy palate shows tannins well tucked in. All the other wines are very well made.

○ Vermentino di Gallura Sup. Costarenas '09	TT	5
● Cannonau di Sardegna '08	TT	5
● Entu '08	T	5
⊙ Rena Rosa '09	T	4
○ Vermentino di Gallura Petrizza '09	T	4
○ Ammentu '07	YY	6
○ Ammentu '05	YY	6
● Entu '07	YY	5
● Entu '06	YY	5
● Mannu '06	YY	8
● Mannu '05	YY	8
○ Vermentino di Gallura Petrizza '08	YY	4*
○ Vermentino di Gallura Petrizza '07	YY	4*
○ Vermentino di Gallura Sup. Costarenas '08	YY	5
○ Vermentino di Gallura Sup. Costarenas '06	YY	5

Mesa

LOC. SU BARONI
09010 SANT'ANNA ARRESI [CA]
TEL. 0781965057
www.cantinamesa.it

CELLAR SALES
PRE-BOOKED VISITS

ANNUAL PRODUCTION 500,000 bottles
HECTARES UNDER VINE 70
VITICULTURE METHOD Conventional

Advertising executive Gavino Sanna directs the Mesa estate on the path to quality wine production. For some years now, high quality has shown across the range from flagship wines to simpler products. The Sant'Anna Arresi winery wagers everything on promoting native varieties, above all carignano, as well as cannonau and vermentino. There are four main vineyards and each is perfect for one specific variety. Those in Su Baroni, mainly sandy, are planted to carignano, and the Bentu Estu vineyard, with clayey, pebble-rich soil, is ideal for vermentino.

The nice red Buio Buio '08 comes from carignano grown in the best vineyards on the estate. The incredible notes on the nose range from spice and forest floor to fruity nuances of blueberry and wild strawberry. The convincing palate has a freshness that tones down the serious structure and body, and the long finish shows deep and extremely clean. The Cannonau di Sardegna Primo Scuro '08, with violet and cherry notes, and Vermentino di Sardegna Opale Bianco '09, with tropical tones and a full-flavoured, progressive palate, are also both worth investigating. The rest of the range is well typed or better.

● Buio Buio '08	TT	5
● Cannonau di Sardegna Primo Scuro '08	TT	3*
● Primo Rosso '08	TT	3*
○ Vermentino di Sardegna Opale Bianco '09	TT	5
● Carignano del Sulcis Buio '08	T	4
○ Opale Dopo '08	T	6
⊙ Primo Rosato '09	T	3
○ Vermentino di Sardegna Giunco '09	T	4
○ Vermentino di Sardegna Primo Bianco '09	T	3
● Buio '07	YY	4*
● Buio Buio '07	YY	5
● Malombra '05	YY	7
○ Vermentino di Sardegna Giunco '08	YY	4*
○ Vermentino di Sardegna Opale '08	YY	5

Mura

LOC. AZZANIDÒ, 1
07020 LOIRI PORTO SAN PAOLO [OT]
TEL. 078941070
www.vinimura.it

CELLAR SALES
PRE-BOOKED VISITS

ANNUAL PRODUCTION 48,000 bottles
HECTARES UNDER VINE 11
VITICULTURE METHOD Conventional

The small, family-run Mura estate, around 11 hectares in the area of Loiri Porto San Paolo, has been producing good wines across the range since 1999. Over the past few years, the quality bar has been raised even further, so Mura has now become one of the benchmark estates on the island. Production is based for the most part on vermentino, skilfully vinified while taking into account the terroir of Gallura, as well as other native varieties such as cannonau and carignano.

Mura wines performed well this year, especially the Vermentino di Gallura Superiore Sienda, which reached our finals. The '09 version gives a complex nose of floral sensations, white peach and aromatic herbs. A soft attack on the palate is refined by acidity that pulls the wine toward a nice almondy finish like the most classic Vermentinos. The Vermentino di Gallura Cheremi '09 is simpler, yet fresh, well made and pleasant. Outstanding among the reds is Cannonau di Sardegna Cortes '08, a heady, savoury wine with varietal rose and violet notes.

○ Vermentino di Gallura Sup. Sienda '09	▼▼	4*
● Cannonau di Sardegna Cortes '08	▼▼	4*
○ Vermentino di Gallura Cheremi '09	▼▼	4*
● Nebidu '06	▼	4
● Baja '05	▽▽	6
● Jara '05	▽▽	4*
○ Vermentino di Gallura Cheremi '08	▽▽	4*
○ Vermentino di Gallura Sup. Sienda '08	▽▽	4*

Pala

VIA VERDI, 7
09040 SERDIANA [CA]
TEL. 070740284
www.pala.it

CELLAR SALES
PRE-BOOKED VISITS

ANNUAL PRODUCTION 450,000 bottles
HECTARES UNDER VINE 68
VITICULTURE METHOD Conventional

Mario Pala is heir to this major winery in Serdiana founded in the 1950s by his father Salvatore. Those days of bulk production are long gone. Now Pala is at the top of its class on the island, thanks to long experience, intelligent investment and quality-oriented decisions. The wide range includes two principal lines, the base Silenzi line and the I Fiori line, which replace the varietal names of the past, plus several selections and some blends from internationals and native varieties. The vineyards in the hills have clay soils and some have old, bush-trained vines.

The excellent Cannonau di Sardegna I Fiori '08 has a nose that focuses on crisp red fruit and a fresh, succulent palate with good acid backbone. The Silenzi Rosso '09 is surprising, especially at this price, and amazes with a heady nose of Mediterranean scrubland, and a long, deep palate. Among the whites, the Vermentino di Sardegna I Fiori '09 is tangy with varietal almond. Finally, a mention goes to the rosé Chiaro di Stelle '09, one of the best rosé-fermented wines from the island.

● Cannonau di Sardegna I Fiori '08	▼▼	4*
⊙ Chiaro di Stelle '09	▼▼	4*
● Silenzi Rosso '09	▼▼	3*
○ Vermentino di Sardegna I Fiori '09	▼▼	4*
● Essentija '07	▼	5
● Monica di Sardegna I Fiori '08	▼	3
○ Nuragus di Cagliari I Fiori '09	▼	3
○ Silenzi Bianco '09	▼	3
○ Vermentino di Sardegna Stellato '09	▼	4
○ Entemari '08	▽▽	5
○ Nuragus di Cagliari Sàlnico '08	▽▽	3*
● S'Arai '06	▽▽	6
● S'Arai '05	▽▽	6
○ Vermentino di Sardegna Crabilis '08	▽▽	3*
○ Vermentino di Sardegna Stellato '08	▽▽	4*

Pedres

Z. I. Settore 7
07026 Olbia
tel. 0789595075
www.cantinapedres.it

CELLAR SALES
PRE-BOOKED VISITS

ANNUAL PRODUCTION 290,000 bottles
HECTARES UNDER VINE 40
VITICULTURE METHOD Conventional

The Pedres estate was founded in 2002 by Giovanni, heir of the Mancini family, who boast a winemaking history in Gallura that goes back to the 19th century. The estate has around 40 hectares of vineyards, all in hilly areas at around 300 metres above sea level, and all in Gallura, in Monti and Calangianus. The subsoil has a sandy, granite quality and gives naturally low grape yields. Work in the cellar is limited to bringing out the best this character.

It is no surprise to find a wine here with great elegance and finesse, complex and respectful of the terroir and variety. The Vermentino di Gallura Superiore Thilibas is truly convincing in the '09 vintage, weaving apricots and white peaches charmingly with nuances of aromatic herbs, curry plant and orange blossom on the nose. The succession of fresh, balsamic, mineral notes on the palate fade into an extremely clean, citrussy finish, all contributing to a first, well-deserved Three Glass prize. There is also an excellent Cannonau di Sardegna Cerasio '08 and a really enjoyable Moscato di Sardegna Spumante Assolo, proof that there is top quality across the entire range.

○ Vermentino di Gallura Sup. Thilibas '09	▼▼▼	5*
● Cannonau di Sardegna Cerasio '08	▼▼	5
● Cannonau di Sardegna Sulitài '08	▼▼	4*
○ Moscato di Sardegna Assolo	▼▼	4*
○ Vermentino di Gallura Jaldinu '09	▼▼	4*
○ Lu Gadduresu Spumante Brut	▼	4
● Muros '07	▼	4
○ Vermentino di Sardegna Colline '09	▼	4
● Cannonau di Sardegna Cerasio '06	▽▽	4*
○ Moscato di Sardegna	▽▽	4*
○ Vermentino di Gallura Jaldinu '08	▽▽	4*
○ Vermentino di Gallura Sup. Thilibas '08	▽▽	4*
○ Vermentino di Gallura Sup. Thilibas '07	▽▽	4*

Cantina Sociale Santa Maria La Palma

loc. Santa Maria La Palma
07041 Alghero [SS]
tel. 079999008
www.santamarialapalma.it

CELLAR SALES
PRE-BOOKED VISITS

ANNUAL PRODUCTION 3,600,000 bottles
HECTARES UNDER VINE 700
VITICULTURE METHOD Certified organic

Santa Maria La Palma deals in big numbers. More than 300 member growers and around 700 hectares under vine produce over three and a half million bottles that bring prestige to wine production in the north-west of the island. This Alghero-based co-operative transforms these numbers into a quality that runs through the entire production with better than honest prices. The varieties grown include traditional grapes as well several international varieties planted for so long here as to be permitted under the Alghero DOC.

The reds were the most convincing from this range. The Cannonau di Sardegna Le Bombarde '09 is a great classic with heady, eucalyptus aromas and a supple, juicy palate. Great for your everyday drinking, and for your budget. The Alghero Rosso Cinquanta Vendemmie '07 is a good, mouthfilling and well structured blend from a careful selection of cagnulari plus a dash of native varieties. The nose has sensations of root vegetables and spice, and the mouthfilling palate caresses with silky tannins. The Alghero Cagnulari '08, with its vegetal nose and deep, savoury palate, is a wine to bank on.

● Alghero Cagnulari '08	▼▼	5
● Alghero Rosso Cinquanta Vendemmie '07	▼▼	6
● Cannonau di Sardegna Le Bombarde '09	▼▼	4*
● Cannonau di Sardegna Ris. '04	▼	5
○ Vermentino di Sardegna Aragosta '09	▼	3
○ Vermentino di Sardegna I Papiri '09	▼	4
● Alghero Cabirol '06	▽▽	4*
● Alghero Cagnulari '07	▽▽	5
● Alghero Cagnulari '06	▽▽	5
● Alghero Cagnulari '05	▽▽	5
● Cannonau di Sardegna Le Bombarde '08	▽▽	4*
● Cannonau di Sardegna Le Bombarde '07	▽▽	4*
● Cannonau di Sardegna Le Bombarde '06	▽▽	4*
● Monica di Sardegna '08	▽▽	3*

★ Cantina di Santadi

VIA CAGLIARI, 78
09010 SANTADI [CI]
TEL. 0781950127
www.cantinadisantadi.it

CELLAR SALES
PRE-BOOKED VISITS

ANNUAL PRODUCTION 1,700,000 bottles
HECTARES UNDER VINE 606
VITICULTURE METHOD Conventional

If any winery knows how to promote an winemaking area and a native variety present only in this corner of Sardinia, it is Santadi. This Sulcis co-operative has operated for many years with a quality-oriented philosophy, presenting local and international markets with well-made wines that respect territory and variety. Obviously, carignano is the variety used for most of the estate reds, though other traditional varieties are present including nasco, an aromatic variety used to make a delicious late-harvest wine.

This year, the '06 Shardana amazed us and deservedly reached the finals. From carignano with a splash of syrah, this varietal wine has Mediterranean sensations of scrubland, red fruit and spicy shades, followed by a gutsy, mouthfilling palate with soft extract. The Grotta Rossa '08 is also good. It's a simpler version of Carignano del Sulcis that knows how to be juicy, long and utterly irresistible. Rounding off the reds is Araja '08, a wine from a special blend of carignano and sangiovese. One final note goes to a white, the Nuragus di Cagliari Pedraia '09, a vibrant, fresh wine with distinctive notes of medlar.

● Shardana '06	🍷🍷	6
● Araja '08	🍷🍷	4
● Carignano del Sulcis Grotta Rossa '08	🍷🍷	4*
○ Nuragus di Cagliari Pedraia '09	🍷🍷	4*
● Cannonau di Sardegna Noras '08	🍷	5
⊙ Cannonau di Sardegna Rosato '09	🍷	4
● Monica di Sardegna Antigua '09	🍷	4
○ Vermentino di Sardegna Cala Silente '09	🍷	4
○ Vermentino di Sardegna Villa Solais '09	🍷	3
○ Villa di Chiesa '08	🍷	6
● Carignano del Sulcis Sup. Terre Brune '05	ΨΨΨ	8
● Carignano del Sulcis Sup. Terre Brune '04	ΨΨΨ	8
● Carignano del Sulcis Sup. Terre Brune '03	ΨΨΨ	7
● Carignano del Sulcis Sup. Terre Brune '01	ΨΨΨ	7
● Carignano del Sulcis Sup. Terre Brune '00	ΨΨΨ	7
○ Latinia '01	ΨΨΨ	5

Sardus Pater

VIA RINASCITA, 46
09017 SANT'ANTIOCO [CI]
TEL. 0781800274
www.cantinesarduspater.com

CELLAR SALES
PRE-BOOKED VISITS

ANNUAL PRODUCTION 600,000 bottles
HECTARES UNDER VINE 300
VITICULTURE METHOD Conventional

The natural landscape in Sant'Antioco features Mediterranean scrubland dense with myrtle, mastic and juniper framing the many vineyards that characterize this wine producing area of the island. The densely planted bush-trained vines, for the most part ungrafted, naturally produce low yields and potentially high quality, potential that is fully exploited by the Sardus Pater winery. Over the past few years, this major co-operative group has produced an impressive range of wines with plenty of peaks of excellence.

Speaking of excellence, Carignano del Sulcis Is Arenas Riserva '07, aided by a great growing year, gives an enormously complex nose run through with sensations of black pepper, myrtle, root vegetables and sweet tobacco. The supple, caressing palate is crossed by a major acid vein, well integrated with creamy, sweet tannins. Three Glasses. On the white front, the two Vermentino di Sardegnas are interesting. The Lugore '09 is grassy with no lack of tropical fruit and the Terre Fenicie '09 has a rich nose and deep, savoury palate. A final mention goes to the Moscato di Cagliari Amentos '09, a fresh, sweet wine that shows extremely clean on the nose.

● Carignano del Sulcis Is Arenas Ris. '07	🍷🍷🍷	5*
○ Moscato di Cagliari Amentos '09	🍷🍷	5
○ Vermentino di Sardegna Lugore '09	🍷🍷	4
○ Vermentino di Sardegna Terre Fenicie '09	🍷🍷	4*
⊙ Carignano del Sulcis Horus '09	🍷	4
● Carignano del Sulcis Nur '09	🍷	4
● Monica di Sardegna Insula '09	🍷	4
● Carignano del Sulcis Arenas Ris. '05	ΨΨΨ	5*
● Carignano del Sulcis Is Arenas Ris. '06	ΨΨΨ	5*
● Carignano del Sulcis Is Solus '08	ΨΨ	4*
● Carignano del Sulcis Is Solus '07	ΨΨ	4*
● Carignano del Sulcis Kanai Ris. '07	ΨΨ	5
● Carignano del Sulcis Kanai Ris. '06	ΨΨ	5
● Carignano del Sulcis Nur '08	ΨΨ	4*
● Carignano del Sulcis Nur '07	ΨΨ	4*
● Carignano del Sulcis Sup. Arruga '04	ΨΨ	6
○ Moscato di Cagliari Amentos '07	ΨΨ	5

Giuseppe Sedilesu

VIA ADUA, 2
08024 MAMOIADA [NU]
TEL. 078456333
www.giuseppesedilesu.com

CELLAR SALES
PRE-BOOKED VISITS

ANNUAL PRODUCTION 60,000 bottles
HECTARES UNDER VINE 15
VITICULTURE METHOD Organic

Traditional viticulture is much discussed, as are wines made "in the vineyard and not in the cellar", and respect for terroirs and native varieties. Unfortunately, few producers really apply this philosophy. One that does, however, is Mamoiada-based Sedilesu, a Cannonau specialist. The most interesting thing is that the traditional approach in the vineyard translates into wines with an extremely clean style, free of defects and capable of transmitting genuine sensations that go beyond mere aromatics.

All three wines from this estate reached our national finals and the masterpiece is Mamuthone. This Cannonau di Sardegna '08 swept up Three Glasses thanks to a nose of incredible complexity and length. Myrtle, rose petals, forest floor and black berry fruit are only some of the nuances in the bouquet, followed by a palate that is succulent yet savoury, fresh and caressing with a silky tannic weave. Other good wines, with very different profiles, include the more full-bodied and structured Carnevale '07 and the S'Annada '08, an only apparently simpler red whose freshness and succulence lend it extraordinary drinkability.

●	Cannonau di Sardegna Mamuthone '08	▼▼▼	4*
●	Cannonau di Sardegna Carnevale '07	▼▼	6
●	Cannonau di Sardegna S'Annada '08	▼▼	4*
○	Perda Pintà '07	▽▽▽	6
●	Cannonau di Sardegna Ballutundu Ris. '06	▽▽	7
●	Cannonau di Sardegna Ballutundu Ris. '05	▽▽	7
●	Cannonau di Sardegna Carnevale '06	▽▽	6
●	Cannonau di Sardegna Mamuthone '07	▽▽	4*
●	Cannonau di Sardegna Mamuthone '06	▽▽	4*
○	Perda Pintà '06	▽▽	6

★ Tenute Sella & Mosca

LOC. I PIANI
07041 ALGHERO [SS]
TEL. 079997700
www.sellaemosca.com

CELLAR SALES
PRE-BOOKED VISITS

ANNUAL PRODUCTION 7,600,000 bottles
HECTARES UNDER VINE 550
VITICULTURE METHOD Conventional

The historic Sella & Mosca label has made Sardinian wine famous worldwide, and continues to promote high quality without compromising its idea of wine. The wide range of wines from Alghero starts with the basic line – always recommended for its value for money – and includes several peaks of Italian and international excellence. The estate operates mainly in north-west Sardinia with the production of Alghero DOC, but has properties in other fine winemaking areas of the island.

Yet again, the Alghero Rosso Marchese di Villamarina '05 is splendid, a wine that can be enjoyed now yet has no fear of ageing. The result of vinifying select cabernet sauvignon, it unfurls a nose rich in vegetal sensations ranging from pine needles to Mediterranean scrub around a well-defined fruity component. The excellent palate shows nicely ripe tannins well integrated into the texture, coupled with tidy, vibrant acidity. A great example of Vermentino di Gallura Superiore is Monteoro '09, an outstanding white with a citrussy, mineral nose and fresh, supple, salty palate. The Alghero Torbato Terre Bianche Cuvée 161 '09 also impresses.

●	Alghero Marchese di Villamarina '05	▼▼▼	7
○	Alghero Torbato Terre Bianche Cuvée 161 '09	▼▼	5
○	Vermentino di Gallura Sup. Monteoro '09	▼▼	4*
○	Alghero Torbato Terre Bianche '09	▼▼	4
●	Cannonau di Sardegna Dimonios Ris. '06	▼▼	5
●	Alghero Anghelu Ruju '03	▼	7
⊙	Alghero Oleandro '09	▼	4
●	Alghero Tanca Farrà '06	▼	5
○	Alghero Thilion '09	▼	5
○	Vermentino di Sardegna Cala Reale '09	▼	4
○	Vermentino di Sardegna La Cala '09	▼	4
●	Alghero Marchese di Villamarina '04	▽▽▽	7
●	Alghero Marchese di Villamarina '03	▽▽▽	7
●	Alghero Marchese di Villamarina '01	▽▽▽	7
○	Alghero Torbato Terre Bianche Cuvée 161 '07	▽▽▽	4*
○	Vermentino di Gallura Monteoro '08	▽▽▽	4*

F.lli Serra

VIA GARIBALDI, 25
09070 ZEDDIANI [OR]
TEL. 0783418276
www.vernacciaserra.it

CELLAR SALES
PRE-BOOKED VISITS

ANNUAL PRODUCTION 40,000 bottles
HECTARES UNDER VINE 14
VITICULTURE METHOD Conventional

Listing small, family-run wineries in this section of the Guide is always a pleasure, especially when they are returning after a few years' absence. Credit goes to the Serra brothers, who courageously carry forward a passion tied to that oenological jewel known as Vernaccia di Oristano. Production is typical for the wine type and involves ageing in large, part-filled barrels for many years, which encourages creation of a yeast flor that is this wine's distinctive feature. The estate has 14 hectares planted to vernaccia as well as the international varieties that go to creating the estate red, Kora Kodes.

The Vernaccia di Oristano Riserva '99 is simply the best we tasted of this wine type. The complex sensations on the nose alternate nuts, bitter honey, apricot and sponge cake. The dry palate has a light sweet touch, and the tangy freshness pulls the wine into a deep finish where signature oxidative shades and almond paste emerge. Three well-deserved Glasses. The cabernet sauvignon Kora Kodes '08 is also great, giving vegetal aromas and a balanced, gutsy palate.

○ Vernaccia di Oristano Ris. '99	YYY (black)	5*
● Kora Kodes Rosso '08	YY (black)	4*
○ Vernaccia di Oristano Ris. '00	YY	4
○ Vernaccia di Oristano Ris. '92	YY	4
○ Vernaccia di Oristano Ris. '86	YY	3

Tenute Soletta

LOC. SIGNOR'ANNA
07040 CODRONGIANOS [SS]
TEL. 079435067
www.tenutesoletta.it

CELLAR SALES
PRE-BOOKED VISITS

ANNUAL PRODUCTION 100,000 bottles
HECTARES UNDER VINE N.A.
VITICULTURE METHOD Conventional

Soletta is a small estate in the north of Sardinia created in the mid 1990s. Over the past few years, it has carved out a major niche in the island's winemaking, thanks to the efforts and dogged perseverance of the three siblings who manage it: Umberto covers production, Pina the sales aspects and Francesco deals with export. All in all, this great winemaking family produces a range of very fine bottles, having put their money on traditional varieties like cannonau, vermentino and moscato.

Two wines impressed us. The Vermentino di Sardegna Chimera '09 has a nose with aromatic herb tones and clear, lingering citrussy sensations. The fresh, dynamic palate has a pleasantly bitterish finish. Among the reds, the typical Cannonau di Sardegna Keramos Riserva '06 shows the profile of a great Mediterranean wine, with charming notes of myrtle shading into nuances of liquorice and pencil lead before the impressive freshness on the palate leaves the mouth balsamic and clean. Also very good is Cannonau di Sardegna Corona Majore '07, which has an intense nose of ripe fruit and a caressing palate. The other wines are all well made.

● Cannonau di Sardegna Keramos Ris. '06	YY (black)	5
○ Vermentino di Sardegna Chimera '09	YY (black)	4*
● Cannonau di Sardegna Corona Majore '07	YY (black)	5
● Cannonau di Sardegna Sardo '08	Y (black)	4
○ Vermentino di Sardegna Sardo '09	Y (black)	4
● Cannonau di Sardegna Keramos Ris. '04	YYY	5
● Cannonau di Sardegna Corona Majore Ris. '06	YY	5
● Cannonau di Sardegna Corona Majore Ris. '05	YY	5
● Cannonau di Sardegna Firmadu '05	YY	4*
● Cannonau di Sardegna Ris. '04	YY	4
○ Dolce Valle Moscato Passito '04	YY	4*
○ Hermes '05	YY	5
○ Kianos '08	YY	5

Cantina Trexenta

v.le Piemonte, 40
09040 Senorbì [CA]
tel. 0709808863
www.cantina-trexenta.it

CELLAR SALES
PRE-BOOKED VISITS

ANNUAL PRODUCTION 1,000,000 bottles
HECTARES UNDER VINE 10
VITICULTURE METHOD Conventional

Trexenta is a major co-operative winery started in the mid 1950s. For some time now it has worked on raising levels of quality. The range is broad and production runs around a million bottles a year. Greatest efforts are dedicated to the reds even though, year after year, the whites have also started to convince us for their stylistic cleanliness and pleasant drinkability. We should also mention the modest price tags, amazingly low even for the top wines from strict selections.

We felt the best bottle was the well-typed, complex Cannonau di Sardegna Bingias '07. The nose has a bouquet of rose and red berries. In the mouth, it is imposing yet never loses its suppleness or the vibrancy of its elegantly refined palate. The other Cannonaus are also interesting, such as the deep, succulent Goimajor '08, the spicy, caressing Tanca su Conti Riserva '07, or the Corte Adua '07, which shows touches of liquorice and cocoa powder. From the whites, we picked out Vermentino di Sardegna Monteluna '09 for its appealing citrussy nose and rosemary nuances, followed by a palate with a savoury, flavourful finish.

● Cannonau di Sardegna Bingias '07	🍷🍷	4*
● Cannonau di Sardegna Corte Adua '07	🍷🍷	3*
● Cannonau di Sardegna Goimajor '08	🍷🍷	2*
● Cannonau di Sardegna Tanca su Conti Ris. '07	🍷🍷	5
● Monica di Sardegna Bingias '07	🍷🍷	4*
○ Vermentino di Sardegna Monteluna '09	🍷🍷	2
● Antigu '06	🍷	6
● Cannonau di Sardegna Baione '07	🍷	4
● Monica di Sardegna Duca di Mandas '07	🍷	3
○ Vermentino di Sardegna Bingias '09	🍷	3
○ Vermentino di Sardegna Contissa '09	🍷	2
○ Vermentino di Sardegna Donna Leonora '09	🍷	2
● Cannonau di Sardegna Baione '06	YY	3*
● Cannonau di Sardegna Bingias '06	YY	3*
● Cannonau di Sardegna Corte Adua '06	YY	2*

Cantina del Vermentino

via San Paolo, 2
07020 Monti [SS]
tel. 078944012
www.vermentinomonti.it

CELLAR SALES
PRE-BOOKED VISITS

ANNUAL PRODUCTION 2,500,000 bottles
HECTARES UNDER VINE 500
VITICULTURE METHOD Conventional

Started up in the mid 1950s, year after year Cantina di Monti has assumed a major role among Gallura co-operatives, which in Sardinia, especially in the north-east of the island, are renowned for their high-quality wines. As the name shows, the estate focuses on vermentino, although the range also features many sound products based on traditional varieties. The rest is provided by granite-based soils and hillside vineyards ideally aspected for viticulture, helping the 350 member-growers to furnish high quality grapes.

Confirming the winery's strong suit were two intriguing Vermentino di Gallura '09s. Funtanaliras has a bouquet of aromatic herbs and citrus, and the fresh, supple palate finishes savoury. The S'Eleme '09 also has a fresh mouthfeel and good drinkability, despite the nose being more centred on ripe, white-fleshed fruit. Reds include the excellent Abbaìa '09, from a cabernet sauvignon base, which shows typical violet and bell pepper touches and offers a juicy, fragrant palate. The rest of the wines are good.

● Abbaìa '09	🍷🍷	3*
○ Vermentino di Gallura Funtanaliras '09	🍷🍷	4
○ Vermentino di Gallura S'Eleme '09	🍷🍷	3*
● Cannonau di Sardegna Tamara '08	🍷	4
● Galana '04	🍷	5
○ Moscato di Sardegna Spumante Vigna del Portale	🍷	4
⊙ Spumante Brut Rosato Vigna del Portale	🍷	4
○ Vermentino di Gallura Sup. Arakena V. T. '08	🍷	5
○ Vermentino di Gallura Funtanaliras '08	YY	5

Cantina del Bovale

loc. S'Isca
09098 Terralba [OR]
tel. 078383462
www.cantinadelbovale.it

Bovale makes did well and presented excellent wines. We felt the most convincing was the Sinnos '08 from cannonau, monica and bovale. The nose has outstanding ripe fruit and spice, and the palate shows fresh and vital, aided by an excellent tannic weave. The Terralba Majorale '08 is also quite good.

● Sinnos '08	YY	4*
● Terralba Majorale '08	YY	5
● Terralba Arcuentu '08	Y	4
O Vermentino di Sardegna Sabbie d'Oro '09	Y	3

Cantina di Calasetta

via Roma, 134
09011 Calasetta [CI]
tel. 078188413
www.cantinacalasetta.com

This small co-operative in Calasetta surprised us this year with excellent wines led by a great Carignano del Sulcis Aina Riserva '07. The nose features notes of spice and red berries, and the fresh, savoury palate flaunts caressing tannins, just what a great Mediterranean wine should be.

● Carignano del Sulcis Aina Ris. '07	YY	5*
● Carignano del Sulcis Piede Franco '08	YY	4*
● Carignano del Sulcis Tupei '08	YY	4*
O Vermentino di Sardegna Cala di Seta '09	Y	3

Silvio Carta

via Roma, 2
09070 Baratili San Pietro [OR]
tel. 0783410314
www.silviocarta.it

Silvio Carta submitted some interesting wines this year, among them a Vernaccia di Oristano Riserva from '01. The nose brims with nuts and sponge cake, and oxidative shades on the palate are softened by freshness and vitality. The rest of the wines are good, especially the Vermentino di Sardegna '09.

O Vernaccia di Oristano Ris. '01	YY	5
● Cannonau di Sardegna Badde Ruja '08	Y	4
O Eleonora Vernaccia '09	Y	4
O Vermentino di Sardegna Badde Alba '09	Y	3

Cantina Sociale di Castiadas

loc. Olia Speciosa
09040 Castiadas [CA]
tel. 0709949004
www.cantinacastiadas.com

Though this Castiadas winery specializes in Cannonau di Sardegna – the Capo Ferrato subzone is in this area – we liked the Vermentino di Sardegna Praidis '09. The nose features outstanding notes of white peach and thyme, and the palate is savoury from start to finish.

O Vermentino di Sardegna Praidis '09	YY	3*
● Cannonau di Sardegna Capo Ferrato Ris. '05	Y	4
● Monica di Sardegna Genis '09	Y	3
● Parolto '06	Y	4

Chessa

via San Giorgio
07049 Usini [SS]
tel. 3283747069
www.cantinechessa.it

Giovanna Chessa, owner of this small operation at Usini, was clear about making top-quality wine right from the start. In confirmation, we tasted an excellent Cagnulari from the '09 vintage that shows clear, clean aromas of spice and myrtle before the fresh, caressing palate signs off deep and full flavoured.

● Cagnulari '09	YY	5*
O Kentàles	Y	6
O Vermentino di Sardegna Mattariga '09	Y	5

Gianluigi Deaddis

loc. San Pietro
SS 134 km 2,2
07030 Bulzi [SS]
tel. 079588314
www.cantinadeaddis.com

Gianluigi Deaddis's estate makes a fine debut in the Guide. Three well-made wines come from six hectares under vine. The most interesting is the Ultana '08, a Bordeaux blend that landed in our finals. B bell pepper and red fruits on the nose return on a fresh, supple palate with excellent drinkability.

● Ultana '08	YY	6
● Padres '08	YY	4
O Vermentino di Sardegna Narami '09	Y	4

Paolo Depperu

LOC. SAS RUINAS
07025 LURAS [OT]
TEL. 079647314
azienda.depperu@tiscali.it

If you are looking for a rich, characteristically Mediterranean white with good structure, go for the Ruinas di Depperu. In the '09 vintage, this Gallura Vermentino shows complex, lingering aromatics of white-fleshed fruits leading into fresh, savoury drinkability on the palate.

○ Ruinas '09	🍷🍷	5

Vigne Deriu

LOC. SIGNORANNA
07040 CODRONGIANOS [SS]
TEL. 079435101
www.vignederiu.it

The Deriu family continues to make high-quality wines. The Cannonau di Sardegna '08 has refined aromas of cherry and violet. Vermentino di Sardegna '09 is zesty and rich in sensations that conjure up ripe, white-fleshed fruits. Finally, the interesting Oro Ere '08 is a sweet white from a moscato base.

● Cannonau di Sardegna '08	🍷🍷	4*
○ Vermentino di Sardegna '09	🍷🍷	4*
○ Oro Ere '08	🍷	6

Fradiles

VIA SANDRO PERTINI, 2
08030 ATZARA [NU]
TEL. 3331761683
www.fradiles.it

Despite specializing in the Mandrolisai DOC, the Fradiles winery amazed us this year with an IGT red from a base of bovale sardo. Bagadiu '08 has a soft, well-structured palate supported by good acid backbone. The nose shows distinctive tones of leather, ripe fruit and medicinal herbs.

● Bagadiu '08	🍷🍷	5

Gostolai

VIA FRIULI VENEZIA GIULIA, 24
08025 OLIENA [NU]
TEL. 0784288417
gostolai.arcadu@tiscali.it

Tonino Arcadu owns this Oliena estate specializing in Nepente. The most convincing wine from the broad range submitted was Su Gucciu, a sweet red where the perception of sugar is well balanced by subtle tannins and good freshness. In addition, the Cannonau di Sardegna Nepente Riserva '05 is well typed.

● Su Gucciu	🍷🍷	5
● Cannonau di Sardegna Nepente di Oliena Ris. '05	🍷	5
● Cannonau di Sardegna Nepente di Oliena Sos Usos de Una la '07	🍷	4

Li Duni

LOC. LI PARISI
07030 BADESI [SS]
TEL. 079585844
www.cantinaliduni.it

This estate in northern Sardinia produces some intriguing wines. Vermentino di Gallura Superiore Rena Bianca '09 has the character of a wine born by the sea, enhancing its aromatics with salty, mineral nuances. The sweet attack on the palate is quickly balanced by a lovely, deep, savoury sensation.

○ Vermentino di Gallura Sup. Rena Bianca '09	🍷🍷	6
● Tajanu '06	🍷	5
○ Vermentino di Sardegna Amabile '08	🍷	5

Li Seddi

VIA MARE, 29
07030 BADESI [SS]
TEL. 079683052
www.cantinaliseddi.it

This small Badesi winery was up to snuff again this year. The best wine is again an IGT red from traditional varieties. The Petra Ruja '08 shows fruit that is ripe but not overripe on the nose, and the palate is complex, long and supple thanks to a nice balance of tannic weave and caressing sensations.

● Petra Ruja '08	🍷🍷	4*
● Lu Ghiali '08	🍷	5
○ Vermentino di Gallura Sup. Li Pastini '09	🍷	5

Lisca

VIA DELOGU, 89
07044 ITTIRI [SS]
TEL. 079442612
antonio.lisca@alice.it

This small operation near Sassari produces traditional, typical wines. The most convincing is the Inchiza '08, set apart by a floral, balsamic, scrubland bouquet, and a palate with a Mediterranean attack that never loses the clean suppleness of the fruit.

● Inchiza '08	🍷🍷	4*
○ Carignos '09	🍷	4
○ Lisca Brut '05	🍷	5

Alberto Loi

SS 125 KM 124,2
08040 CARDEDU [OG]
TEL. 070240866
www.cantina.it/albertoloi

It was only a middling vintage for Alberto Loi's wines, which all seem to share slight hints of overripeness. Among the wines tasted, we mention the two Cannonau di Sardegna Riservas. The Sa Mola '07 features green, spicy notes and the Alberto Loi '06 is well structured with a slightly bitterish finish.

● Cannonau di Sardegna Alberto Loi Ris. '06	🍷	4
● Cannonau di Sardegna Cardedo Ris. '08	🍷	4
● Cannonau di Sardegna Sa Mola Ris. '07	🍷	3
● Tuvara '06	🍷	6

Piero Mancini

LOC. CALA SACCAIA
07026 OLBIA
TEL. 078950717
www.pieromancini.it

Piero Mancini's winery in Gallura did very well. In one of the best versions ever, the Vermentino di Gallura Cucaione '09 has an intriguing nose rich in citrus and aromatic herbs, and a long, savoury palate with appealing progression. The supple, juicy Cannonau di Sardegna Falcale '07 is also quite good.

● Cannonau di Sardegna Falcale '07	🍷🍷	4*
○ Vermentino di Gallura Cucaione '09	🍷🍷	3*
● Scalapetra '08	🍷	3
○ Vermentino di Gallura Primo '09	🍷	5

Cantina Sociale del Mandrolisai

C.SO IV NOVEMBRE, 20
08038 SORGONO [NU]
TEL. 078460113
www.mandrolisai.com

This co-operative winery specializing in bovale continues to turn out well-crafted wines, vinified with respect to tradition and terroir. Aside from a classic Mandrolisai Superiore '05 with grassy, leather tones, we felt the Ternura, an aromatic, flavoursome sweet white, was interesting.

● Mandrolisai Rosso Sup. '05	🍷	4
○ Ternura	🍷	5

Abele Melis

VIA SANTA SUINA, 3
09098 TERRALBA [OR]
TEL. 0783851090
melis.vini@tiscali.it

Abele Melis doesn't restrict himself to Terralba DOC wines. The fresh Cannonau di Sardegna Horreum '08 has cherries and currants while Vermentino di Sardegna Ereb '09 shows upfront aromatic herbs and citrus, a vibrant palate and a salt-edged finish. The flavourful Terralba Dominariu '07 is good.

● Cannonau di Sardegna Horreum '08	🍷🍷	4
○ Vermentino di Sardegna Ereb '09	🍷🍷	5
● Terralba Dominariu '07	🍷	4
○ Vermentino di Sardegna Iocalia '09	🍷	4

Meloni Vini

VIA GALLUS, 79
09047 SELARGIUS [CA]
TEL. 070852822
www.melonivini.com

Top of the list this year were the three organically produced monovarietals from the Selargius estate's Le Sabbie line. The Cannonau di Sardegna '07 has a supple, caressing palate, the Monica di Sardegna '08 shows fruity aromas and serious structure while Vermentino di Sardegna '09 has a citrus tang.

● Cannonau di Sardegna Le Sabbie '07	🍷	4
● Monica di Sardegna Le Sabbie '08	🍷	4
○ Nasco di Cagliari Donna Jolanda '04	🍷	5
○ Vermentino di Sardegna Le Sabbie '09	🍷	4

Murales

via Colcò, 45
07026 Olbia
tel. 078968298
www.vinimurales.it

This young Olbia estate debuted with authentic wines in a personal style. The good Nativo '08 is a red from syrah, cabernet and cannonau with a deep, lean palate and touches of red fruit and scrubland. The Cannonau di Sardegna Arcanos '08 has a persuasive nose hinging on aromatic herbs and spiciness.

	Glasses	Price
● Cannonau di Sardegna Arcanos '08	2	4*
● Nativo '08	2	4*
○ Vermentino di Gallura Miradas '09	1	4
○ Vermentino di Sardegna Tutti i Venti '09	1	4

Cantina Sociale Il Nuraghe

SS 131 km 62
09095 Mogoro [OR]
tel. 0783990285
www.ilnuraghe.it

From the wines produced by the Mogoro co-operative, the most convincingly clean and well made were the Cannonau di Sardegna Vignaruja '07, with a fresh, vital palate preceded by balsam on the nose, and the Vermentino di Sardegna Don Giovanni '09, which shows soft yet with linear development.

	Glasses	Price
● Cannonau di Sardegna Vignaruja '07	2	4*
○ Vermentino di Sardegna Don Giovanni '09	2	4*
● Cannonau di Sardegna Nero Sardo '08	1	4
○ Nasco di Cagliari Villabbas	1	5

Tenuta Nuraghe Crabioni

via Umberto I, 30
07037 Sorso [SS]
tel. 079351217
www.nuraghecrabioni.com

The Nuraghe Crabioni di Sorso estate debuts in the Guide. Terroir and climate are the strong points for these 35 hectares in the north of the island. The compelling Cannonau di Sardegna '08 shows scrubland and spice while the fresh, vital Vermentino di Sardegna '09 has good development.

	Glasses	Price
● Cannonau di Sardegna '08	1	4
○ Vermentino di Sardegna '09	1	4

Cantina Sociale di Ogliastra

via Baccasera, 36
08048 Tortolì [NU]
tel. 0782623228
cantina.ogliastra@live.it

This co-operative winery in Tortolì makes great wines that respect their territory. This year, an excellent '06 Cannonau di Sardegna Riserva won us over with notes of myrtle, spice and Mediterranean herbs, and a palate that is big yet, thanks to its freshness, never loses its refinement.

	Glasses	Price
● Cannonau di Sardegna Ris. '06	2	4*
● Cannonau di Sardegna Su Marchesu '07	1	3

Olianas

loc. Porruddu
09031 Gergei [CA]
tel. 0558300411
www.sardegnavini.eu

Wines from the Olianas estate are again good. In one of the best versions ever, the '09 Cannonau di Sardegna shows surprising complexity on the nose, unwinding spicy aromas of sweet tobacco and leather that find confirmation on the rich depth of the smooth palate.

	Glasses	Price
● Cannonau di Sardegna '09	2	5
○ Vermentino di Sardegna '09	1	4

Cantina Cooperativa di Oliena

via Nuoro, 112
08025 Oliena [NU]
tel. 0784287509
www.cantinasocialeoliena.it

You won't go wrong buying a Cannonau from this co-operative winery in Oliena, specialized in Nepente. The '08 vintage charms on the nose with cherry and morello cherry, and the warm palate is slightly alcoholic yet balanced by measured acidity, tannins well tucked in, finishing clean and savoury.

	Glasses	Price
● Cannonau di Sardegna Nepente di Oliena '08	2	4*
● Cannonau di Sardegna Corrasi Nepente di Oliena Ris. '06	1	5
● Lanaitto '09	1	3

Cantine di Orgosolo

VIA SANTA LUCIA
08027 ORGOSOLO [NU]
TEL. 0784403096
www.cantinediorgosolo.it

This Orgosolo winery, which groups 19 winemakers, has convinced us again this year with excellently made wines. Cannonau di Sardegna Urulu was held back for a year but we were amazed by the fresh, dense palate and excellent drinkability of the Soroi '07, Riserva di Cannonau. Locoe '09 is also nice.

● Cannonau di Sardegna Soroi Ris. '07	2 glasses	6
● Locoe '09	1 glass	4

Pedra Majore

VIA ROMA, 106
07020 MONTI [SS]
TEL. 078943185
www.pedramajore.it

Vermentino di Gallura I Graniti '09 is a classic from Pedra Majore and was well up to expectations again this year, offering mineral, citrus aromas consistent with the fresh, tangy palate. Also quite exciting is Mirju, a sweet wine from overripe grapes with hints of apricot and candied fruit.

○ Mirju	2 glasses	6
○ Vermentino di Gallura I Graniti '09	2 glasses	4
○ Vermentino di Gallura Sup. Hysonj '09	1 glass	5
○ Vermentino di Sardegna Le Conche '09	1 glass	4

Cantine Marcello Puddu

VIA MARZABOTTO, 3A
08025 OLIENA [NU]
TEL. 3498115090
cantine.puddu@tiscali.it

Marcello Puddu's vineyards are mostly planted to cannonau, known hereabouts as nepente. The rich, well-structured Cannonau di Sardegna Nepente di Oliena Mandras '08 has serious body, ripe fruit and medicinal herbs. Good acidity adds suppleness and thrust on the palate, which finishes fresh and balsamic.

● Cannonau di Sardegna Nepente di Oliena Mandras '08	2 glasses	4

F.lli Puddu

LOC. ORBUDDAI
08025 OLIENA [NU]
TEL. 0784288457
azienda.puddu@tiscali.it

The Puddu brothers' Oliena estate carries on the local tradition of making Nepente. Cannonau di Sardegna Nepente di Oliena '08 introduces notes of fruit in alcohol and a warm, embracing palate. The Papalope Rosso is sweet, complex and supple, yet shows big body and structure.

● Cannonau di Sardegna Nepente di Oliena '08	1 glass	4
● Papalope Rosso	1 glass	4

Josto Puddu

VIA SAN LUSSORIO, 1
09070 SAN VERO MILIS [OR]
TEL. 078353329
www.cantinapuddu.it

Established in the early 1960s, the Josto Puddu winery makes a range of interesting wines from traditional varieties. The best is Cannonau di Sardegna Antares '07 with its notes of roses preceding a fresh, vibrant palate.

● Cannonau di Sardegna Antares '07	1 glass	4
● Monica di Sardegna Torremora Sup. '08	1 glass	4
○ Vermentino di Sardegna Maris '09	1 glass	4
○ Vernaccia di Oristano Ris. '01	1 glass	4

Giampietro Puggioni

VIA NUORO, 11
08024 MAMOIADA [NU]
TEL. 0784203516
www.cantinagiampietropuggioni.it

The Puggioni estate in Mamoiada always makes traditional, authentic Cannonau di Sardegnas. The most convincing was Lakana '08, a well-structured wine with distinct red fruits in alcohol and a warm, caressing palate. With its slight hints of overripeness, Ilisi '08 is somewhat penalized by a bitter finish.

● Cannonau di Sardegna Lakana '08	2 glasses	4*
● Cannonau di Sardegna Ilisi '08	1 glass	6

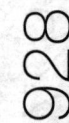

Cantine Surrau

SP Arzachena - Porto Cervo
07021 Arzachena [OT]
tel. 078982933
www.vignesurrau.it

This Arzachena estate did well with a nice range of traditional reds and whites. The most interesting was Barriu '06 IGT, a blend of cannonau, carignano, cabernet and muristellu offering saddle leather and fragrant, flowing drinkability. Branu '09 is the cleanest, most mineral Vermentino di Gallura around.

● Barriu '06	🍷🍷	6
○ Vermentino di Gallura Branu '09	🍷	5
○ Vermentino di Gallura Sciala '09	🍷	5

Tanca Gioia Carloforte

loc. Gioia
09014 Carloforte [CI]
tel. 3356359329
www.u-tabarka.com

The sweet wine was the biggest surprise at this Carloforte estate. U Tabarka Quae '09, from mostly moscato, shows aromas of candied orange, melon, orange blossom and nuts, followed by a fresh, deep, lively palate. The subtle yet well-made U Tabarka Giancu '09 features citrus notes with grassy nuances.

○ U Tabarka Quae '09	🍷🍷	6
○ U Tabarka Giancu '09	🍷	5
● U Tabarka Roussou '08	🍷	5

Cantina Sociale della Vernaccia

loc. Rimedio
via Oristano, 6a
09170 Oristano
tel. 078333155
www.vinovernaccia.com

Vernaccia wines from this Oristano co-operative are always interesting. The Riserva '07 di Cannonau di Sardegna Corash is very good, its nose tempting with crisp fruit and the creamy palate unfurling close-knit tannins and a clean, elegant finish. The other bottles are well crafted.

● Cannonau di Sardegna Corash Ris. '07	🍷🍷	4*
● Cannonau di Sardegna Maiomone '07	🍷	4
⊙ Nieddera Rosato '09	🍷	2
○ Terresinis '09	🍷	3

Villa di Quartu

loc. Cepola
via G. Garibaldi, 90
09045 Quartu Sant'Elena [CA]
tel. 070820947
www.villadiquartu.com

Every year, Villa di Quartu submits a range of sound, whistle-clean wines. The ever-reliable Cepola Rosso '08 is a blend of monica, barbera, cannonau and bovale with a succulent, vibrant fresh palate. Vermentino di Sardegna Poetho '09 is also interesting for its flavourful palate and sea-salt sensations.

● Cepola Rosso '08	🍷🍷	4
● Monica di Sardegna Ammostus '09	🍷	3
○ Vermentino di Sardegna Poetho '09	🍷	5

WINERIES IN ALPHABETICAL ORDER

WINERIES BY REGION

WINERIES IN ALPHABETICAL ORDER

XXI

WINERIES IN ALPHABETICAL ORDER

WINERIES IN ALPHABETICAL ORDER

WINERIES IN ALPHABETICAL ORDER

WINERIES IN ALPHABETICAL ORDER

WINERIES IN ALPHABETICAL ORDER

XXVI

WINERIES IN ALPHABETICAL ORDER

WINERIES IN ALPHABETICAL ORDER

WINERIES IN ALPHABETICAL ORDER

XXIX

WINERIES IN ALPHABETICAL ORDER

WINERIES IN ALPHABETICAL ORDER

WINERIES IN ALPHABETICAL ORDER

WINERIES BY REGION

WINERIES BY REGION

WINERIES BY REGION

XXXV

WINERIES BY REGION

WINERIES BY REGION

LAZIO

WINERIES BY REGION

WINERIES BY REGION

WINERIES BY REGION

WINERIES BY REGION

WINERIES BY REGION

WINERIES BY REGION

XLIII

WINERIES BY REGION

WINERIES BY REGION

WINERIES BY REGION

WINERIES BY REGION

XLVII

WINERIES BY REGION

TRENTINO

WINERIES BY REGION

WINERIES BY REGION

WINERIES BY REGION